The Rough Guide to

Europe

ON A BUDGET

this edition written and researched by

Jonathan Bousfield, Tim Burford, Lucy Cowie, Caroline Daly, Kiki Deere, Jen Foster, Nick Harrison, Hilary Heuler, Daniel Jacobs, Anna Kaminski, Ciara Kenny, Norm Longley, John Malathronas, Neil McQuillian, Sophie Middlemiss, Kathryn Miller, Suzanne Morton-Taylor, Roger Norum, Alice Park, Georgia Platman, Natalia O'Hara, James Rice, Alison Roberts, Rmishka Singh, James Stewart, Emma Thomson, Kate Turner, Steven Vickers, Neville Walker, Luke Waterson, Christian Williams, Matt Willis and Martin Zatko

www.roughguides.com

Contents

Colour section 1

Introduction 4
When to go 8
Ideas 10

Itineraries 17

Basics 27

Getting there 29
Getting around 33
Accommodation 38
Festivals and annual events 40
Work and study 42
Travel essentials 44

Guide 53

1 Albania 53
2 Austria 67
3 Belgium and Luxembourg ... 95
4 Bosnia-Herzegovina 121
5 Britain 137
6 Bulgaria 219
7 Croatia 247
8 Czech Republic 277
8 Denmark 303
10 Estonia 333
11 Finland 353
12 France 373
13 Germany 451
14 Greece 521
15 Hungary 577
16 Ireland 603
17 Italy 639
18 Latvia 719
19 Lithuania 737
20 Macedonia 757
21 Montenegro 771
22 Morocco 785
23 The Netherlands 821
24 Norway 851
25 Poland 881
26 Portugal 911
27 Romania 949
28 Russia 971
29 Serbia 995
30 Slovakia 1013
31 Slovenia 1033
32 Spain 1053
33 Sweden 1145
34 Switzerland 1175
35 Turkey 1203
36 Ukraine 1243

Travel store 1261

Small print & Index 1265

◂◂ LAKE BLED, SLOVENIA ◂ CASA BATTLÓ, BARCELONA

0
500 km
0
250 miles
Metres
4000
2000
1000
400
200
0
below sea level
Arctic Circle
REYKJAVÍK
ICELAND
Faroes
Shetland
Bergen
ATLANTIC OCEAN
NORTH SEA
Edinburgh
Belfast
IRELAND
DUBLIN
York
UNITED KINGDOM
Cardiff
LONDON
NETHERLANDS
AMSTERDAM
DENMARK
Århus
Hamburg
BRUSSELS
BELGIUM
Cologne
GERMANY
LUX.
Frankfurt
PARIS
LUXEMBOURG CITY
FRANCE
Munich
BERN
Zürich
SWITZERLAND
Santiago de Compostela
Bordeaux
Lyon
Bilbao
Milan
Venice
Porto
PORTUGAL
MONACO
SAN MARINO
Marseille
ANDORRA
Florence
MADRID
LISBON
SPAIN
Barcelona
Corsica (Fr.)
ROME
Valencia
Ibiza
Seville
Mallorca
Sardinia
MEDITERRANEAN SEA
Tangier
ALGIERS
Casablanca
RABAT
Fes
TUNIS
MOROCCO
Essaouira
Marrakesh
ALGERIA
TUNISIA

NORWAY
SWEDEN
FINLAND
RUSSIA
OSLO
HELSINKI
St Petersburg
STOCKHOLM
TALLINN
ESTONIA
Gothenburg
BALTIC SEA
RĪGA
LATVIA
MOSCOW
COPENHAGEN
LITHUANIA
VILNIUS
RUSSIA
MINSK
BELARUS
BERLIN
WARSAW
POLAND
KYIV
PRAGUE
Kraków
CZECH REPUBLIC
UKRAINE
SLOVAKIA
BRATISLAVA
VIENNA
MOLDOVA
CHISINAŬ
AUSTRIA
BUDAPEST
HUNGARY
LJUBLJANA
ROMANIA
SLOVENIA
ZAGREB
CROATIA
GEORGIA
BELGRADE
T'BILISI
ADRIATIC SEA
BOSNIA-HERZEGOVINA
BUCHAREST
BLACK SEA
SARAJEVO
SERBIA
BULGARIA
PODGORICA
SOFIA
ITALY
MONTENEGRO
SKOPJE
Istanbul
ALBANIA
MACEDONIA
Naples
TIRANA
Thessaloníki
ANKARA
TURKEY
GREECE
AEGEAN SEA
İzmir
ATHENS
Sicily
SYRIA
MALTA
Crete
CYPRUS
LEBANON
IRAQ

Introduction to

Europe

No continent on Earth packs a punch like Europe. Not only is it rich in beauty, history and romantic appeal, it's also astonishingly diverse. One day you might be strolling along a grand boulevard, absorbing centuries of civilization, and the next you could be skiing headlong down a black run surrounded by snow-capped, saw-toothed mountains. There are ancient forests to explore, super-strong espressos to sip, and incredible architectural wonders that will have you repeatedly grabbing for your camera.

Virtually wherever you end up – on a baking-hot beach in Portugal or knee-deep in the wintry snows of Finland – you're likely to find some surprising common ground that will ease your onward journey. There's the shared currency, for starters (the euro is already used in most EU states), and a unique "open borders" policy that allows hassle-free travel between countries that were once fierce enemies. Back in those days, exploring Europe was only for the wealthy. Not anymore.

In fact, armed with the right know-how, it's possible to see Europe's best sights on a budget, party till you can't party any more, and still have enough cash left for a decent breakfast. You could grab a quick croissant and *café au lait* in Paris or go slow in Copenhagen with a stomach-stretching platter of open sandwiches. Then, check into your hostel (Europe has one of the world's best networks of budget accommodation) and head out in search of fun with the vast student populations that make cities like Rome and Barcelona stand out from the crowd. If culture's more your bag, it's possible to get a free fix in almost every European capital. In London, for example, you can spend days getting lost in stupendous collections of international treasures and it won't cost you a penny.

Free history lessons are everywhere, too. You can wander through sacred grottos on the sun-scorched islands of Greece, or imagine yourself coming face to face with a vampire at "Dracula's" medieval castle in Romania. It seems nowhere is without a story. But for a collection of countries with such rich heritage, Europe doesn't spend much time looking backwards. It's home to some impressively futuristic modern architecture; some of the world's best nightclubs; and fresh, cutting-edge restaurants that set the senses alight.

The key to experiencing all of this on a budget is knowing where to look, and we've packed this book with expert tips to help you make the most of your trip for less. We've covered all of the must-see attractions – from the Vatican to the Brandenburg Gate – as well as cities on Europe's outer fringes, like İstanbul and Marrakesh. Away from the beaten track, there's advice on getting to grips with Norway's majestic fjords, soaring Alpine peaks and the glittering Balkan coastline.

So how do you get from one place to the next? Well, with myriad budget airlines you could fly, but it's hardly the greenest option. And when you think of all the sights and smells you'd miss out on by jumping on a plane (not to mention the hassle of hanging around in airports) travelling overland takes on a whole new appeal. High-speed train lines and spectacular stations are popping up across Europe, and just looking at an arrivals board whirring its way through destinations should be enough to whet your appetite – Paris, Rome, Warsaw and Moscow are

SAILING TO DAMME, THE NETHERLANDS.

Top 5 Hostels

▶▶ **Ostel, Berlin** Experience Iron Curtain retro chic at this GDR-themed hostel (see p.468).
▶▶ **Living Lounge, Lisbon** Packed with contemporary art, this sleek and funky place is half-gallery, half-hostel (see p.925).
▶▶ **Villa St-Éxupéry, Nice** Former monastery beautifully converted into a buzzing hostel close to the beaches of the French Riviera (see p.436).
▶▶ **AF Chapman, Stockholm** A tall, elegant ship festooned with flags could be your home for the night (see p.1156).
▶▶ **Celica Youth Hostel, Ljubljana** Try a night behind bars at this artfully refurbished prison in Ljubljana (see p.1042).

all just a platform away. And thankfully, if you take the train you won't have to spend much either. A range of cheap, convenient rail passes are available for pan-European travel: there's the InterRail pass – now a byword for criss-crossing continents by train – and Eurail, its sister pass for non-Europeans. Both can be tailored to your trip, whether you're staying in one country for a few months or hotfooting your way round the entire continent.

When to go

Europe is a year-round destination, so don't worry too much about what the weather will be doing; good conditions for snowboarding aren't ever going to be ideal for sunbathing. In terms of budget, however, it makes sense to travel in the off season (basically October through to May). Cheaper menus appear on restaurant tables, hotels drop their rates, and haggling over prices becomes a realistic option. This is especially true of tourist hotspots like Paris, Barcelona and Rome, which attract far bigger crowds in July and August.

If you do decide to travel during the peak **summer** season, try heading east – the Balkan coastline, the Slovenian mountains and Baltic cities are all fantastic places for making the most of your money. When tourist traffic dies down as **autumn** approaches, head to the Med. The famous coastlines and islands of southern Europe are quieter at this time of year, and the cities of Spain and Italy begin to look their best. **Wintertime** brings world-class skiing and snowboarding to European mountainsides (though not always) and countless festive markets pop up in the towns and cities below. There are epic New Year parties everywhere from Moscow to Lisbon and, despite the cold weather elsewhere at this time of year, there's still the possibility of sunshine in Turkey and Morocco. While it's no secret that **spring** is the time to hit the French capital, it's also worth heading north to the Netherlands, Scandinavia and the British Isles where you'll find beautifully long days and relatively affordable prices before the summer season kicks in around July.

WALKING IN THE CIRQUE DE GAVARNIE, PYRENEES

While **weather** extremes are not the issue they are in say, Asia or Africa, you should still bear them in mind when planning your trip. The Arctic winter in Scandinavia and Russia can bring temperatures as low as -35°C, with the sun barely rising above the horizon for months at a time. Conversely, summer days in central, southern and eastern parts of continental Europe can be sweltering – temperatures of around 40°C are not unheard of.

FOOD STALLS, DJEMMA EL FNA, MARRAKESH

Ideas Art and culture

MUSEUM ISLAND, BERLIN Five world-class museums crammed onto one small island – a day-trip in itself. **See p.462**

BALLET, RUSSIA The birthplace of this beautiful dance form – admire the tutus, demi-pliés and glorious waltzing music. **See p.986**

THE PARTHENON, ATHENS The iconic image of Western civilization and template for buildings the world over. **See p.532**

SISTINE CHAPEL, THE VATICAN Michelangelo's stupendous ceiling is worth craning your neck for. **See p.652**

AYA SOFYA, İSTANBUL Christianity and Islam meet at this sixth-century architectural marvel. **See p.1210**

MUSEO GUGGENHEIM, BILBAO Europe's most spectacular museum houses work by some of the biggest names in modern art. **See p.1137**

Ideas Outdoor activities

ISLAND-HOPPING, GREECE
Create your own odyssey on board a yacht in the Aegean. **See p.553**

TAKING A SAUNA, FINLAND
Heat yourself to boiling point then take a bone-chilling plunge. **See p.369**

WHITEWATER RAFTING, MONTENEGRO The foaming waters of the Tara River are perfect for rafting and kayaking. **See p.784**

WINDSURFING, MOROCCO Essaouira is the best place to take to the water, with a powerful wind constantly blowing over the almost waveless bay. **See p.818**

SKIING AND SNOWBOARDING, FRANCE The French Alps offer the gnarliest and liveliest skiing and boarding on the continent. **See p.443**

HIKING THE TATRAS, POLAND/ SLOVAKIA World-class hiking in summer and some of Europe's best-value skiing in winter. **See pp.905 & 1028**

Ideas Festivals and events

EDINBURGH FESTIVAL
Comedy, drama, juggling, bagpipes – you'll find them all at this unparalleled arts festival.
See p.204

LA TOMATINA, SPAIN
Indulge your inner naughty child at this enormous food fight.
See p.1104

OKTOBERFEST, MUNICH
Sheer unadulterated beer guzzling at the world's largest public festival.
See p.514

FOOTBALL, BARCELONA The biggest stadium in Europe is home to the all-conquering FC Barcelona and probably the best games of footie you'll ever see. **See p.1058**

THE PALIO, SIENA See the dust fly and the passions rise at the most exciting horse race on earth. **See p.689**

EXIT FESTIVAL, SERBIA A beautiful fortress setting, a thumping sound system and top-name acts – what's not to like? **See p.1008**

ITINERARIES

ITINERARIES

Britain and Ireland 19
France and Switzerland 20
Benelux, Germany and Austria 20
Spain, Portugal and Morocco 21
Italy 22
Central and Eastern Europe 23
Scandinavia 23
Russia and the Baltic coast 24
The Balkan Peninsula 25
Greece and Turkey 25

Europe itineraries

You can't expect to fit everything Europe has to offer into one trip and we don't suggest you try. On the following pages are a selection of itineraries that guide you through the different regions of the continent, taking you from the misty Scottish Highlands to the bazaars of İstanbul. Each itinerary could be done in two to three weeks if followed to the letter but don't push it too hard – with so much to see and do you're going to get waylaid somewhere you love or head off the suggested route.

BRITAIN AND IRELAND

Home to four proud nations, these two small islands pack in a huge amount – from stately castles and windswept moors to theatre, Premiership football and Europe's best music festivals. Don't forget your brolly, drinking hat and sense of humour.

❶ **LONDON** As the saying goes, when a man is tired of London, he is tired of life. One of the world's greatest cities is also one of the most expensive, but follow our tips to emerge with your wallet intact. See p.145

❷ **OXFORD** The famous university town offers the chance to punt along the river, admire the college architecture or down a few in a student pub. See p.174

❸ **SNOWDONIA** Despite the notoriously unpredictable weather, the misty Welsh mountains offer excellent hiking and some of Britain's best hostels. See p.200

❹ **YORK** From a Viking museum and medieval streets to the soaring Gothic Minster, if you want to soak up some British history, York is the place to do it. See p.190

❺ **EDINBURGH** With its stunning cityscape, lively bars and – if you time it right – international festival, the Scottish capital has something for everyone. See p.202

❻ **THE HIGHLANDS** Find your inner Braveheart, knock back some whisky and hike, climb or ski surrounded by Britain's most stunning scenery. See p.216

❼ **BELFAST** A fascinating if troubled history, friendly locals and access point to one of Europe's natural wonders, the Giant's Causeway. See p.632

❽ **DUBLIN** Yep, Guinness really does taste better here though there's a lot more to see and do in Ireland's sophisticated capital. See p.610

❾ **IRELAND'S WEST COAST** From Galway to Cork, Ireland's west coast is studded with buzzing towns and beautiful, windswept beaches. See p.624

FRANCE AND SWITZERLAND

Still the world's number-one tourist destination, France can smugly claim to have it all from mountains and sun-kissed beaches to unrivalled food and fashion. Pricey it may be, but nearby Switzerland is worth the expense for its attractive, appealingly relaxed cities and the jaw-dropping mountain views.

❶ **PARIS** Laze over a coffee in a Left Bank café, arrange a romantic rendezvous or tick off the many museums in Europe's most elegant capital. **See p.380**

❷ **THE LOIRE VALLEY** Bucolic valley that's filled with some of the most impressive chateaux you'll see in the country. **See p.399**

❸ **BORDEAUX** An elegant, bustling city, world-famous wine-growing region and, a short drive away, some of Europe's finest surf beaches. **See p.408**

❹ **THE PYRENEES** Clear your head after all that wine with the fresh air and fine walks of this mountain range bordering Spain. **See p.416**

❺ **THE CÔTE D'AZUR** Nice, Cannes, Monaco – the names alone ooze glamour so get your glad rags on and show the world your fabulous side. **See p.434**

❻ **CORSICA** France's adventure playground, Corsica is home to one of Europe's toughest and most rewarding treks, the GR20. **See p.444**

❼ **LYON** There's no better city in which to indulge your passion for French cuisine than here in the country's gastronomic capital. **See p.438**

❽ **THE ALPS** Try your luck scaling Europe's highest mountains, or spend a season as a ski instructor or chalet monkey. **See p.442 & p.1191**

❾ **ZÜRICH** Laidback Zürich is now one of Europe's clubbing hotspots and has a wonderful riverside setting. **See p.1195**

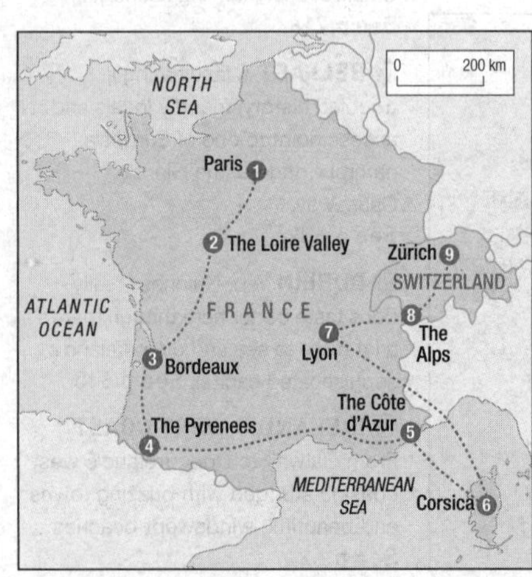

BENELUX, GERMANY AND AUSTRIA

From fine chocolates and champion beers to fairytale castles, dark forests and clinking cowbells, this region has something for most people. The cities can pass in a blur of late nights but try and make time for the scenery too.

❶ **AMSTERDAM** Whatever you're looking for – cannabis, clubs, high culture or cuisine – the Netherlands' largest city will provide it. **See p.828**

❷ **BRUGES** It may be brazenly touristy but this gem of Flemish architecture is still worth a visit for its atmospheric canals and beautiful buildings. **See p.114**

❸ **COLOGNE** Linked to Brussels and beyond by super-fast trains, Cologne makes a perfect first stop in Germany with its spectacular old town and lively festivals. **See p.489**

❹ **HAMBURG** Germany's northern gateway boasts a vast port, magnificent red-brick warehouses and a riotous bar and live music scene. **See p.481**

SPAIN, PORTUGAL AND MOROCCO

Penélope Cruz, Cristiano Ronaldo, tapas, port and Rioja – it's hard not to warm to the Iberian peninsula. To the south, Morocco is just a short hop across the sea but a different planet in many respects.

❶ **BILBAO** Capital of the Basque country, Bilbao is Spain's friendliest city and home to one of Europe's most spectacular buildings: the Guggenheim. **See p.1136**

❷ **BARCELONA** Innovative architecture, city beaches, late-night bars and an atmospheric old town – you'll find it hard to leave the Catalan capital. **See p.1102**

❸ **IBIZA** Europe's clubbing capital packs in more sunburnt skin per square inch of dancefloor than anywhere on earth, but you can also find a secluded beach if you look hard enough. **See p.1107**

❹ **MADRID** Take your cue from the locals in the Spanish capital – if you're

❺ **BERLIN** Over twenty years since the fall of the Wall, Berlin still has a raw, youthful energy that belies its history of division and destruction. **See p.459**

❻ **DRESDEN** Bombed to bits in World War II, Dresden is the classic Phoenix from the flames story and now one of Europe's favourite backpacker hangouts. **See p.472**

❼ **MUNICH** From beer-fuelled thigh-slapping to modern art and mountain scenery, you'll find it all in Bavaria's capital. **See p.509**

❽ **SALZBURG** Hit the Mozart trail, pose Julie Andrews-style in homage to *The Sound of Music* or pull on some skis and head for the mountains. **See p.84**

❾ **VIENNA** Austria's capital is chock-full of palaces, museums and grand boulevards – with coffee and cake in a grand café never too far away. **See p.72**

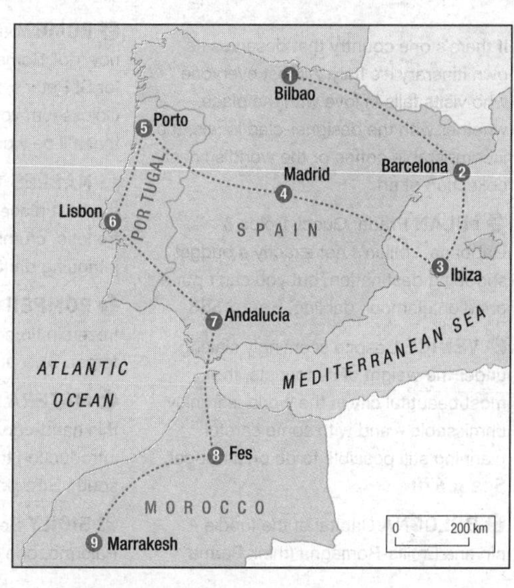

dining before 10pm, dancing before midnight and asleep before dawn, you haven't experienced a truly Madrileño night out. See p.1061

❺ **PORTO** Wander the atmospheric cobbled streets of Portugal's second city – and sample a drop at one (or more) of the countless port lodges. See p.933

❻ **LISBON** Portugal's immediately likeable capital has a great setting, delicious food and a huge amount of historic interest. See p.918

❼ **ANDALUCÍA** Spain in a nutshell – flamenco, fine wines, bullfighting and heat. If you're pushed for time stick to the unmissable cities of Seville and Granada. See p.1082

❽ **FES** Once across the Straits of Gibraltar, dive head first into Morocco with a stay in this medieval city of labyrinthine alleys, souks and mosques. See p.803

❾ **MARRAKESH** Stunning, atmospheric city with the Atlas Mountains as a backdrop and the live circus that is the Djemaa el Fna square at its heart. See p.813

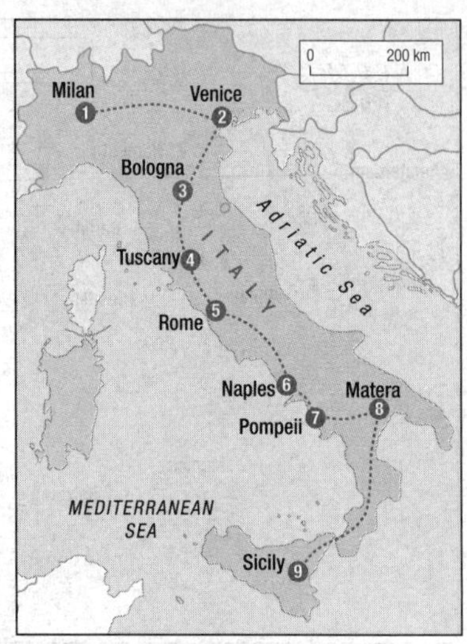

ITALY

If there's one country that deserves its own itinerary it's Italy. Almost everyone who visits falls in love with the place, whether with the designer-clad locals, the incomparable coffee or the world's finest collection of art.

❶ **MILAN** Prada, Gucci, Dolce & Gabbana...Milan's not exactly a budget shopping destination, but you can't put a price on glamour, dahling. See p.658

❷ **VENICE** Despite seemingly sinking under the weight of its tourists, the most beautiful city in the world is frankly unmissable – and with some careful planning still possible to do on a budget. See p.670

❸ **BOLOGNA** Capital of the foodie nirvana Emilia-Romagna (think Parma ham, Parmesan, balsamic vinegar), Bologna is an essential pit stop for anyone with a digestive system. See p.677

❹ **TUSCANY** Birthplace of the Renaissance, Florence rightly pulls in the masses; nearby Siena is just as beautiful, full of fun-loving students and an excellent base to explore the region's hill towns. See p.682 & p.689

❺ **ROME** You can hardly "do" Europe and not "do" Rome. Whether you're queuing for St Peter's, the Sistine Chapel or the Colosseum you can at least rest assured that it'll be worth every minute. See p.647

❻ **NAPLES** The home of pizza – and the best place to eat it – Naples is also a frenetic, crumblingly attractive city with an intriguing dark side. See p.697

❼ **POMPEII** Seeing a Roman town frozen in time is an experience you won't forget. See p.702

❽ **MATERA** Try sleeping in a cave in this hand-carved stone city – the perfect introduction to Italy's captivating far south. See p.706

❾ **SICILY** Beaches, volcanoes and, in Palermo, one of Italy's most in-your-face cities – Sicilians simply do it better. **See p.708**

CENTRAL AND EASTERN EUROPE

Having long shrugged off the Iron Curtain, the region we used to regard as Eastern Europe is now firmly at the beating heart of the continent. With elegant cities and vast tracts of unspoiled countryside, these countries provide a remarkable set of riches.

❶ **PRAGUE** The Czech capital would probably win a pan-European beauty contest for its architecture. As for the beer…well, let's just say you won't be disappointed. **See p.283**

❷ **WARSAW** Beyond the Polish capital's immaculately reconstructed old town there are beautiful palaces and parks – and a restaurant, club and vodka-soaked bar scene – to explore. **See p.888**

❸ **KRAKÓW** Arty and atmospheric, picture-postcard-pretty Kraków should not be missed, though neither should a sobering trip to nearby Auschwitz. **See p.900**

❹ **TATRAS MOUNTAINS** Stretching between Poland and Slovakia the Tatras are that rare thing – majestic wilderness without hordes of Gore-Tex-clad tourists. **See p.905 & p.1028**

❺ **BUDAPEST** Two cities for the price of one: stately, museum-packed Buda and across the not-so-blue Danube, nightlife and restaurant hotspot Pest. **See p.584**

❻ **GREAT PLAIN, HUNGARY** Once you've got over the fact that you're still in Europe rather than Outer Mongolia, it's time to saddle up and explore the wide-open space. **See p.600**

❼ **TRANSYLVANIA** No, you probably won't see any vampires, but this history-steeped region holds myriad other attractions, from fairytale villages and colourful festivals to tracking wolves in the spectacular Carpathians. **See p.962**

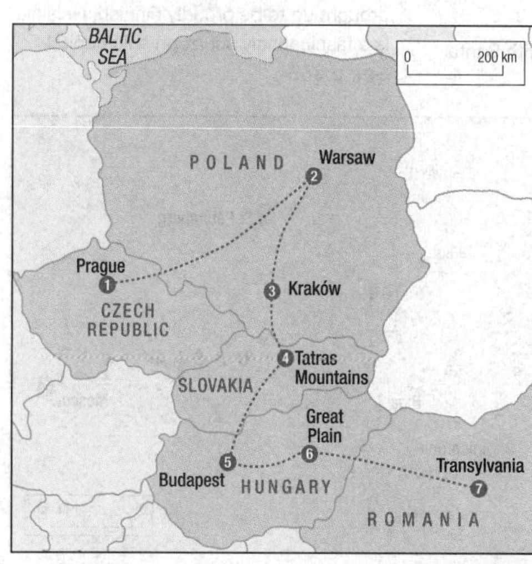

SCANDINAVIA

While it can hit your finances, Scandinavia's worth persevering with. Apart from resembling Europe's answer to Middle Earth it's also full of stylish cities, ingenious design, and friendly if hard to fathom locals.

❶ **COPENHAGEN** Picturesque and user-friendly, the Danish capital is a lively, welcoming introduction to the region. **See p.310**

❷ **GOTHENBURG** Sweden's second city boasts elegant architecture, a fantastic nightlife scene and a fully functioning rainforest among its standout attractions. **See p.1161**

❸ **OSLO** Paying €8 for a beer can put people off the Norwegian capital. If you can get over the prices, though, you'll understand why it frequently tops "best places to live" lists. **See p.858**

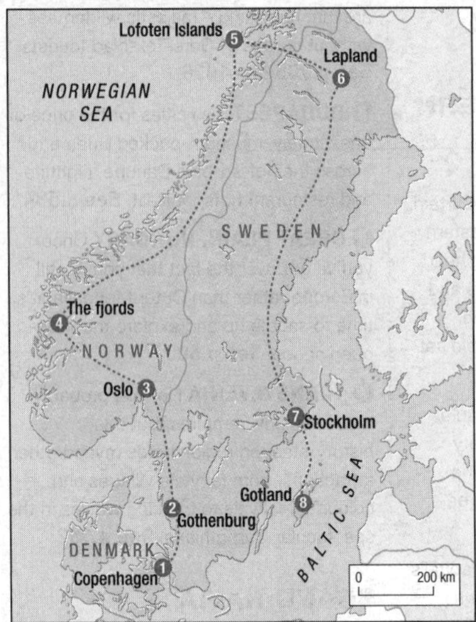

8 GOTLAND Sweden's party island buzzes in summer when the DJs hit the decks in Visby and the beaches fill with bronzed bodies. See p.1169

4 THE FJORDS No trip to Norway would be complete without a visit to the country's western coastline and its magnificent fjords. See p.866

5 LOFOTEN ISLANDS A mild climate, wild scenery and cute, laidback fishing villages pull in the crowds to this remote archipelago in Norway's far north. See p.875

6 LAPLAND Synonymous with Santa, Lapland (whether Swedish or Finnish) fits the winter fantasy perfectly with reindeer, yapping huskies and the staggering Northern Lights. See p.372 & p.1172

7 STOCKHOLM Scandinavia's best-looking capital offers up an unspoilt medieval core, über-hip nightlife and, incongruously enough, some fine beaches. See p.1152

RUSSIA AND THE BALTIC COAST

Big scary bear it may be, but ever-changing Russia should not be missed, even if it's just to dip into its most "European" city, St Petersburg. Its compact Baltic neighbours, meanwhile, provide some of the beautiful – and most fun – cityscapes in Eastern Europe.

1 MOSCOW Big, brash, expensive, surreal and exciting, twenty-first-century Moscow is almost a nation in itself and well worth the effort to get to. See p.978

2 ST PETERSBURG With jaw-dropping architecture and priceless art collections, Russia's second city is at its best during the midsummer White Nights festival. See p.986

3 HELSINKI The love child of the Russian and Swedish empires, since brought up to be proudly Finnish, Helsinki is a fascinatingly schizophrenic capital. See p.366

❹ **TALLINN** Having survived its tenure as a cheap stag- and hen-party venue par excellence, the beautifully preserved Estonian capital still retains a huge amount of charm. See p.339

❺ **RĪGA** Larger and more cosmopolitan that its neighbours, Latvia's atmospheric capital is full of architectural treasures and is the gateway to some wonderful coastal scenery. See p.725

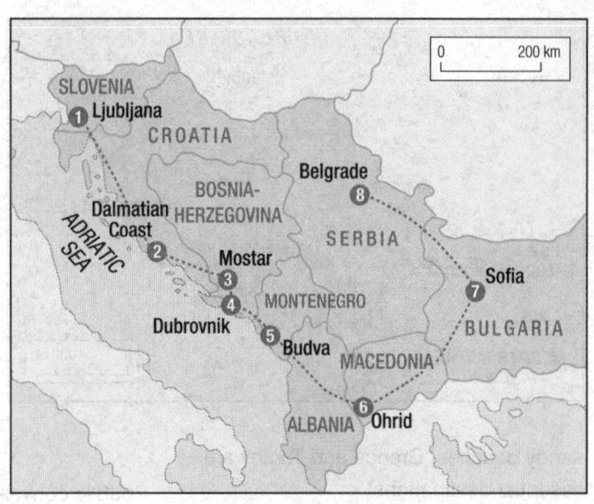

❻ **CURONIAN SPIT** This narrow strip of lofty sand dunes and dense pine forest is the place to get your hiking boots on and strike out on the numerous walking trails. See p.755

❼ **VILNIUS** The friendliest and perhaps prettiest of the Baltic capitals, Vilnius's largely undiscovered status means you can get a break from the crowds. See p.743

THE BALKAN PENINSULA

A fascinating cultural meeting point, the Balkans today are an exciting, safe (mostly) and mercifully cheap place to travel. While Croatia, Slovenia and Bulgaria have been on the scene for a while, send a postcard from Bosnia-Herzegovina or Macedonia and you're bound to have someone at home reaching for an atlas.

❶ **LJUBLJANA** Repeat after me: "Lyoo-bly-AH-nah". It may be hard to pronounce but the Slovenian capital is a small, perfectly formed pit stop between central Europe and the Adriatic. See p.1039

❷ **DALMATIAN COAST** Croatia's dramatic Dalmatian coast and islands are the perfect place to drop out for the summer with watersports, cheap wine and Vitamin D on unlimited offer. See p.261

❸ **MOSTAR** Engineering feat, symbol of Bosnian regeneration and a ridiculously high diving board, Mostar's old bridge is the iconic sight of the region. See p.133

❹ **DUBROVNIK** Rivalling Venice in its day, the "pearl of the Adriatic" has survived centuries of conquest and intrigue, not to mention being on an easyJet flight route. See p.272

❺ **BUDVA** Montenegro's star resort boasts the requisite pretty old town but it's the unspoilt beaches and throbbing open-air bars that pull in the party set. See p.779

❻ **OHRID** Impossibly picturesque, set on the shimmering shores of the eponymous mountain-backed lake, Ohrid is the jewel in Macedonia's crown. See p.768

❼ **SOFIA** While no beauty, Bulgaria's laidback capital is an absorbing mix of cultural influences and boasts some of Eastern Europe's best hostels. See p.226

❽ **BELGRADE** Hectic and hedonistic, the Serbian capital is fast attracting the hip crowd thanks to its adrenaline-charged nightlife. See p.1001

GREECE AND TURKEY

Whether you're interested in classical antiquity and the founding of Western civilization or just sparkling blue seas and

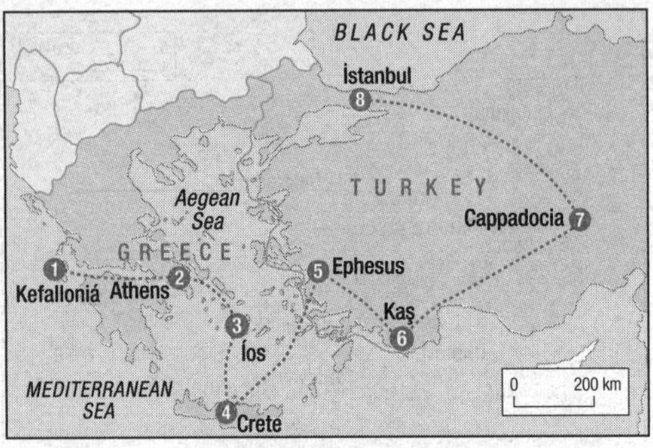

sandy beaches, Greece and Turkey are essential destinations.

❶ **KEFALLONIÁ** Beautiful Kefalloniá is the best place to hop on a moped and find that perfect beach. **See p.570**

❷ **ATHENS** Crowded, noisy and polluted the Greek capital may be, but once you've seen the sun set over the Parthenon you'll be hooked. **See p.529**

❸ **ÍOS** A favourite among hard-partying backpackers, Íos maintains a bohemian, hippie-era charm and is the best stop on the Cyclades island-hopping trail. **See p.558**

❹ **CRETE** Home to the Minotaur and a fair few trashy resorts, Crete also boasts the dramatic Samarian Gorge, Europe's answer to the Grand Canyon. **See p.57**

❺ **EPHESUS** Turkey's best-preserved archeological site is a treasure-trove of ruined temples, mosaics, baths and some spectacular public conveniences. **See p.1228**

❻ **KAŞ** Fill your days mountain biking, paragliding or diving then relive it all in some of the Med's liveliest bars. **See p.1232**

❼ **CAPPADOCIA** It's a long trip east but Cappadocia's unique volcanic landscape has an irresistible allure – stay in a cave hotel and visit a subterranean city. **See p.1239**

❽ **İSTANBUL** Squeeze every kuruş out of your Turkish Lira shopping in the bazaars, having a rub down in a hammam and enjoying the surprisingly hectic nightlife. **See p.1210**

BASICS

BASICS

Getting there 29
Getting around 33
Accommodation....38
Festivals and annual events....40
Work and study....42
Travel essentials....44

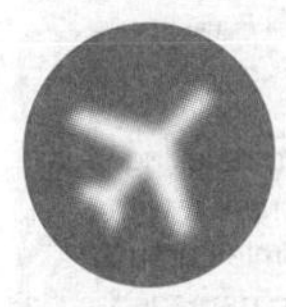

Getting there

Europe can be easily reached by air from just about anywhere in the world, with flights to all major European cities. It's also possible to arrive by ferry from across the Mediterranean, the Black Sea and the Atlantic. The Trans-Siberian railway is the main route into Europe from Asia.

Airfares will always depend on the season; they're usually highest in the summer and over the Christmas period, as well as over public holidays. Note also that flying on weekends or requiring a nonstop journey sometimes adds quite a bit to the round-trip fare. Barring special offers, the cheapest published fares usually require advance purchase of two to three weeks, and impose certain restrictions, such as heavy penalties if you change your schedule. Most cheap fares will only give a partial refund, if any, should you cancel or alter your journey, so check the restrictions carefully before buying.

You can often cut costs by going through a **discount agent**, which in addition to dealing with discounted flights may also offer special student and youth fares and a range of other travel-related services such as travel insurance, rail passes and tours.

If Europe is only one stop on a longer journey, and especially if you are based in Australia or New Zealand, you might consider a **Round-the-World** (RTW) air ticket. Prices increase with the number of stops – figure on around £750–1100/US$1500–2000/Aus$2500/NZ$3350 for a RTW ticket including one or two European stopovers.

FROM BRITAIN AND IRELAND

Heading from Britain to destinations in northwestern Europe, it's not just greener to go by train, long-distance bus or ferry – it can be quicker and cheaper too. However, it's normally cheaper to fly than take the train to most parts of southern Europe. From Ireland, you may save a little money travelling by land, sea or even air to London and buying your flight there, but the difference isn't much. Budget airlines often have special deals and sales, so it's always a good idea to check.

By plane

London is predictably **Britain**'s main hub for air travel, offering the highest frequency of flights and widest choice of destinations from its five airports (Heathrow, Gatwick, Stansted, Luton and City). Manchester also has flights to most parts of Europe, and there are regular services to the continent from Birmingham, Southampton, Bournemouth, East Midlands, Bristol, Cardiff, Glasgow, Edinburgh, Leeds/Bradford and Newcastle. From the Republic of Ireland, you can fly direct to most major cities in mainland Europe from Dublin, Shannon and Cork. From Belfast, there are direct flights with easyJet to a handful of destinations; otherwise, you'll need to change in London or Manchester.

Budget airlines such as easyJet, bmibaby and Ryanair offer low-cost tickets to airports around Europe (though not always the most convenient airports), and they often have some seriously cheap offers in winter; see p.30 for a list of some of the more established operators, though be aware that the budget air travel industry is in a permanent state of flux, and airlines go in and out of business all the time. It's also worth checking with flight agents who specialize in low-cost, discounted flights (charter and scheduled), some of them – like STA Travel and Trailfinders – concentrating on deals for young people and students. In addition, there are agents

A BETTER KIND OF TRAVEL

At Rough Guides we are passionately committed to travel. We feel that travelling is the best way to understand the world we live in and the people we share it with – plus tourism has brought a great deal of benefit to developing economies around the world over the last few decades. But the growth in tourism has also damaged some places irreparably, and climate change is exacerbated by most forms of transport, especially flying. All Rough Guides' trips are carbon-offset, and every year we donate money to a variety of charities devoted to combating the effects of climate change.

specializing in offers to a specific country or group of countries on both charters and regular scheduled departures.

European budget airlines

At the time of writing there were 44 budget airlines serving countries in or near Europe. We've listed the more established operators below but for full details of routes visit ⓦwww.flycheapo.com, ⓦwww.skyscanner.net is an invaluable price comparison resource.

Air Berlin ⓦwww.airberlin.com.
Blue Air ⓦwww.blueair-web.com.
bmibaby ⓦwww.bmibaby.com.
Darwin ⓦwww.darwinairline.com.
easyJet ⓦwww.easyjet.com.
Flybe ⓦwww.flybe.com.
Fly Niki ⓦwww.flyniki.com.
Germanwings ⓦwww.germanwings.com.
Jet2 ⓦwww.jet2.com.
Norwegian Air Shuttle ⓦwww.norwegian.no.
Ryanair ⓦwww.ryanair.com.
Transavia ⓦwww.transavia.com.
TUIfly ⓦwww.tuifly.com.
Vueling ⓦwww.vueling.com.
Wizz Air ⓦwww.wizzair.com.

By train

Direct trains through the **Channel Tunnel** from London to Paris (20 daily, 2hr 15min) and Brussels (9 daily, 1hr 53min) are operated by Eurostar. Tickets for under-26s start at £39 one-way, £59 return. For over-26s, the cheapest and least flexible tickets cost £39 one-way or £69 return. Through-ticket combinations with onward connections from Lille, Brussels and Paris can be booked through International Rail and Rail Europe (see p.37).

Other rail journeys from Britain involve a sea crossing by ferry or, sometimes, catamaran. Tickets can be bought from International Rail, and from most major rail stations or from Dutchflyer (ⓦwww.stenaline.co.uk/ferry/rail-and-sail/Holland) if routed via the Hook of Holland. For some destinations, there are cheaper SuperApex fares requiring advance booking and subject to greater restrictions. Otherwise, international tickets are valid for two months and allow for stopovers on the way, providing you stick to the prescribed route (there may be a choice, with different fares applicable). One-way fares are generally around two-thirds the price of a return fare. If you're under 26 you're entitled to all sorts of special deals, not least cut-price youth fares.

From **Ireland**, direct rail tickets to Europe via Britain generally include both boat connections, and are available from Irish Railways offices in the Republic (ⓣ01/703 1884, ⓦwww.irishrail.ie), or Northern Ireland Railways in the North (ⓣ028/9066 6630, ⓦwww.translink.co.uk).

For rail passes, contacts and other types of discounted rail travel, see p.33.

By bus

If you're really watching your pennies, a long-distance bus is often the cheapest option, although much less comfortable than the train. The main operator is **Eurolines** (ⓦwww.eurolines.co.uk; ⓦwww.eurolines.ie), which has a network of routes spanning the continent. Prices can be up to a third less than by train, and there are marginally cheaper fares on most services for those under 26, which undercut youth rail rates for the same journey. There's usually a discount if you buy your ticket in advance, and bigger discounts for journeys booked a week in

YOU AND THE EU

After a tricky birth in the aftermath of World War II, the EU (European Union) is now reaching maturity. A recent growth spurt has increased the number of member states to 27 and it now stretches from the beaches of Portugal in the west, across the former Iron Curtain to the shores of the Black Sea in Bulgaria, and to Cyprus. So what does this self-styled "family of democratic nations" mean to the average traveller? Well, a key part of it is likely to be in your pocket – the **euro** (see box, p.49) is the currency of seventeen EU countries, and the remainder (apart from the notable exceptions of Britain, Denmark and Sweden) are likely to adopt it once their economies are ready. You'll also find your passport gathering dust as there are no internal border controls between many countries (most of those using the euro plus Switzerland) – although you should carry ID for random checks. If you run into trouble dial ⓣ112 – the universal EU emergency number. If you're lucky enough to hold an EU passport, the continent really begins to open up: you can work, study, shop, receive free healthcare and even take your pet wherever you like across the member states.

advance: as an example, current Eurolines fares from London's Victoria Coach Station to Paris or Amsterdam start at £29 for a one-way ticket or £39 for a return booked at least seven days in advance. Connecting services from elsewhere in Great Britain add £15 each way to the price of the ticket. Eurolines also has **Minipass** return tickets from London to two or more European cities, valid for ninety days. Alternatively, you might consider their fifteen-, thirty- and forty-day passes, or one of the various passes offered by Busabout for their services around the continent (see p.37).

By ferry

There are numerous ferry services between Britain and Ireland, and between the British Isles and the European mainland. Ferries from the southeast of Ireland and the south coast of England connect with northern France and Spain; those from Kent in southeast England reach northern France and Belgium; those from Scotland and the east coast and northeast of England cross the North Sea to Belgium, the Netherlands, Germany and Scandinavia.

Ferry operators

Brittany Ferries UK ⓣ0871/244 0744, ⓦwww.brittany-ferries.co.uk; Ireland ⓣ021/427 7801, ⓦwww.brittanyferries.ie. Cork to Roscoff (April–Oct); Portsmouth to Caen, Cherbourg, St Malo, Bilbao and Santander; Poole to Cherbourg; Plymouth to Roscoff and Santander.

Condor Ferries UK ⓣ0845/609 1024, ⓦwww.condorferries.co.uk. Portsmouth to Cherbourg; Portsmouth, Poole and Weymouth to St Malo via Jersey and Guernsey.

DFDS Seaways UK ⓣ0871/522 9955, ⓦwww.dfdsseaways.co.uk. Harwich to Esbjerg (Denmark); Newcastle to Amsterdam; Dover to Dunkerque.

Irish Ferries UK ⓣ0870/517 1717, ⓦwww.irishferries.com; Ireland ⓣ0818/300 400, ⓦwww.directferries.ie. Dublin to Holyhead; Rosslare to Pembroke, Cherbourg (March–Dec) and Roscoff (May–Sept).

LD Lines UK ⓣ0844/576 8836, ⓦwww.ldlines.co.uk. Portsmouth to Le Havre.

Norfolkline UK ⓣ0844/847 5042 (Dover–Dunkerque), ⓣ0844/499 0007 (Irish Sea); Ireland ⓣ01/819 2999, ⓦwww.norfolkline.com. Dover to Dunkerque; Belfast and Dublin to Birkenhead.

P&O Ferries UK ⓣ0871/664 5645, ⓦwww.poferries.com. Hull to Zeebrugge and Rotterdam; Dover to Calais; Larne to Cairnryan and Troon (March–Oct); Dublin to Liverpool.

SeaFrance UK ⓣ0871/423 7119, ⓦwww.seafrance.com. Dover to Calais.

Stena Line UK ⓣ0870/570 7070, ⓦwww.stenaline.co.uk; Ireland ⓣ01/204 7777, ⓦwww.stenaline.ie. Harwich to Hook of Holland; Rosslare to Fishguard; Dun Laoghaire and Dublin to Holyhead; Belfast to Stranraer.

Superfast Ferries UK ⓣ0870/420 1267, ⓦwww.superfast.ferries.org. Rosyth to Zeebrugge.

Transeuropa Ferries UK ⓣ01843/595522, ⓦwww.transeuropaferries.com. Ramsgate-Ostend.

Transmanche Ferries UK ⓣ0800/917 1201, ⓦwww.transmancheferries.com. Newhaven to Dieppe.

FROM THE US

From the US the best deals are generally from the main hubs such as New York, Washington DC and Chicago to London. Fixed-date advance-purchase tickets for midweek travel to London cost around US$595 in low season (roughly speaking, winter), US$890 in high season (summer, Christmas and Easter) from New York and Washington DC, US$800/1170 from Chicago. A more flexible ticket will set you back around US$1900 out of New York, US$2200 out of Chicago. Fixed-date advance-purchase alternatives include New York to Paris for US$700/1270, US$800/1050 to Frankfurt, US$700/1060 to Madrid, or US$800/1500 to Athens; flying from Chicago, discounted tickets can be had at US$600/1200 to Paris, US$650/1230 to Frankfurt, US$660/1100 to Madrid, or US$900/1500 to Athens. There are promotional offers from time to time, especially in the off-peak seasons; Virgin Atlantic, for example, sometimes has very cheap New York–London fares in late winter with no advance purchase necessary.

From the west coast the major airlines fly at least three times a week and up to twice daily from Los Angeles, San Francisco and Seattle to the main European cities. Flexible economy-class tickets from LA to London will set you back at least US$2800 in high season. If you can buy your tickets in advance and don't need flexibility, you can get to London or Paris for US$780/1320 (low/high season), to Frankfurt for US$660/1180, to Madrid for US$750/1180, or to Athens for US$1200/1700.

FROM CANADA

Most of the big airlines fly to the major European hubs from Montréal and Toronto at least once daily (three times a week for smaller airlines). From Toronto, London is your cheapest option, with the lowest direct round-trip fare around Can$700/940. For a flexible economy-class ticket on the same route, you're looking at around Can$3300. Fares from Montréal to Paris start at Can$700/850. Vancouver and Calgary have daily flights to several European cities, with round-trip fares to London from around Can$920/1440, depending on the season.

FROM AUSTRALIA AND NEW ZEALAND

There are flights from Melbourne, Sydney, Adelaide, Brisbane and Perth to most European capitals, with not a great deal of difference in the fares to the busiest destinations: a return from Sydney to London, Paris, Rome, Madrid, Athens or Frankfurt should be available through travel agents for around Aus$2400 in low season (Australia's summer, Europe's winter) and slightly higher in high season (though you can sometimes get great deals). A one-way ticket costs slightly more than half that, while a return flight from Auckland, Wellington or Christchurch to Europe is approximately NZ$2150 in low season and from around NZ$2700 in high season. Asian airlines often work out cheapest, and may throw in a stopover. Some agents may also offer "open jaw" tickets, flying you into one city and out from another, which needn't even be in the same country. For RTW deals and other low-price tickets, the most reliable operator is STA Travel (see "Agents and operators" below), which also supply packages with companies such as Contiki and Busabout, can issue rail passes, and advise on visa regulations – for a fee they'll even do all the paperwork for you.

FROM SOUTH AFRICA

Many major airlines fly from Johannesburg and Cape Town to a number of European hubs. Flights from Johannesburg cost about ZAR7400 to Frankfurt, and around ZAR7700 to Paris; and slightly more from Cape Town. BA fly direct to London from Johannesburg or Cape Town for a similar price. You might also try flying via the Gulf with Emirates or Etihad.

AGENTS AND OPERATORS

ebookers UK ⓣ020/3320 3320, ⓦwww.ebookers.com; Republic of Ireland ⓣ01/4311 311, ⓦwww.ebookers.ie. Low fares on an extensive selection of scheduled flights to Europe.

North South Travel UK ⓣ01245/608 291, ⓦwww.northsouthtravel.co.uk. Discounted fares worldwide. Profits are used to support projects in the developing world, especially the promotion of sustainable tourism.
STA Travel UK ⓣ0871/230 0040; US ⓣ1-800/781-4040; Australia ⓣ134 STA; New Zealand ⓣ0800/474 400; South Africa ⓣ0861/781781, ⓦwww.statravel.com. Worldwide specialists in independent and student travel; also student IDs, travel insurance, car rental, rail passes, and more.
Trailfinders UK ⓣ0845/058 5858; Republic of Ireland ⓣ01/677 7888; Australia ⓣ1300/780 212, ⓦwww.trailfinders.com. One of the best-informed and most efficient agents for independent travellers.
USIT Republic of Ireland ⓣ01/602 1906, Northern Ireland ⓣ028/9032 7111, ⓦwww.usit.ie. Ireland's main student and youth travel specialists.

Getting around

It's easy to travel in Europe, and a number of special deals and passes can make it fairly economical too, especially for students and those under 26. Air links are extensive and, thanks to the growing number of budget airlines, flying is often cheaper than taking the train, but you'll appreciate the diversity of Europe best at ground level, by way of its enormous and generally efficient web of rail, road and ferry connections.

BY TRAIN

Trains are generally the best way to tour Europe. The rail network in most countries is comprehensive and the continent boasts some of the world's most scenic rail journeys. Costs are relatively low, too – apart from Britain, where prices can be absurdly steep – as trains are heavily subsidized, and prices are brought down further by passes and discount cards. We've covered the various passes here, as well as the most important international routes and most useful addresses; frequencies and journey times are given throughout the guide.

During the summer, especially if you're travelling at night or a long distance, it's best to make **reservations** whenever you can; on some trains (TGV services, for example) it's compulsory. See our "Extra rail charges" box for more on supplements.

If you intend to do a lot of rail travel, the **Thomas Cook European Timetable** (ⓦwww.thomascookpublishing.com) is an essential investment, detailing the main lines throughout Europe, as well as ferry connections, and is updated monthly. Online, ⓦwww.bahn.de is the best resource, with comprehensive domestic and international rail listings across Europe, while ⓦwww.seat61.com is another excellent source of information.

Finally, whenever you board an international train in Europe, check the route of the car you are in, since trains frequently split, with different carriages going to different destinations.

Europe-wide rail passes

InterRail

InterRail passes have long been synonymous with young European backpackers travelling across the continent on the cheap. There are two types of pass available: the **Global Pass** and **One Country Pass**. Both can be bought direct from ⓦwww.interrailnet.com and from main stations and international rail agents in all thirty countries covered by the scheme. To qualify, you need to have been resident in one of the participating countries for six months or more. The only countries in this book not covered by

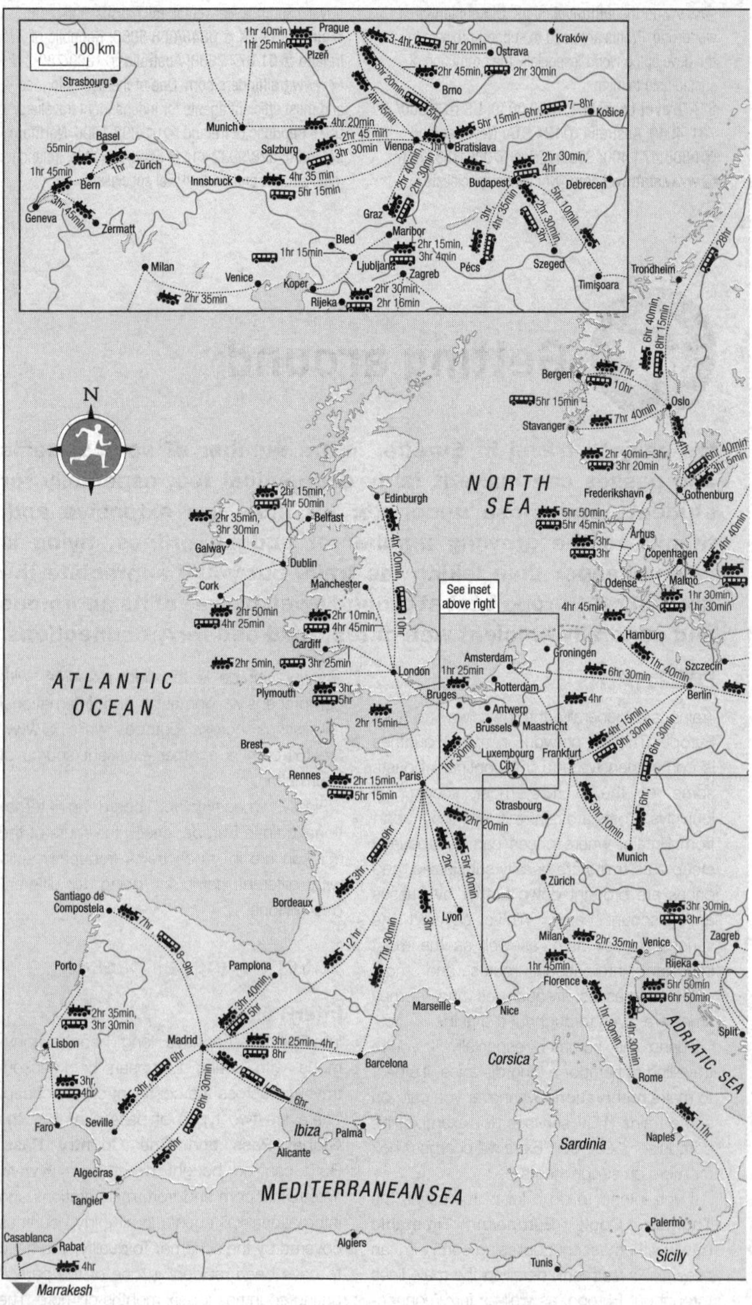

See inset above right
ATLANTIC OCEAN
NORTH SEA
MEDITERRANEAN SEA
ADRIATIC SEA
Corsica
Sardinia
Sicily
Ibiza
Marrakesh

Nordkapp
Tromsø
14hr
Rovaniemi
10hr 20min
13hr 25min
Joensuu
4hr 40min
7hr 10min
3hr 40min
9hr
St Petersburg
2hr,
2hr 30min
Turku
Helsinki
7hr
Stockholm
Tallinn
12–14hr
4–8hr
8hr 30min
BALTIC SEA
10hr
18hr
15hr 45min
5hr
16hr,
17hr
Moscow
Riga
7hr
5hr
35min
1hr
Vilnius
Gdánsk
Minsk
5hr
6hr
5hr 25min
6hr
Warsaw
3hr 10min
6hr
Kiev
Kraków
See inset above left
7hr 20min
Timişoara
8hr 30min–9hr 30min
7–10hr
5–6 hr
Banja Luka
Belgrade
8hr
9hr 15min
5hr
5hr
Bucharest
BLACK SEA
9hr 15min
Sarajevo
8hr
7hr
Varna
3hr,
3hr 30min
Mostar
Sofia
6–7hr,
Burgas
Podgorica
5hr 30min
Dubrovnik
Shkodra
2hr 30min
2hr
Plovdiv
3hr 30min
Skopje
Tirana
3–5hr
3hr
İstanbul
5hr 45min
5hr 30min
6hr 40min
Bitola
Pogradeci
Thessaloníki
6hr 30min
2hr
5hr
Ankara
4hr 15min–6hr,
6hr
7–8hr
Corfu
AEGEAN SEA
11hr
Athens
İzmir
7hr
Antalya
Tbilisi
Yerevan
0
500 km
0
100 km
Groningen
40min,
2–3hr
Amsterdam
2hr 20min,
4hr 12min
Rotterdam
2hr
2hr 35min
Bruges
Antwerp
1hr
Brussels
1hr
30min
Maastricht
3hr
Luxembourg City
JOURNEY TIMES BY TRAIN & BUS

EXTRA RAIL CHARGES

Note that even if you've bought an InterRail or Eurail pass, you will still need to pay extra charges or supplements to travel on many high-speed trains (such as Eurostar, TGV and AVE), night trains and those on special scenic routes. Even where there is in theory no supplement, there's often a compulsory reservation fee, which may cost you double if you only find out about it once you're on the train. For details of charges check the InterRail website under "special trains" or "supplements". You can often avoid these charges if you plan your journey within domestic networks.

the scheme are Albania, Andorra, Estonia, Latvia, Lithuania, Morocco and Russia.

InterRail Global Pass The daddy of all rail passes, offering access to almost the entire European rail network. You can choose between five different time periods – continuous blocks of 15 or 22 days or one month – or set amounts of travel – either five days within ten days or ten days within 22 days. Youth (under-26) passes valid for second-class travel start from €169/£150 for five days up to €409/£362 for a month. Note that you cannot use the pass in the country in which you bought it although discounts of up to fifty percent are usually available.

InterRail One Country Pass Same principle as the Global Pass but valid for just one country (or the Benelux zone of Belgium, the Netherlands and Luxembourg). Time periods and prices vary depending on the country. A three-day second-class youth pass will set you back €34/£31 in Bulgaria, €119/£106 in Spain and €134/£119 in France.

Eurail

Non-European residents aren't eligible for InterRail passes. For them the Eurail scheme (ⓦwww.eurailtravel.com) offers a range of passes giving unlimited travel in twenty-five European countries. There are four types of pass – the **Global Pass**, **Select Pass**, **Regional Pass** and **One Country Pass**, all of which should be bought outside Europe. Apart from some One Country passes, all are available at discounted youth (25 or younger) rates for second-class travel and saver rates for adults travelling in groups.

Eurail Global Pass A single pass valid for travel in 22 countries: Austria, Belgium, Bulgaria, Croatia, Czech Republic, Denmark, Finland, France, Germany, Greece, Hungary, Ireland, Italy, Luxembourg, the Netherlands, Norway, Portugal, Romania, Slovenia, Spain, Sweden and Switzerland. There are seven different time periods available from ten days' travel within two months, up to three months' continuous travel. Prices start at €345/US$449 for a youth pass valid for fifteen days.

Eurail Select Pass Allows you to select three, four or five bordering countries out of the 22 countries above plus Montenegro and Serbia. Prices start at €218/US$305 for a three-country youth pass valid for five days' travel within two months.

Eurail Regional Pass Allows travel within two bordering countries. Prices depend on the country combination; for example an Austria–Czech Republic youth pass valid for five days' travel in two months will cost you €122/US$195 whereas the same period for Germany–Switzerland costs €224/US$289.

Eurail One Country Pass Offers travel within one of the following seventeen countries (or the Benelux zone of Belgium, the Netherlands and Luxembourg): Austria, Croatia, Czech Republic, Denmark, Finland, Greece, Hungary, Ireland, Italy, the Netherlands, Norway, Poland, Portugal, Romania, Slovenia, Spain and Sweden. Prices vary depending on the size of the country and whether youth passes are available: for example a youth pass in Denmark valid for three days' travel costs €69/US$95; the same time period costs €163/US$229 in Spain where special youth passes are not available.

Regional rail passes

In addition to the InterRail and Eurail schemes there are a few regional rail passes which can be good value if you're doing a lot of travelling within one area; we've listed some of the main ones below. National rail passes (apart from InterRail and Eurail) are covered in the relevant chapter of the Guide.

Balkan Flexipass Offers unlimited first-class-only travel through Bulgaria, Greece, Macedonia, Serbia, Montenegro, Romania and Turkey. Prices start at US$270 (youth US$161) for five days' travel in one month.

Brit Rail Pass ⓦ**www.britrail.com.** Allows unlimited travel in Britain, Northern Ireland and the Republic of Ireland. Prices start from US$445 for five days' standard-class travel in one month.

European East Pass Gives five days' travel in a month in Austria, the Czech Republic, Hungary, Poland and Slovakia for US$228, plus up to five additional days at US$31 each.

Rail contacts

UK

European Rail ⓣ020/7619 1083, ⓦwww.europeanrail.com. Independent specialists for continental rail travel.

Eurostar ⓣ0870/518 6186, ⓦwww.eurostar.com. UK to France and Belgium.

International Rail ⓣ0870/084 1410, ⓦwww.international-rail.com. Global rail specialist.

InterRail ⓦwww.interrailnet.com. Main website for buying InterRail passes.

The Man in Seat 61 ⓦwww.seat61.com. Comprehensive informational site set up by a rail enthusiast.

Rail Europe ⓣ0844/848 4064, ⓦwww.raileurope.co.uk. European rail experts.

STA Travel ⓣ0871/230 0040, ⓦwww.statravel.com.

US and Canada

ACP Rail International US & Canada ⓣ1-866-9-EURAIL, ⓦwww.eurail-acprail.com. Eurail agent.

BritRail Travel US & Canada ⓣ1-866-BRITRAIL, ⓦwww.britrail.com. British passes.

Europrail International Canada ⓣ1-888/667-9734, ⓦwww.europrail.net. European and many individual country passes.

Eurail US & Canada ⓦwww.eurail.com.

Flight Centre ⓣ1-866-WORLD-51 (North America only), ⓦwww.flightcentre.com.

Rail Europe US & Canada ⓣ1-800-4-EURAIL, ⓦwww.raileurope.com. Official Eurail agent, with the widest range of regional and one-country passes.

STA Travel ⓣ1-800-781-4040 ⓦwww.statravel.com.

Australia and New Zealand

CIT World Travel Australia ⓣ1300/361 500, ⓦwww.cittravel.com.au. Eurail and Italian rail passes.

Octopus Travel Australia ⓣ1300/727 072; NZ ⓣ0800 450 485, ⓦwww.octopustravel.com/au.

Rail Plus Australia ⓣ03/9642 8644, ⓦwww.railplus.com.au; NZ ⓣ09/377 5415, ⓦwww.railplus.co.nz. Eurail and BritRail passes.

South Africa

Rail Europe ⓣ011/628 2319, ⓦwww.raileurope.co.za. Official distributor for European rail in South Africa.

BY BUS

Long-distance journeys by bus between major European cities are generally slower and less comfortable than by train and – if you have a rail pass – not necessarily cheaper. If you're only travelling to a few places, however, a bus pass or circular bus ticket can undercut a rail pass, especially for over-26s. There's also the option of a bus tour if you're on a tight schedule or simply want everything planned for you.

Eurolines ⓦwww.eurolines-pass.com. Offers the Eurolines pass, valid for travel between 35 cities in sixteen countries. It costs £249/€290 (£289/€345 for over-26s) for fifteen days in high season (late June to mid-Sept as well as Christmas/New Year) and £329/€375 (£389/€455) for 30 days. Prices are around a third lower in low season.

Busabout ⓦwww.busabout.com. Offers a hop-on, hop-off service throughout Western Europe operating May–Oct. There are three "loops" on offer as well as a Flexitrip Pass where you design your own route. Prices start from £365/€408 for a one-loop pass or £319/€357 for the Flexitrip Pass.

Contiki ⓦwww.contiki.com. Long-established operator offering bus tours throughout Europe for 18- to 35-year-olds from three to 46 days. An eleven-day tour from Amsterdam to Barcelona costs £1229/€1375 including hotel accommodation and meals.

BY FERRY

Travelling by ferry is sometimes the most practical way to get around, the obvious routes being from the mainland to the Mediterranean islands, and between the countries bordering the Baltic and Adriatic seas. There are countless routes serving a huge range of destinations, too numerous to outline here; we've given the details of the most useful routes within each chapter. For further details of schedules and operators, see the Thomas Cook European Timetable (see p.33).

BY PLANE

Most European countries now have at least one budget airline selling low-cost flights online, and invariably undercutting train and bus fares on longer international routes. Apart from its environmental impact, travelling by air means you miss the scenery and "feel" for a country that ground-level transport can provide; there's also the inconvenience of getting between airports and the cities they serve, often quite a haul in itself. But, if you're pressed for time, and especially if you want to get from one end of Europe to another, flying is definitely an option. See p.30 for a selective list of budget airlines.

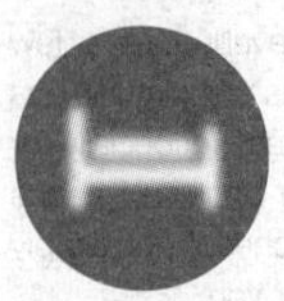

Accommodation

Although accommodation is one of the key costs to consider when planning your trip, it needn't be a stumbling block to a budget-conscious tour of Europe. Indeed, even in Europe's pricier destinations the hostel system means there is always an affordable place to stay. If you're prepared to camp, you can get by on very little while staying at some excellently equipped sites.

The one rule of thumb is that in the most popular cities and resorts – Venice, Amsterdam, Prague, Paris, Barcelona, the Algarve, and so on – things can get very busy during the peak summer months. Be sure to book in advance regardless of your budget.

HOSTELS

The cheapest places to stay around Europe are the innumerable hostels that cover the continent. There is a large number of good-quality independent hostels in most major cities, though the majority of establishments are members of Hostelling International (HI), which incorporates the national youth hostel associations of every country in the world. Most are clean, well-run places, always offering dormitory accommodation, and often a range of private single and double rooms, or rooms with four to six beds. Many hostels also either have self-catering facilities or provide low-cost meals, and the larger ones have a range of other facilities – a swimming pool and a games room for example. There is usually no age limit, but where there is limited space priority is given to those under 26. The best rates are usually available online, on the hostel website or through booking engines such as Hostelworld (Ⓦwww.hostelworld.com) or Hostelbookers (Ⓦwww.hostelbookers.com).

Strictly speaking, to use an HI hostel you have to have membership, although if there's room you can stay at most hostels by simply paying a bit extra. If you do plan to stay in hostels, however, it's certainly worth joining, which you can do through your home country's hostelling association. HI hostels can usually be booked through their country's hostelling association website, almost always over the counter at other hostels in the same country, and often through the international HI website Ⓦwww.hihostels.com. Alternatively try Ⓦwww.hostels.com or Ⓦwww.hostelz.com, which also offer non-HI-affiliated hostels.

Youth hostel associations

US and Canada

Hostelling International-American Youth Hostels Ⓦwww.hiayh.org.
Hostelling International Canada Ⓦwww.hihostels.ca.

UK and Ireland

Youth Hostels Association (YHA) England and Wales Ⓣ01629/592700, Ⓦwww.yha.org.uk.
Scottish Youth Hostels Association Ⓣ01786/891400, Ⓦwww.syha.org.uk.
Irish Youth Hostel Association Republic of Ireland Ⓣ01/830 4555, Ⓦwww.anoige.ie.
Hostelling International Northern Ireland Ⓣ028/9032 4733, Ⓦwww.hini.org.uk.

ACCOMMODATION PRICES

All accommodation prices listed are for high season. The prices we list for hotels, guesthouses, B&Bs, *pensions* and private rooms are for the cheapest double room. For hostels, it is the price of the cheapest dorm bed, and for campsites the cost of a night's stay per person, except where noted.

Australia, New Zealand and South Africa

Australia Youth Hostels Association Ⓦwww.yha.com.au.
Youth Hostelling Association New Zealand Ⓣ0800/278 29, Ⓦwww.yha.co.nz.
Hostelling International South Africa Ⓦwww.hihostels.com.

HOTELS AND PENSIONS

With hotels you can really spend as much or as little as you like. Most hotels in Europe are graded on some kind of star system. One- and two-star category hotels are plain and simple on the whole, usually family-run, and rooms often lack private facilities; sometimes breakfast won't be included. In three-star hotels rooms will nearly always be en suite, prices will normally include breakfast and there may well be a phone or TV in the room; while four- and five-star places will certainly have all these, plus swimming pool, and other such niceties. In the really top-level places breakfast, oddly enough, isn't always included.

Obviously prices vary greatly, but you're rarely going to be paying less than £25/US$35 for a basic double room even in southern Europe, while in the Netherlands the average price is around £50/US$70, and in Scandinavia and the British Isles somewhat higher than that. In some countries a *pension* or B&B (also variously known as a guesthouse, *pensão*, *Gasthaus* or numerous other names) is a cheaper alternative, offering just a few rooms of simple accommodation. In some countries these advertise with a sign in the window; in others they can be booked through the tourist office, which may demand a small fee. There are various other kinds of accommodation – apartments, farmhouses, cottages, *gîtes* in France, and more – but most are geared to longer-term stays and we have detailed them only where relevant.

CAMPING

The **cheapest** form of accommodation is, of course, a campsite, either pitching your own tent or parking your caravan or camper van. Most sites charge per person, with additional charges per plot and/or per vehicle. Facilities can be excellent, especially in countries such as France where camping is very popular, though of course the better the facilities, the pricier the site. If you don't have a vehicle you should add in the cost and inconvenience of getting to the site, since most are on the outskirts of towns, sometimes further. Some sites also have cabins, which you can stay in for a little extra, although these are usually fairly basic affairs, only really worth considering in regions like Scandinavia where budget options are thin on the ground. Tourist offices can often recommend well-equipped and conveniently located sites.

As for **camping rough**, it's a fine idea if you can get away with it – though perhaps an entire trip of rough camping is in reality too gruelling to be truly enjoyable. In some countries it's easy – in parts of Scandinavia it's a legal right, and in Greece and other southern European countries you can usually find a bit of beach to pitch down on – but in others it can get you into trouble with the law.

COUCHSURFING

Couchsurfing (Ⓦwww.couchsurfing.com) is an internet-based hospitality service offering travellers the chance to stay for free with local people. Hosts are verified through references and a vouching system but you should obviously think carefully about whom you are prepared to stay with and have a backup plan if things don't work out (there are plenty of safety tips detailed on their website). There are now almost three million couchsurfer members. Many sites have tried to piggyback on this trend, but few are as popular – one worth checking out though is Room FT (Ⓦwww.roomft.com).

Camping carnets

If you're planning to do a lot of camping, an **international camping carnet**, which gives discounts on member sites, is a good investment. In the US and Canada the carnet is available from home motoring organizations, or from Family Campers and RVers (FCRV; ⓣ1-800/245-9755, ⓦwww.fcrv.org). In the UK and Ireland, the carnet costs £5.50, and is available to members of the AA in Ireland or the RAC in the UK, or for members only from the Camping and Caravanning Club (ⓣ084/5130 7632, ⓦwww.campingandcaravanningclub.co.uk; annual membership £39).

Festivals and annual events

There's always some event or other happening in Europe, and the bigger shindigs can be reason enough for visiting a place. Be warned, though, that if you're intending to visit a place during its annual festival you need to plan well in advance; accommodation can be booked up months beforehand, especially for the most famous events. For a complete guide to world festivals check out ⓦworldparty.roughguides.com.

FESTIVAL CALENDAR

Many of the festivals and annual events you'll come across in Europe have their origin in – and in many cases still represent – religious celebrations, commemorating a local miracle or saint's day. Others are decidedly more secular – from film and music festivals to street carnivals. The following are some of the biggest celebrations, further information on which can be found online or at local tourist offices.

January

Twelfth Night (Jan 6) Rather than Christmas Day, in Spain this is the time for present-giving, while in Orthodox Eastern Europe, Jan 6 is Christmas Day.
La Tamborrada, San Sebastián, Spain (Jan 20) Probably the loudest festival you will encounter as scores of drummers take to the streets of San Sebastián.

February

Berlin Film Festival, Germany (early to mid-Feb) Home of the Golden Bear award, this film bash is geared towards the general public.
Carnival/Mardi Gras (mid-Feb) Celebrated most famously in Venice, but there are smaller events across Europe, notably in Viareggio (Italy), Luzern and Basel (Switzerland), Cologne (Germany), Maastricht (Netherlands) and tiny Binche (Belgium).

March

Las Fallas, Valencia, Spain (March 15–19) The passing of winter is celebrated in explosive fashion with enormous bonfires, burning effigies and plenty of all-night partying.
St Patrick's Day (March 17) Celebrated wherever there's an Irish community, in Dublin it's a five-day festival with music, parades and a lot of drinking.

April

Easter Celebrated with most verve and ceremony in Catholic and Orthodox Europe, where Easter Sunday or Monday is usually marked with some sort of procession; note that the Orthodox Church's Easter can fall a week or two either side of the Western festival.
Feria de Abril, Seville, Spain (mid-April) A week of flamenco music and dancing, parades and bullfights, in a frenzied and enthusiastic atmosphere.
Queen's Day, Amsterdam, Netherlands (April 30) Queen Beatrix's official birthday is the excuse for this anarchic 24-hour drinking and dressing-up binge – remember your orange attire.

May

Cannes Film Festival, France (mid/late May) The world's most famous cinema festival is really more of an industry affair than anything else.
PinkPop Festival, Landgraaf, Netherlands (late May/early June) Holland's biggest pop music festival.

June

Festa do São João, Porto, Portugal (June 23–24) Portugal's second city puts on the mother of all street parties, culminating in revellers hitting each other with plastic hammers.
Glastonbury Festival, England (mid/late June) Despite being one of Europe's largest (most expensive) music festivals, Glastonbury is a surprisingly intimate affair thanks to its beautiful setting and hippie vibe.
Roskilde Festival, Denmark (late June/early July) An eclectic range of music (rock, dance, folk) and performance arts, with profits going to worthy causes.

July

The Palio, Siena, Italy (July 2 & Aug 16) Italy's most spectacular annual event: a bareback horse race between representatives of the different quarters of the city around the main square.
Exit Festival, Novi Sad, Serbia (early July) Europe's hippest music festival held in a beautiful fortress and attracting top DJs and artists from around the world.
Montreux Jazz Festival, Switzerland (early July) These days only loosely committed to jazz, this festival takes in everything from folk to breakbeats.
Fiesta de San Fermín, Pamplona, Spain (July 6–14) Anarchic fun, centred on the running of the bulls through the streets of the city, plus music, dancing and of course a lot of drinking.
Avignon Festival, France (early/mid-July) Slanted towards drama but hosts plenty of other events too.
Dubrovnik Summer Festival, Croatia (July & Aug) A host of musical events and theatre performances against the backdrop of the town's beautiful Renaissance centre.
The Proms, London (July–Sept) World-famous concert series that maintains high standards of classical music at egalitarian prices.

August

Edinburgh Festival, Scotland (last three weeks of Aug) A mass of top-notch and fringe events in every performing medium, from rock to cabaret to modern experimental music, dance and drama.
Locarno Film Festival, Switzerland (early Aug) Movies from around the world compete on the banks of Lake Maggiore.
La Tomatina, Buñol, Spain The last Wednesday in August sees the streets of Buñol packed for a one-hour food fight disposing of 130,000 kilos of tomatoes.
Notting Hill Carnival, London (last weekend of Aug) Predominantly Black British and Caribbean celebration that's become the world's second biggest street carnival after Rio.
Ramadan (July/Aug in 2012 & 2013) Commemorating the revelation of the Koran to the Prophet Mohammed, the month of fasting from sunrise until sunset ends with a huge celebration called Eid el-Fitr. Morocco, Turkey, Kosovo, Albania, Bosnia-Herzegovina, plus Muslim areas of Bulgaria and Greece.

September

Ibiza Closing Parties, Spain (first week in Sept) The summer dance music Mecca goes out with a bang in September with all the main clubs holding closing parties.
Venice Film Festival, Italy (first 2 weeks in Sept) First held in 1932, this is the world's oldest film festival.
Regata Storica, Venice, Italy (early Sept) A trial of skill for the city's gondoliers.
Oktoberfest, Munich, Germany (final 2 weeks of Sept) A huge beer festival and fair, attracting vast numbers of people to consume gluttonous quantities of beer and food.
Galway International Oyster Festival, Ireland (last weekend in Sept) The arrival of the oyster season is celebrated with a three-day seafood, Guinness and dancing shindig.

October

Combat des Reines, Switzerland (mid-Oct) Quirky cow-fighting contest held to decide the queen of the herd in the Valais region of Switzerland. The main event is the copious drinking and betting on the sidelines (and no, the cows don't get hurt).
Mondial du Snowboard, Les Deux Alpes, France (last weekend in Oct) World-class boarders and plenty of hangers-on kick off the snow season at this beautiful Alpine resort.

November

Bonfire Night, Lewes, England (Nov 5) Huge processions and tremendous fireworks light up this sleepy town every year.

Madonna della Salute Festival, Venice, Italy (Nov 21) Annual candlelit procession across the Grand Canal to the church of the Santa Maria della Salute.

December

Christmas Festive markets sprout up across the continent in the run-up to Christmas. One of the best is found in Cologne, Germany.

New Year's Eve Celebrated with fireworks and parties across Europe, it's probably best experienced in Edinburgh where over a hundred thousand cram the streets for Hogmanay.

Work and study

The best way of getting to know a country properly is to work there and learn the language. Study opportunities are also a good way of absorbing yourself in the local culture, though they invariably need to be fixed up in advance; check newspapers for ads or contact one of the organizations listed opposite.

WORKING IN EUROPE

There are any number of jobs you can pick up on the road to supplement your spending money. It's normally not hard to find bar or restaurant work, especially in large resort areas during the summer, and your chances will be greater if you speak the local language – although being able to speak English may be your greatest asset in more touristy areas. **Cleaning jobs**, **nannying** and **au pair** work are also common, if not spectacularly well paid, often just providing room and board plus pocket money. Some of them can be organized on the spot, while others need to be arranged before you leave home.

The other big casual earner is farm work, particularly **grape-picking**, an option from August to October when the vines are being harvested. The best country for this is France, but there's sometimes work in Germany too, and you're unlikely to be asked for documentation. Also in France, along the Côte d'Azur, and in other yacht-havens such as Greece and parts of southern Spain, there is sometimes crewing work available, though you'll obviously need the appropriate experience.

Rather better paid, and equally widespread, if only during the September to June period, is **teaching** English as a foreign language (TEFL), though it's sometimes hard to find English-teaching jobs without a TEFL qualification. You'll normally be paid a liveable local salary, sometimes with somewhere to live thrown in, and you can often supplement your income with more lucrative private lessons. The TEFL teaching season is reversed in Britain and to a lesser extent Ireland, with plenty of work available during the summer in London and on the English south coast (but again, some kind of TEFL qualification is usually required).

A final tip for those hoping to work abroad: buy a book dedicated to the subject. We recommend those published in the UK by Vacation Work; visit Ⓦwww.crimsonpublishing.co.uk for their catalogue. Travel magazines like Wanderlust (Ⓦwww.wanderlust.co.uk) have a Job Shop section which often advertises job opportunities with tour companies, while Ⓦwww.studyabroad.com is a useful website with listings and links to study and work programmes worldwide.

STUDYING IN EUROPE

Studying abroad invariably means learning a language, in an intensive course that lasts between two weeks and three months, and staying with a local family. There are plenty of places you can do this, and you should reckon on paying around £300/US$500 a week, including room and board. If you know a language well, you could also apply to do a short course in another subject at a local university; scan the classified sections of the newspapers back home, and keep an eye out when you're on the spot. The EU runs a programme called Erasmus in which university students from Britain and Ireland can obtain mobility grants to study in one of 32 European countries for between three months and a full academic year if their university participates in the programme. Check with your university's international relations office, or see Ⓦwww.britishcouncil.org/erasmus.

Work and study contacts

AFS Intercultural Programs US Ⓣ1-800/AFS-INFO, international enquiries Ⓣ+1-212/352-9810; Ⓦwww.afs.org. Global UN-recognized organization running summer programmes to foster international understanding.

American Institute for Foreign Study UK Ⓣ020/7581 7300, US Ⓣ1-866/906-2437; Ⓦwww.aifs.com. Language study and cultural immersion for the summer or school year.

ASSE International UK Ⓣ01952/460 733, US Ⓣ1-800/677-2773, Canada Ⓣ1-800/361-3214, Australia Ⓣ03/9775 4711; Ⓦwww.asse.com. International student exchanges and summer language programmes across most of Europe.

Association for International Practical Training US Ⓣ410/997-2200, Ⓦwww.aipt.org. Summer internships in various European countries for students who have completed at least two years of college in science, agriculture, engineering or architecture.

British Council UK Ⓣ0161/957 7775, Ⓦwww.britishcouncil.org. The Council's Recruitment Group recruits TEFL teachers with degrees and TEFL qualifications for posts, while its Education and Training Group runs teacher exchange programmes and enables those who already work as educators to find out about teacher development programmes abroad.

Council on International Educational Exchange (CIEE) US Ⓣ1-800/40-STUDY, Ⓦwww.ciee.org/study. An international organization worth contacting for advice on studying, working and volunteering in Europe. They run summer-semester and one-year study programmes, and volunteer projects.

International House UK Ⓣ020/7611 2400, Ⓦwww.ihlondon.com. Reputable English-teaching organization that offers TEFL training leading to a Certificate in English Language Teaching to Adults (CELTA), and recruits for teaching positions in Britain and abroad.

World Learning US Ⓣ1-800/257-7751, Ⓦwww.worldlearning.org. The Experiment in International Living (Ⓦwww.experimentinternational.org) has summer programmes for high-school students, while the School for International Training (Ⓦwww.sit.edu/studyabroad) offers accredited college semesters abroad, with language and cultural studies, homestay and other academic work.

Travel essentials

COSTS

It's hard to generalize about what you're likely to spend travelling around Europe, but it's by and large **not cheap**. Some countries – Norway, Switzerland, the UK – are among the most expensive in the world, while in others (Turkey, for example) you can live quite well on a fairly modest budget. Remember, however, that all of Europe is modern and well touristed which means higher prices than in the developing world. In general, countries in the north and west of Europe are more expensive than those in the south and east, though keep an eye on exchange rates.

Accommodation will be your largest single expense, and can really determine where you decide to travel. **Food and drink** costs also vary wildly, although again in most parts of Europe you can assume that a cheap restaurant meal will cost £8–15/US$15–25 a head, with prices nearer the top end of the scale in Scandinavia, at the bottom end in eastern and southern Europe, and below that in Turkey and Morocco. **Transport** costs are something you can pin down more exactly if you have a rail pass. Nowhere, though, are transport costs a major burden, except perhaps in Britain where public transport is less heavily subsidized than elsewhere.

The bottom line for an average daily budget touring the continent – camping, self-catering, hitching, etc – might be around £25/US$35 a day per person. Adding on a rail pass, staying in hostels and eating out occasionally would bring this up to perhaps £40/US$60 a day, while staying in private rooms or hotels and eating out once a day would mean a personal daily budget of at least £60/US$90. See the box opposite for tips on keeping your costs down.

PRICES

At the beginning of each chapter you'll find a guide to "rough costs" including food, accommodation and travel. Prices are quoted in euros for ease of comparison. Within the chapter itself prices are quoted in local currency.

CRIME AND PERSONAL SAFETY

Travelling around Europe should be relatively trouble-free, but, as in any part of the world, there is always the chance of petty theft. Conditions vary greatly depending on the country: in Scandinavia, for example, you're unlikely to encounter much trouble of any kind, whereas in the inner-city areas of metropolises such as London, Paris or Barcelona, the crime rate is significantly higher. Finally, in poorer regions such as Morocco, Turkey and southern Italy, street crime tends to be low, but tourists are an obvious target.

Safety tips

In order to minimize the risks, you should take some basic precautions. First and perhaps most important, try not to look too much like a tourist. Appearing lost, even if you are, is to be avoided, and it's not a good idea – especially in southern Europe – to walk around flashing an obviously expensive camera: the professional bag-snatchers who tour train stations can have your valuables off you in seconds.

Be **discreet** about using a mobile phone, and be **sure** to put it back into a secure pocket as soon as you've finished; be similarly protective of your iPod. If you're waiting for a train, keep your eyes (and hands if necessary) on your bags at all times; if you want to sleep, put everything valuable under whatever you use as a pillow. Exercise caution when choosing a train compartment and avoid any situation that makes you feel uncomfortable. **Padlocking** your bags to the luggage rack if you're on an overnight train increases the likelihood that they'll still be there in the morning. It's also a good idea to wear a **money belt**.

GETTING BY ON A BUDGET

Buy a rail pass. Whether you're planning to take in all of Europe or just a few countries, a rail pass will save you a bundle (see p.36).

Find a roommate. Accommodation in hotels, *pensions* and private rooms is cheaper if you share, so buddy up.

Student/youth discounts. If you're a student or under 26, make sure you bring your student or youth card (see p.50) and always ask about discounts.

Head for the countryside. Don't spend more time than you need to in the city – prices will always be highest.

Shun tourist traps. Eat and drink with the locals and try regional food as it'll usually be cheaper.

Self-cater. Markets are full of fresh, seasonal picnic fare which makes self-catering a treat. Take a water bottle. Water's free to refill, after all.

Drink at home. Have a few drinks before you go out – you can usually pick up beer and wine from local shops at a fraction of the price that you'll pay in bars.

Be flexible. Transport is often cheaper in off-peak hours.

Sleep on the train. Make your longest journeys overnight – you'll forego accommodation costs for the night.

Bargain, bargain, bargain. Don't be afraid to haggle (especially in places like Morocco where it's expected), but know when to stop.

If you're staying in a hostel, take your valuables out with you unless there's a very secure store for them on the premises. It's a good idea to take a photocopy of your passport and send it to your email account, as is leaving a copy of your address book with friends or family. If you're driving, don't leave anything valuable in your parked car.

If the worst happens and you do have something stolen, inform the police immediately (we've included details of the main city police stations – and where relevant dedicated tourist police – in the Guide); the priority is to get a statement from them detailing exactly what has been lost, which you'll need for your insurance claim back home. Generally you'll find the police sympathetic enough, sometimes able to speak English, but often unwilling to do much more than make out a report and give you a reference number.

CUSTOMS

Customs and duty-free restrictions vary throughout Europe, but are standard for travellers arriving in the EU at one litre of spirits, four litres of table wine, plus 200 cigarettes (or 250g tobacco, or fifty cigars). There is no duty-free allowance for travel within the EU: in principle you can carry as much in the way of duty-paid goods as you want, so long as it is for personal use. Note that Andorra, Gibraltar, the Canary Islands and Ceuta are outside the EU for customs purposes. Remember that if you are carrying prescribed drugs of any kind, it might be a good idea to have a copy of the prescription to show to suspicious customs officers. Note also that all EU members restrict the importation from outside Europe of meat, fish, eggs and honey, even for personal consumption.

VISA ALERT!

Everyone needs a visa to visit Russia, which must be obtained in advance, and if you're passing through Belarus to get there, you'll need a transit visa for that country as well. Citizens of most countries also need a visa for Turkey, which is available at the border (see p.1204). South Africans need a visa for most European countries so be sure to check with the appropriate embassy before travelling.

DRUGS

It's hardly necessary to state that drugs such as amphetamines, cocaine, heroin, LSD and ecstasy are **illegal** all over Europe, and although use of cannabis is widespread in most countries, and legally tolerated in some (famously in the Netherlands, for example), you are never allowed to possess more than a tiny amount for personal use, and unlicensed sale remains illegal. Penalties can be severe (in certain countries, such as Turkey, even possession of cannabis can result in a hefty prison sentence) and your consulate is unlikely to be sympathetic.

ELECTRICITY

The supply in Europe is 220v (240v in the British Isles), which means that anything on North American voltage (110v) normally needs a transformer – or at least a plug adapter if the power cord has a built-in transformer. Some countries (notably Spain and Morocco) still have a few places on 110v or 120v, so check before plugging in or you could fry your electronics. British and Irish sockets take three rectangular pins, elsewhere they take two round pins. A travel plug which adapts to these systems is useful to carry. See Ⓦwww.kropla.com for more.

ENTRY REQUIREMENTS

Citizens of the UK (but not other British passport holders), Ireland, Australia, New Zealand, Canada and the US do not need a **visa** to enter most European countries (current exceptions are listed in the box on p.45), and can usually stay for between one and three months, depending on nationality. EU countries never require visas from British or Irish citizens. Always check visa requirements before travelling, as they can and do change; this especially applies to Canadian, Australian, New Zealand and South African citizens intending to visit Eastern European countries.

Twenty-five countries (Austria, Belgium, Czech Republic, Denmark, Estonia, Finland, France, Germany, Greece, Hungary, Iceland, Italy, Latvia, Lithuania, Luxembourg, Malta, the Netherlands, Norway, Poland, Portugal, Slovakia, Slovenia, Spain, Sweden and Switzerland), known as the Schengen group, now have joint visas which are valid for travel in all of them; in theory, there are no immigration controls between these countries, but there may be spot-checks of ID within their borders.

GAY AND LESBIAN TRAVELLERS

Gay men and lesbians will find most of Europe a **tolerant** place in which to travel, the west rather more so than the east. Gay sex is no longer a criminal offence in any country covered by this book except Morocco, but some still have measures that discriminate against gay men (a higher age of consent for example). Lesbianism would seem not to officially exist, so it is not generally subject to such laws. For further information, check the International Lesbian and Gay Association's European region website at Ⓦwww.ilga-europe.org.

HEALTH

You won't encounter many health problems in Europe. You don't need to have inoculations for any of the countries covered in this book, although for Morocco and Turkey typhoid jabs are advised, and in south-eastern Turkey malaria pills are a good idea for much of the year – check Ⓦwww.cdc.gov/travel for full details. Remember to keep your polio and tetanus boosters up to date.

EU citizens are covered by reciprocal health agreements for free or reduced-cost emergency treatment in many of the countries in this book (main exceptions are Albania, Morocco and Turkey). To claim this, you will often be asked for your proof of residence or European Health Insurance Card (EHIC), which you can apply for in Britain at Ⓦwww.dh.gov.uk, and in Ireland at Ⓦwww.ehic.ie. Without an EHIC, you won't be turned away from hospitals but you will almost certainly have to pay for any treatment or medicines. Also, in practice, some doctors and hospitals charge anyway and it's up to you to claim reimbursement when you return home. Make sure you are insured for potential medical expenses, and keep copies of receipts and prescriptions.

Doctors, hospitals and pharmacies

For minor health problems it's easiest to go to a pharmacy, found pretty much everywhere. In major cities there should be at least one pharmacy open 24 hours – check any pharmacy window for a rota indicating the branch currently open all night. In cases of serious injury or illness contact your nearest consulate, which will have a list of English-speaking doctors, as will the local tourist office. In the accounts of larger cities we've listed the most convenient hospital casualty units/emergency rooms.

Contraceptives

Condoms are available everywhere, and are normally reliable international brands such as Durex, at least in northwestern Europe; the condoms in eastern European countries, Morocco and Turkey are of uncertain quality, however, so it's best to bring your own.

AIDS is of course as much of a problem in Europe as in the rest of the world, and it hardly needs saying that unprotected casual sex is extremely dangerous; members of both sexes should carry condoms.

The **pill** is available everywhere, too, though often only on prescription; again, bring a sufficient supply with you. In case of emergency, the morning-after pill is available from pharmacies without a prescription in Belgium, Denmark, Finland, France, Greece, Holland, Morocco, Norway, Poland, Portugal, Sweden, Switzerland and the UK.

Drinking water

Tap water in most countries is **drinkable**, and only needs to be avoided in Morocco and parts of Turkey. Unfamiliar food may well give you a small dose of the runs, but this is usually nothing to worry about, and is normally over in a day or two.

INSURANCE

Wherever you're travelling from, it's a very good idea to have some kind of travel insurance. Before paying for a new policy, however, check whether you're already covered: students will often find that their student health coverage extends into the vacations and for one term beyond the date of last enrolment; and some credit cards include travel insurance.

Otherwise you should contact a specialist travel insurance company. A typical policy usually provides cover for the loss of baggage, tickets and – up to a certain limit – cash or cheques, as well as cancellation or curtailment of your journey. Most of them exclude so-called dangerous sports unless an extra premium is paid: in Europe this can mean anything from scuba-diving to mountaineering, skiing and even bungee-jumping. With medical coverage, you should ascertain whether benefits will be paid as treatment proceeds or only after you return home, and whether there is a 24-hour medical emergency number. When securing baggage cover, make sure that the per-article limit will cover your most valuable possession. If you need to make a claim, you should keep receipts for medicines and medical treatment, and in the event you have anything stolen, you must obtain an official statement from the police.

INTERNET AND EMAIL

Internet cafés are widespread across Europe and in major cities you're likely to find many hotels and cafés offering wireless access (wi-fi or WLAN) for those with laptops or smart phones. Obviously the further you get off the beaten track, the slower connection speeds will become and you may even have to resort to somewhat expensive dial-up access.

LEFT LUGGAGE

Almost every train station of any size has facilities for depositing luggage – either lockers or a desk that's open long hours every day. We've given details in the accounts of the major capitals.

MAIL

We've listed the central post offices in major cities and given an idea of opening hours. Bear in mind, though, that in most countries you can avoid long waits in post offices by buying stamps from newsagents, tobacconists and street kiosks. If you know in advance where you're going to be and when, it is possible to collect letters addressed to you, marked "poste restante" and sent to the main post office in any town or city will be kept under your name – for at least two weeks and usually for a month. When collecting mail, make sure you take your passport for identification, and be aware that there's a possibility of letters being misfiled by someone unfamiliar with your language; try looking under your first name as well as your surname.

NEWSPAPERS

British and American newspapers and magazines are widely available in Europe, sometimes on the day of publication, more often the day after. They do, however, cost around three times as much as they do at home. In addition, locally produced English-language papers are often available in major cities, usually on a weekly or monthly basis. These are often a much more engaging way to get your news fix and learn more about local issues and events.

MAPS

Though you can often buy maps on the spot, you may want to get them in advance to plan your trip – if you know what you want, the best advice is to contact a firm such as Stanfords in the UK (Ⓦwww.stanfords.co.uk) or Rand McNally in the US (Ⓦwww.randmcnally.com); both sell maps online or by mail order. We've recommended the best maps of individual countries throughout the book. If you intend to travel mainly by rail, it might be worth getting the Thomas Cook *Rail Map of Europe*. For extensive motoring, it's better to get a large-page road atlas such as Michelin's *Tourist and Motoring Atlas*.

MONEY

The easiest way to carry your money is in the form of plastic. Hotels, shops and restaurants across the continent accept major credit and debit cards, although cheaper places may not. More importantly, you can use them 24/7 to get cash out of ATMs throughout the region, including Morocco and Turkey, as long as they are affiliated to an international network (such as Visa, MasterCard or Cirrus). In some countries banks are the only places where you can legally change money, and they often offer the best exchange rates and lowest commission. Local banking hours are given throughout this book. Outside normal hours you can use bureaux de change, often located at train stations and airports, though their rates and/or commissions may well be less favourable.

PHONES

It is nearly always possible, especially in Western Europe, to make international calls from a public call box. Otherwise, you can go to a post office, or a special phone bureau, where you can make a call from a private booth and pay afterwards. Most countries have these in one form or another, and tourist offices will point you in the right

THE EURO (€)

The euro is the currency of 17 EU countries (and a couple of others). Coins come as 1c, 2c, 5c, 10c, 20c, 50c, €1 and €2, with one side of the coin stating the denomination while the other side has a design unique to the issuing country. Euro notes come as €5, €10, €20, €50, €100, €200 and €500.

At the time of writing, £1 was worth €1.12, US$1 got you €0.70, Can$1 was €0.72, Aus$1 equalled €0.74, NZ$1 was €0.74 and ZAR1 was €0.10. Check ⓦwww.xe.com for the latest exchange rates.

direction. Avoid using the phone in your hotel room – unless you have money to burn.

To call **any country** in this book from Britain, Ireland, South Africa or New Zealand, dial ⓣ00, then the country code, then the city/area code (if there is one) without the initial zero – except for Russia, Latvia and Lithuania, where an initial 8 is omitted; Italy, where the initial zero must be dialled; and Spain, where the initial 9 must be dialled – then the local number. From the US and most of Canada, the international access code is ⓣ011, from Australia it's ⓣ0011; otherwise the procedure is the same.

To **call home** from almost all European countries, including Morocco and Turkey, dial ⓣ00, then the country code, then the city/area code (without the initial zero if there is one), then the local number. The exception is Russia, where you dial ⓣ8, wait for a continuous dialling tone and then dial ⓣ10, followed by the country code, area code and number.

For **collect calls**, use the "Home Country Direct" service. In the UK and some other countries, international calling cards available from newsagents enable you to call North America, Australia and New Zealand very cheaply. Most North American, British, Irish and Australasian phone companies either allow you to call home on a credit card, or billed to your home number (contact your company's customer services before you leave to find out their toll-free access codes from the countries you'll be visiting), or else will issue an international calling card which can be used worldwide, and for which you will be billed at home. If you want a calling card and do not already have one, leave yourself a few weeks to arrange it before leaving.

MOBILE/CELL PHONES

North American cell phones may not work in Europe – for details contact your provider. Mobiles from the UK, Ireland, Australia and New Zealand and South Africa can be used in most parts of Europe, and a lot of countries – certainly in Western Europe – have nearly universal coverage, but you may have to inform your provider before leaving home to get international access switched on, and you will be charged for receiving calls and even voicemail. Also note that it will not always be possible to charge up or replace your pre-paid cards, so again check beforehand and, if necessary, top up your credit before you leave.

The most useful resource for information on phone codes and electrical systems around the world is ⓦwww.kropla.com.

SHOPPING

Europe is a great place to shop – with outlets running the gamut from the souks of Morocco to the high fashion houses of Paris and Milan you'll be spoilt for choice. We've included country-specific information on shopping in each individual chapter, especially in capital cities. See the chart below for size conversions.

STUDENT AND YOUTH DISCOUNTS

It's worth flashing whichever discount card you've got at every opportunity – you never know what you might get. If you're a student, an **International Student Identity Card** (ISIC for short) is well worth the investment. It can get you reduced (usually half-price, sometimes free) entry to museums and other sights, as well as qualifying you for other discounts in certain cities. It can also save you money on some transport costs, notably ferries. The card costs £9 in the UK, €13 in Ireland, US$22 in the US, Can$20 in Canada, Aus$25 in Australia, NZ$25 in New Zealand and

CLOTHING AND SHOE SIZES

Women's dresses and skirts									
American	4	6	8	10	12	14	16	18	
British	8	10	12	14	16	18	20	22	
Continental	38	40	42	44	46	48	50	52	
Women's blouses and sweaters									
American	6	8	10	12	14	16	18		
British	30	32	34	36	38	40	42		
Continental	40	42	44	46	48	50	52		
Women's shoes									
American	5	6	7	8	9	10	11		
British	3	4	5	6	7	8	9		
Continental	36	37	38	39	40	41	42		
Men's suits									
American	34	36	38	40	42	44	46	48	
British	34	36	38	40	42	44	46	48	
Continental	44	46	48	50	52	54	56	58	
Men's shirts									
American	14	15	15.5	16	16.5	17	17.5	18	
British	14	15	15.5	16	16.5	17	17.5	18	
Continental	36	38	39	41	42	43	44	45	
Men's shoes									
American	7	7.5	8	8.5	9.5	10	10.5	11	11.5
British	6	7	7.5	8	9	9.5	10	11	12
Continental	39	40	41	42	43	44	44	45	46

ZAR110 in South Africa. If you're not a student but under 26, get an International Youth Travel Card, which costs the same and can in some countries give much the same sort of reductions. Both cards are available direct from Ⓦwww.isiccard.com or from youth travel specialists such as STA.

As well as the above options, the EURO<26 youth card entitles anyone under 26 (or up to 30 in some countries) to a wide range of discounts on transport services, tourist attractions, activities and accommodation for up to a year. It is available online for people living outside Europe and at designated outlets throughout the continent (apart from France) for residents – you'll need proof of age and a passport-sized photo. Although the card is valid across the region, prices vary across individual countries (from around €9 to €14), as do the relevant discounts (see Ⓦwww.euro26.org for full details).

TIME

This book covers four time zones (see map opposite). GMT (Greenwich Mean Time), aka UTC, or Universal Time, is five hours ahead of Eastern Standard Time, eight hours ahead of Pacific Standard Time, eight hours behind Western Australia, ten hours behind eastern Australia, twelve hours behind New Zealand and two hours behind South Africa. Note that all countries in this book (except Morocco) have daylight saving time from March to October; thankfully, they usually all manage to change at the same time. This change, along with daylight saving in North America, Australia and New Zealand, can affect the time difference by an hour either way.

TOURIST INFORMATION

Before you leave, it's worth contacting the tourist offices of the countries you're intending to visit for free leaflets, maps and brochures. This is especially true in parts of central and eastern Europe, where up-to-date maps can be harder to find within the country, though note that a few countries do not have any official tourist offices abroad.

Once you're in Europe, on-the-spot information is easy enough to find. Most countries have a network of tourist offices that answer queries, dole out a range of (mostly free) maps and brochures, and can often book accommodation, or at least advise you on it. They're better organized in northern Europe – the UK, Scandinavia, the Netherlands, France, Switzerland – with branches in all but the smallest village, and mounds of information; in Greece, Turkey and eastern Europe you'll find fewer tourist offices and they'll be less helpful on the whole, sometimes offering no more than a couple of dog-eared brochures and a photocopied map. We've given further details, including a broad idea of opening hours, in the introduction for each country.

Tourist information websites

If there is no office in your home country, apply to the embassy instead.

Albania ⓦ www.albaniantourism.com.
Andorra ⓦ www.andorra.ad.
Austria ⓦ www.austria.info.
Belgium ⓦ www.visitbelgium.com.
Bosnia-Herzegovina ⓦ www.bhtourism.ba.
Britain ⓦ www.visitbritain.com.
Bulgaria ⓦ www.bulgariatravel.org.
Croatia ⓦ www.croatia.hr.
Czech Republic ⓦ www.czechtourism.com.
Denmark ⓦ www.visitdenmark.com.
Estonia ⓦ www.visitestonia.com.
Finland ⓦ www.visitfinland.com.
France ⓦ www.franceguide.com.
Germany ⓦ www.germany-tourism.de.
Greece ⓦ www.gnto.gr.
Hungary ⓦ www.hungary.com.
Ireland ⓦ www.discoverireland.com.
Italy ⓦ www.enit.it.
Latvia ⓦ www.latviatourism.lv.
Lithuania ⓦ www.lithuaniatourism.co.uk.
Luxembourg ⓦ www.visitluxembourg.com.

BASICS | TRAVEL ESSENTIALS

Macedonia ⓦ www.exploringmacedonia.com.
Montenegro ⓦ www.visit-montenegro.com.
Morocco ⓦ www.visitmorocco.org.
Netherlands ⓦ www.holland.com.
Norway ⓦ www.visitnorway.com.
Poland ⓦ www.poland.travel.
Portugal ⓦ www.visitportugal.com.
Romania ⓦ www.romaniatourism.com.
Russia UK ⓦ www.visitrussia.org.uk;
US ⓦ www.russia-travel.com.
Serbia ⓦ www.serbia-tourism.org.
Slovenia ⓦ www.slovenia.info.
Spain ⓦ www.tourspain.es.
Sweden ⓦ www.visit-sweden.com.
Switzerland ⓦ www.myswitzerland.com.
Turkey ⓦ www.tourismturkey.org.
Ukraine ⓦ www.ukraine.com

TRAVELLERS WITH DISABILITIES

Prosperous northern Europe is easier for disabled travellers than the south and east, but the gradual enforcement of EU accessibility regulations is making life easier throughout the European Union at least. Wheelchair access to public buildings nonetheless remains far from common in many countries, as is wheelchair accessibility to public transport. Most buses are still inaccessible to wheelchair users, but airport facilities are improving, as are those on cross-Channel ferries. As for rail services, these vary greatly: France, for example, provides well for disabled passengers, as do Belgium, Denmark, Switzerland and Austria, but many other countries make little if any provision. For comprehensive info on disabled travel, check out ⓦ www.disabledtravelers.com.

WOMEN TRAVELLERS

One of the major irritants for women travelling through Europe is sexual harassment, which in Italy, Greece, Turkey, Spain and Morocco especially can be almost constant for women travelling alone. By far the most common kind of harassment you'll come across simply consists of street whistles and catcalls; occasionally it's more sinister and very occasionally it can be dangerous. Indifference is often the best policy, avoiding eye contact with men and at the same time appearing as confident and purposeful as possible. If this doesn't make you feel any more comfortable, shouting a few choice phrases in the local language is a good idea; don't, however, shout in English, which often seems to encourage them. You may also come across gropers on crowded buses and trains, in which case you should complain as loudly as possible in any language – the ensuing scene should be enough to deter your assailant.

Albania

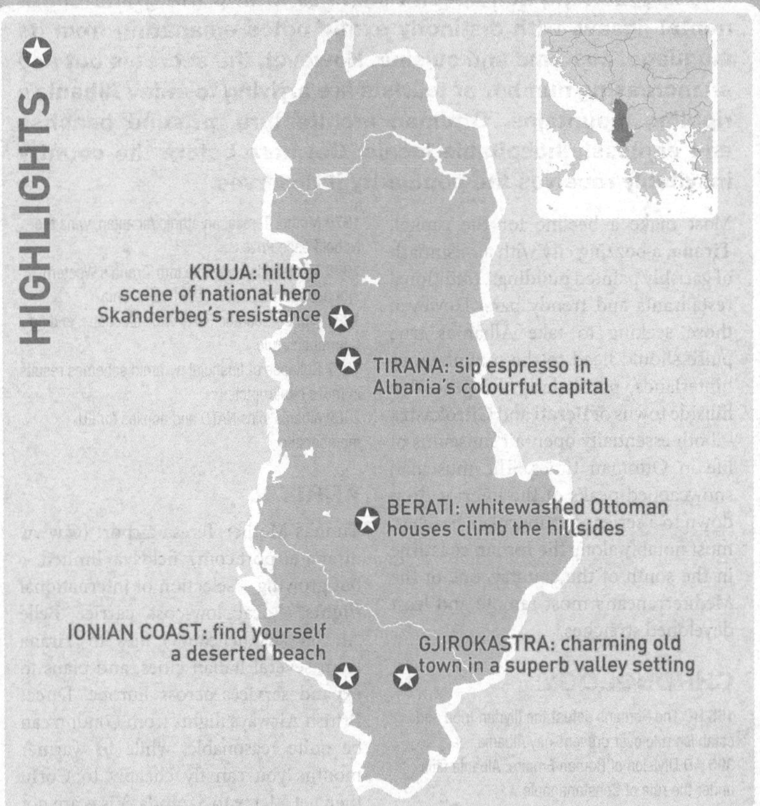

ROUGH COSTS

DAILY BUDGET Basic €20 /occasional treat €35

DRINK Bottle of red €4

FOOD *Qoftë* (lamb rissoles) €2

HOSTEL/BUDGET HOTEL €12/€25

TRAVEL Bus: Tirana–Berati €3.50; train: Tirana–Pogradeci €2

FACT FILE

POPULATION 3.2 million

AREA 28,748 sq km

LANGUAGE Albanian (Shqip)

CURRENCY Lekë

CAPITAL Tirana (population: 700,000)

INTERNATIONAL PHONE CODE ⓣ355

Introduction

Albania is, quite simply, one of Europe's most beguiling corners. Although its years of isolationist rule are long over, this rugged land still doesn't seem to fit into the grand continental jigsaw, with distinctly exotic notes emanating from its language, customs and cuisine. However, the secret is out and an increasing number of tourists are arriving to enjoy Albania's rippling mountains, Ottoman architecture, pristine beaches and endlessly hospitable locals. Get here before the country inevitably receives the popularity it deserves.

Most make a beeline for the capital, **Tirana**, a buzzing city with a mishmash of garishly painted buildings, traditional restaurants and trendy bars. However, those seeking to take Albania's true pulse should head to the mountainous hinterlands, particularly the peaceable hillside towns of **Berati** and **Gjirokastra** – both essentially open-air museums of life in Ottoman times. The muscular, snowcapped peaks of the interior drop down to a series of immaculate beaches, most notably along the **Ionian coastline** in the south of the country, one of the Mediterranean's most remote and least developed stretches.

CHRONOLOGY

168 BC The Romans defeat the Illyrian tribe and establish rule over present-day Albania.
395 AD Division of Roman Empire; Albania falls under the rule of Constantinople.
300s–500s Invasions by Visigoths, Ostrogoths and Huns.
1343 Serbian invasions.
1443–79 Resistance against Ottoman rule, most of it led by national hero Skanderbeg.
1614 Founding of Tirana.
1912 Albania gains independence.
1922 Ahmet Zogu becomes prime minister and president before finally crowning himself King Zog in 1928.
1939 Mussolini annexes Albania; King Zog retreats to the *Ritz* in London.
1946 Proclamation of People's Republic of Albania, led by Enver Hoxha.
1967 "Cultural Revolution" sees agriculture collectivized, religious buildings destroyed and cadres purged.
1979 Mother Teresa, an ethnic Albanian, wins the Nobel Peace Prize.
1990 Thousands scramble into Tirana's Western embassies in an attempt to flee Albania.
1992 The Democratic Party wins elections, ending Communist rule.
1997 Collapse of financial pyramid schemes results in mass bankruptcies.
2009 Albania joins NATO and applies for EU membership.

ARRIVAL

Tirana's Mother Teresa airport (ⓦwww.tirana-airport.com) fields a limited – but growing – selection of international **flights**. Local low-cost carrier Belle Air (ⓦwww.belleair.it) flies to Tirana from several Italian cities, and plans to expand services across Europe. Direct British Airways flights from London can be quite reasonable, while in warmer months you can fly cheaply to Corfu then get a ferry to Saranda. Visas are not required for citizens of most nations; South Africa is a notable exception.

Greece offers by far the simplest international **bus** connections – there are several daily services to Tirana from both Athens and Thessaloniki (from €25), and it's also possible to get direct buses to a number of other Albanian cities. From Macedonia there are direct buses from Skopje (via Struga). Getting there from Montenegro is still a pain, though it's possible to take an early-morning *furgon* (minivan) to Shkodra from Ulcinj.

The most interesting form of arrival is by **ferry**. From May to September, Venezia Lines (Ⓦwww.venezialines.com; €65) runs regular services to Durrësi from Bari; it's also possible to get to Saranda by ferry from Corfu (Ⓦwww.ionian-cruises.com; €19), with at least two ferries per day making the half-hour hop.

GETTING AROUND

Getting from A to B is a little tricky in Albania – you simply need a little time and patience, and to treat travel information as a guideline not gospel.

Most travel is conducted by **bus**; the vehicles are usually fine, fares are cheap, and the roads are continually being improved. However, the authorities have steadfastly refused to build any bus stations – fine in smaller towns, but a nightmare in a city as large as Tirana where matters are utterly confusing. Buses are supplemented by minibuses known as **furgons**, which are more numerous but run to no fixed schedule, and with no obligation to depart until full, drivers tend to roam around town until they have the required number of passengers. Most buses and *furgons* depart in the morning, and tend to dry up by mid-afternoon.

Albania also boasts a limited **train** network. The main line runs from Tirana to Durrësi, then heads south before splitting off to Vlora and Pogradeci; there's also a route heading north to Shkodra. The trains are slow and sport cracked windows, but are worth trying at least once. InterRail passes are not valid in Albania, and would be pretty pointless in any case.

ACCOMMODATION

Accommodation is surprisingly plentiful for a country with such low tourist numbers, and while state-owned monstrosities were once the norm, a recent building boom has unleashed a whole generation of clean, good-value **hotels**. You should be able to find a double room for under €25 (prices are almost always quoted in euros), and breakfast is usually included. There are not usually any set rates for single rooms, but you can expect a small discount from the regular rate. During summer, **private rooms** come into play at beach resorts, and there are now **hostels** in Tirana, Saranda and Berati, all charging €10–14 for dorm beds. There are almost no dedicated **campsites**, though the secluded beaches of the Ionian coast are great for those who can manage without facilities. Wild camping is fine in theory, but leaves you at the mercy of the (occasionally corrupt) local police.

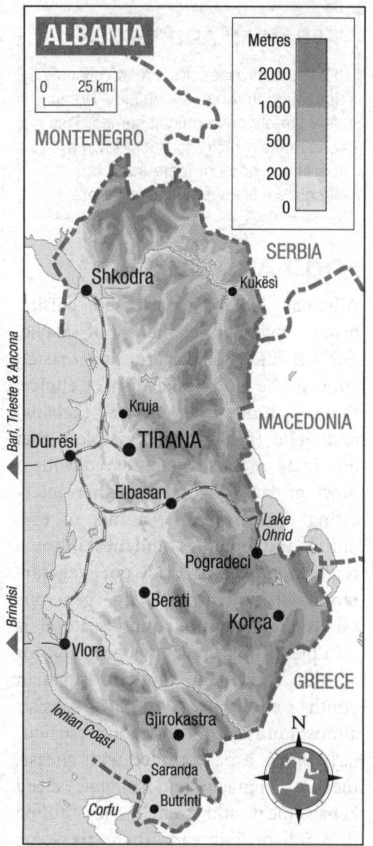

> **ALBANIAN ADDRESSES**
>
> Postal addresses are a relatively new invention in Albania – outside Tirana, few streets have official names. This can make it tricky to track down a particular hotel or restaurant, but locals are always willing to help.

FOOD AND DRINK

Albania's largely meat-based cuisine brings together elements of Slavic, Turkish and Italian fare. Spit-roasted lamb is the traditional dish of choice, though today it's *qebab* (kebabs) and *qoftë* (grilled lamb rissoles) that dominate menus, often served with a bowl of *kos* (yogurt). Another interesting dish is *fergesë*, a mix of egg, onions and tomatoes (and meat in some regions) cooked in a clay pot. **Vegetarians** will find that filling, generous salads are ubiquitous, and seafood is also plentiful around the coast. But for all this choice the modern Albanian youth – and many a tourist – subsists almost entirely on snack food, particularly *burek*, a pastry filled with cheese, meat or spinach; and *sufllaqë*, sliced kebab meat and french fries stuffed in a roll of flatbread. There are some excellent **desserts** on offer, including spongy *shendetlije*, cream-saturated *trilece*, and the usual Turkish pastries.

Drink

As for drinks, **coffee** is king in Albania. Consumed throughout the day, it's traditionally served Turkish-style, with grounds at the bottom (*kafe turke*), though there has recently been a marked shift towards espresso. There are cafés everywhere you look, and it's worth noting that cafés and bars generally melt into the same grey area – what's one by day will usually morph into the other by night.

The alcoholic drink of choice is **raki** – like coffee, this spirit is something of a way of life in Albania, and usually consumed with meals. The country also produces some good **wine**, mostly red, though most locals will own to a preference for Macedonian fare; Rilindja is a good, easy-to-find local label. **Beer** is easy to find, and it's also worth sampling Skënderbeg **cognac**, which is cheap, available in shops everywhere and not too bad at all.

CULTURE AND ETIQUETTE

Albanians tend to go out of their way to welcome foreign guests – partly due to the low number of visitors – and generally do a fine job of eroding popular misconceptions.

Religious practice was largely stamped out following the 1967 Cultural Revolution, meaning that although seventy percent of the population is Muslim, the majority are non-practising; the same can be said of the Christian remainder.

One cultural nicety is that the **body language** used to imply "yes" and "no" is the diametric opposite of what you may be used to – a shake of the head (actually more of a wobble) means "yes", and a nod (actually more of a tilt) means "no". Younger folk and those used to foreigners may well follow international norms, which adds to the confusion.

Tipping at restaurants is generally an exercise in rounding up to the nearest lekë note, but with bigger bills ten percent is the norm. **Smoking** has been officially prohibited in public places since 2007, though the police are too busy smoking to fine anybody, and you'll still see ashtrays on every restaurant table.

SPORTS AND OUTDOOR ACTIVITIES

In a mountainous country with a long coastline, the main attractions are pretty obvious – there are some delightful places to **swim** along the Ionian coast, while the most accessible **hiking** is in the national park area of Mount Dajti. More adventurous activities are thin on the ground, with a monopoly of sorts held by Outdoor Albania (☎04/222 7121, Ⓦwww.outdooralbania.com), an adventurous young team that can organize treks and **ski-shoeing** trips, or more high-octane fun such as **kayaking** and **paragliding**.

COMMUNICATIONS

Albania's network of **post offices** continues to grow, and most are open Monday to Friday from 9am to 5pm. While their quality of distribution is also improving – from a pretty low base – it's still prudent to hang onto any valuable parcels until you're out of the country. Public **phones** are hard to track down, and almost all use cards; you may be offered these on the street but it's safer – and cheaper – to buy from a post office, many of which will also have public phones of their own. **Internet** cafés are surprisingly widespread in urban

ALBANIAN

Note that the dual nature of Albanian nouns – all have definite and indefinite forms – can cause some confusion with place names. Tirana is alternately referred to as Tiranë, Durrësi as Durrës, Berati as Berat, Saranda as Sarandë and Gjirokastra as Gjirokaster.

	Albanian	Pronunciation
Yes	*Po*	Paw
No	*Jo*	Yaw
Please	*Ju lutem*	Yoo lootem
Thank you	*Faleminderit*	Falemin-derit
Hello/Good day	*Tungjatjeta*	Toongya-tyeta
Goodbye	*Mirupafshim*	Meeropafshim
Excuse me	*Më falni*	Muh falni
Where?	*Ku?*	Koo?
Good	*Mirë*	Mir
Bad	*Keq*	Kek
Near	*Afër*	Afur
Far	*Larg*	Larg
Cheap	*I lirë*	Ee lir
Expensive	*I shtrenjtë*	Ee shtrenyt
Open	*I hapur*	Ee hapoor
Closed	*Mbyllur*	Mbeeloor
Today	*Sot*	Sawt
Yesterday	*Dje*	Dye
Tomorrow	*Nesër*	Nesur
How much is...?	*Sa kushton...?*	Sa kushton...?
What time is it?	*Sa është ora?*	Sa ushtu awra?
I don't understand	*Unë nuk kuptoj*	Oonuh nook koop-toy
Do you speak English?	*A flisni anglisht?*	Ah fleesnee anglisht?
One	*Një*	Nyuh
Two	*Dy*	Deeh
Three	*Tre*	Treh
Four	*Katër*	Katur
Five	*Pesë*	Pes
Six	*Gjashtë*	Gyasht
Seven	*Shtatë*	Shtat
Eight	*Tetë*	Tet
Nine	*Nëntë*	Nuhnt
Ten	*Dhjetë*	Dyet

ALBANIA INTRODUCTION

EMERGENCY NUMBERS

Police ⓣ129; Ambulance ⓣ127; Fire ⓣ128.

areas; expect to pay anything from 50 to 200 lekë per hour, though some places charge in 10-minute blocks.

EMERGENCIES

Despite its bad rap, the **crime rate** in Albania is actually quite low by European standards, and you're extremely unlikely to find yourself stumbling into one of the famed blood feuds, some of which still bubble away up north. It is, however, worth being aware of a high **road accident** rate made vividly clear by the alarming number of memorial stones by the roadside.

Albania's **hospitals** are in very poor shape – most locals go abroad for treatment if they can afford it, and you should do likewise if possible. There are very few ambulances, so should you or a friend come across an accident it's usually best to hunt down a cab. **Pharmacies** exist in all urban areas, and are usually open 9am to 7pm.

INFORMATION

There are a few **tourist information offices** dotted around, though hours can be irregular to say the least – they can supply maps and book accommodation, but you're better off asking for information at your hotel or hostel.

MONEY AND BANKS

Albania uses the **lekë**, which is also often used in its singular form, lek. Coins of 1, 5, 10, 20, 50 and 100 lekë are in circulation, as are notes of 200, 500, 1000, 2000 and 5000 lekë. Exchange **rates** are currently around 130 lekë to the euro, 150 lekë to the pound, and 100 lekë to the US dollar. Note that many Albanians haven't yet caught up with the **chopping off of a zero** in the 1970s – you may be quoted 1000 lekë when they mean 100. Accommodation prices are quoted in euros at all but the cheapest places, and some of the more upmarket restaurants do likewise; in these you can pay with either currency, though will usually save a little paying in lekë. **Banks** are the best places to exchange money, and are usually open on weekdays 9am–3pm. **ATMs** are everywhere in Tirana and easy to find in any town, while **credit cards** are increasingly accepted in hotels.

ALBANIA ONLINE

ⓦ**www.albaniantourism.com** Official site of the tourist board.
ⓦ**www.albania-hotel.com** Good for booking rooms online.
ⓦ**www.albanianhistory.net** Collection of historical articles.
ⓦ**www.enverhoxha.info** Detailing the "greatness" of former dictator Enver Hoxha.

OPENING HOURS AND HOLIDAYS

Few **shops** and restaurants in Albania have set **working hours**, though you can expect restaurants to be open from breakfast to supper, and shops daily from 9am to 5pm. **Museums** are usually closed on Mondays.

Most shops and all banks and post offices are closed on **public holidays**: January 1 and 2, January 6, March 14, March 22, May 1, October 19, November 28 and 29 and December 25, as well as at Easter, both Catholic and Orthodox.

Tirana

Albania's quirky capital, **TIRANA**, exudes a youthful energy quite at odds with the potholes, enormous boulevards and brutal architecture it inherited from Hoxha's failed regime. The contrast is a delight; particularly in the central Blloku area, which was off-limits to all but Party members during Communist times. A generation down the line, it now plays host to armies of stylish, fun-loving young locals, sipping espresso before hunting down the latest trendy bar, and slowly fulfilling their city's apparent dream of becoming a "regular" European capital.

Tirana has been a major city since the Ottoman era, though events of the twentieth century eroded much of its legacy. Instead, you'll continually find yourself among buildings that expose influences from Italian to Communist to postmodern. In the 1920s, Italian planners used fascistic templates to create **Skanderbeg Square** and its surrounding area, before dictator Enver Hoxha added his own frills. More recently, charismatic mayor Edi Rama attempted to paint his city into the modern day; the resulting kaleidoscope of **colourful buildings** performs a continuous palette shift from lemon to lime, saffron to cinnamon and burgundy to baby blue, making it appear the beneficiary – some locals say victim – of a made-for-television makeover.

What to see and do

Tirana is better for strolling than sight-seeing, but there's plenty to keep you occupied in the southbound stretch from **Skanderbeg Square** to the **Grand Park**, which narrowly bypasses the trendy **Blloku** district on the way.

Skanderbeg Square

All roads in Tirana lead to **Skanderbeg Square**, centrepoint of the city and, therefore, the nation as a whole. Marked at its southern end by an equestrian statue of national hero Skanderbeg, who led the ultimately unsuccessful resistance to fifteenth-century Ottoman invasions, it was a bit of a mess at the time of writing thanks to major reconstruction efforts that had been indefinitely postponed. They had also seen the temporary closure of the imposing **National History Museum** on the north side of the square (usually Tues–Sat 9am–1pm & 5–7pm, closed Mon; 300 lekë).

Heading clockwise around the square you'll find the **Palace of Culture**, which houses the National Theatre of Opera and Ballet. Then comes the pretty **Et'hem Bey Mosque**, which was closed off during Communist rule; one sunny day in 1991, thousands flocked here to make use of their new-found religious freedom. Right next door is the tall **clock tower**, which can be climbed for views of the square (Mon 9am–1pm, Thurs 9am–1pm & 4–6pm; 100 lekë).

Bulevard Dëshmorët e Kombit and Blloku

Heading south from Skanderbeg Square is the "Boulevard of National Martyrs". The first major sight is the **National Art Gallery** (9am–1pm & 5–8pm, closed Mon; 100 lekë), which is well worth visiting; the most notable exhibitions are Onufri's renowned icons, and a collection of Socialist Realist paintings. Continuing south, the pleasant green verges of the **Lana** are a good place to get a handle on some of Tirana's famed **colourful buildings**. South of the river, any road on the right will take you to the **Blloku** district, while on the left is the distinctive **Pyramid**. Apparently designed by Hoxha's daughter (a disputed assertion), it first fuctioned as a museum dedicated to the leader, and then as a conference centre; it's now defunct, though locals are fond of scaling its walls for a beer. Walking south again, grandiose buildings line

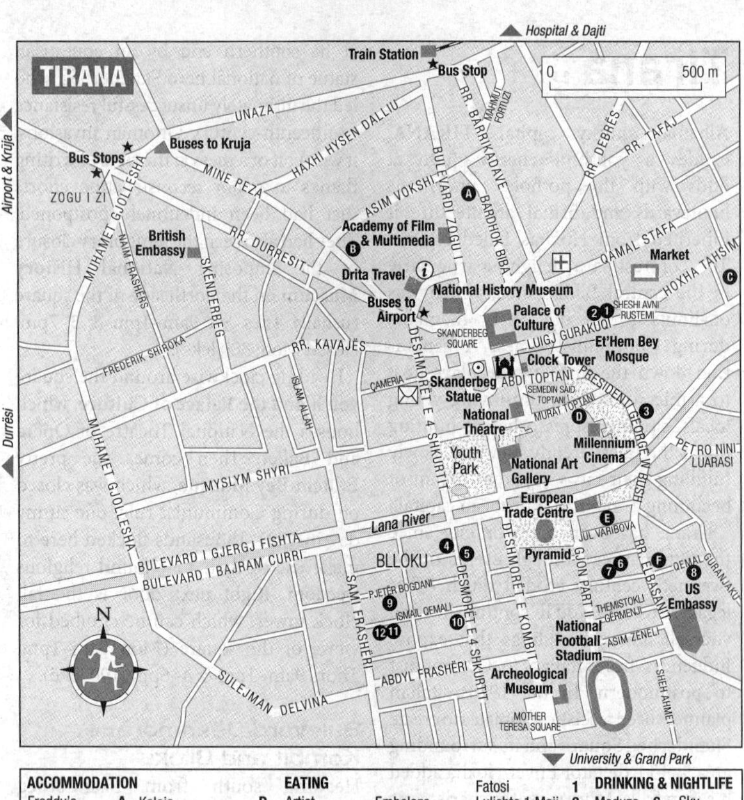

ACCOMMODATION				EATING				DRINKING & NIGHTLIFE	
Freddy's	A	Kalaja	D	Artist Lounge	7	Embelaza Francese	4	Meduza	6
Green House	E	Tirana Backpackers	F	Dani	8	Era	12	Radio	11
Hostel Albania	C	Vila Tafaj	B	Fatosi	1	Lulishte 1 Maji	3	Raum	9
				Oda	2	Quo Vadis	10	Sky Club	5

the road until you emerge in Mother Teresa Square, home to a passable **Archeological Museum** (Mon–Fri 10.30am–2.30pm; free). Further back, though not terribly easy to access, is the **Grand Park**, whose main feature is an artificial lake around which the Tiranese come for a spot of relaxation. Unfortunately swimming here is not advised; the villages on the far side of the lake empty their sewage into it, and the woods are full of snakes.

Arrival

Air Mother Teresa International Airport (also known as Rinas Airport) is located 20km northwest of Tirana. Taxis usually charge around 2500 lekë for the 30min trip into town – haggle in euros and you'll likely pay more – though it's far cheaper to take the hourly Rinas Express bus (6am–6pm; 45min; 250 lekë), which drops off at the north end of Skanderbeg Square.

Bus Arriving in Tirana by bus is something of a Kafkaesque adventure – amazingly, the city has not yet seen the need to build a bus station, so you may be dropped at any one of a dozen places, depending upon your point of embarkation; in addition, legal wrangles between bus companies and *furgon* drivers mean that the latter often have to shift their bases. The most common drop-off point is the Zogu i Zi junction northwest of town, though arrivals from the north often use the train station as a base. In general, if leaving Tirana it's best to ask locals – more than one, preferably, since you're likely to get a few different answers.

Train The station is north of the centre, at the top of Bulevardi Zogu I.

Information

Tourist office There's an office behind the National History Museum on Ded Gjo Luli (Ⓣ04/222 3313), but better advice can be found at one of the hostels, whose staff are more knowledgeable.

Listings *Tirana Times* (Ⓦwww.tiranatimes.com) is best for event listings. The biannual *Tirana In Your Pocket* guide (Ⓦwww.inyourpocket.com) is also a good source of information.

Tours Outdoor Albania (Ⓦwww.outdooralbania.com) and Juicy Tours (Ⓦjuicytours.com.au) both organize fascinating out-of-Tirana excursions.

City transport

Buses run every 15–30min on a few main routes 6am–10pm; 30 lekë one-way.

Taxis should cost 300–500 lekë for a trip within the city centre (none have meters), though central Tirana is just about small enough to cover on foot.

Accommodation

Hostels

Freddy's 75 Bardhok Biba Ⓣ068/203 5261, Ⓦwww.freddyshostel.com. Hotel rooms at hostel prices – some "dorms" in this family home have just two beds, making it a cheap option for those needing a private room. Dorms €12.

Hostel Albania 56 Beqir Luga Ⓣ067/278 3798, Ⓦwww.hostel-albania.com. Friendly, relaxing hostel, tucked into a pleasant residential neighbourhood – a little tricky to find at first, but well worth the effort. Dorms €11.

Tirana Backpackers 85 Elbasanit Ⓣ068/468 2353, Ⓦwww.tiranahostel.com. Comfy dorm rooms arranged around a fragrant garden. Very central, but the road noise can be a bit much for some – a few shots of raki from the on-site bar will see you to sleep. Dorms €12.

Hotels

Kalaja 9 Murat Toptani Ⓣ04/225 0000. Collection of comfy rooms – those downstairs are best – set into a wonderful niche in the old castle walls. There's also a small but pleasant courtyard area for relaxing over morning coffee. Doubles €30.

Vila Tafaj 86 Mine Peza Ⓣ04/222 7581, Ⓦwww.tafaj.com. Fresh, spacious rooms set within a graceful old building; they're justifiably proud of their interior courtyard. Unfortunately, it's not terribly central. Doubles €65.

TREAT YOURSELF

Green House 6 Jul Varibova (Ⓣ04/225 1015, Ⓦwww.greenhouse.al). Artistically designed boutique hotel whose rooms (doubles from €130) are perhaps the trendiest in the whole country – the ones on the ground floor are larger, but cost just the same. There's also a superb restaurant whose prices are within budget reach; 1100 lekë for a veal fillet with truffle sauce.

Eating

Cafés

Artist Lounge 12 Ismail Qemali. This sophisticated den may be a little pricey, but the sumptuous shakes and cakes have many a traveller coming back for more. One of the only places in Tirana to project a trendy vibe without soaking it in deafening music.

Embelaza Franceze 1 Dëshmorët e 4 Shkurtit. Cakes and coffees served up in a lavish interior. Savoury dishes are available but somewhat overpriced (mains 1000 lekë and up).

Quo Vadis 21 Ismail Qemali. Multi-section café-bar that's hugely popular with preening locals. Sit in the front section to soak up views of Hoxha's old house while throwing down your espresso.

Restaurants

Dani Qemal Guranjaku. Working-man's den with a menu full of cheap-but-tasty Albanian staples. Bolognese-topped *pilaf* with a side serving of *kos* costs only 200 lekë.

Era 33 Ismail Qemali. A hugely popular restaurant with locals and visitors alike – it's attractive yet affordable, service is top-notch, and the menu bursting with delectable local fare. Try the lamb with artichoke and goose fillet with mushroom. Meal with wine under 1000 lekë.

Fatosi Luigj Gurakuqi. A cut above most *qoftë* snack-shacks – best evidenced by the fact that they're often grilling over a hundred delicious meat rissoles at once. Ten of them, with some bread and fried onion, will set you back just 310 lekë.

Lulishte 1 Maji Presidenti George W. Bush. Sprawling family restaurant that serves Italian, Albanian and Mexican meals on the ground floor, and Chinese food upstairs. Mains from 500 lekë.

Oda Luigj Gurakuqi. Small, homely place offering you the chance to eat Ottoman-style meals on Ottoman-style sofas. The stuffed eggplant

(700 lekë) is superb, and the offal stew (*tavë dheu*) far better than it sounds; all is best washed down – if you're brave – with a shot of flavoured raki.

Drinking and nightlife

Tirana's nightlife scene moves up a notch with each passing year. Almost everything of note is concentrated in the fashionable Blloku area, which can be busy until midnight on weekdays, and far later on weekends.

Meduza Mustapha Matohiti. Imagine drinking on Downing St, or on the grounds of the White House. In Albania, anything goes... at this ground-level bar you can drain a Guinness while the Prime Minister snoozes away (or parties himself to sleep) upstairs. Burly security chaps ensure that it's also the safest place in the city to have a drink.

Radio 29 Ismail Qemali. Trendy bar that's very popular with the city's artier set, and as such a good place to meet locals.

Raum Pjetër Bogdani. Two upper floors frequented by a young and creative set, who make a sundown shift from coffee to cocktails. Also stages occasional art exhibitions.

Sky Club 5 Dëshmorët e 4 Shkurtit. Okay, so you're basically paying extra for height, but this lofty bar's revolving floor means that you can see the whole of Tirana in one drinking session. There's also a good restaurant one level down.

Entertainment

Usually held in December, the Tirana International Film Festival (Ⓦwww.tiranafilmfest.com) has screenings at the Millennium Cinema and National Theatre. 2011 saw the birth of the Bunker Festival, a wild, bunker-based party set to take place each May – ask at the hostels for details.

Academy of Film and Multimedia Alexsandër Moisiu Ⓣ04/236 5188, Ⓦwww.afmm.edu.al. Occasional free screenings of foreign movies (usually Thurs at 7pm).

Millennium Cinema Murat Toptani. Season-old Hollywood films shown in a wonderful old theatre whose outdoor café is a delight on sunny days. Tickets from 300 lekë.

Shopping

Tirana has a fascinating daily market (6am–10pm), which sprawls over several blocks north of the Sheshi Avni Rustemi roundabout; Sundays are best. Adrion, on Skanderbeg Square, has English-language books, newspapers and magazines.

Directory

Embassies and consulates UK, Skënderbeg Ⓣ04/223 4973; US, Elbasanit Ⓣ04/224 7285.

Exchange It's hard to find yourself outside visible range of an ATM in Tirana. All of the attached banks will be able to exchange cash during banking hours.

Hospital Civilian Hospital, Dibrës.

Internet There are plenty of internet cafés around, usually charging 50–80 lekë/hr.

Pharmacies Bulevardi Zogu I (Mon–Sat 8am–8pm; Ⓣ04/222 2241; closed Sun); Dëshmorët e 4 Shkurtit (Ⓣ04/222 6759, staff on duty 24hr).

Post office Çameria. Mon–Fri 8am–8pm.

Moving on

Train Durrësi (7 daily; 1hr); Pogradeci (2 daily; 6hr 40min).

Bus Athens (daily; 12hr); Berati (hourly; 3hr); Durrësi (hourly; 40min); Gjirokastra (6 daily; 4hr 30min); Saranda (6 daily; 6hr); Skopje (daily; 10hr).

Around Tirana

Local landmarks from which you can peer down on Tirana include the slopes of **Mount Dajti** and the hilltop town of **Kruja**, while also within range is the laidback port of **Durrësi**. All can be visited on a day-trip from the capital.

MOUNT DAJTI

The dark, looming shape of **Mount Dajti** is easily visible from Tirana, a temptation that can prove too much for city-dwellers, who head to the forested slopes in droves on sunny weekends. The mountain's network of paths feel surprisingly remote even though you're only 25km from the capital. There's no public transport to the mountain, but by taxi it should be no more than 500 lekë to the base of the cable car (8am–10pm; 700 lekë return; Ⓦwww.dajtiexspres.com) that whisks passengers to within a slog of the summit. It's a good place to enjoy spit-roasted lamb: try the *Panorama* (Ⓣ067/436 1124) or *Dajti Tower* (Ⓣ067/401 1035; Ⓦdajtitower.com).

KRUJA

Lofty **KRUJA**, 35km from Tirana, was the focal point of national hero Skanderbeg's resistance to the Ottoman invasions of the fifteenth century, and you'll see his likeness all over town. Most people make a beeline straight to the **castle**, which houses a number of restaurants and an excellent **History Museum** (9am–1pm & 3–6pm, closed Mon; 200 lekë), whose diverting collection of weaponry, icons and the like is augmented by an impressive modern interior. Also within the castle walls is the **Ethnographic Museum** (same times; 300 lekë), housed in a gorgeous building with a serene outdoor courtyard. Souvenir salesmen have taken over the town, and the best place to buy your Albania-flag T-shirt, Skanderbeg statuette or Mother Teresa lighter is the restored **Ottoman bazaar**, just below the castle access road. *Furgons* from Tirana (200 lekë) leave regularly from the end of Mine Peza.

DURRËSI

Sitting atop a 10km stretch of Adriatic beach, the port city of **DURRËSI** is the easiest escape route for sea-seeking Tiranese, and on summer weekends there are few better places to party. There may be far nicer beaches down south, but this one is still pretty fun.

Known as Dyrrhachium, the city was already an important port in Roman times, and served as a launchpad for fifth-century Visigoth attacks on Italy; it also served as Albania's capital for a short time after independence. Evidence survives from the city's Roman heyday: a **forum** and **amphitheatre** sit just off opposite ends of the main square, Sheshi i Lirisë, with the latter (8am–8pm; 200 lekë) the largest such construction in the Balkans. In between stands an elegant **mosque**. You can then either follow the old **castle wall** or cobblestoned Tregëtare downhill to the seafront **promenade**; a ten-minute stroll will bring you to the enjoyable **Archeological Museum** (daily except Mon 9am–3pm; 200 lekë).

The **train and bus stations** sit almost side by side within an easy walk of the main square and the ferry terminal, which receives regular services from Italy. Those who don't fancy trawling the beach area – packed in summer – will find good culinary and **sleeping** options around the bottom of Tregëtare; the lofty *Mediterran* (Ⓣ052/227 074, Ⓔmediterran_hotel.dr@hotmail.com; doubles €25) is both the best value and easiest to find, while the *Arvi* (Ⓣ052/230 403, Ⓦwww.hotelarvi.com; doubles €60) is halfway to the museum.

Southern Albania

With its jumble of rugged mountains fringed by pristine curls of beach, Albania's south is the most appealing part of the country. The interior route boasts the rewarding towns of Berati and **Gjirokastra**, each home to whole swathes of Ottoman buildings. Heading on down the Ionian Coast instead, you'll find one of Europe's only unspoilt sections of Mediterranean shore, a near-permanently sunny spot where the twin blues of sea and sky are ripped asunder by a ribbon of grey mountains – on a clear day you'll be able to see Italy from the 1027m-high **Llogaraja Pass**. Both routes converge at the beach town of **Saranda**, while further south are the fantastic ruins of **Butrinti**.

BERATI

A well-preserved relic of Ottoman times, **BERATI** is one of Albania's must-sees. Fish-scaling the slopes of an ancient **citadel** are huddles of **Ottoman houses**, their dark, rectangular windows staring from whitewashed walls like a thousand eyes.

ALBANIA'S BUNKERS

Cross into Albania by land or sea, and you'll soon notice clutches of grey, dome-like structures dotting the countryside. Under Hoxha's rule, these **bunkers** were scattered around the country in tremendous numbers – estimates run as high as 750,000, which would have meant that there was more than one for every four Albanians. These were no family shelters, as might be expected, but strategic positions to which every able-bodied man was expected to head, weapon in hand, at the onset of war. Though Western spies did indeed make attempts to infiltrate the country, the bunkers were never really put to the test. Almost impossible to shift, they're now a semi-permanent part of Albanian life; young, privacy-seeking couples occasionally put them to interesting use, while in 2011 the Bunker festival (see p.62) was created.

While modern-day Berati spreads out for quite some way down the Osumi valley, most of the old buildings come in three central clusters – **Kalasa** is inside the citadel, **Mangalemi** lurks beneath, and sleepy **Gorica** sits across the river.

What to see and do

You'll have great views of Berati from the fourteenth-century **Kalasa**, a citadel (daily 9am–9pm, 100 lekë; free out of hours) towering above town, which is accessed via a steep, cobbled road. Unlike other such places in Albania this is still a functioning part of town and home to hundreds, yet almost nothing dilutes its centuries-old vibe. There were once over thirty **churches** here but just a handful remain; oldest and most beautiful is the thirteenth-century **Church of the Holy Trinity**, sitting on the slope below the inner fortifications. Churches remain locked for most of the year, but you can ask around to find the key-keepers. Also within the grounds is the **Onufri Museum** (daily except Mon 9am–4pm; 200 lekë), dedicated to the country's foremost icon painter, famed for his use of a particularly vivid red. Heading back down the access road you'll come across the diverting **Ethnographic Museum** (Oct–April 9am–4pm, Sun to 2pm; May–Sept 9am–1pm & 4–7pm, Sun 9am–2pm; 200 lekë) and the first of the centre's three main **mosques**.

Arrival and information

Bus The central square acts as a bus station of sorts, though it's also possible to pick up or be dropped off at various locations on the main road.

Tours Rafting excursions (around €50/person) and trips around nearby Mount Tomorri can be organized through Outdoor Albania (Ⓦwww.outdooralbania.com). *Berat Backpackers* also lay on occasional tours.

Accommodation

Berat Backpackers Ⓣ069/306 4429, Ⓦberatbackpackers.com. The default budget location, and with good reason: rooms are cosy, and the garden patio is a delightful place for evening drinks. Located over the river in Gorica. Dorms €10.

Berati Ⓣ032/236 953. Cheap rooms, some with balconies, in a central location just west of the bus station square – look for the sign. Also has a very reasonable in-house restaurant. Doubles €25.

Mangalemi Ⓣ032/232 093, Ⓦwww.hotelmangalemi.com. Traditional guesthouse whose rooms offer excellent value; all are en suite with comfy beds and powerful showers. Near the centre of town, on the road to the citadel. Doubles €30.

Eating and drinking

Ajka Few women in Berati go to bars, but those who do come to this smart place just over the Gorica bridge. Also good for coffee; head on up to the roof terrace for the best views.

Mangalemi Inside the guesthouse of the same name. Professional service, large portions and reasonable prices – 500 lekë can get you nicely full. The salads are great, or give the stuffed liver a try; head up to the terrace if the weather's nice.

Nova Slightly pricey menu (mains 700–1000 lekë) centred on steaks and kebabs, though a romantic hilltop setting near the citadel entrance more than compensates.

Onufri Simple restaurant inside the citadel walls, serving Albanian staples.

White House ⓣ032/234570. Riverside restaurant serving the best pizzas in town (from 450 lekë; delivery service available) as well as seafood dishes and traditional Albanian fare.

Moving on

Bus Gjirokastra (2 daily; 4hr); Saranda (2 daily, 6hr); Tirana (hourly; 3hr).

GJIROKASTRA

Sitting proudly above the sparsely inhabited Drinos valley, **GJIROKASTRA** is one of Albania's most attractive towns, and home to some of its friendliest people. Its days as an Ottoman trading hub have bequeathed it a wealth of sparkling **Ottoman houses**, which line a grey-white-pink tricolore of steep, cobbled streets. Gjiro is also etched into the nation's conscience as the birthplace of former dictator **Enver Hoxha**, and more recently the world-renowned author Ismail Kadare.

What to see and do

The Old Town's centrepiece is its imposing **citadel** (May–Sept 9am–7pm; 200 lekë), which is clearly visible from any point in town. Built in the sixth century and enlarged in 1811 by Ali Pasha Tepelna, it was used as a prison by King Zog, the Nazis and Hoxha's cadres; the interior remains suitably spooky. There are also tanks and weaponry to peruse, but most curious is the shell of an **American jet** which was (apparently) forced down in 1957 after being suspected of espionage by the Communist regime. Other than the castle, Gjiro's most appealing sight is its collection of mainly nineteenth-century **Ottoman houses**; there are some prime examples in Partizani, a steep residential area just west of the castle.

Arrival and information

Bus Buses and *furgons* stop on the highway intersection below the New Town. From here it's a steep, half-hour walk to the Old Town, or a 300-lekë taxi ride.

Tours The *Kotoni* (ⓦwww.kotonihouse.com) can organize a variety of interesting tours, including horseriding and picnics on the nearby hills.

Accommodation

None of these establishments have addresses, but they're easy to find. The *Gjirokastra* is next to the theatre on the road running under the castle wall, where you'll also find signs to the *Kotoni*; the *Kalemi* is further up the same road.

Gjirokastra ⓣ084/265 982. Small but modern guesthouse with an excellent location; discounts available outside peak season. Doubles €25.

Kalemi ⓣ084/263 724, ⓦhotelkalemi.tripod.com. Lofty old building with a variety of pleasant rooms on offer, some with commanding valley views and chunky wooden floors. Doubles €35.

Kotoni ⓣ084/263 526, ⓦwww.kotonihouse.com. Cosy Ottoman-era building whose owners may well be the most amiable – and energetic – couple in Gjirokastra. Homely touches include excellent breakfasts and handmade trimmings in the bedrooms. Doubles €30.

Eating and drinking

Fantazia Uphill from Qafa e Pazarit. Stylish and extremely popular café offering splendid valley views, and a variety of teas, coffees and alcoholic drinks. Espresso 70 lekë.

Kujtimi Qafa e Pazarit. Fantastic Albanian meals dished out under the leaves of a maple tree. A salad and a small main (the *qoftë* is recommended) will set you back 500 lekë.

Moving on

Bus Berati (2 daily; 4hr); Saranda (6 daily; 1hr 30min); Tirana (6 daily; 4hr 30min).

SARANDA AND BUTRINTI

Staring straight at the Greek island of Corfu, and even within day-trip territory, sunny **SARANDA** is perhaps Albania's most appealing entry-point. A recent building boom has eroded some of the town's original genteel atmosphere, but it's still a great place to kick back, stroll along the promenade and watch the sun set over cocktails. There are beaches in town, but better are those near the village of Ksamili, which lies next to the archeological treasure-trove of **Butrinti**.

Butrinti and the Blue Eye

Splendidly sited on an exposed nub of land, the isolated ruins of **Butrinti** (daylight hours; 700 lekë) offer a peek into over 2500 years of history, and are a delight to explore on its eucalyptus-lined trails. The area was first developed by the Greeks in the fourth century BC, and the expansive **theatre** and nearby **public baths** were built soon after. Butrinti then reached its zenith during Roman times – Julius Caesar stopped by in 44 BC – though most of the statues unearthed from this period are now in the museums of Tirana. You can see most of Butrinti's sights on a looped footpath, though do head up to the **Acropolis** for wonderful views. You can pick up *furgons* to Butrinti (six daily; 45min; 100 lekë) at any point on Skënderbeu (the road above the prom), but given the paucity of public transport many opt to shell out for a taxi (around €20 including waiting time). If Butrinti's beauty tempts you to stay, try the superb *Livia* (ⓣ069/205 1263; doubles €35).

On the way from Saranda to Gjirokastra is the wonderful **Blue Eye**, an underwater spring forming a pool of deepest blue. Its setting in a cool, remote grove is quite spectacular – the water is delicious, and you can swim in it until you get the chills (it won't take long). Hop on anything heading from Saranda to Gjirokastra, and ask to be let off at the Syri i Kaltër; the pool is 20min from the road on a decent path.

Arrival and information

Boat The small terminal on the west side of town has at least 2 daily services to Corfu. Tickets can be bought from a small office on the access road.
Bus The bus "station" (you'll see…) is just north of the centre on Vangjel Pando. The harbour is a 5min walk downhill.
Information Useful listings and local information are found on ⓦwww.saranda-guide.com.

Accommodation

Hostels

The Bunker Mitat Hoxha 10 ⓣ069/434 5426, ⓦwww.backpackerssr.hostel.com. Also known as "Backpackers SR", this small but decent hostel is hard to track down, despite a location almost directly opposite the ferry terminal. Dorms €12.
Hairy Lemon Koder 8f ⓣ069/355 9317, ⓦwww.hairylemonhostel.com. Irish-owned hostel a 10min walk west of the centre, past the ferries. Clean and friendly, with very comfy beds and a great chill-out area for meeting new travel buddies. Dorms €12 July–Sept, €10 Oct–June.

Hotels

Hotel Real Off Abedin Dino ⓣ085/226 361. This is a simple place with spotless rooms, but dirt-cheap. Doubles €20.
Kaonia Jonianet 2 ⓣ085/222 600. The best value of the hotels around the harbour, perhaps because of the unfinished shell-building it's attached to. All rooms have balconies, but not all offer sea views so look before you pay. Doubles €40.
Palma Mitat Hoxha 1 ⓣ085/222 929. Spick-and-span hotel next to the ferry terminal – ask for a balcony room, if you don't mind the noise. Room prices can drop as low as €25 off-season. Doubles €60.

Eating and drinking

Bequa Friendship Park. Off the east side of the park below the bus station, with meat dishes from 250 lekë; real penny-pinchers will appreciate the 60 lekë *pilaf*. Try to nab one of the outdoor tables.
Happy Hour Abedin Dino. Peering out over the prom, this fun bar is worth mentioning for its "Sperm of Barman" shots alone. Open until last customer leaves.
Limani Harbour. Literally jutting out into the harbour, this is the most popular place in town by some margin; good for coffee in the morning, pizza for dinner (from 450 lekë), *trilece* for dessert, and ouzo in the evening.
Paradise Abedin Dino. A winning blend of style, service and reasonable prices at this seafront restaurant. East of town off the Butrinti road.
Viljani Abdein Dino. This prom-side cafe-bar serves draught beer in ice-cold glasses – enough said. Don't ask for a large one unless you want a full litre of the stuff.

Moving on

Bus Berati (2 daily; 6hr); Gjirokastra (6 daily; 1hr 20min); Tirana (6 daily; 6hr).

Austria

HIGHLIGHTS

COFFEE AND CAKE, VIENNA: indulge in mouthwatering treats in one of Vienna's ornate coffeehouses

SALZBURG: a fine Baroque city, home to Mozart and, of course, the sound of music

VIENNESE ART: feast your eyes on stunning paintings by Gustav Klimt and Egon Schiele

HALLSTATT: visit this picture-postcard village in the lovely Salzkammergut region

ADVENTURE SPORTS, INNSBRUCK: hiking, mountain-biking, and canyoning in the stunning Austrian Alps

ROUGH COSTS

DAILY BUDGET Basic €55 /occasional treat €75

DRINK Beer (0.5l €3.50), wine or coffee €3

FOOD *Schnitzel* €9

HOSTEL/BUDGET HOTEL €20/€60

TRAVEL Train: Graz–Vienna €31.40; Vienna–Salzburg €44.20

FACT FILE

POPULATION 8.3 million

AREA 83,872 sq km

LANGUAGE German

CURRENCY Euro (€)

CAPITAL Vienna (population: 1.7 million)

INTERNATIONAL PHONE CODE ⓣ43

Introduction

Glorious Alpine scenery, monumental Habsburg architecture, and the world's favourite musical – Austria's tourist industry certainly plays up to the clichés. However, it's not all bewigged Mozart ensembles and schnitzel; modern Austria boasts some of Europe's most varied museums and contemporary architecture not to mention attractive and sophisticated cities whose bars, cafés and clubs combine contemporary cool with elegant tradition.

Long the powerhouse of the Habsburg Empire, **Austria** underwent decades of change and uncertainty in the early twentieth century. Shorn of her empire and racked by economic difficulties, the state fell prey to the promises of Nazi Germany. Only with the end of the Cold War did Austria return to the heart of Europe, joining the EU in 1995.

Politics aside, Austria is primarily known for two contrasting attractions – the fading imperial glories of the capital, and the stunning beauty of its Alpine hinterland. **Vienna** is the gateway to much of central Europe and a good place to soak up the culture of *Mitteleuropa*. Less renowned provincial capitals such as **Graz** and **Linz** are surprising pockets of culture, innovation and vitality. **Salzburg**, between **Innsbruck** and Vienna, represents urban Austria at its most picturesque, an intoxicating Baroque city within easy striking distance of the mountains and lakes of the **Salzkammergut**, while the most dramatic of Austria's Alpine scenery is west of here, in and around **Tyrol**, whose capital, **Innsbruck**, provides the best base for exploration.

CHRONOLOGY

1st century BC Romans take over Celtic settlements in present-day Austria.
788 AD Charlemagne conquers Austrian land.
1156 The "Privilegium Minus" gives Austria the status of Duchy.
1278 The Habsburgs seize control of much of modern Austria (except Salzburg), and retain it until World War I.
1683 The Siege of Vienna – the Habsburgs under Leopold I defeat the Ottoman Turks outside Vienna.
1773 Wolfgang Amadeus Mozart becomes Court Musician in Salzburg.
1797 Napoleon defeats Austrian forces, taking Austrian land.
1814 An Austrian coalition force defeats Napoleon. In the Congress of Vienna the Salzburg lands are given to Austria, ending centuries of independence under Prince-Archbishops.
1866 Austrian territory is lost as a result of the Austro-Prussian war.
1899 Sigmund Freud publishes *The Interpretation of Dreams*, introducing the concept of the ego.
1914 The assassination of the Austrian Archduke, Franz Ferdinand, begins the events that lead to World War I.
1920 A new constitution creates the Republic of Austria.
1938 Hitler incorporates Austria into Germany through "Anschluss".
1945 Austria is occupied by Allied forces as World War II ends.
1965 *The Sound of Music* draws attention to Austria on the big screen.
1980s Protests at election of President Kurt Waldheim, due to rumours implicating him in Nazi war crimes.
1995 Austria joins the EU.
1999 The far-right Freedom Party led by Joerg Haider wins 27 percent of the vote in national elections.
2008 The world is enthralled by the case of Josef Fritzl – who imprisoned his daughter in a cellar for twenty-four years, fathering seven children with her.

ARRIVAL

Austria lies right at the heart of Europe, with seven countries bordering it. Its excellent transport connections make it an easy stopoff on either a north–

south or east–west route through Europe. Vienna has a major international airport, and you can also fly to Salzburg, Innsbruck, Graz and Linz or to the Slovak capital Bratislava, only a 1hr 15min bus journey from Vienna. Vienna is also one of central Europe's major rail-hubs, with **connections** including Budapest, Bratislava and Prague. Trains from Croatia and Slovenia stop in Graz, before also terminating here. Arriving from northern Italy (Venice, for example), it's likely you'll arrive in Innsbruck, which also has good rail connections with Munich, as does Salzburg.

GETTING AROUND

Austria's **public transport** is fast, efficient and comprehensive. ÖBB (ⓦwww.oebb.at) runs a punctual **train** network, which includes most towns of any size. All stations in cities and larger towns have left-luggage lockers. An Austria one-country pass with Eurail starts at €77 (3 days validity in 1 month; under-25s), though it's worth checking individual train prices, which can work out cheaper.

Buses (ⓦwww.postbus.at) serve remoter villages and Alpine valleys; fares are around €10 per 100km. Daily and weekly regional travelcards (*Netzkarte*), covering both trains and buses, are available in many regions.

Austria is bike-friendly, with **cycle lanes** in all major towns. Many train stations rent **bikes** for around €15 per day (€10 with a valid train ticket).

ACCOMMODATION

Outside popular tourist spots such as Vienna and Salzburg, **accommodation** need not be too expensive. Good-value **B&B** is usually available in the many small family-run hotels known as *Gasthöfe* and *Gasthaüser*, with prices from €50 per double. In the larger towns and cities a *pension* or *Frühstuckspension* will offer similar prices. Most places also have a stock of **private rooms** or *Privatzimmer*, although in well-travelled rural areas, roadside signs offering *Zimmer Frei* are common (double room €30–45). Local tourist offices will have lists of these and will often ring around and book something for you.

There are around a hundred **HI hostels** (*Jugendherberge* or *Jugendgästehaus*), run by or affiliated to ÖJHV (ⓦwww.oejhv.or.at) or the ÖJHW (ⓦwww.oejhw.or.at). Rates are €17–24, normally including breakfast (€1–2 extra for non-members). There are also a few excellent **independent hostels**

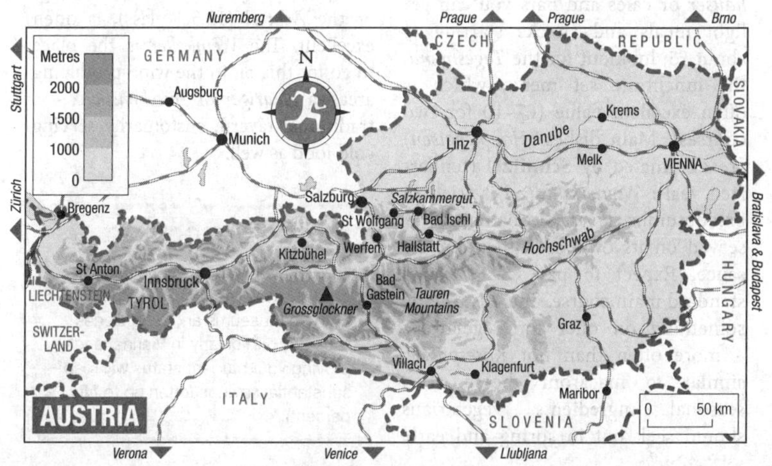

AUSTRIA

INTRODUCTION

> **AUSTRIA ONLINE**
>
> ⓦ **www.austria.info** Austrian Tourist Board website.
> ⓦ **www.oebb.at** Train website; including excellent English-language journey planner.
> ⓦ **www.tiscover.com** Detailed information on all regions of the country.
> ⓦ **www.wienerzeitung.at** Website of the official Vienna city authorities' newspaper.

in Salzburg and Vienna, plus affiliated youth hotel chains.

Austria's numerous **campsites** often have laundry facilities, shops and snack bars. Most open May to September, although some open year-round.

FOOD AND DRINK

Austrian food is hearty and traditional; often of good quality, it makes use of local and seasonal ingredients. For ready-made snacks, try a bakery (*Bäckerei*), confectioner's (*Konditorei*), or local market. **Fast-food** centres on the *Würstelstand*, which sells hot dogs, *Bratwurst* (grilled sausage), *Käsekrainer* (spicy sausage with cheese), *Bosna* (spicy, thin Balkan sausage) and *Currywurst*. In *Kaffeehäuser* or cafés and bars you can get light meals and **snacks** starting at about €5; look out for the *Tagesmenu*, the lunchtime set menu, which is often excellent value (€7–10 for two courses). Main dishes (*Hauptspeisen*) are dominated by **Schnitzel** (tenderized veal): *Wienerschnitzel* is fried in breadcrumbs, *Pariser* in batter, *Natur* served on its own or with a creamy sauce. Expect to pay €8–12 for a standard main course. There is usually something on offer for vegetarians – more often than not *Käsespätzle*, similar to macaroni cheese. Two seasonal ingredients vegetarians should seek out in spring and early summer are *Bärlauch*, wild garlic, delicious in soups and pasta sauces, and *Spargel*, asparagus, typically the white variety and served with hollandaise.

Drink

For Austrians, daytime drinking traditionally centres on the **Kaffeehaus**, relaxed places serving alcoholic and soft drinks, snacks and cakes, alongside a wide range of different coffees: a *Schwarzer* is small and black, a *Brauner* comes with a little milk, while a *Melange* is half coffee and half milk; a *Kurzer* is a small espresso; an *Einspänner* a glass of black coffee topped with *Schlag*: whipped cream. A cup of coffee in one of these places is pricey (€2.50–3), but for this you can linger for hours. Most cafés also offer a tempting array of freshly baked cakes and pastries, as do *Café-Konditorei* (café-patisseries), where the cakes take centre stage.

Night-time drinking centres on **bars** and cafés, although traditional *Bierstuben* and *Weinstuben* are still thick on the ground. Austrian **beers** are of good quality. Most places serve the local brew on tap, either by the *Krügerl* (half-litre, €3), *Seidel* (third-litre, €1.80) or *Pfiff* (fifth-litre, €0.80–1.30). The local **wine**, drunk by the *Viertel* (25cl mug) or the *Achterl* (12.5cl glass), is often excellent. The *Weinkeller* is the place to go for this or, in the wine-producing areas, a *Heuriger* or *Buschenshenk* – a traditional tavern, customarily serving cold food as well.

> **STUDENT DISCOUNTS**
>
> It is definitely worth carrying an **ISIC card** (ⓦ www.isic.org) in Austria. Entry to museums and art galleries is costly, particularly in Vienna, and proving your student status will reap substantial savings (often up to fifty percent).

EMERGENCY NUMBERS

Police ☎133; Ambulance ☎144; Fire ☎122.

CULTURE AND ETIQUETTE

Austrian culture and etiquette is much like the rest of Western Europe, with leisurely café culture a central fixture. In restaurants, bars and cafés modest tipping – around ten percent or rounding up to the nearest euro – is expected (pay the waiter or waitress directly).

SPORTS AND ACTIVITIES

With stunning mountain scenery and beautiful lakes, Austria is an ideal destination for all sorts of outdoor sports. **Skiing** and snowboarding are major national pastimes (see box, p.94) and **hiking** and biking trails are clearly marked and graded. Tourist offices will usually have a surfeit of details on local routes and every other possible local activity.

COMMUNICATIONS

Most **post offices** are open Monday to Friday 8am to noon and 2 to 6pm; in larger cities they do without the lunch break and also open Saturday 8 to 10am. **Stamps** can also be bought at tobacconists (*Tabak-Trafik*). You can make international calls from all public phones, but it's easier to do so from booths at larger post offices. The operator and directory enquiries number is ☎118 11. **Internet access** is widespread (€2–5/hr) and many hostels and hotels have wi-fi.

EMERGENCIES

Austria is law-abiding and reasonably safe. Dial ☎059133 for the nearest police station (*Polizei*). **Pharmacies** (*Apotheke*) follow shopping hours; a rota system covers night-time and weekend opening, with details posted in the window.

LANGUAGE

A high proportion of Austrians speak English, though any attempt at a few phrases of **German** (see p.71) will be heartily appreciated, though Austrian accents and dialects can be tricky – the standard greeting throughout Austria is *Grüss Gott*.

INFORMATION

Tourist offices (usually *Information*, *Tourismusverband*, *Verkehrsamt* or *Fremdenverkehrsverein*) are plentiful, often hand out free maps and almost always book accommodation.

MONEY AND BANKS

Austria's currency is the **euro** (€). Banking hours tend to be Monday to Friday 8am to 12.30pm and 1.30 to 3pm; Thursday until 5.30pm. Post offices charge slightly less commission on exchange than banks, and in larger cities, have longer hours.

OPENING HOURS AND PUBLIC HOLIDAYS

Most shops are open all day Monday to Saturday, though out of cities they can close at lunch and on Saturday afternoons. Many **cafés**, **restaurants** and bars also have a weekly *Ruhetag* (closing day). Shops and **banks** close, and most museums have reduced hours, on **public holidays**: January 1, January 6, Easter Monday, May 1, Ascension Day, Whit Monday, Corpus Christi, August 15, October 26, November 1, December 8, December 25 and 26.

Vienna

Most people visit **VIENNA** (Wien) with a vivid image in their minds: a romantic place, full of imperial nostalgia, opera houses and exquisite cakes. Even so, the city can overwhelm with its eclectic feast of architectural styles, from High Baroque through the monumental imperial projects of the late nineteenth century, to the decorative Jugendstil (Art Nouveau) style of the early twentieth, used to great effect on several of the city's splendid U-Bahn stations.

Vienna became an important centre in the tenth century, then in 1278 the city fell to **Rudolf of Habsburg**, but didn't become the imperial residence until 1683. The great aristocratic families flooded in to build palaces in a frenzy of construction that gave Vienna its **Baroque character**. By the end of the Habsburg era the city had become a breeding ground for the ideological passions of the age, and the ghosts of Freud, Klimt and Schiele are now some of the city's biggest tourist draws.

What to see and do

Central Vienna is surprisingly compact: with the historical centre, or **Innere Stadt**, just 1km wide. The most important sights are concentrated here and along the Ringstrasse – the series of traffic- and tram-clogged boulevards that form a ring road around the centre. Efficient public transport allows you to cross the city in less than thirty minutes, making even peripheral sights, such as the monumental imperial palace at **Schönbrunn**, easily accessible. However, for all the grand palaces and museums, a trip to Vienna that's only frantic sightseeing would miss out on European café culture at its very finest: spending a leisurely afternoon nursing a creamy coffee and a piece of cake in one of the grand, shabby-glamorous coffee-houses that the city is famous for.

Stephansdom

The obvious place to begin exploration is **Stephansplatz**, the pedestrianized central square dominated by the hoary Gothic **Stephansdom** (Mon–Sat 6am–10pm, Sun 7am–10pm, except during services; free, but entry fees to most sections, combined ticket €14.50). It's worth paying to explore the interior more fully, with the highlights of the main section (Mon–Sat 8.30–11.30am & 1–5.30pm, Sun 1–5.30pm; tour with audioguide €4.50; English tours April–Oct daily 3.45pm; €4.50) the Wiener Neustädter Altar, a late Gothic masterpiece, and the tomb of the Holy Roman Emperor Friedrich III. The **catacombs** (tours every 15–30min Mon–Sat 10–11.30am & 1.30–4.30pm, Sun 1.30–4.30pm; €4.50) contain the entrails of illustrious Habsburgs housed in bronze caskets. Stellar views reward those climbing the 137m-high (343 steps) south spire (daily 9am–5.30pm; €3.50); lower, but with a lift, is the north tower (daily 8.15am–4.30pm; July & Aug till 6pm; €4.50). The warren of alleyways north and east of **Stephansdom** preserve something of the medieval character of the city, although the architecture reflects centuries of continuous rebuilding.

Judenplatz

Though one of Vienna's prettiest little squares, **Judenplatz**, northwest of Stephansdom, is dominated by a deliberately bleak concrete **Holocaust Memorial** by British sculptor Rachel Whiteread. The square marks the site of the medieval Jewish ghetto and you can view the foundations of a fourteenth-century synagogue at the excellent **Museum Judenplatz** at no. 8 (Sun–Thurs 10am–6pm, Fri 10am–2pm; €4), which brings something of medieval Jewish Vienna to life. Buy a joint ticket (€10) to also visit the intriguing **Jüdisches Museum**, Dorotheergasse 11 (Sun–Fri

10am–6pm; €6.50; ⓦwww.jmw.at), a museum of Jewish tradition and culture.

Kärntnerstrasse and Graben

From Stephansplatz, pedestrianized Kärntnerstrasse runs south past street entertainers and shops to the illustrious **Staatsoper** (ⓦwww.wiener-staatsoper.at), opened in 1869 in the first phase of the Ringstrasse's development. A more unusual tribute to the city's musical genius is the state-of-the-art **Haus der Musik**, Seilerstätte 30 (daily 10am–10pm; €11; ⓦwww.hausdermusik.com), a hugely enjoyable museum of sound.

Running west of Stephansplatz is the more upscale Graben, featuring an extremely ornate plague column (*Pestsäule*), built to commemorate the 1679 plague.

The Hofburg

The immense, highly ornate **Hofburg** palace (ⓦwww.hofburg-wien.at) houses many of Vienna's key imperial sights. Skip the rather dull **Kaiserappartements** in favour of the more impressive **Schatzkammer** (Mon & Wed–Sun 10am–6pm; €12). Here you can see some of the finest medieval craftsmanship and jewellery in Europe, including relics of the Holy Roman Empire and the Habsburg crown jewels. The Hofburg is also home to two of the most enduring tourist images of Vienna: singing boys and prancing horses. Steps beside the Schatzkammer lead up to the **Hofmusik Kapelle** (Mon & Tues 11am–3pm, Fri 11am–1pm; €1.50), the venue for Mass with the **Vienna Boys' Choir** (mid-Sept to June Sun 9.15am; ⓣ01/533 9927, ⓦwww.wsk.at), for which you can obtain free, standing tickets from 8.30am (otherwise €5–29, book in advance).

On the north side of the Hofburg, the imperial stables are home to the white horses of the **Spanish Riding School**, known for their extraordinary, intricate performances. There are three ways to see them: book for a performance well in advance (Feb–June & late Aug to Dec, usually Sat & Sun or Fri & Sun; standing from €23, seats from €47; ⓦwww.srs.at); attend a morning exercise session (Jan–June & mid-Aug to July usually Tues–Fri, plus occasional Sat 10am–noon, box office at Josefplatz from 9am; the queue is at its worst early on, but by 11am it's usually easy enough to get in; €12); or, join a guided tour of the school and stables (Jan Tues–Sat; Feb, March & Nov Tues–Sun; April–Oct & Dec daily; tours 2pm, 3pm & 4pm; combined tour and training session €26; tickets from visitor centre at Michaelerplatz daily 9am–4pm). Alternatively, if you just want to take a peek at the horses, look into the stables (*Stallburg*) from the glass windows on Reitschulgasse.

Finally, at the Hofburg's easternmost tip, the **Albertina** (daily 10am–6pm, Wed till 9pm; €9.50; ⓦwww.albertina.at), houses one of the world's largest graphic art collections, with works by Raphael, Rembrandt, Dürer and Michelangelo.

VIENNA'S HEURIGEN

If you fancy sampling some Austrian wines and a scenic excursion out of the city, take a trip to one of the wine-producing villages on Vienna's outskirts. To the north of the Danube, **Stammersdorf** (tram #31 from Schottenring; 40min) is surrounded by vineyards and filled with traditional, family-run *Heurigen* (wine taverns). A great place to start is **Wienhof Wieninger**, 21 Stammersdorferstr. 78 (mid-April till mid-Dec Thurs & Fri 3pm–midnight, Sat & Sun midday till midnight; ⓦwww.heuriger-wieninger.at), which has a pleasant garden, a buffet and a good selection of own-label whites available by the glass.

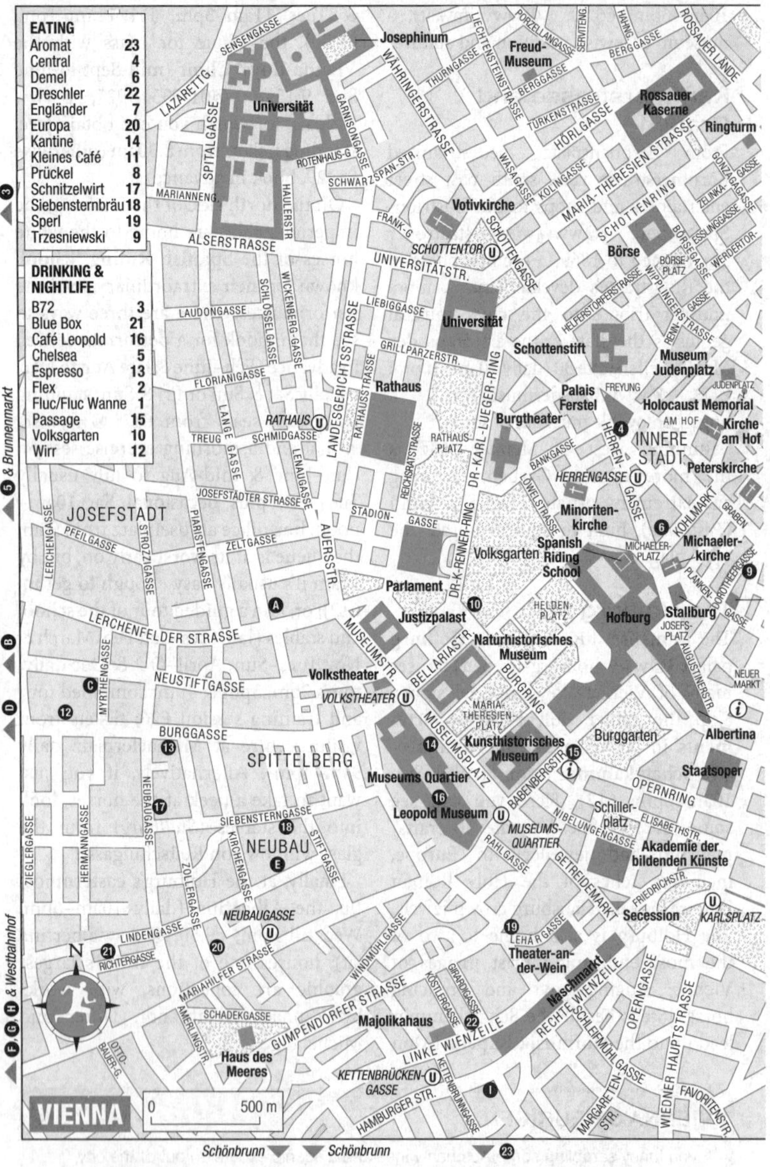

The Ring and Rathausplatz

The Ring, the large boulevard that encircles the Innere Stadt, along with its attendant monumental civic buildings, was created to replace the town's fortifications, demolished in 1857, many of these buildings now house museums. On the western section is the showpiece **Rathausplatz**, a square framed by four monumental public buildings: the Rathaus (City Hall), the Burgtheater, Parlament and the Universität – all completed in the 1880s.

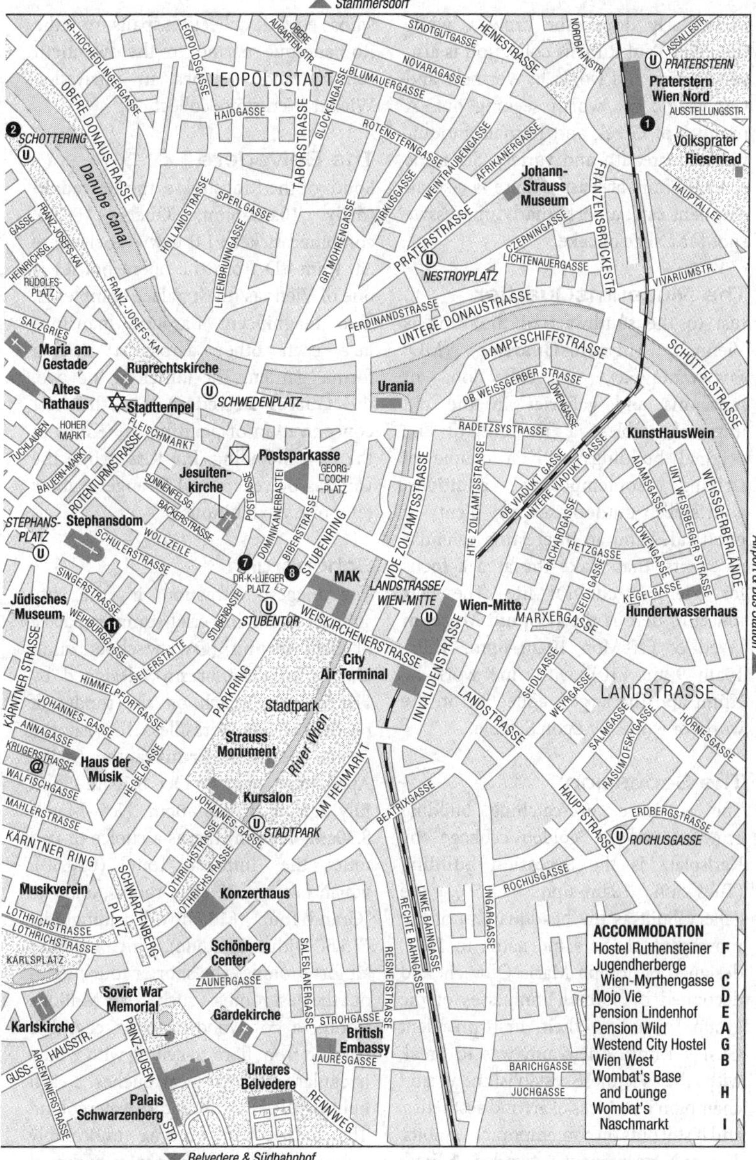

The Kunsthistorisches Museum

Of all Vienna's museums, the **Kunsthistorisches Museum** on Ringstrasse still outshines them all (Tues–Sun 10am–6pm, Thurs till 9pm; June–Aug open daily; €12; Ⓦwww.khm.at). It's one of the world's greatest collections of Old Masters – comparable with the Hermitage or Louvre. An unrivalled collection of sixteenth-century paintings by Bruegel the Elder particularly draws the crowds, while the Peter Paul Rubens collection is also very strong and works by Vermeer and Caravaggio are worth seeking out. A number of Greek and Roman antiquities add breadth and variety. Set aside several hours at least – there is also an excellent café; a particularly impressive spot for a slice of cake.

The MuseumsQuartier

Just to the southwest of the Ring is Vienna's **MuseumsQuartier** (MQ; Ⓦwww.mqw.at), a collection of museums and galleries in the old imperial stables, a mixture of the original buildings with a couple of striking contemporary additions, with stylish outdoor seating, plenty of good cafés and an interesting calendar of events, that make the area a focus for Vienna's cultural life. The best museum here is the **Leopold Museum** (Wed & Fri–Mon 10am–6pm, Thurs 10am–9pm; €10), with fine work by Klimt and the largest collection in the world of works by Egon Schiele.

The Secession

The eccentric, eye-catching building crowned with a "golden cabbage" by Karlsplatz is the **Secession building** (Tues–Sun 10am–6pm; €8.50), the gallery built as the headquarters of the movement of the same name in 1898, designed by Joseph Maria Olbrech, and decorated by several luminaries of the group, including their first president Gustav Klimt. Their aim was to break with the Viennese establishment and champion new ideas of art and aesthetics, and it still puts on contemporary exhibits. The only permanent artwork is Klimt's *Beethoven Frieze* downstairs.

MAK

Beyond Stubenring is the enjoyable **MAK** (Tues 10am–midnight, Wed–Sun 10am–6pm; €9.90, free Sat; Ⓦwww.mak.at), an applied arts museum whose eclectic collection spans from the Romanesque period to the twentieth century and includes an unrivalled Wiener Werkstätte collection.

The Belvedere

South of the Ringstrasse, the **Belvedere** (daily 10am–6pm; Oberes €9.50, combined ticket €14; Ⓦwww.belvedere.at; tram #D from the opera house) is one of Vienna's finest palace complexes. Two magnificent Baroque mansions face each other across a sloping formal garden. The loftier of the two, the **Oberes Belvedere**, has the best concentration of paintings by Klimt in the city, including *The* Kiss, while the Unteres Belvedere and Orangerie show temporary exhibitions.

Schönbrunn

The biggest attraction in the city suburbs is the imperial summer palace of **Schönbrunn** (Ⓦwww.schoenbrunn.at; U4 to Schönbrunn), designed by Fischer von Erlach on the model of residences like Versailles. To visit the palace rooms or **Prunkräume** (daily: April–June, Sept & Oct 8.30am–5pm; July & Aug 8.30am–6pm; Nov–March 8.30am–4.30pm) there's a choice of two tours: the "Imperial Tour" (€10.50), which takes in 22 state rooms, and the "Grand Tour" (€13.50 with audioguide, €15.50 with tour guide), which includes all forty rooms. The shorter tour misses out the best rooms – such as the Millions Room, a rosewood-panelled chamber covered from floor to ceiling with wildly irregular Rococo cartouches, each holding a Persian miniature watercolour. The palace can become unbearably overcrowded at the height of summer, with lengthy queues – it's a good idea to buy tickets in advance online. The splendid Schlosspark (daily dawn–dusk; free) is dotted with attractions, including the Gloriette – a hilltop colonnaded monument, now a café and terrace from which you can enjoy splendid views

(April–June & Sept 9am–6pm; July & Aug 9am–7pm; Oct 9am–5pm; €2.50), fountains, a maze and labyrinth (same hours as Gloriette; €3.50) and Vienna's excellent **Tiergarten** or zoo (daily: Jan, Nov & Dec 9am–4.30pm; Feb 9am–5pm; March & Oct 9am–5.30pm; April–Sept 9am–6.30pm; €14; Ⓦwww.zoovienna.at).

Arrival and information

Air Vienna Airport (Ⓦwww.viennaairport.com) is around 20km southeast of the city. The cheapest way to reach the centre is to take S-Bahn line #S7 to Wien-Mitte station (every 30min; 24min; €3.60 one-way). The City Airport Train (CAT; every 30min; 16min; €10 one-way) to Wien-Mitte is slightly faster. Buses (every 30min; €7 one-way) run to Ⓤ Schwedenplatz (20min) in the centre and Westbahnhof (45min).

Train Vienna's train stations are undergoing major redevelopment, with Südbahnhof being expanded into Wien Hauptbahnhof for 2013; until then, arrival points may change. Trains from the west and Hungary, plus Salzburg, and many domestic destinations, terminate at the Westbahnhof (U3 five stops from the centre); trains from Bratislava arrive at Südbahnhof (Ostbahn; Ⓤ Südtiroler Platz and a 5min walk or tram #D); Vienna-Meidling station serves trains from Graz and the Czech Republic, Poland and Slovenia (U6 four stops south of Westbahnhof).

Bus Vienna International Bus terminal is at Erdbergstr. (Ⓤ Erdberg, southeast of the centre, six stops from Stephansplatz on line U3).

Boat DDSG (Ⓦwww.ddsg-blue-danube.at) from further up the Danube, or from Bratislava, dock at Schwedenplatz.

Tourist office Main tourist office, Albertinaplatz 1, behind the opera house (daily 9am–7pm; Ⓣ01/245 55, Ⓦwww.wien.info) Also airport arrivals (daily 6am–11pm).

City transport

So many attractions are in or around the Innere Stadt that you can do a great deal on foot.

Public transport The network (Ⓦwww.wienerlinien.at) consists of trams (Strassenbahn or Bim), buses, the U-Bahn (metro) and the S-Bahn (fast commuter trains). U-Bahns run around 5/6am–12.30am, Fri & Sat 24hr, around every 20min between 1am & 5am; trams run till around midnight, A network of nightbuses centre on Schwedenplatz and Kärtner Ring/Oper.

VIENNESE ADDRESSES

Vienna is divided into **numbered districts** (*Bezirke*). District 1 is the Innere Stadt; districts 2–9 are arranged clockwise around it; districts 10–23 are a fair way out. Addresses begin with the number of the district, followed by the street name, then the house number and apartment number.

Tickets Buy your ticket from ticket booths or machines at stations, tobacconists or on board trams and buses (more expensive), then validate it at the start of your journey. One-way tickets are €1.80 (€2.20 on board buses and trams) and allow unlimited changes in one direction; day passes are: 24hr €5.70; 48hr €10 & 72hr €13.60. The Vienna Card (€18.50) acts as a 72-hour travel pass and gives discounts at attractions. If you have an ISIC card, simply buying a travel pass is a better bet.

CityBikes Vienna has a very cheap city-wide bike scheme (Ⓦwww.citybikewien.at), with stations all over the city, including behind Stephansdom on Stephansplatz. The first hour is free, second is €1, third is €2. Bikes can be rented with a credit card or with a "tourist card" rented for €2 plus deposit from Royal Tours, Herrengasse 1–3 (daily 9–11.30am & 1–6pm).

Accommodation

For cheaper accommodation booking ahead is essential in summer. Several hostels are near the Westbahnhof, which is an easy few stops into the centre.

Hostels

Hostel Ruthensteiner 15, Robert Hamerlinggasse 24 Ⓣ01/893 42 02, Ⓦwww.hostelruthensteiner.com Ⓤ Westbahnhof. Excellent, friendly and relaxed hostel an easy walk from the Westbahnhof. There's a spacious leafy courtyard, plus bar, musical instruments, kitchen, barbecue, internet, laundry and free wi-fi. Dorms €17, doubles €62.

Jugendherberge Wien-Myrthengasse 7, Myrthengasse 7 Ⓣ01/523 63 16, Ⓦwww.oejhv.or.at. Central HI hostel a short walk up Neustiftgasse from Ⓤ Volkstheater. Book well in advance. Dorms €17.50.

Mojo Vie 7, Kaiserstr. 77/8 ⓣ0676 55 111 55, ⓦwww.mymojovie.at ⓤBurggasse-Stadthalle or tram #5 to Burggasse from Westbahnhof stops outside. Charming, very stylish alternative to the standard hostel. *Mojo Vie* runs a network of apartments dotted around the neighbourhood, with dorms (one four-bed, one six-bed), or private rooms. Excellent communal areas and personal, welcoming vibe. Minimum two nights, maximum four people per group. Dorms from €20, doubles €56.

Westend City Hostel 6, Fügergasse 3 ⓣ01/597 67 29, ⓦwww.westendhostel.at. A few minutes' walk from the Westbahnhof, a refurbished 211-bed former hotel with friendly staff, patio. Dorms €22.50, en-suite rooms €69.

Wombat's "the Base" 15, Grangasse 6 and **Wombat's "The Lounge"** Mariahilferstr. 137 ⓣ01/897 23 36, ⓦwww.wombats.at. A pair of party-orientated *Wombat's* hostels, both near the Westbahnhof. With guest kitchen, laundry and free wi-fi. Dorms €20, doubles €70.

Wombat's Naschmarkt Rechte Wienzeile 35 ⓣ01/897 23 36, ⓦwww.wombats-hostels.com ⓤKettenbrückengasse. It's all about location at this newest branch of the Wombat's chain, which is right by the Naschmarkt and walking distance from the Innere Stadt. This huge huge hostel is slick, well equipped, with all dorms en suite, good bar and communal areas, and convenient, but inevitably a little bland. Dorms €20, doubles €70.

Hotels and pensions

Pension Lindenhof 7, Lindengasse 4 ⓣ01/523 04 98, ⓦwww.pensionlindenhof.at ⓤNeubaugasse. Quirky *pension* in a great location just off Mariahilferstr. The hallway is filled with plants and rooms have creaky parquet flooring. Breakfast is included, but you pay €2 extra per shower in rooms with shared facilities. Singles €37, doubles with shared bathrooms €54.

Pension Wild 8, Lange Gasse 10 ⓣ01/406 51 74, ⓦwww.pension-wild.com ⓤVolkstheater. Friendly, laidback *pension*, a short walk from the Ring in a student district behind the university. Especially popular with gay travellers; booking is essential. Singles €41, doubles (non en suite) €53, en suite shower (shared toilet) €67.

Campsites

Wien West 14, Hüttelbergstr. 80 ⓣ01/914 2314, ⓦwww.wiencamping.at. Bus #148 or #152 from ⓤHütteldorf. In the plush far-western suburbs of Vienna, with two- and four-bed bungalows to rent. Closed Feb. €7.30/person, plus €7/tent.

Eating

Cafés

Central 1, Herrengasse 14 ⓤHerrengasse. Traditional meeting-place of Vienna's intelligentsia, and Trotsky's favourite *Kaffeehaus* – of all Vienna's cafés, perhaps the most ornate. Weekday two-course set lunch €9.60. Daily till 10pm.

Demel 1, Kohlmarkt 14 ⓤHerrengasse. Elaborately displayed, *Café-Konditorei Demel*'s patisseries and cakes are highly prestigious and correspondingly pricey. Closes 7pm.

Dreschler 6, Linke Wienzelle 22 / Girardgasse 1 ⓤKarlsplatz. Takes the best of the classic Viennese café, and adds a contemporary twist – a stylish remodel and relaxed vibe day through into late evening, when there are DJs. Good snacks, and breakfasts (from €6.50). Only shuts for an hour between 2 and 3am.

Engländer 1, Postgasse 2 ⓤStubentor. Great *Kaffeehaus* with a long pedigree and food that has a touch of *nouvelle cuisine*. Snacks €3–10, mains €9–18; two-course lunch menu €9.20, including vegetarian options. Open till 1am.

Europa 7, Zollergasse 8 ⓤNeubaugasse. Lively, modern café hosting a young, trendy crowd. Good breakfast menu, weekend breakfast buffet €10.90 (9am–3pm). Open till 5am.

Kantine 7, Museumsplatz 1 ⓤMuseumsQuartier. One of the MuseumsQuartier's cafés, with a varied menu and free wi-fi. Daily till 2am, Sun till midnight.

Kleines Café 1, Franziskanerplatz 3 ⓤStephansplatz. Tiny café with outside seating, tucked away in a tranquil cobbled square, serving delicious open sandwiches (from €3.50).

Prückel Stubenring 24. You could lose hours of your life in a caffeine- and smoke-filled haze here, one of the best and most relaxed of the classic Viennese coffeehouses, with a stylish 1950s decor.

Sperl 6, Gumpendorferstr. 11 ⓤKarlsplatz/Babenbergerstr. With a slightly faded, *fin-de-siècle* interior this is among the finest of the city's coffeehouses, with reasonably priced food (daily special €7.90) and coffee and cake for around €6. July & Aug closed Sun. Mon–Sat 7am–11pm, Sun 11am–8pm.

Trzesniewski Dorotheergasse 1. Just off Graben, this is a great place for a pit stop – grab a couple of small open sandwiches, with pâté toppings such as herring, egg or spicy pepper for €1 each, washed down with a *pfiff* (0.2l; €1) of beer. Mon–Fri 8.30am–7.30pm, Sat 9am–5pm; other branches, including Marianhilfer Str. 95.

Restaurants

Aromat Margaretenstr. 52 Ⓤ Kettenbrückengasse ⓣ 01 913 24 53. Just eight tables, and a short, daily changing evening menu (mains around €8.50–12) of imaginative Mediterranean-influenced dishes, plus sweet and savoury crêpes, make this a bit of a treat. Tues–Sun 5–11pm.

Schnitzelwirt 7, Neubaugasse 52. Tram #49. Great place for *Wienerschnitzel* – a bargain at €6. Closed Sun.

Siebensternbräu 7, Siebensterngasse 19 Ⓤ Volkstheater/Neubaugasse. Popular modern *Bierkeller* that brews its own beer and serves solid Viennese food from €6.

Drinking and nightlife

If you fancy a bar crawl or live music the string of clubs under the railway arches around Ⓤ Thaliastr., Josefstädterstr. and Alser str. are a good bet.

B72 8, Hernalser Gürtel Bogen 72–73, under the arches ⓦ www.b72.at Ⓤ Alserstr. or Josefstadterstr. (between the two). Dark, designer club featuring a mixture of DJs and often good live indie bands. Open till 4am.

Blue Box 7, Richtergasse 8 ⓦ www.bluebox.at Ⓤ Neubaugasse. *Musikcafé* with resident DJs and a good snack menu (buffet plate €5.60 or €7.60). Open till 2am or later.

Café Leopold 7, Museumsplatz ⓦ www.cafe-leopold.at Ⓤ MuseumsQuartier. Coolest of the MuseumQuartier's cafés, in a very stylish glass-walled space attached to the museum. Chic café during the day, DJs and designer gear come out at night.

Chelsea 8, Gürtelbögen 29–30, Lerchenfelder Gürtel ⓦ www.chelsea.co.at Ⓤ Thaliastr. Popular, grungy rock venue with up-and-coming bands. Situated underneath the railway arches on a stretch with several bars.

Espresso 7, Burggasse 57 Ⓤ Volkstheater. Chilled bar with street terrace and retro furniture. Mon–Fri from 7.30pm, Sat & Sun from 10am.

Flex 1, Am Donaukanal ⓦ www.flex.at Ⓤ Schottenring. Serious dance-music club by the canal, attracting some of the city's best DJs. Open till 4am.

Fluc/Fluc Wanne 2, Praterstern 5 ⓦ www.fluc.at Ⓤ Praterstern. Takes shabby-chic to a new level, upstairs bar (*Fluc*) and underground club (*Fluc Wanne*), inside a former pedestrian tunnel could be mistaken for a stack of disused industrial containers during the day. Come nigh-time they transform into one of the best nights out in the city; *Fluc* opens early evening, and is always free, and both put on interesting electro, house and hip-hop nights.

Passage 1, Babenberger Passage, Burgring/Babenbergerstr. ⓦ www.sunshine.at Ⓤ MuseumsQuartier/Volkstheater. Dressy, futuristic club, in a converted pedestrian underpass. Open till 4am.

Volksgarten 1, Burgring 1 ⓦ www.volksgarten.at Ⓤ Volkstheater. Vienna's longest-running club in the park of the same name – cheesy but fun. Open till 5am.

Wirr 7, Burggasse 70 ⓦ www.wirr.at Ⓤ Volkstheater. Day-into-evening café-bar, and "night café" downstairs, with a host of events, including burlesque nights. Popular for weekend brunches and lunches (from €6.40). Daily till late.

Entertainment

The local listings magazine *Falter* (ⓦ www.falter.at) has comprehensive details of the week's cultural programme. The tourist office also publishes the free monthly *Programm*.

Konzerthaus 3, Lothringerstr. 20 ⓣ 01 242 002. ⓦ www.konzerthaus.at. Major classical venue, which also has performances of jazz and world music.

Musikverein 1, Karlsplatz 6 ⓣ 01 505 81 90 ⓦ www.musikverein-wien.at. Ornate concert hall, home of the Vienna Philharmonic.

Staatsoper 1, Opernring 2 ⓣ 01/513 15 13, ⓦ www.wiener-staatsoper.at. One of Europe's most prestigious opera houses. The season runs from September to June and tickets range from a

VIENNA'S MARKETS

Naschmarkt Ⓤ Karlsplatz. Large famous market with Turkish deli stalls, hip cafés and a plethora of stalls and snack joints, serving everything from falafel to sushi. On Saturday mornings a flea market extends south near Ⓤ Kettenbrückengasse. Mon–Fri 6am–7.30pm, Sat 6am–5pm.

Brunnenmarkt Brunnengasse Ⓤ Josefstädter Strasse. Further out, so with a distinctively local feel, Brunnenmarkt sells everything from homewares to Turkish breads and pastries. At Yppenplatz, its northern end, there's a farmers' market on Saturday mornings, where you can pick up local produce or stop for brunch at one of the many cafés. Mon–Fri 6am–6.30pm, Sat 6am–2pm.

mere €8 to over €240. Tickets often sell out, but the ticket office also sells hundreds of standing-place tickets (*Stehplätze*) each night 1hr 20min before a performance (from €3/4).

Shopping

Mariahilferstr. is best for high-street clothes shops and the big chains, though Neubaugasse, nearby, is more eclectic.

Shakespeare & Co 1, Sterngasse 2 Ⓦ www.shakespeare.co.at Ⓤ Schwedenplatz. Friendly English-language bookshop; also sells translations of Austrian authors.

Directory

Embassies Australia, 4, Mattiellistr. 2–4 ⓣ 01/506 740; Canada, 1, Laurenzerberg 2 ⓣ 01/531 38 30 00; Ireland, 1, Rotenturmstr. 16–18 ⓣ 01/715 42 46; UK, 3, Jauresgasse 12 ⓣ 01/71 61 30; US, 9, Boltzmanngasse 16 ⓣ 01/31 33 90.

Hospital Allegemeines Krankenhaus, 9, Währinger Gürtel 18–20 Ⓤ Michelbeuern-AKH.

Internet Surfland Internet Café, 1, Krugerstr. 10; daily 10am–11pm; 30min/€3.90.

Post offices 1, Fleischmarkt 19; Westbahnhof; Südbahnhof; all 7am–10pm.

Moving on

Train Bratislava (every 30min; 1hr); Budapest (6 daily; 2hr 40min); Graz (hourly; 2hr 30min); Innsbruck (18 daily; 5hr); Linz (every 30min; 1hr 45min); Melk (hourly; 1hr 15min); Prague (5 daily; 4hr 45min); Salzburg (every 30min; 3hr).

Boat DDSG (Ⓦ www.ddsg-blue-danube.at) operates boats between Vienna and Bratislava (April–Oct 4 daily; 1hr 15min).

Central Austria

West of Vienna, the Danube snakes through the Wachau, one of its most scenic stretches, where castles and vineyards cling to steep slopes above quaint villages. The western end of this 40km stretch is marked by a stunning Baroque monastery in **Melk**. Further west the river steadily loses charm, though it's still a focus for several towns and cities, including **Linz**, whose high-tech Ars Electronica museum is particularly enjoyable. South of the Danube region, the land slowly climbs and rolls into the hills of Styria, with its attractive and bustling capital **Graz**. Northwest of here, the land rises again up to the Salzkammergut, a region of fine Alpine scenery and pretty lakes within easy reach of **Salzburg**. Southwest of the Salzkammergut the peaks really start to soar and resorts like **Bad Gastein** take full advantage of the landscape and healthy spring waters to offer great skiing, and first-rate spa facilities.

MELK

For real High Baroque excess, head for the early eighteenth-century **Benedictine monastery** at **MELK** – a pilgrimage centre associated with the Irish missionary St Koloman. The monumental coffee-cake monastery, perched on a bluff over the river, dominates the town. Highlights of the interior (daily: April & Oct 9am–5pm; May–Sept 9am–6pm; tours in English 10.55am & 2.55pm; Nov–March guided tours only (in German): 11am & 2pm; €7.70, €9.50 with guided tour; Ⓦ www.stiftmelk.at) are the exquisite library, with a cherub-infested ceiling by Troger, and the rather lavish monastery church, with similarly impressive work by Rottmayr.

Arrival and information

Train The station is at the head of Bahnhofstr., which leads directly into the old quarter.

Tourist office Babenbergstr. 1 (April & Oct Mon–Fri 9am–noon & 2–5pm, Sat 10am–noon; May & June Mon–Fri 9am–noon & 2–6pm, Sat & Sun 10am–2pm; July & Aug Mon–Sat 9am–7pm, Sun 10am–noon & 5–7pm; Sept Mon–Fri 9am–noon & 2–5pm, Sat 10am–2pm; ⓣ 02752/52 30 74 10, Ⓦ www.stadt-melk.at). Has a substantial stock of private rooms, though few are central.

Accommodation

Junges Hotel Melk Abt Karl-Str. 42 ⓣ02752/526 81, ⓦmelk.noejhw.at. HI hostel ten minutes' walk from the tourist office; March–Oct, reception 4–9pm. Dorms €20.40, doubles €45.80, breakfast included.

LINZ

Away from its industrial suburbs, **LINZ** is a pleasant Baroque city straddling the Danube, which is steadily reinventing itself as a city of technology and innovation, most evident in a couple of show-stopping new museums.

What to see and do

Linz's two most striking contemporary attractions – Lentos Museum and Ars Electronica Center – face each other on either side of the Danube River; make sure you wander up this way after the sun comes down when both are illuminated, their neon facades glowing dramatically opposite each other. To the south of the river is the city's compact Old Town, the hub of which is **Hauptplatz**, with its pastel-coloured facades and central Trinity Column, crowned by a gilded sunburst. Many of the city's liveliest bars are clustered just west of here, around the triangle formed by Hoffgasse, Altstadt and Hahnengasse. Heading south from the Hauptplatz, the busy shopping street Landstrasse leads south towards the train station.

Lentos

A modern addition to the city's cultural scene nestles beside the Danube: the shimmering, hangar-like steel-and-glass **Lentos** (Tues–Sun 10am–6pm, Thurs till 9pm; €6.50; ⓦwww.lentos.at), which houses contemporary and modern art, including Klimt and Schiele.

Ars Electronica Center

Just across the river is Linz's other major attraction, and worth a trip to the city alone, the unusual **Ars Electronica Center**, Hauptstrasse 2 (Tues, Wed & Fri 9am–5pm, Thurs 9am–9pm, Sat & Sun 10am–6pm; €7; ⓦwww.aec.at). A Tardis-like temple to science and technology, inside the glowing box is an impressive series of interactive high-tech exhibits. One highlight is the "CAVE", a virtual-reality room with 3D projections on the walls and floor. Basement areas explore future developments in biology, materials, the brain and robots – set aside several hours and get stuck into the hands-on experiments.

Arrival and information

Train station 2km south of the centre, at the end of Landstr; all trams (lines #1, #2 and #3) from the underground platform at the station (direction "Zentrum") run up Landstr. to Hauptplatz.
Tourist office Alte Rathaus, Hauptplatz 1 (May–Sept Mon–Sat 9am–7pm, Sun 10am–7pm; Oct–April Mon–Sat 9am–5pm, Sun 10am–5pm; ⓣ0732/70 70 20 09, ⓦwww.linz.at); sells the Linz Card (1 day €15, students €10; 3-day €25, students €20) which includes entry to museums and travel.
City transport Useful network of trams and buses: "mini" 4-stop ticket €0.90; single journey ("midi", transferable) €1.90; 24hr "maxi" ticket €3.80, under-21s €1.90. The Pöstlingbergbahn from Hauptplatz is a tourist tram up to the Pöstlingberg on the north side, a hill with good views over the city and a beer garden (every 30min, 25min one-way, €5.60 return).

Accommodation

Herberge Linz Kapuzinerstr. 14 ⓣ0699 11 80 7003, ⓔherberge.linz@aon.at. Very central (5min walk west of Hauptplaz, along Promenade off Landstr. then Klammstr.), but bare-bones hostel, clean basic dorms and kitchens, some nice outdoor space; check-in only 6–8pm. Dorms €17.
Jugendherberge Stanglhofweg 3 ⓣ0732/66 44 34, ⓦwww.jugendherbergsverband.at. Friendly youth hostel 2km from Hauptbahnhof; bus #17, #19, #19a, #45a, or #46 to "Leondingerstr.". All bedrooms are en suite, breakfast included. Dorms €18.50, doubles €47.
Wilder Mann Goethestr. 14 ⓣ0732/65 60 78, ⓦwww.wildermann.cc. Simple, but friendly and convenient hotel, between the station and the centre

(take the tram one stop from the station to Goethestr.); rooms available with shared facilities or with en-suite showers, breakfast extra. Singles €32, doubles €44.

Eating, drinking and nightlife

Alte Welt Hauptplatz 4. Unpretentious bar and wine cellar with tables on a cosy courtyard just off the Hauptplatz and on the main square itself. Hearty, Austrian/Italian-influenced mains; €6.50–15. Open till 2am, with live music and cabaret some nights.

p'aa Altstadt 28. Contemporary vegetarian restaurant, with an imaginative, global menu including curries, Greek, Turkish and Italian-inspired dishes, salads and tasty juices, all using top-quality fresh ingredients. Lunch specials €7; evening mains €12.50–14. Mon–Sat 11am–2.30pm & 5.30pm–midnight. Also has a deli/takeaway place just off the Hauptmarkt at Rathausgasse 5.

Traxlmayr Promenade 16. Traditional coffeehouse; serves an excellent selection of coffees, and is a good place to treat yourself to a slice of *Linzer Torte*, the town's ubiquitous almond-and-jam *torte* (€3.10). Closed Sun.

Moving on

Train Graz (7 daily; 3hr 30min–3hr 45min); Salzburg (every 30min; 1hr 15min); Vienna (every 30min; 1hr 45min).

GRAZ

Austria's second-largest city, **GRAZ**, owes its importance to the defence of central Europe against the Turks. From the fifteenth century, it was constantly under arms, rendering it more secure than Vienna and leading to a modest seventeenth-century flowering of the arts. Today Graz celebrates its reputation as a city of design, thanks to a clutch of modern architectural adventures and a large student population, and it's a fun place to spend a few days without the tourist traffic of Innsbruck or Salzburg.

What to see and do

Graz is compact and easy to explore, with most sights within easy walking distance of its central **Hauptplatz**, with its fantastically decorated Baroque facades.

The Altstadt

From Hauptplatz, it's a few steps to the River Mur and two examples of Graz's architectural renaissance: the **Murinsel** is an ultramodern floating bridge-cum-meeting-place with a café linking the two banks, inspired by an open mussel, while the giant bulbous **Kunsthaus Graz** (Tues–Sun 10am–6pm; €8; Ⓦwww.kunsthausgraz.at), is a museum of contemporary art, video installation and photography. Entrance tickets to the Kunsthaus function as a day-pass for several city museums that form part of the Landesmuseum Joanneum (Ⓦwww.museum-joanneum.at), a city-wide institution.

Among them is the **Landes zeughaus** (Mon & Wed–Sun: April–Oct 10am–6pm; Nov to early Jan & March only with guided tour, on hour 10.15am–2.15pm, Sun also 3.15pm; €8), the city armoury on Herrengasse just south of the Hauptplatz, which bristles with sixteenth-century weapons used to keep the Turks at bay.

Schlossberg

To get a view over the city take a trip up the wooded hill that overlooks the town: either walk up the zigzagging stone stairs from Schlossbergplatz or take the lift (daily 8am–12.30am; €0.80 each way) or funicular (April–Sept Mon–Wed & Sun 9am–midnight, Thurs–Sat 9am–2am; Oct–March daily 10am–10pm; €1.90, included in public transport ticket), from Sackstrasse. The **Schloss**, or fortress, was destroyed by Napoleon in 1809; only a few prominent features survive – noticeably the huge sixteenth-century **Uhrturm** (clock tower), and more distant **Glockenturm** (bell tower).

Schloss Eggenberg

Another part of the Landesmuseum Joanneum is the Baroque **Schloss Eggenberg**, 4km west of the city centre, (tram #1 from the station). Designed in imitation of the Escorial for Hans Ulrich von Eggenberg (1568–1634),

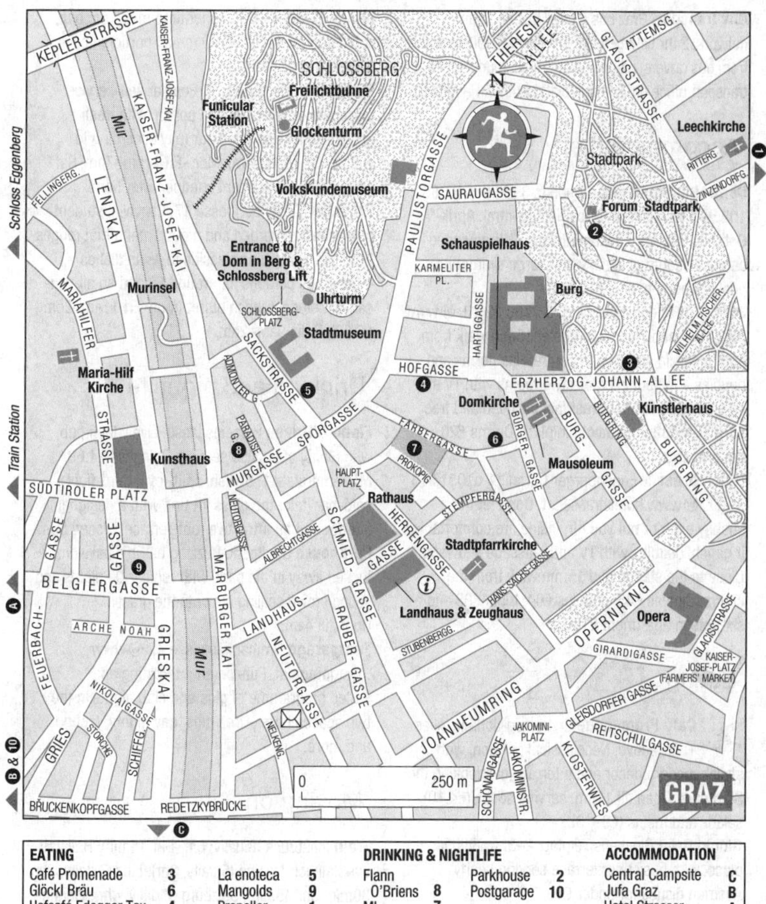

EATING				DRINKING & NIGHTLIFE				ACCOMMODATION	
Café Promenade	3	La enoteca	5	Flann O'Briens	8	Parkhouse	2	Central Campsite	C
Glöckl Bräu	6	Mangolds	9	Ml	7	Postgarage	10	Jufa Graz	B
Hofcafé Edegger Tax	4	Propeller	1					Hotel Strasser	A

chief minister to Ferdinand II, the Schloss houses on one floor the Alte Galerie (March & Nov: Tues–Sun 10am–4pm; April–Oct: Tues–Sun 10am–6pm; €8), whose intelligently curated collection includes thirteenth-century devotional works, and a macabre *Triumph of Death* by Jan Bruegel. The palace rooms can only be visited by guided tour (Prunkräume; hourly: Tues–Sun 10am–4pm, except 1pm; English tours usually available); they were designed as an allegory of the universe (24 rooms, 365 windows on the outside, four towers and so on); the highlight is the "Room of the Planets", a great hall with an elaborate ceiling and wall paintings depicting the zodiac, and also the three Asian rooms, in particular the one decorated with rare Japanese panels from Osaka.

Arrival and information

Train Graz's train station is on the western edge of town, a 15min walk or short tram ride (#1, #3, #6 or #7) from Hauptplatz.

Tourist office Herrengasse 16 (daily: Jan–March & Nov 10am–5pm; April–Sept 10am–6pm; ⓣ0316/807 50, ⓦwww.graztourismus).

City transport Graz has a good bus and tram network. 24hr ticket €4.20; 1hr ticket €1.90, available from bus drivers, machines on trams, tourist office, transport office on Jakominiplatz south of Hauptplatz.

Accommodation

Central Campsite Martinhofstr. 3 ⓣ0676 37 85 102, ⓦwww.tiscover.at/campingcentral; April–Oct; bus #32 from Jakominiplatz. Well-equipped campsite south of Graz, with a large swimming pool. €8/person, plus €13/tent.

Jufa Graz Idlhofgasse 74 ⓣ05/708 32 10, ⓦwww.jufa.at. Friendly, modern hostel 15min walk from both the train station and centre. Has dorms and doubles – including hotel-style rooms with TV and en suite. Good buffet breakfast included and free wi-fi. Bus #32 from Jakominiplatz. Dorms €20, doubles €60.

Hotel Strasser Eggenburger Gürtel 11 ⓣ0316/71 39 77, ⓦwww.hotelstrasser.at. Don't let the shabby exterior put you off; inside are comfortable, if garish, doubles with TV and massage showers. Close to the station and 15min walk from the centre. Singles €45, doubles €64, triple €93 and six-person apartment €180.

Eating

Café Promenade Erzherzog-Johann-Allee 1. Attractive, Neoclassical pavilion, with stylish modern decor and a terrace overlooking the Stadtpark. Open till 11pm, serving soups (€4.10), salads and mains (€9–13).

Glöckl Bräu Glockenspielplatz 2–3. Traditional place, with busy beer terrace serving hearty Austrian dishes for under €10.

Hofcafé Edegger Tax Hofgasse 8. Sedate, genteel little café, adjoined to a long-established city-centre cake shop. Coffee from €2.10. Closed Sun.

La enoteca Sackstr. 14 (in courtyard). This wine shop and restaurant, with a small cosy interior and a few courtyard tables, serves a short menu of delicious pasta dishes and antipasti. Evening dishes €6.50–€11.50, lunchtime menu of soup, salad and pasta for €5.90 (small portions) or €7.40 (large).

Mangolds Griesgasse 11. Popular self-service place and excellent veggie option, with fresh juices and a large salad bar (pay according to weight: €1.18/100gm). Mon–Fri 11am–7pm, Sat 11am–4pm; 20 percent cheaper after 5pm.

Propeller Zinzendorfgasse 17. Convivial student pub, with beergarden and a good menu that ranges from hearty Austrian classics to Asian dishes – generous portions for around €8 and an all-you-can-eat student lunch buffet (Mon–Fri 11am–2pm €6.80). Daily 9am–2am.

Drinking and nightlife

Flann O'Briens Paradiesgasse. Lively Irish pub, with plenty of outside seating. Guinness €4.60.

MI Färberplatz 1. Stylish, split-level third-floor café-bar (take the glass lift up), with a designer interior and an attractive roof-terrace. Closed Sun.

Parkhouse Stadtpark. Buzzing bar in a pavilion, tucked away in the park, with regular DJ nights and young crowd spilling out onto the grass. Open till 4am.

Postgarage Dreihackengasse 42 ⓦwww.postgarage.at. Puts on an interesting and varied programme of gigs and club nights in the two spaces here – free gigs, gay nights, techno and more.

Moving on

Train Innsbruck (8 daily; 6hr–6hr 15min); Hallstatt via Stainach-Irdning (5 daily; 3hr); Linz (7 daily; 3hr 30min–3hr 45min); Salzburg (7 daily; 4hr); Vienna (hourly 2hr 30min).

SALZBURG

For many visitors, **SALZBURG** represents the quintessential Austria, offering ornate architecture, mountain air,

GRAZ FARMERS' MARKET

The region of Styria (Steiermarkt) is known as a wine-growing and farming region, producing local specialities it is proud of, in particular **Kürbiskernöl** (pumpkin seed oil), which has a delicious, nutty flavour and is used in salad dressings and other dishes on many Graz menus. As a result, Graz's **farmers' market** (Kaiser-Josef-Platz; Mon–Sat 6am–1pm) is particularly good, and an excellent place to buy bottles of Kürbiskernöl, local cheeses, breads, meat and other produce. There are also snack stands, coffee joints and fresh juice bars.

and the musical heritage of the city's most famous son, Wolfgang Amadeus **Mozart**. The city and surrounding area were for centuries ruled by a series of independent prince-archbishops, and it is the pomp and wealth of their court that is evident everywhere in the fine Baroque Altstadt.

What to see and do

Salzburg's compact centre straddles the River Salzach, squeezed between two dramatic mountains – Mönchsberg on the west and Kapuzinerberg on the east. The **west bank** forms a tight-knit network of alleys and squares – Alter Markt, Residenzplatz, Mozartplatz (with obligatory statue of the composer) and Domplatz – overlooked by the medieval **Hohensalzburg fortress** high above.

Residenzplatz

The complex of Baroque buildings at the centre of Salzburg exude the ecclesiastical and temporal power of Salzburg's archbishops, whose erstwhile living quarters – the **Residenz** – dominate the west side of Residenzplatz. You can take a self-guided audio-tour of the lavish **state rooms** (daily 10am–5pm; combined ticket with Residenzgalerie €8.50), and then visit the **Residenzgalerie** (closed Mon), one floor above, whose collection includes a few interesting paintings, most notably the small, almost sketch-like *Old Woman Praying* by Rembrandt.

On the east side of Residenzplatz, accessed from Mozartplatz, is the Neue Residenz, built by Archbishop Wolf Dietrich von Raitenau, topped by the **Glockenspiel**, a seventeenth-century musical clock which chimes at 7am, 11am and 6pm. It now houses the excellent Salzburg Museum (Tues–Sun 9am–5pm, Thurs till 8pm; July, Aug & Dec also Mon 9am–5pm; €7; Ⓦwww.salzburgmuseum.at), which as well as showing some of the archbishop's lavish rooms, explores the history of Salzburg, the rediscovery of Salzburg by Romantic painters and the city's tourist industry.

Domplatz and Franziskanerkirche

The pale marble facade of the **Dom** dominates **Domplatz**, while inside, the impressively cavernous Renaissance structure dazzles with its ceiling frescoes. Across Domplatz, an archway leads through to the Gothic **Franziskanerkirche**, which houses a fine Baroque altar around an earlier *Madonna and Child*. The altar is enclosed by an arc of nine chapels, and a frenzy of stucco. Look out for the twelfth-century marble lion that guards the stairway to the pulpit.

Mozarts Geburtshaus and Mozarts Wohnhaus

Getreidegasse, the main street in Salzburg's old town, is lined with opulent boutiques, painted facades and wrought-iron shop signs. At no. 9 is the canary-yellow **Mozarts Geburtshaus** (daily: July & Aug 9am–8pm; Sept–June 9am–5.30pm; €6, joint ticket with Wohnhaus €12; Ⓦwww.mozarteum.at), where the musical prodigy was born (in 1756) and lived until the age of 17. Between the waves of tour parties it can be an evocative place, housing some fascinating period instruments, including one of his baby-sized violins. Over the Salzach River on Makartplatz is **Mozarts Wohnhaus**, the family home from 1773 till 1787 (same hours; €7), containing an engrossing multimedia history of the composer.

Hohensalzburg

Overlooking the city from the rocky mountain, the fortified **Hohensalzburg** (daily: May–Sept 9.30am–7pm; Oct–April 9.30am–5pm; €10.50 including funicular, €7.40 without; Ⓦwww.salzburg-burgen.at) is Salzburg's key landmark. You can get up here using

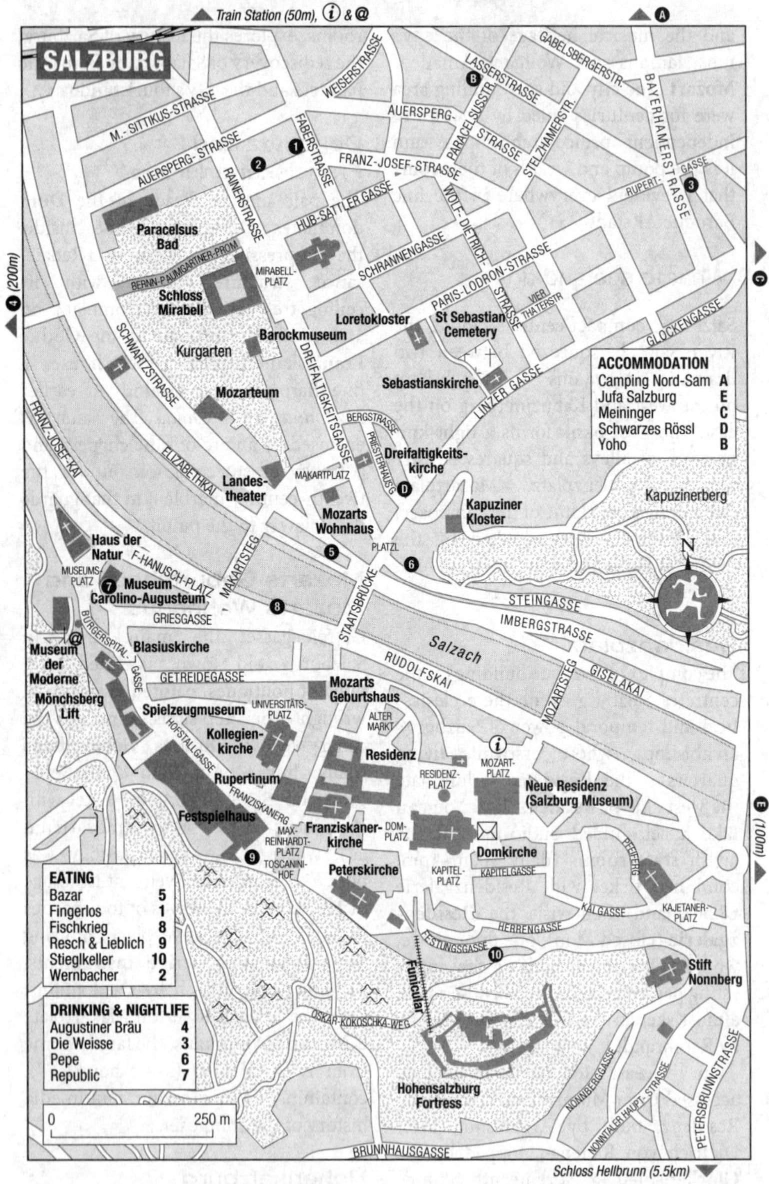

the oldest funicular in Austria (daily: May, June & Sept 9am–8pm; July & Aug 9am–10pm; Oct–April 9am–5pm; every 10min; funicular only, Oct–April from 5pm, May–Sept from 7pm €3.80 return) from Fesstungsgasse behind the Dom, although the walk up isn't as hard as it looks. Begun around 1070, the fortress gradually became a more salubrious courtly seat. Included in the price is an audioguide tour of the observation tower – with spectacular views

– and battlements, separate access to the impressive state rooms and various exhibitions. On summer, evenings (7–9.30pm), entrance to the ramparts is free, providing a good feel for the place.

Mönchsberg

For some of the best views across to the fortress, take the Mönchsberg lift up to the **Mönchsberg** from Anton-Neumayr-Platz (daily 8am–7pm, Wed till 9pm; July & Aug daily till 9pm; €2). At the summit, the sleekly concrete-and-glass Museum der Moderne, which puts on big-name art exhibitions (Tues–Sun 10am–6pm, Wed till 8pm; €8), is a stylish contrast to all the Baroque.

Schloss Mirabell

Across the river from the Altstadt, **Schloss Mirabell** on Mirabellplatz stands on the site of a palace built by Archbishop Wolf Dietrich for his mistress Salome, with whom the energetic prelate was rumoured to have sired a dozen children. The palace's ornate gardens offer a much-photographed view back across the city.

Schloss Hellbrunn and the Untersberg

The Italianate palace **Schloss Hellbrunn** (daily: April, Oct & Nov 9am–4.30pm; May, June & Sept 9am–5.30pm; July & Aug 9am–9pm, only Wasserspile after 6pm; €9.50; Ⓦwww.hellbrunn.at) on Salzburg's southern fringe – 5km from the city centre – was built in the early seventeenth century by Salzburg's decadent archbishop Marus Sitticus as a place for entertaining. The main attraction is the gardens' impressive array of fountains and watery gimmicks, or *Wasserspiele*; guided tours of them depart every 15min, with the tour guide showing off all the tricks and hidden fountains, including an elaborate, water-powered mechanical theatre, with great aplomb (prepare to be splashed). The palace itself features paintings of Sitticus's unusual animal collection, and a lavishly frescoed festival hall and music room.

To get to Schloss Hellbrunn take bus #25 from the train station or Mirabellplatz (every 20–30min). This bus continues to the village of St Leonhard, 7km further south, where the 1853-metre **Untersberg** is climbed by a cable car (March–June & Oct 8.30am–5pm; July–Sept 8.30am–5.30pm; Dec–Feb 9am–4pm; return €20), for impressive views of Salzburg to the north and the Alps to the south, making it a hit with summer hikers and skiers in winter.

Arrival and information

Train The station is 2km north of Mozartplatz; numerous buses run to Mirabellplatz and Altstadt.
Tourist office Mozartplatz 5 (daily: June–Sept 9am–7pm; Oct–May 9am–6pm; Ⓣ0662/88 98 73 30, Ⓦwww.salzburginfo.at); also at the train station (daily: June–Sept 8.30am–8pm; Oct–May 9am–6pm). Both offices sell the **Salzburg Card** (Nov–April €22/24hr, €30/48hr; May–Oct €25/24hr, €34/48hr; 10 percent student discount), which includes public transport and admission to all of the sights – if you go on the Unterbergs cable car it nearly pays for itself.
City transport Bus network centring on the train station and Mirabellplatz. Single ticket from tobacconists and transport offices €1.60 (€1.90 on board).

THE SOUND OF MUSIC

Salzburg certainly wastes no time cashing in on its connection with the legendary singing Von Trapp family, immortalized in the movie *The Sound of Music*. From its kiosk on Mirabellplatz, Panorama Tours (Ⓣ0662/883 21 10, Ⓦwww.panoramatours.com) runs what they dub "**The Original Sound of Music Tour**" (daily 9.30am & 2pm; 4 hr; €37) on which you're bussed to the key film locations, such as Hellsbrun Palace and Mondsee Cathedral, played the soundtrack and sent away with a free *edelweiss* souvenir.

Accommodation

Camping Nord-Sam Samstr. 22a ⓣ0662/64 04 94, ⓦwww.camping-nord-sam.com. The most central campsite, well equipped with a heated outdoor pool. Bus #23 from the train station to stop Mauermannstr. €8/person, plus €5/tent.
Jufa Salzburg Josef Preis Allee 18 ⓣ05/7083 613, ⓦwww.jufa.at. Very central and well-equipped large youth hostel, popular with groups. Includes breakfast. Bus #25 from the train station. Dorms €21, doubles €80.
Meininger Fürbergstr. 18–20 ⓣ0720/88 34 14, ⓦwww.meininger-hotels.com. New, well-equipped and large hostel. Some rooms and the fifth-floor terrace have views over Kapuzinerberg. Located on a busy junction out of the centre, but convenient bus #2 or #4 from Mirabellplatz to Sterneckstr. Dorms from €15, doubles from €64.
Schwarzes Rössl Priesterhausgasse 6 ⓣ0662/87 44 26, ⓦwww.academiahotels.at. Wonderful, creaky old place, in a central location. Great value for money. Rooms available with shared or private facilities. July–Sept. Singles €50, twins €80.
Yoho Paracelsusstr. 9 ⓣ0662/87 96 49, ⓦwww.yoho.at. Very popular and often fully booked hostel near the train station. With sociable bar, internet café and laundry facilities. Dorms €19, doubles €65.

Eating

Cafés

Bazar Schwarzstr. 3. Elegant coffeehouse with a pleasant river-view terrace. Breakfast €4.50–14.
Fingerlos Franz-Josef-Str. 9. Stylish and relaxed *Café-Konditorei*, serving cakes as fine as you'll find in Salzburg, and excellent breakfasts. Coffee €3. Tues–Sun 7.30am–7.30pm.
Wernbacher Franz-Josef-Str. 5. Classic café with a gorgeous plush 1950s interior. Specials (€9.90–16.90) change every week, but expect Austrian classics plus American options such as burgers and club sandwiches.

Restaurants

Fischkrieg Hanuschplatz 4. Self-service riverside place serving fish and seafood in every form: fishburgers (€2.30) or grilled squid with fries €6.50. Mon–Sat till 6.30pm.
Resch & Lieblich Toscaninihof 1. Tucked away near the Festspielhaus, offering good-value Austrian cuisine in dining rooms carved out of the Hohensalzburg cliffs. Daily specials from €7.20. Closed Sun.
Stieglkeller Festungsgasse 10. Enormous brewery with a beer terrace overlooking the town. Solid traditional food from €8.30.

Drinking and nightlife

Augustiner Bräu Augustinerstr. 4–6. Fifteen minutes northwest of the centre, this vast beer hall has a raucous open-air terrace. Own-brewed beer is served in huge glasses – €5.80 for 1l. Mon–Fri 3–11pm, Sat & Sun 2–11pm.
Die Weisse 10 Rupertgasse. Lively micro-brewery, well off the tourist track, with nice little beer garden and great pub food. Goulash and dumplings €11.
Pepe Steingasse 3. Intimate cocktail bar near the river. Open till 3am.
Republic Anton-Neumayr-Platz 2. Stylish restaurant-club, serving food until 11pm (lunch specials €6.90). The wide-ranging DJ and live music programme (anything from salsa to blues or electro) attracts a young, trendy crowd. Open till 4am Friday and Saturday.

Entertainment

The city hosts dozens of concerts all year round; check with Salzburg Ticket Service (ⓦwww.salzburgticket.com), in the tourist office on Mozartplatz.
Salzburg Festival Late July to late Aug; ⓣ0662/804 55 00, ⓦwww.salzburgfestival.at. One of Europe's premier festivals of classical music, opera and theatre, with outdoor concerts

Directory

Consulates UK, Alter Markt 4 ⓣ0664/610 56 17.
Internet Isis in the train station (€3/hr).
Post office Postamt 1010, Residenzplatz 9.

Moving on

Train Bad Gastein (9 daily; 1hr 30min); Graz (7 daily; 4hr); Hallstatt via Attnang-Puchheim (8 daily; 2hr 10min–2hr 40min); Innsbruck (9 daily; 2hr); Linz (every 30min; 1hr 15min); Munich (hourly; 2hr); Werfen (hourly; 40–50min).
Bus Strobl (for St Wolfgang; hourly; 1hr 10min).

WERFEN

With its impressive fortification and spectacular ice caves, **WERFEN**, 40km south of Salzburg, offers a great day of sightseeing, but arrive early to comfortably see both. The moody castle **Festung Hohenwerfen** (April Tues–Sun 9.30am–4pm; May–Sept daily 9am–5pm; mid-July to mid-Aug till 6pm; Oct daily 9.30am–4pm; €10.50, €14 with lift), on an outcrop above town, lies a twenty-minute signed walk from Werfen's train station. Though much modified over the years, it has eleventh-century origins and all the usual components – ornate chapel and torture chamber included – are neatly gathered around a courtyard. There are daily falconry displays (11am & 3pm) too.

Werfen's castle may tower over the town, but up the road at the **Eisriesenwelt ice caves**, it's a mere pimple on the valley floor. The caves are more than two hours' walk from the entrance building, so most visitors take a cable car. Tours (at least hourly: daily July & Aug 9.30am–4.30pm; May, June, Sept & Oct 9.30am–3.30pm; €19 with cable car, €8.50 without) explore the first kilometre of a 40km network and last around 75 minutes. It's cold enough to require a jumper.

Trains from Salzburg frequently arrive at Werfen's station, from where buses to the caves depart daily at 8.20am, 10.20am, 12.20pm & 2.20pm, with more departures from an official departure point across the river. Bus drivers sell a combined ticket for the ride up, the cable car and the cave (€22.60).

THE SALZKAMMERGUT

The **Salzkammergut**, Austria's lake district, features a spectacular series of lakes and mountains. You can get a taster for the area in a day-trip from Salzburg to St Wolfgang, or on a "Sound of Music tour", but if you want to hike, mountain bike or just chill out, head to a lakeside campsite or B&B for a few days relaxation – picture-perfect Hallstatt is a good choice.

St Wolfgang

The pretty little village of **ST WOLFGANG**, on the north shore of Wolfgangersee, is undeniably picturesque, though it can get crowded in summer, and provides a good taster of the region, particularly if you take the vintage train to the top of the **Schafberg** peak (May–Oct; €29 return; to avoid queuing, reserve a seat on ⓣ06138/223 20, ⓦwww.schafbergbahn.at) from a station on the western edge of town.

In town, the **Pfarrkirche**, above the lake shore, houses a high altar, an extravagantly pinnacled structure 12m in height, that was completed between 1471 and 1481, and features brightly gilded scenes of the *Coronation of the Virgin* flanked by scenes from the life of St Wolfgang.

Buses from Strobl (see box below) drop off at both ends of town, before and after the road tunnel that bypasses the centre. The **tourist office** (Mon–Fri 9am–6pm, Sat 9am–noon; ⓣ06138/80 03, ⓦwww.wolfgangsee.at) is at the eastern entrance to the road tunnel.

Hallstatt

The jewel of the Salzkammergut is **HALLSTATT**, which clings to the base of precipitous cliffs on the shores of the Hallstättersee, 20km south of

GETTING AROUND THE SALZKAMMERGUT

A single **train** line runs northen–south from Attnang-Puchheim via **Bad Ischl** (one of the region's main towns) and **Hallstatt** to Stainach Irdning (hourly; 2hr 09min total journey), with easy connections **from Salzburg** and Linz at Attnang-Pucheim and **from Graz** at Stainach Irdning. Buses run from Salzburg to many villages, with Bad Ischl a useful hub for connecting buses. Hourly **buses** between Salzburg and Bad Ischl run east along the southern shore of the Wolfgangersee; for **St Wolfgang** change at Strobl for a connecting bus.

Bad Ischl. With towering peaks and a pristine lake, this is a stunning setting in which to hike, swim or rent a boat. Arriving **by train** is an atmospheric and evocative experience; the station is on the opposite side of the lake, and the ferry, which meets all incoming trains, gives truly dramatic views.

What to see and do

Hallstatt gave its name to a distinct period of Iron Age culture after Celtic remains were discovered in the salt mines above the town. Many of the finds date back to the ninth century BC, and can be seen in the **Museum Hallstatt** (April & Oct daily 10am–4pm; May–Sept daily 10am–6pm; Nov–March Wed–Sun 11am–3pm; €7.50; Ⓦwww.museum-hallstatt.at).

The **Pfarrkirche** has a south portal adorned with sixteenth-century Calvary scenes. In the graveyard outside is a small stone structure known as the **Beinhaus** (daily 10am–5pm), traditionally the repository for the skulls of villagers. The skulls, some quite recent, are inscribed with the names of the deceased and dates of their death, and are often decorated.

The steep Gainswand-Weg starts behind the graveyard to lead up to the **Salzachtal** (1hr 30min of hard hiking), the highland valley where **salt mines** once ensured the area's prosperity, and can still be viewed (guided tour only: late April to late Oct daily 9.30am–3/4.30pm; €18). You can also take the **funicular** (late April to late Oct daily 9am–4.30/6pm; €12 return, combined ticket with tour €24) from the suburb of Lahn.

Arrival and information

Train The station is across the lake; ferries are timed to coincide with trains (€2.20). Return ferry times are posted up at the ferry station and around town; the last train to Hallstatt arrives around 6.30pm.

Bus Stop in the suburb of Lahn, a 10min lakeside walk south of the centre.

Tourist office Seestr. 169 (May, June, Sept & Oct Mon–Fri 9am–1pm & 2–5pm; July & Aug Mon–Fri 9am–5pm, Sat & Sun 9am–4pm; Nov–April Mon–Fri 9am–4pm; Ⓣ06134/82 08, Ⓦwww.hallstatt.net).

Accommodation and eating

Camping Klausner-Höll Lahnstr. Ⓣ06134/83 22, Ⓦwww.camping.hallstatt.net. A short walk from the landing stage at Lahn, on the outskirts of the village. Quiet and well equipped. Mid-April to Oct. €7.50/person, plus €4.50/tent; also has guest rooms from €44.

Gasthaus zur Mühle Kirchenweg 36 Ⓣ06134/83 18, Ⓦwww.hallstatturlaub.at. Welcoming, small bar, restaurant and hostel set back from the landing stage, with a good line in pizzas (from €7). Upstairs are some basic dorm rooms. Dorms €14.

Gasthof Simony Markt 105 Ⓣ06134/8231, Ⓦwww.gasthof-simony.at. Located right by the ferry station and the main square, this relaxed, attractive guesthouse has a good range from singles to quad rooms, with shared or en-suite bathrooms, decorated with traditional wooden furniture and some with balconies overlooking the lake. Also has a lakeside restaurant. Singles €40, doubles from €60; includes a good breakfast.

BAD GASTEIN

Combining the quiet elegance of an old nineteenth-century spa destination with modern trappings and reasonably modest price tags, the resort of **BAD GASTEIN**, 94km south of Salzburg, is one of Austria's best budget mountain getaways. Note, however, it's a seasonal destination for winter skiing and high-summer hiking only.

OUTDOOR ACTIVITIES

Boats can be rented from the boatshed just south of the landing stage (1hr €15). The tourist office can advise on hiking routes and sell local hiking guides. At the southern end of town in Lahn is a "Badinsel", an artificial island for sunbathing and swimming (changing facilities nearby).

What to see and do

The town fills the head of the Gastein valley with most hotels arranged in tiers up either side, with a waterfall running through the centre. There are some elegant Jugendstil buildings, but the overall impression is of distinctly faded grandeur. The mountains are the chief attraction, served by two gondolas, and are a big draw for winter skiers. The four **ski areas** (www.skigastein.com) offer plenty for every standard; day-passes cost €42. In summer, the gondolas serve a web of **hiking trails**, with the 2246-metre Stubnerkogel mountain trail (late May to mid-Oct 8.30am–4pm; €18 return) offering particularly fine views.

Bad Gastein's radon-rich waters have made it a restorative destination since medieval times. To sample them today head to the **Felsentherme**, Bahnhofplatz (daily 9am–9pm; www.felsentherme.com; 3hr €19.50), a spa with a collection of pools and saunas, many with splendid views, and a full menu of beauty treatments.

Arrival and information

Train The station is at the top end of the centre, within walking distance of most central accommodation.
Tourist office Kaiser-Franz-Josef-Str. 1, a short walk downhill from the bus and train station (June to mid-July Mon–Fri 8am–6pm, Sat 9am–noon; mid-July to Sept Mon–Fri 8am–6pm, Sat 9am–3pm, Sun 9am–noon; Oct–May Mon–Fri 8am–6pm; 06432/339 35 60, www.gastein.com). Can book private rooms (from €36).
Gastein Card Given out free by hotels and hostels if you stay, and offers discounts on local transport, services and attractions.

Accommodation

Euro Youth Hotel Krone Bahnhofsplatz 8 06434/23 300, www.euro-youth-hotel.at. Large, sociable hostel close to the station. Offers ski or spa packages. Closes April, May, Oct & Nov. Dorms €16, doubles €50.
Junge Hotel Bad Gastein Ederplatz 2 06434/20 80, www.hostel-badgastein.at. Slick HI hostel, a 10min walk from the train station, away from the centre. Dorms €17, doubles €50.

Eating and drinking

Jägerhäusl Kaiser-Franz-Josef-Str. 9 06434/202 54. A lively, traditional place to eat with a big outdoor terrace. Serves pizzas and Austrian classics like *Schnitzel* and *Käsespätzle* (pasta with cheese; mains €8–15.90).

Western Austria

West towards the mountain province of **Tyrol**, Austria's grandiose Alpine scenery begins to emerge. Most trains from Salzburg travel through a corner of Bavaria in Germany before joining the Inn valley and climbing back into Austria towards **Innsbruck**. A less direct but more scenic route (more likely if you're coming from Graz) cuts by the majestic **Hoher Tauern** – site of Austria's highest peak, the Grossglockner. As Tyrol's main town, Innsbruck offers the most convenient mix of urban sights and Alpine splendour.

INNSBRUCK

Nestled in the Alps and encircled by ski resorts, **INNSBRUCK** is a compact city cradled by towering mountains. It has a rich history: Maximilian I based his imperial court here in the 1490s, placing the city at the heart of European politics for a century and a half. This combination of historical pedigree and proximity to the mountains has put Innsbruck firmly on the tourist trail.

What to see and do

Most attractions are confined to the central **Altstadt**, bounded by the river and the Graben (Marktgraben and

Burggraben), a road that follows the course of the medieval town's moat.

Maria-Theresien-Strasse

Innsbruck's main artery is **Maria-Theresien-Strasse**, famed for the view north towards the great Nordkette, the mountain range that dominates the city. At its southern end the triumphal arch, **Triumphpforte**, was built for the marriage of Maria Theresa's son Leopold in 1756. Halfway along, the **Annasäule**, a column supporting a statue of the Virgin, commemorates the retreat of the Bavarians, who had been menacing Tyrol in 1703. Herzog-Friedrich-Strasse leads on into the centre, opening out into a plaza lined with arcaded medieval buildings. At the plaza's southern end is the **Goldenes Dachl**, or "Golden Roof" (though the tiles are really copper), built in the 1490s to cover an oriel window from which the court of Emperor Maximilian could observe the square below. The **Goldenes Dachl Museum** (May–Sept daily 10am–5pm; Oct & Dec–April Tues–Sun 10am–5pm; €4), is flashy but disappointing, offering a brief glimpse of the balcony.

Domplatz and the Hofburg

Standing on Domplatz, the ostentatious **Domkirche St Jakob** is home to a valuable *Madonna and Child* by German master Lucas Cranach the Elder, although it's buried in the fussy Baroque detail of the altar.

The adjacent **Hofburg**, entered around the corner, has late-medieval roots but was remodelled in the eighteenth century, its Rococo state Kaiserapartments are crammed with opulent furniture (daily 9am–5pm, Wed till 7pm; €5.50).

The Hofkirche and Volkskunstmusemn

At the head of Rennweg, is the **Hofkirche** (Mon–Sat 9am–5pm, Sun 12.30–5pm; €5; ⓦwww.hofkirche.at), which contains the imposing (but empty) **mausoluem of Emperor Maximilian**. This extraordinary project was originally envisaged as a series of 40 larger-than-life statues, 100 statuettes and 32 busts of Roman emperors, but in the end only 32 of the statuettes were completed.

Housed in the same complex, the **Tiroler Volkskunstmuseum** (daily: 9am–5pm; combined ticket €10), features a huge collection of folk art and objects including re-creations of traditional wood-panelled Tyrolean interiors.

Landesmuseum Ferdinandeum

A short walk south, the **Landesmuseum Ferdinandeum**, Museumstr. 15 (Tues–Sun 9am–5pm; combined ticket €10), contains one of the best collections of Gothic paintings in Austria; most originate from the churches of the South Tyrol (now in Italy).

Schloss Ambras

Set in attractive grounds 2km southeast of the centre, **Schloss Ambras** (daily 10am–5pm; Aug till 6pm; closed Nov; €10; tram #6 or #TS bus from the train station) was the home of Archduke Ferdinand of Tyrol. It features the impressive Spanish Hall, built in 1569–71, and exhibitions of armour and curios amassed from around the globe. Don't miss the inner courtyard covered in sixteenth-century frescoes, including depictions of the triumph of Bacchus.

Hungerburg plateau

A good starting point for hikes is the **Nordpark**, on the slopes of the Nordkette range, accessible from the swish Hungerburgbahn cable railway. The Zaha Hadid-designed Congress station is opposite the Hofgarten; take it to Hungerburg, then continue on a two-stage sequence of cable cars to just below the summit (daily 8.30am–5.30pm, Fri also 6–11.30pm; €26 return; ⓦwww.nordkette.com). The rewards are stupendous views of the high Alps and the possibility of all sorts of hikes.

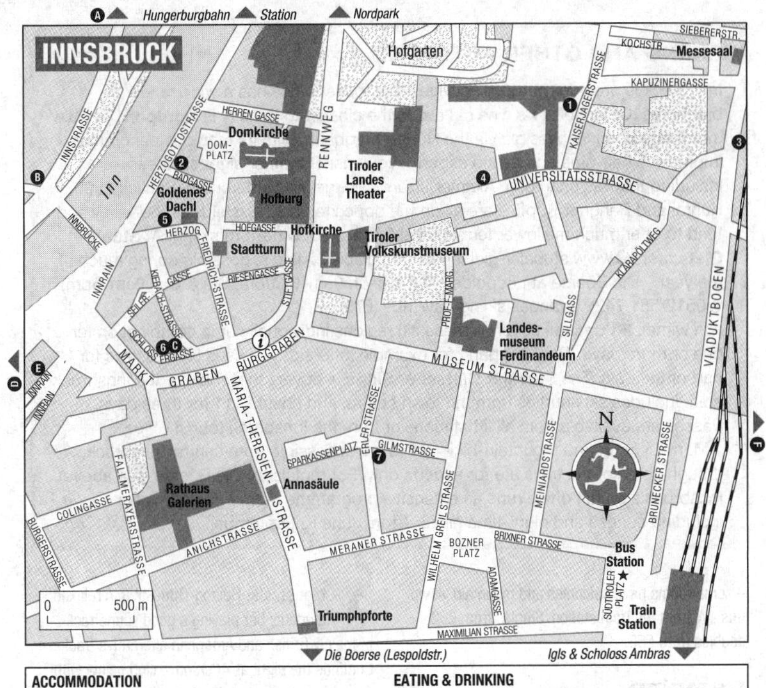

ACCOMMODATION				EATING & DRINKING					
Basic Hotel	E	Innbrücke	B	Café Central	7	Elferhaus	5	Noi	1
Camping Kranebitten	D	Nepomuk's	C	Café-Konditorei		Himal	4	Weli	3
HI Jugendherberge Innsbruck	F	Pension Paula	A	Munding	6	Moustache	2		

Arrival and information

Train The station is on Südtirolerplatz, east of the old town, an easy walk from the centre.
Bus The station is south of the train station.
Tourist office Burggraben 3 (daily 9am–6pm; Ⓣ0512/5356 0 Ⓦwww.innsbruck.info). It sells the Innsbruck Card (24hr/€29; 48hr/€34; 72hr/€39), which includes public transport, one return trip on all cable-car rides and admission to all the sights.
City transport Buses and trams; single tickets €1.90, 24hr/€4.20. The Sightseer bus stops at main sights (#TS; every 40min; €3.20, included with Innsbruck Card).

Accommodation

Hostels

HI Jugendherberge Innsbruck Reichenauerstr. 147 Ⓣ0512/34 61 79, Ⓦwww.youth-hostel-innsbruck.at. Large, functional HI hostel on the outskirts of the city. Bus #0 from Landesmuseum runs every 5–10min during the day. Dorms €20.50, doubles €66.

Nepomuk's Kiebachgasse 16 Ⓣ0512/58 41 18, Ⓦwww.nepomuks.at. Slightly ramshackle one-dorm hostel above *Café Munding*, whose owners also run the hostel and serve its good breakfasts. Also has a couple of doubles, though one is windowless and noisy. Dorms €22, doubles €54.

Hotels and pensions

Basic Hotel Innrain 16 Ⓣ50512/58 63 85, Ⓦwww.basic-hotel.at. Despite the name, not the cheapest or most basic option, but a no-frills take on a business hotel; reception open till 10pm (check in with a credit card after then). Free wi-fi. Front-facing rooms are noisy. Singles from €65, doubles from €90.

Innbrücke Innstr. 1 Ⓣ0512/28 19 34, Ⓦwww.gasthofinnbruecke.at. Plain but comfortable *Gasthof* on the west bank of the Inn, just over the bridge from the Altstadt. More expensive rooms have en-suite facilities, although most are without. Singles €34, doubles without en suite €60.

Pension Paula Weiherburggasse 15 Ⓣ0512/29 22 62, Ⓦwww.pensionpaula.at. Friendly, good-value *pension* in a chalet on a hillside north of the river

SKIING AND OTHER ACTIVITIES

Innsbruck is great for outdoor activities; the tourist office has a wide range of brochures. Of Innsbruck's nine **ski areas** the closest to the city is **Nordpark** (Ⓦwww.nordkette.com), accessible via the Hungerburgbahn, with its fabulous panoramas, impressive half-pipe and taxing expert-level runs. The other eight ski areas – including the Patscherkofel, Axamer Lizum, Glungezer, Muttereralm, Schlick 2000, Kühtai and Rangger Köpfl. – are all on the opposite, southern, side of the valley and tend to offer much mellower terrain ideal for relaxed, wide-turn skiing. At **Stubai Gletscher** (Ⓦwww.stubaier-gletscher.com) glacier skiing is possible during much of the year – Die Böerse at Leopoldstr. 4 (Mon–Fri 9am–6.30pm, Sat & Sun 9am–5pm; Ⓣ0512/581 742), arranges skiing day-trips (€75).

In winter, **lift passes** cover all these ski regions individually or in combination for one or more days. The Nordpark, for example, offers day-passes for €28 (less for part of the day). The **Stubaier Gletscher Skipass** covers the whole of the Innsbruck area, includes ski shuttles from the town centre, and costs €111 for three days. Passes are available from all lift stations or from the Innsbruck tourist office.

Many **cycling** and mountain-bike routes are accessible from central Innsbruck, though some of the trails are for experts only. For rentals try Die Böerse (see above). Innsbruck's tourist office runs an extensive programme of free guided **walks** – including sunrise and night-time hikes – from June to September.

– some rooms have balconies and mountain views. Bus #W from the train station. Singles from €32, doubles from €55.

Camping

Camping Kranebitten Kranebittner Allee 214 Ⓣ0512/54 67 32, Ⓦwww.campinginnsbruck.com. Open May–Oct. Well-equipped campsite 7km west of town. Bus #LK from Boznerplatz, a block west of the station, to Klammstr. €8.30/person, plus €10.50/tent.

Eating and drinking

Café Central Gilmstr. 5. Venerable coffeehouse serving up excellent cakes and decent breakfasts (from €6). Good spot to linger over a coffee and slice of cake (€2.80).

Café-Konditorei Munding Kiebachgasse 16. Superb cakes and pastries, in a bustling local daytime-only café.

Elferhaus Herzog-Friedrich-Str. 11. Popular old-town beer bar, with a lively atmosphere, big selection of beers, serving good basic Austrian food. Daily specials €7.80.

Himal Universitätsstr. 13 Ⓣ0512/588 588. Stylish Nepalese place serving fresh tasty curries, including an excellent-value lunch deal – two courses for €7.10–7.50, with good veggie options. Mon–Sat 11.30am–2.30pm & 6–10.30pm, Sun 6–10.30pm.

Moustache Herzog-Otto-Str. 8. A relaxed, studenty bar playing a good soundtrack of mainly British and American alternative tracks. Continue the night at *Aftershave* club below with something on most nights from 10pm. Bar Tues–Sun 11am–2am.

Noi Kaserjägerstr. 1. Excellent, cheap Thai restaurant around the corner from the Hofkirche with tasty lunch menus from €7.90.

Weli Viaduktbogen 26. Informal, unpretentious café-bar with snacks. Good starting point for exploring the various late-opening bars under the railway arches. Open from 7pm.

Directory

Consulates UK, Kaiserjägerstr. 1 Ⓣ0512/58 83 20.
Hospital Universitätklinik, Anichstr. 35 Ⓣ0512/50 40.
Internet service Bubble Point, Andreas-Hoferstr. 37 & Brixnerstr. 1 (Mon–Fri 8am–10pm, Sat & Sun 8am–8pm; Laundry also available here. 15min €0.50).
Post office Südtiroler Platz 10–12.

Moving on

Train Munich (8 daily; 1hr 50min); Salzburg (9 daily; 2hr); Venice (1 daily; 4hr 40min); Vienna (18 daily; 5hr); Zürich (6 daily; 3hr 30min).

Belgium & Luxembourg

HIGHLIGHTS

BRUGES: discover why everyone raves about this perfect medieval town

GHENT: marvel at the town's castle and lively bars

BRUSSELS: see the most well-preserved square in the country, the Grand-Place

ARDENNES: cycle, kayak or hike through the Ardennes woods

LUXEMBOURG CITY: visit Europe's most dramatically sited capital

ROUGH COSTS

DAILY BUDGET Basic €40 /occasional treat €55

DRINK Jupiler beer €1.60

FOOD Mussels with chips €12–20

HOSTEL/BUDGET HOTEL €20/€50–70

TRAVEL Train: Brussels–Antwerp €6.70; Brussels–Namur €8.20

CURRENCY Euro (€)

FACT FILE

POPULATION Belgium: 10.5 million; Luxembourg: 503,302

AREA Belgium: 30,582 sq km; Luxembourg: 2586 sq km

LANGUAGE Flemish (Belgium), Letzebuergesch (Luxembourg), French, German

CAPITAL Belgium: Brussels; Luxembourg: Luxembourg City

INTERNATIONAL PHONE CODE Belgium: ⓣ32; Luxembourg: ⓣ352

Introduction

A federal country, with three official languages and an intense rivalry between its two main groups – Dutch-speaking Flemish and French-speaking Walloons – Belgium has a cultural diversity that belies its rather dull reputation. Lively, cultured cities in the predominantly urban north give way to beautiful forests and rugged hills in the south; and regular, affordable trains and an impressive range of good-value accommodation make the country a pleasure to travel, as does the Belgians' enthusiasm for fine cuisine and endless varieties of beer.

Roughly in the middle of Belgium lies the capital, **Brussels**, the heart of the EU and a genuinely vibrant and multicultural city. North of here stretch the flat landscapes of Flemish Belgium, whose main city, **Antwerp**, is a bustling old port with doses of high art, high fashion, and twice as many bars as Amsterdam. Further west, also in the Flemish zone, are the charismatic cities of **Bruges** and **Ghent**, each with a stunning concentration of medieval architecture. Belgium's most scenic region, the Ardennes, is, however, in Wallonia, its deep, wooded valleys, high elevations and dark caverns sprawling away to the south, with the town of **Namur** the obvious gateway.

The Ardennes reach across the border into the northern part of the Grand Duchy of Luxembourg, a dramatic landscape of rushing rivers and high hills topped with crumbling castles. The best base for rural expeditions is **Luxembourg City**, an exceptionally picturesque place with a rugged setting.

CHRONOLOGY

Belgium

54 BC Julius Caesar defeats the Belgae tribes.
496 AD The King of the Franks, Clovis, founds a kingdom which includes Belgium.
1400–1500 The Belgian cities of Bruges, Brussels and Antwerp become the European centres of commerce and industry.
1477 Following the marriage of Austrian King Maximilian I and Mary of Burgundy, Belgium becomes part of Austria.
1713 Treaty of Utrecht transfers Belgian territory from French to Austrian rule.
1790 The Belgians form an independent state from Austria, though it does not last long. They are subsequently invaded by Austria, France and the Netherlands in quick succession.
1830 Belgium gains independence from the Netherlands.
1885 King Leopold II establishes a personal colony in the African Congo.
1908 The Belgian government takes over the Congo Free State after reports of Leopold's brutal regime are circulated.
1914–18 Belgium is invaded by Germany, and is the site of heavy fighting, before it is liberated.
1940–44 Nazi invasion, and ultimately liberation by Allied forces.
1957 Belgium is a founder member of the European Economic Community (EEC).
1960 Independence granted to the Congo.
1992 Belgium ratifies the Maastricht Treaty on the European Union.
2007 Following the resignation of Prime Minister Guy Verhofstadt, Belgium is without a government for 100 days.
2011 On February 17, Belgium became the country that has experienced the longest period without an official government – an accolade previously held by Iraq (289 days). At the time of writing Yves Leterme continues to head a caretaker government.

Luxembourg

963 AD Count Siegfried of Ardenne founds the capital of Luxembourg.
1354 Luxembourg's status is raised from fief to duchy by Emperor Charles IV.

1477 The Habsburgs take control of Luxembourg.
1715 Luxembourg integrated into the Austrian Netherlands.
1867 Second Treaty of London ensures Luxembourg's independence and neutrality.
1890 Luxembourg announces its own ruling monarchy, relinquishing its ties to the Netherlands.
1914–1918 German occupation.
1920 Joins the League of Nations.
1939–1945 German occupation.
1957 Luxembourg is a founder member of the EEC.
2000 Grand Duke Jean abdicates, handing responsibility over to his son Henri.
2008 Constitutional crisis is provoked by Grand Duke Henri threatening to block a bill legalizing euthanasia. As a result, Parliament approves a reform which restricts the monarch to a purely ceremonial role.

ARRIVAL

Most airborne travel is into Brussels, which has two **airports**: the closer one is Zaventem (also known as Brussels International), while Charleroi (which serves most budget airlines including Flybe and Ryanair) lies about 55km from the centre. There are frequent **rail** connections from London, Paris, Amsterdam and Luxembourg, with almost all international trains arriving at Bruxelles-Midi (Brussel-Zuid), and frequently also stopping in Ghent or Antwerp. Eurostar tickets are valid to any onward station in Belgium. Eurolines **buses** from Paris, Amsterdam, London and other destinations stop at Brussels-Nord, as well as Antwerp, Ghent and Bruges. Numerous **ferry** services ply between the UK and Belgian ports, including Ramsgate–Ostend (4hr), Rosyth–Zeebrugge (20hr) and Hull–Zeebrugge (15hr).

GETTING AROUND

Travelling around Flanders is rarely a problem. Distances are short, and an efficient train network links all the major and many minor towns and villages. The Ardennes and Luxembourg, on the other hand, can be a little more problematic: the train network is not extensive and bus timetables can demand careful study for longer journeys.

Belgium's railway system (Ⓦwww.b-rail.be) – SNCB in French, NMBS in

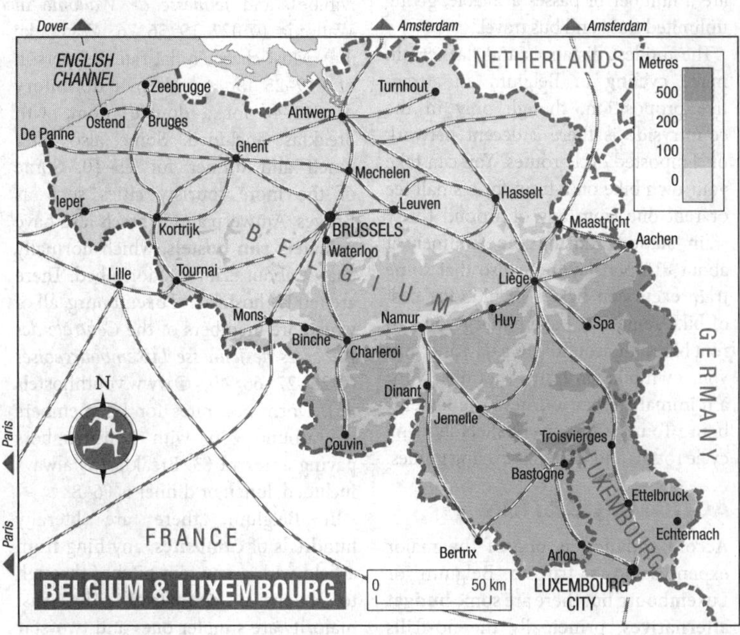

Flemish – is comprehensive and efficient, and fares are comparatively low. If you are under 26, don't have an InterRail or Eurail pass, and are spending some time in Belgium, ask for the **Go-Pass**, which buys you ten journeys between any Belgian stations for €50. (If you are planning on travelling from Belgium to Luxembourg and have a Go-Pass, use the pass to get to the Belgian border town of Arlon and buy an extension from there.) SNCB/NMBS also publishes information on offers and services in their comprehensive timetable book, which has an English-language section and is available at major train stations. **Buses** are only really used for travelling short distances, or in parts of the Ardennes where rail lines fizzle out.

Luxembourg's railways (Ⓦwww.cfl.lu) comprise one main north–south route down the middle of the country, with a handful of branch lines fanning out from the capital, but most of the country can only be reached by **bus**. Fares are comparable with those in Belgium, and there are a number of passes available, giving unlimited train and bus travel.

The modest distances and flat terrain make **cycling** in Belgium an attractive proposition, though only in the countryside is there a decent network of signposted cycle routes. You can take your own bike on a train for a small fee or rent one from any of around thirty train stations during the summer at about €10 per day; note also that some train excursion tickets include the cost of bike rental. In Luxembourg you can rent bikes for around €10 a day, and take your own bike on trains (not buses) for a minimal fee per journey. The Luxembourg Tourist Office has leaflets showing cycle routes and also sells cycling guides.

ACCOMMODATION

Accommodation is one of the major expenses on a trip to Belgium or Luxembourg but there are some **budget alternatives**, principally the no-frills end of the hotel market, private rooms – effectively B&Bs – arranged via the local tourist office, and a plentiful array of hostels. Whichever type of accommodation you choose, it's always a good idea to book ahead, especially in peak season.

In both countries, prices begin at around €60 for a double room in the cheapest one-star **hotel**; breakfast is normally included. Reservations can be made (for free) through most tourist offices on the day itself; the deposit they require is subtracted from your final hotel bill. **Private rooms** can be booked through local tourist offices too. Expect to pay €40–60 a night for a double, but note that they're often inconveniently situated on the outskirts of cities and towns. An exception is in Bruges, where private rooms – many of them in the centre – can be booked direct.

Belgium has around thirty **HI hostels**, run by two separate organizations: *Vlaamse Jeugdherbergcentrale* in Flanders (Ⓣ032 32 72 18, Ⓦwww.vjh.be), and *Jeunesse de Wallonie* in Wallonia (Ⓣ022 19 56 76, Ⓦwww.laj.be). Most charge a flat rate per person of €19–25 for a bed in a dormitory or €42–48 for a double room, with breakfast included. Some also offer lunch and dinner for €5–10. Some of the more touristy cities such as Bruges, Antwerp and Brussels also have **privately run hostels**, which normally charge about €20 for a dorm bed. There are ten HI hostels in Luxembourg, all of which are members of the *Centrale des Auberges de Jeunesse Luxembourgeoises* (Ⓣ26 27 66 40, Ⓦwww.youthhostels.lu). Dorm-bed rates for HI members are around €20, with non-members paying an extra €3. Breakfast is always included; lunch or dinner is €6–8.

In Belgium, there are literally hundreds of **campsites**, anything from a field with a few tent pitches through to extensive complexes. The vast majority are simpler one- and two-star establishments, for which two adults with a tent can expect to pay €10–20 per night, though surprisingly, most four-star sites don't cost much more – add about €5. All of Luxembourg's campsites are detailed in the Duchy's free tourist office booklet. Prices vary considerably, but are usually €5–7 per person, plus €5–7 for a pitch. In both countries, campsite phone numbers are listed in free camping booklets, and in Luxembourg the national tourist board (Ⓣ42 82 82 10, Ⓦwww.ont.lu) will make a reservation on your behalf.

FOOD AND DRINK

One of the great pleasures of a trip to Belgium is the cuisine, and if you stay away from tourist spots, it's hard to go wrong. Southern Belgian (or Wallonian) cuisine is similar to traditional French, retaining its neighbour's fondness for rich sauces and ingredients. The Ardennes region is renowned for its smoked ham and pâté.

Luxembourg's food is less varied and more Germanic, but you can still eat out extremely well. In Flanders the food is more akin to that of the Netherlands, with mussels and French fries the most common dish. Throughout the country, pork, beef, game, fish and seafood are staple items, often cooked with butter, cream and herbs, or sometimes in beer; hearty soups are also common. *Hesprolletjes* (chicory and ham baked in a cheese sauce) and *stoemp* (puréed meat and vegetables) are two traditional dishes worth seeking out. Traditional Flemish dishes such as *waterzooi*, or "watery mess" (fish or chicken stew), and *carbonnade* (beef casserole) are also widely available. There are plenty of good **vegetarian** options too, such as quiche and salad, and you can find vegetarian restaurants in all of the larger cities.

In both countries, bars and **cafés** are a good source of inexpensive meals, at least at lunchtime, serving simple dishes – omelettes, steak, mussels, plus a dish of the day for around €12. **Restaurants** are usually pricier, but the food is generally excellent. **Frituurs** (stands serving chips) are ubiquitous, cheap and usually offer a bewildering variety of sauces.

Belgium is also renowned for its chocolate. The big chocolatiers, Godiva and Leonidas, have shops in all the main towns and cities, but high-quality chocolate is also available in supermarkets at a much lower price – try Jacques or Côte d'Or.

Drink

Beer in Belgium is a real treat. Beyond the common lager brands – Stella Artois, Jupiler and Maes – there are about seven hundred speciality beers, from dark stouts to fruit beers, wheat beers and brown ales – something to suit any palate. The most famous are the strong ales brewed by the country's six **Trappist monasteries**; Chimay is the most widely available. **Luxembourg** doesn't really compete, but its three most popular brews – Diekirch, Mousel and Bofferding – are pleasant enough lagers.

French **wines** are universally sold, but Luxembourg's wines, especially the *crèmant* (sparkling wine), produced along the north bank of the Moselle, are very drinkable. You'll also find Dutch-style **jenever** (similar to gin) in most bars in the north of Belgium, and in Luxembourg home-produced **eau-de-vie**, distilled from various fruits.

STUDENT AND YOUTH DISCOUNTS

Most museums and galleries offer substantial discounts to those under 26, even if you don't have an ISIC card. Train travel is also cheaper for travellers aged under 26 if you buy a **Go-Pass** (see "Getting around", opposite).

CULTURE AND ETIQUETTE

The Belgians' relaxed attitude extends to the service – it's not unusual to be left waiting at the bar while the barman methodically polishes all the glasses. Don't worry about politely drawing some attention to yourself, as they're usually very helpful once they've noticed you. Leaving a ten percent **tip** is common in restaurants, but elsewhere is expected only when service has been exceptional.

SPORTS AND OUTDOOR ACTIVITIES

The Ardennes are ideal for hiking, kayaking, cycling and horseriding (see p.118 for operators); cross-country skiing is also an option. La Roche-en-Ardenne and Bouillon make excellent bases in Belgium, while in Luxembourg the towns of Vianden and Echternach (each about an hour from Luxembourg City) are popular destinations for hikers and cyclists. See p.120 for more on cycling.

COMMUNICATIONS

Post offices are usually open Monday to Friday 9am to noon and 2 to 5pm. Some urban post offices also open on Saturday mornings. Many public **phones** take only phonecards, which are available from newsagents and post offices. **Internet** access is widespread. However, due to more and more hostels, hotels and cafés offering free wi-fi, dedicated cybercafés are disappearing fast.

BELGIUM AND LUXEMBOURG ONLINE

Ⓦ **www.visitflanders.com** Information on Brussels and the Flanders region.
Ⓦ **www.belgiumtheplaceto.be** Information on Brussels and southern Belgium.
Ⓦ **www.visitluxembourg.lu** The Luxembourg tourist board's official site.
Ⓦ **www.use-it.be** Excellent online guide for young travellers on Brussels and the Flanders region.

EMERGENCY NUMBERS

Belgium Police ⓣ101; fire and ambulance ⓣ100.
Luxembourg Police ⓣ113; fire and ambulance ⓣ112.

EMERGENCIES

Both countries are safe. However, if you're unlucky enough to have something **stolen**, report it immediately to the nearest police station and get a report number, or better still a copy of the statement itself, for your insurance claim when you get home. With regard to **medical emergencies**, if you're reliant on free treatment within the EU health scheme, try to remember to make this clear to the ambulance staff and any medics you subsequently encounter. Outside working hours, all **pharmacies** should display a list of open alternatives. Weekend rotas are also listed in local newspapers.

INFORMATION

In both Belgium and Luxembourg, there are **tourist offices** in all but the smallest of villages. They usually provide free local maps, and in the larger towns offer a free accommodation booking service too.

MONEY AND BANKS

Belgium and Luxembourg both use the **euro** (€). **Banks** are the best places to change money and are generally open Monday to Friday 9am to 4/4.30pm in both countries, though some have a one-hour lunch break between noon and 2pm, and some close after lunch on Friday. **ATMs** are commonplace.

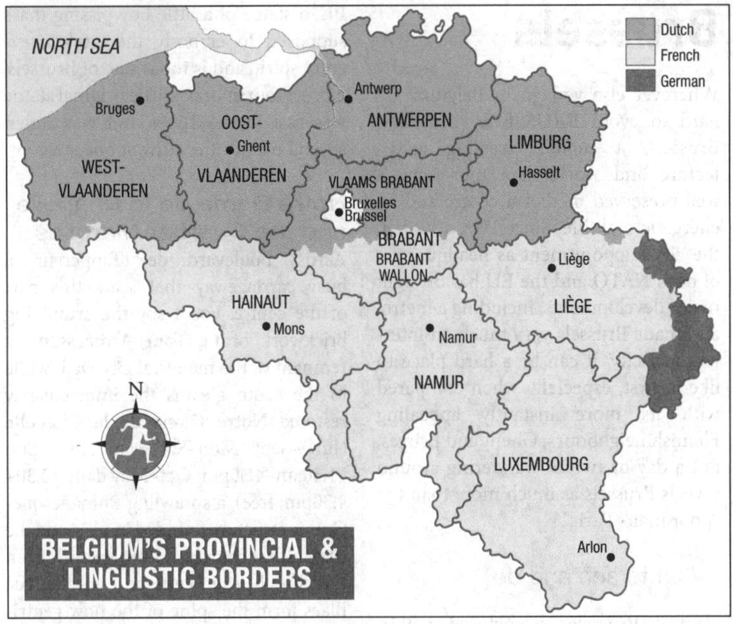

OPENING HOURS AND HOLIDAYS

In both countries, most shops are closed on Sunday with some only reopening on Monday afternoon, even in major cities. Nonetheless, normal **shopping hours** are Monday to Saturday 9/10am to 6/7pm with many urban supermarkets staying open until 8/9pm on Fridays and smaller places shutting early on Saturday. In the big cities, a smattering of convenience stores (*magasins de nuit/nachtwinkels*) stay open either all night or until around 1/2am daily, and some souvenir shops open late and on Sundays too. Most **museums** are closed on Mondays, though look out for occasional late-night openings, especially in Brussels. Restaurants also often close on Mondays. Many **bars** have relaxed closing times, claiming to stay open until the last customer leaves. Less usefully, many restaurants and bars close for at least a couple of weeks in July or August.

Shops, banks and many museums are closed on the following **public holidays**: New Year's Day, Easter Sunday, Easter Monday, May 1, Ascension Day (forty days after Easter), Whit Sunday, Whit Monday, June 23 (Luxembourg only), July 21 (Belgium only), Assumption (mid-Aug), November 1, November 11 (Belgium only), Christmas Day.

LANGUAGE

There are three official languages in **Belgium**: Flemish, French and German. Speaking French in the Flemish north is not appreciated and vice versa. Most Belgians speak English. Natives of **Luxembourg** speak Letzebuergesch, a dialect of German, but most people also speak French and German and many speak English too. See p.378, p.456 and p.826 for some basic French, German and Dutch language tips.

Brussels

Wherever else you go in Belgium, it's hard to avoid **BRUSSELS** (Bruxelles, Brussel), a capital boasting architecture and world-class museums, a well-preserved medieval centre and an energetic nightlife. Since World War II, the city's appointment as headquarters of both NATO and the EU has brought major developments, including a metro, and made Brussels very much an international city. It can be a hard place to like at first, especially when compared with its more instantly appealing Flemish neighbours, Ghent and Bruges, but a day or two of wandering around reveals Brussels as much more than the "poor man's Paris".

What to see and do

Central Brussels is enclosed within a pentagon of boulevards – the **petit ring** – which follows the course of the medieval city walls. The centre is also divided between the Ville Haute and Ville Basse, the former being the traditional home of the city's upper classes who kept a beady eye on the workers down below.

The Grand-Place

The obvious point to begin any tour of the **Ville Basse** is the **Grand-Place**, the commercial hub of the city since the Middle Ages. With its stupendous spired tower, the **Hôtel de Ville** dominates the square; inside you can view various official rooms (tours in English: Wed 3pm, Sun 10am & 2pm; €5). But the real glory of the Grand-Place lies in its **guildhouses**, mostly built in the early eighteenth century, their slender facades swirling with exuberant carving and sculpture.

The Manneken Pis

Rue de l'Etuve leads south from the Grand-Place down to the **Manneken Pis**, a statue of a little boy pissing that's supposed to embody the city's irreverent spirit, and is today one of Brussels' biggest tourist draws. The original statue was cast in the 1600s, but was stolen several times – the current one is a copy.

Notre Dame de la Chapelle and the Quartier Marolles

Across boulevard de l'Empereur, a busy carriageway that scars this part of the centre, you'll spy the crumbling brickwork of **La Tour Anneessens**, a remnant of the medieval city wall, while to the south gleams the immaculately restored **Notre Dame de la Chapelle** (June–Sept Mon–Sat 9am–5pm, Sun 11.30am–4.30pm; Oct–May daily 12.30–4.30pm; free), a sprawling Romanesque-Gothic structure founded in 1134 and the city's oldest church. Running south from the church, rue Haute and parallel rue Blaes form the spine of the now gentrified **Quartier Marolles**, traditionally a working-class neighbourhood. **Place du Jeu de Balle**, the heart of Marolles, has retained its earthy character and is the site of the city's best **flea market** (daily 7am–2pm; busiest on Sun). Return to the Ville Haute using the free glass-walled lift at the junction of rue des Minimes and rue de l'Epee, which drops you off in place Poelaert and offers fantastic views of the city.

The Cathédrale

The **Cathédrale** (Mon–Fri 7am–6pm, Sat 8.30am–3.30pm, Sun 2–6pm; €1), lies a couple of minutes' walk to the east of the Grand-Place, at the east end of rue d'Arenberg. It's a splendid Brabantine-Gothic building begun in 1220. Look out also for the gorgeous sixteenth-century **stained-glass windows** in the transepts and above the main doors.

Place Royale

Climb the Mont des Arts – a wide stairway ascending towards **place Royale** – and on the left is the Old

COMICS IN BRUSSELS

Brussels is a city made for comic-book fans. The **Centre Belge de la Bande Dessinée** (Comic Strip Museum; daily except Mon 10am–6pm; €8) at 20 rue des Sables focuses on Belgian comics such as Tintin, Smurfs and so on. For shopping focus head to **boulevard Lemonnier** which boasts ten comic-book shops. Various walls around the city have been decorated with building-sized scenes from comic strips, and tourist information can supply you with a trail following the major ones.

England Building, one of the finest examples of Art Nouveau in the city. Once a department store, it now holds the **Musée des Instruments de Musique**, at rue Montagne de la Cour 2 (MIM; Tues–Fri 9.30am–5pm, Sat & Sun 10am–5pm; €5/students €4), which contains an impressive collection of musical instruments. The rooftop café has great views of the city. Back on place Royale, at rue de la Régence 3, the **Musées Royaux des Beaux-Arts** (Tues–Sun 10am–5pm; last ticket 4pm; €8) comprise two museums: the Musée d'Art Moderne (closed until 2012) and the Musée d'Art Ancien, which together accommodate a world-class collection of fine art, including works by Bruegel and Rubens. Next door, the **Musée Magritte** (daily except Mon 10am–5pm, Wed till 8pm; €8/€13 combi ticket with Musées Royaux des Beaux-Arts) contains the largest collection of the Surrealist's work in the world.

Outside the petit ring

Brussels by no means ends with the petit ring. To the east of the ring road, are the glass high-rises of the **EU**, notably the winged **Berlaymont** building beside Métro Schuman and, nearby, the lavish **European Union Parliament building** (free guided tours: usually Mon–Thurs 10am & 3pm, Fri 10am, but check website; Ⓦwww.europarl.europa.eu), an imposing structure topped off by a spectacular, curved glass roof.

Just south of the petit ring is the fashionable Ixelles district, filled with excellent examples of Art Nouveau and Art Deco architecture, as well as chic bars and restaurants. Its northern boundary is home to a large African community known as **Matongé**, named after a district of Kinshasa in the Congo. Here you can explore the shops of **Galerie d'Ixelles** and sample fried plantain from one of the cafés on rue Longue Vie. To the southwest is the Saint-Gilles suburb. At 25 rue Américaine, the **Musée Victor Horta** (daily except Mon 2–5.30pm; €7; Ⓦwww.hortamuseum.be), occupies the innovative Art Nouveau architect's former home.

Arrival

Air The main airport is in Zaventem, 13km northeast of the centre, served by regular trains to the city's three main stations (30min; €5.20). No-frills airlines fly into Charleroi, 55km south of Brussels; shuttle buses leave hourly for the city (1hr; €13).

Train Brussels has three main train stations – Bruxelles-Nord, Bruxelles-Central and Bruxelles-Midi, each a few minutes apart. The majority of international trains, including expresses from London, Amsterdam, Paris and Cologne, stop only at Bruxelles-Midi (Brussel-Zuid), south of the city centre. Bruxelles-Central is a 5min walk from Grand-Place; Bruxelles-Nord lies in the business area just north of the main ring-road. To transfer from one of the three main stations to another, simply jump on the next available main-line train.

Bus Eurolines buses arrive at the Bruxelles-Nord station complex.

Information

Tourist information VisitBrussels (formerly Brussels International) has offices on rue Royale 2–4 (daily 10am–6pm; Ⓣ02 513 89 40, Ⓦwww.visitbrussels.be) and in the Hôtel de Ville on the Grand-Place (daily 10am–6pm). There are smaller

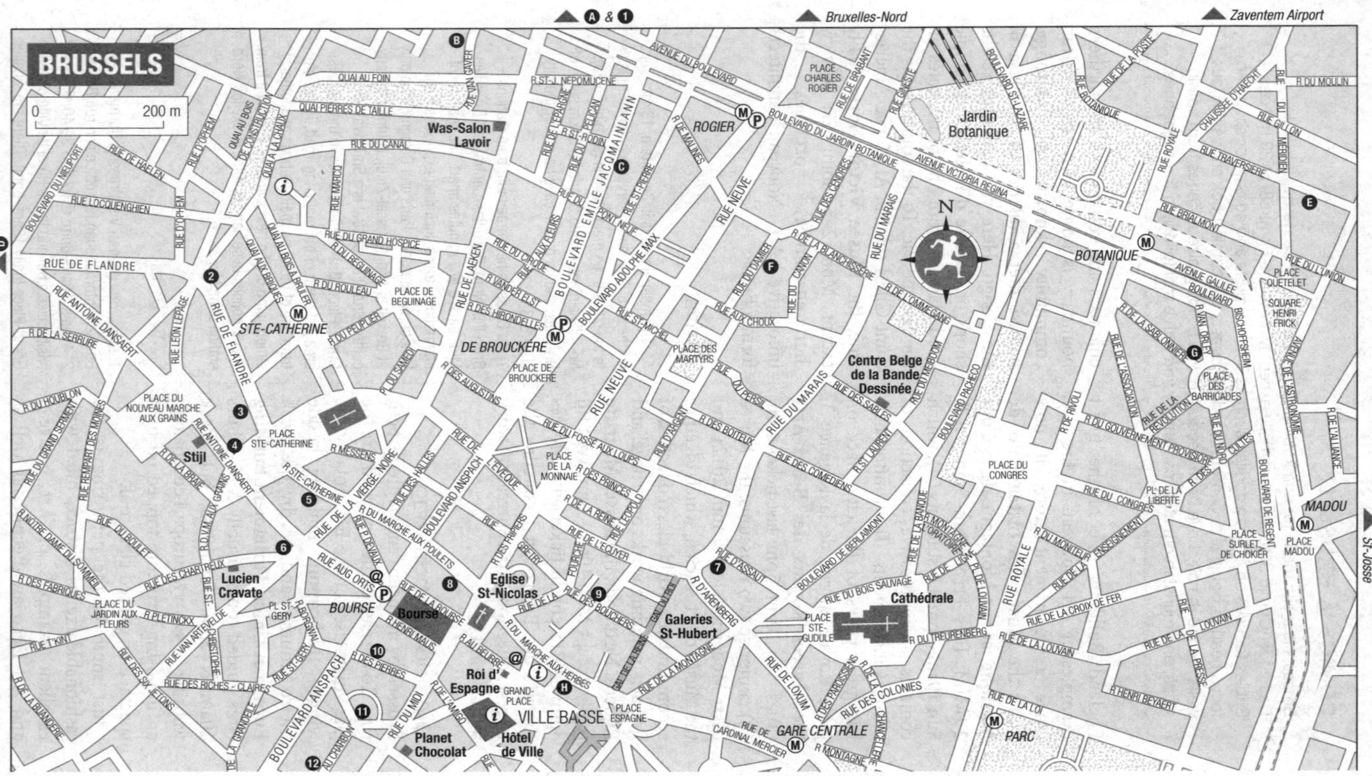
BRUSSELS
0
200 m
A & 1
Bruxelles-Nord
Zaventem Airport
St-Josse
D
Jardin Botanique
ROGIER
PLACE CHARLES ROGIER
BOTANIQUE
MADOU
PLACE MADOU
PLACE SURLET DE CHOKIER
BOULEVARD DU JARDIN BOTANIQUE
AVENUE VICTORIA REGINA
BOULEVARD ST-LAZARE
BOULEVARD DE REGENT
AVENUE DE L'ASTRONOMIE
PLACE DES BARRICADES
PLACE QUETELET
SQUARE HENRI FRICK
PLACE DU CONGRES
PL. DE LA LIBERTE
RUE ROYALE
BOULEVARD PACHECO
Centre Belge de la Bande Dessinée
Cathédrale
PLACE STE-GUDULE
PARC
GARE CENTRALE
Galeries St-Hubert
PLACE DE LA MONNAIE
PLACE DES MARTYRS
RUE NEUVE
RUE DU MARAIS
BOULEVARD ADOLPHE MAX
BOULEVARD EMILE JACQMAINLANN
PLACE DE BROUCKERE
DE BROUCKERE
PLACE DE BEGUINAGE
STE-CATHERINE
PLACE STE-CATHERINE
RUE DE FLANDRE
RUE ANTOINE DANSAERT
PLACE DU NOUVEAU MARCHE AUX GRAINS
Stijl
Lucien Cravate
PLACE DU JARDIN AUX FLEURS
BOURSE
Bourse
Eglise St-Nicolas
Roi d' Espagne
GRAND-PLACE
Hôtel de Ville
VILLE BASSE
PLACE ESPAGNE
Planet Chocolat
BOULEVARD ANSPACH
Was-Salon Lavoir
QUAI AU BOIS A BRULER
QUAI AUX BRIQUES
N

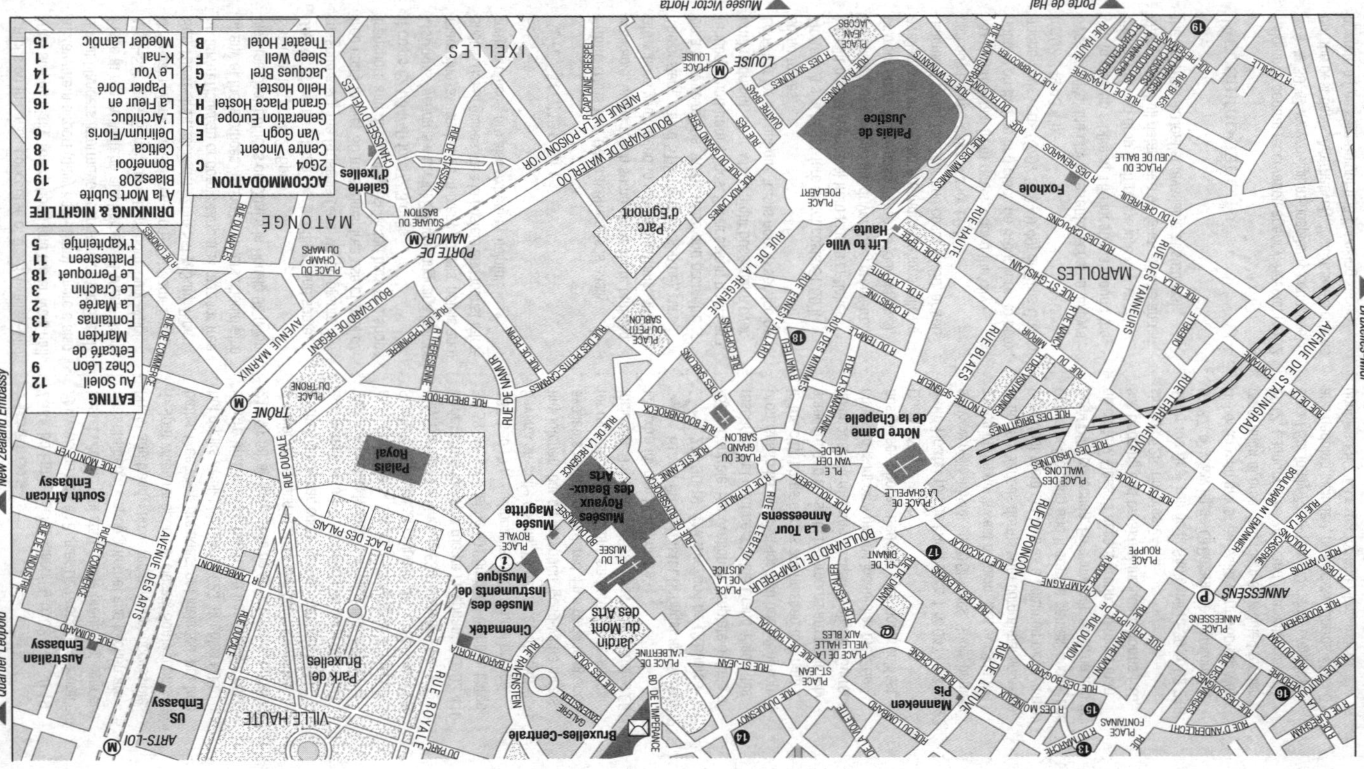
Quartier Leopold
New Zealand Embassy
Musée Victor Horta
Porte de Hal
Bruxelles-Midi
EATING
Au Soleil 12
Chez Léon 9
Eetcafé de Markten 4
Fontainas 13
La Marée 2
Le Crachin 3
Le Perroquet 18
Plattesteen 11
t'Kapiteintje 5
DRINKING & NIGHTLIFE
À la Mort Subite 7
Blaes208 19
Bonnefooi 10
Celtica 8
Delirium/Floris 6
L'Archiduc 16
La Fleur en Papier Doré 17
Le You 14
K-nal 1
Moeder Lambic 15
ACCOMMODATION
2Go4 C
Centre Vincent Van Gogh E
Generation Europe D
Grand Place Hostel H
Hello Hostel A
Jacques Brel G
Sleep Well F
Theater Hotel B
VILLE HAUTE
MATONGÉ
IXELLES
MAROLLES
Park de Bruxelles
Palais Royal
Parc d'Egmont
Palais de Justice
Musées Royaux des Beaux-Arts
Musée Magritte
Musée des Instruments de Musique
Cinematek
Jardin du Mont des Arts
Notre Dame de la Chapelle
La Tour Anneessens
Lift to Ville Haute
Foxhole
Manneken Pis
Galerie d'Ixelles
Australian Embassy
South African Embassy
US Embassy
Bruxelles-Centrale
ARTS-LOI
TRÔNE
PORTE DE NAMUR
LOUISE
ANNEESSENS

offices on the main concourse of the Bruxelles-Midi train station (daily 10am–6pm) and the arrivals hall at Zaventem airport (daily 8am–9pm). There's also a Visit Flanders information centre near the Grand-Place at rue du Marché aux Herbes 61 (April–Sept Mon–Sat 9am–6pm, Sun 10am–5pm; July–Aug daily 9am–7pm; Oct–March Mon–Sat 9am–5pm, Sun 10am–4pm; closed 1–2pm Sat & Sun). Pick up an Art Nouveau or comic-strip trail map for free at any of these offices. Young travellers should also visit the Use-It offices on Quai à la Houille 9a (Mon–Sat 10am–1pm & 2–6pm).

Discount cards All the tourist offices and some museums sell the Brussels Card, which grants free entry to over 30 museums, free use of public transport, and discounts in selected bars and shops. It costs €24/34/40 for 1/2/3 days.

Listings *Agenda* is a useful English-language listings magazine, available free in many hostels, hotels and shops. *Use-It* guides, free in hostels and tourist information offices, are also extremely helpful.

City transport

Public transport Central Brussels is easily walkable, but to reach some of the more outlying attractions you'll need to use public transport. The system, called STIB (Ⓦwww.stib.be), runs on a mixture of bus, tram, métro and prémétro (underground trams) lines. Services run from 6am until midnight, after which night buses take over. Look out for the antique trams now in service on some routes.

Tickets A single flat-fare ticket costs €1.80 if bought before you travel from kiosks or ticket machines, or €2 from the driver (bus, prémétro or tram only). A day-pass (*carte de jour/dagpas*), available at métro and prémétro stations, allows unlimited travel for 24hr and costs €4.50, or you can buy a three-day pass for €9.50.

Taxis Hire a taxi from ranks around the city – notably on Bourse and place de Brouckère; to book, phone Taxis Verts (Ⓣ02 349 49 49) or Taxis Orange (Ⓣ02 349 43 43).

Cycling Villo! the city bike rental scheme, allows you to pick up a bike at 180 locations around the city centre and drop it off elsewhere at a very cheap rate. Full details are on Ⓦen.villo.be and in the *Train & Vélo* leaflet (available at stations).

Accommodation

Belgium's central reservation agency, Resotel (Ⓣ02 779 39 39, Ⓦwww.belgium-hospitality.com), seeks out the best deals. Alternatively, VisitBrussels offices operate a free same-night hotel booking service.

Hostels

2Go4 bd Emile Jacmainlaan 99 Ⓣ02 219 30 19, Ⓦwww.2go4.be Ⓜ Rogier/De Brouckère. Excellent hostel with helpful staff. Large groups (of over six) not admitted. TV snug, internet and kitchen are bright and trendy; however, none are accessible 1–4pm when reception is closed. Some rooms have baths. Free wi-fi. Breakfast not included, but free hot drinks available. Dorms €23, doubles €69.

Centre Vincent Van Gogh rue Traversière 8 Ⓣ02 217 01 58, Ⓦwww.chab.be Ⓜ Botanique. Underwent a major renovation in 2011 and downstairs has a smart black bar, conservatory with pool table and homely wooden kitchen. New bunk beds and mattresses due. Rooms located across the street are a bit soulless. Laundry, internet, wi-fi, no curfew. Sheets and breakfast included. 18- to 35-year-olds only. Dorms €19, singles, €34, doubles €54.

Generation Europe rue de l'Eléphant 4 Ⓣ02 410 38 58, Ⓦwww.laj.be Ⓜ Comte de Flandre. Large 165-bed HI hostel popular with school groups. Several en-suite dorms, TV room, laundry, wi-fi, tiny kitchen, bar on reception, good-value meals available when pre-ordered. Five parking spaces for motorhomes. Bedding and organic breakfast included. Dorms €19.40, singles €35, doubles €51; €3 extra for non HI members.

Grand Place Hostel Haringstraat 6–8 Ⓣ02 219 30 19, Ⓦwww.2go4.be Ⓜ Bourse /Gare Centrale. Renovation incomplete at time of research, but right next to the Grand-Place this promises to be the best-located budget option in the city. Large dorms are finished to a high standard and en-suite bathrooms are positively luxurious. Internet and kitchen available. Currently, check-in is inconveniently located at the *2Go4* hostel (see above). Bedding only, not breakfast. Dorms €25.

Hello Hostel rue de l'Armistice 1 Ⓣ0471 93 59 27, Ⓦwww.hello-hostel.eu Ⓜ Simonis. Snug, homely option in the northwest of town, just outside the petit ring. Various dorms with communal showers. Breakfast room doubles as a common room (a new one is being built) and there are games, books, and huge DVD collection. Free internet, wi-fi, no laundry, no curfew. Doesn't accept groups of more than six. Bedding and breakfast included. Dorms €18, singles €25, doubles €44.

Jacques Brel rue de la Sablonnière 30 Ⓣ02 218 01 87, Ⓦwww.laj.be Ⓜ Botanique. Comfortable HI hostel with mix of en-suite dorm rooms. Major renovation of breakfast room scheduled for Jan 2012. Laundry, free wi-fi and internet, games, *Babel Bar* (daily 7am–1am). Organic breakfast and bedding included, no curfew. Dorms €19.40, doubles €52; €3 extra for non HI members.

Sleep Well rue du Damier 23 ⓣ02 218 50 50, ⓦwww.sleepwell.be Ⓜ Rogier/De Brouckère. Has hostel section with bland but spacious rooms, and "hotel" section with quieter, renovated en-suite rooms. There's a bar, wi-fi, internet, laundry, no curfew. Bedding and breakfast included. Hostel: dorms €19.50, singles €36, doubles €54; hotel: singles €46, doubles €66.

Hotels

Theater Hotel rue van Gaver 23 ⓣ02 350 90 00, ⓦwww.theaterhotelbrussels.com Ⓜ Yser. Hip boutique hotel in the red-light district, but with excellent rooms. Doubles €60.

Eating

Brussels has an international reputation for its food, and even at the dowdiest snack bar you'll find well-prepared *Bruxellois* dishes featuring amalgamations of Walloon and Flemish cuisine.

Cafés

Au Soleil rue du Marché au Charbon 86. Prémétro Bourse. Bohemian bar serving reasonably priced snacks with a lovely terrace overlooking Eglise Notre-Dame du Bon Secours. Mon–Fri 10am–1am, Sat & Sun 10am–2am.

Eetcafé de Markten place du Vieux Marché aux Grains 5 Ⓜ Ste-Catherine. Vibrant café offering no-nonsense, good-quality salads, sandwiches and soups at very reasonable prices. Mon–Sat 8.30am–midnight, Sun 10am–6pm.

Fontainas rue du Marché au Charbon 91. Prémétro Bourse. Changes from chilled-out café in the day to lively gay cocktail bar at night. Free wi-fi. Mon–Fri 10am–1am, Sat & Sun 11am–2am.

Restaurants

Chez Léon rue des Bouchers 18. Touristy, but serves reliably tasty mussels – opt for their mussels, chips and beer "meal deal" for €12.90. Mains €10–20. Daily 11.30am–11pm.

La Marée rue de Flandre 99 Ⓜ Ste-Catherine. Seafood bistro run by husband-and-wife team. The decor is pretty basic, but the food is always creative. Mains €12. Tues–Sat noon–2pm & 6.30–10pm.

Le Crachin rue de Flandre 12. Breton crêperie serving home-made sweet and savoury buckwheat pancakes and mugs of cider. Mains €6. Tues–Thurs noon–2.30pm & 6.30–10.30pm, Fri–Sun noon–10.30pm.

Le Perroquet rue Watteeu 31 Ⓜ Louise. Art Nouveau café serving good-value pittas and salads Mains €7–14. Mon–Sat 9am–6pm.

Plattesteen rue du Marché au Charbon 41. Prémétro Bourse. Typical *Bruxellois* dishes served at this traditional family restaurant, famous for it sunny terrace beneath a cartoon mural. Mains €10. Daily noon–1am.

't Kapiteintje rue St Catherine 30 Ⓜ St-Catherine/Bourse. Grubby café where locals come to watch football and tuck into Flemish specialities like rabbit cooked in Leffe beer. A rare find. Mains €12–17. Mon–Sat 10am–10pm.

Drinking and nightlife

Brussels' bars are a joy. St-Géry is the place to drink especially in the summer when bars spill out into the square. Rue du Marché au Charbon is the hub of gay nightlife.

Bars

À la Mort Subite rue Montagne aux Herbes Potagères 7 Ⓜ Gare Centrale. Legendary 1920s bar famous for its Gueuze and Kriek beers. Mon–Sat 11am–1am, Sun noon–midnight.

Bonnefooi rue des Pierres 8. Prémétro Bourse. Live music every night at this hip bar. Great atmosphere in summer when the crowds spill out onto the street. Jupiler costs €1 until 10pm daily. Daily 5pm–8am.

Celtica rue du Marché aux Poulets 55. Prémétro Bourse. Catch that all-important football match on the big screens here. DJs play every night from 11pm and – in typical Irish fashion – happy-hour prices run from 1pm to midnight. Daily 1pm–late.

Delirium/Floris Impasse de la Fidélité 4a. Ⓜ Gare Centrale. Home of Delirium Tremens – once billed the Best Beer in the World – this bar is a backpacker favourite.

La Fleur en Papier Doré rue des Alexiens 55 Ⓜ Gare Centrale. Infamous "brown" bar that was a favourite haunt of Hergé and Magritte. Serves Lambic beer the traditional way. Tues–Sat 11am–midnight, Sun 11am–7pm.

L'Archiduc rue Antoine Dansaert 6. Prémétro Bourse. Legendary Art Deco jazz bar. Things get going around midnight – ring the doorbell to get in. Daily 4pm–5am.

Moeder Lambic place Fontainas 8. Prémétro Anneessens. Voted 10th Best Bar in the World in 2011, it has 46 beers on tap, including Brussels-brewed Cantillon – all served to snug wooden booths. Daily 11am–1am, till 2am Sat & Sun.

Clubs

Blaes 208 (formerly Fuse) rue Blaes 208 ⓦwww.blaes208.be Ⓜ Porte de Hal. One of Brussels' institutions, with big-name DJs usually lined up for its Sat techno nights. Entry €5 before midnight, €10 after. Usually Wed–Sat, with monthly gay nights.

K-nal ave du Port 1 Ⓦ www.k-nal.be Ⓜ Yser. Huge warehouse overlooking the canal that hosts fashionable parties Entry €5 before midnight, €10 after. Fri & Sat 11pm–6am.

Le You rue Duquesnoy 6 Ⓦ www.leyou.be Ⓜ Gare-Centrale. Club hosting a variety of gay and straight nights including "Gay Tea Dance" on Sun. Entry €10, includes two free drinks. Thurs 11pm–5am, Fri–Sat 11.30pm–6am, Sun 9pm–3am.

Shopping

Aside from the Marolles flea market (see p.102), rue Blaes and rue Haute are lined with a mix of affordable and expensive antiques shops. For vintage, head to **Foxhole** (Thurs–Sun 9.30am–6pm) on rue des Renards 6, and **Lucien Cravate** on rue des Chartreux 24. Rue Antoine Dansaert is home to all the designers – check out **Stijl** at no. 74. High-street labels can be found on and around rue Neuve. For good-quality chocolate try place du Grand Sablon – **Pierre Marcolini** and **Wittamer** both have stores here.

Directory

Embassies Australia, rue Guimard 6–8 Ⓣ 02 286 05 00; Canada, av de Tervuren 2 Ⓣ 02 741 06 11; Ireland, chaussée d'Etterbeek 180 Ⓣ 02 282 34 00; New Zealand, 7th Floor, ave des Nerviens 9–31 Ⓣ 02 512 10 40; South Africa, rue Montoyer 17–19 Ⓣ 02 285 44 00; UK, ave d'Auderghem 10 Ⓣ 02 287 62 11; USA, bd du Régent 27 Ⓣ 02 811 40 00.
Hospital Hôpital St Pierre, rue Haute 322 Ⓣ 02 535 3317.
Internet *Aroma Coffee Lounge*, Grand Place 37 has wi-fi, as does *McDonalds* on place de la Bourse 3.
Left luggage Self-service lockers at all three main train stations; €3/3.50/4 for small/medium/large locker for 24hr.
Pharmacies Agora, rue du Marché aux Herbes 109; Multipharma, rue du Marché aux Poulets 37.
Post office Bruxelles-Central (Mon, Wed–Fri 8.30am–5pm, Tues 9.30am–6pm).

Moving on

Train to: Amsterdam (hourly; 2hr 40min); Antwerp (every 30min; 40min); Bruges (every 30min; 1hr); Ghent (every 30min; 40min); London (every 2hr; 2hr); Luxembourg City (hourly; 2hr 50min); Marloie (for La Roche-en-Ardennes; hourly; 1hr 50min); Namur (every 30min; 1hr); Ostend (hourly; 1hr 20min); Paris (hourly; 1hr 30min).

Northern Belgium

Almost entirely **Flemish**-speaking, the region to the north of Brussels possesses a distinctive and vibrant cultural identity, its pancake-flat landscapes punctuated by a string of fine historic cities. These begin with **Antwerp**, a large old port dotted with many reminders of its sixteenth-century golden age, followed by **Ghent** and **Bruges**, which became prosperous during the Middle Ages on the back of the cloth trade. All three cities have great restaurants and a lively bar scene.

ANTWERP

ANTWERP, Belgium's second city, and the de facto capital of Flemish Belgium, fans out from the east bank of the Scheldt River about 50km north of Brussels. Many people prefer it to the capital; it is an immediately attractive place famous for Rubens, fashion, diamonds and the best nightlife in Belgium.

What to see and do

At the centre of Antwerp is the spacious **Grote Markt**, where the conspicuous

> **FERRIES TO BRITAIN**
>
> Belgium's main international ferry port is **Zeebrugge**, just outside Bruges, with ferries from Hull and Rosyth in Britain. Ferry companies provide bus connections from the port to the train station. Transeuropa ferries run from Ramsgate to the resort town of **Ostend**, from where trains to Bruges take fifteen minutes.

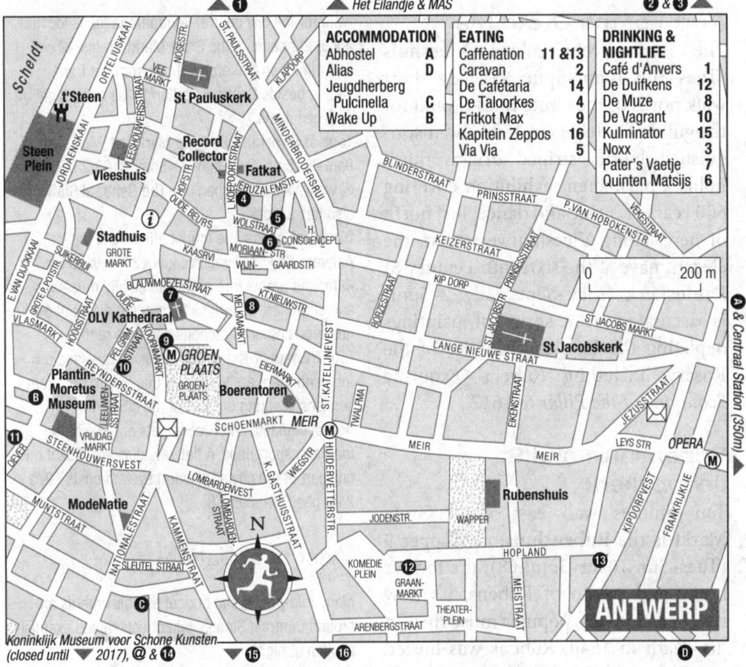

Brabo fountain features a bronze of Silvius Brabo, the city's first hero, depicted flinging the hand of the giant Antigonus – who terrorized passing ships – into the Scheldt. The north side of Grote Markt is lined with daintily restored sixteenth-century **guildhouses,** while the west is hogged by the handsome **Stadhuis**.

Onze Lieve Vrouwe Kathedraal

Southeast of Grote Markt, the **Onze Lieve Vrouwe Kathedraal** (Mon–Fri 10am–5pm, Sat 10am–3pm, Sun 1–4pm; €5) is one of the finest Gothic churches in Europe, dating from the middle of the fifteenth century. Four paintings by Rubens, including his masterpieces *Elevation of the Cross* and *Descent from the Cross*, are displayed here.

Plantin-Moretus Museum

The **Plantin-Moretus Museum** on Vrijdagmarkt 22–23 (Tues–Sun 10am–5.30pm; €8), occupies the grand old mansion of Rubens' father-in-law, the printer Christopher Plantin. It provides a beautiful, richly decorated setting for two of the oldest printing presses in the world.

ModeNatie and Museum voor Schone Kunsten

In the heart of the city's fashion quarter along Nationalestraat, the **ModeNatie** (Ⓦwww.modenatie.com) showcases some of the avant-garde fashion for which the city is famous. Part of the building contains **MoMu** (Mode Museum; Tues–Sun 10am–6pm; €7; Ⓦwww.momu.be), which has some great contemporary fashion displays.

About fifteen minutes' walk further south at Leopold de Waelplaats, the **Koninklijk Museum voor Schone Kunsten** (Royal Museum of Fine Arts; Ⓦwww.kmska.be) has one of the country's best fine-art collections. Unfortunately, it is closed for renovation until 2017.

North of the Grote Markt

The impressively gabled **Vleeshuis** (Tues–Sun 10am–5pm; €5), is a short walk north of the Grote Markt. Built for the guild of butchers in 1503 and distinguished by its striped brickwork; it holds a permanent exhibition covering 600 years of music and dance. Just north of here, along Vleeshouwersstraat, the elegant nave at the sixteenth-century **St Pauluskerk** (May–Sept daily 2–5pm) is decorated by a series of paintings depicting the Fifteen Mysteries of the Rosary, including Rubens' exquisite *Scourging at the Pillar* of 1617.

Rubenshuis and St Jacobskerk

Ten minutes' walk east of the Grote Markt is the **Rubenshuis**, at Wapper 9 (Tues–Sun 10am–5pm; €8); the former home and studio of Rubens, it's now restored as a very popular museum. On his death in 1640, Rubens was buried in the chapel behind the high altar at **St Jacobskerk**, just to the north at Lange Nieuwstraat 73. It includes one of his last works, *Our Lady Surrounded by Saints*, featuring himself as St George, his two wives as Martha and Mary, and his father as St Jerome.

Het Eilandje

The docks north of the city centre, are home to Antwerp's newest museum, **MAS** (Museum aan de Stroom; Tues–Fri 10am–5pm, Sat–Sun 10am–6pm; €5; Ⓦwww.mas.be), which brings together the collections of the former Ethnographic, National Shipping and Folklore museums in a dynamic display spread over floors four to eight. The top floor offers superb panoramic views of the city.

Arrival, information and city transport

Train Antwerp has two main-line train stations, Berchem and Centraal. The latter is the one you want for the city centre. Centraal Station is located about 2km east of the Grote Markt; trams #2 and #15 (direction Linkeroever) run from the tram station beside Centraal Station to the centre; get off at Groenplaats.

Tourist information Grote Markt 13 (Mon–Sat 9am–5.45pm, Sun 9am–4.45pm; Ⓣ03 232 01 03, Ⓦwww.visit.antwerpen.be). The Centraal Station also has a kiosk.

Discount cards The tourist offices sell the Antwerp City Card which costs €31, is valid for 48hr, and grants free access to all city museums and churches, as well as 25 percent discount on numerous other attractions and bike rental.

City transport The centre is easily traversed on foot, and there are very good bus, metro and tram services covering the rest of the city. Franklin Rooseveltplaats and Groenplaats are two of the main transport hubs. A flat-rate one-way ticket on any part of the city's transport system costs €2; a 24hr pass (*dagpas*) €5.

Accommodation

Many mid-priced and budget establishments are around Centraal Station, where you should exercise caution at night.

Abhostel Kattenberg 110 Ⓣ03 473 57 01 66, Ⓦwww.abhostel.com. Chic family-run hostel 15min walk from the centre. Rooftop terrace, kitchen, lounge, free wi-fi, no curfew. Breakfast included. Dorms €19 without bedding, €21 with bedding, doubles €50.

Alias Provinciestraat 256 Ⓣ03 230 05 22, Ⓦwww.wix.com/aliasyouthhostel/home. Previously the *New International Youth Hostel*, it has been given a lick of paint and new beds. There's a homely TV room and adjoining breakfast room, free wi-fi, no curfew. Breakfast (not bedding) included. Dorms €19 (€15 for under-26s), singles €34, doubles €49.

Jeugdherberg Pulcinella Bogaardeplein 1 Ⓣ03 234 03 14, Ⓦwww.vjh.be. Brand-new black-and-white minimalist hostel. Four- and six-bed en-suite

TREAT YOURSELF

Wake Up Hoogstraat 68 (Ⓣ03 225 16 06, Ⓦwww.wake-up.be). Bright, well-located hotel with breakfast in the lovely café downstairs included. The rooms accommodating four are a good deal. Book in advance in summer. Singles €50, doubles €85, quadruples €120. City tax of €2.50 per person not included.

dorms have individual reading lights and lockers. Designer bar downstairs, no kitchen, free wi-fi and internet, no curfew. Breakfast and sheets included. Dorms €22, singles €35.50, doubles €53.

Eating

Antwerp is full of informal café-restaurants. Several of the best are clustered on Suikerrui and Grote Pieter Potstraat near the Grote Markt, and there's another concentration in the vicinity of Hendrik Conscienceplein. For fast food, try the kebab and falafel places on Oude Koornmarkt, or, of course, any of the *frituurs*.

Cafés and snacks

Caffènation Hopland 46. Great coffee, and a nice garden at this café close to Rubenshuis. Mon–Fri 8.30am–7.30pm, Sat 9am–8pm, Sun noon–6pm.

Caravan Damplein 17. Vintage café that puts together picnic hampers and is famous for its weekend *koppijn ontbijt* ("hangover breakfast") served with either a beer or a painkiller. Mains €5–12. Mon–Wed & Sun 10am–9pm, Thurs–Sat 10am–11pm.

De Cafétaria Montignystraat 21. Shabby-chic café serving healthy sandwiches, milkshakes, pastries and excellent coffee. Plenty of magazines strewn around for reading. Mains €5. Daily 9am–6pm.

Fritkot Max Groenplaats 12. Serves the best chips in town. Cornets cost €3. Mon–Thurs & Sun noon–midnight, Fri–Sat noon–3am.

Via Via Wolstraat 43. Popular travellers' café serving dishes from around the world. Mains €10. Mon–Sat 11.30am–late, Sun 3pm–late

Restaurants

De Taloorkes Lange Koepoortstraat 61. Five minutes' walk from Grote Markt but a world away from its touristy offerings, this locals' restaurant serves mouthwatering stews and mussels. Mains €15. Daily noon–10pm.

Kapitein Zeppos Vleminckveld 78. Off-the-beaten-track restaurant with exposed brick walls and chunky wooden tables. Excellent steaks and salads and the *dagschotel* (daily special) is extremely good value for money. Mains €12. Cash only. Mon–Fri 10am–10pm, Sat–Sun 11am–11pm.

Drinking and nightlife

Bars

De Duifkens Graanmarkt 5. A great place to try local beer Bolleke Koninck. Rumour has it the former owner's ashes are stored in the urn sat on top of the fireplace! Mon–Fri 11.30am–late, Sat–Sun 10am–late.

De Vagant Reyndersstraat 25. Specialist gin bar serving Belgian and Dutch *jenevers* in comfortable surroundings. Mon–Fri 11am–11pm, Sat–Sun noon–11pm.

Kulminator Vleminckveld 32. Filled with knick-knacks, this beer café stocks over 600 brands. Mon 8am–midnight, Tues–Fri 11am–midnight, Sat 5pm–midnight.

Pater's Vaetje Blauwmoezelstraat 1. In the shadow of the cathedral, this old-fashioned pub has a great range of beers and is popular with tourists and locals alike. Sun–Thurs 11am–3am, Fri–Sat 11am–5am.

Quinten Matsijs Moriaanstraat 17. Established in 1545, this is Antwerp's oldest bar. The regal dark-wood interior is ideal for a relaxed quiet drink. Tues–Sat noon–late, Sun noon–8pm.

Clubs

Café d'Anvers Verversrui 15. Club housed in a sixteenth-century church in the red-light district. Mainly house music. Thurs 11pm–6am, Fri–Sat 11pm–7.30am.

De Muze Melkmarkt 15. Renowned jazz bar, with free live performances Mon–Sat at 10pm and Sun at 3pm. Daily 11am–late.

Noxx Kotterstraat 1 ⓦ www.noxxantwerp.eu. Club in the Het Eilandje district, north of the city centre. Has four rooms, including the *Salle Noire* with a 360° LED wall. Music varies. Entry on Thurs free, Fri varies, Sat €15. Thurs 10pm–6am, Fri 11pm–6am, Sat 11pm–7am.

Shopping

Most high-street labels can be found along Meir and Huidevettersstraat, while Kammenstraat is good for vintage clothes shops. Lange Koepoortstraat has plenty of secondhand record shops including **FatKat** at no. 51 and **Record Collector** at no. 70. Everything from pricey antique shops to cavernous junk shops can be found along Kloosterstraat.

Directory

Internet Famous Cyber, Nationalestraat 92 (Mon–Thurs & Sun 10am–8pm, Fri 10am–9pm, closed Sat; €1.50/hr).

Left luggage Self-service lockers in the train station under the stairs, €3/24hr.

Post office Groenplaats 43 (Mon–Fri 9am–6pm, Sat 9am–noon).

Moving on

Train Bruges (hourly; 1hr 20min); Brussels (every 30min; 40min); Ghent (every 30min; 50min); Ostend (hourly; 1hr 40min).

GHENT

The largest town in Western Europe during the thirteenth and fourteenth centuries, **GHENT (Gent)** was once at the heart of the medieval Flemish cloth trade. It's now the third largest city in Belgium, and rivals Bruges thanks to its beautiful canals and well-preserved medieval architecture – without the stifling tourism.

What to see and do

A captivating university town with a spirited nightlife and its own **castle**, Ghent's main appeal lies in wandering the cobbled streets which line the canalside and sampling the city's bars.

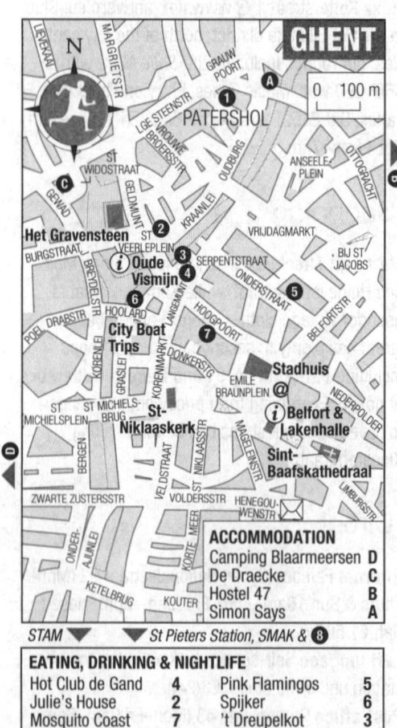

St Baafsplein

Ghent is famous for its three towers in a row. The first of these – and the best place to start exploring is – the mainly Gothic **Sint-BaafsKathedraal**, squeezed into the corner of St Baafsplein (April–Oct Mon–Sat 8.30am–6pm, Sun 1–6pm; Nov–March Mon–Sat 8.30am–5pm, Sun 1–5pm). Inside, a small chapel (April–Oct Mon–Sat 9.30am–5pm, Sun 1–5pm; Nov–March Mon–Sat 10.30am–4pm, Sun 1–4pm; €4 includes audioguide) holds Ghent's greatest treasure, the altarpiece of the *Adoration of the Mystic Lamb,* a wonderful, early fifteenth-century painting by brothers Hubert and Jan van Eyck.

On the west side of St Baafsplein lurks the medieval **Lakenhalle** (Cloth Hall), a gloomy hunk of a building. One of its entrances leads to the adjoining **Belfort** (Belfry; daily 10am–6pm; €5), a much-amended edifice dating from the fourteenth century. A lift climbs up to the roof for excellent views over the city centre. St Niklaaskerk, at the western end of Emile Braunplein, completes the trio.

The Graslei and Patershol

The **Graslei** forms the eastern side of the old city harbour and is home to a splendid series of medieval guild-houses. On warm days it's packed with students sunning themselves. From here you can catch boat tours. Nearby just to the north are the narrow cobbled lanes and alleys of the **Patershol**, a pocket-sized district that was formerly home to the city's weavers, but is now Ghent's main restaurant quarter. To the west, on Sint-Veerleplein, stands **Het Gravensteen** (Castle of the Counts; April–Sept 9am–6pm, final entry at 5pm; Oct–March 9am–5pm, final entry 4pm; €8 includes audioguide), a spectacular twelfth-century castle, now a chilling torture museum.

SMAK and STAM

Strolling south from the centre along Ghent's main shopping street,

Veldstraat, it takes about twenty minutes to reach the old casino, parts of which have been turned into **SMAK** (Citadelpark; Tues–Sun 10am–6pm; €6; ⓦwww.smak.be), a contemporary art museum well known for its adventurous temporary exhibitions.

Just north, across the canal, is **STAM** (Godshuizenlaan 2; Tues–Sun 10am–6pm; €6; ⓦwww.stamgent.be), a new museum detailing the city's history.

Arrival, information and city transport

Arrival Of Ghent's two train stations, St Pieters is the handiest one for town, about 2km to the south of the city centre; trams (#1 direction Evergem or Wondelgem) run up to the Korenmarkt, plumb in the centre of town, every few minutes.

Tourist information Moved from the crypt of the Lakenhalle to the Oude Vismijn (Sint-Veerleplein 5) in Spring 2012 (daily: March 15 to Oct 14 9.30am–6.30pm; Oct 15 to March 14 9.30am–4.30pm; ⓣ09 266 56 60, ⓦwww.visitgent.be).

Discount cards The Museum Pass grants free entry to all Ghent's museums and monuments and free use of public transport. It costs €20 for 3 days and can be bought from the tourist office, hotels, participating museums and De Lijn offices.

City transport Ghent's centre is very compact, so you probably won't need to buy a day-pass. The flat-rate fare for trams is €2/journey; validate the ticket at the machine once you get on.

Accommodation

The tourist office publishes a comprehensive brochure detailing local accommodation, and operates a free hotel booking service.

Camping Blaarmeersen Zuiderlaan 12 ⓣ09 266 81 60. Popular five-star campsite to the west of the town centre, with excellent sports facilities including a lake. July–Aug €5.50/person, plus €5/tent; Sept–June €4.50/person, plus €4/tent.

De Draecke St Widostraat 11 ⓣ09 233 70 50, ⓦwww.vjh.be/gent. Central option with very friendly staff. En-suite rooms are unremarkable, communal areas (bar, TV room) are a bit lacklustre. Things may improve when the extension and courtyard terrace are completed. No kitchen, no curfew. Bedding and breakfast included. Dorms €20.80, singles €35, doubles €50, no city tax; €3 extra for non HI members.

Hostel 47 Blekerijstraat 47 ⓣ0478 71 28 27, ⓦwww.hostel47.com. Trendy hostel in the north of town. Dorm rooms are finished to a high standard and communal showers and sinks are very swanky. Free wi-fi, no laundry, no curfew. Includes breakfast and sheets, but not city tax (€2.50/person). Cash only. Dorms €24, singles €45, doubles €66.

> **TREAT YOURSELF**
>
> **Simon Says** Sluizeken 8 (ⓣ09 233 03 43, ⓦwww.simon-says.be). Located above a cosy coffeehouse in trendy Patershol, this B&B has two very stylish double rooms each with elegant stone-tile en-suite bathrooms. €100 (€95 when staying two nights), includes breakfast and city tax.

Eating, drinking and nightlife

Fancier restaurants are concentrated in Patershol, while less-expensive spots, cluster around the Korenmarkt. Ghent boasts an energetic drinking scene thanks to its student population.

Cafés and restaurants

Julie's House Kraanlei 13. Wonderful artisanal bakery offering home-made cupcakes, brownies and tarts. Good breakfast menus too. Wed–Sun 9am–6.30pm.

> **GHENT FESTIVAL**
>
> For ten days during the second half of July, Ghent transforms into a 24-hour party city as it pulsates with the **Gentse Feesten** (ⓦwww.gentsefeesten.be). Stages are set up in all the town's main squares and blast out every kind of music. Accommodation can get booked up months before the festival, so be sure to make a reservation, and try to avoid the city straight afterwards – everything is shut for the next week or so as the city rests.

Mosquito Coast Hoogpoort 28. Travellers' café with bookshelves of guides, two terraces and a menu of filling wraps and salads. Also serves Ghent-made aperitif *Roomer*. Tues–Sat 11am–late, Sun 3pm–late.

Pane e Vino Nederkouter 9. Cheap and delicious pizza and pasta in a simple, lively setting. Margherita pizza €6.90. Mon–Fri 11.30am–2.30pm & 5.30–10.30pm, Sat 5.30–10.30pm.

Bars

't Dreupelkot Groentenmarkt 12. The city's last traditional *jenever* bar. It stocks over 215 flavours, all kept at icy temperatures. Mon–Sat 4pm–late.

Pink Flamingos Onderstraat 55. Wacky little place stuffed with kitsch paraphernalia. Attracts a hip crowd, and is a great place for an aperitif or cocktails. DJs play every night from 10pm. Thurs–Sat 2pm–3am.

Spijker Pensmarkt 3. Cosy candlelit bar housed in a thirteenth-century leprosy shelter. Terrace out the back with lovely views of the canal. Daily 9am–4am.

Clubs and live music

Hot Club de Gand Schuddevisstraatje Groentenmarkt 15b www.hotclubdegand.be. Hidden down a narrow alley, this is the best jazz spot in town, with jam sessions on Wed evenings. Daily 3pm–late.

The White Cat Drongenhof 40. Funky basement club in the Patershol district – don't miss the aquarium bar. Live jazz/ funk on Fri and Sat. Wed–Sat 8pm–late.

Directory

Internet Coffee Lounge, Botermarkt 6 (Mon & Wed–Sun 10am–7pm; €2.50/hr).

Post office Lange Kruisstraat 55 (Mon–Fri 9am–6pm, Sat 9am–3pm).

Moving on

Train Antwerp (every 30min; 50min); Bruges (every 20min; 25min); Brussels (every 30min; 40min); Ostend (every 30min; 50min).

BRUGES

The reputation of **BRUGES (Brugge)** as one of the most perfectly preserved medieval cities in Europe has made it the most popular tourist destination in Belgium. Inevitably, the crowds tend to overwhelm the city's charms, but you would be mad to come to Belgium and miss the place. Bruges boomed throughout the Middle Ages, its weavers turning English wool into clothing that was exported worldwide. By the end of the fifteenth century, however, Bruges had begun its decline and its development stalled.

What to see and do

The older sections of Bruges fan out from two central squares, Markt and Burg.

Markt, Belfort and Hallen

Markt, edged on three sides by nineteenth-century gabled buildings, is the larger of the two squares, an impressive open space flanked on its south side by the mighty **Belfort** (Belfry; daily 9.30am–5pm; €8), built in the thirteenth century when the town was at its richest. The belfry is attached to the rectangular **Hallen**, a much-restored edifice also dating from the thirteenth century. Entry to the Belfry is via the Hallen; inside, a tapering staircase leads up to the roof from where there are spectacular views over the city.

The Burg and the Heilig Bloed Basiliek

From the Markt, Breidelstraat leads through to the **Burg**, whose finest building is the **Heilig Bloed Basiliek** (Basilica of the Holy Blood; daily: April–Sept 9.30am–noon & 2–6pm; Oct–March Mon, Tues & Thurs–Sun 10am–noon & 2–4pm, Wed 10am–noon; €1.50). Its Upper Chapel holds a phial of the blood of Christ brought back from Jerusalem by the Crusaders. Stored in a grandiose silver tabernacle, the Holy Blood is still venerated on Ascension Day, when it is carried through the town in a colourful but solemn procession.

The Stadhuis

The **Stadhuis** has a beautiful, turreted sandstone facade, behind which is

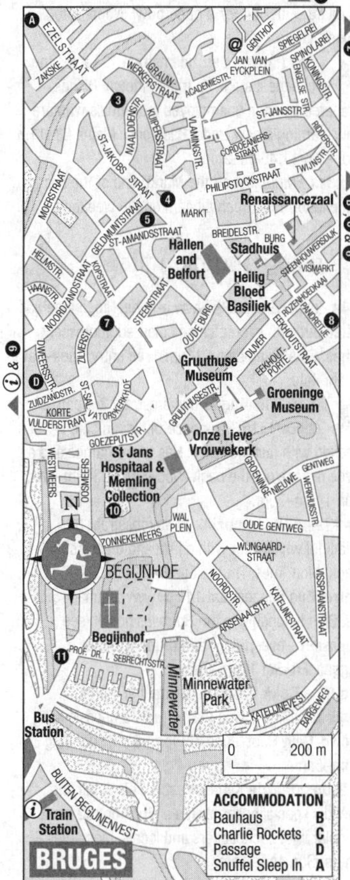

EATING		DRINKING & NIGHTLIFE			
De Stoepa	11	B-in	10	Ma Rica Rokk	9
L'Estaminet	8	Café Vlissinghe	2	't Brugs Beertje	7
Médard	5	De Kleine Nachtmuziek	3		
Pas Partout	1	Entrenous	6		
Pickles	4				

a magnificent **Gothic Hall** (daily 9.30am–5pm; €2). The price of admission covers entry to the nearby former alderman's mansion. Its Renaissance **'tBrugse Vrije** (Tues–Sun 9.30am–12.30pm & 1.30–5pm) dates from the sixteenth century, oozes history and features an enormous oak chimneypiece carved in honour of the ruling Habsburgs.

The Groeninge and Gruuthuse museums

The **Groeninge Museum**, at Dijver 12 (Tues–Sun 9.30am–5pm; €8), houses a superb collection of Flemish paintings, including several canvases by Jan van Eyck. Further along the Dijver, at no. 17, the **Gruuthuse Museum** (Tues–Sun 9.30am–5pm; €6) is sited in a rambling fifteenth-century mansion and holds a varied collection of fine art, including intricately carved altarpieces and locally made tapestries.

Onze Lieve Vrouwekerk

The **Onze Lieve Vrouwekerk** (Tues–Sat 9.30am–5pm, Sun 1.30–5pm; €4), on Mariastraat houses a delicate marble statue of *Madonna and Child* by Michelangelo and, in the chancel (same hours; €2.50) the exquisite Renaissance mausoleums of Charles the Bold and his daughter Mary of Burgundy.

St Jans Hospitaal and Begijnhof

St Jans Hospitaal (Tues–Sun 9.30am–5pm; €8) has been turned into a lavish museum celebrating the city's history in general and the hospital in particular. In addition, the old Hospital chapel displays a small but exquisite collection of paintings by **Hans Memling**.

From St Jans, it's a quick stroll down to the **Begijnhof** (Mon–Sat 10am–5pm, Sun 2.30–5pm; free), a circle of white-washed houses around a tidy green. Nearby is the romantic **Minnewater**, often known as the "Lake of Love".

Arrival and information

Arrival Bruges's train station adjoins the bus station about 2km southwest of the centre. Local buses leave from outside the train station for the main square, the Markt; tickets cost €1.20.

Tourist information The main office is in the city concert hall at 't Zand 34 (daily 10am–6pm; ⓣ 050 44 86 86, ⓦ www.brugge.be). There is a smaller branch inside the train station (Mon–Fri 10am–5pm, Sat & Sun 10am–2pm; ⓣ 050 44 86 86).

Discount card The Brugge City Card (Ⓦwww.bruggecitycard.be) grants free access to the main museums, attractions, includes a free canal boat ride and 25 percent discount on bicycle rental and public transport. It costs €34/39 for 48/72hr, and is cheaper for under-26s.

Accommodation

Bauhaus Langestraat 133–145 Ⓣ050 34 10 93, Ⓦwww.bauhaus.be. Cheerful hostel with its own nightclub (see *Entrenous*, opposite). Ask for a bunk in the new section: "pod" beds have curtains around them for privacy and locker drawers. 10 percent off the bill and free beer at the hostel's excellent bar-restaurant. Free wi-fi, no curfew. Reception located at no. 145. Bedding and breakfast included. Dorms €14, singles €26, doubles €40.

Charlie Rockets Hoogstraat 19 Ⓣ050 33 06 60, Ⓦwww.charlierockets.com. Has 19 rooms above a lively American-style bar-restaurant. Opt for the "new" section if you can. Breakfast €3 extra. Dorms €17, doubles €50.

Passage Dweersstraat 26 Ⓣ050 34 02 32, Ⓦwww.passagebruges.com. Hostel has ten comfortable dormitories; breakfast (€5 extra) is served in the excellent period restaurant. Next door, the *Passage Hotel* offers simple but well-maintained doubles, some with shared facilities. Dorms €16, doubles €52–67.

Snuffel Sleep In Ezelstraat 47–49 Ⓣ050 33 31 33, Ⓦwww.snuffel.be. West of the centre with 4- to 12-bed dorms. Life centres around the laidback, late-opening bar. Free wi-fi, book exchange, kitchen, bike rental (€6/day). Bedding and breakfast included. Dorms €15.

Eating

Most establishments churn our mediocre tourist-orientated fare, though there are some exceptions.

De Stoepa Oostmeers 124. Mediterranean-style bar-café with wood-burning stove in winter and a quiet leafy terrace ideal for a relaxed lunch in summer. Mains €6–8. Tues–Sun 11.45am–2am.

L'Estaminet Park 5. Friendly neighbourhood café-bar with a cosmopolitan clientele, first-rate beer menu and good pasta dishes. Mains €8. Tues–Sun 11.30am–late, Thurs 4pm–late.

Médard Sint-Amandsstraat 18. Family-run Italian restaurant famous for its generous portions of pasta – just €4 for a huge bowl. Noon–late, closed Thurs.

Pas Partout Jeruzalemstraat 1. Serves the cheapest steak en frites in town. Dishes prepared by once unemployed individuals who are now learning a new trade. Cash only. Mains €8–11. Mon–Sat 11.45am–2pm.

Pickles *Frituur* just off the Markt; one of the best options for fries. Open till 4am on the weekend.

Drinking and nightlife

B-in Zonnekemeers Ⓦwww.b-in.be. Hip lounge bar kitted out with eye-catching coloured fluorescent tubes. Gets going about 11pm. Free entry. Tues–Sat 11am–late.

Café Vlissinghe Blekersstraat 2. Open since 1515, this peaceful hidden café is packed with historic relics. Has board games and a large terrace out the back. Wed–Sat 11.30am–late, Sun 11am–7pm.

De Kleine Nachtmuziek St Jakobsstraat 60. Peaceful whisky bar with a jazz and blues sound-track. Mon, Tues, Thurs– Sun 6pm–late.

Entrenous Langestraat 145 Ⓦwww.bauhauszall.be. Club belonging to the *Bauhaus* hostel (see opposite) – everything from drum 'n' bases to reggae. Fri–Sat 11pm–7am.

Ma Rica Rokk t'Zand 6. Central bar with a tropical "holiday" vibe that attracts a good-looking crowd. Daily Sept–June 7.30pm–3am; July–Aug 9pm–5am.

't Brugs Beertje Kemelstraat 5. This small and friendly speciality bar claims a stock of 300 beers. Popular with backpackers and locals. Mon–Tues & Thurs–Sun 4pm–1am.

Directory

Internet The city has free wi-fi zones ("ZapFi") in the t'Zand, Markt and Burg squares. Bean around the World at Genthof 5 (Mon & Thurs–Sun 10am–7pm, Wed noon–7pm; €1/15min) has free wi-fi and an internet terminal.

Left luggage Located at main station entrance on the left; €3/3.50/4 for small/medium/large self-service locker.

Moving on

Train Antwerp (hourly; 1hr 20min); Brussels (every 30min; 1hr); Ghent (every 20min; 25min); Ostend (every 20min; 15min); Zeebrugge (hourly; 15min).

Southern Belgium

South of Brussels lies **Wallonia**, French-speaking Belgium, where a belt of heavy industry interrupts the rolling farmland that precedes the high wooded hills of the **Ardennes**. The latter spreads over three provinces – **Namur** in the west, **Luxembourg** in the south and Liège in the east – and is a great place for hiking and canoeing.

NAMUR

NAMUR is a charming town, whose antique centre boasts a number of first-rate restaurants and lively bars lent vigour by its university students. It is also the ideal base from which to explore the Ardennes forest.

What to see and do

The town occupies an important strategic location, straddling the confluence of the rivers Sambre and Meuse, the main result being the massive, rambling **citadel** – one of the largest in Europe – which overlooks the town. Explore it on foot or take the La Citad'n tourist train (daily June to mid-Sept; weekends only mid-Sept to mid-Nov; €2), which departs every twenty minutes from place de l'Ange and rue du Grognon.

At rue de Fer 24, is the **Musée Provincial des Art Anciens** (Provincial Museum of Ancient Arts; Tues–Sun 10am–6pm; €3, audioguide €2) which now houses the *Trésor du Prieuré d'Oignies* – a spellbinding collection of reliquaries.

In the heart of the old town, at rue Fumal 12, is the **Musée Provincial Félicien Rops** (Tues–Sun 10am–6pm, open Mon July & Aug only; €3; ⓦwww.museerops.be). Sexually liberated for his generation, Rops pushed the boundaries in his sketches and paintings – look for his saucy *Satantic* series on the second floor.

A general **market** is held every Saturday on rue de Fer and a flea market every Sunday on quai de la Meuse (both 7am–1pm).

Arrival, information and city transport

Arrival Namur's train and bus stations are north of the centre on place de la Station.

Tourist information Square Léopold (daily 9.30am–6pm; ⓣ081 24 64 49, ⓦwww.namurtourisme.be). There's also a seasonal office (April–Oct daily 9.30am–6pm; ⓣ081 24 64 48), inside the Halle Al'Chair at rue du Pont 21.

City transport Rent bikes from Maison des Cyclistes inside the train station (€12/day). From June to September Namourette boats taxi passengers across the River Meuse from Grognon to the town of Jambes; €1 one-way.

Accommodation

Auberge de Jeunesse Félicien Rops 8, ave ⓣ081 22 36 88, ⓦwww.laj.be. At the southern edge of town. Main building renovated in 2011; it now offers doubles and 3-, 4- and 5-bed dorms. There's a bar with a terrace overlooking the river, a communal and professional kitchen serving breakfast and evening meals (mains €5), TV room, free internet and wi-fi, laundry and no curfew. It's 3km from the train station: walk along the river or take bus #3 or #4 from the centre (€1.75). Sheets and breakfast included. Dorms €19.50, singles €33, doubles €48; €3 extra if not an HI hostel member.

La Valse Lente quai des Chasseurs Ardennais, ⓣ0479 56 91 16, ⓦwww.lavalselente.be. Converted barge with four clean and cosy en-suite rooms. An excellent breakfast is included. Doubles €70.

Eating and drinking

A Table! rue des Brasseurs 21. Lively café serving organic light bites and veggie options. Tables at the back have views of the Sambre and the citadel. Mains €13. Mon–Thurs 11.30am–2.30pm, Fri–Sat 11.30am–2.30pm & 6.30–9pm.

La Mère Gourmandin rue du Président 13. Serves savoury crêpes and tumblers of home-made cider. Romantic and candlelit at night. Mains €12.

Mon–Thurs noon–2pm, Fri–Sat noon–2pm & 6.30–9.30pm.

Piano Bar place Marché-aux-Légumes. One of Namur's most popular bars. Live jazz Fri & Sat from 10pm.

Soup Shop rue de Bruxelles 35. Rustic café serving hearty home-made soups, quiches and pasta. Mains €4. Mon–Fri 11.30am–3pm, Sat 11.30am–3.30pm.

Moving on

Train to: Brussels (every 30min; 1hr); Luxembourg City (hourly; 1hr 40min); Marloie (for La Roche-en-Ardenne; hourly; 35min); Melreux (for La Roche-en-Ardenne; hourly; 1hr).

LA ROCHE-EN-ARDENNE

If you've had enough of Belgian cities or flat landscape, head to the **Ardennes** for a change of scene. **La Roche-en-Ardenne** is one of the area's best bases for outdoor activities. Admittedly, it's packed in the summer (mostly with young families), but it's easy to escape into the gorgeous woods that surround it. The only downside is that, aside from the town's fairly impressive **castle ruins** (daily 10/11am–4/5pm, 6.30pm in July & Aug; €4.50), there's not too much to amuse you if the weather's bad.

Arrival and information

Train and bus The nearest stations to La Roche are Marloie and Melreux, both around half an hour away; buses leave every 2hr. Catch bus #3 from Melreux or #15 from Marloie (2hr 35min). Buses drop passengers off in the centre of town.

Tourist information place du Marché 15 (daily 9.30am–5pm, till 6pm July & Aug; ⓣ084 36 77 36, ⓦwww.la-roche-tourisme.com). Offers internet access.

Activities

There's no shortage of companies offering kayaking and other activities

Ardenne Aventures rue du Hadja 1 ⓣ084 41 19 00, ⓦwww.ardenne-aventures.be. Long (€21; 5hr) and short (€16; 1hr 30min) kayak trips year-round, leaving hourly in high season; mountain biking (€18; 4hr); horseriding (€35; 2hr); rafting (Nov–April; €19; 1hr 30min). You can get good rates if you combine two activities on one day.

Brandsport *Auberge La Laiterie*, Mierchamps 15 ⓣ084 41 10 84, ⓦwww.brandsport.be. Orienteering (€16.50 for a half-day); kayaking (€13.50 for a half-day); caving (€46.50 for a half-day); archery (€26.50 for a half-day). Horseriding, abseiling and caving can also be organized.

Accommodation, eating and drinking

Camping Le Vieux Moulin Petite Strument 62, about 800m to the south of the town centre along the Val du Bronze ⓣ084 41 15 07, ⓦwww.strument.com. Huge campsite with a picturesque setting beside a stream. Open March–Oct. €8.50/tent, plus €2.50/person.

Domaine des Olivettes chemin de Soeret 12 ⓣ084 41 16 52, ⓦwww.lesolivettes.be. Fifteen minutes out of town, this 1920s villa combines hostel, hotel, restaurant, bar and equestrian centre. Unfortunately, the hostel is only available to large groups. Singles €65, doubles €80.

Le Clos René rue Chamont 30. Delightful pancake house that also serves delicious *cidre de poire*. Pancakes start at €6.

Luxembourg

Famous as a tax haven, financial centre and headquarters for various European institutions, the **Grand Duchy of Luxembourg**, one of Europe's smallest sovereign states, unsurprisingly gets written off by many travellers. However, this is a mistake: **Luxembourg City** is incredibly charming and well worth visiting for a night or two.

LUXEMBOURG CITY

LUXEMBOURG CITY is one of the most spectacularly sited capitals in Europe. The valleys of the rivers Alzette and Pétrusse, which meet here, cut a green swathe through the city, their deep canyons formerly key to the city's defences.

What to see and do

Luxembourg City divides into four distinct sections: the old town (northern side of the Pétrusse valley) holds most of the city's sights and is the most appealing quarter, the modern city home to the train station, the atmospheric valleys of the **Grund** area (east), and the **Kirchberg** section (northeast) home to sleek European Union buildings.

The old town

The UNESCO-listed old town focuses on two squares: the **place d'Armes**, fringed with cafés and restaurants, and the larger **place Guillaume II**, the venue of Luxembourg's main general market (Wed & Sat 7am). Nearby, on rue du St-Esprit, is the **Musée d'Histoire de la Ville de Luxembourg** (Tues–Sun 10am–6pm, Thurs till 8pm; €5; ⓦwww.mhvl.lu). Levels 0–2 house a permanent exhibition explaining Luxembourg's history and there is a glass-walled lift offering dramatic views of the Grund.

Just a few minutes' walk east of the museum on the montée de Clausen lie the **Casemates du Bock** (March–Oct daily 10am–5pm; €3), 17km of underground tunnels, the earliest of which were excavated in 1644 under Spanish control.

The Grund

The dramatic **chemin de la Corniche** tracks the side of the cliff with great views of the slate-roofed houses of the quaint and leafy **Grund** down below. It leads to the gigantic **Citadelle du St-Esprit**, whose top has been levelled off and partly turned into a leafy park. The Grund is especially worth visiting on Wednesday and Friday nights when its bars kick into action.

Kirchberg

Spread over a large area, the east of the city is largely dominated by

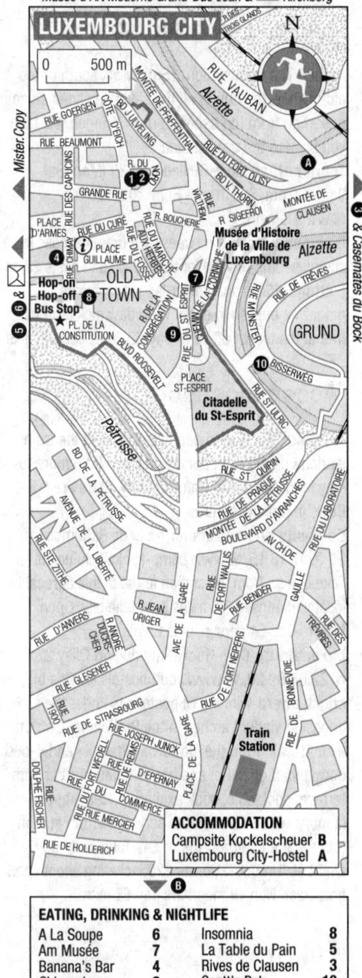

European Union buildings, but among them, at Park Dräi Eechelen 3, is the **Musée d'Art Moderne Grand-Duc Jean** (Mudam; Wed–Fri 11am–8pm, Sat–Mon 11am–6pm, closed Tues; €5; ⓦwww.mudam.lu). A good way to see the area is to take the hour-long tours offered by the hop-on hop-off **sightseeing bus** (April–Oct every 20min from place de la Constitution; €14; valid for 24hr).

Arrival and information

Arrival The train station, 15min walk south of the old town, is the hub of all the city's bus lines. Buses departing from the depot on rue Aldringen will take you back to the train station.
Tourist office place Guillaume II 30 (Mon–Sat 9am–6/7pm, Sun 10am–6pm; ⓣ22 28 09, ⓦwww.lcto.lu).
Discount card The *muséeskaart* grants access to all city museums, is valid for three days and costs €9.
Listings *352* is an English-language events magazine published every Thursday; pick it up for free at the tourist office or pay €2.50 at news kiosks.

Accommodation

There are plenty of cheap hotels around the train station but you're better off paying a little more to stay in the old town. Unfortunately, there are no B&Bs in the city centre.
Campsite Kockelscheuer route de Bettembourg 22 ⓣ47 18 15, ⓦwww.camp-kockelscheuer.lu. Take bus #5 from the station to get to this agreeably located campsite 2.5 miles out of the city. Open March–Oct. €4/person, plus €5/pitch.
Luxembourg City-Hostel rue du Fort Olisy 2 ⓣ22 68 89 20, ⓦwww.youthhostels.lu. This big, bright, award-winning HI hostel sits under the imposing viaduct arches in the Pfaffenthal district, a short walk from the old town. Offers 4- and 6-bed dorms (half en suite) and has a restaurant/bar with terrace, pool table, book exchange, free internet, laundry, no curfew. Shuttle service to/from station (3km; €3) and airport (6km; €4). Take bus #9, alight at "Umboc". Dorms €20 including sheets and breakfast. Non-HI members pay €3 extra.

Eating

French cuisine is popular here, but traditional Luxembourgish dishes, such as neck of pork with broad beans (*judd mat gaardebounen*), are found on many menus too.
A La Soupe rue Chimay 9. Trendy soup bar just off place Guillaume II. Mains €4.50. Mon–Sat 7am–8.45pm, closed Sun.
Banana's Bar ave Monterey 9. Lively American bar-restaurant whose walls are plastered with old advertising posters. Serves burgers, pastas and salads for €12. No credit cards. Mon–Sat noon–10pm, Sun noon–6pm.
Chiggeri rue du Nord 15 ⓣ22 99 36. Bohemian bar-restaurant with funky decor. Famous for its *tartiflette* and Bible-thick wine list. Mains €20. Mon–Fri 10am–1am, Sat & Sun 11am–3am.
La Table du Pain ave Monterey 19 ⓣ24 16 08 Snug bakery offering quiches, soups and salads for around €12. Daily 7am–7pm.
Um Dierfgen Côté d'Eich 6 ⓣ22 61 41. Serves traditional Luxembourgish meals, including *steak cheval* (horse steak) for €20. Daily 11.30am–2.30pm & 6–10pm, closed Sun & Mon evening.

Drinking and nightlife

There's a lively bar scene in the old town and Grund, and the new development of pubs and clubs at *Les Rives de Clausen* (rue Emile Mousel 2; 10min walk from the HI hostel) gets especially busy on Friday evenings.
Am Musée rue du St-Esprit 14. Its quiet, leafy terrace boasts superb views of the Grund and is best enjoyed in summer. Tues–Sun 10am–6pm, Thurs till 8pm.
D'Qliq rue du St-Esprit 17. Music bar highly recommended by locals – hosts live concerts too. Happy hour 5–7pm. Daily 5pm–late.
Insomnia rue Notre Dame 15. A few steps downhill from Place Guillaume II and popular with trendy types. Mon–Fri 9am–1am, Sat & Sun 5pm–3am.
Scott's Pub rue Bisserweg 4. Located in the Grund, this Irish bar has a lovely terrace and attracts a young, expat crowd: the most backpacker-friendly hangout in Luxembourg.

Directory

Bike rental Vél'oh! ⓦwww.veloh.lu. 54 stations dotted across town. Payment with bank card. First 30min free, then €5/24hr.
Internet The entire city has a wi-fi network, access cards can be bought from the tourist office (€5/48hr). Alternatively, try MisterCopy, blvd Prince Henri 9b (Mon–Fri 9am–6pm, Sat 10am–5pm; €6.50/hr).
Luggage storage Located on platform 3CD of the train station; €3/day; daily 6am–9.30pm.
Pharmacies Goedert, place d'Armes 5; um Piquet, rue Aldringen 23.
Post office rue Aldringen 25 (Mon–Fri 7am–7pm, Sat 7am–5pm).

Moving on

Train to: Brussels (on the hour and 20min past the hour; 2hr 50min); Cologne (hourly; 5hr); Namur (hourly; 1hr 40min); Nancy (every 40min; 1hr 30min); Strasbourg (hourly; 2hr).

Bosnia-Herzegovina

HIGHLIGHTS

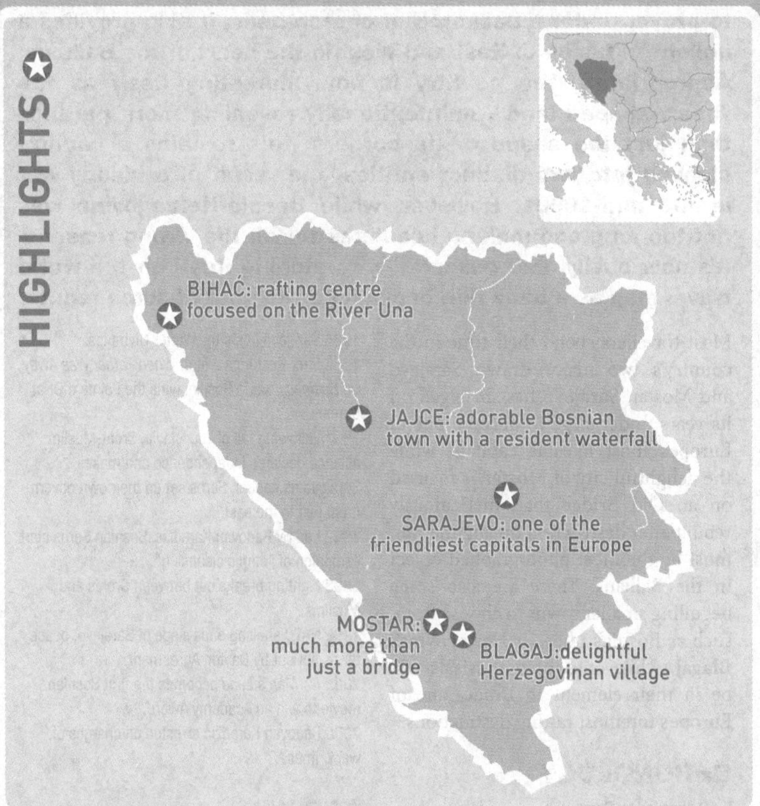

ROUGH COSTS

DAILY BUDGET Basic €25 /occasional treat €40

DRINK Bosnian coffee €0.50–1

FOOD *Čevapčići* (meat rissoles) €2–4

HOSTEL/BUDGET HOTEL €12/€25

TRAVEL Bus: Sarajevo–Bihać €25; train: Sarajevo–Mostar €5

FACT FILE

POPULATION 3.9 million

AREA 51,197 sq km

LANGUAGES Bosnian, Croatian, Serbian

CURRENCY Convertible Mark (KM)

CAPITAL Sarajevo (population: 400,000)

INTERNATIONAL PHONE CODE ⓣ387

Introduction

A land where turquoise rivers run swift and sheep huddle on steep hillsides, Bosnia-Herzegovina is one of Europe's most visually stunning corners. With muezzins calling the faithful to prayer under a backdrop of church bells, it also provides a delightful fusion of East and West in the heart of the Balkans. Appropriately, the country is now marketing itself as the "heart-shaped land", unintentionally revealing more perhaps than just the shape of its borders: this remains a country cleaved into two distinct entities, the result of a bloody war in the mid-1990s. However, while Bosnia-Herzegovina was not too long ago making headlines for all the wrong reasons, it's now busily, and deservedly, re-etching itself on the world travel map as a bona fide backpacker magnet of some repute.

Most travellers spend their time in the country's two major draws: Sarajevo and Mostar. **Sarajevo** has shrugged off its years under siege to become one of Europe's most likeable capitals, while the delightful city of **Mostar** is focused on an Old Bridge that, meticulously rebuilt after destruction during the war, must be the most photographed object in the Balkans. There are also some beguiling smaller towns to choose from, such as Bosnia's **Jajce**, or Herzegovina's **Blagaj**, while outdoor enthusiasts will be in their element in **Bihać**, one of Europe's foremost rafting destinations.

CHRONOLOGY

9 AD Annexed by Rome.
395 Division of Roman Empire; the area that comprises today's Bosnia-Herzegovina stays under the rule of Rome.
553 Emperor Justinian I conquers the area for the Byzantine Empire.
1463 Bosnia falls to the Ottoman Empire.
1482 Herzegovina falls to the Ottoman Empire.
1878 Russian defeat of Turkey sees Bosnia-Herzegovina transferred to Austria-Hungary.
1914 Franz Ferdinand shot in Sarajevo by a Bosnian Serb, eventually leading to World War I.
1918 Bosnia-Herzegovina becomes part of the Kingdom of Serbs, Croats and Slovenes.
1961 Ivo Andrić, born near Travnik, wins the Nobel Prize for Literature.
1984 Sarajevo hosts the Winter Olympics.
1985 Emir Kusturica's film, *When Father Was Away on Business*, set in Bosnia, wins the Palme d'Or at Cannes.
1991 Following fall of Yugoslavia, Croat-Muslim alliance declares independence and makes Sarajevo its capital; Serbs set up their own government just to the east.
1992 Led by Radovan Karadžić, Bosnian Serbs start campaign of "ethnic cleansing".
1993 Fighting breaks out between Croats and Muslims.
1995 NATO shelling ends siege of Sarajevo; peace terms set out by Dayton Agreement.
2001 *No Man's Land* becomes the first Bosnian movie to win an Academy Award.
2008 Radovan Karadžić arrested on charges of war crimes.

ARRIVAL

As close to landlocked as it's possible to get, Bosnia-Herzegovina is fairly easy to enter from all sides. **Trains** from Belgrade and Budapest arrive at Sarajevo, while a daily service between the Croatian cities of Ploče and Zagreb runs through Mostar and Sarajevo on the way. **Bus** connections are more numerous and points of origin include Podgorica, Split and a number of German cities. There are a smattering of international **flights** from Western Europe, but those seeking

A TALE OF TWO ENTITIES

Travellers should be aware that, in many ways, Bosnia-Herzegovina functions as two separate countries. These are not Bosnia and Herzegovina, as one might infer from the name, since these are geographical regions (Bosnia makes up around 80 percent of the country, with Herzegovina a small triangle south of Sarajevo). Rather, the country is split along ethnic lines. To the west, and including Sarajevo, is the **Federation of Bosnia and Herzegovina**, a Muslim-Croat alliance; while to the east and north is the **Republika Srpska**, an ethnic-Serb territory of almost equal size, centred on its capital Banja Luka. To add to the confusion, there are three official languages – all essentially the same – and three presidents. "Most countries just have one idiot in charge", says a local, "but we've got three."

budget carriers must fly in to Zagreb or Dubrovnik (see p.272).

GETTING AROUND

Bosnia-Herzegovina isn't the easiest country to get around, since much of its transport infrastructure – particularly the rail network – was damaged during the war. Things are improving, however, and decent **bus** services will almost always be able to get you where you want to go; it'll just take a little longer than you might expect, and perhaps cost a little more too. See Wbhtourism.ba for schedules. Also note that connections between the Federation and the Republika Srpska aren't regular.

There are also a few **railway** lines across the country, though severe underfunding means that most trains are too slow to be worth considering; the one exception is the twice-daily route linking Sarajevo and Mostar.

ACCOMMODATION

Accommodation is still pretty cheap in Bosnia-Herzegovina – you should always be able to find a **hotel** room in the €20–35 range; there are usually no set rates for single rooms, but ask and you may get €5–10 off. Wi-fi access is becoming widespread, most rooms have cable TV, and breakfast is usually included. **Guesthouses** (*pansiona*) are available in some towns, though are nowhere near as numerous as in neighbouring countries. The **hostel** scene has taken off in Sarajevo and Mostar (dorm beds costing around €12), and **private rooms** are still available in these cities, though they're pretty rare elsewhere. There are quite a few **campsites** dotted around, most with reasonable facilities. The presence of unexploded mines from the war means that wild camping is not a good idea.

FOOD AND DRINK

Centuries of Ottoman rule have left Turkish fingerprints on the nation's **cuisine**. You'll find *čevapčići* joints everywhere, selling grilled meat rissoles that are usually served up with *somun* (spongy bread) and chopped onion. Similarly hard to avoid are stands selling *burek*, greasy pastries filled with meat, spinach, cheese and sometimes pumpkin or potato; many travellers rate Sarajevo as the best *burek* city in the Balkans. Soups (*čorba*) and vegetables pop up all over the place on the country's menus, though more often than not the latter are stuffed with mincemeat; **vegetarians** will often have to satisfy themselves with salads, or certain selections from the ubiquitous pizzerias. Sweeties also have a Turkish ring to them, with syrupy *baklava* pastries available everywhere; added to this are an artery-clogging range of creamy **desserts**, most notable of which is *tufahije*, a marinaded apple topped with walnut and cream.

Drink

The consumption of **coffee** (*kafa*) has been elevated to something approaching an art form (see box opposite). For alcohol, there are a few good domestic **beers** (*pivo*), and Herzegovina produces a lot of **wine** – try Blatina, a local variety of red. There's also rakia, a potent spirit as popular by night as coffee is by day. Locals are also fond of telling guests that Bosnian tap water is safe to drink – evidently a major source of pride.

CULTURE AND ETIQUETTE

It's imperative to note that there are three distinct **ethnicities** in Bosnia-Herzegovina – **Bosnian Serb**, mostly Orthodox; **Bosnian Croat**, mostly Catholic; and Muslims known as **Bosniaks**. Of course, all were constituent parts of the bloody war of the mid-1990s; this affected every single person in the country, and reverberations can still be felt today – it's never too far away from people's minds. Some locals are more than willing to talk about their experiences, particularly in Sarajevo, but of course it's best to let them make the first move.

Also worth noting is the **geographical split** evident in the country's name – you'll find yourself using "Bosnian" as an adjective most of the time, and this is accepted, though in Herzegovina it's a *tiny* bit of a faux pas to tell locals how much you're "enjoying Bosnia".

BOSNIAN COFFEE

Don't dare use the dreaded T-word – although Bosnian coffee is served **Turkish-style**, with hot water poured over unfiltered grounds, locals insist that their variety is unique. It's markedly weaker than Turkish coffee, mainly because of its function as a social lubricant – it's consumed fervidly throughout the day, with different coffee sittings ascribed different terms: *razgalica* in the morning, *razgovoruša* a little later on, and *sikteruša* following a meal. Coffee is **served** on a metal tray from a *džezva*, a cute metal pot, and poured into little tumblers (*fildžan*). Also on the tray will be a *šečerluk*, containing a few cubes of sugar – it's traditional to dip the corner of a sugar cube into your coffee for a flash, nibble it, then let the coffee wash it down. And, most importantly, do as the locals do and take your time.

As for the more regular facets of travel etiquette, you should **dress** conservatively around religious buildings, leave small change or a little more as **tips** in a restaurant, and be aware that for all the ethnic rivalry, **smoking** is perhaps the country's dominant religion.

SPORTS AND OUTDOOR ACTIVITIES

Bosnia-Herzegovina is pretty good for outdoor pursuits. Beefy mountains mean that **hiking** is popular, though the continued presence of **landmines** means that you should seek local confirmation that an area is safe before setting off. During winter, a few **ski** slopes around Sarajevo come to life, while there's year-round **rafting** to be had on several of the country's rushing rivers – the best is the Una, near Bihać.

COMMUNICATIONS

Most **post offices** (*pošta*) are open weekdays from 9am to 5pm, and often on Saturday mornings too. Public **phones** use cards, which can be bought at post offices and kiosks, but it's usually cheaper to make international calls at a post office. **Internet** access is fairly widespread, even in small towns, and you should expect to pay 1–2KM/hr.

BOSNIA-HERZEGOVINA ONLINE

Ⓦ**www.bhtourism.ba** Official tourist board site.
Ⓦ**www.bhmac.org** Contains some useful information about landmine dangers.
Ⓦ**www.sonar.ba** Excellent event listings, mainly focused on Sarajevo.

EMERGENCIES

With the war still fresh in many minds, travellers often arrive expecting Bosnia-Herzegovina to be a dangerous place; it will quickly become clear that this is not the case, and that the **crime rate** is very low by European standards. The country's two **police** forces are usually easy to deal with, but keep your passport or a copy handy in case of a spot check. One very important danger to note is the presence of **landmines**. Strewn liberally during the war, the vast majority have now been cleared, and there's no danger in any urban area. In the countryside, however, it's advisable to stick to clear paths.

Pharmacies usually follow shop hours, though in larger cities you'll find that some stay open until late, and are sometimes open 24 hours.

INFORMATION

Larger cities have **tourist information offices** with English-speaking staff; some can make accommodation bookings. Free city **maps** are handed out at most hotels and all tourist offices.

EMERGENCY NUMBERS

Police ☎122; Ambulance ☎124; Fire ☎123.

MONEY AND BANKS

The currency of Bosnia-Herzegovina is the **convertible mark**, usually abbreviated to KM. Notes of 5, 10, 20, 50, 100 and 200 KM are in circulation, as are coins of 10, 20 and 50 feninga, and 1, 2 and 5 KM. Exchange **rates** are currently around 1.96KM to the euro, 2.28KM to the pound, and 1.39KM to the US dollar. One interesting little quirk of Bosno-Herzegovinan society is an apparent allergy to **large notes** – even paying for a 2KM coffee with a 5KM bill may result in a ten-minute hunt for change, while whipping out a 50KM bill for a small purchase will see you laughed down the road.

Accommodation prices are almost always quoted in euros, as are meals at some upmarket restaurants. In urban areas you won't have to look too far for an **ATM**, and **exchange offices** are plentiful in places used to tourists. **Banks** are usually open weekdays from 9am to 4pm, and often on Saturday mornings too.

BOSNIAN

The Bosnian language is essentially the same as Serbian, which is essentially the same as Croatian (see p.252), and all three are listed as official languages in Bosnia-Herzegovina. Note that the Republika Srpska uses the **Cyrillic alphabet**, which may cause some problems with street signs, menus and timetables.

OPENING HOURS AND HOLIDAYS

Times are less rigid here than in most countries – **shops** usually open when they want to open, which in most cases is from 10am to 7pm, and in larger cities there's little difference on weekends. All banks and post offices will be closed on **public holidays**: January 1, March 1, May 1 and November 25 – though these dates are far from the end of the story as the Catholic and Orthodox churches celebrate Easter and Christmas at different times, and Muslims celebrate a biannual holiday known as *Bajram*.

Sarajevo

With their imaginations and travel memories fired by spiky minarets, grilled kebabs and the all-pervasive aroma of ground coffee, many travellers see in **SARAJEVO** a Slavic mini-Istanbul. The Ottoman notes in the air are most prominent in Baščaršija, the city's delightful Old Town, which is home to umpteen mosques, bazaars, kebab restaurants and cafés. Further afield, burnt-out buildings evoke the catastrophic war of the mid-1990s, though the fun-loving, easy-going Sarajevans do a great job of painting over the scars of those tumultuous years – it's hard to walk around without being offered coffee, and it's hard to be invited for coffee without making friends.

Sarajevo gained importance during **Roman** times, and after a short slumber was reinvigorated as a trading hub during the **Ottoman** period, but sadly its recent history is far more pertinent. The international spotlight fell on the city as the host of the **1984 Winter Olympics**, but less than a decade later the world's eyes were retrained on it during a **siege** that lasted for almost four years – by some estimates, the longest in military history. Bosnian Serb forces made a near-unbroken ring around the city, shelling major buildings and shooting civilians dead on their way to work, while years of litter lay rotting in the streets. When the ceasefire was announced in 1996, around ten thousand people had been killed; on the ground you may notice some of the many **Sarajevo Roses** – flower-like scars of mortar shell explosions, poignantly filled in with red resin.

What to see and do

The central district of **Baščaršija** is Sarajevo's prettiest and contains most of its sights. Heading west from here, the city's history unravels like a tapestry – Ottoman-era mosques slowly give way to the churches and elaborate buildings of the Austro-Hungarian period, before communist behemoths herald your arrival into "Sniper Alley" and its shells of war.

Baščaršija

The pedestrianized streets of **Baščaršija** are a delight to wander around, and the area is filled to the brim with cafés, snack stands and trinket stalls. It's most logical to approach this district from the east, where you'll find the once-glorious **National Library**. In 1992, a single day's shelling destroyed over three million books, but reconstruction of this pink-and-yellow cream cake of faded beauty finally started in 2010. A little way along is the central square, home to **Sebilj**, a small fountain, and **Baščaršija Mosque**. Far more beautiful is the **Gazi Husrev Beg Mosque** just down the way, which is worth a peep inside. Further west, you'll come across the **Bezistan**, an Ottoman-era bazaar now sadly filled with fake football shirts, racks of sunglasses and other goods unsuited to such an elegant structure.

Baščaršija is also home to the six buildings that make up the **Museum of Sarajevo** – by far the largest is located inside the old Bursa Bezistan bazaar (Mon–Sat 10am–4pm; 2KM), just off the main square, which features a whole host of historical relics.

The Latin Bridge and around

Modest in appearance, the **Latin Bridge** has some weighty history behind it – this was the scene of the assassination of Archduke Franz Ferdinand and, by extension, the start of World War I. Off its northern end, a small **museum** commemorates the incident (Mon–Sat 10am–4pm; 2KM). Across the Miljacka River you'll see the fascinating **Papagajka**, a decaying

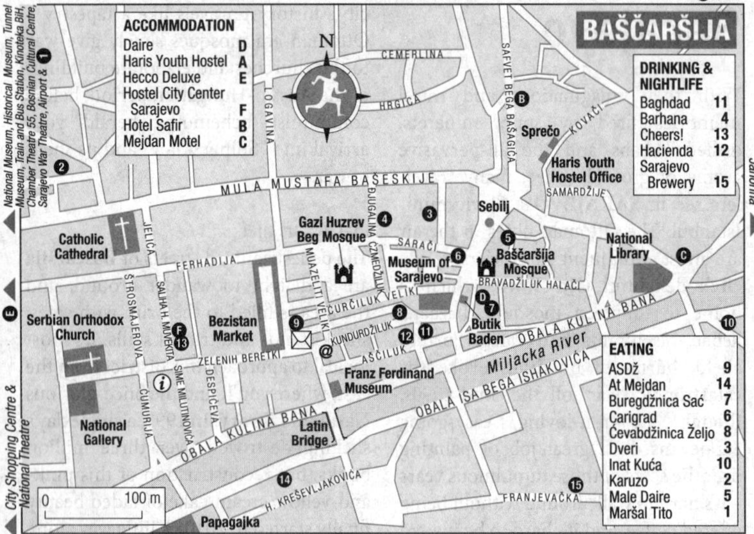

yellow-and-green residential block apparently designed with hovercars in mind – this is how the Jetsons may have lived under Communism.

The church and cathedral

Two glorious religious buildings dominate the skyline just west of central **Baščaršija.** To the north is the twin-turretted Catholic **cathedral** dating from the 1880s, while a short walk to the southwest will bring you to the slightly older Serbian Orthodox **church,** its yellow-and-pink exterior topped with the curvaceous domes typical of the order. West again is the **City Shopping Centre**, which was the only place to buy and exchange goods during the siege. Also in the area is the **National Gallery** (Mon–Fri 10am–6pm; free), whose rolling exhibitions can feature anything from kids' paintings to black-and-white wartime photography.

"Sniper Alley" museums

Within walking distance west of Baščaršija are a pair of museums that count as the city's best. First is the elegant **National Museum** (Tues–Fri & Sun 10am–3pm; 5KM), which has an interesting and varied collection of artefacts amongst its pillars and domes, and puts on good rolling exhibitions. A stone's throw away is the **Historical Museum** (Mon–Fri 9am–4pm, Sat & Sun 9am–1pm; 4KM). Don't be put off by the somewhat brutal exterior and shabby entrance, as there's plenty to see; the permanent exhibition details how Sarajevo functioned during the siege. On the other side of the main road it's worth peeking inside the **Holiday Inn**, a distinctive yellow building that was the city's only functioning hotel during the siege, and as home to foreign journalists was also one of its safest places.

Of even greater importance during the siege was the tunnel under the airport, part of which is now open as the **Tunnel Museum** which can be visited on daily tours (€12; bookable through hotels or travel agencies). During the siege, Sarajevo's UN-held airport was the only break in the city's surrounding ring of Serb forces – an 800m-long tunnel dug underneath the runways provided, for most locals, the only way into or out of the city. At the museum, you'll be played a home-movie-style DVD that describes the tunnel's creation, and the reasoning behind it, before being led through a small section of the now-collapsed route.

Arrival and information

Air Sarajevo's airport is just 7km from the city centre, a trip that will cost 17–20KM by taxi. You can save a bit by taking tram #3 to the final stop, then hiring a cab.

Train and bus The stations are located almost alongside each other west of Baščaršija. It's a half-hour walk into the centre, a short trip on tram #1, or a 7KM cab ride.

Tourist office The official office is at Zelenih Beretki 22 (ⓦsarajevo-tourism.com), but there are travel agencies all over town; almost all will be able to hand out maps and book accommodation.

Tours Both the *Haris* and *City Center* hostels organize popular day-long tours of surrounding sights for about €15, or the slightly overpriced "Tunnel Tours" (see opposite).

Listings Try to pick up a copy of the useful *Sarajevo Navigator*, a monthly booklet available at the tourist office and most hotels, and check out ⓦwww.sonar.ba.

City transport

Public transport An efficient system of buses, trams and trolleybuses operates throughout the city from 5am–1am. Tickets can be bought from a kiosk for 1.60KM, or for 1.80KM from the driver; be sure to validate your ticket on board, as fines are steep and ticket inspectors strict.

Taxis Journey costs start at 2KM, though a ride in the centre is more likely to cost around 5KM.

Accommodation

Hotels have always been a bit pricey in Sarajevo, but the city now has a fair few hostels. If you get stuck, dozens of agencies around Baščaršija will be able to set you up with a private room.

Hostels

Haris Youth Hostel Vratnik Mejdan 29 ⓣ033/232563, ⓦwww.hyh.ba. Super-relaxed hostel a 15min walk uphill from the centre. Check in at their office, near the Baščaršija tram stop, and they'll give you and your bag a free ride up. Evenings can see anything from barbeques to impromptu guitar sessions. Dorms €15.

Hostel City Center Sarajevo Muvekita 2/3 ⓣ033/203213, ⓦwww.hcc.ba. Extremely clean hostel in a very central location, though one too central for some - the street outside can be bursting with noise until the wee hours. Dorms €12.

> **TREAT YOURSELF**
>
> Hovering over the city centre, **Hecco Deluxe** at Ferhadija 2 (ⓣ033/559995, ⓦwww.hotel-hecco.net), is an immaculate boutique hotel occupying the top three floors of a tall block. Its luxurious rooms are a steal. The restaurant is good for coffee (3KM) or a light meal (from 10KM) whether you're staying here or not. Doubles €90.

Hotels

Daire Halači 3 ⓣ033/233310, ⓔidentiko@bih.net.ba. Traditionally-styled, good-value guesthouse in the city centre, though paper-thin walls mean that it can get noisy. Doubles €30.

Hotel Safir Jagodića 3 ⓣ033/475 040, ⓦwww.hotelsafir.ba. The best of a clutch of mid-rangers just north of the centre. Doubles €70.

Mejdan Motel Mustaj-Pašin Mejdan 11 ⓣ033/233 563, ⓦwww.mejdanmotel.com. Tucked into the hillside near the river, this motel feels quite secluded despite its proximity to the centre. Doubles €52.

Eating

It's hard to walk for five metres in Baščaršija without coming across yet another *kebapči* joint. *Burek* is similarly easy to hunt down, and many travellers rate it the best in the Balkans.

Cafés

At Mejdan Obala Isa Bega Ishakovića. Set in, around and on top of a park-centre pavilion near the Latin Bridge, this is a great place for coffee on a summer's day. Also has occasional jazz or orchestral music shows in the evening.

Carigrad Trgovke 2. Mouthwatering selection of rich cakes, syrupy *baklava* and other sweet sins from just 1.50KM. Note that said desserts actually look bigger on your plate than they do behind the counter.

Male Daire Luleđina bb. Peace-out café just behind the Baščaršija Mosque, where you can throw down good Bosnian coffee for 1.50KM, and suck on a

nargileh for just 5KM. *Dibek* is a near-identical place in the same courtyard.
Maršal Tito Bihaćka 19. Military-themed café-bar tucked under a wing of the Historical Museum. With socialist realist pictures on the inside and a gunship sitting outside, it's an interesting place to drink and chat.

Restaurants

ASDž Ćurčiluk Mali 3. Curiously named canteen-style restaurant with rows of simple, tasty local staples to choose from, usually costing 6KM a plate. Service can be gruff.
Buregdžnica Sać Bravadžiluk Halači bb. With something as simple as *burek*, there should be very little to choose between purveyors, but the ones on offer here are simply a cut above the rest. Try the pumpkin (*tykva*) variety, with lashings of cream. 2–3KM/portion.
Ćevabdžinica Željo Kundurdžiluk 12. Other Baščaršija kebab joints may be a little more polished, but this pair – close by each other – are always packed with locals, who know that they provide the most bang for their buck. 6KM for ten *kebapči* and bread.
Dveri Prote Bakovića 12. Traditional Bosnian food in a traditional Bosnian setting, replete with piped Bosnian music. The food is absolutely heavenly - try the polenta with bacon, or the sardines.
Inat Kuća Veliki Alifakovac 1. Riverside restaurant doling out tasty local fare; a filling plate of various stuffed veggies will cost 15KM. It's name means "House of Spite"... Read the menu to find out why.
Karuzo Dženetića Ćikma bb. It's nice to see a chef avoid culinary pigeonholes. Karuzo's Saša brings together meat-free dishes whose variety defies explanation, and sushi. Somehow, it seems to work. Mains around 20KM.

Drinking and nightlife

Sarajevo has a fair few quirky underground bars, which come and go with alarming regularity - ask around. Locals go out late – most bars only start to fill up after midnight.
Baghdad Bazerdžani 6. Elaborate, dimly lit cocktail bar that may well be the best looking in Sarajevo. Drinks are a little pricey, though.
Barhana Đjugalina 8. Set in a tucked-away courtyard and good for a drink, particularly on one of the candlelit outdoor tables.
Cheers! Muvekita 4. The main reason why those staying at Muvekita's various hostels don't get too much sleep - if you can't beat 'em, join 'em. Regular live music nights.
Hacienda Bazerdžani 3. Mexican-themed bar that throws parties most nights; most raucous are the weekend DJ sets.
Sarajevo Brewery Franjevačka 15. If you like Sarajevsko Pivo, why not head straight for the source? Their city-centre factory has a large, ornate bar out back, where it costs 5KM for a large glass of the good stuff. It's also more or less the only place in which you can try their delicious dark variety.

Entertainment

Bosnian Cultural Centre Branilaca Sarajeva 24 ⓦwww.bkc.ba. Large concert venue.
Chamber Theatre 55 Maršala Tita 54 ⓦwww.kamerniteatar55.ba. Homely place used for experimental theatre productions, though rarely in English.
Kinoteka BiH Alipašina 19 ⓦwww.kinotekabih.ba. Interesting mix of subtitled movies shown weekdays at 7pm.
National Theatre Obala Kilina Bala. The largest theatre in the country, and home to Sarajevo's opera and ballet academies.
Sarajevo War Theatre Gabelina 16. Hosts a fascinating clutch of performances from home and abroad.

Shopping

Most useful to the traveller is a small area around Mula Mustafa Bašeskije, where you'll find a couple of appealing **markets** – indoor and outdoor – and a few second-hand clothing stores. The most appealing souvenir purchase is a Bosnian coffee set: while whole teams of Baščaršija stands sell cheap ones, **Sprečo** on Kovači 15 sells beautiful hand-made copper-and-tin sets for €30. Also try tracking down **Butik Badem** on Abadžiluk, which doles out superb Turkish sweets, dried mulberries, and a lot more besides.

SKIING AROUND SARAJEVO

The slopes around Sarajevo are great for skiing: **Jahorina** is the closest resort to town (ⓦwww.oc-jahorina.com), and has over 30km of ski runs; day-passes start at 25MK, equipment can be rented, and there are a fair few hotels and **pansions** around. There is usually one very early bus a day from Sarajevo.

FESTIVALS IN SARAJEVO

Baščaršija Nights Ⓦwww.bascarsijskenoci.ba. Ballet, theatre, music and art exhibitions spread across the month of July.

Jazz Fest Ⓦwww.jazzfest.ba. Decent jazz festival, usually held in November.

MESS Ⓦwww.mess.ba. International, English-centred festival of theatre. October.

Sarajevo Film Festival Ⓦwww.sff.ba. One of the most important film festivals in the Balkans, and largely focused on the region's own output. Held in August.

Saravejo Winter Ⓦwww.sarajevskazima.ba. Artistic festival taking place each November.

Directory

Embassies and consulates Canada, Grbavička 4 ⓣ033/222033; UK, Tina Ujevića 8 ⓣ033/282200; US, Alipašina 43 ⓣ033/445 700.
Money Banks and ATMs are everywhere, and currency can be exchanged in the train station.
Hospital Kranjčevićeva 12 ⓣ033/208 100.
Internet There are cafes all over the city, but Internet Club Click at Kundurdžiluk 1 is a good choice.
Pharmacy Obala Kulina 7 (ⓣ033/272300; daily 8am–8pm) and Zelenih Beretki 28 (ⓣ033/626200; Mon–Sat 9am–8pm).
Post office Zmaja od Bosne 88 (Mon–Sat 7am–8pm).

Moving on

Train Belgrade (daily; 9hr); Budapest (daily; 11hr); Mostar (2 daily; 3hr 30min); Zagreb (2 daily; 9hr).
Bus Belgrade (daily; 7hr); Bihać (3 daily; 7hr); Dubrovnik (3 daily; 6hr); Jajce (5 daily; 3hr 30min); Mostar (hourly; 2hr 30min); Travnik (6 daily; 2hr); Zagreb (3 daily; 8hr).

Bosnia

Occupying roughly four-fifths of the country, mountainous Bosnia contains some of the country's most appealing towns, and helpfully all can be visited on a fairly straight route linking Sarajevo and Zagreb. First up, get a sense of medieval history in **Travnik**, Bosnia's former capital, then head to **Jajce**, a tiny town with a waterfall crashing through its centre. Lastly there's laid-back **Bihać**, one of Europe's best rafting hotspots.

TRAVNIK

Just a couple of hours out of Sarajevo, **TRAVNIK** is a good day-trip target, though its position on a main transport route detracts slightly from a delightful setting. This was the **Bosnian capital** during the latter part of Ottoman rule, and the residence of high-ranking officials known as viziers – you'll see their tombs (*turbe*) dotted around town. More recently, Travnik also gained fame as the birthplace of Ivo Andrić, a Nobel Prize-winning novelist whose *Bosnian Chronicle* was set in his hometown.

The best place to soak up Travnik's history is its majestic fifteenth-century **castle** (10am–6pm; 1.5KM), built to hold off Ottoman forces but completed a few years too late. It's now great for a clamber around, and provides spectacular views of the surrounding mountains. Just under the castle is **Plavna Voda**, a quiet huddle of streamside **restaurants** where you can eat trout caught further upstream.

JAJCE

Whereas Travnik has grown a little too busy for its size, little **JAJCE** is simply adorable – even its name is cute, a diminutive form of the word "egg", and therefore translating as something like "egglet". The name is said to derive from the shape of a hill jutting up in the Old Town, ringed with walls and topped with an impressive **citadel**. In the Middle Ages, Bosnian kings were crowned just down the hill in the **Church of St Mary** (open to the public); the last coronation, of Stjepan Tomašević, took place here in 1461, but two years later the king had his head lopped off during the Ottoman invasion. Opposite the church are the **catacombs** (no set opening hours; 1KM), essentially an underground church, complete with a narthex, nave, presbytery and baptistry; if you're lucky, you'll find the keyholder in the restaurant opposite. Further downhill, the 21-metre-high **waterfalls** are a splendid sight, despite the pounding they took during the Bosnian conflict.

Jajce's **bus station** is a short walk from all the main sights, but there are very few **places to stay**, so book ahead to get a room at the excellent *Stari Grad* (ⓣ030/654006, ⓦwww.jajcetours.com; doubles €42) in the Old Town. Failing that, rooms at the *Hotel Turist* (ⓣ030/654144, ⓦwww.hotel-turist98.com; doubles €42) are far nicer than its horrid exterior might suggest. There are a few **restaurants** dug into the cliffside just over the bridge from the bus station, but most notable is *Vodopad*, just inside the gates, which doles out colossal double-scoop ice creams for just 1KM – don't expect to finish one if the weather's hot.

RAFTING IN NORTHWEST BOSNIA

Rafting in the Bihać area is possible year-round – the continuous flow of tourist traffic means that you'll usually be able to join a group (6–10 per boat) in any month, though the main season runs from March to October. Six kilometres from town, **Una Kiro** (ⓣ037/361110, ⓦwww.una-kiro-rafting.com) is the best established company for foreigners, and has a camping ground next to their base. There are three main routes to choose from; listed per-person prices include equipment and transport, but not meals.

Kostela-Bosanska Krupa An easy 24km, 5hr stretch that's best for novices. €37.

Kostela-Grmuša Short, but packs in a few meaty rapids on a 13km, 3hr course. €27.

Štrbački Buk-Lohovo An absolutely terrifying 15km, 4hr route featuring a 25m rapid. €42.

BIHAĆ

Herzegovina has no shortage of great **rafting** locales, but Bosnia's **BIHAĆ** beats them all. The crystal-clear **River Una** rushes through town, though it's a little further upstream that you'll find the best rafting; the river is highest in the spring and autumn. Adventure sports aside, Bihać is a pleasant, compact town with a cheerful pedestrianized zone in the centre. Here you'll find the **Church of Zvonik** and **Fathija Mosque**, both visitable, but most interesting is the **Captain's Tower**, once a prison, now a museum (Mon–Fri 9am–4pm, Sat 9am–2pm Sat, closed Sun; 1KM).

Central Bihać is small enough to walk around, and the **bus station** is conveniently located at the north of town. The best **accommodation** for budget travellers is just down the road at the switched-on *Villa Una* (ⓣ037/311393; €35), who can help to organize rafting trips; otherwise the area is great for **campsites**, particularly the *Aduna Orljani* (ⓣ037/221431, ⓦwww.aduna.ba; €10 per tent), a riverside site 5km from town. For **food**, try fresh fish at the *River Una*, so close to the water that you can bathe your feet, or good pizza across the bridge in the attractive *Belvedere*.

Herzegovina

Wedged into the far south of the country, little Herzegovina is less known than its big brother, Bosnia, but this land of muscular peaks and rushing rivers arguably has more to see. Pride of place goes to **Mostar** and its famed Old Bridge, but it's worth venturing outside the city to see little **Blagaj**, or absorb the religious curiosities of **Međugorije**. Those on their way to Dubrovnik or Montenegro should also call in at **Trebinje**, by far the most pleasant town in the Republika Srpska.

MOSTAR

On arrival at the train or bus station, you may be forgiven for thinking that the beauty of **MOSTAR** has been somewhat exaggerated. There then begins a slow descent to the Old Town, during which it becomes more and more apparent that it really is a very special place indeed. Attentive ears will pick out rushing streams, salesmen crying their wares, as well as church bells and *muezzins* competing for attention, while steep, cobblestoned streets slowly wind their way down to the fast-flowing, turquoise-blue Neretva River and its Old Bridge, incredibly photogenic even when the Speedo-clad *mostari* – the brave gents who dive from the apex – aren't tumbling into the waters below. The city is becoming ever more popular with tourists, though the dearth of high-end accommodation means that most visit on a day-trip – bad news for anyone on the Old Bridge around lunchtime, though great news for anyone staying the night.

Mostar's history is irrevocably entwined with that of its bridge. Like hundreds of locals, this was to fall victim in 1993 when the Croats and Muslims of the town, previously united against the Serbs, turned on each other: the **conflict** rumbled on for two long years, each side sniping at the other from opposing hills. Locals claim that prior to the war, more than half of the city's marriages were mixed, but the figure has since dwindled to nothing; while relations have started to improve, bitterness remains in the air, and messages of hate are still graffitied onto the walls.

What to see and do

The **Old Town**, spanning both sides of the Neretva, contains most things of interest in Mostar, and in its centre is the **Old Bridge**, focal point of the city and the obvious place to kick off your sightseeing. On the eastern bank is the more interesting Muslim part of town, while the west is mainly home to Catholic Croats.

The east bank

Off the eastern end of the bridge is **Helebija**, a tower that now accom-

THE OLD BRIDGE

Transit point, dungeon, tourist attraction, war victim and macho launchpad, Mostar's small, hump-backed **Stari Most** has led an interesting life. With tradesmen terrified by the rickety nature of its wooden predecessor and the fast-flowing Neretva below, it was built in the 1560s at the instigation of Suleyman the Magnificent. Those employed to guard the bridge were called the **mostari**, a term later borrowed when naming the city, and then used to describe the men who dive from the apex, 21m down into the Neretva. After 427 years in service, the bridge was strategically destroyed by Croat forces in November 1993, symbolizing the ethnic division of the city. There then began the arduous process of rebuilding it piece by piece, following the same techniques used in its initial construction, and it only fully reopened in 2004. The *mostari* are still there, day after day; they'll try to work the crowd into shelling out an acceptable fee – officially a secret, but sneaky investigations have found the precise figure to be €50 – before taking the plunge. Join them if you dare, especially in July, when the annual **diving festival** marks the highlight of Mostar's year.

modates the enlightening **Old Bridge Museum** (daily except Mon 10am–6pm; 5KM), spread over four levels, and topped with a viewing point; you'll be able to see pictures of the bridge's destruction, and footage of its rebirth. Lined with trinket stores, cobblestoned Kujundžiluk then climbs uphill, soon leading to the **Koski Mehmed Paša Mosque** (sunrise–sunset). For all its beauty, the panoply of souvenir sellers shows that tourism, rather than religious endeavour, is the current priority, but it's still worth paying the 8KM to climb the minaret. Passing another mosque, the road segues quickly into modern Mostar, though pay attention to signs pointing out the **Turkish House** (irregular hours; 2KM) on your left, a fascinating peek into the Ottoman traditions of yesteryear. Above Kujundžiluk you'll see the **Cejvan Cehaj Mosque**, Mostar's oldest, on the way to the **Museum of Herzegovina** (Mon–Fri 9am–2pm, Sat 10am–noon; 2KM). Between the two lies a Muslim **graveyard**, and it's hard not to be moved when you notice that almost everybody laid to rest here died the same year, 1993.

The west bank

Tara, the bridge's western tower, was once a dungeon into which prisoners were thrown to die, either from injury, starvation or – in rainy season – drowning. It's now a café, the base of the diving club, and the **War Photo Exhibition** (daily 9am–9pm; 6KM), an array of startling shots taking during the troubles by Kiwi photographer Wade Goddard. A little zigzagging will bring you to the **Crooked Bridge** – apparently built as a warm-up for the big boy, and almost as pleasing – and the **Tabhana**, a former bathhouse now filled with bars and restaurants. Up the hill you'll see the enormous **Catholic Church**, with its even more oversized bell tower, evidently raised to such heights in a fit of religious pride. To reach the church you'll have to cross a main road that, during the war, served as the **front line** – walking along to the north reveals a succession of battered buildings.

Arrival and information

Bus and train The stations are located side-by-side in an ugly area to the east of town, a 20min walk from the Old Bridge.

Tourist office Behind the Tabhana, just west of the Old Bridge, and good at arranging accommodation or city tours (May–Sept 8am–8pm; open irregular hours in other months; ⓣ033/580833). You can also book rooms at travel agencies outside the stations.

Tours The high-octane Bata, of *Hostel Majdas* fame (see below), runs jam-packed full-day tours for €20/person, including hiking and diving in areas unreachable on public transport – guests usually come back in the late evening covered in sweat and mud, yet happy as Larry.

Accommodation

The tourist office can help to organize private rooms, which cost €10–25/person depending upon the season, room size and proximity to the Old Town.

Emen Onešćukova 32 ⓣ036/581120, ⓦwww.motel-emen.com. Rooms in this motel are simply gorgeous, and the Old Town location ideal. Doubles €60.

Hostel Majdas Franje Miličevića 39 ⓣ061/382940, ⓦwww.hostelmajdas.com. Friendly, cosy and within a short walk of the Old Town, this is Mostar's best hostel by a long way. Their day-long tours (see above) are astonishingly

TREAT YOURSELF

Muslibegović House Osman Dikića 32 ⓣ036/551379, ⓦwww.muslibegovichouse.com. A rare and surprisingly affordable chance to stay in a national monument – this home has been in the hands of the noble Muslibegović family for over 300 years. Rooms have been renovated with tasteful, individual designs; doubles cost €90 in peak season – it's worth the extra €10 for the suites.

good, and they now have private rooms on the other side of the river. Dorms €12.50.

Kriva Cuprija Crooked Bridge ☎036/550953, Ⓦwww.motel-mostar.ba. Decent rooms next to the rushing waters that surge beneath the Crooked Bridge – make sure that you're based in this one, and not their sister hotel of the same name, on the other side of the river. Excellent restaurant attached (see below). Doubles €65.

Pansion Oscar Onešćukova 33 ☎036/580237. Rooms at this guesthouse are a little musty, but perfectly adequate for the price. Take a look around as there are several styles available. Doubles €30.

Eating and drinking

Try to avoid eating from 12–2pm, which is when the tour groups are led to their pre-booked seats for pre-cooked meals.

Ali Baba East bank. The word "cavernous" is often misused, but this quirky place – cafe, bar and club all at once – is housed, literally, in a cave. It's the liveliest place in town of an evening, and summer months see DJs come in to spin some vinyl. The "Ali Baba" sign is on the little-used road entrance (the tunnel leading to it is worth a peek); the one at the lower entrance says "Open Sesame!"

Bella Vista West bank. There are a fair few restaurants with a view of the Old Bridge, so which to choose? Firstly, the view from the west bank is better; secondly, this is both cheaper, less crowded and closer to the bridge than its competitors. Good meals including pizzas or schnitzels for 7KM, and trout for 12KM.

Jami Braće Fejića 15. Take-away joint claiming to make the best *burek* in town... If they're not right, they're not far off.

Kriva Cuprija Crooked Bridge. Excellent value, considering the quality of the food, and an excellent location under the Crooked Bridge. Fresh trout with salad and a berry sauce will only cost 10KM, a little more for the "Hercegovinan Plate" of rice, lamb and potatoes.

Restorant Balkan Braće Fejića. Almost next door to the Cejvan Cehaj Mosque, here you can enjoy cheap burek, a couple of pieces of Turkish delight, and some coffee - all for less than 5KM.

Štrbački West bank. Okay, so it's a tourist trap, as evidenced by the traditionally uniformed staff. But it's a very nice trap to fall into, since the food's excellent, and fairly priced to boot: try the stuffed peppers for 8KM. In addition, it's one of the few places in the old town to serve proper Bosnian coffee.

Moving on

Train Sarajevo (2 daily; 3hr 30min).

Bus Dubrovnik (5 daily; 4hr); Sarajevo (hourly; 2hr 30min); Trebinje (3 daily; 3hr 30min).

EXCURSIONS FROM MOSTAR

Using Mostar as a base, you have a whole slew of destinations to choose from. Unfortunately, the paucity of public transport means that it's tough to see more than one in a day, and some places aren't accessible at all, so are best visited on a **tour** from Mostar.

Blagaj

Closest to Mostar is the village of **BLAGAJ**, just 12km to the east and accessible by local buses #10, #11 and #12 (7 services a day; 40min; 3KM). Once you disembark, carry straight ahead through the town to the **Tekija** (daily 8am–8pm; 4MK). Huddled into a niche in the cliff-face, this wonky wooden building was once the residence of dervishes, and the interior is suitably Spartan. Right next to it, a never-ending torrent of water gushes out of the cliff, apparently reaching levels of 43,000 litres per second; some of this is skimmed off to make tea and coffee, which you can order at a waterside table for just 1.5KM, including a free chunk of *lokum* (Turkish delight).

Međugorije

Twenty-six kilometres south of Mostar is the curious village of **MEĐUGORIJE**, a mere non-entity until June 1981, when a group of teenagers claimed to have been spoken to by the **Virgin Mary** here. Unlike Lourdes and Fatima, this has not been officially recognized by the Vatican, but that doesn't stop pilgrims arriving in such numbers that there are now thousands of rooms available to accommodate them. The main sights here are the **Church of St James** and the nearby "Weeping Knee" statue, so named as it apparently flouts the laws of thermodynamics by dribbling out a constant flow of fluid. You can reach here on local bus #48 from Mostar, though – get this – they don't run on Sundays.

Počitelj and the Kravice Waterfalls

A few kilometres south of Međugorije is the hillside village of **POČITELJ**, one of the most traditional in Herzegovina. The place is quite stunning, and dotted with remnants from the fifteenth century, most notably a citadel and a terrific mosque. Unfortunately there are no direct buses here, so it's best to join a tour. Groups heading here will likely swing through to see the nearby **Kravice Waterfalls**, which are not accessible on public transport. High, wide and handsome, the pool below is a great place for a dip.

TREBINJE

The Republika Srpska's most appealing town by a country mile, **TREBINJE** is tucked into Herzegovina's southern extremity, and its proximity to Dubrovnik and the Montenegrin border make it the ideal start or finish line to a race through the country. It's most famed for the Arslanagić Bridge – a longer version of the one in Mostar – which sits a ten-minute walk from the town centre, and a couple of still-functioning **hilltop monasteries**, which are a delight to roam around and well worth the climb.

Back in the centre is the **Old Town**, a pretty warren of streets now largely filled with cafés; better yet for coffee-slurping is elegant **Jovan Dučić Square**, home to a daily market and almost totally cloaked with maple leaves (*platani*). These have given their name to the adjacent *Hotel Platani* (ⓣ059/270420, ⓦwwwhoteplatani.info; doubles €50), by far the best **place to stay** in town and fair value for the price; staff may also be able to advise on finding private rooms in the area. It has a good **restaurant** attached to it, though more elegant is *Porto Bello* in the Old Town, which doles out good steaks for 15KM, and cheaper is *Market 99*, a food court on top of the city supermarket.

Britain

HIGHLIGHTS

OVER THE SEA TO SKYE: craggy peaks, sparkling water and Celtic mystery in the Scottish islands

EDINBURGH FESTIVAL: the world's biggest arts festival

YORK: stunning medieval city packed with cool bars and quirky boutiques

HIKING WALES: from Offa's Dyke and the Black Mountains to Snowdonia and the Brecan Beacons, Wales is hiker's dream

THE BRITISH MUSEUM: arguably the world's finest museum- and its free

BATH: England's most beautiful city full of Regency and Roman Splendour

ROUGH COSTS

DAILY BUDGET basic €50 /occasional treat €75

DRINK Lager €4 per pint

FOOD Fish and chips €8

HOSTEL/BUDGET HOTEL €25/€60–90

TRAVEL Train: London–Brighton €8–25; bus London–Manchester €7–30

FACT FILE

POPULATION 61 million (includes Northern Ireland)

AREA 244,820 sq km

LANGUAGE English

CURRENCY Pound sterling (£)

CAPITAL London (population: 7.5 million)

INTERNATIONAL PHONE CODE ⓣ44

Introduction

A famous British newspaper headline in the 1950s declared: "Fog in Channel, Continent Cut Off". Britain's outlook on the world has always been unique, born of its status as an island nation on the western edge of Europe. And yet within this compact territory there's not just one country but three – England, Wales and Scotland – and a multitude of cultural identities: God forbid you should call a Scot or a Welshman English.

London, the capital, is the one place that features on everyone's itinerary. **Brighton** and **Canterbury** offer contrasting diversions – the former a lively seaside resort, the latter one of Britain's finest medieval cities. The southwest of England holds the rugged moorlands of **Devon**, the rocky coastline of **Cornwall**, and the historic spa city of **Bath**, while the chief attractions of central England are the university cities of **Oxford** and **Cambridge**, and Shakespeare's hometown **Stratford-upon-Avon**. Further north, the former industrial cities of **Manchester**, **Liverpool** and **Newcastle** are lively, rejuvenated places, and **York** has splendid historical treasures, but the landscape, especially the uplands of the Lake District, is the biggest magnet. For true wilderness, head to the **Welsh mountains** or **Scottish Highlands**. The finest of Scotland's lochs, glens and peaks, and the magnificent scenery of the West Coast islands, can be reached easily from **Glasgow** and **Edinburgh** – the latter perhaps Britain's most attractive urban landscape.

CHRONOLOGY

54 BC The Romans attack Britannia but are forced back until a successful invasion in 43 AD.
1066 AD Duke William II of Normandy defeats the last Anglo-Saxon ruler, King Harold II, at the Battle of Hastings.
1215 The Magna Carta forms the basis upon which English law is built.
1301 Edward I conquers Wales, giving his heir the title Prince of Wales.
1534 Henry VIII breaks with the Catholic Church. The Head of State becomes Head of the Church of England.
1603 King James VI of Scotland also becomes James I of England in the Union of the Crowns.
1653–58 A brief period of republicanism under Oliver Cromwell, following the English Civil War.
1707 The Act of Union unites the parliaments of Scotland and England, with the addition of Ireland in 1800.
1800s The Industrial Revolution helps Britain to expand her empire and become a dominant world force.
1914–18 Britain fights in World War I.
1928 Women attain full suffrage after a hard-fought campaign.
1939–45 Britain fights in World War II. London and other major centres are heavily bombed during the Blitz.
1947 Indian independence from British rule heralds the gradual demise of the British Empire.
1960s The Beatles sing their way through the swinging sixties.

"**Great Britain**", or just "Britain", is a geographical term encompassing England, Scotland and Wales, including their islands. However, it can also be used politically, in the context of central government, "British" nationals, or for national teams at sporting events such as the Olympics, in which case it includes Northern Ireland. "**United Kingdom**" is a political term, referring to the sovereign state of England, Scotland, Wales and Northern Ireland. In this guide Northern Ireland is covered with the rest of the island in the Ireland chapter.

1979 Margaret Thatcher becomes Britain's first female Prime Minister.
1998 Devolution in Scotland and Wales.
2005 On July 7 London is rocked by terrorist bombings leaving 52 dead.
2012 London to host the Olympics.

ARRIVAL

If you're travelling from outside mainland Europe or Ireland, clearly the only direct route to Britain is by **air**. Long-haul flights land at a range of destinations throughout the UK, including Manchester, Edinburgh and Glasgow, though most air passengers still find themselves passing through London's main airports – Gatwick, Heathrow, Stansted and Luton – the latter two the principal hubs of no-frills carriers like Ryanair and easyJet, which also operate out of smaller regional airports around the country and provide many internal flights. Greener alternatives for getting to Britain from mainland Europe include the **Eurostar** (Ⓦ www.eurostar.com) high-speed train from Paris or Brussels to St Pancras International in London, Eurolines **bus** (Ⓦ www.eurolines.co.uk), or **ferry**: boats from Ireland, France, Belgium, the Netherlands, Denmark and Spain dock at ports across the UK.

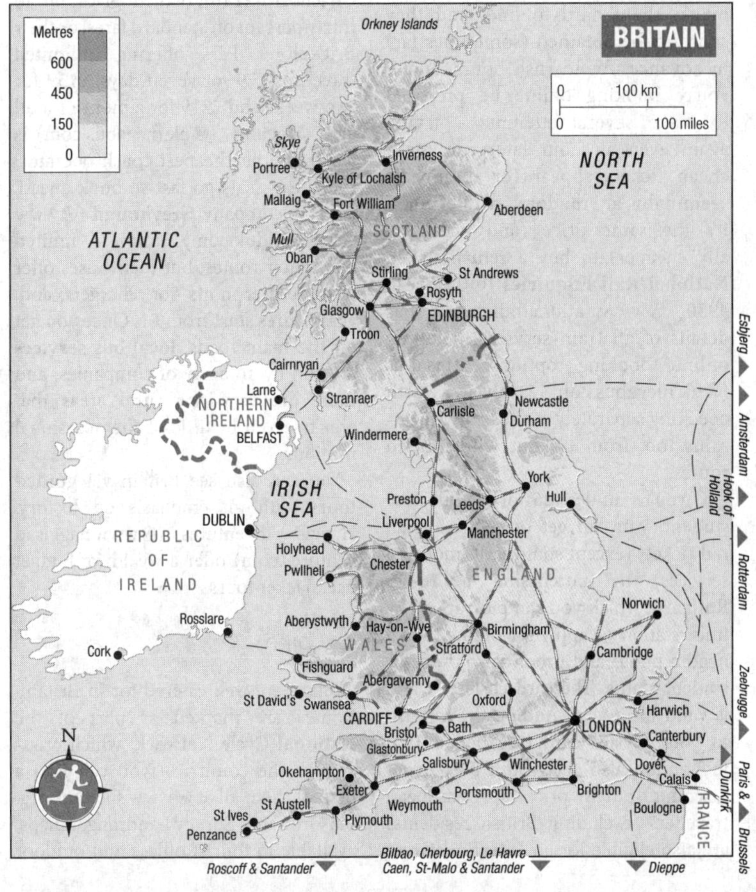

GETTING AROUND

Most places are accessible by train and/or coach (as long-distance buses are known), though costs are among the highest in Europe. **Traveline** (ⓣ0871/200 2233 ⓦwww.traveline.org.uk) is a national service that can advise on trains, coaches, ferries and, most usefully, local buses.

By train

Having suffered decades of chronic under-investment, the British **train** network is slowly beginning to improve, though **fares** remain high. Cheap tickets do exist, but the bafflingly complicated pricing system makes them hard to find, and they can only be obtained (sometimes far) in advance. Avoid rush hours, and if you're booking online be prepared to make several attempts – trying again even an hour later can make cheap tickets appear (or disappear) seemingly at random, while often it's the same price (and occasionally cheaper) to buy a return ticket. **National Rail Enquiries** (ⓣ0845/748 4950, ⓦwww.nationalrail.co.uk) has details of all train services including online booking options. Megabus (ⓦuk.megabus.com) is always worth checking separately as they run Megatrains too, from £1, but with limited routes.

If you're under 26 or a full-time student, you can get one-third off all rail tickets (except some early-morning services) by purchasing a **16–25 Railcard**, which you can pick up at any train station or apply for online. You'll need a photo and proof of your age or student status. The card costs £24 and is valid for a year. Adding the railcard to your Oyster card (see box, p.154) in London also gets you a 34 percent discount on daily price caps. European travellers (excluding British residents) are also eligible for an **InterRail Great Britain Pass** (ⓦwww.interrailnet.com; see p.36). Prices start from €134/£123 for three days train travel in one month for under-25s, and there are pricier adult fares too.

By bus

Long-distance buses are referred to as **coaches** in Britain. Services between cities are frequent and inexpensive especially compared to trains, however, long journeys take considerably longer. **National Express** (ⓣ08717/818181, ⓦwww.nationalexpress.com) serve the most routes, and prices sometimes start from just £1. If you're a student or under 26 you can buy a National Express Coachcard (£10), which gives up to thirty percent off standard fares, or their BritXplorer Pass offering unlimited travel for £79 for seven days, £139 for two weeks and £219 for a month for all ages. **Megabus** (ⓦuk.megabus.com) is generally the cheapest coach operator; the cheap seats go fast so book ahead. The US company **Greyhound** (ⓦwww.greyhounduk.com) have limited commuter routes, but their buses offer wi-fi, powerpoints for chargers and, again, fares start from £1. Once you get off the main roads, **local bus services** are run by an array of companies, and there are very few rural areas that aren't served by at least the occasional minibus.

You can also see Britain via **guided tours** with an emphasis on history. Haggis Adventures (ⓦwww.haggisadventures.com) offer a wealth of budget backpacker tours.

By bike

Cyclists are well catered for in Britain. Routes are marked as part of the **National Cycle Network**, which criss-crosses the country – you can find a map of them all at ⓦwww.sustrans.org.uk. Ordnance Survey Landranger maps, available in tourist offices and outdoor shops, also mark some routes, as well as footpaths and minor roads. Most cities now have some **cycle lanes**, which are often shared with buses and taxis.

Bikes can generally be taken on **trains** (with the exception of the London underground), though some companies may charge you and/or require you to book in advance. National Express **coaches** only take bikes if they can fold and are bagged. Bikes cannot be taken on London buses.

ACCOMMODATION

Accommodation in Britain is expensive and it's a good idea to reserve in advance. Many tourist offices will book rooms for you, although expect to pay a small fee for this, as well as putting down a deposit.

Britain has an extensive network of **HI hostels** operated by the Youth Hostel Association (Ⓦwww.yha.org.uk for England and Wales; Ⓦwww.syha.org.uk for Scotland). A bed for the night with YHA can cost as little as £15, but in cities except to pay up to £25. YHA membership (£15/year) will save you £3 per night. Most places of interest will also have at least one **independent hostel**, which will generally be of a comparable standard and can be several pounds cheaper.

In tourist cities it's hard to find a double room in a **hotel** for less than £60 a night, though there are a few cheaper chain hotels: Premier Inn (Ⓦwww.premierinn.com) sometimes offer identikit rooms from £30 while Travelodge (Ⓦwww2.travelodge.co.uk) can be as low as £20 per room when there are deals on. EasyHotel (Ⓦwww.easyhotel.com) have small rooms decked out in their signature orange; London rooms start at £25, while Edinburgh rooms from £15. A nicer option for budget accommodation, and often cheaper outside London (particularly if you're on your own), are **guesthouses** and **B&Bs** – usually a comfortable room in a family home, plus a substantial breakfast – starting at around £30 a head. Tourist offices often have a list of nearby accredited B&Bs.

There are more than 750 official **campsites** in Britain, charging from around £5 per person. Camping wild in England and Wales requires the landowner's permission, while in Scotland it is mostly legal as long as you're unobtrusive and leave the site as you found it.

FOOD AND DRINK

Long lampooned as a culinary wasteland, Britain has seen a transformation in both the quality and variety of its restaurants over the past two decades. Modern British cuisine – in effect anything inventive – has been at the core of this change, though wherever you go you'll find places serving Indian, Italian and Chinese food, and often plenty of other international cuisines. If you're on a tight budget, the temptation is still to head for the nearest fast-food joint, but with a little effort, alternatives can easily be found, with even higher-end establishments often offering reasonably priced lunchtime or early-evening deals.

Wherever you stay you'll almost certainly be offered an **"English breakfast"** – basically eggs, bacon, sausage, and any combination of fried or grilled sides such as tomatoes, mushrooms, black pudding, bread and baked beans are also usually added; you'll also be given the option of cereal, toast and fruit as well. Every major town will have upmarket restaurants and so-called **gastropubs** serving daintily presented cuisine, but traditional British cooking – the mainstay of pub food – is hearty and filling. Typical dishes include the quintessential fish and chips, steak and kidney pie, shepherd's pie (minced lamb topped with mashed potato), and – mainly on Sundays – roast dinners, served with roast potatoes, veg and (particularly with beef) Yorkshire pudding, made from savoury batter. Britain is one of Europe's better countries for **vegetarians**, and wherever you eat there'll always be at least one veggie choice.

Drink

Drinking traditionally takes place in the **pub**, where beer – sold by the pint or half-pint – generates most of the business, although wine, bottled beer and spirits are also popular. Despite the popularity of cold, fizzy lager, traditional British beer, known as real ale or bitter, is undergoing something of a renaissance; richer and often darker than lager, and served at cellar temperature rather than chilled, it comes in thousands of varieties. In England pubs are generally open Monday to Saturday from 11am to 11pm, and on Sunday from noon to 10.30pm (though changes to licensing laws mean many places now open longer than that at weekends); hours are often longer in Scotland, while Sunday closing is common in Wales.

In Scotland, the national drink is of course **whisky**. The best – and most expensive – are single malts, best drunk neat or with a splash of water to release the flavour.

CULTURE AND ETIQUETTE

Famed for their stiff upper lip and polite reticence, the British do tend to be more reserved than their continental counterparts. Possibly the most cosmopolitan place in Europe – in the larger cities anyway – Britain has developed a reputation for liberal tolerance and benefits from a diverse range of faiths, creeds and colours.

Tipping is expected (if not mandatory) in restaurants; around ten percent of the total is the norm. Technically this is optional, though you will be frowned at if you ask for it to be removed. It's also customary to tip taxi drivers a similar amount, though it is not necessary to tip bar staff at bars and pubs.

SPORTS AND OUTDOOR ACTIVITIES

Football (soccer) is a British obsession. "The beautiful game" was codified here in 1863, and seeing a match is a must for any sports fan, though for top games it can be extremely difficult and costly to acquire tickets. To guarantee seeing a Premier League match choose a lesser-known club: in London, Fulham (Ⓦwww.fulhamfc.com). **Rugby** and **cricket**, though popular, do not generally inspire the same fervent tribalism as football, and consequently can offer a more relaxed spectator experience. You can turn up and buy tickets on the day for domestic matches at Lord's cricket ground in London (Ⓦwww.lords.org) during the season (April–Sept). Tennis fans make a beeline for the world-famous championships at **Wimbledon** (Ⓦwww.wimbledon.com), but it's not a cheap day out.

Britain's diverse geography and geology, with access to large bodies of fresh and salt water, mean that venues for **outdoor pursuits** are easily accessible. **Walking** is one of the finest ways to see the country, and an excellent infrastructure of long-distance footpaths crisscrosses Britain (Ⓦwalkingbritain.co.uk). The uplands of Wales (Ⓦwww.visitwales.co.uk/active), Scotland (Ⓦactive.visitscotland.com) and the English Lake District (Ⓦgolakes.co.uk) are particularly good for hiking, climbing and watersports, while Devon and Cornwall (Ⓦwww.visitsouthwest.co.uk) have the best **surfing** in the UK.

COMMUNICATIONS

Internet cafés and wi-fi are common, and you'll also find access at most

BRITAIN ONLINE

www.visitbritain.com Official tourist board site with links to regional sites.
www.transportdirect.info Information on nationwide transport.
www.backpackers.co.uk The low-down on independent hostels.
www.streetmap.co.uk Detailed UK street maps.

accommodation. Prices vary and are sometimes extortionate; while you may find cheaper, £3–5 per hour is not uncommon. **Post offices** open Monday to Friday 9am to 5.30pm, some open on Saturday 9am–noon. **Public phones** (operated mainly by BT) are disappearing fast; phonecards to make calls to mobiles or internationally can be bought from post offices and newsagents – most also accept credit cards. For the **operator**, call ⓣ100 (domestic) or 155 (international).

EMERGENCIES

Police are approachable and helpful. Tourists aren't a particular target for criminals except in the crowds of the big cities, where you should be on your guard against **pickpockets**. Britain's bigger conurbations all contain areas where you may feel uneasy after dark, but these are usually away from tourist sights.

For health complaints that require immediate attention, go to the **emergency** department of the local hospital (known as A&E). These are run by the **National Health Service** (NHS; ⓦwww.nhs.uk to find your nearest) and will be free at the time of treatment, though depending on your country (some have mutual agreements with Britain) you may get billed later. For minor injuries you can also use NHS **walk-in clinics. Pharmacists** dispense only a limited range of drugs without a doctor's prescription. Most are open standard shop hours, though in large towns there may be ones that stay open late or even 24hr; local newspapers carry lists of late-opening pharmacies.

INFORMATION

Tourist offices exist in virtually every British town, offering information and a basic range of maps. **National parks** (ⓦwww.nationalparks.gov.uk) also have their own information centres, which are better for guidance on outdoor pursuits. The most comprehensive series of **maps** is produced by the **Ordnance Survey** (ⓦwww.ordnancesurvey.co.uk) – essential if you're planning serious hiking.

MONEY AND BANKS

The **pound sterling** (£), divided into 100 pence, remains the national currency. There are coins of 1p, 2p, 5p, 10p, 20p, 50p, £1 and £2; and notes of £5, £10, £20 and £50; notes issued by Scottish banks are legal tender but sometimes not accepted south of the border. At the time of writing, £1 was worth €1.16 and $1.60. Normal **banking hours** are Monday to Friday 9.30am to 5pm, though branches are increasingly open on Saturday mornings. **ATMs** accept a wide range of debit and credit cards, but note that freestanding ATMs usually charge around £2 to take money out on top of your bank charges so try and go to one attached to a bank. Shops, hotels, restaurants and most other places readily accept **credit cards** for payment.

OPENING HOURS AND HOLIDAYS

General **shop hours** are Monday to Saturday 9am to 5.30/6pm, although many places in big towns are also open

EMERGENCY NUMBERS

Police, fire and ambulance ⓣ999 or 112.

Sunday (usually 11am–5pm in England and Wales, longer in Scotland) and till 7/8pm – or later – at least once a week. Thanks to a recent change in law, pubs are now allowed to stay open 24hr with the relevant licence. However, while a few now open for breakfast, or until 1am or 2am, most still follow the traditional pub opening hours of 11am–11pm daily except Sunday when it's noon–10.30pm. Where an establishment's opening hours are not mentioned in the text it can be assumed they follow these.

Public holidays are: January 1, January 2 (Scotland only), Good Friday, Easter Monday (not Scotland), first Monday and last Monday in May, last Monday in August, St Andrew's Day (Nov 30, or nearest Mon if weekend; Scotland only), Christmas Day and Boxing Day (Dec 25 & 26) – though in practice it's only on January 1, January 2 (Scotland only) and Christmas Day that everything shuts down; on other holidays, many shops in larger towns and cities – as well as nearly all sights – remain open.

London

With a population of around 7.5 million **LONDON** sprawls over an area of more than 600 square miles either side of the River Thames. The city exudes an undeniable buzz of success; it is where the country's news, art and money are made, and the pace of life is fast (just watch commuters bolting down the escalators). However, high-octane excitement comes at a price, with accommodation and transport costs among the most expensive in the world. The high living costs are nevertheless put up with by most Londoners precisely because there is just so much to see and do here, much of it free.

Skip exorbitantly priced palaces in favour of London's (mostly free) world-class museums and galleries and be sure to visit at least a couple of the outdoor spaces; London is one of the world's greenest cities with many parks, cemeteries and canals to explore. London's famous department stores and offbeat weekend **markets** offer limitless **shopping**, while its cultural scene caters for all tastes and budgets, churning out everything from musicals to experimental live music. While **food** can be expensive, London's multicultural society means that there is a stunning variety of cuisine, often very affordable.

What to see and do

The majority of sights are north of the **River Thames**, and a good place to start is the political and regal centre; the area around Whitehall, with **Trafalgar Square** at one end, **Parliament Square** at the other and **Buckingham Palace** off to the side.

Trafalgar Square and the National Gallery

Trafalgar Square's focal point is **Nelson's Column**, featuring the one-eyed admiral who died defeating the French at the 1805 Battle of Trafalgar. Extending across the north side of the square is the **National Gallery** (daily 10am–6pm, Fri till 9pm; free; ⓦwww.nationalgallery.org.uk), one of the world's great art collections. Masterpieces include paintings by Raphael, Michelangelo, da Vinci and Rembrandt, along with Van Gogh's *Sunflowers* and Seurat's *Bathers at Asnières*. Round the side of the National Gallery, in St Martin's Place, is the fascinating **National Portrait Gallery** (daily 10am–6pm, Thurs & Fri till 9pm; free; ⓦwww.npg.org.uk), which houses images of the great and good, from Hans Holbein's larger-than-life drawing of Henry VIII and Sam Taylor-Wood's video portrait of David Beckham.

Covent Garden

A minute or so walk northeast of Trafalgar Square between Shaftesbury Avenue and the Strand is **Covent Garden**, a lively area centred around an early seventeenth-century piazza and nineteenth-century market hall, which housed the city's principal fruit and vegetable market until the late 1970s.

THE LONDON PASS

However tight your budget, if you're coming to London, you'll likely want to see at least a few of the most famous sights. Unfortunately many come with whopping entry costs, and this is where **The London Pass** (1/2/3/6-day £44/59/72/95; ⓦwww.londonpass.com) comes in. Saving money from the major attractions like London Zoo, the Tower of London and St Paul's Cathedral, the card will also get you extras like audioguides at galleries, cinema tickets, and you can even turn it into an Oyster card (see box, p.154) by adding the public transport option.

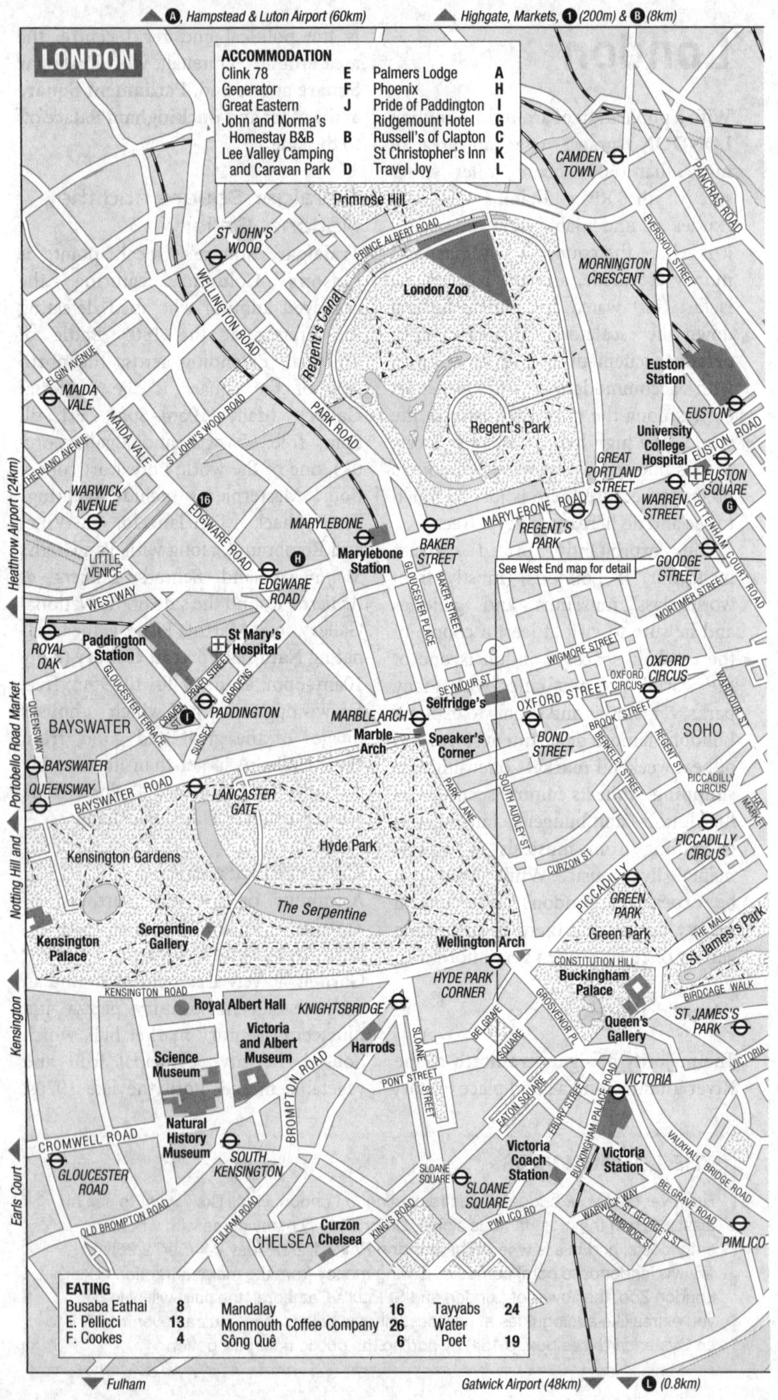

BRITAIN

LONDON

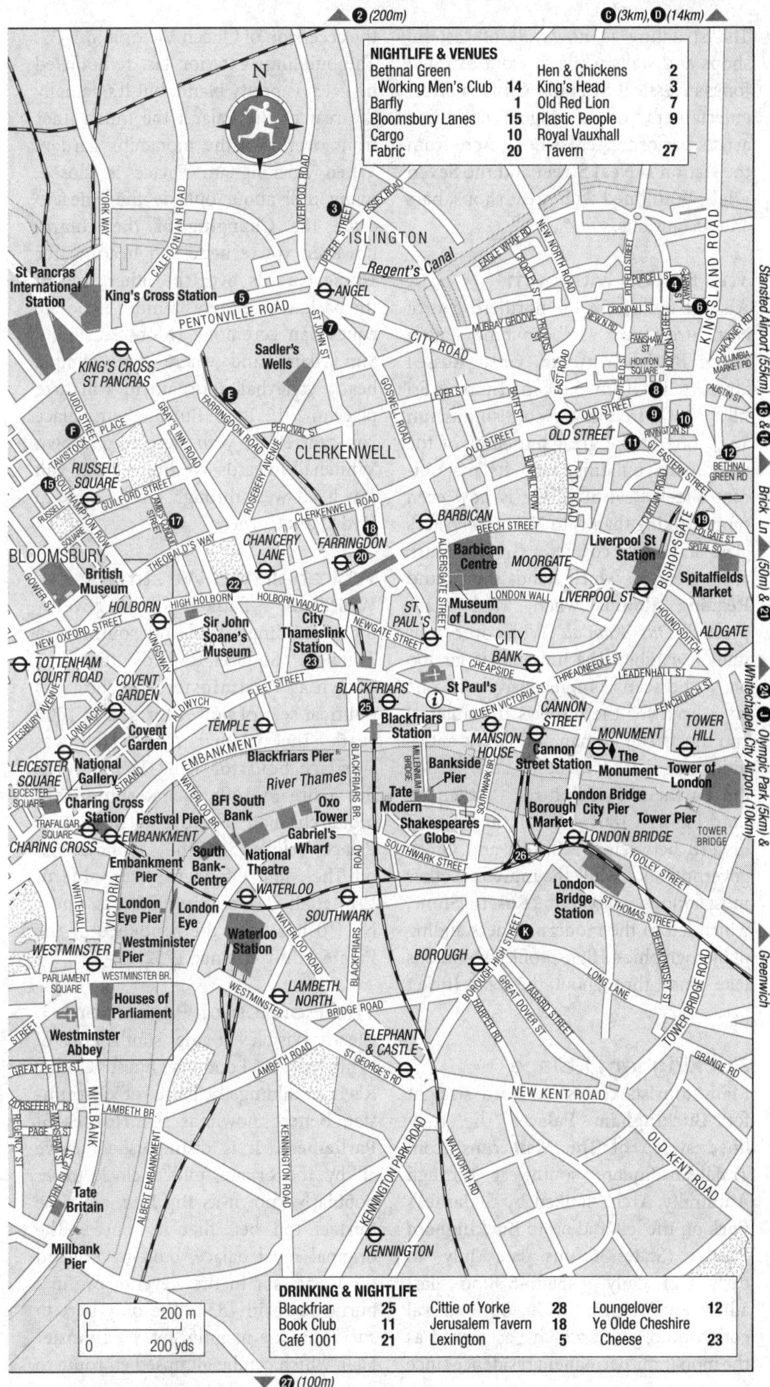
2 (200m)
C (3km), D (14km)
NIGHTLIFE & VENUES
Bethnal Green Working Men's Club 14
Barfly 1
Bloomsbury Lanes 15
Cargo 10
Fabric 20
Hen & Chickens 2
King's Head 3
Old Red Lion 7
Plastic People 9
Royal Vauxhall Tavern 27
N
ISLINGTON
Regent's Canal
ANGEL
St Pancras International Station
King's Cross Station
KING'S CROSS ST PANCRAS
PENTONVILLE ROAD
CITY ROAD
Sadler's Wells
CLERKENWELL
OLD STREET
RUSSELL SQUARE
BLOOMSBURY
British Museum
BARBICAN
Barbican Centre
MOORGATE
Liverpool St Station
LIVERPOOL ST
Spitalfields Market
CHANCERY LANE
FARRINGDON
HOLBORN
Sir John Soane's Museum
City Thameslink Station
ST PAUL'S
Museum of London
CITY
BANK
ALDGATE
TOTTENHAM COURT ROAD
COVENT GARDEN
BLACKFRIARS
St Paul's
TEMPLE
Blackfriars Station
MANSION HOUSE
CANNON STREET
MONUMENT
TOWER HILL
Covent Garden
Blackfriars Pier
Bankside Pier
Cannon Street Station
The Monument
Tower of London
LEICESTER SQUARE
National Gallery
River Thames
Tate Modern
Shakespeares Globe
Borough Market
London Bridge City Pier
Tower Pier
Charing Cross Station
BFI South Bank
Oxo Tower
Festival Pier
Gabriel's Wharf
LONDON BRIDGE
TOWER BRIDGE
CHARING CROSS
EMBANKMENT
Embankment Pier
South Bank Centre
National Theatre
WATERLOO
SOUTHWARK
London Bridge Station
London Eye Pier
London Eye
Westminister Pier
Waterloo Station
WESTMINSTER
BOROUGH
LAMBETH NORTH
Houses of Parliament
Westminster Abbey
ELEPHANT & CASTLE
NEW KENT ROAD
OLD KENT ROAD
MILLBANK
Tate Britain
Millbank Pier
KENNINGTON
0 200 m
0 200 yds
DRINKING & NIGHTLIFE
Blackfriar 25
Book Club 11
Café 1001 21
Cittie of Yorke 28
Jerusalem Tavern 18
Lexington 5
Loungelover 12
Ye Olde Cheshire Cheese 23
27 (100m)
Stansted Airport (55km), 13 & 14
Brick Ln (50m) & 21
24, J, Olympic Park (5km) & Whitechapel, City Airport (10km)
Greenwich

The structure is now full of tasteful shops and stalls while in front of Inigo Jones's classical **St Paul's Church** street entertainers, opera singers or mime artists perform. Across Long Acre from the station is **Neal Street** and the **Seven Dials**, both lined with great shops, bars and restaurants.

The British Museum

A short walk from the northern end of Neal Street near Holborn tube station is the **British Museum**, Great Russell Street (daily 10am–5.30pm, Thurs & Fri till 8.30pm; free; Ⓦwww.britishmuseum.org), one of the great museums of the world. The building, with its magnificent Greek Revival edifice is now even more striking thanks to Norman Foster's glass-and-steel covered Great Court, at the heart of which stands the **Round Reading Room**, where Karl Marx penned *Das Kapital*. With over four million exhibits, the museum is far too big to be seen comprehensively in one go – head for the displays that interest you most. The Roman and Greek antiquities are second to none, and include the **Parthenon Sculptures** – taken by Lord Elgin in 1801 and still the cause of discord between the British and Greek governments – while the museum's other most famous exhibit is the **Rosetta Stone**, which led to the modern understanding of hieroglyphics. High-profile exhibitions take place throughout the year (ticket prices vary).

Buckingham Palace

Many tourists choose to head straight for **Buckingham Palace**. The tree-lined sweep of **The Mall** runs from Trafalgar Square southwest through Admiralty Arch, flanked by **St James's Park** on the left and on to **Buckingham Palace** (State Rooms late July to early Oct daily 9.45am–6.30pm, last admission 3.45pm; £17.50; Ⓦwww.royalcollection.org.uk), which has served as the monarch's permanent residence since the accession of Queen Victoria in 1837. The building's exterior, last remodelled in 1913, is pretty bland, but it's actually the rear of the Palace: the much finer front overlooks the monarch's garden. When Buckingham Palace is closed, many mill about outside the gates to catch the **Changing of the Guard**, however, you're better off heading for **Horse Guards** over the other side of the park, where there's a more elaborate equestrian ceremony (Mon–Sat 11am, Sun 10am) and where the Olympic beach volleyball tournament will take place in 2012. From Buckingham Palace you can retrace your steps to go down Whitehall towards Westminster, or you can head west through Green Park to Hyde Park Corner.

Whitehall and Westminster

Whitehall, flanked by government buildings, leads off south from Trafalgar Square towards the area known as **Westminster**, the country's political seat of power for nearly 1000 years. The original White Hall was a palace built for King Henry VIII, but a fire in 1698 meant subsequent monarchs had to move to St James's Palace (closed to the public), just off The Mall. Off to the west side of Whitehall is **Downing Street**, where No. 10 has been the residence of the Prime Minister since 1732.

The Houses of Parliament

Clearly visible at the south end of Whitehall is London's finest Gothic Revival building, the Palace of Westminster, better known as the **Houses of Parliament**. It is distinguished above all by the ornate, gilded clock tower popularly known as **Big Ben**, after the thirteen-ton bell that it houses. The original royal palace, built by Edward the Confessor in the eleventh century, burnt down in 1834. The only part to survive is the magnificent Westminster Hall, which can be glimpsed en route to

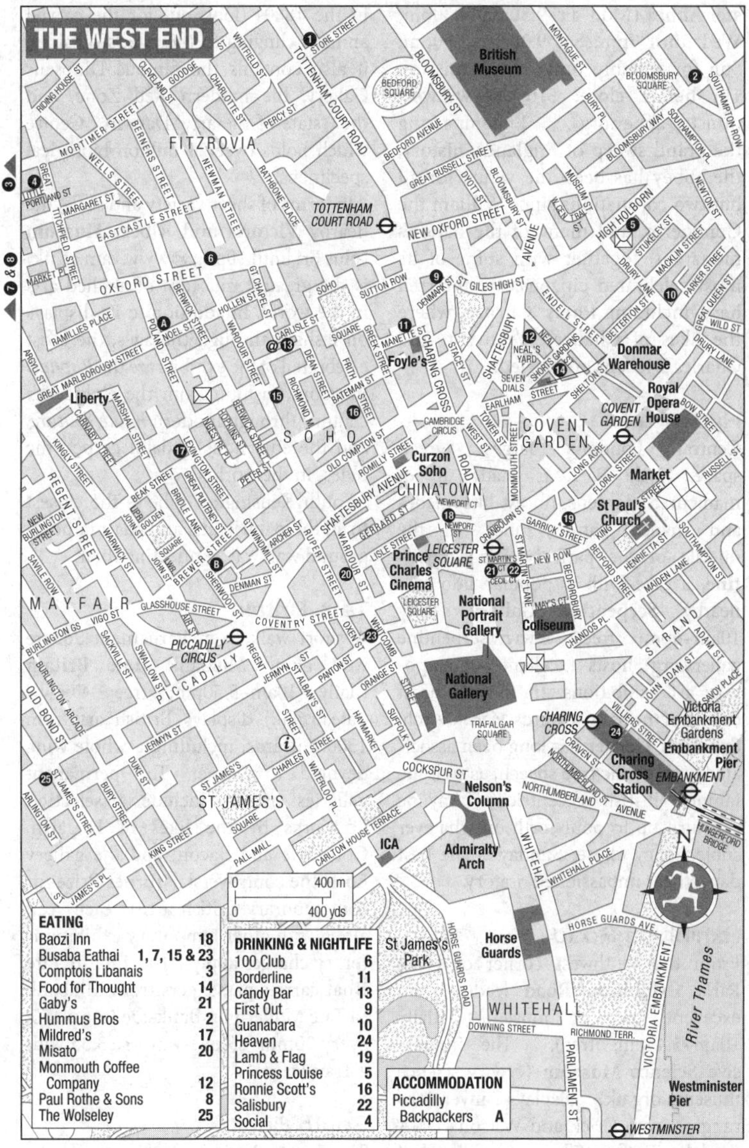

the **public galleries** (free; check parliament is in session; queue 1–2hr before session start outside the Cromwell Green visitor entrance; Ⓦ www.parliament.uk) from which you can watch parliament's proceedings. There's a multitude of different pre-paid tour options available on the website.

Westminster Abbey

The Houses of Parliament overshadow their much older neighbour, **Westmin-**

ster Abbey (Mon–Fri 9.30am–4.30pm; Wed until 7pm; Sat 9.30am–2.30pm; Sun for worship only; last admission 1hr before close; £16; Ⓦwww.westminster-abbey.org). Encompassing the grand sweep of England's history, the abbey has been the venue for all but two coronations since William the Conqueror, and many of the nation's monarchs, together with some of its most celebrated citizens, are interred here, including **Poets' Corner**, where the likes of Chaucer, Tennyson and Charles Dickens are buried.

Hyde Park

Central London's largest green space, **Hyde Park** is made up of manicured gardens, forest-like glades and shaded nature zones. In the middle of the park is **The Serpentine**, a lake with a popular lido; the nearby **Serpentine Gallery** (daily 10am–6pm; free; Ⓦwww.serpentinegallery.org) hosts excellent contemporary art exhibitions. In the northeast corner of the park, towards Marble Arch, **Speakers' Corner** has long been associated with public free speech, as well the famous British eccentricity. Anyone can turn up to pour forth on whatever subject they chose; Sunday is the best day to hear impassioned oratory.

Exhibition Road

From the southwest corner of Hyde Park, **Exhibition Road** leads to an excellent trio of museums (daily 10am–5.45pm; free). The impressive **Science Museum** (Ⓦwww.sciencemuseum.org.uk) displays inventions ranging from Crick and Watson's DNA model to *Puffing Billy*, the world's oldest surviving steam train with many other interactive exhibits. Further south, just off Exhibition Road on Cromwell Road, the **Natural History Museum** (Ⓦwww.nhm.ac.uk) is worth seeing for its marvellous German Romanesque building designed by Alfred Waterhouse in the 1880s (look out for the carved animals clinging to the pillars outside); it also contains the famous Dinosaur Gallery, the modern Red Zone, and the state-of-the-art Darwin Centre which holds over 20 million biological specimens.

In terms of sheer variety and scale, the nearby **Victoria and Albert Museum** (plus Fri until 10pm; Ⓦwww.vam.ac.uk) is the greatest museum of applied arts in the world. In addition to its displays on fashion through the ages, the most celebrated of the exhibits are the *Raphael Cartoons*, fashion from the eighteenth century through modern *haute couture*, and the enormous Ardabil carpet, the oldest in the world.

South Kensington tube is the closest to all three museums and has an underground walkway connecting them.

Tate Britain

A short walk from Parliament Square west along Millbank, **Tate Britain** (daily 10am–5.50pm; free; Ⓦwww.tate.org.uk) displays British art from 1500 onwards, including a whole wing devoted to Turner. The permanent galleries usually include a selection of works by the likes of Hogarth, Constable and Bacon, and the gallery hosts the controversial Turner Prize for contemporary British artists each year, along with other temporary exhibitions (entry charges apply). The **Tate to Tate Boat** carries passengers from Millbank to Tate Modern on Bankside (see p.155; every 30min; £5 one-way or £3.35 with a Travelcard).

South Bank

The **South Bank** forms the stretch by the Thames roughly from Westminster Bridge to London Bridge (a 50min walk). The riverside footpath buzzes with life, as people stroll and jog past street entertainers and art installations, or sit out eating at the many restaurants. The focal point is the **London Eye** (daily 10am–8.30/9.30pm; £18.60; ten percent discount if bought online; Ⓦwww.londoneye.com), a 135m-tall observation wheel that revolves above the river. Head north from here past the brutalist **South Bank Centre** (see p.159) – which encompasses the Royal Festival Hall and the Hayward Gallery – the adjacent **National Theatre** and **British Film Institute**. You'll pass craft shops and restaurants in Gabriel's Wharf and the OXO Tower before reaching Bankside (see below).

Bankside and the Tate Modern

Contemporary **Bankside** is dominated by **Tate Modern** (daily 10am–6pm, Fri & Sat till 10pm; free; Ⓦwww.tate.org.uk), built in a minimalist postwar power station. There are pricey temporary exhibitions (around £10; book ahead for major exhibitions), but as the permanent collection includes works by just about every famous modern artist including Monet, Bonnard, Matisse, Picasso, Dalí, Mondrian, Warhol and Rothko, you should get your fill of modern art for free.

Directly outside Tate Modern is Norman Foster's **Millennium Bridge**, which, with its spectacular views, will take you across the river to the City of London and St Paul's Cathedral.

Globe Theatre to London Bridge

Dwarfed by the Tate Modern is **Shakespeare's Globe** (Ⓦwww.shakespeares-globe.org), a reconstruction of the polygonal playhouse where most of the Bard's later works were first performed. If you're happy to stand in the pit, you can catch a show from as little as £5. A short stroll further east winds away from the river under Victorian railway arches to **London Bridge** and the popular **Borough Market** (see box, p.152), a fantastic place to refuel.

The City of London

Follow the commuters as they trudge over London Bridge to the **City of London**. Despite the newer development of Canary Wharf stealing many companies further east, the area remains the London's financial hub. Out of office hours, the City can feel hauntingly empty but its charm lies in magnificent buildings interspersed with tiny chapels on narrow, winding streets.

St Paul's Cathedral

On the western edge of the City is one of London's most famous landmarks, **St Paul's Cathedral** (Mon–Sat 8.30am–4pm; £14.50; Ⓦwww.stpauls.co.uk). The most distinctive feature of architect Christopher Wren's Baroque edifice is the vast dome, one of the largest in the world. Highlights include the **Whispering Gallery**, up in the dome, so called because words whispered to the wall on one side are clearly audible on the other; the broad exterior Stone Gallery; and the uppermost Golden Gallery, which offers panoramas over London. The **crypt** is the resting place of Wren, Turner, Reynolds and other artists, but the most imposing sarcophagi are those occupied by the Duke of Wellington and Lord Nelson.

Museum of London

Just north of St Paul's, situated in the 1970s-designed **Barbican Centre**, is the **Museum of London** (daily 10am–6pm; free; Ⓦwww.museumoflondon.org.uk). It tells the story of the city, from prehistoric times to the present day with particularly interesting displays on Roman London and the Great Fire, plus the Lord Mayor's state coach dating to 1757. The Barbican Centre itself (Ⓦwww.barbican.org.uk) is one of London's cultural hotspots, housing cinemas, theatres and galleries.

Tower of London

Despite all the hype, and the entrance fee, the **Tower of London** (March–Oct 9/10am–5.30pm; Nov–Feb 9/10am–4.30pm; £19.80 or £17 if booked online; Ⓦwww.hrp.org.uk), on the river a mile southeast of St Paul's by Tower Bridge, remains one of London's most remarkable buildings. Begun by William the Conqueror, and pretty much completed by the end of the thirteenth century, the Tower is the most perfectly preserved (albeit heavily restored) medieval fortress in the country. The central **White Tower** holds part of the Royal Armouries collection, and, on the second floor, the Norman Chapel of St John, London's oldest church. Close by is Tower Green, where two of Henry VIII's wives were beheaded. The Waterloo Barracks house the **Crown Jewels**, among which are the three largest cut diamonds in the world.

The East End

A short walk from the Tower brings you to Aldgate and the start of the **East End**. The area has always drawn large immigrant populations due to its proximity to the river – the area has been in turn Huguenot, Jewish and most recently, Bangladeshi and Pakistani. Walk down Whitechapel Road from Aldgate and you'll pass one of Britain's largest mosques, as well as the excellent **Whitechapel Gallery** (Tues–Sun 11am–6pm, Thurs until 9pm; free; ⓦwww.whitechapelgallery.org), which shows off a cutting-edge mix of contemporary art. **Brick Lane** meanders off to the left (take Osborn St), lined with curry houses, trendy street markets, retro shops and boutiques.

At the other end of Brick Lane, are the funky, creative areas of **Shoreditch**, **Hoxton** and **Old Street**. The area is a fun place to go out in the evening, and is full of boutique restaurants, galleries, cafés and design stores. A two-to-three mile walk further east down Whitechapel Road brings you to, what was, five years ago, a desolate industrial area, now transformed into the **2012 Olympic Park**.

Regent's Park and Camden

As with almost all of London's royal parks, Londoners have Henry VIII to thank for **Regent's Park**, which he confiscated from the Church for yet more hunting grounds. Flanked

MARKETS

At the weekend, visit one of London's high-quality markets: some are well established, some trendy pop-ups, but wherever you go, you're sure to find tasty food and a lively, relaxed atmosphere. Unless specified, markets tend to run 10am–5pm.

Borough Serious foodies stock up on hard-to-source ingredients. Not cheap, but there are free tasters and cheaper gourmet snacks. Thurs–Sat from 8am. ⓤLondon Bridge.

Brick Lane and Spitalfields Technically two separate markets, but punters wander between the two on Sundays, when Brick Lane is thick with food stalls. Spitalfields draws an eclectic mix of artists, jewellers and designers in a restored covered market. Spitalfields market Thurs, Fri & Sun 10am–4pm; closed Sat. ⓤLiverpool St.

Camden Town From its origins as a punk hangout in the 1970s, there are still plenty of Dr. Martens and studded jackets on offer, mixed with every other sub-culture going. Open daily. ⓤCamden Town.

Columbia Road An easy walk from Brick Lane, this lovely plant and flower market is also full of boutique stores and hip coffee shops. Sun 8am–3pm. Shoreditch High Street Overground.

Portobello Road The most iconic London market thanks to the film *Notting Hill*, with a roaring trade in antiques, rare books and vintage finds in genteel surroundings. Best on Saturdays. ⓤNotting Hill.

Greenwich Covered market with quirky handmade gifts, arts and crafts as well as vintage clothes stores and home-made smellies. Cutty Sark DLR.

by some of the city's most elegant residential buildings, the park is home to **London Zoo** (daily 10am–4/6pm; £18.60; Ⓦwww.zsl.org), one of the world's oldest and most varied collections of animals. Take the tube to Baker Street, Regent's Park or Great Portland Street to enter the park at its southernmost edge and walk north to the zoo, or get the tube to **Camden Town** with its famous **market** (see box, p.152) and music scene, and walk west down the **Regent's Canal**, which runs through the middle of the zoo.

Hampstead Heath and Highgate Cemetery

Camden gives way to the affluent suburb of Hampstead and to wild **Hampstead Heath**, which offers the perfect antidote to London's highly manicured parks. East of Hampstead is **Highgate Cemetery**, ranged on both sides of Swains Lane (Ⓤ Highgate/Archway). Karl Marx lies in the East Cemetery (daily 10/11am–4/5pm; £3; Ⓦwww.highgate-cemetery.org); more atmospheric is the overgrown West Cemetery (guided tours only: March–Nov Mon–Fri 2pm, Sat & Sun hourly 11am–4pm; Dec–Feb Sat & Sun hourly 11am–3pm; £5), with its spooky Egyptian Avenue and terraced catacombs.

Greenwich

One of London's most beguiling spots, and offering respite from the frenetic centre, **Greenwich** is worth the short trip. Transport links are good: there are regular riverboats (see p.155), trains from London Bridge, or the DLR scoots from Bank via the redeveloped Docklands south to the *Cutty Sark*, the famous tea clipper (due to reopen in spring 2012 after a devastating fire). Hugging the riverfront to the east is Wren's beautifully symmetrical Baroque ensemble of the **Old Royal Naval College** (daily 10am–5pm; free). Across the road, the **National Maritime Museum** (same hours; free; Ⓦwww.nmm.ac.uk), exhibits model ships, charts and globes. From here Greenwich Park stretches up the hill, crowned by the Wren-inspired **Royal Observatory** (same hours; free), where you can straddle the Greenwich Mean Time meridian.

Arrival by air

Flying into London, you'll arrive at one of the capital's five international airports: Heathrow or Stansted (Ⓦwww.baa.com), Gatwick (Ⓦwww.gatwickairport.com), Luton (Ⓦwww.london-luton.co.uk) or City (Ⓦwww.londoncityairport.com). EasyBus (Ⓦwww.easybus.co.uk) has buses from all the airports, except City, to central London from £2. From Heathrow, Gatwick and Stansted, there are express trains every 15min that will get you there faster than other modes of transport, but at around £20 for a single ticket, it's not cheap.

Heathrow 15 miles west. Served by Piccadilly Line on the Tube (roughly every few minutes from 6am–midnight; 1hr; £5 cash or £4.50/2.70 Oyster peak/off-peak). National Express coaches go to Victoria Coach Station (every 30min; 1hr; £5). After midnight, night bus #N9 runs to Trafalgar Square (every 20min; 1hr; £2.20 cash/1.30 Oyster).

Gatwick 30 miles south. Connected by several train companies: Southern trains run on the same route as the Gatwick Express, but are cheaper (every 15min; 35min; £11.50), and Thameslink trains run to London Bridge, Blackfriars and St Pancras International (every 20min; 45min; around £10).

Stansted 34 miles northeast. National Express services run to Victoria Coach Station or Liverpool Street (every 30min; 1hr 30min; around £12).

Luton 37 miles north. Served by shuttle buses to Luton Airport Parkway station, from there are services to St Pancras (every 10–15min; 30min; £11.50) and other stations on the Thameslink line (see Gatwick). Green Line bus #757/#755 also runs from the airport terminal into central London (every 20min–1hr; 1hr 30min; £16 or £22 return within 3 months).

London City 10 miles east. Served by the Docklands Light Railway (DLR), with regular services to Bank (every 5min; 22min; £4 cash or £2.90/2.50 Oyster peak/off-peak).

Arrival by train and bus

Train Eurostar services from Paris or Brussels terminate at St Pancras International (with a high-

OYSTER CARDS

The cheapest way to pay for all public transport in London is to use an **Oyster** touch card (Ⓦtfl.gov.uk/oyster; £5), valid on the underground, buses, trams, the DLR, the London Overground rail network, National Rail services in London and will give you money off some riverboats. You can store cash on the card ("pay as you go") as well as weekly travel cards, simply "top up" at stations or newsagents (look for the Oyster logo outside). When using an Oyster, one-way bus fares are almost halved (£2.20 to £1.30) and tube fares in Zone 1 are reduced from £4 if paying cash to £1.90. If you pay as you go, you'll be charged no more than the maximum daily cap (currently £8 peak or £6.60 off-peak for Zones 1 and 2). Consider buying a week's travel pass (from £25.80) if you're staying for several days and plan on making lots of journeys. You can buy pre-loaded cards before you come to the UK (Ⓦvisitorshop.tfl.gov.uk). Even without Oyster, a one-day (£8/6.60 peak/off-peak) or seven-day (£27.60) paper travelcard will still save you pounds.

speed link to Stratford International planned for the 2012 Olympics). Trains from the English Channel ports arrive at Victoria, Waterloo or Charing Cross stations, while those from elsewhere in Britain come into one of London's numerous main-line termini (namely Waterloo and Paddington from the southwest, Euston or King's Cross from the north, and Liverpool Street from the east), all of which have tube stations.

Bus Long-distance buses from around Britain and continental Europe arrive at Victoria Coach Station, 500 yards walk south of Victoria train station.

Information

London's flagship information office is the Britain and London Visitor Centre, near Piccadilly Circus at 1 Lower Regent St (Mon 9.30am–6/6.30pm, Tues–Fri 9am–6/6.30pm, Sat–Sun 9am–4pm; Ⓣ08701/566366, Ⓦwww.visitlondon.com), which has multilingual staff, internet facilities, and also acts as a ticket and travel agency. There are other branches all over the city – the website details them on a map. The City Information Centre (Mon–Sat 9.30am–5.30pm, Sun 10am–4pm; Ⓣ020/7332 1456, Ⓦwww.visitthecity.co.uk), opposite St Paul's Cathedral, is another well-run option.

City transport

Transport for London (TfL) oversees the city's public transport and their website (Ⓦtfl.gov.uk) is a vital tool for all Londoners and visitors to help navigate this enormous city by tube, bus, boat or bike. It can even help you plan walking routes or look up reliable taxi companies. TfL's six tourist information centres are in the following major stations: Piccadilly Circus tube station, Heathrow Terminals 1, 2 and 3, Euston, Liverpool Street, Victoria and King's Cross St. Pancras (all daily 9.15am–6pm). There's also a 24-hour phone line for information on all services, including up-to-date closures or diversions (Ⓣ0843/222 1234).

Underground The quickest way to get around is via the London Underground network, known as "the tube" (daily 5.30/7.30am–12.30am approx; check "first and last" tube on TfL website). It can be staggeringly expensive without an Oyster card (see box, above). Tickets must be bought in advance from the machines or booths in station entrance halls and need to be kept until the end of your journey so that you can leave the station. If you use Oyster, be sure to always touch the card reader on the way in and out of each station. If you cannot produce a valid ticket or Oyster card on demand, you'll be charged an on-the-spot penalty fine of £50. Bear in mind that during rush hour the tube is heaving with commuters and best avoided, especially if you are laden with baggage. Within central London always check whether walking will be quicker – Covent Garden and Leicester Square stations are just a 4min walk apart.

Bus A great way to see the city, especially from the top of London's famous red double-deckers. Many run 24hr though be aware night buses prefixed with the letter "N" may not run the same route as their day counterpart. If you don't have an Oyster card, you will need to buy a single ticket (£2.20) from the machine at the bus stop before boarding (in central London), or simply pay the driver outside of the centre (use small change). Hail buses by sticking your arm out. Most buses are modern, but a classic London Routemaster bus (#15) complete with conductor runs from Charing Cross station to the Tower of London.

Boat Riverboat services on the Thames are a pleasant and quick way to get between east and west. Having an Oyster or a paper travelcard will get you a third off riverboat tickets, while if you've a pay-as-you-go Oyster you'll get ten percent off single fares. Westminster Pier, Embankment Pier and Waterloo Pier are the main central embarkation points and there are regular sailings to Bankside, London Bridge, Tower Bridge and Greenwich. Timings and services alter frequently so pick up the *Thames River Services* booklet from a TfL travel information office, phone Ⓣ020/7222 1234 or visit Ⓦwww.thamesclippers.com.

Taxi If you're in a group, London's metered black cabs (just wave to hail one when their orange "taxi" light is illuminated) can be a viable way of travelling. Cost depends on time of day, distance travelled and travel time and there's a minimum £2.20 fare. A two-mile journey (10–20min) should cost around £10 between 6am–8pm. To book in advance, call Ⓣ020/7272 0272. Minicabs look just like regular cars and are considerably cheaper than black cabs (a black cab to Heathrow will cost up to £80, while a minicab will charge around £50–60), but need to be booked by phone in advance. To get numbers for local registered minicab companies, text Cabwise (Ⓣ07797/800229) with your location, or call the travel information number above.

Train and tram There are a variety of different train lines in London. The Overground and the Docklands Light Railway (DLR) are operated by TfL and form part of the Tube map – most interchanges are as simple as on the tube. National Rail services from London out to Greater London suburbs and commuter towns are run by outside agents, but you can now use Oyster cards for most journeys in and around the city (details on TfL website). Oyster can also be used on the trams in south London.

Bike The public bike rental scheme is available to all (Ⓦtfl.org.uk; credit or debit card needed to hire at docking stations found all over central London). The "Boris Bikes", named after the mayor who installed them, cost £1 to rent for the day or £5 for a week, then you pay an hourly incremental charge after that; the first half an hour is free, so long as you keep docking the bikes and picking up new ones it can be a great and cheap way to see London. You can find rental shops through the London Cycling Campaign (Ⓦwww.lcc.org.uk). Pick out cycle-friendly routes using the free guides available from transport information offices, or check the TfL website.

Accommodation

Where to stay can be a difficult question in a city London's size. West London offers easy access to the museums and central London, though it tends to be the most expensive part of town for eating and nightlife. Northeast London is currently London's hippest area and the Olympics will provide even more reason to stay here. Leafy northwest London provides unrivalled access to London's best green spaces, while anywhere near the South Bank will be central enough to walk into the West End while offering the chance to explore off-the-beaten-track neighbourhoods south of the river. The Visit London hotel booking service (Ⓣ0845/644 3010, Ⓦwww.visitlondon.com) will get you the best available prices with no additional charge. Student rooms are also available over the summer vacation from July to Sept; try Imperial College (Ⓣ020/7594 9507, Ⓦwww.imperial.ac.uk/summeraccommodation) or LSE (Ⓣ020/7955 7575, Ⓦwww.lsevacations.co.uk). For classy, modern budget B&Bs, the Bed and Breakfast Club (Ⓦwww.thebedandbreakfastclub.co.uk), collects them under one roof. The following are on the map on pp.146–147 unless otherwise stated.

Hostels

The YHA (see p.38) have eight HI-affiliated London hostels, all in unbeatable locations (Oxford Street, Holland Park, St Pancras, St Paul's, Central, Earls Court and Thameside), and most offer cheap twins and doubles as well as dorms. Prices shown are examples of the cheapest weeknight dorm in high season; in low season beds start from as little as £6. A continental breakfast is included at the hostels below unless specified.

Clink78 78 King's Cross Rd Ⓣ020/7183 9400, Ⓦwww.clinkhostel.com Ⓤ King's Cross. Quirky hostel housed in a Victorian courthouse. Chill-out space is in the actual courtrooms, and for added authenticity you can sleep in the claustrophobic confines of a former police cell. The same team run the cosier *Clink261* nearby at 261 Gray's Inn Rd. Dorms £18, cells £63, doubles £73.

Generator Compton Place Ⓣ020/7388 7666, Ⓦwww.generatorhostels.com Ⓤ Russell Square. Raucous, 837-bed party hostel with neon-lit post-industrial decor and a youthful clientele. Dorms £27, private rooms £30.50/person.

Great Eastern 1 Glenaffric Ave Ⓣ020/7531 6514, Ⓦwww.bestplaceinns.com (others in Marylebone, Waterloo and Victoria). Island Gardens DLR station. Tucked out of the way in Docklands by the Thames, this hostel, one of a growing chain, is a 10min walk from Greenwich via a foot tunnel, and 5min on the DLR to Canary Wharf tube. Above a remodelled pub with sparkling facilities and great lounge area. Dorms £15.

Palmers Lodge 40 College Crescent ⓣ020/7483 8470, ⓦwww.palmerslodge.co.uk ⓤSwiss Cottage. Superb hostel with disabled access in a converted Victorian mansion, retaining much of its period character. Dorms £18, doubles £37.

Piccadilly Backpackers 12 Sherwood St ⓣ020/7434 9009, ⓦwww.piccadillybackpackers.com ⓤPiccadilly Circus. See map, p.149. Incredibly central and cheap, but you'll have to put up with noise. Dorms £12, doubles/twins £69.

Pride of Paddington 1–3 Craven Rd ⓔcontactus@theprideofpaddington.co.uk, ⓦwww.theprideofpaddington.co.uk ⓤPaddington. Opposite Paddington station and great for Hyde Park and central London, this renovated hostel above a pub is basic but spotless. Email for bookings. Cooked breakfast included. Dorms £25, doubles/twins £75.

St Christopher's 121 Borough High St ⓣ020/7407 1856, ⓦwww.st-christophers.co.uk (other branches in Camden, Hammersmith, Shepherd's Bush and Greenwich) ⓤLondon Bridge. Cheerful party hostel in a series of buildings near London Bridge. *The Village* has a nightclub and comedy bar; *The Inn* is above a pub and a little more tranquil, while *The Oasis* is London's only hostel exclusively for women. Dorms £18, doubles/twins £56.

Travel Joy 111 Grosvenor Rd ⓣ020/7834 9689, ⓦwww.traveljoyhostels.com ⓤPimlico or bus #24 from central London. Right on the river in tranquil Pimlico, this delightful pub provides free soft drinks for guests. Dorms £23.50, twins £80.

Hotels and B&Bs

Most budget hotels and B&Bs in central London are grotty or old-fashioned; a short commute from the centre, you get much better value for money. See p.38 for budget chain hotels.

John and Norma's Homestay B&B 74 Coniston Rd ⓣ020/8444 8127, ⓦ74coniston.com ⓤBounds Green. Cosy two-bed B&B in a well-heeled suburb of Muswell Hill with many restaurants and shops nearby. Pleasant owners put on a healthy breakfast spread. Doubles/twins £80.

Ridgemount Hotel 65–67 Gower St ⓣ020/7636 1141, ⓦwww.ridgemounthotel.co.uk ⓤEuston Square. What you sacrifice in style and room size, you make up for in location in Bloomsbury and, as a bonus, you get a spotless and friendly hotel to boot. Doubles/twins £66; en-suites £86.

Russell's of Clapton 123 Chatsworth Rd, Hackney ⓣ0797/666 9906, ⓦrussellsofclapton.com. Homerton Overground or #38 bus from central London. The out-of-the-way location (15min walk from the Overground station) in a formerly insalubrious part of Hackney means you get a boutique B&B offering vintage-style luxury for tiny prices. Doubles £65–95.

Campsites

Lee Valley Camping and Caravan Park Meridian Way, Enfield ⓣ020/8803 6900, ⓦwww.leevalleypark.org.uk. Train from Liverpool St to Edmonton Green then #W8 bus. For a completely different London experience, try a four-person wood cabin (£45/night) or two-person cocoon (£35) in a leisure complex including golf course and cinema in North London. You can pitch your own tent, too (£19.50).

Eating

Few cities can match London for the sheer diversity of eating experiences on offer. You'll find restaurants from every country on earth, with pubs just as likely to offer Thai green curry as steak and ale pie. With so much choice, it's not hard to eat well on a budget, provided you're happy with "ethnic" food. In addition to the places below, there are a handful of good London-based chains with several branches around the city, including *Leon* (ⓦwww.leonrestaurants.co.uk), which offers inventive, health-conscious fast food, Hummus Bros (ⓦwww.hbros.co.uk) serving very cheap dishes based around the Mediterranean staple, Busuaba Eathai (ⓦbusaba.com) which has inventive Thai dishes, and the *S&M Café* (ⓦwww.sandmcafe.co.uk), specializing in sausage and mash. The following are marked on the map on pp.146–147, unless otherwise stated.

Cafés

E. Pellicci 332 Bethnal Green Rd ⓤBethnal Green. Run by the Pellicci family since the 1900s and a favourite haunt of gangster brothers the Krays, this is the most elegant and cosy greasy spoon in town. 7am–4pm; closed Sun.

F. Cookes 150 Hoxton St ⓤOld Street. Get the very traditional London pie, mash & liquor (parsley gravy) with the house chilli vinegar for under £4, or if you dare, a jellied eel in this spit 'n' sawdust family-run place. Mon–Sat 10am–7pm, closed Sun.

Food For Thought 31 Neal St ⓤCovent Garden. See map, p.149. Subterranean vegetarian café serving wholesome salads, soups and mains from £4.50. Daily noon–8.30pm; Sun until 5.30pm.

Gaby's 30 Charing Cross Rd ⓤLeicester Square. See map, p.149. Jewish café serving a wide range

TREAT YOURSELF

Tea at the Wolseley Traditional British afternoon tea doesn't come much more special than this: exquisite cream teas from £9.75 in the beautiful Art Deco surroundings of the opulent *Wolseley* restaurant at 160 Piccadilly. Don't worry about dressing up; the experience is surprisingly relaxed. Daily 7/8am–11pm. See map, p.149.

of home-cooked Mediterranean specialities. Hard to beat for value, choice and location. Mains from £3.80. Mon–Sat 9am–midnight, Sun 11am–10pm.
Monmouth Coffee Company 27 Monmouth St, Seven Dials Ⓤ Holborn. See map, p.149. Also Borough Market Ⓤ London Bridge. *Monmouth* have built a name for themselves for making the best coffee in London – look out for other cafés selling their blends. 8am–6pm; closed Sun.
Paul Rothe & Son 35 Marlyebone Lane Ⓤ Bond Street. Established in 1900 and still run by the Rothes, marvel at the variety of jams in the window, and also at the low prices of their British breakfast and lunches. Sandwich/soup/jacket potato £3. Mon–Fri 8am–6pm, Sun 11.30am–5.30pm.

Restaurants

Baozi Inn 25 Newport Court Ⓤ Leicester Square. See map, p.149. So authentic you may not recognize anything on the menu, but this place serving Beijing and Chengdu street food is a treat for the tastebuds. Mains £6. Daily noon–10.30pm.
Ciao Bella 86–90 Lamb's Conduit St Ⓤ Russell Square/Holborn. Jolly, extremely popular old-style Italian, serving huge plates of pasta or pizza for £7. Daily noon–11.30pm.
Comptois Libanais 65 Wigmore St Ⓤ Bond Street. See map, p.149. Serving incredible Lebanese food at incredible prices at any time of day with design-conscious surroundings. Mains £7. Mon–Sat 9/10am–9/10pm, Sun noon–6pm.
Mandalay 444 Edgware Rd Ⓤ Edgware Road. A real gem, serving pure, freshly cooked, unreconstructed Burmese cuisine. Lunch deal £3.90. Lunch noon–2.30pm, dinner 6–10.30pm.
Mildred's 45 Lexington St Ⓤ Oxford Circus or Piccadilly Circus. See map, p.149. Intimate veggie restaurant and bar with an imaginative menu, featuring burritos, tagines and stir-fries. Light meals £5.50, mains £7.50. Mon–Sat noon–11pm, closed Sun.
Misato 11 Wardour St Ⓤ Piccadilly Circus. See map, p.149. Japanese café known for its converse qualities of enormous portions for miniscule prices. Mains £5. Daily noon–10.30pm.
Sông Quê 134 Kingsland Rd. Hoxton Overground. On a strip of road packed with Vietnamese restaurants, the basic decor here belies the excellent food and efficient service. Mains £7. Lunch noon–3pm; dinner 5.30–11pm.
Tayyabs 83–89 Fieldgate St ☎ 020/72476400 Ⓤ Aldgate East. Close to, but not on, Brick Lane (home to pushy curry touts), this Pakistani restaurant is popular for its grills, naan and bring-your own-alcohol policy. Come early or be prepared to queue. Mains from £6. Daily noon–11.30pm.
Water Poet 9 Folgate St Ⓤ Liverpool Street. Along with fish and chips, the Sunday roast is pretty much the national dish. This pub does both dishes brilliantly. Roast with all the trimmings £11. Sunday lunch noon–5pm; otherwise normal pub opening hours.

Drinking and nightlife

From Victorian pubs serving ale to old gents, to hip bars and clubs frequented by an eternally young, edgy clientele, London has it all. To the east, a thriving bar and club scene around Shoreditch, Hoxton and Old Street is still going strong, though the coolest of the cool are increasingly shifting their parties elsewhere. The following are marked on the map on pp.146–147 unless otherwise stated.

Pubs and bars

Blackfriar 174 Queen Victoria St Ⓤ Blackfriars. One of the capital's most unusual pubs, with marble walls, stained-glass windows and carved or illustrated monks in every nook and cranny.
Book Club100 Leonard St Ⓤ Liverpool Street/Old Street. With a bar serving food, along with cheaper

DRINKING ON A BUDGET

For a break from London's sky-high drink prices check out the sensitively restored Victorian pubs owned by the **Sam Smith's** brewery. Prices are kept low as everything, including spirits and soft drinks come from the same brewery; a pint of lager starts at just £2.15. The *Cittie of York*, 22 High Holborn (Ⓤ Chancery Lane) or *Ye Olde Cheshire Cheese* at 145 Fleet St (Ⓤ Blackfriars), and *The Princess Louise* at 208 High Holborn (Ⓤ Holborn) all have historical interiors, but there are plenty of others.

and better cocktails than other bars in the area, this hip Shoreditch hangout also boasts a ping pong room, film screenings, live music and opens from breakfast until midnight/2am.

Café 1001 91 Brick Lane Ⓤ Aldgate East/Liverpool St. Sprawling, grungy bar above a heaving café. Squishy sofas and free live music and cinema draw a laidback hipster crowd. Café opens from 6am.

Jerusalem Tavern 55 Britton St Ⓤ Farringdon. Cool Clerkenwell's the setting for this packed pub, serving some of the best ales in London from barrels in the wall.

Lamb & Flag Rose St Ⓤ Covent Garden or Leicester Square. See map, p.149. A respite from hectic Covent Garden, this compact pub was once known as the *Bucket of Blood* – after the prize fights held here.

Lexington 96 Pentonville Rd Ⓤ Angel. This luxuriously decorated bourbon joint puts on events like a "Rock 'n' Roll" pub quiz, as well as cheap live music and club nights upstairs. Daily noon–late.

Salisbury 90 St Martin's Lane Ⓤ Leicester Square. See map, p.149. Beautiful old gin palace packed with original features, dark wood, mirrors and glassware in the heart of Theatreland.

Social 5 Little Portland St Ⓤ Oxford Circus. See map, p.149. Cosy retro bar with booths upstairs with a buzzing club below with DJs playing everything from rock to rap for a truly hedonistic crowd. Daily from midday–late or last people leave.

Clubs

Bethnal Green Working Men's Club 42 Pollard Row Ⓦ workersplaytime.net Ⓤ Bethnal Green. East End club seeks "party seekers, creatives, pioneers and luminaries" for cabaret, performance art and theme club nights. Opening times vary; see website.

Bloomsbury Lanes Basement of *Tavistock Hotel*, Bedford Way Ⓦ www.bloomsburylive.com Ⓤ Russell Square. Get your glad rags on for subterranean karaoke, bowling, cocktails and dancing with different nights spinning funk, rockabilly and disco. Daily 1pm–late.

Cargo 83 Rivington St Ⓦ www.cargo-london.com Ⓤ Old Street. Live music bar/club with globally influenced music, trendy crowds and a laidback vibe. Also has a restaurant with a good £5 lunch deal. Daily from noon.

Fabric 77a Charterhouse St Ⓦ www.fabriclondon.com Ⓤ Farringdon. Probably London's most famous club, and one that keeps drawing the crowds despite the hefty entry fee (£10–20) to hear cutting-edge dance music. Get there early or buy your ticket online to avoid queues. Club nights Wed–Sun; see website.

Guanabara Parker St Ⓦ www.guanabara.co.uk Ⓤ Holborn. Nightly samba, bossa-nova and Latin beats keep the punters on the dancefloor at this fun Brazilian club. Free entry before 9pm. Daily from 5pm.

Plastic People 147 Curtain Rd Ⓦ www.plasticpeople.co.uk Ⓤ Old Street/Liverpool Street. An intimate venue playing a mix of house, hip-hop, funk and jazz. Thurs–Sat from around 9.30pm.

> **TREAT YOURSELF**
>
> A cocktail at **Loungelover**, 1 Whitby St (Ⓣ 020/7012 1234 Ⓦ www.loungelover.co.uk; Shoreditch High Street Overground), may not come cheap (£8–12), but it's worth the trip to see the fabulously camp decor of this lavish, bejewelled bar tucked off Bethnal Green Road. It's best to book a table at weekends; otherwise just walk in and stand at the bar. Japanese food served. Daily 6pm–midnight/1am.

Gay and lesbian nightlife

Candy Bar 4 Carlisle St Ⓦ candybarsoho.com Ⓤ Tottenham Court Road. See map, p.149. Britain's first seven-day all-girl bar/club offers a retro-style cocktail bar-cum-pool room upstairs, and a noisy, beery ground level cruising area. Bar from 4pm, club from 10pm.

First Out 52 St Giles High St Ⓤ Tottenham Court Road. See map, p.149. The West End's original gay café-bar, and still permanently packed, serving good veggie food at reasonable prices (mains from £6.50). At weekends, there's music and DJ acts in the downstairs bar. Daily 9am–11pm except Sun 10am–10.30pm.

Heaven Under The Arches, Villiers St Ⓦ www.heaven-london.co.uk Ⓤ Charing Cross/Embankment. See map, p.149. Britain's most popular gay club, this legendary, 2000-capacity club continues to reign supreme. Regular club nights Mon & Thurs–Sat; for other events see website.

Royal Vauxhall Tavern 372 Kennington Lane Ⓦ www.rvt.org.uk Ⓤ Vauxhall. From cabaret to comedy and from bingo to disco, the *RVT* has it all. An international gay institution. Check website for event start times.

Entertainment

Cinemas

BFI Under Waterloo Bridge, South Bank Ⓦ www.bfi.org.uk Ⓤ Waterloo. Serious arts cinema showing up to ten different films each day and screening the

London Film Festival (Oct) and London Lesbian and Gay Film Festival (late March).

Curzon Cinemas 38 Curzon St, 99 Shaftesbury Ave & 206 King's Rd Ⓦ www.curzoncinemas.com. Classy arthouse chain specializing in European cinema.

Prince Charles 2–7 Leicester Place Ⓦ www.princecharlescinema.com Ⓤ Leicester Square. The bargain basement of London's cinemas, with a programme of newish movies and cult favourites.

Live music venues

100 Club 100 Oxford St Ⓦ www.the100club.co.uk Ⓤ Tottenham Court Rd. See map, p.149. Historically important venue – the Sex Pistols played here – in a very central location hosting quality new talent.

Barfly 49 Chalk Farm Rd Ⓦ www.barflyclub.com Ⓤ Camden Town/Chalk Farm. See map, pp.146–147. Where a large array of punk, rock and indie bands make their debut, with club nights too.

Borderline Orange Yard, Manette St Ⓦ venues.meanfiddler.com/borderline Ⓤ Tottenham Court Road. See map, p.149. Count on this intimate venue for live rock and Americana. Good place to catch new bands. Also weekly rock, metal and indie nights.

Ronnie Scott's 47 Frith St Ⓦ www.ronniescotts.co.uk Ⓤ Tottenham Court Rd. See map, p.149. London's most famous jazz club; big-name acts play in the dimly lit, red-velvet downstairs club. Less pricey and great fun is Wed's late-night jam session (from 9.30pm; £5) in the upstairs bar.

South Bank Centre By Waterloo Bridge Ⓦ www.southbankcentre.co.uk Ⓤ Waterloo. Vast arts complex, showcasing high-quality music of all genres; it includes the Royal Festival Hall and the Purcell Room, both top classical music venues.

CULTURE ON THE CHEAP

Many theatres offer student discounts, and have standing, restricted view, or standby tickets available last minute. Try Ⓦ www.lastminute.com who have cheaper tickets for most of the big shows, or there's the TKTS booth in Leicester Square selling half-price tickets (Mon–Sat 10am–7pm, Sun 11am–4pm) for that day's performances. For classical music, between July and September, you can't beat the **Proms** (Ⓦ www.bbc.co.uk/proms), the annual classical music festival held at the Royal Albert Hall, simply queue up a few hours before the performance to get £5 tickets.

Theatres

Dominated by big musicals, there's no shortage of other world-class performances. Another option is theatre pubs, where experimental performances are shown in intimate pub settings before moving on to bigger things. Check out the *Old Red Lion*, 418 St John's St, the *King's Head*, 115 Upper St, or the *Hen & Chickens*, 109 St Paul's Rd, clustered between Angel and Highbury & Islington tubes.

Coliseum St Martin's Lane Ⓤ Leicester Square. Home to the English National Opera, more radical and democratic than the Royal Opera House, with opera (in English) and ballet.

Donmar Warehouse Earlham St Ⓤ Covent Garden. Formerly the spiritual home of director Sam Mendes, and the best bet for a central off-West End show.

Institute of Contemporary Arts (ICA) Nash House, The Mall Ⓤ Charing Cross. Contemporary theatre, dance, films and art at this enduringly cutting-edge venue.

National Theatre by Waterloo Bridge, South Bank Ⓤ Waterloo. The NT has three separate theatres and consistently good productions. With almost half of all tickets for certain plays going on sale at £10, it's no wonder that some performances sell out months in advance. If you haven't booked, ask about discounted day seats or £5 standing tickets.

Sadler's Wells Rosebery Ave Ⓤ Angel. London's biggest dance venue puts on a mix of the best contemporary dance and ballet.

Shopping

London's up there with Paris and New York for the sheer variety of its shopping, and there are many stores and boutiques you simply won't find anywhere else. If you're on a budget, window-shopping is still a great way of spending time; better still, visit one of the capital's many markets (see box, p.152).

Shopping streets

Charing Cross Road Great place to pick up reading material. Rummage in one of the many secondhand bookshops, or browse new titles in Foyles.

Covent Garden Plenty of high street stores, plus independent fashion outlets around the Neal St area, Floral St and Long Acre.

Knightsbridge to Sloane Square Every high-end designer has their flagship store near here.

Oxford Street London's most famous and frequented shopping strip, home to gargantuan branches of high street shops including Topshop, Primark and Niketown.

Soho and Carnaby Street Seedy Soho is crammed with quirky fashion shops, independent record stores and erotica. At its western boundary, Carnaby Street (ⓦwww.carnaby.co.uk) trades heavily on its association with the swinging sixties, but is still a good bet for cool trainers and young fashion.

Directory

Embassies Australia, Corner of Aldwych with the Strand ⓣ020/7379 4334 (ⓤHolborn/Temple); Canada, 1 Grosvenor Square ⓣ020/7258 6600 (ⓤBond Street), from summer 2012 due to relocate to Canada House, Trafalgar Square (opposite National Gallery); Ireland, 17 Grosvenor Place ⓣ020/7235 2171 (ⓤHyde Park Corner); New Zealand, 80 Haymarket ⓣ020/7930 8422 (ⓤPiccadilly Circus); South Africa, South Africa House, Trafalgar Square ⓣ020/7451 7299 (ⓤCharing Cross); United States, 24 Grosvenor Square ⓣ020/7499 9000 (ⓤBond Street).

Exchange Shopping areas such as Oxford St and Covent Garden are littered with private exchange offices, but their rates are usually worse than the banks. Any post office (see below) will exchange money commission-free and any large bank will offer competitive rates.

Hospitals St Mary's Hospital, Praed St ⓣ020/7886 6666 (ⓤPaddington); University College Hospital, 235 Euston Rd ⓣ0845/1555 000 (ⓤEuston Square).

Internet Net Stream in St Anne's Court (off Wardour St) is open 24hr ⓤTottenham Court Road.

Left luggage At all airport terminals and major train stations.

Pharmacy Boots at Piccadilly Circus is open until midnight, or Zafash at 233 Old Brompton Rd is 24hr (ⓤEarls Court).

Post office 24 William IV St (ⓤLeicester Square/Charing Cross). Mon–Fri 9.15am–6.30pm, Sat 9am–5.30pm.

Moving on

Train Bath (every 30min; 1hr 30min); Brighton (every 15min; 1hr 15min); Bristol (every 30min; 1hr 25min); Brussels (9 daily; 3hr10min); Cambridge (every 15min; 45min); Cardiff (every 30min; 2hr 10min); Dover (every 2hr; 1–2hr); Durham (hourly; 2hr 45min); Edinburgh (hourly; 4hr 30min–7hr 30min); Glasgow (hourly; 4hr 30min–5hr 30min); Lille (8 daily; 2hr 45 min); Liverpool (hourly; 2hr 10min); Manchester (every 20min; 2hr 10min); Newcastle (every 30min; 3hr 15min); Oxford (every 20–30min; 1hr); Paris (hourly; 2hr 15min); Penzance (13 daily; 5hr 30min); Stratford-upon-Avon (5 daily; 2hr 15min); York (every 30min; 2hr 20min).

Bus Amsterdam (4 daily; 12hr); Bath (every 30min; 2hr 30min–4hr); Berlin (1 daily; 20hr); Brighton (hourly; 2hr); Bristol (every 1–2hr; 2hr 45min); Cambridge (hourly; 2–3hr); Cardiff (hourly; 3hr 20min–3hr 50min); Dover (1–2 hourly; 2hr 30min–3hr); Dublin (1 daily; 12hr 30min); Durham (4 daily; 6hr–7hr 25min); Edinburgh (6 daily; 8hr 40min–12hr 30min); Glasgow (7 daily; 8hr–10hr 30min); Inverness (2 daily; 12hr 35min–13hr 30min); Liverpool (1–2 hourly; 5hr 10min–6hr 40min); Manchester (1–2 hourly; 4hr 45min–6hr 35min); Newcastle (5 daily; 6hr 40min–7hr 45min); Oxford (every 15min; 1hr 45min); Paris (4 daily; 8hr 30min); Penzance (6 daily; 9hr); Stratford-upon-Avon (4 daily; 3hr 30min); York (5 daily; 4hr 55min–6hr 15min).

Southeast England

Nestling in self-satisfied prosperity, **southeast England** is the richest part of Britain. Swift, frequent rail and coach services make it ideal for **day-trips**

QUINTESSENTIAL LONDON SHOPS

Harrods on Brompton Road (daily 10am–8pm, Sun noon–6pm; ⓤKnightsbridge) is London's grandest department store and a major tourist attraction; check out the incredible food hall with its Arts and Crafts tiling. A better bet for clothes is **Selfridges** (daily 8.30am–9pm, except Sun noon–6pm; ⓤMarble Arch/Bond Street) on Oxford Street. Famous for its creative window displays, it sells pretty much everything from sushi, via stationery. Just off Regent Street is the elegant mock-Tudor department store **Liberty** (daily 10am–9pm except Sun noon–6pm; ⓤOxford Circus) on Great Marlborough Street, famous for its iconic prints with jewellery, scarves, bags and fabrics in rich, and peculiarly calming surroundings.

from London. The medieval ecclesiastical power base of **Canterbury** is full of history, while, on the coast the upbeat, hedonistic resort of **Brighton** is London's summer playground by the sea.

DOVER

DOVER is the main port of entry along this stretch of coast, and the country's busiest. **Ferries** sail to Calais and Dunkirk from the Eastern Docks, which is also the starting point for LD Lines's service to Boulogne. The main **train station**, for services to Canterbury and London (two hourly; 1–2hr), is Dover Priory, ten minutes' walk west of the centre and served by shuttle buses from the Eastern Docks. **Coaches** to London (hourly; 2hr 30min) pick up from both the docks and the town-centre bus station on Pencester Road. The **tourist office** is on Biggin Street (daily 9/10am–4/5.30pm; Oct–March closed Sun; ⓣ01304/205108, ⓦwww.whitecliffscountry.org.uk).

CANTERBURY

CANTERBURY, still home to England's pre-eminent Archbishop, was one of medieval Europe's hottest pilgrimage destinations as Chaucer's *Canterbury Tales* attest. Pilgrims flocked to the shrine of Archbishop Thomas à Becket, who was brutally murdered in the cathedral nave in 1170, victim of an unseemly spat between Church and State. Enclosed on three sides by medieval walls, quaint Canterbury now hosts a sizeable student population and great food and shopping options, but the main draw for visitors is still the towering edifice of the cathedral.

What to see and do

Built in stages from 1070 onwards, **Canterbury Cathedral** (Mon–Sat 9am–5pm, Sun 12.30–2pm; ⓦwww.canterbury-cathederal.org; £9) derives its distinctive presence from the perpendicular thrust of its late Gothic towers, dominated by the central, sixteenth-century Bell Harry tower. In the northwest transept, a modern sculpture, portraying ragged swords, is suspended over the place where Becket met his violent end. You'll also want to see the Romanesque arches of the crypt, one of the few remaining visible relics of the Norman cathedral with religious murals dating back to the 1100s.

East of the cathedral, across the ring road, are the evocative ruins of **St Augustine's Abbey** (April–Aug daily 10am–6pm; Sept–March Sat & Sun 10am–4/5pm; £4.80; EH), on the site of a church founded by St Augustine, who began the conversion of the English in 597.

The best exposition of local history is provided by the interactive Canterbury Heritage Museum, on Stour Street (April–Sept daily 10am–4pm; Oct–March Mon–Sat 11am–4pm; £8, includes up to four children with each adult; ⓦwww.canterbury.gov.uk).

Arrival and Information

Train Canterbury has two train stations: Canterbury East for most services from London Victoria and Dover Priory, and Canterbury West for services from London Charing Cross via Waterloo East and London Bridge, as well as high-speed trains from St Pancras – the stations are 10min south and northwest of the centre respectively.

Bus St George's Lane, below the High St.

Tourist office 12–13 Sun St, opposite the entrance to the cathedral (Mon–Sat 9.30am–5pm, Sun 9.30am–4.30pm; ⓣ01227/378100, ⓦwww.canterbury.co.uk).

Internet Dot Café, first floor, 21 St Dunstan's St (Mon–Sat 9am–9pm; £3/hr).

Accommodation

Arthouse B&B 24 London Rd ⓣ01227/453032, ⓦwww.arthousebandb.com. A ten-minute walk from the centre, this unique arty B&B in an old fire station makes up with character what it lacks in the number of rooms (just two). Doubles £55.

Kipps Hostel 40 Nunnery Fields ⓣ01227/786121, ⓦwww.kipps-hostel.com. Homely independent hostel near Canterbury East station and an easy walk to the centre. There's a communal kitchen, free wi-fi and a garden with space for a couple of tents. Dorms £16, doubles/twins £45.

Eating and drinking

Canterbury can be an expensive town for food if you're trying to avoid the chain restaurants, with some surprisingly upmarket places, but there are some excellent budget finds tucked away.

Boho Café Bar 27 High St. Enter *Boho*'s world of Calavera skulls, flock wallpaper and chandeliers for delicious breakfasts, posh sandwiches, fish dishes and steak. Breakfast from £3. Mon 9am–5pm, Tues–Sat 9am–9pm, Sun 10am–5pm.

The Farmhouse 11 Dover St. Trendy but relaxed bar-restaurant with retro 1950s furniture and statement wallpaper serving Modern British cuisine all day, at some of the best prices in town. Live music and DJs at weekends (small entry fee). Pie and mash £5. Tues–Thurs 9am–midnight, Fri–Sat 9am–2am, Sun 11am–5pm.

Goods Shed Canterbury West station. Top-notch local picnic ingredients and cheap lunch specials in this atmospheric café and farmers' market. Tues–Sat 9am–7pm, Sun till 4pm.

Thomas Becket 21 Best Lane. Lively independent pub, tucked down a backstreet, with guest ales, Sunday roasts and an impressively adorned ceiling dripping with hops. Daily 10am–midnight.

Moving on

Train Brighton (change at Ashford International; hourly; 2hr 15min); Dover (hourly; 30min); London St. Pancras (hourly; 1hr); London Victoria (every 30min; 1hr 45min); London Charing Cross via Waterloo East and London Bridge (every 30min; 1hr 40min).

Bus Dover (hourly; 40min); London (hourly; 2hr).

BRIGHTON

BRIGHTON has been a magnet for day-tripping Londoners since the Prince Regent (later George IV) started holidaying here in the 1770s with his mistress, launching a trend for the "dirty weekend". One of Britain's most entertaining seaside resorts, the city has emerged from seediness to embrace a new, fashionable hedonism, becoming one of the country's gay centres. This factor – along with a large student presence – has endowed Brighton with a buzzing nightlife scene, and there's a colourful music and arts festival (ⓦwww.brightonfestival.org), which runs for three weeks in May.

What to see and do

From the train station on Queen's Road it's a ten-minute stroll straight down to the seafront, a four-mile-long pebble beach bordered by a balustraded promenade.

The seafront

The wonderfully tacky half-mile-long **Palace Pier** is an obligatory call; it's a huge amusement arcade, peppered with booths selling fish and chips, candyfloss and the famous Brighton rock. A less garish option is the oldest electric railway in the world, **Volk's Electric Railway** (Easter to mid-Sept daily 10/11am–5/6pm; every 15min; £3 return), whose antiquated locomotives run eastward towards the marina and the nudist beach.

The Royal Pavilion and around

Inland, wedged between the Lanes and North Laine (see opposite), and flanked by the Theatre Royal is the square known as Pavilion Gardens, home to the flamboyant **Royal Pavilion** (daily: April–Sept 9.30am–5pm; Oct–March 10am–4.30pm; £9.80; ⓣ03000/290900, ⓦwww.brighton-hove-rpml.org.uk). The closest you'll get to the Taj Mahal in Britain, the Royal Pavilion is a wedding-cake confection of pagodas, minarets and domes built in 1817 as a pleasure palace for the Prince Regent. Its interior is even more impressive than the exterior, decorated with ostentatious chandeliers and exotic chinoiserie. Opposite the Pavilion is the **Brighton Museum and Art Gallery** (Tues–Sun 10am–5pm plus Monday bank hols; free; same contact details as the Pavilion), worth a visit for its displays of twentieth-century

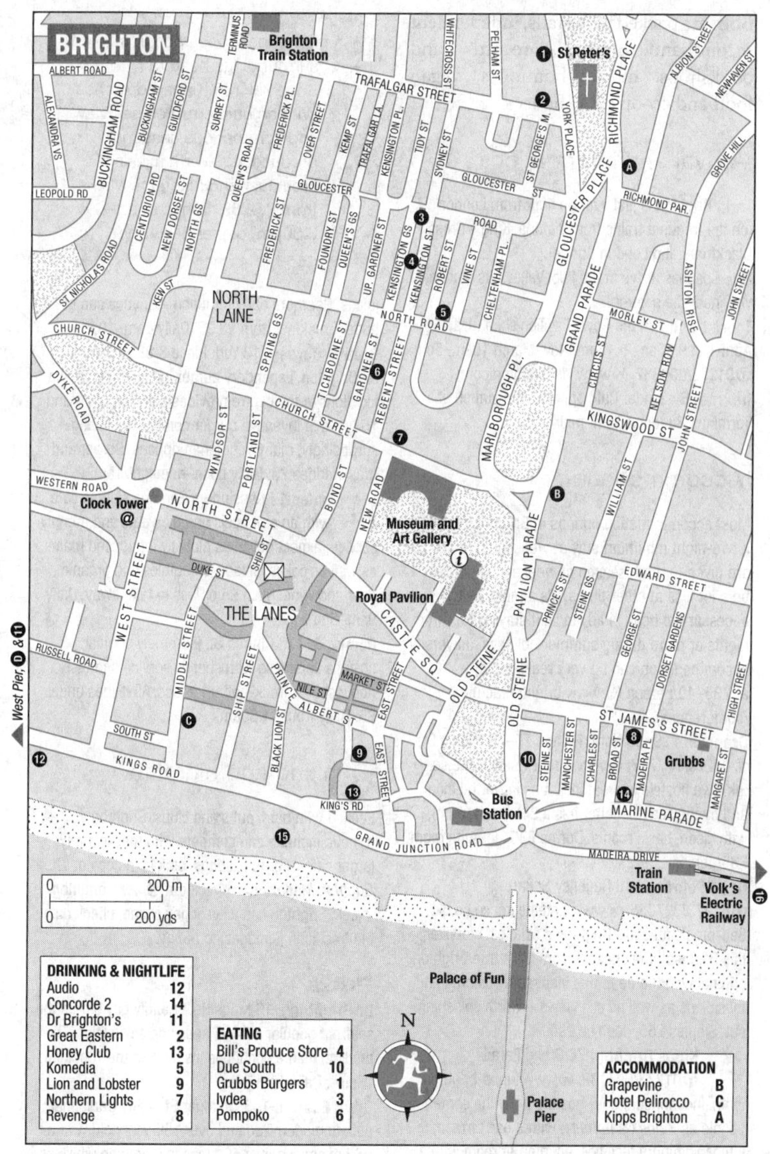

design and a pair of the corpulent Prince Regent's enormous trousers.

The Lanes and North Laine

Between the seafront and Trafalgar Street lie Brighton's "lanes", offering some of the UK's best shopping. The narrow alleys of **The Lanes** preserve the layout of the fishing port that Brighton once was, while to the north the arty, bohemian quarter of **North Laine** is not in fact one road but many thin streets.

Both are packed with stalls, independent secondhand clothes-, record- and bookshops, quirky boutiques, vegan food and co-op coffeehouses.

Arrival and information

Train Brighton is just over an hour from London (on the frequent trains from Victoria, King's Cross, Blackfriars and London Bridge).
Bus Coaches arrive at the Pool Valley bus station, very near the seafront.
Tourist office At the Royal Pavilion shop (daily: April–Oct 9.30am–5.15pm; Nov–March 10am–5pm; ⓣ01273/290337, ⓦwww.visitbrighton.com).
Internet Bystander Café opposite the station at 1 Terminus Rd (open 7am–midnight).

Accommodation

Most accommodation options in Brighton require a two-night minimum stay at weekends. Prices are given for high season at weekends and can be a lot less at other times. It's almost always necessary to book in advance. If staying for three nights or more during summer holidays, university accommodation can be very reasonable, at £35–40/person (ⓦwww.brighton.ac.uk/conferences).

Grapevine 29–30 North Rd and 75–76 Middle St, ⓣ01273/777717, ⓦwww.grapevinewebsite.co.uk. Two hostels in great locations in North Laine and by the sea (the latter has a 24hr restaurant), with clean, basic rooms. Dorms £30, en-suite room £35/person.

Hotel Pelirocco 10 Regency Square ⓣ01273/327055, ⓦwww.hotelpelirocco.co.uk. Self-proclaimed as "Brighton's sauciest stopover" this B&B isn't the cheapest, but it's a true Brighton original with theme rooms inspired by cinema and musicians as well as sea views – worth splashing out. Singles £55, doubles £90.

Kipps Brighton 76 Grand Parade ⓣ01273/604182, ⓦwww.kipps-brighton.com. Independent cosy hostel run by the same people as *Kipps Canterbury*, with a bar, terrace, kitchen, laundry facilities, an internet room with a tropical feel, and wi-fi. Breakfast £2. Dorms £24.50, doubles £72.

Eating

Bill's Produce Store 100 North Rd. Airy warehouse shop/café, popular for its beautifully presented brunches, fresh smoothies and juices. Get there early for lunch – queues can be huge. Breakfast from £3.95. Daily 8am–10pm.

TREAT YOURSELF

For superior seafood in relaxed surroundings head to **Due South** at 139 Kings Rd Arches. With an uninterrupted sea view and scrumptious seasonal produce, it's worth missing breakfast and lunch for. Mains from £12.50. Lunch noon–3.30pm, dinner 6–9.45pm.

Grubbs Burgers 13 York Place & 89 St James' St, Brighton. Legendary burger institution with two locations in the centre provides a choice of around 15 types of inventive burger combos, including, surprisingly, many vegetarian options. Burger and fries/wedges £5. Daily noon–midnight/1am.

Iydea 17 Kensington Gardens. Veggie café with an emphasis on quick eats and friendly service; expect delicious globally influenced mains, as well as cakes, salads, smoothies and organic beer and wine. Main £5 or less to take away. Daily 9am–5pm.

Pompoko 110 Church St. Extremely popular no-frills Japanese with speedy service and tasty rice dishes at rock-bottom prices. All dishes under £5. Daily from 11.30am.

Drinking and nightlife

Packed with bars, pubs and clubs, Brighton's frenetic nightlife can compete with that of many larger cities. For full listings, pick up a copy of *The Brighton Magazine* or check out ⓦwww.brighton.co.uk. Brighton has a lively gay scene; check out the free listings magazine *3Sixty*.

Pubs

Dr Brighton's 16 Kings Rd. Friendly gay bar on the seafront popular with all ages and sexualities. The medical theme continues inside with the "Cocktail Clinic". Daily 1pm–late.

Great Eastern 103 Trafalgar St. A tiny traditional pub, unmodernized and over 150 years old with a USP of serving over 50 types of American whiskies. Live music on Thursday and traditional roast lunches on Sunday. Daily noon–midnight.

Lion and Lobster 24 Silwood St ⓣ01273/327299. A classic pub serving excellent food in rambling dining quarters (book at weekends), and a two-storey outdoor terrace. Mains £8. Mon–Thurs 11am–1am, Fri–Sat 11am–2am, Sun noon–midnight.

Northern Lights 6 Little East St. Eat reindeer pasta and drink Fisherman's-Friend-flavoured vodka under blue and green lights at this compact Scandinavian bar with friendly staff and classic rock. Smörgåsbord for two £9. Mon–Thurs 5pm–midnight, Fri–Sat noon–2am, Sun 3pm–midnight.

Clubs and live music

Audio 10 Marine Parade Ⓦwww.audiobrighton.com. "A clubber's club", it proclaims on its website, and one of Brighton's best; draws some big-name acts and DJs from all genres. Club nights Wed–Sat, bar open daily.

Honey Club 214 Kings Rd Arches, Ⓦwww.thehoneyclub.co.uk. By the seafront near the bottom of Ship St, this attracts a youngish crowd, dancing to garage, house R&B and hip-hop. Club nights Tues & Thurs–Sun.

Komedia 44 Gardner St Ⓦwww.komedia.co.uk. Cool venue offering everything from cabaret and comedy to rock gigs, club nights and spoken word. Café open from 10am daily; for evening event times see website.

Revenge 32 Old Steine Ⓦrevenge.co.uk. Two-floor, predominantly gay venue also featuring cabaret. Bar open daily; club nights Tues & Thurs–Sat.

Moving on

Train Canterbury (change at Ashford International hourly; 2hr 20min); Gatwick airport (every 15min; 25–40min); London (every 15min; 1hr 15min).

Bus Gatwick airport (hourly; 1hr); London (hourly; 2hr).

The West Country

England's **West Country** is not a precise geographical term, but as a broad generalization, the cosmopolitan feel of the southeast begins to fade into a slower, rural pace of life from **Salisbury** onwards, becoming more pronounced the further west you travel. In Neolithic times a rich and powerful culture evolved here, shown by monuments such as **Stonehenge** and **Avebury**. Urban attractions include vibrant **Bristol** and the elegant Regency spa town of **Bath**, while those in search of rural peace and quiet should head for the compelling bleakness and ancient woods of **Dartmoor**. The south-western extremities of Britain include some of the most beautiful stretches of coastline: with rugged, rocky shores and excellent white sandy beaches, **Cornwall** is one of the country's busiest corners over the summer.

SALISBURY

Modern **SALISBURY** was founded after clergy living in the fort at **Old Sarum**, two miles north of the city, moved down the valley and created a walled sanctuary and the magnificent cathedral at the site where five rivers meet. Unlike most British towns, the centre follows a grid pattern, so it is easy to find your way from the train station off Fisherton Street east over the River Avon to the bus station and Market Square (market on Tues & Sat), or to the Cathedral south down the High Street through North Gate.

What to see and do

The city's dominant feature is the elegant spire of its **cathedral** (Mon–Sat 9am–5pm, Sun noon–4pm; £5.50 donation includes 45min tour or £8.50 for 1hr 45min tour including spire; Ⓦwww.salisburycathedral.org.uk), the tallest in the country, rising over 400ft. The cathedral was almost entirely completed in the thirteenth century. Don't miss the world's oldest working clock, dating to 1386, which resides in the north aisle. A lofty octagonal **chapterhouse**, approached via the cloisters (Mon–Sat 9.30/10am–4.30pm, Sun 12.45–3.45pm; free), holds one of the four extant copies of the 1215 **Magna Carta**, England's most famous constitutional document, as well as one of the finest medieval friezes in Europe depicting famous Old Testament stories.

Most of Salisbury's remaining sights are grouped in a sequence of graceful historic houses around **Cathedral Close**. The **Salisbury and South Wiltshire Museum** on West Walk (Mon–Sat 10am–5pm, plus Sun noon–5pm in July–Aug; £6; Ⓦwww.salisburymuseum.org.uk) is a good place to bone up on the Neolithic history of the region before heading out to Stonehenge.

Arrival and information

Train On the northwest edge of town, a 10min walk to the cathedral or a 30min stroll through town to *Salisbury YHA*.
Bus Buses terminate behind Endless St, a short walk northeast of the cathedral.
Tourist office Fish Row, just off Market Square (Mon–Sat 9.30am–5.30pm, plus Sun July–Aug 11am–3pm; Ⓣ01722/334956, Ⓦwww.visitsalisbury.com).

Accommodation

Alderbury Caravan & Camping Park Southampton Rd, Whaddon Ⓣ01722/710125 Ⓦwww.alderburycaravanpark.co.uk. Three miles south of Salisbury, this pleasant and friendly campsite is easily reached on bus #X7 from the city centre (15min). Pitch £13–19.
Salisbury YHA Milford Hill House, Milford Hill Ⓣ0845/371 9537, Ⓦwww.yha.org.uk. Excellent secluded hostel 10min walk east of the city centre. Dorms £21, rooms £51.

Eating and drinking

Gallery Café at Fisherton Mill 108 Fisherton St. Fantastic café-cum-art-and-craft gallery where you'll as likely get a great stone-baked bread sandwich (£5.50) as watch sculptors or milliners at their craft. Tues–Sat 10am–5pm.
Haunch of Venison 1 Minster St. Tiny, atmospheric old pub supposedly home to the ghost of the "Demented Whist Player", whose amputated mummified hand resides in a nook in a side room as a warning to card game cheats everywhere. Also boasts an outstanding whisky selection.
Moloko 5 Bridge St. Self-consciously "cool", this vodka bar opens till late. From 7pm, closed Mon.

Moving on

Train Bath (hourly; 55min); Bristol (hourly; 1hr 10min); Exeter (for Dartmoor; every 1–2hr; 2hr); London (every 25–35min; 1hr 30min).
Bus Bath (1 daily; 1hr 20min); Bristol (1 daily; 2hr 10min); London (3 daily; 2hr 45min).

STONHENGE AND AVEBURY

In deepest darkest Wilshire, between Salisbury and Bath, the countryside was once home to a thriving Neolithic civilization, the greatest legacy of which is **Stonehenge** (daily 9/9.30am–4/7pm; last admission 30min prior to closing time; £7.50; EH). Built in several distinct stages and adapted to the needs of successive cultures, the first stones were raised about 3500 BC and during the next six hundred years, the incomplete blue-stone circle was transformed into the familiar formation observed today. The way in which the sun's rays penetrate the enclosure at dawn on midsummer's day has led to speculation about Stonehenge's role as either an astronomical observatory or a place of sun worship. During normal visiting hours the stones are cordoned off – you see them from about 100m away. The only way to enter the circle itself is to **pre-book** for entry outside standard visiting hours (£13.70; Ⓣ01722/343830, Ⓦwww.english-heritage.org.uk), or to go on the evening of the summer solstice, where tens of thousands of revellers party at the stones until sunrise (see the website for details). Get there from Salisbury on the #X5 bus (hourly; £5.70 return) to Amesbury, then a two-mile walk. More conveniently, hop-on tour buses (every 30min–1hr from 9am–1pm; £11 return, or £18 including admission to both sites) run from Salisbury's train and bus stations.

Salisbury also serves as a base for visiting the Neolithic site around thirty miles north at **AVEBURY**. The **stone circles** were probably erected some 4000 years ago, and the main circle – with a diameter of some 1300ft – easily beats Stonehenge in terms of scale. Catch a guided tour (2 daily; £2; ask at the National Trust museums) to make the site come to life. The National Trust run two small **museums** in the village (daily 10/10.30am–4/6pm; £4.40 for both, £1 off if arriving by public transport) for more on the monoliths. From Salisbury bus station catch the #2 to Devizes, then change for the #49 to Avebury (1hr 30min–2hr). From Bath, try Mad Max tours who'll take you to both sites (daily; £17.50 for half day or £32.50 full day; ⓣ07990/505970, ⓦwww.madmaxtours.co.uk).

BATH

Bath is surely a contender for the prettiest city in Britain. It became an important city under the Romans who worshipped at the hot springs, creating the eponymous **baths**, one of Britain's top sights. Revived and reconstructed in the eighteenth century as a retreat for the wealthy and fashionable, the city has a harmonious and elegant look, constructed from the local honey-coloured sandstone – the city still retains the genteel air of refinement Jane Austen satirized in her novels *Persuasion* and *Northanger Abbey*. However, the large student population makes this a vibrant city and there are numerous festivals throughout the year, such as the eclectic two-week International Music Festival and, naturally, the Jane Austen Festival when a regency dress parade takes place. See ⓦwww.visitbath.co.uk for all festivals.

What to see and do

Bounded on three sides by the River Avon, Bath's core is relatively compact. From Bath Spa train station, head north along Manvers Street which becomes Pierrepoint Street in the direction of Pulteney Bridge and turn off left up York Street to reach the Abbey, Roman Baths and tourist office. Carry on winding northwest from the Abbey until you reach Queen Square and walk through Royal Victoria Park to reach the most famous streets in Bath, the Royal Crescent and Royal Circle.

The Roman Baths and Bath Abbey

The Romans considered natural hot springs a gift from the gods, and Bath's, being the only ones in Britain, received very special treatment when they conquered in 43 AD. Hidden underground for years, the springs were rediscovered by the Victorians and made into the wonderfully interactive **Roman Baths museum** (daily: March–June & Sept–Oct 9am–6pm; July & Aug 9am–10pm; Nov–Feb 9.30am–5.30pm; last entry 1hr before closing; £13; ⓦromanbaths.co.uk). Highlights include the almost perfectly preserved bronze head of Minerva, Roman goddess of the sacred spring, a large portion of the decorative front of the Temple that would have stood as part of the bath complex, as well as the extensive warren of spa rooms. The **Pump Room**, built in the eighteenth century, is now a restaurant and tearoom; the Roman Baths entrance ticket entitles you to a free glass of the tepid ferrous spa water inside.

The Royal Crescent and Assembly Rooms

The best of Bath's eighteenth-century architecture is on the high ground to

TREAT YOURSELF

Follow in the footsteps of the Romans and pamper yourself in stylish, contemporary surroundings at **Thermae Bath Spa** (daily 9am–10pm; ⓦwww.thermaebathspa.com), Britain's only natural hot spa. A two-hour session, with access to the spectacular open-air rooftop pool, costs £25.

the north of the town centre, where the well-proportioned Georgian urban planning is showcased by the elegant **Circus** and adjacent **Royal Crescent**.

It was here that the social calendar of Bath's elite was centred at the **Assembly Rooms** (daily 10.30am–5/6pm; £2, or included with entry to the Fashion Museum), just east of the Circus. The building also houses the fascinating **Fashion Museum** (same hours; £7.25 or joint ticket with Roman Baths £16; ⓦwww.fashionmuseum.co.uk).

Arrival and information

Train and bus The train and bus stations are both on Dorchester St at the end of Manvers St, 5min south of the Abbey.
Tourist office Just off the Abbey churchyard (Mon–Sat 9.30am–5/6pm, Sun 10am–4pm; ⓦvisitbath.co.uk). Free walking tours set off every day from the Pump Room at 10.30am & 2pm (Sat 10.30am only).
Internet @Internet, 13 Manvers St (9am–9pm).

Accommodation

Backpackers' Hostel 13 Pierrepoint St ⓣ01225/446787, ⓦwww.hostels.co.uk. Very shabby but relaxed hostel, centrally located with a party dungeon for nocturnal guests. Dorms £20.
Bath YHA Bathwick Hill ⓣ 0845/371 9303, ⓦwww.yha.org.uk. Stunning HI hillside villa a good mile uphill east of town with restaurant and bar; bus #18 or #U18. Dorms £20.
Bath YMCA Broad St Place ⓣ01255/325900, ⓦwww.ymca.co.uk. Large basic hostel in a pretty enclave in the centre of town, wi-fi and basic breakfast included. Dorms £20, doubles/twins £53.
White Hart Inn Widcombe Hill ⓣ01225/313985, ⓦwww.whitehartbath.co.uk. Well worth the 10min walk from the station, and although it is a bit further out from the centre, this old inn with a restaurant and bar downstairs offers simple but excellent-value accommodation. Dorms £15, twins £40.

Eating and drinking

Cafés and restaurants

Wild Cafe 10a Queen St. A trendy local favourite for brunch with great organic and fairtrade food, low prices and the boast that it is powered by renewable energy. Brunch £5.75. Mon–Thurs 8am–5pm, Fri 8am–7pm, Sat 9am–7pm, Sun 10am–5pm.
Lime Lounge 11 Margarets Buildings off Brock St. Cheap-and-cheerful café in between the Royal Crescent and Royal Circle. From inventive fry-ups to a £7 soup and sandwich deal to 2-4-1 main meals in the evening. Mon–Sat from 8am; Sun from 10am.
Yak Yeti Yak l2 Pierrepont St ⓣ01225/443473. Not the cheapest, but you may not get another Nepalese meal this good in Britain: splash out on the set meal (£12.50 for the vegetarian option) to get a real taste for the cuisine. Booking essential at weekends. Noon–2.30pm for lunch; from 5pm for dinner.

Pubs

The Bell 103 Walcot St. Everything you could want from a neighbourhood pub with a range of beers, a mixed and lively crowd, garden and live music most days, plus bargain wood-fired pizza (£5.50).
The Porter 2 Miles Buildings, George St. Something of a Bath institution with great vegan & vegetarian food and live music downstairs. Next door is *Moles*, the best place to see live music in Bath and with regular club nights.
The Raven 6–7 Queen St. Not content with its reputation for its microbrewed ales, relaxed atmosphere and evening entertainments like storytelling, this pub also serves up fantastic pies.

Moving on

Train Bristol (every 20min; 11–20min); London (every 30min; 1hr 30min); Oxford (change at Didcot Parkway; every 30min–1hr; 1hr 10min–1hr 40min); Salisbury (hourly; 55min).
Bus Bristol (every 20min; 1hr); Glastonbury (1 direct daily from Bath Spa; 1hr), London (every 30min; 2hr 40min–4hr).

BRISTOL

Situated on a succession of chunky hills twelve miles west of Bath and just inland from the mouth of the River Avon, **BRISTOL** grew rich on transatlantic trade – the slave trade, in particular – in the early part of the nineteenth century. It remains a wealthy, commercial centre, and is home to a population of around 450,000, a major university, a thriving music scene that produced some of the most significant bands of the Nineties (Portishead, Tricky, Massive Attack), and Banksy – guerrilla artist and agent provocateur whose subversive stencils adorn neglected city walls throughout the world. More ethnically diverse than other cities in the Southwest, Bristol manages to combine clued-up arty urban culture with enticing green spaces and striking industrial architecture. In August, the city hosts Europe's largest hot-air balloon fiesta – a spectacular sight.

What to see and do

The city centre is an elongated traffic interchange, known as the **Centre Promenade**. Walking from the station, detour via the church of **St Mary Redcliffe** (Mon–Sat 9am–4/5pm), a glorious Gothic confection begun in the thirteenth century, before continuing across the river, through elegant Queen's Square. The southern end of the centre gives way to the city's **Floating Harbour**, an area of waterways that formed the hub of the old port. It is now the location of numerous bars and restaurants as well as two of Bristol's contemporary arts venues: the **Arnolfini** (Ⓦwww.arnolfini.org.uk; free), a cool, white gallery and performing arts space, and the **Watershed Arts Centre** (Ⓦwww.watershed.co.uk), which has an excellent café. Behind the Watershed lies **at-Bristol** (daily 10am–5/6pm; £11.90; Ⓦwww.at-bristol.org.uk), a hands-on science centre and planetarium geared towards kids. Just to the north of here, **College Green** is overlooked by the city's nineteenth-century **cathedral** and the curvaceous red-brick Council House. A short walk west along the southern side of the harbour, or a brief ride on the ferry (70p; 2min), brings you to Isambard Kingdom Brunel's majestic **ss Great Britain** (daily 10am–4.30/5.30pm; £12.50; Ⓦwww.ssgreatbritain.org) the world's first propeller-driven iron ship, which first launched from here in 1843.

The main road leading north from the centre, **Stokes Croft**, has become the city's cultural pulse as artists and creative types have turned what was until recently a grotty road littered with derelict buildings into a buzzing and fashionable part of the city with an array of vintage shops, cool cafés and street art.

Clifton

Reached by #8 bus from the Centre Promenade, genteel **Clifton Village** is a great place to wander with airy terraces, enticing pubs and upmarket antiques shops. Overhanging the limestone abyss of the Avon gorge is the **Clifton Suspension Bridge**, another creation of the indefatigable engineer Brunel. From the Clifton side of the Suspension Bridge, **the Downs**, the city's largest green space, stretches north for a couple of miles. On the way back down to the centre, don't miss the **City Museum and Art Gallery** (daily 10am–5pm; free; Ⓦwww.bristol.gov.uk/museums), home to Banksy's controversial *Paint Pot Angel* sculpture.

Arrival and information

Air Bristol airport is eight miles south of town. Regular buses run to the stations and the city centre.
Train The main station, Bristol Temple Meads, is a 5min bus ride southeast of the centre (bus #8 or # 9), or a 15min walk.
Bus Close to the Broadmead shopping centre on Marlborough St.
Tourist office E Shed, Canons Rd, just off Centre Promenade on the water (daily 10am–5/6pm; Ⓣ0906/7112191, Ⓦvisitbristol.co.uk). Website has a useful "Bristol on a Budget" section including free downloadable audio walking tours.
Internet *Bristol YHA* (see below) has a pleasant café with internet access (£3/hr).

Accommodation

Bristol Backpackers 17 St Stephen's St Ⓣ0117/9257900, Ⓦbristolbackpackers.co.uk (bookings by phone only). Loud, convivial place in the heart of the centre, with late bar and internet access. Dorms £16, twins £38.
Bristol YHA 14 Narrow Quay Ⓣ0845/371 9726, Ⓦwww.yha.org.uk. Splendidly situated hostel in an old wharfside building next to the Arnolfini. Dorms £20, twins £46.

Clifton House 4 Tyndall's Park Rd ⓣ0117/9355407, ⓦcliftonhousebristol.com. Elegant B&B in Clifton behind the museum with triple and quad rooms. Full English breakfast included. Doubles £65.

Eating

For food on the go, try St Nicolas' Market, Corn St (Mon–Sat 9.30am–5pm), with a huge array of local and ethnic food stalls.

Boston Tea Party 75 Park St, 97 Whiteladies Rd & 1 Princess Victoria St, Clifton. Chain of cafés dotted around the Southwest, each with its own personality. With an emphasis on locally sourced produce. Coffee & cake £5. Mon–Sat 8am–6pm, Sun 9am–6pm; Park St branch open till 8pm daily.

Canteen 80 Stokes Croft. In a refurbished 1960s office block this cooperative-run bar with restaurant serves subsidized delicacies such as pan-fried lamb's liver with chorizo or mussels in cider, plus soup, for just £6.50. Plus live alternative music for all tastes in the evening. Sister venue *No. 1 Harbourside*, next to the tourist office at 1 Canon's Rd, serves similarly fantastic and cheap food, also with live music every evening. Both venues open for lunch and music starts around 9.30pm or from 4pm Sun.

Mud Dock 40 The Grove. Bike shed café-restaurant on the quayside, with a bargain £5 weekday lunch and great views from their balcony over the water. Mon 10am–5pm, Tues–Sat 10am–10pm, Sun 10am–5pm.

Thali Cafe 12 York Rd, Montpellier, 1 Regent St, Clifton & 1 William St, across the river from Temple Meads. Colourful mini-chain of Bristol Indian restaurants serving up a fantastic range of street food and thalis on the cheap (£7.95). All branches open daily from 6pm; St Mark's Rd branch open daily from 10am; Regent St branch open from 10am Sat–Sun.

Drinking and nightlife

For nightlife and music listings check out the magazine *Venue* (ⓦwww.venue.co.uk) available at any newsagent. The Arnolfini and Watershed both have superb arts cinemas, and there's a renowned theatre company at the Old Vic on King St (ⓦwww.bristololdvic.org.uk).

Apple Welsh Back, at the end of King St. A fantastic array of West Country ciders, cider cocktails, all served on a floating canal boat on the harbour. Daily 11am–midnight, Sun till 10.30pm.

Coronation Tap 8 Sion Place. A Clifton institution, famous for its Exhibition Cider, a lethal brew restricted to half-pint measures. A must if you want to sample the West Country's regional tipple. Mon–Fri from 5.30pm, Sat & Sun from 7pm.

Croft 117–119 Stokes Croft ⓦwww.the-croft.com. Showcases progressive home-grown bands and DJs from all genres, every night of the week. Small cover charge to get in (from £3).

Old Duke 45 King St. Named after Duke Ellington, this place is a convivial music-lovers' pub with an emphasis on jazz. Near the water with live music every night. Open from noon; bands on from 8.30pm and 12.30pm on Sunday.

Thekla The Grove ⓦtheklabristol.co.uk. Legendary riverboat venue staging eclectic events, gigs and Bristol's best club nights. Thurs–Sat 10pm–3am or later.

GLASTONBURY FESTIVAL

The world-famous **Glastonbury Festival** (ⓦwww.glastonburyfestivals.co.uk; last weekend in June) is one of the West Country's biggest draws. When first hosted in 1970, this small-scale event cost £1, but nowadays it draws 175,000-plus people to its binge of music and hedonism – the £175 tickets sell out in hours. The cost may be exorbitant, but there's still nothing else quite like it.

Moving on

Train Bath (every 20min; 11–20min); Cardiff (every 20min; 35–50min); Exeter for Dartmoor (every 30min; 1hr 15min); Penzance (5 daily; 4hr 15min); Oxford via Reading (every 30min–1hr; Salisbury (hourly; 1hr 10min); York (hourly; 4hr). 1hr 20min),

Bus Bath (every 20min; 1hr); Cardiff (every 1–2hr; 1hr 10min); Glastonbury (some via Wells; every 30min; 1hr 20min); Oxford (1 daily; 2hr 50min); Penzance (5 daily; 7hr); Salisbury (1 daily; 2hr 10min).

DARTMOOR

DARTMOOR, an expanse of uplands some 75 miles southwest of Bristol, is one of England's most beautiful wilderness areas. It's home to an indigenous breed of **wild pony** and dotted with **tors**, natural outcrops of granite. The area is renowned for outdoor pursuits, from cycling and horseriding to canoeing and climbing. Don't go unprepared, especially if you plan to camp, as the moor has an unforgiving weather system and explorers regularly get lost in its thick fogs.

The **northern** part of the moor is more easily accessible from Exeter while the **southern moor** is best approached from Plymouth. Check out ⓦwww.dartmoor-npa.gov.uk to help plan your trip. There are three **tourist offices** in the park: the Haytor information centre (daily April–Sept 10am–5pm; Oct 10am–4pm; Nov–March Thurs–Sun 10.30am–3.30pm; ⓣ01364/661520); Postbridge information centre (April–Sept 10am–5pm; Oct 10am–4pm; ⓣ01822/880272); and the main High Moorland Visitor Centre in Princetown (same hours as Haytor; ⓣ01822/890414). For **accommodation**, try the remote and cosy *YHA* hostel a mile south of Postbridge at Bellever (ⓣ0845/371 9622, ⓦwww.yha.org.uk; dorms £20, small discount for arrival on foot/bike), or *Sparrowhawk Backpackers*, 45 Ford St, Moretonhampstead (ⓣ01647/440318, ⓦwww.sparrowhawkbackpackers.co.uk; dorms £16, rooms £36).

There are **train** stations at Exeter, Newton Abbot, Totnes, Ivybridge and Plymouth, and **buses** run from those towns onto the Moor. The Haytor Hoppa bus runs on a Saturday (May–Oct) from Newton Abbott or Bovey Tracy (both serviced by frequent buses from Exeter) up to the northeast corner of the Moor.

Okehampton

The wildest parts of the moor, around its highest points of **High Willhays** and **Yes Tor** (which at over 2000ft classify them as southern England's only mountains), are a few miles south of the market town of **OKEHAMPTON**, served by regular buses from Plymouth and Exeter. Some of the starkly beautiful terrain around here is used by the Ministry of Defence as a firing range: details of times when it's safe to walk the moor are available from the MOD website (ⓦwww.mod.uk/access) and the **tourist office** (Mon–Sat 10am–4pm; ⓣ01837/53020, ⓦwww.okehamptondevon.co.uk), off Fore Street. Here you'll also find the excellent, if petite, **Museum of Dartmoor Life** (April–Oct 10.15am–4.30pm; Nov–Dec 11am–3pm, call for rest of winter opening hours; £3.50; ⓣ01837/52295). There's a *YHA* hostel and activity centre in a converted goods shed at the station (ⓣ0845/371 9651; camping £8, dorms £21).

PENZANCE AND AROUND

The busy market and port town of **PENZANCE** forms the natural gateway to the westernmost extremity of Cornwall, the Penwith Peninsula, and has the best transport links – all the major sights in the region can be reached on day-trips from here.

What to see and do

Although Penzance itself makes a pleasant base, the real attractions are a bus ride away along the coast.

St Michael's Mount

The view east across the bay is dominated by **St Michael's Mount** (ⓦwww.stmichaelsmount.co.uk), site of a fortified medieval monastery perched

CAMPING ON DARTMOOR

Camping wild on certain common land in Dartmoor is permitted for one or two nights, though you shouldn't pitch on farmland, within 100m of a road, house or on an archeological site; check out ⓦwww.dartmoor-npa.gov.uk/visiting/active-dartmoor/camping for a helpful map. Always obtain consent from the landowner if pitching on private land and follow the backpacking code of conduct.

THE EDEN PROJECT

One of Cornwall's major draws, occupying a 160-foot-deep disused clay pit, the **Eden Project** (April–Oct daily 9am–6pm; Nov–March Mon–Fri 10am–3pm, Sat & Sun 10am–6pm; last entry 1hr 30min before closing; £20; ticket valid for one year, discounts if arriving by public transport or booking online; Ⓦwww.edenproject.com) showcases the diversity of the planet's plant life in a stunningly landscaped site. The centrepiece is two vast geodesic "biomes", or conservatories, one holding plants more usually found in Mediterranean zones, and the larger housing the world's largest indoor rainforest. The Eden Project lies four miles northeast of St Austell in Bodelva (bus #101 from St Austell train station or #527 from Newquay). Arrive early and allow at least half a day for a full exploration.

on an offshore pinnacle of rock. At low tide, the Mount is joined by a cobbled causeway to the mainland village of Marazion (regular buses from Penzance); at high tide, a boat can ferry you over (£1.50 each way). You can amble partway along the Mount's shoreline, but most of the rock lies within the grounds of the **castle**, now a stately home (April–Oct 10.30am–5pm; closed Sat; £7).

The Minack Theatre

Clinging to a craggy cove near Porthcurno beach, seven miles west of Penzance, the **Minack Theatre** (daily: April–Sept 9.30am–5.30pm plus evening performances; Oct–March 10am–3.30pm; £4 entrance to site during day, performance prices vary; Ⓦwww.minack.com) is a splendid sight, a craggy amphitheatre using the sea as a backdrop and with seats carved into the rocks. From Penzance, buses #300 and #1A drop you in Porthcurno, from which it is a 400m steep climb to the theatre, or the #504 will take you all the way.

Arrival and information

Train and bus Both stations are at the north-eastern end of town, a step away from Market Jew St.

Travel card "Ride Cornwall" day ticket (£10; available from ticket offices) gives you unlimited access to buses and trains in the county, and to Plymouth in Devon.

Tourist office Just outside the train and bus stations. At the time of writing, the future of the tourist office in Penzance was uncertain; call ahead (Ⓣ01736/362207, Ⓦvisit-westcornwall.com) or try the Cornwall Information Line (Ⓣ0844/8889275).

Internet Penzance Computers, 36b Market Jew St (Mon–Sat 9am–6pm, Sun 10am–4pm; £3.75/hr).

Accommodation

Penzance Backpackers Alexandra Rd (no number; about halfway up) Ⓣ01736/363836, Ⓦwww.pzbackpack.com. Good independent hostel on a quiet tree-lined road 15min walk from the station. With kitchen and wi-fi. Dorms £16, rooms £36.

Penzance YHA Castle Horneck, Alverton Ⓣ0845/371 9653, Ⓦwww.yha.org.uk. Beautifully converted and refurbished Georgian manor house about a mile from the centre off the Land's End road. Dorms £18.40, rooms £51.

Whitesands Hotel Sennen, near Whitesand Bay and Land's End Ⓣ01736/871776, Ⓦwhitesandslodge.co.uk. In between Penzance and St Ives, this quirky hotel with themed rooms and a cheaper surf lodge with its own kitchen, as well as tipis and yurts. On-site bar, restaurant and barbecue. Buses from Land's End and St Ives stop outside. Tipis £16/person (at least 4 in group), dorms in surf lodge £21, en-suite double B&B £78.

Eating and drinking

Archie Browns Bread St. Welcoming veggie café and health food shop using locally sourced ingredients. Breakfasts and lunches from £4. Daytime only; closed Sun.

The Admiral Benbow 46 Chapel St. Friendly seventeenth-century pub crammed with maritime fittings.

The Turk's Head Chapel St. Ancient inn with a piratical heritage that includes a smugglers' tunnel. Touristy, but fun, and with great food.

Moving on

Train Bristol (5 daily; 4hr 15min), London (13 daily; 5hr 30min); Par (for Newquay; every 30min–1hr; 1hr); St Ives (change at St Erth; every 45min–1hr; 45–55min).
Bus Bristol (5 daily; 7hr); London (6 daily; 9hr); Newquay (3 daily; 2hr); St Ives (hourly; 50min).

ST IVES

Across the peninsula from Penzance, the fishing village of **ST IVES** is the quintessential Cornish resort, featuring a muddle of narrow streets lined with whitewashed cottages, sandy beaches, and squawking seagulls. The village's erstwhile tranquillity attracted several major artists throughout the twentieth century, including Ben Nicholson and Barbara Hepworth, and every other shop in town is a gallery making the most of its arty heritage. There is even a diminutive outpost of the **Tate gallery** empire here overlooking Porthmeor Beach (rotating exhibitions; daily 10am–4.20/5.20pm; closed Mon Nov–Feb; £5.65 or £8.55 combined with Barbara Hepworth Museum; ⓦwww.tate.org.uk/stives). The charming **Barbara Hepworth Museum and Garden** on Barnoon Hill (same hours as Tate St Ives; £4.65) preserves the studio of the modernist sculptor. Of the town's three beaches, the largest, north-facing **Porthmeor** occasionally has good surf; boards can be rented here. Alternatively, ramble along the costal path south towards **Zennor** for beautiful views of craggy coves and wild flowers.

The train **station** is at Porthminster Beach. The **St Ives Visitor and Information Centre** (daily 10am–4/5pm; ⓣ01736/797600; ⓦwww.visit-westcornwall.com), is in the Guildhall and you can find internet at Kawabunga's, 48 Fore St. Nearby, the rambling *St Ives Backpackers* **hostel** (ⓣ01736/799444, ⓦwww.backpackers.co.uk/st-ives; dorms £17.95, twins £40) occupies an enormous old Wesleyan chapel on The Stennack (note it has no internet facilities or locks on doors). Tuck into the best burgers in the southwest at *Blas Burgerworks*, the Warren, with a great choice for vegetarians, too (daily noon–10pm).

NEWQUAY

Buffeted by Atlantic currents, Cornwall's north coast is the area of the West Country most favoured by the **surfing** set. King of the surf resorts is tacky **NEWQUAY,** whose seven miles of golden sands, including Fistral Beach, hosts surfing championships. Equipment can be hired on most beaches or from one of the surf shops around town.

Newquay's **airport** is three miles north of the town; bus #556 runs to the centre. The **train station** (change in Par or Plymouth) is just east of the centre; buses terminate on Manor Road. There's a **tourist office** at Marcus Hill (Mon–Fri 9.15am–5.30pm, Sat–Sun 10am–4pm; ⓣ01637/854020, ⓦvisitnewquay.org) and numerous campsites and **hostels**, including the hospitable if rather cramped *Newquay International Backpackers*, 69 Tower Rd (ⓣ01637/879366, ⓦwww.backpackers.co.uk/newquay; dorms £19.95, twin room £42), and *Matt's Surf Lodge* at 110 Mount Wise (ⓣ01637/874651, ⓦwww.matts-surf-lodge.co.uk; dorms £20, twins £40; breakfast included).

Central England

Encompassing both the old industrial towns and cities of the Midlands and some postcard-pretty countryside, alongside some of England's major cultural landmarks, **CENTRAL ENGLAND** defies easy categorization. With close on a million residents, Birmingham is the Midlands' largest city, but despite boasting one of the best concert halls in the country, is still unlikely to feature on a whistle-stop national tour. More appealing for a quick-fix of history and culture are **Stratford-upon-Avon**, birthplace of William Shakespeare, and the rival university cities of **Oxford** and **Cambridge**.

OXFORD

Thoughts of **OXFORD** inevitably conjure up the university, revered as one of the world's great academic institutions. The city's skyline is dominated by its "dreaming spires", while its streets form a dense maze of historic honey-stone buildings, containing the university's 38 colleges. Although in term time you're never far from the university or its thousands of students, Oxford is a sizeable city, and the combination of workaday vitality with sleepy academic tradition is a distinct part of its appeal. Note that access to colleges may be restricted during examinations – especially in May and June – conferences and functions.

What to see and do

Start by ascending the spire of the University Church, **St Mary the Virgin**, on the High Street (Mon–Sat 9/9.30am–4.30/6pm, Sun 11.30am–5pm; £3; closed for renovation during the first half of 2012) to orientate yourself with fantastic panoramic views.

Christ Church College and the cathedral

One of the wealthiest and most ostentatious of Oxford's colleges, Christ Church (Mon–Sat 9am–4.30pm, Sun 2–4.30pm; £7.50), whose grand **dining hall** (often closed noon–2pm) featured in the *Harry Potter* films. The college chapel is in fact the city of Oxford's **Cathedral**. Christ Church's **Picture Gallery**, through the Canterbury Gate off Oriel Square (May–Sept Mon–Sat 10.30am–5pm, Sun 2–5pm; Oct–April Mon–Sat 10.30am–1pm & 2–4.30pm, Sun 2–4.30pm; £3 or £1.50 if paying to enter the college), is also worth a peek for its prestigious Old Master paintings and drawings.

Christ Church Meadow, Merton and Magdalen

South of Christ Church, **Christ Church Meadow** offers scenic views and gentle walks – either east along Broad Walk to the River Cherwell or south along New Walk to the Thames (referred to hereabouts as the Isis). From the Broad Walk, paths lead to **Merton** (Mon–Fri 2–5pm, Sat & Sun 10am–5pm; £2), among the oldest and prettiest of Oxford's colleges. Nearby Rose Lane emerges at the eastern end of the High Street opposite **Magdalen College** (pronounced "maudlin"; daily 1–4/6pm; £4.50), which boasts its own deer park and a prestigious college choir.

The Bodleian Library and around

Just north of the High Street span the buildings that make up the **Bodleian Library** (Mon–Fri 9am–5pm, Sat 9am–4.30pm, Sun 11am–5pm; by guided tour only, 6 tours daily; from

PUNTING IN OXBRIDGE

Hiring a punt – essentially a flat-bottomed Venetian-style gondola powered by a brave soul brandishing a pole – is one of the finest ways to experience both Oxford and Cambridge. In **Oxford**, Magdalen Bridge Boathouse (@www.oxfordpunting.co.uk), just past the college on the High Street rents punts, rowboats and pedaloes for £16–20 per hour. In **Cambridge**, a side street behind Trinity College has a range of shops offering the cheapest punts in town, at around £14 per hour, perfect for a cruise downstream past the architectural splendours of the college Backs or, for the adventurous, a trip upstream to rural Grantchester.

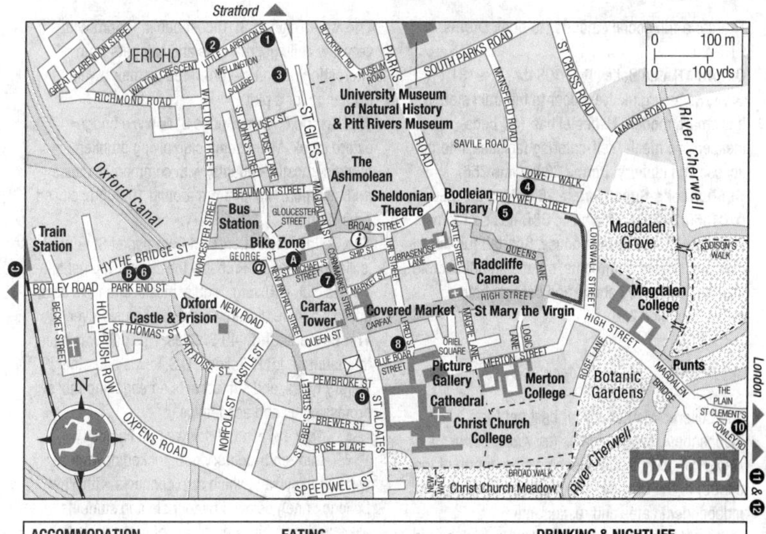

ACCOMMODATION		EATING		DRINKING & NIGHTLIFE	
Oxford Backpackers **B**	St Michael's Guest House **A**	Atomic Burger **11**	Edamamé **4**	The Bear **8**	The Eagle & Child **3**
Oxford YHA **C**		Big Bang **2**	G&D's **1, 9 & 12**	The Bridge **6**	Turf Tavern **5**
			Kazbar **10**	The Cellar **7**	

£4.50; ⓦwww.bodley.ox.ac.uk), the second largest collection of books in the country. The most dramatic library building (although inside it is just a reading room) is the Italianate **Radcliffe Camera** (twice-weekly guided tour only, booking essential £13; ⓣ01865/277224).

University museums

A couple of minutes' walk north along Parks Road and through the Natural History Museum lies the **Pitt Rivers Museum** (Tues–Sun 10am–4.30pm; free; ⓦwww.prm.ox.ac.uk). Its fascinating anthropological hoard includes totem poles, swords and opium pipes. Five minutes west of the Sheldonian is the mammoth Neoclassical edifice containing the **Ashmolean Museum** (Tues–Sun 10am–6pm; free; ⓦwww.ashmolean.org), displaying an array of Islamic, Indian and Oriental antiquities, a good selection of Pre-Raphelite paintings and a Stradivari "Messiah" violin dating to 1716.

Arrival and information

Train From Oxford's train station, it's a 5min walk to the centre.

Bus Long-distance buses terminate at Gloucester Green bus station.

Tourist office 15 Broad St (Mon–Sat 9.30am–5pm, Sun 10am–4pm; ⓣ01865/252200, ⓦwww.visitoxfordandoxfordshire.com).

Bike rental Bike Zone at 28–32 St Michael's St, off Cornmarket St (ⓣ01865/728877), is £18/day.

Internet *Coffee Republic* at the corner of New Inn Hall St and George St does coffee, snacks, free wi-fi or internet booths for £3/hr (daily 7am–8pm, Sun from 9am).

Accommodation

Oxford has a good choice of hostels, and out of term time, some colleges also make student rooms available to tourists (ⓦoxfordrooms.co.uk). Wherever you stay, it's advisable to book in advance.

Oxford Backpackers 9a Hythe Bridge St ⓣ01865/721761, ⓦwww.hostels.co.uk. Very backpacker friendly; no extra charges for anything including internet and wi-fi, lockers, linen, towels, use of the kitchen and breakfast.

There's a full social calendar to boot. Dorms £15–20.

Oxford YHA 2a Botley Rd ⓣ0845/371 9131 ⓦwww.yha.org.uk. Next door to the train station, this smart, modern HI hostel has 184 beds, inexpensive meals, self-catering facilities, internet access and laundry. Dorms £20, twins £56.

St Michael's Guest House 26 St Michael's St ⓣ01865/242101. This basic B&B has six rooms in a three-storey terrace house. Spartan furnishings and shared bathrooms, but it's an unbeatable location. Book well ahead and confirm before arrival. Doubles £56.

Eating

The Covered Market is your best bet for independent, daytime cafés (try *Alpha Bar* or *Georgina's*), while the Jericho district (north of the centre) or the Cowley Rd out east are great for independent cafés and restaurants.

Atomic Burger 96 Cowley Rd. With comic books for wallpaper and breakfasts named after John Hughes characters, this place is an ode to Americana. As for burgers, there's a choice from Magnum P.I. (with pineapple; £8) or the plain Forrest Gump (£6.75). All available in beef, chicken or veggie. Daily 10am–10.30pm.

Big Bang 124 Walton St, Jericho. Good British gourmet sausages and quality mash, as well as great breakfasts. Sometimes accompanied by live jazz. The £6.50 lunch menu's a bargain. Daily from 10am.

Edamamé 15 Holywell St. Terrific Japanese food at modest prices – it's no wonder the queue for this tiny restaurant snakes down the street. Mains from £6. Closed all day Mon & Tues, and Wed & Sun eve.

G&D's *George & Davis* 5 Little Clarendon St, Jericho; *George & Danver* 94 St Aldates; *George & Delila* 104 Cowley Rd. Fantastic Oxford mini-chain of ice-cream cafés – they make their own. Also great bagels & coffee. Daily 8am–midnight.

Kazbar 25–27 Cowley Rd. Authentic Spanish food served in a Morrocan ambience is a very winning combination. The mouthwatering array of tapas (normally £3–5) is half-price between 5–7pm weeknights or 3–4.30pm Sat–Sun. Also great as a bar with exotic cocktails and sangria. Mon–Fri eves only, Sat–Sun from noon.

Drinking and nightlife

For listings of gigs and other events, consult *Daily Info*, a poster put up in colleges and all around town (daily term time, otherwise weekly; ⓦwww.dailyinfo.co.uk).

The Bear 6 Alfred St. Oldest pub in Oxford with very low ceilings, real ales and snippets from interesting neckties – proffered by their owners in exchange for a pint.

The Bridge 6 Hythe Bridge St ⓦwww.bridgeoxford.co.uk. Mainstream club plying drunken punters (mostly students) with commercial dance, r'n'b and pop. Nightly from around 10.30pm; closed Tues & Sun.

The Cellar Frewin Court, off Cornmarket St ⓦwww.cellarmusic.co.uk. Probably the closest you get to a serious club in Oxford. Nightly music, often live acts, attracts a more discerning breed of music lover.

The Eagle & Child 49 St Giles. This pub was once the haunt of J.R.R. Tolkien, C.S. Lewis and other literary types, and still attracts an engaging mix of professionals and academics.

Turf Tavern Off Holywell St. Famous thirteenth-century pub, tucked down a winding alleyway (which also connects with New College Lane), beloved by tourists and students alike, with fine ales and plenty of outdoor seating.

Moving on

Train Bath (change at Didcot Parkway; every 30min–1hr; 1hr 10min–1hr 40min); London (every 20–30min; 1hr); Manchester (every 30min; 3hr); Stratford-upon-Avon (change at Banbury or Leamington Spa; hourly; 1hr 30min).

Bus Cambridge (every 30min; 3hr 20min); Heathrow Airport (every 30min; 1hr 30min); London (every 15min; 1hr 45min); Stratford-upon-Avon (daily; 1hr).

STRATFORD-UPON-AVON

The pretty town of **STRATFORD-UPON-AVON** is synonymous with its famous citizen, William Shakespeare, who was born here in 1564. The town revels in its links to the bard and successfully plays up the "merrie old England" image. Most people come to see the five attractively restored Shakespeare-related properties, but you could save your money and simply soak up the atmosphere by meandering along the river, lined with Tudor buildings.

What to see and do

Top of everyone's Bardic itinerary is **Shakespeare's Birthplace Museum** (daily April–Oct 9am–5/6pm, Nov–March 10am–4pm; £12.50 each or

THE ROYAL SHAKESPEARE COMPANY

Do not go to Stratford without seeing a play at the newly restored Royal Shakespeare Theatre (box office Mon–Sat 9am–8pm; ⓣ0844/800 1110, ⓦwww.rsc.org.uk) home to the fantastically talented **Royal Shakespeare Company**. The Company works on a repertory system, which means you could see three or four different plays in a visit of a few days (though not all by The Bard himself). Tickets start at £5 for standing room, rising to £58 for the best seats in the house. Note that the most popular shows get booked up months in advance.

combined ticket to all five houses £19.50; ⓦwww.shakespeare.org.uk) on Henley Street. Pass through the tacky visitor centre to the heavily restored building where the great man was born to gain some understanding of his beginnings. A short walk away on Chapel Street is **Nash's House**, once the property of Thomas Nash, first husband of Shakespeare's granddaughter, Elizabeth Hall. The house is kitted out with period furnishings and temporary exhibitions. Here there's also the **Dig for Shakespeare at New Place**, Shakespeare's family home when he moved back to Stratford from London. The house is long gone, now replaced with an archeological dig. A five-minute walk away, Old Town Street is home to the beautiful medieval **Hall's Croft**, former home of Shakespeare's eldest daughter, Susanna, and her husband, John Hall.

About half a mile west of the town centre in Shottery is the thatched, wood-beamed **Anne Hathaway's Cottage**, said to be where Shakespeare courted Anne. Two and a half miles from here (clearly signposted) is Shakespeare's mother's family home, now called **Mary Arden's Farm**; a classily recreated Tudor working farm complete with rare breed animals, as well as weavers, falconers and farmers in period costume.

Back in town, a short walk from Hall's Croft towards the river is the handsome **Holy Trinity Church** (Mon–Sat 9am–4/5/6pm winter/spring/summer, Sun 12.30–5pm year-round. William and Anne Shakespeare are buried here in the chancel (£2 donation).

Arrival and information

Train Stratford's train station is on the north-western edge of town, a 10min walk from the centre.

Bus Long-distance buses pull into the Riverside Station on the east side of the town centre, off Bridgeway.

Tourist office 62 Henley St (Mon–Sat 9am–5/5.30pm, Sun 10am–3/4pm; ⓣ01789/264 293 ⓦwww.shakespeare-country.co.uk).

Internet Cyber@Junction, 28 Greenhill St. £3.50/hr.

Accommodation

Hamlet House 52 Grove Rd ⓣ01789/204386 ⓦwww.hamlethouse.com. Friendly B&B 5min walk from the centre, with quirky themed rooms and a resident parrot named Dolly. Free internet, bike hire and jumbo breakfasts. En-suite room £65.

Stratford YHA Hemmingford House, Alveston ⓣ0870/770 6052, ⓦwww.yha.org.uk. Rambling Georgian mansion with its own café-bar on the edge of the pretty village of Alveston, two miles east of town. Buses #X15 and #X18 from Bridge St or bus station (last bus 11.40pm; 10min). Dorms from £10.

Eating and drinking

Hole in the Wall Guild St. Pizza kitchen and bar with a roof terrace and live music weekly. Good-value food and pop art Shakespeares on the walls. Lunch deal pizza & drink £6. Daily noon–late.

Old Thatch Tavern Market Place. The only thatched building in the centre of Stratford, and one of the only historic inns that hasn't lost its character, this independently run pub has good British food and ales.

Real Tea Café 40a Wood St. The perfect antidote to the multitude of twee tearooms, this funky café has 35 types of tea, each brewed to perfection. Mon–Sat 8.30am–6pm, Sun 10am–5pm.

Moving on

Train London Marylebone (5 daily; 2hr 15min); Oxford (change at Banbury or Leamington Spa; hourly; 1hr 30min);
Bus London (4 daily; 3hr 30min); Oxford (daily; 1hr).

CAMBRIDGE

Tradition has it that the University of **CAMBRIDGE** was founded by refugees from Oxford, who fled that town after one of their number was lynched by hostile townsfolk in the 1220s; there's been rivalry between the two institutions ever since, though nowadays it's manifested in the annual boat race. What distinguishes Cambridge from its counterpart is **"the Backs"**, the green swathe of land straddling the River Cam, which overlooks the backs of the old colleges, and provides the town's most enduring image of grand academic architecture. As in Oxford, access to the colleges may be restricted during examinations, conferences and functions. For four days in late July, the town hosts the popular **Cambridge Folk Festival** (Ⓦwww.cambridgefolkfestival.co.uk).

What to see and do

Cambridge city centre is bound to the west by the Cam and is dominated by historic university buildings. One logical place to start a tour is King's Parade, originally the medieval High Street.

King's College

Flanking King's Parade, **King's College** has a much-celebrated, extraordinarily beautiful **chapel** (term time Mon–Fri 9.30am–3.30pm, Sat 9.30am–3.15pm, Sun 1.15–2.30pm; rest of year Mon–Sat 9.30am–4.30pm, Sun 10am–5pm; £6.50; Ⓦwww.kings.cam.ac.uk) and is home to an equally vaunted choir (term time Evensong Mon–Sat 5.30pm, Sun 3.30pm). At the northern end of King's Parade, the **Senate House** is the scene of graduation ceremonies.

Trinity College

Just north of King's, **Trinity College** (Ⓦwww.trin.cam.ac.uk) is the largest of the Cambridge colleges. Beyond the Great Gate lies the vast asymmetrical expanse of Great Court, which displays a fine range of Tudor buildings, the oldest of which is the fifteenth-century clock tower – the annual race against its midnight chimes is now common currency thanks to the film *Chariots of Fire*. The west end of Nevile's Court is enclosed by the beautiful **Wren Library** (term time Mon–Fri noon–2pm, Sat 10.30am–12.30pm; rest of year Mon–Fri only; free). Back outside Trinity, it's a short hop to the River Cam, where you can go **punting** – the quintessential Cambridge pursuit (see box, p.174).

St John's College and the Round Church

Founded by Henry VII's mother, Lady Margaret Beaufort, **St John's College** (daily 10am–3.30/5.30pm, closed Christmas–Jan; £3.20) is worth a quick peek for its chapel ceiling depicting saints and scholars standing shoulder to shoulder, as well as its mishmash of architectural styles. The lovely **Bridge of Sighs**, modelled on its famous counterpart in Venice and built in 1813, links the college's New Court with Third Court. On Bridge Street, the strange and distinctive twelfth-century **Round Church** (Tues–Sat 10am–5pm, Sun 1–5pm; £2.50) is not only the second oldest building in the city, but also directly influenced by the Church of the Holy Sepulchre in Jerusalem.

Kettle's Yard

Kettle's Yard on Castle Street makes a refreshing break from the colleges (summer Tues–Sun 1.30–4.30pm; winter Tues–Sun 2–4pm; free Ⓦwww.kettlesyard.co.uk). The house is actually an amalgamation of four derelict cottages and was the vision of Jim Ede, curator of the Tate Gallery in the 1920s, and his wife Helen, who left it exactly

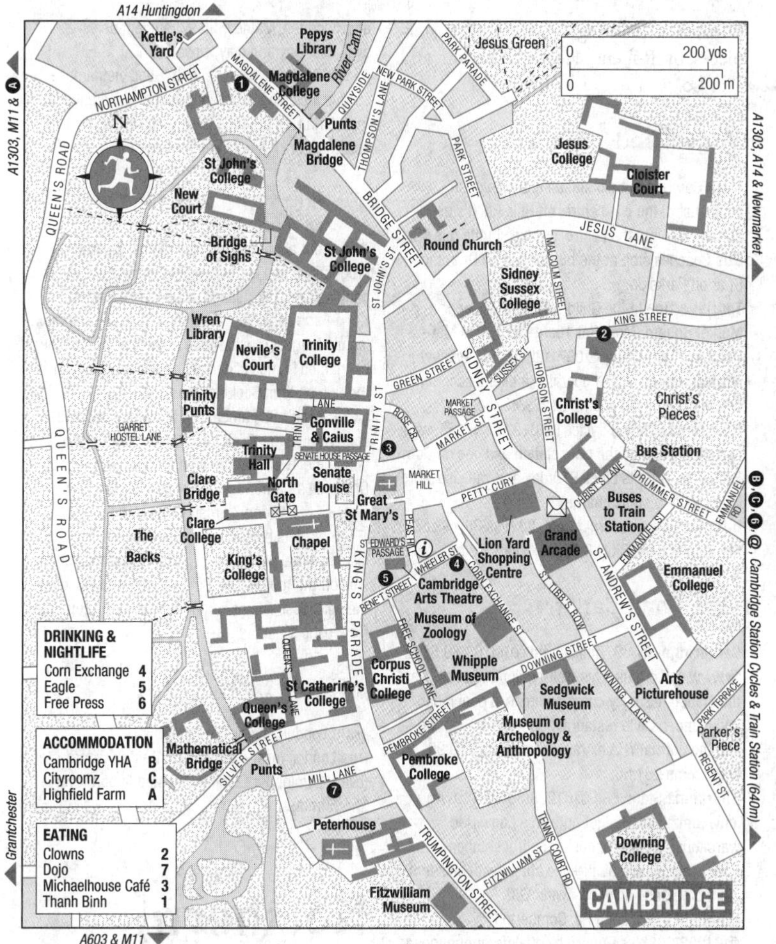

as they had lived in it. Full of art, plants and beautiful furniture, the house also showcases artworks by artists the Edes knew personally, including Ben and Winifred Nicholson, Brancusi, Miró, Hepworth and Braque. There is also an adjacent **gallery** space (Tues–Sun 11.30am–5pm; free).

Queens' College and the Fitzwilliam Museum

Queens' College (daily Jan–March 2–4pm, rest of year 10am–4/4.30pm, closed for exams in May–June; £2.50), with its twin Tudor courtyards, is accessed through the gate on Queen's Lane. Equally eye-catching is the wooden Mathematical Bridge over the Cam, a copy of the mid-eighteenth-century original which, it was claimed, would stay in place even if the nuts and bolts were removed. From Queens', it's a short stroll in the opposite direction from the colleges down Trumpington Street to the excellent **Fitzwilliam Museum** (Tues–Sat 10am–5pm, Sun noon–5pm; free; Ⓦwww.fitzmuseum.cam.ac.uk). The Lower Galleries contain classical antiquities, including a large Egyptian collection, while the Upper Galleries display applied arts and

European painting, including masterpieces by Rubens, Hogarth, Renoir and Picasso.

Arrival and information

Train Cambridge train station is a mile or so southeast of the city centre, off Hills Rd. It's a 20min walk into the centre, or take shuttle bus #3.
Bus Coaches stop at the bus station on Drummer St or on Parkside.
Tourist office In the Guildhall, Peas Hill, near Market Square (Mon–Sat 10am–5pm, plus May–Oct Sun 11am–3pm; ⓣ0871/226 8006, ⓦwww.visitcambridge.org). It operates a useful accommodation booking service (ⓣ01223/457581).
Bike rental Station Cycles (ⓣ01223/307125) with two shops, one by the train station and one on Corn Exchange St rents bikes £10/day and will also store luggage for a small charge.
Internet Budget Internet Café, 30 Hills Rd, close to the train station. Daily 8.30am–10pm; £2/hr.

Accommodation

Cambridge YHA 97 Tenison Rd ⓣ0870/770 5742 ⓦwww.yha.org.uk. This well-equipped hostel near the station has cosy common areas, a pool table and canteen-style restaurant as well as a garden, and the normal YHA extras. Dorms from £19.95, twin rooms £51.50.
Cityroomz Station Rd ⓣ01223/304050 ⓦwww.cityroomz.com. Budget hotel in a converted warehouse, smack opposite the train station. Rooms are simple bunk-style affairs with showers. Light breakfast included. Twins £60.
Highfield Farm Long Rd, Comberton ⓣ01223/262308 ⓦwww.highfieldfarmtouringpark.co.uk. Rural family-run campsite, five miles west of the city (20min by bus #18 or #18A). March–Oct. £12.50 for a small tent.

Eating

Clowns 54 King St. Licensed, day-and-night Italian café with roof garden. Serving cakes (the Rafaele Gateau is heavenly), panini, all-day breakfasts, pasta and daily specials. Pasta from £3. Daily 8am–late.
Dojo 1 Miller's Yard. Extremely popular pan-Oriental noodle bar serving up high-quality Asian dishes (from £7.50). Daily lunch & dinner.
Michaelhouse Café St Michael's Church, Trinity St. Appealing café in a church nave with an emphasis on local produce. Good for breakfast, lunch and afternoon tea. Mains from £7; student deals available. Daytime only; closed Sun.
Thanh Binh 17 Magdalene St. Good Vietnamese cuisine including excellent pork balls and unusual fruit durian ice cream. Lunch menu £7.95 for two courses. Lunch and dinner, closed Sun.

Drinking and nightlife

To find out about current club nights, theatre productions and comedy nights, browse the flyers hanging from the railings down King's Parade.
Corn Exchange Corn Exchange St ⓦwww.cornex.co.uk. Largest music venue in the city with all the big names in music, dance and comedy passing through on tour. Booking essential.
Eagle Bene't St. Famous old inn with a cobbled courtyard where Crick and Watson sought inspiration in the 1950s, at the time of their discovery of DNA; still a Cambridge drinking institution.
Free Press 7 Prospect Row. In the backstreets behind Emmanuel College this tiny local has real ales, a beer garden, great food and is well off the tourist trail. Go up Melbourne Place on the northeast side of Parker's Piece, and keep right for Prospect Row.

Moving on

Train London (every 15min; 45min).
Bus London (every 30min–1hr; 2–3hr); Oxford (every 30min; 3hr 20min); Stansted Airport (every 2hr; 50min).

Northern England

The great outdoors grabs the headlines in lake-laden, mountain-ravined **Northern England**. The best-known area is the **Lake District**, encompassing picturesque stone-built villages, sixteen huge lakes and England's highest mountains. Less explored but equally beautiful is **Northumberland** in the northeast and the southern **Peak District**. Northern England is also home to some of the country's major cities: including **Manchester** and **Liverpool** in the west and **Newcastle** in the northeast – they each combine the ostentatious civic architecture of nineteenth-century capitalism with vigorous twenty-first-century renewal. The ecclesiastical hotbeds of **Durham** and **York** are unmissable, their famous cathedrals providing a focus for fascinating, medieval-themed meanderings.

MANCHESTER

Sprawling northern metropolis **MANCHESTER** has one of the country's most vibrant social and cultural scenes, enlivened by the student population of its two major universities, its stylish Gay Village, the glitzy Curry Mile and its buzzing, bohemian Northern Quarter. In many ways it is the flagship for multifaceted Britishness: it shot to prominence courtesy of its Industrial Revolution riches, later becoming a powerhouse of music and football.

What to see and do

From the main Piccadilly train station, it's a few minutes' walk northwest to **Piccadilly Gardens**, an obvious starting point for an exploration of the city.

Manchester Art Gallery

The **Manchester Art Gallery** (Tues–Sun 10am–5pm; free; Ⓦwww.manchestergalleries.org) has a fine collection of Pre-Raphaelite paintings, Impressionist pictures of Manchester by Adolphe Valette and an excellent interactive gallery. It is located a quarter of a mile from the gardens, on Mosley Street. Just north, the **Town Hall** (daily; free; guided tours Wed & Sat) is the country's pinnacle of Victorian civic aspiration: check out the Ford Madox Brown murals inside.

Royal Exchange Theatre and National Football Museum

St Ann's Square is home to the wonderful **Royal Exchange Theatre** (Ⓦwww.royalexchangetheatre.org.uk). If you don't have time to see a show, pop in and have a look at the building – formerly the Cotton Exchange – whose florid, pink marble columns and lofty cupolas surround the spherical performance space, an egg-like module squatting in the centre. New Cathedral Street runs down to Exchange Square, home of the **Wheel of Manchester**, a huge Ferris wheel offering overpriced views of the whole city (9/10am–11pm/midnight; £6.50). Just round the corner, in Cathedral Gardens, you'll find the **National Football Museum** (Ⓣ0161/870 9275 Ⓦwww.nationalfootballmuseum.com), a spectacular, wedge-shaped glass building due to open in early 2012; it takes a look at links between football and popular culture in the UK.

Museum of Science and Industry

South down Deansgate and right onto Liverpool Road, the superb **Museum of Science and Industry** (daily 10am–5pm; free; Ⓦwww.mosi.org.uk) celebrates the triumphs of industrialization. Exhibits include working steam engines, textile machinery, a hands-on science centre, atmospheric recreations of period rooms and a glimpse of the Manchester sewer system complete with realistic smells.

Salford Quays and Old Trafford

Metrolink trams from Mosley Street and Piccadilly run to Harbour City, jump-off point for the revamped **Salford Quays**, scene of a massive urban renewal scheme in the old dock area. Centrepiece is the spectacular waterfront **Lowry Centre** (daily 9.30/10am–8pm; free; Ⓦwww.thelowry.com), housing theatres and galleries, where room is always made for the work of the artist L.S. Lowry, best known for his "matchstick men" scenes. You can also get here by walking down the docks from the Salford Quays tram stop. A

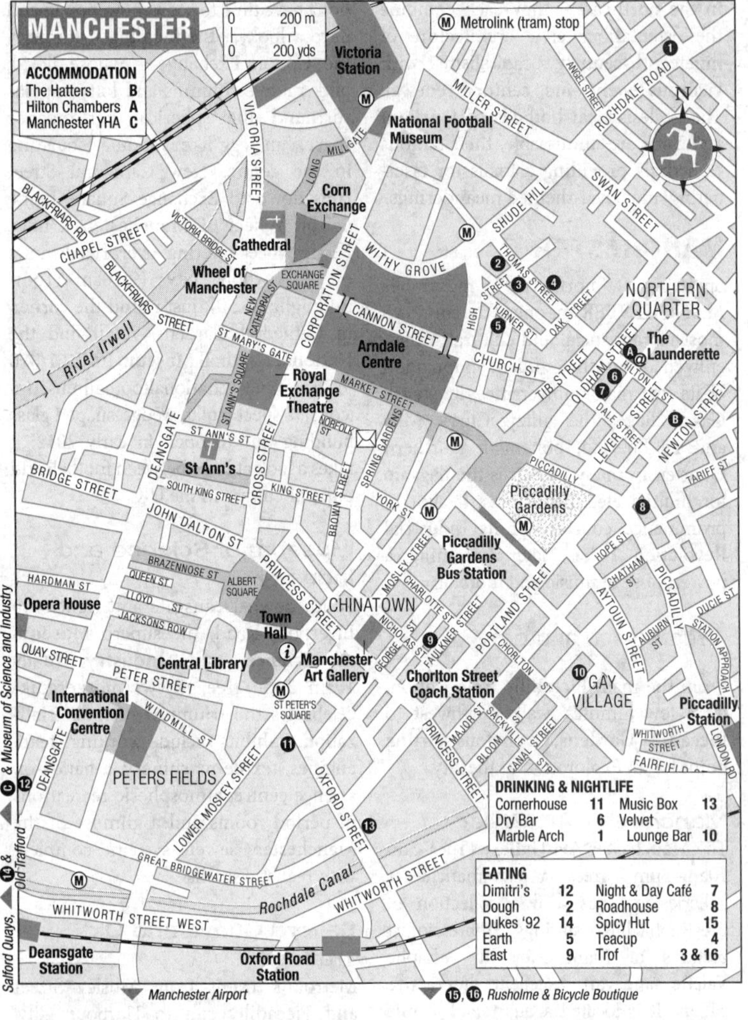

footbridge runs across the docks to the **Imperial War Museum North** (daily 10am–5/6pm; free; ⓦnorth.iwm.org.uk), a striking aluminium-clad building imaginatively exploring the effects of war since 1900. Looming nearby is **Old Trafford**, home of Manchester United Football Club, whose museum, a must-see for any football fan, is sited in the North Stand (daily 9.30am–5pm; museum & tour £13.50, museum only £10.50; advance booking essential for tours ⓣ0161/868 8000, ⓦwww.manutd.com; Metrolink towards Altrincham to Old Trafford, or towards Eccles to Exhange Quay).

Arrival and information

Air The airport is ten miles south, with fast, frequent train service to Piccadilly (15 min; £4.10).

Train Most trains arrive at Piccadilly station, on the city's east side.

Bus Long-distance coaches stop at Chorlton St, just west of Piccadilly station.

Tourist office Manchester Visitor Centre is in Piccadilly Plaza, on Portland St (Mon–Sat 9.30am–5.30pm, Sun 10.30am–4.30pm; ⓣ0871/222 8223, ⓦwww.visitmanchester.com), with branches at the airport and the Lowry too.
Bike rental Bicycle Boutique, Hillcourt St ⓣ0161/273 7801; £15/day (£12/day at weekends).
Internet The Launderette, 19 Hilton St, doubles as a cybercafé and launderette, Mon–Fri 7.30am–7.30pm, Sat 8am–5pm, Sun 10am–4pm; £1/30min.

Accommodation

The Hatters 50 Newton St ⓣ0161/236 9500, ⓦwww.hattersgroup.com. More cheap than cheerful, this hostel, housed in a converted listed building in the fashionable Northern Quarter, is friendly nonetheless. Staff will provide tourist information and book tours. Dorms from £15, singles £27.50, twins £50.
Hilton Chambers 15 Hilton St ⓣ0161/236 4414, ⓦwww.hattersgroup.com. This pleasant, clean Northern Quarter hostel has internet access, a roof terrace, complimentary all-day breakfast and travel information. Prices go up at weekends. Dorms from £15, singles £35, doubles £55.
Manchester YHA Potato Wharf, Castlefield ⓣ0871/371 9647, ⓦwww.yha.org.uk. Opposite the Science and Industry Museum, this swanky HI hostel (all dorm rooms have en-suite bathrooms), has a great canalside location. Dorms from £16.65, doubles £43.

Eating

For cheap eats, head a few blocks east of the Town Hall to Chinatown, or Wilmslow Rd in Rusholme (buses #40–48, except #45), otherwise known as "Curry Mile", featuring some of Britain's best budget Asian cooking.
Dimitri's 1 Campfield Arcade, Deansgate. Serving a medley of Greek, Italian and Spanish cuisine, *Dimitri's* has atmospheric arcade seating and decent-value 3-course meals for £12.50.
Dough 75–77 High St. A stylish yet affordable pizza restaurant, with creations ranging from goat's cheese and chives to Moroccan lamb and mango – from £5.95.
Dukes '92 18–20 Castle St, Castlefield. Former stable block for canal horses, now a large, sociable pub with terrace seating, a wood-fire pizza oven and a great-value range of pâtés and cheeses.
Earth 16–20 Turner St. Veggie food – curries, pies, salads and juices – in a funky Northern Quarter café in the Manchester Buddhist Centre. Mains from £3.50.
East 52–54 Faulkner St. Popular dim sum restaurant in Chinatown. Mains from £4.
Spicy Hut 35 Wilmslow Rd. Garishly decorated, long-standing and unpretentious curry house on the Curry Mile. They do a mean madras. Mains £9.
Teacup 55 Thomas St. Café, deli, gallery, record shop: caffeine and vinyl junkies will love this popular chilled-out Northern Quarter hangout.
Trof 8 Thomas St ⓣ0131/833 3197. Coffee, sandwiches, burgers, beer: whatever your craving, midday or midnight, *Trof* can oblige. Expect eclectic cocktails and events like Sunday's roast dinner-and-vinyl session. The original Fallowfield branch is at 2a Landcross Rd.

Drinking and nightlife

Manchester has no shortage of places to drink. The two best-known areas are the Northern Quarter, around Oldham St, and the Gay Village, around Canal St. For details of nightlife, consult Friday's *Manchester Evening News*.
Cornerhouse 70 Oxford St. With celebrity patrons Danny Boyle and Helen Mirren, this chic venue's status as café, bar, gallery and leading independent cinema seems assured. You could spend hours here.
Dry Bar 28–30 Oldham St. A "Madchester" institution – it was owned by Factory Records – and catalyst for much of what goes on in the Northern Quarter, this cool bar has banned the likes of Liam Gallagher for bad behaviour.

MANCHESTER MUSIC

In 1978, local TV personality Tony Wilson founded **Factory Records** and gave voice to a musical movement that came to define both Manchester and Britain's post-punk musical soundscape. Bands like Joy Division, New Order and the Happy Mondays emerged and embraced the new electronic music that was played at Factory's club, **The Hacienda**, the prototype for the industrial warehouse spaces ubiquitous in club design today. *The Hacienda* closed in 1997 but its legacy lives on, with places like the *Night & Day Café* (16 Oldham St; ⓦwww.nightnday.org) and the *Roadhouse* (8 Newton St; ⓦwww.theroadhouselive.co.uk) providing stages for up-and-coming talent.

Marble Arch 73 Rochdale Rd. Out-of-the-way lavish-looking brewpub with vaulted ceilings and sloping floors, concocting six of its own ales: you can often see the brewing going on outside.

Music Box 65 Oxford St ⓦwww.musicboxmanchester.com. Respected underground club hosting several popular nights and live bands during the week.

Velvet Lounge Bar 2 Canal St. Elegant, opulent Gay Village bar, decorated with plush velvet curtains and zebra-striped chairs on which to sip your cocktails.

Moving on

Train Liverpool (frequent; 45min–1hr); London (every 20min; 2hr 10min); Newcastle (every 30min; 2hr 40min); Windermere (3 direct trains daily; 1hr 45min); York (every 30min; 1hr 30min).

Bus Durham (5–6 daily; 4hr 30min); Glasgow (5 daily; 5hr); Newcastle (9 daily; 4hr 30min–5hr); York (18 daily via Leeds; 3hr).

PEAK DISTRICT

The wild, cavern-riddled **PEAK DISTRICT** lies between Manchester and Sheffield, and is Britain's oldest and most easily accessed national parks. The main centres are **Buxton**, just outside the park boundaries, **Castleton** to the northeast and **Bakewell** in the southeast.

Arrival & information

Train Buxton and Castleton are connected by hourly train to Manchester and Sheffield via the spectacular Hope Valley line. Castleton's train station is two miles out at Hope.

Bus National Express buses stop several times daily in Bakewell and Buxton en route between Manchester and London Victoria. TransPeak buses run hourly between Bakewell and Buxton: other routes include the #173 (Castleton–Bakewell) and the #68 (Buxton–Castleton).

Tourist office The main offices are at Buxton (Pavilion Gardens; daily 9.30am–5pm; ⓣ01298/25106) and Castleton's National Park Centre (Buxton Rd; April–Oct daily 9.30am–5.30pm; Nov–March 10am–5pm; ⓣ01433/620679, ⓦwww.peakdistrict.gov.uk).

What to see and do

The sedate Victorian spa town of **Buxton** should be your first stop if coming by train from Manchester. The town is centred around nineteenth-century pleasure gardens complete with a pavilion theatre and the legendary **St Ann's Well,** where the famous mineral water is sourced. There are spectacular caverns just outside town at **Poole's Cavern** (daily: March–Oct 9.30am–5pm; Nov–Feb Sat & Sun 10am–4pm; ⓦwww.poolescavern.co.uk) but you're better off heading to **Castleton**, a beautiful stone village 10 miles northwest with its three showcaves and dozens more challenging subterranean passageways to explore (details at the visitor centre, see below). A five-mile hike or one stop on the Hope Valley line further brings you to **Edale**, where the area's best hike to **Kinder Scout** (8 miles) begins. From **Bakewell**, famed for its jam-filled pudding, it's three miles on TM Travel buses #181/#240/#241/#242 to **Chatsworth House** (Baslow village; house 11am–5.30pm; garden 11am–6pm; £16; ⓣ01246/565300, ⓦwww.chatsworth.org) one of Britain's grandest country houses set in a 35,000-acre estate with a garden featuring the iconic cascades, as well as woods, valleys, fountains and tumbling rivers.

Accommodation

Castleton YHA Castleton ⓣ01433/620235, ⓦwww.yha.org.uk. YHA in fabulous 42-room Losehill Hall, just outside Castleton: extensive grounds have their own livestock, there's also a planetarium and a Celtic roundhouse for campfires and the like. Dorms from £15.

Youlgreave YHA Fountain Square, Youlgreave ⓣ0845/3719151, ⓦwww.yha.org.uk. 42-bed hostel in a converted Victorian co-op, 3 miles outside Bakewell on bus #170/#171. Dorms £18.40.

Eating and drinking

The George Castle St, Castleton. Wins the highly contested accolade of Castleton's best pub with its cosy bar and real ale selection.

LIVERPOOL

Astounding twenty-first-century revival has left **LIVERPOOL** leading the way as the region's most liveable, loveable big city: a major turnaround from its infamous postwar poverty. The re-discovered sense of cultural pride is almost as palpable as in the days when it was Britain's main trans-atlantic port and the empire's second city. The Albert Dock has been the focus of regeneration, where converted warehouses and glitzy, glassy architecture showcase Liverpool's cultural spoils. Acerbic wit and loyalty to one of the city's two football teams are the linchpins of the city's identity, along with an underlying pride in the local musical heritage – fair enough from the city that produced The Beatles.

What to see and do

From Lime Street train station it's a short walk to William Brown Street and the impressive **Walker Art Gallery** (daily 10am–5pm; free; Ⓦwww.liverpoolmuseums.org.uk/walker), which takes you on a jaunt through British art history: Hogarth, Gainsborough, Hockney and local boy Stubbs are all well represented: be sure to see Ben Johnson's vivid 2008 Liverpool cityscape.

The Waterfront

It's a fifteen-minute walk west from the Walker Art Gallery to the **Pier Head** and Liverpool's waterfront, where it's worth taking a "Ferry 'cross the Mersey" (as sung by Gerry and the Pacemakers) to Birkenhead for the views back towards the city; ferries serve commuters during rush-hours (£2.50 return), but in between there are hourly cruises with commentary (£6.70). Just behind the ferry terminal, but best seen from the river itself, stands the grandiose **Liver Building**, with its enormous clock faces and local mascots – a Liver bird perched on each tower.

A short stroll south is the **Albert Dock** where you'll find the **Tate Liverpool** (daily 10am–6pm; closed Mon Oct–June; free; Ⓦwww.tate.org.uk/liverpool), northern home of the national collection of modern art. Occupying the other side of the dock is the **Maritime Museum** (daily 10am–5pm; free; Ⓦwww.liverpoolmuseums.org.uk/maritime), now incorporating the **International Slavery Museum**.

The cathedrals

To the east of the city, at either end of Hope Street, stand two very different but equally powerful twentieth-century cathedrals: the Roman Catholic **Metropolitan Cathedral** (daily 8am–5/6pm; donation requested), a ten-minute walk up Mount Pleasant, is a vast inverted funnel of a building, while the pale red Anglican **Liverpool Cathedral** (daily 8am–6pm; admission free) is the largest in the country: a muscular, neo-Gothic creation, designed by Sir Giles Gilbert

THE FAB FOUR

Liverpool's most famous sons, The Beatles, account for a large number of the city's tourist attractions, with plenty of pubs and shops providing a high dose of Fab Four nostalgia. Spread over two venues on Albert Dock and Pier Head is **The Beatles Story** (daily 9am–7pm; £12.25), a multimedia attempt to capture the essence of the band's rise. Buses depart from here for a two-hour **Magical Mystery Tour** (book on Ⓣ0151/236 9091 or at tourist offices; £14.95) of sites associated with the band, such as Penny Lane and Strawberry Fields. Real fans will also want to visit **20 Forthlin Rd**, once home of the McCartney family, the **Mendips**, the house where John Lennon lived between 1945 and 1963 and, taking devotees right back to grassroots level, the **Kasbah Coffee Club** where the band first practised together (accessible on pre-booked minibus tour Feb–Nov Wed–Sun; £16; Ⓣ0151/427 7231). Finish your Fab tour with a night at **The Cavern Club** (see p.186).

Scott in 1903 but not completed until 1978. Climb the colossal tower (£5) to get fabulous 360-degree city views.

Arrival and information

Air Liverpool John Lennon airport is eight miles south of the city, with buses heading into town every 30min.
Train Trains arrive at Lime Street station, on the eastern edge of the city centre.
Bus Coaches stop on Norton St, northeast of the station.
Boat Ferries from Dublin and Belfast dock just north of Pier Head.
Tourist office Albert Dock (daily 10am–5.30pm; Ⓣ0151/233 2008, Ⓦwww.visitliverpool.com). There's another branch at 36–38 Whitechapel (closed Sun).
Discount card Liverpool Visitor Card (£24.99/29.99 for 1/3 days), giving admission to all major attractions.
Internet Liverpool Central Library, William Brown St (Ⓣ0151/233 583; free).

Accommodation

Aachen 89–91 Mount Pleasant Ⓣ0151/709 3477, Ⓦwww.aachenhotel.co.uk. The most central and popular budget hotel, with value-for-money rooms and big "eat-as-much-as-you-like" breakfasts. Singles/doubles from £45/65.
Embassie Hostel 1 Falkner Square Ⓣ0151/7071089, Ⓦwww.embassie.com. This nineteenth-century house exudes character, with a games room and a quirky, bohemian ambience. Complimentary breakfast with real coffee. Dorms £17.50 (£22.50 Fri/Sat).
International Inn 4 South Hunter St, off Hardman St Ⓣ0151/709 8135, Ⓦwww.internationalinn.co.uk. Converted Victorian warehouse with en-suite dorms for two to ten people and helpful staff. Adjacent café has internet access; cheap rooms and apartments are also available. Dorms from £15, doubles from £36, apartments from £65.
Liverpool YHA Wapping Ⓣ0845/371 9527, Ⓦwww.yha.org.uk. One of the best HI hostels, just south of Albert Dock. Smart three-, four- or six-bed rooms, all with private bathroom, plus licensed café, laundry and 24hr reception. Dorms from £15.95, triple rooms £93.95.

Eating

Liverpool's Chinatown, around Berry and Nelson sts, is a good place to look for cheap food.

Egg Newington St. Gem of a veggie/vegan café doing mammoth quiches, salads and vegan-friendly cakes. Bring your own wine: it's on the second floor. Mains from £4.95.
Green Days Cafe 13a Lark Lane. Pick of the bunch of brilliant restaurants in the hip Lark Lane area of Liverpool with the coffee, breakfasts and Liverpool's best vegetarian menu as highlights.
Kimo's 38 Mount Pleasant. Moroccan-style café-restaurant serving burgers and pizzas from £3.50 and tasty Moroccan dishes from £5.50.
Yuet Ben 1 Upper Duke St. The celebrated yet reasonably priced Peking cuisine here is authentic, with plenty of vegetarian options – try the set menu for £9.50. Mains from £6.50. Closed Mon.

Drinking and nightlife

The Cavern Quarter around Mathew St is home to myriad pubs, often Beatles-themed, lining pedestrianized streets. The evening paper, the *Liverpool Echo*, has what's-on listings, while annual festivals like the Summer Pops (July) and International Beatles Festival (Aug) are when the city lets its hair down.

The Baltic Fleet 33a Wapping. Restored maritime pub with its own brewery, pub grub (lunchtimes and weekend evenings) and a view out to the docks from the front.
The Cavern Club 10 Mathew St Ⓦwww.cavernclub.org. Rebuilt version of The Beatles' original venue, hosting live bands Thurs–Sun.
Kazimier 4–5 Wolstenholme Square. Offbeat Indie/alternative venue showcasing weekly live acts.
The Magnet 45 Hardman St Ⓦwww.magnetliverpool.co.uk. Blood-red decor, an abundance of history and plenty of soul – there's a funky club downstairs hosting quality live talent.
Nation Wolstenholme Square Ⓦwww.cream.co.uk and Ⓦwww.chibuku.com. Nightclub hosting Liverpool's most infamous nights – Cream and Chibuku.
The Philharmonic 36 Hope St. Fabulous, ornate pub boasting mosaic floors, gilded wrought-iron gates and marble decor in the gents, as well as reasonably priced food.

Entertainment

Everyman Theatre and Playhouse Hope St Ⓦwww.everymanplayhouse.com. Multipurpose venue presenting drama, dance, poetry and music.
FACT 88 Wood St Ⓦwww.fact.co.uk. The Foundation for Art and Creative Technology shelters two galleries showing film/video/new media projects, an arthouse cinema and café-bar.

Liverpool Academy 11–13 Hotham St Ⓦwww.o2academyliverpool.co.uk. The best medium-sized live music venue in town, with good club nights.

Moving on

Train Cardiff (change at Crewe; every 45min–1hr; 4hr); Liverpool (hourly; 2hr 10min); Manchester (every few min; 45min–1hr); York (hourly; 2hr 20min).
Bus Cardiff (4 daily; 6hr 20min); Manchester (hourly; 1hr); Newcastle (6 daily; 6hr 30min); Oxford (5 daily; 5hr 30min); York (3 daily; 3hr 50min).

CHESTER

Genteel **CHESTER** boasts Britain's most intact city walls and unique medieval Rows (covered walkways high above street level lined with shops and cafés). Timber-framed houses sit sedately beside the River Dee, which in Roman times made it a port and one of the most important strongholds in the empire. These days, Chester makes a good base for visiting Liverpool or North Wales.

What to see and do

Walking the 2.5 miles round the Roman **city walls** is the best introduction to the city. Outside the walls to the east on Vicar's Lane is Britain's largest **Roman Ampitheatre** (daily; free) hinting at Chester's former importance within the empire. For more on the Romans, visit the **Grosvenor Museum** (Mon–Sat 10.30am–5pm, Sun 1–4pm; free) on Grosvenor Street or sign up for a guided city tour with a Roman centurion at the **Roman Tours Shop** next door (tours daily at 12pm). The northeastern section of the walls skirts the 1000-year-old **Cathedral** (Mon–Sat 9am–5pm, Sun 1–4pm; £5) a grand monastic complex with wonderfully preserved cloisters. Another fun way to explore is via a river or canal boat: **Roman High Tea Cruises** (4pm daily; £10) run by **Mill Hotel & Spa** (Ⓣ01244/350 035, Ⓦwww.millhotel.com) throw in cakes and sandwiches with their canal cruise, leaving from outside the hotel on Milton Street.

Arrival and information

Train Trains arrive at Lime St station, on the eastern edge of the city 10 minutes' walk from the centre.
Bus Coaches stop on Norton St, northeast of the station.
Tourist office Visitor centre/café/shop on Vicar's Lane, opposite the Roman amphitheatre (daily 9.30am–5pm; Ⓣ01244/401 796). Wi-fi access available.

Accommodation

Chester Backpackers 67 Broughton St. The best budget option in town is a steal: a quirky former pub with dorms from £15 and twins from £40. Long-term rates are available.

Eating and drinking

Blue Moon Cafe 23 The Groves. Down on the riverfront, this 1950's-themed café serves imaginative lunches (£5–7), metamorphosing into a Mediterranean bistro (Thurs–Sat eves).
The Brewery Tap 52–54 Lower Bridge St. Seventeenth-century hall with great cask ales and meals from £8.50.

Moving on

Train Conwy (hourly; 1hr) Liverpool (every 15min; 1hr); Manchester (2–3 hourly; 1hr 15min); .
Bus Liverpool (2 hourly; 1hr 10min); Manchester (4 daily; 1hr 30 min).

LAKE DISTRICT

The site of England's highest peaks and its biggest concentration of lakes, the glacier-carved **Lake District National Park** is the nation's most popular walking area. Weather here in Cumbria changes quickly, but the sudden shifts of light on the bracken-bedaubed moorland, and on the slate of the local buildings, are part of the area's appeal. The region is informally divided into the North Lakes, which include **Keswick**, and the South Lakes, including **Windermere** and **Ambleside**.

Arrival and local transport

Train Use the main-line service from London Euston to Glasgow, disembarking at Lancaster or

Oxenholme. Within the Lake District only Windermere and Kendal are accessible by train, on a branch line from Oxenholme.

Bus National Express coaches run daily from London Victoria and Manchester to the Lake District. Stagecoach buses go everywhere in the region, and offer Explorer Tickets, valid on the whole network, for 1, 4 or 7 days (£9.75/21.50/30). Tourist offices provide a complete list of services, but the main routes are #555 from Lancaster to Kendal, Windermere, Ambleside, Grasmere, Keswick and Carlisle, and the summer-only open-top #599, from Bowness to Ambleside via Windermere and Brockhole.

Windermere

Windermere is the largest of the lakes, with its main town of **WINDERMERE** set a mile or so back from the water. Other than the short climb up to the viewpoint of **Orrest Head** (30min), it offers little to do, but it is the region's main service centre. The **tourist office** is outside the train station (daily 9.30am–4.30/6pm; ⓣ015394/46499). **Bikes** can be rented from Country Lanes at the train station (ⓣ015394/44544, ⓦwww.countrylanes.co.uk). For **food** try *The Elleray* on Victoria Street or *Lazy Daisy's* on Cresent Road.

For trips onto Windermere itself, catch bus #618/#599 from outside

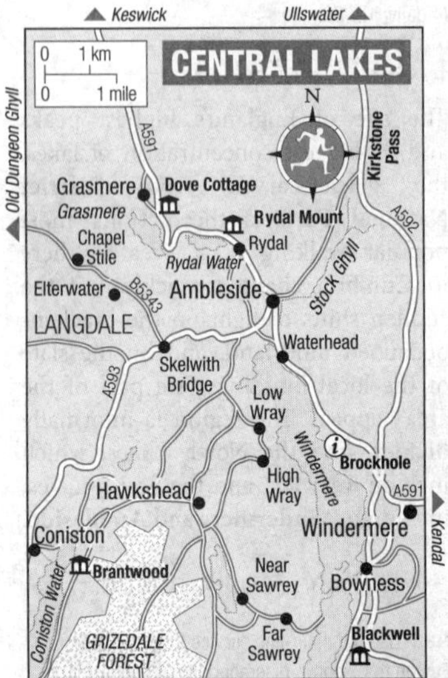

ACCOMMODATION IN THE LAKES

There are 25 YHA **youth hostels** in the region, including one in all the areas listed here, with the exception of Bowness. Go to ⓦwww.yha.org.uk for details – be aware that hostels can get both busy and expensive in summer. **Campsites** also proliferate, some in exceptional locations. For more information visit the official site of the Cumbria Tourist Board, ⓦwww.golakes.co.uk.

Windermere station to the more photogenic, but often more crowded, lakeshore town of **BOWNESS**. Lake **ferries** (ⓣ015394/43360, ⓦwww.windermere-lakecruises.co.uk) run to Lakeside at the southern tip (£9.80 return) or to Waterhead (for Ambleside) at the northern end (£9.50 return); a 24-hour Freedom of the Lake ticket costs £17.25. There are also buses (#555 or #599) to the **Lake District National Park Visitor Centre** at Brockhole, which boasts an excellent information centre as well as exhibitions on the Lake District past, present and future (mid-March to Oct 10am–5pm; Nov to mid-March 10am–4pm; free; ⓣ015394/46601). Boats to the Visitor Centre run from Ambleside (£7). In Bowness, don't miss a drink/meal in *The Hole in't Wall* **pub** behind the church, the town's oldest hostelry.

Accommodation

The accommodation listed below is in Windermere: rooms in Bowness are pricier.

Brendan Chase 1 College Rd ⓣ015394/45638, ⓦwww.placetostaywindermere.co.uk. Backpacker-friendly B&B with rambling en-suite rooms. From £25/person.

Lake District Backpackers' Lodge High St ⓣ015394/46374, ⓦwww.lakedistrictbackpackers.co.uk. This little hostel close to the station is unmanned, so don't turn up without a booking as this provides the code for you to get in. They take cash only, and don't give change. Dorms £14.50.

Ambleside

Pretty but touristy, **Ambleside** is good for stocking up on outdoor gear, and makes a reasonable base between the north and south lakes. The **tourist office** is in the Central Buildings by the Market Cross (daily 9am–5.30pm; ⓣ01539/432582) and the **Ambleside Armitt Museum** (Mon–Sat 10am–4.30pm; £2.50) exhibits items of local geological, archeological and literary interest. *Zeffirelli's*, a cinema on Compston Road, has a daytime café and dinner-only pizza restaurant.

Accommodation

Ambleside Backpackers Old Lake Rd ⓣ015394/32340, ⓦwww.englishlakesbackpackers.co.uk. Independent family-run hostel located in a quiet part of town, with immaculate rooms. Dorms £17.50.

Ambleside Youth Hostel Waterhead ⓣ0845/3719620. Massive 257-bed hostel on the lakeside, often packed with school groups. Rooms are clean and staff helpful. The café serves food until 8pm. Dorms from £14.65.

Linda's Shirland, Compston Rd ⓣ015394/32999. B&B and bunkhouse run by the eponymous indefatigable Linda. Cheaper rates for self-caterers. £50

Elterwater and Langdale

The #516 bus from Ambleside to the *Old Dungeon Ghyll* runs four miles west to the charming hamlet of **ELTERWATER**, boasting the *Britannia Inn*, an old lakeland pub with tasty food. The valley offers dramatic scenery and plenty of good walking, including up to Stickle Tarn and the peaks of **Langdale** (including England's highest point, Scafell Pike). *Sticklebarn Tavern*, two miles beyond Elterwater on the same bus route, is a good place to start from, though you should make sure you have good shoes, waterproofs and a map. It also has a fantastic hikers' bar and a bunkhouse with basic dorm beds (ⓣ015394/37356; dorms £13). Canny campers stay just before the *Sticklebarn* at the *Baysbrown Campsite* in Chapel Stile (ⓣ01539/437150; £5, cars £2.50), which offers stunning views down the valley. Chapel Stile is also home to chic *Brambles Café*, serving coffee and light meals. If you need some relaxation after a long day's walking, the *Langdale Hotel* down the road from *Baysbrown Campsite* lets non-residents use its pool, spa and sauna (£9.75).

LAKE DISTRICT LUMINARIES

The lakeland landscape has been an inspiration to some of England's most revered literary figures. **William Wordsworth** lived at Rydal Mount (March–Oct daily 9.30am–5pm; Nov–Feb Wed–Sun 11am–4pm; £6.50, gardens only £4), three miles northwest of Ambleside on the #555 bus, and the more interesting Dove Cottage, which still holds many of the Wordsworth's possessions (daily 9.30am–4.30/5pm; closed Jan; £7.50) at Grasmere. Wordsworth and his sister Dorothy lie in simple graves in the village churchyard of St Oswald's.

Beatrix Potter, author, illustrator and botanist, lived at Hill Top (mid-Feb to Oct daily except Fri 10.30/11am–3.30/4.30/5pm; £7; ticket numbers limited; ⓦwww.nationaltrust.org.uk), a lovely seventeenth-century house in the hamlet of Near Sawrey. You can take a ferry from Bowness and cover the steep two miles to the house on foot or by minibus. Get there early to beat the crowds.

From the village of Coniston, reached by bus #505 from Windermere or Ambleside, you can take the wooden *Coniston Launch* (£9.50 return; ⓣ01768/775753, ⓦwww.conistonlaunch.co.uk) to the elegant lakeside villa, Brantwood (mid-March to mid-Nov daily 11am–5.30pm; mid-Nov to mid-March Wed–Sun 11am–4.30pm; £6.30, gardens only £4.50), once home of artist and critic **John Ruskin**. The house is full of Ruskin's own drawings and sketches, as well as items relating to the Pre-Raphaelite painters he inspired.

Keswick and Derwent Water

Principal hiking and tourist centre for the northern lakes, **KESWICK** (pronounced "kez-ick") lies on the shores of **Derwent Water**. The **Keswick Launch** (daily mid-March to Nov & school hols; Dec to mid-March Sat & Sun; £9 return trip; ⓣ01768/772263, ⓦwww.keswick-launch.co.uk) runs right around the lake, and you can get off at Hawes End for the climb up **Cat Bells** (1481ft), best of the lakeside vantage points. From Keswick you can hike up to Lattrigg (1203ft; 3hr) for breathtaking views or the more challenging **Skiddaw** (3050ft; 5hr), among the more straightforward of the many true mountain hikes around. Walks round the lake down **Borrowdale**, perhaps the most beautiful valley in England, take three to five hours, depending on whether you stick to the lakeside or climb above it. There's also a bus (#17) along the lakeside road. A mile and a half's stroll eastwards is **Castlerigg Stone Circle**, a Neolithic monument commanding a spectacular view.

Arrival and information

Buses The terminal is behind Booths Foodstore, off Keswick's Main St.
Tourist office Moot Hall, Market Square (Daily 9.30am–4.30/5.30pm; ⓣ01768/772645).
Bike rental Keswick Mountain Bikes, Southey Hill ⓣ01768/775202, ⓦwww.keswickmountainbikes.co.uk.

Accommodation

Bluestones 7 Southey St ⓣ01768/774237, ⓦwww.bluestonesguesthouse.co.uk. This place stands out from the multitude with an welcoming and warm attitude and big buffet breakfasts. Discounted winter rates available. Doubles £58.
Denton House Penrith Rd ⓣ01768/775351, ⓦwww.vividevents.co.uk. This very friendly, laidback hostel focuses on the Lake District's outdoor attractions, and can organize activities in the area. Dorms £15.
Keswick Camping Crow Park Rd ⓣ01768/772392, ⓦwww.campingandcaravanningclub.co.uk. Very convenient location west of town, 5min from the bus station. Booking advised. From £7.65/person plus £7.10/tent.

Eating, drinking and entertainment

Dog and Gun Lake Rd. Keswick's best pub, with local beers and a celebrated goulash (from £4.95).
The George 3 St John's St. Old coaching inn with Jennings ales on tap, serving a much-in-demand Cow Pie (£10.95).
Lakeland Pedlar Henderson's Yard, off Main St. Keswick's most agreeable café: vegetarian-friendly, with excellent home-made cakes and scones, as well as soups and sandwiches.
Theatre by the Lake ⓦwww.theatrebythelake.co.uk. Hosts drama, dance and music.

YORK

Affluent **YORK** is a layer cake of history: the Romans used the city as their capital in northern Britain, as did Edwin of Northumbria, whose conversion to Christianity in 627 granted it huge spiritual importance. Then the Vikings swept through in 866, and ruled until 954, when Eric Bloodaxe lost Jorvik – as it was then known – to King Edred, who brought it into his unified England. Today its sinuous century-old cobbled streets are filled with cafés and craft shops, surrounded by picturesque medieval ramparts and centred on the spectacular Gothic Minster.

What to see and do

Start your sightseeing with a stroll along the **city walls** (daily till dusk), a three-mile circuit that takes in the various medieval "bars", or gates, with fine views of the Minster. Guided walks (daily 10.15am, plus 2.15pm April–Sept & 6.45pm July & Aug; free; 2hr) depart from outside the art gallery in Exhibition Square; just turn up.

York Minster

Ever since Edwin built a wooden chapel on the site, **York Minster** (Mon–Sat 9/9.30am–5pm, Sun noon–3.45pm; £9)

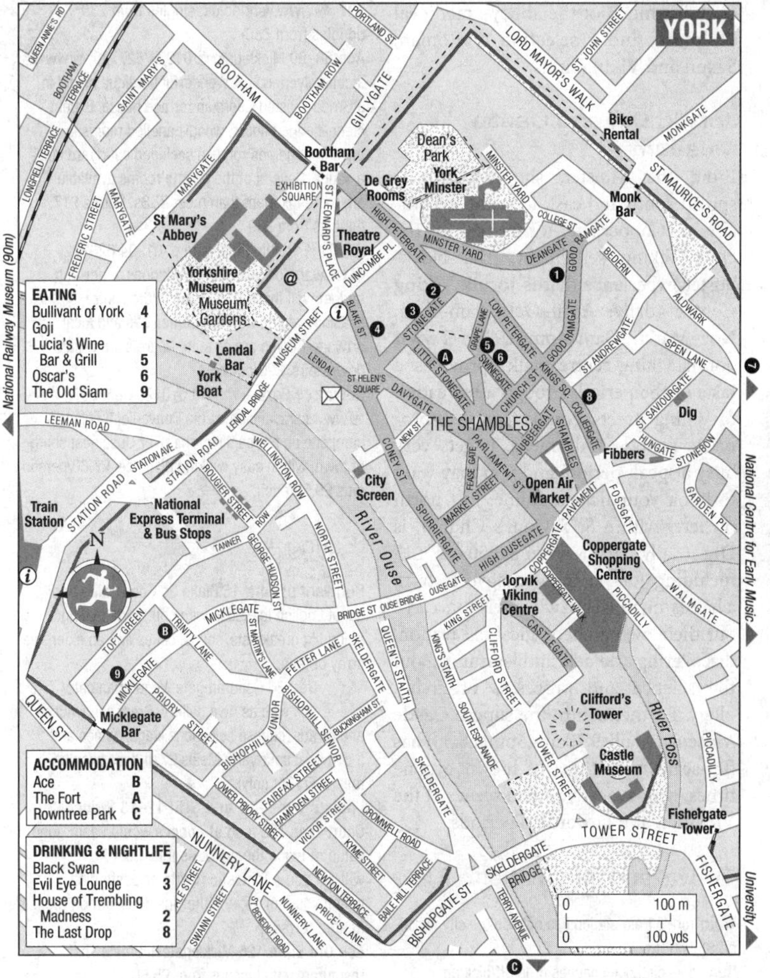

has been the centre of religious authority for the north of England. Most of what's visible now was built in stages between the 1220s and the 1470s, and today it ranks as the country's largest Gothic building. Inside, the scenes of the East Window, completed in 1405, and the abstract thirteenth-century Five Sisters window, represent Britain's finest collection of stained glass. Various parts of the Minster have their own admission charges, though the full £14.40 ticket covers all the attractions – don't miss climbing the central tower, which gives views over the medieval pattern of narrow streets to the south, known as **The Shambles**.

Yorkshire Museum

Southwest of the Minster, just outside the city walls, Museum Gardens leads to the ruins of the Benedictine abbey of St Mary and the **Yorkshire Museum** (daily 10am–5pm; £7.50, or £13 including the Castle Museum; ⓦwww.yorkshiremuseum.org.uk), which contains much of the abbey's medieval sculpture, and a selection of Roman, Saxon and Viking finds.

Jorvik, Dig and Castle Museum

From the Minster, shopping streets spread south and east, focusing eventually on Coppergate, former site of the city's Viking settlement. The blockbuster experience that is **Jorvik Viking Centre** (daily: April–Oct 10am–5pm; Nov–March 10am–4pm; £9.25; Ⓦwww.jorvik-viking-centre.co.uk) provides a taste of the period through a recreation of Viking streets, complete with appropriate sounds and smells. It gets very busy at peak period, and you may want to book your tickets online. Just north of here, within St Saviour's Church, is **Dig** (daily 10am–5pm; £5.50 or £13 including Jorvik; Ⓦwww.digyork.com), a hands-on museum where visitors carry out their own archeological excavation, discovering artefacts and learning about the science and processes of archeology. Further south, the superb **Castle Museum** (daily 9.30am–5pm; £8.50) has full-scale recreations of life in bygone times, with evocative street scenes of the Victorian and Edwardian periods.

Arrival and information

Train York's train station lies outside the city walls on Station Rd.

Bus Long-distance coaches drop off/pick up outside the train station, as well as on Rougier St, 200m northeast, just before Lendal Bridge.

Tourist office 1 Museum St (Mon–Sat 9am–5pm, Sun 10am–4pm; Ⓣ01904/550099, Ⓦwww.visityork.org).

Discount card York Pass (from £30/day), which includes access to nearly all the sights.

Internet *Evil Eye Lounge*, 42 Stonegate, 12 terminals available in this cocktail bar (Mon–Sat 10am–11pm, from 11am Sun; £1/30min).

Accommodation

The University of York offers good-value rooms/self-catering flats out of term time (Ⓣ01904/328431, Ⓦwww.york.ac.uk; singles from £39, doubles from £80).

Ace 88–90 Micklegate Ⓣ01904/627720, Ⓦwww.acehotelyork.co.uk. Wonderful boutique hostel in a Grade 1-listed Georgian terrace house. Expect stone-flagged floors, wood-panelled rooms, a basement games room, a secluded courtyard and a sauna. Several of the private rooms available are more luxuriant than most B&Bs. Dorms £17, doubles from £60.

The Fort 1 Little Stonegate Ⓣ01904/620222 Ⓦwww.thefortyork.co.uk. York does upper-end budget well these days: bang in the centre, spacious rooms with flat-screen TVs and local artwork. Rooms are en suite; there's a bar-café downstairs. £29/person.

Rowntree Park Terry Ave Ⓣ01904/658997, Ⓦwww.caravanclub.co.uk. Conveniently placed campsite on the banks of the river Ouse, just south of town, within easy walking distance. £7.60/person plus £9.50/pitch.

Eating

Bullivant of York 15 Blake St. Good-value traditional English teahouse with courtyard seating doing big breakfasts, soups, cakes and an extensive array of teas.

Goji 36 Goodramgate. Vegetarian café/deli with its own gallery. Great sandwiches and salads, cheese selections, vegan wines and a convivial courtyard. Meals £7. It does evening meals (Fri/Sat only).

Lucia's Wine Bar and Grill 12–13 Swinegate Court East. The food at *Lucia's* would seem good value at twice the price. As it is, £6.45 will get you a fantastic risotto or pasta dish, which you can enjoy either inside or out on the heated terrace.

The Old Siam 126 Micklegate. Intimate Thai restaurant with lunches from £5.50.

Oscar's 27 Swinegate. Lively wine bar and restaurant, with light bites like baguettes for £3.30.

Drinking and nightlife

Black Swan Peasholme Green. York's oldest (sixteenth-century) pub with some superb stone flagging and wood panelling, plus a regular singer-songwriter and folk nights.

Evil Eye Lounge 42 Stonegate. Inviting bar with comfy sofas, an encyclopedic range of spirits, quaffable cocktails and great Thai food. Open until 1am at weekends.

House of Trembling Madness Stonegate. Sequestered away above the Bottled Beer shop and serving a great range of Belgian beers in a medieval hall.

The Last Drop 27 Colliergate. Conveniently located outlet of the York Brewery.

Entertainment

City Screen 13 Coney St (ⓦwww.picturehouses.co.uk). Arthouse cinema with a riverside café-bar and live music.

Music The National Centre for Early Music in St Margaret's Church, Walmgate (ⓦwww.ncem.co.uk) hosts a prestigious early music festival in July, plus world, jazz and folk gigs. Indie and guitar-pop bands play most nights of the week at Fibbers, Stonebow House, Stonebow (ⓦwww.fibbers.co.uk).

Moving on

Train Edinburgh (every 30min; 2hr 25min–2hr 40min); London (every 30min; 2hr–2hr 20min); Manchester (every 15–30min; 1hr 30min); Newcastle (every 30min; 1hr).

Bus Edinburgh (2 daily; 6hr 15min); Glasgow (1 daily; 7hr 30min); London (4 daily; 5hr 15min); Manchester (hourly changing at Leeds; 2hr 35min); Newcastle (4 daily; 2hr 20min).

DURHAM

A "perfect little city" according to travel writer Bill Bryson, **DURHAM** is known for its spectacular cathedral and castle perched high on a bluff enclosed by a loop of the River Wear (pronounced "weer"). Once one of northern England's power bases, today it's a quiet provincial city with a strong student presence. Visit as a day-trip from Newcastle or stay over to soak up the medieval vibe.

What to see and do

Durham hit the limelight after the remains of St Cuthbert, the patron saint of Northumbria, were moved here in the ninth century because of Viking raids. His shrine at the eastern end of the beautiful eleventh-century **cathedral** (Mon–Sat 9.30am–6pm, Sun 12.30–5.30pm; open till 8pm daily mid-July to Aug; £5 donation requested) soon became a pilgrimage site. The cathedral is England's finest example of Norman architecture, and also contains the tomb of the Venerable Bede, the country's first historian. The **Treasures of St Cuthbert** exhibition, which includes his coffin, is in the undercroft (Mon–Sat 10am–4.30pm, Sun 2–4.30pm; included in admission charge), while the **tower** gives breathtaking views (Mon–Sat 10am–3/4pm; £5). On the opposite side of Palace Green is the **castle** (regular guided tours; £5; call ⓣ0191/334 3800 for details), a much refurbished Norman edifice that's now a university hall of residence. A half-hour stroll follows a pathway on the wooded river bank below the cathedral and castle, all the way around the peninsula. South of the centre on Elvet Hill the engrossing **Oriental Museum** (Mon–Fri 10am–5pm, Sat & Sun noon–5pm; £1.50), run by Durham University, is the country's only museum dedicated exclusively to oriental art.

Arrival and information

Train Durham train station is 10min walk from the centre, via either of two river bridges.

Bus The bus station is just south of the train station on North Rd.

Tourist office Millennium Place (Mon–Sat 9.30am–5.30pm, Sun 11am–4pm; ⓣ0191/384 3720, ⓦwww.thisisdurham.com).

Accommodation

Durham University has rooms available – including within the castle – at Easter and from July to Sept (ⓣ0800/289970, ⓦwww.dur.ac.uk/conferences; singles £40, doubles £72).

Castle View Crossgate ⓣ0191/3868852, ⓦwww.castle-view.co.uk. The best-value guesthouse with homely rooms, internet access and great views of Durham. Doubles £80.

Eating, drinking and entertainment

Compared with Newcastle down the road, Durham's no clubbers' paradise but there are plenty of lively bars as well as some nice old-fashioned pubs like the *The Victoria* (86 Hallgarth St) and The Gala Theatre and Cinema at Millennium Place hosts drama, music/comedy/film nights (ⓣ0191/332 4041, ⓦwww.galadurham.co.uk).

Fabio's 66 Saddler St. Lively bar above a popular, good-value Italian restaurant (you can eat your food in either). Pizza/pasta dishes £5.30–7. Jazz on Sunday nights.

Leonard's Café Fowler's Yard. Cosy coffee shop below the indoor market. Across the road are the Fowler's Yard Creative Workshops, where you can see traditional crafts being practised.

Vennel's Café Saddler's Yard, off Saddler St. Café serving everything from cakes to pasta in a lovely little hidden courtyard.

NEWCASTLE-UPON-TYNE

NEWCASTLE-UPON-TYNE has shaken off its image as being all bare-chested football fans and raucous nightlife. While still possessing both in abundance, this formerly industrial city is now as trendy as it is tough, and more about culture than clubbing. It's streets ahead of its rivals in the northeast, and has a slew of fine galleries and arts venues, as well as a handsome Neoclassical downtown area fanning out from the lofty Grecian column of **Grey's Monument**, the city's central landmark. Facing Newcastle across the Tyne is rejuvenated Gateshead, a former industrial area now the hub of the city's art scene.

What to see and do

Arriving by train from the south, your first view is of the **River Tyne**, flanked by redeveloped quaysides and crossed by a series of bridges linking Newcastle to the **Gateshead** side of the river. Most famous is the single steel-arched **Tyne Bridge**, built in 1928 and complemented by the hi-tech "winking" **Millennium Bridge**, a wonderful sweeping arc of sparkling steel channelling pedestrians cross-river. North of the centre is student- and bar-filled Jesmond, while east is the trendy, regenerated area of Ouseburn.

Laing Gallery, BALTIC & The Sage

The northeast's main art collection is housed in the **Laing Gallery** on New Bridge Street (Mon–Sat 10am–5pm, Sun 2–5pm; free; ⓦwww.twmuseums.org.uk/laing), but is overshadowed by the excellent **BALTIC** (Baltic Centre for Contemporary Art; daily 10/10.30am–6/6.30pm; free; ⓦwww.balticmill.com) next to the Millennium Bridge in Gateshead. Second only in size gallery-wise to London's Tate Modern, this converted former flour mill accommodates exhibition galleries, artists' studios, a café-bar and two restaurants. On a similarly ambitious scale, the BALTIC has been joined by the **Sage Gateshead** (daily 10am–late; free; ⓦwww.thesagegateshead.org), a billowing steel, aluminium and glass structure by Norman Foster. The programme of concerts (classical and contemporary) and activities here has transformed this side of the river.

Arrival and information

Air The airport is six miles north, served by the local Metro system (Day Saver for unlimited rides after 9am on weekdays £4).

Train Newcastle's Central Station is a couple of minutes' walk from the centre.

Bus The coach station, on St James's Boulevard, is a few minutes' walk west of the station.

Ferry The ferry port (for crossings from Amsterdam) is in North Shields, seven miles east, with connecting buses running to the centre.

Tourist office The main tourist office is at Central Arcade (Mon–Sat 9/9.30am–5.30pm; Sun 11am–5pm; ⓣ0191/2778000, ⓦwww.newcastlegateshead.com).

Internet Newcastle City Library, 33 New Bridge St West (Mon–Thurs 8am–8pm, Fri & Sat 8.30am–5.30pm, Sun 11am–5pm; ⓣ0191/277 4100, free access for members – join at front desk), plus free wi-fi.

Accommodation

The University of Northumbria (ⓣ0191/227 4209, ⓦwww.northumbria.ac.uk) and Newcastle University (ⓣ0191/222 6000, ⓦwww.ncl.ac.uk) offer good-value, summertime B&B (mostly single rooms) in their halls of residence (£30). Jesmond – a mile north of the centre, on the Metro – is the main location for budget accommodation.

Albatross Backpackers Inn 51 Grainger St ⓣ0191/233 1330, ⓦwww.albatrossnewcastle.co.uk. The most convenient place to stay in Newcastle, this large, friendly hostel is both cheap and central. Dorms £16.50.

Caledonian Hotel 64–68 Osborne Rd ⓣ0191/281 7881. Pleasant hotel in the centre of Jesmond's bar/restaurant scene with large rooms and internet access. Doubles from £60.

Euro Hostel 17 Carliol Square ⓣ0845/490 0371, ⓦwww.euro-hostels.co.uk/newcastle. Clean, smart rooms at this 256-bed converted warehouse hostel top one of the city's best bars. All rooms are en suite with flat-screen TVs. 4-bed dorms from £12.50.

Eating

Many restaurants are grouped around Bigg Market, a block west of Grey St.

Nudo 54–56 Low Friar St. Plush, popular noodle house with sushi from £2 and noodle dishes for £5–8.

Pizzeria Francesca 136–140 Manor House Rd, Jesmond. Bright, family-run pizza place with meals starting at £4.95. Happy hour (Mon–Fri 5–6pm) brings costs down further.

Scrumpy Willow and the Singing Kettle 89 Clayton St. Cool café in a converted house doing a roaring trade in veggie fare, like the infamous dhal, plus great coffee and scrummy cakes.

Side Café Bistro 1–3 The Side. Arty café, gallery and cinema near the quayside.

TREAT YOURSELF

Claiming to be Britain's oldest continually used eatery, **Blackfriars** on Friars Street (ⓣ0191/261 5945, ⓦwww.blackfriarsrestaurant.co.uk) is a thirteenth-century monastery, with several cosy eating areas, one with a monastic-style banqueting table. Overlooking a lush central courtyard, it's the northeast's best restaurant, and somehow prices for delicious main meals like steak or gourmet sausage-and-mash are only £9. Go there for lunch or an early weekday evening to get the best deals. Worth the splurge.

Drinking and nightlife

Free monthly entertainment listings magazine, *The Crack*, available in pubs and record shops, is the best way to find out about what's on.

The Cluny Lime St, Ouseburn. Hip music venue hosting rising music stars from around the globe. Glorious burgers and a good international beer selection.

Digital Times Square ⓦwww.yourfutureisdigital.com. Proud owner of the best sound system in the city, plenty of world-class DJs have headlined here. Music runs the full gamut from eighties cheese through to rave. Thursday night is indie night; last Friday of the month is Turbulence: Northern Englands's best drum and bass DJ night.

The Forth Pink St ⓦwww.theforthnewcastle.co.uk. Great pre-club spot with an innovative food menu, good music, an open fire and a roof terrace.

Powerhouse 7–19 Westmoreland Rd. The north-east's only exclusively gay club, playing something for everyone until 4am over three floors.

Moving on

Train Durham (every few min; 10min); Edinburgh (every 30min; 1hr 30min); Glasgow (every 30min, most via Edinburgh; 2hr 40min–3hr); London (every 30min; 3hr–3hr 15min); York (every 10–30min; 1hr); Manchester (via York; 2hr 35min–3hr 20min).

Bus Durham (2–3 hourly; 30–45min); Edinburgh (3 daily; 2hr 40min–3hr 10min); Glasgow (1 daily; 3hr 55min); Liverpool (6 daily; 5hr 25min–6hr 50min); London (5 daily; 6hr 40min–7hr 45min); Manchester (9 daily; 5hr 30min); York (4 daily; 2hr 20min).

HADRIAN'S WALL

Hadrian's Wall, separating Roman England from barbarian Scotland, can be a wonderfully atmospheric place, especially on a rainy day, when it's not difficult to imagine Roman soldiers gloomily contemplating their bleak northern posting from atop the wall. Nowadays the **Hadrian's Wall Path**, an 84-mile waymarked trail (5–7 days) runs coast to coast across Northumberland and Cumbria. It starts at **Segedunum** at Wallsend, four miles east of Newcastle, the last outpost of Hadrian's great border defence. You can visit the excavations (daily: April–Oct 10am–5pm; Nov–March 10am–3pm; £4.50; ⓜWallsend).

Otherwise, the best jumping-off point and base for longer exploration is the abbey town of **HEXHAM**, 45 minutes west of Newcastle by train or bus. Some of the finest preserved sections of wall include **Housesteads** (daily 10am–4/6pm; £5), the most complete Roman fort in Britain, set in spectacular countryside, and the partly recreated fort and lively museum at **Vindolanda** (daily 10am–5/6pm; £5.20). The circular route starting and finishing at *Once Brewed* provides a decent walk, covering around 7.5 miles and taking in both Housesteads and Vindolanda, as well as some dramatic scenery. For a break from the Romans, visit **All Out Adventures** (ⓦwww.alloutadventures.co.uk) at **Slaley Hall** near Hexham where you can try your hand at a host of outdoor activities from archery to Segweying (£25–60).

Arrival and information

Bus The Hadrian's Wall #AD122 bus (Easter–Oct: 7 daily, though not all services cover the whole route; 1-day ticket £7.50, 3-day £15, 7-day £30) runs between Hexham and Carlisle via all main sites; at least once daily it links through to Newcastle and Wallsend. The year-round #685 bus runs from Carlisle to Housesteads via Haltwhistle (on the Newcastle–Carlisle train line).

Tourist office There's a National Park Centre at *Once Brewed* (Easter–Oct daily 9.30am–5pm; Nov–Easter Sat & Sun 10am–3pm; ⓣ01434/344396, ⓦwww.visitnortheastengland.com). Hexham has a tourist office in the main car park (daily 9/10am–5/6pm; Nov–Easter closed Sun; ⓣ01434/652220).

Accommodation and eating

Hadrians Wall Camping Melkridge, Haltwhistle ⓣ01434/320495, ⓦwww.hadrianswallcampsite.co.uk. Small, level site near the Wall with a centrally heated bunk barn. £2/person plus £8/tent, bunk barn £15/person.

Once Brewed ⓣ0845/371 9753, ⓦwww.yha.org.uk. HI hostel in a modern, purpose-built block 15 miles west of Hexham and within easy walking distance of the wall. Feb–Nov only. Dorms £18.40.

Twice Brewed Inn ⓣ01434/344534, ⓦwww.twicebrewedinn.co.uk. Friendly pub on the same site as *Once Brewed* with simple rooms, food (served till 8.30pm) and local beers. Closed Jan. Rooms £34.

LINDISFARNE (HOLY ISLAND)

Accessed by a sandy causeway at low tide only, magical emerald-green **LINDISFARNE** (ⓦwww.lindisfarne.org), topped by its distinctive, stumpy castle, has been one of Britain's most important pilgrimage destination 635 AD, when St Aidan's monastic order settled here. Tourist information is available at the **Lindisfarne Centre,** Marygate (daily 10am–5pm; exhibition £3). From here it's a short walk to the ruined eleventh-century **Lindisfarne Priory** (Feb–Oct daily 9.30/10am–4/5pm; Nov–Jan Sat–Mon 10am–2pm; £4.80), burial place of St Cuthbert, on the site of St Aidan's original monastery. The island is also Britain's best puffin-spotting site. Bus #505 runs from Newcastle Haymarket (4 daily; 2hr 20min; change at Beal). Connections are dependent on tide times: check before travelling (ⓣ01670/533998, ⓦwww.lindisfarne.org).

Wales

Picturesque **WALES** has long appealed to English holidaymakers, drawn by unspoilt countryside, in which the population of sheep vastly outnumbers that of humans. The relationship between Wales and England, however, has never been entirely easy. Fed up with demarcation disputes, the eighth-century Mercian king Offa constructed a dyke to separate the two countries: the 177-mile **Offa's Dyke Path** still (roughly) marks the border to this day, though Wales passed under English rule in the late thirteenth century. The arrival, in 1999, of the National Assembly for Wales, the first all-Wales tier of government for nearly six hundred years, may

WELSH CULTURE AND LANGUAGE

Indigenous **Welsh culture** survives largely through language and song. Music, poetry and dance is celebrated at Eisteddfod festivals throughout the country; most famous are the annual Royal National Eisteddfod (Ⓦ www.eisteddfod.org.uk) in different locations across the country in early August.

The **Welsh language** has undergone a revival and you'll see it on road signs all over the country, although you're most likely to hear it spoken in the north, west and mid-Wales, where for many, it's their first language. Some Welsh place names have never been anglicized, but where alternative names do exist, we've given them in the text.

Some basics

Hello	*Helo*	Hello
Goodbye	*Hwyl*	huh-will
Please	*Os gwelwch chi'n da*	Oss gway-look un tha
Thank you	*Diolch*	Dee-ol'ch

well indicate that power is shifting back, although so far it's a slow trickle. Regardless, Wales retains a strong national identity, most clearly manifested in the Welsh language (see box above).

Much of the country, particularly the **Brecon Beacons** in the south and **Snowdonia** in the north, is relentlessly mountainous and offers wonderful walking terrain, while **Pembrokeshire** to the west boasts lonely coastline. The biggest towns, including the capital **Cardiff** in the south, **Aberystwyth** in the west, and **Caernarfon** in the north, all cling to the coastal lowlands, but even then the mountains are only a short bus-ride away. **Holyhead**, on the island of **Anglesey**, is the main British port for ferry sailings to Dublin.

CARDIFF

Though once shackled to the fortunes of the coal-mining industry, Wales's capital city, **CARDIFF** (Caerdydd), has been revitalized over the past decade, not least due to the arrival of the Welsh Assembly. The city's narrow Victorian arcades are interspersed with new shopping centres and wide pedestrian precincts.

What to see and do

Cardiff's city centre extends north of Cardiff Central train station. To the west of the centre, overlooking the River Taff, is the gleaming **Millennium Stadium** (Ⓦ www.millenniumstadium.com); Cardiff's main historical landmark, the castle, is a short stroll northeast of here.

Cardiff Castle and the National Museum

Cardiff Castle (daily 9am–5/6pm; £8.95) is the historical heart of the city. Standing on a Roman site developed by the Normans, the castle was embellished by the English architect William Burges in the 1860s, and each room is now a wonderful example of Victorian "medieval" decoration: the Banqueting Hall and Fairytale Nursery steal the show. Five minutes' walk northeast, the **National Museum and Gallery** in Cathays Park (Tues–Sun 10am–5pm; free; Ⓦ www.museumwales.ac.uk) houses a fine collection of Impressionist paintings, together with natural history and archeological exhibits.

Cardiff Bay

A half-hour walk south of the centre is the **Cardiff Bay** area, also reached by bus #7 from Central Station, or a train from Queen Street. Once known as Tiger Bay, the long-derelict area has seen massive redevelopment since the Welsh Assembly opened. The **Wales Millennium Centre** dominates, with its huge theatre inside (see below). Nearby is the Cardiff Bay **Visitor Centre** (see below), known as "The Tube" for its unique, award-winning design. There are also waterfront walks, glittering millennium architecture and an old Norwegian seamen's chapel, converted into a cosy café.

Around Cardiff

The Museum of Welsh Life (daily 10am–5pm; free; Ⓦwww.museumwales.ac.uk) is at St Fagans, four miles west of the centre on bus #32/#320. This 100-acre open-air museum is packed with reconstructed rural and industrial heritage buildings.

Arrival and information

Air Cardiff Airport is around 35min west of the centre; bus #X91 runs hourly to Cardiff Central train station (see below).

Train/bus Long-distance coaches, and buses from the airport, arrive at the bus terminal, right beside Cardiff Central train station, south of the city centre off Penarth Rd. Local trains use Queen St station instead, east of the centre.

Tourist office The Old Library on The Hayes (Mon–Sat 9.30am–6pm, Sun 10am–4pm; Ⓣ029/2087 3573, Ⓦwww.visitcardiff.com), and Cardiff Bay Visitor Centre (daily 10am–6/7.30pm; Ⓣ029/2087 7927).

Internet Cardiff Central Library, The Hayes, Ⓣ029/2038 2116, Ⓦwww.cardiff.gov.uk. Free Internet access for members (one piece of ID required to join).

Accommodation

Big Sleep Hotel Bute Terrace, near Cardiff International Arena Ⓣ029/2063 6363, Ⓦwww.thebigsleephotel.com. Trendy, central budget hotel with clean rooms and a modern interior. Rooms £58.

NosDa at Cardiff Backpackers 98 Neville St Ⓣ029/2034 5577, Ⓦwww.nosda.co.uk. Excellent hostel with a young crowd, barbecues and a bar, west of the centre across the River Taff. Dorms £19.50.

NosDa Studio Hostel 53–59 Despenser St Ⓣ029/2037 8866, Ⓦwww.nosda.co.uk. Sister hostel to *NosDa* on Neville St (across the river from the centre, opposite the Millennium Stadium), this place offers superb facilities at budget prices. Dorms are bright and modern and there's a bar, terrace, internet access, gym and 24hr reception. Dorms £19.50, twin rooms £44.

Eating, drinking and nightlife

Clwb Ifor Bach(The Welsh Club) 11 Womanby St Ⓦwww.clwb.net. Little club playing an eclectic range of music from Motown to punk to indie. Drinks £4.50–6.

Madame Fromage 18 Castle Arcade. Cheese experts, serving up delicious soups, cold platters and larger bites in a pretty Victorian arcade opposite the castle.

Milgi Lounge 213 City Rd Ⓦwww.milgilounge.com. Video-art gallery and cocktail bar in the student district, a mile and a half north of the centre, hosting live music.

Old Arcade 14 Church St. Traditional pub retaining some character – one of the best in the centre.

Zerodegrees 27 Westgate St. Sleek glass-fronted restaurant and microbrewery close to the Millennium Stadium. Stone-fired pizzas from £6.95.

Entertainment

Wales Millennium Centre Ⓣ0870/040 2000, Ⓦwww.wmc.org.uk. Wide-ranging arts programme, including opera, ballet, contemporary dance, music and comedy.

Moving on

Train Abergavenny (every 30min; 40min); Bristol (every 20min; 35–50min); Conwy (5–6 daily; 4hr); London (every 30min; 2hr 10min); Manchester (hourly; 3hr 25min); Pembroke (every 2hr; 3hr 15min).

Bus Abergavenny (hourly; 1hr 30min); Aberyswyth (2 daily; 3hr 50min); Brecon (6 daily; 1hr 25min); Bristol (7 daily; 1hr 15min); London (hourly; 3hr 20min–3hr 50min).

CHEPSTOW AND TINTERN ABBEY

South Wales' main historical treasure is accessible from the sleepy market town of **CHEPSTOW** (Cas-Gwent), bunched around Britain's first stone **castle** (April–Oct daily 9am–5pm; Nov–March Mon–Sat 9.30am–4pm, Sun 11am–4pm; £4; Ⓦwww.cadw.wales.gov.uk), built by the Normans in 1067.

Nothing in town, however, can match the six-mile stroll north along the Wye to the romantic ruins of **Tintern Abbey**, built in 1131 and now in a state of majestic disrepair (same hours as castle; £4). If you don't fancy walking, catch bus #69 (every 2hr), which runs from Chepstow to Tintern and on to Monmouth, eight miles north.

For information on Chepstow and the **Offa's Dyke Path** contact the **tourist office** on Bridge Street (daily: March–Oct 9.30am–5.30pm; Nov–March 10am–3.30pm; ⓣ01291/623772, ⓦwww.chepstow.co.uk). The cheapest place to stay is someway out: the spooky *St Briavels Castle* HI **hostel** (ⓣ0845/371 9042, ⓦwww.yha.org.uk; dorms £14.40) occupies a moated Norman castle seven miles northeast of Chepstow on bus #69.

THE BRECON BEACONS

The **Brecon Beacons National Park** (ⓦwww.breconbeacons.org) is a vast area of rocky uplands that makes perfect walking country, though tough: the SAS use the terrain for training. The Beacons themselves, a pair of 2900ft-high hills accessed from Brecon town, share the limelight with the **Black Mountains** in the park's eastern portion, which rise north of pretty Crickhowell.

There are regular train services from Cardiff to **Abergavenny**, start point of the 100-mile Beacon Way, which traverses the entire national park from Abergavenny to Llangadog (allow 8 days). Sixty Sixty's (ⓦwww.sixtysixty.co.uk) #X43 bus service runs from Cardiff to Brecon (every 2hr; 1hr 25min), Crickhowell (2hr 15min) and Abergavenny (2hr 30min). Buses from Hereford in England (accessible by rail) travel to **Hay-on-Wye** (#39) and Brecon. Check what weather to expect before setting out on the hills as conditions change rapidly.

Crickhowell and around

Friendly **CRICKHOWELL** (Crughywel) lies five miles west of Abergavenny and makes a more picturesque base. A great six-mile hike into the **Black Mountains** from here takes you through remote countryside to tiny **Partrishow Church**; inside, you'll find a rare carved fifteenth-century rood screen complete with a dragon and an ancient mural of the grim reaper. For more dramatic scenery, the six-and-a-half-mile round trip to Table Mountain (1481ft) or the still-longer hike up to **Sugar Loaf** (1955ft), offer great views of the Black Mountains.

Crickhowell's **tourist office** (daily 10am–5pm; ⓣ01873/812105) is on Beaufort Street; the bus stops nearby on the square. The best-value **accommodation** in town is at the *Riverside Campsite* (ⓣ01873/810397; £2 per person, plus £4 per tent) by the impressive seventeenth-century river bridge. *The Bear* on the square is the nicest pub.

Brecon

The largest of the central Brecon Beacons rise just south of **BRECON** (Aberhonddu), a lively little town eight miles west of Crickhowell known for its mid-August international jazz festival. For details of the numerous hiking routes call in at the **tourist office** in the Cattle Market car park (Mon–Sat 9.30am–4.45pm, Sun 10am–4pm; ⓣ01874/622485). There's an HI **hostel** two miles east of Brecon at Groesfford (ⓣ0845/371 9506, ⓦwww.yha.org.uk; dorms £18.40), a mile off the Abergavenny bus route.

Hay-on-Wye

To the north of the Black Mountains, on the border with England, charming **Hay-on-Wye** is famous as the second-hand book capital of the world and is home to Britain's leading literary festival (annually in late May). **Accommodation** is scarce during the festival and prices high, so book ahead: pick of the crop is *The Bridge*, 4 Bridge St (ⓣ01497/822952, ⓦwww.thebridgehay.co.uk; doubles £60), a small, family-run

B&B serving excellent cooked breakfasts. *Kilverts Inn* on The Bullring has superior **pub** food and good cask ales.

PEMBROKESHIRE AND ST DAVID'S

The sleepy town of **Pembroke** (Penfro), accessible by train from Cardiff, is the jumping-off point from which to explore **Pembrokeshire Coast National Park** (Ⓦwww.pcnpa.org.uk), covering some 258 miles of isolated scenic coastline. Walkers can hail buses that run along the coast.

St David's

Around thirty miles north of Pembroke, the city of **ST DAVID'S** (Tyddewi), Britain's smallest, is one of the most enchanting spots in Britain (Ⓦwww.stdavids.co.uk). Its beautiful **cathedral** (£4 donation requested), delicately tinted purple, green and yellow by a combination of lichens and geology, hosts a prestigious classical music festival in late May or early June. Nearby the remains of the magnificent fourteenth-century **Bishop's Palace** (Easter–Oct daily 9.30am–5/6pm; Nov–Easter Mon–Sat 10am–4pm, Sun 11am–4pm; £3.20) add to the wonderful setting.

From Haverfordwest (on the National Express bus network) take hourly bus #411 the sixteen miles west to the city.

FERRIES TO IRELAND

Two ferries to Rosslare in Ireland (4hr) leave from **Pembroke Dock**, two miles north of Pembroke, every day. About 17 miles further north, at the end of the main train line from Cardiff and London – is **Fishguard** (Abergwaun), another embarkation point for Rosslare, with ferries and catamarans departing daily. **Holyhead (Caergybi)**, on Anglesey, is the busiest Welsh ferry port, with several daily ferry and catamaran sailings leaving for Dublin.

St David's HI **hostel** is at Llaethdy, close to Whitesands Beach (Ⓣ0845/371 9141 Ⓦwww.yha.org.uk; dorms £18.40). There's a national park **visitor centre** in town at the Oriel y Parc Landscape Gallery (daily: late March to Oct 9.30am–5.30pm; Nov to late March 10am–4.30pm; Ⓣ01437/720392, Ⓦwww.pembrokeshirecoast.org.uk).

ABERYSTWYTH

ABERYSTWYTH, a lively, thoroughly Welsh seaside resort of neat Victorian terraces, has a thriving student culture. The flavour of the town is best appreciated from the seafront, where one of Edward I's castles bestrides a windy headland to the south. There's also a Victorian **camera obscura,** which can be reached via the clanking **cliff railway** (daily mid-March to mid-Nov 10am–5pm; mid-Nov to mid-March Wed–Sun 10am–5pm; £3.50 return). For a more extended rail trip, you could take the popular **Vale of Rheidol** narrow-gauge steam train to **Devil's Bridge**, a canyon where three bridges span a dramatic waterfall (April–Oct; £14.50).

The **train station** is ten minutes south of the seafront, reached by walking up Terrace Road past the **tourist office** (Mon–Sat 10am–5pm, plus Sun in July & Aug; Ⓣ01970/612125). The town seafront is lined with genteel **guesthouses**: a block back the best deal around is at smart *Maes y Mor*, 25 Bath St (Ⓣ01970/639270, Ⓦwww.maesymor.co.uk; singles £25, doubles £40). A self-catering kitchen is available. *The Treehouse*, on Eastgate, is a great daytime vegetarian **café-deli** with mains from £6.40.

SNOWDONIA AND THE NORTH COAST

Jagged peaks, towering waterfalls and glacial lakes – it's not surprising that walkers congregate in large numbers in **Snowdonia National Park**, (Ⓦwww.visitsnowdonia.info) with a steady stream of tourist traffic even in the bleakest months. The park covers an enormous area stretching from Aberdyfi in the south to Conwy on the north coast; its highlight, though, is the glory of North Wales – **Mount Snowdon**, at 3560ft the highest mountain in England and Wales, and the blue-grey, slate towns and villages that surround the peak.

Whenever you come, make sure you're equipped with suitable shoes, warm clothing, and food and drink to see you through any unexpected hitches. There are two main access routes. From Porthmadog, a few miles north of Harlech (both on the local rail network), **buses** skirt the base of Snowdon north to Caernarfon and Llanberis; main-line **trains** from Crewe and Chester hug the north coast through Bangor to Holyhead, passing through Llandudno Junction and Conwy (the latter is a request stop).

Caernarfon

CAERNARFON is a handy springboard for trips into Snowdonia. **Caernarfon Castle** (daily: April–Oct 9.30am–5pm; Nov–March Mon–Sat 9.30am–4pm, Sun 11am–4pm; £4.95), built in 1283, is arguably one of the most splendid castles in Britain, with atmospheric towers and rambling stone passageways. It's here that heirs to the throne, the princes of Wales, are ceremonially invested.

Buses stop on Penllyn, just across Castle Square from the **tourist office** on Castle Street (April–Oct daily 9.30am–4.30pm; Nov–March Mon–Sat 9.30am–3.30pm; ⓣ01286/672232, ⓦwww.visitcaernarfon.com). *Totters*, a sparkling-clean independent backpacker **hostel** at 2 High St (ⓣ01286/672963, ⓦwww.totters.co.uk; dorms £14) provides excellent budget accommodation, while the *Black Boy Inn* on Northgate Street serves great **pub** food (mains f£6.95) and Welsh cream teas. *Beics Menai* (1 Slate Quay, ⓣ01286/676804, ⓦwww.beicsmenai.co.uk) southeast of the castle offers bike rental for £22 per day.

Llanberis and Snowdon

Regular buses run the seven miles southeast from Caernarfon to lacklustre **LLANBERIS**, a lakeside village in the shadow of **Snowdon** and a convenient base for exploring the area. The longest but easiest ascent of the mountain is the **Llanberis Path**, a signposted five-mile hike (3hr), manageable by anyone reasonably fit. Alternatively, take the generally steam-hauled **Snowdon Mountain Railway** (daily mid-March to October; £25; ⓦwww.snowdonrailway.co.uk), which operates from Llanberis to the summit, weather permitting. The slate quarries that seared Llanberis's surroundings now lie idle, but the **Welsh Slate Museum** (Easter–Oct daily 10am–5pm; Nov–Easter daily except Sat 10am–4pm; free; ⓦwww.museumwales.ac.uk) remains as a memorial to the workers' tough lives.

Buses stop near the **tourist office**, 41 High St (Sun–Wed 9.30am–4.30pm; ⓣ01286/870765, ⓔllanberis.tic@gwynedd.gov.uk). Stodgy caff classics are available at *Pete's Eats*, 40 High St, opposite. There's a good choice of accommodation for walkers. The Sherpa Bus services (from £4 all day) encircle Snowdon, providing access to several well-equipped HI **hostels** (ⓦwww.yha.org.uk), each at the base of a footpath up the mountain. The *Llanberis YHA* (ⓣ0845/371 9645) is closest to amenities and to the fastest path up Snowden; *Bryn Gwynant* (ⓣ0845/371 9108), *Pen-y-Pass* (ⓣ0845/371 9534) and *Snowdon Ranger* (ⓣ0845/371 9659) are more secluded. Dorms at each cost £18.40.

North Wales Coast

From Caernarfon, buses run northwest via Bangor to the pretty little island of **Anglesey** (Ynys Môn), connected to North Wales by the Menai Bridge, built by Thomas Telford in 1826. Beside the bridge is the big draw of **Beaumaris Castle** (April–Oct daily 9am–5pm; Nov–March Mon–Sat 9.30am–4pm,

Sun 11am–4pm; £3.70), reached by bus #53, #57 or #58 from Bangor. The giant castle was built in 1295 by Edward I to guard the straits and has a fairytale moat enclosing its twelve sturdy towers. Eighteen miles east of Bangor, at the medieval walled coastal town of Conwy is another of King Edward's masterpieces, **Conwy Castle** (same hours as Beaumaris; £4.80). Conwy's modern **HI hostel**, *Lark Hill*, is just west of the centre (Ⓣ0845/371 9732, Ⓦwww.yha.org.uk; dorms £18.40, twins £38.95).

Scotland

With its kilted bagpipers, brooding castles on craggy highland hilltops, mystery-steeped lochs and whisky, Scotland has a unique character, which is apparent as soon as you cross the border from England. This is partly due to the Scots, unlike the Welsh, successfully repulsing the expansionist designs of England down the centuries. Although the "old enemies" formed a union in 1707, Scotland retained many of its own institutions, notably distinctive legal and educational systems. However, the most significant reawakening of Scottish political nationalism since then has been 1997's referendum, in which the Scottish people voted in favour of devolution. The Scottish Parliament held its first meeting in 1999, and the 2011 elections saw the Scottish National Party gain a historic majority: a first for a Scottish political party in the modern era and a telling step towards increased independence.

Most of the population clusters around the two principal cities: stately **Edinburgh**, the national capital, with its magnificent architecture and imperious natural setting, and revitalized **Glasgow**, a former Industrial Revolution powerhouse now renowned for its culture, nightlife and cuisine. Outside this Central Belt, Scotland is overwhelmingly rural, and just beyond Glasgow the wild, mountainous, loch-strewn bulk of the **Highlands** rears up and doesn't stop until it hits the north coast. Off the west coast lie the majority of Scotland's beach-lined islands, surviving largely on fishing and agriculture. All this makes for terrific outdoor activities, with many of the most scenic spots – such as the famous **Loch Lomond** and **Loch Ness** – easily accessible.

EDINBURGH

EDINBURGH, so said former resident Robert Louis Stevenson, "is what Paris ought to be". For many centuries Scotland's capital rivalled Europe's greatest cities in terms of learning, cultural clout and setting. It straddles two extinct volcanoes, Castle Rock – topped with an imposing castle – and Arthur's Seat, which shelters the official residence of the Royal Family in Scotland. In between is a beautiful city, made up of steeply twisting alleyways (wynds) and stone-built houses. The 440,000 population swells massively in high season, peaking in August during the **Edinburgh Festival**, but year-round it is far and away Scotland's most popular tourist destination.

What to see and do

The centre has two distinct parts. The castle rock is the core of the medieval city – the **Old Town** – where nobles and servants lived side by side for centuries within tight defensive walls: Edinburgh earned its nickname "Auld Reekie" from the smog and smell generated by the cramped inhabitants. To the north, the **New Town**, designed by eminent architects of the day, was begun in the late 1700s: still largely intact, it's an outstanding example of Georgian town planning.

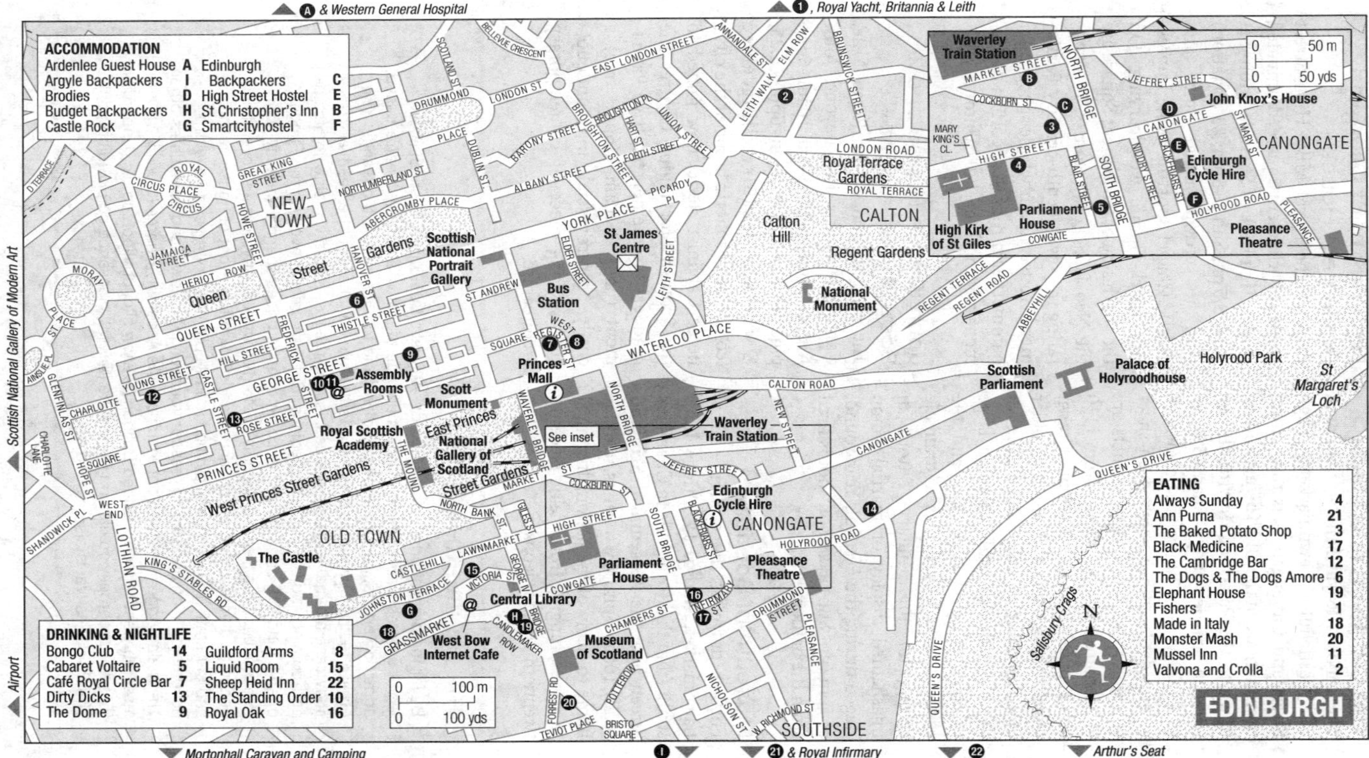

SCOTLAND

BRITAIN

The Old Town and castle

The cobbled **Royal Mile** – composed of Castlehill, Lawnmarket, High Street and Canongate – is the central thoroughfare of the **Old Town**, running down to the Palace of Holyroodhouse from the **castle** (daily 9.30am–5/6pm; £15; ⓦwww.edinburghcastle.gov.uk), a formidable edifice perched on sheer volcanic rock. Within its precincts are St Margaret's Chapel, dating from 1110 and containing the ancient Crown Jewels of Scotland and the even older Stone of Destiny, coronation stone of the kings of Scotland. There's a large military museum here, too, and the castle esplanade provides a dramatic setting for the Military Tattoo, an unashamed display of martial pomp staged during the Festival. Year-round, at 1pm (not Sun) a cannon shot is fired from the battlements.

Museum of Scotland

Further down at the eastern end of Lawnmarket, George IV Bridge leads south from the Royal Mile to Chambers Street; here the **Museum of Scotland** (daily 10am–5pm; ⓦwww.nms.ac.uk) is home to many of the nation's historical treasures, ranging from Celtic pieces to twentieth-century icons.

High Kirk of St Giles and Parliament House

Back on the Royal Mile, High Street starts at Parliament Square, dominated by the **High Kirk of St Giles** (Mon–Sat 9am–5/7pm Sun 1–5pm; £3 donation) with its crown-shaped spire and Thistle Chapel sporting some impressive mock-Gothic woodcarving. On the south side of Parliament Square are the Neoclassical law courts, incorporating the seventeenth-century **Parliament House**, under whose spectacular hammerbeam roof the Scottish parliament met until the 1707 Union.

John Knox's House and Scottish Parliament

The final section of the Royal Mile, Canongate, starts just beyond **John Knox's House** (Mon–Sat 10am–6pm, plus July & Aug Sun noon–6pm; £4.25; ⓦwww.scottishstorytellingcentre.co.uk), atmospheric home of the city's fierce Calvinist cleric, now joined to the Scottish Storytelling Centre. The road leads to the new **Scottish Parliament** (daily 9/10am–4/6pm; free) a costly, controversial but undoubtedly striking piece of contemporary architecture.

THE EDINBURGH FESTIVAL

By far the biggest arts event in Europe, August's **Edinburgh Festival** (ⓦwww.edinburghfestivals.com) is really a multitude of festivals, mostly theatre-based, attracting artists, performers, comedians and tourists in their thousands. **The Fringe** festival, begun as a sideline to the International Theatre Festival to showcase alternative performances, is now the largest draw, mainly for its up-and-coming and big-name comedians. But with a ticket even on the Fringe often hitting £10 or more, and accommodation prices soaring, the only way to experience the Festival cheaply is often to work it. Anything and everything becomes a venue, and every venue needs box office, front of house, technical and bar staff. You won't make much money, but you'll often end up with accommodation and free passes for your venue's shows, and sometimes others. The main Fringe venues to approach are the Assembly Rooms (ⓦwww.assemblyfestival.com), Gilded Balloon (ⓦwww.gildedballoon.co.uk), Underbelly (ⓦwww.underbelly.co.uk) and Pleasance (ⓦwww.pleasance.co.uk/edinburgh). The Book Festival is also a good bet.

HAUNTED EDINBURGH

From serial-killing corpse-dealers Burke and Hare to the malevolent Mackenzie Poltergeist, the winding streets and underground vaults of the Old Town shelter a multitude of spooks, and several entertaining **ghost tours** operate around the High Street. Some favour a historical approach while others lean firmly toward the high theatrical, using "jumper-ooters" – usually costumed students – to scare unsuspecting tour-goers. **The Real Mary King's Close** (£11.50; ⓣ0845/070 6244, ⓦwww.realmarykingsclose.com), off the Royal Mile, is a tour (1hr; daily every 20min Aug 9am–9pm; April–July, Sept & Oct 10am–9pm; Nov–March Sun–Thurs 10am–5pm, Fri & Sat 10am–9pm) of an intact old close built over after the plague, offering a fine balance between the informative and the chilling.

The Palace of Holyroodhouse and Arthur's Seat

The Royal Family's official Scottish residence is the imposing **Palace of Holyroodhouse** (daily: April–Oct 9.30am–6pm; Nov–March 9.30am–4.30pm; £10.50), which has seen entwined with its fair share of historical figures including Oliver Cromwell and Mary Queen of Scots. The public are admitted to the sumptuous state rooms unless the royals are in residence. The **Queen's Gallery** (same hours; £3) displays works of art from the royal collection. The palace looks out over Holyrood Park, from where fine walks lead along the **Salisbury Crags** and up **Arthur's Seat** beyond; a fairly stiff climb is rewarded by magnificent views over the city and the Firth of Forth.

The New Town

The wide grassy valley of Princes Street Gardens marks a clear divide between the Old and New Towns. Along the north side runs **Princes Street**, the main shopping area. Splitting the gardens halfway along is the **National Gallery of Scotland** (daily 10am–5pm, Thurs till 7pm; free; ⓦwww.nationalgalleries.org), an Athenian-style sandstone building. One of the best small collections of pre-twentieth-century art in Europe, it displays works by major European artists including Botticelli, Titian, Rembrandt, Gauguin and Van Gogh. Look out for Sir Henry Raeburn's charming *Reverend Robert Walker Skating* – a postcard favourite. The National is linked, via a Neoclassical underground chamber, to the **Royal Scottish Academy** (same opening hours; free), an exhibition space originally designed in 1826.

The Scott Monument and Calton Hill

East of the National Gallery you can climb the peculiar Gothic spire of the **Scott Monument** (daily: April–Sept 10am–6/7pm; Oct–March 9/10am–4/6pm; £3), a tribute to Sir Walter Scott. Further on down Princes Street **Calton Hill** rises up above the New Town and is worth climbing, both for the citywide views and for the surreal collection of Neoclassical follies, including the unfinished **National Monument**, perched on the very top.

Scottish National Portrait Gallery

North of Princes Street is the broad avenue of Queen Street, at whose eastern end stands the **Scottish National Portrait Gallery** (daily 10am–5pm, Thurs till 7pm; free). The remarkable red-sandstone building is modelled on the Doge's Palace in Venice; inside the collection of portraits offers an engaging procession through Scottish history from Bonnie Prince Charlie to Sean Connery.

Scottish Modern Art Galleries

In the northwest corner of the New Town lies **Stockbridge**, a smart residential suburb with vintage shops, cool cafés and a bohemian vibe. From here Belford Road leads up to the **Scottish National Gallery of Modern Art** and the **Dean Gallery** extension opposite (both daily 10am–5pm; free); the two offer an accessible introduction to all the notable movements of twentieth-century art, with a sculpted garden area designed by Charles Jencks.

Leith

Once rough-round-the-edges Leith, Edinburgh's historic port two miles northwest of the city centre, has been revitalized in recent years and is now a cool collection of lively waterside bars and restaurants. It's home to the Royal Yacht *Britannia* (Ocean Terminal Leith; daily: April–June & Oct 10am–4pm; July–Sept 9.30am–4.30pm; Nov–March 10am–3.30pm; £11; ⓦwww.royalyachtbritannia.co.uk), the Queen's former luxury yacht. The vessel has hosted some of the world's most important figures in its 44 years of service and kickstarted Leith's regeneration when it came to rest in the port here.

Arrival

Air Edinburgh airport is seven miles west of the centre; there are bus connections around the clock to the city, and the new tram line is set to be in operation from the beginning of 2012.
Train Edinburgh's Waverley Station is bang in the centre on Princes St.
Tram The city's tram system is scheduled to be in operation by 2014, connecting Edinburgh Airport with Leith and Newhaven via the city centre.
Bus The coach terminal is on St Andrew Square, just north of Princes St. The best way to get around the city centre is on foot, with the exception of Leith (bus #7/#10/#12/#14/#16 via Leith Walk from Princes St). There's also a good local bus service, although the extensive roadworks in preparation for the trams mean they're often diverted; day-passes are available on board (£3.20, but beware the two firms operating don't take each other's passes – Lothian also don't give change).

EDINBURGH OUTDOORS

Many of Scotland's outdoor features can be enjoyed – albeit on a more limited scale than in the Highlands – within striking distance of the capital. The **Pentland Hills** are ideal for moderate but scenic walking (take Lothian bus #10, #11, #15 or #16). At **Glentress** (ⓦwww.thehubintheforest.co.uk; First bus #62 or #62A), an area of forest near Peebles, about an hour south of Edinburgh, you can rent mountain bikes to enjoy the purpose-built tracks and runs, and follow it up with great cakes at the café. Edinburgh also has some pleasant **beaches**: it's worth making the hour or so trip out along the east coast to find the best ones. First buses #124 and #X5 stop at Longniddry and beautiful Gullane, each with shallow, sandy bays and surprisingly warm water. Also consider the jaunt to Rosslyn Chapel (April–Sept Mon–Sat 9am–6pm, Sun noon–4.45pm; Oct–March Mon–Sat 9.30am–5pm, Sun noon–4.45pm; ⓦwww.rosslynchapel.com) seven miles south of Edinburgh on bus #15, a fifteenth-century mystery-steeped chapel in a wooded glen.

Information and tours

Tourist office 3 Princes St, above the station on the top level of Princes Mall (July & Aug Mon–Sat 9am–8pm, Sun 10am–8pm; Sept–June Mon–Sat 9am–5/7pm, Sun 10am–5/7pm; ⓣ0845/225 5121, ⓦwww.edinburgh.org). There's also one at the airport.
Discount card An Edinburgh Pass secures free airport transfer, unlimited bus travel and access to 27 of the city's attractions (1-day pass/2-day/3-day £29/39/49). The pass can be obtained from the main tourist office.
Bike rental Edinburgh Cycle Hire, 29 Blackfriars St ⓣ0131/556 5560, ⓦwww.cyclescotland.co.uk. This place rents bikes (from £15/70/day/week) and can offer cycling tours of Scotland. Edinburgh itself is hard work, but there's pleasant cycling along the canal as far as Glasgow.

Accommodation

If you want to stay during the Festival (early Aug to early Sept), you'll need to book months in advance and be prepared to pay more than the usual high season prices. Minto St, which starts about a mile and a half south of the train station and Pilrig St, just west of Leith Walk, hold myriad B&Bs.

Hostels and guesthouses

Ardenlee Guest House 9 Eyre Place ⓣ0131/556 2838, ⓦwww.ardenlee.co.uk. Welcoming guesthouse, near the Royal Botanic Garden, with comfortable rooms. Doubles £60.

Argyle Backpackers 14 Argyle Place, Marchmont ⓣ0131/667 9991, ⓦwww.argyle-backpackers.co.uk. Quiet hostel, with small dorms and a dozen double/twin rooms. Pleasant location in studenty Marchmont, off Melville Drive, the road running through The Meadows, a pleasant park. Dorms £13, doubles £44.

Brodies 93 High St ⓣ0131/556 2223, ⓦwww.brodieshostels.co.uk. Tucked down a typical Old Town close, it's cosier than many others, but with limited communal areas. Dorms from £10, doubles from £45.

Budget Backpackers 37–39 Cowgate ⓣ0131/226 6351, ⓦwww.budgetbackpackers.com. Welcoming and relaxed hostel, in a handy location on the Grassmarket, with a great chill-out room and decent rooms. Dorms from £14.

Castle Rock 15 Johnston Terrace ⓣ0131/225 9666, ⓦwww.scotlandstophostels.com. Friendly 200-bed hostel tucked below the castle ramparts. It comes with a comfortable lounge, "period" features and a ghost. Dorms £13.

Edinburgh Backpackers 65 Cockburn St ⓣ0131/220 2200, ⓦwww.hoppo.com. Big hostel with a great central location in a side street off the Royal Mile. Rooms are of a good standard and clean. They also have self-catering apartment-style doubles. Dorms from £15, doubles from £55.

High Street Hostel 8 Blackfriars St ⓣ0131/557 3984, ⓦwww.scotlands-top-hostels.com. Large hostel, in a sixteenth-century building just off the Royal Mile, with basic rooms. Dorms £13, twins from £40.

St Christopher's Inn 9–13 Market St ⓣ0131/226 1446, bookings ⓣ020/7407 1856, ⓦwww.st-christophers.co.uk. 110-bed place with smallish private rooms as well as dorms and a bar downstairs. The bunks are a tad rickety. Dorms from £11.50.

Smartcityhostel 50 Blackfriars St ⓣ0131/524 1989, ⓦwww.smartcityhostels.com. This immaculate modern hostel is definitely flashpacker territory, offering spotless, hotel-standard en-suite accommodation, with a stylish bar, terrace and restaurant. Dorms £18.50, doubles £52.

Campsite

Mortonhall Caravan and Camping 38 Mortonhall Gate, Frogston Rd East ⓣ0131 6641533, ⓦwww.mortonhall.co.uk. Friendly site set in landscaped grounds 6km south of city centre via bus #11 from Princes St. £11/person and tent.

Eating

Edinburgh has one of Britain's best eating scenes, and a thriving café culture.

Cafés

Always Sunday 170 High St. Light, airy café with a great range of gluten-free and dairy-free products, and freshly squeezed juices. A great place for late, lazy breakfasts. Daily until 6pm.

The Baked Potato Shop 56 Cockburn St. The best place in town for tatties (potatoes): try the vegetarian haggis filling. Potatoes around £3. Daily 9am–9pm.

Black Medicine 2 Nicholson St. All totem poles and wooden furniture, this funky café offers cheap panini, wi-fi, great smoothies and delicious "black medicine" (coffee). Mon–Fri 8am–8pm, Sat until 6pm, Sun 10am–4pm.

Elephant House 21 George IV Bridge. Popular café with a cavernous back room, famous as the birthplace of Harry Potter. Mains from £4. Daily 8am–11pm.

Restaurants

Ann Purna 45 St Patrick Square. Swankily decorated vegetarian Indian restaurant: quite possibly Scotland's best. Mains £12–14.

The Cambridge Bar 20 Young St. A wide range of home-made burgers, with more toppings than you could possibly imagine, starting at £5.95.

The Dogs & The Dogs Amore 104 & 110 Hanover St. Two adjacent restaurants offering locally sourced meat and seafood, with an imaginative twist to many dishes. *The Dogs* has a Scottish menu, while *Amore* is Italian-biased. Mains from around £7.50.

Fishers 1 The Shore. Of all the seafood restaurants on this trendy stretch along the Leith docks, *Fishers* keeps its prices most reasonable, its atmosphere most congenial and has high-quality fish dishes sourced from around Scotland's coast. Mains £10–15.

Made in Italy 42 Grassmarket. This place has been dishing up reliably cheap pizzas and Italian sandwiches/salads for years, lovingly decorated in kitsch sourced especially from Milan. Sun–Thurs 8am–11pm, Fri/Sat until late.

Monster Mash 4a Forrest Rd. Hugely popular diner, serving quality renditions of British standards at small cost.

Mussel Inn 61–65 Rose St. Owned by two Scottish shellfish farmers; you can feast here on a kilo of mussels for around £10.

Valvona and Crolla 19 Elm Row. Stylish deli (Scotland's oldest) doing picnic treats with a Mediterranean slant (great Italian wines and cheeses). Mon–Sat 8am–6.30pm, Sun 10am–5.30pm.

Drinking and nightlife

Hardcore clubbers head over to Glasgow, but Edinburgh still has a lively nightlife. Pick up a copy of *The List* to find out what's going on. If you're just out for a drink, you're spoiled for choice with the New Town's glam traditional pubs or snazzy bars along the Shore in Leith. The top of Leith Walk is the place for gay nightlife.

Pubs and bars

Café Royal Circle Bar 19 West Register St. Make a point of visiting this Grade A listed pub, arguably Edinburgh's most beautiful watering hole. There's a pricier restaurant below serving seafood.

Dirty Dicks 159 Rose St. Fun decor, cask-conditioned ales, an animated atmosphere and legendary steak-and-ale pie.

The Dome 14 George St. Opulent bar/restaurant/garden-café with a vast magnificent domed drinking area in Edinburgh's eighteenth-century Physician's Hall.

Guildford Arms 1–5 West Register St. Beautiful New Town Victorian pub, bedecked with chandeliers and serving real ales.

Sheep Heid Inn 43–45 The Causeway, Duddingston. Edinburgh's oldest pub with great ales, tasty food and the world's oldest-known skittle alley, once a stopoff for Mary Queen of Scots. It's a tad out of town, a 20-minute walk around the base of Holyrood Park, but worth it.

The Standing Order 62–66 George St. Former bank-turned-bar still sporting a 30-ton safe. Owned by the Wetherspoons chain and thus cheap.

Live music and clubs

Bongo Club 37 Holyrood Rd Ⓦwww.thebongoclub.co.uk. Top club playing reggae, funk, soul, drum and bass and electro. The big nights go on until 3am.

Cabaret Voltaire 36–38 Blair St Ⓦwww.thecabaretvoltaire.com. Eclectic beats and the occasional live band. You can party until 3am.

Liquid Room 9c Victoria St Ⓦwww.liquidroom.com. Holds house and indie nights; also a popular live venue. Doors close at 3am.

Royal Oak Infirmary St Ⓦwww.royal-oak-folk.com. The venue for Scottish folk music, you'll hear plenty of talented people playing here any night of the week, and it's definitely not all old fogies.

Directory

Embassies and consulates Australia (Honorary Consulate) 5 Mitchell St Ⓣ0131/538 0582; Canada, 50 Lothian Rd, Festival Square Ⓣ0131/473 6320; US, 3 Regent Terrace Ⓣ0131/556 8315.

Exchange Several big bank branches on and around St Andrew's Square, Hanover St and along George St.

Hospital Royal Infirmary, Old Dalkieth Rd Ⓣ0131/536 1000; Western General Hospital, Crewe Rd South Ⓣ0131/537 1000 for minor injuries.

Internet West Bow Internet Café, 98 West Bow (daily 10am–11pm; from £1.20/hr).

Left luggage At Waverley Station and in lockers by St Andrew's Square bus station.

Pharmacy Boots, 101–103 Princes St.

Post office St James' Shopping Centre, near the east end of Princes St.

Moving on

Train Aberdeen (hourly; 2hr 30min); Durham (every 30min; 2hr); Glasgow (every 15min; 50min); Inverness (10 daily; 3hr 50min); Leuchars (for St Andrews; 1–2 hourly; 1hr 10min); London (hourly; 4hr 30min–7hr 30min); Newcastle (every 30min; 1hr 30min); Stirling (every 30min; 50min); York (every 30min; 2hr 30min).

SCOTLAND'S MUSIC FESTIVALS

In recent years several summer festivals have sprung up in Scotland. For mainstream acts, check out **T in the Park**, near Kinross (July; Ⓦwww.tinthepark.com), and **Rock Ness**, near Inverness (June; Ⓦwww.rockness.co.uk). For something more alternative, try **Loopallu**, in the Highlands at Ullappol (June; Ⓦwww.loopallu.co.uk), or the **Wickerman Festival** (July; Ⓦwww.thewickermanfestival.co.uk), near Dundrennan in Dumfries and Galloway, which culminates in the burning of a huge wicker effigy.

Bus Durham (1 daily; 4hr 30min); Glasgow (every 15min; 1hr 15min); Inverness (hourly; 3hr 35 min–4hr 35min); Manchester (2 direct daily; 6hr 25min–9hr 30min); Newcastle (3 daily; 2hr 40min–3hr 10min); St Andrews (every 30min; 2–3hr); Stirling (hourly; 1hr).

GLASGOW

Having shrugged off its post-industrial malaise, rejuvenated **Glasgow**, Scotland's largest city, has undergone a revamp these last two decades and now basks in the light of its outstanding achievement: epitomized in its successful application to host the 2014 Commonwealth Games. The River Clyde on which it sits now bustles again with prosperity; the city's also home to one of the world's best art schools and a fantastic live music scene. The city is rightly favoured by many for its down-to-earth ambience, die-hard "Glesga" party spirit and innovative architecture ranging from lavish eighteenth-century mansions through to cutting-edge twenty-first-century design.

What to see and do

Glasgow's centre lies on the north bank of the River Clyde, around the grandiose **George Square**, a little way east of Central Station. Here, in the West End and on the South Side, lies the legacy of grand civic buildings that led the Victorians to label Glasgow the "second city of the Empire".

The Gallery of Modern Art

Just south of George Square, down Queen Street, is the **Gallery of Modern Art** (Mon–Wed & Sat 10am–5pm, Thurs 10am–8pm, Fri & Sun 11am–5pm; free; Ⓦwww.glasgowlife.org.uk), a lavish eighteenth-century construction housing an exciting collection of contemporary Scots art, notably Toby Paterson and John Byrne.

Cathedral and Necropolis

Northeast of George Square is the **cathedral** on Castle Street (Mon–Sat 9.30am–4/5.30pm, Sun 1–4/5.30pm). Originally built in 1136, it's the only Scottish mainland cathedral to have escaped the country's sixteenth-century religious reformers. The adjacent **Necropolis**, a hilltop cemetery for the magnates who made Glasgow rich; has great views across the city.

Kelvingrove Art Gallery and the West End

The boundaries of the leafy **West End** are marked by the magnificent, Baroque crenellations of **Kelvingrove Art Gallery** (daily 10/11am–5pm; free; Ⓦwww.glasgowlife.org.uk), which boasts pieces by Rembrandt, Degas, Millet, Van Gogh and Monet, as well as an impressive body of Scottish painting. Don't miss Dalí's *Christ of St John of the Cross* – an arresting vision of the Crucifixion.

River Clyde

With the opening of the **Riverside Museum** (Mon–Thurs & Sat 10am–5pm, Fri & Sun 11am–5pm; free; Ⓦwww.glasgowlife.org.uk) at 100 Pointhouse Place, showcasing the city's shipbuilding heritage, the tide continues to turn for Glasgow's redeveloped riverside, which already features the wonderful **Glasgow Science Centre** (50 Pacific Quay; daily 10am–5pm). You can also take a cruise from the quay outside here on the world's last ocean-going paddle steamer (Ⓣ0845/130 1647 Ⓦwww.waverleyexcursions.co.uk). A return trip down the Clyde estuary costs £19.95; summer trips go beyond to the Isle of Bute and the Isle of Arran).

The Burrell Collection

About four miles south of the centre, in **Pollok Country Park** (bus #45/#48/#57 from Union Street, or train to Pollokshaws West), is the astonishing **Burrell Collection**, housed in a custom-built gallery (daily 10/11am–5pm; free; Ⓦwww.glasgowlife.org.uk). Works by Memling, Cézanne, Degas, Bellini and

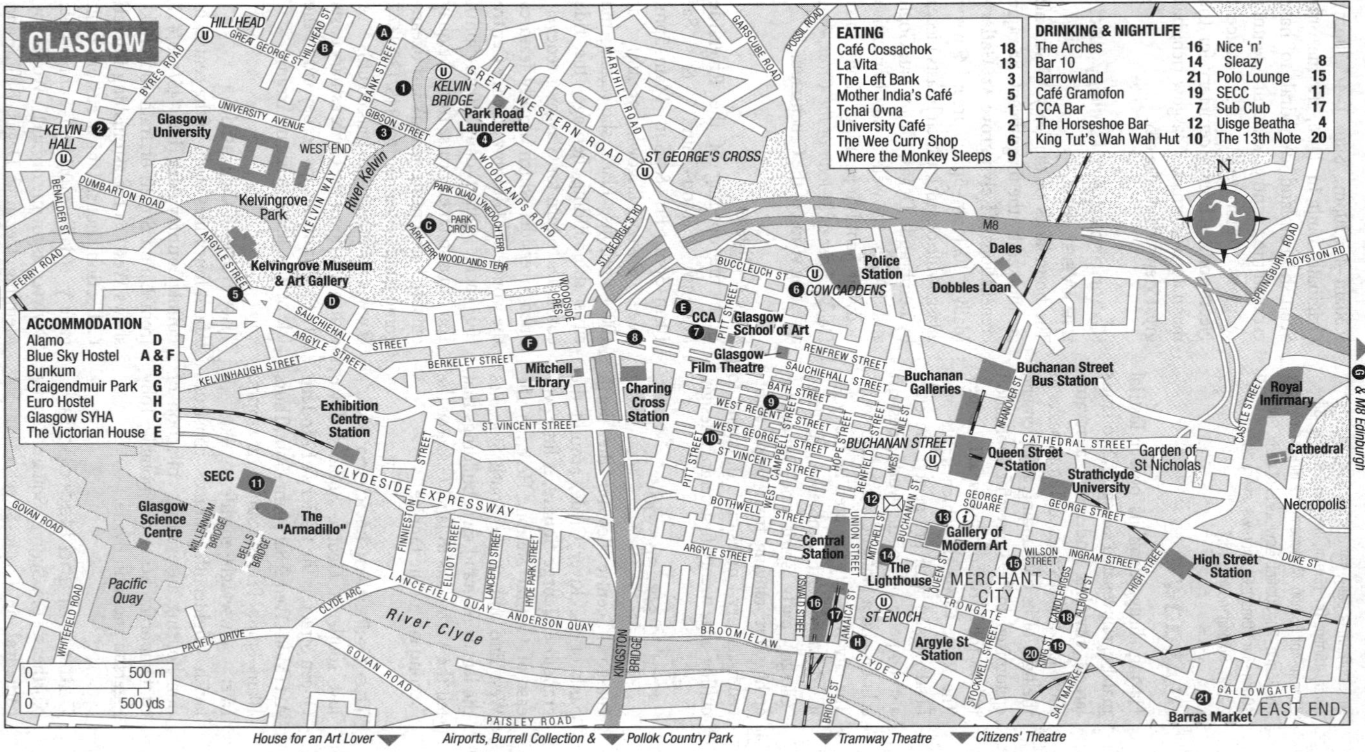

GLASGOW
EATING
Café Cossachok 18
La Vita 13
The Left Bank 3
Mother India's Café 5
Tchai Ovna 1
University Café 2
The Wee Curry Shop 6
Where the Monkey Sleeps 9
DRINKING & NIGHTLIFE
The Arches 16
Bar 10 14
Barrowland 21
Café Gramofon 19
CCA Bar 7
The Horseshoe Bar 12
King Tut's Wah Wah Hut 10
Nice 'n' Sleazy 8
Polo Lounge 15
SECC 11
Sub Club 17
Uisge Beatha 4
The 13th Note 20
ACCOMMODATION
Alamo D
Blue Sky Hostel A & F
Bunkum B
Craigendmuir Park G
Euro Hostel H
Glasgow SYHA C
The Victorian House E
N
0 500 m
0 500 yds
HILLHEAD
KELVIN HALL
KELVIN BRIDGE
ST GEORGE'S CROSS
COWCADDENS
BUCHANAN STREET
ST ENOCH
Glasgow University
Kelvingrove Park
Kelvingrove Museum & Art Gallery
Park Road Launderette
River Kelvin
Police Station
Dales
Dobbles Loan
CCA
Glasgow School of Art
Glasgow Film Theatre
Mitchell Library
Charing Cross Station
Exhibition Centre Station
Buchanan Galleries
Buchanan Street Bus Station
Royal Infirmary
Cathedral
Garden of St Nicholas
Necropolis
Queen Street Station
Strathclyde University
GEORGE SQUARE
Gallery of Modern Art
High Street Station
Central Station
The Lighthouse
MERCHANT CITY
Argyle St Station
Barras Market
EAST END
SECC
The "Armadillo"
Glasgow Science Centre
Pacific Quay
River Clyde
M8
WEST END
BYRES ROAD
GREAT GEORGE ST
HILLHEAD ST
BANK STREET
GIBSON STREET
UNIVERSITY AVENUE
GREAT WESTERN ROAD
MARYHILL ROAD
GARSCUBE ROAD
POSSIL ROAD
WOODLANDS ROAD
PARK QUAD
LYNEDOCH TERR
PARK CIRCUS
PARK TERR
WOODLANDS TERR
WOODSIDE CRES
ST GEORGE'S RD
KELVIN WAY
DUMBARTON ROAD
BENALDER ST
FERRY ROAD
ARGYLE STREET
SAUCHIEHALL STREET
KELVINHAUGH STREET
BERKELEY STREET
ST VINCENT STREET
CLYDESIDE EXPRESSWAY
FINNIESTON STREET
ELLIOT STREET
LANCEFIELD STREET
HYDE PARK STREET
LANCEFIELD QUAY
ANDERSON QUAY
CLYDE ARC
MILLENNIUM BRIDGE
BELLS BRIDGE
GOVAN ROAD
WHITEFIELD ROAD
PACIFIC DRIVE
PAISLEY ROAD
KINGSTON BRIDGE
BROOMIELAW
BUCCLEUCH ST
PITT STREET
RENFREW STREET
BATH STREET
WEST REGENT STREET
WEST GEORGE STREET
WEST CAMPBELL STREET
HOPE STREET
RENFIELD STREET
WEST NILE ST
NILE ST
BOTHWELL STREET
UNION STREET
MITCHELL ST
BUCHANAN ST
QUEEN ST
OSWALD STREET
JAMAICA ST
CLYDE ST
BRIDGE ST
STOCKWELL STREET
TRONGATE
KING ST
SALTMARKET
CANDLERIGGS
ALBION ST
WILSON STREET
INGRAM STREET
HIGH STREET
GEORGE STREET
CATHEDRAL STREET
NHANOVER ST
CASTLE STREET
SPRINGBURN ROAD
ROYSTON RD
DUKE ST
GALLOWGATE
Riverside Museum
G & M8 Edinburgh
House for an Art Lover
Airports, Burrell Collection & Pollok Country Park
Tramway Theatre
Citizens' Theatre

Géricault feature among the paintings, while in adjoining galleries pieces from ancient Rome, Greece, China and medieval Europe are exhibited.

Arrival and information

Air Glasgow International airport lies eight miles west of the city, with regular buses shuttling to Buchanan St bus station; Glasgow Prestwick airport, thirty miles south, is connected to the city centre by train.
Train Glasgow has two main train stations, around 10min walk apart: Central serves all points south and west, as well as Edinburgh on occasion; Queen St serves Edinburgh and the north.
Bus Buchanan St bus station sits at the northern end of Buchanan St.
Tourist office On the south side of George Square, near the top of Queen St (Mon–Sat 9am–7pm, Sun 10am–6pm; ⓣ0141/204 4400, ⓦwww.seeglasgow.com); there's a smaller office at the airport.

City transport

Glasgow's central grid pattern makes navigation by foot relatively simple. The Strathclyde Travel Centre, at Buchanan St bus station (Mon–Sat 6.30am–10.30pm, Sun 7am–10.30pm), has information on all public transport, as well as discount passes.
Underground The Underground is cheap and easy, operating on a circular chain of fifteen stations with a flat fare of £1.20 (Discovery Ticket £3.50 for a day's unlimited travel).
Bike rental Dales, 150 Dobbies Loan ⓣ0141/332 2705.

Accommodation

During summer, the University of Glasgow (ⓣ0141/330 4743) lets out rooms (£20–35 single).

Hostels and hotels

Alamo 46 Gray St ⓣ0141/339 2395, ⓦwww.alamoguesthouse.com. Quiet and attractive option near the university that offers good value for money. Rooms are tastefully furnished and comfy. Doubles £59.
Blue Sky Hostel 65 Berkeley St ⓣ0141/221 1710, ⓦwww.blueskyhostel.com. Lively, friendly hostel within easy walking distance of the town centre, with a huge cuddly canine and free internet access. They also own a more sedate hostel at 3 Bank St in the West End (ⓦwww.glasgowwestendbackpackers.co.uk) with all en-suite, mostly private rooms. Dorms £12, twin rooms from £30.
Bunkum 26 Hillhead St ⓣ0141/581 4481, ⓦwww.bunkumglasgow.co.uk. Welcoming, family-run hostel in a great position close to the university in a stately Victorian terrace. Dorms £16, twins £32.
Euro Hostel 318 Clyde St ⓣ0141/222 2828, ⓦwww.euro-hostels.co.uk/glasgow. There's usually still room at this huge, rather soulless 360-bed hostel when the rest of Glasgow is booked up. There's a bar, chill-out room and a 24hr alcohol licence. Dorms £13, twins £36.
Glasgow SYHA 8 Park Terrace ⓣ0141/332 3004, ⓦwww.glasgowhostel.co.uk. Refurbished hostel in a listed building beside Kelvingrove Park in a good position for going out in the West End. All rooms are en suite and of a high standard. Dorms £14.50.
The Victorian House 212 Renfrew St ⓣ0141/332 0129, ⓦwww.thevictorian.co.uk. B&B with homely pine-furnished en-suite rooms and buffet-style breakfast included. Doubles from £59 if booked online.

CHARLES RENNIE MACKINTOSH

There aren't many architects who have made a bigger impression on a city than Charles Rennie Mackintosh (1868–1928). Little-appreciated in his lifetime, his fascinating, pioneering building designs around the city are among the best examples of early modernist architecture, and are now finally getting the recognition they deserve. See his work for yourself at his first commission, the **Lighthouse** (Mitchell Lane; Mon–Sat 10.30/11am–5pm, Sun noon–5pm; £4; ⓦwww.thelighthouse.co.uk), **Glasgow School of Art** (167 Renfrew St; daily: April–Sept hourly tours 10am–4pm; Oct–March 11am & 3pm; £7.75; ⓣ0141/353 4500, ⓦwww.gsa.ac.uk), **House for an Art Lover** (Bellahouston Park; daily: 10am–5pm; £4.50 ⓦwww.houseforanartlover.co.uk) and the **Willow Tearooms** (217 Sauciehall St; Mon–Sat 9am–5pm, Sun 11am–4.15pm; free) where you can appreciate the architecture over tea and cakes.

Campsite

Craigendmuir Park Clayhouse Rd, Stepps ⓣ0141/779 4159, ⓦwww.craigendmuir.co.uk. Large, well-equipped campsite four miles northeast of the centre; take a train to Stepps, from where it's a 15min walk. £14.25/person and pitch.

Eating

Café Cossachok 38 Albion St. Russian restaurant, gallery and live venue that envelops diners in soft red light with haunting violin music. The menu includes Slavic staples like *borscht*.

La Vita 1–5 St Vincent Place. Italian restaurant spread over three floors on the corner of George Square. The food is excellent and the portions enormous. Bargain lunch menu at £5.95.

The Left Bank 33–35 Gibson St. Airy restaurant with a monumental all-day brunch and innovative mains with a Middle Eastern slant from £5.95.

Mother India's Café 1355 Argyle St. Innovative, tapas-style approach to curry and great value make this bustling place, near Kelvingrove Museum, a winner. Alex "Franz Ferdinand" Kapranos is a fan. Dishes from £3.40.

Tchai Ovna 42 Otago Lane. Enchanting "magic teashop", tucked down a lane in the arty West End. Sample exotic teas in an atmosphere that's part opium den, part hippy commune. Excellent vegetarian food for under £5.

University Café 87 Byres Rd. An original Art Deco-style café – something of an institution. The menu is of the no-frills kind – think steak pie and Knickerbocker Glory. Dishes from £3.50.

The Wee Curry Shop 7 Buccleuch St. Tiny establishment offering excellent-value Indian meals. Dishes for around £6.

Where the Monkey Sleeps 182 West Regent St. Breath of fresh air in the city centre: a basement coffee shop playing great music attracting a bohemian/student crowd.

Drinking and nightlife

Pubs and nightspots cluster around the city centre, the suave Merchant City to the east of Queen St, and the West End around Ashton Lane, a charming cobbled street lined with bars and restaurants.

Pubs and bars

Bar 10 10 Mitchell Lane. A great pre-club bar with DJs. Its industrial interior is the work of Ben Kelly, designer of Manchester's fabled, but now demolished, *Hacienda*.

Café Gramofon 7 King St. Flying the flag for Merchant City's eclectic assortment of hidden-away bars. Romanian wine, Hungarian goulash and weekly live comedy/theatre.

The Horseshoe Bar 17 Drury St. Rarely a quiet moment at this city-centre pub which features the longest bar in the UK and almost perpetual karaoke.

Uisge Beatha 232–246 Woodlands Rd. Warm, candlelit pub with kilted bar staff, stuffed animals and a friendly blend of locals and students supping a vast array of whiskies.

Clubs

The Arches 30 Midland St ⓦwww.thearches.co.uk. Cavernous club and live venue, under Central Station, that pulls off gigs, theatre and lysergic club nights with equal aplomb. The bigger nights can go on past 4am.

Polo Lounge 84 Wilson St. Popular gay club that mixes refined drinking upstairs with a packed, cruisey dancefloor in the basement.

Sub Club 22 Jamaica St ⓦwww.subclub.co.uk. Underground club and purveyor of the finest techno and electro.

Entertainment

Live music

The 13th Note 50–60 King St ⓦwww.13thnote.co.uk. A Glasgow institution hosting up-and-coming bands from metal to indie via acoustic rock. Also serves great veggie food.

Barrowland 244 Gallowgate ⓦwww.glasgow-barrowland.com. Glasgow's most famous live venue, with a medium-size capacity for soon-to-be-big bands and more established acts.

King Tut's Wah Wah Hut 272a St Vincent St ⓦwww.kingtuts.co.uk. Famous as the place where Oasis were discovered, and still hosting excellent gigs.

Nice 'n' Sleazy 421 Sauchiehall St ⓦwww.nicensleazy.com. Late-night bar, with the best jukebox in town and great gigs in its sweaty basement.

SECC Exhibition Way ⓦwww.secc.co.uk. The Scottish Exhibition and Conference Centre, including the famous "Armadillo" building, hosts the big-name touring bands and comedy acts.

Cinema and theatre

Centre for Contemporary Arts (CCA) 350 Sauchiehall St ⓦwww.cca-glasgow.com. Cultural centre that has a reputation for a programme of controversial performances and exhibitions.

Citizens' Theatre 119 Gorbals St ⓦwww.citz.co.uk. South Side theatre famous for sourcing top Scottish talent.

Glasgow Film Theatre 12 Rose St ⓦwww.gft.org.uk. Wonderful cinema showing art films and old favourites.

The Grosvenor Ashton Lane. Independent cinema/café also hosting live music and screenings in Kelvingrove Park.

Directory

Hospital Royal Infirmary, 84 Castle St ⓣ0141/211 4000.
Internet Mitchell Library, North St: wi-fi access and 100 PCs for public use (free for members).
Pharmacy Boots, Buchanan Galleries.
Police Pitt St ⓣ0141/532 2000.
Post office 47 St Vincent St.

Moving on

Train Balloch (every 30min; 45min), Edinburgh (every 15min; 50min); Inverness (every 2hr; 3hr 25min, some change at Perth); Liverpool (via Wigan/Preston; every 30min; 3hr 30min); London (hourly; 4hr 30min–5hr 30min); Mallaig (for Skye; Mon–Sat 3 daily; Sun 1 daily; 5hr 15min); Manchester (2 direct, 23 daily via Preston/Carlisle; 3hr 15min–3hr 45min); Oban (for Mull; Mon–Sat 3 daily; Sun 1 daily; 3hr); Newcastle (every 30min–1hr; 2hr 40min–3hr; most change in Edinburgh); Stirling (every 30min; 30min).
Bus Edinburgh (every 10–15min; 1hr 10min); Inverness (every 1hr 30min; 3hr 30min-4hr 30min); Liverpool (1 daily; 6hr 30min); London (7 daily; 8hr–10hr 30min); Manchester (5 daily; 5hr); Newcastle (1 daily; 4hr); Oban (for Mull; 3 daily; 3hr); St Andrews (hourly; 2hr 20min); Skye (3 daily; Kyle of Lochalsh 5hr, Portree 6hr, Uig 6hr 30min); Stirling (hourly; 45min).

STIRLING

STIRLING's strategic position between the Lowlands and Highlands at the easiest crossing of the River Forth has shaped its major role in Scottish history. Its steep cobbled streets and stupendous castle atop a crag has also earned the city somewhat flattering comparisons to a mini-Edinburgh.

What to see and do

Imperiously set on a rocky volcanic outcrop, the atmospheric **castle** (daily 9.30am–5/6pm; £9) combined regal and military functions. Highlights within the complex are the **Royal Palace**, dating from the late Renaissance, and the earlier **Great Hall**, with its restored hammer-beam roof. The oldest part of Stirling huddles around the streets leading up to the castle. Look out for the Gothic, timber-roofed **Church of the Holy Rude** (daily 10am–5pm), where the infant James VI – later James I of the United Kingdom – was crowned King of Scotland in 1567. From here, Broad Street slopes down to the lower town, passing the **Tolbooth**, the city's arts and cultural centre. Stirling is famous as the scene of Sir William Wallace's victory over the English in 1297, a crucial episode in the Wars of Independence. The Scottish hero was commemorated in the Victorian era with the **Wallace Monument** (daily 10/10.30am–4/5/6pm; £7.75) a bizarre Tolkienesque tower providing stupendous views – finer even than those from the castle.

Arrival and information

Train and bus The train and bus stations are both just east of the centre in the lower part of town.
Tourist office 41 Dumbarton Rd, in the lower part of town (June to mid-Sept daily 9am–6/7pm, Sun 9.30/10am–4pm; mid-Sept to May Mon–Sat 9/10am–4/5pm; ⓣ01786/475 019, ⓦwww.visitscottishheartlands.com).
Internet Lingle's (62 Upper Craigs); £1.50/hr.

Accommodation

Willy Wallace Hostel 77 Murray Place ⓣ01786/446773, ⓦwww.willywallacehostel.com. Lively, welcoming backpacker hostel with a comfortable common room. Dorms £15, doubles £36.
Witches Craig Campsite Off St Andrew's Rd ⓣ01786/474947, ⓦwww.witchescraig.co.uk. Picturesque site three miles east of town; take bus #62. Closed Nov–March. £18 for 2 people plus tent.

Eating

La Ciociara 41 Friars St. Good-value Italian in the heart of Stirling.
The Portcullis Castle Wynd. Right by the castle, this eighteenth-century hotel has one of the city's best bars, complete with beer garden and fire. It serves food too.

ST ANDREWS

The country's oldest university town and a major golfing hotspot, plush **ST ANDREWS** lies on a gorgeous stretch of the Fife coast 56 miles northeast of Edinburgh. With Prince William as a former alumnus and its seven swanky golf courses being both the oldest and most revered in the world, it's unsurprising the town has a self-important air. Having attracted a well-to-do crowd for several centuries, it's on the pricey side, too.

What to see and do

Entering the town from the Edinburgh road, you pass no fewer than four golf links, the last of which is the **Old Course**, the most famous and – in the opinion of Jack Nicklaus – the world's best. At the southern end of the Old Course towards the waterfront, is the **British Golf Museum** (March–Oct daily 9.30/10am–5/5.30pm; Nov–March daily 10am–4pm; £6); if you want to step onto the famous fairways, head to the **Himalayas** putting green, located right by the first hole and only £2 per round. A wonderful crescent of sandy beach sweeps north from the Old Course; immediately south of it runs North Street, one of St Andrews' two main arteries, largely taken up with grand university buildings.

The castle and cathedral

The ruined **castle** (daily: 9.30am–4.30/5.30pm; £5.20, combined ticket with cathedral £7.60) sits on North Street, while a short distance further along the coast is the equally ruined Gothic **cathedral** (same hours; £5.50), the mother church of medieval Scotland and the largest and grandest ever built in the country.

Arrival and information

Train There are no direct trains, though frequent buses connect with the train station five miles away in Leuchars.

Bus The bus station is west of town on City Rd.

Tourist office 70 Market St (Mon–Sat 9.15/9.30am–5/7pm, plus Sun April to mid-Oct 10/11am–4/5pm; ⓣ01334/472021, ⓦwww.standrews.co.uk).

Accommodation

The tourist office will book rooms for a ten percent deposit – worth doing in the summer and during big golf tournaments, when accommodation is in short supply.

Cairnsmill Caravan Park ⓣ01334/473604. A large, family campsite a mile from town with a swimming pool and games room. Bunkhouse accommodation available. £15.

St Andrews Tourist Hostel ⓣ01334/479911, ⓦwww.standrewshostel.com. Nicely decorated hostel with clean, basic dorm rooms, a well-equipped kitchen and comfy lounge. Dorms £14.

Eating

The Lizard *Ogstons*, 147 North St ⓦwww.ogstonsonnorthst.com. This fantastic building contains a great restaurant (mains £8–10), bar and a cosy basement music lounge.

LOCH LOMOND AND THE TROSSACHS

Lying at at the heart of the **Trossachs National Park**, **Loch Lomond** – the largest stretch of fresh water in Britain – is the epitome of Scottish scenic splendour, thanks in large part to the ballad that fondly recalls its "bonnie, bonnie banks". From the main hub at **BALLOCH**, at the loch's southwestern tip, you can take a cruise around the 33 islands nearby (ⓣ01389/752376, ⓦwww.sweeney.uk.com; from £6.50 for a one-hour cruise). The **western shore** is easily accessible by bus from Balloch, with the A82 zipping along its banks. The **eastern shore**, however, is much more peaceful, as large sections of it are only accessible via the footpath which forms part of the West Highland Way. The easiest hike to the graceful peak of **Ben Lomond** (3192ft) is from **Rowardennan** (3hr), accessible in summer by ferry from Inverbeg on the western shore or alternatively by catching the hourly McColls bus #309 from Balloch to Balmaha and hiking the remaining seven miles.

Arrival and information

Train The easiest way to get to the loch is to take one of the frequent trains from Glasgow Queen St Station to Balloch.
Tourist office The vast Gateway Centre at Balloch, incorporating shops, information points and cafés, also has a tourist office (daily 10am–5pm; ⓣ01389/727700, ⓦwww.lochlomond-trossachs.org).

Accommodation

The tourist office has details of the wide choice of campsites and B&Bs in all the villages. The hostels below are open only from March to October.
Loch Lomond Hostel ⓣ01389/850226, ⓦwww.syha.org.uk. A couple of miles northwest of Balloch, this is Scotland's most beautiful HI hostel, and comes complete with resident ghost. Dorms £17.75.
Rowardennan Hostel ⓣ01360/870259, ⓦwww.syha.org.uk. Another alluringly sited HI hostel – see opposite for how to get here. Dorms £16.85, quads £66.

INVERNESS

Lying 160 miles north of Edinburgh, **INVERNESS** is the capital of the Highlands: a grey but affable town with a vibrant dining scene and wonderful setting at the mouth of the River Ness. The chief historical attraction nearby is the ever-popular Culloden Visitor Centre (daily: April–Oct daily 9am–5/6pm; Nov–March 10am–4pm; £10), six miles east on bus line #1A from the city centre. In 1746, Culloden Moor was the scene of the last pitched battle on British soil, when Bonnie Prince Charlie's Jacobite army was crushed in just forty minutes, ending Stuart ambitions of regaining the monarchy forever. Infinitely more dramatic is **Cawdor Castle** (April–Oct daily 10am–5.30pm; £9), twelve miles northeast on Rapsons bus #12 from Inverness, a fairytale fourteenth-century castle and legendary home of Shakespeare's Macbeth.

Arrival and information

Air Inverness airport is seven miles northeast of the town. There's a bus into the city every half-hour, and the journey takes 20min.
Train and bus The train and bus stations are next to each other just northeast of the centre off Academy St.
Tourist office Castle Wynd (April–Oct Mon–Sat 9am–5/6pm Sun 9.30/10am–4/5pm; Nov–March Mon–Sat limited hours; ⓣ01463/234353, ⓦwww.inverness-scotland.com). Will find rooms for a small fee and does bike rent.

Accommodation

Bazpackers 4 Culduthel Rd ⓣ01463/717663 ⓦwww.bazpackershostel.co.uk. The smallest hostel in town, and the best, with an open fire, friendly staff and views over the River Ness. Dorms from £15, doubles £36–44.
Inverness Student Hotel 8 Culduthel Rd ⓣ01463/236556, ⓦwww.invernessstudenthotel.com. This welcoming hostel has great views, an open fire in the common room, internet access and a quiet location by the castle. Dorms £17.
Inverness YHA Victoria Rd ⓣ 0870/004 1127, ⓦwww.syha.org.uk. Large, modern HI hostel with excellent facilities, though it's not the most central option. Dorms £17.50.

Eating and drinking

Hootananny 67 Church St. Lively pub that has live gigs and good Thai food.

MIDGE ALERT

During the summer months, particularly in wetter areas, the Highlands and Islands are blighted by midges – tiny biting insects that appear in swarms. If you're camping or hiking, make sure you have insect repellent – locals swear by Avon's Skin So Soft moisturizer – or a midge hood, a net fitting over a wide-brimmed hat which, while making no concessions to fashion, should protect the face. Even a light breeze will blow the midges away though, so try and pick somewhere that isn't completely still to camp.

THE LOCH NESS MONSTER

Tales of Nessie date back at least as far as the seventh century, when the monster came off second best in an altercation with St Columba. However, the possibility that a mysterious prehistoric creature might be living in the loch only attracted worldwide attention in the 1930s, when sightings were reported during the construction of the road along its western shore. Numerous appearances have been reported since, but even the most high-tech surveys of the loch have failed to come up with conclusive evidence.

La Tortilla Asesina 99 Castle St. Snug Spanish restaurant with tapas from £2.50.

Moving on

Train Aviemore (every 1hr 30min–2hr; 35–45min); Edinburgh (8 daily; 3hr 15min–4hr 45min); Glasgow (3 direct daily, or change at Perth; 3hr 20min); Kyle of Lochalsh (for Skye; Mon–Fri 4 daily; Sat 2 daily; Sun 1 daily; 2hr 30min, weekend trains not direct); Stirling (some change at Perth; 10 daily; 2hr 45min).
Bus Edinburgh (hourly; 3hr 35min–4hr 35min); Fort William (via Loch Ness, every 2hr; 1hr 50min); Glasgow (every 1hr 30min, some change at Perth; 4hr 30min); Stirling (4 daily, change at Perth; 3hr 50min).

LOCH NESS

Loch Ness forms part of the thickly forested natural fault line of the Great Glen, which slices across the southern edge of the Highlands between Inverness and Fort William. Most visitors are eager to catch a glimpse of the elusive **Loch Ness Monster**: to find out the whole story, take a bus to **DRUMNADROCHIT**, fourteen miles southwest of Inverness, where the **Loch Ness Exhibition Centre** (daily: Eater–Oct 9/9.30am–5.30/6pm; Oct–Easter 10am–3.30pm; £6.50; ⓦwww.lochness.com) attempts to breathe life into the old myth. A couple of miles south the ruined **Castle Urquhart** (daily April–Sept 9.30am–6pm; Oct until 5pm; Nov–March until 4.30pm; £7) is one of Scotland's most beautifully sited fortresses.

THE HIGHLANDS

The beguiling **Highlands** are a stunning mix of bare hills, green glens and silvery lochs, which extend up to the country's northern coast. The distances involved, along with scarce public transport, mean that you'll need several days to explore any one part properly. **FORT WILLIAM** is the Highlands' key outdoor base, served by train from Glasgow and bus from Inverness. On the outskirts of town is the **Nevis Range**, with skiing in winter and mountain biking in summer, and, sixteen miles south, **Glen Coe**, where soaring scenery and poignant history combine like nowhere else in the country. If you want to climb **Ben Nevis** (Britain's highest peak), the easiest route (7hr return) begins just outside town but make sure you wear suitable clothing, as capricious weather conditions and poor visibility can combine to make the ill-prepared hiker extremely vulnerable. Fort William also marks one end of the West Highland Way, which runs all the way to Glasgow.

It's better to stay in **Glen Nevis** than Fort William itself: try the SYHA's *Glen Nevis* **hostel** (ⓣ01397/702336 ⓦwww.syha.org; dorms £18.50) at the foot of Ben Nevis, a 2.5-mile walk or £6 taxi ride out of town. **Outdoor activities** are the big draw: most tourist information centres and hostels carry information on local hiking routes and adventure sports. Some scenic spots are served by First ScotRail's train network (ⓦwww.scotrail.co.uk), which has good-value travel passes available.

Aviemore and the Cairngorms

AVIEMORE, at the foot of the looming **Cairngorm** range, now a national park, is a good base for challenging hiking, ancient pine forests and winter sports.

HIGHLAND TOURS

A couple of rival companies offer lively minibus tours designed specifically for backpackers: **Haggis** (Ⓣ0131/557 9393, Ⓦwww.haggisadventures.com) and **Macbackpackers** (Ⓣ0131/558 9900, Ⓦwww.macbackpackers.com) depart from Edinburgh on trips lasting between one and seven days, covering the likes of Loch Ness, Skye and the Highlands. Three-day tours to Skye cost about £90.

Glenmore Lodge (Ⓣ01479/861256, Ⓦwww.glenmorelodge.org.uk), which runs excellent, though expensive, outdoor courses, offers B&B **accommodation** (rooms £50–60). In town, there's an SYHA hostel just south of the train station on Grampian Road (Ⓣ01479/810345, Ⓦwww.syha.org; dorm £17) and the *Cairngorm Hotel* opposite the station serving reasonably priced pub-style food.

THE ISLE OF MULL AND AROUND

The **Isle of Mull** is the most accessible of the Hebridean islands off Scotland's west coast: just 45 minutes by ferry from **Oban**, which is linked by train to Glasgow. Its three hundred miles of rugged coastline is the main draw, peppered with castles, beautiful beaches, idyllic chocolate-box villages like Tobermory and Iona, the birthplace of Christianity in Britain.

Craignure and Tobermory

CRAIGNURE, the ferry terminal for boats from Oban (3–6 daily; 45min; £4.45 one-way), has the island's main **tourist office** (mid-Oct to March Mon–Sat 9am–5pm, Sun 10.30am–noon & 3.30–5pm; April to mid-Oct Mon–Fri 8.30am–5.15/7pm, Sat 9am–5.15/6.30pm, Sun 10/10.30am–5.15/7pm; Ⓣ01680/812377, Ⓦwww.visitscottishheartlands.com), a decent pub, bike rental and a campsite. Just outside is dramatic thirteenth-century **Duart Castle** (April Mon–Thurs & Sun 11am–4pm; May to mid-Oct daily 10.30am–5.30pm; £5), two miles' walk along the bay: you can peek in the dungeons and ascend to the rooftops. Mull's "capital" **TOBERMORY,** 22 miles northwest of Craignure, is easily the most attractive fishing port in the west of Scotland, with brightly coloured houses and boats sheltering in a bay backed by a steep bluff. For a list of the local **B&Bs** head for the **visitor centre** (Tigh Solais; April–Oct daily 9/10am–5/6pm; Ⓣ01688/302 876), in the harbour building at the northern end of the harbour. The **HI hostel** (Ⓣ01688/302481; dorms £16.75, closed Nov–Feb) is on Main Street, along with the *Mishnish Hotel* pub, popular for live folk music at weekends.

Fionnphort and Staffa

Some 35 miles west of Craignure, tiny **Fionnphort** is nevertheless one of Mull's metropolises. A few miles south at Knockvologan is the gorgeous sandy beach of **Erraid**, inspiration for Robert Louis Stevenson's thriller *Kidnapped.* Boats from Fionnphort run to **Staffa**, a moody, uninhabited basaltic island marking the northern end of the Giant's Causeway (see p.636) with the cathedral-like **Fingal's Cave**, whose haunting noises inspired Mendelssohn's *Hebrides Overture* (the *Iolaire*; Ⓣ01681/700358; Ⓦwww.staffatrips.co.uk; £25; also stops on Iona).

Isle of Iona

Serene little **Iona**, served by Calmac ferry (6–10 daily; 10min) from Fionnphort, has been a place of pilgrimage for several centuries: it was here that St Columba fled from Ireland in 563 and established a monastery subsequently responsible for the conversion of more or less all of pagan Scotland. The present **abbey** (daily 9.30am–4.30/5.30pm; £5.50) dates from

ISLAND-HOPPING

The sea off Scotland's west coast is dotted with islands, from tiny rocks to substantial landmasses. The main ferry company, **Caledonian MacBrayne** (CalMac; Ⓦwww.calmac.co.uk), connects most of them, and offers a range of island-hopping trips. **Arran**, **Islay** and the **Small Isles** (Rum, Muck and Eigg) are all worth visiting, too.

1200, while Iona's oldest building, **St Oran's Chapel**, lies just south. It stands at the centre of the burial ground, Reilig Odhrain, which is said to contain the graves of sixty kings. Camping is not permitted, but the excellent *Iona Hostel* (Ⓣ01681/700781, Ⓦwww.ionahostel.co.uk; dorms £19.50), a mile from the ferry, has comfortable beds and superb views.

THE ISLE OF SKYE

The deeply indented coastline, azure water, spectacular summits and bright, clear light of the **Isle of Skye** make it one of the most captivating spots in Britain. The island's stunning topography once shielded Bonnie Prince Charlie from capture by government forces; now the high, jagged peaks of the **Cuillin** ridge are Britain's best (and most demanding) walking and climbing terrain. Equally dramatic are the rock formations of the **Trotternish peninsula** in the north. Skye is connected to the mainland via a bridge to Kyle of Lochalsh, from where several trains daily serve Inverness, and by ferry from Armaldale in south-eastern Skye to Mallaig, from where trains run to Glasgow. Three daily buses also link Skye with Glasgow (Rapsons; Ⓣ0871/200 2233, Ⓦwww.rapsons.com).

Elgol and the Cuillins

The best approach to the **Cuillins** is by #49 bus from Broadford on the dramatic road fourteen miles southwest to **ELGOL**, from where there are boat trips on the *Bella Jane* (March–Oct Mon–Sat; one-way £14, return £22; Ⓣ0800/731 3089, Ⓦwww.bellajane.co.uk) to stunning Loch Coruisk, where there's a seal colony. With adequate planning, you can hike from the loch up into the Cuillins or back to Elgol. Serious hikers also head for **GLENBRITTLE**, west of the Cuillins, where there's an HI hostel (Ⓣ01478/640278, Ⓦwww.syha.org.uk; dorms £16, closed Oct–Feb) and a nearby campsite (Ⓣ01478/640404; £6.40, closed Nov–March).

Portree

Skye's capital **PORTREE**, an attractive fishing port in the north of the island, has the island's main **tourist office** just off Bridge Road (Mon–Sat 9am–5pm, plus April–Oct Sun 10am–4pm; Ⓣ01478/612137). The town has several **hostels**, of which the biggest and best is *Portree Independent Hostel* (Ⓣ01478/613737; Ⓦwww.hostelskye.co.uk; dorm £15). Food-wise the best deal is the excellent fish and chips down by the harbour, and the cheerful *Arriba Inn* just up from the harbour, which does fantastic cakes.

Old Man of Storr and Uig

Some nine miles from Portree on the **Trotternish peninsula**, are Skye's geological highlights: a 165-foot sea-stack called the **Old Man of Storr** and, soaring above Staffin Bay ten miles north, the **Quiraing** – a spectacular forest of rock formations. The tranquil village of **UIG**, on the west coast, has ferries to the islands of the Outer Hebrides, as well as an HI hostel (Ⓣ01470/542746; dorms £16, closed Oct–March). The very friendly, year-round *Uig Bay Campsite* (Ⓣ01470/542714, Ⓦwww.uig-camping-skye.co.uk; £5) rents out bikes.

Bulgaria

HIGHLIGHTS

THE BLACK SEA COAST: white sand and beach bars

ALEXSANDAR NEVSKI CATHEDRAL, SOFIA: the capital's most striking building

RILA MONASTERY: fabulous frescoes deep in the mountains

PLOVDIV'S OLD QUARTER: get lost among the ornate houses and Roman remains

BANSKO: skiing and snowboarding on the cheap

ROUGH COSTS

DAILY BUDGET Basic €25 /occasional treat €40

DRINK Beer (0.5l) €1

FOOD Shopska salad €3

HOSTEL/BUDGET HOTEL €10/€30

TRAVEL Train: Sofia–Plovdiv €5 (2–3hr); bus: €5

FACT FILE

POPULATION 7.3 million

AREA 110,910 sq km

LANGUAGE Bulgarian

CURRENCY Lev (Lv)

CAPITAL Sofia (population: 1.35 million)

INTERNATIONAL PHONE CODE ⓣ359

Introduction

With several dramatic mountain ranges, superb beaches, numerous historic towns and a web of working villages with traditions straight out of the nineteenth century, Bulgaria has a wealth of attractions crammed into a relatively compact country. More than anything else, this is a land of adventures: once you step off the beaten track, road signs and bus timetables often disappear (or are only in Cyrillic), and few people speak a foreign language, but almost everyone you meet will be determined to help you on your way.

Bulgaria's image has altered dramatically in recent years, thanks largely to the modernization of the country's tourist infrastructure coupled with soaring foreign interest in inexpensive rural and coastal properties. Independent travel is common: costs are relatively low, and for the committed there is much to take in. Romantic National Revival era architecture is a particular draw, with **Koprivshtitsa**, **Bansko** and **Plovdiv** foremost amongst examples of the genre. The monasteries are stunning, too – the finest, **Rila**, should be on every itinerary, while for city life aim for **Sofia**, Plovdiv, and the cosmopolitan coastal resorts of **Varna** and **Burgas**.

CHRONOLOGY

4000s BC Thracian tribes settle in the area of present-day Bulgaria.
600s BC Greeks settle in the area of present-day Bulgaria.
100s AD Romans invade the Balkan Peninsula.
200 A popular Roman amphitheatre draws people to Serdica (Sofia).
681 The First Bulgarian Kingdom is formed.
864 Bulgaria accepts the Orthodox Church.
1018 The country falls under Byzantine control.
1185 The Byzantines are repelled and the Second Bulgarian Kingdom is proclaimed.
1396 The Ottomans conquer Bulgaria, ushering in almost five hundred years of Turkish rule.
1876 Revolutionaries based at Koprivshtitsa carry out the ill-fated April Rising, which provokes savage Ottoman reprisals.
1877 War of Liberation sees Russia declare war on Turkey to win freedom for Bulgaria.
1886 The Treaty of Bucharest ends the Serbo–Bulgarian war begun the previous year, and Bulgaria gains territory.
1908 Bulgaria declares itself an independent kingdom.
1912 First Balkan War; Bulgaria sustains heavy losses in victory over the Ottomans.
1913 Second Balkan War; previous allies Serbia and Greece defeat Bulgaria.
1914–18 Bulgaria sides with the Central Powers during World War I.
1945 Soviet army invades German-occupied areas of Bulgaria.
1954 Todor Zhivkov becomes head of the Bulgarian Communist Party in power.
1989 Zhivkov ousted among calls for democratization.
1991 New constitution proclaims Bulgaria a Parliamentary Republic.
2001 Former king Simeon II is elected Prime Minister.
2004 Bulgaria joins NATO.
2007 Bulgaria joins the EU.
2009 Zhivkov's former bodyguard, Boiko Borisov, is elected Prime Minister.

ARRIVAL

The majority of tourists arrive at either of Sofia's two airport terminals, although in summer many fly directly to the coastal cities of Varna and Burgas on charter flights. Frequent **low-cost flights** from London and other European cities to Sofia, are provided by easyJet and Wizz Air, which also has summer services to Varna and Burgas. The national carrier Bulgaria Air (Ⓦwww.air.bg) serves most of Europe but there are no direct flights to or from North America or Australasia.

Bulgaria has land borders with five countries and reliable international **rail** links. Popular routes include from Bucharest to Veliko Tarnovo (5–6hr) or to Sofia (11hr), and from Thessaloniki to Sofia (10hr), while trains from İstanbul traverse the country, stopping at Plovdiv (11hr) and Sofia (14hr) before continuing to Belgrade. Eurolines (Ⓦwww.eurolines.bg) runs frequent **bus** services to Sofia from many major European cities and has booking offices in Sofia, Plovdiv, Varna, and Burgas.

GETTING AROUND

Public transport in Bulgaria is inexpensive but often slow and not always clean or comfortable. Travelling by **bus** (*avtobus*) is usually the quickest way of getting between major towns and cities. Generally, you can buy tickets (*bileti*) at the bus station (*avtogara*) at least an hour in advance when travelling between towns, but on some routes they're only sold when the bus arrives. On rural routes, tickets are often sold by the driver.

Bulgarian State Railways (BDZh; Ⓦwww.bdz.bg) can get you to most towns; trains are punctual and fares low. Express services (*ekspresen*) are restricted to main routes, but on all except the humblest branch lines you'll find so-called Rapid (*burz vlak*) trains. Where possible, use these rather than the snail-like *patnicheski* services. Long-distance or overnight trains have reasonably priced couchettes (*kushet*) and/or sleepers (*spalen vagon*). For these, on all expresses and many rapids, you need seat **reservations** (*zapazeni mesta*) as well as tickets (*bileti*). To ensure a seat in a non-smoking carriage (*myasto za nepushachi*), you will have to specify this when booking. Railway station ticket offices only sell tickets on the day of travel, so at weekends and in the summer it's wise to purchase an advance ticket from a railway booking office (byuro za bileti). **International tickets** must be bought in advance from the Rila Agency (Ⓦwww.bdz-rila.com); branches can be found in all major cities. Most stations have **left-luggage** offices (*garderob*). InterRail and Balkan Flexipass are valid, although it often works out cheaper to buy rail tickets as you go.

Cycling in Bulgaria's congested cities, where cycle lanes are few and far between, is best avoided, but the country's quiet minor roads linking towns and villages are a delight for cyclists. Of the few bike hire outfits in Bulgaria, Zig-Zag Holidays in Sofia (Ⓦwww.zigzagbg.com) is one of the most reliable and also runs organized tours.

ACCOMMODATION

Decent **hostels** charging around 20Lv for a dorm bed and 50–70Lv for double rooms can be found in Sofia, Plovdiv, Veliko Turnovo, Burgas and Varna. Budget **hotels** rent doubles from around 40Lv, a little more in Sofia and Plovdiv, while cosier family-run hotels with similar prices are common on the coast and in touristy towns such as Koprivshtitsa and Bansko.

The best **campsites** (*kamping*; summer only) are dotted along the coast where campers are charged individually (around 7Lv per person) and two-person chalets (25–35Lv per night) are usually available. Camping rough is technically illegal and punishable with a fine, though authorities usually turn a blind eye. A number of hostels also offer camping space.

FOOD AND DRINK

Sit-down meals are eaten in either a **restorant** (restaurant) or a **mehana** (tavern). There's little difference between the two, save that a *mehana* is likely to offer folksy decor and a wider range of traditional Bulgarian dishes. Wherever you go, you're unlikely to spend more than 25Lv for a main course, salad and drink. The best-known traditional dish is *gyuvech* (which literally means "earthenware dish"), a rich stew comprising peppers, aubergines and beans, to which is added either meat or meat stock. *Kavarma*, a spicy meat stew (either pork or chicken), is prepared in a similar fashion. **Vegetarian meals** (*yastia bez meso*) are hard to obtain, although *gyuveche* (a variety of *gyuvech* featuring baked vegetables) and *kachkaval pane* (cheese fried in breadcrumbs) are worth trying.

Foremost among **snacks** are *kebapcheta* (grilled sausages), or variations such as *shishche* (shish kebab) or *kyofteta* (meatballs). Another favourite is the *banitsa*, a flaky-pastry envelope with a filling – usually cheese – sold by bakeries and street vendors in the morning and evening. Elsewhere, *sandvichi* (sandwiches) and *pitsi* (pizzas) dominate the fast-food repertoire. Bulgarians consider their **yogurt** (*kiselo mlyako*) the world's finest, and hardly miss a day without consuming it.

Drink

The quality of Bulgarian **wines** is constantly improving. Among the best reds are the heavy, mellow Melnik, and rich, dark Mavrud, while Dimyat is a good dry white. If you prefer the sweeter variety, try Karlovski Misket (Muscatel) or Traminer. Cheap native **spirits** are highly potent: *mastika* (like Greek *oúzo*) is drunk diluted with water; *rakiya* – brandy made from either plums (*slivova*) or grapes (*grozdova*) – is generally sipped, accompanied by

BODY LANGUAGE

Bulgarians shake their heads when they mean "yes" and nod when they mean "no" – and sometimes reverse these gestures if they know they're speaking to foreigners, thereby complicating the issue further. Emphatic use of the words *da* (yes) and *ne* (no) should help to avoid misunderstandings.

salad. Bulgarian **beer** is as good as any, but local brands such as Kamenitza, Zagorka, and Shumensko must now compete with the likes of Staropramen, Stella Artois and Heineken, which are brewed locally under licence.

Coffee (*kafe*) usually comes *espresso* style. **Tea** (*chai*) is nearly always herbal – ask for *cheren chai* (literally "black tea") if you want the real stuff, normally served with lemon.

CULTURE AND ETIQUETTE

Bulgarians are predominantly Orthodox Christian; Muslims of Turkish descent make up around nine percent of the population. Social etiquette in Bulgaria is still rather formal. Shaking someone's hand is the most common form of **greeting** and you should address someone with their title and surname unless you know them well. It is appropriate to wait for the Bulgarian person to decide when to become less formal with you. When invited to someone's home it is polite to bring a small gift, and something from your own country will be particularly appreciated.

As for **tipping**, leaving a ten percent tip will definitely be well received, although it is not obligatory.

SPORTS AND OUTDOOR ACTIVITIES

Bulgaria's mountainous terrain offers plenty of adventurous options. The **ski season** lasts from December to March, and the country has several well-known resorts. Bansko (ⓦwww.bansko.bg), in the spectacular Pirin mountain range in the southwest, is the best known, with alpine peaks and challenging runs perfect for experienced skiers and snowboarders. Other large resorts include Pamporovo (ⓦwww.winter.pamporovoresort.com) in the Rhodope Mountains, which is the best for beginners, and Borovets (ⓦwww.borovets-bg.com) in the Rila range; for more information see ⓦwww.bulgariaski.com.

Of all Bulgaria's ranges, the Rila Mountains (ⓦwww.rilanationalpark.org) provide some of the country's most attractive **hiking** destinations, including the highest peak – Mount Musala (2925m) – from where a two–three-day trail leads to Rila Monastery. For the best maps, advice and organized hikes visit Zig-Zag Holidays (ⓦwww.zigzagbg.com) in Sofia. **Horseriding** is growing in popularity, and a small number of travel agencies can arrange trips of varying length (see box, p.233).

Despite the popularity of team sports such as basketball, handball and volleyball, none can compete with **football** for the passion with which it is involved. Teams in the premier division ("A" Grupa) play on Saturday or Sunday afternoons. **Tickets** are generally cheap and sold at booths outside the grounds on the day of the match. The Bulgarian Football League maintains an informative website with limited English-language content (ⓦwww.pfl.bg).

> **BULGARIA ONLINE**
>
> **ⓦwww.bulgariatravel.org** Comprehensive travel information.
> **ⓦwww.discover-bulgaria.com** Travel information and hotel booking.
> **ⓦwww.sofiaecho.com** Bulgaria's English-language news site.
> **ⓦwww.travel-bulgaria.com** Information on history and culture, as well as travel.
> **ⓦwww.programata.bg** Up-to-date English-language cultural listings.

COMMUNICATIONS

You'll find that cafés, bars and restaurants generally offer free wi-fi and most hostels have free computer access. **Post offices** (*poshta*) are usually open Mon–Sat 8.30am–5.30pm, longer in big towns. **Phonecards** (*fonokarta*) for both Bulfon's orange phones and Betcom's

EMERGENCY NUMBERS

For any emergency dial ⓣ112

blue phones are available from post offices and many street kiosks and shops. Cheap SIM cards from Bulgaria's three main network providers (Mtel, Globul, and Vivacom) are widely available. The operator number for domestic calls is ⓣ121, for international calls ⓣ123.

EMERGENCIES

Petty theft is a danger on the coast, and the Bulgarian **police** can be slow in filling out insurance reports unless you're insistent. Foreign tourists are no longer a novelty in much of the country, but **women** travelling alone can expect to encounter stares, comments and sometimes worse, and clubs on the coast are pretty much seen as meat markets. A firm rebuff should be enough to cope with most situations. Note that everyone is required to carry some form of **ID** at all times.

If you need a **doctor** (*doktor*) or dentist (*zabolekar*), go to the nearest hospital (*bolnitsa*), whose staff might speak English or German. Emergency treatment is free of charge although you must pay for **medicines** – larger towns will have at least one 24-hour pharmacy.

INFORMATION

Bulgaria's National Tourist Information Centre, located in Sofia at pl. Sveta Nedelya 1 (Mon–Fri 9am–5.30pm; ⓣ02/933 5826, ⓦwww.bulgariatravel.org), is a smart, modern affair offering free maps and travel advice. Most major towns and cities have local **tourist information centres** where staff speak several languages and can provide maps, brochures and leaflets although they aren't usually authorized to make hotel reservations. The best general **maps** of Bulgaria and Sofia are published by Kartografiya and Domino; both are available in Latin alphabet versions and are sold at street stalls, petrol stations and bookshops.

MONEY AND BANKS

Until Bulgaria joins the Eurozone (target date: Jan 1, 2013) the currency remains the **lev** (Lv), which is divided into 100 stotinki (st). There are notes of 2Lv, 5Lv, 10Lv, 20Lv, 50Lv, and 100Lv and coins of 1st, 2st, 5st, 10st, 20st and 50st, and 1Lv. Pegged to the euro, the lev is stable and although hotels and travel agencies frequently quote prices in euros, you will be expected to pay in the local currency. At the time of writing, €1 was equal to 1.95Lv, $1 to 1.35Lv, and £1 to 2.20Lv. Producing a **student ID card** at museums and galleries will often get you a discount of between a third and a half.

Banks are open Monday to Friday 9am to 4pm, and there are ATMs in every town. Private exchange bureaux, offering variable rates, are widespread – but beware of hidden commission charges. Also watch out for black market moneychangers who approach unwary foreigners with offers of better rates; if they sound too good to be true, they are. Many smaller banks and offices won't take traveller's cheques, and credit cards are generally acceptable only at the more expensive shops, hotels, and restaurants.

OPENING HOURS AND HOLIDAYS

Big-city **shops** and **supermarkets** are generally open Monday to Friday 8.30am to 6pm or later; on Saturday they close at 2pm. The massive malls that have sprung up in recent years are usually open daily from 10am to 10pm. In rural areas and small towns, an unofficial siesta may prevail between noon and 3pm. Many shops, offices, banks and museums are closed on the following **public holidays**: January 1, March 3, Easter Sunday and Monday, May 1, May 24, September 6, September 22, December 25 & December 31. Additional public holidays may occasionally be called by the government.

BULGARIAN

Hotel and travel agency staff in Sofia and the larger towns and coastal resorts generally speak some **English**, but knowledge of foreign languages elsewhere in the country is patchy; younger people are more likely to know a few words of English. Most street signs, menus and so on are written in the **Cyrillic** alphabet, but an increasing number have English transliterations.

	Bulgarian	Pronunciation
Yes	Да	Da
No	Не	Ne
Please	Моля	Molya
Thank you	Благодаря	Blagodarya
Hello/Good day	Добър ден	Dobur den
Goodbye	Довиждане	Dovizhdane
Excuse me	Извинявайте	Izvinyavite
Where?	Къде?	Kude?
Good	Добро	Dobro
Bad	Лошо	Losho
Near	Близо	Blizo
Far	Далече	Daleche
Cheap	Евтино	Eftino
Expensive	Скъпо	Skupo
Open	Отворено	Otvoreno
Closed	Затворено	Zatvoreno
Today	Днес	Dnes
Yesterday	Вчера	Vchera
Tomorrow	Утре	Utre
How much is...?	Колко струва...?	Kolko stroova...?
What time is it?	Колко е часът?	Kolko ai chasut?
I don't understand	Не разбирам	Ne razbiram
Do you speak English?	Говорите ли английски?	Govorite li Angleeski?
One	Един/Една	Edin/edna
Two	Две	Dve
Three	Три	Tree
Four	Четири	Chetiri
Five	Пет	Pyet
Six	Шест	Shest
Seven	Седем	Sedem
Eight	Осем	Osem
Nine	Девет	Devet
Ten	Десет	Deset
Do you have any vegetarian dishes?	Имате ли вегетерианска храна?	Imate li vegitarianska hrana?
Cheers	Наздраве	Nazdrave
The bill, please	Може ли сметката	Mozhe li smetkata
Is this the bus for...?	Това ли е автобусът за...?	Tova li avtobusat za...?
Is this the train to...?	Това ли е влакът за...?	Tova li e vlakut za...?
Have you got a single/double	Имате ли единична двойна стая	Imate li edinichna/ dvoyna staya
How much for the night?	Колко струва нощувката?	Kolko struva noshtuvkata?

Sofia

With its drab suburbs and distinct lack of charming old buildings **SOFIA** (София) can appear an uninspiring place to first-time visitors. However, much has been done in recent years to revitalize the heart of the city, and once you've settled in and begun to explore, you'll find it a surprisingly vibrant place, especially on fine days, when its lush public gardens and pavement cafés buzz with life. It also possesses the draw of verdant **Mount Vitosha**, just 8km to the south.

Sofia was founded by a Thracian tribe some three thousand years ago, and various **Roman ruins** attest to its zenith as a regional imperial capital in the fourth century AD. The Bulgars didn't arrive on the scene until the ninth century, and with the notable exception of the thirteenth-century Boyana Church, their cultural monuments largely disappeared during the Turkish occupation (1396–1878), whose own legacy is visible solely in a couple of stately **mosques**. The finest architecture postdates Bulgaria's liberation from the Turks: handsome public buildings and parks, and the magnificent **Aleksandar Nevski Cathedral**.

What to see and do

Most of Sofia's sights are centrally located and within easy walking distance of each other. The pedestrianized Bulevard Vitosha forms the heart of the shopping district and leads north to the Church of Sveta Nedelya, from where bul. Tsar Osvoboditel passes the major public buildings, culminating with the grand Aleksandar Nevski Church.

Sveta Nedelya Church

At the heart of Sofia is **ploshtad Sveta Nedelya**, a pedestrianized square dominated by the distinctive **Sveta Nedelya Church** (daily 7am–7pm), whose broad dome dominates the vast interior chamber. Colourful modern frescoes adorn every square inch of its walls.

The Largo, Party House and Council of Ministers

Laid out in the 1950s to demonstrate the power of Communist rule, the **Largo** is an elongated plaza flanked on three sides by severe monumental edifices built in Soviet Classicist style. They include the towering monolith of the former **Party House**, originally the home of the Communist hierarchy, and now serving as government offices. The plaza extends westwards to the **Sofia Monument,** the city's symbol which represents the eponymous Goddess of Wisdom. On the northern side of the Largo is the **Council of Ministers**, Bulgaria's cabinet offices.

The Banya Bashi Mosque and the mineral baths

The Banya Bashi Mosque was built in 1576 by Mimar Sinan, who also designed the great mosque at Edirne in Turkey. The mosque is not officially open to tourists but modestly dressed visitors may visit outside of prayer times. Behind stand Sofia's **mineral baths**, housed in a splendid yellow-and-red striped *fin-de-siècle* building, closed since 1986 and still being restored. Locals gather daily to bottle the hot, sulphurous water that gushes from public taps into stone troughs outside, opposite ul. Exzarh Iosif.

The Rotunda of St George and the Presidency

Sofia's oldest church is the fourth-century **Rotunda of St George**, built upon the city's oldest Roman foundations and housing frescoes from the eighth century onwards. Surrounding the church is the **Presidency**, guarded by soldiers in colourful nineteenth-

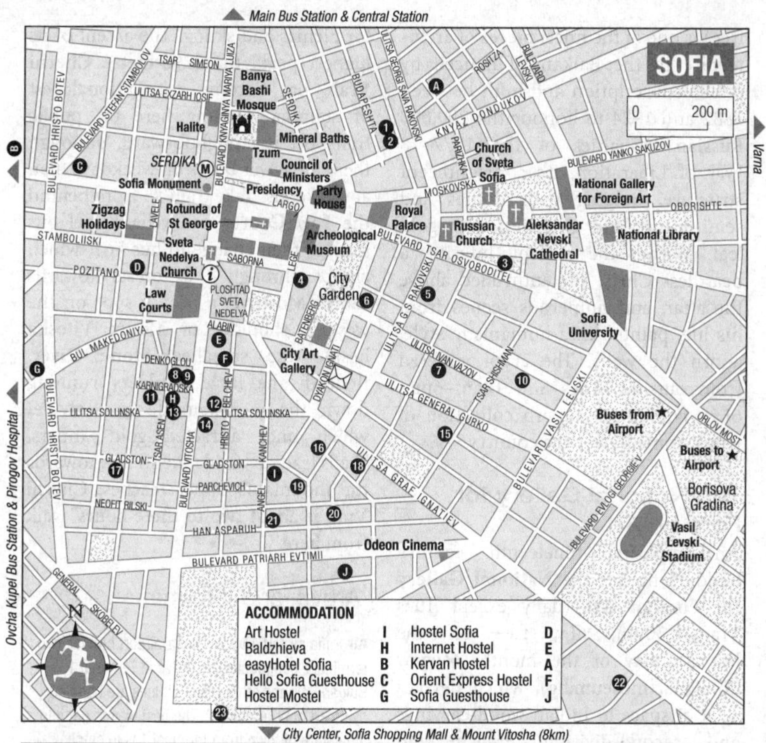

EATING				DRINKING, NIGHTLIFE & ENTERTAINMENT			
Annette	21	Memento Café	9	Alcohol	5	Hambara	18
Art Club Museum Café	4	Pri Yafata	13	Apartment	20	ID Club	8
Baalbek	6	Slunce Luna	17	Bilkovata	15	J.J. Murphy's	11
Before & After	12	Tea House (Chai vuv fabrikata)	1	Blaze	10	My Mojito	7
Divaka	19	Ugo	14 & 16	Chervilo	3	Sofia Live Club	23
Dream House	E			Dada	2	Swingin' Hall	22

century garb (Changing of the Guard hourly).

The Archeological Museum

A fifteenth-century mosque now holds the **Archeological Museum** (daily 10am–6pm; 10Lv), whose prize exhibit is the magnificent Valchitran Treasure, a Thracian gold cauldron plus cups. Also on show is a collection of Thracian armour, medieval church wall paintings and numerous Roman tombstones.

The City Art Gallery

The **City Art Gallery** (Tues–Sat 10am–7pm, Sun 11am–6pm; free) in the City Garden, immediately to the south of pl. Aleksandar Batenberg, stages regular exhibitions of contemporary Bulgarian art.

The Russian Church and Aleksandar Nevski Cathedral

Built on the site of a mosque in the early twentieth century, the **Russian Church** (daily 8am–7pm) is a stunning golden-domed building with an emerald spire and an exuberant mosaic-tiled exterior, which conceals a dark, candle-scented interior. The nearby **Aleksandar Nevski Cathedral** (daily 7am–7pm, liturgy on Sundays at 1pm;

free) is one of the finest pieces of architecture in the Balkans. Financed by public subscription and built between 1882 and 1924 to honour the 200,000 Russian casualties of the 1877–78 War of Liberation, it's a magnificent structure, bulging with domes and semi-domes and glittering with gold leaf. Within the gloomy interior, a beardless Christ sits enthroned above the altar, and numerous scenes from his life, painted in a humanistic style, adorn the walls. The crypt, entered from outside (Tues–Sun 10am–6pm; 6Lv), contains a superb collection of icons from all over the country.

The National Gallery for Foreign Art

An imposing nineteenth century building houses the **National Gallery for Foreign Art** (daily except Tues 11am–6.30pm; 6Lv, free on the last Monday of the month; ⓦwww.foreignartmuseum.bg), which devotes a lot of space to Indian wood-carvings and second-division French and Russian artists, though there are a few minor works by the likes of Rodin, Chagall and Kandinsky. Heading west past Alexander Nevski Cathedral, you'll pass two recumbent lions flanking the Tomb of the Unknown Soldier, set beside the wall of the plain, brown-brick **Church of Sveta Sofia** which gave the city its name in the fourteenth century.

Borisova Gradina

Down bul. Tsar Osvoboditel, past Sofia University, is **Borisova Gradina**, named after Bulgaria's interwar monarch, Boris III. The park – the largest in Sofia – has a rich variety of flowers and trees, outdoor bars, two football stadiums and two huge Communist monuments.

Mount Vitosha

A wooded granite mass 20km long and 16km wide, **Mount Vitosha**, 8km south of the city, is where Sofians go for picnics and skiing. The ascent of its highest peak, the 2290-metre **Cherni Vrah**, has become a traditional test of stamina. Getting here on public transport is straightforward, although there are fewer buses on weekdays than at weekends. Take tram #5 from behind the Law Courts to Ovcha Kupel bus station, then change to bus #61, which climbs through the forests towards **Zlatni Mostove**, a beauty spot on the western shoulder of Mount Vitosha beside the so-called **Stone River**. Beneath the large boulders running down the mountainside is a rivulet which once attracted gold-panners. Trails lead up beside the stream towards the mountain's upper reaches: Cherni Vrah is about two to three hours' walk from here.

Arrival and information

Air Sofia airport (ⓦwww.sofia-airport.bg) has two terminals: budget carriers arrive at Terminal 1; Bulgaria Air and other major airlines are handled by smart new Terminal 2. The best way to get into the centre of town from Terminal 1 is to catch *marshrutka* #30, which runs until around 10pm (every 15–30min; 1.50Lv). Bus #84 leaves from Terminal 1 and #284 from Terminal 2; tickets (1Lv) can be bought from the airport newspaper kiosk – you'll need additional tickets for any oversized bags. Waiting taxis might well try to charge you an exorbitant 40Lv or more, so it's wise to book one at the booth in the arrivals hall (10–15Lv).

Train Trains arrive at Central Station (Tsentralna Gara), a concrete hangar harbouring a number of exchange bureaux and snack bars, but little else to welcome the visitor. It's a 5min ride along bul. Knyaginya Mariya Luiza (tram #1 or #7) to pl. Sveta Nedelya, within walking distance of several hotels and hostels.

Bus Most buses arrive at the new bus station, just next to the train station, although some Bansko services and Blagoevgrad buses (for connections to Rila Monastery) use the Ovcha Kupel terminal, 5km southwest of the centre along bul. Tsar Boris III.

Tourist office Both the National Tourist Information Centre at pl. Sveta Nedelya 1 (see p.226) and the Sofia Tourist Information Centre (Mon–Fri 9.30am–6.30pm; ⓣ02/4918344, ⓦwww.Info-sofia.bg) in the underpass at the Kliment Ochridski metro station, provide city maps and local travel advice.

An excellent alternative is the friendly travel agency Zig-Zag Holidays (Ⓦwww.zigzagbg.com) at bul. Stamboliiski 20 (entrance on ul. Lavele; Mon–Fri 9.30am–6.30pm, daily in summer; Ⓣ02/980 5102, Ⓦwww.odysseia-in.com), which charges a 5Lv consultation fee, although not for accommodation booking.

City transport

Public transport There's a flat fare of 1Lv on all urban routes, whether by bus (*avtobus*), trolleybus (*troleibus*), the one-line metro system, or tram (*tramvai*). Tickets (*bileti*) are sold from street kiosks and occasionally on board, and must be punched as you enter the vehicle (inspections are frequent and there are 10Lv spot fines for fare-dodgers). Kiosks at the main tram stops sell one-day tickets (*karta za edin den;* 4Lv) and a strip (*talon*) of five/ten tickets (4.50Lv/8Lv) – the tickets must be used in sequence by the purchaser. Metro tickets can only be bought from metro stations.

Taxis and minibusesThe most reliable taxi company is OK taxis (Ⓣ02/9732121), charging 59st per kilometre until nightfall, 70st afterwards, and 60st initial fare; make sure the driver has his meter running. Additionally, there's a fleet of private minibuses (*marshrutka*), acting like shared taxis and covering around forty different routes across the city for a flat fare of 1.50Lv. Destinations and routes are displayed on the front of the vehicles – in the Cyrillic alphabet – and passengers flag them down like normal taxis, calling out when they want them to stop.

Accommodation

Sofia has a number of good hostels, and some small, reasonably priced hotels in central locations.

Hostels

Art Hostel ul. Angel Kanchev 21a Ⓣ02/987 0545, Ⓦwww.art-hostel.com. Sofia's trendiest hostel, hosting art exhibitions, live music, resident DJs and occasional drama performances. Guests have access to a kitchen and popular tea room-cum-bar with lovely garden, as well as free wi-fi and computer access. Breakfast included. Dorms 24Lv, doubles with shared bathroom 64Lv.

Hostel Mostel bul. Makedoniya 2A Ⓣ0889/223296, Ⓦwww.hostelmostel.com. Superb hostel located in a historic building a short walk from the centre and offering free wi-fi and computer access, an all-you-can-eat breakfast, a bowl of pasta and a bottle of beer for every night of your stay. The ground floor has a cavernous, comfortable lounge space with flat screen TV, DVDs, and travel library. Just up the road is the hostel's lively *HM bar* where guests are entitled to a free drink. Dorms 20Lv, doubles 54–70Lv.

Hostel Sofia ul. Pozitano 16 Ⓣ02/989 8582, Ⓦwww.hostelsofia.net. Well-established hostel showing signs of wear and tear but still clean, well-run, and enduringly popular. Located behind the Law Courts, with around fifty beds on two floors, shared kitchen, bathroom, cable TV and wi-fi. Breakfast and tea and coffee included. Dorms 20Lv.

Internet Hostel ul. Alabin 50a Ⓣ0889/138298, Ⓔinterhostel@yahoo.co.uk. Friendly hostel with kitchen and wi-fi offering spacious but dated doubles, triples and quads, as well as studio apartments. Located on the second floor of a shopping arcade, above the *Dream House* restaurant. Breakfast included as well as a free drink at the Irish bar downstairs. Dorms 20Lv, doubles 60Lv, studio apartment for two 70Lv.

Kervan Hostel ul. Rositza 3 Ⓣ02/983 9428, Ⓦwww.kervanhostel.com. Bohemian hostel in a quiet area of the centre, close to Nevski Cathedral. There's a kitchen plus computer access and free wi-fi. Breakfast included. Dorms 20Lv, doubles 60Lv.

Orient Express Hostel ul. Hristo Belchev 8A Ⓣ0888/384828, Ⓦwww.orientexpresshostel.com. Small and homely hostel, with high ceilings, modern fittings combined with antique and salvaged furniture, and TVs in every room. Its fifth-floor position makes for great views from the rooms, but some arduous stair climbing as there's no lift. Friendly and helpful staff. Breakfast, free wi-fi and computer access included. Dorms 20Lv, doubles 70Lv, apartment 90Lv.

Sofia Guesthouse bul. Patriarh Evtimiy 27 Ⓣ02/403 0100, Ⓦwww.sofiaguest.com. Large hostel with very central location and clean, bright rooms, plus a garden, TV lounge, free wi-fi and computer access, and free breakfast. Staff can arrange bike rental, day-trips, and a pick up/drop off service from the train and bus station or airport. Dorms 18Lv, double 70Lv, attic apartment 100Lv.

Hotels

Baldzhieva ul. Tsar Asen 23 Ⓣ02/981 1257, Ⓦwww.baldjievahotel.net. Small hotel with a pleasant yard one block west of bul. Vitosha. The en-suite rooms are clean and simply furnished, and come with phone, fridge, TV, and wi-fi. Breakfast not included. Single 48Lv, doubles 70Lv.

easyHotel Sofia ul. Aldomirovska 108 Ⓣ02/920 1654, Ⓦwww.easyHotel.com. Despite being inconveniently located several blocks west of the centre, this is a great deal for anyone in search of a spotless, cheap en-suite room. Prices are per room (small 40–60Lv or standard 50–70Lv) and vary according to availability.

Hello Sofia Guesthouse bul. Stefan Stambolov 12 ⓣ0889/138298, ⓦwww.hellosofia.eu. Situated just a short distance from Sofia's thriving Women's Market (Zhenski Bazaar) this delightful new guesthouse has been thoughtfully designed and features imaginative styling and home comforts that include widescreen TVs, wi-fi, spacious en-suite bathrooms, and a smart shared kitchen and lounge area. Singles 60Lv, doubles 70Lv, triples 85Lv.

Eating

The cheapest places to grab snacks, a beer or a coffee are the many cafés and kiosks around bul. Vitosha or in the city's public gardens. International coffeehouse chains such as Starbucks and Costa have opened a number of cafés in recent years and there are plenty of pricier restaurants offering a range of international cuisine.

Cafés

Art Club Museum Café Corner of ul. Saborna & ul. Lege. Chic café with a pleasant patio, set amid Thracian tombstones next to the Archeological Museum. Live DJs in the basement Thurs, Fri & Sat nights. Serves a variety of light meals, desserts and drinks, such as cappuccino with coconut and banana (4.50Lv). Open 24hr.

Memento Café bul. Vitosha 32 ⓦwww.memento.bg. Tiny yet enormously popular spot with a Mediterranean feel serving top-notch coffee, cakes, and sandwiches.

Tea House (Chai vuv fabrikata) ul. Georgi Benkovski 11. Atmospheric traditional teahouse with a formidable array of teas including "monks' tea", Kashmir *chai* and rose priced from 2 to 7Lv.

Restaurants

Annette ul. Angel Kunchev 27 ⓦwww.annette.bg. An excellent Moroccan restaurant with tree-shaded outdoor seating and a mouth-watering range of exotic dishes that include chicken baked with pear in wine sauce (12.50Lv).

Before & After ul. Hristo Belchev 12 ⓦba.club-cabaret.net. Elegant and popular restaurant near the *Orient Express Hostel*, with a range of Bulgarian, Turkish and Continental dishes, including some fantastic traditional desserts. Also great for vegetarian options, including grilled vegetables in yoghurt and dill (5.50Lv). Hosts tango dances on Sun.

Divaka ul. Gladston 54. Bright and busy restaurant, just west of Graf Ignatiev, behind the *Art Hostel*, serving excellent, meat-heavy Bulgarian dishes. Chicken kebab 7.50Lv, vegetarian shish kebab 5.50Lv. Open 24hr.

Dream House ul. Alabin 50a ⓣ02/9808163, ⓦwww.dreamhouse-bg.com. Intimate, friendly and well-established vegetarian restaurant above a shopping mall. Has a good choice of meals and snacks using seasonal produce, including aubergine couscous (6.80Lv) and Asian bamboo soup (2.90Lv). They also deliver within the city centre area.

Pri Yafata ul. Solunska 28 ⓦwww.pri-yafata.com. Brash but fun take on a traditional *mehana*, complete with live music, costumed staff and a great Bulgarian menu that includes tripe soup (*shkembe churba*; 3.90Lv) and a wide range of grilled meat dishes.

Slunce Luna ul. Gladston 18b ⓦwww.sunmoon.bg. Popular vegetarian restaurant with rustic furniture and a bakery producing great wholemeal bread. Lethargic service is offset by the relaxed atmosphere.

Ugo bul. Vitosha 45 ⓦwww.ugo.bg. One of the better pizza and pasta restaurants in the centre, Ugo offers a broad range of dishes 24 hours a day. There's another branch at ul. Neofit Rilski 68.

Drinking and nightlife

For evening entertainment, there's an ever-growing number of clubs, most playing a mix of pop, retro, rock or the ubiquitous local "folk pop"(*chalga*). Jazz and Latino music are also popular.

Bars

Apartment ul. Neofit Rilski 68. Stylish and laid-back, this eclectic bar-cum-living room occupies a pair of high-ceilinged nineteenth-century flats hung with an intriguing array of artwork. The pricy drinks menu keeps the riff-raff at bay. Daily noon–2am.

Bilkovata ul. Tsar Shishman 22. A buzzing, smoky cellar with decent music and a young crowd, *Bilkovata* is something of a legend in Sofia, fondly remembered by successive generations of students, arty types and young professionals, and still going strong. Packed beer garden in summer. Daily 10am–2am.

Dada ul. Benkovski 10 ⓦwww.dadaculturalbar.eu. A popular new addition to Sofia's nightlife scene, Dada's regular cultural evenings attract a mixed crowd of Bulgarians and expats. Just around the corner from Nevski cathedral. Daily noon–2am.

Hambara ul. 6-ti septemvri 22. Hidden behind an unmarked doorway just off the street, this dark, candle-lit, stone-floored bar is one of the most atmospheric places in the centre for a long night of drink-fuelled conversation. Live jazz several nights a week. Daily 7pm–2am.

J.J. Murphy's ul. Karnigradska 6 Ⓦwww.jjmurphys.net. Sofia's top Irish bar, offering filling pub grub, big-screen sports and live music at the weekends.

Clubs

Entrance fees range from nothing to 20Lv depending on the venue, expect to pay more if a major DJ is manning the decks. A valid ID is compulsory.

Alcohol ul. Rakovski 127 Ⓦwww.clubalcohol.com. Underground nightspot that looks like a huge subterranean barn and has an eclectic something-for-everybody music policy. An Oriental-style chillout room boasts cushions and hubble-bubble pipes. Daily 9pm–5am.

Blaze ul. Slavyanska 36. Lively bar and club near the university, with a good sound system and trendy clientele. Daily 9pm–3am.

Chervilo bul. Tsar Osvoboditel 9 Ⓦwww.chervilo.com. Stylish city-centre club offering the latest in house, techno, Latin and lounge music on two floors. The action spreads out onto the terrace in summer, when it's more like an elite, pay-to-enter pavement café than a club. Café daily 10am–10pm; club Thurs–Sat 10pm–7am.

ID Club ul. Kurnigradska 19B Ⓦwww.idclub.bg. A popular gay club with plenty of dancing space that plays retro, chalga, and pop until the early hours. Face control is strict on busy nights. 9pm–3am.

My Mojito ul. Ivan Vazov 12. One of Sofia's trendiest clubs, with regular DJ slots and a laid-back crowd. Daily 9pm–5am.

Entertainment

Live music

Sofia Live Club National Palace of Culture (NDK). Ⓦwww.sofialiveclub.com. Plush club lying deep beneath the NDK building which has hosted an impressive number of international world music and jazz groups. Daily 8pm–2am.

Swingin' Hall ul. Dragan Tsankov 8 Ⓦwww.swinginghall.com. Cheerful, crowded bar that's been around for years and has live music (usually pop/rock or jazz) on two stages. Tues–Sat 9pm–4am.

Cinema

Cineplex bul. Arsenalski 2 Ⓣ02/964 3007, Ⓦwww.cineplex.bg. Multi-screen cinema in the City Center Sofia shopping mall, with various snack possibilities in the vicinity.

Odeon bul. Patriarh Evtimiy 1 Ⓣ02/969 2469. Shows oldies and prize-winning art films past and present. Small bar in the lobby.

Shopping

The city's main shopping street, bul. Vitosha, is the place where you are most likely to come across familiar high-street shops and brands. In addition to those listed below, the City Center (bul. Arsenalski 2) and Sofia (bul. Stamboliiski 101) malls are characterless yet immensely popular malls stuffed with clothes shops, eateries and bars.

Malls

Halite bul. Knyaginy Mariya Luiza, opposite the Banya Bashi Mosque. This elegant building houses Sofia's central food hall with two floors of shops and food stalls.

Tzum Once the preserve of the party elite, Sofia's premier shopping mall stocks upmarket and luxury goods.

Markets

Aleksandar Nevski Located at the apex of the three central churches on pl. Aleksandar Nevski, this collection of stalls offers an odd mix of religious paintings, Turkish-influenced silver jewellery, traditional Bulgarian peasant clothing, lace and textiles, and antique and replica Communist items. Some may find the large array of Nazi memorabilia on some of the tables in rather bad taste.

Zhenski bazaar One of the city's best outdoor markets is on bul. Stefan Stambolov where trinkets, fresh fruit, vegetables and other foodstuffs are on sale.

Directory

Embassies and consulates Australia, Trakia 37 Ⓣ02/946 1334; Canada, Pozitano 7 Ⓣ02/969 9710; Ireland, Bacho Kiro 26–30 Ⓣ02/985 3425; South Africa, Bacho Kiro 26 (2nd floor) Ⓣ02/939 5015; UK, Moskovska 9 Ⓣ02/933 9222; US, Kozyak 16 Ⓣ02/937 5100.

Gay Sofia Ⓦwww.gay.bg. Site with information about Bulgaria's gay scene.

Hospital Pirogov hospital, bul. General Totleben 21 Ⓣ02/915 4411, Ⓦwww.pirogov.bg. For an ambulance call Ⓣ112.

Pharmacy Aronia 2001, bul Pencho Slaveikov 6 (opposite Pirogov hospital) open 24hr.
Post office ul. General Gurko 6 (daily 7am–8.30pm).

Moving on

Train Bansko (3 daily; 7hr); Belgrade (1 daily; 7hr 30min); Blagoevgrad (6 daily; 2hr 30min–3hr 30min); Bucharest (1 daily; 9hr 30min); Burgas (8 daily; 6hr 30min); Veliko Turnovo via Gorna Oryahovitsa (6 daily; 4hr 30min); Istanbul (1 daily; 11hr); Koprivshtitsa (5 daily; 1hr 40min); Plovdiv (14 daily; 2hr–3hr 30min); Septemvri (hourly; 2hr); Thessaloniki (2 daily; 6hr); Varna (9 daily; 8hr).
Bus Bansko (6 daily; 3hr); Burgas (hourly; 7hr); Koprivshtitsa (2 daily; 2hr); Plovdiv (hourly; 2hr); Rila village (2–3 daily; 2hr); Varna (every 30min; 7hr); Veliko Tarnovo (8–9 daily; 4hr).

Southern Bulgaria

The route south from Sofia skirts the Rila and Pirin mountain ranges, swathed in forests and dotted with alpine lakes, and home to Bulgaria's highest peaks. If time is short, the place to head for is the most revered of Bulgarian monasteries, **Rila**, around 30km east of the main southbound route. **Bansko**, on the eastern side of the Pirin range, boasts a wealth of traditional architecture, as well as being a major ski resort and a good base for hiking. Another much-travelled route heads southeast from Sofia towards Istanbul. The main road and rail lines now linking Istanbul and Sofia essentially follow the course of the Roman Serdica–Constantinople road, past towns ruled by the Ottomans for so long that foreigners used to call this part of Bulgaria "European Turkey". Of these, the most important is **Plovdiv**, Bulgaria's second city, whose old quarter is a wonderful mixture of National Revival mansions and classical remains. Some 30km south of Plovdiv is **Bachkovo Monastery**, containing Bulgaria's most vivid frescoes.

RILA MONASTERY

As the most celebrated of Bulgaria's religious sites, famed for its fine architecture and mountainous setting – and declared a World Heritage site by UNESCO – the **Rila Monastery** receives a steady stream of visitors, many of them day-trippers from Sofia. Joining one of these one-day tours from the capital (which can be arranged with Zig-Zag Holidays; see p.222) is the simplest way of getting here, but can work out expensive (most tours cost around 120Lv p.p.). It's much more economical to get there by public transport, though realistically you'll have to stay the night.

What to see and do

Ringed by mighty walls, the **monastery** (daily dawn–dusk; free; Ⓦwww.rilamonastery.pmg-blg.com) has the outward appearance of a fortress, but this impression is negated by the beauty of the interior, which even the crowds can't mar. Graceful arches above the flagstoned courtyard support tiers of monastic cells, and stairways ascend to wooden balconies. Bold red stripes and black-and-white check patterns enliven the facade, contrasting with the sombre mountains behind and creating a harmony between the cloisters and the **church**. Richly coloured frescoes shelter beneath the church porch and cover much of its interior. The iconostasis is splendid, almost 10m wide and covered by a mass of intricate carvings and gold leaf. Beside the church is **Hrelyo's Tower**, the sole remaining building from the fourteenth century. Cauldrons, which were once used to prepare food for pilgrims, occupy the soot-encrusted kitchen on the ground floor of the north wing, while on the floors above you can inspect the spartan refectory and panelled guest rooms. Beneath the east wing is the **treasury** (daily 9am–4.30pm; 10Lv), where, among other things, you can view a wooden cross carved with more than 1500 miniature human figures during the 1790s.

Arrival

Bus There are 2–3 daily buses from Sofia's Ovcha Kupel terminal (reached by tram #19 from the railway station, or #5 from behind the Law Courts) to Rila village, from where three or four buses a day make the 27km run up to the monastery. Otherwise, you'll need to catch the bus or train to Blagoevgrad in the Struma Valley, and then change to a local bus for Rila village (hourly; 35min).

Accommodation

It's possible to stay in the monastery's reasonably comfortable rooms (ⓣ07054 2208; gates close at 11pm; 40Lv single, 60Lv double).

Zodiac ⓣ0887/362186, ⓦwww.camping-zodiac.com. Pleasant campsite occupying an attractive riverside spot, with smart double bungalows and a good restaurant. Camping 10Lv/person, double bungalow 40Lv.

Eating

For cheap snacks, delicious bread and doughnuts, head for the bakery opposite the east gate.

Drushliavitsa Built over a stream on the hillside just beyond the East Gate, this traditional-style Bulgarian restaurant offers polite service and shaded outdoor seating. The menu features Bulgarian standards and fresh local trout (6.50lv).

Rila Situated behind the bakery. Identical in style to the *Drushliavitsa* with a similar menu and prices, but less enthusiastic service.

Moving on

There are three buses a day from Rila Monastery to Rila village from where hourly buses depart for nearby Blagoevgrad and beyond.

Bus Blagoevgrad to: Bansko (10 daily; 1hr); Sofia (hourly; 2hr).

BANSKO

Lying some 40km east of the main Struma Valley route, **BANSKO** (Банско) is the primary centre for walking and skiing on the eastern slopes of the Pirin mountains. Originally an agricultural centre, it's witnessed massive investment in ski tourism in recent years, resulting in the unappealing sight of apartment blocks and hotels squeezed into the backyards of stone-built nineteenth-century farmhouses. Despite this overdevelopment, the central old town, with its numerous traditional pubs hidden away down labyrinthine cobbled streets, is as attractive as ever and the perfect place to wind down after a hard day on the slopes.

Though connected to Sofia and other towns by bus, Bansko can also be reached by a **narrow-gauge railway**, which leaves the main Sofia–Plovdiv line at Septemvri and forges its way across the highlands. It's one of the most scenic trips in the Balkans, but also one of the slowest, taking five hours to cover just over 100km.

What to see and do

Bansko centres on the modern pedestrianized pl. Nikola Vaptsarov, where the **Nikola Vaptsarov Museum** (daily

HORSERIDING IN THE RILA MOUNTAINS

A unique way to experience the spectacular terrain of the **Rila Mountains** is on horseback. Some of the trails pass through virtually untouched forest areas and alongside staggering glacial lakes; there are also some seriously rocky options for experienced or adventurous riders. The tour operator Horseriding Bulgaria at ul. Orfey 9, Sofia (ⓣ02/400 3095, ⓦwww.horseridingbulgaria.com) offers a number of tour options priced at around €600 for seven days, including individual tours with a guide, out of their Iskar Ranch at the foot of the Rila Mountains.

8am–noon & 2–5.30pm; 4Lv) relates to the local-born poet and socialist martyr. Immediately north of here, pl. Vazrazhdane is watched over by the solid stone tower of the **Church of Sveta Troitsa**, whose interior contains exquisite nineteenth-century frescoes and icons. On the opposite side of the square, the **Rilski Convent** contains an icon museum (Mon–Fri 9am–noon & 2–5pm; 4Lv) devoted to the achievements of Bansko's nineteenth-century icon painters.

From the main square, ul. Pirin leads north towards the **cable car** (Dec–April daily 8.30am–5pm; 20Lv), where there is a buzzing collection of ski-hire shops, bars and restaurants. Ski passes cost 55Lv per day (36Lv for children), and ski and snowboard equipment can be hired for around 30Lv per day. The cable car doesn't operate outside the ski season so the only option for reaching the summit in the summer months is to head west – on foot or by taxi – via a steep fourteen-kilometre uphill climb to the Vihren hut, where cheap dorm **accommodation** (10Lv per person) is available. This is the main trailhead for hikes towards the 2914-metre summit of **Mount Vihren**, Bulgaria's second-highest peak, or gentler rambles around the meadows and lakes nearby.

Arrival and information

Bus and train The bus and train stations are on the northern fringes of town, 10min walk from pl. Vaptsarov.

Tourist office Kandahar Complex, ul. Kralev Dvor 4 (Mon, Wed, Fri, Sat & Sun noon–6pm; ⓣ0886/543262, ⓦwww.banskotouristinformation.com).

Accommodation

Durchova Kushta ul. P R Slavejkov 5 ⓣ0749/88223, ⓦwww.durchova-kashta.com. Comfortable but plain en-suite, pine-furnished rooms with TV, phone and minibar. Also has a sauna. Single 40Lv, double 60Lv without breakfast.

Kadiyata ul. Yane Sandanski 8 ⓣ0899/969370. Family-run place in the heart of the old town, offering smart en-suites with modern furnishings and TV. Single 40Lv, double 60Lv without breakfast.

Roshkova Kashta ul. Mozgovitsa 17 ⓣ0886/840827, ⓦwww.roshkoff-house.netfirms.com. Pleasant hotel situated on a quiet street just outside the centre of Bansko. En-suite rooms, wi-fi and breakfast included. Free daily bus to the lift station. Singles 30Lv, doubles 50Lv.

Eating and drinking

Dedo pene ul. Aleksandar Buynov 1, just south of pl. Vazrazhdane ⓦwww.dedopene.com. The whole range of traditional Bulgarian food and Bansko specialities at mid-range prices in an atmospheric dining room crammed with folksy decorations – and you can sit in the vine-shaded courtyard in summer.

Molerite ul. Glazne 41, just north of pl. Nikola Vaptsarov ⓦwww.molerite.com. Two floors of wooden benches and ethnic textiles, and superb local specialities such as roast lamb (17Lv) and sword-grilled shish kebabs (15Lv). Turns into a folk-pop disco after about 11pm.

Oxygen ul. Stefan Karadzha 27. Basement bar in the town centre with mixed programme of DJ-driven sounds, potent cocktails and good vibes.

Moving on

Train Septemvri (4 daily; 5hr).

Bus Blagoevgrad (hourly; 1hr); Plovdiv (6 daily; 4hr); Sofia (hourly; 3hr).

PLOVDIV

Bulgaria's second largest city, **PLOVDIV** (Пловдив) has more obvious charms than Sofia, which locals tend to look down on. The old town embodies Plovdiv's long history – Thracian fortifications subsumed by Macedonian masonry, overlaid with Roman and Byzantine walls. Great timber-framed mansions, erected during the Bulgarian renaissance, symbolically look down upon the derelict Ottoman mosques and artisans' dwellings of the lower town. But this isn't just another museum town: the city's arts festivals and trade fairs are the biggest in the country, and

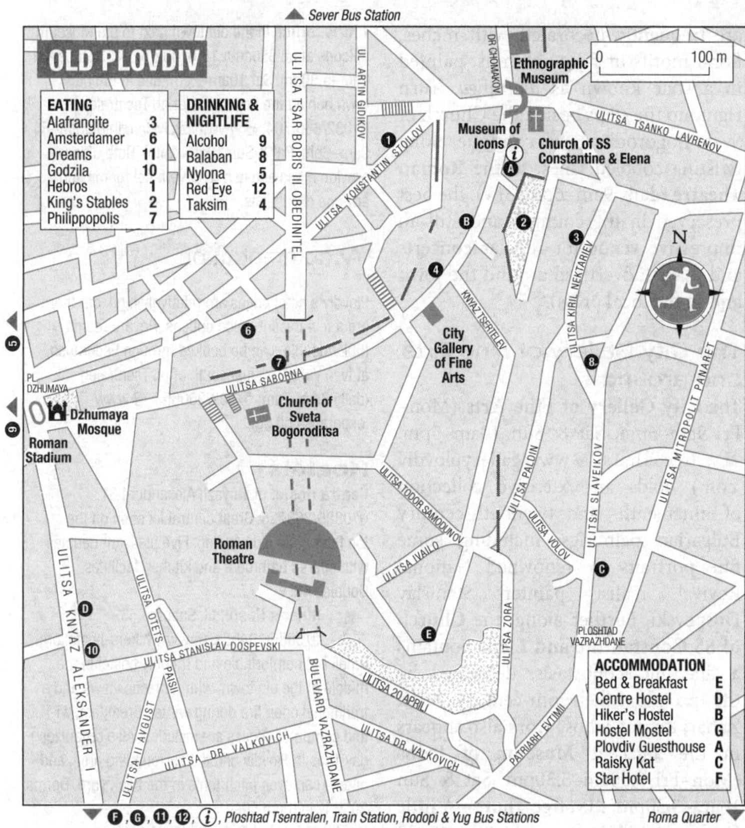

its restaurants and bars are equal to those of the capital.

What to see and do

Plovdiv centres on the large **ploshtad Tsentralen**, dominated by the monolithic *Hotel Trimontium Princess*.

Ploshtad Dzhumaya

Thronged with promenading Plovdivians and lined with shops, cafés, and bars, the pedestrianized ul. Knyaz Aleksandar I leads onto the attractive **ploshtad Dzhumaya** where the substantial ruins of a **Roman stadium** that could hold thirty thousand spectators are on display beneath the square. Among the variously styled buildings here, the renovated **Dzhumaya Mosque**, with its diamond-patterned minaret and lead-sheathed domes, steals the show; it's believed that the mosque dates back to the reign of Sultan Murad II (1359–85).

The Old Quarter

Covering one of Plovdiv's three hills with its cobbled streets and colourful mansions, the **Old Quarter** is a painter's dream and a cartographer's nightmare. As good a route as any is to start from pl. Dzhumaya and head east up ul. Saborna. Blackened fortress walls dating from Byzantine times can be seen around Saborna and other streets, sometimes incorporated into the dozens of timber-framed National Revival houses that are Plovdiv's speciality. Outside and within, the walls are frequently decorated with niches, floral motifs or false columns, painted in a style known as *alafranga*. Turn right, up the steps beside the Church of Sveta Bogoroditsa, and continue, along twisting cobbled lanes, to the **Roman Theatre** (daily 9am–6pm; 3Lv), the best preserved in the country, and still an impressive venue for regular concerts and plays (advertised around the town and in the local press).

The City Gallery of Fine Arts and around

The **City Gallery of Fine Arts** (Mon–Fri 9am–6pm, Sat & Sun 10am–5pm; 2Lv, free Thurs; ⓦwww.galleryplovdiv.com) holds an extensive collection of nineteenth- and twentieth-century Bulgarian paintings, including some fine portraits by renowned National Revival realist painter Stanislav Dospevski. Further along, the **Church of SS Constantine and Elena** contains a fine gilt iconostasis, decorated by the prolific nineteenth-century artist Zahari Zograf, whose work also appears in the adjacent **Museum of Icons** (Mon–Fri 9.30am–5.30pm, Sat & Sun 10am–5.30pm; 2Lv, free Thurs). A little further uphill is the richly decorated Kuyumdzhioglu House, now home to the **Ethnographic Museum** (Tues–Sun 9am–12.30pm & 1.30pm–6pm; 5Lv). Folk costumes and crafts are on display on the ground floor, while upstairs, the elegantly furnished rooms reflect the former owner's taste for Viennese and French Baroque.

Arrival and information

Train Plovdiv's train station is on bul. Hristo Botev, a 10min bus ride (#20 or #26) south of the centre.
Bus Two of Plovdiv's three bus stations are near the train station: Rodopi, serving the mountain resorts to the south, is just on the other side of the tracks; while Yug, serving Sofia and the rest of the country, is one block east. The third bus station, Sever, is north of the river (bus ##3 or #99; 20min) and serves destinations such as Koprivshtitsa and Veliko Tarnovo.
Tourist office In the old town next to the Museum of Icons at ul. Saborna 18 ⓣ032/620453 (Tues–Fri 9am–5.30pm, Sat 10am–2pm) and in the new town behind the post office at pl. Tsentralen 1, ⓣ032/656 794, ⓦwww.plovdiv-tour.info (Mon–Fri 9am–6pm, Sat & Sun 10am–2pm). Both offices provide maps and can reserve hotel rooms and arrange excursions.

Accommodation

Plovdiv's hotel prices are relatively high, but there are a few decent-value options. Private rooms (50Lv/double) can be booked through Esperansa, at Ivan Vazov 14, just south of pl. Tsentralen (daily 8am–7pm; ⓣ032/260653, ⓦwww.esperansa.hit.bg).

Hostels

Centre Hostel ul. Knyazh Alexander I 31, ⓣ0885/868725. Great central location on the top floor of an old building. Five pleasant doubles with shared bathroom and kitchen facilities. Doubles 40Lv.
Hiker's Hostel ul. Saborna 53 ⓣ0885/194553, ⓦwww.hikers-hostel.org. Small but comfortable and friendly hostel in the middle of the old town, with fantastic views and a traditional open fire during winter. Breakfast, wi-fi and computer access are included. Also organizes day-trips in Plovdiv and the surrounding area, and guests can even pitch tents in the back yard. Dorms 20Lv, twin room 50Lv.
Hostel Mostel ul. Petar Parchevich 13, ⓣ0897/100185, ⓦwww.hostelmostel.com. Charming hostel in the new town with wi-fi, computer access, free breakfast, evening meal, and bottle of beer included in the price. Tent space in the yard for 12Lv/person. Dorms 20Lv, twin room 52Lv.
Plovdiv Guesthouse ul. Saborna 20 ⓣ032/622432, ⓦwww.plovdivguest.com. Modern hostel in the old town with six-bed dorms that each have a bathroom. Private en-suite rooms are also available and breakfast and wi-fi are included. Dorms 20Lv, twin room 68Lv.
Raisky Kat ul. Slaveikov 6 ⓣ032/268849, ⓦwww.raiskykat.hostel.com. Dated but welcoming, family-run hostel offering doubles and triples with shared bathroom in the old town. 20Lv/person, doubles 44Lv.

Hotels

Bed & Breakfast ul. Knyazh Tseretelev 24 ⓣ0878/434770, ⓔbedbreakfast@abv.bg. Situated high in the old town, this cosy family-run hotel has

TREAT YOURSELF

For some of the best wine and food that southern Bulgaria has to offer, head to the restaurant of the **Hebros** hotel at ul. Konstantin Stoilov 51 (Ⓣ032/260180, Ⓦwww.hebros-hotel.com). The international menu changes from day to day – look out for their delicious home-made meatballs served with tomato and aubergine purée - and there are always vegetarian options and an array of delicious desserts. Main courses are around 30Lv and appetizers, such as fried frogs legs with parsley, around 15Lv. Tempting as the food is, it is the wine that really earns *Hebros* its stellar reputation, with recommended wines for every dish and a tremendous selection of wines from all over Bulgaria and the world; prices average 30Lv a bottle.

large comfortably furnished en-suites. Single 80LV, doubles 90–120Lv.

Star Hotel ul. Patriarch Evtiimi 13 Ⓣ032/633599, Ⓦwww.starhotel.bg. What was once Plovdiv's top Socialist-era hotel is now offering the very same faded but comfortable rooms with a/c and wi-fi at a fraction of their original price. Very central location. Breakfast not included. Singles 20Lv, doubles 40Lv.

Eating

The most atmospheric restaurants are in the old town, many occupying elegant old houses and serving good, traditional Bulgarian food. In the new town, ul. Knyaz Aleksandar I is awash with cheaper fast-food outlets, though better quality can be found away from the main drag.

Alafrangite ul. Kiril Nektariev 17. Lovely National Revival-style restaurant housed in an old town mansion. Mid-range prices, plus nightly live music in the fig-shaded courtyard.

Amsterdamer ul. Konstantin Stoilov 10. Stylish reproduction of a Dutch restaurant serving reasonably priced international and Bulgarian cuisine.

Dreams ul. Knyaz Aleksandar I 42. A popular central spot for coffee, cocktails and cakes.

Godzila ul. Knyaz Aleksandar I 29a. Pizzeria on the main street that serves a reasonable selection of dishes.

King's Stables ul. Saborna 9a. One of the old town's nicest and most reasonably priced restaurants. Serves large portions of traditional Bulgarian food, including some excellent grilled dishes (3–8Lv). The yogurt with home-made blueberry jam is definitely worth trying. There's also a bar that offers equally generous measures of spirits and weekly live music performances. Summer only.

Philippopolis ul. Saborna 29. 20L Ⓦwww.philippopolis.com. An excellent old town restaurant beneath an art gallery serving well-presented international food in a quiet garden with lovely views.

Drinking and nightlife

The best drinking holes are the pavement cafés of ul. Knyaz Aleksandar I. The Kapana area just north of the Dzhumaya mosque is the best place to head for late-night drinks and dancing.

Alcohol ul. Lady Strangford 5. A vibrant bar-cum-club with frequent live music as well as retro, dance, jazz, and Latino nights. Located up a side street just west of pl. Dzhumaya. Daily 9pm–4am.

Balaban ul. Kiril Nektariev 4. Atmospheric old town bar with low ceilings, wood panelling, and cheap cocktails. Daily 11am–midnight.

Nylona ul. Benkovski 8. Dimly lit and unsigned rock bar in the Kapana area that attracts an alternative crowd and hosts irregular live music performances. Daily 2pm–4am.

THE NIGHT TRAIN TO ISTANBUL

There's a nightly **train** to Istanbul, which leaves Plovdiv at 9pm and arrives at 8am; tickets cost 50Lv and must be bought in advance from the BDZh/Rila office opposite the train station at bul. Hristo Botev 31A (Mon–Fri 8am–6pm, Sat 9am–5pm; Ⓣ032/643120). Australian, US, UK and most EU citizens require Turkish **visas** (see p.1204) which can be bought at the Kapikule frontier and paid for in pounds (£10), dollars ($20) or euros (€15); Canadians are currently charged $60 or €45. Have the exact sum ready in cash, as they don't always have change and won't let you in without the visa. Other nationals should contact the Turkish consulate at ul. Filip Makedonski 10 in Plovdiv (Ⓣ032/632 309) for current visa prices.

Red Eye ul. Gladston 8. Just off pl. Tsentralen, this tiny, but incredibly popular bar is crammed into the first floor of a rickety old building. Features a staple diet of rock and retro. Daily 7pm–2am.
Taksim ul. Saborna 47. Cheap, open-air old town hangout with sweeping views of the city. Daily 10am–11pm.

Directory

Hospital For 24hr emergency treatment try Medicus Alpha at ul. Veliko Tarnovo 21 (☎032/634463, Ⓦwww.medicusalpha.com), alongside the park next to pl. Tsentralen.
Internet Most hostels have computer access and cafés and bars generally offer free wi-fi.
Pharmacy Kamea, ul. Hristo Danov 4, close to pl. Dzhumaya is open 24hr.
Post office pl. Tsentralen 1 (Mon–Sat 7am–7pm, Sun 7am–11am).
Travel agents Several agencies at the Yug bus station sell tickets for international buses. Hebros Bus (daily 8am–7pm; ☎032/626916), a Eurolines agent, can book seats on buses to Greece, Turkey and Western Europe.

Moving on

Train Burgas (6 daily; 4–5hr); Istanbul (1 nightly; 11hr); Koprivshtitsa via Karlovo (3 daily; 3hr); Sofia (15 daily; 2hr 30min); Varna (5 daily; 6hr).
Bus Avtogara Rodopi: Smolyan (via Bachkovo monastery) (hourly; 40min); Avtogara Sever: Koprivshtitsa (1 daily; 2hr 30min); Veliko Tarnovo (4 daily; 4hr); Avtogara Yug: Burgas (4 daily; 4hr); Sofia (hourly; 2hr); Varna (5 daily; 5hr).

BACHKOVO MONASTERY

The most attractive destination around Plovdiv is **Bachkovo Monastery** (daily 7am–8pm; free), around 30km away and an easy day-trip from the city (hourly buses from Rodopi station to Smolyan). Founded in 1038 by two Georgians in the service of the Byzantine Empire, this is Bulgaria's second-largest monastery. A great iron-studded door admits visitors to the cobbled courtyard, surrounded by wooden galleries and adorned with colourful frescoes. Beneath the vaulted porch of Bachkovo's principal church, **Sveta Bogoroditsa**, are frescoes depicting the horrors in store for sinners; the entrance itself is more cheery, overseen by the Holy Trinity.

It's possible to **stay** in refurbished rooms in the monastery (☎03327/2277; 30Lv/person with shared bathroom and cold water, 40Lv/person with hot water and en suite), and there are three **restaurants** just outside; *Vodopada*, with its mini-waterfall, is the best.

Central Bulgaria

For over a thousand years, Stara Planina – known to foreigners as the **Balkan range** – has been the cradle of the Bulgarian nation. It was here that the Khans established the First Kingdom, and here, too, after a period of Byzantine control, that the Boyars proclaimed the Second Kingdom and created a magnificent capital at **Veliko Tarnovo**. The nearby Sredna Gora (Central Mountains) were inhabited as early as the fifth millennium BC, but for Bulgarians this forested region is best known as the Land of the April Rising, the nineteenth-century rebellion for which the picturesque town of **Koprivshtitsa** will always be remembered.

Although they lie a little way off the main rail lines from Sofia, neither Veliko Tarnovo nor Koprivshtitsa is difficult to reach. The former lies just south of Gorna Oryahovitsa, a major rail junction midway between Varna and Sofia, from where you can pick up a local train or bus; the latter is served by a stop on the Sofia–Burgas line, where six daily trains in each direction are met by local buses to ferry you the 12km to the village itself.

KOPRIVSHTITSA

Seen from a distance, **KOPRIVSHTITSA** (Копривщица) looks almost too lovely to be real, its half-timbered houses lying in a valley amid wooded hills. It would be an oasis of rural calm if not for the tourists drawn by the superb architecture and Bulgarians paying homage to a landmark in their nation's history.

What to see and do

All of the town's museums are open 9.30am–5.30pm, with half of them closing on Mondays, and the other half on Tuesdays. You can buy a combined ticket for all six for 5Lv at the tourist office and at any of the museums; individual houses are priced at 2Lv each. It's also possible to hire an English-speaking guide for a two-hour tour (20Lv).

A street running off to the west of the main square leads to the **Oslekov House** (closed Mon). Its summer guest room is particularly impressive, with a vast wooden ceiling carved with geometric motifs. Cross the Freedom Bridge opposite the information centre to reach **Karavelov House** (closed Tues), the childhood home of Lyuben Karavelov, a fervent advocate of Bulgaria's liberation who spent much of his adult life in exile where he edited revolutionary publications. Near the Surlya Bridge is the birthplace of the poet **Dimcho Debelyanov** (closed Mon), who is buried in the grounds of the hilltop **Church of the Holy Virgin**. A gate at the rear of the churchyard leads to the birthplace of **Todor Kableshkov** (closed Mon), leader of the local rebels. Kableshkov's house now displays weapons used in the Rising and features a wonderful circular vestibule. Continuing south, cross the **Bridge of the First Shot**, which spans the Byala Reka stream, head up ul. Nikola Belodezhdov, and you'll come to the **Lyutov House** (closed Tues), once home to a wealthy yogurt merchant and today housing some of Koprivshtitsa's most sumptuous interiors. On the opposite side of the River Topolnitsa, steps lead up to the birthplace of another major figure in the Rising, **Georgi Benkovski** (closed Tues). A tailor by profession, he made the famous silk banner embroidered with the Bulgarian lion and "Liberty or Death!".

Arrival and information

Train Buses to Koprivshtitsa usually meet trains arriving at the station 12km south of town.
Bus The small bus station is 200m south of the main square.
Tourist office The tourist office on the main square, pl. 20th April 7 (daily 10am–7pm; ⓣ07184/2191, ⓦwww.koprivshtitza.com), and a museum centre (Wed–Sun 9.30am–5.30pm); both sell tickets for Koprivshtitsa's six house museums.

KOPRIVSHTITSA AND THE APRIL RISING

From the "Bridge of the First Shot" to the "Place of the Scimitar Charge", there's hardly a part of Koprivshtitsa that isn't named after an episode or participant in the **April Rising of 1876**, a meticulously planned grassroots revolution against Ottoman control that failed within days because the organizers had vastly overestimated their support. Neighbouring towns were burned by the *Bashibazouks* – the irregular troops recruited by the Turks to put the rebels in their place – and refugees flooded into Koprivshtitsa, spreading panic. The rebels eventually took to the hills while local traders bribed the *Bashibazouks* to spare the village – and so Koprivshtitsa survived unscathed, to be admired by subsequent generations as a symbol of heroism. Although the home-grown Bulgarian revolution failed, the barbarity of the Turkish reprisals outraged the international community and led to the 1877–88 War of Liberation which won freedom for Bulgaria from over five hundred years of Ottoman rule.

Accommodation

The tourist office can also book private rooms (40Lv) in charming village houses. Advance reservations are recommended in summer.

Bolyarka ⓣ07184/2043, ⓦwww.kboliarka.hit.bg. Four-room B&B just uphill from the centre, offering bright, pine-furnished rooms and a lovely garden. Singles 30Lv, doubles 50Lv.

Panorama ⓣ07184/2035, ⓦwww.panoramata.com. A well-run complex south of the centre with smart modern rooms on the ground floor and traditional-style rooms above; most have sweeping views of the town. Singles 40Lv, doubles 60Lv.

Trayanova Kashta ⓣ07184/3057. Just up the street from the Oslekov House, with delightful rooms in the National Revival style. Singles 30Lv, doubles 40Lv.

Eating and drinking

Dyado Liben Inn This fine nineteenth-century mansion opposite the main square serves traditional dishes such as *gyuvech* (meat stew) for 5–10Lv.

Lomeva Kashta A folk-style restaurant just north of the square, serving grills and salads from 5Lv.

Moving on

Train Plovdiv (4 daily; 3hr); Sofia (6 daily; 2hr); Veliko Tarnovo (1 daily; 4hr).

Bus Plovdiv (1 daily; 2hr 30min); Sofia (4 daily; 2hr).

VELIKO TARNOVO

With its dramatic medieval fortifications and huddles of antique houses teetering over the lovely River Yantra, **VELIKO TARNOVO** (Велико Търново) holds a uniquely important place in the minds of Bulgarians. When the National Assembly met here to draft Bulgaria's first constitution in 1879, it did so in the former capital of the Second Kingdom (1185–1396), whose civilization was snuffed out by the Turks. It was here, too, that the Communists chose to proclaim the People's Republic in 1944.

What to see and do

Modern Veliko Tarnovo centres on **ploshtad Mayka Balgariya**: from here bul. Nezavisimost (which becomes ul. Stefan Stambolov after a few hundred metres) heads northeast into a network of narrow streets that curve above the River Yantra and mark out the old town and its photogenic houses. From ul. Stambolov, the narrow cobbled ul. Rakovski slopes up into the **Varosh Quarter**, a pretty ensemble of nineteenth-century buildings once home to bustling artisans' workshops and now occupied by clothing and souvenir shops.

Sarafkina House

Clinging to the steep hillside at ul. General Gurko 88 is the **Sarafkina House** (Tues–Sat 9am–6pm; 6Lv), whose elegant restored interior is notable for its splendid octagonal vestibule and a panelled rosette ceiling.

Museum of the Bulgarian Renaissance and Constituent Assembly

Designed by the legendary local architect Kolyo Ficheto (1800-1881), the blue-and-white building where the first Bulgarian parliament assembled in 1879 is now home to the **Museum of the Bulgarian Renaissance and Constituent Assembly** (daily except Tues 9am–6pm; 6Lv), where you can see a reconstruction of the original assembly hall, and a collection of icons.

Tsarevets

Ulitsa Ivan Vazov leads directly from the museum to the medieval fortress, **Tsarevets** (daily: April–Oct 8am–7pm; Nov–March 9am–5pm; 6Lv). A successful rebellion against Byzantium was mounted from this citadel in 1185, and Tsarevets remained the centre of Bulgarian power until 1393, when, after a three-month siege, it fell to the Turks. The partially restored fortress is entered via the **Asenova Gate** halfway along the western ramparts. To the right, paths lead round to **Baldwin's Tower**, where

Baldwin of Flanders, the so-called Latin Emperor of Byzantium, was incarcerated by Tsar Kaloyan. Visitors can climb up to the parapet of the fully renovated tower for sweeping views of the town.

Don't miss the dramatic 20-minute Tsarevets Sound and Light show held most evenings during the summer – it's free on public holidays, but on other days you'll have to wait for a large group to fork out for it. Call ⓣ062/636952 for show times.

Arrival and information

Train All trains between Sofia and Varna stop at Gorna Oryahovitsa, from where local trains and frequent buses cover the remaining 13km to Veliko Tarnovo. From Tarnovo train station, 2km south of the city centre, buses #4 and #13 run to pl. Mayka Balgariya.
Bus Buses to and from Sofia and Varna use the small central bus terminal (*tsentralna avtogara*) just behind the Tourist Information Centre. Buses to Plovdiv, Burgas and Ruse (from where there are buses to Bucharest) use the western terminal (*avtogara zapad*) 4km southwest of town accessed by bus #10 and trolley buses #1 and #3 from the centre. Buses to Athens and Istanbul use the southern bus terminal (*avtogara yug*) which is a 10-minute walk south of the centre along bul. Hristo Botev.
Tourist office bul. Hristo Botev 5 (Mon–Fri 9am–6pm; summer Sat & Sun 9am–5pm; ⓣ062/600768, ⓦwww.velikoturnovo.info).

Accommodation

Comfort ul. Paneyot Tipografov 5 ⓣ062/628728, ⓦwww.hotelcomfortbg.com. A spotless, family-run place, with wi-fi, a/c and splendid views of the Tsarevets. Located just above the Varosh Quarter's bazaar. Breakfast not included. Singles 40Lv, doubles 50Lv.
Hikers Hostel ul. Rezervoarska 91 ⓣ062/604019 or ⓣ0889/691661, ⓦwww.hikers-hostel.org. A friendly hostel tucked away in a narrow street above the Varosh Quarter with striking views of Tsarevets, along with excellent dorm accommodation, tent space, kitchen and free wi-fi, computer access and pick-up service. Dorms 20Lv, twins 50Lv.
Hostel Mostel ul. Iordan Indjeto 10 ⓣ0897/859359, ⓦwww.hostelmostel.com. Located in a beautifully restored 140-year-old Ottoman building south of the road leading to Tsarevets, with comfortable dorms and private en-suite rooms. Pick-up service, wi-fi, computer access, an all-you-can-eat breakfast, an evening meal and a beer for every night of your stay are all included in the price. There's also a barbecue and tent space in the garden. Dorms 22Lv, doubles 60Lv, camping 12Lv/person.
Nomads Hostel ul. Gurko 27 ⓣ062/603092 and ⓣ0886/039705, ⓦwww.nomadshostel.com. A welcoming, cosy hostel with helpful staff who can arrange a variety of trips around the region. Wi-fi, computer access and a great organic breakfast are included. Dorms 20Lv, doubles/twins 45Lv.

Eating and drinking

Mosquito ul. Stefan Stambolov 21. A relaxed café-bar overlooking the gorge, with good coffee and cakes.
Mecha Dupka ul. G.Marmarchev 14. Serves authentic Bulgarian fare (main courses 8–15Lv) in a Varosh Quarter cellar, often with accompanying music and dancing.
Melodie Bar pl. Slaveykov 1. Small, dimly lit jazz bar frequented by locals and expats. Daily 11am–1am.
Shastlivetsa ul. Stambolov 79. Restaurant on the main road towards Tsarevets offering local dishes, as well as a large range of pizzas and pastas. Main courses around 7Lv.

Moving on

International trains must be booked in advance through the Rila/BDZh office behind the tourist office at ul. Kaloyan 1 (Mon–Fri 8am–noon & 1–4.30pm; ⓣ062/622042).
Train Veliko Tarnovo to Gorna Oryahovitsa (3 daily; 15min). Gorna Oryahovitsa to Bucharest (2 daily; 5–6hr); Burgas (1 daily; 7hr); Istanbul (1 daily; 14hr); Sofia (2 daily; 5hr 30min); Varna (2 daily; 4–5hr).
Bus Burgas (4 daily; 4hr 30min); Plovdiv (3 daily; 4hr 30min); Sofia (hourly; 4hr); Varna (hourly; 5hr).

The Black Sea coast

Bulgaria's **Black Sea** resorts have been popular holiday haunts for more than a century, though it wasn't until the 1960s that the coastline was developed for mass tourism, with Communist party officials from across the former

Eastern Bloc descending on the beaches each year for a spot of socialist fun in the sun. Since then, the **resorts** have mushroomed, growing increasingly sophisticated as the prototype mega-complexes have been followed by holiday villages. With fine weather practically guaranteed, the selling of the coast has been a success in economic terms, but with the exception of ancient **Sozopol** and touristy **Nesebar**, there's little to please the eye. Of the coast's two cities – **Varna** and **Burgas** – the former is by far preferable as a base for getting to the less-developed spots.

VARNA

VARNA (Варна) is a cosmopolitan place, and nice to stroll through: Baroque, nineteenth-century and contemporary architecture are pleasantly blended with shady promenades and a handsome seaside park. As a settlement it dates back almost five millennia, but it wasn't until seafaring Greeks founded a colony here in 585 BC that the town became a port. The modern city is used by both commercial freighters and the navy, as well as being a popular tourist resort in its own right.

What to see and do

Social life revolves around **ploshtad Nezavisimost**, where the opera house and theatre provide a backdrop for restaurants and cafés. The square is the starting point of Varna's evening promenade, which flows eastward from here along bul. Knyaz Boris I and towards bul. Slivnitsa and the seaside gardens. Beyond the opera house, Varna's main lateral boulevard cuts through pl. Mitropolit Simeon to the domed **Cathedral of the Assumption**. Constructed in 1886, it contains a splendid iconostasis and bishop's throne. The **Archeology Museum** on the corner of Mariya Luiza and Slivnitsa (summer Tues–Sun 10am–5pm; winter Tues–Sat 10am–5pm; 5Lv; Ⓦwww.amvarna.com) houses one of Bulgaria's finest collections of antiquities. Most impressive are the skeletons adorned with Thracian gold jewellery that were unearthed in Varna in 1972 and date back almost six thousand years.

South of the centre on ul. Han Krum are the extensive remains of the third-century **Roman baths** (summer Tues–Sun 10am–5pm; winter Tues–Sat 10am–5pm; 5Lv). It's still possible to discern the various bathing areas and the once huge exercise hall. At the southern edge of the Sea Gardens, the **Navy Museum** (summer Mon–Sat 10am–6pm; winter Mon–Fri 10am–5pm; 5Lv) is worth a trip to see the boat responsible for the Bulgarian Navy's only victory; it sank the Turkish cruiser *Hamidie* off Cape Kaliakra in 1912.

Beaches

Varna's municipal beach offers a perfunctory stretch of sand but little tranquillity as it's dominated by open-air bars and clubs. The beaches at the busy resorts of **Golden Sands** and **Albena** to the north are hardly any quieter, but are certainly wider and much more attractive. Beyond Albena the coastline turns rocky until the villages at **Krapets** and **Durankulak**, just short of the Romanian border, which boast some wonderful undeveloped sandy beaches.

Arrival and information

Air Varna airport (Ⓦwww.varna-airport.bg) is about a five-minute ride from opposite the Tourist Information Centre (bus #409; every 15min 6am–11pm; 1–3Lv) northwest of the city. Taxis cost 10–15Lv.

Train The train station is a 10-min walk south of the centre along ul. Tsar Simeon.

Bus The bus terminal is a 10min journey (bus #1, #22 or #41) northwest of the centre on bul. Vladislav Varnenchik.

Tourist office pl. Sv. Kiril i Metodi opposite the Cathedral of the Assumption (summer daily

9am–7pm; ⓣ052/608918, ⓦwww.varnainfo.bg). The staff sell city maps, reserve hotel rooms and organize excursions.

Accommodation

Private rooms (doubles 35–60Lv) can be arranged by two accommodation agencies (*kvartirno byuro*) with neighbouring offices in the railway station: Astra Tour (ⓣ052/605861) and Isak Accommodation (ⓣ052/602318) are both open daily from 7am–11pm in summer.

Flag Hostel ul. Bratia Shkorpil 13A ⓣ0897/408115, ⓦwww.varnahostel.com. Located a couple of minutes' walk east of the Cathedral of the Assumption, the hostel occupies the top floor of a nondescript building and offers small dorms with wi-fi, a/c and breakfast included. Dorms 20Lv.

Interhotel Cherno More bul. Slivnitsa 33 ⓣ052/612235, ⓦwww.chernomorebg.com. Once the city's flagship Socialist-era hotel, this central, sixteen-floor concrete monolith now offers its modernized rooms at budget prices. Fabulous views and a top-floor cocktail bar and restaurant. Singles or doubles 70Lv.

Yo Ho Hostel ul. Ruse 23 ⓣ0887/933340, ⓦwww.yohohostel.com. Centrally located just off pl. Nezavisimost, this fun hostel sprawls over several colourful floors and hosts regular live bands and art exhibitions. Breakfast, wi-fi, computer access and pick-up service are included. Helpful staff can arrange day-trips and bike rental. Dorms 24Lv, doubles 56Lv.

Eating and drinking

There are plenty of bars to choose from along bul. Knyaz Boris I, while in summer the beach, reached by steps from the Sea Gardens, is lined with open-air bars, fish restaurants and a seemingly unending strip of nightclubs. Outside high season, though, it's pretty dismal.

Arkitekt ul. Musala 10. A traditionally furnished wooden townhouse west of the centre serving authentic Bulgarian dishes and plenty of grilled meat (6–12Lv), with a pleasant courtyard garden.

Bara bul. Knyazh Boris 24. Quirky first-floor bar with chessboard ceiling lamps, bathroom mosaics, old furniture and a great selection of cocktails.

Happy Bar and Grill pl. Nezavisimost. American-style eatery with a picture menu offering a mixture of Bulgarian and international food. The *kashkaval pane* (battered cheese) is particularly good (4Lv).

Hotel Cherno More bul. Slivnitsa 33. Head to the sixteenth-floor cocktail bar for unrivalled views of the city; cocktails will set you back between 8–10Lv.

Morske Vulk ul. Odrin. Just south of pl. Exarch Yosef, this is one of the friendliest and cheapest restaurants in town, with a vibrant, alternative crowd and brilliant Bulgarian dishes, including vegetarian options such as pizza for around 7Lv.

Three Lions Pub pl. Slaveikov 1. Thriving English-themed pub located 100 metres east of the train station with regular live rock bands, big-screen TVs and good food.

Moving on

Train Plovdiv (4 daily; 6–7hr); Sofia (8 daily; 8–9hr).

Bus Burgas (hourly; 3hr); Golden Sands (every 20–30min; 20min); Sofia (every 30min; 7hr); Sunny Beach (hourly; 2hr 10min); Veliko Tarnovo (8 daily; 4hr).

BURGAS

The south coast's prime urban centre and transport hub, **BURGAS** (Бургас) provides easy access to the picture-postcard town of Nesebar to the north and Sozopol to the south. Bypassed by most tourists, the pedestrianized city centre, lined with smart boutiques, bars and cafés, is pleasant enough, though Burgas's best features are the well-manicured **Sea Gardens** overlooking the beach, and its rusting pier at the eastern end of town.

Arrival and information

Bus and train stations Both are located at the southern edge of town, near the port.

Tourist office Beneath bul. Hristo Botev in the underpass opposite the opera house (Mon–Fri 8.30am–5.30pm ⓣ056/825772, ⓦwww.tic.burgas.bg). Provides maps and can make hotel reservations.

Accommodation

Burgas has long suffered from a shortage of budget accommodation, though the establishment of a small hostel suggests that things may change.

Burgas Hostel Slavyanska 14 ⓣ056/825854 or ⓣ0886/096747, ⓦwww.hostelburgas.com. Central hostel with friendly, helpful staff located 10min from the train station. Offers clean dorms, sea views from its roof terrace, wi-fi, free breakfast, and kitchen and laundry facilities as well as a free pick-up service from the bus and train stations. Dorms 20Lv.

Fors ul. K. Fotinov 17 ⓣ056/828852, ⓦwww.hotelfors-bg.com. Smart central hotel with good service, and spotless en-suite rooms with wi-fi and a/c. Breakfast included Singles 50Lv, doubles 75Lv.

Fotinov ul. K. Fotinov 22 ⓣ0897/834130, ⓦwww.hotelfotinov.com. Pleasant family-run hotel near the *Fors*. Facilities include fitness equipment, wi-fi, sauna and a/c. Breakfast not included Singles 45Lv, doubles 60Lv.

Eating and drinking

Burgas' pedestrianized central boulevards are crammed with bars, cafés and restaurants that spill out onto the streets in summer. There are several pleasant places to eat in the Sea Gardens and plenty more bars along the beach.

Zheleznyat Svetilnik ul. K. Fotinov 28. Great traditional-style restaurant with shaded outdoor seating serving typical Bulgarian dishes at mid-range prices with an emphasis on grilled meat. Excellent wine list.

Zlatna Kotva bul. Bogoridi 64. Popular nautical-themed place serving a broad variety of reasonably priced fish dishes along with Bulgarian and international cuisine.

Moving on

Train Plovdiv (5 daily; 4hr 30min); Sofia (7 daily; 8–9hr).

Bus Nesebar (every 40min; 50min); Istanbul (4 daily; 6hr; departing from Nisikli Turism at ul. Bulair 39); Plovdiv (4 daily; 4hr); Sofia (hourly; 6hr 30min); Sozopol (every 30min; 50min); Varna (hourly; 2hr).

NESEBAR

Famed for its delightful medieval churches, nineteenth-century wooden architecture and labyrinthine cobbled streets, **NESEBAR**'s (Несебър) old town, 35km northeast of Burgas, lies on a narrow isthmus connected by road to the mainland. It was founded by Greek colonists and grew into a thriving port during the Byzantine era; ownership alternated between Bulgaria and Byzantium until the Ottomans captured it in 1453. The town remained an important centre of Greek culture and the seat of a bishop under Turkish rule, which left Nesebar's **Byzantine churches** reasonably intact. Nowadays the town depends on them for its tourist appeal, demonstrated by the often overwhelming stream of summer visitors. Outside the hectic summer season, the place seems eerily deserted, with little open other than a few sleepy cafés.

What to see and do

A man-made isthmus connects Nesebar's old town with the mainland. Standing just inside the city gates, the **Archeological Museum** (daily 9am–6pm; 5Lv) has an array of Greek tombstones and medieval icons on display. Immediately beyond the museum is **Christ Pantokrator**, the first of Nesebar's churches, currently in use as an upmarket art gallery. It features an unusual frieze of swastikas – an ancient symbol of fertility and continual change. Downhill on ul. Mitropolitska is the eleventh-century church of **St John the Baptist** (now also an art gallery), only one of whose frescoes still survives. Overhung by half-timbered houses, ul. Aheloi branches off from ul. Mitropolitska towards the **Church of Sveti Spas** (summer only: Mon–Fri 10am–5pm, Sat & Sun 10am–4pm; 3Lv), outwardly unremarkable but filled with seventeenth-century frescoes.

A few steps to the east lies the ruined **Old Metropolitan Church**, dominating a plaza filled with pavement cafés and street traders. The church itself dates back to the sixth century, and it was here that bishops officiated during the city's heyday. Standing in splendid isolation beside the shore, the ruined **Church of St John Aliturgetos** represents the zenith of Byzantine architecture in Bulgaria. Its exterior employs limestone, red bricks, crosses, mussel shells and ceramic plaques for decoration.

Beaches

Visitors can either head for Nesebar's handful of small beaches or hop on a shuttle bus to the unattractive neighbouring resort of **Sunny Beach** where a great expanse of golden sand studded with thousands of umbrellas stretches for several kilometres along the overdeveloped coastline.

Arrival and information

Bus Buses arrive at either the harbour at the western end of town, or further up Han Krum before turning around to head for the nearby Sunny Beach resort. Bus #1 connects the new and old towns.
Tourist office Located in the centre of the old town at ul. Messemvria 10 (Mon–Fri 10am–6pm ⓣ0554/42611, ⓦwww.visitnessebar.org).

Accommodation

Private rooms (30–60Lv double), many in fine old houses, can be booked through Messemvria Tour at ul. Han Krum 16 (daily 8am–6pm) close to the post office in the new town, near the St John the Baptist church.
Rai ul. Sadala 7 ⓣ0554/46094. A small and comfortable family-run *pension* on the northern side of the peninsula with a/c and wi-fi. Open summer only. Singles 30Lv, doubles 40Lv.
Tony ul. Kraybrezhna 20 ⓣ0554/42403. Nearby the *Rai* hotel in the old town, this hotel's pleasant, a/c rooms have balconies with sea views and wi-fi. Singles 40Lv, doubles 50Lv.

Eating and drinking

There are plenty of places to eat, although most restaurants are aimed at the passing tourist crowd, serving predictably mediocre food. Snacks are available from summertime kiosks along the waterfront.
Kapitanska Sreshta ul. Mena 22. Atmospheric fish restaurant housed in a nineteenth-century building with a lovely shaded terrace overlooking the old town's harbour.
Neptun ul. Neptun 1. Pleasant outdoor spot on the southeastern tip of the old town with great sea views. Serves a reasonably priced selection of Bulgarian standards.

Moving on

Bus Burgas (every 40min; 50min); Sofia (8 daily; 6hr 30min); Varna (6 daily; 2hr 10min).

SOZOPOL

SOZOPOL (Созопол) is a busy fishing port and holiday resort, especially popular with East European tourists. The town's charm owes much to its **architecture**, the old wooden houses jostling for space, their upper storeys almost meeting across the town's narrow cobbled streets. The oldest settlement in Bulgaria, Sozopol was founded in the seventh century BC by Greek colonists.

What to see and do

The **Archeological Museum** (summer Mon–Fri 8.30am–5pm; winter Mon–Fri 8am–noon; 4Lv) behind the library holds a worthwhile collection of ancient ceramics, as well as a number of artefacts uncovered in the local area. Further into the town, follow the signs to the **Southern Fortress Wall and Tower Complex** (10am–7pm; 4Lv), which gives access to a beautifully restored tower dating from the fourth century BC.

Sozopol's two small **beaches** are predictably overcrowded in high season, so it's worth making the short trip north to the emptier beaches around the *Zlatna Ribka* campsite (see p.246).

Arrival and information

Bus Buses from Burgas arrive at pl. Han Krum on the southern edge of the old town. Those from other Bulgarian cities usually arrive and depart from pl. Cherno More in the the new town.
Tourist office In the absence of a municipal tourist office, the best source of information is the Lotos travel agency located high in the new town at ul. Musala 7 (summer daily 8am–7.30pm; ⓣ0550/23925, ⓦwww.aiatour.com).

Accommodation

Accommodation in Sozopol can be even harder to find during summer than in Nesebar, and most places shut down for the rest of the year. The Lotos travel agency (see above) can arrange private rooms of varying standards (16–30Lv/person).

Art ul. Kiril I Metodii 72 ⓣ0550/24081, ⓦwww.arthotel-sbh.com. Smart modern hotel and restaurant perched on a rocky cliff at the northern end of the peninsula. Singles or doubles 75Lv.
Rusalka ul. Milet 36 ⓣ0550/23047. On the south of the peninsula, this is the best-value old-town hotel with comfortable a/c rooms overlooking the sea. Breakfast not included. Singles 60Lv, doubles 80Lv.
Zlatna Ribka ⓣ0550/22427. Popular seaside campsite with great beach 3km north of town on the Burgas bus route. 25–35Lv/tent; camper van 30–50Lv.

Eating and drinking

Art ul. Kiril I Metodii 72. Great restaurant with outdoor tables on the cliff's edge. Serves a mid-priced range of Bulgarian and international meals.
Chuchura ul. Ribarska 10. Situated on the western side of the old town, this is a popular traditional-style restaurant with a particularly good selection of fish dishes (20–30Lv/person).
Vyatarna Melnitsa ul. Morski Skali 27. Similar in style and price to the *Chuchura*, the "Windmill" has excellent service and perches on the northern tip of the peninsula.

Moving on

Bus Burgas (every 30min; 50min); Plovdiv (7 daily; 5hr); Sofia (9 daily; 7hr 15min).

Croatia

HIGHLIGHTS

AMPHITHEATRE, PULA: visit the sixth largest amphitheatre in the world

ZADAR: visit this buzzing town and discover its unique Sea Organ

DIOCLETIAN'S PALACE, SPLIT: be amazed by this extraordinary 1700-year-old palace

VIS ISLAND: relax on the coast's lushest island

DUBROVNIK SUMMER FESTIVAL: enjoy world-class classical music at Croatia's prestigious festival

ROUGH COSTS

DAILY BUDGET Basic €38 /occasional treat €43

DRINK Litre of local wine €7

FOOD *Čevapčići* (mini kebabs) €5

PRIVATE ACCOMMODATION/HOSTEL/CAMPSITE €42/€20/€14

TRAVEL Ferry travel within Dalmatian islands €3–7; Bus: Zagreb–Split €15–20

FACT FILE

POPULATION 4.4 million

AREA 56,594 sq km

LANGUAGE Croatian (Hrvatski)

CURRENCY Kuna (kn)

CAPITAL Zagreb (population: 800,000)

INTERNATIONAL PHONE CODE ⓣ385

Introduction

Croatia's serpentine coastline and sheer natural beauty make it an irresistible European destination. Its tourist industry is now fully fledged, but the accompanying development has been fairly unobtrusive and there are still plenty of secluded rocky beaches and pristine old towns to explore. As well as a stunning array of architecture, the country has a rich cultural heritage and an intimate festival scene – all relatively cheap to enjoy, though Croatia is set to join the EU in mid-2013.

The capital, **Zagreb**, is a lively central European metropolis, combining elegant nineteenth-century architecture with plenty of cultural diversions and a vibrant café scene. The peninsula of **Istria** contains many of the country's most developed resorts, with old Venetian towns like **Rovinj** rubbing shoulders with the raffish port of **Pula**. Further south lies **Dalmatia**, a dramatic, mountain-fringed stretch of coastline studded with islands. Dalmatia's main towns are Italianate **Zadar**, with Croatia's best nightlife, and vibrant **Split**, an ancient Roman settlement and modern port that provides a jumping-off point to a series of enchanting **islands**. South of Split lies the medieval walled city of **Dubrovnik**, site of an important festival in the summer and a magical place to be, whatever the season.

CHRONOLOGY

168 BC The Romans conquer the Illyrians in the area known as present-day Croatia.

600s AD Early Croatian Slavic forefathers settle in the region.

799 Charlemagne invades the Dalmatian area of Croatia, establishing Frankish interest in the area.

925 Tomislav is crowned the first King of Croatia.

1102 Croats are forced to accept Hungarian rule.

1214 The Statute of the Island of Korčula is the first document in Europe to abolish the slave trade.

1526 Habsburg dynasty takes control of Croatia after the Battle of Mohacs.

1918 After the defeat of the Habsburgs in World War I, Croatia joins the Kingdom of the Serbs, Croats and Slovenes.

1929 The kingdom becomes known as Yugoslavia.

1945 General Tito leads successful resistance campaigns against the Nazis.

1980 Tito dies, leading to calls by Balkan countries for independence from Yugoslavia.

1989 The collapse of Communism heightens the call for political and national autonomy.

1990 Conservative Franjo Tudjman is elected President.

1991 Croatia declares its independence, leading to military campaigns by the Serbs against the Croats.

1995 Croat forces take control of large areas, forcing Croatian Serbs to flee Croatia. The Dayton Peace Accords end the war.

2005 Fugitive General Ante Gotovina, wanted for war crimes, is captured in the Canary Islands.

2009 Croatia's accession to the EU is set back due to border disputes with Slovenia.

2011 General Ante Gotovina is convicted of war crimes at The Hague and sentenced to 24 years in jail. Croatia approved for EU accession in mid-2013.

ARRIVAL

The principal international **airports** are Dubrovnik, Pula, Split, Zadar and Zagreb. Ryanair runs services to Pula and Zadar and easyJet fly to Zagreb, Split and Dubrovnik. Wizz Air and Jet2 fly to Split and Dubrovnik, and BA fly to Dubrovnik and Zagreb. The national carrier, Croatia Airlines (Ⓦwww.croatiaairlines.com), operates routes throughout Europe.

Ferry routes to Croatia run frequently from Italy: Split and Zadar from Ancona, Split from Pescara, Rovinj from Trieste and Venice, Pula from Venice and Dubrovnik from Bari. See Ⓦwww.jadrolinija.hr, Ⓦwww.venezialines.com, Ⓦwww.triestelines.it and Ⓦwww.snav.it.

Croatia is served by many international buses, including services from Vienna, Belgrade and Sarajevo, most of them run by Eurolines (Ⓦwww.eurolines.com), who are partnered with AutoTrans (Ⓦwww.autotrans.hr). Several German cities are connected with Croatia too; see Ⓦwww.touring.de. For services from Trieste check Ⓦwww.autostazionetrieste.it

Croatia is also linked with the rest of Europe by **rail**; see Ⓦwww.hznet.hr for timetables.

GETTING AROUND

Croatia's **train** service is pretty limited; you're much more likely to use the excellent **bus** network.

By bus

Croatia has an array of small local bus companies. The leading one is AutoTrans (Ⓦwww.autotrans.hr); services are well integrated and punctual and bus stations tend to be well organized. If you're at a big city bus station, tickets (*karta*) must be bought from ticket windows before boarding the bus. Elsewhere, buy them from the driver. You'll be charged around 7kn for items of baggage to be stored in the hold.

By train

Croatian Railways *(Hrvatske željeznice*; Ⓦwww.hznet.hr*)* runs a smooth and efficient service, but it isn't very extensive. The most useful route is the Zagreb–Split line, which is served by high-speed, tilting trains. Trains (*vlak*, plural *vlakovi*) are divided into *putnički* (slow ones, which stop at every station) and IC (intercity trains that are faster and more expensive). Timetables (*vozni red*) are usually displayed on boards in stations – *odlazak* means departure, *dolazak* arrival. **InterRail** passes are valid, and you must pay a small reservation fee for longer journeys.

By ferry

Jadrolinija (ⓦwww.jadrolinija.hr) operates numerous **ferry** services. The Rijeka–Split–Stari Grad (Hvar)–Korčula Town (Korčula)–Sobra (Mljet)–Dubrovnik route runs twice a week in both directions between May and September. Rijeka to Dubrovnik is a 22hr 30min journey, involving one night on the boat. In addition, ferries and faster catamarans link Split with the islands of Brač, Hvar, Vis and Korčula. **Fares** are reasonable for short trips: Split to Hvar costs 22kn. For longer journeys, prices vary greatly according to the level of comfort. **Book** in advance for longer journeys, wherever possible, and note that ferry timetables change around the end of May and end of September.

ACCOMMODATION

Private rooms (*privatne sobe*) have long been the mainstay of Croatian tourism. Bookings are made through private travel agencies (usually open daily 8am–8/9pm in summer). High-season prices are around €36/265kn per person for a simple double sharing a toilet and bathroom and €42/315kn for an en-suite double; stays of less than three nights are sometimes subject to a surcharge. Places fill up quickly in July and August: arrive early or book ahead. Single travellers will sometimes find it difficult to get accommodation at all at this time, unless they're prepared to pay the price of a double room; at other times, you could expect to get a thirty percent discount. It's very likely you'll be offered a place to stay by elderly ladies waiting outside train, bus and ferry stations, particularly in southern Dalmatia. Don't be afraid to take a room offered in this manner, but be sure to establish the location and agree a price before setting off: expect to pay around twenty percent less than you would with an agency. However you find a room, you can usually examine it before committing to paying for it. Official establishments with rooms should have a blue plaque saying "*sobe*" or "*apartmani*" outside – if they don't, they're not legal.

Independent **hostels** are cropping up more and more in Croatia – especially in the larger towns. The average price for a dorm bed is 150kn and many also offer private rooms. The Croatian Youth Hostel website (ⓦwww.hfhs.hr) also has details and prices of HI-affiliated hostels.

Campsites usually open just for the summer season; see ⓦwww.camping.hr for a list.

FOOD AND DRINK

Croatia has a varied and distinctive range of **cuisine**, largely because it straddles two culinary cultures: the fish- and seafood-dominated cuisine of the Mediterranean and the hearty meat-oriented fare of Central Europe.

For **breakfasts** and **fast food**, look out for bakeries or snack-food outlets selling *burek* (about 10kn), a flaky pastry filled with cheese; or grilled meats such as *ćevapčići* (rissoles of minced beef, pork or lamb sold in a bun with relish; 37kn for a dozen from street stalls). Bread (*kruh*) is bought from a *pekarna* (bakery) or a supermarket.

A **restaurant** menu (*jelovnik*) will usually include starters such as *pršut* (home-cured ham) and *paški sir* (piquant hard cheese). Typical mains include *punjene paprike* (peppers stuffed with rice and meat), *gulaš* (goulash) or some kind of *odrezak* (fillet of meat, often pan-fried), usually either *svinjski* (pork) or *teleški* (veal). On the coast, you'll be regaled with every kind of seafood. *Riba* (fish) can come either *na žaru* (grilled) or *pečnici* (baked). *Brodet* is a hot peppery fish stew. Other main menu items on the coast are *lignje* (squid), *škampi* (unpeeled prawns eaten with your fingers), *rakovica* (crab), *oštrige* (oysters), *kalamari* (squid), *školjke* (mussels) and *jastog* (lobster); *crni rizoto* is risotto with squid. No town is without at least one **pizzeria**, serving good stone-baked pizzas (around 40kn). A **konoba** is a no-frills, often family-run restaurant, usually serving local dishes at low prices.

Typical **desserts** include *palačinke* (pancakes) and *sladoled* (ice cream).

Drink

Croatia is laden with relaxing **cafés** (*kavanas*) for daytime drinking. Coffee (*kava*) is usually served black unless specified otherwise – ask for *mlijeko* (milk) or *šlag* (cream). Tea (*čaj*) is less available and drunk without milk.

Croatian **beer** (*pivo*) is of the light lager variety; Karlovačko and Ožujsko are two good local brands. The local **wine** (*vino*) is consistently good and reasonably cheap: in Dalmatia there are some pleasant, crisp white wines such as Kastelet, Grk and Posip, as well as reds including the dark, heady Dingač and Babić; in Istria, Semion is a bone-dry white and Teran a light fresh red. Local spirits include *medenica*, a honey-based slow-burning nectar; *loza*, a clear grape-based spirit; and *Maraskino*, a cherry liqueur from Zadar.

CULTURE AND ETIQUETTE

With an almost ninety percent Roman Catholic population, religious holidays in Croatia are celebrated with gusto – not least because outward displays of religion were discouraged by Tito, leading to what seems like a "making up for lost time" attitude. A fun-loving people generally, especially among the younger generation, Croatians are welcoming and will happily engage you in conversations about food, wine and politics over a beer or two.

A service charge is not usually added to restaurant bills and it is the norm to leave a **tip** at your discretion (ten percent is quite acceptable).

SPORTS AND OUTDOOR ACTIVITIES

The Dalmatian coast is great for **water-sports**, including windsurfing, kite-surfing, wake-boarding and some less hardcore pursuits, such as banana-boating and renting a motorboat. Brač, Hvar and Vis have plenty of well-marked **cycling** and **hiking** trails.

Football remains the nation's favourite diversion, Dinamo Zagreb being the best-known team internationally.

COMMUNICATIONS

Post offices (*pošta* or HPT) are discernible by their bright yellow signs and open Monday to Friday 7am to 7pm, Saturday 7am to 2pm. In big towns and resorts, some are open daily and until 10pm. Stamps (*marke*) can also be

CROATIA ONLINE

ⓦ **www.adriatica.net** Information on the Adriatic resorts and an accommodation booking service.
ⓦ **www.croatia.hr** Official tourist board site.
ⓦ **www.find-croatia.com** General travel info.
ⓦ **www.istra.com** Official website for the Istrian peninsula.
ⓦ **www.dalmacija.net** Covers Dalmatia.

bought at newsstands, and letterboxes are painted the same yellow as post office signs.

Public **phones** use cards (*telekarta*), which come in denominations of 15kn, 25kn, 50kn and 100kn; buy these from post offices or newspaper kiosks. You can also make international calls from the post office. Croatian SIM cards are available for about 100kn. Even small towns have **internet cafés** (expect to pay around 25kn/hr) and many normal cafés offer wi-fi now too.

CRIME AND SAFETY

The crime rate is low by European standards and **police** (*policija*) are generally helpful when dealing with tourists. They often make routine checks on identity cards and other documents, so always carry your passport. In an **emergency**, call ☎112.

CROATIAN

	Croatian	Pronunciation
Yes	*Da*	Dah
No	*Ne*	Neh
Please	*Molim*	Mo-leem
Thank you	*Hvala*	Hvahlah
Hello/Good day	*Bog/Dobar dan*	Dobahr dan
Goodbye	*Bog/Dovidjenja*	Doh veedehnyah
Excuse me	*Izvinite*	Izvineet
Sorry	*Oprostite*	Auprausteete
Today	*Danas*	Danass
Good	*Dobro*	Dobroh
Bad	*Loše*	Losheh
How much is...?	*Koliko stoji...?*	Koleekoh sto-yee...?
What time is it?	*Koliko je sati?*	Koleekoh yeh satee?
I don't understand	*Ne razumijem*	Neh rahzoomeeyehm
Do you speak English?	*Govorite li engleski?*	Govoreeteh lee ehngleskee?
One	*Jedan*	Yehdan
Two	*Dva*	Dvah
Three	*Tri*	Tree
Four	*Četiri*	Cheteeree
Five	*Pet*	Pet
Six	*Šest*	Shest
Seven	*Sedam*	Sedam
Eight	*Osam*	Osam
Nine	*Devet*	Devet
Ten	*Deset*	Deset
Where is...?	*Gdje je...?*	Gdyeh ye...?
Where are...?	*Gdje su...?*	Gdyeh soo...?
entrance	*ulaz*	oolaz
exit	*izlaz*	eezlaz
Tourist office	*Turistički Ured*	Tooristichkee oored
toilet	*zahod*	zah-haud
private rooms	*sobe*	saubey
I'd like to book...	*Ja bih revervirala...*	Ya bee reserveerahla...
Cheap	*Jeftino*	Yeftinoh
Expensive	*Skupo*	Skoopoh
Open	*Otvoreno*	Otvoreenoh
Closed	*Zatvoreno*	Zatvoreenoh

HEALTH

UK citizens only pay 20 percent of the cost of emergency hospital treatment in Croatia. Travel insurance is highly recommended though, as public facilities are not always available. **Pharmacies** (*ljekarna*) tend to follow normal shopping hours (see below) and a rota system covers nights and weekends; details are posted in the window of each pharmacy.

INFORMATION

Most towns of any size have a **tourist office** (*turističke informacije*), which will give out brochures and local maps. Few offices book private rooms, but they will direct you to an agency that does.

MONEY AND BANKS

The local currency is the **kuna** (kn), which is divided into 100 lipa. There are coins of 1, 2, 5, 10, 20 and 50 lipa, and 1kn, 2kn and 5kn; and notes of 5kn, 10kn, 20kn, 50kn, 100kn, 200kn, 500kn and 1000kn. Accommodation and ferry prices are often quoted in euros, but you still pay in kuna. **Banks** (*banka*) are open Monday to Friday 9am to 5pm (sometimes with longer hours in the summer), Saturday 8am to 1pm. Money can also be changed in post offices, travel agencies and **exchange bureaux** (*mjenjačnica*). Credit cards are accepted in a large number of hotels and restaurants. At the time of writing £1 = 9kn, €1 = 7kn and $1 = 5kn. It's relatively hard to get rid of kuna once you've left Croatia (though exchange offices in neighbouring countries often accept it); spend up or exchange before leaving.

OPENING HOURS AND HOLIDAYS

Most **shops** open Monday to Friday 8am to 8pm, Saturday 8am to 3pm, although many supermarkets, outdoor markets and the like are open daily 7am–7pm. A handful of newagents and supermarkets open on Sundays. Many **museums and galleries** are closed on Mondays. Most shops and banks are closed on the following **public holidays**: January 1, January 6, Easter Monday, May 1, Corpus Christi, June 22, June 25, August 5, August 15, October 8, November 1 and December 25 & 26.

Zagreb

Capital of Croatia since 1991, **ZAGREB** has served as the cultural and political focus of the state since the Middle Ages. The city grew out of two medieval communities, Kaptol, to the east, and Gradec, to the west, each sited on a hill and divided by a river long since dried up but nowadays marked by a street known as Tkalčićeva. Zagreb grew rapidly in the nineteenth century, and the majority of its buildings are relatively well-preserved, grand, peach-coloured monuments to the self-esteem of the Austro-Hungarian Empire. Nowadays, with a population reaching almost one million, Zagreb is the style-conscious, boisterous capital of a newly self-confident nation. A number of good museums and a varied and vibrant nightlife ensure that a few days here will be well spent.

What to see and do

Central Zagreb falls neatly into three parts. **Donji Grad**, or Lower Town, which extends north from the train station to the main square, Trg bana Jelačića, is the bustling centre of the modern city. Uphill from here, to the northeast and the northwest, are the older quarters of **Kaptol** (the Cathedral Quarter) and **Gradec** (the Upper Town), both peaceful districts of ancient mansions, quiet squares and leafy parks.

Trg bana Jelačića and Ilica

Flanked by cafés, hotels and department stores, **Trg bana Jelačića** is hectic with trams and hurrying pedestrians; the statue in the centre is of

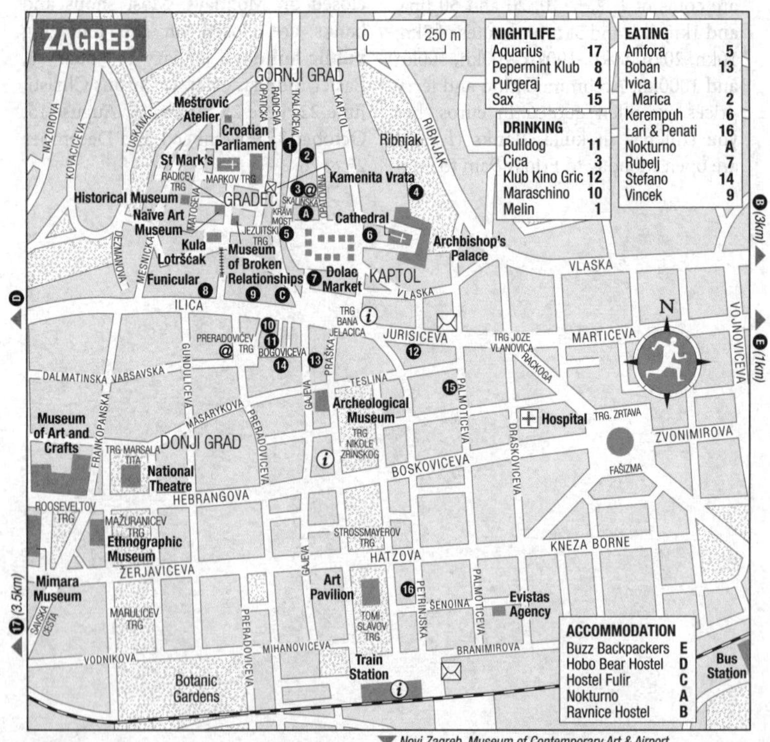

the nineteenth-century governor of Croatia, Josip Jelačića.

Running west from the square, below Gradec hill, is **Ilica**, the city's main shopping street. A little way along it and off to the right, you can take a **funicular** (daily 6.30am–10pm, every 10min; 4kn one-way) up to the Kula Lotršćak (see p.256).

Preradovićev Trg and Trg maršala Tita

Head south of Ilica via **Preradovićev Trg**, a small, café-filled square where there's a flower market, and you will reach **Trg maršala Tita**. This grandiose open space is centred on the late nineteenth-century **National Theatre**, a solid ochre-coloured pile behind a water sculpture by Ivan Meštrović, *The Well of Life*.

The Museum of Arts and Crafts and the Ethnographic Museum

The beautiful **Museum of Arts and Crafts**, just west of the National Theatre (Tues, Wed & Fri–Sun 10am–7pm, Thurs 10am–10pm, Sun till 2pm; 30kn), holds an impressive collection of furniture and textiles dating from the Renaissance to the present day. Nearby on Mažuranićev Trg, the **Ethnographic Museum** (Tues–Thurs 10am–6pm, Fri–Sun till 1pm; 15kn, free Thurs) displays a collection of costumes from every corner of the country and an array of curios brought back by Croatian explorers from all over the world.

Mimara Museum

The **Mimara Museum** at Rooseveltov Trg 5 (Tues, Wed, Fri & Sat 10am–5pm, Thurs till 7pm, Sun till 2pm; 40kn; temporary exhibitions 20kn) houses one of Zagreb's most prized art collections, a treasure-trove belonging to Zagreb-born Ante Topić Mimara. Highlights include Chinese art from the Shang through to the Song dynasty, as well as a fine collection of European paintings, including works by Rembrandt, Rubens, Renoir and Velázquez.

The Art Pavilion and Archeological Museum

Tomislavov Trg, opposite the train station, is the first in a series of three shaded, green squares that form the backbone of the lower town. Its main attraction is the **Art Pavilion** (Tues–Sat 11am–7pm, Sun 10am–1pm; 20kn), built in 1898 and now hosting art exhibitions in its gilded stucco and mock-marble interior. On the western edge of the most northerly square – tree-lined **Trg Nikole Zrinskog** (or Zrinjevac) – stands the **Archeological Museum** (Tues, Wed & Fri 10am–5pm, Thurs till 8pm, Sat & Sun till 1pm; 20kn), which houses interesting artefacts from prehistoric times to the Middle Ages.

Kaptol and the cathedral

The filigree spires of Zagreb's **cathedral** (open daily) mark the edge of the small district (and street) known as **Kaptol**, ringed by the ivy-cloaked turrets of the eighteenth-century **Archbishop's Palace**. Destroyed by an earthquake in 1880, the cathedral was rebuilt in neo-Gothic style, with a high, bare interior. Behind the altar lies a shrine to Archbishop Stepinac, head of the Croat church in the 1940s, imprisoned by the Communists after World War II, and beatified by the pope in 1998.

Gradec and Dolac market

Gradec is the most ancient and atmospheric part of Zagreb, a leafy, tranquil quarter of tiny streets, small squares and Baroque palaces. It begins at the lively **Dolac market** (daily till mid-afternoon), which occupies several tiers immediately behind Trg bana Jelačića; this is the city's main food market, held every morning.

Tkalčićeva

From the far side of Dolac market **Tkalčićeva** spears north along the path of the dried-up river that used to divide Kaptol and Gradec. Nowadays this is the city's prime people-watching spot – grab a seat at one of the many al-fresco bars and cafés for the evening *korzo* (promenade) when well-heeled locals and their pooches strut their stuff.

Entry to Gradec proper from here is by way of **Krvavi Most**, which connects the street with Radićeva. On the far side of Radićeva, the **Kamenita Vrata** is a gloomy tunnel with a small shrine that formed part of Gradec's original fortifications. Close by, the **Kula Lotršćak** (Burglars' Tower; Tues–Sun 11am–7pm; 10kn) marks the top station of the funicular (see p.255) and provides fantastic views over the rest of the city and the plains beyond; a small cannon has been fired from the tower every day at noon since 1877.

The Museum of Broken Relationships

Both moving and entertaining, the **Museum of Broken Relationships**, Cirilmetodska 2 (daily 9am–9pm; 20kn), is an idiosyncratic collection of mementoes from failed relationships. The donated exhibits vary from a prosthetic limb to a garden gnome, each accompanied by a touching background story.

The Naïve Art Museum and Church of St Mark

The **Naïve Art Museum**, Cirilmetodska 3 (Tues–Fri 10am–6pm, Sat & Sun 10am–1pm; closed hols; 20kn), provides a captivating introduction to the world of Croatia's self-taught village painters. Just north of here, the focus of **Markov Trg** is the squat **Church of St Mark**, a much-renovated structure, whose striking tiled roof displays the colourful coats of arms of the constituent parts of Croatia.

The Meštrović Atelier

North of St Mark's, the **Meštrović Atelier** (Tues–Fri 10am–6pm, Sat & Sun 10am–2pm; 20kn), Mletačka 8, is a wonderful exhibition dedicated to Croatia's most famous twentieth-century artist in the sculptor's former home and studio.

Museum of Contemporary Art

One of Zagreb's most stylish attractions is the **Museum of Contemporary Art** (Tues–Fri & Sun 11am–6pm, Sat 11am–8pm; 30kn; tram #14 to Siget stop), occupying a swish modern building on the south side of the River Sava on Avenija Većeslava Holjevaca. The museum showcases home-grown movements in abstract, conceptual and performance art, and there's a strong international collection too, including works by Picasso, Dalí and Miró.

Arrival

Air Zagreb airport is 10km southeast of the city; buses run to the main bus station (7am–8pm; every 30min–1hr; 30kn).

Train Zagreb's central train station (*glavni kolodor*) is on Tomislavov Trg, on the southern edge of the city centre, a 10min walk from Trg bana Jelačića.

Bus The main bus station (*autobusni kolodvor*) is a 10min walk east of the train station, at the junction of Branimirova and Držićeva – trams #2 and #6 run between the two, with #6 continuing to the main square.

Information

Tourist office Trg bana Jelačića 11 (Mon–Fri 8.30am–8pm, Sat 9am–6pm, Sun 10am–4pm; Ⓣ01/48-14-051, Ⓦwww.zagreb-touristinfo.hr); Main railway station (Mon–Fri 8.30am–8.00pm, Sat & Sun 12.30–6.30pm); airport (Mon–Fri 9am–9pm, Sat & Sun 10am–5pm).

Discount cards The tourist office sells the Zagreb Card (24hr/60kn, 72hr/90kn), which offers unlimited city transport and good discounts in museums and restaurants – perfect if you plan to do lots.

Listings Pick up the free monthly *Events and Performances* pamphlet from the tourist office.

City transport

Trams The easiest way to get about, with sixteen routes. Lines #2 and #6 run between the bus and train stations, #6 taking you into Jelačića, the main crossing point in the city. There's also a four-line network of night services.

Bus The bus network serves the capital's peripheries, setting off from the suburban side of the train station.

Tickets Tram and bus tickets (*karte*), valid for 1hr 30min if travelling in one direction, are sold at kiosks (8kn) or from the driver (10kn); day-tickets (*dnevne karte*) cost 24kn. Validate your ticket by punching it in the machines on board. You can also purchase a single ticket (8kn) by sending the message "ZG" to 8585.

Taxis There are ranks at the station and the northeast corner of Trg bana Jelačića. The standard rate is 19kn plus 7kn/km, which goes up by twenty percent early in the morning and late at night, on Sundays and holidays. Luggage costs 5kn/item.

Accommodation

Private rooms Arrange through the Evistas agency at Šenoina 28, midway between the train and bus stations (Mon–Fri 9am–8pm, Sat 9.30am–5pm; ⓣ01/48-39-554, ⓔevistas@zg.t-com.hr). Rooms from 550kn.

Hostels and hotels

Buzz Backpackers Babukićeva 1b ⓣ01/24-20-267, ⓦwww.buzzbackpackers.com. Neat, colourful hostel in a peaceful neighbourhood 5–10min by tram from the centre. Shared kitchen, free wi-fi, small garden and common room. Tram #4 from the train station, or tram #5 or #7 from the bus station, to Mašićeva. Dorms 120kn, twin bunk rooms 330kn, doubles 400kn.

Hobo Bear Hostel Medulićeva 4 ⓣ01/48-46-636, ⓦwww.hobobearhostel.com. Stylish hostel in a great location near Ilica. There's a funky wine-cellar-like common room, free wi-fi and a well-appointed kitchen. Take tram #6 from the bus or train station to Frankopanska. Dorms 110–147kn, doubles 340kn.

Hostel Fulir Radićeva 3a ⓣ01/48-30-882, ⓦwww.fulir-hostel.com. Tucked in a small courtyard off Tkalčićeva, *Fulir* offers homely dorms with a Rough Guides-esque colour scheme, a kitchen, cosy common room and resident cat. Free wi-fi. Dorms 130kn, twins 368kn.

Nokturno Skalinska 2a ⓣ01/48-13-325, ⓦwww.hostel.nokturno.hr. Amazingly central hostel right behind the Dolac. Sunny dorms, free wi-fi and internet, a common room and kitchen all make this a fine choice. Try the restaurant downstairs (see opposite). Dorms 130kn, singles 200kn.

Ravnice Hostel I Ravnice 38b ⓣ01/23-32-325, ⓦwww.ravnice-youth-hostel.hr. Large, clean hostel, which also has space to camp in its pleasant garden, 15min east of the centre by tram, near Maksimir Park (trams #4, #7, #11, #12, to Ravnice stop). All prices include breakfast and free internet. Bright, airy dorms 110–125kn, single rooms 184kn, double rooms 294kn. Tents 60kn/night.

Eating

Zagreb has plenty of cafés and bars with outdoor seating in the pedestrian area around Gajeva and Bogovićeva, and along trendy Tkalčićeva. For picnic food, head to Dolac market (see p.255).

Cafés

Ivica I Marica Tkalčićeva 70. Hansel and Gretel go organic at this gingerbread-house-styled café serving superb wholemeal cakes (10kn/slice). Its restaurant also serves healthy traditional food, including nettle soup and Istrian truffle pasta. Daily noon–11pm.

Vincek Ilica 18. The best place in town to stop for ice cream (6kn/scoop), cakes and hot chocolate. Mon–Sat 8.30am–11pm.

Restaurants

Amfora Dolac 2. Next door to the indoor fish market at the Dolac this cheap-and-cheerful spot serves a fresh fishy menu including fish stew (25kn) and sardines (26kn). Daily, lunch only.

Boban Gajeva 9. In an attractive vaulted basement, *Boban* is a popular spot with pasta and spaghetti dishes from 45–75kn. Daily 10am–11.30pm.

Kerempuh Kaptol 3, Dolac. Above the Dolac market (where ingredients are sourced daily); this is a smart, affordable spot to fill up on traditional Croatian favourites. Lunchtime specials 50kn, soup 20kn, veal liver 35kn. Mon–Sat 7am–11pm, Sun 7.30am–4pm.

Lari & Penati Petrinjska 42a. A small but perfectly formed deli-cum-restaurant with amazingly cheap and classy food, from spare ribs (45kn) to tuna confit and fennel (40kn). All served to a soundtrack of smooth jazz. Mon–Fri 8am–5pm, Sat noon–5pm.

Nokturno Skalinska 4. On a cobbled street off Tkalčićeva, *Nokturno* offers pleasant outdoor seating and tasty pizzas (25–35kn), meat and fish dishes (40–75n) and salads (25kn). Mon–Thurs 8am–midnight, Fri & Sat 8am–1am, Sun 8am–midnight.

Rubelj Dolac market. Cheapest central place for simple but tasty Balkan grilled-meat standards,

with 17 city-wide branches. The mixed grill costs 40kn and *čevapčići* just 28kn. Daily 9am–midnight.
Stefano Bogovićeva 3. Smart but affordable Italian restaurant specializing in quality pasta dishes, pizzas (50kn) and delicious puddings with outdoor seating on the city's buzzing pavement-café strip. Mains 60–80kn. Mon–Fri 9am–midnight, Sat & Sun till 2am.

Drinking and nightlife

Bars

Bulldog Bogovićeva 6. Don't be put off by the name – this is a typically stylish Zagreb bar and pavement café in the town centre, which sometimes features live bands. Daily 9am–1am.
Cica Corner of Tkalčićeva and Skalinska. This café has an eccentric interior filled with washing machines and retro hairdressing chairs, and plenty of outdoor seating. Famous for its potent fruit- and herb-flavoured brandies (12kn). Daily 8am–midnight.
Klub Kino Gric Jurišićeva 6. Boasts both a private arthouse cinema and a small chilled-out bar with stripey walls. Enjoy a White Russian (30kn) in one of its stylish red director's chairs. Daily 7.30am–11.30pm.
Maraschino Margaretska 1. So trendy it hurts this bar/club features live DJs and a bar made of martini glasses. Try a shot of the eponymous cherry brandy from Zadar (12kn). Mon–Thurs & Sun 7am–1am, Sun till 4am.
Melin Kožarska 19. A relaxed, grungey spot on Tkalčićeva with an outdoor terrace. Daytime patrons include coffee-drinking local nuns but in the evenings it attracts a livelier crowd who enjoy the loud music and cheap beers. Mon–Thurs 10am–1am, Fri & Sat till 2am, Sun 5pm–1am.

Clubs

Aquarius Aleja Mira bb Ⓦwww.aquarius.hr. At the eastern end of Lake Jarun, 6km southwest of the centre, this club specializes in techno and drum'n'bass. International headline acts also play here too (tickets from 190kn). Tram #17 from Trg bana Jelačića to Horvati. Cover charge for club nights 30–40kn. Thurs–Sun 10pm–6am.
Pepermint Klub Ilica 24. Look for the long queue of fashionistas on Ilica to find this fresh and trendy club, which plays a mix of music from funk to soul. Daily 10am–4am.
Purgeraj Ribnjak Ⓦwww.purgeraj.hr. In the leafy park behind the cathedral, *Purgeraj* is popular with students who enjoy its varied music and big outdoor terrace in summer. Mon–Thurs 9am–2am, Fri & Sat till 4am.
Sax Palmotićeva 22 Ⓦwww.sax-zg.hr. Fashionable basement club two blocks east of Trg N. Zrinskog, featuring a variety of live music with a jazz bias. Cover charge from 20kn. Tues–Sat 9am–3am.

Shopping and markets

The principal area for **shopping** is along Ilica, off Trg bana Jelačića, which has several independent stores as well as familiar high-street names, punctuated by handsome coffee shops and a few tempting bakeries.

The bric-a-brac **market** in Britanski Trg on a Sunday is a magpie's dream – jewellery, traditional Croatian embroidery, farming implements, binoculars – you name it, it's there. Get there before 2pm.

Directory

Embassies Australia, Nova Ves 11 Ⓣ01/48-91-200; Canada, Prilaz Gjure Deželića 4 Ⓣ01/48-81-200; UK, Ivana Lučića 4 Ⓣ01/60-09-100; US, Thomasa Jeffersona 2 Ⓣ01/66-12-200.
Exchange In the post office on Branimirova or at any bank. Privredna bank at Ilica 5 changes travellers' cheques.
Festivals Zagreb offers an impressive array of annual festivals and events including INmusic (late June; Ⓦwww.t-mobileinmusicfestival.com), a two-day rock-and-pop festival on the shores of Lake Jarun. The 2011 line-up included Arcade Fire, Cypress Hill and Grinderman. Check with tourist information for details of other events.
Hospital For emergencies visit Heinzelova 88 Ⓣ01/63-02-911.
Internet Wi-fi is widespread. The most central internet cafés are VIP internet café, Preradovićev Trg 5 (daily 8am–11pm; 1hr/15kn) and Tobacco, Skalinska 3 (Mon–Fri & Sun 10am–10pm, Sat noon–10pm; 1hr/20kn).
Left luggage At the train (15kn/hr; 24hr) and bus stations (5kn/hr; 24hr). Tobacco, Skalinska 3 (10kn/bag for 24hr).
Pharmacy 24hr pharmacies at Radiceva 3 and Ilica 301.
Post offices Branimirova 4 (24hr); Jurišićeva 13 (Mon–Fri 7am–9pm, Sat till 2pm, Sun 8am–2pm).

Moving on

Train Belgrade (4 daily; 6hr); Budapest (3 daily; 6hr); Ljubljana (7 daily; 2hr 20min); Munich (2 daily; 8hr 45min); Salzburg (2–3 daily; 7hr); Sarajevo (2 daily; 9–10hr); Split (3 daily; 5hr 30min–8hr);

Venice (1 daily; 7hr 15min); Vienna (2 daily; 6hr 30min), Zadar (2 daily; 5–9hr).
Bus Belgrade (daily; 6hr), Dubrovnik (7 daily; 9–11hr); Ljubljana (1 daily; 3hr); Munich (2 daily; 9hr 30min–11hr); Pula (hourly; 4hr–5hr 30min); Rijeka (hourly; 2hr 30min–3hr); Rovinj (7–9 daily; 4hr 30min–6hr); Sarajevo (5 daily; 7–8hr); Split (every 30min; 4hr 45min–8hr 30min); Trieste (1 daily; 4hr); Vienna (3 daily; 5–6hr); Zadar (hourly; 3–5hr).

Istria

A large peninsula jutting into the northern Adriatic, **Istria** is Croatian tourism at its most developed. Many of the towns here were resorts in the nineteenth century and still attract an annual influx of sun-seekers. Yet the growth of tourism has done little to detract from the essential charm and beauty of the region. This stretch of the coast was under Venetian rule for four hundred years and there's still a fair-sized Italian community, with Italian very much the second language. Istria's largest centre is the port city of **Pula**, which, with its Roman amphitheatre and other relics of Roman occupation, is a rewarding place to spend a couple of days. On the western side of the peninsula, the town of **Rovinj**, with its cobbled piazzas and shuttered houses, is almost overwhelmingly pretty.

PULA

Once the chief port of the Austro-Hungarian Empire, **PULA** is an engaging combination of working port, naval base and vibrant riviera town. The Romans put the city squarely on the map when they arrived in 177 BC, transforming it into an important commercial centre.

What to see and do

The chief reminder of Pula's Roman heritage is its impressive amphitheatre; south of here, the town centre circles a pyramidal hill, scaled by secluded streets, dotted with Roman relics and topped with a star-shaped Venetian fortress.

The amphitheatre

The first-century BC **Roman amphitheatre** (daily 8am–8pm; 40kn) is the sixth largest in the world, and once had space for over 23,000 spectators. The outer shell is fairly complete, as is one of the towers, up which a slightly hair-raising climb gives a good sense of the enormity of the structure and a view of Pula's industrious harbour. The amphitheatre hosts the annual **Pula Film Festival** (Ⓦwww.pulafilmfestival.hr) at the end of July, as well as concerts throughout the summer.

The Triumphal Arch and the Temple of Augustus

On the eastern side of the central hill, Istarska – which later becomes Giardini – leads down to the first-century BC **Triumphal Arch of the Sergians**, through which Sergijevaca, Pula's main drag, leads to the town's ancient Roman **Forum**, now the square at the centre of Pula's old quarter. On the far side of here, the slim but impressive **Temple of Augustus** was built between 2 BC and 14 AD to celebrate the cult of the emperor; its imposing Corinthian columns, still intact, make it one of the best examples of a Roman temple outside Italy.

The cathedral and Archeological Museum

Heading north from the Forum along Kandlerova leads to Pula's **cathedral** (daily: June–Aug 10am–1pm & 5–8pm; 5kn), a broad, simple and very spacious structure that displays a mixture of periods and styles: a fifteenth-century renovation of a Romanesque basilica built on the foundations of a Roman temple. Over the road, you can follow streets up to the top of the hill, the site of the original Roman Capitol. It's now the home of a mossy seventeenth-century **fortress** (accessed via the Historical Museum of Istria; daily: summer 8am–5pm; winter 9am–5pm; 10kn), built by the Venetians, behind which are the remains of a small **Roman Theatre** (free) and the **Archeological Museum** (Jan–April & Oct–Dec Mon–Fri 9am–2pm; May–Sept Mon–Sat till 8pm, Sun till 3pm; 20kn), where pillars and toga-clad statues mingle with ceramics, jewellery and trinkets from all over Istria, some of them prehistoric.

Arrival and information

Air Pula's airport is 6km northeast of the city. The bus ride to the centre costs 35kn; taxis are around 100kn.
Train Pula's train station is a 10min walk north of the centre, at the far end of Kolodvorska.
Bus The bus station is 10min northeast of the centre, along Istarska Divizije.
Tourist office In the Forum (daily: June–Sept 8am–10pm; Oct–May 9am–5pm; ⓣ052/212-987, ⓦwww.pulainfo.hr).

Accommodation

Private rooms Book through A Turizam, opposite the cathedral at Kandlerova 24 (closed Sun; ⓣ052/212-212, ⓦwww.a-turizam.hr), or Atlas, Starih Statuta 1 (ⓣ052/393-040, ⓦwww.atlas-croatia.com). Rooms from 100kn.
Pula Art Hostel Marulićeva ⓣ098/874-078, ⓦwww.pulaarthostel.com. Sociable hostel near central Pula with lots of creative touches, including a mosaic staircase. Free wi-fi and internet. Take bus #2a or #3 to Verudela from the bus station and look out for the hostel, which is a distinctive green building. Dorms from 162kn.
Stoja 3km southeast of town ⓣ052/387-144, ⓦwww.arenacamps.com. Simple campsite on a wooded peninsula with beautiful rocky beaches; take bus #1 from Giardini. Pitch 84kn plus 64kn/person. Minimum two nights in summer.

Eating and drinking

The vast market on Narodni Trg (daily till 2pm) is useful for picnics.
Bistro Dva Ferala Kandlerova 32. *Dva Ferala* attracts a lively local crowd to its street-side seating for cheap Croatian cuisine, including *čevapčići*, and pork and chips: both 45kn. Mon–Sat 8am–8pm.
Jupiter Castropola 38. Perched on a hill near the fortress this is a popular pizzeria with pretty Art Deco glass panels and a terrace. Sizeable pizzas from 30kn. Mon–Fri 10am–11pm, Sat noon–11pm, Sun 3–11pm.
Pietas Julia Riva 20 ⓦwww.pietasjulia.com. Grab a sofa and an apple martini (36kn) at this fun lounge bar in a pavilion west of the amphitheatre. Free wi-fi. Daily till 4am.
Uljanik Dobrilina 2. Counter-cultural club of many years standing with a huge beer garden, DJ nights at weekends and live music in the summer. Cover charge varies – often free entry during the summer. Thurs–Sat till late.

Moving on

Train Ljubljana (1 daily; 4hr 30min); Zagreb (3 daily; 7–9hr).
Bus Dubrovnik (1 daily; 15hr); Rijeka (roughly hourly; 1hr 30min–2hr 30min); Rovinj (roughly hourly; 45min); Split (3 daily; 10hr); Trieste (4 daily; 2hr 45min–3hr 45min); Venice (1daily; 5hr); Zadar (3 daily; 7hr); Zagreb (hourly; 3hr 30min–5hr).
Ferry Venice (May–Oct 2 weekly; 3hr): book through Commodore Travel at Riva 14 (ⓣ052/211-631); Zadar (June–Sept 2–5 weekly; 4hr 45min).

ROVINJ

Once an island, charming **ROVINJ** lies 40km north of Pula. Refreshingly free of traffic its hotchpotch of cobbled streets, terracotta roofs and shuttered windows teeter over the clear sea, and the harbour is an attractive mix of fishing boats and swanky yachts.

MOVING ON FROM ISTRIA: RIJEKA

Travelling on from Istria towards Zagreb or Dalmatia, most routes lead through the port city of **RIJEKA**: regular **buses** run from here to Zagreb, Pula, Rovinj, Zadar, Split and Dubrovnik, and it's the starting point for the Jadrolinija coastal **ferry** to Dubrovnik. Rijeka's train and bus stations are about 400m apart, at Krešimirova 5 and at the eastern end of the same street on Trg Žabica. The Jadrolinija ferry office (ⓣ051/666-111) is along the waterfront from the bus station at Riva 16.

What to see and do

From the main square, **Trg maršala Tita**, the Baroque **Vrata svetog Križa** leads up to Grisia Ulica, lined with galleries selling local art. It climbs steeply through the heart of the Old Town to **St Euphemia's Church** (daily: April–June 10am–1pm; July–Sept till 6pm), dominating Rovinj from the top of its peninsula. This Baroque eighteenth-century church has the sixth-century sarcophagus of the saint inside, and you can climb its 58m-high tower (same hours; 10kn). Paths on the south side of Rovinj's busy harbour lead south towards **Zlatni rt**, a densely forested cape, crisscrossed by tracks. The best of the **beaches** – all rocky – are here, but you can also try the two islands just offshore: **Sveta Katarina**, the nearer of the two, and **Crveni otok**, just outside Rovinj's bay (linked by boats from the harbour; every hour; 30kn return).

Arrival and information

Bus Rovinj's bus station is 5min walk southeast of its centre, just off Trg na lokvi, at the junction of Carrera and Carducci.
Tourist office On the waterfront promenade at Obala Pina Budicina 12 (June–Sept daily 8am–10pm; Oct–May Mon–Fri till 3pm, Sat till 1pm; ⓣ052/811-566, ⓦwww.tzgrovinj.hr).

Accommodation

Private rooms Try Natale, opposite the bus station at Carducci 4 (ⓣ052/813-365, ⓦwww.rovinj.com), Globtour, Alda Rismondo 2 (ⓣ052/814-130, ⓦwww.globtour-turizam.hr), and Futura Travel, M. Benussi 2 (ⓣ052/817-281, ⓦwww.futura-travel.hr). Rooms from 145kn.
Porton Biondi Aleja Porton Biondi 1 ⓣ052/813-557, ⓦwww.portonbiondi.hr. A pine-shaded campsite with its own beach, 700m north of town. Mid-March to Nov. Tent 23kn plus 66kn/person.

Eating and drinking

Trg Valdibora is home to a small produce market.
Da Sergio Grisia 11. Great pizzas – baby and normal-sized – from 38kn. Much better value than the harbourfront. Daily noon–midnight.
Maestral Obala V.Nazora. On the seafront towards Zlatni rt there is plenty of pine-shaded outdoor seating here and the fresh seafood (from 40kn) is grilled alfresco. Daily 8am–11pm.
Monte Carlo Svetoga Križa 23. This bar has a gorgeous terrace where you can intersperse drinks with refreshing dips in the sea. Bottled beer 20kn. Daily 8am–1am.

Moving on

Bus Dubrovnik (1 daily; 15hr); Pula (roughly hourly; 45min); Rijeka (5–7 daily; 3hr); Split (1 daily; 11hr); Trieste (2 daily; 2–3hr); Venice (1daily; 5hr 15min); Zadar (1 daily; 8hr); Zagreb (7–8 daily; 4hr 30min–6hr).
Ferry Trieste Lines to Trieste (June–Oct 1–2 daily; 1hr 30min–2hr 15min); Venezia Lines to Venice (summer only, 2 weekly; 3hr 30min).

The Dalmatian Coast

Stretching from Zadar in the north to the Montenegrin border in the south, the Dalmatian Coast is one of Europe's most dramatic shorelines. All along, well-preserved medieval towns sit on tiny islands or just above the sea on slim peninsulas, beneath a grizzled karst landscape that drops precipitously into some of the clearest – and cleanest – water in the Mediterranean. For centuries, the region was ruled by Venice, spawning towns, churches and architecture that wouldn't look out of place on the other side of the water. The busy northern port city of Zadar provides a vivacious introduction to the region. Otherwise, the main attractions are in the south: the lively provincial capital Split, built around a Roman palace, is served by trains from Zagreb and provides onward bus connections with the walled city of Dubrovnik. Ferry and catamaran connections to the best of the islands – Brač, Hvar, Vis and Korčula – are also from Split.

ZADAR

A bustling town of nearly 100,000 people, **ZADAR** has a compact historic centre crowded onto a tapered peninsula jutting into the Adriatic. In recent years, it has made a name for itself as a nightlife hub, with a number of summer festivals taking place in nearby Petrčane (see box opposite).

What to see and do

Zadar displays a pleasant muddle of architectural styles, with Romanesque churches competing for space with modern cafés. The main sights are concentrated in the Old Town, which is hemmed in by the sea; the central Roman Forum is the best place to begin exploring.

The Forum

Zadar's main square – or **Forum** – is dominated by the ninth-century **St Donat's Church** (April–May & Oct daily 9am–5pm; July–Sept till 10pm; 15kn), a hulking cylinder of stone with a vast bare interior, built – according to tradition – by St Donat himself, an Irishman who was bishop here for a time. Opposite, the **Archeological Museum** (summer Mon–Sat 9am–9pm; winter Mon–Fri till 2pm, Sat till 1pm; 15kn), housed in a slick, modern building, has an absorbing collection of Neolithic, Roman and medieval Croatian artefacts.

Behind St Donat's, the twelfth- and thirteenth-century **Cathedral of St Anastasia** has an arcaded west front reminiscent of Tuscan churches. Around the door frame stretches a frieze of twisting acanthus leaves, from which various beasts emerge – look out for the rodent and bird fighting over a bunch of grapes. You can climb the 56m campanile for great views over the city (Mon–Sat 10am–5pm; 10kn).

South of the Forum

Southeast of the Forum lies **Narodni Trg**, an attractive Renaissance square.

> **THE SEA ORGAN**
>
> Zadar's quirkiest feature, the **Sea Organ** consists of wide marble steps leading into the sea, with a set of tubes and cavities carved underneath, which enable the sea and wind to orchestrate a constant harmony. Emitting a strange sound, a bit like panpipes crossed with whale song, the *Organ* is surprisingly melodic and relaxing. Next to it is another public artwork, **A Salute to the Sun**: a huge disc that accumulates solar power during the day and radiates a multicoloured hypnotic glow by night.

A little further southeast, on Trg Petra Zoranića, the Baroque St Simeon's Church houses the exuberantly decorated reliquary of St Simeon, commissioned by Queen Elizabeth of Hungary in 1377 and fashioned from 250kg of silver by local artisans.

Overlooking the harbour at Poljana Zemaljskog odbora 1 is the state-of-the-art **Museum of Ancient Glass** (winter Mon–Sat 9am–4pm; summer till 7pm; 30kn), which contains one of the finest collections of ancient Roman glassware outside Italy and affords wonderful views of the harbour, too.

Arrival and information

Air Zadar's airport is 12km east of town. Buses (25kn) run into town.

Train and bus The train and bus stations are about 1km east of the town centre, a 20min walk or a hop on bus #5 – tickets cost 8kn from the driver or 13kn (valid for two journeys) from kiosks.

Boat Ferries arrive on Liburnska obala, just outside the walls of the Old Town.

Tourist office Narodni Trg (May–June & Sept Mon–Fri 8am–9/10pm, Sat & Sun 9am–2pm; July & Aug 8am till midnight; Oct–April Mon–Fri 8am–8pm, Sat & Sun 9am–2pm; ☎023/316-166, Ⓦwww.tzzadar.hr).

Accommodation

Private rooms Try Aquarius at Nova Vrata bb (☎023/212-919, Ⓦwww.juresko.hr) and Miatours,

Vrata sv. Krševana bb (Ⓣ023/254-300, Ⓦwww.miatours.hr), both under the arches in the town wall, near the ferry quays; rooms from 150kn.

Borik Majstora Radovana 7 Ⓣ023/332-074, Ⓦwww.camping.hr. Well-equipped campsite near *Hostel Zadar* (bus #5 or #8 from the bus and train stations). Summer only. 130kn/person or 160kn with a car.

Hostel Zadar Obala kneza Trpimira 76 Ⓣ023/331-145, Ⓔzadar@hfhs.hr. Large, welcoming youth hostel 5km northwest of town. Dorms 140kn (members 11kn less).

Old Town Hostel Mihe Klaica 5 Ⓣ099/809-3280, Ⓦoldtownzadar.com. In the middle of the Old Town this hostel offers clean pastel-coloured rooms and romantic views over the rooftops. Shared kitchen, free wi-fi and internet access. Dorms 120kn, doubles 280kn.

Eating

There's a Kerum supermarket at Mate Karamana 5.

Konoba Na Po Ure Špire Brusine 8. Popular with locals and visitors alike this homely restaurant is best known for its fish dishes, including heaps of juicy mussels (45kn) and fresh anchovies (25kn). Daily 10am–11pm.

Malo Misto Jurja Dalmatinca 3. This simple restaurant grills a mix of meats on its lovely leafy terrace – mains from 75kn. Through the archway in the corner of Narodni trg. Summer only, daily 7am–midnight.

Trattoria Canzona Stomorica 8. Atmospheric Italian with great-value pizzas (from 36kn) and mains such as rich shrimp gnocchi (65kn). Try to nab one of the tables on the atmospheric alley outside. Mon–Sat 10am–11.30pm, Sun noon–11pm.

Drinking and nightlife

Arsenal Trg Tri Bunara Ⓦwww.arsenalzadar.com. Arts centre, lounge bar, restaurant and concert venue, *Arsenal* is a seriously exciting venue. Housed in a restored Venetian warehouse, you can pop in for a reasonably priced breakfast or catch a concert, film or DJ set. Cover charge for some events. Free wi-fi. Mon–Thurs & Sun 7am–midnight, Fri & Sat 7am–2am.

The Garden Bedemi zadarskih pobuna Ⓦwww.watchthegardengrow.eu. A kind of tree house for grown-ups, this lounge-bar sits high up in the city walls: there are big beds to relax on, cocktail in hand, as well as a dancefloor that regularly boasts big-name DJs (there is a cover charge for popular events). See also box below. Daily till late.

Kult Stormica 6. One of a number of café-bars tucked down winding Stormica this fashionable spot has a large wooden terrace area on which to enjoy the pumping music. Daily 7.30am–1am.

Moving on

Bus Dubrovnik (8 daily; 7hr–8hr 30min); Pula (3 daily; 6hr 30min); Rijeka (9 daily; 4hr 30min);

PETRČANE FESTIVALS

Petrčane, a sleepy 900-year-old fishing village just north of Zadar, may seem an unlikely spot for dusk-to-dawn partying, but in recent years clubbers have tired of Ibiza's crowds and prices, and have been pitching up here for their dose of summertime fun instead. Set up in 2006 by the people behind *The Garden* club (see above), the week-long Garden Festival attracts big-name international DJs and has spawned a host of summer festivals on the same idyllic peninsula. The site is based around a beachfront bar and *Barbarella's*, a club done up in retro Seventies style, and you can also join one of the Argonaughty boat parties (€14) to prolong the fun offshore. **Getting there** from Zadar is easy – it's a twenty-minute taxi ride. There's plenty of **accommodation** too, in Petrčane and Punta Skala, 1km away; contact Generalturist (Ⓣ01/48-05-652, Ⓔinfo@generalturist.com; private rooms from 335kn). There are several **campsites** nearby; *Camping Pineta* (45kn per person plus 20kn per tent; Ⓦwww.camp-pineta.com) is the largest, a short walk from the festival site and right by the sea.

Electric Elephant Mid-July; €97; Ⓦwww.electricelephant.co.uk.

Soundwave Late July; €102; Ⓦwww.soundwavecroatia.com.

Stop making Sense Mid-Aug; €103; Ⓦwww.sms-2010.com.

SuncéBeat Late July to early Aug; €109; Ⓦwww.suncebeat.com.

The Garden Festival Early to mid-July; €103; Ⓦwww.thegardenfestival.eu.

Rovinj (1 daily; 8hr); Split (approx every 30min; 3hr–3hr 30min); Zagreb (hourly; 3–5hr).
Ferry Ancona (1 daily; 6–9hr; book through Jadrolinija); Pula (June–Sept 2–5 weekly; 4hr 45min; book through Miatours, see p.262).
Train Split (2 daily; 5hr), Zagreb (2–3 daily; 5–9hr).

SPLIT

The largest city in the region, and its major transit hub, **SPLIT** is a hectic place, but one of the most enticing spots on the Dalmatian Coast. At its heart lies a crumbling Old Town built within the walls of Diocletian's Palace, and including some of the most outstanding classical remains in Europe.

What to see and do

Diocletian's Palace is still the epicentre of the city – lived in almost continuously since Roman times, it has gradually become a warren of houses, tenements and churches. Almost everything worth seeing is concentrated here, behind the waterfront Riva, while to its west is the lush **Marjan peninsula**.

Diocletian's Palace

Built as a retirement home by Dalmatian-born Roman Emperor Diocletian in 305 AD, **Diocletian's Palace** has been remodelled through the centuries. The best place to start a tour is on its seaward side through the **Bronze Gate**, which once gave direct access to the water. Through the gate, you find yourself in a shady vaulted hall full of souvenir stalls, You can get some idea of the size and layout of Dicoletian's erstwhile home by visiting the atmospheric **subterranean halls** (June–Sept daily 9am–9pm; Nov–March Mon–Sat till 6pm, Sun till 2pm; April, May & Oct Mon–Sat till 8pm, Sun till 6pm; 35kn) that once sat beneath his apartments; the entrance is to your left once you enter the Bronze Gate.

Carry on through the vaulted hallways and up the steps to the **Peristyle**, which these days serves as the main town square. At the southern end, more steps lead up to the **vestibule**, an impressive round building that's the only part of the imperial apartments to be left anything like intact, despite losing its dome.

The cathedral

On the eastern side of the Peristyle stands one of two black granite Egyptian sphinxes, dating from around 15 BC, which flanked the entrance to Diocletian's mausoleum; the octagonal building, surrounded by an arcade of Corinthian columns, has since been converted into Split's **cathedral** (daily 8am–7pm; 15kn; 5kn extra to visit the crypt). The cathedral's striking walnut and oak **doorway** was carved in 1214 and shows scenes from the life of Christ. Inside, the dome is ringed by two series of decorative Corinthian columns and a frieze that contains portraits of Diocletian and his wife. The church's finest feature is a cruelly realistic *Flagellation of Christ* depicted on the Altar of St Anastasius, completed by local artist Juraj Dalmatinac in 1448. To the right of the entrance is the **campanile** (same hours; 10kn), a restored Romanesque structure – from the top, the views across the city are magnificent.

Follow the alleyway directly opposite the cathedral to reach the intriguing **baptistry**, or Temple of Jupiter (same hours as cathedral; 10kn), originally built by a cult in Diocletian's time and later adapted by Christians.

The Golden Gate and Archeological Museum

North of the cathedral, along Dioklecijanova, is the grandest and best preserved of the palace entrances: the **Golden Gate**. Just outside there's a piece by Meštrović, a gigantic statue of the fourth-century Bishop **Grgur Ninski** – rubbing its big toe is said to bring good luck. Fifteen minutes' walk northwest of here, the **Archeological Museum**, at Zrinsko Frankopanska 25 (June–Sept Mon–Sat 9am–2pm & 4–8pm; Oct–May Mon–Fri 9am–2pm &

4–8pm, Sat 9am–2pm; 20kn), contains displays of Illyrian, Greek, medieval and Roman artefacts. Outside, the arcaded courtyard is crammed with gravestones, sarcophagi and decorative sculpture.

The Marjan peninsula

If you want some peace and quiet, and stunning views over the city, head for the woods of the **Marjan peninsula** west of the Old Town. It's accessible via Sperun and then Senjska, which cut up through the slopes of the **Varoš** district. There are tiny rocky **beaches** all round the peninsula.

Meštrović Gallery

The main historical highlight of the Marjan peninsula lies fifteen minutes west of the centre (bus #12 from the seafront). The **Meštrović Gallery**, Ivana Meštrovića 46 (May–Sept Tues–Sun 9am–7pm; Oct–April Tues–Sat till 4pm, Sun 10am–3pm; 30kn, includes entrance to Kaštelet), is housed in the ostentatious Neoclassical building that was built – and lived in – by Croatia's most famous twentieth-century artist, the sculptor Ivan Meštrović (1883–1962). This fabulous collection consists largely of boldly fashioned bodies curled into elegant poses. Meštrović's former workshop, **Kaštelet** (same hours), is 200m up the same road, and contains a chapel decorated with his woodcarved reliefs showing scenes from the Stations of the Cross.

Arrival and information

Air Split airport is 16km west of town; Croatia Airlines buses connect with scheduled flights and run to the waterfront Riva (30kn); their office at Riva 9 has timetables. Alternatively, the #37 Split–Trogir bus runs from the main road outside the airport to the suburban bus station on Domovinskog rata, just north of the Old Town (every 20min; 20kn). A taxi costs 250kn.

Train and bus Split's main bus and train stations are next to each other on Obala Kneza Domagoja, 5min walk round the harbour from the centre.

Boat The ferry terminal and Jadrolinija booking office are both in the harbour.

Discount card The Splitcard, available from the tourist office (35kn/ 72hr; free if you're staying three days or more), gets you free or discounted entrance to several of the sights, plus reductions on hostels and restaurants.

Tourist office In the Peristyle of the Palace (May–Sept Mon–Sat 8am–9pm, Sun till 1pm; Oct–April Mon–Fri 8am–8pm, Sat till 1pm; ⓣ021/345-606, ⓦwww.visitsplit.com).

Accommodation

Private rooms Booked through Turist Biro, Obala narodnog preporoda 12, on the waterfront (ⓣ021/347-100, ⓔturist.biro.split@st.t-com.hr) and Travel 49, Dioklecijanova 5 (ⓣ098/858-141, ⓦwww.travel49.com), who also offer a 15 percent discount for Rough Guide readers on tours and bicycle rental. Rooms from 440kn.

Golly & Bossy Morpurgova Poljana 2 ⓣ021/510-999, ⓦwww.gollybossy.com. Sleek hotel decked out in eye-popping black and yellow, with tongue-in-cheek captions along the floors. Also includes the *De Belly Café,* a stylish restaurant and bar in the pretty courtyard outside (mains from 25kn). The smart dorms are the most affordable option and each one is built into its own cubbyhole. Dorms 210kn. Rooms start at 650kn for a standard double (single-use 580kn).

Silver Central Kralja Tomislava 1 ⓣ021/490-805, ⓦwww.silvercentralhostel.com. A modern, central hostel with a buzzy common area, bright and breezy dorms and free wi-fi and internet. Its sister hostel, *Silver Gate*, is at Hrvojeva 6 (ⓣ021/322-857). Dorms 190kn, rooms at other locations 525kn.

Split hostel booze & snooze Narodni trg 8 ⓣ021/342-787, ⓦwww.splithostel.com. In the middle of the old city, this hostel is run by friendly Croatian-Australians who like partying with their guests. Also has a sister hostel – *Split Hostel Fiesta Siesta* – with on-site bar at Kruževičeva 5. Free internet. Dorms 180kn.

Eating

The daily market at the eastern edge of the Old Town is the place to shop for fruit, veg and local cheeses. There is also a fish market at Obrov 5 and a supermarket in the Old Town at Kraj Sv arije 2.

Bistro Black Cat Cnr of Petrova and Šegvića. Midway to Baćvice beach, this is a popular backpackers' hangout with great soups, quiches and international dishes such as Javanese chicken (55kn). Mon–Sat 8am–11pm.

Buffet Fife Trumbićeva obala 11. Near the seafront this is a no-frills local favourite, serving dishes such as stuffed sweet peppers (35kn) and *pašticada* (beef stew with prunes; 45kn) in huge portions. Daily 6am–midnight.

Galija Kamila Tončića 12. Popular pizzeria with a wood-fired oven and pleasant terrace area. Huge salads for around 50kn and the obligatory pizzas are 32kn–57kn. Mon–Sat 9am–noon, Sun noon–midnight.

Konoba Trattoria Bajamont Bajamontićeva 3. Grab a seat at an old sewing machine table and watch the chef cook tasty Dalmatian dishes such as asparagus risotto (55kn) and calamari (50kn). Daily 8am–11pm.

Drinking and nightlife

The beach at Bačvice, a few minutes' walk south past the train station, is a popular party place in summer.

Bifora Bernardinova 5. An indie bar decorated with psychedelic pixies and mushrooms, *Bifora* is a fun place to enjoy a cocktail (from 30kn). Mon–Thurs & Sun 7am–1am, Fri & Sun till 2am.

Ghetto Club Dosud 10. A great spot for a beer, the arty *Ghetto Club* is a bar, café and gallery in a lovely courtyard with a fountain. Mon–Thurs & Sun 10am–1am, Fri & Sun till 2am.

Puls Buvinina 1. A bohemian café-bar sprawled across steps decorated with bright silk cushions, mini-sofas and tables. Cocktails from 35kn. Mon–Thurs 8am–1am, Fri & Sat till 2am, Sun 4pm–1am.

Teak just off Majstora Jurja. A nicely furnished café-bar with a sleek wood interior. Good for a quiet coffee or some funk and something boozy in the evening. Beers from 11kn. Daily 8am–midnight.

Directory

Exchange At the bus station or any bank.

Hospital Firule, Spinčićeva 1 ⓣ021/556-111.

Internet Backpacker Caffé, Obala kneza Domagoja bb (10kn/20min, half-price 3–5pm). Cyber Club 100, Sinjkska 2 (20kn/hr).

Left luggage At the bus (daily 7am–9pm; 5kn for first hour, then 1.5kn/hr) and train (5.45am–10pm; 15kn/hr; 24hr) stations. Travel 49 (see p.265; 10–15kn/hr; 24hr). Internet Corner (5kn/1hr).

Pharmacy Lučac, Pupačićeva 4 (24hr).

Post office Kralja Tomislava 9 and Obala kneza Domagoja 2.

Moving on

Bus Belgrade (2 daily; 11hr 30min); Dubrovnik (14–17 daily; 4hr–4hr 30min; make sure you take your passport, as you pass through Bosnia on the way); Pula (3 daily; 10hr); Rijeka (12 daily; 8hr); Rovinj (1 daily; 11hr); Sarajevo (5 daily; 6hr 30min–8hr); Trieste (1 daily; 10hr 30min); Zadar (hourly; 3hr–3hr 30min); Zagreb (every 30min; 4hr 45min–8hr 30min).

Ferry Note that services are reduced outside of the summer months. Krilo Jet and SNAV tickets are available from the Jadrolinja ticket office. Ancona (3 weekly; 10hr); Brač (Bol: 1 daily; 55min; Supetar: hourly; 50min); Dubrovnik (2 weekly; 11hr); Hvar (Hvar Town: 1 daily; 1hr; 1 daily Krilo Jet catamaran, 55min; Stari Grad: 7 daily; 2hr); Korčula (Vela Luka: 2 ferries daily; 2hr 45min; 1 catamaran daily; 1hr 45min; Korčula Town: May–Sept 2 weekly ferries, 6hr; 1 daily Krilo Jet catamaran, 2hr 25min); Pescara (1 daily SNAV catamaran; 5hr 30min); Rijeka (2 weekly; 11hr 30min); Vis (daily: 2–3 ferries, 2hr 20min; 1 catamaran, 1hr 15min).

Train Zadar (2 daily; 5hr); Zagreb (2–3 daily; 5hr 30min–8hr).

BRAČ

BRAČ is famous for its milk-white marble, which has been used in buildings as diverse as Berlin's Reichstag and the White House in Washington – and, of course, Diocletian's Palace in Split. In addition to the marble, a great many islanders were once dependent on the grape harvest, though the phylloxera (vine lice) epidemics of the late nineteenth and early twentieth centuries forced many of them to emigrate. Even today, as you cross Brač's interior, the signs of this depopulation are all around. The easiest way to reach Brač is by **ferry** from Split to **Supetar**, an engaging, laidback fishing port on the north side of the island, from where it's an hour's bus journey to **Bol**, a major windsurfing centre on the island's south coast and site of one of the Adriatic's most beautiful beaches, **Zlatni Rat** (Golden Horn).

Supetar

Though the largest town on the island, **SUPETAR** is a rather sleepy village onto which package tourism has been painlessly grafted. There aren't many sights, save for several attractive shingle **beaches** which stretch west from the harbour, and the **Petrinović Mausoleum**, a neo-Byzantine construction 1km west of town, built by sculptor Toma Rosandić to honour a local-born shipping magnate.

The library, Jobova bb (Mon–Sat 8.30am–1.30pm & 2.30–7.30pm; free), houses the Ivan Rendić Gallery, displaying sculptures by this successful Supetar native who worked around the turn of the century.

Arrival and information

Tourist office Beside the ferry dock at Porat 1 (June–Sept daily 8am–10pm; Oct–May Mon–Fri till 3.30pm; ⓣ021/630-551, ⓦwww.supetar.hr).

Accommodation

Private rooms Available from Atlas (ⓣ021/631-105) on the harbourfront at Porat 10, and Start (ⓣ021/757-741), opposite the ferry dock. Rooms from 300kn.

Shangri La Backpackers Ive Jakšića ⓣ021/630-937, ⓔinfo@brachostels.com. A very basic hostel 10min uphill from the harbour. There is a large terrace area with sea views and a shared kitchen. Free wi-fi and internet. Summer only. Dorms 103kn, double rooms 252kn.

Eating and drinking

There's a supermarket in the harbour.

Benny's Bar Put Vela Luke bb. West of town towards the *Supetrus* hotel complex, *Benny's Bar* has a large outdoor terrace with a pool where you can take in the sea air and enjoy live DJs and cocktails. Summer only, daily till 2am.

Bistro Palute Porat 4. The best of the places to eat on the harbourfront: serves good grilled fish from an open wood fire and meat dishes such as mixed skewers with fries (52kn) and goulash (55kn). Daily 8am–midnight.

Konoba Lukin Porat 32. Harbourside seating, a cosy, familial atmosphere and well-prepared local dishes make this the best option for a meal. Cuttlefish salad (60kn) and pizzas (30–40kn). Daily noon–midnight.

Activities

Scuba diving Fun Dive Club in the *Supetrus* hotel complex at Put Vela Luke 4 (closed Oct–April; ⓣ0981/307-384, ⓦwww.fundiveclub.com) rents snorkelling and scuba gear and arranges dives (from 200kn).

Mountain biking ACF at bana J. Jelačića 14 rents out mountain bikes (80kn/day).

Quad biking You can rent quad bikes (185kn/3hr) and scooters (155kn/3hr) from M&B (ⓦwww.mb-rental.com), in the same office as the Start travel agency, opposite the ferry dock.

Moving on

Ferry Split (9–14 daily; 50min).

Bol

Stranded on the far side of the Vidova Gora Mountains, you cannot help but be overwhelmed by the beauty of **BOL**'s setting, or the charm of its old stone houses. However, the main attraction of the village is its beach, **Zlatni Rat**, which lies to the west of the centre along the wooded shoreline. This pebbly spit juts into the sea like a finger, changing shape from season to season as the wind plays across it. Unsurprisingly, it gets very crowded during summer.

Dramatically perched on a bluff just east of central Bol, is the late fifteenth-century **Dominican Monastery** (daily 10am–noon and 5–8pm), which boasts an altar painting by Tintoretto.

Arrival and information

Air Croatia Airlines fly to Bol airport, which is 10km from town, in the summer months.

Bus From Supetar, 14 daily buses (40kn one-way, 50kn return) make the hour-long trip to Bol's harbour. Some buses take a slower route – check before you leave.

Ferry Ferries dock at the end of the harbour in the middle of town.

Tourist office In the harbour (July & Aug daily 8.30am–10pm; June & Sept daily 8.30am–2pm & 4.30–9pm; Oct–May Mon–Fri 8.30am–2pm; ⓣ021/635-638, ⓦwww.bol.hr).

Accommodation

Private rooms Boltours at Vladimira Nazora 18 (ⓣ021/635-693, ⓦwww.boltours.com), arrange private rooms (from 200kn) and apartments (from

415kn for two). Alternatively, try Adria at Bračka Cesta 10 (ⓣ021/635-966, ⓦwww.adria-bol.hr), a 10min walk west.

Kito Camping Bračke ceste bb ⓣ021/635-551, ⓦwww.camping-brac.com. Large, friendly campsite close to the centre of Bol, with kitchens and a nearby supermarket. 8kn/tent plus 57kn/person.

Eating and drinking

There's a Konzum supermarket in the harbour.

Konoba Mlin Ante Starčevića 11. A lovely restaurant in a pretty old stone mill, with live music and an outdoor wood-fired grill where freshly caught fish are cooked to taste. Mains from 70kn. June–Oct only, daily 5pm–midnight.

No. 1 finger food Rudina 32. A minute restaurant with a mix of cakes, snack food and tasty mains (from 15kn), which turns into a bar as the sun goes down. Daily 9am–2am.

Pizzeria Topolino Frane Radića 1. Just metres from the sea, *Topolino* offers gorgeous views and a wide range of breakfast dishes, wood-oven-cooked pizzas, fresh salads (from 50kn) and home-made lemonade (17kn). May–Oct only, daily 8am–11pm.

Varadero Frane Radića. A prime position in the main square with DJs, a twelve-page cocktail menu (from 40kn) and a beach *cabaña feel* – this is the place to be after dark. April–Oct only, daily 7.30am–2am.

Activities

Hiking The 778m peak of Vidova Gora is within easy reach of Bol: a trail (2hr each way) heads uphill just beyond the *Kito* campsite (see above). Check with tourist information for details of the route.

Mountain biking The tourist office has free cycling maps. Next door, *Big Blue Café* rents bicycles (78kn/day).

Watersports Big Blue (ⓣ021/635-614, ⓦwww.big-blue-sport.hr; April–Nov) on the path leading to Zlatni Rat rents windsurfing boards (296kn/half day) and sea kayaks (185kn/day).

Moving on

Ferry Hvar (Jelsa: 1 daily; 20min; note that buses to Hvar Town are not very regular on Sundays), Split (1 daily; 55min).

HVAR

One of the most hyped of all the Croatian islands, **HVAR** is undeniably beautiful – a slim, green slice of land punctuated by jagged inlets and cloaked with hills of lavender. Tourist development hasn't been too overbearing, and the old Venetian charm of the island's main centre, **Hvar Town**, attracts a moneyed yachting crowd.

What to see and do

Hvar's central main square is flanked by the arcaded bulk of the **Venetian arsenal**, the upper storey of which was added in 1612 to house a **theatre** (closed for refurbishment at the time of writing), the oldest in Croatia. At the eastern end of the square is the **cathedral** (open mornings before services), a sixteenth-century construction with an eighteenth-century facade – a characteristic mixture of Gothic and Renaissance styles. Inside, the **Bishop's Treasury** (daily: June–Aug 9am–noon & 5–7pm; Sept–May 10am–noon; 20kn) holds a small but fine selection of chalices and reliquaries. The rest of the Old Town stretches back from the piazza in an elegant confusion of twisting lanes and alleys.

Up above, the **fortress** (daily: April & May 9am–4pm; June–Sept 8am–11pm; 25kn) was built by the Venetians in the 1550s and offers gorgeous sweeping views. From here, you can pick out the attractive fifteenth-century **Franciscan Monastery** (May–Oct Mon–Fri 9am–1pm & 5–7pm; 20kn) to the left of the harbour, and the pleasingly simple monastic church next door.

Beaches and islands

The **beaches** nearest to town are rocky and crowded, so it's best to make your way towards the **Pakleni otoci**. Easily reached by water taxi from the harbour (25–40kn one-way), the Pakleni are a chain of eleven wooded islands, three of which cater for tourists with simple bars and restaurants: Jerolim, a naturist island, is the nearest; next is Marinkovac; then Sv Klement, the largest of the islands. Bear in mind that camping is forbidden throughout the islands, and that naturism is popular.

Arrival and information

Arrival At least one daily hydrofoil from Split arrives at Hvar Town itself; seven other ferries head for Stari Grad, 4km east, from where buses run into Hvar Town. There's also one daily ferry from Bol on Brač to Jelsa in the centre of the island, from where there are buses to Hvar Town (3–4 daily; 30kn one-way) and Stari Grad (5–11 daily; 25kn one-way); times vary.
Tourist office On the waterfront below the theatre at Trg sv. Stjepana bb (July & Aug daily 8am–2pm & 3–10pm; June & Sept Mon–Sat 8am–2pm & 3–8/9pm, Sun 10am–noon & 6–8/9pm; Oct–May Mon–Sat 8am–2pm; ⓣ021/741-059, ⓦwww.tzhvar.hr).

Accommodation

Private rooms Contact Atlas on the harbourfront at Fabrika 27 (ⓣ021/741-911, ⓦwww.atlas-croatia.com), or Pelegrini, by the ferry dock at Riva bb (ⓣ021/742-743, ⓔpelegrini@inet.hr). Rooms from 360kn.
Green Lizard Hostel Lucica ⓣ0981/718-729, ⓦwww.greenlizard.hr. A funky, family-run hostel uphill from the ferry port, with great sea views, fun cocktail evenings and hammocks to chill out in. Shared kitchen, free internet and wi-fi. Easter–Oct. Dorms 150kn, doubles 320kn.
Orange Hostel Vandele Bozitkovic 16 (near *Green Lizard*) ⓣ091/515-7330, ⓦwww.orange.hostel.com. More a peaceful private house than a hostel – there isn't a common room – with a leafy terrace and a mixture of rooms within its tangerine exterior. Twins 470kn, doubles 528kn, triples 705kn.

Eating and drinking

There is a supermarket and a produce market next to the bus station.
Kod Matkovića Godina Tradicije 50. A huge menu with plenty of Dalmatian specialities, and fairly priced too. A lunch menu of soup, schnitzel and salad is only 60kn. Summer only.
Pizza Kogo Trg sv. St Jepana 34. A popular spot with pew-like seating inside and plenty of tables on the main square too. Reasonably priced mains include salads (45–55kn) and pizzas (45–65kn). Daily breakfast, lunch and dinner.
Veneranda Club Gornja Cesta bb, west of the harbour ⓦwww.v-528.com. This monastery-turned-club is where the crowds from *Carpe Diem* come to rip up the dancefloor later on; it offers international DJs (cover charge 150–200kn), an oxygen bar and wallet-busting cocktails (from 60kn). Regular cover charge 50kn. Summer only, daily 9pm–5am.

Activities

Island tours Secret Hvar (ⓣ021/717-615, ⓦsecrethvar.com) offers kayaking (350kn) and hiking trips (300kn), and can also organize private rooms.
Watersports Hvar Adventure at Obala bb, just off the Riva (ⓣ091/15-43-072, ⓦwww.hvaradventure.com), run sailing, climbing and kayaking tours; prices start at 350kn for a sunset sea-kayaking tour.

Moving on

Bus Jelsa (2–4 daily; 50min); Stari Grad (5 daily; 35min).
Ferry Korčula Town (1 daily Krilo Jet catamaran; 1hr 15min; tickets available from Pelegrini Tours); Vela Luka (1 catamaran daily; 45min); Split (daily: 1 ferry, 1hr; 1 Krilo Jet catamaran, 55min); Vis (1 weekly; 1hr 30min). There are also SNAV services (ⓦwww.snav.it) from Stari Grad to Pecara, Italy (July–Sept; 1 daily; 4hr 30min).

VIS

Wild and hilly, **VIS** is situated further offshore than any other of Croatia's inhabited Adriatic islands. Closed to

TREAT YOURSELF

Said to be the best cocktail bar in Croatia, glamorous **Carpe Diem**, on the Riva (summer only, daily 9am–2am; ⓦwww.carpe-diem-hvar.com), is the epitome of jet-set. DJs spin crowd-pleasing tunes on the colonnaded terrace overlooking the harbour till the early hours, while skilled bartenders mix a long list of decadent cocktails (from 50kn). There is no cover charge but it's rumoured that they have a "face control" admissions policy when busy, so it's worth dressing up. They have recently opened another venue – **Carpe Diem Beach** (mid-June to late Aug, daily 10am–5am) – on the island of Marinkovac, which hosts hedonistic full moon parties every night in peak season (cover charge for events 100kn; check website for listings).

foreigners for military reasons until 1989, the island has never been overrun by tourists, and even now depends much more heavily on independent tourism and visiting yachts than its neighbours. Visitors are drawn by its wild mountainous scenery, two good-looking towns, **Vis Town** and **Komiža**, and great beaches and bars.

Vis Town

VIS TOWN is a sedate arc of grey-brown houses on a deeply indented bay, above which loom the remains of abandoned agricultural terraces. A five-minute walk east from the harbour is the town's **history museum** (summer: Tues–Sun 10am–1pm & 5–9pm; 20kn) and not far on from here is the suburb of **Kut**, an atmospheric, largely sixteenth-century tangle of narrow cobbled streets overlooked by summer houses built by the nobles from Hvar. A kilometre further lies a small British war cemetery, and just behind it, a pebbly beach. Heading west around the bay soon brings you to a small peninsula where the campanile of the Franciscan monastery of St Hieronymous rises gracefully alongside a huddle of cypresses. The ruins of an ancient Greek cemetery and nearby Roman baths lie just before the monastery.

Arrival and information

By boat Ferries and catamarans arrive at Vis Town, from where buses depart for Komiža on the western side of the island. Ferries arrive in the Luka area, in the middle of town.

Tourist office Just to the right as you leave the ferry dock (June–Sept daily 8am–8pm; Oct–May Mon–Sat 8.30am–2.30pm; ⓣ021/717-017, ⓦtz-vis.hr).

Accommodation

Private rooms Navigator (ⓣ021/717-786, ⓦwww.navigator.hr), directly in front of the ferry dock, offer a range of rooms and apartments from 200kn with shared bathroom and 330kn with en suite. They also offer island tours, trips to the Blue Cave (see opposite; 200kn) and scooter rental (200kn/hr).

Eating and drinking

There is a small supermarket near the harbour. Note that eating out on Vis is reasonably expensive and the island is extremely seasonable.

Kod Paveta Dinko I Anka Tomić. This charming restaurant, just down from Vis's open-air cinema (summer only), is known for its delicious, well-priced fish dishes. Try the home-made gnocchi (50kn). Summer only.

Konoba Vatrica Kralija Krešimira. Friendly, family-run restaurant in Kut, specializing in fresh fish cooked over a wood fire. More affordable options are the black squid risotto and macaroni in lobster sauce (both 60kn). Lunch & dinner March–Oct.

Lambik Pod Ložu 2. A fun bar with occasional live DJs, set in a gorgeous courtyard and old villa. Pull up a rattan chair and watch the sun go down with a cold beer. Summer only.

Moving on

Bus Komiža (6–8 daily; 15min; 20kn one-way).

Ferry Hvar (1 weekly; 45min); Split (daily: 2–3 ferries, 2hr 20min; 1 catamaran, 1hr 15min).

Komiža

KOMIŽA, 10km from Vis Town, is the island's main fishing port – a picturesque town surrounded by lofty mountains. Dominating the southern end of the harbour is the Kaštel, a stubby sixteenth-century fortress, which now holds a charming **Fishing Museum** (June–Sept Mon–Sat 9am–noon & 6–9pm; 15kn). Komiža's nicest beaches are ten minutes south of here, where you'll find a sequence of pebbly coves. Each morning, small boats leave Komiža harbour for the nearby island of Biševo in order to visit the **Blue Cave**, a grotto filled with eerie shimmering light; expect to pay around 140kn for a half-day trip.

Arrival and information

Bus Buses from Vis Town terminate about 100m behind the harbour.

Tourist office On the Riva just beyond the Kaštel (June–Aug Mon–Sat 8am–9pm, Sun 8.30am–12.30pm; Sept–May Mon–Sat 8am–noon & 5–7pm; ⓣ021/713-455, ⓦwww.tz-komiza.hr).

Accommodation

Private rooms Booked through Darlić & Darlić, (Ⓣ021/713-760, Ⓦwww.darlic-travel.hr), Ulica Hrv. Mučenika, just back from the main square. Try also Alternatura on the same road (Ⓣ021/717-239, Ⓦwww.alternatura.hr), which offers paragliding and sea kayak tours, and Srebrnatours, Ribarska 4 (Ⓣ021/713-668, Ⓦwww.srebrnatours.hr), which organizes diving excursions. Rooms from 250kn.

Eating and drinking

Aquarius Kamenica beach. A popular summertime beach club, with fresh food and cocktails, projections beamed onto the sea, nightly DJs and dancing till dawn. Summer only.

Konoba Bako Gundelićeva 1. Romantic beachside tavern complete with an indoor lobster pond. The fresh fish by the kg is pricey but there are also shrimp skewers (60kn) and *frutti di mare* (86kn) on offer. Open summer only for dinner.

KORČULA

Like so many islands along this coast, **KORČULA** was first settled by the Greeks, who gave it the name Korkyra Melaina or "Black Corfu" for its dark and densely wooded appearance. Even now, it's one of the greenest of the Adriatic islands, and one of the most popular. Medieval **Korčula Town** is the island's main settlement.

What to see and do

KORČULA TOWN sits on a beetle-shaped hump of land, a beautiful walled city ribbed with narrow alleys. The Venetians first arrived here in the eleventh century, and stayed, on and off, for nearly eight centuries, and their influence is particularly evident in the Old Town.

The Cathedral and Bishop's Treasury

The Old Town huddles around the **Cathedral of St Mark** (Mon–Sat: May, June & Oct 9am–2pm; July–Sept same hours & 5–7pm; Oct–April enquire at the tourist office to visit; 5kn), with a facade decorated with a gorgeous fluted rose window and a bizarre cornice frilled with gargoyles. The interior is one of the loveliest in the region – a curious mixture of styles, ranging from the Gothic forms of the nave to the Renaissance northern aisle, tacked on in the sixteenth century.

The best of the cathedral's treasures have been moved to the **Bishop's Treasury** (same hours as cathedral; 20kn, includes entrance to the cathedral), a couple of doors down. This small collection of fine and sacral art is one of the best in the country; look out for the Leonardo da Vinci sketch of a soldier wearing a costume bearing a striking resemblance to that of the Moreška dancers (see box, p.273).

The Town Museum and the House of Marco Polo

On the main square, a former Venetian palace holds the **Town Museum** (Mon–Sat: April to mid-June & mid-Sept to Oct 10am–2pm; mid-June to early July same hours, plus 6–8pm; early July to mid-Sept 10am–9pm; 15kn), which displays a plaster cast of a fourth-century BC Greek tablet from Lumbarda – the earliest evidence of civilization on Korčula. Nearby is another remnant from Venetian times, the **House of Marco Polo** (daily: June, May & Sept 10am–2pm & 4–8pm; July & Aug 9am–9pm; 15kn). Korčula claims to be the birthplace of the explorer, although it seems unlikely that he had any connection with this seventeenth-century house, which is currently being renovated into a museum.

Beaches

Your best bet for **beaches** is to head off by water taxi from the old harbour to one of the **Skoji islands** just offshore. The largest and nearest of these is **Badija** (40kn return), where there are some secluded rocky beaches, a couple of snack bars and a naturist section.

There's also a sandy **beach** just beyond the village of **Lumbarda**, 8km south of Korčula (hourly buses in summer; 15kn one-way; 15min).

Arrival and information

Bus Korčula's bus station is 400m southeast of the Old Town. The bus service from Dubrovnik crosses the narrow stretch of water dividing the island from the mainland by ferry from Orebić.

Boat Ferry and catamaran services from Dubrovnik, Hvar and Split dock in Korčula Town harbour. In addition, there are also ferry and catamaran services from Hvar and Split to Vela Luka at the western end of the island, from where there's a connecting bus service to Korčula Town (3–6 daily; 1hr 10min). The Jadrolinija ticket office in Korčula Town is at Plokata 19.

Tourist office By the western harbour at Obala dr. Franje Tudmana 4 (June–Sept Mon–Sat 8am–3pm & 5–9pm, Sun 9am–1pm; Oct–May Mon–Sat 8am–2pm; ⓣ020/715-701, ⓦwww.visitkorcula.net).

Accommodation

Private rooms Kaleta (ⓣ020/711-282, ⓦwww.kaleta.hr) and Kantun Tours (also left luggage and bike rental; ⓣ020/715-622, ⓦwww.kantun-tours.com), both at Plokata bb, offer rooms from 250kn.

Campsite Kalac ⓣ020/726-336, ⓦwww.korcula-hotels.com. Korčula's largest campsite, just 3km from town and with 600 pleasant pine-shaded pitches and a small sandy beach. 47kn/tent plus 58kn/person.

Onelove Hrvatske Zajednice 6 ⓣ020/716-755, ⓦwww.korculabackpacker.com. The place to party with other travellers, with a huge number of dorms. It's on the doorstep of the Old Town and offers a 24hr bar where films are screened. Dorms 120kn.

Villa Depolo Ul. Svetog Nikole bb ⓣ020/711-621, ⓔegon.depolo@du.t-com.hr. Four enormous, tastefully decorated rooms on the seafront 150m west of the Old Town; several have brilliant sea views. Doubles 290kn; extra bed 50kn.

Eating and drinking

There's a Konzum supermarket in the corner of the harbour.

Arsenal Bistro Vl. Ljiljana Duhović. Just right of the main gate into the Old Town, *Arsenal Bistro* is a real gem, with a changing menu of delicious cooking served in a simple canteen-like interior; try the mouthwatering home-made macaroni and lamb (50kn). Daily 8am–10pm.

Dos Locos Šetalište Frana Kršinića. Live DJs, and an alfresco bamboo bar draw the crowds to this spot behind the bus station, and during happy hour (8–10pm) cocktails are only 40kn. Daily till late.

Massimo Šetalište Petra Kanavelic. This cocktail bar, ensconced in a medieval turret, may be pricey but it's one of the prime spots for admiring a Korčula sunset. You have to go up and down by ladder – worth keeping in mind after a couple of cocktails (from 45kn). Daily 6.30pm–2am.

Planjak Plokata 21. This restaurant lacks a scenic Old Town location, but offers cheap and tasty meals such as grilled calamari (50kn) and goulash (46kn), and a terrace area. Daily 8am–10pm.

Moving on

Bus Dubrovnik (2 daily; 3hr 30min), Zagreb (1 daily; 11hr 30min). Korkyra Info also runs a door-to-door minibus service to Dubrovnik (June–Sept; daily; 2hr; 148kn).

Ferry Note that ferry departures may switch between the west and east harbours in bad weather, so check before you leave. From Vela Luka: Hvar (1 catamaran daily; 45min); Split (daily: 2 ferries, 2hr 45min; 1 catamaran, 2hr). From Korčula Town: Dubrovnik (ferry: May–Sept 2 weekly; 4hr; G&V Line catamaran: July–Aug 4 weekly; 2hr 35min, tickets from Korkyra Info); Hvar (Krilo Jet catamaran: 1 daily; 1hr 15min; tickets available from kiosk at west harbour), Split (ferry: May–Sept 2 weekly; 5hr 40min; Krilo Jet catamaran: 1 daily; 2hr 25min).

DUBROVNIK

The immaculately preserved medieval city of **DUBROVNIK**, at Croatia's southern tip, is the country's irresistibly beautiful star attraction. Lapped by the glittering Adriatic Sea, sturdy walls encircle the city's white marble streets, which are lined with imposing Baroque buildings.

First settled by Roman refugees in the early seventh century and given the name Ragusa, the town soon exploited its favourable position on the Adriatic with maritime and commercial genius. By the mid-fourteenth century it had become a successful and self-contained city-state, its merchants trading far

MOREŠKA

Performances of Korčula's famous folk dance, the **Moreška**, take place outside the main gate to the Old Town throughout the summer, every Monday and Thursday evening (tickets available from several agencies including Kaleta, Katun Tours and Atlas, all at Plokata bb; 100kn). This frantic, sword-based dance is the story of a conflict between the Christians (in red) and the Moors (in black): the heroine, Bula, is kidnapped by the evil foreign king and his army, and her betrothed tries to win her back in a ritualized sword fight which takes place within a shifting circle of dancers.

and wide. Dubrovnik continued to prosper until 1667, when an earthquake devastated the city. Though the city-state survived, it fell into decline and, in 1808, was formally dissolved by Napoleon. An eight-month siege by Yugoslav forces in the early 1990s caused much destruction, but the city swiftly recovered.

What to see and do

Within its fabulous **city walls**, Dubrovnik is a sea of terracotta roofs punctured now and then by a sculpted dome or tower. The best way to get your bearings is by making a tour of the walls (daily: April–Oct 8/9am–6/7.30pm; Nov–March 9/10am–3pm; 70kn), which are 25m high with all five towers still intact. From here, you get spectacular views of the **Old Town**, bisected by the main street, Stradun. The main attractions, all within the walls, can easily be covered in a day and a half.

The Pile Gate

The **Pile Gate**, main entrance to the Old Town, is a fifteenth-century construction complete with a statue of St Blaise, the city's protector, set in a niche above the arch. Just through the gate sits **Onofrio's Large Fountain**, built in 1444, a domed affair at which visitors to this hygiene-conscious city used to have to wash themselves before they were allowed any further.

The Franciscan monastery and Stradun

Opposite Onofrio's Large Fountain, the museum of the peaceful fourteenth-century **Franciscan monastery** complex (daily: summer 9am–6pm; winter till 5pm; 30kn) holds some fine Gothic reliquaries and manuscripts tracing the development of musical scoring, together with objects from the apothecary's shop, dating from 1317; there is still a working on-site pharmacy. From here, **Stradun** (also known as Placa), the city's main street, runs dead straight across the Old Town, its limestone surface polished to a shine by thousands of feet. **War Photo Limited**, at Antuninska 6 (June–Sept daily 10am–10pm; May & Oct Tues–Sun 10am–4pm; 30kn) is a three-storey photo gallery housing raw and moving photographs of the conflict in former Yugoslavia and other global disputes.

The far end of Stradun broadens into airy **Luža Square**, the centre of the medieval town and still a hub of activity. On the left, the **Sponza Palace** was once the customs house and mint, with a facade showing off an elegant weld of florid Venetian Gothic and more sedate Renaissance forms. Nowadays it houses free contemporary art exhibitions and a memorial to those who lost their lives during the Dubrovnik siege (daily: May–Oct 9am–6pm; Nov–April 10am–3pm; free).

The Dominican monastery

North behind the Sponza Palace lies the **Dominican monastery**, with an arcaded courtyard filled with palms and orange trees. It also houses a small **museum**

DUBROVNIK SUMMER FESTIVAL

The prestigious **Summer Festival** (Ⓣ020/326-100, Ⓦwww.dubrovnik-festival.hr) from July 10 to August 25 is an enjoyable time to visit, with classical concerts and theatre performances in most of the city's courtyards, squares and bastions. Book well in advance or you may end up without a proper seat.

(daily: summer 9am–6pm; winter till 5pm; 20kn), with outstanding examples of local sixteenth-century religious art.

The Church of St Blaise and Rector's Palace

Built in 1714, the Baroque-style **Church of St Blaise** serves as a graceful counterpoint to the palace. Outside the church stands the carved figure of an armoured knight – known as **Orlando's Column** it was once the focal point of the city-state. Adjacent sits the fifteenth-century **Rector's Palace**, the seat of the Ragusan government, in which the incumbent Rector sat out his month's term of office. Today it's given over to the rather uninspiring **City Museum.**

The cathedral

The seventeenth-century **cathedral** is a rather plain building, although there's an impressive Titian polyptych of *The Assumption* inside. The **Treasury** (summer daily 8am–5pm; 15kn) boasts a twelfth-century reliquary containing the skull of St Blaise; shaped like a Byzantine crown, it is covered with portraits of saints and frosted with delicate gold and enamel filigree work.

The Fort of St John and Church of St Ignatius

The city's small harbour is dominated by the monolithic hulk of the **Fort of St John**; upstairs it houses a **maritime museum** (Tues–Sun: April–Oct 9am–6pm; Nov–March till 4pm; 40kn), which traces the history of Ragusan sea power through a display of naval artefacts and model boats. Skirting round the city's southern walls you enter one of its oldest quarters, **Pustijerna**, much of which predates

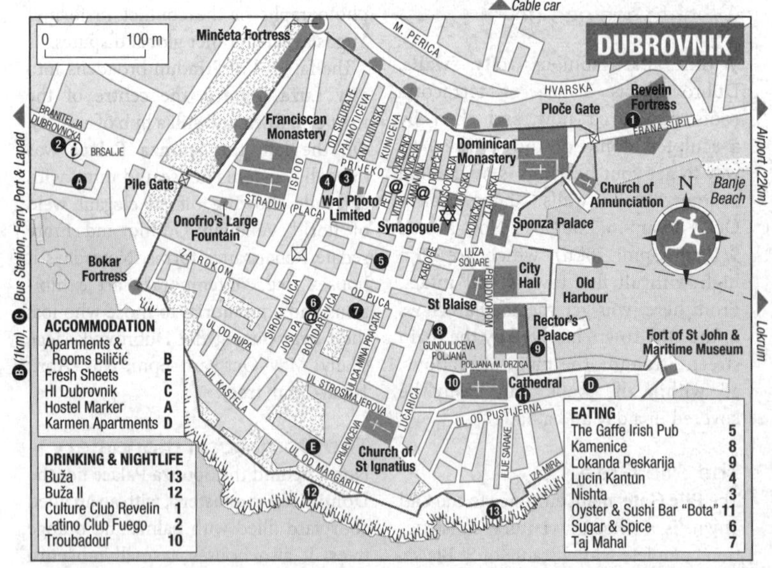

the seventeenth-century earthquake. Uphill sits the **Church of St Ignatius**, Dubrovnik's largest, a Jesuit confection modelled on Rome's enormous Gesù church. Steps sweep down from here to **Gundulićeva Poljana**, the square behind the cathedral, which is the site of the city's morning produce market.

The Dubrovnik Cable Car and beaches

It's possible to escape the crowds via the **Dubrovnik Cable Car**, Petra Krešimira (daily: summer 8am–midnight; winter till 8pm; 74kn return), whose orange pods soar up to the top of Mount Srđ behind the city. The noisy and crowded main city **beach** is a short walk east of the Old Town; less crowded and somewhat cleaner is the beach on the Lapad peninsula, 5km to the west (bus #6 from the Pile Gate). Or you can catch a boat from the old city jetty (April–Oct 8am–6pm, every 30min; journey time 10min; 50kn return) to the wooded island of **Lokrum**. Covered in pine trees, Lokrum is home to an eleventh-century Benedictine monastery-turned-palace and has extensive rocky beaches running along the eastern end of the island – with a naturist section (known as FKK) at the far eastern tip.

Arrival and information

Air Atlas buses (30min; 35kn) to Dubrovnik meet each flight to/from the airport; enquire at the tourist office for times.

Bus and ferry The ferry and bus terminals are located in the port suburb of Gruž, 3km west of town. The main western entrance to the Old Town, the Pile Gate, is a 30min slog along Branitelja Dubrovnika; you're better off catching a bus – #1a or #1b from the ferry terminal or bus station, or #7 towards Lapad. Buy tickets for local buses from the driver (10kn) or from kiosks (8kn).

Tourist office The main branch is on the plaza outside the Pile Gate at Brsalje 5 (June–Sept daily 8am–8pm; Oct–May Mon–Fri 8am–3pm, Sat 9–2pm; Ⓣ020/323-887, Ⓦwww.tzdubrovnik.hr). There's also one opposite the ferry terminal in Gruž (same hours). The one-day Dubrovnik Card (130kn; Ⓦdubrovniktouristcard.com) offers free entry to eight city attractions and 24hr public transport.

Listings Pick up the free, monthly *Dubrovnik Riviera Guide* from the tourist office. You can also find useful information, including a message board, at Ⓦwww.dubrovnik-online.com.

Accommodation

Private rooms Locals offering private rooms meet bus and ferry arrivals. Alternatively, try Atlas, at Đurda 1 (Ⓣ020/442-585, Ⓔatlas.pile@atlas.hr). Central rooms from 400kn, rooms in Gruž and Lapad from 300kn.

Apartments & Rooms Biličić Privežna 2 Ⓣ020/417-152, Ⓦwww.dubrovnik-online.com/apartments_bilicic. Well-equipped rooms a 10min walk uphill from town. There's a gorgeous garden – complete with tortoises – and genial owner Marija offers free picks-ups, internet access and laundry service. Rooms 440kn, four-person apartment 880kn.

Fresh Sheets Vetraniceva 4 Ⓣ091/79-92-086, Ⓦwww.igotfresh.com. A fun, stylish hostel in a great Old Town location with superb views, free wi-fi and internet and a communal kitchen. Breakfast Included. Dorms 222kn, doubles 562kn. Private rooms (singles and doubles) in neighbourhood from 244kn/person.

HI Dubrovnik Vinka Sagrestana 3, follow steps next to *Café Bar Ferrari* on Bana Jelačića Ⓣ020/423-241, Ⓔdubrovnik@hfhs.hr. Connected to the Old Town and bus and ferry terminals by buses #1a and #1b, #3, #4, #5, #6 and #7. Well-run with clean rooms, a leafy courtyard and free breakfasts. Dorms 157kn (10kn less for members).

Hostel Marker Od Tabakarije 20 Ⓣ091/73-97-545, Ⓦwww.apartments-lovrijenac.com. A range of comfortable rooms and apartments spread between five old houses beneath the Lovrjenac Fort. Four-bed apartments 1190kn, six-bed apartments 1040kn, doubles 518kn.

TREAT YOURSELF

Make like a real Ragusan and splash out on a stay at the *Karmen Apartments*, Bandureva 1 (Ⓣ020/323-433, Ⓦwww.karmendu.com; sleeps 2–3; 665–1072kn). Exquisitely and artfully decorated, these four homely apartments are full of personal touches and offer amazing views of the harbour and city walls. Marc, the owner, is a wealth of local information.

Eating

There's a morning market (Mon–Sat) at Gundulićeva Poljana in the Old Town, and a supermarket in the same square.

Kamenice Gundulićeva Poljana 8. A simple fish restaurant where waitresses in white clogs serve cheap portions of whitebait (56kn) and locals sometimes break into song over the delicious *kamenice* (oysters; 10kn each). Summer 8am–midnight; winter till 9pm.

Lokanda Peskarija Right on the old harbour with a huge terrace and great views, this seafood-only restaurant serves up a small but fantastic menu including mussels (60kn) and a fish platter (180kn for two people). Daily 7am till late.

Lucin Kantun Od Sigurate bb ⓣ020/321-003. Amazing Mediterranean tapas dishes such as lamb with honey and lavender (35kn) and monkfish wrapped in bacon (35kn), all cooked in an open kitchen; reserve ahead. Daily lunch and dinner.

Nishta Prijeko bb. A meal at this stylish vegetarian café makes a welcome change from Croatia's meat and fish staples. A healthy portion of vegetable curry will set you back 85kn and there is a fresh salad bar too (30–59kn). Closed Sun.

Oyster & Sushi Bar "Bota" Od Pustijerne bb ⓣ020/324-034. Worth splashing out on, "*Bota*" offers fresh-as-you-like sushi and sashimi for 7kn/piece, and tempura oysters (12kn/piece) straight from the restaurant's renowned oyster farm in Mali Ston. Daily 10am–1am.

Sugar & Spice Ulica Sv. Josipa. A chic and charming café/bakery, whose talented owner makes beautiful cakes (15kn/slice), and savoury breads and muffins to eat in or take away. Closed Mon.

Taj Mahal Nikole Gučetića 2. Don't be fooled by the name – *Taj Mahal*, tucked away off the main drag, offers traditional Bosnian dishes such as stuffed aubergines (40kn), veal in pastry (80kn) and *baklava* (25kn) in an exotic interior. Daily 10am–11pm.

The Gaffe Irish Pub Miha Pracata 4. Ignore the sports pub exterior – *The Gaffe* offers excellent hearty home cooking at reasonable prices. Low season lunch specials such as beef stew and dumplings are only 30kn. Daily, lunch only.

Drinking and nightlife

Buža Accessed from Ilije Sarake. Reached via a hole in the city walls, this is a stunning spot for a dip in the sea and a drink, with a cluster of tables perched on rocky terraces. Its more expensive (34kn/beer) sister bar, *Buža II*, is at Crijeviceva 9. Daily till late, depending on the weather.

Culture Club Revelin Sv. Dominika 3 ⓦwww.clubrevelin.com. The stocky Revelin Fort makes an amazing venue for club nights and gigs, attracting international DJs such as Darren Emerson – check their website and posters for listings and cover charge. Wed–Sat till late.

Troubadour Bunićeva Poljana 2. A buzzing bar run by three musical brothers, with a great view of the cathedral. Live music – usually jazz – every night. Beer 35kn. Daily 9am–2am.

Directory

Consulates UK: Vukovarska 22/1 ⓣ020/324-597.

Hospital Roka Mišetića 2 ⓣ020/431-777.

Internet access Netcafé, Prijeko 21 (10kn/15min), Hugo Internet, Prijeko 13 (7kn/15min, 10kn/30min), Link, next to *Spaghetteria Toni* on Nikole Bozidarevica (10kn/15min).

Left luggage Bus station (daily 4.30am–10.30pm; first hour 5kn, thereafter 1.5kn/hr).

Pharmacy Kod Zvonika, Stradun (Mon–Fri 7am–8pm, Sat 8am–noon).

Post office Široka (Mon–Fri 8am–7pm, Sat 8.30am–3pm).

Watersports Adriatic Kayak Tours, Zrinsko Frankopanska 6, organize kayaking tours (ⓣ020/312-770, ⓦwww.adriatickayaktours.com; from 275kn for a half-day to Lokrum island).

Moving on

Air Atlas buses to the airport pick up at the bus terminal in Gruž and outside the cable-car station on Petra Krešimira.

Bus Korčula (1–2 daily; 3hr); Montenegro (various towns; 2–4 daily); Pula (1 daily; 15hr); Rijeka (4 daily; 11hr 30min–13hr); Rovinj (1 daily; 16hr); Sarajevo (5 daily; 5–6hr); Split (14–17 daily; 4–4hr 30min – take your passport, as you pass through Bosnia); Trieste (1 daily; 15hr); Zadar (6–7 daily; 7–8hr 30min); Zagreb (8 daily; 11hr).

Ferry Bari, Italy (4–6 weekly; 9hr); Korčula (May–Sept 2 weekly; 4hr; G&V Line catamaran July–Aug 4 weekly; 2hr 35min); Rijeka (2 weekly; 22hr 30min); Split (2 weekly; 11hr).

Czech Republic

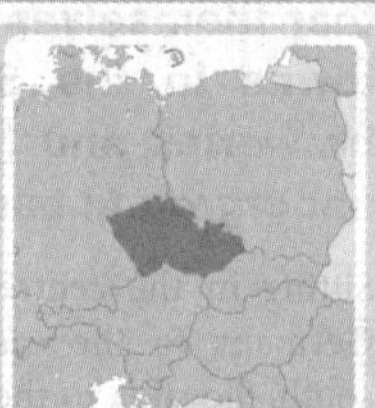

HIGHLIGHTS

KARLOVY VARY: indulge in a some spa treatments at this lovely town in the mountains

PRAGUE: row through the golden city at dusk

SEDLEC OSSUARY: see human bones in the subterranean ossuary at Sedlec

PLZEŇ: visit the home of Pilsner Urquell, the original lager

OLOMOUC: discover the capital of an ancient empire

ČESKÝ KRUMLOV: forget the Renaissance ever ended at this fairytale town

ROUGH COSTS

DAILY BUDGET Basic €35 /occasional treat €45

DRINK Pilsner Urquell €1.50

FOOD Pork and dumplings €3

HOSTEL BED/BUDGET HOTEL €10/€30

TRAVEL Prague–Karlovy Vary: train €10; bus: €6

FACT FILE

POPULATION 10.5 million

AREA 78,866 sq km

LANGUAGE Czech

CURRENCY Czech koruna (Kč)

CAPITAL Prague (population: 1.3 million)

INTERNATIONAL PHONE CODE ⓣ420

Introduction

"Prague never lets you go", said Franz Kafka, "this dear little mother has claws". Prague gets her golden claws into tourists too, and few ever make it outside the capital. But those who tear themselves away won't be sorry; the honey-coloured spa towns in the Sudeten Mountains, Bohemia's Renaissance breweries and hilltop ruins, and the tumbling vineyards and underground bars of Moravia are worth exploring.

Sitting in the centre of Europe, with Germany to the east, Poland to the south, Slovakia to the west and Austria in the north, the Czech Republic has one foot in Western Europe, and one in the Slavic East. Although the country is small, the variety in landscape and architecture is enormous, encompassing the forests and rolling countryside of **Bohemia**, peaceful spa towns like Karlovy Vary, **Moravia's** spectacular karst region and historic towns like **Olomouc** and Český Krumlov.

CHRONOLOGY

Fourth century BC The Celtic "Boii" tribe inhabit the area now known as Bohemia.
500s AD Slavic tribes arrive.
830 AD The Great Moravian Empire is established on the Morava River.
907 Hungarians conquer the Great Moravian Empire.
1355 Charles IV, "the father of the Czech nation", is crowned Holy Roman Emperor.
1415 Protestant reformer Jan Hus is burned at the stake, sparking decades of religious conflict.
1458 George of Poděbrady is crowned.
1526 King Ferdinand I, a Habsburg, takes the Czech throne, and begins a project of re-Catholicization.
1620 The Protestant nobility is defeated by Catholic forces at the Battle of White Mountain.
1800s Rapid growth in nationalism and industrialization.
1918 The independent republic of Czechoslovakia is founded at the end of World War I.
1938 German troops annex Sudetenland in western Czechoslovakia.
1945 German occupation ends as the Allies move in.
1948 The Communist Party seizes control of Czechoslovakia.
1968 The "Prague Spring" sees a brief period of political liberalization, the USSR responds by invading.
1989 The Velvet Revolution. Czechoslovakia becomes a democracy.
1993 The Czech Republic and Slovakia peacefully separate into two states.
2004 The Czech Republic joins the EU.

ARRIVAL

There are direct flights from more than a dozen UK airports, and from New York JFK, to Prague's Ruzyně Airport (Ⓣ220 113 314, Ⓦwww.prg.aero/cs), 10km northwest of the city. Several international routes (including one from London Stansted by Ryanair) serve Brno, and there are a couple of flights a week to and from Karlovy Vary (Ⓦwww.airport-k-vary.cz).

Prague is served by direct **train** services from numerous major European cities, including Bratislava, Berlin, Vienna and Budapest.

Eurolines (Ⓦwww.eurolines.com) runs good international **bus services** to the Czech Republic, as does Student Agency (Ⓦwww.studentagencybus.com), which also runs between Prague and other Czech cities. Tourbus (Ⓦwww.tourbus.cz) goes to Prague, Brno, Olomouc and other major cities.

GETTING AROUND

Czech public transport is affordable and reliable. For train and bus times go to Ⓦwww.idos.cz.

By train

The Czech Republic has one of the most comprehensive **rail** networks in

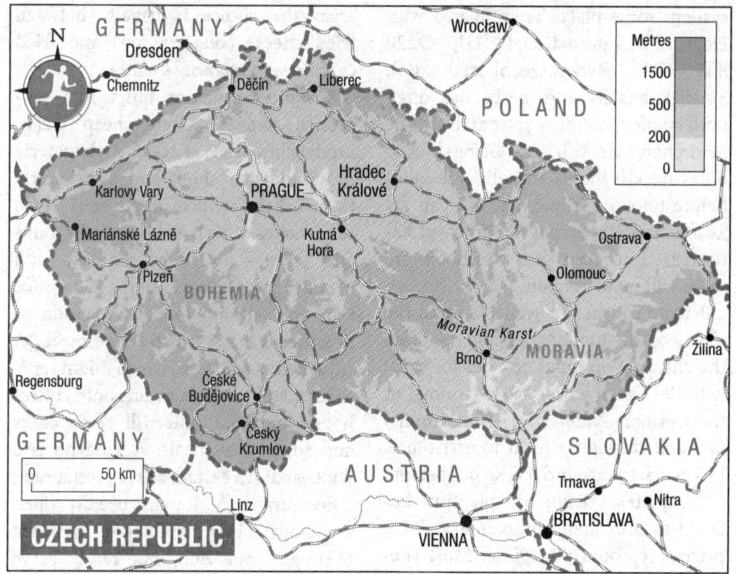

Europe. Czech Railways (České dráhy (ČD); Ⓦwww.cd.cz) runs two types of train: *rychlík* (R) or *spěšný* (Sp) trains are faster, only stopping at major towns, while *osobní* trains stop at every small station, averaging 30km per hour. Fast trains are further divided into SuperCity (SC), which are first-class only, EuroCity (EC) or InterCity (IC), which charge a supplement, and Expres (Ex), which don't. **Tickets** (*jízdenky*) for domestic journeys can be bought at the station (*nádraží*) before or on the day of departure. ČD runs reasonably priced **sleepers** to a number of neighbouring countries, which you should book in advance. **InterRail** and Eurail passes are valid in the Czech Republic.

By bus

Regional **buses** – mostly run by the state bus company, Česká státní automobilová doprava (ČSAD; Ⓦwww.csadbus.cz) go to most places, with private companies like ČEBUS providing an alternative on popular inter-city routes. **Bus stations** are usually alongside train stations; some have ticket offices but you can usually buy tickets from the driver. For long-distance journeys it's a good idea to book your ticket at least a day in advance.

The Student Agency (Ⓣ800 100 300, Ⓦwww.studentagency.cz, Ⓦwww.studentagencybus.com) runs an excellent, reasonably priced bus service, with direct routes between popular destinations. Tourbus also has good domestic bus connections (Ⓦwww.tourbus.cz).

By bicycle

Cycling is popular in the Czech Republic, and the varied countryside provides good terrain whatever your level. Regional cycling maps (Ⓦwww.shocart.cz) are sold in bookshops. There's bike rental in all major cities and some smaller towns. See Ⓦwww.czechcycling.info for more information.

ACCOMMODATION

Accommodation will be the largest chunk of your daily expenditure. Though there isn't an organized hostel system, some places are affiliated with Hostelling International (HI; ⓣ220 805 684, ⓦwww.czechhostels.com). Smaller hostels and B&Bs are often understaffed; confirm your arrival time beforehand or you risk being locked out. Check if there's an online discount before booking in person; you can get as much as 30 percent off. Tourism has decreased in recent years, so hotels are often willing to bargain.

Private rooms are available in all the towns on the tourist trail, and are often the cheapest option. Look out for signs with the Czech word *Pokoje* (rooms) or the German *Zimmer Frei* (free rooms) or book through a local tourist office. Prices start at around 350Kč per person.

Campsites (*kemp*) are plentiful but facilities are often rudimentary. Pitch prices are about 50–100Kč. Most sites have simple **chalets** (*chaty* or *bungalovy*) for around 200Kč per person. The Shocart map *Kempy a chatové osady ČR* lists Czech campsites and is sold in many bookshops. See the Czech Camping Association website (ⓦwww.camp.cz) for more.

The prices we quote are for high season (usually May–Sept), without breakfast, unless otherwise stated.

FOOD AND DRINK

The great mystery of Czech food is where the summer menu went. Pork, game, dumplings and cabbage are perfect in the icy Eastern winters but depressing on a hot day. Czech staples like roast duck (*pečená kachna*), beef in cream sauce (*svíčková na smetaně*) or pork stew (*moravský vrabec*) are omnipresent, and can be delicious or boring, depending on the chef. Desserts include strudel (*závin*), fruit dumplings (*ovocné knedlíky*) and crêpes (*palačinky*).

Prague and bigger towns offer a big choice of non-Czech restaurants, and even small towns have a pizzeria and a Chinese restaurant. **Vegetarian** food is easy to come by in cities, but in rural areas the choice is usually between fried cheese (*smažený sýr*) and fried cauliflower (*smažený květák*).

A **samoobsluha** or **bufet** is a self-service canteen selling cheap meals, sandwiches and snacks. A **bageterie** is a sandwich shop, and a **pekařství** is a bakery, which often sells open sandwiches as well as bread, rolls, buns and cakes – not to be confused with a **cukrárna**, or cake shop. A **pivnice** is a pub without food, a **hospoda** or **hostinec** is a pub which serves meals. A **čajovna** is a teahouse, which might serve snacks, and **kavárna** means both coffee-house and café, and will serve cakes and sometimes meals. A **vinárna** is a winebar and a **restaurace** is a restaurant.

Restaurants and pubs usually open at about 11am and close between midnight and 2am, but rarely serve food in the last few hours of the day. Lunchtime is early – 11.30am–1.30pm; if you arrive late popular dishes will be gone. Many restaurants bring pretzels or a basket of bread to the table, which seem complimentary but appear on the bill if eaten. Most restaurants and pubs do not charge service, and you should tip around ten percent. It's customary to sit with strangers when seats are scarce, especially in pubs and canteens: just ask if the space is free (*Máte tady volno*?), and wish fellow diners a good meal (*Dobrou Chut'*).

Drink

The Czechs drink more **beer** (*pivo*) per capita than anyone else in the world – hardly surprising given the high quality and low price of Czech beer. The most famous brands are Pilsner Urquell, from Plzeň, and Budvar, from České Budějovice. Even small canteens and cafés have **beer** on tap. Southern Moravia is a wine-growing region, and produces some good whites. Other specialities include *slivovice*, devilishly strong plum brandy, and Becherovka, herb liquor.

CZECH

	Czech	Pronunciation
Yes	*Jo*	Yoh
No	*Ne*	Neh
Please/You're welcome	*Prosím*	Pro-seem
Thank you	*Děkuji*	Dye-koo-yi
Good day/Hello	*Dobrý den*	Dob-ree den
Goodbye	*Na hledanou*	Nash-leh-dan-oh
Excuse me	*Promiňte*	Prom-in-teh
Sorry	*Pardon*	Pardon
Where?	*Kde?*	Kde?
Good	*Dobrý*	Dobree
Bad	*Špatný*	Shpatnee
Near	*Blízko*	Bleez-ko
Far	*Daleko*	Dah-lek-o
Cheap	*Levný*	Levnee
Expensive	*Drahý*	Dranee
Open	*Otevřeno*	Ot-evsh-en-o
Closed	*Zavřeno*	Zavsh-en-o
Today	*Dnes*	Dnes
Yesterday	*Včera*	Vch-er-a
Tomorrow	*Zítra*	Zeet-ra
How much is it?	*Kolik to stojí?*	Kol-ik toh sto-yee?
What time is it?	*Kolik je hodin?*	Kol-ik ye hod-in?
I don't understand	*Nerozumím*	Ne-rozoo-meem
Do you speak English?	*Mluvíte Anglicky?*	Mluv-ee-te ang-lit-skee?
I don't know Czech	*Nerozumím Český*	Ne-rozoo-meem Chess-kee
Toilet	*Toaleta*	Toh-aleta
Square	*Náměstí*	Nam–yest-yee
Station	*Nádraží*	Nah-dra-shee
Platform	*Nástupiště*	Nah-stoopish-tyeh
One	*Jeden*	Yed-en
Two	*Dva*	Dva
Three	*Tři*	Trshi
Four	*Čtyři*	Shtiri
Five	*Pět*	Pyet
Six	*Šest*	Shest
Seven	*Sedm*	Sed-um
Eight	*Osm*	Oss-um
Nine	*Devět*	Dev-yet
Ten	*Deset*	Dess-et

COMMUNICATIONS

Most **post offices** (*pošta*) are open Monday to Friday 8am to 5pm, Saturday 8am to noon. Signs over the counters show where to queue: *známky* (stamps), *dopisy* (letters) or *balíky* (parcels). Stamps are sold at newsagents and kiosks. Some **public phones** only take phonecards (*telefonní karty*), available from post offices, kiosks and some shops. You'll find **internet cafés** in bigger towns; they usually charge 60–100Kč per hour.

EMERGENCIES

Like any major city Prague has a **pickpocket** problem. Danger-spots are Old Town Square, Charles Bridge, the #22 tram and in the metro. The area around hlavní nádraží (main station)

CZECH REPUBLIC ONLINE

ⓦwww.czech.cz Basic information on the Czech Republic.

ⓦwww.expats.cz Magazine for Prague's expat community with useful practical information and events listings.

ⓦwww.praguepost.com Online English-language news.

ⓦwww.radio.cz/english News and cultural events.

ⓦwww.ticketpro.cz, **ⓦwww.ticketstream.cz**, **ⓦwww.ticketsbti.cz** Three good sites for finding out what's on in Prague and booking tickets online.

ⓦwww.slovnik.cz Reliable online dictionary.

and the park at Karlovo náměstí (Charles Square) are used by drug addicts and prostitutes at night. By law you should carry your **passport** with you.

Pharmacies (*lékárna*) are easy to find but not always English-speaking. If you need a repeat prescription take the empty bottle or remaining pills.

INFORMATION

Most towns have a **tourist office** (*informační centrum*) with English-speaking staff. You can find **maps** (*mapa*) in tourist offices, bookshops and petrol stations.

EMERGENCY NUMBERS

Police ⓣ158; Fire ⓣ150; Ambulance ⓣ155.

STUDENT DISCOUNTS

Student discounts are up to half-price. Bring an ISIC card, as many places won't recognize university cards.

MONEY AND BANKS

The local **currency** is the Czech crown, or koruna česká (Kč), though some tourist-oriented services list prices in euros. At the time of writing £1 = 27Kč, €1 = 24Kč and $1 = 16Kč. **Banks** are usually open Monday to Friday 8am to 5pm and there are plenty of ATMs.

OPENING HOURS AND HOLIDAYS

Most shops are open Monday to Friday 9am to 5 or 6pm. Smaller shops close for lunch between noon and 2pm and some stay open late on Thursdays. In larger towns some shops stay open all day at weekends, and the corner shops (*večerka*) stay open daily till 10 or 11pm. Museums, galleries and churches are generally open daily; synagogues are closed on Saturdays and Jewish holidays. Many attractions are closed on Mondays.

Public holidays include January 1, Easter Monday, May 1, May 8, July 5 and 6, September 28, October 28, November 17, December 24–26.

Prague

Historical, whimsical, hedonistic and cynical, **PRAGUE** bewilders its visitors and charms them. Since the Iron Curtain fell in 1989, tourism and investment has poured in, turning the previously ramshackle Communist capital into a buzzing Western metropolis.

Prince Bořivoj, an early Christian, founded the first Czech dynasty in 870, and his grandson, Prince Václav (the Good King Wenceslas of the song) became the Czech patron saint before being offed by his younger brother Boleslav I. Prague experienced a golden age under the urbane emperor, **Charles IV**, a polylingual patron of the arts whose court was the heart of fourteenth-century Europe. Charles founded the university and as well as an entire new quarter, Nové Město, built the Charles Bridge and St Vitus'. A long period of Austro-Hungarian rule gave Prague its Teutonic facades and high-minded coffeehouses, while the National Revival reasserted the Slavic identity of the city and the onion dome rose again. The short-lived First Republic, modelled on American democracy, crashed when Nazi troops marched into Czechoslovakia, and President Beneš's decision to accept German "protection" was a dark moment in the nation's history, but saved the city from decimation. In 1948 Communism arrived in a wave of stained concrete, bringing a few architectural pearls along with the swine. The period since '89 has seen rapid construction, but with a few exceptions, such as Jean Nouvel's Golden Angel mall and the playful Dancing House, it's been conservative and timid. Not so the restaurants, hotels, bars and clubs, which have re-awoken Prague's slumbering decadence.

What to see and do

Flowing from the east towards Germany, the Vltava divides Prague in the centre. Hradčany and Malá Strana, once home to the Austro-Hungarian elite, sit primly on the left bank, faced by the noisier commercial quarters, Staré Město, Josefov and Nové Město.

Hradčany, which houses the castle and St Vitus' Cathedral, tumbles into **Malá Strana** (Little Quarter), a maze of cobbles, carved doorhandles and stickleback roofs. The Czech senate's Baroque gardens, which back onto Malostranská metro, are open daily from noon till 4pm.

Over the river is **Staré Město** (Old Town), a delicate web of alleys and passages running towards Staroměstské náměstí, the old market square. Within Staré Město is the old Jewish quarter, **Josefov**, which now encloses a luxury shopping district.

Nové Město (New Town), the most central part of the modern city, spans the largest area of old Prague, with blocks stretching south and east of the old town in long strides.

Prague Castle

Once the heart of the Holy Roman Empire, **Prague Castle** (sights daily 9am–4/5pm; grounds daily 5/6am–11pm/midnight; Ⓦwww.hrad.cz) is home to the Czech president and crown jewels. Wandering is free, but to enter the buildings you need to buy a ticket (250–350Kč) at the Castle Information Centre, opposite the cathedral entrance.

St Vitus' Cathedral

Medieval **St Vitus' Cathedral**, which broods over the Prague skyline, is scarcely visible close up; the Third Courtyard surrounds it too tightly. The **Chapel of sv Václav**, by the south door, was built in the fourteenth century to

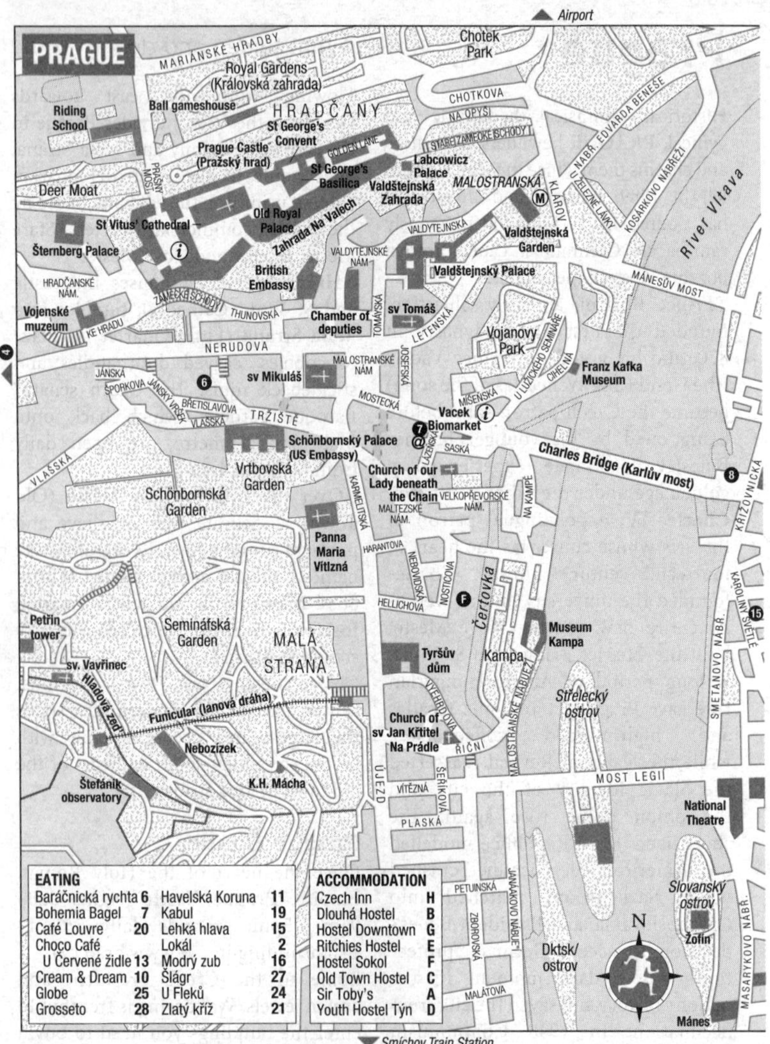

commemorate the Czech prince Saint Wenceslas (Václav), murdered by his brother Boleslav I. A door in the south wall leads to the coronation chamber, which houses the **crown jewels**.

Old Royal Palace

The **Old Royal Palace** (Starý královský palác), across the courtyard from the south door of the cathedral, was home to Bohemian royalty from the eleventh to the seventeenth centuries. The massive **Vladislav Hall** (Vladislavský sál) where the early Bohemian kings were elected, is now used for swearing Czech presidents into office.

Basilica of St George

The Basilica of St George (Bazilika sv Jiří), with its beautiful Romanesque interior, was originally built in 1173. Concerts are often held here. The

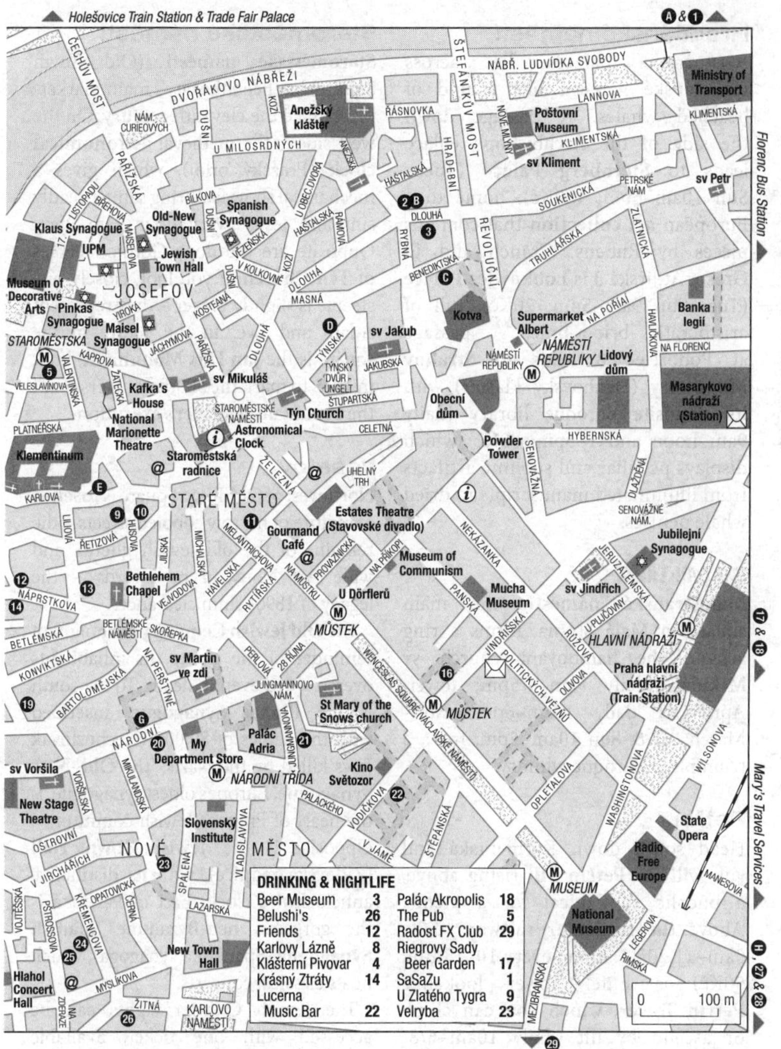

nearby Convent of Saint George houses a collection of sixteenth- to eighteenth-century Czech art.

Golden Lane

Golden Lane (Zlatá ulička), round the corner from the basilica, is a street of toy-sized tradesmens' cottages, as bright and compact as a watercolour box. Franz Kafka briefly lived at no. 22, his sister's house, during World War I. There's a 50Kč entry charge during the day, but after 6pm you can enter for free.

The Royal Gardens

North of the castle walls, cross the **Powder Bridge** (Prašný most) to reach the **Royal Gardens** (Královská zahrada; April–Oct daily 10am–6pm; free), and enjoy the view over Little Quarter surrounded by fountains, sloping lawns and almond trees.

Hradčanské náměstí

Aristocratic palaces lie across Hradčanské náměstí like a pod of beached whales. A passage down the side of the Archbishop's Palace leads to **Šternberg Palace** (Tues–Sun 10am–6pm; 150Kč), home to a European **art collection** that contains pieces by Rubens, Cranch and El Greco. At Jiřská 3 is **Lobkowicz Palace** (Tues–Sun 9am–5pm; 20Kč), full of aristocratic bric-a-brac. A passage at Pohořelec 8 leads to **Strahov Monastery** (Strahovský klášter) with its exquisite Baroque library (daily 9am–noon and 1–5pm; 80Kč) which displays peculiar and sublime artifacts from illuminated manuscripts to dried whale penises.

Sv Mikuláš

Malostranské náměstí, the main square in Malá Strana, forms a ring around the flamboyant church **sv Mikuláš** (daily 9am–4/5pm; tower: April–Oct daily 10am–6pm; Nov–March Sat & Sun 10am–5pm; free), a triumph of Baroque whimsy.

Petřín

Head south down Karmelitská and you will see **Petřín hill** rising above, a bucolic spot ideal for a picnic. Above the **funicular railway** (daily 9am–11.20/11.30pm; every 10–15min; 50Kč) is Eiffel Tower lookalike **Petřín Tower**, which you can climb or ascend by lift (daily 10am–6/8/10pm; 100Kč).

Charles Bridge

Linking Malá Strana to Staré Město is Prague's most celebrated landmark, the **Charles Bridge** (Karlův most), built in 1357. At the centre is Czech patron saint John of Nepomuk, thrown off the bridge by Wenceslas IV for refusing to divulge the queen's confessions. It's best seen at dawn, or late at night, when the crowds are gone.

Staroměstské náměstí

Staroměstské náměstí (Old Town Square) has been the city's main marketplace since the eleventh century. On the west side is the medieval **astronomical clock** (Pražský orloj), which gives a mechanical show featuring saints, deadly sins and Jesus every hour 9am–9pm. Opposite are the dour Gothic steeples of **Týn Church**; if you look closely one steeple is slightly bigger – they represent Adam and Eve. In the centre of the square is the **Jan Hus Monument**, built in 1915 to mark the 500th anniversary of the Protestant reformer's execution.

Josefov

Northwest of Old Town Square is **Josefov**, a mixture of narrow cobbled streets – the remains of the old Jewish ghetto, and wide Art Nouveau boulevards – the legacy of 1890s slum clearance.

The **Old Jewish Cemetery** is a poignant reminder of the ghetto, its inhabitants overcrowded even in death. To the south is the **Pinkas Synagogue**, inscribed with the names of 80,000 Czechoslovak Jews killed by the Nazis. The **Old–New Synagogue**, Europe's oldest synagogue, is the heart of Prague's Jewish community. Opposite is the **Jewish Town Hall** (Židovská radnice), with its distinctive anticlockwise clock. East of Pařížská is the gorgeous neo-Byzantine **Spanish Synagogue** (Španělská synagoga), which hosts classical concerts.

The Jewish Quarter sights can be accessed with one ticket, available from the shop in front of the **Old–New Synagogue entrance** (daily except Sat & Jewish holidays winter 9am–4.30/6pm; summer 9am–6pm; 430Kč, 320Kč for students under 26; Ⓦwww.jewishmuseum.cz).

Museum of Decorative Arts

The **Museum of Decorative Arts** (17. Listopadu 2; Tues 10am–7pm, Wed–Sun 10am–6pm; 120Kč, free entry Tues 5–7pm), a neo-Renaissance palace

FRANZ KAFKA

Franz Kafka was born in 1883 to middle-class Czech Jewish parents who ran a haberdashery in Old Town. His ambivalent relationship with Prague is reflected in his trademark tone of anxious claustrophobia – "A cage went in search of a bird", he once jotted in a notebook. You can see the building where he slaved away as a clerk at **na poříčí 7**, and his homes on **Golden Lane** (no. 22) and **Old Town Square** (Oppelt building). Kafka went to fortnightly meetings at **Café Louvre** (see p.289) and also frequented **Café Savoy** in Malá Strana, where he first met the actor Isaac Lowy, who re-awakened his interest in Jewish culture. At the **Kafka Museum** at Cihelna 2b (daily 10am–6pm; 120Kč) you can see first editions and manuscripts, personal letters, diaries and drawings – a peephole into one of the most intriguing minds of the twentieth century.

opposite the Rudolfinum, shows a splendid collection of glass, clothes, pottery, clocks, dresses and other ephemera of daily life spanning a thousand years.

Mucha Museum

A turning halfway along Na příkopě leads to the **Mucha Museum** at Panská 7 (daily 10am–4/6pm; 120Kč), dedicated to the Czech Art Nouveau designer and painter Alfons Mucha.

Obecní dům

Squatting ponderously on one edge of náměstí Republiky is **Obecní dům** (the Municipal House), a delightful example of Czech Art Nouveau containing a concert hall, restaurant, café and frescoes by Mucha. You can get in by taking the overpriced guided **tour** (two or three daily; 280Kč), or drink tea in the gilded café for rather less.

Museum of Communism

Situated, with delicious irony, above *McDonalds*, the **Museum of Communism** Na Přikopě 10 (daily 9am–9pm; 180Kč) draws a detailed picture of life behind the Iron Curtain in all its grim monotony, from propaganda and labour camps to shopping and TV.

Wenceslas Square

The greasy axle of modern Prague is **Wenceslas Square** (Václavské náměstí), a mass of shabby gift shops and strip clubs. It was here that protesters gathered to topple Communism in the Velvet Revolution. At the top end is a statue of St Wenceslas on his horse. Below is a small **memorial** to 21-year-old student **Jan Palach**, who burnt himself to death in protest against the Russian invasion of '68, becoming a symbol of Czech resistance.

Veletržní palác: The Museum of Modern Art

Take tram #12 from outside Ⓜ Malostranska to **Veletržní palác** (Tues–Wed & Fri–Sun 10am–6pm, Thurs 10am–9pm; 100Kč for each floor or 250Kč for all four), a stately piece of 1920s functionalism housing works by Klimt, Picasso and the French Impressionists.

DOX Centre for Contemporary Art

DOX (Mon 10am–10pm, Wed–Fri 11am–7pm, Sat & Sun 10am–6pm, closed Tues; 180Kč, students 90Kč) showcases modern painting, sculpture, architecture, design and photography. Though still a newcomer, it's hosted the likes of Andy Warhol and Damian Hirst, as well as Czechs like sculptor David Černý and émigré architect Jan Kaplický.

Arrival and information

Air Prague's airport (letiště), Ruzyně (Ⓦ www.csl.cz), is 10km from the city centre. The best way of getting into town is to catch a bus and then a metro. Bus #119 (4am–midnight; every 7–15min; 20min) goes to Ⓜ Dejvická on line A, and bus #179 to Ⓜ Nové Butovice on line B. "Fixed-price" taxis are expensive, at about 700Kč to the centre.

Train If you're coming by train you'll arrive at one of Prague's four stations, Praha hlavní nádraží, (Prague Main Station), where international trains terminate, Praha Holešovice station, Praha Masarykovo or Praha Smíchov. All four are adjacent to metro stations.

Bus The main bus station is Praha-Florenc on the eastern edge of Staré Město, and right next to Ⓜ Florenc (line B). At night it's a shady place, so don't loiter.

Tourist office The Prague Information Service, (Pražská informační služba – PIS) is free and can provide maps, brochures, help with accommodation and tickets. There are several branches around town; the main office is at the bottom of Wenceslas Square at Na příkopě 20 (Mon–Fri 9am–6/7pm, Sat 9am–3/5pm; April–Oct also Sun 9am–5pm; Ⓦ www.pis.cz), other branches are located inside Hlavní nádraží (Main station), at the Charles bridge, Staroměstské náměstí 5 (Old Town Square) and Rytířská 31 near Ⓜ Muztek.

River cruise Prague is most beautiful from the water. Boat trips down the Vltava last between an hour and a day; there are lunch and dinner cruises and jazz and club boats with live music. Buy tickets on the riverbank at Čechův Bridge or Embankment nábřeži, or pre-book with Prague Passenger Shipping (Ⓣ 224 931 013, Ⓦ www.paroplavba.cz; 190Kč/hr), or Jazzboat (Ⓣ 731 183 180, Ⓦ www.jazzboat.cz; 607Kč adults, students 315Kč/2hr 30min).

Bike rental Praha Bike (Dlouhá 24, daily 9am–8pm, Ⓦ www.prahabike.cz) rents bikes and organizes tours around Prague for 440Kč for 6hr. City Bike (Králodvorská, Ⓦ www.citybike-prague.com) offers bike rental with an optional MP3 audio tour; 500Kč for 8hr.

City transport

Metro The metro (daily 5am–midnight Sun–Thurs & 5am–1am Fri & Sat) is fast, reliable and – with only three lines – easy to navigate.

Trams Running every 3–20min, Prague's trams cross the city's hills and cobbles with great dexterity. Tram #22, which runs through Vinohrady and Hradčany, is a option if you want to sightsee. Night trams (numbers #51–#59; midnight–4.30am; every 30min) all pass through Lazarská in Nové Město.

Tickets Buy tickets at tobacconists, kiosks or the ticket machines inside metro stations, and validate them by stamping in the yellow machines on board trams or at the metro entrance. There are two main tickets: the 32Kč ticket is valid for 90min; the 24Kč is valid for 30min. Plain-clothes inspectors check tickets and there is a fine of 800Kč on the spot if you don't have a valid ticket.

Travel passes If you're planning to use public transport regularly you can buy a travel pass (100Kč/24hr, 330Kč/72hr); remember to validate it. Another option is **Praguecard** (Ⓦ www.praguecard.biz), which costs €56 (1358Kč), students €43 (1044Kč), and gives you three days of transport and entry to 50 attractions. It can be bought at tourist offices, the airport or online.

Taxis Prague cabbies are notoriously wily, so it is best to call a taxi – AAA has English-speaking operators (Ⓣ 222 333 222) as does Profi Taxi (Ⓣ 844 700 800). If you have to hail a cab, get a quote beforehand, and ask for a receipt (*účtenka*).

Accommodation

Prague has hundreds of hotels and hostels, and prices are similar to any other European capital. The central hotels are located in Staré Město, Nové Město and Malá strana, or you can go further out to pay less. Vinohrady is picturesque, with great wine bars and restaurants, Žižkov is down at heel but lively at night, Vyšehrad is pretty and sedate. There are plenty of travel agencies, but it's cheaper to book direct. You can find apartments and rooms on Ⓦ www.prague-city-apartments.cz, Ⓦ www.happyhouserentals.com and Ⓦ www.city-info.cz. The Charles University offers student rooms over the summer; contact the booking office at Voršilská 1, Nové Město (Mon–Fri only; Ⓣ 224 930 010; beds July to mid-Sept; from 350Kč).

Hostels and B&Bs

Czech Inn Francouzská 76, Vinohrady Ⓣ 267 267 600, Ⓦ www.czech-inn.com. All oak floors, brushed aluminium and discarded backpacks *Czech Inn* seems like the product of a tryst between a youth hostel and a luxury hotel. It's on the edge of the town centre (10min by tram to Old Town Square) and has free wi-fi, a café-bar with live music, great staff and a 24-hour reception. Go by metro to I.P. Pavlova, then tram #4 or #22 to Krymská. Dorms 450Kč, double en suite 1800Kč.

Dlouhá Pension and Hostel (Travellers' Hostel) Dlouhá 33 Staré Město Ⓣ 224 826 662, Ⓦ www.travellers.cz. Ⓜ Náměstí Republiky. Large party hostel five minutes' walk from Old Town Square with free internet, kitchen and a 24-hour reception, next door to *Roxy* music club. Breakfast included. Dorms 350Kč, doubles 1300Kč.

Hostel Downtown Národní 19, Nové Město Ⓣ 224 240 570, Ⓦ www.hosteldowntown.cz. Clean, garishly decorated HI-affiliated hostel. Bed 500Kč, double en suite 2000Kč.

Hostel Sokol Nosticova 2, Malá strana ⓣ257 007 397, ⓦwww.hostelsokol.cz. Immaculate, spartan dorms full of brass and white linen overlooking the river, originally built for Communist athletes. Dorms 350Kč.

Old Town Hostel Benediktská 2, Staré Město ⓣ224 829 058, ⓦwww.oldpraguehostel.com. Bright, compact hostel on a quiet central street with free wi-fi and a computer room. Breakfast included. Dorms €14.90 (363Kč), doubles €48 (1169Kč).

Ritchie's Hostel Karlova 13, Staré Město ⓣ222 221 229, ⓦwww.ritchieshostel.cz ⓜStaroměstská. Bang in the heart of town, over a souvenir shop, with decent dorms and rooms. Internet access. Dorms 320Kč, doubles 1700Kč.

Sir Toby's Dělnická 24 ⓣ246 032 610, ⓦwww.sirtobys.com ⓜNádraží Holešovice or tram stop Dělnická. Upmarket suburban hostel with a garden, cellar bar, lounge, free internet, large kitchen and dorms that look like pricey hotel rooms stretched. Dorm 350–470Kč, doubles 1840Kč.

Youth Hostel Týn Týnská 19, Staré Město ⓣ224 828 519, ⓦwww.hosteltyn.com ⓜNáměstí Republiky. The bright, shabby look and fried chicken smell of a juvenile detention unit, but it's central and unlikely to be booked up. A useful fallback. Dorms 400Kč, doubles 1200Kč.

Eating

There was a time when Prague food was limited to meat and dumplings, but now you can find anything from French to Korean to Mexican. Restaurants are affordable, especially at lunchtime (11.30am–1.30pm) when pubs and bistros run cheap daily offers. Prices soar in the tourist district but quality lags behind. Prague has a thriving café culture, and watching the city slip by from an old-fashioned coffeehouse, with a slice of strudel or honey cake and a book, is one of the city's great pleasures.

Cafés

Bohemia Bagel Lázeňská 19, Malá strana. Refuel with a quick sandwich, burger or fried breakfast. Free wi-fi. Mon–Fri 7am–midnight, Sat & Sun 8am–midnight.

Café Louvre Národní 22, Nové Město. Lovely Art Nouveau coffeehouse as rich and delectable as the peach cheesecake. There's a billiard hall, lunch menu, English papers and a shady terrace. Mon–Fri 8am–11.30pm, Sat & Sun 9am–11.30pm.

Choco Café U Červené židle Liliová 4, Staré Město. Friendly little Old Town café famous for its hot chocolate. Mon–Fri 9am–8pm, Sat & Sun 10am–8pm.

Cream & Dream Husova 12, Staré Město. The best ice cream in Prague – ask anyone. Daily 10am–10pm.

Šlágr Francouzská 72, Vinohrady. A chocolate-scented, dimly lit, jazz-infused lovesong to the lost coffeehouses of '20s Prague. Delicious home-made cakes. Daily 10am–10pm.

Globe Pštrossova 12, Nové Město. Modern café-bookshop popular with Prague's American crowd, with good food, free wi-fi and an internet café (1Kč/min). Great breakfasts. Sun–Mon 9.30am–midnight, Thurs–Sat 9.30am–1.30am

Zlatý kříž Jungmannovo nám. 19, Nové Město. A meaty slice of real Czech culture, this popular stand-up lunch-bar serves Prague's best *chlebíčky* (ornate open sandwiches) for only 16Kč, plus cold-cuts, rolls and beer on tap. Daily 7am–7pm.

Restaurants

Baráčnická rychta Tržiště 23, Malá strana. Popular local stashed in a back alley in the tourist district. Good food, outdoor seating in the quiet courtyard and Svijany, a superb beer, on tap. Mains 140–295Kč. Mon–Sat 11am–11pm, Sun 11am–9pm.

Grosseto Francouzská 2, Vinohrady. Spacious, bright restaurant serving nice Italian dishes at a reasonable price. Mains 129–330Kč. Daily 11.30am–midnight.

Havelská Koruna Havelská 21, Staré Město. Burly women in smocks dispense stew and beer to local workers. Located two minutes' walk from Old Town Square. Mains 89–150Kč. Daily 10am–8pm.

Kabul Karolíny Světlé 14, Staré Město. Super Afghani restaurant five minutes from Old Town Square with a cheap lunch menu. Mains 90–280Kč, lunch 85Kč. Daily noon–11pm.

Lehká hlava Boršov 2, Staré Město. Cure for Czech pub fatigue – bright, chic, non-smoking and vegetarian. Mains 130–195Kč. Mon–Fri 11.30am–11.30pm, Sat & Sun noon–11.30pm.

Lokál Dlouhá 33, Staré Město. A restaurant chain trying to recreate the charm of a little Czech pub on a grand scale, and against all odds succeeding. Mains 134–142Kč. Mon–Fri 11am–1am, Sat noon–1am, Sun noon–10pm.

Modrý zub Jindřišská 5, Nové Město. Thai noodle bar and takeaway located close to Wenceslas Square, serving inauthentic but likeable food. Mains 145–275Kč. Mon–Fri 10am–midnight, Sat 11am–midnight, Sun 11am–11pm.

U Fleků Křemencova 11, Nové Město. Riddled with arches, beams, Gothic windows and wooden panelling, *U Fleků* brings an antiquarian gravity and lots of meat to the microbrewery concept.

There's a beer garden too. Mains 139–349Kč. Daily 10am–11pm.

Drinking and nightlife

Pubs close between 11pm and 2am so for late-night drinking head to the city centre's bars and clubs. All-night bars with gambling (*herna*) are dotted around Prague, but are grubby and unsafe. Pub crawls are a good way to cover a lot of ground – the best is Prague Underground (Ⓦwww.pragueunderground.com), which meets at the Astronomical Clock at 9pm Mon–Sat and costs 500Kč, or try market leader Prague Pub Crawl (Ⓦwww.pubcrawl cz) for 490Kč.

Bars and pubs

Beer Museum Dlouhá 46, Staré Město. No glass cases or fossils in sight in this relaxed central pub – just a line of taps as long as a Louvre corridor. Daily 10am–11pm.

Belushi's Odborů 4, Nové Město. Trendy, dimly lit bar and music club in the ground floor of *Mosaic House* hostel, which moonlights as a sports bar for the hockey and football and serves decent meals. The stream of hostel guests creates a gregarious atmosphere. Daily 7.30am–2am.

Klášterní pivovar Strahovské nádvoří 301, Hradčany. Reward yourself for the steep walk up Petřin with the delicious beer, dark and light, brewed by the monks at Strahov Monastary. Daily 10am–10pm.

Krásný Ztráty Náprstkova 10, Staré Město. Jolly little café-bar popular with art students and those pretending to be art students. Mon–Fri 9am–1am, Sat & Sun noon–1am.

The Pub Veleslavínova 3, Staré Město. Self-service pub with a tap on every table. The amount of beer (Pilsner Urquell) you've consumed is projected on a big screen to encourage inter-table rivalry. Mon–Fri 11am–2am, Sat noon–2am, Sun noon–midnight.

Riegrovy sady Beer Garden Riegrovy sady, Vinohrady. Pints are sold out of one hut, sausages out of another. There's a big screen for sport, table-football and table-hockey. Alternatively you can buy your beer in a plastic cup and drink it in the park, with cherry blossom rustling above. Daily noon–2am (dependent on weather).

Velryba Opatovická 24, Nové Město. Welcoming, amateurishly frescoed underground bar filled with young intellectuals, debating noisily over beer and a plate of something hot. Daily 9am–6pm.

U Zlatého tygra Husova 17, Staré Město. If you like authenticity, this tobacco-smoked local full of noisy old men is the place for you. Pilsner on tap, located two minutes from Old Town Square. Daily 3–11pm.

Clubs

Friends Náprstkova 1, Staré Město. Low-key gay bar which transforms into a raucous club on Friday and Saturday nights. Daily 6pm–4am.

Karlovy lázně Novotného lávka 1, Staré Město. Hyper-kitsch super-club next to Charles Bridge; techno on the top floor, progressively more retro as you descend towards the internet café in the lobby. Daily 9pm–5am.

Lucerna Music Bar Vodičkova 36, Nové Město. Central club featuring local bands and occasional international acts. There are popular 80s nights on Fridays and Saturdays. Daily 8pm–3am.

Palác Akropolis Kubelíkova 27, Žižkov. Art Deco mammoth *Akropolis*, a maze of live music, theatre, dancing and eating, offering rock, house, pop, hip-hop, reggae and the rest. Daily 8pm–5am.

Radost FX Club Bělehradská 120, Vinohrady. Popular central club decorated like a faux-oriental brothel famous for its Thursday hip-hop night. It doesn't close till 5am and has a good vegetarian café. Daily 10pm–6am.

SaSaZu Bubenské nábřeží 306, Holešovice. Shiny goliath of Prague nightlife modelled on the slick clubs of New York's meatpacking district, with an oriental fusion restaurant. Fri & Sat 10pm–5am.

Entertainment

You can find full entertainment listings on the Prague Events Calendar (Ⓦwww.pragueeventscalendar.cz), Prague Experience (Ⓦwww.pragueexperience.cz), or in the Day&Night section of the rather overpriced English-language paper the *Prague Post* (sold in the kiosks on Wenceslas Square).

Theatre

Lanterna Magika Národní 4 Ⓣ224 931 482 Ⓦwww.blacktheatreprague.cz. A blend of circus, puppetry and dance. Czech theatre minus the language barrier.

National Marionette Theatre Žatecká 1 Ⓣ224 819 323, Ⓦwww.mozart.cz. Giant marionettes miming to a CD of Mozart's *Don Giovanni.*

Cinemas

Kino Lucerna Štěpánská 61, Nové Město Ⓦwww.lucerna.cz/kino. Nestling inside a shopping arcade off Wenceslas Square, Lucerna is a flamboyant, pint-sized Art Nouveau cinema. Czech, international, old, new films and a quiet vintage bar.

Kino Světozor Vodičkova 41, Nové Město Ⓦwww.kinosvetozor.cz. New releases, classics, art-house and documentaries.

Live music

AghaRTA Jazz Centrum Železná 16, Staré Město ⓦwww.agharta.cz. Prague's best jazz club, with a good mix of top international names and local acts. Daily from 9pm.

U Malého Glena Karmelitská 23, Malá Strana ⓦwww.malyglen.cz. Popular jazz venue in a Little Quarter cellar with a restaurant upstairs.

Vagon Národní třída 25, Nové Město, ⓦwww.vagon.cz. Smoky music club playing a mix of rock and reggae, bursting at the seams with long-haired students and ageing rockers.

Classical music, opera and ballet

Small classical concerts are held in churches in the tourist district every night – you'll be pelted with fliers as you walk through town, or you can find listings online (see opposite)

Národní Divadlo (National Theatre) Národní 2, Nové Město ⓦwww.narodni-divadlo.cz. Grand monument to nineteenth-century nationalism, built with a brick from every village in the country. Ballet and opera performed by national and touring companies.

Rudolfinum Alšovo nábřeží 12, Staré Město ⓦwww.rudolfinum.cz. This neo-Renaissance concert hall next to the river houses the Czech Philharmonic Orchestra, creators of a thousand film soundtracks.

Stavovské divadlo (Theatre of the Estates) Ovocný trh 1, Staré Město ⓦwww.narodni-divadlo.cz. A similar programme to the National in one of the loveliest theatres in Europe. Mozart conducted the first performance of *Don Giovanni* here in 1787.

Outdoor activities

Boating Žofín or Střelecký island. Pedalo and rowing boat rental from little firms on the river islands opposite the National Theatre. April–Oct; passport kept as deposit, approx 100Kč/hr.

HC Slavia 02 Arena, Libeň, ⓦwww.hc-slavia.cz. Nothing beats an ice hockey match, beer in one hand and sausage in the other, surrounded by a thousand bellowing Czechs.

Podoli Swimming Complex Podolska 74, ⓦwww.pspodoli.cz. Olympic-sized indoor and outdoor pools, waterslides, saunas and lawn for sunbathing. Take tram #3, #16, #17 or #21 to Kublov.

Shopping

Bontonland Václavské náměstí 1. Music and film emporium buried bunker-like under Wenceslas Square.

Palladium Náměstí Republiky 1. Central mall with major European brands, supermarkets and a food court.

Pařižská This street named "Paris" resembles the broad leafy boulevards of France's capital, and houses Cartier, Hermes, Louis Vuitton et al. More shopping on nearby Celetná and Karlova.

Shakespeare and Sons U lužického semináře 10. Little Quarter English-language bookshop.

Directory

Embassies and consulates Australia (honorary), Klimentská 10, Nové Město ⓣ221729260; Canada, Muchova 6, Hradčany ⓣ272 101 800; New Zealand, Dykova 19, Vinohrady ⓣ222 514 672; Ireland, Tržiště 13, Malá Strana ⓣ257 530 061; UK, Thunovská 14, Malá Strana ⓣ257 402 111; US, Tržiště 15, Malá Strana ⓣ257 022 000.

Hospital Na Františku Hospital, Na Františku 8, Staré Město ⓣ222 311 870 (24hr number, English spoken).

Internet *Bohemia Bagel*, Masná 2. Internet terminals, long-distance calling and bottomless coffee (daily 8am–9.30pm; internet 2Kč/min); Globe Internet terminals (see p.289; Sun–Wed 9.30am–midnight, Thurs–Sat 9.30am–1am; 1.5Kč/min).

Left luggage There are lockers or left-luggage offices at all train stations.

Pharmacies Palackého 5, Nové Město (24hr; ⓣ224 946 982); Štefánikova 6, Malá Strana (24hr; ⓣ257 320 918).

Post office Jindřišská 14, Nové Město (daily 2am–midnight, but service is slow outside office hours).

Moving on

Train Berlin (every 2hr; 4hr 45min); Bratislava (daily; 5hr 20min); České Budějovice (up to 14 daily; 2hr 15min–3hr); Dresden (daily; 2hr 30min); Karlovy Vary (3 daily; 4hr 5min–5hr 10min); Olomouc (1–2 hourly; 3hr 10min–3hr 30min); Plzeň (hourly; 1hr 40min).

Bus Most buses depart from Florenc bus station. For Student Agency buses, book ahead (see p.278); main office in Florenc bus station; ⓣ800 100 300, ⓦwww.studentagencybus.com. Berlin (daily; 6hr 30min); Bratislava (up to 6 daily; 3–6hr); Brno (every 30min–1hr; 2hr 20min–3hr 30min); České Budějovice (up to 8 daily; 2hr 30min–3hr 25min); Český Krumlov (2–6 daily; 2hr 40min–3hr 25min); Karlovy Vary (hourly; 2hr 10min–2hr 40min); Kutná Hora (hourly on weekdays; 1hr 15min).

Bohemia

Prague is circled by the region of **Bohemia**, which covers the western two-thirds of the Czech Republic. To the west of Prague is **Karlovy Vary**, a picturesque spa town in the woody Sudeten hills, while south-east of that is **Plzeň**, brimming with industrial vigour and Pilsner Urquell beer. Travelling east towards Slovakia you'll reach **Kutná Hora**, with its sinister bone church. South of Prague, close to the Austrian border, is another beer-brewing giant, **České Budějovice**, home of Budweiser, and **Český Krumlov**, with its rose-coloured churches and frescoed palaces.

KUTNÁ HORA

A short bus ride from Prague, **KUTNÁ HORA** has a handful of tourist attractions and a sleepy, provincial atmosphere. Beneath the town are miles of exhausted silver and gold mines. From 1308, Bohemia's royal mint at Kutná Hora converted its silver into coins that were used all over Central Europe, but when the mines ran dry the town dwindled.

What to see and do

Kutná Hora's old town is so small it can be explored in a couple of hours. Most of the main attractions sit between main square Palackého náměstí and the Cathedral of Sr Barbora ten minutes to the southeast.

Sedlec Ossuary

The town's most popular attraction is the ghoulish **ossuary** (*kostnice*), which houses 40,000 human skeletons (daily: April–Sept 8am–6pm; Oct–March 9am–noon & 1–4pm; 50Kč, students 30Kč) arranged in intricate patterns by local oddball František Rint, a carpenter, in 1870. Take bus #1 or #4 from Kutná Hora to Sedlec.

Cathedral of sv Barbora

The **Cathedral of sv Barbora** (Tues–Sun: April–Oct 9am–6pm; Nov–March 10am–4pm), a Gothic masterpiece dedicated to the patron saint of miners, is approached by a street lined by Baroque saints and angels. To the right is the former Jesuit College, now the Kutná Hora Arts Centre.

The Italian Court

From Palackého naměstí head down 28 října to the **Italian Court**, where coins were once minted. Exhibits re-create working conditions, and there's an exhaustive collection of Kutná Hora coins. Entrance is by guided tour only (daily: April–Sept 9am–6pm; March & Oct 10am–5pm; Nov–Feb 10am–4pm; 130Kč).

The Mining Museum

In a medieval fort at the junction of Barborská and Ruthardská is the **Mining Museum** (April–Oct Tues–Sun 9/10am–5/6pm; 130Kč), where tourists can stroll the ancient mines in white coats and goggles.

Arrival and information

Train From Prague Main Station (direct trains roughly every 2hr; 55min) the station is out of town, near Sedlec (useful for visiting the ossuary). Take the #1 or #4 bus into the town centre.

Bus From Florenc station, Prague (4 daily; 1hr 30min).

Tourist office Palackého náměstí 377 (April–Sept daily 9am–6pm; Oct–March Mon–Fri 9am–5pm, Sat & Sun 10am–4pm; ⓣ 327 512 378, ⓦ www.kh.cz). Can book private rooms and has internet access.

Eating and drinking

Barborská Barborská 35. Miniature cocktail bar with a friendly, urban vibe. Mon–Thurs 4pm–1am, Fri & Sat 4pm–3am.

Dačický Rakova 8. Meaty Czech comfort food and local dark beer in arched, dimly lit beerhall. Mains 119–499Kč. Daily 11am–11pm.

Kavárna na Kozím Plácku Dačického náměstí 10. Fussy granny decor belies the grave nature of this café's commitment to the coffee bean. Daily 10am–10pm.

ČESKÉ BUDĚJOVICE

ČESKÉ BUDĚJOVICE is a sweet kernel of medieval town inside a tough shell of industrial sprawl. It was built in 1265, and its history has been connected with beer since the beginning, when citizens brewed lager for the Holy Roman Emperor. In the seventeenth century war and fire devastated the town, but it was lavishly rebuilt by the Habsburgs. Today its elegant arcades and winding backstreets are the perfect place to enjoy a Budvar beer – which is, after all, the reason most people come here.

What to see and do

The compact medieval town centre forms a grid around magnificent **Přemysla Otakara II Square**, one of Europe's largest marketplaces. Just off the square is Black Tower (Černá věž; July–Aug Tues–Sun 10am–6pm, Nov–March Tues–Sat 10am–6pm; 30Kč, students 20Kč), which you can climb for good views.

Budvar brewery

The **Budvar brewery** is 2.5km up the road to Prague, on Karolíny Světlé (bus #2). You'll need to book ahead for a one-hour English tour (daily 9am–4pm; 100Kč; ⓣ387 705 341, ⓦwww.budweiser.cz).

Arrival and information

Bus and train The town's train and bus stations are a 10min walk from the old town: from the stations head west along Lannova třída. There are several daily direct trains and buses from Prague; it's possible to visit as a day-trip, but if you want to visit the brewery consider staying overnight.

Tourist office Náměstí Přemysla Otakara II. 1 (May–Sept Mon–Fri 8.30am–6pm, Sat 8.30am–5pm, Sun 10am–4pm; Oct–April Mon–Fri 9am–4pm, Sat 9am–1pm; ⓣ386 801 413, ⓦwww.c-budejovice.cz).

Accommodation

Penzion Centrum Biskupská 103 ⓣ387 311 801, ⓦwww.penzioncentrum.cz. Renovated central townhouse with bright, comfortably furnished rooms. Singles 900Kč, doubles 1200Kč.

U Tří sedláků Hroznová 488 ⓣ387 222 303, ⓦwww.penzionutrisedlaku.cz. Pleasant rooms over a central local pub. The highlight is home-made cake for breakfast around the bar. Breakfast 80Kč. Singles 800Kč, doubles 1200Kč.

Ubytovna u nádraží Dvořákova 14 ⓣ387 203 597, ⓦwww.ubytovna.vors.cz. Cheap, recently refurbished rooms in a dour housing block 10 minutes' walk from the centre. Singles 420Kč, doubles 460Kč.

Eating and drinking

Café au Chat Noir Náměstí Přemysla Otakara II. 21. Relaxed, Parisian-style café on the main square. Mon–Fri 9am–10pm, Sat 10am–10pm, Sun 2–10pm.

Hladový vokno Kněžská 10. When your budget's tight and your belt's loose head to *Hladový vokno* (Hungry Window) for a hefty kebab or burger, 29–62Kč. Mon–Thurs 9am–11pm, Fri–Sat 9am–midnight, Sun 2–10pm.

Indická Resaurace Chelčického 10. Climb a poky private staircase to find this well-loved Indian restaurant, known for warm service and lovingly cooked food. Lunch specials 75–85Kč, mains 75–250Kč. Mon–Sat 11am–11pm.

Masné Krámy Krajinská 13. Locals call it "the beer church" – an arched lofty Renaissance meat-market devoted to local beer. Don't miss the excellent unfiltered yeast beer (*kroužkovaný ležák*). Mon–Sat 10.30am–11pm, Sun 10.30am–9pm.

Oaza Stromovka 8. *Oaza* looks like the kind of parkside shack that doles out orange sausages and warm beer, but its tender char-grilled meat, delicate salads and boozy fruit fools make it one of the most popular restaurants in town. Mains 115–455Kč. Closed Oct–April.

Singer Pub Česká 55. Noisy, affable local frequented by Erasmus students. Mon–Thurs 11am–midnight, Fri 6pm–3am, Sat 6pm–3am, Sun 6pm–midnight.

Moving on

Train Brno (every 2–3hr; 4hr 27min); Český Krumlov (8 daily; 50min); Plzeň (every 2hr; 1hr 57min).

Bus Brno (5 daily; 4hr 5min); Český Krumlov (approx every 30min; 35–45min).

ČESKÝ KRUMLOV

Tiny, red-roofed **ČESKÝ KRUMLOV** nestles between two bends in the Vltava River like a patch of wild strawberries. In summer, tour buses unload crowds of visitors at the city gates at noon and pick them up in the afternoon, creating a five-hour stampede through the narrow streets. The only solution is to stay overnight; there's too much to see in a day anyway. The town's been a UNESCO World Heritage Site since 1992.

What to see and do

The twisting River Vltava divides the town into two: circular Staré Město on the right bank and the Latrán quarter on the left.

Krumlov Chateau

Krumlov Chateau (May, Sept & Oct 9am–5pm; June–Aug 9am–6pm, closed Mon) rises above the Latrán quarter. You can stroll through the castle's grounds and main courtyards day or night, but to go inside you'll have to pay for one of the three guided tours (180–380Kč). Climb the tower for beautiful views and explore the chateau's geometrical gardens and two theatres, the exquisite Rococo Chateau Theatre, and the cunning Communist Revolving Theatre, which spins on a mechanical axis.

The Eggenberg Brewery

A world away from the gleaming, modern breweries at Plzeň and České Budějovice is the **Eggenberg**, which opened in 1630. Tours cost from 100Kč (daily 11am–4pm; ⓣ380 711 225, ⓦwww.eggenberg.cz). The restaurant serves good traditional food.

Egon Schiele Art Centrum

Just off the main square, on Široká, is the wonderful **Egon Schiele Art Centrum** (daily 10am–6pm; 120Kč; ⓣ380 704 011; ⓦwww.schieleartcentrum.cz), devoted to the eponymous Austrian painter, who moved here in 1911 and caused outrage by painting nude teenagers and putting his feet on café tables. There are also temporary exhibitions of contemporary art and design.

Arrival and information

Bus and train The bus station is a 5min walk northeast of the inner town; the train station is 1km from the centre. There are shuttle-buses from Salzburg, Vienna, Linz and Prague. If you come by train you will have to change at České Budějovice.
Tourist office Náměstí Svornosti 2 (daily: April, May & Oct 9am–6pm; June & Sept 9am–7pm; July & Aug 9am–8pm; Nov–March 9am–5pm; ⓣ380 704 622, ⓦwww.ckrumlov.cz). Internet access (5Kč/5min).

Accommodation

Hostel Merlin Kájovská 59 ⓣ606 256 145, ⓦwww.hostelmerlin.cz. Clean, cheap rooms overlooking the river with shared bathrooms and a kitchen. 250Kč/person in a dorm or double.
Hostel 99 Věžní 99 ⓣ775 276 253, ⓦwww.hostel99.cz. A kitchen, table tennis, movies, informative staff, a bar and (overpriced) restaurant. Come summer the dorms resemble high school pyjama parties. The rafting pub crawl is famous. Dorms 300Kč, doubles 700–900Kč.
Krumlov House Hostel Rooseveltova 68 ⓣ380 711 935, ⓦwww.krumlovhostel.com. A renovated Renaissance bakery as warm and cheering as fresh bread. There are private rooms and dorms, a common room, large kitchen, wi-fi and movies. Dorms 300Kč in high season, doubles 400Kč.
U Čerta a Káči Dlouhá 100 ⓣ777 615 903, ⓦwww.certakaca.cz. This central *pension* looks like a dolls' house, with low wooden beams, heart-print curtains and a dwarf-sized kitchen. Breakfast in bed 150Kč. Doubles 800–1300Kč.
Vodácký kemp Nové Spolí ⓣ777 640 946, ⓦwww.kempkrumlov.cz. Basic campsite in a picturesque spot by the river, 2km from the town, reachable by the #3 bus from the train or bus station. 45Kč/person and tent.

Eating and drinking

Antre Horní 2. Dapper 30s cafe and music club in the municipal theatre. Breakfast, snacks and cakes, cocktails, wine, beer and live jazz. Daily 10am–midnight.

Egon Schiele Café Široká 71. A snug sitting-room of a gallery café which locals say serves the best coffee in Krumlov. There's chess, board games, books and wi-fi. The cheesecake (*tvarohový dort*) is a sad dieter's happy dream. Daily 10am–6pm.

Na Louži Kájovská 66. The best Czech cooking in town. Come at lunchtime, as the chef only cooks once a day and popular dishes run out. Don't miss the fruit dumplings (*ovocné knedlíky*), pastry-and-fruit parcels slippery with melted butter and sprinkled with hard sweet cheese and brown sugar. Mains 68–90Kč. Daily 10am–11pm.

Pizzeria Nonna Gina Klášterní 52. Authentic, Italian family-owned restaurant; even the olive oil comes from the family's vineyard in Italy. Mains 90–160Kč. Daily 10am–6pm.

U dwau Maryí/ At the Two Marys Parkán 104. Ye olde Bohemian food as it never was, but who's complaining? Gruel, rabbit, mead and millet on a riverside terrace. Mains 125–160Kč. Daily 11am–11pm.

Entertainment

Cikánská Jizba Dlouhá 31. *Cikánská Jizba* (Gypsy Bar) is a standard Czech pub every night except Fridays, when talented local Roma musicians play. Mon–Thurs 5pm–midnight, Fri 1pm–1am, Sun noon–1am.

Expedicion Soukenická 33 ⓦwww.expedicion.cz. Fishing, horseriding, bike riding, paintballing, dog-sledding, mountain climbing, skijoring, canoeing and expeditions involving combinations of the above. Paintballing 590Kč/person/match, fishing 790Kč/5hr, horseriding 300Kč/hr.

Five Petalled Rose Festival Every June at the solstice. Medieval fair with jousting, fencing and theatre in the park.

International Music Festival Annually July–Aug Large multi-genre music festival which usually attracts a few big names.

Vltava Sport Service Hradební 60. Bikes, scooters, canoes and rafts for rent. Bikes 320Kč/day, kayaks 400Kč/4hr trip.

Moving on

Train České Budějovice (8 daily; 50 min); Prague (8 daily, change at České Budějovice; 3hr 40min), Plzeň (every 2hr, change at České Budějovice; 2hr 57 min).

Bus České Budějovice (3 hourly; 50min); Prague (14 daily; 2hr 55min (Student Agency bus) or 3hr 30min (local bus, involves 1 change)).

PLZEŇ

Tough, industrial **PLZEŇ** (Pilsen) was built on beer and bombs. Founded in 1292, the city swelled in the nineteenth century when the Industrial Revolution brought an ironworks and an armaments factory, and diversified to cars and trams under Communism. Most tourists come to pay their respects to Plzeň's beloved son, Pilsner Urquell. The town's diverse architecture and unpretentious vigour are strong secondary attractions.

What to see and do

The main square, náměstí Republiky is dominated by the Gothic **cathedral** of **sv Bartoloměj**, with the tallest spire in the country (103m). Opposite is the Italianate town hall, built in the Renaissance but sgraffitoed last century. Nearby Velká **synagogue** (April–Sept Mon–Fri & Sun 10am–6pm; Oct Mon–Fri & Sun 10am–5pm; Nov Mon–Fri 10am–4pm, Sun 10am–5pm; 50Kč adults, 35Kč students), the third largest in the world, was once the heart of the town's large Jewish community, decimated by the Holocaust, and now houses exhibitions.

Pilsner Urquell and Brewery Museums

The star attraction in Plzeň is 12° Plzeňský Prazdroj, better known as **Pilsner Urquell** (Original Pilsner; English guided tours daily 10.45am, 12.45pm, 2.15pm or 4.15pm; 70–200Kč). **Pivovarské Brewery Museum**, in the original brewery, provides some history and a film on brewing (daily: April–Dec 10am–6pm; Jan–March 10am–5pm; brewery only 120Kč, museum only 70Kč, combined ticket 200Kč; ⓣ222 710 159, ⓦwww.prazdroj.cz/en).

Plzeň's Historical Underground

While you are at the Brewery Museum don't miss **Plzeň's Historical Underground** (Plzeňské historické podzemí;

daily 10am–6pm; English tour 90Kč, students 60Kč; ⓣ380 704 011, ⓦwww.plzenskepodzemi.cz), 500m of tunnels under the town. The tunnels were once part of an underground network of passages that rivalled the streets above.

Arrival and information

Train and bus You can get to Plzeň from Prague in 1hr 30min by either bus or train (both offering direct service). The main train station (Hlavní nádraží), is just east of the city centre. The bus terminal is on the west side of town. From both, the city centre is only a 10-minute walk.

Tourist office Náměsti Republiky 41 (daily: April–Sept 9am–7pm; Oct–March 9am–6pm; ⓣ378 035 330, ⓦwww.plzen.eu).

Accommodation

Euro Hostel Na Roudné 13 ⓣ377 259 926, ⓦwww.eurohostel.cz. No-frills dorms and doubles ten minutes' walk from the centre. Opt out of breakfast, which is overpriced. Dorms 350Kč, doubles 800Kč.

Pension City Sady 5 května 52 ⓣ377 326 069, ⓦwww.pensioncityplzen.cz. Slightly tired rooms in a convenient location by the river. Breakfast included. Doubles 1450Kč.

Pension V Solní Solní 8 ⓣ377 236 652, ⓦwww.volny.cz/pensolni. Cosy three-room *pension* off the main square. Book in advance. Breakfast included. Doubles 1200Kč.

Pension Stará Plzeň Na Roudné 12 ⓣ 377 259 901, ⓦwww.pension-sp.cz. Rustic house and stables converted into a handsome old-fashioned *pension*. Doubles 800–1200Kč.

Eating and drinking

Anděl Vegetarian Restaurant Bezručova 5–7. Central, good-value vegetarian restaurant open till midnight. Mains 55–120Kč. Mon–Fri 11am–10pm, Sat & Sun noon–10pm.

CrossCafe Anglické nábřeží 1. Fantastic views at this American-style coffee shop at the top of Plzeň's only skyscraper. Mon–Fri 7.30am–9pm, Sat & Sun 11am–9pm.

Francis Náměstí Republiky 3. 50s rock-playing student bar-café with a wood-burning stove for winter, a courtyard for summer, sausages for the hungry and books for the antisocial. Daily 3–10pm.

Měšťanská Beseda Kavárna Kopeckého sady 13. Opulent Art Nouveau interior, beer on tap, old men grimacing over chessboards and delectable honey chocolates (*medový koule*) make this the place for a rainy afternoon. Mon–Fri 9am–10pm, Sat Sun11am–10pm.

Na Parkánu Veleslavínova 4. It's the Brewery Museum pub, but lusty portions, unfiltered beer and decent prices make it popular with locals. Cheap lunch menu 11am–1pm. Mains 75–250Kč. Mon–Wed 11am–11pm, Thurs 11am–midnight, Fri–Sat 11am–1am, Fri 11am–10pm.

Moving on

Train České Budějovice (every 2hr; 1hr 56min); Prague (hourly; 2hr).

Bus Karlovy Vary (8–9 daily; 1hr 30min–1hr 50min); Prague (2 hourly; 1hr–1hr 45min).

KARLOVY VARY

Karlovy Vary residents have a favourite joke. Russian President Medvedev says to Czech President Klaus, "If you get any closer to the USA I'll bomb Prague". President Klaus says, "If you bomb Prague I'll bomb Karlovy Vary". The freshly painted spa town, awash with fur caps and poodles in Dior handbags, feels decidedly un-Czech, largely due to its popularity with Russia's nouveau riche, partly because tourists outnumber locals. Peter the Great, Goethe and Beethoven all visited the town, and the old-style pleasures of spa life – hiking in the forest, bathing in hot spring water, and eating sweet nut wafers (*oplatky*) to chase away the taste of the water – are still the best.

What to see and do

Walking into town with Communist eyesore *Thermal Hotel* on your right, you'll pass a series of slender white colonnades built over the springs, which can be sampled for free. The grandest is **Mill Colonnade** (Mlýnská kolonáda), containing five springs. Further up Lázeňská street are **Market Colonnade** (Tržní kolonáda), a delicate wooden construct, and the Communist-era **Hot Spring Colonnade** (Vřídelní kolonáda), a spring so hot and powerful that spa guests breathe the vapours instead of drinking the water.

Hiking

The cool pine forests surrounding Karlovy Vary are perfect for **hiking**, and there are dozens of well-marked trails. One popular route goes from *Grand Hotel Pupp* to a viewing tower and hilltop restaurant *Diana*, 1.5 km away. If you don't want to walk you can ride the **funicular** (Feb–May & Sept–Dec 9am–6pm; June–Aug 9am–7pm; 60Kč return).

Moser glassworks and museum

Luxury glass manufacturer **Moser** lies in the town's suburbs. You can tour the glassworks and glass museum (Kpt Jaroše 46; tours every 30min; daily 9am–2.30pm; closed July 23 to Aug 7 (dates may change); 180Kč, students 100Kč; ⓣ353 226 252, ⓦwww.moser-glass.com). Take bus #22 or #1 from Tržnice to the Moser stop.

Spa treatments

Sampling the waters is free, but you'll need to buy a drinking cup from a kiosk, or bring a plastic bottle. To avoid the bitter taste, wallow in the waters instead; the cheapest option is *Hotel Thermal*'s springwater hilltop pool (daily 8am–9pm, last entrance 7.45pm; 100Kč for 90min 80Kč with ISIC). Follow the signs reading "bazén" (pool). If you'd prefer to be coated in mud or steamed in brine try the modern spa centre at *Carlsburg Plaza* hotel (Mariánskolázeňská 23; Mon–Fri 7.30am–7.30pm, Sat & Sun 8.30am–7.30pm; ⓦwww.carlsbad-plaza.com).

Arrival and information

Train and bus Trains from Prague arrive at Horní station, to the north of town. Trains from Mariánské Lázně arrive at Dolní station, close to the main bus station and town centre. Buses run to the spa from both stations. If you're bussing from Prague, alight one stop early at Tržnice, right in the centre. There's a Student Agency bus from Prague airport or Florenc (7 daily; 1hr 45min; ⓣ800 100 300, ⓦwww.studentagencybus.com).

Tourist office At Dolní station, Západní 2a (Mon–Fri 8am–6pm, Sat & Sun 10am–5pm (break 11.15–11.45am); ⓣ353 232 838, ⓦwww.karlovy-vary.cz). There's also tourist information at Husovo náměstí 2 and *Thermal Hotel*.

Language The town is orientated to Russian tourists, so finding English speakers is harder than elsewhere; bring your phrasebook.

INTERNATIONAL FILM FESTIVAL

The **Karlovy Vary Film Festival** (ⓦwww.kviff.com) comes to town every July, bringing a smattering of A-listers and a carnival atmosphere. Anyone can buy tickets (65Kč) or day passes (200Kč/day) to the films, which range from Hollywood blockbusters to low-budget European indies. The town gets crowded so book accommodation and travel in advance.

Accommodation

Avoid the hotels that cluster around the spas, they're designed and priced for Russian oligarchs. Guesthouses and B&Bs are located around the bus and train stations. Private rooms are good value and can be booked through the tourist office.

Březový Háj Campsite ⓣ353 222 665, ⓦwww.brezovy-haj.cz. Located on a riverbank, *Březový*, 3km from the centre, has tennis courts, a pool and bungalows. Catch the Březova bus from Tržiště bus station. Bed in bungalow 190Kč, camping 100Kč/person and tent.

Chebský Dvůr/ Egerlander Hof Tržiště 39 ⓣ353 229 332, ⓦwww.egerlanderhof.eu. Clean, basic rooms above a pub in the heart of the spa district. Singles 650Kč, doubles 1000Kč.

Kavalerie T.G. Masaryka, 43 ⓣ353 229 613, ⓦwww.kavalerie.cz. On the main street connecting the bus station and the centre, *Kavalerie* is a B&B over a café with homey rooms. There are two tiers, economy and standard (the difference is mostly in size) plus apartments. For two people with breakfast, 1170Kč for economy, 1320Kč for standard.

Maltézský Kříž Stará Louka 50 ⓣ353 169 011, ⓦwww.maltezskykriz.cz. If you have a little more to spend, this central boutique hotel offers better quality at a lower price than any other central hotel. It's becoming popular so book in advance. Includes breakfast in high season. Singles 1650Kč, doubles 2800Kč.

Eating and drinking

To avoid the overpriced restaurants and pubs, picnicking is the cheapest eating option; there are supermarkets and bakeries on T.G. Masaryka.

Foopa Jaltská 7. The biggest cocktail menu in town at this central bar which moonlights as a club on Friday and Saturday nights.

Kavárna Čas T.G. Masaryka 3. Quiet little cinema coffee shop filled with the scent of popcorn and sweets, free of tour groups, serving excellent Italian espresso.

Kus-Kus Stará Louka 10. Snug cellar café serving organic, vegetarian and vegan sandwiches, salads, cakes and snacks, and a daily 89Kč lunch menu, eat-in or takeaway. Mon 8am–5pm, Tues–Fri 7am–5pm.

Rad's Baguettes Zeyerova 2. The only inexpensive sandwich shop in the centre, with sandwiches, panini and baguettes. Up to 32Kč. Mon–Fri 7am–6pm, Sat 7am–noon.

Tandoor I.P. Pavlova 25. It's hard to find, stashed down a private driveway, but the pleasant food, friendly service and decent prices are worth the effort. Alcohol is served, Ling beer on tap. Mon–Sat noon–10pm, Sun noon–6pm.

U Švejka Stará Louka 10. The least overpriced of the central restaurants. High prices are balanced by large portions. Daily 11am–11pm.

Moving on

Train Plzeň (every 1–2hr; 2hr 52 min, with a change at Mariánské Lázně; 3hr 26 min, direct); Prague (every 2hr; 3hr 20 min).

Bus Plzeň (8–9 daily; 1hr 30min–1hr 50min); Prague (hourly; 1hr 30min– 2hr 10min).

Moravia

Eastern **Moravia** (Morava), is poorer and more provincial than Bohemia, but warmer and more relaxed. It shares borders with Poland to the north, and Slovakia and Austria to the south. In the southeast of Moravia is bustling, industrial **Brno**, with red-brick houses and wide boulevards, and travelling south you'll reach **Olomouc**, an ancient city bursting with youthful energy.

BURČÁK

September ushers in **vinobraní**, a boisterous festival marking the wine harvest. Revellers dance, drink and feast in an event that dates back to the Middle Ages, and the star of the show is **burčák**, white wine fresh from the press. Sweet and bubbly, it's only part fermented so it tastes as innocent as peach juice, but it's up to 8 percent alcohol. It's only available from the end of August to the end of November at festivals, wine bars and markets. There are festivals all over the country (see box, 301), though the best are in wine country, Moravia. For more information, check at Ⓦwww.wineofczechrepublic.cz.

BRNO

BRNO evolved into the handsome, red-brick city of today in the nineteenth century, when it was a major textile producer and known as "rakouský Manchestr" (Austrian Manchester). The capital of Moravia, Brno's vital energy has produced 11 universities, a powerful economy and a number of famous Czechs, including inventor of genetics Gregor Mendel, composer Leoš Janáček and novelist Milan Kundera.

What to see and do

Triangular **Svobody Square** sits funnel-like on the high street, Masarykova. To the right is Zelný trh, the old medieval Cabbage Market, still bustling with vegetable traders hawking onions and daffodils. **Špilberk Castle**, which houses historical exhibitions, dominates the skyline to the west, in a

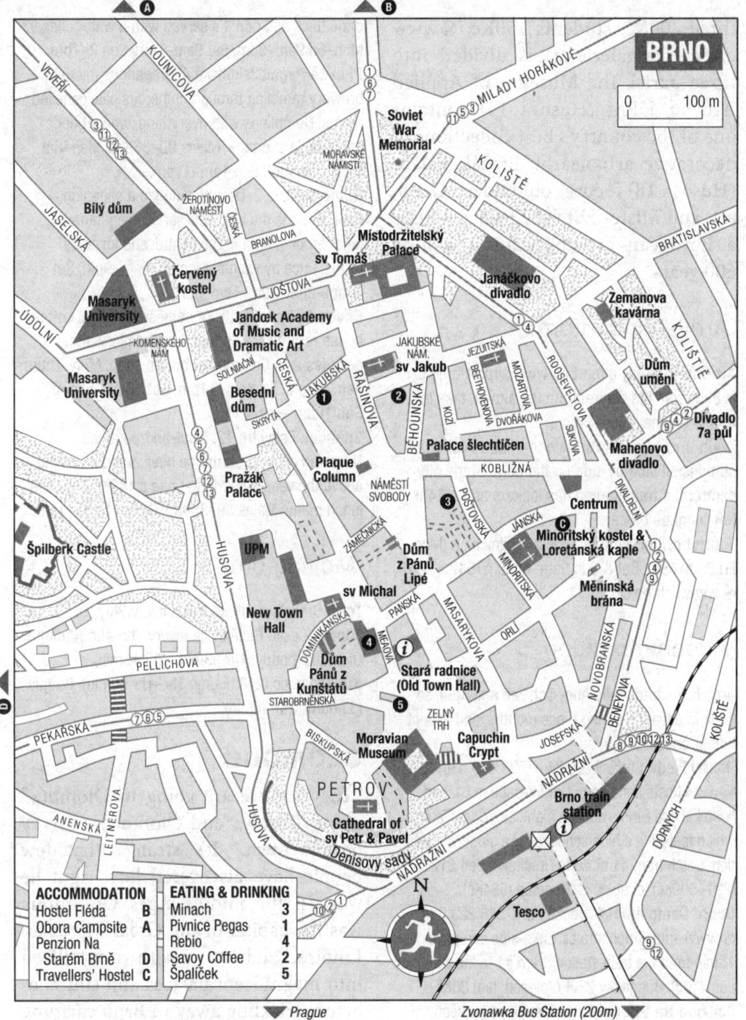

standoff with the hilltop **Cathedral of St Peter and St Paul** to the south.

Capuchin crypt

Below the Cabbage Market is the Capuchin monastery, with its popular crypt (May–Sept Mon–Sat 9am–noon & 1–4.30pm; Oct to mid-Dec closed Mon; closed mid-Dec to mid-Feb), which houses a charming collection of mummified monks.

The Old Town Hall

On Stará Radnice is the **Old Town Hall,** packed with strange artefacts clothed in fantastical legends. The tower (April–Sept daily 9am–5pm; 20Kč) offers panoramic views of Brno.

Moravian Gallery

The second largest art museum in the country, the **Moravian Gallery** (Wed–Sun 10am–6/7pm; entrance to all three 300Kč, students 150Kč; Ⓦwww.moravska-galerie.cz) is divided into three parts: The Museum of Applied Arts or UPM (Husova 14) contains one of the country's best collections of decorative art; nearby Pražák Palace (Husova 18) focuses on modern Czech art; and Místodržitelský Palace houses a European art collection spanning 600 years.

Arrival and information

Air Brno's Tuřany airport (Ⓦwww.airport-brno.cz) is 8km from the centre; from the airport, take bus #76 to the main bus station.
Train and bus Brno's main train and bus stations sit side by side on the edge of the city centre; the train station has lockers and a 24hr left-luggage office.
Tourist office Old Town Hall at Radnická 8 (Mon–Fri 8am–6pm, Sat & Sun 9am–6pm; Ⓣ542 427 15, Ⓦwww.ticbrno.cz).

Accommodation

Brno hosts trade fairs Aug–Oct, Feb and April, so book in advance during those months, and expect higher prices.
Hostel Fléda Štefánikova 24 Ⓣ533 433 638, Ⓦwww.hostelfleda.com. Graffiti-daubed 61-bed hostel above Brno's coolest nightclub, *Club Fléda,* which feels like a high school after a student revolution. Catch tram #1 or #6 to Hrnčířská. Bed €12–20 (291–509Kč), doubles €22/person (534Kč).
Obora Campsite Rakovecká 72 Ⓣ546 223 334, Ⓦwww.autocampobora.cz. Lake-side campsite 15min from the train station (tram #1 to the zoo, then bus #103). Bungalow 230Kč/person, tent 80Kč.
Penzion Na Starém Brně Mendlovo náměsti 1a Ⓣ543 247 872, Ⓦwww.pension-brno.com. Genteel B&B in a former monastery. Go through Vankovka shopping centre from the train and bus stations and take tram #1 to Mendlovo náměsti. Doubles 1150Kč.
Travellers' Hostel Jánská 22 Ⓣ542 213 573, Ⓦwww.travellers.cz. Adequate rooms in university buildings from July 1 to Aug 28. Breakfast included. Dorms 290Kč.

Eating and drinking

Minach Pasáž Alfa, Poštovská 6e. Coffee with a punch, heavyweight brownies and hot chocolate so dark, thick and rich it's served with a water chaser. Mon–Fri 9am–9pm, Sat 9am–7pm, Sun 2–7pm.
Pivnice Pegas Jakubská 4. Gregarious micro-brewery rambling through numerous oak-panelled rooms. Dumplings with everything, wheat beer and a table shortage. Mains 90–365Kč. Mon–Sat 9am–midnight, Sun 1am–11pm.
Rebio Mečová 2. Despite being in a shopping mall, *Rebio* is the best self-service vegetarian diner around, right in the centre, and loved by locals. Price by weight. Mon–Fri 9am–9pm, Sat 11am–9pm, Sun 11am–8pm.
Savoy Coffee Jakubské náměsti. 1. Regal coffee-house returned to its functionalist glory after decades as a Communist button shop. Mon–Thurs 8am–10pm, Fri 8am–11pm, Sat 10am–11pm, Sun 10am–8pm.
Špalíček Zelný trh 12. Meat-and-potatoes Moravian cuisine, Starobrno beer, outdoor seating above the vegetable market and a 149Kč 3-course lunch menu. Mains 89–300Kč. Daily 11am–11pm.

Moving on

Train Bratislava (direct trains every 2hr; 1hr 30min); České Budějovice (every 2hr; 4hr 30min); Olomouc (hourly; 1hr 33min– 2hr 15min).
Bus Olomouc (2–3 hourly; 1hr–1hr 50min); Prague (3 hourly; 2hr 30min).

OLOMOUC

"They say we are going to Olomutz," wrote Tolstoy, "and Olomutz is a very decent town." It's strange that few people have discovered how right he was. In the middle Ages **Oloumouc** was the capital of the Great Moravian Empire, and its wealth crystallized into magnificent palaces and churches before trickling away to Brno carrying a wave of industrial sprawl. The unspoilt city centre is home to 25,000 students, who ensure a rich supply of lively bars, cafés and clubs.

What to see and do

The old town clusters around two adjacent squares, **Horní** (upper) and **Dolní** (lower). The town hall on Horní has an astronomical clock, exuberant Communist kitsch covered with gesticulating blonde peasants. Nearby is the polygonal Holy Trinity Column, protected by UNESCO, the largest plague column in the country.

Cathedral of sv Václav and Přemysl Palace

Dwarfing tiny Václavské square is the **Cathedral of sv Václav,** originally a Romanesque basilica, which contains a **crypt** (Tues & Thurs–Sat 9am–5pm, Wed 9am–4pm, Sun 11am–5pm) packed with reliquaries. Next door is the **Archdiocesan Museum** (in Přemysl Palace; Tues–Sun 10am–6pm; 50Kč, 25Kč with ISIC), showcasing more than a thousand years of local history and a mind-blowing collection of church bling. The highlight is a gold-plated carriage covered with romping cherubs.

Olomouc Museum of Art

The ticket to the Archdiocesan Museum also allows entry to the **Olomouc Museum of Art** on Denisova (same opening hours), an enjoyable stroll through twentieth-century Czech art.

Arrival and information

Train station 1.5km east of the centre; catch tram #2, #4 or #6.
Bus station 3km east; catch tram #4.
Tourist office Town Hall, Horní náměsti (daily 9am–7pm; ⓣ585 513 385, ⓦwww.olomouc-tourism.cz).

Accommodation

Arigone Univerzitní 20 ⓣ585 232 350, ⓦwww.arigone.cz. Excellent boutique hotel in a delightful old house in the heart of the historical centre. Singles 1990Kč, doubles 2290Kč including breakfast.
Pension Moravia Dvořákova 37 ⓣ603 784 188, ⓦwww.pension-moravia.com. Large suburban house converted into a welcoming B&B, 10 minutes from the centre. Singles 600Kč, doubles 800Kč.
Pension U Jakuba 8.května 9 ⓣ585 209 995, ⓦwww.ujakuba.cz. Affordable central hotel so hygenic it must be wrapped in plastic. Doubles 1000Kč, 4-bed apartments 2000Kč.
Poets' Corner Hostel Sokolská 1 ⓣ777 570 730, ⓦwww.hostelolomouc.com. Friendly, laidback central hostel in two brightly painted '30s flats, run by lifelong travellers. 8-bed dorms, double and triple rooms, wi-fi, two kitchens and self-catering facilities, bikes for rent, laundry services, common room, informative staff. Dorms 300–350Kč, doubles 900Kč.

Eating and drinking

Cafés and restaurants

Café 87 Denisova 47. Fresh sandwiches, good coffee, free wi-fi, ideal street-gazing and famous chocolate pie. Mon–Fri 7.30am–9pm, Sat & Sun 8am–9pm.
Fontana Smetanovy sady, Rudolfova alej. Ornate nineteenth century café and restaurant in a leafy central park with an affordable Czech menu. Mains 75–155Kč. Daily 10am–10pm.
Nepálská restaurace Mlýnská 4. Nepalese restaurant with an excellent all-you-can-eat lunchtime

FESTIVAL FRENZY

With its long-held reputation as a centre of culture and the arts, Olomouc is a natural home for festivals. April brings **Academia Film** (ⓦwww.afo.cz), screening international science documentaries, the **Religious Music Festival** and flower festival **Flora Olomouc** (ⓦwww.flora-ol.cz). In May is the **Dvořák Festival**; actually a celebration of all the major Czech composers. In May/June comes **Beerfest** (ⓦwww.beerfest.cz), the biggest beer festival in the country, an enjoyable combination of beer, rock music and gastronomy. The **Olomouc City Festival** (ⓦwww.olomouc.eu) also in June, offers plays, concerts, art exhibitions and a Great Whipped Cream Battle. In the first week of July there's **Zahrada**, the country's biggest folk and world music festival, and in September the **Organ Music Festival**. There are also 8 1-day jazz festivals throughout the year (ⓦwww.jazzclub.olomouc.com).

buffet, with an Irish pub on the same premises. Recommended for vegetarians suffering from fried cheese fatigue. Buffet 100Kč. Mon–Sat 11am–1am.

Moritz Nešverova 2. The finest micro-brewery in Olomouc, serving light, delicate lager and hearty Moravian cuisine. There's a beer garden in the summer with live music. Try the open sandwiches with bitter *tvarůžky* cheese marinated in beer, or the roast duck with cabbage and dumplings. Mains 42–160Kč. Daily 11am–11pm.

Sant' Angelo Nešverova 2. This smart non-smoking cafe has two claims to fame – the best breakfast and the best hot chocolate in town. Mon–Fri 7.30am–9pm, Sat Sun 8am–9pm.

Bars and clubs

15Minut Komenského 31. A few steps away from university dorms and filled with wasted, wildly enthusiastic students every weekend. Their riotous two-day Erasmus Party in September is infamous. Fri–Sat 5pm–4am.

Arktik Music Club Denisova 6. Is it a club, a cinema or a cocktail bar? Drink a few tequila slammers, eat a box of popcorn, have a dance and puzzle it out.

The Black Stuff Irish Pub 1. máje19. Toy-town railway tunnel meets hobbit drinking hole, popular with students. Seven beers on tap. Mon–Thurs 4pm–2am, Fri 4pm–3am, Sat 5pm–3am, Sun 5–11pm.

Metro Chill Out Club Subterranean mural-daubed electro bar with DJs on Friday and Saturday nights. Mon–Thurs 4am–4pm, Fri 4pm–late, Sat 8pm–late.

Vertigo Klub Univerzitní 6. Named after Hitchcock's dreamy noir masterpiece, this atmospheric underground student bar, filled with loquacious philosophy students and a smell that isn't quite tobacco, is open until 2am every night. Mon–Thurs from 7pm, Fri–Sun from 4pm.

Moving on

Train Brno (5 daily; 1hr 30min–2 hr 20 min); Prague (hourly; 2hr 10min; slower trains between).
Bus Brno (hourly; approx 1hr 30min).

Denmark

HIGHLIGHTS ✪

SKAGEN: sample fantastic seafood and see world-class art at this lovely seaside resort

ÅRHUS NIGHTLIFE: Denmark's second city buzzes with trendy riverside bars and live music

TIVOLI, COPENHAGEN: a timeless pleasure park with nightly fireworks

VIKING SHIP MUSEUM,ROSKILDE: take to the seas on board a Viking longboat

ODENSE: quaint, cobbled and home to Denmark's biggest literary export – Hans Christian Andersen

ROUGH COSTS

DAILY BUDGET Basic €50 /occasional treat €80

DRINK Carlsberg (pint) €4.50

FOOD *Pølser* (Danish hot dog) €3.35

HOSTEL/BUDGET HOTEL €23.50/€65

TRAVEL Copenhagen–Århus Train/Bus €47/€39

FACT FILE

POPULATION 5.3 million

AREA 43,094 sq km

LANGUAGE Danish

CURRENCY Danish krone (kr)

CAPITAL Copenhagen (population: 1.2 million)

INTERNATIONAL PHONE CODE: ⓣ45

Introduction

Butter, bacon, Carlsberg, some mean cheeses and the continent's greatest range of pastries: little wonder Denmark is internationally recognized for churning out some phenomenal food and drink; with more Michelin-starred restaurants than the rest of Scandinavia combined, it is renowned for fine dining too. Anyone would be forgiven for thinking the Danes might be content to sit feasting in their trendy restaurants or traditional old bodegas but they're a health-conscious people: a bunch will have jogged past your table before you can say smørrebrød and cycling is inherent – Denmark has one of the world's most integrated cycle networks. With agriculture its primary industry, technological innovation is a big part of the economy and of daily life: fair enough from the country that invented Lego and leads the world's alternative energy production. Expect impeccable design at every turn, and an ultra-efficient transport infrastructure – Denmark definitely is one of Europe's most enjoyable countries to navigate.

Wedged between mainland Europe and the rest of Scandinavia, Denmark has preserved a distinct national identity, exemplified by the universally cherished royal family and the reluctance to fully integrate with the EU (the Danish rejection of the euro was more about sovereignty than economics). There's also a sense of a small country that has long punched above its weight: it once controlled much of northern Europe and still maintains close ties with Greenland, its former colony.

Geographically, three main landmasses make up the country – the islands of Zealand and Funen and the peninsula of Jutland, which extends northwards from Germany. Most visitors make for **Zealand** (Sjælland), and, more specifically, **Copenhagen**, an exciting focal point with a beautiful old centre, a good array of museums and a boisterous nightlife. **Funen** (Fyn) has only one real urban draw, **Odense**, once home to Hans Christian Andersen; otherwise, it's renowned for cute villages and sandy beaches. **Jutland** (Jylland) has, as well as scenery alternating between lonely beaches, gentle hills and heathland, two of the liveliest Danish cities in **Århus** and **Aalborg**.

CHRONOLOGY

400 BC "Tollund Man", a body found preserved in a bog in 1950, provides evidence of habitation during the Iron Age.

500 AD First mention of the "Dani" tribe is made by foreign sources.

695 First Christian mission to Denmark.

825 First Danish coinage introduced.

1397 The Union of Kalmar unites Denmark, Sweden and Norway under a single Danish monarch.

1536 Reformation leads to the establishment of the Danish Lutheran Church.

1629 Sweden heavily defeats Charles IV's Denmark in the Thirty Years' War, resulting in Danish territorial losses.

1814 Denmark cedes Norway to Sweden.

1836 Hans Christian Andersen writes "The Little Mermaid".

1849 Constitutional monarchy established.

1864 Defeat by Prussia results in the loss of much territory.

1914 Neutrality is adopted during World War I.

1918 The vote is granted to all Danes.

1934 Children's playtime is transformed by the invention of Lego by Ole Kirk Christiansen.

1940 Nazi invasion meets minimal resistance.

1945 Denmark is liberated by Allied forces.
1979 Greenland is given greater autonomy by the Danish.
1989 First European country to legalize same-sex marriages.
1991 Danish police fire on protestors demonstrating against the country's acceptance of the Maastricht Treaty.
1992 Denmark wins European Football Championships
2004 Crown Prince Frederick marries Australian Mary Donaldson in a lavish ceremony.
2006 Cartoon depictions of the Prophet Mohammed in Danish newspapers spark mass protests in the Muslim world.

ARRIVAL

Visitors usually arrive in Copenhagen, either flying in to gleaming **Kastrup Airport** or pulling in to the city's **Central Station**, connected with the European rail network via Germany and, across the spectacular Øresund bridge, to Sweden. Most international buses also arrive at Central Station. In addition, the **regional airports** at Aalborg, Århus and Billund handle a growing number of budget flights, mostly operated by Ryanair. There are regular **ferry services** to and from the UK (via Esbjerg), to Sweden/Norway (via Frederikshavn or Hirtshals) and to the Faroe Islands/Iceland (via Hirtshals).

GETTING AROUND

Denmark has a swift, easy-to-use public transport system. Danish State Railways (Danske Statsbaner or DSB; Ⓦwww.dsb.dk) runs an exhaustive and reliable **rail** network supplemented by a few privately owned rail lines. Services range from the large inter-city expresses *(lyntog)* to smaller local trains *(regionaltog)*. InterRail/Eurail passes are valid on all DSB trains, with reduced rates on most privately owned lines. Ticket prices are calculated according to a country-wide zonal system and travel by local transport within the zone of departure and arrival is included in the price.

The **bus** network is also extensive, and often supplements the train timetable, although prices don't work out much cheaper than trains. Some are operated privately and some by DSB itself; InterRail and Eurail passes are not valid. DSB **timetables** or *Køreplan* detail train, bus and ferry services, including the S-train and metro systems in Copenhagen. The only buses not included are those of the few private companies: these are slower but generally cheaper; details can be found at train and bus stations.

All the Danish islands are linked by **ferries** or bridges. Where applicable, train and bus fares include the cost of crossings (although with ferries you can also pay at the terminal and walk on). Routes and prices are covered on the very useful HI map.

Cycling is the best way to appreciate Denmark's flat landscape (maps and information at ⓦwww.dcf.dk). Cycle paths proliferate, country roads have sparse traffic and all large towns have cycle tracks. Bikes can be rented at hostels, tourist offices and some train stations, as well as from bike rental shops (70–90kr/day, 350–400kr/week; 200–500kr deposit). All trains and most long-distance buses accept bikes, but you'll have to pay according to the zonal system used to calculate passenger tickets (12–60kr); 48kr to take your bike from Copenhagen to Århus by train, or 80kr by bus. Reservations (costing around 20kr extra) are recommended.

ACCOMMODATION

Accommodation is a major expense, although there is a wide network of good-quality **hostels**. Most have a choice of private rooms, often with en-suite toilets/showers, as well as dorm accommodation; nearly all have cooking facilities. Rates are around 150kr per person for a dorm bed; non-HI members pay an extra 35kr a night (160kr for one-year HI membership); travellers without bed linen will also need to pay to rent this. Danhostel Danmarks Vandrerhjem (ⓦwww.danhostel.dk) produces a free hostel guide. For a similar price, **sleep-ins** (smaller hostels geared towards backpackers) can be found chiefly in major towns though some are open only in summer. There can be an age restriction (typically 35 or under). Local tourist offices have details.

Rooms at **hotels** can compare pricewise with private rooms in hostels. Expect to pay 550kr as a minimum for a double room, though note that this nearly always includes an all-you-can-eat breakfast. It's a good idea to book in advance, especially during peak season (this can also give you big discounts). Tourist offices can also supply details of **private rooms**, which usually cost 300–400kr a double, plus a 50–70k booking fee. **Farmstays** (*Bondegårdsferie*) are becoming increasingly popular; see ⓦwww.bondegaardsferie.dk.

Camping

If you plan to **camp**, you'll need an international camping carnet, or a Camping Card Scandinavia (100kr), which is available at official campsites. A Transit Pass (35kr) can be used for a single overnight stay. Most campsites are open April to September, while a few stay open all year. There's a rigid **grading system**: one-star sites have toilets and showers; two-stars also have basic cooking facilities and a food shop within 2km; three-stars include a laundry and a TV room; four-stars also have a shop, while five-stars include a cafeteria. Prices are 75–100kr per person. Many campsites also have **cabins** to rent, usually with cooking facilities, for 2000kr–4000kr per week for a six-berth place, although they are often fully booked in summer. Tourist offices offer a free leaflet listing all sites. **Camping rough** without permission is illegal, and an on-the-spot fine may be imposed. Good English-language information is available at ⓦwww.dk-camp.dk.

FOOD AND DRINK

Traditional **Danish food** is characterized by rather stodgy meat or fish and two veg combos, although the quality of ingredients is invariably excellent. Specialities worth seeking out include *stegt flæsk med persille sovs* (thinly sliced fried pork with boiled potatoes and parsley sauce) and the classic *røget sild* (smoked herring). **Breakfast** (*morgenmad*) is a treat, with almost all hotels and hostels offering a spread of cereals, freshly made bread, cheese, ham, fruit juice, milk, coffee and tea, for around 60kr (if not included in room prices). **Brunch**, served in most cafés from 11am until mid-afternoon, is a popular, filling option for late starters and costs 80–100kr. The traditional **lunch** (*frokost*) is *smørrebrød* – slices of rye bread heaped with meat, fish or cheese, and assorted trimmings – sold for 40–80kr a piece and very filling. An excellent-value set lunch can usually be found at restaurants and *bodegas* (bars selling no-frills food). *Tilbud* is the "special", *dagens ret* the "dish of the day"; expect to pay around 80kr for one of these, or 100–170kr for a three-course set lunch. The latest craze is smushi – the Danish take on sushi – (about 50kr per piece).

For daytime **snacks**, there are hot dog stands (*pølsevogn*) on all main streets and at train stations, serving hot dogs (*pølser*), toasted ham-and-cheese sandwiches (*parisertoast*) and chips (*pommes frites*) for around 25kr. Bakeries and cafés sell Danish pastries (*wienerbrød*), tastier and much less sweet than the imitations sold abroad, and *rundstykker* (literally "round pieces"), a type of crispy bread roll. Restaurants are pretty expensive for dinner (reckon on 120–170kr) but you can usually find a Middle Eastern or Thai place offering **buffets** for around 80–100kr. Kebab shops are also very common and often serve pizza slices for around 25kr. If you plan on **self-catering**, head for the good-value Netto or Fakta supermarkets.

Drinking

The most sociable places to **drink** are pubs (variously known as a *værtshus*, *bar* or *bodega*) and cafés, where the emphasis is on **beer**. The cheapest is bottled lager – the so-called gold beer (Guldøl or Elefantøl; 25–35kr/bottle) is the strongest. Draught lager (Fadøl) is more expensive and a touch weaker, but tastes fresher. The most common brands are Carlsberg and Tuborg, although microbreweries are now common with many pubs making their own beer on the premises. Most international **wines** (from 40kr) and **spirits** (20–40kr) are widely available. There are many varieties of **schnapps**, including the potent Aalborg-made Aquavit.

CULTURE AND ETIQUETTE

Denmark is a liberal and tolerant country. The defining aspect of culture here, in fact is "Hygge": spending quality time with friends or loved ones over good food. Remember that the Danish language doesn't have a specific word for "please" so don't be upset if Danes leave it out when talking to you in English (which most Danes speak very well). When wandering about make sure you don't stray into the cycle lanes alongside most roads and note that locals will wait for the green "walk" light at pedestrian crossings even when there isn't a car in sight.

Tipping is not expected as service charges are included in hotel, restaurant and bar bills; however, if you think

DENMARK ONLINE

Ⓦ **www.visitdenmark.com** Excellent Danish tourist board site.
Ⓦ **www.cphpost.dk** News and reviews from the *Copenhagen Post*, the capital's English-language weekly.
Ⓦ **www.aok.dk** Listings for most of Zealand; Danish only.
Ⓦ **www.rejseplanen.dk** Public transport journey planner (with English-language option).

you've had particularly good service it's not unheard of to leave a few kroner. **Smoking** is banned in most restaurants, cafés and bars.

SPORTS AND OUTDOOR ACTIVITIES

Football (soccer) is by far the most popular **sport** in Denmark. The biggest teams are FC Copenhagen and Brøndby (both from the capital) who play in the twelve-team Superliga (Ⓦwww.dbu.dk). As for **outdoor activities**, there's a series of cycle routes and hiking paths (Ⓦwww.dvl.dk). Watersports are also popular. Over 200 beaches having Blue Flag status and the extensive fjords of Zealand and Jutland provide further variety for the recreationally minded; ask at tourist offices where the best swimming is. Klitmøller on Jutland is the surfing capital.

COMMUNICATIONS

Post offices are open Monday to Friday 9.30/10am to 5/6pm and Saturday 9.30/10am to noon/2pm, with reduced hours in smaller communities. You can buy stamps from most newsagents. If you're in Denmark long-term consider buying a **Danish SIM** for your mobile – prepaid cards from operators such as Telmore and CBB are available from petrol stations and post offices from 99kr. **Internet access** is free at libraries and some tourist offices, most towns have internet cafés and ubiquitous coffee chain *Baresso* offer free wi-fi.

EMERGENCY NUMBERS

All emergencies Ⓣ112.

EMERGENCIES

Danish **police** are generally courteous and most speak English. For **prescriptions**, doctors' consultations and dental work – but not hospital visits – you have to pay on the spot.

INFORMATION

Most places have a **tourist office** that can help with accommodation. They're open daily in the most popular spots, but have reduced hours from October to March. All airports and many train stations also offer a hotel booking service.

MONEY AND BANKS

Currency is the **krone** (plural kroner), made up of 100 øre. It comes in notes of 50kr, 100kr, 200kr, 500kr and 1000kr, and coins of 50øre, 1kr, 2kr, 5kr, 10kr and 20kr. **Banking hours** are Monday to Friday 9.30/10am to 4pm, Thursday until 5.30/6pm. Banks are plentiful and are the easiest place to **exchange cash** and travellers' cheques, although they usually charge around 30kr per transaction. Forex bureaux tend to charge 20kr to exchange cash and 10kr per travellers' cheques but are scarce. Most airports and ferry terminals have late-opening exchange

STUDENT AND YOUTH DISCOUNTS

Your **ISIC card** will get you thirty to fifty percent off most museum and gallery admission prices, although free entry is often available on Wednesdays and Sundays. If you're staying long-term a **DSB Wildcard** (180kr) offers fifty percent off train fares for a year (Ⓦwww.dsb.dk).

DANISH

	Danish	Pronunciation
Yes	*Ja*	Ya
No	*Nej*	Nye
Please	*Vær så venlig*	Verso venly
Thank you	*Tak*	Tagg
Hello/Good day	*Goddag*	Go-day
Goodbye	*Farvel*	Fah-vell
Excuse me	*Undskyld*	Unsgul
Good	*God*	Got
Bad	*Dårlig*	Dohli
Near	*Nær*	Neh-a
Far	*Fjern*	Fee-ann
Cheap	*Billig*	Billie
Expensive	*Dyr*	Duy-a
Open	*Åben*	Oh-ben
Closed	*Lukket*	Lohgget
Ticket	*billet*	bill-le
Today	*Idag*	Ee-day
Yesterday	*Igår*	Ee-goh
Tomorrow	*Imorgen*	Ee-mon
How much is...?	*Hvad koster...?*	Val kosta...?
I'd like...	*Jeg vil gerne ha...*	yai vay gerna ha...
What time is it?	*Hvad er klokken?*	Val eayr cloggen?
Where is...?	*Hvor er...?*	Voa eayr...?
A table for...	*et bord till...*	et boa te...
I don't understand	*Jeg forstår ikke*	Yai fusto igge
Do you speak English?	*Taler de engelsk?*	Tayla dee engellsgg?
One	*En*	Ehn
Two	*To*	Toh
Three	*Tre*	Tray
Four	*Fire*	Fee-a
Five	*Fem*	Fem
Six	*Sex*	Sex
Seven	*Syv*	Syu
Eight	*Otte*	Oddeh
Nine	*Ni*	Nee
Ten	*Ti*	Tee

facilities, and ATMs are widespread. At the time of writing, €1 = 7.4kr, US$1 = 5.3kr and £1 = 8.5kr.

OPENING HOURS AND HOLIDAYS

Standard **shop hours** are Monday to Friday 9.30/10am to 5.30/7pm, Saturday 9/9.30am to 2/5pm. Shops are closed on Sundays, with the exception of the first Sunday of each month and Sundays in the run-up to Christmas, although new legislation should see Sunday opening hours increasing from 2012. All shops and banks are closed, and public transport and many museums run to Sunday schedules on **public holidays**: January 1; Maundy Thursday to Easter Monday; Prayer Day (4th Fri after Easter); Ascension (fortieth day after Easter); Whit Sunday and Monday; Constitution Day (June 5); December 24 (pm only); December 25 and 26. On **International Workers' Day**, May 1, many offices and shops close at noon.

Copenhagen

Split by lakes and surrounded by sea, an upbeat waterside vibe permeates **COPENHAGEN** (København), one of Europe's most user-friendly capitals. It's a welcoming, compact city with a centre largely given over to pedestrians (and cyclists) with an emphasis on café culture and top-notch museums by day, and a cracking live music, bar and club scene by night. Festivals like **Distortion** (June) and the **Jazz Festival** (July) show the city off at its coolest and most inventive.

Until the twelfth century, when **Bishop Absalon** built a castle on Christiansborg's present site, there was little more than a tiny fishing settlement to be found here. Trade and prosperity flourished with the introduction of the Sound Toll on vessels in the Øresund, and the city became the Baltic's principal harbour, earning the name **København** ("merchants' harbour"). By 1443 it had become the Danish capital. A century later, Christian IV created Rosenborg Castle, Rundetårn and the districts of Nyboder and Christianshavn, and in 1669 Frederik III graced the city with its first royal palace, Amalienborg.

What to see and do

The historic core of the city is **Slotsholmen** originally the site of the twelfth-century castle and now home to the huge **Christiansborg** complex. Just over the Slotsholmen Kanal to the north is the medieval maze of **Indre By** ("inner city"), while to the south the island of **Christianshavn** is dotted with cutting-edge architecture as well as the alternative enclave of **Christiania**. Northeast of Indre By are the royal quarters of Kongens Have and **Frederiksstaden**, while to the west the expansive Rådhuspladsen leads via Tivoli Gardens to Central Station and the hotspots of **Vesterbro** and **Nørrebro**.

Tivoli

Just off hectic Vesterbrogade outside the station is Copenhagen's most famous attraction, **Tivoli** (mid-April to mid-Sept Sun–Thurs 11am–11pm, Fri & Sat 11am–12.30am; mid-Nov to end Dec closes one hour earlier; 75kr, Fri 120kr; Ⓦwww.tivoli.dk), an entertaining mixture of landscaped gardens, outdoor concerts (every Fri) and fairground rides. You'll probably hear it before you see it thanks to its high perimeter walls and the constant screams from the roller coasters (multi-ride tickets 200kr). On a summer evening when the park is illuminated by thousands of lights and lamps reflected in the lake, it's quite a magical experience.

Ny Carlsberg Glyptotek

Founded by Carlsberg tycoon Carl Jacobsen, the **Ny Carlsberg Glyptotek** (daily 11am–5pm; 75kr, Sun free; Ⓦwww.glyptoteket.dk) is Copenhagen's finest art gallery. There's a knockout selection of Greek and Roman sculpture on the first floor as well as some excellent examples of modern European art, including Degas casts, Monet's *The Lemon Grove* and works by Gauguin, Van Gogh and Danish Golden Age artists like Eckersberg upstairs. Wind up your visit with a slice of delicious cake in the café beside the delightfully domed winter garden.

Thorvaldsens and the National museums

On the north side of Slotsholmen, the **Thorvaldsens Museum** (Tues–Sun 10am–5pm; 20kr, Wed free; Ⓦwww.thorvaldsensmuseum.dk) is the home of an enormous collection of work of Denmark's most famous sculptor, Bertel Thorvaldsen. A short walk away over the Slotsholmen Kanal is the **Nationalmuseet** (National Museum; same hours, with guided tours July–Sept Tues, Thurs & Sun at 11am; free; Ⓦwww.natmus.dk), which has excellent displays on Denmark's history from the Ice Age to the present day. The prehistory section in particular is fascinating, and includes amber animals, gold Viking horns, numerous corpses preserved in bogs and Denmark's oldest coin, struck around 995.

Indre By and the Rundetaarn

West of Kongens Nytorv, the city's largest square and home to some of the best hot dog stalls in town, pedestrianized **Strøget** leads into the heart of **Indre By**. This is Denmark's premier shopping area, with the likes of Prada jostling for space with local giant, Illums Bolighus. The quirky 35-metre-high **Rundetaarn** (Round Tower; June–Sept 10am–8pm; Oct–May 10am–5pm; 25kr; ⓦwww.rundetaarn.dk) dominates the skyline northwest of Strøget. Built as an observatory and finished in 1642, the main attraction is the view from the top reached via a spiral walkway. It's a still-functioning observatory and you can view the night sky through its astronomical telescope (mid-Oct to mid-March Tues & Wed 7–10pm).

Nyhavn and Frederiksstaden

Running east from Kongens Nytorv, a slender canal divides the two sides of **Nyhavn** ("new harbour"), picturesquely lined with colourful eighteenth-century houses – now bars and cafés – and thronged with tourists year-round. Just north of Nyhavn, the royal district of **Frederiksstaden** centres on cobbled Amalienborg Slotsplads, home to the four **Amalienborg** royal palaces. Two remain as royal residences, and there's a changing of the guard at noon if the monarch is home. In the opposite direction is the great marble dome of **Frederikskirken**, also known as Marmorkirken or marble church (Mon–Thurs 10am–5pm, Fri–Sun noon–5pm; admission to dome 1pm & 3pm Sat & Sun, plus Mon–Fri June–Aug; free), modelled on St Peter's in Rome. Further along Bredgade a German armoured car commandeered by the Danes to bring news of the Nazi surrender marks the entrance to the **Frihedsmuseet** (Museum of the Danish Resistance Movement; Tues–Sun 10am–3pm, May–Sept until 5pm; free; ⓦwww.frihedsmuseet.dk).

Kongens Have and Rosenborg Slot

West of Frederikskirken, **Kongens Have** is the city's oldest public park and a popular spot for picnics. Within the park is the fairytale **Rosenborg Slot** (May–Oct daily 10/11am–4/5pm; Nov–April Tues–Sun 11am–2pm; 70kr), the castle that served as the principal residence of Christian IV. The highlight is the downstairs treasury, where the **crown jewels** and rich accessories worn by Christian IV are on display.

COPENHAGEN ON A BUDGET

Europe's third most expensive city, Copenhagen can be a tricky place to get by on a budget but with a bit of planning you can make the most of your wallet. Museums with **free admission** include the National Museum, the Museum of the Danish Resistance and the Statens Museum for Kunst (National Gallery), while many others offer free entry one day per week. Another great free activity in summer is swimming in Copenhagen harbours' outdoor pool on Islands Brygge, southwest across the canal from Indre By. You should also consider buying a CPHCARD (see p.315). As for getting around, you can walk to most places, use the free city bikes or take the harbour bus-boats. The city has plenty of free music on offer, including concerts at Tivoli almost weekly during summer. As for accommodation, having your own bed linen and HI card saves you up to 85kr nightly.

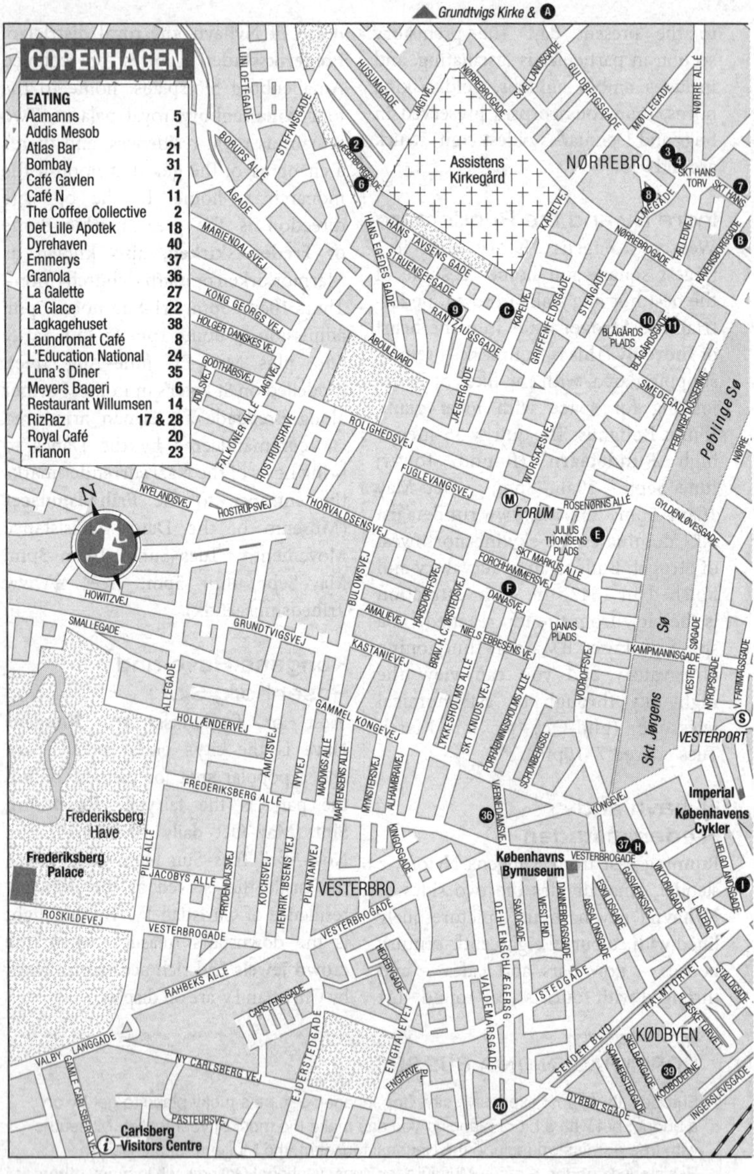

The Botanisk Have and art galleries

The **Botanisk Have** (Botanical Garden; daily 8.30am–4/6pm; winter closed Mon; free), on the west side of Kongens Have, is dotted with greenhouses and rare plants. The neighbouring **Statens Museum for Kunst** (Tues–Sun 10am–5pm, Wed until 8pm; free; Ⓦ www.smk.dk) holds a vast collection of art, from minor Picassos to major works by Matisse and Titian – although

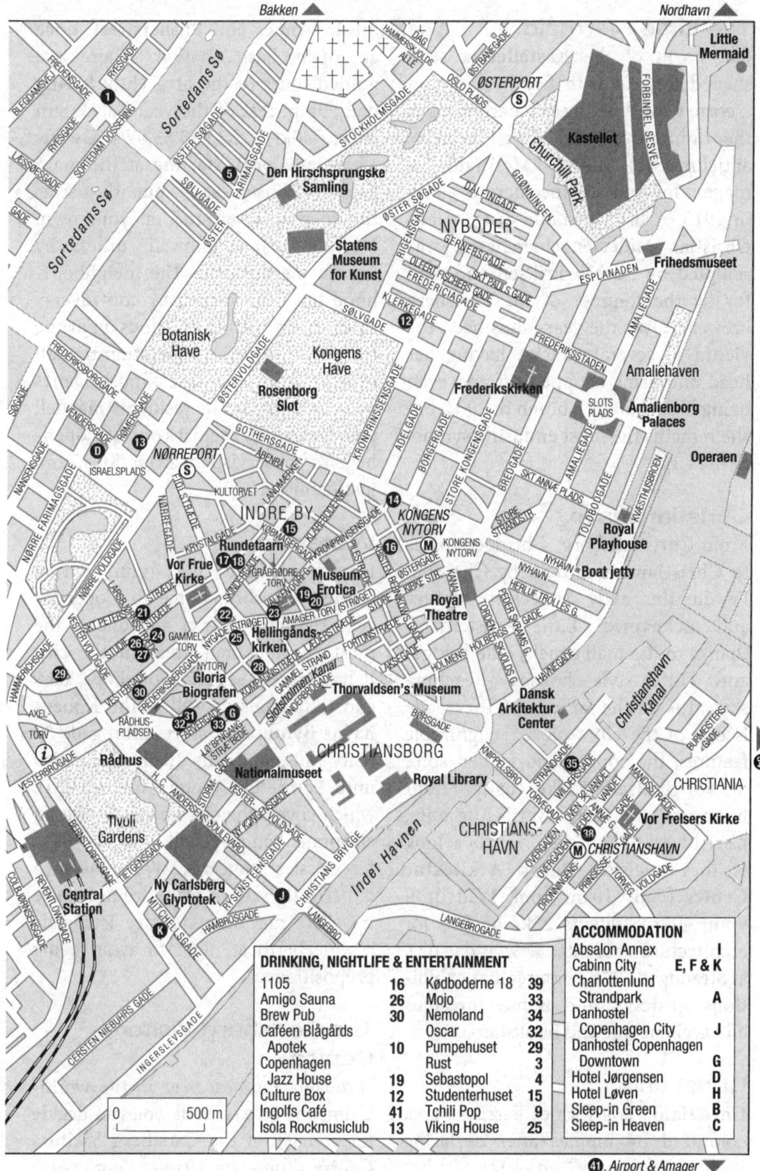

it's the light, spacious architecture of its new wing that steals the show. Across the park on Stockholmsgade, **Den Hirschsprungske Samling** (The Hirschsprung Collection; daily except Tues 11am–4pm; 50kr, free on Wed; Ⓦwww.hirschsprung.dk) holds a collection of twentieth-century Danish art, including work by the Skagen artists (see box, p.332), renowned for their use of light.

The Little Mermaid

Just north of the **Kastellet**, a star-shaped fortress with five bastions on a corner overlooking the harbour, sits the diminutive (and in all honesty anticlimactic) **Little Mermaid**, a magnet for tourists since her unveiling in 1913. A bronze statue of the Hans Christian Andersen character, it was sculpted by Edvard Eriksen and paid for by the founder of the Carlsberg brewery. Over the years she's been the victim of several attacks, having her head and arms chopped off and even being blown up by a bomb in 2003, but she remains the most enduring symbol of the city.

Christianshavn

From Christiansborg, a bridge crosses to **Christianshavn**, built by Christian IV in the early sixteenth century and nicknamed "Little Amsterdam" thanks to its small canals, cute bridges and Dutch-style houses. Reaching skywards on the far side of Torvegade is one of the city's most recognizable features, the copper and golden spire of **Vor Frelsers Kirke** (daily 11am/noon–3.30pm; tower April–Aug only; free, tower 30kr). Also worth a look is the canalside **Dansk Arkitektur Center** (daily 10am–5pm, Wed until 9pm; 40kr; students 25kr or free for architecture students; ⓦwww.dac.dk), at Strandgade 27B, with regular exhibitions on design and architecture plus an excellent café and bookshop.

Christiania

Christiania is a former barracks area colonized by hippies after declaring itself a "free city" in 1971. It has evolved into a self-governing entity based on collective ownership, with quirky buildings housing alternative small businesses such as a bicycle workshop and women's smithy, as well as art galleries, cafés, restaurants, Copenhagen's best falafel stand, music venues and Pusherstreet, once an open hash market. There are guided tours of the area (July & Aug daily 3pm; rest of the year Sat & Sun only; 30kr; ⓣ32.95.65.07, ⓦwww.christiania.org), starting at the main gate by Prinsessegade, but it's just as fun to wander around on your own. No photos are allowed, unless by special permission. The neighbourhood has been racked by controversy since the off, sitting as it does on prime real estate while its population remain exempt from the taxes most Danes pay. Although, as its residents may tell you, it earns its keep: it's one of Copenhagen's most visited attractions, and justifiably so.

Vesterbro

Directly behind the train station begins **Vesterbro**, home to Copenhagen's red-light district and one of the most cosmopolitan areas in the city. It has a great selection of shops, bars and restaurants as well as the **Københavns Bymuseum** at Vesterbrogade 59 (City Museum; daily 10am–4pm, Wed until 9pm; 20kr though free on Fri), which covers the city's history, with an elaborate banquet hall upstairs used for classical concerts. While the area is perfectly safe to walk around, male travellers may want to give Istedgade a wide berth at night to avoid being propositioned.

The Carlsberg Visitors Centre

"Probably the best beer in the world" claims the advert. Well, you can decide for yourself at the **Carslberg Visitors Centre** (Tues–Sun 10am–4/5pm; 65kr; ⓦwww.visitcarlsberg.dk) along Gamle Carlsberg Vej (buses #18 and #26). As well as learning how to create the perfect pint at the Jacobsen Brewhouse, you also get to sample two beers from a choice of Carlsberg, Tuborg and Jacobsen brews.

Nørrebro

Nørrebro, an edgy area northwest across the canal from Indre By (accessible from the centre via buses #3A, #4A or 5A or a 25-minute walk), is crammed with some of Copenhagen's best cafés, bars and clubs, centred on Sankt Hans Torv. Caution is advised, particularly at night: but it's home to most of Denmark's most happening hangouts and the resplendent **Assistens Kirkegård**, a tranquil cemetery which locals use as a park in summer, and that has Hans Christian Andersen among its permanent residents.

Arrival

Air Kastrup airport is 11km southeast of the centre, and is served by a main-line train to Central Station (5am–midnight every 10min; midnight–5am hourly; 12min; 34.50kr).

Train Trains pull into Central Station (Københavns Hovedbanegård or København H on tickets) near Vesterbrogade.

Bus Long-distance buses from elsewhere in Denmark stop at or near the Central Station.

Boat Ferries dock an S-train ride away north of the centre at Nordhavn (two stops from Nørreport station).

Information

Tourist office Vesterbrogade 4a, across from Central Station ⓣ70.22.24.42, ⓦwww.visitcopenhagen.com (May & June Mon–Sat 9am–6pm; July & Aug Mon–Sat 9am–8pm, Sun 10am–6pm; Sept–April Mon–Fri 9am–4pm, Sat 9am–2pm). Accommodation (including private rooms) can be booked for free via their website. Note that pickpockets operate in the tourist office and thefts are common: be vigilant with your possessions (the same applies in the train station).

Discount cards If you're sightseeing on a tight schedule, the CPHCARD (229/459kr for 24/72hr) is valid for the entire public transport network (including all Zealand) and gives entry to most attractions in the area. It's available at tourist offices, hotels, travel agents and the train station.

City transport

Metro, S-tog and bus An integrated network of buses, electric S-trains (S-tog) and an expanding metro covers the city (5am–1am); night buses (*natbus*) take over after 1am, along with metro services on Thurs, Fri and Sat nights, though the latter are less frequent. Night fares are double daytime fares and if you're taking your bike you'll need to buy a special ticket. Free route maps are available from stations.

Tickets The cheapest ticket is the *billet* (24kr for two zones), valid for an hour's unlimited travel. You can also buy a *Klippekort* containing ten *billets* (140kr for two zones). Other options include the CPHCARD (see opposite) and the city card (for the four main city transport zones; 70/180kr for 24/72 hr). 7-day flexicards (different zone combinations available) are good money-saving devices for those on a slightly longer stay. Single *billets* can be bought on board buses; all other tickets can and should be bought at train stations/newsagents. Make sure you validate your ticket before boarding at the yellow ticket-punching machines on the platform. Plainclothes ticket inspectors operate on almost all train routes: there are instant 600kr fines for travelling without a ticket.

Cycling The City Bike scheme (April–Nov; ⓦwww.bycyklen.dk) allows you to borrow bikes from racks across the city for a deposit of 20kr, which is returned when the bike is locked back into any other

COPENHAGEN TOURS

When the weather's good it's worth forking out on a **city tour** to familiarize yourself with Copenhagen. There are hop-on/hop-off open-top **bus tours** around the key city sights (200kr; ⓦwww.sightseeing.dk) and also Netto Boats (March–Oct 10am–5pm; 40kr; ⓦwww.netto-baadene.dk) operating hour-long canal and harbour **boat tours** past the old stock exchange (not open to the public), the island of Holmen and the Little Mermaid, leaving regularly from Nyhavn.

For bike enthusiasts, the best option is Bike Mike (April–Dec 10.30am, plus June–Sept 2.30pm; 260kr for 3hr including bike rental; ⓣ26.39.56.88, ⓦwww.bikecopenhagenwithmike.dk) with themed **cycle tours** departing from Turesensgade near Orstedsparken. See below for more on cycling in Copenhagen.

rack. Bike rental is available from CPH Bike Rental, Turesensgade 10 (from 50kr/6 hr; profits go to helping cycling In Africa) and Københavns Cykelbørs, Gothersgade 157 (from 75kr/day).

Accommodation

Copenhagen has a good selection of hostels, mainly concentrated in the city centre and Nørrebro. Booking ahead is recommended on weekends and during summer months; otherwise turn up as early as possible during the day to ensure a bed. Hotels can be pricey but there are often online deals available and a few cheaper options in the centre. Private rooms (around 400kr) booked through the tourist office are usually an S-train ride away from the centre. Breakfast is not included, unless otherwise stated.

Hostels

Danhostel Copenhagen City H.C. Andersens Boulevard 50 ⓣ33.11.85.85, ⓦwww.dgi-byen.com/hotels/danhostel_copenhagen_city. Priding itself as Europe's largest "designer" youth hostel, this thousand-bed monster is friendly, efficient and centrally located in a multistorey building overlooking the harbour. There's a guest kitchen, a convivial café-bar and free wi-fi. Bikes for 100kr/day. All rooms en suite. Dorms 135–185kr, doubles 540–720kr.

Danhostel Copenhagen Downtown Vandkunsten 5 ⓣ70.23.21.10, ⓦwww.copenhagendowntown.com. Affable hostel with mostly small 4-person dorms and 30 private rooms, along with a cool café-bar, free wif-fi, pool table, chill-out cushions and a bang-in-the-centre location. Dorms from 135kr, doubles 399kr.

Hotel Jørgensen Rømersgade 11 ⓣ33.13.81.86, ⓦwww.hoteljoergensen.dk. Hostel offering 6- to 12-bed dorms and basic rooms (with cable TV; 10 have their own bathroom), with a buffet breakfast included. Common room with TV, pool and table football. A stone's throw from Nørreport station on Israels Plads. Dorms 145kr, doubles 550–650kr.

Sleep-in Green Ravnsborggade 18, Nørrebro ⓣ35.37.77.77. Eco-friendly hostel (solar power, organic breakfasts) with somewhat noisy eight-, twenty- and thirty-bed dorms. Age limit 35; free internet; organic breakfast 50kr. Bus #5a/#16, night bus #81N/#84N from the centre (10min). Closed Sept to mid-June. Dorms 175kr.

Sleep-in Heaven Struenseegade 7, Nørrebro ⓣ35.35.46.48, ⓦwww.sleepinheaven.com. Welcoming hostel in a quiet spot next to Assistens Kirkegård. Six- or twelve-bed mixed dorms, plus double rooms (shared bathroom). Age limit 35; breakfast 40kr. Open 24hr; pool table; free internet. Bus #12/#69, nightbus #92N from the centre (10min). Dorms140kr, doubles 550kr.

Hotels

Absalon Annex Helgolandsgade 15 ⓣ33.24.22.11, ⓦwww.absalon-hotel.dk. Basic, slightly worn rooms with TV and shared bathroom in a one-star annexe of this three-star hotel. Price includes a good breakfast buffet. Singles 450kr, doubles 550kr.

Cabinn City Mitchellsgade 14 ⓣ33.46.16.16, ⓦwww.cabinn.com. Clean cabin-style rooms close to Tivoli and the station. All are en suite and have TV; breakfast is 60kr extra. Two other branches in Frederiksberg. Singles 485kr, doubles 615kr.

Hotel Løven Vesterbrogade 30 ⓣ33.79.67.20, ⓦwww.loevenhotel.dk. A real bargain for such a central location, in a historic nineteenth-century building (ring the bell marked "1st floor Løven" for admittance), with 46 airy and spacious rooms spread over five floors; most have a fridge, and some have a/c and bathroom. No breakfast but has kitchen for self-catering. Reservations essential in summer. Doubles 450kr.

Campsites

Charlottenlund Strandpark Strandvejen 144, Charlottenlund ⓣ39.62.36.88, ⓦwww.campingcopenhagen.dk. Beautifully situated 6km from Copenhagen at Charlottenlund Beach and with good, clean facilities. Very busy in summer. S-train line A, B or C to Svanemøllen then bus #14. Closed mid-Sept to April. 95kr/person, plus 40kr/tent.

Eating

Mixing Michelin-stars with budget bars, Copenhagen delights with its tremendously varied eating scene – which has helped to plan it on the map as Scandinavia's most sophisticated city. Head out of the centre as locals do towards Nørrebro and Vesterbro for the best deals.
For self-caterers, bakeries are a good option, while for takeaway *smørrebrød* try the outlets at Centrum Smørrebrød, Vesterbrogade 6C; or Klemmen at Central Station. There are Netto supermarkets at Nørre Voldgade 94, Nørrebrogade 43 and Landemærket 11.

Cafés

Café Gavlen Ryesgade 1. With delicious cakes (40kr) baked daily on the premises and good *smørrebrød* (45kr), this café is chic enough to grace Montparnasse: at night speciality beers and cocktails replace the delicious coffee as the drink of choice.

The Coffee Collective Jaegersborggade 10. The best café in town. Seriously: the coffee at least cannot be bettered, as this joint is run by a former world champion barista. Ethically sourced coffee, ultra-knowledgeable staff and coffee roasted right in front of you during the day.

Dyrehaven Sonder Boulevard 72. Cool café-bar-restaurant popular with in-the-know locals and expats. It serves real Danish food, as opposed to the gimmicky tourist version, like *kartoffelmed* (black bread with potatoes; 55kr).

Granola Vernedamsvej 5. Feel-good retro coffee bar serving delicious ice cream on one of the city's trendiest streets. Brunch 80kr.

La Galette Larsbjørnsstræde 9. Authentic Breton pancakes made with organic buckwheat and an array of fillings – from ham and eggs to smoked salmon and caviar. Pancakes 35–110kr.

Laundromat Café Elmegade 15. You can tell a good-value, popular café by the crowds, right? They certainly flock to this place, where breakfast goodies start at 48kr and big brunches at 85kr. Great cakes and coffees.

Luna's Diner Sankte Anne Gade 5. Bright little café in Christianshaven with street-front seating, the best milkshakes in town (59kr), burgers (90kr) and a popular weekend veggie brunch (169kr, but you'll never eat it all).

Restaurants

Aamanns Øster Farimagsgade 10. Good place for cheap *smørrebrød* and other Danish dishes (from 44kr). Eat in or take away.

Addis Mesob Fredensgade 11. Now-legendary Ethiopian restaurant: try their spicy stews with flatbread. Mains 79kr; lunchtime buffet 125kr.

Atlas Bar Larsbjørnsstræde 18. Busy basement bar-restaurant with an imaginative range of world food from ostrich and Japanese beef to Mexican vegetarian burritos (kitchen closes 10pm). Mains from 105kr.

Bombay Lavendelstrade 13. The city's best Indian, with curry's to eat in/take away for 111kr.

Café N Blågårdsgade 17. Bargain burgers (69kr) and a "special" dish-of-the-week (from 25kr) make this fabulous veggie/vegan café-restaurant a handy pit stop for budget-conscious travellers. Veggie buffet, home-made bread, great coffee and pavement seating.

Det Lille Apotek Store Kannikestæde 15. "The little pharmacy" claims to be the oldest restaurant in Copenhagen: come here for traditional Danish fare like *smørrebrød*. Main meals can be pricey if you veer away from the veggie options but they serve good-value lunches (90–110kr).

TREAT YOURSELF

Truth be told, Copenhagen's main pedestrian street Strøget can seem bleak compared to the rest of the city but it's worth exploring for the tucked-away gem that Is the **Royal Café** (Amager Torv 6). In a peaceful courtyard off the main drag, this state-of-the-art café is the place to come for *smushi*: a mix of Danish *smørrebrød* and Japanese fusion cuisine. You'll need 130kr to sample three *smushi* (the herring is best); other lunch items are 100–125kr.

L'Education National Larsbjornstrade 12. Cute brasserie with friendly staff: the tasty French food is cheap (mains 125–155kr) but the service and intimate atmosphere (candles and checked tablecloths) make the experience memorable. Sandwiches/quiches 69kr; charcuterie selection 79kr.

Restaurant Willumsen Store Regnegade 26. Initimate restaurant with an antiquarian decor, offering plenty of *smørrebrød*, such as sausage with onion and aspic (58kr) and various herring dishes (52kr). Has live jazz on Wed evenings.

RizRaz Kompagnistræde 20. Stylish, time-tested Mediterranean chain with an excellent vegetarian buffet (lasagne/pizza/salad) for 79kr (89kr after 4pm). Another branch at Store Kannikestræde. Mains around 139kr.

Drinking and nightlife

Nørrebro shares the best nights out with hip Kødbyen just southeast of Tivoli, the city's still-functioning meatpacking district, where arty bars and clubs have taken over old warehouses. Bars across the city are generally open until midnight/1am (Sun–Wed) and until at least 2am (Thurs–Sat).

Bars

1105 Kristen Bernikows Gade 4. It ain't cheap, but then the bartender here is inventor of the "Copenhagen", the city's signature cocktail. Phenomenal drinks and plenty of beautiful people.

Brew Pub Vestergarde 29. Popular micobrewery bang in the centre of town with a range of ales (37/58kr for small/large) and a great beer garden.

Caféen Blågårds Apotek Blågårds Plads 20. Unpretentious bar with a mixed crowd: students like the cheap beer and an older crowd are attracted by the regular live blues/jazz.

COPENHAGEN'S BEST BAKERIES

The Danes take their bakeries seriously and you'll see them all around Copenhagen. The range of loaves and pastries on offer is almost intimidating, but staff will happily advise. As well as *rundstykker* and flaky pastries, most bakeries offer affordable sandwiches. The following five are among the city's best:

Emmerys Vesterbrogade 34, Nørrebrogade 8, and Østerbrogade 51, among others. Trendy bakery chain with organic bread and filling sandwiches (around 60kr).

Lagkagehuset Torvegade 45, Christianshavn. Opposite the metro station, this justifiably popular bakery offers a bewildering range of breads baked in stone ovens, as well as great pastries (from 14kr) and fruit-covered cakes.

La Glace Skoubougade 3, east of Gammel Torv. Copenhagen's oldest confectioner (dating to 1870), this is an essential stop for cake and freshly made hot chocolate.

Meyers Bageri Jaegersborggade 9. The focus is on bread here: It comes out of the oven the moment before the store opens, and the variety of loaves is incredible.

Trianon Hyskenstræde 8, east of Nytorv. Purveyors to the queen – so the standard of breads and pastries here is top-notch.

Ingolfs Café Ingolfs Alle 3. South of the centre in Amager via bus #5a, this is a mellow, Bohemian café-bar serving daytime organic brunches and often erupting into a live music venue at sundown. Come here for recuperation the morning after, then get the party started all over again. Closes 11pm Mon–Fri, midnight Fri/Sat.

Nemoland Christiania. Run by Christiania residents, this is one of the city's most popular open-air bars, with picnic tables and decent café food. In winter, the crowd moves indoors to the pool tables and backgammon boards.

Oscar Rådhuspladsen 77. Café-bar in a perfect location off Rådhuspladsen; popular with a gay clientele. DJs hit the decks at weekends.

Sebastopol Sankt Hans Torv 2. Trendy café-bar with a retro feel on the Sankt Hans Torv square. Small/large beer 28/52kr. Good brunches too.

Studenterhuset Købmagergade 52. Friendly student hangout by the Rundetaarn with table football and pinball machines. Live music Thurs–Sat and an international party every Wed for foreign-exchange students. Sandwich 33kr; large beer 23kr (a student card gets you a third off all prices).

Tchili Pop Rantzausgade 28. *Tchili Pop*'s oh-so-cool clientele keep coming back here for the laidback vibe and great live music sessions from up-and-coming Danish bands. It's one of Nørrebro's best bars.

Viking House Vimmelskaftet 49. Touristy but boisterous joint pumping out rock/heavy metal classics and with live music at weekends. In something of a drinkers wasteland and always lively. Daily noon–5/7am.

Clubs

Culture Box Kronprinsessegade 54A Ⓦwww.culture-box.dk. Stylish basement club and the best electronica venue in town. Cover charge 60–120kr.

Isola Rockmusiclub Linnésgade 16A. Intimate club/bar playing mostly soul, rock and R&B. Free entry. Thurs–Sat 8pm–5am.

Kødboderne 18 Kødboderne 18. Club/live music venue in the heart of Kødbyen hosting everything from electronica to blues/rock, and a renowned Saturday club night. THE place to go out in Copenhagen right now. Cover charge 60kr.

Rust Guldbergsgade 8 Ⓦwww.rust.dk. Popular club and concert venue playing indie, rock and hip-hop. Cover charge 40–60kr.

Shopping

Clothes Istegade and the parallel Vesterbrogade have the best selection of boutiques including vintage and little-known designer wear. Check out Donn Ya Doll at Istedgade 55 for a great range of gadgets and Scandinavian designer labels.

Danish design ILLUM, hard to miss halfway down Strøget at Østergade 52, is Copenhagen's premier department store: worth visiting just to marvel at the interior. Nearby, Bang & Olufsen's flagship store at Kongens Nytorv 26 sells top-end TVs, cordless telephones and so on. The Bodum store at Østergade 10 offers a range of imaginative kitchenware including their classic cafetiere.

Markets The most central market is the celebrated-but-pricey Gammel Strand flea market (every Fri & Sat 8am–5pm), focusing on antiques. It's better to head further out to Nørrebro's

GAY COPENHAGEN

The Danish capital has a small but lively **gay scene** and hosts regular festivals and events including an annual Gay Pride march and one of the world's oldest LGBT film festivals, **MIX**, held each October. There are several gay clubs and numerous bars across the city; the big sauna is **Amigo Sauna** (Studiestrade 21a; ⓦwww.amigo-sauna.dk). Check out ⓦwww.visitcopenhagen.com/gay, ⓦwww.copenhagen-gay-life.dk for more information.

Assistens Cemetery for cheaper deals on everything from porcelain to clothes (every Sat May to mid-Oct 7am–2pm). Copenhagen's new food market, Torvehallerne, should be open by the time you read this (on Israels Plads near Norreport station).

Entertainment

Cinema

Grand Mikkel BryggersGade 8 ⓣ33.15.16 11, ⓦwww.grandteatret.dk. Stylish arthouse cinema with a great café and lively events programme (films around 70kr).

Imperial Ved Vesterport 4 ⓣ70.13.12.11, ⓦwww.kino.dk. Copenhagen's largest cinema, with only one theatre which can fit over 1100 people. Seats around 90kr.

Live music

As well as the options below, check out the programmes at *Vega* at Enghavevej 40 in Vesterbro and *Rust* (see opposite).

Copenhagen Jazz House Niels Hemmingsensgade 10 ⓦwww.jazzhouse.dk. The city's premier jazz venue.

Mojo Løngangsstræde 21C ⓦwww.mojo.dk. Atmospheric, divey blues venue with live acts every night. Happy hour 8–10pm; open until 5am. Entrance free or 60–120kr.

Pumpehuset Studiestræde 52 ⓦwww.pumpehuset.dk. A concert venue in a former salt warehouse, with bars on both floors. Hosts Danish bands and also attracts international names such as Kaiser Chiefs and Röyksopp. Entrance 70–250kr.

Opera and theatre

If you're under 25 (or if you're buying after 4pm on performance day) then you may be able to get tickets at half-price for the venues below: ask at the Royal Theatre box office for details.

Operaen Christianshavns Torv ⓦwww.operaen.dk. The city's spectacular opera house is as much an architectural as a musical attraction. Cheap tickets on the day of the performance can cost as little as 100kr. Guided tours available (advance booking essential, 100kr).

Royal Playhouse Sankt Annæ Plads 36 ⓦwww.kgl-teater.dk. Dramatic new waterside building with three stages, one of which can be opened for alfresco performances. All plays are in Danish; the café has a great harbourside view. Tours in English (100kr).

Royal Theatre Kongens Nytorv ⓦwww.kgl-teater.dk. Denmark's oldest and grandest theatre hosts ballet, opera, drama and concerts.

Directory

Embassies Australia, Dampfærgevej 26 ⓣ70.26.36.76; Canada, Kristen Bernikowsgade 1 ⓣ33.48.32.00; Ireland, Østbanegade 21 ⓣ35.47.32.00; UK, Kastelsvej 36-40 ⓣ35.44.52.00; US, Dag Hammarskjölds Allé 24 ⓣ33.41.71.00.

Exchange Den Danske Bank at the airport (daily 6am–8.30pm); Forex and X-Change at Central Station (daily 7/8am–9pm).

Hospital Rigshospitalet, Blegdamsvej 9 ⓣ35.45.35.45.

Internet The Royal Library's Black Diamond site at Søren Kierkegaards Plads 1 in Slotsholmen has free internet/wi-fi In a hugely impressive harbourside complex.

Left luggage Lockers at Central Station, from 30kr for 24hr.

Pharmacies Steno Apotek, Vesterbrogade 6C; Sønderbro Apotek, Amagerbrogade 158. Both 24hr.

Police In Central Station and at Halmtorvet 20, off Lille Istedgade.

Post office Købmagergade 33 and at Central Station.

Moving on

Train Aalborg (2 hourly; 4hr 25min–4hr 50min); Århus (2 hourly; 2hr 55min–3hr 10min); Hamburg (hourly; 5hr); Helsingør (every 20min; 50min); Malmö (every 30min; 22min); Odense (4 hourly; 1hr 30min); Roskilde (6–8 hourly; 25min).

Bus Aalborg (3–5 daily; 4hr 45min); Århus (6–7 daily; 3hr); Malmö (hourly; 55min).

DAY-TRIPS FROM COPENHAGEN

When the weather's good, you can top up your tan at the **Amager Strand-**

park beach, just 5km from the centre (bus #12 or take the metro to Øresund, Amager Strand or Femøren then a 5min walk). If Tivoli hasn't exhausted your appetite then make for the world's oldest amusement park at **Bakken** (April–Aug daily noon/2pm–10pm/midnight; multi-ride ticket 219kr), close to the Klampenborg stop at the end of lines C and F+ on the S-train. Besides slightly sinister clowns and vintage roller coasters it offers pleasant woods and nearby beaches to wander around.

There are two more excellent attractions on Zealand's north-eastern coast. In the affluent town of **HILLERØD** at the end of S-train line C is the spectacular multi-turreted **Frederiksborg Slot** (April–Oct daily 10am–5pm; Nov–March 11am–3pm; 60kr; Ⓦwww.frederiksborgslot.dk), a seventeenth-century castle built by Christian IV surrounded by an ornamental lake and housing Denmark's national portrait gallery. Further north in **HUMLEBÆK**, and a short walk from its train station, is **Louisiana**, an outstanding modern art gallery, at Gammel Strandvej 13 (Tues–Fri 11am–10pm, Sat–Sun 11am–6pm; 90kr; Ⓦwww.louisiana.dk). The gallery's setting is worth the journey alone – a harmonious blend of art, architecture and the natural landscape.

The rest of Zealand

As home to Copenhagen, **Zealand** is Denmark's most visited region, and, with a swift metropolitan transport network covering almost half of the island, you can always make it back to the capital in time for an evening drink. North of Copenhagen, **Helsingør** (Elsinore) is the departure point for ferries to Sweden and the site of legendary Kronborg Castle. To the west, and on the main train route to Funen, is **Roskilde**, with an extravagant cathedral that served as the resting place for Danish monarchs, and a gorgeous location on the Roskilde fjord, from where five Viking boats were salvaged and are now displayed in a specially built museum.

HELSINGØR

Despite its status as a busy ferry port, **HELSINGØR** is a quiet, likeable town with some major historical attractions. Its position on the narrow strip of water linking the North Sea and the Baltic brought the town prosperity when, in 1429, the Sound Toll was imposed on passing vessels. Today it remains an important waterway, with ferries to Swedish Helsingborg accounting for most of Helsingør's through-traffic and innumerable cheap booze shops.

What to see and do

The town's great tourist draw is **Kronborg Castle** (May–Sept daily 10.30am–5pm; Oct–April Tues–Sun 11am–3/4pm; 95kr; Ⓦwww.kronborgcastle.com), principally because of its literary associations as Elsinore Castle, the setting for Shakespeare's *Hamlet*. There's no evidence Shakespeare ever visited Helsingør, and the tenth-century character Amleth on whom his hero was based long predates the castle. Nevertheless, the Hamlet souvenir business continues to thrive here. The present castle dates from the sixteenth century when it jutted into the sound as a formidable warning to passing ships not to consider dodging the toll, and it remains a grand affair, enhanced immeasurably by its setting; the interior, particularly the royal chapel, is spectacularly ornate. Beneath the castle are the casemates, gloomy cavernous rooms that served as soldiers' quarters during times of war.

The big new attraction just south is the revamped former shipyard area where the recently opened Culture Yard (Mon–Fri 10am–9pm, Sat–Sun 10am–4pm; free; Ⓦwww.kulturvaerftet.dk) is now a theatre, concert venue, library and café-restaurant housed in an innovatively designed glass-steel structure created from old wharf buildings. Its **Varftsmuseum** (Tues–Sat 10am–2pm, Sun/Mon 2–6pm) gives an insight into local maritime heritage. The **National Maritime Museum** (50kr, 95kr joint ticket with Kronborg Castle) is also moving here in 2013 from its current location within the castle complex. Exhibits include relics from Denmark's conquests in Greenland, India, the West Indies and West Africa, as well as the world's oldest surviving ship's biscuit (1852). Note that much of this area is still a construction site until 2013.

The medieval quarter

Helsingør's well-preserved medieval quarter is dominated by **Stengade**, the main shopping street, linked by a number of narrow alleyways to Axeltorv, the town's small market square and a nice place to enjoy a beer. Near the corner of Stengade and Skt. Annagade is Helsingør's cathedral, **Skt. Olai's Kirke** (daily: May–Aug 10am–4pm; Sept–April 10am–2pm; free), while beyond is **Skt. Mariæ Kirke** (daily 10am–2pm, free; guided tours at 2pm Mon–Fri; 20kr), whose Karmeliterklostret, built circa 1400, is now the best-preserved medieval monastery in Scandinavia (guided tours only; arrange via the church office). Its former hospital now contains the **Town Museum** (daily noon–4pm, Sat until 2pm; closed Mon; 20kr), which displays an unnerving selection of surgical tools used in early brain operations.

The northern coast of Zealand is scattered with quaint little fishing villages: consider a trip to **Gilleleje**, where you can buy fresh fish directly from the fishermen (connected by train to Helsingør).

Arrival and information

Train station On Jernbanevej, a 2min walk south of the centre.

Tourist office Havnepladsen 3, just opposite the train station (Mon–Fri 10am–4pm; Ⓣ49.21.13.33, Ⓦwww.visithelsingor.dk).

Accommodation

Danhostel Helsingør Nordre Strandvej 24 Ⓣ49.28.49.49, Ⓦwww.helsingorhostel.dk. Beautifully located hostel in a restored villa right on the beach (suitable for swimming) 2km north of town; bus #340 from the station (8min; get off at Højstrup Trinbraet stop). Rents bikes for 75kr/day. Dorms 175kr, doubles 450kr.

Helsingor Camping Strandalleen 2 Ⓣ49.28.49.50. Near the hostel on the same bus route, this magnificent site has great coastal views across to Kronborg Slot. 60kr/person, plus 30kr/tent.

Eating and drinking

Café Brostraede Brostraede 1. Unpretentious café with limited seating but the best sandwiches around (44kr) and organic beers; on a tiny alley linking the port with the old town.

Chilli Blues Bar Sct. Anna Gade 48. Popular evening hangout, particularly good for blues and rock music; a rear patio adds to the ambience.

Lynhjems eftf. Ole Jensen. Stenegade 19. Don't consider stocking up on picnic items anywhere else. The cheese selection at this supermarket/deli, particularly, will wow you.

Moving on

Train Copenhagen (every 20min; 50min).

ROSKILDE

Once the capital of Denmark, **ROSKILDE** is worth a visit even if you can't make it to its famous rock festival (see p.323). Its Viking Ship Museum is a world-class attraction while the cathedral and old centre are lovely to wander around. One of Denmark's most colourful markets takes place on Wednesday and Saturday on the square outside the cathedral.

FERRIES TO SWEDEN

The main ferry operator between Helsingør to **Helsingborg** in Sweden is Scandlines (Ⓦ www.scandlines.dk), making the twenty-minute crossing every 20–30min (around 50kr return). All services leave from the main terminal by the train station. Eurail is valid on Scandlines while InterRail and the Copenhagen Card give a 25 percent discount.

What to see and do

The fabulous **Roskilde Domkirke** (April–Sept Mon–Sat 9am–5pm, Sun 12.30–5pm; Oct–March Tues–Sat 10am–4pm, Sun 12.30–4pm; 60kr), was founded by Bishop Absalon in 1170 and largely completed by the fourteenth century. It's stuffed full of dead Danish monarchs including twenty kings and seventeen queens. The most impressive chapel is that of Christian IV, full of bronze statues, frescoes and vast paintings of scenes from his reign. The current queen, the charismatic Margrethe II, has also expressed a desire to be buried here.

Next door is Roskilde Palace, housing the diverting **Museum of Contemporary Art** (Tues–Fri 11am–5pm, Sat & Sun noon–4pm when there are exhibitions on; 40kr, Wed free).

The Viking Ship Museum

Fifteen minutes' walk north of the centre on the banks of the fjord is the modern **Viking Ship Museum** (daily 10am–5pm; 100kr May–Sept, otherwise 70kr; Ⓦ www.vikingshipmuseum.dk). Inside, five superb specimens of Viking shipbuilding are displayed: a deep-sea trader, a merchant ship, a warship, a fishing vessel and a longship preserved incredibly from 1042, each retrieved from the fjord where they were sunk to block invading forces. Two life-size models of ships are next door, which you can board after trying on traditional Viking clothes. Outside, you can watch boat-building and sail-making using only tools and materials available during the Viking era; when the weather allows you can also experience a replica ship's seaworthiness on the fjord – you'll be handed an oar when you board and be expected to pull your weight as a crew member (50min; 80kr on top of the museum ticket; minimum 12 people). It's a humbling experience when you consider that similar ships made it all the way to Greenland.

Arrival and information

Train and bus The train station is at the southern edge of town. The bus station is within the same complex.

Tourist office On the main square, Stændertorvet 1 (Mon–Fri 10am–5pm, Sat 10am–1/2pm; Ⓣ 46.31.65.65, Ⓦ www.visitroskilde.com).

Accommodation

Roskilde Camping Baunehojvej 7 Ⓣ 46.75.79.96 Ⓦ www.roskildecamping.dk. 4km north of town via Frederiksborgvej on bus route 603, the campsite here has a gorgeous grassy, woodsy setting on the edge of the fjord. It's quite windy round here. 78kr.

Roskilde Vandrerhjem Vindeboder 7 Ⓣ 46.35.21.84, Ⓦ www.danhostel.dk/roskilde. Beautifully situated modern hostel in the harbour area near the Viking Museum. Free internet access and also rents out bikes (50kr/day or 300kr/week). Dorms 200kr, doubles 600kr.

Eating and drinking

Bavinchi Algade 7. Roskilde's best bakery; breads and cakes 8–15kr.

Café Druedahls Skomagergade 40. Popular café just south of the cathedral, with a range of beers and sandwiches. Offers a good-value brunch for 79kr.

Gimle Helligkorvej 2, a 10min walk east of the tourist office. Café/live music venue serving burgers (75kr) and sandwiches (45kr) noon–midnight; turns into a club Fri & Sat nights (midnight–5am).

Moving on

Train Copenhagen (every 20min; 30min); Odense (every 30min; 1hr 10min).

ROSKILDE FESTIVAL

Book well in advance if you wish to stay during the **Roskilde Festival** (www.roskilde-festival.dk), one of the largest open-air music festivals in Europe, attracting almost 100,000 people annually. Tickets go on sale in December and tend to sell out quickly. The festival usually takes place in early July and there's a special free campsite beside the festival site, to which shuttle buses run from the train station every few minutes.

Funen

Funen is the smaller of the two main Danish islands. The pastoral outlook of the place and the laidback fishing villages along the coast draw many visitors, but the main attraction is **Odense**, Denmark's third city and the birthplace of writer Hans Christian Andersen and composer Carl Nielsen.

ODENSE

Named after Odin, chief of the pagan gods, **ODENSE** (pronounced Own-suh) is over a thousand years old. An attractive little place, with a lush location on the River Odense Å, it has an engaging cultural scene and a surprisingly energetic nightlife with a focus on live music: it's one of Denmark's most enchanting destinations.

What to see and do

The city's inner core is a network of cobbled streets flanked by photogenic medieval houses.

Hans Christian Andersen Hus and Hans Christian Andersens Barndomshjem

The city's (perhaps the country's) best attraction is the **Hans Christian Andersen Hus** at Bangs Boder 29 (June–Aug daily 9am–6pm; Sept–May Tues–Sun 10am–4pm; 60kr), where the writer was born in 1805. The museum includes a library of Andersen's works and audio recordings of some of his best-known fairytales read by the likes of Sir Laurence Olivier. There's also intriguing paraphernalia including school reports, manuscripts, paper cuttings and drawings from his travels. The most striking feature, aside from the diminutive house itself, is the series of murals by Niels Larsen Stevns (1930) depicting different stages of Andersen's life. Check out the telling quotes on Andersen's unconventional looks and talent: "He is the most hideous man you could find but has a poetic childish mind", commented a contemporary.

Down the road at Munkemøllestræde 3–5 is the tiny **Hans Christian Andersens Barndomshjem** (Childhood Home; daily 10/11am–3/4pm; 25kr) where the writer lived between the ages of two and fourteen.

The City Centre

On Skt. Knuds Plads just southwest of the Rådhus (town hall) is the crypt of Gothic **Skt. Knuds Kirke** (Mon–Sat 10am–4/5pm, Sun noon–5pm; free). It holds the remains of King Knud II and his brother Benedikt, both murdered in 1086 at the altar of nearby Skt. Albani Kirke. Don't miss the splendiferous gold-leaf-coated altarpiece inside by Lübeck master Claus Berg.

At Jernbanegade 13, the **Fyns Kunstmuseum** (Funen Art Gallery; Tues–Sun 10am–4pm; 40kr; www.museum.odense.dk) focuses on late nineteenth-century Danish art including stirring works by Vilhelm Hammershøi and Skagen artist P.S. Krøyer.

Over at the Odense Concert Hall the city's other famous son, Carl Nielsen (one of Europe's leading nineteenth-century composers) also has a riveting museum devoted to his life, **Carl Nielsen Museet** (May–Sept Tues–Sun 11am–3pm; 25kr).

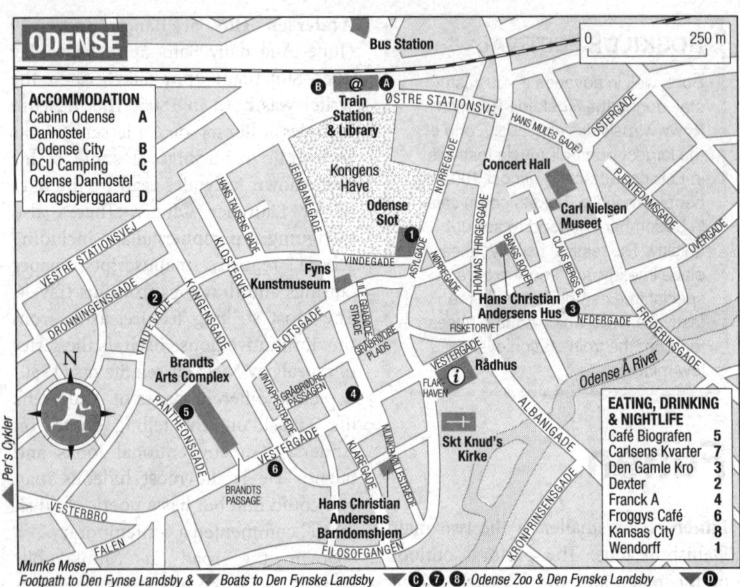

Just off Vestergade, west of the centre is the **Brandts Arts Complex.** Once a large textile mill, the area has been beautifully converted and now features an art school, cinema, music library and three museums (Tues–Sun 10am–5pm; 80kr combined ticket; Ⓦwww.brandts.dk). In the large hall that once housed the huge machinery is the **Kunsthallen**, which displays works by the cream of new talent in art and design, and the **Museet for Fotokunst**, featuring changing photography exhibitions. On the third floor the **Danmarks Mediemuseum** chronicles the development of printing, bookbinding and illustrating from the Middle Ages to the present day.

Den Fynske Landsby and Odense Zoo

South of the centre at Sejerskovvej 20 is **Den Fynske Landsby** (Funen Village; April–Oct Tues–Sun 10am–5/7pm; Nov–March Sun 11am–5pm; 60kr; Ⓦwww.museum.odense.dk), a living, breathing nineteenth-century village made up of buildings brought here from all over Funen, including a windmill and a school. In summer free shows are staged at the open-air theatre. Buses #110 and #111 run to the village from the bus station.

It's infinitely better, however, to walk to the museum by following the river south about 4km via the ornamental park of Munke Mose. Boats also run there hourly (75kr return) via **Odense Zoo** (daily 10asm–6/7pm; 130kr; Ⓦwww.odensezoo.dk), which has Northern Europe's largest exclusively African safari park.

Arrival and information

Train and bus Odense train station is part of a large shopping mall 5min walk north of the centre. Long-distance buses also terminate here.

Tourist office At Vestergade 2 near the Rådhus (Sept–June Mon–Fri 9.30am–4.30pm, Sat 10am–1pm; July & Aug 9.30am–6pm, Sat 10am–3pm, Sun 11am–2pm; Ⓣ63.75.75.20, Ⓦwww.visitodense.com).

Discount card The Odense Card covers most attractions (129kr). Available at the tourist office.

Left luggage At the train station behind the ticket office; 20kr.

Internet Free access in the library at the train station.
Bike rental CSV Cykeludlejning, at Nedergade 36; rents bikes May–Oct (100kr/day, plus 500kr deposit).

Accommodation

Hostels

Danhostel Odense City Østre Stationsvej 31 ⓣ66.11.04.25, ⓦwww.cityhostel.dk. Conveniently located in a former hotel next to the train station, this five-star hostel has clean rooms, wi-fi for 30kr/day and 24hr automated check-in. Also has a good café with buffet breakfast for 65kr. Dorms 235kr, doubles 575kr.

Odense Danhostel Kragsbjerggaard Kragsbjergvej 121 ⓣ66.13.04.25, ⓦwww.odense-danhostel.dk. Sister hostel to the city branch, this one is set in a manor house surrounded by woodland 2km south of the centre (bus #61 & 63 from the station). Breakfast 60kr. Rents on a per-room basis (2- to 8-person rooms available, so works out cheap if you're in a big group. Doubles 570kr.

Hotels

Cabinn Odense Østre Stationsvej 7–9 ⓣ63.14.57.00, ⓦwww.cabinn.com. Budget chain hotel close to the train station. All rooms are short on space but are en suite and have TV. Free internet access; buffet breakfast 60kr. Singles 485kr, doubles 615kr.

Campsite

DCU Camping Odensevej 102 ⓣ66.11.47.02, ⓦwww.camping-odense.dk. Located near Den Fynske Landsby on the outskirts of Odense, this campsite has mini-golf and a heated pool. Take bus #22 from the train station towards Højby. 72kr/person, plus 20kr/tent.

Eating

Café Biografen Brandts Passage 39–41. Trendy bar attached to an artsy cinema. Club sandwich 68kr; coffee 22kr.

Den Gamle Kro Overgade 23. Set within a seventeenth-century courtyard, this traditional restaurant offers perhaps the best gastronomic experience in Demark. There's a basement wine cellar and a host of delicious *smørrebrød* (mostly 71-93kr); mains like the trout fillet start at 208kr.

Franck A Jernbanegade 4. Lively even when the rest of the city centre's shut down, this café-bar has withstood the test of time. Happy-hour brunch 68kr. Live jazz at weekends.

Froggys Café Vestergade 68. Bang-in-the-centre café-bar serving delicious salads (86kr) and the legendary Froggy's burger (99kr). DJs at weekends.

Wendorff Asylgade 16. Wonderful bakery with two counters teeming with bread and cakes (8–14kr).

Drinking and nightlife

Carlsens Kvarter Hunderupvej 19. Cosy bar in the style of a country pub, with a relaxed atmosphere and Odense's best selection of beers (around 30kr), including all the Belgian Trappist ales.

Dexter Vindegade 65. Jazz, blues and folk venue with live music 2–3 times a week (entry 50–60kr) and a free jam night on Mon evenings. Good range of international beers too.

Kansas City Munkebjergvej 140. This old clothes factory is now an experimental music venue epitomizing everything that's great about the local music scene: watch this space for tomorrow's big Danish names in the music biz. It's 2km south of the centre via bus #29 or #63.

Moving on

Train Århus (every 30min; 1hr 40min); Copenhagen (3 hourly; 1hr 35min); Esbjerg (hourly; 1hr 20min).

Jutland

Long ago, the Jutes, the people of **Jutland**, were a separate tribe from the more warlike Danes who occupied the eastern islands. By the Viking era, however, the battling Danes had spread west, absorbing the Jutes, and real power gradually shifted towards Zealand, where it has largely stayed ever since. Nevertheless, **Århus**, Denmark's second city halfway up the eastern coast, and **Aalborg**, capital of northern Jutland, are vibrant, cosmopolitan urban centres. Further inland, the landscape is dramatic – stark heather-clad moors, fjords and dense forests, while north of Aalborg the landscape becomes increasingly wind-battered and stark until it reaches **Skagen**, on the peninsula's tip.

THE FERRY PORTS: ESBJERG AND FREDERIKSHAVN

Jutland has two main international ferry ports. **ESBJERG** has overnight ferries to/from Britain; bus #5 connects the passenger harbour with the centre (a 15min walk). The train station, with trains to/from Copenhagen (3hr 10min), is at the end of Skolegade, and, at no. 33, you'll find the tourist office (Sept–June Mon–Fri 10am–5pm, Sat 10am–1pm, July & Aug Mon–Fri 10am–5pm, Sat 10am–2.30pm; ⓣ75.12.55.99, ⓦwww.visitesbjerg.dk).

FREDERIKSHAVN, in the far north of the region (2hr 45min by train from Århus), has express ferries to Sweden and Norway. Its ferry terminal is near Havnepladsen, not far from the centre, while all buses and most trains terminate at the central train station, a short walk from the town centre; some trains continue to the ferry terminal itself. The tourist office is close by at Skandiatorv 1 (Jan–June & mid-Aug to Dec Mon–Fri 9am–4pm, Sat 10am–1pm, July to early Aug Mon–Sat 9am–4pm, Sun 10am–1pm; ⓣ98.42.32.66, ⓦwww.frederikshavn-tourist.dk).

ÅRHUS

Denmark's second-largest city, **ÅRHUS**, is an instantly likeable assortment of intimate cobbled streets, sleek modern architecture, brightly painted houses and student hangouts. It's small enough to get to grips with in a few hours, but lively enough to make you linger for days – an excellent music scene, interesting art, pavement cafés and energetic nightlife all earn it the unofficial title of Denmark's capital of culture.

What to see and do

Århus's main street, the pedestrianized Ryesgade/Søndergade, leads down from the train station, across the river and into the main town square, Bispetorvet. Running parallel one block west of Rysegade is Park Alle with the functionalist 1941 **Rådhus** (city hall), designed by Arne Jacobsen and Eric Moller (guided tours including bell tower arranged through tourist office). The square itself is dominated by the fifteenth-century **Domkirke** (Mon–Sat 9.30/10am–3/4pm) a massive Gothic church with exquisite frescoes as well as a miniature Danish warship hanging from the ceiling. The area to the north, known as the Latin Quarter, is crammed with browsable shops, galleries and enticing cafés.

ARoS

ARoS (Tues–Sun 10am–5pm, Wed until 10pm; 90kr; ⓦwww.aros.dk) is one of Europe's most beautiful contemporary buildings and a fantastic modern art museum. It contains seven floors of works from the late eighteenth century to the present day accessed from a centrepiece spiral walkway reminiscent of New York's Guggenheim. The Skagen artists head the fine collection of home-grown art: the likes of Warhol are also represented along with the eerie five-metre-high *Boy*, by Australian sculptor Ron Mueck. The latest addition is the remarkable Rainbow Panorama, a circular rooftop walkway, fashioned in all colours of the spectrum, and offering wonderful city views.

Den Gamle By

A short walk northwest of the centre is one of the city's best-known attractions, **Den Gamle By** ("the old town"), on Viborgvej (daily: mid-June to Aug 9am–6pm; Sept to mid-June 10/11am–3/5pm; 100–125kr; ⓦwww.dengamleby.dk), an open-air museum of traditional Danish life, with seventy-odd half-timbered townhouses and actors in contemporary dress. A new town expansion is under construction (due for completion

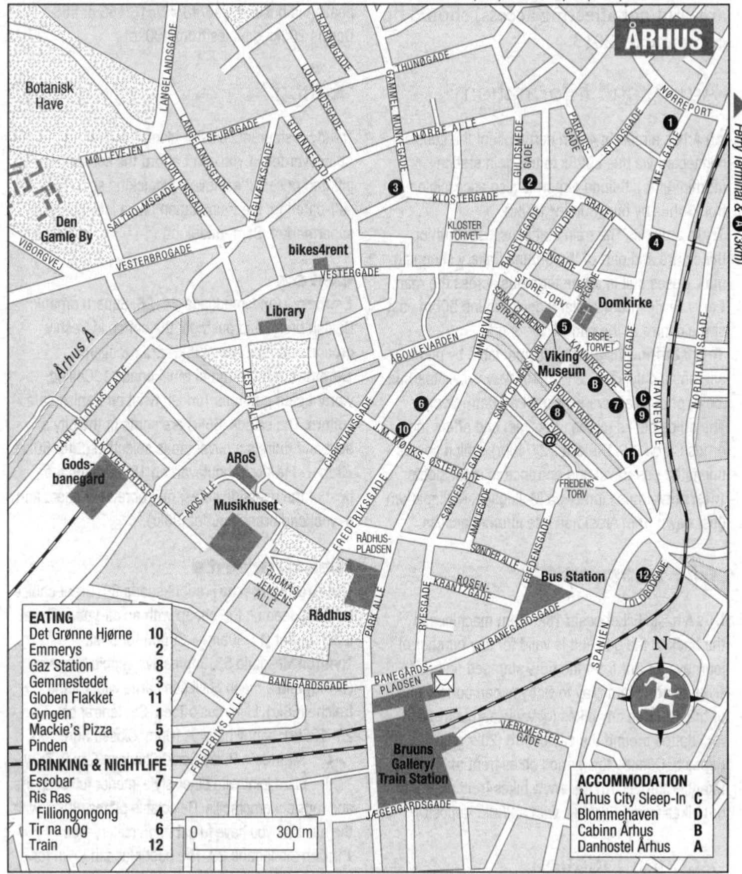

in 2014), which will feature shops and homes from 1900 to 1974 and attractions such as a poster museum. Close by are the pleasant **botanical gardens** (Mon–Sat 1–3pm, Sun 11am–3pm; free).

Marselisborg Palace and Moesgård Museum

Marselisborg Skov, two kilometres south of the centre, is the city's largest park, and home to the summer residence of the Danish royals: its landscaped grounds can be visited when the monarch isn't staying (usually at all times outside Easter, Christmas and late June to early Aug).

Ten kilometres south of Århus, the **Moesgård Museum** (April–Sept daily 10am–5pm; Oct–March Tues–Sun 10am–4pm, closed Mon; 60kr; ⓦwww.moesmus.dk), reached direct by bus #6, details Danish civilizations from the Stone Age onwards. Its most notable exhibit is the "Grauballe Man", an amazingly well-preserved sacrificial victim dating from around 100 BC discovered in a peat bog west of town in 1952. Also remarkable is the Illerup Ådal collection of Iron Age weapons and the scenic "prehistoric trail" which runs 3km to the sea. A striking redesign of the museum (tripling the area but not affecting access) should be complete by 2013.

Arrival and information

Air Århus airport is 44km northeast of the centre, connected via bus #925x to the train station (45min; 90kr). Billund airport is also accessible from Århus by bus (80min; 180kr).
Train and bus The train station is just south of the centre and part of the Bruuns Gallery shopping mall. Buses pull in at the terminus across the road.
Ferry Ferries from Zealand dock around 500m east of the centre at the end of Nørreport.
Tourist office VisitAarhus (contactable by phone and email only; ⓣ87.31.50.10, ⓦwww.visitaarhus.com; phones answered Mon–Fri 10am–3pm). The office books rooms (70kr fee) and offers the Århus Card (119/149kr for 24/48hr), which covers unlimited bus travel and entrance to most sights.
Internet Aarhus Library on Møllegade, Mølleparken (just down from Aros) has free internet access.

City transport

Bus A basic ticket costs 18kr from machines in the back of the bus and is valid for any number of journeys for 2hr from the time stamped on it.
Bike rental From May to Oct you can borrow one of the 400 free city bikes (ⓦwww.aarhusbycykel.dk) dotted around the city centre (20kr coin deposit). Outside this period bikes4rent at Skanderborgvej 107 (ⓦwww.bikes4rent.dk) rents out bikes from 75kr/day, with a 250kr deposit.

Accommodation

Århus City Sleep-In Havnegade 20 ⓣ86.19.20.55, ⓦwww.citysleep-in.dk. The most central hostel, with facilities including a guest kitchen, pool and TV rooms and a courtyard for summer barbecues. Organic breakfast is 65kr; also has free internet access. Dorms 160kr, doubles 420kr.
Blommehaven Ørneredevej 35 ⓣ86.27.02.07, ⓦwww.blommehaven.dk. Overlooking a bay 5km south of the city centre, this campsite has access to a beautiful beach. Closed mid-Oct to mid-March (bus #6 or #19). 72kr/person, plus 20kr/tent.
Cabinn Århus Kannikegade 14 ⓣ86.75.70.00, ⓦwww.cabinn.com. Good-value cabin-style rooms in a bang-in-the-centre location. All rooms are en suite, with TV and telephone. Singles 485kr, doubles 615kr.
Danhostel Århus Marienlundsvej 10 ⓣ86.21.21.20, ⓦwww.aarhus-danhostel.dk. Peaceful hostel set in woods 3km northeast of the centre and close to the popular Den Permanente beach via buses #1/#6/#8/#9/#16/#56 or #58. Dorms 200kr, doubles from 400kr.

Eating

Trendy restaurants cluster along the river on Åboulevarden: if you can't afford the somewhat inflated prices, it's a lovely picnicking spot. For self-catering, the train station has a late-opening supermarket (8am–midnight).

Cafés

Emmerys Guldsmedgade 24–26. Superb organic Danish bread and pastries; the coffee is freshly ground and the cakes (35kr) are excellent.
Gemmestedet Gammel Munkegade 1. Chilled, vibrant café putting a Turkish twist on Danish café culture. The salads (65kr) are some of the city's best and there's a novel tapas selection (2 for 50kr).
Globen Flakket Åboulevarden 18. Perhaps the best of the riverside cafés; microbrewery beers and a weekend brunch buffet (98kr).

Restaurants

Det Grønne Hjørne Frederiksgade 60. Great choice for a big feed on the cheap with an all-you-can-eat lunch buffet (11.30am–4.30pm) for 59kr.
Gyngen Mejlgade 53. Impressive veggie burgers (110kr) and a mean chilli con carne with crème fraîche (68kr). Live music Tues–Sat (entrance 20–125kr); happy hour 9–10pm. Closed Sun.
Mackie's Pizza Sankt Clemens Torv 9. Zany pizza joint with diner-style interior full of sports and music memorabilia. Delectable pizzas (80kr), with the rule that you have to eat them cutlery-free.
Pinden Skolegade 29. The best place in town for traditional Danish food including a knockout *stegt flæsk med persille sovs* (pork in a creamy parsley sauce) for 92kr. All-you-can-eat lunch buffet 125kr, 12.30–3.30pm. Closed Sun.

Drinking and nightlife

Escobar Skolegade 32. Popular student hangout with cheap beer (draught 38kr), loud music and friendly bar staff. Open until 3am.
Gaz Station Åboulevarden 21. Grungy, raucous club playing everything from rock to cheesy Eighties' pop and hosting quality live music/stand-up comedy. Big-screen sports too. Perennially popular with a student clientele. Thurs–Sat 11pm–5am.
Ris Ras Filliongongong Majlegade 24. Chilled student hangout with a vast range of beers. No food served but you're welcome to bring your own.
Tir na nÓg Frederiksgade 40. Large, lively Irish bar with big-screen football and live folk/rock music at

weekends. Pint of Carlsberg 25kr noon–7pm. Open until 3am.

Train Toldbodgade 6 ⓦwww.train.dk. Århus's most popular nightclub is also a concert venue that pulls in some big-name DJs and international acts. Entry fees for club nights 70–100kr, or up to 225kr for concerts.

Moving on

Train Aalborg (every 30min; 1hr 20min–1hr 40min); Copenhagen (every 30min; 3hr–3hr 20min); Odense (every 30min; 1hr 40min).

NORTHWEST OF ÅRHUS

Mainland Denmark's loveliest scenery lies northwest of Aarhus, with the big draw being the country's first national park, **Thy** (ⓦnationalparker.naturstyrelsen.dk), created in 2008. It's a lonely tract of wild beach and inland heath containing the Danish surfing Mecca of **Kirtmøller**, and backing onto vast fjords such as **Limfjorden**, producing some of the world's finest oysters. There's an information centre at **Stenbjerg Landing** (May–Oct 11am–3pm) on bus route #320 from Harup Thy train station. Trains run from Åarhus to Struer (hourly; 2hr 10min) and then on into the park.

AALBORG

North Jutland's main city, **AALBORG** has undergone a renaissance of recent years. Long renowned for its raucous nightlife and nearby Viking burial ground, it's now redeveloped its waterfront with hugely impressive results to showcase its industrial heritage, while not detracting from its substantial medieval core. It's also the main transport terminus for the region, and makes an exciting stopover on the way north to Skagen.

What to see and do

Huge investment on the stretch of Aalborg facing Limfjorden has transformed the once industrial **waterfront** district into a centre for design and entertainment, while there's plenty of historical charm in the sights and cobbled streets of the **old town**.

Kunsten Museum of Modern Art and Aalborg Tower

Those after a culture fix should head to the **Kunsten Museum of Modern Art** (Tues–Sun 10am–5pm; 60kr, free in Dec; ⓦwww.kunsten.dk), a stunning modern art gallery close to a sculpture park (take bus #15 or walk ten minutes west of the train station). Just west of here, up a staircase through woods, is the **Aalborg Tower** (April–Oct 11am–5pm, 10am–7pm in July; 30kr), with spectacular city views and a bistro restaurant.

The Old Town

Aalborg's well-preserved **old town** centres on the Gothic cathedral, the **Budolfi Domkirke** (June–Aug Mon–Fri 9am–4pm, Sat 9am–noon; Sept–May Mon–Fri 9am–3pm, Sat 9am–noon). On the other side of Østerågade, the sixteenth-century **Aalborghus Castle** is notable for its dungeon (May–Oct Mon–Fri 8am–3pm; free) and underground passages (until 9pm).

Leading down to the waterfront is bar-lined **Jomfru Ane Gade,** Aalborg's booziest street.

Waterfront

The waterfront is still in the development phase with a cruise ship terminal, a landscaped park and more restaurants/bars on the cards but for now the showpiece attraction is **Nordkraft** (Kjellerups torv 5; ⓦwww.nordkraft.dk) housed in a former power station five minutes' walk east of the centre near the big new shopping centre Friis, and containing a cinema, theatre/concert venue, several restaurants and the relocated tourist office. A short walk west is the **Utzon Center** (daily 10am–5pm; 60kr; ⓦwww.utzoncenter.dk) designed by the man that gave the world the Sydney Opera House, Jørn Utzon. Utzon was born in Aalborg and left the city this fitting architectural masterpiece, inspired by the old shipyards hereabouts, shortly before his death. It's a showcase for contemporary design and has a wonderful café. A ten-minute walk further west is the distinctive **V&S Distillery** at Olensens Gade 1, home of the potent Scandinavian spirit Aquavit (tours July & Aug Tues & Thurs 10am and 1pm; 50kr; other times by appointment, ask at tourist office).

Lindholm Høje

A few kilometres north of Aalborg via bus #2 (15min), atmospheric **Lindholm Høje** (Lindholm Hills; free) is Scandinavia's largest Viking burial site with more than seven hundred graves. It's best to visit early or late in the day as the slanting sunlight glints off the burial stones, many of which are set in the outline of a Viking ship. It's worth stopping by the site's impressive **museum** (April–Oct daily 10am–5pm; Nov–March Tues–Sun 10am–4pm; 40kr).

Arrival and information

Air Aalborg airport (served by budget airline Norwegian Air Shuttle from London Gatwick) is 7km northwest of the centre and connected by bus #2 (20min).
Train and bus Both terminals are on J.F. Kennedys Plads, 10min walk southwest of the centre. The train station has left-luggage lockers (20kr for 24hr).
Tourist office In the Nordkraft building at Kjellerups torv 5: helpful service and touch-screen information. (Mon–Fri 11am–8pm, Sat 10am–2pm; ⓣ99.31.75.00, ⓦwww.visitaalborg.com). They sell the Aalborg Card here (179/299kr for 24/72hr), which gives you free public transport, free admission to most attractions and discounts in cafés/shops.
Internet There is free access in the city library at Rendsburggade 2.

Accommodation

The tourist office can also book rooms (350kr) in the centre for a 70kr fee.
Cabinn Aalborg Fjordgade 20 ⓣ96.20.30.00, ⓦwww.cabinn.com. Modern hotel with small, clean, en-suite rooms next to the Riis shopping centre. Breakfast 60kr; singles 485kr, doubles 615kr.
Danhostel Aalborg ⓣ98.11.60.44, ⓦwww.danhostelnord.dk/aalborg. Large, well-equipped hostel 3km west of the town on the Limfjord bank beside the marina – take bus #13 to the Egholm ferry junction and continue on foot for 5min following the signs. Dorms 285kr, doubles 478kr.
Strandparken Skydebanevej 20 ⓣ89.12.76.29, ⓦwww.strandparken.dk. Pleasant campsite 2km west of the centre with access to an open-air swimming pool and beach. Closed mid-Sept to mid-March. 77kr/person, plus 20kr/tent.

Eating and drinking

Jomfru Ane Gade is packed with late-opening bars, clubs and restaurants offering bargain food/drink deals.
Den Fede Aeling Strandvegen 12C. "The ugly duckling" perches on the edge of the fjord near the Limfjordsboren bridge: it does great coffees and makes the transition to bar at night. It's the liveliest of the recently sprung-up waterside eating choices.
Irish House Østerågade 25. Popular pub serving traditional Irish food (mains 49–69kr) and ales, with regular drinks deals. Live music Thurs–Sat, jam session on Mon and sport on TV most evenings.
Penny Lane Boulevarden 1. Buzzing café serving filling sandwiches (70kr) and lunches (70–99kr).
Søgaards Bryghus CW Obels Plads 1A. One of Denmark's best brewpubs with tasting samples of any 6 of the 85 brews concocted here (59kr). The food is first-rate too (they do a mean steak). Brunches from 85kr, mains 150kr.
Studenterhuset Gammeltorv 11, opposite Budolfi Domkirke ⓦwww.studenterhuset.dk. Student-run music venue/café: the place to catch local Danish bands. Also has book exchange library and free internet. Coffee 14kr; large beer 29kr. Mon–Sat 11.30am–late.

Moving on

Train Århus (2 hourly; 1hr 20min); Copenhagen (2 hourly; 4hr 30min); Frederikshavn (hourly; 1hr 10min).
Bus Århus (via Hobro; 1–2 daily; 4hr); Copenhagen (3 daily; 5hr 30min); Odense (via Hobro; 4 weekly; 4hr).

THE FAROE ISLANDS

Accessible only via plane or ferry, the remote and otherworldly Faroe Islands are an archipelago of 18 wild, green, steeply pitching isles buffeted by North Atlantic winds, making for an unforgettable adventure and a fascinating insight into Denmark's former colonial territories (islanders prefer the term autonomous region). The islands are characterized by the abundance of sheep (which outnumber humans and have fuelled the trade in Faroese woollen products since they were worn by the cast in the iconic Danish TV-series *The Killing*) and by Denmark's most dramatic scenery. Krone is the currency and Danish/English are understood.

What to see and do

The world's smallest capital city, **Torshavn**, a tranquil port of colourful turf-roofed houses, is the obvious starting point for island explorations. The historic **Tingenes** area by the harbour, is of most interest, along with the islands' now-famous woollen handicrafts showcased at Gudrun & Gudrun (Dalagøta 12; ⓦwww.gudrungudrun.com). Northwest on the island of Eysturoy and connected by bus #400 from Torshavn is **Leirvik**, a fishing village famed for its wonderful **Boat Museum** (harbourfront; May–Sept Mon–Sat 10am–5pm; contact Torshavn tourist office before visiting). Further northwest from Torshavn is **Viðoy**, a wild island boasting some of Europe's highest sea cliffs and a haven for birdlife. To reach the cliffs at **Cape Enniberg**, head to the village of Viðareiði (bus #400 from Torshavn to Klaksvik then bus #500; five daily; 90kr) from where it's a tough, mountainous walk. The remotest inhabited island is spectacular **Mykines**, to the extreme west of the archipelago. Truly lost in time, it has some of the Faroes' best hiking. Get to Mykines via helicopter from Vágar Airport (ⓦwww.atlantic.fo) or boat from nearby Sørvágur (summer only).

Arrival and information

Air Vagar Airport, 30km west of Torshavn, is connected to the capital by bus (ten daily; 45min; 90kr).

Ferry Ferries dock in the centre of Torshavn.

Tourist office Bryggjubakki 12 (ⓦwww.visitfaroeislands.com). Can advise on accommodation/ activities/ transport on all the islands. Pick up the excellent English-language leaflet "Walking The Faroe Islands". Due to extreme conditions a guide for any hike on the Faroes is strongly recommended.

Accommodation, eating and drinking

Áarstova Gongin 1. Brilliant, snug new restaurant in one of Torshavn's oldest houses, specializing in Faroese cuisine. Get your salted fish and wind-dried lamb here. Lunches 90kr, evening mains from 190kr.

Café Natur Aarvegur 7. The liveliest joint in town. Harbourside café-bar sporting the Faroes' best beer selection with live music at weekends.

Kerjaon Hostel Oyggjarvegur 45 ⓣ298.31.75.00, ⓦwww.hotelforoyar.com. The best budget accommodation in Torshavn, located next to the *Hotel Føroyar*. 175kr.

Moving on

Air There are direct flights with Atlantic Airways to Denmark's Copenhagen Kastrup Airport (several daily) and Billund Airport (five weekly). Flights also go to Stavanger in Norway and London Stanstead in the UK (both twice weekly in summer).

Boat Smyril Lines (ⓦwww.smyrilline.com) run the long-but-memorable ferry from Hirtshalls southwest of Skagen on Jutland (2 weekly; 36hr; from 1800kr return). The same company also run weekly boats to Iceland during summer.

SKAGEN

About 100km north of Aalborg, **SKAGEN** sits at the very top of Denmark amid breathtaking heather-topped sand dunes. A popular resort, it attracts thousands of visitors annually thanks to its artistic connections and wonderful seafood restaurants.

What to see and do

Much of Skagen's appeal lies in aimlessly wandering its marina or cycling out to its fabulous beaches. There is one star sight, however – the **Skagen Museum** (signposted from train station; daily

THE SKAGEN ARTISTS

Skagen has long been popular with artists thanks to the warm, golden sunlight that illuminates its coastal scenery. During the 1870s a group of painters inspired by naturalism settled here and began to paint the local fishermen working on the beaches as well as each other. The **Skagen artists**, among them Michael and Anna Ancher and P.S. Krøyer, stayed until the turn of the century and achieved international recognition for their work, now on display at the Skagen Museum.

10am–5pm, May–Aug Wed until 9pm; closed Mon Sept–April; 80kr; Ⓦwww.skagensmuseum.dk), displaying much of the work of the influential Skagen artists (see box above). Nearby, at Markvej 2–4, is the home of one of the group's leading lights and his wife, herself a skilful painter: the **Michael and Anna Anchers Hus** (May–Oct daily 10/11am–3/6pm; Nov–April Sat 11am–3pm; 60kr). Around 1.5km southwest of the hostel is the **Buried Church**, which was engulfed by sand drift in 1795 and subsequently abandoned. Today the white spire is all that remains amid the dunes. **Old Skagen,** 4 kilometres west of the centre, is where Denmark's jet set have their villas: head to the **Solnedgangspladsen** here to watch the spectacular sunsets.

Grenen

Denmark's northernmost tip is at **Grenen**, 3km from Skagen along Strandvej and the beach, where two seas – the Kattegat and Skagerrak – meet, often with a powerful clashing of waves. You can get here by tractor-drawn bus (April to mid-Oct; 25kr return) – although it's an enjoyable walk through beautiful seaside scenery. At the tip you'll find some fascinating World War II heritage, an ambient restaurant and miles of blissful quiescence.

Arrival and information

Train The train station is on Sct. Laurentii Vej, the town's main thoroughfare. It's served by privately operated trains from Frederikshavn (50 percent discount with Eurail/InterRail) roughly once an hour.

Tourist office Vestre Strandvej 10, close to the marina (June–Aug Mon–Sat 9am–6pm & Sun 10am–2pm; rest of year Mon–Fri 9.30am–4pm; Ⓣ98.44.13.77, Ⓦwww.skagen-tourist.dk). Can arrange private rooms (around 350kr for 75kr fee).

Bike rental Skagen Cykeludlegning by the train station (80kr/day, plus 200kr deposit).

Accommodation

Danhostel Skagen Rolighedsvej 2 Ⓣ98.44.22.00, Ⓦwww.danhostelnord.dk/skagen. A little way out of the centre, but the rooms are clean and good value. Breakfast 50kr. The nearest train station is actually Frederikshavnsvej. Reservations essential in summer. Closed Dec- to mid Feb. Dorms 150kr, doubles 600kr.

Grenen Camping Fyrvej Ⓣ98.44.25.46, Ⓦwww.grenencamping.dk. By the beach 1.5km along the road to Grenen. Closed mid-Sept to late April. 75–85kr/person, plus 35–50kr/tent in July/Aug.

Eating, drinking and nightlife

Skagen has fantastic "fresh-off-the-boat" seafood: treat yourself to a blowout meal at one of the marina restaurants, like *Pakhuset* at Rødspættevej 6.

Brøndhums Hotel Anchersvej 3. Near the Skagen Museum and historically more important as it was here that the Skagen Artists met, ate, stayed and socialized. You can do the same in the wonderfully atmospheric hotel restaurant; *smørrebrød* is an affordable 70–80kr.

Buddy Holly Havnevej 16 Ⓦwww.buddy-skagen.dk. Pretty cheesy but this is Skagen's liveliest club with plenty of drinks deals. Daily 10pm–5am in summer.

Jacobs Café Havnevej 4. Lively café-bar with outside seating and free internet access. Sandwiches 75–85kr.

Moving on

Train Frederikshavn (hourly; 35min).

Estonia

HIGHLIGHTS ★

LAHEMAA NATIONAL PARK: pristine wilderness teeming with wildlife on Estonia's north coast

TALLINN'S OLD TOWN: wander this beautifully preserved corner of the city

SAAREMAA: a perfect island getaway with a beautiful castle and relaxing spa hotels

TARTU: party the night away with the student population of Tartu

PÄRNU BEACH: enjoy a bracing dip in the Baltic or take a mud bath in a local spa

ROUGH COSTS

DAILY BUDGET Basic €50 /occasional treat €70

DRINK A. Le Coq beer €2.50

FOOD Blood sausage and *sauerkraut* €5

HOSTEL/BUDGET HOTEL €22/€45

TRAVEL Bus: Tallinn–Saaremaa €16; Tartu–Tallinn €12

FACT FILE

POPULATION 1.4 million

AREA 45,227 sq km

LANGUAGE Estonian

CURRENCY Euro (€)

CAPITAL Tallinn (population: 413, 290)

INTERNATIONAL PHONE CODE ⓣ372

Introduction

Visitors to Estonia encounter a mix of urbanity and wilderness, of the medieval and the contemporary, with crumbling castles and colourful design permeating urban landscapes. An efficient transport system makes it easy to get around, and the tech-savvy, dynamic residents welcome visitors with open arms. Friction between older generations of Russians and Estonians is a throwback to the Soviet era, while younger people mix freely, and those who get past the Estonians' natural reserve find them to be gregarious, uninhibited hosts.

Estonia's capital, **Tallinn**, has a magnificent medieval centre and lively nightlife, rivalled only by that of **Tartu**, an exuberant university town. **Pärnu**, a popular seaside resort, is also worth a short visit. For inexpensive spa treatments, a fine castle and unspoilt countryside head for the island of **Saaremaa**, while **Lahemaa National Park**, outside Tallinn, offers a taste of pristine wilderness.

CHRONOLOGY

100s AD Tacitus refers to the Aestii people – the forebears of the Estonians.
1154 Estonia depicted on a map of the world for the first time.
1219 Danish conquer North Estonia, ushering in over a century of Danish rule.
1227 German crusaders invade the rest of Estonia.
1346 Danish territories in Estonia sold to the German Livonian Order.
1525 First book printed in the Estonian language.
1561 Livonian Order surrender their Estonian territory to Sweden.
1625 Sweden takes control over all Estonia.
1632 Estonia's first university opens in Tartu.
1721 Russia defeats Sweden in the Northern War and takes over Estonia.
1816 Serfdom is abolished in Estonia.
Late 1800s The spread of the Estonian language in schools is instrumental in increasing Estonian nationalism.
1918 Estonia states its claim to independence but is invaded by the Red Army starting the Estonian War of Independence.
1920 The Russians are defeated giving Estonia full independence.
1934 Authoritarian rule is established by Prime Minister Konstantin Pats.
1940 Soviets invade Estonia.
1944 Soviets maintain control by end of World War II, ushering in Communist rule.
1988 The "Singing Revolution" begins with huge crowds gathering to sing national songs.
1991 The fall of the Soviet Union leads to Estonian independence.
2004 Estonia joins NATO and the EU.
2007 Estonia is the first country to introduce internet voting for national elections.
2009 Estonia's economy takes a downturn as a result of the global economic crisis.
2011 The euro becomes Estonia's official currency.

ARRIVAL

The compact and ultramodern **Tallinn Airport** (Ⓦwww.tallinn-airport.ee) is served by fifteen European airlines, including easyJet. Estonian Air (Ⓦwww.estonian-air.ee) offers direct flights from many major capitals including London, Dublin, Frankfurt, Barcelona and Stockholm. International **bus lines**, such as Eurolines (Ⓦwww.eurolines.ee), Ecolines (Ⓦwww.ecolines.net) and Hansabuss (Ⓦwww.hansabuss.ee), connect Tallinn via Tartu or Pärnu to Russia (Kaliningrad, St Petersburg), Latvia (Rīga), Lithuania (Vilnius, Kaunas), Poland (Kraków, Warsaw), and Germany (Berlin, Bonn, Cologne, Hamburg, Munich, Stuttgart), among others. The only international **rail service** from Estonia is the daily overnight train from Tallinn to Moscow – book seats in advance. Tallinn can also be reached by **ferry** from Helsinki, Finland and from Stockholm, Sweden.

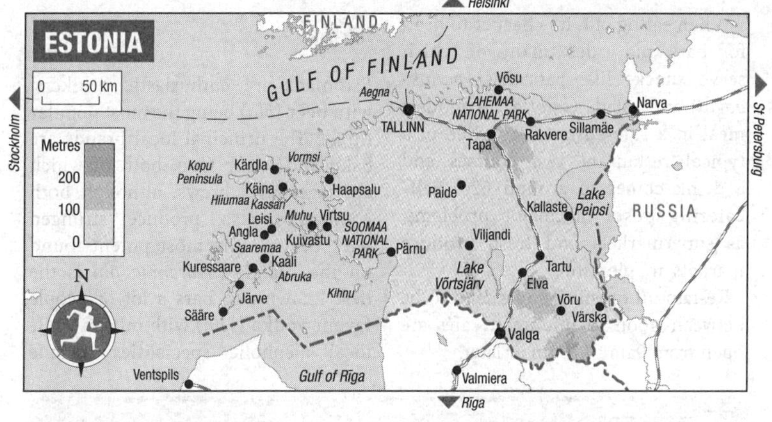

GETTING AROUND

Bus tickets can be bought either from the bus station ticket office or directly from the driver. Online schedules available at ⓦwww.bussireisid.ee; buy tickets in advance if you're travelling in the height of summer or at weekends. **Buses** are also the best method for travelling to neighbouring Baltic countries, with numerous daily services linking Tallinn, Vilnius and Rīga via Pärnu.

The **rail network** is limited, but trains are as fast as buses and slightly cheaper. Check ⓦwww.edel.ee for times and prices; purchase your ticket from the conductor.

The bigger cities have efficient **public transport** systems, and are well geared towards being explored by **bike**, as are the islands such as Saaremaa. Due to the scarcity of public transport on the islands, many locals hitchhike; the usual precautions apply.

ESTONIA ONLINE

ⓦ**www.visitestonia.com** Extensive tourist board site covering all things Estonian.
ⓦ**www.baltictimes.com** English-language weekly newspaper.
ⓦ**www.inyourpocket.com** Excellent guide covering Tallinn, Tartu and Pärnu.

ACCOMMODATION

Though cheaper than in Western Europe, accommodation in Estonia will still take a large chunk out of most budgets. Tallinn has a vibrant **youth hostel** scene, though outside of the capital, some **hostels** are just student dorms converted for the summer. Beds cost €16–22 per person. Youth hostels aside, booking a **private room** is often the cheapest option (€23–27/person). This can be arranged through tourist offices or private agencies. There are also plain guesthouse or *pension* rooms for €25–35 per person including breakfast, though the cheapest of these are not always centrally located.

FOOD AND DRINK

Mainstays of **Estonian cuisine** include soup (*supp*), dark bread (*leib*) and herring (*heeringas*), culinary legacies of the country's largely peasant past. A typical national dish is *verevorst* and *mulgikapsad* (blood sausage and sauerkraut); various kinds of smoked fish, particularly eel (*angerjas*), perch (*ahven*) and pike (*haug*), are popular too, as are **Russian dishes** such as *pelmeenid* (ravioli with meat or mushrooms). Both Tallinn and Tartu also boast an impressive choice of ethnic **restaurants**. Outside these two cities, **vegetarians** will find their choice to be more limited.

When eating out, it's cheaper to head for bars and cafés, many of which serve **snacks** like pancakes (*pannkoogid*) and salads (*salatid*). A modest meal in a café costs €6–8, while in a typical restaurant two courses and a drink comes to around €20. **Self-catering** poses no major problems, as supermarkets and fresh produce markets are plentiful.

Restaurant opening hours tend to be between noon to midnight; cafés are open from 9am to 10pm or later.

Drink

Estonians are enthusiastic drinkers, with **beer** (*õlu*) being the most popular tipple. The principal local brands are Saku and A. Le Coq, both of which are lager-style brews, although both companies also produce stronger, dark beers – the most potent found on the islands (*Saaremaa õlu* is the best known). In bars a lot of people favour **vodka** (*viin*) with mixers while local alcoholic specialities include

ESTONIAN

	Estonian	Pronunciation
Yes	*Jah*	Yah
No	*Ei*	Ey
Please	*Palun*	Palun
Thank you	*Aitäh/tänan*	Ayteh, tanan
Hello/Good day	*Tere*	Tere
Goodbye	*Head aega*	Heyad ayga
Excuse me	*Vabandage*	Vabandage
Where?	*Kus?*	Kus?
Student ticket	*Õpilase pilet*	Ypilahse pilet
Toilet	*Tualett*	Tualet
I'd like	*Ma sooviksin*	Mah sawviksin
I don't eat meat	*Ma ei söö*	Mah ay serr
The bill, please	*Palun arve*	Pahlun ahrrve
Good/Bad	*Hea/Halb*	Heya/Holb
Near/Far	*Lähedal/Kaugel*	Lahedal/Cowgal
Cheap/Expensive	*Odav/Kallis*	Odav/Kallis
Open/Closed	*Avatud/Suletud*	Avatud/Suletud
Today	*Täna*	Tana
Yesterday	*Eile*	Eyle
Tomorrow	*Homme*	Homme
How much is...?	*Kui palju maksab...?*	Kuy palyo maksab...?
What time is it?	*Mis kell praegu on?*	Mis kell prego on?
I don't understand	*Ma ei saa aru*	May saaru
Do you speak English?	*Kas te räägite inglise keelt?*	Kas te raagite inglise kelt?
One	*Uks*	Uks
Two	*Kaks*	Koks
Three	*Kolm*	Kolm
Four	*Neli*	Neli
Five	*Viis*	Vees
Six	*Kuus*	Koos
Seven	*Seitse*	Seytse
Eight	*Kaheksa*	Koheksa
Nine	*Üheksa*	Ooheksa
Ten	*Kümme*	Koome

hõõgvein (mulled wine) and **Vana Tallinn**, a pungent dark liqueur which some suicidal souls mix with vodka. **Pubs and bars** – most of which imitate Irish or American models – are taking over, especially in Tallinn. If you're not boozing, head for a *kohvik* (café); **coffee** (*kohvi*) is usually of the filter variety, and **tea** (*teed*) is served without milk (*piima*) or sugar (*suhkur*) – ask for both if necessary. Bars are usually open from noon until 2 or 4am on weekends.

CULTURE AND ETIQUETTE

Estonians tend to be reserved when you first meet them, though if you are lucky enough to be invited to a local home, you will see their warm and generous side. Unused to loud displays of emotion, they are scandalized by the loutish behaviour of foreign stag parties, although they do enjoy sociable drinking. A ten percent **tip** is sufficient in restaurants to reward good service; otherwise just round up the bill.

SPORTS AND OUTDOOR ACTIVITIES

Football and **basketball** are the national sports; for the former, go to the A. Le Coq Arena (Asula 4c; ⓣ627 9940) whereas Tallinn's Kalev Stadium (Juhkentali 12; ⓣ644 5171) is the best place to see a basketball game. In the summertime, Estonia becomes a haven for **watersports**: windsurfing, kayaking, canoeing or simply hitting the beach. **Hiking**, **biking** and **horseriding** are popular both on the Estonian mainland and on the islands off its coast, such as Saaremaa and Hiimaa. Almost twenty percent of Estonia is protected land, divided between four **national parks** and numerous **nature reserves**, which are home to many species of wild animals and birds. National parks are best visited between May and September; RMK (ⓦwww.rmk.ee) manages the protected areas and campsites.

COMMUNICATIONS

Post offices (*postkontor*) are open Monday to Friday 8am to 6pm and Saturday 9am to 3pm. Most **public phones** take phonecards (available at kiosks and post offices) for local and long-distance calls. Alternatively, you can either purchase a local starter kit (which includes a SIM card and free talk time) for your mobile phone, or use a mobile phone from another European country, since it is relatively inexpensive; consult your service provider about roaming charges. **Internet cafés** have become scarce due to the proliferation of free wi-fi hotspots; free wi-fi is offered by most cafés and restaurants, and by all accommodation options in this chapter.

EMERGENCIES

Theft and street crime are at relatively low levels. The **police** (*politsei*) are mostly young and some speak English. **Emergency health care** is free and, in Tallinn at least, emergency operators speak English.

INFORMATION

Tourist offices (ⓦwww.visitestonia.com) can be useful for booking B&Bs and hotel rooms, as well as good-quality free **maps**; most bookstores also have good map sections. The *In Your Pocket* guides (ⓦwww.inyourpocket.com) are excellent listings guides, available from tourist offices and kiosks for €2.20.

MONEY AND BANKS

Currency is the euro (€), which is divided into 100 cents. Notes come as €5, 10, 20, 50, 100, 200 and 500, and

EMERGENCY NUMBERS

Police ☎110; Fire & ambulance ☎112.

coins as 1, 2, 5, 10, 20, and 50 cents and 1 and 2 euros. Bank (*pank*) opening hours are Monday to Friday 9am to 4pm, with most also open on Saturday from 9am to 2pm. **ATMs** are widely available. **Credit cards** can be used in most hotels, restaurants and stores, but outside urban areas cash is preferred.

OPENING HOURS AND HOLIDAYS

Most **shops** open Monday to Friday 10am to 6pm and Saturday 10am to 3pm, but many larger ones stay open later and are also open on Sundays. **Public holidays**, when most shops and all banks are closed, are: January 1, February 24, Good Friday, Easter Monday, May 1, June 23 and 24, August 20, December 25 and 26.

Tallinn

TALLINN, Estonia's compact, buzzing capital, with its enchanting heart surrounded by medieval walls, has been shaped by nearly a millennium of outside influence. However, once the staple crumbling backdrop for Soviet fairytale films, Tallinn has now reinvented itself as an inexpensive weekend getaway for Europeans, and these days its buzzing cafés, pubs and clubs can offer a variety of hedonistic pursuits on a night out.

What to see and do

The heart of Tallinn is the **Old Town**, still largely enclosed by the city's medieval walls. At its centre is the **Raekoja plats**, the historic marketplace, above which looms **Toompea**, the hilltop stronghold of the German knights who controlled the city during the Middle Ages. East of the city centre there are several places worth a visit such as **Kadriorg Park**, a peaceful wooded area with a cluster of historic buildings and a view of the sea; the forested island of **Aegna** and the **Lauluväljak** amphitheatre.

Raekoja plats

Raekoja plats, the cobbled market square at the heart of the Old Town, is as old as the city itself. On its southern side stands the fifteenth-century **Town Hall** (Raekoda), boasting elegant Gothic arches at ground level, and a delicate steeple at its northern end. Near the summit of the steeple, **Vana Toomas**, a sixteenth-century weathervane depicting a medieval town guard, is Tallinn's city emblem. The well-labelled and informative **museum** inside the cellar hall (May–Sept Mon–Sat 10am–4pm; rest of the year closed weekends; €4) depicts Tallinn town life through the ages, and there is a good view from the belfry. For an even better view of the town square, climb the spiral staircase of the **Town Hall Tower** (Raekoja Torn; May–Sept daily 11am–6pm; €3).

THE TALLINN CARD

To do a lot of sightseeing in a short space of time, it can be really worth your while to pick up a **Tallinn Card** (www.tallinncard.ee; €12/24/32/40 for 6/24/48/72hr), which gives you unlimited free rides on public transport as well as free entry to a plethora of attractions and discounts in shops and restaurants. Check website for details.

Church of the Holy Ghost and St Nicholas's Church

The fourteenth-century **Church of the Holy Ghost** (Puhä Vaimu kirik; May–Sept Mon–Sat 9am–5pm; rest of the year 10am–3pm) on Pühavaimu is the city's oldest church, a small Gothic building with stuccoed limestone walls, stepped gables, carved wooden interior, a tall, verdigris-coated spire and an ornate clock from 1680 – the oldest in Tallinn.

Contrasting sharply is the late Gothic **St Nicholas's Church** (Niguliste kirik; Wed–Sun 10am–5pm; museum €3.20) southwest of Raekoja plats. Dating back to the 1820s and rebuilt after being mostly destroyed in a 1944 Soviet air raid, the church now serves as a museum of church art, including medieval burial stones and the haunting *Danse Macabre* ("Dance With Death") by Bernt Notke. It also hosts free organ recitals (Sat & Sun 4pm).

Toompea and the Aleksander Nevsky Cathedral

Toompea is the hill where the Danes built their fortress after conquering what is now Tallinn in 1219. According to legend, it is also the grave of **Kalev**, the mythical ancestor of the Estonians.

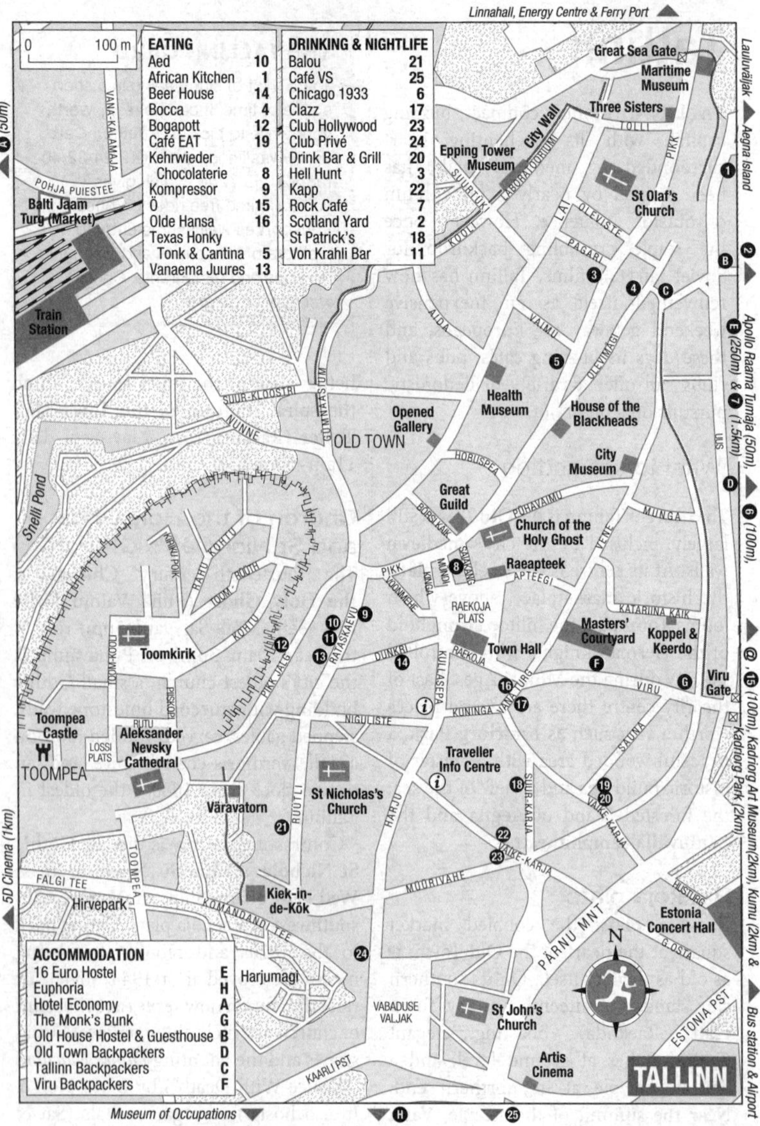

Approach through the sturdy gate tower – built by the Teutonic Knights to contain the Old Town's inhabitants in times of unrest – at the foot of Pikk jalg. This is the cobbled continuation of Pikk, the Old Town's main street, that climbs up to Lossi plats, dominated by the impressive-looking **Aleksander Nevsky Cathedral** (8am–7pm). This imposing onion-domed structure was built at the end of the nineteenth century for the city's Orthodox population – an enduring reminder of the two centuries Tallinn spent under tsarist rule.

At the head of Lossi plats, the pink **Toompea Castle** stands on the original

WACKY TALLINN

Those with a taste for the macabre won't want to miss the **Estonia Health Care Museum** (Tues–Sat 11am–6pm; €2.60) at Lai 28. There are some real gems on display, such as the mummified body of a man. You'll marvel at how a human body could possibly pass the impressive array of kidney stones and peer with horrified fascination at the absorbing collection of this-is-what-happens-if-you-don't-get-that-venereal-disease-seen-to-promptly wax moulds of male and female genitalia.

Danish fortification site. Today's castle is the descendant of a stone fortress built by the Knights of the Sword, the Germanic crusaders who kicked out the Danes in 1227 and controlled the city until 1238 (when the Danes returned). The building is now home to the **Riigikogu**, Estonia's parliament (Mon–Fri 10am–4pm; admission by guided tour only; ☎631 6345).

Kiek-in-de-Kök and Bastion Tunnels

The imposing **Kiek-in-de-Kök tower** (March–Oct Tues–Sun 10.30am–5.30pm; until 4.30pm rest of the year; €4.50; joint ticket with Bastion Tunnels €8.30), dating from 1475, stands on Komandandi tee. It houses interactive displays on the development of the town and its fortifications throughout its history, as well as changing contemporary art displays in the cellar. Below the tower lies the entrance to a network of seventeenth-century **bastion tunnels**, originally built for defence by the Swedes but most recently used as bomb shelters during World War II. Guided tours (twice daily; €5.75 ☎644 6686) initiate you into the tunnels' history and legend; bring warm clothes as the temperature tends to be a cool 6–8°C even in the height of summer.

The Museum of Occupations

South of Lossi plats, on Toompea 8, the airy and modern **Museum of Occupations** (June–Aug daily 10am–6pm; rest of year 11am–6pm; €2) brings to life the personal experience of Estonians under Nazi and Soviet occupation through use of interactive exhibitions, and displays of artefacts from 1940–1991.

Pikk and around

Pikk tänav, running northeast from Pikk jalg gate and linking Toompea with the port area, has some of the city's most elaborate examples of **merchants' houses** from the Hanseatic period, including the **Great Guild** at Pikk 17, headquarters of the German merchants who controlled the city's wealth; the **House of the Blackheads**, Pikk 26, with a lavishly decorated Renaissance facade; and the **Three Sisters**, a gabled group at Pikk 71. Supremely functional with loading hatches and winch-arms set into their facades, these would have served as combined dwelling places, warehouses and offices. Take the parallel street of Vene to the outstanding **Tallinn City Museum** at no. 17 (March–Oct Wed–Mon 10.30am–6.30pm; Nov–Feb 10.30am–5pm; €3.20), which imaginatively recounts the history of Tallinn from the thirteenth century through to Soviet and Nazi occupations and Estonian independence.

St Olaf's Church

At the northern end of Pikk stands the enormous Gothic **St Olaf's Church** (Oleviste kirik), first mentioned in 1267 and named in honour of King Olaf II of Norway, who was canonized for battling against pagans in Scandinavia. The church is chiefly famous for its 124-metre spire, which you can climb for a spectacular view of Old Town and the port (daily 10am–6pm, July & Aug until 8pm; €2).

The Maritime Museum and city wall

The sixteenth-century **Great Sea Gate**, which straddles Pikk at its far end, is flanked by two towers. The larger of these, Fat Margaret Tower, has walls four metres thick and now houses the **Estonian Maritime Museum** (Tues–Sun 10am–6pm; €3.20; some English captioning), a surprisingly entertaining four floors of nautical instruments, scale models of ships and antique diving equipment. Down Gümnaasiumi, is one of the longest extant sections of Tallinn's medieval **city wall**. The 4km of walls that surrounded the Old Town were mostly constructed during the fourteenth century. Today, 1.85km of it still stands, along with twenty of the original 46 towers. You can enter three of the oldest towers, Nunne, Kuldjala and Sauna, from Gümnaasiumi 3 (Mon–Wed & Fri 11am–5pm, Sat & Sun 11am–4pm; €1.30).

Kadriorg Park

Kadriorg Park, a heavily wooded area 2km east of the Old Town along Narva mnt., was laid out according to the instructions of Russian tsar Peter the Great. The main entrance to the park is at the junction of Weizenbergi tänav and J. Poska (tram #1 or #3 from Viru väljak). Weizenbergi cuts through the park, running straight past **Kadriorg Palace**, a Baroque residence designed by the Italian architect Niccolò Michetti, which Peter had built for his wife Catherine. The palace houses the **Kadriorg Art Museum** (May–Sept Tues–Sun 10am–5pm; Oct–April Wed–Sun 10am–5pm; €4.20), with a fine collection of Dutch and Russian paintings. A short walk up Weizenbergi, the immense, futuristic-looking **KUMU** (May–Sept Tues–Sun 11am–6pm; Oct–April Wed–Sun 11am–6pm; €5.50) is a must-see for anyone interested in Estonian art through the ages.

Aegna Island

An hour's ride on the boat from the nearby **Pirita harbour** (take bus #1, #34 or #38 from the underground stop at the Viru Centre; €7.50 return), tiny peaceful **Aegna** is an excellent day-trip destination (May–Sept Mon & Wed–Fri three ferries daily, Sat & Sun four ferries daily; double-check timetable with tourist office). Its forest-covered interior and clean beaches attract locals who camp here in the summer.

Arrival and information

Air The Lennart Meri Tallinn Airport (*lennu jaam*) is 3km southeast of the city centre and linked to Viru väljak by bus #2 (every 20min; 6am–midnight; €1.20). It stops behind the Viru shopping mall, 5min walk from the Old Town's Viru Gate.

Train Tallinn's train station (*balti jaam*) is at Toompuiestee 35, just northwest of the Old Town, 10min walk to the Town Square. There are ATMs by the front doors.

Bus The city's bus terminal (*autobussi jaam*) is at Lastekodu 46, 2km southeast of the centre; there is an ATM and luggage storage. Trams #2 and #4 run from nearby Tartu mnt. to Viru väljak at the eastern

ESTONIA'S SONG FESTIVAL

The **Lauluväljak** at Narva mnt. 95 (ⓦ www.lauluvaljak.ee), just to the northeast of Kadriorg Park, is a vast amphitheatre which is the venue for Estonia's **Song Festivals**. These gatherings, featuring a choir 25-thousand-strong, are held every five years, and have been an important form of national expression since the first all-Estonia Song Festival held in Tartu in 1869. The grounds were filled to their 45,000-person capacity for the 1988 festival when people joined their voices in song as a significant public expression of longing for independence from Soviet rule, in what became known as the **"Singing Revolution"**. The next Song Festival is in July 2014.

TALLINN TOURS

Tallinn can be explored in many different ways. Here are some of the more innovative tours:

City Bike Tours Uus 33 ⓣ511 1819, ⓦwww.citybike.ee. Tours of the Old Town and beyond run by young, energetic guides, as well as a "Legends and Secret Tunnels" afternoon walking tour. Groups can try the weird and wonderful "Conference Bike". Guided and self-guided tours of Lahemaa National Park available.

EstAdventures ⓣ5308 8373, ⓦwww.estadventures.ee. Small-group tours of Tallinn ("Legends of Tallinn" comes particularly recommended), as well as day-trips to Lahemaa National Park.

Hop-on, hop-off bus For easy access to attractions outside the Old Town, such as Kadriorg Park, complete with running commentary, hop on one of the tour buses just outside Viru Gate. Bus passes: adults €16/20/23 for 24/48/72hr; students €13/16/20 for 24/48/72hr.

Tallinn Traveller Info Info Tent opposite the tourist office June–Aug (daily 10am–10pm); otherwise drop by the Traveller Info Centre at Vana Posti 2 (daily 10am–6pm; ⓣ5837 4800, ⓦwww.traveller.ee). The excellent and inexpensive "Chill-out Tour", "Beautiful Bike Tour" or the "Funky Bike Tour" present Tallinn and its environs in a novel way, led by young, knowledgeable, multilingual student guides.

entrance to the Old Town; alternatively, take any bus heading west along Juhkentali.

Boat Arriving by sea, the passenger port (*reisisadam*) is just northeast of the centre at Sadama 25. For updated schedules see ⓦwww.portoftallinn.com.

Tourist office Kullasseppa 4 (May–Sept Mon–Fri 9am–7pm, Sat & Sun 10am–5pm; Oct–April Mon–Fri 9am–5pm, Sat 10am–3pm; ⓣ645 7777, ⓦwww.tourism.tallinn.ee). You can also buy the Tallinn Card here (see box, p.339).

City transport

Public transport Tallinn has an extensive tram, bus and trolleybus network. Tickets (*talongid*) for all three systems are available from kiosks near stops for €0.96 (book of 10 for €6.39) or from the driver for €1.60. Validate your ticket using the on-board punches. Kiosks also stock 24/72hr passes for €4.47/7.35.

Accommodation

Demand for budget accommodation still outstrips supply in summer, so book in advance. You can find central and excellent-value private rooms at Mere 4 with *Bed & Breakfast Rasastra* (Mon–Sat 9.30am–6pm, Sun 9.30am–5pm; ⓣ661 6291, ⓦwww.bedbreakfast.ee), an agency offering singles €16, doubles €34 & triples €40 in family homes throughout the Baltics, and private apartments (€40–165) for longer stays.

16 Euro Hostel Roseni 9 ⓣ501 3046, ⓦwww.16eur.ee. Just outside the Old Town walls, this tastefully decorated cheapie haven offers free use of sauna and swimming pool (9–11am) to complement your stay in one of its en-suite rooms or dorms. Dorms €13, doubles, triples or quads €16–19/person.

Euphoria Roosikrantsi 4 ⓣ5837 3602, ⓦwww.euphoria.ee. A four-storey hostel with a great communal atmosphere, impromptu jamming sessions, clean dorms and a couple of rooms, all with shared facilities. You can smoke a hookah and even paint your own mural in the large common room. Dorms €13–14; private 2/3/4-bed rooms €19/17/16/person.

Hotel Economy Kopli 2c ⓣ667 8300, ⓦwww.economyhotel.ee. Refurbished 1920s hotel offering modern and comfortable rooms overlooking the train station area on the outskirts of the Old Town. Breakfast is included, as is wi-fi in the lobby. Singles €35, doubles €55, triples €80.

The Monk's Bunk Viru 22 ⓣ665 1120, ⓦwww.themonksbunk.com. New hostel that's sociable without being a stag party magnet, whose staff go out of their way to keep guests entertained with a variety of day-trips, tours and pub crawls. Spacious dorms have comfortable beds and good ratio of guests per shower eliminates queuing. Dorms €10–14.

Old House Hostel & Guesthouse Uus 26 ⓣ641 1281, ⓦwww.oldhouse.ee. Renovated, quiet Old Town house with attractive dorms and a handful of cosy twin rooms with shared bath, guest lounge and kitchen. Wi-fi available. Dorms €15, doubles €29, triples €39.

TREAT YOURSELF

FEAST ON TALLINN'S FINEST

The decor at Ö (Mere pst. 6e, ⓣ661 6150) – sedate charcoal and cream - is simplicity itself, so your attention is directed at the exquisitely presented, modern Estonian dishes made from locally sourced, seasonal ingredients. Try the eel poached in apple wine (€13), the venison steak in wild mushroom sauce (€19) and finish off with chocolate fondue with home-made blueberry ice cream (€8).

Old Town Backpackers Uus 14 ⓣ5742 6961. With a vibe like your friend's living room after a party, this central backpacker favourite consists of two large open-plan rooms with bunk beds and additional pull-out couches. Huge guest kitchen, breakfast and free use of sauna included. Dorms €10.

Tallinn Backpackers Olevimägi 11 ⓣ644 0298, ⓦwww.tallinnbackpackers.com. This party spot encourages bonding between fellow international travellers, be it through video screenings, communal dinners or drink-your-own-height-in-beer-cans on "Wizard Wednesdays". Don't count on getting much sleep! Dorms €16–17.

Viru Backpackers Viru 5 ⓣ644 6050, ⓦwww.tallinnbackpackers.com. The calmer sister hostel to *Tallinn Backpackers* with quiet singles, doubles and triples, as well access to all *Tallinn Backpackers* facilities and an invitation to join their raucous parties, but with the option of actually sleeping afterwards. Singles €16, doubles €32, triples €38.

Eating

Self-caterers can try the Rimi supermarket at Aia 7 or else buy some cheap fresh produce at the Balti Jaama Turg (train station market) behind the train station.

Cafés

Bogapott Pikk jalg 9. This tiny family-run Tallinn institution, surrounded by part of the medieval wall, serves delicious sandwiches, coffee and pastries while you look around the art shop and ceramics studio. Coffee €1.50.

Café EAT Sauna 2. Popular with students, this basement establishment offers different kinds of *pelmeenid* (dumplings) and doughnuts, sold by weight (€0.65/100g). Cheap and very filling. Pint of cider €2.50.

Kehrwieder Chocolaterie Saiakang 1. Dark, warren-like cellar café filled with quirky old furniture, famous for its great handmade chocolates and gourmet coffees, though the latter don't come cheap. Coffee €2.40.

Kompressor Rataskaevu 3. Roomy café-bar popular with a youngish crowd, and famous for its wonderfully stodgy Estonian pancakes: a smoked-cheese-and-bacon pancake will set you back €3.50.

Restaurants

Aed Rataskaevu 8. The self-styled "Embassy of Pure Food" delivers delicious and imaginative fusion dishes, including many vegetarian options, such as spelt pasta with tofu (€4) and pumpkin risotto (€6.50).

African Kitchen Uus 34. Wide selection of peanut, coconut and rice dishes, some spicy and many vegetarian, prepared by a Nigerian chef and served in a jungle-themed lounge. Tasty smoothies (€3.50) and mains (€5.50–14).

Beer House Dunkri 5. Busy, roomy beer cellar which brews its own ales and serves up generous portions of imaginative meat dishes, such as elk and wild boar, as well as good, solid sausage-and-mash combos. Mains €8–12. Live music nightly.

Bocca Olevimägi 9. A chic cocktail spot in the evenings, this slick Italian restaurant with superbly executed dishes won't blow a hole in your budget if you stick to the soups and pastas. Try the linguine with grilled prawns and scallops (€12).

Olde Hansa Vana turg 1. Extremely popular yet affordable medieval-style restaurant inside an old tavern. Ask your serving wench for a starter plate to share with some elk/boar/bear sausages (€10) and wash it down with a tankard of honey mead.

Texas Honky Tonk & Cantina Pikk 43. This kitschy, lively Texan saloon attracts a quota of homesick Americans and anyone else hungry for ribs, burritos, tacos and burgers. Mains €6–10.

Vanaema Juures Rataskaevu 10/12. A Tallinn favourite for many years, "Grandma's Place" serves no-nonsense Estonian home food in a cosy cellar setting. Try Grandma's elk roast, the meatballs or the lamb in blue cheese sauce. Mains €5–8. Closes 6pm Sundays.

Drinking and nightlife

Most of Tallinn's popular clubs cater for a mainstream crowd. More underground, cutting-edge dance music events change location frequently and are advertised by flyers, or try asking around in the city's hipper bars; expect to pay €4–10 admission.

Bars

Café VS Pärnu mnt. 28. This hip café by day with purple/silver industrial decor morphs into a chilled out DJ venue by night, randomly complete with great Indian food. Start your day with a masala omelette (€4.80) or bring a friend if you order the chicken biriyani to go with your late-night beats – portions are generous (€7).

Drink Bar & Grill Väike-Karja 8. The patrons at this lively bar are a mixed bunch: locals, backpackers and expats – but all are united in their love of unusual beers, organic ciders and the bar's own house brew.

Hell Hunt Pikk 39. Lively pub packed with expats and locals most nights. It's spacious, friendly and serves its own excellent light and dark Hunt beer.

Scotland Yard Mere pst. 6e. Large, lively pub with live music nightly, a large dancefloor, and a queue to the bar; dress extra pretty to catch the leisurely barman's eye. If after a drink or two you find that the toilets resemble electric chairs, relax: they're supposed to.

St Patrick's Suur-Karja 8. The pick of Tallinn's Irish pubs, set in a beautifully restored medieval house and popular with expats, tourists and locals alike. Your fourth Saku Originaal beer comes free.

Von Krahli Bar Rataskaevu 10/12. "Krahl" to regulars, this large hip hangout is always packed with a mix of local students and bohemian types. Frequent live music – from alternative to reggae to hip-hop. Good, cheap food: huge daily specials €4.

Clubs

Balou Rüütli 18 ⓦ www.balou.ee. Popular subterranean club attracts a young crowd with some very danceable beats. Free or up to €8, depending on the night. Thurs & Fri 11pm–5am, Sat 11pm–6am.

Club Hollywood Vana-Posti 8 ⓦ www.clubhollywood.ee. Large Old Town dance club playing techno, R'n'B and hip-hop. Very popular with a younger crowd as well as tourists. €3–7; free entry for women on Wednesdays. Wed–Sat 11pm–5am.

Club Privé Harju 6 ⓦ www.clubprive.ee. Style-conscious temple to cutting-edge dance culture, often attracting big-name DJs; check the schedule. You have to be 20 years old and above. Entry €7–14. Thurs 11pm–5am, Fri & Sat midnight–6am.

Kapp Vana-Posti 8. *Kapp* (Estonian for "closet") is frequented by a mixed gay and straight crowd for the cocktails, great music, chilled out ambience and good beats. Sun–Thurs 5pm–midnight, Fri & Sat 5pm–4am.

Live music

Chicago 1933 Aia 3 ⓦ www.chicago.ee. The name says it all: this swinging joint successfully recreates the ambience of the 1930s in the Windy City, its patrons sliding into dark wood booths to enjoy some excellent live blues. Entry €14. Sun–Thurs noon–1am, Fri & Sat noon–3am.

Clazz Vana Turg 2 ⓦ www.clazz.ee. One of the most popular venues in the Old Town for nightly live music – from blues to jazz to Latin, Fri & Sat 11am–4am, rest of week until 2am, shorter hours in winter.

Rock Café Tartu mnt 80d, 3rd floor ⓦ www.rockcafe.ee. Two-storey rock club in a warehouse near the bus station, with a superb sound system and excellent live acts on weekends – largely rock, but also occasional blues. Entry €3.20–9.60 Fri & Sat 10pm–3am.

Entertainment

Cinemas

5D Cinema Endla 45 (Kristline Centre) ⓦ www.5dcinema.ee (website in Estonian and

SAUNAS

The first thing to do when you go to an Estonian **sauna** is get completely naked, though in mixed saunas wrapping a towel around you is at your own discretion. Once you get used to the heat, scoop some water onto the hot stones; it evaporates instantaneously, raising the temperature. Once everyone is sweating profusely, some might gently swat themselves or their friends with birch branches; this increases circulation and rids the body of toxins. Don't overdo it – ten minutes should be long enough, but get out immediately if you start to feel dizzy. Locals normally follow up with a plunge into a cold lake, although a cold shower will suffice. A good place to start is **Kalma** at Vana-Kalamaja 9a (Mon–Fri 11am–10pm, Sat & Sun 10am–11pm; men €8–9, women €6.50–8; ⓣ627 1811, ⓦ www.kalmasaun.ee) – Tallinn's oldest public bath (built in 1928), containing private saunas for rent as well as men's and women's general baths (complete with swimming pool).

Russian only). This state-of-the-art cinema drags you right into the movie with its combination of moving seats, 3-D imagery, scents and even water misting. Intense. €5.

Artis Estonia pst. 9 Ⓦ www.kino.ee (website in Estonian only). Shows a full range of independent films. €4.20–4.80.

Shopping

Antiik Kinga 5. Come here for all your collectable Soviet kitsch, including a number of Lenin busts.

Apollo Raamatumaja Viru 23. Large bookstore with numerous English-language books and travel guides.

Koppel & Keerdo Vene 12. Beautiful glasswork to admire and to purchase.

Masters' Courtyard Off Vene. Courtyard housing some of Tallinn's most original art and craft shops and galleries, where you can find some special ceramics, glassware, woodworks and candles for a very reasonable price.

Opened Gallery Lai 11. Psychedelic paintings and other arresting works of art by local artist Neeme Lall.

Directory

Embassies Canada, Toomkooli 13, 2nd floor Ⓣ 627 3311; Ireland, Vene 2, 2nd floor Ⓣ 681 1888; UK, Wismari 6 Ⓣ 667 4700; US, Kentmanni 20 Ⓣ 668 8100.

Exchange Outside banking hours, try Tavia at Aia 5 for good rates, though their overnight rates are not as favourable as their day rates. Beware of Monex exchange offices which offer poor rates.

Hospital Tallinn Central Hospital, Ravi 18 Ⓣ 620 7040. English-speaking doctors available. Or call the Tallinn First Aid hotline on Ⓣ 697 1145 for advice in English.

Internet Kehrwieder, Viru 23 (daily 10am–7pm; €2.50/hr) on the second floor of a bookshop.

Left luggage At the bus station (Mon–Sat 6.30am–10pm, Sun 7.45am–8pm; €4/24hr).

Pharmacies Aia Apteek, Aia 7 (9am–9.30pm); Tõnismäe Apteek, Tõnismägi 5 (24hr).

Police Pärnu mnt. 11 Ⓣ 612 4200.

Post office Narva mnt. 1, opposite the *Viru Hotel*. Mon–Fri 7.30am–8pm; Sat 8am–6pm.

Moving on

Train Moscow (1 daily at 5.20pm; 15hr);Pärnu (2 daily; 2hr 40min); Tartu (3–5 daily; 2hr 30min–3hr 30min).

Bus Kuressaare (up to16 daily; 4hr 30min); Pärnu (every 30min 6.20am–9pm; 2hr); Rīga (11 daily; 4hr 30min); St Petersburg (6–8 daily; 7–9hr); Tartu (every 30min 5.45am–11pm; 2hr 30min); Vilnius (2 daily; 8hr–8hr 30min).

Ferry Helsinki (10–15 daily; 1hr 30min–3hr 30min); Stockholm (1 daily at 6pm; 16hr).

The rest of Estonia

There are several attractions outside Tallinn that are well worth visiting, such as the vast, beautiful expanse of **Lahemaa National Park** and the pretty island of **Saaremaa**, home to the Bishop's Castle. The seaside resort of **Pärnu** is a slightly livelier affair, but outshone in vibrancy by the buzzy university town of **Tartu**.

LAHEMAA NATIONAL PARK

The largest of Estonia's national parks, 72,500-hectare **Lahemaa** lies an hour's drive or bus ride from Tallinn. It stretches along the north coast, comprising lush forests, pristine lakes, and ruggedly beautiful coves and wetlands. The land is dotted with erratic rocks (giant boulders) left over from the last Ice Age and tiny villages throughout, while the forest is home to brown bears, wild boar, moose and lynx. The park is best explored by bicycle, as the villages are all connected by good paved roads. Parts of the park are doable as a day-trip, but you may well be charmed into staying longer.

Exploring the park

If you go with Tallinn's *City Bike* Tours (see p.343), this is the day route that offers an excellent introduction to the park: start in the village of **Palmse**, where you can take in the grand German manor (10am–7pm May–Sept; shorter hours rest of year; €4); and cycle 8.5km northeast to **Sagadi Manor**, a well-preserved eighteenth-century aristocratic home (May–Sept daily 10am–6pm (by prior appointment only)), before heading north for 3km to **Oandu** – the start of several nature trails. Just before the fishing village of **Altja**, 2km to the north, you'll find the 1km **Beaver Trail** where you can see beavers building dams and stop for lunch at *Altja Korts* – an attractive tavern serving tasty fresh dishes, such as grilled salmon with grated potato pancakes (mains €8). From Altja you can cycle around the coast of the **Vergi peninsula**, taking in the picturesque villages (17km) surrounded by pine forest, before ending up on the wide, clean, windswept beach in **Võsu.** A seaside trail heads north from Võsu for 6km before arriving at the attractive village of **Käsmu** which has a superb nautically-themed **museum**, (9am–6pm; donations) started by a local collector many years ago; you'll spot the giant sea mines in the front yard. If you have any energy left, you can then tackle the rugged cycle trails along the western half of the Käsmu peninsula before getting picked up. If you go it alone, you can take the once-daily morning bus from Tallinn to Käsmu, do the above trail in reverse and then cycle up from Palmse to Võsu (6km) for an overnight stay before catching a bus back to Tallinn the following day.

Park practicalities

The **Lahemaa National Park Visitor Centre** (May–Aug 9am–7pm; Sept 9am–5pm; ⓣ329 5555, ⓦwww.lahemaa.ee) is located in tiny Palmse; you can take a Rakvere- or Narva-bound bus from Tallinn to Viitna (hourly; 1hr) and hike or hitchhike the 7.2km to Palmse or else catch a bus from Võsu (1 daily). The helpful staff at the visitor centre can advise on accommodation, biking and hiking trails, and nature tours, and provide a detailed map of the area.

Public transport is infrequent; though there are buses from Tallinn to Võsu (2 daily), Käsmu and Altja (1–2 daily each), cycling is the best way to get around. Locals do hitchhike, but the usual precautions apply.

There are **guesthouses** and places to **eat** in Palmse, Sagadi, Altja, Võsu and Käsmu, as well as **campsites**, **huts** and **forest houses** throughout, maintained by RMK (ⓦwww.rmk.ee). Good places to stay include the *Toomarahva Turismitalu* farmstead in Altja (ⓣ505 0850, ⓦwww.mpm.pri.ee; doubles €40, sleeping on hay bales €5) and *Metsa Puhkemaja* hostel (ⓣ323 8431, ⓦwww.toomarahva.ee; rooms €15 per person) in **Võsu**. You can rent a **bicycle** at the *Palmse Hotel* (€4/hr or €15/day) and Sagadi Manor, though bikes are sturdier and better maintained at Tallinn's *City Bike Hostel* (Uus str. 33; ⓦwww.citybike.ee), which arranges transfers and day-trips to Lahemaa.

SAAREMAA

The island of **SAAREMAA**, off the west coast of Estonia, is claimed by many to be one of the most authentically Estonian parts of the country. Buses from Tallinn, Tartu and Pärnu come here via a ferry running from the mainland village of Virtsu to Muhu Island, which is linked to Saaremaa by a causeway.

What to see and do

The principal attraction is Kuressaare's thirteenth-century castle, one of the finest in the Baltic region, but the rest of the island also deserves exploration; **cycling** is the best way to get around.

Kuressaare

In **Kuressaare**'s Kesk väljak (main square) you'll find the yellow-painted **Town Hall**, dating from 1670, its door guarded by stone lions. From the square, Lossi runs south past a monument commemorating the 1918–20 War of Independence to the magnificent **Bishop's Castle** (Piiskopilinnus), set in the middle of an attractive park and surrounded by a deep moat. The formidable structure dates largely from the fourteenth century and is protected by huge seventeenth-century ramparts. The labyrinthine keep houses the **Saaremaa Regional Museum** (May–August daily 10am–7pm; Sept–April Wed–Sun 11am–6pm; €4; students €2), a riveting collection of displays charting the culture, nature and history of the island (including an excellent section on Soviet occupation) You can also climb the watchtowers, one of which houses stunning contemporary art and photography exhibitions.

Around the island

Cycling is a wonderful way of seeing Saaremaa, with its alternating landscapes of pine forest, tiny villages and vast fields; rent a bike from Bivarix Rattapood (Tallinna 26; Mon–Fri 11am–7pm, Sat 11am–5pm €8/4hr, €15/day). Highlights include the 37km route north from Kuressaare to **ANGLA**, its five much-photographed wooden windmills by the roadside. Halfway along, **KAALI** village, home to a giant meteorite crater thought to be at least 4000 years old, makes a worthy detour.

Ten kilometres southwest of Kuressaare, you can stop at **JARVE**, the local beach hangout, or do the 47km down to the tip of the Torgu peninsula, which ends in an amazing view from the jagged cliffs.

Arrival and information

Bus From the bus station on Pihtla turn left onto Tallinna to reach the main square.
Tourist office The tourist office is in the Town Hall (Tallinna 2; June–Aug Mon–Fri 9am–6pm, Sat & Sun 10am–4pm; Sept–May Mon–Fri 9am–5pm; ⓣ45/33120, ⓦwww.kuressaare.ee & ⓦwww.saaremaa.ee).

Accommodation

Kraavi Holiday Cottage 500m southeast of the castle at Kraavi 1 ⓣ45/55242, ⓦwww.kraavi.ee. Family-run guesthouse offering cosy, spacious doubles and triples with a hearty breakfast included and free wi-fi. Use of sauna and bikes is extra. Little English spoken but hostess is very welcoming. Singles €20–30, doubles €34–40, triples €46–52.
Ovelia Majutus Suve 8 ⓣ45/55732. Friendly and clean guesthouse with basic rooms, some with TVs, some are en suite, and have a shared kitchen. Ten minutes' walk from the bus station. Doubles €40.
Piibelehe Holiday Home Piibelehe 4 ⓣ45/36206, ⓦwww.piibelehe.ee. On the outskirts of town, this place has a number of airy guest rooms, some en suite and with use of a kitchen; camping also available. Discounts for multi-day stays. €3/person, plus €5/tent, singles €23–26, doubles €38–51.

Eating and drinking

Classic Café Lossi 9. A great little spot to sample some of the best coffee and food in town while sitting in a cosy nook, surrounded by black-and-white photos of Kuressaare. Coffee €1.50.
Kodulinna Lokaal Tallinna mnt. 12. Popular café on the main square dishing up inexpensive soups and light meals. Try the Saaremaa-style potato pancake (€2.60).
Veski Pärnu 19. Popular pub in an old windmill serving imaginative dishes. Try the wild boar with ginger and honey on barley mash (€11) or the miller's wife's cottage cheese dessert (€4).

Moving on

Bus Leisi (5–6 daily; 55min); Pärnu (up to 5 daily; 3hr); Tallinn (up to 18 daily; 4hr 30min); Tartu (3 direct daily; 6hr).

PÄRNU

PÄRNU, Estonia's main seaside resort, comes into its own in summer, when it fills up with locals and tourists and hosts daily cultural and musical events.

TREAT YOURSELF

SPA HOTEL RÜÜTLI

Non-guests are welcome to sample a variety of inexpensive "medical" and "wellness" spa treatments at this hotel (Pargi 12 ⓣ45/22133, ⓦwww.sanatoorium.ee) including "Charcot's Shower" – strip naked and be pummelled with strong jets of water (€10). Treatments take place between 8am–3pm; book in advance.

What to see and do

Rüütli, cutting east–west through the centre, is the Old Town's main pedestrianized thoroughfare, lined with shops and a mix of seventeenth- to twentieth-century buildings, while parallel Kuninga boasts the largest concentration of restaurants. The entertaining **Pärnu Museum** is at Rüütli 53 (Mon–Sat 10am–6pm; €2.60/students €1.30), tracing local history from 9000 BC up until World War II; ask for the information sheet in English. The oldest building in town is the **Red Tower** (Punane Torn; Tues–Sun 10am–5pm; free), a fifteenth-century remnant of the medieval city walls at Hommiku 11, a block north from Rüütli.

Follow Nikolai south from the centre and you'll reach the **Kunsti Museum** (daily 9am–9pm; Ⓦwww.chaplin.ee; €3) set in the Communist Party HQ at Esplanaadi 10. It holds regular shows, film festivals and excellent temporary exhibitions of contemporary Estonian art. South of here Nikolai joins Supeluse, which leads to the beach, passing beneath the trees of the shady Rannapark. Just beyond the sand dunes lies Pärnu's main attraction: the wide, clean sandy **beach**, lined with see-saws, changing booths and volleyball nets. During the summer months, the largely Swedish and Finnish crowds have replaced the Soviet ones.

Arrival and information

Train The train station is about 5km east of the centre at Riia mnt. 116.

Bus The bus station is on Pikk in the Old Town (information & ticket office round the corner at Ringi 3; daily 6.30am–7.30pm). Luggage storage by platform 8 (Mon–Fri 8am–7.30pm, Sat–Sun 9am–5pm; €3/day).

Tourist office The tourist office at Uus 4 (June–Aug Mon–Fri 9am–6pm, Sat 10am–4pm, Sun 10am–3pm; Sept–May Mon–Fri 9am–5pm; Ⓣ44/73000, Ⓦwww.parnu.ee) stocks extensive information on Pärnu and surrounding area.

A LIVING MUSEUM

A short boat ride from Pärnu lies an island stuck in a delightful time warp. The four hundred or so inhabitants of **Kinhu** sustain a traditional way of life that you won't find on the Estonian mainland. You'll find young women wearing traditional striped woollen skirts, just like their great-grandmothers, and see little old ladies riding old-fashioned Soviet motorcycles with sidecars (there are no cars on the island). The only place to stay is the **Rock City Guesthouse** (Sääre village Ⓣ5340 2408, Ⓦwww.rockcity.ee; €8); open June–Aug only and must be booked in advance. To get here, take a ferry from the ferry quay at Kalda 2 (1–2 departures Wed–Sun; 2hr 30min; €4.50 one-way).

Accommodation

Hommiku Hostel & Guesthouse Hommiku 17 Ⓣ445 1122, Ⓦwww.hommikuhostel.ee. Both hostel and guesthouse-style accommodation are on offer at this attractive central budget option: all doubles and triples are en suite and have their own kitchenettes; singles share a bathroom. Wi-fi and cable TV throughout. Dorms €20, singles €39, doubles €58, triples €77.

Hostel Lõuna Lõuna 2 Ⓣ443 0943, Ⓦwww.hostellouna.eu. Centrally located, with spartan, spacious dorms and basic rooms with shared facilities, popular with local students, and functional, wi-fi-equipped en suites on the ground floor. Dorms €15–20, singles €30–45, doubles €45–60.

Terve Hostel Ringi 50 Ⓣ529 8168, Ⓦwww.terve.ee. Cosy family-run guesthouse offering airy, clean rooms with shared facilities, plus use of jacuzzi, guest kitchen and wood-fired sauna, just south of the town centre. Doubles €50, triples €60.

Eating and drinking

Club Str& Tammsaare pst. 35. A seafront hotel club with quirky decor attracting a mixed crowd of locals and tourists, and some decent DJs. Fri & Sat 10pm–4am; admission €5. Age 21-plus.

Postipoiss Vee 12. Wooden tavern, invoking nostalgia for tsarist Russia with its decor, and specializing in delicious Russian cuisine. You can't go wrong with home-made *pelmeni* (meat dumplings) in *chanterelle* sauce. Get in early to beat the groups. Mains €4–6.

Rüütlihoov Rüütli 29. This lively pub has friendly service and live music on weekends. The outdoor terrace is a good spot for a cold beer (€2.50).

Si-Si Restaurant and Lounge Supeluse 21. Inside a mansion with an attractive garden, this excellent Italian restaurant serves authentic dishes such as aubergine baked with mozzarella and tagliatelle with shrimp and courgettes to a contented beach crowd. Mains €6–17.

Sõõrikubaar Pühavaimu 15. An essential stop for caffeine addicts, this popular little café also does tasty pastries and *sõõrikud* (Estonian doughnuts).

Steffani Nikolai 24. Extremely popular restaurant with a wide choice of tasty pizza and pasta dishes. Huge *calzones* €7. Runs a popular second branch between Ranna pst. and the beach in the summer, serving similar fare. Closes 2am Fri & Sat.

Moving on

Train to: Tallinn (2 daily; 2hr 30min).
Bus to: Kuressaare (4–5 daily; 3hr); Rīga (3 daily; 2hr 30min); (Tallinn (at least 1 hourly; 4.40am–8.30pm; 2–3hr)); Tartu (up to 16 daily; 2hr 30min).

TARTU

TARTU, less than three hours southeast of Tallinn, is an attractive town, liveliest during term time, with events all year round (Ⓦwww.visittartu.com).

What to see and do

The main sights lie between **Cathedral Hill**, right in the centre, and the **River Emajõgi**, and include the Art Museum, the Cathedral and the colourful Supilinn district.

Town Hall and around

The city's centre is its cobbled Raekoja plats, fronted by the Neoclassical Town Hall, a pink-and-white edifice with the "Kissing Students" statue in the fountain in front of it. The northeast corner features the **Leaning House** – Tartu's answer to the Leaning Tower of Piza and home of the **Tartu Art Museum** (Wed–Sun noon–6pm; €2.25), with edgy temporary exhibitions downstairs and works by Estonian masters upstairs. The Neoclassical theme continues in the cool white facade of the main **Tartu University** building at Ülikooli 18, just north of the square. Upstairs you can look at the Student Lock-up, where students were incarcerated in the nineteenth century for such offences as the late return of library books and duelling (weekdays 11am–5pm; €0.65; joint ticket with the Art Museum on the ground floor €2). About 100m beyond the university is the red-brick Gothic **St John's Church** (Tues–Sat 10am–6pm; €1.60), founded in 1330, and most famous for over one thousand pint-sized terracotta sculptures set in niches around the main entrance.

Cathedral Hill and around

Behind the Town Hall, Lossi climbs Cathedral Hill, a pleasant park with the remains of the red-brick **Cathedral** at the top, housing the University History Museum. Built by the Knights of the Sword in the thirteenth century, it boasts the best view of Tartu from the rooftop terrace (June–Aug daily 10am–5pm; May & Sept Wed–Sun 11am–5pm; Oct–Nov Sat–Sun 11am–5pm; €1.60). Nearby is the **Sacrifice Stone** left over from Estonia's pagan past; students now burn their lecture notes on it after the exams. Behind the stone you'll find **Kissing Hill**, where newlywed grooms carry their brides.

Two blocks west of Cathedral Hill, the infamous "Grey House" at Riia 15b – a place which filled the inhabitants of Tartu with dread in the 1940s and 50s – is now the **KGB Cells Museum** with exhibits on deportations, Estonian resistance and life in the Soviet gulags, summarized in English (Tues–Sat 11am–6pm; €1.30).

Arrival and information

Train The train station is about 900m southwest of the centre at Vaksali 6. There are no facilities at the station.

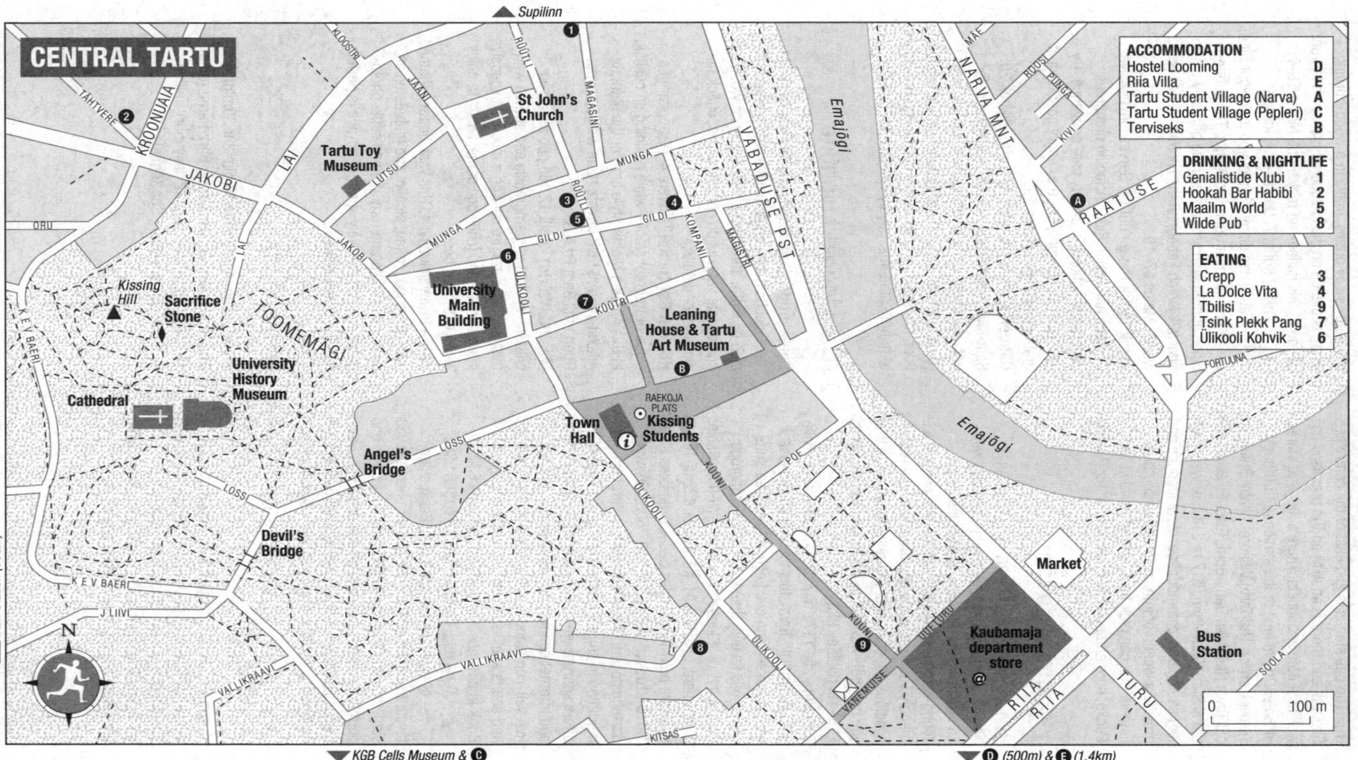
CENTRAL TARTU
ACCOMMODATION
Hostel Looming D
Riia Villa E
Tartu Student Village (Narva) A
Tartu Student Village (Pepleri) C
Terviseks B
DRINKING & NIGHTLIFE
Genialistide Klubi 1
Hookah Bar Habibi 2
Maailm World 5
Wilde Pub 8
EATING
Crepp 3
La Dolce Vita 4
Tbilisi 9
Tsink Plekk Pang 7
Ülikooli Kohvik 6
Supilinn
St John's Church
Tartu Toy Museum
University Main Building
Leaning House & Tartu Art Museum
Kissing Hill
Sacrifice Stone
Toomemägi
University History Museum
Cathedral
Raekoja Plats
Town Hall
Kissing Students
Angel's Bridge
Devil's Bridge
Emajõgi
Market
Kaubamaja department store
Bus Station
Vabaduse pst
Narva mnt
Raatuse
Fortuuna
Turu
Riia
Soola
Küüni
Ülikooli
Vallikraavi
K E V Baeri
J Liivi
Lossi
Jakobi
Lai
Kroonuaia
Tähtvere
Oru
Munga
Gildi
Rüütli
Magasini
Kompanii
Magistri
Küütri
Jaani
Kloostri
Lutsu
Poe
Vanemuise
Uueturu
Kitsas
Roosi
Punga
Kivi
Mäe
Train Station (900m)
KGB Cells Museum & C
D (500m) & E (1.4km)
0 100 m
N

Bus The bus station is just east of the centre at Soola 2, and there is an ATM on the premises as well as a café and toilets. There's luggage storage at *Hotel Dorpat* next to the station (€1.50/bag).
Tourist office The Tartu Visitors' Centre inside the old Town Hall (Mon 9am–6pm, Tues–Fri 9am–5pm, Sat & Sun 10am–2pm; ⓣ744 2111, ⓦwww.tartu.ee) can book accommodation, store luggage and provide a wealth of info on Tartu and southern Estonia. You can pick up a copy of *Tartu in Your Pocket* here and surf the internet (free for 20min).

Accommodation

Hostel Looming Kastani 38 ⓣ5623 9568, ⓦwww.loominghostel.ee. New eco-hostel with an emphasis on recycling located inside the Young Estonian Creativity Centre with bright decor, friendly young staff, comfy, brand-new beds and a spacious guest lounge. The only drawback is that you currently have to go to the loo in pairs. Dorms €15–19, doubles €33–36.
Riia Villa Riia 117a ⓣ738 1300, ⓦwww.riiavilla.ee. West of Old Town, this tranquil guesthouse is well worth seeking out. Each of the six en-suite rooms has its own theme; choose "Glamorous Simplicity" or "Kleopatra's Room". Wi-fi available. To get here, take bus #1, #8, #18 or #22 up Riia to Soinaste bus stop. Singles €26–29, doubles €37–40.
Tartu Student Village ⓣ742 7608, ⓦwww.tartuhostel.eu. Cheap and fairly central accommodation in summer at two locations. Pepleri 14 offers spartan en-suite rooms with kitchenettes and internet connection, while Narva mnt. 27 has five self-contained apartments with TV, internet and sauna access (€6/hr), ideal for a longer stay. Book in advance. Singles €20, doubles €30.
Terviseks Raekoja Plats 10 ⓣ565 5382, ⓦwww.terviseksbbb.com. Backpacker-favourite-turned-B&B run by friendly, energetic young staff, with spacious, brightly decorated doubles and dorms, modern lounge and gleaming kitchen. Special touches include reading lights by each bed and a guitar for guest use. Dorms €15–25, doubles €30.

Eating

Crepp Rüütli 16. Chic and busy café serving delicious salads, baguettes and filling crêpes (€3). The service is sometimes quite leisurely.
La Dolce Vita Kompanii 10 (entrance from Gildi). Life seems pretty sweet when one of the thin-and-crispy pizzas, made in a wood-burning oven, is placed on the chequered tablecloth in front of you at this Italian-run restaurant. Mains €6–7.
Tbilisi Küüni 7. Don't let the kitschy Caucasian decor distract you from your food, which is a genuine Georgian delight. The aubergines stuffed with walnuts and the perfectly grilled *shashlik* (shish kebab) hit the spot as well as your wallet. Mains €7–10.
Tsink Plekk Pang Küütri 6. Serves inexpensive Chinese and Indian food, including numerous vegetarian options, in an arty café ambience. Try the "rusty busty porky" or the "angry cow" or just grab a milkshake. Mains €5.
Ülikooli Kohvik (University Café) Ulikooli 20. Split-level establishment with an elegant café upstairs serving the likes of smoked duck with roast beetroot, and a bargain buffet on the ground floor, dishing up a selection of salads and hot dishes to hungry students; pay by weight. €0.70/100g.

Drinking and nightlife

Genialistide Klubi Magasini 5 ⓦwww.genklubi.ee. Eclectic boho venue that's a café by day and club by night, attracting a mixed, arty crowd. Music and events vary, as do opening times; check the website for details.
Hookah Bar Habibi Tähtvere 4. Disappear in a cloud of fragrant smoke while reclining on cushions at this Arabian Nights-style bar. For the ultimate relaxation, rent their private room with a sauna. Open until 3am Fri & Sat.
Maailm (World) Rüütli 12. Hip pub plastered with travel-related memorabilia and strewn with mismatched furniture serving a mix of inexpensive international food (chilli con carne, tacos) to enjoy along with your beer.
Wilde Pub Vallikraavi 4. This vast, literary-themed pub offers tea, coffee, alcohol and Irish/Estonian pub grub amid grand furniture and sepia photographs, while the lively summer terrace is perfect for beer and snacks.

Moving on

Train Tallinn (4 daily; 2hr 30min–3hr 30min).
Bus Kuressaare (3 direct daily; 6hr); Pärnu (up to 15 daily; 2hr 30min); Rīga (2 daily; 5hr); Tallinn (1–2 hourly 3am–9pm; 2hr 30min).

Finland

HIGHLIGHTS

SÁMI CULTURE, INARI: one of Europe's last frontiers, where nomadic reindeer herders live in harmony with snowmobiles and Nokias

KUOPIO SAUNA: warm your bones at the world's biggest woodsmoke sauna

LENIN MUSEUM, TAMPERE: fascinating museum delving into the relationship between Lenin and Finland

OLAVINLINNA CASTLE, SAVONLINNA: one of the best-preserved medieval castles in northern Europe

DESIGN DISTRICT, HELSINKI: sample the shops, cafés and nightlife of this vibrant and trendy area of the capital

ROUGH COSTS

DAILY BUDGET Basic €40 /occasional treat €65

DRINK *Salmiakki* (liquorice-flavoured vodka) €4–6 a shot

FOOD Reindeer stew with potatoes €9

HOSTEL/BUDGET HOTEL €20/€45

TRAVEL Helsinki–Tampere by bus €25; Helsinki–Rovaniemi by train €84

FACT FILE

POPULATION 5.4 million

AREA 338,145 sq km

LANGUAGE Finnish and Swedish

CURRENCY Euro (€)

CAPITAL Helsinki (population: 590,000)

INTERNATIONAL PHONE CODE ⓣ358

Introduction

Drawing strong influences both from its easterly neighbour, Russia, as well as from the West, Finland remains one of Europe's most enigmatic countries. It's a land best known for its laconic, pithy people with a penchant for kicking back in a sauna sans vêtements, and for its quirky and bizarre annual festivals – its strangeness is a good part of its charm. And while it's far from a budgeteer's paradise, there are definitely ways to save – that is, if you know where to drink.

The Finnish landscape is mostly flat and punctuated by huge forests and lakes, but has wide regional variations. The south contains the least dramatic scenery, but the capital, **Helsinki**, more than compensates, with its brilliant *fin-de-siècle* architecture and superb collections of late modern and contemporary artworks, as does the former capital of **Turku**, with some great museums and nightlife. Stretching from the Russian border in the east to the industrial city of **Tampere**, the vast waters of the **Lake Region** provide a natural means of transport for the timber industry – indeed, water here is a more common sight than land with towns lying on narrow ridges between lakes. North of here, the gradually rising fells and forests of **Lapland** are Finland's most alluring terrain and are home to the Sámi, semi-nomadic reindeer herders. For a few months on either side of midsummer, the midnight sun is visible from much of the region.

CHRONOLOGY

1800 BC Tribes from Russia settle in Lapland.
98 AD Roman historian Tacitus writes first recorded reference of the "Fenni".
1150s Sweden invades southwestern Finland.
1293 Sweden defeats Finland again, establishing dividing lines between the Catholic West and Orthodox East.
1642 First complete Finnish translation of the Bible produced.
1721 In the Treaty of Uusikaupunki, Sweden cedes Finnish land to Russia.
1809 Russians take Finland after military victory over Sweden.
1812 Helsinki is declared capital of Finland.
1858 Confusion caused as Russia forces Finns to drive on the right-hand side of the road.
1860 Finland acquires its own currency, the markka.
1906 Finland gains its own national parliament. Finnish women are the first in the world to receive full political rights.
1917 Finland declares independence from Russia.
1939–40 Soviet troops invade Finland but meet fierce resistance during the "Winter War".
1941 Under the Moscow Peace Treaty, the southeast territory of Karelia is ceded to the Russians.
1952 Helsinki holds the Olympic Games.
1987 Finnish company Nokia begins to make hand-held mobile phones.
1995 Finland joins the EU.
2000 Tarja Halonen becomes the first female president.
2002 Finland adopts the euro.
2006 National celebrations as Finnish death metal group Lordi win Eurovision song contest.
2009 Finnish government sells its share in Santa Park, signalling that the global economic crisis has reached the North Pole.
2011 The conservative National Coalition wins Finland's parliamentary elections, with the populist, anti-immigration and anti-EU True Finns party coming in third, causing alarm around Europe.

ARRIVAL

There are over twenty airports dotted around the country, but you're most likely to arrive at Helsinki Vantaa, Tampere Pirkkala or Lappeenranta Airport, which are the main hubs for **international flights**. BMI (ⓦwww.flybmi.com) and Norwegian (ⓦwww.norwegian.no) fly into Helsinki and

Ryanair into Tampere and Lappeenranta from the UK, but the biggest low-cost airline in Finland is Blue1 (Ⓦwww.blue1.com), which offers routes to and from most major European cities. Finnair (Ⓦwww.finnair.com) is also a good bet for cheap flights. **Ferries** arrive from Tallinn in Estonia or Stockholm at Helsinki and Turku; contact either Silja Line (Ⓦwww.tallinksilja.com) or Viking Line (Ⓦwww.vikingline.fi) for tickets and timetables. Another increasingly popular route into the country is overland by **train** from St Petersburg to Helsinki, which thanks to a new high-speed rail link takes less than three hours.

GETTING AROUND

For the most part trains and buses integrate well, and you'll only need to plan with care when travelling through the more remote areas of the far north and east. **Trains** are operated by Finnish State Railways (VR; Ⓦwww.vr.fi). Comfortable Express and InterCity trains, plus faster, tilting Pendolino trains, serve the principal cities several times a day. If you're travelling by night train, it's better to go for the more expensive sleeper cars if you want to get any rest, as no provision is made for sleeping in the ordinary seated carriages. Elsewhere, especially on east–west hauls through sparsely populated regions, trains are often tiny or replaced by buses on which rail

passes are still valid. InterRail passes are valid on all trains. The best timetable is the *Rail Pocket Guide* published by VR and available from all train stations and tourist offices. **Buses** – privately run, but with a common ticket system – cover the whole country, but are most useful in the north. Tickets can be purchased at bus stations and most travel agents; only ordinary one-way tickets can be bought on board. The timetable (*Pikavuoroaikataulut*), available at all main bus stations, lists all bus routes, or check Ⓦwww.matkahuolto.fi.

Domestic flights can be comparatively cheap as well as time-saving, especially if you're planning to visit Lapland and the far north. Finnair (Ⓦwww.finnair.com) and Blue1 (Ⓦwww.blue1.com) are the main operators, though the cheaper tickets are generally only available if booked well in advance. One-way tickets with Blue1 can be especially good value.

Cycling can be an enjoyable way to see the country at close quarters, particularly because the only appreciable hills are in the farthest stretches of the north. You can take your bike along with you on an InterCity train for a €10 fee (reservations rarely necessary), and most youth hostels, campsites and some hotels and tourist offices offer bike rental from around €10 per day, or €45 per week; there may also be a deposit of around €30.

ACCOMMODATION

There's a good network of 65 official **HI hostels** (Ⓦwww.hostellit.fi) as well as a few independents. Most charge €5–6 for breakfast and bed linen is often extra, too (€4–7), so if you're on a tight budget it's worth bringing your own sheets. Dorms are almost always single-sex. The free *Finland: Budget Accommodation* booklet, available from any tourist office, contains a comprehensive list of hostels and campsites.

Hotels are expensive. Special offers in summer mean that you'll be able to sleep well on a budget in high season, but may have difficulty finding anything affordable out of season – the reverse of the norm. In many towns you'll also find **tourist hotels** (*matkustajakoti*) offering fewer frills for €35–50 per person, and **summer hotels** (*kesähotelli*; June–Aug only), which offer decent accommodation in student blocks for €25–45 per person.

Official **campsites** (*leirintäalue*) are plentiful. The cost to camp is roughly €10–12 per pitch, plus €3–4 per person, depending on the site's star rating. Most open from May or June until August or September, although some stay open longer and a few all year round. Many three-star sites also have cottages, often with TV, sauna and kitchen. To camp in Finland, you'll need a Camping Card Scandinavia, available at every site for €9 and valid for a year. Camping rough is illegal without the landowner's permission – though in practice, provided you're out of sight of local communities, there shouldn't be any problems.

FOOD

Finnish food is a mix of Western and Eastern influences, with Scandinavian-style fish specialities and exotic meats such as reindeer and elk alongside dishes that bear a Russian stamp – pastries, and casseroles strong on cabbage and pork. Also keep an eye out for *karjalan piirakka* – oval-shaped pastries containing rice and mashed potato, served hot with a mixture of finely chopped hard-boiled egg and butter. *Kalakukko* is another inexpensive delicacy, if an acquired one: a chunk of bread with pork and whitefish baked inside it; it's legendary around Kuopio but available almost everywhere. Slightly cheaper but just as filling, *lihapiirakka* are envelopes of sweet pastry filled with rice and meat – ask for them with mustard (*sinappi*) and/or ketchup (*ketsuppi*).

Breakfasts (*aamiainen*) in hotels usually consist of a buffet of herring, eggs, cereals, cheese, salami and bread, while you can lunch on the economical **snacks** sold in market halls (*kauppahalli*) or adjoining cafés. Most train stations and some bus stations and supermarkets also have cafeterias offering a selection of snacks, greasy nibbles and light meals, and street stands (*grillis*) turn out burgers and hot dogs for around €3. Otherwise, campus **mensas** are the cheapest places to get a hot dish (around €4); theoretically, you have to be a student, but you're only asked for ID on occasion. In regular restaurants or *ravintola*, **lunch** (*lounas*) deals are good value, with many places offering a lunchtime buffet table (*voileipäpöytä* or *seisovapöytä*) stacked with a choice of traditional goodies for a set price of around €10. Pizzerias are another good bet, serving lunch specials for €6–9. For **evening meals**, a cheap pizzeria or *ravintola* will serve up standard plates of meat and two veg, while in Helsinki and the big towns there's usually a good range of options, including Chinese and Thai.

Drink

Most restaurants are fully licensed, and many are frequented more for drinking than eating. **Bars** are usually open till midnight or 1am (and clubs until 2am or 3am) and service stops half an hour before closing. You have to be eighteen to buy beer and wine, twenty to buy spirits, and some places have an age limit of twenty-four. The main – and cheapest – outlets for takeaway alcohol are the ubiquitous government-run **ALKO** shops (Mon–Thurs 9am–6pm, Fri 9am–8pm, Sat 9am–4pm).

Beer (*olut*) falls into three categories: "light beer" (I-Olut), like a soft drink; "medium strength beer" (*keskiolut*; III-Olut), perceptibly alcoholic, sold in supermarkets and cafés; and "strong beer" (A-Olut or IV-Olut), on a par with the stronger European beers, and only available at licensed restaurants, clubs and ALKO shops. Strong beers, such as Lapin Kulta and Koff, cost about €1.30 per 300ml bottle at a shop or kiosk. Imported beers go for €2.20–3 per can. Finlandia **vodka** is €19 for a 700ml bottle; Koskenkorva, a rougher vodka, is €15. You'll also find Finns knocking back **salmiakki**, a premixed vodka/liquorice cocktail which looks, smells and tastes like cough medicine, and *fisu*, another inexplicably popular drink that blends Fisherman's Friend lozenges with Koskenkorva.

CULTURE AND ETIQUETTE

To an outsider, the percipient and proud Finns can seem almost alarmingly pithy and withdrawn: little value is put on exuberance, and you can have an entire conversation with a Finn without their making any discernible facial expression. Underneath this reserve, of course, Finnish people are as full of enthusiasm and affection as any other nation. This is a people whose aversion to small talk and affinity for the awkward moment is rivalled only by their remarkable ability to drink several times their body weight in grain alcohol in an evening's sitting. Their underlying bonhomie does come out when there's drink around, but alcohol abuse really has long been a noticeable problem here, and it's wise to

FINLAND ONLINE

- **www.visitfinland.com** The Finnish tourist board site.
- **www.finland.fi** A government information site on Finnish culture and society.
- **www.sauna.fi** The Finnish Sauna Society.
- **www.festivals.fi** A comprehensive listing of festivals throughout Finland.

avoid trying to keep up with the Finnish capacity for drinking.

Tipping is rare in Finland, and **buying rounds** is unheard of. Service is usually included in restaurant bills although it's common to round the bill up to the nearest convenient figure when paying in cash (the same applies for taxi fares).

SPORTS AND OUTDOOR ACTIVITIES

The winter landscape lends itself to **cross-country skiing**, the season lasting from December until January in the south and April in northern and central Finland. There are ski slopes, too – see Ⓦwww.ski.fi for more information – and several operators offering off-piste skiing. Watery pursuits like **kayaking** (or kitesurfing on the frozen lakes in the winter) are a worthwhile option in the lake regions, especially around Lake Inari. Popular national **sports** include the distinctively Finnish *pesäpallo*, similar to baseball, and ice hockey.

COMMUNICATIONS

Communications are dependable and quick. Free **internet access** is readily available, either at the tourist office

FINNISH

Stress on all Finnish words always falls on the first syllable.

	Finnish	Pronunciation
Yes	*Kyllä*	Koo-leh
No	*Ei*	Ay
Thank you	*Kiitos*	Keetos
Hello/Good day	*Hyvää päivää*	Hoo-veh pai-veh
Goodbye	*Näkemiin*	Nek-er-meen
Excuse me	*Anteeksi*	Anteksi
Where?	*Missä?*	Miss-eh?
Good	*Hyvä*	Hoo-veh
Bad	*Paha*	Paha
Near	*Lähellä*	Le-hell-eh
Far	*Kaukana*	Kau-kanna
Cheap	*Halpa*	Halpa
Expensive	*Kallis*	Kallis
Open	*Avoinna*	Avoyn-na
Closed	*Suljettu*	Sul-yet-oo
Today	*Tänään*	Ten-ern
Yesterday	*Eilen*	Aylen
Tomorrow	*Huomenna*	Hoo-oh-menna
How much is...?	*Kuinka paljon maksaa...?*	Koo-inka pal-yon maksaa...?
What time is it?	*Paljonko kello on?*	Palyonko kello on?
I don't understand	*En ymmärrä*	Enn oomerreh
Do you speak English?	*Puhutteko englantia?*	Poohut-tuko englantia?
One	*Yksi*	Uksi
Two	*Kaksi*	Kaksi
Three	*Kolme*	Col-meh
Four	*Neljä*	Nel-yeh
Five	*Viisi*	Veesi
Six	*Kuusi*	Coosi
Seven	*Seitsemän*	Sayt-se-men
Eight	*Kahdeksan*	Cah-deksan
Nine	*Yhdeksän*	Oo-deksan
Ten	*Kymmenen*	Kummenen

or local library (booking sometimes required), and major towns and cities have free, comprehensive wi-fi. **Post offices** are generally open 9am to 6pm Monday to Friday, with later hours in Helsinki. Public **phones** have been swiftly phased out in favour of mobile service; if you plan to make a lot of calls in Finland, invest in a Finnish SIM card for use in your phone. €20 will get you a Finnish number with about sixty minutes of domestic calling time or several hundred domestic text messages. Directory enquiries are ☎118 (domestic) and ☎020208 (international).

EMERGENCIES

You hopefully won't have much cause to come into contact with the Finnish **police**, though if you do they are likely to speak English. As for **health problems**, if you're insured you'll save time by seeing a doctor at a private health centre (*lääkäriasema*) rather than waiting at a national health centre (*terveyskeskus*), though you're going to pay for the privilege. Medicines must be paid for at a **pharmacy** (*apteekki*), generally open daily 9am to 6pm; outside these times, a phone number for emergency help is displayed on every pharmacy's front door.

INFORMATION

Most towns have a **tourist office**, some of which will book accommodation for you, though in winter, their hours are much reduced and some don't open at all. You can pick up the decent map of Finland free from tourist offices.

EMERGENCY NUMBERS

☎112 for all emergency services.

MONEY AND BANKS

Finland's currency is the **euro** (€). Banks are open Monday to Friday 9.30am to 4.15pm. Some **banks** have exchange desks at transport terminals, and **ATMs** are widely available. You can also change money at hotels, but the rates are generally poor. **Credit cards** are widely accepted right across the country.

OPENING HOURS AND HOLIDAYS

Most **shops** generally open Monday to Friday 9am to 6pm, Saturday 9am to 4pm. Along with banks, they close on **public holidays**, when most public transport and museums run to a Sunday schedule. These are: January 1, January 6 (Epiphany), Good Friday and Easter Monday, May 1, Ascension (mid-May), Whitsun (late May), Midsummer (late June), All Saints' Day (early Nov), December 6 and 24 to 26.

Helsinki

Instantly loveable, **HELSINKI** is remarkably different from the other Scandinavian capitals, and closer both in mood and appearance to the major cities of Eastern Europe. For a century an outpost of the Russian Empire, Helsinki's very shape and form derives from its more powerful neighbour. Yet during the twentieth century it became a showcase for independent Finland, much of its impressive architecture reflecting the dawning of Finnish nationalism and the rise of the republic. Today, visitors will find a youthful buzz on the streets, where the boulevards, outdoor cafés and restaurants are crowded with Finns taking full advantage of the short summer. At night the pace picks up in Helsinki's great selection of lounges, cafés, bars and clubs.

What to see and do

Following a devastating fire in 1808, and the city's designation as Finland's capital in 1812, Helsinki was totally rebuilt in a style befitting its new status: a grid of wide streets and Neoclassical brick buildings modelled on the then Russian capital, St Petersburg.

Esplanadi and Senate Square

Esplanadi, a wide tree-lined boulevard across a mishmash of tramlines from the harbour, is Helsinki at its most charming. At its eastern end, the **City Museum** at Sofiankatu 4 (Mon–Fri 9am–5pm, Thurs 9am–7pm, Sat & Sun 11am–5pm; free) offers a record of 450 years of Helsinki life in an impressive permanent exhibition called "Helsinki Horizons".

To the north is Senate Square (Senattintori), dominated by the exquisite form of the recently renovated **Tuomiokirkko** (Cathedral; June–Aug daily 9am–11pm; Sept–May Mon–Sat 9am–6pm, Sun noon–6pm). After the elegance of the exterior, the spartan Lutheran interior comes as a disappointment; more impressive is the gloomily atmospheric **crypt** (same times; entrance on Kirkkokatu), now often used for exhibitions.

Uspenski Cathedral

The square towards the eastern end of Aleksanterinkatu is overlooked by the onion domes of the Russian Orthodox **Uspenski Cathedral** (Mon–Fri 9.30am–4pm, Sat 9.30am–2pm, Sun noon–3pm; Oct–April closed Mon; tram #3). Inside, there's a glitzy display of icons. Beyond is **Katajanokka**, a wedge of land extending between the harbours; with its beautiful Art Nouveau architecture it's one of the city's most atmospheric places to walk around.

Kiasma and Lasipalatsi

Kiasma is Helsinki's museum of contemporary art (Tues 10am–5pm, Wed–Thurs 10am–8.30pm, Fri 10am–10pm, Sat & Sun 10am–5pm; €10; Ⓦwww.kiasma.fi), its gleaming steel-clad exterior and hi-tech interior make it well worth a visit. Temporary exhibitions feature everything from paintings to video installations. Opposite is the **Lasipalatsi**, a multimedia complex situated in a recently renovated 1930s classic Functionalist building, now home to a number of trendy shops and cafés.

Parliament and National Museum

North along Mannerheimintie past the train station and the Kiasma museum is the multi-columned and rather solemn 1931-era **Parliament Building** (guided tours only: free). There's more information on the parliament from the attached visitor centre at Arkadiankatu 3 (July & Aug Mon–Fri 10am–4pm;

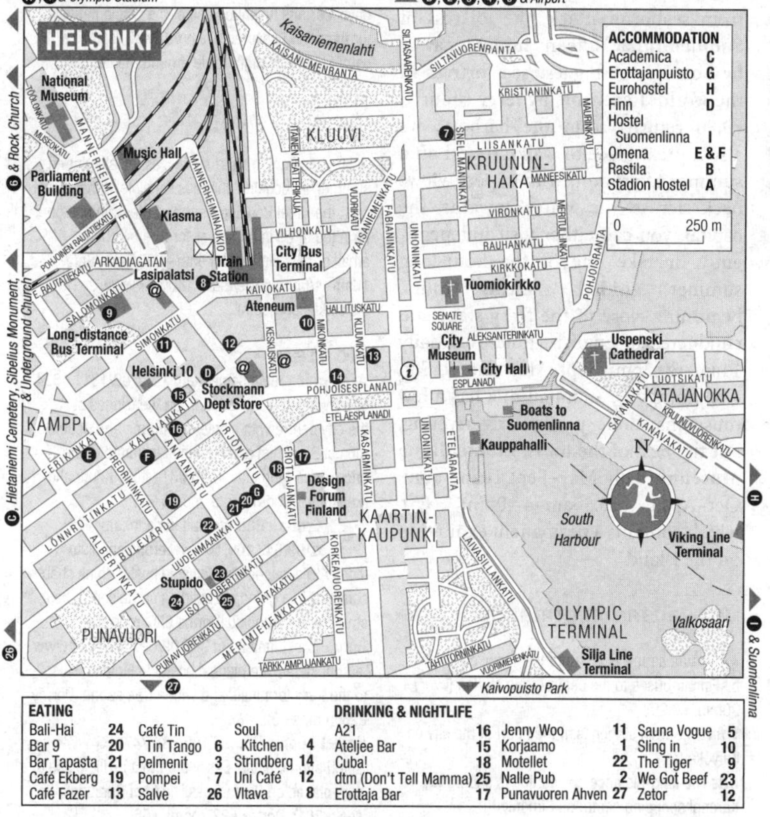

rest of year Mon–Thurs 10am–6pm, Fri closes 4pm; free). North of here is the **National Museum** (Tues 11am–8pm, Wed–Sun 11am–6pm; €7), its design drawing on the country's medieval churches and granite castles. The exhibits, from prehistory to the present, are exhaustive; concentrate on a few specific sections, such as the fascinating medieval church art and the ethnographic displays.

Olympic Stadium

Nearly two miles north of the train station along Mannerheimintie, the recently renovated **Olympic Stadium** is clearly visible; originally intended for the 1940 Olympics, it hosted the second postwar games in 1952. Its **tower** (Mon–Fri 9am–8pm, Sat & Sun 9am–6pm; €2) gives an unsurpassed view over the city and the southern coast.

Rock Church

One mile west of the train station, at Lutherinkatu 3, is the late-1960s **Rock Church** (Temppeliaukio kirkko; Mon & Wed 10am–5pm, Tues 10am–12.45pm & 2.15–5pm, Thurs & Fri 10am–8pm, Sat 10am–6pm, Sun 11.45am–1.45pm & 3.30–6pm; closed during services; tram #3B), blasted from a single lump of granite. Recently restored, it's a thrill to be inside, beneath its domed copper roof.

Suomenlinna

Built on five interconnected islands by the Swedes in 1748 to protect Helsinki from seaborne attack, the fortress of **Suomenlinna**, fifteen minutes away by boat, is the biggest sea fortress in the world. Reachable by ferry (hourly; €3.80 return) from the harbour, it's also a great place to walk around on a summer afternoon, with superb views back across the water towards the capital: you can either visit independently or take one of the hour-long summer **guided walking tours**, beginning close to the ferry stage and conducted in English (June–Aug daily 11am & 2pm; Sept–May Sat & Sun 1.30pm; €8/7). Suomenlinna has a few museums, none particularly riveting, but the best of the lot is **Suomenlinna Museum** (daily May–Sept 10am–6pm; Oct–April 10.30am–4.30pm; €5), which contains a permanent exhibition on the island.

Arrival and information

Air Vantaa airport is 20km to the north, connected by Finnair buses to the central train station (every 20min; €6.20).
Train The train station is in the heart of the city on Kaivokatu.
Bus The long-distance bus station is under the Kamppi shopping centre on Simonkatu
Ferry Terminals are less than 1km from the centre; take tram #3T or #3B.
Tourist office The excellent City Tourist Office at Pohjoisesplanadi 19 (mid-May to mid-Sept Mon–Fri 9am–8pm, Sat & Sun 9am–6pm; mid-Sept to mid-May Mon–Fri 9am–6pm, Sat & Sun 10am–4pm; ⓣ09/3101 3300, ⓦwww.visithelsinki.fi) hands out the useful, free listings magazines *Helsinki This Week* and *City*.
Discount card If you're staying a while, consider purchasing a Helsinki Card (€35/45/55 for 24/48/72hr), giving unlimited travel on public transport and free entry to more than fifty museums.

City transport

The city's transport system (trams, buses and a limited metro) is very efficient. One-way tickets can be bought on board (€2.20) or from the bus station, tourist office or kiosks around the centre, while a tourist ticket (€6.80/13.60/20.40 for one/three/five days) permits unlimited use of the whole network for the period covered. Tram #3T/#3B follows a useful figure-of-eight route around the centre.

Accommodation

Hostel beds are in short supply, especially during summer, so booking ahead is sensible, either direct or at the Hotel Booking Centre at the train station for a fee of €5 in person or for free by phone, email or online (Mon–Fri 9am–4.30/6pm, Sat 10am–4/5pm; ⓣ09/2288 1400, ⓦwww.helsinkiexpert.com).

Hostels

Academica Hietaniemenkatu 14 ⓣ09/1311 4334 ⓦwww.hostelacademica.fi. On the fringes of the city centre with single-sex dorms and double rooms. Breakfast and bed linen included in the price. June–Aug only. Tram #3T (stop "Kauppakorkeakoulu"). Dorms €25, rooms €66.
Erottajanpuisto Uudenmaankatu 9 ⓣ09/642 169, ⓦwww.erottajanpuisto.com. Atmospheric and sociable hostel (think shabby couches) in a grand old building on Helsinki's best street for bar hopping. Dorms €26, rooms €72.
Eurohostel Linnankatu 9 ⓣ09/622 0470, ⓦwww.eurohostel.fi. The biggest hostel in Finland, close to the ferry terminals and with a free sauna. Dorms €26, rooms €52.
Hostel Suomenlinna ⓣ09/684 7471, ⓦwww.snk.fi/suomenlinna. Easily the most idyllic place to stay; placed on the fortress island of Suomenlinna (see p.361). Dorms €22, rooms €55.
Stadion Hostel Olympic Stadium ⓣ09/477 8480, ⓦwww.stadionhostel.com. Some 2km out of the centre and often crowded, but cheap and open all year. Tram #3T, #4, #7 or #10 to the stadium, then follow the signs. Dorms €19, rooms €44.

Hotels

Finn Kalevankatu 3b ⓣ09/684 4360, ⓦwww.hotellifinn.fi. 27 peaceful, modern rooms on the top floor of an office block, virtually in the city centre. Singles €49, doubles €59.
Omena Eerikinkatu 24 & Lönnrotinkatu 13 ⓦwww.omenahotels.com. Helsinki's best deals can often be found at either of these two centrally located, self-service, internet-reserved hotels. Rooms are very sleek. Singles and doubles €45.

Campsite

Rastila Karavaanikatu 4 ⓣ09/3107 8517, ⓦwww.rastilacamping.fi. Great camping spot with cabins and dorms in an attached hostel. It's

13km east of the city centre, near the end of the metro line (Vuosaari) and served by night buses #90N till 1.30am during the week and 4.15am Fri & Sat. Camping €5/person, dorms €20, cabins €50.

Eating

Many places offer good-value lunchtime deals, and there are plenty of affordable ethnic restaurants and fast-food *grillis* for the evenings. At the end of Eteläesplanadi the *kauppahalli* (Mon–Fri 8am–7pm, Sat 8am–4pm) is good for snacks and sandwiches (try, for example, *Soppakeittiö*; ⓣ09/612 3226). Another great bargain are the numerous university student cafeterias around the city.

Cafés

Café Ekberg Bulevardi 9. Nineteenth-century fixtures and a *fin-de-siècle* atmosphere, with starched waitresses bringing expensive sandwiches and pastries to marble tables. Lunch €8.70.

Café Fazer Kluuvikatu 3. Owned by Finland's biggest chocolate company, with celebrated cakes and pastries. Lunch €8.80.

Café Tin Tin Tango Töölöntorinkatu 7. Somewhat quirky café-bar with a laundry machine and sauna (book a day in advance) en route to the Olympic Stadium. Slough off the travel dirt and have a beer at the same time.

Strindberg Pohjoisesplanadi 33. A classic Finnish café: the upstairs restaurant serves contemporary Scandinavian cuisine, while the street level café is one of the places in town to see and be seen. Mains from €15.

Uni Café Mannerheimintie 3. Cheap, filling meals at this university cafeteria right in the centre of town. A great place to meet young people.

Restaurants

Bali-Hai Iso Roobertinkatu 35. One of the hippest little restaurants in town with a spartan, almost Hopper-esque interior. Try the scrumptious house *rödburger*. Big with local celebs.

Bar 9 Though known as a great, unpretentious neighbourhood bar, they also serve excellent food all day. Massive grilled ham and cheese sandwiches, spicy pastas and salads from €5.50.

Bar Tapasta Uudenmaankatu 13. Bustling evening tapas joint with Spanish beers and wine to accompany the fairly authentic food. Tapas from €3.90.

Pelmenit Kustaankatu 7. This hole in the wall of a Russo-Judeo-Finnish restaurant serves great inexpensive home-cooked meals such as dumplings, blinis and borscht. Mains around €6.

Pompei Snellmaninkatu 16. Excellent, down-at-heel neighbourhood Italian restaurant run by a friendly Neopolitan. Really great pizzas from €7.

Salve Hietalahdenranta 11. Unselfconsciously old-school sailors' restaurant at the end of Bulevardi that's been serving up the same heavy Finnish fare for over a century. Well worth a visit. Lunch from €7.30.

Soul Kitchen Fleminginkatu 26–28. American-style restaurant serving southern specialities such as macaroni and cheese and succulent BBQ ribs. Aretha and Ray play the tubes.

Vltava Elielinaukio 2. Pronounced "Valltava", this Czech restaurant just next to the train station serves massive grilled sausage and steak dishes sided with a great collection of pilsners.

Drinking and nightlife

Drinking in Helsinki is about as autonomic an activity as breathing for city residents. Wednesday is a popular night for going out, while on Friday and Saturday it's best to arrive as early as possible to get a seat. Several venues put on a steady diet of live music and there are occasional free gigs on summer Sundays in Kaivopuisto Park, south of the centre. There's also a wide range of clubs and discos, which charge a small admission fee (€5–8). For details of what's on, read the back page of the culture section of *Helsingin Sanomat*, or the free fortnightly English-language paper *City*, found in record shops, bookshops, department stores and tourist offices.

Bars

A21 Annankatu 21. This award-winning bar offers excellent if slightly pricey cocktails, designer seating and cliques of there-to-be-seen clientele.

Ateljee Bar *Hotel Torni*, Yrjönkatu 26. The best views of Helsinki from this stylish (but expensive) rooftop bar. Mon–Thurs 2pm–2am, Fri & Sat noon–2am, Sun 2pm–1am (outside of summer, closes one hour earlier).

Cuba! Erottajankatu 4. Popular bar with a decent-sized dancefloor that puts on electronica, rock, pop and house music in addition to some steamy salsa nights.

Erottaja Bar Erottajankatu 15–17. Stripped-down underground bar that is popular with students from Helsinki's art and design school. Fills up around 6pm, and gets very busy at weekends, when DJs play electro and the like until 3am.

Motellet Annankatu 10. Laidback bar with comfy felt sofas and sticky floors that is immensely popular with Helsinki's chichi media set. Happy hour 8–10pm. Free wi-fi.

Punavuoren Ahven Punavuorenkatu 12. One of Helsinki's best *olutravintoloja* ("beer restaurants"), this tranquil dive is very local, with Finns of all ages sporting berets, moustaches, pipes and various other retro accoutrements.
Sling in Mikonkatu 8. Best – and best-priced – cocktails in Helsinki, with knowledgeable bartenders who do the classics and their own inventive concoctions. Awkwardly located on the second floor of a shopping mall across from the train station. Enter on Kaivokatu. Sat–Thurs opens at 5pm, Fridays opens at 3pm.
We Got Beef Iso Roobertinkatu 21. Reggae, ska and funk are the turntable mainstays at this hipster bar, with a small dancefloor out the back.
Zetor Kaivopiha, Mannerheimintie 3. This classic Finnish bar-restaurant classic is filled with old rusty tractors and serves drinks and eats all day and night until 3.30am. A great place to try *sahti* – Finnish home-brewed ale. Sun–Mon noon–midnight; Tues noon–3am; Wed–Sat noon–4am.

Clubs

Jenny Woo Simonkatu 6. Dark and pop downtown nightclub big among younger Finns and the teenyboppers who linger outside hoping to sneak their way in. Happy-hour bargain cocktails.
Korjaamo Töölönkatu 51B. This excellent cultural centre puts on a series of superb indie rock, electronica and avant-garde concerts throughout the year, and also has a great bar.
The Tiger 1A Urho Kekkosenkatu. This extremely popular sprawling nightclub consists of several levels, multiple black-marble dancefloors, large terrace lounges and VIP rooms. Fri–Sun 10pm–4am.

Gay Helsinki

The gay scene in Helsinki has shrunk somewhat in recent years, but it's still lively. For the latest details, pick up a copy of the widely available monthly *Z* magazine – in Finnish only but with a useful listings section – or drop into the state-supported gay organization SETA, Hietalahdenkatu 2b 16 (☎09/681 2580 Ⓦwww.seta.fi).
dtm (Don't Tell Mamma) Iso Roobertinkatu 32. The capital's legendary gay night club, with occasional drag shows and house music most nights.
Nalle Pub Kaarlenkatu 3–5. The heart of Helsinki's lesbian scene, this apartment-like spot in the Kallio district features a jukebox and a daily happy hour (3–6pm).
Sauna Vogue Sturenkatu 27A. Finland's only gay sauna, with a bar, steamroom, terrace and masseur. €18 entry.

Shopping

Look out for Design District stickers, marking the city's most interesting boutiques and designer shops.
Design Forum Finland Erottajankatu 7. Comprehensive shop, café and studio space devoted to Finnish design: clothes, homeware, ceramics and jewellery.
Helsinki 10 Eerikinkatu 3. Some great clothing brands from Finland and further afield at this lovingly stocked boutique.
Stockmann Department Store Corner of Aleksanterinkatu and Mannerheimintie. Sprawling Constructivist edifice selling everything from bubble gum to Persian rugs. Next door, the Akateeminen Kirjakauppa is the city's best bookstore.
Stupido Iso Roobertinkatu 23. Independent record shop with a dedicated Finnish section featuring a lot of heavy metal and Europop. A good place to pick up flyers and listings.

Directory

Embassies Australia (honorary consulate), Museokatu 25b ☎09/4777 6640; Canada, Pohjoisesplanadi 25b ☎09/228 530; Ireland, Erottajankatu 7A ☎09/646 006; South Africa, Rahapajankatu 1A ☎09/6860 3100; UK, Itäinen Puistotie 17 ☎09/2286 5100; US, Itäinen Puistotie 14a ☎09/616 250.
Exchange Apart from the banks, try Travelex at the airport (5.30am–11.30pm) or Forex at the train station (daily 8am–9pm).
Hospital Marian Hospital, Lapinlahdenkatu 16 ☎09/4716 3339.
Internet Cafe Aalto, Akateeminen Kirjakauppa, Keskuskatu 1; mbar in the Lasipalatsi, Mannerheimintie 22–24; Netcup, Aleksanterinkatu 52.
Left luggage Lockers (€3 and up) in the long-distance bus station (Mon–Thurs & Sat 9am–6pm, Fri 8am–6pm), and in the train station (Mon–Fri 7am–10pm).
Pharmacy Yliopiston Apteekki (☎0300/20 200, toll call), Mannerheimintie 96, is open 24hr; its branch at Mannerheimintie 5/Kaivopiha, is open daily 7am–midnight.
Post office Mannerheiminaukio 1. (Mon–Fri 7am–9pm, Sat & Sun 10am–6pm).

Moving on

Air Ivalo (for Inari; 2–3 daily; 1hr 40min); Oulu (10–15 daily; 1hr); Rovaniemi (5–7 daily; 1hr 20min).
Train Oulu (8 daily; 6–9hr); Rovaniemi (4 daily; 9hr 45min–12hr 45min); St Petersburg (2 daily; 3hr 30min); Tampere (hourly; 2hr); Turku (hourly; 2hr).

Bus Porvoo (15 daily; 1hr); Turku (hourly; 2hr 30min–2hr 50min).
Ferry Stockholm (3 daily; 16hr); Tallinn (15–25 daily; 1hr 40min–4hr).

PORVOO

About 50km east of Helsinki, **PORVOO** is one of the oldest towns on the south coast and one of Finland's most charming. Its narrow cobbled streets, lined by small colourful wooden buildings, give a sense of Finnish life before the capital's bold squares and Neoclassical geometry. Close to the station, the **Johan Ludwig Runeberg House**, Aleksanterinkatu 3 (Mon–Sat 10am–4pm, Sun 11am–5pm; Sept–April closed Mon & Tues; €6), is where the famed Finnish poet lived from 1852; one of his poems provided the lyrics for the Finnish national anthem.

The old town is built around the hill on the other side of Mannerheimkatu, crowned by the fifteenth-century **Tuomiokirkko**, where Alexander I proclaimed Finland a Russian Grand Duchy and convened the first Finnish Diet. The cathedral survived a serious arson attack in 2006 and reopened two years later. The town's past can be explored in the **Porvoo Museum** (May–Aug Tues–Sat 10am–4pm, Sun 11am–4pm; Sept–April Wed–Sun noon–4pm; Sept–April closed Mon & Tues; €6) at the foot of the hill in the main square.

Buses run daily from Helsinki to Porvoo (€11 one-way; 1hr), arriving opposite the **tourist office**, Rihkamakatu 4 (early June to Aug Mon–Fri 9am–6pm, Sat & Sun 10am–4pm; Jan to early June & Sept–Dec Mon–Fri 9am–4.30pm, Sat 10am–2pm; Sept to early June closed Sun; ⓣ019/520 2316, ⓦwww.porvoo.fi). There's a **hostel** at Linnankoskenkatu 1–3 (ⓣ019/523 0012, ⓦwww.porvoohostel.cjb.net; dorms €20, rooms €48) and a **campsite**, *Sun Camping Porvoo Kokonniemi* (ⓣ019/581 967, ⓦwww.suncamping.fi; early June to mid-Aug; €4 per person, plus €14 per tent), 1.5km from the town centre. The cheapest **place to eat** is *Hanna Maria* in the Old Town at Välikatu 6, which has lunches that range from 6€ to 10€.

The southwest

The area immediately west of Helsinki is a region of interminable forests interrupted by modest-sized patches of water and wooden villa towns. The far southwestern corner is more interesting, with islands and inlets around a jagged shoreline, a spectacular archipelago stretching halfway to Sweden and some distinctive Finnish-Swedish coastal communities.

TURKU

Co-host of the European Capital of Culture during 2011 (along with Tallinn), **TURKU** was once the national capital, but lost its status in 1812 and most of its buildings in a ferocious fire in 1827. These days it's a small and sociable city, bristling with history, culture and a sparkling nightlife, thanks to the students from its two universities.

What to see and do

To get to grips with Turku and its pivotal place in Finnish history, cut through the centre to the Aura River which splits the city. This tree-framed space was, before the great fire of 1827, the bustling heart of the community.

Tuomiokirkko

Overlooking the river, the **Tuomiokirkko** (daily 9am–7/8pm except during services) was erected in the thirteenth century and is still the centre of the Finnish Lutheran Church. Despite repeated fires, a number of features survive, and there's a small museum in the south gallery.

Turku Art Museum

The **Turku Art Museum** (Tues–Fri 11am–7pm, Sat & Sun 11am–5pm; €8) is housed in a lovely building constructed in 1904. It contains one of the better collections of Finnish art, with works by all the great names of the country's nineteenth-century Golden Age plus a commendable stock of modern pieces.

Aboa Vetus and Ars Nova

Turku's newest and most splendid museum is the combined **Aboa Vetus and Ars Nova** (daily 11am–7pm, Sept–March closed Mon; €8; guided tours July–Aug daily 11.30am), along the riverbank. Digging the foundations of the modern art gallery revealed a warren of medieval lanes, now on show. The gallery comprises 350 striking works plus temporary exhibits, and there's a great café too.

Turku Castle

Crossing back over Aurajoki and down Linnankatu and then heading towards the mouth of the river will bring you to **Turku Castle** (May to mid-Sept Tues–Sun 10am–6pm; mid-Sept to April Tues 10am–6pm, Wed noon–8pm, Thurs–Sun 10am–6pm; €8). If you don't fancy the walk, hop on bus #1 from the market square. The featureless exterior conceals a maze of cobbled courtyards, corridors and staircases, with a bewildering array of finds and displays – a 37-room historical museum. The castle probably went up around 1280; its gradual expansion accounts for the patchwork architecture.

Arrival and information

Train and bus Both the stations are within easy walking distance of the river, just north of the centre.
Ferry From the Stockholm ferry, take the train to the terminal, 2km west, or catch bus #1 to Linnankatu.
Tourist office Aurakatu 4 (June–Aug Mon–Fri 8.30am–6pm, Sat & Sun 9am–4pm; Sept–May Mon–Fri 8.30am–6pm, Sat & Sun 10am–3pm; ⓣ02/262 7444, ⓦwww.turkutouring.fi).

Accommodation

Campsite Ruissalo ⓣ02/262 5100, ⓦwww.turku.fi/ruissalocamping. On the island of Ruissalo, which has two sandy beaches and overlooks Turku harbour. June–Aug; bus #8. €5/person, plus €15/tent.
Hostel Turku Linnankatu 39 ⓣ02/262 7680, ⓦwww.turku.fi/hostelturku. One of the cleanest, most efficient and best-run hostels in Finland, situated right by the river. Pine floors, comfy sofas as well as three large kitchens, laundry, personal lockers, an internet café and inexpensive bicycle rental service. Take bus #1 or #30. Dorms €18.
Linnasmaki Lustokatu 7 ⓣ02/4123 500, ⓦwww.linnasmaki.fi. Basic 56-room summer hostel in the Christian Institute, 4km from town (bus #14 or #15). Mid-May to mid-Sept only. Dorms €25.
Omena Hotelli Humalistonkatu 7 ⓦwww.omenahotels.com. Alvar Aalto fans might fancy a stay in this building designed by Finland's most famous architect. The hotel is modern and self-service, with an automated reception area. Doubles €45.
River Hostel Turku Linnankatu 72 ⓣ040/689 2541 ⓦwww.turkutouring.fi/s/river-hostel-turku. Permanently docked on the river and opened in June 2011, the *S/S Bore* is now the most exciting place to stay in Turku on a budget. The appeal lies not in the tidy, en-suite cabin rooms, but in the quirky experience of staying on an ex-cruise ship. Doubles €55.
Tuure Bed and Breakfast Tuureporinkatu 17 C ⓣ02/233 0230 ⓦwww.netti.fi/~tuure2. Clean, pleasant little guesthouse with friendly proprietors in the centre of town, located in a drab office building. Free wi-fi and computer stations. Singles €38, doubles €54.

Eating and drinking

Fresh produce is sold in the *kauppatori* (market square), near the tourist office every day; in summer it's full of open-air cafés; nearby, the effervescent market hall or *kauppahalli* (Mon–Fri 8am–5pm, Sat 8am–2pm) offers a slightly more upmarket choice of delis and other places to eat. A drink at one of the many floating bar-restaurants moored along Itäinen Rantakatu is a popular summer tradition.

Cafés and restaurants

Assarin Ullakko Rehtorinpellonkatu 4a. This rock-bottom-priced student cafeteria offers a lively atmosphere great for meeting local students. Lunch costs €5.20 (50 percent discount for students). Closed Sun.

Baan Thai Kauppiaskatu 17. Great Thai food at respectable prices. Mains around €7.

Blanko Aurakatu 1. Popular bar-restaurant just opposite the tourist office. Good lunches and house and electro DJs till 3am at weekends. Lunches from €7.40, dinners double that.

Foija Aurakatu 10. Busy cellar restaurant with vaulted ceilings and great service opposite the market square. Great pastas, salads and pizzas from €6.50.

Herman Läntinen Rantakatu 37. A bright, airy storehouse right on the river dating from 1849, with excellent lunches from €7.50.

Bars and clubs

Baari Kärpänen Kauppiakatu 8. Excellent hard rock bar with lovely embroidered red velvet seating inside and a cobblestone terrace in front. Looks rough, but actually very sociable. Open until 4am.

Dynamo Linnankatu 7. A rocking bar set across two floors, with red velour chairs and olive leather couches. Gets going around 1am, when the dancefloor becomes packed and sweaty.

Klubi Humalistonkatu 8. Cavernous, studenty venue featuring live bands and DJ nights – for listings, check the posters liberally applied to lampposts all over town.

Kuka Linnankatu 17. Furnished with an eclectic mix of classic Finnish design pieces and retro madness, this cool, arty bar attracts Turku's creative types. Live music or DJs several nights a week.

Moving on

Train Helsinki (hourly; 2hr); Turku (8 daily; 1hr 40min).

Bus Helsinki (hourly; 2hr 30min–2hr 50min), Tampere (every 30min; 2hr–2hr 55min.

Ferry Stockholm (4 daily; 10–11hr).

The Lake Region

About a third of Finland is covered by the **Lake Region**, a huge area of bays, inlets and islands interspersed with dense pine forests. Despite holding much of Finland's industry, it's a tranquil, verdant area, and even **Tampere**, a major industrial city, enjoys a peaceful lakeside setting. The eastern part of the region is the most atmospheric: slender ridges furred with conifers link the few sizeable landmasses. The regional centre, **Savonlinna**, stretches gorgeously across several islands and boasts a fine medieval castle, inside which a superb opera festival is held every summer, while bustling **Kuopio** offers a good taste of the region.

TAMPERE

Scandinavia's largest inland city, **TAMPERE** is a leafy place of cobbled avenues, sculpture-filled parks and two sizeable, placid lakes. It was long a manufacturing centre, but thanks to an impressive arts patronage, it has become one of Finland's most enjoyable cities, with free outdoor concerts, a healthy nightlife and one of the best modern art collections in the country.

What to see and do

The main streets run off either side of Hämeenkatu. To the left, up slender Hämeenpuisto, the **Lenin Museum** at no. 28 (Mon–Fri 9am–6pm, Sat & Sun 11am–4pm; €5) commemorates the revolutionary's ties with Finland and his life in general; the absorbing exhibition has a devoted, trainspotter feel. Moomin fans shouldn't miss the adorable **Moomin Museum** (Tues–Fri 9am–5pm, Sat & Sun 10am–6pm; €7) in the basement of the city library at Hämeenpuisto 20, a respectful and exhaustive overview of Tove Jansson's creations. Nearby, at Puutarhakatu 34, the **Art Museum of Tampere** (Tues–Sun 10am–6pm; €6) holds temporary art exhibitions, but if you're looking for Finnish art you might be better off visiting the **Hiekka Art Gallery**, a few minutes' walk away at Pirkankatu 6 (Tues–Thurs 3–6pm, Sun noon–3pm; €7). Better still is the tremendous **Sara**

Hildén Art Museum (daily 11am–6pm, closed Mon Oct–April; €10, includes admission to Särkänniemi amusement park and Näsinneula observation tower), built on the shores of Näsijärvi, a quirky collection of Finnish and foreign modern works; take bus #16 (or #4 in summer) from the centre.

Arrival and information

Air Bus #61 operates between the airport and the city centre, taking 40min.
Train The station's at Rautatienkatu 25, at the end of Hämeenkatu.
Bus The long-distance bus station is in the town centre, off Hämeenkatu.
Tourist office In the railway station (Jan–May Mon–Fri 8.30am–4.30pm; June–Aug Mon–Fri 9am–6pm, Sat & Sun 11am–3pm; Sept–Dec Mon–Fri 8.30am–4.30pm; ⓣ03/5656 6800, ⓦwww.gotampere.fi).

Accommodation

Dream Hostel Åkerlundinkatu 2 ⓣ045/236 0517, ⓦwww.dreamhostel.fi. Voted Finland's hostel of the year in 2011, this cosy spot features modern furnishings and pretty much every amenity you could imagine, including a sauna and gym. Dorms €27.50.
Härmälä Campsite ⓣ020/719 9777. 4km south of the city centre in gorgeous wooded environs with cabins (€48) and rooms (€45); bus #1. Mid-May to mid-Sept. €14/tent, plus €5/person.
Hostel Sofia Tuomiokirkonkatu 12a ⓣ03/254 4020, ⓦwww.hostelsofia.fi. Bright, attractive hostel with rooms that look smack onto the cathedral. Dorms €28.
Omena Hotelli Hämeenkatu 7 & Hämeenkatu 28 ⓦwww.omenahotels.com. These two excellent, self-service hotels have no reception and you must book online, but they offer some of the best deals in town. Doubles €45.

Eating

Coyote Bar and Grill Hämeenkatu 3. Retro dining spot filled with young locals scarfing down burgers and finger food, then lingering on bottles of Karjala IV.
Kahvila Runo Ojakatu 3. With some great Finnish rustic furniture, this bookish, high-ceilinged space has plenty of charm and is the best place for a coffee and cake in town.
Salud Tuomiokirkonkatu 19. A lively Spanish restaurant serving mixed tapas plates and an amply sized weekday lunch buffet, both for under €10.

Drinking

Klubi Tullikamarinaukio 2 ⓦwww.klubi.net. Busy nightclub and concert venue in an old customs house behind the train station. Also serves cheap lunches.
Vanha Monttu Hämeenkatu 17 ⓦwww.vanhamonttu.net. Cellar bar filled with ex-punk and hard-rocker kids and lots of naff memorabilia on the walls. The lively drunken karaoke nights are a particularly good spot to see the Finnish national character up close.

Moving on

Train Helsinki (hourly; 2hr); Kuopio (9 daily; 3hr 35min); Oulu (10 daily; 5hr); Savonlinna (2 daily; 4–5hr); Turku (8 daily; 1hr 40min).

SAVONLINNA AND AROUND

SAVONLINNA is one of the most relaxed towns in Finland, renowned for its **opera festival** (ⓣ015/476 750, ⓦwww.operafestival.fi) in July. It's packed throughout summer, so book well ahead if you're visiting at this time. Out of peak season, its streets and beaches are uncluttered, and the town's easy-going mood and lovely setting – amid a confluence of forests and lakes – make it a pleasant place to linger.

What to see and do

The best locations for soaking up the atmosphere are the **harbour** and **market square** at the end of Olavinkatu, where you can cast an eye over the grand *Seurahuone* hotel, with its Art Nouveau fripperies. At the square, try the Savonlinna specialty known as "*lörtsy*", a delicious meat-and-rice-filled pastry packed with condiments. Follow the harbour around picturesque Linnankatu, or better still around the sandy edge of Pihlajavesi, which brings you to atmospheric and surprisingly well-preserved **Olavinlinna Castle** (guided tours

Jan–May Mon–Fri 10am–4pm, Sat & Sun 11am–4pm; June to mid-Aug daily 10am–6pm; mid-Aug to mid-Dec Mon–Fri 10am–4pm, Sat & Sun 11am–4pm; €6), perched on a small island. Founded in 1475, the castle witnessed a series of bloody conflicts until the Russians claimed possession of it in 1743 and relegated it to the status of town jail.

Nearby is the **Savonlinna Provincial Museum** in Riihisaari (Tues–Sun 11am–5pm, plus Mon same times in July & Aug; €5), which occupies an old granary and displays an intriguing account of the evolution of local life, with rock paintings and ancient amber carved with human figures.

Arrival and information

Train There are two train stations: be sure to get off at Savonlinna-Kauppatori, just across the main bridge from the tourist office.
Bus The bus station is off the main island, but within easy walking distance of the town centre.
Tourist office Puistokatu 1 (July to early Aug Mon–Sat 10am–6pm, Sun 10am–2pm; other times Mon–Fri 9am–5pm; ⓣ015/517 510, ⓦwww.savonlinna.travel).

Accommodation

Perhehotelli Hospitz Linnankatu 20 ⓣ015/515 661, ⓦwww.hospitz.com. Attractive, central hotel. Prices go up during the opera festival. Singles €88, doubles €98.
Savonlinna SKO Hostel Opistokatu 1 ⓣ015/72 910, ⓦwww.sko.fi. Likeable summer hostel in the town's Christian Institute. 6km from the city centre. Rooms €60.
S/S Heinävesi Savonlinna harbour ⓣ015/517 510, ⓦwww.savonlinnanlaivat.fi. In the summer, this steamship offers 34 beds in comfy on-board cabins. Singles €58, doubles €68.
Vuohimäki Camping Vuohimäentie 60 ⓣ015/537 353, ⓦwww.fontana.fi. The nearest campsite, though still a good 7km from the centre. Early June to late Aug; bus #4. €14/tent, plus €4/person (€14 in total for only one person).

Eating and drinking

Good, cheap food is available at the pizza joints along Olavinkatu and Tulliportinkatu.

Majakka Satamakatu 11. Tasty Finnish nosh, with some good deals at lunchtime (from €6.20).
Paviljonki Rajalahdenkatu 4. The restaurant of a local cookery school, serving great €14 lunches (11am–4.30pm) including dessert and coffee.

Moving on

Train Parikkala (for Helsinki; 2 daily; 50min); Punkaharju (3 daily; 20min).
Bus Kuopio (3–7 daily; 2hr 45min–4hr 20min).

KUOPIO

The pleasant lakeside town of **KUOPIO** is best known for its enormous smoke sauna, the biggest in the world, and makes for a worthwhile pit stop on your way north to Lapland. One of the best times to visit is during the annual **Kuopio Dance Festival** (ⓦwww.kuopiodance festival.fi) in mid-June.

What to see and do

Built on a grid system, the centre is easy to navigate. Just south of the train station is the main square, the *kauppatori*. From here Kauppakatu leads east to the **Kuopio Museum** (Tues–Fri 10am–5pm, till 7pm on Wed; Sat & Sun 11am–5pm; €6) at no. 23 with two floors of natural and cultural history. Further up the road, at no. 35, the **Kuopio Art Museum** (same times; €4) is housed in a converted bank. The thoughtfully curated temporary exhibitions focus mainly on modern Finnish art. Around the corner on Kuninkaankatu, the **Victor Barsokevitsch Photographic Centre** (June–Aug Mon–Fri 10am–6pm, Sat & Sun 11am–4pm; Sept–May Tues–Fri 11am–5pm, till 7pm on Wed, Sat & Sun 11am–3pm; summer €5, winter €3) is a real find – one of the best photography galleries in the country, with changing exhibitions.

Kuoipio's **woodsmoke sauna** (Tues year-round, plus Thurs mid-May to mid-Sept; €12; ⓦwww.rauhalahti .fi), set at the *Jätkänkämppä Lumberjack Lodge*, is the main draw in town, and about as quintessentially Finnish an experience as you'll find: there are traditional Finnish evenings each night the sauna is open, which often include a Lumberjack Show and great dinner buffet from mid-May to mid-August (€20). The lodge is located 4km south of the centre in the *Rauhalahti* spa hotel complex.

Arrival and information

Train and bus Kuopio's train and bus stations are located opposite each other just north of the *kauppatori*.

Tourist office Within the City Hall at Haapaniemenkatu 17 (June–Aug Mon–Fri 9.30am–5pm; rest of year Mon–Fri 9.30am–4.30pm; ⓣ017/182 584, ⓦwww.visitlakeland.fi). The Kuopio Card (€12) on sale here, offers free entry to the town's museums as well as admission to the smoke sauna.

Accommodation

Hostelli Hermanni Hermanninaukio 3e ⓣ040/910 9083, ⓦwww.hostellihermanni.fi. Comfortable if basic hostel 1.5km out of town. Dorms €25, doubles €45.

Rauhalahti Katiskaniementie 8, 5km from the city centre ⓣ01/747 3000; ⓣ03/060 830, ⓦwww.rauhalahti.com. Attractive lakeside campsite with cottages (€30), a hotel (singles €77, doubles €92) and space for tents (late May to late Aug). €13/tent, plus €4/person.

Youth Hostel Virkkula Asemakatu 3 ⓣ040/418 2178, ⓦwww.kuopionsteinerkoulu.fi. Summer hostel in a colourful converted school just by the train station. Mid-June to early Aug. Dorms €19.

Eating and drinking

Café Kaneli Pohjolankatu 2a. Charming little café cluttered with knick-knacks and pictures, serving great coffee and cake.

Sampo Kauppakatu 13. Proudly traditional fish restaurant that has been serving Finnish dishes since 1931. Mains around €13.

Wanha Satama At the harbour. Set in a former customs house, this modern Finnish restaurant is popular on sunny summer evenings, serving inexpensive sandwiches and salads and more expensive local dishes.

Moving on

Train Helsinki (5–6 daily; 6hr 50min); Oulu (4 daily; 4hr 30min–6hr 5min); Rovaniemi (2 daily; 8hr 30min); Savonlinna (9 daily; 2hr 45min–4hr); Tampere (7 daily; 5hr 30min).

The north

The northern regions take up a vast portion of Finland: one third of the country lies north of the Arctic Circle. It's sparsely populated, with small communities often separated by long distances. The coast of Ostrobothnia is affluent due to the adjacent flat and fertile farmland; busy and expanding **Oulu** is the region's major city, though it maintains a pleasing small-town atmosphere. Further north is the remote and wild territory of **Lapland**, its wide-open spaces home to several thousand Sámi, who have lived more or less in harmony with this harsh environment for millennia. Up here are two good bases: the buzzing town of **Rovaniemi** and, further north, the quiet village of **Inari**, Lapland's de facto capital and a great jumping-off point for trips to the rest of the region; there is an extensive bus service and regular flights from Helsinki. Make sure you try Lappish **cuisine**, too – fresh cloudberries, smoked reindeer and wild salmon are highlights.

OULU

OULU, with its renowned university, is a leading light in Finland's burgeoning computing industry and a great place to pause on your way up north, with a good collection of restaurants and cafés and a pulsing nightlife, especially in the warmer months. On Kirkkokatu, the copper-domed and stuccoed **Tuomiokirkko** (June–Aug daily 11am–8/9pm; Sept–May Mon–Fri noon–1pm) seems anachronistic amid the bulky blocks of modern Oulu. Across the small canal just to the north, the **Northern Ostrobothnia Museum** (June–Aug Tues–Fri 10am–6pm, Sat & Sun 11am–6pm; Jan–May & Sept–Dec Tues–Sun 10am–5pm; €3) has a large regional collection with a good Sámi section.

Arrival and information

Bus and train The adjacent stations are located a few blocks east of the *kauppatori* and *kauppahalli*.
Tourist office Torikatu 10 (Mon–Fri 9am–4pm; mid-June to Aug until 5pm, plus Sat 10am–4pm; ⓣ08/5584 1330, ⓦwww.oulutourism.fi).

Accommodation

Nallikari Holiday Village ⓣ044/703 1353, ⓦwww.nallikari.fi. Campsite with cabins on Hietasaari Island, 4km from town; take bus #17 from Isokatu in the town centre. Cabins €36; €13/tent, plus €4/person.
Välkkylätalo Ylioppilaantie 2 ⓣ010/272 2987. Fairly central summer hostel near the city centre with bland but acceptable rooms. Doubles €45.

Eating, drinking and nightlife

45 Special Saarisonkatu 12 ⓦwww.45special.com. Legendary rock club with three floors and frequent live bands; the Sunday jams are a good bet.
Finlandia Hallituskatu 31. No-nonsense pizzeria that is one of the cheapest places for a dinner in town.
Never Grow Old Hallituskatu 13–17 ⓦwww.ngo.fi. With swinging wicker bungalow chairs, a painted Caribbean beachscape and reggae music all night long this quirky bar is perfect for late-night dancing.
Valve Café Hallituskatu 7 ⓦwww.oulunelokuvakeskus.fi. Oulu's youth and cultural centre has a relaxed courtyard café that's super in the afternoons. Films are screened every evening in the same building.

Moving on

Train Helsinki (8 daily; 6–9hr); Rovaniemi (7 daily; 3hr 35min); Tampere (6 daily; 8hr 10min–14hr 35min).

ROVANIEMI

Easily reached by train, **ROVANIEMI** is touted as the capital of Lapland, and while its fairly bland shopping streets are a far cry from the surrounding rural hinterland, the town's Arctic sensibility makes it worth spending a day here while gearing up for an exploration of the Northern Finnish hinterland. The best way to prepare yourself for what lies further north is to visit the 172m-long glass tunnel of **Arktikum** at Pohjoisranta 4 (early June to mid-June daily 10am–6pm; mid-June to Aug daily 9am–6pm; early Jan to May and Sept to Nov Tues–Sun 10am–6pm; €12; ⓦwww.arktikum.fi). Subterranean galleries house Sámi crafts, costumes and displays on all things circumpolar. The **midnight sun** is visible from Rovaniemi for several weeks each side of misdummer. The best vantage points are either the striking bridge over the Ounaskoski or atop the forested and mosquito-infested hill, Ounasvaara, across the bridge.

Two of the biggest attractions are outside town. **The Arctic Circle**, 8km north is connected by the hourly bus #8 from the railway station (€6.80 return). A few paces north of the circle is the **Santa Claus Village** (mid-Jan to May 10am–5pm; June–Aug 9am–6pm, Sept–Nov 10am–5pm; Dec to early Jan 9am–7pm; free), a large log cabin where you can meet Father Christmas all year round.

Arrival and information

Air The airport is located 5 miles north of town, and connected by bus (€5).
Train The train station is just outside the town centre, at Ratukatu 3.
Bus The bus station is just west of the centre, off Postikatu, a few minutes' walk east from the train station.
Tourist office Rovakatu 21 (mid-June to mid-Aug Mon–Fri 9am–1pm, Sat & Sun 9am–1pm; rest of the year Mon–Fri 9am–5pm; ⓣ016/346 270, ⓦwww.visitrovaniemi.fi).

Accommodation

Guesthouse Borealis Asemieskatu 1 ⓦwww.guesthouseborealis.com. Wonderful family-run spot with colourful rooms and great service. Singles €47; doubles €58.

Hostel Rudolf Koskikatu 41, book via ⓣ016/321 321, ⓦwww.hotelsantaclaus.fi. Modern hostel with colourful rooms 10min walk from the centre. There are no staff on site; check-in and reservations are handled by the *Hotel Santa Claus*, Korkalonkatu 29. April–Nov. Dorms €28, doubles €44.

Ounaskoksi Camping ⓣ016/345 304. Campsite on the far bank of Ounaskoski, facing town – a 20min walk from the station. Mid-May to late Sept. €13/tent, plus €7.50/person.

Eating and drinking

Kauppayhtiö Valtakatu 24. Unexpectedly fantastic café-bar with a mishmash of retro furniture. DJs at the weekend and a gallery at the back. Free wi-fi. Mon–Thurs 10.30am–8pm, Fri & Sat 10.30am–2am.

Kotileipomo Antinkaapo Rovakatu 13. The best café in town serves a wide range of cakes and pastries.

Monte Rosa Pekankatu 9. Rovaniemi's best Italian restaurant, with excellent pan pizzas and pasta dishes, from around €11.

Zoomit Korkalonkatu 29. Modern, if somewhat gaudy bar popular with local university students.

Moving on

Air Helsinki (4 daily; 1hr 20min).

Train Helsinki (4 daily; 9hr 45min–12hr 45min); Oulu (7 daily; 3hr).

Bus Inari (4 daily; 5hr 15min); Nordkapp, Norway (June to late Aug 1 daily; 10hr 35min).

INARI

A half-day bus ride north of Rovaniemi, **INARI** lies along the fringes of Inarijärvi, one of Finland's largest lakes, and makes an attractive base from which to further explore this part of Lapland. In the town itself, the excellent **SIIDA** (Sámi Museum; Tues–Sun: June to mid-Sept 9am–8pm; mid-Sept to May 10am–5pm; €9; ⓦwww.siida.fi) has an outstanding outdoor section giving you an idea of how the Sámi survived in Arctic conditions in their tepees, or *kota*, while the indoor section has a well-laid-out exhibition on all aspects of life in the Arctic. Towards the northern end of the village, summer **boat tours** (€12) depart from under the bridge to the ancient Sámi holy site on the island of **Ukonkivi**. If walking's your thing then check out the pretty **Pielpajärvi Wilderness Church**, a well-signposted 7km (2hr) hike from the village.

Arrival and information

Air Ivalo airport is a 40min bus ride from town.

Bus Buses stop outside the tourist office, in the centre of town, before continuing to Karasjok in Norway and – from June to late Aug only – Nordkapp, about the most northerly point in Europe.

Tourist office The helpful tourist office (June–Aug daily 9am–8pm; rest of the year Tues–Fri 10am–5pm; ⓣ016/661 666, ⓦwww.inarilapland.org) is in the SIIDA museum complex. Staff here can advise on guided snow-scooter trips in winter and fishing trips in summer – as well as trips across the Russian border to Murmansk.

Accommodation

Finding accommodation should not be too problematic, though Inari does get very busy during the summer.

Lomakylä Inari Inarintie 26 ⓣ016/671 108, ⓦwww.saariselka.fi. A brief walk from town, these lakeside log cabins are open year-round and most have private bath. €38/cabin.

Uruniemi Campsite 2km south of the village ⓣ016/671 331, ⓦwww.uruniemi.com. In a lovely location right by the lake, with cabins and rooms arranged around manicured grounds. Oct–May advanced booking obligatory. €5/tent, plus €5/person. Cottages from €38.

Villa Lanca Opposite the tourist office ⓣ040/748 0984, ⓦwww.villalanca.com. Cheery guesthouse with gorgeous rooms. Singles €55, doubles €79.

Eating

Inarin Kultahovi Saarikoskentie 2. This pricey hotel's restaurant dishes up the best meals in town, including reindeer carpaccio and skewered tiger prawns.

SIIDA The museum restaurant prepares excellent Arctic dishes, including a succulent baked salmon fillet with hollandaise sauce.

Moving on

Bus Ivalo (3–5 daily; 35min); Rovaniemi (3–5 daily; 5hr 15min–7hr 50min).

France

HIGHLIGHTS

MUSÉE D'ORSAY, PARIS: the capital's most enjoyable museum, with an unparalleled collection of Impressionist art

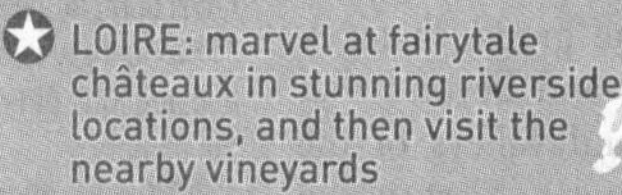

LOIRE: marvel at fairytale châteaux in stunning riverside locations, and then visit the nearby vineyards

LYON: truck into delicious regional specialities in one of the city's excellent bouchons

BORDEAUX: enjoy the superb local wines in one of the many sun-drenched squares

CORSICA: explore the island's rugged mountains and fine sand beaches

ROUGH COSTS

DAILY BUDGET Basic €40 /occasional treat €65

DRINK Glass of wine €2.50, beer €3

FOOD Baguette/sandwich €3–5

HOSTEL/BUDGET HOTEL €16–30/€25–55

TRAVEL Paris–Nice by train €25

FACT FILE

POPULATION 63.4 million

AREA 547,030km

LANGUAGE French

CURRENCY Euro (€)

CAPITAL Paris (population: 9.6 million)

INTERNATIONAL PHONE CODE ⓣ33

Introduction

France is one of Europe's most stylish and dynamic countries. The largest country in Western Europe, it offers a variety of cultural and geographical experiences unmatched across the continent. Yet, despite its size, it's surprisingly easy to explore, with a fantastic high-speed train network which means that within hours of indulging in the café culture of the capital, you could be swimming in the clear waters of the Côte d'Azur.

Paris continues to captivate visitors with its world-class museums, distinctive neighbourhoods and exuberant nightlife. To the west, **Normandy** boasts some of the country's greatest Romanesque architecture, while the lush countryside and rocky coastline of neighbouring **Brittany** provide great surroundings for getting away from it all. Just south lie the grand châteaux of the **Loire valley**, and beyond that the gorgeous hills and valleys of the **Dordogne**. The Atlantic coast has a misty charm, including low-key **La Rochelle** and the surfing capital of **Biarritz**. Though most people push on south to the country's most obvious attractions, there's a lot to be said for exploring the Germanic towns of **Alsace** in the east and the high and rugged heartland of the **Massif Central**. France's gastronomic capital, **Lyon**, acts as a gateway to the heady southern region of **Provence**, characterized by beautiful countryside, charming towns and sublime food. The **Côte d'Azur** retains something of its old glamour, while **Marseille** is more worthy of exploration than its reputation would have you believe. The very south of the country, marked by the canyons of the **Pyrenees**, hides the dream-like fortress of Carcassonne, and provides some of the country's best walking territory, alongside the **Alps.** The student cities of **Montpellier** and **Toulouse** should be stops on any budget traveller's itinerary, boasting cheap restaurants, excellent nightlife and a relaxed ambience.

CHRONOLOGY

51 BC Julius Caesar conquers Gaul.
486 AD Clovis I, leader of the Franks, establishes his rule over Gaul.
800 Charlemagne rules as King of the Franks.
1066 William, the Duke of Normandy, invades England and is crowned King of England.
1337 The Hundred Years' War with England begins.
1431 After leading the French army to victory, Joan of Arc is burnt at the stake for heresy, at the age of 19.
1589 Henry IV is the first of the Bourbon dynasty to become King of France. Enforces Catholicism over the country.
1789 The French Revolution ends the rule of the monarchy and establishes the First Republic.
1804 Napoleon I declares himself Emperor of the French Empire.
1815 Napoleon I is defeated at the battle of Waterloo; the monarchy is restored.
1848 Louis-Napoleon, Napoleon I's nephew, is made President of the Second Republic before declaring himself Emperor a few years later.
1871 Defeat in the Franco-Prussian War leads to the creation of the Third Republic.
1872 Monet ushers in the Impressionist Movement.
1889 Eiffel Tower is built, making it the tallest building in the world.
1905 Church and State are legally separated.
1914–18 World War I – over 1.5 million killed.
1939–44 Nazi Germany occupies France leading to four years of fascist rule under the Vichy regime. France is liberated by Allied forces in August 1944.
1962 Algeria gains independence from French colonial rule.
1995 Jacques Chirac elected President.
2002 The euro replaces the franc.
2005 Civil unrest and riots across the country after the death of two teenagers who were running from police in one of Paris' impoverished housing estates.
2007 Nicolas Sarkozy is elected President, narrowly beating Ségolène Royal, France's first female presidential candidate.
2008 Smoking is banned in bars and cafés.

ARRIVAL

The main hub for arrivals by **air** is Paris Charles de Gaulle, which is served by both major and budget airlines. In addition, there are around 34 other airports, including Lyon, Nice, La Rochelle and Marseille. France has excellent train connections to the rest of continental Europe. The main access point by **train** from most countries is Paris: Gare du Nord links to Amsterdam, Brussels, Germany and the UK; Gare de Lyon to Italy; and Gare d'Austerlitz to Spain. There are also excellent connections from the south of France to Italy and Spain.

The Eurolines **coach service** (ⓦwww.eurolines.com) connects most European countries to France; the main arrival point in Paris is the *gare routière* in the suburb of Bagnolet.

GETTING AROUND

France has the most extensive **rail** network in Western Europe, run by the government-owned SNCF (ⓦwww.sncf.com). The only areas not well served are parts of the Alps and the Pyrenees, where some rail routes are replaced by SNCF buses. Private bus services tend to be uncoordinated and are best used only as a last resort.

Train fares are reasonable, especially if booked well in advance; Paris to Lyon, for example, can cost as little as €19, but four times that if booked on the day of travel. InterRail and Eurail passes are valid on normal trains at all times. The high-speed and very efficient TGVs (*Trains à Grande Vitesse*) require reservations (€3), and there is a supplement to travel on certain other trains (from €1). All tickets (not passes) must be stamped in the orange machines in front of the platform of the train station (*gare*) on penalty of a steep fine. All but the smallest stations have an information desk but only a handful have *consignes automatiques* – coin-operated left-luggage lockers. The word *autocar* on a timetable column indicates that it's an **SNCF bus service**, on which rail tickets and passes are valid.

Bikes that can be dismantled go free on all trains – if you can't collapse your bike then it can still travel free as long as the train doesn't require reservations and there's room. If you're catching a train that requires a reservation, your bike will also need a booking, and you'll have to pay a flat fee of €10 (regardless of distance). The main SNCF stations and larger tourist offices often rent bikes for around €10–15 per day.

ACCOMMODATION

Outside the summer season and school holidays, it's generally possible to turn up in any town and find accommodation. However, many hostels get booked up with school groups, so where possible it's worth reserving in advance.

All **hotels** are officially graded and are required to post their tariffs inside the entrance. Most **hostels** in France are operated by FUAJ, the French youth hostel association (part of the worldwide Hostelling International; Ⓦwww.hihostels.com). Many of the hostels are situated some distance away from the centre of town, and the quality varies widely – from old-fashioned institutional accommodation to bright, modern, well-situated buildings. Many FUAJ hostels close in the middle of the day so you are unable even to leave your bags, and all require that you vacate the rooms by around 10am, even if you're not checking out. Almost all hostels provide bed linen, and most provide free breakfast, with the exception of a few private hostels **Gîtes d'étape** provide bunk beds and simple kitchen facilities in rural areas for climbers, hikers, cyclists, etc – they are listed, along with mountain refuges, on Ⓦwww.gites-refuges.com. Local **campsites** provide a good budget alternative as they are generally clean, well equipped and often enjoy prime locations. Prices are usually for two people plus a tent – we've noted any exceptions. Ask tourist offices for lists of sites or consult Ⓦwww.campingfrance.com.

FOOD AND DRINK

Eating out in France isn't particularly cheap, but the quality of the food is often excellent and, even in the big cities, it's usually easy to find somewhere where you can enjoy a *plat* and a glass of wine for under €15.

Generally the best place to eat **breakfast** (*petit déjeuner*) is in a bar or café. Most serve *tartines* (baguette with butter and/or jam) and croissants, until around 11am. Coffee is invariably served black and strong – *un café* is an espresso, while *un café crème* is made with hot milk. Tea (*thé*) and hot chocolate (*chocolat chaud*) are also available – though the former is served without milk unless you request it on the side.

Cafés are often the best option for a light **lunch**, usually serving omelettes, sandwiches (generally half-baguettes filled with cheese or meat) and *croque-monsieur* (toasted ham and cheese sandwich; €3–6), as well as more substantial meals. Crêperies are ubiquitous throughout France and are usually very reasonably priced (from €5), and Oriental restaurants are also good for a cheap, filling meal (from €7). Most cafés and restaurants have a midday *formule* (set menu) of two or three courses, often including a glass of wine. With *formules* starting at around

€9, it's worth making lunch your main meal to make the most of these offers, which will often allow you to enjoy high-quality restaurant food that you wouldn't otherwise be able to afford. Most restaurants serve food from noon to 2pm and 7 to 11pm, but some cafés serve snacks throughout the day.

Vegetarian restaurants are becoming more common, especially in large cities, and if you make it clear that you're *un végétarien*, something can normally be arranged in all but the most basic of places.

Drink

Drinking is an important part of French life, with the local bar playing a central social role. **Wine** (*vin*) is the national drink, and drunk at just about every meal or social occasion. Even the most basic of cafés usually offer a wide range of wines by the glass, and ordering a *pichet* or a carafe (usually ranging from a quarter bottle to a half bottle) is often great value.

Beer can be very expensive, especially if ordered by the pint. Beer on tap (*à la pression*) is the best value – ask for *une pression* or *un demi* (0.33 litre). Spirits such as **cognac** and **armagnac**, and of course the notorious **absinthe**, are widely drunk but not cheap. A pleasant, inexpensive pre-dinner drink is *un kir*, a mix of white wine and crème de cassis, and if you're in the south of France it's definitely worth sampling the local **pastis**, drunk over ice and diluted with water – very refreshing on a hot day.

CULTURE AND ETIQUETTE

Making an effort to speak French, however dreadful your accent, is always highly appreciated; a few basic words will get you a lot further than any amount of grimacing and pointing.

It's customary to **tip** porters, tour guides, taxi drivers and hairdressers, usually one to two euros. Restaurant prices almost always include a service charge, so there's no need to leave an additional cash tip unless you feel you've received service out of the ordinary.

SPORTS AND OUTDOOR ACTIVITIES

The main sport in France is undoubtedly **football**. The French football league (Ⓦwww.lfp.fr) is divided into Ligue 1 (the highest), Ligue 2 and National; teams playing in the first category include Saint-Étienne, Lyon and Paris Saint-Germain. Match tickets are available from specific club websites, or in the town they are playing – ask at the local tourist office.

Rugby is another major pursuit, especially in southwestern France, and the country often puts up a good showing in the Six Nations Tournament in March and April. Further details of rugby fixtures can be found at Ⓦwww.francerugby.fr. The annual Tour de France, an epic 3000km **cycle** race across the country every July (Ⓦwww.letour.fr), is one of the country's most popular sporting events. The country's best **skiing** is in the Alps, and it's usually possible to ski from November to April. Prices can be high, however, so it's worth checking package prices in resort towns such as Chamonix (see p.443). France is also traced with lots of long-distance

FRANCE ONLINE

Ⓦ**www.tourisme.fr** French Tourist Board.

Ⓦ**www.franceguide.com** Links to many tourist offices.

Ⓦ**www.france.com** Guide on travelling around the country and places to stay, with the opportunity to interact with other travellers.

Ⓦ**www.discoverfrance.net** Useful tourist information, with links to other sites.

Ⓦ**www.viafrance.com** Information on festivals, expos, events and concerts.

FRENCH

	French	Pronunciation
Yes	*Oui*	Whee
No	*Non*	No(n)
Please	*S'il vous plaît*	See voo play
Thank you	*Merci*	Mersee
Hello/Good day	*Bonjour*	Bo(n)joor
Goodbye	*Au revoir/à bientôt*	Orvoir/abyantoe
Excuse me	*Pardon*	pardo(n)
Today	*Aujourd'hui*	Ojoordwee
Yesterday	*Hier*	Eeyair
Tomorrow	*Demain*	Duhma(n)
What time is it?	*Quelle heure est-il?*	Kel ur et eel?
I don't understand	*Je ne comprends pas*	Je nuh compron pah
How much?	*Combien?*	combyen?
Do you speak English?	*Parlez-vous anglais?*	Parlay voo onglay?
One	*Un*	Uh(n)
Two	*Deux*	Duh
Three	*Trois*	Trwah
Four	*Quatre*	Kattre
Five	*Cinq*	Sank
Six	*Six*	Seess
Seven	*Sept*	Set
Eight	*Huit*	Wheat
Nine	*Neuf*	Nurf
Ten	*Dix*	Deess
Where's the...?	*Où est...?*	Oo ay...?
Entrance	*Entrée*	Ontray
Exit	*Sortie*	Sortee
Tourist office	*Office de tourisme*	Ofees der tooreesmer
Toilet	*Toilettes*	Twalet
Hotel	*Hôtel*	Otel
Youth hostel	*Auberge de jeunesse*	obairzh der zherness
Church	*Église*	Ay-gleez
Museum	*Musée*	Mewzay
What time does the...leave?	*À quelle heure part...?*	A kel er par...?
Boat	*Le bateau*	Ler bato
Bus	*Le bus*	Ler bews
Plane	*L'avion*	Lavyon
Train	*Le train*	Ler trun
Ticket	*Billet*	Beelay
Do you have a... room?	*Avez-vous une chambre...?*	avay voo ewn shombrer...?
Double	*Avec un grand lit*	avek un grand lee
Single	*À un lit*	A un lee
Cheap	*Bon marché*	Bo(n) marchay
Expensive	*Cher*	Share
Open	*Ouvert*	Oovair
Closed	*Fermé*	Fermay

footpaths, known as *sentiers de grande randonnée* or GRs, and facilities for **hikers** are generally very good, including mountain refuges and excellent information centres in major hiking regions. The most popular areas for hiking are the Pyrenees and the Alps, though the Massif Central has some impressive, off-the-beaten-track routes.

COMMUNICATIONS

Post offices (*la poste*) are widespread and generally open from 8.30am to 6.30pm Monday to Friday, and 8.30am to noon on Saturday. **Stamps** (*timbres*) are also sold in *tabacs* (tobacconist shops). International **phone calls** can be made from any phone box (*cabine*), using phonecards (*télécartes*), which are available from post offices, *tabacs* and train station ticket counters. For all calls within France you must dial the entire ten-digit number, including area code. The number for directory enquiries is ⓣ12. **Internet access** is widespread, if not especially cheap; prices begin at around €1 per hour and can go up to €6 per hour.

EMERGENCIES

There are two main types of **police**, the Police Nationale and the Gendarmerie Nationale, and you can report a theft, or any other incident, to either.

To find a **doctor**, ask for an address at any *pharmacie* (chemist) or tourist information office. Consultation fees for a visit will be €20–25 and you'll be given a *Feuille de Soins* (Statement of Treatment) for any insurance claims. EU citizens are, with an EHIC, exempt from charges – see p.46.

EMERGENCY NUMBERS

Police ⓣ17; Ambulance ⓣ15; Fire ⓣ18; or ⓣ112 for all three.

INFORMATION

Most towns and villages have an *Office de Tourisme*, giving out local **information** and free maps. The larger ones can book accommodation anywhere in France, and most can find you a local room for the night, albeit with an added service charge.

MONEY AND BANKS

The currency of France is the **euro** (€). Standard **banking hours** are Monday to Friday 9am to noon and 2 to 4.30pm; in cities, some also open on Saturday morning. **ATMs** are found all over France and most accept foreign cards. Credit cards are generally accepted by larger shops, and most restaurants and hotels.

OPENING HOURS AND HOLIDAYS

Basic **working hours** are 9am to noon/1pm and 2/3 to 6.30pm. The traditional closing **days** for shops (and some restaurants) are Sunday and Monday. **Museums** are usually closed on Mondays, with reduced opening hours outside of summer. All shops, museums and offices are closed on the following **national holidays**: January 1, Easter Sunday and Monday, Ascension Day, Whit Monday, May 1, May 8, July 14, August 15, November 1, November 11, December 25.

STUDENT AND YOUTH DISCOUNTS

Most of the museums and attractions listed here offer a student or under-26 discount, which can be anything up to a third off. To make the most of these, buy an **ISIC** (International Student) or **IYTC** (International Youth) card. For more information see ⓦwww.isiccard.com. It's also worth noting that many museums have free entry on the first Sunday of every month.

Paris

All the clichés about **PARIS** are true – stylish, romantic, glamorous and utterly compelling – yet it retains surprises that continue to delight even the most seasoned visitors. Undoubtedly France's jewel in the crown, it is an essential stop on any visit. The landscape of the city changes as you cross from *quartier* to *quartier*, and each area has a distinct style and atmosphere – from cosmopolitan **St-Germain** and the genteel Luxembourg Gardens to the vibrant Marais, abuzz with bars and cafés, and the steep cobbled streets of **Montmartre**. Paris is small for a capital city, and the best way to explore it is on foot – or do as the locals do and rent a bike (see p.388). Of course, it goes without saying that the café, bar and restaurant scene here is among the best in Europe, even for travellers on a budget.

What to see and do

Paris is split into two halves by the Seine. On the north of the river, the **Right Bank** (*Rive droite*) is home to the *grands boulevards* and its most monumental buildings, many dating from the civic planner Baron Haussmann's nineteenth-century redevelopment. Most of the major museums are here, as well as the city's widest range of shops around rue de Rivoli and Les Halles.

The **Left Bank** (*Rive gauche*) has a noticeably different feel. A legendary Bohemian hangout since the nineteenth century, the city's best range of bars and restaurants are based here, as well as some of its most evocative streets, such as the areas around St-Germain and St-Michel. These days much of the area has given in to commerce, with increasingly expensive and chic shops opening up, though it's not hard to discover some of its old spirit if you wander off the main roads.

Parts of Paris, of course, don't sit so easily within such definitions. **Montmartre**, rising up to the north and dominated by the great white dome of Sacré Coeur, has managed to retain a village-like atmosphere despite its tourist popularity, and the islands of the Seine (de la Cité and St-Louis), though touristy themselves, retain a charming old-fashioned atmosphere within their side streets.

The Arc de Triomphe, Champs-Élysées and around

The **Arc de Triomphe** (daily 10am–10.30/11pm; €9.50; M° Charles-de-Gaulle-Etoile), at the head of the Champs-Élysées, is an imposing Parisian landmark, matched only by the Eiffel Tower, and offers panoramic views from the top. The celebrated **avenue des Champs-Élysées** is now, unfortunately, home to little more than a constant stream of tourists and too many fast-food and chain shops. It leads to the vast, usually traffic-clogged **place de la Concorde**, whose centrepiece, a gold-tipped obelisk from the temple of Luxor, was presented to the city by the viceroy of Egypt in 1829. Beyond lies the formal **Jardin des Tuileries** (daily 7/7.30am–7.30/9/11pm; M° Concorde), the perfect place for a stroll with its grand vistas and symmetrical flowerbeds. Towards the river, the **Orangerie** (daily except

PARISIAN ARRONDISSEMENTS

Paris is divided into twenty postal districts, known as *arrondissements*, which are used to denote addresses. The first, or *premier* (abbreviated as 1er), is centred on the Louvre and the Tuileries, with the rest (abbreviated as 2e, 3e, 4e etc) spiralling outwards in a clockwise direction.

Tues 9am–6pm; €7.50; M°Concorde) displays Monet's largest water-lily paintings in a specially designed room, as well as works by Cézanne, Matisse, Utrillo and Modigliani.

The Louvre

On the east side of the Jardin des Tuileries is arguably the world's most famous museum, the **Louvre** (daily except Tues 9am–6pm; Wed & Fri till 9.45pm; €10; M° Palais Royal-Musée du Louvre/Louvre-Rivoli). The building was first opened to the public in 1793 and within a decade Napoleon had made it the largest art collection on earth with the takings from his empire, which explains the remarkably eclectic collection.

The main entrance is via I.M. Pei's iconic glass pyramid, but to avoid the (lengthy) queues, enter through the Louvre Rivoli métro station or through the Louvre Carousel shopping arcade. Most people head straight for Da Vinci's *Mona Lisa*, but it's definitely worth exploring some of the other sections such as **Sculpture**, which covers the entire development of the art in France from Romanesque to Rodin.

The Pompidou Centre

From the Louvre, it's a short walk to the **Pompidou Centre** (place Georges Pompidou; daily except Tues 11am–10pm; free; M° Rambuteau), famous for its striking design, which was masterminded by Renzo Piano and Richard Rogers, who had the innovative idea of turning its insides out to allow for maximum space inside. The main reason to visit is the hugely popular **Musée National d'Art Moderne** (daily except Tues 11am–9pm; €10–12), one of the world's great collections of modern art, spanning from 1905 to the present day, taking in Cubism, Surrealism and much more along the way.

The Marais

Just east of the Pompidou Centre lies the **Marais**, one of Paris's more striking *quartiers*. This very chic area is defined by its designer clothes shops, trendy cafés and bars, and cool nightlife; and it's one of the city's main gay hotspots. The **Musée d'Art et d'Histoire du Judaïsme**, 71 rue du Temple (daily except Sat 10/11am–6pm; €6.80; M° Rambuteau), pays homage to the area's Jewish roots, with a major display of Jewish artefacts and historical documents as well as paintings by Chagall and Soutine. A short walk east brings you to the seventeenth-century Hôtel Juigné Salé, which holds the **Musée Picasso**, 5 rue de Thorigny (daily except Tues 9.30am–5.30/6pm; €6.50; M° St-Sébastien Froissart), housing a substantial collection of the artist's personal property but closed until spring 2013 for a major renovation and extension.

The Bastille and Île St-Louis

Southeast of the Marais is **place de la Bastille**, the site of the Bastille prison that was famously stormed in 1789, beginning the French Revolution. Now the place is marked by the Colonne de Juillet, topped by a green bronze figure of Liberty, and by the strikingly modern Opéra Bastille. A short walk southwest and across the pont de Sully brings you to the peaceful Île St-Louis, its main road, rue St-Louis en l'Île, lined with shops and restaurants.

Île de la Cité

Pont St-Louis bridges the short distance to **Île de la Cité**, where the city first started in the third century BC, when a tribe of Gauls known as the Parisii settled here. The most obvious attraction is the astounding Gothic **Cathédrale de Notre-Dame** (daily 8am–6.45pm; free; M° Cité), which dates from the mid-fourteenth century and was extensively renovated in the nineteenth. It's worth climbing the towers (daily 10am–5.30/6.30/11pm; €8) for an up-close view of the gargoyles and tower architecture.

At the western end of the island lies **Sainte-Chapelle**, 4 bd du Palais (daily

9/9.30am–5/6pm; €8; M° Cité). One of the finest achievements of French Gothic style, it is lent a fragility by its height and huge expanses of glorious stained glass.

The Eiffel Tower

Gustave Eiffel's iconic tower is, rightly or wrongly, the defining image of Paris for most tourists. Hugely controversial on its 1889 debut, it has come to be

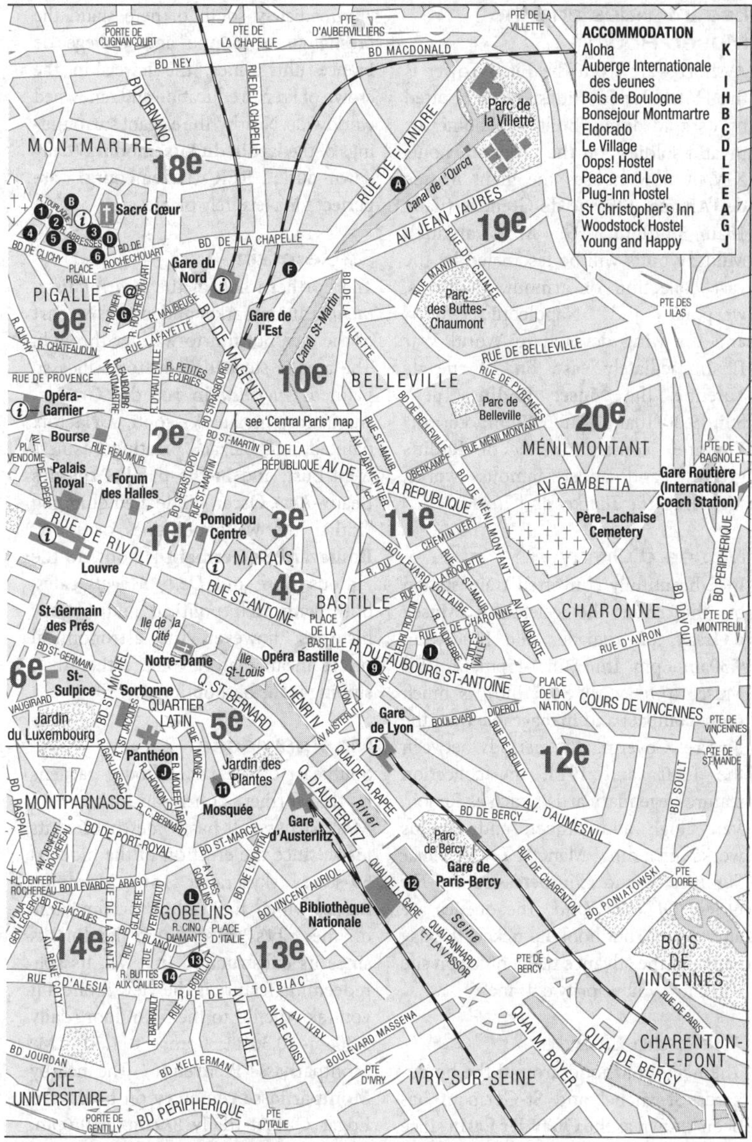

recognized as one of the city's leading sights. If you wish to pay it a visit (daily 9/9.30am–11pm/midnight; €8.20 to second floor, €13.40 to top; M° Bir Hakeim/RER Champ de Mars-Tour Eiffel) be prepared for frustratingly long queues. It's at its most impressive at night, when fully illuminated – especially from the opposite side of the river.

Les Invalides and the Musée Rodin

A short walk from the Eiffel Tower is the Hôtel des Invalides, easily spotted by its gold dome. Built as a home for invalid soldiers on the orders of Louis XIV, it now houses the giant **Musée de l'Armée**, 129 rue de Grenelle (daily 10am–5/6/9pm; €9; M° Varenne). Military buffs will be fascinated by the vast collection of armour, uniforms, weapons and Napoleonic relics, and the wing devoted to World War II. Immediately east, on 77 rue de Varenne, the **Musée Rodin** (Tues–Sun 9.30/10am–4.45/5.45pm; €6; M° Varenne) contains many of Rodin's greatest and most famous works, including *The Thinker* and *The Kiss*.

Musée d'Orsay

In a beautifully converted train station by the river, the celebrated **Musée d'Orsay**, 62 rue de Lille (Tues–Sun 9.30am–6pm, Thurs till 9.45pm; €8; RER Musée d'Orsay/M° Solférino), is much more compact and manageable than the Louvre. Covering the periods between the 1840s and 1914, the collection features legendary artists such as Renoir, Van Gogh and Monet, and famous works including Manet's *Le Déjeuner Sur L'Herbe* and Courbet's striking *The Origin Of The World*. The queues are always long, but booking tickets the day before at the advance ticket office on site will allow you priority entrance.

The Latin Quarter

The neighbourhood around the boulevards St-Michel and St-Germain has been known as the **Quartier Latin** since medieval times, when it was the home of the Latin-speaking universities. It is still a student-dominated area – its pivotal point being **place St-Michel** – and schizophrenic in its mixture of cool hangouts and tacky tourist traps. There are, however, some excellent bars and restaurants.

Immediately south of here stand the prestigious Sorbonne and Collège de France universities, the jewels in the crown of French education and renowned worldwide. Nearby, the elegant surroundings of the **Jardin du Luxembourg** (daily dawn–dusk; RER Luxembourg) are perfect for a leisurely picnic.

St-Germain

The northern half of the 6e *arrondissement* is an upmarket and expensive part of the city, but fun to wander through. The area is steeped in history: Picasso painted *Guernica* in rue des Grands-Augustins; in rue Visconti, Delacroix painted, and Balzac's printing business went bust; and in the parallel rue des Beaux-Arts, Oscar Wilde died quipping "Either the wallpaper goes or I do." **Boulevard St-Germain** is home to the famous *Flore* and *Deux Magots* cafés, both with rich political and literary histories; however, the astronomical prices mean that gawping rather than sipping is the best option.

Montparnasse

Southeast of the Luxembourg gardens is the former bohemian quarter of Montparnasse. It has somewhat lost its lustre since the erection of the hideous 59-storey skyscraper **Tour Montparnasse**, which has rightly become one of the city's most hated landmarks since its construction in 1973. Its sole redeeming feature is the view it offers if you take the lift to the 56th floor (daily 9.30am–10.30/11.30pm; €11.50; M° Montparnasse-Bienvenüe). The nearby **Montparnasse cemetery** on boulevard Edgar Quinet (daily 8/9am–5.30/6pm; free; M° Raspail) offers a little peace in this busy *quartier* and has plenty of illustrious names, including Samuel Beckett and Serge Gainsbourg.

Montmartre

In the far north of the city, in the middle of the 18e *arrondissement*, is the glorious district of **Montmartre**. Though the area around Sacré-Cœur and place du Tertre can be horribly touristy, the quieter streets that surround lively rue des Abbesses are a pleasure to wander around, and still suggest a bygone age. The nineteenth-century neo-Byzantine **Sacré-Cœur** (daily 6am–10.30pm; free; M° Anvers/Abbesses) crowns the Butte Montmartre – to get there, take the funicular from place Suzanne Valadon (ordinary métro tickets and passes are valid) or climb the (very) steep stairs via place des Abbesses. The views from the top of the dome (daily 9am–6/7pm; €5) can be rather disappointing, except on the clearest of days. Off nearby rue Lepic is the **Moulin de la Galette**, the last remaining windmill in Montmartre. Further down the hill, in the seedy district of Pigalle, is the famous Moulin Rouge, though it's not worth going out of your way to see.

Père-Lachaise

To the east of the city lies one of the world's most famous graveyards, the **Père-Lachaise cemetery**, boulevard de Ménilmontant, 20e (daily 8/9am–5.30/6pm; free; M° Père-Lachaise), which attracts pilgrims to the graves of Oscar Wilde (in division 89) and Jim Morrison (in division 6). There are countless other famous people buried here, among them Chopin (division 11) and Edith Piaf (division 97) – pick up a map at the entrance as it's easy to get lost.

Arrival

Air Paris has two main airports: Charles de Gaulle and Orly. A much smaller one, Beauvais, 76km north, is used primarily by the low-cost airlines Ryanair and Wizz Air. Charles de Gaulle (CDG) is 23km northeast and connected to Gare du Nord train station by RER train line B (every 15min, 5am–midnight; 30min; €9.10). There's also the Roissybus, which terminates at M° Opéra (every 15min, 5.45am–11pm; 45min; €10) and two Air France bus lines to M° Charles-de-Gaulle-Étoile (every 20min, 5.45am–11pm; 50min; €15), or to Gare de Lyon and Gare Montparnasse (every 30min, 6am–10pm; 1hr; €16.50). Orly, 14km south of Paris, connects to the centre via Orlybus, a shuttle bus direct to RER line B station Denfert-Rochereau on the Left Bank, from where you can get on the métro (6am–11.20pm; 30min; €6.90) and via Orlyval, a fast shuttle train line to RER line B station Antony with connections to M° Dénfert-Rochereau, St-Michel and Châtelet (every 4–8min, 6am–11pm; 35min; €10.75).

Train Paris has six main-line train stations, all served by the métro. You can buy national and international tickets at any of them. Gare du Nord serves northern France, while trains from nearby Gare de l'Est go to eastern France. Gare St-Lazare serves the Normandy coast; Gare de Lyon the southeast and the Alps; Gare Montparnasse serves Chartres, Brittany, the Atlantic coast and TGV lines to Tours and southwest France; and Gare d'Austerlitz serves the Loire valley and the southwest.

Bus Most international and national long-distance buses use the main *gare routière* at Bagnolet in eastern Paris (M° Gallieni).

Information

Tourist office There are tourist office branches all over the city. The most useful one is at 25 rue des Pyramides 1er (June–Oct daily 9am–7pm; Nov–May Mon–Sat 10am–7pm, Sun 11am–7pm; ⓣ08.92.68.30.00, ⓦwww.parisinfo.com; M° Pyramides/RER Auber) and can help with last-minute accommodation, as can the offices at Gare de Lyon (Mon–Sat 8am–6pm) and Gare du Nord (daily 8am–6pm). You can also book tickets to museums at the tourist offices – handy for skipping the long queues.

Discount passes Many museums offer discounted entry to under-26s (with ID, see p.379), and there are reduced fees for everyone on Sundays. They're also often free on the first Sunday of every month, but they do get very busy because of it. The tourist office sells the Paris Museum Pass (€35 two-day, €50 four-day, €65 six-day), valid for more than 60 museums and monuments in Paris and the surrounding area.

City transport

Tickets Single tickets (€1.70) are valid on buses, the métro and, within the city limits (zones 1–2), the RER rail lines. If you're going to be using a fair bit of public transport, it makes more sense to buy a *carnet* of ten tickets (€12.50).

Métro The métro (abbreviated as M°) is an easy way of travelling around the city. The various lines are colour-coded and numbered, and the name of

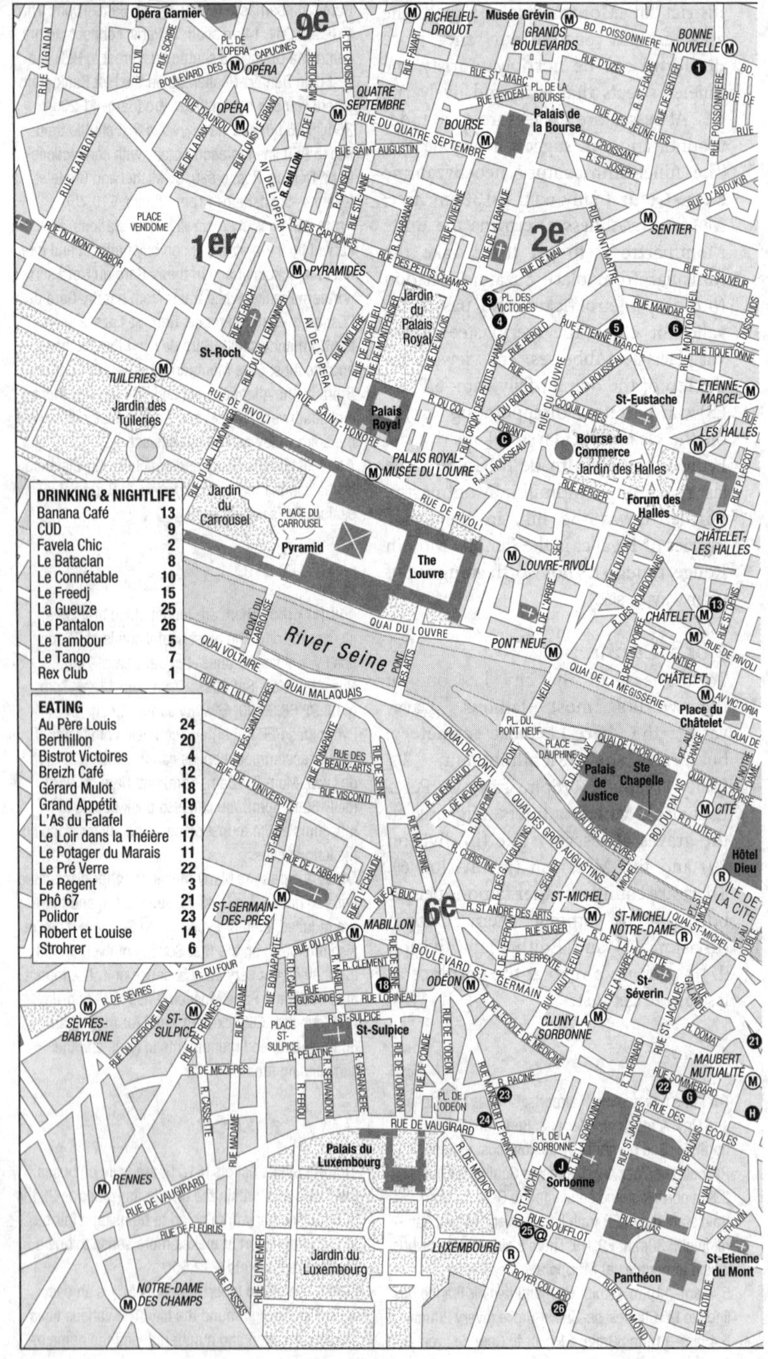
DRINKING & NIGHTLIFE
Banana Café 13
CUD 9
Favela Chic 2
Le Bataclan 8
Le Connétable 10
Le Freedj 15
La Gueuze 25
Le Pantalon 26
Le Tambour 5
Le Tango 7
Rex Club 1
EATING
Au Père Louis 24
Berthillon 20
Bistrot Victoires 4
Breizh Café 12
Gérard Mulot 18
Grand Appétit 19
L'As du Falafel 16
Le Loir dans la Théière 17
Le Potager du Marais 11
Le Pré Verre 22
Le Regent 3
Phô 67 21
Polidor 23
Robert et Louise 14
Strohrer 6
Opéra Garnier
9e
RICHELIEU-DROUOT
Musée Grévin
GRANDS BOULEVARDS
BONNE NOUVELLE
OPÉRA
QUATRE SEPTEMBRE
BOURSE
Palais de la Bourse
PLACE VENDOME
1er
2e
SENTIER
PYRAMIDES
Jardin du Palais Royal
PL. DES VICTOIRES
St-Roch
TUILERIES
Jardin des Tuileries
Palais Royal
St-Eustache
ETIENNE-MARCEL
LES HALLES
PALAIS ROYAL-MUSÉE DU LOUVRE
Bourse de Commerce
Jardin des Halles
Forum des Halles
Jardin du Carrousel
PLACE DU CARROUSEL
Pyramid
The Louvre
LOUVRE-RIVOLI
CHÂTELET-LES HALLES
CHÂTELET
River Seine
PONT NEUF
Place du Châtelet
PL. DU. PONT NEUF
PLACE DAUPHINE
Palais de Justice
Ste Chapelle
CITÉ
Hôtel Dieu
ILE DE LA CITÉ
ST-GERMAIN-DES-PRÉS
MABILLON
6e
ST-MICHEL
ST-MICHEL/NOTRE-DAME
ODÉON
St-Séverin
CLUNY LA SORBONNE
SÈVRES-BABYLONE
ST-SULPICE
St-Sulpice
MAUBERT MUTUALITÉ
PL. DE L'ODEON
Palais du Luxembourg
PL DE LA SORBONNE
Sorbonne
RENNES
LUXEMBOURG
Jardin du Luxembourg
Panthéon
St-Etienne du Mont
NOTRE-DAME DES CHAMPS

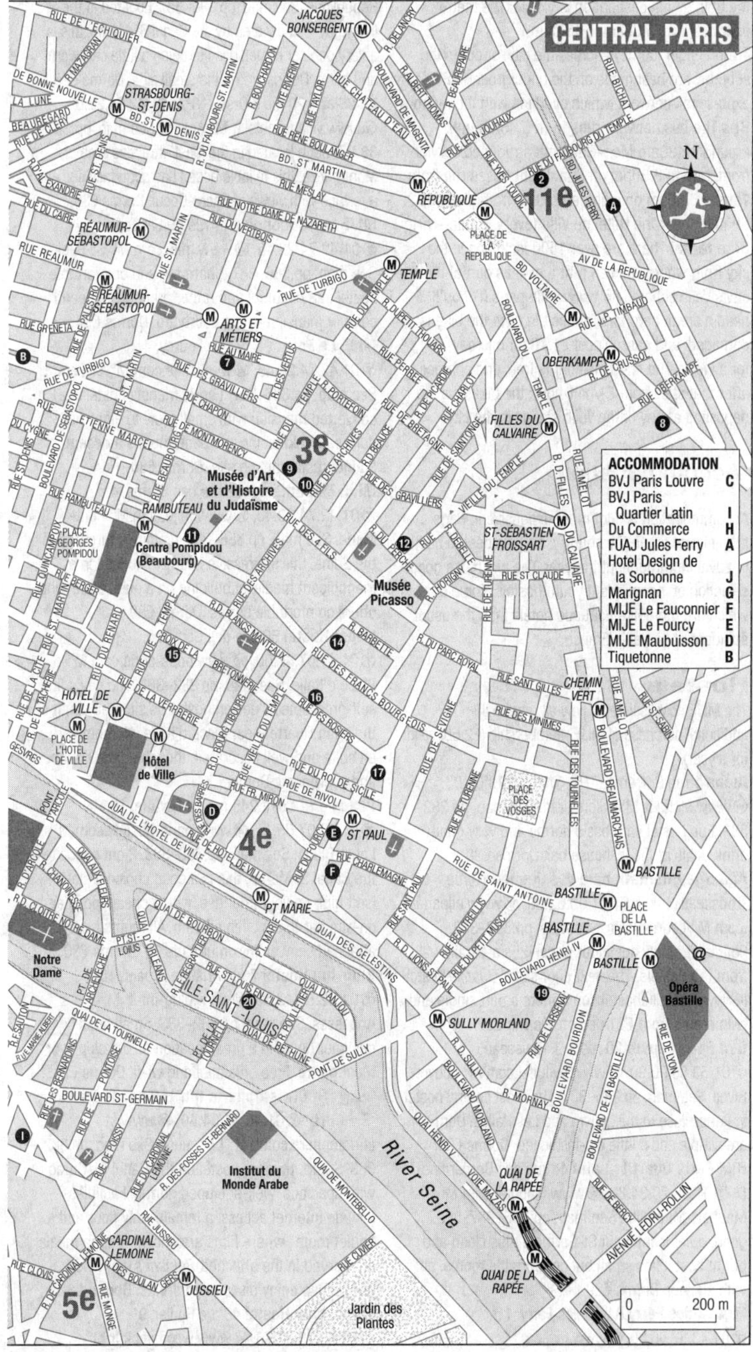
CENTRAL PARIS
ACCOMMODATION
BVJ Paris Louvre C
BVJ Paris Quartier Latin I
Du Commerce H
FUAJ Jules Ferry A
Hotel Design de la Sorbonne J
Marignan G
MIJE Le Fauconnier F
MIJE Le Fourcy E
MIJE Maubuisson D
Tiquetonne B
Centre Pompidou (Beaubourg)
Musée d'Art et d'Histoire du Judaïsme
Musée Picasso
Hôtel de Ville
Notre Dame
Institut du Monde Arabe
Opéra Bastille
Jardin des Plantes
River Seine
Ile Saint-Louis
PLACE DE LA REPUBLIQUE
PLACE DES VOSGES
PLACE DE LA BASTILLE
3e
4e
5e
11e
0 200 m

the train's final destination is visible. The métro operates from 5.20am to 1.20am.

Train Longer journeys across the city, or out to the suburbs, are best made on the underground RER express rail network, which overlaps with the métro.

Bus The bus network runs from 5.45am until around 12.30am Mon–Sat, with a reduced service from 7am to 8.30pm on Sun. Night buses run from 1am to 5.30am on eighteen routes from place du Châtelet near the Hôtel de Ville (every 30min–1hr).

Bike rental There are over 1500 locations in the city from where you can rent a bike as part of the city's Velib scheme (Ⓦwww.velib.paris.fr). You'll need a credit card for a deposit in case the bike is damaged, and passes cost €1.70 for one day, €8 for a week. The first half-hour is free, and charges after that start from €1/half-hour; the bikes can be deposited at any of the Velib stands in the city.

Accommodation

Accommodation is a lot more expensive in Paris than elsewhere in the country, and it's best to book in advance throughout the year. The city has a good selection of independent youth hostels, some of which are more like boutique hotels than the usual standard of hostel in France.

Hostels

The MIJE hostels listed below all require the additional purchase of MIJE membership (€2.50; valid for a year).

Aloha 1 rue Borromée, 15e Ⓣ01.42.73.03.03, Ⓦwww.aloha.fr M° Volontaires. See map, pp.382–383. Fun hostel with basic dorms and very good drink deals at the in-house bar. Dorms €30.

Auberge Internationale des Jeunes 10 rue Trousseau, 11e Ⓣ01.47.00.62.00, Ⓦwww.aijparis.com M° Ledru-Rollin. See map, pp.382–383. Popular, friendly hostel for under-25s a 10min walk from the Bastille. The next door sister *Bastille* hostel (Ⓦwww.bastillehostel.com) offers smart single and twin rooms from €21/person. Dorms €21.

BVJ Paris Louvre 20 rue J. J. Rousseau Ⓣ01.53.00.90.90, Ⓦwww.bvjhotel.com M° Louvre Rivoli. See map, pp.386–387. The most central hostel in Paris, close to the Louvre and Les Halles. Dorms are simple and a little old-fashioned. Dorms €29.

BVJ Paris Quartier Latin 44 rue des Bernardins, 5e Ⓣ01.43.29.34.80, Ⓦwww.bvjhotel.com M° Maubert-Mutualité. See map, pp.386–387. In a good, quiet location in St-Germain, this clean and bright hostel has small but comfortable rooms, all with shower. Dorms €29.

FUAJ Jules Ferry 8 bd Jules-Ferry, 11e Ⓣ01.43.57.55.60, Ⓦwww.fuaj.org M° République. See map, pp.386–387. Located in the lively gay-friendly area by the Canal St Martin, this is a very popular hostel, despite being a little careworn and basic. Dorms are on the small side. Dorms €25.

Le Village 20 rue d'Orsel, 18e Ⓣ01.42.64.22.02, Ⓦwww.villagehostel.fr M° Anvers. See map, pp.382–383. Though located in the least attractive area of Montmartre, this reliable hostel has good facilities and a terrace with views of Sacré-Coeur. Dorms €30.

MIJE Le Fauconnier 11 rue du Fauconnier, 4e Ⓣ01.42.74.23.45, Ⓦwww.mije.com M° St-Paul. See map, pp.386–387. Charming and comfortable hostel in a beautiful and rather grand seventeenth-century mansion with a courtyard. Dorms €30.

MIJE Le Fourcy 6 rue de Fourcy, 4e Ⓣ01.42.74.23.45, Ⓦwww.mije.com M° St-Paul. See map, pp.386–387. Large, friendly hostel in a converted mansion with small four- to eight-bed dorms. Breakfast included and there's a decent, budget restaurant on site. Dorms €30.

MIJE Maubuisson 12 rue des Barres, 4e Ⓣ01.42.74.23.45, Ⓦwww.mije.com M° Pont-Marie. See map, pp.386–387. A stone's throw from the Seine, this impressive hostel is housed in a magnificent medieval building on a quiet street and offers comfortable dorms. Dorms €30.

Oops! Hostel 50 ave des Gobelins, 13e Ⓣ01.47.07.47.00, Ⓦwww.oops-paris.com M° Place d'Italie. See map, pp.382–383. The city's first, self-proclaimed, "design hostel" is situated south of the Latin Quarter near Place d'Italie. All rooms are en suite and well decorated, though a little cramped and overpriced. Dorms €34.

Peace and Love 245 rue La Fayette, 19e Ⓣ01.46.07.65.11, Ⓦwww.paris-hostels.com M° Louis-Blanc. See map, pp.382–383. Right opposite the Canal St Martin, this is a good choice if sleep isn't high on your priorities, with a cheap, popular on-site bar that's open till 2am. All rooms have attached shower. Maximum age 35. Dorms €30.

Plug-Inn Hostel 7 rue Aristide Bruant, 18e Ⓣ01.42.58.42.58, Ⓦwww.plug-inn.fr M° Abbesses. See map, pp.382–383. Small hostel with designer decor in a great location on the slopes of Montmartre. Free breakfast and wi-fi. Dorms €31.

St Christopher's Inn 159 rue de Crimée, 19e Ⓣ01.40.34.34.40, Ⓦwww.stchristophers.co.uk M° Laumière. See map, pp.382–383. Smart, modern hostel on the Canal St-Ourcq with spacious, well-equipped dorms. Facilities include internet access, a female-only floor and a "quiet room" where films are shown. Cheap meals are served in the attached *Belushi's* bar, where guests can enjoy discounted drinks. Dorms €32.

Woodstock Hostel 48 rue Rodier, 9e Ⓣ01.48.78.87.76, Ⓦwww.woodstock.fr M°

TREAT YOURSELF

Hotel Design de la Sorbonne (6 rue Victor Cousin, 5e ☎01.43.54.58.08, Ⓦwww.hotelsorbonne.com M° Luxembourg/Cluny-La Sorbonne; see map, pp.386–387). Situated on a quiet street opposite the Sorbonne and just minutes from the Luxembourg Gardens, this little designer hotel is an excellent choice if you fancy a bit of luxury. Rooms have been strikingly furnished with a mix of old and new styles, and all have IMacs with television, DVD and CD player and free internet access. Book through their website to get the best rates – high-season doubles from as little as €105.

Anvers. See map, pp.382–383. This popular hostel has a great location, just a few streets away from Montmartre and an easy walk from the city centre. Additional €3 for Fri and Sat night stays. Dorms €25.

Young and Happy 80 rue Mouffetard, 5e ☎01.47.07.47.07, Ⓦwww.youngandhappy.fr M° Monge/Censier-Daubenton. See map, pp.382–383. In the heart of a student enclave in the Latin Quarter, this establishment has a youthful atmosphere that more than lives up to its name. Dorms €30.

Hotels

Bonsejour Montmartre 11 rue Burq, 18e ☎01.42.54.22.53, Ⓦwww.hotel-bonsejour-montmartre.fr M° Blanche. See map, pp.382–383. In a fantastic position just off lively rue des Abbesses, this friendly family-run hotel offers exceptional value and a good range of doubles and singles. The best are the double rooms with balcony (€69) – excellent for enjoying a glass of wine before a night out, and a complete steal. Doubles €66.

Du Commerce 14 rue de la Montagne-Ste-Geneviève, 5e ☎01.43.54.89.69, Ⓦwww.commerce-paris-hotel.com M° Maubert-Mutualité. See map, pp.386–387. Welcoming budget hotel on a quiet street in the heart of the Latin Quarter. Rooms are decorated in Provençal colours, and there's a small kitchen/dining room. Doubles €54.

Eldorado 18 rue des Dames, 17e ☎01.45.22.35.21, Ⓦwww.eldoradohotel.fr M° Place de Clichy. See map, pp.386–387. A popular budget hotel near busy Place de Clichy and 5min walk from Montmartre, with a bohemian, laidback atmosphere, comfortable, quirkily decorated rooms, a private garden and a good attached bar. Book well in advance. Doubles €80.

Marignan 13 rue du Sommerard, 5e ☎01.43.54.63.81, Ⓦwww.hotel-marignan.com M° Maubert-Mutualité. See map, pp.386–387. Excellent backpacker-oriented hotel, with free wi-fi, laundry and self-catering facilities; good choice of triples and singles. Special offers available if you book well ahead. Breakfast included. Doubles €68.

Tiquetonne 6 rue Tiquetonne, 2e ☎01.42.36.94.58, Ⓦwww.hoteltiquetonne.fr M° Étienne-Marcel. See map, pp.386–387. Good-value place, set on a small, attractive street that appears not to have been changed for about fifty years, and has great hospitality. Doubles €60.

Camping

Bois de Boulogne Allée du Bord de l'Eau ☎01.45.24.30.00, Ⓦwww.campingparis.fr. See map, pp.382–383. The city's major campsite is situated in the large and beautiful Bois de Boulogne, and offers a range of facilities including showers and a canteen. To get here, take bus #244 from M° Porte Maillot. €18/person and pitch.

Eating

Eating out in Paris need not be an extravagant affair, and even at dinner, it's possible to have a meal for less than €15 in many places. Anyone in possession of an ISIC card is eligible to apply for tickets for the university restaurants run by CROUS – see Ⓦwww.crous-paris.fr for a list of addresses, and buy your ticket from the restaurants themselves.

Cafés

Berthillon 31 rue St-Louis-en-l'Île, 4e M° Pont Marie. See map, pp.386–387. Expect long queues for some of the best ice creams and sorbets in the city; the divine flavours include salted caramel and Earl Grey. Single scoop €2.30. Wed–Sun 10am–8pm.

Café de la Mosquée 39 rue Geoffroy-St-Hilaire, 5e M° Jussieu. See map, pp.382–383. This oasis of calm offers great mint tea and Middle Eastern cakes (€2). Daily 10am–midnight.

Le Duroc 88 rue de Sèvres, 7e M° Duroc. See map, pp.382–383. An excellent café that feels as though it hasn't changed for at least thirty years and is always packed with locals. The good-value lunch menu (€14) is well worth indulging in and usually includes a perfectly cooked steak option.

Le Loir dans la Théière 3 rue des Rosiers, 4e M° St-Paul. See map, pp.386–387. Peaceful, quirky retreat with leather armchairs and a laidback atmosphere. Midday *tartines* and omelettes (€9–12), fruit teas and cakes (€4–6.50) served all day, and a great Sunday brunch. Mon–Fri 11am–7pm, Sat & Sun 10am–7pm.

La Mascotte 52 rue des Abbesses, 18e M° Blanche. See map, pp.382–383. A fantastic, unpretentious locals' bar that's a good choice throughout the day, whether for coffee (€2.20) and a croissant or a glass of wine from their extensive list (from €4). Daily 10am–midnight.

Le Regent 1 rue de la Vrillière, 2e M° Bourse. See map, pp.386–387. This corner café makes a great lunch choice, with an excellent-value *formule* for €13 which includes dishes such as steak *haché* and *saucisse du Cantal*. Mon–Fri.

Restaurants

Au Grain de Folie 24 rue de la Vieuville, 18e M° Abbesses. See map, pp.382–383. This homely Montmartre restaurant specializes in unpretentious and basic vegetarian dishes such as a salad with lentils, vegetables and grilled goat's cheese. *Prix fixe* €12–16.

Au Père Louis 38 rue Monsieur le Prince, 6e ⓣ01.43.26.54.14. M° Odéon. See map, pp.386–387. Usually packed with locals, this cosy, somewhat labyrinthine restaurant is a great choice for a long, enjoyable meal. The menu is packed with classic French dishes, including an excellent *cassoulet* (€16). Save room for the *café gourmand* – espresso served alongside *Viennoiseries* (Viennese pastries) and ice cream (€7). Daily noon–3pm & 7pm–midnight.

Au Virage Lepic 61 rue Lepic, 18e ⓣ01.42.52.46.79 M° Abbesses. See map, pp.382–383. Simple, good-quality food, focusing on meat and game (from €12), served in a noisy, friendly, old-fashioned bistro. Very popular so book ahead.

Bistrot Victoires 6 rue de la Vrillière, 2e ⓣ01.42.61.43.78 M° Bourse. See map, pp.386–387. A convivial local bistro, tucked away near the Palais Royale. The fantastic old bar and big mirrors lend it a timeless appeal, and the food is surprisingly cheap (and excellent) for this part of the city (*confit de canard* €10). Daily noon–3pm & 7–11pm.

Breizh Café 109 rue Vieille du Temple, 3e ⓣ01.42.72.13.77 M° Rambuteau. See map, pp.386–387. On one of the quieter streets in the Marais, *Breizh Café* serves excellent, authentic Breton *galettes* and crêpes in a refreshingly modern interior. The *complète champignon* (ham, cheese, egg and mushrooms; €7.80) is particularly good, as are the dessert crêpes with salted caramel (€4.50). Wed–Sun noon–11pm.

Grand Appétit 9 rue de la Cerisaie, 4e M° Bastille. See map, pp.386–387. Vegetarian and macrobiotic meals for around €15 in this dedicated eco-vegetarian restaurant.

L'As du Falafel 34 rue des Rosiers, 4e M° St-Paul. See map, pp.386–387. Famous throughout the city for its delicious falafel special – pitta bread stuffed full of cabbage, aubergine, hummus, yogurt and falafel (€5); a more extensive menu is available for eating in. Sun–Thurs.

Le Bistrot St-Antoine 58 rue Faubourg Saint-Antoine, 11e M° Bastille. See map, pp.382–383. Close to the Bastille, this popular bistro has a dark, attractive interior in which to enjoy the well-priced (if rather standard) dishes, such as *poulet rôti* (€7.50), as well as sandwiches from €4.50.

Le Mono 40 rue Véron, 18e M° Abbesses. See map, pp.382–383. Togolese restaurant serving delicious grilled fish and meats (from €10) in a boisterous, noisy atmosphere. Save space for the delicious banana desserts. Closed Wed.

TOP THREE PARISIAN PATISSERIES

You can't walk far in Paris without stumbling over a patisserie, many of which have been serving cakes for hundreds of years. Here are three of the best that are worth braving the queues for:

Gérard Mulot 76 rue de Seine, 6e M° Odéon. Expect queues at this justifiably famous patisserie, which is usually crammed with locals. The many delights include a red-fruit millefeuille and lemon meringue tart (from €4).

Ladurée 75 av des Champs-Élysées M° George V. Famous for its delectable macaroons (€2.20), which come in flavours such as violet and blackcurrant, salted caramel, and orange blossom. Indulge in one of their many treats over a cup of their delicate tea in this ornate tearoom, or head to the more intimate branch at 16 rue Royale.

Strohrer 51 rue Montorgueil M° Étienne-Marcel. The city's oldest patisserie serves arguably its most divine selection of cakes – the Rosier (large rose macaroon filled with rose-flavoured cream and raspberries; €4.90) is particularly blissful.

Le Potager du Marais 22 rue Rambuteau, M° Rambuteau. 3ᵉ. See map, pp.386–387. Chic and lively vegetarian restaurant with some great daily specials, such as a brilliant aubergine curry. Set menu €25.

Le Pré Verre 8 rue Thénard, 6ᵉ ⓣ 01.43.54.59.47. M° Maubert-Mutualité. See map, pp.386–387. Informal wine bar-restaurant with an excellent lunch menu (starter, main, glass of wine and a coffee €13.50), which might include dishes such as grilled pork with sautéed potatoes or cumin and pepper soup. Tues–Sat noon–2pm & 7.30–10pm.

Le Temps des Cerises 18–20 rue de la Butte-aux-Cailles, 13ᵉ M° Corvisart. See map, pp.382–383. Homely, good-value neighbourhood bistro with reassuringly traditional dishes such as *steak-frites* and a decent wine list. Lunch menu €16.

Pancake Square 4 rue de Surène, 8ᵉ M° Madeleine. See map, pp.382–383. A nautical-themed crêperie near place de la Madeleine, with decent crêpes such as the *flibustier* (cheese, crème fraîche and mushrooms; €7) and *pichets* of Breton cider (€7.50).

Phô 67 59 rue Galande, 5ᵉ. M° Cluny – La Sorbonne. See map, pp.386–387. Fantastic little Vietnamese restaurant in what is otherwise a very touristy part of town. Most people come here for the exquisite Phô (beef and noodle soup; €9), but it's also worth leaving room for the desserts – especially the taro root in coconut milk (€4).

Polidor 41 rue Monsieur-le-Prince, 6ᵉ M° Odéon. See map, pp.386–387. Historic bistro that was a favourite of James Joyce; short-tempered service but the food is good and reasonably priced (*boeuf à la provençale* €11).

Drinking and nightlife

Drinks are charged in bars according to where you sit, with standing at the bar the cheapest option. The university quarter near St-Germain-des-Prés has some great spots, as does the Marais with its small, crowded café-bars and trendy gay bars. Most places are open all day until around 2am, and many offer an early evening "happy hour" until around 8pm. Be warned that beer is much more expensive than wine and can cost up to €8 for a pint. For listings, the best, inexpensive, weekly guide is *Pariscope*, with a small section in English, and available from newsagents. It's also worth checking out the webzine *Paris Voice* (ⓦ www.parisvoice.com) for the latest events.

> **TREAT YOURSELF**
>
> **Robert et Louise** 64 rue Vieille du Temple (ⓣ 01.42.78.55.89; M° Rambuteau See map, pp.386–387). The unassuming facade of this Marais institution doesn't betray anything of the cosy restaurant's rustic, down-to-earth interior. The ground-floor dining room, where you're likely to be seated shoulder to shoulder with other diners, is permeated by the heady smell of the wood fire, over which the signature dish *côte de boeuf pour deux* (€42) is beautifully cooked.

Bars

La Folie en Tête 33 rue de la Butte-aux-Cailles, 13ᵉ M° Place-d'Italie. See map, pp.382–383. Down-to-earth, fun place, decorated with old musical instruments; happy-hour drinks from €2.50. Mon–Sat 5pm–2am, Sun 6pm–midnight.

La Gueuze 19 rue Soufflot, 5ᵉ M° St-Michel. See map, pp.386–387. Belgian beers aplenty in this somewhat theme-esque bar near the Jardin du Luxembourg. Great happy hour from 4–7pm (two for one on *pression*), and also 11pm–2am Fri–Sun. Daily 9am–2am.

Le Connétable 55 rue des Archives, 3ᵉ M° Rambuteau. See map, pp.386–387. This lively, cosmopolitan bar attracts a mixed crowd of all ages, especially after midnight. Wine from €4. Daily 11am–3pm, 7pm–3am.

Le Divan du Monde 75 rue des Martyrs, 18ᵉ ⓦ www.divandumonde.com M° Pigalle. See map, pp.382–383. Café-bar with an eclectic selection of live music and occasional big-name DJs. Drinks from €5.

Le Pantalon 7 rue Royer Collard, 5ᵉ M° St-Michel. See map, pp.386–387. Eccentrically decorated bar with cheaper-than-average drinks and an absurd daily happy hour from 5.30–7.30pm, when pints cost from €3. Mon–Sat 5.30pm–2am.

Le Tambour 41 rue Montmartre, 2ᵉ M° Sentier. See map, pp.386–387. Lovely bar on a quiet side street which has a great range of wines at reasonable prices, beginning at around €3 a glass. Tues–Sat noon–6am, Sun & Mon 6pm–6am.

Clubs

Autour de Midi…et Minuit 11 rue Lepic, 18ᵉ ⓣ 01.55.79.16.48, ⓦ www.autourdemidi.fr M° Blanche. See map, pp.382–383. A cosy subterranean jazz club which has an excellent and varied programme, including free jam sessions on Tues and Wed.

Batofar quai Francois Mauriac, 13ᵉ M° Quai-de-la-Gare. See map, pp.382–383. A quirky boat venue near the Bibliothèque Nationale, with music ranging from house and techno to hip-hop.

Favela Chic 18 rue du Faubourg de Temple, 11ᵉ M° République. See map, pp.386–387. Brazilian-themed club near the Canal St. Martin, serving good cocktails and attracting a young crowd. Expect table-top dancing and unpretentious fun.

Le Bataclan 50 bd Voltaire, 11e Ⓦwww.bataclan.fr M° Oberkampf. See map, pp.386–387. This old theatre has one of the best line-ups of any venue, covering everything from international and local dance to rock, opera, comedy and techno nights.

Rex Club 5 bd Poissonnière, 2e M° Grands-Boulevards. See map, pp.386–387. One of Paris' best-known clubs, playing electronic music and attracting big-name DJs. Entrance €10–15. Wed–Sat 11pm–5am.

Gay and lesbian Paris

Paris has a well-established gay scene concentrated mainly in the Halles, Marais and Bastille areas. For information, check out *Têtu* (Ⓦwww.tetu.com), France's biggest gay monthly magazine, or visit the main information centre, Centre Gai et Lesbien de Paris, 63 rue Beaubourg, 3e (Ⓣ01.43.57.21.47; M° Ledru-Rollin/Bastille).

Banana Café 13 rue de la Ferronnerie, 1er M° Châtelet. See map, pp.386–387. Seriously hedonistic club-bar, packing in the punters with up-tempo clubby tunes. Daily 6pm–5am; happy hour 6–11pm. Free entry.

CUD 12 rue des Haudriettes, 3e M° Rambuteau. See map, pp.386–387. Inexpensive drinks and a relaxed door policy make this small club-bar a good choice for a stress-free night out. Daily 11pm–7am.

Le Freedj 35 rue Ste-Croix-de-la-Bretonnerie, 4e Ⓣ01.42.78.26.20 M° Hôtel-de-Ville. See map, pp.386–387. A stylish club in the heart of the Marais, which attracts a young, trendy crowd. Daily 6pm–4am.

Le Tango 13 rue au Maire, 3e M° Arts-et-Métiers. See map, pp.386–387. This old dance-hall plays an eclectic range of music, from disco to tango, and also hosts tea dances on Sunday. €8 entrance fee. Thurs–Sun 10.30pm–5am.

Entertainment

Cinema Tickets cost around €9.50 in Paris and discounted tickets are offered across the city on Wednesdays. Films are identified as either *v.o.*, which means they're shown in their original language, or *v.f.*, which means they're dubbed into French.

Theatres Along with concert venues, these offer standby tickets at a reduced rate, which are generally only released around 20min before the performance, and many offer discounted tickets to students. The Cité de la Musique, 221 av Jean-Jaurès, 19e (M° Porte-de-Pantin; from €8; Ⓦwww.cite-musique.fr) has an eclectic music programme that covers Baroque, contemporary works, jazz, chansons and world music, while the city's original opera house, Palais Garnier, place de l'Opéra, 9e (M° Opéra; from €5; Ⓦwww.opera-de-paris.fr) stages operas and ballets within its lavish interior.

TREAT YOURSELF

Hédiard (21 place de la Madeleine, 8e Ⓦwww.hediard.fr M° Madeleine). Gastronomes will be in seventh heaven in this smart shop, where the finest foods have been sold since its foundation in 1854. Fine chocolates and patisseries, great wines and some amazing delicacies are all readily available – and the budget-conscious will be able to find a few less expensive treats too.

Shopping

Galeries Lafayette 40 bd Haussmann, 9e Ⓦwww.galerieslafayette.com M° Auber. This massive department store sells everything from lingerie and designer fashion to books and DVDs. Worth a visit just to gawp at the astonishing architecture.

Marché aux Puces de St-Ouen rue des Rosiers,18e Ⓦwww.les-puces.com M° Porte de Clignancourt. Bargain hunters congregate on this massive flea market (Europe's largest), with over 2500 stalls – be prepared to haggle.

Réciproque 88 & 95 rue de la Pompe, 16e Ⓦwww.reciproque.fr M° Rue de la Pompe. Heavily reduced (up to half-price) *dépôt-vente* selling seconds and old stocks of clothing. Great for accessories and last season's hits.

Directory

Embassies and consulates Australia, 4 rue Jean-Rey, 15e Ⓣ01.40.59.33.00; Canada, 37 av Montaigne, 8e Ⓣ01.44.43.29.00; Ireland, 4 rue Rude, 16e Ⓣ01.44.17.67.00; New Zealand, 7 rue Léonard-de-Vinci, 16e Ⓣ01.45.01.43.43; UK, 35 rue du Faubourg-St-Honoré, 8e Ⓣ01.44.51.31.00; US, 2 av Gabriel, 8e Ⓣ01.43.12.22.22.

Exchange A good *bureau de change* is the Comptoir des Tuileries, near the Louvre at 27 rue de l'Arbre Sec, 1er Ⓣ01.42.60.17.16.

Hospital Contact SOS-Médecins Ⓣ01.47.07.77.77 for 24hr medical help, or dial Ⓣ15 for emergencies.

Internet King Telecom, 66 rue Rodier, 18e; Webcafé Milk, 13 rue Soufflot, 6e.

Left luggage Lockers (€4.50–9.50) are available at all train stations.
Pharmacy Dérhy, 84 av des Champs-Élysées is open 24hr.
Post office 52 rue du Louvre, 1er.

Moving on

Train Avignon (21 daily; 2hr 40min–3hr 30min); Bayonne (6 daily; 4hr 45min); Bordeaux (hourly; 3hr); Boulogne (hourly; 2hr 10min); Carcassonne (12 daily; 5hr 10min–8hr 40min); Dijon (hourly; 1hr 40min); Grenoble (hourly; 2hr 50min–4hr); Le Havre (11 daily; 2hr); Lille (hourly; 1hr); Lyon (hourly; 2hr); Marseille (hourly; 3hr); Montpellier (12–17 daily; 3hr 30min); Nancy (12 daily; 1hr 30min–2hr 20min); Nantes (11 daily; 2hr); Nice (13 daily; 5hr 40min–6hr); Nîmes (16 daily; 3hr); Poitiers (14 daily; 1hr 40min); Reims (12 daily; 45min–1hr 40 min); Rennes (hourly; 2hr 15min); Rouen (hourly; 1hr 15min); Strasbourg (17 daily; 2hr 20min); Toulouse (10 daily; 5hr–6hr 30min); Tours (hourly; 1hr–1hr 30min).

DAY-TRIPS FROM PARIS

Within easy day-trip distance from Paris are three of the country's most popular sights – stately **Versailles**, the cathedral of **Chartres** and Monet's beautiful garden at **Giverny**.

Versailles

The **Palace of Versailles** (Tues–Sun 9am–5.30/6.30pm; €18 palace and gardens, €15 palace only) is the epitome of decadence and luxury, with its staggeringly lavish architectural splendour that is a homage to its founder, the "Sun King" Louis XIV. The **ornamental gardens** (8am–6/8.30pm) are particularly splendid and ostentatious, complete with canals, boating lakes and fountains. The easiest way to get to Versailles is on the half-hourly RER line C5 from Gare d'Austerlitz to Versailles-Rive Gauche (40min; €6.80 return).

Chartres

About 35km southwest of Versailles, an hour by frequent train (€28.80 return) from Paris-Montparnasse, is the modest market town of **CHARTRES**. It's well worth visiting to see the **Cathédrale Notre-Dame** (daily 8.30am–7.30pm), one of Europe's most impressive architectural achievements. A magnificent Gothic structure, it was built in the thirteenth century and has a number of fascinating features, including the tallest Romanesque steeple in existence and the Ste-Voile, reputedly the Holy Veil worn by the Virgin Mary.

Giverny

Less than an hour west of Paris, **GIVERNY** is famous for **Monet's house and gardens**, complete with water-lily pond (April–Oct daily 9.30am–6pm; €8). Monet lived here from 1883 until his death in 1926 and the gardens that he laid out were considered by many – including Monet himself – to be his "greatest masterpiece"; the best months to visit are May and June, when the rhododendrons flower around the lily pond and the wisteria hangs over the Japanese bridge, but it's overwhelmingly beautiful at any time of year. To get here, take a train to nearby **Vernon** from Paris-St-Lazare (3–5 daily; 45min; €26.40 return), then either rent a bike from the station or take the connecting bus #241 from the station (€4 return).

Northern France

Northern France includes some of the most industrial and densely populated parts of the country. However, there are some curiosities hidden away in the far northeastern corner. **Lille** with its *vieux ville* is lovely to amble around and **Boulogne** is by far the prettiest port town. Further south, the *maisons* and vineyards of **Champagne** are the main draw, for which the best base is **Reims,** with its fine cathedral.

BOULOGNE

BOULOGNE is a pleasant Channel port with admirable architecture and good food and drink. Its **ville basse** (Lower Town), where the main port is located, is home to pretty *pâtisseries*, *salons du thé* and a range of contemporary shops and brasseries. Rising above, the **ville haute** (Upper Town) is where you'll find the medieval ramparts surrounding the twelfth-century castle, the cathedral and a range of quaint cafés and restaurants.

The main **tourist office** is in Nausicaá aquarium, boulevard St-Beauve (☎03.21.10.88.10), and there's an annexe office on boulevard de la Poste (both offices: July & Aug daily 9am–7pm; Sept–June Mon–Sat 9.30am–12.30pm & 2–6pm; April–June also Sun 10am–1pm; Ⓦwww.tourisme-boulognesurmer.com). The cheapest **beds** in town are at the friendly *FUAJ Bologne-sur-Mer* in front of Boulogne Ville Gare, 56 place Rouget de Lisle (☎03.21.99.15.30, Ⓦwww.fuaj.org; €20.25). Near the centre of the **ville basse**, *Hôtel Alexandra,* 93 rue Adolphe Thiers, is clean and comfortable (☎03.21.30.20.03, Ⓦwww.hotel-alexandra.fr; €63), while *Hôtel Faidherbe*, 12 rue Faidherbe (☎03.21.31.60.93, Ⓦwww.hotelfaidherbe.fr; €68) is a good base just a few minutes away from the port. For fabulous home-made cakes and a range of tea, try *L'Arbre à Thé*, 91 Grande Rue. Near the cathedral on rue de Lille, *Restaurant de la Haute Ville* offers typical cuisine (*plat du jour* €9) and *Crêperie St-Michel* (next door) serves sweet and savoury crêpes.

CALAIS

CALAIS is one of the main arrival ports for ferries from the UK. Unless you have an early-morning departure there's little reason to make a special stop here, but if you need a place to stay try *Hôtel Bonsai*, opposite the **train station**, 2 quai du Danube (☎03.21.96.10.10, Ⓦwww.bonsai-marmotte.com; €40). The *Centre Européen de Séjour Auberge de Jeunesse*, avenue du Maréchal de Lattre de Tassigny (☎03.21.34.70.20; €20.40) is a fifteen-minute walk away from the station, or take bus #3 from right outside. The majority of **restaurants** are concentrated on place d'Armes – *Bollywood Bar* serves curries from €9 or next-door *Au Coq D'Or* does *plats du jour* from €8.60. For last-minute **ferry** bookings both Sea France (☎03.21.19.42.42) and P&O Ferries (☎0825 120 156) are on opposite sides of the square.

LILLE

LILLE has a lively atmosphere and some good cultural activities making it worth visiting for a day or two. The winding, cobbled streets of the old town are lined with traditional patisseries, brasseries and a range of upmarket shops. The **Grand-Place**, also known as place du Général de Gaulle, is a busy square dominated by the old exchange building (**Vieille Bourse**), which now houses an afternoon book market (Mon–Sat). South of the old quarter lies the modern place Rihour, beyond which is the **Musée des Beaux-Arts**, place de la République (Mon 2–6pm, Wed–Sun 10am–6pm; €5.50; ☎03.20.06.78.00), a notable fine arts museum that's well worth a visit to see its excellent collection of Renaissance art and varying exhibitions.

Arrival and information

Train Gare Lille-Flandres is on place de la Gare where there is a range of hotels and places to eat. Gare Lille-Europe is a couple of minutes' walk further east, and serves London, Brussels, Amsterdam, Lyon and Strasbourg.
Bus All local buses stop outside Gare Lille-Flandres.
Tourist office In the old Palais Rihour on place Rihour (Mon–Sat 9.30am–6.30pm, Sun 10am–noon & 2–5pm; Ⓦwww.lilletourism.com).
Discount vouchers Pick up a free copy of *PiliPili Lille* magazine in any bar or café and make the most of the money-off vouchers.
Internet Allo Monde, 9 rue de Molinel.

Accommodation

Faidherbe 42 place de la Gare ⓣ03.20.06.27.93, ⓦwww.hotel-faidherbe-lille.com. Just opposite the station, this pleasant and well-equipped hotel is clean and welcoming. Doubles €46.
Flandre-Angleterre 13 place de la Gare ⓣ03.20.06.04.12, ⓦwww.hotel-flandre-angleterre.fr. The clean, comfortable rooms are somewhat on the small side but it's a stone's throw from Gare Lille-Flandres. Doubles €69.
FUAJ Lille 12 rue Malpart ⓣ03.20.57.08.94, ⓦwww.fuaj.org. A basic, good-value FUAJ youth hostel, centrally located near the Hôtel de Ville. Breakfast included. Internet facilities and free wi-fi. Dorms €20.40.
Premiere Classe Hotel 19 place des Reignaux ⓣ03.28.36.51.10, ⓦwww.premiere-classe-lille-centre.fr. This cosy, functional hotel is clean and great value if travelling in a group: prices are per room, and each room sleeps up to three people. Free wi-fi. Doubles €58.

Eating and drinking

Aux Moules 34 rue de Béthune. Although a bit on the touristy side, this restaurant serves good-value mussels (€12) in fine Art Deco-style surroundings.
Café Ugo place Rihour. Popular with locals, this relaxed, laidback café is just off the main square. €4.50 for coffee and delicious croissants.
La Pate Brisée Restaurant rue de la Monnaie. Located in the old town, this restaurant serves great warming staples such as baked potatoes and an array of quiches. Main meal plus drink from €8.90; cocktails from €3. Daily 7–10pm.
Les Trois Brasseurs 18–22 place de la Gare. A fun microbrewery (part of a small chain) with good local beers from €4.
So Good Café place de Béthune. Healthy fast-food joint that serves a range of sandwiches (from €3) and salads to eat in or take away, also caters for vegetarians. Daily 8.30am–8.30pm.

Moving on

Train From Gare Lille-Flandres: Calais (hourly; 1hr 10min); Paris (2 hourly; 1hr). From Gare Lille Europe: Brussels (7 daily; 40min); London St Pancras (hourly; 1hr 30min); Lyon (10 daily; 3hr–3hr 50min); Strasbourg (12 daily; 3hr 50min),

REIMS

REIMS is located at the heart of the Champagne region, so if you fancy a tipple or two it's worth stopping by. If culture is more your thing then there's also the Gothic **Cathédrale Notre Dame** (daily 7.30am–7.30pm), one of the most beautiful in France. The interior is renowned for the stained-glass designs by Marc Chagall in the east chapel and glorifications of the champagne-making process in the south transept.

If you're in town for the **champagne**, head to place des Droits-de-l'Homme and place St-Niçaise, around which most of the champagne *maisons* are situated; cellar tours involve a small fee which includes a tasting at the end. Good houses to visit are **Mumm**, 34 rue du Champ-de-Mars (March–Oct daily 9–11am & 2–5pm; Nov–Feb Sat & Sun 2–5pm; €10; ⓦwww.mumm.com), which is informative but informal, while **Tattinger**, 9 place St-Niçaise (March–Nov daily 9.30am–1pm & 2–5.30pm; Dec–Feb Mon–Fri 9.30am–1pm & 2–5.30pm; €10; ⓦwww.tattinger.com), is a bit fancier. You have to book to visit the bigger name brands, **Veuve Clicquot**, 1 place des Droits-de-l'Homme (April–Oct Tues–Sat; Nov–March Tues–Fri; €13; ⓣ03.26.89.53.90, ⓦwww.veuve-clicquot.fr), is the least pompous. All have English-language tours.

The **train station** is on the northwest edge of the town, on square Colbert, just a short walk north of the centre. The **tourist office** is located opposite the cathedral on the main square at 2 rue Guillaume de Machault (May–Sept Mon–Sat 9am–7pm, Sun 10am–6pm; Oct–April Mon–Sat 9am–6pm, Sun 10am–1pm; ⓣ08.92.70.13.51, ⓦwww.reims-tourism.com). The *Alsace Hotel* (6 rue du Général Sarrail; ⓣ03.26.47.44.08, ⓦwww.hoteldalsacereims.com; €50) is the cheapest of the **hotels** in the centre. The *Centre International de Séjour* (Parc Léo Lagrange; ⓣ03.26.40.52.60, ⓦwww.cis-reims.com; €20.40) has the best dorm accommodation although it's a fifteen-minute walk from the station (take tram A or B to "Comédie"). For lunch try

L'Apostrophe at 59 place Drouet d'Erlon, a stylish **brasserie** serving traditional French dishes (from €12) and a delicious assortment of cakes.

Normandy and Brittany

To the French, the essence of **Normandy** is in its food and drink: a gourmand's paradise, this is the land of butter and cream, cheese and seafood, cider and calvados. Many of the towns also have great historic as well as architectural importance: **Rouen** is where Joan of Arc was burned at the stake, **Bayeux** is rightly celebrated for its eponymous tapestry; the 80km stretch of northern coastline was the site of the **D-Day landings**; and the granite spectacle of **Mont St-Michel** dates back to the thirteenth century. The striking coastline, sandy beaches and lush countryside of **Brittany** seem to belong to a very different part of France; it seems almost unbelievable that the verdant pastures are within easy reach of Paris. People here are both fiercely proud and defiantly isolationist; you might be forgiven for thinking at times that you had left France altogether.

ROUEN

ROUEN is a city of impressive churches, half-timbered houses and small cobbled streets. The town's focal point is place du Vieux-Marché, where Joan of Arc was burned at the stake in 1431. The main old market square leads onto rue du Gros-Horloge, which has a colourful one-handed clock arching over the street. Walking along here brings you to the impressive **Cathédrale de Notre-Dame** (Mon 2–7pm, Tues–Sun 7.30/8am–6/7pm; free), a Gothic masterpiece built in the twelfth and thirteenth centuries, which is now best known for Monet's series of paintings of it that explore the interaction between light and shadow.

Arrival and information

Train The main train station, Rouen Rive-Droite, is a 10min walk from the centre.

Bus The bus station is just off the southern end of the main rue Jeanne d'Arc.

Tourist office Opposite the cathedral at 25 place de la Cathédrale (May–Sept Mon–Sat 9am–7pm & 1.30–6/7pm, Sun 9.30am–12.30pm & 2–6pm; Oct–April Mon–Sat 9.30am–12.30pm & 1–6pm; closed Sun; Ⓦwww.rouentourisme.com).

Internet Cyber Net, 47 place du Vieux-Marché (€4/hr).

Accommodation

Des Arcades 52 rue des Carmes ⓉO2.35.70.10.30, Ⓦwww.hotel-des-arcades.fr. Centrally located, near place du Vieux-Marché, this hotel has colourful rooms. Doubles €40.

FUAJ Rouen 251 route de Darnétal Ⓣ02.35.08.18.50, Ⓦwww.fuaj.org. Located in a former dyeworks factory, this modern hostel is friendly and has good communal areas. To get here, take bus #2 or #3 from Théâtre des Arts to "Auberge de Jeunesse". Dorms €21.

Hotel Astrid 11 place Bernard Tissot Ⓣ02.35.71.75.88, Ⓦwww.hotel-astrid.fr. Located right opposite the train station. The en-suite rooms are basic but reasonably priced. Doubles €55.

Eating and drinking

Brasserie Paul 1 place de la Cathédrale. An old-fashioned and very French brasserie where you can have a good meal of calves' liver and *escargots* from €12.

Crêperie la Regalière 12 rue Massacre. Located just off the Rue du Gros Horloge, this is a great place for traditional crêpes with *menus* from €9.50.

La Boîte à Bières 35 rue Cauchoise. The town's best bar, with a great atmosphere and sometimes live music.

Le Taormina 18 rue de Vieux Palais. A great selection of pizzas and large bowls of pasta from €7.50. Value meals including starter, drink and main are available from €10.

Moving on

Train Caen (hourly; 2 hr); Dieppe (12–15 daily; 45min); Le Havre (12–15 daily; 1hr); Paris (6–8 daily; 1hr 10min).

BAYEUX

BAYEUX's world-famous **tapestry** depicting the 1066 invasion of England by William the Conqueror is one of the highlights of a visit to Normandy. The 70m strip of linen, embroidered over nine centuries ago, is housed in the **Centre Guillaume le Conquérant**, rue de Nesmond (daily: 9/9.30am–6/6.30/7pm; mid-Nov to mid-March closed 12.30–2pm; €7.80). The **cathedral**, place de la Liberté (8.30am–6/7pm), is a spectacular thirteenth-century edifice, with some parts dating back to the eleventh century.

Bayeux's **train station** is on the southern side of town, on boulevard Sadi Carnot, and the **tourist office** is at Pont St-Jean (Mon–Sat 9am–7pm, Sun 9am–12.30pm & 2–6.30pm; Oct–June closed Mon–Sat 12.30–2pm & all day Sun; ⓣ02.31.51.28.28, ⓦwww.bayeux-tourism.com). Located fifteen minutes' walk away from the station is the friendly and decent HI **hostel**, *The Family Home*, 39 rue du Général de Dais (ⓣ02.31.92.15.22; dorms €21.20), which also serves three-course meals. The most affordable of the hotels in town are the *Maupassant*, 19 rue St-Martin (ⓣ02.31.92.28.53; doubles from €42), which has small but functional rooms, and *La Gare*, 26 place de la Gare (ⓣ02.31.92.10.70; doubles €32), which is also home to Normandy Tours (see box below). The nearest **campsite** (ⓣ02.31.92.08.43; closed Nov–April; €4.10 per person plus pitch) is on boulevard d'Eindhoven, a fifteen-minute walk from the centre or you can catch bus #3. Most of the **restaurants** are on pedestrianized rue St-Jean, of which the best is *La Table du Terroir* at no. 42, a carnivore's paradise with dishes from €12.

ST-MALO

ST-MALO is a beautiful Breton coastal town with cobbled streets surrounded by medieval ramparts. You can easily spend a lazy day or so ambling through the lanes, strolling along the beaches and taking your chances against the tide to reach some of the old fort islands. The **town museum**, in the castle to the right as you enter the main city gate, Porte St-Vincent (daily 10am–noon/12.30pm & 2–6pm; winter closed Mon; €5.80), covers the city's eventful history, which has encompassed colonialism, slave-trading and privateers, among other initiatives. The **Cathédrale St-Vincent** on place Jean de Châtillon was severely damaged during World War II, as was most of the old town, but has since been restored.

There's plenty of windsurfing, sailing or wakeboarding opportunities. **Surf School St-Malo** is located just off chaussée du Sillon along the bay (2 av de la Hoguette; ⓣ02.99.40.07.47,

D-DAY BEACHES

On June 6, 1944, 135,000 Allied troops stormed the beaches of Normandy in Operation Overlord. After heavy fighting, which saw thousands of casualties on both sides, the Allied forces took command of all the beaches, which was a major turning point of World War II. The 80km stretch of coastline north of Bayeux that saw the D-Day landings includes: **Omaha**, now home to the Musée Mémorial d'Omaha Beach (daily 9.30/10am–6/6.30/7.30pm; €5.90; ⓦwww.musee-memorial-omaha.com), where exhibits include uniforms and a tank; and **Arromanches**, 10km northwest of Bayeux, which was the main unloading point for cargo (some four million tonnes of it). The interesting museum at Arromanches, **Musée du Débarquement**, place du 6 juin (daily 9/10am–5/7pm; €6.50; ⓦwww.musee-arromanches.fr), has further information on France's liberation. One of the best ways to see the beaches is on a **tour**: contact D-Day Tours (ⓣ02.31.51.70.52; €45–90) or Normandy Tours (ⓣ02.31.92.10.70, ⓦwww.normandy-landing-tours.com; €48)

Ⓦwww.surfschool.org); contact them for details of prices and availability.

Arrival and information

Train The station is a 15min walk heading south from the walled city.
Bus Buses from out of town stop at Porte St-Vincent.
Tourist office Esplanade St-Vincent (Mon–Sat 9/10am–12.30pm & 1.30/2.30–6/7.30pm, Sun 10am–12.30pm & 2.30–6pm; winter closed Sun; Ⓦwww.saint-malo-tourisme.com).
Internet Cyber'Com, 26 bd des Talards (€4.50/hr).

Accommodation

Auberge de Jeunesse Éthic Étapes 37 av du Père Umbricht Ⓣ02.99.40.29.80, Ⓦwww.centrevarangot.com. Spotlessly clean and relatively comfortable hostel located 1.5km from the train station and 150m from the beach (take bus #5, #9 or #10). Book well in advance. Dorms €20.50.
Aux Vieilles Pierres 9 rue Thevenard Ⓣ02.99.56.46.80. Centrally located within the ramparts, though the rooms are a bit on the small side. Doubles €35.
Camping Alet Cité d'Alet, Gaston Buy Ⓣ02.99.81.60.91, Ⓦwww.camping-saint-malo.fr. Perfectly positioned campsite on a peninsula by the beach that's also well located for nightlife. Amenities include a café, shop and showers. €13.80 for a pitch and up to 2 people.
Port Malo Hotel 15 rue Ste-Barbe Ⓣ02.99.20.52.99, Ⓦwww.hotel-port-malo.com. Inside the walls, this quaint hotel has surprisingly modern rooms, plus there's a bar right downstairs. Doubles €55.

Eating and drinking

The Carrefour supermarket is centrally located on rue Ste-Barbe.
Coquille d'Oeuf 20 rue de la Corne de Cerfs. A small, cosy restaurant serving great local cuisine. Be prepared for slow service. Menus from €25.
La Java 3 rue Ste-Barbe. A quirky café and cider bar with dolls adorning the walls and swing seats at the bar.
Tam's Kaffe 5 place des Frères Lamenais. This laidback bar has a funky vibe and resident DJs playing on the terrace. Cocktails from €7. Open till 2am.
Tanpopo place de la Poissonnerie. Creative Japanese food, with a good-value lunch menu including a bento box, rice and dessert for €19.
La Terasse du Corps de Garde montée Notre-Dame. Tuck into delicious crêpes while enjoying the fabulous view out to sea from the top of the ramparts. From €2.50.

TREAT YOURSELF

Beaufort 25 chaussée du Sillon (Ⓣ02.99.40.99.99, Ⓦwww.hotel-beaufort.com; €113). Right on the seafront, this cosy boutique hotel has the softest king-size beds and massaging power showers. Enjoy sunset views from the ambient lounge bar.

Moving on

Train Dinan (8 daily; 1hr); Paris (3 daily; 3hr); Rennes (hourly; 1hr).

MONT ST-MICHEL

Although officially part of Normandy, the island of **MONT ST-MICHEL** is easily reached from Brittany and just a short hop from St-Malo. It's also the site of the striking Gothic **Abbaye du Mont-Saint-Michel** (tours daily 9/9.30am–6/7pm; €9), whose church, known as La Merveille, is visible from all around the bay. The granite structure was sculpted to match the contours of the hill, and the overall impression is stunning. It's important to remember to keep an eye on the tide; the Mont can become entirely surrounded by the sea remarkably quickly.

The best way of **getting here** is to take the train to Pontorson, and then take one of the regular buses on to Mont St-Michel. **Accommodation** is quite pricey here; the cheapest hotel inside the walls is *Hôtel du Guesclin* (Ⓣ02.33.60.14.10, Ⓦwww.hotelduguesclin.com; €72). A good place for **lunch** is *Crêperie La Sirène*, serving hearty, unpretentious food from €6.

NANTES

Part of Brittany until the 1960s, **NANTES** has transformed itself in the last decade to become a buzzing riverside metropolis. The star attraction in the city is the **Machines de l'Île** (varied opening hours, see ⓦwww.lesmachines-nantes.fr; €7 for elephant ride), home to the disarmingly realistic mechanical **elephant** which takes regular walks along the riverside. Lining the main road is the high-tech **Musée d'Histoire de Nantes** (daily 10am–6/7pm; €5), located in the **Château des Ducs**, which was built by two of the last rulers of independent Brittany, François II and his daughter Duchess Anne. In 1800 the castle's arsenal exploded, shattering the stained glass of the **Cathédrale de St-Pierre et St-Paul** (9am–6/7pm), 200m away, just one of many disasters that have befallen the church.

The **train station,** on rue de Richebourg, is a short métro ride from the central stop of "Commerce". The **tourist office**, at 2 place Saint-Pierre (daily 10am–1pm & 2–6pm, except Tues 10.30am–6pm; ⓣ08.92.46.40.44, ⓦwww.nantes-tourisme.com) sells a "Nantes Pass" (from €20/day) which gives you free entry to the town's museums, tram travel and boat cruises up the Loire to see the many châteaux. For **accommodation**, try the charming and central *Hôtel Rénova*, 11 rue Beauregard (ⓣ02.40.47.57.03, ⓦwww.hotel-renova.com; doubles €49) or *Hotel du Château*, 5 place de la Duchesse (ⓣ02.40.74.17.16, ⓦwww.hotelduchateau-nantes.fr; doubles €42), just opposite the Château des Ducs. The *FUAJ Nantes Le Manu* **hostel** is at 2 place de la Manu (closed noon–4pm; ⓣ02.40.29.29.20, ⓦwww.fuaj.org; €19.85); take tram #1 to "Manufacture". The place du Commerce is a largely pedestrianized area thronged with decent, inexpensive **bars** and **restaurants**. *Le Bistroquet*, 87 rue du Maréchal Joffre, has an excellent lunch menu (€11), while *Café Cult*, place du Change, has a cool, bohemian atmosphere and some great cheese and cured ham dishes (from €12).

The Loire Valley

With countless **châteaux** overlooking the stunning river and panoramic views over some of France's best vineyards, the Loire Valley is deservedly one of the country's most celebrated regions. Alongside the luxurious châteaux there are numerous lovely towns, including dependably enjoyable **Tours,** laidback **Saumur**, historic **Orléans** and the fairytale town of **Amboise**.

TOURS

The elegant and compact regional capital **TOURS** makes a good base to stay. The city has two main areas, situated on either side of the central rue Nationale. To the east looms the extravagant towers and stained-glass windows of the **Cathédrale St-Gatien** (9am–7pm), with some handsome old streets behind. Adjacent, the **Musée des Beaux-Arts** (9am–12.45pm & 2–6pm, closed Tues; €4), on place François Sicard, has some beautiful paintings in its collection, notably Mantegna's *Christ in the Garden of Olives* and *Resurrection*. The **old town** crowds around medieval place Plumereau, on the west side of the city, its half-timbered houses imposing and neatly ordered.

CYCLING THE LOIRE VALLEY

There are over 300km of safe cycling routes to take you around the highlights of the Loire Valley. Cycle paths meander along the river from Tours to **Château de Villandry** (ⓦwww.loire-a-velo.fr has all the details). You can rent bikes from Detours de Loire, 35 rue Charles Gille (ⓣ02.47.61.22.23), or Velomania, 109 rue Colbert (ⓣ02.47.05.10.11).

Villandry

One of the Loire's most popular châteaux, **Villandry** (daily 9am–5/6.30pm; gardens till 5.30/7.30pm; €9.50, €6.50 gardens only) boasts extraordinary ornamental Renaissance gardens set out on several terraces that have marvellous views over the river. The château dates from 1536 and has a collection of Spanish paintings and a Moorish ceiling from Toledo. There's no public transport here, but it's easy to reach by bike from Tours. Alternatively, shuttle buses operate July to August between Tours and the château (2/3 daily; 35min; timetables at ⓦwww.tourainefilvert.com).

Arrival and information

Train The train station is located to the south of the city, on rue Édouard Vaillant.
Tourist office 78–82 rue Bernard-Palissy, in front of the train station (Mon–Sat 8.30/9am–6/7pm, Sun 10am–12.30pm & 2.30–5pm; mid-Oct to mid-April closed lunch and Sun afternoon; ⓣ02.47.70.37.37, ⓦwww.tours-tourisme.fr).

Accommodation

FUAJ Tours 5 rue Bretonneau ⓣ02.47. 37. 81 58, ⓦwww.fuaj.org. Well-located cheapie with optional extras such as bike rental (€12/day); breakfast is included. Reception closed noon–5pm. Dorms €21.
Saint-Jean 13 place des Halles ⓣ02.47.38.58.77. A decent hotel with mid-sized rooms just a stone's throw from rue de la Monnaie. Doubles €49.
Terminus 7/9 rue de Nantes ⓣ02.47.05.06.24. Clean, comfortable rooms, good if you're catching an early-morning train but a 15min walk from all the action. Doubles €48.
Val de Loire 33 bd Heurteloup ⓣ02.47.05.37.86, ⓦwww.hotel-chambre.hotelvaldeloire.fr. A pleasant and good-value hotel in a very central location. All fourteen rooms are nicely decorated. Doubles €50.

Eating and drinking

Comme Autre Fouée 11 rue de la Monnaie. This charmingly old-fashioned place specializes in the miniature sweet and savoury dough-based snacks, *fouée*, with fillings such as goat's cheese or honey (*menus* from €16).
Et tranche thé 38 rue Bernard Palissy. Café offering all kinds of fruity concoctions – smoothies and the like from €1.50.
Mamie Bigoude 22 rue de Chateauneuf. Outrageous 1950s-style decor coupled with delicious burgers (€10.90) and crêpes (from €6) make this restaurant a good bet.
Les Trois Orfèvres 6 rue des Orfèvres. This bar-club is open from midnight until 5am from Wed–Sun and its proximity to place Plumereau makes it a popular choice for tourists and students alike.

Moving on

Train Amboise (frequent; 22min); Chenonceaux (5–7 daily; 30min); Chinon (5–10 daily; 45min); Orléans (frequent; 1hr–1hr 30min); Paris (frequent; 1hr 15min); Saumur (frequent; 45min).

CHENONCEAUX

Perhaps the finest Loire château is that straddling the river at **Chenonceaux** (daily 9/9.30am–5/8pm; €10.50), about 15km from Villandry and accessible by train from Tours. As with Villandry, the stunning formal gardens and beautiful river views are the highlight. The château's charming interior is preserved in pristine condition.

Chinon

Aruined château (daily 9/9.30am–5/7pm; €7) that's a fascinating relic of France's historic past: parts of it date from the twelfth and thirteenth centuries, and there's even evidence of graffiti carved by imprisoned and doomed Templar knights in the western Tour Coudray. Wedged between the castle and the River Vienne, the ancient town of **Chinon** is an attractive place to stop. The tourist office is on place Hofheim (May–Sept daily 10am–7pm; Oct–April closed 12.30–2.30pm & Sun; ⓣ02.47.93.17.85, ⓦwww.chinon-valdeloire.com). The *Belle Epoque Hotel*, 14 av Gambetta (ⓣ024.7.93.00.86, ⓦwww.garhotel.fr; €48) is a pleasant, central place to stay, while a five-minute walk from the town across the river on Île-Auger is a campsite (ⓣ02.47.93.08.35; €2.20 per person plus €4.70 per pitch) that rents out kayaks in the summer to both guests and visitors. *La Treille* is a wonderfully old-fashioned restaurant that serves excellent game and fish dishes (lunch menu €13).

SAUMUR

SAUMUR is a peaceful, pretty riverside town, and a good place to base yourself, within easy reach of Tours and Chinon. The town is a major centre of absinthe distillation; the **Distillerie Combier**, 48 rue Beaurepaire (€4), offers bilingual tours and tastings. On a more cultural note, the immense **Abbaye de Fontevraud** (daily 9.30/10am–5.30/6.30/7.30pm; €9), 13km on bus #1 from the town centre (4–6 daily; 35min), was founded in 1099 as both a nunnery and a monastery with an abbess in charge. Its chief significance is as the burial ground of the Plantagenet kings and queens, notably Henry II, Eleanor of Aquitaine and Richard the Lionheart; some of the tombs are extraordinarily elaborate.

Arrival and information

Train On the north bank of the river; head over two bridges to get to the south bank and the main part of the town.
Tourist office place de la Bilange (Mon–Sat 9.15am–6/7pm, Sun 10/10.30am–noon/12.30pm & 2.30–5.30pm; ⓣ02.41.40.20.60, ⓦwww.ot-saumur.fr) can help book accommodation.

Accommodation

Camping l'Île d'Offard rue de Verden ⓣ02.41.40.30.00, ⓦwww.cvtloisirs.com. This campsite has a swimming pool, small bar and restaurant. €27 for pitch and up to 2 people.
Centre International de Séjour Île d'Offard ⓣ02.41.40.30.00. Centrally located hostel, which has bright rooms sleeping up to eight-bed dorms. Dorms €16.20.
Le Cristal 10 place de la République ⓣ02.41.51.09.54, ⓦwww.cristal-hotel.fr. A two-star delight with river views from most rooms. Doubles €68.

Eating and drinking

Auberge St-Pierre 6 place St-Pierre. Not good for vegetarians but meat eaters will love the steak (€15.50), frogs' legs with white wine sauce (€12.90) or rich game dishes.
Les Forges de St-Pierre 1 place St-Pierre. Serves good staple meals of lamb and chicken; *plats du jour* from €12.

AMBOISE

AMBOISE is a beautiful town based along the banks of the Loire. The main feature is the **Château Royal d'Amboise** (9am–5/6/7pm; €10), perched up high holding a majestic spot overlooking the river and visible from all points around town. It was built in the eleventh century and saw further additions by successive royals. Leonardo da Vinci's final residence, **Clos-Lucé**, is also located here (2 rue de Clos-Lucé; 9/10am–6/7/8pm; €13), housing a collection of some of his inventions.

Accommodation

Camping de L'Île d'Or Île d'Or ⓣ02.47.57.23.37, ⓦwww.camping-amboise.com. Campsite located just the other side of the island from the hostel with access to a big open-air swimming pool. €2.65/person, plus €3.55/pitch.
Centre Charles Péguy Hostel Île d'Or ⓣ02.47.30.60.90, ⓦwww.mjcamboise.fr. This large hostel has a great location right on the river and is walking distance to the château. Most rooms have fabulous views. Dorms €18.20.
Le Chaptal 13 rue Chaptal ⓣ02.47.57.14.46, ⓦwww.hotel-chaptal-amboise.fr. A good central cheapie with small and somewhat chintzy rooms. Doubles €49.

Eating

Le Parvais 3 rue Mirabeau. Popular with locals, this restaurant off the main drag serves typically French cuisine. *Plats du jour* from €12.50.
The Shaker 3 quai Francois Tissard. Funky bar that's great for late-night alfresco drinks in a picturesque spot – its riverside location is overlooked by the château. Beers from €3, cocktails from €7.50. Open 6pm–3/4am weekends.

Moving on

Train Orleans (frequent; 1hr); Tours (frequent; 20min).

ORLÉANS

Due south of Paris, **ORLÉANS** became legendary when Joan of Arc delivered the city from the English in 1429. Stained-glass windows in the nave of the enormous, Gothic **Cathédrale Sainte-Croix** (daily 9.15am–6.45pm) tell the story of her life, from her childhood through to her heroic military career and her eventual martyrdom. Immediately opposite, the **Musée des Beaux-Arts** (Tues–Sun 10am–6pm; €3) has an excellent collection of French paintings.

The **tourist office** is at 2 place de l'Etape (Mon–Sat 9/9.30/10am–1pm & 2–5/5.30/6/6.30/7pm; July & Aug Sun 10am–1pm & 2–5pm; ⓣ02.38.24.05.05, ⓦwww.tourisme-orleans.fr). The *Auberge de Jeunesse*, 7 av de Beaumarchais (ⓣ02.38.53.60.06, ⓦwww.auberge-crjs-orleans.fr; €14.20) is 10km south of the city; staff are helpful and readily provide good information about the town. For somewhere central try *Hôtel de L'Abeille* (64 rue Alsace-Lorraine ⓣ02.38.53.54.87, ⓦwww.hoteldelabeille.com; €69), a luxurious, traditionally decorated **hotel** with oak wood floors. For **food**, *La Petite Marmite*, 178 rue de Bourgogne, serves traditional dishes such as *carbonnade* and *escargots*; *menus* from €19. *L'Antidote*, 32 rue de l'Empereur, is a good spot for cocktails, with a laidback atmosphere and outdoor seating.

Burgundy

Burgundy has some charming towns and villages, as well as some of the country's finest food and drink. **Dijon**, the capital, is a slick and affluent town with great shops and lovely architecture. Heading south, **Beaune** is a good place to sample the best of the region's famous wine, and to try local specialities such as *escargots à la bourguignonne*, *bœuf bourguignon* and *coq au vin*.

DIJON

DIJON is a smart, modern town based around a range of shop-lined streets. Most famous for its mustard, it also has some beautiful architecture and numerous relaxed and friendly bars.

What to see and do

The Palais des Ducs, in the heart of the city, is notable both for the fifteenth-century **Tour Philippe le Bon** (daily April–Nov 9am–noon & 1.45–5.30pm; Dec–March Sat & Sun 9am–3.30pm, Wed 1.30–3.30pm; tours hourly; €2.30) and the fourteenth-century **Tour de Bar**, which houses the magnificent **Musée des Beaux-Arts** (daily except Tues 9.30/10am–5/6pm; free) with its collection of paintings ranging from Titian and Rubens to Monet and Manet. **Place de la Libération**, a graceful semi-circular space, has beautiful fountains and is lined with a number of coffee bars. Heading up rue Rameau and following the road to the left brings you to the stunning thirteenth-century Gothic **church of Notre-Dame**, the north wall of which holds a small sculpted owl (*chouette*), which people touch for luck.

Arrival and information

Train and bus Dijon's train and bus stations sit next to each other at the end of av Maréchal-Foch, 5min from place Darcy.

Tourist office 11 rue des Forges (April–Sept Mon–Sat 9.30am–6.30pm, Sun 10am–6pm; Oct–March Mon–Sat 9:30am–1pm & 2–6pm, Sun 10am–4pm; ⓣ08.92.70.05.58, ⓦwww.visitdijon.com) and there is another branch at the train station with the same hours.

Internet Cyberspace, 46 rue Monge (€4/hr).

Accommodation

B&B Hotel 5 rue du Chateau ⓣ08.92.70.75.06, ⓦwww.hotel-bb.com. With a fabulous central location, this is a tidy and compact boutique-style hotel with comfortable beds. Doubles €53.

Camping du Lac off bd Chanoine Kir, about 3km from the centre ⓣ03.80.43.54.72, ⓦwww.camping-dijon.info. This pleasant campsite has the usual amenities, such as hot showers, a small café and a shop. To get here take bus #3. Closed Nov–March. €3.80/person, plus €6.50/pitch.

CRISD 1 bd Champollion ⓣ03.80.72.95.20, ⓦwww.cri-dijon.com. The local HI option is comfortable, cheap and has excellent self-catering facilities. Only drawback is that it's 2.5km from the centre – take bus #3 from the station to "CRI-Dallas". Dorms €19.50.

Hotel Le Sauvage 64 rue Monge ⓣ03.80.41.31.21, ⓦwww.hotellesauvage.com. Beautifully restored fifteenth-century hotel in a great central location with a good restaurant. Can be noisy so light sleepers should ask for a room away from the kitchen. Doubles €52.

Le Jacquemart 32 rue Verrerie ⓣ03.80.60.09.60, ⓦwww.hotel-lejacquemart.fr. A basic but adequate small hotel handily located in the centre. Doubles €51.

Eating, drinking and nightlife

A Tout Va Bien 12 rue Quentin. Near the covered market, this inexpensive restaurant is particularly popular on market days and offers a great *menu du jour* for €12.50.

Café de l'Univers 47 rue Berbisey. Head to this place for a night of serious dancing, where there's a variety of music held on different nights of the week. On Saturday and Sunday mornings, things go on until 9am.

Chez Nous Impasse Quentin. In an alleyway just off rue Quentin, this tiny bar is something of a local institution.

L'O Restaurant 14 rue Quentin. Stylish tapas and wine bar with a great range of tasty dishes, from €20 for a selection.

My Wok Big bowls of noodles with a build-your-own choice of ingredients. Also does late-night takeaway. Noodles from €4.90.

Se Bar rue Monge. Late-night drinking spot, popular with a young crowd. Has outdoor seating and a good range of beers on tap.

BURGUNDY VINEYARDS

The Burgundy vineyards are justly famous for their produce. The best way to explore them is on the **Route des Grand Crus** (ⓦwww.route-des-grands-crus-de-bourgogne.com), which takes in such places as **Montrachet** and **Chassagne**, both famous for their high-calibre wines. The wine is cheaper if bought from source – expect to pay around €10 for a good bottle and €20 and upwards for an excellent one. If you fancy learning more about the wines, the **École des Vins de Bourgogne** in Beaune, 6 rue du 16ᵉ Chasseurs (ⓣ03.80.26.35.10, ⓦwww.ecoledesvins-bourgogne.com), offers reasonably priced (from €20) crash courses in wine appreciation, some in English.

Moving on

Train Beaune (frequent; 20min); Bern (daily; 5hr 30min); Lyon (frequent; 1hr 30min–2hr 15min); Milan (daily; 6hr 30min); Paris (frequent; 1hr 45min).

BEAUNE

BEAUNE is the major producer of the region's best wine, and one of the best places in France for tasting it. Its other major attraction is the fifteenth-century multicoloured hospital, the **Hôtel-Dieu** (daily 9am–6.30pm; €6.70), which houses three museums, a number of courtyards and small, dingy cellars with remaining features from the hospices. On nearby rue d'Enfer is the **Musée du Vin** (daily 9.30am–5/6pm; Dec–March closed Tues; €4.50), which does an excellent job of explaining the region's wine history. The **Marché aux Vins** (daily 9.30–11.30am & 2–5.30pm; €10), the town's main wine-tasting establishment, is a rather more taster-friendly experience, allowing you to sample numerous delectable vintages.

Arrival and information

Train From Beaune train station, the town centre is 500m up av du 8 Septembre, across the boulevard and left onto rue des Tonneliers.
Bus Buses leave from rue Maufoux, beyond the walls.
Tourist office 6 bd Perpreuil (Mon–Sat 9/10am–6/7pm, Sun 10am–1pm & 2–5/6pm; ⓣ03.80.26.21.30, ⓦwww.ot-beaune.fr).

Accommodation

Foch 24 bd Maréchal Foch ⓣ03.80.24.05.65, ⓦwww.hotelbeaune-lefoch.fr. This is a pleasant little hotel, run by a charming family. Doubles €43.
Les Cent Vignes rue Auguste Dubois ⓣ03.80.22.03.91. Located just 1km out of Beaune, this good-value campsite has showers and a shop. Walk or take bus #2 from the tourist office. €3.90/person, plus €4.70/tent.

Eating and drinking

Bistrot Bourguignon 8 rue Monge. Tiny but charming restaurant that does a good-value lunch (€13), with wine from €3 a glass.
Pickwick's Pub & Wine Bar 2 rue Notre-Dame. This hilariously tacky would-be English pub is worth a look if you're a whisky connoisseur – they have an excellent range, starting at €5.
Piqu' Boeuf Grill 2 rue du Faubourg Madeleine. Carnivores will love this place, with rich, bloody steaks (€16) and some lovely wines (from €4).

Alsace and Lorraine

Dominated by the remarkable city of **Strasbourg**, the eastern region of Alsace often bears more similarity to Germany or Switzerland than to the rest of the country. The *mélange* of cultures is at its most vivid in the string of little wine towns that punctuate the **Route des Vins** along the eastern margin of the wet and woody Vosges mountains. The province of **Lorraine** is home to elegant eighteenth-century **Nancy**. Food and drink is excellent in the region: from local brew Kronenbourg to delicious white Rieslings and Gewürztraminers, the alcohol is excellent (and relatively inexpensive), and the *winstubs* (or wine rooms) that dominate towns offer inexpensive, unpretentious food based around pork, veal and beef, often in stews or casseroles.

NANCY

NANCY, capital of Lorraine, is a refined and beautiful town, dominated by opulent squares and splendid boulevards. At the centre is **place Stanislas**, a supremely graceful square at the far end of rue Stanislas, dominated by the **Hôtel de Ville**. The roofline of this UNESCO World Heritage Site is topped by florid urns and lozenge-shaped lanterns dangling from the beaks of gilded cockerels. On the west side of the square, the **Musée des Beaux-Arts** (daily except Tues 10am–6pm; €6) boasts work by Caravaggio, Dufy, Modigliani and Matisse. A little to the north is the **Musée Lorrain**, 64 Grande-Rue (daily except Mon 10am–12.30pm & 2–6pm; €5.50), devoted to Lorraine's history. It's housed in the splendid Palais Ducal, which is worth a look on its own merits.

Arrival and information

Train Nancy's train station is at the end of rue Stanislas, a 5min walk from place Stanislas.
Tourist office 1 place Stanislas (Mon–Sat 9am–6/7pm, Sun 10am–1/5pm; ⓣ03.83.35.22.41, ⓦwww.ot-nancy.fr). Buy *Le Pass Nancy* (€10) – this gets you reduced museum entry, a cinema ticket, guided city tour and other goodies.
Internet e-café, 11 rue des Quatre Églises.

Accommodation

Camping de Brabois av Paul-Muller ⓣ03.83.27.18.28, ⓦwww.camping-brabois.com. The nearest campsite to town, with showers, shop and a café on site. Around 2km out of the city; take bus #126 from the train station. Closed mid-Oct to March. €14.60 for pitch and up to 2 people.
Château de Rémicourt 149 rue de Vandoeuvre ⓣ03.83.27.73.67, ⓦwww.fuaj.org. The local hostel is a 20min bus ride (bus #134 or #135 from

TREAT YOURSELF

De Guise 18 rue de Guise (T03.83.32.24.68, Wwww.hoteldeguise.com; doubles €79). An atmospheric choice in the centre of the old town. Ask for one of the traditional rooms, which are themed according to past kings. Book through their website to get the best rates – high-season doubles from €49.

outside the station) but is a respectable and friendly option. Dorms €14.70.

De l'Académie 7 rue des Michottes T03.83.35.52.31, Wwww.academie-hotel.com. Rooms are a little on the small side but this is a cheap, cheerful hotel in the town centre. Doubles €30.

Eating

Grand Café Foy Located in the heart of place Stanislas, this café is popular with locals and serves up typical French cuisine from €12.

Gustatori 40 rue Stanislas. Lovely Italian *épicerie* which serves beautifully fresh pasta dishes. Menus from €9.90.

L'Excelsior 50 rue Henri Poincaré. This stylish Art Deco place is like stepping back into the 1920s. Slightly pricey but an excellent place for a treat; great wine list and set menus from €30/person.

Moving on

Train Lyon (frequent; 4hr 40min); Paris (10 daily; 1hr 30min); Strasbourg (8–13 daily; 1hr 30min).

STRASBOURG

STRASBOURG is a major city with the feel of a charming provincial town. It has one of the loveliest cathedrals in France, an ancient but active university and is the current seat of the Council of Europe and the European Court of Human Rights, as well as part-time base of the European Parliament. Even if you're not planning to spend much time in eastern France, Strasbourg is well worth a detour.

What to see and do

Strasbourg focuses on two main squares, the busy **place Kléber** and, to the south, **place Gutenberg**, named after the fifteenth-century pioneer of printing type.

Cathédrale de Notre-Dame

The major landmark is the **Cathédrale de Notre-Dame** (daily 7–11.30am & 12.40–7pm; free), which beautifully combines ostentatious grandeur with chocolate-box fragility. Climb to the top platform for stunning views to the Black Forest (€4.40), and don't miss the tremendously complicated **astrological clock** (noon–12.30pm; €2), built in 1842. Visitors arrive in droves to witness its crowning performance – striking the hour of noon with unerring accuracy at 12.30pm.

South of the Cathedral

The **Musée de l'Oeuvre Notre-Dame**, 3 place du Château (Tues–Sun midday–6pm; €4), houses the original sculptures from the cathedral exterior, as well as some of Europe's finest collected stained glass. A particular highlight is the *Les Amants Trépassés* in room 23, which shows two lovers being punished, and makes the average Hollywood horror film look mild in comparison.

Grand Île & Petite France

The **Grand Île** section of the city is the most striking, featuring the beautiful **Petite France** area, which has winding streets bordered by sixteenth- and seventeenth-century houses with carved woodwork and decked with flowers. The name Petite France was given to the area by the Alsatians in the seventeenth century, having been a quarantine area for patients of a devastating sixteenth-century venereal disease, attributed to the French. The **Musée d'Art Moderne et Contemporain**, 1 place Jean-Hans Arp (Tues, Wed, Fri & Sat midday–7pm, Thurs midday–9pm, Sun 10am–6pm; €7), stands on the west bank of the river and houses an

impressive collection featuring Monet, Klimt, Ernst and Klee. If your tastes are more alcoholic, pop into **Kronenbourg**, a short way from the centre on 68 route d'Oberhausbergen (Mon–Sat, reservation compulsory; €6), which runs daily **brewery** tours.

Arrival and information

Train The train station is a 15min walk from place Kléber.

Tourist office 17 place de la Cathédrale (daily 9am–7pm; ⓣ03.88.52.28.28, ⓦwww.ot-strasbourg.fr) with another branch in the train station.

Internet Linksys, 22 rue des Frères (€3/hr). Also, plenty of internet places line rue du Maire Kuss, opposite the train station.

Accommodation

It's worth bearing in mind that hotels – never cheap at the best of times – get booked up early when the European Parliament is in session (one week a month); visit ⓦwww.europarl.europa.eu for up-to-date information.

Camping de la Montagne Verte 2 rue Robert Forrer ⓣ03.88.30.25.46, ⓦwww.camping-montagne-verte-strasbourg.com. Just 10min away from the centre (take the tram towards Petit France), this leafy campsite has an on-site shop and bike rental. €9.60 for one person and tent.

Ciarus 7 rue de Finkmatt ⓣ03.88.15.27.88, ⓦwww.ciarus.com. Pleasant and comfortable hostel, with regular social events. In the north of the city, around 15min by foot from place Gutenberg. Dorms €28.50.

Des Deux Rives rue des Cavaliers by the Pont de l'Europe ⓣ03.88.45.54.20, ⓦwww.fuaj.org. Quiet hostel set in a large park on the banks of the Rhine with a 2am curfew; take bus #2 from the station towards Kehl. Dorms €22.20.

Le Colmar 1 rue du Maire Kuss ⓣ03.88.32.16.89, ⓦwww.hotel-lecolmar.com. One of the best budget options just a short walk from the train station, *Le Colmar* is situated on the western edge of the Grande Île with en-suite rooms and a good buffet breakfast. Doubles €37.

Eating and drinking

Au Brasseur 22 rue des Veaux. This studenty bar-restaurant has great drinks deals with half-price beers daily from 5–7pm and free concerts on Friday and Saturday nights. The food is probably best avoided. Beers from €3.

FEC Student Canteen place St-Étienne. Good, unpretentious meals at rock-bottom prices, such as beef stew and grilled or fried fish. A three-course meal costs just €4.80.

L'Académie de la Bière 17 rue Adolphe-Seyboth Frequented by locals and tourists alike, who come to appreciate the fine beer served here; pints from €3.

L'Epicerie 6 rue Vieux Seigle. A lovely café situated in a reconstructed grocers, with vintage decor and serving delicious *tartines* (open sandwiches) from €5.50.

Zanzibar 1 place St-Étienne. Cellar bar with a hip crowd thronging the sweaty dancefloor; admission from €4.

Moving on

Train Basel (frequent; 1hr 15min); Frankfurt (8–9 daily; 2hr 30min); Nancy (frequent; 1hr 15min); Paris (hourly; 2hr 20min).

The southwest

The southwest of France has a varied landscape, stretching from the vast horizons of Poitou-Charente to the ordered rows of Bordeaux's vineyards and the lush, heady green of the Dordogne. The Atlantic coast, lacking the busy glitz of the Côte d'Azur, has a slow, understated charm, best seen in **La Rochelle**. Further south, **Bordeaux**, justifiably famous for its wines, is a cosmopolitan and lively city that's worth a few days' exploration – from here, it's easy to strike east to **Périgueux**, a good base for exploring the nearby prehistoric caves, or south to the Basque coast, home to **Biarritz**, the country's surf capital, and **Bayonne,** with its fine old timber-framed buildings and excellent chocolatiers.

The Pyrenees, marking the very south of France, are home to some of the country's best walking and one of its most vibrant cities, the rose-brick university town of **Toulouse**, whose youthful energy is matched only by **Montpellier**. Medieval **Carcassonne**, between the two, is undoubtedly the biggest tourist trap of the region, but it's hard not to be wowed when you first see its fairy/tale spires rising above the surrounding buildings.

LA ROCHELLE

The lively port town of **LA ROCHELLE** has an exceptionally beautiful seventeenth- and eighteenth-century centre and is a very pleasant place to linger for a few days. Granted a charter by Eleanor of Aquitaine in 1199, it rapidly became a port of major importance, trading in salt and wine. Following a makeover in the 1990s, which established a university, pedestrianized the centre and moved out the fishing operation, La Rochelle has become the largest Atlantic yachting port in Europe, without the exclusivity of some of its Mediterranean counterparts.

What to see and do

The heavy Gothic gateway of the Porte de la Grosse Horloge straddles the entrance to the old town, dominating the pleasure-boat-filled inner harbour, which is guarded by two of La Rochelle's three sturdy towers, **Tour de la Chaîne** and **Tour St Nicholas** (10am–6.30pm; €6, €8 for all three towers). Behind the Grosse Horloge, the main shopping street rue du Palais is lined with eighteenth-century houses and arcaded shop fronts. The **Musée du Nouveau Monde**, 10 rue Fleuriau (Mon & Wed–Sat 10am–12.30pm & 2–6pm, Sun 2.30–6pm; €4), commemorates the town's dubious fortunes from slavery, sugar, spices and coffee. For beaches – and bicycle paths – you're best off crossing over to the **Île de Ré**, a narrow, sand-rimmed island immediately west of La Rochelle (take the Rébus buses from place de Verdun). Out of season it has a slow, misty charm, centred on the cultivation of oysters and mussels; in summer it's packed to the gills.

Arrival and information

Train From the train station, it's a 7min walk down av du Général de Gaulle to the town centre.

Tourist office 2 quai Georges Simenon, Le Gabut (April & May Mon–Sat 9am–6pm & Sun 10am–6pm; June & Sept Mon–Sat 9am–7pm & Sun 10am–6pm; July & Aug Mon–Sat 9am–8pm & Sun 10am–6pm; Oct–March Mon–Sat 9am–6pm & Sun 10am–1pm; ⓣ05 46 41 14 68, ⓦwww.larochelle-tourisme.fr).

Internet Le Continuum, 9 ter rue Amelot, near the market.

Accommodation

FUAJ La Rochelle av des Minimes ⓣ05.46.44.43.11, ⓦwww.fuaj.org. Modern hostel in a good position by the Port des Minimes, 30min walk from the station. The bright, nicely decorated rooms are all en suite and roomy; dinner is available (from €6) and outdoor activities are often organized. To get here from the station, follow signs to Porte des Minimes. Reception open 8am–noon, 2–7pm & 9–10pm. Dorms €16.

Hotel de l'Océan 36 cours des Dames ⓣ05.46.41.31.97, ⓦwww.hotel-ocean-larochelle.com. This small, friendly hotel is decked out in blues and yellows. All rooms have shower and toilet attached, and those at the front have excellent views of the port. Doubles €65.

Le Soleil av Crépeau ⓣ05.46.44.42.53. This municipal campsite has ping-pong, pétanque and hot showers, and allows barbecues. Its best asset is its location; right by the sea, just 800m from the town centre. Open mid-June to mid-Sept. €9.70/person, plus pitch.

Un hôtel en ville 20 place du Maréchal Foch ⓣ05.46.41.15.75, ⓦwww.unhotelenville.fr. Right in the centre but down a quiet side street, this place feels like it should be a lot pricier than it is. Compared to the tired decor of many budget and mid-range hotels this is rather sleek with a cool, modern, boutique look. Doubles €79.

Eating, drinking and nightlife

Corrigans 20 rue des Cloutiers, ⓦwww.corrigans.fr. A low-key but convivial little place down a quiet street near the market. The beer is reasonably priced and there's an Irish music session every Sunday. Tues–Sat 6pm–2am & Sun 7pm–1am.

Isêo Gourmet 2 rue des Cloutiers, Place du Marché. A modern version of the traditional *traiteur* offering *nem* (fried Vietnamese rolls, from €3.20 for two), *maki* (from €4.20 for eight) and sushi (€13.50 for eight). Pan-Asian *formules* (from €6.20) make a nice lunchtime change. Daily 11am–3pm & 5–9pm (10pm Sat).

La Guignette 8 rue Saint Nicolas. Formerly a sailor's haunt (and it still looks like the sort of place a seadog would favour), this is a wine bar beloved of local students, who come at *l'heure de l'apéro for* a glass of its eponymous aperitif – white wine flavoured with fruit.

Le Piano Pub 12 cour du Temple. One of a number of venues on this pleasant *cour*, this is popular with a student-age crowd and hosts the occasional rock gig. Daily 7pm–2am.

Le Soleil Brille Pour Tout Le Monde 13 rue des Cloutiers ⓣ05.46.41.11.42. Opposite *Corrigans*, this is a colourful place as befits its name ("the sun shines for everyone"). It's renowned for its good-value tarts and *plats du jour*. Booking is advisable. Tues–Sat noon–2pm & 7.30–10pm.

Moving on

Train Bordeaux (6 daily; 2hr 20min); Cognac (6 daily; 1hr 20min–2hr); Nantes (4 daily; 1hr 50min); Poitiers (12 daily; 1hr 45min).

BORDEAUX

Though crammed with grand, old buildings, **BORDEAUX** still has a surprisingly youthful feel. Café culture is in full swing here – indeed, one of the most pleasurable things about a visit to the city is sitting out on a sun-drenched terrace enjoying a glass or two of the region's fabulous wines. If you have time, and want to find out more about the justifiably world-famous wines of the region, it's definitely worth doing a wine tour (see box, p.411).

What to see and do

The centre of Bordeaux bends around the east bank of the **Garonne** River in the shape of *un croissant de lune* (a crescent moon) – and is colloquially known as *Porte de la Lune*.

Le Triangle d'Or and Quinconces

The "golden triangle", full of chic Parisian boutiques, runs between **place Gambetta**, with its eighteenth-century Porte Dijeaux, place de la Comédie with the classical 1780 **Grand Théâtre**, and place Tourny at the peak. In a breathtaking nineteenth-century colonial warehouse to the north of the vast Esplanade des Quinconces is the unmissable **CAPC musée**, 7 rue Ferrère (Tues–Sun 11am–6pm, Wed till 8pm; permanent collection free, temporary exhibitions €5). This is the finest contemporary art exhibition space in France, displaying pioneering national and international works with admirable use of space and lighting. The permanent collection includes Richard Long and Gilbert&George, but the temporary installations are often the most exciting.

Sainte-Catherine, Saint Pierre and Place de la Victoire

The central pedestrian artery, **rue Ste-Catherine**, leads down from place de la Comédie to the city's best historical museum, the **Musée d'Aquitaine**, 20 cours Pasteur (Tues–Sun 11am–6pm; free or €5 for temporary exhibitions), which illustrates the history of the region from prehistoric times through to the 1800s. A few streets north stands the **Cathédrale St-André** (Mon–Fri 7.30–11.30am & 2–6pm), with its exquisite stained-glass windows and slender twin spires. Around the corner at 20 cours d'Albret, the **Musée des Beaux-Arts** (daily except Tues 11am–6pm; free or €5 for temporary exhibitions) displays works by Rubens, Matisse and Renoir, as well as Lacour's evocative 1804 Bordeaux dockside scene, *Quai des Chartrons*. To the east lies the striking **place de la Bourse**, best viewed from the river's edge, reflecting in the glassy Font du Miroir, while farther south you'll find the student-friendly **place de la Victoire**, surrounded by cafés, restaurants and late-night bars.

Arrival and information

Air Bordeaux Mérignac airport, 12km west, is connected by regular shuttle bus (daily 7.45am (Sat & Sun 8.30am)–10.45pm; 45min; €7) to place Gambetta, cours du 30-Juillet and Gare St Jean.

Train The station, Gare St Jean, lies 2km southeast of central Bordeaux, easily accessed by tram C from Esplanade des Quinconces (10min; €1.40).

Tourist office 12 cours du 30-Juillet (Nov–April Mon–Sat 9am–6.30pm & Sun 9.45am–4.30pm; May–June Mon–Sat 9am–7pm & Sun 9.30am–6.30pm; July–Aug Mon–Sat 9am–7.30pm & Sun 9.30am–6.30pm; Sept–Oct Mon–Sat 9am–6pm & Sun 9.30am–6.30pm; ⓣ 05.56.00.66.00,

COGNAC

On the La Rochelle to Bordeaux line, the little town of **Cognac** (ⓦ www.tourism-cognac.com) is shrouded in the heady scent of its famous brandy. Of the various cognac *chais* (distilleries) huddled around the end of the Grande-Rue, **Baron Otard is** one of the best choices for a guided tour (April–Oct daily 11am–5pm; Nov & Dec Mon–Fri except bank holidays 11am–5pm; ⓦ www.baronotard.com), which recounts a history of the site, the principles of making cognac and, most importantly, a tasting. A good restaurant choice in town is *Le Coq d'Or*, place François 1er, for its ornate interior and excellent-value *formule* (€8.50). If you get carried away with the brandy and need to stay the night, *L'Oliveraie*, 6 place de la Gare (ⓣ 05.45.82.04.15, ⓦ www.oliveraie-cognac.com; doubles €56), has simple rooms and a swimming pool.

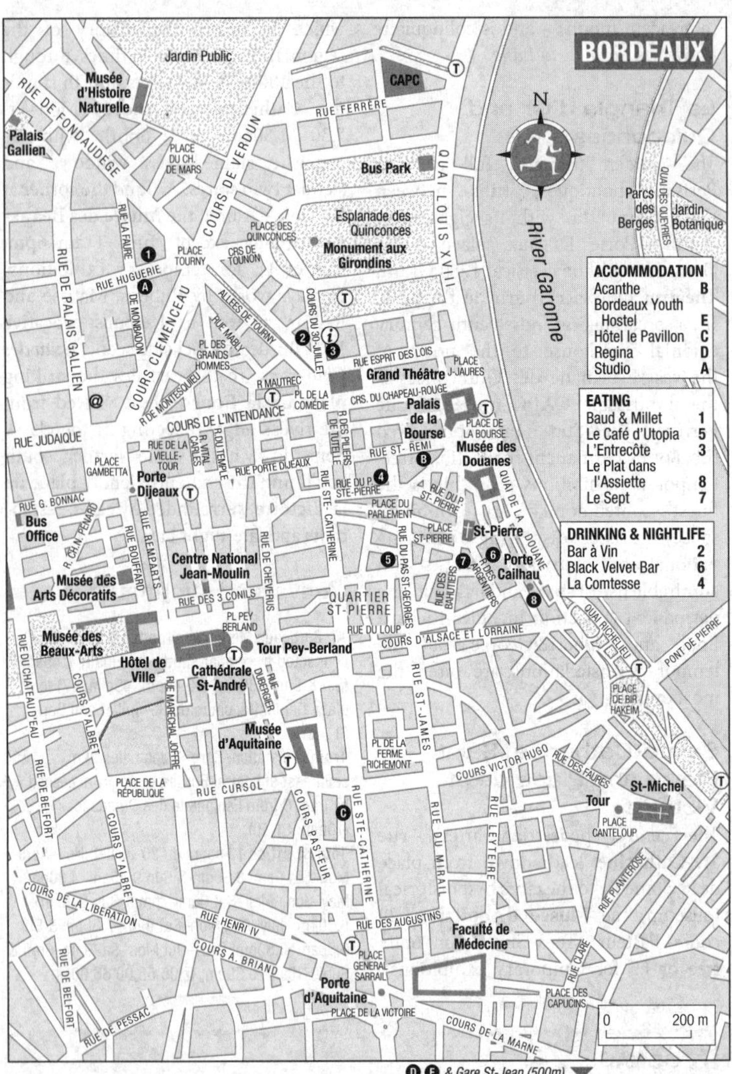

Ⓦ www.bordeaux-tourisme.com). Organizes a plethora of wine and city tours. There are also branches at the train station and at the airport.
Internet Iphone, 24 rue du Palais Gallien.

City transport

Tram/bus The hubs of the comprehensive transport networks are place Gambetta for buses and Esplanade des Quinconces for trams. Buy tickets at the machines on the platforms before boarding and validate them on board; one hour's travel €1.40, day pass €4.10.
Bike rental Liberty Cycles, 104 cours d'Yser (Ⓣ 05.56.92.77.18; €12/day; book in advance).

Accommodation

Acanthe 12–14 rue St-Rémi Ⓣ 05.56.81.66.58, Ⓦ www.acanthe-hotel-bordeaux.com. Centrally located, with brightly decorated, spacious rooms. Doubles €69.

WINE TASTING IN THE BORDEAUX REGION

Along with Burgundy and Champagne, the wines of Bordeaux form the Holy Trinity of French **viticulture**. Bordeaux is mostly a red-wine region, growing high-class (and more expensive) **Cabernet Sauvignon** on the Left Bank (the countryside to the west of the Garonne River and Gironde estuary), while smaller growers make predominantly Merlot-and Cabernet-Franc-based wines on the Right Bank. There are also some very good white wines, mainly from the Pessac and Graves regions to the south and southeast – largely based on **Sauvignon Blanc** and **Semillon**, that come in both dry and sweet forms. The easiest way to taste the wines is in the village of **St Emilion**, to the east of Bordeaux, where there are many wine shops that hold wine tastings. L'Envers du Décor, 11 rue du Clocher (ⓣ05.57.74.48.31), is a good choice and has reasonable prices. The Bordeaux tourist office (see p.409) has information on château visits and wine-tastings, and organizes a good variety of half-and full-day wine tours of the area.

Bordeaux Youth Hostel 22 cours Barbey ⓣ05.56.33.00.70, ⓦwww.auberge-jeunesse-bordeaux.eu. This modern hostel has a slightly impersonal feel but good facilities including free internet. Rooms are clean and large, and most have attached shower or bath. Fifteen minutes from the centre by foot. Dorms €22.50.

Hôtel le Pavillon 6 rue Honoré Tessier ⓣ05.56.91.75.35, ⓦwww.hotelpavillon.com. An incredible bargain right in the centre of town. Each room has been decorated tastefully using original art (the owner is a collector) and antiques. No en-suite toilets or showers, but rooms have sinks. Doubles €30.

Regina 34 rue Charles Dominique ⓣ05.56.91.32.88, ⓦwww.hotelreginabordeaux.com. Opposite the station, this friendly hotel offers bright, good-sized rooms, all with shower or bath. Fifteen minutes' walk to the city centre. Doubles €59.

Studio 26 rue Huguerie ⓣ05.56.48.00.14, ⓦwww.hotel-studio-bordeaux.fr. In an excellent position, this is a big backpackers' favourite with small, clean white rooms, all en suite, and a helpful owner. Doubles €30.

Eating

Baud & Millet 19 rue Huguerie. This fantastic wine shop has tables set up at the back where you can enjoy a leisurely glass of wine (from €4) and a plate of cheese and charcuterie (€12.50). The friendly Monsieur Baud speaks excellent English and delights in helping you with your choice. Mon–Sat 10am–11pm.

Le Café d'Utopia 5 place Camille Jullian. A lively, casual place in a beautiful old building that also houses the Utopia arthouse cinema, popular throughout the day and evening. Try one of their huge hot sandwiches (from €6) or the delicious gourmet salads (from €10). Mon–Fri noon–3pm & 7–10.30pm, Sat & Sun noon–10.30pm Oct–April, daily noon–10.30pm May–Sept.

L'Entrecôte 4 cours du 30 Juillet. Simplicity at its tastiest: two servings of beautifully tender steak, with a fabulous sauce, perfectly cooked chips and a green salad (€17). The dessert menu is extensive – try the profiteroles (€5.50). Expect to queue. Daily noon–2pm & 7.15–10.45pm.

Le Plat dans l'Assiette 8 rue Ausone. One whole menu on a plate – that's the hook here – but it's no haute cuisine gimmick; the cheapest of the assiettes – the *éphémère* at €16.50 – still crams in goats cheese, *magret séché* and Serrano ham in among the relatively healthy stuff. Mon, Wed & Sat 7.30–11pm, Tues, Thurs & Fri noon–2pm & 7.30–11pm.

Le Sept 7 rue de la Tour de Gassies ⓣ05.56.52.30.60. A quiet spot with an interior patio in the middle of the hustle and bustle of surrounding roads. The boss is a charismatic fellow who welcomes each new arrival into the restaurant. The portions are generous, while the *gambas flambées au pastis* are a must. Daily 8–10.30pm.

Drinking and nightlife

Bar à Vin 3 cours du XXX Juillet ⓣ05.56.00.43.47, ⓦbaravin.bordeaux.com. Promoters for Bordeaux wine growers and home to a wine-tasting school, the bar here is a good place to sample the region's excellent wines (from €2.50), best enjoyed with one of the wonderful cheese plates (€7). Mon–Sat 11am–10pm.

Black Velvet Bar 9 rue du Chai des Farines. It's a tough call but this is probably the best of the British/Irish bars in the city if only for the fact that popularity can be self-perpetuating – you're likely

SURFING IN LACANAU

Bordeaux's nearest beach, **Lacanau-Océan** (Ⓦwww.lacanau.com), is well known for its beautiful lake and famous for its world-class **surfing**. If you fancy catching some waves, take bus #702 from opposite gare St Jean (3 daily; 1hr 50min; €14) – once there, you can rent boards and learn to surf at Lacanau Surf Club (Ⓣ05.56.26.38.84, Ⓦwww.surflacanau.com), located on the corner of boulevard Plage and boulevard Liberty. *La Villa Zénith*, 16 av Adjudant Guittard (Ⓣ06.84.60.88.08, Ⓦwww.lacanau-zenith.com; dorms €23), is 200m from the beach and has comfy dorms, garden, cooking facilities and equipment lockers.

to find company here (and if not, then definitely a decent burger). Happy hour 5–8pm. Mon–Sat 5pm–2am, Sun 5pm–midnight.

La Comtesse 25 rue du Parlement-Ste-Pierre. Eclectic music, often samba or electro to shake your *derrière* until the small hours in a retro-Baroque interior. Note the shrine-like display above the door; *demi* €3. Daily 6pm–2am.

Moving on

Train Bayonne and Biarritz (10–12 daily; 1hr 40min–2hr 10min); Marseille (5–6 daily; 6–7hr); Nice (4 daily; 8hr 30min–10hr 10min); Paris (19 daily; 3hr–3hr 30min); Périgueux (10–12 daily; 1hr 10min–1hr 30min); Toulouse (10–17 daily; 2hr–2hr 45min).

PÉRIGUEUX

The bustling market town of **PÉRIGUEUX**, with its beautiful Renaissance and medieval centre, makes a fine base for visiting the **Dordogne's** prehistoric caves.

What to see and do

The centre of town focuses on **place Bugeaud**, west of which is the striking **Cathédrale St-Front** (daily 8am–7pm) – its square, pineapple-capped belfry surging above the roofs of the surrounding medieval houses. During a nineteenth-century restoration, the architect Paul Abadie added five Byzantine domes to the roof, which served as a prototype for his more famous Sacré Coeur in Paris (see p.385). Heading north along rue St-Front, you'll reach the **Musée d'Art et d'Archéologie du Périgord**, at 22 cours Tourny (Mon & Wed–Fri 10.30am–5.30pm, Sat & Sun 1–6pm; €4.50), which boasts some beautiful Gallo-Roman mosaics found locally.

Arrival and information

Train The station is a 10min walk to the west of place Bugeaud.

Tourist office 26 place Francheville (daily 9/10am–12.30pm & 2–6/7pm; Ⓣ05.53.53.10.63, Ⓦwww.tourisme-perigueux.fr). Has a fact sheet detailing how to get to the caves and back in a day (see opposite).

Internet Ouratech, 1 place du Général Leclerc.

Accommodation

Camping Barnabé 80 rue des Bains Ⓣ05.53.53.41.45, Ⓦwww.barnabe-perigord.com. This peaceful campsite enjoys an excellent position on the banks of the River Isle. Plots are shady, and there's a bar, ping-pong and mini-golf on site. To get there cross pont des Barris and follow the south riverbank for 20min. €4.40/person, plus €3.70/tent.

Des Barris 2 rue Pierre Magne Ⓣ05.53.53.04.05, Ⓦwww.hoteldesbarris.com. A lovely little hotel with twelve simple but attractive wood-furnished rooms. All are en suite and the best have views across the river to the cathedral. Doubles €53.

Le Midi 18 rue Denis-Papin Ⓣ05.53.53.41.06, Ⓦwww.hotel-du-midi.fr. Right opposite the station, this bar-hotel offers the cheapest rooms in town. Doubles €45.

Eating and drinking

Cocotte et Cie 17 rue Voltaire. A popular choice, with a lovely terrace that's ideal for enjoying the reasonably priced food, such as *confit de canard* (€9).

L'Eden 3 rue Aubergerie. An intimate restaurant serving up old-style Périgord cooking with great care and skill, using local ingredients. The menus are recommended – €12.50 at lunchtime and €28.50 in the evening. Mon–Sat.

Les Toqués 38 rue Pierre Semard Ⓦwww.publestoques.com. An Irish pub/gig venue with a fine range of bottled beers that accelerates from quiet evening drinks to no-holds-barred rowdiness at the drop of a hat. Tues & Wed 10am–10pm, Thurs–Sat 10am–midnight.

Moving on

Train Bordeaux (13 daily; 1hr 10min–1hr 30min); Les Eyzies (2–6 daily; 35min); Paris (12 daily; via Libourne or Limoges; 4–5hr).

VÉZÈRE VALLEY CAVES

This lavish cliff-cut region, riddled with **caves** and subterranean streams, is half an hour or so by train from Périgueux. Cro-Magnon skeletons were unearthed here in 1868 and since then an incredible wealth of archeological evidence about the life of late Stone Age people has been found. The paintings that adorn the caves are remarkable not only for their age, but also for their exquisite colouring and the skill with which they were drawn.

What to see and do

The centre of the region is **LES EYZIES**, a rambling, somewhat unattractive village dominated by tourism. Worth a glance before or after visiting the caves is the **Musée National de la Préhistoire** (June & Sept daily except Tues 9.30am–6pm; July & Aug daily 9.30am–6.30pm; Oct–May daily except Tues 9am–12.30pm & 2.30–5.30pm; €5). Les Eyzies' **tourist office**, 19 rue de la Préhistoire (June–Sept Mon–Sat 9am–7pm, Sun 9/10am–noon & 2–5/6/7pm; Oct–May Mon–Sat 9am–noon & 2–6pm, closed Sun, except April & May 10am–noon & 2–5pm; Ⓣ05.53.06.97.05, Ⓦwww.leseyzies.com) has information on private rooms in the area, internet and rents out bikes for €14 per day.

Font de Gaume caves

Just outside Les Eyzies, off the road to Sarlat, the **Grotte de Font-de-Gaume** (daily except Sat: mid-May to mid-Sept 9.30am–5.30pm; mid-Sept to mid-May 9.30am–12.30pm & 2–5.30pm; Ⓣ05.53.06.86.00; €7) contains dozens of polychrome paintings, the colour remarkably preserved by a protective layer of calcite. The tours last forty minutes but only two hundred people are admitted each day, so to be sure of a place you should reserve in advance by phone or arrive before 9.30am.

The Cap Blanc frieze

The **Abri du Cap Blanc** (daily: mid-May to mid-Sept 9.30am–5.30pm; mid-Sept to mid-May 9.30am–12.30pm & 2–5.30pm; Ⓣ05.53.06.86.00; €7) is a steep 7km bike ride from Les Eyzies. This is not a cave but a rock shelter, containing a 15,000-year-old frieze of horses and bison, the only exhibited prehistoric sculpture in the world.

Grotte des Combarelles

Three kilometres from Les Eyzies is the **Grotte des Combarelles** (daily except Sat: mid-May to mid-Sept 9.30am–5.30pm; mid-Sept to mid-May 9.30am–12.30pm & 2–5.30pm; €7), whose engravings of humans, reindeer and mammoths from the Magdalanian period (about twenty thousand years ago) are the oldest in the region.

Montignac

Up the valley of the Vézère River to the northeast, **MONTIGNAC** is more attractive than Les Eyzies. Its prime interest is the cave paintings at nearby **Lascaux** – or, rather, the tantalizing replica at Lascaux II (mid-Feb to mid-April & Nov–Dec Tues–Sun 10am–12.30pm & 2–5.30pm; Oct daily

10am–12.30pm & 2–6pm; mid-April to June & Sep daily 10am–12.30pm & 2–6.30pm; July & Aug daily 9am–8pm; 40min guided tour €9); the original has been closed since 1963 due to deterioration caused by the breath and body heat of visitors. Produced seventeen thousand years ago, the paintings are considered the finest prehistoric works in existence. The **tourist office** (Mon/Tues–Fri/Sat 9.30/10/10.30am–12.30pm & 2–5/6pm; July & Aug daily 9am–7pm; ⓣ05.53.51.82.60, ⓦwww.tourisme-vezere.com) is at place Bertrand-de-Born. Montignac is short on moderately priced **accommodation**; the best option is the *Hôtel de la Grotte*, 63 rue du 4 Septembre (ⓣ05.53.51.80.48, ⓦwww.hoteldelagrotte.fr; doubles €30), which has a nice restaurant (*menus* from €12.50). There's also a **campsite**, *Le Moulin du Bleufond* (closed mid-Oct to March; ⓣ05.53.51.83.95, ⓦwww.bleufond.com; €7.40 per person, plus €8.50 per pitch), on the riverbank.

BIARRITZ

A former Viking whaling settlement, **BIARRITZ** became famous in the nineteenth century when Empress Eugénie came here with the last French Emperor, Napoleon III. He built her a seaside palace in 1855 and an impressive list of kings, queens and tsars followed, bringing *belle époque* and Art Deco grandeur to the resort. Today Biarritz is the undisputed surf capital of Europe, hosting the prestigious weeklong Surf Festival in July, which includes a longboard competition and nightly parties on the Côte des Basques beach. The town feels as though its glory days are well past, and now it's a rather traditional (and tacky) seaside resort that can't compete with the Côte d'Azur.

What to see and do

The town's beaches are the main attraction. The best surfing is on the long competition beach, **plage de la Côte des Basques**, to the south – those less interested in surfing should try the intimate **Port-Vieux** beach for a calmer swim. The **Musée de la Mer** (July & Aug daily 9.30am–midnight; Sept & June daily 9.30am–7pm; Oct–March Tues–Sun 9.30am–12.30pm & 2–6pm; €13; ⓦwww.museedelamer.com), opposite Rocher de la Vierge, has an interesting aquarium taken from the Bay of Biscay, and a rooftop seal pool. **Asiatica**, at 1 rue Guy Petit (daily 2–7pm; July & Aug Mon–Fri 10.30am–7pm; €7), uphill and left off avenue Foch, houses one of Europe's most important collections of oriental art.

Arrival and information

Air Aérodrome Biarritz-Bayonne-Anglet is connected to the town centre by Chronoplus line #8A (€1).
Train The station lies 3km from the centre in La Négresse. Bus #2 and the *navette des plages* (see opposite) connect it to square d'Ixelles.
Tourist office 1 square d'Ixelles (Mon–Fri 9am–6pm, Sat & Sun 10am–5pm; ⓣ05.59.22.37.00, ⓦwww.biarritz.fr).
Scooters Rent a Bike, 24 rue Peyroloubilh (ⓣ05.59.24.94.47) rents scooters and beach buggies; ID and credit card required (€12/day).

Accommodation

Atalaye 6 rue des Goélands ⓣ05.59.24.06.76. A fine example of faded seaside glamour with some rooms offering views of the ocean. Doubles €59.

PELOTE BASQUE

The fastest ball game in the world, **pelote** (or *pilota* in Basque) consists, in essence, of propelling a ball (*pelote*) against a wall (*fronton*) so that your opponent cannot return it, sometimes at speeds of over 300km per hour. There are over twenty versions with different courts, rackets and balls.

The biggest tournaments in Biarritz – the Open in July and the Gant d'Or in August, played in the parc Mazon on av Joffre and the Plaza Berri on avenue Foch – are great spectacles.

Biarritz Camping 28 rue Harcet ⓣ05.59.23.00.12, ⓦwww.biarritz-camping.fr. A spacious and well-equipped campsite, just a short walk from the beach and 2km from the centre of town. Prices quoted are for two people so you may be able to get a discount if alone. Open mid-May to mid-Sept. €28 for two people plus pitch.
FUAJ Biarritz 8 rue Chiquito de Cambo ⓣ05.59.41.76.00, ⓦwww.fuaj.org. Just 1.5km from the beach and close to the station and the lake, this comfortable, modern hostel has two- to four-bed dorms, rents out bicycles and has some good deals on surf lessons. To get here, take bus #2, #9, or ligne B bus on Sun to "Bois de Boulogne". April–Sept closed 12.30–6pm; Oct–March closed 11.30am–6pm. Dorms €18.30.
La Marine 1 rue des Goélands ⓣ05.59.24.34.09, ⓦwww.hotel-lamarine-biarritz.com. A fresh-feeling place, painted crisp blue and white. The only downside to its central location is the noise from revellers outside. Doubles €49.
Le Saint Charles 47 av Reine Victoria ⓣ05.59.24.10.54, ⓦwww.hotelstcharles.com. The decor of the rooms in this pretty 1920s house a little way out of the centre is tired, but the lush garden makes up for that. Doubles €60.

Eating and drinking

Bar Jean 5 rue des Halles ⓣ05.59.24.80.38. Don't miss out on this local tapas favourite (from €4.90), which also serves plates of the excellent local ham (€12.50) and sangria (€3.50). Very popular so worth booking ahead. Open daily (closed Tues & Wed Sep–June).
Bleue de toi 30 rue Mazagran. They've done a lot with this crêperie's small size – stylishly decorated, there's a tiny mezzanine space and tables outside. The midday menu crêpe features a glass of cider, a galette (try the *forestière*) and a sweet crêpe for dessert. Open daily.
Casa Juan Pedro Quai Du Petit Port. Occupies a uniquely picturesque spot but doesn't make you pay for the privilege. Try the grilled sardines (€7.50). Open daily.
Les Cent Marches Côte des Basques. A marvellously simple open-sided shack overlooking the ocean. It's a ten- to fifteen-minute walk from the centre but you won't find a better spot in town for a sundowner. Closed Tues Nov–March.
Les Halles place Sobradiel. Most towns have a good *halles* (covered food markets) but this one is excellent. Go for breakfast, a picnic lunch or to indulge in a *gateau Basque* (jam- or custard-filled cake).
Le Surfing 9 bd du Prince-de-Galles ⓦwww.lesurfing.fr. Transformed from a legendary, surfboard-shrewn place to this sleek incarnation, but its location is hard to beat. More expensive these days, but there are lighter dishes such as omelettes from €8.50, or sardines *d'Espagne ortiz* with bread for €11.50. Open daily.
Sideria Hernani 29 av du Maréchal Joffre. Heavy wooden tables, barrels and local warmth accompany excellent Basque cuisine and cider. The *côte de boeuf* (€38 for two people) is huge but well worth it. Open daily from 8pm.

Moving on

Train Bayonne (14 daily; 15–30min); Paris (5 daily, connect in Bayonne; 5hr–6hr 15min).
Bus Bus #1 from square d'Ixelles and #2 from outside the casino both go to Bayonne; in July and August, the *navette des plages* (beach bus) covers all the beaches from Anglet to Ilbarritz, departing from outside the casino. See ⓦwww.chronoplus.eu for further information. Two buses daily to Bilbao (2hr 55min; €17.20) and San Sebastian (1hr 45min; €6.30) depart from rue Joseph Petit at 12.15pm and 6.45pm.

BAYONNE

Capital of the French Basque country and home of the bayonet, **BAYONNE** lies 6km inland at the junction of the Nive and Adour rivers. Having escaped the worst effects of mass tourism, it remains a cheerful and pretty town, with the shutters on the older half-timbered houses painted in the distinctive Basque tones of green and rust-red.

What to see and do

The town's two medieval quarters line the banks of the Nive, whose quays are home to many bars and restaurants. Grand Bayonne on the west bank is the administrative and commercial centre, while Petit Bayonne, to the east, has a more bohemian feel and is full of places to eat and drink.

Petit Bayonne

On **quai des Corsaires,** along the Nive's east bank, stands the **Musée Basque** (April–Sept Tues–Sun 10am–6.30pm; July & Aug daily 10am–6.30pm; Oct–

March Tues–Sun 10.30am–6pm; €5.50), which provides a comprehensive overview of modern Basque culture. The city's second museum, **Musée Bonnat** has an unexpected treasury of art, including works by Goya, El Greco, Rubens and Degas, but is closed until 2014.

Grand Bayonne

The **Cathédrale Ste-Marie** (Mon–Sat 10–11.45am & 3–5.45pm, Sun 3.30–6pm), across the Nive, looks best from a distance, its twin spires rising with airy grace above the houses; the **cloister** (daily 9/9.30am–12.30pm & 2–5/6pm; free) rewards a visit with a good view of the stained glass and buttresses. Chocolate-making technqiues were brought here by Jewish chocolatiers fleeing the Spanish Inquisition. It was here that a devilish brew, hot chocolate, was introduced to the country, much to the distaste of the Catholic church due to its aphrodisiac qualities – the best place in town to try it is *Cazenave* (see opposite).

Arrival and information

Train Bayonne's train station is in the St-Esprit quarter on the opposite bank of the Adour from the centre, 10min walk over the Pont St-Esprit.

Tourist office Take rue Bernède from the Hôtel de Ville, to place des Basques (Sept–June Mon–Fri 9am–6.30pm & Sat 10am–6pm; July & Aug Mon–Sat 9am–7pm & Sun 10am–1pm; ⓣ08.20.42.64.64, ⓦwww.bayonne-tourisme.com); it has an excellent scheme that lends bikes for free.

Internet CyberNetCafé, 9 place de la République.

Accommodation

Hôtel des Arceaux 26 rue Port Neuf ⓣ05.59.59.15.53. Many rooms don't have exterior windows which can prove stuffy on hot days but the building overall has a pleasingly quirky character. Doubles €66.

Hôtel des Basques 4 rue des Lisses ⓣ05.59.59.08.02. The entrance door of this simple place in Petit Bayonne is extremely unpromising but things improve inside (in spite of the sloping floors in parts). Doubles €40.

Monbar 24 rue Pannecau, Petit Bayonne ⓣ05.59.59.26.80. Though a bit fusty and lacking a little in character, this quiet family-run hotel has clean and bright en-suite rooms. Doubles €32.

Temporésidences 4 rue Pontrique ⓣ05.59.59.11.77, ⓦwww.temporesidence.com. This is a good option for longer stays, with apartments sleeping up to five people from €48/night (minimum three nights).

Eating and drinking

Auberge du Petit Bayonne 23 rue des Cordeliers ⓣ05.59.59.83.44. The welcome is warm and the food hearty at this husband-and-wife-run place. Menus are €10–18. The lamb's sweetbreads with cèpes are excellent but you must try the roasted suckling lamb (*agneau de lait*) when it's available. Thurs–Tues noon–2pm & 7.30–9.30pm (Sat 10pm); closed Tues & Sun eve.

Bistrot Ste-Cluque 9 rue Hugues, St-Esprit. Make sure you try the local cured ham (€7.50), flavoured with salt from nearby mines, at this jolly bistro by the station; three-course dinner menu €18. Open daily.

Cazenave 19 Arceaux du Pont-Neuf. The pick of the chocolatiers; try the famous *chocolat mousseux* – delicious, hand-whipped hot chocolate served with chantilly cream (€5.20) – with a serving of their hot, buttered toast (€3). Tues–Sat 9.15am–noon & 2–7pm.

El Asador A well-regarded traditional restaurant in town with a €20 menu. Noon–2.30pm & 7.30–9.30pm, closed Sun evening & Mon.

En Equilibre 19 rue des Cordeliers ⓣ05.59.59.46.98. Decor is all cool tiles and stone with splashes of colour. Try the €12 lunchtime or €18 evening menu. Noon–2.30pm & 7.30–10.30pm, closed Sun & Mon lunch.

Moving on

Train Bordeaux (6–12 daily; 1hr 40min–2hr 10min); Hendaye (14 daily; 35min) on the border with Spain, where the Euskotren makes the crossing to St Sébastien (every 30min; 45min); Lourdes (5–8 daily; 1hr 45min–2hr); Paris (14–16 daily, some indirect; 4hr 45min–6hr); Toulouse (7–12 daily; 3hr 10min–4hr 40min).

LOURDES

In 1858 Bernadette Soubirous, the 14-year-old daughter of a poor local miller in **LOURDES**, had eighteen visions of the Virgin Mary in a spot called the Grotte de Massabielle. Miraculous cures at the grotto soon followed and Lourdes grew exponentially; it now sees six million Catholic pilgrims a year and whole streets are devoted to the sale of religious kitsch. At the **grotto** itself – a moisture-blackened overhang by the riverside with a statue of the Virgin inside – long queues of the faithful process through. Above looms the first, neo-Gothic church built here, in 1871, and nearby the massive subterranean **basilica** has a capacity of twenty thousand. Lourdes **train station** is on the northeastern edge of town. For the **tourist office** (Mon–Sat 9am–noon & 2–5.30/6/6.30/7pm; Easter–Oct also Sun 10am–12.30/6pm; ⓣ05.62.42.77.40, ⓦwww.lourdes-infotourisme.com) on place Peyramale turn right outside the station, then left down Chaussée Maransin. There's an abundance of inexpensive **hotels** in Lourdes, including the simple *Hotel Croix des Nordistes*, 29 bd de la Grotte (ⓣ05.62.94.28.57, ⓦwww.hotelcroixdesnordistes-lourdes.com; doubles €42), and a number of **campsites** in the area, such as *Plein Soleil*, 11 av du Monge (ⓣ05.62.94.40.93, ⓦwww.camping-pleinsoleil.com; €19 for two people plus pitch).

TOULOUSE

TOULOUSE is one of the most vibrant provincial cities in France, thanks to its sizeable student population – second only to that of Paris. The city has long been a centre for aviation – St-Exupéry and Mermoz flew out from here on their pioneering flights over Africa in the 1920s – and has more recently been developed as the country's centre of high-tech industry.

What to see and do

The centre of Toulouse is a rough hexagon clamped around a bend in the wide, brown Garonne River.

Place du Capitole and the old city

The **place du Capitole** is the site of Toulouse's town hall and a prime meeting place, with numerous cafés and a weekday market. South of the square, and east of rue Alsace-Lorraine, lies the **old town**. The predominant building material here is the flat Toulousain brick, whose cheerful rosy colour gives the city its nickname of *ville rose*. Best

HIKING IN THE PYRENEES

From Lourdes train station, several SNCF buses run daily to **Gavarnie** and **Barèges**, two resorts near the heart of the Parc National des Pyrénées Occidentales. From either, a few hours on the Pyrenees-spanning hiking trail, GR10, or the harder HRP (Haute Randonnée Pyrénéenne), brings you to staffed alpine refuges (rough camping is not generally allowed in the park). In summer, serious and properly equipped hikers may wish to continue on the trails, which are well served with refuges, though the weather and terrain make them highly dangerous in winter. The Lourdes and Bayonne tourist offices have information, or check ⓦwww.lespyrenees.net. Gavarnie is smaller and pricier than Barèges, but has an incomparable natural ampitheatre towering above, forming the border with Spain. You can stay in dorms at *Le Gypaëte* (ⓣ05.62.92.40.61; dorms €13), or camp at the primitive but superbly positioned *La Bergerie* (ⓣ05.62.92.48.41, ⓦwww.camping-gavarnie-labergerie.com; €3.70 per person, plus €4 per pitch), towards the cirque. Barèges has more of a real village feel, with a good streamside campsite – *La Ribère* (ⓣ05.62.92.69.01, ⓦwww.laribere.com; €13.40) – and two high-quality gîtes next to each other: *L'Oasis* (ⓣ05.62.92.69.47, ⓦwww.gite-oasis.com; €24 B&B, or €36 half board per person in a variety of dorms) and *L'Hospitalet* (ⓣ05.62.92.68.08, ⓦwww.hospitalet-bareges.com; €44 per person full board).

known of these buildings is the Hôtel d' Assézat, towards the river end of rue de Metz, which houses the marvellous private art collection of the **Fondation Bemberg** (Tues–Sun 10am–12.30pm & 1.30–6pm, Thurs till 9pm; €6), including excellent works by Bonnard.

St-Sernin

Rue du Taur leads northwards from place du Capitole to place St-Sernin and the largest Romanesque church in France, **Basilique de St-Sernin** (Oct–May Mon–Sat 8.30am–6pm & Sun 8.30am–7.30pm; June–Sept Mon–Sat 8.30am–7pm & Sun 8.30am–7.30pm). Dating back to 1080, it was built to accommodate passing hordes of Santiago pilgrims and is one of the loveliest examples of its kind.

Les Jacobins

West of place du Capitole, on rue Lakanal, the church of **Les Jacobins** (daily 9am–7pm) is another impressive ecclesiastical building. This is a huge fortress-like rectangle of unadorned brick, with an interior divided by a central row of slender pillars from whose capitals spring a colourful splay of vaulting ribs.

Across the Garonne

Across the Pont-Neuf on the west bank of the Garonne stands the brick tower of the inspirational **Chateaux d'Eau**, (Tues–Sun 1–7pm; €2.50; Ⓦwww.galeriechateaudeau.org) the first public gallery dedicated to photography in France and holding over four thousand pieces, along with antique equipment. Continue west from the river, then north up Allées de Fitte to the vaulted nineteenth-century slaughterhouse, **Les Abattoirs** (Wed–Sun 11am–7pm; €7), whose comprehensive modern and contemporary art collections include the striking eight-metre-high Picasso theatre screen.

Arrival and information

Air Shuttle buses leave Aéroport Toulouse-Blagnac every 20min and take half an hour to reach Gare Matabiau (€5).
Bus and train Buses and trains arrive at Gare Matabiau, a 15min walk from the city centre down allées Jean-Jaurès.
Tourist office place Charles de Gaulle (Mon–Sat 9am–6/7pm, Sun 10/10.30am–5pm; Oct–May closed Sat–Sun 12.30–2pm; Ⓣ05.61.11.02.22, Ⓦwww.uk.toulouse-tourisme.com).
Bikes Vélô Toulouse bike stands can be found throughout the city – credit card guarantee required, first half-hour free, then from €1.50/30min.
Internet Nethouse, 1 rue de Trois Renards.

Accommodation

Camping le Rupé 21 chemin du Pont de Rupé Ⓣ05.61.70.07.35, Ⓦwww.camping-toulouse.com. The closest campsite, just north of the city in a green park, with waterskiiing and fishing spots nearby. Take métro line B direction Borderouge and get off at La Vache, then take bus #59 to Rupé. €15/person and pitch.
Croix Baragnon 17 rue Croix-Baragnon Ⓣ05.61.52.60.10, Ⓦwww.hotelcroixbaragnon.com. Surprisingly airy rooms in this rare thing, a centrally budget hotel. Be prepared to climb some stairs as there's no lift available. Doubles €55.
Des Arts 1bis rue Cantegril Ⓣ05.61.23.36.21. Lovely little hotel tucked away in the old town. Rooms vary in size and are basic but nicely decorated. The soundproofing between them isn't very effective, though. Doubles €40.
FUAJ Residence Jolimont 2 av Yves Brunaud Ⓣ05.34.30.42.80, Ⓦwww.fuaj.org/toulouse. Though not very central, this hostel is only 1km from the station and offers simple but clean dorm rooms. Dorms €17.
Petite Auberge de Compostelle 17 rue d'Embarthe Ⓣ07.60.88.17.17, Ⓦwww.gite-compostelle-toulouse.com. Four- and six-bed dorms, some of which overlook a public park. There's a pleasingly clean and airy feel to the place. No arrival after 10.30pm. Dorms €20.

Eating

Café Lusso 6 bis, place Saintes Scarbes Ⓣ05.34.31.61.09. A cute restaurant on a serene *place* where you'll enjoy the sound of a tinkling fountain as you dine. Mains are €14–19, and include the occasional French take on British

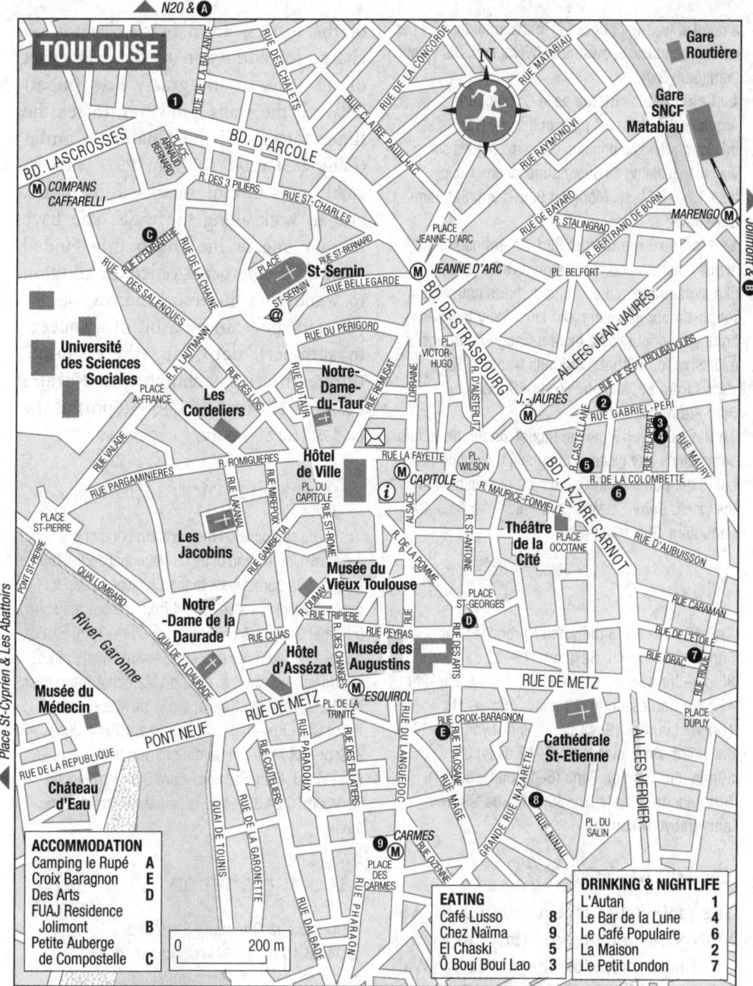

gastropub food – their "fish and chips" (€15.50) is great. Mon & Tues noon–2pm, Wed–Sat noon–2pm & 8–10pm.

Chez Naïma Marché des Carmes. There are better-looking options hereabouts but few can rival Naïma's welcome and home-style (often Moroccan) cooking. Just one or two choices are available, such as rabbit stew (€9) with plentiful sides of fries and green beans. Daily 10.30am until early evening.

El Chaski 6 rue de la Colombette. An unexpected purveyor of the Bolivian pies known as *salteñas* (€3 each or €6.50 with a South American beer), this is a very simple canteen offering something a little out of the ordinary.

Ô Bouí Bouí Lao 30 rue Palaprat. A really popular little Thai/ Lao restaurant. The evening *menu gourmet* is good value at €19. Mon–Fri noon–3pm & 7.30pm–midnight, Sat 7.30pm–midnight.

Drinking and nightlife

L'Autan 58 bd Arcole. A satisfyingly dingy option with a bric-a-brac-stuffed interior, and frequented by the city's mods and rockers (getting along famously). The pavement terrace is a fine spot for a daytime coffee. Daily 11am–2am.

Le Bar de la Lune 22 rue Palaprat. Relax with one of 120 types of beer (bottles such as Duvel from €5, a *demi* of well-kept beer €2) in this friendly little bar where the music allows for conversation. Daily until 2am (3am Sat).

Le Café Populaire 9 rue de la Colombette. Arguably the cheapest pints in the city (€2.50) at this long-standing drinking den, which goes some way to explaining its buzzy atmosphere. Happy hour 7.30–8.30pm. Mon–Sat 9am–2am (Sat 3am). Closed Aug.

La Maison 9 rue Gabriel Péri. An atmospheric, artfully dishevelled place with a retro cinema-like sign outside, mismatched chairs and tables, rough-timbered ceiling and knowingly tacky fairy lights. It's doubtless a hipster hangout but not exclusive for all that. Cocktails from €7.50, *demis* from €3, *assiettes* from €8. Daily 5pm–2am (later Sat).

Le Petit London 7 bis rue Riquet. An unofficial hub of the city's arty types (and punks) the action spills out of the pub onto the pavement most nights of the week. *Demi* €2. Mon 5pm–midnight, Tues–Sat 9am–2am, Sun 10am–8pm.

Moving on

Train Barcelona (3 daily, via Narbonne; 4hr 50min–5hr 45min); Bayonne (18–22 daily; 2hr 30min–3hr 45min); Bordeaux (16 daily; 2hr–2hr 45min); Carcassonne (18 daily; 45min–1hr 15min); Lourdes (9–14 daily; 2hr); Lyon (10–14 daily; 4hr–6hr); Marseille (9–12 daily; 3hr 50min–5hr 50min); Paris (8–12 daily; 5–7hr).

Bus Andorra (2 daily; 3hr 30min). See Ⓦwww.andorrabybus.com.

CARCASSONNE

The fairytale aspect of **CARCASSONNE**'s old town (la Cité), was the inspiration for the castle in Walt Disney's *Sleeping Beauty*. Viollet-le-Duc rescued it from ruin in 1844, and his rather romantic restoration has been furiously debated ever since. Unsurprisingly, it's become a real tourist trap, its narrow lanes lined with innumerable souvenir shops and regularly crammed with hordes of day-trippers.

What to see and do

The **Cité** is a twenty-five-minute walk from the station (20min from the new town) – well worth it to get a full view of the fortress from below. There's no charge for admission to the main part of the Cité, or the grassy *lices* (moat) between the walls. However, to see the inner fortress of the **Château Comtal** (daily 9.30am–5/6.30pm; €9), with its small museum of medieval sculpture, and to walk along the walls, you have to join one of the half-hourly guided tours from the ticket office. In addition to wandering the town's narrow streets (though they can be a bit of a squeeze in summer), don't miss the beautiful, thirteenth-century church of **St-Nazaire** (daily 9–11.45am & 1.45–5/6pm) at the end of rue St-Louis.

Arrival and information

Train The station is on the northern edge of the new town, at the end of av du Maréchal Joffre, from where it's a 35min walk to the Cité (very steep for the last 5min) or catch ligne 4 from the bus stop on bd Omer Sarraut (Mon–Sat hourly 7am–7pm; €1.20).

Tourist office Three branches, the main one at 28 rue de Verdun; another at av du Maréchal Joffre near the station and the third at the Porte Narbonnaise in the Cité (July–Aug daily 9am–7pm; April–June & Sept–Oct Mon–Sat 9am–6pm Sun 9am–1pm; Nov–March Mon–Sat 9am–6pm Sun 9am–noon; Ⓣ04.68.10.24.30, Ⓦwww.carcassonne-tourisme.com).

Accommodation

Campéole la Cité route St-Hilaire Ⓣ04.68.10.01.00, Ⓦwww.campingcitecarcassonne.com. This campsite has a well-shaded riverside location and good sporting facilities, and is less than 10min walk from the Cité. Accommodation in sturdy fixed tents or mobile homes €23–41 (min two nights July & Aug); one pitch for one/two people €24.90.

FUAJ Carcassone rue du Vicomte Trencavel Ⓣ04.68.25.23.16, Ⓦwww.fuaj.org. A fantastic hostel in an unsurpassable position in the heart of la Cité. Dorms are comfortable and have attached shower, and there's also table tennis, themed nights in the bar, bike rental and organized trips to the surrounding countryside. Dorms €22.

Hotel du Pont Vieux 32 rue Trivalle Ⓣ04.68.25.24.99, Ⓦwww.hoteldupontvieux.com. Tired decor but atmospheric in spite of it, with a lovely garden behind ivy-covered walls, and the more expensive rooms offering views of the Cité. Doubles €56.

Notre Dame de l'Abbaye 103 rue Trivalle ⓣ04.68.25.16.65, ⓦwww.abbaye-carcassonne.com. If the FUAJ is full, this is the second best bargain, with a beautiful garden and spick-and-span dorms. Doubles €47 (with shared bathroom), dorms (includes breakfast) €23.

Eating and drinking

Comptoir des Vins et Terroirs 3 rue du Comte Roger. Just around the corner from the youth hostel, this smart but unpretentious wine bar offers a great opportunity to try the best of the region's wines. It's €10 for a three wine *dégustation* (with an explanation of the region's winemaking traditions) or €17 with three complimentary cheeses. Daily 10.30am–10.30pm.

La Tête de l'Art 37 bis rue Trivalle. Decent modern art adorns this place just outside the battlements, and the owner/chef runs the art gallery opposite. Dishes include onion soup, garlic-roast chicken stuffed with pork, and fruit tart; there's a vegetarian menu for the same price (€16). Daily 10am–midnight.

L'Auberge des Lices 3 rue Raymond-Roger Trencavel. Set nicely apart from the main tourist traffic in the Cité, the cheapest menu (€19) features cassoulet. Thurs–Tues noon–2pm & 7.30–10pm (open Wed eve July & Aug).

Les Buissonnets 6 rue Cros Mayrevieille. The Cité is awash with cassoulet but here it's the real deal, with good-quality charcuterie. They cook their *frites* in goose fat, too. *Menus* run €17–21. Daily noon–2pm (closed Mon low season).

Moving on

Train Barcelona (6 daily, via Narbonne; 4hr–5hr 10min); Montpellier (14 daily, 1hr 15min–1hr 45min); Nice (6 daily, via Marseille; 4–5hr); Paris (11–16 daily; 3–6hr); Perpignan (13 daily; 1hr 30min–2hr 15min); Toulouse (18–22 daily; 45min–1hr 15min).

MONTPELLIER

MONTPELLIER is a vibrant city, renowned for its ancient university, once attended by such luminaries as Petrarch and Rabelais. Most of the central area is pedestrianized, which lends itself to unhurried exploration and many enjoyable evenings at terrace cafés.

What to see and do

At the town's hub is place de la Comédie, a grand oval square paved with cream-coloured marble and surrounded by cafés. The Opéra, an ornate nineteenth-century theatre, presides over one end, while the other end leads onto the pleasant Champs de Mars park. Nearby, the much-vaunted **Musée Fabre** (39 bd Bonne Nouvelle; Tues, Thurs, Fri & Sun 10am–6pm, Wed 1–9pm, Sat 11am–6pm; €6) has a wide art collection stretching from the Renaissance to the modern day, housed in a number of exceptionally beautiful buildings. The tangled, hilly lanes of Montpellier's old quarter lie behind the museum, and are full of seventeenth- and eighteenth-century mansions and small museums. The **Jardin des Plantes** (Tues–Sun noon–6/8pm; free), just north of the old town, with its alleys of exotic trees, is France's oldest botanical garden, founded in 1593. Opposite the gardens lies the **university quarter**, with its beautiful old buildings and lively café life.

Arrival and information

Air The airport is 8km to the west of Montpellier, by the beaches, connected to the city by *navettes* (€2.40, including one bus or tram connection in town).

MONTPELLIER MARKETS

"Allez-allez-allez!" is the call of Montpellier's stallholders in the many markets around the town. Here are three of the best: **Les Halles Jacques-Coeur** (Tues–Sat 8am–8pm, Sun 8am–2pm) opposite the tram on boulevard Antigone has quality home-made food; across the *place*, the **Marché Paysan** (Sun 9.30am–1.30pm) sells all local produce; **Plan-Cabanes**, at Faubourg du Courreau and Gambetta (daily 7.30am–1.30pm) is the most fun – here you can eat Arab and African cuisine for next to nothing.

Bus and train The bus and train stations are on the southern edge of town, a short walk down rue de Maguelone from the centre.
Tourist office Near place de la Comédie (Sept–June Mon–Wed & Fri 9am–6.30pm, Thurs 10am–6.30pm, Sat 10am–6pm, Sun 10am–5pm; July–Aug Mon–Fri 9.30am–7.30pm, Sat & Sun 9.30am–6.30pm; Ⓣ04.67.60.60.60, Ⓦwww.ot-montpellier.fr).
Internet Cyberstade, 6 rue Jules-Ferry.

Accommodation

FUAJ Montpellier rue des Écoles-Laïques Ⓣ04.67.60.32.22, Ⓦwww.fuaj.org. Housed in a handsome building in the old town, this helpful hostel offers pretty standard FUAJ accommodation, and has a lounge with table football and a pool table. Closed noon–3pm. Dorms €19.
Les Étuves 24 rue des Étuves Ⓣ04.67.60.78.19, Ⓦwww.hoteldesetuves.fr. A small family-run hotel, full of *belle époque* touches. The spotless, white rooms have en-suite showers or baths. Doubles €39.
Le Mistral 25 rue Boussairolles Ⓣ04.67.58.45.25, Ⓦwww.hotel-le-mistral.com. Central and budget, that rare combination. There are newly renovated rooms and tired-looking, cheaper options. Doubles €55.
Majestic 4 rue du Cheval Blanc Ⓣ04.67.66.26.85, Ⓔmajesticmontpellier@yahoo.fr. Though it hardly lives up to its name, this friendly hotel offers simple, surprisingly spacious rooms in a great position in the old town, close to the place de la Comédie. Doubles €38.

Eating and drinking

Barberousse 6 rue Boussairolles. Wooden from top to toe, with barrels for tables, this place feels a little like a ship's hold. Given that it's a *rhumerie* with nearly 80 kinds available, you might find the floor starts listing, too. Mon–Sat 6pm–2am.
La FaBRik 12 rue Boussairolles. Live music (think rock, blues, jazz and Irish), Belgian beers, whiskies from around the world, and the occasional indoor boules tournament at this hipster hotspot. Tues–Sat 5pm–1am.
La Tomate 6 rue Four des Flammes. Truly a city institution, not least because of the prices – a midday menu is just €9.10, while the €12.95 evening menu offers fish soup and cassoulet among its options. It's wood-panelled inside with a fireplace in one of the rooms. Tues–Sat noon–2pm & 7.30–10.30pm.
Le Bec de Jazz rue Gagne Petit. Most people are on the *rhum arrangé* or ginger-flavoured punch (both €3/glass, €20/bottle) at this intimate, stone-walled place owned by Malian Omar. There's no obvious signage, just an advertising sign for Fischer beer. Daily 7.30pm–1am.
Pourquoi Pas 3 rue Jules Latreilhe, place Saint Côme. The slightly wonky pavement terrace has a certain charm while the good value two-course menu (€12) has plenty of choices, such as red mullet and leeks as a starter and a bountiful carpaccio with excellent *frites* for main. They also serve an English-style brunch (€12) on Sundays. Tues–Sat lunch and supper, & Sun 11am–3pm.

Moving on

Train Avignon (12 daily; 1hr); Barcelona (4 daily, 2 via Port-Bou; 4hr 20min–7hr); Carcassonne (9 daily; 1hr 25min–1hr 45min); Marseille (10 daily; 1hr 30min–2hr 20min); Nîmes (frequent; 30min); Paris (12 daily; 3hr 30min); Perpignan (16 daily; 1hr 30min–2hr).

PERPIGNAN

This far south, climate and geography alone ensure a palpable Spanish influence, but **PERPIGNAN** is actually Spanish in origin and home to the descendants of refugees from the Spanish Civil War. It's a cheerful city, with Roussillon's red and yellow striped flag atop many a building, and makes an ideal stopoff en route to Spain or Andorra.

What to see and do

The centre of **Perpignan** is marked by the palm trees and smart cafés of **place Arago**. From here rue d'Alsace-Lorraine and rue de la Loge lead past the massive iron gates of the classical **Hôtel de Ville** to the tiny **place de la Loge**, the focus of the old heart of the city. Just north up rue Louis-Blanc is one of the city's few remaining fortifications, the crenellated fourteenth-century gate of **Le Castillet**, now home to the **Musée de l'Histoire de la Catalogne Nord**, a fascinating museum of Roussillon's Catalan folk culture (daily except Mon 10.30am–6pm; €4).

Arrival and information

Train The station is a 15min walk from the city centre.
Bus The bus station is by Pont Arago, on av du Général Leclerc.
Tourist office In the Palais des Congrès at the end of bd Wilson (Mon–Sat 9am–6/7pm, Sun 10am–1/4pm; ⓣ04.68.66.30.30, ⓦwww.perpignantourisme.com).
Internet GamesNet at 45 bis av du Général Leclerc.

Accommodation

Camping Catalan route de Bompas ⓣ04.68.63.16.92, ⓦwww.camping-catalan.com. A lively campsite 5km from the centre, with washing machines, a swimming pool and frequent pétanque competitions. Ask for shade as not all pitches have it. €15.40/person and pitch (€21.40 for two people/one pitch).
FUAJ Perpignan Parc de la Pépinière ⓣ04.68.34.63.32, ⓦwww.fuaj.org/perpignan. Badly situated as it backs onto a very busy major road, but convenient for the train station (5min). Dorms are bright but basic and meals are available. Closed from 10am–5pm. Dorms €18.
Hotel de la Loge 1 rue des Fabriques d'en Nabot ⓣ04.68.34.41.02, ⓦwww.hoteldelaloge.fr. A charming hotel with antiques scattered around, wooden ceiling beams and really amenable staff. Some rooms look out onto the lovely inner courtyard – all in all, a bargain. Doubles €55.
Hotel du Berry 6 av du Général de Gaulle ⓣ04.68.34.59.02, ⓦwww.hotelduberry.com. Close to the station, the rooms (all en suite) really are basic but a night's sleep doesn't come much cheaper. Doubles €40.

Eating and drinking

La Cafétière 17 rue de l'Ange. A small but rather distinguished café serving up top-quality brews from the bean-filled drawers and tins of tea, which line its walls. The on-site antique roaster is a lovely object. Mon 2–7pm & Tues–Sat 7.30am–7pm.
Crêperie Bretonne 8 rue du Maréchal Foch. Even if you're underwhelmed by the prospect of a crêperie, consider giving this one a chance. The decor alone is worth a visit – you may find yourself eating at an old sewing machine table. Crêpes and gallettes are €3.20–8.90. The *magret de canard* filling is excellent. Mon–Sat noon–2.30pm & 7–11.30pm.
El Serrano 16 rue de la Cloche d'Or. Tiny deli-café on a side street near Musée Rigaud offering excellent plates (€4–7.50) of *manchego*, *jambon* serrano and *pata negra salamanca*, alongside *pichets* of wine (€4) or sangria (€5). Tues–Sun 8am–7pm.
VIP 4 rue Grande des Fabriques. Not easy to find though its quality means that plenty of locals will be able to direct you. Crisp white tablecloths and a strong meat presence on the menu. You won't go wrong with the *plat du jour* (€9.50).

THE CÔTE VERMEILLE

The **Vermilion Coast** (ⓦwww.collioure.com) is named for its richly coloured rocks, which attracted artists such as Picasso, Dalí and Matisse. The latter's 1905–06 paintings of Collioure saw the birth of Fauvism, the forerunner to Cubism. Aside from these colourful rocks, the coast is also home to some lovely beaches and charming fishing towns. Over ten trains a day run between Perpignan and Collioure (25min).

Moving on

Train Barcelona (5 daily; 2hr 50min–5hr); Carcassonne (via Narbonne; 13–16 daily; 1hr 30min–2hr); Montpellier (16–20 daily; 1hr 30min–2hr); Paris (10–16 daily; 5hr–9hr 20min); Toulouse (16 daily; 1hr 30min–2hr).

Provence and the Côte d'Azur

Provence is held by many to be the most irresistible region in France, with attractions that range from the high mountains of the southern Alps to the wild plains of the **Camargue**. Though technically part of the neighbouring region of Languedoc, the old Roman town of **Nîmes** is a good place to start exploring, as is nearby **Arles**, most famous for van Gogh's paintings and a great place to indulge in the area's café

PONT DU GARD

This stunning vestige of the 50km aqueduct built in the first century AD to carry spring water from Uzès to Nîmes is a poignant memorial to the hubris of Roman civilization. It sits peacefully in the valley of the Gardon River, and is a great place to cool off on hot summer days. Tours are run from the informative museum on the left side of the valley; to get there, take a bus from Nîmes to Uzès, where six *navettes* run to the Pont each day; bring a swimsuit, walking shoes and a picnic. Ⓦwww.ot-pontdugard.com.

culture. **Avignon**, home of a wonderful summer festival, is so crammed full of history that it can sometimes feel like a living museum, while just to the north lies Europe's best-preserved Roman theatre, in **Orange**. Most of the region's towns are full of cobbled streets lined with brightly coloured, shuttered buildings, which are a delight to explore, and none more so than **Aix-en-Provence.**

By contrast, **Marseille,** France's second city, still hasn't shaken off its gritty image. Yet it rewards a little exploration and is home to some of the area's finest food. It also makes a good base for exploring the stunning **Calanques**. The Côte d'Azur certainly lives up to its name – taking a train along the coast reveals sparkling turquoise sea, packed in many places with the glitzy yachts of the rich and famous. **Nice** has all the trappings of a jet-set lifestyle, yet it feels a little more down-to-earth than nearby **Cannes**, and makes a great base for exploring small villages in the hills and other seaside towns.

NÎMES

NÎMES is intrinsically linked to two things: ancient Rome – whose influence is manifest in some of the most extensive **Roman remains** in Europe – and denim, a word corrupted from *de Nîmes*. First manufactured as *serge* in the city's textile mills, denim was exported to America to clothe workers, where a certain Mr Levi Strauss made it world famous. These days, the town has a relaxed charm, and with an excellent hostel makes for a good place to relax for a few days.

What to see and do

The old centre of Nîmes spreads northwards from place des Arènes, site of the magnificent first-century **Les Arènes** (daily 9/9.30am–5/6/7pm; €7.80), one of the best-preserved Roman arenas in the world. Turned into a fortress by the Visigoths while the Roman Empire crumbled, the arena went on to became a huge medieval slum before it was fully restored. Now, with a retractable roof, it hosts opera, an international summer jazz festival and bullflights during the high-spirited Ferías on Pentecost and the third weekend of September. Another Roman survivor can be found northeast along boulevard Victor Hugo – the **Maison Carrée** (daily: April–Sept 10am–6.30/7pm; Oct–March 10am–4.30/6pm; €4.50), a compact temple built in 5 AD and celebrated for its harmony of proportion – the entrance price includes a 3-D film about Roman Nîmes.

Arrival and information

Air The airport is 8km to the south, accessible by *navettes* leaving from av Feuchères, in front of the station.

Bus and train Nîmes' bus and train stations are at the end of av Feuchères, just a few minutes' walk southeast from the amphitheatre. Regional buses leave from bays situated out the back.

Internet Nîmes Internet Centre, 4 rue des Greffes; Net@games, 25 rue de l'Horloge.

Tourist office 6 rue Auguste, by the Maison Carrée (Mon–Sat 8.30/9am–6.30/7/8pm, Sun 10am–5/6pm; Ⓣ04.66.58.38.00, Ⓦwww.ot-nimes.fr); buy the monument and museum pass (€9.90) here, which gives access to the town's attractions for three days.

Accommodation

Acanthe du Temple 1 rue Charles Babut ⓣ04.66.67.54.61, ⓦwww.hotel-temple.com. The rooms are basic but it's the service provided by owner Eric (who speaks English) that makes this place the pleasure that it is. Doubles €55.

FUAJ Nîmes 257 chemin de l'Auberge de Jeunesse, Cigale ⓣ04.66.68.03.20, ⓦwww.fuaj.org. Set in a beautiful arboretum, in the hills 2km west of Nîmes, this friendly hostel offers modern two-, four- or six-bed dorms. There's a great bar on site serving cheap drinks, as well as good kitchen facilities and bike rental. Take bus #i (Alès or Villeverte direction) from the station to Stade. Dorms €14.90.

Hotel des Tuileries 22 rue Roussy ⓣ04.66.21.31.15, ⓦwww.hoteldestuileries.com. In an excellent location and run by an English couple who are gradually renovating the somewhat tired decor, this is a solid option. Doubles €66.

Eating and drinking

À la Tchatche 4 rue Saint-Antoine. A wonderful *bistrot à vins* with a young, convivial owner fiercely proud of the local provenance of all his produce, not least his mother's cured duck (€6.50). The *champignons à la brandade* (€4.50) are superb as is the pélardon cheese with herbed honey (€6). Tues noon–2pm & Wed–Sat noon–2pm, plus evening.

Café Latin 29 place de la Maison Carrée. The terrace is a marvellous spot come evening when Maison Carrée is illuminated. The *pichets* of wine are good value.

Fox Tavern 18 rue de l'Horloge. Ironically British, with a photo of the Queen above the bar, this is a fun live music venue and drinking den. Pints €5.

Le Petit Mas corner of rue Fresque and rue de la Madeleine. Generous salads are the thing at this buzzing little spot. The €13.50 midday *formule* of tapas and a *plat du jour* or salad is excellent value – the "Petit Mas" salad features Serrano ham, smoked duck and pélardon cheese atop a mound of greenery.

Wine Bar "Le Cheval Blanc" 1 place des Arènes. With a terrace overlooking the arena this Parisian-brasserie-style place is perfect for a tipple. The €12.50 lunch menu is excellent value. Mon–Sat noon–2pm & 7–11pm/midnight.

Moving on

Train Arles (6 daily; 25min); Avignon (16 daily; 30min); Clermont-Ferrand (3 daily; 5hr); Lyon (9 daily; 1hr 20min); Marseille (14 daily; 50min–1hr 20min); Montpellier (frequent; 30min); Nice (6 daily, via Marseille; 4–5hr); Paris (11 daily; 3hr); Perpignan (13 daily; 2hr 10min–2hr 40min).

ARLES

ARLES is a lovely, relaxed little Provençal town, steeped in Roman history. In 1888, Vincent Van Gogh was drawn in by the picturesque town, where he painted *Starry Night* and *Night Café*, but also got into a drunken argument with Gauguin and cut off the lower part of his left ear. Today, Arles is the centre of French photography as home to the École Nationale de Photographie and host to the summer photographic **festival**, Les Rencontres (July to mid-Sept; ⓦwww.rencontres-arles.com).

What to see and do

The focal point for tourists in Arles is the striking **amphitheatre** (Arènes), at the end of rue Voltaire (daily: April–Sept 9am–7pm; Oct–March 9am–6pm; €6), built at the end of the first century. The surrounding Rond-Point des Arènes is crammed full of touristy shops, cafés and restaurants, and can get very crowded on summer days. No original Van Gogh paintings remain in Arles, but the Fondation Van Gogh – which moved in 2010 from the Palais de Luppé to a temporary space at 17 rue des Suisses before moving again in spring 2012 to a new permanent home at the Hôtel Léautaud de Donines (5 place Honoré Clair) – exhibits works based on his masterpieces by well-known contemporary artists, such as Hockney and Bacon. On place de la République you'll find the **Cathédrale St-Trophime**, whose doorway is one of the most famous examples of twelfth-century Provençal carving, depicting a Last Judgement trumpeted by rather enthusiastic angels.

Cirque Romain

The best insight into Roman Arles is at the **Musée de l'Arles Antique**

(Wed–Mon 10am–6pm; €6), west of the town centre, by the river. The fabulous mosaics, sarcophagi and sculpture illuminate Arles' early history.

Place Constantin

Housed in a splendid medieval building once used by the Knights of the Order of Malta, the **Musée Réattu** (10 rue du Grand Prieuré; Tues–Sun: July–Sept 10am–7pm; Oct–June 10am–12.30pm; €7; Ⓦwww.museereattu.arles.fr) hosts a fine collection of modern art, including sketches and sculptures by Picasso. Opposite are the remains of the fourth-century **Roman baths** (daily: March–April 9am–noon & 2–6pm; May–Sept 9am–noon & 2–7pm; Oct 9am–noon & 2–6pm; Nov–Feb 10am–noon & 2–5pm; €3).

Arrival and information

Train The train station is 5min walk from the amphitheatre on av Paulin.
Tourist office Opposite rue Jean Jaurès on bd des Lices (Jan–March & Nov–Dec Mon–Sat 9am–4.45pm Sun 10am–1pm; Oct Mon–Sat 9am–5.45pm Sun 10am–1pm; April–Sept daily 9am–6.45pm; Ⓣ04.90.18.41.20, Ⓦwww.arlestourisme.com), and provides a hotel booking service. There's also a handy tourist office in the station (April–Sept Mon–Fri daily 9.30am–1.30pm & 2.30–6pm).
Internet Cyber City, 31 rue Voltaire.

Accommodation

De la Muette 15 rue des Suisses Ⓣ04.90.96.15.39, Ⓦwww.hotel-muette.com. A bargain smack bang in the centre of the old town, and recently refurbished, it's all cool greys and browns with bare stone walls. Doubles €58.
Du Musée 11 rue du Grand Prieuré Ⓣ04.90.93.88.88, Ⓦwww.hoteldumusee.com. There's a warm Spanish feel to the decor of this hotel set in a seventeenth-century building. Breakfast on the inner courtyard sets you up perfectly for the day. Check the rooms as some are more spacious than others. Doubles €60.
FUAJ Arles 20 av du Maréchal-Foch Ⓣ04.90.96.18.25, Ⓦwww.fuaj.org. The dorms are somewhat old-fashioned, but clean and airy, and there's a small bar on site. Often gets overrun with noisy school kids, but the location is good – just 5min from the centre of town and 15min walk from the train station. Closed 10am–5pm. Dorms €18.

VAN GOGH'S ARLES

The tourist office (see below) issues a good booklet of themed **walking tours** in Arles (€1). The best of these is the Van Gogh trail which, by following various markers on the pavements, takes you to the sites of his most famous paintings – it's fascinating to see how the town has changed since he was here.

Eating and drinking

Bar le Baroque 4 bd Georges Clemenceau. Sink into one of the cosy armchairs in this modern café, which serves three variations of lasagne (salmon and spinach; aubergine; bolognese; €9).
Chez Néné et Bébé 12 impasses du Forum. Tucked away off busy place du Forum, with a friendly, chatty owner and a constant stream of locals popping in for a drink. The pizzas (all €10) are excellent and drinks are very reasonably priced (*pastis* €2, wine €2) – a great place to finish the day.
Cuisine de Comptoir 10 rue Liberté. A simple but smart place serving up excellent tartines on fine *poilâne* bread. It's no sandwich bar, though – served with soup (often gazpacho) and salad they're worth savouring with a glass of wine. €10–15. Mon 10am–midnight & Tues–Sat 8.30am–midnight.
L'Entrevue 23 Quai Marx Dormoy. A Moroccan restaurant on the riverbank with an attached hammam – a session in the latter followed by a plate of couscous is an unusual but delightful combination (€28). Mon–Sat 9.30am–midnight & Sun 9.30am–5pm.

Moving on

Train Avignon (11–16 daily; 20min–1hr); Lyon (7–9 daily; 2hr 20min–2hr 55min); Marseille (15–20 daily; 45min–1hr); Montpellier (15–20 daily; 55min); Nîmes (8–11 daily; 25min).

THE CAMARGUE

The flat, marshy delta immediately south of Arles – **the Camargue** – is a beautiful area, used as a breeding-ground for the bulls that participate in local *corridas*

Le Calendal Hotel 5 rue Porte de Laure (Ⓣ04.90.96.11.89, Ⓦwww.lecalendal.com; doubles €119). Mere steps from the amphitheatre, this sunny hotel is a great choice if you feel like splashing out. Rooms are bright and decorated in traditional Provençal colours without being twee; all are en suite, with air conditioning and satellite television. The real selling point is the gorgeous garden at the back. Prices occasionally include use of the Roman baths-inspired spa – check ahead.

(bullfights), and the white horses ridden by their herdsmen. The wildlife of the area also includes flamingos, marshbirds and sea birds, and a rich flora of reeds, wild flowers and juniper trees. The only town is **SAINTES-MARIES-DE-LA-MER**, best known for the annual Gypsy Festival held each May, and which is linked by a regular bus service to Arles (5–7 daily from bd Georges Clemenceau; 1hr; €2.60). It's a pleasant, if touristy place, with some fine sandy beaches. If you're interested in birdwatching or touring the lagoons, your first port of call should be the **tourist office** on 5 av Van Gogh (daily: July & Aug 9am–8pm; Sept–June 9am–5/7pm; Ⓣ04.90.97.82.55, Ⓦwww.saintesmaries.com), which can tell you where to rent bicycles, horses or 4x4s, if you prefer to explore the delta alone.

AVIGNON

AVIGNON, great city of the popes and for centuries one of the major artistic centres of France, is today one of the country's biggest tourist attractions and is always crowded in summer. It's worth putting up with the inevitable queues and camera-wielding hordes to enjoy the unique stock of monuments, churches and museums of this immaculately preserved medieval town. During the **Avignon festival** in July, it's the only place to be – around 200,000 spectators come here for the show, though, so doing any normal sightseeing becomes virtually impossible.

What to see and do

Central Avignon is enclosed by thick medieval walls, built by one of the nine popes who based themselves here in the fourteenth century, away from the anarchic feuding and rival popes of Rome. Place de l'Horloge is lined with cafés and market stalls on summer evenings, beyond which towers the enormous **Palais des Papes** (daily: March–June 9.30am–7pm; July & Aug 9am–8/9pm; Sept & Oct 9am–7pm; Nov–Feb 9.30am–5.45pm; €10.50, joint ticket with Pont St-Bénézet €15). Save your money though: the denuded interior gives little indication of the richness of the papal court, although the building is impressive for sheer size alone. The nearby **Musée du Petit Palais** (daily except Tues 9.30/10am–1pm & 2–5.30/6pm; €6) houses a collection of religious art from the thirteenth to sixteenth centuries. Jutting out halfway across the river is the famous **Pont St-Bénézet** (also known as Pont d'Avignon; same hours as Palais des Papes; €5.50). The struggle to keep the bridge in good repair against the ravages of the Rhône was finally abandoned in 1660, three and a half centuries after it was built, and today just four of the original 22 arches survive.

Arrival and information

Train Avignon's main train station is opposite the porte de la République on bd St-Roch, just 5min from the central place de l'Horloge. A regular shuttle bus runs to the separate TGV station, 3km to the southeast, from just inside porte de la République (2–4 hourly; 13min; €1.20).
Tourist office 41 cours Jean-Jaurès (April–Oct Mon–Sat 9am–6pm, Sun 10am–5pm; Nov–March Mon–Fri 9am–6pm, Sat 9am–5pm, Sun 10am–noon; Ⓣ04.32.74.32.74, Ⓦwww.avignon-tourisme.com); accommodation booking service and English-language tours.

Internet Cybert Média at 22 rue Portail Matheron. Daily 9.30am–11pm (Aug 10am–9pm).

Accommodation

Bagatelle 25 allée Antoine-Pinay ⓣ04.90.86.30.39, ⓦwww.campingbagatelle.com. Well located on Île de la Barthelasse, just 20min walk from the station, this is the nearest campsite to town. It also has a busy hostel with clean but small dorms and a handful of private rooms. There's a bar and restaurant on site, but they have the feel of a rather old-fashioned holiday camp. Camping €18; dorms €18.

Le Splendid 17 rue Agricol Perdiguier ⓣ04.90.86.14.46, ⓦwww.avignon-splendid-hotel.com. One of several hotels on this pretty side street at the heart of the old town but the staff's friendliness sets *Le Splendid* apart. Doubles €59.

Médiéval 15 rue Petite-Saunerie ⓣ04.90.86.11.06, ⓦwww.hotelmedieval.com. A former aristocratic townhouse with a grand staircase. Though the bedroom decor is a little tired, it's all kept very clean and the studios are particularly good value for longer stays. Doubles €66.

Mignon 12 rue Joseph Vernet ⓣ04.90.82.17.30, ⓦwww.hotel-mignon.com. This little hotel has rooms decked out in Provençal colours, all with satellite TV, a/c and wi-fi. Breakfast is included in the price and can be enjoyed in your room for no extra charge. Doubles €64.

Monclar 13–15 av Monclar ⓣ04.90.86.20.14, ⓦwww.hotel-monclar.com. An attractive eighteenth-century house with a pleasant garden, situated outside the town walls, close to the train station. Rooms are clean and bright and there is free internet access. Doubles €60.

Eating

Au Tout Petit 4 rue d'Amphoux ⓣ04.90.82.38.86. This gem of a restaurant is so small that the chef is also the waiter. The truly creative fusion cuisine includes such options as duck tartare with sesame, *za'atar* and curry and a cold Mexican-style soup with pepper sorbet. Two-course lunch menu €11, two-course dinner €16. Tues–Sat afternoon and evening.

Crêperie du Cloître 9 place du Cloître Saint-Pierre. Tucked away in a peaceful square behind St-Pierre, this is a lovely spot to enjoy generously filled sweet and savoury crêpes (from €6).

Ginette & Marcel 25 place des Corps Saints. Famed for their *tartines*, charming location on a pretty *place* and grocery-style interior decor. The three-cheese-and-pear *tartine* (€6.20) is particularly delicious. Daily from 11am.

AVIGNON FESTIVAL

During Avignon's three-week July **festival** (ⓣ04.90.27.66.50, ⓦwww.festival-avignon.com), over one hundred venues show multiple plays every day, alongside opera, classical music and film. The most popular aspect of the festival is probably the **street performers** – musicians, magicians, dancers, jugglers, clowns, artists and mime acts – who bring great colour and noise to the city. Make sure you book your hotel early.

Mamma Corsica 35 rue Saint Jean le Vieux. A truly atmospheric place, its ceiling hung with fishing paraphernalia and a chef who occasionally comes out at the end of service to sing Corsican songs. A two-course menu is €18 with dishes featuring Corsican flavours such as brocciu cheese and wild boar. Mon–Fri from 7.30pm; Sat & Sun from noon.

Drinking and nightlife

AOC Cave & Bar à vins 5 rue Trémoulet. The friendly staff will guide you through the selection of over 150 wines, much of which is the local Côtes du Rhône. Prices start from €2.50 a glass. Tues–Fri noon–2pm & 6pm–1am, Sat 6pm–1am.

Pub Z 58 rue Bonneterie. Owned by a zebra-loving rocker, the animal's print is everywhere in this frequently rowdy bar with an eclectic clientele and good (alternative) music on the stereo. Daily until 1.30am.

Redzone 25 rue Carnot. Popular club, with a good range of themed nights, from salsa to electro and hip-hop. Open till 3am; free entry.

Moving on

Gare SNCF Arles (frequent; 20–40min); Lyon (10 daily; 2hr 20min); Nîmes (15 daily; 20–40min); Toulouse (11 daily, 8 via Nîmes or Montpellier; 3hr 10min–4hr 30min).

Gare TGV Lyon (2 hourly; 1hr 5min–1hr 30min); Nice (12 daily; 3hr–4hr 10min); Paris (15 daily; 2hr 40min–3hr 30min).

AIX-EN-PROVENCE

For many visitors, **AIX-EN-PROVENCE** is the ideal Provençal

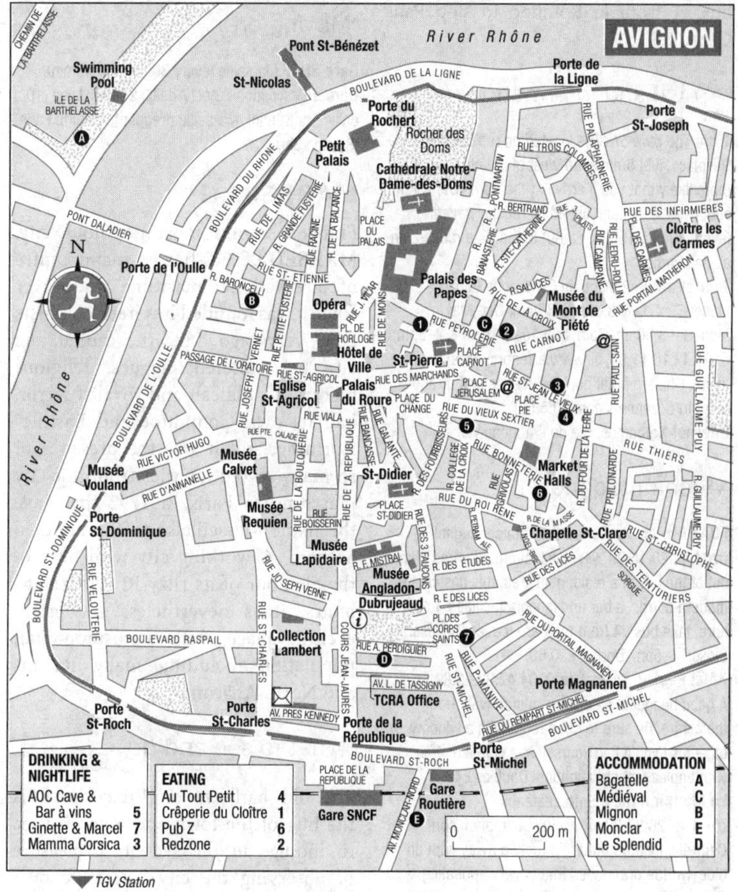

city, the cobbled streets of its old town still retaining the romance of days past, especially when lit by the sun. The city has a (not entirely unfair) reputation for snobbishness, but it is still a relaxed and enjoyable place, where the greatest pleasure is in winding through the streets and relaxing in a shady place over a *pastis*.

What to see and do

Aix's old town stretches back from the leafy expanse of cours Mirabeau, and it's easy to spend a few hours just exploring the atmospheric streets, which are dotted with interesting shops and cafés. The only museum worth heading to is the **Musée Granet** (daily 11am/noon–6/7pm; €6), whose permanent collection includes some minor works by the town's most famous painter, Paul Cézanne, and a number of archeological finds from the region; it's the interesting and often inventive temporary exhibitions, however, that make a visit worthwhile. To find out more about Cézanne, you can visit the **Atelier Cézanne** (daily: July & Aug 10am–6pm; Sept–June 10am–noon & 2–5/6pm; €5.50), his studio, which looks exactly the same as it did at the time of his death. To get there, catch bus #1 from la Rotondo to stop Paul Cézanne.

Arrival and information

Train The *gare SNCF* is located on rue Gustavo-Desplace, just 5min southwest of the old town. It's more likely that you'll arrive at the *gare TGV*, 13km southwest of Aix and linked by regular *navette* (every 20min; 15min; €3.80) to the *gare routière* on av de l'Europe.
Tourist office 2 place du Général de Gaulle (June–Sept daily 8.30am–8/9pm; Oct–May Mon–Sat 8.30am–7pm, Sun 10am–1pm & 2–6pm; ⓣ04.42.16.11.61, ⓦwww.aixenprovencetourism.com). Offers a hotel booking service and arranges tours to Cézanne's home (€5.50).
Internet Netgames, rue de l'Aumone Vielle.

Accommodation

FUAJ Aix-en-Provence 3 av Marcel Pagnol ⓣ04.42.20.15.99, ⓦwww.fuaj.org. Situated 2km out of the city in a residential area, this hostel offers modern dorms, a bar and laundry facilities. To get here, take bus #4 from the *gare routière* to Vasarely. Closed 1–5pm. Dorms €20.60.
Hôtel Paul 10 av Pasteur ⓣ04.42.23.23.89. A good budget choice a ten-minute walk from the centre. Be sure to get a room with a window otherwise you'll find yourself in a cell-like affair with unpleasant strip lighting. Doubles €48.
Le Manoir 8 rue d'Entrecasteaux ⓣ04.42.26.27.20, ⓦwww.hotelmanoir.com. Centrally located but feels tucked away with an olde-worlde grandness that is very appealing, even if the rooms have a slight fustiness and certain of the staff are very far from friendly. Breakfast is served in the fourteenth-century cloister. Doubles €67.

Eating and drinking

Bar Brigand Place Richelme (Place des Sangliers). A satisfyingly grungy little pub so beloved of the town's hipsters they spill out onto the pavement across the street. Daily from 9am (Sun from 2pm).
La Brûlerie Place Richelme. It's not as easy as you'd think to get good coffee in France, but they serve the good stuff here, plus it's cheap.
La Calèche 10 rue de la Masse. The menu is wide-ranging but really it's all about the excellent pizza here, with bases singed just so in the wood-fired oven. Daily noon–3pm & 7pm–midnight.

Moving on

Gare SNCF Marseille (every 30min; 30–45min).
Gare TGV Avignon TGV (17 daily; 20min); Lyon (10 daily; 1hr 30min); Marseille (frequent; 15min); Paris (8 daily; 3hr).

MARSEILLE

France's second most populous city, **MARSEILLE** has been a major centre of international maritime trade ever since it was founded by Greek colonists 2600 years ago. Like the capital, the city has suffered plagues, religious bigotry, republican and royalist terror, had its own Commune and Bastille-storming, and it was the presence of so many revolutionaries from this city marching to Paris in 1792 that gave the name Marseillaise to the national anthem. A working city with little of the glamour of its ritzy Riviera neighbours, it is nevertheless a vibrant, exciting place, with a cosmopolitan population including many Italians and North Africans.

What to see and do

The old harbour, or **Vieux Port**, is the hub of the town and a good place to indulge in the sedentary pleasure of observing the city's streetlife over a *pastis*. Two fortresses guard the entrance to the harbour and the town extends outwards alongside the harbour from its three quais.

Le Panier

On the northern side of the harbour is the original site and former old town of Marseille, known as **Le Panier**. During the occupation, large sections were dynamited by the Nazis to prevent resistance members hiding in the small, densely populated streets, which in turn prompted a mass deportation of residents from the northern docks. Rebuilt and repopulated in the 1950s, today's Le Panier is full of a young, fashionable and bohemian working class. The quarter's main attraction is La Vieille Charité, a Baroque seventeenth-century church and hospice complex, on rue de la Charité, now home to several museums, including the **Musée d'Archéologie Méditerranéenne** (Tues–Sun 10/11am–5/6pm; €3), housing a superb collection of Egyptian mummified animals.

La Canebière

Leading east from the Vieux Port is La Canebière, Marseille's main street. Just off the lower end, in the Centre Bourse shopping mall, is a museum of finds from Roman Marseille, the **Musée d'Histoire de Marseille** (closed until end 2012; €3), which includes the well-preserved remains of a third-century Roman merchant vessel. South of La Canebière are Marseille's main shopping streets, rue Paradis, rue St-Ferréol and rue de Rome, and the **Musée Cantini**, 19 rue Grignan (Tues–Sun 10/11am–5/6pm; €3), which houses a fine collection of twentieth-century art with works by Dufy, Léger and Picasso.

South of the Vieux Port

The **Abbaye St-Victor** (daily 8.30am–6.30pm) is the city's oldest church. It looks and feels like a fortress – the walls of the choir are almost 3m thick. Dominating the skyline to the south, astride a rocky hill, is the marble and porphyry basilica of Marseille's most famous landmark, the cathedral of **Notre-Dame de la Garde** (daily 7am–7/8pm). Crowning the high belfry, and visible across most of the city is a 9m gilded statue of the Virgin Mary, known locally as the *Bonne Mère* (Good Mother). Inside are beautiful mosaics and shrines covered in ex-votos – trinkets, plaques, paintings and, more recently, football shirts – offered to the Saints for good luck.

Chateau d'If, les Calanques and the beach

A twenty-minute boat ride takes you to the **Château d'If** (daily 9.30am–5.30/6.30pm; Oct–March closed Mon; €5), the notorious island fortress that figured in Dumas' great adventure story, *The Count of Monte Cristo*. In reality, no one ever escaped, and most prisoners, incarcerated for political or religious reasons, ended their days here. Boats (€10 return; Ⓦwww.frioul-if-express.com) leave hourly for the island from the Quai des Belges.

Twenty minutes southeast of Marseille (bus #21), **Les Calanques**, beautiful rocky inlets carved from white limestone, provide fine bathing, diving and walking – note that smoking and fires are prohibited during summer because of the fire risk. To reach the **plage du Prado**, Marseille's main sand beach, take bus #83 or #19 to the Promenade Pompidou (20min).

Arrival and information

Air Marseille Airport is 25km away, connected by shuttle buses to the train station (every 20min; €8.50).
Train Gare St-Charles is a 15min walk from the city centre.
Public transport Buses and the métro cover the city: *solos* (singles) €1.50, *cartes journées* (day passes) €5 from métro stations and on buses. The bus station is on place Victor Hugo.
Tourist office 4 La Canebière (Mon–Sat 9am–7pm, Sun 10am–5pm; Ⓣ08.26.50.05.00, Ⓦwww.marseille-tourisme.com). Free accommodation booking service (Ⓦwww.resamarseille.com).
Internet Alpha.net at 22 rue Coutellerie. Daily 7.30am–midnight.

Accommodation

FUAJ Bonneveine impasse Dr Bonfils, off av Joseph Vidal Ⓣ04.91.17.63.30, Ⓦwww.fuaj.org. Five kilometres from the city, but in a fantastic location near Les Calanques and just 200m from the beach, this is a fun hostel, with clean dorms of between two and six beds. Tours, sea kayaking, bike rental and horseriding can be arranged, and there's a bar on site. Take bus #44 to the Bonnefon stop. Dorms €20.

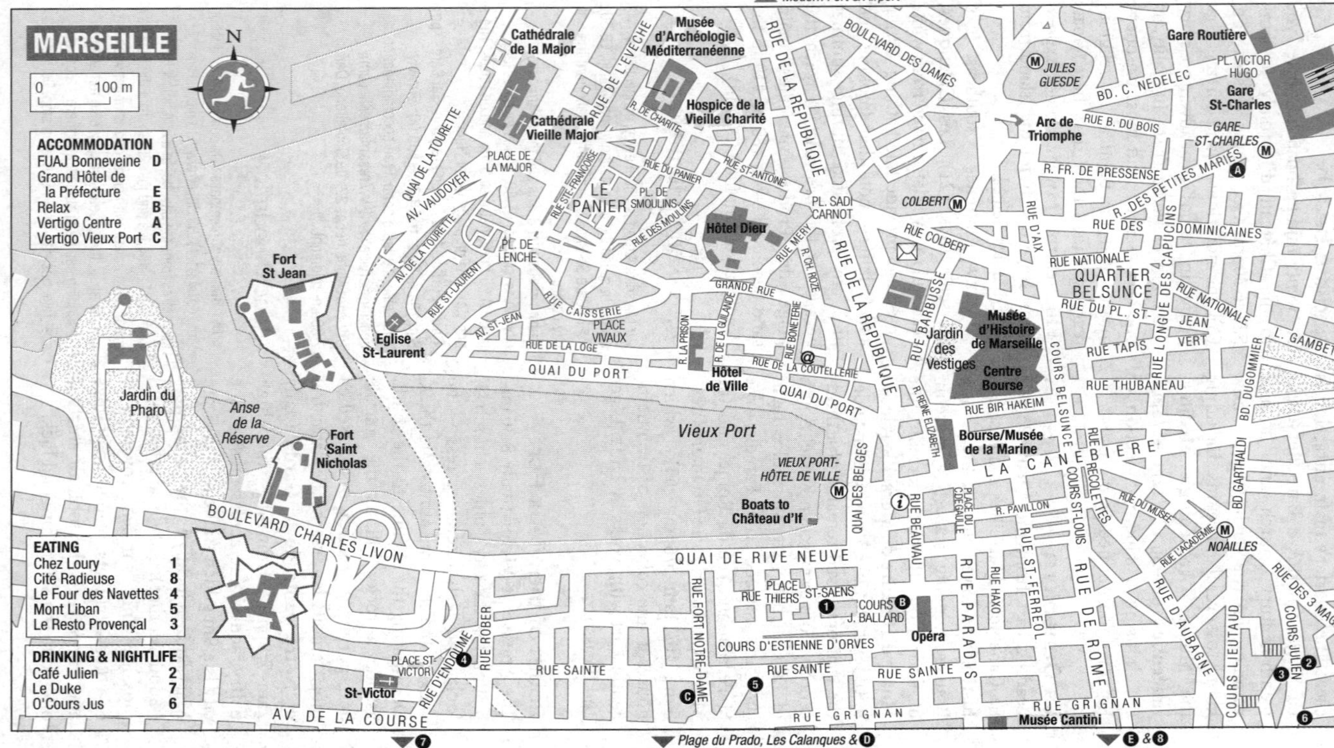
MARSEILLE
0 100 m
N
ACCOMMODATION
FUAJ Bonneveine D
Grand Hôtel de la Préfecture E
Relax B
Vertigo Centre A
Vertigo Vieux Port C
EATING
Chez Loury 1
Cité Radieuse 8
Le Four des Navettes 4
Mont Liban 5
Le Resto Provençal 3
DRINKING & NIGHTLIFE
Café Julien 2
Le Duke 7
O'Cours Jus 6
Modern Port & Airport
Plage du Prado, Les Calanques & D
E & 8
7
Cathédrale de la Major
Cathédrale Vieille Major
Musée d'Archéologie Méditerranéenne
Hospice de la Vieille Charité
Hôtel Dieu
LE PANIER
Fort St Jean
Eglise St-Laurent
Jardin du Pharo
Anse de la Réserve
Fort Saint Nicholas
Vieux Port
Boats to Château d'If
VIEUX PORT-HÔTEL DE VILLE
Hôtel de Ville
Jardin des Vestiges
Musée d'Histoire de Marseille
Centre Bourse
Bourse/Musée de la Marine
QUARTIER BELSUNCE
Arc de Triomphe
Gare Routière
Gare St-Charles
GARE ST-CHARLES
JULES GUESDE
COLBERT
NOAILLES
Opéra
Musée Cantini
St-Victor
BOULEVARD CHARLES LIVON
QUAI DE RIVE NEUVE
QUAI DU PORT
RUE DE LA REPUBLIQUE
LA CANEBIERE
RUE PARADIS
RUE DE ROME
RUE ST-FERREOL
RUE SAINTE
RUE GRIGNAN
AV. DE LA COURSE
COURS JULIEN
COURS LIEUTAUD
RUE D'AUBAGNE
BOULEVARD DES DAMES
COURS BELSUNCE
QUAI DES BELGES
COURS D'ESTIENNE D'ORVES
RUE FORT NOTRE-DAME

Grand Hôtel de la Préfecture 9 bv Louis Salvator ⓣ04.91.33.99.81, ⓦwww.hoteldelaprefecture.fr. A once-grand place with a rich history now providing bargain rooms just minutes from the Vieux Port. Doubles €45.

Relax 4 rue Corneille ⓣ04.91.33.15.87, ⓦwww.hotelrelax.fr. A big hotel in a great spot overlooking the grand place and just 100m from Vieux Port. The rooms are fine, though mostly small, while the reception doubles as the owners' living room. Doubles €60.

Vertigo Centre 42 rue Petits Mariés ⓣ04.91.91.07.11, ⓦwww.hotelvertigo.fr. Mere steps from the train station, this excellent hostel has bright, spacious dorms, all en suite, as well as a number of private rooms – the "deluxe" have private balconies. Staff are friendly and helpful, and there's a good kitchen, garden and a cheap bar. Dorms €25, doubles €60.

Vertigo Vieux Port 38 rue Fort Notre Dame ⓣ04.91.54.42.95, ⓦwww.hotelvertigo.fr. A marvellous hostel spread across two former warehouses, each with quality modern art (all local commissions) on display. The communal spaces are very well conceived, the dorms are airy and breakfast is included.

Eating

Chez Loury 3 rue Fortia. There's cheaper bouillabaisse in the city, but this place offers a good compromise between cost and quality. The €28 menu includes an aperitif of *kir*, the famous soup with authentic weever, tub gurnard and eel, followed by dessert.

Cité Radieuse 280 bd Michelet. Head to the third floor of Le Corbusier's magnificent apartment building (see box below) and have a drink on the terrace of the retro-futuristic café.

Le Four des Navettes 136 rue Sainte. A beautiful old bakery – their famous, orange-flavoured *navette* biscuits are a must for a Marseille picnic. Daily from 7am (Sun from 9am).

Le Resto Provençal 64 Cours Julien ⓣ04.91.48.85.12. The cooking is traditionally Provençal, the edgy Cours Julien setting is decidedly not, which makes for a satisfying overall experience. The meat dishes are especially good – try the *pieds-paquets* when available. Menus at lunchtime (€13) and evening (€24). Wed noon–2pm, Tues, Thurs, Fri noon–2pm & 7.30–10.30pm, Sat 7.30–10.30pm; closed Sept.

Mont Liban 63 rue Sainte. This little hole in the wall serves Lebanese flavoured *chaussons* (with cheese or spinach), which are cheap and delicious. Should you wish to eat in, there's a funny little sitting area cluttered with the family's domestic odds and ends.

LE CORBUSIER

If you're interested in architecture, it's definitely worth taking the short bus journey out to Le Corbusier's **La Cité Radieuse**. Completed in 1952, this seventeen-storey block of flats is surprisingly striking even today, and you can take the lift up to the rooftop to enjoy fantastic views of the city and the surrounding area. To get here, take bus #21 from Centre Bourse to Le Corbusier.

Drinking and nightlife

Café Julien 39 Cours Julien. A popular bar at the town's best music venue, orientated towards reggae, world music and hip-hop.

Le Duke 59 rue d'Endoume. A hipster bar with bright colours, crisp graphics and a few nods to the 1950s – nab the old Chesterfield sofa and order a bottle of wine (€16). Tues–Sat 6pm–midnight.

O'Cours Jus 67 Cours Julien. This tiny place's terrace is the perfect spot to take in the atmosphere of Cours Julien, a place that manages to feel both cool and friendly at once.

Moving on

Train Arles (frequent; 40min–1hr); Avignon (12–15 daily; 1hr 10min); Cannes (15 daily; 2hr); Lyon (8–12 daily; 1hr 40–3hr 30min); Montpellier (18–23 daily; 1hr 30min–3hr); Nice (15 daily; 2hr 20min–2hr 45min).

Ferry Ajaccio (10 weekly; 10–12hr); Bastia (10 weekly; 10–12hr).

CANNES

Fishing village turned millionaires' playground, **CANNES** is best known for the International Film Festival, held in May, during which time it is overrun by the denizens of Movieland, their hangers-on, and a small army of paparazzi. The seafront promenade, **La Croisette**, and the Vieux Port form the focus of Cannes' eye-candy life, while the old town, **Le Suquet**, on the steep hill overlooking the bay from the west, with its quaint winding streets and eleventh-century castle, is a pleasant place to wander.

Arrival and information

Train The station is on rue Jean-Jaurès, a short walk north of the centre.
Tourist office The main office is in the Palais des Festivals on the waterfront (daily 9/10am–7/8pm; ⓣ04.92.99.84.00, ⓦwww.cannes.travel). There is also a booth at the station (Mon–Sat 9am–1pm & 2–6pm).
Internet Dre@m, 6 rue du Commandant Vidal.

Accommodation

Albe 31 rue du Bivouac Napoléon ⓣ04.97.06.21.21, ⓦwww.albe-hotel.fr. A good-value two-star with bright and clean rooms with a/c, just one street from the Palais and the beach. Doubles €65.
Cybelle 14 rue du 24 août ⓣ04.93.38.31.33, ⓦwww.hotelcybelle.fr. Excellent value considering the location and the price-hiking reputation of this town. The decor is by no means chic but rooms feel clean and crisp. Doubles €68.
Parc Bellevue 67 av Maurice Chevalier ⓣ04.93.47.28.97, ⓦwww.parcbellevue.com. The nearest campsite is in the suburb of La Bocca, 3km to the west of Cannes; most plots are shaded and there is a 40m pool. Take bus #2 from the train station. Dorms €17.
PLM 3 rue Hoche ⓣ04.93.38.31.19, ⓦwww.hotel-cannes-plm.com. A comfortable little hotel in a good location close to the station and a short walk from the beachfront. Rooms are decorated in soothing, neutral colours and there's free wi-fi. Doubles €85.

Eating and drinking

Café Lalu 32 rue du Commandant André. A lovely little place for an early evening *apéro* after a stroll along La Croisette. Daily 11am–9pm.
La Crêperie 66 rue Meynadier. Cheerful little crêperie with a good-value menu that is served all day (a savoury and a sweet crêpe, plus a glass of cider or wine; €11).
Le Bistrot Gourmand 10 rue Docteur Pierre Gazagnaire. A couple of minutes northwest of the marina, this place offers film-star food on a budget – truffle-infused dishes are one of their hallmarks. *Formules* €15–30. Tues–Sat lunch and dinner, Sun lunch only.
Lemonot 12 rue Hélène Vagliano. A few minutes southeast of the train station, fabulously fresh ingredients and excellent Lebanese meze. *Formules* €10–19. Tues–Sat.
Morrison's Irish Pub 10 rue Teisseire. As is frequently the case in France, the most popular bar in town is Irish, and this down-to-earth place makes a pleasant change from Cannes' A-list ambience. Gigs are held here, too. It can get a little too rowdy when live sports are televised. Mon–Sun 5pm–2.30am.
Zanzibar 85 rue Félix-Faure. One of the oldest gay bars in France, this wood-panelled spot is fun and also hetero-friendly.

Moving on

Train Marseille (frequent; 2hr); Monaco (frequent; 1hr–1hr 10min); Nice (frequent; 25–35min).

NICE

NICE, capital of the French Riviera and France's fifth-largest city, grew into a major tourist resort in the nineteenth century, when large numbers of foreign visitors – many of them British – were drawn here by the mild Mediterranean climate. The most obvious legacy of these early holidaymakers is the famous **promenade des Anglais** stretching along the pebble beach, which was laid out by nineteenth-century English residents to facilitate their afternoon stroll by the sea. These days, Nice is a busy, bustling city, but it's still a lovely place, with a beautiful location and attractive historical centre.

What to see and do

Vieux Nice and La Plage

The old town, a rambling collection of narrow alleys lined with tall, rust-and-ochre houses, centres on place Rossetti and the Baroque **Cathédrale Ste-Réparate**. It's worth making the nearby Parc du Château one of your first stops to take in the view, which stretches across the town and west over the bay. It's a steep walk up, or there's a lift, tucked just under the stairs (free) on the western side. A short walk north through the old town takes you to the promenade des Arts, where the **Musée d'Art Moderne et d'Art Contemporain** (daily except Mon 10am– 6pm; free) has

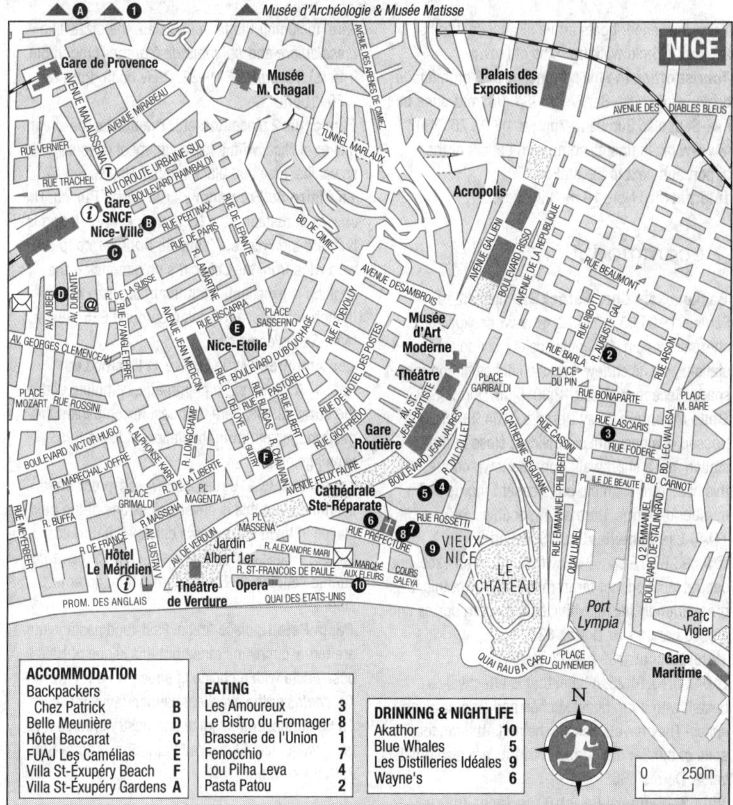

a collection of Pop Art and neo-Realist work, including pieces by Andy Warhol and Roy Lichtenstein.

Cimiez

Up above the city centre is Cimiez, a posh suburb that was the social centre of the town's elite some seventeen centuries ago, when the city was capital of the Roman province of Alpes-Maritimae. To get here, take bus #15 from in front of the train station. The **Musée d'Archéologie**, 160 av des Arènes (daily except Tues 10am–6pm; free) houses excavations of the Roman baths, along with accompanying archeological finds. Overlooking the museum is the wonderful **Musée Matisse** (daily except Tues 10am–6pm; free): Nice was the artist's home for much of his life and the collection covers every period. Nearby, the beautiful **Musée Chagall**, 16 av du Docteur Ménard (daily except Tues 10am–5/6pm; €7.50–9.50), exhibits dazzlingly colourful biblical paintings, stained glass and book illustrations.

Arrival, information and city transport

Air Nice airport is 6km southwest of the city, connected to the train station by bus #23 (every 30min; daily 6am–9pm; €1).

Train The main train station, Nice-Ville, is a 10min walk northwest from the centre, on av Thiers.

Bus and tram Single tickets for both cost €1, and one-day tickets (€4) are also available.

Ferry Passenger boats arrive at quai de l'Amiral Infernet, a 5min walk from the old town.
Tourist office The main branch is at 5 promenade des Anglais (Mon–Sat 8/9am–6/8pm; mid-June to mid-Sept also Sun 9am–7pm; ⓣ08.92.70.74.07, ⓦwww.nicetourisme.com), with outlets at the airport and next to the station.
Internet Nice Nett, 19 rue Paganini.

Accommodation

Backpackers Chez Patrick First floor, 32 rue Pertinax ⓣ04.93.80.30.72, ⓦwww.backpackers chezpatrick.com. A friendly hostel close to the station, with no curfew. Lacks a kitchen or communal space. Reception closed 12.30–5pm. Dorms €28.
Belle Meunière 21 av Durante ⓣ04.93.88.66.15. Housed in a beautiful old building close to the station and a short walk from the town centre, this hotel offers simple but pleasant rooms and a number of dorms. Dorms €17, doubles €49.
FUAJ Les Camélias 3 rue Spitalieri ⓣ04.93.62.15.54, ⓦwww.fuaj.org. In an excellent, central location, not far from the old town, this is a great, friendly hostel with clean, modern dorms and a good bar on site. Dorms €25.
Hôtel Baccarat 39 rue d'Angleterre ⓣ04.93.16.14.25. A hotel that is effectively a hostel, with dorm beds, kitchen and a communal space. They have a flexible, helpful attitude, too, in spite of the 3–6am curfew. Privates are also good value. Dorms €35.
Villa St-Éxupéry Beach 6 rue Sacha Guitry ⓣ04.93.16.13.45, ⓦwww.villahostels.com. Another excellent hostel from the people behind the *Gardens* venue (below). This one doesn't have quite the same buzz or charm as the other, though its location can't be beat. Tram stop "Massena". Dorms €30.
Villa St-Éxupéry Gardens 22 av Gravier ⓣ04.93.84.42.83, ⓦwww.villahostels .com. Housed in a beautiful old monastery above town, this is a real party hostel, and deservedly popular. Most dorms are en suite and a few have terraces with views over the city. The bar, housed in the old chapel, serves beer and wine for €1 and is packed every night, and there's also free internet, cheap dinners, and an excellent breakfast spread (included). Take the tram from the station towards Las Planas and get off at "Comte de Falicon". Dorms €30.

Eating

Brasserie de l'Union 1 rue Michelet. It's a bit of a schlep but there's true Niçois cuisine on offer here, including the famous salad, the pizza-like *pissaladière* and *beignets de légumes* (vegetable fritters). *Formules* €11–22. Daily noon–2pm & 7.30–10pm.
Fenocchio 2 place Rossetti. The master ice-cream maker of Nice, with a huge variety of flavours, such as vanilla, rose and black pepper. One scoop €2.
Le Bistro du Fromager 29 rue Benoît Bunico. The cheesiest restaurant in Nice, their every offering is built around France's fantastic *fromage*, coupled with wine from the cellar. It's no gimmick – the cooking is excellent, and the atmosphere buzzy, though you'll have to bank on around €25/person. Mon–Sat, evening only.
Les Amoureux 7 rue Fodéré. Is this Nice or Napoli? A site of pizza pilgrimage, complete with the buzzy atmosphere that best accompanies this gastronomic gift from the Italians. Closed Sun; evenings only.
Lou Pilha Leva 10 rue Collet. A self-proclaimed institution, but this is nevertheless one of the best places in town to try *socca* chickpea flatbreads (€2.50) – classic Nice fast food – and *petits farcis* stuffed vegetables. Daily 10am–10pm (later in summer).
Pasta Patou 2 place Arson. Fast-food pasta joints are ten-a-penny in France but this is one of Nice's best. Pasta with a choice of sauce is €6 (€7 for *fiocchettis* or the excellent salmon ravioli). The €3.50 coffee, orange juice and pastry breakfast is good value, too. Mon–Wed 8am–5pm, Thurs–Sat 7.30am–9.30pm.

Drinking and nightlife

Akathor 32 cours Saleya. The fifty different European beers attract both locals and tourists in their droves. Regular live music; pint €4–6.
Blue Whales 1 rue Mascoïnat. A relaxed place, with a long happy hour, from 5.30–9.30pm, and live music throughout the week from DJs or bands.
Les Distilleries Idéales 40 rue de la Préfecture. A good place for a pint and a catch-up. With a fine terrasse, its corner location lends itself to a little people watching, too.
Wayne's 15 rue de la Préfecture. Live music every night at this bar, which heaves with backpackers. Some may well find it a little much – dancing on the table is a nightly ritual. Daily 2.30pm–12.30am, happy hour 7–9pm Mon–Fri.

Moving on

Train Avignon TGV (10 daily; 2hr 50min–3hr 35min); Genoa (7 daily via Ventimiglia; 3–4hr

30min); Lyon (hourly, some via Marseille; 4hr 15min–5hr 15min); Marseille (16 daily; 2hr 30min); Milan (7 daily via Ventimiglia; 4hr 50min–6hr 10min); Monaco (frequent; 15min); Paris (14 daily; 5hr 45min–6hr 25min).

MONACO

The tiny independent principality of **MONACO** rears up over the rocky Riviera coast like a Mediterranean Hong Kong. The three-kilometre-long state consists of the old town of Monaco-Ville; Fontvieille; La Condamine by the harbour; Larvotto, with its artificial beaches of imported sand; and, in the middle, **MONTE CARLO**. There are relatively few conventional sights – indeed, Monaco seems composed of little other than roads, fast cars and apartment blocks – but one worth heading to is the superb (though expensive) **Musée Océanographique** on avenue St-Martin (daily 9.30/10am–6/7/7.30pm; €14), which displays a living coral reef, transplanted from the Red Sea into a 40,000-litre tank. If you want to try your luck at the famous **casino** (over-18s only; open from 2pm daily), you'll have to dress smartly – no shorts or T-shirts – and show your passport.

Arrival and information

Train Monaco train station is underground, reached from av Prince-Pierre. Bus #4 (direction Larvotto) takes you from the train station to the Casino-Tourism stop, near the tourist office.
Bus The bus station is on place d'Armes.
Tourist office 2a bd des Moulins (Mon–Sat 9am–7pm, Sun 10am–noon; Ⓣ92.16.61.16, Ⓦwww.monaco-tourisme.com).

Accommodation

Hôtel de France 6 rue de la Turbie Ⓣ03.77.93.30 24.64, Ⓦwww.monte-carlo.mc/france. Comfortable and clean, this is as cheap as they get for a double room in the centre, though planned improvement works may push prices up. Doubles €116.
RIJ Villa Thalassa Ⓣ04.93.78.18.58, Ⓦwww.clajsud.fr. This clean and welcoming hostel is a great choice and just 2km away from Monte Carlo along the coast near a good beach at Cap d'Ail. You can walk here in 30min from the city, or get the train to Cap d'Ail. Dorms €18.50.

Eating and drinking

Arlecchino 6 rue Notre Dame de Lorette. For a cheap (daytime) bite to eat, this little café does sandwiches from €3.90, among other Italian treats. To find it, take the first set of stairs up from rue Portier.
Stars 'n' Bars 1er, 6 quai Antoine. This feisty, well-known bar on the quai serves up good-value food (for Monaco). Pizzas from €9; happy hour 5.30–7.30pm.
Virage 1 quai Albert 1er. For an affordable glimpse of this town's bling soul you could try the weekly €17 lunchtime menu (main course, dessert, drink) at this fancy ice-white bar-restaurant with excellent harbour views.

The southeast

The southeast of France encompasses a geographically varied area, from the thick forests of the Massif Central to the dramatic peaks of the Alps. The Massif Central, not the most accessible part of the country, is worth going out of your way for, especially to see the dramatic landscape that surrounds **Le Puy-en-Velay**, which makes an excellent base for exploration. Most travel in the region will require passing through **Lyon**, a beautiful city that's worth lingering over, especially to sample some of its exquisite restaurants. From here, a few hours on a train will take you to **Grenoble**, hemmed in by snow-capped mountains, and to **Chamonix**, which really comes alive during the ski-season, and a great place for extreme sports throughout the year.

LE PUY-EN-VELAY

LE PUY sprawls across a broad basin in the mountains, a muddle of red roofs and poles of volcanic rock;

both landscape and architecture are completely theatrical. The town is a good base for explorations of the Massif Central – the tourist office (see below) is well stocked with information to help you plan your visit.

The **cathedral**, at the top of Mont Corneille, with its small, almost Byzantine cupolas and Romanesque facade, dominates the old town. The nearby **church of St-Michel** (daily: May–Sept 9am–6.30pm; Oct–April 9.30am–noon & 2–5.30pm; €2.75), at the top of Rocher d'Aiguilhe, is an eleventh-century construction that appears to have grown out of the rock.

The main **bus stop and train station** are on place du Maréchal Leclerc, a fifteen-minute walk from the **tourist office** on place du Clauzel (July & Aug daily 8.30am–7.30pm; Sept–June daily 8.30am–noon & 1.30–6.15pm, closed Sun Oct–Easter; ⓣ04.71.09.38.41, ⓦwww.ot-lepuyenvelay.fr).

The *Régional*, 36 bd du Maréchal Fayolle (€24.50 for shared bathroom; ⓣ04.71.09.37.74) is a basic **hotel** attached to a friendly bar, with cheap and comfortable doubles; even cheaper are the old but clean dorms in the *FUAJ Centre Pierre Cardinal*, 9 rue Jules Vallès (ⓣ04.71.05.52.40; reservations compulsory for weekend stays; check-in from 2–11.30pm only, Sun from 6–9pm; €11.20) which has basic breakfasts (€3) and cooking facilities. The municipal **campsite**, *Bouthézard* (ⓣ04.71.09.55.09; mid-March to mid-Oct; €6.10), is half an hour's walk north from the station, or take bus #6 from chemin de Roderie. For inexpensive regional **food** and a good cheeseboard, sit out on the beautiful terrace of the *Âme des Poètes*, by the cathedral on rue Séguret, or try *Marco Polo*, an Italian restaurant at 46 rue Raphaël.

There are ten trains to Lyon daily (2hr 20min) and eight to Paris (4hr 25min–5hr 30min) via St Etienne and/or Lyon.

LYON

It's hardly surprising that **LYON** is France's gastronomic capital, with more restaurants per square metre here than anywhere else on earth. Lyon also has a vibrant nightlife and cultural scene, the highlight of which is the summer-long festival Les Nuits de Fourvière, celebrating theatre, music and dance.

What to see and do

The city is split into three by its two rivers – the Saône and the Rhône. The elegant city centre, **Le Presqu'Île**, is made up of grand boulevards and public squares, while across the Saône lies the beautifully preserved and atmospheric old Renaissance quarter of Vieux Lyon.

Le Presqu'Île

North from Gare de Perrache, the pedestrian rue Victor-Hugo opens out onto the vast place Bellecour, which dwarfs even its statue of Louis XIV on horseback. On rue de la Charité, the **Musée des Tissus et des Arts Decoratifs** (Tues–Sun 10am–5.30pm; €7; ⓜAmpère Victor-Hugo), has an interesting collection of fabrics, clothes and tapestries dating from ancient Egypt to the present, alongside a collection of period furnishings. Northwest of place Bellecour, on the east bank of the Saône, the quai St-Antoine is lined every morning with a colourful food market; a book market takes place just upriver on Sundays.

North and inland from the river, Place des Terreaux is home to the **Musée des Beaux-Arts** (daily except Tues 10/10.30am–6pm; €7 for permanent collections, €9 for temporary exhibitions, €12 for both; ⓜHôtel de Ville). This absorbing collection includes ancient Egyptian, Greek and Roman artefacts as well as works by Rubens, Renoir and Picasso.

La Croix-Rousse

North of place des Terreaux, the old silk weavers' district of **La Croix-Rousse** has an authentic, creative feel to it. It is still a working-class area, but today only twenty or so people work on the computerized looms that are kept in business by the restoration and maintenance of tapestries within France's palaces and châteaux. The famous *traboules*, or covered alleyways, that run between streets were originally used to transport silk safely through town, later serving as wartime escape routes and hideouts for la Résistance. Look out for small signs dotted about on walls in this area – follow the arrows to do a self-guided walking tour.

Vieux Lyon

The streets on the left bank of the Saône form an attractive muddle of cobbled lanes and Renaissance facades. The **Musée des Marionnettes du Monde**, in the **Musée Gadagne** (Wed–Sun 11am–6.30pm; €6; Ⓜ Vieux Lyon), place du Petit Collège, is well worth an hour or two of your time, containing not just Lyon's famous puppets but also a collection of puppets from around the world. At the southern end of the rue St-Jean lies the **Cathédrale St-Jean**; though damaged during World War II, its thirteenth-century stained glass is in perfect condition.

Lyon Romain

Just beyond the cathedral, at Ⓜ Vieux Lyon on avenue Adolphe-Max, is a funicular station, from which you can ascend (€2.40/return) to the two **Roman theatres** on rue de l'Antiquaille (daily 7am–7/9pm; free), and the excellent **Musée de la Civilisation Gallo-Romaine**, 17 rue Cléberg (Tues–Sun 10am–6pm; €4), containing mosaics and other artefacts from Roman Lyon. Crowning the hill, the **Basilique de Notre-Dame** (daily 9am–7pm) is a gaudy showcase of multicoloured marble and mosaic, and there are fantastic views over the city from the gardens at the back of the church.

Elsewhere in the city

Reminders of the war are never far away in France and the **Centre d'Histoire de la Résistance et de la Déportation**, 14 av Berthelot (Wed–Sun 9/9.30am–5.30/6pm; €4), tells of the courage and ingenuity of the French Resistance. It also serves as a poignant memorial to the city's deported Jews. To the southeast of town, the **Musée Lumière**, 25 rue du Premier-Film (Tues–Sun 10am–6.30pm; €6; Ⓜ Monplaisir-Lumière), houses the Lumière brothers' cinematograph, which in 1895 projected the world's first film.

Arrival and information

Air Tram–train *le Rhône Express* runs from Part-Dieu main-line station to Lyon-St-Exupéry airport (every 15min, 6am–9pm; every 30min 5am–6am & 9pm–midnight; €13).

Train The main TGV train station, Part-Dieu, is on bd Marius-Vivier-Merle, in the heart of the commercial district on the east bank of the Rhône, and connected to the centre by métro. Other trains arrive at the Gare de Perrache, to the southern edge of the centre on the Presqu'île.

Tourist office place Bellecour (daily 9am–6pm; Ⓣ 04.72.77.69.69, Ⓦ www.en.lyon-france.com).

Internet Raconte-moi La Terre, 38 rue Thomassin, with a bookshop specializing in travel literature (closed Sun); Le République, Place de l'Hôpital.

City transport

Bus-train-métro Tickets for all city transport cost a flat €1.60, or buy the tourist office's *liberté* ticket for a day's unlimited travel on trams, buses and métro (€4.50).

Bikes Velo-V is a citywide cycling scheme where you take and leave a bike from one of about a hundred sites around town for €1/2 an hour (depending on length of rental; first half-hour free); credit card authorization required.

Accommodation

Camping Indigo Porte de Lyon Ⓣ 04.78.35.64.55, Ⓦ www.camping-lyon.com. The closest campsite,

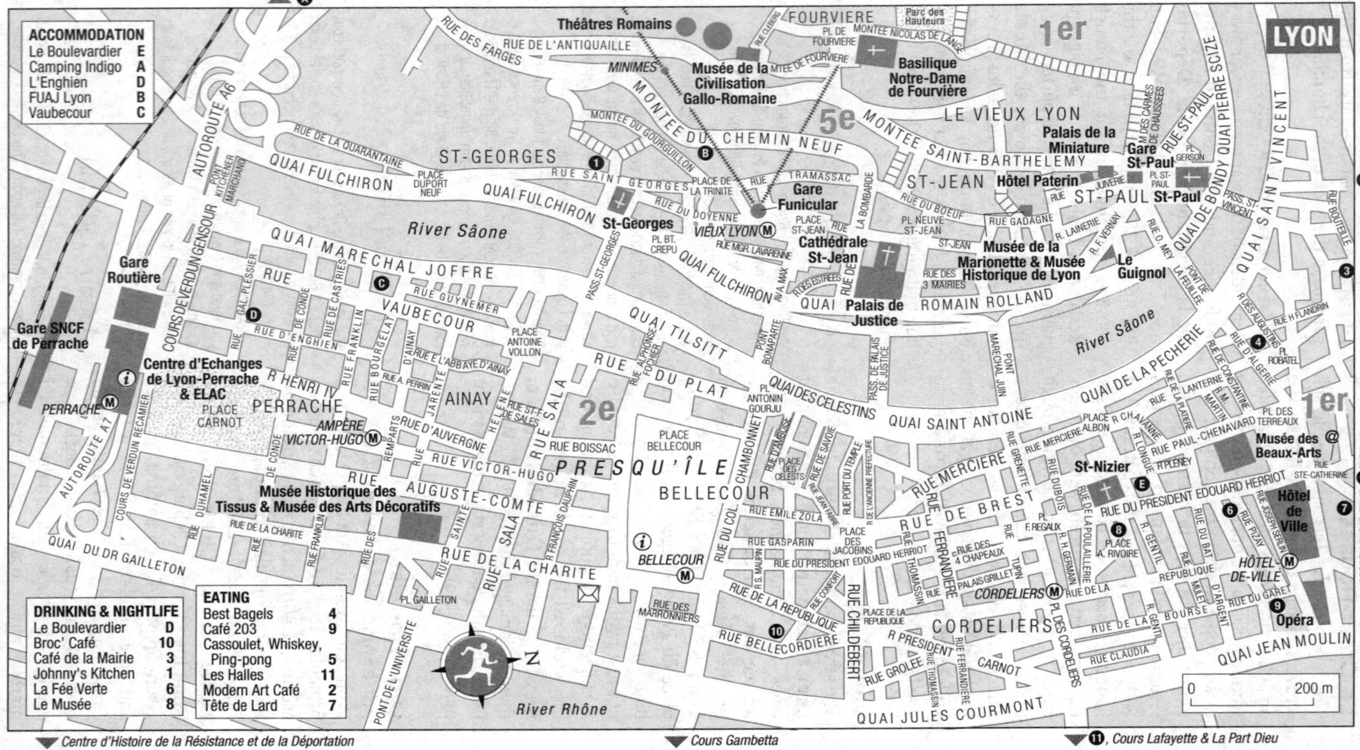
LYON
ACCOMMODATION
Le Boulevardier E
Camping Indigo A
L'Enghien D
FUAJ Lyon B
Vaubecour C
DRINKING & NIGHTLIFE
Le Boulevardier D
Broc' Café 10
Café de la Mairie 3
Johnny's Kitchen 1
La Fée Verte 6
Le Musée 8
EATING
Best Bagels 4
Café 203 9
Cassoulet, Whiskey, Ping-pong 5
Les Halles 11
Modern Art Café 2
Tête de Lard 7
Théâtres Romains
Musée de la Civilisation Gallo-Romaine
Basilique Notre-Dame de Fourvière
FOURVIERE
Parc des Hauteurs
LE VIEUX LYON
Palais de la Miniature
Gare St-Paul
St-Paul
Hôtel Paterin
ST-JEAN
ST-PAUL
ST-GEORGES
St-Georges
Gare Funicular
VIEUX LYON
Cathédrale St-Jean
Palais de Justice
Musée de la Marionette & Musée Historique de Lyon
Le Guignol
River Saône
Gare SNCF de Perrache
Gare Routière
Centre d'Echanges de Lyon-Perrache & ELAC
PERRACHE
PLACE CARNOT
AINAY
AMPÈRE VICTOR-HUGO
Musée Historique des Tissus & Musée des Arts Décoratifs
PRESQU'ÎLE
PLACE BELLECOUR
BELLECOUR
St-Nizier
Musée des Beaux-Arts
Hôtel de Ville
HÔTEL-DE-VILLE
Opéra
CORDELIERS
River Rhône
0 200 m
Centre d'Histoire de la Résistance et de la Déportation
Cours Gambetta
11, Cours Lafayette & La Part Dieu
5 & La Croix-Rousse

with a bar, restaurant, internet and a summer swimming pool. Ten minutes by bus #89 from the bus station in Gare de Vaise, north of the city. €18.90/person and pitch.

FUAJ Lyon 41–45 montée du Chemin Neuf ⓣ04.78.15.05.50. An excellent hostel, well worth the hike up from the métro station (Vieux Lyon) for the fantastic views of the city from its terrace. Dorms are comfortable and clean, the staff are very friendly and helpful, and there's a good bar. To avoid the walk up, catch the funicular to Minimes and walk down from there. Dorms €21.

L'Enghien 22 rue d'Enghien ⓣ04.78.37.42.63, ⓦwww.enghien-lyon.fr. A surprisingly smart budget choice, with brightly decorated, spacious rooms, some with attached toilet and all with private showers. Very close to Gare de Perrache. Doubles €55 (with shared bathroom), €60 (with bathroom).

Le Boulevardier 5 rue de la Fromagerie ⓣ04.78.28.48.22, ⓦwww.leboulevardier.fr. In a great, central location, this peaceful and friendly hotel offers simple but comfortable rooms that are a real bargain. Worth staying for the attached bar alone (see opposite). Doubles €49.

Vaubecour 28 rue Vaubecour ⓣ04.78.37.44.91. Very handy for Gare de Perrache and housed in a lovely old building, though the rooms are rather basic and now looking quite dated. Doubles €44 (with shared bathroom), €52 (with shower), €55 (with shower and toilet).

Eating

Best Bagels place Robatel. This café lives up to its name – try the pepper-filled "Louisiana Fire". The attached shop sells a good range of American food brands, from Oreos to Dr Pepper. Bagel, drink and accompaniment €6.95.

Café 203 9 rue du Garet. This delightful café attracts a young crowd and has an excellent €13 *formule – plat au choix* (such as *terrine de poisson* or an oriental-inspired prawn pasta) plus one of their absolutely scrummy desserts.

Cassoulet, Whiskey, Ping-pong 4ter rue de Belfort. Apart from offering what it says on the sign – the owner's three favourite things – this little bar has good jazz, cheap beer and wine and a great atmosphere. Cassoulet €10, whiskey from €2.

Le Musée 2 rue Forces ⓣ04.78.37.71.54. How the owner maintains this level of personal service is a marvel. He comes to each table and explains what's on the menu then, at the end of each service, takes guests out to the back of the restaurant to see the *traboule*. As for the food, well it's simple *bouchon* cooking at its best: *quenelle*, pig's cheek *à la lyonnaise*, *escargots* with *pistou*. Tues–Sat, afternoon & evening.

Les Halles 102 cours Lafayette. Lyon's covered market has enough gorgeous produce to keep a gourmand happy for weeks – a great stop on sunny days when you can pick up everything you need for a picnic. Tues–Sat 7am–noon & 3–7pm, Sun 7am–noon.

Pignol 17 rue Emile Zola. Justifiably famous Lyonnaise patisserie, serving a mouthwatering array of sweet treats to eat in or take away, and a number of savoury lunch dishes such as *croque-monsieur* (€6.80).

Tête de Lard 13 rue Désiré. A meat-heavy restaurant with a €24 menu – fancy *tête de veau* (braised calf's head) with *gribiche* sauce? Tues–Sat noon–1.30pm & 7.30–9.30pm.

Drinking and nightlife

Broc' Café 2 place de l'Hôpital. The cosy, dark interior of this busy bar-café makes a great stop for a drink or two – or to watch the world go by on the place. *Demi* €2.50. Mon–Sat 8am–1am.

Café de la Mairie 4 place Sathonay. One of a number of low-key places on this pleasant place which is a lovely spot for an early-evening sundowner. Mon–Sat from 7am.

Johnny's Kitchen 48 rue St Georges. There's a natural sort of feel to this little pub, unlike some of the other English- or Irish-style venues in old Lyon where the atmosphere can seem a little phoney. And sure, you're in gastronomic Lyon, but don't be embarrassed to order one of the good burgers (€10 with fries and salad). Pints €4.50. Daily noon–2.30am.

La Fée Verte 4 rue Pizay. A small dedicated absinthe bar where DJs play accessible hip-hop and electro. Absinthe €2.70.

Le Boulevardier 5 rue de la Fromagerie. A great little bar, with a charming, relaxed feel that matches the jazz played here (both live and recorded). A good place to start or finish your night off (wine €2.50, *demi* €2.70). Mon–Sat 7/8am–8pm (open until 3am if there's a concert Fri & Sat) & Sun 9am–2pm.

Modern Art Café 65 bd de la Croix Rousse ⓦwww.modernartcafe.net. Recline on a deckchair or retro leather sofa in this unpretentious bar where the friendly owner organizes original art exhibitions and brilliant DJs. Cocktails from €7 and a midday *formule* (the bruschetta is good) for €12. Mon–Fri noon–2pm & 4pm–2am, Sat & Sun 4pm–3am; closed Wed afternoon.

Moving on

Train Arles (7 daily; 2hr 40min); Avignon TGV (16 daily; 1hr 10min); Dijon (17 daily; 1hr 40min–2hr

45min); Geneva (13–15 daily; 1hr 45min–2hr 50min); Grenoble (frequent; 1hr–2hr 10min); Marseille (frequent; 1hr 45min–3hr 45min); Paris (every 30min; 1hr 50min–2hr 10min); Turin (via Chambery; 4 daily, 4–5hr).

GRENOBLE

The economic and intellectual capital of the French Alps, **GRENOBLE** is a thriving city, beautifully situated on the Drac and Isère rivers and surrounded by mountains. The old centre, south of the Isère, focuses on place Grenette and place Notre-Dame, both popular with local students, who lounge around in the many outdoor cafés. The central **Musée de Grenoble**, 5 place Lavalette (daily except Tues 10am–6.30pm; €5, free first Sunday each month), is considered, by dint of its twentieth-century masterpieces, to be one of the best in Europe and includes works by Matisse, Chagall and Gauguin. Grenoble's highlight, however, especially in good weather, is the trip by **téléphérique** from the riverside quai Stéphane Jay up to Fort de la Bastille on the steep slopes above the north bank of the Isère (daily May–Sept; Oct–April Tues–Sun; first ascent between 9.15am and 11am, last descent between 6.30pm and 12.15am according to the season; €4.70/6.80 one-way/return). It's a hair-raising ride to an otherwise uninteresting fort, but the views over the mountains and down onto the town are stunning, and the walk down is lovely and tranquil.

Arrival and information

Bus and train The train and bus stations are on the northwestern edge of the city, at the end of av Félix Viallet, a 10min walk to the centre.
Tourist office 14 rue de la République, near place Grenette (Mon–Sat 9am–6.30pm, Sun 9am–2pm; ⓣ04.76.42.41.41, ⓦwww.grenoble-tourisme.com).
Internet Celsius Café, 11 rue Guétal.
Hiking information Maison de la Montagne, 3 rue Raoul Blanchard (Mon–Fri 9.30am–12.30pm & 1–6pm, Sat 10am–1pm & 2–5pm; ⓦwww.grenoble-montagne.com).

Accommodation

Alizé 1 place de la Gare ⓣ04.76.43.12.91, ⓦwww.hotelalize.com. Just across the road from the station, Grenoble's cheapest hotel offers a friendly welcome and basic but surprisingly spacious and airy rooms. Doubles €39.

FUAJ Grenoble 10 av du Grésivaudan ⓣ04.76.09.33.52. This smart, modern, eco-friendly hostel has ultra-clean dorms and a good atmosphere. There's excellent information about hiking in the area and skiing in winter; unfortunately it's 5km from the centre of town. Take bus #1 to la Quinzaine (the best option) or tram A to la Rampe. Dorms €21.

Hôtel de l'Europe 22 place Grenette ⓣ04.76.46.16.94, ⓦwww.hoteleurope.fr. Faded grandeur in a seventeenth-century building with a central location overlooking the square. Rooms are generally small, and the cheapest have shared bathrooms. Doubles €50.

Hôtel Gambetta 59 bd Gambetta ⓣ04.76.87.22.25, ⓦwww.hotel-gambetta-grenoble.com. The once-cheerful rooms are now a little tired, but overall this is a fine budget choice. Some of the top-floor rooms have excellent views,

HIKING IN THE ALPS

There are six **national and regional parks** in the Alps – Vanoise, Écrins, Bauges, Chartreuse, Queyras (the least busy) and Vercors (the gentlest) – each of which covers ideal walking country, as does the **Route des Grandes Alpes**, which crosses all the major massifs from Lake Geneva to Menton and should only be attempted by seasoned hikers. All walking routes are clearly marked and equipped with refuge huts, known as **gîtes d'étape** (ⓦwww.gites-refuges.com). The Maisons de la Montagne in Grenoble and Chamonix (see above and p.444) provide detailed information on GR paths (an abbreviation of Grande Randonnée meaning "long ramble"), and local tourist offices often have maps of walks in their areas. Bear in mind that anywhere above 2000m will only be free of snow from early July until mid-September.

though the free wi-fi doesn't quite reach this high. Doubles €63.

Les Trois Pucelles ⓣ04.76.96.45.73, ⓦwww.camping-trois-pucelles.com. Four kilometres from Grenoble, in Seyssins, this campsite has 65 pitches, two swimming pools and a restaurant in an arboretum by the Drac River. Open all year; to get here take tram C in the direction of Le Prisme and get off at Mas des Îles; from here it's 400m south at the river's edge. €10/person and pitch.

Eating and drinking

Café des Arts 36 rue St-Laurent. An intimate venue with an excellent programme of live music, mainly jazz. Daily 8pm–midnight.

Ciao a Te 2 rue de la Paix ⓣ04.76.42.54.41. The interior of this family-run ristorante may be a little dated but then classic Italian cuisine is hardly avant-garde. From *panzarotti* to pasta to octopus salad, it's nonetheless consistently excellent, though not cheap. Book in advance. Tues–Sat, lunch and dinner.

Indira Gandhi 152 Cours Berriat. This simple but smart restaurant is particularly strong on tandoori dishes. Curries from €10, lunchtime/evening menus €8/18. Open daily.

K Fée des Jeux 1 quai Stéphane Jay. A unique place specializing in board games, Sunday brunch and, strangely, mead. The food is good value too, particularly the €7.50 salads. Wed–Fri 6pm–1am, Sat 2pm–1am, Sun 2–6pm. Kitchen open these days noon–2pm except Sun 10.30am–noon.

Mark XIII 8 rue Lakanal. A two-floor bar and venue that draws in an exciting depth and variety of underground electronic DJ talent (progressive house, drum'n'bass, techno, ambient).

Tarteline 6 Grande Rue. Cute little place with a country feel offering delicious savoury and sweet tarts, such as the Reblochon (potato, reblochon cheese and bacon, €6.50) as well as a good-value lunch menu for €11.50. Tues–Sat 10am–7pm.

Moving on

Train Chamonix (5–9 daily with connections; 4hr 15min); Lyon (frequent; 1hr 15min–1hr 45min); Paris (9 daily direct; 3hr); Turin (2–3 daily, via Chambéry; 3hr 30min–3hr 50min).

CHAMONIX AND MONT BLANC

At 4810m, **Mont Blanc** is both Western Europe's highest mountain and the Alps' biggest draw. Nestled at its base, the town of **CHAMONIX** is lively year-round; in summer it's popular for rock climbing and hiking, while in winter its draw is the area's vast skiing possibilities. The pricey **téléphérique** (daily, every 15min: mid-May to mid-June & late Aug to mid-Sept 8.10am–4.30/5pm; mid-June to early July & mid- to late Aug 7.10am–4.30/5pm; early July to mid-Aug 6.30am–5/5.30pm; mid-Sept to Oct 8.30am–3.30/4pm; closed Nov to mid-Dec & five days in mid-May; ⓣ04.50.53.22.75; €42.50 return) soars to the Aiguille du Midi (3842m), a terrifying granite pinnacle on which the cable-car station and a restaurant are precariously balanced. Here, the view of Mont Blanc, coupled with the altitude, will literally leave you breathless. Book the téléphérique ahead to avoid the queues and get there early, before the clouds and the crowds close up.

TREAT YOURSELF

One of the most exhilarating experiences you can have in the Alps is not on the ground, but in the air. A number of companies operate **tandem paragliding flights**, which allow you to take in the fantastic scenery from a different perspective. Fly Chamonix (ⓣ610.28.20.77, ⓦwww.fly-chamonix.com) offers tandem flights from €100 – for more information, or to book a flight, head to Chamonix Freeride Centre, 280 rue Paccard, Chamonix (daily 9am–noon & 3–7pm).

Arrival and information

Train Chamonix station is 3min walk from the centre, down av Michel Croz. Behind it, at Montvers station, a mountain train serves only the glaciers.

Bus Buses leave from in front of the train station.

Tourist office 85 place du Triangle-de-l'Amitié (late June to mid-Sept daily 9am–7pm; mid-Sept to late June daily 9am–12.30pm & 2–6pm; closed Sun Oct & Nov; ⓣ04.50.53.00.24, ⓦwww.chamonix.com); able to book accommodation, provides good information on local activities and advises on weather and snow conditions.

Hiking information The Maison de la Montagne on place de L'Église is the place for organizing climbing, trekking, mountain biking and parapenting. On the top floor, l'Office de Haute Montagne (daily 9am–noon & 3–6pm; ⓣ04.50.53.22.08, ⓦwww.ohm-chamonix.com) offer general advice on mountain conditions and activities. They also have good information about the Gîtes de Montagne that are situated along the major hiking trails.

Accommodation

Camping Les Marmottes 140 chemin des Doux ⓣ04.50.53.61.24 or ⓣ04.50.53.41.06, ⓦwww.camping-lesmarmottes.com. Situated off the main road, south of Chamonix, this campsite is linked to the town via a free bus service. Facilities include a games room, use of barbecues and a laundry, and you can enjoy great views of Mont Blanc. €5.90/person plus €5.20/pitch.

Du Louvre Impasse de l'Androsace ⓣ04.50.53.00.51. Right in the centre of the village, this renovated hotel offers simple but clean rooms. Doubles €90.

FUAJ Chamonix-Mont Blanc 127 Montée J. Balmat, les Pélerins d'en Haut ⓣ04.50.53.14.52, ⓦwww.fuaj.org. Situated in a traditional chalet, 2km out of the centre, this hostel has good dorms and a friendly atmosphere, but no on-site kitchen. Take bus #3 from the town centre or the train to Les Pélerins. Closed noon–5pm & 7.30–8.30pm. Dorms €19.90.

Gîte Vagabond 365 av Ravanel-le-Rouge, ⓣ04.50.53.15.43 ⓦwww.gitevagabond.com. This lively and friendly hostel is a good choice year-round and invaluably cheap for the ski-season (book ahead). Dorms €21.

Hôtel de l'Arve 60 impasse des Anémones, ⓣ04.50.53.02.31. Open year-round with an excellent, central location this chalet-style accommodation is a relative snip. Doubles €82.

Eating and drinking

Chambre 9 272 av Michel Croz. A renowned, loud and lively bar on the ground floor of the *Gustavia* hotel, full of young, dancing tourists.

La Calèche 18 rue Paccard. The decor, chock-a-block with traditional paraphenalia from ice picks to stuffed animals provides a truly atmospheric backdrop for the rich regional cuisine, though it's slightly overpriced.

MBC 350 Route du Bouchet. This microbrewery is perfect for those who find *bière blonde* doesn't quite hit the spot in the mountain air. Burger lovers will be satisfied, too.

Poco Loco 47 rue Paccard. It doesn't look like much but this sliver of a snack bar does what it does – toasted sandwiches and other *sur le pouce* goodies – very well and very generously.

Tigre, Tigre 239 av Michel Croz. Warm up with this likeable Indian restaurant's large curries (€12–16) after coming down the mountain.

Moving on

Train Grenoble (2 daily, via St Gervais; 6hr 10min); Lyon (8 daily, via St Gervais; 4–5hr).

Bus Courmayeur, Italy (2–6 daily; 45min); Geneva (2–5 daily; 2hr).

Corsica

Known to the French as the "île de beauté", Corsica has an amazing diversity of natural landscape. Being one-third national park, its magnificent rocky coastline is interspersed with outstanding beaches, while the interior mountains soar as high as 2706m. Two French *départements* divide Corsica, each with its own capital: Napoleon's birthplace, **Ajaccio** on the southwest coast; and **Bastia**, which faces Italy in the north. The old capital of **Corte** dominates the interior, backed by a formidable wall of mountains. Of the coastal resorts, **Calvi** draws tourists with its massive citadel and long sandy beach; while **Bonifacio**'s Genoan houses perch atop limestone cliffs, overseeing the clearest water in the Mediterranean, on the island's southernmost point. Still more dramatic landscapes lie around the **Golfe de Porto** in the far northwest, where the famous red cliffs of the **Calanches de Piana** rise over 400m.

AJACCIO

Set in a magnificent bay, **AJACCIO** has all the ingredients of a Riviera-style town with its palm trees, spacious squares, glamorous marina and street cafés. **Napoleon** was born here in 1769, but did little for the place except to make it the island's capital for the brief period of his empire. It is, however, a lovely place to spend time, particularly around the harbour and narrow streets inland from the fifteenth-century **Genoese** citadel. The **Musée Fesch**, rue Cardinal-Fesch (Mon, Wed & Sat 10/10.30am–5/6pm, Thurs & Fri noon–5/6pm; Oct–April open third Sun of month noon–5pm; May–Sept Sun noon–6pm; July & Aug Fri noon–8.30pm; €8) is home to the country's most important collection of Renaissance paintings outside Paris, including works by Botticelli, Titian and Poussin. The best beach to head to is **plage Trottel**, ten minutes southwest from the centre along the promenade.

Arrival and information

Air The airport, Napoleon Bonaparte, is 8km southeast and connected to the town by shuttle bus (*navette*; €5); taxis cost around €25.

Train The train station is a 10min walk north along the seafront.

Bus and ferry The ferry port and bus station occupy the same building off quai L'Herminier.

Tourist office 3 bd du Roi Jérôme (April–June, Sept & Oct Mon–Sat 8am–7pm, Sun 9am–1pm; July & Aug Mon–Sat 8am–8pm, Sun 9am–1pm & 4–7pm; Nov–March, Mon–Fri 8am–12.30pm & 2–6pm, Sat 8.30am–12.30pm & 2–5pm; ⓣ04.95.51.53.03, ⓦwww.ajaccio-tourisme.com).

Internet Cyber Espace (wi-fi and computers), 1 rue Dr Versini.

Accommodation

Budget accommodation in Ajaccio is hard to find and hotels get booked up quite quickly. The tourist office can provide a list of those available as well as private apartments to rent.

Camping de Barbicaja route des îles Sanguinaires ⓣ04.95.52.01.17. The most convenient campsite is 3km out of town, near the beach, and has a bar and hot showers. It's a short bus ride away from place Général-du-Gaulle on bus #5. Closed Oct–April. €8.60/person and pitch.

Kallisté 51 cours Napoléon ⓣ04.95.51.34.45, ⓦwww.hotel-kalliste-ajaccio.com. This tastefully renovated nineteenth-century building has seen better days, but there are rooms here that are worth the slightly inflated price – take a look around before choosing one. Extras include scooter rental and free internet. Doubles €95.

Marengo 2 rue Marengo ⓣ04.95.21.43.66, ⓦwww.hotel-marengo.com. A sweet little hotel with spacious, clean rooms. The cheapest have showers but shared toilets, while some lead onto a floral courtyard. €63.

Eating and drinking

Le 20123 2 rue Roi de Rome ⓣ04.95.21.50.05. Cute and twee Corsican village-themed bar with

GETTING TO CORSICA

Air France (ⓦwww.airfrance.fr) and its partner company **Air Corsica** (CCM; ⓦwww.aircorsica.com) have regular flights to Corsica's four airports at Ajaccio, Bastia, Calvi and Figari (near Bonifacio). It's often possible to get discounts if you are under 25.

The three principal **ferry companies** serving the island are Corsica Ferries (ⓦwww.corsica-ferries.com), Moby (ⓦwww.moby.it) and SNCM (ⓦwww.sncm.fr). Prices are between €30 and €80, with the cheapest from the Italian ports. From October to March routes are scaled back to several journeys a week; check websites for details.

Nice to: Ajaccio (6 weekly; 6hr 15min–7hr); Bastia (8 weekly; 5hr 20min–7hr 30min); Calvi (1 daily; 5hr 45min).

Marseille to: Ajaccio (10 weekly; 11–12hr); Bastia (14 weekly; 11–13hr).

Livorno to: Bastia (22 weekly; 4hr).

Genoa to: Bastia (1 daily; 4hr 45min).

Savona to: Bastia (14 weekly; 6hr).

Santa-Teresa-di-Gallura to: Bonifacio (2–8 daily; 1hr).

Porto Torres to: Ajaccio (1 weekly; 4hr 30min).

traditional singers. Generous evening menu €33. Book in advance. Open from 7pm.

Le Glacier du Port 6 Quai Napoléon. A prime spot with good, home-made ice cream on offer. You get a lot for your money, but it's not cheap.

Marché Campinchi place César Campinchi. This market is open 8am–noon Tues–Sun, and is a great place to stock up in fresh fruit and veg, plus cheese and Corsica's famed charcuterie at its cheapest.

Vino de Diablo Port de l'Amirauté. A party place with live music and a lovely expansive terrace on the port. Three tapas and a drink for €13 – lunch menu at around the same price – is good.

Moving on

Train Bastia (2–4 daily; 3hr 30min); Calvi (change at Ponte Leccia; 1–2 daily; 4hr 30min); Corte (2–4 daily; 2hr).

Bus Bastia (2 daily; 3hr); Bonifacio (1–2 daily; 3hr 15min); Corte (2 daily; 1hr 45min).

LE GOLFE DE PORTO

Corsica's most startling landscapes surround the **Golfe de Porto**, on the west coast. A deep blue bay enfolded by outlandish red cliffs, among them the famous **Calanches de Piana** rock formations, the gulf is framed by snow-topped mountains and a vast pine forest. The entire area holds endless possibilities for outdoor enthusiasts, with a superb network of marked trails (free maps available from the Ajaccio tourist office) and **canyoning** routes, perfect bays for **kayaking** and some of the finest **diving** sites in the Mediterranean.

Less adventurous visitors can explore the coast on one of the excursion boats from the village of **PORTO**, the gulf's main tourist hub, where there's a **tourist office** (Ⓣ04.95.26.10.55, Ⓦwww.porto-tourisme.com) and a huge range of **accommodation**. Best value among the cheap **hotels** is *Le Vaïta*, a fifteen-minute walk from the centre (Ⓣ04.95.26.13.33; Ⓦwww.le-vaita.com; €75). *Camping Oliviers*, situated just along from the supermarket on the main road east from the village (Ⓣ04.95.26.14.49, Ⓦwww.camping-oliviers-porto.com; €9.80 per person plus €3.50 per tent) is lovely, with pitches under the shade of olive trees. Amenities include a bar, swimming pool, gym, hot tub, a hammam and massages. The campsite also has wooden chalets with terrace, private bathroom and double room (€111). For an inexpensive **meal**, try one of the pizzerias lining the roadside above the marina.

CALVI

Seen from the water, the great citadel of **CALVI** resembles a floating island, defined by a hazy backdrop of snow-capped mountains. The island's third port, the town draws thousands of tourists for its 6km of sandy beach. The

BASTIA: COMING AND GOING

Bastia is the island's main transport hub – while there's little of particular interest here, there's a good chance that you'll pass through the town at least once during your visit.

Air Bastia's airport, Poretta, is 20km south of town. Shuttle buses (35–40min; €9) meet all flights and stop outside the train station in the centre of town.

Ferry The port is in the north of town, a five-minute walk from the centre. See the box on p.445 for ferry routes and journey times. Services include Nice (5hr 20min–7hr 30min), Marseille (11–13hr) and Livorno (4hr).

Train The station, west of place St-Nicolas, serves: Ajaccio (2–4 daily; 3hr 30min); Calvi (1–2 daily; 3hr, change Ponte Leccia); and Corte (2–4 daily; 1hr 45min).

Bus run from the train station to Calvi (Mon–Fri 4.30/5pm, Sat noon; 2hr) and Corte (3 weekly, Mon, Wed & Fri 12.10pm; 1hr 20min–1hr 45min), and from rue du Nouveau Port to Ajaccio (Mon–Sat 7.45am & 3pm; 3hr), Corte (Mon–Sat 7.45am & 3pm; 1hr 15min) and Porto Vecchio (2 daily June–Sept only, 8.30am & 4pm; 3hr).

ville haute, a labyrinth of cobbled lanes and stairways encased by a citadel, rises from **place Christophe Colomb**, which links it to the town and marina of the *ville basse*. The square's name derives from the local belief that the discoverer of the New World was born here, in a now ruined house on the edge of the citadel. To reach the public **beach**, keep walking south, past the boats in the marina, and – unless you want to pay for a lounger and waited service – past the private beach bars.

Arrival and information

Air Calvi's Ste-Catherine airport is 7km southeast of the town, connected only by taxis (€17–19).
Train The train station, on av de la République, is just off the marina to the south of the town centre.
Bus Buses to and from Bastia and Calenzana stop in place Porteuse d'Eau, next to the station. Porto buses stop outside the Super U supermarket 200m south of the train station.
Ferry The ferry port is on the opposite side of the marina, below the citadel.
Tourist office Port de Plaisance (April–Oct daily 9am–5/7pm; Nov–March Mon–Sat 9am–noon & 2–5pm; ⓣ04.95.65.16.67, ⓦwww.balagne-corsica.com).

Accommodation

Du Centre 14 rue Alsace-Lorraine ⓣ04.95.65.02.01. The most convenient budget accommodation, hidden away in the *ville basse*, with modest and well-kept rooms. Doubles €59.
La Pinède ⓣ04.95.65.17.80, ⓦwww.camping-calvi.com. One of the smartest of several campsites that are sheltered in the pine forest behind the public beach, with tennis, a bar and a good shop. It's a 2km walk along av de la République or take the infrequent beach train (*ferrovière*; around five daily) that serves Île Rousse and get off at the "Tennis" stop; open mid-March to mid-Nov. €9.50/person plus €3.50/tent.
U Carabellu route de Pietra-Maggiore ⓣ04.95.65.14.16. Hostels are a rare breed in Corsica, so book ahead for this one, whose dorms are tidy and have plenty of room. It also has a great out-of-town spot overlooking the bay; from the station, turn left down av de la République, then right at the Total garage after 500m and keep walking for 3.5km. Also offers full- (€33) and half-board (€28) options. Dorms €18.50.

Eating and drinking

Bar de la Tour quai Landry. A lovely spot overlooking the water, it's a great place for an early evening beer.

ISLAND TRANSPORT

Corsica is somewhat difficult to navigate if relying on public transport, with services slow and infrequent. The unofficial websites ⓦwww.corsicabus.org and ⓦwww.train-corse.com are helpful for train and bus timetables.
Train Corsica's narrow-gauge railway crosses the mountains to connect the island's main towns along the most scenic of lines. Lines run from Calvi–Ponte Leccia in the interior and from Ajaccio–Bastia. InterRail and other cards reduce the fare to half for all services, or you could buy a **Carte Zoom**, which gives one week's unlimited train travel for €49. The cards are available from any station. For up-to-the-minute timetable information call the stations at Calvi (ⓣ04.95.65.00.61), Bastia (ⓣ04.95.32.80.61) or Ajaccio (ⓣ04.95.23.11.03).
Bus Buses are infrequent between the larger towns and rarely reach the interior villages; main routes include Bastia–Porto Vecchio, Ajaccio–Bastia and Calvi–Bastia. Services are scaled back drastically between November and May.
Scooter With little public transport and many secluded beaches to visit, the roads that undulate and meander around Corsica mean it's a great place to rent a scooter. Try Scootloc at Place du Marché in Ajaccio (ⓣ06.26.17.31.07; €39–45/day), Scoot Rent at 3 quai Banda del Ferro in Bonifacio (ⓣ06.25.44.22.82/06.25.75.88.71; €45/day) or Garage d'Angeli at 4 rue Villa St-Antoine in Calvi (ⓣ04.95.65.02.13; €35–50/day).
Car This is by far the most convenient way to get around Corsica. Hertz (ⓦwww.hertz.fr), Europcar (ⓦwww.europcar.com) and Avis (ⓦwww.avis.fr) all have offices in the big towns and airports, with prices starting from €70 per day.

Chez Tao rue Ste-Françoise. A famous, beautiful and expensive piano bar, set in a sixteenth-century former bishop's palace. It's a romantic place to share a bottle of wine on the terrace and enjoy impressive views of the bay. Open 8pm–5am.
Pizzeria Cappuccino quai Landry. This restaurant has a great atmosphere and serves up good-value *calzones* (from €11.50) and pasta.
U Fanale route de Porto ⓣ04.95.65.18.82. Overlooking the bay with excellent local cuisine, this is worth the (appetite-building) walk from the town centre. The €24 menu (including a Corsican cheese course) is recommended. Book ahead. Open March–Dec.

Moving on

Train All services go via Ponte Leccia; Ajaccio (1–2 daily; 4hr 45min); Bastia (1–2 daily; 3hr 15min); Corte (1–2 daily; 3hr).
Bus Bastia (daily 6.30/7.15am except Sun; 2hr 15min); Porto: (July to mid-Sept daily 3.30pm; May–June & mid- to late Sept Mon–Sat 3.30pm; no service late Sept to May; 2hr 30min).

CORTE

Perching on the rocky crags of the island's spine, **CORTE**, the island's only interior town, is regarded as the spiritual capital of Corsica, as this is where **Pasquale Paoli** had his seat of government during the brief period of independence in the eighteenth century. Paoli founded a university here and its student population adds some much-needed life. For outdoor enthusiasts, this is also an ideal base for **trekking** into the island's steep valleys, with two superb gorges stretching west into the heart of the mountains.

What to see and do

The main street, **cours Paoli**, runs the length of town, culminating in **place Paoli**, a pleasant market square lined with cafés. A cobbled ramp leads up to the **ville haute**, where you can still see the bullet marks made by Genoese soldiers during the War of Independence in tiny **place Gaffori**. Continuing north you'll soon come to the gates of the **citadelle**, whose well-preserved ramparts enclose the **Museu di a Corsica** (Nov–March Mon–Sat 10am–5pm; April to mid-June Tues–Sun 10am–6pm; mid-June to mid-Sept daily 10am–8pm; mid-Sept to Oct daily 10am–6pm; closed first half Jan; €5.30). The best views of the citadel, the town and its valley are from the **Belvédère**, a man-made lookout post on the southern end of the ramparts.

Arrival and information

Train Corte's train station is 1km south east of town at the foot of the hill near the university.
Bus Some buses stop at the south end of cours Paoli, others go to the station.
Tourist office In the *citadelle* (Mon–Fri 9am–noon & 2–5pm in winter, Mon 10am–1pm & 3–6pm & Tues–Sat 9am–6pm in summer; ⓣ04.95.46.26.70, ⓦwww.corte-tourisme.com).

Accommodation

Ferme Équestre l'Albadu Ancienne route d'Ajaccio ⓣ04.95.46.24.55. The nicest of the local campsites, located 15min walk from town – follow the main road south down the hill from place Paoli and take the second right after the second bridge. €5/person, plus €2.50/tent.
HR allée du 9 Septembre ⓣ04.95.45.11.11, ⓦwww.hotel-hr.com. Cheap and cheerful rooms in an old converted police station southwest of the station and just 10min from the centre. €40.
Le Torrent Santo Pietro di Venaco ⓣ04.95.47.00.18, ⓦwww.hotel-letorrent.fr. In a village just outside Corte, this hotel in a nineteenth-century building on a hillside has seen better days but is certainly atmospheric. Doubles €73.

Eating and drinking

Café du Cours 22 rue Paoli. Student nights and well-priced drinks at this busy bar which also has internet access, some live Corsican bands and daytime left-luggage facilities; *demi* €3.
Le Nicoli 4 av Jean Nicoli. Corsican produce, Italian techniques, all beautifully presented in an elegant setting. The €19.50 menu represents excellent value. Closed Sun.
U Museu 1 rampe Ribanelle. Huddled beneath the citadel walls, this place serves a superb goat's cheese salad and tasty wild-boar stew; three-course menu €15.

THE GR20

The GR20 hiking trail stretches across Corsica's dramatic granite spine from Calenzana in the north to Conza in the south. Covering a breathtaking landscape, the route takes you through some lush countryside and over the snowcapped peaks of the heart of island. It is manageable for anyone in reasonable shape with basic trekking common sense, but proper hiking equipment is essential, as are nerves of steel for the ropes and vertical staircases built into the mountainside. Covering a distance of 180km, it takes around two weeks to complete, walking 2–6hr per day; red and white waymarks show the route, which is well serviced with bunked **mountain refuges**. Although the refuges cook and sell food, several days' supplies and a good stock of water are recommended. Do not attempt the route outside of the summer months; even then there is some residual snow in parts.

Buses go from Calvi to Calenzana (July & Aug 2 daily; Sept–June 4 weekly Mon, Tues, Thurs & Fri; 30min; €8), where the walk begins.

Accommodation and more detailed information about the route can be found at Ⓦwww.corsica.forhikers.com/gr20. Detailed maps can be obtained from the tourist office.

Moving on

Train Ajaccio (2–4 daily; 2hr); Bastia (2–4 daily; 1hr 30min); Calvi (1–2 daily via Ponte Leccia; 2hr 30min).

Bus Ajaccio (2 daily except Sun, 9am & 4.15pm; 1hr 45min); Bastia (3 daily except Sun, 7.45am, 9.30am & 4.40pm; 1hr 15min).

BONIFACIO

The port of **BONIFACIO** has a superb, isolated position on a narrow peninsula of dazzling white limestone at Corsica's southernmost point, only an hour away by boat from Sardinia. For hundreds of years the town held the most powerful **fortress** in the Mediterranean and was a virtually independent republic. Nowadays, people are met with sights of precariously balanced houses edging their way into the sea. Bonifacio has become a chic holiday spot, sailing centre and deluxe day-trip.

What to see and do

The **ville haute** is connected to the marina by a steep flight of steps at the west end of the quay, at the top of which you can enjoy glorious views across the straits to Sardinia. Within the massive fortifications of the citadel is an alluring maze of cobbled streets which bring you back down to the marina, where a **boat excursion** (around €17.50; try company Rocca Croisières) round the base of the cliffs gives a fantastic view of the town and the **sea caves**. Some outstanding beaches lie near Bonifacio, most notably the shell-shaped **plage de la Rondinara**, 10km north; further north still, off the main Porto-Vecchio road, the **plages de Santa Giulia** and **Palombaggia** wouldn't look out of place in the Maldives. In July and August four buses daily (7.20am, 8.30am, 12.45pm, 5pm; 30min; Sept–June 3 daily except Sun 7.20am, 8.30am, 12.50pm) make the journey from Bonifacio to Porto Vecchio, passing the turn off for la Rondinara. From Porto Vecchio a beach bus runs in July and August (daily 10am, 2pm, 4.30pm; 30min) to Palombaggia and another to Santa Giulia (daily in July, Mon–Sat in Aug, 9.50am, 12.10pm, 3.05pm, 6.30pm; 20min).

Arrival and information

Bus Buses stop in the car park at the base of the harbour.

Ferry Boats from Santa-Teresa-di-Gallura on Sardinia dock at the far end of the quay at the bottom of the hill.

Tourist office The tourist office is based in the *ville haute*, at the bottom of rue Fred Scamaroni (June & Sept daily 9am–7pm; July & Aug daily 9am–8pm; ⓣ04.95.73.11.88, ⓦwww.bonifacio.fr).
Internet Scara Lunga, quai Jérôme Comparetti.

Accommodation

L'Araguina 33 av de Bonifaccio, ⓣ04.95.73.02.96, ⓦwww.camping-araguina-bonifacio.com. The only campsite close to the town has lumpy and sandy pitches but loans out tents and sleeping bags for those unprepared. It's north from the marina, 1km out of town. €6.60/person, plus €2.70/tent.
Royal 8 rue Fred Sacramoni ⓣ04.95.73.00.51, ⓦwww.hotel-leroyal.com. A good option in the centre of town, only minutes away from the tourist office. Don't let slightly faded blue carpet and curtain-less showers put you off – the beds are comfy and it offers a decent night's sleep. Doubles €60.

Eating and drinking

B'52 quai Camparetti. A laidback and tasteful late-night bar (open until 2am), with tapas bites to accompany the house cocktails.
Cantina Doria rue Doria ⓣ04.95.73.40.59. Serving traditional, hearty, Corsican specialities - try the fish soup and charcuterie (maybe not together) in particular. Three-course menu for €16.50.
Kissing Pigs 15 quai Banda del Ferro. In spite of the prevailing pig theme (excellent *charcuterie)*, the *aubergine à la bonifacienne* is one of the highlights. Worth reserving a table on the terrace for a dreamy view of the port. The €19 "chestnuts" (*châtaignes*) menu is a steal.

Moving on

Bus Ajaccio (1–2 daily except Sun; 3hr 30min); Porto Vecchio, for connections to Bastia (Sept–June Mon–Sat 7.20am, 8.30am & 12.50pm; July & Aug 7.20am, 8.30am, 12.45pm & 5pm; 30min).
Ferry Santa-Teresa-di-Gallura in Sardinia (2–8 daily with Moby or Saremar; 1hr).

Germany

HIGHLIGHTS

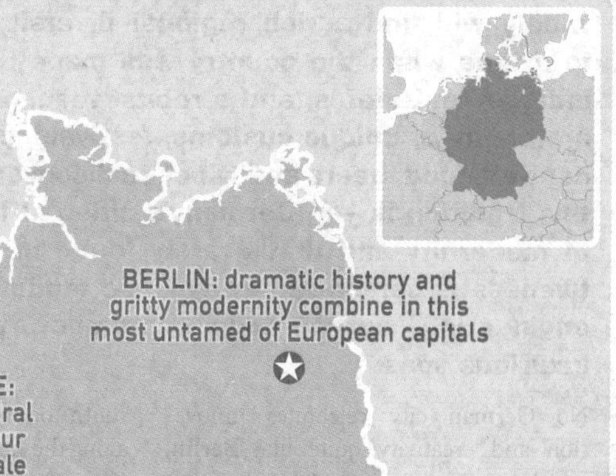

BERLIN: dramatic history and gritty modernity combine in this most untamed of European capitals

DOM, COLOGNE: Cologne's cathedral is Gothic grandeur on a massive scale

DRESDEN: glorious Baroque architecture by day; decadent bar-crawling by night

FREIBURG: mosaic streets, a majestic setting and one of Germany's most beautiful churches

OKTOBERFEST, MUNICH: the world's most famous beer festival

ROUGH COSTS

DAILY BUDGET Basic €41/ occasional treat €57

DRINK Beer (half-litre €2.70)

FOOD *Schnitzel* €8

HOSTEL/BUDGET HOTEL €18/ €40–70

TRAVEL Train: Munich–Berlin €44–139

FACT FILE

POPULATION 81.8 million

AREA 357,021 sq km

LANGUAGE German

CURRENCY Euro (€)

CAPITAL Berlin (population: 3.4 million)

INTERNATIONAL PHONE CODE ⓣ49

Introduction

Berlin and Munich deservedly draw the crowds, but the rest of Germany is often underrated as a destination, despite its picture-postcard medieval villages, dynamic modern cities and swathes of idyllic countryside. But those who do explore more widely will find a rich regional diversity, which harks back to a time when the country was made up of a patchwork of independent states, and a robust respect for the past. There are plenty of unique customs, festivals, castles, historic town centres, food, beers and wines to discover. Juxtaposed with all this tradition is – in Germany's cities at least – an embracing of modernity and that's rarely found in Europe. Here inventiveness is celebrated in dynamic modern architecture, slick engineering, cutting-edge contemporary art museums and luxurious spas.

No German city celebrates innovation and creativity quite like **Berlin,** which bursts with youth, art and energy. Counter-culture also thrives in the other great eastern German city of **Dresden**, which is also known for its Baroque finery. This too, is a key draw in the many palaces of **Potsdam**, while small but cultured **Weimar** is another significant town that rewards travel in this region.

In northern Germany the large, bustling harbour city **Hamburg** with its rambunctious nightlife is a key draw. Further south, straddling the banks of the River Rhine, **Cologne** is another dynamic city, famed for a skyline dominated by a spectacular cathedral begun in 1248, and its huge and decidedly impious Carnival celebrations.

Munich is the key city in southern Germany, with its fine museums and bustling beer halls, but in general the region is best appreciated in smaller towns which preserve the pastoral and romantic side of Germany. Among them are the university town of **Heidelberg**; **Trier** with its many Roman remains; the spa town of **Baden-Baden**; and the attractive and youthful Black Forest town of **Freiburg**. Many of Germany's scenic highlights can be found in the south too; including the **Bavarian Alps** along the Austrian border; the **Bodensee** (Lake Constance) near the Swiss border; the **Black Forest** and the **Rhine Valley** – whose majestic sweep has spawned a rich legacy of legends and folklore.

CHRONOLOGY

57 BC Julius Caesar invades and conquers "Germania Inferior".

800 AD Charlemagne, the Frankish ruler over territory including Germany, is crowned Holy Roman Emperor.

1438 Habsburg dynasty rules over Germany with election of Albert I.

1517 Martin Luther writes his *95 Theses* against corruption in the Catholic Church, a protest that culminates in the Protestant Reformation.

1648 End of the Thirty Years' War between European Catholic and Protestant powers leads to the division of Germany into princely states.

1871 Unification of Germany under Chancellor Otto von Bismarck, after German success in the Franco-Prussian War.

1880s Bismarck establishes German colonies in Africa.

1918 Germany is defeated in World War I; the Treaty of Versailles enforces heavy reparation payments upon Germany.

1919 The Weimar Republic is established.

1923 Hyperinflation causes economic meltdown.

1933 Hitler becomes Chancellor of Germany.

1939 World War II begins as Germany invades Poland.

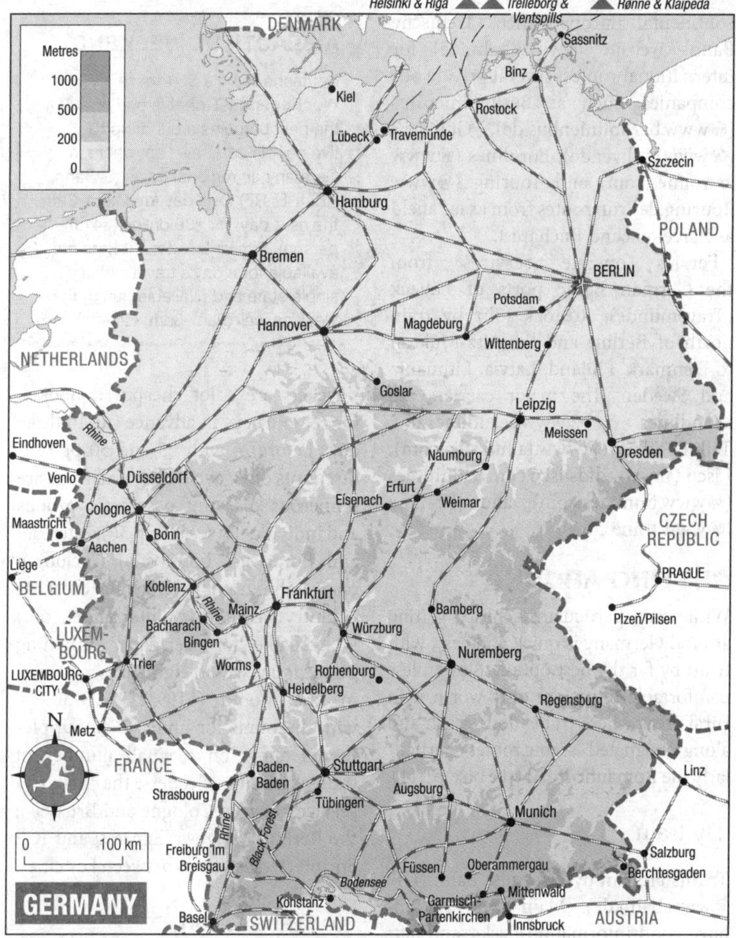

1939–45 Millions die in Nazi concentration camps during the Holocaust.
1945 Germany is defeated, the Allies occupy the country.
1949 Germany is divided between Communist East and Democratic West.
1961 The Berlin Wall is constructed.
1989 Following mass protests, the Berlin Wall is torn down.
1990 The two Germanys are reunited.
2005 Angela Merkel becomes first female – and first eastern – Chancellor.
2006 Germany hosts the Football World Cup.
2009 Germany celebrates twenty years since the fall of the Wall; Angela Merkel is re-elected as chancellor.
2011 In the wake of Japanese nuclear disaster and a wave of anti-nuclear protests, a Green government is elected in the state of Baden-Württemberg.

ARRIVAL

Flying is the cheapest and most convenient way to get to Germany from outside Europe and even from many other European countries thanks to the proliferation of discount airlines. The largest airport is Frankfurt Airport (FRA), and there are over forty others to choose from. Germany is well connected by **bus and train** with destinations throughout continental Europe. Check Deutsche Bahn's website (ⓦwww.bahn.de) for international routes; several private bus companies, such as BerlinLinienBus (ⓦwww.berlinlinienbus.de), Gulliver's (ⓦwww.gulliver.de), Eurolines (ⓦwww.eurolines.com) and Touring (ⓦwww.touring.de) run routes from as far afield as Barcelona and Bucharest.

Ferries operate services from the German Baltic ports of Lübeck (Travemünde), Rostock (3hr by train north of Berlin) and Sassnitz-Mukran to Denmark, Finland, Latvia, Lithuania and Sweden. The major carriers are Scandlines (ⓦwww.scandlines.de), Tallink/Silja (ⓦwww.tallinksilja.com), Lisco (ⓦwww.dfdslisco.com), Finnlines (ⓦwww.finnlines.com) and TT-Line (ⓦwww.ttline.com).

GETTING AROUND

While not particularly cheap, getting around Germany is quick and easy, with **train** by far the best option. Slower, less comfortable **buses** are only worth it in rural areas where trains don't reach and along designated "scenic routes", particularly the Romantic Road (see box, p.511).

By train

Trains are run by Deutsche Bahn (DB; ⓦwww.bahn.de). Main train stations have good information desks, and left-luggage lockers (€1.50–€5). The fastest and most luxurious service is the InterCityExpress (ICE). InterCity (IC) and EuroCity (EC) trains are next in line. Slower Regional trains (RE/RB) run on lightly used routes and are often significantly cheaper. Major cities often have an **S-Bahn** commuter rail network.

With **standard tickets**, valid for two days, you can make as many stops along the way as you'd like. So if you're heading to Berlin from Cologne, you can take a day in Hannover on your way for no extra charge. A return ticket costs the same as two one-way tickets.

A BEAUTIFUL WEEKEND

Deutsche Bahn's **Schönes-Wochenende-Ticket** is one of the best bargains around: up to five people can travel anywhere in Germany on regional trains (S-Bahn, RB, IRE, RE) for a day (midnight–3am the next day) for €39 online (€41 in person). Similar **Länder-Tickets** are available for a day's travel within a single state and available during the week as well (9am–3am; €20–34).

Tickets are a lot cheaper if booked for set journeys in advance (up to three days before) – with 25 and 50 percent discounts often available – and there are numerous discount passes for groups and individuals (see box, p.36). InterRail and Eurail are both valid (including on S-Bahn trains). The InterRail One Country Pass (ⓦwww.interrailnet.com) is available for Germany, providing three, four, six or eight days of travel in one month (€199/219/279/309 – with discounts for under-26s). **Supplements** apply on a small number of trains including sleepers; the Thalys (a service between Cologne and Brussels); the Berlin–Warszawa Express; and ICE Sprinters – fast trains between key cities.

Local transport

All cities have reliable local **buses**, though in more rural areas they can be infrequent. You can usually buy tickets from the driver; stops are marked "H" for *Haltestelle*. Major cities also have a **U-Bahn**, or metro/tram system, where you'll normally need to buy and validate your ticket before boarding, although some trams have ticket machines on board. U-Bahns are patrolled, albeit infrequently, by plain-clothes ticket inspectors who will levy on-the-spot fines of around €40 on passengers without valid tickets.

By bicycle

Cyclists are well catered for: many smaller roads have cycle paths, and bike-only lanes are ubiquitous in cities, where it's often a great way to get around. There are also some excellent long-distance cycle routes. Many train stations have bicycle rental outlets (around €12/day), including DB's "Call a Bike" scheme (Ⓦwww.callabike.de); hostels also often rent bikes. Bikes need their own ticket (*Fahrradkarte*) on a train: €4.50 on regional trains and €9 on IC/EC trains. Bikes are not allowed on ICE services.

ACCOMMODATION

It's often best to reserve **accommodation** in advance, especially in the cities, where trade fairs and seasonal tourism can create high demand. Nearly all tourist offices will reserve accommodation for a fee.

You're never far away from a large, functional **HI hostel** (*Jugendherberge*) run by DJH (Ⓦwww.jugendherberge.de) – but they are often block-booked by school groups, so reserve in advance, and they aren't particularly cheap (around €22, including breakfast and sheets). Non-HI members pay an extra €3.10 per night (until you have six stamps, which gives you membership); people aged 27 and over also pay around €3 extra. There are usually no curfews or lockouts, but reception hours may be limited. **Independent hostels** are usually a better choice in cities – friendly, relaxed and often an excellent source of local advice. Expect to pay €15–22; breakfast and sheets are not always included. The Backpacker Network Germany (Ⓦwww.backpackernetwork.de) lists many options.

Hotels are graded, clean and comfortable. In rural areas, prices start at about €30 for a double room; in cities, about €40–50. *Pensions* and **B&Bs** are plentiful; local tourist offices will have a list (or look for signs saying *Fremdenzimmer* or *Zimmer frei)*; rates start at around €20 for a double.

Even the most basic **campsites** have toilets, washing facilities and a shop. For a complete list of campsites see Ⓦwww.bvcd.de.

FOOD AND DRINK

German **food** is both good value and high quality, and though traditionally solid and meat-heavy, at least in cities there's often a wide range of international choices: Italian restaurants are the most reliable, but Balkan, Greek, Turkish and Chinese places are also common. Most hotels and guesthouses include **breakfast** in the price of the room – typically including cold meats and cheeses, bread and jam.

Traditionally **lunch** tends to be treated as the main meal, with good-value daily menus on offer. Pubs and inns – a **Gaststätte**, **Gasthaus** or **Gasthof** – are usually cosy and serve hearty home cooking, particularly pork and sausages along with distinct regional variations.

The distinction between café, restaurant and bar is often blurred, with many offering good simple breakfasts, salads and some mains. The easiest option for snacks, however, is to head for the ubiquitous **Imbiss** street stalls and shops, which range from traditional *Wurst* sellers to popular *döner kebap* places.

Traditional German cuisine generally offers little for **vegetarians**, but there's usually something on the menu – such as *Maultaschen* (similar to ravioli) and *Käsespätzle* (like macaroni cheese) – and anywhere more contemporary should have a veggie choice or two.

Drink

For **beer** drinkers, Germany is paradise. Munich's beer gardens and beer halls are the most famous drinking dens in the country, offering a wide variety of premier products, from dark lagers through tart *Weizens* to powerful *Bocks*. Cologne holds the world record for the number of city breweries, which all produce the beer called *Kölsch*, but wherever you go you can be fairly sure of getting a locally brewed beer. There are many high-quality German **wines**, especially those made from the Riesling grape. **Apfelwein** is a variant of cider beloved in and around Frankfurt.

CULTURE AND ETIQUETTE

Most Germans are friendly, hospitable and helpful, and if you stand at a corner long enough with map in hand, someone's bound to volunteer help. **Jaywalking** is illegal in Germany; you could be fined if caught, but are most likely to get off with disapproving looks from passers-by (less so in large cities).

The German approach to paying at a café is a little different. If you're in a group, you'll be asked if you want to pay individually (*getrennt*) or all together (*zusammen*). To **tip in a café**, round your bill up to the next €0.50 or €1 and give the total directly to the waiter; at restaurants you'll be expected to leave around 10 percent of the bill.

SPORTS AND OUTDOOR ACTIVITIES

Bundesliga football (Ⓦwww.bundesliga.de/en) is the major spectator sport in Germany, with world-class clubs playing in top-notch stadiums. Tickets can be purchased from the clubs' websites; important matches sell out well in advance.

Germany's great outdoors has a lot to offer, particularly to **hikers** and **cyclists**. The most popular regions for hiking are in the Black Forest and the Bavarian Alps, but there are well-maintained, colour-coded hiking routes all over Germany. The country is crisscrossed with long-distance cycling routes. The cycling page on Germany's tourism website (Ⓦwww.germany-tourism.de/cycling) is excellent for planning.

GERMANY ONLINE

Ⓦ**www.germany.travel/en/index.html** Official tourist board site.

Ⓦ**www.stadtplandienst.de** City maps.

Ⓦ**www.webmuseen.de** Information on the country's museums.

EMERGENCY NUMBERS

Police ⓣ110; Fire & Ambulance ⓣ112.

COMMUNICATIONS

Post offices are open Monday to Friday 8am to 6pm and Saturday 8am to 1pm. Call shops are the cheapest way to phone abroad, though you can also **phone** abroad from all payphones except those marked "National"; phonecards are widely available. The operator is on ⓣ03. Internet access is widespread; expect to pay €2–4 per hour.

EMERGENCIES

The **police** (*Polizei*) usually treat foreigners with courtesy. Reporting thefts at local police stations is straightforward, but there'll be a great deal of bureaucracy to wade through. Doctors generally speak English. **Pharmacies** (*Apotheken*) can deal with many minor complaints; all display a rota of local pharmacies open 24hr.

INFORMATION

You'll find a good **tourist office** in every town, with a large amount of literature and maps; town and regional tourist websites are usually excellent. City tourist offices often offer discount cards, which typically cover public transport and free or discounted entry to major sights. These can be worthwhile, but check first what discounts are offered – sometimes they're no better than the student price.

MONEY AND BANKS

German currency is the **euro** (€). **Exchange facilities** are available in most banks, post offices and commercial exchange shops called *Wechselstuben*. The Reisebank has branches in the train stations of most main cities (generally open daily, often till 10/11pm). Basic **banking hours** are Monday to Friday 9am to noon and 1.30 to 3.30pm, Thursday till 6pm. **Credit cards** are fairly widely accepted – but certainly not universally – with budget restaurants, cafés and most shops often not accepting them. There can also be a surcharge in

GERMAN

Pronunciation Consonants: "w" is pronounced like the English "v"; "sch" is pronounced "sh"; "z" is "ts". The German letter "ß" is a double "s". Vowels: "ei" is "eye", "ie" is "ee", "eu" is "oy".

	German	Pronunciation
Yes	*Ja*	Yah
No	*Nein*	Nine
Please	*Bitte*	Bitteh
Thank you	*Danke*	Duhnkeh
Hello/Good day	*Güten Tag*	Gooten tahg
Goodbye	*Tschüss, ciao, or auf Wiedersehen*	Chuss, chow, or owf veederzain
Excuse me	*Entschuldigen Sie, bitte*	Enshooldigen zee bitteh
Today	*Heute*	Hoyteh
Yesterday	*Gestern*	Gestern
Tomorrow	*Morgen*	Morgan
I don't understand	*Ich verstehe nicht*	Ich vershtayeh nicht
How much is...?	*Wieviel kostet...?*	Vee feel costet...?
Do you speak English?	*Sprechen Sie Englisch?*	Sprechen zee aing-lish?
I'd like a beer	*Ich hätte gern ein Bier*	Ich hetteh gairn ein beer
Entrance /exit	*der Eingang/der Ausgang*	dare eingahng/ dare owsgahng
Toilet	*das WC/die Toilette*	dahs vay-tsay/dee toyletteh
HI hostel	*die Jugendherberge*	dee yougendhairbairgeh
Main train station	der *Hauptbahnhof*	howptbahnhof
Bus	*der Bus*	dare boos
Plane	*das Flugzeug*	das floog-tsoyg
Train	*der Zug*	dare tsoog
Cheap/expensive	*Billig/teuer*	Billig/toy-er
Open/closed	*Offen/auf geschlossen/zu*	Uhffen/owf gehshlossen/tsoo
One	*Eins*	Einz
Two	*Zwei*	Tsvi
Three	*Drei*	Dry
Four	*Vier*	Fear
Five	*Fünf*	Foonf
Six	*Sechs*	Zex
Seven	*Sieben*	Zeeben
Eight	*Acht*	Ahkt
Nine	*Neun*	Noyn
Ten	*Zehn*	Tsain

hostels and smaller hotels. **ATMs** are widespread.

OPENING HOURS AND HOLIDAYS

Shops open at 8am and close around 6 to 8pm weekdays and 2 to 4pm on Saturdays; they are generally closed all day Sunday, though regulations vary by state. Exceptions are pharmacies, petrol stations and shops in and around train stations, which stay open late and at weekends. **Museums** and **historic monuments** are, with few exceptions (mainly in Bavaria), closed on Monday. **Public holidays** are: January 1, January 6 (regional), Good Friday, Easter Monday, May 1, Ascension Day, Whit Monday, Corpus Christi (regional), August 15 (regional), October 3, November 1 (regional) and December 25 and 26.

Berlin

Energetic and irreverent, **BERLIN** is a welcoming, exciting city where the speed of change in the past decades has been astounding. With a long history of decadence and cultural dynamism, the revived national capital has become a magnet for artists and musicians. Culturally, it has some of the most important archeological collections in Europe, as well as an impressive range of galleries and museums and an exuberant, cutting-edge nightlife.

The city resonates with modern European history, having played a dominant role in Imperial Germany, during the Weimar Republic after 1914, and in the Nazis' Third Reich. After 1945, the city was partitioned by the victorious Allies, and as a result was the frontline of the Cold War. In 1961, its division into two hostile sectors was given a very visible expression by the construction of the notorious Berlin Wall. After the Wall fell in 1989, Berlin became the national capital once again in 1990. These days, parliament (**Bundestag**) sits in the renovated Reichstag building, and the city's excellent museum collections have been reassembled. The physical revival of Berlin has put it at the forefront of contemporary architecture, and there is a plethora of dramatic new buildings around the city.

What to see and do

Most of Berlin's main sights are in the central **Mitte** district, focused around the leafy boulevard of Unter den Linden. A bustling area of restaurants, shops and bars around Hackescher Markt lies a short walk northeast, while to the south lies Potsdamer Platz and the museums of the Kulturforum. This overlooks the Tiergarten park while further west lies the adjacent area City West, a neighbourhood known for its shopping, particularly along the Ku'damm. The residential city districts encircling Mitte–particularly of **Kreuzberg**, **Prenzlauer Berg** and **Friedrichshain**–have many of the city's liveliest hangouts.

The Brandenburg Gate and the Reichstag

The most atmospheric place to start a tour of Berlin is the **Brandenburg Gate**, the city-gate-cum-triumphal-arch built in 1791. To its north stands the **Reichstag**, the nineteenth-century home of the German parliament,

WALKING TOURS

In recent years **walking tours** of Berlin have become the most popular way for budget travellers to begin exploring the city. They can be a great way to not only get a handle on the place but also to meet other travellers. All companies offer general four-hour city tours for around €12 plus more specialized ones such as Third Reich sites; Cold War Berlin; Jewish life; Potsdam; and Sachsenhausen. Operators include **Original Berlin Walks** (Ⓣ030/301 91 94, Ⓦwww.berlinwalks.com); **Insider Tours** (Ⓣ030/692 31 49, Ⓦwww.insiderberlintours.com); and **New Berlin Tours** (Ⓣ0030/510 50 03 01, Ⓦwww.newberlintours.com), whose city-centre tour is technically free, though generous tips are expected. One company offering something a bit different is **Alternative Berlin** (Ⓣ0162/81 98 264, Ⓦwww.alternativeberlin.com), which tours the graffiti art and squats of Berlin's underbelly. And finally, one tour not to miss is the chance to visit various underground installations such as a World War II bunker, with **Berliner Unterwelten** (Ⓣ030/49 91 05 17, Ⓦwww.berlinerunterwelten.de), whose ticket office is in the southern entrance hall of the Ⓤ Gesundbrunnen station.

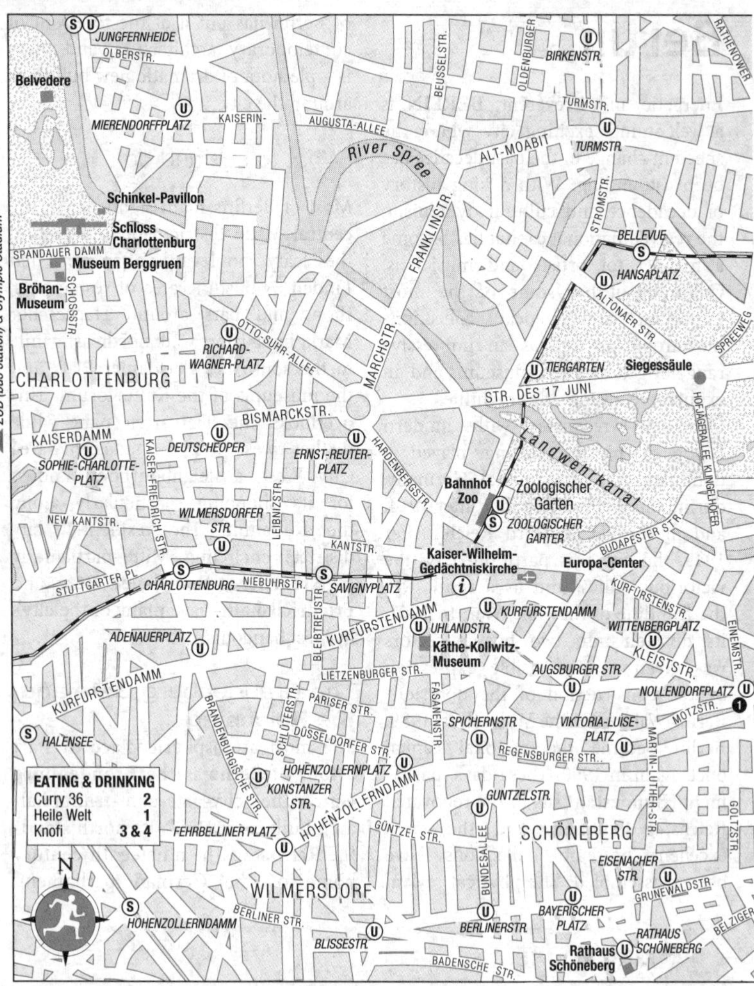

which was remodelled by Norman Foster for the resumption of its historic role in 1999, when the much-photographed glass cupola was added. Pre-booked groups (☎030/22 73 21 52; registration required weeks ahead) and visitors with reservations for its gourmet rooftop restaurant (daily 9am–4.30pm & 6.30pm–midnight; ☎030/22 62 99 33) can make the trip to the top for fine views over the surrounding government quarter and Tiergarten park as well as much of central Berlin.

The Holocaust Memorials

The bold **Holocaust Memorial** (officially the "Memorial to the Murdered Jews of Europe"), lies south of the Brandenburg Gate, where 2711 upright concrete slabs of varying height have been arranged in a dizzying grid. The exhibition in its underground information centre (*Ort der Information*; Tues–Sun: April–Sept

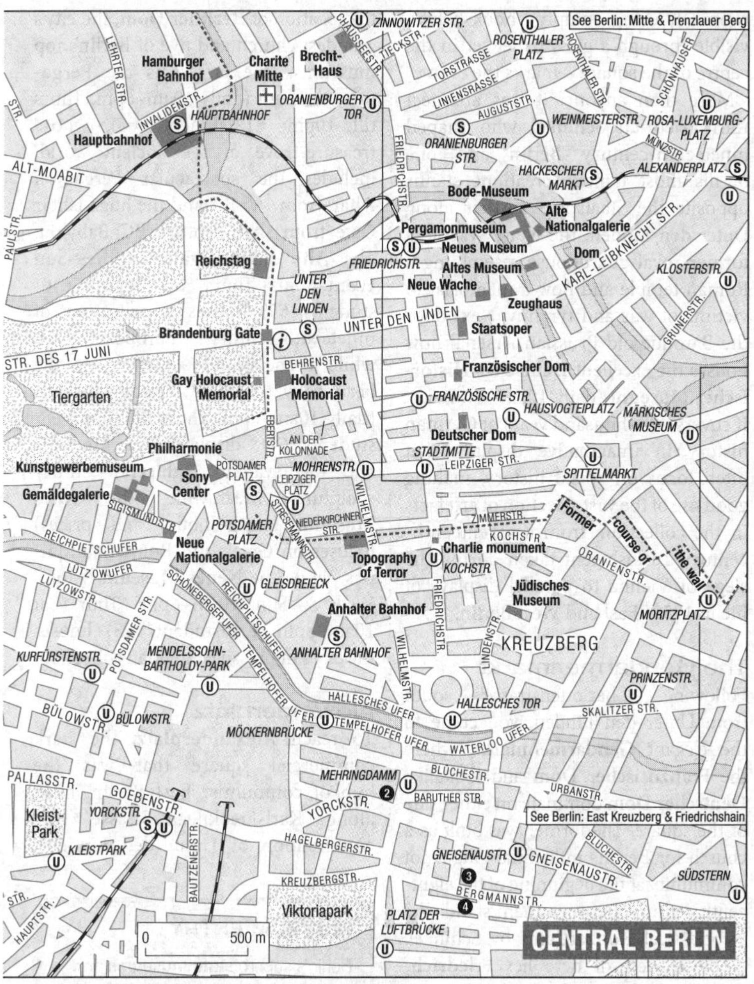

10am–8pm; Oct–March 10am–7pm; free) is carefully presented and moving.

Over the road, on the fringes of the Tiergarten park, another concrete oblong, forms the **Gay Holocaust Memorial**, which remembers those convicted of homosexual acts under the regime. The whole construction leans to one side, so is defiantly not straight, and has a small window behind which a film of two men kissing permanently plays.

Unter den Linden

East of the Brandenburg Gate stretches broad and stately **Unter den Linden**, once Berlin's most important thoroughfare. Post-unification renewal, including over-sized embassies and museums flanking the boulevard, only hint at its former grandeur.

Bebelplatz, at Unter den Linden's eastern end, was the site of the infamous Nazi book-burning of May 10, 1933; an unusual memorial – an underground room housing empty bookshelves, visible through a glass panel set in the centre of the square – marks the event.

More than anyone, it was architect Karl Friedrich Schinkel who shaped nineteenth-century Berlin and one of his most famous creations stands opposite the Staatsoper further along Unter den Linden: the **Neue Wache**, a former royal guardhouse resembling a Roman temple and now a memorial to victims of war and tyranny. Next door the Baroque old Prussian Arsenal now houses the excellent **Deutsches Historisches Museum** (daily 10am–6pm; €6). It covers two thousand years of German history in imaginative displays that often focus on social history, making good use of the vast selection of artefacts in the collection: from a seventeenth-century Turkish tent taken during the siege of Vienna to parallel displays of life in 1950s East and West Berlin.

The Gendarmenmarkt

Following Charlottenstrasse south from Unter den Linden, you come to the elegant **Gendarmenmarkt**, where the **Französischer Dom** and lookalike **Deutscher Dom** dominate on either side of the square. The former was built as a church for Berlin's influential Huguenot community at the beginning of the eighteenth century. Between them stands the Neoclassical **Konzerthaus** by Schinkel. A block west of here lies **Friedrichstrasse**, a high-class shopping street.

Schlossplatz and Museuminsel

At the eastern end of Unter den Linden is the **Schlossplatz**, former site of the imperial palace, then of the GDR's Palast der Republik (parliament), which was dismantled in 2008 to make way for transitional projects and ultimately a re-creation of the Schloss, due for completion in 2018. The Platz stands at the midpoint of the Spree island whose northern half, **Museuminsel**, is the location of **Berliner Dom**, the city's grandest church and five of Berlin's top museums. The largest is the **Pergamonmuseum** (daily 10am–6pm, Thurs till 10pm; €12/students €6), whose treasure-trove of the ancient world, includes the spectacular Pergamon Altar, from 160 BC and the huge Ishtar Gate from sixth-century BC Babylon. The **Alte Nationalgalerie** (Tues–Sun 10am–6pm, Thurs till 10pm; €10/students €5) houses a collection of nineteenth-century European art, while at the island's northern tip the beautifully restored **Bode-Museum** (daily 10am–6pm, Thurs till 10pm; €8/students €4), displays Byzantine art and medieval to eighteenth-century sculpture. Meanwhile, the **Altes Museum** (same hours and prices) focuses on Greek and Roman antiquities, while the **Neues Museum** (Mon–Wed & Sun 10am–6pm; Thurs–Sat 10am–8pm; €10/students €5) houses the city's impressive Egyptian collection.

Alexanderplatz

To reach **Alexanderplatz**, the stark commercial square that was the hub of communist East Berlin, head along Karl-Liebknecht-Strasse (the continuation of Unter den Linden),

MUSEUM ENTRY

Berlin's superb **state museums and galleries** (including all Museuminsel and Kulturforum museums; Ⓦwww.smb.museum) are all free from four hours before closing on Thursdays. As well as the basic museum entrance ticket, day-tickets for each cluster of museums can be bought; called a **Bereichskarte** (literally "area ticket"; €8–16). Meanwhile, a three-day ticket for all Berlin's state-owned museums, and dozens of others including the Jewish Museum, is a steal at €19/students €9.50. With a **student ID card** almost all sights and museums give up to fifty percent discounts.

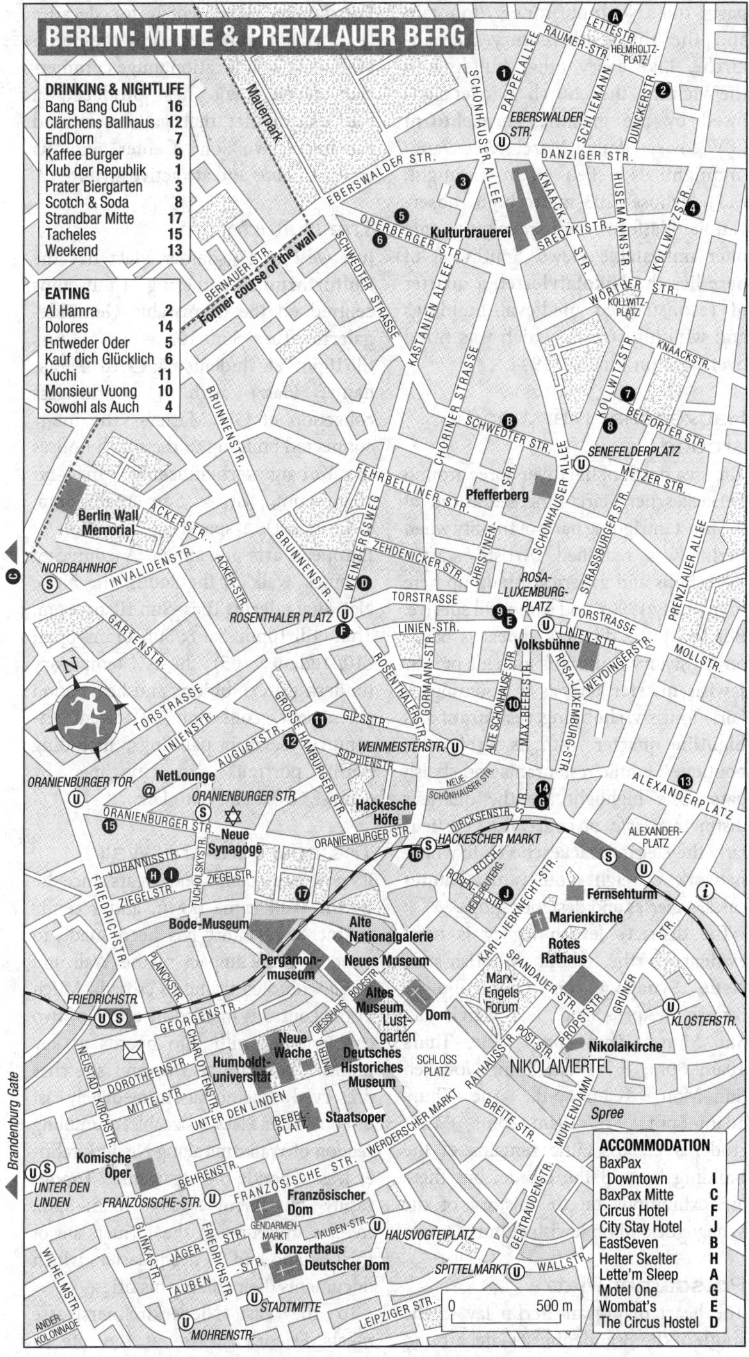

GERMANY

BERLIN

past the Neptunbrunnen fountain and the thirteenth-century Marienkirche. Like every other building in the vicinity, the church is overshadowed by the gigantic **Fernsehturm** (TV tower; daily: March–Oct 9am–midnight; Nov–Feb 10am–midnight; €11), whose 203-metre-high observation platform and revolving café offer unbeatable views. Southwest of here lies the **Nikolaiviertel**, a quarter of reconstructed medieval buildings and winding streets, which was razed overnight on June 16, 1944.

Hackescher Markt and around

The area north of the River Spree around Ⓢ Hackescher Markt emerged as one of the most intriguing parts of the city when Berlin was reunified. Artists' squats, workshops and galleries sprang up here in the early 1990s, and some still survive. But today the district's appeal is based on its history as Berlin's affluent prewar **Jewish quarter** and as a booming, if fairly touristy, **shopping**, **restaurant** and **nightlife quarter**, with its fashionable boutiques, ethnic restaurants and stylish bars. One highlight are the quarter's distinctive *Höfe*, or courtyards; particularly the elegant **Hackesche Höfe** whose network of eight courtyards features cafés, galleries and designer shops.

The district's Jewish legacy is most evident in the rebuilt Moorish-style **Neue Synagoge** on Oranienburger Strasse (April–Sept & March–Oct Sun–Mon 10am–8pm, Tues–Thurs 10am–6pm, Fri 10am–5pm; Nov–Feb Sun–Mon 10am–6pm, Tues–Thurs 10am–6pm, Fri 10am–2pm; €3.50/students €2.50). Little remains of the building beyond the facade, but there are exhibitions on the history of the synagogue and on Jewish culture.

Potsdamer Platz

The heart of prewar Berlin lay to the south of the Brandenburg Gate, around **Potsdamer Platz**, which for decades lay dormant and bisected by the Berlin Wall. Post-reunification, huge commercial development has produced a business district that gathers around the impressive Sony Center, with its cinema, shops and attractive atrium.

The Kulturforum

Just west of Potsdamer Platz lies the **Kulturforum**, a gathering of museums centred on the unmissable **Gemäldegalerie** (Tues–Sun 10am–6pm, Thurs till 10pm; €8/students €4; Ⓢ & Ⓤ Potsdamer Platz), with its world-class collection of Old Masters. The interconnected building to the north houses the **Kunstgewerbemuseum** (Tues–Fri 10am–6pm, Sat & Sun 11am–6pm; same ticket), a sparkling collection of European arts and crafts. A couple of minutes' walk to the south, the **Neue Nationalgalerie** (Tues–Sun 10am–6pm, Thurs till 10pm, Sat & Sun 11am–6pm; €10/students €5) hosts temporary modern art exhibitions and has a good permanent collection of twentieth-century German paintings, including Berlin portraits and cityscapes by George Grosz and Otto Dix.

The course of the Wall

It's now more than twenty years since the **Berlin Wall** came down, and recently an increased effort has been made to remember the impact of the Wall and those who died trying to cross it. Much of the course is marked by a row of two cobblestones, with info boards at key points. There are also several stretches preserved as memorials. Immediately east of Potsdamer Platz, a sizeable, crumbling section of Wall runs along Niederkirchnerstrasse, beside the captivating, **Topography of Terror** (daily 10am–8pm; free), a museum on the former site of the Gestapo and SS headquarters which documents their chilling histories.

To the east Niederkirchnerstrasse meets Friedrichstrasse at the site of the Wall's most infamous crossing: **Checkpoint Charlie**. Here, along with a reconstruction of the checkpoint, is a fascinating open-air display on the Wall's history.

At Bernauer Strasse, just north of Mitte, there's a short stretch of wall that has been preserved as the **Berlin Wall Memorial**. This is the only section where the two parallel walls plus "death strip" between remain, viewable from a lookout at the small documentation centre over the road (Tues–Sun: April–Oct 9.30am–7pm; Nov–March 9.30am–6pm; free; Ⓢ Nordbahnhof/Ⓤ Bernauer Str.).

Stretching along the River Spree, near Friedrichshain, a 1.3-kilometre-long section of the Wall known as the **East Side Gallery** (Ⓢ Ostbahnhof) is covered with paintings by international artists, originally done in the months after the fall of the Iron Curtain, but touched-up since. At Bernauer Strasse, Checkpoint Charlie and the Brandenburg Gate there are kiosks where you can pick up a GPS audioguide to follow the course of the Wall (4hr €8, day €10/students €5/€7; Ⓦ www.mauerguide.com).

Jüdisches Museum

Daniel Libeskind's striking zinc-skinned **Jüdisches Museum**, Lindenstr. 9–14 in west Kreuzberg (Jewish Museum; Mon 10am–10pm, Tues–Sun 10am–8pm; €5/students €2.50; Ⓤ Hallesches Tor/Kochstr.), is part museum, part memorial. Its lower ground level is Libeskind's reflection on three strands of the Jewish experience in Berlin: exile, Holocaust and continuity, and is a disorientating but compelling experience. You are then directed to the upper two floors, a more conventional exhibition which documents the culture, notable achievements and history of Berlin's Jewish community.

Ku'damm and around

A short walk south of Bahnhof Zoo station, at the focus of the city's western side, is the start of the Kurfürstendamm, or **Ku'damm**, a 3.5-kilometre strip of ritzy shops, cinemas, bars and cafés. Western Berlin's most famous landmark here is the **Kaiser-Wilhelm-Gedächtnis-kirche**, mostly destroyed by British bombing in 1943, the broken spire left as a reminder of the horrors of war, with a modern church built alongside.

Tiergarten

Berlin Zoo, beside Zoo Station, forms the beginning of the giant **Tiergarten**, a restful expanse of woodland and a good place to wander along the banks of the Landwehrkanal. Strasse des 17 Juni heads all the way through the Tiergarten to the Brandenburg Gate, with the **Siegessäule**, the iconic victory monument, at the central point.

Schloss Charlottenburg

The sumptuously restored **Schloss Charlottenburg** is on Spandauer Damm 10–22 (Old Palace; Tues–Sun: April–Oct 10am–6pm; Nov–March 10am–5pm; €12/students €8; New Wing; Wed–Mon: April–Oct 10am–6pm; Nov–March 10am–5pm, €6/students €5; 10min walk from Ⓢ Westend or bus #M45 from Zoo). Commissioned by the future Queen Sophie Charlotte in 1695, it was added to throughout the eighteenth and early nineteenth centuries. Admission to the Old Palace includes a tour of the main state apartments and self-guided visits to the private chambers, while the New Wing includes an array of paintings by Watteau and other eighteenth-century French artists. South of the Schloss complex, the **Museum Berggruen** (Tues–Sun 10am–6pm; €8/students €4) exhibits a large Picasso collection, among others.

The Olympiastadion

Located at the west of the city is the site of the 1936 Olympics, and of the 2006

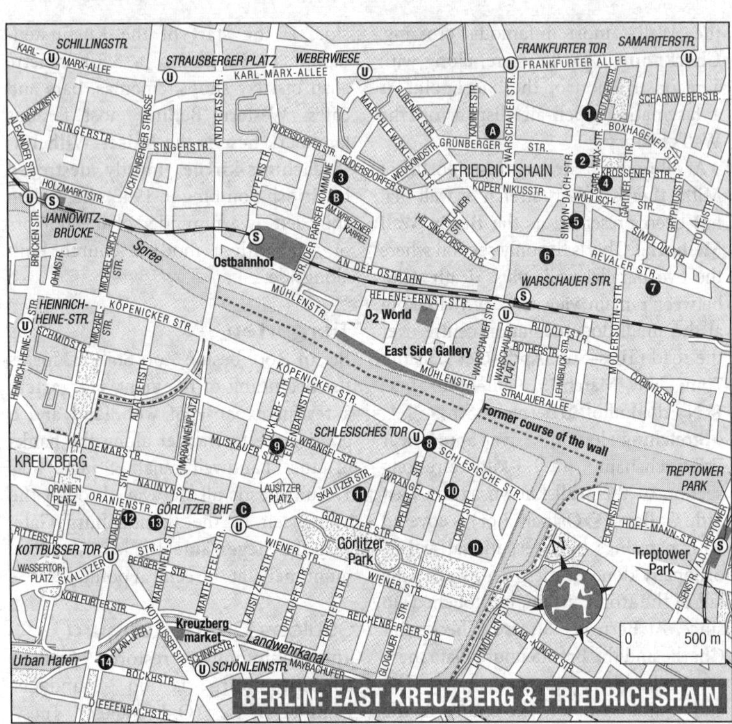

ACCOMMODATION		EATING		DRINKING & NIGHTLIFE			
BaxPax Kreuzberg	C	Burgeramt Fruhstücksklub	4	Astro	2	Lurette	1
Odysee Globetrotter	A	Burgermeister	8	Berghain	3	Privatclub	9
Ostel	B	Il Casolare	14	Cassiopeia	6	Rosi's	7
Jetpak Alternative	D	Knofi	12	Kptn A. Müller	5	SO 36	13
		Kvartira Nr. 62	11			Watergate	10

Football World Cup final, the **Olympiastadion**, one of the very few impressive Nazi-era buildings to have survived. If you can't make it to a Hertha BSC (Ⓦwww.herthabsc.de) match, you can visit at other times (daily 9am–4/7/8pm; €4/students €3; various tours available €8.50–10; Ⓦwww.olympiastadion-berlin.de; Ⓤ or ⓈOlympiastadion); check online or at the tourist office first.

Arrival

Air Berlin's two international airports (Ⓦwww.berlin-airport.de) both lie within easy reach of the city centre via public transport. The closer of the two is Tegel airport (TXL) from which a frequent #TXL express bus runs to the Hauptbahnhof and Alexanderplatz, while #X9 express or local #109 buses run to Bahnhof Zoo. A public transport zone AB ticket (€2.30) covers this.

Tegel is due to shut in 2012 and all traffic will land at Berlin Brandenburg International (BBI) – which will incorporate Berlin's other airport: Schönefeld (SXF). From S-Bahn line S9 runs to Alexanderplatz, the Hauptbahnhof and Bahnhof Zoo (every 30min; 30min); bus #X7 runs to nearby ⓊRudow. A public transport zone ABC ticket (€3) covers journeys from Schönefeld into the centre.

Train The huge Hauptbahnhof northeast of the Brandenburg Gate is well connected to the rest of the city by S- and U-Bahn.

Bus Most international buses stop at the bus station (ZOB), which is linked to the Ku'damm area by many buses, including the #M49 service, and Ⓤline #2 from Kaiserdamm station.

Information

Tourist offices At the Hauptbahnhof (daily 8am–10pm; ⓣ030/25 00 25, ⓦwww.visitberlin.de). Also at: Brandenburg Gate (daily 10am–7pm); Kurfürstendamm 21 (Mon–Sat 10am–8pm, Sun 9.30am–6pm); and in the ALEXA shopping centre, Alexanderplatz (Mon–Sat 10am–8pm).

Discount passes The WelcomeCard (Berlin AB: 48hr/€16.90/72hr/€22.90/5-day/€29.90; Berlin and Potsdam ABC: 48hr/€18.50/72hr/€24.90/5-day/€34.90; ⓦwww.berlin-welcomecard.de) provides free travel and up to fifty percent off at many of the major tourist sights, though not those on the Museuminsel, and many of the discounts are the same as student prices.

City transport

BVG (ⓦwww.bvg.de) operate an efficient, integrated system of U- and S-Bahn train lines, buses and trams, though cycling in Berlin is also very easy (see p.470 for bike rental outlets).

U- and S-Bahn Trains run daily 4.30am–12.30am (Fri & Sat all night).

Bus and tram The city bus network – and the tram system in eastern Berlin – covers the gaps left by the U-Bahn; several useful tram routes centre on Hackescher Markt, including the #M1 to Prenzlauer Berg. Night buses and trams operate, with buses (around every 30min) generally following U-Bahn line routes; free maps are available at most stations.

Tickets Available from machines at Ⓤ-Bahn stations, on trams or from bus drivers: zone AB single ticket €2.30; zone ABC single €3; short-trip ticket (*Kurzstreckentarif*) for 3/6 train or bus/tram stops €1.40; zone AB day ticket €6.30; for 2/3/5 days the WelcomeCard (see above) is good value. Validate single tickets in the yellow or red machines on platforms before travelling.

Accommodation

Berlin has plenty of great hostels, primarily in Mitte, Prenzlauer Berg, Kreuzberg and Friedrichshain; several new options are more like budget hotels and are often the best choice for private rooms. Try to book at least a couple of weeks in advance in high season. A few of the larger hostels vary their prices considerably depending on demand; high-season prices are quoted.

Hostels

BaxPax ⓦwww.baxpax.de. Trio of backpacker outfits with clean, bright-as-a-button rooms. *Kreuzberg* (Skalitzer Str. 104 ⓣ030/695 183 22; Ⓤ Görlitzer Bahnhof; dorms €15–21, twin €66, doubles €98; see map opposite) and *Mittes Backpacker* (Chausseestr. 102, Ⓤ Zinnowitzer Str; ⓣ030/283 909 65; dorms €18–25, doubles €86; see map, p.463) are laidback, offering cooking facilities, bike rental and (in Kreuzberg only) a rare chance to sleep in a VW Beetle. The *Downtown BaxPax* (Ziegelstr. 28, ⓣ030/278 748 80; Ⓢ & Ⓤ Friedrichstr; dorms €23–30, singles €70, doubles €99; see map, p.463), in the best location, is a little more hotel-like, with most rooms en suite; sheets €2.50.

The Circus Hostel Weinbergsweg 1a, Mitte ⓣ030/20 00 39 39, ⓦwww.circus-berlin.de Ⓤ Rosenthaler Platz. See map, p.463. Welcoming, clean, fun and deservedly popular base in a great location between Mitte and Prenzlauer Berg, with helpful staff and it's own bar. Dorms €19–25, doubles €56, en suite €70.

City Stay Hotel Rosenstr. 16, Mitte ⓣ030/23 62 40 31, ⓦwww.citystay.de Ⓢ Hackescher Markt. See map, p.463. Bright and airy hostel in the bustling heart of Mitte which, thanks to its off-street location, is a peaceful and safe base for travellers. Dorms €17–21, doubles €50, en suite €64.

EastSeven Schwedter Str. 7, Prenzlauer Berg ⓣ030/936 222 40, ⓦwww.eastseven.de Ⓤ Senefelderplatz. See map, p.463. Cosy, small, independent hostel with kitchen and pretty garden, including a barbecue. Some nice touches, such as communal meals on Monday, discounts in local shops and good tips on nearby clubs. Dorms €19, doubles/twins €56.

Helter Skelter Kalkscheunenstr. 4–5, Mitte ⓣ030/280 44 997, ⓦwww.helterskelterhostel.com Ⓢ Friedrichstr. See map, p.463. Lively and central old-school backpackers' place with kitchen and sheets included – and breakfast too if you stay three nights. Dorms €15–22, singles €35, doubles €63.

Jetpak Alternative Görlitzerstr. 38 ⓣ030/62 90 86 41 ⓦwww.jetpak.de Ⓤ Schlesisches Tor. See map opposite. Attractive high-end hostel in a gritty neighbourhood close to all the action in Kreuzberg and Friedrichshain. Perks include free internet, a buffet breakfast and underfloor heating, along with bicycle rental, laundry facilities and cheap beer. Dorms €27.

Lette'm Sleep Lettestr. 7, Prenzlauer Berg ⓣ030/44 73 36 23, ⓦwww.backpackers.de Ⓤ Eberswalder Str. See map, p.463. Chilled-out hostel with free internet, a kitchen and a good location, on a particularly attractive square in Prenzlauer Berg. Dorms €16–21, twins €49, doubles €69.

Odyssee Globetrotter Hostel Grünberger Str. 23, Friedrichshain ⓣ030/29 00 00 81, ⓦwww.globetrotterhostel.de Ⓤ Frankfurter Tor. See map opposite. Young, well-organized hostel with quirky, individually designed rooms and a guest kitchen, ideally situated for the Friedrichshain nightlife scene – though a touch far from the sights. Dorms €12.50–19.50, doubles €47, en suite €54.

Ostel Wriezener Karree 5 ⓣ030/25 76 86 60, ⓦwww.ostel.eu Ⓢ Ostbahnhof. See map, pp.466–467. Novelty *Ostalgie*-themed hostel and hotel, all authentically decked out GDR-style, though with some very modern facilities such as free wi-fi. Breakfast €7.50. Dorms €22, doubles €71.

Wombat's Alte Schönhauser Str. 2 ⓣ030/847 108 20, ⓦwww.wombats-hostels.com/berlin Ⓤ Rosa-Luxemburg-Platz. See map, p.463. Bright, friendly and well-equipped new hostel, in a great location near some good bars. All dorms are en suite, the spacious apartments with kitchens are particularly stylish, and the roof bar has superb views over the city. Breakfast €3.70. Dorms €24, doubles €70, double room apartment €80.

Hotels

Circus Hotel Rosenthalerstr. 1 ⓣ030/20 00 39 39, ⓦwww.circus-berlin.de Ⓤ Rosenthaler Platz. See map, p.463. Fantastic and stylish budget-hotel run by the *Circus Hostel* over the road. Helpful staff provide tons of local advice and some nice extras like free loans of laptops to take advantage of the hotel's free wi-fi. Good breakfasts (€8) are also offered and all rooms are en suite, though those overlooking the street a little noisy. Singles €70; doubles €90.

Motel One Berlin-Alexanderplatz Dircksenstr. 36 ⓣ030/20 05 40 80, ⓦwww.motel-one.com Ⓢ Alexanderplatz. See map, p.463. A ubiquitous chain hotel, but the location of this one is unbeatable and the rooms stylish. Breakfast €7.50. Singles €69, doubles €84.

Eating

Many cafés, bars and restaurants serve food, with plenty offering a good weekend brunch. The bustling Kreuzberg/Neukölln market (Tues & Fri noon–6pm) on the Maybach Ufer (Ⓤ Schönleinstr. or Kottbusser Tor), is great for cheap breads, vegetables, meat and Turkish sweets.

Al Hamra Raumerstr. 16, Prenzlauer Berg Ⓤ Eberswalder Str. or Ⓢ Prenzlauer Allee. See map, p.463. Relaxed, extremely popular Arabian-style café-bar. Good food and cheap drinks every day – Sunday brunch until 5pm is especially tasty (€9).

Burgeramt Frühstücksklub Krossener Str. 22, on Boxhagener Platz Ⓤ Frankfurter Tor or Ⓢ Warschauer Str. See map, pp.466–467. *Imbiss* place with a slightly eccentric line in burger toppings – pineapple, teriyaki and gouda appear together – but there are plenty of classic and veggie versions, making it a perfect bar-hopping pit stop in Friedrichshain. Open till midnight. Burgers €2–5.

Burgermeister Oberbaumstr. 8 Ⓤ Schlesisches Tor. See map, pp.466–467. Cult burger joint in converted old Prussian public toilets by the elevated underground station at Schlesisches Tor serving fresh and delicious burgers (€2–3.50) that could hold their own in far classier surroundings. Has a couple of places to sit, but mostly it's standing room only and often packed. Mon–Thurs 11am–2am, Fri & Sat 11am–4am, Sun 3pm–2am.

Curry 36 Mehringdamm 36, west Kreuzberg Ⓤ Mehringdamm. See map, p.460–461. One of the best places to try Berlin *Currywurst* (€1.60) – a traditional fast-food combo of grilled sausage, hot tomato sauce and curry powder. Open daily until 4am.

Dolores Rosa-Luxemburg-Str. 7, Mitte Ⓢ & Ⓤ Alexanderplatz. See map, p.463. Mouthwatering California-style Mexican fast food, complete with San Francisco decor and a predictable concentration of expats. Burritos from €3.90.

Entweder Oder Oderberger Str. 15, Prenzlauer Berg Ⓤ Eberwelder Str. See map, p.463. Friendly, typically Prenzlauer Berg café-bar, with a tasty menu of German dishes that's perfect for a hangover-beating breakfast: either a big platter for two for €13.50, or the "Italian" option – an espresso and a cigarette (€2).

Il Casolare Grimmstr. 30, Kreuzberg Ⓤ Schönleinstr. See map, p.466. Always-packed Italian restaurant in a lovely, leafy canalside spot that's famous for its great wafer-thin pizzas (from €7) and brusque service.

Kauf dich Glücklich Oderberger Str. 44, Prenzlauer Berg Ⓤ Eberwelder Str. See map, p.463. Super-cute, café-bar-shop waffle and ice-cream parlour combination, all done out in Fifties retro furniture (that's for sale).

Knofi Bergmannstr. 11 & 98, west Kreuzburg Ⓤ Mehringdamm. See map, p.466. The *Gössies* – filled Turkish crêpes – are cheap (€4), huge and delicious at this lively local Mediterranean café (no. 11) and deli (no. 98); there's the same menu of soups, salads and some hot dishes at both, and a smaller choice at their other deli at Oranienstr. 179 (Ⓤ Kottbusser Tor), where you can get a plate of salads and pâtés for €7.

Kuchi Gipsstr. 3, Mitte Ⓤ Weinmeister Str. See map, p.463. Deliciously fresh, imaginative sushi, all prepared in front of you, is the speciality at this stylish Mitte restaurant. Well worth the slightly higher prices: sushi selection from around €9, stir-fried noodles with tofu €10.

Kvartira Nr. 62 Lübbener Stra. 18 ⓣ0179/134 33 43 Ⓤ Schlesisches Tor. See map, p.466.

Atmospheric Russian cafe in 1920s-era dark red and gold decor serving Russian classics such as *borscht* (€3), delicious *pelimi* (dumplings; €4.50) and tea flavoured with jam – as well as some great chocolate cake.

Monsieur Vuong Alte Schönhauser Str. 46, Mitte Ⓤ Weinmeisterstr. See map, p.463. Small, hip and popular Vietnamese place with a high-quality, low-price menu that changes daily. Meals €8.

Sowohl als Auch Kollwitzstr. 88, Prenzlauer Berg Ⓤ Eberswalder or Senefelderplatz. See map, p.463. Excellent cake selection, with an extensive coffee and tea menu to boot; also popular for breakfast.

Drinking and nightlife

Berlin's nightlife ranks among the best in the world and is centred on several different neighbourhoods. As Hackescher Markt and Oranienburger Str. become more upmarket, and touristy, the best bars tend to be in the inner-city residential areas: in Prenzlauer Berg, try the area around Kastanienallee for places with a relaxed, neighbourhood feel; in Friedrichshain, the Simon-Dach-Str. is a premier twenty-something late-night hangout; while many of the city's best clubs and prime alternative hangouts are in the vicinity or in the adjoining ramshackle district of Kreuzberg. If you fancy exploring Berlin's legendary nightlife in the company of other young travellers, consider joining a pub crawl tour. For around €12 you'll be taken to half a dozen watering holes and a club (cover included). All companies offering walking tours (see p.470) also organize pub crawls.

Bars

Astro Simon-Dach-Str. 40, Friedrichshain Ⓤ Frankfurter Tor. See map, p.466. Always packed pre-club kitsch bar with different DJs nightly.

EndDorn Belforter Str. 27, Prenzlauer Berg Ⓤ Senefelderplatz. See map, p.463. Cosy, brick-walled bar, which also does cheap food, for around €5. Closed Sun, drinks only Sat.

Klub der Republik Pappelallee 81, Prenzlauer Berg Ⓤ Eberswalder Str. See map, p.463. Cheap drinks and frequent live DJs in this fabulous chilled-out lounge-bar that gets the shabby-retro look just right. Fire-escape steps up to the entrance.

Kptn. A. Müller Simon-Dach-Str. 32 Ⓤ & Ⓢ Warschauer Str. See map, p.466. Ramshackle, sociable and very popular budget bar, with a neighbourhood feel and free table football. Daily 6pm until late.

Lurette Str. 105, Friedrichshain Ⓤ Frankfurter Tor & Ⓢ Warschauer Str. See map, p.466. Retro bar-club, complete with 1960s wall projections, dishing up cheap cocktails to an upbeat crowd.

Prater Biergarten Kastanienallee 7–9 Ⓤ Eberswalder Str. See map, p.463. Large and relaxed Prenzlauer Berg beer garden. April–Sept daily from noon (weather permitting). The attached *Gaststätte* serves German classics year-round.

Scotch & Sofa Kollwitzstr. 18, Prenzlauer Berg Ⓤ Senefelderplatz. See map, p.463. Trendy, relaxed pre-club bar with free internet and a loyal crowd.

Strandbar Mitte Monbijoustr. 3, Mitte Ⓢ Hackescher Markt. See map, p.463. Seasonal (April–Oct), popular city beach bar with sand and deckchairs overlooking the River Spree.

Tacheles Oranienburger Str. 54–56, Mitte Ⓤ Oranienburger Tor. See map, p.463. Now a bit of a counter-culture theme park, this huge squat-style arts centre is something of an institution. It includes a cinema, three bars and beer garden. Its *Café Zapata* gets some good bands in.

Clubs

Don't bother turning up before 1am at Berlin's clubs. To find out what's on, pick up one of the listings magazines, *Zitty* (Ⓦ www.zitty.de), *Tip* (Ⓦ www.tip-berlin.de), or the English-language *Exberliner* (Ⓦ www.exberliner.com).

Bang Bang Club Choriner Str. 34. Mitte Ⓦ www.bangbang-club.de Ⓢ Hackescher Markt. See map, p.463. Studenty indie club, which is one of the locations of the excellent *Karrera Klub* (Ⓦ www.karreraklub.de), and puts on good gigs.

GAY BERLIN

Berlin's diverse **gay scene** is spread across the city, but there's a discernible gay village just south of Ⓤ Nollendorfplatz in Schöneberg. Here you'll find bars like *Heile Welt at* Motzstr. 5 (daily 6pm–late see map, p.470), one of Berlin's youngest and trendiest gay bars with great cocktails and a convivial atmosphere. This is one place to pick up gay listings magazine *Siegessäule* (Ⓦ www.siegessaeule.de), also available in many local cafés and shops. Look out for Club nights by GMF (Ⓦ www.gmf-berlin.de) at various venues, including Sundays at *Weekend* (see p.470), and visit *Berghain* (see above), a mixed venue with a strong gay presence. The Christopher Street Day Gay Pride festival takes place every year in June (Ⓦ www.csd-berlin.de).

Berghain Am Wriezener Bahnhof, Friedrichshain Ⓦwww.berghain.de Ⓢ Ostbahnhof. See map, p.466. Legendary techno club in a huge former power station, which attracts a mixed gay–straight crowd; entrance policy is strict and generally turns away anyone who looks like a foreign backpacker. Upstairs *Panorama Bar* Fri & Sat, *Berghain* usually Sat only, until well into Sun.

Cassiopeia Revaler Str. 99 Ⓦwww.cassiopeia-berlin.de Ⓢ & Ⓤ Warschauer Str. See map, p.466. Shambolic former squat with a mad combination of skate-park, climbing wall, cinema, beer garden and four dancefloors. Always worth a look.

Clärchens Ballhaus Auguststr. 24 Ⓦwww.ballhaus.de Ⓢ Hackescher Markt. See map, p.463. Dancehall that harks back to 1913 which hosts a range of dance nights, with instruction – check website for times and styles. Also dishes up great pizzas.

Kaffee Burger Torstr. 60, Mitte Ⓦwww.kaffeeburger.de Ⓤ Rosenthaler Platz/Rosa-Luxemburg-Platz. See map, p.463. Small, former GDR bar decorated in deep flushed red, with an eclectic range of live music, spoken word events and club nights, including the infamously funky Russian disco twice monthly.

Privatclub Pücklerstr. 34, Kreuzberg Ⓦwww.privatclub-berlin.de Ⓤ Görlitzer Bhf. See map, p.466. Intimate basement club (under *Markthalle*, a more sedate café) with an eclectic range of nights, including soul, Balkan-electronica and indie. Open Fri & Sat; other nights for the occasional live gig.

Rosi's Revalerstr 29, Friedrichshain Ⓦwww.rosis-berlin.de Ⓢ Warschauer Str. See map, p.466. Quirky and hugely fun with Berlin's hallmark unfinished and improvised feel. There's a sense of crashing a house party here, with a small kitchen and living room to hang out in between bouts on dancefloors where indie or techno pounds. Outdoor table tennis too.

SO 36 Oranienstr. 190, Kreuzberg Ⓦwww.so36.de Ⓤ Görlitzer Bhf. See map, p.466. Cult Punk club with a large gay and lesbian following. Sunday's *Café Fatal* – ballroom dance class at 7pm, dancing from 8pm – is a fantastically friendly gay and mixed free-for-all. Also frequent live music.

Watergate Falckensteinstr. 49 Ⓦwww.water-gate.de Ⓤ Schlesisches. See map, p.466. Tor. Futuristic club with impressive light installations with a glorious riverside location; music is varied but mostly electronic.

Weekend Alexanderplatz 7, Mitte Ⓦwww.week-end-berlin.de Ⓤ & Ⓢ Alexanderplatz. See map, p.463. Floors 12, 15 and the roof of a GDR-era tower block (the one with the Sharp sign at the top) are taken over by this techno club – great views, particularly from the roof, but slightly posey.

Entertainment

If you're hunting for cut-rate last-minute tickets to just about any kind of show or event, try Hekticket, which sells half-price tickets from 2pm and has two locations: Hardenberg Str. 29a, Charlottenburg, opposite the main entrance to Ⓤ & Ⓢ Zoologischer Garten (Ⓣ030/230 99 33 33, Ⓦwww.hekticket.de); and Karl-Liebknecht-Str. 12, Mitte, north of the TV tower, Ⓤ & Ⓢ Alexanderplatz (Ⓣ030/24 31 24 31, Ⓦwww.hekticket.de).

CineStar Potsdamerstr. 4 Ⓦwww.cinestar.de Ⓤ & Ⓢ Potsdamer Platz. Cinema in the Sony Center on Potsdamer Platz that screens films in English; €8/€6.50 students.

Philharmonie Herbert-von-Karajan-Str. 1 Ⓣ030/25 48 80, Ⓦwww.berliner-philharmoniker.de Ⓤ & Ⓢ Potsdamer Platz. Custom-built home of the world's most celebrated orchestra, the Berlin Philharmonic.

Staatsoper Unter den Linden 7 Ⓣ030/20 35 40, Ⓦwww.staatsoper-berlin.org Ⓢ & Ⓤ Friedrichstr. Excellent operatic productions in one of central Berlin's most beautiful buildings.

Shopping

Clothes Boutiques and local designers are in good supply in Berlin, though bargains are rare. The area just northeast from Ⓢ Hackescher Markt is the best place for shoe boutiques. Head to Prenzlauer Berg (from Kastanienallee to Helmholzplatz) for high-quality, high-priced local designers, and to the Boxhagener Platz area of Friedrichshain for the latest hipster apparel.

Markets Flea markets (*Flohmärkte*) abound in Berlin; head to the Mauerpark in Prenzlauer Berg on Sunday from 8am–6pm (tram #M10 to Bernauer Str./Wolliner Str.) for the best bargains.

Directory

Bike rental and tours Many hostels rent out bikes for around €12/day, as do Fat Tire (daily: 9.30am–6pm, to 8pm April–Sept; Ⓣ030/24 04 79 91, Ⓦfattirebiketours.com/berlin), beneath the TV tower at Alexanderplatz. They also offer bike tours (€22/students €20 for 4hr 30min).

Embassies and consulates Australia, Wallstr. 76–79 Ⓣ030/880 08 82 31; Canada, Leipziger Platz 17 Ⓣ030/20 31 20; Ireland Jägerstr. 51 Ⓣ030/22 07 20, Ⓦwww.embassyofireland.de; New Zealand, Friedrichstr. 60 Ⓣ030/20 62 10, Ⓦwww.nzembassy.com; South Africa, Tiergartenstr. 18 Ⓣ030/22 07 30, Ⓦwww.suedafrika.org; UK, Wilhelmstr. 70–71 Ⓣ030/20 45 70,

Ⓦwww.britischebotschaft.de; US, Clayallee 170 Ⓣ030/830 50, Ⓦwww.germany.usembassy.gov.

Exchange ATMs and exchange at the airports, and major stations including Reisebank, at the Hauptbahnhof (daily 8am–10pm).

Hospitals There's an emergency room at Campus Charité Mitte, entrance Luisenstr. 65/66, Mitte Ⓣ030/450 50.

Internet Free wi-fi at the Sony Center; internet access in all hostels (around €2/30min) and also at NetLounge, Auguststr. 89.

Pharmacy Apotheke Haupbahnhof, at the Hauptbahnhof. Open 24/7.

Post office The post office (Postämt) with the longest hours is at Bahnhof Friedrichstr., at Georgenstr. 12 (Mon–Fri 6am–10pm, Sat & Sun 8am–10pm).

Moving on

Train Cologne (hourly; 5hr 20min); Dresden (every 2hr; 2hr); Frankfurt (hourly; 4hr); Hamburg (hourly; 1hr 40min); Hannover (hourly; 2hr); Leipzig (hourly; 1hr 15min); Munich (hourly; 6hr); Paris (4 daily, including overnight; 8–10hr); Prague (every 2hr; 4hr 40min); Warsaw (5 daily; 5hr 25min); Weimar (every 2hr; 2hr 20min).

DAY-TRIPS FROM BERLIN

Easy and engaging day-trips using the S-Bahn include the town of **Potsdam**, just southwest of Berlin, that's famous for the lavish summer palaces and gardens of the Prussian royalty at Sanssouci. Just beyond Berlin's northern edge lies the sombre site of the former **Sachsenhausen** concentration camp.

Potsdam: Park Sanssouci

Stretching west from **POTSDAM**'s town centre is Park Sanssouci (park entry free, but €2 donation requested for which you get a useful map; day ticket for all sights €19/students €14), a dazzling collection of eighteenth- and nineteenth-century Baroque and Rococo palaces and ornamental gardens that were the fabled retreat of the Prussian kings. Dotted with follies, fountains and themed gardens, you could easily lose a day exploring the extensive park. **Schloss Sanssouci** (April–Oct Tues–Sun 10am–6pm; €12/students €8; Nov–March Tues–Sun 10am–5pm; €8/students €5), the star attraction, was a pleasure palace completed in 1747, where Frederick the Great could escape the stresses of Berlin and his wife. Head here first, as tickets are timed and sell out fast. East of the palace is the **Bildergalerie** (May–Oct Tues–Sun 10am–6pm; €3/ students €2.50), a restrained Baroque creation with paintings by Rubens, Van Dyck and Caravaggio. On the opposite side of the Schloss, the **Neue Kammern** (April Wed–Mon 10am–6pm; May–Oct Tues–Sun 10am–6pm; Nov–March Wed–Mon 10am–5pm; €4/students €3) was originally used as an orangerie and later converted into a guest palace in similar lavish Rococo style. West of here, the **Orangerie**, (April Sat & Sun 10am–6pm; May–Oct Tues–Sun 10am–6pm; €4/students €3, tower €2), a later, Neoclassical palace built by Frederick William IV in 1826 features the astonishing Raphael Hall, covered with quality copies of many of Raphael's most famous works. At the west end of the 1.5km-long stylized gardens, stands the massive Rococo **Neues Palais** (Wed–Mon: April–Oct 10am–6pm; Nov–March 10am–5pm; €6/students €5), which has an exquisitely opulent interior.

Arrival and information

Arrival Ⓢ#7 (every 10min; 35min; zone C) or a regional train to Potsdam. From Potsdam train station bus #695 (every 20min) or #X5 to Schloss Sanssouci (2km); #695 also stops at the Neues Palais, the Orangerie and the Dachhaus.

Information Potsdam tourist office is in the train station (April–Oct Mon–Sat 9.30am–8pm, Sun 10am–4pm; Nov–March Mon–Fri 9.30am–6pm, Sun 10am–4pm). Sanssouci's main information office is by the windmill (Historische Mühle; daily: March–Oct 8.30am–5pm; Nov–Feb 9am–4pm) near the Schloss Sanssoucci entrance.

Gedenkstätte Sachsenhausen

Over 200,000 people were imprisoned at **Sachsenhausen concentration camp** between 1936 and 1945, of which many tens of thousands died at the hands of the Nazis. Some original buildings have been turned into a memorial with exhibitions (daily: mid-March to mid-Oct 8.30am–6pm; mid-Oct to mid-March 8.30am–4.30pm; free audio tour €3; leaflet €0.50; Ⓦwww.stiftung-bg.de/gums/en/index.htm). Take Ⓢ #1 to Oranienburg (every 10min; 50min; zone C), and then bus #804 or #821 or walk for twenty minutes, following the signs to Sachsenhausen.

Eastern Germany

Berlin stands apart from the rest of the East, but its dynamism finds an echo in the two other main cities in the region: particularly in **Dresden**, the beautiful Saxon capital so ruthlessly destroyed in 1945, now rebuilt and thriving, and **Leipzig**, which provided the vanguard of the 1989 revolution. Both combine some interesting sights and excellent museums and galleries, with a fun, irreverent bar and club scene. Equally enticing are some of the smaller places, notably the beautiful, diminutive **Weimar**, the fountainhead of much of European art and culture, while small-town **Meissen** retains the appearance and atmosphere of prewar Germany.

DRESDEN

Once generally regarded as Germany's most beautiful city, **DRESDEN** survived World War II largely unscathed until the night of February 13, 1945. Then, in a matter of hours, it was reduced to ruins in saturation bombing, with around 18,000 to 25,000 people killed. Post-reunification, the city has slotted easily into the economic framework of the reunited Germany, and most of the historic buildings have been brilliantly restored in an ambitious and hugely successful project. Its physical revival is reflected in its resurgent nightlife, its thriving Neustadt-centred scene is a hedonistic surprise.

What to see and do

The city's main sights are in the picturesque **Altstadt**, which stretches along the southern bank of the River Elbe. The grand Baroque set pieces are centred on **Theaterplatz** – with the Zwinger, Residenzschloss and Semperoper (the grand opera house) – and **Neumarkt** further east. Between the two is Augustusstrasse, along which runs a porcelain-tiled mural, while the formal **Brühlsche Terrasse** is an elegant promenade along the river. The southern part of the Altstadt is more prosaic, though the large 1960s Prager Strasse, which runs down to the Hauptbahnhof, is useful for high-street shopping, while north of the river the **Neustadt** is the best place to eat, drink and sleep.

The Frauenkirche

Dominating Dresden Altstadt's skyline is the elegant, soaring dome of the Baroque **Frauenkirche** (Mon–Fri 10am–noon & 1–6pm; occasionally closed for special events), on the **Neumarkt**. Only a fragment of wall was left standing after the war, and in 1991 the decision was taken to rebuild the church, using many of the original stones, creating a chequerboard of light and dark stones in places. The inside is gloriously light, with an impressive 37-metre-high interior dome. You can climb up the dome for a close-up look and stunning views across town (March–Oct Mon–Sat 10am–6pm, Sun 12.30–6pm; Nov–March till 4pm; €8/students €5). There's a Frauenkirche information centre at Galeriestr. 1 (Mon–Sat 9.30am–6pm) and a ticket office for concerts at Georg-Treu-Platz 3 (Mon–Fri 9am–6pm).

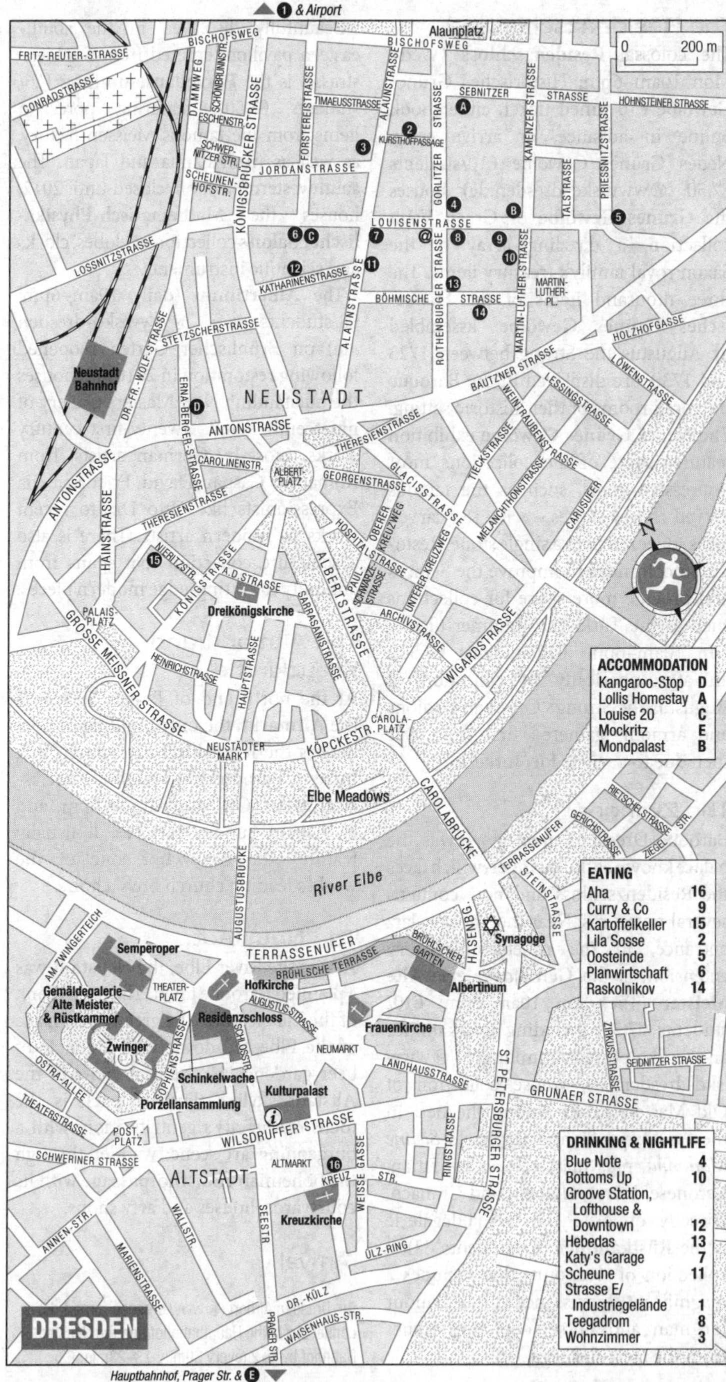
DRESDEN
1 & Airport
Hauptbahnhof, Prager Str. & E
NEUSTADT
ALTSTADT
River Elbe
Elbe Meadows
Alaunplatz
Neustadt Bahnhof
Dreikönigskirche
Semperoper
Gemäldegalerie Alte Meister & Rüstkammer
Zwinger
Hofkirche
Residenzschloss
Frauenkirche
Albertinum
Synagoge
Schinkelwache
Porzellansammlung
Kulturpalast
Kreuzkirche
ACCOMMODATION
Kangaroo-Stop D
Lollis Homestay A
Louise 20 C
Mockritz E
Mondpalast B
EATING
Aha 16
Curry & Co 9
Kartoffelkeller 15
Lila Sosse 2
Oosteinde 5
Planwirtschaft 6
Raskolnikov 14
DRINKING & NIGHTLIFE
Blue Note 4
Bottoms Up 10
Groove Station, Lofthouse & Downtown 12
Hebedas 13
Katy's Garage 7
Scheune 11
Strasse E/ Industriegelände 1
Teegadrom 8
Wohnzimmer 3

The Residenzschloss

The colossal **Residenzschloss** (Wed–Mon 10am–6pm; Historisches Grünes Gewölbe €10 timed ticket, either book online in advance, or arrive early; Neues Grünes Gewölbe €10/students €7.50; Ⓦwww.skd-dresden.de) houses the **Grünes Gewölbe** or Green Vault collection, a dazzling array of the Saxon royal family's treasury items. The three thousand items of the **Historisches Grünes Gewölbe**, assembled by Augustus the Strong between 1723 and 1730, are displayed in the Baroque mirrored rooms of their historic setting. The **Neues Grünes Gewölbe** exhibition features some of the collection's most impressive items, such as the famous carved cherry stones – with 185 carved faces squeezed onto a single stone. Restoration continues to improve the Schloss and provide more space for collections such as the Türkische Kammer (Tues–Sun 10am–6pm; €10/students €7.50), an atmospherically lit collection of Augustus the Strong's Ottoman fashions and armour, gathered first from war then due to a vogue for "turkerie".

The Zwinger

Baroque Dresden's great glory was the palace known as the **Zwinger**, which faces the Residenzschloss and now contains several museums. Near the Theaterplatz entrance, in the nineteenth-century extension, is the **Gemäldegalerie Alte Meister** (Tues–Sun 10am–6pm; €10/students €7.50, including Rüstkammer and Skulpturensammlung; Ⓦwww.skd-dresden.de), whose collection of Old Masters ranks among the best in the world: you'll find Raphael's *Sistine Madonna*, plus masterpieces by Titian, Veronese, Dürer, Holbein and Cranach. Directly opposite the Gemäldegalerie is the **Rüstkammer** (€3/students €2), a collection of weaponry that includes a magnificent Renaissance suit of armour for man and horse, depicting scenes from the Hercules saga.

Beautifully displayed in the southeastern pavilion, entered from Sophienstrasse, is the **Porzellansammlung** (€6/students €3.50), featuring porcelain items from the famous Meissen factory, as well as from China and Japan. The southwestern pavilion, closed until 2012, houses the **Mathematisch-Physikalischer Salon**'s collection of globes, clocks and scientific instruments.

The **Albertinum** (daily 10am–6pm; €8/students €6; Ⓦwww.skd-dresden.de) on Brühlischer Garten reopened following restoration in 2010 and houses the outstanding New Masters Gallery of nineteenth- and twenty-first-century works, most by German artists: from Romantic Caspar David Friedrich via Expressionists like Otto Dix to recent works by modern artists. There is also a sculpture collection that spans from antiquity to cutting-edge modern pieces.

The Altmarkt and Kreuzkirche

At the north end of Prager Strasse is the **Altmarkt**; the only building of note here is the **Kreuzkirche**, a church that mixes a Baroque body with a Neoclassical tower. On Saturdays at 6pm, and at 9.30am Sunday services, it usually features the Kreuzchor, one of the world's leading church boys' choirs.

The Neustadt

Across the River Elbe, the **Neustadt** was a planned Baroque town. The north bank of the Elbe features the green open space of the Elbe Meadows, with a couple of beer gardens and the best views of the Altstadt skyline. Further back is the focus of the city's gentrification, with a burgeoning art scene; wander through the bohemian **Kunsthofpassage** with its courtyards, houses and arty shops.

Arrival

Air Dresden Airport (Ⓦwww.dresden-airport.de) is connected to the Hauptbahnhof and the Neustadt Bahnhof by Ⓢ2 (every 30min; 13–23min; €2).

Train Dresden has two main train stations – the Hauptbahnhof, south of the Altstadt, and Neustadt Bahnhof, at the northwestern corner of the Neustadt.

Information

Tourist office In the Kulturpalast on Altmarkt (Mon–Fri 10am–7pm, Sat 10am–6pm, Sun 10am–3pm; ⓣ0351/50 160 160, ⓦwww.dresden-tourist.de).
Discount passes The good-value Dresden-City-Card (€24/48hr) covers public transport, entrance to all Dresden state museums, except the Historiches Grünes Gewölbe, and sundry discounts. The Dresden Regio-Card (€75/5-day) extends to regional transport.

City transport

Public transport The network of trams, buses and S-Bahn is frequent and reliable, though the main sights are easily walkable. For getting between the Neustadt and Altstadt trams #8 (to Theaterplatz) and #7 (to Synagoge by Brühlischer Garten) are useful. One-way €2; day ticket €5.

Accommodation

Kangaroo-Stop Erna-Berger-Str. 8–10, Neustadt ⓣ0351/314 34 55, ⓦwww.kangaroo-stop.de. Cheap, spacious hostel with a kitchen on a quiet street 3min from the Neustadt Bahnhof, 10min from the bar district. Dorms in one building and apartments and private rooms in another. Dorms €12.50–17.50, doubles €40, apartments €74–88.
Lollis Homestay Görlitzer Str. 34, Neustadt ⓣ0351/810 84 58, ⓦwww.lollishome.de. This wonderfully cosy hostel is in the centre of the lively Neustadt, with friendly staff, quirky rooms, a kitchen (plus free communal dinners weekly) and bikes for rent – though the central location means it can be loud at night. Tram to Alaunplatz or 20min from Neustadt Bahnhof. Sheets €2 extra. Dorms €13–19, doubles €44 (both €2 extra at weekends).
Louise 20 Louisenstr. 20, Neustadt ⓣ0351/889 48 94, ⓦwww.louise20.de. Bright, quiet, though slightly bland, hotel-quality hostel in a courtyard in the bar district. Dorms €16–17, doubles €40–44.
Mockritz Boderitzer Str. 30 ⓣ0351/47 15 250, ⓦwww.camping-dresden.de. This campsite is open year-round. Reception 8–11am & 4–9pm. Bus #76 from the Hauptbahnhof. €5.50/person, plus €3.50 for a small tent.
Mondpalast Louisenstr. 77, Neustadt ⓣ0351/56 34 050, ⓦwww.mondpalast.de. Another great backpackers' place with a kitchen and en-suite doubles on one of the Neustadt's main thoroughfares. Bike rentals €8/day. Tram to Louisenstr., Pulsnitzerstr. or a 20min walk from the Neustadt Bahnhof. Sheets €2. Dorms €14–19.50, doubles €44–52.

Eating

Aha Kreuzstr. 7, Altstadt. Slightly hippy-ish fair-trade café and shop, with a good-value menu of soups and healthy mains.
Curry & Co Louisenstr. 62, Neustadt. Ultra-hip, minimalist *Currywurst* joint. *Currywurst* and fries €4.
Kartoffelkeller Nieritzstr. 11, Neustadt. Potato served in myriad ways, in a beautiful cellar space, at good rates. Roast potatoes with herring fillets €9. Closed Sun.
Lila Sosse Kunsthof alleyway, Alaunstr. 70, Neustadt. A cool bistro in a pretty courtyard that prepares modern German dishes from €11.
Oosteinde Preissnitzstr. 18, Neustadt. Delicious, good-value food served under a low-vaulted roof or outside in a peaceful beer garden. Burgers from €6, mains from €7.50.
Planwirtschaft Louisenstr. 20, Neustadt. Popular café-bar-restaurant and *Biergarten* with great breakfast buffet (Mon–Fri €9, Sat & Sun €11).
Raskolnikov Böhmische Str. 34, Neustadt. A large, rambling, bohemian Russian bar-café and restaurant. Great food and atmospheric beer garden.

Drinking and nightlife

With over 130 bars and clubs clustered around a handful of narrow streets, the Neustadt provides something for everyone. For nightlife listings, pick up a copy of *Sax* or *Dresdner*, (German only) from kiosks or backpacker hostels. Most bars open daily from around 8pm till 3am or later at weekends, also the main clubbing nights.

Bars

Blue Note Görlitzer Str. 2b, Neustadt ⓦwww.bluenote-dresden.de. Dark, smoke-filled and boozy jazz bar, packed to the gills every night for its live music.
Bottoms Up Martin-Luther-Str. 31, Neustadt. Down a quiet backstreet away from the main action, this easy-going café-bar and beer garden is an unpretentious favourite with good weekend breakfasts.
Hebedas Rothenburger Str. 30, Neustadt. Grungy atmospheric bar that epitomizes the Neustadt alternative scene.
Scheune Alaunstr. 36–40, Neustadt ⓦwww.scheune.org. Neustadt arts centre with a welcoming bar, large beer garden, live music,

theatre and gay and lesbian nights; the *Scheune Café* serves Indian food (from €11).

Teegadrom Louisenstr. 48, Neustadt. An alternative to the Neustadt hipster scene: calm and candlelit, with board games.

Wohnzimmer Alaunstr. 27/Jordanstr. 19, Neustadt. Two levels of living-room-themed bar, with comfy couches and good cocktails.

Clubs

Groove Station, Lofthouse & Downtown Katherinenstr. 11–13, Neustadt ⓦwww.groovestation.de, ⓦwww.lofthouse-dresden.de & www.downtown-dresden.de. Set around a courtyard, this rough-and-ready rock, hip-hop and dance bar and live music complex has been a Neustadt cornerstone for years.

Katy's Garage Alaunstr. 48, Neustadt ⓦwww.katysgarage.de. Neustadt institution – and one of the few clubs to open daily – with a chilled beer garden at the front, and club behind (from 8pm); Monday is student night.

Strasse E/Industriegelände Werner-Hartmann-Str. 2 ⓦwww.strasse-e.de. Industrial area turned club/venue mini-city north of the Neustadt, where there's always something on; next door *Strassencafe* (Thurs–Sun from 6pm) with board games, pool, table football and darts, is good for a pre-club drink. Tram #7 or #8 to Industriegelände, along Hermann-Mende-Str. then right onto Werner-Hartman-Str.

Moving on

Train Berlin (every 2hr; 2hr 15min); Frankfurt (hourly; 4hr 45min); Leipzig (every 30min; 1hr 15min–1hr 40min); Meissen (every 30min; 40min); Prague (every 2hr; 2hr 10min); Weimar (hourly; 2hr 10min); Wrocław (3 daily; 3hr 30min).

DAY-TRIPS FROM DRESDEN

Around Dresden there is stunning scenery in **Saxon Switzerland** and the quaint unspoilt town of **Meissen**, making the city a good base for exploring the region. Both are within Dresden's regional transport network, and the three-day Dresden Regio-Card is good value for week-long stays (see p.475).

Sächsische Schweiz (Saxon Switzerland)

The **Sächsische Schweiz** (Saxon Switzerland) region southeast of Dresden is a natural wonderland of majestic sandstone mountains, offering ample opportunities for hiking, cycling and climbing. One classic route is the 115-kilometre Malerweg (Painter Route), overnighting in the tourist-friendly villages along the way. There are countless day hikes as well, such as Königstein to Rathen via Lilienstein (7km), through woods and open vistas.

It's easy to visit this region from Dresden; just take Ⓢ#1 (every 30min; three-zone ticket €5.60) to Kurort Rathen, Königstein or Bad Schandau and follow trailheads from there; local buses also connect these towns. The tourist office in Dresden (see p.475) sells maps and gives information on the Sächsische Schweiz, or check out ⓦwww.saechsische-schweiz.de.

Meissen

The cobbled square and photogenic rooftop vistas are reason enough to visit the porcelain-producing town of **MEISSEN,** which, unlike its neighbour Dresden, survived World War II almost unscathed.

Walking towards the centre from the **train station** (a 20min walk over the railroad bridge or the Altstadtbrücke; both are signposted), on the opposite side of the River Elbe, you see Meissen's commandingly sited castle almost immediately, rising just back from the Elbe's edge. The **Albrechtsburg** (daily: March–Oct 10am–6pm; Nov–Feb 10am–5pm; €8/students €4) is a late fifteenth-century combination of military fortress and residential palace, which housed a porcelain factory in the eighteenth and nineteenth centuries. Much of its current interior is nineteenth century, with murals celebrating Saxon history. Cocooned within the castle precinct is the Gothic **Dom** (daily: April–Oct 9am–6pm; Nov–March 10am–4pm; €3/students €2); inside, look out for the brass tomb-plates of the Saxon dukes.

The **Staatliche Porzellan-Manufaktur Meissen** is at Talstr. 9 (daily: May–Oct 9am–6pm; Nov–April 9am–5pm; €9/students €5), about 1.5km south of the central Markt. This is the most famous factory to manufacture Dresden china, whose invention came about when Augustus the Strong imprisoned the alchemist Johann Friedrich Böttger, ordering him to produce gold. Instead, he accidentally invented the first true European porcelain. You can view many of the factory's finest creations in the **museum** or in a shop (free).

Meissen's **tourist office** is located on Markt 3 (April–Oct Mon–Fri 10am–6pm, Sat & Sun 10am–3pm; Nov–March Mon–Fri 10am–5pm, Sat 10am–3pm, Jan closed weekends; Ⓣ03521/41 940, Ⓦwww.touristinfo-meissen.de).

LEIPZIG

LEIPZIG has always been among the most dynamic of German cities. With its influential and respected university, and a tradition of trade fairs dating back to the Middle Ages, there was never the degree of isolation from outside influences experienced by so many cities behind the Iron Curtain. Leipzigers have embraced the challenges of reunification, and the city's imposing monuments, narrow cobbled backstreets and wide-ranging nightlife make for an inviting visit.

What to see and do

Most points of interest lie within the old centre, a compact mix of traditional and often strikingly modern, with several *Passagen*, covered shopping arcades, often with stylish Art Nouveau touches running between the main streets.

Nikolaikirche and Markt

Following Nikolaistrasse due south from the train station brings you to the **Nikolaikirche**, a rallying point during the collapse of the GDR, when its weekly peace prayers, which had been going on for several years, escalated into large protests. Although a sombre medieval structure outside, inside the church is a real eye-grabber thanks to rich decoration, works of art and pink columns with palm-tree-style capitals. A couple of blocks west is the Markt, whose eastern side is entirely occupied by the **Altes Rathaus**, built in the grandest German Renaissance style with elaborate gables and an asymmetrical tower. To the rear of the Altes Rathaus is the Baroque **Alte Handelsbörse**, formerly the trade exchange headquarters. South of the Markt is **Mädler Passage**, an elegant arcade famous for the restaurant *Auerbach's Keller*, which features in Goethe's *Faust*.

Museum der bildenden Künste

Immense and striking, the modern perspex-skinned cube of the **Museum der bildenden Künste**, at Katharinenstra. 10 (Tues & Thurs–Sun 10am–6pm, Wed noon–8pm; €5/students €3.50), houses a distinguished collection, from Old Masters through to twentieth-century artists, and is particularly strong on Leipzig-born Max Beckmann. Traditional galleries are interspersed with airy, two-storey spaces that feature contemporary pieces, many by local artists. The result is imaginative and playful, and showcases some of the work of a thriving local art scene. To explore it further, check out the excellent **Galerie für Zeitgenössische Kunst**, Karl-Tauchnitz-Str. 11, just outside the Ring southwest of the centre (Gallery for Contemporary Art; Tues–Fri 2–7pm, Sat–Sun noon–6pm; €5/students €3); it has a second gallery in the **Spinnerei** galleries complex in an old cotton mill west of the centre (Ⓢ Plagwitz; Ⓦwww.spinnerei.de).

The Thomaskirche and Bach-Museum

Just southwest of the Markt, on Thomaskirchof, stands the

Thomaskirche, where Johann Sebastian Bach served as cantor for the last 27 years of his life. Predominantly Gothic, the church has been altered through the centuries. The most remarkable feature is its musical tradition: the Thomanerchor choir, which Bach once directed, can usually be heard on Fridays (6pm), Saturdays (3pm) and during the Sunday service (9.30am). Directly across from the church is the **Bach-Museum** (Tues–Sun 10am–6pm; €6/students €4), which showcases Bach relics such as his manuscripts and evokes his period and music through modern displays.

Runde Ecke and Zeitgeschichtliches Forum

In the autumn of 1989 Leipzig was at the forefront of protests against the GDR, and one focus for this was the **Runde Ecke**, at Dittrichring 24, the city's headquarters for the Stasi, East Germany's secret police (daily 10am–6pm; free; helpful English audioguide €3). Much of it has been preserved as it was, complete with a Stasi official's office, making it a fascinating trawl through the methods and machinery of the Stasi.

Less atmospheric but slicker is the **Zeitgeschichtliches Forum** (Tues–Fri 9am–6pm, Sat & Sun 10am–6pm; free; ask for English notes), just south of the Markt at Grimmaische Str. 6, a multimedia museum on the history of the GDR.

The Grassi museums

Just east of the centre is the **Grassi museum** complex, which houses a trio of museums at Johannisplatz 5–11 (Tues–Sun 10am–6pm; combined ticket €12/students €9; tram #4, #7, #12 or #15 to Johannisplatz), with the **Museum für Angewandte Kunst** (Applied Arts; €5/students €3.50), the star, a huge and well-displayed collection of decorative arts. The other two are the **Museum für Völkerkunde** (Ethnology; €6/students €3) and the **Museum für Musikinstrumente** (Musical instruments; €5/students €3).

Arrival and information

Air Leipzig-Halle Airport (www.leipzig-halle-airport.de) is connected with the main train station by the Airport Express train (every 30min; 15min).
Train Leipzig's enormous Hauptbahnhof is at the northeastern corner of the Ring, which encircles the old part of the city.
Tourist office Beside the Museum der bildenden Künste at Katharinenstr. 8 (Mon–Fri 9.30am–6pm, Sat 9.30am–4pm, Sun 9.30am–3pm; Nov–Feb opens Mon–Fri at 10am; 0341/71 04 260, www.leipzig.de); staff can book private rooms (free service). Their Leipzig Card (1-day €8.90/3-day/€18.50), which covers public transport and various discounts, is unlikely to work out as good value – particularly if you get student discounts, which are often the same.
City transport A network of trams and buses centring on the Hauptbahnhof covers places outside the city centre; trams #9 and #11 are useful for Karl-Liebknecht-Str. Up to four stops (Kurzstrecke) €1.50, one-way ticket €2, day ticket €5.

Accommodation

Auensee Gustav-Esche-Str. 5 0341/46 51 600, www.camping-auensee.de. This campsite is open year-round, with bungalow rooms available (€30). Reception daily: April–Oct 8am–1pm & 2–9.30pm; Nov–March 8am–1pm & 2–5.30pm; tram #10 or #11 (direction Wahren/Schkeuditz) to Annaberger Str., then bus #80 to Auensee. €6/person, plus €3.50/small tent.
Central Globetrotter Kurt-Schumacher-Str. 41 0341/14 98 960, www.globetrotter-leipzig.de. Popular backpacker spot 3min walk north of the station. Sheets €2.50, sleeping bags not allowed. Dorms €12.50–19 (€2 extra at weekends), double rooms €38–44.
Rizz City Karl-Liebknecht-Str. 40 0341/2 11 33 05, www.ritz-city.de. Excellent *pension* between the hip Südvorstadt neighbourhood and the centre, though front rooms can suffer traffic noise. Quads available, breakfast not included. Tram #10 or #11 to Südplatz. Doubles €70.
Sleepy Lion Jacobstr. 1 0341/99 39 480, www.hostel-leipzig.de. In a renovated building since 2011, this is a spacious, well-run hostel west of the centre, 15min walk from the station. Sheets €2.50, sleeping bags not allowed. Dorms €12.50–€16 (€2 extra at weekends), doubles €42–54, apartments €55–80.

Eating and drinking

Gottschedstr., just west of the Thomaskirche, is lined with attractive cafés and bars, while Karl-Liebknecht-Str. a couple of tram stops south of the centre (#10 or #11), is lively and studenty.

Kickers in Karl-Liebknecht-Str. 82. Small, relaxed bar with free table football; open till 3am at weekends. Tram #10 or #11 to Südplatz.

Luise Bosestr. 4, corner of Gottschedstr. Chic café-bar with an attractive vaguely Pop Art decor, that serves excellent breakfasts (from €4.50) and pasta dishes.

Maga Pon Gottschedstr. 11. One of the oddest spots in town may just be this well-located and eccentrically decorated *Waschcafé* – scrambled eggs and a load of laundry, €3 each; also has a small beer garden.

Zur Pleissenburg Ratsfreichulstr. 2, just south of Thomaskirche off Burgstr. Great-value pub-restaurant in the centre serving hearty German food daily until late at night. Daily specials from €5.

Nightlife

Ilses Erika Bernhard-Göring-Str. 152, Südvorstadt ⓦwww.ilseserika.de. Indie bar, club and music venue Thurs–Sat; beer garden all summer long. Tram to Connewitz Kreuz.

Moritzbastei Universitätsstr. 9 ⓦwww.moritzbastei.de. A cavernous student cellar bar and club in the centre, with lots of events on, including live music, and with beer gardens and a cheap student canteen.

naTo Karl-Liebknecht-Str. 46, Südvorstadt ⓦwww.nato-leipzig.de. Popular bar, live music venue and cinema. Tram #10 or #11 to Südplatz.

Moving on

Train Berlin (hourly; 1hr 20min); Dresden (every 30min; 1hr 15min–1hr 40min); Frankfurt (hourly; 3hr 30min); Meissen (hourly; 1hr 20min); Weimar (hourly; 1hr).

WEIMAR

Despite its modest size, **WEIMAR** has played an unmatched role in the development of German culture: Goethe, Schiller and Nietzsche all made it their home, as did the architects and designers of the Bauhaus school. The town was also chosen as the drafting place for the constitution of the democratic republic established after World War I, a regime whose failure ended with the Nazi accession. Add to this the town's cobbled streets and laidback, quietly highbrow atmosphere and Weimar makes an attractive stop for a day or two.

What to see and do

Weimar's main sights are concentrated in the city's walkable centre, south of the main train station and on the west side of the River Ilm. The meadow-like **Park an der Ilm** stretches 2km southwards from the **Schloss** on both sides of the river. The former concentration camp at **Buchenwald** is a bus ride to the northwest.

The Schloss and Markt

Weimar's former seat of power was the **Schloss**, set by the River Ilm at the eastern edge of the town centre, a Neoclassical complex of a size more appropriate for ruling a mighty empire. It's now a museum (Tues–Sun: April–Oct 10am–6pm; Nov–March 10am–4pm; €3/students €2.50), with a collection of Old Masters on the ground floor, including pieces by both Cranachs and Dürer, while the first-floor rooms are grand Neoclassical chambers, with lavish memorial rooms to great poets – most notably Goethe and Schiller. South of nearby Herderplatz is the spacious **Markt**, lined with a disparate jumble of buildings, the most eye-catching of which is the green and white gabled Stadthaus on the eastern side, opposite the neo-Gothic Rathaus.

The Goethewohnhaus und Nationalmuseum

On Frauenplan, south of the Markt, is the **Goethewohnhaus und Nationalmuseum** (Tues–Sun: April–Sept 9am–6pm, Sat till 7pm; Oct 9am–6pm; Nov–March 9am–4pm; combined €8.50/students €7; Nationalmuseum only €3/students €2.50). Goethe lived here for some fifty years until his death in 1832, and the house is atmospherically preserved as it was in his lifetime, complete with his extensive collections and the chair in which he died.

Theaterplatz and around

Weimar's most photographed symbol is the large double statue of Goethe and Schiller. It stands in the centre of Theaterplatz, a spacious square west of the Markt. The **Nationaltheater** on the west side of the square was founded and directed by Goethe, though the present building is a modern copy. Directly opposite is the small but interesting **Bauhaus museum**, with a collection of artefacts from the school (daily 10am–6pm; €4.50/students €3.50).

Schillerstrasse snakes away from the southeast corner of Theaterplatz, with **Schillerhaus** at no. 12 (Tues–Sun: April–Sept 9am–6pm, Sat till 7pm; Oct 9am–6pm; Nov–March 9am–4pm; €5 /students €4), the home of the poet and dramatist for the last three years of his life.

Konzentrationslager Buchenwald

The **Konzentrationslager Buchenwald** (Tues–Sun: April–Oct 10am–6pm; Nov–March 10am–4pm; free; www.buchenwald.de) is situated north of Weimar on the Ettersberg heights, and can be reached by bus #6 (hourly from Goetheplatz and the train station). Over 240,000 prisoners were incarcerated in this concentration camp, with 65,000 dying here. Very few original buildings remain, but an audioguide (€3) and the historical exhibition paint a vivid picture of life and death in the camp.

Arrival and information

Train Weimar's train station, on the Leipzig line, is a 20min walk north of the main sights.

Tourist office Markt 10 (April–Oct Mon–Sat 9.30am–7pm, Sun 9.30am–3pm; Nov–March Mon–Fri 9.30am–6pm, Sat & Sun 9.30am–2pm; ☎03643/54 54 07, www.weimar.de).

Accommodation

DJH Germania Carl-August-Allee 13 ☎03643/85 04 90, www.djh-thueringen.de. Neat and tidy HI hostel between the station and the centre. There's another DJH on the other side of the centre at Humboldt Str. 17 (☎03643/85 07 92). Dorms €27.

Labyrinth Hostel Goetheplatz 6 ☎03643/81 18 22, www.weimar-hostel.com. Fantastic, central and friendly hostel each of whose attractive spotless rooms were individually designed by different local artists. There's a good kitchen, a relaxed communal area and a courtyard. Dorms €14–21, doubles €46.

Savina Meyerstr. 60 ☎03643/8 66 90, www.pension-savina.de. Convenient *pension* where all rooms have en-suite bathrooms and kitchenettes. Doubles from €60, singles €45.

Eating and drinking

There's a market on the Markt (Mon–Sat 9am–4.30pm).

ACC Burgplatz 1. A relaxed bar and restaurant with quiet candlelit tables lining a cobbled side street, free internet and an upstairs gallery. Mains from €7.

Estragon Herderplatz 3. Small café that's part of an organic supermarket, with a daily changing menu of tasty, filling soups (€2.80–5.30) and a salad bar (pay by weight). Mon–Fri 10am–7pm, Sat 10am–4pm.

Giancarlo's Schillerstr. 11. Gloriously old-fashioned Italian ice-cream parlour, with over sixty home-made flavours – try the bitter chocolate – or there are extravagant sundaes and waffles. The €1 breakfast (9–11am) of coffee and a croissant, doughnut or roll is unbeatable value.

Kasseturm Goetheplatz 10. Student club in an atmospheric brick tower, which has some good live music nights.

Moving on

Train Dresden (hourly; 2hr 10min); Eisenach (every 30min; 45min–1hr 10min); Frankfurt (hourly; 2hr 30min); Leipzig (hourly; 1hr).

EISENACH: THE WARTBURG

A small town on the edge of the Thuringian Forest, **EISENACH** is home to the best-loved medieval castle in Germany, the **Wartburg**. The castle complex, first mentioned in 1080, includes one of the best-preserved Romanesque palaces this side of the Alps, as well as newer additions, including the Festsaal, a nineteenth-century interpretation of medieval grandeur so splendid that Ludwig II of Bavaria had it copied for his fairytale palace, Neuschwanstein. The tour takes you through the ornately decorated rooms. Also on view is a small exhibition of paintings – including some elegant portraits by Cranach – and, the **Lutherstube**, the room in which Martin Luther translated the New Testament into the German vernacular while in hiding in 1521–22. The castle can only be viewed on **guided tours** (every 15min; daily: April–Oct 8.30am–5pm; Nov–March 9am–3.30pm; €9/students €5); ask for an English translation of the guide's script.

Arrival and information

Arrival Eisenach is 45min–1hr 10min from Weimar by train, and can be done as a day-trip. The Wartburg is a good hour's walk from the train station (you can get a map from DB information at the train station or tourist office). From the station head southwest along Wartburgallee; after 20–30min at Reuter Villa there's a signposted footpath up to the Wartburg – it's a pretty steep 30min climb from here. From April–Oct bus #10 runs hourly from the train station to the Eselstation (donkey station), it's a 15min steep climb to the castle from here.

Tourist information Markt 9 (Mon–Fri 10am–6pm, Sat & Sun 10am–5pm; ⓣ03691/79 230, ⓦwww.eisenach.de).

Accommodation and eating

There's a traditional restaurant at the Wartburg, cheap and tasty Thuringian *Rostbratwurst* stalls near the donkey station, and a dozen or so cafés and restaurants around the Markt in the town centre.

DJH Artur Becker Mariental 24 ⓣ03691/74 32 59, ⓦwww.djh-thueringen.de. Clean and friendly hostel, a 30min walk from the station, or take bus #3 or #10; it's on the Wartburg side of town (at the bottom of the hill; about 30min walk from the top). Dorms €22.

Northern Germany

Hamburg, Germany's second city, is infamous for the sleaze and hectic nightlife of the Reeperbahn strip – but it is far more than this, with a sophisticated cultural scene, handsome warehouse quarter and big city allure. Another maritime city, **Lübeck**, has a strong pull, with a similar appeal to the mercantile towns of the Low Countries. To the south lies **Hannover**, worth a visit for its museums and gardens. The province's smaller towns present a fascinating contrast – the former silver-mining town of **Goslar**, in particular, is unusually beautiful.

HAMBURG

Stylish media centre and second-largest port in Europe, **HAMBURG** is undeniably cool – more laidback than Berlin or Frankfurt, more sophisticated than Munich, and with nightlife to rival the lot. Its skyline is dominated by the pale green of its copper spires and domes, but a few houses and churches are all that's left from older times. Though much of the subsequent rebuilding isn't especially beautiful, the result is an intriguing mix of old and new, coupled with an appealing sense of open space – two-thirds of Hamburg is occupied by parks, lakes or canals.

What to see and do

Much of the fun of Hamburg is in exploring different quarters, each with a distinct feel and purpose. The centre, defined by the Binnenalster and Aussenalster lakes to its northeast, and the docks and port to the south, is focused on the oversized **Rathaus**. The streets that span north, particularly **Jungfernstieg** and around, are classy and commercial. But the focus of Hamburg

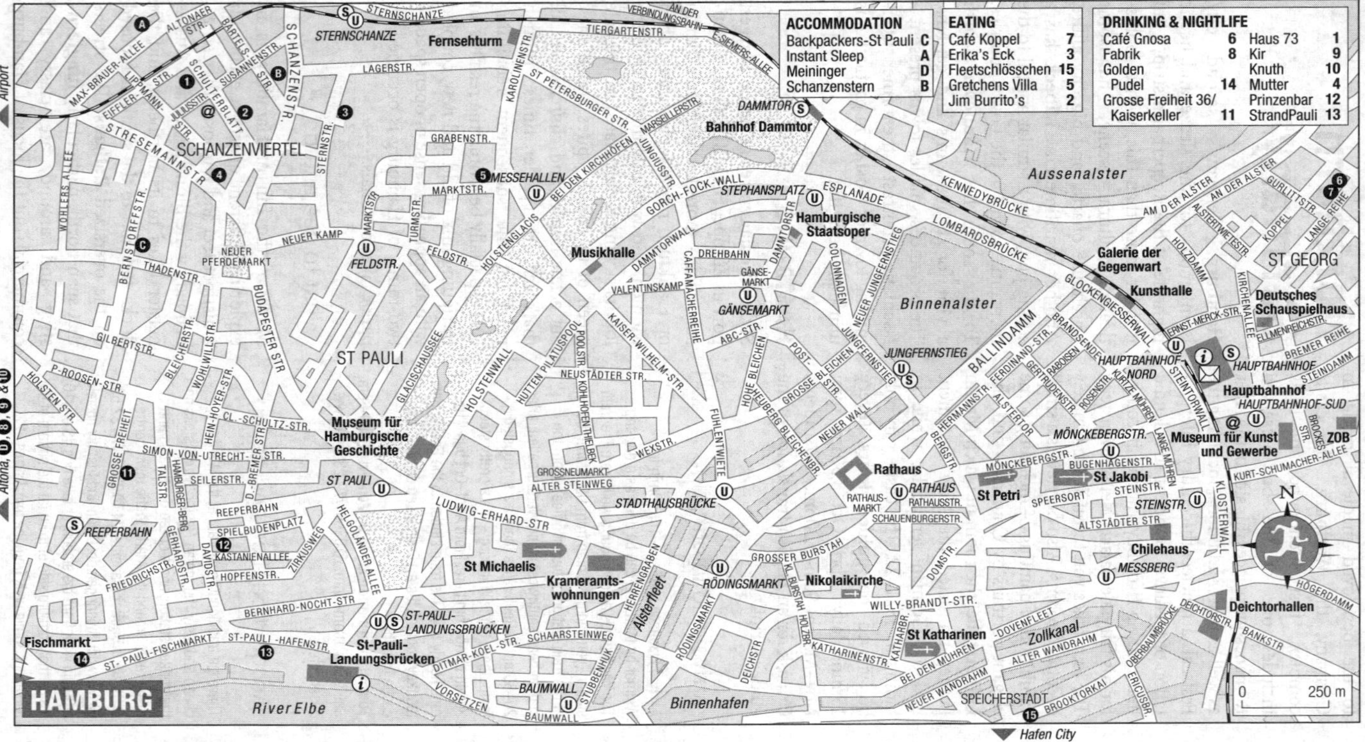
HAMBURG
ACCOMMODATION
Backpackers-St Pauli C
Instant Sleep A
Meininger D
Schanzenstern B
EATING
Café Koppel 7
Erika's Eck 3
Fleetschlösschen 15
Gretchens Villa 5
Jim Burrito's 2
DRINKING & NIGHTLIFE
Café Gnosa 6
Fabrik 8
Golden Pudel 14
Grosse Freiheit 36/Kaiserkeller 11
Haus 73 1
Kir 9
Knuth 10
Mutter 4
Prinzenbar 12
StrandPauli 13
Airport
Altona, D, 8, 9 & 10
Hafen City
SCHANZENVIERTEL
ST PAULI
ST GEORG
Aussenalster
Binnenalster
River Elbe
Binnenhafen
Zollkanal
Alsterfleet
Fernsehturm
Bahnhof Dammtor
Hamburgische Staatsoper
Musikhalle
Galerie der Gegenwart
Kunsthalle
Deutsches Schauspielhaus
Hauptbahnhof
Museum für Kunst und Gewerbe
ZOB
Museum für Hamburgische Geschichte
Rathaus
St Petri
St Jakobi
Chilehaus
Deichtorhallen
St Michaelis
Krameramtswohnungen
Nikolaikirche
St Katharinen
St-Pauli-Landungsbrücken
Fischmarkt
SPEICHERSTADT
0 250 m
N

is the **docks** and **warehouses** along the Elbe River. North from the port are the best neighbourhoods after dark: **St Pauli** and its infamous Reeperbahn, the studenty **Schanzenviertel** further north, and chic **Altona** off to the west.

The Rathaus

The commercial and shopping district centres on **Binnenalster** lake and the neo-Renaissance **Rathaus** (guided tours several times a day in English: Mon–Thurs 10am–3pm, Fri 10am–1pm, Sat 10am–5pm, Sun 10am–4pm; €3), a magnificently pompous demonstration of the city's power and wealth in the nineteenth century.

Nikolaikirche and St Michaelis

Hamburg's skyline is punctuated by a series of church spires – it's worth climbing one to appreciate the surrounding watery expanses. The most dramatic ascent is the glass lift up through the skeletal spire of **Nikolaikirche** on Willy-Brandt-Strasse, which is pretty much all that remains of the church, the rest having been destroyed in 1943. A small, poignant exhibition is displayed in the crypt (daily: May–Sept 10am–8pm; Oct–April 10am–5pm; €3.70 for spire and exhibition). Hamburg's city church is the elegant Baroque **St Michaelis**, on Englische Planke. Its interior is whiter than ever following restoration and you can go up the tower (daily: May–Oct 9am–7.30pm; Nov–April 10am–5pm; €4/students €3.50) for a panorama over the docks.

The waterfront

From the red-brick **Speicherstadt** immediately south of the Markt, via eye-catching new developments of the **HafenCity** area to the impressive utilitarian **port** to the west, Hamburg's waterfront is its most distinctive area. With its tall, ornate warehouses, the nineteenth-century Speicherstadt quarter is the most attractive part to wander and crisscross the bridges at will – Hamburg has more of them than Venice or Amsterdam. Its modern counterpart behind is HafenCity, a 25-year docklands development project with futuristic architecture like the Elbephilharmonie concert hall.

Further west, the harbour area is dominated by the solid wharf building of **St Pauli Landungsbrücken**, while west again along Hafenstrasse is the lcoation for the legendary **Fischmarkt**. Come early on Sunday and you'll find yourself in an amazing trading – and drinking, it's a post-club institution – frenzy; everything is in full swing by 6am then all over by 10am. Around the harbour you can pick up many one-hour **boat tours** (prices start at €12), giving an intriguing look at the port and its industrial containers.

St Pauli and the Schanzenviertel

The former dockers' quarter, **St Pauli**, is now the red-light district and nightlife centre. Its main artery is the **Reeperbahn** – ugly and unassuming by day, blazing with neon at night. Running off here is Grosse Freiheit, the street that famously hosted The Beatles' first gigs – the junction of the two is now Beatles-Platz, with a sculpture of the Fab Four and a nearby museum, Beatles Mania, with memorabilia (daily 11am–6pm; €12/students €9).

The neighbourhood north of here, centred on Schulterblatt, is the **Schanzenviertel**, (or Schanze), home to a riotously good fun, scruffy and studenty bar scene and cool urban ateliers.

The Kunsthalle

Just northeast of the Hauptbahnhof on Glockengiesserwall, is the **Kunsthalle**, Hamburg's unmissable art collection (Tues–Sun 10am–6pm, Thurs till 9pm; €10/students €5). The main building features an outstanding collection, ranging from Old Masters to twentieth century, and includes works by Rembrandt and Munch. An attached glass cube, reached via an underground passageway, houses the **Galerie der Gegenwart** (Contemporary Art; same ticket), with late twentieth-century works plus big temporary exhibitions and installations.

Arrival

Air Ⓢ line S1 connects Hamburg Airport with the main train station (every 10min; 25min; €2.70). The Lübeck Airport (served by Ryanair and Wizz Air) is connected to Hamburg bus station by a shuttle bus (timed to flights; 1hr 15min; €9).
Train The Hauptbahnhof is at the eastern end of the city centre.

Information

Tourist office In the Hauptbahnhof (Mon–Sat 9am–7pm, Sun 10am–6pm; ⓣ040/30 05 13 00, ⓦwww.hamburg-tourismus.de). Also at the airport (daily 5.30am–11pm) and St Pauli–Landungsbrücken 4/5 (Mon–Wed 9.30am–6pm, Thurs–Sat 9.30am–7pm, Sun 9am–6pm).
Discount pass The Hamburg Card (€8.90/20.50/35.90 for 1/3/5 days) gives reduced admission to some of the city's museums as well as free use of public transport.

City transport

Hamburg is big, so its extensive public transport network, made up of U-Bahn, S-Bahn and buses, can come in handy. A short trip costs €1.60, a one-way trip €2.70, a day ticket €5.50 (after 9am, €6.80 before), a day ticket for up to five people is €9.60, and a three-day ticket €16.50.

Accommodation

Backpackers-St Pauli Bernstorffstr. 98 ⓣ040/23 51 70 43, ⓦwww.backpackers-stpauli.de Ⓤ Feldstr. Small backpacker hostel run by St Pauli locals, well located for both St Pauli and the Schanze, with good communal area and bar next door. Sheets €2 (own sleeping bags not permitted), dorms €19.50–25, doubles €60.
Instant Sleep Max-Brauer-Allee 277 ⓣ040/43 18 23 10, ⓦwww.instantsleep.de Ⓢ & Ⓤ Sternschanze. Located in the lively Schanze area, this laidback, basic hostel has the cheapest beds in town, and a kitchen and internet access, though it's on a noisy corner above a bar. Dorms €16.50–21, doubles €52.
Meininger Goetheallee 9–11 ⓣ040/414 31 40 08, ⓦwww.meininger-hostels.com. Slick, large, hotel-standard hostel from this growing chain. All dorms are en suite, the communal areas are stylish, and it's 5min walk from Altona station (Max-Brauer-Allee exit). Prices vary considerably depending on demand, and are cheaper online. Dorms €18–33, doubles from €64.
Schanzenstern Bartelsstr. 12 ⓣ040/439 84 41, ⓦwww.schanzenstern.de Ⓢ & Ⓤ Sternschanze. Eco-hostel in the Schanze area, with an attached organic restaurant. Sheets included. Second comfortable branch in Altona (Kleine Rainstr. 24–26; ⓣ040/3991 91 91; Ⓢ Altona). Dorms €19, doubles from €54.

Eating

Café Koppel In Koppel 66, Lange Reihe 75, northeast of the train station in St Georg district. Relaxed but classy vegetarian café-restaurant that's part of an arts centre, with a small menu of home-made daily specials (around €7), delicious cakes and a pretty summer garden.
Erika's Eck Sternstr. 98 Ⓤ & Ⓢ Sternschanze. This is a firm student favourite, serving huge portions of traditional German dishes almost round the clock, making it popular post-clubbing. Daily from 5pm, till 2pm the next day Mon–Fri, till 9am Sat & Sun.
Fleetschlösschen Brooktorkai 17 Ⓤ Messberg. Atmospheric little café in a small building in the Speicherstadt – worth stopping at to browse through its collection of books on Hamburg and the harbour. Short menu of fairly standard pasta dishes and good coffee.
Gretchens Villa Marktstr. 142 Ⓤ Messehallen. Cute, bright little café with a short daytime menu and heavenly cakes – a good spot for people-watching on this street of stylish shops. Tues–Fri 10am–7pm, Sat–Sun 11am–7pm.
Jim Burrito's Schulterblatt 12, Schanzenviertel Ⓤ & Ⓢ Sternschanze. Laidback Schanze take on Mexican: tasty, cheap and filling, if not particularly spicy (a range of chilli sauces are to hand), and with a nicely shabby charm to the place. Burritos €3.50–7.90.

Drinking and nightlife

Hamburg's nightlife is outstanding: the Schanzenviertel for studenty bar-crawling; St Pauli for clubs and live music venues; while Altona attracts an older, more relaxed crowd. For information on the gay scene check *Hinnerk* (German only) magazine, available from the tourist office, cafés and bars.

Bars

Café Gnosa Lange Reihe 93. Well-known gay bar-café northeast of the train station. Packed at weekends. Marvellous cakes for €3, and good breakfasts.

Knuth Grosse Rainstr. 21 Ⓢ Altona. Relaxed but stylish neighbourhood café-bar.

Mutter Stresemannstr. 11 Ⓤ & Ⓢ Sternschanze. Small, atmospheric (and smoky) retro-styled bar that's often the last to shut.

StrandPauli Hafenstr. 89 Ⓤ & Ⓢ Landungsbrücken. Cool urban beachbar on the old wharf, with cocktails, Carribean vibes and an unrivalled view of the port. Opens midday, closes at midnight.

Clubs and live music

Fabrik Barnerstr. 36 Ⓦ www.fabrik.de. Ⓢ Altona. Major live music and club venue in Altona, with a huge range of music and occasional mixed gay nights. Usually open nightly.

Golden Pudel Am St Pauli Fischmarkt 27 Ⓦ www.pudel.com Ⓢ Reeperbahn or Ⓤ & Ⓢ Landungsbrücken, Often packed and raucous club in what looks like a squat on the harbour, that gets some great local DJs playing electro, dub and hip-hop.

Grosse Freiheit 36/ Kaiserkeller Grosse Freiheit 36 Ⓦ www.grossefreiheit36.de Ⓤ St Pauli or Ⓢ Reeperbahn. A tourist attraction in itself, *Grosse Freiheit 36* books major acts most weekends. Emphasis on goth and rock. The massive *Kaiserkeller* below plays mostly alternative music, and is famous for hosting The Beatles in the early 1960s. Closed Tues & Sun.

Haus 73 Schulterblatt 73 Ⓦ www.dreiundsiebzig.de Ⓤ & Ⓢ Sternschanze. There's always something going on in this ramshackle building, somewhere between a community centre and a club, from dance classes to film and reggae club nights.

Kir Barnerstr. 16 Ⓦ www.kir-hamburg.de Ⓢ Altona. Dance club spinning indie and electro with occasional mixed gay and lesbian nights. Closed Tues and Sun.

Prinzenbar Kastanienallee 20 Ⓦ www.prinzenbar.net Ⓤ St Pauli or Ⓢ Reeperbahn. This wonderfully atmospheric venue, all crumbling Baroque cherubs, chandeliers and dark corners, hosts small club nights and live gigs; mainly indie.

Directory

Bike rental Fahrradladen St Georg, Schmilinskystr. 16, 10min from Hauptbahnhof (Mon–Fri 10am–7pm, Sat 10am–1pm); Fahrradstation, Schlüterstr. 11 Ⓢ Dammtor (Mon–Fri 9am–6pm).

Consulates New Zealand, Domstr. 19 Ⓣ 040/442 55 50; UK, Neuer Jungfernstieg 20 Ⓣ 040/448 032 36; US, Alsterufer 28 Ⓣ 040/41 17 11 00.

Exchange Reisebank, at the train station.

Internet In the basement of the Saturn department store, southern building of the main train station (Hauptbahnhof-Süd; 30min/€1.50). Also Teletime on Schultterblatt (30min/€1).

Pharmacy At the train station. Daily 7am–11pm.

Post office At the train station. Mon–Fri 8am–6pm, Sat 8am–12.30pm.

Moving on

Train Århus (2 daily; 5hr); Berlin (hourly; 1hr 40min); Copenhagen (4 daily; 5hr); Frankfurt (hourly; 4hr); Hannover (every 30min; 1hr 35min); Lübeck (every 30min; 40min); Munich (hourly; 6hr–6hr 30min).

LÜBECK

Just an hour from Hamburg, **LÜBECK** makes a great day-trip. Set on an egg-shaped island surrounded by the water defences of the River Trave and the city moat, the pretty Altstadt is a compact place to wander, with many small lanes and courtyards to explore.

What to see and do

The city's emblem – and your first view of the Altstadt as you approach from the station – is the twin-towered, leaning **Holstentor** (daily: Jan–March 11am–5pm; April–Dec 10am–6pm; €5/students €2.50), with a small city museum inside. Straight ahead, over the bridge and up Holstenstrasse, the first church on the right is the Gothic **Petrikirche**; an elevator goes to the top of its spire (daily 9am–9pm, from 10am Oct–March; €3/students €2) for great views over the town. Back across Holstenstrasse is the Markt and the elaborate **Rathaus**. Just behind, you'll find *Konditorei-café* **Niederegger**, a renowned shop crammed with marzipan products and a free museum dedicated to the sugary substance.

Behind the north wing of the town hall stands the **Marienkirche**, Germany's oldest brick-built Gothic church. The interior makes a light and lofty backdrop for treasures like a 1518 high altar. The church's huge bells remain embedded in the floor where they fell when the church was bombed in 1942.

Katharinenkirche, on the corner of Königstrasse and Glockengiesserstrasse, has three sculptures on its facade by Ernst Barlach; only these of the nine commissioned in the early 1930s had been completed when his work was banned by the Nazis. To the north at Königstrasse 9–11 are the **Behnhaus** and the **Drägerhaus**, two patricians' houses now converted into a museum (Tues–Sun: Jan–March 11am–5pm; April–Dec 10am–5pm; €5/students €2.50) housing modern and nineteenth-century paintings. More art – excellent medieval plus modern exhibitions – can be found in the St Annen Museum (April–Dec Tues–Sat 10am–5pm, Jan–March from 11am; €5/students €2.50) in a former convent, which also has good displays on merchant life in Lübeck.

Arrival and information

Air Bus #6 goes from Lübeck airport to the train station (every 20min; 25min; €2.70).
Train station 5min west of the Altstadt: walk down Konrad-Adenauer-Str. to the Holstentor.
Ferry Lübeck's port, Travemünde, is 20min by train from Lübeck.
Tourist office Holstentorplatz 1 (June–Sept Mon–Fri 9.30am–7pm, Sat 10am–3pm, Sun 10am–2pm; Oct–May Mon–Fri 9.30am–6pm, Sat 10am–3pm; Dec also Sun 10am–2pm; ⓣ01805/889 97 00, ⓦwww.luebeck.de). It has internet terminals (€3/hr), a café, arranges walking tours and has information on boat tours.
Discount passes The Happy Day Card (€10/12/15 for 24/48/72hr) covers public transport and up to a fifty percent discount at museums. Combined museum tickets are also available: two museums in three days €8/students €4, three in three days €12/students €6, all museums in one week €17/students €8.

Eating

Hüxstr. which runs east from the Markt, has several good cafés and bars.
Cole Street Beckergrube 18, west of the Markt, off Breite Str. Named after a south London street where the owner once lived, this shabby-chic café and bar is good for a light bistro lunch or a drink.

Moving on

Train Copenhagen (4 daily; 4hr 20min); Hamburg (every 30min; 40min).
Ferry Lisco Baltic Service (ⓣ04502/88 66 90, ⓦwww.dfdslisco.com) travel to Rïga (2 weekly; 35hr; €74). Finnlines (ⓣ04502/805 43, ⓦwww.ferrycenter.fi): to Helsinki (9 weekly; 28hr) and Malmö (3 daily; 8–9hr). TT-Line (ⓣ04502/ 801 81, ⓦwww.ttline.com) to Trelleborg (4 daily; 7hr).

HANNOVER

HANNOVER is a major transport hub and trade-fair city and, unfortunately, it looks the part, too. The city's showpiece – refreshingly – is not a great cathedral, palace or town hall, but a series of **gardens** and first-class **museums**. Hannover's location at the intersection of major cross-country rail lines and its lack of budget accommodation make it a perfect candidate for a pit stop – on your way to somewhere else.

What to see and do

Hannover's commercial centre is a short walk southwest of the train station. The best **museums** are further south, on the other side of Friedrichswall, while the splendid **royal gardens** are northwest of the centre. The centre is pretty bland, but there are some attractive corners and interesting neighbourhoods if you explore a bit further out.

The Altes Rathaus and Marktkirche

A short distance southwest of the train station, a few streets of rebuilt half-timbered buildings convey some impression of the medieval town. The elaborate brickwork of the high-gabled fifteenth-century **Altes Rathaus** is impressive, despite the modern interior. Alongside is the fourteenth-century red-brick Gothic **Marktkirche**, with some miraculously preserved stained glass.

Niedersächsisches Landesmuseum and Sprengel Museum

Southeast of the Marktkirche, across Friedrichswall on Willy-Brandt-Allee, is the **Niedersächsisches Landesmuseum** (Tues–Sun 10am–5pm, Thurs till 7pm; €4/students €3, Fri 2–5pm free; Ⓤ Aegidientorplatz), housing a fine collection of paintings from the Middle Ages to the early twentieth century, plus archeology and ethnology collections. A bit further down the road lies the **Sprengel Museum** (Tues–Thurs & Sun 10am–8pm, Fri & Sat 10am–10pm; €7/students €4, higher during special exhibitions; Ⓦ www.sprengel-museum.de), with a first-rate collection of twentieth- and twenty-first-century painting and sculpture.

The Neues Rathaus

West of the Landesmuseum on Friderichswall is the vast, green-domed **Neues Rathaus**, built at the start of the twentieth century. In the foyer are four models of Hannover in 1689, 1939, 1945 and today, illuminating the extent of wartime loss, something that is all too clear as you look over the city from the top of the town hall's **dome** (Mon–Fri 9am–6pm, Sat & Sun 10am–6pm; €2.50/students €2), reached via a curved lift.

The gardens

The royal gardens of **Herrenhausen**, featuring Europe's biggest fountain, stretch out northwest of the centre. Proceeding north from town along Nienburger Strasse, the **Georgengarten**, an English-style landscaped garden, is to the left, a foil to the city's pride and joy, the magnificent formal **Grosser Garten** beyond (daily 9am till dusk; May–August till 8pm; €5; trams #4 and #5 to Herrenhäuser Gärten, main entrance just by the stop on Herrenhäuser Str.). If possible, time your visit to coincide with the fountain displays (late March to late Oct daily 11am–noon & 2/3–5pm). Directly opposite, on Herrenhäuser Strasse, is the entrance to **Berggarten**, the botanic garden (same hours and ticket).

Arrival and information

Airport Ⓢ #5 (every 30min; 20min; €3.20) runs between Hannover Airport and the train station.
Train and bus The train station is in the centre of town, just northeast of main shopping district Kröpke; behind is the bus station.
Tourist office Across from the train station, Ernst-August-Platz 8 (Mon–Fri 9am–6pm, Sat 9am–2pm; May–Sept also Sun 9am–2pm; Ⓣ 0511/12 34 51 11, Ⓦ www.hannover-tourism.de); they'll book you into a hotel for a €2.50 fee.
Discount pass The Hannover Card (individual €9.50/16, up to 5 people €18/31 for 1/3 days), covers public transport and provides discounts to the main museums and sights.
Internet Inside the *Burger King* in the train station (€2/hr); there are also cheap phone and internet places around Steintor.

City transport

The best of Hannover is outside the centre, so its excellent transport network of tram/U-Bahn, S-Bahn and buses is centred on the Hauptbahnhof, Kröpke and Aegidientorplatz is useful. The tram/U-Bahn network has some overground tram lines (like #17 and #10) and some hybrid tram/U-Bahn lines where central stops are underground, with lines emerging above ground to become street-level trams further out (such as #4 and #5). One-way tickets €2.30, day tickets €4.30.

Accommodation

There are very few budget options in Hannover, and prices double or more during trade fairs.
Flora Heinrichstr. 36 Ⓣ 0511/38 39 10, Ⓦ www.hotel-flora-hannover.de. Spotless hotel behind

the train station, with breakfast included. Singles €38–49, doubles €59–75.

Hostel Hannover Lenaustr. 12 ⓣ0511/131 99 19, ⓦwww.hostelhannover.de. Basic but friendly, this slightly old-fashioned hostel has decent communal areas but packed dorms. Outside the centre, but good for the Linden-Limmer nightlife. Trams #10 and #17 to Goetheplatz. Check-in 8–11am & 5–8pm. Sheets €3. Dorms €15–25 (€5 more at weekends and trade fairs).

Eating and drinking

In the centre, slightly twee, touristy Kramerstr. and Knochenhauerstr. near the Markt, are your best options. More fun for nightlife is the sprawling Linden-Limmer district west of the centre, particularly around Goetheplatz or midway along Kötnerholzweg. Lister Meile, behind the station, is also a good bet.

Café Glocksee Glockseestr. 35 ⓦwww.cafe-glocksee.de. Great, scruffy little club and venue. Tram #10 to Goetheplatz; head along Lenaustr. and it's the graffitied building at the end (entrance round the back).

Café Safran Königsworther Str. 39, corner of Braunstr. This laidback café-bar has some sort of cheap deal every day, such as beer and a pizza for €6. Tram #10 to Glocksee.

Markthalle Karmaschstr. 49, near the Markt. The indoor market is packed full of dozens of food stalls – German, Italian, Spanish, Turkish and Japanese, and even a cocktail bar – selling good-value meals. Mon–Wed 7am–8pm, Thurs & Fri 7am–10pm, Sat 7am–4pm.

Spandau Projekt Engelbosteler Damm 30 ⓤChristuskirche. Cool retro-styled café-bar on a street of restaurants north of the centre with Italian and Thai veggie curries at fair prices plus organic breakfast buffets at weekends.

Moving on

Train Amsterdam (every 2hr; 4hr 20min); Berlin (hourly; 1hr 40min); Cologne (hourly; 2hr 40min); Frankfurt (hourly; 2hr 20min); Goslar (hourly; 1hr); Hamburg (every 30min; 1hr 35min); Munich (hourly; 4hr 20min–4hr 40min).

BREMEN

Famous for a fairytale of four animal musicians, **BREMEN** is an attractive small city located about an hour from Hannover and Hamburg. Maritime trade via the Weser River led to it becoming a wealthy medieval merchant city with a liberal mindset, something for which Bremen remains famous today. Their legacy is such attractive architecture as one of the finest town squares in North Germany, listed as a UNESCO World Heritage Site, and a small but enjoyable nightlife district.

What to see and do

The town's geographic and cultural heart is the **Markt**, with a **Rathaus** fronted by a fabulous Renaissance facade of ornate allegorical carving. Rooms within (Mon–Sat hourly 11am–6pm except 2pm, Sun 11am; €5) live up to the looks, especially the Güldenkammer with gilded Jugendstil leather wall-hangings. Outside a statue of Roland, a chivalric knight and protector of civic rights, brandishes a sword at the **Dom** opposite to champion the citizens' independence from the archbishops; a church lackey burned down its wooden predecessor. Running south off the Markt, **Böttcherstrasse** was remodelled in the 1920s from a decaying alley into a "Kunst Schau" (Art Show) by a team of avant-garde artists, notably sculptor Bernhard Hoetger. Here, the **Paula-Modersohn-Becker Museum** (Tues–Sun 11am–6pm; €5/students €3) contains artworks by an artist from a local art colony at Worpswede while revamped Gothic merchant's house **Roselius-Haus** (same ticket) displays late-medieval art and furniture.

South of the Dom is the **Schnoorviertel**, the traditional quarter of fishermen, sailors and craftsmen on the Weser's banks at the edge of the old town. Today the cottages contain upmarket boutiques, galleries and restaurants – touristy, certainly, but cute nonetheless. East of the Schnoor, the **Kunsthalle** (Tues 10am–9pm, Wed–Sun 10am–5pm; €6) has an excellent gallery of German and international art, including works by Rubens and Delacroix, alongside works by Worpswede artists.

Arrival and information

Train Head straight out of the train station; it's a 10min walk into the centre.
Tourist office Just off Markt on the corner of Obernstr. and Liebfrauenkirchof (Mon–Fri 10am–6.30pm, Sat–Sun 10am–4pm; ⓣ 0421/30 800 10, ⓦ www.bremen-tourism.de). Smaller office in the train station (Mon–Fri 9am–7pm, Sat–Sun 9.30am–6pm).

Accommodation, eating and drinking

In the centre, Schlacte is a line of bars on the riverbank, the main bar and nightlife district is the Ostertorviertel east of the old town.
Lila Eule Bernhardstr. 10. Once a 50s jazz den, this grungy dive-club hosts gigs and student clubs several nights a week, with entry either for free or at low prices.
Piano Fehrfeld 64. Lazy-paced café-bar at the heart of the Ostertorviertel whose menu of pizzas, pastas and steaks, all priced under €10, is popular with everyone from families to friends.
Ratskeller Am Markt 21. Touristy and not cheap at around €14 a main, but the cellar restaurant beneath the Rathaus is one of the most famous in Germany for historic atmosphere as much as traditional cooking.
Townhouse Am Dobben 62. ⓣ 0421/78 015, ⓦ www.townside.de. Friendly modern hostel in Bremen's nightlife district with eco ethics such as rainwater collection and Fairtrade products. Kitchen and women's dorm. Dorms €14–21, double rooms €50. Tram #6 from the train station.

Moving on

Train Hamburg (every 30min; 1hr); Hannover (hourly–1hr 20min).

Central Germany

Central Germany is the country's most populous region and home to its industrial heartland – the Ruhrgebiet. **Cologne** stands out here, with its reminders of long centuries as a free state, cheek-by-jowl bars and a populace that's legendary for its friendliness. Neighbouring **Bonn**, Beethoven's birthplace, is venerable yet surprisingly hip for its size, while nearby **Aachen** is of interest as the first capital of the Holy Roman Empire. To the south the Rhineland-Palatinate is famed for the Romantic Rhine: a vineyard-lined stretch of the river which passes through a gorge of impressive rock outcrops, studded with the sort of castles that have given rise to many a tall tale. Nowadays pleasure cruisers – and a railway line – make the attractive journey through the **Gorge**, and beyond to the state capital of **Mainz**, where the printing press was invented, as celebrated in the excellent Gutenberg Museum. The Mosel River, which joins the Rhine near the city of Koblenz, has a similar parade of vineyards and ruined castles leading south to the ancient town of **Trier**, with its extraordinarily well-preserved Roman remains – some of the best outside Italy. To the northeast, in the province of Hesse, dynamic **Frankfurt** dominates, with its financial sector providing the region's economic base.

COLOGNE (KÖLN)

COLOGNE (Köln) has a population of a million, and its huge Gothic Dom is the country's most visited monument. Despite its long history much of the city is modern – the legacy of World War II – but though it's not the most beautiful city in Germany it's certainly one of the liveliest and most friendly. Try to catch the annual pre-Lent **Carnival** – when huge parties fill the streets – or the summer Christopher Street Day (Gay Pride) celebrations, which can attract up to a million visitors. Cologne has a long and glorious history – as a Roman colony (Colonia), a pilgrimage centre, trading city, marketer of eau de Cologne and, most recently, as Germany's broadcasting capital.

What to see and do

Cologne's major sights are all within walking distance of the train station, in a dense centre on the west bank of the Rhine.

The Dom

One of the largest Gothic buildings ever built, Cologne's gigantic **Dom** (daily May–Oct 6am–9pm; Nov–April 6am–7.30pm) once symbolized its power – its archbishop was one of the seven Electors of the Holy Roman Empire – and the Dom remains the seat of the Primate of Germany. Begun in 1248, building stopped in 1560, resuming only in the nineteenth century, when the towers were completed. Climb the 509 steps to the top of the south tower (Tower daily: March–April & Oct 9am–5pm; May–Sept 9am–6pm; Nov–Feb 9am–4pm; €3 or combination ticket with Schatzkammer €6) for a breathtaking panorama over the city and the Rhine. The **Domschatzkammer** (daily 10am–6pm; €5) in the vaults on the north side of the building contains a stunning array of treasury items,

Museum Ludwig and the Römisch-Germanisches Museum

In a modern building next to the Dom, the spacious **Museum Ludwig** (Tues–Sun 10am–6pm, first Thurs in month 10am–10pm; €10, first Thurs in month €5; ⓦwww.museenkoeln.de) is one of Germany's premier collections of modern art, particularly strong on American Pop Art and German Expressionism. The neighbouring **Römisch-Germanisches Museum** (Tues–Sun 10am–5pm, first Thurs in month 10am–10pm; €7; ⓦwww.museenkoeln.de) was built directly over its star exhibit, the Dionysus Mosaic, which can be viewed *in situ*. The finest work of its kind in northern Europe, it was created for a patrician villa in about 200 AD.

Gross St Martin and the Rhine

For nearly six hundred years, the tower of **Gross St Martin**, one of Cologne's twelve Romanesque churches, was the dominant feature of the city's skyline. Just behind it is the best spot to enjoy the Rhine, a grassy promenade stretching between the Hohenzollern (railway) and Deutzer bridges. For the best view of the Altstadt, cross the river by the footway along the railway bridge to reach the **KölnTriangle** skyscraper, which has an observation deck (Ottoplatz 1: May–Sept Mon–Fri 11am–10pm, Sat & Sun 10am–10pm; Oct–April Mon–Fri noon–6pm, Sat & Sun 10am–6pm; €3).

Wallraf-Richartz-Museum and Schokoladenmuseum

Southwest of Gross St Martin is the **Wallraf-Richartz-Museum** (Tues, Wed & Fri–Sun 10am–6pm, Thurs 10am–9pm; €7 for permanent collection only or €9.50 including temporary exhibitions; ⓦwww.museenkoeln.de), whose holdings centre on the fifteenth-century Cologne school as well as a fine Impressionist collection. Further south, on the banks of the Rhine, is the **Schokoladen Museum** (Tues–Fri 10am–6pm, Sat & Sun 11am–7pm, last entry 1hr before closing; €7.50; ⓦwww.schokoladenmuseum.de), a thoroughly enjoyable museum focusing on the history and production of chocolate.

Arrival

Air Cologne/Bonn Airport is connected to the train station by Ⓢ line S13 (every 20min; 15min; €2.50). Düsseldorf Airport has its own train station, with frequent connections to Cologne main station (every 30min; 40min; €18.50). Bohr Omnibus (ⓦbohr.de) operates a shuttle bus between Cologne main station and Airport Weeze (aka Düsseldorf-Weeze; 8 daily; 2hr 15min; €21 one-way) and from Frankfurt-Hahn Airport (5 daily; 2hr 15min; €16 one-way).
Train The Hauptbahnhof is immediately north of the Dom in the centre of the city.
Bus The bus station (ZOB) is directly behind the train station on Johannisstr.

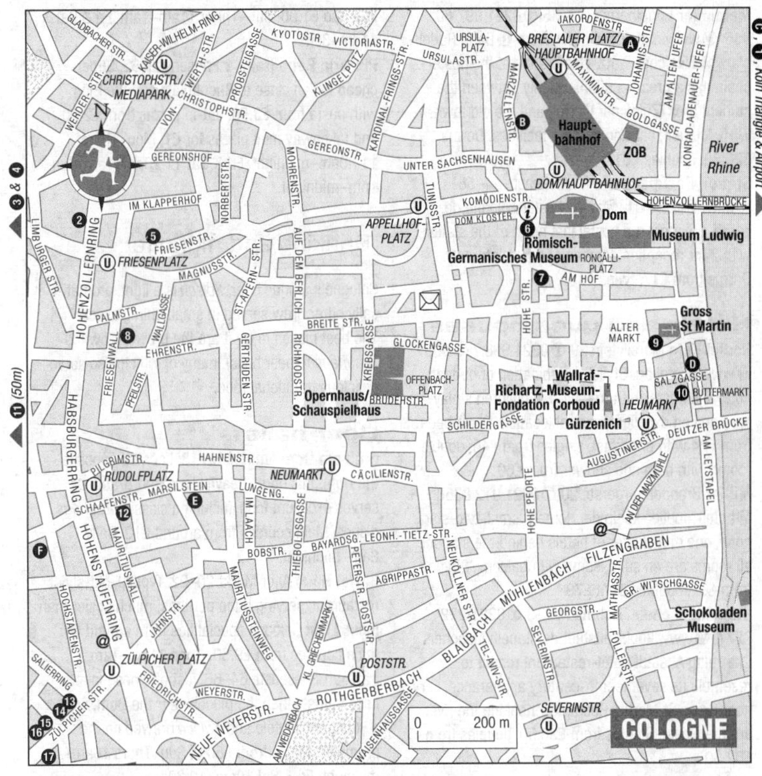

ACCOMMODATION		EATING		DRINKING & NIGHTLIFE			
Hostel Köln	E	Bella Rosa	15	Biermuseum	10	Live Music Hall	3
Köln-Deutz City Hostel	C	Café Reichard	6	Ex-Corner	12	MTC	13
Meininger	F	Habibi	16	Filmdose	17	Nachtflug	2
Müller	A	In Bauturm	11	Früh am Dom	7	Päffgen	5
Stapelhäuschen	D	Pizzeria Bella		Gaffel Haus	9	Stiefel	14
Station Backpacker's	B	Italia 1	8	Gebäude 9	1	Underground	4

Information

Tourist office Main office opposite the Dom (Mon–Sat 9am–8pm, Sun 10am–5pm; ⓣ0221/22 13 04 00, ⓦwww.koelntourismus.de). Staff can book hotel rooms (doubles from around €40). You can pick up the free listings magazine *Choices* (ⓦwww.choices.de) in their basement ticket office and hire an electronic iGuide for a self-guided tour of the city (€8).

Discount passes The WelcomeCard is valid for 24hr: €9 (Cologne city)/€12 (Cologne plus surrounding district)/€22 for entire Cologne/Bonn region) and provides free transport and substantial price reductions for many sights.

City transport

The public transport network (ⓦkvb-koeln.de) is a mixture of buses and trams/U-Bahn. Short trip €1.70, one-way trip €2.50, day-pass €7.30 and a strip of four one-way trips €7.30.

Accommodation

Hostels

Köln Deutz City Hostel Siegesstr. 5 ⓣ0221 81 47 11, ⓦkoeln-deutz.jugendherberge.de. Large and functional HI hostel close to Deutz station, directly across the Rhine from the Altstadt. Dorms €20.30, twin rooms from €51.

Meininger Engelbertstr. 33–35 ⓣ0221 997 60 965, ⓦwww.meininger-hotels.com Ⓤ Bahn Rudolfplatz or Zülpicher Platz. This branch of the hostel chain has a great location, roughly between the student area (Zülpicher Viertel) and the old town. Wi-fi, kitchen, bar and laundry facilities. Dorms €20.50, doubles €61.

Station Backpacker's Marzellenstr. 44–56 ⓣ0221 912 53 01, ⓦwww.hostel-cologne.de. Large, privately run hostel just north of the station, with 24hr reception, kitchen and free internet. Dorms from €17, twins €48.

Hotels and guesthouses

Hostel Köln Marsilstein 29 ⓣ0221 998 776 00, ⓦwww.hostel.ag. Stylish combination of budget hotel and hostel with free wi-fi, a children's play area and an excellent, central location. Dorm beds from €24 with breakfast, singles from €45, double rooms with bath and shower from €60.

Müller Brandenburgerstr. 20 ⓣ0221 912 8350, ⓦhotel-mueller-koeln.de. Homely, small two-star hotel, one of a cluster of hotels behind the station; all rooms are en suite, some with balcony. Singles from €64, doubles from €79.

Stapelhäuschen Fischmarkt 1–3 ⓣ0221/272 7777, ⓦwww.koeln-altstadt.de/stapelhaeuschen. Charming Altstadt hotel-restaurant rebuilt to resemble its seventeenth-century appearance, very near Gross St Martin. Rooms overlooking the river are the nicest. Singles from €38.50, doubles from €62.30.

Eating

Cafés

Café Reichard Unter Fettenhennen 11 Ⓤ Rudolphplatz. Local institution serving delicious cakes (around €5) in elegant surroundings; fine Dom views from the terrace too. Daily 8.30am–8pm.

Im Bauturm Aachener Str. 24. Build your own breakfast at this lovely bohemian café-by-day, bar-by-night. Breakfasts from €3.90. Mon–Fri 8am–3am, Sat & Sun 9am–3am.

Restaurants

Bella Rosa Heinsberger Str. 11a, corner Zülpicherstr. ⓣ0221 476 75 016. One of a handful of good-value Italian restaurants in the student area. Big portions and a young, friendly crowd. Pizza and pasta from €4. Sun–Thurs 8am–1am, Fri & Sat 8am–3am.

Habibi Zülpicher Str. 28. Serving arguably the best falafel in Germany, this Lebanese restaurant in the student neighbourhood stays open for the late-night munchies. Takeaway falafel in bread €1.90. Sun–Thurs 11am–1am, Fri & Sat 11am–3am.

Pizzeria Bella Italia 1 Friesenwall 52. Super-cheap Italian close to Rudolfplatz and the Ring, with pasta from €3.50, eat-in pizzas from €2.90 and takeaway mini pizzas for €1. Mon–Thurs 11.30am–midnight, Fri & Sat 11.20am–1am, Sun 1pm–midnight.

Drinking and nightlife

Cologne's unique beer, *Kölsch* is a light, aromatically bitter brew served in small, thin glasses. The best places to try it are the brewery-owned *Brauhäuser* (beer halls), many of which also serve delicious traditional food.

Beer halls

Früh am Dom Am Hof 12–18. Located opposite the Dom, this huge, heavily touristed *Brauhaus* serves excellent food, including classic *brauhaus* dishes. Main courses from around €10. Daily 8am–midnight.

Gaffel Haus Alter Markt 20–22. Typical, old-style restaurant, serving huge portions; much cosier than most. Light Cologne specialities from around €4; main courses from €9.50. Open 11am–1am.

Päffgen Friesenstr. 64–66, just off Friesenplatz. Less touristy than the places near the Dom, with a younger clientele and *Kölsch* brewed on the premises. Mains from €8.20. Sun–Thurs 10am–midnight, Fri & Sat 10am–12.30am.

Bars

Biermuseum Buttermarkt 39. Small, loud Altstadt bar tucked away near the river, serving countless types of beer on tap and in bottles. The surrounding area is the main focus of nightlife for visitors, though locals tend to prefer the western part of the city along the Ring.

Ex-Corner Schaafenstr. 57–59. The absolute lynchpin of the gay scene's so-called "Bermuda Triangle", this corner bar is one of a cluster just south of Rudolfplatz and is busy every night of the week. Daily 7pm–5am.

Filmdose Zülpicher Str. 39 ⓦwww.filmdose-koeln.de. Tram stop Dasselstr/Bhf Süd. Fun café-bar that's packed with students enjoying a post-lecture *Kölsch*; it has a cabaret stage used for live theatre during term time. Breakfasts from €3.90. Mon–Fri 9am–1am, Fri & Sat until 3am.

Stiefel Zülpicher Str. 18. Dilapidated and relaxed punk-rock bar in a student quarter that's packed with cheap restaurants and lively bars. A great place to nurse a beer or shoot pool. Open 8pm–2am, Fri & Sat until 3am.

Clubs

Gebäude 9 Deutz-Mühlheimer-Str. 127–129 ⓦgebaeude9.de ⓤKölnMesse. Intimate bar, club and theatre hall where events and exhibitions take place. Club nights blend everything from indie, northern soul and ska to dancehall and electro.

Live Music Hall Lichtstr 30, Ehrenfeld ⓦlive musichall.de ⓤVenloer Str. Don't let the name fool you – music here at weekends is primarily from DJs, with regular pop, rock and 80s nights, with live gigs on Wednesdays and Thursdays. Concerts start at 8pm; Fri & Sat club nights from 9 or 10pm.

MTC Zülpicher Str. 10 ⓦmtcclub.de ⓤZülpicher Platz. Studenty venue featuring rock and metal bands live, plus DJ nights. Concerts Fri & Sat at 8pm.

Nachtflug Hohenzollernring 89 ⓦnachtflug.com. Probably the best of several fairly mainstream clubs on the Ring between Zülpicher Platz and Christophstr., with DJs spinning mainly house, dance & R&B. Best for the monthly pan-sexual after-hours club *Greenkomm* which runs from 6am on Sunday morning – if you've still got the legs for it. €13.

Underground Vogelsanger Str. 200 ⓤVenloer Str. ⓦwww.underground-cologne.de. Great for live gigs, especially rock and punk, the *Underground* has a beer garden and a big indie/alternative following. Wed–Sat from 6.30pm; beer garden from 6pm in summer. Concerts usually 8pm.

Directory

Bike rental At the Radstation by the north (Breslauer Platz, ⓣ0221 139 7190) exit from the Hauptbahnhof (Mon–Fri 5.30am–10.30pm, Sat 6.30am–8pm, Sun 8am–8pm; €5/3hr, €10/1 day, €20/3 days) or at Markmannsgasse, (on the banks of the Rhine before the Deutzer Brücke ⓣ0171/629 87 96); same prices, though they also do 1hr rental (€2).

Cinema Metropolis, Ebertplatz 19 ⓦwww.metro polis-koeln.de ⓤEbertplatz. Small cinema showing English-language films.

Internet Microcall, Hohenstaufenring 5 ⓣ0221 420 4796. Daily 10am–11pm; €1/hr.

Medical services Emergencies ⓣ112; out of hours medical service ⓣ01805 044100. There is a full list of Cologne hospitals on the city website ⓦstadt-koeln.de.

Left luggage At the train station (€5/24hr, €2.50/2hr) and at ⓤFriesenplatz (€2).

Pharmacy At the north exit from the train station (Mon–Fri 6am–10pm, Sat 8am–10pm, Sun 10am–6pm); there's also a digital notice board giving details of out-of-hours service.

Post office Breite Str. 6-26, Mon–Fri 9am–7pm, Sat 9am–2pm.

COLOGNE'S CARNIVAL

Though Cologne's **carnival** actually begins as early as November 11, the real business starts with Weiberfastnacht on the Thursday prior to Lent. The city goes wild for the next five days until Ash Wednesday; prepare yourself for drunken dancing in the streets and wild costumes. The best of the numerous parades are the alternative **Geisterzug Saturday night**, complete with fire-juggling and drumming, and the spectacular **Rose Monday Parade**, which features music, floats and political caricatures.

Moving on

Train Aachen (every 30min; 52min); Amsterdam (every 2hr; 2hr 40min); Berlin (hourly; 5hr 12min); Bonn (frequent; 20–30min); Brussels (4 daily; 1hr 44min); Frankfurt (approx. hourly; 1hr 10min); Heidelberg (every 30 min–1hr 30 min; 2hr 40min); Luxembourg (every 2 hr; 3hr 16min); Mainz (1–2/hour; 1hr 45min); Paris (3 daily; 3hr 17min); Stuttgart (2/hour; 2hr 13min).

River cruise K-D ⓦwww.k-d.com to Bonn (April–Oct 1 daily; 3hr).

BONN

A great day-trip from Cologne, lovely, riverside **BONN** was West Germany's unlikely capital from 1949 until unification in 1990. But even with its role diminished, Bonn is still worth a visit to see the birthplace of Ludwig van Beethoven, a string of top-rated museums, an attractive Old Town, and to experience its exuberant student-centred nightlife.

What to see and do

The small pedestrianized **Altstadt** centres on two spacious squares. The square to the south is named after the **Münster**, whose central octagonal tower and spire is the city's most prominent landmark. The Markt square is dominated by the pink Rococo **Rathaus** and hosts a market every day except Sunday.

The Beethoven-Haus and the Schloss

A couple of minutes' walk north of Markt, at Bonngasse 20, is the **Beethoven-Haus** (April–Oct Mon–Sat 10am–6pm, Sun 11am–6pm; Nov–March Mon–Sat 10am–5pm, Sun 11am–5pm; €5; Ⓦ www.beethoven-haus-bonn.de), where the composer was born in an attic room in 1770. Beethoven left Bonn for good aged 22, but the city nevertheless has the best collection of memorabilia of its favourite son. To the east is the enormously long Baroque **Schloss**, once the seat of the Archbishop-Electors of Cologne and now part of the university.

The Museumsmeile

The **Museumsmeile** (Ⓤ Heussallee/Museumsmeile) is home to the **Kunstmuseum** (Tues–Sun 11am–6pm, Wed till 9pm; €7; Ⓦ www.kunstmuseum-bonn.de), with its fine Expressionist collection. Next door is the **Kunst- und Ausstellungshalle** (Tues & Wed 10am–9pm, Thurs–Sun 10am–7pm; day ticket for one exhibition €8, all exhibitions and roof garden €14; Ⓦ www.bundeskunsthalle.de), a postmodern arts centre hosting major temporary exhibitions. The Kunstmuseum's other neighbour is the **Haus der Geschichte** (Tues–Fri 9am–7pm, Sat & Sun 10am–6pm; free; Ⓦ www.hdg.de), a fascinating museum exploring German history from the end of World War II to the present.

Arrival and information

Train and bus Bonn's train station lies in the middle of the city; just to the east is the bus station, whose local services, along with the trams (which become U-Bahns in the city centre), form part of a system integrated with Cologne's (see p.490).
Tourist office Windeckstr. 1, near Münsterplatz (Mon–Fri 10am–6pm, Sat 10am–4pm, Sun 10am–2pm; Ⓣ 0228/77 50 00, Ⓦ www.bonn-region.de).
Discount pass The Bonn Regio WelcomeCard (valid 24hr: €9 city of Bonn/€12 greater Bonn/€22 Cologne-Bonn region) is a great deal in Bonn, providing free travel and free admission to almost all museums and sights.

Eating and drinking

Cassius Garten Maximilianstr. 28d, across from the station. Offers daily-changing hot vegetarian specials, buffet-style meals (pay by weight: 100g costs €1.60), and great cakes, including vegan options, from €1.80. Coffee €2.20. Mon–Sat 11am–8pm.
Pawlow Heerstr 64. Funky, studenty café-bar in the bohemian Nordstadt district a short walk from the old town, with benches outside, great milky coffees and small measures of wine for tight budgets – from €1.50. Daily 10am–1am.
Zebulon Stockenstr. 19. This Altstadt bar is a big favourite with students, especially of the American-study-abroad variety. Mon–Fri 4pm–1am, Sat noon–1am, Sun 5–11pm.

AACHEN

AACHEN has a laidback atmosphere that reflects its large student population, making it a good day-trip from Cologne or a stopoff between countries. Bordering Belgium and the Netherlands, it was the hub of Charlemagne's Europe-wide eighth-century empire. The choice was partly strategic but also because of the presence of hot springs. Relaxing in these waters was one of the emperor's favourite pastimes, and they remain a major draw at the luxurious **Carolus Thermen** (daily 9am–11pm, last entry at 9.30pm; €14 a day; Ⓦ www.carolus-thermen.de), a spa northeast of the centre.

What to see and do

The surviving architectural legacy of Charlemagne is small, but its crowning jewel, the former **Palace chapel**, has pride of place at the heart of the **Dom** (Jan–March Mon–Fri 11am–6pm, Sat & Sun 1–6pm; April–Dec Mon–Fri 11am–7pm, Sat & Sun 1–7pm; Ⓦ www.aachendom.de), a Unesco World Heritage Site. At its end, the gilded shrine of Charlemagne, finished in 1215 after fifty years' work, contains the emperor's remains, while the gallery has the imperial throne, viewable only on a tour (English tour daily at 2pm; €4; tickets from Dominformation opposite Schatzkammer). Next to the Dom is the dazzling treasury or **Schatzkammer** (Jan–March Mon 10am–1pm, Tues–Sun 10am–5pm; April–Dec Mon 10am–1pm, Tues–Sun 10am–6pm, last entry 30min before closing; €5; entrance on Johannes-Paul-II-Str.). Its highlights are the tenth-century Lothar Cross and a Roman sarcophagus once used as Charlemagne's coffin. The emperor's palace once extended as far as the expansive **Markt**. Here two of the palace towers remain, incorporated into the fourteenth-century **Rathaus**, whose facade is lined with the figures of fifty Holy Roman Emperors, 31 of whom were crowned in Aachen. The glory of the interior (daily 10am–6pm; €5) is the much-restored Kaisersaal, repository of the crown jewels – in reproduction.

Arrival and information

Train The centre is 10min walk from the train station – down Bahnhofstr., then left into Theaterstr.

Tourist office In the Elisenbrunnen on Friedrich-Wilhelm-Platz (Jan–Easter Mon–Fri 9am–6pm, Sat 9am–2pm; Easter–Dec Mon–Fri 9am–6pm, Sat 9am-3pm, Sun 10am–2pm; ⓣ0241/180 29 60, ⓦwww.aachen.de).

Eating and drinking

The student quarter centres on Pontstr. – which leads northeast out of the Markt – and is lined with bars and cheap cafés and restaurants.

Kittel Pontstr. 39. Relaxed bohemian café with daily student breakfast specials and great inexpensive food, with pasta or chilli from €5. Daily 10am until at least 1am.

Leo van den Daele Büchel 18. Venerable wood-clad café with great cakes and particularly good *Printen*, a spiced gingerbread that's the main local speciality. Breakfasts from €6. Mon–Fri 9am–6.30pm, Sat 9am–6pm, Sun 10am–6pm.

Ocean/Sowiso Pontstr. 164–166. One of a cluster of lively sports and cocktail bars, with student-friendly prices, plentiful outdoor seating and a cheerful atmosphere. 9.30am until late.

Moving on

Train Brussels (hourly; 1hr 15min); Cologne (every 20min; 35–55min); Liège (hourly; 25–55min); Maastricht (via Heerlen: hourly; 1hr 12min); Paris Gare du Nord (every 2hr; 2hr 36min).

MAINZ

At the confluence of the Rhine and Main rivers, **MAINZ** is an agreeable mixture of old and new, with an attractive restored centre and a jovial populace who are responsible for Germany's second biggest carnival bash (after Cologne). Its long-standing ecclesiastical power aside, Mainz is also famous for Johannes Gutenberg, who pioneered printing here in the sixteenth century.

What to see and do

Rearing high above central Mainz, the **Dom** (March–Oct: Mon–Fri 9am–6.30pm, Sat 9am–4pm, Sun 12.45–3pm & 4–6.30pm; Nov–Feb Mon–Fri & Sun till 5pm) is unusual for sharing its outer walls with rows of eighteenth-century houses. Inside, the choirs at both ends indicate it as an imperial cathedral, with one for the emperor and the other for the clergy. The bustling **market square** outside (markets: Tues, Fri & Sat mornings) adjoins Liebfrauenplatz and the fascinating **Gutenberg Museum** (Tues–Sat 9am–5pm, Sun 11am–3pm; €5; ⓦwww.gutenberg-museum.de), paying tribute to one of the greatest inventions of all time, which enabled the mass-scale production of books. Its extension next door is the **Druckladen** (Printing shop; Mon–Fri 9am–5pm Sat 10am–3pm; €5; ⓦwww.druckladen.mainz.de), where visitors are shown how to hand-set type, and can buy posters, cards and the like.

Arrival and information

Train The station is a 15min walk northwest of the city centre; head down Bahnhofstr. or take a tram or bus to Höffchen.

Tourist office Brückenturm am Rathaus (Mon–Fri 9am–6pm, Sat 10.30am–4pm, Sun 11am–3pm; ⓣ06131/28 62 10, ⓦwww.info-mainz.de). Tricky to find, with an isolated position: it's elevated above the street beside a pedestrian bridge. Offers a free accommodation booking service, with rooms from €54.

Accommodation

DJH Otto-Brunfels-Schneise 4 ⓣ06131/853 32, ⓦwww.diejugendherbergen.de. Modern HI hostel, with single, twin and four-bed rooms, in the wooded heights of Weisenau. Buses #62 & #63 from the Hauptbahnhof will take you to stop "Am Viktorstift/*Jugendherberge*" within 400m of it. Dorms €19.90, twins €50.80.

Stadt Coblenz Rheinstr. 49 ⓣ06131/629 04 44, ⓦwww.stadtcoblenz.de. Conveniently located and comfy hotel near the Dom, though some rooms suffer from street noise. Singles €45, doubles €55.

Eating, drinking and nightlife

Mainz boasts more vineyards on its outskirts than any other German city; its many lovely wine bars are the best places to sample their produce.

Altdeutsche Weinstube Liebfrauenplatz 7. The oldest wine bar in town, offering cheap daily dishes. Evenings only; local wine from €2.60.

Eisgrub-Bräu Weisslilengasse 1a. Microbrewery with an accomplished range of its own beers and a good line of inexpensive food (mains average €8).

Heiligeist Rentengasse 2. Attractive and inexpensive bistro in the Gothic vaults of a fifteenth-century hospital; mains (average €9) are international and feature several Italian options.

Kuz Dagobertstr. 20b ⓣ06131/28 68 60, ⓦwww.kuz.de. Mainz's most dependably happening club with a sociable beer garden and busy events list which often involves live music, particularly world music. Cover charge around €8. Usually busy until at least 4am at the weekend.

Moving on

Train Cologne (frequent; 1hr 45min); Frankfurt (frequent; 40min); Heidelberg (frequent; 1hr 20min); Koblenz (every 30min; 1hr); Stuttgart (every 30min; 1hr 30min); Trier (hourly; 2hr 30min).

River cruises K-D ⓦwww.k-d.com sail along the Rhine between Mainz and the city of Koblenz: Bacharach/Kaub (April–Oct 1–2 daily; 2hr 30min).

THE RHINE GORGE

North of Mainz, the Rhine snakes west to **BINGEN**, where the spectacular eighty-kilometre-long **Rhine Gorge**, begins. Its most famous sight is the **Lorelei**, a rocky projection between Oberwesel and St Goar, where, legend has it, a blonde maiden would lure passing mariners to their doom with her song. The region is best visited by boat or by bike, spending a night in Bacharach, but if you're pressed for time, the train will do. The railway between Mainz and the city of Koblenz runs along the riverbank, offering wonderful gorge views from the windows on the train's eastern side. Some **river cruises** (mainly April–Oct) depart from Mainz, but more begin at Bingen. The full one-way boat fare from Bingen to Koblenz is €29.60.

Bacharach

Pretty, half-timbered **BACHARACH**, 15km from Bingen, huddles behind a fourteenth-century wall, which you can walk along for a brilliant overview of the town that's chock-full of alleyways and quirky buildings like the celebrated **Altes Haus** at Oberstrasse 61, which is so wonky it seems to lean in all directions at once. Many of them house *Weinstuben* (wine bars), where you should try local favourite *Hahnenhof* Riesling. The twelfth-century castle of Burg Stahleck above town houses the *Jugendherberge Bacharach* (ⓣ06743/12 66, ⓦwww.djh.de; dorms €18.90, twins €48.80) – probably Germany's most atmospheric hostel. It's a steep uphill climb to get there, but the views of the Rhine Valley are worth it. The best budget hotel is the lovely half-timbered *Im Malerwinkel* (ⓣ06743/12 39, ⓦwww.im-malerwinkel.de; singles €40; doubles €65), built into the old town wall. There's also a **campsite** at Strandbadweg 9 (ⓣ06743/17 52, ⓦwww.camping-sonnenstrand.de; €5 per person, plus €3 per tent), 5min south of the station.

TRIER

Birthplace of Karl Marx, and the oldest city in Germany, **TRIER** was once the capital of the Western Roman Empire. Nowadays, it's merely a regional centre for the upper Mosel valley, giving it a relaxed air. Despite a turbulent history, the city's past is well preserved here; particularly in the impressive group of Roman remains north of the Alps.

What to see and do

The centre corresponds roughly to the Roman city and can easily be covered on foot. From the train station, it's a few minutes' walk down Theodor-Heuss-Allee to the **Porta Nigra**, Roman Trier's northern gateway. From here, Simeonstrasse runs down to the **Hauptmarkt**, a busy pedestrian area, where market stalls sell groceries and flowers. At the southern end of the Hauptmarkt, a half-hidden Baroque portal leads to the exquisite Gothic church **St Gangolf**, built by the burghers of Trier to aggravate the archbishops, whose political power they resented.

The Dom and Konstantinbasilika

Up Sternstrasse from the Hauptmarkt, the magnificent Romanesque **Dom** (daily: April–Oct 6.30am–6pm; Nov–March 6.30am–5.30pm) lies on the site of the one built in the fourth century by Emperor Constantine. The present church dates from 1030, and the original facade has not changed significantly since then. From here, take Liebfrauenstrasse past the ritzy wine bar *Palais Kesselstatt* and turn left on An der Meerkatz, to the **Konstantinbasilika** (April–Oct Mon–Sat 10am–6pm, Sun noon–6pm; Nov–March Tues–Sat 11am–noon & 3–4pm, Sun noon–1pm). Built as Constantine's throne hall, its dimensions are awe-inspiring: 30m high and 67m long, it is completely self-supporting. It became a church for the local Protestant community in the nineteenth century.

The Rheinisches Landesmuseum and the Kaiserthermen

Just beyond some formal gardens southwest of the Konstantinbasilika, the **Rheinisches Landesmuseum** (Tues–Sun 10am–5pm; €6; Ⓦwww.landesmuseum-trier.de) is easily the best of Trier's museums, with a collection that conveys the sophistication and complexity of Roman civilization; the prize exhibit is the *Neumagener Weinschiff*, a Roman sculpture of a wine ship. A few minutes' walk further south, the **Kaiserthermen** (daily: March & Oct 9am–5pm; April–Sept 9am–6pm; Nov–Feb 9am–4pm; €2.10) was once one of the largest bath complexes in the Roman world. The extensive underground heating system has survived, and you can walk its passages.

BOAT TRIPS ON THE MOSEL

The final 195km-long stretch of the Mosel connecting Trier with the city of Koblenz cuts a sinuous and attractive gorge that gives Germany some of its steepest vineyards and best full-bodied wines. **Boats** offer an ideal way to explore the valley: the Personen-Schiffarht Gebrüder Kolb (Ⓦwww.moselfahrplan.de) offer regular sailings from Trier to Bernkastel-Kues; the Mosel-Schiffs-Touristik (Ⓦwww.moselpersonenschifffahrt.de) concentrate on the middle leg around Traben-Trarbach and Bernkastel-Kues; while Köln-Düsseldorfer (Ⓦwww.k-d.com) cover the northern stretch between Cochem and Koblenz. Pick up the latest timetables for all three companies at the tourist information offices in Trier or Koblenz.

The Karl-Marx-Haus

Southwest of the Hauptmarkt, the **Karl-Marx-Haus,** Brückenstrasse 10 (April–Oct daily 10am–6pm; Nov–March Mon 2–5pm, Tues–Sun 11am–5pm; €3; Ⓦwww.fes.de/marx/index.htm), is where Karl Marx was born. It now houses a modern three-storey museum on his life and work, as well as a general history of Communism up to the present day.

Information

Tourist office At An der Porta Nigra (Jan & Feb Mon–Sat 10am–5pm, Sun 10am–1pm; May–Oct Mon–Sat 9am–6pm, Sun 10am–5pm; Nov, Dec, March & April Mon–Sat 9am–6pm, Sun 10am–3pm; Ⓣ0651/97 80 80, Ⓦwww.tourist-information-trier.de). It sells the Trier-Card (€9/3 days), which covers transport and provides discounts at the museums.

Bike rental At the train station by platform 11. Mid-April to Oct daily 9am–7pm; Nov to mid-April Mon–Fri 10am–6pm. €10/day.

Accommodation

DJH An der Jugendherberge 4 Ⓣ0651/14 66 20, Ⓦwww.djh.de. Spotless modern HI hostel, with games rooms and sports facilities. Bus #12. Dorms €19.90, twin rooms €50.80.

Camping Treviris Luxemburger Str. 81 Ⓣ0651/820 09 11, Ⓦwww.camping-treviris.de. Campsite on the western bank of the Mosel, over the Konrad-Adenauer bridge. Open April–Oct. €6.30/person; plus €4.50–9/tent.

Hille's Gartenfeldstr. 7 Ⓣ0651/710 27 85, Ⓦwww.hilles-hostel-trier.de. Homely, clean and sociable independent hostel a 10min walk south of the station. Reception Nov–June 4–6pm, July–Oct 2–8pm. €15, singles €28, doubles €28.

Eating, drinking and nightlife

Alt Zalawen Zurlaubener Ufer 79, north of the Kaiser-Wilhelm-Brücke. This traditional tavern, complete with outdoor seating overlooking the Mosel, makes an excellent place to try out the local cider, Viez. Meat platter €6. Daily 3pm until late.

Astarix Karl-Marx-Str. 11. This relaxed student bar is your best bet for good and inexpensive food, and there's often live music at night. Pizza €3.50–5. The entrance is down an alley.

Forum Hindenburgstr. 4 Ⓦwww.forum-trier.com. An invariably packed café-bar-club spinning Latin, house and hip-hop to a younger crowd. Occasional live shows. Wed–Sat 10pm–late.

Weinstube Palais Kesselstatt Liebfrauenstr. 10. Late-opening, well-known wine bar – the best choice among the many possibilities for tasting local wines. Wine from €4.

Moving on

Train Cologne (hourly; 2hr 45min); Frankfurt (hourly; 3hr); Luxembourg (hourly; 50min).

FRANKFURT

Straddling the River Main just before it meets the Rhine, **FRANKFURT AM MAIN** is known as Germany's financial capital and the home of the European Central Bank. But it also has some of Germany's best museums and some excellent (if expensive) nightlife. Over half of the city, including almost all of the centre, was destroyed during the war and the rebuilders often opted for innovation over restoration, resulting in an architecturally mixed skyline – part skyscraper, part quaint, Germanic red sandstone.

What to see and do

Frankfurt's centre is defined by its old city walls, now a semicircular stretch of public gardens. Presided over by the gabled **Römer** or town hall, the broad, irregular piazza of **Römerberg** is the historical and geographical heart of the Altstadt, where Charlemagne built his fort to protect the original *frankonovurd* (Ford of the Franks). The whole quarter was flattened by bombing in 1944, but the most significant landmarks were rebuilt or restored afterwards and there are now moves to rebuild more of the original houses. Each December, Römerberg is the focus for Frankfurt's delightful **Christmas Market.**

Kaiserdom

The Altstadt's most significant survivor is the thirteenth-century church

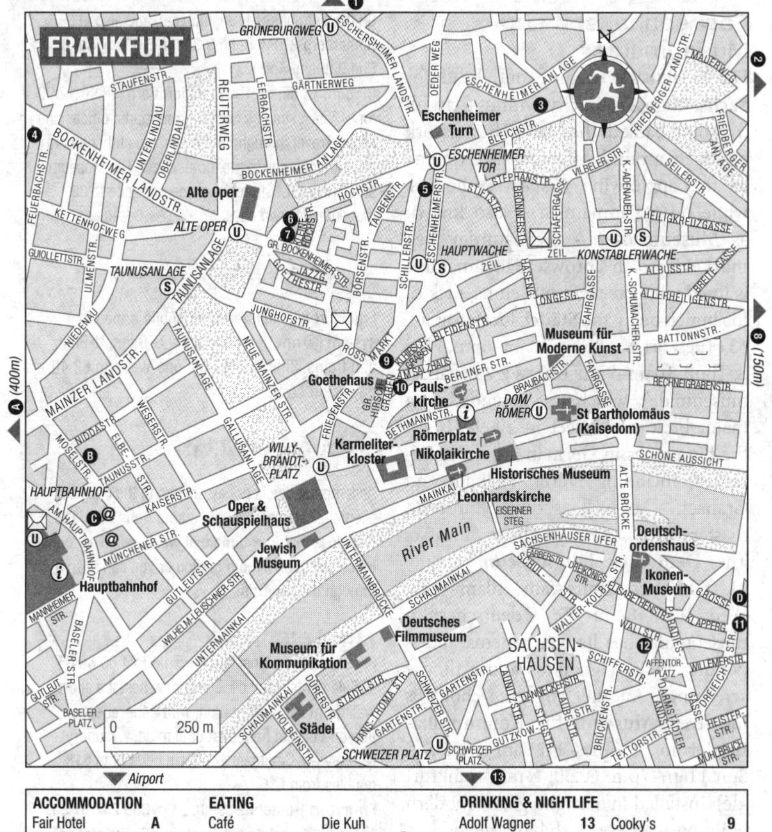

ACCOMMODATION		EATING				DRINKING & NIGHTLIFE			
Fair Hotel	A	Café Karin	10	Die Kuh die Lacht	5	Adolf Wagner	13	Cooky's	9
Five Elements	B	Café Laumer	4	Mirador	2	Batschklapp	1	Fichtekränzi	12
Frankfurt Hostel	C			Vinum	6	Club Voltaire	7	Pulse	3
Primus	D					Cocoon	8	Zum Eichkatzerl	11

of St Bartholomäus, known as the **Kaiserdom** (daily Sun–Thurs 9am–noon & 2.30–6pm, Fri 2.30–6pm; tours Tues–Sun at 3pm; €3), where for two centuries Holy Roman Emperors were crowned. To the right of the choir is the restored **Wahlkapelle** (electoral chapel), where the seven Electors would choose the Holy Roman Emperor.

Museum für Moderne Kunst

Dividing Braubachstrasse from Berliner Strasse at the eastern end of the Altstadt is the **Museum für Moderne Kunst** (MMK, Domstrasse; Tues & Thurs–Sun 10am–6pm, Wed 10am–8pm; €12, Ⓦmmk-frankfurt.de), a three-storey affair featuring major modern artists such as Lichtenstein and Beuys, alongside innovative temporary exhibitions.

Jewish Museum

A short distance to the west of the Römerberg – in a mansion on Untermainkai that once belonged to the Frankfurt-based Rothschild family – is the **Jewish Museum** (Tues & Thurs–Sun 10am–5pm, Wed 10am–8pm; €4; Ⓦjuedischesmuseum.de), which examines the city's Jewish community, 10,000 of whom died in Nazi hands.

Sachsenhausen and Museumsufer

For a laidback evening out, head for **Sachsenhausen**, the city-within-a-city on the south bank of the Main. The network of streets around Affentorplatz is home to the apple-wine (*Ebbelwei*) houses, while on Schaumainkai – also known as **Museumsufer** – the Saturday **flea market** is worth a browse. Schaumainkai is lined with excellent museums, pick of the bunch being the **Städel**, located at no. 63 (Tues, Fri, Sat & Sun 10am–6pm, Wed & Thurs 10am–9pm; €10; Ⓦwww.staedelmuseum.de), which was extended in a major building project in 2009–11. All the big names in German art are represented, including Dürer, Holbein and Cranach – as well as other European masters from Rembrandt to Picasso. The **Deutsches Filmmuseum** at no. 41 (Tues & Thurs–Sun 10am–6pm, Wed 10am–8pm; €5; Ⓦdeutschesfilmmuseum.de) has its own cinema and is popular for foreign films and arthouse screenings. Another engaging choice is the lively **Museum für Kommunikation** at no. 53 (Tues–Fri 9am–6pm, Sat, Sun 11am–7pm; €2.50; Ⓦmfk-frankfurt.de), installed in a bright, glassy modern building, whose exhibits include a Salvador Dalí lobster telephone.

Arrival

Air Frankfurt Airport (Ⓦfrankfurt-airport.com) has its own long-distance train station, with regular rail links to most German cities and Frankfurt's Hauptbahnhof (frequent; 11min; €3.90), to which it is linked by two S-Bahn lines. The deceptively named Frankfurt Hahn Airport (Ⓦwww.hahn-airport.de) actually lies midway between Trier and Koblenz but is connected to Frankfurt by bus (every 30 min–1hr 30min; 1hr 45min; €13).
Train From the Hauptbahnhof it's a 15min walk to the centre, or take Ⓤ line #4 or #5, or tram #11 or #12. There is a left-luggage facility here.

Information

Tourist office In the train station (Mon–Fri 8am–9pm, Sat & Sun 9am–6pm; Ⓣ069 21 23 88 00, Ⓦfrankfurt-tourismus.de), and also at Römerberg 27 (Mon–Fri 9.30am–5.30pm, Sat & Sun 9.30am–4pm).
Discount passes The Frankfurt Card (€8.90/12.90 for 1/2 days) can be bought from tourist offices and allows travel throughout the city, plus fifty percent off entry charges to most museums. The Museumsufer Ticket (€15) provides free entrance to 33 museums for two days.

City transport

Frankfurt has an integrated public transport system (Ⓦrmv.de) made up of S-Bahn, U-Bahn and trams. Short trip €1.50, one-way trip €2.40, day ticket €6.20.

Accommodation

Accommodation is pricey, thanks to the business clientele; rates can double during trade fairs. The flipside is that they tumble at weekends. The tourist office will book a room for you or you can search through their website.

Hostels

Five Elements Moselstr. 40 Ⓣ069 24 00 58 85, Ⓦ5elementshostel.de. Lively new hostel a short walk from the main station, with 24hr reception, all-you-can-eat breakfast until midday, laundry & free wi-fi. Breakfast €4. Dorm beds from €18, doubles from €36.
Frankfurt Hostel Kaiserstr. 74 Ⓣ069 247 51 30, Ⓦfrankfurt-hostel.com. Very close to the station with free wi-fi and 24hr bar and reception. Sheets and breakfast included. Dorms from €19, doubles from €65.

Hotels

Fair Hotel Mainzer Landstr. 120 Ⓣ069 74 26 28, Ⓦfairhotelfrankfurt.de. Pleasant budget hotel just north of the train station, away from the sleazier streets. Singles €40, doubles €75.
Primus Grosse Rittergasse 19–21 Ⓣ069 62 30 20, Ⓦhotel-primus.de. Good-value three-star hotel close to the Sachsenhausen *apfelwein* taverns. All rooms en suite. Singles €52, doubles €72.

Eating

Café Karin Grosser Hirschgraben 28. Frankfurt institution that's friendly, unpretentious and well worth a visit. Breakfast all day (from €3) and bistro-bar in the evenings; pasta €9.80. Mon–Sat 9am–midnight, Sun 10am–7pm.

Café Laumer Bockenheimer Landstr. 67 Ⓦ cafe-laumer.de. Dignified old café in a fine old villa, halfway up the Westend's main thoroughfare, with a leafy terrace at the front. Daily specials €6.40. Daily 11.30am–6pm.

Die Kuh die Lacht Schillerstr. 28. Excellent burgers – including meat-free falafel and nut options – with side dishes ranging from fries to salad or veggie tempura. Classic burger €6.50. Mon–Sat 11am–11pm, Sun noon–10pm; also at Friedensstr. 2.

Mirador Bergerstr. 65 Ⓤ Merianplatz. Trendy café-bar with gold-dusted decor on a street lined with such places. Beers from €2.50, cocktails from €7.80; food from around €10. Sun–Thurs 10am–1am, Fri & Sat 10am–3am.

Vinum Kleine Hochstr. 9 Ⓣ 069 29 30 37. Pretty brick-vaulted wine cellar close to the Alte Oper and Börse, with local Rheingau wines to try (from €4) and main courses from around €10.

Drinking and nightlife

Apfelwein (cider) is Frankfurt's speciality, and Sachsenhausen's apple-wine taverns are the most atmospheric places to try it. Many taverns also offer hearty traditional food. Alt-Sachensenhausen has plenty of clubs and bars too; there are more in the city centre and around Hanauer Landstr.

Apple-wine taverns

Adolf Wagner Schweizer Str. 71, Sachsenhausen. One of the best of the taverns, with a lively clientele of all ages and a cosy terrace. Meals from €9, *Apfelwein* €1.80. Daily 11am–midnight.

Fichtekränzi Wallstr. 5. Lovely tavern with a tree-shaded courtyard, wood-panelled interior and a more extensive menu than many. "Frankfurt slaughter platter" (consisting of almost every part of the pig) €6.90. Open 5pm; kitchen closes at 11.30pm.

Zum Eichkatzerl Dreieichstr. 29, Sachsenhausen. An excellent, traditional tavern with a large courtyard and some veggie options; main courses from €8. Mon–Fri 5pm–1am, Sat & Sun 4pm–1am.

Bars

Club Voltaire Kleine Hochstr. 5. Politically committed bar and club with various events from art exhibitions to debates and live music. Mon–Sat 6pm–1am, Sun 6pm–midnight.

Pulse Bleichstr. 38a. Stylish but friendly lounge, cocktail bar & restaurant that is the focus of Frankfurt's gay and lesbian scene, with a wonderful garden at the back and a club downstairs. Cocktails €8. Mon–Fri from 11am, Sat & Sun from 10am.

Clubs

Batschkapp Maybachstr. 24 Ⓦ www.batschkapp.de Ⓢ #6 to Eschersheim or Ⓤ #1, #2 or #3 to Weisser Stein. Grimy, sweaty venue for top-rank indie bands – avoid the school-age club nights though. Concerts usually start at 8pm.

Cocoon Carl-Benz-Str. 21 Ⓦ www.cocoonclub.net Ⓤ #4 to Gwinnerstr. then bus #F-41 to Carl Benz Str. or night bus #N63 from Konstablerwache. Techno legend Sven Väth's slick superclub is Frankfurt's best-known dance venue; entry is occasionally free before midnight. Fri & Sat 9pm–6am.

Cooky's Am Salzhaus 4 Ⓦ www.cookys.de. Stylish hip-hop, house and soul club north of Berliner Str., hosting popular DJ nights plus occasional live acts. Cover varies: €5–10. Tues–Sun from 10pm.

Directory

Consulates Australia, Main Tower, 28th floor Neue Mainzer Str. 52–58 Ⓣ 069/90 55 80; UK, Barclays Capital, Bockenheimer Landstr. 38–40 Ⓣ 069 7167 5345; US, Giessenerstr. 30 Ⓣ 069/753 50.

Exchange Reisebank, at the train station.

Hospital Bürgerhospital, Nibelungenallee 37–41 Ⓣ 069/15 00 00.

Internet Internet Callshop, Kaiserstr. 70. Open 9am–midnight; Internet Phoneshop, Kaiserstr. 81, Mon–Sat 9am–11pm, Sun 10am–11pm.

Pharmacy At the train station, lower concourse (Mon–Fri 6.30am–9pm, Sat 8am–9pm, Sun 9am–8pm).

Post office Branch at the train station (Mon–Fri 7am–7pm, Sat 9am–4pm) and Goetheplatz 6 (Mon–Fri 9.30am–7pm, Sat 9am–2pm).

Moving on

Train Berlin (hourly; 4hr 45min); Cologne (1–2/hour; 1hr–1hr 25min); Hamburg (hourly; 3hr 55min); Heidelberg (hourly; 1hr–1hr 35min); Munich (hourly; 3hr 15min); Nuremberg (2/hour; 2hr 5min); Würzburg (every 20 min–1hr; 1hr 10min).

Baden-Württemberg

The southwestern state of **Baden-Württemberg** is Germany's most prosperous. The motorcar was invented here in the late nineteenth century, and the region has stayed at the forefront of technology ever since, with **Stuttgart** still the home of Daimler (Mercedes) and Porsche. Baden-Württemberg is also home to the famous university city of **Heidelberg**, and the elegant spa resort of **Baden-Baden**, which remains evocative of its nineteenth-century heyday as a playground for European aristocracy. **Baden-Württemberg**'s scenery is wonderful: its western and southern boundaries are defined by the Rhine and its bulge into Germany's largest lake, the **Bodensee** (Lake Constance). Within the curve of the river lies the **Black Forest**, source of another of the continent's principal waterways, the Danube.

HEIDELBERG

Home to Germany's oldest university, **HEIDELBERG** is majestically set on the banks of the swift-flowing Neckar, 70km south of Frankfurt. For two centuries, it has seduced travellers like no other German city. The centrepiece is the Schloss, a compendium of magnificent buildings, made more atmospheric by their ruined condition – this is one castle where you won't end up traipsing through over-decorated bedchambers. The rest of the city has some good museums, but the main appeal lies in its picturesque cobbled streets, crammed with traditional restaurants and student pubs. In spring and early summer the streets hum with activity and late-night parties – by July and August, most students have left, to be replaced by swarms of visitors.

What to see and do

The dominating **Schloss** can be reached from the Kornmarkt by the *Bergbahn* funicular (€5 return), which continues to the Königstuhl viewpoint (€8 return); you can also walk up in ten minutes via the Burgweg. At the southeastern corner is the most romantic of the ruins, the Gesprengter Turm; a collapsed section lies intact in the moat, leaving a clear view into the interior. The **Schlosshof** (daily 8am–5.30pm; €5, grounds free from 6pm until dusk; Ⓦwww.schloss-heidelberg.de) is a group of Renaissance palaces that now contains the diverting Pharmacy Museum and the Grosses Fass, an eighteenth-century wine barrel capable of holding 220,000 litres.

The Altstadt

The **Altstadt**'s finest surviving buildings are grouped around the sandstone **Heiliggeistkirche** on Marktplatz. Note the tiny shopping booths between its buttresses, a feature ever since the church was built. The striking Baroque **Alte Brücke** is reached from the Marktplatz down Steingasse; dating from the 1780s, it was painstakingly rebuilt after being blown up during World War II. The **Palais Rischer** on Untere Strasse was the most famous venue for the university's *Mensur*, or fencing match; wounds were frequent and prized as badges of courage – for optimum prestige, salt was rubbed into them, leaving scars that remained for life. Universitätsplatz, the heart of the Old Town, is flanked by the eighteenth-century **Alte Universität** (April–Sept Tues–Sun 10am–6pm; Oct Tues–Sun 10am–4pm; Nov–March Tues–Sat 10am–4pm; €3) and the **Neue Universität**, erected with US funds in 1931. The oddest of Heidelberg's traditions was that its students didn't used to come under civil jurisdiction: offenders were dealt with by the university authorities, and could serve their punishment at leisure. The **Studentenkarzer** (Students' Prison) around the corner at Augustinergasse 2 (Studentenkarzer; same hours and ticket as Alte Universität) was used from 1778 to 1914; its spartan cells are covered with graffiti.

Arrival and information

Air The Baden-Airpark (Ⓦwww.badenairpark.de) is connected to Heidelberg train station by bus (2 daily; 1hr 30min; €20).
Train and bus Heidelberg's train and bus stations are in an anonymous quarter west of the centre a 20min walk west of the Altstadt. Trams #5 and #21 run into the centre.
Tourist office On the square outside the station (April–Oct Mon–Sat 9am–7pm, Sun 10am–6pm; Nov–March Mon–Sat 9am–6pm) and in the Rathaus on Marktplatz (Mon–Fri 8am–5pm, Sat 10am–5pm; Ⓣ06221/194 33, Ⓦwww.cvb-heidelberg.de).
Discount pass The HeidelbergBeWelcomeCARD (one day €11, two days €13, four days €16) provides free entrance to some sights, including the Schloss, and transport.
City transport Heidelberg is small, but the bus and tram system is useful for journeys from the train or bus stations. One-way trip €2.20, day ticket €5.30.
Internet Heidelberger Internet Café, Plöck 101 (up the road from Essighaus). Daily 10am–10pm, €1/hr.

Accommodation

Hotels are often booked solid and are fairly expensive; the chart outside the tourist office lists vacancies.
DJH Tiergartenstr. 5 Ⓣ06221/65 11 90, Ⓦwww.jugendherberge-heidelberg.de. This hostel is on the north bank of the Neckar, about 4km from the centre. Take bus #31 from Bismarkplatz to "*Jugendherberge*". Dorms €24.10.
Hotel Central Kaiserstr. 75 Ⓣ06221/206 41, Ⓦwww.hotel-central-heidelberg.de. Sparkling and airy, but rather bland, modern hotel near the train station. One of the best-value places in town that's likely to have a bed. Singles €65, doubles €75.
Jeske Mittelbadgasse 2 Ⓣ06221/237 33, Ⓦwww.pension-jeske-heidelberg.de. This is a good, central option, a few steps off Marktplatz. Breakfast not included. Rooms €55.

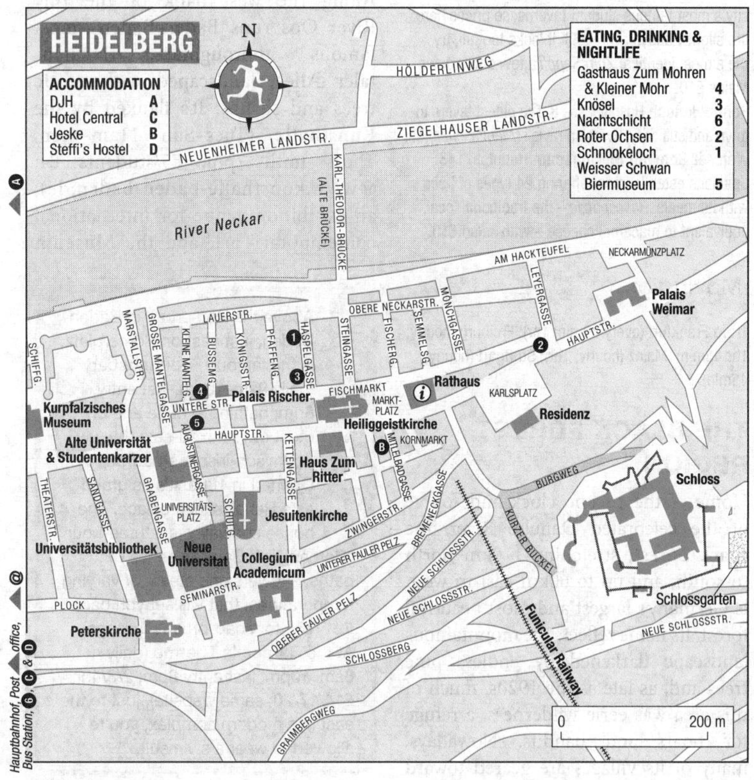

GERMANY
BADEN-WÜRTTEMBERG

Steffi's Hostel Alte Eppelheimer Str. 50 ⓣ6221/778 27 72, ⓦwww.hostelheidelberg.de. Independent hostel in a former brick factory a short walk from the train station. Perks include kitchen, free wi-fi and bike rental. Dorms €18, doubles €52.

Eating, drinking and nightlife

Some of the best places to eat are the city's atmospheric student taverns, known for their basic dishes at reasonable prices.

Gasthaus Zum Mohren & Kleiner Mohr Untere Str. 5. One of several hip, young drinking spots along this alley, with various nightly events until 3am. Bar food includes *Bratwürste* with fries for €8.

Knösel Haspelgasse 16. Try the famous *Heidelberger Studentenkuss*, a dark chocolate filled with praline and nougat (€2.15), at this chic café or at the shop next door. Coffee €2.

Nachtschicht Bergheimer Str. 147 ⓦwww.nachtschicht.com. Popular club in a former factory with hip-hop, disco and house nights. Just north of the train station. Wed–Sat.

Roter Ochsen Hauptstr. 217. This is one of the city's most famous student taverns, so prices here are slightly above average. If it looks too full, try the almost identical *Zum Sepp'l* a few doors down. Mains €10.

Schnookeloch Haspelgasse 8. The oldest tavern in town and still cosy. Swabian ravioli (*Maultaschen*) €8.

Weisser Schwan Biermuseum Hauptstr. 143. Spacious establishment offering 24 types of beer with its meals. *Käsespätzle* – the traditional local equivalent to macaroni cheese – with salad €10.

Moving on

Train Frankfurt (every 30min; 1hr); Freiburg (hourly; 1hr 45min); Mainz (hourly; 1hr); Stuttgart (hourly; 45min).

THE BLACK FOREST REGION

Home of the cuckoo clock and source of the celebrated Danube River, the **Black Forest**, stretching 170km north to south, and up to 60km east to west, is Germany's largest and most beautiful forest. Its name reflects the mountainous landscape darkened by endless pine trees and, as late as the 1920s, much of this area was eerie wilderness, a refuge for boars and bandits. Nowadays, many of its villages are geared toward tourism, brimming with tacky souvenir shops, while old forest trails provide easy hiking. Most of the Black Forest is associated with the Margravate of Baden, whose old capital, **Baden-Baden**, is at the northern fringe of the forest, in a fertile orchard and vine-growing area. **Freiburg im Breisgau**, doubtless one of Germany's most enticing cities, is surrounded by the forest.

Baden-Baden

The therapeutic value of the town's hot springs, first discovered by the Romans, is still the main draw in **BADEN-BADEN** – hardly the recipe for a party atmosphere– but nevertheless, it's a pretty town for a stroll.

What to see and do

Along the west bank of the tiny River Oos runs Baden-Baden's most famous thoroughfare, Lichtentaler Allee, landscaped with exotic trees and shrubs. It's flanked by the **Kunsthalle** (Tues–Sun 11am–6pm, Thurs until 7pm; €5/students €4; ⓦwww.kunsthalle-baden-baden.de), an exhibition venue for international contemporary art, and the **Museum**

TREAT YOURSELF

Above the Römerbad in Baden-Baden, just east on Römerplatz, is the famous **Friedrichsbad** (daily 9am–10pm, last entry 8pm; bathing is nude and on most days mixed-sex; ⓦwww.roemisch-irisches-bad.de). Opened in 1869, it's as grand as a Renaissance palace. The house speciality is a three-hour "Roman-Irish Bath", a series of baths, showers and steam of varying temperatures, that will set you back €21 (€31 for soap-brush massage). At the **Caracalla Therme** (daily 8am–10pm, last entry 8pm; 2/3/4hr €14/17/20; same website), just to the east in a modern complex, you're allowed to wear a swimsuit.

Frieder Burda (Tues–Sun 10am–6pm; €10/students €8, combined ticket with Kunsthalle €12; ⓦwww.museum-frieder-burda.de), which contains an excellent collection including several works by Beckmann, Kirchner, Picasso and de Kooning. Just north at Kaiserallee 1 is the famously opulent **Casino**, the oldest in Europe, whose gilded frescoes and chandeliers are well worth a peek (*Kurhaus*; visit in the evening for a flutter; €5 – ID required; ⓦwww.casino-baden-baden.de). For women, dresses or skirts are obligatory, while men need a jacket and tie (rentals: €8 and €3 respectively), and while smart jeans are permitted, sports shoes aren't.

Arrival and information

Air The Karlsruhe/Baden-Baden (FKB) airport (ⓦwww.badenairpark.de) is connected to the Baden-Baden train station by the Hahn-Express and bus #140 (€9).
Train The station is located 4km northwest in the suburb of Oos; bus #201 goes to the centre, "Leopoldplatz".
Tourist office In the Trinkhalle on Kaiserallee (Mon–Sat 9am–6pm, Sun 9am–1pm; ⓣ07221/27 52 00, ⓦwww.baden-baden.de); staff can book rooms.

Accommodation

Deutscher Kaiser Hauptstr. 35 ⓣ07221/721 52, ⓦwww.hoteldk.de. Pleasant, family-run hotel 2km from the centre in the lovely suburb of Lichtental. Take bus #201 to "Eckerlestr." Singles €35, doubles €52.
DJH Hardbergstr. 34 ⓣ07221/522 23, ⓦwww.jugendherberge-baden-baden.de. Uninspiring HI hostel between the train station and the centre. Take bus #201 to "Grosse-Dollenstrasse"; from there it's a signposted 10min climb. Reception open 5–10pm. Dorms €21.30 including breakfast.

Eating and drinking

Baden Baden's centre is full of cheap snack joints.
Leo's Luisenstr. 10. A trendy café-bar serving huge, delicious salads (€12). Open until 3am.
Löwenbräu Gernsbacher Str. 9. If you're sick of Swabian fare, head to Löwenbräu and eat like a Bavarian (mains average €16). Boisterous summer beer garden. Traditional breakfast (*Weisswurst*, *brezn* & beer) €6.
Rathausglöckel Steinstr. 7 ⓣ07221/906 10. Traditional favourites like venison goulash (€9) and winter-warmer potato soup (€6) are served in this cosy sixteenth-century house on a side street off the Marktplatz.

Moving on

Train Freiburg (hourly; 1hr); Heidelberg (every 30min; 1hr 10min); Strasbourg (every 30min; 1hr).

FREIBURG IM BREISGAU

FREIBURG IM BREISGAU – midway between Strasbourg (France) and Basel (Switzerland) – basks in the laidback atmosphere you'd expect from Germany's sunniest city. It's been a university town since 1457 and its youthful presence is maintained all year round with a varied programme of festivals. It's a thoroughly enjoyable place to visit, and makes the perfect urban base for exploring the surrounding Black Forest.

What to see and do

The city's most impressive sight is the dark-red sandstone **Münster**, with its impressively intricate openwork spire. Begun in about 1200, the church has a masterly Gothic nave, with flying buttresses, gargoyles and statues – the magnificent sculptures of the west porch are among the most important German works of their time. From the tower (Tues–Sat 9.30am–5pm, Sun 1–5pm; €2) there's a fine panorama of the city and the surrounding forest-covered hills. Walking south from here on Kaiser-Josef-Strasse, Freiburg's central axis, you come to the **Martinstor**, one of two surviving towers of the medieval fortifications. Just southeast of here is the main channel of the Bächle; follow it along Fischerau (the old fishermen's street) and Gerberau, to the **Schwaben Tor**, the other thirteenth-century tower.

Schauinsland

The hills of the Black Forest almost rise out of Freiburg's Altstadt, giving the town a hugely convenient outdoorsy playground for hikers and mountain bikers, and the tourist information office has an abundance of good maps, as well as suggestions for numerous trailheads accessible by public transport. The largest of these forested peaks, **Schauinsland**, lies 7km south of the city and is easily ascended, thanks to the Schauinslandbahn cable car (daily: Jan–June & Oct–Dec 9am–5pm; July–Sept 9am–6pm; one-way €8.50/ return €12; ⓣ0761/451 17 77, ⓦwww.bergwelt-schauinsland.de; tram #2 to Günterstal terminus then bus #21). From its summit a five-minute walk leads to a lookout tower and the top of several well-marked trails. These offer first-class hiking and mountain biking – partly because almost the entire 14km journey back to Freiburg is downhill – with great views along the way.

Arrival and information

Train and bus The train station, with the bus station on its southern side, is about a 10min walk west from the city centre.

Tourist office Following Eisenbahnstrasse, you come to the tourist office in the Altes Rathaus at Rathausplatz 2–4 (June–Sept Mon–Fri 8am–8pm, Sat 9.30am–5pm, Sun 10am–noon; Oct–May Mon–Fri 8am–6pm, Sat 9.30am–2.30pm, Sun 10am–noon; ⓣ0761/388 18 80, ⓦwww.freiburg.de). For €3, they'll find you a room (doubles from €34).

Internet Internet Cafe Freiburg, Bismarckallee 5, is a cheap internet café near the station (daily 10am–10pm).

Accommodation

Black Forest Hostel Kartäuserstr. 33 ⓣ0761/881 78 70, ⓦwww.blackforest-hostel.de. Buzzing backpackers' hostel in an old factory, and by far the best place to stay in town. Well-equipped kitchen, internet, and bikes for €5/ day. Sheets €3. Tram to Schwabentorbrücke or 30min walk east from the station. Dorms €14, singles €30, doubles €50.

Hirzberg Kartäuserstr. 99 ⓣ0761/35 054, ⓦwww.freiburg-camping.de. The most convenient of Freiburg's three campsites, between the two hostels to the east of the centre. Open all year round. Tram to Stadthalle, then head north across the Dreisam. €6.50/person, plus €4–5/tent.

Schemmer Eschholzstr. 63 ⓣ0761/20 74 90, ⓦwww.hotel-schemmer.de. West of the train station, this is the cheapest central hotel. Tram to Eschholzstr. or a 10min walk. Singles €45, doubles €58.

Eating, drinking and nightlife

Nightlife revolves around the junction of Universitätstr. and Niemenstr.; pick up a free *Freiburg Aktuell* magazine to see what's on.

Jazzhaus Schnewlinstr. 1 ⓣ0761/292 34 46, ⓦwww.jazzhaus.de. Club in an old wine cellar that hosts all manner of musical events, from world music concerts to blues, jazz, rock and hip-hop, to busy, fairly mainstream weekend club nights, attracting a range of ages. Big names occasionally play here, when tickets run to around €10–30; otherwise the cover is about €7. Open until at least 3am most nights.

Karma Bertoldstr. 51–53 ⓦwww.karma-freiburg.de. The *Karma* complex has everything you need: a café-bar daily till 3am, a restaurant (closed Sun) with weekday lunch specials (around €6) and a club in the cellar playing funk and house on Fri & Sat.

Markthalle Martinsgässle 235 & Grünewalderstr. 4. Food court that bustles with locals visiting different kiosks for quality regional Swabian, Mexican, Indian, Asian, French and Italian dishes. It's standing only, but the food is excellent value and service quick. One entrance lies at the end of an alley just east of the Martinstor; the main entrance is barely more obvious and off Grünewalderstr.

Onkel Wok Belfortstr. 57 ⓣ0761/38 09 78 88. Hectic Asian place with an open kitchen and the kind of great, freshly prepared food that keeps it busy around the clock. Fill up from as little as €4.

Weinstube Oberkirch Münsterplatz 22. Pricey but excellent restaurant, serving local specialities. Ox with *Spätzle* €14.

Moving on

Train Basel (hourly; 45min); Frankfurt (hourly; 2hr 10min); Heidelberg (hourly; 1hr 45min); Strasbourg (hourly; 1hr 20min); Stuttgart (hourly; 2hr); Zürich (hourly; 2hr).

STUTTGART

In the centre of Baden-Württemberg, 85km southeast of Heidelberg, **STUTTGART** is home to the German success stories of Bosch, Porsche and Mercedes. Founded around 950 as a stud farm (*Stutengarten*), it became a town only in the fourteenth century. Though not the most beautiful of cities, it has a range of superb museums and a sophisticated cultural scene and nightlife.

What to see and do

From the train station, Königstrasse passes the dull modern Dom and enters Schlossplatz, on the south of which is the **Altes Schloss**, home to the **Landesmuseum Württemberg** (Tues–Sun 10am–5pm; €5; Ⓦwww.landesmuseum-stuttgart.de). This large and richly varied museum explores the history of the region from the Stone Age to the present through archeological exhibitions as well as arts and crafts. However, large parts of the collection will be inaccessible until 2014, in the meantime access to remaining exhibits is free. Northeast of Schlossplatz at Konrad-Adenauer-Strasse 30–32 is the **Staatsgalerie** (Tues & Thurs 10am–9pm, Wed & Fri–Sun 10am–6pm; €5.50/students €4; Wed & Sat free; Ⓦwww.staatsgalerie.de). There's an Old Masters section as well as a New Gallery focusing on various schools within twentieth-century art movements.

The Mercedes-Benz-Museum and the Porsche Museum

As much as they are collections of vintage cars, the Mercedes and Porsche museums are also temples to fine engineering, human ingenuity and thousands of hours of careful hard work. So slick are the museums – their modern architecture airy and futuristic, the displays self-confident, seamless and high-tech – that they can't fail to inspire. As corporate propaganda they are hard to beat and it's almost impossible to decide which is better. The **Mercedes-Benz-Museum** (Tues–Sun 9am–6pm; €8/students €4; Ⓢ#1 to Gottlieb-Daimler-Stadion; Ⓦwww.mercedes-benz.com/museum) is strong on the early parts of motoring history, since its founders invented both the motorbike and motor car. However, the earliest examples of each are eclipsed by the rest of the museum that's chock-full of luxury cars and the machines designed for world-record attempts. The **Porsche Museum** (Tues–Sun 9am–6pm; €8/students €4; Ⓢ#6 to Neuwirtshaus; Ⓦwww.porsche.com/international/aboutporsche/porschemuseum/) is no less flashy. Dozens of priceless, highly polished examples of engineering at its finest are explained by an intelligent audioguide (free) and touch-screen monitors. Racing driver video testimonials help bring the vehicles to life as do recordings of engine noises. The success of the brand is underlined by a display of some of Porsche's 28,000 trophies.

Arrival and information

Air Stuttgart Airport is linked to the train station by Ⓢ#2 and #3 (frequent; 30min).

Train and bus Stuttgart's train and bus stations are in the centre of town. A day ticket for the extensive integrated public transport network costs €6.10, a one-way ticket is €2.

Tourist office Opposite the train station at Königstr. 1a (Mon–Fri 9am–8pm, Sat 9am–6pm, Sun 1–6pm; Ⓣ0711/222 82 53, Ⓦwww.stuttgart-tourist.de). Another branch at the airport, in Terminal 3 (Mon–Fri 8am–7pm, Sat & Sun 9am–noon & 1–6pm).

Discount passes The StuttCard (€9.70/three days) covers admission to most museums and numerous freebies; the combination StuttCard (€18/three days) also includes use of local public transport.

Internet and bike rental Tips'n'Trips, Lautenschlagerstr. 22 (Mon–Fri noon–7pm, Sat 10am–2pm; Ⓦwww.jugendinformation-stuttgart.de), offers both Internet and bike rental 200m southwest of the station. Internet €2/hr; bike rental for 24hr: €15/students €11.

Accommodation

Alex 30 Alexanderstr. 30 ⓣ0711/838 89 50, ⓦwww.alex30-hostel.de ⓤOlgaeck or 20min walk southeast from the station. Convenient independent hostel near the Bohnenviertel. Has a bar, café, kitchen and tiny terrace, and free wi-fi and sheets are included. Dorms €23, singles €35, doubles €56.

DJH Haussmannstr. 27 ⓣ0711/664 74 70, ⓦwww.jugendherberge-stuttgart.de. Large, well-organized standard DJH hostel. Take tram #U15 to Eugensplatz and then continue 5min uphill. Dorms €24.10, singles €34.10, twins €58.20

Museum-Stube Hospitalstr. 9 ⓣ0711/29 68 10, ⓦwww.museumstube.de. Spotless guesthouse above a Croatian restaurant, and one of the few central bargains. Some rooms are en suite. Singles €35, doubles €70.

Eating, drinking and nightlife

Stuttgart is surrounded by vineyards, and its numerous *Weinstuben* are excellent places to try good-quality, traditional, noodle-based dishes and local wines at low cost. *Lift* and *Prinz Stuttgart*, available from newsagents, have complete nightlife listings.

Calwer-Eck-Bräu Calwerstr. 31. Microbrewery with good beer and food. Mains €9, beer €3. ⓢStadtmitte.

Die Röhre Willy-Brandt-Str. 2 ⓦwww.die-roehre.com. Legendary local club in an old tunnel with an industrial feel. Music from across the board, with everything from more mainstream alternative and drum'n'bass to death metal, played to three dancefloors. Cover €7. Fri & Sat 10pm–5am.

Dilayla Eberharstr. 49. Dimly lit basement that bustles with a broad spectrum of people dancing to Seventies and Eighties hits or lounging on couches; open until 4am week nights, 6am weekends; get there after midnight.

Palast der Republik Friedrichstr. 27. Offbeat cult place – a former public loo that's now a beer kiosk – on sunny days drinkers line the pavement outside.

Weinhaus Stetter Rosenstr. 32. A lovely atmosphere, excellent service and the widest choice of wines in town await you at this family-run *Weinstube*. The lentil soup with sausages (€6) is outstanding. Wine from €3.

Moving on

Train Konstanz (6 daily; 2hr 20min); Munich (every 30min; 2hr 20min); Zürich (every 2hr; 2hr).

KONSTANZ AND THE BODENSEE

In the far south, hard on the Swiss border, **KONSTANZ** lies at the tip of a tongue of land sticking out into the huge **Bodensee** (Lake Constance). The town itself is split by the lake giving Konstanz the air of a sea town. The town's convivial atmosphere is best experienced in the summer, when street cafés tempt prolonged stays and the water is a bustle of sails.

What to see and do

Konstanz's most prominent building is the **Münster** church, dating from the Romanesque period and located in the heart of the Altstadt. The regional highlights are two small Bodensee islands. The nearby **Insel Mainau** (daily dawn–dusk; €15.90/€8.50 students; ⓦwww.mainau.de) has a royal park featuring magnificent floral displays, formal gardens, greenhouses, forests, a butterfly house and a handful of well-placed restaurants. The other island, **Reichenau**, preserves three stunning Romanesque churches. You can reach this tranquil island 8km west of Konstanz by bike, ferry (summer only; hourly; 1hr; €11.10; will take bikes too) or public transport: take a regional train to Reichenau station, then change to bus #7372 to "Mittelzell" (frequent; 20min).

Information

Tourist office Beside the train station at Bahnhofplatz 43 (April–Oct Mon–Fri 9am–6.30pm, Sat 9am–4pm, Sun 10am–1pm; Nov–March Mon–Fri 9am–6pm; ⓣ07531/13 30 30, ⓦwww.konstanz-tourismus.de); staff can book private rooms (€55).

Bike rental Kultur-Rädle, Bahnhofplatz 29 ⓦwww.kultur-raedle.de (Mon–Fri 9am–12.30pm & 2.30–6pm, Sat 10am–4pm; Easter–Oct also Sun 10am–12.30pm; €12/day).

Accommodation

Campingplatz Bruderhofer Fohrenbühlweg 45 ⓣ07531/313 88, ⓦwww.campingplatz-konstanz.de. One of two pleasant neighbouring campsites on the lakeshore 3km northeast of the centre and around 1km from the car-ferry dock. A 10min walk from bus #1 (to Tannenhof). €4.50/person, plus €6.80/tent.

DJH Konstanz Zur Allmannshöhe 18 ⓣ07531/322 60, ⓦwww.jugendherberge-konstanz.de. Excellent hostel uniquely located in an old water tower, but 5km out of town. Take bus #4 to Jugendherberge. Dorms €22.60.

Lake cruises

You can get information on cruises and ferries from the Bodensee-Schiffsbetriebe at Hafenstr. 6 (ⓣ07531/364 00, ⓦwww.bsb-online.com). Ferries run regularly around the lake and scenic trips are offered to Switzerland.

Moving on

Train Basel (every 30min; 2hr 20min); Freiburg (hourly; 2hr 20min); Munich (every 30min; 4hr 15min); Stuttgart (hourly; 2hr 45min); Zürich (frequent; 1hr 20min).

Bavaria

Bavaria (Bayern), Germany's largest federal state, fills the southeast of the country, providing its entire border with Austria. It's the home of almost all German clichés: beer-swilling men in *Lederhosen*, piles of *sauerkraut* and sausages galore. But that's only a small part of the picture, and one that's almost entirely restricted to the Bavarian Alps that lie south of the magnificent state capital, **Munich**. Eastern Bavaria – whose capital is **Regensburg** – is dominated by rolling forests where life revolves around logging and minor industries like glass production. To the north, **Nuremberg** is the hub of Protestant **Franconia** (Franken), a region known for its vineyards and natural parks as well as the beautifully preserved and atmospheric medieval towns – notably Rothenburg ob der Tauber, which is but a highlight among the glut of attractive places that dot Bavaria's Romantic Road.

MUNICH

Founded in 1158, **MUNICH** (München) has been the capital of Bavaria since 1504, and as far as the locals are concerned it's the centre of the universe. Impossibly energetic, it bursts with a good-humoured self-importance that is difficult to dislike. After Berlin, Munich is Germany's most popular city – and with its compact, attractive old centre it's far easier to digest. It has a great setting, with the mountains and Alpine lakes just an hour's drive away. The best time to come is from June to early October, when the beer gardens, cafés and bars are in full swing – not least for the world-famous **Oktoberfest** beer festival.

What to see and do

Just ten minutes' walk east of the train station, the twin onion-domed towers of the red-brick Gothic Frauenkirche (**Dom:** Mon–Wed & Sat 7am–7pm, Thurs 7am–8.30pm, Fri 7am–6pm; tower April–Oct Mon–Sat 10am–5pm; €3) form the focus of the city's skyline. The pedestrian shopping street **Kaufingerstrasse**, just below, heads east to the centre and the main square, the Marienplatz.

Marienplatz

The **Marienplatz** is the bustling heart of Munich, thronged with crowds being entertained by street musicians and artists. At 11am and noon (and 5pm March–Oct), the square fills with tourists as the tuneless carillon in the **Neues Rathaus** (Marienplatz 8; Tower May–Oct daily 10am–7pm; Nov–April Mon–Fri 10am–5pm; €2.50) jingles into action. To the right is the plain Gothic tower of the **Altes Rathaus**, which now houses a vast toy collection in the **Spielzeugmuseum** (daily 10am–5.30pm; €4).

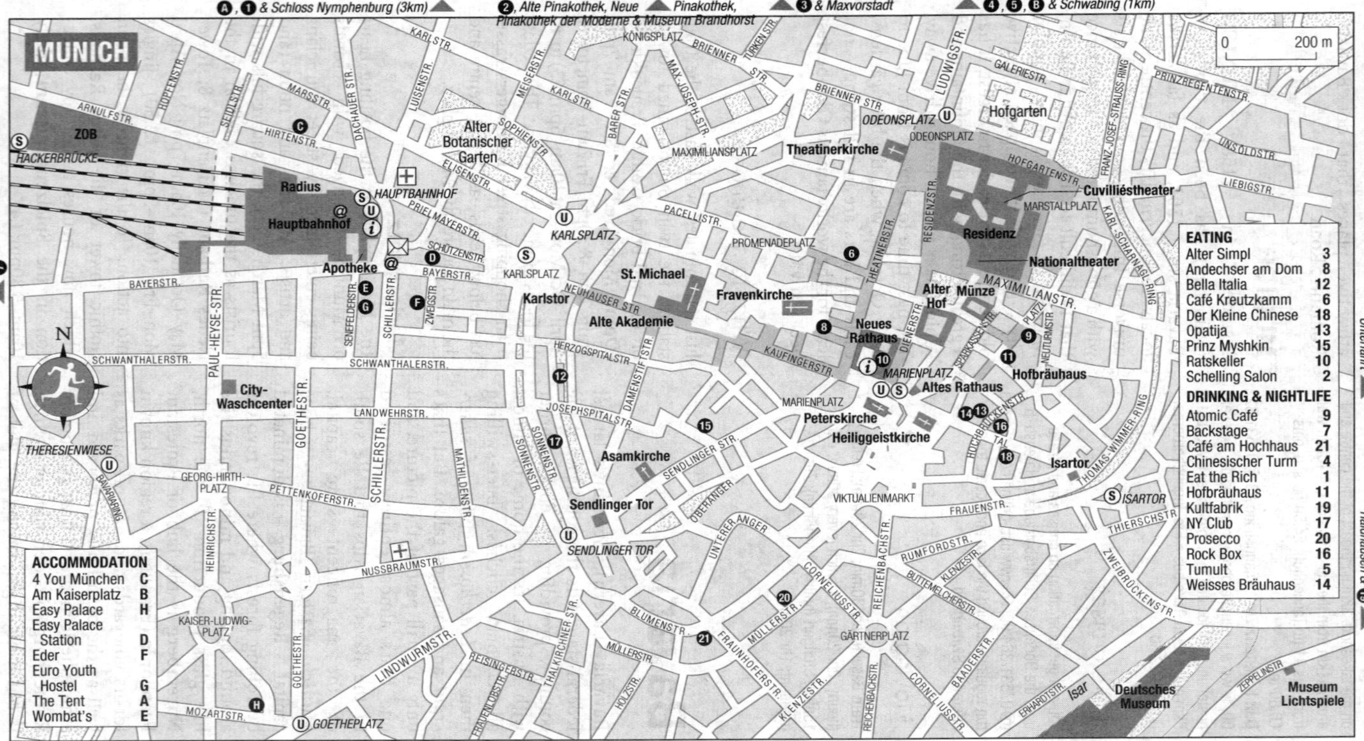
MUNICH
A, 1 & Schloss Nymphenburg (3km)
2, Alte Pinakothek, Neue Pinakothek, Pinakothek der Moderne & Museum Brandhorst
3 & Maxvorstadt
4, 5, B & Schwabing (1km)
Unterfahrt
Haidhausen & 19
7
0 200 m
ZOB
HACKERBRÜCKE
Radius
Hauptbahnhof
HAUPTBAHNHOF
Apotheke
Alter Botanischer Garten
KARLSPLATZ
Karlstor
St. Michael
Alte Akademie
Fravenkirche
Theatinerkirche
ODEONSPLATZ
Hofgarten
Residenz
Cuvilliéstheater
Nationaltheater
Alter Hof
Münze
Neues Rathaus
MARIENPLATZ
Altes Rathaus
Hofbräuhaus
Peterskirche
Heiliggeistkirche
VIKTUALIENMARKT
Asamkirche
Sendlinger Tor
SENDLINGER TOR
Isartor
ISARTOR
City-Waschcenter
THERESIENWIESE
GOETHEPLATZ
GÄRTNERPLATZ
KAISER-LUDWIG-PLATZ
Deutsches Museum
Museum Lichtspiele
Isar
EATING
Alter Simpl 3
Andechser am Dom 8
Bella Italia 12
Café Kreutzkamm 6
Der Kleine Chinese 18
Opatija 13
Prinz Myshkin 15
Ratskeller 10
Schelling Salon 2
DRINKING & NIGHTLIFE
Atomic Café 9
Backstage 7
Café am Hochhaus 21
Chinesischer Turm 4
Eat the Rich 1
Hofbräuhaus 11
Kultfabrik 19
NY Club 17
Prosecco 20
Rock Box 16
Tumult 5
Weisses Bräuhaus 14
ACCOMMODATION
4 You München C
Am Kaiserplatz B
Easy Palace H
Easy Palace Station D
Eder F
Euro Youth Hostel G
The Tent A
Wombat's E

THE ROMANTIC ROAD

The **Romantic Road** (Romantische Str.; ⓦ www.romantischestrasse.de) is perhaps Germany's most famous and best-loved tourist route, running from the vineyards of Würzburg in northern Bavaria over 385km of pastoral scenery and quaint medieval villages to the fairytale castles of Füssen in the south. Cheesy as it sounds, the Romantic Road harbours the charming, picturesque Germany promised by brochures.

Bus From April to October, Touring (ⓣ 069 719126 268, ⓦ www.touring-travel.eu) runs one bus daily in each direction between Frankfurt and Füssen via Munich, up and down the Road, with short stops in many of the towns.

Train Not all points on the Road are served by the Deutsche Bahn, but going by train to one or two towns (like Rothenburg or Füssen) is a great way to avoid the bus crowds and get a feel for the route.

Bicycle Touring by bike is the most scenic way to explore the region. The well-maintained cycling route stretches 460km from the Main to Bavarian Alps – order GPS data online (ⓦ www.romantischestrasse.de), or pick up information from tourist offices along the way.

Alter Peter and the Viktualienmarkt

On the south side of Marienplatz, the **Peterskirche** tower (summer Mon–Sat 9am–7pm, Sat & Sun 10am–7pm; winter Mon–Sat 9am–6pm, Sat & Sun 10am–6pm; €1.50) offers the best views of the Altstadt. Directly below, you'll find the **Viktualienmarkt**, an open-air food market selling everything from *Weisswurst* and beer to fruit and veg. West of here, at Sendlinger Str. 62, stands the pint-sized **Asamkirche** (daily except Fri 9am–6pm; Fri 3.30–6pm; free. Guided tours Tues at 4pm; €5), one of the most splendid Rococo churches in Bavaria.

The Hofbräuhaus and the Residenz

Northeast of Marienplatz is the **Hofbräuhaus**, Munich's largest and most famous drinking hall (see p.513). North of here, on Residenzstrasse, is the entrance to the palace of the Wittelsbachs, the immense **Residenz** (daily: April to mid-Oct 9am–6pm; mid-Oct to March 9am–5pm; €7; ⓦ www.residenz-muenchen.de). One of Europe's finest Renaissance buildings, it was so badly damaged in the last war that it had to be almost totally rebuilt. The splendid 66m-long Antiquarium, the oldest part of the palace, is the highlight of the visit. A separate ticket is necessary to see the fabulous treasures of the **Schatzkammer** (same hours as the Residenzmuseum; €7/€11 combined ticket with Residenz); the star piece is the dazzling stone-encrusted statuette of St George, made around 1590. Across Odeonsplatz from the Residenz is one of the city's most regal churches, the **Theatinerkirche**, whose golden-yellow towers and green copper dome add a splash of colour to the roofscape.

The Pinakothek museums and the Museum Brandhorst

For art lovers, it's the galleries around Barerstrasse in the Maxvorstadt that are the city's main draw. The **Alte Pinakothek** (Tues 10am–8pm, Wed–Sun 10am–6pm; €7/€12 day ticket with other Pinakothek museums and Brandhorst; entry to each is €1 on Sundays; ⓦ www.pinakothek.de) is one of the largest galleries of Old Masters in Europe, housing the world's finest assembly of German art. The **Neue Pinakothek** (Wed 10am–8pm, Mon & Thurs–Sun 10am–6pm; €7) holds a fine collection of nineteenth-and early twentieth-century art. The **Pinakothek der Moderne** (Tues, Wed & Fri–Sun 10am–6pm, Thurs 10am–8pm; €10) is worth visiting for its stark modern architecture alone, but the collection is impressive too, from Dalí and Picasso to German greats such as Beckmann and Polke. It hosts exhibitions of design, architecture and graphics. Close by is the equally striking **Museum Brandhorst** (Tues–Sun 9am–6pm; Thurs until 8pm; €7 inc. free English audioguide), housing a world-class modern art collection, including works by Andy Warhol and Cy Twombly.

The Deutsches Museum

Munich's most impressive museum – the **Deutsches Museum** at Museumsinsel 1 (daily 9am–5pm; €8.50; ⓦwww.deutsches-museum.de) – occupies a midstream island in the Isar, southeast of the centre. Covering every conceivable aspect of scientific and technical endeavour, from historical scientific instruments to the latest medical research, this is the most compendious collection of its type in Germany.

Arrival

Air Munich's airport, Franz Josef Strauss Flughafen (ⓦwww.munich-airport.de), is connected to the Hauptbahnhof by Ⓢ#1 and #8.
Train The Hauptbahnhof is at the western end of the city centre.
Bus The ZOB is on Arnulfstr., behind the train station.

Information

Tourist office There are tourist offices at Bahnhofplatz 2 (Mon–Sat 9am–8pm, Sun 10am–6pm; ⓣ089/23 39 65 00, ⓦwww.muenchen.de) and in the Neues Rathaus on Marienplatz (Mon–Fri 10am–8pm, Sat 10am–5pm, Sun 10am–2pm), either of which can book rooms (from around €50).

City transport

U-bahn, trams & buses Short trips (*kurzstrecke*: up to two S- or U-Bahn stops, or up to four bus or tram stops) on Munich's public transport system (ⓦwww.mvv-muenchen.de) cost €1.20, one-way trips €2.50 (€2.40 if you pay by card). One-day passes, valid for all public transport in the central city area, are a good investment at €5.40 (single) and €9.80 (up to five people). Also available are strip cards (€12 for 10); stamp two strips for every zone crossed – the zones are shown on maps at stations and tram and bus stops. For short trips, only one strip needs to be cancelled.

Accommodation

Cheap accommodation can be hard to find, especially during Oktoberfest, when prices can double – book well in advance.

Hostels

4 you München Hirtenstr. 18 ⓣ089/552 16 60, ⓦwww.the4you.de. Lively eco-friendly hostel very close to the main station, with some singles and doubles, as well as standard dorms. Linen and breakfast included, but there's a small charge for towels. Dorms from €19 summer/€16 winter, doubles €42.
Easy Palace Mozartstr. 4 ⓣ089/558 79 70, ⓦwww.easypalace.de. Welcoming hostel within spitting distance of the Oktoberfest grounds; 15min walk south from the train station or U-Bahn to Goetheplatz. Sheets included. Dorms €14.90, doubles €79.40.
Euro Youth Hotel Senefelderstr. 5 ⓣ089/599 08 80 11, ⓦwww.euro-youth-hotel.de. Good atmosphere and location with late-closing bar and helpful staff. Dorms €21, twins €72.
The Tent In den Kirschen 30 ⓣ089/141 43 00, ⓦwww.the-tent.com. Top budget digs – bed down in a vast circus tent, located a 15min tram ride from the Hauptbahnhof (#17 – runs all night), or pitch your own tent. Beds €7.50.
Wombat's Senefelderstr. 1 ⓣ089/59 98 91 80, ⓦwww.wombats-hostels.com. The pick of the backpackers' bunch. Modern, lively and central with a great bar, winter garden and friendly staff. Sheets included. Dorms from €20, private rooms from €70.

Hotels and guesthouses

Am Kaiserplatz Kaiserplatz 1 ⓣ089/34 91 90. ⓦwww.amkaiserplatz.de Ⓤ Münchener Freiheit. Good-value *pension* in Schwabing: rooms are individually decorated if rather chintzy, with high ceilings. Some are en suite but most share shower and WC. Three-, four- or five- bed rooms available. Singles from €33, doubles with shared bathroom from €49.
Easy Palace Station Schützenstr. 7 ⓣ089/552 52 10, ⓦwww.easypalace.de. Between the station

and the centre; what this clean, basic hotel lacks in charm it makes up for in convenience. Singles €44, doubles €54.

Eder Zweigstr. 8 ⓣ089/55 46 60, ⓦwww.hotel-eder.de. Cosy family-owned hotel in one of the quieter side streets near the train station. Singles €47, doubles €62.

Eating

Gaststätten and the brewery-affiliated *brauhäuser* offer filling soups, salads and sandwiches – look out too for the *brotzeit* section on many menus for simpler and lighter – but often still filling – snack dishes. An excellent place to fuel up is the bustling Viktualienmarkt, which has an array of outdoor or stand-up eating options.

Cafés

Alter Simpl Türkenstr. 57. Famous literary café-bar and student haunt named after the satirical magazine *Simplicissimus*, with salads, pasta or meat dishes for less than €10. Weekdays 11am–3am, weekends 11am–4am.

Café Kreutzkamm Maffeistr. 4. Airy and elegant; one of the best *Kaffee-und-Kuchen* establishments – it also does good home-made ice cream. Cake €3.50. Mon–Fri 8am–7pm, Sat 9am–7pm; Sun noon–6pm; closed Sun from Oct–April.

Schelling Salon Schellingstr. 54. Huge, atmospheric old café in the Maxvorstadt, with various games including billiard tables, table tennis and chess, plus cheap hot food from around €5. 10am–1am; closed Tues & Wed.

Restaurants

Andechser am Dom Weinstr. 7a, behind the Dom ⓣ089 29 84 81. Traditional place serving beer from the Andechs monastic brewery and solid Bavarian fare to a cheerful crowd. Mains €12; half-litre of Helles beer €3.60. Daily 10am–1am.

Bella Italia Herzog-Wilhelm-Str. 8 ⓣ089 593 259. One of a small chain of cheap Italian restaurants, with a central location close to Stachus. Pasta dishes from €3.80. Daily 11am–12.30am.

Der Kleine Chinese Im Tal 28 ⓣ089 29 16 35 36. Cheap, filling Chinese dishes served all day in this tiny eatery near Marienplatz. Mains €5.50–7.50. Daily 11am–10pm.

Opatija Hochbrückenstr. 3 ⓣ089 26 83 53. Excellent, cosy Croatian restaurant with good prices, despite its proximity to Marienplatz. Simple mains from €6. Open daily.

Prinz Myshkin Hackenstr. 2 ⓣ089 26 55 96. Best vegetarian in the city, with international dishes served beneath a high vaulted ceiling. Lunch special €6.50. Open 11am–12.30am

Ratskeller Marienplatz 8 ⓣ089 219 98 90. The labyrinthine cellar of the Neues Rathaus is always full – by no means just with tourists. Serving everything from *Bratwurst* with *Sauerkraut* to elegant seasonal dishes including game, the food is hearty and good. Main courses from around €11; daily 10am–midnight.

> **BREAKFAST OF CHAMPIONS**
>
> *Weisswurst* (white veal sausage), *Brezen* (bready pretzels eaten with sweet mustard) and *Weissbier* (wheat beer) make up a typical **Bavarian breakfast**. Traditionally, the highly perishable *Weisswurst* isn't to be eaten past noon.

Drinking and nightlife

Drinking is central to social life in Munich and, apart from the *Gaststätten* and beer gardens, the city has a lively café-bar culture. North of the centre, hip student bar-cafés in the Maxvorstadt fade into the glitz of Schwabing; lesbian and gay nightlife clusters in the Isarvorstadt between the Altstadt and the river, while the main focus for clubbers is Haidhausen, across the river. For listings check out the English-language *Munich-Found* (ⓦwww.munichfound.de).

Bars and beer halls /gardens

Chinesischer Turm Englischer Garten 3. Huge beer garden in the lovely Englischer Garten, with Hofbräu beers. Occasional live entertainment including folk bands. Lunch specials €6.90. Daily 10am–11pm.

Eat the Rich Hessstr. 90, Maxvorstadt. The cocktails are served in half-litre measures at this packed party locale near the university, which at least eases pressure on the bar. Tues–Thurs 7pm–1am; Fri & Sat 7pm–3am.

Hofbräuhaus Platzl 9. The most famous and touristy of the beer halls, but beer and food prices are reasonable. Mass (1L beer) €7.30. Open 9am–11.30pm.

Tumult Blütenstr. 4 ⓦtumult-in-muenchen.de ⓤUniversität. Packed Fifties-burlesque-themed bar in the Maxvorstadt, catering to a friendly and hip rockabilly-punk crowd. May–Sept from 9pm, Oct–April from 8pm.

Weisses Bräuhaus Im Tal 7. Famous for its *Weissbier* (€3.60) and a little cosier than the *Hofbräuhaus*. Daily 8am–1am.

Clubs

Most of Munich's clubs are either east or west of the centre; expect to pay €5–15.

Atomic Café Neuturmstr. 5 ⓦ www.atomic.de. Bar, club and live music venue near the *Hofbräuhaus* catering to a fashionable, rock-loving crowd, with an emphasis on live gigs by indie bands. Tues–Thurs 10pm–4am, Fri & Sat 10pm–5am; open from 9pm when bands are playing.

Backstage Reitknechtstr. 6 ⓦ www.backstage.eu. One of the best clubs in town, with nightly DJs spinning everything from hip-hop and electro to rock. Plenty of live shows as well. Tram #16 or #17 to Steubenplatz.

Kultfabrik Grafinger Str. 6, Haidhausen ⓦ www.kultfabrik.de Ⓢ & Ⓤ Ostbahnhof. Along with adjacent *Optimolwerke* at Friedenstr. 10 (ⓦ www.optimolwerke.de), this mini-city of clubs and bars housed in a network of old factory buildings attracts upwards of 30,000 at weekends. A mix of musical genres and locales makes this Munich's premier nightspot.

Rock Box Im Tal 15, entrance on Hochbrückenstr. Lounge-club in a small tried-and-tested venue opposite *Opatija*. Mon–Wed 3pm–1am, Thurs–Sat 3pm–3am, Sun 7pm–2am, with DJs on Fri & Sat.

Lesbian and Gay Munich

Munich has an active and visible gay scene, with venues scattered throughout the Isarvorstadt. *Rosa München* (German only) is an excellent free gay guide, available from bars and other venues.

Café am Hochhaus Blumenstr. 29. More bar than café, attracting a young, hip crowd to a prominent site opposite Munich's only Weimar-era skyscraper. From 8pm.

NY Club Sonnenstr 25. Munich's only full-time lesbian and gay disco, with slick decor and a variety of events, including *Amazonas* women's night on Wed. From 10pm Wed & Fri, 11pm Sat.

Prosecco Theklastr. 1. Tiny, camp bar that blends Alpine kitsch with every other variety of decorative excess. The music is a mix of German *Schlager* tunes (schmaltzy German pop) and made-in-Munich Eurodisco hits. Great fun. Wed–Sat from 9pm.

OKTOBERFEST

The huge **Oktoberfest**, held on the Theresienwiese fairground for sixteen days following the penultimate Saturday in September, is an orgy of beer drinking spiced up by fairground rides that are so hairy they're banned in the US. The event began with a fair held to celebrate a Bavarian royal wedding in October 1810; it proved so popular that it's been repeated ever since. For more information, check out ⓦ www.oktoberfest.de.

Entertainment

Munich has four symphony orchestras – the Münchener Philharmoniker, the Symphonie-orchester des Bayerischen Rundfunks, the Münchner Rundfunkorchester and the orchestra at the Staatsoper – as well as the respected Münchner Kammerorchester. The most prestigious theatre company is the Bayerisches Staatsschauspiel, which plays at the Residenztheater, but there are many more, including a sizeable fringe element. Advance tickets for plays and concerts can be bought at the box offices, at the tourist offices at Marienplatz and the Hauptbahnhof or online (ⓦ www.muenchenticket.de).

Museum-Lichtspiele Lilienstr. 2, Haidhausen ⓦ www.museum-lichtspiele.de. Small cinema showing English-language films.

Olympiapark ⓦ www.olympiapark-muenchen.de Ⓤ Olympiazentrum. Free lakeside concerts – from rock to classical – at the Theatron daily in July and August.

Unterfahrt Einsteinstr. 42, Haidhausen ⓦ www.unterfahrt.de Ⓤ Max-Weber-Platz. Showcase for avant-garde jazz, with many big names.

Directory

Bike rental Radius, at the train station near platform 32 (daily: mid-March to mid-Oct 9.30am–6pm; mid-Oct to mid-March weather dependent; €14.50/day; ⓣ 089/54 34 87 77 30; ⓦ www.radiustours.com). Also offers bike and walking tours.

Consulates Canada, Tal 29 ⓣ 089/219 95 70; Ireland, Denningerstr. 15 ⓣ 089/20 80 59 90; South Africa, Sendlinger-Tor-Platz 5 ⓣ 089/231 16 30; UK, Möhlstr. 5 ⓣ 089/21 10 90; US, Königinstr. 5 ⓣ 089/288 623.

Exchange Reisebank, at the train station and airport.

Hospital Rotkreuz Krankenhaus Nymphenburger Str. 163 (ⓣ 089/1303 2543); Medical emergency ⓣ 112.

Internet Internetcafé München, in the Hauptbahnhof.

Left luggage At the train station.
Pharmacy Check ⓦwww.lak-bayern.notdienst-portal.de for information on the out-of-hours service.
Post office Bahnhofplatz 1 (Mon–Fri 8am–8pm, Sat 9am–4pm).

Moving on

Train Augsburg (every 10–20min; 36–43min); Berchtesgaden (via Freilassing; 4 daily; 3hr); Berlin (2/hour; 6hr–6hr 40min); Garmisch-Partenkirchen (hourly; 1hr 30min); Innsbruck (every 2hr; 1hr 52min); Nuremberg (2/hour; 1hr 14min); Regensburg (hourly; 1hr 27min); Salzburg (1–2/hour; 1hr 30min–2hr); Vienna (every 2hr; 4hr 17min).

DAY-TRIPS FROM MUNICH

Schloss Nymphenburg (daily: April to mid-Oct 9am–6pm; mid-Oct to March 10am–4pm; €6/€11.50 combined ticket for all Nymphenburg attractions [€8.50 in winter]; ⓦwww.schloss-nymphenburg.de**)**, the summer residence of the Wittelsbachs, is reached by tram #17 from the train station. Its kernel is a small Italianate palace begun in 1664 for the Electress Adelaide, who dedicated it to the goddess Flora and her nymphs – hence the name. More enticing than the palace itself are the wonderful park and its four distinct pavilions (combined ticket for all pavilions: daily: April to mid-Oct 9am–6pm; closed mid-Oct–March; €4.50); in particular, don't miss the stunning **Amalienburg**, the extravagant Rococo-style hunting lodge built behind the south wing of the Schloss by court architect François Cuvilliés.

KZ-Gedenkstätte Dachau

On the northern edge of Munich, the town of **Dachau** was the site of Germany's first **concentration camp** (Tues–Sun 9am–5pm; free; English audioguide €3.50; maps free. Documentary film in English at 11.30am & 3.30pm**)**, and the motto that greeted arrivals has taken its chilling place in the history of Third Reich brutality: *Arbeit Macht Frei*, "Work Sets You Free". Many original buildings still stand, including the crematorium and gas chamber; a replica hut gives an idea of the conditions prisoners endured. In the former maintenance building there's a sobering exhibition in English detailing the history of the camp, including graphic colour film shot at liberation. Dachau's S-Bahn station is on line S2 from Munich; from the S-Bahn take bus #726 to the KZ-Gedenkstätte (Mon–Fri & peak time Sat every 20min; Sun every 40min). There is parking a short walk from the camp.

THE BAVARIAN ALPS

It's amid picture-book mountain scenery that you'll find the classic Bavarian folklore and customs, and the **Bavarian Alps** encompass some of the most famous places in the province, such as the fantasy castle of **Neuschwanstein** and Hitler's **Eagle's Nest** near Berchtesgaden. Visit these hotspots outside the July–August peak season and you'll find the crowds less oppressive.

Neuschwanstein and Schloss Hohenschwangau

Lying between the Forggensee reservoir and the Ammer mountains, **FÜSSEN** and the adjacent town of **SCHWANGAU** are the bases for visiting Bavaria's two most popular castles. **Schloss Hohenschwangau** (guided tours daily: April–Sept 9am–6pm; Oct–March 10am–4pm; €10.50/€21.50 combined ticket with Neuschwanstein; ⓦwww.hohenschwangau.de), originally built in the twelfth century but heavily restored in the nineteenth, was where "Mad" King Ludwig II spent his youth. Ludwig's stamp is firmly imprinted on **Schloss Neuschwanstein** (guided tours daily: April–Sept 9am–6pm; Oct–March 10am–4pm; €12/€21.50 combined ticket with Schloss Hohenschwangau; tickets for both castles can only be bought at the ticket centre at

Alpseestrasse 24 in Hohenschwangau village; ⓦwww.neuschwanstein.de), the storybook castle which he had built on a crag overlooking Hohenschwangau. The inspiration for Disneyland's castle, it's an architectural hotchpotch with a stunning Byzantine throne hall. Still incomplete at Ludwig's death, it's a monument to a sad and lonely man. Take the train to Füssen (every 2hr from Munich; 2hr) and then bus #73 or #78 to Hohenschwangau. The nearest HI **hostel** is in Füssen, a ten-minute walk from the train station at Mariahilferstr. 5 (ⓣ08362/77 54, ⓦwww.fuessen.jugendherberge.de; dorms €19.20), otherwise the **tourist office**, Kaiser-Maximilian-Platz 1 (Mon–Fri 9am–5pm, Sat 10am–2pm; ⓣ08362/938 50, ⓦwww.fuessen.de) in Füssen, can book accommodation. Füssen is also the end of the **Romantic Road** from Würzburg via Augsburg (see box, p.511), served by special tour buses in season.

Mittenwald

Cuddled up against the Austrian border and just 15km from Garmisch-Partenkirchen, pretty **MITTENWALD** makes a lovely base for hiking and cycling. The **Karwendel mountain** towering above is a popular climb, and the view from the top is exhilarating; it's reachable by cable car (€22 return). The **tourist office**, at Dammkarstr. 3 (ski season & summer Mon–Fri 8.30am–6pm, Sat 9am–noon, Sun 10am–noon; spring & autumn low season Mon–Fri 8.30am–5pm; ⓣ08823/339 81, ⓦwww.mittenwald.de) provides free maps of the area. The hostel, *Jugendherberge Mittenwald*, Buckelwiesen 7 (ⓣ08823/17 01, ⓦwww.mittenwald.jugendherberge.de; dorms €17.20), is 4km north of the town. There are plenty of good **guesthouses**, such as the outdoorsy *Bergzauber*, Klausnerweg 26 (ⓣ08823/939 60, ⓦwww.bergzauber.de; doubles €52, singles €32), and the central *Alpenrose* (Obermarkt 1 ⓣ08823/927 00, ⓦwww.alpenrose-mittenwald.de), a rustic *gasthof* with lovely *lüftmalerei* paintings on the facade and some singles, including cheaper options with shared facilities from €29.

Berchtesgaden

Almost entirely surrounded by mountains at Bavaria's southeastern extremity – but easily reached by rail from Munich – the area around **BERCHTESGADEN** has a magical atmosphere, especially in the mornings, when mists rise from the lakes and swirl around lush valleys and rocky mountainsides.

A star attraction is the stunning emerald **Königssee**, Germany's highest lake, which bends around the foot of the towering **Watzmann** (2713m), 5km south of town – regular buses run out here – and there are year-round **cruises** (8am–5.15pm April–Oct; limited winter service; €16 return). Berchtesgaden is indelibly associated with **Adolf Hitler**, who rented a house in the nearby village of Obersalzberg, which he later enlarged into the **Berghof**, a stately retreat where he could meet foreign dignitaries. High above the village, Hitler's *Kehlsteinhaus*, or "**Eagle's Nest**", survives as a restaurant, and can be reached by bus and lift from Obersalzberg (mid-May to late-Oct; €15 return; ⓦwww.kehlsteinhaus.de). Berchtesgaden has some great **mountain walks** to take you away from the summer crowds – there are maps at the **tourist office** (June to mid-Oct Mon–Fri 8.30am–6pm, Sat 9am–5pm, Sun 9am–3pm; mid-Oct to May Mon–Fri 8.30am–5pm, Sat 9am–noon; ⓣ08652/96 70, ⓦwww.berchtesgadener-land.info), opposite the train station. Berchtesgaden is also home to an unexpected diversion, the **Salzbergwerk** (daily: May–Oct 9am–5pm; Nov–April 11.30am–3pm; €14.90; ⓦwww.salzzeitreise.de), a historic salt mine that's been refurbished with an hour-long amusement-park-like ride/tour through its underground caverns.

Berchtesgaden's **youth hostel**, the *DJH Berchtesgaden*, Struderberg 6

(Ⓣ08652/943 70, Ⓦwww.berchtesgaden.jugendherberge.de; dorms €16.90 with breakfast), in the Strub district west of the town centre, has views of the Watzmann massif. The *Haus Achental* (Ⓣ08652/45 49, Ⓦwww gaestehaus-achental.de; doubles from €40 with breakfast, singles €26) is a friendly alternative close to the station on Ramsauer Strasse. Try the lively *Bräustüberl (*Bräuhausstr. 13 Ⓣ08652/97 67 24), next to the *Berchtesgadener Hofbräuhaus* brewery downhill from the Altstadt, for food.

REGENSBURG

The undisturbed medieval ensemble of central **REGENSBURG**, stunningly located on the banks of the Danube midway between Nuremberg and Munich, can easily be visited as a day-trip, but it makes a tempting overnight stop too. Getting lost in the web of cobbled medieval lanes, nursing a drink in one of the sunny squares or cycling along the Danube are the main draws here. It's also a university city, with a lively nightlife scene for its size.

What to see and do

A good place to start is the twelfth-century **Steinerne Brücke**, the only secured crossing along the entire length of the Danube at the time it was built. At the southern end of the bridge, it's worth climbing the **Brückturm** (April–Oct Tues–Sun 10am–5pm; €2), the last survivor of the bridge's watchtowers, for excellent views of the old town and river. Just south, the Gothic **Dom** (daily: April–Oct 6.30am–6pm; Nov–March 6.30am–5pm) was begun in 1273, has some beautiful fourteenth-century stained-glass windows. Regensburg's medieval **Rathaus** contains the magnificent fourteenth-century Gothic Reichssaal, which was from 1663 to 1806 the fixed venue for the imperial Diet or Reichstag of the Holy Roman Empire. It can now be visited as part of the **Reichstagsmuseum** (April–Oct guided tours in English daily at 3pm; Nov, Dec & March at 2pm; €7.50). There's also a prison and torture chamber in the basement. In the southern part of the Altstadt is **Schloss Thurn und Taxis** (guided tours: in English July to mid-Sept daily at 1.30pm; €11.50; Ⓦwww.thurnundtaxis.de), one of the largest inhabited palaces in Europe, occupying the converted monastic buildings of the abbey of St Emmeram.

Arrival and information

Train Maximilianstr. leads straight from the train station north to the centre.

Tourist office At Rathausplatz 4 (April–Oct Mon–Fri 9am–6pm, Sat 9am–4pm, Sun 9.30am–4pm; Nov–March Mon–Fri 9am–6pm, Sat 9am–4pm, Sun 9.30am–2.30pm; Ⓣ0941/507 44 10, Ⓦwww .regensburg.de).

Bike rental Bikehaus, Bahnhofstr. 18 (Ⓣ0941/599 88 08), on the left as you leave the Hauptbahnhof on the northern (Altstadt) side. €12/24hr.

Accommodation

Brook Lane Hostel Obere Bachgasse 21 Ⓣ0941 690 09 66, Ⓦwww.hostel-regensburg .de. Independently run hostel in the Altstadt, with accommodation in snug dorms (from €15) or spartan singles (€35) and doubles (€50). Open 24hr.

DJH Regensburg Wöhrdstr. 60 Ⓣ0941/4662830, Ⓦwww.regensburg.jugendherberge.de. Youth hostel on an island in the Danube, within easy walking distance of the Altstadt. Breakfast including Dorms €21.

Eating and drinking

Dicker Mann Krebsgasse 6 Ⓣ0941 57370. Vine-covered and candlelit café-restaurant on a tiny side street off Haidplatz serving delicious, good-value meals. Breakfast from €3.30, dinner specials from around €6. Daily 9am–1am.

Fürstliches Brauhaus Waffnergasse 6–8. The Thurn und Taxis' *brauhaus*, with a copper micro-brewery behind the bar, a shady beer garden and own-brew Helles, Marstall Dunkell and Braumeister Weisse beers. Light meals from €5, main courses around €8.50. Mon–Fri 11am–midnight, Sat & Sun 10am–midnight.

Wurstkuchl Historische Wurstküche Thundorfer Str. 3 ⓣ 0941/466 210. Next to the Steinerne Brücke and looking like somewhere a hobbit might grill sausages, this institution originally functioned as the stonemasons' and dock workers' kitchen and has a menu dominated by the delicious Regensburg sausages (plate of 6 €7.50). Daily 8am–7pm.

Moving on

Train Munich (hourly; 1hr 33min); Nuremberg (hourly; 1hr); Vienna (every 2hr; 4hr).

NUREMBERG

In many minds, the medieval town of **NUREMBERG** (Nürnberg) conjures up images of the Nazi rallies, the 1935 "Nuremberg Laws" which deprived Jews of their citizenship and forbade them relations with Gentiles, and then the war-crime trials. Yet all this infamy is a world away from the friendly, bustling city of today. Nuremberg's relaxed air makes a day spent exploring its half-timbered houses, fine museums and beer halls hard to beat.

What to see and do

Meticulous postwar rebuilding means you'd never guess that World War II bombs reduced ninety percent of Nuremberg's centre to rubble. The reconstructed medieval core is compact, surrounded by ancient city walls and neatly bisected by the River Pegnitz.

The Kaiserburg

The **Kaiserburg** (imperial castle: guided tours daily: April–Sept 9am–6pm; Oct–March 10am–4pm; €7/€5.50 for Palas and museum alone), which forms the northwest corner of the Medieval fortifications, was where Holy Roman Emperors held their "Reichstag" or imperial diet in the Middle Ages. Guided tours visit the Palas or castle keep and the Tiefer Brunnen – the castle's 47m-deep well. Tickets are also valid for the castle museum and the **Sinwellturm tower** (Sinwellturm and Tiefer brunnen without museum & Palas €3.50), which can be climbed for great views.

The Germanisches Nationalmuseum

The sprawling **Germanisches Nationalmuseum,** Kartäusergasse 1 (Tues & Thurs–Sun 10am–6pm, Wed 10am–9pm; €6; ⓦ www.gnm.de) presents the country's cultural history through its large, important collection of artefacts and art from German central Europe, from the Bronze Age to the present. Look out for the first globe, made by Martin Behaim in 1492 – just before Columbus "discovered" America.

The Fascination and Terror exhibition

The Nazi Party rallies were held on the Zeppelin and March fields in the suburb of Luitpoldhain. Here, the gargantuan but never-completed Congress Hall houses the **Documentation Centre Nazi Party Rally Grounds** (Mon–Fri 9am–6pm, Sat & Sun 10am–6pm; €5; tram #9 to Doku-Zentrum; ⓦ www.museen.nuernberg.de), an unmissable multimedia exhibition documenting the history of the rally grounds and the ruthless misuse of power under National Socialism.

Arrival and information

Air The U2 underground service connects Nürnberg airport with the train station (every 10min; 13min).

Train The Hauptbahnhof is just outside the southern edge of the city walls; follow Königstr. into the centre.

Tourist office At the entrance to the Altstadt opposite the train station (Mon–Sat 9am–7pm, Sun 10am–4pm; ⓣ 0911/233 60, ⓦ tourismus-nuernberg.de). Smaller office at Hauptmarkt 18, in the Altstadt (Mon–Sat 9am–6pm; May–Oct also Sun 10am-4pm; Dec Mon–Sat 9am–7pm, Sun 10am–7pm; ⓣ 0911/233 60).

Discount pass The Nürnberg Card (€21/2 days) covers public transport plus entrance to museums.

City transport There are U-Bahn, tram, and bus systems; a one-way trip costs €2.10, a day ticket (or both Sat & Sun) €4.20. Nuremberg also has a Parisian-style public bike hire network, NorisBike (ⓦ norisbike.de), with 66 rental points across the city; €1/30 min, €8/24hr. You can register as a user and pay by credit card at the rental station.
Internet Flat-S, on the top floor of the train station's middle hall; open 24hr; €4/hr.

Accommodation

DJH Burg 2 ⓣ 0911 230 93 60, ⓦ nuernberg .jugendherberge.de Ⓤ #2 to Rathenauplatz, then bus #36 to Burgstr. or 25min walk from the station. The HI hostel has a wonderful location in the fifteenth-century imperial stables next to the Kaiserburg, overlooking the Altstadt. Closed for refurbishment at time of writing, but due to reopen; check website for latest details. Dorms €23.10.
Lette'm Sleep Frauentormauer 42 ⓣ 0911 992 81 28, ⓦ backpackers.de. This friendly and popular hostel offers free internet access, a kitchen and secure storage. Dorms €16, plus €3 for bed linen, private rooms €49.
Pension Vater Jahn-Parma Jahnstr. 13 ⓣ 0911/44 45 07, ⓦ hotel-vaterjahn-parma.de. Immaculate and friendly guesthouse just south of the Opernhaus on the other side of the railway tracks, close to the Hauptbahnhof and Altstadt. Doubles from €47, with bathroom from €65, singles from €26.50.

Eating and drinking

There are plenty of snack stops in the pedestrian shopping zone and at the Hauptbahnhof; bars and cafés are scattered throughout the Altstadt.
Barfüsser Hallplatz 2. This popular beer hall in cavernous cellars brews its own beer and serves good food. Daily specials from €8; six *bratwurst* €6.40. Daily 11am–1am.
Bratwurst Herzle Brunnengasse 11. A bit less obviously tourist-oriented than some options, *Herzle* is a great place for sampling Nuremberg's mini-sausages. Six *bratwürste* €6.60. Mon–Sat 11am–10pm.
Club Stereo Klaragasse 8 ⓦ club-stereo.net. This lounge-style club is more relaxed than most and hosts indie and pop nights. Thurs–Sat from 11pm.
Mach 1 Kaiserstr. 1–9 ⓦ www.mach1-club .de. Stylish club with a main floor pumping house and electro sounds, a futuristic tunnel and a more intimate lounge area. Thurs–Sat from 10pm.
Souptopia Lorenzerstr. 27. If you're sick of sausage, head for this little wonder, where seven types of soup are on offer daily, including at least

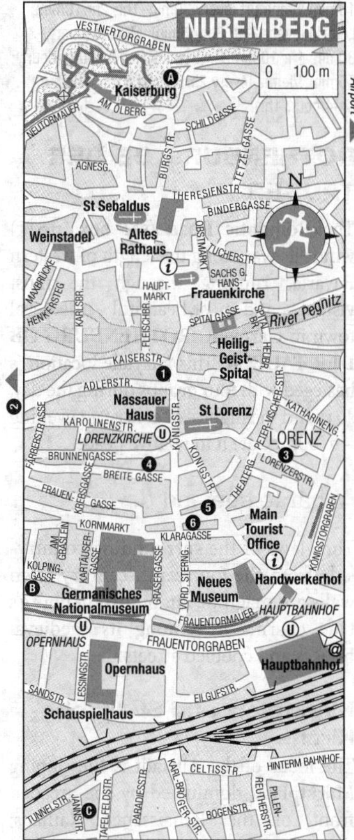

ACCOMMODATION		EATING & DRINKING			
DJH	A	Barfüsser	5	Mach I	1
Lette'm Sleep	B	Bratwurst Herzle	4	Souptopia	3
Pension Vater Jahn-Parma	C	Club Stereo	6	Treibhaus	2

one vegan option. Large bowl of soup from €5.80. Mon–Fri 11am–7.30pm, Sat 11am–5pm.
Treibhaus Karl-Grillenberger-Str. 28. Refreshingly out of the way yet still in the Altstadt (close to Ⓤ Weisser Turm) this hip café-bar offers everything you need from morning to night, with breakfasts from €1.90, salads from €5 and cocktails from €4.10. Mon–Wed 8am–1am, Thurs & Fri 8am–2am, Sat 9am–2am, Sun 9.30am–1am.

Moving on

Train Augsburg (every 30min–1hr 30min; 1hr 10min); Berlin (every 30 min–1hr 30min; 5hr

10min); Frankfurt (every 30min–1hr; 2hr 10min); Leipzig (every 2 hr; 3hr 45min); Munich (every 30min; 1hr 10min–1hr 25min); Regensburg (hourly; 55min); Vienna (every 2hr; 4hr 56min); Würzburg (2–4/hour; 1hr).

ROTHENBURG OB DER TAUBER

The **Romantic Road** (see box, p.511) winds its way along the length of western Bavaria, running through the most visited – and most beautiful – medieval town in Germany: **ROTHENBURG OB DER TAUBER**. This fairytale location is besieged with tour groups during the day, so spend the night – or at least an evening – to appreciate it in relative peace.

What to see and do

The views of the surrounding countryside from the fourteenth-century town walls are magnificent, but Rothenburg's true charms lie among its medieval houses and cobbled streets.

Marktplatz and St Jakobs-Kirche

The focus of the Altstadt is the sloping **Marktplatz**, dominated by the arcaded front of the Renaissance Rathaus; the narrow, sixty-metre tower of the Altes Rathaus (daily: April–Oct 9.30am–12.30pm & 1–5pm; Dec daily 10.30am–2pm & 2.30–6pm; Fri & Sat until 8pm; Nov & Jan–March weekends only noon–3pm; €2) provides the best views. The other main attractions on the Marktplatz are the mechanical figures on the facade of the **Ratsherrntrinkstube**. Eight times a day these figures re-enact an episode in which former mayor Nusch allegedly saved Protestant Rothenburg from the wrath of Catholic General Tilly during the Thirty Years' War, by downing three litres of wine in one. Northwest of the Marktplatz is the impressive Gothic **St Jakobs-Kirche** (April–Oct 9am–5pm; Nov & Jan–March 10am–noon & 2–4pm; Dec 10am–4.45pm; €2). Don't miss the exquisite Heilig-Blut-Altar, a masterpiece of woodcarving by Tilman Riemenschneider, tucked away on an upper level.

The Mittelalterliches Kriminalmuseum

Of the local museums, the most interesting is the Mittelalterliches **Kriminalmuseum** (Burggasse 3–5. Daily: Jan, Feb & Nov 2–4pm; March & Dec 1–4pm; April 11am–5pm; May–Oct 10am–6pm; €4; Ⓦwww.kriminalmuseum.rothenburg.de.), which contains collections of medieval torture instruments and related objects, such as the beer barrels that drunks were forced to walk around in.

Arrival and information

Train Ten-minute walk east of the centre. From the station head left on Bahnhofstr., then right on Ansbacherstr., which takes you straight through Röder city gate.

Tourist office In the Ratsherrntrinkstube on Marktplatz (April–Oct & Dec Mon–Fri 9am–6pm, Sat & Sun 10am–3pm; Nov & Jan–March Mon–Fri 9am–5pm, Sat 10am–1pm; Ⓣ09861 40 48 00, Ⓦwww.rothenburg.de). Organizes daily English-language tours at 2pm €7/90min.

Accommodation and eating

DJH Mühlacker 1 Ⓣ09861 941 60, Ⓦrothenburg.jugendherberge.de. Housed in two beautifully restored houses and a modern annexe off the bottom of Spitalgasse. Dorms €22.40.

Gästehaus Raidel Wenggasse 3 Ⓣ09861 31 15, Ⓦromanticroad.com/raidel. A wonderfully creaky 600-year-old house, this guesthouse oozes character. Singles €45, doubles €69.

Roter Hahn Obere Schmiedgasse 21 Ⓣ09861 97 40. Franconian regional specialities in the historic setting of a fourteenth-century inn, with main courses from €9.

Moving on

Train Würzburg (hourly; 1hr 10min).

Greece

HIGHLIGHTS

THESSALONIKI: the springboard to Northern Greece & Vergina

METEORA: awe-inspiring Byzantine monasteries in a magical setting

ATHENS: roam the Acropolis and hit the capital's clubs

OLYMPIA: discover where the games were born

SANTORÍNI: take in the sunset from this spectacular island

KNOSSOS: visit the home of the Minotaur

ROUGH COSTS

DAILY BUDGET Basics €30 /occasional treat €40

DRINK Oúzo €3

FOOD *Souvláki* (shish kebab) €3

HOSTEL/BUDGET HOTEL €15/€40

TRAVEL Bus: Athens–Delphi €15; ferry: Athens–Crete €36

FACT FILE

POPULATION 11.2 million

AREA 131,900 sq km (including 6000 islands)

LANGUAGE Greek

CURRENCY Euro (€)

CAPITAL Athens (population: 4 million)

INTERNATIONAL PHONE CODE ⓣ30

Introduction

With 227 inhabited islands and a landscape that ranges from Mediterranean to Balkan, Greece has enough appeal to fill months of travel. The beaches are distributed along a convoluted coastline, with cosmopolitan resorts lying surprisingly close to remote islands where boats may call only once or twice a week. The initial glimpse of sapphire water or the discovery of millennia-old ruins bordered by ancient olive groves is intoxicating, and it's the mingling of history and hedonism that ensures Greece's enduring appeal. Island-hopping is still popular, but if you're on a tight budget, consider exploring the mainland or the Peloponnese by bus, or save on multiple ferry trips by focusing on a few highlights.

The country is the sum of an extraordinary diversity of influences. Romans, Arabs, Frankish Crusaders, Venetians, Slavs, Albanians, Turks, Italians, as well as the thousand-year Byzantine Empire, have all been and gone since the time of Alexander the Great. Each has left its mark: the **Byzantines** through countless churches and monasteries; the **Venetians** in impregnable fortifications such as Monemvasiá in the Peloponnese; the **Franks** with crag-top castles, again in the Peloponnese but also in the Dodecanese and east Aegean. Most obvious, perhaps, is the heritage of four hundred years of **Ottoman Turkish** rule which exercised an inestimable influence on music, cuisine, language and way of life.

Even before the fall of Byzantium in the fifteenth century, Greek peasants, fishermen and shepherds had created one of the most vigorous and truly **popular cultures** in Europe, which found expression in song and dance, costumes, embroidery, furniture and the distinctive whitewashed houses. Though having suffered a decline under Western influence, Hellenic culture – architectural and musical heritage in particular – is undergoing a renaissance.

CHRONOLOGY

c. 800 BC Homer writes *The Iliad* and *The Odyssey*.
776 BC First Olympic Games are held in Olympia.
438 BC The building of the Parthenon is completed.
399 BC The trial and execution of Socrates, the founding father of philosophy, takes place.
387 BC Plato establishes the Athens Academy.
323 BC Alexander the Great dies heralding the beginning of the Hellenistic period.
146 BC Greece becomes a province of the Roman Empire.
330 AD The Roman capital moves to Constantinople and Byzantine Empire established. Christianity becomes dominant religion.
1453 Ottoman Turks invade Constantinople. End of the Byzantine Empire.
1821 Greek National Revolution against Ottoman rule.
1832 The Treaty of London recognizes Greek Independence. Greece becomes a monarchy under King Otto I.
1833 Athens becomes the capital of modern Greece.
1864 King Otto ousted, King George I introduces parliamentary democracy.
1896 The first modern Olympic Games are held in Athens.
1912–13 During the Balkan wars Greece doubles its size, gaining Salonika and parts of Macedonia and Thrace.
1940–41 Greece is invaded and occupied by German, Italian and Bulgarian armies. Liberation comes four years later with the help of heavy resistance fighting.
1945–49 Greek Civil War between Communists and pro-Western forces.
1952 A new constitution is passed which retains the monarchy as head of state.

1967 Military coup led by Colonel George Papadopoulos.
1974 Turkish invasion of Cyprus. The colonels' junta collapses. New constitution established and the monarchy abolished with a referendum.
2002 Greece adopts the euro.
2010 The economic crisis forces the Greek government to seek help from the European Union and the IMF.

ARRIVAL

There are international **airports** on the mainland at Athens and Thessaloníki, both well connected with their respective cities. Other destinations served by budget flights include Crete, Corfu and Rhodes, as well as numerous other mainland and island destinations. By **boat**, there are regular ferries from Ancona, Bari, Brindisi, Trieste and Venice in Italy, arriving at Corfu, Kefalloniá, Igoumenítsa and Pátra. Eurail and InterRail pass holders may travel with Superfast Ferries (Ⓦwww.superfast.com) at **discounted fares** from Ancona and Bari. You can also travel by boat from Turkey to the Dodecanese and the northern Aegean islands (Rhodes, Kós, Sámos, Híos and Lésvos), and from Albania to Corfu. By **land**, crossing into Greece is possible from Albania, Macedonia, Bulgaria, Romania and Turkey by bus arriving in Thessaloníki. Note that since January 2011 there are no more international trains into Northern Greece. However, if you arrive overland at Thessaloníki, onward travel to the rest of the country is easy and straightforward.

GETTING AROUND

The limited **rail** network (Ⓦwww.osenet.gr) has become even more so with the financial crisis, and trains are slower than the equivalent buses – except on the showcase IC (intercity) lines. However, most trains are cheaper than buses, and some of the routes are highlights in their own right. **Eurail** and **InterRail** are valid, though pass holders must reserve like everyone else, and there's a small supplement on the intercity services. It is essential to validate your train ticket on the platform before you board the train.

Buses form the bulk of public land transport, and service on the major routes is efficient, with companies organized nationally into a syndicate called **KTEL**. If starting a journey from a bus station, you will be issued with a ticket with a seat number. Return tickets are open-ended and must be validated at the box office before you board the bus.

Schedules for **sea transport** are notoriously erratic. Regular ferry tickets are best bought on the day of departure, unless you need to reserve a cabin – although in high season and over the Orthodox Easter period it's best to book several days in advance. The cheapest ticket is "deck class". Leave plenty of time for your journey as ferries are often late, or take longer to reach their destinations than scheduled. Hydrofoils and high-speed catamarans are roughly twice as fast and twice as expensive as ordinary ferries. In season, *kaïkia* (caïques) sail to more obscure islets.

Once on the islands, almost everybody rents a **scooter** or a **bike**. Scooters cost from €12 a day, mountain bikes a bit less. To rent a scooter or bike, you must produce a motorcycle licence from your country of origin.

ACCOMMODATION

Most of the year you can turn up pretty much anywhere and find a **room**. Only around Easter (Orthodox) and during July and August are you likely to experience problems; at these times, it's worth booking well in advance.

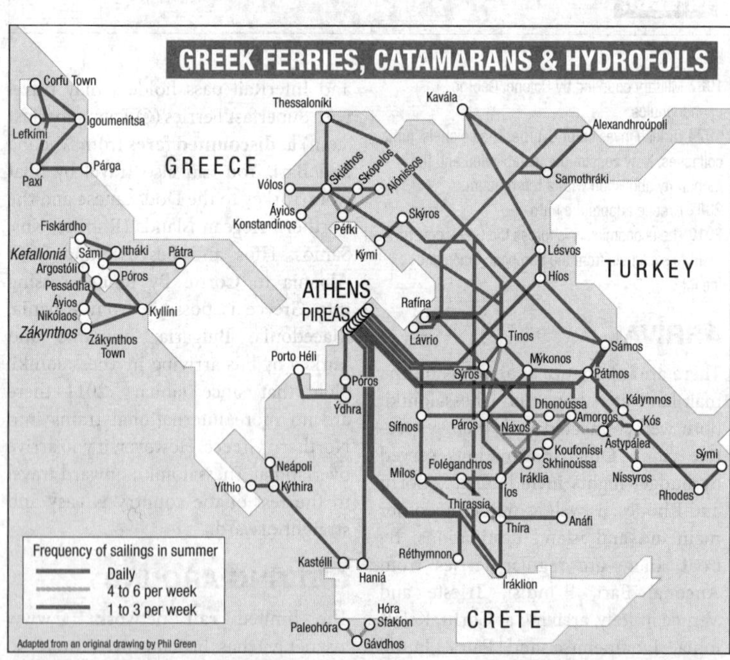

Hotels are categorized from "Luxury" down to "E-class", but these ratings have more to do with amenities and number of rooms than pricing – a budget hotel will typically cost €30–60 for a double. Throughout Greece, you have the additional option of **privately let rooms** (*dhomátia*). These are divided into three classes (A–C), and are usually cheaper than hotels. As often as not, rooms find you: owners descend on ferry and bus arrivals to fill any space they have. On the islands, minibuses from campsites and hotels meet new arrivals for free transfers. Increasingly, rooms are being eclipsed by **self-catering facilities**, which can be equally good value. If signs or touts are not apparent, ask for studios at travel agencies, which usually cluster around arrival points. Note that hotels and hostels do not normally include breakfast in their prices; an extra charge of €5 is standard.

Bringing a tent increases your options for cheap accommodation. Official **campsites** range from basic island compounds to highly organized complexes, mostly closed in winter (Nov–April). Many sites rent tents or have more permanent accommodation in the form of cabins and bungalows. Rough camping is forbidden.

FOOD AND DRINK

Eating out in Greece is popular and reasonably priced: €10–15 per person for a meal with beer or cheap wine. Typical **taverna** dishes to try include *moussakás* (aubergine and meat pie), *yígandes* (giant haricot beans in tomato sauce), *tzatzíki* (yogurt, garlic and cucumber dip), *melitzanosaláta* (aubergine dip), *khtapódhi* (octopus) and *kalamarákia* (fried baby squid). Quintessentially Greek **ouzerí** and **mezedhopolía** serve filling *mezédhes* (the Greek version of tapas) with drinks, adding up to a substantial meal. Note that people eat late: 1.30–3pm for lunch & 9–11.30pm for dinner, although plenty of places serve food all day.

BUDGET EATING

Head to a supermarket and stock up on Greek yogurt and honey for breakfast and buy *tyrópites* and *spanakópites* (cheese and spinach pies respectively) from a bakery for lunch. **Snacks** are one of the pleasures of Greek eating. Good budget food chains include *Woodys* and *Everest*.

As for **drinks**, the traditional coffee shop or **kafenío** is the central pivot of rural life; like tavernas, these range from the sophisticated to the old-fashioned. Their main business is sweet Greek coffee, but they also serve spirits such as aniseed-flavoured *oúzo* and brandy, as well as beer and soft drinks. Islanders take pre-dinner *oúzo* an hour or two before sunset: you'll be served a glass of water alongside, to be tipped into your *oúzo* until it turns milky white. **Bars** are ubiquitous in the largest towns and resorts. Drinks, at €5.50–10, are invariably more expensive than at a *kafenío*.

CULTURE AND ETIQUETTE

It is important to be respectful when visiting one of Greece's many **churches** or **monasteries**, and appropriate clothing should be worn – covered arms and legs for both sexes. The more popular sites often provide such clothing, should you be without it. Photography is also banned in sacred places. Another important part of Greek life is the afternoon **siesta**, when peace and quiet are valued. In restaurants, **tipping** is normally expected and usually customers leave a little more for service. **Topless bathing** is the norm on virtually all Greek beaches but, especially in smaller places or town beaches, check first before stripping off. Full nudity is tolerated only at designated or isolated beaches.

SPORTS AND OUTDOOR ACTIVITIES

The larger islands and resorts on the mainland have countless opportunities for **watersports** – including waterskiing, windsurfing, diving and snorkelling. There are usually information kiosks at the main beaches. The country's mountainous landscape provides plenty of **walking** and **climbing** options. The most rewarding areas are in northern Greece, concentrating around Mount Olympus to the east and the Epirus region to the northwest. Always wear sturdy walking boots for long treks, and carry plenty of water. If you want to do some serious hiking, it's worth buying a specialist map.

COMMUNICATIONS

Post offices operate Monday to Friday 7.30am to 2pm. The Central GPO at Syndagma Square in Athens is open until 8pm in the evening and also 7.30am–2pm during weekends. **Stamps** can also be bought at designated postal agencies inside newsstands or stationers. **Public phones** are mainly card-operated; buy phonecards from newsagents and kiosks. It's possible to make collect (reverse-charge) or charge-card calls from these phones, but you need €2.5 credit on a Greek phonecard to begin. The operator is on ⓣ129 (domestic) or ⓣ139 (international). If you're in the country for more than a week or so it's worth buying a **pay-as-you-go SIM card** available from mobile-phone shops; you can get your phone unlocked here, too. All big towns have **internet cafés**, and there's usually at least one place on the more visited islands. Expect to pay around €1–3 per hour.

GREECE ONLINE

ⓦ**www.culture.gr** Ministry of Culture site, with information on ruins and museums.
ⓦ**www.athensnews.gr** Useful and literate English-language weekly.
ⓦ**www.visitgreece.gr** Greek National Tourist Organization site.
ⓦ**www.gtp.gr** Information on all ferry and hydrofoil schedules except some minor lines.

PERÍPTERO PAVEMENT KIOSKS

You can't walk far in Greece without coming across a *períptero* pavement kiosk. Selling everything from bus tickets to condoms, razors and stationery, they're often the first port of call for directions, too. Many are open 24 hours.

EMERGENCIES

The most common causes of a run-in with the **police** are drunken loutishness and camping outside an authorized site. For minor medical complaints go to the local **pharmacy**, usually open Monday to Friday 8am to 2pm. Details of pharmacies open out-of-hours are posted in all pharmacy windows. For serious medical attention you'll find English-speaking doctors in all bigger towns and resorts; consult the tourist police for names. Emergency treatment is free in state hospitals, though you'll only get the most basic level of nursing care.

INFORMATION

There are **National Tourist Organization (EOT)** offices in most larger towns and resorts; in other places, try the municipal tourist offices, which are mostly open only in the summer. The

EMERGENCY NUMBERS

Police ⓣ100; Ambulance ⓣ166; Fire ⓣ199; Tourist police ⓣ171.

GREEK

	Greek	Pronunciation
Yes	*Ναί*	Né
No	*Οχι*	Óhi
Please	*Παρακαλώ*	Parakaló
Thank you	*Ευχαριστώ*	Efharistó
Hello/Good day	*Γειά σας/Χαίρετε*	Yá sas/Hérete
Goodbye	*Αντίο*	Adío
Excuse me	*Συγνώμη*	Signómi
Sorry	*Λυπάμαι*	Lipáme
When?	*Πότε;*	Póte?
Where?	*Πού;*	Poú?
Good	*Καλό*	Kaló
Bad	*Κακό*	Kakó
Near	*Κοντά*	Kondá
Far	*Μακριά*	Makriá
Cheap	*Φτηνό*	Ftinó
Expensive	*Ακριβό*	Akrivó
Open	*Ανοιχτό*	Anikhtó
Closed	*Κλειστό*	Klistó
Today	*Σήμερα*	Símera
Yesterday	*Χθές*	Khthés
Tomorrow	*Αύριο*	Ávrio
How much is...?	*Πόσο κάνει;*	Póso káni…?
What time is it?	*Τί ώρα είναι;*	Tí óra íne?
I don't understand	*Δέν καταλαβαίνω*	Thén katalavéno
Do you speak English?	*Ξαίρετε Αγγλικά;*	Xérete angliká?
Do you have a room?	*Εχετε ένα ελεύθερο δωμάτιο;*	Éhete éna eléfthero domátio?
Where does this bus go to?	*Πού πηγαίνει αυτό τό λεωφορείο;*	Poú piyéni aftó tó leoforío?
What time does it leave?	*Τί ώρα φεύγει;*	Tí óra févyi?
A ticket to...	*Ενα εισιτήριο γιά...*	Éna isitírio yiá…
I'm going to...	*Πάω στό...*	Páo stó…
Can I have the bill please?	*Τό λογαριασμό παρακαλώ;*	Tó loghariazmó, parakaló?
One	*Ενα /Μία*	Éna/mía (for 1:00)
Two	*Δύο*	Dhío
Three	*Τρία/Τρείς*	tría/trís(for 3:00)
Four	*Τέσσερα/Τέσσερεις*	Téssera/tésseris (for 4:00)
Five	*Πέντε*	Pénde
Six	*Εξι*	Éxi
Seven	*Εφτά*	Eftá
Eight	*Οκτώ*	Októ
Nine	*Εννέα*	Enéa
Ten	*Δέκα*	Théka

tourist police often have lists of rooms to let, but are really there to assist if you have a serious complaint about a hotel or restaurant.

MONEY AND BANKS

Greece's currency is the **euro** (€). **Banks** are normally open Monday to Thursday 8am to 2.30pm, Friday 8am to 2pm.

STUDENTS AND YOUTH DISCOUNTS

Many state-owned **museums and sites** are free for students from EU countries (a valid card is required, but not necessarily an ISIC). Non-EU students generally pay half-price. Holders of the ISIC card may also be eligible for ferry discounts; check Ⓦwww.greekferries.gr for details.

They charge a flat fee (€2–3) to change money, the National Bank usually being the cheapest; travel agencies and designated exchange booths give a poorer rate, but often levy a sliding two percent commission, which makes them better than banks for changing small amounts. Most **ATMs** accept foreign cards; in isolated areas cash rather than travellers' cheques will prove useful. **Credit cards** are generally accepted in most hotels, restaurants and shops.

OPENING HOURS AND HOLIDAYS

Shops generally open at 8.30/9am to 2.00/2.30pm Mondays to Saturdays with afternoon shopping 5.30/6pm–8.00/8.30pm on Tuesdays, Thursdays and Fridays. Tourist areas have shops and offices that often stay open right through the day. On Sundays many shops are closed. In rural areas **public transport** reduces dramatically or ceases completely, so be careful not to get stranded. Opening hours for **museums** and **ancient sites** change with exasperating frequency, although many are closed on Mondays. Smaller sites generally close for a long siesta (even when they're not supposed to), as do monasteries. Most museums and archeological sites are free on the following days: Sundays November to March; first Sunday in April, May, June and October; second Sunday in July to September; all national holidays. There's a vast range of **national holidays** and **festivals**. The most important, when almost everything will be closed, are: January 1 and 6, first Monday of Orthodox Lent (March 5 2012, March 18 2013), March 25, May 1, Orthodox Easter Sunday and Monday, Pentecost/Whit Monday (June 4 2012, June 24 2013), August 15, October 28, December 24–27.

Athens

Chaotic and exhilarating, **ATHENS** has been inhabited continuously for over seven thousand years. Vastly improved by a vigorous scrub before the Olympics in 2004, it has an efficient, user-friendly metro and its mix of contemporary culture, nightlife and heritage rivals that of almost any European city. Part of Athens' charm is the mix of retro and contemporary: cutting-edge clothes shops and designer bars stand by the remnants of the Ottoman bazaar, while Brutalist 1960s apartment-blocks dwarf crumbling Neoclassical mansions.

Athens' Acropolis, protected by a ring of mountains and commanding views of all seagoing approaches, was a natural choice for prehistoric settlement. Its development as a city-state reached its zenith in the fifth century BC with a flourish of art, architecture, literature and philosophy that has pervaded Western culture ever since. The **ancient sites** are the most obvious of Athens' attractions, but the attractive cafés, markets and landscaped stair-streets, the startling views from the hills of Lykavitós and Filopáppou, and, around the foot of the Acropolis, the scattered monuments of the Byzantine and nineteenth-century town all have their appeal.

What to see and do

Pláka is the best place to begin exploring the city. One of the few parts of Athens with charm and architectural merit, its narrow streets and stepped lanes are flanked by nineteenth-century Neoclassical houses. The interlocking streets provide countless opportunities for watching the world – or at least, the tourists – go by. While the Acropolis complex is an essential sight, it can be rewarding to stumble across smaller and more modest relics, such as the fourth-century Monument of Lysíkratos, or the first-century Tower of the Winds. Or take a walk through the pleasant National Gardens, away from the chaos of Athens' traffic-choked streets. Save some energy for the balmy evenings, however – with fantastic restaurants and funky bars, Athens knows how to juxtapose the ancient with the modern.

ANCIENT MONUMENTS ENTRY

The **ticket** to the Acropolis (€12, non-EU students €6, EU students free) is valid for four days and allows free access to all the other ancient sites in Athens. Otherwise, minor sites charge a separate €2 admission fee if you haven't visited the Acropolis. All the sites have the same hours (April–Sept 8am–7pm; Oct–March 8am–sunset).

The Acropolis

A rugged limestone outcrop, watered by springs and rising abruptly from the plain of Attica, the **Acropolis** (April–Sept 8am–7pm; Oct–March 8am–sunset) was one of the earliest settlements in Greece, supporting a Neolithic community around 5000 BC. During the ninth century BC, it became the heart of the first Greek city-state, and in the fifth century BC, Pericles had the complex reconstructed under the direction of architect and sculptor Pheidias, producing most of the monuments visible today, including the Parthenon. Having survived more or less intact for over two millennia, the Acropolis finally fell victim to the vagaries of war. In 1811 Lord Elgin removed parts of the frieze (the "Elgin Marbles"), which he later sold to the British Government and which has caused much controversy ever since. While the original religious significance of the Acropolis is now nonexistent, it

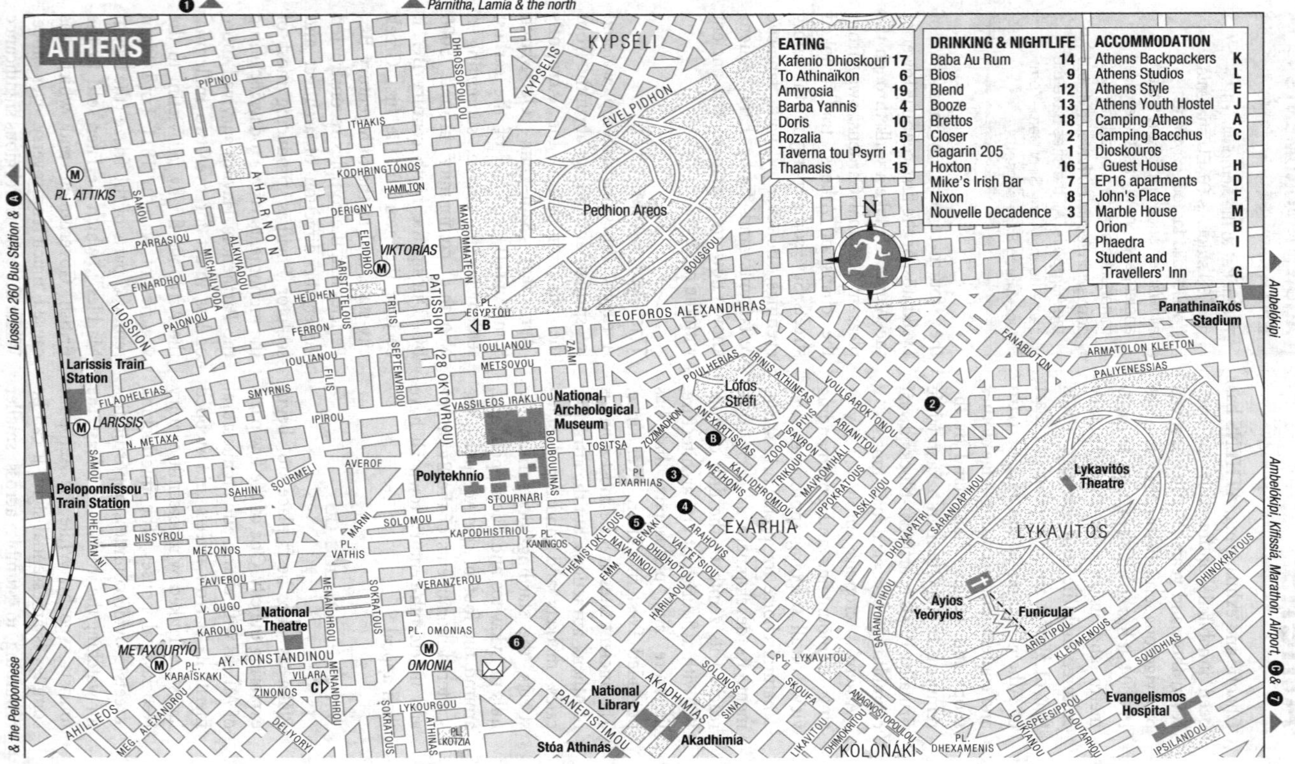
Párnitha, Lamía & the north
Liossíon 260 Bus Station & A
& the Peloponnese
Ambelókipi
Ambelókipi, Kifissiá, Marathon, Airport, C & 7
ATHENS
EATING
Kafenio Dhioskouri 17
To Athinaïkon 6
Amvrosia 19
Barba Yannis 4
Doris 10
Rozalia 5
Taverna tou Psyrri 11
Thanasis 15
DRINKING & NIGHTLIFE
Baba Au Rum 14
Bios 9
Blend 12
Booze 13
Brettos 18
Closer 2
Gagarin 205 1
Hoxton 16
Mike's Irish Bar 7
Nixon 8
Nouvelle Decadence 3
ACCOMMODATION
Athens Backpackers K
Athens Studios L
Athens Style E
Athens Youth Hostel J
Camping Athens A
Camping Bacchus C
Dioskouros Guest House H
EP16 apartments D
John's Place F
Marble House M
Orion B
Phaedra I
Student and Travellers' Inn G
KYPSÉLI
Pedhion Areos
LEOFOROS ALEXANDHRAS
Panathinaïkós Stadium
Lófos Stréfi
National Archeological Museum
Polytekhnío
EXÁRHIA
LYKAVITÓS
Lykavitós Theatre
Áyios Yeóryios
Funicular
Evangelismos Hospital
KOLONÁKI
Akadhimía
National Library
Stóa Athinás
National Theatre
OMONIA
PL. OMONIAS
METAXOURYÍO
VIKTORÍAS
LARISSIS
PL. ATTIKIS
Larissis Train Station
Peloponnissou Train Station
PATISSION (28 OKTOVRIOU)
AY. KONSTANDINOU
AKADHIMIAS
PANEPISTIMIOU
AHARNON
LIOSSION
PL. EXARHIAS
PL. LYKAVITOU
PL. DHEXAMENIS
PL. KANINGOS
PL. VATHIS
PL. KARAÏSKAKI
PL. EGYPTOU

ATHENS

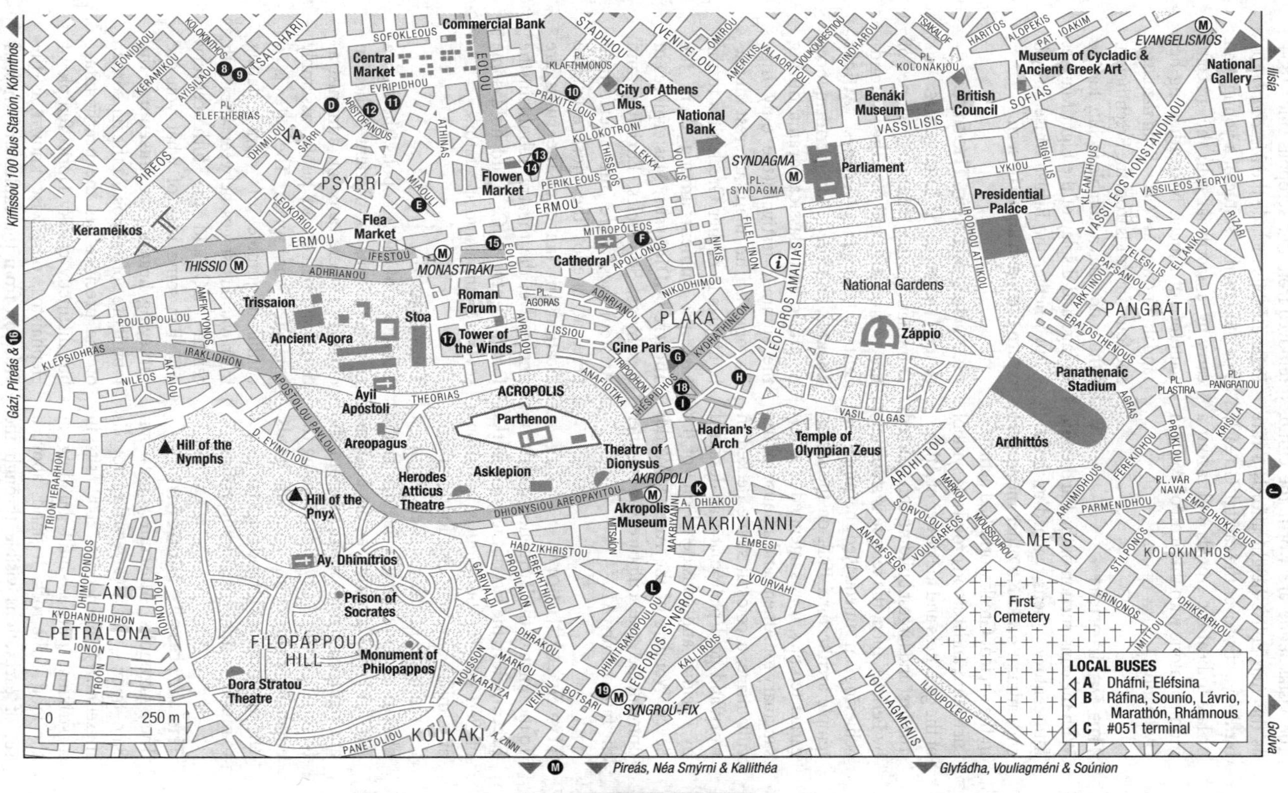

GREECE

is still imbued with a sense of majesty. The vistas alone are worth the climb, as the Acropolis's height affords a rare bird's-eye view over the capital. Go early or late to beat the crowds and savour a moment alone with this icon of Western civilization.

The Parthenon

With the construction of the **Parthenon**, fifth-century Athens reached an artistic and cultural peak. No other monument in the ancient Greek world had achieved such fame, and it stood proud as a symbol of the greatness and the power of Athens. The first and largest building constructed by Pericles' men, the temple is stunning, achieving an unequalled harmony in temple architecture. Built on the site of earlier temples, it was intended as a new sanctuary for Athena and a house for her cult image, a colossal statue decked in ivory and gold plate that was designed by Pheidias and considered one of the Seven Wonders of the Ancient World; unfortunately the sculpture was lost after the fifth century AD.

The Erechtheion

To the north of the Parthenon stands the **Erechtheion**, the last of the great works of Pericles. The building is intentionally unlike anything else found among the remnants of ancient sites. The most bizarre and memorable feature is the Porch of the Caryatids, as the columns are replaced by six maidens from the town of Caryae (Caryatids) holding the entablature gracefully on their heads. The significance of this design continues to puzzle both historians and visitors.

The Acropolis Museum

The **Acropolis Museum** (Tues–Sun 8am–8pm; €5; ⓦwww.theacropolismuseum.gr), opened in 2009, sits in a striking, purpose-built building at the foot of the rock. It stands above a set of excavations visible through the see-through floor (opening in 2012). It contains nearly all the portable objects removed from the Acropolis since 1834. Prize exhibits include the *Moschophoros*, a painted marble statue of a young man carrying a sacrificial calf; the graceful sculpture of Athena Nike adjusting her sandal, known as *Nike Sandalízoussa*; and four Caryatids from the Erechtheion. Athens now has a suitable facility for the storage and display of the Elgin Marbles – but whether the British Museum will return them remains to be seen.

Herodes Atticus Theatre and Theatre of Dionysus

Dominating the southern slope of the Acropolis hill is the second-century Roman **Herodes Atticus Theatre**, restored for performances of music and classical drama during the summer festival (the only time it's open). The main interest hereabouts lies in earlier Greek sites to the east, pre-eminent among them the **Theatre of Dionysus**. Masterpieces of Aeschylus, Sophocles, Euripides and Aristophanes were first performed here, at one of the most evocative locations in the city. The ruins are impressive; the theatre, rebuilt in the fourth century BC, could hold some seventeen thousand spectators.

The Agora

Northwest of the Acropolis, the **Agora** was the nexus of ancient Athenian city life, where acts of administration, commerce and public assembly competed for space. The site is a confused jumble of ruins, dating from various stages between the sixth century BC and the fifth century AD. For some idea of what you are surveying, head for the **museum** in the rebuilt Stoa of Attalos. At the far corner of the precinct sits the nearly intact but distinctly clunky Doric Temple of Hephaistos, otherwise known as the **Thissíon** from the exploits of Theseus depicted on its friezes.

The Roman Forum

The **Roman Forum**, or Roman agora, was built as an extension of the Hellenistic Agora by Julius Caesar and Augustus. The best-preserved and most intriguing of the ruins, though, is the graceful, octagonal structure known as the **Tower of the Winds**. It was designed in 50 BC by the Macedonian astronomer Andronicus, and served as a compass, sundial, weather vane and water clock powered by a stream from one of the Acropolis springs. Each face of the tower is adorned with a relief of a figure floating through the air, personifying the eight winds.

Sýndagma Square and the National Gardens

All roads lead to Platía Syndágmatos – **Sýndagma Square** – with its pivotal metro station. It is geared to tourism, with a main post office, banks, luxury hotels and travel agents grouped around. Behind the Neoclassical parliament buildings off the square, the **National Gardens** provide the most refreshing spot in the city, a shady oasis of trees, shrubs and creepers. South of the gardens stands **Hadrian's Arch**, erected by the Roman emperor to mark the edge of the classical city and the beginning of his own. Directly behind are sixteen surviving columns of the 104 that originally comprised the **Temple of Olympian Zeus** – the largest in Greece, dedicated by Hadrian in 132 AD.

Town museums

At the northeastern corner of the National Gardens is the fascinating and much-overlooked **Benáki Museum**, Koumbári 1 (Mon, Wed, Fri & Sat 9am–5pm, Thurs 9am–midnight, Sun 9am–3pm; €6, students €3), with a well-organized collection that features Mycenaean jewellery, Greek costumes, memorabilia of the Greek War of Independence and historical documents, engravings and paintings.

Taking the second left off Vassilísis Sofías after the Benáki Museum will bring you to the **Museum of Cycladic and Ancient Greek Art**, Neofýtou Dhouká 4 (Mon & Wed–Sat 10am–5pm, Thurs 10am–8pm, Sun 11am–5pm; €5, Sat €2.50, 18–26 years €1), impressive for both its subject and the quality of its displays.

To the northwest, beyond Omónia, the fabulous **National Archeological Museum**, Patissíon 44 (Mon 1.30–8pm, Tues–Sun 3pm; €7, students €3), contains gold from the grave circle at Mycenae, including the so-called Mask of Agamemnon, along with an impressive classical art collection and findings from the island of Thíra, dating from around 1450 BC, contemporary with the Minoan civilization on Crete.

Arrival and information

Air The Suburban Rail line whisks you from Eleftherios Venizélos airport to Baríssis train station (hourly; 5.10am–11.30pm; €8), involving a change at Nerantziotissa, where you can also transfer to the Line #1 metro. Although this is the quickest mode of transport, the airport is also directly connected to the Line #3 metro (every 30min; 6.35am–11.35pm; €8). The #X93 serves the bus station at Kifissoú 100 (every 30min; 24hr). The #X94 (every 15–30min; 24hr) heads for Ethnikí Ámyna metro station. The #X95 (every 10min; 24hr) from outside Arrivals goes direct to Sýndagma Square. The #X96 (every 30min; 24hr) runs to Pireás port and the #X97 every (30–40min; 24hr) to Dafni Metro station. All tickets cost €5 one-way.

Train Salonika trains arrive at the Laríssis train station to the northwest of the city centre, with its own metro station on Line #2. From here, there are trains to all parts of Greece, although for some destinations in the Peloponnese you may need to take the Suburban Rail to Kórinthos and change there.

Bus Buses from northern Greece and the Peloponnese arrive at Kifissoú 100 bus station, 10min from the centre by bus #051 (5am–midnight). Buses from central Greece arrive closer to the centre at Liossíon 260, north of the train station. From here bus #024 goes to Sýndagma (5am–midnight). Most international buses drop off at the train station or Kifissoú 100; a few will drop you right in the city centre.

Boat If you arrive by boat at Pireás, the easiest way to get to the centre is by metro on Line #1, with the station being a few steps from the quay.

Tourist office The city's main EOT office is at Leofóros Amálias 26 (Mon–Fri 9am–7pm, Sat & Sun 10am–4pm; ⓣ210 3310 392, ⓔinfo@gnto.gr).

Crime Though safer than many European cities, Athens has seen a crime rise in the last few years as the result of tensions between a new, immigrant community and the police, an increase in drug use and unemployment and an anti-establishment protest history. It's hard to speak of no-go areas, but avoid walking in parks after dark (especially Pedion tou Areos), Omónia, and the streets behind the Athens Polytechnic. Motorcycle bag snatching is also on the up especially in the centre and around Ⓜ Victoria.

City transport

Bus and trolley Athens' bus and trolley network is extensive but very crowded at peak times. Tickets for buses must be bought in advance from kiosks and validated once on board.

Tram A tram line runs from Sýndagma to the seaside resorts of Glyfádha and Faliro.

Metro Line #1 of the metro runs from Pireás to Kifissiá, with central stops at Thissío, Monastiráki and Omónia; Line #2 runs from Áyios Andónios to Áyios Dhimítrios via Sýndagma and a station at the foot of the Acropolis; Line #3 heads east from Monastiráki to Dhoukíssis Plakendías (with special metro cars continuing direct to the airport). Tickets (€0.80) are available at all stations from automatic coin-op dispensers or staffed windows. They must be validated before boarding.

Tickets For €4 you can buy a ticket valid on all public transport for 24hr. You can also buy a single-journey ticket valid on all forms of transport for €1. All public transport operates daily from 5am–midnight. At the weekend (Fri–Sat), metro operates to 2am; trams operate 24hr.

Taxis can be surprisingly difficult to hail and fairly expensive. Taxi drivers will often pick up several passengers along the way, each paying the full fare for their journey – so if you're picked up by an already occupied taxi, memorize the meter reading; you'll pay from then on, including a €1.50 minimum charge.

Accommodation

The city can be deserted in August when a lot of establishments close for vacations and the nightlife moves to the islands and to the seaside.

Hostels

Athens Backpackers Makri 12, Makriyiánni ⓣ210 9224 044, ⓦwww.backpackers.gr. Relaxed hostel in a prime location with clean, simple dorms, internet access, rooftop bar with Acropolis views and a buzzing atmosphere. The free walking tour and organized bar crawl make it a great place to meet fellow travellers. Very popular, so best to book first. Dorms €24.

Athens Style Agias Theklas 10, Monastiráki ⓣ210 3225 010, ⓦwww.athenstyle.com. Pleasant hostel with roof terrace, wi-fi, free breakfast and a great location a few minutes' walk from Monastiráki metro. Private rooms and studio apartments (three beds) available. Dorms €25, doubles €50, 4-bed apartments €120.

Athens Youth Hostel Dhamáreos 75, Pangráti ⓣ210 7519 530, ⓦwww.athens-yhostel.com. In a congenial (if remote) neighbourhood – trolleys #2 or #11 stop nearby – with cooking and laundry facilities. Dorms €12.

Dioskouros Guest House Pittakou 6 ⓣ210 3248 165, ⓦwww.hotelfivos.gr. Very basic and cheap hostel in the Pláka area, good at organizing further trips to the islands. Prices include continental breakfast. No private bathrooms. Dorms from €20, doubles €55.

Student and Travellers' Inn Kydhathinéon 16, Pláka ⓣ210 3244 808, ⓦwww.studenttravellersinn.com. Popular, clean and well-run hotel-cum-hostel in a prime location close to nightlife. Official HI hostel. Cheerful rooms, as well as luggage storage, free wi-fi access and a garden bar with big screen. Dorms €21, double rooms €35.

FERRY PORTS

The port of **Pireás**, effectively an extension of Athens, is the main terminus for international and inter-island ferries. Get there from Athens by metro: Pireás is the last stop on Line #1 heading southwest from Monastiráki. Once there, blue-and-white buses shuttle passengers around the port for free. The other ports on the east coast of the Attic peninsula, **Rafína and Lávrio**, are alternative departure points for many of the Cycladic and northeastern Aegean islands. Frequent buses connect them with Platia Egyptou in central Athens.

Hotels

John's Place Patróöu 5, Pláka ☎210 3229 719. Dark rooms with shared bath, but neat and well kept. Centrally located, it is in a peaceful backstreet off Mitropóleos, with a cheap restaurant on the ground floor. Doubles €40–50.

Marble House Cul-de-sac off Anastasíou Zínni 35, Koukáki ☎210 9228 294, Ⓦwww.marblehouse.gr. Peaceful, welcoming *pension* south of the Acropolis. Most rooms en suite and with balcony; all rooms have fans and fridge. Free wi-fi. Closed Jan and Feb. Doubles with private bath €40–50.

Orion Emmanouíl. Benáki 105, and Dryadon 4, Exárhia ☎210 3827 362, Ⓦwww.orion-dryades.com. Quiet, well-run budget hotel across from the Lófos Stréfi park – a steep final walk to get there, yet close to many attractions. Rooftop kitchen and common area with an amazing view. Doubles €55–75.

Phaedra Adhriánou & Herefóndos 16, Pláka ☎210 3238 461, Ⓦwww.hotelphaedra.com. Cheerful and clean rooms with a/c, just over half en suite. Excellent location on a pedestrianized street overlooking a Byzantine church and the Acropolis. Doubles €60.

Studios

Athens Studios Veikou 3a, Makriyiánni ☎210 9235 811, Ⓦwww.athensstudios.gr. Well-priced serviced studios run by the team at *Athens Backpackers*. Simple, spacious and clean with kitchen, TV and wi-fi. Extra sleepers can be accommodated on fold-out beds. Six-bed apartment €155.

Campsites

Camping Athens Leofóros Athinón 198–200 ☎210 5814 114, Ⓦwww.campingathens.com.gr. 7km west of Athens, this is the closest campsite to the city. Decent facilities, mini-market and snack bar. €8.50/person, plus €5/tent.

TREAT YOURSELF

Stay in considerable style at **EP16 apartments** (Epikourou 16, Psyrrí; ☎6976 484 135, Ⓦwww.EP16.com). Cool, contemporary apartments in a refurbished 1930s block with sleek furnishings, a well-stocked beer fridge (drinks included) and a shady roof terrace with Acropolis views. Apartments for 2–3 people €90–120 per night.

Camping Bacchus 4km from Lavrio signposted on the road to Sounion ☎22920 39571. Very convenient for the ferries. €7.50/person, plus €7/tent.

Eating

Despite the touts and tourist hype, Pláka provides a pleasant evening's setting for a meal, but for good-value, good-quality cuisine, outlying neighbourhoods such as Psyrrí, Sýndagma, Gazi and Exárhia are better bets. Note that Athens sells some of Europe's most expensive coffee, at €3 for an espresso even at an ordinary café: developing a taste for Greek coffee (*ellinikós*) will prove slightly cheaper.

Cafés and ouzerí

Kafenio Dhioskouri Dhioskoúron 13, Pláka. Popular, shady bar-café with an unbeatable view of the ancient agora, where cold drinks and coffees take precedence over slightly pricey snacks. Also serves absinthe. *Mezédhes* €5–9.

To Athinaïkon Themistokléous 2, corner with Panepistimíou. Established since 1932, this is a sophisticated *ouzerí* with marble tables and old posters, popular with local workers at lunch; strong on fresh seafood. Mon–Sat 11.30am–12.30am; closed Sun.

Restaurants

Amvrosia Dhrákou 3–5, right by Ⓜ Syngroú-Fix, Veïkoú. The best grill on this pedestrian street, always packed. Good takeaway *ghýros* (Greek kebabs), or enjoy a whole roast chicken at outdoor tables. Kebabs €6–9.

Barba Yannis Emmanouíl Benáki 94, Exárhia. Vast menu of inexpensive oven-cooked food, served both indoors – in a charmingly old-fashioned interior – and out. Food is best at lunch, but it's open until 1am Mon–Fri, until 6pm Sat. Mains €5–8.

Doris Praxitelous 30. Daytime-only restaurant with a loyal local clientele. Ignore the dodgy decor and tuck into hearty stews and cheap pasta. Greek doughnuts (*loukoumades*) are a speciality. Mains from €6.

Rozalia Valtetsíou 58, Exárhia. A great all-round *mezédhes*-and-grills taverna with an extensive menu. There's also a garden, open in summer. *Mezédhes* €5.

Taverna tou Psyrri Aischýlou 12, Psyrrí. Straightforward taverna that excels in grilled/fried seafood, vegetable starters and wine from basement barrels. Arrive early (remember Greeks eat late) or wait for a table. Mains €10.

Thanasis Mitropóleos 69, Monastiráki. Reckoned the best *souvláki* and Middle Eastern kebabs in this district. Always packed with locals at lunchtime, but worth the wait. Take out or eat in. Kebabs €8. Open till 2am daily.

Drinking and nightlife

Many bars are open as cafés during the day, serving snacks and coffees, but transform themselves in the evenings, often with live music. The bars in Exárhia are popular with local students and are relaxed and more affordable, while those in Kolonáki are cool and hip, and more expensive. All clubs charge admission fees, sometimes as much as €15–20, although this usually includes a free drink. Clubs do not start filling up until after midnight but stay open until dawn. In summer much of Athens' nightlife moves to larger outdoor venues on the southern coast, easily accessible by tram which operate round the clock at weekends.

Bars

Baba Au Rum Kleitíou 6, Sýndagma. This trendy bar has a colourful decor, and offers a great selection of cocktails at reasonable prices. Daily 8pm–late.

Booze Kolokotróni 57–59. Cavernous, dark space with a cool daytime crowd draped at long tables supping draft beer and playing board games. Stick around at night for DJs, exhibitions and the latest from the Athens avant-garde. Daily 10am–late.

Brettos Kydathinéon 41, Pláka. With colourful bottles and wooden barrels lining the walls, this is a sophisticated spot which oozes reminders of its hundred-year-plus history. *Oúzo* €3; cocktails €7. Daily 10am–2am.

Closer Ippokrátous 150 & Vatatzi 69, Exárhia. The entrance looks like a normal house door, but walk up the stairs where the DJs play some of the latest and most innovative rock/indie music. It gets busier after 1am. Daily 10pm–6am.

Hoxton Voutadon 42, Gazi. Hip, industrial-style bar-club playing rock, electro and pop to Gazi scenesters. Daily 9pm–3am.

Mike's Irish Bar Sinópis 6, Pyrgos Athinón, Ambelókipi. A lively watering hole which has something to suit everyone, including karaoke, live music and big screens for sport. Guinness drinkers are especially well catered for. Daily 8pm–4am.

Nixon Agisilaou 61b, Gazi. One of Athens' trendiest and busiest, bars, where you can meet young locals sipping cocktails at €8 a go. Tourist-free – so far. Daily 8pm–late.

Clubs and live music

Bios Peireós 84, Gazi www.bios.gr. Around the corner from *Nixon* (see above), *Bios* comprises a small, cosy bar upstairs, and a raw, minimalist club downstairs with an adjoining terrace. From the Stereo MCs to Performance Art – you'll find it here. Daily 10pm till late.

Blend Aristofánous 11, Psyrri www.blendathens.com. Athens' prime techno club with well-known international DJs every week. Midnight–late. Cover charges vary.

Gagarin 205 Liossíon 205, near Ⓜ Attikís www.gagarin205.gr. The place to watch the best international up-and-coming bands and more established acts.

Nouvelle Decadence Emmanouíl Benáki 87, Exárhia, opposite *Barba Yannis* (see p.535). Athens' top alternative venue with theme nights. Daily 10pm–5am.

THE ATHENS FESTIVAL

The **Athens Festival** (☎210 327 2000, www.greekfestival.gr), from June to late August, encompasses classical Greek theatre, contemporary dance, classical music, big-name jazz, traditional Greek music and a smattering of rock shows. Most performances take place at the Herodes Atticus Theatre – an atmospheric venue on a warm summer's evening. There are also bus excursions to the great ancient theatre at Epidaurus (see p.541). The main festival box office is at Panepistimou 39; tickets cost from €15.

Entertainment

For up-to-the-minute listings, get yourself a copy of the English-language weekly *Athens News* (www.athensnews.gr), which has details of clubs, galleries, concerts and films and check out the website www.secret-athens.gr.

Dora Stratou Theatre Filopáppou Hill ☎210 3244 395, www.grdance.org. Dancers, singers and folk musicians unite to give spectators an insight into continuing local Greek traditions. Tickets from €15. Late May to mid-Sept Tues–Sat 9.30pm & Sun 8.15pm.

Shopping

Books and maps Compendium (Nikodimou 5, off Sýndagma) has books on Greece, travel guides, magazines and a secondhand section. Eleftheroudhakis (Panepistimíou 17 plus other branches) has the largest foreign-language stock in town, plus maps.

Clothes For high-street shopping, head to the stores around Kolonáki square.

Markets The Monastiráki flea market is open daily and has an interesting selection of weird and wonderful goods for sale. Sunday is the best time for a visit, as the market expands into the surrounding streets. The nearby Central Market sells local foods.

Souvenirs Tourists head to Pláka where souvenir shops abound, and where leather goods and jewellery take precedence.

Directory

Embassies and consulates Australia, Kifissiás & Alexandras Level 6 Thon Bldg ⓣ210 8704 000; Canada, Ioánni Yennadhíou 4 ⓣ210 7273 400; Ireland, Vassiléos Konstandínou 7 ⓣ210 7232 771/2; New Zealand, Kifissiás 76 ⓣ210 6924 136; UK, Ploutárhou 1, Kolonáki ⓣ210 7272 600; US, Vassilísis Sofías 91 ⓣ210 7212 951/9.

Hospitals Evangelismós, with its own metro stop, is the most central, but KAT, way out in Maroússi, is the designated Greater Athens emergency ward.

Internet Free wi-fi access around Syntagma Square, Ⓜ Thissíon and at Platía Kotziá.

Left luggage Many hotels store luggage for free. Or try Pacific Travel Services, Níkis 26, Syntagma (Mon–Fri 9am–8pm, Sat & Sun 9am–2pm; ⓣ210 3241 007).

Post offices Main branch on Mitropóleos, corner of Syntagma.

Moving on

Train Kórinthos (7/8 daily; 1hr 20min); Pátra (8/9 daily; 3hr 20min–4hr); Pýrgos (5 daily; 5–6hr); Thessaloníki (8 daily; 4–7hr); Vólos (1 daily; 4hr 30min).

Bus Corfu (3 daily; 11hr); Delphi (6 daily; 3hr); Igoumenitsa (4 daily; 7hr); Ioánnina (8 daily; 8hr); Kalamáta (9 daily; 2hr 30min–3hr 30min); Kefaloniá (6 daily; 8hr); Kórinthos (every 30min; 1hr 20min); Kými, for Skýros ferries (5 daily; 3hr 30min); Mycenae-Fíkhti (hourly; 2hr 30min); Náfplio (hourly; 2hr 30min); Pátra (every 30min; 2hr 30min–3hr); Pýrgos (10 daily; 5hr); Rafína (every 30min; 1hr–1hr 30min); Sounion (hourly; 2hr); Spárti (12 daily; 4hr); Thessaloníki (12 daily; 6hr 30min); Tríkala (8 daily; 4hr 30min); Tripoli (12–15 daily; 2hr 15min); Vólos (12 daily; 5hr); Zákynthos (4 daily; 6hr).

Ferry (from Pireás) to: Crete (5–7 daily; 12hr); Híos (1–3 daily; 6–9hr); Íos (2–3 daily; 3hr 30min–10hr); Kós (2 daily; 7–12hr); Lésvos (1–2 daily; 9–13hr); Mýkonos (4 daily; 3hr 30min–5hr 30min); Náxos (5–7 daily; 5–8hr); Páros (3–4 daily; 3–7hr); Pátmos (4–5 weekly; 7–12hr); Rhodes (1–3 daily; 11–23hr); Santoríni (4–5 daily; 4–16hr); Sífnos (4–6 daily; 2–7hr); Sýros (4–6 daily; 3–5hr) and many other destinations.

DAY-TRIPS FROM ATHENS

The 70km of shoreline south of Athens has good but highly developed beaches. At weekends the sands fill fast, as do innumerable bars, restaurants and clubs. But for most visitors, this coast's attraction is at the end of the road. **Cape Sounion** is among the most imposing spots in Greece, and on it stands the fifth-century BC **Temple of Poseidon** (daily 9.30am–sunset; €4, students €2), built in the time of Pericles as part of a sanctuary to the sea god. In summer you've faint hope of solitude unless you arrive before the tours do, but the temple is as evocative a ruin as Greece can offer. Doric in style, it preserves sixteen of its thirty-four columns, and the view is stunning. Below the promontory lie several coves, the most sheltered of which is a five-minute walk east from the car park and site entrance. The main Sounion **beach** is more crowded, but has a group of tavernas

STARLIT CINEMA

Outdoor cinema is a charming Greek tradition and there are hundreds of al-fresco screens throughout the country. A balmy evening watching a classic in a bougainvillea-draped courtyard with a few beers is hard to beat. Try the centrally located Cine Paris (ⓣ210 3222 071, ⓦwww.cineparis.gr) in Athens or the Cinema Kamari (ⓣ22860 31974, ⓦwww.cinekamari.gr) on Santoríni (see p.559). Both open May–Sept.

at the far end, which – considering the location – are reasonably priced. Buses to Sounion leave every hour from the KTEL terminal on Mavromatéon at the southwest corner of the Pédhion Áreos park in central Athens. They alternate between coastal and inland services, the latter slightly longer and more expensive. Take the coastal route that takes around two hours.

The Peloponnese

The appeal of the **Peloponnese** is hard to overstate. The **beaches** of this southern peninsula are among the finest and least developed in the country, while its ancient sites include the Homeric palace of Agamemnon at **Mycenae,** the Greek theatre at **Epidaurus** and the sanctuary of **Olympia**, host to the Olympic Games for a millennium. Medieval remains run from the fabulous castle at **Acrocorinth** and the strange tower-houses and frescoed churches of the **Máni**, to the extraordinary Byzantine towns of **Mystra** and **Monemvasiá**. The Peloponnese also boasts Greece's most spectacular train route, an hour-long journey on the **rack-and-pinion rail line** from Dhiakoftó to Kalávryta (see box, p.535).

PÁTRA

The city of **PÁTRA** is the third largest in the country, and connects the mainland to Italy and the Ionian Islands. Unlike many other destinations in the Peloponnese, Pátra is a thriving working city and has a life of its own which extends far beyond tourism, despite the number of travellers passing through. There are enough sites and museums to fill a day's sightseeing, though most people choose to pass through rather more quickly.

GETTING TO THE PELOPONNESE

The usual approach from Athens is on the frequent buses and trains that run via modern **Kórinthos** (Kórinthos). From Italy and the Adriatic, **Pátra** is the main port of the Peloponnese, although some ferries from the Ionian Islands arrive at Kyllíni.

The city is best enjoyed in the evening, when thousands of party-going university students transform the streets. At the heart of the drinking scene is Agíou Nikoláou, a pedestrian street crammed with bars. The Patras Carnival (Ⓦwww.carnivalpatras.gr) is the best-known in Greece.

Arrival and information

Train The train station is by the port on Óthonos Amalías.

Bus Buses arrive at the KTEL Achaia bus station 200m north of the train station.

Ferry Ferries from all departure points arrive at the port close to the bus and train stations.

Tourist office Agorá Argýri, Agiou Andréou & Arátou, (daily 8am–10pm; Ⓣ2610 461 740/1, Ⓦwww.infocenterpatras.gr).

Tourist Police Goúnari 52, by the Italian ferry terminal Ⓣ2610 455 833.

Accommodation

Pension Nicos Patréos 3 and Agíou Andhréou 121 Ⓣ2610 623 757. Rooms (some en suite) are a little small but this hotel is convenient for the port, train and bus stations and there's a rooftop bar. Doubles €20–35.

Youth Hostel Iróön Polytekhníou 62 Ⓣ2610 427 278, Ⓦwww.patrasrooms.gr. Located 800m north of the bus terminal on the coastal road and it does have the cheapest beds in town. The hostel also rents apartments behind the bus station. Dorms €12.

Moving on

Train Athens (8–9 daily; 3–4hr); Kórinthos (3 daily; 2hr 30min); Pýrgos (4 daily; 1hr 30min–2hr).

Bus Athens (every 30min; 2hr 30–3hr); Ioánnina (2 daily; 5hr); Kalamáta (2 daily; 4hr); Nafpaktos/Delifi (4–6 daily; 3hr); Pýrgos (6–10 daily; 2hr).
Ferry Ancona (2–3 daily; 20–21hr); Bari (1–2 daily; 16hr); Brindisi (3–7/week; 13–16hr); Corfu (1 daily; 6–7hr); Igoumenítsa (1 daily; 8–10hr); Itháki (2 daily; 6hr); Kefalloniá (2 daily; 2hr 30min–5hr); Venice (4–6/week; 30–32hr).

ANCIENT KÓRINTHOS

Whoever possessed **Kórinthos** – the ancient city that displaced Athens as capital of the Greek province in Roman times – controlled both the trade between northern Greece and the Peloponnese, and the short cut between the Ionian and Aegean seas. It's unsurprising, therefore, that the city's history is a catalogue of invasions and power struggles, until it was razed by the Romans in 146 BC. The site lay in ruins for a century before being rebuilt, on a majestic scale, by Julius Caesar in 44 BC. St Paul stayed for 18 months and preached there in 51/52 AD.

What to see and do

Nowadays, the remains of the city occupy a rambling site below the acropolis hill of Acrocorinth, itself littered with medieval ruins. To explore both you need a full day, or better still, to stay close by. The modern village of **ARHÉA KÓRINTHOS** spreads around the main archeological zone, where you'll find plenty of places to eat and sleep, including a scattering of **rooms** to rent in the backstreets.

DHIAKOFTÓ TO KALÁVRYTA RAILWAY

A contender for one of Europe's quirkiest railway journeys, the **rack-and-pinion rail line** (Odontotós; Ⓦwww.odontotos.com) from Dhiakoftó to Kalávryta is a must for any visitor to the region (€19 return). Trains grind their way up vertiginous slopes, rattle through tunnels and clank over crazily narrow bridges on their way through the dramatic Vouraikós Gorge.

The main site

The main excavated site (daily 8am–3/7.30pm; €6, Sun free) is dominated by the remains of the Roman city. You enter from the south side, which leads straight into the **Roman agora**. The real focus, however, is a survival from the classical Greek era: the fifth-century BC **Temple of Apollo**, whose seven austere Doric columns stand slightly above the level of the forum.

Acrocorinth

Towering 575m above the lower town, **Acrocorinth** (summer: daily 8.30am–7pm; winter: Tues–Sun 8.30am–3pm; free) is an amazing mass of rock still largely encircled by 2km of wall. During the Middle Ages this ancient acropolis of Kórinthos became one of Greece's most powerful fortresses. It's a 4km climb up (about 1hr), but well worth it. Amid the sixty-acre site, you wander through a jumble of semi-ruined chapels, mosques, houses and battlements, erected in turn by Greeks, Romans, Byzantines, Franks, Venetians and Ottomans.

Arrival

Bus and train Frequent bus and train services run from Athens and Pátra to modern Kórinthos, from where you can catch a local bus from KTEL Kórinthos or the main square to Arhéa Kórinthos and the adjacent site (hourly; 20min; €1.20).

Accommodation

Hotel Korinthos Damaskenou 26 Ⓣ27410 26710, Ⓦwww.korinthoshotel.gr. One block from the port and three blocks from the bus station, this small but friendly hotel is very popular with local students. Free wi-fi. Doubles €50.
Marinos Rooms Arhéa Kórinthos, Sysyphus St Ⓣ2741 031 209, Ⓦwww.marinosrooms.com. Very popular, family-run hotel in Ancient Kórinthos with comfortable rooms. Book in advance. Restaurant downstairs. Doubles €35.

Moving on

Train Athens (12/13 daily; 1hr 30min); Dhiakoftó (3 daily; 1hr 15min–1hr 30min); Pátra (6 daily; 45min–1hr 30min).
Bus (KTEL bus station) Ancient Kórinthos (hourly; 20min); Árgos (hourly; 1hr); Kalamáta (7 daily; 3hr 15 min–4hr); Mycenae-Fíkhti (hourly; 30min); Náfplio (7 daily; 1hr 20min); Spárti (8 daily; 4hr).

MYKÍNES (MYCENAE)

Southwest of Kórinthos, the ancient site of **MYCENAE** is tucked into a fold of the hills just 2km northeast of the modern village of **Mykínes**. Agamemnon's citadel, "well-built Mycenae, rich in gold", as Homer wrote, was uncovered in 1874–76 by the German archeologist Heinrich Schliemann, who was convinced that Homer's epics had a factual basis. Brilliantly crafted gold and sophisticated architecture bore out the accuracy of Homer's words. The buildings unearthed by Schliemann show signs of having been occupied from around 1950 BC until 1100 BC, when the town, though still prosperous, was abandoned. No coherent explanation has been found for this event, but war between rival kingdoms was probably a major factor.

What to see and do

You enter the **Citadel of Mycenae** (summer Mon 12.30–7.30pm, Tues–Sun 8am–7.30pm; winter daily 8.30am–3.30pm; €8, EU students free) through the mighty **Lion Gate**. Inside the walls to the right is **Grave Circle A**, the cemetery which Schliemann believed contained the bodies of Agamemnon and his followers, murdered on their triumphant return from Troy. In fact the burials date from about three centuries before the Trojan war, but they were certainly royal, and the finds are among the richest yet unearthed. Schliemann took the extensive **South House**, beyond the grave circle, to be the Palace of Agamemnon. But a much grander building was later discovered on the summit of the acropolis. Rebuilt in the thirteenth century BC, it is, like all Mycenaean palaces, centred on a **Great Court**. The small rooms to the north are believed to have been royal apartments and in one of them the remains of a red stuccoed bath have led to its fanciful identification as the place of Agamemnon's murder.

Outside the walls of the citadel lay the main part of the town, and extensive remains of **merchants' houses** have been uncovered near to the road. A few minutes' walk down the road is the astonishing **Treasury of Atreus**, a royal burial vault entered through a majestic fifteen-metre corridor.

Arrival

Orientation The modern village of Mykínes has one main street, where all accommodation and places to eat are located. You will need to travel onward from Fíkhti or the ancient site to get there.
Train There's a train station at Fíkhti, 2km west of Mykínes. If you don't want to walk you can catch a local bus.
Bus Most long-distance KTEL buses will drop you off at Fíkhti, while three daily buses from Náfplio stop at the site entrance.

Accommodation

Belle Hélène ⓣ27510 76225. Once the home of Schliemann, this hotel looks a bit run-down, but it's full of history. Furthermore, its rooms are spacious and the shared bathrooms are clean. Breakfast included. Doubles €40.
Camping Atreus ⓣ27510 76221. This shady campsite comes equipped with clean facilities, a swimming pool, and a restaurant on site. March to early Oct. €6/person, €4/tent.

Eating

Taverna O Spiros. Surrounded by flowers and foliage, enjoy traditional Greek dishes at this friendly local taverna. Mains €6.

Moving on

Bus Árgos (5 daily; 30min); Náfplio (3 daily; 1hr).

NÁFPLIO

NÁFPLIO, a lively, beautifully sited town with a faded elegance, inherited from when it was briefly modern Greece's first capital, makes an attractive base for exploring the area or for resting up by the sea.

What to see and do

The main fort, the **Palamídhi** (daily: summer 8am–7pm; winter 8am–sunset; €4), is most directly approached by 999 stone-hewn steps up from Polyzoïdhou Street. Within its walls are three self-contained castles, all built by the Venetians in the 1710s. To the west, the **Acronafplía** fortress occupies the ancient acropolis, whose walls were adapted by successive medieval occupants. The third fort, the photogenic **Boúrtzi**, occupies the islet offshore from the harbour and allowed the Venetians to close the shallow shipping channel with a chain. In the town itself, Platía Syndágmatos, the main square, is a great place to relax over a coffee. There's also a thriving nightlife, with a string of bars along the waterfront at Bouboulínas.

Arrival and information

Train The train station is on the waterfront, 600m north of the bus station.

Bus Buses arrive on Syngroú, just south of the interlocking squares Platía Trión Navárhon and Platía Kapodhístria.

Tourist office 25-Martíou 2 (daily 9am–1pm & 4–8pm; ⓣ2752 024 444).

Accommodation

Dimitris Bekas Rooms Efthimiopoúlou 26 ⓣ27520 24594. Don't be disheartened by the stone steps leading up to this welcoming *pension* – the views from the roof terrace are stunning. It is located close to the centre of the old town. Doubles €25.

Hotel Economou Argonaftón 22 ⓣ27520 23955. A 15min walk out of town and in need of modernizing, but this hotel is one of only a few budget options. Even when it's full, you'll be squeezed in somewhere. Dorms €15, doubles €30.

Eating

Old Mansion Siokóu 7. Bustling taverna serving up Greek favourites to the accompaniment of live traditional music (Fri–Sun). Mains €8–15.

Moving on

Bus Árgos (every 30min; 30min); Athens (hourly; 3hr); Epidaurus (4 daily; 45min); Mycenae (3–4 daily; 1hr); Trípoli (2–4 daily; 1hr).

EPIDAURUS

From the sixth century BC to Roman times, **EPIDAURUS**, 30km east of Náfplio, was a major spa and religious centre; its **Sanctuary of Asclepius** was the most famous of all shrines dedicated to the god of healing. The magnificently preserved 14,000-seat theatre (daily 8am–5/7pm; €6, Sun free) is the venue for evening classical-theatre **performances** (June–Aug Fri & Sat; ⓦwww.greekfestival.gr) during the Athens and Epidaurus Festival. If you want to camp, *Camping Nicholas I&II.* in Paleá Epidaurus (ⓣ27530 41297/41445, ⓦwww.nicolasgikas.gr; €6 per person, €5 per tent), has wonderful pitches among orange and mulberry groves, right on the beach. Elsewhere, try *Hotel Alkyon*, Asklipíou 195 (ⓣ27530 22002; €35), 5km north of the theatre at **Lygourió**.

MYSTRA

A glorious, airy place, hugging a steep flank of the Taïyetos mountains, **MYSTRA** is an astonishingly complete Byzantine city that once sheltered a population of some twenty thousand. The castle on its summit was built in 1249 by Guillaume II de Villehardouin, fourth Frankish Prince of the Morea (as the Peloponnese was then known), and together with the fortresses of Monemvasiá and the Máni it guarded his territory. In 1262 the Byzantines drove out the Franks and established the Despotate of Mystra.

To explore the site of the **Byzantine city** (daily: summer 8am–7pm; winter 8am–3pm; €5), it makes sense to take the bus from Spárti (10 daily; €1.20), which stops at Néos Mystrás and then continues up the hill. Make for the top entrance, then explore a leisurely downhill route. Following this course, the first identifiable building you come to is the fourteenth-century church of **Ayía Sofía**. The **Kástro**, reached by a path that climbs directly from the upper gate, maintains the Frankish design of its thirteenth-century construction, though modified by successive occupants. Heading down from Ayía Sofía, there are two possible routes. The right fork winds past the ruins of a Byzantine mansion, while the left fork passes the massively fortified **Náfplio Gate** and the vast, multistorey complex of the **Despots' Palace**. At the **Monemvasiá Gate**, linking the upper and lower towns, turn right for the **Pandánassa convent**, which is perhaps the finest that survives in the town. Further down on this side of the lower town make sure you see the diminutive **Perívleptos monastery**, whose single-domed church, partly carved out of the rock, contains Mystra's most complete cycle of frescoes. The **Mitrópolis**, or cathedral, immediately beyond the gateway, ranks as the oldest of Mystra's churches, built from 1270 onward.

SPÁRTI

SPÁRTI (ancient Sparta, though there's little left to see) is a good alternative base to Mystra, with cheaper accommodation. Spárti has everything you would expect from a town of its size, including vibrant bars and cafés. If you want to see Mystra without sacrificing an evening's worth of entertainment, then make it a day-trip from Spárti.

Arrival

Bus The KTEL bus station is at the far eastern end of Lykoúrgou, a 10min walk from the centre. Buses for Mystra leave from here.

Internet Ladas Lykoúrgou 130 ⓣ2731 083 016; €1.50/hr.

Accommodation

Apollon Thermopýlon 84 ⓣ27310 22491. This friendly hotel has plenty of clean and comfortable en-suite rooms. Doubles €55.

Castle View Néos Mystrás ⓣ27310 83303, ⓦwww.castleview.gr. Shady and quiet, this campsite is within walking distance of the village. April–Oct. €7/person, plus €4/tent.

Hotel Cecil Paleológou 125 ⓣ27310 24980. A warm welcome awaits at this centrally located small hotel, with clean en-suite rooms equipped with a/c and TV. Doubles €55.

Paleologio Mystras 2.5km from Spárti, halfway to Néos Mystrás ⓣ27310 22724. Well-run campsite with good facilities. Buses to Néos Mystrás stop at the entrance. Open all year. €6.50/person, plus €3.50/tent.

Eating and drinking

Diethnes Paleológou 105. The garden here is an oasis of calm, especially atmospheric in the evenings. Hearty Greek favourites are dished up to the sound of birdsong. Meal around €12–15.

Ministry Music Hall Paleológou 84. One of the most popular bars in town, with tables spilling onto the pavement and a sophisticated, cocktail-quaffing crowd.

Moving on

Bus Areópoli (2 daily; 2hr); Athens (10 daily; 4hr); Kalamáta (2 daily; 2hr 30min); Kórinthos (8 daily; 2hr); Monemvasiá (3 daily; 2hr 30min); Yíthio (5 daily; 1hr).

MONEMVASIÁ

Set impregnably on a great eruption of rock connected to the mainland by a causeway, the Byzantine seaport of **MONEMVASIÁ** is a place of grand, haunted atmosphere. At the start of the thirteenth century it was the Byzantines' sole possession in the Morea, eventually being taken by the Franks in 1249 after three years of siege. Regained by the Byzantines as part of the ransom for the captured Guillaume de Villehardouin, it served as the chief commercial port of the Despotate of the Morea. At its peak in the Byzantine era, Monemvasiá had a population of almost sixty thousand.

What to see and do

A causeway connects mainland **Yéfira** to Monemvasiá. The twenty-minute walk provides some wonderful views, but there is also a free shuttle bus in season. The **Lower Town** once sheltered forty churches and over 800 homes, though today a single main street harbours most of the restored houses, plus cafés, tavernas and a scattering of shops. The foremost monument is the **Mitrópolis**, the cathedral built by Emperor Andronikos II Komnenos in 1293, and the largest medieval church in southern Greece. Across the square, the tenth-century domed church of **Áyios Pétros** was transformed by the Ottomans into a mosque and is now a small **museum** of local finds (Tues–Sun 8am–7.30pm, Wed till 11pm; free). Towards the sea is a third church, the **Khrysafítissa**, with its bell hanging from an old acacia tree in the courtyard. The climb to the **Upper Town** is highly worthwhile, not least for the solitude. Its fortifications, like those of the lower town, are substantially intact; within, the site is a ruin, though infinitely larger than you could imagine from below.

Arrival and information

Bus Buses arrive in the village of Yéfira on the mainland, where most accommodation is located. The bus stop is outside Malvasia Travel.

Information There is no tourist office, but Malvasia Travel (see above) is helpful. It also sells bus tickets.

Accommodation

Akrogiali Yéfira ⓣ2732 061 360. The best budget option: nine spotless rooms in the centre of town. Doubles €45.

TREAT YOURSELF

If Monemvasiá has cast its enchanting spell over you, then splash out to stay on the rock itself. **Malvasia** (ⓣ2732 063 007/8, ⓦwww.malvasia-hotel.gr; €85) is a peaceful hotel full of charm, retaining many traditional features, and the views are breathtaking.

Dina's House Kastro ⓣ27320 -61311, ⓦgr.monemvasia-online.com/dina. Self-contained apartments with all mod cons inside a part of the old castle. Top marks for atmosphere. €55–65 but haggle and you could get them cheaper.

Eating

Matoula Monemvasiá. This long-running family restaurant has plenty of fresh fish on offer, and a shady terrace on which to enjoy the food and the views. Mains €8–12.

To Kanoni Monemvasiá. A small and friendly place inside the castle with split-level seating, offering a variety of vistas. Also open for breakfast. Mains €7–10.

Moving on

Bus Athens (4–6 daily; 5hr); Kórinthos (3 daily; 4hr 30min); Spárti (5–6 daily; 1hr 30min); Trípoli (3 daily; 2hr 30min).

YÍTHIO

YÍTHIO, Sparta's ancient port, is the gateway to the dramatic Máni peninsula and one of the south's most attractive seaside towns. Its low-key harbour, with occasional ferries, has a graceful nineteenth-century waterside, while out to sea, tethered by a long narrow causeway, is the islet of **Marathoníssi** (ancient Kranae), where Paris and Helen of Troy spent their first night after her abduction from Sparta.

Arrival

Bus Buses from Athens and Spárti drop you close to the centre of town, at the bus station located on Vassiléos Pávlou.

Accommodation

Meltemi On the Yíthio–Areópoli road ⓣ27330 23260, ⓦwww.campingmeltemi.gr. Good facilities including free wi-fi. April–Oct. €6/person, plus €5/tent, bungalow rent (€15/person).

Rooms Matina Vassiléos Pávlou 19 ⓣ27330 22518. Little English is spoken but the staff are welcoming. Rooms are spacious and airy, and there's a small terrace too. Doubles €50.

Saga Pension Tzanetáki ⓣ27330 23220, ⓦwww.sagapension.gr. Spacious and comfortable rooms, most with balconies towards the sea. There's also a popular restaurant downstairs. Doubles €50.

Eating

Barba Sideris Ermou & Xanthaki. A taverna right by the sea, specializing in skewered and grilled meat dishes. Pig out for €15–20.

To Korali Plateia Yíthiou. This is the place to do as the locals do – order some *oúzo* and watch the world go by from the corner of the square. Mains €10–15.

Moving on

Bus to: Areópoli (4 daily; 30min); Athens (4–6 daily; 5hr); Kórinthos (6 daily; 2hr 45min); Spárti (6 daily; 50min); Trípoli (3 daily; 2hr 30min).

THE MÁNI PENINSULA

The southernmost peninsula of Greece, the **Máni peninsula**, stretches from Yíthio in the east and Kalamáta in the west down to Cape Ténaro, mythical entrance to the underworld. It's a wild and arid landscape with an idiosyncratic culture and history: nowhere else in Greece seems so close to its medieval past. There are numerous opportunities for outdoor activities too. The quickest way into it is to take a bus from Yíthio to **AREÓPOLI**, gateway to the so-called Inner Máni. For onward travel to the Outer Máni, a change at Oítylo is involved. Check ⓦwww.messinianmani.gr.

Arrival

Bus Buses from Yíthio drop you in the centre of town, by the main square. The bus station is behind the small church – look for the KTEL sign outside.

Accommodation

Hotel Kouris Main Square ⓣ27330 51340. All rooms are en suite and have balconies, and it's the cheapest option in town. Doubles €40–50.

Tsimova Behind the Church of Taxiárhes ⓣ27330 51301. A renovated tower-house in the old lower town, full of character and charm. Doubles €50.

Moving on

Bus Oítylo (3 daily; 20min); Yíthio (4 daily; 30min).

Outer Máni

Various attractions lie to the north of Areópoli, along the eighty-kilometre road to Kalamáta, which has views as dramatic and beautiful as any in Greece. There are numerous cobbled paths for hiking and a series of **small beaches**, beginning at **NÉO ÍTILO** with its fine sandy beach, and extending more or less through to Kardhamýli. The fishing village of **ÁYIOS NIKÓLAOS**, has the best fish tavernas and rooms. **STOÚPA**, with possibly the best beach, is now geared towards British tourism, with several small hotels, two **campsites**, supermarkets and tavernas. **KARDHAMÝLI**, 8km north, remains a beautiful place despite its commercialization and busy road, with a long pebbly beach and the restored tower-house quarter of **ANO KARDHAMÝLI**.

Arrival

Bus Buses stop in Kardhamýli next to the main square. There is no KTEL office as such, but Wunder Travel (ⓣ27210 73141) has bus timetables.

Accommodation

Iphigenia Rooms Kardhamýli ⓣ27210 73648. A wonderful base for exploring the area. Apartments with small kitchenettes and balconies. €50–70 depending on season.

Lela's Kardhamýli ⓣ27210 73541, or mobile ⓣ6977 716 017 in winter. Tucked away (look for signs from the main road), these rooms occupy prime position beside the sea. There's also a good taverna (see opposite). Doubles €50.

Eating and drinking

Aman Café Kardhamýli. Next to *Lela's*, this lively bar, open all day, is the perfect place to watch the sunset from the leafy terrace. Cocktails €7.50.

Lela's Kardhamýli. With an ever-changing menu, *Lela's* is ideal for a delicious, home-cooked meal. Go early to grab a table with the best views. Mains €8.

Moving on

Bus Kalamáta (4 daily; 1hr).

OLYMPIA

The historic resonance of **OLYMPIA**, which for over a millennium hosted the Panhellenic Games, is rivalled only by Delphi or Mycenae. Its site, too, ranks with this company, for although the ruins are confusing, the setting is as perfect as could be imagined: a luxuriant valley of wild olive and plane trees beside the twin rivers of Alfiós and Kladheós, overlooked by the pine-covered Mount Kronion.

What to see and do

The entrance to the **ancient site** (May–Oct daily 8am–7pm; Nov–April Mon–Fri 8am–5pm, Sat & Sun 8.30am–3pm; €6, or €9 with museum) leads along the west side of the sacred precinct wall, past a group of public and official buildings. Here the fifth-century BC sculptor Pheidias was responsible for creating the great gold-and-ivory cult statue in the focus of the precinct, the great Doric **Temple of Zeus.** The smaller **Temple of Hera**, behind, was the first built here; prior to its completion in the seventh century BC, the sanctuary had only open-air altars. Rebuilt in the Doric style in the sixth century BC, it's the most complete structure on the site. However, it's the 177-metre track of the **Stadium** itself that makes sense of Olympia: the start and finish lines are still there, as are the judges' thrones in the middle and seating banked to each side, which once accommodated up to thirty thousand spectators. Finally, in the **archeological museum** (May–Oct Mon 12.30–7.30pm, Tues–Sun 8am–7.30pm; Nov–April Mon 10.30am–5pm, Tues–Sun 8.30am–4/5pm; €6, or €9 with site), the centrepiece is the statuary from the Temple of Zeus, displayed in the vast main hall. Most famous of the individual sculptures is the **Hermes of Praxiteles**, dating from the fourth century BC; one of the best preserved of all classical sculptures, it retains traces of its original paint.

Arrival and information

Train and bus Most people arrive at Olympia via Pýrgos, which has frequent buses and trains to the site. The train station is close to the town's centre. The bus stop is at one end of Praxitéles Kondhýli.

Tourist office On Praxitéles Kondhýli (daily June–Sept 8am–3pm; ☎26240 22262).

Accommodation

Camping Diana ☎26240 22314. The closest campsite, 1km from the site, has a pool and good facilities. March–Dec. €7/person, plus €5/tent.

Youth Hostel Praxitéles Kondhýli 18 ☎26240 22580. This dingy hostel is in the centre of town but this is its only selling point. There's hot water only

ONWARD TRAVEL

Igoumenítsa is Greece's third passenger port after Pireás and Pátra, with almost hourly ferries to Corfu; several daily to and from Italy (Ancona, Bari, Brindisi and Venice) make it a likely arrival point. The tourist office is next to the customs house on the old quay (daily 8am–2pm; ☎26650 22227), while the bus station sits two blocks back from here in the town centre, on Kyprou. There are frequent bus and train services **from Thessaloníki** on to Bulgaria, Romania or Turkey, though you should get any necessary visas in Athens.

in the mornings and evenings, and an 11pm curfew. Dorms €10.

Eating

Symposio Karamanli. This taverna is located away from the neon lights of the main drag, and this is reflected in the prices. Good food, welcoming atmosphere. Grills €6–8.

Moving on

Bus Pýrgos (hourly; 45min); Trípoli (1–3 daily; 3hr 30min).

The centre and north

Central and northern Greece has a multifaceted character, encompassing both ancient and modern, from the mythical home of the gods on **Mount Olympus** to the urban splendour of **Thessaloníki**, and a plethora of landscapes. The highlights lie at the fringes: site of the ancient oracle **Delphi**, and further northwest at the otherworldly rock-monasteries of **Metéora**. Access to these monasteries is through **Kalambáka**, beyond which the **Katára pass** over the Píndhos mountains provides a stunning backdrop. En route lies **Métsovo**, perhaps the easiest location for a taste of mountain life, though blatantly commercialized. Nearby **Ioánnina**, once the stronghold of the notorious Ali Pasha, still retains a lot of character. To the south, closer to Athens, is the monastery of **Ósios Loukás**, one of Greece's finest Byzantine buildings and worth a detour en route to Delphi.

DELPHI

With its position on a high terrace overlooking a great gorge, in turn dwarfed by the ominous crags of Parnassós, it's easy to see why the ancients believed the extraordinary site of **DELPHI** to be the centre of the Earth. But what confirmed this status was the discovery of a chasm that exuded strange vapours and reduced all comers to frenzied, incoherent and obviously prophetic mutterings. For over a thousand years a steady stream of pilgrims toiled their way up the dangerous mountain paths to seek divine direction, until the oracle eventually expired with the demise of paganism in the fourth century AD.

What to see and do

You enter the **Sacred Precinct of Apollo** (daily: summer 8am–7pm; winter 8.30am–3pm; €6, or €9 with museum) by way of a small agora, enclosed by ruins of Roman porticoes and shops selling votive offerings. The paved **Sacred Way** begins after a few stairs, zigzagging uphill between the foundations of memorials and treasuries to the **Temple of Apollo**. The theatre and stadium used for the main events of the Pythian games are on terraces above the temple. The **theatre**, built in the fourth century BC, was closely connected with Dionysus, god of drama and wine. A steep path leads up through pine groves to the stadium, which was banked with stone seats in Roman times.

The **museum** (Tues–Sun 8.30am–3pm) contains a collection of ancient sculpture matched only by finds on the Acropolis in Athens; the most famous exhibit is *The Charioteer*, one of the few surviving bronzes of the fifth century BC. Following the road east of the sanctuary towards Aráhova, you reach a sharp bend. To the left, the celebrated **Castalian spring** still flows from a cleft in the cliffs, where visitors to Delphi were obliged to purify themselves. Across and below the road from the spring is the **Marmaria** or Sanctuary of Athena Pronoia (same hours as main site; free), the "Guardian of the Temple". The precinct's most conspicuous building is the **Tholos**, a fourth-century BC rotunda whose purpose remains a mystery. Above the Marmaria, a **gymnasium** also dates from the fourth century BC, though it was later enlarged by the Romans.

Arrival and information

Delphi is 150km northwest of Athens – an easy enough day-trip by bus.

Bus The small bus station is on Pávlou & Fridheríkis, at the opposite end of the town to the archeological site.

Tourist office Above the town hall at Pávlou & Fredheríkis 12 (Mon–Sat 8am–3pm; ⓣ 22650 82900).

Accommodation

Apollon Camping 1.5km west towards Ámfissa ⓣ 22650 82750, ⓦ www.apolloncamping.gr. A good camping option, and the closest to Delphi. Open all year. €7/8/person, plus €3.50/4/tent.

Athina Pávlou & Fredheríkis 55 ⓣ 22650 82239. Most rooms at this guesthouse face the valley for spectacular views, and all have fans. Breakfast included. April–Oct. Doubles €60–70.

Sibylla Pávlou & Fredheríkis 9 ⓣ 22650 82335, ⓦ www.sibylla-hotel.gr. The rooms are spotless and comfortable and the staff are helpful. Close to the site. Doubles €45.

Eating

I Skala On the stair-street opposite the *Sibylla*. A small taverna serving a good selection of set menus (€8–10).

Taverna Vakchos Apóllonos 31 ⓦ www.vakchos.com. This taverna combines a wonderful setting and mouthwatering food. The menu includes plenty of home-made fare, including wine and baklava. Mains €6–8.

Moving on

Bus Athens (6 daily; 3hr); Pátra (1 daily; 3hr); Thessaloníki (2 daily; 5hr).

KALAMBÁKA AND METÉORA

Few places are more exciting to arrive at than **KALAMBÁKA** and the neighbouring village of **Kastráki**. Your eye is immediately drawn to the weird grey cylinders of rock overhead – these are the outlying monoliths of the extraordinary valley of **Metéora**. The earliest religious communities in the valley emerged during the late tenth century, when hermits made their homes in the caves that score many of the rocks. In 1336 they were joined by two monks from Mount Áthos, one of whom established the first monastery here.

> **ÓSIOS LOUKÁS**
>
> The UNESCO site of the monastery of **Ósios Loukás** may be remote, but its Byzantine mosaics – the finest in the country – are definitely worth seeking out. From Delphi, take the bus to Livadhiá and then on to Dhistomo, from where you can take a taxi the remaining 8km. Free.

What to see and do

Today, put firmly on the map by films such as the James Bond classic *For Your Eyes Only*, the four most visited monasteries are essentially museums. Only two others, Ayías Triádhos and Ayíou Stefánou, continue to function with a primarily religious purpose. Each monastery levies an **admission charge** of €2 and operates a strict **dress code**: skirts for women (supplied at the monasteries), long trousers for men and covered arms for both sexes.

Beyond the monastery of **Ayíou Stefánou**, firmly planted on a massive pedestal, stretches a chaos of spikes, cones and stubbier, rounded cliffs. Visiting the monasteries demands a full day, which means staying two nights nearby.

Ayíou Nikoláou Anápavsa and Varlaám

From Kastráki, the fourteenth-century **Ayíou Nikoláou Anápavsa** (summer only, daily 9am–6pm) is reached first.

Some 250m past the car park and stairs to Ayíou Nikoláou, a clear path leads up a ravine between assorted monoliths; soon, at a fork, you've the option of bearing left (for Megálou Meteórou; see below) or right to **Varlaám** (9am–1pm & 3–6pm, closed Thurs; Nov–April to 5pm also closed Fri), which is one of the oldest and most beautiful monasteries in the valley.

Megálou Meteórou and Roussánou

From the fork below Varlaám the path also takes you northwest to **Megálou Meteórou** (same times as Varlaám; closed Tues; Nov–April also closed Wed), the grandest of the monasteries and also the highest. Next you follow trails until you reach the signed access path for the tiny, compact convent of **Roussánou** (same times as Varlaám, closed Wed).

Ayías Triádhos and Ayíou Stefánou

It's less than a half-hour from Roussánou to the vividly frescoed **Ayías Triádhos** (same times as Varlaám; Nov–April closed Thurs), approached up 130 steps carved through a tunnel in the rock. **Ayíou Stefánou** (same times as Varlaám, closed Mon), the last of the monasteries, lies a further fifteen minutes' walk east of Ayías Triádhos; bombed in World War II, it's the one to omit if you've run out of time.

Arrival and information

Train The train station is 100m south of the bus station in Kalambáka.

Bus Buses arrive at the bus station in Kalambáka on Ikonomou. All long-distance buses from Thessaloníki or the south involve a change at Tríkala (total: 2hr 45min). To get to Kastráki, 1km away, you can either walk for 20min along the signposted road, or take one of the hourly buses (in season only) from Platía Dhimarhíou, at the fountain, two of which continue to Metéora (9am & 1.30pm).

Tourist office Next to the Kalambáka bus stop.

Internet All Time Café, on the Metéora road, Kastráki (daily 8pm–3am).

Accommodation

Hotel Meteora Ploutárhou 13 ⓣ24320 22367. The pick of the Kalambáka hotels. En-suite rooms, delicious breakfasts and great value for the high standard. Doubles €40.

Hotel Tsikeli Kastráki ⓣ24320 22438, ⓦwww.tsikelihotel.gr. A wonderful, relaxing guesthouse, with simple rooms and stunning views. Free wi-fi. Breakfast is served in the lush garden. Doubles €45.

Plakias Not far from the square, Kastráki ⓣ24320 22504, ⓦwww.meteora-plakias.gr. A homely feel accompanies these clean and crisp en-suite rooms, although the ground-floor rooms sacrifice their views of Metéora. Doubles €25.

Vrachos ⓣ24320 22293, ⓦwww.campingkastraki.gr. A well-equipped campsite with a large swimming pool and caravans to rent. Also offers rock-climbing lessons and bike rental. €6/person, plus €4/tent.

Eating

Bakaliarákia Below the square and behind the church in Kastráki, a traditional taverna, with cheap fried cod and house wine. Mains €5–7.

Parádhissos Kastráki. This taverna offers a spacious terrace with beautiful views and a variety of barbecued specialities. Mains €5–8.

Moving on

Train Athens (direct 2 daily; 5hr); easier to go to Larissa (10/11 daily; 3hr 30min) and onwards to Kalambáka (10 daily; 1hr 15min).

Bus Ioánnina (2–3 daily; 3hr); Métsovo (3 daily; 1hr 30min); Tríkala (hourly; 30min).

IOÁNNINA

The fortifications of **IOÁNNINA**'s old town, former capital of the Albanian Muslim chieftain Ali Pasha, are punctuated by towers and minarets. From this base Ali, "the Lion of Ioánnina", prised from the Ottoman Empire a fiefdom encompassing much of western Greece. Disappointingly, most of the city is modern and undistinguished; however, the fortifications of Ali's citadel, the **Kástro**, survive more or less intact. Apart from this, the most enjoyable quarter is the old **bazaar** area, outside the citadel's main gate.

On the far side of the lake from Ioánnina, the island of **Nissí** is served by water-buses (every 30min; €1.70) from the quay northwest of the Froúrio. Its village, founded during the sixteenth century, is flanked by several beautiful, diminutive monasteries, with the best thirteenth-century frescoes in **Filanthropinón**.

Arrival and information

Bus The main bus station is at Zozimádhon 4, serving most points north and west; a smaller terminal at Bizaníou 19 connects villages south and east.
Tourist office Dhodhónis 39 ⓣ26510 41868, 48442 or 48866 (Mon–Fri 8am–2.30pm, also open eves and Sat morn in summer), south of the centre; can provide information on the whole Epirus region.
Internet The Web at Pyrsinélla 21 ⓣ26510 26813 (24hr; €2.50/hr).

Accommodation

Filyra Andhroníkou Paleológou 18 ⓣ2651 0 83 560, ⓦhotelfilyra.gr. Four modern, bright studios with individual touches located in the historic Kástro. Small kitchenettes are ideal for self-catering. €65.
Limnopoula Kanari 10 ⓣ26510 25265. This pleasant lakeshore campsite is 2km out of town on the Pérama/airport road. April–Oct. €9/person, plus €2/tent.

Eating

Fysa Roufa Georgiou Avéroff 55. Open 24 hours a day, this popular restaurant serves oven-baked dishes. Mains €5–8.
To Souvlaki tou Vounou Amfithea. Ten minutes from the centre by taxi, this taverna/grill is in a fantastic location by the lake. Mains €10–12. Open daily till 2am.

Moving on

Bus Athens (9–10 daily; 7hr); Igoumenítsa (9 daily; 2hr 30min); Métsovo (4 daily; 1hr 30min); Pátra (3 daily; 3hr 30min); Thessaloníki (4–6 daily; 3hr).

THESSALONÍKI

Second city of Greece, **THESSALONÍKI** feels more Central European and modern than Athens. With a student population of 120,000, the city's **nightlife** is buzzing, with many bars and clubs concentrated either in the regenerated warehouse area of Ladhádhika by the port or further up in Valaoritou Street. During the Byzantine era, it was the second city after Constantinople, reaching a cultural "Golden Age" until the Ottoman conquest in 1430. As recently as the 1920s, the city's population was as mixed as any in the Balkans: besides the Greeks there were Turks, who had been in occupation for close on five centuries, Slavs, Albanians, and the largest European **Jewish** community in the Mediterranean – 80,000 at its peak.

What to see and do

Today, Thessaloníki boasts many excellent sights – including a superb Archeological Museum and some lovely frescoed Byzantine churches – but the most obvious pleasures of Greece's second city are in its street-life: its myriad bars, first-rate restaurants and pumping clubs.

The Archeological Museum

The renovated **Archeological Museum** (Tues–Sun 8am–3pm; May–Sept to 8pm; €6) is a few paces from the White Tower. The museum's highlights are the "Macedonian gold" rooms on the ground floor, containing precious finds from various tombs in the area. There are startling amounts of gold and silver – masks, crowns, necklaces, earrings, bracelets – all of extraordinary craftsmanship.

The Museum of Byzantine Culture and White Tower

The well-curated **Museum of Byzantine Culture** (same hours as the Archeological Museum; €4), just east of the archeological museum, is also worth a look for its finely preserved tombs, splendid mosaics, icons and jewellery. Close

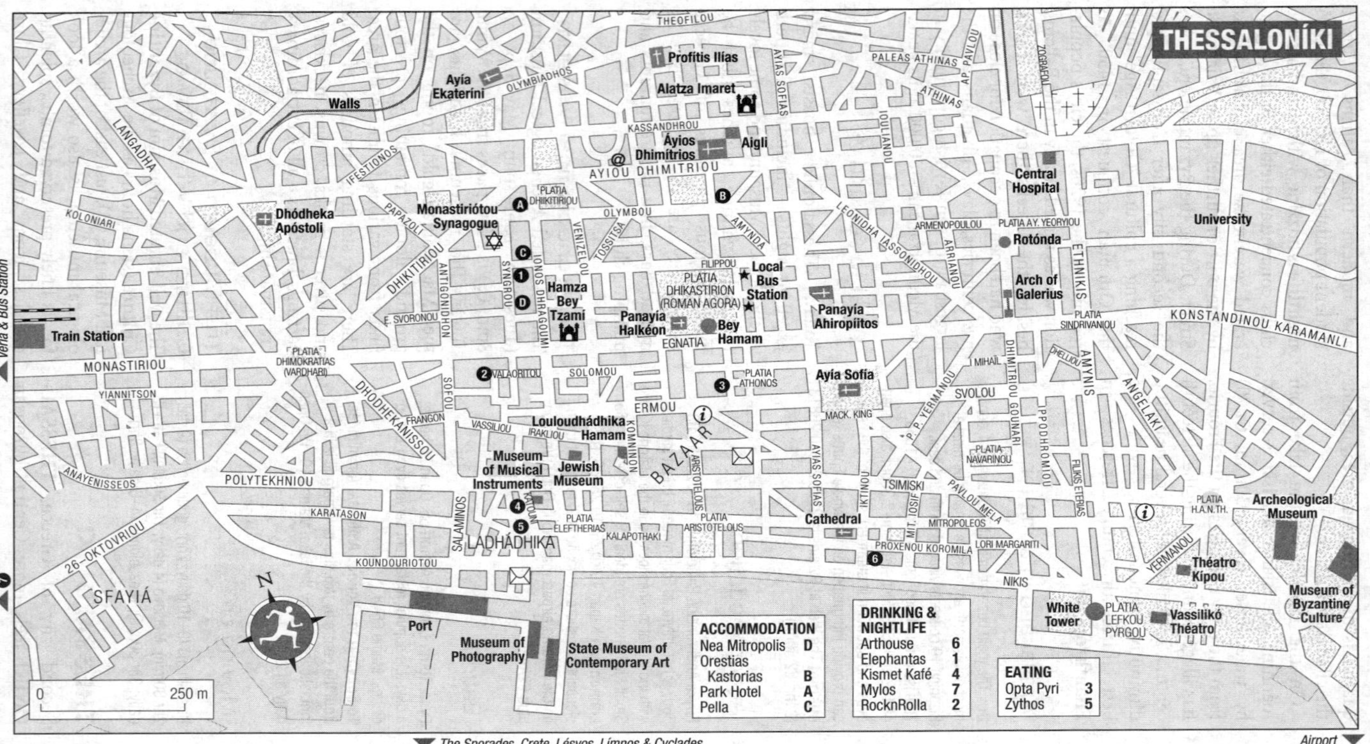
THESSALONÍKI
ACCOMMODATION
Nea Mitropolis D
Orestias Kastorias B
Park Hotel A
Pella C
DRINKING & NIGHTLIFE
Arthouse 6
Elephantas 1
Kismet Kafé 4
Mylos 7
RocknRolla 2
EATING
Opta Pyri 3
Zythos 5
Profítis Ilías
Ayía Ekateríni
Walls
Alatza Imaret
Áyios Dhimítrios
Aigli
Central Hospital
University
Dhódheka Apóstoli
Monastiriótou Synagogue
Rotónda
Arch of Galerius
Local Bus Station
Hamza Bey Tzami
Panayía Halkéon
Bey Hamam
Panayía Ahiropiítos
Train Station
Ayía Sofía
Louloudhádhika Hamam
Museum of Musical Instruments
Jewish Museum
Cathedral
LADHÁDHIKA
BAZAAR
Archeological Museum
Théatro Kípou
Museum of Byzantine Culture
White Tower
Vassilikó Théatro
Port
Museum of Photography
State Museum of Contemporary Art
SFAYIÁ
0 250 m
Véria & Bus Station
The Sporades, Crete, Lésvos, Límnos & Cyclades
Airport
THEOFILOU
OLYMBIADHOS
PALEAS ATHINAS
AP. PAVLOU
ATHINAS
ZOGRAFOU
AYIAS SOFIAS
KASSANDHROU
IOULIANDU
AYIOU DHIMITRIOU
LANGADHA
IFESTIONOS
KOLONIARI
PAPAZOLI
OLYMBOU
AMYNDA
LEONIDHA IASSONIDHOU
ARMENOPOULOU
PLATIA AY. YEORYIOU
ETHNIKIS
KONSTANDINOU KARAMANLI
DHIKITIRIOU
ANTIGONIDHON
SYNGROU
IONOS DHRAGOUMI
VENIZELOU
TOSSITSA
FILIPPOU
PLATIA DHIKASTIRION (ROMAN AGORA)
EGNATIA
ARRIANOU
PLATIA SINDRIVANIOU
DHELLIOU
AMYNIS
ANGELAKI
MONASTIRIOU
YIANNITSON
PLATIA DHIMOKRATIAS (VARDHARI)
E. SVORONOU
VALAORITOU
SOLOMOU
SOFOU
PLATIA ATHONOS
ERMOU
MACK. KING
I. MIHAIL
DHIMITRIOU GOUNARI
SVOLOU
P. P. YERMANOU
IPPODHROMIOU
PLATIA NAVARINOU
FILIKIS ETERIAS
DHODHEKANISSOU
FRANGON
VASSILIOU
IRAKLIOU
KOMNINON
ARISTOTELOUS
AYIAS SOFIAS
IKTINOU
TSIMISKI
PAVLOU MELA
ANAYENISSEOS
POLYTEKHNIOU
KARATASON
SALAMINOS
KATOUNI
PLATIA ELEFTHERIAS
KALAPOTHAKI
PLATIA ARISTOTELOUS
MIT. IOSIF
MITROPOLEOS
PROXENOU KOROMILA
LORI MARGARITI
PLATIA H.A.N.TH.
YERMANOU
NIKIS
PLATIA LEFKOU PYRGOU
26-OKTOVRIOU
KOUNDOURIOTOU

by, on the waterfront, Thessaloniki's enduring landmark, the **White Tower** (Tues–Sun 8.30am–3pm; €3), the last surviving bastion of the city's medieval walls, tells the story of the city through a high-tech multimedia exhibit. Go to the top for an unforgettable view of the city.

Churches

Among the city's many **churches**, the unmissable ones are Áyios Geórgios, originally a Roman rotunda built in 306 AD, decorated with golden mosaics; Áyios Dhimítrios (built originally in 413 AD though the current building dates from 1948) with several seventh-century mosaics and the relics of the saint; the eighth-century Ayía Sofía, with superb mosaics of the Ascension and the Virgin Enthroned; and Panayía Acheiropíitos (fifth-century AD) the largest Palaeochristian church in the Balkans.

The Photography and Contemporary Art museums

If, after all the icons and alabaster you feel like something a little more contemporary, the excellent portside **Museum of Photography** (Tues–Sun 11am–7pm, Fri & Sat to 9pm; €2) is worth a few hours' exploration. In 2012 and 2014 it will be hosting the international Photo Biennale with talks and presentations in various languages.

Arrival and information

Air From the airport, 16km out at Mikrá, buses #78 (every 15–20min; 5.30am–11pm) and #78N (every 30min; 11pm–5.30am) run to the train station and KTEL terminal. Taxi €20.
Train The train station at Monastiriou 28 on the west side of town is a short walk from the central grid of streets and the waterfront.
Bus Buses use a KTEL terminal 3km southwest of the centre; city buses #8 & #31 go there from Egnatía St (€0.90). Taxi from centre €6.
Ferry The port is at the southern edge of the city, close to Ladhádhika.
Tourist office Tsimiskí 136 (Mon–Sat 9am–9pm & Sun 9am–3pm; ⓣ2310 221 100) and also at Platía Aristotelous 8 ⓣ2310 222 935, same hours.

Accommodation

Nea Mitropolis Syngroú 22 ⓣ2310 530 363, ⓦwww.neametropolis.gr. The drab paint job doesn't do it many favours but the sense of faded grandeur has a certain charm. Not sure about the surly staff though. Doubles €45–55.
Orestias Kastorias Agnóstou Stratiótou 14 ⓣ2310 276 517, ⓦwww.okhotel.gr. Housed in a recently renovated Neoclassical building, the simple rooms have balconies with views towards the Roman Forum or Áyios Dhimítrios. Doubles €50.
Park Hotel Ionos Dragoumi 81 ⓣ2310 524 121, ⓦwww.parkhotel.com.gr. Clean, central and spacious, this is an old business hotel with friendly and efficient staff. Free wi-fi, smoking floors, breakfast included. Doubles €45.
Pella Íonos Dhragoúmi 63 ⓣ2310 524 221. A friendly hotel with small but well-equipped, spotless rooms. Free wi-fi. Doubles €50.

Eating

You can eat well and cheaply in the many *Goody's* takeaways scattered around the city. If you fancy sitting down try the *ouzerís* around Platía Áthonos.
Opta Pyri Platía Áthonos. This two-floor establishment packs them in every night. Live music every night after 8pm. *Souvláki* with all trimmings €7.
Zythos Platía Katoúni 5. A hip bar-restaurant, with dozens of well-kept foreign beers and an innovative menu. Mains €6–8. Daily noon–2am.

Drinking and nightlife

Arthouse Vogatsikou 4. An excellent, small club hosting the coolest nights in town and playing everything from reggae to techno with aplomb. Top international DJs occasionally pass through. Don't go before 11pm.
Elephantas Corner of Syngroú and Filíppou 2. Relaxed, alternative bar with chilled sounds and quality cocktails. A laidback place to kick off an evening.
Kismet Kafé Katoúni 11. Intimate and cosy, with hard DJ sounds inside, and candlelit tables, perfect for a relaxed drink outside.
Mylos Andhréou Yeoryíou 56. The main indoor music venue is the multidisciplinary complex *Mylos*, out in an old flourmill, where you'll find more bars, a summer cinema and exhibition galleries.
RocknRolla Valaoritou 31. Dead in the middle of the hip Valaoritou area and flanked by many more bars, this is the one with the most innovative sounds.

Directory

Consulates Canada, Tsimiskí 17 ⓣ2310 256 350; UK, Aristotélous 21 ⓣ2310 278 006; US, Tsimiskí 43 ⓣ2310 242 907/8. If you need a visa for onward Balkan travel, it's best to get it in Athens.
Hospital Yenikó Kendrikó, Ethnikís Amýnis 41 ⓣ2313 308 100.
Internet IQ Net, Ágiou Dhimítriou corner Pasteur St; Vittas, Plateia Navarinou 5.
Post office Vasileos Irakliou 38; Mon–Fri, 7.30am–8pm Sat, 7am–2pm, Sun 9am–1.30pm.

Moving on

Train Alexandroupolis (2 daily; 6hr); Athens (10 daily; 5–6hr); Kateríni (13 daily; 40min–1hr); Larisa (8 daily; 2hr); Veria-Edessa (12 daily 1–2hr).
Bus Athens (11/day; 7hr); Ioánnina (5 daily; 3hr); İstanbul (3 daily; 12hr); Kalambáka (4 daily; 3hr); Korytsa (3 daily; 4hr); Litóhoro (14 daily; 1hr 5min); Larisa (5 daily 2hr); Sofia (every Fri 1.30pm); Tríkala (5 daily; 3hr); Véria (hourly; 1hr 15min); Vólos (9 daily; 2hr).
Note that there are numerous private companies offering bus journeys to various Balkan destinations around the train station.
Ferry Híos (1–4 weekly; 18–20hr); Iráklion (daily; 30–33hr); Kós (1 weekly; 24hr); Mýkonos (1–4 weekly); Mytilini 1–2 weekly; 14hr); Náxos (1 weekly; 24hr); Páros (1 weekly; 22hr); Santoríni (1–4 weekly; 24hr); Skópelos (4 weekly; 7–9hr).

HALKIDHIKÍ

Many travellers insist that no other place in Greece can boast beaches like those of Halkidhikí and with 550km of coastline over its three peninsulas of Kassándhra, Sithonía and Mount Athos, they may well be right. Although monastic Mount Athos is out of bounds to women – a ban that extends to all female animals such as chickens and cows – the other two "feet" of Halkidhikí certainly make up for it. Kassándhra, being closer to Thessaloníki, is the more developed while Sithonía, further out, is the quieter location.

Although for quite some time Halkidhikí has been the exclusive domain of package tourists, recent initiatives by local tour operators have developed a range of backpacker-oriented activities including mountain biking, watersports, hiking and horseriding (ⓦwww.gohalkidiki.com).

Several archeological sites aside – including Stáyira, the birthplace of Aristotle – the most interesting cultural event in Halkidhikí is the Sani Festival in the town of Sáni (July–Aug; ⓦwww.sanifestival.gr), which brings together world-class rock and jazz acts, as well as Greek superstars.

Accommodation

Camping Blue Dream Sáni ⓣ23750 41449, ⓦwww.campingbluedream.gr. High-quality campsite dead on the beach with restaurant and lively beach bar; conveniently situated for the Sani Festival. May–Sept €8/person, plus €7/tent.
Camping Valti Sykiá ⓣ23750 41449, ⓦwww.camping-valti.com. Shaded leafy family campsite on a superb beach on the eastern side of Sithonía. May–Oct €5/person, plus €4/tent.

VERGÍNA (ANCIENT AEGAE)

In 1977, archeologists discovered the burial sanctuary of the ancient Macedonian dynasty, including Alexander the Great's father and son, at the village of **VERGÍNA**. The four **Royal Tombs** (mid-May to Oct Tues–Sun 8am–7.30pm; winter to 3pm; €8) constitute the focus of an unmissable underground museum. It features delicate gold and silver funerary artefacts, the facades of the tombs, the kings' armours, frescoes (uniquely, with perspective) and the ashes of the deceased royals in ornate ossuaries. It's easy to make this a day-trip from Thessaloníki: hourly buses run to Véria (€9 return), from where eleven onward buses per day cover the final 20 minutes to modern Vergína village (€3.20 return, taxi €15 one-way).

MOUNT OLYMPUS

Highest, most magical and most dramatic of all Greek mountains, **Mount**

Olympus – the mythical seat of the gods – rears straight up nearly 3000m from the shores of the Thermaïkos Gulf. Dense forests cover its lower slopes and its wild flowers are gorgeous. If you're well equipped, no special expertise is necessary to reach the top between mid-June and October, though it's a long hard pull, and its weather is notoriously fickle. You can buy a proper **map** of the range in Athens, Thessaloníki or Litóhoro.

Litóhoro

The usual approach to Mount Olympus is via **LITÓHORO** on the eastern slopes, a pleasant village in a magnificent mountain setting. The easiest way to reach the village is to travel by bus from Salonika from where hourly buses make the 1hr 15min journey. Best-value **accommodation** is the hotel *Enipeas*, with balconied rooms and a central location (Ⓣ23520 84328; €50) or further out by the sea at Gritsa, 5km from Litóhoro, the *Seaside Hostel* (Ⓣ23520 61406; Ⓦwww.summitzero.gr; €15). The best **restaurants** are *To Pazari*, uphill from the main square, and the innovative *Gastrodrómio en Olympo* (Ⓣ23520 21300) on the square itself. You can splash out on casseroles with locally sourced meats and mountain herbs, fresh fish and a platter with thirty different types of Greek cheeses.

The ascent

Four to five hours' walking along the well-marked, scenic E4 long-distance path up the Mavrólongos canyon brings you to **Priónia**, from where there's a sharper three-hour trail-climb to the *Spilios Agapitos* **refuge** (Ⓣ23520 81800; €10 per person, plus €4.20 per tent; mid-May to mid-Oct). It's best to stay overnight here, as you need to make an early start for the three-hour ascent to **Mýtikas**, the highest peak (2917m) – the summit frequently clouds over towards midday. The path continues behind the refuge, reaching a signposted fork above the tree line in about an hour; straight on, then right, takes you to Mýtikas via the ridge known as Kakí Skála, while the abrupt right reaches the *Yiosos Apostolidhis* **hut** in one hour (no phone; €10 per person; mid-June to mid-Sept). From the hut there's an enjoyable loop down to the **Gortsiá** trailhead and from there back down into the Mavrólongos canyon, via the medieval monastery of Ayíou Dhionysíou. If you are short of time, you can hike the short 30-minute trail along Enipéas Gorge to the village's water reservoir.

The Cyclades

The **Cyclades** is the most satisfying Greek archipelago for island-hopping, with its vibrant capital on **Sýros**. The majority of the islands are arid and rocky, with brilliant-white, cuboid architecture, making them enormously popular with tourists. **Íos**, the original hippie island, is still a backpacker's paradise, while **Mýkonos** – with its teeming old town, nudist beaches and highly sophisticated clubs and bars (many of them gay) – is by far the most visited (and most expensive) of the group. Arriving by ferry at the partially submerged volcanic caldera of **Santoríni**, meanwhile, is one of the world's great travel adventures. **Páros**, **Náxos** and **Sífnos** are nearly as popular, while the one major ancient site worth making time for is **Délos**, the commercial and religious centre of the classical Greek world. Almost all of the Cyclades are served by boats from Pireás, but there are also ferries from Rafína, one hour by bus north of Athens.

SÝROS

Home to the capital of the Cyclades, **Sýros** is the most populous island in the archipelago. The main town and port of **ERMOÚPOLIS** is a lively spot, bustling with a commercial life that extends far beyond tourism. Crowned by two imposing churches, the Catholic Capuchin **Monastery of St Jean** in the medieval quarter of Ano Sýros and the Orthodox **Anástasis**, the city is one of the most religiously and culturally diverse places in the whole of Greece.

Accommodation

Kastro Rooms Kalomenopoúlou 12 ⓣ 22810 88064. Spacious rooms in a beautiful old mansion house near the main square, with access to a communal kitchen. Doubles €35.

Palladion Proïou 3 ⓣ 22810 86400, ⓦ www.palladion-hotel.com. Quiet, clean, recently renovated and with rooms overlooking a garden – this place is excellent value. Doubles €55.

Eating

Stin Ithaki tou Aí Klonos & Stefanou. Tucked down a side street, this welcoming taverna has all the Greek classics and vibrant bougainvillea overhead. Mains €10.

Yiannena Platía Kanári. Popular, friendly spot, seemingly unchanged since the 1950s, serving great seafood and other Greek standards. Mains €7.

Moving on

Ferry Íos (5–6 weekly; 4–7 hr); Mýkonos (3–5 daily; 50min); Náxos (1–2 daily; 1hr 30min–2hr); Pireás (3–5 daily; 2hr 30min–4hr); Santoríni (1–2 daily; 3–6hr); Sífnos (2–3 weekly; 2hr 30min).

SÍFNOS

Although **Sífnos** – notable for its classic Cycladic architecture and pottery – often gets crowded, its modest size makes exploring the picturesque island a pleasure, whether by the excellent in-season bus service or on foot over a network of old stone pathways.

KAMÁRES, the port, is tucked at the base of high bare cliffs in the west. A steep twenty-minute bus ride takes you up to **APOLLONÍA**, a rambling collage of flagstones, belfries and flowered courtyards. The island bank, post office and tourist police are all here, while the Aegean Thesaurus agency (ⓣ 22840 33151, ⓦ www.thesaurus.gr) should be able to help with rooms. As an alternative base, head for **KÁSTRO**, a regular bus ride below Apollonía on the east coast; built on a rocky outcrop with an almost sheer drop to the sea on three sides, this medieval capital of the island retains much of its character. The island's finest beach is, however, **VATHÝ**, a fishing village regularly connected by bus to and from Apollonía.

Accommodation

Hotel Stavros Kamáres ⓣ 22840 33383, ⓦ www.sifnostravel.com. These crisp en-suite rooms have balconies with sea views. There's also a decent book exchange in the reception. Doubles €50.

Makis Camping Kamáres ⓣ 22840 32366, ⓦ www.makiscamping.gr. A campsite with excellent facilities – including a laundry open to non-guests – as well as studios. May–Sept. €8/person, plus €4/tent; studios €50.

Moving on

Boat Íos (1–3 weekly; 3hr); Mýkonos (1 weekly; 5hr); Pireás (2–4 daily; 3–5hr); Santoríni (2 weekly; 4hr 30min); Sýros (2–3 weekly; 2hr 30min–5hr).

MÝKONOS

Mýkonos has become the most popular and expensive of the Cyclades,

DÉLOS

Boats from the west end of Mýkonos harbour (€38 return) leave for ancient **Délos**, the sacred isle, where Leto gave birth to Artemis and Apollo. It's worth a half-day trip for the magnificent views across to the nearby Cyclades from Mount Kýnthos (a 15min walk to the top), and for the archeological site (Tues–Sun 8.30am–3pm; €5) with remains of ancient temples, mosaics and its monumental lion avenue.

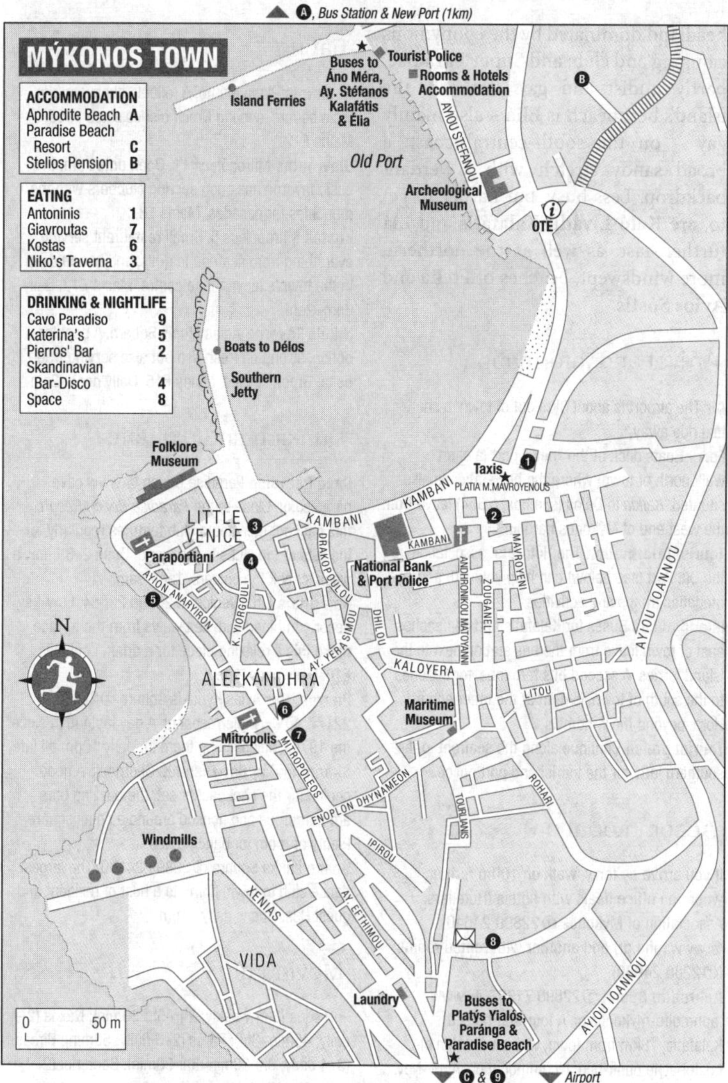

visited by several million tourists a year. If you don't mind the crowds, the upmarket capital, **MÝKONOS TOWN** (also known as **HÓRA**), is still the most beautiful and vibrant of all island capitals. Dazzlingly white, it's the archetypal Greek island town with sugar-cube buildings stacked around a cluster of seafront fishermen's dwellings.

The closest **beach** is **Áyios Stéfanos**, 4km north and connected by a very regular bus service, though **Platýs Yialós**, 4km south, is marginally less crowded. A bus service from Mykonos town and a *kaïki* service from **Órnos** 2km south connects almost all the beaches east of Platýs Yialós: gorgeous, pale-sand **Parága** beach, popular with campers; **Paradise**, well sheltered by its headland dominated by the eponymous camping and club; and **Super Paradise**, partly nudist and gay. Probably the island's best beach is **Eliá** – also mainly gay – on the south-central coast: a broad sandy stretch with a verdant backdrop. Less busy, but harder to get to, are **Kaló Livádi, Kalafátis** and **Liá** further east, as well as the northern, more windswept, beaches of **Fteliá** and **Áyios Sóstis**.

Arrival and information

Air The airport is about 3km out of town, a short taxi ride away.
Ferry Boats dock at the "new" port (a short walk north of town) where the bus station is also situated. *Kaïkia* to Délos (see box, p.554) leave from the west end of Mýkonos harbour.
Tourist information The Hoteliers' association in the Old Port (see below) can help you with accommodation, maps and activities.
Island buses Buses for Kalafátis and all beaches east of town leave from the bus station next to the Island ferries. A second bus terminus, for beaches to the south of town, is right at the other end of Hóra, beyond the windmills.
Tourist police Continue along the seafront to the southern jetty for the tourist and port police.

Accommodation

If you arrive by ferry, walk on 100m further, where an office deals with hotels (Hoteliers Association of Mykonos ⓣ22890 24540, ⓦwww.mha.gr) and another with rented rooms (ⓣ2280 24860).
Aphrodite Beach ⓣ22890 71367, ⓦwww.aphrodite-mykonos.gr. A four-star hotel at Kalafátis, 18km from town, with a selection of hostel-style bunk-bed accommodation. April–Nov. Four-person dorms €140.
Paradise Beach Resort ⓣ2289 022 129, ⓦwww.paradise-greece.com. An industrial-size (and feel) campsite, also offering cabins and bungalows. April–Oct. Camping €10/person, plus €5/tent, cabins €30, bungalows €54.
Stelios Pension ⓣ22890 24641or 22890 26779. A whitewashed Mykonian-style building, with comfortable rooms. On steps leading up from behind the OTE telecommunications office. April–Oct. Doubles €90.

Eating

Antoninis Platía Mantó. A reliable choice on the main square, serving Greek dishes since 1955. Mains €12.
Giavroutas Mitropóleos 11. Open until 7am, this basic taverna has been serving clubbers with the munchies for decades. Mains €8.
Kostas Mitropóleos 5. Small restaurant serving everything from seafood to grills, and buried deep in the town's labyrinthine centre. Mains €12. Daily 6pm–2am.
Niko's Taverna Agias Monis Square. A popular option, strong on fresh fish but also serving traditional Greek cuisine. Mains €15. Daily noon–2am.

Drinking and nightlife

Cavo Paradiso Paradise Beach ⓦwww.cavoparadiso.gr. Close to the *Paradise Beach Resort*, this packed after-hours club features regularly in the lists of top clubs in the world. Open 2–3 times a week, check the posters. 1am–9am.
Katerina's Little Venice ⓣ22890 23084. Low-key decor combined with sea views from the terrace make this a relaxing place for a drink. Cocktails €10. Daily noon–late.
Pierros' Bar Ayias Kyriakis Square ⓣ22890 22177, ⓦwww.pierrosbar.gr. A gay institution since the 1970s, still packing them in. Daily 10pm till late.
Skandinavian Bar-Disco K. Georgouli. A good choice for the backpacker set, the buzzing bars are numerous and housed around a small square. Plenty of room for dancing, too.
Space Lákka Square ⓣ22890 24100. The largest dance club in town, home to a host of resident and guest DJs. Opens daily 11pm.

Moving on

Ferry Íos (3–4 weekly; 2hr–5hr 30min); Náxos (2–4 daily; 45min–3hr); Páros (2–3 daily; 50min); Pireás (3–4 daily; 3hr 30min–5hr 30min); Santoríni (2–4 daily; 2hr 15min–7hr); Sífnos (0–1 weekly; 3hr 30min); Sýros (1–3 daily; 45min–1hr 15min).

PÁROS

With its old villages, monasteries, fishing harbour and labyrinthine capital, **Páros** has everything one expects from a Greek island, including a vibrant nightlife, four blue flag beaches and boat connections to virtually the entire Aegean.

PARIKIÁ, the main town, has ranks of white houses punctuated by the occasional Venetian-style building and church domes. Just outside the centre, the town also has one of the most interesting churches in the Aegean – the sixth-century **Ekatondapylianí**, or "Church of One Hundred Gates". The town culminates in a seaward Venetian **kastro**, whose surviving east wall incorporates a fifth-century BC round tower. The second largest village of Páros, **NÁOUSSA** retains much of its original character as a fishing village with winding, narrow alleys and simple Cycladic houses.

Arrival and information

Ferry All ferries dock at Parikiá, the main town.
Tourist information Located in the windmill in the centre of the roundabout opposite the quay (summer only, during ferry arrivals).
Island buses The bus stop is centrally located in Parikiá next to the quay. There are buses to Náoussa every 30min in July–Aug.

Accommodation

Captain Manolis Market St, Parikiá ⓣ22840 21244, ⓦwww.paroswelcome.com. Central but unbelievably quiet and freshly renovated; all rooms have garden views. May–Oct. Doubles €40.
Dina Market St, Parikiá ⓣ22840 21325, ⓦwww.hoteldina.com. Small family *pension*, obsessively clean and right in the middle of the action. Doubles €50.
Krios Beach Camping 2km from Parikiá ⓣ22840 21705, ⓦwww.krios-camping.gr. Excellent facilities in a shady site. Occasional parties that include plate smashing. Free wi-fi and pool. May–Sept. €6/person, plus €2/tent.
Young Inn Náoussa ⓣ6976 415 232, ⓦwww.young-inn.com. Comfortable en-suite bedrooms, some with kitchenettes, with free transfers to the port. A sociable place, as there are all kinds of organized activities. April–Oct. Dorms €8, doubles €25.

Eating

Happy Green Cows Just behind the National Bank in Parikiá, this place serves excellent, inventive vegetarian food in kitsch, colourful surrounds. Carnivore concessions include fish and chicken. Mains €12.
Trata Parikiá. Down a side street off the road heading east out of town, this popular taverna specializes in seafood. Mains €8.

Drinking and nightlife

Dubliner By the bridge, Parikiá. Young, brash and OTT, this is where you will probably end up dancing after a night drinking in town. Cocktails €7–8. Daily 11pm–6am.

Moving on

Ferry Íos (2–3 weekly; 2hr–3hr); Mýkonos (1–2 daily; 45min–1hr); Náxos (2–3 daily; 35min); Pireás (3–5 daily; 3–4hr); Santoríni (1–3 daily; 3hr); Sífnos (2 weekly; 2hr 45min); Sýros (6–8 weekly; 2hr 40min).

NÁXOS

Náxos is the largest and most fertile of the Cyclades with high mountains, intriguing central valleys, a spectacular north coast, sandy beaches in the southwest, and Venetian towers and fortified mansions scattered throughout.

What to see and do

A long causeway protecting the harbour connects **NÁXOS TOWN** with the islet of Palátia, where the huge stone portal of an unfinished sixth-century BC **Temple of Apollo** still stands. Most of the town's life goes on down by the port or in the streets just behind it; the quaint Old Market Street has narrow, stone paths leading to small shops and a handful of restaurants and cafés. From here, stepped lanes lead up past crumbling balconies and through low arches to the fortified medieval **kastro**, near the **Archeological Museum** (Tues–Sun 8.30am–2.30pm; €3), with its important Early Cycladic collection. The town has a laidback feel, with unashamedly long happy hours which last for most of the day. There's a thriving nightlife, with plenty of bars scattered along the waterfront.

Beaches

The island's best **beaches** are regularly served by buses in season. Within Náxos Town itself is **Áyios Yeóryios**, a long sandy bay, part of the hotel and restaurant quarter. A short bus ride south, however, you'll find the more inviting **Áyios Prokópios** and **Ayía Ánna** beaches, with plenty of rooms to let and many good tavernas. Beyond the headland stretches **Pláka** beach, a 5km-long vegetation-fringed expanse of white sand, which comfortably holds the summer crowds of nudists and campers from its two friendly campsites: *Marágas* (Ⓣ22850 24552; April–Oct; €7 per person and tent), which also has rooms (€45), and the newer *Pláka* (Ⓣ22850 42700, Ⓦwww.plakacamping.gr; April–Oct; €7 per person, plus €2 per tent) flanked by the imaginatively named *Pláka I* and *Pláka II* hotels (€45 and €60 respectively).

Arrival and information

Ferry Boats dock at the quay at the northern end of Náxos Town.

Tourist information You can obtain Information at Zas Travel or Auto Tour car rental opposite the quay; you can pick up leaflets or leave your luggage here (daily 9.30am–9.30pm).

Island buses The bus stop in Náxos Town is opposite the quay. There are buses to Ayía Ánna (every 30min), Áyios Prokópios (every 30min) and Pláka (every 30min).

Accommodation

Despina's Rooms Náxos Town Ⓣ22850 22356. Hidden (but well signposted) beneath the castle In the Bourgos, the rooms are small but clean and airy, with shared bathroom and balconies with sea views. Doubles €35.

Hotel Grotta Kambanelli 7, Grotta Ⓣ22850 22215, Ⓦwww.hotelgrotta.gr. Welcoming hotel in a good location and maybe the best breakfast in the Cyclades. Free wi-fi and jacuzzi. Doubles €75.

Soula Hotel Áyios Yeóryios beach Ⓣ22850 23196, Ⓦwww.soulahotel.com. A family-run budget hotel close to both the beach and the town, with free internet access and free transfers. Dorms €13, doubles €40, a/c €6/day extra.

Eating and drinking

Elia Old Market St, Náxos Town. Housed in a beautiful stone building, this smart café-bar has live music and an enticing atmosphere. Also serves breakfast and lunch. Daily 9am–3pm & 7pm–late. Cocktails €8.

Manolis Garden Old Market St, Bourgos. A peaceful spot for an evening meal, with traditional Greek dishes. May–Oct Daily 6pm–1am. Mains €8–10.

Molos Ayios Prokópios. Commanding the best part of the beach and serving traditional Greek fare, this is the pick of the seaside tavernas. Mains €8. May–Oct Daily 9am–1am.

Moving on

Ferry Íos (4–5 weekly; 1hr 30min); Mýkonos (1–3 daily; 3hr); Páros (2–3 daily; 45min); Pireás (2–3 daily; 4hr–5hr 30min); Santoríni (1–2 daily; 1hr 15min–3hr 30min); Sífnos (1 weekly; 3hr 30min); Sýros (4–5 weekly; 2hr 30min).

ÍOS

Once a hippie hangout, the island remains popular with a younger crowd seeking fun and sun, which **Íos**, party capital of the Aegean, provides in abundance. However, although no other island attracts more under-25s, Íos has miraculously maintained much of its traditional Cycladic charm, with picture-perfect whitewashed houses and churches. Íos's lively nights lead to lazy days, perfect for exploring the island beaches.

What to see and do

Don't expect a quiet stay in the town of **HÓRA**, as every evening the streets throb to music with the larger **clubs** clustered near the bus stop. To get the most out of the nightlife, start around 11pm with the bars and clubs around the central square, which tend to close at 3am. Around this time the larger clubs on the main street begin to liven up, and the party continues (even if you don't) until 9am.

Mylopótas and Manganári

The most popular stop on the island's bus routes is **MYLOPÓTAS**, site of a magnificent beach where there's a mini-resort (run by Far Out Camping, see below) offering plenty of activities on offer, including quad biking, watersports and diving, as well as parties. It gets very crowded, so for a bit more space, head away from the Mylopótas bus stop, where there are dunes behind the beach. From Yialós, boats depart daily at around 10am to **MANGANÁRI** on the south coast, where there's a superb blue flag beach.

Arrival

Ferry Boats dock at the quay in Yialós. Regular buses connect the port to Hóra and Mylopótas (every 15min; 8am–12.30am) and many hotels and hostels offer a free transfer.

Accommodation

Far Out Camping Mylopótas ⓣ22850 91468, ⓦwww.faroutclub.com. By far the most popular campsite, thanks to its facilities and fun factor. Also has bungalows to rent. April–Sept. Camping €12, bungalows €20.

Francesco's Hóra Old Town ⓣ22860 91223, ⓦwww.francescos.net. A favourite option with the backpacker set, with the only dorm beds in town as well as private rooms. Lively bar and terrace with sea views and a pool. Dorms €17, doubles €50.

Lófos Hóra ⓣ22860 9148. Right up from the archeological site, this family-owned, shaded complex with basic but well-furnished rooms is very convenient for access both to the bus stop and the Hóra nightlife opposite. May–Oct. Doubles €40.

Marko's Village Hóra ⓣ22860 91059, ⓦwww.markosvillage.com. Tastefully decorated rooms set around a pool and noisy bar, a short stumble from the nightlife. Doubles €35.

Eating

Ali Baba's Hóra. Thai chefs dish up generous portions of authentic Thai food, served with the famous fishbowl cocktails. Stir-fries €10. Open daily from 6pm.

Lord Byron Hóra. An intimate restaurant with funky decor, serving generous meze plates to share (€12). A restaurant for those with an appetite. Daily 6pm–1am

Mario's Top of the stairs from Mylopótas beach. Perched at a curve on the road to Hóra with spectacular views and enormous pizzas (€9). Daily noon–midnight.

Drinking and nightlife

Íos Club Top of the stairs from Yialós. Kicks off the evening with its sunset viewing. Daily 6pm–late.

Red Bull Bar Main square. Small bar specializing in dance music – and the well-known energy drink, mixed with large doses of spirits. Daily 10pm–3am. Cocktails €7.

Scorpion Main street. Huge nightclub, packed to the rafters, and with a dancefloor that throbs well beyond dawn. Entry €10 including a free drink. Daily 1am–late.

Slammer Bar Main square ⓦwww.slammerbar.com Legendary bar, although beware of saying the word "slammer" too loudly. Plays popular music from the Eighties to current tunes. Entry €5 including a free drink. Daily 10pm–3am.

Sweet Irish Dreams Main street, in front of the church. Satisfy your cravings for a pint of the black gold here and dance till dawn on the tables. Entry €7 including a free drink.

Moving on

Ferry Mýkonos (1–2 daily; 1hr 40min); Náxos (4–5 weekly; 45min–3hr); Páros (2–4 weekly; 5hr); Pireás (1–2 daily; 3hr 20min); Santoríni (2–3 daily; 35min–1hr 30min); Sífnos (2–3 weekly; 3–5hr); Sýros (3–5 weekly; 5hr 30min).

SANTORÍNI (THÍRA)

Santoríni is the epitome of relaxation, with its sun-drenched beaches and ambling whitewashed stone paths. The island (a partially submerged volcanic caldera poking above the ocean's surface in five places) is a welcome destination to those who have spent too many nights partying on Íos. As the ferry manoeuvres into the great bay, gaunt, sheer cliffs loom hundreds of feet above. Nothing grows to soften the view, and the only colours are the reddish-brown, black and grey pumice strata layering the cliff face of **Thíra**, the ancient name of Santoríni. Despite a past every bit as turbulent as the geological conditions that formed it, the island is now best known for its spectacular views, dark-sand beaches and light, dry white wines.

What to see and do

Regular buses meeting the ferries at **Órmos Athiniós** make their way to the island's capital **FIRÁ**; half-rebuilt after a devastating earthquake in 1956 and lurching dementedly at the cliff's edge. Besieged by day-trippers from cruise-ships, it's somewhat tacky and commercialized, though watching the sunset from a cliff-hugging terrace of any of the overpriced restaurants you'll understand why it's so popular. There's no shortage of **rooms** in the area, though most are expensive. The town boasts a couple of **museums** (Tues–Sun 8.30am–3pm; €3 for both): the Archeological Museum, near the cable car to the north of town, and the Museum of Prehistoric Thíra, between the cathedral and the bus station.

Around the island

Near the northwestern tip of the island is one of the most dramatic towns of the Cyclades, **ÍA**, a curious mix of pristine white reconstruction and tumbledown ruins clinging to the cliff face. With a post office, travel agencies and an excellent **youth hostel** (see below), it makes a good base from which to explore the island. Santoríni's **beaches** are bizarre: long black stretches of volcanic sand that get blisteringly hot in the afternoon sun. There's little to choose between **KAMÁRI** and **PERÍSSA**, the two main resorts: both have long beaches and a mass of restaurants, rooms and apartments, although Períssa gets more backpackers.

At the southwestern tip of the island, evidence of a Minoan colony was unearthed at **Akrotíri** (summer Tues–Sun 8.30am–3pm; €5; bus from Firá or Períssa), a town buried under banks of volcanic ash. Nearby is the spectacular, red-sand **Kókkini Ámmos** beach.

BOAT TRIPS TO THE VOLCANO

Take a **boat trip** (€10–30) from Firá or Ía to explore the magma-encrusted islets of the caldera and to swim in the sulphurous hot springs. You can book trips of varying lengths from your accommodation or a travel agent.

Arrival

Ferry Most boats arrive at the somewhat functional port of Órmos Athiniós from where buses meeting the ferries make their way to the island's capital.

Island buses Bus services are plentiful enough between Firá and other destinations around the island.

Accommodation

Kykladonisia Firá ⓣ22860 22458, ⓦwww.santorinihostel.com. Sleek, upmarket hostel with a swimming pool and free wi-fi. Try to get one of the rooms with a sunset view. Dorms €25, doubles €45.

San Giorgio Firá ⓣ22860 23516, ⓦwww.sangiorgiovilla.gr. Tucked away to left of the parking next to the main square, this hotel has clean, excellent-value rooms (discount for Rough Guide readers). April–Nov. Doubles €50.

Santorini Camping Firá ⓣ22860 22944, ⓦwww.santorinicamping.gr. A shady campsite with a pool, restaurant and internet access. Camping €9/person and tent; March–Nov €12.50.

Youth Hostel Ía ⓣ22860 71465. An excellent hostel with a terrace and shady courtyard, a bar and clean dorms, but with a short season: mid-June to mid-Sept. Dorms €16.

Moving on

Ferry Íos (1–3 daily; 30min–1hr); Iráklion (1–2 daily; 1hr 30min–5hr); Mýkonos (1–3 daily; 2hr 30min); Náxos (2–4 daily; 1hr 20min); Páros (2–3 daily; 3hr 30min–6hr); Pireás (3–5 daily; 4–9hr); Sífnos (1–2 weekly; 4–5hr); Sýros (5–6 weekly; 5–8hr).

The Dodecanese

The **Dodecanese** islands lie so close to the Turkish coast that some are almost within hailing distance of the shore. They were only included in the modern Greek state in 1948 after centuries of occupation by Crusaders, Ottomans and Italians. Medieval **Rhodes** is the most famous, but almost every one has its classical remains, its Crusader castles, its traditional villages and grandiose, Italian-built Art Deco public buildings. The main islands of Rhodes, **Kós** and **Pátmos** are connected almost daily with each other, and none is hard to reach. Rhodes is the principal transport hub, with ferry services to Turkey, as well as connections with Crete, the northeastern Aegean islands, selected Cyclades and the mainland.

RHODES

It's no surprise that **Rhodes** is among the most visited of Greek islands. Not only is its east coast lined with sandy beaches, but the core of the capital is a beautiful and remarkably preserved medieval city.

What to see and do

RHODES TOWN divides into two unequal parts: the compact old walled city and the new town sprawling around it in three directions. There's plenty to explore in the rest of the island too, not least charming **Haráki** and lively **Líndhos**.

Rhodes Town

First thing to meet the eye, and dominating the northeast sector of the city's fortifications, is the **Palace of the Grand Masters** (Tues–Sun 8am–7.30pm; winter till 3pm; €6, or €10 combina-

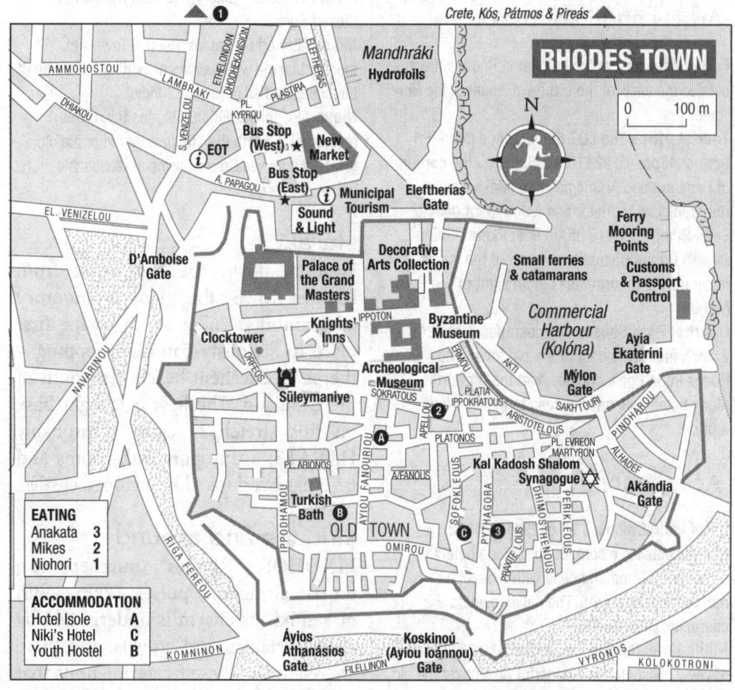

tion ticket with other museums). Two excellent **museums** occupy the ground floor: one devoted to medieval Rhodes, the other to ancient Rhodes. The heavily restored **Street of the Knights** (Odhós Ippotón) leads due east from the front of the palace. The "Inns" lining it housed the Knights of St John for two centuries, and at the bottom of the slope the Knights' Hospital now houses the **Archeological Museum** (Tues–Sun 8.30am–7pm; €6, or €10 combination ticket), where the star exhibit is the famous statue of *Aphrodite of Rhodes*. Across the way St Mary's church houses the **Byzantine Museum** (Tues–Sun 8.30am–2.40pm; €2, or €10 combination ticket for the 3 museums), housed in the Knights' chapel and highlighting the island's icons and frescoes. Heading south, it's hard to miss the most conspicuous Ottoman monument in Rhodes, the candy-striped **Süleymaniye Mosque** (ask at tourist office for hours; free).

Arrival and information

Ferry Boats dock at the harbour in Rhodes Town outside the walls of the Old Town, south of the New Town.

Tourist office The EOT tourist office (Mon–Fri 8am–2.45pm; ⓣ22410 44330) is on the corner of Papágou and Archiepiskopou Makaríou; the municipal tourist office (June–Sept daily 9am–8pm; ⓣ22410 3545) is at Platia Rimini.

Island buses Buses for the rest of the island leave from two terminals within sight of the New Market.

Internet Rock Style at Dhimokratías 7 ⓣ22410 27502, just southwest of the old town, and Rodos Iróon Polytechniou 11 at the far north. Many hotels will offer access to their wi-fi at a price.

Accommodation

Hotel Isole Evdhóxou 75 ⓣ22410 20682, ⓦwww.hotelisole.com. Simple, clean hotel in a converted Ottoman house with a beautiful roof terrace. Free wi-fi. The Italian owners are charming. Doubles €50.

Niki's Hotel Sofokléous 39 ⓣ22410 25115, ⓦwww.nikishotel.gr. Wonderful views over the old town from the roof garden, and breakfast served outside on a lovely patio. Free wi-fi. Doubles €40–50.

Youth Hostel Ergíou 12 ⓣ22410 30491. A friendly hostel with dorm beds, double rooms and studios. The dorms are basic, but the studios are carefully restored in a separate building, with original features retained. Dorms €10, doubles €30–35.

TREAT YOURSELF

Nireas (Sofokléous 22 ⓣ22410 3378). Occupying a lovely, leafy courtyard in the Old Town, a world away from the tourist traps, *Nireas* serves up tasty, fresh seafood with panache. A meal will cost about €30 but the setting and the quality are worth skipping breakfast and lunch for.

Eating

Anakata Pythagora 79, Rhodes Town. Enjoy a light lunch or a coffee in this shady garden surrounded by vibrant pink flowers. Take a peek at the art gallery, too. Sandwiches €3. Closed Sun.

Mikes Alley off Sokrátous, Rhodes Town. This modest taverna with pavement seating has some of the cheapest fish in town (€20/kilo).

Niohori Ioánni Kazoúli 29, Rhodes Town. This restaurant is worth the 10min walk out of the old town, as it serves Greek cuisine at reasonable prices. Mains €5–7.

Haráki

Heading down the east coast from Rhodes Town, the giant promontory of **Tsambíka**, 26km south, is the first place to seriously consider stopping – there's an excellent beach just south of the headland. The best overnight base on this stretch of coast is probably **HARÁKI**, a tiny port with rooms and tavernas overlooked by a ruined castle.

Líndhos and around

LÍNDHOS, Rhodes' number two tourist attraction, pulses 12km south of Haráki. Its charm is undermined by commercialism and crowds, and there are relatively few self-catering units that aren't block-booked through package companies – find vacancies through Pallas Travel (☎22440 31 4949). On the hill above the town, the Doric **Temple of Athena** and Hellenistic stoa (porch-like building used for meetings and commerce) stand inside the inevitable Knights' Castle (Tues–Sun 8am–7pm; winter Tues–Sun 8am–3pm; €6). Líndhos's beaches are crowded and overrated; you'll find better ones heading south past Lárdhos, the start of 15km of intermittent coarse-sand beach up to and beyond the growing resort of **Yennádhi**. Inland near here, the late-Byzantine frescoes in the village church of **Asklipió** are among the best on Rhodes.

Moving on

Air Athens (6–7 daily; 1 hr); Iráklion (daily; 55min); Thessaloniki (daily; 1hr 15min). Rhodes is also connected directly with many European capitals via charter flights.
Ferry Iráklion (1–2 weekly; 10–14hr); Kós (2–4 daily; 2hr 30min–3h); Marmaris (1–2 daily; 1–2hr); Pátmos (2 daily; 5hr); Pireás (9–12 weekly; 10–20hr); Santoríni (4–5 weekly; 6–7hr); Sýros 3–4 weekly; 9hr).

KÓS

Kós is the largest and most popular island in the Dodecanese after Rhodes, and there are superficial similarities between the two. Like its rival, the harbour here is also guarded by a castle of the Knights of St John, the streets are lined with ambitious Italian public buildings, and minarets and palm trees punctuate extensive Greek and Roman remains.

What to see and do

Mostly modern **KÓS TOWN**, levelled by a 1933 earthquake, fans out from the harbour. Apart from the castle, the town's main attraction is its wealth of Hellenistic and Roman remains. It's also one of the few spots in Greece where cycling is positively encouraged, and cycle lanes traverse the whole of Kós Town.

The Archeological Museum and castle

The **Archeological Museum** at Platia Eleftherías (Tues–Sun 8am–6.30pm; €3) holds ancient mosaics and statues. Next to the **Castle** (Tues–Sun 8am–2.30pm; €4), scaffolding props up the branches of the so-called Hippocrates plane tree, which does have a fair claim to being one of the oldest trees in Europe.

The Asklepion and Platáni

Hippocrates is honoured by the **Asklepiíon** (Tues–Sun 8am–7.30pm; winter 3pm; €4), a temple to Asklepios and renowned centre of Hippocratic teaching, 45 minutes on foot (or a short bus ride) from town. The road to the Asklepiíon passes through the village of **PLATÁNI**, where Turkish owners run the popular *Arap* and *Sherif* tavernas (summer only), serving excellent, affordable food.

Beaches

To get to the **beaches** you'll need to use buses or rent scooters or bikes. Around 12km west of Kós Town, **Tingáki** is easily accessible but busy. **Mastihári**, 30km from Kós Town, has a decent beach and private rooms for hire. Continuing west, buses run as far as **Kéfalos**, which covers a bluff looking back along the length of Kós. Well before Kéfalos are **Áyios Stéfanos**, where the exquisite remains of a mosaic-floored fifth-century basilica overlook tiny Kastrí islet, and **Kamári**, the package resort just below Kéfalos. Beaches begin at Kamári and extend east past Áyios Stéfanos for 7km, almost without interruption; **Paradise** has the most facilities, but **Magic** (officially Polémi) and **Langádhes** are calmer and more scenic.

Arrival and information

Ferry Boats arrive at the harbour, to the north of the centre in Kós Town.

Tourist office 500m south of the ferry dock (Mon–Fri: May–Oct 8.30am–3pm; Nov–April 8.30am–2.30pm; ⓣ22420 24460).

Island buses Buses arrive 500m west of the tourist office. From the centre there are buses to Paradise (6 daily); Platáni (15 daily); Tingáki (12 daily); Mastihári (7 daily).

Accommodation

Hotel Afendoulis Evripýlou 1, Kós Town ⓣ22420 25321, ⓦwww.afendoulishotel.com. Homely en-suite rooms with balconies are set around a mezzanine floor, and there's a warm family welcome. Doubles €30–50.

Pension Alexis Irodhótou 9, Kós Town ⓣ22420 28798, ⓦwww.pensionalexis.com. Set around a shady garden with a veranda and freshly renovated place with informative owners, who also welcome late arrivals. Doubles €35–50.

Eating

Ambavris 1.5km inland in the eponymous hamlet on the road to Platáni. This taverna may be some distance out of town, but it has an excellent selection of *mezédhes* and is popular with the locals. Dinner only. Mains €6–8.

Koakon Artemisías 56. Located in a residential area by the marina, this restaurant has a varied Greek menu, including fish dishes. Mains €6–8.

Moving on

Air Athens (daily; 1hr); Iráklion (daily; 1hr).

Ferry Bodrum (1–2 daily; 30–45min); Pátmos (1–3 daily; 2hr 30min); Pireás (1 daily; 15hr); Rhodes (1–4 daily; 3hr).

PÁTMOS

St John the Apostle reputedly wrote the Book of Revelation in a cave on **Pátmos**, and the monastery that commemorates him, founded here in 1088, dominates the island both physically and politically. Although the monks no longer run Pátmos as they did for more than six centuries, their influence has stopped most of the island going the way of Rhodes or Kós.

What to see and do

SKÁLA, the port and main town, is the only busy part of the island, crowded with day-trippers from Kós and Rhodes. **HÓRA** is a beautiful little town whose antiquated alleys conceal over forty churches and monasteries, plus dozens of shipowners' mansions dating from the seventeenth and eighteenth centuries.

Monastery of St John

The **Monastery of St John** (daily 8am–1.30pm, Tues, Thurs & Sun also 4–6pm; monastery free, treasury €3) shelters behind massive defences in the hilltop capital of Hóra. Buses go up, but the thirty-minute walk along a beautiful old cobbled path is much more worthwhile.

Monastery of the Apocalypse

Just over halfway up the hill to Hóra is the **Monastery of the Apocalypse**, built around the cave where St John heard the voice of God issuing from a cleft in the rock. This is merely a foretaste, however, of the main monastery, whose fortifications guard a dazzling array of religious treasures dating back to medieval times.

Beaches

The bay north of the main harbour in Skála shelters **Méloï beach**, with a well-run campsite. For swimming, the second beach north, **Agriolivádhi**, is usually less crowded. From Hóra a good road runs above the package resort of Gríkou to the isthmus of **Stavrós**, from where a thirty-minute trail leads to the excellent beach, with one seasonal taverna, at **Psilí Ámmos** (summer *kaïki* from Skála). There are more good beaches in the north of the island, particularly **Livádhi Yeránou**, shaded by tamarisk groves and with a decent taverna, and **Lámbi** with volcanic pebbles and another quality taverna, *Leonidas*.

Arrival and information

Ferry Boats arrive at the harbour, in the middle of Skála.
Tourist office Close to the police station opposite the harbour, the tourist office (summer only; hours vary) can assist with accommodation.
Island buses The bus stop is next to the harbour. There are buses to Hóra (11 daily) and Gríkou (8 daily).

Accommodation

Pension Maria Paskalides ⓣ22470 33262, ⓦwww.sirocostudios.gr. Situated five minutes from the port, these fully equipped self-contained apartments have large balconies and sunset views. Doubles €60
Stefanos Camping Meloï ⓣ22470 31821. Well-equipped campsite, with many facilities and a taverna. Mid-May to mid-Sept. €2/person, plus €8/tent.

Eating

Art Café Skála, behind the post office. Excellent bar-café with flickering candles, views to the harbour and the monastery, draft beer and a breezy roof garden.
Ouzerí To Hiliomodhi Skála. As the nautical decor suggests, this is the place for fish and seafood dishes. Open daily from 5pm. Mains €5–7.

Moving on

Ferry Kós (1–3 daily; 2hr 30min); Pireás (4–5 weekly; 6–10hr); Rhodes (2–4 daily; 5–9hr); Sámos (1–2 daily; 3hr); Syros (1–2 weekly; 4hr).

Northeastern Aegean

The seven scattered islands of the **northeastern Aegean** form a rather arbitrary archipelago. Local tour operators do a thriving business shuttling passengers for absurdly high tariffs between the easternmost islands and the Turkish coast. The most-visited island, Sámos, is overrun with package tours in summer; tranquil **Lésvos** has a more low-key appeal.

LÉSVOS

Lésvos, birthplace of Sappho, the ancient world's foremost woman poet, may not at first seem particularly beautiful, but the craggy volcanic landscape of pine and olive groves grows on you. Despite the inroads of tourism, this is still essentially a working island, with few large hotels outside the capital, Mytilíni, and the resorts of Skála Kallonís and Mólyvos.

What to see and do

Few people stay in **MYTILÍNI**, but do pause long enough to peek at the **Archeological Museum**, with its superb Roman mosaics (Tues–Sun 8.30am–3pm, 7pm in summer; €3). Sleepy **MÓLYVOS**, also known as Mithymna, on the northwestern coast, is easily the most attractive spot on Lésvos, and much more appealing than its touristy neighbour, Petra. Tiers of sturdy, red-tiled houses mount the slopes between the picturesque harbour and the Genoese castle. Wandering through the cobbled streets is a pleasure, since the town's hillside location provides plenty of stunning vistas across the sweeping bay. If the exploration has worn you out, reward yourself with a visit to the **hot springs** of Eftaloú (daily: old baths 6–8am & 6–10pm; €3.50; new baths 9am–6pm; €5; ⓣ22530 71245). The main lower road, past the tourist office, heads towards the picturesque harbour, where there are some good-quality seafood tavernas. Lésvos's best beach is at **SKÁLA ERESSOÚ** in the far southwest, with rooms far outnumbering hotels (except during the International Women's Festival in September; ⓦwww.womens festival.eu). Tavernas with wooden terraces line the beach – try *Eressos*

Palace or *Blue Sardine*. **PLOMÁRI** in the southeast, long the *oúzo* capital of Greece, is another good base, though it lacks beaches within walking distance.

Arrival and information

Ferry Boats arrive at the quay in Mytilíni. On arrival, turn left to reach the town centre.

Tourist office The office in Mytilíni is located at Aristárhou 6 near the quay (Mon–Fri 9am–1pm; ⓣ22510 42511). The office in Mólyvos is close to the bus stop (May, June & Sept: Mon–Sat 10am–3pm; July–Aug also 4–9pm & Sun 10am–3pm; ⓣ22530 71347, ⓦwww.mithymna.gr) and can help with accommodation.

Island buses The bus station in Mytilíni (ⓣ22540 28873) is located at the southwestern end of the waterfront, slightly inland near Platía Konstandinopóleos. There are buses to Mólyvos (5 daily), Plomári (5 daily), and Skála Eressoú (3 daily).

Accommodation

Molivos Camping Mólyvos ⓣ22530 71169, ⓦwww.molivos-camping.com. A shady campsite with good facilities, 800m from town. May–Oct. €10/person and tent.

Nassos Guest House Mólyvos, up from the tourist office ⓣ69420 46279, ⓦwww.nassosguesthouse.com. A charming, converted Turkish house built around 1900. There are fine views of the town from the rooms and the terrace. Doubles €35.

Pension Lida Plomári ⓣ22520 32507. A fine restoration inn occupying old mansions, with sea-view balconies, 300m from the beach. Doubles €30.

Eating

The Captain's Table Mólyvos. Set among the fishing boats in the picturesque harbour, with good fish as well as traditional dishes. Fish €7–8. Daily from 5.30pm.

To Hani Mólyvos. Near the market, this restaurant-grill serves delicious meals, complemented by a wonderful terrace with views over the town towards the sea. Mains €6–8.

Moving on

Air Athens (5 daily; 50min); Iráklion (2–3 weekly; 1hr 15min); Thessaloniki (2 daily; 50 min).

Ferry Ayvalik/Dikili, Turkey (daily; 1hr 30min); Pireás (1–2 daily; 8–10hr); Thessaloníki (1–2 weekly; 15hr);

The Sporades

The **Sporades**, scattered across the northwestern Aegean, are an easy group to island-hop. The three northern islands – package-tourist haven Skiáthos, Alónissos and **Skópelos**, the pick of the trio – have good beaches, transparent waters and thick pine forests. **Skýros**, the fourth of the Sporades, is isolated from the others and less scenic, but with perhaps the most character; for a relatively uncommercialized island within a day's travel of Athens it's unbeatable.

SKÓPELOS

More rugged yet better cultivated than neighbouring Skiáthos, **Skópelos** is also very much more attractive. **SKÓPELOS TOWN** slopes down one corner of a huge, almost circular bay. There are dozens of rooms to let – take up one of the offers when you land or visit the Roomowners Association (see opposite) for vacancies. Within the town, spread below the oddly whitewashed ruins of a Venetian *kastro*, are an enormous number of churches – 123 reputedly, though some are small enough to be mistaken for houses.

Beaches

Buses run along the island's one asphalt road to Loutráki about seven times daily, stopping at the turn-offs to all the main beaches and villages. **Stáfylos** beach, 4km out of town, is the closest, but it's small, rocky and increasingly crowded; the overflow, much of it nudist, flees to **Valanió**, just east. Much more promising, if you're after relative isolation, is sandy **Limnonári**, a fifteen-minute walk or

GETTING TO THE SPORADES

The **Sporades** are well connected to Athens by air (Skiáthos) or by bus and ferry via Áyios Konstandínos or Vólos (for Skiáthos and Skópelos). The only way to get to Skýros is from the port of Kimi or by air from Athens and Thessaloníki.

short *kaïki* ride from **AGNÓNDAS** (which has tavernas and rooms). The large resort of **Pánormos** has become overdeveloped, but slightly further on, **Miliá** offers a tremendous 1500m sweep of tiny pebbles beneath a bank of pines.

Arrival and information

Ferry Boats arrive at the quay in the middle of Skópelos Town. The island also has another port at Loutráki.

Island buses The bus stop is next to the quay, near the taxi rank. There are buses to Agnóndas (6–8 daily), Miliá (3–5 daily) and Loutráki (4–6 daily) also stopping at Pánormos, Agnóndas and Stáfylos.

Accommodation

The Roomowners Association, opposite the quay (daily 9.30am–2pm; ☎ 24240 24576), has lists of the island's accommodation.

Archontiko Skópelos Town ☎ 24240 22765. This welcoming guesthouse has traditional decor and a homely atmosphere, situated on a quiet, cobbled street. Doubles €35.

Hotel Regina Skópelos Town ☎ 24240 22138. Close to the waterfront, these spacious en-suite rooms have large double beds and balconies. Breakfast included. Doubles €55.

Eating

Alexander Skópelos Town. A delightful garden restaurant, serving traditional Greek food alongside more unusual local specials, such as pork with plums. Mains €7–12. Open daily from 7pm.

O Molos Old Harbour, Skópelos Town. A reliable taverna on the waterfront, serving typical Greek cuisine. Mains €7–8. Daily noon–midnight.

Moving on

Ferry Áyios Konstandínos (4 daily; 1hr 20min); Skiáthos (6 daily; 45min–1hr); Vólos (4–6 daily; 1hr 30min–3hr).

SKÝROS

Skýros remained until the 1980s a very traditional and idiosyncratic island. Some older men still wear the vaguely Cretan costume of cap, vest, baggy trousers, leggings and clogs, while the women favour yellow scarves and long embroidered skirts. Skýros also has a particularly lively *Apokriátika* or pre-Lenten **carnival**, featuring the "Goat Dance", performed by masked revellers in the village streets.

What to see and do

A **bus** connects Linariá – a functional little port with a few tourist facilities – to **SKÝROS TOWN**, spread below a high rock rising precipitously from the coast. Traces of classical walls can still be made out among the ruins of the Venetian *kastro*; within the walls is the crumbling, tenth-century monastery of **Áyios Yeóryios**. Despite the town's peaceful afternoons, the narrow streets come alive in the evening, as the sun sets behind the hills, bathing the white buildings in a soft light. There are several hotels and plenty of **rooms** to let in private houses; you'll be met with offers as you descend from the bus. The campsite is down the hill at the fishing village of **MAGAZIÁ**, with rooms and tavernas fronting the island's best beach.

Arrival and information

Ferry Boats arrive at the functional port of Linariá. Buses meet the boats and connect the port to Skýros Town.

Information There is no tourist office, but Skýros Travel on the main street (☎ 2222 091123, Ⓦ www.skyrostravel.com) or Ⓦ www.skyros.gr can help with accommodation.

Accommodation

Hotel Elena Skýros Town ⓣ 22220 91738. With tiled floors, white walls and wooden furniture, these rooms are clean, comfortable and centrally located. €45.

Eating

Liakos Skýros Town. Tasty local dishes are served on a rooftop terrace with a panoramic view over the town. Mains €6–11. Mon from 6pm, Tues–Sun from 1pm.

Nostos Café Skýros Town. On the central square above the bank, this is the perfect place for a pre-dinner drink as you watch the sunset from the terrace.

O Pappous k'Ego Skýros Town. This popular spot opens for dinner only and serves Skyrian specialities such as goat in lemon sauce. Tables spill out onto the cobbled pavement. Mains €5–9.

Moving on

Air Athens (3 weekly; 1hr 40min); Thessaloníki (3 weekly; 1hr 40min).

Ferry Kými (2–4 daily; 1hr 40min).

Ionian islands

The six **Ionian islands** are geographically and culturally a mixture of Greece and Italy. Floating on the haze of the Adriatic, their green silhouettes come as a surprise to those more used to the stark outlines of the Aegean. The islands were the Homeric realm of Odysseus and here alone of all modern Greek territory the Ottomans never held sway. After the fall of Byzantium, possession passed to the Venetians, and the islands became a keystone in that city-state's maritime empire from 1386 until its collapse in 1797 when they passed to the French, the British and finally the Greeks in 1864. Tourism has hit **Corfu** in a big way but none of the other islands has endured anything like the same scale of development. For a less sullied experience, head for **Kefalloniá**.

CORFU (KÉRKYRA)

A visit to **Corfu** is an intense experience, if sometimes a beleaguered one, for it has more package hotels and holiday villas than any other Greek island. The commercialism is apparent the moment you step ashore at the ferry dock, or cover the 2km from the airport. That said, **KÉRKYRA TOWN**, the capital, has a lot more going for it than first exposure to the summer crowds might indicate.

What to see and do

Although unavoidably touristy, **Kérkyra Town** has a buzzy appeal: cafés on the Esplanade and in the arcaded Listón have a civilized air, and become lively bars when the sun sets. The rest of the island is dotted with some lovely beaches and appealing villages.

Kérkyra Town and around

In Kérkyra Town, the Palace of Sts Michael and George at the north end of the Spianádha is worth visiting for its **Asiatic Museum** (Tues–Sun 8.30am–7.30pm; till 2.30pm winter; €4) and **Municipal Art Gallery** (daily 9am–5pm; €1.50). The **Byzantine Museum** (summer Tues–Sun 8am–7pm; winter 8.30am–2.30pm; €2) and the cathedral are both interesting, as is the **Archeological Museum**, Vraíla Armeni 1 (Tues–Sun 8.30am–3pm; €4) where the small but intriguing collection features a 2500-year-old Medusa pediment. The island's patron saint, Spyrídhon, is entombed in a silver-covered coffin in his own church on Vouthrótou, and four times a year, to the accompaniment of much celebration and feasting, the relics are paraded through the streets. Some 5km south of town lies the picturesque convent of **Vlahérna**, which is joined to the plush mainland suburb of Kanóni by a short causeway; the tiny islet of **Pondikoníssi** in the bay is visited by frequent *kaïkia* (€1.50 return).

Vátos and Pélekas

Much of the island's coastline has been remorselessly developed; the tiny village of **VÁTOS**, just inland from west-coast Érmones, is the one place within easy reach of Kérkyra Town that has an easy, relaxed feel to it and reasonable rooms and tavernas. Nearby **PÉLEKAS** is rather busy and also inland but it's a good alternative base. The best option for independent travellers is to stay in the village, which has a free bus service to the beach of Glyfadha. Thanks to the village's hilltop location, there are some fine views over the surrounding countryside towards the coast.

Áyios Górdhis and around

Further south, **ÁYIOS GÓRDHIS** beach is more remote but that hasn't spared it from the crowds who come to admire the cliff-girt setting. **Áyios Yeóryios**, on the southwest coast, consists of a developed area just before its beautiful beach, which extends north alongside the peaceful Korissíon lagoon. **Kávos**, near the cape itself, rates with its many clubs and discos as the nightlife capital of the island; for daytime solitude and swimming, you can walk to beaches beyond the nearby hamlets of Sparterá and Dhragotiná.

Arrival and information

Air The airport is 2km from town. Local buses #2 and #3 leave from 500m north of the terminal gates. A taxi should cost €10.
Ferry Boats arrive at the new port, 1km west of town.
Tourist office There's an information booth at Platía Saróko (summer only: Mon–Sat 8am–11pm, Sun 8am–4pm).

Island transport

Local buses The bus stop is at Platía Saróko, where there's also a kiosk with timetable information. Bus #11 goes to Pélekas (7 daily).
Long-distance buses The bus station is on Avramiou, near the new fortress and the new port.

Accommodation

The Roomowners Association at D. Theotóki 2a near the Archeological Museum (daily 9am–1.30pm) is the best source of independent accommodation.

Kérkyra

Dionysus Camping Village Dhassiá, 8km north of Kérkyra Town ⓣ26610 91417, ⓦwww.dionysuscamping.gr. Campsite with good facilities and sporting activities. Also has bungalows to rent for an extra €10/person. Take bus #7. April–Oct. €6.50/person, plus €4.50/tent.
Europa Yitsiáli 10 ⓣ26610 39304. By the new port, these are the cheapest rooms in town, although hot water and cleanliness are not guaranteed. Doubles €40.

Around the island

Corfu Traveler's Inn Áyios Górdhis ⓣ26610 53935, ⓦwww.corfubackpackers.com. Beachside accommodation with plenty of activities on offer. Prices include breakfast and dinner. Dorms €25.
Pension Martini Pélekas ⓣ26610 94326, ⓦwww.pensionmartini.com. Simple rooms have balconies with great views, and there's a lush garden too. Doubles €30.
The Pink Palace Áyios Górdhis ⓣ26610 53103/4, ⓦwww.thepinkpalace.com. An enormous, youth-orientated holiday complex with jacuzzis, club, sports facilities, hairdressers, money exchange and more. Prices include breakfast and dinner. Dorms €23, doubles €45–55.

Eating and drinking

Kérkyra

Aleko's Beach On the jetty below the Palace of Sts Michael and George, serving typical Greek cuisine and seafood. Go later in the evening to soak up the atmosphere. Mains €7–9.
Mikro Café Theotóki & Kotárdou 42. A delightful café-bar with an inviting garden, perfect for an evening drink. Beers €3, cocktails €6.50.
To Paradosiakon Solomoú 20. This colourful restaurant with pavement seating serves traditional dishes. Mains €7–9. Open daily from 10am.

Pélekas

Jimmy's ⓣ26610 94284, ⓦwww.jimmyspelekas.com. Opposite a tiny, yellow church near the crossroads of the roads to the beach and Kaiser's Throne lookout point, this friendly taverna serves excellent food all day, including vegetarian dishes and local specials. Mains €7–9.

Zanzibar By the small town square. Small, popular café-bar with an extensive cocktail menu and live music in the evenings. Beers €2, cocktails €4.50.

Moving on

Air Athens (2–3 daily; 1hr).

Bus Athens (3 daily; 11hr).

Ferry Albania (1 daily; 30min); Ancona (2 weekly; 5hr); Brindisi (3–5 weekly; 6–11hr); Igoumenítsa (8–10 daily; 1hr 30min); Pátra (6–8 weekly; 6hr 30min–8hr); Venice 1–2 weekly; 26hr).

KEFALLONIÁ

Kefalloniá is the largest, and, at first glance, least glamorous, of the Ionian islands; the 1953 earthquake that rocked the archipelago was especially devastating here, with almost every town and village levelled. Since the 2001 film adaptation of Louis de Bernières' novel, *Captain Corelli's Mandolin*, the island has attracted increasing numbers of tourists.

What to see and do

There's plenty of interest: beaches to compare with the best on Corfu or Zákynthos, good local wine, and the partly forested mass of Mount Énos (1628m). The island's size, skeletal bus service and shortage of summer accommodation make renting a motorbike or car a must for extensive exploration.

Argostóli

ARGOSTÓLI, with daily ferries to Kyllíni on the mainland, is the bustling, concrete, island capital. The town's **Archeological Museum** (Tues–Sun 8.30am–3pm; €3) is second only to Corfu's in the archipelago.

North of the island

Heading north, you come to the beach of **Mýrtos**, considered the best on the island, although lacking in facilities; the closest places to **stay** are nearby Dhivaráta and almost bus-less **Ássos**, a beautiful fishing port perched on a narrow isthmus linking it to a castellated headland. At the end of the line, pretty **Fiskárdho**, with its eighteenth-century houses, is the most expensive place on the island; the main reason to come would be for the daily **ferry** to Lefkádha island, and crossings to Itháki.

The east coast

Busy **SÁMI**, set against a natural backdrop of verdant, undulating hills, nestles itself into a sweeping bay. The town is the second port on the island, with boats to Itháki and Pátra. However, **AYÍA EFIMÍA**, 10km north, makes a far more attractive base. Between the two towns, 3km from Sámi, the **Melissáni cave** (daily 9am–sunset; €6), a partly submerged Capri-type "blue grotto", is well worth a stop. Southeast from Sámi are the resorts of **PÓROS**, with regular ferries to Kyllíni.

Arrival and information

Ferry Ferries from Kyllíni mostly dock at Póros, although a daily ferry docks at Argostóli. Ferries from Pátra dock at Sámi.

Tourist offices The waterfront tourist office is in Argostóli (Mon–Fri 7am–3pm).

Island buses The bus station in Argostóli is just past the causeway, on I. Metaxa. There are buses to Ayía Efimía (4 daily); Fiskárdho (2 daily); Póros (2 daily); and Sámi (4 daily). There is no bus service on Sundays.

Accommodation

Hotel Melissani Sámi ⊕26740 22464. An interestingly, if wackily, decorated hotel. The thirteen en-suite rooms have balconies or verandas. May–Oct. Doubles €50.

Karavomilos Beach Sámi ⊕26740 22480, ⓦwww.camping-karavomilos.gr. A shady campsite near the beach, 1km from town. May–Sept. €8.50/person, plus €6/tent.

Olga A Tritsi 82, Argostóli ⊕26710 24981, ⓦwww.olgahotel.gr. Centrally located, beautiful Neoclas-

GREECE IN THE MOVIES

It's no surprise that Greece's photogenic sea, sands and dazzling light have provided the set for numerous films. Worth seeking out before your trip are **Shirley Valentine** (1989), the story of a downtrodden housewife's discovery of Mýkonos (see p.554) and alfresco love; the romantic musical comedy **Mamma Mia** (2008), filmed on Skópelos (see p.556) and the Bond film **For Your Eyes Only** (1981), set amid the spectacular cliff-top monasteries of the Metéora (see p.547).

sical hotel with large rooms by the quayside. Doubles €50.

Eating and drinking

Captain's Table Cnr I. Metaxa & 21 Maïou, Argostóli. A waterfront restaurant with a nautical theme serving everything from home-made pizza to fresh fish. Mains €6–9.
Mermaid Restaurant Sámi. In a wonderful location on the seafront, this friendly restaurant uses local produce to create hearty dishes. Mains €6–9.
Phoenix Vergoti 2, Argostóli. Just off the central square, this enclosed garden is a peaceful spot for a coffee by day, and a popular bar by night.

Moving on

Bus Athens (6 daily; 7hr)
Ferry Brindisi (0–1 weekly; 12hr); Itháki (3–5 daily; 45min); Kyllíni (5–7 daily; 1hr 30min); Pátra (1–2 daily; 2hr 30min).

Crete

CRETE is distinguished as the home of the **Minoan** civilization, Europe's earliest, which made the island the centre of a maritime trading empire as early as 2000 BC and produced artworks unsurpassed in the ancient world. The capital, **Iráklion**, is not the prettiest town on the island, although visits to its superb Archeological Museum and the Minoan palace at nearby **Knossos** are all but compulsory. There are other great Minoan sites at **Mália** on the north coast and at **Phaestos** in the south. Near the latter are the remains of the Roman capital at **Gortys**.

Historical heritage apart, the main attractions are that inland this is still a place where traditional rural life continues, and that the island is big enough to ensure that, with a little effort, you can still get away from it all. There's also a surprisingly sophisticated club scene in the north-coast cities, and plenty of manic, beer-soaked tourist fun in some resorts in between.

IRÁKLION

The best way to approach bustling **IRÁKLION** is by sea; that way you see the city as it should be seen, with Mount Ioúktas rising behind and the Psiloritis range to the west. As you get closer, it's the fifteenth-century city walls that first stand out, still dominating and fully

TRANSPORT AND ORIENTATION ON CRETE

Crete's **transport connections** are excellent. There are regular ferries from Pireás to Iráklion, Réthymnon, Haniá and Áyios Nikólaos, as well as regular connections to Kastélli and Sitía (all on the north coast), a constant stream of buses running between these places, and onward bus connections from these main centres to much of the rest of the island. Thanks to the tourists, there are also plenty of **day-trips** available in season, and small boats linking villages on the south coast. Rather than head for Iráklion, you're better off basing yourself initially in the beautiful city of Haniá (for the west, the mountains and the famous Samarian Gorge), in Réthymnon (only marginally less attractive, and handy for Iráklion, the major Minoan sites and the south), or Sitía to explore the far east.

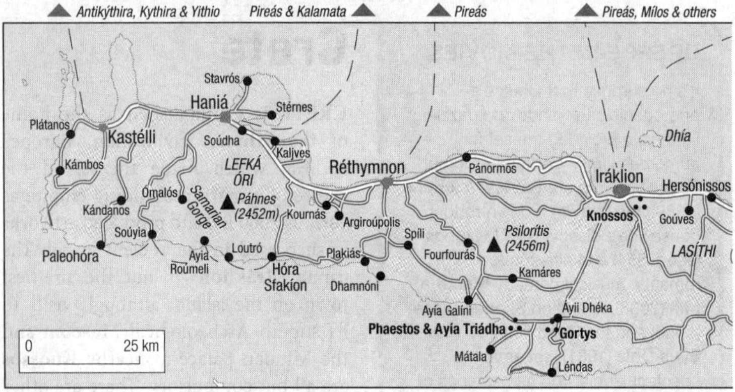

Antikýthira, Kythira & Yithio · Pireás & Kalamata · Pireás · Pireás, Mílos & others

Stavrós · Haniá · Stérnes · Plátanos · Kastélli · Soúdha · Kalíves · Dhía · Kámbos · LEFKÁ ÓRI · Réthymnon · Pánormos · Iráklion · Hersónissos · Omalós · Samarian Gorge · Páhnes (2452m) · Kándanos · Kournás · Argiroúpolis · Knossos · Goúves · Soúyia · Spíli · Psiloritís (2456m) · Paleohóra · Ayía Roúmeli · Loutró · Hóra Sfakíon · Plakiás · Fourfourás · LASÍTHI · Dhamnóni · Kamáres · Ayía Galíni · Áyii Dhéka · Phaestos & Ayía Triádha · Gortys · Mátala · Léndas · 0 · 25 km

encircling the oldest part of town, and finally you sail in past the great Venetian fort defending the harbour entrance. With few sights to trek around, Iráklion is best enjoyed as a centre of great **café** life: the pedestrianized alleys off Dedhálou, especially Koráï, are crammed with tables and packed evenings and weekends. One thing not to miss is the excellent **Archeological Museum**, just off the north side of the main square, Platía Eleftherías. It hosts a collection that includes almost every important prehistoric and Minoan find on Crete. A new building is being constructed, due to open in 2012, and in the meantime only a temporary exhibition is open (summer Mon 1.30–8pm; Tues–Sun 8am–8pm; winter to 3pm; €4).

Arrival and information

Bus For all points along the north-coast highway and Knossos use Bus Station A close to the ferry dock; services on inland routes to the south and west (for Phaestos, for example) leave from a terminal outside the city walls at Haniá Gate.

Ferry Boats dock at the quay at the eastern end of town. As you arrive, turn right to reach the centre.

Tourist office Opposite the museum (Mon–Sat 8.30am–8.30pm; ⓣ2810 246 298/9, ⓦwww.heraklion-city.gr). There is also an office at the airport.

Internet Gallery Games Net, Koráï 14 (daily until 4am; €1.50/hr).

Accommodation

Hellas Rent Rooms Hándhakos 24 ⓣ2810 288 851. A popular option, with a roof garden, cheap breakfasts, a snack bar and panoramic views. Dorms €12, doubles €30.

Rea Kalimeráki 1 ⓣ2810 223 638, ⓦwww.hotelrea.gr. A clean and comfortable *pension* in a quiet location, with friendly staff. April–Oct. Doubles €35.

Youth Hostel Víronos 5 ⓣ2810 286 281, ⓔheraklioyouthhostel@yahoo.gr. Shabby and none too clean, but spacious rooms and you won't find anything cheaper. Inexpensive meals are served in the restaurant, with home-grown ingredients. Dorms €10.

Eating

Ippokambos Sofokli Venizelou 3. The locals' choice for *mezedhes* and the freshest seafood. Authentic and delicious. Mains €6–9.

Peri Orexeos Koráï 10. A good choice for typical Cretan cuisine. There's a pleasant terrace too, for lazy breakfasts and snacks. Mains €6–9.

Moving on

Bus Áyios Nikólaos (every 30min until 10.30pm; 1hr 30min); Haniá (18 daily; 3hr); Hersónissos (every 15–30min; 40min); Knossos (every 10min; 20min); Mália (every 15–30min; 1hr); Phaestos (8 daily; 1hr); Réthymnon (hourly; 1hr 30min); Sitía (4 daily; 3hr 15min).

Ferry Mýkonos (1–2 daily; 5hr); Iráklion to Páros & Cyclades (1–2 daily; 4hr); Iráklion to Pireás (5–7 daily; 6–10hr); Iráklion to Rhodes (2 weekly; 12–13hr); Kastélli to Yíthio (2 weekly; 7–8hr).

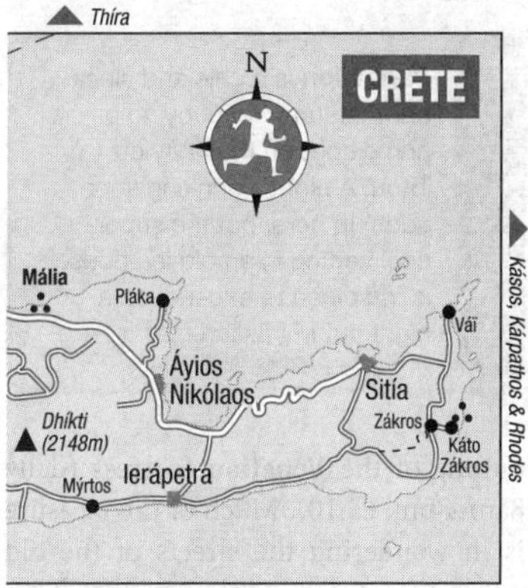

KNOSSOS

The largest of the Minoan palaces, **KNOSSOS** (daily: April–Sept 8am–7.30pm; Oct–March 8.30am–5pm; €6; frequent buses from Iráklion) reached its cultural peak over 3500 years ago. Evidence of a luxurious lifestyle is plainest in the **Queen's Suite**, off the grand **Hall of the Colonnades** at the bottom of the stunningly impressive **Grand Staircase** (which visitors are no longer allowed to use but which can be viewed from above). Most extraordinary is the fact that until just over 100 years ago, Knossos was known only as a mythical place, the court of King Minos; the site was excavated by Sir Arthur Evans from 1900 onwards.

GORTYS

About 1km west of the village of Áyii Dhéka, where the bus drops you off, **GORTYS** (daily 8am–7.30pm; €4) is the ruined capital of the Roman province of Cyrenaica, which included not only Crete but also much of North Africa. If you walk here from Áyii Dhéka you'll get an idea of the huge scale of the place at its height in the third century AD. At the main entrance to the fenced site, north of the road, is the ruined but still impressive basilica of **Áyios Títos**, the island's first Christian church and burial place of the saint (Titus) who converted Crete and was also its first bishop. Beyond this is the **Odeion**, which houses the most important discovery on the site, the **Law Code** – ancient laws inscribed on stones measuring about 10m by 3m.

KNOSSOS AND THE MINOTAUR

Legend has it that King Minos built the labyrinth at Knossos to contain the **minotaur**. This terrifying creature with a man's body and a bull's head fed on fresh maidens and young men – until Theseus, prince of Athens, arrived to slay the monster, and, with Minos's daughter Ariadne's help, successfully escaped the maze.

HERSÓNISSOS AND MÁLIA

The coast east of Iráklion was the first to be developed, and is still the domain of the package tourist. There are some good beaches, but all of them fully occupied. The heart of the development lies around **HERSÓNISSOS** and **MÁLIA**, which these days form virtually a single resort. If it's the party-holiday spirit you're after, this is the place to come. Hersónissos is perhaps slightly classier, but Mália was a bigger place to start with, which means there's a real town on the south side of the main road, with more chance of reasonably priced food and accommodation. Wherever you go, you'll have no problem finding bars, clubs and English (or Irish or even Dutch) pubs. Some of the better beaches stretch east from Mália, where the atmospheric ruins of the **Palace of Mália** (Tues–Sun 8.30am–3pm; €4), much less visited than Knossos or Phaestos, boast a virtually intact ground plan.

SITÍA

Sleepy **SITÍA**, the port and main town of the relatively unexploited eastern edge of Crete, may be about to wake up. For the moment, though, it still offers a plethora of waterside restaurants, a long sandy beach and a lazy lifestyle little affected by the thousands of visitors in peak season. There are several cheap **rooms** around Kondhiláki, a few streets back from the harbour. At the eastern end of the island, **VÁÏ BEACH** is the most famous on Crete thanks to its ancient grove of palm trees. In season, though, its undoubted charms, now fenced off, are diluted by crowds of day-trippers. Other beaches at nearby **Ítanos** or **Palékastro** – Crete's main windsurfing centre – are less exotic but emptier. Or head further south – at **Káto Zákros** the pebbly beach is right by another important Minoan palace.

Arrival and information

Bus The bus station is on the southern edge of town, a short walk from the town's centre.
Ferry The harbour is centrally located.
Tourist office On the seafront (Mon–Fri 9.30am–2.30pm & 5–9pm & Sat 9.30am–2.30pm; ⓣ28430 28300).

Accommodation and eating

Hotel Arhontiko Kondhiláki 16, Sitía ⓣ28430 28172. This welcoming family-run guesthouse has clean and simple rooms, and a leafy garden at the front. Doubles €25.
Taverna Mihos Kornárou 117, Sitía ⓣ28430 22416. A traditional taverna with seating along the waterfront. There's a varied menu, including seafood and Cretan specialities. Mains €5–9.

Island transport

Bus Áyios Nikólaos (7 daily; 1hr 30min); Iráklion (4 daily; 3hr 15min); Mália (7 daily; 2hr 15min).

RÉTHYMNON

West of Iráklion, the old town of **RÉTHYMNON** is a labyrinthine tangle of Venetian and Turkish houses set around an enclosed sixteenth-century harbour and wide sandy beach. Medieval minarets lend an exotic air to the skyline, while dominating everything from the west is the superbly preserved outline of the **Venetian fortress** (daily 8am–8pm; €3.10). Much of the pleasure is in wandering the streets of the old town once the sun has set; there's an unbroken line of tavernas, cafés and cocktail bars right around the waterside and into the area around the old port. Better-value places are found around the seventeenth-century Venetian **Rimóndi Fountain**, an easily located landmark. The heart of Réthymnon's nightlife – which, although abundant, doesn't warm up until midnight – centres on the Venetian port.

TREAT YOURSELF

Pagopiíon is a chic and sleek bar-restaurant occupying a prime spot on Platía Ayíou Títou. A night's drinking soon adds up here, but the super-cool setting in an old ice house is *the* place to experience a night out in Iráklion.

Arrival and information

Bus From the bus station, head around the inland side of the fortress to reach the beach and the centre.
Tourist office Located right on the beach on Sofokli Venizelou (Mon–Fri 8am–2.30pm, Sat 10am–4pm; ⓣ28310 29148).

Accommodation

Barbara Dokimaki Rooms Dambérgi 14 ⓣ28310 22607. Pleasant en-suite rooms with kitchenettes, set around a small courtyard or terrace area. Doubles €40.
Camping Elizabeth Missiria, 4km east of Réthymnon ⓣ28310 28694, ⓦwww.camping-elizabeth.net. This campsite is in the hotel strip along the beach, served by frequent buses from the main bus station. April–Oct. €7.50/person, plus €5.40/tent.
Olga's Pension Souliou 57 ⓣ28310 53206. Small but attractive rooms are individually decorated, and there's a flower-filled roof garden. A gem. Doubles €35–50.
Youth Hostel Tombázi 41 ⓣ28310 22848, ⓦwww.yhrethymno.com. This friendly and relaxed hostel has clean facilities, cheap breakfasts and free wi-fi access. Dorms €11.

Eating, drinking and nightlife

Rock Club Cafe Ioulias Petichaki 6 Ⓦwww.rockcafe-rethymno.com. A long-standing favourite near the harbour, this club kicks off around midnight and plays mainstream sounds.

Metropolis Nearchou 15 Ⓦwww.metropolis-crete.com. A funky bar with a scattering of themed events, karaoke and live music. Free entry.

Stella's Kitchen Souliou 55, at *Olga's Pension*, see opposite. Popular with the locals, this café is good for breakfasts and great-value daily specials, a couple of which are always vegetarian. Mains €5–6. Daily 8am–9pm.

To Pigadi Xanthoúdhidhou 31. Despite the well-dressed clientele, this unpretentious restaurant is great value. There's an atmospheric garden and excellent food with attentive service. Mains €7–12.

Moving on

Bus Haniá (hourly; 1hr); Iráklion (hourly; 1hr 30min).

PLAKIÁS

Réthymnon lies at one of the narrower parts of Crete, so it's relatively quick to cut across from here to the south coast. The obvious place to head is **PLAKIÁS**, a growing resort that's managed to retain a small-town atmosphere. There are numerous **rooms**, very busy in August, as well as a relaxed and friendly youth **hostel** (Ⓣ28320 32118, Ⓦwww.yhplakias.com; dorms €10) at the back of the town, and *Camping Appollonia* (April–Oct; Ⓣ28320 31507; €7 per person, plus €4 per tent) on the road in from Réthymnon.

HANIÁ

HANIÁ is the spiritual capital of Crete; for many, it is also the island's most attractive city – especially in spring, when the snowcapped peaks of the Lefká Óri (White Mountains) seem to hover above the roofs.

What to see and do

The **port area** is the oldest and the most interesting part of town. The little hill that rises behind the landmark domes of the quayside Mosque of the Janissaries is called **Kastélli**, site of the earliest Minoan habitation and core of the Venetian and Turkish towns. Beneath the hill, on the inner harbour, the arches of sixteenth-century Venetian arsenals survive alongside remains of the outer walls. Behind the harbour lie the less picturesque but livelier sections of the old city. Around the cathedral on Halídhon are some of the more animated shopping areas, particularly leather-dominated **Odhós Skrydhlóf**.

Beaches

Haniá's **beaches** all lie to the west: the packed city beach is a ten-minute walk beyond the Maritime Museum, but for good sand you're better off taking the bus from the east side of Platía 1866 along the coast road to Kalamáki. In between you'll find emptier stretches if you're prepared to walk some of the way.

HIKING THE SAMARIAN GORGE

The **Samarian Gorge** – one of Europe's longest – is an easy day-trip from Haniá (May–Oct only), as there are regular buses. If you do it, though, be warned that you will not be alone: dozens of coachloads set off before dawn from all over Crete for the dramatic climb into the White Mountains and the long (at least 4hr) walk down. At the bottom of the gorge is the village of Ayía Roúmeli from where boats will take you east to Hóra Sfakíon and your bus home, or west towards the pleasant resorts of Soúyia and Paleohóra. The mountains offer endless other **hiking challenges** Soúyia and Paleohóra are both good starting points, as is Loutró, a tiny place halfway to Hóra Sfakíon, accessible only by boat.

Arrival and information

Bus The bus station is on Odhós Kydhonías, within easy walking distance of the centre.

Ferry Ferries dock about 10km away at the port of Soúdha: there are frequent city buses that will drop you by the market on the fringes of the old town.

Tourist office In the *Dhimarhío* (town hall) at Kydhonías 29, four blocks east of the bus station (summer only: Mon–Fri 8am–2.30pm; ⓣ 28210 36155).

Internet Triple W, at Balantinou 4 (ⓣ 28210 93478; 24hr).

Accommodation

Camping Hania 5km west of town ⓣ 2821 031 138, ⓦ www.camping-chania.gr. Small site, but it has a pool and is close to the beaches. Get there by city bus from Platía 1866. March–Oct. €5/adult, plus €4/tent.

Earini Rooms Halídhon 27 ⓣ 2821 057 666, ⓦ www.earini.gr. A hospitable welcome and decent rooms are found at this well-situated guesthouse. There's also a large apartment. Doubles €35–45, 2-bed apartment €150.

Mme Bassia Betólo 45–51 ⓣ 2821 055 087, ⓦ www.mmebassia.gr. A charming *pension* with a homely atmosphere. Traditionally decorated rooms are a good size, and there's a tiny roof garden too. Doubles €45.

Pension Nora Theotokopoúlou 60 ⓣ 2821 072 265, ⓦ www.pension-nora.com. Charming a/c en-suite rooms in an old wooden Turkish house, with access to a shared kitchen. Doubles €40.

Eating and drinking

Ababa Tapas Café Eisodion 12. Secreted off a side street behind the harbour, this warm, alternative bar lures with twinkling lights, decent tunes and charming staff. Tapas dishes from €6.

Ellotia 1st Sidestreet, Pórtou 6. This cosy garden taverna serves delicious traditional fare in a leafy setting. Grills €6–9.

Metropolitan Betólo 28. Food is pricey, but come to this American-style bar in the evenings for live music from 10pm. Cover charge €1.50.

Tamam Zambelíou 49. A converted Turkish bathhouse houses this restaurant which has an adventurous menu. Especially popular with vegetarians and wine-lovers. Mains €5–9.

Moving on

Bus Iráklion (hourly; 3hr); Omalos (for the Samarian Gorge; 4 daily when the gorge is open; 1hr); Réthymnon (hourly; 1hr).

Hungary

HIGHLIGHTS

SZÉPASSZONY VALLEY, EGER: taste Bull's Blood (a famous Hungarian wine) at the valley's miniature cellars

THERMAL BATHS, BUDAPEST: wallow in hot thermal waters in one of Budapest's grand historic baths

CASTLE HILL, BUDAPEST: you literally can't miss this: the heart of the historic Buda side of the city

BADACSONY: enjoy local wines and long walks in this gorgeous wine-growing region

PÉCS: explore the student bars by night and the town's many historic treasures by day

ROUGH COSTS

DAILY BUDGET Basic €30 /occasional treat €45

DRINK Beer (large) €1–2

FOOD Goulash €3

HOSTEL/PENSION €10–30

TRAVEL Budapest–Eger €8 by train; Pécs–Keszthely €10 by bus

FACT FILE

POPULATION 10 million

AREA 93,000 sq km

LANGUAGE Hungarian

CURRENCY Forint (Ft)

CAPITAL Budapest (population: 2.5 million)

INTERNATIONAL PHONE CODE ⓣ36

Introduction

Bordered by countries as diverse as Austria, Serbia and Ukraine, Hungary is a crossroads at the centre of the continent - what was once known as Mitteleuropa – and it fuses old Europe and new in its mix of Hapsburg grandeur and Communist-era grittiness. There is a Central European solidity to its food, buildings and culture, but the more exotic, and undeniably romantic, founding myth of the nomadic, warrior Magyars from the Central Asian steppe is also key to Hungarians' fiery national pride.

Budapest, the capital, is a city of imposing scale and wide Danube vistas, split by the river into historic Buda and buzzy Pest, and offering both the old (imperial-era boulevards, Art Nouveau coffeehouses, bubbling Turkish baths) and the new (quirky warehouse bars and summer riverboat clubs). A few hours' travel beyond Budapest is enough to access Hungary's other key charms, from Serb-influenced **Szentendre**, a short way north along the Danube bend, to the lush wine-growing **Badacsony** region on the shores of **Lake Balaton** to the southwest. Balaton, the "nation's playground", also plays host to crowded summer party resorts such as **Siófok**, or gentler **Keszthely**. Hungary's three most culture-rich towns beyond Budapest are scattered across the country but not to be missed: **Sopron**, close by the border with Austria; **Pécs**, on the far southern tip, ringed by alpine hills; and **Eger**, just northeast of Budapest, a mellow, historic city famous for its Bull's Blood wine. Across southeast Hungary stretches the enormous Great Plain, covering half the country and home to some beautiful national parks and the cities of **Szeged** and **Kecskemét**.

CHRONOLOGY

9 BC Area around the Danube is conquered by the Romans.

434–453 AD Attila the Hun's feared empire is centred in modern-day Hungary.

568 The Avars, nomads from Inner/Central Asia, arrive.

Around 896 The Magyars in Hungary begin the *honfoglalás* or land-taking (conquest of the region).

1000 Kingdom of Hungary established by King Stephen.

1242 The Mongols attack Hungary.

1526 The Hungarian army is defeated by the Ottomans in the Battle of Mohács and the country is split into three regions, under different forms of government.

1552 The Hungarians hold back the Turks at the Eger fortress – a major date in national consciousness.

1699 The Turks are defeated and expelled from Hungary by the Austrian Habsburgs.

1867 In order to quell separatist calls, Austria accepts greater Hungarian autonomy – in what is known as the Compromise – and the dual monarchy of Austria-Hungary is formed.

1896 Huge celebrations across Hungary for the millennial anniversary – 1000 years since the arrival of the Magyars.

1918 After World War I, Austria-Hungary is split into two countries.

1920 Treaty of Trianon in which Hungary loses two-thirds of its prewar territory.

1919–41 The right-wing dictatorship of Admiral Horthy.

1938 Hungarian journalist László Bíró invents the ballpoint pen.

1944 Germany occupies Hungary and installs the Arrow Cross party (Hungarian fascists) in government.

1944–45 Hungary's large prewar Jewish community is decimated as Jews are deported and ghettoized under Nazi occupation.

1945 Soviets invade Hungary.

1947 Soviets consolidate their postwar power in Hungary.

1956 National uprising against Soviet occupation is brutally repressed.

1989–91 Collapse of Communism in the Soviet Union and the eastern bloc.
1990 Hungary's first free elections held.
2004 Hungary joins the EU.

ARRIVAL

Flights to Budapest arrive at Ferenc Liszt (formerly Ferihegy) airport, 20km from the centre; bus and metro connect into Budapest, but most convenient is the airport bus that will take you straight to your accommodation. Several budget airlines now fly to Balaton airport – the closest town is Keszthely, with a regular bus service to and from Balaton Airport.

Most international **trains** arrive at Keleti pu in Budapest, although Nyugati pu and Déli pu also handle international arrivals (see "Arrivals" in the Budapest section). Global or One Country InterRail passes are valid on all trains. International **buses** are generally operated by Eurolines, or Volánbusz, its Hungarian associate, with their two main terminals in Budapest.

GETTING AROUND

Public transport in Hungary is cheap, clean and fairly reliable. The only problem can be getting information, as English is by no means uniformly spoken.

Intercity **trains** are the fastest way of getting to the major towns (marked "IC" on the timetable), though seat reservations, a separate numbered piece of card available at any MÁV office (Ⓦwww.mav-start.hu), are compulsory for services marked Ⓡ on timetables, and cost around 480Ft extra. You can buy **tickets** (*jegy*) for domestic services at the station (*pályaudvar* or *vasútállomás*) on the day of departure, but it's best to buy tickets for international trains (*nemzetközi gyorsvonat*) at least 36hr in advance. When buying your ticket, specify whether you want a one-way ticket (*egy útra*), or a return (*retur* or *oda-vissza*). For a journey of 100km, travelling second-class on an express train, expect to pay around 1600Ft.

Volánbusz (Ⓦwww.volanbusz.hu) runs the bulk of Hungary's **buses**, which are often the quickest way to travel between the smaller towns. Arrive early to confirm times and get a seat. For **long-distance services** from Budapest and the major towns, you can book a seat up to 30min before departure; after that, you get them from the driver (and

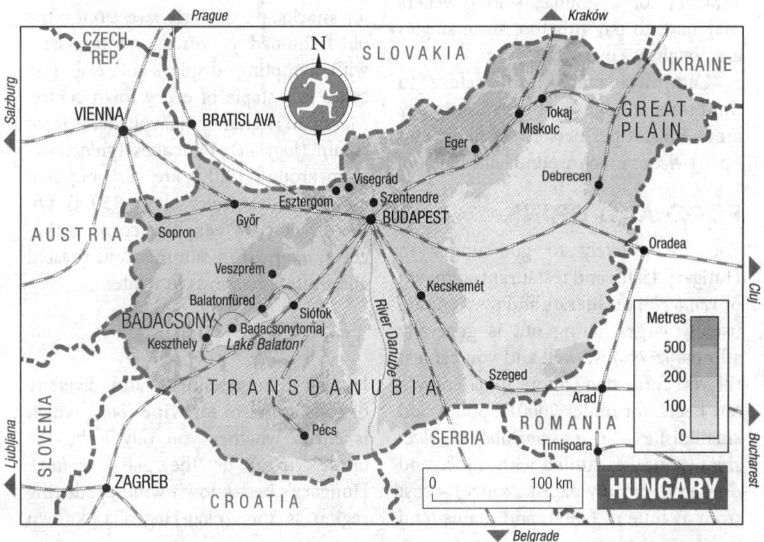

risk standing). For a journey of 100km, expect to pay around 1600Ft.

ACCOMMODATION

Accommodation tends to fill up during high season, so you should aim to **book ahead**. **Hostels** are increasingly common in the main tourist destinations, while across the country, the tradition of the homely *pension* (*panzió*) or **guesthouse** (*vendégház*) still thrives, ranging from rooms in private homes to more professional outfits. Here, expect to pay from 8000Ft for a double. If you're really strapped for cash, try for **university dorms** – rooms are rented out in July and August, and often available at weekends year-round; local tourist offices can assist with bookings. **Private rooms** (*vendégszoba*) and apartments are also affordable and can be arranged through Ibusz, the nationwide agency (ⓦwww.ibusz.hu), or local tourist offices. Doubles range from 4000Ft in provincial towns to around 6000Ft in Budapest. Budget **hotels** are often rather old-fashioned; outside Budapest and Lake Balaton (where prices are thirty percent higher), a three-star **hotel** (*szálló* or *szálloda*) will charge from around 12,000Ft for a double; solo travellers may have to pay this too, since singles are not always on offer.

Campsites range from deluxe to third class. In high season, expect to pay around 800Ft per person per night, and up to twice as much around Lake Balaton.

FOOD AND DRINK

You are unlikely to go hungry in Hungary. Cafés and restaurants (*étterem* or *vendéglő*) proliferate and portions are usually large. Eating out is generally affordable: choose well and you can eat till you can eat no more, plus enjoy a few beers, for under 2000Ft. Soups and small dishes – such as *hortobágyi palacsinta* (pancakes stuffed with mince and doused in creamy paprika sauce) – cost from as little as 600Ft, and mains tend to start around 1200Ft (or 1800Ft in higher-end eateries).

For foreigners, the archetypal **Hungarian dish** is goulash (*gulyásleves*) – a stew including meat and potatoes, brilliantly coloured with paprika and traditionally served in a cauldron (*bogrács*). Hungarians are fond of frying meat in breadcrumbs and stuffing it with other types of meat and cheese. The Mangalica pig, a hairy boar with a curly sheep-like fleece, is a particular (if fatty) delicacy. Choices for **vegetarians** in Hungarian restaurants tend to be limited to the salads or starters sections of menus – for example, fried cheese, mushrooms or cauliflower (*rántott sajt/gomba/karfiol*).

Hungarians like a protein-heavy **breakfast** (*reggeli*) featuring cheese, eggs and salami, plus bread and jam. **Coffeehouses** (*kávéház*) are increasingly trendy and you'll find many serving breakfast and coffee with milk (*tejeskávé*) or whipped cream (*tejszínhabbal*). Most Hungarians take their coffee short and strong (*eszpresszó*).

Traditionally, **lunch** is the main meal of the day, and lunch set menus (*napi menű*) can be a highly affordable way of eating out. You won't want for **snacks**, particularly sweet ones: the old-fashioned *cukrászda* or patisserie with tempting displays of elaborate cakes is a staple of every town centre. Marzipan is a national favourite, as is ice cream (*fagylalt*). **Pancakes** (*palacsinta*, from around 150Ft) are very popular, as are strudels (*rétes*; about 350Ft). On the streets you can buy corn-on-the-cob (*kukorica*) in summer and roasted chestnuts (*gesztenya*) in winter.

Drink

Hungary's mild climate and diversity of soils are ideal for **wine** (*bor*), which is cheap whether you buy it by the bottle (*üveg*) or the glass (*pohár*). Hungary's best-known wine-producing region is the Tokaj-Hegyalja, known predominantly for dessert wine. *Bikavér*, produced around Eger and meaning "Bull's Blood", is a robust red. Good whites can be found around the Badacsony in the Balaton region.

Wine bars (*borozó*) are common, but the best way to taste is at source at the wine cellars (*borpince*) around Pécs and Eger. Harder drinkers favour **brandy** (*pálinka*), with popular flavours being distilled from apricots (*barack*) and plums (*szilva*). Local **beers** (*sör*) to try are Soproni Ászok and Pécsi Szalon *sör*.

CULTURE AND ETIQUETTE

Hungarians are generally very ready to help if you need directions or assistance. The biggest barrier can be language – in Budapest you can survive on English but elsewhere you will likely need to muster a little German, as well as the polite basics in Hungarian. When **tipping** waiters and taxi-drivers, roughly ten percent is more or less expected.

Hungary's dominant **religion** is Catholicism but there are many Protestant churches. Respectful clothing is expected in places of worship. **Women travellers** should not expect any particular hassle in Hungary.

SPORTS AND OUTDOOR ACTIVITIES

Hungary is a predominantly rural country, one-fifth covered in forests. The Great Plain, especially the area around Kecskemét and the Kiskunság National Park, offers some of the best **horse-riding** in Europe as well as fantastic horse-shows during the summer. It's cheapest to select an independent horseriding operator (see section on Kecskemét on p.601).

Cycling is very well provided for: Tourinform can provide cycling maps with recommended routes, and bikes can be rented in most towns at reasonable prices. Particularly scenic cycling routes can be found in the vineyard-covered hills around the Badacsony, where cycling routes run alongside the small winding roads. There are also plenty of **hiking** opportunities in Hungary; walks in the Badacsony region offer stunning views over Lake Balaton. Again Tourinform can provide maps and information.

HUNGARY ONLINE

Ⓦ **www.tourinform.hu** National tourist office.
Ⓦ **www.ibusz.hu** Handy portal for viewing and booking cheap private rooms all across Hungary.
Ⓦ **www.budapestinfo.hu** Comprehensive site with up-to-the-minute listings.
Ⓦ **www.funzine.hu** Fantastic English-language site with information on gigs, nights out, culture and more in Budapest.
Ⓦ **www.mav-start.hu** Train timetables and information.

COMMUNICATIONS

Post offices (*posta*) are usually open Monday to Friday 8am to 6pm, Saturday 8am to midday. You can make local calls from **public phones**, where 20Ft is the minimum charge, or from cardphones; cards come in 50 and 120 units and can be bought from post offices and newsstands. To make national calls, dial Ⓣ06, wait for the buzzing tone, then dial the area code and number. You can make international calls from most public phones: dial Ⓣ00, wait for the buzzing tone, then dial the country code and number as usual. **Internet access** is widely available (usually 400–700Ft/hr) in most towns; many *pensions*, as well as cafés and bars, have wi-fi.

EMERGENCIES

Tourists are treated with respect by the **police** (*rendörség*) unless they're suspected of smuggling drugs or driving

HUNGARIAN

	Hungarian	Pronunciation
Yes	*Igen*	I-gen
No	*Nem*	Nem
Please	*Kérem*	Kay-rem
Thank you	*Köszönöm*	Kur-sur-nurm
Hello/Good day	*Jó napot*	Yo nopot
Goodbye	*Viszontlátásra*	Vee-sont-lar-tarsh-rar
Excuse me	*Bocsánat*	Botch-ah-not
Good	*Jó*	Yo
Bad	*Rossz*	Ross
Today	*Ma*	Ma
Yesterday	*Tegnap*	Teg-nop
Tomorrow	*Holnap*	Hall-nop
How much is...?	*Mennyibe kerül...?*	Men-yi-beh keh-rool...?
What time is it?	*Hány óra van?*	Hine-ora von?
I don't understand	*Nem értem*	Nem ear-tem
Do you speak English?	*Beszél Angolul?*	Beh-sail ong-olool?
One	*Egy*	Edge
Two	*Kettö*	Ket-tur
Three	*Három*	Hah-rom
Four	*Négy*	Naidge
Five	*Öt*	Urt
Six	*Hat*	Hot
Seven	*Hét*	Hait
Eight	*Nyolc*	Nyolts
Nine	*Kilenc*	Kee-lents
Ten	*Tíz*	Teez
Where is/are?	*Hol van/vannak?*	Hawl-von/von-nok?
Entrance	*bejárat*	beyah-ro
Exit	*kijárat*	kiyah-rot
Women's toilet	*női*	nuy
Men's toilet	*férfi mosdó*	fayr-fi maws-daw
Toilet	*WC*	vait-say
Hotel	*szálloda*	sahlaw-da
Railway station	*vasútállomás*	voh-sootal-law-mass
Bus/train stop	*megalló*	meh-gall-o
Plane	*repülőgép*	repoo-lur-gepp
Near	*közel*	kur-zel
Far	*távol*	tav-oll
Single room	*egyágyas szoba*	edg-yahg-yos saw-ba
Double room	*kétágyas szoba*	kay-tadg-yas soba
Cheap	*Olcsó*	Ol-cho
Expensive	*Drága*	Drah-ga
Open	*Nyitva*	Nyeet-va
Closed	*Zárva*	Zah-rva

under the influence of alcohol. Most police have some German, but rarely any other foreign language. Always carry a photocopy of your passport.

All towns listed in this chapter have at least one **pharmacy**, identifiable by their green cross signs. Opening hours are generally Monday to Friday 9am to 6pm, Saturday 9am to noon or 1pm; signs in the window give the location of all-night pharmacies (*ügyeletes gyógyszertár*). Tourist offices can direct

EMERGENCY NUMBERS

Police ⓣ107; Ambulance ⓣ104; Fire ⓣ105.

you to local medical centres or doctors' surgeries (*orvosi rendelő*); these will probably be in private (*magán*) practice, so be sure to carry health insurance. EU citizens have reciprocal arrangements for emergency treatment, but only at state hospitals.

INFORMATION

You'll find branches of **Tourinform** (ⓣ01/438-8080, ⓦwww.tourinform.hu) Hungary's national tourist office, in most towns. They don't usually book accommodation, but do have information on rooms if you haven't booked ahead. **Ibusz** (ⓦwww.ibusz.hu) is the nationwide agency which can help you book accommodation online or on the spot. There are also **local tourist offices** in larger towns (such as Balatontourist around Lake Balaton), which can book rooms.

MONEY AND BANKS

Currency is the **forint** (Ft or HUF), which comes in notes of 200Ft, 500Ft, 1000Ft, 2000Ft, 5000Ft, 10,000Ft and 20,000Ft, and in coins of 1Ft, 2Ft, 5Ft, 10Ft, 20Ft, 50Ft, 100Ft and 200Ft. At the time of writing, €1=265Ft, US$1=185Ft, and £1=300Ft. Standard **banking hours** are Monday to Thursday 8am to 5pm, Friday 8am to 2pm. **ATMs** are widespread, and you can use a **credit/debit card** to pay in many hotels, restaurants and shops.

OPENING HOURS AND HOLIDAYS

Shops are generally open Monday to Friday 10am to 6pm, Saturday 10am to 1pm, and closed on Sundays and public holidays including January 1, March 15, Easter Monday, May 1, Whit Monday, August 20, October 23, November 1, December 25 and 26. Shopping centres operate later hours and are generally open every day, and Tesco – now seemingly everywhere in Hungary – is often open 24/7.

Budapest and around

Over two million people – one-fifth of Hungary's population – live in **BUDAPEST**, and it is the political, cultural and commercial heart of the country. After the 1867 Compromise, which gave the Hungarian monarchy equal status with Austria under the final half-century of the Hapsburg Empire and ushered in a high age of Hungarian nationalism, the city was rapidly developed to become a standing celebration of Hungarian culture and power, and the sheer scale of its vast iconic buildings, from the castle to the Parliament to the Gellert Baths, testifies to Hungary's central role in European history.

Since the unification of Buda and Pest in the nineteenth century, the **Danube** (Duna) is less a dividing line, more the heart of the city itself - providing its most splendid vistas, from both banks. **Pest** is on the eastern bank of the Danube and **Buda** on the hilly west bank. Each of Budapest's 23 districts (*kerületek*) is designated on maps and at the beginning of addresses by a Roman numeral; "V" is Belváros (inner city), on the Pest side; "I" is the Castle district in Buda.

What to see and do

Castle Hill (Várhegy) is the crowning feature of the **Buda** side; a plateau one mile long, it rises steeply from the Danube bank, bearing the imposing Buda Palace, a web of cobbled streets and the Mátyás Church, symbolic of Hungarian nationalism. **Pest** is thick with hip cafés and bars, as well as home to the historic Belváros (central old town) and the intimate Jewish district.

Buda: Castle Hill

Castle Hill stands on the western bank of the **Chain Bridge** (Széchenyi lánchíd), opened in 1849, and – amazingly – the first permanent bridge between Buda and Pest. From Clark Ádám tér on the Buda side, you can reach Castle Hill on the dinky nineteenth-century funicular or **Sikló** (daily 7.30am–10pm; 840Ft up or 1450Ft return), or simply walk the winding, leafy path up from Clark Ádám tér.

Mátyás Church and Fishermen's Bastion

On **Szentháromság tér**, the busy square at the heart of Buda, stands the bright-roofed **Mátyás Church** (Mon–Sat 9am–5pm, Sun 1–5pm; 990Ft). Inside, the church is fabulously exuberant, with the original thirteenth-century structure used as the base for a late nineteenth-century redesign in a Romantic Nationalist style. The splendid gold leaf and nationalist motifs clearly reclaimed the church as Hungarian – it had been a mosque for a time under Ottoman rule. A statue of **King Stephen** (Szent Istvan) on horseback stands outside - he is revered as the founder of the Hungarian state and the one responsible for converting Hungarians to Christianity. Behind the church is the neo-Romanesque **Fishermen's Bastion** or Halászbástya, constructed in 1902 on the spot supposedly defended in the past by the guild of fishermen against would-be invaders. Today it's an excellent place for looking out across the river to the splendid Parliament building rising up on the east bank.

Buda Palace

Topping the crest of Castle Hill, close by the point where the funicular railway emerges, stands **Buda Palace**. The fortifications and interiors have been endlessly remodelled, with the palace's destruction in World War II only the latest in a long line of onslaughts since the thirteenth century. The **National Gallery** (Tues–Sun 10am–6pm; 1000Ft; half-price

BUDAPEST

ACCOMMODATION	
Ábel Panzió	G
Back Pack Guesthouse	H
Csilleberc Camping	A
Mandala Hostel	F
Marco Polo Youth Hostel	B
Mária & István	I
Museum Guest House	E
Nightingale Mini Hotel	C
Red Bus Hostel	D

EATING	
Centrál	19
Duran Sandwich Bar	11
Falafel Faloda	7
Gerbeaud	17
Govinda	12
Hummus Bar	9
Kádár étkezde	14
Kőleves	15
M	8
Menza	5
Müvész	6
Ruszwurm	10

DRINKING & NIGHTLIFE	
Castro Bizstro	16
Darshan Udvar	20
Gusto's	1
Instant	3
Karma Café	4
Kiado Kocsma	2
Lánchíd Söröző	13
Szimpla Kert	18

for students; Ⓦwww.mng.hu), which occupies the central wings B, C and D of the palace compound, contains Hungarian art from the Middle Ages onwards including heavily symbolic nineteenth-century representations of idealized national myths. On the far side of the Lion Courtyard, the **Budapest History Museum** in Wing E (daily 10am–6pm, closed Mon; 1400Ft, half-price for students under 26 Ⓦwww.btm.hu) gives some further historical context with a gathering of artefacts from Budapest's dark ages and medieval past, but is rather old-fashioned, and arguably underwhelming for the price.

Gellért Hill

Close by the Szabadság híd (Liberation bridge) on the Buda side is **Gellért Hill** (Gellérthegy), home to the best known of the city's baths, Gellért Baths (see box opposite) and topped by the **Liberation Monument**, constructed in 1947 to commemorate Hungary's liberation from Nazi rule. Depicting a woman holding aloft the palm of victory, it is one of the few Soviet monuments to survive the fall of the Iron Curtain *in situ* (most have been destroyed or moved out of town to the Memento Park). Below, the **Citadella**, a mock-medieval fortress built by the Habsburgs to cow the population after the 1848–49 revolution, hugs the west bank of the Danube.

Communist Memento Park

The **Memento Park** (Szoborpark; daily 10am–sunset; 1500Ft, Ⓦwww.mementopark.hu), on the Buda side of the river 15km south of town, houses statues of Marx, Engels, Lenin and friends, as well as heroic scenes from Communist legend, and is a lively glimpse into the Communist past of eastern Europe for the uninitiated. It is not easily accessed by public transport, unfortunately: the easiest option, but far from cheap, is to take the Statue Park bus from Deák tér (daily at 11am; July 16 to Aug 28 also at 3pm; 4500Ft return, includes entry fee).

Pest: around Vörösmarty tér

Central **Vörösmarty tér** is flooded with crowded café terraces; it's worth stopping to savour the sweet delights on offer at the **Gerbeaud** patisserie, a favourite *fin-de-siècle* high-society haunt. By *Gerbeaud*'s terrace is the entrance to the Underground Railway (Földatti Vasút), the first metro line on the continent, and the second in the world after London's, when it opened in 1896.

Váci utca, a mix of chic shops and tourist tat stalls, runs south from **Vörösmarty tér**. Past the Pesti Theatre, where the twelve-year-old Frank (Ferenc) Liszt made his concert debut, Váci utca continues south to the **Central Market** (Mon 6am–5pm, Tues–Fri 6am–6pm, Sat 6am–2pm), a grand high-roofed hall whose stalls are laden with paprika, *pálinka*, local wines and enough sausages and hams to satisfy the most voracious meat-eater.

National Museum

Just off Múzeum körút (the road named after it), and easily accessed by Ⓜ Kálvin tér, is the grandiose Neoclassical **National Museum** (Wed–Sun 10am–6pm; 1100Ft or 550Ft for EU citizens under 26; Ⓦwww.hnm.hu), which gives a comprehensive overview of Hungarian history from the Magyar tribes' arrival to the collapse of Communism.

The Great Synagogue and Jewish quarter

On the corner of Wesselényi and Dohány utca stands the **Great Synagogue** or Dohány Street synagogue (March–Oct: Sun–Thurs 10.30am–5.30pm, Fri 10am–3.30pm; Nov–Feb: Sun–Thurs 10am–3.30pm, Fri 10am–1.30pm; 2000Ft for entrance to synagogue and garden). It is the world's second-largest synagogue (the largest is in New York) and the central place of worship for what remains – despite the devastation of the Holocaust – Central Europe's largest Jewish community. The Byzantine-Moorish interior is worth a look, but the history is the powerful part: Theodor (Tividar) Herzl, father of Zionism, was born on this site, and in the courtyard are buried the bodies of more than 2000 people who died here in 1944–45 when the synagogue was part of the Budapest ghetto. Take the time to look at the beautiful silver tree in the "garden of remembrance", named after Raoul Wallenberg, the Swedish diplomat who rescued many Jews during World War II. Behind the synagogue lies Pest's old Jewish quarter, today dotted with trendy cafés and snug little patisseries.

St Stephen's Basilica

Looming over the rooftops to the north of Vörösmarty tér is the dome of **St Stephen's Basilica** (ⓦwww.basilica.hu), an assertive nineteenth-century cathedral whose heavy ornamentation inspires awe more than contemplation. The dome collapsed shortly after building but is now sturdy enough to climb for its panoramic views of Budapest (dome: April–Oct Mon–Sat 10am–6pm; 500Ft). On St Stephen's Day, August 20, the mummified hand of St Stephen – Hungary's most revered relic – is brought out of a side-chapel and paraded round the building.

Parliament and the Danube east bank

The east bank of the Danube is peppered with beautiful buildings, notably the Art Nouveau Gresham Palace (now the *Four Seasons Hotel*) on **Roosevelt tér** and the unmissable **Parliament**, Hungary's biggest building. The Parliament houses the old **Coronation Regalia**, including national hero St Stephen's crown, sceptre and orb, and its impressive interior features sweeping staircases and a 96m-high gilded central dome. There are daily **tours** of the building – in English – if parliamentary business allows (10am, noon, 2pm; free for EU citizens, 2950Ft for others; tickets from Gate X on Kossuth Square; ⓦwww.parlament.hu).

BATHING IN STYLE: BUDAPEST'S SPA SCENE

Budapest has some of the grandest **baths** in Europe, and they are much more affordable than you might expect: Hungarians see it as practically their democratic right to wallow in the thermal waters bubbling up from subterranean springs. A Budapest spa visit is one of the city's must-do experiences, fantastically restorative and sure to ease any aches and pains from pounding the city streets. A basic ticket covers three hours in the pools, sauna and steam rooms (*gözfürdo*). You pay more to access extra services such as mud baths (*iszapfürdo*) or massages (*masszázs*).

Built in 1913, the magnificent **Gellért baths**, with original Art Nouveau furnishings, awesome mosaics, sculptures and stained glass offer the most exclusive experience (daily 6am–8pm; 3600Ft pool and cabin). You can get cheaper tickets just for the stunning thermal baths (which close earlier at weekends; separate baths for men and women). The popular **Széchenyi Baths** in Pest (ⓦwww.szechenyifurdo.hu) are the hottest in the capital, and strongly recommended. Right by Heroes' Square, they boast large outdoor pools where old men play chess on floating boards, and fun features like water rapids and underwater bubble jets (May–Sept daily 6am–10pm, Oct–April 6am–5pm; from 2250Ft). The atmospheric **Rudas baths**, meanwhile, house a charming octagonal pool under a characteristic Turkish dome (men only Mon & Wed–Fri 6am–8pm, women only Tues 6am–8pm, mixed Sat & Sun 6am–7pm and Fri–Sun 10am–4pm; from 1500Ft).

Andrássy út

To the east of St Stephen's basilica, **Andrássy út** runs dead straight for 2.5km, a wide avenue lined with grand if sometimes tumbledown buildings. Look out for the magnificent Opera House at no. 22. At no. 60, out east towards Hosök tere, is the **House of Terror** (Tues–Sun 10am–6pm; 1800Ft, 900Ft for students under 26; Ⓦwww.terrorhaza.hu). Once the headquarters of the fascist Arrow Cross and later of the Communist secret police (the ÁVO), the House of Terror is now a hard-hitting museum to the "dual terror" of Fascism and Communism. Original footage, photographs and interviews with survivors are powerfully used to tell the story of the twin tyrannies that Hungary suffered in the twentieth century. Not to be missed.

Hosök tere – Heroes' Square

The bombastic **Hosök tere** (Heroes' Square) was created to mark the 1000th anniversary of the Magyar conquest in 1896, and its triumphant conquerors and rearing horses recall a time when Hungarian nationalism was at full throttle. Its centrepiece is the **Millenary Monument**, portraying the Magyar leader Prince Árpád, and the surrounding semicircle of greats of Hungarian history include King Stephen and Lajos Kossuth, who headed Hungary's short-lived independent government after the 1848 revolution. Also on **Heroes' Square** is the **Museum of Fine Arts** (Tues–Sun 10am–5.30pm, late opening to 9pm on Thurs; 1600Ft/800Ft if 26 or under; Ⓦwww.szepmuveszeti.hu), with a good, but not hugely extensive, collection of paintings by big names including Bruegel, Rembrandt and El Greco. Behind the museum lies **Budapest Zoo** (daily 9am–6.30pm; 2100Ft), which may not top the city's attractions for grown-ups but does feature some striking architecture; let's hope its animal inhabitants appreciate it. Opposite the zoo are the yellow neo-Baroque **Széchenyi baths** (see box, p.587).

The Városliget and Petőfi Csarnok

The **Városliget** (City Park), which starts just behind the Hősök tere, holds the **Vajdahunyad Castle**, a somewhat kitsch imitation Transylvanian castle which incorporates no less than 21 architectural styles from across Hungary's regions and was built in 1896 as a celebration of Hungarian art and design. In the courtyard is a statue of the monk Anonymus – a celebrated twelfth-century chronicler of Hungarian history. An artificial lake at the foot of the castle is filled with water for rowing and pedaloes in summer and an ice-rink in winter.

Arrival and information

Air From Ferihegy airport (Ⓣ01/296-9696), an airport minibus (signed as Airport Shuttle Minibusz) will deliver you to any address you ask for (2900Ft one-way, 4900Ft return; office in the terminal building). The journey is cheaper but not as quick or convenient by public transport; take airport bus #200 to Kobánya-Kispest metro station, and from there it's ten metro stops to the centre (Deák tér station). Tickets for both legs of the journey will cost 290Ft if you buy bus/metro tickets from the newsagents at the airport terminals. Airport taxi-drivers are notorious sharks and better avoided.

Train There are three main train stations, all of which are directly connected by metro with the central Deák tér metro station in the Belváros. Keleti station (Eastern station; Ⓣ01/313-6835) handles most international trains, including those from Vienna (Westbahnhof), Belgrade, Bucharest, Zagreb and Bratislava, as well as domestic arrivals from Sopron and Eger; Nyugati station (Western station; Ⓣ01/349-0115) receives trains from Prague and Bratislava, some from Bucharest, and domestic ones from the Danube Bend; and Déli station (Southern station Ⓣ01/355-8657) has one train a day from Vienna (Südbahnhof), the occasional train from Zagreb, and domestic services from Pécs and Lake Balaton. General train information at Ⓦwww.mav.hu; you can book tickets in advance from abroad on Ⓣ01/371-9449.

Bus The central international bus station is at Népliget (blue metro), serving international destinations and routes to Transdanubia. Volánbusz (☎01/382-0888, Ⓦwww.volanbusz.hu) services international routes including to and from the Czech Republic, Croatia, Poland, Serbia and the Ukraine. Also in Pest, Stadionok bus station (red metro) serves areas east of the Danube; and Árpád híd bus station (blue metro) serves the Danube Bend.
Boat Passenger boats from Vienna, Bratislava and other international destinations run from April–Oct, operated by Mahart (Ⓦwww.mahartpassnave.hu). International boats dock at quays along the Danube between the Lanchíd bridge and Szabadság bridge.
Tourist office There are three major Tourinform offices in Budapest: Sütọ utca 2, just around the corner from Deák tér metro (this branch also houses the Tourist Police office; daily 8am–8pm; ☎01/438-8080, Ⓦwww.tourinform.hu); other branches are at Liszt Ferenc tér 11 (April–Oct daily noon–8pm; Nov–March Mon–Fri 10am–6pm), and Ferihegy Airport (Terminal 1: daily 9am–10pm; Terminal 2A: daily 8am–11pm; Terminal 2B: daily 9.30am–9.30pm). Tourist information stands are also found in handy locations such as in the Castle District on Szentháromság tér, at the Central Market, Budapest Airport (at both terminals), and Keleti Railway Station. The official Budapest website is at Ⓦwww.budapestinfo.hu.
Discount passes A Budapest Card (5500/6900/8300Ft for 24/48/72 hr; Ⓦwww.budapest-card.com), available at the airport and town centre tourist offices, hotels and major metro stations, and available to order online at Ⓦwww.budapestinfo.hu, gives unlimited travel on public transport, free museum admission, and discount on the airport minibus. Many museums offer half-price entry to students or those under 26 – a welcome discount as entry prices are often steep.

City transport

See Ⓦwww.bkv.hu for comprehensive info on Budapest city transport. If you don't have the correct ticket you can be fined up to 12,000Ft.
Tickets A basic 320Ft ticket is valid for a journey along one metro line, and also for a single journey on buses, trolleybuses, trams and the HÉV suburban train as far as the city limits. Books of 10 tickets (2800Ft) or passes (1550/3850Ft for one/three days) offer better value and convenience; buy tickets from metro stations, and punch in the machines at the station entrance before the journey starts (or on board buses, trolleybuses and trams). You must use a new ticket for each connection if you are changing lines.
Metro The metro (daily 4.30am–11.15pm) has three lines (yellow, red and blue) intersecting at Deák tér; services run every 2–15 min.
Bus and tram Buses (*busz*) generally run every 10–15 min. Express buses, with the red suffix "E", go nonstop between termini. Trams (*villamos*) and trolleybuses (*trolibusz*) run regularly throughout the day. Most nightbuses have three-digit numbers which begin with a 9 (apart from the #6), and run every 30–60min between around midnight and dawn along routes with a night service. Full information at Ⓦwww.bkv.hu.
Taxi Avoid hailing a taxi on the street; you are liable to get ripped off. Try Főtaxi (☎01/222-2222, Ⓦwww.fotaxi.hu) or the English-speaking Citytaxi (☎01/211-1111, Ⓦwww.citytaxi.hu): both charge a basic fee of around 300Ft plus around 250Ft/kilometre.

Accommodation

If you want to be close to Budapest's nightlife, cafés and central sights, the best places to stay are districts V, VI and VII in Pest. Buda's lush residential district (XI) is quieter and less hectic – as long as you're game for a sprightly half-hour walk to get to downtown Pest. Hostels can be booked through their individual websites.

Hostels

Back Pack Guesthouse XI, Takács Menyhért utca 33 ☎01/385-8946, Ⓦwww.backpackersbudapest.hu. Budapest's oldest hostel, situated on a tree-lined residential street in Buda, has a grungy, alternative feel. The doubles are in better nick than the dorms. Garden where visitors can pitch tents and a yurt which sleeps 7–8 in summer. Tram #49 or bus #7 to Tétényi út stop. Dorms 3800Ft (2800Ft off-season), doubles 11,000Ft (9000Ft off-season), camping 3000Ft/person.
Mandala Hostel VIII, Krúdy Gyula 12 ☎01/789-9515. Beautifully decorated boutique hostel in a central old-town location; lots of fresh pine. Large dorm €10, doubles from €23.
Red Bus Hostel V, Semmelweis utca 14 ☎01/266-0136, Ⓦwww.redbusbudapest.hu. 2min from Deák tér, a small, friendly, quiet hostel with reasonably modern decor. Dorms 4000Ft, doubles 11,000Ft.

Hotels and pensions

Ábel Panzió XI, Ábel Jenő utca 9 ☎01/381-0553, Ⓦwww.abelpanzio.hu. Fantastic 1913 Art Nouveau villa, under family management, in a green residential street a 30min walk from the Belváros. Just ten rooms, so it's essential to book in advance. Singles €50, doubles €60.

Mária & István IX, Ferenc körút 39 ⓣ01/216-0768, ⓦwww.mariaistvan.hu. Friendly couple who rent out rooms in their Hungarian-decorated flat. They also have two private apartments for rent sleeping up to 5 (see website). Singles from €18, doubles from €30.
Nightingale Mini Hotel VIII, József Körút 5 (at Blaha Lujza Square) ⓣ709/479-694, ⓦnightingale-minihotel-budapest.freeblog.hu. Very fresh, chic decor in this "mini-hotel" offering doubles and three-bed rooms in a central location. Each room has its own bathroom. Doubles €30 (high season).

Campsites

Csillebérc Camping XII, Konkoly Thege Miklos út 21 ⓣ01/395-6537, ⓦwww.csilleberciszabadido.hu. Large, well-equipped site in the Buda hills offering a range of bungalows. Bus #90 from Moszkva tér to the Csillebérc stop. Open all year. Camping 800Ft/person, plus 1400Ft/tent; bungalows 10,000Ft.

Eating

There are some great eating-out options in Budapest, and it's also easy to refuel cheaply and on-the-go at the growing numbers of cafés serving falafel, sandwiches and hummus-based snacks. Patisseries are also – as everywhere in Hungary – ubiquitous. By Western European standards prices are very reasonable.

Patisseries

Centrál V, Károlyi Mihály utca 9. Grand old coffee-house 3min walk south from Ferenciek tére. Gundel pancake – a flambéed Hungarian classic involving chocolate and nuts – 980Ft.
Müvész VI, Andrássy út 29. Classic old coffeehouse, across from the Opera House, decorated in the old style with chandeliers and dark furnishings.
Ruszwurm I, Szentháromság utca 7 ⓦwww.ruszwurm.hu. Delightful bijoux patisserie in the heart of the Castle Hill's cobbled streets – it's been running for almost 200 years, and offers delicious breakfast goods and sweet treats. *Mandulas kifli* (a large crescent almond biscuit) 250Ft.

Snacks

Duran Sandwich Bar V, Október 6 utca 15. If you're hungry on the go near St Stephen's, this remains, it seems, one of Hungary's only sandwich bars. Open sandwiches from 190Ft apiece. Closed Sun.
Falafel Faloda VI, Paulay Ede utca 1. Perennially popular falafel vendor. Good side-salads on offer. Basic falafel 780Ft. Closed Sun.
Hummus Bar VII, Kértész utca 39. Perfect for a speedy, healthy meal. Several outlets around Budapest (see ⓦwww.hummusbar.hu). Hummus with pitta, omelette, salad and drink deal, 790Ft.

TREAT YOURSELF

Gerbeaud (V, Vörösmarty tér 7–8; daily 9am–9pm; ⓦwww.gerbeaud.hu) is a Budapest institution, the archetype of the much-loved Hungarian patisserie, specializing – as they all do – in cream-laden confections with coffee. A coffee and sweet treat will set you back around 1500Ft (cakes start at 950Ft, two to three times their price elsewhere).

Restaurants

Govinda V, Vigyázó Ferenc utca 4 (side street, just north of Roosevelt tér), and V, corner of Papnövelde utca and Veres Pálné utca ⓦwww.govinda.hu. Vegetarian Indian dishes at low prices. Ayurvedic meal including main, salad and drink, 1450Ft
Kádár étkezde VII, Klauzál tér 9. Highly affordable, heart-warming home-cooking in the old Jewish quarter – a truly authentic experience, with a daily menu in Hungarian only. You will be asked how many pieces of bread you ate as you leave, and charged accordingly. Lamb stew with potatoes will set you back 1200Ft. Tues–Sat 11.30am–3.30pm; closed Sun & Mon.
Kőleves Dob utca/Kazinczy utca (next to Klauzál tér). Fun, upbeat restaurant using fresh, high-quality ingredients in inventive Hungarian fusion dishes – great for lunch or a light dinner in the Jewish quarter. Mains 2000Ft.
M Kersetz út (off Liszt Ferenc tér). ⓣ01/322-3108 (after 5pm only). Cosy little restaurant that feels at once low-key and very special (great for a romantic meal), with quirky interior design (pencil sketches on brown paper walls) and delicious Hungarian-inspired food. The desserts, such as cheesecake with dates, are particularly generous. Mains from 1500Ft.
Menza VI, Liszt Ferenc tér. Stylish, if self-consciously so: offers Hungarian dishes alfresco on the see-and-be-seen Liszt Ferenc Square. Try stuffed paprika for 1700Ft.

Drinking and nightlife

The **floating party scene** (held on river boats on the Danube) comes alive in the summer: check flyers and posters around town. *Budapest*

Official Guide provides practical info on sights and transport. The fortnightly *Budapest Funzine* (ⓦwww.funzine.hu) is the best publication in English for nightlife and events updates. *Pestiest* (Hungarian only) has comprehensive events listings. All are available from hotels, cafés and tourist information points.

Bars and clubs

Castro Bizstro V, Madách Imre tér 3. Shabby-chic café-bar close to Deák tér, with laidback feel and eclectic decor including chintzy floral tablecloths. Serves Serbian food, including "pig-feast plate" (sausage, *liverwurst* and blood-pudding) 1250Ft; stuffed cabbage 1590Ft.

Darshan Udvar VIII, Krúdy Gyula utca 7. Part of a cluster of bars in a courtyard off a charming pedestrianized street. Oriental decor and world music.

Gusto's II, Frankel Leó utca. This tiny, civilized wine bar near the Buda side of Margit Bridge has tons of personality and is much loved by Budapest residents. Large glass of wine 500Ft.

Instant VI, Nagymező utca 38 ⓦwww.instant.co.hu. Labyrinthine venue set around an open courtyard with an offbeat energy and surreal, arty decor.

Karma Café VI, Liszt Ferenc tér 11. High-end bar/restaurant with oriental-inspired decor, on one of Pest's most popular squares. Cocktails from 1300Ft.

Kiado Kocsma VI, Jókai tér 3. Intimate, dark bar akin to a British pub in a great location.

Lánchíd Söröző I, Fő utca 4 ⓦwww.lanchidsorozo.hu. Fantastic pub and café with a loyal local following, equally good for a morning coffee, afternoon beer or last drink of the night. Close to the Lanchid Bridge on the Buda side. Daily 11am–1am.

Szimpla Kert VII, Kazinczy utca 14 ⓦwww.szimpla.hu. The original *kert* (warehouse bar) occupies a chaotic warehouse space set just off a street in the Jewish quarter, adorned with art and antiques. Until 2am.

Entertainment

Tickets for most music in Budapest events can be bought through Ticket Express (VI, Andrássy út 18; ⓣ01/312-0000, ⓦwww.eventim.hu).

Peţofi Csarnok Városliget ⓦwww.petoficsarnok.hu. Folk music and big international acts in the City Park.

Trafó IX, Liliom utca 41 ⓦwww.trafo.hu. Theatre, music and dance venue in Pest.

Shopping

Market The Central Market Hall in Pest (ⓦwww.piaconline.hu), open Mon–Fri 6am–5/6pm, Sat 6am–3pm is crammed with gift potential, from bottles of Tokaj to giant hams, and good value too: Budapest residents shop here, which is always a good sign.

Shops Malls with high-street names in Budapest include Mammut and Mammut II by Moskvá tér (ⓦwww.mammut.hu). The main shopping area is south of Vörösmarty tér in central Pest.

Directory

Embassies and consulates Australia, XII, Király-hágó tér 8–9 ⓣ01/457-9777, ⓦwww.australia.hu; Canada, XII, Ganz u. 12–14 ⓣ01/392-3360; Ireland, V, Szabadság tér 7 ⓣ01/301-4960,

FESTIVALS IN BUDAPEST

See ⓦwww.festivalcity.hu for information on all Budapest's festivals.

Budapest Spring Festival Last two weeks in March ⓦwww.btf.hu. Jazz, folk, opera, chamber music, flamenco and theatre takes place in venues across the capital.

Summer on the Chain Bridge Every weekend in July–Aug. Scores of classical and popular concerts; the famous bridge is jam-packed with market stalls and musicians. Ask at Tourinform for details.

Sziget Festival Mid-Aug ⓦwww.sziget.hu. The week-long Sziget (meaning "island") Festival is an open-air pop and rock fest fondly known as the "Hungarian Woodstock".

St Stephen's Day Aug 20. Craft fairs, folk dancing, river parades and fireworks launched from barges on the river to celebrate the nation's founding father.

Autumn Festival Mid-Oct ⓦwww.bof.hu. Music, ballet, theatre and film from Hungarian and international artists.

Ⓦwww.embassyofireland.hu; New Zealand, VII, Nagymező utca 47, Ⓣ01/302-2484; UK, V, Harmincad utca 6 Ⓣ01/266-2888, Ⓦwww.britishembassy.hu; US, V, Szabadság tér 12 Ⓣ01/475-4400, Ⓦwww.usembassy.hu.

Exchange The best places for exchange are larger banks such as Magyar Külkereskedelmi Bank at V, Türr István utca 9 at the top of Váci utca, central Pest.

Hospitals 24-hour medical help at V, Semmelweis utca 14/b (entrance on Gerlóczy utca), near Astoria, Ⓣ01/311-6816; and at weekends at II, Ganz utca 13–15 Ⓣ01/202-1370.

Internet Electric Café, VII, Dohány utca 37 (daily 9am–midnight); Fougou, VII, Wesselenyi utca 57 (daily 7am–2am); Yellow Zebra Bikes store, behind Opera House, VI, Lázár utca 16.

Maps Tourist offices supply free maps. If you want more detail, try the wire-bound 1:25,000 Budapest Atlas (1700Ft), from newsstands and Tourinform.

Pharmacies Alkotás utca 1b, opposite Déli station, and Teréz körút 41, near Oktogon, are both open 24hr.

Police The tourist police office is located inside the main Tourinform office, V, Sútő utca 2. The 24-hour police phone information service is on Ⓣ01/438-8080. Multiple police stations offer 24-hour tourist assistance, including V, Szalay utca 11–13 and XI, Bocskay út 90.

Post office V, Petőfi utca 13; with extended opening hours: VI, Teréz körút 51, Mon–Fri 10am–7pm, Sat 8am–1pm.

Moving on

Train Balatonfüred (every 1–2hr; 2hr 30min); Eger (8 daily; 1hr 50min–2hr 20min); Kecskemét (12 daily; 1hr 30min); Pécs (11 daily; 3hr); Siófok (14 daily; 2hr); Sopron (7 daily; 3hr); Szeged (12 daily; 2hr 30min); Szentendre (every 10–20min; 40min).

Bus Balatonfüred (5 daily; 2hr 15min–3hr); Eger (hourly; 2hr–3hr 20min); Hévíz (4 daily; 3hr 20min–4hr); Keszthely (4 daily; 3hr 15min–4hr 15min); Pécs (5 daily; 4hr); Siófok (7 daily; 1hr 35min–2hr 10min); Sopron (3–5 daily; 3hr 45min); Szentendre (every 30min; 30–45min).

Ferry/Hydrofoil Usually operating April–Oct/Nov, weather permitting; Ⓣ01/484-4013. Szentendre (1–3 daily; 1hr 40min); Vienna (1–2 daily; 6hr 20min).

SZENTENDRE

To escape the humid Budapest summers, many people head north of the city to the **Danube Bend**, a grand stretch of the river heading out towards Estergom, cradle of Hungarian Christianity. **SZENTENDRE** on the west bank of the Danube Bend is a popular day-trip from Budapest (40min by HÉV train from Batthyány tér; 1hr 30min by boat from Vigadó tér pier), a picturesque if rather touristy "town of artists" with narrow cobbled streets and quaint houses.

What to see and do

Szentendre was originally populated by Serbs seeking refuge from the Ottomans in the late seventeenth century and the Serbian cultural imprint remains, particularly in the atmospheric, incense-filled **Blagovestenska Church** (Tues–Sun 10am–5pm; winter open for worship only; 300Ft), on the north side of the main square, **Fő tér**. Just around the corner at Vastagh György utca 1 is the **Margit Kovács Museum** (daily 10am–6pm; 1000Ft), displaying the lifetime work of Hungary's greatest ceramicist and sculptor, born in 1902. There's a charming view over Szentendre's steeply banked rooftops and gardens from the hilltop **Templom tér**, above Fő tér, where the **Serbian Orthodox Cathedral** is visible inside its walled garden; tourists are generally not admitted, but you can see the cathedral iconostasis and treasury in the adjacent museum (Tues–Sun 10am–6pm in high season, Tues–Sun 10am–4pm in low season; 500Ft). Beyond that, the town's chief attractions consist of wandering along the riverside or poring over the offerings at the many tourist-oriented stalls.

Arrival and information

Bus and train stations Both located a 5min walk south of town. Local buses run in along Dunakanyar körút.

Ferry port 100m north of the town centre.

Tourist office Tourinform, Bercsényi st 4; entrance from Duna Korzó (Mon–Fri 9am–4.30pm,

Sat & Sun 10am–4pm; ⓣ26/317-965, ⓦwww.szentendreprogram.hu).
Listings There are regular pop concerts in the centre of town, and open-air theatre in the summer: ask Tourinform for details.

Accommodation

Centrum Panzió Duna korzó, ⓣ26/302-500, ⓦwww.hotelcentrum.hu. Homely, moderately plush rooms with modern bathrooms, just opposite the riverbank. Singles 11,000Ft, doubles 13,000Ft (high season).
Ilona Panzió Rákóczi utca 11 ⓣ26/313-599. Simple rooms in a pleasant location in the heart of the old quarter. Singles 5800Ft, doubles 8000Ft.
Pap-Sziget Pap Island, 1.5km north of town ⓣ26/310-697, ⓦwww.pap-sziget.hu. Take any bus heading towards Visegrád or Esztergom and get off by the *Danubius Hotel*. May–Sept only. Camping 1380Ft/person, plus 3600Ft/tent; double bungalows 9000Ft, hostel dorm 2500Ft.

Eating and drinking

Avakumica Alkotmány 4. Elegant cellar café opposite the Serbian Orthodox cathedral on Templom tér.
Görög Kancsó Görög utca. A Greek restaurant with a summer-holiday feel and sophisticated decor; offers glass-enclosed seating along the main *korzo*. Stuffed vine leaves 2190Ft.
Palapa Dumtsa Jenő utca 22. Brightly decorated Mexican outfit with lively garden and cocktails. Mains from 1600Ft.
Rab Ráby Kucsera Ferenc utca 1. Traditional, filling Magyar cuisine in a tavern restaurant. Hearty mains from 1500Ft.

Western Hungary

The major tourist attraction to the west of the capital is **Lake Balaton**, dubbed the "Hungarian sea", and all that remains of the Pannonian Sea which once covered this part of Europe. Its built-up southern shore features loud resorts such as Siófok, which brands itself as the "Capital of Summer", while gentler **Keszthely** perches on the western tip. Worth a visit if you fancy a spot of swimming, windsurfing or sailing while in Hungary, **Siófok** in particular is perhaps better avoided if you are looking for a restful or scenic break. By contrast, the four villages that cluster around the **Badacsony**, a hulk of volcanic rock on the northern shore of the lake, are very charming indeed and the perfect starting point for walks and wine tasting in the Balaton region.

The western region of **Transdanubia** is the most ethnically diverse in the country. Its valleys and hills, forests and mud flats have been settled by Magyars, Serbs, Slovaks and Germans and occupied by Romans, Ottomans and Habsburgs. Its towns have been through multiple evolutions and it shows: the delightful **Sopron** has a gorgeous medieval centre, Roman ruins and Baroque finery to its name, while **Pécs** boasts the country's best-preserved Ottoman mosque as well as some fascinating early Christian excavated finds.

SIÓFOK

The biggest, trashiest resort on Balaton, in summer **SIÓFOK** throbs with crowds intent on sunbathing, boozing and clubbing. The two main resort areas are Aranypart (Gold Shore) to the east of the Sió Canal, and Ezüstpart (Silver Shore) to the west. Though the central stretch of shoreline consists of paying **beaches** (daily mid-May to mid-Sept 7am–9pm; 1000Ft), there are free beaches 1km further along at both resort areas (the Hungarian for beach is *strand*). You can rent windsurfing equipment and wakeboards from 1700Ft per hour and small sailing boats (from €120 – excluding tax – for up to six people for one day) at most beaches.

Arrival and information

Bus and train stations Next to each other in the centre of town on Fő utca.

Tourist office Tourinform office at Fő utca 174–176, in the Atrium Shopping Centre (Mon–Fri 8am–4pm; ⓣ84/310-117, ⓦwww.siofokportal.com). They can book private rooms.

Accommodation

Aranypart Camping Szent László utca 183–185 ⓣ84/353-899. Five kilometres east of the centre (bus #2) is this large, well-equipped campsite. Mid-April to mid-Sept. 1200Ft/person, plus 600Ft for tent; chalets sleeping four from 9000–24,000Ft.
Touring Hostel Cseresznye utca 1/0 ⓣ84/310-551, ⓦwww.siofokhostel.com. Large, slightly dated hostel 2km from the centre; all rooms are twin rooms. May–Sept. Twin room, 5000Ft/person/night.
Város Kollégiuma Petőfi Sétány 1 ⓣ84/312-244, ⓦwww.siofokvaroskollegiuma.sulinet.hu. Large student residence open year-round. On the shore of Golden Beach. Dorms 3500Ft/person.

Eating and drinking

Amigo Fő utca 99. Fast-food-style pizza café. Pizzas from 1800Ft.
Café Roxy Szabadság tér 1. Very pleasant wood-panelled café-restaurant; great for a relaxed glass of wine, mid-morning coffee or oven-baked pizza. Pizzas from 900Ft.
Flört Just off Fő utca ⓦwww.flort.hu. High-energy techno and club anthems from 10pm–7am.
Palace Dance Club West of town at Deák Ferenc utca 2 ⓦwww.palace.hu. Siófok's most notorious club has two floors of house, dance, techno, and lays on foam parties. Open until dawn. Special designated buses will whisk you to the palace every hour from 9pm outside the Víztorony (water tower) in the centre.

Moving on

Bus Keszthely (2 daily; 1hr 40min).
Ferry Badacsony (July & Aug 4 daily; 4hr 20min).

KESZTHELY

KESZTHELY is a gentler counterpart to brash Siófok, with a pleasant waterfront with two bays (one for swimming, the other for ferries) with stretches of grass and small beaches that give peaceful views over the seemingly never-ending lake. Less likely to detain you are its "Africa Museum" (an open-air collection of grass huts), horror museum and "sex panopticon".

What to see and do

Walking up from the train station along Martírok útja, you'll pass the **Balaton Museum** at the junction with Kossuth Lajos utca (May–Oct Tues–Sun 10am–6pm; Nov–April Tues–Sat 9am–5pm; 500Ft), hosting exhibits on the region's history and wildlife. Kossuth utca, swarming with cafés and vendors, leads up towards the beige, Baroque **Festetics Palace** (Sept–June Tues–Sun 10am–5pm; July & Aug 9am–6pm; 2000Ft basic ticket, 3300Ft for all exhibitions; ⓦwww.helikonkastely.hu). Created in 1745 by Count György Festetics, the palace attracted the leading lights of the eighteenth-century literary scene and high society. Highlights include the mirrored ballroom, but given the entry fee, on a budget you may prefer to admire the exterior and pretty surrounding gardens. The palace stages regular summer concerts – check with Tourinform (ⓦwww.keszthely.hu) – and also houses the **Wines of Balaton Region museum** in its cellars (daily 10am–6pm; 2700Ft including wine tasting).

Arrival and information

Train and bus stations Both 5min walk southwest of the cluster of lakeside hotels along Kazinczy utca. Some buses drop off on Fő tér, halfway along Kossuth utca, the main drag.
Boat dock 10min walk south of the centre, along Erzsébet királyné útja.
Tourist information Tourinform, Kossuth Lajos utca 30 (Mon–Fri 9am–5pm, Sat 9am–12.30pm; ⓣ83/314-144, ⓦwww.keszthely.hu).

Accommodation

Private rooms can be booked through Keszthely Tourist, Kossuth utca 25 (July–Aug daily 9am–9pm; Sept–June 9am–4.30/5.30pm; ⓣ83/312-031, ⓦwww.keszthelytourist.hu). For information on rooms in college dorms (July & Aug only), check with Tourinform (see opposite).

Abszolut Vendeghaz Katona Josef utca 27, ⓣ30/346-6477. Lovely, friendly *pension* with free use of tennis courts and large kitchen. Doubles 9000Ft.

Ambient Hostel Sopron utca 10 ⓣ30/460-3536, ⓦwww.freeweb.hu/keszthely-apartman/index-a.html. Clean and bright dorms, en-suite doubles and small apartments are offered in this handily located hostel next to the Festetics Palace. Dorms 3000Ft, doubles 8000Ft.

Castrum Camping Móra Ferenc utca 48, ⓦwww.castrum-group.hu. Over 300 pitches in this large campsite ten minutes from the lakefront – and hedges and trees provide plenty of shade. 750Ft/person, plus 700Ft/tent.

Műzeum Panzió Műzeum utca 3 ⓣ83/313-182, ⓦwww.balatonhostels.hu. Well-run lemon-yellow *pension* near the station. Singles 4000Ft, doubles from 9000Ft.

Eating and drinking

Close to Kossuth Lajos utca is the daily market (off Bem József utca) selling fresh fruit and traditional Hungarian foodstuffs.

Ánizs Art Café Városház utca 6. Spacious bar with "wild west" decor. Beers 450Ft.

John's Pub Kossuth Lajos utca 46. Saloon-style bar with long affordable cocktail list, and music late into the night.

Margaretta Bercsényi Miklós utca 60 Charming service and an excellent, varied Hungarian menu. Eat inside or out. Mains from 1400Ft include a "shepherd's special" – pork stuffed with sausage, ewe's cheese and bacon.

Oázis Rákóczi tér 3, down Szalasztó utca from the palace. Vegetarian lunch restaurant – serve yourself from a salad bar and your plate is then weighed. A plate costs about 1000Ft. Mon–Fri 11am–4pm.

Moving on

Bus Badacsony (8 daily; 1hr); Hévíz (every 15min; 10–20min).

Ferry Badacsony (July & Aug 4 daily; 2hr).

BADACSONY

The **BADACSONY** – a hefty hunk of volcanic rock, forming a plateau visible from miles around – is the iconic centre-point of the beautiful wine-growing region that is named after it. Four villages nestle at its feet, and **Badacsony village** (technically Badacsonytomaj, but often known in the short form) is a lovely base for walks, wine tasting and visiting the lake.

What to see and do

The table-top peak of the Badacsony rock draws the eye from the vineyard-strewn hills all around it, and is the heart of this undeniably pretty area – best visited out of the high season when, like all of Balaton, it tends to get overrun by visitors. **Badacsony village** has a small-scale sweetness, being easily navigable on foot, and its charms are only enhanced by sampling a glass of local wine – never hard to come by given the abundance of small cellars and roadside bars (*borozó*) hereabouts. Its cultural sights include the **Rósa Szegedy House** and **Rose Rock** among the vineyards uphill from the village. You can rent bikes

WALKING AROUND THE BADACSONY

Badacsony village is a superb base for **wine tasting** and **walking** up onto, and around, the Badacsony rock. Simply get the walking-route map from the helpful TourInform in the village, which shows the various colour-coded walking routes in the area. They are also marked well on the route, with painted arrows on trees and rocks. To scale the hill itself, take a right from Római utca, which cuts through Badacsony village, onto Kisfaludy utca, then ascend first on a sloped road, then a path, and finally stone steps (or a smaller path, depending on your route). Once on top of the Badacsony plateau, you can meander through the woods, which are strewn with wild flowers and popular with butterflies, and eventually descend along a number of routes cutting back down through the vineyards.

at various points along Park utca, the main road by the lake.

Róza Szegedy House and Rose Rock

The **Róza Szegedy House** (May–Sept only, Tues–Sun 10am–6pm; 500Ft) is on Kisfaludy utca, reached by turning right from Római utca. The walk is a reasonably steep 2.5km through the vineyards, or an easy ride in an open-top jeep taxi (600Ft per person) from Park utca – the main street by the lake. Róza Szegedy met her future husband, the poet Sándor Kisfaludy, here in 1795, and he wrote some of his most beautiful works from the house, which contains some of his work and their original furniture. Up a path a little further is **Rose Rock** (Rókzako), where it's said that if a man and woman sit together with their backs facing Lake Balaton and think about each other, they will marry within a year.

Kisfaludy and the Stone Gate

The Rose Rock is a great starting point for an invigorating hike to the Kisfaludy lookout tower (437m) and, twenty minutes further north, the Stone Gate formed from two great basalt towers. Both points offer splendid views of the lake and the patchwork of Badacsony's vineyards. If you fancy a plunge in the lake afterwards, it's a 20-minute walk downhill. Badacsony has clean, paying beaches (Strandfürdő, 400Ft) - cross the railway tracks and Park utca to reach them.

Arrival and information

Train station In the village, just up from the ferry pier.
Bus stop On the main street by the lake, Park utca.
Tourist information Park utca 14 (May to mid-June & mid-Sept to Oct Mon–Fri 9am–5pm & Sat 9am–1pm; mid-June to mid-Sept 9am–6/7pm; Nov–April 9am–3pm; ⓣ87/431-046, ⓦwww.badacsonytomaj.hu).

Accommodation

Balatontourist (next door to Tourinform) can book private rooms (May, June & Sept Mon–Fri 8.30am–3.30pm, Sat 8am–noon; July & Aug Mon–Sat 8am–9pm, Sun 8am–noon; ⓣ87/531-021, ⓦwww.balatontourist.hu).
Borbaratok panzio Római utca 88 ⓣ87/471-000 ⓦwww.borbaratok.hu. Outstanding *panzió*, with large, beautifully comfortable rooms, superb food and the chance to taste fine local wines – bliss. Singles 9800Ft, doubles 12,600Ft.
Hotel Neptun Római utca 170 ⓣ87/531-032 ⓦwww.borbaratok.hu. Tastefully decorated rooms in a beautifully renovated old building. Includes a filling buffet breakfast. Singles 6500Ft, doubles 11,000Ft.
Tomaj Camping Balaton utca 13 ⓣ70/947-9739, ⓦwww.tomajcamping.hu. Pretty campsite by the lakeside, also known as the "Riviera". Open April to Oct. It's around five minutes' walk south from the centre of Badacscony. 900Ft/person, plus 1400Ft/tent.

Eating and drinking

Bacchus Kossuth Lajos utca 1. Open May–Oct. With gorgeous views over the lake, *Bacchus* is a perfect spot for sampling local wines. Mains at 2000Ft.
Borbaratok panzio (details above). Superb Hungarian dishes, with real variety and fresh ingredients. Options include a four-cheese platter at 1400Ft, home-made elderberry juice, and honeyed local wines.
Neptun (part of the *Hotel Neptun*), Római utca 170. Tasty salads, soups, fish and meat dishes from 900Ft.

SOPRON

SOPRON – a captivating town close to the Austrian border – retains its original medieval layout, as well as no less than 240 listed buildings. From its fourth-century Roman-era town walls to its Baroque central squares, it is steeped in history.

What to see and do

The horseshoe-shaped **Belváros** (inner town) is north of Széchenyi tér and the main train station. At its southern end, beautiful **Orsolya tér** (Bear Square) features Renaissance edifices and the white and cream Gothic church. Heading north towards the main square, **Új utca** (New Street – actually one of the town's oldest thoroughfares) is a gentle curve of perfectly preserved homes painted in red, yellow and pink. At no. 22 stands a **medieval synagogue** (May–Sept Tues–Sun 10am–6pm; 600Ft) that flourished when the street was Zsidó utca (Jewish Street); Sopron's Jewish community dates back to the tenth century but was almost completely wiped out in the Holocaust.

Fő tér and the Goat Church

Fő tér features an exquisite assembly of Gothic and Baroque architecture. Its centrepiece is the **Goat Church** (Mon–Sat 8am–6pm) – so called because, legend has it, its construction in the thirteenth century was financed by a goatherd whose flock unearthed a cache of loot. The attached **Chapter house** (March–Oct 10am–noon & 2–5pm), which served as a prayer house and burial chapel, is thought to be one of Hungary's best examples of Gothic religious architecture.

Storno House and Firewatch Tower

The Renaissance **Storno House**, also on the square, exhibits Roman, Celtic and Avar relics, plus mementoes of Liszt (Tues–Sun: April–Sept 10am–6pm; Oct–March 10am–2pm; 1200Ft). North of here rises Sopron's symbol, the **Firewatch Tower** (April, Sept & Oct Tues–Sun 10am–6pm; May–Aug daily 10am–8pm; 900Ft), founded upon the stones of a fortress originally laid out by the Romans. From the top there's a stunning bird's-eye view of the town. The "**Gate of Loyalty**" at the base of the tower commemorates the townfolk's decision to remain part of Hungary when offered the choice of Austrian citizenship in 1921.

Arrival and information

Train station Mátyás Király utca, 500m south of Széchenyi tér and the old town; Sopron is linked to Vienna by a fast intercity service, though it's not on the main Budapest–Vienna route.

Bus station Northwest of the old town, a 5min walk along Lackner Kristóf utca from Ógabona tér.

Tourist office Tourinform is inside the Liszt Cultural Centre at Liszt Ferenc utca 1 (mid-June to mid-Sept Mon–Fri 9am–7pm, Sat & Sun 9am–3pm; mid-Sept to mid-June Mon–Fri 9am–5pm, Sat 9am–3pm; ⓣ99/517-560, ⓦwww.tourinform.sopron.hu).

Accommodation

Jégverem Panzió Jégverem utca 1 ⓣ99/510-113, ⓦwww.jegverem.hu. Pleasant if twee little rooms in an inn. The food at the attached restaurant is better avoided. Doubles 9000Ft, single person in double room 6900Ft.

Vacáció Youth Hostel Ady Endre utca 31 ⓣ20/933-8502, ⓦwww.vakacio-vendeghazak.hu. Large fresh yellow-and-pine hostel opposite the Erzsébet Kert (Elizabeth Gardens), 15min walk from the centre, or take bus #1 or #10. Dorms 2800Ft.

Eating and drinking

Cézár Cellar Hátsókapu utca 2. A shabby exterior hides a cosy candlelit medieval cellar serving local beers, wines and meat and cheese boards.

Fórum Pizzeria Szent György utca 3. Good pizzas in a pleasant setting. From 900Ft.

Liszt Szalon Szent György utca 12. Slightly twee interior but charming courtyard and wonderful blends of tea including cherry-chocolate, apple-strudel and marzipan flavourings. Pitcher of tea 450Ft.

PÉCS

PÉCS is one of Hungary's finest towns, with a strong religious and scholarly heritage (Hungary's first university was founded here in 1367) and remarkable history, today captured by its landmark mosque, synagogue and cathedral and clutch of fascinating Roman-era finds. The surrounding Mecsek hills help create a warm microclimate in the Pécs basin.

What to see and do

Pécs is a small and navigable town, its cultural attractions concentrated in the **Belváros** (Old Town), radiating outwards from Széchenyi tér: start with the synagogue by Kossuth tér, then head through charming Jokai tér towards the leafy western side, where you'll find the magnificent Peter and Paul cathedral.

Synagogue and Mosque of Gázi Kászim Pasha

Heading up Bajcsy-Zsilinszky utca from the bus terminal you'll pass the imposing **synagogue**, which dominates Kossuth tér (May–Oct Sun–Fri 10am–5pm; 300Ft). The beautiful nineteenth-century interior is hauntingly impressive; over 4000 Pécs Jews died in the Holocaust and only a tenth of that number live in Pécs today. During the Ottoman occupation (1543–1686), Pécs' chief church, in a commanding position on Széchenyi tér, was converted into the **Mosque of Gázi Kászim Pasha**, which now stands as the last remaining of 17 mosques the Ottomans built in Pécs (mid-April to mid-Oct Mon–Sat 10am–4pm, Sun 11.30am–4pm; mid-Oct to mid-April Mon–Sat 10am–noon, Sun 11.30am–2pm; donations). The building has again been converted to serve as a church – and a cross placed atop the crescent on its roof – but the underlying design is unmistakably Islamic.

Archeological World Heritage Sites and cathedral

From the centre of town, follow either Káptalan or Janus Pannonius utca towards the pristine white **Peter and Paul cathedral** (April–Oct Mon–Sat 9am–5pm, Sun 1–5pm; Nov–March Mon–Sat 10am–4pm, Sun 1–4pm; 800Ft). Topped with all 12 Apostles, it is built on an epic scale inside. Nearby at Szent Istvan tér 17 (in the gardens just below the steps to the cathedral) is the **Cella Septichora visitor centre**, giving access to a wealth of Roman early Christian archeological remains (Tues–Sun: April–Oct 10am–6pm; Nov–March 10am–4pm; 1600Ft). Pécs fell under Roman rule as the empire expanded into the Balkans in the second century, and became Christian with the conversion of the Emperor Constantine in 313 AD. The excavated rooms include the Peter and Paul burial chamber and a Christian cemetery site, and visitors can get a 360-degree view through glass panels placed above, below and on the side of the chambers.

Arrival and information

Train station 20min walk south of the centre on Indoház tér.
Bus station Northeast of the train station on Zsolyom utca.
Tourist office Tourinform is at Széchenyi tér 7 (June–Sept Mon–Fri 9am–6pm, Sat 9am–2pm, closed Sun; Oct–May Mon–Fri 9am–4/6pm; ⓣ72/213-315, ⓦwww.iranypecs.hu). The excellent monthly English-language *Time Out Pécs* is available from Tourinform.
Taxi Volán ⓣ72/555-555, speak English and are affordable.

Accommodation

You can book a private room or student hostel bed through Ibusz, Király utca 11 (Mon–Fri 9am–6pm, Sat 9am–1pm; ⓣ72/212-157, ⓦpecs@ibusz.hu).
Berg Toboz Panzió Fenyves sor 5 ⓣ72/510-555. ⓦwww.tobozpanzio.hu. *Pension* in the Mecsek hills – a breath of fresh alpine air, although a bit of hike, or taxi ride, out of town. Singles €38, doubles €50.
Főnix Hotel Hunyádi utca 2 ⓣ72/311-680, ⓦwww.fonixhotel.com. Just north of Széchenyi tér, the simple en-suite rooms in this hotel offer good value. Singles 7450Ft, doubles 11,300Ft.
NAP Hostel Kiraly utca 23–25 ⓣ72/950-684, ⓦwww.naphostel.com. Centrally located hostel with bright dorms and graffiti-style decor. Dorms from €10, doubles €44.

Eating and drinking

Az Elefántos Jokai tér 6. Excellent Italian serving delicious thin-crust pizzas on Pécs' best square for people-spotting. All ingredients are imported from Italy, which drives the prices up a bit. Beers 550Ft, pizzas 1500Ft.
Áfium Irgalmasok utcája 2. Cellar restaurant selling filling, affordable food. The broadly nostalgia-themed

decor includes nineteenth-century family photos and retro posters for *Unicum* (a medicinal-tasting Hungarian spirit). Bean soup with smoked pork knuckle 990Ft.

Café Zacc Mátyás király 2. Affordable, studenty underground bar.

Fresco Ferencesek utcája 1. Hip café on corner of Jokai tér Square, hawking smoothies as well as coffee.

Kanta Bár Irgalmasok utcája 6. Arty café-bar, with a brooding, cramped interior and courtyard bar. Free wi-fi. Open until 2am Mon–Sat, till midnight Sun.

Kioszk Szent Istvan tér. Elegant terrace café in a plum location next to the cathedral.

Kulturkert Summer-only courtyard bar and music venue off the western side of Szent Istvan tér, with stunning views of the surrounding hills.

Moving on

Train Budapest (9 daily; 3hr); Sarajevo (1 daily; 9hr).
Bus Budapest (5 daily; 4hr); Szeged (8 daily; 4hr).

Eastern Hungary

The gorgeous town of **Eger**, set among the rolling Bukk hills, is an absolute must on any trip to Hungary long enough to allow you to foray beyond Budapest. The nearby "Valley of the Beautiful Woman" is crammed with miniature wine cellars clustered close together, and is an integral part of a trip to Eger.

EGER

Atmospheric **EGER** boasts a fabled fortress which famously repulsed Ottoman attack in 1552, expansive cobbled streets, and a feeling of bonhomie which must have something to do with its famous Bull's Blood wine (Egri Bikavér).

What to see and do

Eger's historic centre stretches either side of the main square, **Dobó István tér**, extending to the compact, cobbled streets around the castle, northeast of the centre. Near the centre, on Knézich utca, is the elegant fourteen-sided minaret that is an iconic memento of Eger's years under Ottoman occupation.

Cathedral

The splendid Neoclassical **cathedral** or basilica (free to enter) is the country's second largest church after Estergom. Painted the favourite Hungarian yellow, it is five minutes' walk southwest from the main square, approached by a grand set of steps. Inside, it is cheerfully decorated with toffee-coloured columns and pastel frescoes. The **Lyceum** opposite the cathedral is worth visiting for its library (March to mid-Nov Tues–Sun 9.30am–3.30pm; mid-Nov to Feb Sat & Sun only 9am–1pm; 700Ft). The **observatory**, at the top of the tower in the east wing of the Lyceum (same hours; 800Ft), houses a nineteenth-century camera obscura.

Archbishop's Palace

On pleasant, pedestrianized Széchenyi Istvan utca 3 stands the **Archbishop's Palace** (8am–4pm Nov–March; 9am–5pm April–Oct; 400Ft), a U-shaped Baroque building whose right wing houses the treasury and a history of the bishopric of Eger. Cross the bridge and head to the left to see Eger's iconic minaret extending skyward, and looking rather lonely without its mosque attached.

Castle

Uphill from Dobó István tér is the castle (daily March–Oct 8am–6/7/8pm; Nov–Feb 8am–5pm; 700Ft castle grounds only; 1400Ft with exhibitions). You may baulk at the cost of the exhibitions here, but it is certainly worth paying to enter the castle grounds – you get a powerful sense from the inside of the sheer scale of the fortress, which is very well preserved. You can easily imagine the soldiers and local women (who volunteered to join in) in 1552 seeing off a Turkish force allegedly six times their number.

Arrival and information

Train station Állomás tér; to reach the centre, walk up the road to Deák Ferenc utca, catch bus #10 or #12, and get off when you see the cupola of the cathedral.
Tourist office Tourinform office at Bajcsy-Zsilinszky utca 9 (Mon–Fri 9am–5pm, Sat 9am–1pm; ⓣ36/517-715, ⓦwww.eger.hu).

Accommodation

For student hostels and private rooms, contact Ibusz, Széchenyi utca 9 (ⓣ36/312-652, ⓔeger@ibusz.hu).
Garten Guesthouse Legányi Ferenc utca 6 ⓣ36/420-371, ⓦwww.gartenvendeghaz.hu. Very homely guesthouse just above the city, with charming doubles and a lush garden. Doubles from 8000Ft.
Tourist Motel Mekcsey utca 2–4 ⓣ36/411-101, ⓦwww.wix.com/touristmoteleger/home. Basic motel just along from the castle, with good-value rooms sleeping 2–3. Doubles from 7000Ft.
Tulipán Szépasszonyvölgy 71 ⓣ36/311-542, ⓦwww.tulipancamping.com. Campsite in the Szépasszony Valley; open all year. 800Ft/person, plus 840Ft/tent.

Eating and drinking

Kürtős kalács Szent Janos utca 10, off Széchenyi utca. Hole in the wall luring passers-by with the waft of freshly made *kürtős kalács* – "chimney-cakes", a sort of thin, spun cylindrical doughnut encrusted with sugar or nuts. 370Ft each.
Market hall Katóna tér (June–Sept Mon–Fri 6am–6pm, Sat 6am–1pm, Sun 6am–10am; Oct–May 6am–5pm, 6am–1pm, 6am–10pm). The (very central) Eger market is an excellent place to pick up fruit or veg, home-made honey, craft goods or flowers.
Palacsintavár Dobó utca 9. A true Eger institution, with a terrific range of extremely filling pancakes and a diverting interior filled with displays of retro cigarette packets. Large savoury pancake 1600Ft. Daily noon–11pm.
Várkert Étterem Dózsa György tér 8. Traditional Hungarian fare in the pedestrianized area below the castle walls. Mains 1800Ft.

Moving on

Train Budapest (9 direct trains daily; 2hr).
Bus Budapest (more than 20 daily; 3hr).

The Great Plain

Spanning half of Hungary, the **Great Plain** is home to Hungary's national parks and its key horseriding region – horseriding being a core part of Magyar folklore: this warrior people's stunning success in conquering this part of Europe is often attributed to their skill and agility as archers on horseback. Between the Danube and the Tisza rivers are **Kecskemét** and **Széged**, both towns with some interesting bits of turn-of-the-century architecture, and well worth a stop (**Széged** in particular) if you are travelling in the area.

KECSKEMÉT

Possible as a day-trip from Budapest, **KECSKEMÉT** is a small town chiefly remarkable for a few striking pieces of architecture from Hungary's "Romantic Nationalist" period at the turn of the twentieth-century. Its name comes from the Hungarian for goat, *kecske*, as its thirteenth-century bishop apparently used to give the cloven-footed creatures to each new Christian convert. It is also the gateway to **Kiskunság National Park**.

What to see and do

Kecskemét's main attraction is the ornate **Cifra Palace** – a large building on a street corner that you might overlook were it not for the daring Art Nouveau design. Designed by Géza Markus in 1902, it now houses the **Kecskemét Art Gallery** (Tues–Sun 10am–5pm; 320Ft), whose collection of bold, stylized pre-World War I art is well worth a look. South of Szabadság tér is the **Town Hall** – another piece of Romantic Nationalist architecture, with the added charm of a musical clock which pops out hourly. The **Hungarian**

WINE TASTING IN THE VALLEY OF THE BEAUTIFUL WOMAN

Just west of Eger, in the Szépasszonyvölgy – "Valley of the Beautiful Woman" – local **vineyards** produce *Bikavér* (Bull's Blood – smooth, spicy and ruby red), so called because the Ottomans believed the deep red liquid Hungarians drank to steel themselves for battle was bull's blood rather than wine. Other Hungarian varieties cultivated in the region, and on sale here, include *Muskotály* (semi-sweet Muscatel), *Leányka* (medium-dry white) and *Medoc Noir* (rich, dark, sweet red). Sample them all in the string of small cellars built into the hillside a twenty-minute walk from Eger (go west along Király utca to Szépasszonyvölgy). Finding your favourite cellar is a matter of luck and taste, but you may like Kiss Pinceszet at Cziky Sandor utca 15. Cellars close by 8pm.

Photography Museum at Katona József tér 12 (Wed–Sun 10am–5pm; 400Ft; ⓦwww.fotomuzeum.hu) has excellent exhibitions of photography from the nineteenth century to the present day.

Arrival and information

Bus and train stations Next to one another north of the centre. Head down Nagykőrösi utca or Rákóczi utca from the station towards the main square, Szabadság tér.

Tourist information Tourinform is situated in the corner of the Town Hall (Sept–May Mon–Fri 8am–4/5pm; mid-June to Aug Mon–Fri 9am–6pm, Sat & Sun 9am–2pm; ⓣ76/481-065, ⓦwww.kecskemet.hu). They can give detailed information on horseriding operators and trips to the Kiskunság National Park, and also offer bike rental (350Ft/hr).

Accommodation, eating and drinking

Private apartments can be booked with Ibusz in the Malom shopping centre, first floor (Mon–Sat 10am–7pm, Sun 10am–2pm). During the summer rooms are available at the colleges at Jókai tér 4 (ⓣ76/486-977) and Izsáki utca 10 (ⓣ76/506-526).

Fábián Panzió Kápolna utca 14 ⓣ76/477-677, ⓦwww.panziofabian.hu. Very friendly *pension* with smart, spacious rooms and excellent breakfast. Singles from 7800Ft, doubles 11,800Ft.

Kecskemeti Csarda Kölsey utca 7. Perhaps the best restaurant in town for dinner, with a lovely spacious garden; traditional mains 1800Ft.

Vincent Bar and Pastry Szabadság tér 6. This chic café-bar does excellent coffees, cakes and cocktails – a cut above the rest. Fruit tarts 450Ft; baguettes 500Ft.

Moving on

Train Budapest (10 daily; 1hr 30min); Szeged (12 daily; 1–2hr).

Bus Budapest (every 1hr–1hr 30min; 1hr 45min); Szeged (10 daily; 1hr 30min).

SZEGED

SZEGED, the most sophisticated city in the Great Plain, straddles the River Tisza as it flows south towards Serbia. The present layout of the city, and its beautiful Art Nouveau architecture, date from after the great flood of 1879, when Szeged was rebuilt with strapping new buildings and squares thanks to foreign funding. The student population gives the city a real energy, and it's more than pleasant for a day or two's stopover.

What to see and do

Szeged's biggest monument is **Dom tér**, ringed by scholarly cloisters and busts of celebrated Hungarians. It was created in 1920 to accommodate the enormous double-spired **Votive Church** (Mon–Sat 9am–5.30pm, Sun 1–5pm; 400Ft), which leading townspeople pledged to erect after the great flood. At 12.15pm and 5.45pm, the **Musical Clock** on the south side of the square comes alive, as figurines from inside pop out and trundle around to the chiming of bells.

Móra Ferenc Museum

The **Móra Ferenc Museum** (Roosevelt tér 1–3; Tues–Sun 10am–5pm; 700Ft; Ⓦwww.mfm.u-szeged.hu) contains folk art, fine art and archeological remains offering insight into the Avars, the people who ruled much of the Central-Eastern European Pannonian plain from the sixth to ninth centuries. From the museum, it's a short walk to green, pretty Széchenyi tér, home to the neo-Baroque **town hall** with its decorative tiled roof. Look out for the "Bridge of Sighs", modelled on the Venetian original, which links the hall to a neighbouring house.

Great Synagogue

The **Great Synagogue** (Új Zsinagóga), built between 1900 and 1903 by architect Lipót Baumhorn, is one of Hungary's most beautiful buildings, with a blue glass dome with stars picked out in gold, and a stunning interior that is full of life: the frescoes and stained glass replicate exactly the plants and flowers that the then chief rabbi, a keen botanist, estimated would have grown in ancient Jerusalem. It conjures the sense of a Promised Land poignantly. The entrance is on Jósika utca 10 not far from Klauzál tér (Sun–Fri 10am–noon & 1–5pm; closed Jewish holidays; 400Ft).

Arrival and information

Train station South of the Belváros, a short tram ride on the #1.

Bus station Mars tér, a 5min walk to the heart of the Belváros (old city).

Tourist information Tourinform, Dugonics tér 2 (June–Sept Mon–Fri 9am–6pm, Sat 9am–1pm; Sept–May Mon–Fri 9am–5pm; Ⓣ62/488-690, Ⓦwww.szeged.hu).

Festivals The Szeged Open Air Festival (Ⓦwww.szegediszabadteri.hu) each July and August. Stages open-air opera, classical concerts and theatre. For two weeks in mid-May, Széchenyi tér is crammed with wine stalls and trestle tables for the merry Szeged Wine Festival (http://Ⓦborfesztival.blog.hu).

Accommodation

Private rooms can be booked through Ibusz on Oroszlán utca 3 (Mon–Fri 9am–6pm, Sat 9am–1pm; Ⓣ62/471-177, Ⓔszeged@ibusz.hu).

Marika Panzió Ⓣ62 443-861, Ⓦwww.marika.hu. Beautifully run, clean and cosy *pension* with lovely garden. Twenty minutes' walk out of town. Singles 6700Ft, doubles 12,000Ft.

Partfürdő Camping Középkikötő sor Ⓣ62/430-843, Ⓦwww.szegedkemping.hu (May–Sept). On the riverbank in Újszeged, 5min walk from the centre, with its own thermal bath. 1000Ft/person, plus 390Ft/tent.

Eating and drinking

The daily fruit and veg market (from dawn to midday) is just behind Mars tér, with tumbling piles of paprika and seasonal fruits.

A Capella Kávéház Kárász utca 6. Spacious coffeehouse hawking enormous cream and custard cakes; a prime spot for watching the world go by. Treats from 300Ft.

Corzo Café Kárász utca 16. Open-fronted café where students stop for coffee or late-afternoon drinks in Szeged's pedestrianized heart.

Halászcsárda Roosevelt tér 14. A Szeged riverside institution: beautiful high-ceilinged restaurant, where a cauldron of brilliant-red fish goulash with a glass of local white wine goes down swimmingly. Mains from 800Ft; half-price half-portions available.

Matusalem Étterem Széchenyi tér 13. A simple pub-style eating option in the centre serving Hungarian staples. Mains around 1700Ft.

Moving on

Train Budapest (11 daily; 2hr).

Bus Budapest (7 daily; 3hr); Kecskemét (10 daily; 1hr 30min).

Ireland

HIGHLIGHTS

GIANT'S CAUSEWAY: marvel at the astonishing basalt columns

SLIEVE LEAGUE: witness astounding views from Europe's highest sea cliffs

ARAN ISLANDS: be amazed by spectacular archeological remains

DUBLIN: visit the home of world-famous Guinness

COUNTY CLARE: enjoy traditional Irish music in Clare's pubs

ROUGH COSTS

DAILY BUDGET Basic €50 /occasional treat €70

DRINK Guinness €4.50/pint

FOOD Irish stew €10

HOSTEL/BUDGET HOTEL €16 /€35–45

TRAVEL Bus: Kilkenny–Dublin €10.80

FACT FILE

POPULATION 6 million (Republic: 4.2 million; N. Ireland: 1.8 million)

AREA 70,300 sq km

LANGUAGE English; Gaelic

CURRENCY Euro € (Republic); pound sterling £ (N. Ireland)

CAPITALS Dublin (Republic: 1.2 million); Belfast (N. Ireland: 270,000)

INTERNATIONAL PHONE CODE ⓣ353 (Republic); ⓣ44 (N. Ireland)

Introduction

In both Northern Ireland and the Republic, Ireland's lures are its landscape and people – the rain-hazed loughs and wild coastlines, the talent for conversation and wealth of traditional music. While economic growth has transformed Ireland's cities, the countryside remains relatively unchanged.

Ireland's west draws most visitors; its coastline and islands – especially **Aran** – combine vertiginous cliffs, boulder-strewn wastes and dramatic mountains. The interior is less spectacular, though the southern pastures and low wooded hills are classic landscapes. Northern Ireland's principal highlight is the bizarre basalt formation of the **Giant's Causeway**.

Dublin is an extraordinary mix of youthfulness and tradition, of revitalized Georgian squares and vibrant pubs. **Belfast** has undergone a massive rejuvenation, while the cities of **Cork** and **Galway** sparkle with energy.

No introduction can cope with the complexities of Ireland's **politics**, which still permeate most aspects of daily life in many areas in the North. However, regardless of partisan politics, Irish hospitality is as warm as the brochures say, on both sides of the border.

CHRONOLOGY

c. 3000 BC Neolithic tombs first constructed.
c. 500 BC Celts arrive heralding the Iron Age.
c.100 BC Romans refer to Ireland as "Hibernia".
432 AD Saint Patrick arrives in Ireland, converting pagans to Christianity.
795 Viking raids on Ireland.
1167 Arrival of Anglo-Norman invaders, ushering in eight hundred years of English rule.
1558–1603 Policy of Plantation of Irish lands under Queen Elizabeth I.
1649–53 Cromwell re-conquers Ireland, after a bloody campaign against Irish Catholics and English Royalists.
1690 Battle of the Boyne marks decisive victory by the Protestant king William of Orange over Catholic James II of England, as he attempted to regain the crown.
1704 Penal Code introduced, barring Catholics from voting, education and the military.
1759 Arthur Guinness begins to brew his famous stout in Dublin.
1798 Rebellion of the United Irishmen led by Wolfe Tone and supported by French troops is suppressed.
1801 Act of Union makes Ireland officially part of Great Britain.
1803 Second United Irishmen Rebellion under Robert Emmet defeated.
1845–49 Potato famine causes widespread starvation and prompts mass migration to the United States.
1879–82 Land War increases support for the Home Rule movement led by Charles Stewart Parnell.
1916 Easter Rising by Irish nationalists is brutally repressed by the British.
1922 Irish War of Independence ends with secession of 26 Irish counties from the UK to form the Irish Free State. Six counties in the North remain part of Great Britain.
1922 James Joyce's *Ulysses* is published.
1949 The Republic of Ireland is declared.
1970s The Provisional IRA steps up violent campaigns in Northern Ireland and the UK.
1972 British troops kill thirteen civilians in Derry, Northern Ireland in an event known as Bloody Sunday.
1973 Ireland joins the European Community.
1998 Good Friday Agreement signed by the British and Irish governments heralding a new era of peace and cooperation in Northern Ireland.
2002 The euro is introduced in the Republic of Ireland.
2005 The Provisional IRA announces a full ceasefire.
2007 Agreement between rival party leaders, Ian Paisley and Gerry Adams, to share power in an elected assembly for Northern Ireland.
2008 Crisis in the Irish banking system combines with a worldwide recession, bringing an end to economic prosperity.
2010 Police and justice powers for Northern Ireland transferred from London to Belfast; the EU and International Monetary Fund approve an €85billion loan to bail out the Irish economy.
2011 Queen Elizabeth makes historic first State visit to Ireland.

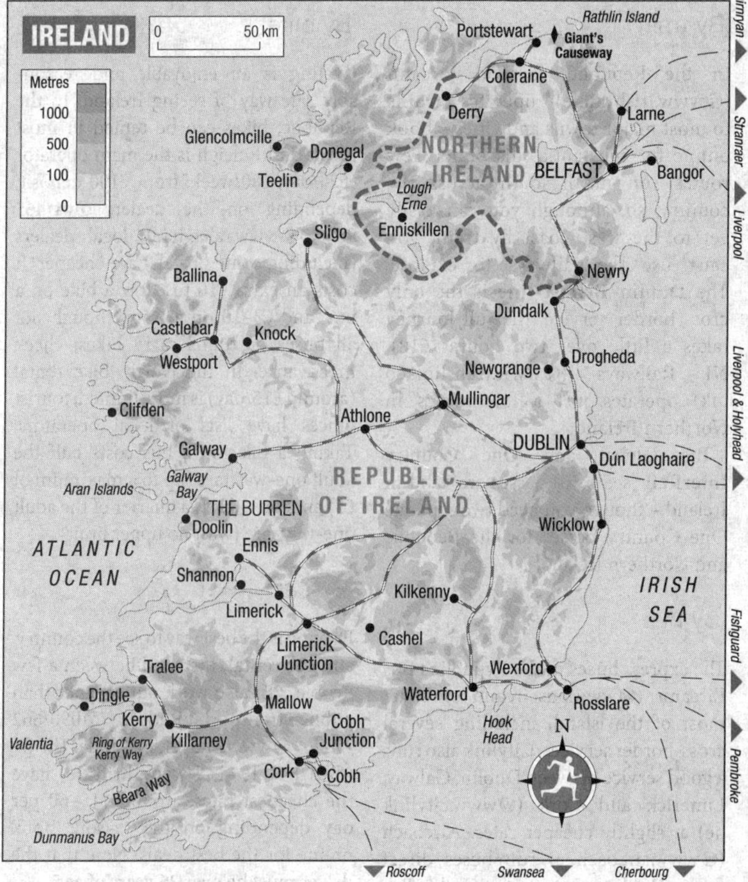

ARRIVAL

Ireland has five international **airports**: Dublin, Cork, Shannon and Knock in the Republic, and Belfast International in the North. Regional airports, which also serve the UK, are Belfast City, Derry, Donegal, Galway, Kerry and Sligo.

Ferry routes from the UK comprise Cairnryan–Larne, Fishguard–Rosslare, Fleetwood–Larne, Holyhead–Dublin, Holyhead–Dún Laoghaire, Isle of Man–Belfast, Isle of Man–Dublin, Liverpool–Belfast, Liverpool–Dublin, Pembroke–Rosslare, Stranraer–Belfast and Troon–Larne. Travelling by ferry without a vehicle is not expensive (about €60 return), but taking a car is pricey (€200–300 in high season).

GETTING AROUND

You can **save money** on rail and bus services by booking online and buying multi-journey tickets in advance; the **Freedom of Northern Ireland/Irish Rover** tickets give you unlimited bus/rail travel for three, five, eight or fifteen days. See ⓦwww.translink.co.uk or ⓦwww.buseireann.ie.

By train

In the Republic, Iarnród Éireann (ⓦwww.irishrail.ie) operates **trains** to most major towns and cities – book online for substantial discounts. Few routes run north–south across the country, so, although you can easily get to the west coast by train, you can't use the railways to explore. The **Dublin–Belfast line** is the only cross-border service, the full journey takes a little over two hours (€18). NI Railways (ⓦwww.translink.co.uk) operates just a few routes in Northern Ireland.

The Global and One Country **InterRail** (see p.36) passes are valid in Ireland – though you need two separate One Country passes for the Republic and Northern Ireland.

By bus

The express **buses** of the Republic's Bus Éireann (ⓦwww.buseireann.ie) cover most of the island, including several cross-border services. Citylink also runs a good service between Dublin, Galway, Limerick and Cork (ⓦwww.citylink.ie) at slightly cheaper rates. Aircoach (ⓦwww.aircoach.ie) run buses direct from Dublin airport to Cork. Bus **fares** are generally cheaper than trains, especially midweek. Remote villages may only have a couple of buses a week, so it's essential to find out the times – major bus stations stock free timetables. Private buses operate on major routes throughout the Republic and are often cheaper than Bus Éireann: J.J. Kavanagh & Sons, for instance, provide an efficient service from Dublin airport to Shannon airport, Limerick, Galway, Kilkenny and Waterford (ⓣ056/883 1106, ⓦwww.jjkavanagh.ie). In the North, Ulsterbus (ⓦwww.translink.co.uk) runs regular and reliable services.

By bike

Cycling is an enjoyable and reasonably safe way of seeing Ireland. In the Republic, bikes can be rented in most towns and Raleigh is the main operator (€20/day, €80/week; from €100 deposit, depending on the dealer; ⓣ01/465 9659, ⓦwww.raleigh.ie); local dealers (including some hostels) are cheaper. It costs an extra €10 to carry a bike on a bus, and €3–10 on a train, though not all buses or trains carry bikes; check in advance. In the North, bike rental (around £15/day) is more limited; tourist offices have lists of local operators. Taking a bike on a bus costs half the adult one-way fare (up to a maximum of £5) and, on a train, a quarter of the adult one-way fare (with no upper limit).

By car

Driving is the best way to see the country, and **car rental**, if shared between a few people, can also work out cheaper than public transport. Budget (ⓣ090/662 7711, ⓦwww.budget.ie) and Thrifty (ⓣ01/844 1944, ⓦwww.thrifty.ie) have the cheapest rates, around €15–60 per day depending on the season. Book online for the best deals. Note that the driver must be over 25 years of age.

ACCOMMODATION

Hostels run by **An Óige** (Irish Youth Hostel Association; ⓦwww.anoige.ie) and **HINI** (Hostelling International Northern Ireland; ⓦwww.hini.org.uk) are affiliated to Hostelling International. Overnight prices start at €11–17 in the Republic and £9.50–13 in the North. Most Irish hostels are **independent hostels**, which usually belong to either Independent Holiday Hostels (ⓣ01/836 4700, ⓦwww.hostels-ireland.com) or the Independent Hostels network (ⓣ074/973 0130, ⓦwww.independenthostelsireland.com). In the Republic, expect to pay

€10–18 for a dorm bed, €17–32 (rising to €46 in some Dublin hostels) per person for private rooms where available; in the North, it's £7–12/£14–25.

B&Bs vary enormously, but most are welcoming, warm and clean. Expect to pay from around €25/£22 per person sharing; most **hotels** are a little pricier but you can find bargains online. Single travellers are usually charged a supplement of about €12/£10. Booking ahead is always advisable during high season and major festivals.

Camping usually costs around €8 a night in the Republic, £7 in the North. In out-of-the-way places it may be possible to camp in the wild, but ask the landowner's permission first: farmers in popular tourist areas may ask for a small fee. Some hostels also let you camp for around €8/£5 per person.

FOOD AND DRINK

Irish **food** is meat-orientated. B&Bs usually provide a "traditional" **Irish breakfast** of sausages, bacon and eggs (although many offer vegetarian alternatives). **Pub lunch** staples are usually meat or fish and two veg, with a few veggie options, while specifically vegetarian places are sparse outside major cities and popular tourist areas. All towns have fast-food outlets, but traditional fish and chips is a better bet, especially on the coast. For the occasional treat, there are some very good seafood restaurants, particularly along the southwest and west coasts. Most towns have daytime cafés serving a selection of affordable hot dishes, salads, soups, sandwiches and cakes.

Drink

The stereotypical view of the "Irish national pastime" has a certain element of truth; especially in rural areas, the **pub** is the social heart of the community and the focus for the proverbial **craic** (pronounced "crack"), a particular blend of Irish fun involving good company, witty conversation and laughter, frequently against a backdrop of music. The classic Irish drink is **Guinness**, best in Dublin, home of the brewery, while the Cork stouts, Beamish and Murphy's, have their devotees. For English-style keg **bitter**, try Smithwicks. Irish **whiskeys** are world famous – try Paddy's, Jameson's or Bushmills.

CULTURE AND ETIQUETTE

With the huge influx of visitors to Ireland in recent years, the country has acquired an increasingly **cosmopolitan** feel, particularly in the big cities, but the sense of national identity and heritage remains strong. Traditional music sessions are still the primary form of evening entertainment in pubs, especially in rural areas.

Despite the decreasing influence of Catholicism in Ireland, family values still reign. It's hard to miss the hospitality and friendliness that most clearly define the Irish.

Smoking is banned in all indoor public places. In restaurants and cafés, a ten percent **tip** is generally expected.

SPORTS AND OUTDOOR ACTIVITIES

Walking and **cycling** in Ireland are great ways of enjoying the country's beautiful landscapes (see Ⓦwww.irishtrails.ie for suggested routes). There are great opportunities for **horseriding** (see Ⓦwww.discoverireland.ie); a lovely ride is along the white sands of Connemara. **Watersports** are popular: Ireland is increasingly praised for its surfing spots, such as Portrush in the north, Bundoran in Donegal, and Lahinch in Clare (see Ⓦwww.isasurf.ie).

The two great Gaelic sports, **hurling** (the oldest field game in Europe, and similar to hockey) and **Gaelic football** (a mixture of soccer and rugby, but predating both these games), are very popular spectator sports. Croke Park Stadium in Dublin is home to the big fixtures (see Ⓦwww.gaa.ie and Ⓦwww.crokepark.ie for information and tickets).

Horse racing (Ⓦwww.goracing.ie) looms large on the sporting agenda: you'll never be far from a race in Ireland, whether it's a big racecourse like Galway or a soggy village affair in the middle of nowhere.

COMMUNICATIONS

Main **post offices** are open Monday to Friday 9am to 5.30pm, Saturday 9am to 1pm. Stamps and phonecards are also often available in newsagents. **Public phones** are everywhere, and usually take **phonecards**; coin-operated phones are rare in rural areas. **International calls** are cheaper at weekends or after 6pm (Mon–Fri). To call the Republic from Northern Ireland dial Ⓣ00353 followed by the area code (without the initial 0) and the local number (note cross-border calls are charged at the international rate). Call centres offer cheaper international rates than public telephones. To call the North from the Republic use the code Ⓣ048, followed by the eight-digit local number. **Internet access** is widely available and costs about €3/£2.50 per hour; it's generally cheaper in big towns and cities.

IRELAND ONLINE

Ⓦwww.discoverireland.ie Fáilte Ireland website with comprehensive tourist information.
Ⓦwww.discovernorthernireland.com Northern Ireland Tourist Board.
Ⓦwww.heritageireland.com Information on Ireland's main heritage sites.
Ⓦwww.ireland.com *Irish Times* site with up-to-date info on Dublin.
Ⓦwww.ntni.org.uk Details of the National Trust's properties in Northern Ireland.

EMERGENCY NUMBERS

In the Republic Ⓣ112 or 999; in Northern Ireland Ⓣ999.

EMERGENCIES

The Republic's police are known as the **Gardaí** (pronounced "gar-dee"), while the **PSNI** (Police Service of Northern Ireland) operates in the North. **Hospitals** and medical facilities are high quality; you'll rarely be far from a hospital, and both Northern Ireland and the Republic are within the European Health Insurance Card scheme. Most **pharmacies** open standard shop hours, though in large towns some may stay open until 10pm; they dispense only a limited range of drugs without a doctor's prescription.

INFORMATION

Tourist offices are abundant in Ireland, in the smaller as well as larger towns on the tourist trail. **Bord Fáilte** provides tourist information in the Republic; the **Northern Ireland Tourist Board** in the North. They provide free maps of the city/town and immediate vicinity, and sell a selection of more extensive and specialized maps.

MONEY AND BANKS

Currency in the Republic is the **euro** (€), in Northern Ireland the **pound sterling** (£). Standard **bank hours** are Monday to Friday 9.30am to 4.30pm (Republic and Northern Ireland). There are **ATMs** throughout Ireland – though not in all villages – and most accept a variety of cards. The exchange rate at the time of writing was €1.11/£1.

OPENING HOURS AND HOLIDAYS

Business hours are roughly Monday to Saturday 9am to 6pm, with some late evenings (usually Thurs) and Sunday

STUDENT DISCOUNTS

A **student card** usually gives reduced entrance charges of up to fifty percent and, if you're visiting sites run by the Heritage Service in the Republic (Ⓦwww.heritageireland.ie), it's worth buying a **Heritage Card** (€21, students €8), which provides a year's unlimited admission.

opening. **Museums** and attractions are usually open regular shop hours, though outside the cities, many only open during the summer. **Cafés** usually open daily from 8am–6pm, and most **restaurants** from noon–10pm, with some closed on a Monday. **Pubs** operate strict trading hours, and those without a late-night licence must close at 11.30pm Sunday to Thursday and 12.30am on Friday & Saturday. **Nightclubs** close at 2.30am.

Public holidays in the Republic are: Jan 1, St Patrick's Day (March 17), Easter Monday, May Day (first Mon in May), June Bank Holiday (first Mon in June), August Bank Holiday (first Mon in Aug), October Bank Holiday (Halloween, last Mon in Oct), December 25 and 26. Note that some places may also close on Good Friday. In the North: January 1, St Patrick's Day (March 17), Good Friday, Easter Monday, May Day (first Mon in May), Spring Bank Holiday (last Mon in May), July 12, August Bank Holiday (last Mon in Aug), December 25 and 26.

THE IRISH LANGUAGE

Though **Irish** is the first language of the Republic, you'll rarely hear it spoken outside the areas officially designated as *Gaeltacht* ("Irish-speaking"), namely West Cork, West Kerry, Connemara, some of Mayo and Donegal, and a tiny part of Meath. However, two important words you may encounter sometimes appear on the doors of pub toilets *Fir* (for men) and *Mná* (for women). You'll also find the word *Fáilte* (welcome) popping up frequently as you enter towns and tourist spots. A few other words to get your tongue round:

Sláinte	cheers, good health
Gardaí	police
An lár	city centre
Dia dhuit	hello
Slán	goodbye

More information on the Gaeltacht areas is available at Ⓦwww.gaelsaoire.ie.

Dublin and around

Set on the banks of the River Liffey, **DUBLIN** is a splendidly monumental city with a cosmopolitan feel and an internationally renowned nightlife. It was the centre of Ireland's booming economy during the "Celtic Tiger" years up to 2007, which brought rejuvenation and renewed energy, which still remains despite high unemployment.

Dublin began as the Viking trading post **Dubh Linn** (Dark Pool), which soon amalgamated with the Celtic settlement of **Baile Átha Cliath** (Town of the Hurdle Ford) – still the Irish name for the city. The city's fabric is essentially **Georgian**, hailing from when the Anglo-Irish gentry invested their income in new townhouses. After the 1801 Act of Union, Dublin entered a long economic decline, but remained the focus of much of the agitation that eventually led to independence.

Dublin city is also an excellent base for excursions to the picturesque mountains, lakes, forested estates and rural villages of County **Wicklow**, or to the five-thousand-year-old passage tombs at Newgrange in the Boyne Valley, County Meath.

What to see and do

Dublin's fashionable **Southside** is home to the city's trendy bars, restaurants and shops – especially in the cobbled alleys of **Temple Bar** leading down to the **River Liffey** – and most of its historic monuments, centred on **Trinity College**, **Grafton Street** and **St Stephen's Green**. But the **Northside**, with its long-standing working-class neighbourhoods and inner-city communities, is the real heart of the city. Across the bridges from Temple Bar are the shopping districts around **O'Connell Street**, where you'll find a flavour of the old Dublin. Here, you'll also find a fair amount of graceful – if slightly shabby – residential streets and squares, with plenty of interest in the museums and cultural hotspots around the elegant **Parnell Square**.

The Vikings sited their assembly and burial ground near what is now **College Green**, a three-sided square where Trinity College is the most famous landmark.

Trinity College

Founded in 1592, Trinity College played a major role in the development of a Protestant Anglo-Irish tradition: right up to 1966, Catholics had to obtain a special dispensation to study here, though now they make up the majority of the students. The stern grey and mellow red-brick buildings are ranged around cobbled quadrangles in a larger version of the quads at Oxford and Cambridge. **The Old Library** (May–Sept Mon–Sat 9.30am–5pm, Sun 9.30am–4.30pm; Oct–April daily noon–4.30pm; €9, students €8; Ⓦwww.bookofkells.ie) owns numerous Irish manuscripts; pride of place goes to the illustrated ninth-century **Book of Kells**, which contains the four Gospels written in Latin on vellum, the script adorned with patterns and fantastic animals intertwined with the text's capital letters. The first of the great Irish illuminated manuscripts, the **Book of Durrow**, which dates from between 650 and 680, is also on display.

Grafton Street and around

Just south of College Green, the streets around pedestrianized **Grafton Street** frame Dublin's quality shopping area – featuring boutiques, department stores and designer outlets, as well as some secondhand, more alternative shops. At the southern end of Grafton Street lies **St Stephen's Green**, whose pleasant gardens and ponds are a pleasant picnic spot on a sunny day. Running

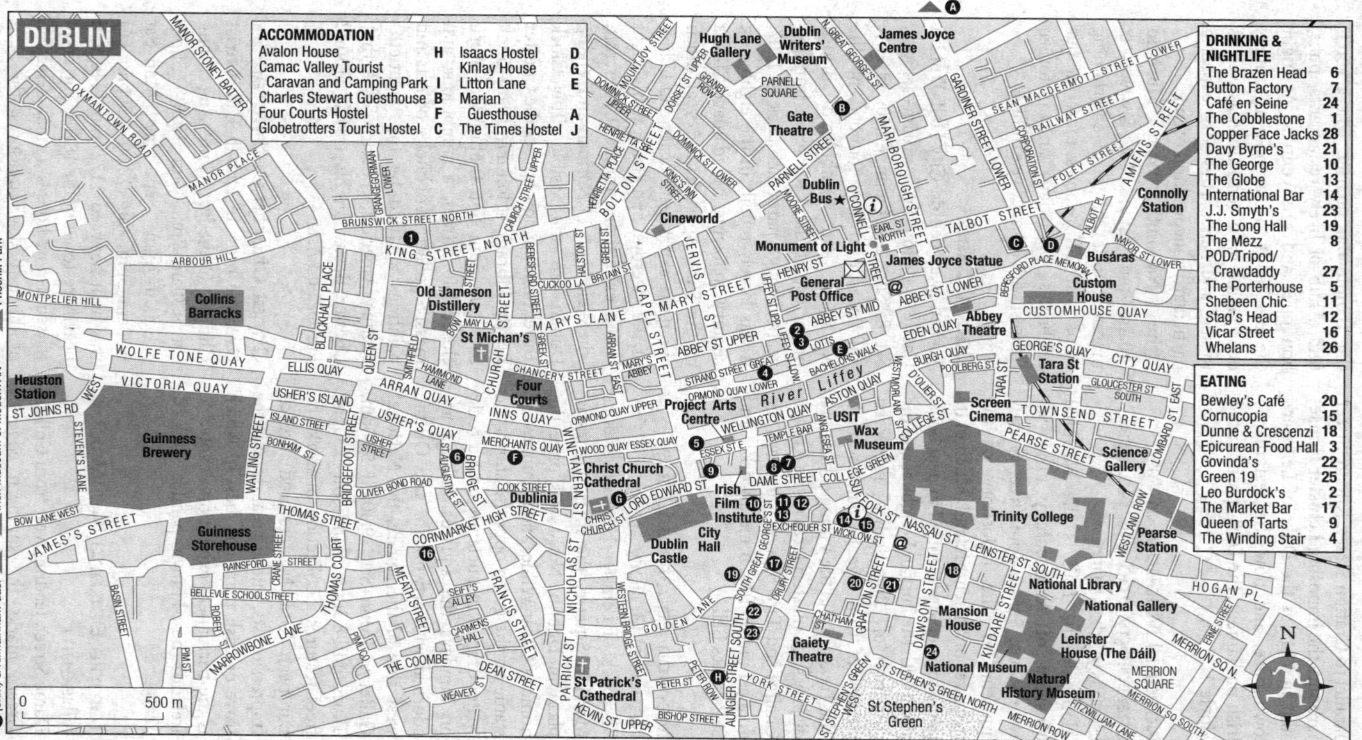
DUBLIN
ACCOMMODATION
Avalon House H
Camac Valley Tourist Caravan and Camping Park I
Charles Stewart Guesthouse B
Four Courts Hostel F
Globetrotters Tourist Hostel C
Isaacs Hostel D
Kinlay House G
Litton Lane E
Marian Guesthouse A
The Times Hostel J
DRINKING & NIGHTLIFE
The Brazen Head 6
Button Factory 7
Café en Seine 24
The Cobblestone 1
Copper Face Jacks 28
Davy Byrne's 21
The George 10
The Globe 13
International Bar 14
J.J. Smyth's 23
The Long Hall 19
The Mezz 8
POD/Tripod/Crawdaddy 27
The Porterhouse 5
Shebeen Chic 11
Stag's Head 12
Vicar Street 16
Whelans 26
EATING
Bewley's Café 20
Cornucopia 15
Dunne & Crescenzi 18
Epicurean Food Hall 3
Govinda's 22
Green 19 25
Leo Burdock's 2
The Market Bar 17
Queen of Tarts 9
The Winding Stair 4
Hugh Lane Gallery
Dublin Writers' Museum
James Joyce Centre
Gate Theatre
Cineworld
Dublin Bus
Monument of Light
James Joyce Statue
General Post Office
Busáras
Connolly Station
Custom House
Abbey Theatre
Tara St Station
Screen Cinema
Science Gallery
Trinity College
Pearse Station
Project Arts Centre
USIT
Wax Museum
Irish Film Institute
City Hall
Dublin Castle
Christ Church Cathedral
Dublinia
Four Courts
St Michan's
Old Jameson Distillery
Collins Barracks
Heuston Station
Guinness Brewery
Guinness Storehouse
St Patrick's Cathedral
Gaiety Theatre
Mansion House
National Library
National Gallery
Leinster House (The Dáil)
National Museum
Natural History Museum
St Stephen's Green
Merrion Square
River Liffey
Phoenix Park
Irish Museum of Modern Art
I (8km) & Kilmainham Gaol
J, 25 & 26
27 & 28
0
500 m
N

parallel to Grafton Street, Kildare Street harbours the imposing **Leinster House**, built in 1745 as the Duke of Leinster's townhouse, and now the seat of the Irish parliament, the **Dáil** (pronounced "doyle").

National Museum of Archaeology and the Natural History Museum

Alongside the Dáil is the **National Museum of Archaeology** (Tues–Sat 10am–5pm, Sun 2–5pm; free; Ⓦwww.museum.ie), the repository of the treasures of ancient Ireland. Much of its prehistoric gold was found in peat bogs, along with the Lurgan Longboat and the collection of "Bog Bodies", preserved victims of Iron Age human sacrifice. The Treasury and the Viking exhibitions display such masterpieces as the Ardagh Chalice and Tara Brooch – perhaps the greatest piece of Irish metalwork – and St Patrick's Bell.

Merrion Square and the National Gallery

The back of Leinster House overlooks **Merrion Square**, the finest Georgian plaza in Dublin. No. 1 was once the home of Oscar Wilde, and a flamboyant statue on the green opposite shows the writer draped insouciantly over a rock; on Sundays the square's railings are adorned with artwork for sale. On the west side of the square, the **National Gallery** (Mon–Sat 9.30am–5.30pm, Thurs until 8.30pm, Sun noon–5.30pm; free) features a collection of works by European Old Masters and French Impressionists, but the real draw is the trove of Irish paintings, best of which is the permanent exhibition devoted to Ireland's best-known painter, Jack B. Yeats.

Temple Bar and the Wax Museum

Dame Street, leading west from College Green, marks the southern edge of the **Temple Bar** quarter, where you'll find a hub of lively restaurants, pubs, boutiques and arts centres. At night the area tends to play host to tourists out looking for a good time, as well as to stag and hen parties – so expect a particularly raucous kind of fun.

The **National Wax Museum** (10am–7pm daily; €10; Ⓦwww.waxmuseumplus.ie) hosts an entertaining who's who of Ireland's most famous celebrities, politicians and historical figures, with interactive exhibits.

Dublin Castle

Tucked away behind City Hall, **Dublin Castle** (Mon–Fri 10am–4.45pm, Sat & Sun 2–4.45pm; €4.50; Ⓦwww.dublincastle.ie) was founded by the Normans, and symbolized British power over Ireland for seven hundred years. Though parts date back to 1207, it was largely rebuilt in the eighteenth century following fire damage. Tours of the State Apartments reveal much about the extravagant tastes and foibles of the viceroys, and the real highlight is the excavations in the Undercroft, where elements of Norman and Viking Dublin are still visible. The Clock Tower building now houses the **Chester Beatty Library** (Mon–Fri 10am–5pm, Sat 11am–5pm, Sun 1–5pm; Oct–April closed Mon; free), a sumptuous and massive collection of books, objects and paintings amassed by the twentieth-century American collector Sir Arthur Chester Beatty on his travels around Europe and Asia.

Christ Church Cathedral

Over the brow of Dublin Hill, **Christ Church Cathedral** (June–Aug Mon–Sat 9.30am–7pm, Sun 12.30–2.30pm & 4.30–7pm; Sept–May Mon–Sat 9.30am–5pm, Sun 12.30–2.30pm; €6) was built between 1172 and 1240 and heavily restored in the 1870s. The crypt museum now houses a small selection of the cathedral's treasures, the least serious of which include a mummified cat and rat, found trapped in an organ pipe in the 1860s.

St Patrick's Cathedral

Five minutes' walk south from Christ Church is Dublin's other great Norman edifice, **St Patrick's Cathedral** (daily 9am–5.30pm; Nov–Feb Sun closes 3pm; €5.50), founded in 1191, and replete with relics of Jonathan Swift, author of *Gulliver's Travels*, its dean from 1713 to 1747.

Guinness Brewery

West of Christ Church, the **Guinness Brewery** covers a large area on either side of James's Street. Guinness is the world's largest single beer-exporting company, dispatching some 300 million pints a year. Set in the centre of the brewery, the **Guinness Storehouse** (daily 9.30am–5pm; July & Aug until 7pm; €15, ten percent discount if you book online; Ⓦwww.guinness-storehouse.com) serves as a kind of theme park for Guinness-lovers – and even if you're not a fan, you can't fail to be entertained by the interactive displays and activities, which include learning how to pour the perfect pint and watching some of those great Guinness TV ads again. Visits to the Storehouse end with reputedly the best pint of Guinness in Dublin, in the panoramic *Gravity Bar* at the top of the building, with amazing views over the city.

Irish Museum of Modern Art

Regular buses (#26, #51, #79 and #90) run along The Quays to Heuston Station from where it's a five-minute walk to the **Royal Hospital Kilmainham**, Ireland's first Neoclassical building, dating from 1680, which now houses the **Irish Museum of Modern Art** (Tues–Sat 10am–5.30pm, Wed opens 10.30am, Sun noon–5.30pm; free). Its permanent collection of Irish and international art includes works by Gilbert and George, Damien Hirst, Sean Scully, Francesco Clemente and Peter Doig.

General Post Office and the Monument of Light

Halfway up O'Connell Street looms the **General Post Office** (Mon–Sat 8am–8pm; free), the insurgents' headquarters in the 1916 Easter Rising; only the frontage survived the fighting, and you can still see where bullets were embedded in the pillars. The building is still a functioning post office, and home to an interesting new **museum** (Mon–Fri 10am–5pm, Sat 10am–4pm; €2) documenting the history of the postal service in Irish society. Across the road on the corner of Essex Street North is a **statue of James Joyce**. At the same junction, where the city's most famous landmark, Nelson's Pillar, once stood (it was blown up by the IRA on the fiftieth anniversary of the Easter Rising in 1966), stands a huge, illuminated stainless-steel spire – the **Monument of Light** – representing the city's hopes for the new millennium.

Parnell Square

At the northern end of O'Connell Street lies Parnell Square, one of the first of Dublin's Georgian squares. Its plain red-brick houses are broken by the grey-stone **Hugh Lane Gallery** (Tues–Thurs 10am–6pm, Fri & Sat until 5pm, Sun 11am–5pm; free; Ⓦwww.hughlane.ie), once the Earl of Charlemont's townhouse and the focus of fashionable Dublin. The gallery exhibits work by Irish and international masters, and features a reconstruction of Francis Bacon's working studio. Almost next door, the **Dublin Writers Museum** (Mon–Sat 10am–5pm, Sun 11am–5pm; €7.50; Ⓦwww.writersmuseum.com) whisks you through Irish literary history from early Christian writings up to Samuel Beckett. Two blocks east of Parnell Square, at 35 North Great George's

St, the **James Joyce Centre** (Tues–Sat 10am–5pm, Sun noon–5pm; €5; Ⓦwww.jamesjoyce.ie) runs intriguing walking tours of the novelist's haunts (summer only; €10; Ⓣ01/878 8547); combined tickets with the Dublin Writers Museum are available.

Old Jameson Distillery

Fifteen minutes west of O'Connell Street, on Bow Street, is the **Old Jameson Distillery** (daily 9am–6.30pm, last tour 5.30pm; €13.50; Ⓦwww.jamesonwhiskey.com). Tours cover the history and method of distilling what the Irish called *uisce beatha* (anglicized to whiskey and meaning "water of life") – which differs from Scotch whisky by being three times distilled and lacking a peaty undertone – and end with a tasting session. The Distillery also has two **bars**, which pride themselves on their Jameson cocktails, and a **restaurant** that serves breakfast and lunch (9am–4.45pm; light lunch €7).

Phoenix Park

Phoenix Park is one of the world's largest urban parks, a great escape from the hustle and bustle of the centre (bus #10 from O'Connell Street or #25 from Wellington Quay); originally priory land, it's now home to the Presidential Lodge, Áras an Uachtaráin (free tours every Sat 10.30am–4.30pm) and **Dublin Zoo** (Feb 9.30am–5pm; March–Sept 9.30am–6pm; Oct 9.30am–5.30pm; Nov–Jan 9.30am–4pm; €15; Ⓦwww.dublinzoo.ie).

Arrival and information

Air The airport is 10km north of the city; Airlink buses #747 and #748 run to Busáras bus station (every 10–20min; 30min; €6 one-way, €10 return), or there are regular Dublin Bus services #16A, #41, #41B & #41C (every 10–20min; €1.85). Aircoach (Ⓦwww.aircoach.ie) run services to the city centre and South Dublin (€7–13 one-way/€12–20 return depending on distance travelled), and a cheap, comfortable coach all the way to Cork (€15/22). A taxi to Dublin centre should cost €25–30.

Train Trains terminate at either Connolly Station on the Northside, or Heuston Station on the Southside.

Bus Bus Éireann coaches arrive at Busáras bus station, off Beresford Place, just behind The Custom House; private buses use a variety of central locations.

Boat Ferries dock at either Dún Laoghaire, 10km south of the city centre, from where DART railway connects to the city (every 20min; €2; 20min), or at the closer Dublin Port, where a Citybus service (€2.50; 15min) – or the local bus #53 – meets arriving ferries; through-coaches from Britain usually drop you at Busáras.

Tourist office Suffolk St, off College Green (Sept–June Mon–Sat 9am–5.30pm, Sun 10.30am–3pm; July–Aug 9am–7pm, Sun 10.30am–3pm; Ⓦwww.visitdublin.com), with branches at 14 Upper O'Connell St, the Dún Laoghaire ferry terminal and the airport.

Travel agency USIT on Aston Quay, by O'Connell Bridge (Mon–Fri 10am–6.30pm, Thurs till 7pm, Sat 9.30am–5pm; Ⓣ01/602 1904, Ⓦwww.usit.ie).

City transport

Bus Dublin has an extensive route network and all buses are exact fare only. Fares are €1.20–2.30, a one-day bus pass is €6, or there are bus and rail passes (including DART or LUAS) for one day/three days (€10.70/€21). Free bus timetables are available from Dublin Bus, 59 Upper O'Connell St. Nitelink night buses cost €5.

Tram The LUAS tram service operates along two routes: from Connolly Station to Tallaght via Abbey St to Heuston Station, and from St Stephen's Green to Sandyford. Tickets cost €1.50–2.70 one-way, €2.90–5 return.

Train The DART railway links Howth and Malahide to the north of the city with Bray and Greystones to the south via Pearse, Tara St and Connolly stations in the city centre (maximum fare €4). A trip on the DART is an activity in itself, affording stunning views of the Dublin suburbs and coastline. Get off at Howth, Malahide, Sandymount, Dún Laoghaire, Killiney, Bray or Greysones for pleasant seaside walks.

Bike rental Cycle Ways, 185 Parnell St Ⓣ01/873 4748.

City tours

Bus tours City Sightseeing (Ⓦwww.citysightseeingdublin.com) and Dublin Bus Tours (Ⓦwww.dublinsightseeing.ie) run similar hop-on, hop-off tours to all the major sights in the city (€16); both collect from the front of Trinity College.

Walking tours Tour Gratis (Ⓦwww.neweuropetours.eu) operate free walking tours, picking up from all of the listed hostels (see below) every morning. The fantastic 1916 Rebellion walking tours (Mon–Sat 11.30am, Sun 1pm, meet at the *International Bar*, 23 Wicklow St; €12; Ⓦwww.1916rising.com) visit sights of interest relating to the 1916 Rising.

Organized pub crawls Dublin Literary Pub Crawl (April–Oct daily 7.30pm; Nov–March Thurs–Sun 7.30pm; meet at *The Duke Pub*, 9 Duke St; €12); and the more raucous Backpacker Pubcrawl (May–Sept daily 8pm; Oct–March Thurs–Sat 8pm; meet Trinity College Front Gates; €10; Ⓦwww.backpackerpubcrawl.com).

Accommodation

Although Dublin has stacks of accommodation, anywhere central will probably be full at weekends, around St Patrick's Day (March 17), at Easter and in high summer so it's wise to book ahead (preferably online). The cheaper places are generally north of the river, especially around the bus and train stations northeast of the centre. All hostels listed provide free breakfast.

Hostels

Avalon House 55 Aungier St Ⓣ01/475 0001, Ⓦwww.avalon-house.ie. Bustling and friendly hostel with slightly cramped dorms but plenty of twin or four-bedded rooms. Performers get a free night's accommodation for an evening recital in the café. Dorms from €16, doubles €50.

Four Courts Hostel 15–17 Merchants Quay Ⓣ01/672 5839, Ⓦwww.fourcourtshostel.com. In a very central location, this hostel is housed in Georgian buildings overlooking the River Liffey. Excellent facilities and helpful staff. Dorms from €15, doubles €55.

Globetrotters Tourist Hostel 46 Gardiner St Lower Ⓣ01/873 5893, Ⓦwww.globetrottersdublin.com. Upmarket hostel where security-locked dorms and individual bed lights make for a peaceful night's sleep. There's a pretty Japanese garden, and all prices include a full Irish breakfast. Dorms from €16, doubles €80.

Isaacs Hostel 2–5 Frenchman's Lane Ⓣ01/855 6215, Ⓦwww.isaacs.ie. Housed in an eighteenth-century wine warehouse with its own restaurant and a free sauna in the basement. Close to the bus station. Dorms from €12, singles €40.

Kinlay House 2–12 Lord Edward St Ⓦwww.kinlaydublin.ie. Large, friendly and popular hostel right beside Christ Church Cathedral. Dorms from €12.50, doubles and twins €60.

Litton Lane 2–4 Litton Lane Ⓣ01/872 8389, Ⓦwww.littonlanehostel.ie. Located in a former recording studio, with great facilities and friendly staff. Adorned with colourful murals and posters depicting Irish rock stars. Dorms from €10, doubles and twins from €45.

The Times Hostel 8 Camden Place Ⓣ01/475 8588, Ⓦwww.timeshostels.com. Small and convivial hostel close to some of the city's best pubs and restaurants, with free pancake breakfasts and organized tours, pub crawls and game nights. Dorms from €15, doubles and twins from €40.

Guesthouses

Charles Stewart Guesthouse 5/6 Parnell Square Ⓣ01/878 0350, Ⓦwww.charlesstewart.ie. Very reasonably priced accommodation in elegant Georgian surroundings, opposite the Gate Theatre. Doubles €80.

Marian Guesthouse 21 Upper Gardiner St Ⓣ01/874 4129, Ⓦwww.marianguesthouse.ie. Welcoming family-run guesthouse, kitschly decorated with plenty of fake flowers and ornaments. Singles €40, doubles €70.

Camping

Camac Valley Tourist Caravan and Camping Park Naas Rd, Clondalkin Ⓣ01/464 0644, Ⓦwww.camacvalley.com. The most convenient campsite, with excellent facilities, located on the N7, a 35min drive from the centre. Bus #69 from the centre (Aston Quay, near O'Connell Bridge), stops right outside the campsite. The last bus is at 11.15pm, so if you're any later, a taxi (around €25) is your only option. €10/person.

Eating

Bewley's Café 78 Grafton St. An old Dublin institution, and a favourite haunt of Ireland's literary luminaries, including Joyce, Kavanagh, Beckett and O'Casey. Lounge over a coffee and croissant for breakfast or enjoy good pasta, pizza or salad for lunch or dinner. Mains from €9.50. You can also catch a lunchtime play or music recital in the theatre upstairs. Daily 8am–10pm.

Cornucopia 21 Wicklow St. One of the city's few vegetarian cafés and very popular for its generous portions of home-made soups, salads, curries and gratins. Mains €8–12. Mon–Sat 8.30am–9pm, Sun noon–8.30pm.

Dunne & Crescenzi 14–16 South Frederick St. Authentic Italian restaurant serving delicious bruschetta, antipasti, panini and simple pasta dishes, washed down by the cheapest (yet very

TREAT YOURSELF

For high-end organic Irish food, it is hard to beat **The Winding Stair** (40 Ormond Quay; ⓣ01/8727320, ⓦwww.winding-stair.com). Dishes are thoughtfully prepared using ingredients from small, carefully selected producers. The menu changes daily but expect dishes like wild Irish venison with creamy potato bake, or hand-smoked haddock poached in milk with white cheddar mash. The dining room is bright and airy, with gorgeous views over the River Liffey. Mains €22. Daily noon–10.30pm.

palatable) house wine in Dublin. Mains €6–15. Daily 8am–late.

Epicurean Food Hall Lower Liffey St. Collection of deli counters and food stands offering lunches from around the world in a communal dining area. Mon–Sat 9.45am–7pm, Sun 11.30am–7pm.

Govinda's 4 Aungier St. Huge helpings of dhal and rice and tasty vegetarian curries, plus daily veggie specials, served by very friendly staff. €7–10. Mon–Sat noon–9pm.

Green 19 19 Camden St. Simple yet top-quality dishes like slow-braised pork belly with a chorizo cassoulet or corned beef with mash and parsley sauce, all priced at €10. Excellent cocktails and a funky vibe completes the picture. Mon–Sat 10am–11pm, Sun noon–10pm.

Leo Burdock's 2 Werburgh St. Dublin's best fish and chips – takeaway only. Fresh cod is €5.75. There's another branch on Liffey St Lower.

The Market Bar 14 Fade St. Dublin's first gastro-bar serving tapas with an Irish twist in a converted abattoir. Tapas €4–12. Daily noon–midnight.

Drinking and nightlife

Most of Dublin's eight hundred pubs serve food as well, and can be the best place to sample traditional Irish food. The music scene – much of which is pub-based – is changeable, so it's always best to check the listings magazines. Check the free *Event Guide* (ⓦwww.eventguide.ie), *In Dublin* (ⓦwww.indublin.ie) and *Totally Dublin* (ⓦwww.totallydublin.ie) or, for music events, *Hot Press* (€3.50). Camden St is the best place to find live rock; hit Temple Bar for clubs playing pop and dance music and touristy traditional sessions. See p.608 for information on opening hours.

Bars

Café en Seine 40 Dawson St. Sip on a cocktail or two at Dublin's classiest establishment, an Art Nouveau-style café-bar with three floors and five bars.

Davy Byrne's 21 Duke St. An object of pilgrimage for *Ulysses* fans, since Leopold Bloom stopped here for a snack. Attracts a sophisticated crowd and also serves good food (traditional Irish stew €12).

The Globe 11 South Great George's St. Trendy, dimly lit bar with loud music and lots of space. Backs onto *RíRá*, a cavernous club with nightly DJs.

The Long Hall 51 South Great George's St. Victorian pub encrusted with mirrors and antique clocks.

Shebeen Chic 4 South Great George's St ⓦwww.shebeenchic.ie An eclectic array of secondhand furniture and bric-a-brac decorates one of Dublin's newest and trendiest hangouts. Lounge over a good burger by day or dance to retro disco tunes by night.

Stag's Head 1 Dame Court, Dame St, almost opposite the Central Bank. Wonderfully intimate pub, full of mahogany, stained glass and mirrors. Very popular with local Dubliners, and does good pub lunches.

Clubs

Button Factory Curved St ⓦwww.buttonfactory.ie. Housed in the refurbished Temple Bar Music Centre, this is the place to find top Irish and international DJs in the Thurs–Sun club till 2.30am.

Copper Face Jacks 29–30 Harcourt St. The most popular of several similar venues along Harcourt St, and notorious for its pop tunes and groups of single lads and lasses looking for a good time. Daily 9pm–2.30am.

The George South Great George's St ⓦwww.thegeorge.ie. Dublin's oldest and most popular gay bar and club. Daily till late.

POD/Tripod/Crawdaddy 35 Harcourt St ⓦwww.pod.ie. Multiple venues housed in an old train station, famously photographed in 1900 with a train crashed through its walls. Local house DJs are a regular feature, with occasional international guests.

Live music

The Brazen Head 20 Lower Bridge St ⓦwww.brazenhead.com. The oldest pub in Dublin, with traditional music nightly from 9.30pm.

The Cobblestone 77 King St North ⓦwww.cobblestonepub.ie. Atmospheric pub on the edge of the Smithfield Plaza, famous for its nightly traditional sessions.

International Bar 23 Wicklow St Ⓦwww.international-bar.com. Large saloon with rock bands and a comedy club upstairs or in the cellar.
J.J. Smyth's 12 Aungier St Ⓦwww.jjsmyths.com. One of the few places to catch local jazz and blues talent.
The Mezz 23–24 Eustace St Ⓦmezz.ie. Café-bar with live rock, jazz, blues funk, soul and reggae every night. Bar food served 2.30–9.30pm. Mains from €6.50.
Vicar Street 58–59 Thomas St Ⓦwww.vicarstreet.com. One of the city's finest music venues, offering a varied programme of major music and comedy acts.
Whelans 25 Wexford St Ⓦwww.whelanslive.com. Notorious music pub and club attracting a host of up-and-coming international stars as well as local talent. Open late every night.

Entertainment

Theatres

Dublin's theatres are among the finest in Europe, offering a good mix of classical and more avant-garde performances. Tickets start at around €20, with concessions offered on Mon–Thurs nights and for matinees. Check the *Event Guide* (Ⓦwww.eventguide.ie) for performances.
The Abbey Lower Abbey St Ⓦwww.abbeytheatre.ie. Ireland's most historic theatre, founded in 1899 by W.B. Yeats to promote Irish culture and drama.
The Gaiety South King St Ⓦwww.gaietytheatre.ie. Dublin's oldest and most ornate theatre, showing pantomimes and popular plays.
The Gate 1 Cavendish Row Ⓦwww.gate-theatre.ie. Showcases contemporary Irish drama, alongside European classics.

Cinemas

Cineworld Parnell St Ⓣ1520/880 444, Ⓦwww.cineworld.ie. Seventeen-screen multiplex.
Irish Film Institute 6 Eustace St, Temple Bar Ⓣ01/679 5744, Ⓦwww.irishfilm.ie. Shows classics and new independent films, and has a good bar and restaurant.
Screen D'Olier St Ⓣ0818/300 301, Ⓦwww.screencinema.ie. Arthouse and independent films.

Shopping

Charity and secondhand Camden St has some good charity shops, while Harlequin, Castle Market, and Wild Child on Drury St sell good-quality vintage gear.
High street and department stores Try Grafton St and Henry St for high-street shops, including Topshop (top of Grafton St) and Penny's (37 O'Connell St), which sells ridiculously cheap clothes, shoes and accessories. Dundrum (Mon–Fri 9am–9pm, Sat 9am–7pm & Sun 10am–7pm) is home to the biggest shopping centre in Europe; take LUAS from St Stephen's Green to Balally.
Markets You can pick up some great bargains on retro clothes and accessories and Irish designer goods at Cow's Lane Market in Meeting House Square in Temple Bar (Sat). George's St Arcade (daily) also has some interesting buys – books, vinyl artwork and clothes.

Directory

Embassies Australia, Fitzwilton House, Wilton Terrace Ⓣ01/664 5300; Canada, 7–8 Wilton Terrace Ⓣ01/234 4000; UK, 29 Merrion Rd Ⓣ01/205 3700; US, 42 Elgin Rd, Ballsbridge Ⓣ01/668 8777.
Exchange Thomas Cook, 118 Grafton St; General Post Office O'Connell St; most city centre banks.
Hospitals Southside: St James's, James St Ⓣ01/410 3000; Northside: Mater Misericordiae, Eccles St Ⓣ01/885 8888.
Internet Central Cybercafé, 6 Grafton St; Global Internet Café, 8 Lower O'Connell St.
Left luggage Busáras, Heuston and Connolly stations.
Pharmacy Dame Street Pharmacy, 16 Dame St; O'Connell's, 55 O'Connell St.
Post office GPO O'Connell St (Mon–Sat 8am–8pm); St Andrew's St (Mon–Fri 9am–6pm, Sat 9am–1pm).

Moving on

Train (Connolly) Belfast (8 daily Mon–Sat, 5 Sun; 2hr 10min); Drogheda (33 daily; 30min–1hr); Rosslare (3–6 daily; 3hr); Sligo (6–11 daily; 3hr 10min–3hr 30min).
Train (Heuston) Cork (12–15 daily; 2hr 50min); Ennis (4 daily, via Limerick; 2hr 55min–3hr 40min); Galway (9–11 daily; 2hr 20min–2hr 50min); Kilkenny (6 daily Mon–Sat, 4 on Sun; 1hr 40min–1hr 50min); Killarney (7 daily; 3hr 30min–3hr 50min); Westport (3 daily; 3hr 20min–3hr 40min).
Bus Belfast (20 daily; 2hr 55min); Cashel (6 daily; 2hr 50min); Cork (6 daily; 4hr 25min); Derry (11 daily; 4hr); Donegal town (11 daily; 3hr 45min–4hr 10min); Doolin (2 daily; 6hr 15 min); Drogheda (35 daily; 1hr 20min); Ennis (13 daily; 4hr 20min–6hr

50min); Enniskillen (11 daily; 2hr 20min–3hr); Galway (15 daily; 3hr 30min); Kilkenny (6 daily; 2hr 10min–2hr 30min); Killarney (5 daily; 6hr 10min); Newgrange (3 daily; 1hr 40min–1hr 55min); Portrush (1–2 daily; 5hr 40min); Rosslare Harbour (18 daily; 3hr 20min); Sligo (7 daily; 4hr); Westport (4 daily; 5hr–5hr 40min).

COUNTY WICKLOW

Referred to as the "Garden of Ireland", the picturesque mountains, lakes, forested estates and rural villages of **County Wicklow** provide a stunning backdrop for a bracing country walk or scenic drive. Given its proximity to the capital, the region is easily visited on a day-trip from Dublin, but there are plenty of B&Bs and hostels in the area.

The wonderfully unspoilt 127km mountain trail, the **Wicklow Way**, bisects the Wicklow Mountains, looping through glacial valleys, farmland and forests. The trail passes through the villages of **Roundwood**, **Rathdrum** and **Enniskerry** (bus #44 from Townsend St in Dublin city centre), from where the eighteenth-century **Powerscourt Estate** gardens and waterfall (house and gardens daily 9.30am–5.30pm, €8; €5; ⓦwww.powerscourt.ie) are easily accessible.

Some 30km south of Enniskerry, the beautifully tranquil monastic site of **Glendalough** ("valley of the two lakes") forms one of the most dramatic landscapes in the country. The monastery was founded in the sixth century by St Kevin, and the 30m-high tapering round tower on the bank of the Lower Lake has epitomized mystical Ireland in tourist brochures for decades. The **visitor centre** (Lower Lake; daily 9.30am–6pm, closed 5pm March–Oct; €3) runs tours (daily 2pm) of the monastic site, and the **Wicklow Mountains National Park Information Centre** (Upper Lake; May–Sept daily 10am–5.30pm; Oct–Feb Sat–Sun 10am–dusk) can provide information on walking routes. Several companies run day-tours to Glendalough from Dublin (including Over the Top Tours, ⓦwww.overthetoptours.com, and Wild Wicklow Tours, ⓦwildwicklow.ie; both €25–28), but you can make your own way by taking the St. Kevin's bus (4 daily; €13 one-way/€20 return; ⓦwww.glendaloughbus.com) from outside the Mansion House on Dawson Street. *The Glendalough Hostel* is ideally located near the monastic settlement (ⓣ0404/45342, ⓦwww.glendaloughinternationalhostel.com; dorms €20, doubles €55), and has its own restaurant.

NEWGRANGE

One of the foremost visitor attractions in the country, **Brú na Bóinne** ("the palace of the Boyne") encompasses the 5000-year-old passage graves of **Newgrange**, Knowth and Dowth. Three rotund mounds of earth rise above these Neolithic graves, south of the River Boyne in County Meath. The tombs have been excavated and reconstructed, and the **guided tour** of Newgrange (from the visitor centre) includes a simulation of the rising sun during the winter solstice, during which the rays of light enter through a strategically positioned slit above the entrance, casting first light on the burial chamber before spreading along the nineteen-metre length of the passage. The exhibition in the **visitor centre** (May–Sept 9am–6.30pm; Oct–April 9.30am–5pm; €3, €6 with entrance to Newgrange; ⓦwww.newgrange.com) includes information on the sites, how they were built and the artwork of enigmatic spirals carved into the stone walls. There is also a full-scale replica of the five-thousand-year-old chamber at Newgrange as well as a model of one of the smaller tombs at Knowth. To get to the site, take the Bus Éireann service #100 from the Busáras bus depot in Dublin city centre (see p.614) to Drogheda, from where a shuttle bus #163 connects to the visitor centre.

The southeast

The southeast is Ireland's sunniest and driest corner. The region's medieval and Anglo-Norman history is richly concentrated in **Kilkenny**, a bustling, quaint inland town, while to the west, at the heart of County Tipperary is the **Rock of Cashel**, a spectacular natural formation topped with Christian buildings from virtually every period. In the southwest, **Cork** is both relaxed and spirited, the perfect place to ease you into the exhilarations of the west coast.

KILKENNY

KILKENNY is Ireland's finest medieval city, its castle set above the broad sweep of the River Nore and its narrow streets laced with carefully maintained buildings. In 1641, the city became the virtual capital of Ireland, with the founding of a parliament known as the Confederation of Kilkenny. The power of this short-lived attempt to unite resistance to English persecution of Catholics had greatly diminished by the time Cromwell's wreckers arrived in 1650. Kilkenny never recovered its prosperity, but enough remains to indicate its former importance.

What to see and do

Left at the top of Rose Inn Street is the broad **Parade**, which leads up to the castle. To the right, the High Street passes the eighteenth-century **Tholsel**, once the city's financial centre and now the town hall. Beyond is **Parliament Street**, the main thoroughfare, where the **Rothe House** (April–Oct Mon–Sat 10.30am–5pm, Sun 3–5pm; Nov–March Mon–Sat 10.30am–4.30pm; €5) provides a unique example of an Irish Tudor merchant's home, comprising three separate houses linked by cobbled courtyards. The thirteenth-century **St Canice's Cathedral** (June–Aug Mon–Sat 9am–6pm, Sun 2–6pm; Sept–March Mon–Sat 10am–1pm & 2–4/5pm, Sun 2–4/5pm; €4) has a fine array of sixteenth-century monuments, many in black Kilkenny limestone. The **round tower** next to the church (same hours; €3; combined ticket with cathedral €7) is the only remnant of a monastic settlement reputedly founded by St Canice in the sixth century; there are superb views from the top. It's the imposing twelfth-century **Castle**, though, which defines Kilkenny (tours daily: 9/9.30am–4.30/5.30pm; €6; Ⓦwww.kilkennycastle.ie). Its library, drawing room, bedrooms and Long Gallery of family portraits are open for viewing, as is the **Butler Gallery** (daily 10am–1pm & 2–4.30/5.30pm; free), housing exhibitions of modern art.

Arrival and information

Train and bus Both stations are just north of the centre, off John St. Some services stop on Patrick St.
Tourist office Rose Inn St, in the sixteenth-century Shee Alms House (May–Sept Mon–Sat 9am–6pm, Sun 11am–5pm; Oct–April Tues–Sat 9am–1pm & 2–5pm; Ⓣ056/775 1500).
Listings The weekly *Kilkenny People* (€1.80) and *Whazon?* (free; Ⓦwww.whazon.com) has listings information. See also Ⓦwww.kilkenny.ie.
Festivals The town is renowned for The Cat Laughs comedy festival in June (Ⓦwww.thecatlaughs.com) and its Arts Festival in August (Ⓦwww.kilkennyarts.ie).

Accommodation

Banville's 49 Walkin St Ⓣ056/777 0182, Ⓔmbanville@eircom.net. Very pleasant and friendly B&B, a 5min walk from the town centre. Doubles from €60.

Kilkenny Tourist Hostel 35 Parliament St Ⓣ056/776 3541, Ⓦwww.kilkennyhostel.ie. An excellent budget option in a rambling Georgian building. Dorms €14–19, doubles from €36.

Tree Grove camping Danville House, New Ross Rd Ⓣ056/777 0302, Ⓦwww.treegrovecamping.com. March–Nov 15. Campsite 1.5km south of the city on the R700. Bike rental available. €8.

Eating

Billy Byrne's 39 John St ⓣ056/772 1783. Fine pub lunches for €9.

Café Sol William St ⓣ056/776 4987. Award-winning café-restaurant particularly good for salads and light mains (from €8).

Gourmet Store 56 High St. Hummus, panini, bagels and wraps made to order at this little deli. From €3. Mon–Sat 8am–6pm.

Kyteler's Inn St Kieran St. Decent pub grub in medieval surroundings, accompanied by regular traditional music sessions.

Drinking and nightlife

Parliament St and Ormonde St are best for live traditional and rock music; John St has a more commercial feel with clubs and pop music.

Edward Langton's 69 John St. Swanky hotel with four bars and a popular club on Tues, Thurs and Sat from 10pm. There's a swing club on Thurs–Sat in the *67 Bar* and regular comedy nights in the new Set Theatre. Also serves good pub grub (mains €12).

The Pumphouse 26–28 Parliament St. Popular with young and old, locals and travellers alike. Music most nights, and there's also a pool table.

Ryans 62 Friary St. Intimate, candlelit bar with traditional music on Thurs and jazz, blues, rock and open-mic sessions other nights.

Tynan's 2 Horseleap Slip, St John's Bridge. Riverside bar with cosy Victorian interior and beer garden; there are still relics from its days as a pharmacy and grocery store.

Moving on

Train Dublin (6 daily; 1hr 40min–2hr).

Bus Cork (3 daily; 2hr 50min); Dublin (6 daily; 2hr 15min–2hr 45min).

THE ROCK OF CASHEL

The extraordinary **ROCK OF CASHEL** (daily: March–April 9am–5.30pm; June–Sept 9am–7pm; Oct 9am –5.30pm; Nov–Feb 9am–4.30pm; €6) appears as a mirage of crenellations rising bolt upright from the vast encircling plain and is where St Patrick reputedly used a shamrock to explain the doctrine of the Trinity. **Cormac's Chapel**, built in the 1130s, is the earliest and most beautiful of Ireland's Romanesque churches and the limestone **Cathedral**, begun in the thirteenth century, is a fine example of Anglo-Norman architecture, with its Gothic arches and lancet windows. The tapering **round tower** is the earliest building on the Rock, dating from the early twelfth century. The **Cashel Heritage Centre** (daily 9.30am–5.30pm; closed Sat & Sun Nov–Feb; free) on Main Street has a small exhibition that covers the history of the town.

Cashel is most often visited as a day-trip from Cork or Kilkenny; buses from Cork drop off and outside *The Bakehouse* bakery, those from Kilkenny and Dublin on the other side of the street. The *Cashel Lodge* (Dundrum Rd; ⓣ062/61003, ⓦwww.cashel-lodge.com; dorms €20, doubles €65, camping €8) is a beautifully renovated coach house blessed with spectacular views and located close to the rock. *Ryan's* on Ladyswell Street and *Davern's* on Main Street are atmospheric traditional **pubs** which also serve food, and *The Bakehouse* on Main Street is a cosy place for a light lunch.

CORK

Everywhere in **CORK** there's evidence of its history as a great mercantile centre, with grey-stone quaysides, old warehouses, and elegant, quirky bridges spanning the River Lee to each side of the city's island core – but the lively atmosphere and large student population, combined with a vibrant social and cultural scene, are equally powerful draws. Massive stone walls built by invading Normans in the twelfth century were destroyed by William III's forces during the **Siege of Cork** in 1690, after which waterborne trade brought increasing prosperity, as witnessed by the city's fine eighteenth-century bow-fronted houses and ostentatious nineteenth-century churches.

What to see and do

The graceful arc of **St Patrick's Street** – which with **Grand Parade** forms the commercial heart of the centre – is crammed with major chain stores. Just off here on Princes Street, the **English Market** (Mon–Sat 9am–5.30pm) offers the chance to sample local delicacies like *drisheen* (a peppered sausage made from a sheep's stomach lining and blood). On the far side of St Patrick's Street, chic Paul Street is a gateway to the bijou environs of French Church Street and Carey's Lane. The west of the city is predominantly residential, though Fitzgerald Park is home to the **Cork Public Museum** (Mon–Fri 11am–1pm & 2.15–5pm, Sat 11am–1pm & 2.15–4pm, plus April–Sept Sun 3–5pm), which focuses on Republican history.

Shandon area

North of the River Lee is the historic **Shandon area**, a reminder of Cork's eighteenth-century status as the most important port in Europe for dairy products. The striking **Cork Butter Exchange** survives, stout nineteenth-century Neoclassical buildings given over to craft workshops. At one corner of the old butter market is the **Cork Butter Museum** (O'Connell Square; March–June & Sept–Oct 10am–5pm; July & Aug 10am–6pm; €4; ⓦcorkbutter.museum), which exhibits, amongst other items, a keg of thousand-year-old butter. Behind the square is the pleasant Georgian church of **St Anne's Shandon** (March–Oct Mon–Sat 10am–4pm, Sun 11.30am–3.30pm; June–Sept Mon–Sat 10am–5pm, Sun 11.30am–4.30pm; Nov–Feb Mon–Sat 11am–3pm, closed Sun; €6), easily recognizable from all over the city by its weather vane – an eleven-foot salmon. The church tower gives excellent views over the city and an opportunity to ring the famous bells.

Around 2km west along North Mall in the Sunday's Well area of the city, is the nineteenth-century **Cork City Gaol** (March–Oct 9.30am–5pm; Nov–Feb 10am–4pm; €8; ⓦwww.corkcitygaol.com), with wax figures and an excellent audioguide focusing on social history.

Arrival and information

Train station 1km east of the city centre on Lower Glanmire Rd.
Bus station On Parnell Place by Merchant's Quay.
Ferry Boats from Swansea and Roscoff arrive at Ringaskiddy, 13km from town. A shuttle bus runs regularly to the centre.
Tourist office Grand Parade (Mon–Sat 9.15am–5pm, July & Aug also Sun 10am–5pm; ⓣ021/425 5100, ⓦwww.discoverireland.ie/southwest).
Internet Internet Exchange, Wood St.
Festivals There's an international jazz festival in late October (ⓦwww.corkjazzfestival.com) and a film festival in November (ⓦwww.corkfilmfest.org).

Accommodation

Hostels

Aaran House Tourist Hostel Lower Glanmire Rd ⓣ021/455 1566, ⓔtracy_flynn3@hotmail.com. Friendly and very convenient for train and bus stations. Dorms €12, doubles €38.
Brú Hostel 57 McCurtain St ⓣ021/455 9667, ⓦwww.bruhostel.com. Modern facilities with a bar attached, where guests can claim a free pint. Live music every night. Dorms €16–21, doubles €48–60.
Kinlay House Bob & Joan's Walk, off Upper John St, Shandon ⓣ021/450 8966, ⓦwww.kinlayhousecork.ie. With great facilities, this large but friendly hostel is in a lovely part of town near St Anne's Shandon. Dorms €15, doubles €44.
Sheila's 4 Belgrave Place, Wellington Rd ⓣ021/450 5562, ⓦwww.sheilashostel.ie. Set back from the hustle and bustle of town, *Sheila's* is comfortable, clean and well run with extras such as a small cinema room and a sauna (€2). Dorms €14, doubles €35.

B&Bs

Gabriel House Summerhill North ⓣ021/450 0333, ⓦwww.gabrielhousebb.com. This old Christian Brothers building has been beautifully renovated and now offers quality accommodation with sweeping views of the city. Doubles €80, singles €55.

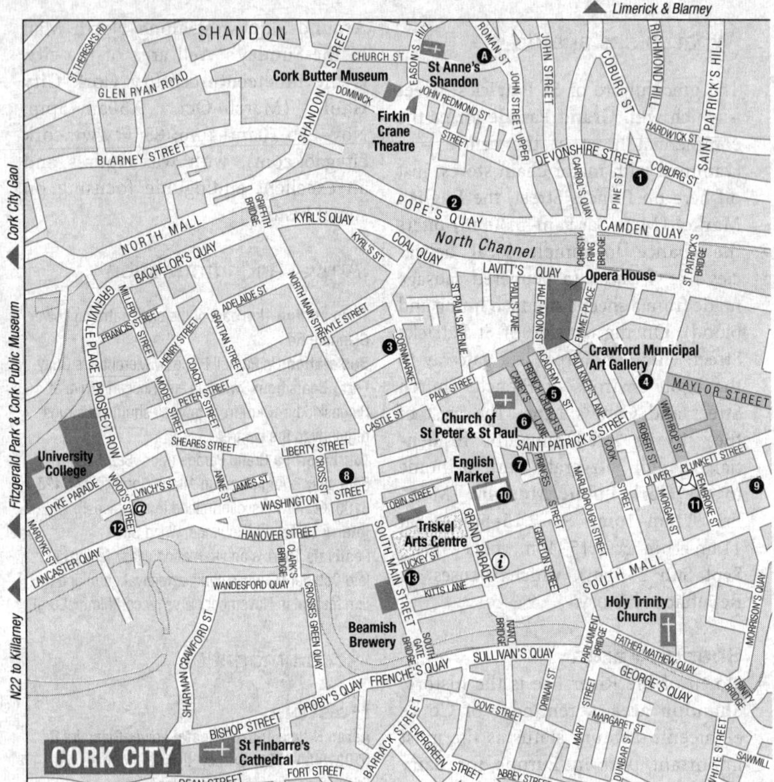

Eating

Café-Bar-Deli 18 Academy St. This ever-popular restaurant serves delicious pasta dishes (€13) and pizza (from €9). Mon–Sat 12.30pm–late, Sun 1–8pm.

Farmgate Café English Market. Enjoy wholesome, fresh food sourced from the surrounding market in a bustling atmosphere. Mains €9–14, gourmet sandwiches €7. Mon–Sat 9am–5pm, closed Sun.

The Fish Hatch *Imperial Hotel*, Pembroke St. Cook-to-order takeaway offering premium fresh fish, hand-cut chips and mushy peas with a hint of mint. Cod meal €8.50. Daily noon–late.

Liberty Grill 32 Washington St. Brunch (served till 5pm Mon–Sat) and burgers are this restaurant's specialities. Mains from €10. Mon–Sat 8am–9pm, closed Sun.

Uncle Pete's Pizzeria 31 Pope's Quay. Grab a €2 slice of thin-crust pizza from this quality Italian takeaway. Daily noon–late.

Nightlife

For listings, pick up the free *Whazon?* (Ⓦ www.whazon.com).

Bodega Nights Cornmarket St, Coal Quay Ⓦ www.bodegacork.ie. Popular club with regular DJs and salsa on Wed. Wed–Sun 11pm–late.

Mutton Lane Inn 3 Mutton Lane. Cosy candlelit pub open since 1787, down a laneway painted with colourful murals. Plays funk and soul, with occasional trad sessions.

The Pavilion 13 Carey's Lane Ⓦ www.pavilioncork.com. Live music venue with regular jazz and blues sessions in the downstairs bar (free) and r'n'b, soul, funk and electro DJs in the upstairs club from 11pm Fri–Sun.

The Savoy St Patrick St Ⓦ www.savoytheatre.ie. Cork's premier club, open from 10pm Thurs–Sat, with DJs and live music. Famous for its Eighties night on the first Fri of every month.

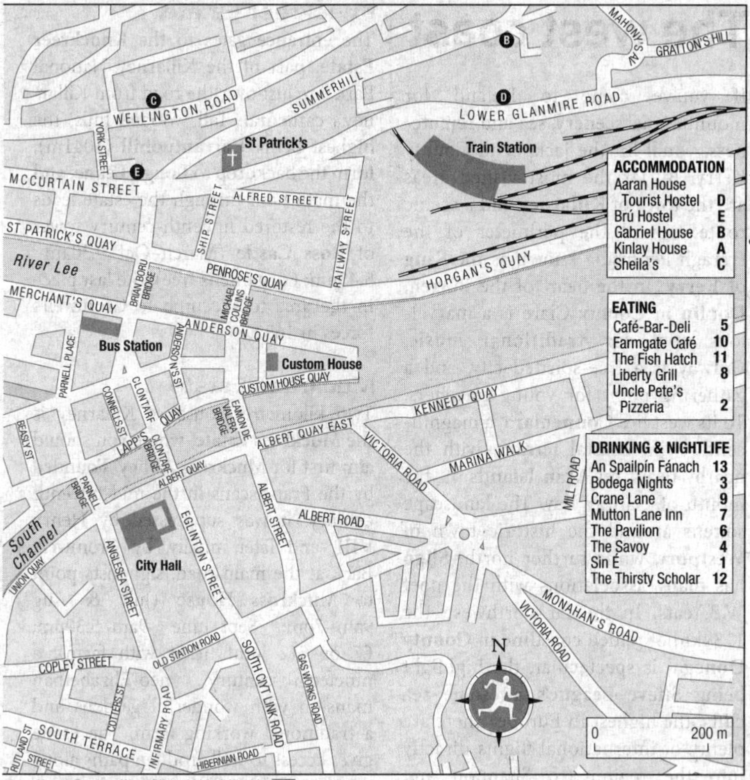

N8 to Dublin, N25 to Youghal & Waterford

ACCOMMODATION

Aaran House Tourist Hostel	D
Brú Hostel	E
Gabriel House	B
Kinlay House	A
Sheila's	C

EATING

Café-Bar-Deli	5
Farmgate Café	10
The Fish Hatch	11
Liberty Grill	8
Uncle Pete's Pizzeria	2

DRINKING & NIGHTLIFE

An Spailpín Fánach	13
Bodega Nights	3
Crane Lane	9
Mutton Lane Inn	7
The Pavilion	6
The Savoy	4
Sin É	1
The Thirsty Scholar	12

Airport, Passage West, Ringaskiddy & Kinsale

The Thirsty Scholar 17 Lancaster Quay. As its name suggests, this great pub is close to the university and accordingly popular with students in term time.

Entertainment

Live music

An Spailpín Fánach South Main St. Traditional music every night, except Saturday, in this famous bar.

Crane Lane Phoenix St Ⓦwww.cranelanetheatre.ie. Billed as the "House of Jazz, Blues and Burlesque", this theatre has a late bar, regular shows and gigs, and is open daily.

Sin É 8 Coburg St. Intimate music bar, usually packed for its traditional sessions and other live music on Tues–Thurs from 9.30pm and Fri and Sun at 6.30pm.

Theatre and cinemas

Triskel Arts Centre Tobin St Ⓣ021/427 2022, Ⓦwww.triskelart.com. A lively spot with cinema, exhibitions, readings and concerts.

Moving on

Train Dublin (15 daily Mon–Sat, 12 Sun; 2hr 35min–3hr 35min); Killarney (9 daily; 1hr 30min–2hr).

Bus Cashel (8 daily; 1hr 35min–1hr 50min); Dublin (6 daily; 4hr 25min); Galway (12 daily; 4hr 25min); Kilkenny (7 daily, only 2 direct; 3hr 10min–4hr 15min); Killarney (13 daily; 2hr).

The west coast

If you've come to Ireland for mountainous scenery, sea and remoteness, you'll hit the jackpot in County Kerry. By far the most visited areas are the town of **Killarney** and a scenic route around the perimeter of the Iveragh Peninsula known as the **Ring of Kerry**. In the heart of the Burren, **Doolin** in County Clare is a marvellous spot for **traditional music**. **Galway** is a free-spirited city, and a gathering point for young travellers. To its west lies **Connemara**, a magnificently wild coastal terrain, with the nearby beautiful **Aran Islands**, in the mouth of Galway Bay. The landscape softens around the historic town of **Westport**, while further north, **Sligo** has many associations with the poet W.B.Yeats. In the far northwest, the 1134km of folded coastline in **County Donegal** is spectacular, the highlight being **Slieve League**'s awesome sea cliffs, the highest in Europe. There are plenty of international flights directly into the region (to Shannon and Knock airports).

KILLARNEY AND AROUND

KILLARNEY town has been heavily commercialized and has little of architectural interest, but surrounding **Killarney National Park**, with some of the best lakes, mountains and woodland in Ireland definitely compensates. **Cycling** is a great way of seeing the terrain, and makes good sense – local transport is sparse.

What to see and do

Around the town, three spectacular **lakes** – Lough Leane, Muckross Lake and the Upper Lake – form an appetizer for MacGillycuddy's Reeks, the highest mountains in Ireland.

Knockreer Estate

The entrance gates to the **Knockreer Estate**, part of the Killarney National Park, are just over the road from Killarney's cathedral. Tall wooded hills, the highest being **Carrantuohill** (1041m), form the backdrop to **Lough Leane**, and the main path through the estate leads to the restored fifteenth-century tower of **Ross Castle** (March–Oct 9.30am–5.45pm; €6, gardens free), the last place in the area to succumb to Cromwell's forces in 1652.

Muckross Estate

Two kilometres south of Killarney is the **Muckross Estate**, where you should aim first for **Muckross Abbey**. Founded by the Franciscans in the mid-fifteenth century, it was suppressed by Henry VIII, and later, finally, by Cromwell. Back at the main road, signposts point to **Muckross House** (July & Aug 9am–7pm; Sept–June 9am–5.30pm; €7 or €12 joint ticket with farm), a nineteenth-century neo-Elizabethan mansion with wonderful gardens and a traditional working farm. The estate gives access to well-trodden paths along the shores of Muckross Lake where you can see one of Killarney's celebrated beauty spots, the **Meeting of the Waters**. Close by is the massive shoulder of Torc Mountain, shrugging off **Torc Waterfall**. The Upper Lake is beautiful, too, with the main road running along one side up to **Ladies' View**, from where the view is truly spectacular.

Gap of Dunloe and the Black Valley

West of Killarney lies the **Gap of Dunloe**, a natural defile formed by glacial overflow that cuts the mountains in two. *Kate Kearney's Cottage*, a pub located 10km from Killarney at the foot of the track leading up to the Gap, is the last fuelling stop before *Lord Brandon's Cottage*, a summer tearoom (June–Aug 10am–5pm), 11km away on the other side of the valley. The track winds its way up the desolate valley between high rock cliffs and waterfalls, past a chain of icy loughs and tarns to the top, to what feels like one of the most remote places in the world: the **Black Valley**, named after its entire population perished during the famine (1845–49). There's a wonderfully isolated *An Óige* **hostel** here too (Ⓣ064/34712, Ⓦwww.anoige.ie; dorms €17). The quickest way to Killarney from here is to carry on down to *Lord Brandon's Cottage* and take the boat back across the Upper Lake.

Arrival and information

Train and bus stations Next to each other on Park Rd, a short walk east of the centre.

Tourist office Beech Rd off New St (daily 9am–6/8pm; Ⓣ064/31633, Ⓦwww.discoverireland.ie/southwest).

Internet Leaders, 9 Beech Rd; Web-Talk, 53 High St.

Listings *The Kerryman* (€1.80) Ⓦwww.kerryman.ie.

Accommodation

Hostels

Killarney Railway Hostel Fair Hill Ⓣ064/663 5299, Ⓦwww.killarneyhostel.com. Clean and friendly and opposite the station. Dorms €15, doubles €46–60.

Neptune's Town Hostel Bishop's Lane, off New St Ⓣ064/663 5255, Ⓦwww.neptuneshostel.com. Large, welcoming hostel with colourful rooms. Breakfast not included. Dorms €15, doubles €45.

The Súgan Hostel Lewis Rd Ⓣ064/663 3104, Ⓦwww.killarneysuganhostel.com. Cosy family-run hostel with colourful decor. There's also bike rental, cheaper if you're a guest. Dorms €14, doubles €40.

Camping

Flesk Caravan and Camping Muckross Rd Ⓣ064/663 1704, Ⓦwww.killarneyfleskcamping.com. 1.5km south of the centre on the N71 Kenmare road. €8/tent plus €8/person.

Eating and drinking

The Country Kitchen 17 New St. Cheap, hearty food, including full Irish breakfast (€9).

Courtney's 24 Plunkett St. Huge but informal bar popular with young people for its midweek traditional sessions, live bands on Fri and DJ sets on Sat.

McSorley's 10 College St. Traditional music in the main bar every night in summer, followed by a live band. The upstairs club is the biggest in Killarney, open till 2am nightly.

O'Connor's Bar 7 High St. Old and intimate little pub with local Irish musicians on Thurs and Fri. You can also book Gap of Dunloe tours here (see opposite).

Moving on

Train Cork (9 daily; 1hr 20min–1hr 40min); Dublin (7 daily; 3hr 15min–3hr 30min).

Bus Cork (13 daily; 1hr 35min–1hr 50min); Dingle (2–5 daily; 2hr–2hr 40min); Dublin (10 daily; 6hr 10min–7hr 30min); Waterville (1 daily; 1hr 55min).

THE RING OF KERRY

Most tourists view the spectacular scenery of the 179km **Ring of Kerry**, west of Killarney, without ever leaving their tour coach or car – so anyone straying from the road or waiting until the afternoon, will experience the slow twilights of the Atlantic seaboard in perfect seclusion. **Cycling** the Ring takes three days and provides access to mountain roads. **Buses** from Killarney circle the Ring in summer (May–Sept 2 daily; from €20 return). The public bus departs from the bus station and private tour operators (book through the tourist office) from their respective offices in town. For the rest of the year, buses travel only the largely deserted mountain roads, as far as Cahersiveen.

DINGLE

The fishing village of **DINGLE** is the best base for exploring the peninsula. Formerly Kerry's leading port in medieval times, then later a centre for smuggling, the town's main attractions nowadays are aquatic: the star of the show is undoubtedly **Fungi** the dolphin who's been visiting the town's harbour for more than 25 years (boats offer trips out to see him from around €15).

Housed in a former hotel, the *Hideout Hostel* is the best budget **accommodation** in town (Dykegate St; ⓣ066/915 0559, ⓦwww.thehideouthostel.com; dorms €17, doubles from €40), or try the laidback *Rainbow Hostel*, 1km west of the centre in Miltown (ⓣ066/915 1044, ⓦwww.rainbowhosteldingle.com; dorms €16, doubles €40, camping €9).

The *Goat Street Café* on Upper Main Street offers international lunches using fresh ingredients, while *John Benny's* on Strand Street is a popular pub renowned for its excellent seafood. For live traditional music in the evenings, try *An Droichead Beag* on Main Street or *O'Flaherty's* on Bridge Street.

SLIGO

SLIGO is, after Derry, the biggest town in the northwest of Ireland. The legacy of **W.B. Yeats** – perhaps Ireland's best-loved poet – is still strongly felt here: the **Yeats Memorial Building** on Hyde Bridge (Mon–Fri 10am–5pm; free) features a photographic exhibition and film on his life, while the poet's Nobel Prize for Literature and other memorabilia are on show in the **Sligo County Museum** in the library on Stephen Street (Mon–Fri 10am–4.45pm; free). **The Model Arts Centre** on The Mall (Tues–Sat noon–6pm, Sun noon–4pm; free) has works by the poet's brother, **Jack B. Yeats**, along with a broad collection of modern Irish art.

The *Railway Hostel* is a small and homely place beside the train station (1 Union Place; ⓣ071/914 4530, ⓦwww.therailway.ie; dorms €20, doubles €45), while *Tree Tops B&B* (Cleveragh Rd, 1km southeast along Pearse Rd; ⓣ071/916 0160, ⓦwww.sligobandb.com; doubles €74) has bright and comfortable rooms, great breakfasts and friendly hosts. For a unique eco-lodge experience, head for the *Gyreum* (Riverstown, 20km south of Sligo town ⓣ071/916 5994, ⓦwww.gyreum.com; dorms from €17) a giant green mound rising out of the Sligo hills, modelled as a "modern-day cairn" with spectacular views spanning five counties.

Café Society (3 Teeling St) has an eclectic menu of burgers, curries and sandwiches served until 9pm, or try *The Gateway Bar* (17–19 Lord Edward St) for filling pub grub. There are regular traditional music sessions in *Earley's* and *Furey's* on Bridge Street or *Shoot the Crows* on Gratton Street.

DINGLE PENINSULA

The **Dingle Peninsula** is a place of intense, shifting beauty: spectacular mountains, long sandy beaches and splinter-slatted rocks. The highlight is the stunning promontory of **Slea Head**, which has fabulous views over to the **Blasket Islands**.

The Irish-speaking area west of Dingle is rich in relics of the ancient Gaelic and early Christian cultures. The spectacular fort of **Dún Beag** (daily Feb–Nov 10am–5pm; €3) is about 6km west of Ventry village, and has four earthen rings as defences and an underground escape route by the main entrance. West of the fort, the hillside above the road is studded with stone beehive huts, cave dwellings, forts, churches, standing stones and crosses – over five hundred in all. The beehive huts were built and used for storage up until the late nineteenth century, but standing among ancient buildings – such as the **Fahan group** – you're looking over a landscape that's remained essentially unchanged for centuries.

Public transport in the west of the peninsula amounts to a very irregular **bus** from Dingle to Dunquin, making **cycling** the best way to explore (see p.606 for bike rental).

COUNTY CLARE

Some 40km northwest of Ennis in **County Clare** is the tiny seaside village of **DOOLIN**, famed for a steady, year-round supply of **traditional music**.

The village is the perfect base from which to explore the mystically barren expanse of **The Burren**, a vast landscape of cracked limestone terraces stretching to the wild Atlantic Ocean. The area is dotted with well-preserved megalithic remains such as the **Poulnabrone Dolmen** (on the R480, 20min drive from Doolin), an imposing tomb constructed from three massive limestone slabs dating from 2500 BC. **The Cliffs of Moher**, 4km south of Doolin, are the area's most famous tourist attraction, with their great bands of shale and sandstone rising 660 feet above the waves. The visitors' centre beside the car park (March & Oct 9am–6pm; April 9am–6.30pm; May & Sept 9am–7pm; June 9am–7.30pm; July & Aug 9am–9.30pm; Nov–Feb 9.15am–5pm; €6; Ⓦwww.cliffsofmoher.ie) can organize tours to O'Brien's Tower, built in 1835 as a viewing point for visitors.

A **ferry** (April–Sept) runs from Doolin pier to the **Aran Islands** (see p.629). **LAHINCH**, a small village 20km south of Doolin, attracts hordes of surfers for its famous beach break. *Lahinch Hostel* (Church St; Ⓣ065/708 1040, Ⓦhomepage.eircom.net/~patshostel/; dorms €15) provides decent dormitory accommodation, and you can rent boards from Lahinch Surf Shop (Ⓣ065/708 1543, Ⓦwww.lahinchsurfshop.com) or organize lessons at the Lahinch Surf School (Ⓣ087/960 9667, Ⓦwww.lahinchsurfschool.com).

Accommodation

Aille River Hostel Ⓣ065/707 4260, Ⓦwww.ailleriverhosteldoolin.ie. Renovated three-hundred-year-old cottage with camping facilities, beautifully located overlooking the Aille River in the centre of Doolin village. Dorms €16, rooms €23/person.

Half Door Ⓣ065/707 5959, Ⓦwww.halfdoordoolin.com. Luxury B&B with sitting room and conservatory for guest use. Doubles from €62.

Rainbow Hostel Ⓣ065/707 4415, Ⓦwww.rainbowhostel.net. A welcoming, family-run place offering bike rental (€8–12/day) and free guided walks of the area. Dorms €16, doubles €40–48.

Eating and drinking

All three of Doolin's pubs, *O'Connor's*, *McGann's* and *McDermott's*, have nightly traditional music sessions, and serve excellent food. *O'Connor's* is particularly recommended for its fresh cod and giant portions of mussels.

GALWAY

County **GALWAY** is home to the country's largest Irish-speaking Gaeltacht region, and as a lively university city, its reputation as party capital of Ireland is well justified. University College Galway guarantees a high number of young people in term time, but the energy is most evident during Galway's **festivals**, especially the **Arts Festival** in the last two weeks of July (Ⓦwww.galwayartsfestival.com), and the Galway Races in the last week of July (Ⓦwww.galwayraces.com).

What to see and do

Granted city status in 1484, **Galway** developed in the Middle Ages into a flourishing centre of trade with the Continent, a period of prosperity that is evident in its impressive architecture. Merchant townhouses line pedestrianized Shop Street, where buskers perform at all hours of the day and night outside some of the city's liveliest bars and cafés. **Lynch's Castle** on Shop Street, which now houses the Allied Irish Bank, dates from the fifteenth century and is a fine example of a medieval townhouse, with its stone facade decorated with carved panels, gargoyles and a lion devouring its prey.

Down by the River Corrib stands the **Spanish Arch**, a sixteenth-century structure that was used to protect galleons unloading wine and rum. Across the river lies the **Claddagh**

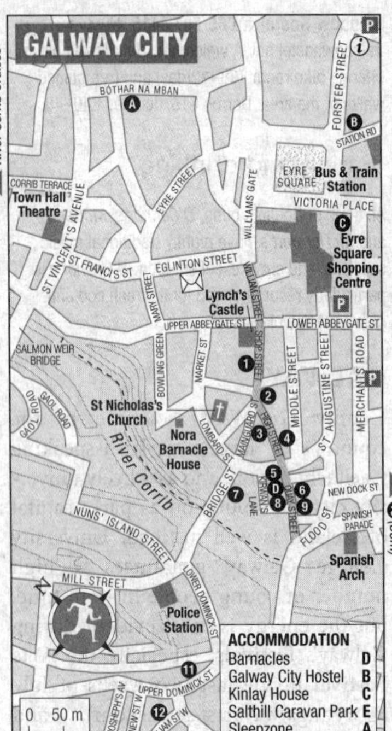

EATING		DRINKING & NIGHTLIFE	
Da Tang Noodle House	4	Blue Note	12
Eight Bar and Restaurant	10	Crane Bar	13
Fat Freddy's	9	The Living Room	7
La Salsa	3	Neachtain's	5
McCambridges	1	The Quays	6
McDonagh's	8	Róisín Dubh	11
		Taaffe's	2

district, the old fishing village that once stood outside the city walls and gave the world the Claddagh ring as a symbol of love and fidelity. Past the Claddagh the river widens out into **Galway Bay**; for a pleasant sea walk follow the road until it reaches **Salthill**, the city's seaside resort. There are several beaches along the promenade, though for the best head 5km from Salthill to **Silverstrand** on the Barna road.

Arrival and information

Train and bus stations Off Eyre Square, on the northeast edge of the city centre.

Tourist office Forster St (daily 9am–5.45pm; ⓣ091/537 700, ⓦwww.irelandwest.ie).

Internet Café 4, High St.

Accommodation

Barnacles 10 Quay St ⓣ091/568 644, ⓦwww.barnacles.ie. Buzzing hostel conveniently located for pubs and cafés on Quay St; the larger dorms are a little crowded, but smaller ones are bright and comfortable. The pretty double overlooking the street is excellent value. Dorms €10–25, doubles €47–70.

Kinlay House Merchant's Rd ⓣ091/565 244, ⓦwww.kinlaygalway.ie. Enormous, impersonal hostel just off Eyre Square. Day-trips to the Aran Islands, the Cliffs of Moher and Connemara depart right outside the door. Dorms €16–25, doubles €50–70.

Sleepzone Bóthar na mBan, Wood Quay ⓣ091/566 999, ⓦwww.sleepzone.ie. Ultramodern hostel with a mini-hotel feel, bright en-suite rooms, a huge communal kitchen and a free internet café. Dorms €15–20, doubles €50–60.

Camping

Salthill Caravan Park Ballyloughlane, Renmore ⓣ091/523 972, ⓦwww.salthillcaravanpark.com. Family-run park located right on the beach, less than 2km from the centre. April–Sept. €10/person.

Eating

Da Tang Noodle House 2 Middle St. Excellent noodle dishes in pretty surroundings. Lunch €6–9, dinner €12–14. Daily noon–10pm.

Eight Bar and Restaurant 8 Dock Rd ⓣ091/565111. With a focus on locally sourced seasonal ingredients and a menu that changes daily, this place caters for serious foodies, with fresh seafood, quality cuts of meat, hearty stews and innovative salads. Mains €15. Daily noon–3pm & 6–10pm.

Fat Freddy's The Halls, Quay St. Good pizzas, salads and antipasti at this fun, colourful bistro. Mains €10–15. Daily noon–10pm.

La Salsa 6 Mainguard St. Mexican takeaway offering giant burritos, nachos and burgers. €4–7. Daily noon–midnight.

McCambridges 38–39 Shop St. The queues run out the door every lunchtime at this gourmet deli renowned for their sandwiches, wraps and rolls. €2.50–5. Mon–Sat 8am–7pm, Sun noon–6pm.

McDonagh's 22 Quay St. A must for the freshest seafood at any time of day. The takeaway next door has a few informal tables and is much cheaper than the restaurant. Mains €8–34. Mon–Sat 5–10pm; takeaway daily noon–midnight.

Drinking and nightlife

See the weekly *Galway Advertiser* (free; www.advertiser.ie/galway) or *Galway City Tribune* (€1.60) for listings.

The Quay St area leading down to the river is known as the "Left Bank" due to the proliferation of popular pubs, restaurants and cafés.

Blue Note 3 West William St. Atmospheric pub with intimate booths and snugs, a heated smoking garden, and DJs most nights.

Crane Bar 2 Sea Rd. Holds revered traditional music sessions nightly from 9pm.

The Living Room 5 Bridge St. Popular late-night bar on three levels with retro decor. DJ Thurs–Sun.

Neachtain's 17 Cross St. Old-fashioned pub that attracts an eccentric, arty crowd.

The Quays Quay St. One of the city's best-loved pubs, whose atmospheric interior was taken from a medieval French church.

Róisín Dubh Dominick St. Popular music bar and venue which plays host to top-class Irish and international acts.

Taaffe's 19 Shop St. One of the best places to hear traditional music, where there are nightly sessions.

Moving on

Train Dublin (9–11 daily; 2hr 30min–3hr).

Bus Cork (12 daily; 4hr 25min); Doolin (4 daily; 1hr 40min–2hr 50min); Dublin (15 daily; 3hr 30min–3hr 45min); Killarney (7 daily; 4hr 40min); Westport (6 daily; 1hr 35min–3hr 45min).

THE ARAN ISLANDS

The **Aran Islands** – **Inishmore**, **Inishmaan** and **Inisheer**, 50km out across the mouth of Galway Bay – are spectacular settings for a wealth of early remains and some of the finest archeological sites in Europe. The isolation of the Irish-speaking islands prolonged the continuation of a unique, ancient culture into the early twentieth century.

Inishmore

Inishmore is a great tilted plateau of limestone with a scattering of villages along the sheltered northerly coast. The land slants up to the southern edge, where dramatic cliffs rip along the entire shoreline. As far as the eye can see is a tremendous patterning of stone, the bare pavements of grey rock split into bold diagonal grooves and latticed by dry-stone walls.

What to see and do

Most of Inishmore's sights are to the northwest of **KILRONAN**, the island's principal town, where minibuses and ponies and traps offering island tours wait by the pier. Past the *American Bar* and up the hill to the west of Kilronan is a small settlement called Mainistir, from where it's a short signposted walk to the twelfth-century **Teampall Chiaráin** (Church of St Kieran). 5km west along the main road from here is Kilmurvey, a small cluster of houses with a sandy beach which is a fifteen-minute walk from the most spectacular of Aran's prehistoric sites, **Dún Aonghasa**, accessed via its **visitor centre** (March–Oct 10am–6pm; Nov–Feb 10am–4pm; €3). The spectacular fort, which is two and a half thousand years old, is perched on the edge of a sheer cliff, beaten relent-

GETTING TO THE ISLANDS

Daily ferries to Inishmore run year-round (less frequent to the other islands), departing from Galway city, Rossaveal (30km west by bus) and Doolin in County Clare. A return trip costs around €25. Book tickets in Galway city through Aran Island Ferries, 4 Forster St (091/568 903, www.aranislandferries.com); or O'Brien Shipping (065/707 4455, www.doolinferries.com) – both companies have desks in the Galway tourist office. You can also fly with Aer Árann Islands (091/593 034, www.aerarannislands.ie) for €45 return.

lessly by the Atlantic Ocean below. The **Seven Churches**, just east of the village of Eoghanacht, is a monastic site dating from the ninth-century, believed to be one of the most significant medieval pilgrimage destinations in the west of Ireland.

Arrival and information

Bus Seasonal minibuses (€10) run tours up through the island's villages. Pony-and-trap tours depart from the pier (€40 for a group of up to 4 people).
Ferry Boats from Galway city, Rossaveal and Doolin (see box, p.629) dock at Kilronan.
Tourist office Just west of where the ferry docks at Kilronan (daily: March–Oct 10am–5pm; Nov–Feb 11am–5pm; ⓣ099/61263).
Bike rental Mullin's and BNN's near the pier (€10/day).

Accommodation

Accommodation can be booked through the Kilronan tourist office, or when you buy your ferry ticket in Galway.
Kilronan Hostel Kilronan ⓣ099/61255, ⓦwww.kilronanhostel.com. Cheery hostel with great facilities, including free internet and wi-fi. Very convenient for the ferry. Dorms €17, doubles €45.
Mainistir House Hostel Mainistir ⓣ099/61318, ⓦwww.mainistirhousearan.com. A 20min walk west from the pier, this peaceful hostel offers a renowned "all you can eat" buffet every night for €15. Dorms €16, doubles €50.

Eating and drinking

Seafood is the island's great speciality, with most of the popular restaurants located in Kilronan.
An tSean Ceibh (The Ould Pier). Simple and cheap place serving fresh fish and chips and seafood chowder, with a few outdoor tables. Daytime only. Closed Nov–Feb.
Joe Watty's Bar A great pub with traditional music most nights; serves good soups and stews, from €6.

Inishmaan

Compared to Inishmore, **Inishmaan** is lush, with stone walls forming a maze that chequers off tiny fields of grass and clover. The island's main sight is **Dún Chonchubhair**: built sometime between the first and seventh centuries, its massive oval wall is almost intact and commands great views. Ask at the *Teach Ósta* pub for information (ⓣ099/73003) – it's a warm and friendly place that also serves snacks in summer. For **accommodation**, try the B&B *Ard Álainn* (April–Sept; ⓣ099/73027, ⓦwww.galway.net/pages/ard-alainn; doubles €50–65) or *An Dún* (ⓣ099/73047; doubles €50–65), both near Dún Chonchubhair.

Inisheer

Inisheer, less than 3km across, is the smallest of the Aran Islands, and tourism plays a key role here. A great plug of rock dominates the island, its rough, pale-grey stone dripping with greenery, topped by the fifteenth-century **O'Brien's Castle**, standing inside an ancient ring fort. Set around it are low fields, a small community of pubs and houses, and windswept sand dunes. The **Inisheer Island Cooperative** hut by the pier (Mon–Thurs 9am–5pm, Fri 9am–4pm; ⓣ099/75008) will give you a map and a list of **B&Bs**; *Radharc an Chláir*, by the castle (ⓣ099/75019; doubles €70), is a good bet. There's also a **hostel**, *Brú Radharc na Mara* (ⓣ099/75024, ⓔradharcnamara@hotmail.com; dorms €15, doubles €40; mid-March to Oct), and a free **campsite** with toilets and washing facilities near the pier. Meals are available at the *Óstán Inis Oírr* hotel. For **music**, head for *Tigh Ned's* bar.

DONEGAL TOWN

DONEGAL TOWN is focused around its old marketplace – The Diamond – and makes a fine base for exploring the stunning coastal countryside and inland hills and loughs. Just about the only sight in the town itself is the well-preserved shell of **O'Donnell's Castle** on Tírchonaill

Street by The Diamond (April–Oct daily 10am–6pm; Nov–March daily 9.30am–4.30pm; €4), a fine example of Jacobean architecture. On the left bank of the River Eske stand the few ruined remains of **Donegal Friary**, while on the opposite bank a woodland path known as Bank Walk offers wonderful views of **Donegal Bay** and the **Blue Stack Mountains**.

Arrival and information

Bus The stop for Bus Éireann departures and arrivals is outside the *Abbey Hotel*.
Tourist office The Quay (June–Aug Mon–Sat 9am–6pm, Sun 11am–3pm; Sept–May Mon–Fri 9.15am–5pm, Sat 11am–5pm; ⓣ074/972 1148, ⓦwww.discoverireland.ie/northwest).

Accommodation

There are dozens of B&Bs in Donegal – book at the tourist office.
Atlantic Guesthouse Main St ⓣ074/972 1187, ⓦwww.atlanticguesthouse.ie. Family-run establishment in the centre of town with bright and cheery rooms. Doubles €50–80.
Donegal Town Independent Hostel ⓣ074/972 2805, ⓦwww.donegaltownhostel.com. Just past the roundabout on the Killybegs Rd, a 5min walk from town, this peaceful and very friendly hostel also has camping (€9). Dorms €16, doubles €38.

Eating and drinking

The Blueberry Tea Room Castle St. Good-quality, reasonably priced food served in a very cosy atmosphere. It has an internet café upstairs. Mains up to €12.
The Reel Inn Bridge St. A lively bar packed with local old-timers, even at midday. Traditional music every night.
Simple Simon The Diamond. Deli in an organic food store offering healthy takeaway lunches. €2–5.

Moving on

Bus Derry (3–7 daily; 1hr 30min); Dublin (9–11 daily; 3hr 30min–5hr 55min); Glencolmcille (2 daily; 1hr 25min); Sligo (8 daily; 1hr).

SLIEVE LEAGUE

To the west of Donegal town lies one of the most stupendous landscapes in Ireland. There are two routes up to the ridge of **Slieve League**: a back way following the signpost to Baile Mór just before Teelin, and the road route from Teelin to Bunglass, a thousand sheer feet above the sea. The former path has you looking up continually at the ridge known as One Man's Pass, on which walkers seem the size of pins, while the front approach swings you up to one of the most thrilling cliff scenes in the world, the **Amharc Mór**. On a good day you can see a third of Ireland from the summit.

GLENCOLMCILLE

Since the seventh century, following Columba's stay in the valley, **GLENCOLMCILLE** has been a place of pilgrimage: every June 9 at midnight the locals commence a three-hour barefoot itinerary of the cross-inscribed slabs that stud the valley basin, finishing up with Mass at 3am in the small church. If you want to attempt *Turas Cholmcille* ("Columba's Journey") yourself, get a map of the route from the Glencolmcille Hill Walkers Centre, which also has lovely modern budget accommodation (ⓣ074/973 0302, ⓦwww.ionadsuil.ie; doubles €40), or the **Folk Village Museum** (Easter–Sept Mon–Sat 10am–6pm, Sun noon–6pm; €3), a cluster of replica, period-furnished thatched cottages. A path to the left of the museum leads to the wonderfully positioned *Dooey Hostel* (ⓣ074/973 0130; dorms €15, doubles €30, camping €8.50). *Biddy's Bar* and *Roarty's* in the village are good for a drink and lively traditional music sessions, while the best **food** on offer is at *An Cistin*, part of the Foras Cultúir Uladh Irish language and culture complex.

Northern Ireland

Both the pace of political change and the uncertainty of its future continue to characterize Northern Ireland. In 1998, after thirty years of the Troubles, its people overwhelmingly voted in support of a political settlement and, it was hoped, an end to political and sectarian violence. For a time the political process gradually inched forwards, hampered by deep mistrust and suspicion on both sides. In recent years, however, considerable headway has been made in the peace process, with the resumption of devolved government in Northern Ireland, and a greater sense of hope evident on both sides of the community. **Belfast** and **Derry** are two lively and attractive cities, and the northern coastline – especially the bizarre geometry of the **Giant's Causeway** – is as spectacular as anything in Ireland.

BELFAST

A quarter of Northern Ireland's population lives in the capital, **BELFAST**. While the legacy of **the Troubles** is clearly visible in areas like West Belfast – peace walls, derelict buildings and political murals on every corner – security measures have been considerably eased, though there are certain flashpoints such as the Short Strand and the Ardoyne, which remain inadvisable to visit.

The city is going from strength to strength with a flourishing arts scene and many new restaurants and clubs. Despite its turbulent history, the city is imbued with a new zest for life, and a palpable cross-community desire for a peaceful future.

What to see and do

City Hall is the central landmark of Belfast, and divides the city conveniently into north and south. The northern section and the immediate environs around City Hall contain most of Belfast's official buildings, as well as the main shopping areas. The southern section of the city, especially down University Road and Botanic Avenue, leading to Queen's University ("The Golden Mile"), is the centre of Belfast's arts scene and nightlife.

Donegall Square and around

Belfast City Hall, presiding over central Donegall Square, is an austere Presbyterian building (tours Mon–Fri 11am, 2pm & 3pm, Sat 2pm & 3pm; free). At the northwest corner of the square stands the **Linen Hall Library** (Mon–Fri 9.30am–5.30pm, Sat 9.30am–4pm; free; Ⓦwww.linenhall.com), entered on Fountain Street,

SECTARIAN MURALS

The Republican and Loyalist **murals** on the Falls and Shankill roads in West Belfast are a must-see. There are over two thousand examples of this political artwork in Northern Ireland altogether, mostly painted during the height of the Troubles to represent the political and religious loyalties of the respective communities. The open-topped Belfast City Sightseeing buses include the murals in their tour of Belfast, departing every 30–45min from Castle Place (£12.50, student £10.50). Taxi Trax (Castle Junction on King St, near City Hall; £25/car; Ⓣ028/9031 5777, Ⓦwww.taxitrax.com) offer bespoke taxi tours including West Belfast, but the most interesting way of viewing the murals is to take a walking tour with political ex-prisoners, who present both Republican and Loyalist viewpoints. Tours (Mon–Sat 11am & Sun 2pm; 2hr; £8; assemble at the bottom of Divis Towers, Falls Rd; Ⓣ028/9020 0770, Ⓦwww.coiste.ie).

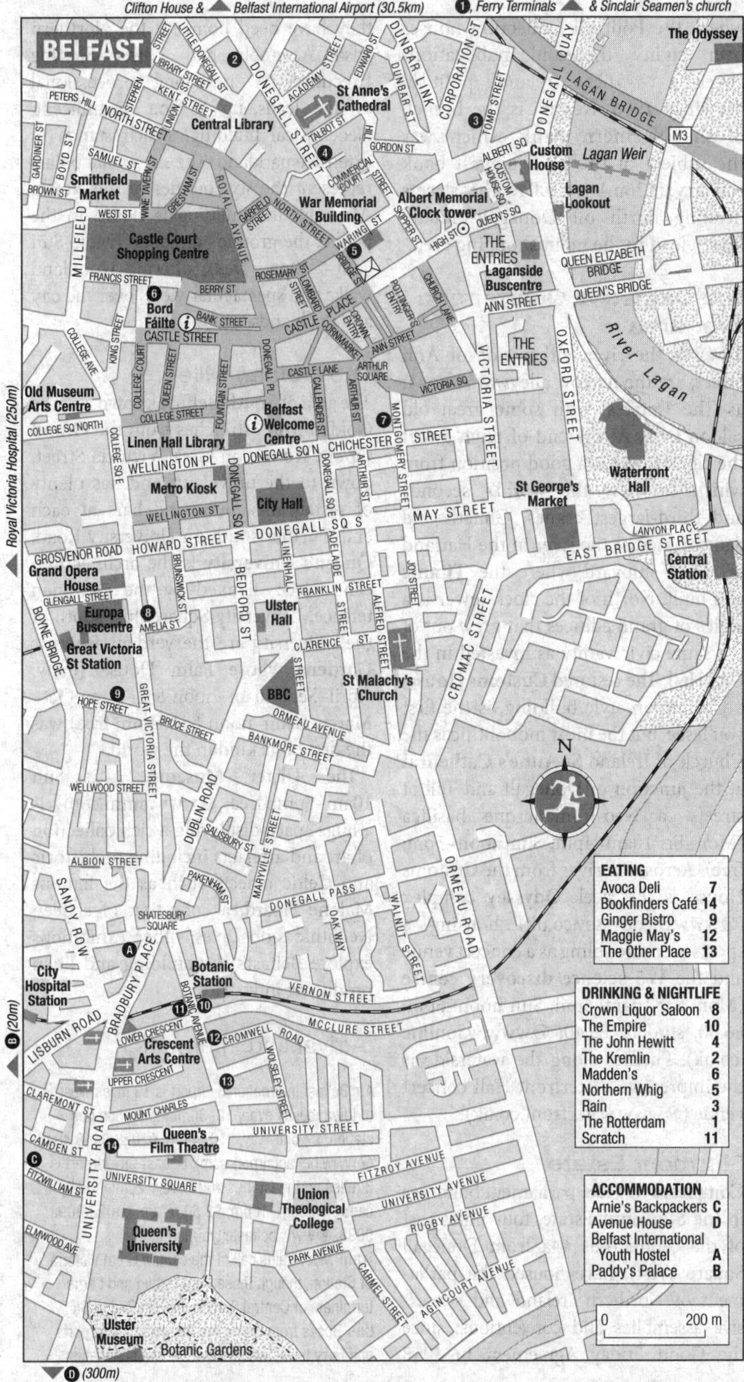

Clifton House & Belfast International Airport (30.5km)
1, Ferry Terminals & Sinclair Seamen's church
BELFAST
The Odyssey
St Anne's Cathedral
Central Library
Smithfield Market
Castle Court Shopping Centre
War Memorial Building
Albert Memorial Clock tower
Custom House
Lagan Weir
Lagan Lookout
THE ENTRIES
Laganside Buscentre
Bord Fáilte
Old Museum Arts Centre
Belfast Welcome Centre
Linen Hall Library
Metro Kiosk
City Hall
St George's Market
Waterfront Hall
Central Station
Grand Opera House
Europa Buscentre
Great Victoria St Station
Ulster Hall
BBC
St Malachy's Church
City Hospital Station
Botanic Station
Crescent Arts Centre
Queen's Film Theatre
Union Theological College
Queen's University
Ulster Museum
Botanic Gardens
River Lagan
Royal Victoria Hospital (250m)
Belfast City Airport (4.8km)
Stormont Estate
B (20m)
D (300m)
N
EATING
Avoca Deli 7
Bookfinders Café 14
Ginger Bistro 9
Maggie May's 12
The Other Place 13
DRINKING & NIGHTLIFE
Crown Liquor Saloon 8
The Empire 10
The John Hewitt 4
The Kremlin 2
Madden's 6
Northern Whig 5
Rain 3
The Rotterdam 1
Scratch 11
ACCOMMODATION
Arnie's Backpackers C
Avenue House D
Belfast International Youth Hostel A
Paddy's Palace B
0 200 m

where the Political Collection houses over eighty thousand publications covering Northern Ireland's political life since 1966. Nearby is the branch of the **Northern Bank** which was the subject of the UK's biggest bank robbery (£26m) in 2004. The streets heading north off Donegall Square North lead to the main shopping area.

The Cathedral Quarter and river area

Towards the river, either side of Ann Street, are the narrow alleyways known as **The Entries**, with some great old saloon bars. At the end of High Street the clock tower is a good position from which to view the world's second- and third-largest cranes, Goliath and Samson, across the river in the Harland & Wolff shipyard where the **Titanic** was built. North of the clock tower is a series of grand edifices that grew out of the same civic vanity as invested in the City Hall. The restored **Customs House**, a Corinthian-style building, is the first you'll see, but the most monolithic is the Church of Ireland **St Anne's Cathedral** at the junction of Donegall and Talbot streets, a Neo-Romanesque basilica (Mon–Fri 10am–4pm, Sun noon–3pm; free). Across the river from the Customs House is the sleek **Odyssey** complex (Ⓦwww.theodyssey.co.uk) housing a sports arena doubling as a concert venue and the **W5 science discovery centre** (Mon–Sat 10am–6pm, Sun noon–6pm; £6.80, student £5.40; Ⓦwww.w5online.co.uk). Further along the waterside is the impressive Waterfront Hall concert venue (Ⓦwww.waterfront.co.uk).

Stormont Estate

Completed in 1938, parliament buildings in the **Stormont Estate**, four miles east of the centre (bus #4a from Donegall Square West), have housed the parliament of Northern Ireland and successive assemblies and conventions; since the Good Friday Agreement in 1998 they have been home to the Northern Irish Assembly and Power Sharing Executive. A mile-long processional avenue leads up to the magnificent, Neoclassical building, which stands in extensive parkland. The six frontal pillars represent the six counties of the North. Although the building is closed to the public, the grounds are open (Mon–Sun 7am–7.30pm; free), offering woodland walks and spectacular views over the city and docklands.

The Golden Mile

The area of **South Belfast** known as "The Golden Mile" stretches from the **Grand Opera House**, on Great Victoria Street, down to the university, and has plenty of restaurants, pubs and bars at each end. Further south on University Road, **Queen's University** is the architectural centrepiece, flanked by the Georgian terrace, University Square. Just south of the university are the verdant **Botanic Gardens** whose Palm House (daily: April–Sept 10am–noon & 1–5pm; Oct–March 10am–noon & 1–4pm; free) was the first of its kind in the world.

The **Ulster Museum** (Tues–Sun 10am–5pm; free; Ⓦwww.nmni.com) is a huge space displaying a rich collection of art and artefacts including prehistoric and Celtic objects such as the famous Malone Hoard, a collection of sixteen Neolithic stone axes; other exhibitions explore Belfast's shipbuilding and linen producing industries.

Arrival and information

Air Belfast International Airport is 19 miles west of town (buses every 10–30min to Europa bus station; £7 one-way, £10 return; Ⓣ028/9448 4848, Ⓦwww.belfastairport.com); Belfast City Airport is 3 miles northeast (bus #600 every 20min to city centre 5.30am–10pm; £2.50 return; Ⓣ028/9093 9093, Ⓦwww.belfastcityairport.com).
Train Most trains call at the central Great Victoria St Station, though those from Dublin and Larne terminate at Central Station on East Bridge St.
Bus Buses from Derry, the Republic, the airports and ferry terminals arrive at Europa bus station

beside Great Victoria St train station; buses from the north coast use Laganside Bus Centre in Queen's Square. A regular Centrelink bus connects all bus and train stations.
Boat Ferries from Stranraer dock at Corry Rd (taxi £9), and those from Liverpool further north on West Bank Rd (taxi £8); while ferries from Cairnryan dock 30km north at Larne (bus or train to centre).
Tourist office The Belfast Welcome Centre, 47 Donegall Place (Mon–Sat 9am–5.30/7pm, Sun 11am–4pm; ⓣ028/9024 6609, ⓦwww.gotobelfast.com).

City transport

Information on all buses and trains is available at ⓣ028/9066 6630 or ⓦwww.translink.co.uk.
Bus The city is served by Metro bus service. Day tickets for the whole network cost £3.50 Mon–Sat; £2.70 after 10am Mon–Sat and all day Sun. One-way tickets cost £1.20–1.80. The metro kiosk in Donegall Square West provides free bus maps. Ulsterbus serves outlying areas.
Bike rental Lifecycles, Unit 35, Smithfield Market (£10/day, £16 for 2hr guided tour).

Accommodation

Hostels

Arnie's Backpackers 63 Fitzwilliam St ⓣ028/9024 2867, ⓦwww.arniesbackpackers.co.uk. Cheerful and relaxed independent hostel with a homely atmosphere and colourful garden, near the university. Dorms £10–12.
Belfast International Youth Hostel 22–32 Donegall Rd ⓣ028/9031 5435. Large, well-equipped but characterless modern HINI hostel, just west of Shaftesbury Square. Dorms £10–15, doubles £35.
Paddy's Palace 68 Lisburn Rd ⓣ028/9033 3367, ⓦwww.paddyspalace.com. Convivial hostel in an old Georgian building, with a large garden and party atmosphere. Dorms £8–13, doubles £38.

B&Bs

Avenue House 23 Eglantine Ave ⓣ028/9066 5904, ⓦwww.avenueguesthouse.com. A homely guesthouse in a red-brick Victorian townhouse, with a warm welcome, pretty garden and great breakfasts. Doubles £60, triples £70.

Eating

Many of the best places to eat and the liveliest pubs are around Great Victoria St and in the university area.
Avoca Deli Arthur St. Gourmet deli counter in the centre of town offering quality soups, salads and mains to eat in or take away. £4–9. Mon–Sat 9.30am–6pm, Sun 12.30–6pm.
Bookfinders Café 47 University Rd. Bohemian café at the back of a charmingly messy bookshop. Poetry nights on Fridays from 8pm. Lunch from £3. Mon–Sat 10am–5.30pm.
Ginger Bistro 7–8 Hope St. Fresh seasonal ingredients are sourced locally from farmers and fishermen, and whipped into tasty and imaginative dishes with an international twist. Mains £13–20. Tues–Sat noon–3pm & 5–9.30pm.
Maggie May's 45 Botanic Ave. Huge, economically priced portions in this cosy café with lots of veggie choices, open for lunch and dinner. Sandwiches from £3, mains £5. Daily 8.30am–10.30pm.
The Other Place 78 Botanic Ave. Fine breakfasts, and plenty of pizzas, pastas and baked potatoes. £5–10. Daily 8am–10pm.

Drinking and nightlife

Belfast's best entertainment is pub music, though there's also a vibrant club scene and plenty of DJ bars. For listings check *The Big List* (free; ⓦwww.thebiglist.co.uk), available in pubs, record shops and hostels, and the *Belfast Evening Telegraph*.

Pubs

Crown Liquor Saloon 46 Great Victoria St. The city's most famous pub, decked out like a spa bath, with a good range of Ulster food, such as champ and colcannon (both potato dishes) and Strangford oysters in season.
The Empire 42 Botanic Ave. Music hall and cellar bar in a converted church, with nightly live music or comedy.
The John Hewitt 53 Donegall St. Owned by Belfast Unemployed Resource Centre, this popular bar has some of Belfast's best traditional music sessions on Tues, Wed and Sat evenings, blues on Thurs and jazz on Fri.
Madden's 52–74 Berry St. Unpretentious and atmospheric pub, with regular traditional music sessions (Fri & Sat).
The Rotterdam 54 Pilot St. Names big and small play in this docklands venue, plus traditional music on Thurs (9.30pm).

Clubs and bars

The Kremlin 90 Donegall St ⓦwww.kremlin-belfast.com. Ireland's biggest gay venue with a host of events throughout the week.

Northern Whig 2–10 Bridge St ⓦwww.thenorthernwhig.com. Massive upmarket bar in the premises of the old newspaper, featuring pre-club DJs most nights.
Rain 10–14 Tomb St ⓦrainnightclub.co.uk. Popular and packed club playing dance music for a young crowd every night.
Scratch 5–6 Lower Crescent. Belfast's flashiest club – two floors of pop music and pitchers of cocktails. Wed–Sun 9pm–late.

Shopping

High Street The main shopping area is the long stretch of Donegall Place and Royal Ave, where you'll find big fashion and retail names. The big shopping centre Castle Court is on Royal Ave.
Arcades and markets Away from main thoroughfare Royal Ave are more alternative and more locally inspired outlets. Haymarket Arcade houses some great film and music stores. East of City Hall off Oxford St is St George's Market, which displays all sorts of delicacies (Fri & Sat).
Vintage/alternative Unsurprisingly, things get more alternative in the university area: The Rusty Zip, 28 Botanic Ave, is full of vintage gems, and No Alibis, 83 Botanic Ave, is a great bookstore which specializes in crime and often holds music events in the evening.

Directory

Exchange Thomas Cook, 10 Donegall Square West (ⓣ0845/308 9139); and the Belfast Welcome Centre (see below).
Hospitals Belfast City Hospital, Lisburn Rd (ⓣ028/9032 9241); Royal Victoria, Grosvenor Rd (ⓣ028/9024 0503).
Internet Belfast Welcome Centre, 47 Donegall Place.
Left luggage Belfast Welcome Centre, 47 Donegall Place.
Police North Queen St ⓣ028/9065 0222.
Post office Castle Place.

Moving on

Train Coleraine (9–10 daily; 1hr 20min–1hr 45min); Derry (5–9 daily; 2hr 30min); Dublin (8 daily; 2hr 20min); Larne Harbour (9–25 daily; 1hr 10min).
Bus Derry (11–32 daily; 1hr 50min); Dublin (20 daily; 3hr); Enniskillen (5–16 daily; 2hr–2hr 20min).

THE MOURNE MOUNTAINS

If you're based in Belfast but fancy a day-trip out of the metropolis, the beautiful **Mourne Mountains** provide the perfect escape. The mountain range comprises twelve peaks, of which Slieve Donard, at 850m, is the highest in Northern Ireland. From Belfast, buses #20, #720 and #237 run from the Europa bus station to Newcastle (up to 15 daily; 1hr); from Newcastle, the Mourne Rambler service (June–Aug) tracks a loop through the area (£4.50 day-ticket; ⓦwww.discovernorthernireland.com).

THE GIANT'S CAUSEWAY

Since 1693, when the Royal Society publicized it as one of the great wonders of the natural world, the **Giant's Causeway** has been a major tourist attraction. Lying 65 miles northwest of Belfast, it consists of an estimated 37,000 polygonal basalt columns; it's the result of a massive subterranean explosion some sixty million years ago which spewed out a huge mass of molten basalt onto the surface and, as it cooled, solidified into massive polygonal crystals. Taking the path down the cliffs from the visitor centre (new centre due to open in summer 2012; hours roughly daily 9.30am–4/5/6/7pm, check the website for current hours; free; car parking £6; ⓦwww.giantscausewayireland.com), or the shuttle bus (every 15min; £2 return) brings you to the most spectacular of the blocks where many people linger, but if you push on, you'll be rewarded with relative solitude and views of some of the more impressive formations high in the cliffs. One of these, **Chimney Point**, has an appearance so bizarre that the ships of the Spanish Armada opened fire on it, believing that they were attacking Dunluce Castle, a few miles further west. An alternative two-mile circuit follows the spectacular cliff-top path from the visitor centre, with views across to Scotland, to a flight of 162 steps leading down the cliff to a set of basalt columns known as the **Organ Pipes**.

Carrick-a-Rede

Don't miss the **Carrick-a-Rede Rope Bridge**, which sits 13km east of the Causeway (March–Oct daily 10am–6/7pm, weather permitting; £5.60). For the past two hundred years, fishermen had reputedly erected a bridge from the mainland cliffs to Carrick-a-Rede island over a vast chasm, so they could check their salmon nets. Now, the National Trust is in charge. Venturing across the swaying rope bridge high above the water is an exhilarating experience, but not for the faint-hearted. Ulsterbus #402 runs between Bushmills and the rope bridge via the Causeway in summer months.

PORTSTEWART

PORTSTEWART is a pleasant coastal resort ten miles west of the Giant's Causeway, with a sandy beach and good surf. There's an IHH **hostel**, *Rick's Causeway Coast Hostel*, at 4 Victoria Terrace (Ⓣ028/7083 3789, Ⓔrick@causewaycoasthostel.fsnet.co.uk; dorms £12, rooms £36) and several **B&B** options. The bus stop for the Giant's Causeway is 100m from the hostel. There are some reasonable **bars**, including *Shenanigans* on the Promenade, which is open till 1am. **Surfing** can be organized at Ocean Warriors (Ⓣ028/7083 6500, Ⓦwww.oceanwarriors.co.uk) on the Promenade.

DERRY

DERRY lies at the foot of Lough Foyle, less than three miles from the border with the Republic. The city presents a beguiling picture, its two hillsides terraced with pastel-shaded houses punctuated by stone spires, and, being seventy percent Catholic, has a very different atmosphere from Belfast. Despite the Catholic dominance, from Partition in 1921 until the late 1980s, the Protestant minority maintained control of all important local institutions. The situation came to a head after the Protestant Apprentice Boys' March in August 1969, when the police attempted to storm the Catholic estates of the Bogside. In the ensuing tension, British troops were widely deployed for the first time in Northern Ireland. On January 31, 1972, the crisis deepened when British paratroopers opened fire on civilians, killing thirteen unarmed demonstrators in what became known as **Bloody Sunday**.

Derry is now greatly changed: tensions eased considerably here long before Belfast, although defiant murals remain and marching is still a contentious issue. The city centre has undergone much regeneration, and Derry has a justifiable reputation for innovation in the arts.

What to see and do

You can walk the entire mile-long circuit of Derry's seventeenth-century **city walls** – some of the best-preserved defences in Europe. Reinforced by bulwarks, bastions and an earth rampart with parapet, the walls encircle

GETTING TO THE GIANT'S CAUSEWAY

Trains from Belfast go to Coleraine, where there's a regular connection to Portrush; from either, you can catch the "open-topper" bus (July & Aug 4 daily; £4.30) to the Causeway, or from Portrush there's bus #172, both running via Bushmills. A restored **narrow-gauge railway** runs between Bushmills and the Causeway (July–Aug 7 daily, plus some days in other months; 20min; one-way £5.25, return £6.75; Ⓣ028/2073 2844). The **Antrim Coaster coach** (Goldline Express #252) runs from Larne direct to the Causeway (2 daily; Oct–June not Sun; 2hr 30min; £4.30) and on to Coleraine via Bushmills, Portrush and Portstewart, Antrim Glens and stunning seascapes en route.

the original medieval street pattern with four gateways – Shipquay, Butcher, Bishop and Ferryquay. City Tours offer walking tours of the walls (11 Carlisle Rd; daily 10am, noon & 2pm; £4; ⓣ0771/293 7997, ⓦwww.derrycitytours.com) and taxi tours (£25/hr for 4 people), which explore fifteen hundred years of history and an introduction to the Bogside murals.

These murals are in the streets that were once the undisputed preserve of the IRA, and **Free Derry Corner** marks the site of the original barricades erected against the British army at the height of the Troubles. Nearby are the Bloody Sunday and Hunger Strikers' memorials. Further along the city wall is the **Royal Bastion**, former site of the Rev. George Walker statue which was blown up in 1973. It is in Walker's and their predecessors' memory that the Protestant Apprentice Boys march around the walls every August 12.

Arrival and information

Air City of Derry airport (ⓣ028/7181 0784, ⓦwww.cityofderryairport.com) is 7 miles northeast, connected to the centre by bus.
Train Trains from Belfast arrive on the east bank of the Foyle with a free connecting bus to the bus station.
Bus station Foyle St beside Guildhall Square.
Tourist office 44 Foyle St (July–Sept Mon–Fri 9am–7pm, Sat 9am–6pm, Sun 10am–5pm; Oct–June Mon–Fri 9am–5pm, Sat 10am–5pm, Sun 10am–4pm; ⓣ028/7126 7284, ⓦwww.derryvisitor.com).
Internet Webcrawler Cyber Café, 52 Strand Rd.

Accommodation

Derry City Independent Hostel 44 Great James St ⓣ028/7128 0524, ⓦwww.derry-hostel.co.uk. A friendly, bohemian hostel with furniture from around the world. Hosts regular barbecues in the summer. Dorms £13.

Dolce Vita 46 Great James St ⓣ028/7137 7989. Run by the people at *Derry City* hostel, the adjacent building has private double and twin rooms in a similar style. Doubles £34.

The Saddler's House 36 Great James St ⓣ028/7126 9691, ⓦwww.thesaddlershouse.com. Beautifully decorated Georgian townhouse run by knowledgeable hosts and serving excellent breakfasts. This, together with its sister B&B *The Merchant House*, is a real treat. They also have self-catering cottages and 2-bed apartments available to rent. Late-night revellers not welcome. Doubles from £50.

Eating

Café del Mondo The Craft Village, Shipquay St. Not-for-profit café and restaurant serving excellent-value stews, soups and salads from around the world. Mains £3.50–8. Café daily 8.30am–6pm, restaurant daily 6pm–midnight.

Halo Pantry and Grill New Market St ⓣ028/71271567. Housed in a former shirt factory, this excellent restaurant on two floors serves top-quality food using locally sourced ingredients at very reasonable prices. *Pantry* mains £7, *Grill* mains £15. Daily noon–10pm.

Drinking and nightlife

Bound for Boston 27–31 Waterloo St. This live music venue has a great beer-garden and seven pool tables.
Peadar O'Donnell's/The Gweedore Bar 59–63 Waterloo St ⓦwww.peadars-gweedorebar.com. Traditional and contemporary music every night.
Sandino's Café Bar Water St ⓦwww.sandinos.com. Intimate candlelit café-bar with a Che Guevara theme downstairs, and a live music venue upstairs, which opens late. Traditional music on Sun from 5pm.

Moving on

Train Belfast (4–9 daily; 2hr 30min); Coleraine (5–9 daily; 1hr).
Bus Donegal (3–7 daily; 1hr 25min–1hr 45min); Dublin (11 daily; 4hr); Enniskillen (5–15 daily; 2hr–4hr 20min); Sligo (3–5 daily; 2hr 30min).

Italy

HIGHLIGHTS

VENICE: catch a waterbus at night for some utterly romantic views

SIENA: attend the Palio, a frenetic and fiercely partisan horse race

ROME: see the spectacular Colosseum up close

NAPLES: eat pizza in its home town

POMPEII: explore the evocative remains of a city buried by ash

PALERMO: prepare to be dazzled by the Sicilian capital's unique architectural mix

ROUGH COSTS

DAILY BUDGET Basic €35 /occasional treat €50

DRINK Wine €2.50/glass

FOOD Local pasta dish €5–8; pizza slice €2

HOSTEL/BUDGET HOTEL €15–30/€25–45

TRAVEL Train: Rome–Naples; bus: €15

FACT FILE

POPULATION 60 million

AREA 301, 230 sq km

LANGUAGE Italian

CURRENCY Euro (€)

CAPITAL Rome (population: 2.7 million)

INTERNATIONAL PHONE CODE ⓣ39

Introduction

Of all the countries in Europe, Italy is perhaps the hardest to classify. A modern industrialized nation and a harbinger of global style, its designers lead the way with each season's fashions. But it is also a Mediterranean country, with all that that implies. If there is a single national characteristic, it is to embrace life to the full, manifest in its numerous local festivals and in the importance placed on good food. There is also, of course, the country's enormous cultural legacy: Tuscany alone has more classified historical monuments than any country in the world, and every region holds its own treasures.

Italy wasn't unified until 1861, a fact that's borne out by the regional nature of the place today. The well-to-do cities of **Turin** and **Milan** epitomize the wealthy, industrial north; to their south is **Genoa**, a bustling port with a long seafaring tradition. By far the biggest draw in the north is **Venice**, a unique and beautiful city – though you won't be alone in appreciating it. The centre of the country, specifically **Tuscany**, boasts classic, rolling countryside and the art-packed towns of Florence, Pisa and Siena, while neighbouring **Umbria** has a quieter appeal. **Rome**, the capital, harbours a dazzling array of ancient and Renaissance gems. South of here in Campania, **Naples**, a vibrant, unforgettable city, is the spiritual heart of the economically undeveloped Italian south, while close by are fine ancient sites and the spectacular **Amalfi Coast**. Puglia, the "heel" of Italy, has underrated pleasures – most notably Lecce, a Baroque gem of a city. **Sicily** is a law unto itself, with attractions ranging from Hellenic remains to the drama of Mount Etna, and the beguiling city of Palermo. **Sardinia**, too, feels far removed from the mainland, especially in its relatively undiscovered interior.

CHRONOLOGY

753 BC Rome founded by Romulus and Remus.
509 BC The city becomes a Republic.
49 BC Julius Caesar wages war against the Senate and extends the Roman Empire across Europe.
80 AD Building of the Colosseum.
476 Last Roman Emperor Romulus Augustus overthrown by barbarians.
756 Papal States created after Frankish forces defeat the Lombards.
1173 Building of the Tower of Pisa begins.
1512 Michelangelo completes his frescoes in the Sistine Chapel, as the Italian Renaissance flourishes.
1804 Napoleon declares himself emperor of Italy.
1814 Following Napoleon's defeat, Italy is divided into various states.
1861 Unification of Italian states into a Kingdom by Giuseppe Garibaldi.
1898 First Italian football league established.
1915 Italy joins World War I on the side of the Allies.
1922 Fascist Benito Mussolini becomes Prime Minister.
1929 The Lateran Treaty declares Vatican City an independent state. It is the smallest state in the world.
1940 Italy enters World War II on the side of the Nazis.
1943 Allies capture Sicily and imprison Mussolini. Italy declares war on Germany.
1945 Mussolini is captured and executed by Italian Communists.
1946 Republic replaces the monarchy.
1957 The Treaty of Rome establishes the European Economic Community.
2007 Silvio Berlusconi wins a third term as prime minister, amid persistent allegations of corruption.
2009 Earthquake in L'Aquila, around 100km east of Rome, kills over 260 people and leaves thousands homeless.

ARRIVAL

The majority of tourists arrive at the **airports** of Rome or Milan, although low-cost European airlines Ryanair

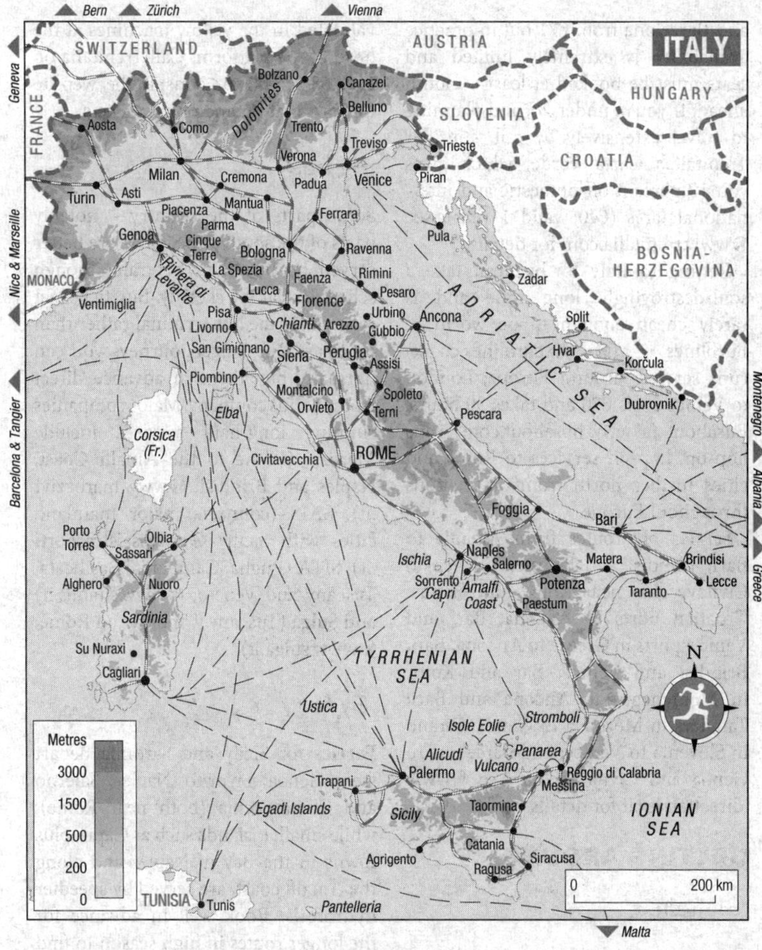

and easyJet also offer services to Bari, Bologna, Brindisi, Genoa, Naples, Palermo, Parma, Perugia, Pisa, Rimini, Turin and Venice, plus destinations in Sardinia and Sicily. Budget Italian airline blu-express (ⓦwww.blu-express.com) flies from France, Spain, Greece and Turkey to Rome, as well as between many Italian cities; Meridiana (ⓦwww.meridiana.it) has routes between many European and Italian cities. From North America, national carrier Alitalia (ⓦwww.alitalia.com) runs direct flights to Milan, Rome and Venice, with numerous connecting flights to other cities, although you may find cheaper deals with US airlines such as Delta and American Airlines. Meridiana operates direct flights from New York to Rome, Naples and Palermo. The cheapest option, though, can be to fly to London and get a budget flight onward from there.

Train travel from the UK often works out more expensive, but there is a vast choice of routes, mostly arriving in Milan. From elsewhere in Europe, look into Trenitalia's Smart Price fares; in theory you can travel from Paris for €30, Vienna and Budapest from €29 and Barcelona from €71 but in practice availability is extremely limited and seats must be booked at least a month ahead. If you're under 26, and planning to travel extensively by rail, consider Trenitalia's Carta Verde, which gives you 10 percent off domestic and international fares (€40; valid 1 year); see Ⓦwww.trenitalia.com for details.

Getting to Italy **by bus** can take a soul-destroyingly long time and is rarely cheap enough to be worth it. Eurolines (Ⓦwww.eurolines.co.uk) runs services around Europe; London to Venice costs €70 and takes 30 hours. Busabout (Ⓦwww.busabout.com) runs hop-on, hop-off services to Rome and cities further north from destinations throughout Europe.

Ferries ply routes from Albania to Bari, Brindisi and Trieste; Corsica to Civitavecchia near Rome and Genoa; Croatian ports to Ancona, Bari and Venice; ports in Greece to Ancona, Bari, Brindisi and Venice; Bar and Kotor in Montenegro to Ancona and Bari; Tangiers in Morocco to Genoa; Pirano in Slovenia to Venice; and Barcelona to Genoa and Civitavecchia. See Ⓦwww.directferries.it for details.

GETTING AROUND

By train

The rail network is extensive, though delays are common. **Trains** are operated by Italian State Railways (Ferrovie dello Stato or FS; Ⓦwww.ferroviedellostato.it). For most journeys you'll have a choice between Eurostar – expensive but fast – the slower, mid-priced Intercity and the cheap, snail-paced Diretto, Interregionale and Regionale. Seat reservations are obligatory on Eurostar and Intercity lines, and should be made a week in advance on busy routes. **InterRail** and **Eurail** passes are valid on the whole FS network, though you'll pay supplements for the fast trains and most long-distance trains. **Tickets** must be validated in the yellow machines at the head of the platform. Call Trenitalia on Ⓣ06.6847.5475 or consult the website for information and online tickets.

By bus

Some parts of the country – notably parts of the south and Sicily – are better served by **bus** than by train, though schedules can be sketchy. Buy tickets at *tabacchi* or the bus terminal rather than on board; for longer journeys you can normally buy them in advance direct from the bus company. Major companies running long-haul services include Marozzi (Rome to the Amalfi Coast, Naples and Brindisi; Ⓦwww.marozzivt.it), SAIS (connects major mainland cities with Sicily; Ⓦwww.saistrasporti.it), SITA (Puglia, Campania, Basilicata, Tuscany and Veneto; Ⓦwww.sitabus.it) and Sulga (Tuscany, Umbria and Rome; Ⓦwww.sulga.it).

By ferry

Ferries for Sicily and Sardinia depart from Genoa, Livorno, Naples, Salerno and Civitavecchia (both near Rome), while smaller islands such as Capri, plus towns in the Bay of Naples and along the Amalfi coast, are served by speedier **hydrofoils**. Book well in advance for the longer routes in high season to find the cheapest fares; for timetables, see Ⓦwww.directferries.it.

ACCOMMODATION

Book **hotels** in advance in the major cities and resorts, especially in summer. Rates vary greatly but on average you can expect to pay €60 for a double without private bathroom (*senza bagno*) in a one-star hotel, and at least €80 for a double in a three-star. Very busy places might ask you to book a minimum of three nights.

B&Bs and **agriturismi** (farmstays) can make a good-value alternative.

They are often in spectacular locations and provide excellent Italian home cooking, though you may need a car to get to them: ask for a list from the local tourist office.

There are **hostels** in every major Italian city, charging €15–30 per person for a dorm bed, though for two people travelling together, this isn't much cheaper than a budget hotel room. You can see the full list of Italy's HI hostels on Ⓦwww.aighostels.com. Alternatively, **student accommodation** is a popular budget option in university towns (July and August only), or ask the tourist board about local **case per ferie**, usually religious houses with rooms or beds to let. They can be better value than hostels but often have curfews.

There are plenty of **campsites** and in most cases you pay for location rather than facilities, which can vary enormously. Daily prices are around €7 per person, plus €10 for a two-person tent. See Ⓦwww.camping.it for information.

FOOD AND DRINK

There are few places in the world where you can eat and drink as well as in Italy. If you eat only pizza and panini, you'll be missing out on the distinctive **regional cuisines**; don't be afraid to ask what the *piatti tipici* (local dishes) are. Most Italians start their day in a bar, with a cappuccino and a *cornetto* (croissant), a **breakfast** that should cost around €2 if you stand at the counter – or at least double that if you take a seat. At **lunchtime**, bars sell *tramezzini*, sandwiches on white bread, and panini. Another stopgap are *arancini*, fried meat- or cheese-filled rice balls, particularly prevalent in the south. Italian ice cream (*gelato*) is justifiably famous and usually costs €1.50–2.50 a cup or cone. **Markets** sell fresh, tasty produce for next to nothing, and work out much cheaper than supermarket shopping.

The ultimate budget option for sit-down food is **pizza**. Although trattorias or restaurants often offer a fixed-price *menu turistico*, but it's generally better to steer clear if you want an authentic experience. A **trattoria** is traditionally cheaper than a restaurant, offering *cucina casalinga* (home-style cooking). But in either, pasta dishes go for around €5–9; main fish or meat courses between €7–15. Order vegetables (*contorni*) separately. Afterwards there's fruit (*frutta*) and desserts (*dolci*).

APERITIVO TIME

When you're strapped for cash but want to have a good time, it's worth remembering that between about 6 and 9pm, most bars either bring you **snacks** or have an *aperitif* buffet if you buy a drink. These snacks are often substantial enough to fill you up, so you'll be able to save on buying dinner.

Drink

Bars are less social centres than functional places for a quick coffee or beer. You pay first at the cash desk (*la cassa*), present your receipt (*scontrino*) and give your order. Coffee comes small and black (*caffè*), with a dash of milk (*macchiato*), iced (*shakerato*) in summer, or there's the ever-popular *cappuccino*. Tea (*tè*) comes with lemon (*con limone*) unless you ask for milk (*con latte*); it's also served cold (*tè freddo*). A *spremuta* is a fresh orange juice; crushed-ice fruit *granite* are refreshing in summer.

Wine is invariably drunk with meals, and is very cheap. Go for the local stuff: ask for *un mezzo* (a half-litre) or *un quarto* (a quarter) *della casa* (house). Bottles are pricier but still good value; expect to pay at least €12 in a restaurant. The cheapest and most common brands of **beer** (*birra*) are the Italian Peroni and Moretti. Draught beer (*alla spina*) is served in measures of a pint (*una media*) and half-pint (*piccola*). A generous shot of spirits, limoncello, or grappa – made from grape pips and stalks – costs from €2. Amaro is a bitter after-dinner liqueur. Drinking in bars (*locali*) can be pricey – around €5 for a beer and €5–9 for a cocktail – while drinking in clubs can be ruinous, although the entrance fee of €10–15 usually includes one drink.

Most places will be happy to serve you **tap water** (*acqua dal rubinetto*). For bottled water, ask for *acqua naturale* (still) or *acqua frizzante* (sparkling).

CULTURE AND ETIQUETTE

Italy remains strongly **family-oriented**, with an emphasis on the traditions and rituals of the Catholic Church, and it's not unusual to find people living with their parents until their early thirties. While the north is cosmopolitan, the south can be rather provincial; women travelling on their own may attract unwanted attention in smaller areas. When entering churches, ensure that your knees and shoulders are covered. In towns and villages all over the country, life stops during the middle of the day for a long lunch.

Tipping is not a big deal in Italy; in restaurants – if a service charge is not included – it's acceptable to reward good service with a couple of euros. In bars, you may see some Italians leave a coin on the counter after finishing their coffee – a convenient way of ridding themselves of small change, but by no means expected. Likewise, taxi drivers will not expect a tip. **Smoking** is outlawed in all enclosed public places.

STUDENT AND YOUTH DISCOUNTS

Entrance to many of Italy's state-owned museums and archeological sites is free or reduced for EU citizens aged under 25. Students are often eligible for discounts too; carry a valid ISIC card or equivalent. For one week each year, usually in April, publicly owned museums and sites open their doors for free for the Settimana della Cultura (Cultural Heritage Week).

SPORTS AND OUTDOOR ACTIVITIES

Spectator sports are popular here, particularly **football** (*calcio*), though cycling, motorcycling and motor racing are also high-profile sports. A football match in Italy can be an exhilarating experience. The season runs from the end of August to June; ⓦwww.lega-calcio.it for details of matches; tickets cost from €20.

Campania, Sardinia and Sicily, with their pristine coastlines and clear waters, provide excellent conditions for **scuba diving** and **snorkelling**, while Rome, Milan, Turin, Venice and, at the other end of the country, Mount Etna in Sicily, are within easy reach of **ski resorts**. The same mountainous terrain is perfectly suited to summertime **hiking**; ask at local tourist offices for maps and itinerary information.

COMMUNICATIONS

Post office opening hours are Monday to Friday 8am to 6.30pm, with branches in larger towns sometimes also open on Saturdays. Stamps (*francobolli*) can also be bought at *tabacchi* – ask for *posta prioritaria* if you want letters to arrive home before you do. Public **phones** are card-operated; get a phonecard (*scheda telefonica*) from *tabacchi* and newsstands for €5/10. For land-line calls – local and long-distance – dial all digits, including the area code. International directory enquiries (ⓣ176) are pricey. Most towns have at least one place with **internet** access; hourly rates are around €2–4.

ITALIAN

	Italian	Pronunciation
Yes/No	*Sì/No*	See/Noh
Please	*Per favore*	Pear fah-vure-ay
You're welcome	*Prego*	Pray-goh
Thank you	*Grazie*	Grraat-see-ay
Hello/Good day/Hi	*Ciao/buongiorno/salve*	Chow/boo-on jawr-noh/salvay
Goodbye	*Ciao/arrivederci*	Chow/arrivi-derchee
Excuse me	*Mi scusi*	Mee scoo-see
Good	*Buono*	Bwo-noh
Bad	*Cattivo*	Cat-ee-voh
Near	*Vicino*	Vih-chee-noh
Far	*Lontano*	Lont-ah-noh
Today	*Oggi*	Ojj-ee
Yesterday	*Ieri*	Ee-air-ee
Tomorrow	*Domani*	Doh-mahn-ee
How much is...?	*Quanto è...?*	Cwan-toe ay...?
What time is it?	*Che ore sono?*	Keh orr-ay son-noh
I don't understand	*Non ho capito*	Non oh kapee-toe
Do you speak English?	*Parla Inglese?*	Parr-la inglay-zay?
One	*Uno*	Oo-noh
Two	*Due*	Doo-ay
Three	*Tre*	Tray
Four	*Quattro*	Cwattr-oh
Five	*Cinque*	Chink-way
Six	*Sei*	Say
Seven	*Sette*	Set-tay
Eight	*Otto*	Ot-toe
Nine	*Nove*	Noh-vay
Ten	*Dieci*	Dee-ay-chee
Ticket	*Biglietto*	Bil-yettoh
Where is...?	*Dov'è...?*	Doh-vay...?
Entrance	*L'ingresso*	Lingress-oh
Exit	*L'uscita*	Loo-shee-tah
Platform	*Il binario*	Il bin-ah-ree-oh
Toilet	*Il bagno*	Il ban-yo
Ferry	*Il traghetto*	Il trag-ettow
Bus	*L'autobus*	Lout-o-boos
Plane	*L'aereo*	Lah-air-ay-oh
Train	*Il treno*	Il tray-no
I would like a...	*Vorrei...*	Vorr-ay...
Bed	*Letto*	Lett-oh
Single/double room	*Camera singola/doppia*	Cam-errah singolah/doppiah
Cheap	*Economico*	Eck-oh-no-micoh
Expensive	*Caro*	Car-oh
Open	*Aperto*	Apairt-oh
Closed	*Chiuso*	Queue-zoh
Breakfast	*Colazione*	Coll-ats-ioh-nay
Hotel	*L'hotel*	Lott-ell
Hostel	*L'ostello*	Lost-ellow

ITALY ONLINE

Ⓦ **www.goitaly.about.com** Guide to sites, attractions and events in Italy.

Ⓦ **www.paginegialle.it** Italian directory of phone numbers.

EMERGENCIES

Most of the **crime** you're likely to come across is small-time. You can minimize the risk of this by being discreet, not flashing anything of value and keeping a firm hand on your camera and bag, particularly on public transport. The police come in many forms: the *Vigili Urbani* deal with traffic offences and the *Carabinieri* with public order and drug control; report thefts to the *Polizia di Stato*. Italy treats soft and hard drugs offences with equal severity.

Pharmacies (*farmacie*) can give advice and dispense prescriptions; there's one open all night in towns and cities (find the address of the nearest on any pharmacy door). For serious ailments, go to the *Pronto Soccorso* (casualty) section of the nearest hospital (*ospedale*).

INFORMATION

Most towns, major train stations and airports have a **tourist office** (*ufficio turistico*), which will give out maps for free. Studio FMB has excellent hiking maps covering the north of the country, as does Club Alpino Italiano, available throughout Italy.

EMERGENCY NUMBERS

Police Ⓣ112 for all emergencies.

MONEY AND BANKS

Italy's currency is the euro (€). You'll get the best rate of exchange at a **bank**; hours are Monday to Friday 8.30am to 1.30pm and 2.30 to 4pm. ATMs (*bancomat*) are widespread. The Italian way of life is cash-based, and many smaller restaurants and B&Bs will not accept credit cards.

OPENING HOURS AND HOLIDAYS

Most shops and businesses open Monday to Saturday 8/9am to 1pm and 4–7/8pm, though in the north, offices work a 9am to 5pm day. Just about everything, with the exception of bars and restaurants, closes on Sunday. Most churches keep shop hours. Museums traditionally open Tuesday to Sunday 9am to 7pm. Most archeological sites open daily from 9am until an hour before sunset.

Many of Italy's inland towns close down almost entirely for the month of August, when Italians head for the coast. Everything closes for national holidays: January 1, January 6, Easter Monday, April 25, May 1, June 2, August 15, November 1, December 8, December 25 and 26.

Rome

Of all Italy's historic cities, **ROME** (Roma) exerts the most fascination. Its sheer weight of history is endlessly compelling. Classical features – the Colosseum, the Roman Forum, the spectacular Palatine Hill – stand alongside ancient basilicas containing relics from the early Christian period, while Baroque fountains and churches define the city centre. But it's not all history and brickwork: Rome has a vibrant, chaotic life of its own, its crowded streets thronged with traffic, locals, tourists and students.

What to see and do

Rome's city centre is divided into distinct areas. The **centro storico** (historic centre) occupies a hook of land on the east bank of the River Tiber, bordered to the east by Via del Corso and to the north and south by water. The old Campus Martius of Roman times, it became the heart of the Renaissance city and is now an unruly knot of narrow streets holding some of the best of Rome's classical and Baroque heritage, as well as much of its nightlife.

From here, Rome's central core spreads east, across Via del Corso to the major shopping streets around the **Spanish Steps** and the main artery of Via Nazionale, and south to the **Roman Forum**, **Colosseum** and **Palatine Hill**. The west bank of the river is home to the **Vatican** and **St Peter's** and, to the south of these, charming **Trastevere**. East of Termini Station is student-hub San Lorenzo, home to Rome's main university and some of its best nightlife.

The Roman Forum

The best place to start a tour of the city is the **Roman Forum** (daily 8.30am–1hr before sunset; 2-day joint ticket with Colosseum and Palatine Hill, who operate same opening hours, €12), the bustling centre of the ancient city. It's worth getting the audioguide (€5, must be returned by 4.30pm) as there is next to no textual information displayed on site.

Running through the heart of the Forum, the **Via Sacra** was the best-known street of ancient Rome, lined with its most important buildings, such as the Curia – begun in 45 BC, this was the home of the Senate during the Republican period. Next to the Curia is the **Arch of Septimius Severus**, erected in the Early third century AD to commemorate the Emperor's tenth anniversary in power. In the centre of the Forum is the **House of the Vestal Virgins**, where the six women charged with keeping the sacred flame of Vesta alight lived. On the far side of the site, the towering **Basilica of Maxentius** is probably the Forum's most impressive relic. From the basilica, the Via Sacra climbs to the **Arch of Titus** on a low arm of the Palatine Hill, its reliefs showing the spoils of Jerusalem being carried off by eager Romans.

Palatine Hill

From the Forum, turn right at the Arch of Titus to reach the **Palatine Hill** (hours and price as per Roman Forum) now a beautiful archeological garden. In the days of the Republic, the Palatine was the most desirable address in Rome. From the **Farnese Gardens**, on the right, a terrace looks back over the Forum, while the terrace at the opposite end looks down on the alleged centre of Rome's ancient beginning – an Iron Age hut, known as the **House of Romulus**, the best-preserved part of a ninth-century village.

Close by, steps lead down to the **Cryptoporticus**, a passage built by Nero to link the Palatine with his palace on the far side of the Colosseum. A left turn leads to the **House of Augustus** (Mon, Wed, Thurs, Sat & Sun 8.30am–7.30pm), which holds beautiful frescoes

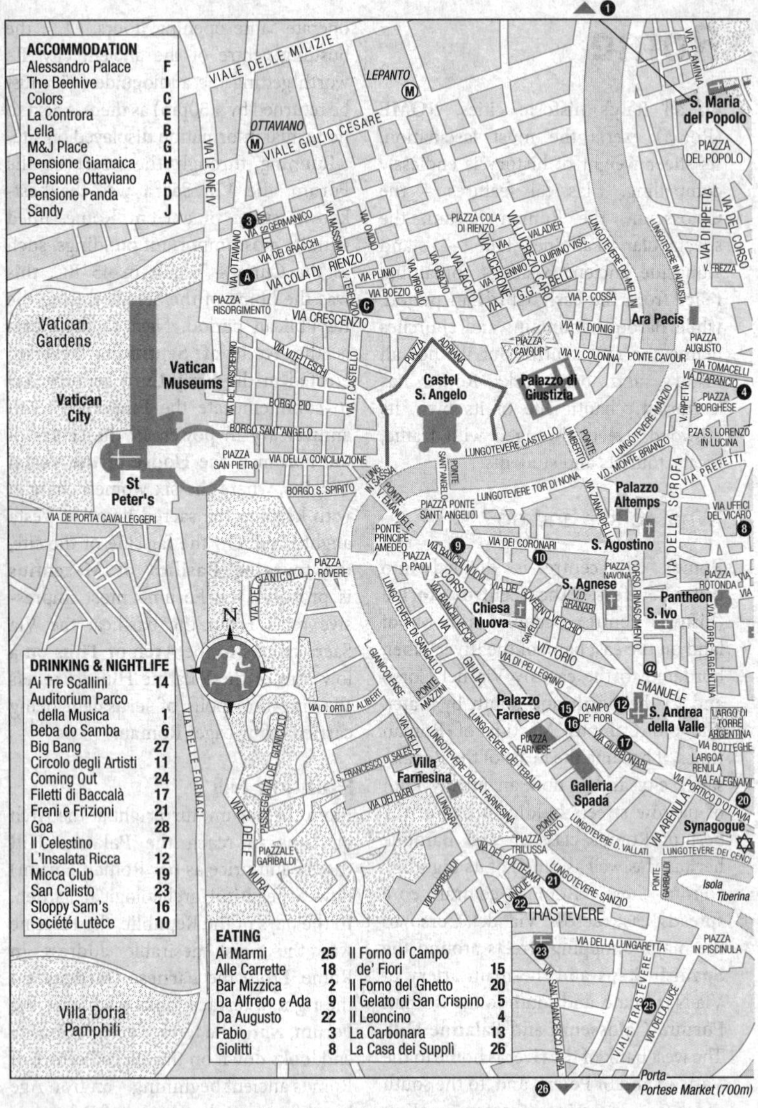

dating back to 30 BC and considered to be among the most magnificent examples of Roman wall paintings anywhere; even the builders' ancient graffiti has been meticulously preserved.

The Capitoline Hill

Formerly the spiritual and political centre of the Roman Empire, the Capitoline Hill lies behind the Neoclassical Vittoriano monument on Piazza Venezia. Atop the Capitoline is **Piazza del Campidoglio**, designed by Michelangelo in the 1530s and flanked by the two wings of one of the city's most important museums of ancient art – and the oldest public gallery in the world, dating back to 1471 – the **Capitoline Museums** (Tues–Sun

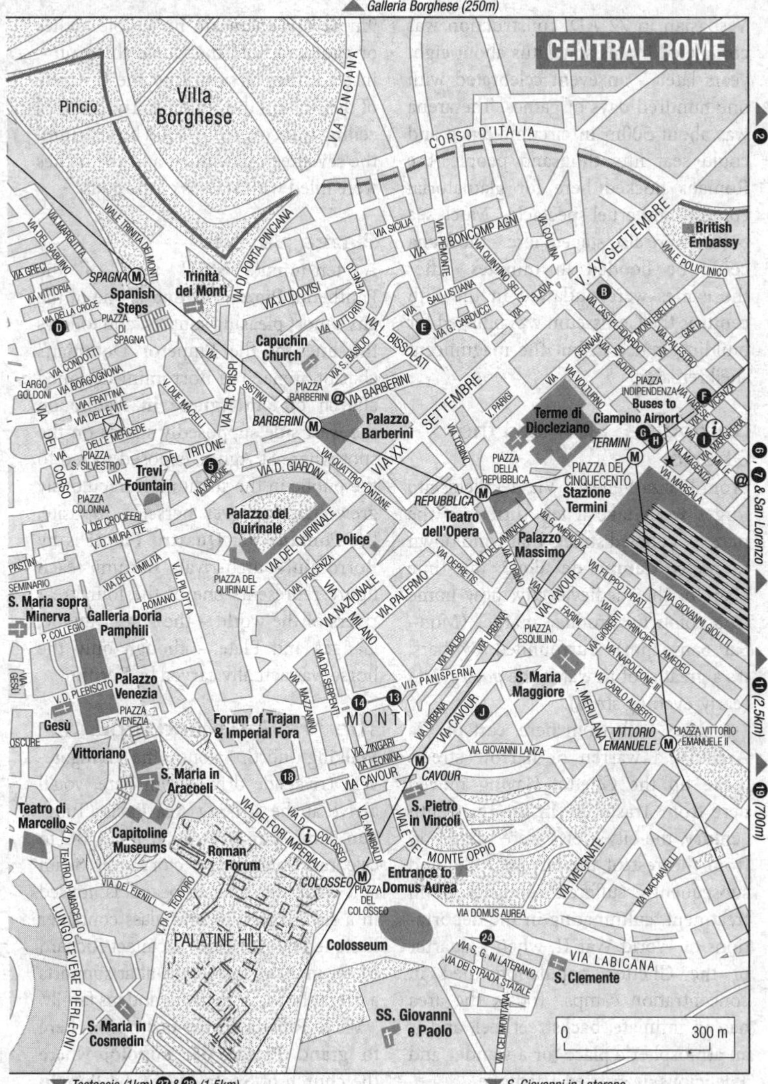

9am–8pm; €12). The Palazzo Nuovo, the museum's left-hand wing, contains some of the best of the city's Roman and Greek sculpture. Highlights of the Palazzo dei Conservatori opposite include various parts of the colossal statue of the Emperor Constantine which once stood in the Forum, and sixteenth-century frescoes.

Colosseum

Immediately outside the Forum, the fourth-century **Arch of Constantine** marks the end of the Via Sacra. Across from here is Rome's most awe-inspiring ancient monument, the **Colosseum** (hours and price as per Roman Forum; bypass queues by buying tickets at the Palatine Hill). Begun by the Emperor

Vespasian in 72 AD, construction was completed by his son Titus about eight years later – an event celebrated with one hundred days of games. The arena was about 500m in circumference and could seat fifty thousand people; the Romans flocked here for gladiatorial contests and cruel spectacles. Mock sea battles were also staged here – the arena could be flooded in minutes. After the games were outlawed in the fifth century, the Colosseum was pillaged for building material, but the magnificent shell remains.

Campo de' Fiori and the Ghetto

From Piazza Venezia, Via del Plebiscito forges west; take a left turn into the maze of cobbled streets that wind down to pretty **Campo de' Fiori**, one-time heart of the medieval city, now home to a colourful produce market (Mon–Sat 6am–2pm). Surrounded by bars, it's a great spot to watch the *passeggiata* (early-evening stroll).

A short walk from here, east of Via Arenula, a warren of narrow streets make up the Ghetto. Having moved here from Trastevere in the thirteenth century, the city's Jews were walled off from the rest of the city in 1556, and subsequently suffered centuries of ill treatment, culminating in the deportations of World War II, when a quarter of the Ghetto's population died in concentration camps. Today, the area has an intimate, backstreet feel, and is an atmospheric place for a wander and a delicious deep-fried artichoke.

Pantheon

One of the centro storico's main draws is the **Pantheon** (Mon–Sat 8.30am–7.30pm, Sun 9am–6pm; free), the most complete ancient Roman structure in the city, finished around 125 AD. Inside, the diameter of the dome and height of the building are precisely equal, and the hole in the dome's centre is a full 9m across; there are no visible arches or vaults to hold the whole thing up – instead, they're sunk into the concrete of the walls of the building. The coffered ceiling was covered in solid bronze until the seventeenth century, and the niches were filled with statues of the gods.

Piazza Navona

A ten-minute stroll west of the Pantheon, **Piazza Navona** is one of the city's most pleasing squares, and follows the lines of the Emperor Domitian's chariot arena. The Borromini-designed church of **Sant'Agnese in Agone** on the west side supposedly stands on the spot where St Agnes, exposed naked to the public in the stadium, miraculously grew hair to cover herself. Opposite, the **Fontana dei Quattro Fiumi** is by Borromini's arch-rival, Bernini; each figure represents one of the four great rivers of the world – the Nile, Danube, Ganges and Plate – though only the horse was actually carved by Bernini.

The Ara Pacis and around

Walking north along the Lungotevere (riverside drive) from here, you'll arrive at the striking **Ara Pacis** (Tues–Sun 9am–7pm; €11). Built in 13 BC to celebrate Augustus's victory over Spain and Gaul, the "altar of peace" is housed in a slick travertine and glass container designed by American architect Richard Meier in 2006. Inside, the altar supports a frieze showing Augustus and his family.

Via di Ripetta arrows north from here to grand **Piazza del Popolo**, where the church of **Santa Maria del Popolo** (daily 7am–noon & 4–7pm) holds some of the best Renaissance art of any Roman church. Two pictures by Caravaggio attract the most attention – the *Conversion of St Paul* and the *Crucifixion of St Peter*.

Villa Borghese

Leafy **Villa Borghese,** just a few minutes' stroll east of Piazza del Popolo, is a tranquil haven from the noise of the city. It harbours several fine museums, not least the **Galleria Borghese** (Tues–Sun 8.30am–7.30pm; timed entry every 2hr; ⓣ06.32.810; call to book at least a day in advance; €8.50), a dazzling collection of mainly Italian art and sculpture. Highlights include Canova's sculpted marble *Pauline*, the sister of Napoleon portrayed as a reclining Venus, in Room 1; spectacular sculptures by Bernini in rooms 2–4; and the six Caravaggios in Room 8.

The Spanish Steps and Trevi Fountain

The area immediately southeast of Piazza del Popolo is historically the artistic quarter of the city, with a distinctly cosmopolitan air. At the centre of the district, **Piazza di Spagna** features the distinctive boat-shaped Barcaccia fountain, the last work of Bernini's father. The **Spanish Steps** – a venue for international posing – sweep up from the piazza to the sixteenth-century church of **Trinità dei Monti**. From the top of the Spanish Steps, narrow Via Sistina winds down to Piazza Barberini, dominated by Bernini's Fontana del Tritone, its muscular Triton held up by four dolphins. West down Via del Tritone, hidden among a web of narrow streets, is one of Rome's more surprising sights – the **Trevi Fountain**, a deafening gush of water over Baroque statues and rocks built onto the back of a Renaissance palace; legend has it that throwing a coin over your shoulder into the pool guarantees your return to Rome.

San Lorenzo

Packed in around Via Tiburtina is the edgy **San Lorenzo** district, a tight grid of streets named after ancient Italian tribes. The area badly suffered the Allied bombing of 1943, and it still has a slightly unkempt air to it. Banksy-style street art and posters advertising upcoming gigs form a constantly evolving backdrop on every inch of spare wall space, interspersed with vintage shops, cool bars and hole-in-the-wall pizza takeaways. It's the place to go to for cheap eats and a night out; young people gather at Piazza dell'Immacolata and surrounding streets for drinks in the early evening, before heading to one of the many busy bars and live music venues.

Trastevere

Over on the Tiber's west bank, picturesque **Trastevere**, once the city's shabby bohemian quarter, is now somewhat gentrified, and home to vibrant nightlife and some of the city's best restaurants.

The hub of the area is **Piazza di Santa Maria in Trastevere**, and the magnificent twelfth-century church of the same name on the western side of the square. Held to be the first official church in Rome, built on a site where a fountain of oil is said to have sprung on the day of Christ's birth, it is resplendent with thirteenth-century mosaics. The square is a good starting point for a mooch through the district's crisscrossing alleys, lined with enticing cafés, bars, markets, boutiques and gelaterias.

St Peter's basilica

The **Vatican City**, a tiny territory north of Trastevere, is partly hemmed in by high walls, but opens its doors to the rest of the city in the form of Bernini's **Piazza San Pietro**. **St Peter's Basilica** (daily 7am–6pm; free) was built to a plan initially conceived at the end of the fifteenth century by Bramante and finished off over a century later by Carlo Maderno, bridging the Renaissance and Baroque eras. The first thing you see, on the right, is Michelangelo's moving *Pietà*, completed when he was just 24. On the right-hand side of the nave, the bronze statue of St Peter was cast in the thirteenth century by Arnolfo di Cambio. Bronze was also used in Bernini's imposing 28m-high *baldacchino*, the centrepiece of the sculptor's embellishment of the interior. To the right of the main doors, you can ascend by stairs or lift to the **roof**, from where there's a steep walk up 320 steps to the **dome** (daily 8am–5pm; €6, €7 with lift), well worth the effort for its glorious views over the city.

The Vatican Museums

A ten-minute walk from the northern side of Piazza San Pietro takes you to the **Vatican Museums** (Mon–Sat 9am–6pm; last admission 4pm; €15, students under 26 €8; last Sun of the month 9am–2pm; last admission 12.30pm; free) – quite simply the largest, richest museum complex in the world, stuffed with treasures from every period of the city's history. The queues to get in can be daunting so it's best to book ahead online (Ⓦmv.vatican.va). Highlights include the **Stanze di Raffaello**, a set of rooms decorated for Pope Julius II by Raphael among others, including the *School of Athens* fresco, which depicts his artistic contemporaries as classical figures: Leonardo is Plato and Michelangelo Heraclitus. Further on is the **Galleria Chiaramonte**, a superb collection of Roman statues, and the **Galleria delle Carte Geografiche** a stunning corridor adorned with incredibly precise, richly pigmented maps of Italy.

The **Sistine Chapel**, of course, is the main draw. Built for Pope Sixtus IV in 1481, it serves as the pope's private chapel and hosts the conclaves of cardinals for the election of each new pope. The paintings down each side wall depict scenes from the lives of Moses and Christ by Perugino, Botticelli and Ghirlandaio, among others. But it's Michelangelo's ceiling frescoes of the *Creation* that everyone comes to see, executed almost single-handedly over a period of about four years for Pope Julius II. The *Last Judgment*, on the west wall of the chapel, was painted by Michelangelo over twenty years later. The nudity caused controversy from the start, and the pope's zealous successor, Pius IV, insisted that loincloths be added – removed in a recent restoration.

Arrival

Air Rome has two airports. Leonardo da Vinci, better known as Fiumicino, and Ciampino, which is exclusively for low-cost flights. Two train services link Fiumicino to Rome: the Leonardo Express to Termini (every 30min until 11.37pm; 30min; €14), and the FMI to Trastevere, Ostiense and Tiburtina stations (every 30min until 11.27pm; €8). Terravision coach services (Ⓦwww.terravision.eu) travel to Termini station (1hr 5min; €6). From Ciampino Terravision (€4) and SIT bus (€4) make the 40min trip to Termini station. The cheapest way of getting into town is to take an Atral bus to Anagnina metro stop, then a metro to Termini station (€2.20), though this will take twice as long.

Train The main train station is Termini, meeting point of the metro lines and city bus routes. Some long-distance services use Stazione Tiburtina, particularly at night. The two stations are connected by metro and bus.

Bus Domestic bus services arrive at the bus terminal outside Stazione Tiburtina.

Information

Tourist office Enjoy Rome (Mon–Fri 8.30am–6pm, Sat 8.30am–2pm; Via Marghera 8a Ⓣ06.445.0734, Ⓦwww.enjoyrome.com) is a friendly, independently run tourist office, staffed by English-speakers, which offers a free accommodation-finding service. Near the Colosseum on Via dei Fori Imperiali, I Fori di Roma (daily 9.30am–6.10pm; Ⓣ06.679.7702) is an information centre with plenty of maps and pamphlets. There's also a tourist information booth at Termini Station (daily 7.45am–9pm), and green tourist information kiosks (PIT) near every major sight (daily 9am–6pm). Ⓦwww.060608.it is a council-run tourist website; you can also call Ⓣ06.0608 for advice in English (daily 9am–9pm).

Discount passes The Roma Pass (€25 for three days; Ⓦwww.romapass.it) gives you free access to all public transport within the city, as well as free entry to the first two sites you visit, plus many further discounts. Buy the pass from tourist information kiosks or from participating sites.

City transport

Public transport is cheap and reasonably reliable. A day-pass (BIG; €4), one-way ticket (BIT; valid for

75min on all public transport, including one trip on the metro; €1), 3-day pass (BTI; €11) or 1-week ticket (CIS; €16) for the metro and bus network can be bought from most newspaper stalls and *tabacchi*, from ticket machines in metro stations and outside Termini station. Stamp tickets to validate them at the entrance gates to metros and on board buses and trams.

Bus The bus network is extensive; useful routes include the #40 from Termini station, which passes through the centre en route to the Vatican, and #116 from the Ⓜ Barberini, which serves both Villa Borghese and the centro storico. A network of night buses (*bus notturni*) serves most parts of the city, running until about 5.30am. #N1 follows metro line A; #N2 calls at all stops along metro line B; and #N8 runs from Trastevere to Termini station.

Metro The quickest way to get around, with trains every 3–5min. The city's two metro lines, A and B, meet beneath Termini station and run 5.30am–11.30pm (Fri & Sat till 1.30am).

Taxi Meters start at €2.80 by day (€4 on Sun) and €5.80 after 10pm. Depending on luggage and the time of travel, it should cost around €10 to get from Termini to the centre. You can hail one in the street, or the ranks at Termini or Argentina (opposite Feltrinelli), or call Ⓣ 06.3570.

Accommodation

In high season (April–July, Sept & major religious holidays) Rome is very crowded, so book accommodation as far in advance as possible. If you arrive without a booking, make straight for Enjoy Rome (see opposite). Many of the city's cheaper hotels are located close to Termini station, but it's pretty insalubrious; pay a bit more to stay in the centre if you can.

Hostels

Alessandro Palace Via Vicenza 42 Ⓣ 06.446.1958, Ⓦ www.hostelalessandro.com. Buzzing hostel with a bar and lively international staff on hand to recommend nightlife options. Dorms €26–35, doubles €110.

The Beehive Via Marghera 8 Ⓣ 06.4470.4553, Ⓦ www.the-beehive.com. Funky hotel with designer furnishings, spotless rooms, a café and a tranquil garden. Dorms €25, shared bathrooms €80, rooms in shared apartments nearby €70.

Colors Via Boezio 31 Ⓣ 06.687.4030, Ⓦ www.colorshotel.com. All rooms and dorms have a/c and are decorated in zingy colours. Guests have the use of the terrace, two common areas and wi-fi. Breakfast included for private rooms only. Dorms €23–29, doubles with shared bathroom €85, with bathroom €95.

La Controra Via Umbria 7 Ⓣ 06.9893.7366, Ⓦ www.lacontrora.com. For the traveller seeking friendliness without riotousness. There's a chilled-out living area, kitchen and clean 4- to 6-bed dorms. Dorms €30–40, doubles €45–60.

M&J Place Via Solferino 9 Ⓣ 06.446.2802, Ⓦ www.mejplacehostel.com. Quirky murals of Rome decorate the walls of this popular hostel, whose dorms sleep up to 10 people. 5 percent discount for Rough Guide readers. Dorms €25–37.50, shared bath doubles €90.

Pensione Ottaviano Via Ottaviano 6 Ⓣ 06.3973.8138, Ⓦ www.pensioneottaviano.com. The dorms are simply furnished and on the cramped side, but *Ottaviano* is a good place to meet other travellers, and there are views of St Peter's from some rooms. Dorms €20–35, twins €40–90.

Sandy Via Cavour 136 Ⓣ 06.488.4585, Ⓦ www.sandyhostel.com. Laidback, conveniently located hostel near the Colosseum. Dorms €20–40.

Hotels

Lella Via Palestro 9 Ⓣ 06.484.940, Ⓦ www.solomonhotels.com. *Lella*'s spacious, warmly decorated en suites offer good value for money – some come with baths, and some with a terrace. Some rooms also operate as dorms with shared bathroom for €25–30. Doubles €85.

Pensione Giamaica Via Magenta 13 Ⓣ 06.490.121, Ⓔ md0991@mclink.it. If you can look beyond the pea-green walls and old-fashioned decor, this family-run *pensione* with shared bathrooms in a quiet street near Termini is a bargain. Breakfast is €6 extra, but there is a fridge for guests' use and plenty of bars nearby. Singles €35, doubles €60.

Pensione Panda Via della Croce 35 Ⓣ 06.678.0179, Ⓦ www.hotelpanda.it. Ideally placed near the Spanish Steps, with neat shared bathrooms and the novelty of a radio in the rooms, this hotel is in high demand. No breakfast. Doubles €78.

Eating

All of Rome's neighbourhoods have at least one food market (generally Mon–Sat 7am–2pm); Campo de' Fiori is the most famous, while Piazza Vittorio Emanuele near Termini sells African fruits and Asian food too. Conad is a 24hr supermarket in the mall underneath Termini station.

Snacks and ice cream

Bar Mizzica Via Catanzaro, 30. Ⓜ Bologna. The best *arancini* this side of Sicily: chunky *ragù*, mozzarella and peas in risotto rice, deep-fried. Snacks (around €2) don't get any better. Open daily.

Fabio Via Germanico 43. Organic fresh juices made with fruit and/or vegetables for €3.50 and zingy salads with ingredients like tofu, lentils and lovely dressings for €4 are the perfect antidote to too much pizza and sun. Good vegetarian choices. Closed Sun.

Giolitti Via degli Uffici del Vicario 40. Fight your way through the hordes at this Roman institution, with a choice of seventy ice cream flavours. Closed Mon.

Il Forno del Ghetto Via del Portico d'Ottavia 1. Historic Jewish bakery with marvellous ricotta and dried fruit-filled cakes. Closed Sat.

Il Forno di Campo de' Fiori Campo de' Fiori 22. This takeaway sells filling slices of pizza for about €1.50 a slice – try the potato and rosemary. The bakery next door serves large filled focaccia sandwiches for about €2.70. Closed Sun.

Il Gelato di San Crispino Via della Panetteria 42. Close to the Trevi fountain and selling some of Rome's best ice cream using all-natural ingredients and in-season fruit. Closed Tues.

La Casa del Supplì Via San Francesco a Ripa, 137. Understandably popular takeaway offering fresh *supplì* (mozzarella and tomato rice balls, €1), *arancini*, pizza and rotisserie chicken. Closed Sun.

Restaurants and pizzerias

The centro storico, Trastevere and Testaccio are full of small, family-run restaurants.

Ai Marmi Viale di Trastevere 53. Nicknamed *l'orbitorio* – the graveyard – for its marble slab tables, this extremely popular pizzeria has excellent *filetto di baccalà* (battered cod), hearty bean dishes and fabulous pizzas (€5–8). You can sit outside. Closed Wed.

Alle Carrette Via Madonna dei Monti 95. Typical Roman pizza is cooked fresh in the wood-fired oven at this welcoming place right by the Forum. The *calzone* are especially good (€7). Open daily, evening only.

Da Alfredo e Ada Via dei Banchi Nuovi 14. Genuine home cooking at great prices, in a cosily wood-panelled dining room. Three courses cost less than €20. Dinner only, Mon–Fri.

Da Augusto Piazza de' Renzi 15. The service may be slapdash, but the setting (an enchanting cobbled piazza) and the food (hearty, cheap Roman staples) are what make this rowdy trattoria special. Opens at noon/1pm for lunch and 8pm for dinner; the queue forms well before. Mains €7/8. Closed Aug.

> **WATER FOUNTAINS**
>
> All over Rome, there are small water fountains from which you can drink. The water is ice-cold, clean and free, so bring a water bottle and fill up.

Filetti di baccalà Largo dei Librari 88. A true Rome experience: chaotic and delicious. As you'd expect from the name, you should order fried fish (€5), along with whatever salad is in season. Closed Sun.

Il Leoncino Via del Leoncino 28. An antidote to the tourist traps in the Spagna area, this is a family-run option with tasty thin-crust pizzas. The Tuscan dish *fagioli all'uccelletto* (cannellini beans baked in tomato with sage) are unmissable for bean lovers. Pizza €6–9. Closed Wed.

L'Insalata Ricca Largo dei Chiavari 85, Via Giulio Cesare Santini 12 and other locations. If you can't face another pizza, this quality chain offers over thirty types of salad (around €7), all freshly prepared and served in huge portions. Open daily.

La Carbonara Via Panisperna 214. A lively, popular restaurant in buzzing Monti, right by *Ai Tre Scallini* (see opposite). Try the signature carbonara and mark your visit on the wall of graffiti. Closed Sun.

Drinking and nightlife

The two main areas to go for a drink are Trastevere and the centro storico, particularly around Campo de' Fiori. Bohemian Monti, near the Colosseum, and studenty San Lorenzo are full of bars frequented by locals. There's a concentration of clubs in Testaccio, though beware of the sleaziness that accompanies a widespread "free for girls" policy; the door charge can be anything from €5 to €25.

Bars

Ai Tre Scallini Via Panisperna 251. Perfect for a glass of wine early evening – moreish snacks included– after traipsing around the Colosseum. Chilled out from lunch until about 8pm, when Monti's cool crowd arrives and spills out into the street. Closed Sun.

Freni e Frizioni Via del Politeama 17. This ex-garage (the name means "Brakes and Clutches"), cluttered with vintage machinery, is a popular early-evening hangout, thanks to its generous *aperitivo* buffet – just buy a drink (from €6) and dig in. Open daily from 6.30pm.

Il Celestino Via degli Ausoni 64. A San Lorenzo hotspot with great coffee by day and a torrent of young people drinking for cheap and making the most of the generous *aperitivo* snacks by night. Closed Sun.

San Calisto Piazza San Calisto. The hub of Trastevere, with the best people watching in the city. Cheap beer, amazing home-made ice cream and eccentric characters make it what it is. Closed Sun.

Sloppy Sam's Campo de' Fiori 10. All the bars on Campo de' Fiori are busy with a mainly expat or traveller crowd. *Sam's* is the most popular and offers huge cocktails and a reasonable dinner menu. Closed Mon.

Société Lutèce Piazza di Montevecchio 17. A 10min walk from Piazza Navona in a picturesque piazza, this laidback bar makes delicious cocktails to go with home-made tapas as well as sushi on certain days. Closed Mon.

Clubs and music venues

For up-to-date info in English, check the Entertainment section of *WHERE Rome* magazine Ⓦwww.wheretraveler.com. Much of the club scene moves down to the beach at Ostia in the summer – look for posters around town and check the listings in Roma *C'è*.

Auditorium Parco della Musica Viale P. de Coubertin ⓣ06.808.2058, Ⓦwww.auditorium.com. Bus #M from Termini. See big international acts in this magnificent venue, one of the few modern constructions in the city. From June–Aug a summer festival is held in the outdoor amphitheatre.

Beba do Samba Via de' Messapi 8. Ⓦwww.bebadosamba.it. From acoustic samba nights to wild funk bands, this colourfully decorated San Lorenzo bar frequented by Brazilians and Italians has a holiday atmosphere and cheap caipirinhas. Closed end July to early Sept, otherwise open nightly.

Big Bang Via Monte Testaccio 22. Popular venue for live acts and club nights, with a happy hour from 10pm till midnight. DJs play anything from rock to new wave to indie. Fri & Sat only.

Circolo degli Artisti Via Casilina Vecchia 42 Ⓦwww.circoloartisti.it. Huge bar, disco and garden with live rock, blues and electro; good vintage market some Sundays. Bus #105 from Termini. Closed Mon.

Coming Out Via San Giovanni in Laterano 8. Ⓦwww.comingout.it. One of Rome's original gay bars and still among the best. Expect live music, karaoke and a friendly crowd. Open daily 5pm–5am.

Goa Via Libetta 13. One of Rome's historic clubs, with ethno-industrial decor and big-name DJs. Closed Mon.

Micca Club Via Pietro Micca 7a Ⓦwww.miccaclub.com. DJ sets, live acts, monthly burlesque nights and a Sunday vintage market in a cool, brick-vaulted space. Closed Mon, Tues & June–Aug.

Entertainment

Cinemas The Nuovo Olimpia (Via in Lucina 16g, off Via del Corso) is the main English-language cinema. *RomaC'è*, a comprehensive listings guide (out Wed, €1), contains a short English section.

Classical music The city's churches host a wide range of concerts, many of them free. The Auditorium

FESTIVALS

Festival delle Letterature Ⓦwww.festivaldelleletterature.it. The floodlit Basilica of Maxentius provides a stunning backdrop to readings by international authors. May & June.

Estate Romana & Expo Tevere Ⓦwww.estateromana.comune.roma.it. Events include concerts and cultural happenings – many of them free – in parks and piazzas around town, plus buzzing bars, restaurants and an outdoor cinema set up along the riverbank around Trastevere and the Tiber Island. "Gay Village" (Ⓦwww.gayvillage.it) runs through the summer with music and club nights. June–Sept.

La Festa di Noantri Piazza Santa Maria in Trastevere and around. Trastevere's traditional summer festival in honour of the Virgin, with street stalls selling snacks and trinkets, and a grand finale of fireworks. Last two weeks of July.

RomaEuropa Festival Ⓦwww.romaeuropa.net. A cutting-edge performing arts festival, generally with some big-name acts, in locations around town. Mid-Sept to Nov.

Rome Film Festival Ⓦwww.romacinemafest.it. A host of film stars descend on the city for its annual film festival, and there are English-language screenings all around town. Mid- to end Oct.

Parco della Musica hosts the Accademia di Santa Cecilia, the city's prestigious classical academy.
Opera The opera scene is concentrated on the Teatro dell'Opera, Piazza B. Gigli in winter (Ⓣ06.4816.0255, Ⓦwww.operaroma.it) and moves to the spectacular Terme di Caracalla in summer.

Shopping

Shops With the exception of the Galleria Alberto Sordi on Via del Corso, malls and department stores are few and far between. The boutiques around Piazza di Spagna are for big-spenders only, but nearby Via del Corso is lined with shops selling cheap to mid-range clothing, books and CDs. Other mainstream outlets can be found along Via Cola di Rienzo near the Vatican, and Via Nazionale, off Piazza della Repubblica. Via del Governo Vecchio off Piazza Navona has a string of great vintage stores; the alleys off Campo de' Fiori and streets of San Lorenzo harbour independent jewellery and clothing shops.
Markets Porta Portese flea market is the city's best known (Sunday mornings; catch the #H from Termini to Porta Portese), but Via Sannio (Mon–Sat 9am–1.30pm; metro San Giovanni) is also a great place to find vintage bargains.

Directory

Embassies Australia, Via Antonio Bosio 5 Ⓣ06.852.721; Canada, Via Salaria 243 Ⓣ 06.854.441; New Zealand, Via Clitunno 44 Ⓣ06.853.7501; UK, Via XX Settembre 80 Ⓣ06.4220.0001; US, Via V. Veneto 119 Ⓣ06.46.741.
Exchange Offices at Termini station operate out of banking hours; also Yex (see "Internet" below).
Hospitals Ambulance Ⓣ118; central hospital: Policlinico Umberto I Ⓣ06.49.971; International Medical Center Ⓣ06.488.2371.
Internet Yex (Corso Vittorio Emanuele 106; daily 8am–2am; €2.90/30min).
Left luggage At Termini station (daily 6am–midnight; €4 for the first 5hr, then €0.60/hr).
Pharmacies PIRAM, Via Nazionale 228 (24hr), near Termini. Rota posted on pharmacy doors.
Police Emergencies Ⓣ112; main police station (*questura*) at Via S. Vitale Ⓣ06.46.861.
Post office Piazza San Silvestro 19 (Mon–Fri 8am–6.30pm, Sat 8am–1pm).

Moving on

Air Cagliari (several daily; 1hr 05min).
Train Bologna (every 15min; 2hr 20min–4hr); Florence (every 15min; 1hr 20min–3hr); Milan (every 15min; 3hr–6hr 30min); Naples (every 30min; 1hr 10min–2hr 50min); Paris (9 daily; 11–20hr); Turin (12 daily; 4hr 20min–6hr); Vienna (5 daily; 11hr 45min–15hr 45min); Zurich (15 daily; 7hr 45min–15hr).
Bus Agrigento (1 daily; 14hr); Amalfi (summer 1–2 daily; 5hr); Lecce (4 daily; 7–8hr 30min); Palermo (1 daily; 12hr); Perugia (7 daily; 2hr 15min); Sorrento (2 daily; 3hr 45min).

Northwest Italy

The northwest of Italy is many people's first experience of the country, and while it often represents its least stereotypical "Italian" aspect, there are some iconic towns in the area. The vibrant city of **Turin** was the first capital of Italy after the Unification in 1860, and still holds many reminders of its past. **Milan**, the upbeat capital of the heavily industrial region of **Lombardy**, continues to be taken seriously for its business and fashion credentials, the region of **Liguria** to the south is home to the country's most spectacular stretch of coastline. The chief town of the province is the sprawling port of **Genoa**, while southeast, towards Tuscany, the **Cinque Terre**'s rugged stretch of coastline continues to wow travellers with its cliff-top villages and clear blue waters.

TURIN

Following the 2006 Winter Olympics, **TURIN** (Torino) – a virtual Fiat company town and the home of Vermouth and Lavazza coffee – has emerged resplendent with gracious avenues, opulent palaces and splendid galleries. It's a lively, bustling place with cafés, a fun nightlife and enough contemporary art to rival any European city.

What to see and do

The grid plan of the Baroque centre makes finding your way around easy.

Via Roma is the central spine, a grand affair lined with designer shops and ritzy cafés and punctuated by the city's most elegant piazzas, notably **Piazza San Carlo**. A ten-minute walk northwest brings you to the fifteenth-century **Duomo**, home of the Turin Shroud, which is kept under wraps and away from the public's eyes. This piece of cloth, imprinted with the image of a man's body, had long been claimed as the shroud in which Christ was wrapped after his crucifixion, although 1989 carbon-dating tests suggested that it was a medieval fake, made between 1260 and 1390.

The **Palazzo Madama**, looming over **Piazza Castello**, is architecturally stunning, and has a collection of Baroque, Gothic, Renaissance and decorative art on show (Tues–Sat 10am–6pm, Sun 10am–8pm; €7.50). East of Via Roma, is the **Mole Antonelliana**, which Turin residents proudly call the "Eiffel Tower of Turin", boasting great views over the city from the top of its panoramic lift. The building also contains the excellent **Cinema Museum** (Mon–Fri & Sun 9am–8pm, Sat 9am–11pm; €5 for panoramic lift only; €9 including museum).

Museums

Turin has a good selection of modern art museums: the **Galleria Civica d'Arte Moderna e Contemporanea** (**GAM**), on Via Magenta 31 (Tues–Sun 10am–8pm; €7.50), holds works dating from the eighteenth century to the present day, by artists such as Giorgio de Chirico and Lucio Fontana. For more contemporary art, it is worth the journey to the **Castello di Rivoli**, 20km outside Turin (Tues–Sun 10am–5pm; €6.50), home to the most important collection of postwar art in Italy, with works by Jeff Koons, Carl Andre and Mario Merz. On weekdays, take the metro to Paradiso, then bus #36 to Piazza Martiri Della Liberte then walk for fifteen minutes.

Arrival and information

Air Turin airport is 16km north of the city. The best way to reach the centre is by the Terravision bus (Mon–Sat every 15–30min; Sun every 45min; €5).
Train The station is in Porta Nuova, a 15min walk from Piazza Castello.
Tourist office Piazza Castello (daily 9am–7pm; ⓣ011.530.070, ⓦwww.turismotorino.org). There is a smaller centre at the train station (daily 9am–7pm and also at the airport (daily 9am–8pm).
Discount passes Pick up a Torino & Piedmonte Card (€22/2 days, €27/3 days) for free travel on all buses, trams and on the panoramic lift. Also includes entrance to over 180 museums and discounts on theatre and concert tickets.
Internet 1pc4u on Via Verdi 20/g offers cheap access.
Post office Via San Domenico 19.

Accommodation

Many of Turin's budget hotels are off Via Nizza, just one block over from the train station.
Bella Vista Via Galliari 15 ⓣ011.669.8139, ⓦwww.bellavista-torino.it. This bustling and friendly top-floor hotel has rooms with big windows and a huge communal balcony; it is just a short walk from the station. Doubles €50.
Hotel Due Mondi Via Saluzzo 3 ⓣ011.650.5084, ⓦwww.hotelduemondi.it. Spacious, comfortable rooms in an old fashioned boutique-style hotel. Discounts are available. Doubles €60.

SKIING THE MILKY WAY

The snowcapped peaks surrounding Turin are home to some of the best ski slopes in the region. Known collectively as the **Milky Way**, the five Italian resorts hosted the 2006 Winter Olympics. Sestriere is the most sophisticated, while Sauze d'Oulx is great for its après-ski scene. All the towns are linked by ski lifts, and a daily ski pass costs an affordable €41. Getting to the slopes involves a train from Turin to Oulx (hourly; 1hr 15min), and then a bus to your chosen destination.

Open 011 Corso Venezia 11 ⓣ011.250.535. Welcoming hostel with helpful staff and large, spotless rooms. Take the train to Torino Dora, or get bus #46 (Dora stop), #52 (Viba stop) or #10 from Porto Nuova station. Dorms €18.
Paradiso Via Berthollet 3 ⓣ011.669.8678, ⓦwww.albergo-paradiso-torino.it. This clean one-star has private bathrooms for every room. The pick of the cheaper hotels in this unappealing district near the train station. Doubles €45.

Eating

Foccareia Tipica Ligure Saint Agostino 6. Part of a chain of restaurants. Local specialities served in a rustic cosy atmosphere. *Farinata* and wine for €4.
Gran Bar Piazza Gran Madre di Dio 2. Cool wine and coffee bar close to the river and the magnificent Vittorio Veneto Piazza. Expresso is cheap at €1.
San Augusto Via San Quintino 9/bis ⓣ011.562.3173. Simply the best pizzeria in Turin (large pizzas from €6). Get there early if you want a table outside or book ahead. Closed Sat lunch.
Urbani Via Saluzzo 3. A hit with with locals, this big, classy place in a shabby part of town. Start talking football with the owner and staff and you will never leave. Pastas from €8 and pizzas from €5.

Drinking and nightlife

The liveliest areas are Il Quadrilatero, a few minutes west of Piazza Castello, Via San Quintino, and the Murazzi on the edge of the River Po, where people congregate at outside tables.
AEIOU Via Spanzotti 3. Big warehouse-style club for dancing all night; features rock, Cuban, jam sessions, art and theatre projects. Entrance usually free.
Arancia di Mexxarate One of the best bars on the lively Piazza Emanuele Filiberto. Buzzy place with tables crammed together outside. Tues–Sun 5pm–4am.
Jamoff Bar Arcate Murazzi del Po. This attractive outdoor bar right next to the river serves drinks all day on barrel tables. Beer €4.
KM5 Bar Via San Domenico 14. Not the most glamorous location but locals flock here for the generous and good-value *aperitivo*. Lots of outdoor seating with DJ every Thursday. Open till 2am.

Moving on

Train Geneva (1 daily; change 3 times; 12hr); Genoa (hourly; 1hr 45min); La Spezia (every 2hr; 3hr 30min); Lyon (twice daily; change at Chambery; 4hr); Milan (frequent; 1hr 50min); Nice (hourly; change at Ventimiglia; 5hr); Paris (2 direct daily; 5hr 45min); Rome (frequent; 4hr 30min); Venice (frequent; 4hr 30min).

MILAN

MILAN (Milano) is the capital of Italy's fashion and design industry, with the reputation as a fast-paced and somewhat unfriendly business city ruled by consumerism and the work ethic. But don't be put off, coupled with the swanky shops and excellent nightlife, Milan boasts a lovely canal area, friendly suburbs and unmissable historical sites – the Gothic cathedral has few peers in Italy, while Leonardo da Vinci's iconic fresco of *The Last Supper* is a must.

What to see and do

Piazza del Duomo

A good place to start a tour of Milan is **Piazza del Duomo**, the city's historic centre and home to the world's largest Gothic cathedral (daily 7.30am–6.45pm; free to enter), begun in 1386 and not completed till almost five centuries later. The gloomy interior gives access to the cathedral's fourth-century **baptistery** (Tues–Sun 9.45am–12.45pm & 2–5.45pm; €4) and the **cathedral roof** (Tues–Sun 9am–6pm; €8 by elevator, €5 on foot), where you are surrounded by a forest of lacy Gothic carving and subjected to superb views of the city. On the north side of the piazza, the opulent **Galleria Vittorio Emanuele II** is a cruciform glass-domed gallery designed in 1865 by Giuseppe Mengoni, who was killed when he fell from the roof a few days before the inaugural ceremony. The Galleria leads through to the world-famous eighteenth-century **La Scala** opera house.

Pinacoteca di Brera

At the far end of Via Brera is Milan's most prestigious gallery, the awe-inspiring **Pinacoteca di Brera** (Tues–Sun 8.30am–7.30pm; €7.50), filled with works looted from the churches and aristocratic collections of French-occupied Italy.

Castello Sforzesco

The **Castello Sforzesco** (castle grounds 7am–7pm) rises imperiously from the mayhem of **Foro Buonaparte**, laid out by Napoleon as part of a grand plan for the city. The castle houses the **Museo d'Arte Antica** and **Pinacoteca** (both Tues–Sun 9am–5.30pm; €3) – the former contains Michelangelo's *Rondanini Pietà,* the latter paintings by Vincenzo Foppa, the leading Milanese artist before Leonardo da Vinci.

Santa Maria delle Grazie and the Last Supper

South of the Castello, the church of **Santa Maria delle Grazie** is Milan's main attraction. A Gothic pile, partially rebuilt by Bramante (who added the massive dome), it is famous for its fresco of *The Last Supper* by Leonardo da Vinci, which covers one wall of the refectory. Advance booking is essential (viewing Tues–Sun 8am–7pm; €8; ⓦwww.milan-museum.com).

Arrival and information

Air Linate is Milan's closest airport, 7km from the city centre and connected by the airport bus to Stazione Centrale (every 30min, 6.05am–11pm; 30min; €4). Ordinary city buses (#73; €1) also run every 15min until around midnight from Linate to Piazza San Babila. Malpensa airport is 45km away towards Lago Maggiore and connected by train to Cadorna station (every 30min; €9) and by bus with Stazione Centrale (until 11.15pm; 1hr; €7.50).

Train Most international trains pull in at the Stazione Centrale, northeast of the centre on Piazza Duca d'Aosta (metro lines MM2 or MM3).

Bus Buses arrive at and depart from Lampugnano bus station. Bus company Sena runs services to Siena, Florence, Rome and locations further south ⓦwww.sena.it.

Tourist office Piazza Castello 1 (Mon–Sat 9am–6pm, Sun 9am–1pm & 2–5pm; ⓣ02.7252.4301/2/3, ⓦwww.provincia.milano.it). There is also a small kiosk in the middle of Stazione Centrale, but it is often impossibly packed. Both have the ever-helpful free listings guide, *Milanomese*, in Italian and English and *Hello Milano.*

City transport

Bus, metro and tram An efficient network of trams, buses and the metro (stations denoted on map as M) runs 6am–12.30pm. There are interconnecting stations so you can change from the metro onto the overground and back. For detailed maps and route information head to the ATM office in Duomo metro station.

Night bus These take over after the other options close, and run until 1am following the train routes, or until about 3am following alternative routes. Buses #90 & #91 operate 24 hours covering Milan's external ring road.

Tickets Tickets (normally valid 1hr 15min; €1) can be used for one journey only on the metro or as many bus and tram journeys as you can make in that time, or a 48hr ticket (€5.50), valid on metro, tram and buses, available from any metro station or *tabacchi.*

Accommodation

There are plenty of one-star hotels, mostly concentrated in the area around Stazione Centrale, and along Viale Vittorio Veneto and Corso Buenos Aires. When there is an "exposition" on (there are about 25 a year, lasting 2–3 days each) prices rocket.

ACISJF Corso Garibaldi 123 ⓣ02.2900.0164, ⓦwww.acisjf.it. Run by nuns and open to women under 25 only; it's in a great location on an eclectic bar-lined street. Singles €30.

Ciao Bella Via Balzaretti 4 ⓣ02.2395.1135, ⓦwww.ciaobellamilan.hostel.com. A welcoming hostel with large en-suite rooms. There is a big colourful sitting room and kitchen as well as a private garden. Take the metro three stops to Piola and walk for 10min. Dorms €30.

Hotel Due Gardini Via B Marcello 47, ⓦwww.hotelduegiardini.it. This friendly spot has a lovely breakfast conservatory and a small garden, and is just a 10min walk from the station. Doubles €70.

La Cordata Casa Scout Via Burigozzo 11 ⓣ02.5831.4675, ⓦwww.lacordata.It. Well-equipped hostel superbly located in a vibrant canal area; free internet and no curfew. Dorms €21.

Piero Rotta HI Hostel Via Martino Bassi 2 ⓣ02.3926.7095, ⓦwww.ostellionline.org. Huge, friendly HI Hostel. There is a public swimming pool

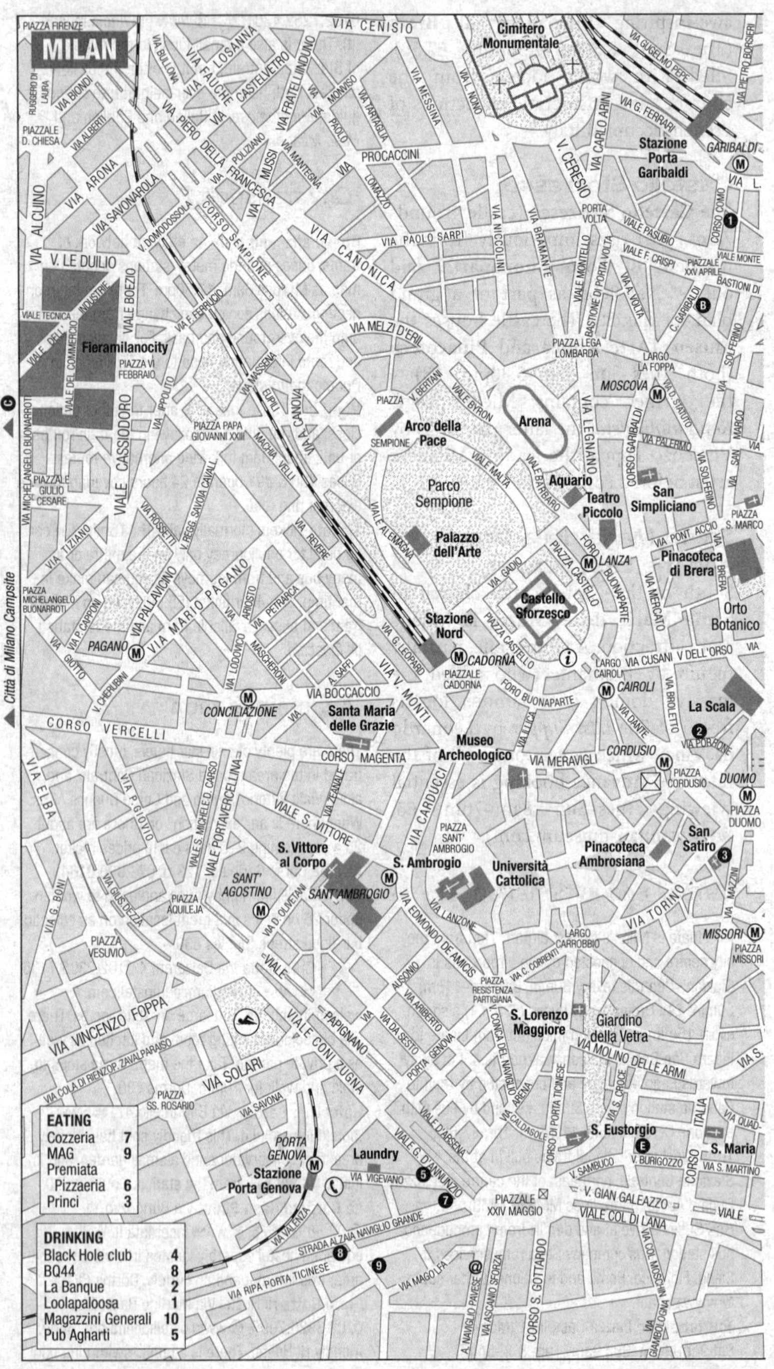
MILAN
Cimitero Monumentale
Stazione Porta Garibaldi
Fieramilanocity
Arco della Pace
Arena
Parco Sempione
Aquario
Teatro Piccolo
San Simpliciano
Palazzo dell'Arte
Pinacoteca di Brera
Castello Sforzesco
Orto Botanico
Stazione Nord
La Scala
Santa Maria delle Grazie
Museo Archeologico
Pinacoteca Ambrosiana
San Satiro
S. Vittore al Corpo
S. Ambrogio
Università Cattolica
S. Lorenzo Maggiore
Giardino della Vetra
S. Eustorgio
S. Maria
Laundry
Stazione Porta Genova
Città di Milano Campsite
VIA CENISIO
CORSO SEMPIONE
VIA CANONICA
VIA PAOLO SARPI
VIA MELZI D'ERIL
VIA MARIO PAGANO
CORSO VERCELLI
CORSO MAGENTA
VIA CARDUCCI
VIA TORINO
VIA SOLARI
VIA VINCENZO FOPPA
VIALE CONI ZUGNA
VIA MOLINO DELLE ARMI
VIALE COL DI LANA
CORSO S. GOTTARDO
CORSO DI PORTA TICINESE
CORSO ITALIA
STRADA ALZAIA NAVIGLIO GRANDE
VIA RIPA PORTA TICINESE
PIAZZALE XXIV MAGGIO
PIAZZA DUOMO
EATING
Cozzeria 7
MAG 9
Premiata Pizzaeria 6
Princi 3
DRINKING
Black Hole club 4
BQ44 8
La Banque 2
Loolapaloosa 1
Magazzini Generali 10
Pub Agharti 5

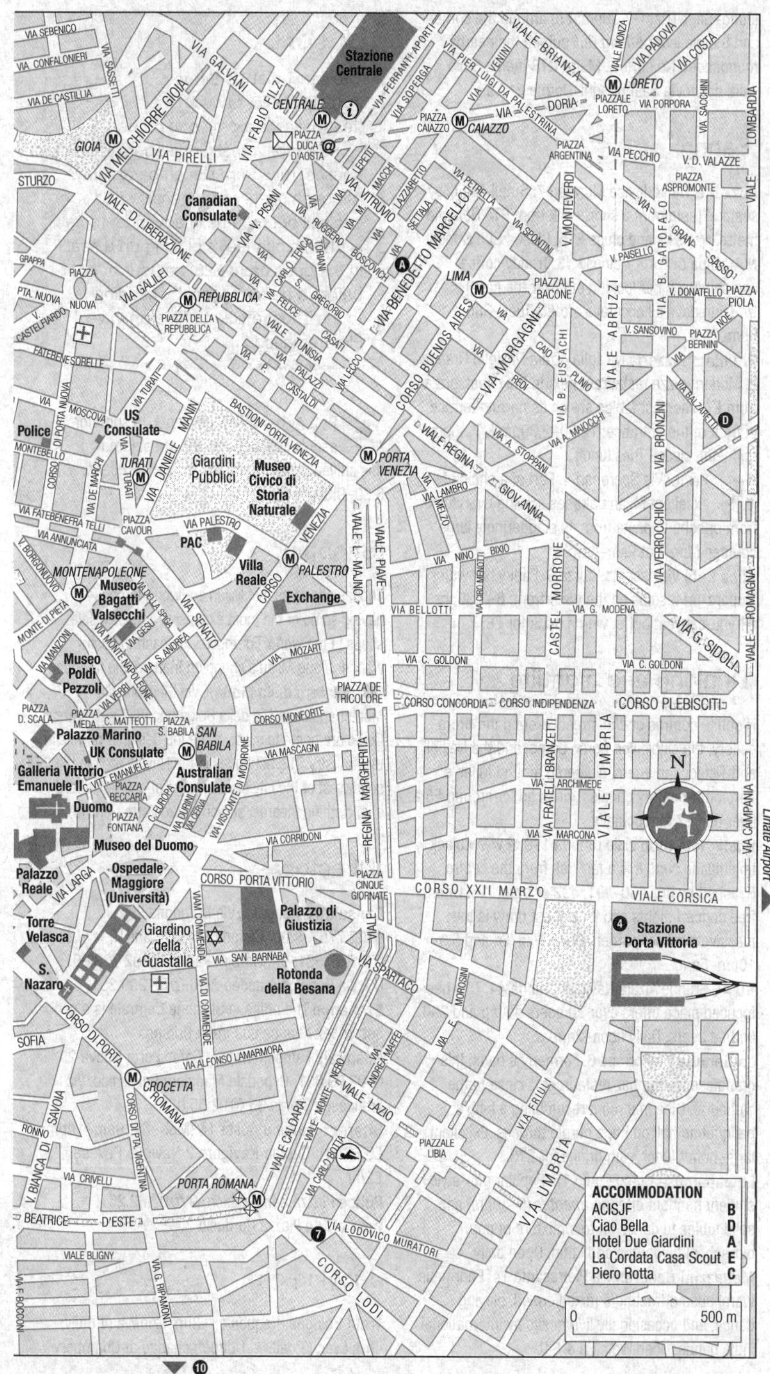

ITALY

NORTHWEST ITALY

(June–Sept 10am–7.30pm; €5) around the corner and the pleasant *Sitting Bull* pub on the nearby roundabout. No curfew. Metro QT8 then a 5min walk down Via Salmoiraghi. Dorms €19.50.

Eating

Cozzeria Via Lodovico Muratori 7. Small and cosy seafood restaurant a short walk from PTA Romano metro. Mussels and chips €15. Closed Sun & Mon.
MAG Ripa di Porta Ticinese 43. Trendy coffee and sandwich bar looking out over the canal. On Thursdays all cocktails are €5. Tues–Sun 6pm–2am.
Premiata Pizzeria Naviglia Alzaia Naviglio Grande 2. Modern pizza restaurant next to the canal; pizzas from €7. The best tables are on its narrow terrace in front of the entrance. 12.30–2.30pm & 7.30pm–midnight, closed Tues lunch.
Princi Via Speronari 4. Part of a chain of excellent Milan bakeries serving everything from brioche to pasta from its staggeringly large counter. Mon–Sat 9am–6pm.
Slice Café Via Ascanio Sforza 9. Funky bar with leopard-print sofas on the waterfront; 6–9.30pm all-you-can-eat buffet with a drink for €8.

Drinking and nightlife

Nightlife centres on the streets around the Brera gallery, the club-filled Corso Como, and the Navigli and Ticinese quarters, clustered around Milan's thirteenth-century canals. Drinks go for around €5 a beer and €7 for cocktails.
Black Hole Club Viale Umbria 118 Ⓦwww.blackholemilano.com. It is a fair trek from the centre. Reached by bus #90, #91, #92 or tram #16. Offers free concert nights and its biggest draw is the massive summer garden. Open Wed, Fri and Sat 10pm–5am.
BQ 44 Grande Alzaia Naviglio Grande 44. This beer-focused place offers over 20 beers on tap and 200 bottled beers. Daily noon–2am.
La Banque Via Porrone 6. Formerly a bank, this grandiose lounge bar-restaurant is close to the cathedral. Dine in a room resembling a king's banqueting hall on huge purple thrones. Excellent large buffet lunch with drinks for €13.
Loolapaloosa Corso Como 15. Popular pub-style student hangout offering *aperitifs* (5–10pm) and solid tables to dance on to a mixture of pop, old-school favourites and Latin. Open daily.
Magazzini Generali Via Pietrasanta 14. Enormous warehouse attracting a mixed crowd, playing dance, and occasionally live music by international indie bands. Open Wed, Fri & Sat.

LA SCALA

The season at **La Scala** (Ⓣ02.860.775, Ⓦwww.teatroallascala.org), one of the world's most prestigious opera houses, runs from December to July. Although seats are expensive and can sell out months in advance, there is often a chance of picking up a seat in the gods (from €25) an hour or so before a performance, by heading to the Theatre ticket office on Via Filodramatico 2.

Pub Agharti Via Vigevano 1. In summer people spill out onto the streets from this chilled popular bar near the canal. *Aperitif* 6.30–9.30pm €6.

Shopping

The fashion streets of Milan are world famous for having some of the most expensive and exclusive shops in the world. For those with cash to flash, wander along Milan's shopping triangle, the famous **Quadrilatero della Moda** – Via Manzoni, Via Montenapoleone, Via della Spiga and Via Sant Andrea Corso are home to some of the top designer names in the industry. The boutiques in the Navigli area in the southwest of the city have a range of quirkier, affordable clothing (nearest station metro Porto Genova).

Directory

Consulates Australia, Via Borgogna 2 Ⓣ02.7767.4200; Canada, Via V. Pisani 19 Ⓣ02.67.581; UK, Via San Paolo 7 Ⓣ02.723.001; US, Via Principe Amedeo 2/10 Ⓣ02.290.351.
Exchange The office in Stazione Centrale is a good bet, or Yex Xhange on Piazza Duomo.
Hospitals Fatebenefratelli, Corso Porta Nuova 23 Ⓣ02.63.631; Ospedale Maggiore Policlinico, Via Francesco Sforza 35 Ⓣ02.55.031.
Internet Piazza d'Aosta 14 (Mon–Sat 9am–10pm; €5.60/hr); Cabine/Navigore 2 Naviglio Pavese €2/hr.
Police Piazza San Sepolcro 9 Ⓣ02.62.261.
Post office Piazza Cordusio 2.

Moving on

Train Bologna (frequent; 1–3hr); Geneva (4 daily; 4hr); Lyon (3 daily – 1 direct; change at Chambery

A DAY-TRIP TO LAKE COMO

Trains leave for Como San Giovanni regularly from Milan's Grand Central station and take 35min, but it is a fair walk to the lake. Cheaper trains from Milan's Cadorna (every 30min; 1hr 15min; last return train Milan is around 9pm) station head to the more convenient North Lake Como station, which is only a five-minute walk from the lake. You can take a cruise (hop-on, hop-off ticket €8; ⓦwww.navigazionelagh.it) which stops at five points around the lake, and don't miss a wander round the enchanting, relaxed village of Torno in the southeast corner of the lake. If you fancy a picnic on Como's beautiful waterfront, drop by the supermarket opposite the North Como train station. Como's tourist offices are on Piazza Matteoti and on Via Maestri Comacini.

or Dijon; 5hr 30min); Paris (4 daily; 7–10hr); Rome (frequent; 3–4hr); Venice (every 30min; 2hr 30min–3hr 30min); Verona (every 30min; 1hr 30min); Vienna (5 daily; 11–14hr; 2 changes); Zagreb (1 daily; 11hr; change at Venice Mestre); Zurich (every 2hr; 3hr 45min).

GENOA

GENOA (Genova) has retained its reputation as a tough, cosmopolitan port but combines the beauty of Renaissance palaces dotted along the small, winding streets. The birthplace of Christopher Columbus, it was one of the five Italian maritime republics, and reached the height of its power in the fifteenth and sixteenth centuries. After a long period of economic decline, Genoa is successfully cleaning itself up, and the city now offers an interesting mix of ultra-modern architecture and amenities, and old-style streets and restaurants.

What to see and do

Genoa spreads outwards from its old town around the port in a confusion of tiny alleyways and old palaces. It is one of the oldest historical centres in Europe with the buzzing Piazza de Ferarri as the heartbeat of the city. Its people speak a near-impenetrable dialect – a mixture of Neapolitan, Calabrese and Portuguese.

Palazzo Ducale

From 1384 to 1515, except for brief periods of foreign domination, the doges ruled the city from the ornate, stuccoed **Palazzo Ducale** in Piazza Matteotti (Tues–Sun 10am–7pm; €4). Decorated with elaborate frescoes, the rooms are a sight to behold. Walk up the tower to the palace's cramped prison cells, which still contain the shackles and scrawled graffiti of prisoners past.

Cattedrale di San Lorenzo

The Gothic **Cattedrale di San Lorenzo** (daily 8am–noon & 3–7pm), complete with Baroque chancel, is home to the Renaissance chapel of St John the Baptist, whose remains once rested in the thirteenth-century sarcophagus. After a particularly bad storm, priests carried his casket through the city to placate the sea, and a commemorative procession takes place each June 24 to honour him. His reliquary is in the **treasury** (tours available Mon–Sat 9am–noon & 3–6pm; €4.50), along with a polished quartz plate on which, legend says, Salome received his severed head.

The waterfront

After generations of neglect Genoa's waterfront has recently undergone restoration and is gaining tourist appeal with a huge aquarium and lively markets and cafés near Piazza Caricamento.

Piazza Banchi and around

Behind Piazza Caricamento is a thriving commercial zone centred on **Piazza Banchi**, formerly the heart of the medieval city, off which the long **Via San Luca** leads north to the **Galleria**

Nazionale di Palazzo Spinola (Tues–Sat 8.30am–7.30pm, Sun 1.30–7.30pm; €6.50), displaying work by the Sicilian master Antonello da Messina. North of here is the wonderful **Via Garibaldi,** lined with frescoed and stuccoed Renaissance palaces; a walk down the street at night is a must. Two palaces are now museums housing Genoese paintings: the **Palazzi Bianco and Rosso** (Tues–Fri 9am–7pm, Sat & Sun 10am–7pm; joint ticket €8, ticket also includes Palazzi Torsi), adorned with fantastic chandeliers, mirrors, gilding and frescoed ceilings.

Christopher Columbus House

The childhood home and museum dedicated to the man who discovered the New World is on Piazza Dante. It is small but gives a fascinating insight into Columbus's life. Highlights include a bell reputedly from his flagship the *Santa Maria* (Sat & Sun 10am–6pm; €4).

Arrival

Air Genoa's airport is only a 20min bus ride from Stazione Principe, and buses run every 45min; tickets for the Volabus, a coach running to and from the airport, are €4 and are available from stations, *tabacchi* and aboard the bus itself.
Train Most trains stop at Milan's two stations, Stazione Principe in Piazza Acquaverde and Stazione Brignole in Piazza Verdi. It is an easy walk to the centre from either. There Is a metro system that connects the centre with Principe. If you have to travel between the two, take bus #28 or #33.
Bus Buses arrive at the main bus terminal outside Stazione Principe. From Principe the metro goes to the centre.
Ferry Ferries arrive at Ferry Terminale, a 10min walk downhill from Stazione Principe. Cruise ships arrive at Stazione Marittima.

Information

Tourist office Piazza de Ferrari, in the Felici Carlo theatre building (daily 9am–1pm & 2.30–6.30pm; ⓣ010.860.6122); a second is on Via Garibaldi (daily 9am–6.30pm; ⓣ010.248.5710). There are also small kiosks at the airport (9am–1pm & 1.30–5.30pm) and on Piazza Caricamento.
Discount passes The tourist office sells a Genoa pass, which gives you free use of all transport in the city, including lifts and funiculars (€4.50/24hr). The Museum Card gives access to most of the cities museums and free bus travel (€20/2 days).
Internet Internet Oblo, Magazzini del Cotone 3 (daily 11am–midnight; €2/hr).

Accommodation

The best areas to stay are the roads bordering the old town, and Piazza Colombo and on Via XX Settembre, Genoa's main shopping street which is near Stazione Brignole.
Astro Via XX Settembre 3/21 ⓣ010.581.533, ⓦwww.albergo-astro.com. Friendly one-star hotel on the seventh floor and very close to Stazione Brignole. The best rooms are the African or flower-themed rooms. Doubles €50.
Barone Via XX Settembre 2/23 ⓣ010.587.578, ⓦwww.hotelbaronegenova.it. Small hotel with light rooms and welcoming owners, 200m from Stazione Brignole. Doubles €55.
Genova Passo Costanzi 10 ⓣ010.242.2457, ⓦwww.hihostels.com. Friendly, clean and well-run HI hostel a 30min bus ride from centre with great views over the port. Single-sex dorm beds and internet access. Take bus #40 or (evening) #640 from Stazione Brignole. From Stazione Principe take bus #35 to Via Napoli and change to bus #40 or #640, alight at the stop on Via Constanzi, last bus departs Via Napoli around midnight. Dorms €16.50.
Villa Doria Via al Campeggio Villa Doria 15, Pegli ⓣ010.696.9600, ⓦwww.camping.it/liguria/villadoria. Leafy campsite 8km from Genoa, with its own café, shop and solarium: take a train to Pegli and then bus #93. €9/person, plus tent €10.

Eating and drinking

For cheap lunches, snacks and picnic ingredients, try the huge covered Mercato Orientale, halfway down Via XX Settembre in the cloisters of an Augustinian monastery. There are lots of restaurants and bars down Via Ravecca, a few hundred metres southeast of the port. For late-night drinking, head to the bars around Piazza delle Erbe, just south of Palazzo Ducale.
Exultate Piazza Lavagna 12. Popular pizzeria that brews its own beer. Lots of tables outside in an intimate piazza. Mon–Fri noon–2.30pm & 7pm–1am, Sat & Sun noon–2am.

Gloglo Piazza Lavagna 19r. *Aperitifs* come with tasty snacks at this relaxed place on a square. Staff are chatty and drinks are generous. Beer €5.

Il Clan Salita Pallavicini 16. Trendy bar packed to the rafters with the young and hip. Arrive early to bag one of the loft bed-seats. Closed Sun.

Louisiana Jazz Club Via S. Sebastiano 36r ⓦwww.louisianajazzclub.com. A drum reveals the entrance to this established and excellent jazz venue.

Sa Pesta Via Giustiniani 16 ⓣ010.246.8336. Extremely popular with locals, this place is well known for its good local cooking. Dishes from €9. Booking a table is essential. Closed Sun & Mon.

Trattoria da Maria Via Testadoro 14/b, just off Via XXV Aprile. No-nonsense, endearingly chaotic place up a grubby side street, which serves up simple Ligurian cooking at rock-bottom prices. Pasta €4.50. Dinner only on Thurs and Fri, lunch Mon–Sat, closed Sun.

Moving on

Train Bologna (frequent; 2–3hr); Milan (hourly; 1hr 30min); Naples (direct 2 daily; 8hr); Pisa (frequent; 2hr); Rome (every 2hr; 5–6hr).

Ferry Bastia (weekly, daily during summer; 4hr 45min); Olbia (daily in summer; 10hr); Palermo (6 weekly; 20hr); Porto Torres (daily; 11hr).

THE RIVIERA DI LEVANTE

A superb stretch of lush green hills sheltering beautiful seaside resorts, the **RIVIERA DI LEVANTE** stretches eastwards from Genoa. The ports that once survived on navigation, fishing and coral diving are now well versed in the ways of tourism, and while the resorts are hectic during summer months, the towns are still charming enough to ensure they're worth visiting. The coastline is wild and beautiful in parts and a coastal path meanders over the cliff-tops to each of the resorts. All the towns can be reached by train and boat.

Santa Margherita Ligure

Pretty **SANTA MARGHERITA LIGURE** is a small, palm-tree-lined resort, with a small pebble beach and concrete jetties to swim from. **Accommodation** options include the cheap, comfortable and friendly *Annabella*, Via Costasecca 10, just off Piazza Mazzini (ⓣ0185.286.531; €62) and *Istituto C.Colombo* (ⓦwww.casaferiecolombo.com; dorms €20), a large hostel on Via Dogali 2a. For good local **food**, try *Il Faro*, Via Marigliano 24a (closed Tues), the long-established *Da Pezzi* (closed Sat), at Via Cavour 21, a canteen-like locals' hangout serving pasta, grills and takeaway snacks, or *Osteria 7* (closed Wed) on Via Jacopis Ruffin 36, where great pastas are served on long wooden tables. The **tourist office** is in the middle of Piazza Vittorio Veneto (daily 9.30am–12.30pm & 2.30–5.30pm; ⓣ0185.287.485, ⓦwww.turismoinliguria.it). **Scooters** and **bikes** are a fun way of getting around: go to Via XXV Aprile 11 (ⓣ0185.284.420, ⓦwww.gmrent.it). Boats depart regularly in summer for Rapallo and the millionaires' playground that is the small village of Portofino (return €8).

Rapallo

RAPALLO is a lovely Riviera town just a forty-minute train ride from Genoa. Brightly coloured beach huts line parts of the pebbled shore, backed by an intriguing tangle of narrow lanes that are well worth a wander. The **tourist office** is at Lungo Vittorio Veneto 7 (Mon 9.30am–1pm, Tues–Fri 9.30am–1pm & 3.30–5.30pm, Sat 9.30am–1pm & 3.30–5.30pm, closed Sun; ⓣ0185.230.346). For decent **accommodation**, *Albergo Fernanda*, 9 Via Milite Ignoto (ⓣ0185.502.44, ⓦwww.hotelfernando.com; doubles €75) is a five-minute walk from the station and is close to a tiny beach. There are a couple of **campsites** – try the large, grassy *Rapallo* at Via San Lazzaro 4 (ⓣ0185.262.018, ⓦwww.campingrapallo.it; €6.50 per person, plus €10 per tent). The best place to **eat** is the authentic *Bansin*, at Via Venezia 105 (closed Sun lunch) in the heart of the old town. For a drink, head to *Enoteca Castello 10* on Lungamare Castello 6, which has lovely views of the castle and sea as well as an enormous menu of bruschetta (€4).

Cinque Terre

The **CINQUE TERRE** (Ⓦwww.parcnazionale5terre.it) is a series of five beautiful villages – **Monterosso**, **Vernazza**, **Corniglia**, **Manarola** and **Riomaggiore** – perched on tiny cliff-bound inlets lapped by azure-blue sea and linked by a coastal pathway. Trains from La Spezia in the south and Levanto in the north run three times an hour and stop at each of the villages. It's possible to visit all the villages in one day via the pathway, although it can get busy at peak seasons. Each village has a tourist office at its train station. The **Cinque Terre Card** (validity available for 1 weekday (€5) or 2 weekdays (€9), is sold at the tourist offices, (it is slightly more expensive on weekends). The card gives access to the paths and village lifts (where available). Other cards include train and hiking combos (1 day/€10; 2 days/€19). There's also a boat that stops at each of the villages every hour (€15/day; one-stop ticket €7). The liveliest of the villages is probably Monterosso, with its excellent large beach; a good place for a drink is *Ca Du Sciensa*, on leafy Piazza Garibaldi 17 just a stone's throw from the beach.

Accommodation tends to be expensive in summer months, at about €120 for a double room, or there are rental apartments that have to be taken for a week at a time. Tiny Manarola is the best of the villages for budget accommodation: the clean *Ostello Cinque Terre* on Via Riccobaldi 21 (Ⓣ0187.920.215, Ⓦwww.hostel5terre.com; €20) offers gorgeous views, delicious food and chilled-out communal spaces. To get there, head to the top of the town and turn left; it's the green building behind the church. For great views over Manarola and good local food take the steep walk up to *Trattoria Billy* on Via Aldo Rollando 122 (Ⓣ0187.920.628; booking recommended).

Northeast Italy

Venice, the premier draw in Northeast Italy, is one of Europe's most stunning –and unmissable – cities. The region around it, the **Veneto**, still bears the imprint of Venetian rule and continues to prosper. Gorgeous, vibrant **Verona** plays on its Shakespeare connections and centres on a fairly intact Roman amphitheatre, while nearby **Padua** hums with student activity and has some artistic and architectural masterpieces. South, between Lombardy and Tuscany, **Emilia-Romagna** is the heartland of northern Italy, a patchwork of ducal territories formerly ruled by a handful of families, whose castles and fortresses still stand proudly in well-preserved medieval towns. **Parma** is a wealthy provincial town worth visiting for its easy-going ambience and delicious food as well as masterful paintings by Parmigianino and Correggio. The coast is less interesting but, just south of the Po delta, **Ravenna** boasts probably the finest set of Byzantine mosaics in the world.

VERONA

The romantic city of **VERONA**, with its Roman sites and cobbled streets of impressive medieval buildings, stands midway between Milan and Venice. It reached its zenith as an independent city-state in the thirteenth century under the Scaligeri family, who were energetic patrons of the arts; many of Verona's finest buildings date from their rule.

What to see and do

The city centre nestles in a deep bend of the River Adige, and the main sight of

> **TREAT YOURSELF**
>
> Nowadays the Roman Arena is used as an **opera venue** for big summer productions. The sight of the stands lit up by the thousands of candles handed out to the audience is a pretty special one. The ticket office (☎045.800.5151, Ⓦwww.arena.it) is outside the arena. Prices begin at €23.

its southern reaches is the central hub of **Piazza Bra** and its mighty **Roman Arena** (Mon 1.30–7.30pm, Tues–Sun 8.30am–7.30pm; July & Aug closes 3.30pm; €4.50). Dating from the first century AD, this Roman amphitheatre originally held seating for twenty thousand (although now it houses the largest outdoor Opera stage in the world, see box above), and offers a tremendous panorama from the topmost of the 44 marble tiers.

Historical centre

To the north of the Roman amphitheatre, Via Mazzini, a narrow traffic-free street lined with expensive clothes shops and pricey *gelaterias* leads to a number of squares. The biggest and most appealing is Piazza Erbe, a pretty square with a market in the middle and cafés lining either side. From Erbe most of the major sights are within an easy walk. The adjacent Piazza dei Signori is flanked by the medieval **Palazzo degli Scaligeri**. At right angles to this is the fifteenth-century **Loggia del Consiglio**, the former assembly hall of the city council and Verona's outstanding early Renaissance building while, close by, the twelfth-century **Torre dei Lamberti** (same hours as Arena; €4.50 to walk or by lift) gives dizzying views of the city; be prepared to block your ears for the hourly ringing of the tower's bells. Juliet's house is situated on the nearby Via Capello 23 (Mon 1.30–7.30pm; Tues–Sun 8.30am–7.30pm; €6) – even if you don't want to pay to go inside the house, you can see the famous balcony, rub the right breast of her statue (supposedly for luck) and read some of the thousands of love messages dotted around the place.

Arche Scaligere and the Duomo

In front of the Romanesque church of **Santa Maria Antica**, the **Arche Scaligere** are the elaborate Gothic funerary monuments of Verona's first family, set in a wrought-iron palisade decorated with ladder motifs, the emblem of the Scaligeri. Nearby, on Via Arche Scaligere 4 is **Romeo's House**, marked by a lopsided sign. Verona's **Duomo**, with its unfinished bell tower (Tues–Sat 10am–6pm, Sun 1.30–5.30pm; €2.50) lies just around the river's bend, a mixture of Romanesque and Gothic styles that houses an *Assumption* by Titian.

Roman theatre

The **Roman theatre** (€4.50), on the north side of the river, is worth climbing up to for its gorgeous views. In July and August, a Shakespeare festival (in Italian, but it's still great to soak up the atmosphere) and a jazz festival make use of this amazing venue. There is a box office on Via Pallone 12 ☎045.8011.154 or you can buy at the venue; Ⓦwww.getticket.it. Ticket prices start at €10. If you want even better views of the city head up to Castelo San Pietro for the ultimate views of Verona.

Basilica di San Zeno Maggiore

A kilometre or so northwest, the **Basilica di San Zeno Maggiore** (Mon–Sat 8.30am–6pm, Sun 12.30–6pm; €2.50) is one of the most significant Romanesque churches in northern Italy. Its rose window, representing the Wheel of Fortune, dates from the twelfth century, as do the magnificent portal and medieval frescoes.

Arrival and information

Train The train station is connected with Piazza Bra by bus #11, #12, or #13. Alternatively, it's a straightforward 15min walk down Corso Porta Nuova.
Tourist office Via degli Alpini 9 Ⓦ www.tourism.verona.it (Mon–Sat 9am–7pm, Sun 9am–4pm).
Discount passes The Verona Card (€15/2 days or €20/5 days) covers most of Verona's museums and churches and can be purchased at the tourist offices, *tabacchis* and most museums.
Exchange Via Cappello 3 (Mon–Sat 9am–8.30pm), or at the station (daily 7.30am–8.30pm).
Internet The Internet Train on Via San Vitale 5/b (daily 7am–9pm, Sat & Sun 2–8pm) or Khan's services on Vicolo Ghaia 1f.

Accommodation

ACISJF-Protezione Della Giovane Via Pigna 7 Ⓣ 045.596.880, Ⓦ www.protezionedellagiovane.it. For women under 26 only, this simple, friendly and clean hostel is right in the old centre. The curfew is 11pm unless you're going to the opera. Take bus #73 or #96/#97 at night from the station to Piazza Erbe, from where it's a 5min walk. Dorms €22.

B&B Casa Nuvola Adigetto 21 Ⓣ 377.441.1906. This excellent B&B Is run by a friendly owner and the rooms are tastefully decorated, some with small balconies. Breakfast is particularly good. Doubles €50.

HI Hostel Via Fontana del Ferro 15 Ⓣ 045.590.360. One of Italy's best hostels, housed In a frescoed *palazzo* on the north side of the river, and surrounded by grandiose gardens. Take bus #72, #73 or #90 from the station. Dorms €20.

Eating and drinking

Retro Gusto Via Berni Francesco 1–3. This restaurant-deli serves wonderful home-made dishes, and has a fantastic wine list. Cheese-tasting platters & other mains from €9. Mon–Sat noon–3.30pm & 7–11pm.
Sottoriva 23 Via Sottoriva 42/a. This bar–restaurant on a lovely quiet street near the river has outdoor seating and serves cheap pizzas and good salads as well as a large choice of beers. Salads €6.50.
Square Via Sottoriva 15. Modern chic bar strong on cocktails. There's a DJ every Thursday evening. Beer and wine €3. Open from 6.30pm, earlier on weekends.

Trattoria Dal Ropetan Via Fontana Del ferro 1 Ⓣ 045.803.0040. Small restaurant tucked away among a maze of streets on the north side of the Po. The food is excellent and the friendly owner a law unto himself. Try the *penne del Ropetan* (€7). Booking recommended.
Trattoria Il Colonne Via Tezone 1. This place has a real community spirit and is a real family affair. No English spoken but this only adds to the charm. They serve an excellent daily pasta for €7.

Moving on

Train Milan (frequent; 1hr 30min–2hr); Padua (frequent; 45min–1hr 30min); Rome (8 direct daily; 3hr); Venice (every 30min; 1–2hr).

PADUA

Extensively rebuilt after World War II bomb damage and hemmed in by industrial sprawl, **PADUA** (Padova) is not the most alluring city in northern Italy. However, it's a particularly ancient city with a relaxed air and a sense of the real Italia. Donatello and Mantegna both worked here, and in the seventeenth century Galileo researched at the university.

What to see and do

Cappella degli Scrovegni

Just outside the city centre, through a gap in the Renaissance walls off **Corso Garibaldi**, the stunning Giotto frescoes in the lapis-ceilinged **Cappella degli Scrovegni**, affectionately referred to as the "scrawny chapel" for its diminutive size (slots for a 15 or 20min viewing must be booked, but bookable on the day if there is space; €13; Ⓣ 049.201.0020, Ⓦ www.cappelladegliscrovegni.it), are the main reason for coming to Padua. Commissioned in 1303 by Enrico Scrovegni in atonement for his father's usury, the chapel's walls are covered with breathtakingly detailed and largely well-preserved illustrations of the life of Mary, Jesus and the story of the Passion. It's a bit of a rush to see forty masterpieces in fifteen minutes, but well worth it.

Piazza del Santo

In the southwest of the city, down Via Zabarella from the *cappella*, is the starkly impressive **Piazza del Santo**. The main sight here is Donatello's **Monument to Gattamelata** of 1453, the earliest large bronze sculpture of the Renaissance. On one side of the square, the basilica of San Antonio, or **Il Santo**, was built to house the body of St Anthony (a famous disciple of St Francis of Assisi); the **Cappella del Tesoro** at the far end of the Duomo (daily 8am–12.45pm & 2.30–6.30pm) houses the saint's tongue and chin in a head-shaped reliquary.

The university

From the basilica, **Via Umberto** leads back towards the university, established in 1221, and older than any other in Italy except Bologna. The main block is the **Palazzo del Bo**, where Galileo taught physics from 1592 to 1610. The major sight is the sixteenth-century **anatomy theatre** (March–Oct tours Mon, Wed & Fri at 3.15pm, 4.15pm & 5.15pm, Tues, Thurs & Sat at 9.15am, 10.15am & 11.15am; Nov–Feb tours Mon, Wed & Fri at 3.15pm & 4.15pm, Tues, Thurs & Sat at 10.15am & 11.15am; €5; ⓣ049.827.3047, booking possible only for groups of ten or more).

Arrival and information

Air The best way to reach Venice Airport from Padua is by bus. There are hourly buses that go to Marco Polo airport via central Venice (1hr; €8). Tickets are bought from the kiosk in the bus station.
Train Padua train station is next to the bus station and is at the far end of Corso del Popolo, a five-minute walk north of the city walls or a short tram stop away. Padua also has a good tram system.
Tourist office Galleria Pedrocchi, just off Via 8 Febbraio (Mon–Sat 9am–1.30pm & 3–7pm; ⓣ049.876.7927, ⓦwww.turismopadova.it), plus another at the station (Mon–Sat 9am–7pm, Sun 9am–noon) and a small kiosk in Piazza Del Santo.
Discount passes The tourist office sells the 48hr Padova Card (48hr/€11; 72hr/€21), which gives access to certain museums (including Scrovegni Chapel frescoes), free bus travel and a parking space.

Accommodation

Albergo Verdi Via Dondi dall'Orologio 7 ⓣ049.836.4163, ⓔinfor@alberghoverdipadova.it. While it doesn't look much from the outside, *Albergo Verdi* has spacious rooms that are stylish and comfortable. There's a lovely breakfast terrace. Doubles €40.
Dante Via San Polo 5 ⓣ049.876.0408, ⓦwww.hoteldante.eu. This old-fashioned hotel could do with a facelift, however, it is one of the cheaper options and only a stone's throw from the sights. Doubles €65.
HI Hostel Via A. Aleardi 30 ⓣ049.875.2219. A large, somewhat soulless hostel, but the cheapest accommodation in town and near all the major sites. 11pm curfew. Bus #12 or #18 from the station (stop at Via Cavalletto). Dorms €19.
Sporting Center Via Roma 123 ⓣ049.793.400, ⓦwww.sportingcenter.it. Extremely well equipped, spacious campsite 15km away in Montegrotto Terme, with a reasonable two-star hotel on site (€64). Also a restaurant, large swimming pool and thermal spa. Served by frequent trains (15min). Per person and tent €16.50.

Eating and drinking

For eating on the go, there's a daily fruit market on Piazza Erbe, which also has a few cheap restaurants and bars. There is a supermarket, Pam, at Garzeria Piazzata 3 (Mon–Sat 8am–9pm, Sun 8am–2pm). On summer evenings, people sit in the centre of the scruffy Prato della Valle.
Cacao Café Via San Francesco 69. A good place for an evening drink with award-winning wines run by the friendly Andrea. Mon–Sat 5–10pm.
La Folperia Piazza della Fruitta. Max and Barbara bring their seafood stall to the square every night between 6.30–9pm. Mouth-watering and generous portions of *gamberi fritta*, calamari and other seafood served on paper plates. Portion around €4.
Osteria L'Anfora Via dei Soncin 13 ⓣ049.656.629. Fantastic *osteria* near Piazza Erbe and one of the few places you want to eat inside rather than outside even on a warm day. Delicious fresh pasta (from €9) is served in a large ramshackle room decorated with the owner's passions in mind. Booking recommended. Closed Sun.
Rossosapore Via Umberto I 6. There can't be many bakeries with a happy hour – between 9–11pm many delicious treats are reduced to only €1. Closed Mon.

Moving on

Train Bologna (frequent; 1hr–1hr 30min); Milan (frequent; 2–3hr); Parma (hourly; 2hr 30min; change at Bologna); Venice (every 10min; 45min); Verona (every 20min; 45min–1hr 30min).

VENICE

The first-time visitor to **VENICE** (Venezia) arrives with a heavy load of expectations, most of which won't be disappointed. It is an extraordinarily beautiful city, and the major sights are all they are cracked up to be. The downside is that Venice is very expensive and deluged with tourists. Twenty million come here each year, most seduced by the famous motifs – Carnival time (see p.677), glass ornaments and singing gondoliers. To avoid the mêlée, stroll down one of the intriguing and peaceful side streets or take a boat across to the Lido and relax on its lovely beach.

What to see and do

Piazza San Marco

Flanked by the Grand Canal, **Piazza San Marco** is probably the busiest square in the whole of Italy, let alone Venice. It's lined with some stunning architecture such as the dominating **Campanile** (Oct–March 9.45am–4pm; April–June 9am–7pm; July–Sept 9.45am–8pm; €8), which began life as a lighthouse in the ninth century, but is in fact a reconstruction: the original tower collapsed on July 14, 1902. It is the tallest structure in the city, and the 98m-high tower provides magnificent views of the neighbouring islands and lagoons, as well as the red-clay rooftops of the city.

Basilica di San Marco

Across the piazza, the **Basilica di San Marco** (March–Nov Mon–Sat 9.45am–5pm, Sun 2–5pm; Nov–March Mon–Sat 9.45am–5pm, Sun 2–4pm) is the most exotic of Europe's cathedrals, modelled on Constantinople's Church of the Twelve Apostles, finished in 1094 and embellished over the succeeding centuries with trophies brought back from abroad. Inside, a steep staircase leads from the church's main door up to the **Museo di San Marco** and the **Loggia dei Cavalli** (March–Oct 9.45am–4.45pm; April–Sept 9.45am–5pm; €4), where you can enjoy fine views of the city and the Gothic carvings along the apex of the facade. However, it's the **Sanctuary**, off the south transept (March–Nov Mon–Sat 9.45am–5pm, Sun 2–5pm; Nov–March Mon–Fri 9.45am–4pm, Sun 2–4pm; €2), that holds the most precious of San Marco's treasures, the **Pala d'Oro**, or golden altar panel, commissioned in 976 in Constantinople. This mind-blowingly intricate explosion of gold, enamel, pearls and gemstones is generally considered to be one of the greatest accomplishments of Byzantine craftsmanship. The **Treasury** (same times; €3) is a similarly dazzling warehouse of chalices, reliquaries and candelabra, while the tenth-century **Icon of the Madonna of Nicopeia** (in the chapel on the east side of the north transept) is the most revered religious image in

VENICE ORIENTATION

The 118 islands of central Venice are divided into six districts known as *sestieri*, with that of **San Marco** (enclosed by the lower loop of the Canal Grande) home to most of the essential sights. On the east it's bordered by **Castello**, to the north by **Cannaregio**. On the other side of the Canal Grande is **Dorsoduro**, which stretches from the fashionable quarter at the southern tip of the canal to the docks in the west. **Santa Croce** roughly follows the curve of the Canal Grande from Piazzale Roma to a point just short of the Rialto, where it joins the smartest of the districts on this bank, **San Polo**.

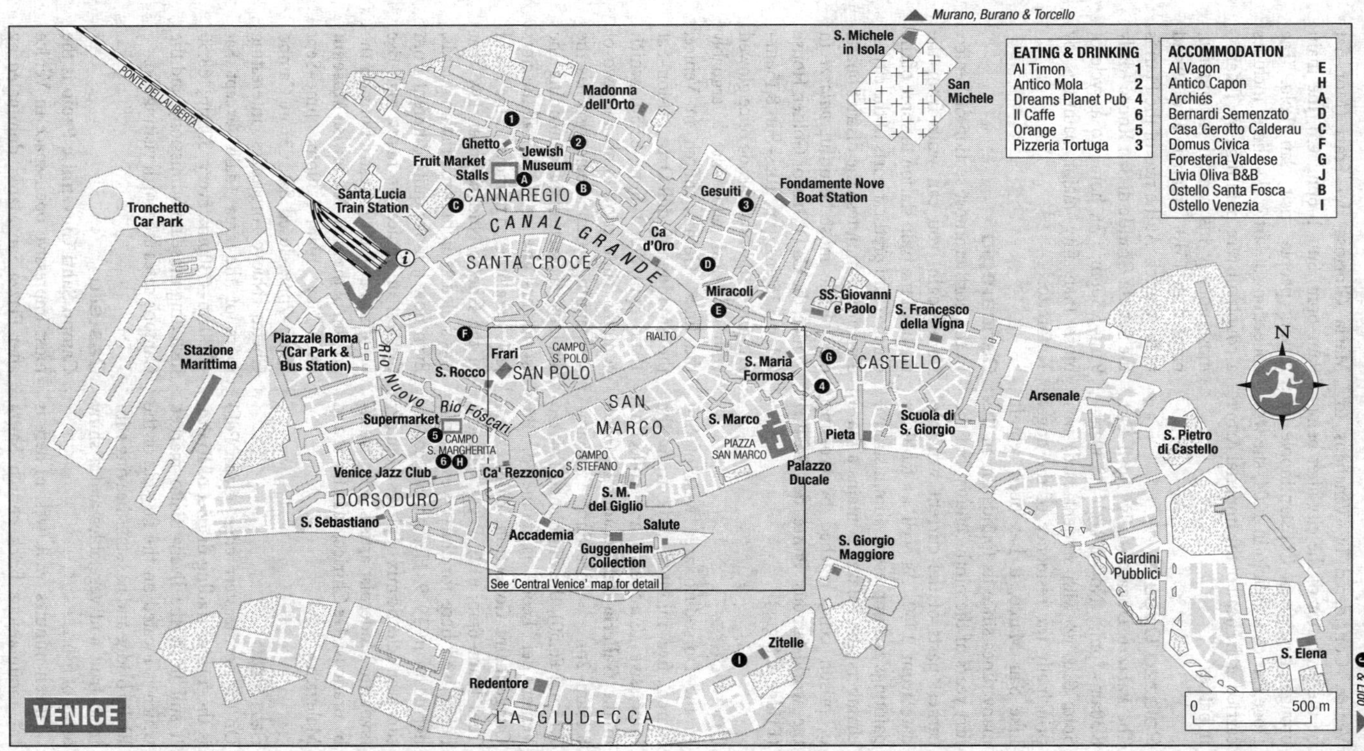
VENICE
Murano, Burano & Torcello
EATING & DRINKING
Al Timon 1
Antico Mola 2
Dreams Planet Pub 4
Il Caffe 6
Orange 5
Pizzeria Tortuga 3
ACCOMMODATION
Al Vagon E
Antico Capon H
Archiés A
Bernardi Semenzato D
Casa Gerotto Calderau C
Domus Civica F
Foresteria Valdese G
Livia Oliva B&B J
Ostello Santa Fosca B
Ostello Venezia I
S. Michele in Isola
San Michele
PONTE DELLA LIBERTÀ
Tronchetto Car Park
Madonna dell'Orto
Ghetto
Jewish Museum
Fruit Market Stalls
Santa Lucia Train Station
CANNAREGIO
CANAL GRANDE
Gesuiti
Fondamente Nove Boat Station
Ca d'Oro
SANTA CROCE
Miracoli
SS. Giovanni e Paolo
S. Francesco della Vigna
Stazione Marittima
Piazzale Roma (Car Park & Bus Station)
Rio Nuovo
Frari
CAMPO S. POLO
RIALTO
SAN POLO
S. Rocco
S. Maria Formosa
CASTELLO
N
Arsenale
SAN MARCO
Rio Foscari
Supermarket
S. Marco
PIAZZA SAN MARCO
Pieta
Scuola di S. Giorgio
S. Pietro di Castello
CAMPO S. MARGHERITA
CAMPO S. STEFANO
Venice Jazz Club
Ca' Rezzonico
Palazzo Ducale
DORSODURO
S. M. del Giglio
S. Sebastiano
Accademia
Salute
Guggenheim Collection
S. Giorgio Maggiore
Giardini Pubblici
See 'Central Venice' map for detail
Zitelle
S. Elena
Redentore
J & Lido
LA GIUDECCA
0
500 m

Venice. Considered by Venetians to be the protector of the city after being brought here from Constantinople by Doge Enrico Dandolo in 1204, she was carried at the head of the Imperial Army in battles.

Palazzo Ducale

The **Palazzo Ducale** (daily: April–Oct 8.30am–7pm; Nov–March 8.30am–5pm; €14, €8 with student card) was principally the residence of the doge. Like San Marco, it has been rebuilt many times since its foundation in the first years of the ninth century, but the earliest parts of the current structure date from 1340. As well as fabulous paintings and impressive administrative chambers, the Palazzo contains a maze of prison cells, reached by crossing the world-famous **Ponte dei Sospiri** (Bridge of Sighs).

Dorsoduro

In the Dorsoduro area west of San Marco, five minutes' walk from the impressive European art collection in the **Galleria dell'Accademia** (Mon 8.15am–2pm, Tues–Sun 8.15am–7.15pm; €6.50), the unfinished Palazzo Venier dei Leoni is home of the **Guggenheim Collection** (daily except Tues 10am–6pm; €12). Peggy Guggenheim lived here for thirty years until her death in 1979. Her private collection is an eclectic mix of pieces from her favourite Modernist artists, with works by Brancusi, De Chirico, Max Ernst and Malevich.

San Polo

On the northeastern edge of **San Polo** is the former trading district of **Rialto**. It still hosts the lively Rialto market, which is located on the far side of the Rialto bridge and has stalls heaving with fresh fruit and vegetables and a shiny array of fish.

Fifteen minutes' walk west of here is the mountainous brick church **Santa Maria Gloriosa dei Frari** (Mon–Sat 9am–6pm, Sun 1–6pm; €3), the main reason people visit San Polo. The collection of artworks here includes a couple of rare paintings by Titian – most notably his radical *Assumption*, painted in 1518. Titian is also buried in the church. At the rear of the Frari is the **Scuola Grande di San Rocco** (daily 9am–5.30pm; €7), home to a cycle of more than fifty major paintings by Tintoretto.

Cannaregio

In the northernmost section of Venice, **Cannaregio**, you can walk from the bustle of the train station to some of the quietest and prettiest parts of the city in a matter of minutes. The district boasts one of the most beautiful *palazzi* in Venice, the **Ca D'Oro**, or Golden House (Mon 8.15am–2pm, Tues–Sun 8.15am–7.15pm; €9), whose facade once glowed with gold leaf, and what is arguably the finest Gothic church in Venice, the **Madonna dell'Orto** (Mon–Sat 10am–5pm, Sun 1–5pm; €2.50), which contains Tintoretto's tomb and two of his paintings. Cannaregio also has the dubious distinction of containing the world's first **ghetto:** in 1516, all the city's Jews were ordered to move to the island of the **Ghetto Nuovo**, an enclave that was sealed at night by Christian guards. Even now it looks quite different from the rest of Venice, its many high-rise buildings a result of restrictions on the growth of the area. The **Jewish Museum** (Oct–May 10am–5.30pm; June–Sept 10am–7pm; closed Sat; €3) in Campo Ghetto Nuovo organizes interesting tours of the area (daily except Sat 10.30am–4.30pm; every 30min; €8.50 including museum admission), and the Campo's **cafés** are worth visiting too.

Castello

Campo Santi Giovanni e Paolo is the most impressive open space in Venice after Piazza San Marco, dominated by the huge brick church of **Santi Giovanni e Paolo** (San Zanipolo), founded by the Dominicans in 1246 and best known for its funeral monuments to 25 doges. The other essential sight in **Castello** is the **Scuola di San Giorgio degli Schiavoni** (Mon 2.45–6pm, Tues–Sat 9.15am–1pm & 2.45–6pm, Sun 9.15am–1pm; €3), to the east of San Marco, set up by Venice's Slav population in 1451. The building has a superb cycle by Vittore Carpaccio on the ground floor.

Venice's other islands

Immediately south of the Palazzo Ducale, Palladio's church of **San Giorgio Maggiore** (daily: Oct–April 9.30am–12.30pm & 2.30–4.30pm; May–Sept 9.30am–12.30pm & 2.30–6pm; €5) stands on the island of the same name and has two pictures by Tintoretto in the chancel – *The Fall of Manna* and *The Last Supper*. On the left of the choir a corridor leads to the **Campanile** (same hours as San Giorgio Maggiore), one of the best vantage points in the city. The long island of **La Giudecca**, to the west, was where the wealthiest aristocrats of early Renaissance Venice built their villas. The main reason to come today is the Franciscan church of the **Redentore** (Mon–Sat 10am–5pm; €3), designed by Palladio in 1577 in thanks for Venice's deliverance from a plague that killed a third of the population. The **Lido**, home to the world's oldest film festival, is a ten-minute boat ride from San Marco (take traghetto #1 or #51) and in summer is a great place to escape the crowds. The quietest stretch of free beach is at the Ospedale Al Mare end of Lungomare Gabriele D'Annunzio.

Arrival and information

Air The city's Marco Polo airport is on the edge of the lagoon, linked to the city centre by ACTV bus #5 (€5) and ATVO bus (€5) across Ponte della Libertà, and the more expensive waterbus run by Alilaguna Ⓦwww.alilaguna.it (from €15).

Train Santa Lucia train station is on the north side of the canal, to the west of the city centre. Waterbus services run to San Marco, and you can cross over the Ponte degli Scalzi bridge to reach San Polo or follow the canal along to get to Cannaregio.

Bus All road traffic comes into the city at Piazzale Roma, at the head of the Canal Grande, from where waterbus services run to all parts of Venice.

Tourist office There are many tourist offices in Venice, many of which become impossibly busy; they include San Marco 71/f (daily 9am–3.30pm; Ⓣ041.529.8711, Ⓦwww.turismovenezia.it) and another on Ex Giardini Reali (daily noon–6pm). There are also desks at the train station (close to platform 1), on Piazza Roma and at the airport.

Discount passes Available at the tourist offices (see above) or online at Ⓦwww.veniceconnected.com. The Museum Pass (€18, valid 6 months) gives entry to most of the main civic museums (it does not include the Accademia or Guggenheim); the Museum Card (valid 3 months; €14), gets you into the museums on Piazza San Marco; and the Chorus Pass (€10), provides entry to fourteen churches. There's also the Venezia Card, available from any of the numerous HelloVenezia outlets in the city (Ⓦwww.venicecard.it; €39.90, valid for 7 days) and covering most museums and 16 churches.

City transport

Despite its tangle of narrow, people-choked streets, walking is the fastest way of getting around Venice – you can cross the whole city in an hour.

Gondola The *traghetti* (ferries) that cross the Canal Grande (€0.50 for the 3-minute trip, finish around 9pm) are a cheap way of getting a ride on a gondola. These old gondolas, stripped of their finery and rowed by two oarsmen, cross from five piers between the station and the Bacino San Marco (the stretch of water along San Marco), look out for signs reading "traghetto Gondola". Otherwise, the boats are ludicrously expensive, though split between six people they become more affordable: the official tariff is €80 for 40min but you may be quoted up to €100 for 45min and an extra €100 for a singer.

Waterbus Waterbuses (*vaporetto*) vary in comfort and get packed during peak seasons (school holiday times and summer in particular) but they are a fun way to see the city. Many have small areas of outdoor seating, but you need to be at the front of the queue to get these. In winter blankets are issued on some routes. Tickets are available from most landing stages and from any Hellovenezia kiosk. They can also be bought In advance at Ⓦwww.veniceconnected.com. Flat-rate fares are

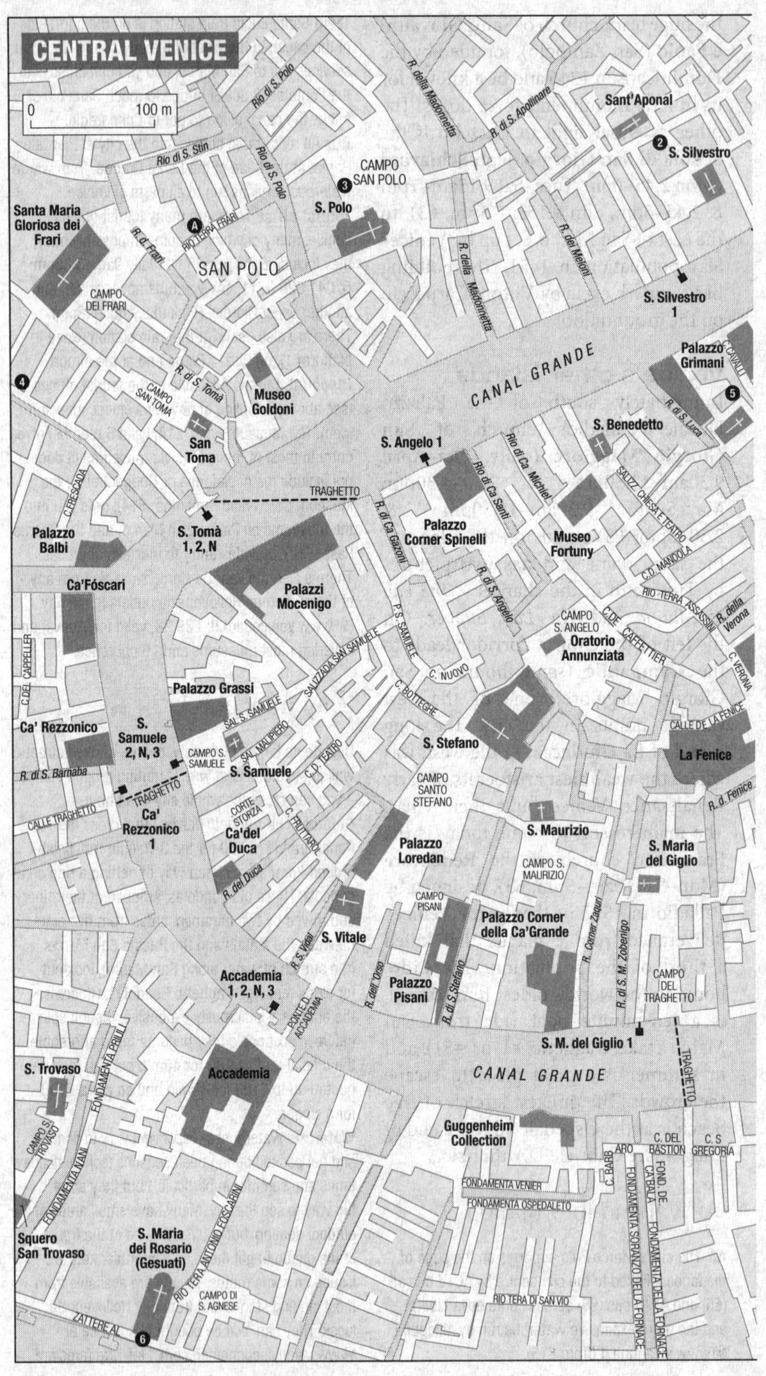
CENTRAL VENICE
0
100 m
Sant'Aponal
S. Silvestro
CAMPO SAN POLO
S. Polo
Santa Maria Gloriosa dei Frari
SAN POLO
CAMPO DEI FRARI
S. Silvestro 1
Palazzo Grimani
CANAL GRANDE
Museo Goldoni
CAMPO SAN TOMÀ
San Toma
S. Benedetto
S. Angelo 1
TRAGHETTO
Palazzo Balbi
S. Tomà 1, 2, N
Palazzo Corner Spinelli
Museo Fortuny
Ca'Fóscari
Palazzi Mocenigo
CAMPO S. ANGELO
Oratorio Annunziata
Palazzo Grassi
Ca' Rezzonico
S. Samuele 2, N, 3
CAMPO S. SAMUELE
S. Samuele
S. Stefano
La Fenice
CAMPO SANTO STEFANO
Ca' Rezzonico 1
Ca'del Duca
Palazzo Loredan
S. Maurizio
CAMPO S. MAURIZIO
S. Maria del Giglio
CAMPO PISANI
Palazzo Corner della Ca'Grande
S. Vitale
Accademia 1, 2, N, 3
Palazzo Pisani
CAMPO DEL TRAGHETTO
S. M. del Giglio 1
S. Trovaso
Accademia
CANAL GRANDE
Guggenheim Collection
FONDAMENTA VENIER
FONDAMENTA OSPEDALETO
Squero San Trovaso
S. Maria dei Rosario (Gesuati)
CAMPO DI S. AGNESE
RIO TERA DI SAN VIO
ZATTERE AL
RIO TERA ANTONIO FOSCARINI
FONDAMENTA PRIULI
FONDAMENTA NANI
FONDAMENTA SORANZO DELLA FORNACE
FONDAMENTA DELLA FORNACE

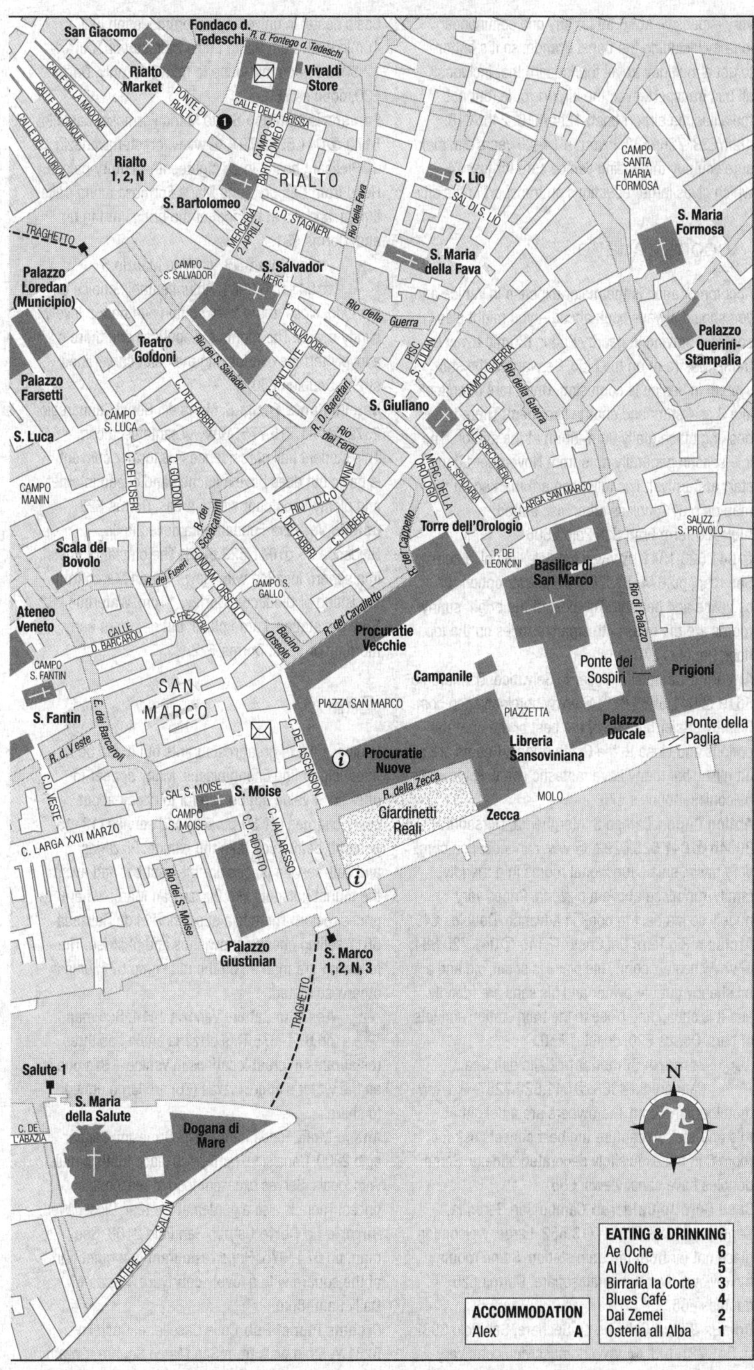
San Giacomo
Fondaco d. Tedeschi
Rialto Market
Vivaldi Store
Rialto 1, 2, N
RIALTO
S. Bartolomeo
S. Lio
CAMPO SANTA MARIA FORMOSA
S. Maria Formosa
TRAGHETTO
Palazzo Loredan (Municipio)
S. Salvador
S. Maria della Fava
Teatro Goldoni
Palazzo Querini-Stampalia
Palazzo Farsetti
S. Giuliano
S. Luca
CAMPO S. LUCA
CAMPO MANIN
Torre dell'Orologio
Scala del Bovolo
Basilica di San Marco
Ateneo Veneto
Procuratie Vecchie
Campanile
Ponte dei Sospiri
Prigioni
S. Fantin
SAN MARCO
PIAZZA SAN MARCO
PIAZZETTA
Palazzo Ducale
Ponte della Paglia
Libreria Sansoviniana
Procuratie Nuove
S. Moise
Giardinetti Reali
Zecca
MOLO
Palazzo Giustinian
S. Marco 1, 2, N, 3
Salute 1
S. Maria della Salute
Dogana di Mare
ZATTERE AL SALON
ACCOMMODATION
Alex A
EATING & DRINKING
Ae Oche 6
Al Volto 5
Birraria la Corte 3
Blues Café 4
Dai Zemei 2
Osteria all Alba 1

very expensive at €6.50 for any one continuous journey including the Canal Grande, so it's better to get a multiday travel tourist card that includes all bus transport, even the airport route (but not the alilaguna airport boat) 12hr /€16; 24hr/€18, 48hr/€28, 72hr/€33. If you're 14–29 years old, make sure you buy the Rolling Venice card for just €4, which gives large reductions on transport in the city.

Accommodation

Accommodation is the major expense in Venice and you should always book ahead – you might also consider staying in nearby Padua (30min away by train), Mestre or on the Lido. Be warned the star system in Venice is confusing. One-stars often look like 3 or 4 stars and charge like them. There is a booking office (daily 9am–8pm) at the station. The low season generally runs from November till the start of Carnival. The following are marked on the map on p.671, unless otherwise stated.

Alex Rio Terra Frari San Polo 2606 ⓣ041.523.1341, ⓦwww.hotelalexinvenice.com. See map, pp.674–675. Cosy one-star option run by Velice and her son. The best of the bright sunny rooms are the ones with small terraces on the top floor. Doubles €70.

Al Vagon Campiello Riccardo Selvatico, Cannaregio 5619 ⓣ041.5285.626, ⓦwww.hoteloalvagon.com. Slightly pricier but one of the best of the one-star options and close to the Rialto bridge. Rooms are a bit glitzy, but many have fantastic canal views and balconies. Doubles €70.

Antico Capon Campo S. Margherita, Dorsoduro 3004b ⓣ041.528.5292, ⓦwww.anticocapon.com. Very basic, small, functional rooms in a friendly, family-run place above a pizzeria. Prices vary hugely so it's best to book in advance. Doubles €45.

Archie's Rio Terra Del Cristo 1814b ⓣ041.720.884, ⓦwww.hostelz.com. This place is small, old and a bit shabby but the owner and his sons are friendly and it is cheap and close to the train station and lots of bars. Dorms €20, doubles €50.

Bernardi Semenzato Calle dell'Oca, Cannaregio 4366 ⓣ041.522.7257, ⓦwww.hotelbernardi.com.The owners are a delight at this one-star. To capture the best sunsets ask for room 8 in the exquisitely decorated annexe. Some doubles have canal views, €55.

Casa Gerotto Calderan Campo San Geremia, Cannaregio 283 ⓣ041.715.562. Large, welcoming place not far from the train station. Some rooms have views over the small square. Dorms €25, doubles €65.

Domus Civica Calle De Le Sechere, San Polo 3082 ⓣ041.721.103, ⓦwww.domuscivica.com. Very basic hostel in university accommodation just a 10min walk from Santa Lucia train station. Curfew 12.30am. Open mid-June to mid-Sept only. Dorms €30, doubles €60.

Foresteria Valdese Santa Maria Formosa, Castello 5170 ⓣ041.528.6797, ⓦwww.foresteriavenezia.it. Pleasant hostel in an eighteenth-century palace. Head from Campo Santa Maria Formosa along Calle Lunga, and it's at the foot of the bridge at the far end. Dorms €31.

Livia Oliva B&B Via Aldo Mauzio 5 ⓣ041.526.2981. An unbeatable choice on the Lido, close to the ferry station and near a lovely sandy beach. The rooms are spotless and there's a lovely terrace overlooking the quiet canal-lined street. Doubles €50.

Ostello Santa Fosca S. Maria dei Servi, Cannaregio 2372 ⓣ041.715.775, ⓦwww.santafosca.com. This student hall of residence in a former convent is basic but does have a kitchen and cheap internet and plenty of outdoor sitting areas. Dorms €23.

Ostello Venezia Fondamenta delle Zitelle, Giudecca 86 ⓣ041.523.8211. The official HI hostel, in a superb location with views of San Marco from the island of Giudecca. Curfew 11pm. Waterbus #82 from the station. Large place, but get there early morning or book. Dorms €22.

Eating

Venice is full of great restaurants but it can be a minefield to find cheap places. Many appear to offer good value but be careful to check about cover charges (€1.50/person) and service (12–15 percent) before you take the plunge. Pizzerias and self-service places are the best bet and avoid the tourist hotspots like Piazza San Marco where prices rocket. There is a supermarket on Salizada 5817 selling cheap sandwiches and pastries. The following are marked on the map on p.671, unless otherwise stated.

Ae Oche Zattere Venezia 1414. See map, pp.674–675 This pizzeria chain has three restaurants in great locations in Venice – this one is on the water's edge. Pizzas (€6) are large enough to share.

Antico Mola Fondamenta degli Ormesini, Cannaregio 2800. Canalside, family-run place that's popular with locals. Serves excellent food at reasonable prices. There Is also a garden at the rear. Closed Wed.

Birraria La Corte Campo San Polo 2168. See map, pp.674–675. Huge restaurant in a quiet part of the square with a lovely courtyard. Pizzas €7. Daily 9am–8pm.

Dreams Planet Pub Calle Casellerie, Castello 5281. A 5min walk from San Marco Square, *Dreams*

Planet is an international pub that screens sporting events open until 2am. Serves a vast range of pizzas and delicious seafood. A bit pricey but the tourist menus are good value.

Pizzeria Tortuga Campo dei Gesuiti, Cannaregio 4888. Excellent pizzeria-bar located near the waterfront. Serves a large choice of bruschetta and speciality salads. Pizzas from €6. Closed Mon.

Drinking and nightlife

Venice is short on clubbing action, however, there are plenty of bars, particularly around Campo Santa Margherita and Campo San Giacomo, where you can relax and enjoy some evening drinks. Many bars close around 8pm. The following are marked on the map on p.671, unless otherwise stated.

Al Timon Fondamenta degli Ormesini, Cannaregio 2754. Great late-night bar by the water's edge that has a wonderful wine selection (glass from €5). Closed Mon.

Al Volto Calle Cavalli, San Marco 4081, near Campo S. Luca. See map, pp.674–675. Stocks over one hundred wines from Italy and elsewhere and serves up a different risotto every day at lunchtime for €6. No credit cards. Closes 11pm, closed Sun.

Blues Café Dorsoduro 3778, near Frari Church. See map, pp.674–675. One of the few places you can enjoy a burger in Venice. Good coffee and large choice of bottled beers. There is live music on Fri & Sat nights. Burgers, wraps and sandwiches €6.50. Mon–Fri 10am–2am, Sat & Sun 3pm–2am.

Dai Zemei off the Rughetta del Ravano, San Polo 1045. See map, p.674–675. Run by the twins who give this place its name this traditional *enoteca* on a tiny side street serves a huge range of great *cechetti*. Beer €3.

Il Caffe Campo Santa Marguerita 2963. This tiny bar draws a large crowd. Either stand outside or join the chilled out throng who sit in the square. Medium beer €4. Closed Sun.

Orange Campo Santa Margherita, Dorsoduro 3054. As the name implies this place is bright orange. A laidback, modern bar in a lively, atmospheric square. Buffet served between 6–8pm. Medium beer €5.

Osteria All Alba San Marco 5370/71. See map, p.674–675. Popular wine bar by the Rialto bridge; pick from their large wine menu or scribble a message on the tastefully graffitied walls inside. Glass of wine from €3. Tues–Sun 9am–1am.

Entertainment

The city's opera house, La Fenice, has been completely rebuilt after a calamitous fire in 1996 (Ⓣ041.786.511, Ⓦwww.teatrolafenice.it) and puts on excellent performances. The most famous celebrated annual event is **Carnival** (Carnevale), which occupies the ten days leading up to Lent, finishing on Shrove Tuesday with a masked ball, dancing in the Piazza San Marco, street parties, pageants and performances. There's also live jazz throughout the year at the popular Venice Jazz Club (Fondamenta dello Squero 3102 Ⓣ340.150.4985, Ⓦwww.venicejazzclub.com). To find out about **concerts and events** going on throughout the city head to one of the tourist offices. Alternatively, check out websites Ⓦwww.hellovenezia.com, Ⓦwww.musicinvenice.co or Ⓦwww.veniceconcerts.com.

Directory

Exchange Strada Nuova 4194 (daily 9am–6.30pm).

Hospital Ospedale Civili Riunti di Venezia, Campo Santi Giovanni e Paolo (Ⓣ041.523.0000).

Internet Calle delle Occa, Cannaregio 4426a (Mon–Sat 10am–10.30pm; €3/hr).

Police Fondamenta di San Lorenzo (Ⓣ041.270.5511).

Post office Salizada del Fontego dei Tedeschi 5554, by the Rialto bridge (Mon–Fri 8.30am–2pm, Sat 8.30am–1pm).

Moving on

Train Bologna (frequent; 1–2hr); Florence (hourly; 2hr); Milan (every 30min; 2hr 30min–3hr 30min); Padua (every 10min; 15–45min); Trieste (frequent; 2hr); Verona (frequent; 1hr 30min).

BOLOGNA

BOLOGNA is the oldest university town in Europe (the institution dates back to the eleventh century) and teems with students and bookshops. Known for its left-wing politics, "Red Bologna" has long been the Italian Communist Party's spiritual home. The birthplace of Marconi boasts some of the richest food in Italy, a busy cultural life and a convivial café and bar scene.

What to see and do

The compact, colonnaded city centre is famous for its 38km of covered arcades, built to cover the horses brought to Bologna by the first university students, and is still startlingly medieval in plan.

Piazza Maggiore and around

Buzzing **Piazza Maggiore** is the heart of the city, dominated by the basilica of **San Petronio**, which was originally intended to have been larger than St Peter's in Rome. On the piazza's western edge, the Palazzo D'Accursio holds the **Museo Morandi** (Tues–Fri 9am–6.30pm, Sat & Sun 10am–6.30pm; free), dedicated to the works of one of Italy's most important twentieth-century painters. Just north of the square, in the centre of Piazza del Nettuno, is the marble and bronze **Fountain of Neptune**, a famous emblem of the city. Created by Giambologna in the late sixteenth century, it shows the sea-god lording it over an array of cherubs, mermaids and dolphins. There's a free open-air **cinema** in Piazza Maggiore in the summer (June–Sept) showing arty and black and white films – ask at the tourist office (see opposite) for details.

Archiginnasio

Bologna's university – the **Archiginnasio** – was founded at more or less the same time as the Piazza Maggiore, though it didn't get a special building until 1565. The most interesting portion is the **Teatro Anatomico** (Mon–Fri 9am–6.45pm, Sat 9am–1.45pm; €6), the original medical faculty dissection theatre, whose tiers of seats surround a professor's chair, covered with a canopy supported by figures known as *gli spellati* – the skinned ones.

Piazza San Domenico

South, down Via Garibaldi, **Piazza San Domenico** is the site of the church of **San Domenico**, built in 1251 to house the relics of St Dominic. The angel and figures of saints Proculus and Petronius were the work of a very young Michelangelo. It also holds a crucifix by Pizzano.

Due Torri

At Piazza di Porta Ravegnana, the **Torre degli Asinelli** (daily 9am–6pm; €3) and perilously leaning **Torre Garisenda** are together known as the Due Torri, the only significant survivors of 180 towers that were scattered across the city during the Middle Ages, when possession of the towers determined the ranks of power within the city. Superstition holds that any student who enters these towers before graduation won't graduate at all. The climb up the 498 steps to the top of the Torre degli Asinelli is tough and takes about fifteen minutes but you'll be rewarded with spectacular views over Bologna's rooftops.

Arrival and information

Air Bologna's airport is northwest of the centre, linked by Aerobus (every 15min; 25min; €6) to the train station and Via dell' Indipendenza in the centre of town.

Train The train station is on Piazza delle Medaglie d'Oro – about a 20min walk to the centre along Via dell'Indipendenza, or take bus #30 or #25 (€1.20).

Bus All long-distance buses terminate in Piazza XX Settembre, next to the train station. Bus company Sena runs services to Naples, Rome and Siena Ⓦwww.sena.it.

Tourist office Piazza Maggiore 1e (daily 9am–7pm; Ⓣ051.239.660); provides the free bi-monthly English-language magazine *L'Ospite di Bologna*.

Internet Internet Point at Via San Vitale 27a (daily 9am–10pm; €1/hr).

City transport

Walking is the best way to see Bologna, as the compact centre can be crossed in under 30min.

Bike rental Autorimessa Pincio, Via dell' Indipendenza 71z Ⓣ051.24.90.81 (4min walk from the train station; €1.50/hr, €15/day).

City Red Bus Ⓦwww.cityredbus.com. Offers a day ticket for just €12 and is a great way to explore Bologna outside the city centre.

Accommodation

Trade fairs take place several times a year (March to early May & Sept–Dec are peak times), during which prices can double – so it's best to book ahead. There's a free accommodation booking service in the tourist office (Ⓣ051.648.7607).

Albergo Pallone Via del Pallone 4 Ⓣ051.421.0533, Ⓦwww.albergopallone.it. Basic but clean place in a somewhat unattractive building. Rooms a bit clinical, but it has a friendly hostel feel and good staff. No breakfast. Doubles €50.

Hostel San Sisto-Due Torri Via Viadagola 5 & 14 ⓣ051.501.810. A 25min bus ride from town (#93 from Via Dei Mille or Via Irenenio from 6am–8pm, every 30min; at night hourly 8pm–12.40am take bus #21/B from across the road from the station or Via Marconi; the hostel's stop is San Sisto). This large friendly HI hostel is in a quiet location well out of the centre. It has big dorms, sitting room and lots of outdoor space. Dorms €17, doubles €40.

Panorama Via Livraghi 1 ⓣ051.221.802, ⓦwww.hotelpanoramabologna.it. Friendly mother-and daughter-run place. Located near Piazza Maggiore, rooms are spacious and bright and some have lovely views over the hills. They also have a 4-bed room at €22/person. Doubles €59.

Pensione Marconi Via Marconi 22 ⓣ051.262.832, ⓦwww.pensionemarconi.it. This one-star doesn't look particularly inviting, but the 44 rooms inside are clean if basic. Ask for a room at the back, as it's on a major road. Doubles €55.

Eating

There's a central supermarket at Via Garibaldi 1, 5min south of Piazza Maggiore, as well as some great food markets: the Mercato delle Erbe at Via Ugo Bassi 25 is a covered produce market, while the lively street markets that cram Via Drapperie and Via Orefici, just off Piazza Maggiore, are perfect for snacks and picnics. Many cheap restaurants are in the popular student streets around Piazza Verdi.

AF Tamburini Via Drapperie 2. This renowned deli, its ceiling thick with hanging sausages and hams, sells no end of picnic food. The deli also has an Indoor self-service restaurant that does pastas at €5.

Altero Via dell' Indipendenza 33. This popular chain of pizza takeaways does excellent square-shaped pizza by the slice (€2) till 1am.

Il Doge Via Caldarese 5. Backstreet pizzeria close to the Due Torri which doles out pizzas for around €7, as well as regional specialities. Tues–Sun noon–3pm & 7pm–midnight.

ITIT Lago Resighi 2f. Modern coffee and sandwich establishment has great comfy seating and cheap sandwiches. Closed Mon.

Osteria al 15 Via Mirasole 13. A lovely old-fashioned trattoria with no menu (the waiter recites the day's specials), enormous portions and very fair prices. Full meal €15. Closed Sun.

Drinking

One of the cheapest and liveliest areas is the pub and bar-lined Via Zamboni, where the university students hang out. It is also worth heading to Via Mollini, Via Righi as well as Via dei Pratello for a more local feel.

Bounty Pub Via Delle Moline 6b. This place does a good value *aperitivo* buffet and has cheap lunchtime deals.

English Empire Via Zamboni 24/a. A lively English-style pub; during happy hour (daily 7–9pm), the *aperitivo* buffet is sufficient to make up dinner. Jamming sessions every Monday night from 7–10pm. Beer €4. Open till 3am.

La Scuderia Piazza Verdi 2. Occupying a former stable block on a rough-and-ready square, this huge bar is aimed squarely at students, with occasional live acts, cheap drinks and plenty of room to dance. Closed Sun.

Mutenye Bar Via Del Pratello 44. A bit of a jaunt from the centre, but the reward is an unfussy tourist-free bar that has a great choice of beers. Most people stand on the small pavement outside. Happy hour 5.30–8.30pm. Daily 5.30pm–2.30am.

Moving on

Train Ferrara (every 30min; 30min–1hr); Florence (frequent; 30min–1hr); Genoa (hourly; 3–4hr); Milan (every 30min; 2–3hr); Rimini (every 30min; 1hr 30min); Rome (frequent; 2hr–2hr 30min); Turin (10 direct daily; 2hr 30min–3hr 30min); Venice (frequent; 1hr 30min–2hr); Verona (hourly; 1hr–1hr 30min).

Bus Rome (1 daily; 5hr 45min); Siena (2 daily; 2hr 40min).

PARMA

PARMA is an extremely pleasant town, with dignified streets, large green spaces, a wide range of good restaurants and an appealing air of provincial affluence. The home of Parmesan and Parma ham also offers plenty to see, not least the works of two key late-Renaissance artists – Correggio and Parmigianino.

What to see and do

Piazza Garibaldi is the fulcrum of Parma, and its cafés and surrounding alleyways are liveliest at night. The mustard-coloured **Palazzo del Governatore** flanks the square, behind which stands the Renaissance church of **Madonna della Steccata**. Inside there are frescoes by a number of sixteenth-century painters, notably Parmigianino. It's also worth visiting the **Duomo**, on Piazza del Duomo in the northeast of the city centre, to see the octagonal **Baptistery** (Mon–Sun 9am–12.30pm & 3–6.45pm; €5), considered to be Benedetto Antelami's finest work, built in 1196. Frescoes by Correggio are in the **Camera di San Paolo** (Tues–Sun 8.30am–1.45pm; €2), in the former Benedictine convent off Via Melloni, a few minutes' walk north.

East of the cathedral square, it's hard to miss Parma's biggest monument, the **Palazzo della Pilotta**, begun for Alessandro Farnese in the sixteenth century and rebuilt after World War II bombing. It now houses the city's main art gallery, the **Galleria Nazionale** (Tues–Sun 8.30am–1.30pm; €6), whose extensive collection includes more works by Correggio and Parmigianino. The grassy area around the Palazzo is a popular place for a picnic. If you've had enough of all things cultural and fancy checking out some shopping streets, stroll down the wide and laidback **Strada della Repubblica**, or alternatively people watch from a café on Via Farini, take a walk along the river or escape the heat of the day at the Parco Ducale.

Arrival and information

Train Parma's train station is a 15min walk from Piazza Garibaldi and most of the buses in the city pass through it, bus #8 is the most direct.

Tourist office Via Melloni 1a ⓣ0521.218.889, ⓦwww.turismo.comune.parma.it (Tues–Sat 9am–7pm; Mon 9am–1pm & 3–7pm; Sun 9am–1pm).

Internet Polidoro 11, Via Maestri 4b (Mon–Fri 10am–1pm & 4–7.30pm; €5/hr). There's also a number of wireless hotspots around the town – ask the tourist office for a map.

Accommodation

Albergo Amorini Via Gramsci 37 ⓣ0521.983.239. Near the nighltife of Strada D'Azeglio and a 5min walk from the Parco Ducale, this one-star hotel isn't anything special, but it is cheap, cheerful and opposite a large supermarket. Doubles €55.

Foresteria Delle Colonne Via Malfald Di Savoia 17a 9a ⓣ0521.924.368, ⓦwww.solaresdellearti.it. An arts foundation that offers simple accommodation. To get here take bus #2 from the Teatro Regio to the *capolinea* (the end of the line) and head right – it's round the back of the building opposite the theatre. Reception open 8.30am–12.30pm & 8pm–midnight. Dorms €20.

La Pilotta Room & Breakfast Strada Garibaldi 31 ⓣ0521.281 415, ⓔinfo @lapilotta.it. Duck through the comically small entrance door to this B&B bang in the centre of Parma. Run by the jolly Clementina, rooms are large and clean. There is a kitchen, washing machine and a great balcony with lovingly tended cacti. March–Aug only. Doubles €65.

Leon d'oro V.Le Fratti 4a ⓣ0521.773.182 ⓦwww .leondoroparma.com. Simple one-star B&B above a great restaurant. It is a bit out of the centre, but the rooms are clean if a bit old-fashioned. Doubles €60.

Ostello della Gioventù Via San Leonardo 86 ⓣ0521.191.7547, ⓦwww.ostelloparma.it. Excellent large hostel with big rooms and helpful staff. A 25-minute walk from the centre or take bus #2 or #13 from the train station to Centro Torri. Dorms €19.50, doubles €43.

Eating

The more expensive restaurants are on Piazza Garibaldi, while the cheaper options are found along the busy Via Farini. There's a supermarket (Billa) on M.D'Azeglio.

Bottiglia Azzura Borgo Felino 63 ⓣ0521.285.842. The "Blue Bottle" offers great lunch deals and cosy upstairs dining. Owner Adriano also arranges piano concerts and displays local artwork throughout the year. Closed Sun.

Formaggi & Salumi 65b Strada Garibaldi. Brilliantly stocked-up deli. The friendly staff here will soon have you loaded up with treats for the perfect picnic. Open until 7.45pm, closed Thurs.

Il Gallo D'Oro Borgo Salina 3 (just off Via Farini). A bit touristy but serves superb unfussy local fare at inexpensive prices. Mains €8. Closed Sun eve.

Sorelle Pichi Via Farini 28. Part of an establishment that includes an excellent deli this restaurant specializes in cured meats; try the spectacular ravioli. Mains €10. Mon–Sat noon–3pm.

Tonic Via Nazaro Sauro 5 ⓣ 0521.508.426. Run by the friendly Edward, this modern bar serves large pastas for great prices. They have regular Indie nights. Pasta €6, mains €7. Closed Sun & Mon eves.

Drinking

In the evening, the best place to head to is lively Via Farini or Strada D'Azeglio, which has a buzzy, youthful atmosphere.

Le Malve Café Via Farini 12b. At night customers overflow into the streets from this popular hangout. During the day the purple seats outside are the perfect places to people watch. Beer €4, cappucino & snack €1.30. Closed Sun.

Peter Pan Strada Luigi Carlo Farini 92. On weekends people of all ages head to this relaxed bar at the far end of Via Farini. Get there early to get tables outside or join the masses on the wide street. *Aperitif* €7. Closed Sunday afternoons.

Surfer Den Via D'Azeglio 62/b. Although nowhere near the sea this place does feel like a beachside café. This tiny place draws a friendly crowd and serves good cocktails.

Entertainment

Events include the annual Verdi festival in October (ⓦ www.teatroregioparma.org or ask at the tourist office), held at the Teatro Regio on Via Garibaldi (ⓣ 0521.039.300), while in summer (normally July) the city hosts the wonderful Sotto Il Cielo festival, a month-long music and dance celebration (ⓦ www.commune.parma.it or ask at the tourist office).

Moving on

Train Bologna (every 30min; 1hr–1hr 30min); Florence (frequent; 1hr 30min–2 hr); La Spezia (frequent; 2hr); Milan (frequent; 1hr 30min); Padua (hourly; 2hr 30min; change at Bologna); Torino (frequent; 3hr–3hr 30min; some change at Milan); Venice (every 30min; 3–4hr; change at Bologna or Brescia).

RAVENNA

RAVENNA's colourful sixth-century mosaics are one of the crowning achievements of Byzantine art – and undoubtedly the main reason for visiting the town. The mosaics are the legacy of a quirk of fate 1500 years ago, when Ravenna briefly became capital of the Roman Empire, and can be seen in a day. The **basilica of San Vitale**, ten minutes northwest of the centre, was completed in 548 AD. Its mosaics, showing scenes from the Old Testament and the life of Christ, are in the apse. Across from the basilica is the tiny **Mausoleo di Galla Placidia**, whose mosaics glow with a deep-blue lustre. Galla Placidia was the daughter, sister, wife and mother of various Roman emperors, and the interior of her fifth-century mausoleum, whose cupola is covered in tiny stars, is breathtaking. East of here, on the **Via di Roma,** is the sixth-century basilica of **Sant'Apollinare Nuovo**. Mosaics run the length of the nave, depicting processions of martyrs bearing gifts. Five minutes' walk up Via di Roma, the **Arian Baptistery** has a fine mosaic ceiling. A **combined ticket** (€11.50) is valid for 7 days and covers most of Ravenna's sights; it's available from any of the participating museums, and is valid for a week. Opening times for all the sights are daily 9am–5pm. Ravenna does have other strings to its bow, as well, including some lovely, sandy beaches (take bus #70 from the station).

The **train station** is a 5min walk from the centre, with the **tourist office** on Via Salara 8 (Mon–Sat 8.30am–7pm, Sun 10am–6pm). There is a large HI **hostel**, *Hostel Dante* 2km away from the centre on Via Aurelio Nicolodi (ⓣ 0544.421.164; March–Nov; dorms €16; a 15min walk east of the town centre or take Metrobus Rosso from opposite the station), which has sparse rooms, but friendly staff and a good, free breakfast. For **food**, there are small delis near the hostel, which sell good picnic grub. There are a few smart **bars** on Piazza del Popolo but drinks here are expensive: *Babaleus Pizzeria* on Vicolo Gabbiani 7 is a better bet – it serves cheap meals (pizza €5) and does a good-value lunch buffet (€7).

Central Italy

The Italian heartland of **Tuscany** is one mass of picture-postcard landscapes made up of lovely, walled hill-top towns and rolling, vineyard-covered hills. **Florence** is the first port of call, home to a majestic Duomo, the extensive Uffizi gallery and the elegant Ponte Vecchio. **Siena**, one of the great medieval cities of Europe, is also the scene of Tuscany's one unmissable festival – the Palio – which sees bareback horseriders careering around the cobbled central square, while **Pisa**'s leaning tower, a feat of engineering against gravity, and intricately decorated cathedral justifiably attract hordes of tourists. To the east lies **Umbria**, a beautiful region of thick woodland and undulating hills; the capital, **Perugia**, is an energetic student dominated town, while **Assisi** is famed for its gorgeous setting and extraordinary frescoes by Giotto.

FLORENCE

FLORENCE (Firenze) is undoubtedly the highlight of Tuscany. Its chapels, galleries and museums are works of art in themselves, and every corner brings you face to face with architectural splendour. Some of the most famous pieces in Western art are on display here, including Michelangelo's *David* in the Accademia and Botticelli's *Birth of Venus* in the Uffizi.

What to see and do

Florence's major sights are contained within an area that can be crossed on foot in a little over half an hour. From Santa Maria Novella train station, most visitors gravitate towards **Piazza del Duomo**, beckoned by the pinnacle of the dome. **Via dei Calzaiuoli**, which runs south from the Duomo, is the main catwalk of the Florentine *passeggiata*, a broad pedestrianized avenue lined with shops. It ends at Florence's other main square, the **Piazza della Signoria**, fringed on one side by the graceful late fourteenth-century **Loggia della Signoria** and dotted with statues, most famously a copy of Michelangelo's *David*.

The Duomo

The **Duomo** (Mon–Sat 10am–4.30/5pm, Sun 1.30–4.45pm) was built between the late thirteenth and mid-fifteenth centuries. The fourth largest church in the world, its ambience is more that of a great assembly hall than of a devotional building. The seven stained-glass roundels, designed by Uccello, Ghiberti, Castagno and Donatello, are best inspected from a gallery that forms part of the route to the top of the dome (€6), from where the views are stupendous. Next door to the Duomo stands the **Campanile** (daily 8.30am–7.30pm; €6) begun by Giotto in 1334. As well as offering an impressive bird's-eye view of Florence, this contains several enormous bells and more than fifty intricately carved marble reliefs. Opposite, the **Baptistery** (Mon–Wed 12.15–7pm, Thurs, Fri & Sat 12.15–10.30pm, Sun 8.30am–2pm; €4), generally thought to date from the sixth or seventh century, is the oldest building in the city. Its gilded bronze doors were cast in the early fifteenth century by Lorenzo Ghiberti, and described by Michelangelo as "so beautiful they are worthy to be the gates of Paradise". Inside, it is equally stunning, with a thirteenth-century mosaic floor and ceiling and the tomb of Pope John XXIII, the work of Donatello and his pupil Michelozzo.

The Palazzo Vecchio

The tourist-thronged **Piazza della Signoria** is dominated by the colossal **Palazzo Vecchio**, Florence's fortress-like town hall (daily 9am–7pm, Thurs closes 2pm; €6), begun in the last year of the thirteenth century as the home of the Signoria, the highest tier of the city's republican government.

The Uffizi

Immediately south of the Piazza Vecchio, the **Galleria degli Uffizi** (Tues–Sun 8.15am–6.50pm; booking advisable at Ⓦwww.uffizi.com; €11 before 4pm & €10 after 4pm) is the greatest picture gallery in Italy. Highlights include Filippo Lippi's *Madonna and Child with Two Angels* and some of Botticelli's most famous works, notably the *Birth of Venus*. While the Uffizi doesn't own a finished painting that's entirely by Leonardo da Vinci, there's a celebrated *Annunciation* that's mainly by him, and Michelangelo's *Doni Tondo*, found in Room 18, is his only completed easel painting.

Bargello

The **Bargello museum** (Tues–Sun 8.15am–4.50pm; €7) lies just northwest of the Uffizi in Via del Proconsolo. The collection contains numerous works by Michelangelo, Cellini and Giambologna. Upstairs is Donatello's sexually ambiguous bronze *David*, the first freestanding nude figure since classical times, cast in the early 1430s.

North: San Lorenzo

The church of **San Lorenzo** (daily 10am–5.30pm, Sun 1.30–5.30pm; €3.50), north of Piazza del Duomo, has a strong claim to be the oldest church in Florence. At the top of the left aisle and through the cloisters, the **Biblioteca Medicea-Laurenziana** (Mon–Sat 9am–1.30pm; free) was designed by Michelangelo in 1524; its most startling feature is the vestibule, a room almost filled by a flight of steps resembling a solidified lava flow. Just east of here, the **Accademia** (Tues–Sun 8.15am–6.50pm; €11 before 4pm & €10 after 4pm), Europe's first school of drawing, is swamped by people in search of Michelangelo's *David.* Finished in 1504, when the artist was just 29, and carved from a gigantic block of marble, it's an incomparable show of technical bravura.

East: Santa Croce

Down by the river, to the southeast of the centre, the church of **Santa Croce** (Mon–Sat 9.30am–5.30pm, Sun 1–5.30pm; €5, including museum), begun in 1294, is full of tombstones and commemorative monuments, including Vasari's memorial to Michelangelo and, on the opposite side of the church, the tomb of Galileo, built in 1737 when it was finally agreed to give the scientist a Christian burial. Most visitors, however, come to see the dazzling frescoes by Giotto.

South: Oltrarno and beyond

The photogenic thirteenth-century **Ponte Vecchio**, loaded with jewellers' shops overhanging the water, leads from the city centre across the river to the district of **Oltrarno**. Head west, past the relaxed, café-lined square of **Santo Spirito**, to the church of **Santa Maria del Carmine** – an essential visit for the superbly restored frescoes by Masaccio in its **Cappella Brancacci** (Mon & Wed–Sat 10am–5pm, Sun 1–5pm; €4).

Palazzo Pitti

South of Santo Spirito is the massive bulk of the fifteenth-century **Palazzo Pitti**. Nowadays this contains six separate museums, the best of which, the **Galleria Palatina** (Tues–Sun 8.15am–6.50pm, summer Sat till 10pm; €13 before 4pm & €12 after 4pm, price includes the Galleria d'Arte Moderna), houses some superb Raphaels and Titians. The rest of the first floor is dominated by the state rooms of the **Appartamenti Monumentali** (included in the Galleria Palatina ticket). The Pitti's enormous formal garden, the delightful **Giardino di Boboli** (Tues–Sun 8.15am–4.30/7.30pm; €6), is also worth a visit. Beyond here, the multicoloured facade of **San Miniato al Monte** (daily 8am–12.30pm & 3–5.30pm; free) lures troops of visitors up the hill. The interior is like no other in the city, and

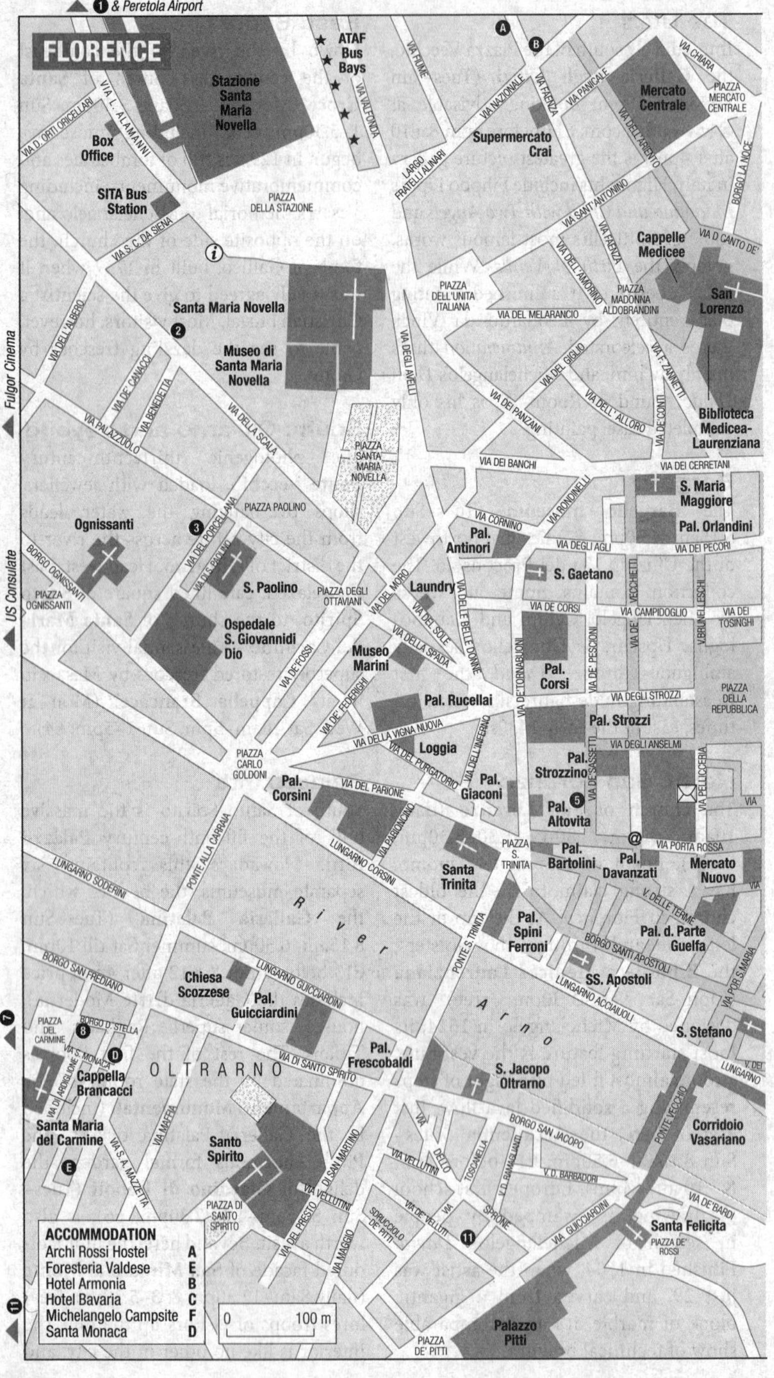
1 & Peretola Airport
FLORENCE
ATAF Bus Bays
Stazione Santa Maria Novella
Box Office
SITA Bus Station
PIAZZA DELLA STAZIONE
Supermercato Crai
Mercato Centrale
PIAZZA MERCATO CENTRALE
Cappelle Medicee
San Lorenzo
Biblioteca Medicea-Laurenziana
PIAZZA DELL'UNITA ITALIANA
PIAZZA MADONNA ALDOBRANDINI
LARGO FRATELLI ALINARI
Santa Maria Novella
Museo di Santa Maria Novella
PIAZZA SANTA MARIA NOVELLA
PIAZZA PAOLINO
Ognissanti
PIAZZA OGNISSANTI
S. Paolino
PIAZZA DEGLI OTTAVIANI
Ospedale S. Giovannidi Dio
Museo Marini
Laundry
Pal. Antinori
S. Gaetano
S. Maria Maggiore
Pal. Orlandini
Pal. Corsi
Pal. Rucellai
Loggia
Pal. Strozzi
Pal. Strozzino
PIAZZA DELLA REPUBBLICA
PIAZZA CARLO GOLDONI
Pal. Corsini
Pal. Giaconi
Pal. Altovita
Pal. Bartolini
Pal. Davanzati
Mercato Nuovo
Santa Trinita
PIAZZA S. TRINITA
Pal. Spini Ferroni
Pal. d. Parte Guelfa
SS. Apostoli
S. Stefano
River Arno
Chiesa Scozzese
Pal. Guicciardini
Pal. Frescobaldi
S. Jacopo Oltrarno
OLTRARNO
PIAZZA DEL CARMINE
Cappella Brancacci
Santa Maria del Carmine
Santo Spirito
PIAZZA DI SANTO SPIRITO
Corridoio Vasariano
Santa Felicita
PIAZZA DE' ROSSI
Palazzo Pitti
PIAZZA DE' PITTI
Fulgor Cinema
US Consulate
VIA L. ALAMANNI
VIA D. ORTI ORICELLARI
VIA S. C. DA SIENA
VIA FIUME
VIA VALFONDA
VIA NAZIONALE
VIA FAENZA
VIA PANICALE
VIA CHIARA
VIA DELL'ARIENTO
BORGO LA NOCE
VIA SANT'ANTONINO
VIA D CANTO DE'
VIA DELL'AMORINO
VIA DEL MELARANCIO
VIA DEGLI AVELLI
VIA DEL GIGLIO
VIA F. ZANNETTI
VIA DEI PANZANI
VIA DELL'ALLORO
VIA DE'CONTI
VIA DEI BANCHI
VIA DEI CERRETANI
VIA DELL'ALBERO
VIA DE' CANACCI
VIA BENEDETTA
VIA PALAZZUOLO
VIA DELLA SCALA
VIA DEL PORCELLANA
VIA D. S. PAOLINO
BORGO OGNISSANTI
VIA CORNINO
VIA RONDINELLI
VIA DEGLI AGLI
VIA DEI PECORI
VIA DEL MORO
VIA DEL SOLE
VIA DELLE BELLE DONNE
VECCHIETTI
VIA DE CORSI
VIA CAMPIDOGLIO
V. BRUNELLESCHI
VIA DEI TOSINGHI
VIA DELLA SPADA
VIA DE' FOSSI
VIA DE' FEDERIGHI
VIA DE' TORNABUONI
VIA DE' PESCIONI
VIA DEGLI STROZZI
VIA DELLA VIGNA NUOVA
VIA DEL PURGATORIO
VIA DELL'INFERNO
VIA DE' SASSETTI
VIA DEGLI ANSELMI
VIA PELLICCERIA
VIA DEL PARIONE
VIA PARIONCINO
VIA PORTA ROSSA
PONTE ALLA CARRAIA
LUNGARNO SODERINI
LUNGARNO CORSINI
V. DELLE TERME
BORGO SANTI APOSTOLI
LUNGARNO ACCIAIUOLI
VIA POR S. MARIA
PONTE S. TRINITA
BORGO SAN FREDIANO
LUNGARNO GUICCIARDINI
BORGO D. STELLA
VIA S. MONACA
VIA DI SANTO SPIRITO
VIA DI CADIGLIONE
VIA MAFFIA
VIA S. A. MAZZETTA
VIA DI SAN MARTINO
VIA DELLO
VIA VELLUTINI
TOSCANELLA
V. D. RAMAGLIANTI
BORGO SAN JACOPO
V. D. BARBADORI
PONTE VECCHIO
LUNGARNO
VIA DE'BARDI
VIA DEL PRESTO
VIA MAGGIO
SDRUCCIOLO DE' PITTI
VIA DE' VELLUTI
SPRONE
VIA GUICCIARDINI
ACCOMMODATION
Archi Rossi Hostel A
Foresteria Valdese E
Hotel Armonia B
Hotel Bavaria C
Michelangelo Campsite F
Santa Monaca D
0 100 m

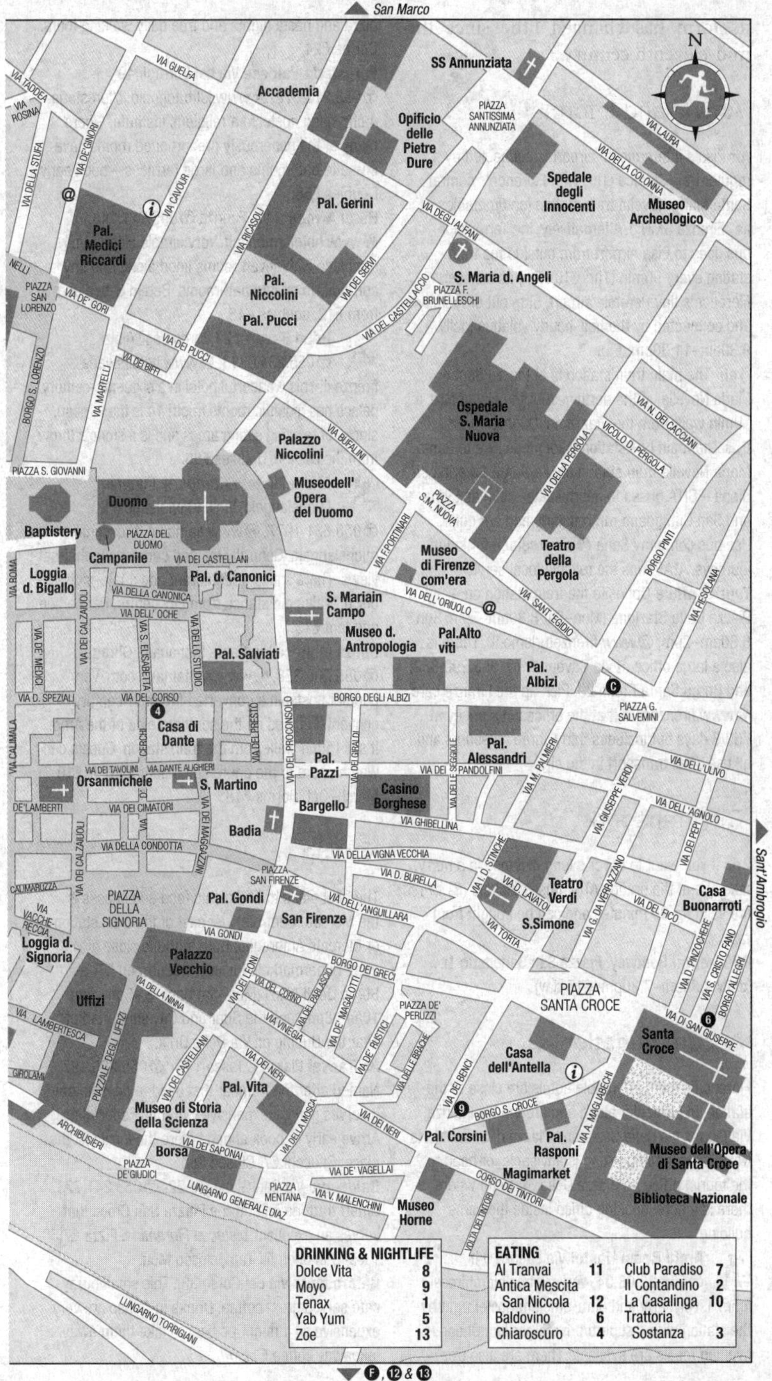

ITALY

CENTRAL ITALY

its form has changed little since the mid-eleventh century.

Arrival and information

Air Pisa's international airport is connected by a regular train service (1hr) with Florence's central Santa Maria Novella train station (on timetables as "Firenze SMN"). Alternatively, the Terravision bus goes to Pisa Airport from outside the train station every 90min (1hr; €10). Flights also serve Florence's tiny Peretola airport, 5km out of the city and connected by the half-hourly Volabus (daily 9.30am–11.30pm; €5).
Train The main train station is at Piazza Santa Maria Novella, in the northwest of the city centre, a 10min walk from the Piazza del Duomo.
Bus The main bus station is located close to Santa Maria Novella train station on Via Santa Caterina da Siena – SITA buses to nearby cities such as Siena and San Gimignano run regularly and are quick. Use bus company Sena ⓦwww.sena.it for longer journeys. ATAF runs the reliable local service.
Tourist office Opposite the train station on 4 Piazza Della Stazione (Mon–Sat 8.30am–7pm, Sun 8.30am–2pm, ⓦwww.firenzeturismo.it). There is also a large office at Via Cavour 1r (ⓣ055.290.832) and Borgo Santa Croce 29. Pick up the Firenze card ⓦwww.firenzecard.it at the offices; it's pricey at €50/3 days but includes thirty-three museums and all use of all transport in the city.

City transport

Bus If you want to cover a long distance in a hurry, take one of the orange ATAF buses; tickets (€1.20) are valid for 90 minutes and can be bought from *tabacchi*.
Bike rental Rentway, Piazza San Benedetto 1r (daily 9.30am–7.30pm; €15/day).

Accommodation

Florence's most affordable hotels are close to the station, in particular along and around Via Faenza, Via Fiume, Via della Scala and Piazza di Santa Maria Novella. Advance booking is advisable, or head to the tourist office on Piazza Della Stazione where there is a hotel booking office inside the same building.
Archi Rossi Hostel Via Faenza 94r ⓣ055.29.08.04, ⓦwww.hostelarchirossi .com. Lively, arty and ultra-efficient hostel right by the station with a superb private garden. Cheap evening meals are available.There are also free pizza and pasta nights and free daily walking tours. Dorms €24.
Foresteria Valdese Via dei Serragli 49 ⓣ055.212.576, ⓦwww.istitutogould.it/foresteria. A charming hostel in a religious institute, where many of the generously proportioned rooms have en-suite bathrooms and large terraces – book early. Doubles €56.
Hotel Armonia Via Faenza ⓣ055.211.146, ⓦwww.hotelarmonia.it. Very simple clean family-run place with seven rooms lined along one tiny corridor. No private bathrooms. Bed in 6-bed dorm from €12, doubles €45.
Hotel Bavaria 26 Borgo degli Albizi ⓣ055.234.0313, ⓦwww.hotelbavaria firenze.it. This wonderful hotel in a sixteenth-century palace has gigantic rooms (room 14 is the largest), stacks of relaxing sitting areas and is a stone's throw from the Duomo. Doubles €55.
Michelangelo Campsite Piazzale Michelangelo, Viale Michelangelo 80 ⓣ055.681.1977, ⓦwww.camping.it/toscana/ michelangelo. Centrally located campsite with great views. There's also a restaurant and a late-night disco. Walking distance from city centre. Per person and tent €13.
Santa Monaca Via Santa Monaca 6, Oltrarno ⓣ055.268.338, ⓦwww.santamaria.com. Very popular hostel in a converted fifteenth-century convent. Located on the southern side of the Arno, it's a 15min walk from the train station. Guests can watch opera at the church next door for only €10 March–Oct. Dorms €18.

Eating

The best place to find picnic food and snacks is the Mercato Centrale, just east of the train station or Mercato Ambroglio. Both markets close at 2pm. Supermarkets include Il Centro on 57r at Borgo Degli Albizi (Mon–Sat 9am–8.45pm, Sun 10am–8pm) and the Spar and City supermarkets near the Duomo on Via Della Orillul.
Al Tranvai Piazza T. Tasso 14/r ⓣ055.225.197. Named after the tramcar that used to pass nearby it serves good, inexpensive Florentine specialities. Arrive early or book ahead before the locals fill the place. Gnocchi €7. Closed Sun.
Baldovino Via San Giuseppe 22r ⓣ055.241.773. Smart trattoria just off the Piazza San Croce that serves an excellent *bistecca Fiorentina*. Pizza €7.50. Tues–Sun open till 1am, closed Mon.
Chiaroscuro Via del Corso 36r. This small buzzy café serves great coffee. Drinks in-house are very expensive so it might be best to take them away; takeaway coffee €1.50.

Club Paradiso Via dell'orto 24. Relax and enjoy the hospitality of the chatty and friendly owner Andrea at this simple restaurant serving great food at low prices. Main meals €6. Closed Sun & Sat lunch.

Il Contandino Via Palazzuolo 69–71r ⓣ055. 238. 2673. This small place is an excellent choice for lunch. For €11 you get a 2-course meal, water and wine.

La Casalinga Via Michelozzi 9r. People are willing to queue a long time for a table at this great-value trattoria that serves old-style family Italian cooking. Pasta €6.

Trattoria Sostanza 25 Via Porcellana ⓣ055.238.2673. Affectionately known as "the trough" this is where the real Florentines have been going for the best *bisteca* (€25) in town since 1869. A simple, no-frills affair, with hearty portions of superlative food. Booking recommended. Closed Sat & Sun.

Drinking and nightlife

Mercato Generale, just east of the train station, has some of Florence's cheapest bars.

Dolce Vita Piazza del Carmine 5. Trendy cocktail and wine bar that also stages small-scale art exhibitions. Cocktails €8. Mon–Sat open till 2am, closed Sun.

Moyo Via dei Benci 23r. This chilled-out café and bar on a busy street serves great cocktails; food on offer includes good breakfasts and lunchtime salads, and drinks with buffet until 2am. Large beer/cocktail €6. Food served till 5pm.

Tenax Via Pratese 46 ⓦwww.tenax.org. Bus #29 or #30. The city's biggest club and one of its leading venues for new and established bands, playing an eclectic mix of indie, trance, modern pop and old classics. Fri & Sat from 10pm.

Yab Yum Via de' Sassetti 5r ⓦwww.yab.it. City-centre club, near the Duomo, playing new dance music. Mon–Sat from 8pm.

Zoe Via Dei Renai 13. Atmospheric, chic and modern cocktail bar, with small-scale painting exhibitions, outdoor seating and snack food during the day. Cocktails €7. Daily 9am–3am.

Entertainment

For listings information, call in at the box office, Via Delle Vecchie Carceri 50 (ⓣ055.210.804), or consult *Firenze Spettacolo* (€1.80), the *Informa Città* or the *Florentine* (available at the tourist offices). As for **festivals**, in May the Maggio Musicale (ⓦwww.maggiofiorentino.com) puts on concerts, gigs and other events throughout the city, while the Festa di San Giovanni (June 24; ⓦwww.fierasangiovanni.it) sees the city's saint honoured with a massive fireworks display. Free concerts and events take place around Florence throughout the summer – see the tourist office for details.

Directory

Consulates UK, Lungarno Corsini 2 ⓣ055.284.133; US, Lungarno A Vespucci 38 ⓣ055.266.951.

Exchange The city is full of ATMs and exchange bureaux; there is one at 7 Piazza Santa Croce.

Hospitals Santa Maria Nuova, Piazza Santa Maria Nuova 1 ⓣ055.27.581. English-speaking doctors are on 24hr call at the Tourist Medical Service, Via Lorenzo il Magnifico 59 ⓣ055.475.411.

Internet Internet Train is at Portarossa, Via Porta Rossa 38r & Via dell'Oriuolo 40r. Also Euro Bangla International on Via Ginori 59r (€1.50/hr).

Police Via Zara 2 ⓣ055.49.771.

Post office Via Pellicceria 3 (daily except Sun 8.30am–12.30pm & 3–6pm).

Moving on

Train Bologna (frequent; 30min–1hr); Genoa (hourly; 4hr; change at Pisa); Milan (frequent; 1hr 45min); Naples (hourly; 3hr); Nice (every 2 hr; 8–10hr; change at Pisa); Paris (1 direct daily; 12hr 50min); Perugia (every 2hr; 2hr); Pisa (every 20min; 50min–1hr 30min); Rome (frequent; 1hr 30min); Venice (hourly; 2hr); Verona (every 1hr–2hr; 2hr).

Bus Siena (hourly; 1hr 30min).

PISA

The Leaning Tower in **PISA** is an iconic image, yet its stunning beauty is often underrated, with its intricate carvings appearing as though they are icing details on a very large wedding cake. It's set alongside the **Duomo** and **Baptistery** on the manicured grass of the lovely **Campo dei Miracoli**, whose buildings date from the twelfth and thirteenth centuries, when Pisa was one of the great Mediterranean powers. Beyond this pretty square, the city synonymous with Galileo, Shelley and Byron may lack the polish of a Siena or a Florence but it is still definitely worth a meander along its charming narrow streets.

PISA'S FESTIVALS

Pisa is known for its **Gioco del Ponte**, held on the last Sunday in June, when teams from the north and south banks of the city stage a series of "battles", including pushing a seven-tonne carriage over the Ponte di Mezzo. But the town's most magical event is the **Luminara** on June 16, when buildings along the river are festooned with candles to celebrate San Ranieri, the city's patron saint.

What to see and do

Leaning Tower

Perhaps the strangest thing about the **Leaning Tower** (daily 8.30am–8.30pm; €15; it is advisable to book ahead ⓦwww.opapisa.it/boxoffice), begun in 1173, is that it has always tilted; subsidence disrupted the foundations when it had reached just three of its eight storeys. For the next 180 years a succession of architects were brought in to try to correct the tilt, until 1350 when the angle was accepted and the tower completed. Eight centuries after its construction, it was thought to be nearing its limit, and the tower, supported by steel wires, was closed to the public in the 1990s – though it's open for visits once again now that the tilt (and 5m overhang) has been successfully halted.

Duomo

The **Duomo** (Mon–Sat 10am–7.30pm, Sun 1–7.30pm; €2, free before 1pm on Sun) was begun a century earlier than the Tower, its facade – a delicate balance of black and white marble, and tiers of arcades – setting the model for Pisa's highly distinctive brand of Romanesque. The third building of the Miracoli ensemble, the circular **Baptistery** (daily 8am–7.30pm; €5), is a slightly bizarre mix of Romanesque and Gothic, embellished with statues (now largely copies) by Giovanni Pisano and his father Nicola. The originals are displayed in the Opera del Duomo **museum** (March–Sept daily 8am–7.30pm; Oct–Feb daily 9am–4.45pm; €5) to the east of the Piazza del Duomo.

Camposanto

Along the north side of the Campo is the **Camposanto** (same hours; €5), a cloistered cemetery built towards the end of the thirteenth century. Most of its frescoes were destroyed by Allied bombing in World War II, but two masterpieces survived relatively unscathed in the Cappella Ammanati – a fourteenth-century *Triumph of Death,* and *The Last Judgement*, a ruthless catalogue of horrors painted around the time of the Black Death.

Arrival and information

Air Pisa's airport is only 1km from the city centre. The best way to the city is by bus. The LAM Rosso (single €1.10) leaves every 10–15min to all major points in the city, including the train station.

Train Pisa's picturesque train station is south of the centre on Piazza della Stazione, a 30min walk from Campo dei Miracoli. Take bus LAM Rosso for the 10min journey to the Leaning Tower.

Tourist office 16 Piazza Vittorio Emanuele II (Mon–Sat 9am–7pm; Sun 9am–4pm; ⓣ050.42.291, ⓦwww.pisaunicaterra.it) and at the airport (daily 9.30am–11.30pm).

Discount card A tourist ticket (€10) gives admission to most of Pisa's museums, but not the Leaning Tower. Available from the main ticket office at Campo Dei Miracoli.

Internet Koine on 5 Via G Carducci (Mon & Fri 10am–8pm, Tues–Thurs 10am–10pm & Sun 2–10pm).

Accommodation

Campeggio Torre Pendente Viale delle Cascine 86 ⓣ050.561.704, ⓦwww.campingtorrependente.it. Large, well-maintained campsite 1km west of Campo dei Miracoli, with a restaurant, shop and large outdoor swimming pool. Closed Nov–March. Per person, plus tent & car from €24.

HI Hostel Via Philippo Corridoni 29 ⓣ0505.201.841. An excellent modern hostel a 5min walk from the train station. Great courtyard and facilities. Take advantage of the free walking tours of the city every Tues–Sun at 9am. Dorms €15.

Hotel Galileo Via S.maria 12 ⓣ050.402.21. Excellent budget choice only a short walk from the tower. Staff speak English. Doubles from €48.

Michele Guest House Via Vespucci 103 ⓣ333.701.483, ⓦwww.guest-house.it. Run by photographer Michele, this excellent B&B has luxurious rooms full of his work. Take advantage of the owner's extensive knowledge of the area. Doubles €60.

Eating

Avoid eating around the Tower if you can, as prices here are sky-high for tourists. Most restaurants close on Sundays in Pisa. The best area for restaurants is around the Piazza delle Vettovaglie, and there are fruit markets around Via D. Cavalca.

Caffeteria delle Vettovaglie Piazza delle Vetto vaglie 33. Trendy bar-restaurant with a different menu every day. Mains €8. Closed Sun.

Chapeau Rouge Piazza Vettovaglie 21. Excellent basic home-cooked food in a charmingly ramshackle setting with friendly owners. Mains €6. Open daily.

La Bottega del Gelato Piazza delle Garibaldi. Great *gelato* and a convenient pit stop midway between the station and the Duomo, eat perched on the wall by the river.

Pizzeria il Montino Via del Monte 1. Super-value pizzeria that serves generous pizzas. It is worth queuing for a table at this popular restaurant. Closed Tues.

Vineria di Piazza Piazza delle Vettovaglie 13. Good soups at decent prices. Soup and fresh bread €6. Closed Sun.

Moving on

Train Florence (every 15min; 1hr–1hr 30min); Lucca (every 30min; 25min); Siena (frequent; 1hr 45min).

Bus Florence, from Pisa Airport (hourly; 1hr 10min).

SIENA

SIENA, 78km south of Florence, is the perfect antidote to its better-known neighbour. Self-contained behind excellently preserved medieval walls, its cityscape is a majestic Gothic attraction that you can roam around and enjoy without venturing into a single museum. During the Middle Ages, Siena was one of the major cities of Europe – the size of Paris, it controlled most of southern Tuscany and developed a highly sophisticated civic life, with its own written constitution and a quasi-democratic government.

What to see and do

The **Campo** is the centre of Siena in every sense: the main streets lead into it, the Palio (see box below) takes place around its café-lined perimeter, and it's the natural place to gravitate towards. It deserves its reputation as one of Italy's most beautiful squares and taking a picnic onto the red stones to watch the

THE SIENA PALIO

The **Siena Palio** is the most spectacular festival in Italy, a minute-and-a-half-long bareback horse race around the Campo contested twice a year (July 2 at 7.45pm and Aug 16 at 7pm) between the seventeen ancient wards – or *contrade* – of the city. Even now, a person's *contrada* frequently determines which churches they attend and where they socialize. There's a big build-up, with trials and processions for days before the big event, and traditionally all Sienese return to their *contrada* the night before the race; emotions run too high for rivals to be together, even if they're husband and wife. The Palio itself is a hectic spectacle whose rules haven't been rewritten since the race began – thus supposedly, everything is allowed except to gouge your opponents' eyes out. On occasions it can take up to an hour to even start the race due to false starts. For the best view, you need to have found a position on the inner rail by 2pm and to keep it for the next seven hours. Beware that toilets, shade and refreshments are minimal, the swell of the crowd can be overwhelming, and you won't be able to leave the Campo for at least two hours after the race. If you haven't booked a hotel room, reckon on staying up all night.

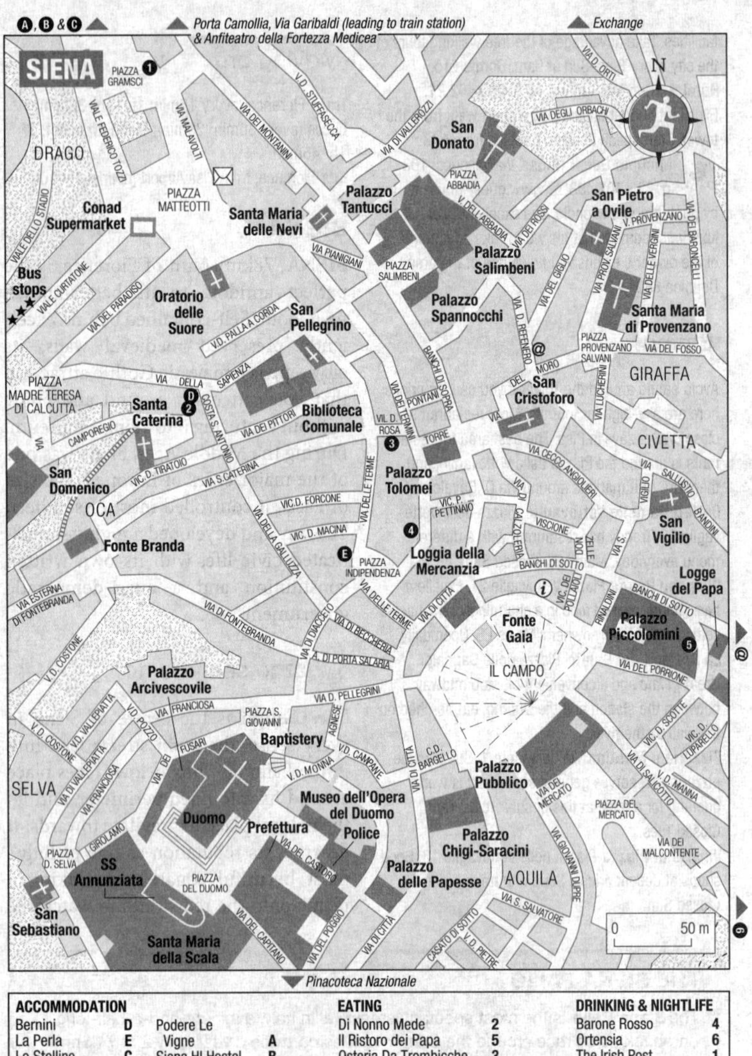

shadows move around the square is a good way to while away an afternoon.

The Palazzo Pubblico

The **Palazzo Pubblico** (daily 10am–6/7pm) – with its 107m-high bell tower, the **Torre del Mangia** (€8) – occupies virtually the entire south side of the square, and although it's still in use as Siena's town hall, its principal rooms have been converted into a **museum** (€8), frescoed with themes integral to the secular life of the medieval city.

Around the Campo

Between buildings at the top end of the Campo, the fifteenth-century **Loggia di Mercanzia**, built as a dealing room for merchants, marks the intersection of the city centre's principal streets. From here **Via Banchi di Sotto** leads east to the **Palazzo Piccolomini** and on into the workaday quarter of **San Martino**. From the Campo, Via di Città cuts west across the oldest quarter of the city, fronted by some of Siena's finest private *palazzi*. At the end of the street, Via San Pietro leads to the **Pinacoteca Nazionale** (Mon 9am–1pm, Tues–Sat 10am–6pm, Sun 9am–1pm; €4), a fourteenth-century palace housing a roll call of Sienese Gothic painting.

The Duomo

Alleys lead north from here to the **Duomo**, completed to virtually its present size around 1215; plans to enlarge it withered with Siena's medieval prosperity. The building is a delight, its style an amazing mix of Romanesque and Gothic, delineated by bands of black and white marble on its facade. Inside, a startling sequence of 56 panels, completed between 1349 and 1547, feature virtually every artist who worked in the city. Midway along the nave, the **Libreria Piccolomini** (daily 10.30am–7.30/8pm; €3), signalled by Pinturicchio's brilliantly coloured fresco of the *Coronation of Pius II*, has superbly vivid frescoes.

Museums

Opposite the Duomo is the complex of **Santa Maria della Scala** (daily 10.30am–6.30pm; €6), the city's hospital for over eight hundred years and now a vast museum that includes the frescoed Sala del Pellegrinaio. The **Museo dell'Opera del Duomo** (Mon–Fri 9.30am–7/8pm; €6), tucked into a corner of the Duomo extension, offers a fine perspective: follow the "Panorama dal Facciatone" signs to steep spiral stairs that climb up to the top of the building; the views are sensational but the topmost walkway is narrow and scarily exposed.

Arrival and information

Train The train station is down in the valley 2km northeast of the centre; an escalator from the shopping centre opposite the train station makes reaching the centre easy; it arrives at Antiporto Di Camolia, at the end of Viale Vittoria Emmanuelle 11 and from here it is a pleasant 10min walk to the Campo.

Bus Buses stop along Piazza Gramchi, by the Basilica of San Domenico, and are much faster and more frequent from Florence than the trains (for which change at Empoli). The journey time is 1hr 10min. See Ⓦwww.sita.It for more information.

Tourist office Piazza del Campo 56 (daily 9am–7pm; Ⓣ0577.280.551/283.040, Ⓦwww.terresiena.it). You can also book train tickets here.

Discount passes If you plan on doing a lot of sightseeing, there are a whole host of combined ticket options ranging from €10–17. Ask at the tourist office for more details.

Exchange Piazza Tolone 4 (Fri 9.30am–7.30pm, Sat 10am–6pm & Sun 10am–2pm, 4–7pm).

Internet Netrunner at Via Pantaneto 54 (Mon–Sat 10am–10pm, Sun 3–8pm; €4/hr); Refe Nero, Via Del Refe Nero 18 (Mon–Fri 10am–7.30pm, Sat 9.30am–5pm; €1.70/hr).

Post office Piazza Matteotti 36/37 (Mon–Fri 8.15am–7pm, Sat 8.15am–1.30pm, closed Sun).

FESTIVALS

Open-air film festival **Cinema in Fortezza** runs from the end of June until the beginning of September. Screenings of the films, varying from slapstick American comedies and world arthouse to old Italian classics, begin at 9.45pm at the Anfiteatro della Fortezza Medicea (€5; Ⓦwww.cinemanuovopendola.it). There are also a number of open-air jazz concerts (Ⓣ0577.271.401, or check out Ⓦwww.sienajazz.it for more details) and wonderful operas held in different evocative settings all over Siena and the surrounding areas (see Ⓦwww.chigiana.it).

Accommodation

In summer, Siena gets ridiculously booked up; it's worth phoning ahead for accommodation, or booking rooms at the Siena Hotels Promotion at Piazza Madre Theresa Di Calcutta 5 (Ⓣ0577.288.084, Ⓦwww.hotelsiena.com).

Bernini Via della Sapienza 15 Ⓣ0577.289.047, Ⓦwww.albergobernini.com. Charming one-star hotel run by a friendly family;

the views from the huge windows and wonderful breakfast terrace are breathtaking. Midnight curfew. Doubles €65.

La Perla 25 Via delle Terme ⓣ057.747.144. Small, one-star *pensione* in a great central location. Rooms 26 and 28 are the newest and best, but be warned they are reached by a steep spiral staircase. Doubles €60.

Lo Stellino Via Fiorentina 95 ⓣ0577.588.926, ⓦwww.sienaholidays.com. Pretty hotel with beautifully decorated rooms, next to the HI hostel, with kitchen facilities and a garden. Doubles €60.

Podere Le Vigne Le Vigne 56 ⓣ0577.286.952, ⓦwww.poderelevigne.it. Picturesque B&B in a typical Tuscan farmhouse a 20min walk from the centre. There is lots of outdoor space to enjoy and the charming Federica also offers cooking lessons. Take bus #54 from the centre. Doubles €65.

Siena HI Hostel Via Fiorentina 89 ⓣ0577.52.212. A friendly and comfortable hostel. It is 2km northwest of the centre; take bus #10 from the train station or Piazza Gramsci, or bus #15 from Piazza Gramsci. If you're coming from Florence, ask the bus driver to let you off at "Lo Stellino". Midnight curfew. Dorms €18.50.

Eating

There is a weekly market at Fortezza Medici every Wed. For good picnic supplies try Conad supermarket on Piazza Matteotti, the shopping arcade or one of the many pizza takeaway outlets, the best of which is near the Campo on Via Rinaldini 12.

Di Nonno Mede Via Camporegio 21. Popular pizzeria (pizza €5.50) down a quiet street near San Domenica Church. The views from the terrace are unbeatable.

Il Ristoro del Papa Logge del Papa 1, between Banchi di Sotto and Bia del Porrione. Friendly, unpretentious pizzeria (pizza €6.50) and restaurant with outdoor seating area and lively atmosphere. Closed Sun.

Osteria Da Trombicche 66 Via Da Terme. Small, cosy place with two tables outside; serves delicious home-made pasta (€6) in big brown bowls. Look out for the porcupine on the wall. Mon–Sat 11am–3pm & 5.30–10pm.

Drinking and nightlife

The lively bars around the Campo, though a bit pricier than elsewhere, are open until late and drinks come with great snacks early in the evening.

Barone Rosso Via Dei Termini 9. This fun bar is a hit with locals and tourists alike. At the weekends local musicians strike up a tune.

Ortensia Via di Pantaneto 95. Small student bar with barely enough room to swing a cat but a good vibe and a friendly hippy owner add appeal. Lasagne €5, beer €2. Open from 6pm.

The Irish Post Piazza Gramschi 20/21. This Irish pub is right next to the bus station and has three wonderfully cosy rooms and outdoor seating; beer €3. Daily from noon till late.

Moving on

Train Florence (hourly; 1hr 30min); Perugia (every 90min; 3hr); Pisa (every 30min; 1hr 50min); Rome (every 2hr; 3–4hr).

Bus Florence (hourly; 90min); San Gimignano (hourly; 1hr; except Sun – involves a change at Poggibonsi).

SAN GIMIGNANO

One of the best-known villages in Tuscany, **SAN GIMIGNANO**'s skyline of towers, framed against the classic rolling hills of the Tuscan countryside, has justifiably caught the tourist imagination, and in high season can get uncomfortably busy. The village was a force to be reckoned with in the Middle Ages: it had a large population of fifteen thousand but was hit hard by the Black Death and never quite recovered – today there's half that number.

You can walk across the town in fifteen minutes and around the walls in an hour. The main entrance gate, facing the bus terminal on the south side of town, is **Porta San Giovanni,** from where **Via San Giovanni** leads to the town's interlocking main squares, **Piazza della Cisterna** and **Piazza del Duomo**. The more austere Piazza Duomo, off to the left, is flanked by the **Collegiata Cathedral** (Mon–Fri 10am–7pm, Sat 10am–5.30pm, Sun 12.30–7.30pm; buy tickets at the office on Piazza Luigi Recori €3.50), frescoed with Old and New Testament scenes. The **Palazzo del Popolo**, next door (daily 9.30/10am–5.30/7pm; €5, includes Tower, Pinoteca and Palazzo Communale), gives you the chance to climb the 218 steps of the **Torre Grossa,** the town's highest surviving tower. North from Piazza Duomo, **Via San Matteo** is one of the grandest and best preserved of the city streets, with quiet alleyways running down to the walls. The small **Wine Museum** (€3 per glass; wine-tasting evenings every Friday 6–8pm; €6 for drink and snacks; call ⓣ0577.941.267 for details) at the Parco della Rocca, is free to enter and you can enjoy a glass of wine at the adjoining bar while admiring some of the most spectacular views the city has to offer.

Arrival and information

Train The nearest train station is Poggibonsi, on the Siena–Empoli line; buses run to San Gimignano every hour (€1.60).
Bus is the best way to get here from Florence (hourly; 1hr 20min) or Siena (hourly; 1hr).
Tourist office Piazza del Duomo 1 (daily 9am–1pm & 3–7pm; ⓣ0577.940.008, ⓦwww.sangimignano.com).
Discount passes Two combined museum tickets are available (€5 or €7.50) at any of the participating sites and at the tourist office.
Internet Café just outside Porta San Mateo (€2/20min).

Accommodation

Accommodation is expensive, and it's advisable to book in advance. The tourist office can offer assistance in booking rooms or try ⓦwww.sienahotelpromotions.com. Finding house numbers in Siena can be difficult as numbers are not clearly marked.
Foresteria del Monastero S Girolamo Via Folgore 30 ⓣ0577.940.573, ⓦwww.monasterosangirolamo.it. Run by Benedictine monks this basic but excellent budget choice in a quiet monastery has comfortable rooms. Booking essential. Dorms €27.
Il Boschetto Loc. Santa Lucia 38c ⓣ0577.940.352, ⓦwww.boschettodipiemma.it. Well-equipped campsite 3km downhill in the village of Santa Lucia. Has a swimming pool and on-site restaurant. €10.50/person, plus €7/tent.
Le Vecchie Mura 15 Via Piandornella 15 ⓣ0577.940.270. The most fabulous restaurant in San Gimignano (see opposite) also rents out private rooms with a/c, and dinner on your doorstep. Doubles €60.
Milena Rossi Via Matteoti 3 ⓣ0577.941.609. A cheap option run by a mother and daughter, who also own *Al Taglio* pizza joint. Three-person apartment €70, doubles €50.

Eating and drinking

Take a picnic up to the Parco Della Rocca or the Parco di Montestaffoli and enjoy the views of the village and surrounding countryside.
Di Vinorum Piazza Cisterna 30/Via degli Innocenti 5. Despite the inauspicious entrance on the Piazza this is a lovely spot for an early evening drink. The bar is built into the town wall and has a cool stone interior. The outdoor tables have fantastic views. Wine from €3. Bruschetta from €5. Reduced opening times in winter.
Gelateria di Piazza Piazza Cisterna 1. Award-winning *gelateria* right on the piazza. Big queues build up here in high season for the former Gelato World Champion establishment.
Le Vecchie Mura Via Piandornella 15 ⓣ0577.940270. Romantic restaurant with wonderful views of the Tuscan hillside from its well-kept terrace. Only open for dinner, closed Tues. Booking essential.
Lucia & Maria Via San Matteo 55 17 ⓣ0577.940.379. The home-made cakes are a delight and the large portions of tasty bruschetta and hearty soups are good value at €6. Closed Wed.
Pizza al Taglio Via San Giorgio 110. In a city full of pizza outlets this is ranks as one of the best takeaways; slice & soft drink €3.

PERUGIA

PERUGIA, the Umbrian capital perched on a hill, is an attractive medieval university town dominated by young people of every nationality, many at the Università per Stranieri (Foreigners' University). It's a good place to for nightlife, people-watching, and eating chocolate – Italy's best-known chocolate, Perugini, is made here.

What to see and do

Perugia hinges on a single street, **Corso Vannucci**, a broad pedestrian thoroughfare. At the far end, the austere **Piazza Quattro Novembre** is backed by the plain-faced **Duomo San Lorenzo** (daily 8am–noon & 4pm–sunset) and is interrupted by the thirteenth-century Fontana Maggiore. The lavishly decorated **Collegio di Cambio** (daily 9am–12.30pm & 2.30–5.30pm; €4.50) sits at Corso Vannucci 25. This is the town's medieval money exchange, frescoed by the famous architect Perugino and said to be the most beautiful bank in the world. The Palazzo dei Priori houses the **Galleria Nazionale di Umbria** (daily 8.30am–7.30pm, closed first Mon of each month; €6.50), one of central Italy's best galleries, whose collection includes statues by Cambio, frescoes by Bonfigli and works by Perugino. **Via dei Priori** is a lovely, winding, cobbled street that gently bends through the rambling white buildings. This leads down to Agostino di Duccio's colourful **Oratorio di San Bernardino**, whose richly embellished facade is by far the best piece of sculpture in the city. On the southern side of town, along Corso Cavour, the cloisters of the large church of **San Domenico** hold the **Museo Archeologico Nazionale dell'Umbria** (Mon 10am–7.30pm, Tues–Sun 8.30am–7.30pm; €4), home of one of the most extensive Etruscan collections around.

Arrival and information

Train Trains arrive well away from the centre of Perugia on Piazza Vittorio Veneto; buses go from outside the station to Piazza Italia or Piazza Matteotti (20min). Tickets can be bought from the ticket stand for €1.50.

THE UMBRIA JAZZ FESTIVAL

One of the most prestigious jazz events in Europe, the **Umbria Jazz Festival** has featured stars such as Dizzy Gillespie and Keith Jarrett. It takes place in July and while the main events tend to be in Perugia, there are offshoots – performances and workshops that often make use of stunning churches, courts and open-air spaces – in towns across the region (see Ⓦ www.umbriajazz.com).

Bus Buses arrive at Piazza Partigiani; follow the bank of escalators up to Piazza Italia. Umbria Mobilita Ⓦ www.apmperugia.it are the biggest bus operators in Perugia and the surrounding area. Bus #TD,# TS, #R or #G run from the bus terminal to the train station.

Tourist office Piazza Matteotti 18 (daily 8.30am–6.30pm; Ⓣ 075.573.6458, Ⓦ www.perugiaonline.com).

Internet Coffee Break at Via Danzetta 22 (daily 11am–1am; €1/hr).

Accommodation

Hotel Rosalba Via del Circo 7 Ⓣ 075.572.0626, Ⓦ www.hotelrosalba.com. Standing alone and impossible to miss with its pink facade, the eccentric and friendly owner runs a great hotel with fresh rooms in a quiet but central location. Doubles €70.

Ostello Della Gioventù Via Bontempi 13 Ⓣ 075.572.2880, Ⓦ www.ostello.perugia.it. Welcoming hostel 2min from the Duomo, with a 1am curfew. Closed between 9.30am and 4pm. Dorms €15.

San Ercolano Via Del Bovaro 9 Ⓣ 075.572.4650, Ⓦ www.santercolano.com. Great budget option, this small hotel in the old town has small clean rooms and friendly staff. Doubles from €50.

Spagnoli Via Cortonese 4 Ⓣ 075.501.1366. Located near the train station, this basic hostel is a handy option to save the walk up the hill into town. Dorms €16.

Eating

Being a student city there are plenty of cheap cafés and takeaways. Co-op (daily 9am–8pm) supermarket is on Piazza Matteotti 15 while Mercato Coperto (Mon–Sat 8am–2pm) is a covered market off Piazza Matteotti, next to the information centre.

Antica Salumeria Granieri Amato Piazza Matteotti. A stall selling sandwiches stuffed with hot roast pork (€2.50). Mon–Sat till 9pm.

Dal Mi'Cocco Corso Garibaldi 12 Ⓣ 075.573.2511. They keep it beautifully simple at this local favourite. The four-course meal costs €13 and the portions are large and hearty. It's best to book. No credit cards.

Il Gufo Via della Viola 18. Run by Italian and German chefs, the "Owl" tavern specializes in using seasonal ingredients in their unpredictable menu that changes daily. Closed Mon.

Mediterranea Piazza Piccinino 11/12 Ⓣ 075.572.1322. Perugia's best pizzeria and possibly Umbria's finest. It serves a vast selection of tasty, cheap pizzas (€5). Booking recommended.

FESTIVALS

As well as its jazz festival, Perugia has a stream of eclectic events throughout the year that are well worth looking up in advance. In mid-October there's a **chocolate festival** (Ⓦwww.eurochocolate.com) that lasts for ten days, while the **Christmas market** is splendid in its scale and opulence. See Ⓦwww .regioneumbria.eu for details.

Drinking and nightlife

Frequented by both local and international students, Perugia's nightlife is varied and lively. If you are not a fan of students nocturnal Perugia is not for you.

Il Birraio Via Del Sole 18. This eclectic pub and brewery serves a large selection of beer and food in differently styled rooms that cater for all moods.

La Terraza Via Matteotti, next to tourist office. Outdoor bar with sweeping views over the Umbrian countryside. Cocktails from €5. Open late May–Sept.

Le Caffe Di Roma Piazza Matteoti 32. A great café for people watching with outdoor seating; cappuccino only €1.

L'Officina Borgo XX Gingro 56. Tucked away so you hardly notice it, this modernist *enoteca*'s centrepiece is a glass-walled kitchen. The staff are extremely friendly and the wine is fantastic. Glass of wine €3. Closed Sun.

Punto di Vista Viale dell'Indipendenza 2. Extremely popular bar with beautiful views of the rolling countryside and snowcapped peaks in the distance. Daily 11pm–2.30am; closed in winter. Beer €4.

Moving on

Train Assisi (hourly; 20min); Florence (every 2hr; 2hr); Rome (frequent; 2–3hr).

Bus Siena (1 daily; 1hr 30min).

ASSISI

ASSISI is Umbria's best-known town thanks to St Francis, Italy's premier saint and founder of the Franciscan order. It has a medieval hill-town charm and is easy to navigate around in just a few hours.

The **Basilica di San Francesco**, now restored to its former glory after a devastating earthquake in 1997, is at the end of Via San Francesco (daily 8.30am–6pm). It houses one of the most overwhelming collections of art outside a gallery anywhere in the world. St Francis lies under the floor of the Lower Church, in a crypt only brought to light in 1818. The walls have been lavishly frescoed by artists such as Cimabue and Giotto, and the stained-glass windows cast a dim light that enhances the magical atmosphere. The Upper Church, built to a light and airy Gothic plan, is richly decorated too, with dazzling frescoes about the life of St Francis. A short trek up the steep Via di San Rufino leads to the thirteenth-century **Duomo** (Mon–Fri 7am–12.30pm & 2.30–7pm), which holds the font used to baptize St Francis.

From the train station, there are half-hourly buses into town. The **tourist office** is on Piazza del Comune 12 (Mon–Sat 8am–2pm & 3–6.30pm, Sun 9am–1pm). There is an excellent small **hostel**, *Ostello della Pace*, run by a very friendly couple (177 Via Di Valecchie; Ⓣ075. 816.767, Ⓦwww.assisihostel.com; dorms €17), located on a beautiful hillside just below the town. For **lunch** or a snack, head to *Il Duomo* on Via Porta Perlici 11, which does tasty, stone-oven pizzas (€4) or the small *Pizzeria Otello* on Via S. Antonio. Alternatively, if you feel like splashing out, book a table at the romantic and candlelit pizzeria (pizzas €8) *Lanterna* on Via S.Rufino 39.

SPOLETO

SPOLETO is a tiny hill-top town adorned with small and winding cobbled streets, beautiful Romanesque churches and the remains of an ancient amphitheatre. **Piazza della Libertà** is where you will find the **Museo Archeologico** (Mon–Sun 8.30am–7.30pm; €4), and where you can also glimpse the ancient arena. From here it's a short walk to the elegant **Duomo** (8.30am–12.30pm

& 3.30–7pm). Inside, the apse frescoes were painted by the fifteenth-century Florentine artist Fra Lippo Lippi – he died shortly after their completion amid rumours that he was poisoned for seducing the daughter of a local noble family. The **Ponte delle Torri**, a photo-favourite, is an astonishing piece of medieval engineering, best seen as part of a circular walk (Mon 9am–2pm & Tues–Sun 9am–6pm) around the base of the **Rocca**. **Piazza del Mercato** and its surrounding streets are a great place to head for a spot of lunch, where there are numerous restaurants offering fixed-price lunch deals: try Trattoria del Festivale on Via Brignole 6, or the excellent *Pizzeria Zeppelin* at Piazza della Republica.

There is a small **hostel**, *Villa Redenta* at 1 Via di Redenta (ⓣ0743.224.936, ⓦwww.villaredenta.com; rooms from €30) just a short walk from the station in the lower town. If you're looking for somewhere closer to the action try *Hotel due Porte* (doubles €55) on Piazza della Vittoria run by a cheery owner.

URBINO

URBINO boasted one of the most prestigious courts in Europe in the fifteenth century, and today the highlight of a visit to this small and stunning hill-top town is the magnificent Palazzo Ducale and its impressive collection of Renaissance paintings. Urbino is hard to reach; the best options are either indirect bus from Perugia (daily; 1hr 50min; €13) or from Pésaro (every 30min, last bus around 9.30pm; 1hr; €2.75). All buses stop in Borgo Mercatale; from here follow Via Mazzini to the city's main square the Piazza della Repubblica. From the piazza all the main sights are a steep but short walk away. The **tourist office** is on Via Puccinotti 3 opposite the Palazzo Ducale, itself built by the extravagant Federico da Montefeltro, the fifteenth-century Duke of Urbino. It is now home to the excellent **Galleria Nazionale delle Marche** (Mon 8.30am–2pm, Tues–Sun 8.30am–7.15pm; €5). Among the paintings in the Appartamento del Duca is Piero della Francesca's strange *Flagellation* and the portrait of the Mute by Raphael, who was born in Urbino. The most interesting of the Palazzo's rooms is Federico's Studiolo, a triumph of illusory perspective.

Buzzy Piazza della Repubblica is a great place for **lunch** or a **drink** – try *Dolce Vita*, which has tables on the square, or the nearby *Pizzeria Il Buco*, tucked under the wall on Via Battisti 1. For **accommodation** *Hotel San Giovanni* on Via Barocci 13 (ⓣ0722.2827, ⓦwww.albergosangiovanniurbino.it; doubles €46) is a good, centrally located option, while there's the smarter but pricier *Albergo Italia* on Corso Garibaldi 32 (ⓣ0722.2701, ⓦwww.albergo-italia-urbino.it; doubles €80).

Moving on

Bus Perugia (daily; 1hr 50min); Pésaro (every 30min; 1hr).

FROM ITALY AND BEYOND

The main arrival and departure port on the eastern coast is the transit town of **Ancona**, with ferries taking you to Croatia, Albania, Greece and Turkey. Ferries leave from Stazione Marittima, a few kilometres north of the train station (take bus #1). All of the ferry companies have ticket offices dotted around the port, plus there are dozens of agencies around town if these happen to be closed. Destinations include: Corfu, Greece (weekly; 15hr); Durrës, Albania (3 weekly in summer; 19hr); Igoumenítsa, Greece (daily; 15hr); Pátra, Greece (daily; 21hr); Split, Croatia (daily; 4hr 30min–10hr); Stari Grad, Croatia (July & August only; 2 weekly; 10hr); Vis, Croatia (weekly; 9hr); Zadar, Croatia (daily; 9hr).

Southern Italy

The Italian **south** (*mezzogiorno*) offers quite a different experience from that of the north; indeed, few countries are more tangibly divided into two distinct, often antagonistic, regions. **Naples** is the obvious focus of the south, an utterly compelling city just a couple of hours south of Rome. In the **Bay of Naples**, highlights are the resort of Sorrento and the island of **Capri**, crawling with tourists but beautiful enough to be worth your time, while the ancient sites of **Pompeii** and **Herculaneum** are Italy's best-preserved Roman remains. South of Naples, the **Amalfi Coast** is a contender for Europe's most dramatic stretch of coastline. In the far south, **Matera**, jewel of the Basilicata region, harbours ancient cave dwellings dug into a steep ravine. Puglia – the long strip of land that makes up the "heel" of Italy – boasts the Baroque wonders of **Lecce,** and is also useful for ferries to Greece and Croatia.

NAPLES

Wherever else you travel south of Rome, the chances are that you'll wind up in **NAPLES** (Napoli). It's the kind of city people visit with preconceptions, and it rarely disappoints: it is dirty and overbearing; it is crime-ridden; and it is most definitely like nowhere else in Italy – something the inhabitants will be keener than anyone to tell you. One thing, though, is certain: a couple of days here and you're likely to be as staunch a defender of the place as its most devoted inhabitants.

What to see and do

The area between the vast and busy Piazza Garibaldi, the city's transport hub, and Via Toledo, the main street a mile or so west, makes up the old part of the city – the **centro storico**, whose buildings rise high on either side of the narrow, crowded streets. South of here is the busy port, and to the northwest, Naples' finest museums.

The Duomo

From Piazza Garibaldi, Via dei Tribunali cuts through to Via Duomo, where you'll find the tucked-away **Duomo**, a Gothic building from the early thirteenth century dedicated to San Gennaro, the patron saint of the city, martyred in 305 AD. Two phials of his blood miraculously liquefy three times a year – on the first Saturday in May, on September 19 and on December 16. If the blood refuses to liquefy, disaster is supposed to befall the city. The first chapel on the right as you walk into the cathedral holds the precious phials, as well as Gennaro's skull.

MADRE

A short walk up Via Duomo, Naples' superb modern art museum, **MADRE**, at Via Settembrini 79 (Wed–Mon 10.30am–2.30pm; €7, Mon free), shows off works by some big-name contemporary artists. The most prominent of these is by Francesco Clemente, a New York-based Neapolitan artist who created the huge, vibrant mural of Naples. The museum also holds works by the likes of Jeff Koons, Anish Kapoor and Gilbert and George, as well as Damien Hirst's famous dot paintings and a massive anchor – symbolizing the city's maritime roots – by Jannis Kounellis.

Spaccanapoli and around

Busy Via dei Tribunali and its parallel, Via San Biagio dei Librai – commonly known as **Spaccanapoli** – make up the heart of the old city and Naples' busiest and architecturally richest quarter. A maelstrom of hurrying pedestrians, revving cars and buzzing scooters, this is the best place to get a sense of the city and its inhabitants. At 253

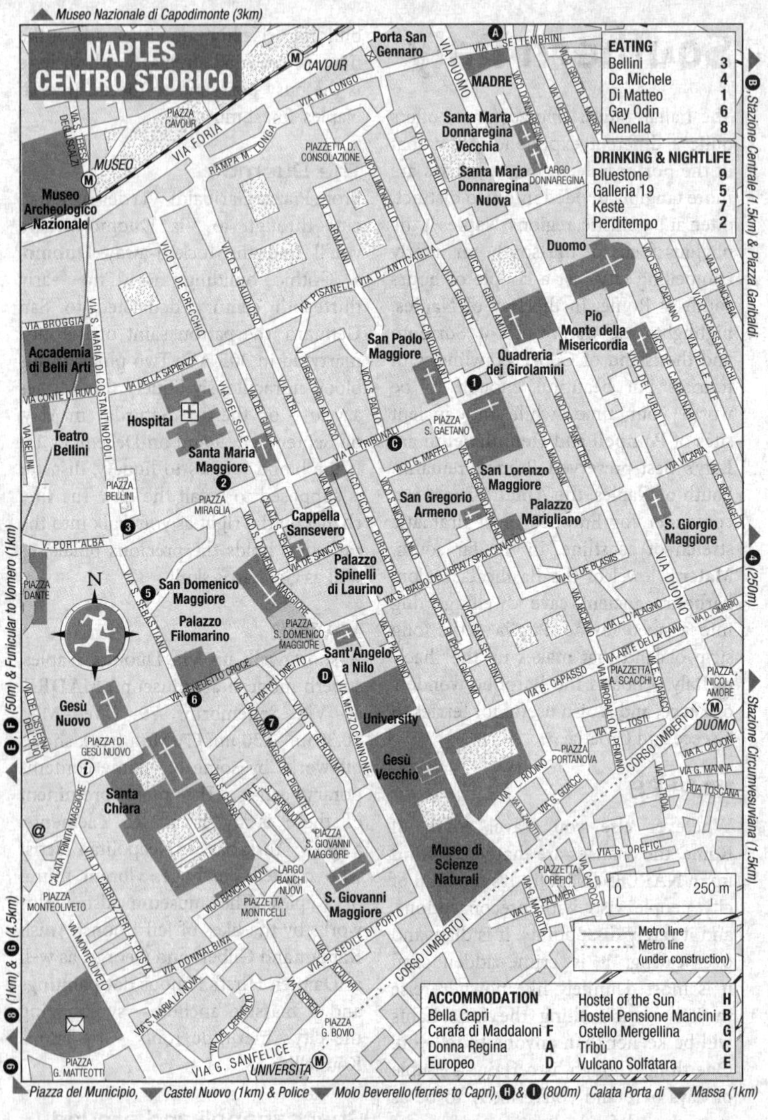

Via dei Tribunali is the **Pio Monte della Misericordia** (Thurs–Tues 9am–2.30pm; €5, free audioguide), an unassuming jewel of a church thanks to its breathtaking altarpiece: Caravaggio's *Seven Works of Mercy* which elegantly juxtaposes warm acts of charity with ribald picaresque street-life, reflecting something of Naples's own appeal. The picture gallery is well worth a visit, containing works by Francesco de Mura, Ribera and others.

Gesù Nuovo and Santa Chiara

West up Spaccanapoli is the **Gesù Nuovo** church, distinctive for its lava-stone facade, prickled with pyramids that give it an impregnable, prison-like air. Facing the Gesù Nuovo, the church of **Santa Chiara** is quite different, a Provencal-Gothic structure built in 1328 (and rebuilt after World War II). The attached **cloister** (Mon–Sat 9.30am–5.30pm, Sun 10am–2.30pm; €5), covered with colourful majolica tiles depicting bucolic scenes, is one of the gems of the city.

Castel Nuovo

A ten-minute walk south of Santa Chiara, **Piazza del Municipio** is a busy traffic junction that stretches down to the waterfront, dominated by the brooding hulk of the **Castel Nuovo**. Built in 1282 by the Angevins and later the royal residence of the Aragon kings, it now contains the **Museo Civico** (Mon–Sat 9am–7pm; €5), which holds periodic exhibitions – but it's the views from the top terrace that make the entrance fee worthwhile.

Palazzo Reale and around

Some 500m west of the castle, **Piazza del Plebiscito**, with its impressive sweep of columns, was modelled on Bernini's Piazza San Pietro in Rome. On one side of the square, the dignified **Palazzo Reale** (Thurs–Tues 9am–7pm; €4) was built in 1602 to accommodate a visit by Philip III of Spain. Upstairs, the first-floor rooms are sumptuously decorated with gilded furniture, *trompe-l'oeil* ceilings, and seventeenth- and eighteenth-century paintings.

Just beyond the castle, the opulent **Teatro San Carlo** is the largest opera house in Italy, and one of the most distinguished in the world. The cheapest seats you can book are €25 for opera, €20 for ballet.

Museo Archeologico Nazionale

Arrowing north from the Piazza del Plebiscito, Via Toledo leads to the **Museo Archeologico Nazionale** (Wed–Mon 9am–7.30pm; €6.50), home to the best of the finds from the nearby Roman sites of Pompeii and Herculaneum. The ground floor concentrates on sculpture, the mezzanine houses the museum's collection of mosaics, while upstairs, wall paintings from the villas of Pompeii and Herculaneum are the museum's other major draw. Don't miss the "secret" room of erotic Roman pictures and sculptures, once thought to be a threat to public morality.

Museo Nazionale di Capodimonte

At the top of the hill is the city's second major museum, the **Museo Nazionale di Capodimonte** (Thurs–Tues 8.30am–7.30pm; €7.50; bus #R4 from Via Toledo or #178 from the Museo Archeologico), the former residence of the Bourbon King Charles III, built in 1738. This has a huge and superb collection of Renaissance and Flemish paintings, including a couple of Brueghels, canvases by Perugino and Pinturicchio, an elegant *Madonna and Child with Angels* by Botticelli and Lippi's soft, sensitive *Annunciation*.

Vomero

Vomero, the district topping the hill immediately above the old city, can be reached by funicular from Corso Vittorio Emanuele, west of the Gesù Nuovo, or Piazza Augusteo near the Teatro San Carlo. A five-minute stroll from the station, the star-shaped fortress of **Castel Sant'Elmo** (Wed–Mon 8.30am–7.30pm; €5) was built in the fourteenth century and hosts occasional exhibitions. Occupying Naples' highest point, its lovely views are only topped by those from the terraced gardens of the **Certosa e Museo di San Martino** (Thurs–Tues 8.30am–7.30pm; €6), a former Carthusian monastery. Now a museum, it contains seventeenth- and eighteenth-century Neapolitan painting and sculpture.

Arrival and information

Air The red-and-white official airport bus Alibus (every 20min; €3) runs from Naples' Capodochino Airport to Piazza Garibaldi and then Piazza Municipio.

Train Trains arrive at Piazza Garibaldi, the main hub of all transport services.

Bus Most long-distance, inter-regional buses and local buses use Piazza Garibaldi, but some (for Amalfi, Sorrento and Pompeii) use Piazza Immacolatella, in the port area.

Ferry Hydrofoils dock at Molo Beverello, a short bus ride or a 15min walk from the centre; ferries arrive at Calata Porta di Massa, connected with Molo Beverello by free shuttle bus.

Tourist information At the train station (daily 9am–8pm) and airport (daily 9am–7pm), but the main tourist office is at Piazza del Gesù Nuovo (Mon–Sat 9am–7pm, Sun 9am–2pm; ⓣ081.551.2701, ⓦwww.inaples.it). Pick up the free listings booklet *Qui Napoli*, handy for events and transport times.

Discount cards If you are around for more than a day, invest in the Artecard (from €12; sold in the station, museums and online at ⓦwww.campaniartecard.it), which is valid on various combinations of city transport, along with free and discounted museum entrance.

City transport

Tickets Buy tickets – valid on all city transport – from *tabacchi*. €1.20 tickets are valid for 1hr 30min, €3.60 ones for the day. A 24hr, Unico Costiera ticket also allows you to travel on SITA buses (to Amalfi, for example) and Circumvesuviana trains (for Pompeii). Prices vary depending on your destination and costs less on weekends. Stamp tickets on board to validate them.

Bus and metro Walking is the best option in the centre, but an extensive bus and metro network is available for the footsore. Useful routes include #R2 between the port, station and the centro storico–Piazza del Gesù, Via Santa Chiara and Via Tribunale. Underground metros – indicated by a red M symbol – are fast but only run every 10min or so. Stops include Piazza Garibaldi, Piazza Cavour, Piazza Dante and Piazza Vanvitelli in Vomero.

Funicular Funicular railways run up to Vomero and the suburbs of Chiaia and Mergellina.

Accommodation

Many of the cheaper hotels are unappealingly sited around Piazza Garibaldi, near the station. If you can afford it, shell out a few extra euros to stay in one of the budget hotels in the historic centre instead. Breakfast is included in all options below, unless stated otherwise.

> If you're going to splurge on accommodation anywhere in Italy, Naples is the place: your money will go a lot further and the city's clutch of boutique B&Bs make memorable places to stay. Choose between arty **Tribù** (Via Tribunali 339; ⓣ081.454.793, ⓦwww.tribunapoli.com; €80), with a cool, designer feel; **Donna Regina** (Via Settembrini 80; ⓣ081.446.799, ⓦwww.discovernaples.net; €92), a beautifully restored ex-convent run by a family of artists; and **Carafa di Maddaloni** (Via Maddaloni 6; ⓣ081.551.3691, ⓦwww.bb-carafa.com; €65–75), with beautiful, frescoed rooms filled with antiques.

Hostels and hotels

Bella Capri Via Melisurgo 4 ⓣ081.552.9494, ⓦwww.bellacapri.it. Right by the port, with bright common areas and small, a/c dorms. It's also a hotel, with simple rooms overlooking the bay. Ten percent discount with this book. Dorms €20, doubles €60–70.

Europeo Via Mezzocannone 109/c ⓣ081.551.8691, ⓦwww.sea-hotels.com. Although small, rooms are central, great value and has a/c. No breakfast, though biscuits are presented on your bed on your arrival. Doubles €50–65.

Hostel of the Sun Via Melisurgo 15 ⓣ081.420.6393, ⓦwww.hostelnapoli.com. Colourful hostel next to the port. The friendly staff are full of advice and organize nightlife tours and pasta parties. Free internet and a bar with a happy hour. Dorms €20; ten percent discount on doubles (€60–70) with this book.

Hostel Pensione Mancini Via Mancini 33 ⓣ081.553.6731, ⓦwww.hostelpensionemancini.com. Right across from the station with kitchen, a/c in all rooms and free luggage storage. Ten percent discount with this book. Dorms €16, rooms €45–55.

Ostello Mergellina Salita della Grotta 23 ⓣ081.761.2346, ⓔnapoli@ostellionline.org. Metro to Mergellina or bus #R3 from Piazza Municipio. HI hostel some way out of the centre with a view of the bay. Breakfast included. Dorms €17, doubles €42.

Camping

Vulcano Solfatara Via Solfatara 161, Pozzuoli ⓣ081.526.2341, ⓦwww.solfatara.it. Metro to Pozzuoli, then a 10min walk uphill. This well-equipped campsite, on the edge of a volcanic crater, has a swimming pool, mini-market and takeaway. €9.90/person, plus €5.40/tent; 2-person bungalows €51.

Eating

Spaccanapoli and Via Tribunali are full of grocery stores, which make up panini for a few euros, and there's a central supermarket, Fior do Cafè, near the university at Via Mezzocannone 99. Colourful produce markets are found all over the centre; one of the best (daily 8am–1pm) takes up the streets around Via Pignasecca, a few streets west of the Gesù Nuovo.

Bellini Via Costantinopoli 79-80. Signature dish *linguine al cartocchio* is unmissable for seafood lovers– fresh clams, mussels, prawns and squid are cooked with tomato, herbs and pasta in a grease-proof paper bag, served with a little ceremony at your table (€11). Pizzas are also good (€6–9). Closed Sun evening.

Da Michele Via Cesare Sersale 1–3. Closed Sun. One of Naples' best pizzerias, serving three options: marinara, margherita or double margherita, from €2.50. Queues can get epic (get a ticket from the cash desk) so order to take away if you can't wait.

Di Matteo Via Tribunali 94. Brilliant pizza. Give your name to the waiters when you arrive then grab a *frittatina* for €1 while you await your table – it's a heavenly bundle of pasta, mince, peas, cheese and black pepper, deep-fried. Closed Sun.

Gay Odin Via Benedetto Croce 61 (plus other branches around the city). Absolutely incredible *gelateria* and chocolate shop. The plain yogurt flavour is lovely. €1.50 cup or cone.

Nennella Vico Lungo Teatro Nuovo 103–105. Authentic Neapolitan cuisine like *pasta e fagioli* (soup with pasta and beans) and sautéed *friarelli* (local chicory-like greens) are served up in this entertaining trattoria, which is always heaving at lunchtime. Full meals €10–12. Closed Sun.

Drinking and nightlife

Most clubs close in July and August and move to the beach; the Neapolitans who remain congregate for a beer in the studenty bars around Piazza del Gesù Nuovo. The rest of the year, the bars and clubs along Via Cisterna dell'Olio, just off the piazza, are a good bet.

Bluestone Via Alabardieri 10. A trendy bar in the Chiaia district, by the water, a favourite hangout for hip Neapolitans. There's often a band with the occasional international act.

Galleria 19 Via S. Sebastiano 19. One of the coolest clubs in Naples, with a velvet Baroque interior, great cocktails, live music and a friendly crowd. Closed mid-May to Sept.

Kestè Largo San Giovanni Maggiore Pignatelli 26–27. A buzzy bar with DJs and live music. Go early for the *aperitivo* buffet and stay for the band or DJ set. Closed Aug.

Perditempo Via San Pietro a Maiella 8. Tiny bar with stacks of new and used CDs and LPs, live music and a cool crowd. Closed Sun & Aug.

Directory

Consulates UK, Via dei Mille 40 ⓣ081.423.8911; US, Piazza della Repubblica 2 ⓣ081.583.8111.
Exchange At Stazione Centrale (daily 8am–7.30pm).
Hospital Ambulance ⓣ118; the Guardia Medica Permanente in Palazzo Municipio is open 24hr.
Internet Lemme Lemme (Piazza Bellini 74; Mon–Sat open all day until 2am, Sun 6.30pm–2am; €0.05/min).
Pharmacy At the train station (24hr).
Police ⓣ113. Main police station is at Via Medina 75 ⓣ081.794.1111.
Post office Piazza Matteotti Giacomo 2 (Mon–Fri 8am–6.30pm, Sat 8am–12.30pm).

Moving on

Air Palermo (several daily; 55min).
Train Lecce (5 daily; 5hr 30min); Palermo (3 daily; 9hr 30min–11hr); Pompeii (from Stazione Circumvesuviana; every 30min; 40min); Rome (every 20min; 1hr 10min–2hr 40min); Siracusa (3 daily; 8hr 30min–10hr 30min); Sorrento (every 20min; 1hr 05min; reach Amalfi by bus or ferry from Sorrento).
Bus Assisi (2 daily; 5hr); Atrani (2 daily; 2hr 30min); Lecce (3 daily; 5hr 30min); Perugia (2 daily; 4hr 30min); Pompeii (hourly; 35min); Sorrento (2 daily; 1hr 20min).
Ferry Capri (10 daily; 1hr 20min); Palermo (2 daily; 8–10hr 30min).
Hydrofoil Capri (every 30min–1hr; 40min); Sorrento (6 daily; 50min).

THE BAY OF NAPLES

Of the islands that dot the bay, **Capri** is the best place to visit if you're here for a short time. **Sorrento**, the brooding presence of **Vesuvius** and the incomparable Roman sites of **Herculaneum** and **Pompeii** are further draws.

Vesuvius

Its most famous eruption, in 79 AD, buried the towns and inhabitants of Pompeii and Herculaneum, and **VESUVIUS** has long dominated the lives of those who live on the Bay of Naples. It's still an active volcano – the only one on mainland Europe – and there have been hundreds of (mostly minor) eruptions over the years. The people who live here fear its reawakening, and with good reason – scientists calculate it should erupt every thirty years or so, and it hasn't done so since 1944. Catch the Circumvesuviana to Pompeii and then the Unico Campania bus to 1000m up the volcano (10 daily between 8am & 3.30pm; last bus down 5.40pm; €11). Alternatively, Vesuvio Express minibuses run from Ercolano Scavi (Ercolano; see opposite) train station roughly every half-hour (daily 9.30am–4.30pm; 1hr 30min; €10 return; ⓣ0817.393.666) to a car park and huddle of souvenir shops and cafés. The walk up to the **crater** from the bus stop takes about half an hour on marked-out paths. At the top (admission €8), the crater is a deep, wide, jagged ashtray of red rock emitting the odd plume of smoke. You can walk most of the way around, but take it easy – the fences are old and rickety. See ⓦwww.vesuviopark.it for information on trails around the volcano.

Pompeii

Destroyed by Vesuvius, **POMPEII** (daily: 8.30am–7.30pm; ticket office closes 6pm; €11) was, in Roman times, one of Campania's most important commercial centres. Of a total population of twenty thousand, it's thought that two thousand perished in the great eruption of 79 AD, asphyxiated by the toxic fumes of the volcanic debris, their homes buried under several metres of ash and pumice. The full horror of their death is apparent in plaster casts made from the shapes their bodies left in the volcanic ash – gruesome, writhing figures, some with their hands covering their eyes.

Seeing the site will take you half a day at least. Entering from the Pompeii-Villa dei Misteri side, you come across the **Forum**, a slim open space surrounded by the ruins of some of the town's most important official buildings. North of here lies a small baths complex, and beyond, the **House of the Faun**, its "Ave" (Welcome) mosaic outside beckoning you in to view the atrium and the copy of a tiny bronze dancing faun. A few streets southwest, the **Lupanare** was Pompeii's only purpose-built brothel, worth a peek for its racy wall paintings. A short walk from the Porta Ercolano is the **Villa dei Misteri**, the best preserved of all Pompeii's palatial houses, which contains frescoes depicting the initiation rites of a young woman into the Dionysiac Mysteries, an orgiastic cult transplanted to Italy from Greece in the Republican era.

On the other side of the site, the **Grand Theatre** is still used for performances, as is the **Little Theatre** on its far left side. From here, it's a short walk to the **Amphitheatre**, one of Italy's most intact and also its oldest, dating from 80 BC.

Herculaneum

The town of **Ercolano**, a 15-minute hop on the train from Naples on the Circumvesuviana line (€2.10 one-way), is the modern offshoot of the ancient site of **HERCULANEUM** (daily: April–Oct 8.30am–7.30pm; ticket office shuts 6pm; €11), situated at the seaward end of Ercolano's main street. A residential town destroyed by the eruption of Vesuvius on August 2, 79 AD, it's much smaller than Pompeii, and as such is a more manageable site – less architecturally impressive, but with better-preserved buildings. Highlights include the **House of the Mosaic Atrium**, with its mosaic-laid courtyard, the large baths complex and the **Casa del Bel Cortile**, which contains a group of skeletons, poignantly lying in the pose they died in. Ercolano's tourist office is at Via IV Novembre 82 (Mon–Sat 8am–2pm; ⓣ081.788.1243).

SORRENTO

Topping the rocky cliffs close to the end of its peninsula, **SORRENTO**'s inspired location and pleasant climate has drawn travellers from all over Europe for two hundred years. Nowadays it caters mostly to the package-tour industry, but this bright, lively place retains its southern Italian roots. Accommodation and food, though not exactly cheap, are much better value than most of the other resorts along the Amalfi Coast, making it a good base from which to explore the area. Sorrento's centre, **Piazza Tasso**, makes a lively focus for the evening *passeggiata*. The town isn't well provided with beaches: most people make do with the rocks and a tiny, crowded strip of sand at **Marina Grande** – fifteen minutes' walk or a short bus ride from Piazza Tasso.

Arrival and information

Train Circumvesuviana trains from Naples (every 30min; 1hr; €4) arrive at the train station, a 5min walk from the centre.

Bus Autolinee Curreri coaches from Naples Airport (6 daily; 1hr 15min; €10) stop at Via degli Aranci, near the train station; SITA buses (every 45 min; 1hr 40min; €3.60) from Amalfi arrive at the station.

Ferry Metrò del Mare operates high-season connections from Naples (4 daily; 1hr; €6.50) to Sorrento's port, an uphill walk or short bus ride (buy tickets from *tabacchi*; €1) from the centre.

Tourist office In the large yellow Circolo dei Foresteri building at Via de Maio 35, just off Piazza Sant'Antonino (Mon–Fri 8.30am–4.15pm; ⓣ081.807.4033, ⓦwww.sorrentotourism.com).

Accommodation

Camping Nube d'Argento Via del Capo 21 ⓣ081.878.1344, ⓦwww.nubedargento.com. A 15min walk from Piazza Tasso towards Marina Grande, this campsite has a pool, restaurant and sea views. €11/person, plus €6/tent, two-person bungalows €70 (€85 in Aug). Closed Nov–Feb.

Hostel Le Sirene Via degli Aranci 160 ⓣ081.807.2925, ⓦwww.hostellesirene.com. 300m from the station, this hostel is a little cramped, but there's a kitchen. Dorms €18–27.50, doubles €45–65.

Ulisse Via del Mare 22 ⓣ081.877.4753, ⓦwww.ulissedeluxe.com. A 5min walk from the centre and just 300m from the sea, this "deluxe hostel" has plush a/c en suites, some of which have been converted into 6-person dorms. Continental breakfast included. Dorms €25–28, doubles €70–90 (half-price for single occupancy).

Eating

There's a Standa supermarket at Corso Italia 223, and Ortofrutticola da Armando, near the station at Via degli Aranci 72, makes panini to order.

Giardiniello Via Accademia 7. Just off Corso Italia, this restaurant-pizzeria with a small garden specializes in fish and barbecued meats, and also does cheap pasta; pizza and drink €5.

Mami Camilla Via Cocumella 4 ⓣ081.878.2067, ⓦwww.mamicamilla.com. Call before 6pm to book a four-course dinner at this cookery school for just €18.

Trattoria Emilia dal 1947 Via Marina Grande 62 ⓣ081.807.2720. This family-run trattoria has prime position on a jetty over the water. Brilliant mixed fried fish (€11) and seafood spaghetti (€9) are cooked by the original Emilia's proud descendants.

Drinking and nightlife

In summer, all the clubbing action takes place at venues out of Sorrento, along the coast. Promoters distribute tickets from midnight onwards in Piazza Tasso; clubs are a 10min taxi ride from here.

Bar Syranuse Piazza Tasso. A lively bar with a terrace that hangs over the edge of the piazza surrounded by a cluster of discos and karaoke clubs.

Mannekin Pis Strada Fuoro/Strada Tasso. A friendly pub with plenty of outdoor seats and whatever English food you're missing. If there's a football match you want to watch, it'll be on here.

Moving on

Train Naples (every 30min–1hr; 50min).

Bus Amalfi (every 40min–1hr; 1hr 30min); Rome (1–2 daily; 4hr).

Ferry Capri (4 daily; 25min); Amalfi (2 daily; 60min)
Hydrofoil Capri (every 30min–1hr; 20min); Naples (6 daily; 50min).

CAPRI

Rising from the sea off the far end of the Sorrentine peninsula, the island of **Capri** is the most sought-after destination in the Bay of Naples. During Roman times the Emperor Tiberius retreated here to indulge in debauchery; more recently the Blue Grotto and the island's remarkable landscape have drawn tourists in their droves. Capri is a busy and expensive place, but it's easy enough to visit as a day-trip (and there's no budget accommodation on the island). In July and August, however, you may prefer to give it a miss rather than fight through the crowds.

What to see and do

CAPRI TOWN is a very pretty place, with winding alleyways converging on the tiny main square of Piazza Umberto. The Giardini di Augusto give tremendous views of the coast below and the towering jagged cliffs above. Opposite, take the hairpin path, Via Krupp, down to **MARINA PICCOLA**, a huddle of houses and restaurants around a few patches of pebble beach – pleasantly quiet out of season, though in summer it's heaving. You can also reach the ruins of Tiberius' villa, the **Villa Jovis**, from Capri town (daily 9am–5.30/6pm; €2), a steep thirty-minute trek east. The site is among Capri's most exhilarating, with incredible views.

ANACAPRI, the island's other main settlement, though less picturesque is the starting point for some worthwhile excursions: from here a chairlift (daily: March–Oct 9am–5pm; Nov–Feb 9am–3.30pm; €10 return) carries you up 596m **Monte Solaro**, the island's highest point, where there's a pricey but picturesquely sited café. The island's most famous attraction, the **Blue Grotto**, is an hour's trek down Via Lo Pozzo, but it's best to take a bus from the main square. At €12.50 it's a bit of a rip-off, with boatmen whisking visitors through the grotto in five minutes flat, but the intense, glowing blue of the cave is undeniably beautiful.

Arrival and information

Ferry Ferries and hydrofoils dock at Marina Grande, the waterside extension of Capri Town, which perches on the hill above, connected by funicular. Buses link the island's main centres – Marina Grande, Capri Town, Marina Piccola and Anacapri – every 10min (€1.40, or €6.90 for a day ticket).
Tourist office Piazza Umberto in Capri town (June–Sept Mon–Sat 8.30am–8.30pm, Sun 9am–3pm; Oct–May Mon–Sat 9am–1pm & 4–7.15pm, Sun 9am–3pm; ⓣ081.837.0686, ⓦwww.capritourism.com).

Eating

Picnics are a good way to avoid paying Capri's inflated restaurant prices. Alimentari da Brioches (Via Fuorlovado 5, Capri Town) makes up panini to order for about €4.
Le Arcate Via Tommaso de Tommaso, Anacapri. Family-run trattoria-pizzeria with a terrace right by the cable-car stop. Wood-fired pizza and a drink €11.
Buonocore Via Vittorio Emanuele, Capri Town. Affordable, good-quality takeaway with tasty fried snacks (€3) and hearty pasta (€8) plus delicious biscuits and cakes. Does a roaring trade in *gelato* served in waffle-cups made before your eyes.

THE AMALFI COAST

Occupying the southern side of Sorrento's peninsula, the **Amalfi Coast** is one of Europe's most beautiful stretches of coast, its corniche road winding around the towering cliffs. There are no trains; buses from Sorrento and Naples take the coast road – a spectacular ride of hairpin bends with fantastic views of the undulating coastline.

Amalfi

In Byzantine times, **AMALFI** was an independent republic and a naval superpower, with a population of some seventy thousand. Vanquished by the

Normans in 1131, it was then devastated by an earthquake in 1343. A few remnants of Amalfi's past glories survive, and its narrow alleyways and tucked-away piazzas make it fun to wander through. The **Duomo** dominates the main piazza, its toy-town facade topped by a glazed-tiled cupola. St Andrew is buried in its crypt, though the most appealing part of the building is the cloister (daily 9am–7.45pm, earlier in winter; €3) – Arabic in feel, with its whitewashed arches and palms. Opposite Piazza Gioia, the **Arsenale** (daily 10am–8.30pm; €2) displays the Tavole Amalfitane – the book of maritime laws that governed the Republic, and the rest of the Mediterranean, until 1570, as well as an exhibition about the evolution of the compass, which was said to have been invented by Amalfitan Flavio Gioia in 1302. Beyond these, the focus is the busy seafront, where there's a crowded **beach**.

Arrival and information

Train The nearest major train station is at Salerno, from where there are SITA buses and ferries to Amalfi.

Bus SITA buses from Sorrento and Naples and Marozzi buses from Rome (June–Sept 1 daily; 5hr 30min) arrive in Piazza Flavio Gioia, on the waterfront.

Ferry Ferries and hydrofoils from Naples, Capri and Sorrento arrive in the tiny harbour.

BARI AND BRINDISI TRANSPORT

Numerous ferries arrive at the busy ports of **Bari** and **Brindisi** on a daily basis, and the two cities are also served by budget airlines Ryanair and easyJet.

Bari

Ferries serve Albania (Durrës: daily; 9hr); Croatia (Dubrovnik: daily; 8–9hr); Montenegro (Bar: 1–2 daily; 8–9hr); and Greece (Igoumenítsa: 2–3 daily; 8–10hr; Corfu: 2 weekly; 8hr; Pátra: daily, 15–16hr). The port is connected with the train station by bus #20/ (every 40min; €0.90).

Trains to Naples (4 daily; 3hr 50min–5hr) and Lecce (15 daily; 1hr 10min–2hr 15min) leave from the central station in Piazza Aldo Moro; trains to Matera (hourly; 1hr 30min) use the private FAL line, leaving from the small station on the corner of the same piazza.

Buses Marinobus services to Naples depart from Piazza Aldo Moro (4 daily; 3hr–3hr 30min). From the **airport**, the Pugliarbus runs to Brindisi airport (3–4 daily; 1hr 40min) and to Matera (2 daily; 1hr 15min); bus #16 goes to the central station (every 40min–1hr; €0.90).

Tourist office Piazza Aldo Moro (Mon–Sat 9am–7pm; Sun 9am–1pm; ⓣ0809.909.341).

Brindisi

Ferries The central Porto Interno, used by ferries from Albania (Valona: daily; 8hr 30min; Vlore: 1 daily; 7hr 30min), is a 10min walk from the centre of town; ferries from Greece (Corfu: 3–5 weekly; 7hr 30min; Igoumenítsa: daily; 9hr; Pátra: 6 weekly; 17hr 30min; Kefalloniá: 4–7 weekly; 10–14hr) dock at Costa Morena, 3km southeast of town but linked by free shuttle bus.

Trains to Lecce (9 daily; 30min); Naples (5 daily; 4hr 50min–6hr 30min). The station is a 20min walk west of the port, on Piazza Crispi.

Buses Miccolis buses to Lecce (3 daily; 35min) and Naples (3 daily; 6hr) and Marozzi buses to Rome (5 daily; 4hr 30min–6hr 30min) all depart from Viale Togliatti in the new town. From the **airport** (buses €3) meet arrivals and run into town via the port and train station. COTRAP buses run from the airport to Lecce (40min; €6).

Tourist office Lungomare Margherita 43/44 (April–Oct daily 9am–1pm & 3–11pm; Nov–March Mon–Fri 9am–1pm & 3–8pm, Sat 9am–1.30pm; ⓣ0831.523.072).

Tourist office Corso delle Repubbliche Marinare 27 (Mon–Fri 9am–1pm & 2–6pm, Sat 9am–1pm; ⓣ089.871.107, ⓦwww.amalfitouristoffice.it).

Accommodation

Almost all the hotels in Amalfi are expensive; it makes sense to base yourself in a hostel in one of the nearby towns, such as Atrani or Positano, a short bus ride from Amalfi.

A' Scalinatella Piazza Umberto I 5–6, Atrani ⓣ089.871.492, ⓦwww.hostelscalinatella.com. SITA bus to Atrani or 1km walk from Amalfi. This popular hostel-cum-hotel has beds and rooms in buildings around Atrani, some overlooking the main square. Dorms €25, doubles €70–90.

Beata Solitudo Piazza G. Avitabile 4, Agerola ⓣ081.802.5048, ⓦwww.beatasolitudo.it. SITA bus to Agerola. This basic hostel 16km north of Amalfi has a small campsite attached, with 5- to 8-bed dorms and a few private en suites. €5.50/person, plus €4/tent, dorms €13, bungalows €55, doubles €80.

Sant'Andrea Via Costanza d'Avalos ⓣ089.871.145, ⓦwww.albergosantandrea.it. One of the cheaper options in town, this pretty hotel on the central square has views of the Duomo from most rooms. Doubles €70, €90 in August.

Eating

There's a Dogi supermarket at Piazza dei Dogi 29, a 2min walk from Piazza Duomo.

Cuoppo d'Amalfi Via Supportico dei Ferrari 10, just off Piazza dei Dogi. A mouthwatering *cuoppo* of fresh fried calamari, octopus, squid and prawns will set you back just €6 (€8 with fish): take it to the sea with a glass of white wine (€2) and enjoy.

Le Arcate Largo Buonocore, Atrani ⓣ089.871.367. A seafront restaurant and pizzeria with beautiful views of sleepy Atrani behind and the horizon ahead. Book to sit right by the sea. Pizza €8, seafood pasta €11. Closed Mon.

Moving on

Bus Ravello (every 30min; 30min); Sorrento (hourly; 1hr 40min).

Ferry Salerno (6 daily; 35min); Sorrento (2 daily; 60min).

Ravello

The best views of the coast are inland from Amalfi, in **RAVELLO**. For a time an independent republic, nowadays it's little more than a large village. What makes it more than worth the thirty-minute bus ride up from Amalfi, however, is its unrivalled location, spread across the top of one of the coast's mountains. The **Duomo** (daily 9.30am–noon & 5.30–7pm) is a bright eleventh-century church with a richly ornamented interior, but Ravello's real draws are its two villas: a two-minute walk from the Duomo are the gardens of the **Villa Rufolo** (9am–8pm, earlier in winter; €5), the spectacular venue for a renowned arts festival in the summer (tickets from €10, some events free; ⓦwww.ravellofestival.com); a ten-minute walk south is the equally stunning **Villa Cimbrone** (daily 9am–sunset; €6).

Tourist information is at Via Roma 18 (daily: March–Oct 9am–6pm; Nov–Feb 9am–4pm; ⓣ089.857.096, ⓦwww.ravellotime.it).

MATERA

Tucked into the instep of Italy in the Basilicata region, **Matera** is one of the south's most fascinating cities. The main point of interest is its *sassi*, rock dwellings dug out of a ravine. During the 1950s and 1960s the residents were forcibly evicted, as the city had degenerated into a slum. New blocks were constructed outside the town to house the population and the *sassi* were left empty, but in 1993 the area was declared a World Heritage Site and has since been slowly repopulated with hotels, restaurants and workshops, as well as starring as the set of many a film, including *The Passion of The Christ*.

The focus of the Sassi district, a warren of rock streets, is the **chiese rupestri** or rock-hewn churches, of which you can visit two, the spectacular Madonna de Idris, with frescoes dating from the fourteenth century and, adjacent, Santa Lucia alle Malve (Tues–Sun: April–Oct 10am–1pm & 2.30–7pm; Nov–March 10.30am–1.30pm; €3 each, or €5 for both). For an insight into what life was like for the *sassi*-dwellers, stop by the **Casa Grotta**, just below Madonna de Idris (daily: April–Oct 9.30am–8pm; Nov–March 9.30am–5pm; €1.50), or the **C'era una Volta** exhibition at Via Fiorentini 251 (daily: 9am–1pm & 3–6.30pm; €1.50), a *sassi* dwelling with its life-size inhabitants and their furniture sculpted out of the local tufa by generations of the same family.

Arrival and information

Air Matera is 60km southwest of Bari airport. Buses operated by Pugliairbus (5 daily; 1hr 15min; €5) run to Piazza Moro in Matera.
Train The train station, on Piazza Matteotti, is served by the private FAL rail line (Ⓦwww.fal-srl.it) from Bari.
Bus Direct coach services from Rome (Mon–Sat 1 daily; 5hr 45min; run by Autolinee Liscio) and from Naples (2 daily; 5hr; run by Autolinee Marino) stop at the Matera Villa Longo station, a 20min walk out of town but connected by bus and the FAL rail line. Trains from Naples run to Potenza from where you can catch the bus to Matera (4 daily; 1hr 15min).
Tourist office Via de Viti de Marco 9, off Via Roma (Mon & Thurs 9am–1.30pm & 4–6.30pm, Tues, Wed & Fri 9am–1.30pm; ⓣ0835.331.983, Ⓦwww.aptbasilicata.it). The infopoint on Via Ridola is more central though (daily 10am–7pm; ⓣ083.531.1645).

TREAT YOURSELF

If you're going to splash out on one of the atmospheric cave hotels, the **Antica Locanda San Martino** (Via Fiorentini 71; ⓣ0835.256.600, Ⓦwww.locandadisanmartino.it; doubles €89–109) is a special choice: a cool, fragrant *sassi* conversion with individual terraces and an underground swimming pool and sauna. The **Hotel Sassi** (Via S. Giovanni Vecchio 89; ⓣ0835.331.009, Ⓦwww.hotelsassi.it; doubles €90, extra beds €20 each) has gorgeous rooms with film-set-worthy views, some of which can sleep large groups on request to make it more affordable.

Accommodation

Casa Per Ferie Sacro Cuore Recinto Mario Pagano 11 ⓣ0835.336.451, Ⓦwww.sacrocuoremt.it. Run by nuns and surrounded by lovely gardens, this makes a restful place to stay. The large rooms do have a rather institutional feel, however. €35/person with breakfast.
Le Monacelle Via Riscatto 9/10 ⓣ0835.344.097, Ⓦwww.lemonacelle.it. This ex-friary is now a smart hotel, with two dorm rooms available. They sleep 14 & 16, but different areas are partitioned off, and they are nicely decorated, with solid wooden bunks. Dorms €16 without breakfast, €20 with. Family room for four €25/person.

Eating and drinking

There's a large market with fresh produce, dried fruit and nuts and cheese just behind Piazza Vittorio Veneto (until 2.30pm).
Il Terrazzino Vico S. Giuseppe 7. A *sassi* restaurant with great views and a cheap tourist menu; try the *orecchiette* pasta with sausage, tomato and mozzarella (€7), or if you can't decide from the many pizza options, go for the *Sorpresa*: a "surprise", with toppings chosen by the pizza-maker (€8). Margherita €3.50, *calzone* €5. Closed Tues.
Mammaliturchi Via delle Beccherie 59. If you need a change from pizza and pasta follow the crowds and get a freshly made kebab with falafel, meat, chips and salad for €4. Closed Mon.

LECCE

LECCE, 40km south of Brindisi port, is often called the "Florence of the south". These alleys may be well trodden, but a real sense of discovery still accompanies a visit to the city's vine-enveloped stonework. Carved from soft sandstone, these buildings were built for wealthy families, churchmen and merchants during the fifteenth to seventeenth centuries, and are among the most beautiful examples of the style. A short walk from the central Piazza Sant'Oronzo is **Santa Croce** (daily 9am–noon & 5–8pm, earlier in winter), the most famous of Lecce's churches, where delicate engravings soften the Baroque outline of the building. Inside, the excess continues with a riot of stars, flowers and foliage covering everything from the top of columns to chapel altarpieces. Lecce's other highlight is the **Piazza del Duomo**, an elegantly proportioned square surrounded by Baroque *palazzi*. The **Duomo** itself (daily 8.30am–12.30pm & 4–7.30pm, earlier in winter) is an explosion of Baroque detail.

Arrival and information

Air Lecce is 40km from Brindisi Airport; from here, COTRAP buses (6 daily; 40min; €5) run to the centre.
Train The train station is 1km south of the centre on Via Oronzo Quarta.
Bus Buses arrive at the City Terminal, a 10min walk from the centre, and at the train station.
Tourist office Via Vittorio Emanuele II 18 (Mon–Sat 9am–1pm & 4.30–7.30pm; ⓣ0832.332.463, ⓦwww.viaggiareinpuglia.it).

Accommodation

B&B Azzurretta Via Vignes 2b ⓣ0832.242.211 ⓦwww.bblecce.it and **Centro Storico B&B** ⓣ0832.242.727, ⓦwww.bedandbreakfast.lecce.it. Both places occupy the top floors of a sixteenth-century *palazzo* boasting a glorious terrace available for lounging or bringing your own *aperitivo. Azzuretta* has large wooden beds and airy rooms (doubles €55–70), while *Centro Storico* is sumptuously furnished (doubles €60).
Abaca Lecce Viale F. Cavalotti ⓣ0832.240.548, ⓦwww.a-abaca.it. Central, friendly B&B with a/c rooms, some with terraces. €20–40/person.

Eating and drinking

Caffè Letterario Via G. Paladini 46. This café-bar organizes a wealth of arty events, including DJ sets and live music nights, usually on Wednesday or Friday. Daily 7.30am–2am.
Guido e figli Via XXV Luglio 14. A restaurant at the front and cheaper self-service canteen at the back with a wide range of *primi* (€5) and *secondi* (€6) based on fresh, in-season produce. Closed Mon.
Le Zie Via Costadura 19 ⓣ0832.245.178. A simple trattoria serving *cucina casareccia* – home-style cooking. Taste Puglia's famous *orecchiette* pasta at its best. The home-made liqueurs at the end are a must-try. *Primi* €6, *secondi* €7. Booking is advisable. Closed Sun eve & Mon.

Moving on

Train Bari (9 daily; 1hr 20min–1hr 50min); Bologna (9 daily; 7–9hr); Brindisi (every 30min–1hr; 25min); Naples (5 daily; 5–7hr); Rome (5 daily; 5–9hr).

Sicily

Perhaps the most captivating of Italy's islands, **SICILY** (Sicilia) feels socially and culturally separate from the rest of Italy. Occupying a strategically vital position, the largest island in the Mediterranean has a history and outlook that has less in common with its modern parent than with its erstwhile rulers – from the Greeks who first settled the east coast, in the eighth century BC, through a bewildering array of Romans, Arabs, Normans, French and Spanish, to the Bourbons, seen off by Garibaldi in 1860. Substantial relics remain, and temples, theatres and churches are scattered across the island.

The capital, **Palermo**, is a bustling city with an unrivalled display of Norman art and architecture and Baroque churches. The most obvious other target is the chic eastern resort of **Taormina**. From here you can visit **Mount Etna**, or travel south to the ancient Greek centre of **Siracusa**. To the west, the greatest draw is the grouping of temples at **Agrigento**, the largest concentration of the island's Greek remains.

PALERMO

In its own wide bay beneath the limestone bulk of Monte Pellegrino, **PALERMO** is stupendously sited. Originally a Phoenician, then a Carthaginian colony, this remarkable city was long considered a prize worth capturing, and under Saracen and Norman rule in the ninth to twelfth centuries it became the greatest city in Europe, famed for the wealth of its court and peerless as a centre of learning. Nowadays it's a brash, exciting city, whose uniquely varied architecture and museums are well worth exploring.

What to see and do

Around the Quattro Canti

The heart of the old city is the Baroque **Quattro Canti** crossroads, with **Piazza Pretoria** and its racy fountain just around the corner. In nearby Piazza Bellini, the church of **La Martorana** (closed for restoration at time of writing) is one of the finest survivors of the medieval city. Its slim twelfth-century campanile and spectacular mosaics make a marked contrast to the adjacent squat chapel of **San Cataldo** (Mon–Sat 9am–2pm & 3.30–7pm, Sun 9am–2pm; €2.50) with its little Saracenic red golfball domes.

Alberghiera

In the district of Alberghiera, a warren of narrow streets to the southwest, you'll find the deconsecrated church of **San Giovanni degli Eremiti** (Via dei Benedettini; daily 9am–6.30/5pm in winter; €6), built in 1148. Built on the remains of a mosque, it's topped with five rosy domes and holds late thirteenth-century cloisters. From here it's a few paces north to the **Palazzo dei Normanni** (Mon–Sat 8.15am–5.45pm, Sun 8.15am–1pm; entrance on Piazza Indipendenza; Fri–Mon €8.50, Tues–Thurs €7), the seat of the Sicilian regional parliament. It was originally built by the Saracens and was enlarged by the Normans, under whom it housed the most magnificent of medieval European courts. The beautiful **Cappella Palatina** (closed to visitors Sun from 9.45am–11.15am), the private royal chapel of Roger II, is almost entirely covered in glorious twelfth-century mosaics. The Norman **Cattedrale** (March–Oct Mon–Sat 9.30am–5.30pm, Sun 7am–1pm & 4–7pm; Nov–Feb Mon–Sat 9.30am–1pm, Sun 7.30am–1.30pm & 4–7pm) boasts a fine portal and tombs containing the remains of some of Sicily's most famous monarchs.

The Museo Archeologico Regionale, Vucciria and around

To the northeast, off Via Roma, the **Museo Archeologico Regionale** (closed for restoration at time of writing) is a magnificent collection of artefacts, mainly from the island's Greek and Roman sites. Two cloisters hold anchors, Bronze Age pottery, coins and jewels retrieved from the sea off the Sicilian coast.

Southeast of here the **Vucciria market** area (daily from 8am) offers glimpses of the Palermo of old. You can cut through to Sicily's **Galleria Regionale** (Tues–Fri 9am–5.30pm, Sat & Sun 9am–12.30pm; €8), on Via Alloro, in the rough-and-ready La Kalsa district. It's a stunning art collection, with works from the eleventh to the seventeenth centuries.

Arrival and information

Air Prestia e Comandè buses meet arrivals and stop at the train station and Piazza Politeama (50min; €5.80). Trinacria Express run trains to the central station (closed for maintenance at time of writing).

Ferry and hydrofoil Services from Naples dock just off Via Francesco Crispi, from where it's a 10min walk up Via E. Amari to Piazza Castelnuovo.

Train Trains arrive at Stazione Centrale, at the southern end of Via Roma – buses #101 and #102 run to the centre. Buy tickets (€1.30; valid for 1hr 30min) at *tabacchi* shops or the booth outside the station; they cost more to buy on board. Red line and yellow line buses start at the station and do circuits of the centre for €0.52/day. There's a left-luggage office at the station (daily 7am–11pm; €4/5hr).

Tourist office The main tourist office is at Piazza Castelnuovo 34 (Mon–Fri 9am–2pm & 2.30–6pm; ⓣ091.605.8351, ⓦwww.palermotourism.com). There's a smaller branch at the airport (Mon–Fri 8.30am–7.30pm; Sat 8.30am–2pm).

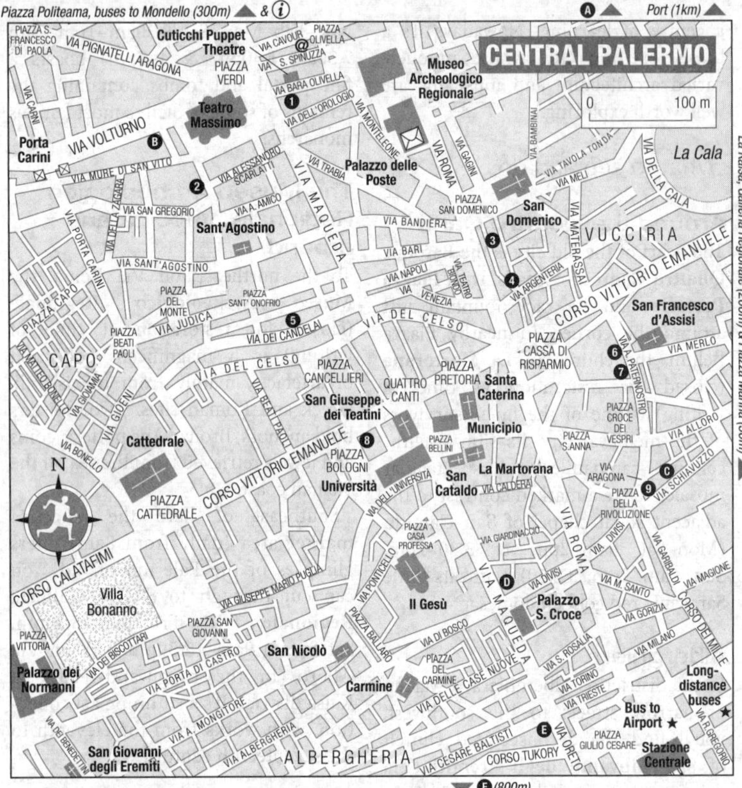

ACCOMMODATION				EATING				DRINKING & NIGHTLIFE	
A Casa di Amici	B	Baia del Corallo	A	Ai Maccheronai	4	Pasticceria del Massimo	2	Bar Libreria Garibaldi	7
Ai Quattro Canti	D	San Saverio	F	Antica Focacceria	6	Trattoria Primavera	8	I Candelai	5
Albergo Paradiso	C	Vittoria	E	Basile	1			Maggiore	3
								Qvivi	9

Internet Punto Pizzo Free, Corso Vittorio Emanuele, 172 (Mon–Sat 10am–1pm then 4–8pm; Sun 9.30am–1.30pm; €0.50/min).

Accommodation

Most of Palermo's budget hotels are situated around the southern ends of Via Maqueda and Via Roma, near the train station – a rather sleazy area at night. It's worth spending a bit more to stay in one of the modern B&Bs in the centre of town.

A Casa di Amici Via Volturno 6 ⓣ091.584.884, ⓦwww.acasadiamici.com. A colourful haven by Teatro Massimo with welcoming staff, use of a kitchen and exotic instruments lying around. Dorms €23, doubles €56.

Ai Quattro Canti Via Maqueda, 124 ⓣ339.266.0963 or 091.6116737, ⓦwww.aiquattrocanti.hostel.com. The super-friendly owners will take care of you like an old friend. Terrace, lofty views and organized nights out and in complete the convivial picture. Dorms €18.

Albergo Paradiso Via Schiavuzzo 65 ⓣ091.617.2825. The rooms at this welcoming family-run hotel share bathrooms, but are light and airy. No breakfast. €45

Baia del Corallo Via Plauto 27, Sferacavallo ⓣ091.679.7807, ⓦwww.ostellopalermo.it. Bus #101 from the station to Piazza De Gasperi, then bus #628. A decent HI hostel 12km northwest of the city, by the sea. Buses only run until 11.30pm though – and a taxi will cost about €35. Dorms €19, doubles €56.

San Saverio Via G. Di Cristina 39 ⓣ091.654.7099, ⓦwww.ostellopalermo.com. Typically no-frills student accommodation a 10min walk from the station. Mid-July to early Sept only. Dorms €22, doubles €40.

Vittoria Via Maqueda 8 ⓣ091.616.2437. Simple, family-run hotel near the station with friendly owners. All rooms are en suite and breakfast is included. Doubles €50.

Eating

The city's markets are a great place to pick up a picnic; try Ballarò, between Piazza Carmine and Piazza Ballarò in the Alberghiera district. There's a GS supermarket in Piazza Marina.

Ai Maccheronai Via Maccheronai 47. Fresh fish from the nearby fish market cooked expertly by good-natured Palermitans. Pasta from €5. Closed Sun.

Antica Focacceria Via A. Paternostro 58. A feast of *panelle*, *arancini*, *polpo* (octopus) and tasty sweet *cannoli* will set you back just €6 at this popular backstreet takeaway. Also serves pasta from €4.

Basile Via Bara 76. Closed Sun. This lunch-only *tavola calda* is crammed with locals on weekdays, who fill up on its enormous plates of pasta (€2.50) and various meat and fish options. You can get a full meal for under €10.

Pasticceria del Massimo Via Alberto Favara 14–16. Head here at breakfast or teatime for perfect *cannoli*, cassata and fruit-shaped marzipan too pretty to eat.

Trattoria Primavera Piazza Bologni 4. Near the cathedral and with outdoor seating, this trattoria serves great home-style cooking like *pasta alla norma*. Meat and fish dishes start at €7. Closed Mon.

Drinking and nightlife

In summer, nightlife shifts to the beach resort of Mondello, which is full of lively bars, a half-hour bus ride from Palermo (#806 from Teatro Politeama). The clubs around Piazza dell'Unità d'Italia, northwest of central Palermo, are open year-round; entrance €5–15. There are plenty of studenty bars in the side streets of the centro storico, especially on Via dei Candelai.

Bar Libreria Garibaldi Via A. Paternostro 46. A laidback bar-café-gallery-bookshop with crooked outdoor tables to watch the world pass by. Have a glass of red with a boiled egg for €2.

I Candelai Via dei Candelai 65. Some of the hottest live music and DJs in Palermo. Attracts a studenty crowd. Closed Mon.

Maggiore Via dei Maccheronai 13. A rustic bar with barrels of marsala lining the walls, cheap beer and wild crowds spilling into the streets every Saturday.

Qvivi Piazza della Rivoluzione 5. One of the square's many bars, this one offers cocktails, wine, beer and groovy outdoor sofas. Music is mixed, from rockabilly to live jazz.

Moving on

Buses (services run by SAIS and Interbus) are quicker than trains in Sicily, taking scenic cross-country routes rather than lumbering round the coast. Buy bus tickets from the agencies in Via Balsamo, by the station.

Air Bologna (2 daily; 1hr 30min); Cagliari (1 daily; 1hr 15min); Milan (several daily; 1hr 30min); Rome (several daily; 1hr).

Train Agrigento (8 daily; 2hr 15min); Siracusa (change at Messina; 4 daily; 6hr 30min–7hr); Taormina (change at Messina; 8 daily; 3hr 45min–5hr 20min).

Bus Agrigento (6–9 daily; 2hr); Florence (1 daily; 17hr); Naples (1 daily; 12hr); Rome (1–2 daily; 13hr); Siracusa (2–4 daily; 3hr 15min); Taormina (change at Catania; 9–16 daily; 4hr).

Ferry Genoa (1 daily; 20hr); Naples (1–2 daily; 8–10hr); Rome (Civitavecchia; 4–6 weekly; 12–14hr).

TAORMINA

On Sicily's eastern coast, and dominating two grand sweeping bays, **TAORMINA** is the island's best-known resort. The outstanding remains of its classical theatre, with Mount Etna as an unparalleled backdrop, arrested passing travellers when Taormina was no more than a medieval hill village. Nowadays it's rather chichi, full of designer shops and pricey cafés, but still has plenty of charm. Its pedestrianized main street, Corso Umberto I, is lined with fifteenth- to nineteenth-century *palazzi* interspersed with intimate piazzas. The **Teatro Greco** (daily 9am–1hr before sunset; €8) is the only real sight, founded by the Greeks in the third century BC, though most of what's left is a Roman rebuilding from the first century AD, when a deep trench was dug in the orchestra to accommodate animals and gladiators.

The closest beach to Taormina is at **MAZZARÓ**, with its much-photographed islet, **Isola Bella**: it's a scenic thirty-minute descent on foot, or use the cable car (every 15min; €3.50 return) from Via Pirandello.

Arrival and information

Air Catania airport is 45km from Taormina; buses run from here to the centre of town.
Train The train station, Taormina-Giardini Naxos, is way below town – it's a steep 30min walk up or a short bus ride to the centre (€1.50).
Bus The bus terminal is in Via Pirandello, a 5min walk from the centre.
Tourist office Palazzo Corvaja, Piazza Santa Caterina (Mon–Sat 8.30am–1.30pm & 4–7pm; ⓣ0942.23.243, ⓦwww.gate2taormina.com). Also at the train station (same hours).

Accommodation

Casa Grazia Via Iallia Bassia 20 ⓣ0942.24.776, ⓔcasagrazia@libero.it. A 5min walk from the Teatro Greco, this family-run hotel has neat rooms, some en suite, all with balcony. No breakfast. March–Oct only. Doubles €60–70.
Taormina's Odyssey Via Paterno di Biscari, 13 ⓣ0942.24.533, ⓦwww.taorminaodyssey.com. A pretty guesthouse-cum-hostel with bright private rooms, two dorms (4- & 6- bed), a large terrace, kitchen and laundry facilities. 50 metres from Corso Umberto. Breakfast included. Dorms €20–24, doubles €45–70.

Eating

There's a mini-market that can make up panini for a couple of euros at Via Bagnoli Croce 68; eat them over the road in the leafy Giardini Pubblici.
Arancini in Corso Piazzetta Leone 2, above the restaurant *Ciclope* on Corso Umberto #203. *Arancini* are freshly fried here; in addition to the usual *ragù* variety you can try pistachio, butter and cheese and even nutella.
Rosticceria di Cateno Aucello Via Cappuccini 8 and **La Cucina di Riccobono** Via Costantino Patricio 24 are both excellent value takeaway options a stone's throw apart, with dishes like aubergine *parmigiana* (€4), chicken and chips (€6) and daily pastas.

Drinking and nightlife

In town, the action takes place in picturesque but posey Piazza Paladini, off the Corso. Alternatively, the summer beach-bars of nearby Spisone are reachable by path from Taormina or by bus from Via Pirandello.
Déjà vu Piazza Garibaldi 2. Young, hip lounge bar that attracts a dressed-up crowd.
Re di Bastoni Corso Umberto 1. A retro-feel bar at odds with the glitz and glamour of the Corso. Grab an outdoor table to watch the evening *passeggiata* along the main drag. Closed Mon in winter.

Moving on

Train Catania (15 daily; 40–50min); Palermo (via Messina; 12 daily; 4hr 30min–5hr 40min); Siracusa (6 daily; 2hr–2hr 50min).
Bus Catania (every 30min; 1hr 10min); Palermo (via Catania; hourly; 3hr 40min).

MOUNT ETNA

Mount Etna's massive bulk looms over much of the coastal route south of Taormina. At 3340m, it is a substantial mountain and the **ascent** is a spectacular trip; the fact that it's also one of the world's biggest volcanoes (and still active) only adds to the draw. Getting up can be costly and is weather-dependent (don't attempt to do it if conditions are cloudy), so get as much advice as possible on the ground beforehand. There are many tour operators based in Taormina offering package deals which, while seeming less pioneering, can work out easier and not too much more expensive.

On **public transport**, you'll need to come via Catania by bus (daily, leaves 8am; 1hr) from Catania train station up to the huddle of souvenir shops and restaurants at the *Rifugio Sapienza* (ⓣ095.915.321; ⓦwww.rifugiosapienza.com; B&B €55 per person), a cosy, chalet-style hotel which marks the end of the drivable road up the south side of Etna. To get as high up as possible, you can either take a cable car then a jeep (9am–5pm; €53.30 return), or, if you are an experienced walker, go on foot (the trip up will take four hours, the return a little less). Take warm clothes, good shoes and glasses to keep the flying grit out of your eyes. The return bus to Catania leaves at 4.30pm, so if you want to walk all the way you'll have to stay the night in the *Rifugio*.

If you don't have the time or funds to reach the summit, the **Circumetnea rail**

service (€6.85; no service on Sundays; InterRail passes not valid) trundles around the base from **GIARRE-RIPOSTO**, thirty minutes by train or bus from Taormina. The whole tour takes three and a half hours and ends in Catania, which is an attractive place (and the home of *pasta alla norma*) dotted with lava-encrusted relics and splendid Baroque *palazzi*. The cheapest accommodation is *Agora*, Piazza Currò 6, near the cathedral (Ⓣ095.723.3010; Ⓦwww.agorahostel.com; dorms €20, doubles €50).

SIRACUSA

Further down Sicily's eastern seaboard, **SIRACUSA** (ancient Syracuse) was first colonized by the Greeks in 733 BC and grew to become their main power base in Sicily. Today, the city boasts some of the best Greek archeological remains anywhere, and also has a strong Baroque character in its old town, squeezed onto the island of **Ortygia**, and connected to the new town by two bridges.

What to see and do

Ortygia

Near the bridge that connects Ortygia to the mainland, the **Temple of Apollo**, built in the sixth century BC, is probably Sicily's most ancient Doric temple. Over the years, it was transformed into a Byzantine church, then an Arab mosque, and into a church again under the Normans. At the centre of the island, the most obvious attraction is the **Duomo** (daily 8am–7pm), set in a piazza studded with Baroque architecture, and itself incorporating twelve fluted columns from the fifth-century BC temple that originally stood here. At the other end of the square, the church of **Santa Lucia** (Tues–Sun 11am–2pm & 5–7pm) harbours a Caravaggio painting, the *Burial of Santa Lucia*. Round the corner at Via Capodieci 16 is the severe thirteenth-century facade of the **Galleria Regionale di Palazzo Bellomo** (Tues–Sun 9am–7pm; €8), an outstanding collection of medieval art, and paintings by Antonello da Messina.

The Archeological Museum

North of the train station the city is mainly new, though the best of Siracusa's archeological sights are also here. It's a twenty-minute walk to Viale Teocrito (or take bus #12 from Riva Nazario Sauro), from where you walk east for the **Museo Archeologico Regionale** (Tues–Sat 9am–7pm, Sun 9am–2pm; €9 includes entrance to Parco Archeologico, valid 2 days), housing a wealth of material from the early Greek colonies; the collection's highlight is a headless marble *Venus*, sculpted rising from the sea. Round the corner, the ruined **Basilica di San Giovanni** has interesting catacombs (daily 9.30am–12.30pm & 2.30–5.30pm; €6).

The Archeological Park

Siracusa's extensive **Parco Archeologico** (daily 9am–2hr before sunset) is a ten-minute walk west of the archeological museum. Here, the **Ara di Ierone II**, an enormous third-century BC altar, is the first thing you see, though the main highlight is the **Teatro Greco**. Cut out of the rock and looking down towards the sea, it hosts a summer season of Greek plays (Ⓦwww.indafondazione.org). Nearby, the **Latomia del Paradiso**, a leafy quarry, is best known for the **Orecchio di Dionigi**, an S-shaped cave, 65m long and 20m high, that Dionysius is supposed to have used as a prison.

Hourly buses make the 55min journey to the tumbledown town of **NOTO** – a good day-trip. The town's crumbling suburbs give way to a lovely Baroque centre. Also within easy reach of town are the sandy **beaches** of Fontane Bianche (bus #21 or #22 from Via Crispi; hourly Mon–Sat, 2 daily Sun; 25min).

Arrival and information

Air Interbus run services from Catania airport to Siracusa.
Train Siracusa's train station is on Via Crispi, a 20min walk from Ortygia and connected with the island by free shuttle bus (#20, every 30min until 9pm; 5min).
Bus Interbus services from Palermo, Rome, Pisa, Florence and Genoa stop in Corso Umberto, near the station.
Tourist office Via Roma 31 (Mon–Fri 9am–1pm & 3–6pm, Sat & Sun 9am–1pm; ⓣ8000.55500, toll-free).

Accommodation

B&B Artemide Via V. Veneto 9 ⓣ338.373.9050, ⓦwww.bedandbreakfastsicily.com. A comfortable B&B with stylish, spacious rooms. If full, there are plenty of others on Via Veneto for similar prices. Doubles €50.
Casa Cristina Via Chindemi 8 ⓣ0931.62.205, ⓦwww.casacristinasr.it. The lovely, airy rooms at this welcoming B&B are a bargain, with dead-ahead views of the Temple of Apollo; one has a lovely frescoed ceiling. Doubles €70.
Casa Mia Corso Umberto 112 ⓣ0931.463.349, ⓦwww.bbcasamia.it. This B&B, in an old *palazzo* not far from Ortygia, has pleasant rooms, a sunny breakfast terrace and helpful owners. Doubles €70.
Lolhostel Via F. Crispi 92/96 ⓣ0931.465.088, ⓦwww.lolhostel.com. Siracusa's only hostel, just a 10min walk from Ortygia, offers 4- to 20-bed dorms and private en suites. Breakfast included. Dorms €22, doubles €65.

Eating

Da Seby Via Mirabella 21. This hole-in-the-wall *tavola calda* with a handful of tables is great value, with a range of tasty hot meals such as swordfish with salad for €5. Closed Sun.
Samouar Via della Maestranza 124–128. A light and airy café-restaurant, serving refreshing lemon, basil and parmesan pasta for just €5 and huge, satisfying salads (€6). Closed Sun.
Spaghetteria Do Scogghiu Via D Scina 11. Bawdy and popular, run by a hilarious father-and-sons team, the spaghetti here comes in dozens of varieties from seafood to *alla norma*, and several twists on the classics. Pasta €8. Closed Mon.

Drinking and nightlife

Nightlife centres on the lively Piazzetta San Rocco in Ortygia and the nearby Via delle Vergini and Via Roma.
Enoteca Solaria Via Roma 86. Laidback, rustic bar with good Sicilian wines and a simple menu of fresh, in-season dishes. Closed Sun.
Il Sedano Allegro Via delle Vergini 5. Bohemian bar with cheap light bites and a friendly atmosphere. Closed Tues.
Tinkitè Via della Giudecca 63, corner of Via Minniti. A hidden treasure, serving lovely cakes for breakfast and delicious snacks come *aperitivo* hour. Closed Wed.

Moving on

Train Agrigento (2–3 daily; 5–6hr); Palermo (5 daily; 5hr 30min–7hr 30min).
Bus Agrigento (Via Catania; 9–15 daily; 4hr 30min); Palermo (2–4 daily; 3hr 15min).

AGRIGENTO

Halfway along Sicily's southern coast, **AGRIGENTO** is primarily of interest for its substantial Greek remains, strung out along a ridge facing the sea a few kilometres below town. The series of Doric temples here, mostly dating from the fifth century BC, are the most evocative of Sicily's remains. They are also the focus of a constant procession of tour buses, so budget accommodation should be booked in advance (though Agrigento could be a day-trip from Palermo). A road winds down from the modern city to the **Valle dei Templi**; buses from the station drop off at a car park between the two separate zones of **archeological remains** (daily 8.30am–7pm; joint ticket with museum €10). The eastern zone is home to the scattered remains of the oldest of the temples, the **Tempio di Ercole**, probably begun in the last decades of the sixth century BC, and the better-preserved **Tempio della Concordia**, dated to around 430 BC, with fine views of the city and sea.

The western zone, back along the path and beyond the car park, is less impressive but still worth wandering around. The mammoth construction that was the **Tempio di Giove**, the largest Doric temple ever known, was in fact never completed, left in ruins by the Carthaginians and further damaged by earthquakes. Via dei Templi leads back to the town from the car park via the excellent **Museo Archeologico Regionale** (Tues–Sat 9am–1.30pm & 4–6pm, Sun & Mon 9am–1.30pm; joint ticket with Valle dei Templi €10) – an extraordinarily rich collection devoted to local finds. From June to mid-September the Valle dei Tempi usually opens at **night**: once the sun has set over the ruins, they're spectacularly illuminated by floodlights.

Arrival and information

Air SAIS buses run to Agrigento from Catania airport, and Sal buses from Palermo airport.
Train Trains arrive at Agrigento Centrale at the edge of the old town (don't get out at Agrigento Bassa). Buses #1, #2 and #3 from outside the station (€1.10 from *tabacchi*, unavailable to buy on board) go to the temples.
Bus SAIS buses from Rome and Naples arrive in Piazzale Rosselli, near the train station.
Tourist office Via Empedocle 73 (second floor of building; Mon–Sat 8am–2.30pm, Wed 8am–2.30pm & 3.30–7pm; ⓣ800.236.837).

Accommodation

Camere a Sud Via Ficani 6 ⓣ349.638.4424, ⓦwww.camereasud.it. In an excellent location just off Agrigento's main drag, this friendly B&B has bright, spacious rooms and a roof terrace. Free internet. Book ahead. Doubles €70.
Letto e Latte Via Cannatello 101 ⓣ092.265.1945, ⓦwww.lettolatte.com. This tranquil B&B 1km from the Valle dei Templi (the bus stops just outside) has six clean, tastefully furnished en-suite rooms. Doubles €55–65.
Piccolo Gellia Via Atenea 220 ⓣ0922.27157, ⓦwww.piccologellia.com. An enchanting B&B run by a charming pair: artsy photos grace the walls, a convivial breakfast table with home-made jam is laid out in the morning and the sweet cat makes you feel right at home. Doubles €49–79.

Eating and drinking

Most of the cheap pizzerias are at Villagio Mosè, east of town, below the temples. In town, lively Via Atenea is the best place for a drink.
Ambasciata di Sicilia Via Giambertoni 2. This folksy trattoria has lovely views from its terrace and reasonably priced dishes. Closed Mon.
Le Cuspidi Piazza Cavour 19. The best ice creams in town, with unusual flavours such as fresh ricotta and almond, as well as the classics.
Terra e Mare Piazza Lena 7 (Via Bic Bac). A homely restaurant to head to after a day of archeology. Hearty pastas like *norma* and meat and seafood mains go for €6–9. Closed Mon.

Sardinia

Just under 200km from the Italian mainland, **SARDINIA** (Sardegna) is often regarded as the epitome of Mediterranean Europe. Its blue seas, white sands and rolling hills are beautiful and its way of life relaxed. Sardinia also holds fascinating vestiges of the various powers – Roman, Carthaginian, Genoese and Pisan – that have passed through, alongside striking remnants of Sardinia's only significant native culture, known as the Nuraghic civilization, in the seven thousand tower-like *nuraghi* that litter the landscape. The capital, **Cagliari**, is worth exploring for its excellent museums and some of the island's best nightlife. From here, it's only a short trip to the renowned ruined city at **Nora**, and the quieter beaches at **Chia**. The other main ferry port and airport is Olbia, in the north, little more than a transit town for the exclusive resorts of the Costa Smeralda. There's a third airport at the relaxed resort of **Alghero** in the northwest.

CAGLIARI

Rising up from its port and crowned by an old citadel squeezed within a protective ring of fortifications, **CAGLIARI** has been Sardinia's capital since at least Roman times and is still the island's biggest town. Nonetheless, its centre is easily explored on foot, with almost all the wandering you will want to do encompassed by the citadel.

What to see and do

The citadel

The most evocative entry to the **citadel** is from the monumental **Bastione San Remy** on Piazza Costituzione. From here, you can potter in any direction to enter its intricate maze. The citadel has been altered little since the Middle Ages, though the tidy Romanesque facade on the mainly thirteenth-century **cathedral** (June–Sept 7.30am–8pm; Oct–May 7.30am–noon & 4–8pm; Mass on Sun 9am, 10.30am, noon & 7pm) in Piazza Palazzo is in fact a fake, added in the twentieth century in the old Pisan style.

Piazza dell'Arsenale

At the opposite end of Piazza Palazzo, a road leads into the smaller **Piazza dell'Arsenale,** site of several museums including the **Museo Archeologico Nazionale** (Tues–Sun 9am–8pm; currently free to enter). In the same complex, the **Pinacoteca Nazionale** (same hours; currently free to enter) features some glowing fifteenth-century altarpieces, while the **Museo delle Cere** (Tues–Sat 9am–1pm & 4–9pm, Sun 9am–1pm & 4–7pm; €1.50) displays a series of thought-provoking anatomical waxworks executed by Clemente Susini for nineteenth-century medical students.

Towers

Off the piazza stands the **Torre San Pancrazio,** (Tues–Sun: April–Oct 9am– 1pm & 3.30–7.30pm; Nov–March 9am–4.30pm; €4), the best preserved of Cagliari's fortified towers, from where it's a 10min walk to the **Torre dell'Elefante** (hours and price as San Pancrazio), named after the small carving of an elephant on one side; climb to the top of either for stupendous views over the city and coast.

Beaches

To get to **Poetto Beach**, the long stretch connected to Cagliari, take bus #PF or #PQ from outside the train station – and, in the summer, #PN – for the 15min ride and get off wherever a patch takes your fancy.

Arrival and information

Air The airport sits beside the Stagno di Cagliari, the city's largest lagoon, a 10min bus ride west of town (€4 one-way, tickets purchased from airport bookshop or coin-only machine in arrivals hall).

Boat Cagliari's port lies in the heart of the town, opposite Via Roma. There is a Tirrenia ticket office close to the port (daily 8.30am–12.20pm & 4–6pm; ⓦ www.tirrenia.it).

Tourist office There are tourist offices at the airport and port (Via Roma 145), and opposite the train and bus stations on Piazza Matteotti (daily: April–Sept 8am–8pm; Oct–March 9am–1.30pm & 2–6pm; ⓣ 070.669.255, ⓦ www.commune.cagliari.it).

Internet *Lamari*, a pleasant café at Via Napoli 43 (€3/hr). Great breakfast offer at €3 for drink, pastry and 30min internet.

Accommodation

Albergo Aurora Salita S. Chiar 19 ⓣ 070.658.625, ⓦ www.albergo-aurora.com. Fantastic location near the buzzing Piazza Yenne. Rooms are slightly shabby, but friendly staff and cheap prices make up for this. Ask for room 112; it is large and has the best views. Doubles €60.

Hostel Marina Piazza San Sepolcro 2 ⓣ 070.450.9709, ⓔ cagliari@aighostels.com. This excellent hostel is located in the heart of the old town, only a short walk from the train station. Enthusiastic staff, an outdoor café and a cinema room. Dorms €22, doubles from €40 (room 108 is the best).

La Terraza Sul Porto Largo Carlo Felice 36 ⓣ 070.658.997, ⓦ www.laterrazzasolporto.com. This fabulous B&B close to the centre has a huge kitchen, cheery decor and a stunning roof terrace. Doubles €40.

Rosso e Nero Via Savoia 6 ⓣ 070.656.673. Ideally located for the restaurants of the Stampace area, this small B&B has clean tastefully decorated rooms. Doubles €50.

Eating

Piazza Yenne is full of outdoor cafés and has a great *gelateria, L'Isola del Gelato.* The best restaurants are around the streets surrounding Via Sardegna.

Illicu Via Sardegna 78. Locals cram into this excellent trattoria that serves traditional Cagliari food often at shared long wooden tables.

The large portions, excellent seafood and singing waiters make this an unforgettable experience. Pasta and beer €10. Closed Sun.

La Damigiana Corso Vittorio Emanuele 115. A simple trattoria a 5min walk from Piazza Yenne run by a mother and son. Mains €10. No credit cards.

Le Patate & Co Scalette San Sepolcro 1. Cheap fast-food restaurant with cosy upstairs seating or tables outside. Calamari and potatoes (potatoes feature heavily on the menu) €7.50. Closed Mon.

Serofino Via Lepanto 6. This large restaurant in the Marina area serves up the cheapest pasta in town. Ragu pasta €4.50. Closed Thurs.

Drinking and nightlife

Caffe Librarium Nostrum Via Sante Croce 33/35. One of the best places in Cagliari for a cocktail at sunset. Open till 2am, closed Mon.

Degli Spiriti Via Canelles 34/San Lorenzo 10. This trendy restaurant, bar and nightclub on Bastion San Remy serves great pizzas (€7) and cocktails and the views over the city are spectacular. Open until 3am.

Mojito Salita Santa Chiara 25. Tiny, red-draped bar just off Piazza Yenne, with outdoor couches and beanbags in the summer. Beer €4. Closed Mon.

Moving on

Train Alghero (3 daily via Sassari; 4hr 30min); Olbia (1 direct daily; 4hr).

Bus Chia (hourly; 1hr 15min); Pula (hourly; 50min). For more information on buses in Sardinia, see ⓦwww.arst.sardegna.it.

Ferry Civitavecchia (1 daily; 15hr); Naples (2 weekly; 16hr); Palermo (1 weekly; 14hr 30min); Trápani (1 weekly; 10hr).

NORA AND AROUND

The charming little town of **PULA**, an hour south of Cagliari, is a great base to explore **Nora** and the stunning southern beaches. *Hotel Quattro Mori*, a basic but clean hotel at Via Cagliari 10, is the cheapest **accommodation** option (ⓣ070.920.9124; €40) – otherwise, your best bet is to ask at the helpful tourist information centre, located right in the middle of the jolly Piazza del Popolo, the central piazza. The piazza is full of little cafés; one of the best is the cheap-and-cheerful *Mr Jingle's Café* at no. 5, which serves main dishes from €5, and has a lovely upstairs balcony. Outside of the summer months some establishments may be shut.

Nora Archeological Centre

To get to fascinating **NORA** from Pula, take an eight-minute ride on the Follesa bus from Piazza Giovanni XXIII, or follow the signs and walk 25min to get here. Nora is the site of an **ancient city** (daily 9am–sunset; ⓣ070.920.9138; €5.50; excellent guides available) thought to date from the eighth century BC. An administrative, religious and commercial centre for over 1000 years, it was abandoned around the seventh century AD when the Arab invasion forced the inhabitants to retreat inland. The monuments – a theatre, thermal baths (which made use of the natural springs to be found here), a forum, a temple, an aqueduct and noble houses – suggest a sophisticated people, and many of the intricate mosaics decorating the town remain intact.

Laguna di Nora

Next to the archeological centre is the **lagoon** (July & Aug daily 10am–5pm; June & Sept daily 10am–4pm; ⓣ070.920.9544, ⓦwww.lagunadinora.it; €8), originally a fish farm and now an environmental park where you can observe nesting birds and local wildlife, paddle around in a **canoe** (€25/3hr, including entry to the lagoon park), or take a **snorkelling** trip to see the Roman remains on the bed of the bay (€25/3hr). Nora beach itself, flanked by the **Torre del Coltellazzo** and the **Torre di Sant Efisio** (which you can climb up for a view over to the mountains of Santa Margherita), is a lovely, family-orientated place for a swim.

Chia

For more secluded beaches, take a bus from Pula's Via Lamarmora to **CHIA** (hourly; 25min); Chia beach is a five-minute walk from where the bus terminates. From here, white sands lapped by turquoise-blue waters stretch along the west coast for about 4km. *Campeggio Torre Chia* is a large **campsite** just a stone's throw from the beach, and has a small on-site shop and restaurant; take a left off the main road from the Chia junction and head towards the sea (Ⓣ070.923.0054, Ⓦwww.rentocamp.com; €9 per person, plus €9 per tent).

ALGHERO

In the northwest of Sardinia, **ALGHERO** is a lively resort with a Catalan flavour. From the **Giardino Pubblico**, the **Porta Terra** is the first of Alghero's seven defensive towers, erected by the prosperous Jewish community before their expulsion in 1492. **Via Roma** runs down from here through the old town's puzzle of lanes to the pedestrianized **Via Carlo Alberto**, home to most of the bars and shops. Turn right to reach **Piazza Cìvica**, the old town's main square, at one end of which rises Alghero's mainly sixteenth-century **cattedrale** (guided tours Feb–Oct Mon–Fri 10am–noon & 4–6pm; free). The best excursions are west along the coast, past the long bay of **Porto Conte** to the point of **Capo Caccia**, where the spectacular sheer cliffs are riddled by deep marine caves. The most impressive of these is the Grotta di Nettuno, or **Neptune's Grotto** (daily: April–Sept 9am–7pm; Oct 9am–5pm; Nov–March 9am–2pm; €12), a long snaking passage that delves far into the rock and is full of stalagmites and stalactites. To get there join a boat trip from the port (€15, entrance to the caves not included; 2hr 30min; Ⓦwww.navisarda.it), or take the bus from the Giardino Pubblico to Capo Caccia and walk the 654 steps down to the caves (June–Sept 3 daily from 9am; Oct–May 1 daily). If you do have time for another excursion head down the coast to the picturesque town of Bosa. There are 4 daily buses to this beautiful town and it takes an hour.

Arrival and information

Air Fertilia airport is 12km north of the town, and served by the #AA bus, for which you can buy tickets in any *tabacchi* (takes 30min; €1).
Train Trains arrive 3km north of the centre and are connected to the port by regular local buses.
Bus Long-distance buses arrive in Via Catalogna, on the Giardino Pubblico.
Tourist office 9 Piazza Porta Terra (April–Sept Mon–Sat 8am–8pm, Sun 9am–1pm; Nov–March Mon–Sat 8am–2pm; Ⓣ079.979.054, Ⓦwww.comune.alghero.ss.it).

Accommodation

Alguer Via Parenzo 79 Ⓣ079.930.478. This slightly shabby HI hostel is located in a fairly distant but tranquil spot 6km along the coast at Fertilia, reachable by hourly local bus from Alghero (€0.70). Dorms €18.
La Mariposa Ⓣ079.950.480, Ⓦwww.lamariposa.it. Popular, friendly well-equipped campsite 2km north of town, with direct access to the seaweed-covered beach. April to mid-Oct. €13/person, plus tent from €14.
L'loc D'or B&B Via Logudoro 26, Ⓣ347.076.3412. A 2min walk to the beach and a short distance from the old town. Owner Gemma provides a true Sardinian hospitality and a great breakfast. Doubles €60.
Mario & Giovanna's B&B Via Canepa 51 Ⓣ339.890.3563. Unmissable with its bright facade this small family-run B&B has with just three rooms. 15min walk from the old town. Doubles €55.

Eating and drinking

Alghero's restaurants are renowned for seafood, at its best in spring and winter. There's also a supermarket, Conad, at Via Mazzini 1a, and a great covered food market on Via Sassari.
Casablanca Via Umberto 76. Don't expect top-notch service but the fresh, large and tasty pizzas (€5) more than make up for this.
Poco Loco Via Gramsci 8. Superb modern pizzeria with live music and bowling. Try the testing metre-long pizza (€20, serves 4). Large screens showing sport. Open until 1am.
Trattoria Maristella Via Kennedy 9. Tasty, reasonably priced fish restaurant popular with locals. Seafood pasta €10. Closed Sun eves.

Moving on

Train Cagliari (5 daily via Sassari; 4hr 30min); Sassari (frequent; 35min).

Latvia

HIGHLIGHTS

SIGULDA: explore the castle ruins and hiking trails of the gorgeous Gauja Valley

JŪRMALA: join the Latvian summer beach party at this string of seaside resorts

VENTSPILS: vibrant port city with bizarre cow statue parade and one of the Latvia's best beaches

RIGA: view the exquisite Jugendstil architecture, and party in the many bars

KOLKA: get away from it all amid tiny seaside villages and windswept coast

ROUGH COSTS

DAILY BUDGET Basic €45 /occasional treat €60

DRINK Aldaris beer €2.50

FOOD Pork with potatoes and sauerkraut €6

HOSTEL/BUDGET HOTEL €18 /€30–45

TRAVEL Bus: Rīga–Liepāja €8.50; train: Rīga–Sigulda €3

FACT FILE

POPULATION 2.3 million

AREA 64,589 sq km

LANGUAGE Latvian; Russian also widely spoken

CURRENCY Lats (Ls)

CAPITAL Rīga (population: 706,413)

INTERNATIONAL PHONE CODE ⓣ371

Introduction

Since becoming a member of the European Union in 2004, Latvia has enjoyed impressive economic growth, although the legacy of Soviet occupation, which left the country with a large Russian minority population, means it has entered the new era as a culturally divided country. Unlike their Baltic neighbours, Latvians are a minority in their country's larger cities; they are more withdrawn and harder to win over. Although visitors are most likely to be attracted to the lively capital of Rīga, to experience the true spirit of Latvia you'll need to head into the vast countryside, with its parks, lakes and forests.

The most obvious destination is the capital, **Rīga**. Its architectural treasures, lively nightlife and countless eating options make it a prime destination for budget travellers, and it's also popular with stag parties. Places within easy reach of the capital include the palace of **Rundāle**, while those wishing to hit the beach can head either to the nearby resort area of **Jūrmala** or to the port city of **Ventspils**. In the scenic **Gauja Valley**, the attractive small towns of **Sigulda** and **Cēsis** can both be used as bases for hiking, biking, canoeing and other outdoor pursuits.

CHRONOLOGY

800s AD Vikings seize the areas around present-day Latvia.
1201 German traders found the city of Rīga.
1285 Rīga joins the Hanseatic League, bringing the Baltic region closer economic ties with the rest of Europe.
1330 Rīga Castle is built for the Livonian Knights (it now houses the President of Latvia).
1561 Southern Latvia is conquered by Poland; Catholicism is adopted.
1629 Parts of Latvia are conquered by Sweden.
1793 Latvian land is taken by Russia, following the partition of Poland.
1816 The system of serfdom is abolished.
Late 1800s Cultural and intellectual movements led by the "Young Latvians" increase Latvian national self-consciousness.
1905 Peasant revolt against the rich, land-owning German nobility in Latvia. Brutal repression follows.
1920 Latvia gains independence, despite German and Soviet military attempts to prevent it.
1940 Latvia is taken by the Soviets at the beginning of World War II, as well as by the Germans a year later. Both occupations cause horrendous suffering for Latvians.
1945 By the end of the war the Soviets are still in control, and Communism rules.
1991 Collapse of the Soviet Union brings about the Latvian restoration of independence.
1999 Vaira Vike-Freiberga, the first female President of Latvia, takes office.
2004 Latvia joins the EU.
2007 After centuries of disputes, Latvia's borders with Russia are set under a treaty signed by both countries.
2008–11 Following a period of rapid economic growth, Latvia has been affected by worldwide recession and has high unemployment levels.

ARRIVAL

Rīga International Airport (Lidosta Rīga) is served by numerous European airlines, including easyJet, Ryanair, Aer Lingus, Lufthansa, Air France, KLM, Turkish Airlines and Austrian Airlines, as well as Latvia's airBaltic (Ⓦwww.airbaltic.com). You can easily get to the city centre by taking bus #22 (0.70Ls) or a taxi, which should cost no more than 15Ls.

Options for cross-border **train** travel are fairly limited, with connections to Vilnius, Lithuania, and Moscow, Russia, but not to Tallinn, Estonia. Both Eurolines (Ⓦwww.eurolines.ee) and Ecolines (Ⓦwww.ecolines.net) offer frequent **bus services** linking

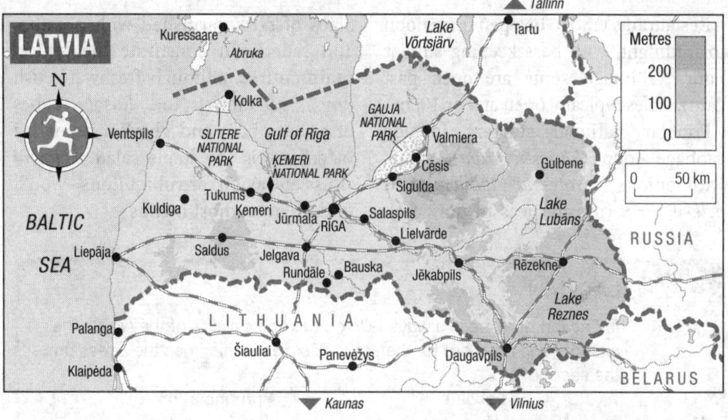

Rīga with Tallinn, Vilnius and St Petersburg, among other international destinations. A daily **ferry** service runs from the Rīga terminal to Stockholm, Sweden; as well as daily from Ventspils to Nynäshamn, Sweden (60km from Stockholm), St Petersburg, Russia, and Lübeck, Germany.

GETTING AROUND

Buy **train** tickets in advance: stations have separate windows for long-distance (*starpilsetu*) and suburban (*pirpilsetu*) trains. Long-distance services are divided into "passenger" (*pasazieru vilciens*) and "fast" (*ātrs*) – both are quite slow but the latter, usually requiring a reservation, stops at fewer places. On timetable boards, look for *atiet* (departure) or *pienāk* (arrival). Check train timetables online at ⓦwww.ldz.lv.

Buses are slightly quicker than trains, though marginally more expensive. Buy long-distance tickets in advance from the ticket counter and opt for an express (*ekspresis*) bus if possible.

Rīga has plentiful and cheap public transport. A new BalticBike borrowing system (ⓦwww.balticbike.lv) allows you to pick up and drop off **bicycles** from various points around Rīga and Jūrmala for as little as 0.70Ls per hour. Cycling is a particularly good way of getting around the resort areas and small towns.

ACCOMMODATION

Outside Rīga and Jūrmala, you won't find many youth hostels, though inexpensive guesthouses and campsites are found in many Latvian towns. **Youth hostels** are particularly prolific in the centre of Rīga (check ⓦwww.hostellinglatvia.com or ⓦwww.hostels.com). A number of small-sized, good-value **hotels** and **guesthouses** are also available, but rooms are in short supply during peak season and advance reservations are required in summer. In Rīga and Jūrmala there are agencies offering well-priced **private rooms** (*istabas*) of a reasonable standard. There's a handful of decently equipped **campsites** in Rīga, Jūrmala, Sigulda, Cēsis and Ventspils. Prices are normally quoted in Lats, though some are provided in euros.

FOOD AND DRINK

While meat or fish and potatoes remain the bedrock of Latvian cuisine, Rīga has something to suit every palate, with a lot of good international cuisine and vegetarian options. **Eating out**, particularly in the capital's classier joints, is fairly expensive, but there are plenty of self-service fast-food places, offering filling meals for around 4Ls. Numerous supermarkets and markets make **self-catering** a viable option too.

Restaurants tend to be open from noon to midnight, with bars keeping similar hours (although some are open past 2am). Cafés typically open at 9 or 10am.

Popular national **starters** include cabbage soup (*kāpostu zupa*), sprats with onions (*sprotes ar sīpoliem*) and *pelēkie zirņi* (mushy peas in pork fat). Slabs of pork garnished with potatoes and sauerkraut constitute the typical **main course**, although freshwater fish (*zivs*) is common too. *Rasols* (cubes of potato, ham and gherkin drenched in cream) is the staple salad. *Pelmeni* (Russian ravioli) are ubiquitous – you'll find them on most menus.

LATVIAN

In Latvian, the stress always falls on the first syllable of the word. The exception is the word for thank you (*paldies*), which has the stress on the second.

	Latvian	Pronunciation
Yes	*Jā*	Jah
No	*Nē*	Neh
Please	*Lūdzu*	Loodzoo
Thank you	*Paldies*	Paldeeass
Hello/Good day	*Labdien*	Labdeean
Goodbye	*Uz redzēsanos*	Ooz redzehshanwas
Excuse me	*Atvainojiet*	Atvainoyet
Today	*Sodien*	Shwadien
Yesterday	*Vakar*	Vakar
Tomorrow	*Rīt*	Reet
What time is it?	*Cik ir pulkstenis?*	Tsik ir pulkstenis?
Open/Closed	*Atvērts/Slēgts*	Atvaerts/Slaegts
Good/Bad	*Labs/Slikts*	Labs/Slikts
Do you speak English?	*Vai jūs runājat angliski?*	Vai yoos roonahyat angliski?
I don't understand	*Es nesaprotu*	Es nesaprwatoo
How much is...?	*Cik tas maksā...?*	Tsik tas maksah...?
Cheap/Expensive	*Lēts/Dārgs*	Laets/Dahrgs
Student ticket	*Studentu biļeti*	Studentu bilyeti
Boat	*Kuģis*	Kugyis
Bus	*Auto*	Owto
Plane	*Lido*	Lidaw
Train	*Dzelzceļa*	Dzelzcelyuh
Where is the...?	*Kur atrodas...?*	Kur uhtrawduhs...?
Near/Far	*Tuvs/Tāls*	Tuvs/Taals
I'd like...	*Es vēlos...*	Es vaalaws...
I'm a vegetarian	*Es esmu veģetārietis/te(m/f)*	Es asmu vejyetahreatis/te
The bill, please	*Lūdzu rēķinu*	Loodzu rehkyinu
Toilet	*Tualete*	Tuuhlete
One	*Viens*	Viens
Two	*Divi*	Divi
Three	*Trīs*	Trees
Four	*Četri*	Chetri
Five	*Pieci*	Pietsi
Six	*Sesi*	Seshi
Seven	*Septiņi*	Septinyi
Eight	*Astoņi*	Astonyi
Nine	*Deviņi*	Devinyi
Ten	*Desmit*	Desmit

Drinks

Rīga has excellent **bars**, though some are expensive. Imported **beer** (*alus*) is widely available, but the local brews are fine and also cheaper – the most common brands are Aldaris and Cēsu. Worth trying once is *Rīga Melnais Balzāms* (Rīga Black Balsam), a kind of bitter liqueur (45 percent) made from a secret recipe of roots and herbs and supposed to cure all ailments.

Coffee (*kafija*) and tea (*tēja*) are usually served black – ask for milk (*piens*) and/or sugar (*cukurs*).

CULTURE AND ETIQUETTE

Latvians are rather reserved and tend to greet each other with solemn handshakes rather than effusive hugs. The distinctive Russian and Latvian communities do not mix much and some resent being mistaken for the other. In the workplace **women** still tend to fill more traditional roles, and the general attitude to women travelling alone tends to be mildly sexist, although there is little risk of harassment. A ten percent **tip** is appropriate for good service in a restaurant.

SPORTS AND ACTIVITIES

Ice hockey is the national sport, and the revered national team plays at the 12,500-seat Arena Rīga (Skanstes 21, ⓣ6738 8200, ⓦwww.arenariga.com). You'll need to book in advance for important games.

Outside Rīga there is plenty of scope for **outdoor pursuits**. A number of beautiful **national parks**, best visited in the summer and home to dozens of protected species, offer extensive hiking and biking trails ripe for exploration. Canoeing, rafting and extreme sports such as mountain boarding, quad biking and bungee jumping are on offer around Cēsis and Sigulda in the Gauja Valley. Skiing and snowmobiling take over in winter while the port of Ventspils attracts kitesufrers.

LATVIA ONLINE

ⓦ**www.latviatourism.lv** Detailed website with helpful information on Latvia's attractions, accommodation and transport.

ⓦ**www.inyourpocket.com/latvia/riga** Excellent, regularly updated listings and all sorts of practical information about Rīga.

ⓦ**www.rigathisweek.lv** Extensive website of *Rīga This Week*, a free listings magazine.

EMERGENCY NUMBERS

Police ⓣ02; Ambulance ⓣ03; Fire ⓣ01.

COMMUNICATIONS

Post offices (*pasts*) are generally open from 8am to 7pm during the week and from 8am to 3pm on Saturdays. Modern **public phones** are operated with either credit cards or magnetic cards (*telekarte*), which come in 2 and 5Ls denominations, and are sold at post offices and most newsagents. Using mobile phones from other European countries is fairly inexpensive, but check roaming charges with your phone company. **Internet cafés** in the capital are becoming obsolete due to ever-increasing number of **wi-fi hotspots** and free internet and wi-fi offered by guesthouses, hotels and youth hostels.

EMERGENCIES

Theft is the biggest hazard. If you're staying in a cheap hotel, don't leave valuables in your room. Muggings and casual violence are not unknown in Rīga; avoid parks and backstreets after dark. **Police** (*policija*), who are unlikely to speak much English, will penalize you if you're caught drinking in public – expect

STUDENT AND YOUTH DISCOUNTS

ISIC cards will get you a fifty percent discount off entry to most museums and attractions, and even some restaurants – look for the ISIC sign on doors. HI-affiliated hostels offer discounts for **YHA** card holders.

a stiff fine. Some **strip clubs** are notorious for ripping off drunk foreign males.

Pharmacies (*aptieka*) are well stocked with over-the-counter painkillers, first aid items, sanitary products and the like. In larger cities, they tend to be open from 8am until 8pm. There are 24-hour pharmacies in the capital, where, with some luck, you'll find an English speaker. **Emergency medical care** is free, but if you fall seriously ill, try and head for home, as many Latvian medical facilities are still lagging behind those in Western Europe.

INFORMATION

Tourist offices run by the Latvian tourist board (ⓦwww.latviatourism.lv) are located at the centre of most major cities and well-touristed towns. Jāņa Sēta (Elizabetes iela 83–85, Rīga) is well stocked with guides, and publishes its own maps. *Riga in your Pocket* (ⓦwww.inyourpocket.com; 2.20Ls) is an excellent English-language **listings** guide. *The Baltic Times* (ⓦwww.baltictimes.com) provides weekly updates on current affairs and events in English while *Rīga This Week* is a detailed listings guide.

MONEY AND BANKS

Latvia's currency is the lats (plural lati) – normally abbreviated to Ls – which is divided into 100 santīmi (s). Coins come in 1, 2, 5, 10, 20 and 50 santīmi, and 1 and 2 lati, and notes in 5, 10, 20, 50, 100 and 500 lati. **Bank** (*banka*) **hours** vary, but in Rīga many are open Monday to Friday from 9am to 5pm, and on Saturdays from 10am to 3pm. Outside the capital, many close at 1pm and most are closed on weekends. **Exchanging cash** is straightforward, even outside banking hours, as Rīga is full of currency exchange offices (*valktas apmaiņa*); shop around to get the best rate. **ATMs** are plentiful nationwide and accept most international cash cards. At the time of writing, €1 = 0.7Ls, $1 = 0.5Ls and £1 = 0.8Ls. Major banks such as the Hansa Banka and SEB will cash **travellers' cheques** (TravelEx Visa and American Express preferred) and give advances on **credit cards**. In Rīga the bigger hotels will also cash travellers' cheques. Credit cards are accepted in an increasing number of establishments.

OPENING HOURS AND HOLIDAYS

Shops are usually open weekdays from either 8 or 10am to 6 or 8pm, and on Saturdays from 10am to 7pm. Some food shops are open until 10pm and are also open on Sundays. In Rīga there are a few 24-hour shops, which sell food and alcohol. Most shops and all banks close on the following **public holidays**: 1 January, Good Friday, Easter Sunday, Easter Monday, May 1, the second Sunday in May, June 23 and 24, November 18, December 25, 26 and 31.

Rīga

RĪGA is the largest, liveliest and most cosmopolitan of the Baltic capitals, with a great selection of accommodation to suit any budget and a wide variety of world cuisine. A heady mixture of the medieval and the contemporary, the city has much to offer architecture and history enthusiasts in the narrow cobbled streets of Old Rīga and the wide boulevards of the New Town, where beautiful examples of Jugendstil Art Nouveau architecture – "music in stone" – line Strēlnieku iela and Alberta iela.

The city also has all the trappings of a modern capital, with efficient and affordable public transportation, excellent shopping, and a notoriously exuberant nightlife.

What to see and do

Old Rīga (Vecrīga), centred around Cathedral Square (Doma laukums) and bisected from east to west by Kaļķu iela, forms the city's nucleus and is home to most of its historic buildings. With its cobbled streets, medieval buildings, narrow lanes and hidden courtyards, it gives the impression of stepping back in time. To the east, Old Rīga is bordered by Bastejkalns Park, beyond which lies the **New Town** (Milda). Built during rapid urban expansion between 1857 and 1914, its wide boulevards are lined with four- and five-storey apartment buildings, many decorated with extravagant Jugendstil motifs.

Town Hall Square

From the doors of St Peter's Church, **Rātslaukums** (Town Hall Square) is straight ahead and dominated by the **House of the Blackheads** (Melngalvju nams; Tues–Sun 10am–5pm; 2Ls), an opulent masterpiece of Gothic architecture. Once serving as the headquarters of Rīga's bachelor merchants, and largely destroyed in 1941, it was lovingly reconstructed for the 800th anniversary of Rīga's foundation in 2001.

Next door, an imposing concrete structure accommodates the unmissable **Occupation Museum** (Latvijas okupācijas muzejs; May–Sept daily 11am–5pm; Oct–April Tues–Sun 11am–5pm; donations), devoted to atrocities committed against Latvia's population by the Nazis and Soviets. Emotion-inducing exhibits include reconstructed gulag barracks and letters to loved ones thrown from trains by Latvians forcibly removed to Siberia.

The Cathedral, the Castle and the Three Brothers

Cathedral Square is dominated by the towering red-brick **Rīga Cathedral** (daily 10am–5pm; 2Ls), established in 1211 and featuring one of the biggest organs in Europe. On the other side of the cathedral, at Palasta 4, is the worthwhile **Museum of Rīga's History and Navigation**, featuring Bronze

LOFTY VIEWS

If you want to see the city unfold before you, with its melange of church domes, vast parks, ribbon of river and squat Soviet creations, follow the urban throng to Šķūņu iela to **St Peter's Church** (Pēter baznīca; winter Tues–Sun 10am–5pm; summer Tues–Sun 10am–6pm), a large red-brick structure with a graceful three-tiered spire and climb the tower (3Ls) for excellent panoramic views of the city. Battling the church for the finest views of Rīga is "Stalin's Birthday Cake" – the **Academy of Sciences** (10am–6pm; 2Ls), a 1950s Empire State Building lookalike at Akadēmijas laukums 1. The 65m skyscraper, adorned with hammers and sickles near the top, has a 360-degree viewing platform on the 17th floor.

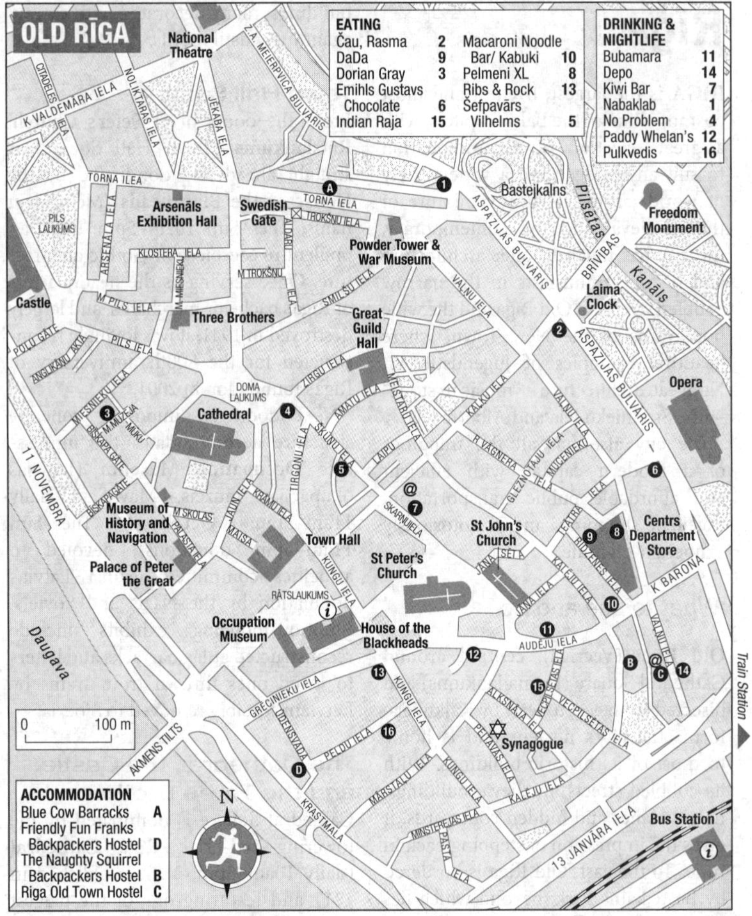

Age and medieval artefacts, such as a mummified criminal's hand, as well as temporary art exhibitions (Wed–Sun 11am–5pm; 3Ls).

From Cathedral Square, Pils iela runs down to Castle Square (Pils laukums) and **Rīga Castle** (Rīgas pils), built in 1515 and now home to the Latvian president. Follow Mazā Pils iela from Pils laukums to see the **Three Brothers** (Trīs brāli), three charming medieval houses, one of which, built in the fifteenth century, is thought to be the oldest in Latvia.

Swedish Gate and the Powder Tower

On Torņa iela, you'll find the seventeenth-century **Swedish Gate** (Zviedru vārti), the sole surviving city gate. At the end of Torņa iela is the Powder Tower (Pulvertornis), a vast, fourteenth-century bastion, home to the excellent **War Museum** (Kara muzejs; daily 10am–5pm; free) – nine floors of the country's turbulent history, from medieval weaponry to world wars I and II and Latvia's struggle for independence.

Bastion Hill and the Guild Hall

Bastion Hill (Bastejkalns) – the park that slopes down to the city canal at the end of Torna iela – is a reminder of the city's more recent history: on January 20, 1991, four people were killed by Soviet fire during an attempted crackdown on Latvia's independence drive. Stones bearing the victims' names mark where they fell near the Bastejas bulvāris entrance to the park.

The Freedom Monument

The modernist **Freedom Monument** (Brīvības piemineklis), known affectionately as "Milda", dominates the view along Brīvības bulvāris as it enters the **New Town**, holding aloft three stars symbolizing the three regions of Latvia. Incredibly, the monument survived the Soviet era, and nowadays two soldiers stand guard here in symbolic protection of Latvia's independence.

National Art Museum

Esplanade Park runs north from Brīvības bulvāris. At the far end of the park, the worthwhile **Latvian National Art Museum** (Valsts mākslas muzejs; Valdemāra iela 10; daily except Tues 11am–5pm; Fri until 8pm; 1.50–3Ls; Ⓦwww.lnmm.lv), housed in a grandiose Neoclassical building, displays an impressive array of nineteenth- and twentieth-century Latvian paintings, sculptures and drawings by Rosentāls, Padegs, Valters and others, as well as changing modern art exhibitions. In a separate building on Torņa iela 1, the **Arsenāls Exhibition Hall** (Tues, Wed & Fri noon–6pm, Thurs noon–8pm, Sat & Sun noon–5pm; 2.50Ls) stages cutting-edge temporary exhibitions by contemporary artists.

Rīga Art Nouveau Museum

The **Rīga Art Nouveau Museum** at Alberta iela 12 (Tues–Sun 10am–6pm; 2.50Ls), housed in the former apartment of renowned artist and engineer Konstantīns Pēkšēns, is a must for anyone with an interest in Art Nouveau. You can view original period furniture and some of Pēksēns' work and the visit culminates in the viewing of a short video which will enable you to tell the difference between "romantic" and "vertical" Art Nouveau facades on the city's streets.

Rīga Motor Museum

It's worth travelling 8km out of town to seek out one of Rīga's odder attractions – the **Motor Museum** (Rīgas motormuzejs; Tues–Sun 10am–6pm; 1.50Ls). Home to an impressive collection of

JEWS IN LATVIA

Jews living in Rīga and other parts of Latvia suffered the same fate as Jews in other parts of Eastern Europe when Latvia was overrun by Nazis. The **Rīga Ghetto Museum** (Maskavas 14a; entry from Krasta; Mon–Fri 10am–5pm; donation) built on the site of the Jewish ghetto behind the Central Market consists of two outdoor exhibits: a seemingly endless wall of victims' names, and photographs and text illustrating the life of the Jewish community in different parts of Latvia before World War II. On Peitavas iela 6/8, you'll find the last surviving **synagogue** in Rīga; when all the synagogues in the city were burned down by the Nazis in 1941, this synagogue and its treasures – the sacred scrolls – escaped destruction due to its close proximity to other buildings. There's a memorial on Gogoļa iela where the **Great Choral Synagogue** was burnt down in July 1941 with its 300-strong congregation trapped inside. At Skolas 6, you will find a small but gritty and informative **Jews In Latvia Museum** (Sun–Thurs noon–5pm; donation) on the history of Jewish life in Latvia from the eighteenth century onwards, including persecution by both Nazis and Soviets, and the survival and "rebirth" of Judaism in independent Latvia.

vehicles through the ages, its pride and joy are the vehicles belonging to Soviet heads of state: see Stalin lounging in the back seat of his bulletproof ZIS. To get here, take bus #21 east along Brīvibas to the Pansionāts stop (20min), cross the road and take the main road that runs to the right of the housing development (5min).

Arrival and information

Air Rīga Airport (Lidosta Rīga; ⓦ www.riga-airport.com) is located about 13km west of the city centre. Bus #22 (every 20min; 70Ls) drops passengers at Strēlnieku laukums, just west of Rātslaukums, and by the train station. A taxi from the airport should cost no more than 12Ls.

Train Rīga's main train station (Centrālā stacija) is just south of Old Rīga on 13 Janvāra iela; it takes about 15min to walk to Rātslaukums from here. Facilities include ATMs, currency exchange and an information centre.

Bus Rīga's bus station (*Autoosta*) is 5min walk west of the train station along 13 Janvāra iela; luggage storage, ATM and tourist information available. To get to Old Rīga, turn left out of the front entrance and use the underpass next to the Coca-Cola Plaza to cross 13 Janvāra iela.

Ferry The ferry terminal (*Jūras pasazieru stacija*) is to the north of Old Rīga. Tram #5, #7 or #9 runs from the stop in front of the terminal on Ausekļa iela to Aspazijas bulvāris in the city centre (two stops; 70Ls).

Tourist office Main office at Rātslaukums 6 in the centre of the Old Town (daily 10am–7pm; ⓣ 6703 7900, ⓦ www.rigatourism.com). It has plentiful information on Latvia's attractions and sells copies of *Rīga In Your Pocket* (2.20Ls) as well as the Rīga Card (10/14/18Ls for 24/48/72hr; ⓦ www.rigacard.lv), which gives unlimited use of public transport plus museum discounts.

City transport

Bikes Lime green Baltic Bikes (ⓦ www.balticbike.lv), can be found at 11 pick-up/drop-off points around the capital and also in Jūrmala. Register online and call ⓣ 6778 8333 when you want to borrow a bike to receive the key code. To return the bike, lock it to any Baltic Bike stand and call the above number again; rent is 0.70Ls/hr.

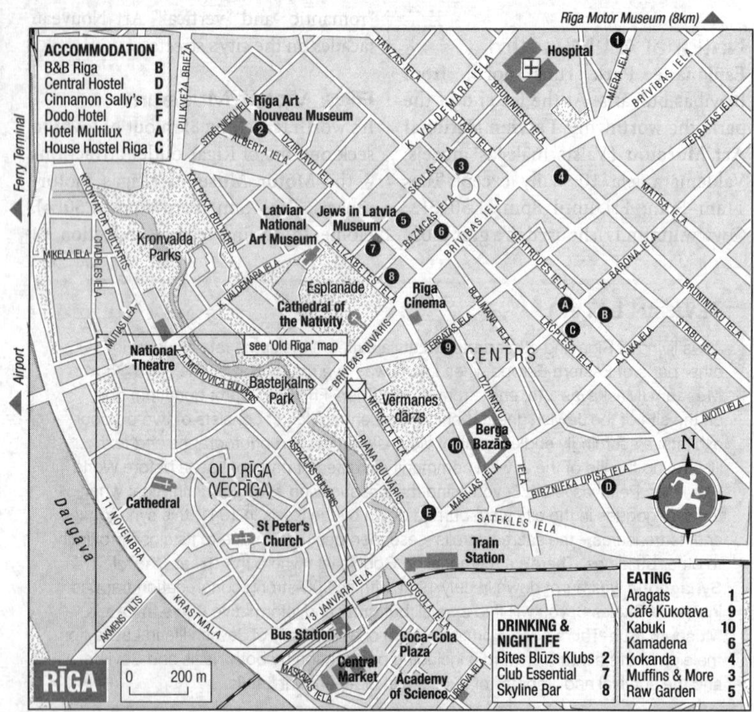

Public transport Both Old Rīga and the New Town are easily navigated on foot, and you can reach outlying attractions by frequent and efficient public transport – buses, trams and trolleybuses – running between 5.30am and midnight. Buy flat-fare one-way tickets from the driver for 0.70Ls or purchase cheaper *e-talons* for one (0.50Ls), four (2Ls), 10 (4.75Ls) and 20 rides (9Ls) as well as one- and three-day travel cards (1.90/5.70Ls) either from public transport ticket machines or from Narvesen and Plus Punkts newsstands. For routes and timetables check Ⓦ www.rigassatiksme.lv.

Accommodation

Rīga has extensive budget accommodation, mostly concentrated in the southern half of Old Rīga, with a few options in nearby New Town and by the Central Market. Reserve in advance in summer. The following are marked on the map opposite, unless otherwise stated.

Hostels

Blue Cow Barracks Torna iela 4-2B, 3rd floor Ⓣ 2773 6700, Ⓦ www.bluecowbarracks.com. See map, p.726. Luxurious touches at this beautifully-decorated, 16-bed hostel include excellent mattresses and cow-themed decor in honour of Latvia's unique breed of blue cows. Two nights' minimum stay required. Let the staff know your arrival time, as the hostel is not always manned. Dorms 14Ls, singles 30Ls, doubles 31–32Ls.

Central Hostel E. Birznieka-Upīša iela 20 Ⓣ 2232 2663, Ⓦ www.centralhostel.lv. The staff are friendly and helpful and the beds (including private rooms) are among the cheapest in the capital, which explains its popularity with local travellers and the odd middle-aged Russian man. Dorms 5.50–8.50Ls, singles 10Ls, doubles 20Ls.

Cinnamon Sally's Merkela iela 1, 3rd floor Ⓣ 2204 2280, Ⓦ www.cinnamonsally.com. More like the luxury apartment of a good friend than a hostel, this hostel has spacious dorms (with extra touches such as the make-up table in the girls' dorm); the combined lounge/kitchen is a great place to socialize and the incomparable Sally herself is always ready for a chat with her guests. Dorms 7.50–10Ls, doubles 30Ls.

Friendly Fun Franks Backpackers Hostel Novembra krastmala 29 Ⓣ 6722 0040, Ⓦ www.franks.lv. See map, p.726. Clean, Aussie-run, laddish hostel for those seeking crush-your-beer-can-against-your-forehead action. Perpetually full and not shying away from hosting stag parties, this firm favourite welcomes you on arrival with a free beer at its 24-hour bar. Raucous fun. Dorms 5.90–10.90Ls, doubles 28–36Ls.

House Hostel Rīga Barona iela 44 (entrance from Lāčplēša iela) Ⓣ 6735 0227, Ⓦ www.riga-hostels.com. Run by Rīga Out There (see p.731), an expat tour operator, this newly revamped boutique hostel offers individually themed private rooms to adventurous travellers. Guest kitchen and lounge available and breakfast is in the popular *Café Osiris*. Singles 25Ls, doubles 30Ls.

The Naughty Squirrel Backpackers Hostel Kalēju iela 50 Ⓣ 2722 0073, Ⓦ www.thenaughtysquirrel.com. See map, p.726. One of the most sociable places to stay in the Old Town, with daily tours and themed nights – from Movie Night to Latvian Food Night. Lockers are provided, and the location is hard to beat. Dorms 9–12Ls, doubles 30–36Ls.

Riga Old Town Hostel Valņu iela 43 Ⓣ 6722 3406, Ⓦ www.rigaoldtownhostel.lv. See map, p.726. Congregate around the bar/reception with fellow international travellers, join in one of their quirky walking tours or relax in the on-site sauna. Dorms 7–12Ls, doubles 34Ls.

Guesthouses and hotels

B&B Rīga Ģertrūdes iela 43 Ⓣ 6727 8505, Ⓦ www.bb-riga.lv. A friendly family-run guesthouse in Central Rīga offering en-suite rooms equipped with cable TV, fridges and microwaves. Breakfast vouchers and airport transfers available. Singles 32Ls, doubles 39Ls.

Dodo Hotel Jersikas iela 1 Ⓣ 6724 0220, Ⓦ www.dodohotel.com. Budget hotel offering tastefully decorated, spacious en-suite rooms with flat-screen TVs and free wi-fi, as well as a French pancake breakfast (3.20Ls), all just a 15min walk or short tram ride from Old Rīga. Doubles 23–28Ls.

Hotel Multilux Barona iela 37 (entrance from Ģertrūdes) Ⓣ 6731 1602, Ⓦ www.multilux.lv. This Art Nouveau building in Central Rīga boasts thoroughly modern en-suite rooms with cable TV, wi-fi, and breakfast buffet included in the price. Singles 14–18Ls, doubles 18–24Ls, triples 28–35Ls.

Eating

Many bars and cafés offer cheap and filling food and there are also plenty of reasonably priced restaurants serving international cuisine. The following are marked on the map opposite, unless otherwise stated.

Cafés and snack bars

Café Kūkotava Tērbatas iela 10/12. Cosy new café that not only serves some of the city's best coffee but also tantalizes you with its delectable home-made cakes.

Emihls Gustavs Chocolate Teatra iela at Aspazijas bulvāris. See map, p.726. Try the exquisite chocolate truffles or sip the bliss-in-a-cup white and dark molten chocolate (with a glass of water on the side in case it proves too rich for you). Hot chocolate 1.50Ls. Daily until 9pm.

Muffins and More Ģertrūdes iela 9. You'll smell the delicious muffins even before you set foot in this tiny, welcoming café. There are more than a dozen varieties and the blueberry ones just might be the best in Eastern Europe. The "More" consists of soup and baguettes. Muffins 0.60Ls; soup 2.50Ls.

Pelmeni XL Kaļķu iela 7. See map, p.726. Popular canteen-style eatery offering six types of *pelmeni* (Russian ravioli) filled with meat or cheese, plus soups and drinks. Gourmet cuisine it ain't but it *will* fill your belly. 1Ls/200g. Also at Audēju 16 (entrance from Vaļņu).

Šefpavārs Vilhelms Šķūņu iela 6. See map, p.726. Self-service, create-your-own-sweet-or-savoury-pancake place near Cathedral Square. 3.50Ls.

Restaurants

Aragats Miera eila 15. The effusive hostess won't have to tell you off for not finishing your food, because you will: the Armenian-style grilled meats and stews, with the fresh herbs chopped up right at your table, are the best in the city. Mains 6–10Ls.

Čau, Rasma Aspazijas bulvaris 20. The decor is rather tacky, but you can't beat the large portions of hearty traditional Latvian cooking. Pigs' ears with crackling, blood sausage and grey peas with bacon are all on the menu here, as are local beers. Mains 3.50–6Ls.

DaDa Audēju iela 16 (Galerija Centrs). See map, p.726. Its decor reflects the anarchist art movement, but *DaDa* specializes in Mongolian barbecue. Fill up a bowl with fresh meat, seafood, vegetables and noodles, pick a sauce and have it cooked in front of you. Small/large bowl 4.50–6.50Ls.

Dorian Gray Mazā Muzeja iela 1. See map, p.726. This newcomer delights with its innovative dishes such as the honey-and-black-pepper-glazed duck and its weekday two-course lunch special is an absolute steal at 3.99Ls. After one of their indulgent desserts, there'll be a portrait of you growing thinner in an attic somewhere.

Indian Raja Vecpilsētas iela 3. See map, p.726. Authentic, flavourful Indian food in a cosy cellar setting – an expat favourite. Huge mains 5.50–8Ls.

Kokanda Bruņinieku 12. This is an excellent choice for inexpensive Central Asian cuisine; try any of the grilled meats or the large, spicy dumplings. Weekday business lunch 3.50Ls.

Macaroni Noodle Bar/Kabuki Audēju 14. See map, p.726. Stylish twin restaurant with minimalist decor offering an extensive menu of excellent home-made pasta and noodle dishes, as well as sushi and sashimi platters and bento box weekday lunch specials (3.99Ls). Mains 5.50–8Ls. Larger *Kabuki* branch at Barona iela 14.

Ribs & Rock Grēcinieku iela 8. At this carnivore central, ribs are the star. Whether you order the ones in caraway marinade or the more peculiar "Dark Side of the Moon", featuring Rīga Black Balsam, you can't go wrong: the tender, flavourful meat just melts off the bone. Mains 8–14Ls.

Drinking and nightlife

The Old Town offers innumerable opportunities for bar hopping, with a wide range of watering holes (many serve decent food too) filling up with fun-seeking locals seven nights a week. Many double as restaurants during the day but close at 1/2am. The following are marked on the map on p.728, unless otherwise stated.

Bars

Kiwi Bar Skārņu iela 7. See map, p.726. Appropriately staffed by Kiwis (and Brits), this sports bar's

VEGGIE RĪGA

The forces of vegetarianism have successfully stormed this bastion of stodgy meat dishes over the last few years. Still, it takes guts to open **Raw Garden**, a stylish vegan non-dairy restaurant (Skolas iela 12). No dish is cooked above 45°C, and you'll either join the crowd of satisfied patrons clamouring for more Thai cucumber soup and papaya-mango cake or leave the premises like Samantha from *Sex and the City*, exclaiming: "I've eaten a f***ing cactus!" Less extreme is **Kamadena** (Lāčpleša 12), where you pick a selection of Indian, Thai and Tibetan dishes, as well as pastas and salads, from a menu filled with quotes from philosophers (closed Sun).

post-hangover Kiwi breakfasts and drink selection are an instant hit with the international backpacker set and expats.

No Problem Tirgoņu 5/7. See map, p.726. The best of the capital's beer gardens, *No Problem* boasts a prime spot overlooking Doma laukums (Cathedral Square), over 20 beers on tap, live music nightly and some of the best burgers in town, served by friendly, efficient staff.

Paddy Whelan's Grēcinieku iela 4. See map, p.726. Big, lively Irish pub/sports bar bursting at the seams whenever a big match is on, offering 18 kinds of beer and cider on tap, as well as great curry from its Indian menu.

Skyline Bar Elizabetes iela 55. Behold Rīga's splendour from a window seat on the 26th floor of the *Reval Hotel Latvija* while sipping a strawberry daiquiri.

Clubs

Club Essential Skolas iela 2 ⓦ www.essential.lv. Adventurous music with DJs from all over Europe and a funky chill-out zone. Dress well and prepare for expensive drinks. Wed, Thurs & Sun 10pm–5am, Fri & Sat 10pm–9am; 3–10Ls.

Depo Vaļņu iela 32 ⓦ www.klubsdepo.lv. See map, p.726. Post-industrial cellar space with alternative DJ nights, live garage bands and an eclectic mix of experimental, reggae, punk, metal and other genres. Noon–5am; 3–5Ls.

Nabaklab Z. A. Mierovica bulvāris 12 ⓦ www.nabaklab.lv. See map, p.726. Part art gallery, part bohemian club with live bands, DJs and a summer terrace for enjoying their own *Nabaklab* brew. Noon–2am. Thurs, Fri & Sat noon–6am.

Pulkvedis (Nobody Writes to the Colonel) Peldu iela 26/28 ⓦ www.pulkvedis.lv. See map, p.726. The sounds at this split-level former bastion of edgy music sometimes degenerate into 80s pop, but when a good DJ is in the house, this easy-going venue filled with a fun-seeking young crowd is the place to be. Entry 3Ls. Mon–Thurs 8pm–3am; Fri & Sat 8pm–5am.

Entertainment

Live Music

Bubamara Audēju 8 ⓦ www.bubamara.lv. See map, p.726. Underground music bar with acts varying from DJs to rock bands, and themed music evenings. Cheap beer and cocktails, too.

Bites Blūzs Klubs Dzirnavu iela 34a, ⓦ www.bluesclub.lv. Laidback, unpretentious blues pub festooned with photos of musicians. There are regular live acts, sometimes international.

Cinemas

Forum Cinemas (Coca-Cola Plaza) 13 Janvāra iela 8 ⓦ www.forumcinemas.lv. Second-largest cinema in northern Europe with 14 screens. 4–6.50Ls.

Riga Cinema Elizabetes iela 61 ⓦ www.kino.riga.lv. Rīga's oldest cinema, showing foreign films as well as blockbusters. 3Ls.

Shopping

Art Nouveau Rīga Strēlnieku iela 9 ⓦ www.artnouveauriga.lv. Dedicated entirely to Art Nouveau merchandise, such as small plaster faces copied from the decorations on Rīga's facades. 10am–6pm.

Berg's bazaar Elizabetes iela 83/85. Soviet kitsch, freshly baked bread, organically grown produce and gourmet food samples. Second and last Saturday of each month. 9am–3pm.

Central Market (Centrāltirgus) A row of massive 1930s former Zeppelin hangars next to the bus station is worth visiting just to appreciate the sheer size of it. It sells everything from half a cow to bread, smoked meats and fake designer watches.

Directory

Embassies Canada, Baznīcas iela 20/22 ⓣ 6781 3945; Ireland, Alberta iela 13 ⓣ 6703 9370; UK, Alunāna iela 5 ⓣ 6777 4700; US, Raiņa bulvāris 7 ⓣ 6703 6200.

Exchange Marika: Brīvības bulvāris 30 and Dzirnavu iela 96 (both 24hr).

Hospital ARS, Skolas iela 5 ⓣ 6720 1007. Some English-speaking doctors. 24-hour medical consultation ⓣ 6720 1003.

Internet All accommodation options listed offer internet and wi-fi; otherwise, try Interneta Planeta Kafe, Vaļņu iela 41 (24hr).

Left luggage At the bus station (daily 6.30am–11pm), from 25–50Ls/hr, depending on weight, 25Ls each additional hour. Lockers at the left-luggage office (Rokas Bagāžas) in the train station basement (1.50Ls/day, 4.30am–midnight).

Pharmacy Ģimenes aptieka, Talinas iela 57b, and Saules aptieka, Brīvības 68 (both open 24hr).

Post office Brīvības bulvāris 32 (Mon–Fri 7am–10pm, Sat & Sun 8am–8pm).

Tours Rīga Out There, at *House Hostel Rīga* (see p.729; ⓣ 2938 9450, ⓦ www.rigaoutthere.com), organizes off-the-wall activities, such as AK-47 shooting in an underground bunker and bobsleighing, as well as excellent nightlife and sightseeing tours, all with an English-speaking guide.

Moving on

Train Liepāja (1 daily Fri & Sun at 6.30pm; 3hr); Majori, Jūrmala (every 30min; 40min); Moscow (1 daily at 4.20pm; 16hr); St Petersburg, (1 daily at 6.50pm; 14hr); Salaspils (1–2 hourly; 15 min); Sigulda (8–10 daily; 1hr); Vilnius (1 every other day – odd dates; 7hr).

Bus Bauska (every 30min; 1hr 10min–1hr 30min); Kaunas (1–2 daily; 4hr 30min); Klaipēda (3 daily; 5hr); Liepāja (at least 12 daily; 3hr–4hr 30min); Moscow (1 daily 17hr); Pärnu (9–11 daily; 3hr 30min); Sigulda (at least 8 daily; 1hr 15min); St Petersburg (4 daily; 12–14hr); Tallinn (9–11 daily; 5hr 30min); Tartu (3 daily; 5hr); Vilnius (4–5 daily; 4hr–4hr 30min).

The rest of Latvia

In summer, the whole of Latvia seems to head to the beach – be it **Jūrmala**, the lively string of seaside resorts near Rīga, or the picturesque port of **Ventspils**, with its unspoiled stretch of sand and its music festival. Nature lovers can head inland to the picturesque little town of **Sigulda**.

JŪRMALA

A 20-kilometre string of small seaside resorts lining the Baltic coast west of Rīga, **JŪRMALA** was originally favoured by the tsarist nobility and later drew tens of thousands of holiday-makers from all over the USSR; it continues to be a popular beach resort today. Its wide, clean, sandy **beach** is backed by dunes and pine woods, and dotted with beer tents and climbing frames. It pulses with sun worshippers during the summer, especially during the week-long **music festival** in July.

What to see and do

Jomas iela, the pedestrianized main street running east from the station square, teems with people and has a number of excellent restaurants and cafés, as well as craft stalls and art exhibitions. A few paths lead to the beach from Jūras iela, north of Jomas iela. The beach aside, Jūrmala's attractions include the wonderful new interactive **Jūrmala City Museum** (Wed–Sun 11am–5pm; 3Ls) which charts the town's history as a popular beach resort. Upstairs is reserved for excellent temporary art and photography exhibitions. Another Jūrmala gem is the **"Inner Light" art gallery** at Omnibusa iela 19 (June–Aug 11am–6pm; Sept–May Sat & Sun only noon–5pm; 1Ls; Ⓦwww.jermolajev.lv). Local artist Vitaly Yermolayev specializes in the use of eerie glow-in-the-dark paint. Near the beach, at Turaidas iela 1, you'll find the Dzintari (Ⓣ6776 2117 Ⓦwww.dzk.lv), an open-air, 2000-capacity concert venue which hosts regular music events in the summer.

Arrival and information

Trains Trains leave Rīga's station from platforms 3 and 4 (0.90Ls one-way). Majori is the main stop for Jūrmala, eleven stops from Rīga.

Minibuses Minibuses depart from the Central Minibus Station (opposite the train station; 75Ls one-way) every 10min between 6am and midnight in the summer. Take either the Rīga–Sloka or the Rīga–Dubulti minibus and get off in front of the Majori train station.

Tourist office Lienes iela 5 (Mon–Fri 9am–7pm, Sat 10am–5pm, Sun 10am–3pm; Ⓣ6714 7900, Ⓦwww.jurmala.lv). Helpful staff have info on the town's attractions and accommodation. There's a Baltic Bikes stand (see p.721) just outside.

Accommodation

Elina Lienes iela 43 Ⓣ6776 1665, Ⓦwww.elinahotel.lv. This popular guesthouse has clean rooms 5min walk from the beach. Singles 35–45Ls, doubles 40–60Ls, quads 50–65Ls.

Kempings Nemo Atbalss iela 1, Vaivari Ⓣ6773 2350, Ⓦwww.nemo.lv. Large campsite popular with caravans and families in a pleasant middle-of-the-forest location just behind the beach, with reasonably clean facilities and a water park on site

(3–5Ls). 2Ls/person, plus 5Ls/tent; rooms in cabins 9–35Ls.

Riga Beach Hostel Dzintaru prospects 50, Dzintari ⓣ2837 4185, ⓦwww.rigabeachhostel.lv. Popular both with local families and international backpackers, this HI-affiliated hostel is a stone's throw from the beach, with spacious, clean dorms and internet access. Dorms 11–15Ls; doubles 28–30Ls.

Eating and drinking

Picērija Ripo Tirgoņu 21. Step inside this London-double-decker-bus-cum-pizzeria for the best pizza in town – from the classic pepperoni to the more exotic Subaru (horseradish-mayo sauce, minced meat, bacon and pickles). Small pizza 4.90–8.40Ls.

Sue's Asia Jomas iela 74. Busy restaurant serving large portions of excellent Indian, Thai and Chinese cuisine. The *Tom yum kuung* is spicy and flavoursome (5.50Ls).

Zangezur Jomas iela 80. Popular Armenian restaurant specializing in grilled meats and other tasty dishes, such as aubergines with garlic and walnuts. Try the *hinkale* – large meat dumplings (3.50Ls).

Moving on

Train Rīga (at least two hourly between 5.40am and 10.30pm; 30min); Ķemeri (15 daily between 6.20am and 00.10am; 35min).

SALASPILS

The concentration camp at **SALASPILS**, 14km southeast of Rīga, is where most of Rīga's Jewish population perished during World War II. One hundred thousand people died here, including prisoners of war and Jews from other countries, who were herded into the Rīga Ghetto after most of the indigenous Jewish population had been liquidated. The site is marked by monumental sculptures, with the former locations of the barracks outlined by white stones. Look for the offering of toys by the children's barracks and the bunker, inscribed with the words "Behind this gate the earth groans" – home to a haunting exhibition (free) about the camp.

To get here take a **suburban train** from Rīga central station in the Ogre direction and alight at **Dārziņi** (0.80Ls one-way; at least one train hourly from Rīga) from where a clearly signposted path leads to the clearing, fifteen minutes' walk through the forest. The stop itself is not well signposted; it's the first one to be completely surrounded by pine forest.

RUNDĀLE PALACE

One of the architectural wonders of Latvia, Baroque **Rundāle Palace** (Rundāles Pils; daily May–Oct 10am–6pm; Nov–April 10am–5pm; combined ticket to the palace, exhibitions and gardens 6.50Ls/students 5.50Ls; ⓦwww.rundale.net) is 77km south of Rīga. Its 138 rooms were built in two phases during the 1730s and 1760s and designed by **Bartolomeo Rastrelli**, the architect responsible for the Winter Palace in St Petersburg. It was privately owned until 1920 when it fell into disrepair, but has largely been returned to its former glory through meticulous restoration. Each opulent room is decorated in a unique fashion and there are changing art exhibitions both inside the palace and in the

LEARN TO FLY

Aerodium (Tues–Fri 4–8pm, Sat & Sun noon–8pm; 17/22Ls for two minutes; 6/7Ls per minute thereafter on weekdays/weekends; ⓣ2838 4400, ⓦwww.aerodium.lv), 5km outside Sigulda, lets you experience the intense adrenaline rush of skydiving without jumping out of a plane. You hover atop an air current created by a powerful wind tunnel; beginners fly up to 5m above the fan, while professionals reach heights five times that. Book your time slot online. Take any Rīga-bound bus and ask to be dropped off at the Silciems stop; 0.70Ls.

vast landscaped gardens. There are frequent buses from Rīga to **Bauska** (every 30min between 7am–8pm; 1hr 30min; 2Ls); then take a local service to Pilsrundāle (up to 9 buses daily from Bauska; 30 min; 0.45Ls). The palace is across the street from the bus stop.

SIGULDA

Dotted with parks and clustered above the southern bank of the River Gauja around 50km northeast of Rīga, **SIGULDA** is Gauja National Park's main centre and a good jumping-off point for exploring the rest of the **Gauja Valley**.

What to see and do

From the train station, Raiņa iela runs north into town, passing the bus station. After about 800m a right turn into Baznaca iela brings you to the impressive seven-hundred-year-old **Sigulda Church** (Siguldas baznīca). Sigulda is home to three castles: Krimulda Castle (Krimuldas pilsdrupas) and Sigulda Castle (Siguldas pilsdrupas), a former stronghold of the German Knights of the Sword, from which you can see **Turaida Castle** (Turaidas pilsdrvpas), the most impressive of the three.

West of the train station along Ausekļa iela is the **bobsleigh track** where you can hurtle down a concrete half-tube at 80km per hr during the summer months (Sat & Sun 11am–6pm; 7Ls/person/ride), try the exhilarating professional winter bob (Oct–March noon–7pm; 35Ls) or check out the view of the Gauja Valley from the top of the tower (daily; 0.50Ls).

Turaida Castle

You can reach **Turaida Castle** by bus #12 (for Turaida or Krimulda) from Sigulda bus station (several daily; 0.50Ls). Alternatively, take the cable car (every 30min; 10am–6.30pm; 2.50Ls) across the Gauja River (Fri–Sun, daredevils can bungee jump from the cable car at 6.30pm; 20Ls; Ⓦ www.bungee.lv) to Krimulda Castle, descend the wooden staircase signposted "Gūtmaņis Cave", then follow the path past the cave – the setting for a legend of "star-crossed lovers". The path turns to the right before rejoining the main road just short of Turaida itself. Built on the site of an earlier stronghold by the bishop of Rīga in 1214, the castle was destroyed when lightning hit its gunpowder magazine in the eighteenth century. These days, its cellar exhibitions chart the castle's history (daily 10am–5/7pm; 3.50Ls) and it's possible to climb up the main tower for 360 degree views of the valley below.

Information

Tourist office Raiņa iela 3, just to the left of the entrance to the bus staion (Mon–Fri 8am–7pm, Sat 9am–2pm; Ⓣ 6797 1335, Ⓦ www.tourism.sigulda.lv). Helpful multilingual staff can book you into private rooms and provide information on exploring the Gauja Valley. They can also arrange hot-air ballooning (book in advance, Ⓣ 2928 8448, Ⓦ www.altius.lv) and bungee jumping from the cable car.

Gauja National Park Administration Baznīcas iela 7 (Mon–Fri 8.30am–5pm Ⓣ 6750 9545; Ⓦ www.gnp.gov.lv). North of the bus and train stations along Raiņa iela, this helpful office provides information on hiking trails in the Gauja National Park, including the popular trail from Sigulda to the village of Ligatne. Hiking map 2Ls.

Accommodation

Līvkalns Pēteralas iela 4b Ⓣ 6797 0916, Ⓦ www.livkalns.lv. This charming hotel's appeal lies in its secluded location, attractive rooms (the more luxurious doubles have own jacuzzis), some with a/c and satellite TV, and a splendid cellar restaurant serving regional cuisine. Breakfast included. Singles 15–22Ls, doubles 25–45Ls.

Melnais Kaķis Pils iela 8 Ⓣ 6797 0272. Spotless, compact rooms with a bar and canteen-style restaurant next door. The disco may keep you awake on Fridays and Saturdays. Doubles 20–26Ls.

Siguldas Pludmale Peldu iela 2 Ⓣ 2924 4948, Ⓦ www.makars.lv. Large campsite (open May–Sept) in a shady riverside spot northwest and downhill from the town centre; the only drawback is the queues to the bathroom. Arranges canoeing and rafting trips. 4Ls/person, plus 2Ls/tent.

Eating and drinking

Kaķu Māja Pils iela 8. The *Black Cat* café offers large helpings of inexpensive canteen-style food and a tempting range of cakes in the bakery next door. Main and a drink: 3.50Ls.

Zalumnieku Piestātne Kafejnīca Pils iela 9. Another canteen-style place with a roomy, rustic interior serving large portions of Latvian food; pay by weight. Complete meal 3Ls. There's also a separate pizza restaurant; medium pizza 3.70Ls.

Moving on

Train Rīga (up to 9 daily; 1hr 15min).
Bus Rīga (at least hourly; 1hr 15min).

GAUJA NATIONAL PARK

Encompassing a diverse range of flora and fauna, **Gauja National Park** (ⓦwww.gnp.lv) covers over 920 square kilometres of near-pristine forested wilderness, bisected by the 425-kilometre Gauja River. The valley is ideal for exploring by bike, as most of the hiking trails are accessible to cyclists. Numerous "wild" campsites are located along the river's banks, and major campsites in Sigulda, Cēsis and Valmiera, at the north end of the park, arrange overnight canoeing and rafting trips.

VENTSPILS

An attractive seaside city, **VENTSPILS**, 200km northwest of Rīga, is also Latvia's biggest port and strategic naval settlement since the twelfth century until the end of Soviet occupation in 1991. The city's Old Town with its cobbled streets, its beach – the best in Latvia – and handful of museums make Ventspils a great place to while away a couple of days.

What to see and do

One of the city's main draws is the long stretch of clean white-sand **beach** at the town's western end – a worthy recipient of the Blue Flag and popular with sun worshippers, volleyball players and kitesurfers in summer. Still, it's so big that you needn't jostle other beach-goers for elbow space even at the height of peak season. In Jūrmalas parks near the beach, you'll find the popular **Beach Aquapark** and also the **open-air museum**, its ethnographic expositions featuring traditional fishermen's dwellings and equipment.

At the northern end of the beach, a long boardwalk, overlooked by a viewing tower, stretches towards the lighthouse. Here you can spot one of several specimens from Ventspils' bizarre **Cow Parade** – the Sailor Cow. Other cow sculptures are found along the Ostas iela promenade that leads east towards the ferry port; don't miss the **Travelling Cow**, shaped like a giant suitcase. South of the promenade lies the Old Town, with its Art Nouveau buildings and its attractive **main square**, overlooked by the jolly yellow **Nicholas Evangelical Lutheran Church** and featuring a giant quill sculpture due to the town's popularity with international writers. The Old Town's most interesting feature is the thirteenth-century **Castle of the Livonian Order** (Jāņa iela 17; May–Oct 9am–6pm; Nov–April Tues–Sun 10am–5pm; 1Ls), home to an excellent interactive museum featuring the history of the city and port and a disturbing exhibit on the Soviet prison in the barracks.

Arrival and information

Bus station The bus station in the town centre at Kuldīga iela 5.

Ferry terminal Ferries from Travemünde and Lübeck in Germany, Nynashamn in Sweden, St Petersburg in Russia, and Saaremaa in Estonia arrive at the ferry terminal at Dārza iela 6. Check ⓦwww.scandlines.lt and ⓦwww.finnlines.com for updated schedules.

Tourist office At the ferry terminal building at Dārza iela 6 (May–Sept Mon–Fri 8am–7pm, Sat 10am–5pm, Sun 10am–3pm; Oct–April Mon–Fri

CAPE KOLKA – THE END OF THE WORLD

To really get away from it all, take a trip to the village of Kolka at the northernmost tip of **Cape Kolka**, where the Gulf of Rīga meets the Baltic Sea, passing through pine forest and numerous coastal villages along the way. Kolka is part of **Slītere National Park**, former Soviet military base turned protected nature reserve and there are a number of nature trails to be hiked, not to mention the seemingly endless expanse of virtually deserted beach. In 2005, the coast suffered from an enormous storm and the tangle of fallen trees, strewn across the deserted beach, is testimony to that. Even at the height of summer, you'll have the place almost to yourself; you can stay at the friendly **Ūši** guesthouse (Ⓣ2947 5692, Ⓦwww.kolka.info; singles 19Ls, doubles 28Ls, triples 35Ls), or pitch a tent in the meadow next to the guesthouse. Meals are provided on request, or you can track down a local fisherman to buy some excellent smoked fish from. To get here, take a direct bus from Rīga (3 daily; 3hr 45min) or from Velspils (change at Talsi; 3 daily; 1hr 15min–2hr, plus travel time from Ventspils) and disembark at "Kolka", the very last stop, NOT "Ūš". From here, it's a 10-minute walk north (the same way the bus was heading, only further) past the church on your left before you see the guesthouse in the field to your right.

8am–5pm, Sat & Sun 10am–3pm; Ⓣ6362 2263, Ⓦwww.tourism.ventspils.lv). Friendly staff have a plethora of leaflets on Ventspils and western Latvia.

Accommodation

Kupfernams Kārļa iela 5 Ⓣ6362 6999, Ⓔkupfernams@inbox.lv. Delightful, centrally located guesthouse with funky en-suite attic rooms with sloping roofs. Wi-fi and breakfast included and there's a good restaurant downstairs. Singles 26Ls, doubles 37Ls.

Ventspils Piejūras Kempings Vasarnicu iela 56 Ⓣ6362 7925, Ⓦwww.camping.ventspils.lv. To the southwest of the city centre, right next to its white sandy beach, this large popular campsite offers tent spaces and fully-equipped holiday cottages, as well as guest kitchen and sauna. 2Ls/person, plus 3Ls/tent; cottages 22– 52Ls.

Eating and drinking

There are several supermarkets for self-caterers, the largest one being at Leilais prospekts and Ganību iela.

Buginš Lielā iela 1/3. Hearty soups, grilled meats, pastas and more served amide some of the most chaotic decor you're ever likely to see on one place; think taxidermist gone wild in an antique shop. The outdoor terrace makes a good beer garden in summer. Mains 3–7Ls.

Julius Meinl Kārļa iela at Kuldigas iela. You'll smell it before you see it; this tiny bakery's the best place for fresh bread and for the most amazing cinnamon and poppy seed swirls in Latvia.

Kumfernams Kārļa iela 5. Cosy café and restaurant serving tasty local staples such as grilled fish with grated potato pancakes and crêpes with a variety of fillings. Mains 3.50–5Ls.

Moving on

Bus Liepāja (6 daily; 2hr 45min–3hr); Rīga (13–16 daily; 2hr 45min–4hr); Talsi (4–5 daily; 1hr 40min).

Ferry Lübeck, Germany (daily Thurs and Mon; 7–9hr); Nynashamn, Sweden (daily Tues–Thurs and Sat & Sun; 10hr); St Petersburg, Russia (Fri 6am; 14 hr); Saaremaa, Estonia (check schedule with tourist office); Travemünde, Germany (1 daily Tues & Fri; 27hr 30min).

Lithuania

HIGHLIGHTS

PALANGA: Lithuania's premier beach resort; the place to hear live music and party all night

Hill of Crosses: a spiritual monument to Lithuanian identity

CURONIAN SPIT: a wild, beautiful national park on the Baltic coast

GENOCIDE MUSEUM, VILNIUS: a haunting reminder of man's inhumanity

TRAKAI: a fairytale medieval castle sitting on its own little island

ROUGH COSTS

DAILY BUDGET Basic €35 /occasional treat €50

DRINK Utenos beer €1.70

FOOD *Cepelinai* (potato and meat parcels) €3.50

HOSTEL/BUDGET HOTEL €12/€40

TRAVEL Bus: Kaunas–Klaipeda €15; train: Vilnius–Kaunas €5

FACT FILE

POPULATION 3.2 million

AREA 65,200 sq km

LANGUAGE Lithuanian

CURRENCY Litas (Lt)

CAPITAL Vilnius (population: 560,000)

INTERNATIONAL PHONE CODE ⓣ370

Introduction

Lithuania is a vibrant and quirky country, which has undergone rapid modernization since becoming independent from the Soviet Union in 1990. You'll find a lively nightlife, both in Vilnius and on the coast, ample grounds for outdoor pursuits in the as yet unspoiled national parks and a number of good beaches, as well as a stark contrast between city life and rural poverty. Fiercely proud of their country, Lithuanians are more exuberant and welcoming than their Baltic neighbours and you are likely to encounter their hospitality everywhere.

Lithuania's small size makes getting around inexpensive; even in well-trodden destinations the volume of visitors is low, leaving you with the feeling that there's still much to discover here. **Vilnius**, with its Baroque Old Town, is the most architecturally beautiful of the Baltic capitals, and boasts a boisterous nightlife, while the second city, **Kaunas**, also has an attractive centre and a couple of interesting museums, along with some excellent restaurants and bars. The port city of **Klaipėda** is a convenient overnight point en route to the resorts of **Neringa** (the Curonian Spit), a unique sliver of sand dunes and forest that shields Lithuania from the Baltic Sea, or to **Palanga**, Lithuania's party town, where everyone flocks in the summer for a good time.

CHRONOLOGY

2000 BC The ancestors of the Lithuanians settle in the Baltic region.
1009 AD First recorded mention of the name Lithuania in the Quedlinburg Annals.
1236 Grand Duke Mindaugas unites Lithuania to ward off German crusaders.
1253 Mindaugas is crowned King of Lithuania.
1386 After an arranged marriage between the King of Lithuania and the Queen of Poland, Lithuania officially converts to Christianity.
1410 The Polish–Lithuanian alliance defeats the Teutonic Knights, increasing their military influence in the Baltic region.
1547 First Lithuanian book, *The Simple Words of Catechism*, is published.
1795 Russia takes control of Lithuania.
1865 Growth of the Lithuanian liberation movement leads to violent repression by the Russians.
1900 Mass Lithuanian emigration across the world to escape Russian repression.
1920 Lithuania gains independence from Russia after heavy fighting.
1939 Lithuania is invaded by Nazi Germany.
1945 During both German and Soviet occupation, thousands of Lithuanian Jews are killed while thousands of other Lithuanians are deported.
1990 Following the success of the nationalist "Sajudis" movement, Lithuania is the first Soviet Republic to declare its independence from Moscow.
1991 Lithuanian independence is recognized by the USSR before its collapse.
2004 Lithuania joins the EU; thousands emigrate to work in Western Europe.
2009 Dalia Grybauskaite becomes Lithuania's first female president.

ARRIVAL

Most tourists arrive by **air**; Vilnius airport is served by sixteen European airlines, including budget airlines Wizz Air (Ⓦwww.wizzair.com), Norwegian Air Shuttle (Ⓦwww.norwegian.com) and Ryanair (Ⓦwww.ryanair.com); the latter also flies to Kaunas. Lithuania has good **rail** connections to neighbouring countries, with direct trains arriving in Vilnius from Riga, Warsaw and Moscow, among others. Several **bus** companies, including Eurolines (Ⓦwww.eurolines.com), provide regular services to Vilnius's central bus station. There are also frequent **ferries** from Kiel in

Germany, and Karlshamn in Sweden, to Klaipėda on Lithuania's Baltic coast (Ⓦwww.krantas.lt).

GETTING AROUND

Buses are slightly quicker, more frequent and more expensive than trains. It's best to buy long-distance bus tickets in advance, and opt for an express (*ekspresas*), to avoid frequent stops. You can also pay for your ticket on board, although this doesn't guarantee you a seat. There are plenty of buses travelling to Lithuania's Baltic neighbours.

You should also buy long-distance **train** tickets in advance – stations have separate windows for long-distance and suburban (*priemiestinis* or *vietinis*) trains. Long-distance services are divided into "passenger" (*keleivinis traukinys*) and "fast" (*greitas*); the latter usually require a reservation. On timetable boards, look for *isvyksta* (departure) or *atvyksta* (arrival).

In Vilnius and Kaunas public transport is frequent and efficient: buses, trolley-buses and route taxis cover most of the city. Smaller places, such as the Curonian Spit, are best explored by **bicycle**; bike rentals are inexpensive and plentiful.

ACCOMMODATION

A good way to keep accommodation costs down is by staying in **private rooms**, which typically cost 100–120Lt with breakfast. The most reliable agency for these is Litinterp (Ⓦwww.litinterp.com), which has offices and guest-houses in Vilnius, Kaunas and Klaipėda; the latter can book rooms in Palanga and on the Curonian Spit. Spartan double rooms in **budget hotels** can cost as little as 80Lt; smarter mid-range places charge 120–200Lt.

There are an increasing number of **hostels**, especially in Vilnius and Kaunas, usually charging 30–45Lt per night for a dorm bed; it's best to reserve in advance. There are plenty of **campsites** in rural areas; expect to pay 10–20Lt per person, and the same per tent.

FOOD AND DRINK

Lithuanian **cuisine** is based on traditional peasant dishes. Typical starters include marinated mushrooms (*marinuoti grybai*), herring (*silkė*) and smoked sausage (*rukyta desra*) along with cold beetroot soup (*saltibarsčiai*). A popular **national dish** is *cepelinai*, or zeppelins – cylindrical potato parcels stuffed with meat, mushrooms or cheese. Others include potato pancakes (*bulviniai blynai*), and *koldųnai* – boiled or fried dumplings with meat or mushroom filling. Popular **beer snacks** include deep-fried sticks of black bread with garlic (*kepta duona*) and smoked pigs' ears. Pancakes (*blynai*, *blyneliai* or *lietiniai*) come in a plethora of sweet and savoury varieties.

Most cafés and bars serve reasonably priced food. Well-stocked supermarkets, such as Iki and Maxima, are found in the main cities and towns. Many restaurants are open between 11am and midnight daily, with cafés open from 8/9am and bars closing at 2am at the earliest.

Beer (*alus*) is popular, local brands being Švyturus, Utenos and Kalnapilis, and so is **mead** (*midus*), Lithuania's former nobleman's drink. The leading local **firewaters** are Starka, Trejos devynerios and Medžiotojų – invigorating spirits flavoured with herbs. Many lively bars in Vilnius and Kaunas copy American or Irish models, although there are also plenty of folksy Lithuanian places, while cafés (*kavinė*) come in all shapes and sizes. Coffee (*kava*) and tea (*arbata*) are usually served black; ask for milk (*pienas*) and/or sugar (*cukrus*).

CULTURE AND ETIQUETTE

Many city dwellers enjoy a thoroughly modern lifestyle, but there is a stark difference between the towns and the far poorer rural Lithuania, where traditional culture remains firmly in place. If eating with locals, it is rude to refuse second helpings of food; when toasting someone, always look them in the eye. Always give an odd number of flowers when visiting Lithuanians, as even numbers are for the dead. Shaking hands across the threshold is bad luck. Family ties are strong, and extended family gatherings are common. Women tend to fill traditional roles. Only tip in restaurants to reward good service; ten percent is fair.

LITHUANIA ONLINE

Ⓦ**www.lithuaniatourism.co.uk** National tourist board site with useful information.

Ⓦ**www.tourism.vilnius.lt** Vilnius tourist information.

Ⓦ**www.muziejai.lt** Portal for Lithuanian museums.

Ⓦ**www.lietuva.lt** General information about the country.

EMERGENCY NUMBERS

Fire ⓣ01; Police ⓣ02; Ambulance ⓣ03. For general emergencies call ⓣ112.

SPORTS AND ACTIVITIES

Lithuania's top sport is **basketball**, and locals religiously follow the matches on TV. Try to catch a game at Vilnius's Siemens Arena. Lithuania's **national parks**, as well as the Curonian Spit, offer various opportunities for **outdoor activities** such as hiking, biking and canoeing.

COMMUNICATIONS

In major towns, **post offices** (*pastas*) are open Mon–Fri 8am–6pm and Sat 8am–3pm; in smaller places hours are more restricted. **Stamps** are also available at some kiosks and tourist offices. **Public phones** operate with cards (*telefono kortelė*), which you can purchase at post offices and kiosks. Getting a prepaid SIM card for your mobile with either Bitė, Omnitel or Tele 2 (10Lt) is a good way of avoiding roaming charges, though using another European mobile in Lithuania is relatively inexpensive. There are a few **internet cafés** in Vilnius and Kaunas; many cafés and restaurants also have free **wi-fi**.

EMERGENCIES

You're unlikely to meet trouble in Lithuania; pickpocketing, car theft and late-night mugging are the most common crimes. You should be aware that a scam operates in Vilnius, whereby drunk foreign men are sought out by beautiful women who lure them into bars run by unsavoury characters, who then charge the men extortionate amounts for drinks and beat them up if they refuse to pay. The **police** expect to be taken seriously, so be polite if you have dealings with them. **Emergency health care** is free but if you get seriously ill, head home.

INFORMATION

Most major towns have **tourist offices**, often offering accommodation listings and event calendars in English. The **In Your Pocket** guides to Vilnius, Kaunas and Klaipėda (available from bookshops, newsstands, tourist offices and some hotels; ⓦwww.inyourpocket.com; 6Lt)

LITHUANIAN

	Lithuanian	Pronunciation
Yes	*Taip*	Tape
No	*Ne*	Ne
Please	*Prašau*	Prashau
Thank you	*Ačiu*	Achoo
Hello/Good day	*Labas*	Labass
Goodbye	*Viso gero*	Viso gero
Excuse me	*Atsiprašau*	Atsiprashau
Sorry	*Atleiskite*	Ahtlayskita
Where?	*Kur?*	Kur?
Can you show me?	*Galėtumėt man parodyti?*	Gahlehtumet mahn pahrawdeeteh?
Student ticket	*Studento billetas*	Studantoh bileahtahs
Toilet	*Tualeto*	Tuahlataw
I'd like to try...	*Aš norėčiai išbandyti*	Ahsh nawrehchow ishbahndeeteh
I don't eat meat	*Aš nevalgau mėsos*	Ahsh navahlgow mehrsaus
Bill	*saskaita*	sahskaitah
Good/Bad	*Geras/Blogas*	Gerass/Blogass
Near/Far	*Artimas/Tolimas*	Artimass/Tolimass
Cheap/Expensive	*Pigus/Brangus*	Piguss/Branguss
Open/Closed	*Atidarytas/Uždarytas*	Atidaritass/Uzhdaritass
Today	*Siandien*	Shyandyen
Yesterday	*Vakar*	Vakar
Tomorrow	*Rytdiena*	Ritdyena
How much is...?	*Kiek kainuoja...?*	Kyek kainwoya...?
What time is it?	*Kiek valandų?*	Kyek valandoo?
I don't understand	*Nesuprantu*	Nessuprantoh
Do you speak English?	*Ar jųs kalbate angliškai?*	Ar yoos kalbate anglishkay?
One	*Vienas*	Vyenass
Two	*Du/dvi*	Doh/Dvee
Three	*Trys*	Triss
Four	*Keturi*	Keturee
Five	*Penki*	Penkee
Six	*Šeši*	Sheshee
Seven	*Septyni*	Septinee
Eight	*Aštuoni*	Ashtuonee
Nine	*Devyni*	Devinee
Ten	*Dešimt*	Deshimt

STUDENT AND YOUTH DISCOUNTS

An ISIC or an IYTC card will usually get you fifty percent discount on museums and sights, as well as on public transport and some long-distance trains during term time. A YHA card gets discounts at HI-affiliated youth hostels, while ISIC/IYTC cards are accepted at any hostel.

are indispensable sources of practical information. Regional **maps** and detailed street plans of Vilnius are available in bookshops and kiosks.

MONEY AND BANKS

Lithuania's currency is the **Litas** (usually abbreviated to Lt), which is divided into 100 centai. Coins come as 1, 2, 5, 10, 20 and 50c, and 1, 2 and 5Lt, with notes of 10, 20, 50, 100, 200 and 500Lt. The litas is pegged to the euro (€1= 3.45Lt). **Bank** (*bankas*) opening hours vary, though branches of Vilniaus Bank are usually open Mon–Fri 8am–3/4pm. If you're looking to exchange money or get a cash advance outside banking hours, find an **exchange office** (*valiutos keitykla*). There are plentiful **ATMs** in all major towns as well as the Curonian Spit; **credit cards** are widely accepted.

OPENING HOURS AND PUBLIC HOLIDAYS

Opening hours for **shops** are 9/10am to 6/7pm. Outside Vilnius, some places take an hour off for lunch; most usually close on Sunday (though some food shops stay open). Most shops and all banks are closed on the following **public holidays**: January 1, February 16, March 11, Easter Sunday, Easter Monday, May 1, July 6, August 15, November 1, December 25 and 26.

Vilnius

VILNIUS is a cosmopolitan and thoroughly modern city that is relatively compact and easy to get to know, with a variety of inexpensive attractions and a lively nightlife. Its numerous Baroque churches jostle for space amid glitzy restaurants and dilapidated old buildings that line its cobbled streets, while the student population lends the place a tangible air of energy and optimism. Beguiling, and sometimes downright odd, Vilnius has an addictive quality.

What to see and do

At the centre of Vilnius, poised between the medieval and nineteenth-century parts of the city, is **Cathedral Square** (Katedros aikštė). To the south of here along Pilies gatvė and Didžioji gatvė is the **Old Town**, containing perhaps the most impressive concentration of Baroque architecture in northern Europe. West of the square in the **New Town** is Gedimino prospektas, a nineteenth-century boulevard and the focus of the city's commercial and administrative life. The traditionally **Jewish areas** of Vilnius between the Old Town and Gedimino prospektas still retain some sights, such as the synagogue.

Cathedral Square

Cathedral Square is dominated by the Neoclassical **cathedral** (daily 7.30am–7.30pm), dating from the thirteenth century when a wooden church was built here on the site of a temple dedicated to Perkųnas, the god of thunder. The highlight of the airy, vaulted interior is the opulent **Chapel of St Casimir**, the patron saint of Lithuania. Next to the cathedral on the square is the white belfry, once part of the fortifications of the vanished Lower Castle. Between the cathedral and the belfry lies a small coloured tile with *stebuklas* (miracle) written on it, marking the spot from where, in 1989, two million people formed a human chain that stretched all the way to Tallinn, Estonia, to protest against Soviet occupation.

Gediminas Castle and Museum

Rising behind the cathedral is the tree-clad Castle Hill, its summit crowned by the red-brick **Gediminas Castle** – one of the city's best-known landmarks – founded by Grand Duke Gediminas, the Lithuanian ruler who consolidated the country's independence. The tower houses a little **museum** (May–Sept daily 10am–7pm; Oct–April Tues–Sun 11am–5pm; 5Lt), with displays of armour and models showing the former extent of Vilnius's medieval fortifications. The view of Old Town from the top is unparalleled. Take the funicular (Tues–Sun 10am–5pm; 3Lt return) from the courtyard of the Applied Art Museum.

The Lithuanian National Museum

About 100m north of the cathedral is the **Lithuanian National Museum**, at Arsenalo 1 (Lietuvos Nacionalinis Muziejus; Tues–Sat 10am–5pm, Sun 10am–3pm; 5Lt; Ⓦwww.lnm.lt), which traces the history of Lithuania from prehistoric times to 1940 through an interesting collection of artefacts, paintings and photographs, including a display of wooden crucifixes and ethnographic reconstructions of peasant life. A little further north on Arsenalo, a separate department houses the much snazzier **Prehistoric Lithuania Exhibition** (same hours; 5Lt), displaying flint, iron, bronze and silver objects and covering the history of Lithuanians up to the Middle Ages.

The National Art Gallery

On the north side of the River Neris, on Konstitucijos 22, the **National Art Gallery** (Nacionalinė Dailės Galerija;

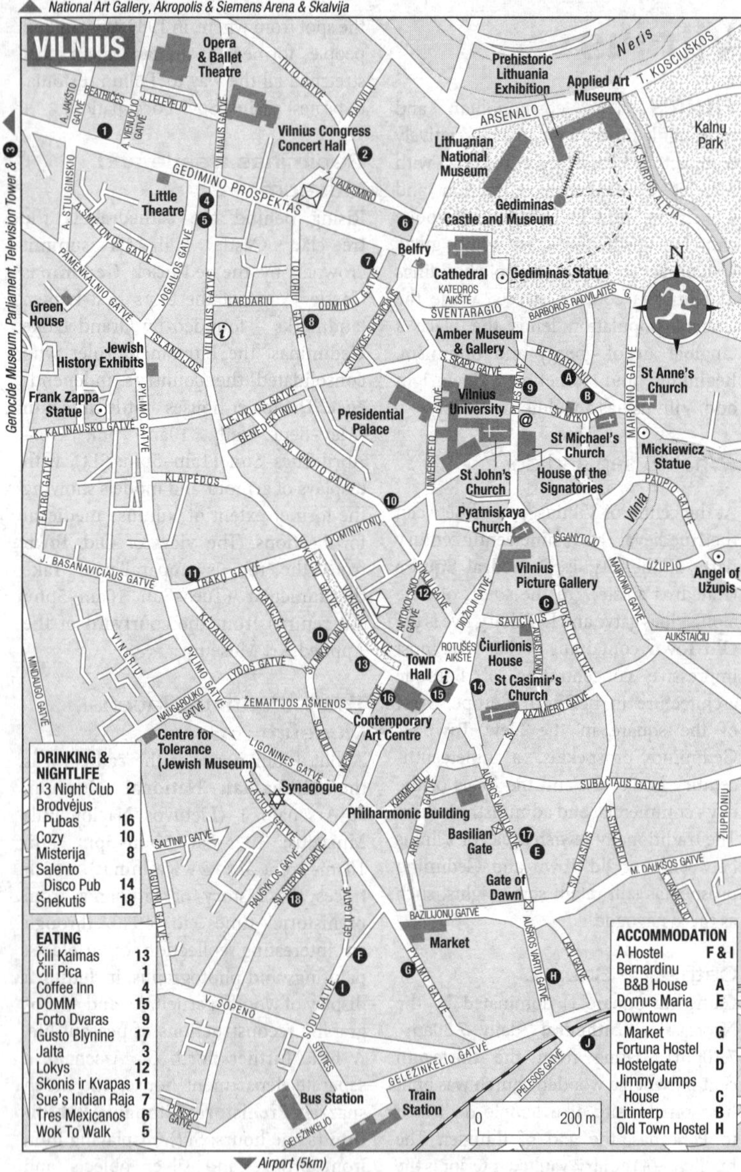

Tues, Wed, Fri & Sat noon–7pm, Thurs 1–8pm, Sun noon–5pm; 6Lt) houses a permanent display of eleven galleries of Lithuanian art since 1900, as well as temporary exhibitions. The works are organized to indicate how art changed in response to political circumstances such as World War II and Soviet repression; check out the photo documentaries of Antanas Sutkus in particular.

The Old Town

The **Old Town**, just south of Cathedral Square, is a network of narrow, often cobbled streets that forms the Baroque heart of Vilnius, with the pedestrianized Pilies gatvė cutting into it from the southeastern corner of the square. To the west of this street is **Vilnius University**, constructed between the sixteenth and eighteenth centuries around nine linked courtyards that extend west to Universiteto gatvė. Within its precincts is the beautiful Baroque **St John's Church** (Šv Jono baznyčia), founded during the fourteenth century, taken over by the Jesuits in 1561 and given to the university in 1737.

St Anne's Church and Užupis

Napoleon Bonaparte, who stayed in Vilnius briefly during his ill-fated campaign against Russia in 1812, is said to have been so impressed by **St Anne's Church** (Šv. Onos Bažnyčia; May–Sept Tues–Sun 10am–6pm), on Maironio gatvė, that he wanted to take it back to Paris on the palm of his hand. Studded with skeletal, finger-like towers, its facade overlaid with intricate brick traceries and fluting, this late sixteenth-century structure is the finest Gothic building in the capital. Just south of St Anne's a bridge over the River Vilnia forms the border of the self-declared independent republic of **Užupis**, home to a flourishing population of artists, bohemians and yuppies (note the locks on the bridge: lovers fasten them here and then throw the key in the river to symbolize their union). Stroll up from *Užupio Café* across the bridge to see the psychedelic art gallery with weird and wonderful creations suspended above the river. Some of the buildings here are in dire need of repair, but there is a trendy feel to the area.

Town Hall Square and around

West of Užupis, Pilies gatvė becomes Didžioji gatvė as it heads south, with the restored Baroque palace at no. 4 housing the **Vilnius Picture Gallery** (Vilniaus Paveikslų Galerija; Wed–Sat 11am–6pm, Sun noon–5pm; 6Lt), with a marvellous collection of sixteenth- to nineteenth-century paintings and sculptures from around the country. The colonnaded Neoclassical building at the end of **Town Hall Square** (Rotušės aikštė) is the **Town Hall** itself. The **Contemporary Art Centre** (Suolaikinio meno centras or SMC; Tues–Sun noon–8pm; 8Lt) lies behind it, hosting modern art exhibitions with interactive elements and a good café. East of the square is the striking **St Casimir's Church** (Šv. Kazimiero Bažnyčia; Mon–Fri 4.30–6.30pm, Sun 8am–1.30pm), the oldest Baroque church in the city, dating from 1604, and possessing a beautiful interior including a marble altarpiece. South of here, Didžioji becomes Aušros Vartų gatvė, leading to the **Gate of Dawn** (Aušros Vartų), the sole survivor of the nine city gates. A chapel above the gate houses the image of the Madonna of the Gates of Dawn, said to have miraculous powers and revered by Polish Catholics; open-air Mass is held on Sundays.

The synagogue

Today the Jewish population of Vilnius numbers only five thousand and, out of over 100 that once existed, the city has just one surviving **synagogue**, built in 1903, at Pylimo 39 (open for services Mon–Fri 8–9.30am & 7.30–8.20pm; Sat 10am–2pm; Sun 8.45–9.45am & 7.30–8pm).

Jewish Museum

The **Vilna Gaon Jewish State Museum** (Valstybinis Vilniaus Gaono Žydų Muziejus; 5Lt; Ⓦwww.jmuseum.lt) is housed in three separate branches. The

Jewish History Exhibits at Pylimo 4 (Mon–Thurs & Sun 10am–2pm; free) has displays upstairs on Jewish partisan resistance, life in the Vilnius ghetto, and an exhibit on Lithuanians who risked their lives to save Jews during the Nazi occupation. The **Green House**, slightly uphill at Pamėnkalnio 12 (Mon–Thurs 9am–5pm, Fri 9am–4pm, Sun 10am–4pm; 5Lt), contains a harrowing display on the fate of Vilnius and Kaunas Jews during World War II, including eyewitness accounts, and many extremely disturbing photographs with some captions in English. Guided museum tours in English can be arranged (30Lt), as well as "history of Jewish Vilnius" tours (Ⓣ5/262-0730). The Centre for **Tolerance**, at Naugarduko 10/2 (Mon–Thurs 10am–6pm, Fri & Sun 10am–4pm; 5Lt), inside a restored former Jewish theatre, houses some excellent twentieth-century Jewish artwork, as well as fine religious items and an excellent display in English on the second floor charting the history of Jews in Lithuania from the fourteenth century until the present day.

Frank Zappa statue

On Kalinausko Street, the bronze head of rocker **Frank Zappa** is perched on a column against a backdrop of street art. Civil servant Saulis Paukstys founded the local Zappa fan club and, in 1992, commissioned the socialist-realist sculptor Konstantinas Bogdanas to create this unique sculpture.

Gedimino prospektas and the Genocide Museum

Gedimino prospektas, running west from Cathedral Square, is the most important commercial street. On the southern side of **Lukiskių aikštė**, a square around 900m west of Cathedral Square, is Gedimino 40, Lithuania's former KGB headquarters. The building also served as Gestapo headquarters during the German occupation and, more recently, the Soviets incarcerated political prisoners in the basement. It's now the **Genocide Museum** (Genocido aukų muziejus; entrance at Aukų 2a; Wed–Sat 10am–6pm, Sun 10am–5pm; 6Lt; Ⓦwww.genocid.lt/muziejus), its torture cells and execution chamber making a grim impression. Well-labelled, detailed exhibits on Soviet occupation, deportation and Lithuanian partisan resistance are upstairs; the optional English-language audiotape commentary (8Lt) is worthwhile if you want a detailed prison tour.

Arrival and information

Air The airport is 5km south of the centre; trains to the central station run every 30min 6.30am–7.30pm (7min; 2.50Lt) or buses #1 and #2 depart every 30min to the centre (20min; 2.50Lt). A taxi costs around 50Lt.

JEWISH VILNIUS

Before World War II, Vilnius was one of the most important centres of Jewish life in eastern Europe. The Jews – first invited to settle in 1410 by Grand Duke Vytautas – made up around a third of the city's population, mainly concentrated in the eastern fringes of the Old Town around present-day Vokiečių gatvė, Zydų gatvė and Antokolskio gatvė. Massacres of the Jewish population began soon after the Germans occupied Vilnius on June 24, 1941, and those who survived the initial killings found themselves herded into two **ghettos**. The smaller of these ghettos centred on the streets of Zydų, Antokolskio, Stiklių and Gaono, and was liquidated in October 1941, while the larger occupied an area between Pylimo, Vokiečių, Lydos, Mikalojaus, Karmelitų and Arklių streets, and was liquidated in September 1943. Most of Vilnius's 80,000 Jewish residents perished in Paneriai forest, 10km southwest of the city.

Bus and train The main train station is at Geležinkelio 16, with 24hr luggage storage in the basement, a 24hr currency exchange, ATMs, detailed timetables, information office and a Maxima supermarket. The bus terminal, just across the road, has luggage storage and an ATM.
Tourist information The multilingual staff at the two main branches at Vilniaus 22 (Mon–Fri 9am–6pm, Sat & Sun 10am–4pm; ⓣ5/262-9660, ⓦwww .vilnius-tourism.lt) and Didžioji 31, in the town hall (ⓣ5/262-6470; same hours), offer advice on accommodation, attractions and festivals (ⓦwww .vilniusfestivals.lt). The best source of listings is the *Vilnius in Your Pocket* city guide (6Lt).

City transport

Bus Tickets cost 2Lt from newspaper kiosks or 2.50Lt from the driver. You can buy a one-/three-/ten-day ticket from the kiosk just to the left of the train station near the trolleybus stop for 13/23/46Lt. Validate your ticket by punching it in the machine on board. Alternatively, hail a minibus (normally yellow) at any bus stop in the direction you're going, pay the driver 3–4Lt and you'll be dropped off at the stop you require.
Taxi Prices are usually reasonable and fares should cost no more than 2Lt/km. Phoning ahead guarantees you a better rate; try Ekipažas (ⓣ5/239-5539).

Accommodation

Hostels

A Hostel Sodų 17 ⓣ5/213-9994, ⓦwww.ahostel .lt. Clean, bright Japanese-style sleeping cubicles, dorms and private rooms, with kitchen and wi-fi. Dorms can be noisy. Five minutes' walk from the train and bus stations and the Old Town, with a sister hostel at Sodų 8. Dorms 28Lt, rooms 80Lt.
Hostelgate Šv. Mikalojaus 3 ⓣ6/383-2818, ⓦwww.hostelgate.lt. This bustling central hostel run by outgoing, helpful staff, offers clean dorms, kitchen, table football and wi-fi. Organized excursions include sauna tours and trips to fire weaponry in the countryside. Dorms 39Lt, rooms 120Lt.
Jimmy Jumps House Savičiaus 12 ⓣ6/078-8435, ⓦwww.jimmyjumpshouse .com. Difficult to find but worth it, this backpackers has a great party feel and offers free walking tours of Vilnius as well as machine-gun tours in the same vein as Hostelgate's, in case you need to let off steam. Kitchen, wi-fi and great waffle breakfast included. Dorms 40Lt, rooms 120Lt.
Old Town Hostel Aušros Vartų 20–10 ⓣ5/262-5357, ⓦwww.oldtownhostel.lt. Cramped, rowdy, but comfortable HI-affiliated hostel near the train and bus stations. Free internet; and wi-fi; breakfast 5Lt extra. A sister hostel, *Fortuna Hostel* (ⓦwww.fortunahostel.lt), is 50m south at Liepkaino 2. Dorms 35Lt, rooms 110Lt.

TREAT YOURSELF

Domus Maria Aušros Vartų 12 ⓣ5/264-4880, ⓦwww .domusmaria.lt. An oasis of calm in the heart of the city, this hotel has been converted from a seventeenth-century monastery and has a large courtyard to relax in. Some of the bright en-suite rooms look out onto the Gate of Dawn. 221Lt.

Hotels and guesthouses

Bernardinu B&B House Bernardinų 5 ⓣ5/261-5134, ⓦwww.bernardinuhouse .com. Great-value B&B with spacious, tastefully decorated rooms, all with cable TV and some en suite. Offers excursions throughout Lithuania. Breakfast 10Lt extra. 170Lt.
Downtown Market Pylimo 57 ⓣ6/798-5476, ⓦwww.downtownmarket.lt. A quirky, friendly boutique hotel close to the Gate of Dawn. The six en-suite rooms are each decorated in market themes (flower market, flea market etc). Organic breakfast included. 170Lt.
Litinterp Bernardinų 7 ⓣ5/212-3850, ⓦwww .litinterp.lt. Stay in the central guesthouse with airy, comfortable rooms and shared bathrooms and kitchenettes, or ask the helpful multilingual staff to book you a private room in the Old Town with a host family (around 180Lt). Book in advance in summer. Breakfast included. 140Lt.

Eating

There's a fast-growing range of eating options in Vilnius and a variety of cuisines to match. Bars and cafés serve both snacks and meals, and often represent better value for money than restaurants.

Cafés and snack bars

Coffee Inn Vilniaus 17. Café chain that's popular with a young crowd, serving excellent coffee and smoothies plus muffins, sandwiches and wraps (including some veggie options). Also at Pilies 3, Gedemino 9 and Trakų 7. Mon–Wed 7am–10pm, Thurs 7am–11pm, Fri 7am–midnight, Sat 9am–midnight, Sun 9am–10pm.

TREAT YOURSELF

DOMM R Didžioji 31 (Town Hall) ⓣ6/867-7707. This is a meal you will remember for the rest of your life. Not only is it the ultimate in modern luxurious dining, the presentation and creativity goes above and beyond anything else Vilnius has to offer. Tuck into dishes that come with their own MP3 soundtrack or emerge from a cloud of smoke, as if in a magician's act. Mains (eg lamb cooked for 24hr with chickpeas, lavender and orchids) around 90Lt; tasting menus from 100Lt. Mon–Sat 6pm–midnight.

Gusto Blynine Aušros Vartų 6. Substantial, tasty-crêpes with every imaginable sweet or savoury filling (6Lt). Daily 9am–10pm.

Skonis ir Kvapas Trakų 8. The most beautiful vaulted interior in town. Big pots of tea, Arabian rugs and an affordable range of cakes and hot meals. Drinks 7Lt; mains 8–15Lt. Daily 10am–10pm.

Restaurants

Čili Kaimas Vokiečių 8. Faux-traditional restaurant whose pub-like interior is decorated with agricultural tools, antlers and even a whole tree. The vast menu of Lithuanian dishes includes *cepelinai* (13Lt) and salads (10Lt). Sun–Thurs 11am–midnight, Fri & Sat 11am–4am.

Čili Pica Gedimino 23. Popular place for inexpensive thin-crust and deep-pan pizzas. Twelve more branches, including one at the Europa shopping mall. Medium pizza 15–18Lt. Thurs–Sat 7.30am–6am, Sun–Wed 7.30am–3am.

Forto Dvaras Pilies 16 ⓦwww.fortodvaras.lt. An excellent place to try fairly authentic *cepelinai* (12Lt) or stuffed potato pancakes (10Lt). Cheap, tasty and filling. Daily 11am–10pm.

Lokys Stiklių 8/10 ⓣ5/262-9046, ⓦwww.lokys.lt. Cosy Lithuanian cellar restaurant specializing in well-cooked game dishes that are worth the splurge. Beaver stew 30Lt; quail with blackberry sauce 40Lt. Daily noon–midnight.

Sue's Indian Raja Odminių 3 ⓣ5/266-1888, ⓦwww.sues-lt.com. One of the best restaurants in town, this place is popular with expats and locals alike. Gorge yourself on excellent curry (around 30Lt), though be warned that the dishes are authentically spicy. Tues–Sat 11am–11pm, Mon & Sun 11am–10pm.

Tres Mexicanos Tilto 2 ⓣ6/741-8600, ⓦwww.tresmexicanos.lt. Run by Mexicans and it shows: try the chocolate chicken (22Lt) or fajitas (24Lt), and wash it down with the house margarita (12Lt). Daily 11am–midnight.

Wok To Walk Vilniaus 19. A great little spot where you choose from an array of noodles, rice, vegetables and sauce and it's all wok-fried in front of you. Quick and tasty. Mains 12Lt. Mon–Thurs 11am–10pm, Fri 11am–3am, Sat noon–midnight, Sun noon–8pm.

Drinking and nightlife

Vilnius has a growing club scene well worth trying, though you may have just as good a time (and cheaper too) in some of the bars mentioned below.

Bars

Brodvėjus Pubas Mėsinių 4. Popular drinking/dancing venue with live bands (Thurs–Sun) and DJs, and a full menu of snacks and hot meals including lunch specials. Beer 8Lt. Daily 8pm–2am or later. Entry 10Lt upwards on music nights.

Cozy Dominikonų 10. Chilled-out cellar bar with a choice of three rooms, DJ appearances, extensive drinks menu (beers 8Lt) and a bargain two-course business lunch (16Lt). Mon–Thurs 9am–2am, Fri 9am–4am, Sat 10–4am, Sun 10–2am.

Misterija Totorių 18 ⓦwww.misterija.lt. Lively pub with themed parties, board games and a weekly quiz. A great place to make new friends. Beers 6Lt, cocktails from 10Lt. Mon–Thurs 11am–4am, Fri 11am–6am, Sat 6pm–6am, Sun 6pm–4am.

Šnekutis Šv. Stepono 8. An excellent place to sample microbrews and ales from all over Lithuania (5Lt) plus traditional dishes (around 12Lt). The rustic decor and tasty beer snacks are a nice touch. Mon–Sat 11am–11pm.

Clubs

13 Night Club Tilto 13 ⓦ13nightclub.lt. Cellar club with a relaxed, studenty atmosphere and a relaxed entrance policy. Has regular themed nights. Thurs–Sat 10pm–6am. Entry 20Lt.

Salento Disco Pub Didžioji 28. Various themed nights (most involving foam), cheesy pop tunes, large TV screens and a young and up-for-it crowd. Daily 9pm–6am. Entry 20Lt.

Entertainment

Cinemas

Forum Cinemas Akropolis Ozo 25, ⓦwww.forumcinemas.lt. Modern, multi-screen cinema in

Vilnius's largest shopping mall, showing the latest blockbusters in original language, with subtitles. 14–20Lt.
Skalvija Goštauto 2/15 ⓣ5/261-0505, ⓦwww.skalvija.lt. Foreign films are shown in this central venue by the river. 6–12Lt.

Live music

Opera & Ballet Theatre Vienuolio 1 ⓣ5/262-0727, ⓦwww.opera.lt. Stunning building featuring well-attended performances by local opera and ballet companies.
Siemens Arena Ozo 14 ⓣ5/247-7576, ⓦwww.siemens-arena.com. Top venue for sports and concerts featuring international stars.
Vilnius Congress Concert Hall Vilniaus 6/14 ⓣ5/261-8828, ⓦwww.lvso.lt. Chamber music, orchestra performances and ballet.

Shopping

Akropolis Ozo 25. Huge shopping complex around 3km north of town with a variety of clothing and jewellery shops, plus an indoor ice rink and the Vichy Aqua Park with water slides (65Lt).
Amber Aušros Vartų 9. An extensive array of amber jewellery and handicrafts.
Senamiesčio Krautuvė Literatų 5. Fresh Lithuanian fare including pickles, sausages and cakes, all laid out in baskets for you to sample.

Directory

Banks and exchange ATMs are plentiful. Parex, outside the station at Geležinkelio 6 (24hr), changes money at decent rates.
Embassies and consulates Australia, Vilniaus 23 ⓣ5/212-3369; Canada, Jogailos 4 ⓣ5/249-0950; Ireland, Gedimino 1 ⓣ5/262-9460; UK, Antakalnio 2 ⓣ5/246-2900; US, Akmenų 6 ⓣ5/266-5500.
Hospital Vilnius University Emergency Hospital, Šiltnamių 29 ⓣ5/216-9212.
Internet Collegium, at Pilies 22 (Mon–Fri 10am–6pm; 8Lt/hr).
Left luggage Train station: 24hr luggage storage in the basement. Bus station: baggage room open 5.30am–9.45pm.
Pharmacy Eurovaistinė, Ukmergės 282 (Maxima), 24hr; Gedimino Vaistinė, Gedimino 27, Mon–Fri 7.30am–8pm, Sat & Sun 10am–5pm.
Police Jogailos 3 ⓣ5/261-6208.
Post office Gedimino prospektas 7 (Mon–Fri 7am–7pm, Sat 9am–4pm).

Moving on

Train Kaunas (every 30min; 1hr 15min–1hr 45min); Klaipėda (6 daily; 5hr); Moscow (2–3 daily; 16hr); Paneriai (every 30min; 10min); St Petersburg (1–2 daily; 14hr); Warsaw (1 daily; 9hr).
Bus Kaunas (every 20–30min; 1hr 30min–2hr); Klaipėda (hourly; 4hr); Nida (via Klaipėda; 1 daily at 7am; 5hr 50min); Palanga (8 daily, 5hr); Rīga (9–13 daily; 5hr–5hr 30min); Tallinn (1 daily at 9pm; 11hr 40min); Trakai (every 30min; 30min); Warsaw (4 weekly; 9hr).

TRAKAI

Around 30km west of Vilnius lies the little town of **TRAKAI**, a mix of concrete Soviet-style buildings merging with the wooden cottages of the Karaite community. The former capital of the Grand Duchy of Lithuania, Trakai was founded during the fourteenth century and, standing on a peninsula jutting out between two lakes, it's the site of two impressive medieval castles and makes for a worthwhile day-trip from the capital.

What to see and do

Once you arrive, follow Vytauto gatvė and turn right down Kęstučio gatvė to reach the remains of the **Peninsula Castle**, now partially restored after having been destroyed by the Russians in 1655. Skirting the ruins along the lakeside path, you will see the spectacular **Island Castle** (Salos pilis), one of Lithuania's most famous monuments, accessible by two wooden drawbridges and preceded by souvenir and rowing-boat rental (15Lt) stalls. You can also rent yachts here (80Lt for 40min cruise with skipper). Built around 1400 AD by Grand Duke Vytautas, under whom Lithuania reached the pinnacle of its power during the fifteenth century, the castle fell into ruin from the seventeenth century until a 1960s restoration returned it to its former glory (May–Sept 10am–7pm; Oct–April 10am–6pm;

14Lt, students 6Lt, permission to take photos 4Lt). The history museum inside displays artefacts discovered while excavating the site.

Trakai is home to three hundred Karaim, Lithuania's smallest ethnic minority – a Judaic sect of Turkish origin whose ancestors were brought here from the Crimea by Grand Duke Vytautas to serve as bodyguards. You can learn more about their cultural contribution to Trakai at the **Karaite Ethnographic Exhibition** (22 Karaimų gatvė; Wed–Sun 10am–6pm; 4Lt). You can sample *kibinai* (5–7Lt), the Karaite culinary speciality – a mincemeat pasty – served up at **cafés** such as *Senoji Kibininė*, at Karaimų 65, and *Kybynlar*, at Karaimų 29; wash it down with *gira*, a semi-alcoholic drink made from fermented bread. To **get to Trakai**, take a bus from Vilnius's main bus station (at least one hourly; 6Lt; last bus from Trakai at 8.45pm) or a train (hourly; 6.20Lt).

The rest of Lithuania

Lithuania is predominantly rural – a gently undulating, densely forested landscape scattered with lakes, and fields dotted with ambling storks in the summer. The major city of **Kaunas**, west of the capital, rivals Vilnius in terms of its historical importance. Further west, the main highlights of the coast are the **Curonian Spit**, whose dramatic dunescapes can be reached by ferry and bus from **Klaipėda**, and **Palanga**, which fills up in summer with thousands of people looking for fun.

KAUNAS

KAUNAS, 98km west of Vilnius and easily reached by bus or rail, is Lithuania's second city, seen by many Lithuanians as the true heart of their country; it served as provisional **capital** during the interwar period of 1920–1939. It is undergoing rapid modernization, with the mirror-like exteriors of new buildings reflecting parts of the medieval city wall. While much of Kaunas is a busy urban sprawl, visitors will invariably be drawn to the old heart of the city where the main attractions lie.

What to see and do

The most picturesque part of Kaunas is the **Old Town** (Senamiestis), centred on **Town Hall Square** (Rotušės aikštė), on a spur of land between the Neris and Nemunas rivers. The square is lined with fifteenth- and sixteenth-century merchants' houses in pastel stucco shades, but the overpowering feature is the magnificent Town Hall itself, its tiered Baroque facade rising to a graceful 53m tower.

The cathedral and castle

Occupying the northeastern shoulder of the square, the red-brick tower of Kaunas's austere **cathedral** stands at the western end of Vilniaus gatvė. Dating back to the reign of Vytautas the Great, the cathedral was much added to in subsequent centuries. After the plain exterior, the lavish gilt-and-marble interior comes as a surprise; the large, statue-adorned Baroque high altar (1775) steals the limelight. Predating the cathedral by several centuries is **Kaunas Castle**, whose scant remains survive just northwest of the square. Little more than a restored tower and a couple of sections of wall are left, with temporary art exhibitions inside (6Lt), but in its day the fortification was a major obstacle to the Teutonic Knights.

The New Town

The main thoroughfare of Kaunas's New Town is **Laisvės alėja** (Freedom Avenue), a broad, pedestrianized shopping street

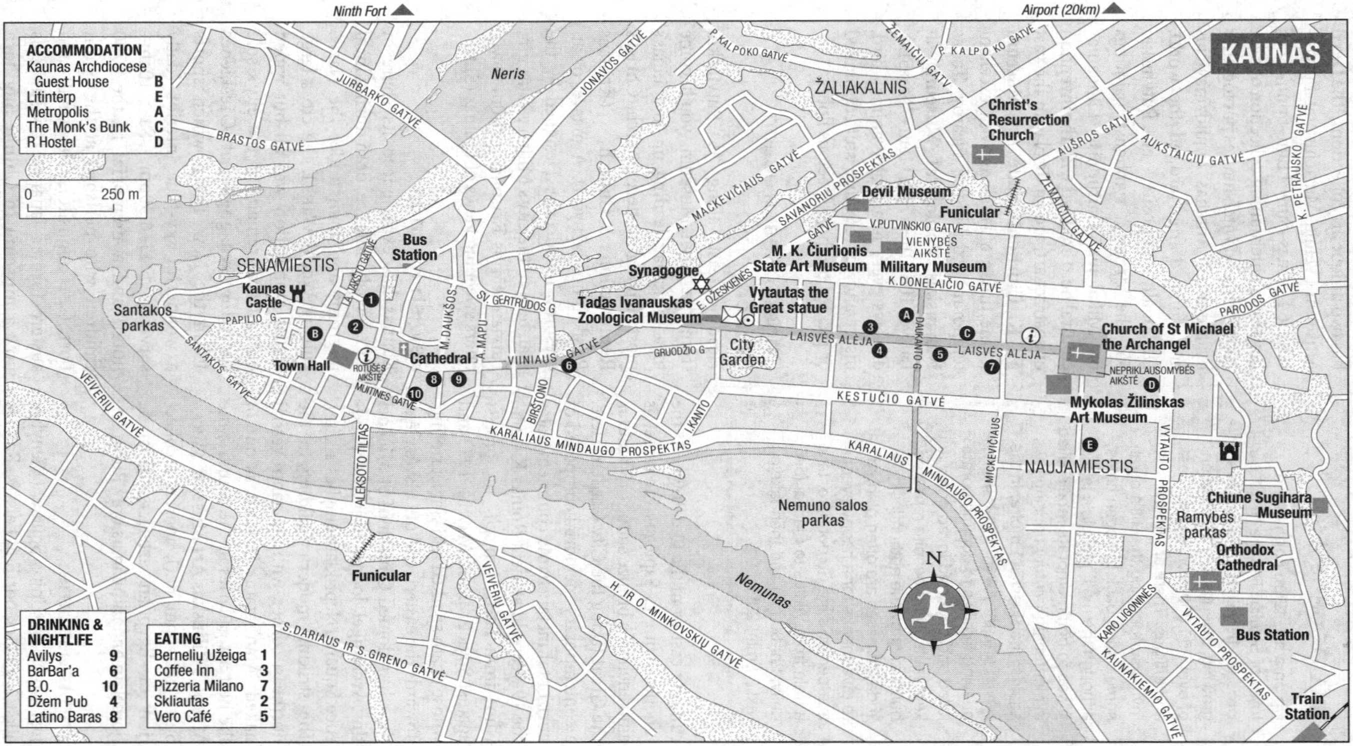

KAUNAS

ACCOMMODATION

Kaunas Archdiocese Guest House	B
Litinterp	E
Metropolis	A
The Monk's Bunk	C
R Hostel	D

EATING

Bernelių Užeiga	1
Coffee Inn	3
Pizzeria Milano	7
Skliautas	2
Vero Café	5

DRINKING & NIGHTLIFE

Avilys	9
BarBar'a	6
B.O.	10
Džem Pub	4
Latino Baras	8

0 250 m

Ninth Fort
Airport (20km)
Neris
Nemunas
Jurbarko Gatvė
Brastos Gatvė
Jonavos Gatvė
P. Kalpoko Gatvė
Žemaičių Gatv
P. Kalpo ko Gatvė
Žaliakalnis
Christ's Resurrection Church
Aušros Gatvė
Aukštaičių Gatvė
K. Petrausko Gatvė
A. Mackevičiaus Gatvė
Savanorių Prospektas
Devil Museum
Funicular
Žemaičių Gatvė
V.Putvinskio Gatvė
Vienybės Aikštė
M. K. Čiurlionis State Art Museum
Military Museum
Gatvė
Synagogue
K. Donelaičio Gatvė
Parodos Gatvė
Senamiestis
Bus Station
Kaunas Castle
La. Jakšto Gatvė
Santakos parkas
Papilio G.
Sv. Gertrūdos G
M. Daukšos
A. Mapu
Tadas Ivanauskas Zoological Museum
E. Ožeškienės
Vytautas the Great statue
Laisvės Alėja
Daukanto G
Church of St Michael the Archangel
Nepriklausomybės Aikštė
Town Hall
Rotušės Aikštė
Cathedral
Vilniaus Gatvė
Gruodžio G
City Garden
Muitinės Gatvė
Santakos Gatvė
Veiverių Gatvė
Birštono
I. Kanto
Kęstučio Gatvė
Mykolas Žilinskas Art Museum
Karaliaus Mindaugo Prospektas
Aleksoto Tiltas
Mickevičiaus
Naujamiestis
Vytauto Prospektas
Nemuno salos parkas
Chiune Sugihara Museum
Ramybės parkas
Orthodox Cathedral
Funicular
Veiverių Gatvė
H. ir O. Minkovskių Gatvė
N
S. Dariaus ir S. Girėno Gatvė
Karo Ligoninės
Kaunakiemio Gatvė
Vytauto Prospektas
Bus Station
Train Station

HILL OF CROSSES

Up on a hill, 12km north of the town of Šiauliai, lies the **Hill of Crosses** (Kryžių Kalnas), an ever-growing, awe-inspiring collection of over 200,000 crosses, statues and effigies. There are many myths surrounding the Hill's origin, some dating back to pagan times, although the most plausible is that it was to commemorate rebels killed in nineteenth-century uprisings against the Russian Empire. In the Soviet era, they were planted by grieving families to commemorate killed and deported loved ones, and kept multiplying despite repeated bulldozing by the authorities. Today, crosses are often planted to give thanks for a happy event in a person's life. To get here, take a train from Vilnius to Šiauliai (5–8 daily; 2hr 30min) and then take a taxi (15min; 25Lt).

running east from the Old Town. At the junction with L. Sapiegos the street is enlivened by a bronze statue of **Vytautas the Great** facing the City Garden. Here, a contemporary memorial composed of horizontal metal shards commemorates the 19-year-old student Romas Kalanta, who immolated himself in protest against Soviet rule on May 14, 1972 and whose death sparked anti-Soviet rioting. Towards the eastern end of Laisvės alėja, the silver-domed **Church of St Michael the Archangel** looms over Independence Square (Nepriklausomybės aikštė). The striking modern building in the northeast corner, with the controversial naked "Man" statue in front, is one of the best art galleries in the country, the **Mykolas Žilinskas Art Museum** (Tues-Sun 11am–5pm; 6Lt), housing a collection of Egyptian artefacts, Japanese porcelain and Lithuania's only Rubens.

The museums

Just north of Unity Square (Vienybės aikštė), a block north of Laisvės, Kaunas has two unique art collections. The **Devil Museum** (Velnių Muziejus), at Putvinskio 64 (Tues–Sun 11am–5pm; 6Lt), houses an entertaining collection of over 2000 devil and witch figures put together by the artist Antanas Žmuidzinavičius and donated from around the world. Diagonally opposite, at Putvinskio 55, the dreamy, symbolist paintings of Mikalojus Čiurlionis, Lithuania's cultural hero credited with the invention of abstract art, are on display in the vast **M. K. Čiurlionis State Art Museum** (same times; 6Lt), along with excellent temporary exhibitions. Nearby, **Tadas Ivanauskas Zoological Museum**, at Laisvės 106 (Tues–Sun 11am–7pm; 5Lt), displays every imaginable animal, bird, insect and sea creature stuffed, pinned or pickled on three spacious floors.

Christ's Resurrection Church

Heading east along V. Putvinskio from the Devil Museum, you'll come to a funicular, leading up to Kaunas's most striking modern church, **Christ's Resurrection Church** (Kristaus Prisikėlimo Bažnyčia). A marvel or an eyesore? You decide. Designed by the man behind the city's Military Museum, Latvian Kārlos Reisons, its 70m tower offers sweeping views of Kaunas (5Lt).

Jewish Kaunas

Kaunas has experienced its share of anti-Jewish violence, both during local pogroms and then under the Nazis. During World War II, the city's large Jewish population was all but wiped out; all that remains is the city's sole surviving **synagogue** at Ožeškienės 13 in the New Town, which sports a wonderful sky-blue interior (daily services 5.45–6.30pm, Sat 10am–noon) and a **memorial** to the 1700 children who perished at the Ninth Fort (see opposite). The small and austere former Japanese consulate is now a **museum to Chiune Sugihara**

(Vaižganto 30; May–Oct Mon–Fri 10am–5pm, Sat & Sun 11am–4pm; Nov–April 11am–3pm; 10Lt), the consul who saved thousands of Jewish lives during the war by issuing Japanese visas against orders.

To reach the Ninth Fort, take bus #35 from Kaunas bus station (every 30min) and get off at the IX Fortas stop. The **Ninth Fort Museum**, at Žemaičių plentas 73 (daily except Tues 10am–6pm; 5Lt), is housed in the tsarist-era fortress where the Jews were kept by Nazis while awaiting execution in the killing field beyond; exhibits cover extermination of Jews and deportation of Lithuanians by the Soviets. A massive, jagged stone memorial crowns the site.

Arrival and information

Air Kaunas's international airport is located around 20km north of Kaunas. Bus #29 (2Lt) passes through the Old Town and stops at the main bus and train stations.

Bus and train Kaunas's bus and train stations are both along Vytauto at the southeastern end of the centre, a 10min walk from Laisvės alėja; take any trolleybus passing in front of the stations to the Old Town (2Lt). There is luggage storage at both, and an ATM out on the main street.

Internet Internet Copy 1, at Kęstučio 54/7 (Mon–Fri 7.45am–7pm, Sat 9am–4pm; 5Lt/hr).

Tourist information Laisvės 36 (June–Aug Mon–Fri 9am–7pm, Sat 10am–6pm, Sun 10am–3pm; Sept–May Mon–Thurs 9am–6pm, Fri 9am–5pm; ⓣ37/323-436, ⓦwww .kaunastic.lt). Provides useful maps and copies of *Kaunas in Your Pocket* (6Lt). There's another office at Rotušės aikštė 29 (same hours).

Accommodation

Kaunas Archdiocese Guest House Rotušės 21 ⓣ37/322-597, ⓦkaunas.lcn.lt /sveciunamai. With a location between two churches that's hard to beat, this charming place has clean doubles and free internet. Consumption of alcohol is forbidden. A real bargain. 80Lt.

Litinterp Gedimino 28–7 ⓣ37/228-718, ⓦwww .litinterp.lt. Ever-reliable guesthouse option offering basic en-suite rooms with kitchenettes. They can also arrange rooms in private residences. 140Lt.

Metropolis Daukanto 21 ⓣ37/205-992, ⓦwww .metropolishotel.lt. Grand old Soviet hotel in a great location with 75 inexpensive en suites. Free wi-fi and breakfast included. 145Lt.

The Monk's Bunk Daukanto 21 ⓣ62/099-695, ⓔkaunashostel@gmail.com. Relaxed, traveller-friendly hostel with a great kitchen, poker nights and free wi-fi. Offers free walking tours of the city. Dorms 35Lt.

R Hostel Daukanto 21 ⓣ69/045-329, ⓦwww .r-hostel.com. A welcome addition to Kaunas's hostel scene, offering a lounge with table football, beer tasting evenings and barbecues. Free wi-fi, book exchange and airport pick-up for 17Lt. Dorms 35Lt, rooms 110Lt.

Eating

Cafés

Coffee Inn Laisvės 72. Great coffee (5Lt), smoothies (7.50Lt) and wraps (8Lt), plus cosy sofas and free wi-fi. Mon–Fri 7am–10pm, Sat 10am–10pm, Sun 10am–9pm.

Vero Café Laisvės 75. Good espresso, cakes and hot chocolate (6Lt) in this modern chain, popular with students. Mon–Fri 7.30am–9pm, Sat & Sun 10am–9pm.

Restaurants

Bernelių Užeiga Valančiaus 9 ⓣ37/200-913. Dine on huge portions of meaty Lithuanian staples in an attractive rustic interior. Mains 10–20Lt. Sat–Wed 11am–10pm, Thurs 11am–11pm, Fri 11am–1am.

Pizzeria Milano Mickevičiaus 19. Tucked away in what looks like a former Soviet administrative office, this busy but informal restaurant serves up fairly authentic pizzas (8–11Lt) and pasta dishes (12Lt). Daily 10am–1am, Fri & Sat until 2am.

Skliautas Rotušės 26. Set in a courtyard near the town hall, this small bar/restaurant has a brick-vaulted ceiling and evokes the atmosphere of the 1940s with old clocks, photos, candles and interwar music. Pork with cranberry sauce 13Lt. Mon–Thurs 10am–midnight, Fri 10am–2am, Sat 11am–2am, Sun 11am–11pm.

Drinking and nightlife

Bars

Avilys Vilniaus 34. Excellent microbrewery in a cosy cellar offering two types of honey-flavoured beer (8Lt), beer soup and a range of standard meat dishes and beer snacks. Wash down a plate of smoked pigs' ears with a pint of grog (warmed honey beer with extra honey and lemon). Mon–Fri noon–midnight, Fri & Sat noon–2am.

B.O. Muitinės 9. This friendly, popular and unpretentious bar is one of the best places to hook up

with a young, arty crowd. Mon–Thurs 9.30am–2am, Fri 9.30am–3am, Sat 11am–3am, Sun 3pm–2am.
Džem Pub Laisvės 59. Take the lift up to this cosy bar with regular live bands, a good range of beers and a superb view of the city. Tues–Thurs 4pm–3am, Fri & Sat 4pm–4am.

Clubs

BarBar'a Vilniaus 56 Ⓦwww.barbarabar.lt. Dress smart, look beautiful and if you make it in, enjoy some cocktails along with Kaunas's pretty young things. Wed & Thurs 10pm–3am, Fri & Sat 10pm–5am.
Latino Baras Vilniaus 22. Small and bustling, with consistently good Latin music, this club is a great place to mingle and show off your moves. Dance lessons offered. Fri & Sat 8pm–4am; entry 20Lt.

Moving on

Train Vilnius (hourly; 1hr 15min–1hr 45min).
Bus Klaipėda (hourly; 3hr); Nida (1 daily at 7am; 4hr 10min); Palanga (7 daily; 3hr 30min); Rīga (9–14 daily; 4hr–4hr 30min); Tallinn (1 daily via Rīga at 9pm; 9hr); Vilnius (every 20–30min; 1hr 30min–2hr); Warsaw (4 weekly; 7hr).

KLAIPĖDA

KLAIPĖDA, Lithuania's third-largest city and most important port, lies on the Baltic coast, 275km northwest of Vilnius. Though it has a handful of sights, the city is of more interest as a staging post en route to the Curonian Spit, or to the party town of Palanga.

The **tourist office** in the Old Town at Turgaus 7 (June–Aug Mon–Fri 9am–7pm, Sat & Sun 10am–4pm; Sept–May Mon–Fri 9am–6pm, Sat 10am–4pm; Ⓣ46/412-186, Ⓦwww.klaipedainfo.lt) has internet access (2Lt/30min), rents bikes for 30Lt per day and stocks the excellent *Klaipėda in Your Pocket* (6Lt). The **old ferry terminal** at Pilies 4 – which you'll want instead of the new ferry terminal at Nemuno 8 if you don't have a car – has regular departures to Smiltynė, the gateway to the Curonian Spit (Lt2.90, return is free).

If you arrive late, the HI-affiliated *Klaipėda Hostel*, at Butkų Juzės 7–4 (Ⓣ46/211-879, Ⓦwww.klaipedahostel.com; dorms 44Lt), is a basic but friendly **hostel** right next to the bus station. Better is *Litinterp Guest House* at Puodzių 17 (Mon–Fri 8.30am–7pm, Sat 10am–3pm; Ⓣ46/410-644, Ⓦwww.litinterp.lt; 140Lt), a 15min walk west along S. Daukanto gatvė from the stations. It has clean, attractive rooms and can book private rooms in Klaipėda or Nida (see p.756).

Good **places to eat** include *Navalis*, at Manto 23, a modern café with tasty sandwiches (10Lt), salads and coffee; and *Ararat*, an outstanding Armenian establishment on Liepų 48a, serving tender, delicately spiced grilled meats (from 22Lt) and excellent red wine.

Moving on

Train Vilnius (3 daily; 5hr).
Bus Kaunas (hourly; 3hr); Liepāja (1 daily at 8.35am; 2hr 35min); Nida (direct: 1–2 Fri–Sun; from Smiltynė: 8 daily; 50min); Palanga (every 30min; 30min); Rīga (6 daily; 4–5hr); Vilnius (hourly; 4–5hr).
Ferry Smiltynė (June–Aug every 30min, 5am–2am; 15min; rest of year at least one hourly, 7am–9pm).

PALANGA

Around 25km north of Klaipėda, **PALANGA** is Lithuania's top seaside resort – party central in the summer.

What to see and do

Palanga's biggest attraction is its 18km white sandy **beach**; throughout the summer months it hosts a number of outdoor all-night music events. The wooden **pier**, jutting into the sea at the end of Basanavičiaus gatvė, is where families and couples gather to watch the sunset (around 10pm in July).

From the beach, head east along pedestrian **Basanavičiaus** with the rest of the human tide, past the street musicians and vendors, countless restaurants, arcade games, amusement park rides and amber stalls. Get fired out of a bungee catapult (50Lt) or dance until morning at one of the clubs on

Vytauto gatvė, the main street, or on S. Darius ir S. Girėno gatvė, which leads off Vytauto gatvė to the beach.

The lush Botanical Garden (Botanikos Sodas) houses a fascinating **Amber Museum** (June–Aug Tues–Sat 10am–midnight, Sun 10am–7pm; Sept–May Tues–Sat 11am–5pm, Sun 11am–4pm; 4Lt; ⓦwww.pgm.lt) with around 25,000 pieces of "Baltic Gold", many with insects and plants trapped inside. The **Anatanas Mončys House Museum** at S. Daukanto 16 (Wed–Sun 11am–5pm; 4Lt) displays unique wooden sculptures, collages and masks made by the twentieth-century Lithuanian sculptor. Visitors are allowed to handle all the exhibits due to the sculptor's will specifying that others can touch his work.

Arrival and information

Bus The bus station on Kretingos gatvė is a couple of blocks away from Basanavičiaus gatvė, the main tourist street.

Tourist information Kretingos 1 (June–Aug daily 9am–7pm, Sat & Sun 10am–4pm; rest of the year Mon–Fri 9am–5pm, Sat 10am–2pm; ⓣ460/48811, ⓦwww.palangatic.lt). Multilingual and helpful staff can book private rooms, organize excursions and provide information on events in and around town.

Accommodation

Due to the town's immense summertime popularity, advance bookings are essential. The cheapest option is to haggle with the locals holding up "Nuomojami kamberiai" (rooms for rent) signs as the bus enters Palanga, although the quality may vary considerably. Outside of the high season prices can be as much as half of those quoted below.

Ema Jurates gatvė 32 ⓣ460/48608, ⓦwww.ema.lt. This brightly painted guesthouse has seven cosy rooms with TV, plus a crêperie on site. 95Lt.

Vandenis Birutės 47 ⓣ460/53530, ⓦwww.vandenis.lt. A comfortable hotel away from the bustle, home to a good café-restaurant with outdoor seating and a live music club. All rooms have cable TV and are en suite. Breakfast included. 300Lt.

Vila Ramybė Vytauto 54 ⓣ460/54124, ⓦwww.vilaramybe.lt. A great boutique hotel with colourful themed rooms, all en suite and some with kitchen or balcony. The restaurant-bar downstairs is one of the best in town. Breakfast included. 200Lt.

Eating, drinking and nightlife

1925 Basanavičiaus 4. Bar-restaurant resembling a log cabin, with a rustic wooden interior and an open fire in winter. Also has a pleasant patio garden. Mains around 30Lt. Daily 10am–midnight.

Čagino Basanavičiaus 14. Come to this bright Russian restaurant for good people-watching and ample portions of hearty meat dishes (20Lt), soups and pancakes. Daily noon–midnight.

Exit Nėries 39. Two-tiered entertainment: lively disco with kitschy decor upstairs (Mon–Thurs & Sun 7pm–3am, Fri & Sat 9pm–6am), and packed nightclub downstairs (daily 10pm–6am).

Laukinių Vakarų Salūnas Basanavičiaus 16. Packed with a young crowd and offering nightly karaoke, wet T-shirt competitions and the occasional live band. Cocktails around 14Lt. Sun–Thurs 9pm–5am, Fri & Sat 9pm–6am.

Žuvinė Basanavičiaus 37a. Fish restaurant with books on the shelves and a smart interior; the generous portions of well-prepared seafood dishes, such as scorpion fish in orange sauce (25Lt) or spaghetti marinara (36Lt), cannot be faulted. Daily 11am–midnight.

Moving on

Bus Kaunas (9 daily; 3hr 30min); Klaipėda (every 30min; 30min); Rīga via Liepāja (1 daily at 9am; 4hr 30min); Vilnius (7 daily; 6hr).

THE CURONIAN SPIT

NERINGA, or the **Kursių Nerija National Park**, is the Lithuanian section of the Curonian Spit, a 98km sliver of land characterized by vast sand dunes and pine forests. Some of the area can be seen as a day-trip from Klaipėda, though it really warrants a stay of several days to soak up the unique atmosphere. Ferries from the quayside towards the end of Žvejų gatvė in Klaipėda (2.90Lt return) sail to **Smiltynė** on the northern tip of the spit. From the landing stage, frequent **minibuses** (9Lt) run south towards more scenic parts of the spit, stopping at the villages of **Juodkrantė**, **Pervalka** and **Preila**, and terminating at **Nida**, 35km south.

CYCLING THE SPIT

The best way to explore the Curonian Spit is by **cycling** (bike rental 8Lt/hr, 30Lt/day) along well-marked biking trails that meander through pine forest and along the sand dunes. **Juodkrantė**, 30km away, is home to **Witches' Hill** (Raganų kalnas), an entertaining wooden sculpture trail in the woods with wonderfully macabre statues of devils, witches and folk heroes. *Vila Flora*, along the waterfront, serves simple but excellent fresh fish (25Lt) and pancakes (12Lt). Heading back towards Nida, stop off at the side of the road to catch a glimpse of the huge **heron and cormorant colony** in the trees. When passing through **Preila**, look for the *rųkyta žuvis* signs and stop at a smokery for some delicious smoked fish, which is much cheaper than in Nida.

NIDA

NIDA is the most famous village on the spit – a small fishing community boasting several streets of attractive blue- and brown-painted wooden houses. Although there are plenty of visitors in the summertime it never feels crowded. There are several good **restaurants** on Naglių gatvė and Lotmiškio gatvė, as well as along the waterfront. From the end of Naglių, a shore path runs to a flight of wooden steps leading up to the top of the **Parnidis dune** south of the village. From the summit you can gaze out across a Saharan sandscape stretching to Russia's Kaliningrad province. Retrace the trail along the waterfront to see elaborate **weather vanes** with unique designs – each village has its own. Stop by the **Neringa History Museum** (Pamario 53; June–Sept daily 10am–6pm; Oct–May Tues–Sat 10am–5pm; 3Lt), which traces the village's heritage through photos of crow-eating locals and fishing paraphernalia. Also along Pamario is the church cemetery with traditional **krikštas** – carved wooden headstones – placed upright at the foot of the resting body. Nida's long, luxuriant **beach** is on the opposite side of the spit, a 30min walk through the forest from the village.

Arrival and information

Bus Buses from the mainland and from Smiltynė stop on Naglių, Nida's main street. Everything in Nida is within walking distance.
Tourist information Taikos 4 ⓣ469/52345, ⓦwww.visitneringa.com (June–Aug Mon–Sat 10am–7pm, Sat 10am–6pm, Sun 10am–3pm; Sept–May Mon–Thurs 9am–1pm & 2–5pm, Fri 10am–3pm); has info on lodging and events.

Accommodation

Nida has a few budget guesthouses, but as they tend to fill up in the summer, advance reservations are required. Private rooms (120–150Lt) and local B&Bs (160–200Lt) can be booked via tourist info.
Inkaro Kaimas Naglių 26 ⓣ469/52123, ⓦwww.inkarokaimas.lt. A beautifully decorated double, quad and a two-room apartment are on offer at this welcoming seaside guesthouse. All are en suite and have satellite TV and kitchenette. 200Lt.
Misko Namas Pamario 11 ⓣ469/52290, ⓦwww.miskonamas.com. Colourful house with a range of en-suite rooms and apartments, communal kitchen and a lovely private garden. Breakfast 22Lt; bike rent 17Lt/day. 215Lt.

Eating and drinking

Baras Bangomūša Naglių 5. Homely, informal place, and one of the best spots in Nida to try the local smoked fish. *Koldūnai* (ravioli-like meat parcels; 12Lt) and other Lithuanian dishes also available. Daily 10am–midnight.
In Vino Taikos 32. Enjoy the best views in Nida from the terrace of this popular hilltop wine bar. Extensive drinks menu. Daily 10am–midnight.
Kuršis Naglių 29. Cosy restaurant offering the gamut of Lithuanian dishes, including roast pike-perch (30Lt) and excellent *šaltibarščiai* (cold beetroot soup; 6Lt). Daily 9am–midnight.

Moving on

Bus Kaunas (via Klaipėda; Fri & Sun 1/day at 2.45pm; 4hr 30min); Smiltynė (7 daily; 1hr 30min); Vilnius (via Klaipėda; Mon, Fri & Sun 1/day at 3.15pm; 5hr 50min).

Macedonia

HIGHLIGHTS

SKOPJE: charming historic centre and beautifully ugly Yugoslav buildings

ŠUTKA: immerse yourself in Europe's largest Roma community

SVETI JOVAN BIGORSKI: the best of Macedonia's many monasteries

OHRID: large, mountain-ringed lake with the country's most beautiful town on its shore

BITOLA: Macedonia's appealing second city

ROUGH COSTS

DAILY BUDGET Basic €25 /occasional treat €35

DRINK Wine from €1.60 per bottle

FOOD *Tavče gravče* (bean casserole) €1.25

HOSTEL/BUDGET HOTEL €12/€25

TRAVEL Bus: Skopje–Ohrid €7.30; train: Skopje–Bitola €4.

FACT FILE

POPULATION 2 million

AREA 25,738 sq km

LANGUAGE Macedonian

CURRENCY Denar (MKD)

CAPITAL Skopje (population: 600,000)

INTERNATIONAL PHONE CODE ⓣ389

Introduction

It's easy to see why the French refer to a mixed salad as a macédoine: this hotchpotch of Ottoman rule, Yugoslav domination, Orthodox faith and Albanian influence represents one of Europe's most varied societies. While traditional tourist sights are thin on the ground, this land of vineyards and rolling fields is a grand place to kick back, and refreshingly places more emphasis on free time than profit margins. In few countries would you have your bus journey interrupted for a spot of apple-picking, or find a stranger cooking you a mountaintop meal during your hike. This, however, is Macedonia.

The capital, **Skopje**, is something of a Yugoslav symphony in grey, though one whose brutal architecture is softened by friendly locals and an appealing Ottoman centre. Most travellers prefer to base themselves around **Lake Ohrid**, a delightful, mountain-fringed expanse straddling the Albanian border. Between Skopje and Ohrid, a glut of immaculately painted **monasteries** compete for your attention; **Sveti Jovan Bigorski** is the most enjoyable, and lies within **Mavrovo**, a national park that provides great hiking opportunities, as well as skiing in the winter.

CHRONOLOGY

168 BC The Macedonian area is absorbed by the Roman Empire.
395 AD The Roman Empire splits, Macedonia falls under Byzantine rule.
447 Attila the Hun rampages through the area.
1394 Five hundred years of Ottoman rule begin.
1878 Russian victory over the Ottoman Empire; Macedonia is ceded to Bulgaria, though soon returned at the instigation of Western powers.
1910 Gonxha Agnesë Bojaxhiu, an ethnic Albanian, now known to the world as Mother Teresa, is born in Skopje.
1912 The Turks are ousted in the Balkan Wars; Macedonia is shared between Serbia and Greece.
1918 The Serb-ruled area that comprises today's Macedonia is given to the Kingdom of Serbs, Croats and Slovenes.
1945 Macedonia becomes part of socialist Yugoslavia.
1963 Over one thousand people killed by an earthquake in Skopje.
1991 Macedonia gains independence from Yugoslavia.
1993 Admitted to the UN as "Former Yugoslav Republic of Macedonia".
2001 Civil war between government and ethnic Albanian insurgents.
2005 Macedonia becomes an official candidate for EU membership.

ARRIVAL

Skopje **airport** (Ⓦwww.airports.com.mk) handles a few international flights, with Wizz Air (Ⓦwizzair.com) the only regular budget airline, making seasonal flights from London and Venice. Ohrid also has an international airport but flights are few and far between; Thessaloniki and Sofia are also within swiping distance. Most, however, make their way to Macedonia overland. There are a couple of daily **bus** services from Tirana in Albania (via Ohrid), but poor neighbourly relations mean that there are very few direct services from Greece. In summer you may be able to catch a minibus from Thessaloniki to Skopje; this was once easier by train but the Greek government, in its wisdom, cut off all international services in 2011. Mercifully, the two daily services from Belgrade to Skopje are still running. Lastly, it's possible to get all the way to Lake Ohrid from Tirana by train – a daily service runs to Pogradec, from

"THEN WHAT ARE WE? FYROMANIANS?"

As soon as Macedonia declared independence from Yugoslavia, a different kind of battle broke out along the Greek border, one regarding two matters integral to a new country: **name** and **flag**. Athens objected to the use of the name – the bulk of historical Macedonia now lies under Greek control – and also to a flag featuring the ancient kingdom's sixteen-pointed Vergina Sun. The new nation squeezed into the UN as the "former Yugoslav Republic of Macedonia", or FYROM for short, and later changed their flag to end a Greek economic blockade. Many nations now recognize the "Republic of Macedonia", but this battle of nomenclature remains locked in stalemate, and is unlikely to end anytime soon.

which the Macedonian border is just 10km away.

Citizens of some countries (notably South Africa), still need **visas** to enter Macedonia, though it's now part of the Schengen zone; check Ⓦwww.mfa.gov.mk for more information.

GETTING AROUND

Almost all travel in Macedonia is by **bus**. Services are punctual and reasonably frequent, and the vehicles themselves are really not that bad. Note that buses take one of two routes between Skopje and Ohrid, one through Bitola, and a more picturesque trip through Kičevo. There is also a limited **train** network, though it suffers from slow and irregular services and is rarely used by travellers. The best domestic line is the thrice-daily service between Skopje and Bitola, which passes through wonderful mountain scenery.

ACCOMMODATION

Accommodation is not terribly varied but generally quite affordable. Skopje's overpriced **hotels** are now supplemented by a few cut-price alternatives (from around €30), while in the hinterlands – including Ohrid – you'll be able to make use of **private rooms**, known as *sobi*; you'll often be met at bus stations by homeowners with rooms to spare. Prices vary wildly depending upon location and facilities, but generally expect to pay from €10 to €30 for a double room. There are now a few **hostels** in Skopje and Ohrid, each costing around €12 for a dorm bed, while **campsites** can be found around the lakes of Ohrid and Prespa; the cost of camping is usually less than €10 per tent.

FOOD AND DRINK

The Macedonian diet is dominated by barbecued **meat** (*skara*), of which the most popular variety are sausage-shaped kebabs (*kebapči*), usually served with chopped onion and spongy, freshly baked bread. Other items to look out for on a regular menu are soups (*čorba*) and *tavče gravče*, a bean casserole served in a hot plate. The ubiquitous *burek* – a pastry filled with meat, cheese or spinach – is a good, cheap **breakfast** choice. **Vegetarians** can find solace in excellent salads and *ajvar* – a meze-like starter made from red peppers – while pizzerias are everywhere and always offer veggie choices. You'll find baklava – syrupy Turkish **sweets** – all over the country.

Drink

The consumption of **coffee** (*kafa*) seems almost obligatory, and it's traditionally served Turkish-style (black, with grounds at the bottom), though espresso is now gaining currency. More local in nature is **boza**, a refreshing millet-based drink available in cake shops. There are some good domestic **beers**, or *pivo* (Skopsko is the most popular

brand) but Macedonia is most famed for uniformly good **wines**. Vranec (red) and Smederevka (white) are two local grape varieties worth trying; you may be lucky enough to find shops selling fresh, home-made concoctions for just 60MKD per litre, but otherwise Tikveš is a reliable, easy-to-find bottled brand. After 9pm alcohol can only be bought in bars and licensed restaurants.

CULTURE AND ETIQUETTE

Macedonia is a real mishmash of cultures, and it's very important to make a few cultural notes. **Political and ethnic issues** still dominate – taking Greece's side in the country's naming dispute won't win you any friends, and neither will promoting Albanian or Macedonian nationalism to the "wrong" side. Only two-thirds of the population are Macedonians of Slav ethnicity – the vast majority of whom belong to the **Orthodox Church** – while most of the remaining third are ethnic Albanian. Tensions still run high between the two groups – 2001 saw a civil war between the government and Albanian insurgents – though travellers are unlikely to notice.

You'll find yourself **smoking** a lot in Macedonia – either your own fumes or secondhand – while **tipping** at restaurants is generally a simple exercise in rounding up. Don't feel that you're being booted out if your waiter stomps over to ask for money mid-meal, as

MACEDONIA ONLINE

ⓦ **www.exploringmacedonia.com** National tourism portal.
ⓦ **www.culture.in.mk** Information about music, film and performing arts.
ⓦ **www.culturalcornerstones.org** Photos and pictures of Šutka's Roma music.
ⓦ **faq.macedonia.org** Frequently asked questions, and some useful answers.

they're often required to settle accounts at the end of their shift.

SPORTS AND OUTDOOR ACTIVITIES

Activities in Macedonia centre around the mountains. The national parks of Mavrovo, Galičica and Pelister are excellent for **hiking** – Mavrovo and Pelister also offer good **skiing** opportunities – while the crystal waters of Lake Ohrid make it good for **diving** and **swimming**. The country's empty roads are ideal for **cycling**, but since there are precious few places to rent bikes it makes sense to bring your own.

COMMUNICATIONS

Most **post offices** (*pošta*) are open Monday to Friday 7am to 5pm, and sometimes also on Saturday mornings. These are the best places from which to make **phone calls** or purchase phonecards. International calls are often best

MACEDONIAN

Macedonia uses the **Cyrillic alphabet**, which poses inevitable problems with street signs, train and bus timetables. For most of these there's no transliteration into Latin script, but many restaurants have dual-language menus, and a decent level of English is spoken across the country.

	Macedonian	Pronunciation
Yes	Да	Da
No	не	Ne
Please	молам	Molam
Thank you	благодарам	Blago-daram
Hello/Good day	здраво	Zdravoh
Goodbye	до гледање	Dog-led-anyeah
Excuse me	извинете	Eezvee-neteh
Where?	каде?	Ka-deh?
Good	добар	Dobar
Bad	лош	Losh
Near	блиску	Bleeskoo
Far	далеку	Dalekoo
Cheap	евтин	Evteen
Expensive	скап	Skal
Open	отворен	Otvoren
Closed	затворен	Zatvoren
Today	денес	Denes
Yesterday	вчера	Vchera
Tomorrow	утре	Ootre
How much is…?	колку чини тоа…?	Kolkoo chinee toe-ah…?
What time is it?	колку е часот?	Kolkoo eh chasot?
I don't understand	не разбирам	Ne razbee-ram
Do you speak English?	зборувате ли англиски?	Zvo-roo-vateh lee Angliskee?
One	еден	Eh-den
Two	два	Dva
Three	три	Tree
Four	четири	Cheh-tee-ree
Five	пет	Pet
Six	шест	Shest
Seven	седум	Sedum
Eight	осум	Ossum
Nine	девет	Devet
Ten	десет	Deset

STUDENT AND YOUTH DISCOUNTS

Many museums and galleries offer cut-price student tickets; in practice, a youthful appearance will be acceptable in lieu of an ISIC card. InterRail and Balkan Flexipass tickets are valid on Macedonian trains.

made from **internet cafés**, which are now easy to find in cities and larger towns; expect to pay around 40MKD per hour.

EMERGENCIES

The crime rate is pretty low by European standards, even in Skopje. However, it's prudent to carry your passport, or a photocopy of the picture page, at all times. You'll find **pharmacies** (*apteka*) in all major towns and cities, and a surprising number have English-speaking staff; opening hours vary but some are 24hr. For more serious matters head to a **hospital**; outside Skopje taxis may be faster than ambulances, and hospitals can be poor.

INFORMATION

There are now a few **tourist information offices** dotted around the country, and though they're slowly starting to learn what travellers require, many don't keep regular hours.

EMERGENCY NUMBERS

For police, ambulance or the fire department call ⓣ112.

MONEY AND BANKS

The currency is the **denar** (usually abbreviated to MKD), comprising coins of 1, 2, 5, 10 and 50MKD, and notes of 10, 50, 100, 500, 1000 and 5000MKD. Exchange **rates** are currently around 60MKD to the euro, 70MKD to the pound, and 43MKD to the US dollar.

Accommodation prices are usually quoted in euros, though you can also pay in denar. Money can be **exchanged** at an exchange office or bank; the latter are usually open Monday to Friday 8am to 5pm. **ATMs** are easy to find in urban areas, though stock up on cash if you're heading into the sticks.

OPENING HOURS AND HOLIDAYS

Most **shops** stay open until 8pm on weekdays, and mid-afternoon on Saturdays. Sundays are still special in Macedonia – don't expect too much to be open, even in central Skopje. Things also grind to a halt on **public holidays**: January 1, 2 and 7, Orthodox Easter (March or April), May 1 and 24, August 2, September 8 and October 11.

Skopje

Still largely off the radar of budget travellers, **SKOPJE** (Скопје) certainly deserves a little more attention. It's one of those places that can be described as "appealingly ugly", with brutal Yugoslav-era designs augmenting the mazy lanes of **Čaršija**, the charming old Ottoman centre. The city was ravaged by an earthquake in 1963, and it's once again in the process of turning itself inside out: at the time of writing, the area around the river was subject to one of the most ambitious renovation schemes in Europe, and by 2014 an all-new stretch of half a dozen large, Baroque-style buildings should have been completed.

What to see and do

The **Čaršija** district north of the river contains the bulk of Skopje's sights, and is the obvious place from which to kick off a trip around the city.

Čaršija and the Kale

Turkish times linger on in the shape of several mosques – **Mustapha Pasha** is the largest and most intricately decorated – and two former bathhouses, the copper-domed **Daud Pasha** (daily except Mon 9am–3pm; 100MKD) and the **Čifte Amam** (Mon–Sat: April–Sept 10am–9pm; Oct–March 10am–6pm; 50MKD). These splendid structures are sadly long out of use as hammams, and both now used as repositories of contemporary art; those seeking history instead can head to the **Museum of Macedonia** (daily except Mon 9am–3pm; 100MKD; Sun to 1pm, free), which is well worth an hour or two. All are outdone, however, by wonderful little **Sveti Spas** (Tues–Fri 9am–5pm, Sat & Sun 9am–3pm; 120-MKD), a secluded fourteenth-century monastery. Its church was built mostly underground – under Ottoman rule churches were not allowed to be higher than mosques – and its carved-walnut iconostasis is jaw-dropping.

Northwest of Čaršija, and up from the eastern ramparts of the old castle (now closed to visitors), is the excellent **National Museum of Contemporary Art** (Tues–Sat 10am–5pm, Sun 9am–1pm; free), from where you can see the whole of Skopje. The collection, which is mainly of local art, is not bad, either.

Mount Vodno

Look south from any vantage point in Skopje and you'll see Mount Vodno, within walking distance of the city and topped with a huge cross. The mountain is great for hiking – the 1066m peak is only a couple of hours' walk from central Skopje. In 2011 a new cable car entered service from the base of the mountain whisking visitors to the top in just 7min (8am–6pm, closed Mon; 100-MKD). To reach the cable car costs 100-MKD by taxi and 30MKD on hourly buses from the bus station.

South of the Vardar

Cross the **Stone Bridge** (Kamen Most) and you'll find yourself in Skopje's main

ŠUTKA

The Skopje district of Šuto Orizari, more commonly referred to as **Šutka**, is home to Europe's largest **Roma** community. The area is impoverished and dilapidated, but a visit can be quite fascinating – colourful buildings, litter-lined streets and a bustling daily market make it feel something like an Indian town transported to the Balkans. It's also one of Macedonia's foremost centres of song and dance, but events run to no schedule – sunny summer afternoons are your best bet. Buses #19 and #20 run here from the post office and train station respectively, or it's only 200MKD by cab.

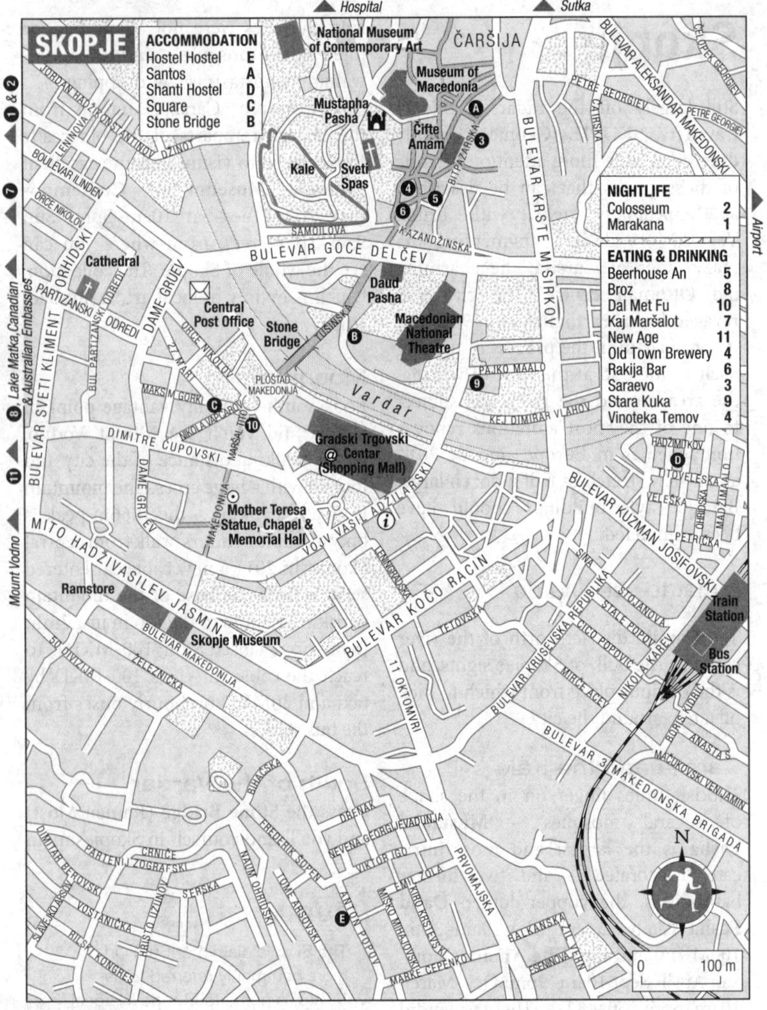

square, **Ploštad Makedonija**. You won't be able to miss the recently erected gigantic equestrian statue of the original Ali G, Alexander the Great; the largest of a bewildering number of statues in the area. Just west of the bridge's southern end are two of the most distinctively Yugoslav buildings in the city – both were, however, designed by Kenzo Tange, a Japanese architect. The **Mepso building** is a fusion of Le Corbusier-style design and Communist-era factory, now used as office space; behind it is the **Central Post Office**, a bizarre concrete spaceship whose lavish interior counts as a Skopje must-see.

Marking the start of largely pedestrianized **Makedonija**, a crescent of elegant buildings – survivors of the 'quake – provides some much-needed respite. **Mother Teresa** was born further down the road, and a memorial hall, chapel and statue have been placed here in her honour. At the very end of the road, you'll see the imposing **Skopje Museum** (Tues–Sat 9am–5pm, Sun 9am–1pm; free); fronted by a large clock that stopped during the earthquake. The exhibitions themselves – usually a bewildering amalgam of photography, artefacts and modern art – are worth a quick look.

Arrival and information

Air Skopje's Alexander the Great airport is 21km east of the city, though as there's no public transport a taxi is the only option. Aim for €20 (1200MKD).
Train and bus The main train and bus stations – don't be too put off by the former – are located right next to each other, a 20min walk or 100MKD taxi ride southeast of the centre.
Tourist office Moše Pijade (9am–5pm, closed Sun; ⓣ02/311 6854). Can hand out pamphlets and give practical advice.

City transport

Bus Tickets for central rides cost 20–30MKD.
Taxi Journey costs start at a very reasonable 50-MKD, and a city-centre trip will rarely cost more than 150-MKD. It's the normal way of getting around, even for locals.

Accommodation

Hostels

Hostel Hostel Ognjan Prica 18 ⓣ02/322 2321. A decent place to stay, though quality has been on the wane of late. The artistic owners stage occasional events and can point you to other ones. Dorms €8.
Shanti Hostel Rade Jovcevski Koragin 11 ⓣ02/609 0807, ⓦwww.shantihostel.com. Super-friendly hostel which makes the most of its small space. There's *burek* and yoghurt for breakfast, and even with the biggest backpack it's an easy walk from the stations. Dorms €8.

Hotels

Santos Bitpazarska 125 ⓣ02/322 6963. Very central, and its cute little rooms represent excellent value. You'll see it signed off Bitpazarska. Doubles €30.
Square Nikola Vapcarov 2 ⓣ02/322 5090, ⓦwww.hotelsquare.com.mk. Stylish mini-hotel set atop a building with echoes of the Communist era. The thoroughly modern rooms are a pleasant surprise. Doubles €60.
Stone Bridge Kej Dimitar Vlahov 1 ⓣ02/324 4900, ⓦstonebridge-hotel.com. Classy hotel just off the north end of the famous bridge. The construction going on nearby will enable you to swipe a fair bit from the rack rates – under €100 should be your target. Doubles €120.

Eating and drinking

The terms "café" and "bar" are somewhat fuzzy; what passes for the former during the day will generally morph into the latter by night. The Čaršija area has become the most buzzing part of town – great news for travellers.

Cafés and bars

Broz Crvena Voda 4. A bizarre Communist-themed coffee-chain parody – Starbuckski? – whose walls are lined with subtle revolutionary pictures. Upstairs seats have good mountain views.
New Age Kosta šahov 9. A little hard to find, but worth the effort – dim lighting and floor cushions make this the kind of place to while away a whole rainy day. Coffee, cocktails and shakes abound, while the range of teas is immense.
Old Town Brewery Gradište 1. Drink Skopsko from a 3-litre tank, while admiring the southern wall of Sveti Spas monastery. They often have bands performing in the evening.
Rakija Bar Podgradje 14. You'll never guess what they serve here. The most expensive *rakija* at this buzzing bar costs 120MKD a glass and tastes quite good, the cheapest goes for 50MKD and may well make you heave. Either way, you won't remember in the morning.

Restaurants

Beerhouse An Kapan An, off Bitpazarska. Don't let the name deceive you – this is a classy restaurant in the charming ground level of Kapan An, a former traders' hostel. Extensive and inventive local menu, with grills starting at around 190MKD – the sausages are particularly good.
Dal Met Fu Makedonia 1. Hugely popular with locals – you may well struggle to get a seat. Order a

Vinoteka Temov Gradište 1a ⓣ02/321 2779. Sophisticated yet rustic wine bar that puts on live traditional music (Wed–Sat, from 9pm). A full range of local wines are available, from 500–3000MKD per bottle; you can also buy by the glass. Booking advisable.

pizza for 220MKD and up, or something more interesting like breaded mozzarella with saffron.

Kaj Maršalot Guro Gakovik 8. Take a trip back to Tito times at this Yugoslav-themed restaurant. The food is little different to that you'll find elsewhere in the city, but where else would you be served by students dressed as Young Pioneers?

Saraevo Bitpazarska 86. Working-man's den with snack-style mains. Ten bite-size *kebapči* with bread and onions will set you back just 120MKD, or try a *tavče gravče* for 70MKD.

Stara Kuka Pajko Maalo 14. Traditional restaurant serving hearty meals that are worth splashing out on; the casseroles are excellent. Walking distance from the centre, and taxi drivers know the name. Mains 250–600MKD.

Nightlife

Clubs in Skopje don't really get going until after midnight; the following stay open much, much later than that.

Colosseum Železnička 66. House venue that regularly ropes DJs in from overseas. Surprisingly polished, and you're almost obliged to pop some moves. In summer they host outdoor events in Gradski Park. Admission 200MKD.

Marakana Gradski Park. Youngish club near the stadium that features live jazz or cover bands almost every night. Admission 50–100MKD.

Entertainment

Macedonian National Theatre Kej Dimitar Vlahov. One of Skopje's very best concrete monstrosities – quite a claim – plays host to ballet and operatic performances; at least it will until moving to a new venue by the river, before 2014. TIcket office 1–8pm; tickets from 200MKD.

Premium Cinema in the Ramstore shopping mall; tickets 150MKD.

Shopping

The streets of Čaršija are a good place to hunt for souvenirs. For shopping malls you can choose between the Gradski Trgovski Centar (CIty Shopping Centre), a relic of years gone by just off the north end of Makedonija, and the shiny new Ramstore, at the end of Makedonija to the south.

Directory

Embassies and consulates Australia, Londonska 11b ⓣ02/306 1114; Canada, Bulevard Partizanski 17a ⓣ02/322 5630; UK, Salvador Aljende 73 ⓣ02/329 9299; US, Samoilova 21ⓣ02/311-6180.

Hospital Re-Medika, Makedonska Brigada 18 ⓣ02/260 3100.

Internet Gradski Trgovski Centar (9am–10pm; 120-MKD/hr).

Money There are ATMs dotted around the city centre, and in the bus station, which also has exchange booths. Otherwise all banks can exchange money.

Pharmacy Dimitri Čupovski 13; 24hr.

Post office Orce Nikolov (Mon–Sat 7am–7.30pm, Sun 8am–2pm).

Moving on

Train Belgrade (2 daily, 9hr); Bitola (3 daily; 3hr–3hr 50min).

Bus Belgrade (12 daily; 7hr); Bitola (12 daily; 2hr 40min); İstanbul (5 daily; 12hr); Mavrovi Anovi (7 daily; 1hr 45min); Ohrid (12 daily; 3–4hr); Sofia (5 daily; 8hr); Tirana (2 daily; 10hr).

LAKE MATKA

A mere half-hour drive from Skopje, pretty **LAKE MATKA** (Матка езеро)

SKOPJE'S FESTIVALS

Buskerfest ⓦwww.buskerfestmakedonija.com. Over a week of eclectic street performances in late May or early June.

Pivo-Lend ⓦwww.pivolend.com.mk. Beer festival held each September within the fortress walls.

Skopje Jazz Festival ⓦwww.skopjejazzfest.com.mk. Acclaimed event featuring musicians from around the world, spread over a week each October.

Skopje Film Festival ⓦwww.skopjefilmfestival.com.mk. Well worth checking out. Screenings in the Kultura cinema at Luj Paster 2.

Vino-Skop ⓦwww.vinoskop.com. Wine festival offering the opportunity to taste local produce, usually held in October.

provides an easy break from – or alternative to – the grey of the capital. The artificial lake is surrounded by richly forested peaks, and its edges are dotted with cute restaurants, many of which can only be accessed by **boat**. You'll be approached by boat owners, who typically charge €10 for a short ride around, and a trip to either a restaurant or some nearby **caves**. It's also possible to stay by the lake in an easy-to-find mountaineering hut named *Matka* (☎02/305 2655; dorms €7), highly recommended since evenings occasionally see the nearby slopes illuminated by fireflies. Bus access has been in a state of flux for some years; it's best to take #5 from the stations to the end, then board #60 to the lake. It's a lot easier by cab (450MKD).

Western Macedonia

Travellers heading from Skopje to Ohrid have two bus routes to choose from. The first heads south through the major – for Macedonia – city of **Bitola**, a pleasant place with some interesting nineteenth-century architecture. Heading west instead will bring you close to the national park of **Mavrovo**, good for hiking in summer and skiing in winter. This latter route also takes an hour less. **Ohrid** itself is Macedonia's prime attraction, the name referring both to a large, mountain-ringed lake, and the beautiful old town that sits on its northern shore. Just to the east, and sitting next to another pristine lake, is charming **Pelister National Park**.

MAVROVO NATIONAL PARK

Mavrovo National Park (Националниот Парк Маврово; Ⓦwww.npmavrovo.org.mk) spreads its wings over one of Macedonia's most beautiful corners, a rich and rugged land where rushing streams tumble down slopes cloaked with pine and birch. There are a wealth of sights and activities to choose from – the wonderful monastery of **Sveti Jovan Bigorski** is a particular delight to visit. **Camping** and **hiking** are possible most of the year, while winter snows make for some of the most affordable **skiing** and **snowboarding** in Europe.

Mavrovo

Most travellers base themselves in the little town of **Mavrovo** (Маврово). This charming resort sits next to a lake of the same name, but is sadly not accessible on public transport; to get here head by bus to **Mavrovi Anovi**, 8km away on the other side of the lake, from where it'll be a 150MKD taxi ride. *Hotel Bistra* (☎042/489002, Ⓦwww.bistra.com; doubles €80) is right next to the ski slopes and good value for the price; they can also help to organize cheaper accommodation for impoverished backpackers.

Sveti Jovan Bigorski

Macedonia has no shortage of wonderful monasteries, but **Sveti Jovan Bigorski** (Свети Јован Бигорски; free) takes the biscuit. Tucked away in delightfully bucolic countryside near the Albanian border, its whitewashed buildings are edged with dark wood, and should the fireflies come out to play in the evening it will feel like you've stepped into a Hayao Miyazaki anime. Most of the older buldings were

SKIING IN MAVROVO

The **Zare Lazarevski** resort (Ⓦwww.zarelaz.com) is the place to head for wintertime fun. The season lasts from Nov 15 to mid-April, day-passes cost just 1100MKD (half-day 850MKD), and skis can be rented for a similar price.

destroyed in a catastrophic fire in 2009, though reconstruction was swift; in due course, travellers will once again be able to stay for a nominal fee. To get here, jump on any bus heading between Debar and Gostivar (both accessible from Skopje and Ohrid), and ask to be let off at the monastery.

BITOLA

Pretty little **BITOLA** (Битола) is one of Macedonia's only attractive urban centres; you'll doubtless wonder if it can really be the second-largest city in the country. Its laidback air also disguises some historical pedigree – in the Ottoman era, such was the importance of this trading hub that a string of **consulates** set up on the main thoroughfare. Amazingly, some remain: the Turkish one still functions because of Bitola's sizeable Turkish minority, while both the British and French ones are still kicking around too. All are housed in splendid nineteenth-century buildings, more of which line the city's pedestrianized main road, Maršal Tito.

Bitola's **train** and **bus** stations sit side by side in contrasting states of disrepair, a fifteen-minute walk south of the centre. There's no real reason to stay overnight, but it makes a convenient break on the Skopje–Ohrid route. The most appealing **rooms** are the splendid collection on offer at the *Hotel De Niro* (Ⓣ047/229656, Ⓦwww.hotel-deniro.com; doubles €54), though those looking for a *sobi* will find one easily.

PELISTER NATIONAL PARK

A pristine national park between Bitola and Ohrid, **Pelister** (Националниот парк пелистер) overlooks **Lake Prespa**, a shimmering expanse that, while nowhere near as deep as Ohrid, boasts surrounding mountain scenery every bit as beautiful. On the northern side of the park sits a small **ski resort**, accessible from Bitola; take a bus to Turnovo and a taxi the rest of the way (€20 all in). From here a spine trail zigzags south to Malo Ezero, a picturesque lake at the park's centre. The lake can also be approached from the wonderfully unspoilt village of **Brajčino** (Брајчино), a great hiking base to the southwest. With its hand-stacked rock walls it shows almost no signs of the modern day. The only official accommodation in the village is at a motel known to locals as *Nikolina*'s (Ⓣ047/482222; doubles €25), though it's quite easy to score a *sobi* (private room), especially in summer when you'll likely be met coming off the bus. Buses to Brajčino leave on the half-hour from Resen, a town on the main Ohrid–Bitola stretch. Just off this latter route is **Malovište** (Маловиште), a gorgeous old village whose population has nosedived to almost nothing. Now being thrown funds to polish up and lure people back, it's well worth a visit to walk the cobbled streets, breathe some fresh air and admire this relic of a bygone age.

OHRID

Vast almost to the point of appearing sea-like, **Lake Ohrid** (Охридско езеро) is Macedonia's major draw. A backdrop of **mountains** encircles the lake like a torn sky, looping through Albanian territory on the way back around. This is the only place in the country that can be described as touristy, but even in peak season the combination of genteel streets and quietly lapping waves lends a relaxed air to proceedings. Locals are friendly and the nightlife is surprisingly lively for a small town.

Lake Ohrid is not only one of the **deepest lakes** in Europe – over 300m in places – but also one of the oldest. Appropriately, it has played host to lakeside communities since the **Neolithic period**, but it was not until Roman times that **OHRID** (Охрид) developed as a town. Large basilicas were constructed from the fifth century, and Slavic tribes started moving in shortly after that. Ohrid's importance as a religious centre was maintained under Ottoman rule, and the town became a popular tourist destination during the Yugoslav period.

What to see and do

Most sights are located within the walls of the **Old Town**, whose steep lanes are home to a glut of churches, museums and galleries. There are a couple of monasteries in the area, but most are here for the timeless majesty of **Lake Ohrid** itself – locals swear that the water remains clean enough to drink, and with visibilty of up to 20m they may well be right. Motorized "water-taxis" are available for 300MKD and up for a 10-minute ride, though since they dilute both the clarity of the water and the beauty of the lake you may prefer to use the **rowing boats** available for hire at various lakeside points (from €2 for 10min).

The Old Town

The best place from which to commence a tour around the Old Town is the **Upper Gate**. In the area immediately to the south you'll find a fascinating **icon gallery** (Tues–Sun 10am–2pm & 6–9pm; 100MKD), home to some of the best examples found in the Ohrid area. Staff here should also be able to open up the adjacent **Sveta Bogorodica**, a thirteenth-century church with wonderful interior frescoes.

West of the gate you've a choice of uphill paths; one heads to the **Fortress of Tsar Samoil** (daily 8am–5pm; 30-MKD), which has a messy interior and is more interesting from the outside. The other path leads past an old **Roman amphitheatre** to **Sveti Kliment** (daily 8am–5pm; 100MKD), a large, modern church. This is built next to the ruins of the oldest church in Ohrid – dating from the fifth century, its foundations are on display under a rather ugly shelter.

From Sveti Kliment it's a hop and a skip down the slopes to **Sveti Jovan Kaneo** (daily 8am–5pm; 100MKD), whose lakeside setting makes it Ohrid's most appealing church. The walk east back into town is rather lovely, and passes the tranquil residential enclave of **Kaneo**; it's also possible to go by boat for 300MKD. Back in the centre you'll find the **National Museum** (Tues–Sun 10am–3pm; 100MKD), full of historical relics and an interesting place to while away an hour or two.

The monasteries

Heading around the eastern shore of the lake will bring you to the wonderful monastery of **Sveti Naum,** which lies within walking distance of the Albanian border. Magical grounds surround the seventeenth-century building, whose interior (daily 7am–7pm; 100MKD) is filled with vivid frescoes. In the summer you can get here by boat from Ohrid town, and buses (110MKD) run every couple of hours during the day; it'll cost the same in a shared taxi. The road heads between the lake and **Galičica**

THE REPUBLIC OF VEVČANI

Fancy a quirky half-day trip? Head to **Vevčani**, a village that declared tongue-in-cheek independence after the fall of Communism. The only real evidence of this are its weird banknotes, and even these are rarely available; ask at *Domanska Kuka*, a terrific restaurant. Instead, it's best to come here for the pleasant **springs** area, signed uphill from town – the water here may be the best in the Balkans, and the energetic can start a 5.2km mountain hike here. To get here you'll need to take a bus from the town of Struga, located on Lake Ohrid.

National Park (Ⓦwww.galicica.org.mk); a great place for a hike; on the way you'll pass the village of Gradište, which boasts remains of a Bronze Age village hauled from the bottom of the lake. You can also dive into the crystal waters around here from €50 per person - check Ⓦwww.amfora.com.mk for details.

Heading instead around the western shore of the lake will eventually bring you to the wonderful monastery of Kališta, where monks once lived in caves dug into the cliffs – these, and other mural-lined halls, are open for visitors (100MKD), though you'll probably have to ask around for the key.

Arrival and information

Air A 14km, 300MKD taxi ride from town.
Bus The station is inconveniently located a 50–70MKD cab ride north of the Old Town.
Tourist office The one inside the bus terminal isn't very helpful, but there's a better one at Partizanska 6 (Ⓣ046/260423).

Accommodation

There are some great places to stay in Ohrid, but *sobi* (private rooms) are also an option, especially when the hotels are booked up in summer months. You're likely to be met at the bus station by those with rooms to spare. Camping is possible at three sites along the lake between Ohrid and Sveti Naum (around 400MKD/tent).

Sunny Lake Klimentov Univerzitet 38 Ⓣ075/629571, Ⓦwww.sunnylakehostel.com. Superb hostel that strikes the tough balance between comfort and party-place. The common areas are great places to meet people, especially in the summer over barbecued meat and a few glasses of *rakija*. Dorms €12.

Vila Lucija Kosta Abraš 29 Ⓣ046/265608, Ⓦvilalucija.com.mk. So close to the lake that you may wake to see your ceiling ashimmer with reflected sunlight. The spick-and-span rooms are excellent value, and come with almost painfully powerful showers. Doubles €30.

Vila Sofija Kosta Abraš 64 Ⓣ046/254370, Ⓦwww.vilasofija.com.mk. Well-equipped boutique rooms set in a beautiful, traditionally styled building – great value, especially for the €29 single rooms. Doubles €49.

Eating and drinking

Ohrid's culinary scene is terribly uninspired for a place with such tourist appeal. In summer, a curl of lakeside café-bars open up in Kaneo (see p.769). More interesting, for some, will be the Skovin Winery behind *Restorant Neim*, where a litre of freshly made wine – fired into plastic bottles from petrol-station-like pumps – will only cost 65MKD.

Jazz Inn Kosta Abraš 80. Not always as mellow as the name might suggest: sometimes there's nobody there, at other times it'll stay open very, very late. Occasional live music.
Liquid Kosta Abraš 52. Bar that's busy most nights with a young and fun-loving clientele – a good place to make new friends, get drunk with existing ones, or a mixture of the two.
Pandanog Local meals in a superb location overlooking the amphitheatre. Mains aren't the cheapest (300MKD and up), but there are some bargains on the menu; it's quite possible to fill up on their delicious appetizers alone.
Restorant Neim One of the only Old Town restaurants cheap enough to be popular with locals; the stuffed peppers (140MKD) are recommended, as are the kebabs (120MKD). A bottle of red will only set you back 300MKD.

Moving on

Bus Bitola (6 daily; 1hr 30min); Resen (6 daily; 50min); Skopje (12 daily; 3–4hr).

Montenegro

HIGHLIGHTS

DURMITOR: kayak through Europe's grandest canyon

KOTOR: beguiling historic centre on a bay circled by gargantuan cliffs

CETINJE: former royal capital, now delightfully sleepy town

BUDVA: the most appealing of Montenegro's many beach towns

STARI BAR: centuries-old ruins set in tranquil countryside

ROUGH COSTS

DAILY BUDGET Basic €30/ occasional treat €50

DRINK Nikšičko Tamno beer €1 (bottle from shop)

FOOD *Sarma* €2.50–4

GUESTHOUSE/BUDGET HOTEL €20/€50

TRAVEL Bus: Budva–Kotor €3; train: Podgorica–Virpazar €1.80

FACT FILE

POPULATION 630,000

AREA 13,812 sq km

LANGUAGE Montenegrin

CURRENCY Euro (€)

CAPITAL Podgorica (population: 180,000)

INTERNATIONAL PHONE CODE ⓣ382

Introduction

The tiny new state of Crna Gora is better known under its Italian name, Montenegro. When translated into English – "Black Mountain" – this may sound somewhat dull, but Montenegro is a land exploding with colour. Carpeted with flowers for much of the year, the country's muscular peaks are dappled with the dark greens of pine, beech and birch from which rushing turquoise streams drop down to a tantalizingly azure blue sea. Fringing it, the coastline is dotted from border to border with beaches of yellow and volcanic grey, and huddles of picturesque, orange-roofed houses – a postcard come to life.

Its beaches and idyllic old towns make the **coastline** most appealing for the traveller, though its most precious jewel – phenomenally photogenic **Kotor** – sits just a little inland at the end of a fjord-like bay. Beach-fringed **Budva** is the other real highlight, but you should also try to make time for the ruins of **Stari Bar**. Inland pleasures are mainly confined to the mountains, particularly the spectacular national park of **Durmitor**, while the old Montenegrin capital of **Cetinje** is also well worth a visit.

CHRONOLOGY

9 AD Roman annexation of the region incorporates most of present-day Montenegro into the province of Dalmatia.
395 The Roman Empire splits into eastern and western halves, with Montenegro lying on the line of division.
990 Slav state of Duklja established.
1190 Successor state of Zeta annexed by Serbia.
1499 Much of Montenegrin interior falls to the Ottoman Empire; the Venetian Empire controls the coast.
1697 Ottomans defeated in the Great Turkish War; Petrović clan assumes control.
1797 Venice falls to Napoleon, who transfers the Gulf of Kotor to Austrian rule.
1878 Montenegro granted independence following the Congress of Berlin.
1918 Kingdom of Serbs, Croats and Slovenes formed, incorporating Montenegro.
1929 Montenegro becomes part of the new Kingdom of Yugoslavia.
1945 Tito becomes prime minister (president from 1953) and ushers in the era of Communist rule; Podgorica renamed Titograd.
1979 Coast between Bar and Ulcinj damaged by earthquake.
1991 Break-up of Yugoslavia; Montenegro votes to stay with Serbia in a referendum.
2006 Montenegro gains independence following a second referendum.

ARRIVAL

Flights to Montenegro are in pretty short supply, but Montenegro Airlines (Ⓦwww.montenegroairlines.com) flies to Podgorica and Tivat (near Kotor) from several European destinations. The state is also easily reached overland from any of its neighbouring countries. From Croatia, there are **buses** along the coast from Dubrovnik – also home to the closest budget flights – and there are a couple of services from Split too; some of these will require a bus change after a short walk across the border. From Serbia, there are several daily buses between Belgrade and the Montenegrin coast, via Podgorica; daily **trains** – including a night service – also run from Belgrade to Bar along the same route. From Bosnia-Hercegovina there are direct buses to Podgorica from Trebinje and Sarajevo.

Perhaps the most romantic way to arrive in Montenegro is by **ferry** from Italy. Between April to September, Montenegro Lines (Ⓦwww.montenegrolines.net) runs

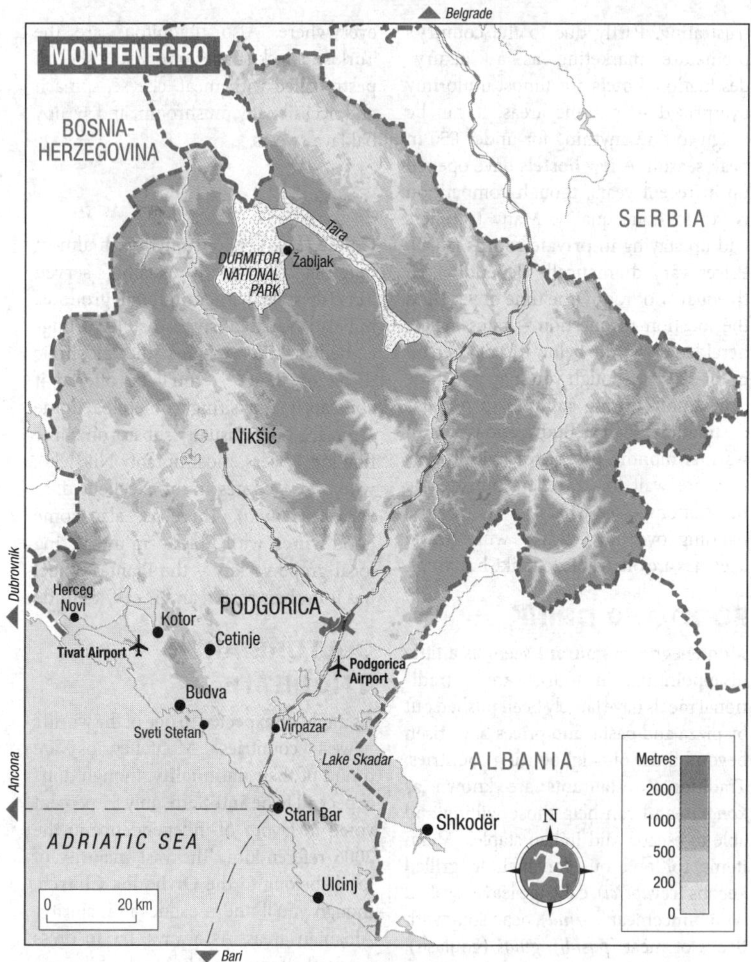

between two and six weekly services to Bar from Bari (from €50).

Note that citizens of some countries, notably South Africa, still need **visas** to enter Montenegro. You may have to apply at a Serbian embassy, since not all Montenegrin ones are up and running yet.

GETTING AROUND

For a country with such a small population, the frequency of intercity **buses** is quite remarkable. In addition, Montenegro has poured substantial funds into the upgrading of its main travel arteries, and travel times are accordingly short. A **train** line heads to Bar from the Serbian border – a beautiful journey. While services are infrequent, prices are dirt-cheap and almost every inch of track affords breathtaking views, especially the run into Podgorica from the Serbian border – be sure to sit on the western side of the train.

ACCOMMODATION

The accommodation scene in Montenegro can be somewhat

frustrating. Partly due to the country's premature marketing as a "luxury" destination, **hotels** are almost uniformly overpriced – in some areas, it can be tough to find anything for under €50 in peak season. A few **hostels** have opened up in recent years, though competition is yet to hone quality. Many travellers end up staying in **private rooms** (*sobe*). Prices vary dramatically depending on the quality of room, the time of year and the location in question – rates in less heralded towns dip below €10 per person in off-season, though you may pay three times more during summer in popular destinations such as Budva and Kotor. In warmer months, proprietors with rooms to spare wait for travellers outside the bus stations – see what's on offer before handing over any cash – while travel agencies are often able to make bookings.

FOOD AND DRINK

Montenegro's **restaurant** scene is a little disappointing. In tourist areas, traditional meals have largely been pushed out by pizza and pasta, and prices have risen beyond those of neighbouring countries. Traditional restaurants are known as *konoba*, and can help those willing and able to escape said Italian staples. Menu items to look out for include grilled kebabs (*čevapčići*), cabbage leaves stuffed with mincemeat (*sarma*), bean soup with flecks of meat (*pasulj*), *gulaš* (goulash), and the artery-clogging *karađorđe vasnicla*, a breaded veal cutlet roll stuffed with cheese. **Vegetarians** can take refuge in the hearty salads available almost everywhere. Also ubiquitous are the Turkish snack staples of *burek*, a slice of pastry filled with meat, cheese, spinach and occasionally mushroom, and syrupy baklava sweets.

MONTENEGRO ONLINE

Ⓦ **www.montenegro.travel** Official tourist board site.
Ⓦ **www.themontenegrotimes.com** Homepage of an interesting English-language weekly.
Ⓦ **www.rivijera.net** Useful listings of coastal accommodation, often including pictures.

Drink

Coffee (*kafa*) is consumed with almost religious fervour, usually served Turkish-style with unfiltered grounds, but also available espresso-style. Strong-as-hell **rakija** remains the alcoholic drink of choice – you'll be offered it constantly if visiting someone's home – but travellers usually subsist on some fine local beers, most notably Nikšićko, which also comes in an excellent dark variety (*tamno*). There are also some good **wines**, with Vranac an interesting local grape variety – the Plantaže label has it in their roster, and is easy to find.

CULTURE AND ETIQUETTE

As might be expected in one of the world's newest countries, Montenegrins are proud of their **nationality**, though don't expect all to be anti-Serb: only 55 percent voted in favour of independence in the 2006 referendum. The vast majority of locals belong to the **Orthodox Church**, though you'll find mosques in majority-Albanian areas. As always, try to dress modestly if visiting religious buildings.

Tipping at restaurants is becoming more common; smaller places will expect to keep small change, and posh restaurants to receive up to ten percent of the bill. Despite an official **smoking** ban, Montenegrins still do much of their breathing through small, tobacco-filled cylinders: non-smokers may have a tough time avoiding the fumes.

SPORTS AND OUTDOOR ACTIVITIES

Outdoor activities come in two main flavours: mountain and coastal. **Hiking**

EMERGENCY NUMBERS

Police ☎92; Ambulance ☎94; Fire ☎93.

is a joy around the peaks of Montenegro's national parks, most notably Durmitor, which is also good for **kayaking**, and **skiing** in winter. On the beach it's a different story, with **watersports** including jetskiing, parasailing and zorbing available at various points along the coast – Budva is the prime spot, though kayaking around Kotor Bay is a delight.

COMMUNICATIONS

Most **post offices** (*pošta*) are open Monday to Friday 8am to 7pm, Saturday 8am to noon. These are also your best bet for **phone calls** as public phones are in extremely short supply; local landlines are cheap to call, though calls to mobile phones are usually €1 per minute. Getting **online** can also be tricky as there are surprisingly few internet cafés; where they do exist, prices are generally €1–2 per hour.

EMERGENCIES

Montenegro has a pretty low crime rate as far as muggings and petty theft go, though of course it pays to be vigilant, especially around bus stations. The

STUDENT AND YOUTH DISCOUNTS

Quite a few sights and museums now offer discounted fares to students (an ISIC card may be useful, but is not essential), and for what it's worth, **InterRail** tickets are valid on Montenegro's single line (which never costs more than a few euros anyway).

MONTENEGRIN

Montenegrin is the official language, though it's essentially the same as Serbian (except that it uses the Roman alphabet rather than Cyrillic). You should be able to get by using Croatian (see box, p.252), with which it has strong similarities.

police (*policija*) are generally easy-going, and some speak basic English.

Pharmacies (*apoteka*) tend to follow shop hours, though you'll find emergency 24-hour telephone numbers posted in the windows. If they can't help, you'll be directed to a **hospital** (*bolnica*), the majority of which are pretty good.

INFORMATION

Many towns and resorts now have a **tourist information office**, though hours can be infrequent and staff do not always speak English. Though they can advise on local accommodation, it's unlikely that they'll book rooms for you – head to a travel agent instead.

MONEY AND BANKS

Though not yet a member of the EU, Montenegro uses the **euro** (€). **Banks** are generally open Monday to Friday 9am to 6pm, Saturday 9am to noon, and **ATMs** are widespread.

OPENING HOURS AND HOLIDAYS

Most **shops** open Monday to Saturday 9am to 8pm – **banks** follow similar hours – many shops close on Sundays. Museums are usually closed on Mondays, and all shops and banks shut down on **public holidays**: January 1, 6 and 7, Orthodox Easter (April or May), May 1 and 21, and July 13.

The coast

Blessed with sunshine, pristine beaches lapped by clear Adriatic waters, and appealing, whitewashed old towns, the **Montenegrin coast** has become one of Europe's hottest properties. Heading north–south from Croatia to the Albanian border, you'll first hit charming **Herceg Novi**, before the coast ducks inland to swallow up magnificent **Kotor** – without doubt the most picturesque town in the land. South of here, the littoral swings back out to the beaches of **Budva**, something of a party capital during the summer. It's then mountain-edged coast all the way to **Bar**, home to some terrific ruins.

HERCEG NOVI

Little **HERCEG NOVI** is a thoroughly likeable town – and, intriguingly, one usually bypassed by tourists. Developed as a coastal resort during eighteenth-century Austro-Hungarian rule, its steep maze of lanes is lined with stately, crumbling villas, and decades of international sailors have bequeathed unto it plants and flowers from around the world. Nearby **beaches** are good for swimming.

What to see and do

Most sights are concentrated within Herceg Novi's appealing, walled **Old Town**. At its centre you'll find the **Church of Archangel Michael**, just over a hundred years old but perhaps looking a few decades more than that. From here you can climb the steps to take in views from the "bloody tower" of **Kanli Kula** (daily 8am–10pm; €1). Downhill, the seafront **promenade** makes for a delightful walk. Head east for twenty minutes, then turn inland to find the elegant, seventeenth-century **Savina Monastery** (daily 6am–8pm; free).

Arrival and information

Bus There's a small station on Jadranski put; turn right then walk downhill and you'll be in the Old Town in about 5min.
Information and tours Tours can be booked at the bus station, or through the Black Mountain agency (daily 8am–8pm; ⓣ 067/640869, ⓦ www.montenegroholiday) at Pet Danica 21, who also arrange great tours of the local area, as well as rafting trips to Durmitor (see box, p.784).
Internet There are a couple of cafés at the north end of the Old Town's main square; €2/hr.

Accommodation and eating

There's a dearth of good-value accommodation in town, though the Black Mountain agency (see above) can book private rooms from €10/person.
Autocamp Zelenika Sunčana obala ⓣ 067/678631. Campsite 3km east of town; open April–Oct. €12/tent.
Centar Sava Ilića 7 ⓣ 031/332442. A short way west of the centre, with just about the cheapest non-*sobi* rooms in town. Open April–Oct. Doubles €45.
Kafana Pod Lozom Trg Nikole Đurkovića. A 2min walk from the church (past the clock tower and turn right), this restaurant cooks up cheap local specialities – you'll be able to fill up for €5. Try the *gulaš*, or the *sarma*.

Moving on

When heading south, most buses cut out the Bay of Kotor loop with a quick ferry ride (no extra charge). Travelling via Kotor will increase the following journey times – excepting Kotor – by around 45min.
Bus Bar (6 daily; 2hr 30min); Budva (every 30min–1hr; 1hr 15min); Kotor (hourly; 45min); Podgorica (hourly; 2hr).

KOTOR

Perched on the edge of a majestic bay, the medieval Old Town of **KOTOR** is the undisputed jewel in Montenegro's crown. Though no longer Europe's best-kept secret, Kotor's sudden elevation to the tour-bus league has failed to dim the timeless delights of its maze of cobbled alleyways and secluded piazzas. Enclosing cafés and churches galore, the town **walls** are peered down upon by a series of hulking peaks.

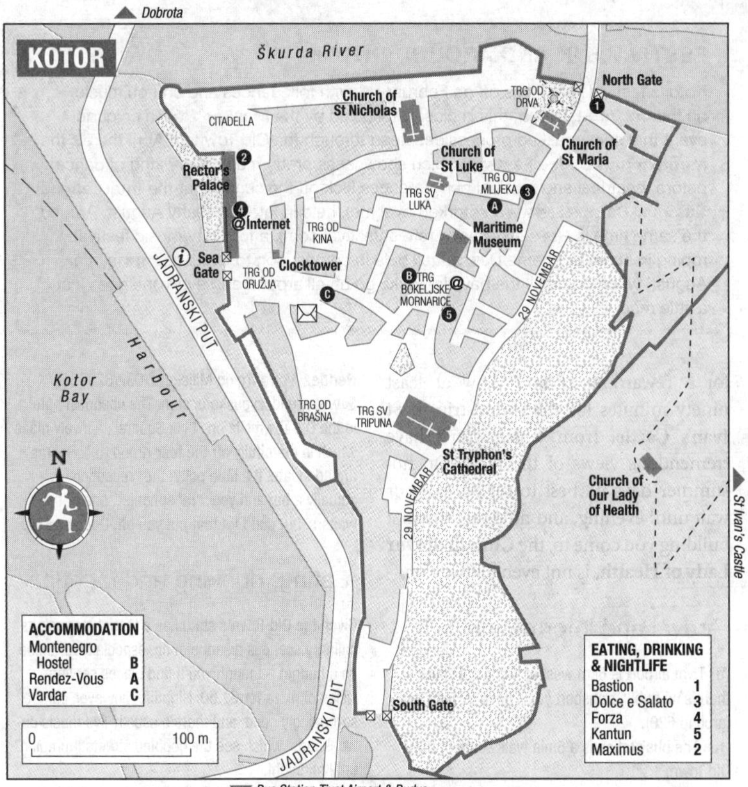

Down below, a harbour now bustling with sleek yachts marks the end of the **Bay of Kotor**, made fjord-like by the thousand-metre cliffs that rise almost vertically from the serene waters.

First colonized by the Greeks, Kotor came to prominence in the twelfth century, then passed through Serb, Austro-Hungarian and Bosnian hands before fifteenth-century Ottoman conquests forced it under the protective wing of Venice. Its period under Venetian rule ended in 1797, the shape of today's Kotor having been laid out in the intervening years.

What to see and do

Kotor's charms are best appreciated by heading to the **Old Town**, *sans* map, and getting lost in the maze of streets. You'll likely enter through the Sea Gate, next to the harbour, and emerge onto the main square, Trg od Oružja. Cafés spill out from glorious buildings, the most notable of which are the old **Rector's Palace**, and a leaning **clock tower**. Burrow through the streets and before long you'll end up at **St Tryphon's Cathedral** (daily 8am–7pm; €2), backed by a wall of mountains and perfect for photos; it's well worth the entry fee for a peek inside. Elsewhere there are several churches worth looking at, as well as a fascinating **Maritime Museum** (Mon–Fri 8/9am–5/8pm; Sat 8/9am–noon; €2), a repository of nautical maps, and model ships.

The old **fortress walls** (daily 8am–8pm; €3) sit proudly above the town, and make

FESTIVALS IN AND AROUND KOTOR

Kotor's festival year kicks off on February 1, with folk dances and church music on the **day of St Tripun**; this is closely followed by the **Masked Ball**, a colourful event that sees masked processions head through the Old Town. In April there's the **Montenegrin Dance Festival**, which showcases pretty much every kind of dance, before theatrical and musical performances kick off the summer at the **International Summer Carnival** (Ⓦwww.kotorkarneval.me), held in late July/early August. Around the same time is **Refresh** (Ⓦwww.refreshfestival.com), a four-day music festival roping in some big-name DJs, but all pale in comparison to **Boka Nights** in late August, when boats fill the bay, fireworks go off all around and everyone goes just a little mad.

for a rewarding climb. Allow at least ninety minutes for the round-trip to **St Ivan's Castle**, from which you'll have tremendous views of the fjord. On hot summer days it's best to set off early or wait until evening, and note that the first building you come to, the **Church of Our Lady of Health**, is not even halfway up.

Arrival and information

Air Tivat airport is 6km west of Kotor, but since there's no public transport you'll have to get a cab (around €20).
Bus The bus station is a 5min walk south of the Old Town.
Internet There are a couple of terminals inside the *Forza* café and a few cafés dotted around the old town (usually €2/hr).
Tourist office Located just outside the main entrance to the Old Town (daily 8am–5pm; July & Aug to 9pm; Ⓣ032/322 886, Ⓦtokotor.me), and able to book accommodation.

Accommodation

At all times of year, you're likely to be approached by *sobe*-owners as you get off the bus. Alternatively, the tourist office can book rooms from €20/person. Rooms are mainly grouped in two areas: Škaljari, uphill from the industrial mess near the bus station, and the more pleasant area of Dobrota, on the bayside just north of the Old Town.
Montenegro Hostel Trg od Muzeja Ⓣ069/039751, Ⓦwww.montenegrohostel.com. Finally, a hostel in the Old Town, and a fairly attractive one at that. There's a bit of noise from bars at night and churches in the morning; also note that you'll be charged if you want to leave your bag before taking the bus out of town. Dorms €12.
Rendez-Vous Trg od Mlijeka Ⓣ032/323931, Ⓦwww.rendezvouskotor.com. The cheapest hotel in the Old Town sits on "Milk Square", a lovely place which is mercifully off the tour-group trail. Rooms are adequate, if a little poky; the "reception" is actually a bar and your "receptionist" one of the waiters, but don't let that put you off. Doubles €50.

Eating, drinking and nightlife

Given the Old Town's status as a tourist magnet, its culinary scene is disappointing, especially for those on a budget – though you'll find places serving slices of pizza for €1.50. Nightlife, however, can be surprisingly good, and there's usually live music on weekends, which see the cobbled streets thumping until midnight.
Bastion Trg od Drva. Seafood restaurant offering a more authentic Old Kotor atmosphere than you'll find elsewhere; the interior is far from showy, and there are great views from the terrace. Squid filled with ham and cheese €12, fish salad €5.
Dolce e Salato Trg od Mlijeka. Outdoor seats in this quiet square are a perfect place for breakfast – a slice of *burek*, a Turkish coffee and a piece of strudel will come to just €3.40.
Forza Trg od Oružja. The best of a whole clutch of cafés on the main square, and a perfect place to

TREAT YOURSELF

Vardar Trg od Oružja (Ⓣ032/326084, Ⓦhotelvardar.com). Rooms in Kotor's plushest hotel are large and immaculately designed, and there's even a Turkish bath in the wellness centre. At €185 for a double you'd really be pushing the boat out, but prices drop to €125 for much of the year.

watch Kotor strolling by. Don't dare step inside to peek at their cakes – you'll almost certainly emerge €3 lighter and a little heavier elsewhere.

Kantun Trg Bokeljske Mornarice. Perhaps the best of Kotor's glut of pizzerias, with particularly good *calzone*. You may struggle to find a seat at mealtimes. Pizzas from €6.

Maximus Citadella. Take your pick from several music-themed floors at the biggest nightclub in the country, occasional host to big-name DJs. Entry can be €10–15 on weekends.

Moving on

Bus Bar (6 daily; 1hr 45min); Budva (every 30min; 30min); Cetinje (hourly; 1hr); Podgorica (hourly; 1hr 30min).

BUDVA

Of Montenegro's seemingly never-ending chain of picturesque coastal towns, **BUDVA** is by far the most popular. Filled to the brim with bars, restaurants and limestone houses, its Old Town is almost as pretty as the one in nearby Kotor, and there's plenty of fun to be had on the beaches, as well as at the seafront bars which pop up in the summer.

What to see and do

Budva's focal point is the **Old Town** – more of a place to stroll and sip coffee than sightsee – though most travellers are here for the **beaches**, and there are plenty to choose from.

The Old Town

The highlight of the Old Town is the area around the **Church of the Holy Trinity**, itself home to frescoes that, while far from ancient, are rather

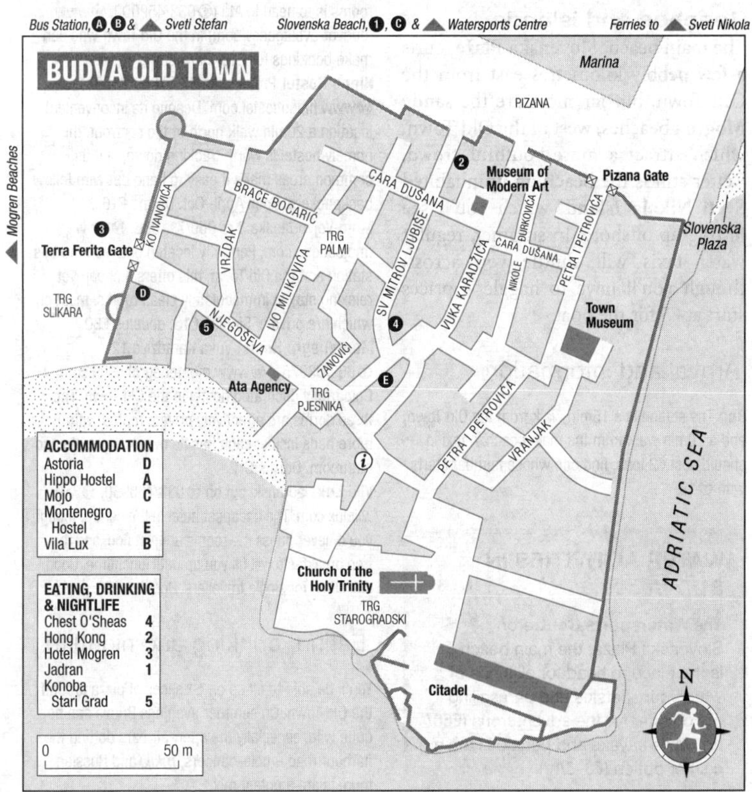

beautiful. Looming over this is the fifteenth-century **citadel** (April–Oct 9am–7pm; €2), which offers splendid views of the Adriatic waves pummelling in. Still, you're best advised to save your money and try to hunt down the entrances to the **Old City wall**, which boasts even better views. There are only two of these, meaning that almost no tourists ever get up there – one is just to the left when you enter through the Terra Ferita gate, and the other is an alley off *Hong Kong* restaurant. Also in the Old Town are the **Town Museum** (Tues–Fri 8am–8pm, Sat & Sun 2–8pm; €2), which houses Greek and Roman booty from the ruins being unearthed beneath the citadel, and a **Museum of Modern Art** (Mon–Sat 8am–2pm & 4–7pm; free).

Beaches and islands

The main beach, **Slovenska Plaža**, curls a few pebbly kilometres east from the Old Town, but far nicer are the sandy **Mogren** beaches, west of the Old Town, which attract a more youthful crowd. Better still is the beach on uninhabited **Sveti Nikola Island**, which you'll see jutting up offshore. In summer, regular water taxis will shuttle you across, though you'll have to haggle – prices start at €5 for the boat.

Arrival and information

Bus The station is a 15min walk from the Old Town, and a 10min walk from the main beach. A taxi in should cost €2 tops; find one whose number starts with ⓣ19.

WATER ACTIVITIES IN BUDVA

The **Watersports Centre** on Slovenska Plaža, the main beach, is the place to head for all kinds of watery fun. Jetskis and parasailing are on offer for the adventurous (€60/hr), while kayaks and pedaloes are a calmer option (€3–5/hr).

TREAT YOURSELF

Astoria Njegoševa 4 (ⓣ033/451110, ⓦwww.hotelastoria.co.me). Friendly boutique hotel just inside the Old Town walls, offering artistically designed rooms and wonderful views from a rooftop terrace. Doubles from €129, though off-season you may get a suite for the same price. They also have a hugely popular restaurant, spilling outside the town wall.

Tourist office Njegoševa 28 (daily 9am–6pm; ⓣ033/402550). They won't advise on accommodation, but not bad for maps and travel information.

Accommodation

If you're not met at the bus station – almost a certainty in summer – your best option for private rooms is to head to Ata (ⓣ033/452000, ⓦwww.budvatravelagency.com) in the Old Town who can make bookings for €15–35/room.

Hippo Hostel Proletarska 37 ⓣ069/253631, ⓦwww.hippohostel.com. Despite its inconvenient location a 20min walk north of the seafront, this homely hostel is worth tracking down, and its common areas make it easy to hang out with fellow backpackers. Open April–Oct. Dorms €16.

Mojo Vojvođanska 3 ⓣ069/711986, ⓦwww.mojobudva.com. Perfectly located between the bus station and the Old Town, this offers a cheap yet relaxing stay in immaculately clean rooms, most of which are private. Singles €15, doubles €30.

Montenegro Hostel Vuka Karadzića 12 ⓣ069/039751, ⓦwww.montenegrohostel.com. Colourfully decorated hostel in the Old Town. The three dorms are effectively private rooms with more beds inside; each has its own kitchenette and bathroom. Dorms €12.

Vila Lux Jadranski put bb ⓣ033/455950, ⓦwww.vilalux.com. The cheapest hotel in the centre, though you'd never guess it – rooms are just fine, and the free breakfasts will fill you up until lunchtime. Good discounts for single travellers. Doubles €52.

Eating, drinking and nightlife

You'll be able to fill up on €1 slices of pizza around the Old Town. On summer evenings Budva can be quite wild, especially the open-air bars dotting the harbour road – pole-dancers, *rakija* and Russian tourists are a potent mix.

Chest O'Sheas Mitrov Ljubiše. Small but appealing Irish pub smack in the middle of the Old Town, with sports events on screen and Guinness on tap.

Hong Kong Cara Dušana 17. The cheapest place to fill up in the Old Town, though one whose terrace directly faces the most expensive visiting yachts. Rice and noodle dishes from just €3; more elaborate mains are available, though they're not terribly authentic.

Hotel Mogren Outside the main Old Town gate. Now here's where the locals go to eat. Burrow down inside the *Hotel Mogren* and you'll find a canteen-style area, where filling local dishes go from just €3; for good measure, you can scoff them down next to a fountain.

Jadran Slovenska Obala 10. Hugely popular waterfront restaurant whose international menu includes *schnitzels* for €8 and mussels for €9. In the summer, they even have a bunch of tables on the beach itself.

Konoba Stari Grad Njegoševa. May look like nothing special from outside, but the seafood served here is excellent (if a little pricey). There's a grand beach terrace outside (one of the few stretches that doesn't charge for entry), which makes this one of the most appealing places for coffee.

Moving on

Bus Bar (hourly; 1hr); Cetinje (every 30min; 1hr); Kotor (every 30min–1hr; 30min); Podgorica (every 30min; 1hr 30min).

BAR

The pleasant town of **BAR** is literally the first port of call for many visitors to Montenegro, thanks to regular ferry connections with Italy. While the beach is rocky and there are no real attractions in the centre, it's worth at least an afternoon thanks to the magnificent ruins of **Stari Bar** (8am–8pm; €1) – *stari* means old – which sit 5km up the hill. The beauty of its setting is quite staggering – sheer cliffs surround this old town on all sides, and tiny farming communities dot the valleys below. Fragments of pottery found in the area date it as far back as 800 BC, though it wasn't until the **sixth century** that the Byzantine Empire created what you see today; the destruction also in evidence was caused during the Ottoman resistance battles of the 1870s. A trip to Stari Bar should set you back no more than €5 by taxi.

The train station is located in the south of town and the bus station lies 300m further along. The ferry terminal is immediately west of the centre, while there's a tourist office on the opposite side of the main road.

Accommodation

There are few *sobe* rooms in central Bar, so it's best to head to Šušanj, a pleasant district hanging over the almost unpronounceable beach of Zukotrlica. It's a 20min walk north along the seafront, or a €2 cab ride.

Sidro Obala ⓣ030/312200. The cheapest hotel in central Bar. Rooms are overpriced but perfectly adequate. Doubles €44.

Val Mila Damjanovića ⓣ067/206603. Block of comfy apartments located in the Šušanj district. Doubles €30.

Eating and drinking

Kaldrma Stari Bar. Adorable veggie restaurant – think cushions and rugs – near the entrance to the ruins. Often closed in the winter.

Karađuzović Stari Bar. Small café near the ruins that's great for breakfast; €3 will buy you a slice of *burek*, a Turkish sweetie and an espresso.

Pulena Vladimira Rolovića 11. Popular pizza-pub tucked into the fantastic Yugoslav-era Robna Kuka centre. Service ranges from slow to lightning-fast.

SVETI STEFAN

A few kilometres south of Budva (most easily accessed by taxi), and visible from the road if you're heading to or from Bar, is the incredibly picturesque island of **Sveti Stefan**, an old fishing village fishscaled with orange roofs. It's now cordoned off as luxury accommodation, but never mind – all the tourist brochure shots are taken from the road anyway, and you can do the same for free.

Moving on

Train Podgorica (4 daily; 1hr); Virpazar (4 daily; 25min).
Bus Budva (hourly; 1hr); Kotor (8 daily; 1hr 45min); Podgorica (7 daily; 1hr 45min).

The interior

The mountains visible from the Montenegrin coast hint at the beauty of its interior, an area sadly bypassed by most travellers. The capital, **Podgorica**, is one of the most natural in Europe but gets almost no backpackers. **Cetinje**, the former capital, makes a delightful stopover. Best of all is the mountainous north, particularly **Durmitor**, a spectacular national park where you can hike though unspoilt pastureland, ski past 2000-metre-plus peaks, or raft through the colossal Tara Canyon.

CETINJE

Sleepy **CETINJE** sits just over the mountainous crest from Budva and Kotor, and is well placed for a visit if you're heading between coast and interior. Cetinje became Montenegro's **capital** on independence in 1878, and of the clutch of embassies that were established, many remain visible today as faded relics of the city's proud past. Though the status of capital has long been passed to Podgorica, many government offices – and, in fact, the presidential seat – remain in Cetinje.

What to see and do

Central Cetinje is small enough to walk around in an hour or two, and almost all sights are located on or near **Njegoševa**, a mostly pedestrianized central thoroughfare. The sights listed below are all open daily 9am–5pm, and can be visited on a €10 combined ticket, or cost from €3 to €5 each.

Trg Dvorski and Trg Revolucije

The **Palace of King Nikola** sits at the southern end of Trg Dvorski. Prior to becoming king in 1910, Nikola was a military leader and poet (as well as a prince, of course), and his old palace is full of regal bric-a-brac. Opposite this is the **Ethnographic Museum**, which mainly features nineteenth-century costumes. Down the road in Trg Revolucie you'll find the **Biliarda**, once the residence of King Petar II, and named after a billiard table – still visible today – that he once had hauled here from Kotor. Near the Biliarda you'll find the **National Museum**, worth visiting for its first-floor art gallery, and nestled into the hillside across the square is **Cetinje Monastery**.

The embassies

Cetinje's former **embassies** are quite fascinating, and it's fun to track them down – basically, look for any oldish building sporting a crest. Nearest the bus station is the grey **French embassy**, covered with an assortment of lemon and blue tiles. Down on Trg Dvorski, the **Serbian embassy** contains the aforementioned ethnographic museum, and the **Bulgarian** one is now a great café. Further down the road, the crumbling **British embassy** is now a music academy; turn left for the **Turkish embassy**, now home to the Faculty of Drama, and the pick of the bunch – the gorgeous, peach-coloured **Russian embassy**.

Buses pull into a tiny terminal next to the *Sport* hotel. From here it's a 10min walk into town. Note that there's no tourist office in Cetinje.

Accommodation and eating

Grand Njegoseva st. 1 ⓣ041/231652, ⓦhotel-grand.tripod.com. Yugoslav-era beast at the end of Njegoševa, full of hairdressers, souvenir shops and the like, but the rooms are somewhat bare. Doubles €60.
Restoran Vinoteka Vasa Raičovića. Rich and varied menu of local specialities, including delicious

gulaš and *sarma*. There's a grand view from the outdoor seats. Mains €4–10.

Sport ⓣ041/231177. Reasonably attractive hotel in the long building next to the bus station; rooms are fresher than you'd expect from the outside. Doubles €51.

Moving on

Bus Budva (every 30min; 1hr); Kotor (hourly; 1hr 15min); Podgorica (every 30min; 45min).

PODGORICA

The Montenegrin capital of **PODGORICA** gets precious few backpackers – there's very little cheap accommodation, and not much to see. However, this is the newest capital city in Europe, one of the smallest, and quite possibly the least visited. It also might be the only European capital in which the river water looks positively drinkable – the city centres on the canyon-like **Morača**, a fast-flowing turquoise river edged by parkland and spanned by a couple of pedestrian bridges. One of these, the Gazela, dives down below street level, and there's a great café-bar a little further south (see opposite) at the confluence with the Morača's tributary, the **Ribnica**; there are also some interesting fortress remains in this area. Also worth a visit is **Gorica Forest Park**, which has some pleasant walking trails; it's behind the easy-to-find national stadium.

Arrival and information

Airport 11km south of the city. No public transport; taxis €15 (set fare) to the centre.

Train and bus The main train and bus stations are located adjacent to each other a 15min walk from the centre.

Tourist office Slobode 47. Pretty good for information, and can advise on accommodation. (Mon–Fri 8am–8pm, plus Sat [same hours] June–Oct; ⓣ020/667535, ⓦwww.podgorica.travel).

Accommodation

Since it can be tough to find a double for under €100, it's important to remember that buses to cheaper towns – anywhere, in other words – run until fairly late, and trains to the coast even later.

Evropa Orahovačka 16 ⓣ020/623444, ⓦwww.hotelevropa.co.me. How convenient – Podgorica's cheapest hotel is located right next to the train and bus stations. Rooms are good and there's a restaurant downstairs. Doubles €70.

Montenegro Hostel Djecevica 25 ⓣ069/039751, ⓦmontenegrohostel.com. Yet another addition to the chain, and they certainly have an eye for location – it's just a few minutes from the stations, in a calm neighbourhood. Dorms €10.

Eating and drinking

Restaurants in Podgorica are better value than the hotels, and *burek*-serving snack bars are easy to find. For nightlife, the best place to head is Njegoševa and the surrounding area.

Duchovny Centar Njegoševa 27. Scoff down cheap, tasty local fare – mostly veggie – in this church-like restaurant; try the salty pancakes with cream. You can eat for under €5.

Karver Obala Ribnice. Charming riverside café set inside an old Turkish bath, whose top was lopped off to make room for a bridge. Squashed it may be, but this is as cool as Podgorica gets - a great hangout for evening drinks, and also has a bookshop selling a few English-language cheapies. Latte €1.

Restoran Nino Right around the corner from the stations, and a perfect place to fill up between rides – five *Čevapi* and bread will only set you back €2.60, and bottles of Nik are under half that.

Skaline Inside the Ribnica gorge. What a location – look one way over the crystalline waters of the Morača, or the other at an Ottoman-era bridge. Great for coffee in the day or a beer in the evening; when it's hot you can strip off and have a swim.

Directory

Embassies and consulates UK, Bulevar Sveti Petra Cetinjskog 149 ⓣ020/205460; US, Džona Džeksona 2 ⓣ020/410500.

Hospital Podgorica Hospital, Ljubljanska 1 ⓣ020/225125.

Internet The www.klub at Bokeška 4 has a few terminals, as does *Karver* café (both €2/hr).

Post office Slobode 1 (Mon–Sat 8am–8pm). Has telephones for public use.

Moving on

Train Bar (10 daily; 1hr); Virpazar (10 daily; 35min).

Bus Bar (7 daily; 1hr 45min); Budva (every 30min;

ACTIVITIES IN DURMITOR

Durmitor is perhaps most famed for its **rafting**, which is among the best in Europe. This can be arranged though agencies on the coast or in Žabljak – try Summit, Njegoševa bb (☎052/360082), or Žabljak Tourist, Svetog Save 37 (☎052/361115) – which charge around €50 per person for a half-day trip. **Hiking** is great from June to September, though since this is a wild area do come prepared, and be warned that the weather can change rapidly, even in summer. The aforementioned agencies can provide maps. Wintertime opens up **skiing** possibilities, and **snowboarding** is on the rise too; the main slopes are accessible from Žabljak, with day-passes costing €15, and ski hire almost the same.

1hr 30min); Cetinje (every 30min; 30min); Herceg Novi (hourly; 2hr); Kotor (hourly, 1hr 30min).

LAKE SKADAR

Oozing over the Albanian border, beautiful **Skadar** is the largest lake in the Balkans, and also one of its most untouched. However, since it lies on the train line, it's easily accessible and can make a good stopoff on your way to or from the coast. The main jump-off point is **Virpazar**, a cute little fishing village at the northern end of the lake, a kilometre back down the line to Podgorica from the station. From here it's a pleasant walk along the lake's western shore, and though there's nowhere to rent bikes, if you've brought one along you'll be in heaven – an hour's ride will bring into sight a clutch of **offshore monasteries**, though to get any nearer you'll have to search for a boat. Accommodation is available in Virpazar at the *Pelikan* (☎020/711107, ⓦwww.pelikan-zec.com; doubles €60), which also has an excellent restaurant.

DURMITOR NATIONAL PARK

A land of jagged, pine-cloaked mountains and alpine pastureland, **Durmitor** is the most scenic place in inland Montenegro, and a hive of **outdoor activity** throughout the year. Dozens of 2000-metre-plus peaks drop down to the spectacular **Tara Canyon**, a kilometre-deep rip in the Earth bisected by a crashing river. Durmitor is a prime spot for skiing, hiking, camping, rafting and far more.

Durmitor is centred on the mountain town of **Žabljak**, accessible by bus along a bumpy, winding road that can turn even the stomachs of the locals. There's plenty of **accommodation** here, though as elsewhere in the country the hotels are a little dear; best value are the *Enigma* (☎052/360130; doubles €60) and the *Javor* (☎052/361337; doubles €60). Better for budget travellers are private rooms – from €10 per person – which you'll be offered on exiting the bus. Durmitor is also a great place for **camping**, and there are a number of sites around the park.

Morocco

HIGHLIGHTS

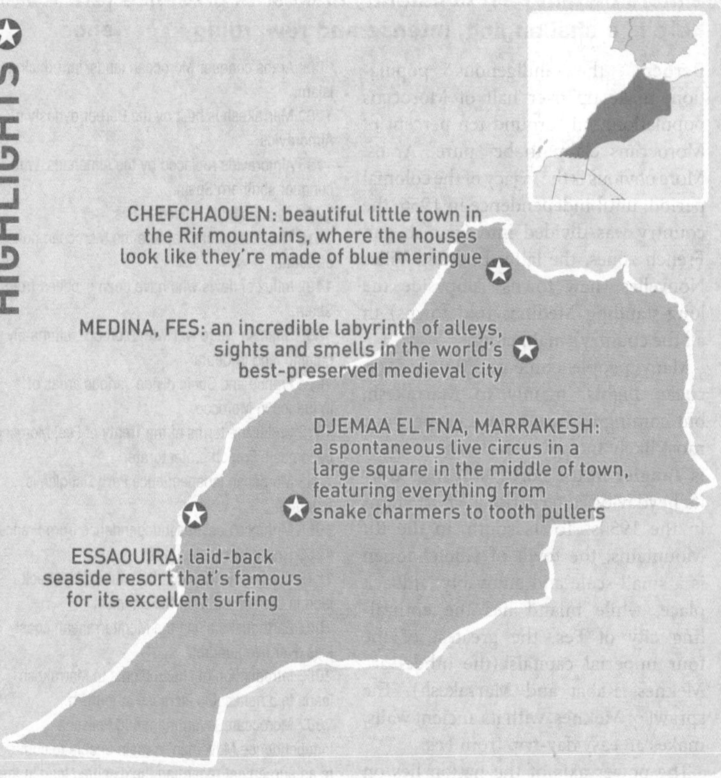

CHEFCHAOUEN: beautiful little town in the Rif mountains, where the houses look like they're made of blue meringue

MEDINA, FES: an incredible labyrinth of alleys, sights and smells in the world's best-preserved medieval city

DJEMAA EL FNA, MARRAKESH: a spontaneous live circus in a large square in the middle of town, featuring everything from snake charmers to tooth pullers

ESSAOUIRA: laid-back seaside resort that's famous for its excellent surfing

ROUGH COSTS

DAILY BUDGET basic €25/ occasional treat €35

FOOD *Tagine* €4–5

DRINK Pot of mint tea €1

HOSTEL/BUDGET HOTEL €10–15

TRAVEL Marrakesh–Casablanca: train €8–12; bus €5–8

FACT FILE

POPULATION 34.3 million

AREA 446,550 sq km

LANGUAGES Arabic, Berber languages, French

CURRENCY Dirham (dh)

CAPITAL Rabat (population: 2 million)

INTERNATIONAL PHONE CODE ⓣ212

Introduction

Just an hour's ferry ride from Spain, Morocco seems worlds away from Europe. It has a deeply traditional Islamic culture and, despite its 44 years of French and Spanish colonial rule, a more distant past constantly makes its presence felt. A visit here is a challenging, intense and rewarding experience.

Berbers, the indigenous population, make up over half of Morocco's population; only around ten percent of Moroccans claim to be "pure" Arabs. More obvious is the legacy of the colonial period: until independence in 1956, the country was divided into Spanish and French zones, the latter building Villes Nouvelles (new towns) alongside the long-standing Medinas (old towns) in all the country's main cities.

Many people come to Morocco on cheap flights, mainly to Marrakesh, but coming by boat from Europe, your most likely introduction to the country is **Tangier** in the north, still shaped by its heyday of "international" port status in the 1950s. To its south, in the Rif Mountains, the town of **Chefchaouen** is a small-scale and enjoyably laidback place, while inland lies the enthralling city of **Fes**, the greatest of the four imperial capitals (the others are Meknes, Rabat and Marrakesh). The sprawl of **Meknes**, with its ancient walls, makes an easy day-trip from Fes.

The power axis of the nation lies on the coast in **Rabat** and **Casablanca**. "Casa" looks a lot like Marseille, while the elegant, orderly capital, **Rabat**, has some gems of Moroccan architecture. Further south, **Marrakesh** is an enduring fantasy that won't disappoint. The country's loveliest resort, **Essaouira**, a charming walled seaside town, lies within easy reach of both Marrakesh and Casablanca.

CHRONOLOGY

42 AD Romans take control of the coastal regions of Morocco.

600s Arabs conquer Moroccan lands, introducing Islam.

1062 Marrakesh is built by the Berber dynasty of Almoravids.

1195 Almoravids replaced by the Almohads, who conquer southern Spain.

1269 The capital is moved to Fes.

1415 The Portuguese capture the Moroccan port of Ceuta.

1492 Influx of Jews who have been expelled from Spain.

1860 Spanish wage war with Morocco, ultimately gaining land in Ceuta.

1904 France and Spain divide various areas of influence in Morocco.

1912 Under the terms of the Treaty of Fes, Morocco becomes a French protectorate.

1943 Moroccan Independence Party, Istiqlal, is founded.

1956 Morocco declares independence from France.

1963 First general elections.

1975 Clashes as Morocco forcefully takes back land in the Sahara from the Spanish.

2004 Earthquake along the Mediterranean coast kills over five hundred.

2006 Introduction of cheap flights to Marrakesh leads to a noticeable increase in tourism.

2007 Moroccan Government and Polisario Independence Movement remain unable to come to an agreement regarding the disputed land in the Western Sahara.

2011 Bomb in Marrakesh kills fifteen people – Islamist militants are suspected of involvement.

ARRIVAL

To reach Morocco from Europe you can either fly or take a ferry. The main airports are in Casablanca, Fes and Marrakesh, the last of which is served regularly by budget airlines from UK and European airports. Ryanair (Ⓦwww.ryanair.com) and easyJet (Ⓦwww.easyjet.com) both sell cheap online tickets.

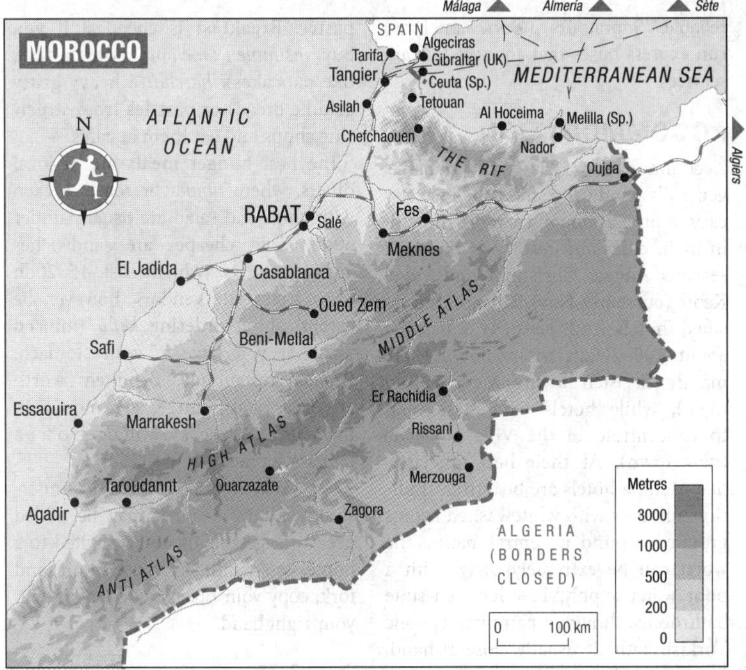

The ports of Ceuta and Tangier are both on the north coast of Morocco and ferries arrive from France (Sète), Italy (Genoa, one per week) and Spain (Algeciras, Tarifa). From Ceuta you can catch buses on to Chefchaouen and Tangier. From Tangier you can catch trains and buses to all of the major cities in Morocco. Boat tickets can be booked online (ⓦwww.comanav.co.uk, ⓦwww.euroferrys.com and ⓦwww.nautasferry.com) or at the ports themselves.

GETTING AROUND

For travel between the major cities, **trains** are the best option. A table of direct and connecting services to any other station is available at any station ticket office or on the ONCF (national rail company) website (ⓦwww.oncf.ma). Couchettes (160dh extra) are available on trains from Tangier to Marrakesh (9hr 30min), and are worth the money for extra comfort and security. Only direct trains are listed in this chapter.

Collective **grands taxis** are usually big Peugeots or Mercedes, plying set routes for a set fare and are much quicker than buses, though the drivers can be reckless. Make clear you only want *une place* (one seat), otherwise drivers may assume you want to charter the whole car. Expect to wait until all six places in the taxi are taken, though you can pay for the extra places if you are in a hurry. Within towns **petits taxis** do short trips, carrying up to three people. They queue in central locations and at stations and can be hailed on streets when they're empty. Payment – usually no more than 15dh – depends on distance travelled.

Buses are marginally cheaper than grands taxis, and cover longer distances, but are slower. CTM (the national company; ⓦwww.ctm.ma) is the most reliable. Supratours (Ⓦwww.oncf.ma) run express buses that connect to train services.

ACCOMMODATION

Accommodation is **inexpensive**, generally good value and usually pretty easy to find, although it's more difficult in main cities and resorts in the peak seasons: August, Christmas, and Aïd el Kebir (currently Nov). Cheap, unclassified hotels and *pensions* (charging about 100–200dh for a double) are mainly in each town's Medina (old town), while hotels with stars tend to concentrate in the Ville Nouvelle (new town). At their best, unclassified Medina hotels are beautiful, traditional houses with whitewashed rooms grouped around a central patio. The worst can be extremely dirty, with a poor water supply. Few have en-suite bathrooms, though a hammam (public Turkish bath) is usually close at hand. Except in Marrakesh, most hotels do not include breakfast in their room price. HI hostels (*auberges de jeunesse*), often bright, breezy and friendly, generally require you to be in by 10 or 11pm and out by 10am daily. Campsites are usually well out of town and tend to charge around 20dh per person plus the same again for your tent.

FOOD AND DRINK

Moroccan cooking is wholesome and filling. The main dish is usually a **tajine** (casserole). Classic *tajines* include chicken with lemon and olives, and lamb with prunes and almonds. The most famous Moroccan dish is **couscous**, a huge bowl of steamed semolina piled with vegetables, mutton, chicken or fish. Restaurant starters include *salade marocaine*, a finely chopped salad of tomato and cucumber, or soup, most often the spicy, bean-based *harira*. Dessert will probably be fruit, yogurt or a pastry. **Breakfast** is cheapest if you buy *msimmen*, *melaoui* (which taste like pancakes), *harsha* (a heavy gritty griddle bread) or pastries from street-side shops and eat them at cafés.

The best **budget meals** are at local diners, where *tajines* or roast chicken with chips and salad are usually under 50dh. Even cheaper are sandwiches and *shwarmas*, which cost 15–20dh from street-side vendors, however, be careful about ordering *kefta* (minced meat) if you have a weak stomach. Fancier restaurants, definitely worth an occasional splurge, are mostly in the Ville Nouvelle and will often offer a bargain set menu at 65–150dh.

Vegetarianism is not widely understood and meat stock may be added even to vegetable dishes. If invited to a home, you're unlikely to use a knife and fork; copy your hosts and eat only with your right hand.

Drink

The national drink is **thé à la menthe** – green tea with a large bunch of mint and a massive amount of sugar. Coffee (*café* in French; *qahwa* in Arabic) is best in French-style cafés. Moroccans tend to take their coffee with half milk and half coffee (*nus-nus*) in a glass. Many cafés and street stalls sell freshly squeezed orange juice, and mineral water is readily available. As an Islamic nation, Morocco gives **alcohol** a low profile, and it's generally impossible to buy in the Medinas; however, bars are always around in the Ville Nouvelle. Moroccan wines, usually red, can be very drinkable, while the best-value **beer** is Flag Speciale. Most local bars are male domains; hotel bars, on the other hand, are more mixed and not much more expensive. The big supermarkets sell alcohol; ask a petit taxi to take you to the nearest Acima or Marjane.

CULTURE AND ETIQUETTE

Morocco is a Muslim country, and in rural areas particularly, people can be quite **conservative** about dress and displays of affection. It's not the done thing to kiss and cuddle in public, nor even for couples to hold hands. Dress is more conservative in rural areas, though even in the cities you can feel uncomfortable in sleeveless tops, short shorts or skirts above the knee. The heat can be oppressive so long, light, loose clothing is best. A shawl allows women to cover up while wearing sleeveless tops.

Be sensitive when taking **photographs**, and always ask permission. In certain places, particularly the Djemaa el Fna in Marrakesh, people may demand money from you just for happening to be in a shot you have taken. Also note that it is illegal to photograph anything considered strategic, such as an airport or a police station.

When invited into people's homes, remove footwear before entering the reception rooms. If invited for a meal, take a gift: a box of sweets from a posh patisserie usually goes down well.

It is acceptable (and a good idea) to try **bargaining** at every opportunity (see box below). If you do it with a smile, you can often get surprising reductions.

Morocco is inexpensive but poor, and **tips** can make a big difference; it's customary to tip café waiters a dirham or two.

SPORTS AND ACTIVITIES

Casablanca and Essaouira cater to **surfers**: the former has better waves while the latter is excellent for windsurfing. Tangier and Rabat have decent beaches but with less developed services. **Mohammedia**, a thirty-minute ride from both Rabat and Casablanca, is a great destination for surfers.

The Moroccan mountain ranges offer great **hiking** opportunities. Good starting points include: Chefchaouen, in the Rif; Fes and Meknes near the Middle Atlas; and Marrakesh, two hours away from Mount Toubkal – the second highest mountain in Africa. Consult local tourist information offices or hotels for advice and details of the trails.

Horseriding is an expensive but increasingly popular way of seeing Morocco. *La Roseraie Hotel*, located in the High Atlas, 60km from Marrakesh, is a great place from which to hire horses and venture into the mountainous countryside. Prices depend on your itinerary but it's not cheap (Ⓣ0524 439128, Ⓦwww.laroseraiehotel.com).

Football is Morocco's most popular sport. You will see it being played in every conceivable open space. If you start up a game on a beach it won't be long before you are joined by some

SHOPPING

You can pick up bargains throughout Morocco, and you will kick yourself if you go home empty-handed. However, getting a price you can brag about in the hostel requires a willingness to enter into the spirit of **haggling**. The first price you will be given will often be at least three and up to ten times more than you should pay. Though quality makes a difference, we've included rough prices for some popular goods you could reasonably fit into a backpack. Fixed-price shops in the Ville Nouvelle also give a good approximation of what you should be paying in the Medina.

- Small kilims (coarse rugs) 500–1500dh
- Leather bags (cheaper in Fes than Marrakesh) 150–300dh
- Leather baboush (slippers) 70–150dh
- Silk scarves 50–100dh
- Jelaba (traditional Moroccan dress) 100–150dh

MOROCCO ONLINE

Ⓦ **www.visitmorocco.com** Moroccan tourist board's website.

Ⓦ **www.babelfan.ma** Arts and culture, including information on festivals throughout Morocco, but in French only.

Ⓦ **www.morocco.com** Huge collection of links to sites about every aspect of Morocco.

Moroccans; equally you'll usually be welcome in pick-up games. All the major cities have teams and money is being poured into new stadiums. For league tables see Ⓦwww.maroc.net/sports and for information on stadiums see Ⓦwww.maroc-football.com.

COMMUNICATIONS

Post offices (PTT) are open Monday to Friday 8am to 4.15pm; larger ones stay open until 6pm, and also open Saturday 8am to noon. You can also buy stamps at postcard shops and sometimes at tobacconists. Always post items at a post office. International phone calls are best made with a phonecard (from post offices and some tobacconists). Alternatively, there are privately run *téléboutiques*, open late. You must dial all ten digits of Moroccan phone numbers. Internet access is available pretty much everywhere, and at low rates: 7–10dh per hour is typical.

EMERGENCIES

Street robbery is rare but not unknown, especially in Tangier and Casablanca. Hotels are generally secure for depositing money; campsites less so. There are two main types of **police** – grey-clad *gendarmes*, with authority outside city limits; and the navy-clad *sûreté* in towns. There's sometimes a brigade of "tourist police" too. Moroccan **pharmacists** are well trained and dispense a wide range of drugs. In most cities there is a night pharmacy, often at the town hall, and a rota of *pharmacies de garde* that stay open till late and at weekends. You can get a list of English-speaking doctors in major cities from consulates. Steer clear of marijuana (*kif*) and hashish – it's illegal, and buying it leaves you vulnerable to scams, as well as potentially large fines and prison sentences.

INFORMATION

There's a **tourist office** (Délégation du Tourisme) run by the Office National Marocain du Tourisme (ONMT) in every major city, and sometimes also a locally funded Syndicat d'Initiative. They stock a limited selection of leaflets and maps, and can put you in touch with official guides. Travel agencies tend to have a fuller range of brochures regarding local activities. There are scores of "unofficial guides", some of whom are genuine students, while others are out-and-out hustlers (though these have been clamped down on). If they do find you, be polite but firm. Note that it's illegal to harass tourists. Tourist offices are usually understocked and often can't give away maps; local bookshops and street-side kiosks are a better bet.

MONEY AND BANKS

The unit of currency is the **dirham** (dh), divided into 100 centimes; in markets, prices may well be in centimes rather than dirhams. There are coins of 10c, 20c, 50c, 1dh, 5dh and 10dh, and notes of 20dh, 50dh, 100dh and 200dh. At the time of writing, £1 = 12.68dh, $1 = 7.87dh, €1 = 11.33. You can get dirhams in Algeciras (Spain) and Gibraltar, and can usually change foreign notes on arrival at

EMERGENCY NUMBERS

Police – Sûreté Ⓣ19, Gendarmes Ⓣ177; Fire and ambulance Ⓣ15.

MOROCCAN ARABIC

Moroccan Arabic is the country's official language, and there are three Berber languages, but much of the country is bilingual in French. For some useful French words and phrases see p.378.

	Moroccan Arabic
Yes	Eyeh
No	La
Please	Afek/Minfadlik
Thank you	Shukran
Hello	Assalam aleikum
Goodbye	Bissalama
Excuse me	Issmahli
Where?	Fayn?
Good	Mezziyen
Bad	Mish Mezziyen
Near (here)	Krayb (min hina)
Far	Baeed
Cheap	Rkhis
Expensive	Ghalee
Open	Mahlul
Closed	Masdud
Today	El Yoom
Yesterday	Imbarih
Tomorrow	Ghedda
How much is...?	Shahal...?
What time is it?	Shahal fisa'a?
I (m) don't understand	Ana mish fahim
I (f) don't understand	Ana mish fahma
Do you (m) speak English?	Takellem ingleezi?
Do you (f) speak English?	Takelma ingleezi?
One	Wahad
Two	Jooj
Three	Tlata
Four	Arba'a
Five	Khamsa
Six	Sitta
Seven	Seba'a
Eight	Temeniya
Nine	Tisaoud
Ten	Ashra

major sea- and airports. For exchange purposes, the most useful and efficient chain of banks is the **BMCE** (Banque Marocaine du Commerce Extérieur). Post offices will also change cash, and there are **bureaux de change** in major cities and tourist resorts. Many banks give cash advances on credit cards, which can also be used in tourist hotels (but not cheap unclassified ones) and the ATMs of major banks. Banking hours are Monday to Friday 8.15am to 3.45pm (Mon–Fri 9.30am–2pm during the holy month of Ramadan).

OPENING HOURS AND HOLIDAYS

Shops and stalls in the souk (bazaar) areas open roughly 9am to 1pm and 3 to 6pm. Ville Nouvelle shops are also likely to close for lunch, and also once a week, usually Sunday. Islamic religious holidays are calculated on the lunar

STUDENT AND YOUTH DISCOUNTS

It is always worth pointing out that you are a student when you are bargaining. However, the informality of most transactions means that there are not many established student discounts. There are a few exceptions, though: ONCF, the train network, has a card for young people that can be purchased for 99dh, which gives you fifty percent reductions on sixteen trips. **Student cards** entitle you to cheaper entry at some museums and other sights, and a small discount on some ferry tickets. They're not worth going out of your way to get, but if you have one you might as well bring it along.

calendar and change each year. In 2012 they fall (approximately) as follows: Feburary 5 is Mouloud (the birthday of Mohammed); Ramadan (when all Muslims fast from sunrise to sunset) roughly July 20 to August 19; the end of Ramadan is celebrated with Aïd es Seghir (aka Aïd el Fitr), a two-day holiday; October 26 is Aïd el Kebir (when Abraham offered to sacrifice his son for God); November 15 is the Muslim New Year. Non-Muslims are not expected to observe Ramadan, but should be sensitive about not breaking the fast in public. Secular holidays are considered less important, with most public services (except banks and offices) operating normally even during the two biggest ones – the Feast of the Throne (July 30), and Independence Day (Nov 18).

Northern Morocco

The northern tip of Morocco contains enough on its own to justify the short ferry ride over from Spain: in three days or so you could check out the delightfully seedy city of **Tangier** and the picturesque little mountain town of **Chefchaouen** in the Rif Mountains.

TANGIER

For the first half of the twentieth century **TANGIER** (Tanja in Arabic; Tanger in French) was an "International City" with its own laws and administration, attracting notoriety through its flamboyant expat community. With independence in 1956, this special status was removed and the expat colony dwindled. Its mixed colonial history and proximity to Spain means that Spanish is a preferred second language. Today Tangier is a grimy but energetic port, mixing modern nightclubs and seedy Moroccan bars with some fine colonial architecture.

What to see and do

The **Grand Socco**, or Zoco Grande – once the main market square (and, since Independence, officially Place du 9 avril 1947) – offers the most straightforward approach to the Medina. The arch at the northwest corner opens onto Rue d'Italie, which leads up to the **Kasbah**. To the right, Rue es Siaghin leads to the atmospheric but seedy **Petit Socco**, or Zoco Chico, the Medina's main square.

ARRIVING IN MOROCCO

From Algeciras (Spain) you can arrive in Morocco either at Tangier or Ceuta. Tangier is the better option as it allows you to connect to all the major transport links, and is itself worth a visit. Ceuta is a dull Spanish enclave with Fnideq, a small but charming Moroccan border town, 3km away. From here you'll have limited transport options.

The Kasbah

To get to the **Kasbah** you can walk from the Petit Socco. Rue des Almohades (aka Rue des Chrétiens) and Rue Ben Raisouli lead to the lower gate. The Kasbah (citadel), walled off from the Medina on the highest rise of the coast, has been the palace and administrative quarter since Roman times. The main point of interest is the former Sultanate Palace, or **Dar el Makhzen** (Mon, Wed, Thurs, Sat & Sun 9am–4pm, Fri 9am–noon & 1.15–4pm; 10dh), now converted into a museum of crafts and antiquities, which gives you an excuse to look around, though the exhibits are rather sparse.

Beaches

Tangier's best **beaches** are a twenty-minute bus ride out of town. There are few vendors selling refreshments, so it's best to bring your own food and drink. **Plage Sidi Kacem** has a trendy beach restaurant, *L'Océan*, that rents out deckchairs and serves hamburgers and European food, as well as being licensed. To get here, take a bus with Route Card Achkar from the Grand Socco; hop off at the *Hotel Mirage* and from here take a petit taxi to the beach (60dh).

Caves of Hercules

Perhaps the area's most popular tourist attraction is the **Caves of Hercules** (Grottes d'Hercule), where the sea has eroded the cave entrance to form the shape of Africa. Buses with Route Card Achkar depart from the Grand Socco; ask the driver to tell you where to get off. The caves (9am–sunset; free) have been occupied since prehistoric times, later serving as a quarry for millstones (you can see the erosion on the walls)

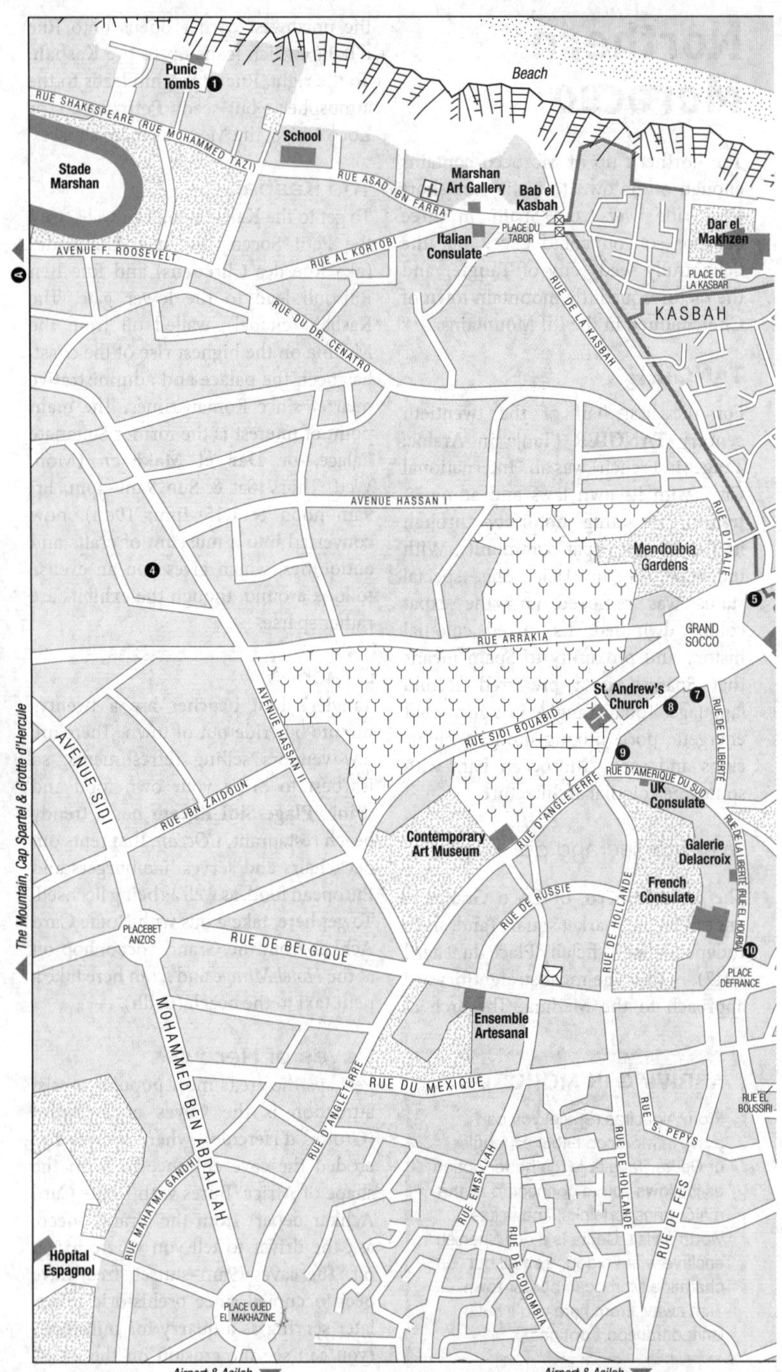
Punic Tombs
1
Beach
RUE SHAKESPEARE (RUE MOHAMMED TAZI)
School
Stade Marshan
RUE ASAD IBN FARRAT
Marshan Art Gallery
Bab el Kasbah
PLACE DU TABOR
Italian Consulate
Dar el Makhzen
PLACE DE LA KASBAR
KASBAH
AVENUE F. ROOSEVELT
RUE AL KORTOBI
RUE DU DR. CENATRO
RUE DE LA KASBAH
A
AVENUE HASSAN I
RUE D'ITALIE
Mendoubia Gardens
4
5
GRAND SOCCO
RUE ARRAKIA
St. Andrew's Church
8
7
9
RUE SIDI BOUABID
AVENUE HASSAN II
RUE DE LA LIBERTE
RUE D'AMERIQUE DU SUD
UK Consulate
AVENUE SIDI
RUE IBN ZAIDOUN
RUE D'ANGLETERRE
Contemporary Art Museum
RUE DE LA LIBERTE (RUE EL HOURIA)
Galerie Delacroix
French Consulate
RUE DE RUSSIE
RUE DE HOLLANDE
10
PLACE DEFRANCE
PLACEBET ANZOS
RUE DE BELGIQUE
The Mountain, Cap Spartel & Grotte d'Hercule
Ensemble Artesanal
MOHAMMED BEN ABDALLAH
RUE D'ANGLETERRE
RUE DU MEXIQUE
RUE EL BOUSSIRI
RUE S. PEPYS
RUE DE HOLLANDE
RUE EMSALLAH
RUE MAHATMA GANDHI
RUE DE FES
RUE DE COLOMBIA
Hôpital Espagnol
PLACE OUED EL MAKHAZINE
Airport & Asilah
Airport & Asilah

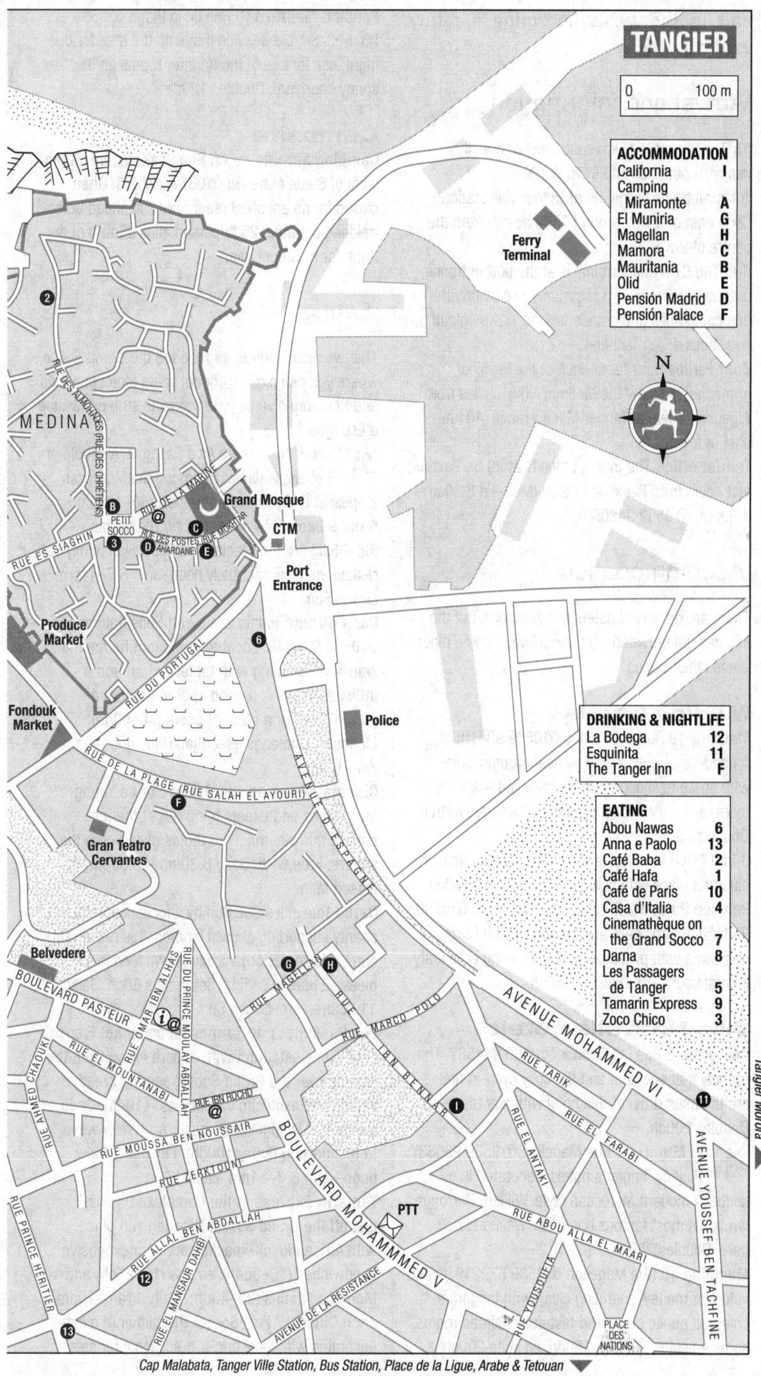
TANGIER
0 100 m
ACCOMMODATION
California I
Camping Miramonte A
El Muniria G
Magellan H
Mamora C
Mauritania B
Olid E
Pensión Madrid D
Pensión Palace F
DRINKING & NIGHTLIFE
La Bodega 12
Esquinita 11
The Tanger Inn F
EATING
Abou Nawas 6
Anna e Paolo 13
Café Baba 2
Café Hafa 1
Café de Paris 10
Casa d'Italia 4
Cinemathèque on the Grand Socco 7
Darna 8
Les Passagers de Tanger 5
Tamarin Express 9
Zoco Chico 3
Ferry Terminal
MEDINA
Grand Mosque
CTM
Port Entrance
Produce Market
Fondouk Market
Police
Gran Teatro Cervantes
Belvedere
PTT
PETIT SOCCO
RUE DES ALMOHADES (RUE DES CHRÉTIENS)
RUE DE LA MARINE
RUE DES POSTES (RUE MOKHTAR AHARDANE)
RUE ES SIAGHIN
RUE DU PORTUGAL
RUE DE LA PLAGE (RUE SALAH EL AYOURI)
AVENUE D'ESPAGNE
BOULEVARD PASTEUR
RUE OMAR IBN ALHAS
RUE DU PRINCE MOULAY ABDALLAH
RUE MAGELLAN
RUE MARCO POLO
RUE IBN BENNAR
AVENUE MOHAMMED VI
RUE TARIK
RUE EL FARABI
RUE EL ANTAKI
RUE EL MOUNTANABI
RUE IBN ROCHD
RUE AHMED CHAOUKI
RUE MOUSSA BEN NOUSSAIR
RUE ZERKTOUNI
BOULEVARD MOHAMMED V
RUE ABOU ALLA EL MAARI
AVENUE YOUSSEF BEN TACHFINE
RUE ALLAL BEN ABDALLAH
RUE EL MANSOUR DAHBI
AVENUE DE LA RESISTANCE
RUE YOUSSOUFIA
RUE PRINCE HERITIER
PLACE DES NATIONS
Tangier Morora
Cap Malabata, Tanger Ville Station, Bus Station, Place de la Ligue, Arabe & Tetouan

and in the 1920s becoming a rather exotic brothel.

Arrival and information

Air The airport is 15km southwest of the city centre. A petit taxi into town is 100dh.
Train All trains terminate at Tanger Ville station (2km east of town), around 15dh by cab from the centre of town.
Bus The CTM bus terminal is at the port entrance, but the gare routière bus station used by private bus companies and grands taxis is 1.5km inland on Ave Youssef Ben Tachfine.
Boat Ferries from Tarifa dock at the terminal immediately below the Medina, while ferries from Algeciras arrive at Tanger Mediterranée, 40 km east of town.
Tourist office The tourist office is at 29 Bd Pasteur, just down from Place de France (Mon–Fri 8.30am–4.30pm; ⓣ0539 948050).

Accommodation

There are dozens of hotels and *pensions*, but the city can get crowded in summer, when some places double their prices.

Medina hotels

Mamora 19 Rue des Postes ⓣ0539 934105. A good-value option with pleasant rooms, some with en-suite showers; make sure you ask for a room facing the mosque, as the views are worth it. Doubles 250dh.
Olid 12 Rue des Postes ⓣ0539 931310. Intensely colourful place with basic rooms. Doubles 150dh.
Pension Palace 2 Rue Mokhtar Ahardane ⓣ0539 936128. Rooms here are simple, all with basins and some with passable showers, giving off a leafy central courtyard. Doubles 150dh.

Ville Nouvelle hotels

California 8 Rue Ibn Bennar ⓣ0539 944587. The friendly management and the cosy lived-in feel are the main draw at this hotel with airy rooms. Doubles 200dh.
El Muniria 1 Rue Magellan ⓣ0539 935337. Pick of Tangier's hotels, decorated in a laidback modern Moroccan style. William Burroughs wrote his most famous book, *The Naked Lunch*, here. Doubles 250dh.
Magellan 16 Rue Magellan ⓣ0539 372319. Great value for money, sparkling clean with tangerine-coloured public areas and tastefully painted rooms, some en suite. Doubles 150dh, en suite 200dh.
Pension Madrid 140 Rue de la Plage ⓣ0539 931693. Simple *pension* that'll do the trick for one night; ask for one of the brighter rooms on the sunny courtyard. Doubles 120dh.

Campsite

Camping Miramonte off Rue Shakespeare, 300m west of Stade Marshan ⓣ0672 207055. Often closed for no apparent reason, so call ahead before trekking out here. 25dh/person, plus 25dh/tent or 30dh for a camper van.

Eating

The two main centres for food are the Grand Socco, where you can pick up cheap, filling Moroccan food and the more diverse (and licensed) strip on Avenue d'Espagne.
Abou Nawas 30 Av d'Espagne. A couple of Lebanese dishes in among the Moroccan staples at this place near the port (60–100dh).
Anna e Paolo 77 Prince Heritier. The pastas (65–85dh) are the speciality at this Italian family-run restaurant. Licensed. Daily noon–3pm & 7–11pm; closed Sun.
Casa d'Italia Palais des Institutions Italiennes ⓣ0539 936348. Located in a beautiful Andalusian-style building with tables set around a little patio, this is a good spot to dig into a pizza (75dh) or a plate of pasta (40–60dh). Licensed. Bookings essential. Daily noon–3pm & 7–11pm.
Cinemathèque on the Grand Socco Young Moroccans and expats hang out at the hip café of this cinema, with tables giving onto the square. Free wi-fi. Daily 8.30am–10.30pm, closed Mon.
Darna Rue Jules Cot. Run by a local nonprofit charity supporting abused women, this restaurant-cum-café serves organically grown food in a pleasant garden setting. Set menus 60dh. Daily 11.30am–4pm, closed Sun.
Les Passagers de Tanger An upmarket French café-cum-restaurant with superb views from the terrace over the Grand Socco, serving creative salads and exquisite carpaccios (110dh). Once a month DJs spin some music from new wave to techno-pop (entry 100dh). Licensed. Daily noon–4pm & 7–11pm, closed Sun.
Tamarin Express in the Complexe Dawliz, just off the Grand Socco. Nigerian-run place with African knick-knacks serving inexpensive sandwiches (10–30dh), salads (10–25dh) and Moroccan mains (25–40dh). Daily 11am–10pm.
Zoco Chico 17 Petit Socco. This slither of a café decorated with local bric-a-brac, some for sale,

TANGIER'S CAFÉ CULTURE

Tangier is best enjoyed from a café and the Petit Socco is packed with them, each offering the opportunity to relax and observe the hustle on the street. Don't miss these two further-flung places: **Café Hafa** is cut into the cliff face and looks across the Mediterranean to Spain; **Café Baba** (take the street into the Dar el Makhzen and turn down the right-hand fork at Place Amrah where it's signposted). Both cafés are very popular with locals and frequented by Ludo-playing Moroccans. For a more upmarket choice, head for Tangier's most famous and reputedly oldest café, the **Café de Paris** on Place de France.

serves hummus and falafel, as well as smoothies (25dh) and refreshing iced teas. Daily 9am–8pm.

Drinking and nightlife

Many of Tangier's nightlife venues attract a rather seedy crowd; the places listed below are the most dependable.

Esquinita Av Mohammed VI. This bar with DJ gets lively on weekends and is one of the few places along the seafront that doesn't attract a seedy crowd. Daily 7pm–4am.

La Bodega 5 Av Allal Ben Abdallah. Cosy bar-restaurant with red undertones; serves decent tapas (50dh). Daily 11am–4pm & 5pm–2am.

The Tanger Inn Mingle with young Moroccans at this lively joint which was once frequented by the Beat Generation authors (Burroughs, Ginsberg and Kerouac); beers 25dh, mixers 45dh. Thurs, Fri & Sat are best, closed Sun off-season. Daily 10pm–1.30am.

Directory

Consulates UK, Trafalgar House, 9 Rue de l'Amérique du Sud ⓣ0539 936939 or 40.

Exchange BMCE, 19 Bd Pasteur has a bureau de change and ATM. Bureaux de change on Rue es Siaghin between the Grand and Petit Socco.

Internet Teleboutique, Bd Pasteur (daily 8am–1am; 10dh/hr); Cyber Adnan, rue de la Marine, Medina (daily 3pm–2am; 10dh).

Pharmacies There are several English-speaking pharmacies on Place de France and Bd Pasteur.

Post office Main PTT, 33 Bd Mohammed V.

Police The Brigade Touristique are based at the former train station by the port ⓣ0539 940477.

Moving on

The overnight train from Tangier to Marrakesh allows you to venture south without losing time. If you want to go east (such as to Chefchaouen) take a bus.

Train Casablanca Voyageurs (8 daily; 5hr); Fes (4 daily; 4hr); Marrakesh (7 daily; 11hr); Meknes (4 daily; 3hr 55min); Rabat (8 daily; 4hr).

Bus Casablanca (41 daily; 6hr); Chefchaouen (7 daily; 3hr 30min); Fes (17 daily; 5hr 45min); Fnideq (for Ceuta) (15 daily; 1hr); Marrakesh (11 daily; 10hr); Meknes (9 daily; 7hr); Rabat (39 daily; 5hr); Tetouan (50 daily; 1hr 30min).

Ferry Algeciras, Spain (18–25 daily; 1hr–2hr 30min); Genoa (1 weekly; 48hr), Gibraltar (1 weekly; 1hr 30min), Sète (1 every 4–5 days; 36hr); Tarifa, Spain (8 daily; 35min).

CEUTA/FNIDEQ

Due to the fast ferry, the drab Spanish enclave of **CEUTA** is a popular entry point for travellers coming from Spain. On disembarking you have to catch a taxi or local bus to the Moroccan border. Once across the border there are lots of grands taxis that will take you the 3km to the Moroccan town of **FNIDEQ** (3dh). Arrive early to leave time for moving on.

Fnideq has some pleasant **hotels** along the one main road, Mohammad V; *Hotel Nador* at no. 134 (ⓣ0539 675345; doubles 150dh) is the cheapest option while *Hotel Fnideq* at no. 172 (ⓣ0539 675467; 250dh) is far cleaner and more comfortable. If you're looking for a restaurant, try the moderately priced seafood restaurant *La Costa* at 232 Mohammad V.

Moving on

The bus station is signposted at the roundabout where the seafront and Av Mohammad V meet, marked by a fountain. Buses are infrequent, so it's often quicker and similarly priced to get a grand taxi to Tetouan or Tangier for better connections.

Bus Casablanca (6 daily; 8hr); Marrakesh (2 daily; 11hr); Meknes (1 daily; 7hr); Rabat (6 daily; 7hr); Tangier (15 daily; 1hr); Tetouan (8 daily; 30min).
Ferry Algeciras, mainland Spain (16–20 daily; 35min; €36). Tickets can be booked at Ceuta port; it is advisable to arrive an hour early. Times to avoid are at the end of Easter week and the last week of August due to a huge increase in demand.
Taxi Those to Tetouan and Chefchaouen are at Fnideq bus station, while those for Tangier can be picked up by 280 Av Mohammed V.

TETOUAN

Coming from Ceuta, you usually need to pick up onward transport at **TETOUAN**, a rather dull town with nothing much to do or see – but a grand taxi from Fnideq will leave you close enough to Tetouan's bus station, a twenty-minute walk southeast of town, to head straight out again. There are regular buses to Meknes, Fes and destinations nationwide. For Tangier, Chefchaouen or Ceuta it's easiest to travel by grand taxi. The ONCF office on Avenue 10 Mai, alongside Place Al Adala, sells train tickets that include a shuttle bus to Tangier from where you can catch a connecting train service. There aren't any hotels by the bus station but if you're stuck in Tetouan, there's the inexpensive *Principe*, 20 Av Youssef Ibn Tachfine (ⓣ0533 113128; doubles 140dh), on the corner of Boulevard de Mouquaouama.

Moving on

Bus Casablanca (31 daily; 6hr); Chefchaouen (19 daily; 2hr); Fes (14 daily; 5hr 20min); Fnideq (for Ceuta) (8 daily; 1hr); Marrakesh (8 daily; 10hr); Meknes (6 daily; 6hr); Rabat (25 daily; 5hr); Tangier (50 daily; 1hr 30min).

CHEFCHAOUEN

Shut in by a fold of the Rif Mountains, **CHEFCHAOUEN** (sometimes abbreviated to Chaouen or Xaouen) had, until the arrival of Spanish troops in 1920, been visited by just three Europeans. It's a town of extraordinary light and colour, its whitewash tinted with blue and edged by golden stone walls. *Pensions* are friendly and cheap and Chefchaouen is one of the best places to spend your first few days in Morocco.

The main entrance to the Medina is a tiny arched entrance, Bab el Ain, but the quickest way to negotiate your way to the centre is to get a petit taxi to **Place el Makhzen** (ask for the Kasbah), where you will find *Hotel Parador*, an expensive hotel, but a good place to pop into for a beer (23dh) or a swim (100dh). From here it is only a two-minute walk to **Place Outa el Hammam**, where most of the town's evening life takes place. By day the town's focus is the **Kasbah** (Mon, Wed, Thurs, Sat & Sun 9am–1pm & 3–6.30pm, Fri 9am–noon & 3–6.30pm, Tues 3–6.30pm; 10dh), a quiet ruin with shady gardens and a small museum, which occupies one side of the square.

Chefchaouen is best enjoyed pottering around the Medina and relaxing at coffee shops or on your terrace. For the more adventurous there are **hiking** trails that start from the town. Or you can catch a grand taxi from Place el Makhzen to go to the **Oued Laou beach** (250dh), about sixty kilometres away, or hike along rivers and waterfalls at **Akchour**, a 30min grand taxi ride away.

Arrival and information

Arrival Buses arrive at the station southwest of town; it's a 15min uphill walk into the centre, or a 10dh petit taxi ride. Grands taxis drop you outside the town walls.
Tourist office There is no tourist office in Chefchaouen, but your hotel should be able to help with general information.

Accommodation

Hostel

HI hostel Rue Sidi Abdelhamid ⓣ0666 865355, ⓔsarham03@live.fr. A very inexpensive but basic and somewhat inconveniently located hostel, fifteen minutes' walk uphill from town, just by the campsite. Dorms 40dh.

Hotels

Hotel Andaluz 1 Rue Sidi Salem ⓣ0539 986034. The sombre colours of the entrance and the simple rooms make this the least appealing of the cheap options; staff are friendly though, and there's a very decent English-language book collection. Doubles 120dh.

Hotel Ouarzazat Avde Alkharazine ⓣ0539 988990. Rooms are decked out in local furniture and bathrooms are pretty spick and span. Doubles 120dh.

Pension La Castellena 4 Sidi Ahmed El Bouhali ⓣ0539 986295. The entire hotel is done out in Chefchaouen's gentle blue and white, while the beautifully decorated rooms are all individually furnished and painted by hand with colourful motifs. Doubles 150dh.

Campsite

Camping Azilan Rue Sidi Abdelhamid ⓣ0539 986979, ⓦwww.campingchefchaouen.com. Located up on the hill above town, by the modern *Hôtel Asma*. Chefchaouen's campsite is inexpensive but can be crowded in summer. 25dh/person, plus 20dh/tent.

Eating and drinking

Café Restaurant Chams Place Outa El Hammam. A laidback joint perfect to stop by for a tea (10dh) mid-afternoon or a *tajine* (30dh) in the evening; head up to the roof terrace for a view of the square and a welcome breeze on a hot day. Daily 8am–11pm.

Casa Aladin Rue Targi 17, off the north end of Place Outa El Hammam. Two floors and a terrace, beautifully done out in *Arabian Nights* style, as its name suggests, serving great *tajines*, couscous (including vegetarian) and other staple fare (mains 45dh, set menus 75dh). Daily noon–11pm.

Restaurant Al Kasba North end of Place Outa El Hammam. Cushioned partitions and fun decor make this a relaxed place to have a decent spot of food for lunch or dinner (mains 30–50dh, menu 60dh). Daily 8am–11pm.

Moving on

Buy tickets a day in advance for Fes and Meknes.

Bus Casablanca (4 daily; 9hr); Fes (7 daily; 5hr); Meknes (3 daily; 5hr 30min); Rabat (4 daily; 8hr); Tangier (7 daily; 3hr 30min); Tetouan (19 daily; 2hr).

Central Morocco

Between the mountain ranges of the Rif to the north and the Atlas to the south lie the cities that form Morocco's heart: the great imperial cities of **Meknes** and **Fes**, the modern capital, **Rabat**, and the country's largest city and commercial capital, **Casablanca**.

MEKNES

More than any other Moroccan town, **MEKNES** is associated with a single figure, the Sultan Moulay Ismail, during whose reign (1672–1727) the city went from provincial centre to spectacular capital showcasing over fifty palaces and fifteen miles of exterior walls. Today Meknes is a more sedate and calm version of Marrakesh, where the Medina's palaces and monuments reward a day's exploration. The town also serves as a perfect base to explore the ancient sites of **Volubilis** and **Moulay Idriss** nearby.

What to see and do

The heart of the town, **Place El Hedim** originally formed the western corner of the Medina, but Moulay Ismail had the houses here demolished to provide a grand approach to his palace quarter. There are a fair few sights to explore leading off the *place*.

The Dar Jamaï and the souks

The **Dar Jamaï** (daily except Tues 9am–6pm; 10dh), at the back of Place El Hedim, is a superb example of a nineteenth-century Moroccan palace, and the museum inside is one of the best in Morocco, with a fantastic display of Middle Atlas carpets. The lane immediately to the left of the Dar Jamaï takes you

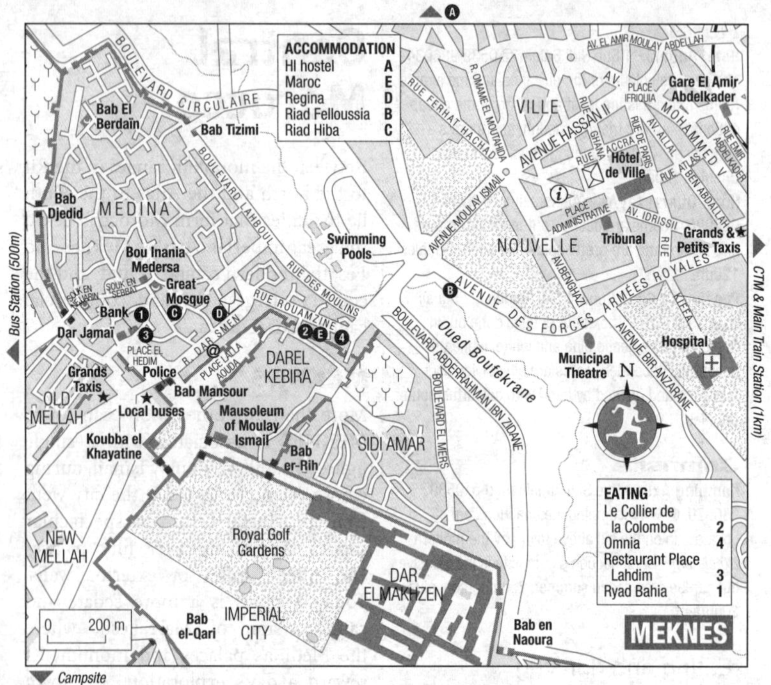

to the Medina's major market street: on your left is **Souk en Nejjarin**, the carpet souk; on your right, leading to the Great Mosque and Bou Inania Medersa, are the fancier goods offered in the **Souk es Sebbat**. The **Bou Inania Medersa** (daily 9am–6pm; 10dh), constructed around 1340–50, has an unusual ribbed dome over the entrance hall and from the roof you can look out to the tiled pyramids of the Great Mosque.

The Koubba el Khayatine and Moulay Ismail's Mausoleum

Behind the magnificent Bab Mansour (open for occasional exhibitions) is Place Lalla Aouda. Straight ahead and bearing left, you come into another open square, on the right of which is the green-tiled dome of the **Koubba el Khayatine**, once a reception hall for ambassadors to the imperial court (daily 9am–5pm; 10dh). Below it a stairway descends into a vast series of subterranean vaults, known as the **Prison of Christian Slaves**, though it was probably a storehouse or granary. Nearby is the entrance to **Moulay Ismail's Mausoleum** (daily except Fri 9–11.30am & 2.30–6.30pm; 10dh donation expected), where you can approach the sanctuary.

Volubilis and Moulay Idriss

A short grand taxi ride from Meknes (300dh for return trip plus 2 hr waiting time) takes you to two of the most important sites in Morocco's history. **Volubilis** (daily 8am–7pm; 10dh) was once the Roman capital of the province; it is still possible to follow the outline of the old city and walk among some well-preserved ruins. At the time of research an on-site museum was under construction, where Roman artefacts housed across Morocco are to be reunited in their place of origin. **Moulay Idriss** was established by the Prophet's great-grandson who is credited with bringing Islam to Morocco. Today, it is a small but bustling town, which Moroccans treat with great respect. It is worth a trip for the views from the top of the town and for an insight into the religious heart of Morocco (particularly true in the festival that takes place in the second week of August). However, non-Muslims are barred from visiting the religious shrines of Moulay Idriss for which the town is famous.

Arrival and information

Train Meknes has two train stations, both in the Ville Nouvelle. All trains stop at Gare de Ville, but Gare El Amir Abdelkader (some services only) is more central.

Bus and taxi Private buses and most grands taxis arrive west of the Medina by Bab el Khemis; CTM buses arrive at their terminus on Avde Fès, near the Gare de Ville, and grands taxis from Fes will drop you in town on their way through.

Tourist office on Place Hedim, Medina (daily 10am–1pm & 4–6pm; ⓣ0535 531733) and at 27 Place Administrative, Ville Nouvelle (Mon–Fri 8.30am–4.30pm; ⓣ0535 516022).

Accommodation

The most atmospheric place to stay is in the Medina, where everything is on your doorstep. All places listed below are in the Medina, unless stated otherwise.

Hostel

HI hostel Ave Okba Ben Nafi, Ville Nouvelle ⓣ0535 524698, ⓔaubergejeune_meknes@hotmail.fr. A 1.5km walk northwest of the city centre, or a 10dh taxi ride. Small rooms, but the place is relatively well maintained and friendly. Breakfast included. Dorms 60dh, twins 75dh.

Hotels

Maroc 7 Rue Rouamzine ⓣ0535 530075. The spartan rooms on the interior courtyard benefit from a welcome cross-breeze, while the hole-in-the-floor bathrooms could do with similar ventilation. Those on restricted budgets can sleep on the rooftop beds for 50dh. Doubles 200dh.

Regina 19 Rue Dar Smen ⓣ0535 530280. A smile at reception helps compensate for the dingy rooms where the bedsprings may well have supported the weight of one too many *tajine*-fed guests. Laundry 50dh. Doubles 120dh.

Riad Hiba 20 Rue Lalla Aicha Addouya ⓣ0535 460109, ⓦwww.riadhiba.com. Heavy ornate furnishings and added bonuses like flat-screen cable TV, a/c and wi-fi. Doubles 330dh.

TREAT YOURSELF

Riad Felloussia 23 Derb Hammam Jdid (ⓣ0535 530840, ⓦwww.riadfelloussia.com). The quaint labyrinthine corridor leads you to a beautiful indoor garden with a tiled fountain and cedar beams, and the riad's five large rooms are beautifully decorated with local fabrics and materials. Breathtaking views from the rooftop terrace, too. Doubles 770dh.

Eating

There are cheap eats on Rue Rouamzine near *Hôtel Maroc* and you can also pick up inexpensive bites from one of the many restaurants in Place Hedim.

Le Collier de la Colombe 67 Rue Driba. The speciality here is Atlas mountain trout (90dh), to be savoured on the rooftop terrace with sunset views over the golden Medina. Daily 11.30am–4pm & 6.30–11pm.

Omnia 8 Derb Ain El Fouki. Friendly, welcoming restaurant set in a family home courtyard brimming with local knick-knacks. Sit in one of the little cushioned salons as fresh aromas from the menu of the day (65dh) waft out of the kitchen. Daily 10am–11pm.

Restaurant Place Lahdim North corner of Place El Hedim. Tuck into some generous portions of tasty Moroccan food (50dh) or unwind on the terrace with some mint tea as you ponder daily life in the square below. Daily 10am–11pm.

Ryad Bahia Tiberbarine. Dig into some home-made food at this pleasant, family-style riad; the friendly, well-travelled owners will make you feel at home as the delicious traditional food is prepared (from 70dh). Daily noon–4pm & 7–10.30pm.

Moving on

Train Casablanca Voyageurs (11 daily; 3hr 20min); Fes (11 daily; 35min); Marrakesh (7 daily; 6hr 30min); Rabat (11 daily; 2hr 10min); Tangier (4 daily; 4hr).

Bus Casablanca (20 daily; 4hr 30min); Chefchaouen (4 daily; 5hr 30min); Fes (roughly every 30min; 1hr); Marrakesh (6 daily; 9hr); Rabat (hourly; 3hr); Tangier (9 daily; 7hr); Tetouan (6 daily; 6hr).

FES (FEZ)

The most ancient of the imperial capitals, **FES** (Fez in English) stimulates the senses and seems to exist somewhere between the Middle Ages and the modern world. Some two hundred thousand of the city's half-million inhabitants (though actual figures are probably much higher than official ones) live in the oldest part of the Medina, Fes el Bali.

What to see and do

Getting lost is one of the great joys of the Fes Medina. However, if you want a more informed approach, pick up a small green book called "Fes" from the paper kiosks; this book corresponds to the tourist trails within the Medina that are marked out by coloured stars. Tour guides also can be employed at the Bab Boujeloud; the official ones wear medallions to identify themselves. One excellent registered local guide is Younes Darif who speaks impeccable English (Ⓣ668741402, Ⓔyounesdarif@hotmail.fr).

Talâa Kebira

Talâa Kebira, the Medina's main artery, is home to the most brilliant of Fes's monuments, the **Medersa Bou Inania** (daily 9am–5pm; closes 4pm during Ramadan; 10dh), which comes close to perfection in every aspect of its construction, with beautiful carved wood, stucco and *zellij* tilework. Continuing down Talâa Kebira you reach the entrance to the **Souk el Attarin** (Souk of the Spice Vendors), the formal heart of the city. To the right, a street leads past the charming **Souk el Henna** – a tree-shaded square where traditional cosmetics are sold – to Place Nejjarin (Carpenters' Square). Here, next to the geometric tilework of the Nejjarin Fountain, is the imposing eighteenth-century **Nejjarin Fondouk**, now a woodwork museum (daily 9am–5pm; 20dh), though the building is rather more interesting than its exhibits. Immediately to the right of the fountain, Talâa Seghira is an alternative route back to Bab Boujeloud, while the alley to the right of that is the aromatic **carpenters' souk**, ripe with the scent of sawn cedar, and top on the list of great Medina smells.

Zaouia Moulay Idriss II

The street opposite the Nejjarin Fountain leads to the **Zaouia Moulay**

FES ORIENTATION

Fes can be difficult to get to grips with, orientation-wise. The Medina in Fes is uniquely vast and beautiful, with two distinct parts: the newer section, **Fes el Djedid**, established in the thirteenth century, is mostly taken up by the Royal Palace; the older part, **Fes el Bali**, founded in the eighth century on the River Fes, was populated by refugees from Tunisia on one bank – the **Kairaouine** quarter – and from Spain on the other bank – the **Andalusian** quarter. In practice, almost everything you will want to see is in the Kairaouine quarter. There are several different gates through which you can enter the old city. **Bab Boujeloud** is the most popular and recognizable entry point and is a useful landmark. From here you can turn left at the *Restaurant La Kasbah* to get on to Talâa Kabira, the Medina's main thoroughfare. From the north, **Bab el Guissa** offers another port of entry. For views of the Medina have a drink at the *Hotel Palais Jamaï* (next to Bab Jamaï) or *Hotel les Merenides*. There's an impressive view from the Arms Museum in the fort above the bus station (daily except Mon 8.30am–6pm; 10dh).

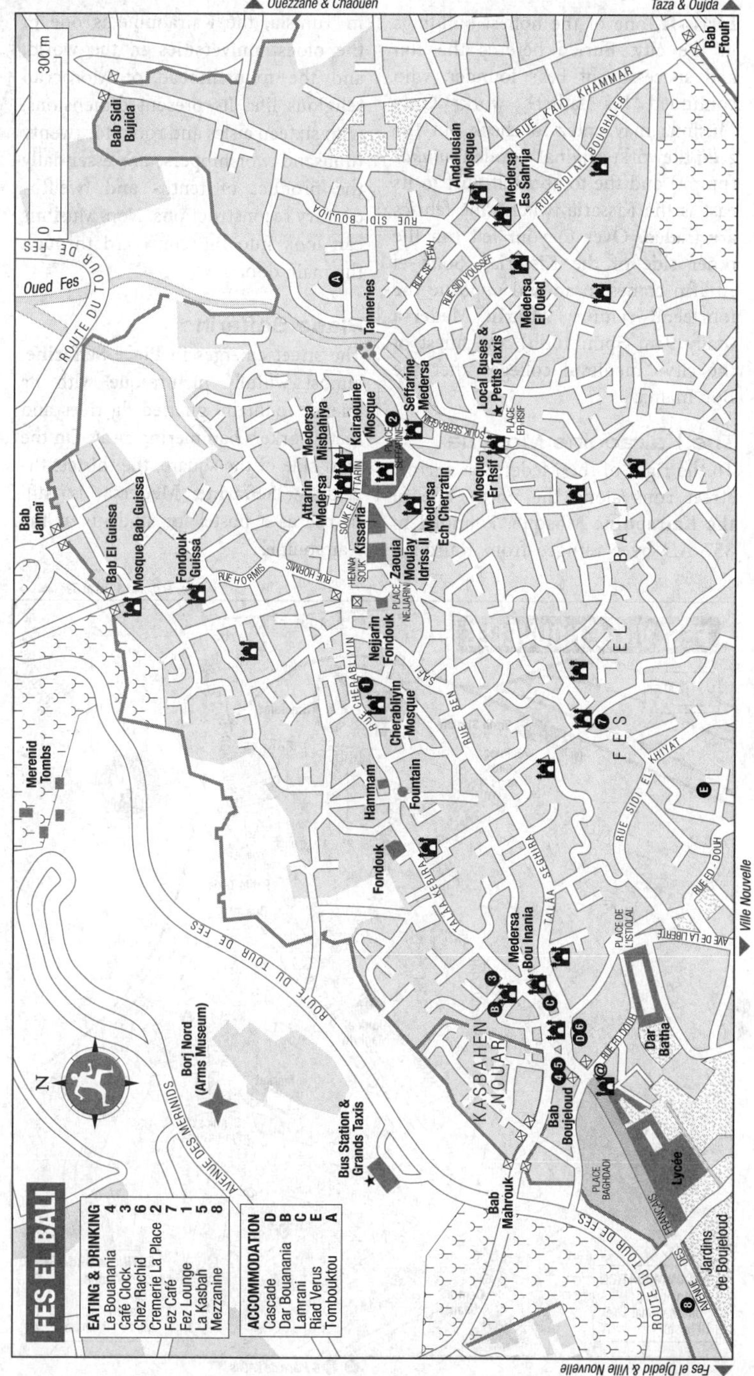
FES EL BALI
EATING & DRINKING
Le Bouanania 4
Café Clock 3
Chez Rachid 6
Cremerie La Place 2
Fez Café 7
Fez Lounge 1
La Kasbah 5
Mezzanine 8
ACCOMMODATION
Cascade D
Dar Bouanania B
Lamrani C
Riad Verus E
Tombouktou A
0
300 m
Ouezzane & Chaouen
Taza & Oujda
Fes el Djedid & Ville Nouvelle
Ville Nouvelle
Bab Sidi Bujida
Bab Ftouh
Oued Fes
Route du Tour de Fes
Avenue des Merinids
Merenid Tombs
Borj Nord (Arms Museum)
Bus Station & Grands Taxis
Bab Mahrouk
Bab Boujeloud
Kasbahen Nouar
Place Baghdadi
Lycée
Jardins de Boujeloud
Dar Batha
Place de l'Istiqlal
Ave de la Liberte
Rue Fd Douh
Medersa Bou Inania
Talâa Kebira
Talâa Seghira
Fondouk
Hammam
Fountain
Cherabliyin Mosque
Rue Cherabliyin
Rue Ben Safi
Neijarin Fondouk
Place Nejjarin
Henna Souk
Zaouia Moulay Idriss II
Kissaria
Souk el Attarin
Attarin Medersa
Medersa Misbahiya
Kairaouine Mosque
Place Seffarine
Seffarine Medersa
Medersa Ech Cherratin
Souk Sebbaghin
Mosque Er Rsif
Place Er Rsif
Local Buses & Petits Taxis
Tanneries
Medersa El Oued
Rue Sidi Youssef
Rue Se Ffah
Rue Sidi Boujida
Andalusian Mosque
Medersa Es Sahrija
Rue Sidi Ali Boughaleb
Rue Kaid Khammar
Rue Sidi el Khiyat
Fes el Bali
Rue Hormis
Fondouk Guissa
Mosque Bab Guissa
Bab El Guissa
Bab Jamaï

Idriss II, one of the holiest buildings in the city. Buried here is the son and successor of Fes's founder, who continued his father's work. Only Muslims may enter to check out the *zellij* tilework, original wooden *minbar* (pulpit) and the tomb itself. Just to its east is the Kissaria, where fine fabrics are traded. Over to your left (on the other side of the Kissaria), Souk el Attarin comes to an end opposite the fourteenth-century **Attarin Medersa** (daily 9am–5pm; 10dh), the finest of the city's medieval colleges after the Bou Inania.

The Kairaouine Mosque

To the right of the Medersa, a narrow street runs along the north side of the **Kairaouine Mosque**. Founded in 857 AD by a refugee from Kairouan in Tunisia, the Kairaouine is one of the oldest universities in the world, and the fountainhead of Moroccan religious life. Its present dimensions, with sixteen aisles and room for twenty thousand worshippers, are essentially the product of tenth- and twelfth-century reconstructions. Non-Muslims can look into the courtyard through the main door.

Place Seffarine

The street emerges in **Place Seffarine**, almost wilfully picturesque with its faïence fountain, gnarled fig trees and metalworkers hammering away. On the west side of the square, the thirteenth-century **Seffarine Medersa** is still in use as a hostel for students at the Kairaouine.

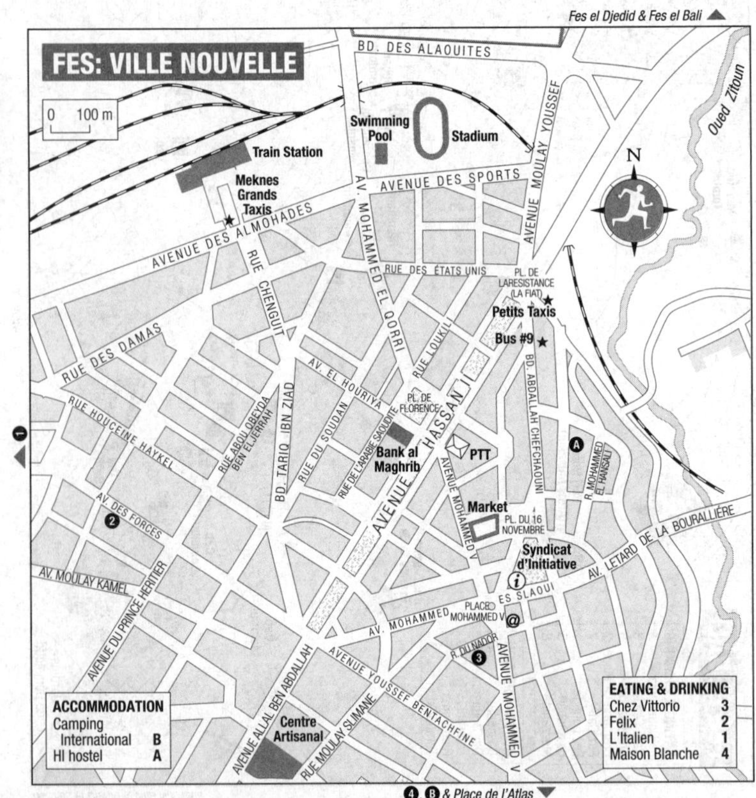

Souk Sabbighin

If you're beginning to find the medieval prettiness of the central souks and *medersas* slightly repetitive, then the area beyond the square should provide the antidote. The dyers' market – **Souk Sabbighin** – is directly south of the Seffarine Medersa, and is draped with fantastically coloured yarn and cloth drying in the heat. Below, workers in grey toil over cauldrons of multicoloured dyes. **Place er Rsif**, nearby, has buses and taxis to the Ville Nouvelle.

The tanneries

The street to the left (north) of the Seffarine Medersa leads to the rather smelly tanneries, constantly visited by tour groups with whom you could discreetly tag along if you get lost. Inside the tanneries water deluges through holes that were once windows of houses. Hundreds of skins lie spread out on the rooftops, above vats of dye and the pigeon dung used to treat the leather. Straight on, the road eventually leads back round to the Attarin Medersa.

Arrival and information

Train The train station is in the Ville Nouvelle, 15min walk north of the hotels around Place Mohammed V. If you prefer to stay in the Medina, take a petit taxi (10dh), or take bus #19 which will drop you off at R'Cif in the Medina; alternatively, walk down to Place de la Résistance (aka La Fiat) and pick up bus #9 to Dar Batha/Place de l'Istiqlal, near the western gate to Fes el Bali, Bab Boujeloud.

Bus The bus station is just outside the walls near Bab Boujeloud. The terminal for CTM buses is off Rue de l'Atlas, which links the far end of Av Mohammed V with Place de l'Atlas.

Taxi Grands taxis mostly operate from the bus station; exceptions include some of those serving Meknes (from the train station).

Tourist office Place Mohammed V (Mon–Fri 8.30am–4.30pm; ⓣ0535 623460) can tell you about June's seven-day Festival of World Sacred Music (ⓣ0535 740535, ⓦwww.fesfestival.com) and the five-day cherry festival which usually follows immediately after it in nearby Sefrou.

Accommodation

There's a shortage of hotel space in all categories, so be prepared for higher-than-usual prices; booking ahead is advisable. For atmosphere and character, the Medina is the place to be. The following are marked on the map on p.803, unless otherwise stated.

Hostels

HI hostel 18 Rue Abdeslam Seghrini, Ville Nouvelle ⓣ0535 624085. See map opposite. One of Morocco's best hostels – well kept, friendly and spotlessly clean. Breakfast included. Dorms 55dh.

Riad Verus 1 Derb Arset Bennis, Batha, Medina ⓣ0535 741941 ⓦwww.riadverus.com. A snazzy riad-cum-hostel with immaculate rooms, most with en suite, as well as a roof terrace and soundproof music lounge. Dorms 220dh, doubles 880dh.

Medina hotels

Cascade Just inside Bab Boujeloud, Fes el Bali ⓣ0535 638442, ⓔcascadasplaza@gmail.com. An old building with a useful public hammam (bathhouse) just behind. Rooms are small and basic, but management friendly; the fantastic view from the terrace, where you can drink if you bring your own, is the real draw. Doubles 180dh.

Dar Bouanania 21 Derb ben Salem (signposted on Talâa Kebira) ⓣ0535 637282, ⓔdarbouanania@gmail.com. Not quite a riad, but the budget equivalent, with spacious rooms and traditional decor for reasonable enough prices. Doubles 400dh.

Lamrani Talâa Seghira, Fes el Bali ⓣ0535 634411. Friendly and by far the best of the cheapie options just opposite a hammam, Doubles 120dh.

Tombouktou 32 Bis Ouad Zhoune ⓣ0535 638851. Moroccan bling is the decor of choice at this clean hotel with a/c and cable TV. The patio with antique collectible cars gives the place a pinch of fun. Doubles 250dh.

Campsite

Camping International Route de Sefrou ⓣ0535 618061. See map opposite. Some 4km south of town, this site is pricey for a campsite but has good facilities, including a pool in summer. Take bus #38 from Place de l'Atlas. 40dh/person, plus 30dh/tent.

Eating

Fes el Bali has two main areas for cheap local food: around Bab Boujeloud and along Rue Hormis (running from Souk el Attarin towards Bab Guissa), while the Ville Nouvelle is mainly home to pricier Western-style restaurants serving European cuisine.

Fes el Bali

Café Clock 7 Derb El Magana. A maze of little comfy salons lead off the three-tiered courtyard; forget *tajines* – you're here for the camel burger (95dh) or the falafel with hummus and tabbouleh (55dh). Daily 8.30am–10pm.

Chez Rachid Inside Bab Boujeloud. One of the friendlier and most welcoming of the numerous street restaurants, with tasty *brochettes* and the usual nosh from 40dh. Daily 11am–11.30pm.

Cremerie La Place On the northeast corner of Place Seffarine. Tiny café perfect to enjoy a tea (10dh) and delectable patisseries (15dh) as you watch the coppersmiths hammering and shaping merchandise under the shade of the picturesque plane tree. Daily 8am–8pm, closed Fri.

Fez Café 13 Akbat Sbaa. Walk through a beautiful oasis of greenery to reach the shady patio of this quiet café where you can enjoy a detox tea (20dh) or a fresh juice (25dh); hungry bellies should come by for a Sunday pizza (60–80dh) or try the fixed menu which changes daily (from 70dh). Daily noon–2pm & 7–10pm.

La Kasbah inside Bab Boujeloud. The draw here is the roof terrace overlooking the blue gate and the windy Medina alleyways below; the *tajines* can be a little insipid though (40dh). Menus 70dh. Daily 9am–midnight.

Le Bouanania inside Bab Boujeloud. Friendly restaurant located in a beautiful building with a cushioned Moroccan salon on the first floor and a roof terrace with commanding views over the ramparts and the blue gate. Mains 40dh, set menu 60dh. Daily 8am–11pm.

Ville Nouvelle

Chez Vittorio Pizzeria 21 Rue Ibrahim Roudani, nearly opposite *Hôtel Central*. Italian restaurant with a wood-fired oven although the pizzas (55–75dh) and pastas are not their strong point; try the steaks and meat dishes instead. Daily noon–3pm & 5–midnight.

L'Italien Ave Omar Ibnou Khattab, Champs de Course, Ville Nouvelle. Fun and fashionable restaurant that is by far the best Italian in town, with proper wood-fired pizzas (60–100dh) and exquisite pastas. Daily noon–midnight.

> **TREAT YOURSELF**
>
> **Maison Blanche** 12 Rue Ahmed Chaouki, Ville Nouvelle (☎0535 622727; see map, p.804). Paris's trendy sister restaurant has made its way to Fes, with sleek couches and illuminated stone walls. Ditch the trainers and head over for some elegant French cuisine with an ever so slight touch of Moroccan. Mains from 180dh. Daily noon–3pm & 6pm–1am.

Drinking and nightlife

There's a lack of drinking places in the Medina itself – those listed below are by far the safest bet, with *Felix* being in the Ville Nouvelle.

Felix Off Av des Forces Armées Royales, Ville Nouvelle. See map, p.804. Moroccan DJs behind the decks do a pretty good job at mixing house, dance and Arabic music. Drinks are a bit pricey with beers at 100dh. Daily midnight–4am.

Fez Lounge 95 Zkak Rouah Tala Kbira. See map, p.803. The tanneries are not far, yet faux leather rules at this Medina hideout where you can sit back and enjoy a *shisha* over a *tartine* (60dh), burger (50dh) or the usual fare (50–80dh). Daily 11am–10pm.

Mezzanine 17 Ksbat Chams. See map, p.803. Sun yourself on the funky lounge terrace at lunchtime or soak in the trendy atmosphere over a chilled beer (35dh) or dinner (40–120dh) as you peer over the city ramparts at the spectacular gardens below. Daily 11am–1am.

Directory

Banks and exchange ATMs in R'Cif and Bab Boujeloud in the Medina; plenty of banks (all with ATMs) on Mohammed V in the Ville Nouvelle, including BMCE on Place Mohammed V; also on Place de l'Atlas and Place Florence.

Hospital Clinique Agdal, by the French Consulate in the Ville Nouvelle.

Internet Cyber Club, corner of Av Mohammed V and Rue el Moujahid el Ayachi, opposite *Hôtel Central* (daily 9am–10pm; 10dh); Cyber Bab Boujeloud, just outside Bab Boujeloud (daily 10am–midnight; 10dh).

Pharmacy Phramacie Bab Boujeloud, just outside Bab Boujeloud (Mon–Fri 8.30am–12.30pm & 3.30–8pm, Sat 8.30am–1pm). Night pharmacy in the *baladiya* (town hall) on Av Moulay Yousef (daily 9.30pm–8.30am).

Police 24/7 at Bab Boujeloud in the Medina; the Commissariat Central is on Av Mohammed V in the Ville Nouvelle behind the post office.

Post office Corner of aves Mohammed V and Hassan II, Ville Nouvelle; also in Place Batha and Place des Alaouites, Medina.

Moving on

Train Casablanca Voyageurs (hourly; 3hr 20min; 110dh); Marrakesh (7 daily; 7hr 15min; 195dh); Meknes (hourly; 30min; 20dh); Rabat (hourly; 2hr 50min; 80dh); Tangier (4 daily; 5hr 35min; 105dh).
Bus Casablanca (30 daily; 5hr 30min); Chefchaouen (7 daily; 5hr); Marrakesh (5 daily; 10hr); Meknes (approximately every 30min; 1hr); Rabat (hourly; 4hr); Tangier (17 daily; 5hr 45min); Tetouan (14 daily; 5hr 20min).

RABAT

Often undervalued by tourists, Morocco's capital city, **RABAT** has a modern political centre (with elegant French architecture), several historical monuments, accessible bars and an ancient Kasbah overlooking a sandy beach. Though it should not take priority over Fes, Marrakesh or Chefchaouen, it is worth a visit if you have the time.

What to see and do

Rabat's compact Medina – the whole city until the French arrived in 1912 – is wedged on two sides by the sea and the river, on the others by the twelfth-century Almohad and fifteenth-century Andalusian walls. Laid out in a simple grid, its streets are very easy to navigate.

Kasbah des Oudaïas and around

North lies the **Kasbah des Oudaïas**, a charming and evocative quarter whose principal gateway – **Bab el Kasbah** or Oudaïa Gate, built around 1195 – is one of the most ornate in the Moorish world. Its interior is now used for art exhibitions. Down the steps outside the gate, a lower, horseshoe arch leads directly to **Moulay Ismail's Palace** (daily except Tues 9.30am–4.30pm; 10dh), which hosts quite an interesting Jewellery Museum. The adjoining **Andalusian Garden** – one of the most delightful spots in the city – was actually constructed by the French in the last century, though true to Arab Andalusian tradition, with deep, sunken beds of shrubs and flowering annuals.

The Hassan Mosque

The most ambitious of all Almohad buildings, the **Hassan Mosque** (daily 8am–7pm; free), with its vast minaret, dominates almost every view of the city. Designed by the Almohad ruler Yacoub el Mansour as the centrepiece of the new capital, the mosque seems to have been more or less abandoned at his death in 1199. The minaret, despite its apparent simplicity, is among the most complex of all Almohad structures: each facade is different, with a distinct combination of patterning, yet the whole intricacy of blind arcades and interlacing curves is based on just two formal designs. Facing the tower are the Mosque and Mausoleum of Mohammed V, begun on the sultan's death in 1961 and dedicated six years later.

The Archeological Museum

On the opposite side of the Ville Nouvelle from the mausoleum is the **Archeological Museum** on Rue Brihi (daily except Tues 9am–4.30pm; 10dh), the most important in Morocco. Although small, it has an exceptional collection of Roman-era bronzes, found mainly at Volubilis.

Chellah

The royal burial ground, **Chellah** (daily 8am–6pm; 10dh), is a startling sight as you emerge from the long avenues of the Ville Nouvelle, with its circuit of fourteenth-century walls, legacy of Abou el Hassan (1331–51), the greatest of the Merenid rulers. Off to the left of the main gate are the partly excavated ruins of the Roman city that preceded the necropolis. A set of Islamic ruins are further down to the right, situated within a second inner sanctuary, approached along a broad path through half-wild gardens.

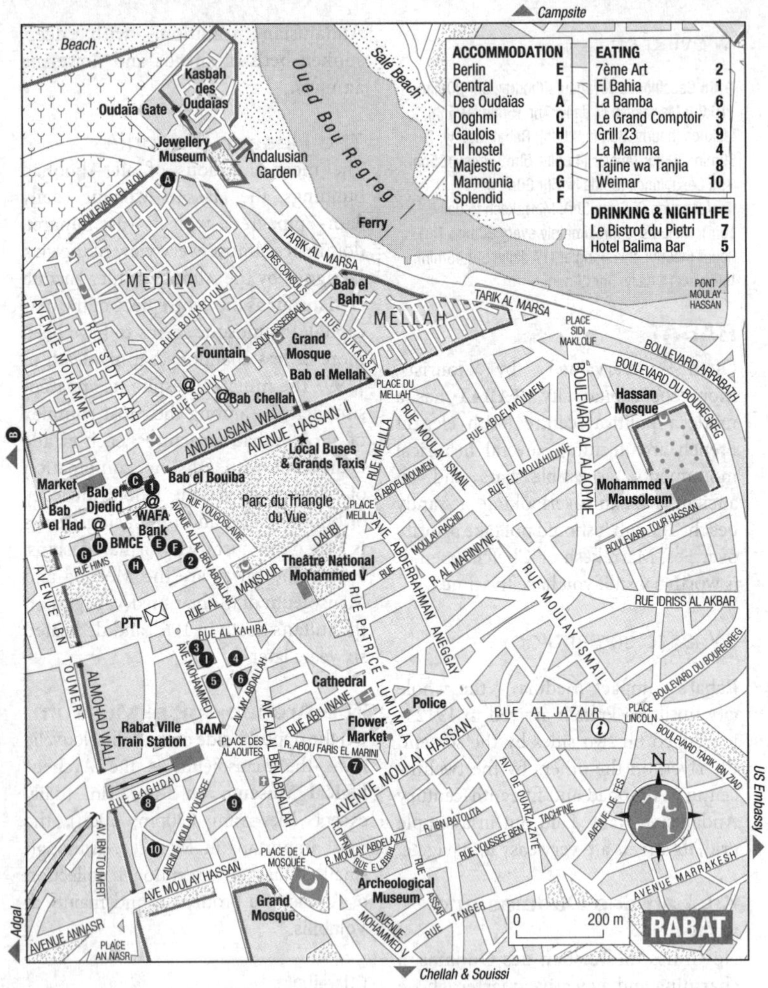

Arrival and information

Train Rabat Ville train station is at the heart of the Ville Nouvelle; don't get off at Rabat Agdal station, 2km from the centre.

Bus The main bus terminal is 3km west of the centre, served by local buses #17, #30 and #41, and by petits taxis. It's easier, if you're arriving by bus from the north, to get off in Salé across the river, and take a grand taxi from there into Rabat.

Taxi Grands taxis for most intercity destinations operate from outside the main bus station; those to Casablanca cost only a couple of dirhams more than the bus and leave more or less continuously. Meknes grands taxis run from Av Hassan II with Av Chellah.

City transport Local bus services radiate from Av Allal Ben Abdallah, Place Melilla and Av Hassan II, where petits taxis and local grands taxis gather.

Tourist office 22 Rue d'Alger, near Place Lincoln ☎0537 660663.

Accommodation

Accommodation can fill up in midsummer and during festivals; it's best to phone ahead.

Hostel

HI hostel 43 Rue Marrassa ☎0537 725769, ✉auberge.jeunes.rbt@hotmail.fr. Just outside the Medina walls north of Av Hassan II, this centrally located hostel has plain and simple dorms with shared bathroom facilities. Dorms 55dh.

Hotels

Des Oudaïas 132 Bd Laalou ⓣ0534 283959. Rooms are comfortable and spacious at this hotel overlooking the Kasbah with ornate whitewashed walls and stone-cased windows. Doubles 200dh.
Doghmi 313 Av Mohammed V, just inside Bab Djedid ⓣ0537 723898. Clean but darkish rooms give off a pleasant white and azure veranda, all with shared bathrooms. Doubles 130dh.
Gaulois 1 Rue Hims (corner of Av Mohammed V) ⓣ0537 723022. Two-star with grand entrance and decent rooms, some en suite. Pricier than other options if the cheap rooms have gone, but can be good value for money. Wi-fi. Doubles 220dh.
Majestic 121 Av Hassan II ⓣ0537 722997, ⓦwww.hotelmajestic.ma. Excellent option for female travellers, with a 24-hour reception and porter; rooms are bright and spotless. Singles 284dh, doubles 348dh.
Mamounia 10 Rue Mamounia ⓣ0537 724479, ⓔhotel_mamounia@hotmail.fr. Andalusian-style faux flowerpots give a touch of fun to the hallway while the clean rooms of this friendly and centrally located hotel are decked out in scarlet. Doubles 130dh.
Splendid 8 Rue Ghazza ⓣ0537 723283. A great option with a leafy courtyard to sit back after a day of exploring the city; some of the clean rooms give onto the central patio. Hot water evenings only. Doubles 230dh.

Eating

Rabat has a wide range of good restaurants serving both Moroccan and international dishes. The cheapest ones are in the Medina.
7ème Art Av Allal Ben Abdallah. Trendy good-value café with tables set around a garden area with a fountain serving all sorts of goodies from hamburgers to ice creams (25–60dh). Daily 7.30am–11pm.
El Bahia Av Hassan II, built into the Andalusian wall, near the junction with Av Mohammed V. Sit at one of the tables that line the Andalusian wall or retreat to the leafy inner patio for reasonably priced *tajines*, kebabs and salads, though service can be slow (45–60dh). Daily 8am–10pm.
Grill 23 386 Av Mohammed V. Cheap but delicious *shwarma* (24–34dh), hamburgers (20–32dh) and panini (24–26dh). Convenient for a takeaway to carry with you on a train journey (it's just up the street from the station). Daily 7am–1am.
La Mamma 6 Rue Tanta, behind the *Hôtel Balima*. Good pasta dishes and wood-oven pizzas (48–78dh) in a rustic trattoria setting. *La Dolce Vita*, next door, is owned by the same family and serves up luscious Italian-style ice cream (32dh) for afters. Daily noon–3pm & 7.30pm–midnight.
Tajine wa Tanjia 9 Rue Baghdad. A lovely little place with low cushioned seating and Moroccan paintings serving a wide range of excellent *tajines* and *tanjia* (jugged beef or lamb) for around 76–96dh. Mon–Fri noon–3pm, 7–11.30pm, Sat noon–4pm.
Weimar 7 Rue Sana'a, inside the Goethe Institute. Studenty, expat hangout serving pastas (45dh), salads (48dh) and meats (69dh), washed down with German beer. Mon–Fri noon–2.30pm & 7–11pm, Sat dinner only.

Drinking and nightlife

Avenues Mohammed V and Allal Ben Abdallah have some good cafés, but the best bars are situated in Agdal, a bit of a trek from the centre. Those itching for a boogie should head to the Centre Commercial Prestige along the Route des Zaers, a 10min taxi ride out of town, home to a cluster of nightclubs.
Hotel Balima Bar Av Mohammed V. This bar is conveniently located in the centre of town and has a terrace overlooking the Parliament; closes at 11pm.
Le Bistrot du Pietri 4 Rue Tobrouk ⓣ0537 707820. Outstanding jazz and world music bands; delicious bistro-style food to accompany the show but book ahead as it's a popular venue. Free entry. Tues, Fri & Sat 7pm–1am.

Directory

Embassies Australia represented by Canada; Canada, 13bis Rue Jaâfar as Sadiq, Agdal ⓣ0537 687400; New Zealand represented by the UK; UK, 28 Av SAR Sidi Mohammed, Souissi ⓣ0537 633333; US, 2 Av Mohammed el Fassi (Av Marrakech) ⓣ0537 762265. Irish citizens are covered by their embassy in Lisbon (ⓣ00-351-

TREAT YOURSELF

Le Grand Comptoir 279 Av Mohammed V (ⓦwww.legrandcomptoir.ma). Classy, Parisian-style brasserie with wonderful 1920s-style decor and live music that ranges from jazz to traditional Moroccan. Serves excellent meat and seafood dishes and a decent selection of wines. A meal with wine will set you back 250–300dh.

1/396 9440), but have an honorary consul in Casablanca (☎0522 272721).
Exchange Along Av Allal Ben Abdallah and Av Mohammed V. BMCE and Wafa Bank at the northern end of Av Mohammed V have bureaux de change open weekdays till 8pm and on Saturday mornings.
Internet Cheapest places are on or off Rue Souika in the Medina (4dh/hr); also on Av Hassan II by *Hôtel Majestic* (Mon–Sat 9am–8pm; 8dh/hr).
Police Av Tripoli, near the Cathedral. Police post at Bab Djedid and north end of Rue des Consuls.
Post office Halfway down Av Mohammed V.

Moving on

Train Casablanca Port (every 30min; 1hr); Casablanca Voyageurs (hourly; 1hr;); Fes (hourly; 3hr 15min); Marrakesh (9 daily; 4hr); Meknes (hourly; 2hr); Tangier (4 daily; 4hr 40min; 95dh).
Bus Casablanca (frequent; 1hr 20min); Essaouira (13 daily; 7hr 30min); Fes (hourly; 4hr); Marrakesh (hourly; 5hr 30min); Meknes (hourly; 3hr); Salé (frequent; 15min); Tangier (39 daily; 5hr).

CASABLANCA

Morocco's main city and economic capital, **CASABLANCA** (or "Casa") is also North Africa's largest port. Casa's Westernized image does not fit with most travellers' stereotype of Morocco but the city offers good food, beaches and fun nightlife.

What to see and do

Casablanca's Medina, above the port and recently gentrified, is largely the product of the late nineteenth century, when Casa began its modest growth as a commercial centre. Film buffs will be disappointed to learn that Bogart's *Casablanca* wasn't shot here (it was filmed entirely in Hollywood) – *Rick's Bar* (expensive) commemorates it as a gimmick at 248 Bd Sour Jedid.

Grande Mosquée Hassan II

The awe-inspiring **Grande Mosquée Hassan II** (guided tours only; summer Sat–Thurs 9am, 10am, 11am, noon & 3pm, Fri 9am, 10am & 3pm; winter Sat–Thurs 9am, 10am, 11am & 2pm, Fri 9am & 2pm; 120dh, students 60dh) is a must-see for all visitors to Casablanca. After Mecca and Medina, it is the world's third largest mosque, with space for one hundred and five thousand worshippers and a minaret soaring 200m. Commissioned by the last king, who named it after himself, it cost an estimated US$800m. It's a short taxi ride northeast of the centre.

The beaches

The **Ain Diab beach**, to the west of Mosque Hassan II, is one of Morocco's best and easily accessible beaches. Surf lessons and equipment are readily available along the corniche, which runs alongside the beach. Mohammedia, 30km from Casa, is a less crowded option, with better surf. Take the train (14dh) from Casa Port station.

Jewish Museum of Casablanca

Five kilometres south of town, in the suburb of Oasis, the **Jewish Museum of Casablanca** at 81 Rue Chasseur Jules Gros (Mon–Fri 10am–6pm; 20dh; wheelchair accessible; ☎0522 994940, Ⓦwww.casajewishmuseum.com) is the only Jewish museum in any Muslim country. Many Moroccan Muslims are proud of the fact that Jewish communities have, historically, been protected in Morocco. The museum gives an insight into the disproportionate role that Jews have played in Moroccan life.

Arrival and information

Casablanca has been the victim of bombings directed at Western institutions, so it is worth checking your embassy websites for current information.
Air Catch a train into Casa Voyageurs train station from the airport. Grands taxis are extortionately expensive (250–300dh) for the 45min drive.
Train Some trains stop only at Casa Voyageurs (2km southeast of the centre) rather than continuing to the Gare du Port, between the town centre and the port. Bus #2 runs into town from Casa Voyageurs; otherwise, it's a 20min walk or a petit taxi ride.
Bus Take the CTM if possible as it drops you downtown on Rue Léon l'Africain by the *Sheraton*

Hotel; other buses arrive at the bus station (Gare Ouled Ziane) southeast of town on Route des Ouled Ziane.

Taxi Most grands taxis arrive at the bus station; some from Rabat arrive a block east of the CTM terminal; those from Essaouira come into a station south of the centre on Bd Brahim Roudani in Maarif.

Tourist office The best information office is the Syndicat d'Initiative at 98 Bd Mohammed V (Mon–Fri 8.30am–4.30pm, Sat 8.30am–noon; ⓣ0522 221524), where you can also arrange a three-hour guided tour by car for 500dh. The Delegation de Tourisme is south of the centre at 55 Rue Omar Slaoui (Mon–Fri 8.30am–4.30pm; ⓣ0522 271177). Further info can be found at ⓦwww.casablanca.ma, a useful site for news and listings (in French).

Accommodation

There are plenty of hotels, though they are often near capacity; cheaper rooms in the centre can be hard to find by late afternoon.

Hostel

HI Hostel (Auberge de Jeunesse) 6 Place Ahmed Bidaoui ⓣ0522 220551, ⓔlesauberges@menara.ma. A friendly, well-maintained place just inside the Medina and signposted from the nearby Gare du Port (70dh/person). Breakfast included. Doubles 150dh.

Hotels

Colbert 38 Rue Chaouia ⓣ0522 314241 ⓦwww.hotelcolbert.ma. Huge (103 rooms) well-priced hotel with decent rooms, some with shower, 3 gardens and 2 terraces. Doubles 130dh.

Du Centre Rue Sidi Balyout ⓣ0522 446180, ⓔhotelducentrecasablanca@hotmail.fr. A warm welcome at reception, along with clean and pleasant-honey hued rooms with en suite, make this an excellent option in the centre. Doubles 240dh.

Galia 19 Rue Ibnou Batouta ⓣ0522 481694, ⓔgalia_19@hotmail.fr. Wooden artefacts liven up the stairwell at this friendly hotel with welcoming rooms. Free wi-fi. Doubles 220dh.

Miramar 22 Rue León l'Africain ⓣ0522 310308. Cheapest of the little hotels in the city centre, with shared bathroom facilities (shower 10dh). Doubles 140dh.

Mon Rêve 5 Rue Chaouia ⓣ0522 311439, ⓔhmonreve@gmail.com. Long-standing budget travellers' favourite popular among locals as well as the odd tourist. Book ahead. Doubles 220dh.

Touring 87 Rue Allal Ben Abdallah ⓣ0522 310216. Refurbished old French hotel that's friendly and excellent value; the best option in an area of cheap hotels. Doubles 130dh.

Campsite

Camping Oasis Dar Bouazza Rte d'Azzour, 18km from town ⓣ0522 290767. This campsite is run by the Syndicat d'Initiative, but is rather a long way from town. 40dh/person and a tent.

Eating

There are plenty of student cafés along the southern end of Moulay Youssef serving cheap-and-cheerful grub at excellent prices. In the central *marché*, it is possible to bring fish for the outdoor restaurants to cook for you.

Café Casablanca 61 Bd. Moulay Youssef at corner of Av Hassan Souktani. Bogart's legendary work comes to life at this pleasant French café with photos, posters and memorabilia scattered about. Superb *harira* soups (20dh), coffees (10dh). Daily 6am–11pm.

La Bodega 127 Rue Allal Ben Abdallah. Jam-packed with Latino and Spanish memorabilia as well as a large TV screen for sporting events, this lively place serves a decent selection of tapas (35–45dh); once the drinks (45–100dh) start flowing the downstairs bar and little dancefloor liven up a fair amount. Daily noon–4pm & 6pm–1am, closed Sun lunch.

La Ligue Arabe On the southern end of Bd. Moulay Youssef. Students sip tea (10dh) in the open air as they discuss their latest school day, while others take their mind off their studies with a game of pool or mini football. Games room, too. Daily 7.30am–11pm.

La Taverne du Dauphin 115 Bd Felix Houphouët Boigny. One of Casa's most famous and popular spots, with great seafood served in the restaurant and bonhomie dished up in the cramped bar. Mains 46–120dh, menu 115dh. Mon–Sat noon–11.30pm.

Port de Pêche By the main entrance of the port. A true local and a real treat for fish lovers with fresh sardines (20–40dh) grilled before your very eyes, not to be confused with the upmarket restaurant next door with a similar name. Daily 7am–3am.

Snack Yasmina On the southern end of Bd. Moulay Youssef. A real student hangout, this place swarms with youngsters swapping school notes as they feast on panini or more substantial mains (22–30dh). Daily 7am–midnight.

Drinking & nightlife

There are scores of bars and clubs along the Corniche, ten minutes' west of the centre, playing all sorts from hip-hop to house music.

Bao on the Corniche African beats and a laidback atmosphere make this a popular spot to get down to the sound of West African rhythms. Entry 100dh. Fri & Sat are the best days. Daily until 4am.

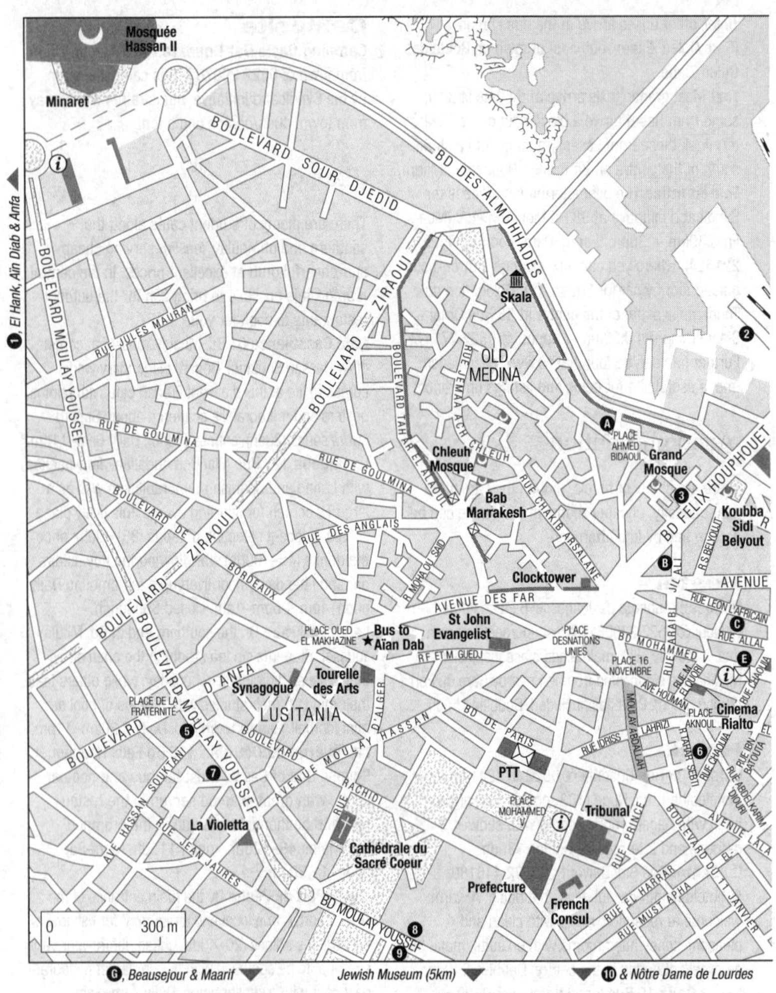

La Cigale 10 Bd Brahim Roudani. The room at the back is where it all takes place – once the first tune is on the jukebox, the night has begun. Beers 20dh, spirits 40dh. Free couscous Friday lunchtime. Daily 9am–1am.

Trica Bar 5 Rue al Moutanabi You could nearly be in NYC at this stylish warehouse bar with brick walls and old school tunes in the background; if you're seriously thirsty try the two-litre giant mojito (400dh). Daily noon–3pm & 7pm–12.30am.

Directory

Internet Cyber, 12 Rue du Gabon (daily 9.30am–11pm; 7dh/hr).

Police Tourist Police on Bd Felix Houphouët Boigny (☎ 0522 220393).

Moving on

Train (Port station) to: Rabat (every 30min 6.30am–8.30pm; 1hr).

Train (Voyageurs station) to: Fes (hourly; 3hr 55min); Marrakesh (every 2hr; 3hr 15min); Meknes (hourly; 3hr 15min); Mohammed V airport (hourly 6am–10pm; 35min); Rabat (every 30min; 1hr); Tangier (6 daily; 4hr 45min).

Bus to: Essaouira (26 daily; 6hr); Fes (28 daily; 5hr 30min); Marrakesh (every 30min; 4hr); Meknes

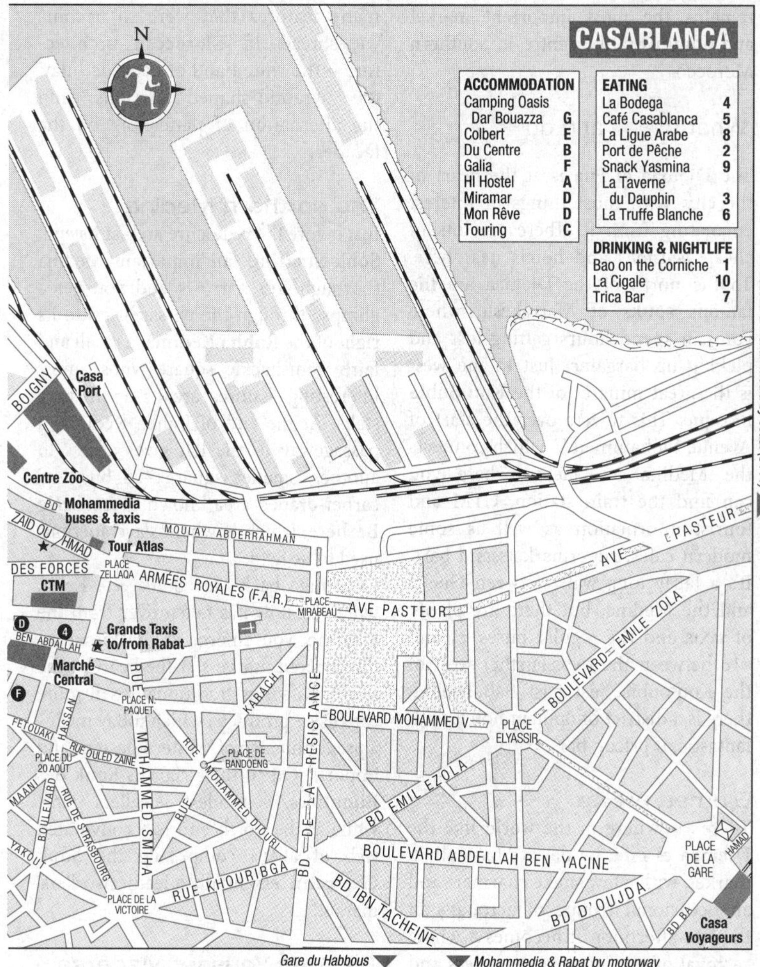

(16 daily; 4hr); Rabat (frequent; 1hr 20min); Tangier (41 daily; 6hr); Tetouan (31 daily; 6hr 30min).

Southern Morocco

Few places on earth can better the abiding memory of the Sahara desert meeting the Atlantic while **Marrakesh**, with its colourful Medina, is undoubtedly Morocco's most well-known city; further south loom the scenic **Atlas Mountains** and west lies the coastal city of **Essaouira**, the country's best windsurfing spot.

MARRAKESH

MARRAKESH (Marrakech in French) is a city of immense beauty; low, pink and tent-like before a great range of mountains. It's an immediately exciting place, especially its ancient Medina. Marrakesh's population is growing and it has a thriving industrial area; the city remains the most important market and administrative centre in southern Morocco.

What to see and do

The **Djemaa el Fna** is at the heart of the city, with most things of interest emanating from it. There are lots of cheap *pensions* and hotels near here. To the north of the Djemaa are the famous **souks** of Marrakesh, where you can spend hours getting lost and picking up bargains. Just to the west is the great minaret of the **Koutoubia** mosque. This towers over the start of Avenue Mohammed V, which connects the Medina to Gueliz, where you can find the train station, CTM and tourist information as well as some modern cafés, supermarkets and bars. It's a fairly long walk between Gueliz and the Medina, but there are plenty of taxis and the regular buses #1 and #16 between the two. Further west of the Koutoubia, just past Bab Djedid, there is a district of opulent hotels with fantastic, if pricey, bars.

Djemaa el Fna

There's nowhere in the world like the **Djemaa el Fna**: by day it's basically a market, with a few snake charmers and an occasional troupe of acrobats; in the late afternoon it becomes a whole carnival of musicians, storytellers and other entertainers; and in the evening dozens of stalls set up to dispense hot food to crowds of locals, while the musicians and performers continue. If you get tired of the spectacle, or if things slow down, you can move over to one of the numerous cafes rooftop terraces.

The Koutoubia

Nearly 70m high and visible for miles, the **Koutoubia Minaret** was begun shortly after the Almohad conquest of the city, around 1150, and displays many features that were to become widespread in Moroccan architecture – the wide band of ceramic inlay, the pyramid-shaped merlons, and the alternation of patterning on the facades.

The northern Medina

Just before the red ochre arch at its end, **Souk Smarine** (an important Medina thoroughfare) narrows and you get a glimpse through the passageways to its right of the **Rahba Kedima**, a small and fairly ramshackle square whose most interesting features are its apothecary stalls. At the end of Rahba Kedima, a passageway to the left gives access to another, smaller square – a bustling, carpet-draped area known as **La Criée Berbère**, which is where slave auctions used to be held.

Cutting back to Souk el Kebir, which by now has taken over from the Smarine, you emerge at the **kissarias**, the covered markets at the heart of the souks. Kissarias traditionally sell more expensive products, which today means a predominance of Western designs and imports. Off to their right is **Souk des Bijoutiers**, a modest jewellers' lane, while at the north end is a convoluted web of alleys comprising the **Souk Cherratin**, essentially a leatherworkers' market.

The Ben Youssef Medersa

If you bear left through the leather market and then turn right, you should arrive at the open space in front of the **Ben Youssef Mosque**. The originally fourteenth-century **Ben Youssef Medersa** (daily 9am–6pm; 50dh; combined ticket for this, the Marrakesh Museum and Almoravid Koubba 60dh) – the annexe for students taking courses in the mosque – stands off a side street just to the east. It was almost completely rebuilt in the sixteenth century under the Saadians, with a strong Andalusian influence.

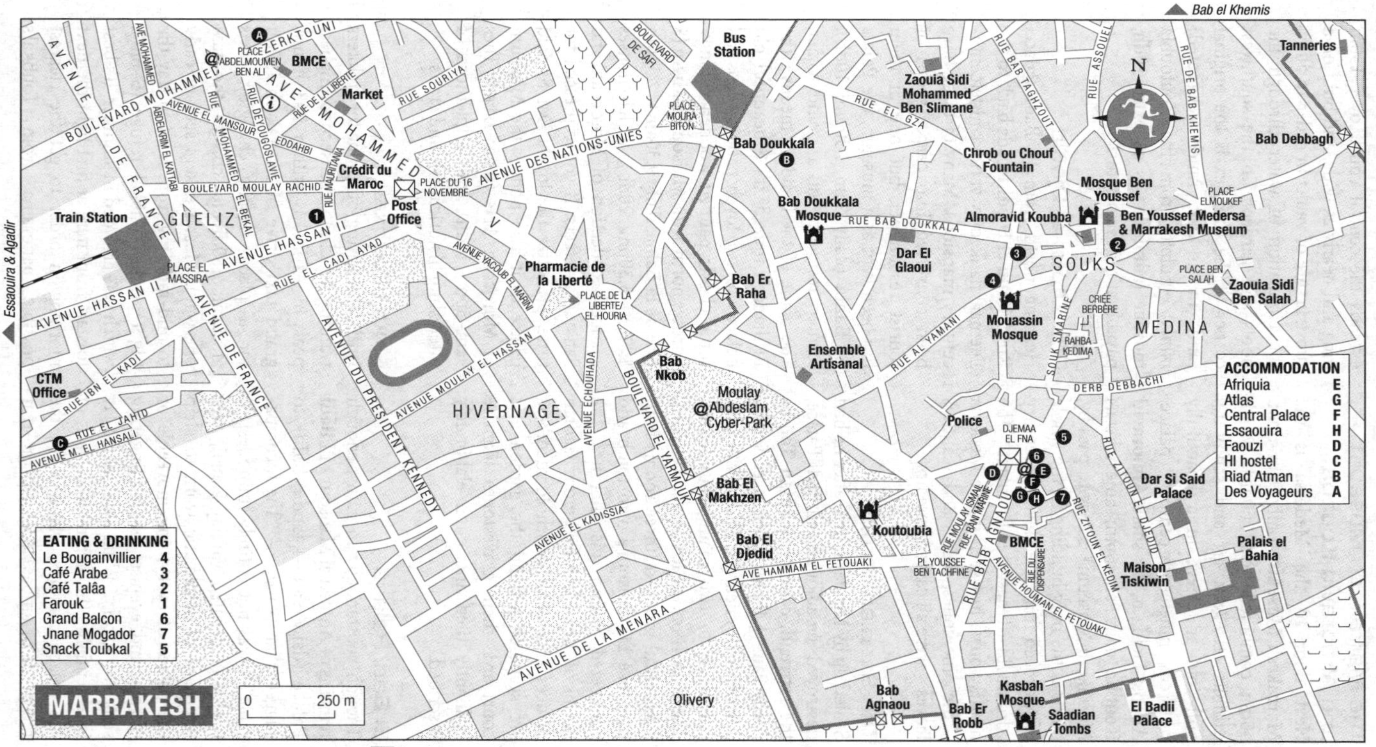
MARRAKESH
EATING & DRINKING
Le Bougainvillier 4
Café Arabe 3
Café Talâa 2
Farouk 1
Grand Balcon 6
Jnane Mogador 7
Snack Toubkal 5
ACCOMMODATION
Afriquia E
Atlas G
Central Palace F
Essaouira H
Faouzi D
HI hostel C
Riad Atman B
Des Voyageurs A
0 250 m
Bab el Khemis
Essaouira & Agadir
Airport
N
Train Station
GUELIZ
HIVERNAGE
SOUKS
MEDINA
Bus Station
Bab Doukkala
Bab Doukkala Mosque
Zaouia Sidi Mohammed Ben Slimane
Chrob ou Chouf Fountain
Mosque Ben Youssef
Almoravid Koubba
Ben Youssef Medersa & Marrakesh Museum
Tanneries
Bab Debbagh
Zaouia Sidi Ben Salah
Dar El Glaoui
Bab Er Raha
Pharmacie de la Liberté
Crédit du Maroc
Post Office
Market
BMCE
CTM Office
Bab Nkob
Moulay Abdeslam Cyber-Park
Ensemble Artisanal
Mouassin Mosque
Police
DJEMAA EL FNA
Bab El Makhzen
Bab El Djedid
Koutoubia
Dar Si Said Palace
Maison Tiskiwin
Palais el Bahia
El Badii Palace
Saadian Tombs
Kasbah Mosque
Bab Er Robb
Bab Agnaou
Olivery
AVENUE DE FRANCE
BOULEVARD MOHAMMED V
AVE MOHAMMED V
PLACE ABDELMOUMEN BEN ALI
ZERKTOUNI
RUE DE LA LIBERTÉ
RUE SOURIYA
AVENUE EL MANSOUR
ABDELKRIM EL KATTABI
RUE MOHAMMED EL BEKAL
RUE DEYOUGOSLAVIE
EDDAHBI
BOULEVARD MOULAY RACHID
RUE MAURITANIA
PLACE DU 16 NOVEMBRE
AVENUE DES NATIONS-UNIES
AVENUE HASSAN II
PLACE EL MASSIRA
RUE EL CADI AYAD
AVENUE YACOUB EL MARINI
PLACE DE LA LIBERTE/ EL HOURIA
AVENUE DU PRESIDENT KENNEDY
AVENUE MOULAY EL HASSAN
AVENUE ECHOUHADA
BOULEVARD EL YARMOUK
AVENUE EL KADISSIA
AVE HAMMAM EL FETOUAKI
AVENUE DE LA MENARA
RUE IBN EL KADI
RUE EL JAHID
AVENUE M. EL HANSALI
BOULEVARD DE SAFI
PLACE MOURA BITON
RUE EL GZA
RUE BAB TAGHZOUT
RUE ASSOUEL
RUE DE BAB KHEMIS
PLACE ELMOUKEF
RUE BAB DOUKKALA
PLACE BEN SALAH
CRIÉE BERBÈRE
RAHBA KEDIMA
SOUK SMARINE
RUE AL YAMANI
DERB DEBBACHI
RUE ZITOUN EL DJEDID
RUE ZITOUN EL KEDIM
RUE MOULAY ISMAIL
RUE BANI MARINE
RUE BAB AGNAOU
RUE DU DISPENSAIRE
AVENUE HOUMAN EL FETOUAKI
PL.YOUSSEF BEN TACHFINE

The Marrakesh Museum and Almoravid Koubba

Next door to the Medersa is the **Marrakesh Museum** (daily 9am–6pm; 40dh; combined ticket 60dh), which exhibits jewellery, art and sculpture, both old and new, in a beautifully restored nineteenth-century palace. Almost facing it, the small **Almoravid Koubba** (daily 9am–6pm; same ticket as Marrakesh Museum) is easy to pass by, but it is the only building in the whole of Morocco from the eleventh-century Almoravid dynasty still intact. The motifs you've just seen in the Medersa – the pine cones, palms and acanthus leaves – were all carved here first.

The Saadian Tombs

Sealed up by Moulay Ismail after he had destroyed the adjoining El Badi Palace, the sixteenth-century **Saadian Tombs** (daily 9am–4.45pm; 10dh), accessed by a narrow alley near the Kasbah Mosque, are home to two main mausoleums. The finer is on the left as you come in, a beautiful group of three rooms built to house El Mansour's own tomb and completed within his lifetime. The tombs of over a hundred more Saadian princes and royal household members are scattered around the garden and courtyard, their gravestones likewise brilliantly tiled and often elaborately inscribed.

El Badi Palace

Though substantially in ruins, enough remains of Ahmed el Mansour's **El Badi Palace** (daily 9am–4.45pm; 10dh) to suggest that its name – "The Incomparable" – was not entirely immodest. It took a later ruler, Moulay Ismail, over ten years of systematic work to strip the palace of everything moveable or of value and, even so, there's a lingering sense of luxury. What you see today is essentially the ceremonial part of the palace complex, planned for the reception of ambassadors. To the rear extends the central court, over 130m long and nearly as wide, and built on a substructure of vaults in order to allow the circulation of water through the pools and gardens. In the southwest corner of the complex is the original (and, in its day, much celebrated) *minbar* (pulpit) from the Koutoubia mosque (admission is an extra 10dh, payable at the main gate).

Rue Zitoun el Djedid

Heading north from El Badi Palace, **Rue Zitoun el Djedid** leads back to the Djemaa, flanked by various nineteenth-century mansions. Many of these have been converted into carpet shops or tourist restaurants, but one of them has been kept as a museum, the **Palais El Bahia** (daily 9am–4.30pm; 10dh), former residence of a grand vizier. The name of the building means "The Brilliance"; indeed, it's a beautiful old palace with two lovely patio gardens and some classic painted wooden ceilings. Further north is the **Maison Tiskiwin** (8 Rue de la Bahia; daily 9.30am–12.30pm & 2.30–5.30pm; 20dh), which houses a superb collection of Moroccan and Saharan artefacts. If you're pressed for time, prioritize the lovely Dar Si Said palace as it also houses the **Museum of Moroccan Arts** (daily except Tues 9am–5pm; 10dh) with a plethora of interesting historical arts and crafts.

Mount Toubkal

Imlil, the setting-off point for trekkers wanting to climb the second highest peak in Africa, is within 2–3 hours' grand taxi drive of Marrakesh (30dh for a place, usually changing taxis at Asni; 180dh to charter the taxi one-way). Most trekkers set out early to mid-morning from Imlil to stay the night at the Toubkal refuge (5–6hr), which gets crowded in summer. It's best to start from here at first light the next morning in order to get the clearest possible panorama from Toubkal's

heights (afternoons can be cloudy). The ascent is not difficult if you are fit, but it can be very cold.

Arrival and information

Air The airport, 4km southwest, is served by bus #19 (every 30min; 20dh) – petits taxis (100dh by day, 120dh by night) are a more convenient option.
Train From the train station, west of Gueliz, cross Ave Hassan II and take bus #3/#4/#8/#10/#14/#66 or a petit taxi (10–15dh) for Place Foucauld by the Djemaa.
Bus The bus terminal is just outside the north-western walls of the Medina by Bab Doukkala; from here it's a 20min walk to the Djemaa, or take bus #3/#4/#5/#8/#10/#14/#16/#17/#26/#66 (opposite Bab Doukkala), or a petit taxi (8–10dh). CTM buses take you to their office south of the train station.
Tourist office Place Abdelmoumen Ben Ali (Mon–Fri 8.30am–4.30pm; ⓣ0524 436131) keeps limited details of services you might need; it's best to rely on your hotel. ⓦwww.ilove-marrakech.com is a good source of information.

Accommodation

The Medina has the main concentration of cheap accommodation – most places quite pleasant – and, unusually, has a fair number of classified hotels too. Given the attractions of the Djemaa el Fna and the souks, this is the first choice. Booking in advance is advisable. All our recommendations are in the Medina unless stated otherwise.

Hostel

HI hostel Rue El Jahid, Gueliz ⓣ0524 447713, ⓔaubergemarrakech@hotmail.fr. Neat and tidy single-sex dorms, good for those with an early start as it's close to the train station. Hot water extra 7dh. Dorms 70dh.

Hotels

Afriquia 45 Sidi Bouloukate ⓣ0524 442403. Basic but hospitable rooms with a Gaudíesque top-floor terrace. The shady orange trees twitter with swallows, but this means an early-morning wake up call. Free wi-fi. Singles 150dh, doubles 350dh.

Atlas 50 Rue Sidi Bouloukate ⓣ0524 39 105, ⓦwww.hotel-atlas-marrakech.com. Calm and clean hotel set around two courtyards, with decorative iron and woodwork throughout; there's an appealing rooftop chill-out lounge for the weary tourist. Excellent rates for single travellers (70dh). Doubles 250dh.

Central Palace 59 Sidi Bouloukate ⓣ0524 440235, ⓦwww.lecentralpalace.com. A peaceful haven set in a leafy three-tiered courtyard with pleasantly decorated rooms, some with en suite. There's also a couscous restaurant on the roof terrace. Doubles 155dh.

Des Voyageurs 40 Av Zerktouni, Gueliz ⓣ0524 447218. Old-fashioned hotel with welcoming management, spacious rooms and a little patio-cum-garden. Doubles 200dh.

Essaouira 3 Derb Sidi Bouloukate ⓣ0524 443805. The entrance opens onto a beautiful courtyard with intricately painted woodwork, where vibrant but tastefully tiled rooms might make you dizzy after a heavy night. Doubles 100dh.

Faouzi 67 Derb Sidu Bouloukate ⓣ05 24 390176, ⓦwww.faouzihotel.com. Sparkling, excellent-value rooms with luxurious marble plaster walls and modern fittings; the sole drawback is the rather uninspiring roof terrace. Doubles 180dh.

Eating and drinking

The most atmospheric place to eat is the Djemaa el Fna, where food stalls set up around sunset and serve up everything from *harira* soup and couscous to stewed snails and sheep's heads, all eaten at trestle tables. Cheap restaurants gather in the Medina, with more upmarket places uptown in Gueliz, along with French-style cafés and virtually all the city's bars.

Café Arabe 184 Rue Mouassine Ideal for a beer at sunset, the roof bar teems with foreigners itching for their thirst-quenching snifter (35dh). Daily 10am–11pm.

Café Talâa By the Talâa souk entrance. Coffees (10dh), juices (15dh) and teas (10dh) as well as substantial fare (*tajines* from 30dh) at this café with straw stools and parasols. Daily 8am–9pm.

Farouk 66 Av Hassan II, Gueliz. Excellent-value set menu with soup or salad, then couscous, *tajine* or *brochettes*, followed by a choice of desserts, for 40dh. Mains 25–40dh.

TREAT YOURSELF

Riad Atman 12 Derb Alaka, Bab Doukkala (ⓦwww.riadatman.com). A peaceful oasis in the heart of the Medina, this welcoming riad has four beautifully furnished rooms, all with en suite, a/c and cable TV, with cedar wood and intricate ironwork throughout. Breakfast included. Doubles €50.

Grand Balcon On top of the *Café Glacier* on Demaa el Fna. "Obligatory consumption" is what it says and so it is – you won't be allowed in unless you pay for your drinks or passable grub (45dh) at the door. The incredible view over the square attracts a large crowd though. Daily 10am–midnight.

Jnane Mogador in the *Jnane Mogador*, Derb Sidi Bouloukat by 116 Rue Riad Zitoun el Kedim. The food is decent (mains from 40dh) and the pretty rooftop terrace will provide a welcome respite from the hustle and hassle of the nearby streets. Daily 8am–11.30pm.

Le Bougainvillier Rue El Mouassine 33. Old French crooners set the mood at this atmospheric café with a leafy sunny patio and little salons, serving panini (50dh), sandwiches (40–50dh) and pizzas (45–60dh). Daily 11am–midnight.

Snack Toubkal in the southeast corner of Djemaa el Fna. Despite its touristy appearance, the food here is popular with locals and tourists alike. Try the delicious *tajines* (22–35dh). Open 24hr.

Directory

Exchange BMCE has branches with adjoining bureaux de change and ATMs in the Medina (Rue Moulay Ismail, facing Place Foucauld) and Gueliz (114 Av Mohammed V).

Internet Moulay Abdeslam Cyber-Park on Av Mohammed V opposite the Ensemble Artisanal (daily 9.30am–6.30pm; 5dh/hr); Cyber Siroua, Bd Mohammed (daily 8.30am–10pm; 7dh/hr).

Pharmacy and doctor Pharmacie du Progrès, Place Djemaa el Fna at the top of Rue Bab Agnaou; Pharmacie La Liberté, just off Place de la Liberté (both Mon–Fri 7.30am–12.30pm & 3.30am–7.30pm, Sat 7.30am–1pm). If you're in need of a doctor try Dr Abdelmajid Ben Tbib, 171 Av Mohammed V ⓣ 0524 431030.

Police 24/7 tourist police on Djemaa el Fna (ⓣ 0524 384601).

Post office Place du 16 Novembre, midway along Av Mohammed V, and on the Djemaa el Fna (Mon–Fri 8am–6pm, Sat 10am–6pm).

Moving on

Air Bus #19 shuttles between the city centre and the airport, leaving from opposite the Koutobia by Jemaa el Fna (every 30min between 6.15am & 9.15pm).

Train Casablanca Voyageurs (9 daily; 3hr 10min; 90dh); Fes (8 daily; 7hr 10min); Meknes (8 daily; 6hr 35min); Rabat (9 daily; 4hr 15min); Tangier (1 daily; 9hr).

Bus Casablanca (every 30min 4am–9pm; 3hr; 60dh); Essaouira (10 daily; 3hr 30min); Fes (5 daily; 7hr; 130dh); Meknes (5 daily; 6hr); Rabat (every 30min; 5hr 30min; 80dh); Tangier (3 daily; 10hr).

ESSAOUIRA

ESSAOUIRA, the nearest beach resort to Marrakesh, is a lovely eighteenth-century walled seaside town. A favourite with the likes of Frank Zappa and Jimi Hendrix back in the 1960s, its tradition of hippy tourism has created a much more laidback relationship between local residents and foreign visitors than you'll find in the rest of Morocco. Today Essaouira is a centre for arts and crafts in addition to being the country's top windsurfing spot.

What to see and do

Essaouira is a great place in which to wander and the **ramparts** are the obvious place to start. Heading north along the lane at the end of Place Prince Moulay el Hassan, you can access the **Skala de la Ville**, the great sea bastion topped by a row of cannons, which runs along the northern cliffs. At the end is the circular **North Bastion**, with panoramic views (closes at sunset).

SHOPPING IN THE SOUKS

Marrakesh is famous for its **souks**, where you can buy goods from all over Morocco. Prices are rarely fixed so before you set out, head to the supposedly fixed-price Ensemble Artisanal (Mon–Sat 9am–8pm, Sun 9am–2pm), on Avenue Mohammed V, midway between the Koutoubia and the ramparts at Bab Nkob, and get an idea of how much things are worth. It pays to bargain hard as the first price you are told can easily be five or ten times the going rate, with the most obscene prices to be found around the edges of the souks.

ESSAOUIRA ORIENTATION

Still largely contained within its ramparts, Essaouira is a simple place to get to grips with. At the northeast end of town is the Bab Doukkala; at the southwest is the town's pedestrianized main square, Place Prince Moulay el Hassan, and the fishing harbour. Between them run two main parallel streets: Avenue de l'Istiqlal/Avenue Mohammed Zerktouni and Rue Sidi Mohammed Ben Abdallah.

Along the Rue de la Skala, built into the ramparts, are the woodcarving workshops, where artisans use **thuja**, a distinctive local hardwood. You can find another impressive bastion by the harbour, the **Skala du Port** (daily 9am–5.30pm; 10dh).

The souks

The town's **souks** spread around and to the south of two arcades, on either side of Rue Mohammed Zerktouni, and up towards the **Mellah** (former Jewish ghetto), in the northwest corner of the ramparts. Don't miss the **Marché d'Épices** (spice market) and **Souk des Bijoutiers** (jewellers' market). Art studios and hippie-style clothing shops cluster around Place Chefchaouni by the clock tower.

The beaches

The southern **beach** (the northern one is less attractive) extends for miles, past the Oued Ksob riverbed and the ruins of an old fort known as the Bordj el Berod. If you're after **watersports**, Club Mistral (ⓣ0524 783934) on the south beach rents out surfboards out kayaks, and wind- and kitesurfing gear, and offers lessons too. For those wanting to spice up their **culinary** skills, Atelier Madada (7 bis, rue Youssef El Fassi ⓣ0524 475512, ⓦwww.lateliermadada .com) offers cookery classes in local specialities.

Arrival and information

Bus The bus station is about 500m (10min walk) northeast of Bab Doukkala. Especially at night, it's worth taking a petit taxi (about 7dh).
Taxi Grands taxis also operate from the bus station, though they may drop arrivals at Bab Doukkala or Place Prince Moulay el Hassan.
Tourist office Av du Caire (Mon–Fri 9am–4.30pm; ⓣ0524 783532).

Accommodation

Accommodation can be tight over Easter and in summer, when advance booking is recommended.

Hotels

Central 5 Rue Dar Eddhab, off Av Mohammed Ben Abdallah ⓣ0524 783623. Sadly the rooms aren't as attractive as the quaint colonnaded interior patio; it's worth paying extra for en suite and make sure you ask for the more spacious rooms on the first floor. 100dh.
Riad Essalam Place My Hassan ⓣ0524 475548, ⓔm.eloujibi@menara.ma. The tiled floors, snug rooms and incredible views from the watch-tower make this an ideal stop for bigger groups. Excellent-value rooms sleeping four 500dh; pricier doubles at R400dh.
Sahara Av Okba Ibn Nafia ⓣ0524 475292, ⓕ0524 476198. The entrance hall and living area are jam-packed with knick-knacks, while the rooms are fun and colourful with attractively uneven walls and a cosy feel. Breakfast included. Doubles 350dh.
Tafraout 7 Rue Marrakech ⓣ0524 476276, ⓦwww.hoteltafraout.com. Negotiate the alley of carpets to enter this calm riad with pleasant, clean rooms, some with en suite. Doubles 150dh.

Campsite

Camping Sidi Magdoul 1km south of town behind the lighthouse ⓣ0524 472196. Clean, friendly and well managed, with hot showers, bungalows in spring and summer (120dh) and an area of soil and trees for pitching tents in. 12dh/person, plus 15–25dh tent.

Eating and drinking

For an informal meal, you can do no better than eat at the line of grills down at the port. Restaurants can be a bit expensive, but there are plenty of places to pick up cheap sandwiches.
After 5 7 Rue Youssef El Fassi. Vaulted brick ceilings, enormous lamps and subdued lighting

give this place a trendy feel. Good-value club sandwiches and fries (70dh) for lunch, splash out a bit more for a cool fusion dinner. Daily noon–11pm.

Café des Arts 56 Av Lisriqlal. Sit at one of the individually painted tables at this little café-cum-restaurant with local argan oil flasks and wooden guitars. Live traditional *gnawa* music from 8pm. Mains 50dh. Daily 10am–4pm & 6pm–midnight.

Dar Al Houma 9 Rue El Hajjali. Tuck into some home-style cooking at this vaulted restaurant with heavy drapery. Soups (10–25dh), *tajines* (45–70dh) and salads (12–55dh). Daily 11.30am–3.30pm & 6–10.30pm.

La Petite Perle 2 Rue el Hajjalli. Sit on cushioned benches in this Berber-like tent and dig into a good-value *tajine* (30–50dh) or couscous (35–70dh). Daily noon–3pm & 7–10.30pm.

Place Marché aux Grains Off Av de l'Istiqlal. This little square is home to some pleasant luncheonettes with outdoor seating serving excellent-value food fresh from the fish market. Three-course set menus from 65dh. Daily 8am–6pm.

Taros Place Moulay Hassan. Along the theme of a boat deck of a Greek island tour, with palm parasols and patio furniture, this is a perfect spot to enjoy an early-evening beer (35dh) or a glass of wine (40dh). Head next door to the terrace at *Casa Vera* for some upbeat DJ tunes from 8pm. Daily 6pm–midnight.

Moving on

Bus Casablanca (26 daily; 6hr); Marrakesh (25 daily; 3hr 30min); Rabat (13 daily; 8hr 30min).

The Netherlands

HIGHLIGHTS

AMSTERDAM: experience canals, coffeeshops and world-famous art

DELFT: enjoy wonderful apple cake in Vermeer's home town

ROTTERDAM: a buzzing port with great nightlife

HOGE VELUWE NATIONAL PARK: cycle through woods to the world's best collection of Van Goghs

MAASTRICHT: a cosmopolitan university town with a tranquil old quarter

ROUGH COSTS

DAILY BUDGET Basic €55 /occasional treat €75

DRINK Beer €2

FOOD Pancake €8

HOSTEL/BUDGET HOTEL €20–35/€70–95

TRAVEL Train: Amsterdam–Maastricht €22.80

FACT FILE

POPULATION 16.5 million

AREA 41,526 sq km

LANGUAGE Dutch

CURRENCY Euro (€)

CAPITAL Amsterdam (population: 1 million)

INTERNATIONAL PHONE CODE ⓣ31

Introduction

Despite the popular reputation of its most celebrated city, Amsterdam, the Netherlands is not all sex and drugs (there's little rock'n'roll). Delve deeper and you will find a diminutive country packed with unique, iconic images: flat, fertile landscapes punctuated by tulips, windmills and church spires; ornately gabled terraces flanking peaceful canals; and mile upon mile of grassy dunes, backing onto stretches of pristine sandy beach.

Though most people travel only to atmospheric **Amsterdam**, nearby is a group of worthwhile towns known collectively as the **Randstad** (literally "rim town"), including **Haarlem** and **Delft** with their old canal-girded centres, and **Den Haag** (The Hague), a stately city with fine museums and easy beach access. The dynamic port city of **Rotterdam** is a showcase for noteworthy architecture and alternative art. Outside the Randstad, life moves more slowly. To the south, the landscape undulates into heathy moorland, best experienced in the **Hoge Veluwe National Park**. Further south lies the compelling city of **Maastricht**, squeezed between the German and Belgian borders.

CHRONOLOGY

58 BC Julius Caesar conquers the area of the present-day Netherlands.
1275 Amsterdam is founded by Count Floris V of Holland.
1477 The Austrian Habsburgs take control.
1500s Protestant Reformation spreads through the Netherlands, leading to wars against the Catholic Habsburg rulers based in Spain.
1579 The Union of Utrecht is signed by seven provinces to form the United Provinces against Spain, and declaring independence for the Netherlands in 1581, heralding a "Golden Age" of trade and colonial expansion.
1603 The Dutch East India Company establishes its first trading post in Indonesia, an area that it would gradually colonize.
1806 Napoleon annexes the Kingdom of Holland for France.
1813 The French are driven out and the Prince of Orange becomes sovereign of the United Netherlands.
1853 Vincent Van Gogh is born.
1914–18 The Netherlands remains neutral during World War I.
1940 Nazi Germany invades the Netherlands, forcing the deportation and murder of Dutch Jews including Anne Frank's family.
1945 Germany is expelled by Allied forces.
1947 Anne Frank's diary is published.
1975 Cannabis is decriminalized – tourism booms.
1992 The Maastricht Treaty is signed, transforming the European Community into the European Union.
1997 Treaty of Amsterdam clears the way for the introduction of a single European currency.
2003 The permanent International Criminal Court is established in The Hague to try war criminals.
2007 Controversial government plans to ban the burka (Islamic dress for women) in public places gains Cabinet support.
2010 The Party for Freedom (PVV) led by the controversial Dutch politician Geert Wilders who campaigns against the "Islamisation of The Netherlands" becomes the third-largest political party, forming a "toleration agreement" with the more traditional CDA and VVD.

ARRIVAL

Most tourists arrive at Amsterdam's **Schiphol** airport, one of Europe's busiest and a mere 15-minute train ride from central Amsterdam, which is served by over seventy budget airline routes and well connected by train to many Dutch cities. Some international flights also land at Rotterdam airport. There are good train links to the UK, France, Belgium and Germany. High-speed trains frequently travel to Amsterdam from Paris, Brussels and Frankfurt (Ⓦwww.nsinternational.nl), and InterRail passes (Ⓦwww.raileurope.co.uk) are

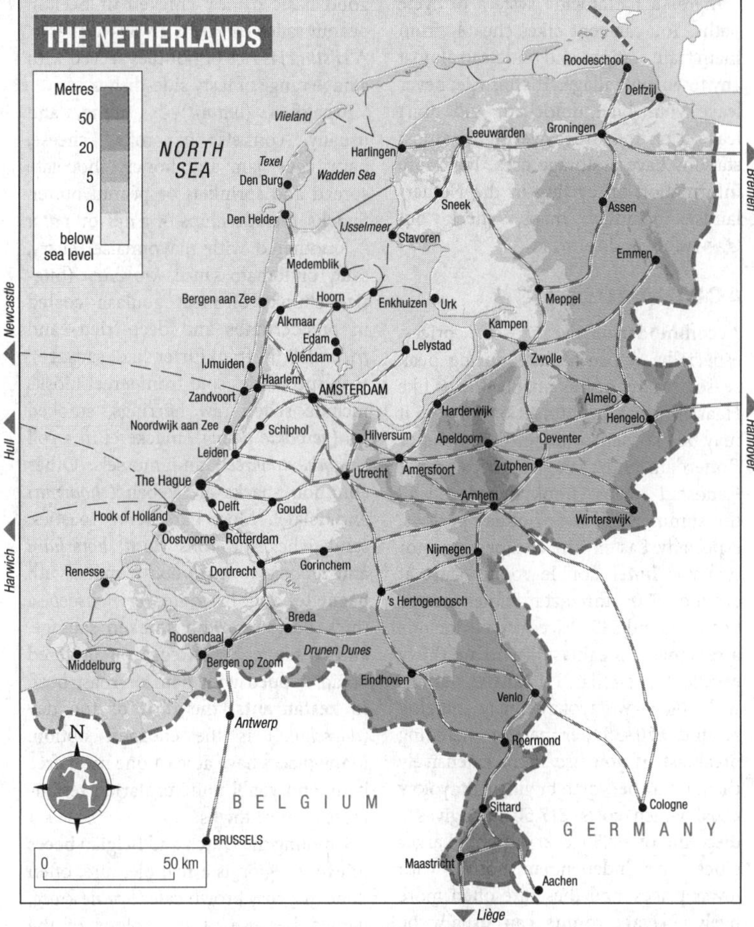

accepted. The Dutchflyer (Ⓦwww.dutchflyer.co.uk) connects London with Amsterdam Centraal by train and boat, while Stenaline ferries (Ⓦwww.stenaline.co.uk) travel between Harwich and the Hook of Holland. P&O ferries (Ⓦwww.poferries.com) leave from Hull and dock in Rotterdam.

GETTING AROUND

Trains (Ⓦwww.ns.nl) are fast and efficient, fares relatively low, and the network comprehensive. With any ticket, you're free to stop off en route and continue later that day. Various **passes** cut costs – ask at the station.

Urban **buses** and **trams** are very efficient. Most cities have recently introduced the public transport chip card, replacing the old "strippenkaart" system. You can buy a disposable card valid from one hour to a couple of days from the bus or tram driver or at a vending machine at the station. Prices vary per type of card and city but count on paying between €2.50 and €3.50 for an hour of unlimited bus or tram use. If you plan on doing extensive travelling, consider buying a day card for around €7.

There's a nationwide system of **cycle** paths. You can rent bikes cheaply from main train stations and outlets in almost any town and village. Theft is rife: never leave your bike unlocked, and don't leave it on the street overnight – most stations have a storage area. For more information on cycling in the Netherlands, including maps, check out Ⓦwww.holland.com/uk.

ACCOMMODATION

Accommodation can be pricey, especially in Amsterdam during peak season. Many of the smaller towns like Haarlem have few budget options, so it may be cheaper to stay in Den Haag or Rotterdam and make day-trips to the Randstad towns. Book ahead during the summer and over holiday periods, especially Easter. The cheapest one- or two-star **hotel** double rooms start at around €70; three-star hotel rooms begin around €85. Prices usually include a reasonable breakfast. There are thirty excellent, if similar, HI **hostels** nationwide (Ⓦwww.stayokay.com), charging around €20–35 per person including breakfast. If you use them extensively then it may be worth buying a **Stayokay Card** which costs €17.50 and gives a discount of €2.50 every night. Larger cities have independent hostels with lower prices, and these are often more lively. **Private rooms** can usually be arranged through the VVV office (see opposite) in town, and usually cost around €25–30 including breakfast. There are plenty of well-equipped **campsites**: expect to pay around €6 per person, plus €3–5 for a tent. Some sites also have **cabins** for up to four people, for around €40 a night.

FOOD AND DRINK

Dutch **food** tends to be plain but thanks to its colonial history, the Netherlands boasts the best **Indonesian cuisine** outside Indonesia. *Nasi goreng* and *bami goreng* (rice or noodles with meat) are good basic dishes; chicken or beef in peanut sauce (*sateh*) is always available. A *rijsttafel* is rice or noodles served with a huge range of tasty side-dishes.

Breakfast (*ontbijt*) is filling, and usually consists of rolls, cheese, ham, eggs, jam and honey, chocolate spread and sprinkles or peanut butter. **Snacks** include chips – *frites* or *patat* – smothered with mayonnaise, curry, satay or tomato sauce, *kroketten* (bite-size chunks of meat goulash coated in breadcrumbs and deep-fried) and *fricandel* (a frankfurter-like sausage). **Fish** specialities sold from street kiosks include salted raw herrings, smoked eel (*gerookte paling*), mackerel in a roll (*broodje makreel*) and mussels. Other common snacks are kebab (*shoarma*) and falafel. Most bars serve toasties, sandwiches and rolls (*tosti, boterham* and *broodjes* – *stokbrood* if made with baguette) and, in winter, *erwtensoep*, a thick pea soup with smoked sausage, and *uitsmijter*: fried eggs on buttered bread, topped with ham or roast beef. In **restaurants**, the dish of the day (*dagschotel*) is the cheapest option. Many places have at least one meat-free item, and you'll find vegetarian restaurants in most towns.

Sampling the Dutch and Belgian **beers** in every region is a real pleasure, often done in a cosy brown café (*bruine kroeg*, named because of the colour of the tobacco-stained walls); the big brands Heineken, Amstel, Oranjeboom and Grolsch are just the tip of the iceberg. A standard, small glass is *een fluitje*; a bigger glass is *een vaasje*. You may also come across *proeflokalen* or tasting houses, small, old-fashioned bars that close around 8pm, and specialize in **jenever**, Dutch gin, drunk straight; *oud* (old) is smooth, *jong* (young) packs more of a punch. **Coffee** is normally good and strong, while **tea** comes in many different blends. **Chocolate** (*chocomel*) is also popular, served hot or cold.

DRUGS

Purchases of up to 5g of cannabis, and possession of up to 30g (the legal limit) are tolerated; in practice, many "**coffeeshops**" offer discounted bulk purchases of 50g with impunity. Coffeeshops in city centres – neon-lit dives pumping out mainstream rock, reggae or techno – are worth avoiding. Less touristy districts house more congenial, high-quality outlets. When you walk in, ask to see the **menu**, which lists the different hashes and grasses on offer. Take care with spacecakes (cakes or biscuits baked with hash), mainly because you can never be sure what's in them, and don't ever buy from street dealers. All other narcotics are illegal, and don't even entertain the notion of taking a "souvenir" home with you.

CULTURE AND ETIQUETTE

The Dutch are renowned for their liberal and laidback attitude, so there isn't much in the way of etiquette to observe. Don't be embarrassed about speaking to locals in English – unlike many of their fellow Europeans, the Dutch are happy to converse in English and are generally helpful. A five to ten percent **tip** is generally expected in cafés and restaurants.

SPORTS AND ACTIVITIES

The Netherlands is a nation of **cyclists**, and you won't have any problems finding cycle paths or bikes for rent. With most of the country's major towns sat cheek by jowl in the Randstad, cycling from city to city is very easy. If you're looking for a more rural experience, the island of Texel and the Hoge Veluwe National Park near Arnhem are ideal, with the park even providing free bicycles for visitors. **Football** is also extremely popular, with the season running from September to May and matches held on Sunday at around 2.30pm, with occasional games on Wednesday too. The major teams are PSV Eindhoven, Feyenoord in Rotterdam, and Amsterdam's Ajax.

COMMUNICATIONS

Most official post offices have recently closed down; all **postal transactions** are now carried out by stores carrying the TNT logo. **Stamps** are sold in most supermarkets, book stores and hotels. Post international items in the "Overige" slot. **Public phones** are rapidly disappearing with only a few of them left near train stations mainly for tourists. Phonecards are available from TNT stores and VVVs (see below) – or credit cards. The operator is on ⓣ0800/0410 (free). Many cafés and public libraries offer **internet access**.

EMERGENCIES

As long as you're wary of pickpockets and badly lit streets at night, you're unlikely to come into contact with the police. **Pharmacies** (*apotheek*) are open Monday to Friday 8.30am to 5.30pm; if they are closed there'll be a note of the nearest open pharmacy on the door. When in need of a doctor, enquire at the reception of your accommodation; otherwise head for any hospital (*ziekenhuis*). If you need the emergency services, police, ambulance and fire are all on ⓣ112.

INFORMATION

VVV tourist offices are usually in town centres or by train stations and have information in English, including maps

THE NETHERLANDS ONLINE

ⓦ**www.holland.com** National tourist board.
ⓦ**www.ns.nl** Train information.
ⓦ**www.9292ov.nl** Door-to-door public transport information.

and accommodation lists; they will also book rooms for a small charge.

MONEY AND BANKS

The Dutch currency is the **euro** (€). **Banking hours** are Monday 1 to 5/6pm, Tuesday to Friday 9am to 5/6pm; in larger cities some banks also open Thursday 7 to 9pm and occasionally on Saturday mornings. **GWK exchange offices** at train stations open late daily. You can also change money at most VVV tourist offices, post offices and bureaux de change, though rates are worse. **ATMs** are widespread.

OPENING HOURS AND HOLIDAYS

Many **shops** stay closed on Monday morning, although markets open early. Otherwise, opening hours tend to be 9am to 5.30/6pm, with many shops closing late on Thursdays or Fridays. Sunday opening is becoming increasingly common with many shops open between noon and 5pm. In major cities,

DUTCH

	Dutch	Pronunciation
Yes	*Ja*	Yah
No	*Nee*	Nay
Please	*Alstublieft*	Alstooblee-eft
Thank you	*Dank u/Bedankt*	Dank yoo/Bedankt
Hello/Good day	*Hallo*	Halloh
Goodbye	*Dag/Tot ziens*	Dahg/Tot Zeens
Excuse me	*Pardon*	Pardon
Where?	*Waar?*	Waah?
Good	*Goed*	Gud
Bad	*Slecht*	Slecht
Near	*Dichtbij*	Dichtbye
Far	*Ver*	Vare
Cheap	*Goedkoop*	Gudkoop
Expensive	*Duur*	Dooer
Open	*Open*	Open
Closed	*Gesloten*	Gesloten
Push	*Duwen*	Doowen
Pull	*Trekken*	Trekken
Today	*Vandaag*	Vandahg
Yesterday	*Gisteren*	Histehren
Tomorrow	*Morgen*	Morgen
How much is...?	*Wat kost…?*	Wat kost…?
I don't understand	*Ik begrijp het niet*	Ick bechripe het neet
Do you speak English?	*Spreekt u Engels?*	Spraicht oo Engells?
One	*Een*	Ayn
Two	*Twee*	Tway
Three	*Drie*	Dree
Four	*Vier*	Veer
Five	*Vijf*	Vife
Six	*Zes*	Zess
Seven	*Zeven*	Zayven
Eight	*Acht*	Acht
Nine	*Negen*	Nehen
Ten	*Tien*	Teen

STUDENT AND YOUTH DISCOUNTS

CJP is part of the European Youth Card Association and is a worthwhile investment. Costing €15, it offers countless discounts to under-30s for one year (www.cjp.nl). Buy it online at www.europeanyouthcard.org or in person at Stayokay hostels or VVV offices. Discounts include most museums, galleries and tourist attractions throughout the country, as well as theatre, film and other leisure activities. If you are over 30, then the nationwide **Museum Card** (*Museumkaart*), costing €44.90 for one year, may be more suitable. It is readily available at museums, many of which offer free entry to card holders.

night shops (*avondwinkels*) open 4pm to 1/2am. **Museum** times are generally Tuesday to Saturday 10am to 5pm, Sunday 1 to 5pm, although these vary widely. Shops and banks are closed, and museums adopt Sunday hours, on **public holidays**: January 1, Good Friday, Easter Sunday and Monday, April 30, May 5, Ascension Day, Whitsun and Monday, December 25 and December 26.

Amsterdam

AMSTERDAM is a charming capital, with a beguiling mix of the provincial and the cosmopolitan and an enduring appeal for backpackers. For many, its array of world-class museums and galleries – notably the **Rijksmuseum**, **Anne Frank House** and the **Van Gogh Museum** – are reason enough to visit.

The city started out as a fishing village at the mouth of the River Amstel, and subsequently grew as a major European trading centre. Amsterdam accommodated its expansion with the cobweb of **canals** that gives the city its distinctive and elegant shape today, and around which a *gezellig* café culture has been established.

Amsterdam emerged as the fashionable centre for the alternative movements of the 1960s, a reflection on the long-standing tolerant attitudes of the Dutch. This bestowed a unique character on the city, which still takes a progressive approach to social issues and culture, with a buzz of open-air summer events and intimate clubs and bars. Although government plans to close coffeeshops and Red Light District windows leaves Amsterdam with uncertainties, its ever-youthful atmosphere and a club scene that has recently come of age will makes sure the city keeps rocking.

What to see and do

Amsterdam's compact centre contains most of the city's leading attractions, and it takes only about forty minutes to stroll from one end to the other. Centraal Station lies on the centre's northern edge, and from here the city fans south in a web of concentric canals, surrounded by expanding suburbs.

At the heart of the city is the **Old Centre**, an oval-shaped area with a jumble of streets and beautiful narrow canals. This is the unlikely setting for the infamous **Red Light District**. Forming a ring around it is the first of the major canals, the **Singel**, followed closely by the **Herengracht**, **Keizersgracht** and **Prinsengracht**, created during the city's expansion in the seventeenth century. Development was strictly controlled, resulting in the tall, very narrow residences with decorative gables. This is the Amsterdam you see in the brochures: still, dreamy canals, crisp reflections of seventeenth-century town-houses and cobbled streets. For shops, bars and restaurants, you're better off exploring the crossing-streets that connect the canals.

To the south is the city's main square and energetic party venue, **Leidseplein**, with the leafy **Vondelpark** nearby. The **Jordaan** to the northwest features mazy streets and narrow canals, and offers perfect strolling territory. To the east is the **Old Jewish Quarter**.

Centraal Station and the Damrak

The medieval core fans south from the nineteenth-century **Centraal Station**, one of Amsterdam's most resonant landmarks. From here, the busy thoroughfare **Damrak** marches into the heart of the city, lined with overpriced restaurants and bobbing canal boats, and flanked on the left first by the Modernist stock exchange, the **Beurs van Bevrlage** (now a concert hall), and then by the enormous De Bijenkorf department store. The **Sexmuseum**, Damrak 18 (daily 9.30am–11.30pm; €4), presents the "art of loving" throughout the ages for your viewing pleasure.

The Red Light District

East of Damrak, the infamous **Red Light District**, stretching across two canals – Oudezijds Voorburgwal and Oudezijds Achterburgwal – is one of the real sights of the city. The atmosphere is undeniably sleazy, but it's perhaps more fun to visit the place at night, when the

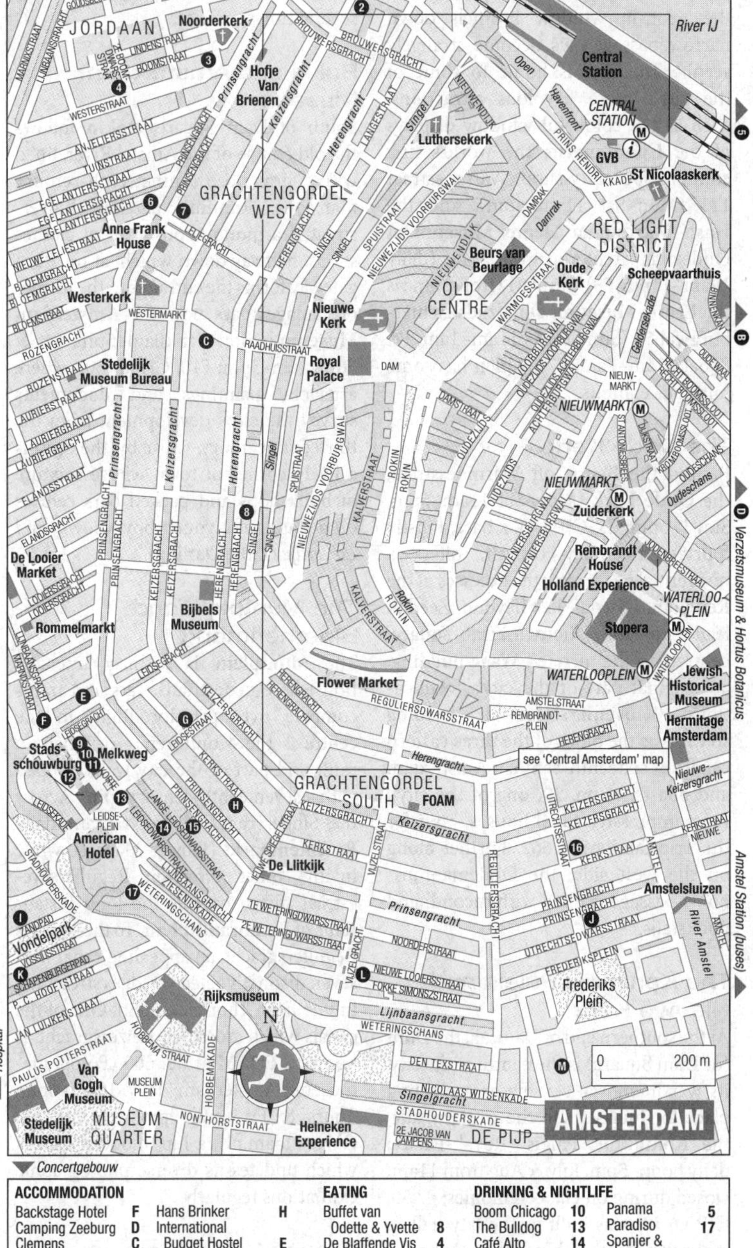

ACCOMMODATION

Backstage Hotel F
Camping Zeeburg D
Clemens C
Coco Mama M
Euphemia L
Flying Pig Uptown K
Golden Bear G
Hans Brinker H
International Budget Hostel E
Prisenhof J
Stayokay Vondelpark I
Stayokay Zeeburg B
Vliegenbos A

EATING

Buffet van Odette & Yvette 8
De Blaffende Vis 4
Il Tramezzino 2
Piccolino 15
Soenda Kelapa 16
Winkel 3

DRINKING & NIGHTLIFE

Boom Chicago 10
The Bulldog 13
Café Alto 14
De Twee Zwaantjes 6
Jimmy Woo 9
Melkweg 11
Panama 5
Paradiso 17
Spanjer & van Twist 7
Sugar Factory 9
Thÿssen 1
Weber 12

seediness is somehow less glaring and the neon-lit window brothels down narrow passageways become strangely scenic. The area is home to some of the city's more frivolous attractions, such as the colourful window displays of the **Condomerie**, the world's first condom speciality shop, Warmoestraat 141 (Mon–Sat 11am–6pm), and the **Hash Marihuana Hemp Museum** at Oudezijds Achterburgwal 148 (daily 10am–11pm; €9). Similarly frolicsome is the **Erotic Museum**, Oudezijds Achterburgwal 54 (Sun–Thurs 11am–1am, Fri & Sat 11am–2am; €7), which has some hilarious exhibits.

The Oude Kerk

Behind the Beurs, off Warmoesstraat, the **Oude Kerk** (Mon–Sat 11am–5pm, Sun 1–5pm; €5, CJP €4), a bare, mostly fourteenth-century church, offers a reverential peace after the excesses of the Red Light District. Just beyond, Zeedijk leads to the **Nieuwmarkt square**, centred on the turreted **Waag** building, an original part of the city's fortifications. **Kloveniersburgwal**, heading south, was the outer of the three eastern canals of sixteenth-century Amsterdam and boasts, at no. 29, one of the city's most impressive canal houses, built for the Trip family in 1662. Further along on the west side, the Oudemanhuispoort passage is filled with secondhand bookstalls.

The Koninklijk Paleis and Nieuwe Kerk

At the southern end of Damrak, the **Dam** (or Dam Square) is the centre of the city, its war memorial serving as a meeting place for tourists. On the western side, the **Koninklijk Paleis** (Royal Palace; daily noon–5pm, July & Aug from 11am, closed during official ceremonies; €7.50, CJP €6.50) was built as the city hall in the mid-seventeenth century. Vying for importance is the adjacent **Nieuwe Kerk** (open for exhibitions, daily 10am–5pm; €8), a fifteenth-century church rebuilt several times.

Rokin and Amsterdam Museum

South of Dam Square, **Rokin** follows the old course of the Amstel River, lined with grandiose nineteenth-century mansions. Running parallel, Kalverstraat is a monotonous strip of clothes shops, halfway down which, at no. 92, a gateway forms the entrance to the former orphanage that's now the **Amsterdam Museum**. (Mon–Fri 10am–5pm, Sat & Sun 11am–5pm; €10, CJP €7.50), where artefacts, paintings and documents survey the city's development from the thirteenth century. Close by, the **Spui** is a lively corner of town whose mixture of bookshops and packed bars centres on a statue of a young boy known as *'t Lieverdje* (Little Darling).

The Muntplein and Bloemenmarkt

The **Muntplein** is a busy intersection where pedestrians, cars and trams compete over priority. Right in the centre is the Munttoren – originally a mint and part of the city walls, topped with a seventeenth-century spire. Across the Singel canal is the fragrant daily **Bloemenmarkt** (Flower Market), while in the other direction Reguliersbreestraat turns towards the loud restaurants of **Rembrandtplein**. To the south is Reguliersgracht, an appealing canal with seven distinctive steep bridges stretching in line from Thorbeckeplein. One of the canals which crosses it, Keizersgracht, is home to **FOAM** at no. 609 (Fotografiemuseum Amsterdam; daily: 10am–6pm, Thurs & Fri until 9pm; €8, CJP €4; Ⓦwww.foam.nl), a hip, modern gallery which updates its diverse photographic exhibitions regularly.

Around Leidseplein

From the Spui, trams and pedestrians cross Koningsplein onto Amsterdam's

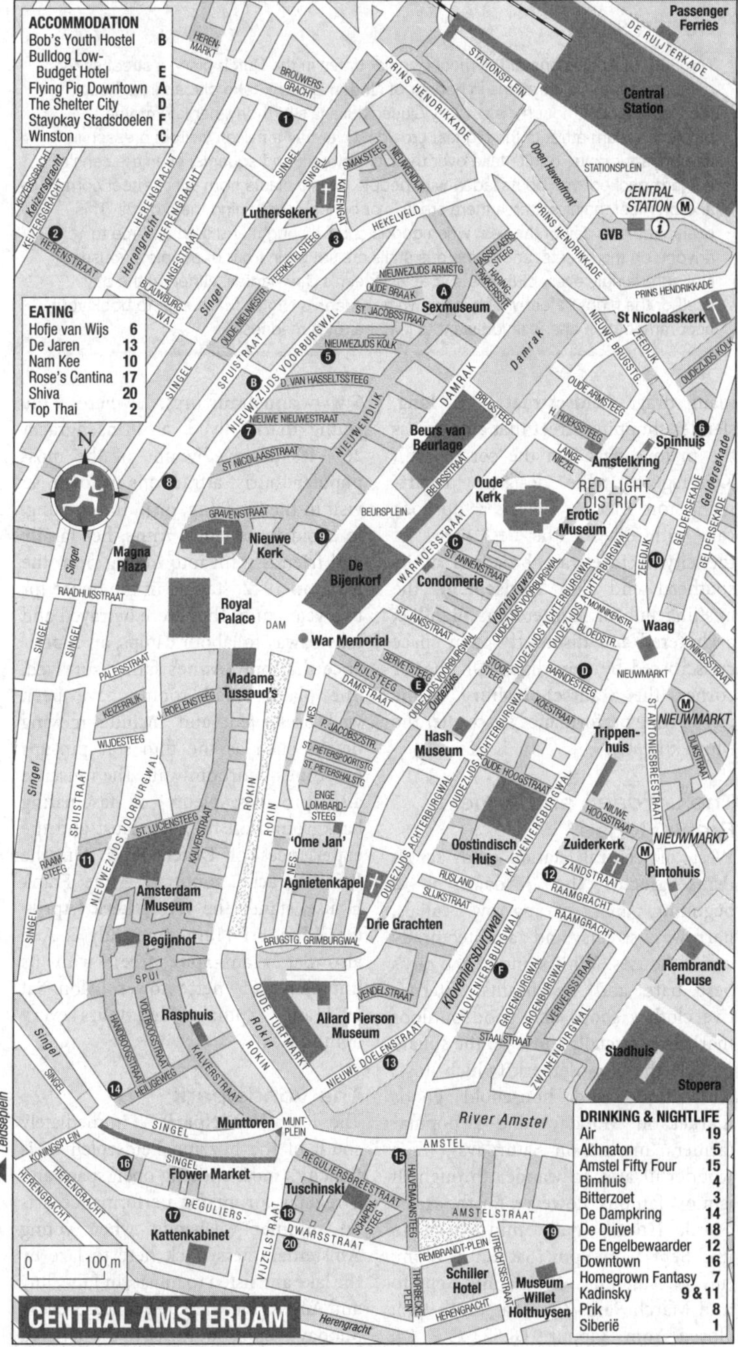
ACCOMMODATION
Bob's Youth Hostel B
Bulldog Low-Budget Hotel E
Flying Pig Downtown A
The Shelter City D
Stayokay Stadsdoelen F
Winston C
EATING
Hofje van Wijs 6
De Jaren 13
Nam Kee 10
Rose's Cantina 17
Shiva 20
Top Thai 2
DRINKING & NIGHTLIFE
Air 19
Akhnaton 5
Amstel Fifty Four 15
Bimhuis 4
Bitterzoet 3
De Dampkring 14
De Duivel 18
De Engelbewaarder 12
Downtown 16
Homegrown Fantasy 7
Kadinsky 9 & 11
Prik 8
Siberië 1
Central Station
Passenger Ferries
De Ruijterkade
Stationsplein
Prins Hendrikkade
Open Havenfront
GVB
St Nicolaaskerk
Luthersekerk
Sexmuseum
Damrak
Beurs van Beurlage
Oude Kerk
Red Light District
Erotic Museum
Spinhuis
Amstelkring
Nieuwe Kerk
Magna Plaza
De Bijenkorf
Condomerie
Royal Palace
Dam
War Memorial
Madame Tussaud's
Waag
Nieuwmarkt
Trippenhuis
Hash Museum
Oostindisch Huis
Zuiderkerk
Pintohuis
'Ome Jan'
Agnietenkapel
Drie Grachten
Amsterdam Museum
Begijnhof
Rasphuis
Allard Pierson Museum
Rembrandt House
Stadhuis
Stopera
River Amstel
Munttoren
Flower Market
Tuschinski
Kattenkabinet
Schiller Hotel
Museum Willet Holthuysen
Rembrandtplein
Leidseplein
0 100 m
CENTRAL AMSTERDAM

QUEEN'S DAY

The 30th of April is one of the most popular dates in the Dutch diary, a street event *par excellence*. Celebrations in honour of **Queen Beatrix** take place throughout the Netherlands (though it's actually Queen Juliana's birthday, her late mother), but Amsterdam attracts the biggest crowds. Over half a million visitors dressed in flamboyant orange outfits take over the city's streets and squares; even the canals are jam-packed with boats laden with people. Music blasts from every street corner and on most major squares there are DJs or bands entertaining the crowds. This is also the one day of the year when goods can be bought and sold tax-free to anyone on the streets, and numerous stalls are set up in front of people's houses. Not surprisingly every club hosts special Queen's Day parties, either on the day itself or the night before which is known as **Queen's Night**. Make sure to book your accommodation ahead if you want to join the royal madness.

main drag, **Leidsestraat** – a long, slender shopping street that cuts across the main canals. On the corner with Keizersgracht, the designer department store Metz & Co has a top-floor café with one of the best views of the city. Leidsestraat broadens at its southern end into **Leidseplein**, the bustling hub of Amsterdam's nightlife, a cluttered and disorderly open space crisscrossed by tram lines. On the far corner, the **Stadsschouwburg** is the city's prime performance space after the Muziektheater.

The Jordaan and Anne Frank House

West of central station and across Prinsengracht, the **Jordaan** is a beguiling area of narrow canals, narrower streets and architecturally varied houses. With some of the city's best bars and restaurants, alternative clothes shops and good outdoor markets, especially those on the square outside the Noorderkerk (which hosts an antique and household goods market on Mondays and a popular farmers' market on Saturdays), it's a wonderful area to wander through. It is most famous, however, for the **Anne Frank House** (daily mid-March to mid-Sept 9am–9pm, Sat until 10pm; July & Aug until 10pm; mid-Sept to mid-March 9am–7pm, Sat until 9pm; closed Yom Kippur; €8.50, CJP €4; Ⓦwww.annefrank.org), where the young diarist lived, at Prinsengracht 267. It's deservedly one of the most popular tourist attractions in town, so visit in the morning, or in the evening, to avoid the queues. Anne, her family and friends went into hiding from the Nazis in 1942, staying in the house for two years until they were betrayed and taken away to labour camps, an experience that only Anne's father survived. The plain, small rooms have been well preserved, and include moving details such as the film star pin-ups on Anne's bedroom wall. The museum also provides plenty of fascinating background on the Holocaust and the experiences of Dutch Jews. On the Prinsengracht, south of Anne Frank House, stands the **Westerkerk** (April–Oct Mon–Fri 11am–3pm; July & Aug also Sat 11am–3pm; free), with its impressive 85-metre tower (Mon–Sat 10/11am–6/8pm; guided tours every 30min; €7).

The Vondelpark

The lush **Vondelpark** – immediately south of the buzzing Leidseplein – is the city's most enticing open space and a regular forum for performance arts on summer weekends, when young Amsterdammers flock here to laze by the lake and listen to music; in June, July and August there are free concerts every Sunday at 2pm. Southeast of the park is a residential district, with designer shops and delis along chic **P.C. Hooftstraat** and **Van Baerlestraat**, and some of the city's major museums grouped around the grassy wedge of **Museumplein**.

The Rijksmuseum

The **Rijksmuseum**, at Jan Luijkenstraat 1 (daily 9am–6pm; €12.50, CJP €6.25; ⓦwww.rijksmuseum.nl), has fine collections of medieval and Renaissance applied art, displays on Dutch history, a fine Asian collection and an array of seventeenth-century Dutch paintings that is among the best in the world. Most people head straight for one of the museum's great treasures, Rembrandt's *The Night Watch*, but there are many other examples of his work, along with portraits by Frans Hals, landscapes by Jan van Goyen and Jacob van Ruisdael, the riotous scenes of Jan Steen and the peaceful interiors of Vermeer and Pieter de Hooch.

The Van Gogh Museum and Stedelijk Museum

For the popular **Van Gogh Museum** at Paulus Potterstraat 7 (daily 10am–6pm, Fri until 10pm; €14, CJP €11.50; ⓦwww.vangoghmuseum.nl), it's best to arrive early in high season, as long queues can be a problem. The collection includes the early years in Holland, continuing to the brighter works he painted after moving to Paris and then Arles, where he produced vivid canvases like *The Yellow House* and the *Sunflowers* series. Along the street, at Paulus Potterstraat 13, the **Stedelijk Museum of Modern Art** (Tues–Sun 10am–5pm, Thurs until 10pm; €10, CJP €5; ⓦwww.stedelijk.nl) has temporarily opened part of the museum which is undergoing major refurbishments with long delays. At the time of writing the museum was scheduled to reopen late 2012 but – as this date has been pushed back frequently – check the website for current information.

The Heineken Experience and De Pijp

The rather disappointing **Heineken Experience** at Stadhouderskade 78, east from the Rijksmuseum (daily 11am–7pm, last entry 5.30pm; €15), provides an overview of Heineken's history and the brewing process, with a couple of free beers thrown in afterwards. South of here is the neighbourhood known as **De Pijp** (The Pipe) after its long, sombre canyons of brick tenements. This has always been one of the city's closest-knit communities, and one of its liveliest, with numerous inexpensive Surinamese and Turkish restaurants and a cheerful hub in the long slim thoroughfare of **Albert Cuypstraat**, whose food and clothes **market** (Mon–Sat 9.30am–5pm) is the largest in the city.

East of the centre

East of Rembrandtplein across the Amstel, the large, squat **Muziektheater** and **Stadhuis** (commonly known as Stopera) flank **Waterlooplein**, home to the city's excellent **flea market** (Mon–Sat). Behind, Jodenbreestraat was once the main street of the Jewish quarter (emptied by the Nazis in the 1940s); no. 6 is **Het Rembrandthuis** (Rembrandt House; daily 10am–5pm; €10, CJP €7), which the painter bought at the height of his fame, living here for over twenty years. It displays a large number of the artist's engravings and paintings, plus a number of archeological findings from the site.

The Jewish Quarter

The excellent, award-winning **Joods Historisch Museum**, at Nieuwe Amstelstraat 1 (Jewish Historical Museum; daily 11am–5pm; closed Yom Kippur; €9, CJP €6), is cleverly housed in a complex of Ashkenazi synagogues dating from the late seventeenth century and gives an imaginative introduction to Jewish life and beliefs. Photographs and film footage give a vivid impression of Amsterdam's long-gone Jewish ghetto, while interactive pieces explain Jewish customs.

Down Muiderstraat, the prim **Hortus Botanicus**, at Plantage Middenlaan 2 (Mon–Fri 9am–5pm, Sat & Sun 10am–5pm; July & Aug until 7pm; Dec & Jan until 4pm; €7, CJP €3.50), is a pocket-sized botanical garden with eight thousand plant species; stop off for a relaxed coffee and cakes in the orangery. The eye-catching Plancius Building at Plantage Kerklaan 61 houses the first-rate **Verzetsmuseum** (Dutch Resistance Museum; Tues–Fri 10am–5pm, Sat–Mon 11am–5pm; €7.50, CJP €4), where a variety of exhibits depict the ways in which the Dutch people opposed Nazi oppression. From here it's a short stroll towards the River Amstel to the **Hermitage Amsterdam** at Amstel 51 (daily 10am–5pm, Wed until 8pm; €15, CJP €12; ⓦwww.hermitage.nl), the first foreign branch of Russia's leading art museum in St Petersburg possessing an extensive collection of paintings of Old Masters, as well as Oriental art and Post-Impressionist work.

Arrival and information

Air Schiphol airport is connected by train to Centraal Station (every 10min, hourly at night; 15min; €3.70).

Train Centraal Station is the hub of all bus and tram routes and just 5min walk from central Dam Square.

Bus International buses arrive at Amstel Station, 10min south of Centraal Station by metro.

Tourist office The main VVV is outside Centraal Station, at Stationsplein 10 (Mon–Wed 9am–6pm, Thurs–Sat 9am–7pm, Sun 9am–5pm; ⓣ0900/400 4040, ⓦwww.iamsterdam.nl) and there's an office in the airport arrivals hall (daily 7am–10pm).

Discount card The Iamsterdam Card from the VVV (€39/49/59 for 24/48/72hr; ⓦwww.iamsterdam.nl), gives free or reduced entry to major museums and attractions, unlimited public transport and selected restaurant discounts.

City transport and tours

Public transport There's an excellent network of trams, buses and the metro (all daily 6/7am–midnight). The GVB public transport office in front of Centraal Station (Mon–Fri 7am–9pm, Sat & Sun 10am–6pm; ⓣ0900/8011, ⓦwww.gvb.nl) has free route maps and sells chip cards (see p.823). After midnight, night buses take over, running roughly hourly from Centraal Station to most parts of the city (one-way ticket €4).

Bike rental From Centraal Station or from a number of firms around town: Bike City, Bloemgracht 70 ⓣ020/626 3721, ⓦwww.bikecity.nl; Damstraat Rent-a-Bike at Damstraat 20 ⓣ020/625 5029, ⓦwww.bikes.nl; or MacBike (ⓣ020/620 0985, ⓦwww.macbike.nl) at Waterlooplein 199, Weteringschans 2, and Stationsplein 5. All charge around €13 a day, plus €50 deposit with ID.

Bike tours Yellow Bike, at Nieuwezijds Kolk 29 (ⓣ020/620 6940, ⓦwww.yellowbike.nl), organizes a three-hour city tour for €23.50/person. Mike's Bike Tours, at Kerkstraat 134 (ⓣ020/622 7970, ⓦwww.mikesbiketoursamsterdam.com), offers a similar tour at a better rate, with student discounts.

Walking tours There are interesting free walking tours of the main sights (daily 11.15am & 1.15pm from the National Monument in Dam Square; 3hr; ⓦwww.neweuropetours.eu).

Accommodation

In high season, and weekends throughout the year, it's always worth booking ahead, or you'll find almost everywhere full. The following are marked on the map on p.829, unless otherwise stated.

Hostels

Bob's Youth Hostel Nieuwezijds Voorburgwal 92 ⓣ020/623 0063, ⓦwww.bobsyouthhostel.nl. See map, p.831. Lively and smoky, this is an old backpackers' favourite. Also has apartments with kitchens. 10min walk southwest from Centraal Station. Dorms €23.

Bulldog Low-Budget Hotel Oudezijds Voorburgwal 220 ⓣ020/620 3822, ⓦwww.bulldog.nl. See map, p.831. Part of the *Bulldog* coffeeshop chain, this super-smart hostel has a bar, DVD lounge, roof terrace and laundry facilities. There are dorms with TVs and showers, doubles and apartments. Dorms €32, doubles €105–120.

Coco Mama Westeinde 18 ⓣ020/627 2454, ⓦwww.cocomama.nl. Located in a former brothel, this self-proclaimed boutique hostel with themed dorms sleeping up to six people has a pleasant common area and cute little garden – which includes a house cat. Dorms €36, doubles €120.

Flying Pig Downtown Nieuwendijk 100 ⓣ020/420 6822, ⓦwww.flyingpig.nl. See map, p.831. Clean, large establishment run by ex-backpackers, with free kitchen, internet, an all-night bar and no curfew; not for faint-hearted non-smokers. 5min walk from Centraal Station. There's also the slightly quieter *Flying Pig Uptown* by the Vondelpark at Vossiusstraat 46 (ⓣ020/400 4187; tram #1/#2/#5 to Leidseplein, then a 5min walk). Both dorms €30, doubles €95.

Hans Brinker Kerkstraat 136 ⓣ020/622 0687, ⓦwww.hans-brinker.com. Well-established and raucously popular cheapie with a bright café attached (meals €5–7). Tram #1/#2/#5 to Prinsengracht. Dorms €25, doubles €80.

International Budget Hostel Leidsegracht 76 ⓣ020/624 2784, ⓦwww.internationalbudgethostel.com. Excellent, homely budget option on a peaceful little canal in the heart of the city. Tram #1/#2/#5 to Prinsengracht. Dorms €18–35.

Stayokay Three HI hostels in town ⓦwww.stayokay.com. *Stadsdoelen* (see map p.831) at Kloveniersburgwal 97 (ⓣ020/624 6832), *Vondelpark* at Zandpad 5 (ⓣ020/589 8996) and *Zeeburg* at Timorplein 21 (ⓣ020/551 3190) all of high standard. *Stadsdoelen* is easiest accessible, *Vondelpark* most atmospheric and *Zeeburg* most modern. Prices vary but expect to pay between €24–33 for a dorm bed and between €75–115 for a double.

Winston Warmoesstraat 129 ⓣ020/623 1380, ⓦwww.winston.nl. This self-consciously young and cool hostel has funky rooms individually decorated with alternative art and a busy ground-floor bar that has occasional live music. Ten minutes' walk from Centraal Station. Dorms €34, doubles €90.

Hotels

Backstage Hotel Leidsegracht 114 ⓣ020/624 4044, ⓦwww.backstagehotel.com. Hotel aimed to accommodate musicians playing at the nearby *Melkweg* or *Paradiso* with theatre mirrors, PA spotlights and flight cases as furniture. Facilities include free internet, a 24-hour bar and pool table. Tram #1, #2 or #5 to Prinsengracht. Singles €59, doubles €90.

Clemens Raadhuisstraat 39 ⓣ020/624 6089, ⓦwww.clemenshotel.com. Clean, neat and good value for money, with breakfast included. Ask for a quieter room at the back. Tram #13/#17 to Westermarkt. Singles €60, doubles €80.

Euphemia Fokke Simonszstraat 1 ⓣ020/622 9045, ⓦwww.euphemiahotel.com. A likeable, laidback atmosphere, and big, basic rooms at reasonable prices, which means it's usually full. Tram #16 or #24 to Weteringcircuit. Singles €70, doubles €80.

Golden Bear Kerkstraat 37 ⓣ020/624 4785, ⓦwww.goldenbear.nl. The first gay hotel in the city, with clean and spacious rooms. Minimum stay of three nights if the weekend is included, March–Nov. Trams #1, #2 & #5 to Kerkstraat. Singles €65, doubles €90.

Prinsenhof Prinsengracht 810 ⓣ020/623 1772, ⓦwww.hotelprinsenhof.com. Housed in an eighteenth-century canal house. Only two rooms are en suite, but a hearty breakfast is included and service couldn't be friendlier. Singles €49, doubles €69.

Campsites

Camping Zeeburg Zuider IJdijk 20 ⓣ020/694 4430, ⓦwww.campingzeeburg.nl. Located on an island amid trees and with free wi-fi. Tram #26 from Centraal Station to Zuiderzeeweg or night bus #359 to Flevoweg. Open all year. €11.50; two-person cabin €45.

Vliegenbos Meeuwenlaan 138 ⓣ020/636 8855, ⓦwww.vliegenbos.com. Well equipped with homely restaurant and lots of shade. In Amsterdam North, a 10min ride on bus #32, #33 or night bus #361 from Centraal Station. Closed Oct–March. €8.70/person, plus €2.50/tent.

Eating

Amsterdam has many ethnic restaurants, especially Indonesian, Chinese and Thai, as well as *eetcafés* that serve decent, well-priced food in an unpretentious setting. The following are marked on the map on p.829, unless otherwise stated.

Cafés

Buffet van Odette & Yvette Herengracht 309. Crowded little place selling home-made quiches, salads and soups as well as mouthwatering cakes to satisfy the sweetest tooth. Open until 4.30/5.30pm.

De Jaren Nieuwe Doelenstraat 20–22, near Muntplein. See map, p.831. Modern, grand café with a waterside terrace – a perfect place for people-watching and newspaper-browsing in the sun. *Appeltaart* €4.

Hofje van Wijs Zeedijk 43. See map, p.831. This lunchroom tucked away in an eighteenth-century courtyard is a true hidden treasure selling countless different coffee and tea blends and home-made delicacies, mainly organic.

Il Tramezzino Haarlemmerstraat 79. Richly filled sandwiches (€2.95) according to the old Venetian recipe to be washed down with a superb espresso in an up-to-the-minute setting.

Winkel Noordermarkt 43, opposite the Noorderkerk. Popular local hangout on Saturday mornings during the farmers' market. Famously delicious apple cake. Mains €12.

Restaurants

De Blaffende Vis Westerstraat 118 ⓣ020/625 1721. Great bar-restaurant in the Jordaan. Popular with students and gets raucous at weekends. Dagschotel around €8–9.

Nam Kee Zeedijk 111–113 ⓣ020/624 3470. See map, p.831. Simple but always bustling Chinese eatery located in Chinatown. Expect to queue up. Mains from €9.

Piccolino Lange Leidsedwarsstraat 63 ⓣ020/623 1495. One of Amsterdam's oldest Italian restaurants, known for its cheap pizzas (from €5) and a 4-course meal for €16.

Rose's Cantina Reguliersdwarsstraat 40 ⓣ020/625 9797. Long-established Mexican restaurant with attractive garden. Fajitas from €16 and a wicked cocktail selection.

Shiva Reguliersdwarsstraat 72 ⓣ020/624 8713. See map, p.831. Outstanding Indian restaurant, with well-priced, expertly prepared food, and veggie options. Mains €15.

Soenda Kelapa Utrechtsestraat 89 ⓣ020/627 9416. A small Indonesian restaurant with no frills but generous portions of excellent food. Chicken *sateh rijsttafel* €17.50. Daily from 6pm.

Top Thai Herenstraat 28 ⓣ020/623 4633. See map, p.831. Some of the best-value authentic Thai food in Amsterdam. Popular and friendly. Pad thai €10. Daily from 4pm.

Drinking and nightlife

There is a distinction between bars and coffeeshops, where smoking dope is the primary pastime (ask to see the menu). You must be 18 or over to enter these, and don't expect alcohol to be served. Most are open 9am–1am (2/3am at weekends). Most clubs are open between 10/11pm–4/5am Drinks cost around fifty percent more than in a bar, but entry prices are low and there's rarely any kind of door policy. The following are marked on the map on p.829, unless otherwise stated.

Bars

De Duivel Reguliersdwarsstraat 87. See map, p.831. Amsterdam's only hip-hop café, with hip-hop and funk from midnight. Daily 8pm–3/4am.

De Engelbewaarder Kloveniersburgwal 59. See map, p.831. Relaxed and informal haunt of Amsterdam's bookish types, with live jazz on Sunday afternoons.

De Twee Zwaantjes Prinsengracht 114. Tiny oddball Jordaan bar where locals sing along raucously to accordion music – you'll either love it or hate it.

Spanjer & van Twist Leliegracht 60. A popular place which is perfect for laidback summer afternoons, with chairs overlooking the quietest canal in Jordaan. Also serves lunch and dinner.

Thijssen Brouwersgracht 107. An old-time local favourite, perfect to linger over coffee or fresh mint tea with a magazine. The tiny terrace gives good views of the bustling market.

Weber Marnixstraat 397. Popular hangout, just off the Leidseplein, attracting musicians, students and young professionals. Crowded and noisy on weekends. Daily 8pm–3/4am.

Coffeeshops

The Bulldog Leidseplein 15–17 and other central outlets. More like a dodgy club than a coffeeshop, and certainly not the place for a thoughtful smoke. The dope is reliably good though, if expensive.

De Dampkring Handboogstraat 29. See map, p.831. With colourful decor and a refined menu, this coffeeshop is known for its good-quality hash.

Homegrown Fantasy Nieuwezijds Voorburgwal 87a. See map, p.831. Part of the Dutch Passion seed company, selling the widest range of (mostly Dutch) marijuana in Amsterdam.

Kadinsky Zoutsteeg 9 & Rosmarijnsteeg 9, both in the old centre. See map, p.831. Sensational chocolate-chip cookies, scrupulously accurate deals and a background of jazz dance.

Siberië Brouwersgracht 11. See map, p.831. Slightly off the beaten tourist track, very relaxed and friendly – worth a visit whether you want to smoke or not.

Clubs

Air Amstelstraat 24 ⓦwww.air.nl. See map, p.831. Amsterdam's newest addition to the club scene hosting everything from hardcore techno DJs to nineties dance nights.

Bitterzoet Spuistraat 2 ⓦwww.bitterzoet.com. See map, p.831. Club with an eclectic mix of nights, featuring live bands as well as DJs.

Jimmy Woo Korte Leidsedwarsstraat 16 ⓦwww.jimmywoo.com. A chic, loungey club where East meets West. It's a favourite of stylish Amsterdammers, so dress well. Thurs–Sun 11pm–3/4am.

Panama Oostelijke Handelskade 4 ⓦwww.panama.nl. Cool club-cum-restaurant overlooking the IJ with frequent live music, salsa and DJ nights.

Sugar Factory Lijnbaansgracht 238 ⓦwww.sugarfactory.nl. A "night theatre" featuring everything from spoken word to cabaret, including straightforward club nights.

Entertainment

Amsterdam buzzes with places offering a wide and inventive range of entertainment. The best source of listings information is the Uitburo (Leidseplein 26; Mon–Fri 10am–7.30pm, Sat 10am–6pm, Sun noon–6pm) or AUB (Ⓦwww.aub.nl). Saturday's *Het Parool* newspaper has a good entertainment supplement, *PS van de Week* or pick up a copy of the NL20 magazine, available at most bars and supermarkets. The following are marked on the map on p.829, unless otherwise stated.

Cinemas and comedy

Boom Chicago Leidseplein 12 Ⓣ020/423 0101, Ⓦwww.boomchicago.nl. Amsterdam's popular, multi-media comedy show combines sketches and rapid-fire improv. The show is energetically performed by Americans who delve deep into the Dutch, and indeed their own, psyche with hilarious results. Tickets are €22/26 for the weekday/weekend shows.

Cinecenter Lijnbaansgracht 236 Ⓣ020/788 2150, Ⓦwww.cinecenter.nl. Shows the big blockbusters alongside foreign-language films. Tickets €9, CJP €8.

De Uitkijk Prinsengracht 452 Ⓣ020/623 7460, Ⓦwww.uitkijk.nl. The oldest film theatre in Amsterdam, and one of the more intimate. Tickets €9, CJP €8.

Live music venues

Akhnaton Nieuwezijds Kolk 25 Ⓣ020/624 3396, Ⓦwww.akhnaton.nl. See map, p.831. Specializes in African and Latin American music and dance parties.

Bimhuis Piet Heinkade 3 Ⓣ020/788 2188, Ⓦwww.bimhuis.nl. See map, p.831. Premier jazz venue. Free improv sessions on Tues from 8pm. Take tram #25/#26 to stop Muziekgebouw/Bimhuis from Centraal Station.

Café Alto Korte Leidsedwarsstraat 115 Ⓦwww.jazz-cafe-alto.nl. Legendary jazz café-bar, with free live music every night from 10pm. Big on atmosphere, though not space. Daily 9pm–3/4am.

Melkweg Lijnbaansgracht 234 Ⓣ020/531 8181, Ⓦwww.melkweg.nl. Amsterdam's famous entertainment venue which combines music, theatre, photography, film and media arts under one roof. There are quality DJs playing at the weekend, a monthly film programme, theatre, gallery, bar and restaurant.

Paradiso Weteringschans 6–8 Ⓦwww.paradiso.nl. The most atmospheric music venue located in a converted church near the Leidseplein hosting local as well as international acts with frequent DJs to top the night off.

Classical music and opera

Beurs van Berlage Damrak 277 Ⓣ020/530 4141, Ⓦwww.beursvanberlage.nl. The splendid interior of the former stock exchange hosts a wide selection of music from the Dutch Philharmonic and Dutch Chamber orchestras.

Concertgebouw Concertgebouwplein 2–6 Ⓣ020/671 8345, Ⓦwww.concertgebouw.nl. Catch world-renowned orchestras playing amid wonderful acoustics. Summer concerts and free lunchtime performances on Wednesdays. There are CJP discounts, and "Sprint Seats" for under-30s sold 45min before the start of each concert for €10.

Gay Amsterdam

Amsterdam has one of the biggest and best-established gay scenes in Europe: attitudes are tolerant and facilities unequalled. The nationwide organization COC, at Rozenstraat 14 (Ⓣ020/626 3087, Ⓦwww.cocamsterdam.nl), can provide information, and has a café and popular club nights. For further advice contact the English-speaking Gay & Lesbian Switchboard (Mon–Fri noon–6pm; Ⓣ020/623 6565, Ⓦwww.switchboard.nl) or check Ⓦwww.gayamsterdam.com. The gay and lesbian bookshop Vrolijk is just behind Dam Square at Paleisstraat 135 (Mon–Fri 11am–6pm, Sat 10am–5pm, Sun 1–5pm; Ⓦwww.vrolijk.nu).

Gay cafés and bars

Amstel Fifty Four Amstel 54. See map, p.831. Perhaps the best-established bar, at its most vivacious in summer when the punters spill out onto the street.

Downtown Reguliersdwarsstraat 31, off Rembrandtplein. See map, p.831. A favourite with visitors. Relaxed and friendly, with inexpensive meals. Daily 10am–8pm.

Prik Spuistraat 109. See map, p.831. Frequently voted as Amsterdam's best gay bar with tasty cocktails, smoothies and snacks, and DJs on weekends. Daily 4pm–1/3am.

Directory

Bookshop The American Book Center, Spui 12 (Mon 11am–8pm, Tues, Wed, Fri & Sat 10am–8pm, Thurs 10am–9pm, Sun 11am–6.30pm), is central and well stocked, including travel guides.

Embassies and consulates Note that most are in Den Haag, not Amsterdam. Australia, Carnegielaan 4, Den Haag Ⓣ070/310 8200; Canada, Sophialaan 7, Den Haag Ⓣ070/311 1600; Ireland, Dr Kuyperstraat 9, Den Haag Ⓣ070/363 0993; New Zealand, Eisenhowerlaan 77N, Den Haag Ⓣ070/346 9324; UK,

Lange Voorhout 10, Den Haag ⓣ070/427 0427; US, Lange Voorhout 102, Den Haag ⓣ070/310 2209.
Exchange GWK Travelex in Centraal Station and on Damrak 1-5 and 86, Kalverstraat 150, Leidsestraat 103 and Leidseplein 31a.
Hospital De Boelelaan 1117 ⓣ020/444 4444.
Left luggage Centraal Station €3. 40–5 for a locker.
Police ⓣ0900/8844 and the operator will direct you to the nearest police office.

Moving on

Train Arnhem (for Hoge Veluwe National Park; every 15min; 1hr 10min); Berlin (every 2hr; 6hr 30min); Brussels (hourly; 2hr 45min); Den Haag HS (every 10min; 45min); Haarlem (every 10min; 15min); Leiden (every 15min; 35min); Maastricht (every 30min; 2hr 35min); Rotterdam (every 10min; 1hr); Schiphol airport (every 10min; 15min); Texel (via Den Helder; every 30min; 1hr 15min); Utrecht (every 15min; 30min).

The Randstad

The string of towns known as the **Randstad**, or "rim town", situated amid a typically Dutch landscape of flat fields cut by canals, forms the country's most populated region and still recalls the landscapes painted in the seventeenth-century heyday of the provinces. Much of the area can be visited as day-trips from Amsterdam, but it's easy and more rewarding to make a proper tour. **Haarlem** is worth a look, while to the south, the university centre of **Leiden** makes a pleasant detour before you reach the refined tranquillity of **Den Haag** (The Hague) and the busy urban centre of **Rotterdam**. Nearby **Delft** and **Gouda** repay visits too, the former with one of the best-preserved centres in the region.

HAARLEM

Just over fifteen minutes from Amsterdam by train, **HAARLEM** is a handsome, mid-sized city that sees itself as a cut above its neighbours. It makes a good alternative base for exploring northern Holland, or even Amsterdam itself, especially if you can't find a bed in the city or would rather be somewhere less hectic.

What to see and do

The core of the city is **Grote Markt** and the adjoining Riviervischmarkt, flanked by the gabled, originally fourteenth-century **Stadhuis** and the impressive bulk of the **Grote Kerk** or **Sint Bavokerk** (entrance at no. 23; Mon–Sat 10am–4pm; €2.50). Inside, the mighty Christian Müller organ of 1738 is said to have been played by Handel and Mozart. The town's main attraction is the outstanding **Frans Hals Museum**, at Groot Heiligland 62 (Tues–Sat 11am–5pm, Sun noon–5pm; €10, CJP €4.50), a five-minute stroll from Grote Markt in the Oudemanhuis almshouse. It houses a number of his lifelike seventeenth-century portraits, including the *Civic Guard* series, which established his reputation.

Arrival and information

Train and bus The train station is north of the centre, about 10min walk from the Grote Markt; buses stop outside.
Tourist office In the Millennium Monument, Verwulft 11 (April–Sept Mon–Fri 9.30am–6pm, Sat 9.30am–5pm; Oct–March Mon 1–5.30pm, Tues–Fri 9.30am–5.30pm, Sat 10am–5pm; ⓣ0900/616 1600, ⓦwww.vvvhaarlem.nl).

Accommodation

Carillon Grote Markt 27 ⓣ023/531 0591, ⓦwww.hotelcarillon.com. A friendly hotel with decent rooms and a good bar downstairs, which serves a tasty breakfast. Excellent location on the Markt. Ask for a room with a view. Singles €45, doubles €80.

Malts Hotel Zijlstraat 56–58 ⓣ023/551 2385, ⓦwww.maltshotel.nl. B&B style hotel located in a monumental building with reasonable-sized modern rooms and friendly service. Hearty breakfast included. Singles €64, doubles €69–95.

Stayokay Haarlem Jan Gijzenpad 3 ⓣ023/537 3793, ⓦwww.stayokay.com. Inconveniently located out of town on a main road, but otherwise this HI hostel is of the usual high standard. From the station it's 15min on bus #2, direction Noord. Dorms €17–35, doubles €95.

Eating and drinking

De Blauwe Druif Lange Veerstraat 7. This intimate *proeflokaal* dates back to 1863 and still boasts oodles of atmosphere. A typical local hangout.
Grand Café Fortuyn Grote Markt 21. Cosy café-bar whose 1930s decor creates an ambience of faded opulence. Atmospheric spot for a drink.
In den Uiver Riviervischmarkt 13. A traditional "brown" café which serves up live jazz alongside their beer at the weekend.
Jacobus Pieck Warmoesstraat 18 ⓣ023/532 6144. Simple yet elegant bistro with steaks aplenty for around €17 and better-value meals served at lunchtime. Closed Sun.
Restaurant La Plume Lange Veerstraat 1 ⓣ023/531 3202. Popular spot serving traditional Dutch dishes and pasta. Mains €16.
XO Grote Markt 8. Up-to-the-minute café serving a youthful clientele. Great terrace and DJs on weekends.

Moving on

Train Amsterdam CS (every 10min; 15min); Amsterdam Schiphol (via Amsterdam; every 10min; 30min); Delft (every 30min; 40min); Den Haag HS (every 30min; 30min); Den Helder (every 15min; 1hr 20min); Leiden (every 10min; 20min).
Bus Schiphol airport (every 10min; 45min; bus #300).

LEIDEN AND THE BULBFIELDS

The charm of **LEIDEN** lies in the peace and prettiness of its gabled streets and canals, though the town's museums are varied and comprehensive enough to merit a visit.

What to see and do

The most appealing quarter is **Rapenburg**, a peaceful area of narrow pedestrian streets and canals that is home to the country's principal archeological museum, the **Rijksmuseum Van Oudheden** (National Museum of Antiquities; Tues–Sun 10am–5pm; €9, CJP €8). Outside sits the first-century AD Temple of Teffeh, while inside are more Egyptian artefacts, along with classical Greek and Roman sculptures and exhibits from prehistoric, Roman and medieval times. Across Rapenburg, a network of narrow streets converges on the Gothic **Pieterskerk**. East of here, Breestraat marks the start of a vigorous **market** (Wed & Sat), which sprawls right over the sequence of bridges into Haarlemmerstraat, the town's major shopping street. Close by, the **Burcht** (daily 10am–10pm; free) is a shell of a fort, whose battlements you can clamber up for views of the town centre. The **Molenmuseum de Valk**, on Molenwerf at 2e Binnenvestgracht 1 (Tues–Sat 10am–5pm, Sun 1–5pm; €3), displays the history of windmills. Walk west along the 2e Binnenvestgracht and soon you'll hit the Rijksmuseum voor Volkenkunde (National Museum of Ethnology; Tues–Sun 10am–5pm; €8.50, CJP €6) with an impressive collection of artefacts from every continent.

The bulbfields

Along with Haarlem to the north, Leiden and Delft are the best bases for seeing the Dutch **bulbfields** that flourish here in spring. The view from the train as you travel from Haarlem to Leiden can be sufficient in itself as the line cuts directly through the main growing areas, the fields divided into stark geometric blocks of pure colour. Should you want to get closer, make a beeline for **LISSE**, home to the **Keukenhof** (mid-March to mid-May daily 8am–7.30pm; €14.50; ⓦwww.keukenhof.nl), the largest flower gardens in the world. Some six million blooms are on show for their full flowering period, complemented by five thousand square metres of greenhouses. Buses (every 30min; #54; 25min) run to the Keukenhof from Leiden bus station. Connexxion's combined bus and entry ticket costs €21 and can be bought at

ⓦwww.connexxion.nl/keukenhof or at the VVV.

Arrival and information

Train and bus stations Both no more than 10min walk north of the centre.
Tourist office Right outside the train station at Stationsweg 41 (Mon–Fri 8am–6pm, Sat 10am–4pm, Sun 11am–3pm; ⓣ071/516 6000, ⓦwww.leiden.nl).

Accommodation

Flying Pig Beach Hostel Parallel Boulevard 208 ⓣ071/362 2533, ⓦwww.flyingpig.nl. A 30min bus ride from Leiden in the beach town of Noordwijk, this place is the antidote to the bland-but-comfortable hostels found all over the Netherlands and your best bet for visiting Leiden on a budget. The bar is a real traveller hangout; you could be forgiven for thinking you were in South America. Take bus #40 or #44 from Leiden to the lighthouse square in Noordwijk. Dorms €25, doubles €95.
Nieuw Minerva Boommarkt 23 ⓣ071/512 6358, ⓦwww.nieuwminerva.nl. Cosy and central canalside hotel with some interesting Dutch-themed rooms, including "Delftware" and "Rembrandt". Singles €72, doubles €121.

Eating and drinking

Barrera Rapenburg 56. Buzzy canalside café-bar with big sandwiches for €5. Daily 10am–1am, Fri & Sat until 2am.
De Bonte Koe Hooglandsekerk-choorsteeg 13. Typical "brown" café tucked away in a narrow alley with tiled walls and a large beer selection.
De Twee Spieghels Nieuwstraat 11. An intimate jazz café with frequent live music, jam sessions and a decent wine selection. Mon–Fri from 4pm, Sat & Sun from 3pm.
La Bota Herensteeg 9–11 by the Pieterskerk. Hidden studenty spot which serves great-value food and beers. Daily 5–10pm. Dagschotel €6.50. No reservations.

Moving on

Train Amsterdam CS (every 15min; 35min); Amsterdam Schiphol (every 10min; 20min); Delft (every 15min; 20min); Den Haag HS (every 10min; 10min); Haarlem (every 10min; 20min); Rotterdam (every 10min; 30min); Utrecht (every 30min; 1hr).

DEN HAAG

With its urbane atmosphere, **DEN HAAG (THE HAGUE)** is different from any other Dutch city. Since the sixteenth century it has been the Netherlands' political capital, though its older buildings are a rather subdued collection with little of Amsterdam's flamboyance. Diplomats and multinational businesses ensure that many of the city's hotels and restaurants are in the expense-account category, and the nightlife is similarly packaged. But among all this, Den Haag does have cheaper and livelier bars and restaurants, as well as some excellent museums.

What to see and do

The modern and historical centres of the city interweave about a kilometre north of Den Haag HS station, with the main sights clustered together. More attractions – including the seaside at **Scheveningen** – are further north, all of which are easily accessible on public transport.

The Binnenhof and Mauritshuis

Right in the centre, the **Binnenhof** is the home of the Dutch parliament and incorporates elements of the town's thirteenth-century castle. The present complex is a rather mundane affair, the small **Hofvijver** lake mirroring the symmetry of the facade. Inside there's little to see except the **Ridderzaal**, a slender-turreted structure that can be viewed on regular guided tours from the information office at Binnenhof 8a (Mon–Sat 10am–4pm; €4). Immediately east of the Binnenhof, the **Mauritshuis** at Korte Vijverberg 8 (Tues–Sat 10am–5pm, Sun 11am–5pm; €12, CJP €6.75; ⓦwww.mauritshuis.nl), located in a magnificent seventeenth-century mansion, is of more interest, famous for its extensive range of Flemish and Dutch paintings including work by Vermeer, Rubens, Bruegel the Elder and

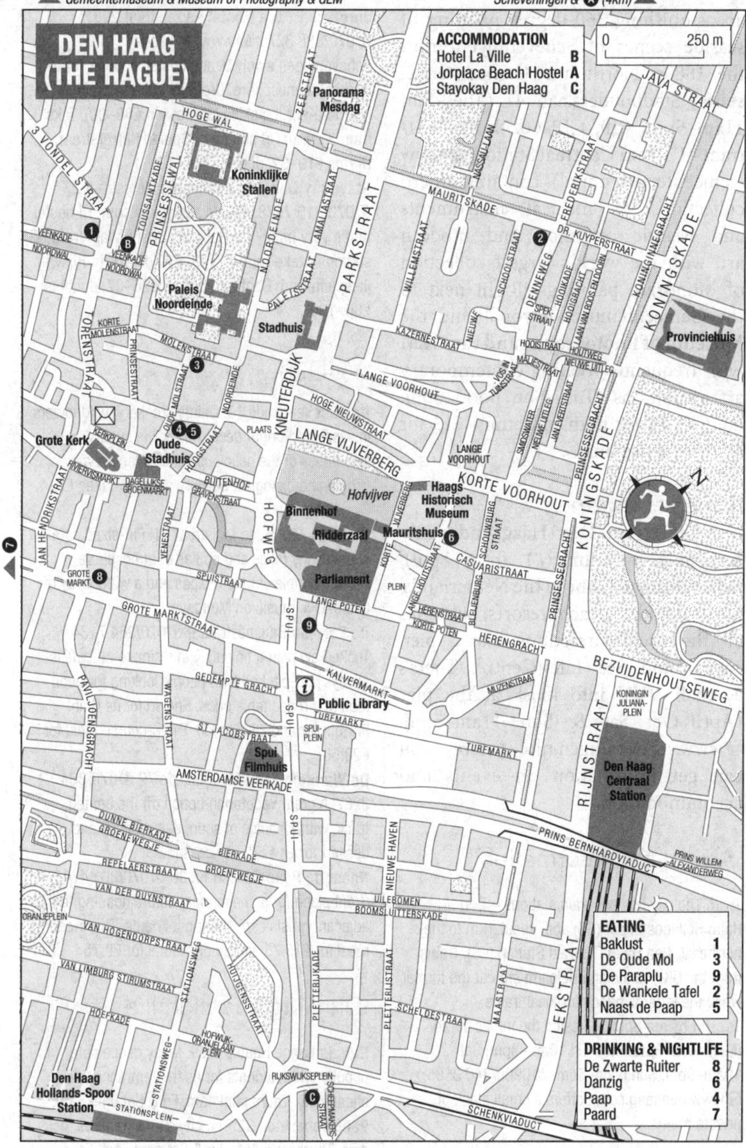

Van Dyck. Take note that from April 2012 until mid-2014 the Mauritshuis will be closed for major renovations. During this period, the museum's highlights will be on display at the Gemeentemuseum (see opposite).

Panorama Mesdag and the Gemeentemuseum

Panorama Mesdag, just west of the pedestrianized shopping area of town at Zeestraat 65 (Mon–Sat 10am–5pm, Sun noon–5pm; €6.50, CJP €5.50) is an astonishing 360-degree painting of seaside scenes of Scheveningen from the 1880s. North, the **Gemeentemuseum**, Stadhouderslaan 41 (Tues–Sun 11am–5pm; €10, CJP €6.50; bus #24/ tram #17 from Centraal Station; ⓦwww.gemeentemuseum.nl), contains superb collections of musical instruments and Islamic ceramics, and modern art, with the world's largest collection of Mondrian paintings. Right next to the Gemeentemuseum you'll find the **Museum of Photography and the GEM** with frequently rotating contemporary art exhibitions (Tues–Sun noon–6pm; €6, CJP €4 for both museums, €13 for all three museums).

Scheveningen

Just 4km from Den Haag and easily accessible by tram (#1 from Spui), **Scheveningen** is one of the Netherlands' most popular beach resorts, and has all the usual attractions like a pier, casino and Sea Life Centre. There's a small VVV info kiosk at the pier (April–Oct Sat & Sun 11am–5pm, ⓦwww.scheveningen.nl) where you can get information on events and accommodation.

Arrival and information

Train The city has two train stations – Den Haag Hollands Spoor (HS) and, about 1km to the northeast, Den Haag Centraal Station (CS). Trains from the UK, France and Belgium stop at the former, while the latter is handy for local trains.

Tourist office Spui 68, inside the public library (Mon noon–8pm, Tues–Fri 10am–8pm, Sat 10am–5pm, Sun noon–5pm; ⓣ0900/340 3505, ⓦwww.denhaag.com); offers a small stock of private rooms.

Accommodation

Hotel La Ville Veenkade 5 ⓣ070/346 3657, ⓦwww.hotellaville.nl. Recently renovated and well-located hotel near the Paleis Noordeinde. Tram #17 from Centraal Station or Holland Spoor to Noordwal. Singles €59, doubles €95, apartments with kitchenette €105.

Jorplace Beach Hostel Keizerstraat 296 ⓣ070/338 3270, ⓦwww.jorplace.nl. Scheveningen's only beach hostel, popular for its laidback atmosphere. Great location to practise your kite-surfing skills (3hr lesson €80–90). Take tram #1 from HS station or Spui to Keizerstraat. Dorms €19–32, doubles €59–67.

Stayokay Den Haag Scheepmakersstraat 27 ⓣ070/315 7878, ⓦwww.stayokay.com. HI hostel that's very handy for Hollands Spoor. Walk from HS station or take tram #1, #9, #12 or #16 to Rijswijkseplein from Centraal. Dorms €26–37, doubles €80–100.

Eating

Baklust Veenkade 19. Dainty crockery, wildflowers in vases and bright decor mirror the sugary sweetness of the delicious cakes. Also serves veggie and biological savoury snacks. Cakes €2–4. Closed Mon.

De Oude Mol Oude Molstraat 61. Pin-sized café with kitschy relics and oodles of atmosphere serving simple yet tasty tapas and a wide array of beers. Live music on Mondays.

De Paraplu Bagijnestraat 9 ⓣ070/364 7134. Tucked away in a tiny alley this simple *eetcafé* is always jam-packed with people looking for good food at a reasonable price. Known for its Giant Plu-burger and juicy *sateh*. Three-course meal for €23.50.

De Wankele Tafel Mauritskade 79 ⓣ070/364 3267. A great vegetarian option off the beaten track, with a choice of soup, daily special and dessert for €14.50. Closed Sun.

Naast de Paap Papestraat 30 ⓣ070/361 4745. Great place for a cheap meal before heading to the adjacent music café sharing its name. Three-course meal for €15.75 and a dagschotel for €9.75.

Drinking and nightlife

Danzig Lange Houtstraat 9. Noisy dance café popular with students for its free entrance and cheap beer. Thurs until 4am, Fri & Sat until 5am.

Paap Papestraat 32. The city's most famous rock café. Thurs until 4am, Fri & Sat until 5am. Free entrance.

Paard Prinsegracht 12, ⓦwww.paard.nl. The main music venue featuring (inter-)national artists as well as frequent DJ nights.

De Zwarte Ruiter Grote Markt 27. Your best bet on the popular Grote Markt square serving a more alternative crowd with frequent live music and a great terrace. Daily 11am–1am.

Moving on

Trains from HS Amsterdam CS (every 10min; 50min); Amsterdam Schiphol (every 15min; 30min); Delft (every 10min; 10min); Gouda (every 15min; 40min); Haarlem (every 30min; 30min); Leiden (every 10min; 15min); Rotterdam (every 10min; 20min).

DELFT

DELFT, 2km inland from Den Haag, is perhaps best known for **Delftware**, the delicate blue and white ceramics to which the town gave its name in the seventeenth century, and as the home of the painter **Johannes Vermeer**. With its gabled red-roofed houses standing beside tree-lined canals, the town has a faded tranquillity – though one that can suffer beneath the tourist onslaught during summer.

What to see and do

A good starting point is to follow the Historic Walk around the old town with a map from the VVV (€3.50). A fifteen-minute walk south of the centre at Rotterdamsweg 196 is the **Koninklijke Porceleyne Fles**, a factory producing Delftware (daily 9am–5pm; Nov to mid-March closed Sun; €8). The **Markt** is also worth exploring for its collection of small speciality art shops and galleries, with a food market every Thursday. The **Nieuwe Kerk** (April–Oct Mon–Sat 9am–6pm; Nov–March Mon–Fri 11am–4pm, Sat 10am–5pm; €3.50, tower €3.50) and the Renaissance **Stadhuis** opposite frame the square. William the Silent – leader of the struggle for Dutch independence in the sixteenth century – is buried in this fine old church and you can climb the 370 steps of the tower for spectacular views. West of here, **Wynhaven**, an old canal, leads to Hippolytusbuurt and the Gothic **Oude Kerk** (same hours and ticket as Nieuwe Kerk), perhaps the town's finest building, with an unhealthily leaning tower. Vermeer fans should check out the **Vermeer Centrum** (daily 10am–5pm; €7) at Voldersgracht 21. Although there are no actual Vermeer paintings, only reproductions, the studio space explaining Vermeer's technique is worth a visit.

Arrival and information

Train From Delft's train station, aim for the big steeple you see on exit and it's a 10min walk north to the Markt.

Tourist office Delft's VVV, called TIP, is just north of the Markt at Hippolytusbuurt 4 (April–Sept Mon & Sat 10am–5pm, Tues–Fri 9am–6pm, Sun 10am–4pm; Oct–March Mon 11am–4pm, Tues–Sat 10am–4pm, Sun 10am–3pm; ⓣ0900/515 1555, ⓦwww.delft.com).

Accommodation

Delftse Hout Campsite Korftlaan 5 ⓣ015/213 0040, ⓦwww.delftsehout.nl. All kinds of accommodation, from chalets to grass huts and eco-homes. Take bus #64 from the station. Camping huts €43.50.

The Soul Inn Willemstraat 55 ⓣ015/215 7246, ⓦwww.soulinn.nl. A small hotel, with imaginative, artistic decor and quirky rooms. Handy location for the station. Singles from €55, doubles from €60.

Eating and drinking

Kleyweg's Stads-Koffyhuis Oude Delft. A bustling café which serves delicious sweet and savoury pancakes and has a canalside terrace. Pancakes €6–11.

Kobus Kuch Beestenmarkt 1. A gem of a café-restaurant – don't miss the famous *appeltaart met slagroom* (apple pie with cream) dished up in cosy surroundings for €3.40.

Locus Publicus Brabantse Turfmarkt 67. Popular local bar, serving a staggering array of beers as well as a good selection of cheap snacks. Sandwiches €3.

Uit de Kunst Oude Delft 140, near Oude Kerk. Charming little café decorated with 1940s memorabilia and offering home-made cakes and cheap snacks. Closed Mon & Tues.

Moving on

Train Amsterdam (every 30min; 1hr); Den Haag HS (every 10min; 10min); Rotterdam (every 10min; 12min).

ROTTERDAM

Just south of Delft lies **ROTTERDAM**, at the heart of a maze of rivers and artificial waterways that together form the outlet of the rivers Rijn (Rhine) and Maas (Meuse). After devastating damage during World War II, Rotterdam has grown into a vibrant city dotted with premier cultural attractions and built around Europe's busiest port. Fortunately redevelopment hasn't obliterated the city's earthy character: its grittiness is part of its appeal, as are its boisterous bars and clubs. An enchanting day-trip from Rotterdam is **GOUDA**, a pretty little city some 25km northeast with the largest Markt in the Netherlands where a touristy **cheese market** is held every Thursday morning from June to August. Gouda can also easily be reached from Utrecht and The Hague.

What to see and do

You can get a feel for the city by walking from the station (or taking tram #7 from just outside) down to the Museumpark along Mauritsweg. More

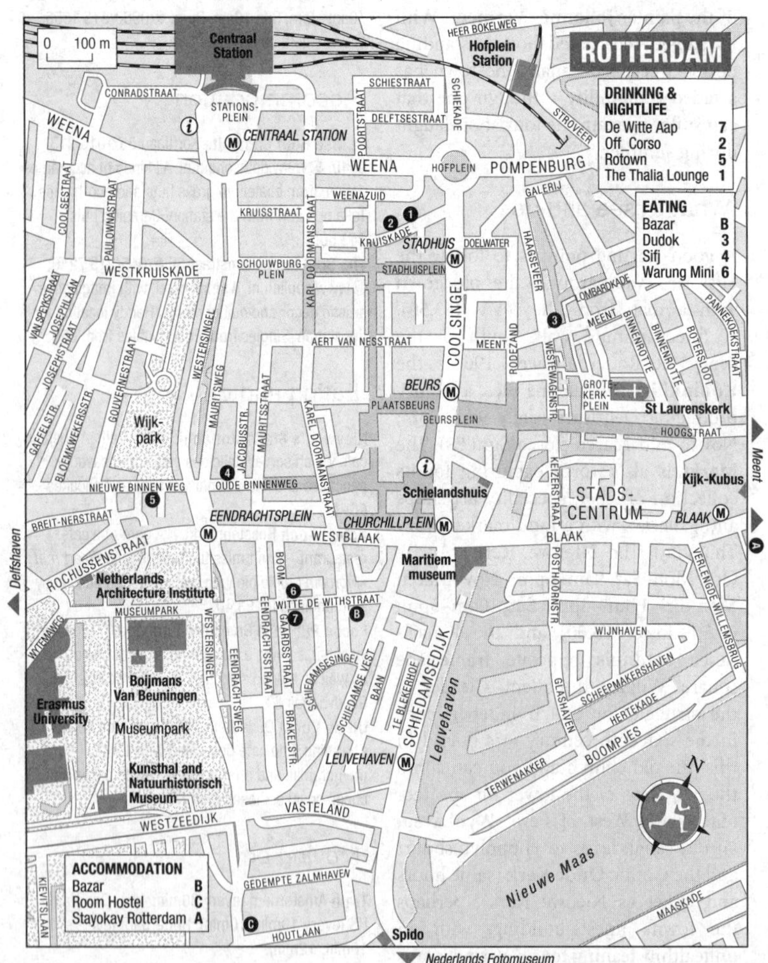

idiosyncratic attractions lie further east, while Delfshaven is a short, and rewarding, journey southwest.

The Museumpark and around

The enormous **Boijmans Van Beuningen Museum**, at Museumpark 18–20 (Tues–Sun 11am–5pm; €10, CJP €7.50, free on Wed; Ⓦwww.boijmans.nl), has a superb collection of works by Monet, Van Gogh, Picasso, Gauguin and Cézanne, while its earlier canvases include several by Bosch, Bruegel the Elder and Rembrandt. A stroll through the Museumpark brings you to the **Kunsthal** (Tues–Sat 10am–5pm, Sun 11am–5pm; €10, CJP €5.50; Ⓦwww.kunsthal.nl) which showcases first-rate exhibitions of contemporary art, photography and design. Also in the park are the **Netherlands Architecture Institute** (Tues–Sat 10am–5pm, Sun 11am–5pm; €8, CJP €5; Ⓦwww.nai.nl), with regularly changing exhibitions focusing on particular architects or areas and the **Natuurhistorisch Museum** (Tues–Sat 10am–5pm, Sun 11am–5pm; €5; Ⓦwww.nmr.nl) with a big collection of stuffed animals. For alternative art, you can't do better than a wander along **Witte de Withstraat,** just east of the Museumpark, with its tiny, inexpensive galleries (check Ⓦwww.tentrotterdam.nl, Ⓦwww.wdw.nl or Ⓦwww.showroommama.nl for current exhibitions).

The Maritiem Museum and Blaak

Near the Leuvehaven is the entertaining **Maritiem Museum** (Maritime Museum; Tues–Sat 10am–5pm, Sun 11am–5pm; July & Aug also Mon 10am–5pm; €7.50, CJP €3). A short walk away is **Blaak**, a pocket-sized area that was levelled in World War II, but has since been rebuilt. The architectural highlight is a remarkable series of topsy-turvy, cube-shaped houses, the *kubuswoningen*, completed in 1984. At Overblaak 70 is the somewhat outdated **Kijk-Kubus** (Show Cube; daily 11am–5pm; Jan & Feb Sat & Sun 11am–5pm; €2.50), which offers a disorientating tour of the house. Nearby, the Binnenrotte **market** (Tues & Sat 8am–5pm) sells cheese, fish and flowers.

Delfshaven

If little in Rotterdam city centre can exactly be called picturesque, **DELFSHAVEN**, a couple of kilometres southwest of Centraal Station, makes up for it (tram #4 or #8 direction Schiedam to Spanjaardstraat or take the metro). Once the harbour that served Delft, it was from here that the Pilgrim Fathers set sail for the New World in 1620. Most of the buildings lining the district's two narrow canals are eighteenth- and nineteenth-century warehouses. Formerly a *jenever* distillery, the **Museum de Dubbelde Palmboom**, Voorhaven 12 (Tues–Sun 11am–5pm; €5), is now a wide-ranging historical museum.

Arrival and information

Train Centraal Station is just north of the centre, and is the hub of a useful tram and metro system, though best avoided late at night.

Tourist office Main VVV at Coolsingel 195–197 (Mon–Fri 10am–7pm, Sat 9.30am–6pm, Sun 10am–5pm; Ⓣ0900/403 4065, Ⓦwww.rotterdam.info). There's a VVV info café on the right as you leave the train station at Stationsplein 45 (Mon–Sat 9am–5.30pm, Sun 10am–5pm). On both locations you can pick up the Rotterdam Welcome discount card from €9, public city transport included.

Use-It Schaatsbaan 41 (mid-May to mid-Sept Tues–Sun 9am–6pm; July & Aug also Mon noon–5pm; mid-Sept to mid-May Tues–Sat 9am–5pm; Ⓣ010/240 9158, Ⓦwww.use-it.nl). Very useful information centre for budget travellers located close to the station. Their free "Do-It-Yourself" tours are particularly handy.

Accommmodation

Bazar Witte de Withstraat 16 Ⓣ010/206 5151, Ⓦwww.hotelbazar.nl. A superb hotel on one of the hippest streets in the city, with an excellent restaurant. Each floor is decorated in the style of

BOAT TRIPS

A fun way to see the city is from the water. One possibility is to take an exhilarating trip in a **water taxi** from the Leuvehaven (€3.60; also from the Veerhaven for a much shorter journey for €2.90; ⓦwww.watertaxirotterdam.nl) to the splendid *Hotel New York*, which occupies the building where transatlantic cruise liners once docked. Close by is the **Nederlands Fotomuseum**, Wilhelminakade 332 (Tues–Fri 10am–5pm, Sat & Sun 11am–5pm; €7, CJP €3.50; ⓦwww.nederlandsfotomuseum.nl), where there's a small exhibition on Rotterdam photography as well as changing exhibitions. From here you can walk back to the centre over the futuristic bridge, the **Erasmusbrug**, an ideal spot for photos. There are also numerous **boat trips** from the Leuvehaven through the harbour (year-round; 1hr 15min; €9.75). In July and August, **day-trips** run to Dordrecht, Schoonhoven, the nineteen windmills at Kinderdijk, and the Delta Project, from €50–52 per person; contact the VVV or Spido for details (ⓣ010/275 9988, ⓦwww.spido.nl).

a different continent – the rooms are unique so choose your favourite from the website before you book. From the station take tram #7 or #20 to Museumpark or tram #8 to Churchillplein. Singles €75, doubles €80.

Room Hostel Van Vollenhovenstraat 62 ⓣ010/282 7277, ⓦwww.roomrotterdam.nl. Very funky hostel with a vibrant bar and quieter lounge. Extremely helpful staff organize events for guests. From Centraal Station take tram #7 to Westerstraat or tram #8 to Vasteland. Dorms from €23, doubles €60.

Stayokay Rotterdam Overblaak 85–87 ⓣ010/436 5763, ⓦwww.stayokay.com. This HI hostel is located inside the famous cube houses so make sure your stomach can handle the disorientating experience after one beer to many. Take the metro to Blaak station, then it's a short walk. Dorms €26, doubles €95.

Eating

The best places for cheap and tasty food are Oude and Nieuwe Binnenweg and Witte de Withstraat.

Bazar Witte de Withstraat 16 ⓣ010/206 5151. Popular bar/restaurant serving excellent Middle Eastern food with colourful surroundings and a lively atmosphere. Mains €10–15.

Dudok Meent 88 ⓣ010/433 3102. An expansive grand café with slick service and the city's most famous apple pie (€3.40).

Sijf Oude Binnenweg 115 ⓣ010/433 2610. One of the many agreeable pub-style places along this stretch. Mains are reasonable: €14.50, including unlimited fries and salad, or cheaper daily specials for €10–12.

Warung Mini Witte de Withstraat 47. A cheap-and-cheerful canteen dishing up hefty portions of decent Surinamese and Chinese. Open until 6am at the weekend to satisfy those late-night cravings. Mains €7–12.

Drinking and nightlife

De Witte Aap Witte de Withstraat 78. Small but bustling café – extremely popular with students – with DJs on weekends and rotating art exhibitions.

Off_Corso Kruiskade 22 ⓦwww.offcorso.nl. ⓂStadhuis. Arty club in an old cinema, specializing in electro and techno. Thurs–Sat 11pm–5am.

Rotown Nieuwe Binnenweg 17–19 ⓦwww.rotown.nl. A pre-party bar with gigs by up-and-coming bands. Also serves food; open until 2am.

The Thalia Lounge Kruiskade 31 ⓦwww.thaliarotterdam.nl. A style-conscious club best known for its frequent Latin house nights. Dress to impress. Fri & Sat 11pm–4/5am.

Moving on

Train Amsterdam CS (every 10min; 1hr); Amsterdam Schiphol (every 10min; 50min); Delft (every 10min; 15min); Den Haag HS (every 10min; 20min); Gouda (every 10min; 20min); Leiden (every 10min; 30min); Utrecht (every 15min; 45min).

UTRECHT

"I groaned with the idea of living all winter in so shocking a place", wrote Boswell in 1763, and the university town of **UTRECHT**, surrounded by shopping centres and industrial developments, still promises little as you approach. But the centre, with its distinctive sunken canals – whose brick cellar warehouses have been converted into chic cafés and restaurants – is one of the country's most pleasant.

What to see and do

For a place of its size, there's surprisingly little in the way of sights and museums in Utrecht. The focal point is the **Dom Tower**, built between 1321 and 1382, which at over 110m is the highest church tower in the country. A guided tour (April–Sept Mon & Sun noon–4pm, Tues–Sat 11am–4pm; Oct–April Mon–Fri noon–4pm, Sat 11am–4pm, Sun noon–4pm; €8, CJP €6.50) takes you unnervingly close to the top, from where you can see Rotterdam and Amsterdam on a clear day. Below is the Gothic **Dom Kerk**; only the eastern part of the cathedral remains after the nave collapsed in 1674, but it's worth peering inside (May–Sept Mon–Fri 10am–5pm, Sat 10am–3.30pm, Sun 2–4pm; Oct–April Mon–Fri 11am–4pm, Sat 11am–3.30pm, Sun 2–4pm; donation requested) and wandering through the Kloostergang, the fourteenth-century cloisters that link the cathedral to the chapterhouse.

Arrival and information

Train and bus stations Both lead into the Hoog Catharijne shopping centre.

Tourist office Close to the Dom Tower at Domplein 9 (Mon–Fri 10am–6pm, Sat 10am–5pm, Sun noon–5pm; ⓣ0900/128 8732, ⓦwww.utrechtyourway.nl).

Accommodation

Stayokay Utrecht-Bunnik Rhijnauwenselaan 14 ⓣ030/656 1277, ⓦwww.stayokay.com. Peaceful, family-orientated HI hostel located a good 5km out of the centre in an old country manor house. Take bus #40 or #41 from the train station to Rhijnauwen. Dorms €26–32, doubles €95.

Strowis Boothstraat 8 ⓣ030/238 0280, ⓦwww.strowis.nl. A pleasant guesthouse with a fresh feel, a kitchen and free internet access in the relaxing lounge. Take a short ride on bus #3/#4/#8/#11 to the Janskerkhof stop. Dorms €16, doubles €62.50.

Eating

Broodje Mario Oudegracht 132. This market stall selling pizza slices and the famous Mario sandwich with cheese, salami and red pepper is a local institute. Fill up for only €3.

De Oude Muntkelder Oudegracht 112. A good option among the many cafés on this busy stretch by the canal; serves inexpensive pancakes for around €8.

De Soepterrine Zakkendragerssteeg 42 ⓣ030/231 7005. An intimate, homely restaurant which serves hearty food including home-made soup and cheese fondue. Mains €11–15.

Van Buuren Drieharingstraat 16 ⓣ030/321 7503. Popular concept where main dishes are divided in two portions to satisfy fussy tastebuds. Usually jam-packed so book ahead.

Drinking and nightlife

Club Monza Potterstraat 16–20 ⓦwww.clubmonza.nl. Popular club with a youthful clientele dancing to up-to-the-minute beats. Open Thurs–Sat.

De Winkel van Sinkel Oudegracht 158. The hippest bar in town with regular dance nights and a chill-out room downstairs.

Ekko Bemuurde Weerd WZ 3 ⓦwww.ekko.nl. Alternative rock and dance venue with live performances by (inter-)national artists and DJs. The café serves a well-priced veggie 3-course meal for €12.50 on Thurs & Fri.

Moving on

Train Amsterdam (every 15min; 30 min); Arnhem (every 15min; 35min); Gouda (every 10min; 20min); Maastricht (every 30min; 2hr); Rotterdam (every 15min; 40min).

Beyond the Randstad

Outside the Randstad towns, the Netherlands is relatively unknown territory to visitors. To the north, there's superb cycling and hiking to be had through scenic **dune reserves** and delightful villages, with easy access to pristine beaches, while the island of **Texel** offers the country's most complete beach experience, and has plenty of birdlife. The **Hoge Veluwe National Park**, near Arnhem, boasts one of the country's best modern art museums and has cycle paths through a delightful landscape. Further south the landscape slowly fills out, moving into a rougher countryside of farmland and forests and eventually into the hills around **Maastricht**, a city with a vibrant, pan-European feel.

TEXEL

The largest of the islands off the north coast – and the easiest to get to (2hr from Amsterdam) – **TEXEL** (pronounced "tessel") offers diverse and pretty landscapes, and is one of Europe's most important bird-breeding grounds.

What to see and do

Texel's main settlement, **DEN BURG**, makes a convenient base and has bike rental outlets. On the coast 3km southeast of Den Burg is **OUDESCHILD**, home to the **Maritiem en Juttersmuseum** (Beachcombers' Museum; Tues–Sat 10am–5pm, Sun noon–5pm; July & Aug also Mon 10am–5pm; €6.50), a fascinating collection of marine junk from wrecks. In the opposite direction is **DE KOOG**, with a good sandy beach and the **EcoMare nature centre**, at Ruijslaan 92 (daily 9am–5pm; €9; Ⓦwww.ecomare.nl), a bird and seal sanctuary as well as natural history museum: from here you can visit the **Wad**, the banks of sand and mud to the east of the island, where seals and birds gather.

Arrival and information

Boat Ferries from the town of Den Helder on the mainland (take bus #33 from the station to the port) depart every hour (20min; €2.50 return ticket). Once on Texel, various buses greet the ferry's arrival and depart for destinations across the island.

Tourist office Den Burg's VVV is at Emmalaan 66 (Mon–Fri 9am–5.30pm, Sat 9am–5pm; Ⓣ0222/314 741, Ⓦwww.texel.net) where you can pick up leaflets, maps and information on cycling routes.

Accommodation

Camping is the most popular option here, with good campsites dotted around the island.

De Koorn Aar Grensweg 388 Ⓣ0222/312 931, Ⓦwww.koorn-aar.nl. Small, well-run campsite (with chalets) close to Den Burg. Closed Nov–March. €30 for a tent for two people.

Kogerstrand Badweg 33 Ⓣ0222/317 208, Ⓦwww.texelcampings.nl. Campsite set among the beachside dunes in De Koog, the island's busiest resort. Closed Nov–March. €3/person, plus €11/tent.

Stayokay Texel Haffelderweg 29 Ⓣ0222/315 441, Ⓦwww.stayokay.com. HI hostel on the outskirts of Den Burg that's more suited to families and groups, although it has a big bar and terrace. Dorms €33, doubles €92.

Eating and drinking

De Pangkoekehuus Kikkertstraat 9, De Cocksdorp. Cosy place serving delicious filled pancakes for around €8.

Freya Gravenstraat 4 Ⓣ0222/321 214. Be sure to book ahead for Den Burg's best restaurant, which serves a delicious three-course set menu each night for €24.50.

HOGE VELUWE NATIONAL PARK

Some 70km southeast of Amsterdam, and just north of the town of **ARNHEM**, is the huge and scenic **Hoge Veluwe National Park** (daily: Nov–March 9am–6pm; April 8am–8pm; May & Aug 8am–9pm; June & July 8am–10pm; Sept 9am–8pm; Oct 9am–7pm; €8 park only, €16 with Kröller-Müller museum; Ⓦwww.hogeveluwe.nl). Formerly the estate of wealthy local couple Anton and Helene Kröller-Müller, it has three entrances – one near the village of **Otterlo** on the northwest perimeter, another near **Hoenderloo** on the northeast edge, and a third to the south at **Rijzenburg**, near the village of Schaarsbergen. The park can easily be reached by bus from either Arnhem (bus #105 to Otterlo) or Apeldoorn (bus #108 to Hoenderloo) from where it's a short walk to the entrance of the park. From either entrance you can pick up free white bicycles, by far the best way to explore the park.

What to see and do

Within the park is the **Museonder** (daily 9.30am–5/6pm), an underground natural history museum, and the **St Hubertus Hunting Lodge** (guided tours only; €3), the former Art Deco home of the Kröller-Müllers. The park's unmissable highlight is the **Kröller-Müller Museum** (Tues–Sun 10am–5pm; €16 including park admission; ⓦwww.kmm.nl), a superb collection of fine art including nearly three hundred paintings by Van Gogh, plus works by Picasso, Seurat, Léger and Mondrian. Behind the museum is a lovely and imaginative **sculpture garden** (Tues–Sun 10am–4.30pm; same ticket).

Arrival and information

Train and bus From nearby Arnhem's or Apeldoorn's train stations, you can catch a bus to the park (see opposite).

Tourist office Arnhem's VVV office is near the station, at Stationsplein 13 (Mon–Fri 9.30am–5.30pm, Sat 9.30am–5pm; ⓣ0900/112 2344, ⓦwww.vvvarnhem.nl).

Accommodation

Hoge Veluwe Campsite ⓦwww.hogeveluwe.nl. Official campsite by the park's northeastern Hoenderloo entrance. It's not possible to make a reservation but there is plenty of space. Closed Nov–March. €7.

Pension Warnsborn Schelmseweg 1 ⓣ026/442 5994, ⓦwww.pensionwarnsborn.nl. A cheap and decent option just north of the centre of Arnhem and near the park entrance. This family-run B&B in an eighteenth-century house has spacious rooms, some with private balconies. Singles €40, doubles €65 with private facilities, €55 when shared and breakfast included.

Moving on

Train Amsterdam (every 15min; 1hr 10min); Utrecht (every 30min; 40min).

MAASTRICHT

Squashed between the Belgian and German borders, **MAASTRICHT** is one of the most delightful cities in the Netherlands. A cosmopolitan place, where three languages happily coexist, it's also one of the oldest towns in the country.

What to see and do

The busiest of Maastricht's many squares is **Markt**, at its most crowded during the Wednesday and Friday morning **market**, with the mid-seventeenth-century **Stadhuis** (Mon–Fri 9am–12.30pm & 2–5pm; free) at its centre. Just west, **Vrijthof** is a grander open space flanked by a line of café terraces on one side and on the other by **St Servaaskerk** (daily 10am–5pm, Sun from 12.30pm; €4), a tenth-century church. Next door is **St Janskerk** (Easter–Oct Mon–Sat 11am–4pm; free), with its tall fifteenth-century Gothic tower (Mon–Sat 11am–4pm; €1.50). On the other side of the square lies the appealing district of **Stokstraat Kwartier**, with narrow streets winding out to the fast-flowing River Jeker and the **Helpoort** fortress gateway of 1229. South of here, the **casemates** in the **Waldeck Park** (guided tours: July–Sept daily noon & 2.30pm; Oct–June Sat & Sun 2pm; €5.25) are further evidence of Maastricht's once-impressive fortifications. Fifteen minutes' walk south is the 110m hill of **St Pietersberg**. Of the two ancient defensive tunnel systems under the hill, the **Zonneberg** is the better, situated on the far side of the hill at Casino Slavante (guided tour: July–Aug daily 1.50pm; €5.25).

Bonnefantenmuseum

On the east side of the river is the city's main art gallery, **Bonnefantenmuseum** at Avenue Céramique 250 (Tues–Sun 11am–5pm; €8, CJP €4; ⓦwww.bonnefanten.nl). Designed by Aldo Rossi, it's situated in the newest part of Maastricht, **Céramique**, which offers a complete contrast to the feel of the historic city. The collection ranges from Old Masters to contemporary artists, but is less of an attraction than the building itself.

Arrival and information

Train and bus The centre of Maastricht is on the west bank of the river. You're likely to arrive, however, on the east bank, in the district Wyck, home to the train and bus stations and many of the city's hotels.

Tourist office The VVV, Kleine Straat 1, at the end of the main shopping street (May–Oct Mon–Sat 9am–6pm, Sun 11am–3pm; Nov–April Mon–Fri 9am–6pm, Sat 9am–5pm; ⓣ043/325 2121, ⓦwww.vvvmaastricht.eu), has copies of a tourist guide (€4.95) with a map and a list of private rooms.

Accommodation

Botel Maastricht Maasboulevard 95 ⓣ043/321 9023, ⓦwww.botelmaastricht.nl. Moored on the river not far from the Helpoort, this is a fun place – there's a huge difference in cabin size for the same price, so ask for a larger one when you book. Singles €29, doubles €44.

Camping De Bosrand Moerslag 4 ⓣ043/409 1544, ⓦwww.campingdebosrand.nl. Campsite 25min south of town on bus #57. Closed Nov–March. €5.75/person, plus €2,70/tent.

Stayokay Maastricht Maasboulevard 101 ⓣ043/750 1790, ⓦwww.stayokay.com. HI hostel with a big riverside terrace done up in a funky retro style, but it can feel soulless. A few minutes' walk from the centre and 15min from the station. Dorms €33, doubles €93.

Eating and drinking

Café Sjiek Sint Pieterstraat 13. Don't be put off by the simple interior; the food in this little *eetcafé* is absolutely superb. Of the many traditional delicacies on the menu, the *Zoervleis* (meat stew) is your best pick. Great terrace in summer. No reservations.

Coffeelovers Dominican Square 1. A stylish café within a bookshop in a beautiful converted church. The great coffee is a perfect accompaniment to browsing the books. Closed Sun.

In de Karkol Stokstraat 5. For a truly authentic experience, this tiny café is the place to be, with music in dialect performed by regional artists and loudly sung along to by the local crowds. Ask for a *sjoes*, a local speciality.

Lunch & Zo Sint Amorsplein 2. A hip and modern café. The decor is minimalist, but the coffee, served with sugary surprises, is far from it. High tea €14.50.

Zondag Wijckerbrugstraat 42. A bustling and bright café-bar near the station, serving snacks, soups and salads until 10pm. Sandwiches €6. Also live DJs at weekends and stiff cocktails.

Moving on

Train Amsterdam (every 30min; 2hr 35min); Liège (hourly; 30min); Utrecht (every 30min; 2hr).

Norway

HIGHLIGHTS

TROMSØ: enjoy the lively nightlife and first-class aquarium in Northern Norway's most picturesque city

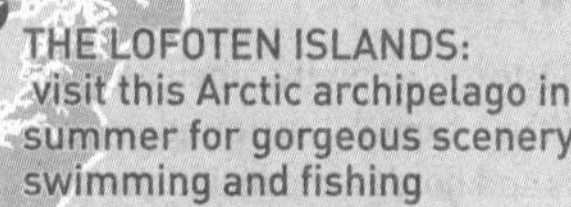

THE LOFOTEN ISLANDS: visit this Arctic archipelago in summer for gorgeous scenery, swimming and fishing

GEIRANGERFJORD: take the Trollstigen Highway to this glorious fjord

GRUNERLØKKA: this former working class district of Oslo is now home to a buzzing collection of bars, clubs and boutique shops

STAVANGER: a little gem of a university town, with great bars and restaurants and one of Norway's greatest natural attractions, Pulpit Rock nearby

ROUGH COSTS

DAILY BUDGET Basic €80 /occasional treat €105

DRINK Beer €8

FOOD Meatballs with potatoes €20

HOSTEL/BUDGET HOTEL €35–45/€80

TRAVEL Train: Oslo–Bergen €35–95; bus: Oslo–Trondheim €65

FACT FILE

POPULATION 4.9 million

AREA 385,252 sq km

LANGUAGE Norwegian

CURRENCY Norwegian krone (kr)

CAPITAL Oslo (population: 605,000)

INTERNATIONAL PHONE CODE ⓣ47

Introduction

Norway's extraordinary landscape will lift your heart while high prices squeeze your wallet. The payoff is the country's mix of likeable, easy-going cities and breathtaking wilderness – during summer, you can hike up a glacier in the morning and thaw out in an urban bar in the evening, watching the sun dip below the horizon for all of half an hour, if at all. Deeper into the countryside, you'll find vast stretches of distinctive glacier-formed landscapes. And because of Norway's low population, it really is possible to travel for hours in this natural grandeur without seeing a soul.

Beyond **Oslo** – a pretty, increasingly cosmopolitan capital surrounded by mountains and fjords – the major cities of interest are historic **Trondheim**, **Bergen**, on the edge of the fjords, and northern **Tromsø**. Anyone with even a passing fondness for the great outdoors should head to the **western fjords**: dip into the region from Bergen or **Åndalsnes**, or linger in one of the many quiet waterside towns and villages. Further north, deep in the Arctic Circle, the astounding **Lofoten Islands** have some of the most striking mountain scenery and clearest water in Norway. To the north of here, the tourist trail focuses on the long journey to **Nordkapp**, the northernmost accessible point in Europe; the route leads through **Finnmark**, one of the last strongholds of the Sámi and their herds of reindeer. Tourism reaches its height from June to August when opening hours are long and activities plentiful; the rest of the year you'll find many establishments closed unless you're in major towns.

CHRONOLOGY

10,000–2000 BC Seal- and reindeer-hunting tribes move into present-day Norway.

800–1050 AD Norwegian Vikings become a dominant force in Europe.

900 King Harald becomes the first ruler of a united Norway.

1030 The Norwegians adopt Christianity.

1262 Norway increases her empire, forming unions with Greenland and Iceland.

1350 Almost two-thirds of the population die during the Black Death.

1396 The Kalmar Union unites Norway with Denmark and Sweden under a single ruler.

1536 Sweden leaves the Kalmar Union, leaving Norway under Danish control.

1814 Norwegian hopes of independence are dashed after Sweden invades and takes control.

1905 Parliament declares independence from Sweden. Haakon VII is crowned the first king of an independent Norway in 525 years.

1911 Explorer Roald Amundsen's expedition is the first to reach the South Pole ahead of the ill-fated Scott expedition.

1913 Norway becomes one of the first countries in the world to give women the vote.

1914 Norway remains neutral during World War I.

1940–45 German forces overrun Norway in 60 days and exterminate half of Norway's Jewish population, before the country is liberated in May 1945.

1960s The discovery of oil and gas in the North Sea leads to greater economic prosperity.

1981 Gro Harlem Brundtland becomes Norway's first female prime minister.

2005 Prime Minister Kjell Bodevik is defeated in the general elections, and is replaced by Labour candidate Jens Stolenberg.

2011 Right-wing extremist Anders Breivik kills 77 people in Oslo in a shooting spree and the bombing of a government building.

ARRIVAL

The four busiest **airports** for budget travellers are Oslo, Bergen, Trondheim and Stavanger. The main low-cost carriers are Ryanair, which serves Oslo, and Norwegian (Ⓦwww.norwegian.no), which covers all main Norwegian

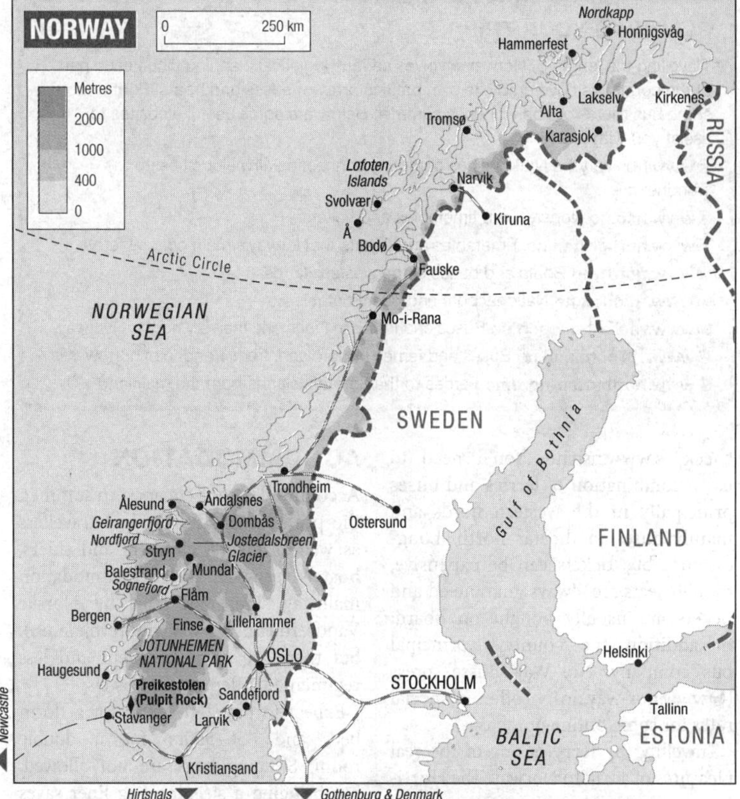

cities. SAS (ⓦwww.sas.no) also flies to most main destinations in the country, with partner airline Widerøe (ⓦwww.wideroe.no) covering the smaller towns.

Norway's long coastline is served by Color Line (ⓦwww.colorline.com), DFDS Seaways (ⓦwww.dfdsseaways.com) and Fjordline (ⓦwww.fjordline.com) **ferry** companies; between them, they ply routes between Oslo, Kiel and Copenhagen, Bergen, Stavanger and Hirtshals.

There are international **trains** to Oslo from Stockholm and Gothenburg in Sweden and to Trondheim from Östersund. International **buses** run from various Swedish cities to Oslo, Narvik and Bodø (ⓦwww.swebusexpress.se and ⓦwww.gobybus.se), and from northern Finland to northern Norway (ⓦwww.eskelisen-lapinlinjat.com).

GETTING AROUND

Public transport is very reliable but in the winter (especially in the north), services can be cut back severely. Regional bus, ferry and train timetables are available at all tourist offices.

There are four main **train** routes, linking Oslo to Stockholm in the east, to Kristiansand and Stavanger in the southwest, to Bergen in the west and to Trondheim and on to Bodø in the north. InterRail and Eurail **rail passes** are valid in Norway, and also give substantial discounts on some major ferry crossings and certain long-distance bus routes. For timetables,

PLANNING YOUR TRIP

Travelling the length of Norway involves serious logistical planning since each part of the country is covered by its own baffling array of buses and boats. Furthermore, some bus routes are only open in summer. Below are some useful websites to assist you with planning.

Ⓦ **www.nor-way.no** National bus company connecting all major cities up to Trondheim.

Ⓦ **www.nsb.no** Norway train timetables and tickets.

Ⓦ **www.hurtigruten.no** Timetables and tickets for Norway's main coastal ferry.

Ⓦ **www.fjord1.no** Boats and buses in the western fjords.

Ⓦ **www.rutebok.no** National boat and bus timetables.

Ⓦ **www.veolia-transport.no** Buses and ferries in Finnmark, the very north of Norway.

Ⓦ **www.177nordland.no** Buses and ferries in Nordland, from Trondheim northwards.

Ⓦ **www.torghatten-nord.no** Ferries to the Lofoten Islands from the mainland.

check Ⓦwww.nsb.no. You'll need to use a combination of ferries and **buses** principally in the western fjords and mainly buses in the far north. Long-distance bus tickets can be expensive, though seats are always guaranteed and tickets are usually bought on board; in addition the country's principal bus company, Nor-Way Bussekspress (Ⓦwww.nor-way.no), offers special rates for some online purchases.

Travelling by **ferry** is one of the real pleasures of a trip to Norway. The **Hurtigruten** – "rapid route" (Ⓦwww.hurtigruten.no) ferry still retains its traditional role of connecting remote coastal towns, linking Bergen with Kirkenes, on the Russian border in the far north. If you purchase a relatively inexpensive deck ticket, you can roll out your sleeping bag in the lounge at night and use the showers. The Hurtigbåt (fast coastal ferry) runs along part of this route.

Flying, if you book in advance and particularly if you are travelling long distances, is far quicker and often cheaper than taking a bus; check Ⓦwww.wideroe.no or Ⓦwww.norwegian.no for offers.

Norway is a great place for **cycling**, but be prepared for narrow mountain roads, long distances and many tunnels, which are closed to non-motorized traffic. Bike Norway (Ⓦwww.bike-norway.com) has all the information you need.

ACCOMMODATION

Accommodation is cheapest in summer, the peak season. For budget travellers as well as hikers, climbers and skiers, **hostels** provide the accommodation mainstay; most are run by Norske Vandrerhjem (Ⓦwww.vandrerhjem.no), but there are some excellent and less regimented independent hostels.

Expect to pay 250–300kr for a dorm bed, and 450–550kr for a double room. Sleeping bags are not allowed, but bringing a sleeping bag liner saves paying bed linen costs (50kr). The more expensive hostels nearly always include breakfast in the price of the room. HI members get a 15 percent discount. Some HI hostels close between 11am and 4pm, there's often an 11pm/midnight curfew and most hostels tend to be inconveniently located. Many hostels close altogether during the winter months.

There are around four hundred official **campsites** around the country (Ⓦwww.camping.no), plenty of them easily reached by public transport. Expect to pay 120–160kr per night for two people using a tent. Sites also often have **cabins** (*hytter*), usually four-bedded affairs with kitchen facilities, with prices ranging between 250 and 750kr. Many campsites come equipped with a guest kitchen, lounge, wi-fi access and sauna. A Camping

MINIPRIS

If you book train and bus tickets and internal flights online, well enough in advance, the **Minipris**, or budget price, can enable you to travel long distances, such as Oslo to Bergen or Trondheim to Bodø, for as little as 199Kr.

Card Scandinavia (CCS); available from campsites or online (ⓦwww.camping.no) gives you numerous discounts. DNT (Norwegian Mountain Touring Club; ⓦwww.turistforeningen.no) maintains 460 **mountain huts** along popular wilderness routes in Norway's national parks, which range from staffed lodges to unmanned huts with kitchen facilities (pick up the key at the nearest DNT office). You can **camp rough** in any wild area in Norway as long as you are at least 150m from houses or water sources, and leave no trace.

Hotels are generally pricey, although summer discounts can net you a double room for as little as 650kr. **Guesthouses** (*pensjonat* or *gjestehus*) cost around 650kr a double, and B&Bs (ⓦwww.bbnorway.com) can offer even better deals. Tourist offices in larger towns can often fix you up with a **private room** in someone's house for around 400–500kr a double. Finally, in the Lofoten Islands, **sjøhus** (literally "sea houses") and **rorbus** (converted fishermen's cabins) can be rented from 550kr per cabin and sleep between 2 to 8 people.

FOOD AND DRINK

Norwegian **food** can be excellent: fish is plentiful, as is the controversial whale meat, while reindeer steak and elk can be sampled in the north. However, eating well on a tight budget can be difficult. Breakfast (*frokost*) – bread, cheese, eggs, jam, cold meat and fish buffet, washed down with unlimited tea and coffee – is usually decent at hostels, and very good in hotels. If it isn't included in the room rate, reckon on an extra 55–75kr.

Picnic food is the best stand-by, and most supermarkets sell disposable barbecues for spontaneous fry-ups. **Fast-food** alternatives include kebab and burger joints, *pølse* (hot dogs) and pizza slices at any Narvesen or 7-Eleven, and sandwiches and cakes at Deli de Luca branches in Oslo, Bergen and Stavanger. Food markets sell *smørbrød*, huge open sandwiches heaped with a variety of garnishes. In the larger towns, traditional cafés (*kaffistovas)* serve high-quality Norwegian food at reasonable prices. At lunchtime (*lunsj*), most restaurants offer a separate lunch menu (mains 140–180kr) or cheaper daily specials (*dagens rett*), while dinner (*middag*) can be prohibitively expensive. All large towns have authentic Thai, Chinese and Indian restaurants which offer cheaper meals than their Norwegian equivalents. Restaurant business hours are 11am/noon to 3pm for lunch and 4/6 to 11pm for dinner.

Drink

Due to heavy regulation and taxing, alcohol prices are among the highest in Europe. Buying from the supermarkets and **Vinmonopolet** (state-run off-licences) is cheapest: in a bar, **beer** costs around 70kr for 500ml. It comes in three strengths: class I is light, class II is what you get in supermarkets, while class III is the strongest and only available at Vinmonopolet. In the cities, bars stay open until at least 1am if not later; in the smaller towns, they tend to close at 11pm. Look out for the national drink, *aquavit*, served ice-cold in little glasses; at forty percent ABV, it's real headache stuff. Outside bars and restaurants, **wines** and **spirits** can only be purchased from Vinmonopolet; opening hours are usually Mon–Wed 10am–4/5pm, Thurs 10am–5/6pm, Fri 9am–4/6pm, Sat 9am–1/3pm. You have to be 18 to buy wine and beer, 20 to buy spirits. No shop will sell you alcohol on a Sunday.

CULTURE AND ETIQUETTE

Norwegian people are generally scrupulously polite, helpful and self-deprecating. The famous **Nordic reserve** is apparent, but usually evaporates under the influence of direct friendliness or, failing that, alcohol – which Norwegians consume in large quantities.

In most restaurants it's common to round up the bill, whereas in upmarket places a 10 percent **tip** is generally expected. Almost everyone speaks excellent English, even in the most isolated towns.

SPORTS AND OUTDOOR ACTIVITIES

Every kind of snow-based sport is represented in Norway, but **skiing** (cross-country and downhill) is the national winter pastime and is taken very seriously indeed. In the north of the country, **dogsledding** and **snowmobile trips** can also help you make the most of the snow, though you pay dearly for the

NORWEGIAN

	Norwegian	Pronunciation
Yes	*Ja*	Ya
No	*Nei*	Ney
Please	*Vær så snill*	Veyr saw snil
Thank you	*Takk*	Takk
Hello/Good day	*God morgen/God dag*	God mor-gan/Go-daag
Goodbye	*Adjø*	Ad-yur
Excuse me	*Unnskyld*	Ewn-shewl
Where is?	*Hvor er…?*	Vor ayr…?
Good	*God*	God
Bad	*Dårlig*	Dawr-lig
Near	*Nær*	Neyr
Far	*Langt*	Laangt
Cheap	*Billig*	Billig
Expensive	*Dyrt*	Deert
Open	*Åpen*	Aww-pen
Closed	*Stengt*	Stengt
Today	*I dag*	Ee-daag
Yesterday	*I går*	Ee-gawr
Tomorrow	*I morgen*	Ee maw-ren
How much is it?	*Hvor myer koster det?*	Vor mew-e kaws-ter de?
What time is it?	*Hva er klokka?*	Vaa eyr klaw-ka?
I don't understand	*Jeg forstår ikke*	Yai fawr-stawr ik-ke
Do you speak English?	*Snakker du engelsk?*	Snack-er doo eyng-elsk?
One	*En*	En
Two	*To*	Taw
Three	*Tre*	Trey
Four	*Fire*	Fee-reh
Five	*Fem*	Fem
Six	*Seks*	Seks
Seven	*Sju*	Shoo
Eight	*Åtte*	Aw-teh
Nine	*Ni*	Nee
Ten	*Ti*	Tee
Help!	*Hjelp!*	Yelp!
Cheers!	*Skål!*	Skol!

privilege, while **sailing** and **kayaking** are great ways to enjoy the western fjord region. The chill, clear waters around the Lofoten Islands are prime **snorkelling**, **diving** and **whale-watching** territory, while Norway's vast national parks are a hiker's dream. There are plentiful hiking and climbing routes, as well as glacier walk excursions, with transport details and maps available from local tourist offices and DNT offices.

COMMUNICATIONS

Most accommodation options offer (usually) **free wi-fi** access, and most libraries have free internet access for 15min. **Post office** opening hours are Monday to Friday 9am to 5pm, Saturday 10am to 2pm. Most public phones only accept **phonecards**, available in a variety of denominations from kiosks.

EMERGENCIES

Violent crime is extremely rare, hence the national shock at the 2011 massacre of 77 civilians by a right-wing extremist. Hotels, pharmacies and tourist offices have lists of local **doctors** and dentists. Norway is not in the EU but reciprocal health agreements mean EU citizens get free hospital treatment with an EHIC card.

INFORMATION

Every town has a helpful **tourist office** (ⓦwww.visitnorway.com). Many book accommodation, some rent out bikes and change money. During the high season – late June to August – they normally open daily for long hours; outside of these months they mostly adopt shop hours and many close down altogether in winter. Some cities, such as Oslo, Bergen and Stavanger, also have local DNT offices (Den Norske Turistforening; ⓦwww.turistofreningen.no) which stock hiking maps and information on Norway's national parks.

EMERGENCY NUMBERS

Police ⓣ112; Ambulance ⓣ113; Fire ⓣ110.

STUDENT AND YOUTH DISCOUNTS

Students and under-26s nearly always get a discount on transport on presentation of an **ISIC** card, as well as about 30 percent off most sights and museums and inexpensive meals in some student restaurants.

MONEY AND BANKS

Norway's currency is the **krone** (kr), divided into 100 øre. Coins come in 50 øre, 1kr, 5kr, 10kr and 20kr denominations; notes are in 50kr, 100kr, 200kr, 500kr and 1000kr denominations. At the time of writing €1 = 7.74kr; £1 = 8.60kr; and US$1 = 5.35kr.

Banking hours are Monday to Friday 8.15am to 3pm, Thursday till 5pm. Most airports and some train stations have exchange offices, open evenings and weekends. **ATMs** are commonplace even in the smaller towns and credit cards are accepted pretty much everywhere.

OPENING HOURS AND HOLIDAYS

Supermarkets are open Monday to Friday 9am to 9pm and on Saturdays 9am to 6pm. Opening hours for **shops** are Monday to Wednesday and Friday 10am to 5pm, Thursday 10am to 7pm, Saturday 10am to 2pm. Almost everything is closed on Sunday, the main exceptions being newspaper and snack-food kiosks (*Narvesen*) and takeaway food stalls. Most businesses are closed on **public holidays**: January 1, Maundy Thursday, Good Friday, Easter Sunday and Monday, May 1 (Labour Day), Ascension Day (mid-May), May 17 (Norway's National Day), Whit Monday, December 25 and 26.

Oslo

Today's **OSLO** is largely the work of the late nineteenth and early twentieth centuries, an era reflected in the wide avenues, dignified parks and gardens, solid buildings and long, classical vistas. Oslo's residents enjoy the trappings of metropolitan life within easy reach of dense forest and sandy beaches.

What to see and do

Unfairly dubbed one of the world's most boring capitals, Oslo is blessed with a clutch of first-rate museums and sights, plentiful (if generally expensive) cafés and restaurants and a lively bar and clubbing scene, all of which will keep you happily occupied for a few days.

Oslo Cathedral and Stortinget

The **cathedral** (Domkirke; Mon–Thurs 10am–5pm, Fri 3.30pm–midnight, Sat midnight–8pm, Sun 10am–8pm) is located just off Karl Johans gate. Its elegant interior, and striking altarpiece are well worth a visit. From here it's a brief stroll up Karl Johans gate to the **Stortinget**, the parliament building, an imposing chunk of neo-Romanesque

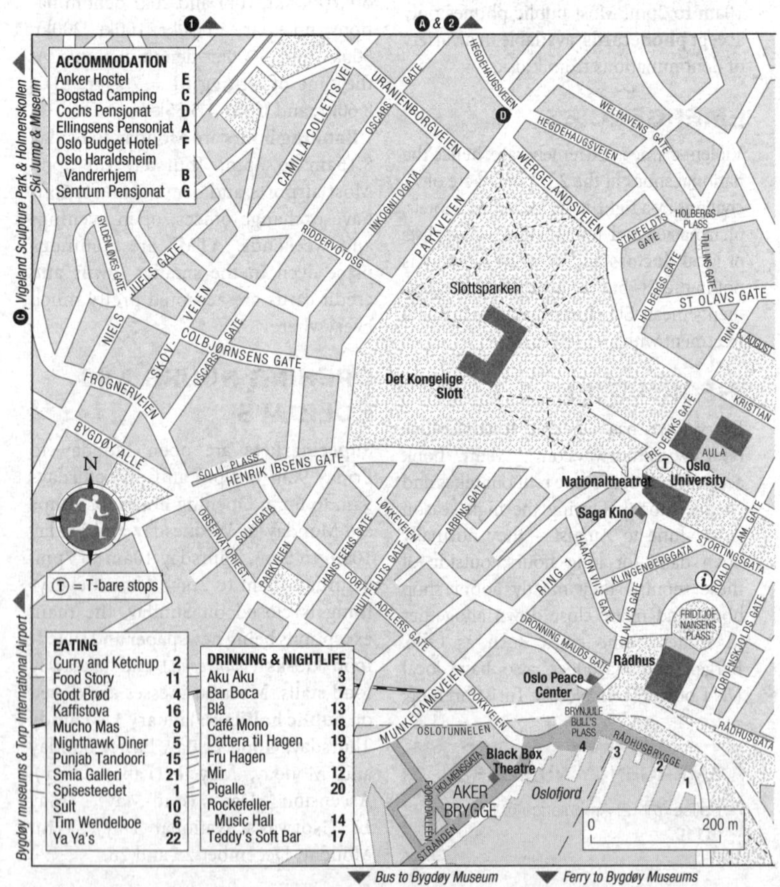

architecture that was completed in 1866. In front of the parliament, a narrow park-piazza flanks Karl Johans gate; in summer it teems with promenading city folk, while in winter people flock to its floodlit open-air skating rinks.

The National Gallery

At Universitetsgata 13, you'll find the **National Gallery** (Nasjonalgalleriet; Tues, Wed & Fri 10am–6pm, Thurs 10am–7pm, Sat & Sun 11am–5pm; free; ⓦwww.nasjonalgalleriet.no), home to Norway's largest and best collection of fine art. A room devoted to Edvard Munch features the original version of the famous *Scream* and there are also wonderfully striking landscapes by Johan Christian Dahl, Caspar David Friedrich and Thomas Fearnley.

City Hall

You can't miss the monolithic brickwork of the massive City Hall near the waterfront. The **Rådhus** (daily 9am–6pm; guided tours Mon–Sat 10am, noon & 2pm, Sun also 4pm in summer, otherwise Wed only; free), opened in 1950 to celebrate the city's 900th anniversary. Venture inside to admire some beautiful carved-wood depictions of Norse myths and an enormous hall decorated with a mural by several prominent Norwegian artists – this is where the Nobel Peace Prize is awarded on December 10 each year.

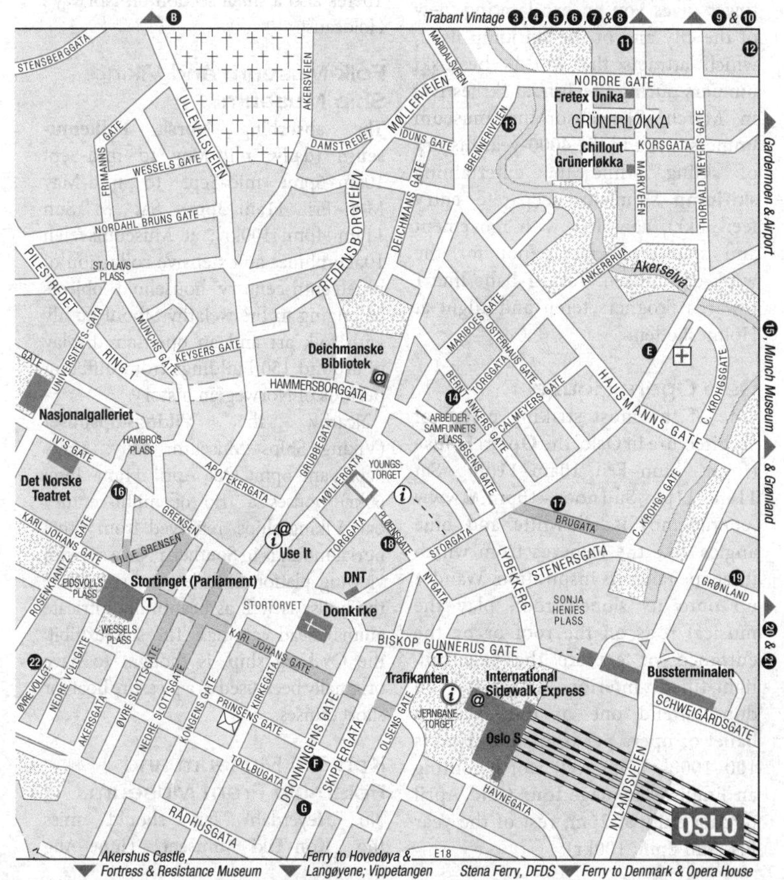

Nobel Peace Center

No visitor to Oslo should miss the **Nobel Peace Center** (mid-May to Sept daily 10am–6pm, closed Mon rest of year; 80kr; ⓦwww.nobelpeacecenter.org), a state-of-the-art interactive museum charting the history of the world's most prestigious prize and the lives and work of its winners. The excellent temporary exhibitions have recently included a powerful photographic display on the plight of refugees.

Holmenkollen Ski Jump & Museum

At the revamped **Ski Jump & Museum** (June–Aug daily 9am–8pm, rest of year 10am–4/5pm; 100kr), the ski-jump tower gives you an exhilarating view of the city and of the ski jump itself, which attracts the world's best ski jumpers during the annual ski festival in March. The absorbing museum immerses you in the 4000-year history of skiing, while the entertaining **ski-jump** simulator (separate entry fee: 50kr), complete with movement and sound effects, is not for the weak of stomach. Take T-bane line 1 towards Frognerseteren and alight at Holmeskollen.

Oslo Opera House

One of the most striking pieces of architecture in Oslo, the **Opera House** (foyer Mon–Fri 10am–11pm, Sat 11am–11pm, Sun noon–10pm; ⓦwww.operaen.no) is all white and blue angles, like the icebergs from which its shape takes its inspiration. Wander up onto its sloped roof, play the musical rods on the roof or by the entrance, or explore the beautiful, light-filled interior. Even if you don't attend one of the excellent ballet or opera performances (tickets 100–1000kr), it's well worth joining an English-language **tour** (mid-April to Aug daily at 2pm; rest of the year Fri–Sun 2pm; 100kr).

Akershus Castle & Fortress

On the eastern side of the harbour, the thirteenth-century **Akerhus Fortress** (May–Aug Mon–Sat 10am–4pm, Sun 12.30–4pm; rest of year Sat & Sun noon–5pm; 70kr; ⓦwww.akershusfestning.no), featuring a seventeenth-century Renaissance castle, is particularly worth visiting for the excellent **Norwegian Resistance Museum** (May–Aug Mon–Sat 10am–5pm, Sun 11am–5pm; rest of year Mon–Fri 10am–4pm Sat & Sun 11am–4pm; 50kr), with its detailed and unbiased treatment of the five years of Norway's occupation by Nazi Germany in World War II, combining documents, photos, posters and artefacts in one absorbing display. There's also a small section on Norway's Holocaust.

Folk Museum and Viking Ship Museum

The absorbing **Norsk Folkemuseum** (daily: mid-May to mid-Sept 10am–6pm; mid-Sept to mid-May Mon–Fri 11am–3pm, Sat & Sun 11am–4pm; 100kr), at Museumsveien 10, combines an extensive collection of nineteenth-century household objects belonging to the welathy Siboni family with folk art and an open-air display of around 150 buildings from different periods of Norwegian history.

Nearby, the **Vikingskipshuset** (Viking Ships Museum: daily: May–Sept 9am–6pm; Oct–April 11am–4pm; 60kr) houses a trio of ninth-century oak Viking ships, retrieved from ritual burial mounds in Southern Norway, with viewing platforms to let you see inside the hulls, as well as beautifully intricate animal head carvings. The star exhibit, the **Oseberg ship**, is thought to have originally been used as a pleasure boat for short cruises.

Kon-Tiki Museum and Polarship Fram Museum

No Heyerdahl fan should miss the **Kon-Tiki museet** (June–Aug

GETTING TO THE BYGDØY PENINSULA

The leafy **Bygdøy peninsula**, is easily reachable by **ferry**, which leaves from the Rådhusbrygge (pier 3; April–Oct every 20min 8am–8.45pm; shorter hours outside summer months; 40kr on board or 27kr from kiosk), stopping first at Dronningen pier (15min from Rådhusbrygge) for the Viking Ship and Folk museums, and then the Bygdøynes piers (20min) for the Kon-Tiki and Fram Polarship museums. Alternatively, take **bus** #30 (every 15min), which runs from Oslo S.

9.30am–5.30pm, rest of year 10am–4pm; 65kr; Ⓦwww.nasjonalgalleriet.no), which displays the balsawood raft on which Thor Heyerdahl made his now legendary, utterly eccentric 1947 journey across the Pacific to prove the first Polynesian settlers could have sailed from pre-Inca Peru, alongside accounts of his other journeys and his life's work.

Inside the **Frammuseet**, next to the Bygdøynes dock (daily: June–Aug 9am–6pm; rest of year 10am–4pm; 60kr; Ⓦwww.nasjonalgalleriet.no), you can clamber aboard the most famous Norwegian ship, the polar vessel *Fram*; this was the ship originally used by Fridtjof Nansen, explorer-turned-ambassador and Nobel Peace Prize winner, and which later carried Roald Amundsen to Antarctica in 1912, allowing him to beat the ill-fated Robert Falcon Scott to the South Pole. Complete with most of its original fittings, the interior gives a superb insight into the life and times of these early polar explorers.

Munch Museum

The **Munch-museet**, Tøyengata 53 (June–Aug daily 10am–6pm; Sept–May Tues–Fri 10am–4pm, Sat & Sun 11am–5pm; 75kr; Ⓦwww.munch.museum.no), is reachable by T-bane or bus #20: get off at Tøyen. Born in 1863, **Edvard Munch** is Norway's most famous painter. His lithographs and woodcuts are on display here, as well as his early paintings and the great signature works of the 1890s. The museum owns one of two versions of *The Scream*, stolen in 2004 and returned about two years later in mysterious circumstances. The museum is set to move to a new home near the Opera House in December 2013.

OSLO PASS

Given the average cost of a museum in Oslo, if you're planning on much sightseeing, an **Oslo Pass** can save you a considerable amount of money. Available at the tourist offices, the Oslo Pass is valid for 24/48/72hr, and costs 230/330/430kr. Students with valid ID get an additional 20 percent off.

Vigeland Sculpture Park

Reachable by tram #12 from the centre (get off at Vigelandsparken), Frogner Park's star feature is the open-air **Vigeland Sculpture Park** (free access), which commemorates another modern Norwegian artist, Gustav Vigeland. Vigeland started on the sculptures in 1924 and was still working on them when he died in 1943. A long series of life-size bronze and granite figures frowning, fighting and playing lead up to the central fountain, an enormous bowl representing the burden of life, supported by straining, sinewy bronze Goliaths, with an intricately carved obelisk towering behind it.

Arrival

Air Oslo Gardermoen International Airport is located 50km north of the city centre. It's served by the FlyToget express train (4.18am–midnight; every 10min; 20min; 190kr; Ⓦwww.flytoget.no), though the cheaper and slower NSB (Norwegian rail) intercity and local trains also stop at Gardermoen

(hourly; fewer on Sat; 30min; 120kr). The Flybussen airport bus (3–4 hourly; 40min; 150kr one-way, 250kr return; Ⓦwww.flybussen.no) runs to the bus terminal at Galleri Oslo. Ryanair flights land at Torp airport, located 110km southwest. Torp-Ekspressen buses connect arriving flights (1hr 30min; 200kr one-way, 330kr return; Ⓦwww.torpekspressen.no) and the Galleri Oslo bus terminal.
Train All trains arrive at Oslo Sentralstasjon (Oslo S), at the eastern end of the city centre.
Bus The Galleri Oslo bus terminal is connected to Oslo S by a pedestrian bridge; it handles long-distance and international buses.
Ferry DFDS Ferries (Ⓦwww.dfdsseaways.com) from Denmark arrive at the Vippetangen quay, a 15min walk south of Oslo S (take bus #60 to the centre), while Colour Line Ferries (Ⓦwww.colorline.no) from Germany dock at Hjortneskaia, some 3km west of the city centre; take tram #13 or bus #33 to the centre.

Information

Tourist office The main branch is at Fridtjof Nansens plass 5 (June–Aug daily 9am–7pm; April, May & Sept Mon–Sat 9am–5pm; shorter hours rest of year; Ⓣ8153 0555 Ⓦwww.visitoslo.com), with a second branch just outside Oslo S in the Trafikanten centre (Mon–Fri 7am–8pm, Sat & Sun 8am–6/8pm) which supplies a comprehensive timetable booklet for Oslo. Both issue free city maps and sell the useful Oslo Pass (see box, p.861).
Youth information The youth information office, Use It, at Møllergata 3 (Ⓣ24 14 98 20, Ⓦwww.use-it.no) aimed at backpackers under the age of 26, provides free luggage storage and internet, and books inexpensive accommodation.
Hiking information Den Norske Turistforening (DNT), has an office in the centre at Storgata 3 (Ⓣ22 82 28 22, Ⓦwww.turistforeningen.no), selling hiking maps, equipment and DNT membership, and giving general advice and information on route planning.
City listings All information offices provide *Streetwise* – a free budget guide to Oslo – as well as the excellent English-language *Oslo Official Guide* and *What's on in Oslo.*

City transport

Trams and buses Trams run on six lines, crossing the centre from east to west. Most bus routes converge at Oslo S and Carl Berners plass.
Underground The *Tunnelbanen* (T-bane) has six lines, all of which also run along the loop of track circling the centre from Majorstuen in the west to Tøyen in the east.
Ferry Numerous local ferries cross the Oslofjord to the south of the centre, connecting the city with its outlying districts and archipelagoes.
Tickets Local transport tickets cost a flat-fare of 27kr; a 24hr travel pass, available from Trafikanten, as well as ticket machines at many stops and Narvesen and 7-Eleven kiosks, is 70kr. Night buses cost 55kr.

Accommodation

Book in advance, particularly in August and September. Private rooms in family-run B&Bs (from 300kr for a single & 450kr for a double) can be booked by the Trafikanten tourist office or Use-It.

Hostels

Anker Hostel Storgata 55 Ⓣ22 99 72 00, Ⓦwww.ankerhostel.no. Enormous, clean and friendly hostel on the edge of the hip Grunerløkka district, attracting an international clientele. Amenities include guest kitchens and a bar. Breakfast 55kr. Dorms 210–250kr; doubles 580kr.
Oslo Haraldsheim Vandrerhjem Haraldsheimveien 4, Grefsen Ⓣ22 22 29 65, Ⓦwww.haraldsheim.no. Best of the HI hostels, 4km northeast of the centre, consisting mostly of four-bed dorms, many en suite. Take tram #15 or bus #31 from the bottom of Storgata to the Sinsenkrysset stop, from where it's a signposted 5–10min walk. Dorms 255kr, singles 415kr, doubles 540kr; breakfast included.
Sentrum Pensjonat Tollbugaten 8 Ⓣ22 33 55 80, Ⓦwww.sentrumpensjonat.no. This friendly hostel has a super-central location and the most comfortable beds of all of Oslo's hostels, though the train station area does get a little dodgy at night. Dorms 290kr, singles 500kr, doubles 750kr.

Hotels and guesthouses

Cochs Pensjonat Parkveien 25 Ⓣ23 33 24 00, Ⓦwww.cochspensjonat.no. Pleasant guesthouse just north of the royal palace, with spartan rooms, some with kitchenettes. The cheapest rooms have shared bathrooms. Triples & quads 320kr/person, singles from 490kr, doubles from 690kr.
Ellingsens Pensonjat Holtegata Ⓣ25 22 60 03 59, Ⓦwww.ellingsenspensjonat.no. Lovely B&B in a nineteenth-century home, with bright, high-ceilinged rooms, some with shared bathrooms. Look for the big white house. Singles 400–480kr, doubles 580–670kr.
Oslo Budget Hotel Prinsens gate 6 Ⓣ22 41 36 10, Ⓦwww.budgethotel.no. Central, spotless rooms decorated in white and cream featuring either two bunk beds or a double, TV, wi-fi and desks.

"Standard" are en suite; "budget" rooms share facilities. Singles 510–610kr, doubles 610–710kr.

Campsite

Bogstad Camping Ankeveien 117 ⓣ22 51 08 00, ⓦwww.bogstadcamping.no. Large, busy campsite in a good location by a lake, 9km from the city centre, with guest kitchen and nearby restaurant. Take bus #32 from Oslo S. Two-person tent 185kr, four-bed huts 1000kr.

Eating

For those carefully counting their kroner, United Bakeries (Karl Johans gare 37) and Godt Brød (Thorvald Meyersgate 49) are best for freshly baked bread and doorstop sandwiches. You can also buy a bag of freshly cooked prawns from a fishing boat at the Rådhusbrygge pier, or head to the open-air market on Youngstorget (Mon–Sat 7am–2pm).

Food Story Thorvald Meyersgate 61. Organic deli and stylish café specializing in seasonal dishes such as fish and shellfish stew, American pancakes with maple syrup and open sandwiches with juniper-smoked salmon. Mains from 129kr.

Kaffistova Rosenkrantz gate 8. This self-service café feels a bit like a school cafeteria but serves burgers, open sandwiches and traditional Norwegian dishes such as meatballs and reindeer cakes at very fair prices. Sandwiches from 79kr; mains 149kr.

Mucho Mas Thorvalds Meyersgate 36. Cute, relaxed bar-restaurant that does a roaring trade in less-than-authentic but still tasty Mexican food. The portions are enormous. Mains 150kr.

Nighthawk Diner Seilduksgata 15. Immensely popular replica 1930s diner complete with original jukebox. The burgers are not cheap (179kr) but they are truly excellent; most dishes are organic and the blueberry milkshakes are to die for.

Punjab Tandoori Grønland 24. Superb curries at bargain prices served at this simple, canteen-style restaurant in Grønland; mains from 75kr.

Spisestedet Hjelmsgate 3. A central vegetarian restaurant with a 30-year reputation; there's an emphasis on organic produce and mostly vegan dishes. Meal 50–100kr. Closed Sat & Sun.

Sult Thorvald Meyersgate 26. This hip restaurant serves seasonal, organic food and their three-course menus (from 410kr), comprising imaginative fish and meat dishes, are well worth the splurge. The attached bar *Tørst* is popular too.

Tim Wendelboe Grünersgata 1. Run by an award-winning barista, this café serves high-quality coffee that's slightly above average in price.

TREAT YOURSELF

Smia Galleri (Oplandsgata 19 ⓣ2219 5920, ⓦwww.smiagalleri.no), with quirky decor – and wrought metal sculptures on the patio, is a local favourite, its imaginative dishes including reindeer heart with lingonberry-aquavit jelly and grilled monkfish with chorizo and gnoccin. Their three-, four- and five- course dinner specials (400/465/525kr) are a real highlight of eating in Oslo. To get here, take bus #37 from Oslo S towards Helsfyr T-bane and disembark at Vålerenga.

Ya Ya's Øvre Vollgate 13. The *som tum* (green papaya salad) at this superb Thai restaurant is spicy enough to satisfy the harshest of critics, the red curry is authentic down to the tiny pea aubergines and the decor (complete with artificial thunderstorm during meal) manages to convince you that you're in a tropical Thai garden. Mains 149kr. Daily 4–10pm.

Drinking and nightlife

Oslo's hippest cafés and bars can be found in the trendy Grünerløkka area as well as the immigrant district of Grønland. The capital also has a lively music scene, with everything from local bluegrass bands to metal to clubs featuring top DJs. For entertainment listings, consult the *Streetwise* guide, published by Use-It (see opposite).

Bars

Aku Aku Thorvald Meyersgate 32. Tiki bar with a South Pacific vibe, great tropical cocktails and a boat strapped to the ceiling that belonged to Thor Heyerdahl, on loan from the Kon-Tiki Museum. Try their signature Chilli Punch.

Bar Boca Thorvald Meyers gate 30. Tiny, friendly 1950s retro bar in Grünerløkka, with great cocktails. Get there early.

Dattera til Hagen Grønland 10. This multi-faceted Grønland gem is a café by day and a lively tapas bar at night, sometimes with a DJ on its small, upstairs dancefloor. There's a massive beer garden and great food.

Fru Hagen Thorvald Meyersgate 38. Faded-grandeur chic: battered upholstery, dark red walls plus good sandwiches and burgers. In good weather, the outdoor tables are perpetually busy. Open till 3am most nights.

Mir Toftesgate 69. Adorably oddball bar tucked away in a courtyard, complete with old aeroplane seats, candlelight and even a book exchange, popular with local rockers. Live music three or four nights a week.
Teddy's Soft Bar Brugata 3. A local stalwart, this genuine 1950s US dive bar is a good place to wind down with a beer or a milkshake.

Clubs

Café Mono Pløensgate 4 ⓦwww.cafemono.no. Popular rock 'n' roll bar-club just by Youngstorget. Decor and music are rock-themed; you can often catch local and international bands here. Open till 3am.
Pigalle Grønlandleiret 15 ⓦwww.olympen.no. Hit the dancefloor at this popular nightclub – the first in Oslo – or enjoy a sedate drink at the adjoining *Olympen* bar, decked out like an old courtroom with chandeliers.

Live Music

Blå Brenneriveien 9c ⓦwww.blaaoslo.no. Cultural nightspot that's rated in the top 100 jazz clubs in the world, featuring primarily live jazz but DJs, salsa and metal nights, public debates and poetry readings feature too. Open till 3.30am at weekends.
Rockefeller Music Hall Torggata 16 ⓦwww.rockefeller.no. One of Oslo's major concert venues, hosting well-known and up-and-coming bands – mostly rock or alternative.

Entertainment

Black Box Theatre Stranden 3 ⓦwww.blackbox.no. Cutting-edge alternative dance and theatre at this arty venue in Aker Brygge.
Saga Kino Stortingsgata 28 ⓦwww.oslokino.no. Six-screen cinema showing the latest Hollywood blockbusters and other international films.

Shopping

Chillout Grünerløkka Markveien 55. Excellent travel shop stocking a wide range of guidebooks, maps and travel gear, with a little café serving perk-me-ups to assist with the browsing.
Fretex Unika Markveien 51. Special branch of the national charity shop, with added cool – the clothes and furniture on sale here are hand-picked, and there are some genuine treasures to be found.
Trabant Vintage Markveien 56. Pick up vintage and vintage-inspired fashions at this impeccably cool Grünerløkka boutique. Other location at Youngstorvet 4 specializes in rock-related designs.

Directory

Embassies and consulates Canada, Wergelandveien 7, 4th Floor, ⓣ22 99 53 00; Ireland, Håkon VII's gate 1, 5th Floor ⓣ22 01 72 00; UK, Thomas Heftyes gate 8 ⓣ23 13 27 00; US, Henrik Ibsens gate 48 ⓣ22 44 85 50.
Exchange Forex, Fridtjof Nansens plass 6 & Oslo S.
Hospital Oslo Kommunale Legevakten, Storgata 40 ⓣ22 93 22 93. 24hr emergency clinic.
Internet International Sidewalk Express (Oslo S, next to west exit; 24hr; 30kr/hr).
Left luggage Oslo S (daily 4.30am–1am) has luggage lockers, as does Use-It (see p.862); 24hr from 50kr.
Pharmacy Jernbanetorgets Apotek (24hr), Jernbanetorget 4b, opposite Oslo S.
Post office Prinsens gate and Kikegate (Mon–Fri 8am–5pm, Sat 9am–2pm).

Moving on

Train Åndalsnes (3–4 daily; 5hr 30min); Bergen (4–5 daily including overnight sleeper train; 6hr

JOTUNHEIMEN NATIONAL PARK

North of Oslo, 1151-square-km **Jotunheimen** is the country's largest and most popular national park. Its valleys, lakes and mountains are a veritable playground for hikers and climbers. The park boasts northern Europe's highest peak, Galdhøppigen (2469m), Sognefjellet – thought to be Norway's most scenic road (and a tough challenge for serious cyclists) and numerous trails with DNT staffed huts along most of them. Popular hikes include the precarious Besseggen ridge, which scythes its way between two glacial lakes; the Hurrungane massif, with fabulous views from the summit of Funnaråken (2069m); and Galdhøppigen, a tough day hike showcasing some dramatic glaciers. You'll need to equip yourself with Staten kartveerk's *Jotunheimen Aust* and *Jotunheimen Vest* maps and Oslo's DNT office (see p.863) can help you with trip planning. Public transport to the park only runs between late June and mid-August, so check schedules in advance.

30min–8hr); Gothenburg (up to 3 daily; 4hr); Stavanger via Kristiansand (3–5 daily, including overnight sleeper train; 7hr 30min–8hr 40min); Stockholm (up to 3 daily; 6hr–7hr 30min); Trondheim (2–4 daily; 6hr 40min–8hr).
Bus Ålesund (2 daily; 10hr); Åndalsnes (2 daily; 8hr); Bergen (3–4 daily; 10hr–11hr 30min).

Southern Norway

Regular trains run from Oslo to the lively harbour town of **Stavanger** on the south coast via Kristiansand. Near Stavanger, the spectacular **Lysefjord** accounts for some of the most dramatic landscape in this half of the country and features one of Norway's biggest hiking attractions: **Preikestolen (Pulpit Rock)** – a dramatic clifftop viewpoint overlooking the fjord far below. The region's forests provide ample opportunity for camping and walking, while watersports, sailing in particular, are popular on the many lakes and beaches; and Stavanger has a vibrant bar and restaurant scene.

STAVANGER

STAVANGER is a breezily charming seaside city that has grown sleek and prosperous as the hub of Norway's oil industry. The presence of a thriving university gives the town a real buzz, and there's a number of excellent but unpretentious bars that wouldn't be out of place in the capital.

What to see and do

The heart-shaped pond, **Breiavatnet**, in the compact town centre is a helpful reference point; the twelfth-century **Norman cathedral** (June–Aug daily 11am–7pm; Sept–May Mon–Sat 11am–4pm; free) is just north of here and the pretty harbour is visible from the cathedral steps.

Stavanger's delightful **old town** is just northwest of the cathedral – stroll around the charming cobbled streets and unique shops or drop into the entertaining **Norwegian Canning Museum** at Øvre Strandgate 88 (daily 11am–4pm; 60kr), part of the multi-site **Stavanger Museum** (Ⓦwww.museumstavanger.no), which takes you through the 12-step process of canning fish – a traditional local industry – from the salting to the smoking and packing; freshly smoked sardines are available to taste. Further east along the harbour, the superb **Norwegian Petroleum Museum** (daily June–Aug 10am–7pm; Sept–May 10am–4/6pm; 100kr; Ⓦwww.norskolje.museum.no) is a slick, well-designed, interactive space lovingly

PREIKESTOLEN (PULPIT ROCK)

The region's biggest highlight, **Pulpit Rock** is responsible for one of Norway's most arresting images: people balancing precariously on the edge of the sheer cliff with a 604m drop into Lysefjord below. In the summer months, two separate companies – **Østerhuss Buss** (Ⓦwww.osterhusbuss.no) and **Tide Reiser** (Ⓦwww.tideresier.no) run combination boat-and-bus return trips to the start of the trail (200kr). Ferries leave for Tau from the Stavanger pier (12 daily; 40min; 41kr one-way), followed by buses (75kr one-way) to the *Preikestolhytta Fjellstue & Vandrerhjem*, Preikestolen's lodge/youth hostel at the foot of the trail. The hike up to Pulpit Rock consists of an uneven, sometimes steep, path strewn with large rocks, along with stretches of boggy ground. The highest section of the trail runs right by the cliff edge and the view of Lysefjord from the top of the cliff is vertigo-inducingly incredible. Reasonably fit hikers can make it to the top in an hour and a half; sturdy footwear is essential and hiking poles a boon.

detailing the history of Norway's most important industry. A must.

Arrival and information

Air The airport, 15km south of the city, is connected to the bus station by regular *flybussen* (daily from 4.30am–8.45pm, Sat till 5.35pm; 2–3 hourly; 30min; 95kr one-way, 150kr return).

Train and bus The train and bus stations are next door to each other on Jernbaneveien, facing Breiavatnet, in the city centre by the small lake.

Ferry International ferries from Denmark arrive at the town's northernmost quay, by Sandvigå. Domestic ferries to Bergen and nearby towns leave from Jorenholmen on the eastern side of the harbour.

Tourist office Opposite the cathedral at Domkirkeplassen 3 (June–Aug daily 9am–8pm; Sept–May Mon–Fri 9am–4pm, Sat 9am–2pm; ⓣ51 85 92 00, ⓦwww.regionstavanger.com).

Accommodation

Budget accommodation anywhere near the centre is hard to come by; book ahead.

Mosvangen Vandrerhjem Henrik Ibsengate 19 ⓣ5154 3636, ⓦwww.vandrerhjem.no. Basic but comfortable hostel (summer only), right next to *Stavanger Camping Mosvangen*. Free internet; breakfast 60kr. Dorms 275kr; singles 450kr, doubles 525kr.

Stavanger Bed and Breakfast Vikedalsgate 1a ⓣ5156 2500, ⓦwww.stavangerbedandbreakfast.no. Extremely popular B&B near the centre with cosy rooms (some with own showers), the best breakfast in town, a book exchange and nightly waffles and coffee for guests. Singles 690–790kr, doubles 790–890kr.

Stavanger Camping Mosvangen Thensvoll 1b ⓣ5153 2971, ⓦwww.mosvangencamping.no. Campsite by a lake, 25min walk from the centre (take bus #4 and ask for directions). Open April–Sept. 40kr/person, plus 80kr/tent, cabins 450–650kr for up to four people.

Eating

Akropolis Greek Restaurant Sølvberggata 14. Authentic Greek spot for those hankering for *moussaka*, grilled meats, big salads and more. The Sunday lunch buffet is particularly good value (190kr).

Bøker & Børst Øvre Holmegate 32 ⓦwww.bokerogborst.com. Relaxed, book-lined café-bar on a street of candy-coloured houses. There's a regular calendar of events with jazz nights, local folk-pop bands and DJs every Sat.

Food Story Hospitalgata 15. Deli and café specializing in organic food and innovative dishes, such as salad with marinated beef and baked cod in blood orange butter sauce, as well as focaccia and sandwiches. Mains 135–195kr. Until 6pm weekdays & 5pm Sat.

Naree Thai Breigata 22. Cheap and cheerful Thai restaurant that's popular with the visitors and the local Thai population. For authentic spice levels, check out the "menu for Thai folk". Lunch mains 75–95kr; dinner mains from around 150kr.

Drinking and Nightlife

B.broman B.bar Skansegata 7. Chic bar frequented by a crowd in their late twenties and early thirties; decorated with works by local artists and serving good value pints (65kr) as well as award-winning cocktails.

Checkpoint Charlie Larshertevigsgate 5. Student favourite, combining Eastern-bloc chic and loud indie and rock music, as well as DJs and live music several nights a week. The monthly "Forbidden Emotions" night, playing songs you'd otherwise be too embarrassed to request, is a highlight.

Sting Valberget 3 ⓦwww.cafe-sting.no. This charming café-bar serves wine by weight, as well as decently priced food. Live music, poetry readings, art exhibitions and jazz in the tiny downstairs club.

Moving on

Train Oslo via Kristiansand (2–4 daily; 8–9hr).

Bus Bergen (up to 12 daily; 5hr 15min–6hr); Kristiansand (2–4 daily; 4hr 15min).

Flaggruten express boat Bergen (1–3 daily; 4hr).

Bergen and the fjords

The **fjords** are the most familiar and alluring image of Norway – huge forested clefts in the landscape which dwarf the large ferries that pass along them. Bergen is a handy springboard for the fjords, notably the **Flåm valley** and its inspiring mountain railway, which trundles down to the Aurlandsfjord, a tiny arm of the mighty **Sognefjord** – Norway's longest and deepest. North of the Sognefjord, **Nordfjord** is the smaller and less stimulating, though there's superb compensation in the **Jostedalsbreen** glacier (Europe's largest), which nudges the fjord from the east. The tiny S-shaped **Geirangerfjord**, further north again, is magnificent too – narrow, sheer and rugged.

BERGEN

BERGEN is the second biggest city in Norway but somehow doesn't feel like it, perhaps because of its air of calm, the cobbled streets of its centre are remarkably easy to walk around. It's one of the rainiest places in rainy Norway, but benefits from a spectacular setting among seven hills and is altogether one of the country's most enjoyable cities, with a lively student scene.

What to see and do

There's plenty to see in Bergen, from fine old buildings to a series of good museums. The city is also in the heart of **fjord country**, within easy reach of some of Norway's most spectacular scenic attractions.

Torget and Bryggen

The obvious place to start a visit is **Torget**, an appealing harbourside plaza that's home to the best fish market in the country. From here, it's a short stroll round to **Bryggen**, where a string of distinctive, brightly painted wooden buildings (now a UNESCO protected site) line the waterfront. These once housed the city's merchants and now hold shops, restaurants and bars. Although most of the original structures were destroyed by fire in 1702 – they carefully follow the original Hanseatic German design. Among them, the **Hanseatic Museum** (mid-May to mid-Sept daily 9am–5pm; rest of year Tues–Fri 11am–2pm, Sat & Sun 11am–4pm; 55kr), an early eighteenth-century merchant's dwelling kitted out in late Hansa style, is the most diverting.

Nearby, the **Bryggens Museum** (mid-May to Aug daily 10am–4pm; Sept to mid-May Mon–Fri 11am–5pm, Sat noon–3pm, Sun noon–4pm; 60kr) features a series of imaginative exhibitions that attempts to recreate local medieval life. To get the most out of these two museums, it's worth taking the **tour** (daily at 11am & 1pm at Bryggen Museum; 100kr).

Rasmus Meyer Samlinger

The pick of Bergen's four art museums is the **Rasmus Meyer Samlinger**, Rasmus Meyers Allé 7 (daily 11am–5pm; closed Mon mid-Sept to mid-May; 60kr), which holds an extensive collection of Norwegian paintings from the eighteenth to early twentieth centuries, including several works by Edvard Munch and beautiful landscapes by Thomas Fearnley and J.C. Dahl.

LOFTY VIEWS

If it's not raining, take a ride on the **Fløibanen**, a funicular railway (every 15min: Mon–Fri 7.30am–11pm/midnight, Sat 8am–11pm/midnight, Sun 9am–11pm/midnight; 75kr return), which runs to the top of **Mount Fløyen** (320m), from where there are incredible panoramic views over the city and the fjord beyond. For even better views, take the shuttle bus from Torget (May–Sept 9am–9pm) to the **Ulriksbanen cable car** (with/without bus 145/245kr), which takes you up Mount Ulriken (620m). From here, you can hike the well-marked trail to the top of Mount Fløyen and come back down on the funicular.

Aquarium and VilVite

Bergen's other attractions include the large **Aquarium** at Nordnessbakken 4 (daily 9am–7pm May–Aug; Sept–April 10am–6pm; 210kr; ⓦwww.akvariet.no), featuring a shark tunnel and fish and sea mammals from around the world. For hands-on fun, it's well worth heading to **VilVite** at Thormølensgate 51 (daily 10am–5pm; 160kr; ⓦwww.vilvite.no), a superb interactive science museum where you can defy gravity by riding a bicycle upside down.

Arrival

Air The airport, 20km south of the city, is connected to the bus station by regular *flybussen* (every 15–20min: 5am–9pm, Sat till 4pm; 45min; 95kr; ⓦwww.flybussen.no), which stops at Torget, the main bus station and the *Radisson SAS Royal Hotel.*

Train and bus The train and bus stations face Strømgaten, a 5min walk southeast of the head of the harbour.

Ferry International ferries and cruise ships arrive at Skoltegrunnskaien quay on the east side of the harbour; domestic Fjord1 (ⓦwww.fjord1.no) and Flaggruten (ⓦwww.flaggruten.no) ferries and catamarans line up on the opposite side of the harbour at the Strandkaiterminalen. A bus (5pm daily; 45kr) runs to the Hurtigruten ferry terminal near Nøstebryggen, a 25min walk from the *Radisson SAS Royal Hotel.*

Information

Tourist office Vågsallmenningen 1 (May & Sept daily 9am–8pm; June–Aug daily 8.30am–10pm; Oct–April Mon–Sat 9am–4pm; ⓣ55 55 20 00, ⓦwww.visitbergen.com). Issues maps and the excellent *Bergen Guide* booklet, books Norway in a Nutshell and other trips, and sells the very worthwhile Bergen Card (200kr/24hr 260kr/48hr), which allows travel on all the city's buses and free entrance to (or discounts for) most of the city's sights, including sightseeing trips.

Hiking information The Bergen Turlag DNT office at Tverrgaten 4–6 (Mon–Wed & Fri 10am–4pm, Thurs 10am–6pm, Sat 10am–2pm; ⓣ55 33 58 10, ⓦwww.bergen-turlag.no) can advise on hiking trails and mountain huts in Western Norway and also sells hiking maps.

Accommodation

Book ahead in summer, especially if you want to stay in the town centre. Private rooms (from around 450kr) can be booked through the tourist office.

Hostels

Bergen Vandrerhjem Montana Johan Blyttsveie 30, Landås ⓣ55 20 80 70, ⓦwww.montana.no. A good spot for active travellers, this large, well-run hostel 4km east of the city centre has hiking trails on its doorstep, bikes for rent, a gym and a great view over the city. Breakfast buffet included. Take bus #31. Dorms 200–275kr, doubles 820kr.

Bergen Vandrerhjem YMCA Nedre Korskirkeallmenningen 4 ⓣ55 60 60 55, ⓦwww.bergenhostel.no. The super-central location, mini kitchenettes in each room, sociable atmosphere and free wi-fi make up for the size of the rooms. Dorms 180kr, doubles 450kr/person, quadruple rooms 320/per person.

Marken Gjestehus Kong Oscarsgate 45 ⓣ55 31 44 04, ⓦwww.marken-gjestehus.com. Bright, modern decor and helpful staff make this 21-room hostel one of Bergen's best accommodation options. Dorms 185– 225kr (bed linen 65kr); singles 795kr, doubles 895kr.

Hotels and guesthouses

City Box Nygårdsgaten 31 ⓣ55 31 25 00, ⓦwww.citybox.no. *City Box*'s slick, modern design extends to its booking system; you book online and use your booking number to check yourself in and print your key card at the door. Rooms are chic with minimalist decor (the cheaper ones share bathrooms); there's free wi-fi too. Singles 500–600kr, doubles 700–900kr.

Skansen Pensjonat Vestrelidsallmenningen 29 ⓣ55 31 90 80, ⓦwww.skansen-pensjonat.no. This attractive seven-room B&B inside a nineteenth-century stone house sits just above the funicular entrance. Excellent views, a Norwegian breakfast and the welcoming couple who run it make it a top place to stay. Singles 450–500kr, doubles 700–800kr.

Eating

Naboen Restaurant Sigunds gate 4. Excellent, innovative Swedish dishes at manageable prices. Try the meatballs with lingonberry preserve or the venison steak in vanilla and port sauce. Mains from 198kr.

Pingvinen Vaskerelven 14. Informal local favourite specializing in small-town Norwegian cooking. Lunch specials include hearty pea soup with bacon, while more substantial dinner dishes feature whale, reindeer and Norwegian meatballs. Lunch mains from 70kr; dinner mains from 170kr.

Pygmalion Nedre Korskirkeallmenningen 5. Cosy organic café with modern art on the walls and a good choice of vegetarian dishes, including salads, pancakes and ciabattas. Salads 120–150kr, pancakes from 80kr.

Taste of Indian Tandoori Marken 12. Authentic, inexpensive Indian food with a number of vegetarian dishes. Three dishes (including one vegetarian) are picked daily for the 79kr lunchtime special.

Torget Fish Market Torget. Feast your eyes on the colourful displays of fish and seafood, shop for local smoked salmon, venison salami and cloudberry jam, or grab one of the delicious open sandwiches (50kr).

Zupperia Vaskerelven 12. Choose from an almost endless menu of soups including Thai chicken, Vietnamese *Pho*, and reindeer with wild mushrooms. More solid dishes include salads, burgers and meat and fish mains. Soups from 59kr.

Drinking and nightlife

Café Opera Engen 18. Arty café by day that serves some of the city's best coffee transforms into a hot nightspot, playing soul, blues and funk on Wed & Thurs, hip-hop on Fri and reggae on Sat.

Garage Christies gate 14. Near-darkness and sticky floors in the club downstairs, playing anything from rockabilly to soul, and a friendly bar upstairs. Look out for the unusual door handles – they're trophies handed out in the Norwegian equivalent of the Grammies, donated by musicians.

Moving on

Train Flåm (via Myrdal and Voss; up to 6 daily; 3hr 10min–4hr 30min); Oslo (up to 5 daily; 6hr 30min–7hr 40min).

Bus Ålesund (1 daily at 8am; 9hr 30min); Flåm (up to 6 daily; 3hr); Oslo (express 3 weekly, 9hr; otherwise 1–3 daily, 11hr); Stavanger (up

BERGEN'S FESTIVALS

Bergen International Festival (@www.festspillene.no) Twelve days of music, ballet, folklore and drama in May/June.

Borealis (@www.borealisfestival.no) A big music festival in late March, celebrating all genres of music.

Octoberfestival Beer-related festivities at Bergen's version of Oktoberfest.

to 12 daily; 5hr); Trondheim (1 daily at 4.20pm; 14hr 20min).

Ferry Fjord1 high-speed ferry to Balestrand (1 daily at 8am; 4hr); Flåm (July–Sept only; 1 daily via Balestrand at 8am; 5hr 30min); Hurtigruten coastal ferry to Ålesund (nightly at 8pm; 12hr 45min).

FLÅM VALLEY

One of the most spectacular attractions in the region is the **Flåmsbana**, a remarkable railway line that plummets 866m from the village of Myrdal into the verdant, mountainous **Flåm valley** and the **Aurlandsfjord**. The track is one of the steepest anywhere in the world, making a wondrously dramatic journey, stopping en route at the spectacular Kjosfoss waterfall. You can take one of the daily trains from Bergen to Flåm via Myrdal and sometimes also Voss (up to 7 daily; 3hr 15min–4hr 30min; from 500kr) or alternatively combine the Flåmsbana with a fjord cruise with Norway in a Nutshell (see box opposite).

Flåm

The village of **FLÅM**, the train's destination, lies alongside meadows and orchards on the Aurlandsfjord, a matchstick-thin branch of the Sognefjord. There are some excellent hiking trails: hikers can get off the train at **Berekvam** station, the halfway point, and stroll down from there, or else walk from Flåm to Berekvam and then hop on the train. Flåm itself is a tiny village that has been developed for tourism to within an inch of its life, but out of season – or on summer evenings, when the day-trippers have gone – it can be a pleasantly restful place. The **tourist office** (daily: May & Sept 8.30–11.30am & noon–4pm; June–Aug 8.30am–4pm & 4.30–8pm; ⓣ57 63 33 13, @www.visitflam.com) by the train station can book ferry tickets and provide information on local hikes. If you're staying overnight, the excellent *Flåm Camping* (ⓣ57 63 21 21, @www.flaam-camping.no; May–Sept only; camping 85kr per person, dorms 220kr, singles 330kr), across the river, has a large campsite and sparkling hostel facilities. You can pick up groceries at the Coop behind the tourist office or grab a large helping of Norwegian staples at the dockside café (mains 139kr).

SOGNEFJORD AND JOSTEDALSBREEN

With the exception of Flåm, the southern shore of the **Sognefjord** remains sparsely populated and relatively inaccessible, whereas the north shore boasts a couple of very appealing villages. Pretty **Balestrand** makes an ideal base for excursions to the breathtaking **Jostedalsbreen glacier**.

Balestrand

BALESTRAND, a scenic tourist destination since the mid-nineteenth century, makes a very pretty base. The beauty of the fjord aside, there is little to see in town apart from the quaint little stave church of **St Olaf**, though Fjærland and Jostedalsbreen (see box, p.812) are within easy striking distance; daily excursions from Balestrand will take you to the village, glacier museum and glacier itself for around 525kr. Buses from Bergen (via Vadheim) and Flåm (via Sogndal) and express Fjord1 boats from Bergen and Flåm arrive at Balestrand's minuscule harbourfront. You'll also find the **tourist office** here (mid-June to mid-Aug Mon–Sat 7.30am–6pm; rest of year Mon–Fri

NORWAY IN A NUTSHELL

If you're short of time, **Norway In a Nutshell** (Ⓦwww.fjordtours.com) specializes in coordinating tours of the fjord country, using either Bergen or Oslo as the starting/finishing point. These range from day-trips to the Flåm valley, Sognefjord and Hardangerfjord to multi-day excursions up and down the coast. Guides are not provided; Norway In a Nutshell simply save you the trouble of trying to coordinate the complex local boat and bus timetables by booking the relevant transport for you. Pick up the tickets at the train station or the Bergen tourist office using the reference number provided.

10am–5.30pm; Ⓣ57 69 12 55, Ⓦwww.visitbalestrand.no); it provides a map of hikes around the village. *Sjøtun Camping* (June to mid-Sept; Ⓣ950 67 261, Ⓦwww.sjotun.com), ten minutes' walk along the shoreline road, is a fully equipped campsite (camping 30kr per person, plus 80kr per tent; 4-person cabin 270kr). *Kafé Me Snakkast*, behind the tourist office, serves inexpensive Norwegian specials, while *Cider House* (Sjøtunsvegen 32) specializes in innovative dishes made from organic produce and home-made cider (from 4pm).

ÅLESUND

An overnight ferry ride from Bergen, the fishing and ferry port of **ÅLESUND**, which many Norwegians consider to be the best place to live in the country, is immediately – and obviously – different from any other Norwegian town. In 1904, a disastrous fire destroyed the town centre, which was then speedily rebuilt largely in the German Jugendstil (Art Nouveau) style, though with original touches, such as the recurring dragon motif. The finest buildings are concentrated on the main street, **Kongensgate**, and around the slender, central harbour and the **Brosundet**. The excellent **Jugendstil Art Nouveau Centre** (June–Aug 10am–5pm; Sept–May Tues–Sun 11am–4pm; 60kr; Ⓦwww.jugendstilsenteret.no) tells the story of Art Nouveau and the rebuilding of the city through the entertaining visual "From Ashes to Art Nouveau" exhibition.

Not to be missed is the vast **Atlantic Ocean Park** (June–Aug Sun–Fri 10am–7pm, Sat until 4pm; Sept–May Tues–Sun 11am–4pm; 130kr; Ⓦwww.atlantenhavsparken.no), 3km from the town centre. As one of the best aquariums in Norway, it provides a comprehensive introduction to the North Atlantic undersea world. In summer, a special bus runs from a bus stop just south of St Olaf's plass (Mon–Sat hourly from 9.55am–3.55pm; 37kr).

Arrival and information

Air Ålesund's airport is located on Vigra island just outside of town. *Flybussen* (120kr; 20min) are timed to correspond with flight arrivals and departures.

Bus The town's bus station is by the waterfront on Sjørgata, a few metres south of the Brosundet.

Ferry The Hurtigruten ferry docks just north of the tourist office by the harbour.

Tourist office On the harbourside at Skaregata 1 (June–Aug daily 9am–6pm; Sept–May Mon–Fri 9am–4pm; Ⓣ70 15 76 00, Ⓦwww.visitalesund-geiranger.com), this branch hands out the free walking tour booklet covering Ålesund's architectural highlights.

Accommodation

Ålesund Vandrerhjem Parkgata 14 Ⓣ70 11 58 30, Ⓦwww.vandrerhjem.no. Central HI hostel in a creaky but clean old building, with self-catering facilities and 3-tier bunk beds in the girls' dorm. Dorms 260kr, singles 580kr, doubles 800kr.

Prinsen Strandcamping Grønvika 15 Ⓣ70 15 21 90. Attractive, fully equipped lakeside campsite 5km east of town, with guest kitchen, lounge and wi-fi access (50kr/24hr). Camping 45kr/person, cabins from 400kr. Take bus #613 (30kr) and ask the driver where to get off.

Eating and drinking

Lille Løvenvold Løvenvold gate 2. Cool but comfy red-walled café/bar with retro furniture, great coffee and cheap sandwiches to soak up the beer. There's a nice little garden and DJs playing Thurs–Sun nights.

Lyspunktet Kipervik gate 1. Modern café with a massive chandelier and generous coffees. Big slouchy sofas, burgers, pasta and imaginative meaty dishes at low prices too.

Ta Det Piano Kipervik gate 1b. Cool little alternative bar and gallery with graffiti-style art on the walls and the odd live band playing on the roof.

XL Diner Skaregata 1.Excellent fish restaurant overlooking the harbour. Their speciality is *bacalao* (salted cod), offered with a variety of sauces. Mains 250kr; Mon–Sat 5pm–midnight.

Moving on

Air Bergen (3 daily; 45min); Edinburgh (1 daily via Oslo); London Gatwick (2 daily via Oslo); Oslo (up to 10 daily; 55min); Trondheim (2 daily; 40min).

Bus Åndalsnes (2 daily; 2hr 20min); Bergen (at least 2 daily; 7hr); Trondheim (2–3 daily; 7hr 30min).

Ferry Hurtigruten ferry to: Bergen (daily at 00.45am; 13hr); Geiranger (mid-April to mid-Sept daily at 9.30am; 3hr 45min); Trondheim (April to mid-Sept daily at 9.30am; 23hr; rest of year daily at 3pm; 15hr).

THE GEIRANGERFJORD

Inland from Ålesund lies the S-shaped **Geirangerfjord**, one of the region's smallest and most breathtaking fjords. It cuts deeply inland, before ending at the small village of **Geiranger**, which is invaded daily by cruise ship passengers in summer. Many impressive waterfalls can be seen throughout the fjord and the sheer cliffs rising on either side dwarf the cruise ships passing through. It's best to approach the Geirangerfjord by bus from the north if you can as the views are prettiest from this direction. From Åndalsnes (see opposite), the nerve-racking hairpin bends of the wonderfully scenic **Trollstigen Highway** climb through some of the country's highest mountains before sweeping down to the tiny Norddalsfjord. From here, it's a quick ferry ride and dramatic journey along the Ørnevegen, the Eagle's Highway, for a first view of the Geirangerfjord. The twice-daily bus only runs between Geiranger and Åndlasnes from late June to August (currently at 12.25 and 6.10pm; check timetables in advance; 3hr). Another wonderful alternative is to take the Hurtigruten ferry from Ålesund (summer months only; daily at 9.25am; 3hr 45min); the same ferry heads back to Ålesund at 1.30pm.

ÅNDALSNES

Whether you're coming from the south via treacherous Trollstigen,

VISITING THE JOSTEDALSBREEN GLACIER

The **Jostedalsbreen glacier** is a vast ice plateau that dominates the whole of the inner Nordfjord region. The glacier's 24 arms – or nodules – melt down into the nearby valleys, giving the local rivers and glacial lakes their distinctive blue-green colour. The glacier is protected within the **Jostedalsbreen Nasjonalpark**, and it's possible to organize **glacier walks** on Nigardsbreen, its longest arm, with Jostedalen Breførarlag, based in Jostedalen village (June–Sept; from 445kr; Ⓦwww.bfl.no). Walks range from two-hour excursions to all-day, fully equipped hikes. If you just want to see the glacier, it's possible to do so on a day-trip from Bergen (the ferry from Balestrand to Fjærland – Norway's book capital - from where the bus takes you to the glacier, is timed to meet the boat from Bergen), though an overnight stay in Balestrand is highly recommended. Along the way, the bus makes a stop at the diverting **Glacier Museum** (April, May, Sept & Oct 10am–4pm; June–Aug 9am–7pm; 110kr; Ⓦwww.bre.museum.no), which features an interesting panoramic film on the glacier and climate change.

or from Oslo by train (via Dombås) on the incredible Rauma line to the **Isfjord**, arriving in **ÅNDALSNES** is nothing short of spectacular. Its wonderful setting amid lofty peaks and looking-glass water makes for a good day hike up a mountain overlooking the town. The train station and tourist office (mid-June to mid-Aug daily 9am–7pm, rest of the year Mon–Fri 9am–3pm; ⓣ71 22 16 22, ⓦwww.visitandalsnes.com) are in the north of town on Jernbanegata with frequent services to Dombås (2 daily; 1hr 40min) and Oslo (4 daily via Dombås or Lillehammer; 5hr 40min–6hr). The adjoining bus station has services to Ålesund (2 daily; 2hr 10min) and Geiranger (mid-June to late Aug only; daily at 8.20am; 3hr 10min). The HI-affiliated *Åndalsnes Hostel*, 1.5km outside of town (ⓣ71 22 13 82, ⓦwww.aandalsnesvandrerhjem.no) is a great place to stay overnight (dorms 290kr, doubles 720kr); the bus to and from Geiranger stops there.

Northern Norway

The long, thin counties of **Trøndelag** and **Nordland** mark the transition from pastoral southern to blustery northern Norway. Trondheim, Trøndelag's appealing main town, is easily accessible from Oslo by train. In **Nordland** you reach the **Arctic Circle**, beyond which the land becomes ever more spectacular, not least on the exquisite, mountainous **Lofoten Islands**. Further north still, the provinces of **Tromsø** and **Finnmark** appeal to those who appreciate untamed, severe natural beauty, with **Tromsø**, a lively university town, the obvious stopping point. As for Finnmark, many visitors head straight for **Nordkapp**, from where the midnight sun is visible between early May and the end of July, while those interested in Sámi culture go east towards Finland and the Sámi town of **Karasjok.**

TRONDHEIM

TRONDHEIM, a loveable and atmospheric city with much of its partly pedestrianized eighteenth-century centre still intact, has been an important Norwegian power base for centuries, its success guaranteed by the excellence of its harbour. The early Norse parliament, or **Ting**, met here, and the city was once a major pilgrimage centre.

What to see and do

Easy-going Trondheim possesses a marvellous cathedral and several low-key sights, as well as a clutch of good restaurants and popular student bars.

Nidaros Cathedral and Archbishop's Palace

The colossal **Nidaros Domkirke** – Scandinavia's largest medieval building, gloriously restored following the ravages of the Reformation and several fires – remains the focal point of the city centre (Mon–Sat 9am–3pm, Sun 9am–5pm; 60kr; joint ticket with Archbishop's Palace 120kr; ⓦwww.nidarosdomen.no). Taking Trondheim's former name (Nidaros means "mouth of the River Nid"), the cathedral is dedicated to King Olav, Norway's first Christian ruler, who was buried here. Thereafter, it became the traditional burial place of Norwegian royalty and, since 1814, the place of coronation for Swedish and Norwegian monarchs. Highlights of the interior include the Gothic choir and the gargoyles on the pointed arches.

Behind the Domkirke lies the heavily restored twelfth-century Archbishop's Palace (mid-June to mid-Aug Mon–Fri 10am–5pm, Sat 10am–3pm, Sun noon–6pm), home to the **Norway Crown Regalia** (70kr) – the crowns, sceptres and ermine ceremonial robes are beautifully presented in the atmospheric cellar. Another wing of the palace houses the absorbing **Army and Resistance Museum** (Mon–Sat 10am–4pm, Sun noon–4pm; free). Its most interesting section is on the top floor and sensitively recalls the German occupation during World War II.

Torvet

Torvet is the main city square, a spacious open area anchored by a statue of Olav Tryggvason, perched on a stone pillar. The broad and pleasant avenues of Trondheim's centre that radiate out from here date from the late seventeenth century.

Sverresborg Trøndelag Folkemuseum

One of the best open-air museums in Norway, the **Folk Museum** (June–Aug 11am–6pm, to 3pm rest of year; 85kr; Ⓦwww.sverresborg.no) is worth the short bus ride from the centre. You can ramble along the paths that take you through the vast outdoor exhibition, which consists of beautifully preserved old buildings from different parts of Norway, including a twelfth-century stave church and tiny houses with grass growing on roofs. There's also a superb restaurant next door. Take Stavset-bound bus #8 along Dronningens gate.

Munkholmen

If you have an extra day in Trondheim and the weather's fine squeeze in a day-trip by ferry (mid-May to Aug at least hourly between 10am–4/6pm; 60kr return) to the "Monk's Island" from the harbour. This lovely island with a great beach has a rich history: it was originally the town's execution grounds, but later housed a monastery, which then became a prison and finally a customs house before becoming the recreation spot that it is today.

Arrival and information

Train and bus The bus terminal (Rutebilstasjon) and train terminal (Sentralstasjon) are next to each other just north of the town centre, across the bridge.
Ferry The Hurtigruten ferry docks at the Pirterminalen Quay, about 600m north of the train/bus stations.
Tourist office On Torvet, the main square (June–Aug Mon–Fri 8.30am–6pm, Sat & Sun 10am–4pm; rest of year Mon–Fri 9am–4pm, Sat 10am–2pm; Ⓣ73 80 76 60, Ⓦwww.trondheim.no).

Accommodation

The tourist office can book private rooms from 400kr.
Pensjonat Jarlen Kongens gate 40 Ⓣ73 51 32 18, Ⓦwww.jarlen.no. Friendly central guesthouse, each of its rooms bar the single have a gleaming bathroom, a kitchenette, a comfortable armchair and free wi-fi. Single 520kr, doubles 650kr.
Singsaker Sommerhotell Rogertsgata 1 Ⓣ73 89 31 00, Ⓦsommerhotell.singsaker.no. Charming summer-only hotel/hostel with a nice courtyard a short walk or bus ride on bus #63 from the centre. Dorms 240kr, singles from 445kr, doubles from 685kr.
Trondheim InterRail Centre Elgesetergate 1 Ⓣ73 89 95 38, Ⓦwww.tirc.no. Easy-going summer hostel (July to early Aug) in the Trondheim University student union – a cavernous network of bars, theatres and music venues – established and run by local students. The café-bar on the premises is famous for its chocolate cake. Dorms 180kr.

Eating and drinking

Baklandet Skydsstasion Øvre Bakklandet 33. Charming café, restaurant and bar housed in an eighteenth-century coach inn in the lovely Bakklandet area. Serves up tasty traditional dishes and is particularly famous for its *bacalao* (mains 149kr).
Choco Boco Nedre Bakklandet 5. Hugely popular, laidback café specializing in interesting coffees (try the chilli one; 43kr) and serving inexpensive salads and sandwiches.
Den Gode Nabo Øvre Bakklandet 66. A huge selection of international beers and a glorious, floating beer garden make this one of Trondheim's best-loved pubs. The food is good too, with a daily fish dish supplied by sister restaurant *Chablis* just upstairs.

Sushi Bar Munkegata 39. This stylish and popular sushi bar's location right near the fish market ensures that the excellent sushi is super-fresh. Sets from 59kr. Takeaway available.

Vertshuset Tavern Sverresborg Allé 11. Next door to the Folk Museum, this creaky wooden tavern with tiny rooms serves up superb traditional Norwegian dishes – from the meatballs with lingonberry sauce to huge plates of smoked salmon with warm potato salad. Mains from 169kr. Open from 2pm weekends; from 4pm weekdays.

Moving on

Train Bodø (2 daily; 9hr 50min); Dombås (2–4 daily; 2hr 30min–3hr); Oslo (2–4 daily; 6hr 40min–7hr 30min).
Bus Ålesund (2–3 daily; 7hr); Bergen (1 daily at 10.30pm; 14hr).
Ferry Hurtigruten coastal ferry to: Ålesund (daily at 10pm; 14hr); Bodø (daily at noon; 24hr 30min).

BODØ

North of Trondheim, it's a long, 730km haul beyond the Arctic Circle to **BODØ**, literally the end of the line: this is where all trains and many long-distance buses terminate. The nine-hour train trip is a rattling good journey, with the scenery becoming wilder and bleaker the further north you go. Bodø is also a stop on the Hurtigruten coastal boat route and the main port of departure for the Lofoten Islands (see box, p.876). The **bus station** (Sentrumsterminalen) at Sjøgata 3 is also home to the **tourist office** (mid-May to Aug Mon–Fri 9am–8pm, Sat 10am–6pm, Sun noon–8pm; Sept to mid-May Mon–Fri 9am–3.30pm; ⓣ75 54 80 00, Ⓦwww.visitbodo.com). The nearby **backpacker service** (Sjøgata 15–17; late June to mid-August 10am–6pm; ⓣ75 65 02 89) provides travel info, luggage storage, printing and wi-fi for free. Most days, it's possible to get off a night train from Trondheim and catch a ferry to the Lofoten Islands straight away, but if you have to stay overnight, the *City Hotel* (ⓣ75 52 04 02 Ⓦwww.cityhotellbodo.no), located by the train station, offers dorms as well as standard rooms (dorms 200kr; singles 600kr, doubles 700kr). A good option for **food** is the inexpensive *Løvolds Kafeteria* (Mon–Fri 9am–6pm, Sat 9am–3pm), down by the quay at Tollbugata 9: its Norwegian menu features local ingredients, with cheap daily specials. There are buses north to Narvik via Fauske (2 daily; 6hr 30min) and southbound trains to Trondheim (2 daily; 9hr 45min).

THE LOFOTEN ISLANDS

Stretched out in a skeletal curve across the Norwegian Sea, the **Lofoten Islands** rise dramatically out of the clear waters as you approach. Snow-covered mountains loom behind tidy little fishing villages with cod drying on traditional wooden racks. Life moves more slowly here, but there's plenty to keep an active traveller occupied: the islands are perfect for rambling, cycling, sea kayaking, diving, snorkelling and even whale watching. The weather is exceptionally mild, and there's plentiful **accommodation** (Ⓦwww.lofoten.info) in *rorbuer* (originally fishermen's huts), hostels and campsites.

Austvågøy

The main town on **Austvågøy**, the largest and northernmost island of the group, is **SVOLVÆR**, a transport hub and home to the excellent **War Memorial Museum** (Fiskergata 12; June–Sept 10am–4pm & 6.15–10pm; evenings only rest of year; 60kr), a well-presented private collection of rare World War II objects (ask the proprietor to tell you about Hitler's last drawings). Nearby **Magic Ice** (mid-June to mid-Aug noon–10.30pm; rest of year 6–10pm; 100kr) is a warehouse ice bar filled with otherworldly sculptures, many carved anew annually by international ice artists. **Passenger ferries** from Bodø dock about 1km west of the town centre, whereas the Hurtigruten docks in the centre, next to the **bus station**. The **tourist office** at Torget (mid-June

GETTING TO THE LOFOTEN ISLANDS

The **Hurtigruten coastal boat** calls daily at two ports, Stamsund and Svolvær (daily from Bodø: 3pm; 4/6hr; daily from Tromsø: 1.30am; 17/19hr; 300kr) while the southern Lofoten car **ferry** (Ⓦwww.torghatten-nord.no) leaves Bodø for Moskenes, Værøy and Røst (June–Aug 1–2 daily except Sunday; 3hr 30min/5hr 15min/7hr 15min; 163kr per person) as well as Moskenes only (June–Aug 6 daily, 1 on Sun at 1.45am; 4hr). By **bus** the main long-distance services from the mainland to the Lofoten are the indirect buses from Bodø to Svolvær via Fauske and other towns and direct buses from Narvik to Svolvær (2 daily; 6hr 15min). Finally you can **fly** from either Bodø or Tromsø with Widerøe (Ⓦwww.wideroe.no). Outside the summer months, transport to and from the islands is reduced, so check the timetables.

to July 9am–8/10pm; rest of year Mon–Fri 9am–4pm, Sat 10am–2pm; Ⓦwww.lofoten.info), has detailed information and transport schedules for all the Lofoten Islands.

Two pleasant places **to stay** are the seafront *Svolvær Sjøhuscamp* (Parkgata 12; Ⓣ76 07 03 36, Ⓦwww.svolver-sjohuscamp.no; double room 550kr, triple room 690kr, quadruple room 880kr) and *Svinøya Rorbuer* (Ⓣ76 06 99 30, Ⓦwww.svinoya.no) a traditional *rorbuer* (1200kr for two people), across the causeway on the slender islet of Svinøya. You can eat decent salads, sandwiches and more substantial fishy mains at *Bacalao*, further along the seafront from the tourist office. Alternatively, treat yourself to dinner at *Børsen*, located in a creaky old former fish house on Svinøya islet, with fabulous fish dishes (from 270kr) accompanied by music in the evenings (open from 5pm).

Vestvågøy

The next large island to the southwest, **Vestvågøy**, is the one that really captivates most travellers, due in no small part to the atmospheric village of **STAMSUND**, whose older buildings are strung along a rocky, fretted seashore. The scenery on this island is truly spectacular and hikers are rewarded with stunning views.

The smashing HI-affiliated *Justad Rorbuer og Vandrerhjem* (Ⓣ76 08 93 34, Ⓦwww.hihostels.no/stamsund; dorms 140kr, singles 335kr, doubles 445kr, cabins from 570kr; closed mid-Oct to early March) consists of several cosy *rorbuer* perched over a pint-sized bay, about 1km up the road from the port and 150m from the nearest bus stop – ask the driver to tell you where to get off. Fishing around here is first-class: the hostel rents out rowing boats and lines; afterwards, you can cook your catch on the hostel's wood-burning stoves. Bikes are also available for rent (120kr) – the friendly owner will suggest cycle routes. For great fish soup, smoked whale – and very friendly service – head to the *Skjaerbrygga* restaurant, right in the centre of town near the supermarket. Regular buses run to Leknes (3–7 daily; 25min) where you can catch another bus to Å or Svolvær.

Flakstadøya and Moskenesøya

By any standard the two Lofoten Islands, **Flakstadøya** and **Moskenesøya**, are extraordinarily beautiful, their rearing peaks crimping a sea-shredded coastline studded with a string of fishing villages. Remarkably, the E10 road travels along almost all of this dramatic shoreline, by way of tunnels and bridges, to **MOSKENES**, the **ferry port** midway between Bodø and the remote, southernmost islands of **Værøy** and **Røst**.

Some 6km further on, the road ends at the delightful village of Å, its huddle of old houses on stilts wedged in tight between the grey-green mountains and the surging sea. Highlights include the **Norwegian Fishing Village Museum** (daily: mid-June to mid-Aug 10am–6pm; rest of the year Mon–Fri 11am–3.30pm; 50kr), a collection of buildings devoted to traditional trades, such as the 1844 bakery which still bakes amazing cinnamon buns (15kr), and the excellent **Lofoten Stockfish Museum** (June–Aug 11am–4pm; 50kr), overseen by the enthusiastic owner who can explain every stage of Lofoten's traditional cod fishing industry.

You can stay at HI-affiliated *Å-Hamna Rorbuer & Vandrerhjem* (ⓣ76 09 12 11, ⓦwww.lofotenferie.com; hostel: singles 300kr, doubles 400kr, triples 540kr, 4-bed *rorbuer* 800kr), or camp at the clifftop *Moskenesstraumen Camping* (ⓣ76 09 11 48; camping from 90kr; 2-/4-person cabin from 450/650kr). *Brygga* is Å's only **restaurant**; it serves excellent fish dishes (lunch from130kr, dinner from 210kr).

Local **buses** run the length of the E10 from Å to and from Leknes (late June to late Aug 2–7 daily; 1hr 45min) and Svolvær via Leknes (2–5 daily; 3hr 15min); less frequently the rest of the year. They don't always coincide with sailings to and from Moskenes, so if you're heading from the ferry port to Å, time your arrival correctly or you'll have to take an expensive taxi.

TROMSØ

Friendly **TROMSØ**, the "gateway to the arctic", is the de facto capital of northern Norway. Set on an island, connected to the mainland by large bridges, and surrounded by dramatic mountains and craggy shoreline, it offers easy access to the plethora of winter and summer activities on offer.

What to see and do

TROMSØ has two cathedrals, a clutch of interesting museums and a lively nightlife, patronized by its significant student population.

Domkirke and the Polar Museum

In the centre of town you can't miss the striking woodwork of the **Domkirke**. From the church, it's a short walk north along the harbourfront to one of the most diverting museums in the city, the **Polar Museum**, Søndre tollbodgate 11 (daily: mid-June to mid-Aug 10am–7pm; rest of year 11am–3pm; 50kr; ⓦwww.polarmuseum.no), whose varied displays include skeletons retrieved from the permafrost of Svalbard and accounts of expeditions by polar explorers Fridjof Nansen and Roald Amundsen.

Polaria

Also on the waterfront, **Polaria**, Hjalmar Johansengate 12 (daily: mid-May to Aug

THE NORTHERN LIGHTS AND THE MIDNIGHT SUN

Tromsø's northerly location but relatively mild climate has made it one of the most popular spots in the world from which to view the **Northern Lights**, or Aurora Borealis, which are seen here almost daily between November and April. Caused by solar winds as they hit the Earth's atmosphere, they light up the sky in shimmering waves of blue, yellow and green – a spectacle of celestial proportions.

In the summertime there's an entirely different Arctic phenomena to behold: the breathtaking **midnight sun**. In Tromsø you're so far north that the sun never actually dips beneath the horizon. Head for Fjellheisen, a cable car that runs to the top of **Mount Storsteinen** (take bus #26 and ask for a cable-car return ticket; late May to mid-Aug 10am–1am; rest of the year 10am–5pm; 140kr) between May 18 and July 25 around midnight and you'll see the sun, hovering over the horizon in the west, setting the sky spectacularly aglow.

10am–7pm; rest of year noon–5pm; 105kr), the city's star attraction, draws coach-loads of tourists to see the 3pm feeding of the bearded seals. This state-of-the-art aquarium combines its tanks of cold-water fish with a walk-through seal tunnel, displays about the region's fragile ecosystem and a stunning panoramic film on Svalbard.

Arctic Cathedral

Across the long Tromsø Bridge from the centre, the white, pointy, ultramodern **Ishavskatedralen** (June to mid-Aug Mon–Sat 9am–7pm, Sun 1–7pm; 35kr midnight sun concerts in summer; 110kr; bus #20, #24, #26 or #28 from city centre) is spectacular, its shape inspired by the Hoja mountain in the sea near Tromsø. It's made up of eleven immense triangular concrete sections representing the eleven Apostles left after the betrayal, with a stunning stained-glass window.

Tromsø University Museum

This excellent anthropological and geological **museum** (daily 9am–4.30/6pm; 30kr) should not be missed by anyone with an interest in all things northern. Apart from the excellent displays on both traditional and modern Sámi culture, complete with ceremonial objects, traditional dress and household implements, downstairs you can learn about the Aurora Borealis phenomenon – how it works – as well as create your own. Take bus #37 from the centre.

Arrival and information

Bus Long-distance buses arrive and leave from the Prostneset (car park adjacent to the tourist office).
Boat The Hurtigruten coastal boat docks in the centre of town at the foot of Kirkegata.
Tourist office Kirkegate 2, near the Domkirke (mid-May to Aug Mon–Fri 9am–7pm, Sat & Sun 10am–6pm; rest of year Mon–Fri 9am–4pm, Sat 10am–4pm; ⓣ77 61 00 00, ⓦwww.visittromso.no); produces a comprehensive Tromsø guide and has two free internet terminals (15min).

ART IN TROMSØ

Tromsø has a couple of excellent art museums which are both free. The **Art Museum of Northern Norway** (Sjørgata 1; Tues–Sun noon–5pm) focuses on beautiful landscape paintings by northern Norwegian artists, as well as modern sculpture and photography exhibitions, while **Perspektivet** (Storgata 95; Tues–Sun 11am–5pm) stages cutting-edge photography exhibitions, the most recent including "Last Days of the Arctic".

Accommodation

The tourist office has a small supply of private rooms from 350kr.
ABC Hotell Nord Parkgate 4 ⓣ77 66 83 00, ⓦwww.hotellnord.no. Basic but comfortable budget hotel with an all-day buffet, comfortable guest lounge, fridges in rooms and bike rental (150kr/day), 400m from the centre of town. Free wi-fi and student discounts available. Singles from 650kr, doubles from 700kr.
AMI Hotell Skolegate 1 ⓣ77 62 10 00, ⓦwww.amihotel.no. Good-value family-run hotel up the hill from the centre of town, with free wi-fi, free tea and coffee in the communal lounges, and discounts for longer stays and for students. Singles from 60kr, doubles from 820kr.
Tromsø Vandrerhjem Åsgårdsveien 9 ⓣ77 65 76 28, ⓦwww.vandrerhjem.no. Frugal, no-frills summer hostel some 2km west of the quay with fully equipped guest kitchens; hop on bus #26 from the centre. Mid-June to mid-Aug only. Dorms 240kr, doubles 570kr.

Eating

You can buy freshly caught cooked prawns straight off the boats at the Stortorget pier and on weekdays, a Thai food stall on Stortorget sells succulent spicy chicken and pork skewers (25kr).
Aunegården Sjøgata 29. Ultra-popular restaurant in a gorgeous old building serving good sandwiches, salads, plus coffee and heavenly cakes fresh from the on-site bakery (try the chocolate with champagne and strawberry mousse).
Café De 4 Roser Grønnegate 38–46. The best coffee in Tromsø is served in this refined café

whose award-winning baristas specialize in latte art.

Globus Café Storgata 30. Popular Eritrean café with a global menu, though its *tour de force* is the *injera* - a large sponge-like pancake topped with mounds of spicy beef curry, lentils and wilted spinach (165kr). Closed Sun & Sat afternoon.

Verdensteatret Storgata 93b. Popular café-bar housed in Norway's oldest movie theatre that attracts an arty young crowd with its cheap lunch food, drinks, independent film screenings and pumping DJ nights.

Drinking and nightlife

Bastard Bar Strandgata 22. This dark industrial cellar joint is the stage for the city's new bands as well as a sports bar. Monday nights are good for cheap beer and there's bottomless black coffee (no sugar) during the day.

Blå Rock Café Strandgate 14/16 Ⓦwww.blarock.no. Much-loved multistorey bar covered with rock memorabilia; doubles as a chilled café serving sumptuous burgers during the day and a hot DJ venue Thursday to Saturday.

Driv Tollbugata 3 Ⓦwww.driv.no. Cosy student café-bar in a waterfront warehouse near the polar museum where the food and beer is cheap and the company cheerful and welcoming.

Ølhallen Pub With its cosy cellar decor and winning location (attached to the Mack Brewery), the city's favourite pub serves a full range of microbrews (67kr/pint). Daytime only: Mon–Sat from 9am.

Moving on

Bus All southbound buses go via Narvik (4hr 30min), though for Svolvær it's possible to change at Bjerkvik: Alta (late June to mid-Aug daily at 4pm; 6hr 30min); Bodø (daily at 10am; 12hr 30min); Svolvær (daily at 10am; 9hr 20min).

Ferry Hurtigruten ferry to: Honningsvåg (daily at 6.30pm; 17hr); Svolvær (daily at 1.30am; 17hr 30min).

TREAT YOURSELF

Emma's Drømekjokken
Kirkegata 8. "Emma's Dream Kitchen" serves sublime locally sourced fare from Arctic char to reindeer at prices to match. At the downstairs café, *Emma's Under*, prices are slightly lower but the dishes, such as whale steak in peppercorn sauce or grilled fish are just as delicious. Lunch mains from 129kr.

FINNMARK, MAGERØYA AND NORDKAPP

Beyond Tromsø, the northern tip of Norway, **FINNMARK**, enjoys no less than two and a half months of permanent daylight on either side of the summer solstice. Here, the bleak and treeless island of **Magerøya** is connected to the northern edge of the mainland by an ambitious combination of tunnels and bridges.

Alta

If you're heading north from Tromsø towards Nordkapp, you have no choice but to stay overnight in the spread-out town of **ALTA**, since there is only one bus daily (4pm; 6hr 30min; 510kr). Long-distance **buses** arrive at the tourist office in the centre of Alta; a good place to stay is *Bårstua Gjestehus*, just off the E6 main road at Konglev-eien 2a (Ⓣ7843 3333, Ⓦwww.baarstua.no; singles 630–900kr, doubles 830–1200kr). The popular *Alfa-Omega* **restaurant** (Markedsgata 14–16) serves pasta, salads and enormous reindeer steak sandwiches, while *Restaurant*

TROMSØ FESTIVALS

Northern Lights Festival Ⓦwww.nordlysfestivalen.no. Six days of music, held at the end of January.

Sámi Week Early February festival which includes reindeer racing, rope tossing and traditional Sámi food and handicrafts.

Midnight Sun Marathon Ⓦwww.msm.no. Held on a Saturday in June; there's also a half-marathon.

THE SÁMI IN NORWAY

Norway's original inhabitants, the Sámi, have herded reindeer in the north of the country for over 11,000 years. Though their traditions and culture were under threat for a long time, today's Sámi are very much alive and kicking; they have their own independence day, their own flag and even their own parliament in the town of **Karasjok**. A detour to Karasjok, linked by twice-daily buses from Alta and Lakselv, is particularly worthwhile and you can take a free guided tour of the **Sámi Parliament** (Kautokeinoveien 50; late June to mid-August hourly from 8.30am–2.30pm; rest of the year Mon–Fri 1pm), visit the **Sámi National Museum** (Museumgata 17; June–Aug 9am–6pm; rest of year 9am–3pm; 80kr), with its displays of traditional clothing, tools and art by contemporary Sámi artists, or take a more light-hearted look at Sámi culture at the **Sápmi Park** (Porsangerveien; June–Aug Mon–Fri 9am–4pm, Sat & Sun 9am–7pm; rest of year Mon–Fri 10am–2pm; 170kr), an excellent high-tech theme park. A great place to stay is the *Engholm's Design Lodge* (Ⓦwww.engholm.no), a collection of rustic cabins 6km south of Karasjok along the Rv92, which doubles as the town's HI hostel and arranges husky safaris in winter; hearty meals available.

Haldde at the *Hotel Vica* is a fantastic place to sample the best of regional cuisine (lunch mains 110–200kr).

Honningsvåg

The fishing village of **HONNINGSVÅG**, Magerøya's only significant settlement, is your last port of call before Nordkapp – the North Cape – just 34km away. Long-distance **buses** arrive at the waterside by the tourist office in the centre of the village. *North Cape Guesthouse* (mid-May to late August), just behind the seafront at Elvebakken 5a, is the best budget **accommodation** option (Ⓣ92 82 33 71, Ⓦwww.northcapeguesthouse.com; dorms 200kr, singles 550kr, doubles 700kr). For **food**, the excellent *Corner*, near the tourist office, serves grilled fish, reindeer stew and pizza (mains 165–210kr).

Nordkapp

While the 307m-high cliff known as Nordkapp isn't actually the northernmost point of Europe (that honour belongs to Knivskjellodden, reached along an 18km signposted track from highway E69), it's as far north as you can get by public transport. It's a hassle to reach, but there *is* something exhilarating about this bleak, wind-battered promontory, dotted with grazing reindeer. It the only viewpoint in Norway that you have to pay to visit, though officially you're paying to enter the blight on the landscape that is **Nordkapphallen** (North Cape Hall; daily: early to mid-May & Sept to mid-Oct 11am–3pm; mid-May to Aug 11am–1am; mid-Oct to April 12.30–2pm; 235kr), a flashy tourist centre that contains Europe's northernmost souvenir shop, café, restaurant, bar, panoramic movie theatre, chapel and post office.

To reach Nordkapp, there's a limited **bus** service from Honningsvåg (late June to mid-Aug 1–2 daily; 45min; 100kr); the road is closed throughout the winter and often in spring too. The Hurtigruten **ferry** offers its passengers an excursion to Nordkapp from Honningsvåg. If you wish to avoid the long and expensive bus journey back to Tromsø, another option is bussing it from Honningsvåg to Lakselv (1–2 daily except Sat; 3hr 30 min), and then flying back with Widerøe (1–2 daily; 45min).

Poland

HIGHLIGHTS

SOPOT: relax on the vast stretch of white sand near this lively summertime resort

NIGHT OUT IN WARSAW: live it up among the glass skyscrapers and abandoned factories of the country's dynamic capital

WROCŁAW: discover this elegant gem of a city, with gorgeous architecture unspoilt by tourist hordes

KAZIMIERZ, KRAKÓW: explore Poland's Jewish heritage in the ancient synagogues and winding alleyways of this now hip neighbourhood

TATRA MOUNTAINS: hike among jagged alpine peaks, swim in crystal-clear lakes and enjoy the unique mountain culture

ROUGH COSTS

DAILY BUDGET Basic €25 /occasional treat €35

DRINK Vodka (50ml shot) €1

FOOD *Żurek* soup €2–3

HOSTEL/BUDGET HOTEL €10/€30

TRAVEL Train: Warsaw–Kraków €13; bus: €10

FACT FILE

POPULATION 38.5 million

AREA 312,685 sq km

LANGUAGE Polish

CURRENCY Złoty (zł/PLN)

CAPITAL Warsaw (population: 1.7 million)

INTERNATIONAL PHONE CODE ⓣ48

Introduction

Poland has long been a nation steeped in tradition and history, although the past twenty years have witnessed such dizzying economic development that the country is starting to feel more and more like the West. Still, beneath the gleaming surface lies a culture firmly rooted in Eastern hospitality and community values, and fascinating reminders of the turbulent past are everywhere. Poland is also a land of considerable natural beauty, whose idyllic lakes, beaches and mountains provide a nice contrast to the cultural rigours of the cities.

Much of **Warsaw**, the capital, conforms to stereotypes of Eastern European greyness, but it does boast an historic centre, beautiful parks and vibrant nightlife. **Kraków**, the ancient royal capital in the south, is the real crowd-puller, rivalling the elegance of Prague and Vienna, while **Gdańsk** on the Baltic Sea offers an insight into Poland's dynamic politics as well as the golden beaches at the nearby resort of **Sopot**. In the west, stately **Wrocław** charms visitors with its architecture and vibrant student life, while quintessentially Polish **Poznań** is still revered as the heart of the nation. Outdoorsy types can enjoy fantastic kayaking in the lake district of Mazury, while the **Tatra Mountains** on the Slovak border offer exhilarating hiking and affordable skiing.

CHRONOLOGY

966 AD Mieszko I creates the Polish state.
1025 Bolesław I, Mieszko's son, is crowned the first King of Poland.
1300s Gdańsk and several other northern cities join the Hanseatic League, and trade prospers.
1385 The Union of Krewo unites the countries of Poland and Lithuania through an arranged marriage.
1410 United Polish and Lithuanian forces defeat the occupying military-religious order, the Teutonic Knights, at the Battle of Grunwald.
1500s The Renaissance sweeps through Poland, giving it significant cultural importance in Europe.
1569 The Lublin Union establishes the Polish–Lithuanian Commonwealth.
1700s Russia, Prussia and Austria divide Polish–Lithuanian land between them in the three Partitions.
1863 The January Uprising against Russian authority is brutally repressed.
1918 An independent Polish state is created following the defeat of Germany, Russia and Austria-Hungary in World War I.
1939 Poland is invaded by Nazi Germany, beginning World War II.
1945 By the end of the war more than six million Poles are dead. Soviets drive out the Nazis and occupy large parts of Poland; the country's borders shift 200km west.
1947 Poland becomes a Communist state.
1978 Karol Wojtyła, Archbishop of Kraków, is elected Pope, taking the name John Paul II.
1980 A workers' uprising in Gdańsk, led by Lech Wałęsa, sweeps through Poland. He forms the Solidarity Party, an important anti-Communist movement.
1990 Wałęsa becomes the first popularly elected president of Poland.
2004 Poland accedes to the EU.
2007 Parliamentary elections overturn the conservative government led by the controversial Kaczyński twins. Moderate Donald Tusk becomes prime minister.
2010 A plane carrying conservative President Lech Kaczyński and a number of Poland's elite crashes near Smolensk, Russia, killing everyone on board. Later that year, moderate Bronislaw Komorowksi is elected president.

ARRIVAL

Several budget **airlines** fly into Warsaw and Kraków, Poland's two most popular cities, but there are also an increasing number of flights into Gdańsk, Wrocław and Poznań from major Western European destinations.

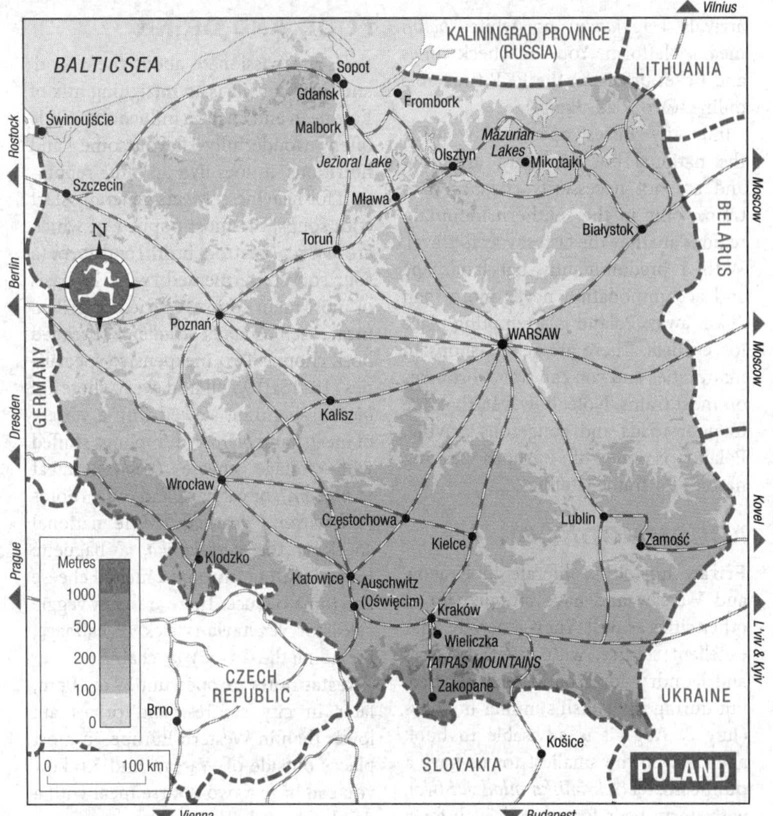

Poland has **rail** connections with all its neighbouring countries. Several direct trains arrive daily in both Kraków and Warsaw from Prague, Budapest and Vienna, while Poznań, Wrocław and Warsaw all have regular connections to Germany.

Several Polish **bus** companies, including Eurolines (Ⓣ22/621 3469, Ⓦwww.eurolines.pl), provide services from all major European capitals to Warsaw, Kraków, Gdańsk and other Polish cities. On the southern border, there are daily public buses to Zakopane from the Slovakian resort of Poprad.

GETTING AROUND

The primary means of transport for budget travellers in Poland is by train, and the PKP **railway** system runs three main types. Express services (*ekspresowy*), particularly IC (*intercity*) or EC (*eurocity*), stop at major cities only, and seat reservations (*miejscówka*; 10–12.50zł) are compulsory. "Fast" trains (*pospieszny*) are less costly, but not necessarily slower. The cheapest services (*osobowy*) are less predictable – some are quick, while others stop at every haystack. Seats come in two classes, with first-class simply meaning a six- rather than eight-seat compartment; it's rarely worth the extra cost. **InterRail passes** – including the "one-country" pass – are valid, though you'll still have to pay for seat reservations. The main city stations are generally termed *główny*; departures (*odjazdy*) are printed on yellow posters;

arrivals (*przyjazdy*) on white; *peron* means platform. You can check times and ticket prices on the PKP timetable online (Ⓦrozklad-pkp.pl).

Inter-city **buses** operated by PKS, the national bus company, are slow, and are not necessarily cheaper than trains; only in the southern mountain regions are they the fastest way to travel. With a predominantly flat landscape and accommodation never more than 50km away, Poland is a tempting place for **cyclists**. There are repair shops in many cities and you can transport bikes on most trains. Note, however, that due to poor roads and dangerous driving, Poland is one of Europe's leading nations for traffic fatalities.

ACCOMMODATION

Private hostels proliferate in Kraków and Warsaw and have cropped up in other cities as well. They generally offer excellent service, with internet access and laundry, for around 45zł per bed, but during the Polish summer holidays (July & Aug) it is advisable to book ahead. Even the smallest towns have a **public hostel** (*schroniska młodzieżowe*), with dorm beds for around 30zł; for a complete list check Ⓦwww.ptsm.org.pl. In large cities they're centrally located and open year-round, though often with lockouts and curfews. There is at least one **budget hotel** in every town, with 120zł normally enough to get you a Spartan but habitable room with communal toilet and shower. Many tourist offices can also find you cheap rooms in **private houses** (*kwatera prywatna*; 70–80zł).

Polish **campsites** are often a fair distance from town centres and are not always much cheaper than a hostel dorm bed (20–40zł). Though some of these sites have excellent facilities, in others you'll find a toilet and little else. For a list of campsites in Poland, check Ⓦwww.eurocampings.co.uk/en/europe/poland.

FOOD AND DRINK

Poles are passionate about their food, and their cuisine is an intriguing mix of European and Eastern influences. While often wonderfully flavoursome and nutritious, it does live up to its reputation for heaviness. **Meals** generally start with soups, the most popular of which are *barszcz* (beetroot broth) and *zurek* (a sour soup of fermented rye). The basis of most main courses is fried or grilled meat, such as *kotlet schabowy* (breaded pork chops). Two inexpensive specialities (10–15zł) you'll find everywhere are *bigos* (sauerkraut stewed with a variety of meats) and *pierogi*, dumplings stuffed with cottage cheese (*ruskie*), meat (*z mięsem*), or cabbage and mushrooms (*z kapustą i grzybami*). The national snack is the *zapiekanka*, a baguette topped with mushrooms, melted cheese and tomato sauce. There are a few veggie cafés for **vegetarians** sick of cabbage, including the *Green Way* chain.

Restaurants are open until 9 or 10pm, later in city centres, and prices are lower than in Western Europe: in most places outside of Warsaw and Kraków you can have a two-course meal with a drink for 40zł. The cheapest option is the local **milk bar** (*bar mleczny*; usually open from breakfast until 6/7pm), which provides fast and filling meals for workers, students and anyone else looking for affordable Polish food.

Drink

The Poles can't compete with their Czech neighbours when it comes to **beer** (*piwo*), but a range of microbreweries (*browars*) supplement the drinkable national brands. Even in Warsaw, you won't pay more than 12zł for a half-litre. Tea (*herbata*) and coffee (*kawa*) are both popular; the former comes with lemon rather than milk. But it's **vodka** (*wódka*), ideally served neat and cold, which is the national drink. As well as the clear variety, it's well worth trying the flavoured types – king among Polish vodkas is the legendary Żubrówka, infused with bison grass. But it's **vodka** (*wódka*), ideally served neat and cold, which is the national drink (see box on p.892 for more information).

CULTURE AND ETIQUETTE

As a nation in which around 75 percent of people are practising Roman Catholics, Poland maintains fairly conservative religious and social customs, especially in the countryside where men are often still seen as the breadwinners. Poland's young, urban population tend to be both more relaxed and wilder than their parents. Yet Poles of all ages are also warm, passionate people, fond of handshakes and of lively, informal conversation over a vodka. Table manners follow the Western norm and it is common to reward good service with a ten percent **tip**, though Poles will sometimes leave less.

SPORTS AND OUTDOOR ACTIVITIES

The most popular **sport** is soccer and the national and top league teams often attract sell-out crowds, but even local village matches invariably draw gangs of enthusiasts. Co-hosting the Euro 2012 with Ukraine has been enough to make a soccer fan out of nearly everybody, and has thrown the country into a frenzy of stadium construction. Despite lacking any international stars, the Poles also enjoy tennis and cycling while American sports – especially basketball – are starting to make an impact. For most **hikers**, the highlight of Poland is the Tatra Mountains in the south, though the country's 23 national parks offer plenty of opportunities for beautiful walks and horseriding. **Watersports** are concentrated around Sopot in the north and Mazury in the northeast, while the **skiing** season (Nov–Feb) brings tourists flocking to southern mountain resorts like Zakopane.

EMERGENCY NUMBERS

Police ⓣ997 (ⓣ112 from mobile phones); fire service ⓣ998; ambulance ⓣ999.

COMMUNICATIONS

Internet cafés charging 4–6zł per hour are present in all towns. Main **post offices** (*Poczta*) are usually open Monday to Saturday 8am to 8pm; branches close earlier. For **public phones** you'll need a card (*karta telefoniczna*), available at post offices and RUCH newsagent kiosks.

EMERGENCIES

Poland is a very safe country to travel in, though inevitably thefts from dorms and pickpocketing do occur. Safely store your valuables whenever possible and, on night trains, lock your compartment when you sleep. Polish **police** (*policja*) are courteous but unlikely to speak English. **Medical care** can be basic and most foreigners rely on the expensive private medical centres run by Medicover (ⓣ500 900 500, ⓦwww.medicover.pl). For non-prescription medication, local pharmacists are helpful and often speak English.

POLAND ONLINE

ⓦ**www.poland.travel/en** The official tourist website with general details on Poland's major sights and visa information.
ⓦ**www.thenews.pl** Polish radio's English-language service, focusing on national news and current events.
ⓦ**www.culture.pl** News and essays on Polish cultural events and history.

POLISH

	Polish	Pronunciation
Yes	*Tak*	Tahk
No	*Nie*	Nyeh
Please	*Proszę*	Prosh-eh
Thank you	*Dziękuję*	Djen-ku-yeh
Hello/Good day	*Dzień dobry*	Djen doh-brih
Goodbye	*Do widzenia*	Doh veed-zen-yah
Excuse me/Sorry	*Przepraszam*	Psheh-pra-shahm
Today	*Dzisiaj*	Djyish-eye
Yesterday	*Wczoraj*	Vchor-eye
Tomorrow	*Jutro*	Yoo-troh
What time is it?	*Która godzina?*	Ktoo-rah go-djee-nah?
I don't understand	*Nie rozumiem*	Nyeh roh-zoom-yem
How much is...?	*Ile kosztuje…?*	Ill-eh kosh-too-yeh…?
Do you speak English?	*Pan/i/mówi po angielsku?*	Pahn/ee/movee poh ahn-gyel-skoo?
Where is the...?	*Gdzie jest…?*	G-djeh yest…?
entrance	*wejście*	vey-shche
exit	*wyjście*	viy-shche
toilet	*toaleta*	to-a-le-ta
hotel	*hotel*	ho-tel
hostel	*schronisko/hostel*	sro-nees-ko
church	*kościoł*	kosh-choow
What time does the... leave/arrive?	*O ktorej odchodzi/ przychodzi…?*	O ktoo-rey ot-ho-djee/ pshih-ho-djee…?
boat	*łódź*	woodj
bus	*autobus*	aw-tow-boos
plane	*samolot*	sa-mo-lot
train	*pociąg*	po-chonk
I would like a...	*Proprozę…*	Po-pro-she…
Bed	*Łóżko*	woosh-ko
Single room	*Pokoj jednoosobowy*	Po-koi yed-no-o-so-bo-vi
Double room	*Pokoj lózkiem*	Po-koi woosh-kyem
Cheap	*Tani*	Tah-nee
Expensive	*Drogi*	Droh-gee
Open	*Otwarty*	Ot-var-tih
Closed	*Zamknięty*	Zahmk-nee-yen-tih
One	*Jeden*	Yed-en
Two	*Dwa*	Dvah
Three	*Trzy*	Trshih
Four	*Cztery*	Chter-ih
Five	*Pięć*	Pyench
Six	*Sześć*	Sheshch
Seven	*Siedem*	Shedem
Eight	*Osiem*	Oshem
Nine	*Dziewięć*	Djyev-yench
Ten	*Dziesięć*	Djyesh-ench

STUDENT AND YOUTH DISCOUNTS

The major cities offer **tourist cards** (available for one day or longer) that give discounts on transport and at the main sights. Your ISIC card can halve entry prices for museums and city transport, especially in Warsaw, and cut inter-city train fares by a third. A Hostelling International card can earn you up to 25 percent off at public hostels.

INFORMATION

Most cities have a **tourist office** (*informacja turystyczna*, or IT), usually run by the local municipality, though some are merely private agencies selling tours.

MONEY AND BANKS

Currency is the **złoty** (zł/PLN), divided into 100 groszy. Coins come in 1, 2, 5, 10, 20 and 50 groszy, and 1, 2 and 5 złoty denominations; notes as 10, 20, 50, 100 and 200 złoty. At the time of writing, €1=4zł, US$1 = 2.8zł and £1= 4.4zł. **Banks** (usually open Mon–Fri 7.30am–5pm, Sat 7.30am–2pm) and exchange offices (*kantors*) offer similar exchange rates. Major credit cards are widely accepted, and **ATMs** are common in cities. Euros are not widely accepted, even in Warsaw.

OPENING HOURS AND HOLIDAYS

Most shops open on weekdays from 10am to 6pm, and all but the largest close on Saturday at 2 or 3pm and all day Sunday. RUCH kiosks, selling public transport tickets (*bilety*), open at 6 or 7am. Most museums and historic monuments are closed once a week. Entrance tends to be inexpensive, and is often free one day of the week. **Public holidays** are: January 1, Easter Monday, May 1, May 3, Corpus Christi (May/June), August 15, November 1, November 11, December 25 and 26.

Warsaw

Packed with a bizarre mix of gleaming office buildings and grey, Communist-era apartment blocks, **WARSAW** (Warszawa) often bewilders backpackers. Yet if any city rewards exploration, it is the Polish capital. North of the lively centre are stunning Baroque palaces and the meticulously reconstructed Old Town; to the south are two of Central Europe's finest urban parks; and in the east lie reminders of the rich Jewish heritage extinguished by the Nazis.

Warsaw became the capital in 1596 and initially flourished as one of Europe's most prosperous cities. In 1815, however, the Russians conquered the city and, despite a series of rebellions, it was not until the outbreak of World War I that this control collapsed. Warsaw again became the capital of an independent Poland in 1918, but the German invasion of 1939 meant this was to be short-lived. Infuriated by the 1944 Warsaw Uprising, Hitler ordered the total destruction of the city, leaving 850,000 Varsovians dead and 85 percent of Warsaw in ruins. Rebuilding is an ongoing process.

What to see and do

The main sights are on the western bank of the Wisła (Vistula) River where you'll find the central business and shopping district, **Śródmieście**, grouped around Centralna station and the nearby Palace of Culture. The more picturesque **Old Town** (Stare Miasto) is just to the north.

The Old Town

The title **Old Town** (Stare Miasto) is, in some respects, a misnomer for the historic nucleus of Warsaw. After World War II the beautifully arranged Baroque streets were destroyed, only to be painstakingly reconstructed so accurately that the area has been named a UNESCO World Heritage Site. The Old Town comes alive in the summer, as tourists, street performers and festivals take over the cobblestone streets. Plac Zamkowy (Castle Square), on the south side of the Old Town, is the obvious place to start a tour.

Royal Castle

On the east side of Castle Square is the thirteenth-century **Royal Castle**, now home to the Castle Museum (May–Sept daily 10am–6pm; Oct–April Tues–Sat 10am–4pm, Sun 11am–4pm; 22zł, Sun free; Ⓦwww.zamek-krolewski.pl). Though the structure is a replica, many of its furnishings are originals. After passing the lavish Royal Apartments of King Stanisław August, you visit the Lanckoranski Gallery, which contains a fascinating range of aristocratic portraits including two paintings – *Girl in a Picture Frame* and *Scholar at His Desk* – by Rembrandt.

Old and New Town squares

On ul. Świętojańska, north of the castle, stands St John's Cathedral, the oldest church in Warsaw. A few yards away, the **Old Town Square** (Rynek Starego Miasta) is one of the most remarkable bits of postwar reconstruction anywhere in Europe. Flattened during the Uprising, its three-storey merchants' houses have been rebuilt in near-flawless imitation of the Baroque originals. It's also home to the **Warsaw Historical Museum** (closed at the time of writing, due to reopen by early 2012; Ⓦwww.mhw.pl), where an English-language film shows poignant footage of the vibrant, multicultural 1930s city and the ruins left in 1945. Crossing the ramparts heading north brings you to the **New Town Square** (Rynek Nowego Miasta) at the heart of the so-called New Town (Nowe Miasto), the town's commercial hub in the fifteenth century but now a quiet spot to escape the bustling Old Town.

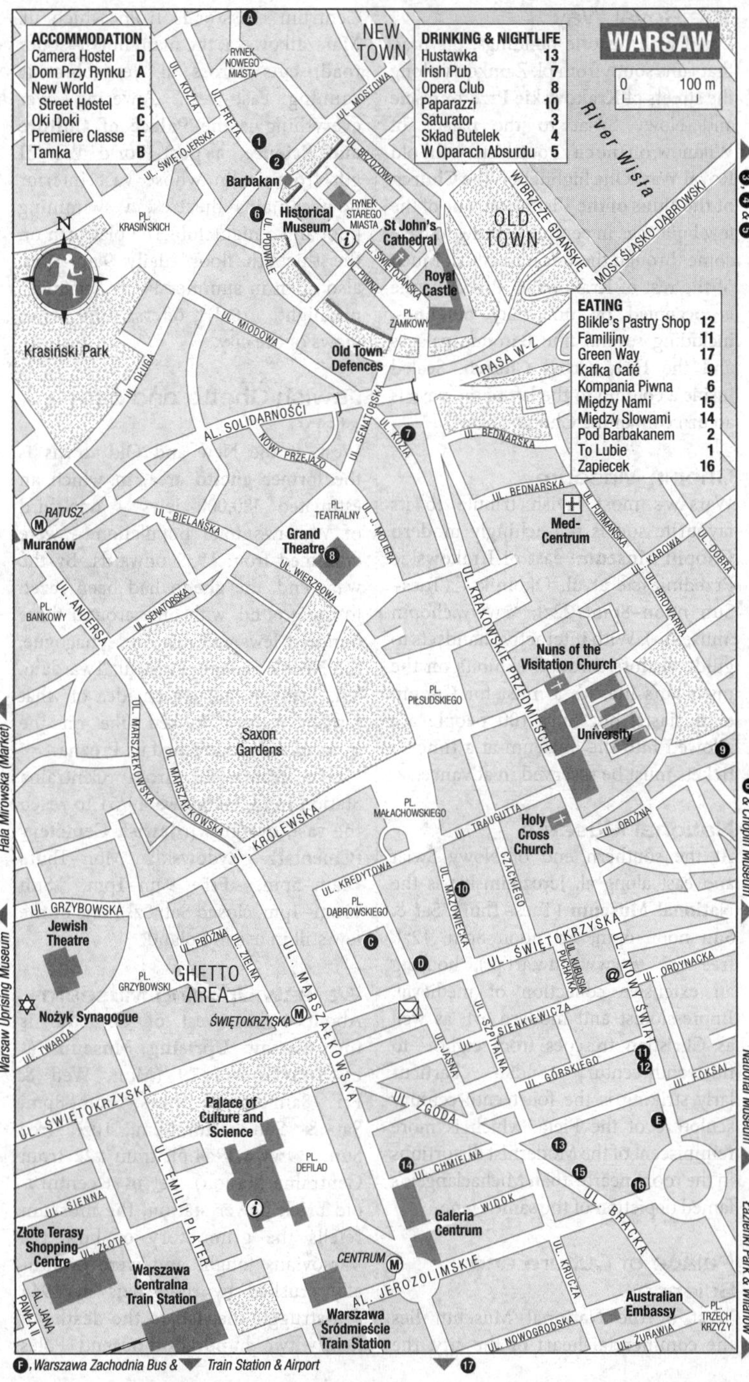
WARSAW
0 100 m
ACCOMMODATION
Camera Hostel D
Dom Przy Rynku A
New World Street Hostel E
Oki Doki C
Premiere Classe F
Tamka B
DRINKING & NIGHTLIFE
Hustawka 13
Irish Pub 7
Opera Club 8
Paparazzi 10
Saturator 3
Skład Butelek 4
W Oparach Absurdu 5
EATING
Blikle's Pastry Shop 12
Familijny 11
Green Way 17
Kafka Café 9
Kompania Piwna 6
Między Nami 15
Między Slowami 14
Pod Barbakanem 2
To Lubie 1
Zapiecek 16
NEW TOWN
OLD TOWN
River Wisła
Barbakan
Historical Museum
St John's Cathedral
Royal Castle
Old Town Defences
Krasiński Park
Grand Theatre
Med-Centrum
Nuns of the Visitation Church
University
Saxon Gardens
Holy Cross Church
Jewish Theatre
GHETTO AREA
Nożyk Synagogue
Palace of Culture and Science
Galeria Centrum
Złote Terasy Shopping Centre
Warszawa Centralna Train Station
Warszawa Śródmieście Train Station
Australian Embassy
Muranów
RATUSZ
ŚWIĘTOKRZYSKA
CENTRUM
3, 4 & 5
B & Chopin Museum
National Museum
Łazienki Park & Wilanów
Hala Mirowska (Market)
Warsaw Uprising Museum
F, Warszawa Zachodnia Bus & Train Station & Airport
17

The Royal Way

Lined with historic buildings, the road that runs south from pl. Zamkowy along the streets of **Krakowskie Przedmieście** and Nowy Świat to the palace of Wilanów, on the city's outskirts, is the old **Royal Way**. One highlight is the **Church of the Nuns of the Visitation**, one of the few buildings in central Warsaw to have come through the war unscathed. Much of the rest of Krakowskie Przedmieście is occupied by university buildings, including several fine Baroque palaces and the **Holy Cross Church**. Sealed inside a column to the left of the nave is an urn containing Chopin's heart.

Chopin Museum

Warsaw's most lavish tribute to its favourite son is the achingly modern **Chopin Museum**, east of Krakowskie Przedmieście at ul. Okolnik 1 (Tues–Sun noon–8pm; 22zł; Ⓦwww.chopin.museum). With interactive handsets to guide visitors through exhibits on the musician's life, it's a must for Chopin enthusiasts, but only 100 people are allowed into the museum at a time so tickets must be reserved in advance.

National Museum

At the southern end of Nowy Świat and east along al. Jerozolimskie is the **National Museum** (Tues–Thurs, Sat & Sun noon–6pm, Fri noon–8pm; 12zł, free Fri; Ⓦwww.mnw.art.pl), housing an extensive collection of medieval, Impressionist and modern art, as well as Christian frescoes from eighth- to thirteenth-century Sudan. Particularly striking is the fourteenth-century sculpture of the Pietà, which is more reminiscent of the Modernist distortions in the room nearby than Michaelangelo's famed depiction of the same scene.

Palace of Culture and Science

West of the National Museum lies the commercial heart of the city, the Centrum crossroads from which ul. Marszałkowska, the main north–south road, cuts across al. Jerozolimskie running east–west. Towering over everything is the **Palace of Culture and Science**, a post-World War II gift from Stalin whose vast interior now contains theatres, a swimming pool and a nightclub. The platform on the thirtieth floor (daily 9am–6pm; also open in summer Fri & Sat 8pm–midnight; 20zł) offers impressive views of the city.

Jewish Ghetto and cemetery

West of the New and Old towns is the former **ghetto** area, in which an estimated 380,000 Jews – one-third of Warsaw's total population – were crammed from 1939 onwards. By the war's end, the ghetto had been razed to the ground, with only around three hundred Jews and just one synagogue, the **Nożyk Synagogue** at ul. Twarda 6, left. You can still get an idea of what Jewish Warsaw looked like on the miraculously untouched ul. Próźna.

Take tram #22 from Centralna Station to ul. Okopowa 49/51 to reach the vast, overgrown **Jewish Cemetery** (Cmentarz Zydowski; Mon–Thurs 10am–5pm, Fri 9am–1pm, Sun 11am–4pm, closed Sat; 8zł), one of the few still in use in Poland.

Warsaw Uprising Museum

About 1.5km west of Centrum is the **Warsaw Uprising Museum** at ul. Grzybowska 79 (Mon, Wed & Fri 8am–6pm, Thurs 8am–8pm, Sat & Sun 10am–6pm; 10zł, free Sun; Ⓦwww.1944.pl; tram #22 from Centralna Station). Set in a century-old brick power station, the museum retells the grim story of how the Varsovians fought and were eventually crushed by the Nazis in 1944 – a struggle that led to the deaths of nearly two hundred thousand Poles and the destruction of most of the city. Special attention is given to the equivocal role played by Soviet troops, who watched passively from the other side of the Wisła as the Nazis defeated the Polish insurgents. Only after the city was a charred ruin did they move across to "liberate" its few remaining inhabitants.

Łazienki Park

About 2km south of the commercial district, on the eastern side of al. Ujazdowskie, is the much-loved **Łazienki Park** (bus #116, # 180 or #195 from Nowy Świat). Once a hunting ground, the area was bought in the 1760s by King Stanisław August, who turned it into a park and built the Neoclassical **Łazienki Palace** (Tues–Sun 9am–4pm; 12zł) across the lake. But the park itself is the real attraction, with its oak-lined paths alive with peacocks and red squirrels.

Wilanów Palace

The grandest of Warsaw's palaces, **Wilanów** (May–Sept Mon, Wed & Sat 9.30am–6pm, Tues, Thurs & Fri 9.30am–4pm, Sun 10.30am–6pm; Oct–April Mon & Wed–Sat 9.30am–4pm, Sun 10.30am–4pm; 20zł, free Sun Oct–April; ⓦwww.wilanow-palac.pl), makes an easy excursion from the centre: take bus #180 south from Krakowskie Przedmieście or Nowy Świat to its terminus. Converted in the seventeenth century from a small manor house into the "Polish Versailles", the palace displays a vast range of decorative styles, a mixture mirrored in the delightful palace **gardens** (daily 9am–sunset; 5zł, free Thurs).

Arrival and information

Air Okęcie airport is 8km southwest of the Old Town: avoid the rip-off taxi drivers and take bus #175 (#N32 at night) into town.

Train The main train station, Warszawa Centralna, is in the modern centre just west of the Centrum crossroads.

Bus The main bus station, Międzynarodowa Dworzec PKS, is located right next to the Warszawa Zachodnia train station, 3km west of Centralna Station. Catch eastbound buses #127, #130, #158 or #517 into town.

Tourist office In the Old Town Square at 19/21 (daily: May–Aug 9am–9pm; March & April, Sept & Oct 8am–7pm; Nov–Feb 8am–6pm; ⓣ22/19431, ⓦwww.warsawtour.pl). There are also IT offices at the Palace of Culture and the airport.

Travel agents STA Travel, ul. Krucza 41/43 (ⓣ22/201 1167) can reserve international or domestic flights and train tickets, and sells ISIC Cards.

City transport

Tickets for trams, buses and the metro (single trip 2.80zł; 1hr 4zł) are available at green RUCH kiosks or automatic ticket machines. Always punch your tickets in the machines on board, as Warsaw's inspectors are extremely thorough. There are also good-value 1-day/3-day/week passes available (9zł/16zł/32zł), which should be punched the first time you use them. Tickets for students (*ulgowy*) are half-price, but you need to show ID.

Bus Well-developed if busy system that runs until around 11pm; after that, night buses leave every 30min from behind the main train station.

Trams A crowded but efficient means of transport, running till 11pm.

Metro A small subway system running north–south through the centre of town is the fastest way to get around; at the moment its route is very limited, but a new east–west line should be operational by 2013.

Taxis Generally cost 1.50–2.60zł/km, with a minimum fare of 6zł, but only take taxis that have the company name and price/kilometre clearly marked. English is spoken at Ele (ⓣ22/811 1111) and Glob (ⓣ19668).

Accommodation

Warsaw has many good private hostels, mainly in Śródmieście; all the hostels listed below offer free internet, breakfast and free/cheap laundry services unless otherwise stated. Hotels tend to be pricier than elsewhere in Poland.

Hostels

Camera Hostel ul. Jasna 22 ⓣ22/828 8600, ⓦwww.camerahostel.com. Slightly dingy, but the film-themed decor is original and the central location is hard to beat. Dorms 39zł, singles 100zł, doubles 145zł.

Dom Przy Rynku Rynek Nowego Miasta 4 ⓣ609 260 625, ⓦwww.cityhostel.net. Small and friendly place with the most affordable rooms in the Nowe Miasto. Open daily July–Aug, only on weekends the rest of the year. Dorms 60zł, doubles 120zł.

New World Street Hostel ul. Nowy Świat 27 ⓣ22/828 1282, ⓦwww.nws-hostel.pl. Friendly staff and a cosy common room (complete with board games and books) make this the pick of Warsaw's hostels, though it might be too quiet for hard-core partiers. Dorms 49zł, doubles 168zł.

Oki Doki pl. Dąbrowskiego ⓣ22/826 5112, ⓦwww.okidoki.pl. With its eccentric Communist-era interior and bar (0.5lt beer 7zł), this hostel has the liveliest feel of any in town. Dorms 46zł, singles 153zł, doubles170zł.

Tamka ul. Tamka 30 ⓣ22/826 3095, ⓦwww .tamkahostel.pl. Colourful (if basic) dorms and a garden that's handy for a summer barbecue. Dorms 30zł, singles 130zł, doubles 150zł.

Hotel

Premiere Classe ul. Towarowa 2 ⓣ22/624 0800, ⓦwww.premiereclasse.com.pl. The city's best budget hotel provides spacious rooms with satellite TV. Breakfast not included (20zł). Rooms (for up to three people) 169zł.

Eating

Milk bars

Familijny ul. Nowy Świat 29. Conveniently located milk bar serving good soups for just a couple of złoty. Mains 4–8zł.

Pod Barbakanem ul. Mostawa 27–9. Popular milk bar just outside the Old Town with wholesome, home-cooked grub. Mains 4–8zł.

Cafés

Blikle's Pastry Shop ul. Nowy Świat 35. Mouth-watering array of pastries, cakes and chocolates. Cake slices 3.50zł.

Kafka Café ul. Obozna 3. Tasty sandwiches and strong coffee make this stylish café popular with a student crowd, who spill out onto the lawn chairs outside in the summer. Sandwiches 10zł.

Między Slowami ul. Chimielna 30. Set back from the street in a small courtyard, this is a great chilling spot after a hard day's shopping. Sandwiches 15zł.

To Lubie ul. Freta 4/6. Invitingly warm interiors and delicious cakes – try the apple pie with ice cream – make this place a good choice for an afternoon break. Cakes 10zł.

Restaurants

Green Way ul. Marszalkowska 28. Locals pack out this fun, inexpensive veggie canteen, which serves inventive mains for around 10zł. Portions are generous, and dishes could feature vegetable dumplings and koftas.

Kompania Piwna ul. Podwale 25. Good-value Bavarian-style restaurant near the Old Town Square, with large beers, huge steaks and cheap, tasty fish dishes. Mains 22–40zł.

Między Nami ul. Bracka 20. Cultured, gay-friendly bar-restaurant that's excellent for a light meal, with some innovative vegetarian choices and a pleasant summer patio. Mains 18–35zł.

Zapiecek ul. Jerozolimskie 28. A wide variety of *pierogis*, *golabki*, *nalesniki* and other traditional Polish specialities, served by waitresses decked out in folk costumes. *Pierogis* 20zł.

Drinking and nightlife

The bar scene in Warsaw has really taken off over the last decade, and the city now genuinely provides a great night out that rivals Prague and needn't blow your budget. Praga, across the river, is a formerly dangerous neighbourhood that now boasts a lively, bohemian bar scene – an interesting alternative to the more glitzy hangouts you'll find downtown. Check out the English-language *Warsaw Insider* (available in most

> The tipple most associated with Poland, **vodka** is actually in danger of being eclipsed in popularity by beer among young Poles, so it's well worth seeking out the varieties you can't find abroad before they disappear from Polish shops and bars completely. Traditionally served chilled and neat – although increasingly mixed with fruit juice –vodka can be **clear** or **flavoured** with anything from bison grass to mountain herbs to juniper berries or honey. There's even been a revival of kosher vodkas, although whether their rabbinic stamps of approval are kosher themselves or just a marketing gimmick isn't always obvious.

hotels; ⓦ www.warsawinsider.pl) for more information on nightlife and a monthly list of events.

Bars

Irish Pub ul. Miodowa 3. For those seeking a pint of the black stuff and live Irish folk and rock music (8–11pm on most nights). 1lt Guinness 38zł. Daily 11am–late.

Paparazzi ul. Mazowiecka 12. One of the flashiest bars in town, featuring an after-work crowd and an impressive list of creative cocktails (22zł). Mon–Fri noon–late, Sat & Sun from 6pm.

Skład Butelek ul. 11 Listopada 22. Wonderfully quirky gathering place for Warsaw's creative types, serving obscure Ukrainian beers in an old factory. 0.5lt beer 9zł. Wed–Sat 7pm–3am.

W Oparach Absurdu ul. Zabkowska 6. Chaotic, lively and decorated with all the haphazard charm of a flea market. 0.5lt beer 8zł. Daily till 3am.

Clubs

Hustawka ul. Bracka 20a. Artistically renovated old palace transformed into a nightclub, drawing in both hipsters and young professionals. Cocktails from 15zł. Mon–Fri noon–late, Sat & Sun from 4pm.

Opera Club pl. Teatralny 1. Dancefloors and semi-private rooms scattered through the cavernous chambers beneath the Grand Theatre, making for a novel night out. Cocktails 19–25zł. Fri & Sat from 10pm.

Saturator ul. 11 Listopada 22. Pulling in adventurous souls from all over town with its anything-goes attitude, this place grooves well into the wee hours. Cocktails 12zł. Daily from 7pm.

Entertainment

The city's festivals enhance the celebratory vibe, especially the Warsaw "Summer Jazz Days" Festival, a series of outdoor concerts held throughout July and August.

Cinema

Films are usually shown in their original language with Polish subtitles. Tickets 17–30zł.

Kinoteka pl. Defilad 1 ⓦ www.kinoteka.pl. Multiplex in the Palace of Culture and Science showing the latest blockbusters.

Muranow ul. Gen. Andersa 1 ⓦ www.muranow.gutekfilm.pl. Art-house cinema that screens a range of films from around the world.

Music

Live bands are apt to appear in bars without any warning; *W Oparach Absurdu* and the *Irish Pub* are your best bets.

Grand Theatre (Teatr Wielki) pl. Teatralny 1 ⓣ 22/692 0200, ⓦ www.teatrwielki.pl. Worth visiting just for its Neoclassical facade, but it also hosts the best of Poland's National Opera. 20–130zł depending on seats.

Theatre

Jewish Theatre (Teatr Żydowski) pl. Grzybowski ⓣ 22/620 6281, ⓦ www.teatr-zydowski.art.pl. The most striking of Warsaw's several small theatres, specializing in productions (often given in Yiddish) that depict Jewish life in Warsaw before the Holocaust. English translations via headphones are available.

Shopping

Malls For flashy boutiques and department stores, first explore the gleaming Złote Terasy shopping centre (replete with such Western titles as H&M and Zara), opposite the Palace of Culture and Science on ul. Emilii Plater, before passing through to the mainly pedestrianized streets of ul. Chimielna and ul. Nowy Świat.

Markets The Hala Mirowska market on al. Jana Pawła II is the place to go for fresh fruits and vegetables (daily); antique hunters should head for the Kolo Antique Market on ul. Obozowa (trams #13 & #23 from the Old Town; Sun 7am–2pm), where you'll find everything from war medals to old Christian icons.

Directory

Embassies and consulates Australia, ul. Nowogrodzka 11 ⓣ 22/521 3444; Canada, ul. Matejki 1/5 ⓣ 22/584 3100; Ireland, ul. Mysia 5 ⓣ 22/849 6633; New Zealand, al. Ujazdowskie 51 ⓣ 22/521 0500; South Africa, ul. Koszykowa 54 ⓣ 22/625 6228; UK, ul. Kawalerii 12 1 ⓣ 22/311 0000; USA, ul. Ujazdowskie 29/31 ⓣ 22/504 2000.

Exchange The Old Town has a host of *kantor* stores that exchange foreign cash, though you will have to shop around for the best rates. Interchange Poland at ul. Chmielna 30 (ⓣ 22/826 3169; Mon–Fri 8am–10pm, Sat & Sun 9am–10pm) is also a reliable option.

Hospitals The nearest public hospital to the centre is the Praski, al. Solidarności 67 (ⓣ 22/818 5061). In emergencies, many backpackers use the private Med-Centrum, ul. Bednarska 13 (ⓣ 22/826 3886; Mon–Fri 8am–6pm).

Internet There is a 24hr internet café below the Centralna station near the exit onto al. Jana Pawla II (4.50zł/hr), or try Eccoms Internet, Nowy Świat 53 (9am–11pm daily; 5zł/hr).

Left luggage Centralna Station has a 24hr left-luggage room and lockers with storage for up to ten days.
Pharmacies There is a pharmacy at Franciszanska 14 near the New Town Square (24hr), and another at ul. Nowy Świat 18/20 (Mon–Fri 8am–9pm, Sat 9am–5pm).
Post office ul. Świętokryszka 31/33 (24hr).

Moving on

Train Berlin (10 daily; 6hr); Budapest (2 daily; 11hr); Gdańsk (14 daily; 5hr); Kraków (hourly; 2hr 30min); Poznań (hourly; 3hr); Prague (3 daily; 11hr); Sopot (14 daily; 5hr 20min); Toruń (11 daily; 3hr); Vienna (2 daily; 8hr); Wrocław (hourly; 6hr); Zakopane (3 daily; 6–10hr).
Bus PKS (ⓦwww.pks.warszawa.pl) runs regular long-distance services to major Polish cities from the main terminal.

Northern Poland

Even in a country accustomed to shifting borders, **northern Poland** presents an unusually tortuous historical puzzle. Successively the domain of the Teutonic Order, Hansa merchants and the Prussians, it's only in the last seventy years that the region has become definitively Polish. The conurbation of **Gdańsk**, **Sopot** and **Gdynia** known as the Tri-City, lines the Baltic coast with its dramatic shipyards and sandy beaches, while highlights inland include the medieval centres of **Malbork** and **Toruń**. Meanwhile the northeastern region of **Mazury**, with its seemingly endless networks of lakes and rivers, is a natural wonderland for kayakers and outdoor enthusiasts. Many of the area's bucolic villages, with their wooden churches and folk traditions, appear to have barely changed since the nineteenth century.

GDAŃSK

Both the starting point of World War II and the setting of the famous strikes against Communist control, **GDAŃSK** has played more than a fleeting role on the world stage. Traces of its past are visible in the steel skeletons of shipyard cranes and the Hanseatic architecture of the old town. After all the social and political upheavals of the last century, the city is now busy reinventing itself as a tourist hub.

What to see and do

With its medieval brick churches and narrow eighteenth-century merchants' houses, Gdańsk certainly looks ancient. But its appearance is deceptive: by 1945, the core of the city lay in ruins, and the present buildings are almost complete reconstructions.

The Main Town (Główne Miasto)

Huge stone gateways guard both entrances to ul. Długa, the main thoroughfare. Start from the sixteenth-century gate at the top, **Brama Wyżynna**, and carry on east through the nearby Brama Zlota. You'll soon come across the imposing Town Hall, which houses a **Historical Museum** (June–Sept Mon 10am–3pm, Tues–Sat 10am–6pm, Sun 11am–6pm; Oct–May Tues 10am–3pm, Wed–Sat 10am–4pm, Sun 11am–4pm; 10zł, free Mon June–Sept & Tues Oct–May) with shocking photos of the city's wartime destruction. Further down, the street opens onto the wide expanse of ul. Długi Targ, where the ornate facade of **Arthur's Court** (same hours as Historical Museum; 10zł) stands out among the fine mansions. The surrounding streets are also worth exploring, especially ul. Mariacka, brimming with amber traders, at the end of which stands **St Mary's Basilica** (Mon–Sat

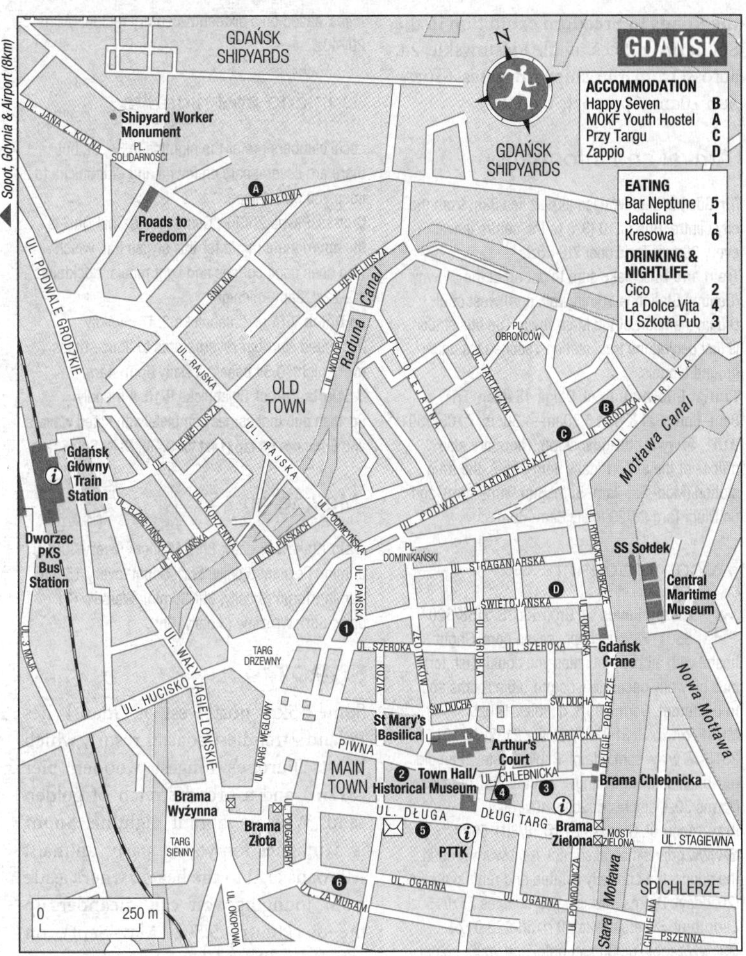

7.30am–6pm, Sun noon–6pm), the largest church in Poland.

The waterfront and shipyards

At the end of ul. Długi Targ the archways of **Brama Zielona** open directly onto the waterfront. Halfway down is the fifteenth-century **Gdańsk Crane**, the biggest in medieval Europe, part of the **Central Maritime Museum** (July & Aug daily 10am–6pm; Jan–June & Sept–Nov Tues–Sun 10am–4pm; Dec Tues–Sun 10am–3pm; 8zł; ⓦ www.cmm.pl) spread over both banks of the river. Highlights include an exhibition of primitive boats; for an extra 8zł you can also tour the cargo ship SS *Sołdek* docked outside. Further north loom the cranes of the famous Gdańsk **shipyards**, crucible of the political strife of the 1980s. Poignantly set outside the shipyard gates is the monument to the workers who formed the anti-Communist Solidarity movement, many of whom were killed during riots in the 1970s. It was here that Poland's struggle to topple Communism began, a story detailed in the **Roads to Freedom** exhibition in the Solidarity offices at ul. Piastowskie 24, across from the shipyard gates (Tues–Sun 10am–5pm; 6zł; Wed 2zł).

Arrival and information

Air Gdańsk Lech Wałęsa airport lies 8km from the city centre. Bus #210 (3zł) to the centre leaves every 20min. Taxis cost 70–80zł.
Train and bus Make sure to get off at the Główny (Central) Station, a 10min walk northwest of ul. Długa, the heart of the Main Town. The bus station is just behind the train station, reached via underground tunnels.
Tourist information ul. Długa 45 (Mon–Fri 8am–6pm, Sat & Sun 8.30am–4.30pm; ⓣ058/301 9151, ⓦwww.pttk-gdansk.pl). There are also offices at the airport (daily 9am–5pm), the train station (Mon–Sat 9am–5pm, Sun 9am–4pm), and on Dlugi Targ 28/29 (daily 8am–6pm).

Accommodation

Happy Seven ul. Grodzka 16 ⓣ58/320 8601, ⓦwww.happyseven.com. Bright hostel with all the amenities you could wish for, plus playfully decorated, comfortable rooms and free internet. Dorms 45zł, doubles 140zł.
MOKF Youth Hostel ul. Walowa 21 ⓣ58/301 2313, ⓦwww.ssm.gda.pl. Public hostel in an old red-brick school building – institutional, but clean. Dorms 30zł, singles/doubles 40zł/80zł.
Przy Targu ul. Grodzka 21 ⓣ58/301 5627, ⓦwww.gdanskhostel.com.pl. A bit worn around the edges, but centrally located and rents out bikes (20zł/day). Dorms 55zł, singles/doubles 75zł/150zł.
Zappio ul. Swietojanska 49 ⓣ58/322 0174, ⓦwww.zappio.pl. Budget hotel and youth hostel in a beautiful prewar building, with big windows and period woodwork. Dorms 45zł, singles 95zł, doubles 158zł.

Eating

Bar Neptune ul. Długa 33/34. Spruced-up milk bar with the usual Polish fare, along with some pre-assembled meals. Mains 5zł.
Jadalina ul. Panska 69. This popular cellar comes with cheap beer and hearty Polish meals. 0.5lt beer 5zł; mains 12–22zł.
Kresowa ul. Ogarna 12. Cuisine from the so-called Lost Territories (*kresy*) to the east of Poland, served in a refined atmosphere for a reasonable price. Don't miss out on the *bigos*, based on a sixteenth-century recipe. Mains 20–40zł.

Drinking and nightlife

Local clubbers prefer the nightlife in Sopot, but there are several bars on Piwna and Chlebnicka to keep you entertained.
Cico ul. Piwna 28/30. "Come in and Chill Out" is the appropriate motto for this stylish bar, which also does good coffees and light meals. Cocktails 15–22zł. 8am–midnight.
La Dolce Vita ul. Chlebnicka 2. This wildly decorated club-bar reverberates to house tunes every night. 0.5lt beer 7zł. Daily 6pm–4am.
U Szkota Pub ul. Chlebnicka 9/10. A friendly Scottish pub that comes complete with kilted waiters and Guinness on tap (14zł for 0.4lt). Daily 3pm–1am.

Moving on

Train Kraków (5 daily; 8hr); Malbork (every 30min; 50min); Poznań (5 daily; 5hr); Sopot (every 15min; 20min); Toruń (9 daily; 3hr 30min); Warsaw (11 daily; 5hr); Wrocław (3 daily; 8hr).

SOPOT

Some 15km northwest of Gdańsk lies Poland's trendiest coastal resort, which boasts Europe's longest wooden pier (512m) and a broad stretch of golden sand. With its vibrant nightlife, **Sopot** is a magnet for young party animals. All roads lead to the beach, where aside from lounging you can meander up the pier (entry 5.50zł May–Sept), on which you'll find boat tours operating in summer.

Arrival and information

Train The train station lies 400m west of the beach and a 5min walk from the main street, ul. Monte Cassino.
Tourist office Opposite the train station at ul. Dworcowa 4 (daily: June to mid-Sept 9am–8pm; mid-Sept to May 10am–6pm; ⓣ58/550 3783, ⓦwww.sopot.pl), with another branch by the pier at pl. Zdrojowy 2 (same hours). Helps with accommodation, which books up quickly in summer.
Internet Net Cave, ul. Pułaskiego 7a (noon–8pm, closed Sun).

Accommodation

Cheap accommodation can be hard to find in Sopot. Your best bet is to look for "Wolny Pokoj" (free room) signs in private houses, where you can rent rooms for around 50zł/person.

Central Hostel ul. Monte Casino 15 ⓣ530 858 717, ⓦwww.hostelcentral.pl. Bang in the centre of town, this hostel is sparsely furnished but has a lively party atmosphere and sunny rooms. Dorms 55zł, doubles 230zł.

Siesta Hostel ul. Krasickiego 11 ⓣ790 639 011, ⓦwww.siestahostel.pl. A homey hostel five minutes from the train station, with a big garden strung with hammocks, and bicycles for rent (20zl/day). Dorms 60zł, doubles 160zł.

U Rybaka pl. Rybakow 16 ⓣ058/551 2302, ⓦwww.urybaka.republika.pl. Several well-furnished rooms with TVs, each sleeping three to four, set in a quiet courtyard 5min from the beach. Triples 255zł.

Eating

For best value, avoid ul. Monte Cassino and head for the restaurants around 1km south along the beach.

Bar Przystan al. Wojska Polskiego 11. A touristy but great-value fish restaurant right on the beach. Fish 5–9zł/100g.

Dobra Kuchnia ul. Jagiełły 6/1. The best place for reasonably priced Polish classics in the centre. Mains 10–20zł.

Drinking and nightlife

Czekolada ul. Bohaterow Monte Cassino 63 ⓦwww.klubczekolada.pl. The most trendy club in town for the well-dressed student crowd. Wed–Sun 9pm–late.

Soho ul. Monte Cassino 61. Along the main drag not far from the pier, with colourful interiors that draw in the punters all night long. Fri & Sat from 10pm.

MALBORK

The spectacular fortress of **MALBORK** (Tues–Sun: mid-April to mid-Sept 9am–7pm, rest of year 10am–3pm; high season 47zł, low season 37zł; ⓦwww.zamek.malbork.pl) was built as the headquarters of the Teutonic Order in the fourteenth century and still casts a threatening shadow over an otherwise sleepy town. As the Teutonic Knights sank into deep financial crises, they were eventually forced to sell the castle in the mid-fifteenth century. The castle was then employed as a royal residence and a stopover for Polish monarchs en route between Warsaw and Gdańsk.

You enter over a moat and through the daunting main gate, before reaching an open courtyard. Brooding above is the **High Castle**, which harbours the centrepiece of the Knights' austere monasticism – the vast **Castle Church** with its faded chivalric paintings. You'll be given an English audioguide for the 3-hour self-guided tour, or, in July and August, you can opt for a live tour instead (both are included in the ticket price). Also during the summer months (June or July), the so-called Siege Days (ⓦwww.oblezenie.malbork.pl) take place, involving locals dressing up in period costume to re-enact the siege of the fortress; there are jousting tournaments, craft fairs and music concerts.

The **train station** is about ten minutes' walk south of the castle; there are trains every thirty minutes from Gdańsk (50min).

KAYAKING IN MAZURY

Known as the "land of a thousand lakes", Mazury is one of the best **kayaking** spots in Europe. The hundreds of kilometres of signposted trails can keep you paddling for days, through sun-dappled forests and lakes filled with swans. The best known is the **Krutynia Trail**, which begins near the village of Sorkwity and ends 115km later in the town of Ruciana-Nida. A number of companies rent kayaks and canoes; the English-speaking AS Tour (ⓣ89/742 1430, ⓦwww.masuria-canoeing.com) rents boats from 20zł per day, and offers a pick-up and drop-off service. Stay at campsites scattered along the kayak trails, or in village guesthouses en route – the tourist office (see opposite) can help with this.

OLSZTYN

The main town in the **Mazury** region, **OLSZTYN** is first and foremost a transport hub and a handy springboard for forays into the countryside. You probably won't want to linger too long here, but the historical centre is picturesque and there are enough sights to keep visitors entertained for a day or two.

What to see and do

Olsztyn's most distinctive landmark is the **Wysoka Brama** (High Gate) at the entrance to the old town on ul. Staromiejska, an imposing red-brick edifice from the fourteenth century that was once part of the city walls and has served as an armoury and a prison. Olsztyn was once home to Nicolaus Copernicus, and you can see one of his sun dials embedded in the walls of the **castle** on ul. Zamkowa, now the town's historical **museum** (Tues–Sun: June–Aug 9am–5pm; Sept–May 10am–4pm; 9zł). At the eastern edge of the old town stands the elegant Gothic **St Jacob's Cathedral**, in which Napoleon's troops once imprisoned 1500 Russian soldiers – the prisoners burnt most of the cathedral's original wooden furnishings to keep warm.

Arrival and information

Train and bus The train and long-distance bus stations lie side by side on ul. Partyzanow, a 20min walk east of the centre; bus #7 runs to the old town.

Tourist office Next to the Wysoka Brama at ul. Staromiejska 1 (daily: May–June & Sept 8am–5pm; July & Aug 8am–6pm; Oct–April 8am–4pm; ⓣ89/535 3565, ⓦwww.mazury.travel). Can provide information about accommodation and outdoor activities in the area.

Accommodation

Hotel Wysoka Brama ul. Staromiejska 1 ⓣ89/527 3675, ⓦwww.hotelwysokabrama.olsztyn.pl. The rooms here have seen better days, but they are cheap, clean enough and very central. Dorms 20zł, singles 55zł, doubles 70zł.

Szkolne Schronisko Mlodziezowe ul. Kosciuszki 72/74 ⓣ89/527 6650, ⓦwww.ssmolsztyn.pl. Basic public hostel a 10min walk east of the centre, with en-suite dorms and kitchen facilities. Dorms 25zł, singles 50zł, doubles 80zł.

> **PIERNIKI**
>
> You can't leave Toruń without trying the local **pierniki**, or gingerbread, which has been made here since the town was founded. *Pierniczek* on Żeglarska 25 offers a mouthwatering range.

Eating and drinking

Awangarda Film Herbaciarnia Rynek 22. Cosy café attached to a prewar art-house cinema, with a pleasant summer balcony, good sandwiches (10zł) and decor that makes you feel you've stepped back in time.

Pomarancza pl. Jednosci Slowianskiej 9. Colourful café serving sweet and savory *nalesniki* (crêpes) from 6zł, with dozens of fillings to choose from.

Weranda Grill ul. Kollataja 15. Good Balkan and Mediterranean food served on a lovely balcony overlooking the creek. Mains 18–26zł.

THE MAZURIAN LAKES

The heart of Mazury lies in the vast expanse of lakes, rivers and forests to the north and east of Olsztyn, a land of tiny villages and unspoilt nature. It's paradise for hikers, and offers perfect conditions for sailing and kayaking (see box, p.897). Because of the absence of large towns, Mazury can be tricky to explore if you don't have your own wheels. In summer, the biggest lakes – Mamry and Śniardwy – attract the biggest crowds. One option is to base yourself in the lakeside village of **MIKOLAJKI**, from where you can set off into the countryside or onto surrounding lakes – the smaller ones will inevitably be quieter: as a general rule, tranquillity increases as you travel east.

Buses from Olsztyn run to Mikolajki six times a day. The tourist office is on pl. Wolnosci (April–June & Sept Sat

& Sun 10am–6pm; July & Aug daily 10am–6pm; ⓣ87/421 6850). There's no shortage of accommodation in the village itself, although some guesthouses are only open in the summer. You'll find dozens of small *pensjons* on ul. Kajki running eastward along the lakefront; try *Krol Sielaw* at no.5 (ⓣ87/421 6323, ⓦwww.krolsielaw.mazury.info; 150zł), a friendly place with en suites above a popular pizzeria. A number of bars and inexpensive restaurants pop up in the summer along the waterfront, and you can get fresh bread and tasty pastries at *Cukiernia* on ul. 3 Maja.

TORUŃ

Once one of the most beautiful medieval towns in Central Europe, **TORUŃ** was founded by the Teutonic Knights and is still rich with their architectural legacy. It's also famous for being the birthplace of Nicolaus Copernicus, whose house still stands. Now a friendly university city, with bars and cafés sprinkled throughout the compact streets, Toruń combines lively nightlife with a status as a UNESCO World Heritage Site.

What to see and do

The highlight of Toruń is the mansion-lined Market Square (Rynek) and its fourteenth-century Town Hall, now the **District Museum** (Tues–Sun: May–Sept 10am–6pm; Oct–April 10am–4pm; 10zł), with a fine collection of nineteenth-century paintings and intricate woodcarvings. South of the Rynek at ul. Kopernika 15/17, the **Copernicus Museum** (same hours as District Museum; 10zł), in the house where the great man was born, contains a fascinating model collection of his original instruments as well as facsimiles of the momentus *De Revolutionibus* and a selection of early portraits. The large, Gothic **St John's Cathedral** (Mon–Sat 8.30am–7.30pm, Sun 4.30–7.30pm; 3zł), at the eastern end of ul. Kopernika, has a tower offering panoramic views over the city (April–Oct only; 3zł extra). Further northeast lies the **New Town** district, its opulent commercial residences grouped around Rynek Nowomiejski.

Arrival and information

Train Toruń Główny, the main train station, is 2km south of the river; buses #22, #25 and #27 (every 10min; 2.50zł) run from outside the station to pl. Rapackiego on the western edge of the Old Town, the first stop after crossing the bridge.

Bus The bus station is on ul. Dąbrowskiego, just north of the centre.

Tourist office Rynek Staromiejski 25 ⓣ56/621 0931, ⓦwww.it.torun.pl (Mon & Sat 9am–4pm, Tues–Fri 9am–6pm; May–Sept also Sun 10am–2pm).

Internet Ksero, ul. Franciszkanska 5 (Mon–Fri 8am–7pm, Sat 9am–4pm).

Accommodation

Orange Plus ul. Jeczmienna 11 19 ⓣ56/651 8457, ⓦwww.hostelorange.pl. A bright, cosy hostel with friendly staff and comfortable dorms. Dorms 30zł, doubles 90zł.

Tor-Host ul. Prosta 2/25 ⓣ788 685 820. Nicely renovated top-floor apartment with kitchen facilities and attractive single and double rooms, good value for solo travellers. Singles 50zł, doubles 90zł.

Eating

Manekin ul. Wysoka 5. The perfect place for pancake lovers, specializing in innovative meat, veg and sweet fillings (from 6zł).

Oberza ul. Rabiańska 9. Cosy restaurant near the Market Square offering quick, traditional buffet meals in a farmhouse interior. Mains 13zł.

Pierogarnia Most Paulinski 2/10. Specializes both in standard *pierogi* and the giant oven-baked variety (10–17zł) in a creative range of flavours.

Pod Arkadami ul. Rozana 1. Clean, bright milk bar on the Market Square serving filling soups and potato dishes. Mains 6zł.

Drinking and nightlife

Bar Mockba Rynek Staromiejski 22. There's a fun mix of hip-hop and rock in this cellar club on the main square. 0.5lt beer 6zł. Daily 1pm–late.

THE HEJNAŁ

Legend has it that during one of the thirteenth-century Tatar raids, a guard watching from the tower of St Mary's Church saw the invaders approaching and blew his trumpet, only for his alarm to be cut short by an arrow through the throat. Every hour a local fireman now plays the sombre melody (*hejnał*) from the same tower, halting abruptly at the point when the guard is supposed to have been hit.

Café Faijka ul. Małe Garbary 1. Chilled-out place filled with cushions, offering a huge range of cocktails and shishas that bubble milk or gin instead of water. Cocktails from 10zł. Sun–Wed till 2am, Thurs–Sat till 3am.

Moving on

Train Gdańsk (9 daily; 3hr 30min); Kraków (3 daily; 8hr); Poznań (9 daily; 2hr 30min); Warsaw (12 daily; 2hr 30min); Wrocław (4 daily; 5hr 30min).

Southern Poland

Southern Poland attracts more visitors than any other region in the country, and its appeal is clear from a glance at the map. The **Tatra Mountains** bordering Slovakia are the most spectacular in the country, snowcapped for much of the year and markedly alpine in feel. The former royal capital of **Kraków** is an architectural gem and the country's intellectual heart. Pope John Paul II was archbishop here until his election in 1978, but equally important are the city's Jewish roots: before the Holocaust, this was one of Europe's most vibrant Jewish centres. This multicultural past echoes in the old district of Kazimierz, and its culmination is starkly enshrined at the death camps of **Auschwitz-Birkenau**, 50km west of the city.

KRAKÓW

KRAKÓW was the only major city in Poland to come through World War II essentially undamaged, and its assembly of monuments has since been hailed as one of Europe's most compelling by UNESCO. The city's Old Town (Stare Miasto) swarms with visitors in summer, but retains an atmosphere of *fin-de-siècle* stateliness, its streets a cavalcade of churches and palaces. A university centre, Kraków has a tangible buzz of arty youthfulness and enjoys a dynamic nightlife.

What to see and do

Kraków is bisected by the River Wisła, with virtually everything of interest on the north bank. At the heart of the **Old Town** is the Main Square, with **Wawel** Hill, ancient seat of Poland's kings and Church, and the rejuvenated **Kazimierz** lying to the south.

The Market Square

The largest square in medieval Europe, the Market Square (Rynek Glówny) is now a broad expanse with the vast **Cloth Hall** (Sukiennice) at its centre, ringed by magnificent houses and towering spires. Originally a collection of outdoor market stalls, the Cloth Hall was first built in 1300 and reconstructed during the Renaissance, and still houses a bustling covered market. To its south is the tiny copper-domed **St Adalbert's**, the first church to be founded in Kraków. On the east side is the Gothic **St Mary's Church** (Mon–Sat 11.30am–6pm, Sun 2–6pm; 6zł), the taller of its two towers, which you can climb during the summer months (May–Aug: Tues, Thurs & Sat 9–11.30am & 1–5.30pm; 5zł), topped by

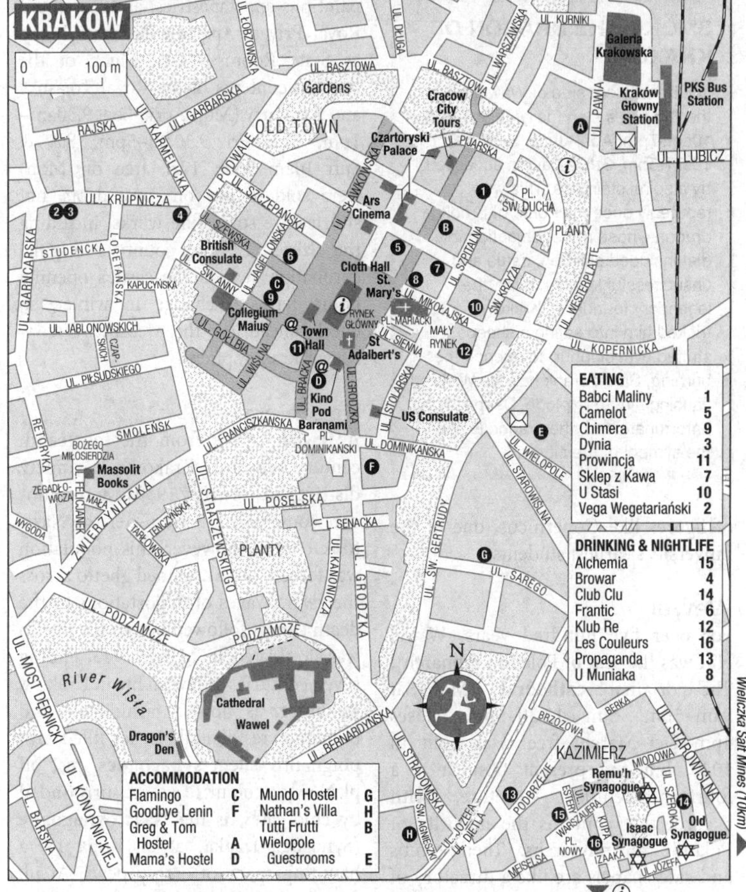

an amazing ensemble of spires. Inside is the stunningly realistic triptych high altar (1477–89), an intricate woodcarving depicting the Virgin Mary's Quietus among the apostles.

Czartoryski Palace

A few blocks north of the Rynek on ul. Pijarska sits the **Czartoryski Palace**, usually home to Kraków's finest art collection, although it is closed until 2013 for renovation. When it reopens, highlights will include Rembrandt's brooding *Landscape with Merciful Samaritan* and Leonardo da Vinci's *Lady with an Ermine*.

The university

West from the Rynek is the university area, whose first element was the fifteenth-century **Collegium Maius** building at ul. Jagiellońska 15. Now it's the **University Museum**, open for guided tours only (Mon, Wed & Fri 10am–3pm, Tues 10am–6pm, Thurs 10am–6pm, Sat 10am–2pm; 16zł; ☎12/422 0549). Most tours are in Polish but there are daily English tours at 1pm, and more in summer – ask in the morning for a schedule of tours for the day. Inside, the ground-floor rooms retain the mathematical and geographical murals once used for the teaching

SMOK – THE DRAGON OF KRAKÓW

On the western side of Wawel Hill is the **Dragon's Den** (daily: July & Aug 10am–7pm; April–June, Sept & Oct 10am–5pm; 3zł), a cavern accessed by a spiral staircase. This was reputedly once the home of Smok, a dragon whose rather objectionable diet included children, cattle and unsuccessful knights. Krak, the legendary founder of Kraków, tricked him into eating a sheep stuffed with sulphur; to quench the burning, Smok drank half the Wisła, causing him to explode. Despite his unfortunate end, the dragon is now the symbol of the city.

of figures like Copernicus, one of the university's earliest students.

Wawel

For over five hundred years, Wawel Hill was the seat of Poland's monarchy. The original **cathedral** (Mon–Sat 9am–5pm, Sun 12.30–5pm; closes 4pm Oct–March; free) was built in 1020, but the present basilica is a fourteenth-century structure, with a crypt that contains the majority of Poland's 45 monarchs. Their tombs and side chapels are like a directory of European artistic movements, not least the Gothic Holy Cross Chapel and the Renaissance Zygmuntówska chapel. The excellent **Cathedral Museum** (closed Sun, otherwise same hours as cathedral; 12zł) features religious and secular items dating from the thirteenth century, including all manner of coronation robes.

Visitor numbers are restricted, so arrive early or book ahead to visit the various sections of **Wawel Castle** (ticket office Mon–Fri 9am–5.45pm, Sat & Sun 9.45am–5.45pm; ⓣ12/422 1697), including the State Rooms (Tues–Fri 9.30am–5pm, Sat & Sun 10am–5pm; 17zł), furnished with Renaissance paintings and tapestries, and the grand Royal Private Apartments (same hours as State Rooms; 24zł). Much of the original contents of the Royal Treasury and Armoury (Mon April–Sept 9.30am–1pm, Tues–Fri 9.30am–5pm, Sat & Sun 10am–5pm; 17zł, free on Mon) were sold to pay off royal debts, but still feature some fine works, including the Szczerbiec, the country's original coronation sword. The castle's opening hours tend to change in winter, so check ahead on the website: ⓦwww.wawel.krakow.pl/en/.

Kazimierz

A **Jewish** centre from the fourteenth century onwards, Kraków's Kazimierz district had grown by 1939 to accommodate some 65,000 Jews. After the Nazis took control, however, this population was forced into a cramped ghetto across the river. Waves of deportations to the death camps followed before the ghetto was liquidated in March 1943, ending seven centuries of Jewish life in Kraków. Kazimierz is now a fashionable and bohemian residential district, filled with poignantly silent **synagogues**. Just off pl. Nowy, a colourful square surrounded by chic cafés, is the **Isaac Synagogue** (Synagoga Izaaka) at ul. Kupa 18, a haunting space of empty pews. At ul. Szeroka 24 is the **Old Synagogue** (Mon 10am–2pm, Wed, Thurs & weekends 9am–4pm, Fri 10am–5pm; 8zł), the oldest surviving example of Jewish religious architecture in Poland and home to the **Museum of Kraków Jewry**, with its traditional paintings by the area's former inhabitants.

Wieliczka salt mines

Ten kilometres from Kraków is the "underground salt cathedral" of **Wieliczka**, 300km of subterranean tunnels that have been used to mine salt since the thirteenth century (daily: April–Oct 7.30am–7.30pm; Nov–March 8am–5pm). The ticket price includes a

TREAT YOURSELF

If you want a break from hostel parties and busy city streets, try the stylish **Wielopole Guestrooms** (ul. Wielopole 3; ⓣ12/422 1475, ⓦwww.wielopole.pl), ideally poised between the Old Town and Kazimierz. Here you'll find spacious but cosy apartments, satellite TV and free internet access. Singles 318zł, doubles 438zł – breakfast included.

tour (68zł English, 49zł Polish), which passes by an underground lake and a number of impressive statues and edifices – including chandeliers – carved out of rock salt. To get there, catch bus #304 from ul. Kurniki next to the main train station (every 20min; 3zł).

Arrival and information

Air Kraków airport is situated 15km west of the city centre. It's easiest to catch the free shuttle bus to the airport's train station, which has trains twice an hour to Kraków Główny (18min; 5.14am–10.44pm; 10zł). The equivalent taxi ride is 50zł.

Train and bus Kraków Główny, the central train station, and the main PKS bus station just opposite, are a 5min walk northeast from the city's historic centre.

Tourist office The most central tourist office is in the Cloth Hall (daily: May–Sept 9am–7pm; Oct 10am–6pm; Nov–April 9am–5pm; ⓣ12/433 7310). There is also a smaller outlet between the train station and the Old Town (ul. Szpitalna 25 ⓣ12/432 0110) as well as one in the Kazimierz district (ul. Jozefa 7 ⓣ12/422 0471). Their website (ⓦwww.krakow.pl) provides the latest information regarding festivals and accommodation.

Tours You'll be bombarded with tour offers for the city and surrounding sights, but these are often rushed and cost four times as much as public transport. If you do want a tour, try Cracow City Tours at ul. Floriańska 44 (daily 9am–9pm; ⓣ12/421 1327, ⓦwww.cracowcitytours.pl), which offers a wide range of itineraries and discounts for students.

Tourist card The Kraków Tourist Card (2/3 days, 50/65zł; ⓦwww.krakowcard.com) gives you free entrance to all the major museums, as well as discounts at some of the city's pricier restaurants, shops and tour providers.

Accommodation

The number of hostels has mushroomed in the last few years, but it is still worth booking ahead if you want to stay in the most central spots. All hostels have free internet, breakfast and cheap laundry services.

Flamingo ul. Szewska 4 ⓣ12/422 0000, ⓦwww.flamingo-hostel.com. A clean, colourful place attracting a lively party crowd. Dorms 45zł, doubles 160zł.

Goodbye Lenin ul. Grodzka 34 ⓣ12/430 3053, ⓦwww.goodbyelenin.pl. Funky, mural-adorned backpacker base with a full kitchen and bright, spacious rooms. There's also another branch at Berka Joselewicza 23. Dorms 40zł, doubles 150zł.

Greg & Tom Hostel ul. Pawia 12 ⓣ12/422 4100, ⓦwww.gregtomhostel.com. Lively, youthful place right across from the train station, with single beds in all the dorms (no bunks) and nightly activities like vodka tasting and Polish dinners. Dorms 55zł, doubles 170zł.

Mama's Hostel ul. Bracka 4 ⓣ12/429 5940, ⓦwww.mamashostel.com.pl. This chilled-out hangout comes with friendly staff and has a great position above the Bracka café scene. Bring earplugs – there's a club downstairs. Dorms 50zł, doubles 180zł.

Mundo Hostel ul. Sarego 10 ⓣ12/422 6113, ⓦwww.mundohostel.eu. Probably the most beautiful hostel in Kraków, with each room decorated according to a different national theme. Dorms 50zł, doubles 160zł.

Nathan's Villa ul. Św. Agnieszki 1 ⓣ12/422 3545, ⓦwww.nathansvilla.com. The popular villa has a bar and cinema, and is handily located between the Old Town and Kazimierz. Dorms 47zł, doubles 164zł, 4-bed apartments 308zł.

Tutti Frutti ul. Floriańska 29 ⓣ12/428 0028, ⓦwww.tuttifruttihostel.com. This welcoming hostel does the basics (especially breakfast) very well and also provides guides for guests seeking the best places to go out. Dorms 45zł, 4-bed apartments 230zł.

Eating

Kraków's centre is renowned for its restaurants and cafés, which offer much beyond the Polish culinary staples.

Milk bars

Babci Maliny ul. Szpitalna 38. Upmarket milk bar with a mountain hut interior, serving suitably wholesome Polish classics. Mains 9–18zł.

U Stasi ul. Mikolajska 16. Milk bar favoured by locals, hidden behind a pizzeria, with unusually friendly service and delicious *knedle* (dumplings) stuffed with plums (7zł).

Vega Wegetariański ul. Krupnicza 20. Inexpensive but innovative veggie dishes; think tofu, beans and lots of greens. Mains 9–12zł.

Cafés and restaurants

Camelot ul. Św. Tomasza 15. A chic, artsy café with excellent desserts, including the best apple pie in town (12.50zł).

Chimera ul. Św. Anny 3. Popular salad bar that charges by the scoop (4–16zł). Around 30 salads are on offer, based on everything from couscous to cottage cheese and radish sprouts.

Dynia ul. Krupnicza 20. The city's most stylish student hangout has some delicious smoothies (7zł) and amazing breakfasts (10–21zł).

Prowincja ul. Bracka 3. Homey, relaxed café owned by local musical legend Grzegorz Turnau, with a wonderful wooden loft, thick hot chocolate and Kraków's best lattes (8zł).

Sklep z Kawa ul. Św. Tomasza 21. Had enough of terrible coffees while on the road? Then head to this fabulously old-fashioned café, which has an array of exotic coffee-bean varieties. Drinks and cakes from 6zł.

Drinking and nightlife

For best value head to Kazimierz or the student quarter to the west of the Old Town.

Bars

Alchemia ul. Estery 5. Murky, quirky and always packed, this candlelit rabbit warren has live jazz on the weekends and a stuffed crocodile over the bar. 0.5lt beer 7.50zł. Mon–Wed till 2am, Thurs–Sat till 4am.

Browar ul. Podwale 6. A German-style beer hall serving home-made *piwo*, including an intriguing ginger brew. 0.5lt beer from 6.50zł. Daily 9am–late.

Les Couleurs ul. Estery 10. A smoky and colourful Parisian-style café-bar serving light meals and alcoholic beverages of every description. Cocktails around 14zł. Daily 11–2am.

Propaganda ul. Miodowa 20. The People's Republic lives on in this popular hangout, cluttered with propaganda posters, old uniforms and antique radios. 0.5lt beer 7zł. Daily 11am–late.

Clubs

Club Clu ul. Szeroka 10/2. Cellar club with chart dance tunes in the heart of Kazimierz. Cocktails around 15zł. Daily 6pm–late.

Frantic ul. Szewska 5. With two dancefloors, there's plenty of space here for grooving to a mix of r'n'b and old school hits. Cocktails from 15zł. Daily 7pm–4am.

Klub Re ul. Krzyza 4. This hip central spot features basement caves to dance in and a cool outdoor courtyard in the summer. 0.5lt beer 10zł. Daily noon–2am.

U Muniaka ul. Floriańska 3. The city's best live jazz from 9.30pm every night. 0.33lt beer 9zł.

Entertainment

Cinema tickets are 11–19zł throughout the city.

Ars ul. Św. Jana 6 ⓦ www.ars.pl. Offers the latest blockbusters, though don't expect all of them to be in English.

Kino Pod Baranami Rynek Główny 27 ⓦ www.kinopodbaranami.pl. Screens a range of Western, Polish and Bollywood titles.

Shopping

Arts and crafts Touristy Floriańska and the boutiques in the Rynek contain a few bargain art dealers among the overpriced souvenirs. Kazimierz is filled with reasonably priced galleries and secondhand shops and, on Sundays, pl. Nowy becomes a colourful flea market of cheap clothes and jewellery.

Books You can find a good selection of English used books, including translations of Polish authors, at the café/bookshop Massolit on Felicjanek 4 (Sun–Thurs 10am–8pm, Fri & Sat 10am–9pm), where you can also trade in your old books for new reading material.

Clothes and food For a Western "mall experience", head for Galeria Krakowska (Mon–Sat 9am–10pm, Sun 10am–9pm), just next to the train station. It has all the fashionable Western brands that you could wish for, in addition to a large Carrefour supermarket.

GETTING TO AUSCHWITZ

You can catch one of the regular buses (2–3 every hour; 1hr 40min; 10zł) to the main camp from Kraków's PKS Terminal. There's an hourly shuttle-bus service to the Birkenau section from the car park at Auschwitz from April to October. Taxis are also available; otherwise it's a 3km walk.

Directory

Consulates UK Św. Anny 9 ☎12/421 7030; US ul. Stolarska 9 ☎12/424 5100.
Exchange To avoid the large commission charged at the banks, check the *kantor* exchanges that fill the streets around the Rynek for the best rates.
Festivals Jewish Cuture Festival (June/July); Summer Jazz Festival (July/Aug).
Hospital Krakówski Szpital Specjalistyczny, Pradnicka 80 ☎12/614 2000.
Internet Cafés are common all over the centre and generally charge 5zł/hr. Two slightly cheaper places are: Pl@net, Rynek 24 (daily 10am–10pm; 4zł/hr), and Hetmanska, ul. Bracka 4 (24hr; 4zł/hr).
Left luggage The train station has a left-luggage depot (7am–10pm; 5zł/24hr).
Pharmacies Apteka, ul. Szpitalna 38 (Mon–Fri 8am–8pm, Sat 9am–4pm).
Post office ul. Westerplatte 20.

Moving on

Train Berlin (1 daily; 10hr); Bratislava (1 daily; 8hr); Budapest (1 daily; 10hr 30min); Gdańsk (6 daily; 8hr); Poznań (10 daily; 7hr 30min); Prague (1 daily; 9hr 30min); Oświęcim/Auschwitz (15 daily; 1hr 45min); Toruń (3 daily; 8hr); Warsaw (hourly; 2hr 30min); Wrocław (hourly; 5hr); Zakopane (12 daily; 3hr 30min).
Bus Zakopane (every 20min; 2hr). Eurolines (see p.883) runs services to all major European capitals from near the main station at ul. Bosacka 18.

OŚWIĘCIM (AUSCHWITZ-BIRKENAU)

A visit to the Auschwitz camps provides an emotive, day-trip from Kraków. In 1940, **OŚWIĘCIM**, a small town 70km west of Kraków, became the site of the Oświęcim-Brzezinka concentration camp, better known by its German name of **Auschwitz-Birkenau**. Of the many camps built by the Nazis, this was the largest and most horrific: something approaching two million people, 85 percent of them Jews, died here. You can join a tour (hourly in English in summer, 3 daily in winter; 38zł) but a detailed guidebook (5zł) is just as helpful.

Auschwitz

Most of the Auschwitz buildings have been preserved as the **Museum of Martyrdom** (daily: March & Nov 8am–4pm; April & Oct 8am–5pm; May & Sept 8am–6pm; June–Aug 8am–7pm; Dec–Feb 8am–3pm; free; Ⓦwww.auschwitz.org.pl). The bulk of the camp consists of the prison cell blocks, with the first section dedicated to “exhibits” found in the camp after liberation: rooms full of clothes and suitcases, toothbrushes, glasses, shoes and a gruesome mound of women’s hair. Other barracks are given over to national memorials, and the blocks terminate with the gas chambers and the ovens where the bodies were incinerated.

Birkenau

The huge **Birkenau** camp (same hours) is less visited, though it was here that the majority of executions took place. Birkenau was designed purely as a death camp, and the huge gas chambers at the back of the camp were damaged but not destroyed by the fleeing Nazis in 1945. Victims arrived in closed trains on the platform, where those who were fit to work (around 25 percent) were separated from those who were driven straight to the gas chambers. The railway line is still there, just as the Nazis abandoned it. Allow 1–2 hours to fully explore the 175-hectare site.

THE TATRAS AND ZAKOPANE

Some 80km long, with peaks of up to 2500m, the **Tatras** are the most spectacular part of the mountain range extending along Poland’s border with Slovakia. They are as beautiful as any mountain landscape in northern Europe, the ascents leading along boulder-strewn trails beside woods and streams and culminating in breathtaking, windswept peaks. The

INTO SLOVAKIA

The coach company Strama runs 5 daily buses to **Poprad** (2hr; 20zł; ⓦwww.strama.eu), a Slovakian skiing and hiking centre. In July and August, you can also spend a day at the spa at **Oravice** (book tours at the tourist office; 110zł).

peaks are topped with snow for most of the year, making it a great area for skiing (from mid-Dec to March). The mountains are a protected national park and as such harbour lots of wildlife: if you're lucky you could glimpse rare species such as lynx, golden eagles and brown bear.

The main base for skiing and hiking on the Polish side is the extremely popular and lively resort of **Zakopane**. There are good road and rail links with Kraków 60km to the north, as well as several mountain resorts across the border in Slovakia.

What to see and do

Skiing here is cheap, with the premier slopes of Kasprowy Wierch just a few minutes out of town, and plenty of places in the centre to rent equipment. **Hikers** may want to avoid the 9km path to the lovely but busy Morskie Oko Lake in high season, but there's no shortage of other, more secluded trails. Świat, at ul. Zamoyskiego 12 (ⓣ693 022 944, ⓦwww.swiat.biz.pl), organizes **rafting** tours (with English-speaking guides) on the nearby Dunajec River. Zakopane's **market** at the bottom of ul. Krupówki sells a wide range of traditional local goods, including *oscypek* (smoked sheep's cheese) and small woodcarvings. This latter local tradition is intriguingly displayed in the whimsical wooden tombs of the nearby Old Cemetery (Stary Cementarz).

Arrival and information

Train and bus Both stations are next to one another on ul. Kosciuszki, a 10min walk east of the pedestrianized main street, ul. Krupówki.
Tourist office Just west of the stations at ul. Kościuszki 17 (daily July & Aug 9am–5pm; Mon–Fri March–June & Sept to mid-Dec 9am–5pm; closed Sun mid-Dec to Feb; ⓦwww.zakopane.pl).
Hiking information The Tatra National Park Information Centre, near the park entrance at ul. Chałubińskiego 44 (daily: Jan–April & Oct 7am–4pm; May & June 7am–5pm; July–Aug 7am–6pm; Nov & Dec 7am–3pm; ⓣ18/202 3300, ⓦwww.tpn.pl), provides good-quality maps and information on routes.
Internet Ksero, ul. Galicy 8 (Mon–Fri 7.30am–10pm, Sat & Sun 10am–9pm; 5zł/hr).

Accommodation

Finding a place to stay is rarely a problem in Zakopane as, in addition to the hostels, many homeowners in town offer private rooms.
Flamingo ul. Krupówki 24 ⓣ18/200 0222, ⓦwww.flamingo-hostel.com. Clean, modern hostel on the party strip for those who like to be in the thick of things. Dorms 35zł, doubles 120zł.
Goodbye Lenin ul. Chłabówka 44 ⓣ18/200 1330, ⓦwww.goodbyelenin.pl. Lying 3.5km out of town, this cosy house in the woods is the perfect place to focus on hiking and skiing. Call ahead for a ride from the bus station. Dorms 35zł, doubles 120zł.
Hotel Fian ul.Chałubińskiego 38 ⓣ600 400 200, ⓦwww.fian.pl. With a sauna and jacuzzi to ease hiking aches, this place also prides itself on the "gastronomic experience" offered by its resident Polish chef. Singles 105zł, doubles 205zł – price includes breakfast.
Stara Polana ul. Nowotarska 59 ⓣ18/206 8902, ⓦwww.starapolana.pl. A warm wood-panelled interior, satellite TV and friendly service make this hostel excellent value. Dorms 35zł, singles 60zł, doubles 100zł.

Eating and drinking

Head to the area around ul. Krupówki where you'll find plenty of lively bars and restaurants.
Bar Mleczny ul. Krupówki 1, entrance from ul. Nowotarska. Pricey for a milk bar, but still the cheapest eats in town with hearty Polish mains for 9–15zł.
Genesis pl. Niepodległości 1. The town's lager-and-lasers-type club attracts Poland's top DJs at

weekends. 5zł cover (more on weekends). Summer daily 9pm–5am; winter Thurs–Sun.

Owczarnia ul. Galicy 4. Giant grilled steaks, *kielbasa* (sausage) and local trout are the specialities in this lively grill-house. Mains 12–35zł.

Paparazzi ul. Galicy 8. This chic cocktail bar has some leafy outdoor seating and fruity drinks (from 17zł). Mon–Fri 4pm–1am, Sat & Sun from noon.

Moving on

Train Gdańsk (2 daily; 17hr); Kraków (9 daily; 3hr 30min); Warsaw (2 daily; 6–10hr).

Bus Kraków (approx 30min, 5am–9pm; 2hr) leaves from the PKS Terminal.

Western Poland

Tossed for centuries back and forth between the Poles, Germans and Czechs, Poland's southwestern province of Silesia is a fascinating blend of cultures, languages and architectural styles. Its main city, **Wrocław**, is the focus of Poland's new economic dynamism. Vibrant **Poznań** to the north, the heart of the original Polish nation, is one of the country's oldest cities and a key commercial link to Western Europe.

WROCŁAW

WROCŁAW (pronounced "vrots-waf"), the fourth largest city in Poland, is used to rebuilding. For centuries – as Breslau – it was largely dominated by Germans, but this changed after the war, as thousands of displaced Poles flocked to the decimated city. The various influences are reflected in Wrocław's architecture, with its mammoth Germanic churches, Flemish-style mansions and Baroque palaces. The latest rebuilding came after a catastrophic flood in the early 1990s, which left most of the centre underwater. Fortunately, the reconstruction that followed has left the pretty Old Town rejuvenated and without the tourist mobs of Kraków. The city has also been actively reaching out to foreign investors in both technology and finance. This, along with a lively university scene, lends Wrocław a vigorous air of economic and cultural well-being.

What to see and do

Wrocław's historical centre is delineated by the former city walls, bordered by a moat and a shady park, and by the River Odra to the north, whose pretty islands are home to a handful of churches.

The Market Square

In the heart of the town is the vast **Market Square** (Rynek) and the thirteenth-century town hall, with its magnificently ornate facades. The hall is now the **Town Museum** (Wed–Sat 10am–5pm, Sun 10am–6pm; 15zł). In the northwest corner of the square are two curious Baroque houses known as **Jaś i Małgosia** (Hansel and Gretel), linked by a gateway giving access to **St Elizabeth's**, the finest of Wrocław's churches. Its ninety-metre tower (Mon–Sat 10am–6pm, Sun 1–6pm; 5zł) is the city's most prominent landmark.

Jewish quarter

Southwest of the square lies the former **Jewish quarter**, whose inhabitants were driven from their tenements during the Third Reich. One of the largest synagogues in Poland, the **Synagoga pod Białym Bocianem** (Synagogue Under the White Stork), lies hidden in a courtyard at ul. Włodkowica 9. Visits can be arranged through the Jewish Information Centre (Mon–Thurs 9am–5pm, Fri 9am–3pm; 6zł; ☎71/787 3902).

The Racławice Panorama and the National Museum

East of the city centre, a rotunda houses the famous **Panorama of the Battle**

TREAT YOURSELF

A meal at the renowned **JaDka restaurant** on ul. Rzeznicza 24/5 may not be cheap (though some classics like *pierogi* come in at only 20–26zł), but you can be assured of world-class Polish cuisine and excellent service.

of Racławice (mid-April to June & Sept daily 9am–5pm; July & Aug daily 9am–5.30pm; Oct Tues–Sun 9am–5pm; Nov to mid-April Tues–Sun 9am–4pm; shows every 30min but expect queues; 22zł, including entrance to the National Museum). This painting – 120m long and 15m high – was commissioned in 1894 for the centenary of the Russian army's defeat by Tadeusz Kościuszko's militia at Racławice, a village near Kraków. You can also visit the nearby **National Museum** (Wed–Fri & Sun 10am–5pm, Sat 10am–6pm; closes 1hr earlier Oct–March; 15zł, Sat free), with its fun and colourful exhibition of twentieth-century Polish installation artists like Jozef Szajna.

University quarter

North of the Market Square is the historic and buzzing **university quarter**, full of bargain eateries and tiny bookshops. At its centre is the huge Collegium Maximum, whose Aula Leopoldina assembly hall, upstairs at pl. Uniwersytecki 1 (daily except Wed 10am–3.30pm; 10zł), is one of the greatest secular interiors of the Baroque age.

Wyspa Piasek and Ostrów Tumski

Northeast from the Market Hall, the Piaskowy Bridge leads to the attractive island of **Wyspa Piasek** and the fourteenth-century church of St Mary of the Sands, with its majestically vaulted ceiling. Two elegant little bridges connect the island with **Ostrów Tumski**, the city's ecclesiastical heart, home to several Baroque palaces and the vast Cathedral of St John the Baptist.

Arrival and information

Air Take bus #406 to the train station from the airport (30min; 2.40zł). The equivalent taxi ride costs 30–40zł.

Train The main train station, Wrocław Główny, faces the broad boulevard of ul. Piłsudskiego, a 15min walk south of the Market Square.

Bus The main station is just to the south of the train station.

Tourist office Rynek 14 (daily: April–Oct 9am–9pm; Nov–March 9am–7pm; ⓣ71/344 3111, ⓦwww.wroclaw-info.pl). Books accommodation.

Internet Internet Navigator, ul. Igielna 14 (daily 9am–midnight; 4zł/hr).

Accommodation

Babel ul. Kołłątaja 16/3 ⓣ71/342 0250, ⓦwww.babelhostel.pl. Close to the train station, this small hostel has friendly staff and cheerful rooms. Dorms 45zł, doubles 140zł.

Boogie Hostel ul. Ruska 35 ⓣ71/342 4472, ⓦwww.boogiehostel.pl. Spacious and colourful, with clean, modern rooms and a tendency to attract a party crowd. Dorms 40zł, singles 110zł, doubles 140zł.

Cinnamon ul. Kazimierza Wielkiego 67 ⓣ71/344 5858, ⓦwww.cinnamonhostel.com. Pleasant, airy rooms and friendly staff make this spice-themed hostel a winner. Dorms 35zł, doubles 135zł.

Mleczarnia ul. Wlodkowica 5 ⓣ71/787 7570, ⓦwww.mleczarniahostel.pl. Comfortable, bohemian hangout, situated in an old building above a candlelit coffee bar. Dorms 45zł, doubles/apartment 220zł.

Savoy pl. Kościuszki 19 ⓣ71/340 3219, ⓦwww.savoy.wroc.pl. With a TV and bathroom included, these are the best budget hotel rooms in town, though internet access and breakfast are extra. Singles 135zł, doubles 162zł.

Eating

Bazylia ul. Kuźnicza 42. Stylishly minimalist canteen, with a wonderful view onto the Collegium and food priced by weight. 2.29zł/100g. Expect tasty soups, vegetable side dishes, chicken escalopes and lots of salads.

Kuchnia Marche ul. Świdnicka 53. Excellent range of international cuisine in a lively, family-friendly setting. Mains 10–20zł.

Mis ul. Kuźnicza 48. Extremely popular and well-known milk bar that provides quick, filling grub for the student crowd. Mains 4zł.

Pod II Strusiem ul. Ruska 61. Set in a rejuvenated former lavatory, this place dishes out some tasty pizzas (9zł). Particularly good for those who like their pizzas hot – the "Fiery One" comes in three varying levels of spiciness; Level Three is definitely a challenge.

Drinking and nightlife

Bezsennosc ul. Ruska 51. Just 10min away from the Rynek, this graffiti-lined cellar resounds to a fun mix of electronic and reggae tunes. Cocktails 14–17zł. Daily from 7pm.

Kalambur ul. Kuznicza 29a. This ornate Art Nouveau pub, with its period bronzework and retro vibe, is a hangout for theatre types and hosts occasional live music. 0.5lt beer 7.50zł. Daily till midnight.

PRL Rynek 10. Festooned with portraits of Lenin and Mao, this popular Communist-themed bar also has a dancefloor downstairs. 0.5lt beer 8.50zł. Daily noon–late.

Moving on

Train Berlin (1 daily; 6hr); Dresden (3 daily; 3hr); Gdańsk (3 daily; 8hr); Kraków (hourly; 5hr); Poznań (hourly; 3hr); Toruń (4 daily; 5hr 30min); Warsaw (15 daily; 6hr).

POZNAŃ

Thanks to its position on the Berlin–Warsaw–Moscow rail line, **POZNAŃ** is many visitors' first taste of Poland. Long identified as the cradle of Polish nationhood, today it's an economically dynamic city with stunning architectural diversity.

What to see and do

The sixteenth-century **town hall** that dominates the **Old Town Square** (Stary Rynek) has a striking eastern facade, which frames a frieze of notable Polish monarchs. Inside is the **Poznań Historical Museum** (mid-June to mid-Sept: Tues–Thurs 11am–5pm, Fri noon–9pm, Sat & Sun 11am–6pm; mid-Sept to mid-June: Tues–Thurs 9am–3pm, Fri noon–9pm, Sat & Sun 11am–6pm; 7zł; Sat free), worth visiting for the Renaissance Great Hall on the first floor. East of the Old Town Square, a bridge crosses to the quiet holy island of **Ostrów Tumski**, dominated by Poland's oldest cathedral, the **Cathedral of St John the Bapist**. Most of the structure was reconstructed after the war, and Poland's first two monarchs are buried in the crypt. Anyone with even a passing interest in architecture should also take a look at the wonderfully renovated **Stary Browar** southwest of the centre at Półwiejska 32 (Mon–Sat 9am–9pm, Sun 10am–8pm; ⓦstarybrowar5050.com), a nineteenth-century brewery intriguingly transformed into a shopping and cultural centre.

Arrival and information

Air Poznań's airport is 7km west of the Old Town and is served by bus #59 (30min; 3zł), which runs to the Rondo Kaponiera just north of the train station, and by bus #L to the station itself (4.40zł). The 10min taxi ride from the airport is 30–40zł.

Train The main train station, Poznań Główny, is 2km southwest of the historic quarter; tram #5 runs from the western exit on ul. Glogowska to the city centre.

Bus The PKS Terminal is a 15min walk south from the Old Town Square, at the intersection of ul. Ratajczaka and ul. Królowej Jadwigi.

Tourist information ul. Ratajczaka 44 (Mon–Fri 10am–7pm, Sat 10am–5pm; ⓣ61/851 9645, ⓦwww.poznan.pl). There is also a handy Provincial Tourist Office on the Old Town Square at no. 59/60 (May–Oct Mon–Fri 9am–8pm, Sat 10am–8pm, Sun 10am–6pm; Nov–April Mon–Fri 10am–8pm, Sat & Sun 10am–5pm).

Public transport Poznań's public transport works on a timed basis; a 15min (2zł) ticket should be adequate for any travel within the centre.

Accommodation

The city's trade fairs, which take place throughout the year (July & Aug excepted), can cause hotel prices to double, so always book ahead.

Frolic Goats ul. Wrocławska 16/6 (entry at ul. Jaskolcza) ⓣ61/852 4411, ⓦwww.frolicgoats hostel.com. This unassuming central hostel has all the facilities a backpacker could need. Free internet access and breakfast are included. Dorms 45zł, doubles 170zł.
Melange ul. Rybaki 6a ⓣ507 070 107, ⓦwww .melangehostel.com. In a slightly derelict old building 10min south of the centre, but the rooms are comfortable and nicely decorated, and the staff are friendly. Dorms 45zł, singles 110zł, doubles 130zł.
Mini Hotelik al. Niepodległości 8a ⓣ61/633 1416. This little place not far from the train station may look a bit tattered, but its rooms are clean, good value and have TVs. The nicest rooms look out onto a small park. Singles 91zł, doubles 129zł.

Eating

Café Ptasie Radio ul. Kościuszki 74. A favourite with the arty elite, this sophisticated and cosy café provides cheesy pasta dishes and salads. Mains 19zł. For dessert try the creamy vanilla cheesecake with ice cream.
Pod Kuchcikiem Św. Marcin 75. This canteen provides classic milk bar grub alongside some nice salads and milkshakes. Mains from 5zł.
Republica Roz pl. Kolegracki 2a. Pretty little café, all teapots and florals, serving cakes, tea and an assortment of hot drinks to warm body and soul. Drinks 6zł.
Spaghetti Bar Piccolo ul. Rynkowa 1. The buffet here comprises simple but tasty spaghetti dishes that are ready as you enter. Mains from 4zł.

Drinking and nightlife

Brovaria Stary Rynek 73. This bar in the Old Town Square may be predictably pricey, but the home-made *piwo* makes a trip irresistible. 0.5lt mulled honey beer 9zł. Daily till 1am.
Cuba Libre ul. Wroclawska 21. A Latin dance club popular with the student crowd, offering the best late-night party in town. 0.5lt beer 7zł. Daily from 7pm.

Moving on

Train Berlin (4 daily; 2hr 30min); Gdańsk (5 daily; 5hr); Kraków (10 daily; 7hr 30min); Toruń (9 daily; 2hr 30min); Warsaw (hourly; 3hr); Wrocław (hourly; 2hr 30min).

Portugal

HIGHLIGHTS

PORT WINE LODGES, PORTO: numerous lodges here offer free tours and tastings

THE DOURO RAIL ROUTE: beautifully scenic line along the foot of the steep Douro river valley

QUIEMA DAS FITAS, COIMBRA: join in this university town's renowned end-of-term celebrations in May

A NIGHT OUT IN LISBON: check out the Bairro Alto and dance till dawn

THE ALGARVE BEACHES: the Ilha de Tavira has some of the best

ROUGH COSTS

DAILY BUDGET Basic €60 /occasional treat €80

DRINK *Vinho verde* €8 a bottle

FOOD Grilled sardines €8

HOSTEL/BUDGET HOTEL €18/€45

TRAVEL Train: Lisbon–Faro €18–19.50; bus: Porto–Lisbon €17.50

FACT FILE

POPULATION 10.6 million

AREA 92,391 sq km

LANGUAGE Portuguese

CURRENCY Euro (€)

CAPITAL Lisbon (population: 564,500)

INTERNATIONAL PHONE CODE ⓣ351

Introduction

Although Portugal is perhaps best known for the "fun in the sun" resorts of the Algarve, there's much more to the Iberian peninsula's lesser-visited country than beautiful beaches. Portugal is geographically diverse yet small enough to travel around easily, with lively cities, mountain ranges, rural villages and a stunning coastline all within rapid reach of each other. Another draw is the relaxed, laidback pace of life, meaning that even in the biggest metropolises, stress and bustle is remarkably rare. And most importantly for the budget traveller, Portugal is still relatively cheap to visit.

Scenically, some of the most interesting parts of the country are in the north: the **Minho**, a verdant area home to Portugal's only national park; and the sensational gorge and valley of the **Douro**, followed along its course by the railway, off which antiquated branch lines edge into remote countryside. For contemporary Portugal, spend some time in **Lisbon** and **Porto**, the two major cities, both treasure-troves of cultural attractions with a vibrant nightlife to boot. And if it's monuments you're after, head to the centre of the country – above all, **Coimbra** and **Évora** – which retain a faded grandeur. The coast is virtually continuous beach, and apart from the **Algarve** and a few pockets around Lisbon and Porto, resorts remain low-key. The loveliest are the wild, isolated beaches of the southern **Alentejo**.

CHRONOLOGY

219 BC The Romans capture the Iberian Peninsula from the Carthaginians, taking the settlement of "Portus Cale" in the process.

711 The Islamic Moors take control of large parts of present-day Portugal.

868 Establishment of the First County of Portugal, within the Kingdom of León.

1095 Crusaders help Portuguese to defeat the Moors.

1139 Afonso I, of the Burgundy dynasty, declares himself king of an independent Portugal.

1386 The Treaty of Windsor, the oldest diplomatic alliance in the world, is signed between England and Portugal securing mutual military support.

1500s Portugal builds a large empire with colonies across the world including Mozambique, Goa and Brazil.

1580 During a succession crisis, Philip II of Spain invades and crowns himself Philip I of Portugal.

1703 The Methuen trade treaty with England, following which port wine becomes popular internationally.

1755 An enormous earthquake destroys much of Lisbon.

1822 Brazil declares independence from Portugal.

1916 Portugal joins World War I on the side of the Allies.

1926 Military coup, led by Antonio de Oliveira Salazar, sweeps control of the country; he remains in power until 1968.

1939 Portugal remains neutral during World War II.

1974 Government overthrown in a near bloodless coup.

1975 Independence is granted to all Portuguese African colonies.

1976 First free elections are held.

1986 Portugal joins the European Community.

2007 Mass demonstrations against the Portuguese government's economic reforms.

ARRIVAL

Portugal's three international **airports** are in Faro, Lisbon and Porto. Faro and Lisbon in particular are well linked to the rest of Europe by the budget airlines (notably easyJet), with services to and from Faro increasing during summer. **Bus** is the quickest and most convenient method of overland transport from Spain, particularly if you are arriving from the south. Common daily routes

include Sevilla–Faro, Sevilla–Lisbon and Madrid–Lisbon. **Trains** are a more costly but usually more comfortable option; the Madrid–Lisbon *trenhotel* runs nightly.

GETTING AROUND

CP (Ⓦwww.cp.pt) operates Portugal's **trains**, which are very reasonably priced – particularly in the case of suburban services from Porto and Lisbon. Those designated *Regionais* stop at most stations. *Intercidades* are twice as fast and more expensive. The fastest and most luxurious are the *Rápidos* (known as "Alfa"), which speed between Lisbon, Coimbra and Porto. **InterRail passes** are valid, though supplements must be paid on *Intercidades* and *Rápidos*. You can check timetables online (select "*Horários y preços*") or call the information line on Ⓣ808 208 208.

The **bus** network, made up of many regional companies, is more comprehensive and services are often faster, while for long journeys buses can sometimes be slightly cheaper than trains. On a number of major routes (particularly Lisbon–Algarve), express coaches can knock hours off standard multiple-stop bus journeys; Rede Expressos (Ⓦwww.rede-expressos.pt) is the largest bus operator. Other key operators include

Rodonorte in the north (Ⓦwww.rodonorte.pt), Rodotejo in the Ribatejo (Ⓦwww.rodotejo.pt), Rodoviária do Alentejo in the Alentejo (Ⓦwww.rodalentejo.pt) and EVA in the Algarve (Ⓦwww.eva-bus.com). For 24hr national bus information call Ⓣ707 22 33 44.

Cycling is popular, though there are few facilities to support cyclists. In the north and centre of the country the terrain is rather hilly, flattening out south of Lisbon. Bikes can be transported on any *Regional* train for €1.50–2.50 (free if the bike is dismantled) as long as there is space. Bus companies' policies vary so enquire before travelling.

ACCOMMODATION

There are over forty state-owned **youth hostels** (*Pousadas de Juventude*; Ⓦwww.pousadasjuventude.pt); most stay open all year and some impose a curfew. All require a valid HI card; for details see Ⓦwww.hihostels.com. Alternatively, hostels in Portugal can provide you with a guest card, which must be stamped every night that you stay (€2 per stamp); once you have five stamps you're a fully paid-up member of HI. A dormitory bed costs €11–18, depending on season and location; doubles in a hostel cost €22–45. There is also a growing number of **independent hostels**, particularly in Lisbon and Porto; they're a pricier alternative to official youth hostels but tend to be more conveniently located, and are often well equipped, with kitchen facilities and internet access.

In almost any town you should be able to find a single room for €30 and a double for under €50; cities are slightly more expensive. The main budget stand-bys are *pensions*, or *pensões* – hotels, often present only in larger towns and cities tend to be rather pricier. Seaside resorts invariably offer cheaper **rooms** (*quartos*) in private houses; tourist offices have lists. At the higher end of the scale are **pousadas** (Ⓦwww.pousadas.pt), often converted from old monasteries or castles, which charge at least four-star hotel prices. No matter what type of accommodation you select, **breakfast** will usually be included (exceptions are noted in this chapter).

Portugal has around two hundred **campsites**, most small, low-key and attractively located, and all remarkably inexpensive – you'll rarely pay more than €5 a person. You can get a map list from any tourist office, or find details online at Ⓦwww.roteiro-campista.pt. Camping rough is banned; beach areas are especially strict about this.

FOOD AND DRINK

Portuguese **food** is cheap and served in plentiful portions. Virtually all cafés dish up a basic meal for under €10, and for a little more you have the run of most of the country's restaurants. **Snacks** include *tosta mistas* (cheese and ham toasties); *pastéis de bacalhau* (cod fishcakes); and *sandes* (sandwiches). In **restaurants** you can usually have a substantial meal by ordering a *meia dose* (half-portion), or *uma dose* (one portion) between two. Most serve an *ementa turística* (set meal), which can be good value, particularly in *pensões* that serve meals, cheaper workers' cafés or *churrasqueiras* (grill restaurants serving meat and fish dishes). It's often worth opting for the *prato do dia* (dish of the day), usually the cheapest dish on the menu, and, if you're on the coast, going for fish and seafood.

Meals usually begin with uninvited appetizers (from bread, butter and olives to more elaborate entrées), which often carry a hefty price tag; if in doubt ask, and don't be afraid to send these items back or ignore them. Typical **dishes** include *sopa de marisco* (shellfish soup); *caldo verde* (finely shredded kale leaves in broth); and *bacalhau* (dried cod, cooked in myriad different ways). *Caldeirada* is a fish stew cooked with onions and tomatoes, *arroz marisco* a similar stew cooked with seafood and rice. *Cabrito assado* (roast kid) is common in the north

SURFING IN PORTUGAL

Portugal is a surfer's paradise, with some of Europe's best beaches for catching waves. Popular spots include **Peniche** in central Portugal, **Guincho beach** near **Cascais** in Lisbon, the **Alentejo coast**, and **Lagos**, and the wilder waters of Sagres in the **Algarve**. First-timers should try a **surf school** such as Peniche Surf Camp (ⓦwww.penichesurfcamp.com; €453 for a week in high season) or The Surf Experience in Lagos (ⓦwww.surf-experience.com; €580 for a week's boot camp); accommodation is included in courses. For those with a bit more experience, equipment is available for rent in all popular surfing spots (around €60 for a week's board rental).

of the country, while down south you're sure to see chicken piri-piri (chicken with chilli sauce) on the menu. **Puddings** include *arroz doce* (rice pudding) and *pudím molotoff* (a kind of lightly toasted meringue drenched in caramel sauce). **Cakes** – *bolos* or *pastéis* – are often at their best in *pastelarias* (patisseries), though you'll also find them in cafés and *casas de chá* (tearooms). Among the best are custard tarts (*pastéis de nata*).

Drink

Portuguese **wines** (*tinto* for red, *branco* for white) are very inexpensive and of high quality. The fortified **port** (*vinho do Porto*; see p.935) and madeira (*vinho da Madeira*) wines are the best known. The light, slightly sparkling **vinhos verdes** are produced in the Minho, and are excellent served chilled. **Brandy** is available in two varieties, Macieiera and Constantino, while Lisbon specializes in the cherry brandy *Ginjinha*, which is served at tiny hole-in-the-wall bars throughout the city. The two most common Portuguese **beers** (*cervejas*) are Sagres and Super Bock.

CULTURE AND ETIQUETTE

Portugal is a **Catholic** country, so it's wise to show respect when visiting churches (bare shoulders should be covered up and short skirts may be frowned upon), and avoid visiting during services, which take place on Sundays and sometimes on other days at around 9.30am. It's also a good idea to learn a few basic phrases in **Portuguese** (see p.916); it will certainly endear locals to you, and outside the main tourist areas English may not be widely understood. In restaurants, it is usual to **tip** five percent to ten percent if you're satisfied with the service.

Lone women travellers should face no problems, but might attract a bit of curiosity from locals.

SPORTS AND OUTDOOR ACTIVITIES

In Portugal, **football** isn't just a sport: it's a national passion. During all major matches, the country goes quiet as people flock to restaurants and bars to watch them on television. The three biggest and most successful football clubs are FC Porto, Sporting Lisbon and Benfica. **Surfing** is also popular (see box above). Portugal's **natural parks** (*parques naturais*) and its one **national park**, the Parque Nacional de Peneda-Gerês in the Minho, are a hiker's paradise. More information about the parks can be found at ⓦwww.icn.pt, and tourist offices located near parks can provide maps and other details. In the Algarve, pick up a copy of the excellent *Trails in the Algarve* booklet, a guide to walking routes in the region, available for €5 from tourist offices.

EMERGENCY NUMBERS

All emergencies ⓣ112.

PORTUGUESE

	Portuguese	Pronunciation
Yes	*Sim*	Sing
No	*Não*	Now
Please	*Por favor*	Por favor
Thank you	*Obrigado* [said by men]/ *Obrigada* [said by women]	Obrigado/obrigada
Hello/Good day	*Olá*	Orla
Goodbye	*Adeus*	Adayoosh
Excuse me	*Desculpe*	Deskulp
Where?	*Onde?*	Ond?
Good	*Bom*	Bom
Bad	*Mau*	Maw
Near	*Perto*	Pertoo
Far	*Longe*	Lonje
Cheap	*Barato*	Baratoo
Expensive	*Caro*	Karoo
Open	*Aberto*	Abertoo
Closed	*Fechado*	Feshardoo
Today	*Hoje*	Oje
Yesterday	*Ontem*	Ontaygn
Tomorrow	*Amanhã*	Amanya
How much is...?	*Quanto é...?*	Kwantoo eh...?
What time is it?	*Que horas são?*	Kay orash sow?
I don't understand	*Não compreendo*	Now comprendoo
Do you speak English?	*Fala Inglés?*	Farla inglayz?
One	*Um/Uma*	Oom/ooma
Two	*Dois/Duas*	Doysh/dooash
Three	*Três*	Treysh
Four	*Quatro*	Kwatroo
Five	*Cinco*	Sinkoo
Six	*Seis*	Saysh
Seven	*Sete*	Set
Eight	*Oito*	Oytoo
Nine	*Nove*	Nove
Ten	*Dez*	Desh
Where is the station?	*Onde é a estação?*	Ond e a estasow?
On the left/right	*A esquerda/direita*	A eeshkerdah/deeraitah
A ticket to...	*Um bilhete para...*	Oom beelyet para...
What time is the train/ bus to...?	*A que horas é o comboio/ autocarro para...?*	A kay oras e o convoyo/ autocarro para...?
I would like a room (single/double)	*Queria um quarto individual/casal*	Kereea um kwarto individooal/cazal
May I see the room?	*Posso ver o quarto?*	Posso ver o kwarto?
At the restaurant		
A table for one/two	*Uma mesa para uma pessoa/duas pessoas*	Uma mehzah para ooma pessoa/duash pessoash
I'm a vegetarian	*Sou vegetariano/a*	So vejetarianoh/ah
A bottle of water/wine	*Uma garrafa de água/vinho*	Ooma garrafuh de aigua/vinyo

PORTUGAL ONLINE

Ⓦ**www.visitportugal.com** Tourist board site, with information and advice.
Ⓦ**oportocool.wordpress.com** The latest hip hangouts in Porto.
Ⓦ**www.spottedbylocals.com/lisbon** Up-to-the minute recommendations from Lisbon residents.
Ⓦ**www.algarveuncovered.com** Detailed site dedicated to the Algarve region.

COMMUNICATIONS

Internet cafés are common (€1.50–3/hr). **Post offices** (*correios*) are normally open Monday to Friday 9am to 6pm, Saturday 9am to noon. International **phone calls** can be made direct from any phone booth; phonecards cost €3, €6 or €9, from post offices, larger newsagents and tobacconists. The operator is on Ⓣ118 (domestic), Ⓣ098 (international).

EMERGENCIES

Lisbon and the larger tourist areas have seen increases in **petty crime**, such as street theft. Pilfering from dorms is relatively rare, but it's always wise to use the lockers provided or buy a padlock for your luggage. Travel on trains and buses is safe, with thefts a rarity. Portuguese **police** are stationed in most towns, and can be recognized by their dark blue uniforms. Lisbon and Porto have separate **tourist police** to deal with issues affecting visitors.

For minor health complaints go to a **pharmacy** (*farmácia*); pharmacists are highly trained and can dispense many drugs without a prescription. Normal opening hours are Monday to Friday 9am to 1pm and 3 to 7pm, Saturday 9am to 1pm. A sign at each one will show the nearest 24hr pharmacy. You can get the address of an English-speaking doctor from a pharmacy or consular office.

INFORMATION

You'll find a **tourist office** (*turismo*) in almost every town. Staff can help you find a room, and provide local maps and leaflets.

MONEY AND BANKS

Currency is the euro (€). **Banks** are open Monday to Friday 8.30am to 3pm; in Lisbon and in the Algarve, **exchange offices** may open in the evening to change money. ATMs are all over and credit cards are widely accepted.

OPENING HOURS AND HOLIDAYS

Shop **opening hours** are generally Monday to Friday 9am to 12.30/1pm and 2/2.30 to 6/6.30pm, Saturday 9am to 12.30/1pm. Larger supermarkets tend to stay open until 8pm, but most shops are closed on Sunday, with some exceptions in the Algarve. Museums, churches and monuments open from around 10am to 6pm, with many state institutions free from 10am until 2pm on Sunday; almost all, however, close on Mondays and at Easter; smaller places often close for lunch. Restaurants often close on Sunday evenings. The main **public holidays** are: January 1, February carnival, Good Friday, April 25, May 1, Corpus Christi, June 10, June 13 (Lisbon only), August 15, October 5, November 1, December 1, December 8 and December 25.

STUDENT AND YOUTH DISCOUNTS

If you're under 26 it's worth investing in a Euro 26 card (Ⓦwww.euro26.org), which often gives the holder sixty percent off admission costs, plus discounts on train and bus travel and accommodation in official youth hostels. Some sights offer a less significant discount on production of a valid university card.

Lisbon and around

There are few more immediately likeable European capitals than **LISBON** (*Lisboa*). A lively city, it remains in some ways curiously provincial, and rooted as much in the 1920s as the 2010s. Wooden trams clank up outrageous gradients, past mosaic pavements, Art Nouveau cafés and the medieval quarter of Alfama, which hangs below the São Jorge castle. The city invested heavily for Expo 98 and the 2004 European Football Championships, reclaiming run-down docks and improving communication links, and today it combines an easy-going pace and manageable scale with a vibrant, cosmopolitan identity.

Lisbon has a huge amount of historic interest. Though the **Great Earthquake** of 1755 (followed by a tidal wave and fire) destroyed most of the grandest buildings, several monuments from Portugal's sixteenth-century golden age survived and frantic reconstruction led to the building of many impressive new palaces and churches across the city's seven hills.

What to see and do

Many of Lisbon's historical sights, such as the Sé (cathedral) and the Castelo de São Jorge, are located in the centre's eastern portion, best reached by following Rua de Conceição and its continuations as they wind away from the **Baixa**, the city's eighteenth-century core, towards the ancient district of **Alfama**. The city centre can be explored on foot, but a quick hop on a **tram** or **elevador** is definitely a less strenuous way of scaling Lisbon's hills. Public transport is also necessary to reach outlying sights such as those located in **Belém**, 6km west of the centre, and the **Fundação Calouste Gulbenkian**, north of the city's main artery, the Avenida da Liberdade. The Baixa is the city's principal shopping district, with more elegant and trendy boutiques located in **Chiado** and **Bairro Alto** respectively. Bairro Alto is also the area to head for food, *fado* and fun, as it is home to many of the city's bars and restaurants.

Baixa

The heart of the capital is the lower town – the **Baixa** – Europe's first great example of Neoclassical design and urban planning. It's an imposing quarter of rod-straight streets, some streaming with traffic, but most pedestrianized with mosaic cobbles. The Baixa's northenmost boundary is **Rossio Square** (officially Praça dom Pedro IV), the area's hub, busy at almost all hours of the day and night and housing some old-style cafés and the grand **Teatro Nacional**. At the waterfront end of the Baixa lies the city's other main square, the beautiful arcaded **Praça do Comércio**. Between the two on Rua Augusta is **MUDE** (Design and Fashion Museum; Tues–Thurs & Sun 10am–8pm; until 10pm Fri & Sat; free), an evolving exhibition space which takes its name from the Portuguese word for movement. MUDE features changing temporary exhibitions as well as a permanent collection giving an excellent overview of modern design and fashion.

The Sé

Lisbon's **Sé** or cathedral (Tues–Sat 9am–7pm, Sun & Mon 9am–5pm) stands on Largo da Sé in the city centre's eastern portion. The oldest church in Lisbon, it was founded in 1147 to commemorate the city's reconquest from the Moors, and occupies the site of the principal mosque of Moorish Lishbuna. Like so many of Portugal's cathedrals, it is Romanesque and restrained in both size and decoration. It was damaged in the 1755 earthquake, and was extensively restored in the 1930s.

Castelo de São Jorge

East of the Baixa, Rua Augusto Rosa and its continuations wind up towards the castle, past the **Miradouro de Santa Luzia**, which offers spectacular views over the River Tejo. The **Castelo de São Jorge** (daily April–Sept 9am–9pm; Oct–March 9am–6pm; €7) contains the restored remains of the Moorish palace that once stood here, and its ramparts and towers boast some excellent views of the city, particularly from the **camera obscura**, which has half-hourly viewings in summer.

Alfama

The **Alfama quarter**, tumbling from the walls of the Castelo to the banks of the Tejo, is the oldest part of Lisbon, and one of its most beautiful, thanks to its picturesque narrow alleyways and breathtaking hilltop views. Despite a definite tourist presence, the quarter retains a largely traditional feel. The **Feira da Ladra**, Lisbon's rambling flea market, fills the Campo de Santa Clara, at the northeastern edge of Alfama, every Tuesday and Saturday. Also worth a visit is the nearby church of **São Vicente de Fora** (Tues–Sun 10am–6pm; €4), a former monastery containing some exquisite eighteenth-century *azulejos* (tiles). The church also houses, in almost complete sequence, the bodies of all Portuguese kings from João IV, who restored the monarchy in 1640, to Manuel II, who lost it and died in exile in England in 1932.

Chiado

Between the Baixa and Bairro Alto, halfway up the hill, lies an area known as **Chiado**, which suffered much damage in a fire in 1988 but has been elegantly rebuilt by Portugal's premier architect, Álvaro Siza Viera. It remains the city's most affluent quarter, centred on **Rua Garrett** and its fashionable shops and chic cafés. The **Elevador de Santa Justa** (€2.80 return), built by Eiffel disciple Raul Mésnier de Ponsard, is an elaborate wrought-iron lift which transports passengers from Rua de Santa Justa in the Baixa to a platform next to the ruined Gothic arches of the **Convento do Carmo**. Once Lisbon's largest church, it was half-destroyed by the 1755 earthquake, becoming perhaps even more beautiful as a result, its vaulted arches reaching dramatically towards the sky. It now houses an **archeological museum** (daily except Sun: June–Sept 10am–7pm; Oct–May 10am–6pm; €3.50) which, alongside sculptures from the original church, also contains an eclectic assortment of treasures from prehistoric times to the modern day.

TREAT YOURSELF

Ride the gold mesh lift to the top floor of the boutique **Bairro Alto Hotel** (Praça Luis de Camões 2) for classic cocktails with a view (€10). The pint-sized terrace is an ideal spot to watch the sunset; gaze over the Tejo to the Ponte 25 de Abril and the statue of Christ the Redeemer on the opposite bank. The exclusive elegance of the setting justifies the cost of that cosmopolitan.

Bairro Alto

High above and to the west of the Baixa is the vibrant quarter of **Bairro Alto**, Lisbon's after-dark playground. Its narrow streets are lined with trendy clothing outlets, *fado* clubs, and a multitude of bars and restaurants. The district can be reached by two funicular-like **trams** – the Elevador da Glória from Praça dos Restauradores or the Elevador da Bica from Rua de São Paulo (both €1.50 one-way).

The Fundação Calouste Gulbenkian

The **Fundação Calouste Gulbenkian** is a ten-minute walk north of Lisbon's main park, the Parque Eduardo VII

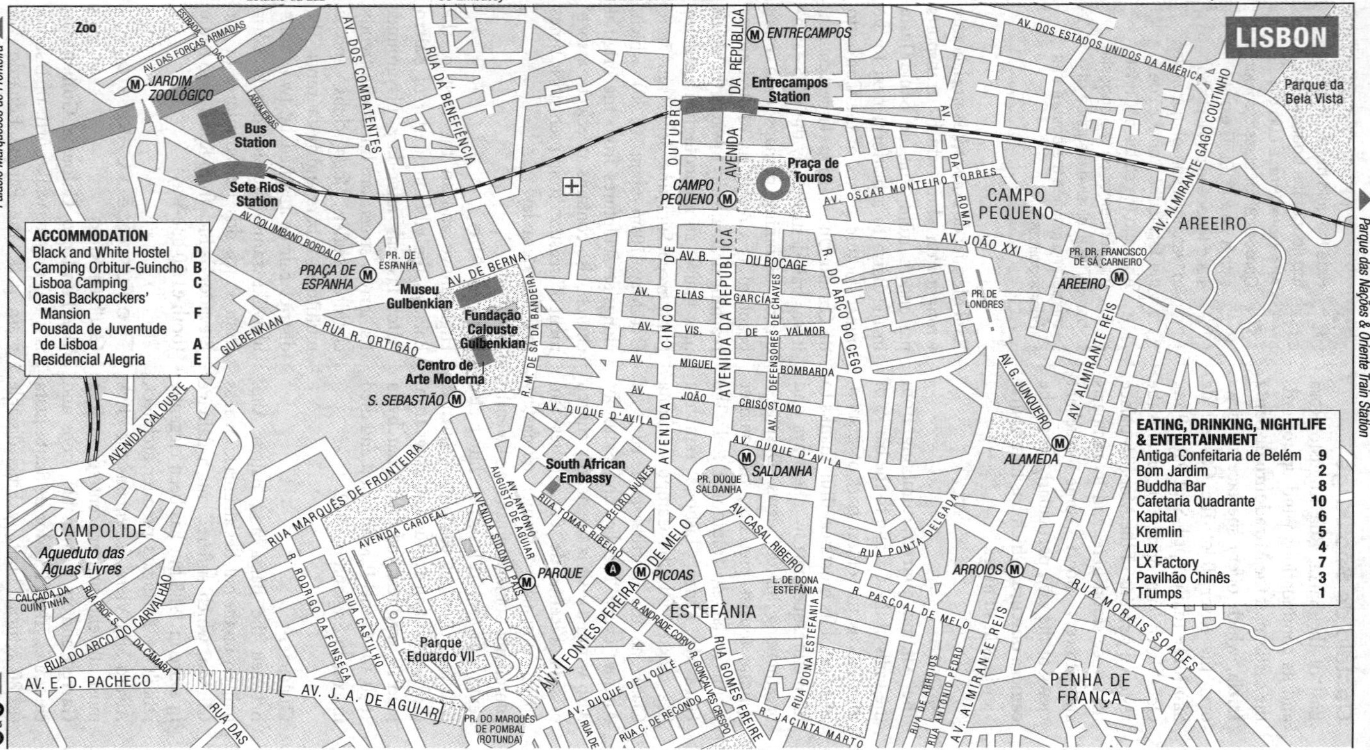
LISBON
Estádio da Luz
US Embassy
Estádio Jose Alvalade
Airport
Parque das Nações & Oriente Train Station
Palacio Marquêses de Fronteira
B & C
Zoo
JARDIM ZOOLÓGICO
Bus Station
Sete Rios Station
Entrecampos Station
ENTRECAMPOS
Praça de Touros
CAMPO PEQUENO
AREEIRO
Parque da Bela Vista
PRAÇA DE ESPANHA
PR. DE ESPANHA
Museu Gulbenkian
Fundação Calouste Gulbenkian
Centro de Arte Moderna
S. SEBASTIÃO
South African Embassy
PARQUE
PICOAS
SALDANHA
PR. DUQUE SALDANHA
ESTEFÂNIA
L. DE DONA ESTEFÂNIA
ALAMEDA
ARROIOS
PENHA DE FRANÇA
PR. DR. FRANCISCO DE SÁ CARNEIRO
PR. DE LONDRES
CAMPOLIDE
Aqueduto das Águas Livres
Parque Eduardo VII
PR. DO MARQUÊS DE POMBAL (ROTUNDA)
AV. DOS ESTADOS UNIDOS DA AMÉRICA
AV. ALMIRANTE GAGO COUTINHO
AV. DA ROMA
AV. OSCAR MONTEIRO TORRES
AV. JOÃO XXI
AV. ALMIRANTE REIS
AV. G. JUNQUEIRO
AVENIDA DA REPÚBLICA
AVENIDA CINCO DE OUTUBRO
R. DO ARCO DO CEGO
DU BOCAGE
GARCÍA
DEFENSORES DE CHAVES
VALMOR
BOMBARDA
CRISÓSTOMO
AV. DUQUE D'AVILA
AV. B. ELIAS
AV. VIS.
AV. MIGUEL
AV. JOÃO
AV. DOS COMBATENTES
RUA DA BENEFICÊNCIA
AV. DAS FORÇAS ARMADAS
ESTRADA DAS LARANJEIRAS
AV. COLUMBANO BORDALO
AV. DE BERNA
RUA R. ORTIGÃO
GULBENKIAN
AVENIDA CALOUSTE
R. M. DE SÁ DA BANDEIRA
RUA PEDRO NUNES
RUA TOMÁS RIBEIRO
AV. FONTES PEREIRA DE MELO
AV. ANTÓNIO AUGUSTO DE AGUIAR
AVENIDA SIDÓNIO PAIS
AV. CASAL RIBEIRO
RUA PONTA DELGADA
R. PASCOAL DE MELO
RUA MORAIS SOARES
RUA DE ARROIOS
RUA ANTÓNIO PEDRO
R. JACINTA MARTO
RUA DONA ESTEFANIA
RUA GOMES FREIRE
R. GONÇALVES CRESPO
R. ANDRADE CORVO
RUA C. DE RECONDO
AV. DUQUE DE LOULÉ
RUA DE
RUA MARQUÊS DE FRONTEIRA
AVENIDA CARDEAL
R. RODRIGO DA FONSECA
RUA CASTILHO
AV. J. A. DE AGUIAR
AV. E. D. PACHECO
RUA DO ARCO DO CARVALHÃO
RUA PROF. S. DA CÂMARA
CALÇADA DA QUINTINHA
RUA DAS
ACCOMMODATION
Black and White Hostel D
Camping Orbitur-Guincho B C
Lisboa Camping C
Oasis Backpackers' Mansion F
Pousada de Juventude de Lisboa A
Residencial Alegria E
EATING, DRINKING, NIGHTLIFE & ENTERTAINMENT
Antiga Confeitaria de Belém 9
Bom Jardim 2
Buddha Bar 8
Cafetaria Quadrante 10
Kapital 6
Kremlin 5
Lux 4
LX Factory 7
Pavilhão Chinês 3
Trumps 1

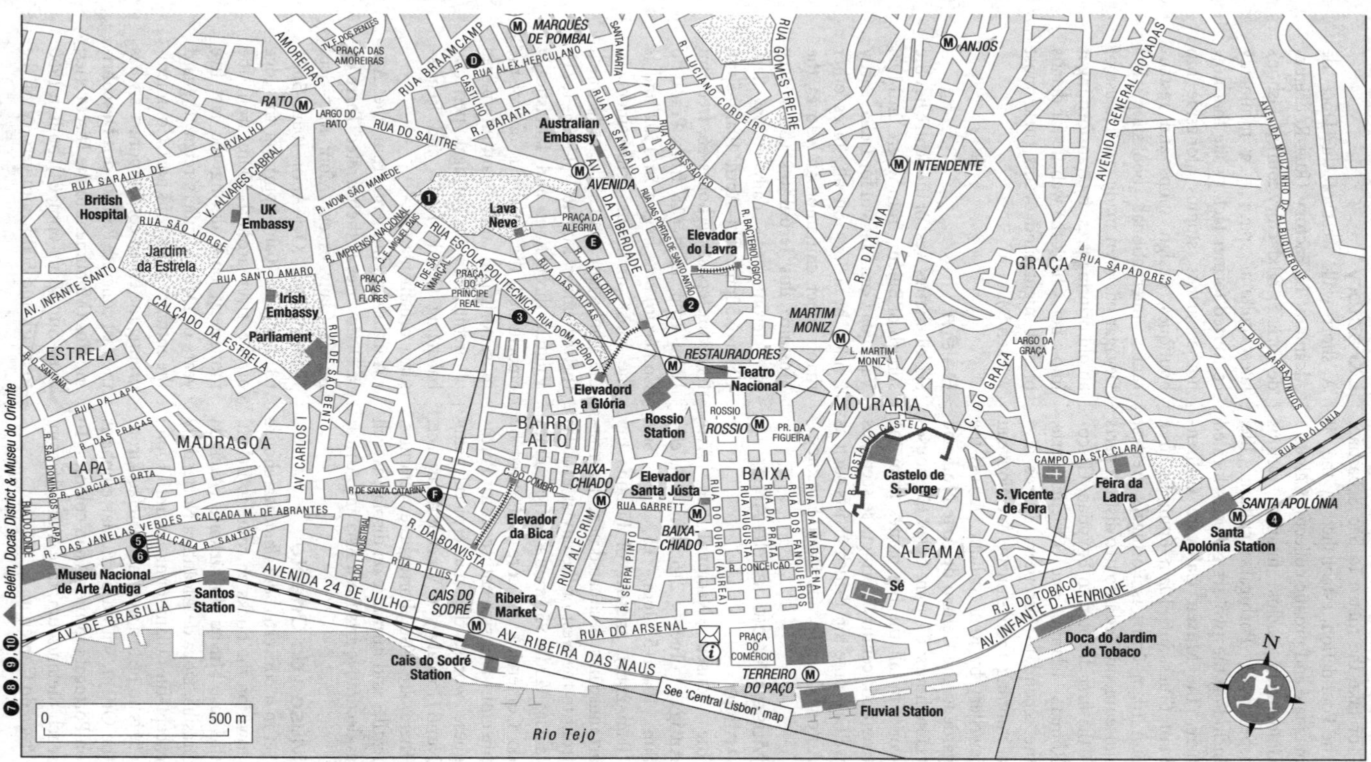
MARQUÊS DE POMBAL
ANJOS
INTENDENTE
AMOREIRAS
PRAÇA DAS AMOREIRAS
RUA BRAAMCAMP
RUA ALEX HERCULANO
RATO
LARGO DO RATO
RUA DO SALITRE
R. BARATA
Australian Embassy
AVENIDA DA LIBERDADE
RUA GOMES FREIRE
R. LUCIANO CORDEIRO
AVENIDA GENERAL ROÇADAS
AVENIDA MOUZINHO DE ALBUQUERQUE
British Hospital
UK Embassy
Jardim da Estrela
Lava Neve
PRAÇA DA ALEGRIA
Elevador do Lavra
R. DAALMA
GRAÇA
RUA SAPADORES
AV. INFANTE SANTO
RUA SANTO AMARO
Irish Embassy
Parliament
PRAÇA DAS FLORES
PRAÇA DO PRÍNCIPE REAL
RUA ESCOLA POLITECNICA
RUA DOM PEDRO V
MARTIM MONIZ
RESTAURADORES
Teatro Nacional
MOURARIA
LARGO DA GRAÇA
C. DO GRAÇA
ESTRELA
CALÇADO DA ESTRELA
RUA DE SÃO BENTO
Elevadord a Glória
Rossio Station
ROSSIO
PR. DA FIGUEIRA
BAIRRO ALTO
MADRAGOA
LAPA
AV. CARLOS I
BAIXA-CHIADO
Elevador Santa Jústa
BAIXA
Castelo de S. Jorge
S. Vicente de Fora
Feira da Ladra
CAMPO DA STA CLARA
SANTA APOLÓNIA
Santa Apolónia Station
Elevador da Bica
ALFAMA
Sé
Museu Nacional de Arte Antiga
Santos Station
AVENIDA 24 DE JULHO
CAIS DO SODRÉ
Ribeira Market
RUA DO ARSENAL
PRAÇA DO COMÉRCIO
AV. INFANTE D. HENRIQUE
Doca do Jardim do Tobaco
AV. DE BRASILIA
AV. RIBEIRA DAS NAUS
Cais do Sodré Station
TERREIRO DO PAÇO
See 'Central Lisbon' map
Fluvial Station
N
0 500 m
Rio Tejo
7, 8, 9, 10, Belém, Docas District & Museu do Oriente

– or take the metro to São Sebastião. The Foundation, established by the oil magnate and prolific collector Calouste Gulbenkian, helps finance various aspects of Portugal's cultural life, including the two art galleries located here. The **Museu Calouste Gulbenkian** (Tues–Sun 10am–6pm; €4, free Sun 10am–2pm) is Portugal's greatest museum, divided into two distinct parts – the first devoted to Egyptian, Greco-Roman, Islamic and Oriental arts, the second to European. There's also a stunning room full of Art Nouveau jewellery by René Lalique. Across the gardens, the **Centro de Arte Moderna** (same hours; €4, joint ticket €7) houses works by all the big names from the twentieth-century Portuguese scene, as well as some top British artists such as Antony Gormley and David Hockney.

Museu Nacional de Arte Antiga

The **Museu Nacional de Arte Antiga** (Tues 2–5.30pm, Wed–Sun 10am–5.30pm; €5, free Sun 10am–2pm), another of Lisbon's top art museums, is situated near the riverfront to the west of the city at Rua das Janelas Verdes 95 (tram #15 from Praça do Comércio). Its core is formed by fifteenth- and sixteenth-century Portuguese works, the masterpiece being Nuno Gonçalves' St Vincent Altarpiece. There are also Portuguese ceramics, textiles and furniture on display, as well as decorative arts from Asia and Africa.

Museu do Oriente

Set in a converted *bacalhau* warehouse down on the docks en route to Belém, the vast **Museu do Oriente** (Avenida Brasília, Doca de Alcântara Norte; daily except Tues 10am–6pm, Fri until 10pm; €5) is home to a wealth of artefacts from the Orient, with a particular emphasis on Portugal's former Asian colonies. To reach the museum, take tram #15 from Praça do Comércio.

LXFactory

A short walk west of the Doca de Alcântara, **LXFactory** (Rua Rodrigues de Faria 3; Ⓦlxfactory.com) is Lisbon's latest cultural space – a minimally converted former factory site that now houses artists' studios alongside hip boutiques, design shops and restaurants. International bookshop Ler Devagar has even made creative use of an old printing press by transforming it into a bar. Check the website for details of club nights and events (held most weekends).

Belém

Six kilometres west of the centre lies the suburb of **Belém**, from where, in 1497, Vasco da Gama set sail for India. Partly funded by a levy on all spices other than pepper, cinnamon and cloves, the **Mosteiro dos Jerónimos** (Monastery of Jerónimos; daily May–Sept 10am–6.30pm; Oct–April 10am–5pm; free; cloisters same hours €6, free Sun 10am–2pm; tram #15 from Praça do Comércio) was begun in 1502 and is the most ambitious achievement in the flamboyant late Gothic style which thrived under Manuel I (1495–1521). Vaulted throughout and fantastically embellished, the cloister is one of the most original and beautiful pieces of architecture in Portugal, perfectly balancing Gothic forms and Renaissance ornamentation.

Another monument from the Age of Discoveries is the turreted **Torre de Belém** (daily except Mon: May–Sept 10am–6.30pm; Oct–April 10am–5pm; €3, free Sun 10am–2pm), on the edge of the river around 500m from the monastery, built during the last five years of Dom Manuel's reign to guard the entrance to Lisbon's port. Commemorating the era in contemporary style is the vast concrete **Padrão dos Descobrimentos** (Monument to the Discoveries; Tues–Sun 10am–6pm; €4), built in 1960 to mark the 500th anniversary of the

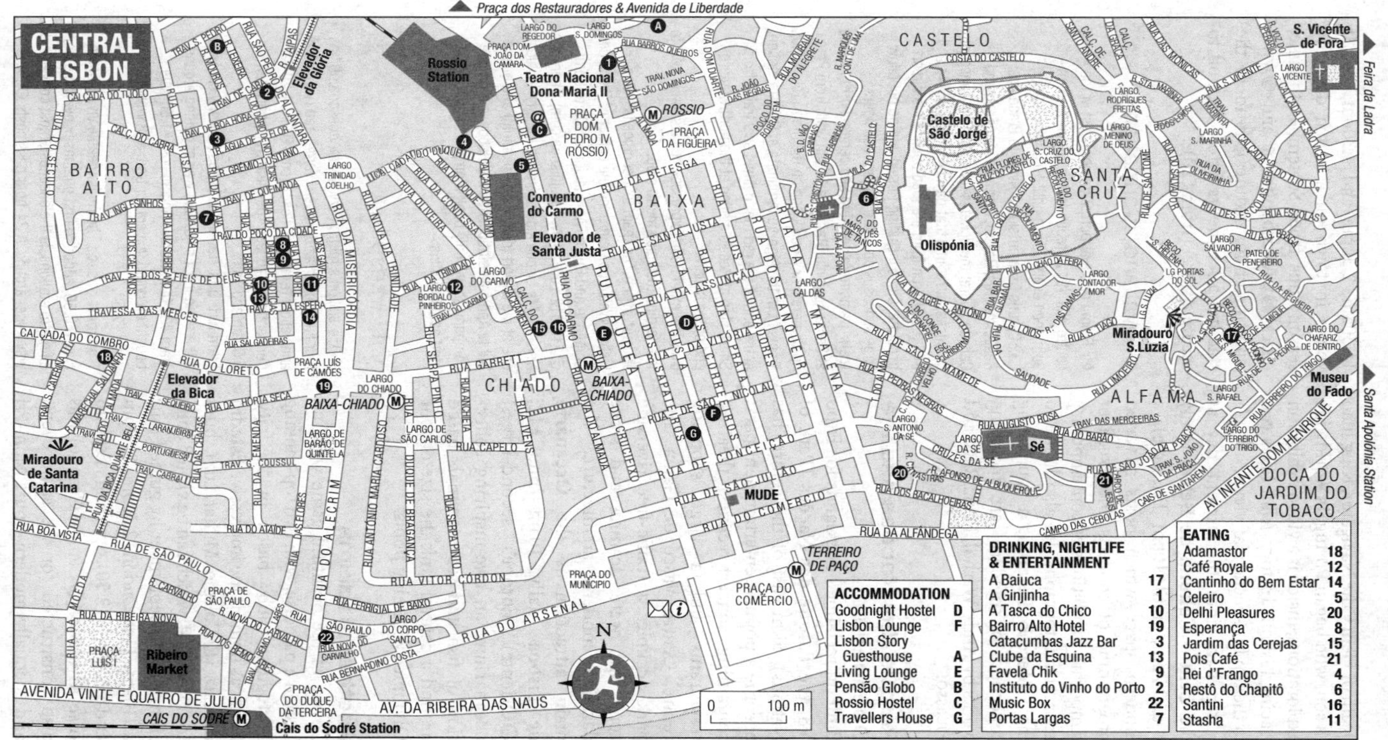
CENTRAL LISBON
Praça dos Restauradores & Avenida de Liberdade
Feira da Ladra
Santa Apolónia Station
CASTELO
BAIRRO ALTO
SANTA CRUZ
BAIXA
CHIADO
ALFAMA
DOCA DO JARDIM DO TOBACO
Castelo de São Jorge
Olispónia
Rossio Station
Teatro Nacional Dona Maria II
Convento do Carmo
Elevador de Santa Justa
Elevador da Glória
Elevador da Bica
Miradouro de Santa Catarina
Miradouro S.Luzia
Museu do Fado
S. Vicente de Fora
Sé
MUDE
Ribeiro Market
Cais do Sodré Station
ROSSIO
BAIXA-CHIADO
TERREIRO DE PAÇO
CAIS DO SODRÉ
PRAÇA DO COMÉRCIO
PRAÇA DO MUNICÍPIO
PRAÇA DOM PEDRO IV (RÓSSIO)
PRAÇA DA FIGUEIRA
PRAÇA LUÍS DE CAMÕES
PRAÇA LUÍS I
PRAÇA DE SÃO PAULO
PRAÇA DO DUQUE DA TERCEIRA
RUA AUGUSTA
RUA DO OURO
RUA DA PRATA
RUA DOS FANQUEIROS
RUA DA MADALENA
RUA GARRETT
RUA DA MISERICÓRDIA
RUA DO ALECRIM
RUA DO ARSENAL
AV. DA RIBEIRA DAS NAUS
AVENIDA VINTE E QUATRO DE JULHO
AV. INFANTE DOM HENRIQUE
RUA DA ALFÂNDEGA
RUA DE SÃO PAULO
CALÇADA DO COMBRO
RUA DO SÉCULO
0 100 m
N
ACCOMMODATION
Goodnight Hostel D
Lisbon Lounge F
Lisbon Story Guesthouse A
Living Lounge E
Pensão Globo B
Rossio Hostel C
Travellers House G
DRINKING, NIGHTLIFE & ENTERTAINMENT
A Baiuca 17
A Ginjinha 1
A Tasca do Chico 10
Bairro Alto Hotel 19
Catacumbas Jazz Bar 3
Clube da Esquina 13
Favela Chik 9
Instituto do Vinho do Porto 2
Music Box 22
Portas Largas 7
EATING
Adamastor 18
Café Royale 12
Cantinho do Bem Estar 14
Celeiro 5
Delhi Pleasures 20
Esperança 8
Jardim das Cerejas 15
Pois Café 21
Rei d'Frango 4
Restô do Chapitô 6
Santini 16
Stasha 11

death of Henry the Navigator, King João I's son, who began Portugal's worldwide explorations; inside is a video exhibition tracing Lisbon's history. A lift takes you to the top for spectacular views.

Step back into the present day at the **Centro Cultural de Belém** (daily 10am–7pm, until 10pm Fri; free), a modern space which hosts a varied programme of concerts and excellent temporary exhibitions of contemporary art and photography. It's also home to the **Colecçao Berardo**, a captivating collection of modern art including works by Andy Warhol, Paula Rego and Picasso.

Parque das Nações and the Oceanarium

Built on reclaimed docklands for Expo '98, the **Parque das Nações** (Park of Nations), 5km east of the centre, has become a popular entertainment park, containing concert venues, theatres, restaurants and a large shopping centre, Centro Vasco de Gama. The park occupies a traffic-free riverside zone with water features and some dazzling modern architecture. The main attraction is the **Oceanário de Lisboa** (daily 10am–7pm; €12; Ⓜ Oriente), Europe's second-largest oceanarium, an awe-inspiring collection of fish and sea mammals based around a central tank the size of four Olympic swimming pools.

Football stadiums

Lovers of the beautiful game will find Lisbon a paradise, with two top-ranking Portuguese clubs based in the city. Benfica's home is the impressive **Estádio da Luz** (Ⓜ Colegio Militar/Luz), built for Euro 2004, which can be visited daily from May to September by guided tour at 10am, 11am, noon, 2.30pm, 3.30pm and 4.30pm (€12.50). Sporting's **Estádio Jose Alvalade** (Ⓜ Campo Grande) was also constructed for the same event, and is equally modern (tours Mon–Fri 11.30am, 2.30pm and 4.30pm; €9). If you're in town on a match day (the season runs from September to June; check Ⓦ www.slbenfica.pt and Ⓦ www.sporting.pt for fixtures), head to the stadium a few hours before kick-off to secure a ticket (from €20).

Arrival and information

Air From Portela airport, 7km northeast of the centre, the #91 Aerobus (every 20min 7.45am–9pm, then every 30min until 10.30pm; 20min; €3.50) runs from outside arrivals to Praça dos Restauradores, Rossio, Praça do Comércio and Cais do Sodré; the ticket is then valid for transport on buses and trams that day. Local buses #44 and #45 (€1.50) run from the road outside the airport to central stops including Rossio, but do not allow large suitcases on board during rush hours.

Train Trains from northern and central Portugal stop at Santa Apolónia Station, a 15min walk from Praça do Comércio or a quick hop on the metro (blue line). Trains from the Algarve terminate at Oriente station, at the end of the red metro line. Local trains from Sintra stop at Rossio station at the northwestern end of the square.

Bus The main Rede Expressos bus station is next to the Jardim Zoológico metro stop.

Tourist office The main tourist office is the Lisboa Welcome Centre, on the corner of Praça do Comércio and Rua do Arsenal (daily 10am–8pm; Ⓣ 210 312 700, Ⓦ www.visitlisboa.com). There are also Ask Me Lisboa kiosks around the city, including one at the airport (daily 6am–midnight) and one at Santa Apolónia station. Ask Me Lisboa is a private company so will only book rooms with its associated partner hotels.

City transport

Metro Lisbon's metro (Ⓦ www.metrolisboa.pt) has four lines, blue (*azul*), green (*verde*), red (*vermelha*), and yellow (*amarela*); tickets cost €0.90/1.20 each (for central/all zones). The metro runs between 6.30am and 1am.

Tram and bus Trams and buses (Ⓦ www.carris.pt) are the most enjoyable way of getting around. Tram #25 to Prazeres. Tickets cost €1.50 when bought on board, except for tram #28 which costs €2.50.

Transport passes The rechargeable Viva Viagem card (€0.50, added to first purchase), available from all metro stations, is the cheapest, most convenient way to get around. A 24-hour pass costs €3.95

TRAM #28 TO PRAZERES

The picture-book tram #28 is one of the city's greatest rides, but because it's so popular there are usually queues to get on and most likely only standing room. Built in England in the early twentieth century, the trams are all polished wood and chrome but give a distinctly rough ride up and down Lisbon's steepest streets, at times coming so close to shops that you could almost take a can of sardines off the shelves. From Graça, the tram plunges down through Alfama to the Baixa and up to Prazeres, to the west of the centre. Take care of belongings as pickpockets also enjoy the ride. If you fancy a tram ride without the crowds, try the equally attractive #25, which heads from Casa dos Bicos along the waterfront and up through Lapa and Estrela to Prazeres.

and allows unlimited travel on buses, trams, metro and *elevadores*. The cards can also be loaded with single journeys (singles purchased in a metro station may only be used on the metro).

Taxi A short taxi journey within the city centre shouldn't cost more than €10, but taxis can be hard to find at night – if you're leaving a bar or club book one by phone from Rádio Táxis de Lisboa (Ⓣ218 119 000) or Teletáxis (Ⓣ218 111 100).

Accommodation

Although prices have risen recently, Lisbon still has plenty of small, cheap *pensions*, many of which are around Rua das Portas de Santo Antão and Rua da Glória, and boasts a good selection of well-equipped modern hostels. Accommodation is easy to find outside Easter and midsummer, when prices rise by up to fifty percent. Addresses below written as 53-3°, for example, describe the street number followed by the floor. The following are marked on the map on p.923, unless otherwise stated.

Hostels

Black and White Hostel Rua Alexandre Herculano 39-1°, Avenida Ⓣ213 462 212, Ⓦwww.costta.com Ⓜ Marquês de Pombal. See map, pp.920–921. Small, stylish hostel with a chilled-out atmosphere and friendly staff. Dorms €15.

Goodnight Hostel Rua dos Correeiros 113-2° Ⓣ213 430 139, Ⓦwww.goodnighthostel.com Ⓜ Rossio. Funky, friendly and well-designed hostel in the heart of the Baixa. Dorms €18, twins €50.

Lisbon Lounge Rua de São Nicolau 41, Baixa Ⓣ213 462 061, Ⓦwww.lisbonloungehostel.com Ⓜ Rossio. Upmarket hostel near Rossio with spacious, airy dorms and an impressive kitchen where nightly 3-course meals are served for €9. Dorms €24, twins €64.

Living Lounge Rua do Crucifixo 116-2°, Baixa Ⓣ213 461 078, Ⓦwww.lisbonloungehostel.com Ⓜ Baixa-Chiado. *Lisbon Lounge's* conveniently located sister hostel has huge individually designed rooms, a luggage lift & bike rental are all part of the excellent offer. Dorms €24, twins €64.

Oasis Backpackers' Mansion Rua de Santa Catarina 24, Chiado Ⓣ213 478 044, Ⓦwww.oasislisboa.com Ⓜ Baixa-Chiado. See map, pp.920–921. Lively, well-equipped hostel with its own bar, located below the Miradouro de Santa Catarina. Dorms €19.

Pousada de Juventude de Lisboa Rua Andrade Corvo 46 Ⓣ213 532 696, Ⓦwww.pousadasjuventude.pt Ⓜ Picoas. See map, pp.920–921. Well-run hostel with good facilities, located near Parque Eduardo VII. Dorms €18, en-suite twin €46.

Rossio Hostel Calçada do Carmo 6 Ⓣ213 426 004 Ⓜ Rossio. Immaculately clean, efficiently run and well-designed hostel with large dorms and excellent doubles. Dorms €20, doubles €65.

Travellers House Rua Augusta 89 Ⓣ210 115 922, Ⓦwww.travellershouse.com Ⓜ Baixa-Chiado. Designed by the same folk as *Rossio*, this larger hostel is another slick operator, with nice touches such as personal safes, a library of travel guides and organized events. Dorms €24.

Pensions and hotels

Lisbon Story Guesthouse Largo de São Domingos 18, Baixa Ⓣ211 529 313, Ⓦwww.lisbonstoryguesthouse.com Ⓜ Rossio. Combining the best of hostel and hotel, *Lisbon Story* offers eight simple yet stylish private rooms with a Lisbon theme, a kitchen and a lounge stocked with travel books. Great breakfast. Singles €40, doubles €50.

Pensão Globo Rua do Teixeira 37, Bairro Alto Ⓣ213 462 279, Ⓦwww.pensaoglobo-lisbon.com. Pleasant *pension* with clean, well-renovated rooms in a variety of shapes and sizes. Singles €40, doubles €45–75.

Residencial Alegria Praça da Alegria 12 Ⓣ213 220 670, Ⓦwww.alegrianet.com Ⓜ Avenida. See map, pp.920–921. Friendly French owners have transformed a standard *residencial* into a comfortable, well-decorated haven in this quiet square. Worth treating yourself. Doubles €70.

Campsites

Camping Obitur-Guincho Lugar da Areia, Guincho ⓣ214 870 450, ⓦwww.orbitur.pt. See map, pp.920–921. A well-located site 12km out of the city in surfer's paradise Guincho, boasting a restaurant, supermarket, and sports facilities. Train from Cais do Sodré to Cascais, then bus to Guincho. €5/person, plus €6.90/tent.

Lisboa Camping Parque Florestal Monsanto ⓣ217 623 100, ⓦwww.lisboacamping.com. See map, pp.920–921. Well-equipped campsite in a large park 6km west of the centre, with pool and shops. The entrance is on Estrada da Circunvalação on the park's west side. Bus #43 from Cais do Sodré. €7/person, plus €5/tent.

Eating

Lisbon has some great cafés and restaurants serving large portions of food at reasonable prices, although these are creeping upwards. Lunch is particularly good value, with plenty of bargain dishes of the day and set menus on offer. Alongside the usual Portuguese restaurants serving grilled meat and fish, there are lots of seafood places, and inexpensive restaurants featuring food from Portugal's former colonies (including Angola, Goa and Macau). Many restaurants are closed on Sundays. The best food market is Mercado da Ribeira, Av 24 de Julho, Cais do Sodré (Mon–Sat 10am–11pm).

Cafés

Antiga Confeitaria de Belém Rua de Belém 90, Belém. See map, pp.920–921. Historic café famous for its delicious *pastéis de nata* (€0.95) – better than all the imitations.

Café Royale Largo Rafael Bordalo Pinheiro 29. See map, p.923. Cosy but chic Chiado café with light home-cooked meals and indulgent treats such as the chocolate and macadamiacrêpe (€3.75).

Cafetaria Quadrante Centro Cultural de Belém. See map, pp.920–921. The cultural complex's self-service café serves hearty salads by weight (€1.65/100g), with the bonus of a large terrace by the Tejo.

Pois Café Rua São João da Praça 93, Baixa. See map, p.923. Eclectically furnished café with a relaxed atmosphere and plenty of international books and papers to peruse. Serves brunch, quiche (€6.50), sandwiches and daily specials (including vegetarian options). Closed Mon.

Santini Rua do Carmo 9, Chiado. See map, p.923. Italian-American-style ice-cream parlour serving divine home-made flavours. Pay before ordering.

Restaurants

Adamastor Rua Marechal Saldanha 24. See map, p.923. Cheerful place with some outdoor seats serving up cheap Portuguese dishes. Closed Sun. Roast chicken €6.

Bom Jardim Trav. De Santo Antão 11–18. See map, pp.920–921. A bit of a Lisbon institution thanks to its spit-roast chickens and now so popular that it has spread into three buildings on either side of a pedestrianized alley. There are a few tables outside, too. Half-chickens are €6; other mains are slightly pricer. Daily noon–11.30pm.

LX Factory Rua Rodrigues de Faria 103. See map, pp.920–921. Former factory canteen serving tasty tapas-style treats (such as goat's cheesecrêpe with apple and raisins in port sauce) and creative mains. Many dishes are cooked in the huge wood-fired oven.

Cantinho do Bem Estar Rua do Norte 46, Bairro Alto. See map, p.923. The service may be erratic, but this tiny place is great value for money – its portions of Portuguese classics (around €12.50) feed two with ease. Go early.

Celeiro Rua 1 de Dezembro 65. See map, p.923. Just off Rossio, this inexpensive self-service restaurant sits in the basement of a health-food supermarket and offers tasty vegetarian spring rolls, quiches, pizza and the like from around €6. There's also a streetside café offering drinks and snacks. Mon–Sat noon–6pm, café 8am–6pm.

Delhi Pleasures Rua da Padaria 18. See map, p.923. Friendly, excellent-value Indian restaurant near the Sé, offering a varied menu of curry classics from €7. Try the cumin-spiced rice.

Esperança Rua do Norte 95, Bairro Alto. See map, p.923. Trendy trattoria with an extensive and reasonably priced menu of pasta, pizza and risotto. Wine is also good value. Pizza from €8.

Jardim das Cerejas Calçado do Sacramento 36. See map, p.923. Vegetarian restaurant with a tasty buffet of hot dishes, soup and salads. Fill up for €7.50 at lunch, €9.50 in the evening. Closed Sun.

Rei d'Frango Calçada do Duque 5, Baixa. See map, p.923. A bargain in the Baixa, this workers' café serves up plentiful portions of Portuguese dishes such as grilled sardines and chicken. Lunchtime dishes of the day are only €5. Closed Sun.

Restô do Chapitô Rua Costa do Castelo 7, Castelo. See map, p.923. Two-in-one venue, with tapas and barbecued meat served in a buzzing courtyard, and more expensive international dishes on offer in the upstairs restaurant. Both have excellent river views. Dinner only.

Stasha Rua das Gaveas 33, Bairro Alto. See map, p.923. Quirky place with indoor streetlamps and friendly staff. The menu is international, with a variety of well-priced meat, fish and vegetarian options. Grilled salmon with sesame seeds and wild mushroom risotto is a bargain at €8.

Drinking and nightlife

The densest concentration of bars and clubs is in Bairro Alto. In summer, crowds spill out of bars and into the streets, creating a festive atmosphere. More expensive late-night action can be found in the Docas (Docklands) district, just east of the 25 de Abril bridge (take tram #15), where the Doca de Alcântara and the Doca de Santo Amaro (further from the city) house waterfront bars and clubs in converted warehouses. Lisbon's gay scene centres around Praça do Príncipe Real in the north of Bairro Alto. Clubs don't really get going until at least 2am and tend to stay open till 6am. Admission fees range from €10 to €20 (usually including a drink).

Bars

A Ginjinha Largo de São Domingos 8, Baixa. See map, p.923. The original *ginjinha* (cherry brandy) bar, this small stand-up place located in lively Largo de São Domingos is a great place to start a night out in Lisbon. *Ginjinha* €0.90.

Clube da Esquina Rua da Barroca 30–32, Bairro Alto. See map, p.923. Popular bar with a chilled-out atmosphere. Old radios decorate the walls; diverse punters prop up the bar.

Favela Chik Ruado Diário de Notícias 66, Bairro Alto. See map, p.923. Funky and friendly little bar with great cocktails and a DJ spinning old-school tunes.

Instituto do Vinho do Porto Rua de São Pedro de Alcântara 45, Bairro Alto. See map, p.923. Over 200 types of port, from €1 a glass. Closed Sun.

Pavilhão Chinês Rua Dom Pedro V 89, Bairro Alto. See map, pp.920–921. Ideal for a chic cocktail, this famous (and pricey) drinking den is decorated with a unique selection of kitsch artefacts.

Portas Largas Rua da Atalaia 105, Bairro Alto. See map, p.923. "Big doors" is a popular spot for a pre-club *caipirinha* or two.

Clubs

Buddha Bar Rua Gare M Alcântara. See map, pp.920–921. The pick of the docklands nightspots, boasting a roof terrace with views of the 25 de Abril bridge.

Kapital Av 24 de Julho 68, opposite Santos station. See map, pp.920–921. Smart club popular with trendy (and wealthy) young Lisboetas.

Kremlin Escadinhas da Praia 5. See map, pp.920–921. Down on the docklands, this former clubbing destination remains the place to head for house tunes. Closed Sun.

Lux Av Infante Dom Henrique Armázem A, opposite Santa Apolónia station. ⓦwww.luxfragil.com. See map, pp.920–921. The city's best and most fashionable club, often hosting top DJs. Closed Mon.

Trumps Rua da Imprensa Nacional 104b, Rato ⓦwww.trumps.pt. See map, pp.920–921. The biggest gay venue in Lisbon. Closed Mon.

Entertainment

To hear some *fado* (see below), head for Bairro Alto, where many restaurants put on performances (from €15 upwards, including dinner). What's-on listings can be found in the monthly *Agenda Cultural*, available free at tourist offices, or at ⓦlisbon.angloinfo.com.

Fado and live music

A Baiuca Rua de São Miguel 20, Alfama. See map, p.923. Tiny bar/restaurant with a family atmosphere and *fado vadio* (amateur) performances.

A Tasca do Chico Rua do Diário de Noticíias 39. See map, p.923. Make like the locals and catch

FADO

Difficult to classify but often described as falling somewhere between the blues and flamenco, the emotional and melodramatic musical genre of **fado** (literally "fate") is as typically Portuguese as custard tarts and Cristiano Ronaldo. *Fado* has its roots in early nineteenth-century Alfama, where it thrived until the early twentieth century, when it was subject to censorship. Despite the authorities' efforts, the genre continued to develop, and still features in the charts today thanks to a new generation of performers. Lisbon is the best place to hear *fado*, although Coimbra also has its own style (see p.931). To get the most out of a show, first visit the modern **Museu do Fado** at Largo do Chafariz de Dentro 1 (daily except Mon 10am–6pm; €4), which gives an excellent audioguide introduction to the history of the genre and its brightest stars, including *grande dame* Amália Rodrigues and rising talent Joana Amendoeira.

some amateur *fado* in this bar on Mon and Wed. Free entry.

Catacumbas Jazz Bar Travessa da Água da Flor 43, Bairro Alto. See map, p.923. Popular little bar with jazz, blues and Brazilian beats concerts from Mon–Thurs.

Music Box Rua Nova do Carvalho 24 Ⓦwww.musicboxlisboa.com. See map, p.923. Live music venue near Cais do Sodré, with a schedule packed full of DJs and bands playing almost every musical style imaginable.

Shopping

The trendy Bairro Alto shops tend to open from early afternoon until midnight; elsewhere, opening hours are standard.

A Vida Portuguesa Rua Anchieta 11, Baixa. From tiles to sardines, if it's Portuguese, you'll find it here.

El Dorado Rua do Norte 23, Bairro Alto. Funky store with a great selection of vintage and new clothes and music.

Mercado da Ribeira Av 24 de Julho, Cais do Sodré. The city's main food market, which is also home to a variety of craft stores.

Outra Face da Lua Rua da Assunçao 22, Baixa. Vintage emporium stocking a mishmash of goodies, from clothing to toys. There's also an in-store café.

Directory

Embassies Australia, Av da Liberdade 198-2° ⓣ213 101 500; Canada, Av da Liberdade 196–200 ⓣ213 164 600; Ireland, Rua da Imprensa à Estrela 1-4° ⓣ213 929 440; South Africa, Av Luis Bívar 10 ⓣ213 535 713; UK, Rua de São Bernardo 33 ⓣ213 924 000; US, Av das Forças Armadas ⓣ217 273 300.

Exchange Main bank branches in the Baixa. Exchange office at the airport (24hr) and at Santa Apolónia station (daily 8.30am–3pm).

Hospital British Hospital, Rua Saraiva de Carvalho 46 ⓣ213 955 067.

Internet PT Comunicaçoes, Praça Dom Pedro IV 68, Baixa.

Left luggage Available at Oriente and Santa Apolónia stations.

Pharmacy Throughout the city, including Farmácia Estácio, Rossio Square (Mon–Sat 9am–1pm & 2.30–7pm).

Post office Praça do Comércio.

Tourist police Praça dos Restauradores.

Moving on

Train Braga (13 daily; 3hr 30min–4hr 30min); Coimbra (17 daily; 2hr–2hr 45min); Faro (4 daily; 3hr 20min–4hr); Madrid (nightly; 11hr 30min); Porto (hourly; 2hr 45min–3hr 10min); Sintra (every 20min; 40min); Tavira (4 daily; 4hr 30min–5hr 30min); Tomar (hourly; 2hr).

Bus Alcobaça (7 daily; 2hr); Coimbra (hourly; 2hr 20min); Évora (hourly; 1hr 30min); Faro (12 daily; 4hr); Lagos (7–10 daily; 4hr–4hr 30min); Madrid (3 daily; 7hr 45min–11hr 30min); Porto (hourly; 3hr 30min–4hr); Porto Côvo (2–3 daily; 3hr 30min); Sevilla (6 weekly; 7hr); Tomar (2–4 daily; 1hr 45min–2hr); Vila Nova de Milfontes (3–4 daily; 3hr 30min–4hr).

BEACHES AROUND LISBON

The coast around Lisbon offers ample opportunities to escape from the summer heat of the capital. Half an hour south of Lisbon, dunes stretch along the **COSTA DA CAPARICA**, a thoroughly Portuguese resort popular with surfers and crammed with restaurants and beach cafés. Solitude is easy enough to find though, thanks to the **transpraia** (mini-railway) that runs along the 8km of dunes in summer. Take the ferry from Cais do Sodré to Cacilhas (every 10 min; €0.81), then the 135 TST bus (every 20 min; €2.75). Buses stop along Rua dos Pescadores by the beach, which leads to the main square, Praça da Liberdade.

Another popular seaside escape is the former fishing village of **CASCAIS**, forty minutes to the west of the city, which boasts three beaches and a campsite (see p.926). To get here, take the train from Cais do Sodré (every 20–30min; €1.70). Cascais has a particular appeal to surfers due to its proximity to Guincho beach (see box, p.915), reached by local bus, which has hosted the World Surfing Championships.

SINTRA

The cool, hilltop woodland setting of **SINTRA** once attracted Moorish lords and the Portuguese kings from Lisbon during the summer months, and the palaces they constructed remain among Portugal's most spectacular attractions. Sintra is best seen on a day-trip from

Lisbon, as its hotels and restaurants are pretty pricey. That said, there are certainly enough sights to keep you occupied for several days. Combined tickets bring the price of admission to the sights down; enquire at the tourist office for the latest offers.

What to see and do

An amalgamation of three villages, Sintra can be confusing, but there are plenty of local buses connecting the sights.

Palácio Nacional

The **Palácio Nacional** (daily except Wed 10am–5.30pm; €7; free Sun until 2pm), about fifteen minutes' walk from the train station, is an obvious landmark, with its distinctive conical chimneys. The palace probably existed under the Moors, but takes its present form from the rebuilding commissioned by Dom João I and his successor, Dom Manuel, in the fourteenth and fifteenth centuries. Its style is a fusion of Gothic and the latter king's Manueline additions. The **chapel** and its adjoining chamber are well worth seeing, as is the curious Magpies Room, decorated with hundreds of paintings of the birds with the motto "*Por Bem*" ("For the good") in their beaks.

Quinta da Regaleira

Also within walking distance of the centre is another must-see site, the beautiful **Quinta da Regaleira** (daily: Feb, March & Oct 10am–6.30pm; April–Sept 10am–8pm; Nov–Jan 10am–5.30pm; €6, or €10 for guided visits booked in advance on ⓣ219 106 650). One of Sintra's most elaborate private estates, it lies ten minutes' walk west of the Palácio Nacional on the Seteais–Monserrate road. The house and its fantastic gardens were built at the beginning of the twentieth century by an Italian theatrical set designer for one of the richest industrialists in Portugal. One highlight is the **Initiation Well**, inspired by the initiation practices of the Knights Templar and Freemasons. The vast gardens are full of surprising delights, with chapels, follies and fountains at every turn.

Monserrate

Beyond Quinta da Regaleira, the road leads past a series of beautiful private estates to recently renovated **Monserrate** (park 9.30am–8pm; palace 9.30am–12.45 pm & 2–6.45pm; €6) – about an hour's walk – a Moorish-style folly of a palace whose 30-hectare **garden**, filled with exotic trees and subtropical shrubs and plants, extends as far as the eye can see.

Moorish castle and Palácio de Pena

Two of Sintra's main sights can be reached on bus #434 – the €4.80 ticket allows you to hop on and off at each one. Starting at the train station, the bus stops outside the Praça da República tourist office before proceeding to the ruined ramparts of the **Castelo dos Mouros** (Moorish castle; daily 9.30am–7pm; €6), from where the views over the town and surrounding countryside are extraordinary. Further on, the bus stops at both entrances to the immense **Pena Park**, at the top end of which rears the fabulous **Palácio da Pena** (Tues–Sun April–Sept 10am–7pm; Oct–March 10am–5.30pm; €9), a wild, nineteenth-century fantasy of domes, towers and a drawbridge that doesn't draw. The cluttered, kitschy interior has been preserved as left by the royal family on their flight from Portugal in 1910.

Arrival and information

Train Trains run every 20min to Sintra from Lisbon's Rossio station (40min; €4.20 return).

Tourist office There's one tourist office at the station, and a larger one (daily 9am–7/8pm; ⓣ219 231 157) just off the central Praça da República.

Accommodation and eating

Casa Piriquita Rua das Padarias 1. Cosy café just south of Praça da República, serving snacks and Sintra's famous *queijadas* (cheese cakes). Sandwiches from €3.

Estrada Velha Rua Consiglieri Pedroso 16. On the road to the Quinta da Regaleira, this good-value café serves sandwiches (from €2), crêpes and other snacks.

Piela's Av Desiderio Cambournac 1 ⓣ219 241 691, ⓦwww.cafepielas.com Pleasant *pension* in Estefania, above central Sintra. Singles €45, doubles €55.

Central Portugal

The Beiras, Estremadura and Ribatejo regions that comprise central Portugal have played crucial roles in each phase of the nation's history – and the monuments are here to prove it. The vast plains of the Beiras are dominated by **Coimbra**, an ancient university town and Portugal's former capital, perched high above the Beira Litoral. Below the Beiras lie Estremadura and Ribatejo, both comparatively small areas of fertile rolling hills, which boast an extraordinary concentration of vivid architecture and engaging towns. **Alcobaça** in Estremadura and **Tomar** in the wine-producing Ribatejo are two of the most striking, both housing famously grand religious monuments.

ALCOBAÇA

The pretty town of **Alcobaça** is dominated by the vast, beautiful **Mosteiro de Santa Maria de Alcobaça** (daily: April–Sept 9am–7pm; Oct–March 9am–5pm; €5, free Sun until 2pm). From its foundation in 1147 until its dissolution in 1834, this Cistercian monastery was one of the greatest in the world. Its **church** (free) is one of the largest in Portugal, with a Baroque facade that conceals an interior stripped of most of its later adornments and restored to its original simplicity. The monastery's most precious treasures are the fourteenth-century **tombs** of Dom Pedro and Dona Inês de Castro, sculpted with incredible detail to illustrate the story of Pedro's love for Inês, the daughter of a Galician nobleman. Pedro's father, Afonso V, forbade their marriage, which nevertheless took place in secret. Afonso ordered Inês's murder, and Pedro waited for his succession to the throne before exhuming her corpse and forcing the royal circle to acknowledge her as queen by kissing her decomposing hand. Their tombs have been placed foot to foot so that on Judgement Day, the lovers may rise and immediately see one another. The monastery's most impressive room is the **kitchen**, featuring a gigantic conical chimney, and a stream tapped from the river to provide Alcobaça's famously gluttonous monks with a constant supply of fresh fish.

Arrival and information

Bus Alcobaça's bus station is 5min walk from the monastery in the centre of town, across the bridge.

Tourist office Opposite the monastery on Praça 25 de Abril (daily 10am–1pm & 2/3–6/7pm; ⓣ262 582 377).

Accommodation and eating

Parque de Campismo Av Professor Vieira Natividade ⓣ262 582 265. Small municipal site 10min north of the bus station. Closed Jan. €4/person.

Pensão Corações Unidos Rua Frei António Brandão 39 ⓣ262 582 142. Neat, clean *pension* with modern bathrooms facing the monastery. The restaurant below the *pensão* serves good-value regional cooking. Singles €35, doubles €45.

Ti Fininho Rua Frei António Brandão 34. Offers reasonably priced grilled fish and meats, omelettes, and wine by the jug.

Moving on

Bus Coimbra (1 daily; 2hr 30min); Tomar (3 daily; 2hr).

TOMAR

Riverside **TOMAR** is famous for its spectacular headquarters of the Portuguese branch of the Knights Templar, which overlooks the town from a wooded hill. It's also an attractive town in its own right – especially during the lively **Festa dos Tabuleiros**, a festival of music and dancing, held the first week in July.

What to see and do

Built on a simple grid plan, Tomar's centre preserves its traditional charm, with whitewashed houses lining narrow cobbled streets. West of the central Praça da República is the former Jewish quarter, where at Rua Joaquim Jacinto 73 you'll find an excellently preserved fourteenth-century synagogue, now the **Museu Luso-Hebraicoa Abraham Zacuto** (daily 10am–1pm & 2–6pm; free), one of the few surviving synagogues in Portugal. There's a bit of contemporary interest at **NAM** (Rua Gil de Avô; Tues–Sun; Nov–March 10am–5pm; April–Sept until 7pm; free) a three-floor modern art gallery exhibiting works mostly by Portuguese artists. A fifteen-minute walk uphill from the town centre, the **Convento de Cristo** (daily: June–Sept 9am–6pm; Oct–May 9am–5pm; €5) is set among pleasant gardens with excellent views of the surrounding woodland. Founded in 1162 by Gualdim Pais, first Master of the Knights Templar, it was the Order's headquarters. At the heart of the complex, surrounded by serene cloisters, is the **Charola**, the high-ceilinged, sixteen-sided temple from which the knights drew their moral conviction. The beautiful adjoining two-tiered **Principal Cloister** is one of the purest examples of the Renaissance style in Portugal.

Arrival and information

Train and bus The stations are located next to each other on Av dos Combatentes de Grande Guerra, 10min south of the town centre.

Tourist office At the top of Av Dr Cândido Madureira (April–Sept Mon–Fri 10am–7pm, Sat & Sun 10am–1pm & 2–6pm; Oct–March daily 10am–1pm & 2–6pm).

Accommodation

Café Paraiso Rua Serpa Pinto 127. A Tomar institution with mirrored walls and a quirky vibe, ideal for a drink at any time of day.

Parque de Campismo ⓣ249 329 824. Tomar's campsite is a short walk east of Rua Marquês de Pombal. €4/person, plus €5/tent.

Residencial União Rua Serpa Pinto 94 ⓣ249 323 161. Faded but passable *pension* on the main street. Good breakfast. Singles €35, doubles €45.

Eating

Restaurante O Tabuleiro Rua Serpa Pinto 148. Friendly restaurant offering a daily menu of delicious regional dishes, served in large portions. *Arroz de peixe* €6.80.

Moving on

Train Coimbra (2 daily; 2hr 30min); Lisbon (15 daily; 2hr).

Bus Alcobaça (3 daily; 2hr); Porto (1 daily; 4hr).

COIMBRA

COIMBRA was Portugal's capital from 1143 to 1255 and ranks behind only Lisbon and Porto in historic importance. Its university, founded in 1290, was the only one in Portugal until the beginning of the twentieth century.

What to see and do

For a provincial town Coimbra has significant architectural riches. Its many students create a rather vivacious atmosphere during term time – especially in May, when they celebrate the end of the academic year with the **Queima das Fitas**, a symbolic tearing or burning of their gowns and faculty ribbons followed by some serious partying. This is when you're most likely to hear the Coimbra *fado*, distinguished from the Lisbon version by its mournful pace and complex lyrics. During the summer months, the atmosphere is rather more subdued.

The old town

Old Coimbra sits on a hill on the right bank of the River Mondego, with the university crowning its summit. The main buildings of the **Old University** (March–Oct daily 9am–7pm; Nov–Feb Mon–Fri 9am–5pm, Sat & Sun 10am–4pm; €7), dating from the sixteenth century, are set around a courtyard (entrance free) dominated by a Baroque clock tower and a statue of João III. The **chapel** is covered with *azulejos* and intricate decoration, but takes second place to the **library**, a Baroque fantasy with *trompe-l'oeil* ceilings. It also has some unusual inhabitants: a colony of bats. Other areas included in the visit are the graduation hall and the academic prison. Halfway down the hill towards the centre stands the solid and simple **Sé Velha** (Old Cathedral; Mon–Thurs 10am–1pm & 2–6pm, Fri 10am–1pm, Sat 10am–5pm; €2), one of Portugal's most important Romanesque buildings.

Central Coimbra

Restraint and simplicity certainly aren't the chief qualities of the flamboyant **Igreja de Santa Cruz** (Mon–Fri 7.30am–6.30pm, Sat 7.30am–12.30pm & 2–7.30pm, Sun 8.30am–12.30pm & 4–7.30pm; €2.50), at the bottom of the hill on Praça 8 de Maio. It houses the tombs of Portugal's first kings, Afonso Henriques and Sancho I, and an elaborately carved pulpit.

Across the river, the beautifully restored convent of **Santa Clara a Velha** (Tues–Sun; May–Oct 10am–7pm; Nov–April 10am–5pm; €5) is worth seeing now you have the chance: a century ago, it had all but disappeared under the rising tide of the Mondego. The nuns moved to higher and higher floors before abandoning the convent for **Santa Clara a Nova** up the hill in 1677. There's now a visitor centre detailing life in medieval Portugal as well as a film of the restoration process (with English subtitles).

Other areas of interest include the epicentre of the students' social scene, **Praça da República**, a ten-minute walk from Praça 8 de Maio up Rua Olímpio Nicolau Rui Fernandes, and the rambling **Botanic Garden** (Mon–Sat: April–Sept 9am–8pm; Oct–March 9am–5.30pm; €1.50) which sits in the shadow of the sixteenth-century **aqueduct** to the east of Praça da República.

Arrival and information

Train Intercity trains stop at Coimbra B, 3km north of the city, from where there are frequent connecting services to Coimbra A in the town centre.
Bus The bus station is on Av Fernão de Magalhães, 15min walk from the centre – turn right out of the bus station and head down the main road. Some buses from the north stop on Av Emídio Navarro.
City transport The main hub for Coimbra's local buses is Av Emídio Navarro near train station A. A one-way journey paid for on board costs €1.50; 3 tickets bought in advance at a newsstand cost €2.20. Bus #1, #3, #7, #8, #10 and #11 run from here to Praça da República.
Tourist office Opposite the bridge on Largo da Portagem (Mon–Fri 9.30am–1pm & 2–5.30pm, Sat & Sun 10am–1pm & 2.30–5.30pm; ⓣ239 488 120, ⓦwww.turismodecoimbra.pt).

Accommodation

Casa Pombal Rua das Flores 8 ⓣ239 835 175, ⓦwww.casapombal.com. The only accommodation option in the old town is this quirky, comfortable *residencial* run by a friendly, helpful owner. Great breakfast. Doubles €50.
Grande Hostel de Coimbra Rua Antero de Quental 196 ⓣ239 108 212, ⓦwww.grandehostelcoimbra.com. Hippyish hostel near Praça da República, set in a big old house with a garden, lounge and kitchen. A good place to meet fellow travellers. Dorms €18, doubles €40.
Pousada de Juventude Rua Henrique Seco 14 ⓣ239 822 955, ⓦwww.pousadasjuventude.pt. Basic but cheap hostel 10min north of Praça da República. Buses #7 and #29 from Av Emídio Navarro pass close by. Dorms €12, twins €28.

Eating, drinking and nightlife

Most of the town's restaurants can be found tucked away in the alleys between Largo da Portagem – the place to head for cafés – and Praça 8 de Maio.

Adega Paço do Conde Rua Paço do Conde 1. Atmospheric, locally renowned *churrasqueira* serving tasty barbecued meat and fish. Meat and vegetable skewer €7.
Associação Académica de Coimbra Praça da República. If you can befriend a student and tag along, you'll get access to the outdoor union bar, a lively place serving snacks and bargain drinks (beer €1).
Café Tropical Praça da República. A favourite haunt of students, with outdoor tables and cheap drinks. Closed Sun.
Jardim da Manga Rua Olímpio Nicolau Rui Fernandes. Self-service café serving up good-value meals in a pretty spot.
Justiça e Paz Bar Rua Couraça de Lisboa 30. The law faculty's canteen offers a cheap no-frills lunch, with meat, fish and vegetarian options. €4.50.
Via Latina Rua Almeida Garrett 1. Popular club playing international hits. Tues–Sat from midnight onwards.

Moving on

Train Lisbon (hourly; 2–3hr); Porto (hourly; 1hr 20min–2hr); Tomar (2 daily; 2hr 30min).
Bus Alcobaça (2 daily; 2hr 30min); Lisbon (hourly; 2hr 20min); Porto (8–10 daily; 1hr 30min).

Northern Portugal

Porto, the country's second largest city, is an attractive and convenient centre from which to explore this region. Magnificently set on a rocky cliff astride the River Douro, it is perhaps most famous for the port-producing suburb of **Vila Nova de Gaia**, supplied by vineyards further inland along the river. The **Douro Valley** is traced by a spectacular rail route, with branch lines following valleys north along the River Tâmega to **Amarante** and along the Corgo to the pretty town of **Vila Real** – a good base for exploration of the Parque Natural do Alvão, and the main centre for transport connections into the isolated rural region of **Trás-os-Montes** – literally "behind the mountains". In the northwest, the **Minho**, considered by many to be the most beautiful part of the country, is a lush wilderness of rolling mountain forests and rugged coastlines (the Costa Verde), with some of the most unspoilt beaches in Europe. A quietly conservative region, its towns have a special charm and beauty, among them the religious centre of **Braga**, and the self-proclaimed birthplace of the nation, **Guimarães**, both of which can be visited by day-trip from Porto, but also make good bases from which to explore the rest of the Minho.

PORTO

Capital of the north, **PORTO** (sometimes called "Oporto" in English) is very different from Lisbon – unpretentious and unashamedly commercial, yet extremely welcoming. As the local saying goes: "Coimbra sings; Braga prays; Lisbon shows off; and Porto works." Already possessing considerable appeal, the city received something of a makeover thanks to funding received for Euro 2004, and now boasts an efficient metro system, state-of-the-art football stadium and a top concert venue, the Casa da Música.

What to see and do

The waterfront Ribeira district is Porto's historic heart, with narrow, winding alleys so picturesque that the area has been declared a UNESCO World Heritage Site. **Boat trips** up the Douro (around €10) depart regularly from Cais da Estiva and, across the river, Cais de Gaia, and are a great way to observe Porto's beauty.

Ribeira

Despite being Porto's most touristy quarter, life in the **Ribeira** continues unaffected by visitors, as a wander through its alleyways will soon reveal.

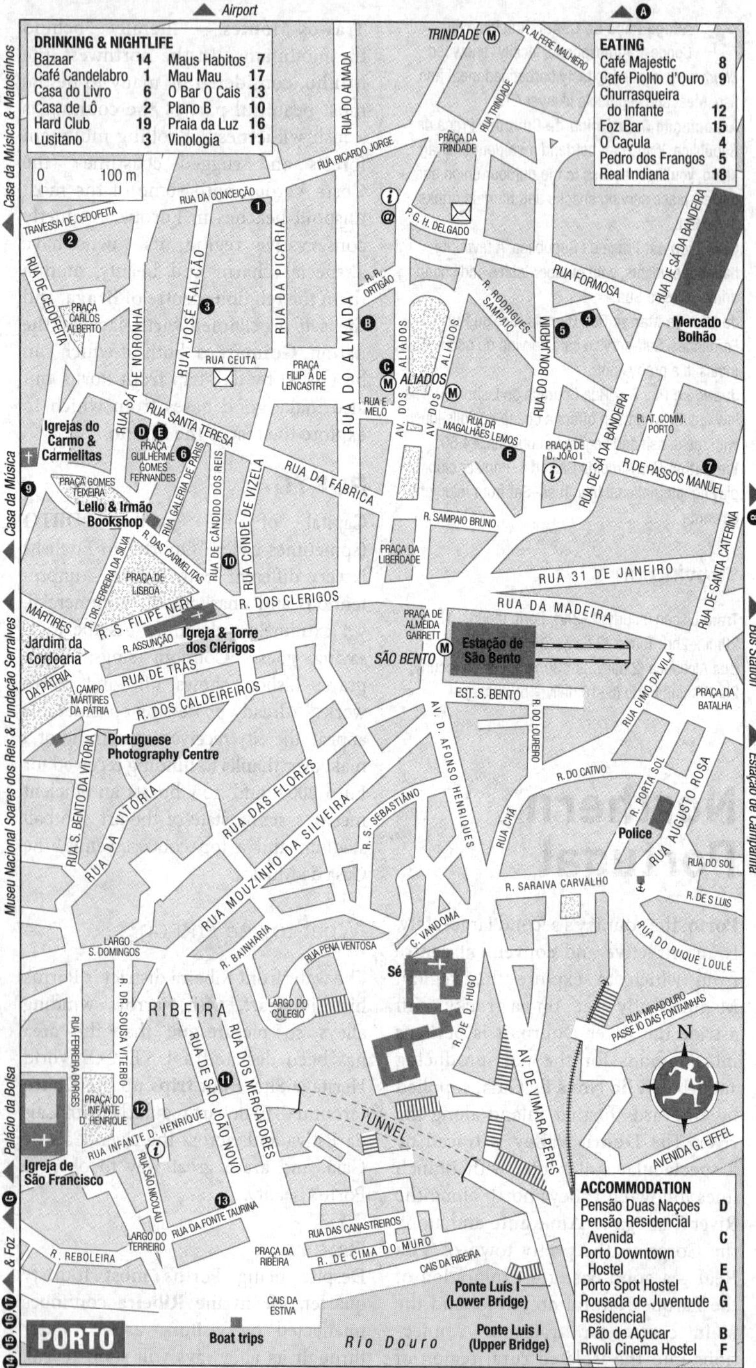
PORTO
DRINKING & NIGHTLIFE
Bazaar 14
Café Candelabro 1
Casa do Livro 6
Casa de Lô 2
Hard Club 19
Lusitano 3
Maus Habitos 7
Mau Mau 17
O Bar O Cais 13
Plano B 10
Praia da Luz 16
Vinologia 11
EATING
Café Majestic 8
Café Piolho d'Ouro 9
Churrasqueira do Infante 12
Foz Bar 15
O Caçula 4
Pedro dos Frangos 5
Real Indiana 18
ACCOMMODATION
Pensão Duas Naçoes D
Pensão Residencial Avenida C
Porto Downtown Hostel E
Porto Spot Hostel A
Pousada de Juventude G
Residencial Pão de Açucar B
Rivoli Cinema Hostel F
0 100 m
Airport
A
Casa da Música & Matosinhos
Casa da Música
Museu Nacional Soares dos Reis & Fundação Serralves
Palácio da Bolsa
G
& Foz
14, 15, 16, 17
Bus Station
Estação de Campanhã
8
Port Lodges, 18 & 19
Vila Nova de Gaia
TRINDADE
R. ALFERE MALHIERO
RUA TRINDADE
PRAÇA DA TRINDADE
RUA DO ALMADA
RUA RICARDO JORGE
RUA DA CONCEIÇÃO
TRAVESSA DE CEDOFEITA
P. G. H. DELGADO
RUA FORMOSA
RUA DE SÁ DA BANDEIRA
Mercado Bolhão
RUA DE CEDOFEITA
PRAÇA CARLOS ALBERTO
RUA DE JOSÉ FALCÃO
RUA DA PICARIA
R. R. ORTIGÃO
R. RODRIGUES SAMPAIO
RUA DO BONJARDIM
AV. DOS ALIADOS
RUA SÁ DE NORONHA
RUA CEUTA
PRAÇA FILIP A DE LENCASTRE
RUA DO ALMADA
ALIADOS
RUA E. MELO
RUA DR MAGALHÃES LEMOS
R. AT. COMM. PORTO
RUA SANTA TERESA
Igrejas do Carmo & Carmelitas
PRAÇA GUILHERME GOMES FERNANDES
RUA DA FÁBRICA
PRAÇA DE D. JOÃO I
R DE PASSOS MANUEL
PRAÇA GOMES TEIXEIRA
Lello & Irmão Bookshop
RUA GALERIA DE PARIS
RUA DE CÂNDIDO DOS REIS
RUA CONDE DE VIZELA
R. SAMPAIO BRUNO
RUA DE SANTA CATERINA
R. DAS CARMELITAS
PRAÇA DE LISBOA
R. DR. FERREIRA DA SILVA
PRAÇA DA LIBERDADE
RUA 31 DE JANEIRO
R. DOS CLERIGOS
RUA DA MADEIRA
MÁRTIRES
R. S. FILIPE NERY
Igreja & Torre dos Clérigos
PRAÇA DE ALMEIDA GARRETT
Estação de São Bento
Jardim da Cordoaria
R. ASSUNÇÃO
SÃO BENTO
RUA DE TRÁS
DA PÁTRIA
CAMPO MÁRTIRES DA PÁTRIA
R. DOS CALDEIREIROS
EST. S. BENTO
RUA CIMO DA VILA
PRAÇA DA BATALHA
AV. D. AFONSO HENRIQUES
R. DO LOUREIRO
Portuguese Photography Centre
RUA S. BENTO DA VITÓRIA
RUA DA VITÓRIA
RUA DAS FLORES
R. S. SEBASTIÃO
R. DO CATIVO
R. PORTA SOL
RUA AUGUSTO ROSA
RUA MOUZINHO DA SILVEIRA
RUA CHÃ
Police
RUA DO SOL
R. SARAIVA CARVALHO
R. DE S LUIS
RUA DO DUQUE LOULÉ
C. VANDOMA
LARGO S. DOMINGOS
R. BAINHARIA
RUA PENA VENTOSA
Sé
R. DE D. HUGO
LARGO DO COLEGIO
RIBEIRA
RUA MIRADOURO
PASSE IO DAS FONTAINHAS
N
RUA FERREIRA BORGES
R. DR. SOUSA VITERBO
RUA DE SÃO JOÃO NOVO
RUA DOS MERCADORES
AV. DE VIMARA PERES
PRAÇA DO INFANTE D. HENRIQUE
TUNNEL
RUA INFANTE D. HENRIQUE
AVENIDA G. EIFFEL
Igreja de São Francisco
RUA SÃO NICOLAU
RUA DA FONTE TAURINA
LARGO DO TERREIRO
RUA DAS CANASTREIROS
R. REBOLEIRA
PRAÇA DA RIBEIRA
R. DE CIMA DO MURO
CAIS DA RIBEIRA
Ponte Luís I (Lower Bridge)
CAIS DA ESTIVA
Boat trips
Rio Douro
Ponte Luís I (Upper Bridge)

The district is also home to many restaurants and bars, as well as the extraordinary **Igreja de São Francisco** on Rua Infante Dom Henrique (daily: March, April & Oct 9am–6pm; June–Sept 9am–7pm; Nov–Feb 9am–5.30pm; €3.50 including museum). Now deconsecrated, its rather plain facade conceals a fabulously opulent, gold-covered interior, refurbished in the eighteenth century. Around the corner on Rua Ferreira Borges is the **Palácio da Bolsa** (Stock Exchange; daily: April–Oct 9am–6.30pm; Nov–March 9am–12.30pm & 2–5.30pm; €7), which ceased trading a few years ago and now offers informative tours every half-hour. The highlight is the ornate *Salão Arabe* (Arab Room), its Moorish style emulating that of the Alhambra palace in Granada, Spain.

Cordoaria to Mercado de Bolhão

The **Museu Nacional Soares dos Reis** at Rua Dom Manuel II (Tues 2–6pm, Wed–Sun 10am–6pm; €5, free Sun 10am–2pm) lies a few minutes' walk west of Aliados, in the Cordoaria area. It was Portugal's first national museum, and contains an impressive selection of works by home-grown artists. The museum is named after local nineteenth-century sculptor António Soares dos Reis, and it's here that you'll find his *O Desterrado* ("The Exiled"), probably the best-known work in Portugal. There's also a vast collection of applied and decorative arts. A short walk away in Campo Mártires da Pátria, you'll find the **Centro Português de Fotografia** (Portuguese Photography Centre; Tues–Fri 10am–12.30pm & 3–6pm, Sat & Sun 3–7pm; free), a former prison which now houses changing photography exhibitions. East of the centre, superb views of the city are on offer at the **Torre dos Clérigos** (April–July, Sept & Oct 9.30am–1pm & 2.30–7pm; Aug 10am–7pm; Nov–March 10am–noon & 2–5pm; €2) attached to the Baroque Igreja dos Clérigos. Nearby on Rua das Carmelitas, **Lello & Irmão** bookshop (closed Sun) is worth a quick browse for its stunning Art Nouveau interior (which appears in the *Harry Potter* films), featuring a fabulously ornate staircase, carved wood panelling and stained glass. Downhill from here is the city's biggest boulevard, the transport hub of **Avenida dos Aliados**, a short walk east of which is the **Mercado de Bolhão** which sells fresh produce every day except Sunday, while the city's main shopping area is located a little further east around Rua de Santa Catarina.

Casa da Música

The west of the city is home to some of Portugal's most exciting cultural centres, not to mention some daring architecture. Dominating the Avenida da Boavista and accessible by metro, 3km west of the centre, **Casa da**

PORT

If you thought port was just an after-dinner tipple reserved for stuffy suppers, think again. Port wine comes in a variety of types and ages, as you'll discover on an afternoon tour of Gaia's port lodges. The relatively little-known **white ports** are served as an aperitif, and can be dry or sweet; another refreshing option is Croft's "Pink", which was one of the first **rosé** ports on the market. After dinner come either tawny or ruby ports: nutty-tasting **tawnies** are made from a blend of different barrel-aged wines, while deep red **rubies** age in the bottle. Further varieties include Late Bottled Vintage (**LBV**), made from good-quality grapes gathered in a single harvest and aged for five years, and the crème de la crème, **Vintage** port, which uses only the best grapes from a particularly fine harvest.

Música (Ⓦwww.casadamusica.com) is a vast, irregularly shaped, and strangely beautiful white concrete confection designed by Rem Koolhaas. Concerts are held here almost every night of the year (see website for details), though you can have a peek at its impressive interior for free. For a more in-depth exploration, there are guided tours in English every day at 4pm (€3).

Fundação Serralves

Three kilometres west of Casa da Música is another architectural gem and one of Porto's key attractions, the **Fundação Serralves** (Tues–Sun 10am–5pm, until 8pm Sat & Sun April–Oct; €7, park only €3; free Sun 10am–1pm; bus #201 from Aliados to Avenida Gomes da Costa), which comprises the modernist **Museum of Contemporary Art**, hosting an exciting array of temporary exhibitions by Portuguese and international artists, and the Art Deco **Serralves Villa** (which also hosts occasional exhibitions), set in a vast, beautiful park. If the exhibition isn't to your taste, skip it and head straight for the **park**: encompassing everything from formal gardens to wild woods, and even a farm featuring species from northern Portugal.

Foz do Douro

The coastline at **Foz** makes an easy escape from the city, reached via tram #1 from Rua Nova da Alfândega. The old wooden tram clanks along the coastline to Passeio Alegre, from where you can take a one-hour stroll along the beachside promenade to the curiously named **Castelo do Queijo** (Cheese Castle) before taking bus #502 back to the centre For much of the year the Atlantic Ocean is too chilly for all but the hardiest of swimmers, but the beaches fill up with sun-worshippers once summer rolls round. Foz is also home to a buzzing nightlife scene.

Vila Nova de Gaia

South of the river and essentially a city in its own right, **Vila Nova de Gaia** (usually referred to as Gaia) is dominated by the port trade. From the Ribeira, the names of the various companies, spelled out in neon letters above the terracotta roofs of the wine lodges, leave you in no doubt as to what awaits you. You can walk to Gaia across the **Ponte Dom Luis I**: the most direct route to the lodges is across the lower level from the Cais da Ribeira, but taking the metro across the top level to the Jardim do Morro stop has the bonus of breathtaking views. The lodges offer **tours**, which generally explain the histories of both the company and of port production, and end in a tasting. Croft and Taylor's offer free tours while other companies charge up to €4. Tours conclude with tastings of one or two ports, with more expensive options such as vintage ports available for an extra fee. It's well worth the trek up the hill to Taylor's, as the free tasting includes a Late Bottled Vintage. The tourist information kiosk on Avenida Diogo Leite has the helpful *Caves do Vinho do Porto* leaflet, which outlines timetables and prices of tours. If all this sampling whets your appetite, head to *Vinologia* (see p.938) to learn and taste more.

Arrival and information

Air From the Francisco Sá Carneiro airport, 10km north of the city, take metro line E (€2, including purchase of rechargeable Andante card) to the centre. Service runs until 1am.

Train Most trains from the south stop at the distant Estação de Campanhã; you may need to change here for a connection to the central Estação de São Bento (5min). Metro line B will also take you into the centre from Campanhã.

Bus The main bus terminal (Rede-Expressos) is on Rua Alexandre Herculano, a short walk east of São Bento, while the Rodo Norte terminal Is on Rua de Passos Manuel.

Tourist office The tourist office is just north of Av dos Aliados on Rua Clube dos Fenianos 25 (summer daily 9am–7pm; winter Mon–Fri 9am–5.30pm, Sat & Sun 9am–4.30pm; ⓣ 222 393 472, ⓦ www.portoturismo.pt). There's also a branch (same hours) at Rua do Infante Henrique 63.

Tourist passes All tourism offices sell the Porto Card, which offers free public transport and free or discounted entry to most of the city's sights. Available in 1-, 2-, and 3-day versions (€8.50, €13.50 and €17.50 respectively).

Internet Onweb, Praça Humberto Delgado 291. Just off Av dos Aliados.

Tourist police Rua Clube dos Fenianos 11.

City transport

Tickets The Andante card covers metro, tram, the funicular from opposite the Ponte Luis I to Praça da Batalha, and most bus lines. It costs €0.50, added to the price of your first ticket, and is available at the airport, in all metro stations and in the main tourist office. Once purchased, it can be recharged with one-way journeys or 24hr passes. Cards must be validated on each trip. You can change transport for free within the hour.

Metro Porto's sleek, five-line metro system (daily 6.30am–1am) is cheap and efficient. The lines meet at Trindade station, which also houses an Andante shop. A single trip in the centre costs €1, and a 24hr pass, valid on all forms of transport, costs €3.60.

Bus One-way bus tickets can be purchased on board for €1.50, but the Andante scheme offers better value.

Taxi Taxis are cheap and plentiful; two useful ranks are located at Praça da Ribeira and the Rotonda da Boa Vista, near Casa da Música.

Accommodation

Well-located, good-value rooms are on offer in the streets to the east and west of Av dos Aliados. There are also some bargain rooms in the slightly seedy area around Praça da Batalha, east of Estação de São Bento. In addition to *residenciais* and *pensões*, Porto now boasts a number of central, well-equipped backpacker hostels.

Hostels

Porto Downtown Hostel Praça Guilherme Gomes Fernandes 66, 1° ⓣ 220 018 094, ⓦ www.portodowntownhostel.com. Friendly, spotlessly clean and central place with different-sized dorms and three double rooms. There's also an inviting lounge, kitchen facilities and free internet. Dorms €17, doubles €42.

Porto Spot Hostel Rua Gonçalo Cristovao 12 ⓣ 22 408 52 05 Ⓜ Trindade. A little further out, this smart and sociable hostel has key-card access, clean minimalist rooms, a garden and nightly meals for €7. Dorms €18, twins €44.

Pousada de Juventude Rua Paulo Gama 552 ⓣ 226 177 257, ⓦ www.pousadasjuventude.pt. Large, clean and modern, with a great view of the mouth of the Douro. It's 20min from the centre: take bus #207 from São Bento or #500 from Casa da Música. Dorms €16, twins €42.

Rivoli Cinema Hostel Rua Dr Magalhães Lemos 83 ⓣ 220 174 634, ⓦ rivolicinemahostel.com. Efficiently run cinema-themed hostel which offers dorms and spacious twin rooms. There's also a roof terrace. Dorms €20, twins €46.

Pensions and hotels

Pensão Duas Nações Praça Guilherme Gomes Fernandes 59 ⓣ 222 081 616, ⓦ www.duasnacoes.com.pt. A deservedly popular option, with bright, decently sized rooms, most of which are en suite. No breakfast. Singles €20–25, doubles €27–32.

Pensão Residencial Avenida Av dos Aliados 141 ⓣ 222 009 551, ⓦ pensaoavenida.planetaclix.pt. Sparklingly clean rooms with smart, modern bathrooms. Singles €35, doubles €45.

Residencial Pão de Açucar Rua do Almada 262 ⓣ 222 002 425, ⓦ www.residencialpaodeacucar.com. Neat and comfortable wooden-floored rooms in a 30s building near the town hall. Singles €35, doubles €45.

Eating

Porto's culinary speciality is the mighty *francesinha* – a gut-busting sandwich of steak, ham and *Linguiça* sausage, covered in a layer of melted cheese and a spicy beer and tomato sauce; an acquired taste. Restaurants are good value; particularly the workers' cafés, which usually offer a set menu at lunchtime (but close around 7.30pm and at weekends). Prime areas are Rua do Almada and Rua de São Bento da Vitória. For international options, head to the trendy riverside Cais de Gaia complex which offers Italian, Indian and other world cuisines.

Café Majestic Rua de Santa Catarina 112. Voted one of the world's most beautiful cafés, with *belle époque* mirrors and cherubs adorning its walls. Perfect for an elegant afternoon tea.

Café Piolho D'Ouro Praça de Parada Letão. Near the university, this diner is popular with students and serves incredibly cheap food throughout the day, before morphing into a packed bar at night. Closed Sun. Squid and rice €5.

Churrasqueira do Infante Praça Infante Dom Henrique. A wide selection of good-value grilled meat and fish makes this *churrasqueira* a great budget option in the Ribeira. Closed Sun. Grilled hake €8.

Foz Bar Praia do Molhe, Foz An informal spot for a cheap bite on the beach, serving burgers and Portuguese staples such as *pastéis be bacalhau* (€5.80).

O Caçula Travessa do Bonjardim 20. Smart spot near Aliados serving a select menu of inventive international fish, meat and vegetarian dishes in generous portions. The €6.50 lunch menu (Mon–Fri) is excellent value.

Pedro dos Frangos Rua do Bonjardim 219. Cheap-and-cheerful café serving spit-roasted chicken. Open until 7pm; closed Tues.

Real Indiana Cais de Gaia 360. Tasty Indian dishes served in a modern space with beautiful views. Good for vegetarians. *Bengan bharta* (aubergine curry) €10.

Drinking and nightlife

The Ribeira area offers a fairly laidback drinking scene, while Cais de Gaia is a good option for sophisticated sipping. More lively late-night bars (open until around 4am at weekends) can be found around Rua de Cândido dos Reis, near Aliados. Most of the city's big clubs are in the outlying Matosinhos district or near Foz.

Bars

Café Candelabro Rua do Conceição 3. Low-key and cool with bookcase-lined walls and huge glasses of quality wine for €1.50. Closed Sun.

Casa do Livro Rua Galeria de Paris 85. Gilded mirrors and gold-striped wallpaper might suggest pretension, but the glitterball reveals the truth: a fun but sophisticated spot.

Casa de Ló Travessa de Cedofeita 20a. A former bakery turned laidback café bar offering tea and cake by day and stronger stuff at night.

Lusitano Rua José Falcão 137. Fun and lively mixed gay/straight bar.

Maus Habitos Rua Passos Manuel 178. Soak up some culture as you drink at this multipurpose venue, with art exhibitions, live bands and DJs.

O Bar O Cais Rua da Fonte Taurina 2. Relaxed bar with a clientele as varied as the soundtrack. Serves a variety of foreign beers, and jugs of cheap sangria.

Plano B Rua de Cândido dos Reis 30. A café by day, this place turns into a popular late-night bar with weekend DJs and a programme of live music and performance art.

Praia da Luz Av do Brazil, Foz. Classy beachside bar strewn with outdoor sofas and sunloungers, ideal for a relaxed sunset cocktail.

Vinologia Rua de São João Nov. 46. Innovative bar offering port tastings with knowledgeable, friendly staff. Even an expert could learn a lot here.

Clubs

Porto's clubs are outside the city centre; catch the #500 to Foz or one of the night buses from Aliados or Casa da Música if you can't afford a taxi.

Bazaar Rua de Monchique 13. Out near Foz, this fashionable split-level club plays mostly house music.

Hard Club Cais de Gaia, Vila Nova de Gaia Ⓦwww.hard-club.com. Porto's main venue for international DJs.

Mau Mau Rua do Outeiro 4, Foz. Popular with locals, this club offers a mixture of house and R&B, with occasional guest DJs. Wed–Sat until 4am.

Moving on

Train Braga (hourly; 1hr 15min–1hr 40min); Coimbra (hourly; 1hr 30min–2hr 30min); Guimarães (13 daily; 1hr 30min); Lisbon (hourly; 3hr–3hr 30min).

Bus Amarante (15 daily; 50min); Braga (hourly; 1hr 30min); Coimbra (8–10 daily; 1hr 30min); Guimarães (12 daily; 1hr 40min); Lisbon (hourly; 3hr 30min).

BRAGA

Capital of the Minho, **BRAGA** is also Portugal's religious capital – the scene of spectacular **Easter celebrations** with torchlight processions. But it's not all pomp and ceremony; it's also a lively university town, with a compact and pretty historical centre.

What to see and do

Rua Andrade Corvo leads from the train station to the centre, entered via the sixteenth-century **Arco da Porta Nova.**

The City

Just beyond the city gate lies the oldest cathedral in the country, the extraordinary **Sé** (daily 8am–6.30pm), which dates back to 1070 and encompasses Gothic, Renaissance and Baroque styles. The most impressive areas of the Sé, the Gothic chapels – especially the *Capela dos Reis* (Kings' Chapel), built to house the tombs of Henry of Burgundy and his wife Theresa, the cathedral's founders – and the upper choir may only be visited by guided tour (9am–12.30pm & 2–5.30pm; €3 including museum). Nearby is the **Palácio dos Biscaínhos** (Rua dos Biscaínhos; Tues–Sun 10am–12.10pm & 2–5.30pm; €2), a beautiful seventeenth-century mansion housing a collection of decorative arts, painting and sculpture. Just behind the palace lies the lovely **Jardim de Santa Bárbara**, an oasis of topiary and rose gardens. Braga's main square, the buzzing, café-lined **Praça da República**, is a short walk northwest of the garden.

Bom Jesus do Monte

Braga's real gem is **Bom Jesus do Monte**, set on a wooded hillside 3km above the city – its glorious ornamental stairway is one of Portugal's best-known images. A monumental place of pilgrimage, Bom Jesus was created by Braga's archbishop in the early eighteenth century. The #2 bus runs from Avenida da Liberdade in Braga to Bom Jesus twice every hour (€1.20). Save the ancient wooden funicular (€1.10) for the return journey and ascend the wide, tree-lined staircases to watch Bom Jesus's simple allegory unfold. Each landing holds a small fountain and a chapel containing rather crumbling tableau depictions of the life of Christ, leading up to the Crucifixion scene on the altar of the Neoclassical church which sits atop the staircase. Beyond the church are wooded gardens and a number of hotels and restaurants.

Arrival and information

Train Braga's train station is almost 1km from the centre, down Rua Andrade Corvo.

Bus The bus station, a regional hub, is east of the centre on Av General Norton de Matos.

Tourist office At the corner of Praça da República and Av da Liberdade (June–Sept Mon–Fri 9am–9pm, Sat & Sun 9am–12.30pm & 2–5.30pm; Oct–May Mon–Fri 9am–12.30pm & 2–6.30pm, Sat & Sun 9am–12.30pm & 2–5.30pm; ⓣ253 262 550, ⓦwww.cm-braga.pt).

Accommodation

Campismo Parque da Ponte ⓣ253 273 355. Cheap, basic campsite 2km south of central Braga. Bus #9, #18 or #56 from Av da Liberdade. €4/person, plus €6/tent.

Pousada de Juventude Rua de Santa Margarida 6 ⓣ253 616 163, ⓦwww.pousadasjuventude.pt. Fairly basic but good value, with eight-bed dorms and en-suite twins. Dorms €13, twin €27.

Residencial Dora Largo da Senhora a Branca 92–94 ⓣ253 200 180, ⓦwww.residencialdora.com. Close to Praça da República, this excellent-value option has a dozen sunny en-suite rooms, with breakfast provided by the owners' next-door bakery. Singles €30, doubles €40.

Eating and drinking

A Brasileira Largo Barão de São Marinho. Bustling café with pavement tables serving drinks and light meals. Sandwich €3.50.

Anjo Verde Largo da Praça Velha 21. Trendy vegetarian restaurant near the Sé dishing up cheap, delicious daily specials such as spinach and mushroom roll (€6.50).

PARQUE NACIONAL DA PENEDA-GERÊS

Encompassing mountains, valleys and moors, Portugal's only designated national park is heaven for nature lovers, with ample opportunities for hiking, as well as more extreme sports. The main bases for exploration are the spa town of **Vila do Gerês** and **Ponte da Barca**, where the park's Regional Development Association, Adere-PG, is located. It's worth visiting them at Largo da Miséricordia 10 (Mon–Fri 9am–12.30pm & 2.30–6pm) or online at ⓦwww.adere-pg.pt for information on walking routes and accommodation, including a booking service. Vila do Gerês is easily reached by bus from Braga, though to get to Ponte da Barca you'll need your own transport.

Churrasqueira da Sé Rua dom Paio Mendes 25. Popular little grill restaurant dishing up Portuguese classics such as sardines (€6.50).

Moving on

Train Lisbon (13 daily; 3hr 30min–4hr 30min); Porto (hourly; 1hr 15min–1hr 40min).
Bus Guimarães (hourly; 30min–1hr); Porto (hourly; 1hr 23min); Vila do Gerês (Mon–Fri hourly, Sat & Sun 6 daily; 1hr 30min).

GUIMARÃES

The first capital of Portugal, **GUIMARÃES** remains an atmospheric and beautiful university town. The town's chief attraction is the hilltop **castle** (daily 9.30am–12.30pm & 2–5.30pm; free), whose square keep and seven towers are an enduring symbol of the emergent Portuguese nation. Built by the Countess of Mumadona and extended by Henry of Burgundy, it became the stronghold of his son, Afonso Henriques, Portugal's first independent king. Afonso launched the Reconquest from Guimarães, which was replaced by Coimbra as the capital city in 1143.

Other key sights include the **Archbishop's Palace** (daily except Mon 9.30am–12.30pm & 2–5.30pm; €3, free Sun 10am–2pm) near the castle, a fifteenth-century building which was perfectly restored and used as a presidential residence for Salazar, Portugal's former dictator; and the **Igreja de Nossa Senhora da Oliveira** on Largo da Oliveira (7.15am–noon & 3.30–7.30pm), a beautiful convent church founded by Countess Mumadona, in the picturesque medieval centre. The pretty **Praça de Santiago** is a popular spot for an alfresco coffee during the day, and comes alive again at night as its bars (such as *Tunel* at no. 29) fill with students.

Arrival and information

Train The train station is south of town, connected to the centre by Av D. Afonso Henriques.
Bus Guimarães's bus station is 15min walk west of town in a vast shopping centre. Follow Av Conde de Margaride to reach the town centre.
Tourist office On the corner of Av D. Afonso Henriques and Alameda de São Damaso (Mon–Fri 9.30am–6.30pm, Sat 10am–6pm, Sun 10am–1pm; Ⓣ253 412 450, Ⓦwww.guimaraesturismo.com); also in Praça de Santiago (Mon–Fri 9.30am–6.30pm, Sat 10am–6pm, Sun 10am–1pm; Ⓣ253 518 790).

Accommodation and eating

Cozinha Regional Santiago Praça de Santiago. Lovely little restaurant offering regional specialities at fair prices, set in a pretty square.
Pousada de Juventude Largo da Cidade Ⓣ253 421 380, Ⓦwww.pousadasjuventude.pt. Stylish new hostel with excellent facilities: the best-value accommodation in town. Dorms €14, twins €35.
Residencial das Trinas Rua das Trinas 29 Ⓣ253 517 358, Ⓦwww.residencialtrinas.com. Another good option in the town centre, with clean, comfortable en-suite rooms. Singles €30, doubles €40.

Moving on

Train Porto (hourly; 1hr 30min).
Bus Braga (hourly; 30min–1hr); Coimbra (2–6 daily; 2hr).

THE DOURO RAIL ROUTE

The Douro Valley, a narrow, winding gorge for the majority of its route, offers some of the most spectacular scenery in Portugal. The **Douro Rail Route**, which joins the river about 60km inland and then sticks to it across the country, is one of those journeys that needs no justification other than the trip itself.

Porto is a good place to begin a trip, though there are also regular connections along the line as far as **Peso da Régua**; beyond Régua, there are less frequent connections to **Tua** and **Pocinho**, which marks the end of the line. The trip from Porto to Pocinho takes 3hr 15min (€10.75), but the best way to experience the rail route is to take one of the branch lines which lead away from the main track at Regua and Tua (sadly the line connecting Livraçao and Amarante is no more).

Amarante

Set above pine woods and vineyards, the riverside town of **AMARANTE** makes a relaxing day-trip from Porto. Much of Amarante's history revolves around the thirteenth-century hermit **Gonçalo**, the Portuguese equivalent of St Valentine, who is credited with founding just about everything in town. Although it has a nice church and unusual modernist museum (the **Museu Amadeo de Souza-Cardoso**; Tues–Sun 10am–12.30pm & 2–5.30pm; €2), the main attraction is the riverside setting, the peaceful atmosphere and picturesque old streets.

The **tourist office** (July–Sept 9am–7pm; Oct–June 9am–12.30pm & 2–5.30pm) is on Alameda Teixeira de Pascoaes. Good, cheap **rooms** can be found at *Albergaria Dona Margarita*, Rua Cândido dos Reis 53 (☎255 432 110; doubles €40); for **food**, try the locally renowned *Adega A Quelha* on Rua de Olivença.

Vila Real

Shortly after Livração, the main line finally reaches the Douro and heads upstream to **Peso da Régua**, the depot through which all port wine must pass on its way to Porto. From here, the narrow-gauge Corgo train line branches off through the mountains destined for **VILA REAL** (station closed for renovation at the time of writing). The gateway to Trás-os-Montes – and the closest this rural province gets to a city – Vila Real is a lively little spot with an invitingly laidback atmosphere and some surprisingly sophisticated shopping. It also makes a great base for exploration of the nearby **Parque Natural do Alvão**, a mountainous park containing an impressive variety of flora and fauna given its petite size (only 72 sq km). Also close to Vila Real, reached by bus #1 from Rua Gonçalo Cristóvão (direction UTAD; ask driver where to get off), is the **Palacio de Mateus** (March–May & Oct 9am–1pm & 2–6pm; June–Sept 9am–7.30pm; Oct–May 10am–1pm & 2–5pm; house and gardens €8.50, gardens only €5), instantly recognizable as the house depicted on labels of Mateus Rosé wine. This palatial Baroque residence is still inhabited by the Mateus family, but certain rooms (including the well-stocked library) can be visited by guided tour. The mansion is set in well-tended formal gardens.

Vila Real's **tourist office** (June–Sept Mon–Fri 9.30am–7pm, Sat & Sun 9.30am–12.30pm & 2–6pm; Oct–May Mon–Sat 9.30am–12.30pm & 2–6pm) is at Av Carvalho Araújo 94. The best-value **accommodation** in the centre of Vila Real is the charming, well-kept *Residencial Real* at Rua Central 5 (☎259 325 879; €40), with the bonus of breakfast in the downstairs *pastelaria*. Other options are the campsite (€4 per person plus €5 per tent), fifteen minutes northeast of the centre up Avenida 1 de Maio (☎259 324 724), and the *Pousada de Juventude* 1km northeast of town on Rua Dr Manuel Cardona (☎259 373 193, Ⓦwww.pousadasjuventude.pt; dorms €10, twins €22–25). The bulk of the town's **restaurants** are on Rua Teixeira de Sousa; a good budget option is *Churrasqueira Real* at no. 14 (half a roast chicken €4.50).

Southern Portugal

The huge, sparsely populated plains of the **Alentejo**, southeast of Lisbon, are overwhelmingly agricultural, dominated by vast cork plantations. This impoverished province provides nearly half of the world's cork but only a meagre living for its rural inhabitants. Visitors to the Alentejo often head for **Évora**, the province's dominant and most historic town. But the **Alentejo coast**, the Costa Azul, is a breath of fresh air after the stifling plains of the inland landscape, and offers a low-key alternative to the busy Algarve.

With its long, sandy beaches and picturesque rocky coves, the southern coast of the **Algarve** is the most visited region in the country. West of **Faro**, the region's capital, you'll find the classic postcard images of the Algarve – a series of tiny bays and coves, broken up by rocky outcrops and fantastic grottoes, which reach their most spectacular around the resort of **Lagos**. To the east of Faro lie the less-developed sandy offshore islets, **the Ilhas** – which front the coastline for some 25 miles – and the lower-key towns of **Olhão** and **Tavira**. In summer it is wise to book accommodation in advance, as the Algarve is a popular package holiday destination.

ÉVORA

ÉVORA, a UNESCO World Heritage Site, is one of southern Portugal's most attractive towns and worth a day's exploration. The Romans and the Moors were in occupation for four centuries apiece, leaving their stamp in the tangle of narrow alleys that rise steeply among the whitewashed houses. Most of the monuments, however, date from the fourteenth to the sixteenth centuries, when, with royal encouragement, the city was one of the leading centres of Portuguese art and architecture.

What to see and do

The **Templo Romano** in the central square is the best-preserved Roman temple in Portugal, its remains consisting of a small platform supporting more than a dozen granite columns with a marble entablature. Next to the temple lies the church of the **Convento dos Lóios**. The convent is now a luxury *pousada*, but the church (Tues–Sun 9.30am–12.30pm & 2–5pm; €3), dedicated to São João Evangelista, contains beautiful *azulejos* and an ossuary under the floor. Nearby, the Romanesque **cathedral** (daily 9am–12.30pm & 2.30–5pm; cloisters and museum €3; museum closed Mon), was begun in 1186, about twenty years after the reconquest of Évora from the Moors. The most memorable sight in town is the **Capela dos Ossos** (daily; Oct–April 9am–1pm & 2.30–5.15pm; May–Sept 9am–1pm & 2.30–5.45pm; €2) in the church of **São Francisco**, just south of Praça do Giraldo. A gruesome reminder of mortality, the walls and pillars of this chilling chamber are covered with the bones of more than five thousand monks; an inscription over the door reads, *Nós ossos que aqui estamos, Pelos vossos esperamos* – "We bones here are waiting for your bones". Just below the church lies a beautiful, shady park with resident peacocks, a duck pond and a small café.

Arrival and information

Bus and train Évora's bus and train stations are 1km west of the old town, a 20min walk from the central Praça do Giraldo. The train station was closed for renovation at the time of writing.

Tourist office Praça do Giraldo (May–Sept Mon–Fri 9am–7pm, Sat & Sun 9.30am–12.30pm & 2–5.30pm; Oct–April 9.30am–12.30pm; ⓣ 266 730 030).

Accommodation

Évora's tourist appeal pushes accommodation prices over the norm. In addition to the places listed below, there are also some attractive *turismo rural* properties in the nearby countryside; the tourist office has details.

Parque de Campismo Estrada de Alcáçovas ⓣ 266 705 190. This well-equipped campsite is 2km out of town on the Alcáçovas road; take bus #5 or #8 from Praça 1 de Maio. €5/person plus €5/tent.

Pensão Giraldo Rua dos Mercadores 27 ⓣ 266 705 833. Clean, comfortable rooms; those with en suite (€65) are more spacious. Prices rise in Aug and Sept. Doubles €52.

Pousada de Juventude Rua Miguel Bombarda 40 ⓣ 217 232 100, ⓦ www.pousadasjuventude.pt. Extensively renovated in 2008, this central hostel is an excellent budget option. Dorms €16, twins €42.

Residencial Policarpo Rua Freiria de Baixo 16 ⓣ 266 702 424, ⓦ www.pensaopolicarpo.com. Beautiful, rambling old place full of rustic charm. Also has rooms sleeping three or four. Doubles €40–60.

Eating and drinking

Bar Oficin@ Rua da Moeda 27. Friendly, laidback bar open until 2am. Closed Sun.
Casa dos Sabores Rua Miguel Bombarda 50. Pleasant café offering inexpensive sandwiches, salads and pastries. Sandwich €2.50.
Dom Joaquim Rua dos Penedoa 6. Smart restaurant near the city walls offering more creative cuisine than most in Évora. Anyone fancy "rancid lard of the saint" for dessert?
O Antão Rua João de Deus 5. The place to come for regional specialities such as rabbit. Closed Wed.

Moving on

Bus Albufeira (for the Algarve, 2 daily, 3hr 30min); Lagos (1 or 2 daily In high season; 4hr–4hr 30min); Lisbon (14 daily; 2hr).

THE ALENTEJO COAST

Starting south of Lisbon, the **Alentejo coast** features towns and beaches as inviting as those of the Algarve. Some of the most attractive are the pint-sized resort of **Vila Nova de Milfontes**, and the surfers' haven of **Zambujeira do Mar**, at the southern point of the coastline stretch. Though exposed to the winds and waves of the Atlantic, with colder waters, the Alentejo coast is fine for summer swimming and far quieter than the Algarve. Outside the summer season, the area is blissfully quiet.

Local **bus** services and express buses from Lisbon take you within easy reach of the whole coastline, stopping at Vila Nova de Milfontes (4hr) and Zambujeira do Mar (4hr 15min). **Accommodation** is plentiful in these resorts, but it's wise to book ahead during the summer months. **Surfing** is popular along the Alentejo coast; first-timers can have lessons at Surf Milfontes in Vila Nova de Milfontes (Ⓣ919 922 193, Ⓦwww.surfmilfontes.com).

Vila Nova de Milfontes

The attractively low-key resort of **VILA NOVA DE MILFONTES** sits on the estuary of the River Mira, whose sandy banks merge into the coastline. This is the most popular as well as one of the most beautiful resorts in the region, its streets lined with houses and hotels painted in the typical Alentejan white and blue. Adding to the charm is a handsome little castle and an ancient port, reputed to have harboured Hannibal and his Carthaginians during a storm.

Dorm beds, attractive en-suite rooms and a guest kitchen can be found at backpackers' favourite *Casa Amarela* on Rua Dom Luis Castro e Almeida (Ⓣ283 996 632, Ⓦwww.casaamarelamilfontes.com; dorms €20, twin or double €45), and there are a couple of large **campsites** to the north of town: the well-equipped *Parque de Campismo Milfontes* (Ⓣ283 996 140, Ⓔparquemilfontes@netc.pt; €7 per person) and the more modest *Campiférias* (Ⓣ283 996 409, Ⓔnovafeiras@oninet.pt; €5 per person). **Bars and restaurants** largely lie between the castle and Largo de Rossio, with smart *Pica Tapa* on Travessa de Sociedade serving up delicious Portuguese cuisine with a twist either à la carte or on set menus priced from €17. Opposite lies *Pacific Bar*, a key fixture of the town's nightlife.

Zambujeira do Mar

Southwest of Odemira southern Alentejo's main inland town, is the tiny village of **ZAMBUJEIRA DO MAR**, where a large cliff provides a dramatic backdrop to the beach, which is prime **surfing** territory. Zambujeira do Mar certainly livens up in summer, with a music festival featuring mostly Portuguese bands held every August, but it's still quieter than Vila Nova de Milfontes. There are only a few small *pensions*, such as the well-run *Mar-e-Sol* (Ⓣ283 961 171; doubles €55), a few private rooms to rent and a pleasant **campsite** (Ⓣ283 961 172, Ⓦwww.campingzambujeira.com.sapo.pt; €5.50 per person, plus €6.50 per tent), about 1km from the cliffs. Restaurants are concentrated around Rua Miramar;

Estibeira is reasonably priced and welcoming.

There are no direct **transport** connections between Zambujeira and the Algarve; the best way to get there is to take a local bus to Odemira (40min), then a bus to Faro (2hr). However, these connections can be erratic; check Ⓦwww.rodalentejo.pt for details.

FARO

FARO is the capital of the Algarve, with excellent beaches within easy reach, but as regional capitals go, it's surprisingly laidback. While its suburbs may be modern, Faro retains an attractive historic centre south of the marina.

What to see and do

The **Cidade Velha**, or Old Town, is a semi-walled quarter entered through the eighteenth-century town gate, the **Arco da Vila**. Here you'll find the majestic **Sé** (Mon–Sat 10am–6pm; €3 including cathedral museum and outdoor bones chapel), which offers superb views from its bell tower. The nearby **Museu Municipal** (opening hours vary, check with tourist office; €2) is housed in a sixteenth-century convent on Largo Dom Alfonso III; the most striking exhibit is a third-century Roman mosaic of Neptune and the four winds, unearthed near Faro train station. Faro's most curious sight is the Baroque **Igreja do Carmo** (Mon–Fri 10am–1pm & 3–5pm, Sat 10am–1pm) near the central post office on Largo do Carmo. A door to the right of the altar leads to a macabre **Capela dos Ossos** (€1), its walls decorated with bones disinterred from the adjacent cemetery. The nearby **beach** (Praia de Faro) can be reached by bus from the Avenida stop opposite the bus station, or by boat from the harbour. Five boats a day also go to the more tranquil **Ilha do Farol**; the tourist information office has timetables.

TREAT YOURSELF

In Serra de Monchique above Portimão (60km north of Faro) nestles the hamlet of **Vila Termal das Caldas de Monchique** (Ⓣ282 910 910, Ⓦwww.monchiquetermas.com) a tiny spa resort centred around natural thermal springs. Weary travellers can lounge in the spa for €15 per day, but staying overnight can also be a bargain: out of season, luxurious hotel rooms are available for as little as €40. Buses run between Monchique and Portimão up to 8 times daily (30 min; €3.95).

Arrival and information

Air Taxis from the airport, 6km west of town, to the centre cost around €12, or take bus #16 or #14 (up to 24 daily; 7am–9.40pm; €1.50), a 20min journey to town. To get to the airport, catch the bus from the stop opposite the bus station.

Train A few minutes beyond the central bus station, up Av da República.

Bus Right in the centre, behind the *Hotel Eva*, north of the marina.

Tourist office The main office is near the harbour at Rua da Misericórdia 8 (Mon–Fri 9.30am–5.30/7pm, Sat & Sun 9.30am–12.30pm & 2–5.30/7pm; Ⓣ289 803 604, Ⓦwww.turismodoalgarve.pt); there's also a branch at the airport.

Accommodation

Pensão São Filipe Rua Infante Dom Henrique 55 Ⓣ289 824 182, Ⓦwww.guesthouse-saofilipe.com. The neat rooms are on the small side, but are immaculately clean. Free wi-fi. No breakfast. Singles €46, doubles €56.

Pousada de Juventude Rua da Polícia de Segurança Pública 1 Ⓣ289 826 521, Ⓦwww.pousadasjuventude.pt. Basic but friendly hostel a 10min walk east of the centre; some rooms have en suite (€40). Dorms €15, twins €42.

Residencial Adelaide Rua Cruz dos Mestres 7 Ⓣ289 802 383, Ⓦwww.adelaideresidencial.com. Smart a/c rooms. Singles €50, doubles €60.

Residencial Madalena Rua Conselheiro Bivar 105 Ⓣ289 805 807, Ⓦwww.residencialmadalena.com.

Old-fashioned but comfortable and good-value rooms in the centre. Singles €35, doubles €40.

Eating and drinking

Adega Nova Rua Francisco Barreto 24. A good-value restaurant which is always crammed with locals. Pork chops €7.50.

Café do Coreto Jardim Manuel Bívar. Right next to the marina, this café is open all day serving sandwiches, pizza and drinks. Pizza from €8.

Columbus Rua Dr Francisco Gomes. Late-night disco bar with a relaxed, friendly atmosphere.

Faz Gostos Rua do Castelo 13. Upmarket but good-value restaurant using locally sourced ingredients to create interesting international dishes (around €12).

Upa Upa Café Bar Rua Conseilheiro de Bívar 51. Chilled-out spot perfect for a drink before hitting the bars and clubs around nearby Rua do Prior.

Moving on

Train Lagos (7 daily; 1hr 40min); Lisbon (4 daily; 5hr 30min–6hr); Olhão (16 daily; 10min); Tavira (12–17 daily; 35–45min).

Bus Évora (2–4 daily; 4hr–4hr 30min); Lagos (8 daily; 2hr 15min); Lisbon (7–9 daily; 4hr–4hr 30min); Olhão (12 daily; 20min); Sevilla, Spain (2 daily; 4hr 40min); Tavira (7–11 daily; 1hr).

LAGOS

The seaside town of **LAGOS** is one of the Algarve's most popular destinations and attracts large numbers of visitors each summer, drawn by its beautiful beaches and lively nightlife. Lagos was also favoured by Henry the Navigator, who used it as a base for African trade. Europe's first slave market was built here in 1441 in the arches of the Customs House, which still stands in the Praça da República near the waterfront.

What to see and do

On the waterfront and to the rear of the town are the remains of Lagos's once impregnable fortifications, devastated by the Great Earthquake. One rare and beautiful church which did survive was the **Igreja de Santo António**; decorated around 1715, its gilt and carved interior is wildly obsessive, every inch filled with cherubic youths struggling with animals and fish. The church forms part of a visit to the adjacent **Museu Municipal** (daily except Mon 9.30am–12.30pm & 2–5pm; €2), housing an eclectic collection of artefacts including Roman busts and deformed animal foetuses.

Lagos's main attraction, however, is its splendid beaches, the most secluded of which lie below extravagantly eroded cliff faces south of town. **Praia de Dona Ana** is considered the most picturesque, though its crowds make the smaller coves of **Praia do Pinhão**, down a track just opposite the fire station, and **Praia Camilo**, a little further along, more appealing. Over the river east of Lagos is a splendid sweep of sand – **Meia Praia** – where there's space even at the height of summer. Meia Praia is an ideal destination for **watersports** enthusiasts, as various companies based here offer sailing, sea kayaking and water-skiing lessons, and it's also popular with surfers. Those who like to keep their feet dry might prefer an excursion to the extraordinary rock formations around **Ponta da Piedade**, a headland that can be viewed by boat (from €10 for an hour) from the marina. Smaller boats have the advantage of gaining access to some of the smaller grottoes.

Arrival and information

Train The train station is across the river, a 15min walk from the centre across the swing bridge to the marina.

Bus The bus station is slightly closer to the town centre, just off the main Av dos Descobrimentos.

Tourist office On Largo Marquês de Pombal in the central pedestrian zone (April & May and Oct–March Mon–Fri 10am–6pm & Sat 10am–2pm; June & Sept Mon–Sat 10am–6pm; July & Aug daily 10am–8pm; ☎ 282 764 111).

Accommodation

Angela Guesthouse Loteamento da Ameijeira, Rua Teixeira Gomes Bloco AN1-2 ☎ 962 616 552,

Ⓔ angelaguesthouse@hotmail.com. Comfortable rooms with shared bathroom in a private apartment just outside the city walls. Doubles €45.

Campismo da Trindade Rossio da Trindade Ⓣ 282 763 893. Small, busy campsite close to the sea. To reach it, follow the main road 200m beyond the fort. €8/person.

Gold Coast Hostel Rua Gil Vicente 48 Ⓣ 916 594 225, Ⓔ goldcoast_hostel@yahoo.com. Friendly, relaxed hostel with a shared kitchen and outdoor terrace. Dorms €23.

Pensão Caravela Rua 25 de Abril 16 Ⓣ 282 763 361. Well-kept rooms right in the centre of town. Doubles €35.

Pousada de Juventude Rua Lançarote de Freitas 50 Ⓣ 282 761 970, Ⓦ www.pousadasjuventude.pt. Busy, well-equipped hostel in a central location. Dorms €18, twins €45.

Rising Cock Hostel Travessa do Forno 14 Ⓣ 968 758 785, Ⓦ www.risingcock.com. Tackily named but popular party hostel. Dorms €30.

Eating, drinking and nightlife

Key areas for restaurants and nightlife are the streets around central Praça Gil Eanes, with more low-key and sophisticated drinking around the marina. Thanks to Lagos's tourist appeal, prices here can be higher than other towns in the Algarve.

Bon Vivant Rua 25 de Abril 105. Multistorey bar-club with a "tropical" roof terrace.

Eddie's Bar Rua 25 de Abril 99. Friendly bar with loud music and cheap drinks.

Meu Limão Rua Silva Lopes 40. Popular bar with some outdoor seating and a wide selection of tapas from €4, as well as some international main dishes.

Mullens Bar Rua Cândido dos Reis. Atmospheric bar-restaurant with lively music until 2am.

No Patio Rua Lançarote de Freitas 46 Ⓣ 282 763 777. Run by a British expat chef, *No Patio* ("on the patio") offers beautifully prepared fusion cuisine at a reasonable price. Prawn and monkfish curry €15. Reservations recommended. Open Thurs–Sun.

O Alcaide Rua Porta da Vila 18. Cheaper than the international restaurants, this Portuguese-run place serves up huge portions of fish and meat dishes.

Moving on

Train Faro (7 daily; 1hr 40min); Lisbon (4 daily; 5hr 15min).

Bus Évora (1 daily; 4hr 30min); Faro (8 daily; 2hr 15min); Sevilla, Spain (2 daily; 6hr 30min).

OLHÃO AND THE ISLANDS

OLHÃO, 8km east of Faro, is the largest fishing port in the Algarve and an excellent base for visiting the local sandbank islands. The pedestrianized centre, close to the seafront, is pretty yet free of tourist hordes, and ensures Olhão retains an unspoilt traditional charm.

What to see and do

Although Olhão has no sights to speak of, its café-strewn centre is worth a wander, and there's a bustling market on Avenida 5 de Outubro. The town's main attraction, however, is its close proximity to and good connections with two of the sandbank islands which comprise the **Ria Formosa Natural Park**. The islands of Armona and Culatra boast some superb, spacious beaches, so expansive that they still feel uncrowded even at the height of summer. Ferries to the islands operate year-round, and depart regularly from the jetty to the left of the municipal gardens. The service to **Armona** (30min; €3.20 return) drops you off at a long strip of holiday chalets and huts that stretches right across the island on either side of the main path. On the ocean side, the beach disappears into the distance and a short walk will take you to totally deserted stretches of sand. Boats to **Culatra** (30min; €3.20 return) call first at Praia da Culatra, a vast expanse of sand stretching away from Culatra town. The same service then makes its way to **Praia do Farol** (1hr; €4 return), considered to be one of the most beautiful beaches on the sandbank islands. Heading east, away from the holiday homes, the beach becomes quieter, and eventually leads to the peaceful Praia dos Hangares.

Arrival and information

Train and bus The train station is east of Av da República northeast of town, while the bus station is nearby, to the west of the Avenida.

TREAT YOURSELF

Aquasul Rua Dr Augusto Carvalho 13 (☎281 325 166). Perfectly cooked international dishes, stonebaked pizzas and changing daily specials are the order of the day at friendly *Aquasul*. Seasonal starters include beetroot carpaccio with goat's cheese and rocket (€6.50), with mains ranging from pizza margehrita (€9.50) to sea bream *en papillote* (€15). The setting is pretty and peaceful, with pastel-coloured tables spilling out of the restaurant into a pedestrianized cobbled street. Dinner Tues–Sun.

Tourist office Largo Sebastião Martins Mestre (May–Sept Mon–Fri 9.30am–7pm; Oct–April Mon–Fri 9.30am–noon & 1–5.30pm; ☎289 713 936).

Accommodation and eating

Camping Olhão ☎289 700 300. Large, well-equipped campsite 2km east of town. In summer a bus runs from near the municipal garden. €5/person, plus €8/tent.

Pensão Bela Vista Rua Teófilo Braga 65 ☎289 702 538. Offers neat and tidy en-suite rooms with a/c; the restaurant beneath offers excellent local dishes. Singles €40, doubles €50.

Pensão Bicuar Rua Vasco da Gama 5 ☎289 714 816, ⓦwww.pension-bicuar.com. Friendly guest-house with a kitchen, roof terrace, and pleasant rooms with shower and sink which sleep up to four. €40 shared bathroom, €50 en suite.

Ria Formosa Av 5 de Outubro 14. Popular restaurant with tasty seafood and rice dishes.

TAVIRA

TAVIRA is a handsome little town made up of cobbled streets, and split into two pretty halves by the River Gilão. The Romans and Moors who once ruled Tavira left behind monuments that contribute to the town's appeal, but the main tourist attractions, the superb island beaches of the **Ilha de Tavira**, actually lie offshore. Boats to the island depart from the quayside on Rua do Cais from July to mid-September (12 daily; 20min; €2 return), with year-round boats from Quatro Águas (up to 12 daily; 5min; €1.50 return), 2km east of town. The beach is backed by dunes and stretches west almost as far as Fuzeta, 14km away. Despite some development – a small chalet settlement, a **campsite,** and a handful of bars and restaurants facing the sea – it's still easy to find your own peaceful patch of sand. Back in central Tavira, it's worth wandering up to the remains of the **Moorish castle** (Mon–Fri 8am–5pm, Sat & Sun 9am–7pm; free), perched high above the town, with its walls enclosing a pretty garden that affords splendid views. Close to the castle, at Calçada da Galeria 12, a former water tower has been converted into a **camera obscura**, offering views of the town (Mon–Sat 10am–5pm; €4).

Arrival and information

Train 1km from the centre of town, at the end of Rua da Liberdade.

Bus Buses pull up at the terminal by the river, a 2min walk from the central square, Praça da República.

Tourist office Rua da Galeria 9, southwest of Praça da República (July & Aug Mon–Fri 9am–7pm; Sept–June Mon–Fri 9.30am–1pm & 2–5.30pm; ☎281 322 511).

Accommodation

Camping Tavira Ilha de Tavira ☎281 324 455, ⓦwww.campingtavira.com. Busy campsite with a great location on the Ilha de Tavira; follow the path opposite the ferry dock to reach it. Open April–Sept. €12/tent plus one camper, €5.50/additional person.

Por do Sol Travessa do Livramento 4 ☎281 321 811, ⓦwww.tavirasol.com. Well-designed *residencial* with friendly owners, spacious rooms and extra touches such as in-room kettles. Doubles €65.

Pousada de Juventude Rua Miguel Bombarda 36 ☎217 232 100, ⓦwww.pousadasjuventude.pt. Brand-new hostel with excellent facilities. Dorms €17, en-suite twin €47.

Eating and drinking

Arco Rua Almirante Cândido dos Reis 67. Friendly, laidback bar on the far side of the river, which attracts both locals and visitors. Closed Mon.

Bica Rua Almirante Cândido dos Reis 22–24. Basic setting, but the food speaks for itself: tasty portions of Portuguese classics such as grilled sardines, from €7.

Rive Gauche Rua Dr Augusto Carvalho 22. Bistro with art-splashed walls and a French-Influenced menu of meat, fish and vegetarian dishes. Vegetarian filo parcel €8.50.

UBI Rua Vale Caranguejo. Tavira's only club is a warehouse-like space reached by following Rua Almirante Cândido dos Reis to the outskirts of town. Closed Mon in summer, open Fri & Sat only in winter.

Moving on

Train Faro (12–17 daily; 35–45min); Olhão (12–17 daily; 15 min).

Bus Lisbon (1 daily; 6hr).

Romania

HIGHLIGHTS

THE CARPATHIANS: stunning mountain scenery, under two hours from the capital

SIGHISOARA: beautiful medieval citadel in the heart of Transylvania, with authentic Dracula connections

MUSEUM OF FOLK CIVILIZATION, SIBIU: a fascinating open-air museum of Romanian village architecture, set in a scenic landscape

BUCHAREST: hectic traffic, Stalinist architecture, pretty residential streets and good dining and nightlife

ROUGH COSTS

DAILY BUDGET Basic €25 /occasional treat €35

DRINK Beer €1–2; bottle of Romanian wine €5

FOOD *Tochitura moldoveneasca* €2

HOSTEL/BUDGET HOTEL €10–15/€30–40

TRAVEL Bucharest–Braşov by train €8; by bus €10

FACT FILE

POPULATION 22,215 million

AREA 237,500 sq km

LANGUAGE Romanian

CURRENCY New leu (RON); plural: lei

CAPITAL Bucharest (population: 2 million)

INTERNATIONAL PHONE CODE ⓣ40

Introduction

Nowhere in Eastern Europe defies preconceptions quite like Romania. The country suffers from a poor image, but don't be put off – outstanding landscapes, a surprisingly efficient train system, a huge diversity of wildlife and rural communities and traditions that at times seem little changed since the Middle Ages.

Romanians trace their ancestry back to the Romans, and they like to stress their Latin roots, although they have Balkan traits too. They see their future as firmly within the Euro-Atlantic family and were delighted to join NATO and then, in 2007, the European Union.

The capital, **Bucharest**, is perhaps daunting for the first-time visitor – its savage history is only too evident – but parts of this once-beautiful city retain a voyeuristic appeal. More attractive by far, and easily accessible on public transport, is **Transylvania**, a region steeped in history, offering some of the most beautiful mountain scenery in Europe as well as a uniquely multi-ethnic character. Its chief cities, such as Braşov, Sibiu and Sighişoara, were built by Saxon (German) colonists, and there are also strong Hungarian and Roma (Gypsy) presences here. In the border region of the **Banat**, also highly multi-ethnic, Timişoara is Romania's most Western-looking city and famed as the birthplace of the 1989 revolution.

CHRONOLOGY

513 BC The Dacian tribe inhabit the area of present-day Romania.
106 AD The Roman Emperor Trajan conquers the Dacian tribe.
271 Following attacks from the Goths, the Romans withdraw from the area.
1000s Hungary conquers and occupies parts of present-day Romania.
1200s Division of Romanian population into different principalities including Wallachia, Moldavia and Transylvania.
1400s Principalities of Moldavia, Transylvania and Wallachia come under attack from the Turkish Ottomans but remain independent.
1448 Vlad "the Impaler" becomes Prince of Wallachia; he is later credited as the inspiration for the character of Dracula.
1700s The Austrian Habsburgs take control of large parts of the Romanian principalities after military successes over the Ottomans.
1862 After battling for independence, Wallachia and Moldavia unite to form Romania. Bucharest is declared the capital.
1878 Romania's claim to independence is formalized by the Treaty of Berlin.
1881 Carol I is named the first King of Romania.
1918 After invasion by the central powers during World War I, Romania is freed and her borders increased.
1939–45 Romania sides with Germany at start of World War II, but changes allegiance to the Allies towards the end. Soviets take large parts of Romanian territory.
1947 Soviet influence remains and the Communist Party comes into power in Romania.
1965 Nicolae Ceauşescu becomes Communist Party leader and adopts a foreign-policy stance independent of the Soviets.
1989 Revolution leads to the overthrow of the Communist regime.
2004 Romania joins NATO.
2007 Romania joins the European Union.

ARRIVAL

Arriving by **air**, most airlines serve Bucharest's Otopeni (Henri Coandă) or Băneasa airports, but there are half a dozen regional airports (of which Timişoara and Cluj-Napoca are the most important), served by a growing number of budget airlines such as Wizz Air (Ⓦwww.wizzair.com), Blue Air (Ⓦwww.blueairweb.com) and Carpatair (Ⓦwww.carpatair.com).

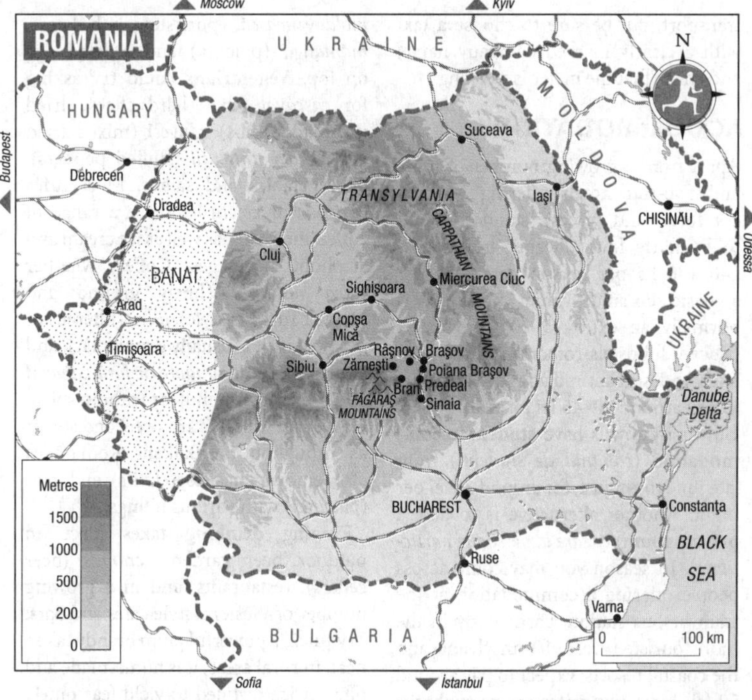

Travelling to Romania by **train** is fairly simple via Paris, Vienna and Budapest, and there are also through trains from Prague, Belgrade, Sofia and Kiev. This will usually cost more than flying into the country, but works well as part of a larger Europe-wide trip using a pass or point-to-point ticket options offered by the rail contacts listed on p.36, including **InterRail** (for European residents) and **Eurail** (for non-European residents).

GETTING AROUND

InterCity **trains** are the most comfortable; they're followed by Rapid and Accelerat services, which stop more often. Personal trains stop everywhere and are generally grubby and crowded. Some overnight trains have **sleeping carriages** (*vagon de dormit*) and **couchettes** (*cuşet*) for a modest surcharge. Seat reservations are required for all fast trains, and are automatically included with locally purchased tickets. You'll also need a reservation for **international trains** even if you do not require one before entering Romania, so be sure to book a seat before departure or face a fine. The best place to **buy tickets** and book seats is at the local Agenţia SNCFR (generally open Mon–Fri 7.30am–7.30pm, Sat 8am–noon; ⓦwww.cfr.ro); at the station tickets are slightly cheaper but available only one hour in advance. Wasteels, a Europe-wide youth rail travel agency (ⓦwww.triptkts.ro), available in some major stations, offers discounts for under-26s. Both **InterRail** and **Eurail** are valid.

The **bus** (*autobuz*) network is confusing and chaotic, while there are also **minibus** (*maxitaxi*) services on the busy routes; although fast and frequent, they are often crowded and the driving can be manic. Maxitaxis also make quite a few surprisingly long inter-city journeys; expect to pay the same as the Accelerat train fare or a bit more. **Taxis** are cheap and an attractive alternative to crowded public transport, but be sure to choose a taxi with a clearly marked company name, and check that the meter is working.

ACCOMMODATION

Apart from a growing number of four- and five-star hotels offering Western comforts (and prices), standards tend to be fairly low. Cheaper **hotels** cost 140–180 lei per person per night, for a basic en-suite room; breakfast is normally an extra 15–20 lei. **Hostels** (Ⓦwww.hihostels-romania.ro) are now fairly widespread, and you should expect to pay around 40–45 lei for a dorm bed. University towns have **student accommodation** (*caminul de studenţi*) from late June to August, for around 30 lei per night. Another alternative is to take a **private room** (*cazare la persoane particulare*). In season you may come across people offering accommodation at the train or bus station, particularly in the more touristed areas of Transylvania and the coastal resorts; expect to pay around 50 lei. Most **campsites** are pretty basic; expect to pay around 20 lei per night for tent space. Outside national parks, most officials will turn a blind eye if you are discreet about camping wild.

FOOD AND DRINK

Breakfast (*micul dejun*) is typically a light meal of bread rolls, butter and jam and an omelette washed down with a coffee (*cafea*). The most common **snacks** are bread rings (*covrigi*), flaky pastries (*pateuri*) filled with cheese (*cu brânză*) or meat (*cu carne*), and a variety of spicy grilled sausages and meatballs such as *mici* and *chiftele*. Menus in most **restaurants** concentrate on grilled meats, or *friptura*. *Cotlet de porc* is the common pork chop, while *muşchi de vacă* is fillet of beef.

Traditional **Romanian dishes** can be delicious. The best known of these is *sarmale* – pickled cabbage stuffed with rice, meat and herbs, usually served with sour cream – and *tochitură moldovenească*, a pork stew, with cheese, *mămăligă* (polenta) and a fried egg on top. **Vegetarians** could try asking for *caşcaval pane* (hard cheese fried in breadcrumbs); *ghiveci* (mixed fried veg); *ardei umpluţii* (stuffed peppers); or vegetables and salads. Most **cafés** (*cafénea* or *cofetărie*) serve a range of coffee and cakes, as well as ice cream and alcoholic beverages. Coffee, whether *cafea naturală* (finely ground and brewed Turkish-style), *filtru* (filtered) or *nes* (instant), is usually drunk black and sweet; ask for it *cu lapte* or *fără zahăr* if you prefer it with milk or without sugar. **Cakes** and **desserts** are sweet and sticky, as throughout the Balkans. Romanians also enjoy pancakes (*clătite*) and pies (*plăcintă*) with various fillings.

Evening **drinking** takes place in outdoor beer gardens, *cramas* (beer cellars), restaurants, and in a growing number of Western-style cafés and bars. Try **ţuică**, a powerful plum brandy taken neat; in rural areas, it is home-made and often twice distilled to yield fearsomely strong *palincă*. Most **beer** (*bere*) is German-style lager. Romania's best **wines** are Grasa and Feteasca Neagră, and the sweet dessert wines of Murfatlar.

CULTURE AND ETIQUETTE

Generally speaking, Romanians tend to be very open and friendly people. They will think nothing of striking up a conversation on buses and trains,

ROMANIA ONLINE

Ⓦ**www.romaniatourism.com** Official tourism site.
Ⓦ**www.mountainguide.ro** Hiking information and links.
Ⓦ**www.eco-romania.ro** Association of ecotourism operators.
Ⓦ**www.inyourpocket.com** Online guide to Bucharest.
Ⓦ**www.sapteseri.ro** Online listings guide for most large cities.

even if they don't speak much English, and will try their best to communicate through any language barrier.

When speaking to older people, it is respectful to address them using either *Domnul* (Mr) or *Doamnă* (Mrs), while shaking someone's hand is the most common and familiar way of **greeting** – although bear in mind that a Romanian man may well kiss a woman's hand on introduction. The welcoming attitude of the Romanians may mean you are **invited to someone's home**; it is considered polite to bring a small gift with you, which you should also wrap. A bottle of wine, chocolates or flowers are all appropriate – although if you do bring flowers you should ensure an odd number of blooms, as even-numbered bouquets are strictly for funerals.

Tipping in restaurants is not necessary, although it will be appreciated.

SPORTS AND OUTDOOR ACTIVITIES

Romania's landscape is dominated by the spectacular Carpathian Mountains. A continuation of the Alps, they encircle Transylvania and provide the country with a rocky backbone perfect for activities ranging from hiking and skiing to caving and mountain biking.

The main mountain ranges, the Bucegi, the Făgăraş, the Apuseni and the Retezat, provide the best-known destinations for **hiking**. There are numerous well-marked trails allowing day-trips or longer expeditions, sleeping in a mountain refuge or *cabana* – these are usually very friendly and sociable places, and make good bases for hiking, caving or climbing. All of the trails are marked on the excellent Hartă Turistica (Ⓦwww.harta-turistica.ro) maps, which can be found in hiking shops and bookshops in most major towns. Some *cabanas* also sell maps. Spring and summer are the best seasons to explore the mountains, and a large number of trails should only be attempted in warmer weather.

Romania also offers some of Europe's cheapest **skiing** and **snowboarding** between November and April (Ⓦwww.ski-in-romania.com). There are several major ski and snowboarding resorts in Romania, the most popular of which is Poiana Braşov, near Braşov. Other resorts include Sinaia, Buşteni and Predeal – all on the main road north from Bucharest – Păltiniş near Sibiu, Borşa to the north in Maramureş, and Ceahlău and Durău on the border of Moldavia. Although Borşa is arguably the best resort for beginners, the larger resorts all have a number of easy and medium pistes and one or more black run.

COMMUNICATIONS

Post offices (*poşta*) in major cities are open Monday to Friday 7am to 8pm, Saturday 8am to noon; in smaller places they may close an hour or two earlier. You can **phone** from the orange cardphones or post offices. Phonecards (10 or 15 lei – get the latter for international calls) are available from post offices and news kiosks. **Wi-fi** is available in many cafés and hotels, though you will have to buy a drink or pay a small fee in cafés. **Internet cafés**, meanwhile, are few and far between.

EMERGENCIES

Watch out for pickpockets in crowded buses and trams. Do not believe anyone claiming to be a policeman and asking to see your passport and/or the contents of your wallet. Make sure you have health insurance. Bucharest's central emergency **hospital** is up to Western standards, while Medicover Unirii, 64–66 Marasesti Blvd (Ⓣ021/335 3900, Ⓦwww.medicover.com), also offers

EMERGENCY NUMBER

In all emergencies call Ⓣ112.

ROMANIAN

	Romanian	Pronunciation
Yes	*Da*	Da
No	*Nu*	Noo
Please	*Vă rog*	Ve rog
Thank you	*Mulţumesc*	Mult-sumesk
Hello/Good day	*Salut/bună ziua*	Saloot/boona zhewa
Goodbye	*La revedere*	La re-ve-dairy
Excuse me	*Permiteţi-mi*	Per-mi-tets-may
Where?	*Unde?*	Oun-day?
Good	*Bun/bine*	Boon/Bee-ne
Bad	*Rău*	Rau
Near	*Apropriat*	A-prope-reeat
Far	*Departe*	D'par-tay
Cheap	*Ieftin*	Yeftin
Expensive	*Scump*	Scoomp
Open	*Închis*	Un-keez
Closed	*Deschis*	Des-keez
Today	*Azi*	Az
Yesterday	*Ieri*	Ee-airy
Tomorrow	*Mâine*	Mwee-ne
How much is...?	*Cât costa...?*	Cuut costa...?
What time is it?	*Ce ora este?*	Che ora est?
I don't understand	*Nu înţeleg*	Noo unts-eledge
Do you speak English?	*Vorbiţi Englezeste?*	Vor-beetz eng-lay-zeste?
One	*Un, una*	Oon, oona
Two	*Doi, doua*	Doy, doo-a
Three	*Trei*	Tray
Four	*Patru*	Pat-ru
Five	*Cinci*	Chinch
Six	*Şase*	Shass-er
Seven	*Şapte*	Shap-tay
Eight	*Opt*	Opt
Nine	*Nouă*	No-ar
Ten	*Zece*	Zay-chay

Western-standard care, with English-speaking doctors. **Pharmacies** (*farmacie*) are open Mon–Sat 9am–6pm, though most towns and cities should have one that's open 24 hours.

INFORMATION

Outside the main cities, **tourist offices** remain few and far between. Otherwise, there are plenty of privately run **tourist agencies**, which should be able to furnish you with a basic map and information.

MONEY AND BANKS

Romania's currency is the new **leu** (plural lei, international code RON), comprising coins of 1, 5, 10 and 50, and notes of 1, 5, 10, 50, 100, 200 and 500 lei. At the time of writing exchange rates were around €1=4.10 lei, £1=4.60 lei and US$=12.90 lei. Some hotels, rental agencies and other services quote prices in euros. There are plenty of **ATMs** everywhere. **Changing money** is best done at banks, which are generally open Monday to Friday between 9am and 4pm; you will need your passport.

Never change money on the streets. **Credit cards** are accepted in most hotels, restaurants and shops.

OPENING HOURS AND HOLIDAYS

Shop **opening hours** are Monday to Friday 9am to 6pm, Saturday 9am to 1pm, with many food shops open until 10pm (or even 24hr), including weekends. Museums and castles also open roughly 9am to 6pm, though most are closed on Mondays; **admission charges** are minimal, so they are only quoted in this chapter unless they are above the norm. **National holidays** are: January 1 and 2, Easter Monday, May 1, December 1, December 25 and 26.

Bucharest

Arriving in **BUCHAREST** (Bucureşti), most tourists want to leave as quickly as possible, but to do so would mean missing the heart of Romania. Bucharest does have its charm and elegance – it just needs digging for. Among the ruptured roads and disintegrating buildings you'll find leafy squares, beautiful, if crumbling, eclectic architecture and dressed-up young Romanians adding a touch of glamour to the surroundings. What's more, it's a dynamic city, changing faster than any other in Romania as new office-towers sprout and shops and bars appear all over.

Head south of the centre into the Centru Civic and you'll come across myriad unfinished projects from Ceauşescu's reign – seeing the true scale of what a dictatorship can do is something you won't forget, and reason enough to spend a day or two in the capital.

What to see and do

The heart of the city lies to the north of the **Dâmboviţa River**, between two north–south avenues; it's a jumble of modern hotels, ancient Orthodox churches, and decaying apartment blocks, relieved by the buzzing **historic quarter** and some attractive parks. Beyond here lies Ceauşescu's monstrously compelling **Centru Civic**, centred on the extraordinary **Palace of Parliament**. Freezing in winter and hot and dusty in the summer, the northern outskirts are cooled by woodlands and a girdle of lakes.

Piaţa Revoluţiei

Most inner-city sights are within walking distance of Calea Victoriei, an avenue of vivid contrasts, scattered with vestiges of *ancien régime* elegance interspersed with apartment blocks, glass and steel facades and cake shops. Fulcrum of the avenue is **Piaţa Revoluţiei**, created during the 1930s on Carol II's orders to ensure a field of fire around the Royal Palace.

On the north side of the square is the **Athénée Palace Hotel** (now a Hilton), famous for its role as an "intelligence factory" from the 1930s until the 1980s, with its bugged rooms, tapped phones and informer prostitutes. To its east are the grand **Romanian Atheneum**, the city's main concert hall, and the **University Library**, torched, allegedly by the Securitate, in the confusion of the 1989 revolution, but since rebuilt and reopened.

To the southeast of the square is the former Communist Party HQ, now the **Senate**, where Nicolae Ceauşescu made his last speech from a low balcony on December 21. His speech drowned out by booing, the dictator's disbelief was broadcast to the nation just before the TV screens went blank. He and his wife Elena fled by helicopter from the roof, but were captured and executed on Christmas Day.

The Royal Palace

The **Royal Palace**, on the western side of Piaţa Revoluţiei, now contains the excellent **National Art Museum** (Wed–Sun: May–Sept 11am–7pm; Oct–April 10am–6pm; 15 lei, free on first Wed of month), the highlight of which is a marvellous collection of medieval and modern Romanian art, featuring the country's most revered painter, Grigorescu, and the great modern Romanian sculptor Brâncuşi; there are also impressive works by El Greco, Rembrandt and Brueghel.

The Creţulescu Church and Cişmigiu Park

Standing opposite the Senate, the eighteenth-century **Creţulescu Church** is the city's most celebrated historic building. Badly damaged during the 1989 fighting, but now handsomely

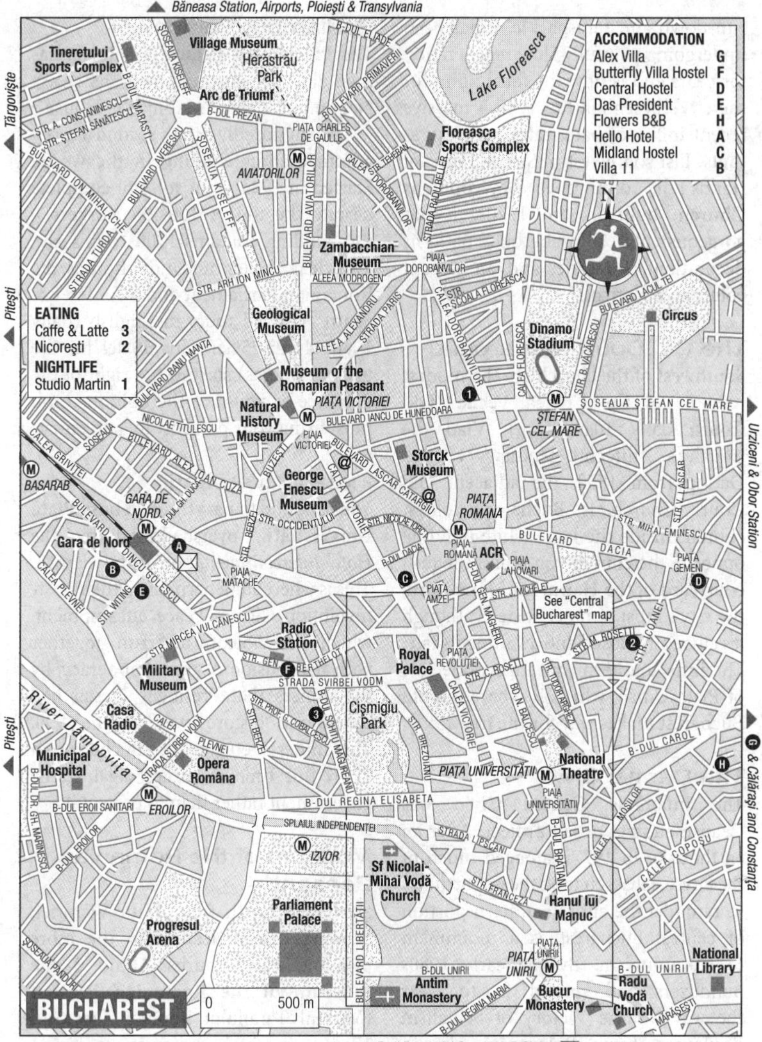

restored, it fronts a tangle of streets wending west towards **Cişmigiu Park**, Bucharest's oldest, containing a boating lake, playgrounds, summer terrace cafés and animated chess-players.

The Military Museum

West of Cişmigiu Park, near the Gara de Nord station, the **Military Museum** (Tues–Sun 9am–5pm; 6 lei) has a fine display on the army's role during the 1989 revolution. Among the most moving exhibits are the personal belongings of both civilians and soldiers, including the blood-splattered uniform worn by the then Minister of Defence, General Vasile Milea, who was executed after refusing to carry out orders to shoot civilians.

The historic centre

At the southern end of B-dul Brătianu is Bucharest's **historic centre**: mostly run-down and ramshackle, it has been undergoing painfully slow regeneration for years and is now the focal point for the city's best nightlife, with a massive recent influx of bars, cafés and restaurants. Just southwest of Strada Lipscani stands the diminutive **Stavropoleos Church**; built in the 1720s, it has gorgeous, almost arabesque, patterns decorating its facade, and an elegant columned portico.

The Old Court and around

Southwest of the church are the modest remains of the **Curtea Veche** (Old Court; daily 10am–4pm), Vlad the Impaler's fifteenth-century citadel. Dating from 1559, the adjacent Old Court Church is Bucharest's oldest church. Inside the large white building opposite the church you'll find the lush courtyard of the **Hanul lui Manuc Inn**, the city's most famous hostelry, though it's currently closed and awaiting its fate. The inn's southern wall forms one side of Piața Unirii, which is where the old Bucharest makes way for the new.

The Centru Civic

The infamous **Centru Civic** was Ceaușescu's pet urban project. After an earthquake in 1977 damaged much of the city, Ceaușescu took the opportunity to remodel the entire southern portion of central Bucharest as a monument to Communism. By the early 1980s bulldozers had moved in to clear the way for the Victory of Socialism Boulevard (now Bulevardul Unirii), taking with them thousands of architecturally significant houses, churches and monuments. Now colossal apartment blocks line Bulevardul Unirii, at 4km long and 120m wide slightly larger – intentionally so – than the Champs-Elysées on which it was modelled. The eastern end of the boulevard is now a banking district, while the other end is dominated by the Parliament Palace.

Parliament Palace

The **Parliament Palace** (Palatul Parlamentului) – also known as Casa Nebunului (The "Madman's House") – is supposedly the second-largest administration building in the world. Started in 1984 – but still not complete despite the toil of 100,000 workers – the building contains 1100 rooms and a nuclear shelter, and now houses the Romanian Parliament and a conference centre. Guided tours in English (daily 10am–4pm; 25 lei, plus 30 lei for the use of cameras) start to the right of the entrance as you face the building. You must bring your passport to gain entry.

Piața Universității

You're bound to pass through busy **Piața Universității**, overshadowed by the *Hotel Intercontinental* on B-dul Carol I. This is where students pitched their post-revolution City of Peace encampment, which was violently overrun, together with the illusion of true democracy, by the miners that President Iliescu had called in to "restore order" in June 1990. The miners returned to Bucharest in 1991, this time in protest against the government rather than to protect it.

Museum of the Romanian Peasant

Stretching north from Piața Victoriei, Șoseaua Kiseleff leads into the more pleasant, leafy suburbs. At no. 3, the **Museum of the Romanian Peasant** (Muzeul Țăranului Român; Tues–Sun 10am–6pm; 6 lei) is a must-see, giving an insight into the country's varied rural traditions, with exhibits on everything from costume and textiles to glass painted icons; to the rear there's a beautiful wooden church, as well as an excellent souvenir shop. Don't miss, in the basement, a curious exhibition of Communist iconography, featuring one of the very few pictures still remaining of Ceaușescu.

SCAMS

Despite Bucharest's reputation for **scams**, it's safer than it was. Still, never pay for anything in advance, never change money without knowing the exchange rate, and never hand your passport or wallet to anyone claiming to be a policeman. Ignore any approaches from taxi drivers and be extremely vigilant with your belongings on public transport.

Herăstrău Park and the Village Museum

Just to the north of the museums, traffic heading for the airports and Transylvania swings around a familiar-looking Arc de Triumf, commemorating Romania's participation on the side of the Allied victors in World War I. To the right, in **Herăstrău Park**, the city's largest, is the **Village Museum** (Muzeul Satului; daily 9am–5pm; 6 lei), a fabulous ensemble of wooden houses, churches, windmills and other structures from various regions of the country.

Arrival and information

Air Otopeni (Henri Coandă) airport is 17km north of the centre; ignore all offers of a taxi within the terminal and instead head through to departures and grab one as it drops someone off – the most reputable firms are Meridian (Ⓣ9444) and Cristaxi (Ⓣ9461), who will charge around 30 lei to the centre; alternatively, head for the #783 bus stop just outside – buy your two-ride ticket (8 lei) from the RATB kiosk. An hourly rail service also connects the airport with Gara de Nord station (50min including transfer between arrivals and the airport train station). Aurel Vlaicu (Băneasa) airport is 8km north of the centre. Buses #131, #335, #780 and #783 leave from the road across from the airport exit.
Train Virtually all trains terminate at the Gara de Nord, from where it's a 30min walk into the centre, or a short ride on the metro (change lines at Piața Victoriei to reach Piața Universității). Taxi drivers are ready to pounce at the main entrance, but only use a reliable company (see above).
Tourist information The main tourist information office is in the Piața Universității underpass (Mon–Fri 9am–6pm, Sat 9am–1pm; Ⓣ021/305 5500), with another, much smaller booth on the main concourse in the Gara de Nord (daily 9am–8pm); while here pick up a free copy of the English-language listings magazine *Bucharest in Your Pocket* (also free in hotels).

City transport

Public transport Although crowded, public transport is efficient and very cheap. The most useful lines of the metro system (3 lei for two journeys, 9 lei for ten) are the M2 (north–south) and M3 (a near-circle). There's also an array of trams, buses and trolleybuses (1.50 lei for one journey).
Tickets Must be bought from kiosks located near the bus stops, and validated in the machine on board.
Taxi After 11.30pm you'll have to depend on taxis, which are very cheap, at about 2 lei/km; the most reputable companies are Cristaxi (Ⓣ9461), Cobalcescu (Ⓣ9451) or Meridian (Ⓣ9444) – make sure the meter is running.

Accommodation

Private apartments generally represent good value in Bucharest – try RoCazare (Ⓣ031/805 1940, Ⓦwww.rocazare.ro) or Professional Realty (Ⓣ021/232 0406, Ⓦwww.accommodation.com.ro), both of which have centrally located rooms and apartments from around 180 lei/day. The following are marked on the map on p.957, unless otherwise stated.

Hostels

Alex Villa Str Avram Iancu 5 Ⓣ021/313 3198, Ⓦwww.alexvilla.ro. This bright and lively hostel has a/c rooms sleeping 2 to 9, free internet and a common room with cable TV. Take trolleybus #85 from Piața Universității east to the Calea Moșilor stop, and continue on foot past the roundabout, turning right at the Greek church. Dorms 40 lei, doubles 100 lei, singles 70 lei.
Butterfly Villa Hostel Str Stirbei Voda 96 Ⓣ021/314 7595, Ⓦwww.villabutterfly.com. Friendly, intimate hostel close to Cişmigiu Park, with two- to eight-bed rooms split over four levels. Price includes breakfast, internet and lockers; laundry is extra and there's often a barbecue in the garden during summer. Bus #178 from Gara de Nord. Dorms 50 lei, doubles 120 lei.
Central Hostel Str Salcamilor 2 Ⓣ021/610 2214, Ⓦwww.centralhostel.ro. Clean and simple place with two- to eight-bed rooms; breakfast and internet is included while laundry is extra. Take bus #79, #86 or #133 from Gara de Nord to Piața

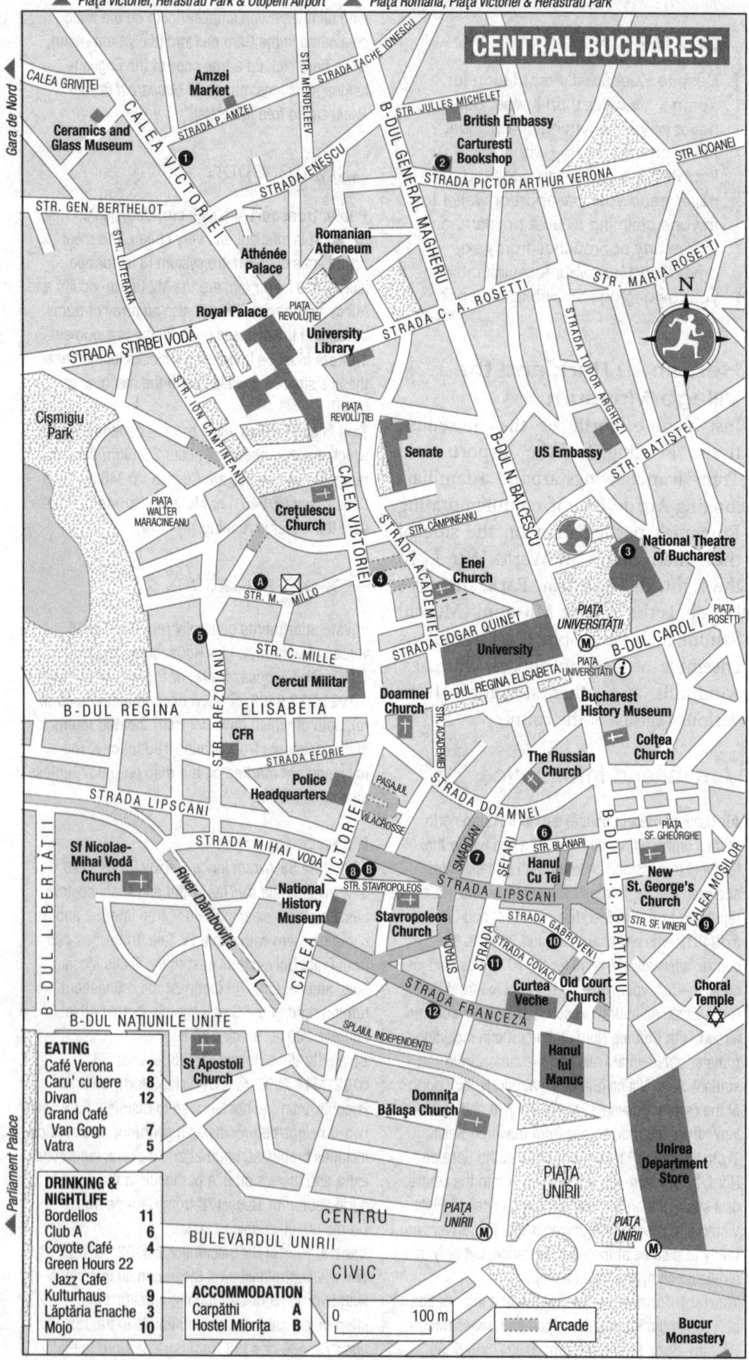

CENTRAL BUCHAREST
Piaţa Victoriei, Herăstrău Park & Otopeni Airport
Piaţa Romană, Piaţa Victoriei & Herăstrău Park
Gara de Nord
Parliament Palace
Amzei Market
Ceramics and Glass Museum
British Embassy
Carturesti Bookshop
Romanian Atheneum
Athénée Palace
Royal Palace
University Library
Cişmigiu Park
Senate
US Embassy
Creţulescu Church
National Theatre of Bucharest
Enei Church
University
Cercul Militar
Doamnei Church
Bucharest History Museum
CFR
Colţea Church
The Russian Church
Police Headquarters
Sf Nicolae-Mihai Vodă Church
Hanul Cu Tei
New St. George's Church
National History Museum
Stavropoleos Church
Curtea Veche
Old Court Church
Choral Temple
Hanul lui Manuc
St Apostoli Church
Domniţa Bălaşa Church
Unirea Department Store
PIAŢA UNIRII
CENTRU
CIVIC
Bucur Monastery
EATING
Café Verona 2
Caru' cu bere 8
Divan 12
Grand Café Van Gogh 7
Vatra 5
DRINKING & NIGHTLIFE
Bordellos 11
Club A 6
Coyote Café 4
Green Hours 22 Jazz Cafe 1
Kulturhaus 9
Lăptăria Enache 3
Mojo 10
ACCOMMODATION
Carpăthi A
Hostel Mioriţa B
0 100 m
Arcade

Gemeni, two stops after Piaţa Romană; then take the first right off B-dul Dacia into Str Viitorului. Dorms 45–60 lei, doubles 150 lei.

Midland Hostel Str Biserica Amzei 22 ⓣ021/314 5323, ⓦwww.themidlandhostel.com. Great central location for this modern hostel, with large dorms sleeping between six and fourteen; breakfast, internet and lockers included. Laundry is extra. Dorms 50–60 lei.

Villa 11 Str Institutul Medico-Militar 11 ⓣ0722/495 900, ⓔvila11bb@hotmail.com. Friendly, family-run hostel just 5min walk from Gara de Nord, with two-, three- and six-bed rooms, some with bathroom. Price includes a pancake breakfast. Laundry and bike hire available. Dorms 45 lei, doubles 120 lei, singles 80 lei.

Hotels

Carpâti Str Matei Millo 16 ⓣ021/315 0140, ⓦwww.hotelcarpatibucuresti.ro. See map opposite. Near Cişmigiu Park, quiet and with helpful staff. Singles and doubles available, some with shared showers or toilet and some en suite, all with TV. Doubles 210–260 lei.

Das President B-dul Golescu 29 ⓣ021/311 0535, ⓦwww.daspresident.ro. Situated across from the train station, this good-value place offers clean, light rooms with flat-screen TVs and modern furnishings, with private and shared bathrooms. Breakfast included. Doubles 150–170 lei.

Flowers B&B Str Plantelor 2 ⓣ021/311 9848, ⓦwww.flowersbb.ro. First-class and very hospitable bed and breakfast, with elegant en-suite rooms and a lovely summery terrace. Bus #65 or #85 to B-dul Carol I from where it's a five-minute walk. Breakfast included. Doubles 190 lei.

Hello Hotel Calea Grivitei 43 ⓣ0372/121 800, ⓦwww.hellohotels.ro. A two-minute walk from the train station, this large, modern hotel has colourful, good-sized rooms with wall-mounted TVs. Breakfast is extra. Doubles 270 lei.

Hostel Mioriţa Str Lipscani 12 ⓣ021/312 0361, ⓦwww.hostel-miorita.ro. See map opposite. A hotel rather than a hostel, the homely *Mioriţa* has a great central location, with six spacious en-suite rooms and cable TV. Breakfast included. Doubles 170 lei.

Eating

Bucharest's restaurant scene has improved dramatically in recent years, and there's now a wide selection of ethnic cuisines to choose from, as well as the traditional Romanian fare. Look out for restaurants offering daily set menus; these three-or four-course meals are typically available Monday to Friday between noon and 5pm and cost around 15–20 lei. The following are marked on the map opposite, unless otherwise stated.

Cafés and restaurants

Café Verona Str Pictor Arthur Verona 13. Located inside the Cărtureşti bookshop, this sophisticated coffeehouse is one of Bucharest's best and is a great place to relax with a coffee, book or laptop. Daily till midnight.

Caffe and Latte B-dul Schitu Măgureanu 35. See map, p.957. Small, colourful café opposite Cişmigiu Park serving a fabulous range of coffees, shakes, sandwiches and cakes. They sell alcoholic drinks too. Daily 8am–10pm.

Caru' cu bere Str Stavropoleos 5. Superb restaurant housed in a spectacular nineteenth-century beer-house replete with carved wooden balconies, stained-glass windows and uniformed waiters. The menu features a broad range of Romanian dishes (15–40 lei), and beer is still brewed on the premises. Daily till midnight.

Divan Str Franceză 46–48. Fabulous Turkish/Middle Eastern restaurant in the heart of the Old Town, doling out authentic and beautifully presented mezes (15 lei), pittas (25 lei) and mains such as lamb kebabs (25–30 lei). Round it all off with a water pipe. Daily noon–11.30pm.

Grand Café Van Gogh Str Smărdan 9. Effortlessly cool Old Town café with a smart orange tinted interior, smooth wooden tables and big bay windows, not to mention a fabulous terrace. Excellent drinks menu (including wine) as well as breakfasts (9 lei), toasted sandwiches (8 lei) and platters (25 lei). Daily 10am–1am.

Nicoreşti Str Maria Rosetti 40. See map, p.957. Unassuming place serving traditional Romanian dishes, such as *ciorba* (thick soup) and pork knuckle with beans, at rock-bottom prices with accompanying live music. Mains 15–20 lei. Daily 11am–11pm.

Vatra Str Brezoianu 23. Very central, very affordable, with simple but tasty Romanian dishes such as *ciorba* (8 lei) and *mici* (12 lei). Daily till midnight.

Drinking and nightlife

Bucharest's historic quarter is now awash with bars, pubs and clubs, and in summer, the clubs and restaurants around the lake in Herăstrău Park are popular. For more detailed information on the city's nightlife check out *Bucharest in Your Pocket* (ⓦwww.inyourpocket.com/romania/bucharest). The following are marked on the map opposite, unless otherwise stated.

Bars and clubs

Bordellos Str Selari 9–11. One of the burgeoning Old Town hangouts, this vibrant pub has good draught beers, great tapas and big screens for all your sporting kicks. Daily 10am–5am.

Club A Str Blănari 14. Catering to a studenty crowd, this is the city's most established venue, a good-time party place with music, theatre and cheap drinks. Mon–Fri 10.30am–5am, Sat 9pm–5am, Sun 5pm–5am.

Coyote Café Calea Victoriei 48–50 (Pasajul Victoriei). Warren-like basement bar renowned for staging some of the city's best gigs; otherwise, a cool place to kick back in and down a beer or two. Tues–Sun 6pm–2am.

Green Hours 22 Jazz Cafe Calea Victoriei 120. Cramped cellar-bar with frequent live music and arty theatre shows that attract a lively alternative crowd. In summer, the action moves outdoors to the leafy courtyard. Open 24hr.

Kulturhaus Str Sf. Vineri 4. Slightly leftfield but massively popular club, with tunes to suit many tastes including folk rock, new wave, punk and indie; there's usually a live band once a week. Thurs–Sat 9pm–5am.

Lăptăria Enache 4th floor of the National Theatre, Piaţa Universităţii. One of Bucharest's most popular bars, with live music in winter, and free films on the rooftop terrace in summer. Entrance is to the left of the theatre as you face it. Daily noon–2am (Fri & Sat till 4am).

Mojo Str Gabroveni 14 Ⓦwww.mojomusic.ro. Cracking Old Town venue offering three floors of fun; the basement Brit Room for gigs (by both the resident house band and visiting groups), a ground-floor bar, and a top-floor acoustic room for karaoke, comedy and the like. Daily 8pm–5am.

Studio Martin B-dul Iancu de Hunedoara 61, near Piaţa Victoriei Ⓦwww.studiomartin.ro. See map, p.957. For serious clubbers, this place brings in the ravers with its international guest DJs (playing techno and house) and gay-friendly atmosphere. Fri & Sat 10pm–5am.

Shopping

Unirea department store Piaţa Unirii 1. Central, enormous and a good place to find familiar labels. Daily 10am–10pm.

Cartureşti bookshop Str Pictor Arthur Verona 13. Superb for English-language books (including Romanian history and literature) and all kinds of music. Daily 10am–10pm.

Hanul cu Tei bazaar Str Lipscani 63–65. Romanian antiques and souvenirs. Mon–Sat 10am–6pm. Also for souvenirs, try the Museum of the Romanian Peasant and the Village Museum.

Târgul Vitan flea market Calea Vitan (metro Dristor I). Sun only.

Piaţa Dorobanţi and Piaţa Matache The best of the city's daily food markets. Both 6am–2pm.

Directory

Embassies and consulates Australia, 5th floor, Str Buzesti 14–18 ⓣ021/316 7558; Canada, Str Tuberozelor 1–3 ⓣ021/307 5000; Ireland, Str Buzesti 50–52 ⓣ021/310 2161; UK, Str J. Michelet 24 ⓣ021/201 7200; US, Str T. Arghezi 7–9 ⓣ021/200 3300.

Gay and lesbian For information, contact Accept ⓣ021/252 9000, Ⓦwww.accept-romania.ro.

Hospital Spitalul Clinic de Urgenţa, Calea Floreasca 8 ⓣ021/599 2300. Medicover Unirii, 64–66 Marasesti Blvd ⓣ021/310 1599, Ⓦwww.medicover.com.

Internet Most hotels and upmarket cafés offer free wi-fi. The best internet point is the Orange Studio at B-dul Lascăr Catargiu 51 (Mon–Fri 9am–9pm, Sat 9am–4pm); also Acces Internet at B-dul Lascăr Catargiu 6 (24hr).

Left luggage *Bagaj de mână* (8 lei; open 24hr) at the Gara de Nord, opposite platforms 4 and 5.

Pharmacy Sensiblu has pharmacies throughout the city. Its 24hr branches are at B-dul Ion Mihalache 106 and Str Radu Beller 6. Helpnet has 24hr pharmacies at B-dul Ion Mihalache 92 and B-dul Unirii 27.

Police B-dul Lascăr Catargiu 22 ⓣ021/212 5684.

Post office Str M. Millo 10 (Mon–Fri 7.30am–8pm) and Str Gara de Nord (Mon–Fri 7.30am–8pm, Sat 8am–2pm).

Moving on

Train Braşov (every 45min–1hr; 2hr 30min–4hr 45min); Sibiu (3 daily; 4hr 45min–5hr 50min); Sighişoara (8 daily; 5hr 15min–6hr); Timişoara (6 daily; 8hr 15min–9hr 30min).

Bus Braşov (hourly; 2hr 45min); Sibiu (hourly; 4hr 30min).

Transylvania

From Bucharest, trains carve their way north through the spectacular **Carpathian mountain range** into the heart of **Transylvania.** The Carpathians offer Europe's cheapest skiing in winter and wonderful hiking during the summer, along with caves, alpine meadows, dense forests sheltering bears, and lowland valleys with quaint villages.

The population is a mix of Romanians, Magyars, Germans, Roma and others, thanks to centuries of migration and colonization. The Trianon Treaty of 1920 placed Transylvania within the Romanian state, but the character of many towns still reflects past patterns of settlement. Most striking are the former seats of Saxon power with their defensive towers and fortified churches. Sighişoara is the most picturesque but could be the Saxons' cenotaph: they have left their houses and churches but their living culture has evaporated, as it threatens to do in Braşov and Sibiu.

BRAŞOV

With an eye for trade and invasion routes, the medieval Saxons sited their largest settlements near Transylvania's mountain passes. **BRAŞOV**, which they called Kronstadt, grew prosperous as a result, and Saxon dominance lasted until the Communist government brought thousands of Moldavian villagers to work in the new factories. As a result, there are two parts to Braşov: the Gothic and Baroque centre beneath Mount Tâmpa, which looks great, and the surrounding sprawl of flats, which doesn't. The central square, surrounded by restored merchants' houses, is now the heart of a buzzing city with a raft of exciting bars and restaurants.

What to see and do

Buses from the station will leave you near the central square, **Piaţa Sfatului**. Leading northeast from the square the pedestrianized **Strada Republicii** is the hub of Braşov's social and commercial life.

Piaţa Sfatului

Piaţa Sfatului is overshadowed by the Gothic pinnacles of the city's most famous landmark, the **Black Church** (Mon–Sat 10am–5pm; 6 lei), which stab upwards like a series of daggers. An endearingly monstrous hall-church that took almost a century to complete (1383–1477), it is so called for its soot-blackened walls, the result of being torched by the Austrian army in 1689. Inside, by contrast, the church is startlingly white, with oriental carpets creating splashes of colour along the walls of the nave. In summer (June–Sept Tues, Thurs & Sat at 6pm), the church's 4000-pipe organ is used for concerts.

The fifteenth-century council house (Casa Sfatului) in the centre of Piaţa Sfatului now houses the **History Museum**, which has a small exhibition dedicated to the Saxon guilds that dominated Braşov in medieval times (Tues–Sun 10am–5pm; 6 lei).

Mount Tâmpa

A length of fortress wall runs along the foot of **Mount Tâmpa**, behind which

THE FORTIFIED CHURCHES OF TRANSYLVANIA

Transylvania's Saxon legacy is clearly apparent in the fortified churches erected throughout the region's villages following the migration of the Saxons to Romania under King Géza II in 1150. The Mioritics Association, in conjuction with UNESCO, is dedicated to preserving the fortified churches and developing tourism around them (Ⓦwww.fortified-churches.com). Despite this, most are not well known and there is little information available. However, most are accessible with their original gate-key, which is usually kept by one of the elder villagers for safekeeping. Simply ask in the village for the key-holder, who should be able to open up the church and show you around. It is normal to pay them a small amount (about 5 lei) for their trouble.

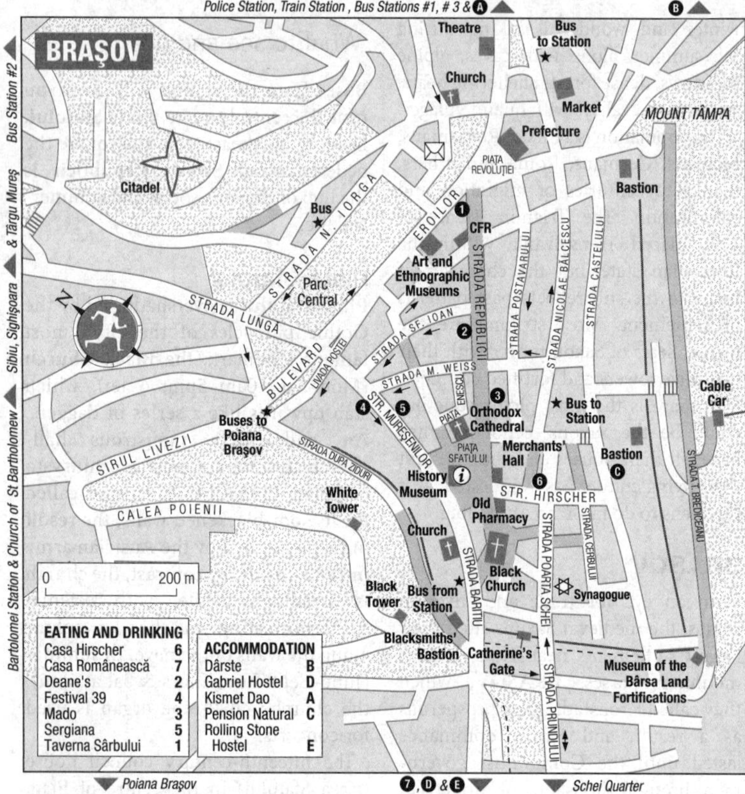

a **cable car** (Tues–Sun 9am–6pm; 8 lei) whisks tourists up to the summit. However, the trails to the top offer a challenging walk (1hr) and some fantastic views.

Museum of the Bârsa Land Fortifications

Of the original seven bastions (towers maintained by the city's trade guilds), the best preserved is that of the weavers, on Str Coşbuc. This complex of wooden galleries and bolt holes now contains the **Museum of the Bârsa Land Fortifications** (Tues–Sun 10am–5pm; 6 lei). Inside are models and weaponry recalling the bad old days when the region was repeatedly attacked by Tatars, Turks and by Vlad the Impaler, who left hundreds of captives on sharp stakes to terrorize the townsfolk. The Saxons' widely publicized stories of Vlad's cruelty unwittingly contributed to Transylvania's dark image and eventually caught Bram Stoker's attention as he conceived *Dracula*.

Arrival and information

Train Braşov's train station is northeast of the old town, 2km from the centre – take bus #4 into town or spend around 8 lei on a taxi.

Tourist office In the History Museum, Piaţa Sfatului 30 (daily 9am–5pm; ⓣ0268/419 078, ⓦwww.brasov.ro).

Internet Cyber Café, Str Republicii 58 (daily 11am–9pm); Internet Café, Str Michael Weiss 11; and on the mezzanine floor of the train station.

Accommodation

Dârste 6km southeast of Braşov at Calea Bucureşti 285 ⓣ0268/339 967, ⓦwww.campingdirste.ro.

Modern campsite with cabins; bus #17 from the centre or #35 from the station. Camping 13 lei, double cabins 55–120 lei.

Gabriel Hostel Str Vasile Saftu 41a ⓣ0744/844 223. One of two hostels in the historic Schei district (bus #51), this quiet, pleasant place has small dorms with segregated male and female bathrooms, a kitchen and internet. Breakfast not included. Dorms 50 lei.

Kismet Dao Str Neagoe Basarab 8 ⓣ0268/514 296, ⓦwww.kismetdao.com. Busy, popular hostel just 5 min from the centre, with decent dorms and private rooms, and a large kitchen. Breakfast, laundry and wi-fi included. Dorms 40 lei, doubles 130 lei.

Pension Natural Str Castelului 58 ⓣ0744/321 273, ⓦwww.pensiuneanatural.ro. Immaculate family-run *pension* with a tranquil garden beside the city walls. Breakfast included. Doubles 200 lei, singles 170 lei, apartment 250 lei.

Rolling Stone Hostel Str Piatra Mare 2a ⓣ0268/513 965 or 0744/816970, ⓦwww.rollingstone.ro. Friendly, sociable hostel with clean, attractive dorms, private rooms and immaculate bathrooms. Pleasant garden terrace with pool and basement bar. Breakfast included. Dorms 42 lei, doubles 150 lei.

Eating and drinking

Casa Hirscher Piaţa Sfatului 12–14. This lovely restaurant, housed in an atmospheric seventeenth-century building, serves quality Romanian and international specialities. Mains 20–40 lei. Daily 9am–11.30pm.

Casa Românească Piaţa Unirii 15. Friendly and cheap restaurant convenient for the hostels, with a courtyard offering views of the *piaţa*. Traditional Romanian fare, and good-sized portions. Mains 15–25 lei. Daily 11am–midnight.

Deane's Str Republicii 19. Eternally popular Irish boozer which puts on some form of entertainment most evenings (music, comedy, karaoke, quizzes). Live sport on TV and a darts room too. Daily 10am–midnight.

Festival 39 Str Republicii 62. A great place to drink, Braşov's most well-known bar is full of the strangest things – from badly stuffed animals to plastic trophies.

Mado Str Republicii 10. Popular restaurant with outdoor seating and a spacious interior. The dishes include traditional Romanian and Turkish specialities; you can also try some Romanian wines, such as the hearty and spicy hot wine favoured in rural Transylvania during winter. Home-made cakes too. Mains 15–30 lei. Daily 10am–midnight.

Sergiana Str Mureşenilor 27. Serves wholesome and tasty Transylvanian food in its warren of atmospheric cellars. Mains 15–30 lei. Daily 11am–1am.

Taverna Sârbului Str Republicii 55. Capacious brick-cellar restaurant dishing up gut-busting portions of meat-heavy Serbian food. Mains 15–25 lei. Daily 9am–11pm.

Moving on

Train Bucharest (every 45min–1hr; 2hr 30min–4hr 45min); Sibiu (8 daily; 2hr 15min–3hr 55min); Sighişoara (10 daily; 1hr 40min–3hr); Timişoara (2 daily; 8hr 45min).

Bus Bran (every 30min Mon–Fri, hourly Sat & Sun; 45min); Bucharest (hourly; 2hr 45min); Zărneşti (hourly Mon–Fri, 8 Sat, 2 Sun; 1hr).

BRAN

Cosy little **BRAN**, 28km southwest of Braşov, is situated at the foot of the stunning Bucegi Mountains. Despite what you may hear, its **castle** (Mon noon–6pm, Tues–Sun 9am–6pm; 20 lei) has only tenuous associations with Dracula, aka Vlad the Impaler, who may have attacked it in 1460. Hyperbole is forgivable, though, as Bran really does look like a vampire count's residence. The castle was built in 1377 by the Saxons of Braşov to safeguard what used to be the main route into Wallachia, and it rises in tiers of towers and ramparts from among the woods, against a glorious mountain background. A warren of stairs, nooks and chambers around a small courtyard, the interior is filled with elaborately carved four-poster beds, throne-like chairs and portraits of grim-faced boyars.

Arrival

Bus Services from Braşov to Bran and Zărneşti leave from bus station 2, 3km north of central Braşov at the end of Str Lungă; take bus #12 from the centre of Braşov or bus #10 from the train station, and get off opposite the stadium.

Accommodation

Private rooms *Ovi-Tours* Str Bologa 16 (ⓣ0268/236 666) have some clean and rustic-style rooms. 80 lei.

The Guesthouse Str General Traian Mosoiu 365B ⓣ0745/179 475, ⓦwww.guesthouse.ro. A comfortable alternative run by an affable British expat, set in a large garden, with kitchen facilities and immaculate en-suite doubles. 120 lei.

Moving on

Bus Braşov (every 30min Mon–Fri, hourly Sat & Sun; 45min); Zărneşti (8 daily; 30min).

RÂŞNOV AND ZĂRNEŞTI

For a more low-key, but no less satisfying, experience than Bran, jump off the Braşov bus in nearby **RÂŞNOV**, where the hilltop fortress (daily 8am–8pm; 6 lei) and the views are stunning. North of Bran is **ZĂRNEŞTI**, a charming small town that is the perfect jumping-off point for trips into the Făgăraş Mountains. You can stay at the homely *Pensiunea Mosorel*, Str Dr Senchea 162 (ⓣ0744/368 432, ⓦwww.pensiuneamosorel.ro; 60 lei), where you can also pitch a tent for the night (12 lei). For a near-medieval mountain escape, spend a night at *Cabana Montana* (ⓣ0744/801 094; 50 lei), in the picturesque hamlet of **MAGURĂ**, on the flanks of the Piatra Craiului Mountains just south of Zărneşti. Phone ahead and they'll pick you up from Zărneşti's bus station.

SIGHIŞOARA

A forbidding silhouette of battlements and needle spires looms over the citadel of **SIGHIŞOARA**, perched on a hill overlooking the Târnave Mare valley; it seems fitting that this was the birthplace of Vlad Ţepeş, the man known to posterity as **Dracula**. Look out for the Medieval Arts and the Inter-ethnic Cultural **festivals** held annually in July and August, when Sighişoara may be overrun by thousands of beer-swillers.

What to see and do

The route from the train station to the centre passes the **Romanian Orthodox Cathedral**, its gleaming white, multifaceted facade a striking contrast to the dark interior. Across the **Târnave Mare** River, the **citadel** dominates the town from a hill whose slopes support a jumble of ancient houses. Steps lead up from the lower town's main square, Piaţa Hermann Oberth, to the main gateway, above which rises the mighty **clock tower**. This was built in the fourteenth century when Sighişoara became a free town controlled by craft guilds – each of which had to finance the construction of a bastion and defend it in wartime.

Sighişoara grew rich on the proceeds of trade with Moldavia and Wallachia, as attested by the regalia and strongboxes in the tower's **museum** (Tues–Fri 10am–5.30pm, Sat & Sun 9am–4.30pm). The ticket also gives access to the seventeenth-century **torture chamber** and the **Museum of Armaments** next door,

WOLF AND BEAR TRACKING IN THE CARPATHIANS

Romania has the largest **wolf** and **brown bear** populations in Europe. Transylvanian Wolf (ⓣ0744/319 708, ⓦwww.transylvanianwolf.ro) is an organization offering guided walks (around 300 lei for up to 5 people, 65 lei for each extra person) tracking wolves, bears, red deer and lynx under the eagle eye of Dan Marin, an award-winning tracker who works closely with conservation organizations and the new Piatra Craiului National Park.

In winter there's also the chance to see some spectacular snow-covered landscapes, and take part in sleigh rides and cross-country skiing. Treat yourself and stay in the Marins' spectacular family guesthouse (Str I. Metianu nr. 108, Zărneşti; 200 lei), where all meals (breakfast, dinner and packed lunch) are home-cooked and included in the price.

with its small and poorly presented "Dracula Exhibition".

In 1431 or thereabouts, the child later known as Dracula was born at Str Muzeului 6 near the clock tower. At the time his father – Vlad Dracul – was commander of the mountain passes into Wallachia, but the younger Vlad's privileged childhood ended eight years later, when he and his brother Radu were sent to Anatolia as hostages to the Turks. There Vlad observed the Turks' use of terror, which he would later turn against them, earning the nickname of "The Impaler". Nowadays, Vlad's birthplace is a mediocre tourist restaurant.

Arrival and information

Train Sighişoara's train station is on the northern edge of town, on Str Libertăţii.
Tourist office There's tourist information at Piaţa Goga 8 (☎0265/770 415) and the more useful Cultural Heritage Info Center, opposite the clock tower at Piaţa Muzeului 6 (☎0788/115 511).

Accommodation

Private rooms Backpackers are met at the station by runners for the town's many excellent private rooms; the best are with the Faur family in the citadel at Str Cojocarilor 1 (☎0744/119 211, ©cristinafaur2003@yahoo.de); guests have use of a kitchen. Dorms 45 lei, doubles 105 lei.
Burg Hostel Str Bastionului 4–6 ☎0265/778 489, ⓦwww.burghostel.ro. Centrally located with clean dorms, doubles and triples. There is a bar in the cellar, internet access and free wi-fi. Breakfast isn't included, but there is a good-value restaurant in the courtyard. Dorms 40 lei, doubles 90 lei.
Nathan's Villa Str Libertăţii 8 ☎0265/772 546, ⓦwww.nathansvilla.com/sighisoara.html. Friendly, popular hostel with bright, airy dorms sleeping ten and four people, in addition to one en-suite double. Breakfast and laundry are included. Dorms 45 lei, doubles 110 lei.

Eating and drinking

Casa cu Cerb Str Şcolii 1. In the hotel of the same name, this is one of the best restaurants in the citadel, with good breakfasts, light meals and more expensive dinners. There's also a lovely, sunny outdoor seating area. Mains 20–35 lei.

TREAT YOURSELF

Casa cu Cerb Str Şcolii 1 (☎0265/774 625, ⓦwww.casacucerb.ro; 250 lei). This extremely classy hotel is a good choice for romantics, with bathtubs big enough for two, while the most expensive rooms have four-poster beds. Breakfast included.

Culture Pub In the basement of the *Burg Hostel* (see below), with some live rock/pop music, mainly weekend evenings. Open till 3am.
International Café Piaţa Cetăţii 8. A cosy café serving delicious and filling sandwiches and cakes (8 lei), and just about the only quiche (10 lei) in Transylvania. Mon–Sat 8am–9pm in summer, 10am–6pm in winter.
Quattro Amici Str Octavian Goga 12. In the lower town, this enjoyable pizzeria offers fabulous oven-baked pizzas and fresh salads, and there's outdoor seating facing the field. Mains 10–20 lei. Daily 10am–11pm.
Rustica Str 1 Decembrie 1918 no. 58. Hearty, wholesome Romanian food – *mititei*, *sarmalute* and the like – in nice surroundings and a popular bar at night. Good breakfast menu. Mains 15–25 lei. Daily 10am–11pm.

Moving on

Train Braşov (10 daily; 1hr 45min–2hr 45min); Bucharest (8 daily; 5hr 15min–6hr 15min); Sibiu (change at Copşa Mică or Mediaş; 15 daily; 2hr 5min–2hr 45min).

SIBIU

The narrow streets and old gabled houses of **SIBIU**'s older quarters seem to have come straight off the page of a fairytale. Like Braşov, Sibiu was founded by Germans invited by Hungary's King Géza II to colonize strategic regions of Transylvania in 1143. Its inhabitants dominated trade in Transylvania and Wallachia, but their citadels were no protection against the tide of history, which eroded their influence after the eighteenth century. Within the last decades almost the entire Saxon community has left Romania. Sibiu still has stronger and more lucrative links with Germany than any Transylvanian town, and its stint as European Capital of Culture in 2007 left its buildings handsomely refurbished. The city also stages some cracking festivals, not least the International Theatre Festival in late May, with open-air stages across all the main squares.

What to see and do

To reach the old town cross the square from the train station and follow Str Gen. Magheru to **Piaţa Mare** – one of three conjoined squares that form the centre.

Piaţa Mare

On the western side of Piaţa Mare stands the handsome eighteenth-century **Brukenthal Palace**, housing the eponymously named **museum** (Tues–Sun 10am–6pm; 12 lei), one of the finest in Romania with an evocative collection of works by Transylvanian and Western painters – look out for Jan van Eyck's *Man in Blue Turban*. The city's **History Museum** (Tues–Sun 10am–6pm; 12 lei) is nearby in the impressive Old City Hall. On the northern side of Piaţa Mare, the huge Catholic church stands next to the **Council Tower** (daily 10am–6pm), which offers fine views to the Carpathians.

The cathedral

Just beyond the Council Tower, on Piaţa Huet, the **Evangelical Cathedral** (Mon–Sat 9am–8pm, Sun from 11am) is a massive hall-church raised during the fourteenth and fifteenth centuries. Climb the tower (Mon–Sat noon–4pm), or descend to the crypt, which contains impressive tombstones of local notables as well as of Mihnea the Bad, the Impaler's son, stabbed to death outside here in 1510.

Museum of Traditional Folk Civilization

Set aside most of a day to explore Sibiu's wonderful open-air **Museum of Traditional Folk Civilization** (Muzeul Astra; Tues–Sun 10am–8pm; 15 lei) on Calea Răşinari, south of the centre; take trolleybus #1 to the end of the line. Set against a mountain backdrop, the museum offers a fantastic insight into rural life, with authentically furnished wooden houses, churches and mills; there's also a traditional inn serving local food and drink.

Arrival and information

Train and bus Sibiu's train and bus stations are next to each other on Piaţa 1 Decembrie 1918, 400m northeast of the main square.

Tourist office Sibiu's tourist office, inside the City Hall at Str Samuel Brukenthal 2 (Mon–Sat 9am–5pm & Sun 9am–1pm; ⓣ0269/208 913, ⓦwww.sibiu.ro), also sells maps.

Internet Silence Internet Café, Str Mitropoliei 27 (daily 9am–10pm).

Accommodation

Ela Str Nouă 43 ⓣ0269/215 197, ⓦwww.ela-hotels.ro. A friendly, family-run hotel, with a pleasant garden, eight spotless en-suite rooms and guest kitchen. From the train station take Str 9 Mai, turn right onto Str Rebreanu, then first left onto Str Nouă. Breakfast is 15 lei. Singles 80 lei, doubles 100 lei.

Evangelisches Pfarrhaus Piaţa Huet 1 ⓣ0269/211 203, ⓔgast@evang.ro. Next to the cathedral, the Lutheran parish house (daily 8am–3pm, or call in advance so a key can be left for you) has a hostel with simple rooms sleeping two to four. No breakfast. Dorms 40 lei.

Old Town Hostel Piaţa Mică 26 ⓣ0269/216 445, ⓦwww.hostelsibiu.ro. Located above a historic pharmacy in a 450-year-old building, the hostel has three large, airy dorms and also offers en-suite doubles at a different location. Breakfast is not included but there is a kitchen, plus free tea and coffee and internet access. The hostel can also arrange bike rental. Dorms 45 lei, doubles 150 lei.

Pensiune and Camping Sălişteanca at Str Băii 13, Sălişte ⓣ0269/553 121, ⓦwww.salisteanca.com. A fantastic choice in summer, this riverside campsite is a lovely place to stay, and has clean, modern facilities. There are also a few large en-suite rooms available, furnished in traditional Transylvanian style. Breakfast 12 lei. dinner is available in the *pensiune* on request. Camping 15 lei per person plus tent, doubles 90 lei.

Podul Minciunilor Str Azilului 1 ⓣ0269/217 259, ⓦwww.ela-hotels.ro. A small, family-run guesthouse near the Liar's Bridge, with five en-suite doubles and one triple. No breakfast. Singles 70 lei, doubles 100 lei.

Eating and drinking

Crama Sibiu Vechi Str Ilarian 3. This cellar restaurant decorated in local style is the best place for something typically Romanian, complete with live folk music and staff dressed in traditional costume. They also have cheap wine on tap. Mains 12–30 lei. Daily noon–11.30pm.

Imperium Club Str Bălcescu 24 Ⓦwww.imperiumclub.eu. Cool, classy brick-cellar bar with regular jazz sessions, piano concerts on Sundays, and evenings of stand-up comedy. Good beer too.

La Turn Piața Mare 1. In a central location next to the Council Tower, this place has a decent range of grilled and barbecued dishes. Mains 15–35 lei. Daily 10.30am–11pm.

Mara Str Bălcescu 21. Excellent local food is served up here, including some superb game, and they also have a large selection of wines, including Romanian varieties. Mains 15–40 lei. Daily 10am–midnight.

Trej Stejari Str Fabricii 2. Enormous summer terrace from which to enjoy big jugs of beer brewed just next door, as well as grilled meats from the barbecue.

Moving on

Train Braşov (7 daily; 2hr 10min–3hr 50min); Bucharest (3 daily; 5hr 25min); Sighişoara (change at Copşa Mică or Mediaş; 16 daily; 2hr 15min–3hr); Timişoara (2 daily; 5hr 10min–6hr).

Bus Bucharest (hourly; 4hr 30min).

The Banat

Once a much larger territory that now lies between Romania and neighbouring Hungary and Serbia, the featureless plains of **Banat** were ruled from **Timişoara** until the Turks conquered it in 1552; they governed until 1716 when they were ousted by the Habsburgs. The region's current frontiers were drawn up during the Versailles conference of 1918–20. Today, Romanian Banat is still home to a diverse population that for centuries has included Slovaks, Bulgarians, Ukrainians and Germans living alongside Serbians, Romanians and Hungarians.

TIMIŞOARA

The engaging city of **TIMIŞOARA**, 250km west of Sibiu near the Serbian border and the rail junction at Arad, is Romania's most Westward-oriented city, its good location and multilingual inhabitants attracting much foreign investment. The city's fame abroad rests on its crucial role in the overthrow of the Ceauşescu regime. A Calvinist minister, Lászlo Tőkes, stood up for the rights of the Hungarian community, and when the police came to evict him on December 16, 1989, his parishioners barred their way. The riots that ensued inspired the people of Bucharest to follow, so that Timişoara sees itself as the guardian of the revolution.

What to see and do

Approaching from the train station, you'll enter the centre at the attractive pedestrianized Piața Victoriei, with fountains and flowerbeds strewn along its length. North of here, antique trams trundle past the Baroque **Town Hall** on the central Piața Libertății, while two blocks further north is the vast Piața Unirii.

Piața Victoriei

The focal point of Piața Victoriei is the huge **Romanian Orthodox Cathedral**, completed in 1946 with a blend of neo-Byzantine and Moldavian architectural elements – this is where most of the protesters were gunned down in 1989. At the opposite end, the unattractive Opera House stands near the **castle**, which now houses the **Museum of the Banat**'s (Mon–Sat 10am–4pm) broad collection of archeological and historical artefacts.

Piața Unirii

Piața Unirii is dominated by the monumental **Roman Catholic** and **Serbian Orthodox cathedrals**. Built between 1736 and 1773, the former (to the east) is a fine example of Viennese Baroque; the latter is roughly contemporaneous and almost as impressive.

The Museum of the Revolution

Just off Piaţa Unirii, at Str Ungureanu 8, is the superb **Museum of the Revolution** (Tues–Sun 10am–4pm), which soberly documents the remarkable events of December 1989, courtesy of photos, newspaper cuttings and film footage, including the extraordinary moment when the Ceauşescu's were informed of their impending execution.

The Ethnographic Museum

In 1868, the municipality demolished most of the redundant citadel, leaving two bastions to the east and west of Piaţa Unirii. The eastern one is occupied by the **Ethnographic Museum** (Tues–Sun 10am–4.30pm; entrance at Str Popa Şapcă 4). Varied folk costumes, painted glass icons and furnished rooms illustrate the region's ethnic diversity, but don't provide a comprehensive history – for example, there's no mention of the thousands of Serbs deported in 1951 when the Party fell out with Tito's neighbouring Yugoslavia.

Arrival and information

Train Timişoara Nord train station is a 15min walk west of the centre along B-dul Republicii.

Tourist office The tourist office (Mon–Fri 9am–8pm, Sat 9am–5pm; ⓣ0256/437 973), on the ground floor of the opera building at Str Alba Julia 2, has maps and copies of the free English-language listings magazine *Timişoara What Where When*.

Internet Club Internet, Str Eminescu 5 (24hr).

Accommodation

Camping International 4km west of town on Aleea Pădurea Verde ⓣ0256/217 096, ⓦwww.campinginternational.ro. Open all year, the well-kept campsite also has huts sleeping one to four people. Take trolleybus #11 from the train station or centre. Camping 10 lei/person plus tent, huts from 110 lei.

Casa Politehnica B-dul Ferdinand 2 ⓣ0256/496 850. Hostel-like accommodation right in the centre of the city, with simple singles and doubles. It's the building with the black door. Breakfast included. Singles 100 lei.

Hotel Nord B-dul Gen, Dragalina 47 ⓣ0256/497 504, ⓦwww.hotelnord.ro. The hotel is conveniently located opposite the train station, but can get a bit noisy outside at night. Inside it is bright and clean with en-suite rooms. Breakfast included. Singles 100 lei, doubles 120 lei.

Eating, drinking and nightlife

There's a useful 24hr supermarket, Stil, on Str Mărăşeşti (at Str Lazăr), a short walk northwest of Piaţa Libertăţii. During the summer party animals should head for the plethora of canalside bars behind the cathedral.

Baroque Piaţa Unirii 14. This place lives up to its name, with wrought-iron tables and chairs outside and a decadent array of teas, coffees, milkshakes and hot chocolate – both alcoholic and non-alcoholic. Breakfasts for around 15 lei, hot drinks from 5 lei. Daily 8am–1am.

Club 30 Piaţa Victoriei 7 ⓦwww.club30.ro. In the Cinema Timiş, this small basement club has good jazz and blues, often live. Daily 6pm–3am.

Da Toni Str Daliei 6. First-rate pizzeria located in the heart of the student quarter, serving an extensive range of pizzas and pasta dishes (15–30 lei). Daily 10am–midnight.

Harold's Aleea Studenţilor 17. Simple, understated and surprisingly classy restaurant, with a wide selection of international and vegetarian options, including the large "Harold's Vegetarian Plate" – to share for 52 lei. Most mains about 20 lei. Daily 11.30am–midnight.

Java Coffee House Str Rodnei 6. This dark bar on the southeastern corner of Piaţa Unirii is a good place for a coffee or something stronger. Drinks range from the classic to the more inventive, including their "ice cream chocolate coffee". Drinks 7–18 lei.

Piranha Club Str Alecsandri 5. A popular drinking den with a range of cocktails and truly eye-catching surroundings, complete with fish tanks, live lizards and snakes. Open around the clock, it's also a pleasant place for morning coffee.

Moving on

Train Braşov (1 daily; 9hr); Bucharest (6 daily; 7hr 30min–8hr 45min); Sibiu (1 daily; 5hr 5min–6hr 30min).

Russia

HIGHLIGHTS

THE HERMITAGE: view thousands of priceless treasures at Russia's premier museum

KUNSTKAMMER: don't miss Peter the Great's eighteenth-century collection of curiosities

PETER AND PAUL FORTRESS: caper along the battlements in period costume and take a dip in the Neva River

BANYA: purge your pores in style at Moscow's Sandunovsky baths

THE KREMLIN: see the Orlov Diamond, the world's largest cannons and stunning churches at the historical and political heart of Russia

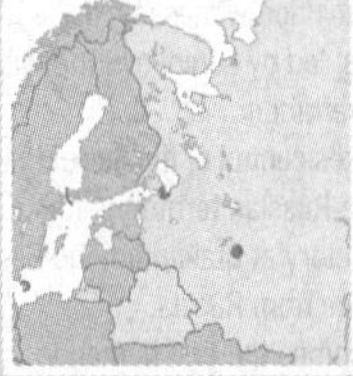

ROUGH COSTS

DAILY BUDGET Basic €55 /occasional treat €75

DRINK Beer (*pivo*) €2.50

FOOD Pancake (*blini*) €1.50

HOSTEL/BUDGET HOTEL €15–25/€45

TRAVEL Train: Moscow–St Petersburg from €25

FACT FILE

POPULATION 142 million

AREA 17,075,400 sq km (including six thousand islands)

LANGUAGE Russian

CURRENCY Ruble (R)

CAPITAL Moscow (population: 10.5 million)

INTERNATIONAL PHONE CODE ⓣ7

Introduction

European Russia stretches from the borders of Belarus and Ukraine to the Ural mountains, over 1000km east of Moscow; even without the rest of the vast Russian Federation, it constitutes by far the largest country in Europe. Formerly a powerful tsarist empire and a Communist superpower, Russia continues to be a source of fascination for travellers. While access is still made relatively difficult by lingering Soviet-style bureaucracy – visas are obligatory and accommodation usually has to be booked in advance – independent travel is increasing every year, and visitors are doubly rewarded by the cultural riches of the country and the warmth of the Russian people.

Moscow, Russia's bustling capital, combines the frenetic energy of an Eastern city with the cosmopolitan feel of a Western one. With its show-stopping architecture – from the tsarist palaces of the Kremlin and the onion domes of St Basil's Cathedral, through the monumental relics of the Communist years, to the massive building projects of today – and the impersonal human tide that packs its streets and subways, the metropolis can feel rather overwhelming. By contrast, **St Petersburg**, Russia's second city, is Europe at its most gracious, an attempt by the eighteenth-century tsar Peter the Great to emulate the best of Western European elegance in what was then a far-flung outpost. Its people are more relaxed and friendly, and its position in the delta of the River Neva is unparalleled, giving it endless watery vistas. Visible – often ostentatious – but uneven wealth creation in both cities has made them twin figureheads for Russia's recent high-speed renaissance.

CHRONOLOGY

862 AD A Scandinavian warrior, Rurik, founds the state of "Russ".
989 Grand Duke Vladimir I adopts Orthodox Christianity.
1552 Ivan the Terrible conquers the Tatars and builds the famous domed St Basil's Cathedral in Red Square, Moscow.
1613 Michael Romanov is elected as Tsar of Russia, ushering in 300 years of Romanov rule.
1725 Peter the Great builds the new capital of St Petersburg after defeating Sweden in the Great Northern War.
1751 First recorded reference to "vodka" is made in a decree made by Empress Elizabeth.
1812 Napoleon invades Russia but is defeated.
1869 Tolstoy writes *War and Peace*.
1892 Tchaikovsky composes the famous ballet, *The Nutcracker*.
1905 Revolution leads to the masses gaining both a constitution and a parliament.
1914 Russia enters World War I on behalf of the Allies.
1917 The October Revolution witnesses the Communist Bolsheviks, led by Lenin, overthrowing the monarchy and government.
1924 Joseph Stalin takes control of the Soviet Union.
1941 The Nazis invade Russian territory; after intense fighting and victory at Stalingrad, the Red Army repel the Germans from Russia.
1961 Yuri Gagarin becomes the first human to travel into space aboard the *Vostok*.
1962 The Cuban Missile Crisis heightens tensions with the US during the Cold War.
1991 The Soviet Union collapses; many former Soviet countries declare independence. Boris Yeltsin is elected President.
1999 Yeltsin resigns and is replaced by Vladimir Putin.
2007 Russian relations with the US deteriorate over their plans to install anti-missile launchers around Russia's borders.
2008 Russia goes to war with Georgia over Georgia's offensive against Southern Ossetia.
2009 President Medvedev announces Russia's rearmament plan, which includes nuclear force.
2011 Russia wins bid to host the football World Cup in 2018.

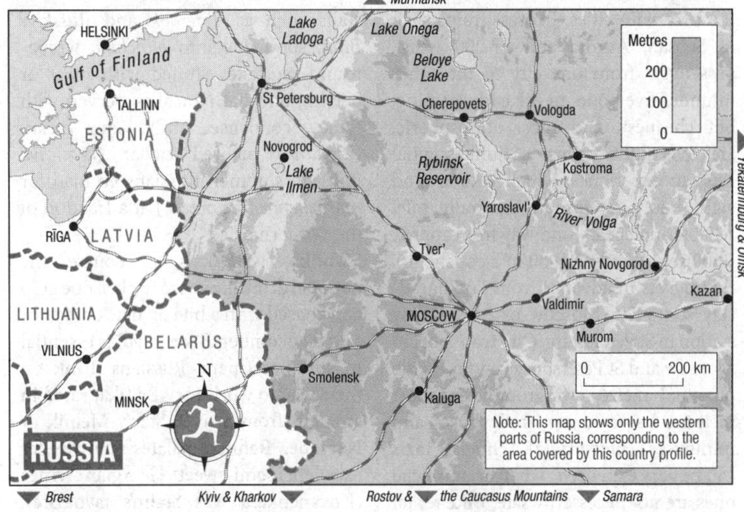

ARRIVAL AND VISAS

Moscow's Sheremetyevo and Domodedovo airports and St Petersburg's Pulkovo Airport are all served by numerous international flights. All **airports** are connected with their respective cities by regular and efficient public transport. Besides being the main hub for all domestic **trains**, including the trans-Siberian ones, Moscow is served by trains from Rīga, Tallinn, Warsaw, Berlin and Budapest, while European train routes into St Petersburg include arrivals from Helsinki, Rīga and Vilnius. Train stations in both Moscow and St Petersburg are well connected to the metro; all Moscow's "vokzals" (train stations) link to a stop on the (brown) circle line. The most convenient way to come to St Petersburg for travellers coming from the Baltic States may be by **bus**, as they are more frequent than trains. **Ferries** into St Petersburg from Helsinki and Tallinn arrive at the Vasilyevskiy Island ferry terminal.

Anyone travelling on a **tourist visa** to Russia must (nominally) have **accommodation** arranged before arrival. If you book a hostel in advance you can request visa support before you go. If you haven't yet decided where to stay when you get your visa, tourist agents in your home country are often prepared to arrange visa "invitations" in which they state that you will be staying at a randomly selected hotel. There is no obligation to actually do so once in Russia. If you book your hostel on arrival, request visa assistance – most hostels can register you or will be able to direct you to a visa registration agency. Note that it's important to **register your visa** within three working days of your arrival. On arrival you will be given an immigration card which you must keep and present on departure.

GETTING AROUND

The **train** and **bus** network is extensive and largely efficient, with up to twenty trains a day in each direction connecting

VISA CONTACTS

www.russianembassy.net Russian embassies and consulates.
www.scottstours.co.uk Visa service, handy for travellers combining Russia with Ukraine, Belarus, the Baltics or Central Asia.
www.visatorussia.com Outstanding visa service.

the two main cities. Express trains such as Sapsan, Aurora and Er-200 whisk passengers from one city to the other in under five hours in the early evening, but cheapest, and most atmospheric, are **overnight trains**, a quintessential Russian experience, which take around eight hours. Trains are generally safe, reliable and cheap (one-way from approx R600 seated only, R1000 in a couchette). Buy tickets in advance from Leningradskiy station in Moscow or Moskovskiy station in St Petersburg. **City transport** in Moscow and St Petersburg centres on the punctual metro; overground transport includes buses, trams, trolleybuses and minibuses (*marshrútki*). Official taxis can be very expensive, whereas unofficial ones are not necessarily safe. **Bike** rental in St Petersburg offers a pleasant way to see the city's quieter outer corners, but cycle around Moscow at your peril.

ACCOMMODATION

Hostels tend to be safer, cleaner and more pleasant than cheap **hotels**, many of which have "economy" rooms unaltered since Soviet times. The standard rate is around R700–800 a night; aim to reserve three to four weeks in advance in the summer. Booking ahead by phone or with Ⓦwww.hostels.com will guarantee you a bed for the night.

FOOD AND DRINK

Moscow and St Petersburg are bursting at the seams with cafés and restaurants covering everything from budget blowouts to *elitni* (elite) extravagance. Japanese is the favoured cuisine, so sushi abounds, but traditional Russian food is still at the heart of many locals' everyday diets. **National dishes** worth tasting include *borshch* (beetroot soup), *shchi* (cabbage soup) and *pirogi* (small pies stuffed with potato, cabbage or *tvorog*, a kind of cottage cheese). Try these at one of the *stolovaya* (canteen-style) restaurants, such as *Moo-Moo* (see p.984). Cheap *blini*, available from street stalls such as *Teremok* and *Russkiye Blini*, subdivide into *blinchiki*, wrap-around pancakes stuffed with meat or berries, and flat pancakes, served with honey, condensed milk, sour cream (*smetana*) or red caviar (*krasnaya ikra*). In summer, Russians go mad for *morozhenoe* (ice cream) at a fraction of the Western price.

Vodka (*vódka*) is, of course, the national drink, knocked back in one gulp and chased with a bite on black bread or salted cucumber. **Beer** (*pivo*) is essential in summer (many Russians drink on their way to work); try Baltika, rated in strength from 3 to 9, Stariy Melnik or Nevskoe. Refined palates may prefer excellent semi-sweet Georgian **wines** (Khvanchkara was Stalin's favourite). For cheap eating and drinking, stock up at a *produkti* (product store), or at *rynki* (markets), scattered across both cities, though concentrated in the suburbs. These sell the full range of Russian dairy delights (try *kefir* – sour milk), salami, sausages and cheap fresh fruit and veg. Traditionally, breakfast is eaten at 8am and lunch between 1 and 2pm; evening meals tend to be eaten around 8pm.

CULTURE AND ETIQUETTE

Though the Western practice of eating out is now widespread, Russians love to entertain at home, and if you're invited over always bring a small present, be it some flowers (if you're male) or some chocolates (if female). **Tipping** is in vogue only at high-end eating and drinking establishments, and five to ten percent should cover it. In **churches**, women should cover their head and shoulders, and men in shorts may be refused entry; you'll also notice that Russians avoid turning their back to the iconostasis that screens the altar. Russians are rather superstitious; you'll see people rubbing the noses of the dog statues at the Metro Ploshad Revolutsii in Moscow for good luck. Old-fashioned chivalry is alive and well, with men opening doors for women and offering to help with heavy lifting. You'll notice young people giving up their seats to the elderly on public transport; follow their example before being told to.

SPORTS AND ACTIVITIES

Spectator sports centre on **football**, with Moscow's biggest teams being Dinamo (Leningradskiy prospekt 36 ⓣ495/612-7172, ⓦwww.fcdynamo.ru; Ⓜ Dinamo) and Spartak (Luzhniki Stadium, Luzhnetskaya nab. 24 ⓣ495/168-2173, ⓦwww.spartak.com; Ⓜ Sportivnaya), while Petersburgers support Zenit (Petrovskiy stadium, 2nd Petrovskiy Island ⓣ812/535-4613 ⓦwww.fc-zenit.ru; Ⓜ Sportivnaya).

Skating is as much part of Russian culture as drinking vodka or eating *blinis* – everyone knows how to. Moscow has plenty of spots for a skate in winter, including the frozen-over paths at the vast Gorky Park, Krymskiy Val ul. 9, Ⓜ Park Kultury or the smaller, more intimate Hermitage garden at ul. Karetniy Ryad 3, Ⓜ Pushinkskaya. You can also skate year-round at the covered rink in Gorky Park. Winter **sledging** in Moscow benefits from good verticals on the Sparrow Hills (Vorobyovye gory; Ⓜ Universitet), where you can overlook Moscow State University, the largest of the "seven sisters", the city's collection of 1950s Stalinist-Gothic skyscrapers. Summer or winter, **swim** in the open air at Chayka, Tuchaninov per. 1/3, Ⓜ Park Kultury, or Luzhniki, Luzhnetskaya nab. 24, Ⓜ Sportivnaya. Cycling enthusiasts can see St Petersburg year-round with a **bike tour** (Skatprokat Rent a Bike, Goncharnaya ul. 7, Ⓜ Pl. Vosstaniya) or **walking tour** (Peter's Walking Tours, through International Youth Hostel, ⓦwww.peterswalk.com; R650 for 4–5hr).

COMMUNICATIONS

Most **post offices** are open Monday to Saturday 8am to 7pm, and blue postboxes are affixed to walls across both cities. However, local mail is slow and not particularly reliable, so for urgent letters use **express companies** such as WestPost, which let you obtain a Finnish PO address, then receive your post in Russia as poste restante, or DHL. **Internet cafés** are abundant and cheap; most hostels offer internet access on a limited number of screens for free or for R1 per minute, and virtually all cafés and restaurants have wi-fi. For **international calls** get a pre-paid international phonecard such as the Zebra Telecom card or Evroset card, usable from any phone. Ask at a bank or telecoms kiosk for a *telefonnaya karta*. ⓦwww.waytorussia.net lets you buy a card pin online, which you can use to make instant international calls. Non-Russian **mobiles** work on roaming via local providers, but you'll pay an arm and a leg. Get a local SIM card for R200–400 (bring your passport with you to buy one), or stick to SMS.

EMERGENCIES

Beware of **petty crime**, particularly pickpockets in the metro and in bus and train stations during rush hour. Don't leave valuables in your hotel room. If you have a dark complexion exercise extra caution, especially at night, as racist attacks are not unknown. Your embassy will be able to advise you on what to do if you get robbed. The **police** (полиция) wear blue-grey uniforms; always make sure you have photocopies of your passport and visa on you, as they do stop people at random and often look for an excuse to fine you. When traversing busy

EMERGENCY NUMBERS

Police ⓣ02; Ambulance ⓣ03; Fire ⓣ01. Moscow rescue service (for help with any incidents while holidaying in Moscow) ⓣ495/937 9911. You'll be connected to an English-speaking operator.

roads, look for an underground crossing – (*perekhod*) переход – as many drivers do not honour zebra crossings. High-street **pharmacies** (*aptéka*) offer many familiar medicines over the counter. Foreigners tend to rely on expensive **private clinics** for treatment, so travel insurance is essential. St Petersburg

RUSSIAN

	Russian	Pronunciation
Yes	да	Da
No	нет	Nyet
Please	пожалуйста	Pazháaloosta
Thank you	спасибо	Spaséeba
Hello/Good day	здравствуйте	Zdrávstweetye
Goodbye	до свидания	Da svidáaneya
Excuse me	извините	Izvinéetye
Sorry	простите	Prostitye
Where?	где?	Gdye?
Good/Bad	хороший/плохой	Khoróshee/Plokhóy
Near/Far	близко/далеко	Bléezki/Dalyekó
Cheap/Expensive	дешевый/дорогой	Deshóvy/Daragóy
Open/Closed	открыто/закрыто	Otkryto/Zakryto
Today	сегодня	Sevódnya
Yesterday	вчера	Vcherá
Tomorrow	завтра	Závtra
How much is...?	сколько стоит...?	Skólka stóyit...?
What time is it?	Который час?	Katóree chass?
I don't understand	я не понимаю	Ya ne ponimáyou
Do you speak English?	вы говорите по-английски?	Vwee gavoréetye po angliyski?
Where are the toilets?	где туалет?	Gdye tualyét?
My name is...	меня зовут...	Menyá zavóot...
What is your name?	как вас зовут?	Kak vas zavóot?
I don't speak Russian	я не говорю по-русски	Ya nye gavaryóo pa-róosski
Can I have....	можно...	Mózhna...
Tea	чай	Chay
Beer	пиво	Péeva
Juice	сок	Sok
I am a vegetarian	я вегетарианец	Ya vegetariyánets
The bill, please	счет пожалуйста	Shchyot, pazhálooista
Men's toilet (often seen as M)	мужчины	moózhshini
Women's toilet (often seen as Z)	женщины	zhénshini
Breakfast	завтрак	Závtrak
One	один	Adéen
Two	два	Dva
Three	три	Tree
Four	четыре	Chetéeri
Five	пять	Pyat
Six	шесть	Shest
Seven	семь	Syeem
Eight	восемь	Vósyem
Nine	девять	Déyvyat
Ten	десять	Déysyat

STUDENT AND YOUTH DISCOUNTS

"Foreigner prices" at museums and galleries are often steeper than for Russian citizens, though most museums offer tickets for foreign **students** which cost half or two-thirds of the full price. An ISIC card is your best bet, though other student cards often work too. Ask for *adeen studyencheskiy bilyet* (one student ticket) in your most authentic accent.

water contains the giardia parasite, which can cause severe diarrhoea – metranidazol is the cure. Moscow's tap water is laden with heavy metals, so it's best to buy bottled water.

INFORMATION

Tourist offices are few and far between. At the time of writing, there was no existing official tourist office in Moscow. St Petersburg's Tourist Information Office (Sadovaya ul. 14, Ⓜ Nevski Prospekt) will be able to point you in the right direction; for the latest restaurant and bar listings pick up the excellent *In Your Pocket* guide (Ⓦ www.inyourpocket.com/russia). Hostel and hotel receptions carry leaflets and maps, and you can get up-to-date bar, restaurant and entertainment listings and reviews from **English-language papers**. The *Moscow Times* and the more ponderously pro-Kremlin *Moscow News* are well established; *Element* is directed at young city-dwellers (Ⓦ www.elementmoscow.ru). Find **maps** in English at bookstores like Dom Knigi stores (larger stores in Moscow at Tverskaya ul. 8/7, Ⓜ Tverskaya and ul. Novy Arbat 8, Ⓜ Arbatskaya).

RUSSIA ONLINE

Ⓦ **www.sptimesrussia.com** English-language online newspaper, with useful tourist information and current listings.
Ⓦ **www.moscowcity.com** Official Moscow city guide.
Ⓦ **www.waytorussia.net** Outstanding, detailed practical advice.

MONEY AND BANKS

Russia's currency is the **ruble**, divided into 100 kopeks. There are coins of 1, 5, 10, 20 and 50 kopeks and 1, 2 and 5 rubles, and notes of 5, 10, 50, 100, 500 and 1000 rubles. Everything is paid for in rubles, although some hostels make a habit of citing prices in either euros or dollars. At the time of writing £1=R45, €1=R40 and US$1=R28. Only **change money** in an official bank or currency exchange. Most **exchange offices** are open Monday to Saturday 10am to 8pm or later, and **ATMs** are plentiful. In general, prices in both cities range from "new Russian" prices down to what the average Russian salary will cover, making many shops, bars and cafés affordable for the budget-conscious traveller.

OPENING HOURS AND HOLIDAYS

Most **shops** are open Monday to Saturday 8am to 7pm or later; Sunday hours are slightly shorter. **Museums** tend to open 9am–5pm, with last ticket sales an hour before closing time, and they are invariably closed one day a week, with one day a month put aside as a "cleaning day". **Churches** are accessible from 8am until the end of evening service. **Clubs** open late – many until 6am – or don't close at all, morphing into early-morning cafés. Russian **public holidays** fall on January 1, 6, 7 and 19, February 23 (Defender of the Motherland Day), March 8 (Women's Day), May 1 and 2 (Labour Day), May 9 (Victory Day), June 12 (Russia Day), and November 4 (Day of Popular Unity).

Moscow

To Westerners, **MOSCOW** (Москва) may look European, but its chaotic spirit is never far beneath the surface. Far removed from its beginnings as a humble wooden town in 1147, today Moscow is Russia's New York City – its residents brash and opinionated, and its glitzy, cosmopolitan heart catering to a well-heeled elite, with the odd pocket of extreme urban poverty. Like its American counterpart, the city never sleeps; you can get anything you want around the clock. Above all, Moscow is an assault on all the senses: a relentless crush of people on the subway, cliquey nightspots, designer shops, any cuisine you can think of, heavy traffic, endless queuing, golden-domed churches and historical treasures.

What to see and do

Moscow's general **layout** is a series of concentric circles and radial lines emanating from Red Square and the Kremlin, and the centre is compact enough to explore on foot. Moscow's sights can also be mapped as strata of its history: the old Muscovy that Russians are eager to show; the now retro-chic Soviet-era sites such as VDNK and Lenin's Mausoleum; and the exclusive restaurants and shopping malls that mark out the new Russia.

Red Square

Every visitor to Moscow is irresistibly drawn to **Red Square**, the historic and spiritual heart of the city. The name (*Krasnaya ploshchad*) derives from *krasniy*, the old Russian word for beautiful. The Lenin Mausoleum squats beneath the ramparts of the Kremlin and, facing it, sprawls **GUM** – the State Department Store in Soviet times – and now devoted to costly fashion outlets. At the southwest end stands the incomparable St Basil's Cathedral. Opposite it you'll find the Historical Museum, directly behind which a golden circle on the ground marks Moscow's Kilometre Zero. In front of St Basil's Cathedral is the fenced-off Lobnoe Mesto (Place of Executions) where Ivan the Terrible and Peter the Great presided over public beheadings and hangings during their respective reigns.

The Lenin Mausoleum and Kremlin wall

In post-Communist Russia, the **Lenin Mausoleum**, which houses Vladimir Ilyich Ulianov's embalmed corpse (daily except Mon & Fri 10am–1pm; free; queue at the Alexander Gardens entrance to Red Square), can be seen as either an awkward reminder of the old days or a cherished relic. Descend past stony-faced guards into the dimly lit chasm where the leader's body lies. Stopping or giggling will earn you stern rebukes. Behind the Mausoleum, the **Kremlin wall** – 19m high and 6.5m thick – contains a **mass grave** of Bolsheviks who perished during the battle for Moscow in 1917. The ashes of an array of luminaries, including writer Maxim Gorky and the first man in space, Yuri Gagarin, are here too. Beyond lie

TREAT YOURSELF

Get the city grit out of your skin at the exquisitely elaborate **Sandunovsky baths** (Neglinnaya ul. 14 bldg 3–7 Ⓦwww.sanduny.ru; Ⓜ Teatralnaya), patronized by Muscovites since 1896. Join Russian businessmen and socialites in the *banya*, a wooden hut heated with a furnace, where you are invited to sweat out impurities, get beaten energetically with birch twigs, and finally plunge into ice-cold water. Men's and women's baths are separate, with the women's section more like a modern spa. A three-hour session costs R1000. Daily 8am–10pm.

the graves of a select group of Soviet leaders, each with his own bust; Stalin still gets the most flowers.

St Basil's Cathedral

No description can do justice to **St Basil's Cathedral** (daily 11am–5.30pm, winter months until 4.30pm, closed Tues; R150, student R50) – perhaps the most famous symbol of Russia – its multicoloured onion domes silhouetted against the skyline where Red Square slopes down towards the Moskva River. The exterior is far more impressive than the interior, which consists of a stone warren of small chapels and souvenir stalls. Built in 1561 to celebrate Ivan the Terrible's capture of the Tatar stronghold of Kazan in 1552, its name commemorates St Basil the Blessed, a "holy fool" who foretold the fire that swept through Moscow in 1547.

The Kremlin

Brooding and glittering in the heart of the capital, the **Kremlin** (Aleksandrovsky Sad; 10am–5pm, closed Thurs; R350, student R100; Ⓦwww.kreml.ru; Ⓜ Borovitskaya) is both the heart of historical Moscow and home to its present-day parliament, the Duma. Its founding is attributed to Prince Yuriy Dolgorukiy, who built a wooden fort here in about 1147. Look out for the **Tsar Cannon**, cast in 1586: one of the largest cannons ever made, this was intended to defend the Saviour Gate, but has never been fired. Close by looms the earthbound, broken **Tsar Bell**, the largest bell in the world, cast in 1655. **Cathedral Square** is the historic heart of the Kremlin, dominated by the magnificent, white **Ivan the Great Bell Tower**. Of the square's four key churches, the most important is the **Cathedral of the Assumption**, with a spacious, light and echoing interior, walls and pillars smothered with icons and frescoes, and temporary exhibitions housed in its belfry. The **Cathedral of the Archangel** houses the tombs of Russia's rulers from Grand Duke Ivan I to Tsar Ivan V, while the golden-domed **Cathedral of the Annunciation** (closed for renovations at time of writing) hides some of Russia's finest icons, including works by Theophanes the Greek and Andrey Rublev.

The Armoury Palace

The unmissable **Armoury Palace** (ticketed entry at 10am, noon, 2.30pm and 4.30pm; R700, student R200), inside the Kremlin, boasts a staggering array of treasures – among them the tsars' coronation robes, jewellery and armour. A separate part of the Armoury Palace houses the Diamond Fund (daily sessions 10am and noon; buy tickets in Aleksandrovsky Sad) – a priceless collection of jewels, including the 190-karat Orlov Diamond, which belonged to Catherine the Great, and the world's largest sapphire.

The Museum of Modern History

The **Museum of Modern History** at Tverskaya ul. 21 (Tues, Wed, Fri 10am–6pm, Thurs & Sat 11am–7pm, Sun 10am–5pm, closed last Fri of the

KREMLIN ETIQUETTE

You may only purchase **tickets** for the set entry times to the Armoury and the Diamond Fund an hour before the session; Soviet-style bureaucracy prevents you from purchasing a ticket in advance. Even if you are in possession of a ticket, you will still have to queue for both attractions separately and watch tour groups and people with connections being ushered in before you. It's all part of the experience...

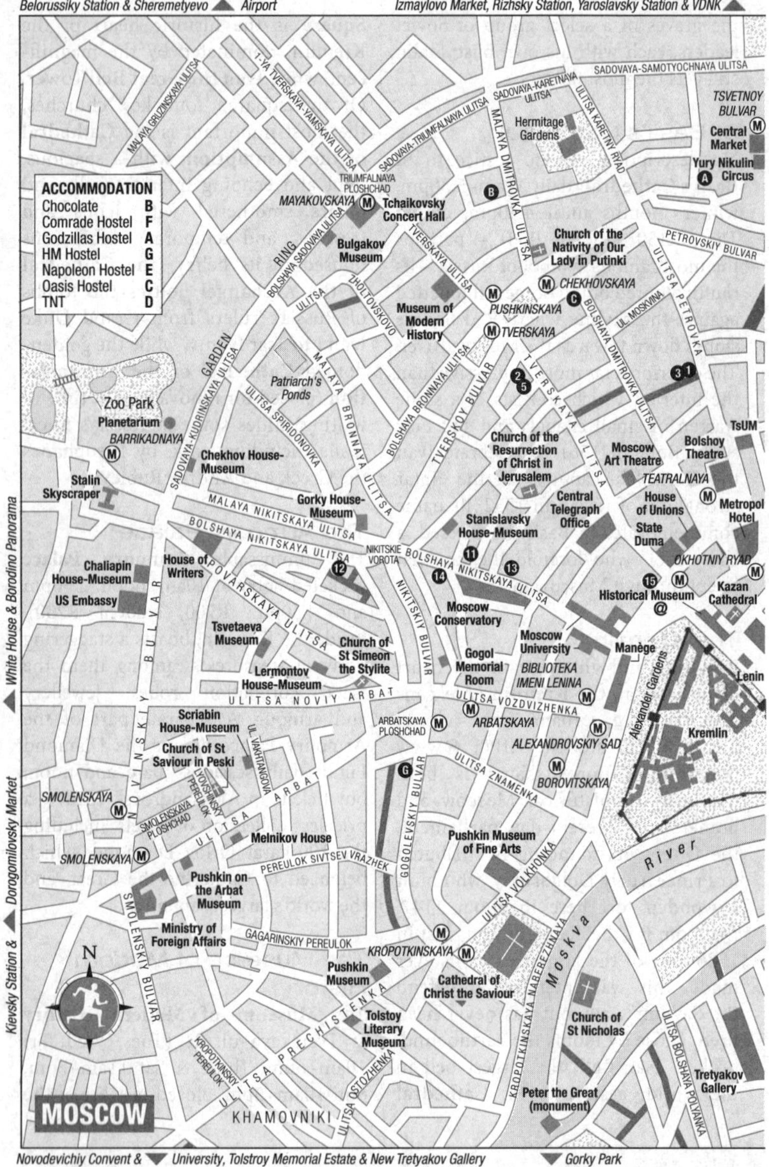

month; R100; Ⓜ Tverskaya) brings the Communist past alive with striking displays of Soviet propaganda posters, photographs and state gifts, although there's a frustrating lack of English translation.

The Pushkin Museum of Fine Arts

Founded in 1898 in honour of the famous Russian poet, the **Pushkin Museum of Fine Arts** at Volkhonka ul. 12 (Tues–Sun 10am–7pm; R150–300,

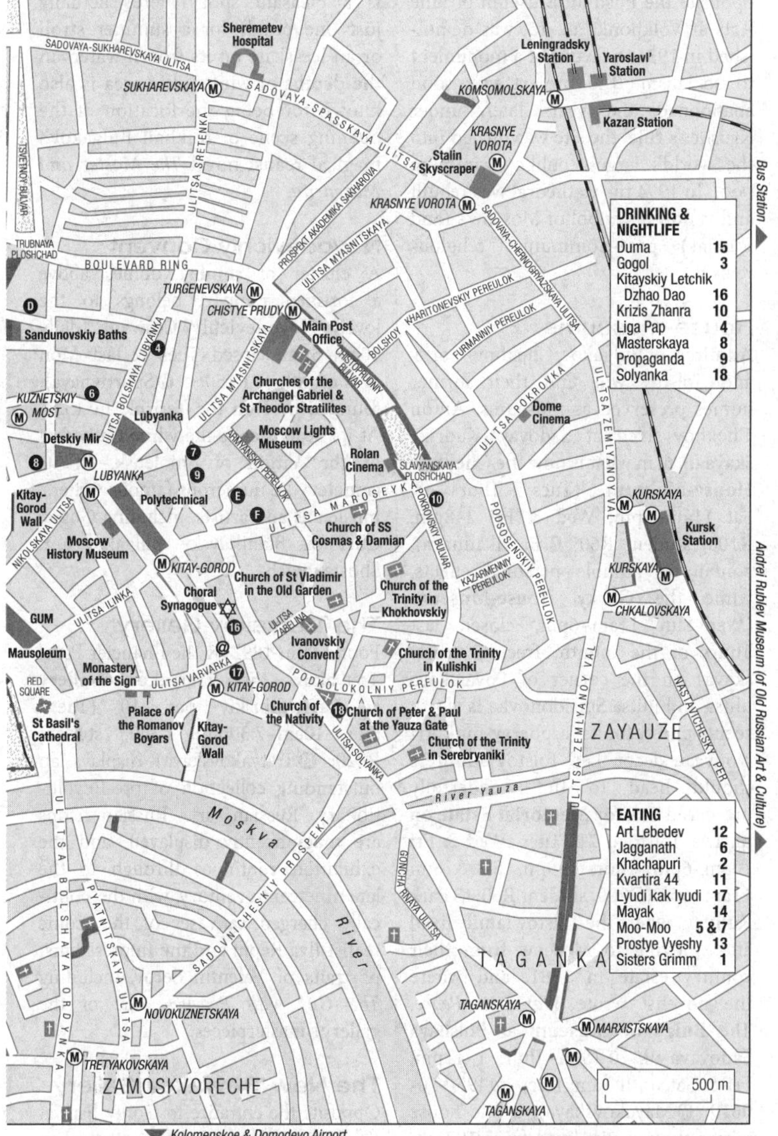

separate fee for Impressionist wing; Ⓜ Kropotkinskaya) holds a hefty collection of **European paintings**, from Italian High Renaissance works to Rembrandt, and an outstanding display of Impressionist works.

Cathedral of Christ the Saviour

Built as a symbol of gratitude to divinity for having aided the Russians' defeat of Napoleon in 1812, the **Cathedral of Christ the Saviour** (daily 10am–6pm), opposite the Pushkin Museum of Fine Arts at Volkhonka ul. 15, was demolished in 1931 in favour of a monument to socialism. The project was soon abandoned and years later, under Krushev's rule, the site was turned into the world's largest public swimming pool. In 1994 the Cathedral was rebuilt and is now a symbol of Moscow's (and Russia's) post-Communist religious revival.

House-museums

Admirers of Bulgakov, Chekhov, Gorky and Tolstoy will find their former homes preserved as museums. Anton Chekhov lived at Sadovaya-Kudrinskaya ul. 6, in what is now the **Chekhov House-Museum** (Tues, Thurs & Sat 11am–6pm, Wed & Fri 2–8pm; R100, student R60; Ⓜ Barrikadnaya), containing humble personal effects, while the **Gorky House-Museum** (Wed–Sun 11am–6pm, closed last Thurs of the month; free; Ⓜ Arbatskaya) on the corner of Povarskaya ulitsa and ulitsa Spiridonovka is worth seeing purely for its raspberry-pink Art Nouveau decor. Leo Tolstoy admirers should head to the wonderfully preserved **Tolstoy Memorial Estate** on ul. Lva Tolstogo 21 (Tues, Wed & Fri 10am–6pm, Thurs 1–9pm, Sat & Sun 11am–6pm; R200, student R60; Ⓜ Park Kultury) where the Tolstoy family lived after moving to Moscow from their country estate in 1881, and where the novelist wrote *War and Peace*. The **Bulgakov Museum** at Bolshaya Sadovaya ul. 10 (Sun–Thurs 1–11pm, Fri & Sat until 1am; free; ⓣ495/970-0619; Ⓜ Mayakovskaya), is the house where the novelist lived from 1921 to 1924. There are nightly tours (1–6am; R550; phone a week in advance for tour in English).

Patriarch's Ponds

One of Moscow's most exclusive neighbourhoods, **Patriarch's Ponds** is a pleasant spot (there's actually just one pond) for a summer stroll or an ice-skate on its frozen waters in the depths of winter. The area is also known for being the location of the opening scene of Mikhail Bulgakov's magical realist novel *The Master and Margarita*.

Novodevichiy Convent

A cluster of shining domes above a fortified rampart belongs to the lovely **Novodevichiy Convent** (daily 10am–5pm; closed Tues & last Mon of month; R150; Ⓜ Sportivnaya), founded by Ivan the Terrible in 1524. At its heart stands the white Cathedral of the Virgin of Smolensk. In its **cemetery** lie numerous famous writers, musicians and artists, including Gogol, Chekhov, Stanislavsky, Bulgakov and Shostakovich.

The Tretyakov Gallery

Founded in 1892 by the financier Pavel Tretyakov, the **Tretyakov Gallery** at Lavrushinskiy per. 10 (Tues–Sun 10am–7.30pm; R360, student R220; Ⓜ Tretyakovskaya) displays an outstanding collection of pre-Revolutionary Russian art. Russian icons are magnificently displayed, and the exhibition continues through to the late nineteenth century, with the politically charged canvases of the iconic realist Ilya Repin and the Impressionist portraits of Valentin Serov, including *The Girl with Peaches*, one of the gallery's masterpieces.

The New Tretyakov Gallery

Opposite the entrance to Gorky Park at Krymskiy Val 10, the **New Tretyakov Gallery** (Tues–Sun 10am–7.30pm; R360, student R220; Ⓜ Park Kultury) takes a breakneck gallop through twentieth-century Russian art, from the avant-garde of the 1910–1920s to contemporary artists. Full and illuminating commentary in English is a bonus.

Gorky Park

Gorky Park on ul. Krymskiy Val 7 (R100; Ⓜ Park Kultury) is a large park occupying an area of 300 acres along the river. In the winter the frozen-over paths become one of the city's largest ice rinks, while in the summer Muscovites stroll the area savouring an ice cream. There's also a popular amusement park within the grounds, which has somewhat passed its sell-by date.

VDNK

To see Soviet triumphalism at its most prolific, visit the Exhibition of Economic Achievements, or **VDNK** (Prospekt Mira; Ⓜ VDNK/Prospekt Mira), with its statue upon statue of ordinary workers in heroic poses. Adding to the scene is the permanent trade-fair-cum-shopping-centre housed in the grandiose Stalinist architecture of the All-Union Agricultural Exhibition of 1939, and the People's Friendship Fountain, flanked by Soviet maidens, each symbolizing a Soviet republic. One of the most hubristic Soviet monuments ever built is the **Space Obelisk**, which bears witness to Soviet designs on the stratosphere. Unveiled in 1964 – three years after Gagarin orbited the earth – it's a sculpture of a rocket blasting nearly 100m into the sky on a plume of energy clad in shining titanium. Moscow's giant Ferris wheel, small amusement park and numerous food vendors help to create a fairground-like atmosphere. For a fantastic view over the VDNK, take the lift to the 25th floor of *Hotel Cosmos* across Prospekt Mira.

Arrival and information

Air Flights from Western Europe arrive either at Sheremeyetevo, or the more efficient Domodedovo. From Sheremetyevo you can take the Aeroexpress train to Belorusky station on the green and brown lines (every 30min between 5am & 12.30am; 35min; R320). From Domodedovo, Aeroexpress trains run to Paveletsky station (every 30min between 7am–midnight; 45min; R320); otherwise take a shuttle bus (every 15min between 6am–midnight; 30min; R80) to Ⓜ Domodedovskaya.

Train All stations are conveniently located by a metro station. Trains from Berlin, Vilnius and Warsaw arrive at Belorusskiy station (Belorusskiy vokzal, Tverskaya Zastava ploshchad' 7; Ⓜ Belorusskaya) while Rizhsky station (Rizhsky vokzal, Rizhskaya ploshchad' 79/3; Ⓜ Rizhskaya) serves Latvian destinations such as Rīga. Leningradsky (Leningradsky vokzal, Komsomolskaya ploshchad 3; Ⓜ Komsomolskaya) is the departure point for frequent trains to St Petersburg; Kievsky station. (Kievsky vokzal, Kievskogo vokzala ploshchad 2; Ⓜ Kievskaya) is the final destination for trains from Kiev and Odessa, while Yaroslavsky station (Yaroslavsky vokzal, Komsomolskaya ploshchad 5; Ⓜ Komsomolskaya) is the starting point for trans-Siberian adventures.

Bus Ecolines buses from Germany and the Baltic States terminate at 37 Leningradskiy pr. (near Ⓜ Dinamo). Eurolines runs from European destinations including Berlin, Rīga, Tallinn and Helsinki to both St Petersburg and Moscow. Moscow's main bus station with intercity departures is at Uralskaya ul. 2; Ⓜ Shcholkovskaya.

Tourist office At the time of research, there was no tourist office in Moscow; there are plans to open an information centre in 2012.

City transport

Bus Bus stops are marked with yellow signs.

Metro With its Soviet mosaics, murals and statuary, Moscow's Metro (5.30am–1am) is world-famous. Stations are marked with a large "M" and you can plan your journey on Ⓦ www.metroway.ru. One-way fare costs R28; buy a card for 5 (R135) or 10 (R265) journeys (ask at the *kassa* for *pyat/dyéssiyet póezdok*).

Minibus *Marshrutkas* are cheap (around R25 a journey). They wait to fill up with passengers, then take the route advertised on the side. You can ask to get out at any point. Pay the driver on board.

Tram and trolleybus Often the best way to tackle a big road like a section of the Garden Ring. Trolleybus stops have blue-and-white signs. Most routes operate from 5am to 1am; fares cost R28 on board; same tickets are used for buses.

Accommodation

Hostels

Chocolate Degtyarniy per. 15, ap.4 Ⓣ 495/971-2046, Ⓦ www.chocohostel.com Ⓜ Tverskaya or Mayakovskaya. True to its name, bars of chocolate are scattered around the kitchen shelves and hall – but sadly they're only for ornamentation. Staff here are friendly, rooms are clean, breakfast is included and the location is superb. Dorms R700, twin room R2400 (no doubles).

Comrade Hostel Maroseyka ul. 11, 3rd floor ⓣ495/628-3126, ⓦwww.comradehostel.com ⓜKitai Gorod. This little hostel only sleeps twenty – the two dorm rooms are pretty spacious nonetheless, and there's a small kitchen and communal area, as well as free wi-fi. Dorms R600.

Godzillas Hostel Bolshoi Karetniy 6 ⓣ495/699-4223, ⓦwww.godzillashostel.com ⓜTsvetnoy Bulvar/Tverskaya. Relaxed, popular hostel a short walk from the centre. Rooms are pleasantly decorated with fun wallpaper, minimalist furniture and parquet floors; the doubles are a bit of a squeeze, though. Helpful staff provide lots of Moscow information. Dorms US$16, doubles US$70.

HM Hostel Maly Afanasyevskiy per. 1/33 ⓣ495/778-8501 ⓜArbatskaya. Cute little hostel smack in the centre of town, with a homely feel – there are only three dorms (2 single-sex, 1 mixed). Kitchen, living room, free laundry and wi-fi. Dorms R890.

Napoleon Hostel Maly Zlatoustinskiy per 2, 4th floor ⓣ495/628-6695, ⓦwww.napoleonhostel.com ⓜKitay Gorod. Fun and lively hostel with a welcoming, lived-in feel; it's in an excellent location to sample the city's nightlife. The spacious dorms (R1000) with quirky floral wallpaper are all named after Russian cities; all have lockers too, and there's a/c for the summer, as well as free wi-fi and laundry facilities.

Oasis Hostel Strastnoy bulvar 4/3, 2nd floor ⓣ495/650-2374, ⓦwww.oasishostel.ru ⓜChekhovskaya. HI-affiliated hostel in the centre of town; the clean dorms (R700) and the one double room (R2200) have flowery babushka-esque bedspreads and Soviet chandeliers. Staff are friendly and the location spot on.

TNT 5 Zvonarskiy per. 5 ⓣ495/973-0501, ⓦwww.tnthostel.com ⓜTrubnaya or Kuznetskiy Most. The decor isn't very exciting, with bare walls, but the unbelievably cheap dorms (R450) are light and welcoming and staff helpful.

Eating

For cheap eats head to a canteen, where you can compile a tray of dishes smorgasbord-style. Take advantage of the great-value business lunches offered by cafés and restaurants during the week between noon and 4pm.

Canteens and cafés

Art Lebedev Bol. Nikitskaya 35 ⓣ495/778-7015 ⓜArbatskaya. This itty-bitty café seating about 15 attracts a literary crowd. Light breakfasts (R170) and salads (R190) as well as heavier dishes like *pelmeni* and *vareniki* (Russian dumplings; both R250). Mon–Fri 9am–11pm, Sat & Sun 11am–11pm.

Jagganath Kuznetskiy Most ul. 11 ⓜKuznetskiy Most. Make your way through a little health food shop to get to this veggie canteen. Curries, light cakes and fresh salads (from R80) as well as soups (from R35) make a nice change from the unrelenting carb-heavy and dairy dishes. Daily 10am–11pm.

Lyudi kak lyudi Solyanskiy Tupik 1/4 ⓣ495/621-1201 ⓜKitay Gorod. Small café with a cosy wine cellar feel. Feast on tasty sandwiches (R150) and pies (R130) as well as more substantial dishes like lasagne (R120). Mon–Wed 8am–11pm, Thurs 8am–3am, Fri 8am–6am, Sat 11am–6am, Sun 11am–11pm.

Moo-Moo Ul. Arbat 4 ⓜArbatskaya. Warm and welcoming canteen decked out with rustic decor and serving a range of cheap tasty Russian grub, all in cow-themed crockery – soups (R69), salads (R30), mains (R39.50) and grilled meats (R129). Just point at what you want. Other locations at Maly. Gnezidnikovskiy per. 9, ⓜTverskaya; Ul. Myasnitskaya ul. 14 ⓜLubyanka. Daily 9am–11pm.

Khachapuri B. Gnezdnikovskiy 10, Pushkinskaya ⓣ985/764-3118, ⓦwww.hacha.ru ⓜTverskaya. Some of the city's tastiest Georgian grub at this cosy, inexpensive café with live piano recitals in the evenings. The exquisite meat *khinkali* (large dumplings) and the *khachapuri* (baked bread with oozing cheese; R120) are unmissable. Superb-value business lunches (R180–500). Mon–Fri 9am–midnight, Sat & Sun 10am–1am.

Restaurants

Kvartira 44 Bol. Nikitskaya 22/2 ⓣ495/691-7503 ⓜArbatskaya. Wooden furniture and a crimson decor give this place a Parisian, intimate feel. Live piano music on Friday nights. Mains from R310. Daily noon–2am.

Mayak Bol. Nikitskaya 19, Arbatskaya ⓣ495/691-7449, ⓜArbatskaya. This popular restaurant located above a theatre is set out like an oversized Soviet drawing room complete with heavy furnishings, a convivial vibe and an international crowd of bohemian Muscovites. Try the beef strogonoff (R490). Daily noon–6am.

Prostye Vyeshy Bol. Nikitskaya 14 ⓣ495/629-3494 ⓜArbatskaya or Okhotny Riad. Step down into a mock cellar with vaulted brick ceilings to get to this little restaurant-cum-wine bar. The food is unpretentious, tasty and seasonal (mains from R290), but if you think this place really is too simple (it translates as "simple things"), then get scribbling on the tables with the pencils provided. Daily 10am–late.

Sisters Grimm Stoleshnikov per.11 ⓣ495/628-8975 Ⓜ Teatralnaya. Tucked away in a courtyard, this quiet little place is a perfect spot for a bite before heading to its next-door neighbour *Gogol* (see below) until the early hours. The international menu includes big juicy burgers (R325) as well as lighter meals such as salads (R190) and soups (R240). Mon–Fri noon–midnight, Sat & Sun until 2am.

Drinking & nightlife

Moscow's famous nightlife is marred by the practice of "face control", excluding the not-so-beautiful people from *elitni* clubs. The venues listed here are largely accessible. There are scores of trendy bars and clubs on Krasny Oktyabr, a former chocolate factory building located across the river from Ⓜ Kropotkinskaya and now home to some of Moscow's hippest nightlife.

Bars

Gogol Stoleshnikov per. 11 Ⓜ Teatralnaya. Fun, friendly and good value place hosting edgy unconventional bands (gigs R200–1000). It's best in summer when you can flavour grilled *shashlik* in the courtyard at the back, and sip on a cocktail or two (R160–300). Daily noon–5pm, Fri & Sat 24hr.

Kitayskiy Letchik Dzhao Dao Lubyanskiy proezd 25/12 ⓦwww.jao-da.ru Ⓜ Kitay Gorod. Descend to the artfully scuffed-up basement labyrinth, where some outstanding alternative bands play at weekends (R200–500). Mon–Fri 10am–6am, Sat & Sun 1pm–6am.

Liga Pap Ul. Bolshaya Lubyanka 24 ⓣ495/624-3636, ⓦwww.liga-pap.ru Ⓜ Turgenevskaya. Trendy sports bar with a large projector as well as an array of plasma TVs dotted around the faux-vaulted brick and wooden interior. Pint of beer (from R130). Daily 24hr.

Clubs

Note that all the venues listed below act as a café by day, restaurant in the early evening, and both bar and club at night. All have free entry unless otherwise stated.

Duma Mokhovaya ul 11, bld 3b ⓣ495/692-1119, ⓦwww.clubduma.ru Ⓜ Teatralnaya. This relaxed, laidback haunt is tucked away in a series of courtyards and set in a modern-age cave with vaulted ceilings. DJs and live bands, from jazz to bossa nova. Vodkas R160, cocktails R230. Mon–Sat 9am–6am, Sun 11am–6am.

Krizis Zhanra Ul Pokrovka 16/16, bld 1 ⓣ965/623-2594, ⓦwww.krizis-zhanra.ru Ⓜ Kitay Gorod. Peer over the split-level balustrade of this popular indie haunt at expats and Russians alike stomping around to 90s classics. Live bands, too. Daily 11am–6am.

Masterskaya Treatralny Proezd 3, bld.3 ⓣ495/625-6838, ⓦwww.mstrsk.ru Ⓜ Lubyanka. Alternative club that attracts a bohemian young crowd. Live concerts at weekends (R100–800). Daily noon–6am.

Propaganda Bolshoy Zlatoustinsky per. 7 ⓣ495/624-5732, ⓦwww.propagandamoscow.com Ⓜ Kitay Gorod. Brick walls along with contrasting dim and bright lights make you feel you're backstage in a Hollywood film set at this popular club. Mild face control so best to book a table for dinner to ensure entry. Gay nights on Sun. Mon–Fri 11.30am–6am, Sat & Sun noon–6am.

Solyanka Solyanka ul. 11/6 ⓣ495/221-7557, ⓦwww.s-11.ru Ⓜ Kitay Gorod. Stylish, trendy club attracting renowned DJs spinning minimal house and electro beats. Mixers from R250. Free entry before 11pm, R500 after. Mon–Fri 10am–6am, Sat 11am–7am, Sun 11am–6am.

Entertainment

Theatre, classical music and ballet all have superb vintages in Russia, and can be surprisingly cheap, provided you ask for the cheapest ticket available (*samiy deshoviy bilyet*).

Cinema

The cinemas listed below screen films in their original language.

Dome Cinema 18/1 Olimpiyskiy pr. ⓦwww.domecinema.ru Ⓜ Prospekt Mira. Latest blockbuster films as well as occasional independent screenings.

35MM Pokrovka ul. 47/24 ⓦwww.kino35mm.ru Ⓜ Chistye Prudy. Specializing in independent foreign films.

Rolan Cinema Chistoprudny Boulevard 12a ⓦwww.5zvezd.ru Ⓜ Chistye Prudy. Art-house films, mainly new classics, including festival screenings.

Music

B2 Bol. Sadovaya ul. 8 ⓦwww.b2club.ru Ⓜ Mayakovskaya. With a capacity of 2000 people, *B2* is a staple venue on the live music scene, hosting all sorts of bands playing anything from jazz to ska music. Daily noon–6am. Thurs R300 after 10pm, Fri & Sat R300–500 after 8pm. Concert admission from R300.

Tchaikovsky Concert Hall Triumfalnaya ploshchad 4/31 ⓦ www.meloman.ru Ⓜ Mayakovskaya. Pick a night when Russian music heads the bill and admire the view; the hall is festooned with red stars. Tickets start at R100.

Theatre

Bolshoy Theatre Teatralnaya pl. 1 ⓣ 499/250 7317, ⓦ www.bolshoi.ru Ⓜ Teatralnaya. The world's most famous ballet.

Shopping

Dorogomilovsky Market ul. Mozhaisky Val 10 Ⓜ Kievskaya. Plenty of fresh produce on offer, including cheeses, meats, fish and seafood as well as an excellent selection of fruit and veg. Daily 7am–8pm.

Izmaylovo Market Izmailovksy Park Ⓜ Partizanskaya. Open-air market with Moscow's best (and cheapest) Soviet paraphernalia and memorabilia including coins, fur hats, *matrioshka* dolls, Soviet posters and postcards. In winter make sure you get there before 3pm. Weekends are best 6am–5pm.

Directory

Embassies Australia, Podkolokolny per. 10a/2, ⓣ 495/956 6070, Ⓜ Kitay Gorod Canada, Starokonyushenny per. 23, Ⓜ Kropotkinskaya ⓣ 495/925 6000; Ireland, Grokholski per. 5, Ⓜ Prospekt Mira ⓣ 495/937 5911; New Zealand, ul. Povarskaya 44, Ⓜ Barrikadnaya, ⓣ 495/956 3579; UK, Smolenskaya nab.10, Ⓜ Smolenskaya ⓣ 495/956 7200; US, Novinskiy bulvar 19, Ⓜ Smolenskaya ⓣ 495/728 5577.

Health European Medical Center, Spiridonovskiy per. 1, ⓣ 495/933-6655, ⓦ www.emcmos.ru; Ⓜ Ushkinskaya; ZAO International Medical Clinic, 31 Grokholskiy per. 31, 10th floor, Ⓜ Prospekt Mira ⓣ 495/937 5760, ⓦ www.sosclinic.ru. Both recognized by international insurance companies.

Internet Centre Internet Club, Kuznetskiy Most 12 Ⓜ Kuznetskiy Most (Mon–Fri 9am–midnight, Sat & Sun 10am–midnight; R90/hr); Site Cafe, Okhotni Ryad shopping centre, basement level to the right of the escalators, Ⓜ Okhotni Ryad (daily 10am–10pm; R150/hr).

Pharmacy Stariy Arbat 25 Ⓜ Arbatskaya; 24hr pharmacy 36.6 at Tverskaya ul. 25/9 Ⓜ Tverskaya.

Post office Central Telegraph Office, Tverskaya ul. 7; Main Post Office, Myasnitskaya ul. 26/2, 9am–6pm. Express postal services via Westpost, ⓦ www.westpost.ru; Courier Service, Bolshaya Sadovaya 10 Ⓜ Mayakovskaya. DHL, 1st Tverskaya Yamskaya ul. 11 Ⓜ Belorusskaya.

Moving on

Train Berlin (1 daily except Wed; 26hr); Budapest (1 daily; 39hr); Helsinki (1 daily; 14hr); Rīga (1 daily; 16hr); St Petersburg (13 daily; 7–9hr and up to 5 Sapsan express trains (4hr); Tallinn (1 daily; 15hr 30min); Vilnius (1 daily; 14hr); Warsaw (1 daily; 17hr 30min).

Bus Rīga (2 daily; 20hr); St Petersburg (1 daily; 13hr); Tallinn (1 daily; 18hr 30min).

St Petersburg

ST PETERSBURG (Санкт-Петербург), Petrograd, Leningrad and St Petersburg again – the city's succession of names mirrors Russia's turbulent history. Founded in 1703 by **Peter the Great** as a "window in the West", three hundred years later St Petersburg, a self-assured and future-focused city, still retains more of a Western European feel than Moscow. A sophisticated capital of the tsarist Empire, the cradle of the Communist Revolution of 1917, and a symbol of Russian stoicism due to the city's heroic endurance of a three-year Nazi siege during World War II, present-day St Petersburg has eased into modernity without sacrificing any of its old-world magnificence and charm, its shopping malls and nightclubs sitting alongside its opulent palaces. The city is easy to navigate and the pace of life is relaxed. The best **time to visit** is during the midsummer White Nights (mid-June to mid-July), when darkness never falls. From May to October all bridges across the Neva are raised from 1am to 5am – a beautiful sight, best seen from a boat.

What to see and do

St Petersburg's centre lies on the south bank of the River Neva, with the curving River Fontanka marking its southern boundary. The area within the Fontanka is riven by a series of avenues

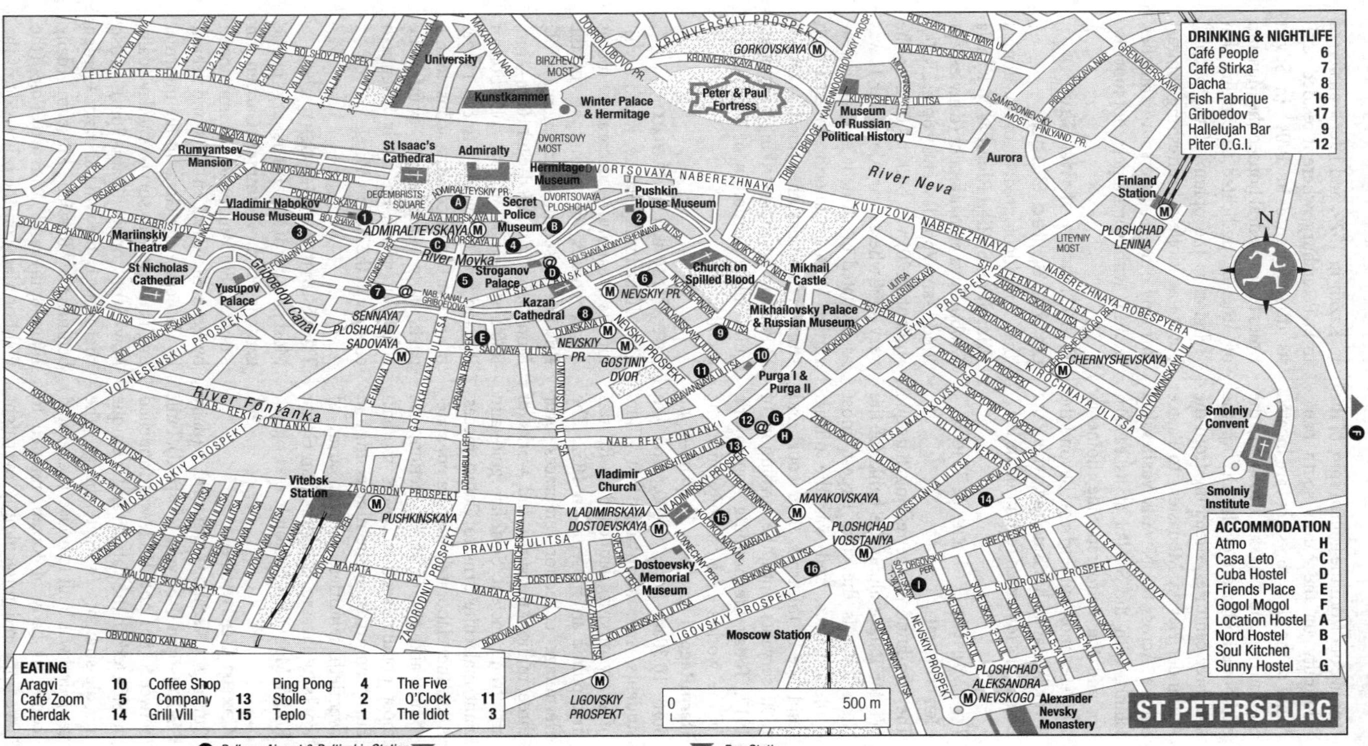
ST PETERSBURG
DRINKING & NIGHTLIFE
Café People 6
Café Stirka 7
Dacha 8
Fish Fabrique 16
Griboedov 17
Hallelujah Bar 9
Piter O.G.I. 12
ACCOMMODATION
Atmo H
Casa Leto C
Cuba Hostel D
Friends Place E
Gogol Mogol F
Location Hostel A
Nord Hostel B
Soul Kitchen I
Sunny Hostel G
EATING
Aragvi 10
Café Zoom 5
Cherdak 14
Coffee Shop Company 13
Grill Vill 15
Ping Pong 4
Stolle 2
Teplo 1
The Five O'Clock 11
The Idiot 3
0
500 m
17, Pulkova Airport & Baltiyskiy Station
Bus Station
N
University
Kunstkammer
Winter Palace & Hermitage
Peter & Paul Fortress
Museum of Russian Political History
Aurora
River Neva
Finland Station
PLOSHCHAD LENINA
Rumyantsev Mansion
St Isaac's Cathedral
Admiralty
Hermitage Museum
Pushkin House Museum
Vladimir Nabokov House Museum
Secret Police Museum
Mariinskiy Theatre
St Nicholas Cathedral
Yusupov Palace
Gribоedov Canal
River Moyka
Stroganov Palace
Kazan Cathedral
Church on Spilled Blood
Mikhail Castle
Mikhailovsky Palace & Russian Museum
SENNAYA PLOSHCHAD/ SADOVAYA
NEVSKIY PR.
GOSTINIY DVOR
Purga I & Purga II
River Fontanka
CHERNYSHEVSKAYA
Smolniy Convent
Smolniy Institute
Vitebsk Station
PUSHKINSKAYA
Vladimir Church
VLADIMIRSKAYA/ DOSTOEVSKAYA
Dostoevsky Memorial Museum
MAYAKOVSKAYA
PLOSHCHAD VOSSTANIYA
Moscow Station
LIGOVSKIY PROSPEKT
PLOSHCHAD ALEKSANDRA NEVSKOGO
Alexander Nevsky Monastery
GORKOVSKAYA
ADMIRALTEYSKAYA
NEVSKIY PROSPEKT
LITEYNIY PROSPEKT
VOZNESENSKIY PROSPEKT
MOSKOVSKIY PROSPEKT
ZAGORODNIY PROSPEKT
SUVOROVSKIY PROSPEKT
KUTUZOVA NABEREZHNAYA
DVORTSOVAYA NABEREZHNAYA
KRONVERSKIY PROSPEKT
TRINITY BRIDGE
LITEYNIY MOST
DVORTSOVY MOST
BIRZHEVOY MOST
SAMPSONIEVSKIY MOST

fanning out from the golden spire of the Admiralty, on the Neva's south bank. Many of the city's top sights are located on and around **Nevsky Prospekt**, the backbone and heart of the city for the last three centuries, stretching from the Alexander Nevsky Monastery to Palace Square. Across the Neva is **Vasilevskiy Island**, with the Strelka at its eastern tip, and the Petrograd Side, home to the Peter and Paul Fortress. Beyond the River Fontanka lies **Smolniy**, where the Bolsheviks fomented revolution in 1917.

The Winter Palace & The Hermitage

The two-hundred-metre-long Baroque **Winter Palace** along the banks of the Neva River is the city's largest, most opulent palace, and was the official residence of the tsars, their court and 1500 servants until the revolution of 1917. Today the building houses one of the world's greatest museums, the **Hermitage** (Tues–Sat 10.30am–6pm, Sun 10.30am–5pm; R400, free to students, free admission first Thurs of every month), launched as Russia's first public art museum in 1852. The Hermitage collection embraces over three million treasures and works of art, from ancient Scythian gold and giant malachite urns to Cubist pieces. After the elaborately decorated state-rooms and the Gold Collection, the most popular section covers modern European art from the nineteenth and twentieth centuries, with an array of works by Picasso, Gauguin, Van Gogh, Rodin, Monet and Renoir.

Kazan Cathedral

Curving **Kazan Cathedral** (daily 8.30am–6pm Ⓜ Nevsky Prospekt), built between 1801 and 1811, was modelled on St Peter's in the Vatican and is unique in die-straight St Petersburg. The cathedral was built to house a venerated icon, Our Lady of Kazan, reputed to have appeared miraculously overnight in Kazan in 1579, and later transferred to St Petersburg, where it resided until its disappearance in 1904. In Soviet times the cathedral housed the Museum of Atheism, dedicated to proving that "religion is the opium of the people", but today it offers a refreshing contrast to many other St Petersburg churches, teeming with worshippers, not tourists.

The Church of the Saviour on the Spilled Blood

The multicoloured, onion-domed **Church on Spilled Blood** at 26 Kanala Groboedova embankment (daily except Wed 11am–7pm, last entry 6pm; , R200, student R120) was built in 1882 on the very spot where Tsar Alexander II was assassinated by student radicals a year earlier. With an interior covered with stunning mosaics, the church is one of St Petersburg's most striking landmarks, quite unlike the dominant Neoclassical architecture.

The Russian Museum

The Mikhailovsky Palace, worth a visit for its beautifully decorated rooms alone, houses the main part of the **Russian Museum** (4 Inzhenernaya ul.; Mon 10am–5pm, Wed–Sun 10am–6pm; R300, student R150). Its collection of Russian art, the world's finest, ranges from fourteenth-century icons to the particularly impressive avant-garde collection from the early twentieth century in the Benois Wing.

The Summer Garden

Most popular of all St Petersburg's public gardens is the **Summer Garden** on Kutuzov Embankment, commissioned by Peter the Great in 1704 and rebuilt by Catherine the Great in the informal English style that survives today (daily May–Sept only, 10am–9pm). Also charming is the Mikhailovsky Garden behind the Russian Museum (daily 10am–8pm) and Marsovo Pole (the Field of Mars) on the other side of the

River Moyka where a flame burns for the fallen of the Revolution and civil war (1917–21).

The Admiralty and Decembrists' Square

The **Admiralty**, perched at the western end of Nevsky Prospekt, was founded in 1704 as a fortified shipyard. It extends 407m along the waterfront from Palace Square to **Decembrists' Square**, named after a group of reformist officers who, in December 1825, marched three thousand soldiers into the square in a doomed attempt to proclaim a constitutional monarchy. Today, Decembrists' Square is dominated by the *Bronze Horseman*, Falconet's 1778 statue of Peter the Great and the city's unofficial symbol.

St Isaac's Cathedral

Looming above Decembrists' Square, **St Isaac's Cathedral** (daily except Wed 11am–7pm, colonnade till 6pm; R200, student R120, colonnade R100; Ⓜ Nevsky Prospekt) is one of the glories of St Petersburg's skyline, its gilded dome the third largest in Europe. The opulent interior is equally impressive, decorated with fourteen kinds of marble. Climb the 262 steps to the outside colonnade to appreciate the cathedral's height (101.5m) and for an expansive view of the city.

The Peter and Paul Fortress

Across the Neva from the Winter Palace stands the **Peter and Paul Fortress**, built to secure Russia's hold on the Neva delta. The Fortress (daily 6am–10pm; free; Ⓜ Gorkovskaya) shelters a cathedral as well as rotating exhibitions in the Engineers' and Commandant's House. The Dutch-style Peter and Paul Cathedral (daily except Wed 10am–7pm; R170–350), completed in 1733, remained the tallest structure in the city until the 1960s. Sited around the nave are the tombs of **Romanov monarchs** from Peter the Great onwards, excluding Peter II, Ivan VI and Nicholas II. The Nevskaya panorama roof walk (10am–8pm) gives an excellent view of the Winter Palace, and you can spot sunbathers by the Neva Curtain Wall from March onwards. Inside the fortress, period dress is available for rent by the hour for those interested in some costumed capering.

Cruiser Aurora

Anchored a short walk along the Neva from the Peter and Paul fortress is the **Cruiser Aurora** (Petrogradskaya nab., daily except Mon & Fri 10.30am–4pm; free; Ⓜ Gorkovskaya), the famous battle ship that fired the opening shot of the revolution of 1917.

Kunstkamera

Don't miss the **Kunstkamera** at Universitetskaya nab. 3, Vasilevsky Island (11am–6pm, closed Mon & last Tues of the month; R200; Ⓜ Vasileostrovskaya), Russia's oldest public museum, founded by Peter the Great in 1714 in order to promote scientific research and educate the general public in the sphere of medical research. All sorts of monstrosities are on display, from malformed fetuses to infants' hearts, carefully preserved in vinegar or vodka.

Museum of Russian Political History

The **Museum of Political History** at Kuibysheva ul. 2/4 (daily except Thurs 10am–6pm; R200; closed last Mon of the month; free entry on public holidays; Ⓜ Gorkovskaya) gives an insight into Soviet-era political and social life, displaying children's textbooks reworked to demonize the *kulaks* (moneyed peasants), appalling photographic evidence of Stalin's purges, and film footage recalling how Western culture enthralled

Soviet youngsters in the 1960s and 1970s. Helpful attendants can provide English-language booklets.

House-museums

St Petersburg was home to some of the greatest writers of Russian literature, including Pushkin, Dostoevsky and Nabokov. The **Pushkin House Museum** at Moyki Reki nab. 12 (daily except Tues 10.30am–5pm; closed every last Fri of the month; R200; Ⓜ Nevsky Prospekt) was where the poet wrote his last poem and letter before the duel that killed him two days later – you can see the pair of duelling pistols and the waistcoat he wore on that tragic day. Dostoevksy enthusiasts should head to the **Dostoevsky Memorial Museum** at Kuznechny per. 5/2, (Tues–Sun 11am–6pm; R160, student R80; Ⓜ Vladimirskaya), where the novelist lived briefly in 1846 and then again from 1878 until his death three years later. Here he initially worked on his first story *The Double*, and later on his last novel *The Brothers Karamazov*. The former home of the prose master behind *Lolita* is the **Vladimir Nabokov House Museum** at ul. Bolshaya Morskaya 47 (Tues–Fri 11am–6pm, Sat noon–5pm; Ⓜ Admiralteskaya), where the novelist lived until 1917. You can watch a video interview with Nabokov as well as peruse curious memorabilia including part of his butterfly collection that was the inspiration behind many of his novels.

Smolniy Convent and Institute

Smolniy Convent (3/1 Rastrelli Square, daily except Wed 11am–7pm, R150, student R90; Ⓜ Chernyshevskaya), a peerless ice-blue Rastrelli Baroque creation that's now a concert and exhibition hall (concerts R100–600; exhibitions R70–200), is the focal point of the Smolniy district. The neighbouring **Smolniy Institute** (pl. Proletarskoy diktaturi 3) is the headquarters of St Petersburg's Governor, but was built between 1806 and 1808 to house the Institute for Young Noblewomen; Lenin orchestrated the October Revolution of 1917 from here. A statue of the man himself still stands in front of the building, and as you enter the Institute's grounds look out for the now familiar Communist slogan: "Workers of the World, Unite!" (Пролетарии всех стран, соединяйтесь!).

Alexander Nevsky Monastery

At the eastern end of Nevsky Prospekt lies the **Alexander Nevsky Monastery** (daily June–Aug 6am–9pm; rest of the year till 8pm; free; Ⓜ Ploshchad' Aleksandra Nevskogo), founded in 1713 by Peter the Great and one of only four monasteries in the Russian Empire with the rank of *lavra*, the highest in Orthodox monasticism. Two famous **cemeteries** lie in the monastery grounds: the Necropolis for Masters of the Arts, where Dostoyevsky, Rimsky-Korsakov, Tchaikovsky and Glinka lie, and, directly opposite, the Lazarus Cemetery, the oldest in the city with elaborately decorated tombs. Tickets are required for entry to both (April–Oct 9.30am–6pm; Nov–March 9.30am–5.30pm, closed Thurs; R200).

Rumyantsev Mansion

Along the Neva embankment to the west of the Admiralty, the focal point of the **Rumyantsev Mansion** (Angliyskaya nab. 44; daily except Wed 11am–6pm, Tues until 5pm; R110, student R70; Ⓜ Sadovaya) is the exhibition on Leningrad during the Great Patriotic War, which details the horrors of life in a desperate city, besieged by the Nazis between 1941 and 1944. The most harrowing exhibit is the diary of 11-year-old Tanya Savicheva, who continued going to school as, one by one, her entire family died of starvation.

Yusupov Palace

Purchased by the aristocratic Yusupov family in 1830, the elaborately decorated **Yusupov Palace** on the Nab. Reki Moiky 94 (daily 10.45am–5pm; R500, student R380, including audioguide; Ⓜ Nevsky Prospekt) was the scene of the murder of the sinister monk, Rasputin, deemed to have had undue influence over the royal family. In 1916, Felix Yusupov and his associates poisoned Rasputin in the cellar (where you can see a wax likeness of the man). When the poison failed to take effect, they shot him, rolled him up in a carpet and threw him in the river; he finally died from drowning, having clawed his way through much of the ice.

Arrival and information

Air International flights arrive at Pulkovo Airport (Ⓣ812/704-3444), Terminal 2. Have some rubles on you when you arrive as the ATM is not always working. Take a shuttle bus (#K3, #39A or #113; R30) or city bus #13 all departing around every 15min to the end of the metro line (Moskovskaya). Shuttle bus Ploschad #K3 continues on to Ⓜ Sennaya in the centre of town.

Train Services from Helsinki arrive at Finland station (Findlyanskiy vokzal), at Ploshchad' Lenina 6 Ⓜ Ploshchad' Lenina. Trains from Rīga and Vilnius terminate at Vitebsk station (Vitebskiy vokzal) Ⓜ Pushkinskaya. Trains from Moscow (up to 18 daily) draw into Moscow station (Moskovskiy vokzal) Ⓜ Ploshchad Vosstaniya.

Bus Most buses arrive at the Central Bus Station, Obvodnovo kanal 36 Ⓜ Obvodny Kanal. Buses from the Baltic States stop at St Petersburg's Baltiyskiy station at Obvodnogo kanal 120 Ⓜ Baltiskaya. See timetables at Ⓦ www.eurolines.eu.

Ferry In the summer months (when the ice melts) there are ferries from Tallinn, Helsinki and Rostock, operated by Silja Line (Ⓦ www.silja .com) and Estonian operator Tallink (Ⓦ www .tallink.ee). They arrive at the Morskoy vokzal, Prospekt Morskoy Slavy 1 Ⓜ Vasilieostrovskaya, at the western end of Vasilevskiy Island (bus #22 or minibus to the centre).

Tourist office The main centre at Sadovaya ul. 14 (Mon–Fri 10am–7pm, Sat noon–6pm; Ⓣ812/982-8253, Ⓦ www.visit-petersburg.com; Ⓜ Nevsky Prospekt) has plenty of material in English.

City transport

Metro The St Petersburg metro, the deepest in the world, runs from 5.30am to midnight. Small numbers of journeys (R25 a journey) are sold using tokens (*zhetoni*), which you feed into ticket machines. For 10 or more rides to be used over a fixed number of days, buy a plastic card.

Bus and trolleybus Often the best way to tackle a big road like Nevsky Prospekt, overground transport is more useful in the city centre than the metro. Buy tickets from the driver (R19).

Minibus *Marshrutkas* (yellow in St Petersburg) are cheap (R30 a journey) and cheerful. The #K-147 goes from Moskovskiy vokzal right to the upper end of Nevsky Prospekt.

Boat One of the best ways to see the city is by boat (May–Oct) – either a private motorboat from any bridge on Nevsky Prospekt (from R1800/hr/boat), or a large tour boat from behind the Hermitage (R250/person). AngloTourismo (Ⓦ www.angloturismo .com) offer guided tours in English (R500) from the pier on Fontanka next to Shuvalovsky Palace at no. 27; Ⓣ921/989-4722. Try the excellent "St Petersburg by Night" boat tour (R600); it takes in the more spectacular of the city's bridges, all lit up, as they are raised for the night.

Accommodation

Hostels

Atmo Liteyniy Propekt 64 Ⓣ911/928-5118, Ⓦ www.atmohostel.ru Ⓜ Mayakovskaya. The psychedelic decor of this hostel eases off as you approach the kitchen and lounge at the back; dorms are spacious and the place is pretty clean. Continental breakfast included. Dorms R600.

Cuba Hostel Kazanskaya ul. 5, 4th floor Ⓣ812/921 7115, Ⓦ www.cubahostel.ru Ⓜ Nevsky Prospekt. Vibrantly decorated hostel in an unbeatable location behind Kazan Cathedral. Dial 41 at the buzzer downstairs. Mixed/single-sex dorms R490–800, doubles R1300/person.

Friends Place Bankovskiy per. 3 Ⓣ812/310-4955 Ⓦ www.friendsplace.ru Ⓜ Spasskaya/Gostiniy Dvor. The Russians' obsession with the TV series *Friends* comes alive at this HI-affiliated hostel, with pictures of the show scattered around, as well as a mock brick wall like the programme's apartment block. Cosy kitchen, clean male and female dorms and a mini foot-ball table. Dorms R900.

Gogol Mogol ul. Stahanovcev 9a, flat 15 Ⓣ921/186-3036, Ⓦ www.gogolmogolhostel.com Ⓜ Novocherkasskaya. Intimate, cosy and spotless, this pleasant, peaceful hostel in a verdant residential area a couple of metro stops from the centre only sleeps fifteen. Dorms R650.

Location Hostel Admiralteisky Prospekt 8 ⓣ812/490-6429, ⓦwww.location-hostel.ru Ⓜ Admiralteyskaya. Funky HI hostel with modern amenities, a friendly atmosphere and helpful staff. The dorms all have lockers, and the brick walls and wooden beams give it a cosy touch. Wi-fi, laundry facilities and light breakfast included. Dorms R600, doubles R1500.

Nord Hostel Bolshaya Morskaya ul. 10 ⓣ812/571 0342, ⓦwww.nordhostel.com Ⓜ Admiralteyskaya. In a beautiful building, this hostel couldn't be more central, but the kitchen/communal area closes at 10pm so if you're up for a party maybe head elsewhere. The dorms are comfortable with shared facilities; internet access. Breakfast included. Dorms €24, doubles €65.

Soul Kitchen 1-ya Sovietskaya ul. 12 ⓣ964/3789-445, ⓦwww.soulkitchenhostel.com Ⓜ Vosstaniya. Snug, homely hostel with comfy dorms; there's also a little love-nest double (R2400) only for couples. Book ahead. Dorms R550.

Sunny Hostel Liteyniy Prospekt 61, apt.31 ⓣ812/942-8082, ⓦwww.sunny-hostel.ru Ⓜ Mayakovskaya. Framed discs decorate the hallway of this pleasant hostel with clean and colourful rooms. To get there, take the second courtyard on your left coming from Nevsky Prospekt; head to the door straight in front of you and dial 31B to be buzzed in. Dorms R600; doubles R2000.

Eating

Canteens and cafés

Café Zoom ul. Gorokhovaya 22 ⓣ812/448-5001 Ⓜ Nevsky Prospekt. Sit back with a good book and unwind at this student café. Hearty breakfast omelettes (from R80), as well as tasty soups (R110). Mon–Fri 9am–midnight, Sat 11am–midnight, Sun 1pm–midnight.

TREAT YOURSELF

Casa Leto (Bol Morskaya 34, ⓣ812/600-1096, ⓦwww.casaleto.com Ⓜ Admiralteyskaya) Intimate high-end family-run B&B comprising five spacious rooms, all individually decorated with antique furniture, adding to the mini-hotel's unique and sophisticated touch. Good discounts in low season (doubles from R4500).

Cherdak Ligovsky per. 17 ⓣ812/272-5564 Ⓜ Plashchad Vosstaniya. Hats, ties and antique sports equipment are apparently what you'd find if you rummaged around a Russian *cherdak* (attic), according to this cosy café. *Blinis* (pancakes) from R50, soups from R130. Daily noon–11.30pm, Fri & Sat noon–2pm.

Coffee Shop Company Nevsky Prospekt 47 Ⓜ Mayakovskaya. Despite this place being part of a chain (there are fourteen others in town) it's got a unique, trendy feel to it. Bargain breakfasts from R135. Mon–Fri 9am–2am, Sat & Sun 24hr.

Stolle Konushenny per. 1/6 ⓣ812/312-1862 Ⓜ Nevsky Prospekt. Parisian bistro-style chain serving delicious, freshly baked pies (from R35). No table service so head to the bar to pick your pie. Daily 9am–9pm.

The Five O'Clock Ul. Karavannaya 11/64 ⓣ812/315-5888 Ⓜ Gostiny Dvor. *Alice in Wonderland*-inspired café, perfect for a quick tea stop. Teas from R90, cakes R130. Daily 9.30am–11pm.

Restaurants

Aragvi Nab. Reki Fontanky 9 ⓣ812/570-5643 Ⓜ Gostiny Dvor. One of the most popular Georgian restaurants in the city, and deservedly so. Their selection of *lobio* starters is superb; the *khachapuri* (R290), oozing cheese, is enough for two; and the generous mains (R350) include delicately spiced grilled meats, and baked sheeps' brains with coriander for the more adventurous. Daily 11am–midnight, Sat & Sun from noon.

Grill Vill Ul. Kolokolnaya 12 ⓣ812/713-3776 Ⓜ Mayakovskaya. Good-value, tasty fast food, as well as business lunches noon–5pm (R200), in a simple setting with wooden interiors; it's a good pit stop before heading to the Dostoevsky Museum nearby. Try the Italian taco (R160). Mon–Fri 11am–10pm, Sat & Sun noon–10pm.

Ping Pong Bol. Morskaya 16 ⓣ812/315-8256 ⓦwww.pingpongcafe.ru Ⓜ Admiralteyskaya. If you're craving Southeast Asian food head to this bright and spacious café-cum-restaurant and tuck into hearty portions of noodles (R240). Business lunches (R290) noon–3.30pm. Daily noon–midnight.

Teplo Bol. Morskaya 45 ⓣ812/570-1974 Ⓜ Admiralteyskaya. Relaxed place with a cosy fireplace and squashy sofas. Soups R140, mains from R180. Mon–Thurs 9am–midnight, Sat 11am–midnight, Sun 1pm–midnight.

The Idiot Nab. Reki Moyki 82 ⓣ812/315-1675 Ⓜ Sadovaya. Soak up the the Soviet atmosphere at this veggie restaurant named after Dostoevsky's novel; the antique heavy furniture nearly makes it feel like you're sitting in his very dining room. Food is adequate (mains from R300) but you do get a free vodka shot upon arrival, and it's happy hour 6.30–7.30pm. Daily 11am–1am.

Drinking

Bars

Café People Ul. Italyanskaya 2 Ⓜ Gostiny Dvor. Hip café-cum-bar with 1960s theme. Enjoy a cocktail (R300) or two on a warm summer evening in the huge marquee at the back. DJs and the latest bands on Fri & Sat add to the cool atmosphere. Beers R150. Daily 8am–6am.

Café Stirka Ul. Kazanskaya 26 Ⓜ Sennaya. Small grungy haunt attracting an alternative crowd; worn-out sofas and good beats from the decent sound system or live bands. Beers (R120). Daily 11am–late.

Dacha D-3, Ul. Dumskaya 9 Ⓜ Gostiny Dvor. Underground joint that gets packed and pretty messy at weekends, popular with the city's young artsy set. Table football in the little side room. Beers and shots both R70. Daily noon–6am.

Piter O.G.I. Fontanky Reky nab. 40 Ⓦ www.piterogi.ru Ⓜ Mayakovskaya. Café, restaurant, bar, club, concert and exhibition hall, this 24/7 place attracts a young, laidback studenty crowd. Great-value grub (mains R179) and drinks (cocktails R130). Music varies from rock to dance.

Clubs

Fish Fabrique Ligovskiy. 53e. Ⓜ Ploschad' Vosstaniya. Grungy venue in the heart of the city's largest centre for artists, hosting regular live gigs (admission R100–300); live music usually on Thurs, Sat & Sun 5pm–6am.

Griboedov Voronezhskaya ul. 2a Ⓜ Ligovskiy Prospekt. An underground club in a former bomb shelter, hosting a range of DJs and alternative bands. Regular parties on Mon (jazz/hop/funk) and Sat (hip-hop/reggae). Mon–Fri noon–6am, Sat & Sun 1pm–6am. Entry R300.

Hallelujah Bar Inzhenernaya ul. 7 Ⓜ Gostiny Dvor. This little joint goes nuts on the weekends when students dance to the cheesy 80s, 90s and Russian tracks. Daily 8pm–6am. Entry R100–150.

Purga Nab. Reki Fontanky 11 Ⓜ Mayakovskaya. You'll either love or hate the two *Purga* clubs; *Purga I* hosts New Year celebrations nightly, complete with address by a Soviet leader, while next door, *Purga II* is the place to go with your other half for a mock wedding. Rowdy fun. *Purga I* daily 4pm–6am, *Purga II* Wed–Sun 8pm–4am. R200 after 8pm, R400 Fri & Sat.

Entertainment

Theatres tend to close for the summer until mid-September. For listings and events pick up the quarterly freebie *Where St Petersburg, In your Pocket* or the Friday *St Petersburg Times*.

Classical, opera and ballet

Mariinskiy Theatre Teatralnaya pl. 1 Ⓣ 812/326 4141, Ⓦ www.mariinsky.ru Ⓜ Sadovaya. Tickets €8–120. Performances at 7pm, matinees at noon.

Philharmonia Mikhaylovskaya ul. 2 Ⓣ 812/710 4257 Ⓦ www.philharmonia.spb.ru. Ⓜ Nevsky Prospekt. Draws international classical musicians as well as Russia's finest. Performances at 7pm.

Live music

JFC Jazz Club Shpalernaya ul. 33 Ⓣ 812/272-9850, Ⓦ www.jfc-club.spb.ru Ⓜ Chernyshevskaya. The city's most exciting, intimate jazz club, tucked away in a courtyard; nightly performances from experimental jazz to blues. Music 7–11pm. Admission from R200.

Shopping

Kuznechny market 3 Kuznechniy per. Ⓜ Vladimirskaya. Shop for Russian speciality foods here, such as mouthwatering displays of sweets and cakes, salted cucumbers, sausages, plaited cheese rinds and caviar. Daily 8am–8pm, Sun 8am–7pm.

Nevsky Souvenir Nevsky Prospekt 3 Ⓜ Nevsky Prospekt. Pick up high-quality (though not cheap) Russian souvenirs here, as well as the obligatory *matrioshka* dolls. There's also stunning amber jewellery by local artists, as well as Fabergé-style eggs made from real eggs. Daily 10am–9pm.

Souvenirs Fair Nab. Kanal Griboedova 1, opposite the Church of the Saviour on the Spilled Blood Ⓜ Nevsky Prospekt. Nearly 200 stalls open all year round with plenty of souvenirs from paintings to handicrafts. Daily 9am–6pm.

Directory

Consulates Australia: Nab. Reky Moiki 11, Ⓣ 812/315 1100 Ⓜ Nevsky Prospekt; UK: pl. Proletarskoy Diktatury 5, US: Ⓣ 812/320 3245 Ⓜ Chernyshevskaya; Furshtadtskaya ul. 15, Ⓣ 812/331 2600 Ⓜ Chernyshevskaya.

Internet Internet Centre, Nevsky Prospekt 17 Ⓜ Nevsky Prospekt (daily 10am–10pm; closed 1.30–2.15pm; R70/hr); Tvoe Café, Liteyniy Prospekt

63 Ⓜ Mayakovskaya (daily 24hr; R70/hr); 59°57", ul. Kazanskaya 26 Ⓜ Sennaya (daily 24hr; R100/hr).
Health MEDEM International Clinic & Hospital, ul. Marata 6, Ⓜ Mayakovskaya ⓣ 812/336 3333; American Medical Clinic, Nab. Reki Moyky 78, Ⓜ Sadovaya ⓣ 812/740 2090.
Pharmacy Petropharm, at Nevsky pr. 22–24 (24hr).
Post office Main office at Pochtamskaya ul. 9, Ⓜ Nevsky Prospekt (Mon–Sat 9am–8pm, Sun 10am–6pm). Express letter post: Westpost, Nevsky Prospekt 86, ⓦ www.westpost.ru (Mon–Fri 9.30am–8pm; Sat noon–8pm). DHL: Nevsky pr. 10 (Mon–Fri 9am–9pm, Sat & Sun 10am–4pm), ⓦ www.dhl.ru.

Moving on

Train Helsinki (1 daily, 6.5hr; 2 express Sapsan trains 3.5hr); Moscow (13 daily; 7–9hr; up to 5 express Sapsan trains, 4hr); Rīga (1 daily; 13hr); Vilnius (1 daily; 13hr).
Bus You can purchase bus tickets online via Lux Express (ⓦ www.luxexpress.eu) to the Baltic States including Rīga (9 daily; 10hr); Tallinn (10 daily; 6hr); Tartu (3 daily; 6hr); Warsaw (5 daily; 26hr). Sovavto (ⓦ www.sovavto.ru) and Finnord run buses to Helsinki (3 daily; 8hr 30min).

DAY-TRIPS FROM ST PETERSBURG

The Imperial palaces of **Peterhof** and **Tsarskoe Selo**, half an hour to an hour outside the city, are both splendid day-trips. Although entering the palaces is increasingly expensive, you can slip away from the crowds into the surrounding parks. As you leave St Petersburg on the bus, look out for the awe-inspiring war monument to Leningrad's World War II sacrifice, and Lenin "hailing a taxi" near Finland station.

The Peterhof

Most visitors with time for just one day-trip opt for **Peterhof** (Great Palace 10.30am–6pm, closed Mon & last Tues of month, R520, student R250; park 9am–7pm; R350, student R180), 29km west of St Petersburg, known as the "Russian Versailles" and famed for its marvellous fountains and impressive cascades. Though originally built between 1709 and 1724 for Peter the Great, each of the subsequent rulers made their mark here. Travel by hydrofoil in summer (at least one hourly 10am–6pm; R200 each way; 30–40min) from outside the Winter Palace or take minibus #224 or #424 from Ⓜ Avtovo (R30), or #103 or #420 from Ⓜ Leninsky Prospekt. Trains also run from Baltiyskiy station in the capital to Noviy Peterhof station.

Tsarskoe Selo and Pavlovsk

Tsarskoe Selo (also known as Pushkin, after the "Russian Shakespeare" who was schooled at the neighbouring Lyceum school), 17km southeast of St Petersburg, centres on the **Catherine Palace** (palace 10am–6pm, closed Tues & last Mon of the month; R550, student R280; park daily 9am–7pm, R200, student R100). The ostentatious blue-and-white Baroque structure built by Catherine the Great is surrounded by a richly landscaped park. Scottish architect Charles Cameron's elegant Neoclassical Gallery stretches high above it. To get to Pushkin, take minibus #299 (R30) from Ⓜ Moskovskaya behind the Lenin monument or #286 from Ⓜ Kupchino; alternatively, take a train to Detskoe selo from Vitebsky station.

The same minibuses take you to the more intimate **Pavlovsk Palace** (10am–6pm, closed Fri & first Mon of the month; palace R500, student R300, park R150, student R80), its magnificent Neoclassical interior set amid luxurious 1500-acre grounds.

Serbia

HIGHLIGHTS

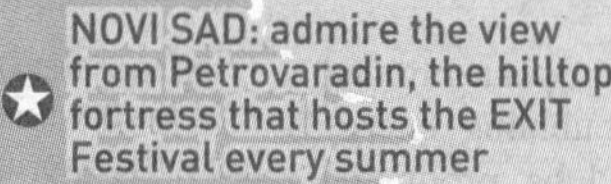

SUBOTICA: enjoy the city's unspoilt feel and fantastical Secessionist architecture

NOVI SAD: admire the view from Petrovaradin, the hilltop fortress that hosts the EXIT Festival every summer

BELGRADE: explore the nightlife and café culture of Serbia's hectic, hedonistic capital city

STUDENICA MONASTERY: the finest of Serbia's fresco-laden, medieval monastic churches

ROUGH COSTS

DAILY BUDGET basic €25 /occasional treat €35

DRINK Beer (half-litre) €1

FOOD *Pljeskavica* (hamburger) €1–2

HOSTEL/BUDGET HOTEL €12/€35

TRAVEL Belgrade–Novi Sad €6 by bus; Belgrade–Niš €6 by train

FACT FILE

POPULATION 7.5 million (excluding Kosovo)

AREA 88,361 sq km

LANGUAGE Serbian

CURRENCY Dinar (din)

CAPITAL Belgrade (population: 1.6 million)

INTERNATIONAL PHONE CODE ⓣ381

Introduction

Serbia is a buzzy and boisterous country, compact enough for visitors to sample both Belgrade's urban hedonism and the gentler pace of the smaller towns or national parks within a few days – and it's one of Europe's most affordable destinations to boot. Grittier than its blue-eyed neighbour Croatia, it is nevertheless an integral part of any backpacker's Balkan tour: at the heart of the region, it gives easy access to the cluster of cultures and histories crammed into this small corner of Europe.

Serbia's young, European-minded population brings a bubbling energy to its bars, cafés and clubs, producing an adrenaline-charged nightlife unmatched anywhere else in the Balkans. The general determination to have a good time confounds the expectations of many a traveller, arriving with memories of the 1990s, when Serbia's name was not often off war reporters' lips. Today, it's just as likely to attract headlines for its crop of world-class tennis players or the annual EXIT festival in Novi Sad.

Serbia's capital, **Belgrade**, is a sociable, hectic city that energizes and exhausts by turns. Northwest of the city on the iron-flat Vojvodina Plain sits lovely **Novi Sad**, window to the **Fruška Gora** hills, while further north – a stone's throw from the border with Hungary – enchanting **Subotica** is sprinkled with early twentieth-century Secessionist architecture. Deep in the mountainous tract of land to the south of Belgrade are three key struts of Serbia's religio-cultural heritage – Žiča, Studenica and Sopoćani **monasteries**. East of here, **Niš** is a pleasant small city to pause in en route to or from Bulgaria or Macedonia.

CHRONOLOGY

168 BC The Romans defeat the Illyrian tribe and establish their rule of the area of present-day Serbia.
630 AD Serbs settle in the region.
1166 Stefan Nemanja, leader of the Serbs, declares independence from Byzantine rule.
1219 The Serbian Orthodox Church is established.
1389 The Ottomans defeat the Serbs in the Battle of Kosovo, ushering in four centuries of direct rule.
1804 National hero Karađorđe ("Black George") begins the First Serbian Uprising against the Ottomans.
1913 The Ottomans lose their remaining authority in Serbia during the Balkan wars.
1918 Following World War I the Kingdom of Serbs, Croats and Slovenes is formed.
1929 The Kingdom is renamed Yugoslavia.
1945 Following World War II, Serbia is absorbed into Socialist Yugoslavia.
1989 Slobodan Milošević, a Serbian communist, becomes President of Serbia.
1992 The wars of the disintegration of Yugoslavia begin. Fighting ends three years later.
1993 The International Criminal Tribunal for the former Yugoslavia is set up in The Hague to try those accused of war crimes.
1998 Serbia launches a violent campaign against the ethnic Albanian community in Kosovo, costing thousands of lives.
1999 NATO's "Operation Merciful Angel" – a ten-week war from the air to end Milošević's ethnic cleansing campaign – drives Yugoslav National Army forces out of Kosovo.
2000 Mass protests lead to the resignation of Milošević.
2003 Serbian prime minister, Zoran Đinđić, is assassinated in Belgrade.
2006 Milošević dies in prison, awaiting trial at the International Criminal Tribunal for the former Yugoslavia on charges of genocide.
2006 Montenegro peacefully gains independence from Serbia.
2008 Kosovo declares independence from Serbia after nine years under UN administration. Serbia does not recognize Kosovo as an independent state.

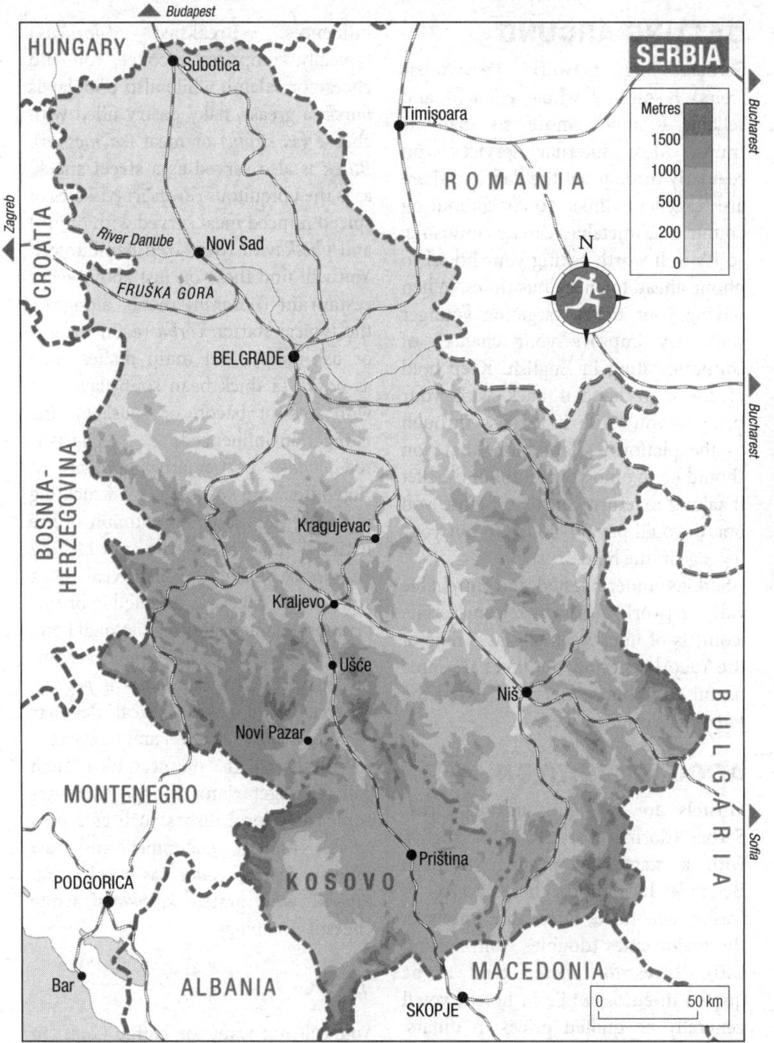

ARRIVAL

Flight operators from the UK include Wizz Air (Ⓦwww.wizzair.com) and the Yugoslav national airline JAT (Ⓦwww.jat.com), inherited by Serbia – the air hostesses' mandatory blue eyeshadow and severe manner evoke times gone by. Serbia's location at the heart of the Balkans means that there are good **rail** connections with all the neighbouring countries, particularly Hungary (via Subotica), Bulgaria (via Niš), Romania (via Timisoara), Croatia, Bosnia-Herzegovina and Montenegro. No visas are needed for nationals of the US, Canada, Australia, New Zealand, UK, Republic of Ireland, or any EU country staying in Serbia for up to ninety days.

GETTING AROUND

Serbia's **bus** network (Ⓦwww.bas.co.rs) is on the whole efficient and reliable – much more so than its trains. Most internal services run regularly throughout the day, and there are excellent links to neighbouring countries. Timetables can be confusing, so it's well worth asking your hostel to phone ahead to check bus times. When buying your ticket, targeting younger staff may improve your chances of communicating in English. Keep hold of the coin handed back with your ticket – you'll use it to pass through to the platform – and note that you should hang onto your outbound ticket if taking a return journey. Before you board, you'll pay 30–40din to put your luggage in the hold.

Serbia's underinvested and unreliable **rail** network (Ⓦwww.zeleznicesrbije.com) is of interest chiefly as a relic of the Yugoslav period, but there are some useful cross-border services. Avoid the *putnički* (slow) services.

ACCOMMODATION

Hostels are springing up all across Serbia (dorms cost €10–20 a night), with a staggering number now in Belgrade. In addition there's a crop of freshly decorated, affordable **hotels** in the major cities (doubles from around €40). Prices for hostels tend to be quoted in euros, while in hotels, you'll generally be quoted prices in dinars. **Rooms** in people's homes (*sobe*) are less commonly offered than in Croatia or Bosnia-Herzegovina, but **apartmani** (furnished individual rooms or suites) are available, with doubles starting at around €40.

FOOD AND DRINK

In common with other Balkan countries, Serbian **cuisine** is overwhelmingly dominated by meat, and many dishes manifest Turkish or Austro-Hungarian influences. **Breakfast** (*doručak*) typically comprises a coffee, roll and cheese or salami, while also popular is *burek*, a greasy, flaky pastry filled with cheese (*sa sirom*) or meat (*sa mesom*). *Burek* is also served as a **street snack**, as is the ubiquitous *čevapčići* (rissoles of spiced minced meat served with onion) and *pljeskavica* (oversized hamburger). You will find these on just about every **restaurant** (*restoran*) menu, alongside the typical starter, *čorba* (a thick meat or fish soup), and **main dishes** such as *pasulj* (a thick bean soup flavoured with bits of bacon or sausage), the Hungarian-influenced paprika-red *gulaš*, particularly popular in Vojvodina, and *kolenica* (leg of suckling pig). But the crowning triumph of the national cuisine is the gut-busting *karađorđe šnicla*, a rolled veal steak stuffed with cheese and coated in breadcrumbs – named after the national hero, Karađorđe Petrović. A popular accompaniment to all these dishes is *pogača*, a large bread cake. Typical **desserts** include *strudla* (strudel) and baklava.

With the reliance on meat, it's a tough call for **vegetarians**, though there are some tasty local dishes such as *srpska salata* (tomato, cucumber and raw onion), *šopska salata* (as *srpska*, but topped with grated *kashkaval* white cheese), and *burek*.

Drink

You will not want for **coffee** (*kafa*) in Serbia, but sadly the traditional Turkish kind (thick, black, with grounds in) can be hard to come by, as many youngsters prefer to drink the Western variants. Balkan **beer** (*pivo*) brands like Lav, Jelen and Montenegrin Nikšićko are very palatable. On the whole **wine** tends to be disproportionately pricey on restaurant menus, but Montenegrin Vranac and Macedonian Tikveš are more affordable. Everyone should sample *slijvovica* – plum *rakija* – but pace yourself to avoid waking up with a shocked head and raw throat.

CULTURE AND ETIQUETTE

Even though tourists are quite a rarity in some parts, part of the charm of travel in Serbia is a sense of "live and let live" – you are unlikely to be quizzed intrusively or pestered to buy wares. Serbian culture as a whole is far from conservative – a fact you'll quickly grasp from the fashion choices youngsters make. You should cover arms and legs in Orthodox churches, however. **Tipping** in restaurants is not essential, but in the nicer places you should leave ten percent.

SPORTS AND OUTDOOR ACTIVITIES

Serbia's countryside is beautiful, varied and never more than a short bus ride away. In the summer, **hike** or walk in the Fruška Gora National Park (Ⓦwww.npfruskagora.co.rs); in winter hit the **ski** slopes with Balkan daredevils at Kopaonik National Park (Ⓦwww.eng.infokop.net). The locals are passionate about **football**, and a derby between Belgrade's Red Star (Ⓦwww.redstarbelgrade.com) and FK Partizan (Ⓦwww.partizan.rs) is invariably a fiery – and rarely violence-free – affair. For something more sedate, head to Novi Sad's FK Vojvodina (Ⓦwww.fkvojvodina.com).

COMMUNICATIONS

Wi-fi is available in a good number of cafés, though you will be expected to buy a drink. **Internet cafés** are not so common, but where you do find one, expect to pay around 100din per hour.

EMERGENCY NUMBERS

Police Ⓣ92; Ambulance Ⓣ94; Fire Ⓣ93; Road assistance Ⓣ987.

SERBIA ONLINE

Ⓦ**www.belgradeeye.com** Excellent English-language site aimed at younger visitors; includes information on a fast-changing club scene.
Ⓦ**www.b92.net** Venerable broadcasting station and the driving force behind anti-Milošević demonstrations during the 1990s; it remains the country's most newsworthy site.
Ⓦ**www.serbia-tourism.org** Official tourist board site.

Public phones use Halo cards, sold with 300din and 600din credit at post offices, kiosks and tobacconists. Most **post offices** (*pošta*) are open Monday to Friday 8am to 7pm. **Stamps** (*markice*) can also be bought at newsstands.

EMERGENCIES

The **crime** rate, even in Belgrade, is low by European standards, though the usual precautions apply. **Identity checks** are not uncommon, so carry a photocopy of your passport.

Pharmacies (*apoteka*) tend to follow shop hours of around Monday to Friday 8am to 8pm, Saturday 8am to 3pm.

INFORMATION

All the towns covered in this chapter have a **tourist information office** (*turističke informacije*), stocking some good-quality materials in English. Another good source of information is *In Your Pocket* (Ⓦwww.inyourpocket.com), which currently publishes both print and online guides to Belgrade, Novi Sad and Niš.

MONEY AND BANKS

The currency is the **dinar** (usually abbreviated to din), comprising coins of 1, 2, 5, 10 and 20din (and also 50 para coins – 100 para equals 1din), and notes of 10, 20, 50, 100, 200, 1000 and 5000din. At the time of writing exchange rates were

SERBIAN

Serbia uses the **Cyrillic alphabet** as well as the Latin one. Many street signs (see p.1003) and bus and train timetables are in Cyrillic only, so it's worth being able to decode at least the first few letters of a word. Serbian, like Bosnian, is very closely related to Croatian (see p.252) and all three languages will be understood in all three countries.

€1 = 100din, £1 = 115din, and US$1 = 70din. **Exchange offices** (*menjačnica*) are everywhere, while **ATMs** are widely available in towns. Credit/debit cards are accepted in most hotels, restaurants and shops.

OPENING HOURS AND HOLIDAYS

Most **shops** open Monday to Friday 8am to 7/8pm (sometimes with a break for lunch), plus Saturday 8am to 2pm, and sometimes later in Belgrade. Most **museums** are open Tuesday to Sunday 9/10am to 5/6pm. Shops and banks close on **public holidays**: January 1, 2 and 7, February 15, and May 1 and 2. The Orthodox Church celebrates Easter between one and five weeks later than the other churches.

Belgrade

BELGRADE (Београд; Beograd) is a vigorous, high-energy city, where throughout spring and summer all ages throng the streets at all hours. With a seemingly endless supply of bars and clubs, its nightlife is one of the unexpected high points on any European itinerary.

The city sits at a strategic point on the junction of the Danube and Sava rivers – something that has proved a source of weakness as well as strength over the ages: Belgrade has been captured as many as sixty times by Celts, Romans, Huns, Avars and more. The onslaught continued right through the twentieth century, when the city suffered heavy shelling during World War II and in 1999 withstood 78 days of NATO airstrikes.

All that considered, contemporary Belgrade is pretty picturesque. The mingling and merging of styles can be off-putting, particularly when a row of beautiful older frontages is interrupted by a postwar interloper, but the grand nineteenth-century buildings and delicate Art Nouveau facades still stand alongside the Yugoslav experimentation, eloquent witnesses of the city's time under the Ottoman and Austro-Hungarian empires.

What to see and do

The city's most attention-grabbing attraction is the **Kalemegdan Fortress**. Just outside the park boundary is the **Old City**, whose dense lattice of streets conceals Belgrade's most interesting sights. South of here is Belgrade's central square, **Trg Republike**, and the old bohemian quarter of **Skadarlija**, beyond which lie several more sights worth seeing, including one of the world's largest Orthodox churches. For a spot of rest and recuperation, head west across the Sava to the verdant suburb of **Zemun**, in New Belgrade, or further south towards the island of **Ada Ciganija**, Belgrade's own miniature beach resort.

Kalemegdan Fortress

Splendidly sited on an exposed nub of land overlooking the confluence of the Sava and Danube rivers is **Kalemegdan Park**, dominated by the **fortress** of the same name. The whole complex is a paean to Serbian heroism, topped with the proud Victory Monument of 1912. Originally built by the Celts in the third century BC, before expansion by the Romans, the fortress has survived successive invasions; most of what remains is the result of a short-lived Austrian occupation in the early eighteenth century. The best of the attractions is the **Military Museum** (Tues–Sun 10am–5pm; 100din), where a history thick with conflict is divertingly presented.

The Orthodox Cathedral and museum

Leaving the park and crossing Pariska, you'll find yourself in the oldest part of the city. At Kralja Petra 7 is the **Orthodox Cathedral**, a rather stark Neoclassical edifice built in 1840 featuring a fine Baroque tower. Built around the same time is the **"?" café**, or *Znak Pitanje* (see p.1005), whose noncommittal name was originally adopted as an interim solution after a spat with church officials over its first choice, *Café at the Cathedral*. Opposite, at Kralja Petra 5, stands the **Museum of the Serbian Orthodox Church** (Mon–Fri 8am–3pm, Sat 9am–noon, Sun 11am–1pm; 50din), where a small collection of bejewelled Bibles and other gorgeously decorated paraphernalia is housed in the HQ of the Patriarchate.

Konak of Princess Ljubica

Just around the corner at Sime Markovića 8 is the **Konak of Princess Ljubica** (Tues–Sat 10am–5pm, Thurs

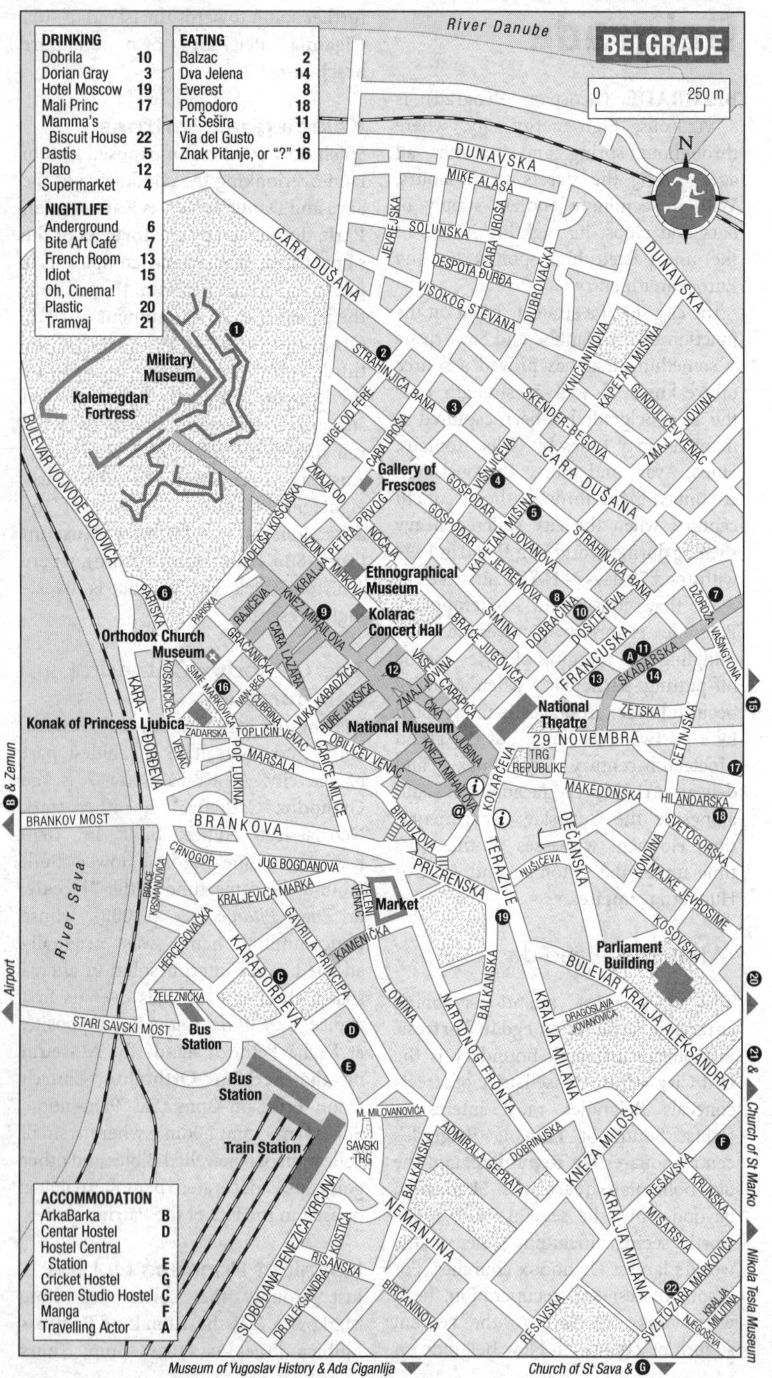

SERBIA

BELGRADE

noon–8pm, Sun 10am–2pm; 100din), the abode of a nineteenth-century noblewoman that underlines the Balkans' position as a cultural crossroads: a Napoleon III-themed room sits alongside a Turkish-style room with a Koran stand. It seems nineteenth-century Belgraders loved socializing too: there's a big semicircular sofa for chatting guests in nearly every room.

The Ethnographical Museum and Gallery of Frescoes

A short walk northeast of the Konak lie two more interesting museums. At Studentski trg 13, the **Ethnographical Museum** (Tues–Sat 10am–5pm, Sun 9am–2pm; 150din) is a lively people's history of crafts and clothes in the Balkans. Beyond here, at Cara Uroša 20, the **Gallery of Frescoes** (Tues, Wed & Fri 10am–5pm, Thurs & Sat noon–8pm, Sun 10am–2pm; 100din) houses replicas of 1200 of the country's most fêted medieval frescoes – a must if you don't have the opportunity to visit the originals at the monasteries of southern Serbia, Macedonia and Kosovo. The style is fresh and colourful – lots of puce and blue.

Trg Republike and around

The main street leading south from Kalemegdan is Kneza Mihailova, a pedestrianized *korzo* (promenade) with narrow, pretty fronts. It becomes more commercialized and hulkish at its southern end as it approaches **Trg Republike** (Republic Square), the city's main square. An irregularly shaped space, it's dominated by the imperious National Museum (which has remained closed for years awaiting renovation), in front of which is a grand statue of Prince Mihailo on horseback – this is the traditional meeting place for Belgraders.

East of Trg Republike is **Skadarlija**, the former bohemian district that centres on charming, cobbled Skadarska. South of Trg Republike is the wide swathe of **Terazije**, which slices through the commercial and business hub of the city.

BELGRADE STREET NAMES

Трг Републике	Trg Republike
Трг Слободе	Trg Slobode
Краља Петра	Kralja Petra
Краља Милана	Kralja Milana
Кнез Михаилова	Knez Mihailova
Француска	Francuska
Добрачина	Dobračina
Змај Јовина	Zmaj Jovina

Parliament Building

A left turn partway down Terazije brings you to the **Parliament Building** (Skupština), a building that has seen its fair share of drama. In October 2000, after Milošević tried to claw back the presidential election he'd lost, hundreds of demonstrators forced their way into the parliament building and threw fake ballot papers out of the windows as the building blazed inside. The Parliament was again the scene of protests after Kosovo's declaration of independence in 2008.

Church of St Marko

Around five minutes' walk along Kralja Aleksandra beyond the Parliament Building is the **Church of St Marko**, a grandiose, five-domed neo-Byzantine structure modelled on the revered monastery of Gračanica in Kosovo. It holds the tomb of the Serbian Emperor, Tsar Dušan, protected by muscled stone guards.

Church of St Sava

Dominating the skyline south of Terazije is the magnificent gilded dome of the **Church of St Sava**, at Svetosavski trg in the Vračar district. Built on the spot where the Turks supposedly burnt the bones of the founder of the Serbian Orthodox Church in 1594, it is a perfect example of the way religious and national identities fuse here. It also stakes a fair claim to be one of the largest Orthodox churches in the world, with a cavernous interior that has been under stop-start construction for over a hundred years. The church is a twenty-minute walk south of Trg Republike.

Nikola Tesla Museum

A short walk north of the Church of St Sava, at Krunska 51, is the engaging **Nikola Tesla Museum** (Tues–Fri 10am–6pm, Sat & Sun till 4pm; 150din), which celebrates the pioneering work of the eponymous nineteenth-century inventor and engineer. Tesla is credited with inventing the AC current, while other notable achievements include the development of wireless communications and remote control technologies. Alongside papers, tools and personal effects, the museum contains the urn with his ashes.

The Museum of Yugoslav History

Well worth the trip is the **Museum of Yugoslav History** (Tues–Sun 10am–4pm; 200din; bus #40 or #41 from Kneza Miloša), located around 1.5km south of the centre on Botićeva 6. The centrepiece of the complex is the House of Flowers, designed in 1975 as Tito's winter garden and now housing the former president's tomb. The adjoining **museum** holds a wealth of exhibits, including gifts presented to Tito by foreign dignitaries, and thousands of batons used in the annual "relay of youth" which took place on 25 May each year to celebrate Tito's birthday.

Ada Ciganlija

In the summer months Belgraders flock to **Ada Ciganlija** (literally, "gypsy island"), a stretch of wooded park along the bank of the Sava just south of the centre. The island's sandy beaches have earned it the local nickname "Belgrade's seaside", and city-dwellers enjoy its giant water slides, waterskiing and naturist area; there's even bungee-jumping. To get here, take bus #53 or #56 from Zeleni Venac.

Zemun

If you're after peace and quiet, head across the Sava River to New Belgrade and the west bank suburb of **Zemun**, a jumble of low-slung houses and narrow winding streets centred around the hilly waterside district of Gardoš, which holds the Baroque **Nikolajevska Church**, the city's oldest Orthodox church. To get here take bus #15 from Zeleni Venac, or bus #83 from outside the train station, and alight on Glavna, the main street.

Arrival and information

Air Belgrade's Nikola Tesla airport is 18km northwest of the city in Surčin, and connected to the centre by bus #72 (5.15am–midnight, Mon–Fri every 30min, Sat & Sun hourly; 120din), which terminates at the Zeleni Venac market. A taxi should cost no more than 1500din but avoid the sharks in the arrivals hall.
Train and bus The main train station (*železnička stanica*) and bus station (*autobuska stanica*) are adjacent to each other on Savski trg and Železnička, 15min walk southwest of the centre.
Tourist office The main information centre is at Knez Mihailova 6 (Mon–Sat 9am–9pm; ⓣ11/328 1859, ⓦwww.tob.rs/en), with other branches in the subway under Terazije (Mon–Fri 9am–8pm, Sat 9am–5pm) and in arrivals at the airport (daily 9am–10pm). You can pick up *Belgrade in Your Pocket* here.

City transport

Public transport Buses, trolleybuses and trams operate throughout the city; tickets can be bought from a kiosk or newsstand (50din) or on board (80din) – either way, they must be validated in the machine on board. Night buses operate between midnight and 4am (100din payable on the bus).
Taxis Affordable and frankly the easiest way to get to the few places that are too far to walk from the centre, like New Belgrade. Flag fall is 140din, after which it's around 55din/km. Aim to catch a taxi from the street or small rank; sharks operate around bus or train stations and at the airport.

Accommodation

Belgrade's hostel scene has grown exponentially over the last couple of years, while many of the city's hotels are now much more affordable.

Hostels

ArkaBarka Bulevar Nikole Tesle bb ⓣ64/925-3507, ⓦwww.arkabarka.net. This floating hostel is a cool concept exactingly executed, with snug cabin-like rooms, on-board entertainment (playlists on the laptop), and drinks on deck (the small balcony edging the raft). To reach it, head towards the river through Ušće Park. Breakfast included. Dorms €15, doubles €38, triples €50.

Centar Hostel Gavrila Principa 46a ⓣ11/761-9686, ⓦwww.hostelcentar.com. Compact, quiet hostel near the bus and train stations, with four-to seven-bed dorms, triples, doubles and singles; every room has a TV and computer, while each floor has its own bathroom and kitchen. Dorms €13–17, singles €28, doubles €40.

Cricket Hostel Makenzijeva 46 ⓣ11/244-1966, ⓦwww.crickethostel.com. Small, warm and friendly hostel with doubles, triple and quads, each with TV and some with balcony. There are laptops for use and wi-fi throughout. A 20min walk south of the stations, or bus #83 to Slavija Square. Breakfast not included. Dorms €15.

Green Studio Hostel Karađorđeva 69 ⓣ11/263-3626, ⓦwww.greenstudiohostel.com. Directly opposite the bus station drop-off point, this welcoming hostel, in an airy loft conversion, has neat rooms and a cool, convivial communal space. Laundry is free. Breakfast not included. Dorms €10–12, doubles €32.

Hostel Central Station Karađorđeva 87 ⓣ11/268-5087, ⓦwww.hostelcentralstation.com. Although a bit shabby looking from the outside, this is a decent hostel offering spotless rooms and bathrooms. Cracking location opposite the bus station. Breakfast not included. Dorms €12, doubles €40.

Manga Resavska 7 ⓣ11/324-3877, ⓦwww.mangahostel.com. Opened by enthusiastic couchsurfers, *Manga* occupies a small chalet of its own, with a range of colourfully decorated dorms and a cosy exposed-brick cellar where guests share dinner with the staff. Free *rakija* on arrival. Dorms €12–18, doubles €40.

Furnished rooms

Travelling Actor (Serbian: *Putujući Glumac*) Gospodar Jevremova 65 (corner of Skadarska) ⓣ11/323-4156, ⓦwww.travelling actor.rs. If you're starting to tire of life on the road, a couple of nights here will set you straight: soft beds, spankingly clean bathrooms and an outstanding location. Breakfast included. Twins and doubles €88.

Eating

For serious nights out, you need serious fuel, and the best place to eat traditional Serbian food is Skadarska, where live music and open-air dining are perfect accompaniments.

Balzac Strahinjića Bana 13. A good spot for al-fresco dining, this sparky little place has a range of differently priced dishes, from pork risotto (600din) to salmon fillet (1150din). It also offers a cracking-value two-course menu of the day (noon–5pm) for 580din. Mon–Sat 10am–midnight.

Dva Jelena Skadarska 32. With singers belting out classic local tearjerkers in its grand salon, *The Two Deer* combines old-world charm with authenticity. Try the restaurant's signature dish, *Jagnjece pecenje* (roast lamb) for 750din. Daily 11am–1am.

Everest Gospodar Jevremova 47a (corner with Dobraćina). This soothing, veggie café is an ideal antidote to hedonistic Belgrade. Take your pick from oatmeal with fruit, fresh soup of the day, salads and sandwiches, or home-made apple pie; alternatively just kick back with a cup of tea and a book on the sofas upstairs.

Pomodoro Hilandarska 32. This fairly simple-looking place knocks up the city's best pizzas (600din) from its wood-burning stove, in addition to some terrific pasta dishes and cooked breakfasts. Mon–Sat 9am–midnight, Sun noon–midnight.

Tri Šešira Skadarska 29. Skadarlija's oldest restaurant, *The Three Hats* is a great place to be introduced to the rough charms of Serbian dining: the mixed grill includes no less than six types of meat. Live folk music 8pm–1am. Grilled pork 620din.

Via del Gusto Knez Mihailova 48. Grab a tasty Italian bite at this cosy trattoria-style establishment located midway along Belgrade's busy main shopping street. Pasta 700din. Daily 9am–midnight.

Znak Pitanje, or **"?"** Kralja Petra 6. The city's oldest, most atmospheric inn (see p.1001), furnished with low wooden tables and stools, is the best place to get stuck into a gut-busting *pljeskavica* (500din).

Drinking and nightlife

There are a staggering number of places to drink and dance, with heavy concentrations along posers' paradise Strahinjića bana ("Silicon Valley"), Obilićev venac and Njegoševa. In summer, it's all aboard the *splavovi* – floating bars and clubs – to dance the night away. Most are concentrated on the bank of the Danube behind the *Hotel Jugoslavija* – a conspicuous block on the main road towards Zemun – and along the Sava around the Brankov Bridge; two of the most popular are *Freestyler* and *Blaywatch*. Most clubs stay open until 4am.

Bars and cafés

Dobrila Dobračina 30. Neat venue with bare-brick walls, funky square bar, cushioned wooden benches and a small stage for regular evenings of live music. Daily 10am–2pm.

Dorian Gray Kralja Petra 87–89. Patrons sip champagne cocktails under a spidery iron awning in this grown-up, glamorous bar.

Hotel Moscow Balkanska 1. Enjoy the ambience of the city's most historic hotel over an afternoon coffee; each one comes with a tasting miniature of the sumptuous cream cakes on offer.

Mali Princ Palmotićeva 27. In the shadow of a giant linden tree, this refined little coffeehouse makes for a relaxing stop, with a range of coffees and some delectable cakes and chocolates. Mon–Sat 8am–midnight, Sun 10am–midnight.

Mamma's Biscuit House Njegoševa 9. By day this cool, contemporary café satisfies those seeking great coffee, and by night it services a more boisterous drinking crowd. Daily 9am–2am.

Pastis Strahinjića Bana 52b. Sophisticos huddle round wooden tables in this French-style bistro bar. Decorative baguettes and a mini *bicyclette* complete the look. Daily 10am–2am.

Plato Akademski Plato 1. Serbs are a literary lot, and this bookstore-cum-café by the philosophy faculty is a Belgrade institution. The loungey outdoor terrace is a fun place to kick back, and there's live jazz at weekends. Mon–Sat 10am–2am, Sun noon–2am.

Supermarket Corner of Strahinjića Bana and Višnjića. If Belgrade hasn't already sharpened your sense of the surreal, check out this vast "concept store", a warehouse with a futuristic aesthetic. Snack on sushi (600din), sip a freshly squeezed juice (300din) or down a cocktail (450din). Daily 9am–2am.

Clubs and live music

Anderground Pariska 1. A warren of vast rooms under the fortress, which has successfully been pounding out house, hip-hop and techno for years.

Bite Art Café Skver Mire Trailović 1. Ever-popular café offering a regular and energetic programme of live funk, soul and jazz in a converted Evangelical church.

French Room Francuska 12. Superb underground venue, blasting out dub and techno at weekends, and more straightforward rock and pop during the week. There are no signs – it's through a courtyard next to a residential building.

Idiot Dalmatinska 13, 1km southeast of Džordža Vašingtona, off Ruzveltova. Students and artists swarm into this small basement club by the Botanic Gardens. Until 2am.

Oh, Cinema! Gračanička 18. Views of the Danube and live music draw crowds on summer weekends, when the club stays open till dawn.

Plastic Takovska 34. Massively popular split-level club, with the lower larger level pumping out mainstream house, and the upper level dispensing electronica; often visited by international DJs.

Tramvaj Ruzveltova 2. Fuggy hideaway more than public catwalk, this grungy watering hole has live bands playing every night. Cheap beer, too.

Entertainment

Tickets for events at major arts venues are on sale at the Bilet Servis ticket agency at Trg Republike 5 (Mon–Sat 9am–8pm).

Kolarac Concert Hall Studentski trg 5, Ⓦwww.kolarac.rs. Hosts many of the concerts of the Beogradska Filharmonija. Box office 10am–2pm & 2.30–7.30pm; tickets 200–500din.

National Theatre Francuska 3 Ⓦwww.narodnopozoriste.co.rs. Tickets to opera, ballet and plays are a snip at 100–800din. Box office 11am–3pm & 5pm till performance.

Shopping

Kalenić Pijaca Maksima Gorkog bb. Belgrade's biggest open-air market, a 20min walk southeast of Trg Republike in the Vračar district (just east of St Sava's). You can stock up on edible souvenirs or essentials for hostel cooking: smallholders sell enormous fresh veg, honey and *ajvar* (pepper-aubergine puree).

Ušće Shopping Centre Across the river in New Belgrade, this is the city's premier shopping complex, harbouring some 150 shops, as well as a host of entertainment facilities.

Directory

Embassies and consulates Australia, Vladimira Popovića 38–40 Ⓣ11/330-3400; Canada, Kneza Miloša 75 Ⓣ11/306-3000; Ireland, Kosančićev venac 2/1 Ⓣ11/263-5911; UK, Resavska 46 Ⓣ11/264-5055; US, Kneza Miloša 50 Ⓣ11/361-9344.

Exchange There are "Menjačnica" signs everywhere.

Hospitals Emergency Centre, Pasterova 2 Ⓣ11/361-8444 (24hr).

Internet Cyber Shark, Tržni Centar on Trg Republike (one floor up; 100din/hr); Vulcan Bookshop, near tourist information at Sremska 4 (130din/hr).
Left luggage (пртљаг – *prtlag*). At bus station (around 150din/day).
Pharmacy Prvi Maj, Kralja Milana 9 ☎11/324-1349; Sveti Sava, Nemanjina 2 ☎11/264-3170. Both 24hr.
Police Savski trg 2 ☎11/645-764.
Post office Zmaj Jovina 17 (Mon–Sat 8am–7pm).

Moving on

Train Budapest (2 daily; 8hr); Kraljevo (2 daily; 4hr); Ljubljana (4 daily; 10hr); Niš (10 daily; 4hr); Novi Sad (10 daily; 1hr 30min); Skopje (2 daily; 8hr 30min); Split (3 night trains; 9hr); Subotica (7 daily; 3hr 30min–5hr); Ušće (2 daily; 5hr); Zagreb (5 daily; 7hr).
Bus Kraljevo (every 1hr–1hr 30min; 2hr); Niš (every 30–45min; 3hr); Novi Sad (every 30–45min; 1hr 20min); Novi Pazar (every 1hr–1hr 30min; 3hr); Sarajevo (9 daily; 7hr); Subotica (hourly; 3hr 30min); Zagreb (5 daily; 5–6hr).

Northern Serbia

North of Belgrade, stretching up towards the Hungarian border and spanning the southern part of the fertile Pannonian Plain, is **Vojvodina**, one of Serbia's most ethnically eclectic regions, with a large Hungarian minority. The region's capital, **Novi Sad**, is a charming spot that's a feasible day-trip from the capital or a handy springboard north to Subotica and Hungary. It's also an ideal base for forays into **Fruška Gora**, the gently undulating hills to the south peppered with medieval Orthodox monasteries.

NOVI SAD AND AROUND

Situated on the main road and rail routes towards Budapest some 75km northwest of Belgrade, **NOVI SAD** (Нови Сад) has long charmed visitors with its comely buildings – remnants of Austro-Hungarian rule. But today it's an emphatically young town – especially in the summer, when thousands of international revellers swarm to Petrovaradin Fortress for the four-day EXIT festival.

What to see and do

Novi Sad developed in tandem with the huge **Petrovaradin Fortress** (open access) on the Danube's south bank. The fortress rises picturesquely from rolls of green hillside, its delicate lemon-yellow buildings set inside sturdy fortifications. It took its present shape in the eighteenth century when the Austrians tried to create an invincible barrier against the Turks. Unfortunately its defences quickly became outdated, and the authorities decided to imprison independent-minded troublemakers here instead – including Karađorđe and, a century later, a young Tito. The fortress **museum** (Tues–Sun 10am–6pm; 100din) relays the history of both the fortress and the town, though is more interesting for its wealth of eighteenth-and nineteenth-century applied art.

As you approach from town, look out for the **plaque** on the right of the bridge commemorating Oleg Nasov, who was killed during the NATO bombing – Novi Sad was one of the cities hardest hit in the spring of 1999, losing all its bridges. Once on the south bank, go on a little further and climb the steps to the right of the church; you'll arrive just under the **clock tower**. The functional twentieth-century architecture of Novi Sad itself looks less alluring than the fortress does from the opposite bank, but the views of the surrounding countryside are magnificent.

Across the river, the hub of the city is **Trg Slobode** (Freedom Square), a spacious plaza bounded on either side by the neo-Gothic **Catholic Church of the Virgin Mary** and the neo-Renaissance town hall. Running east from here is bustling Zmaj Jovina which, together with the adjoining bar-filled alleyway Laze Telečkog and wide, pedestrianized

Dunavska, forms the town's central nexus of streets for eating, drinking and socializing. At the bottom end of Dunavska (nos 35–37) is the excellent **Museum of Vojvodina** (Tues–Sun 10am–6pm; 100din), spread across two buildings. It delves first into Serbia's archeology and ethnography, then comes closer to home with the traumas of two world wars.

Finally, sun-lovers should head for the **Štrand** (May–Sept; 50din), a sandy beach on the Danube's north bank, opposite the fortress, which has bars, cafés and a "school's out" vibe.

Sremski Karlovci

On the eastern fringes of the Fruška Gora National Park, the enchanting small town of **Sremski Karlovci** (**Сремски Карловци**) is a great little trip out of Novi Sad. Its main square, Branka Radičevića, with the Orthodox and Catholic churches side by side and the Four Lions fountain, is highly picturesque, but Sremski Karlovci's status as a national treasure comes courtesy of its speciality wine, **Bermet**, made exclusively here since 1770. Drunk with desserts or as an aperitif, Bermet was popular in the Austro-Hungarian court and served on board the *Titanic*'s maiden voyage. The tourist information office on the main square can point you to the delightful **wine cellar** owned by the Živanović family at Mitropolita Stratimirovića 86b (daily 10am–7pm), where you can buy your own supplies – swing open the side-gate to enter their orchard; there's also a quaint beekeeping museum. Alternatively, relax with a glass or two on the civilized outdoor decking of the hotel of the same name on the main square.

Sremski Karlovci is a ten-minute taxi ride from Novi Sad (around 400din); catch a cab from the rank on Ilije Ognjanovića.

Arrival and information

Train and bus The adjacent bus and train stations are 1km north of the centre on Bulevar Jaše Tomića. The easiest way into town is to hop in a taxi (around 200din) or take bus #4 (40din) from in front of the train station. Walking takes about 30min; head straight down Bulevar Oslobođenja and turn left into Jevrejska at the market.

Tourist office Mihaila Pupina 9 and Modena 1 (Mon–Fri 7.30am–8pm, Sat 10am–3pm; ⓣ21/421-811, ⓦwww.turizamns.rs).

Accommodation

Hostel Downtown Njegoševa 2 ⓣ21/524-818, ⓦwww.hotelnovisad.com. A quiet, unassuming hostel just a few paces along from the main square, with large dorms, kitchen and laundry facility. Breakfast not included. Dorms €10, doubles €30.

Hotel Mediteraneo Ilije Ognjanovića 10 ⓣ21/427-135, ⓦwww.hotelmediteraneo.rs. Bright, fresh, nautical-themed hotel. Spacious, a/c rooms decorated in a fetching lime green and chocolate brown colour. Breakfast included. Doubles €65, 3-person apartments €85.

Lazin Hostel Laze Telečkog 10 ⓣ63/443-703, ⓦwww.lazinhostel.org. Handily located for the nearby bars, the welcoming and clean *Lazin* has six-bed dorms and a couple of doubles, as well as spacious communal areas and a kitchen. Breakfast not included. Dorms €10, doubles €30.

Sova Hostel Ilije Ognjanovića 26 ⓣ21/527-556, ⓦwww.hostelsova.com. Novi Sad's most appealing hostel offers funky four- to ten-bed

THE EXIT FESTIVAL

For four days at the beginning of July the grounds of Petrovaradin Fortress are overrun by **EXIT Festival** revellers (ⓦwww.exitfest.org). Established as one of the premier music events in Europe, EXIT now attracts some of the very biggest names in pop, techno and hip-hop (the 2011 line-up included Arcade Fire, Pulp and Portishead). Buy tickets and camping passes via the website. You can rent rooms in Novi Sad for the duration: check ⓦwww.exittrip.org, which helps with booking accommodation and transport.

rooms, a cosy communal space, kitchen and internet. Breakfast not included. Dorms €12, doubles €36.

Eating

Alla Lanterna Dunavska 27. The decor is a tad faux-rustic but the big plates of pasta and pizza are scrumptious. Pasta 450din.

Foody Modena 1–3. Committed costcutters will warm to this bright, functional canteen, with soups, sandwiches and *pljeskavica.* Sit down or takeaway. 200din.

Kuća Mala Laze Telečkog 4. The *Little House*, with its homely decor and checked tablecloths, is great for a hot sandwich, pizza or bowl of pasta. Mon–Sat 8am–11pm.

Pivnica Gusan Zmaj Jovina 4. Narrow brick-vaulted cellar restaurant doling out juicy mixed grills and kebabs; alternatively just stop by for a beer at the long wooden bar. It's through a passageway by the Diesel shop sign. Daily 8am–midnight.

Drinking

Divan Dućan Laze Telečkog 6. This tiny, original café-bar is crammed with eye-catching art and antiques; it's rather like drinking cocktails in a toy-box. Soya caramel macchiato 115din; Opal Martini 230din. Daily 9am–midnight.

Jelisavetin Bastion Petrovaradinska tvrđava. International DJs draw the crowds at this massive, multi-room club in the fortress's underground chambers. Summer only Fri & Sat until 5am.

Moving on

Train Belgrade (every 2hr; 2hr); Budapest (2 daily; 6hr); Subotica (10 daily; 2hr).

Bus Belgrade (every 30–45min; 1hr 20min); Subotica (hourly; 1hr 30min).

TREAT YOURSELF

Zak Šafarikova 6 (☎021/447-545; Mon–Fri 8am–11pm, Sat 10am–1am, Sun 11am–11pm). Novi Sad's finest restaurant, with exquisitely thought-out dishes such as deer fillet with red cabbage and juniper sauce, and chocolate leaves with white mousse and morello cherries. Fine wines and impeccable service round things off beautifully. 800–1800din.

SUBOTICA

Some 175km north of Belgrade, Vojvodina's second city, **SUBOTICA** (Суботица; Hungarian: Szabadka), is a wonderful counterpoint to the capital, its Secessionist buildings, green spaces, wide pavements and burghers riding around on old-fashioned bicycles all contributing to its unspoilt, wholesome air. Just a stone's throw from Hungary, Subotica feels tangibly more like its northern neighbour. Historically, the ties are close: Subotica reached its apotheosis in the years of the Austro-Hungarian Empire, when it was granted the status of a Royal Free Town.

What to see and do

The heart of the town is grassy **Trg Republike,** fronted by a hulking city hall built in 1912; its gingerbread-like windows and colourfully patterned roof are almost too gaudy to look at in full sunlight. In front stands a brilliant blue fountain added in 2001. Adjoining Trg Republike is Trg Slobode, behind which runs the Korzo, a busy pedestrianized street featuring the fairytale **Piraeus Bank** building, with its door and windows straight out of a medieval castle, created by architects Dezsó Jakab and Marcell Komor at the start of the twentieth century.

Passing through the courtyard by *Boss Pizzeria*, you'll come out onto Rajhlov Park Square; immediately to your right, and occupying the wildly colourful 1904 mansion of architect Ferenc Raichle, is the **Likovni Susret Contemporary Art Gallery** (Mon 8am–2pm, Tues–Fri 8am–6pm, Sat 9am–noon; 50din), exhibiting work by local artists. The real draw however is the attention-seeking interior decor, from the cutesy hearts at the entranceway to the bulbous alcoves upstairs.

Further out, northwest of the city centre is another Jakab/Komor

MONASTERIES AROUND NOVI SAD

Shadowing the city to the south are the low rolling hills of the **Fruška Gora**, once an island in the now evaporated Pannonian Sea. These days, its orchards and vineyards comprise a national park carved up by a web of simple hiking trails. The hills – known among devotees as the Holy Mountain – also house sixteen monasteries (there were once 35). About 15km south of Novi Sad, just off the main road before the village of Irig, is **Novo Hopovo**, where a Byzantine church is housed within a picturesque monastery. Not far off are two more sixteenth-century monastic churches: elegant white **Krušedol** and **Vrdnik-Ravanica**, which has Tsar Lazar's collarbone on display.

Hiring a car is the most practical way to access the monasteries, which are all within 50km of town. With a European or international driver's licence you can hire a vehicle from Ki-Ki (Bulevar Kralja Petra 13; ⓣ21/446-470, ⓦwww.kiki021.com) or Autotehna (Balzakova 29; ⓣ21/474-516, ⓦwww.autotehna.com) in Novi Sad. Alternatively, contact the tourist office in Sremski Karlovci (see p.1008), who can, with some warning, organize group sightseeing tours of the main monasteries (1200din) or arrange for a driver (around 2000din for 3hr).

collaboration: the dignified but now deserted 1902 **synagogue**, where a moving plaque remembers the "4000 Jewish citizens with whom we lived and built Subotica".

Back in the centre, reached by walking west from Trg Republike to Trg Kathedrale, is the 1779 Catholic **Cathedral of St Theresa**. The cathedral is starting to show its age and is a curiously moving place; in the surrounding square, the scattered statues are a poignant mix of classical piety (the two hands clasped in prayer) and postwar brutalism (the enormous monument to the "victims of fascism" who died during World War II).

Arrival and information

Train The train station dominates one side of Rajhlov Park.
Bus The bus station is on Senćanski Put, a 15min walk from the centre on the road to Novi Sad.
Tourist office Trg Slobode 1, to the rear of the City Hall (Mon–Fri 8am–6pm, Sat 9am–1pm; ⓣ24/670-350, ⓦwww.visitsubotica.rs The helpful staff can provide lots of brochures and maps on both the town and Lake Palić.

Accommodation

Hotel Patria Đure Đakovića bb ⓣ24/554-500, ⓦwww.hotelpatria.rs. Between the bus station and the centre, this budget four-star hotel proves you get more bang for your buck outside Belgrade; rooms have modern bathrooms, TV and cable internet. Breakfast included. Doubles 6200din.
Incognito Huga Badalića 3, left off Maksima Gorkog ⓣ62/666-674, ⓦwww.hostel-subotica.com. This large hostel is a 5min walk from the central square, with basic but clean rooms, all with TV and wi-fi. Breakfast not included. Dorms €10, apartment for 2–4 people €20.

Eating and drinking

Boss Matije Korvina 7–8. Just behind the Likovni Susret mansion, this atrium pizzeria and bar is where people come to be seen; the adjoining statue-strewn courtyard is a fabulous place to sup a beer.
Népkör Žarka Zrenjanina 11. Outstanding Hungarian food in a lovely townhouse 5min north of the cathedral. Someone's had fun with the menu (fancy "a pageant of local cheeses" or "concealed brains"?). *Gulaš* to share 150din; set menu 300din.
Stara Picerija Matije Korvina 5. Opposite *Boss*, on a cute cobbled alleyway, this place excels at delivering pizza, hot sandwiches and much more besides; attractive interior and cheerful feel-good classics on the stereo. Large pizza 450din.
Trubadur Rajhlov Park 11. Atmospheric alternative bar lit by soft Victorian-style streetlamps in the shadow of a Gothic mansion.

Moving on

Train Belgrade (6 daily; 3hr 30min–5hr); Budapest (2 daily; 2hr 30min); Novi Sad (10 daily; 2hr).
Bus Belgrade (hourly; 3hr 30min); Novi Sad (hourly; 1hr 30min); Szeged, Hungary (every 2hr; 1hr 30min).

Southern Serbia

South of Belgrade, the softly rolling hillsides studded with low red-roofed houses are the setting for three of the country's most precious medieval monasteries: **Žiča**, **Studenica** and **Sopoćani**. Elsewhere, the south's main city, **Niš**, conveniently straddles major road and rail routes to Bulgaria and Macedonia, and is an attractive small town with some fascinating sights.

ŽIČA, STUDENICA AND SOPOĆANI

In the hilly stretch from the town of Kraljevo, itself some 170km south of Belgrade, south to Novi Pazar lie some of Serbia's most impressive **monasteries**. **Žiča**, just 4km southeast of Kraljevo, was a thirteenth-century creation of St Sava – Serbia's patron saint and the first archbishop of the independent Serbian Church – with a vivid red exterior that evokes the red Serbs use to paint eggs at Easter.

Set against the wild, roaming slopes some 12km (and accessible by bus) from the village of Ušće is **Studenica**. The first and greatest of the Serbian monasteries, it was established in 1190 by Stefan Nemanja, founder of the Nemanjić dynasty, whose marble tomb lies in the Church of the Virgin Mary. Studenica's **superb frescoes** were the work of an innovative but still anonymous Greek painter who created *trompe-l'oeil* frescoes to resemble mosaics.

Around 16km from Novi Pazar is the **Sopoćani**, a thirteenth-century construction that once stretched across a whole complex but of which only the Holy Trinity Church remains. The *Assumption of Virgin Mary* is the most famous of its unusually large Byzantine frescoes; the bright colours and expressive faces are said to prefigure the Italian Renaissance.

NIŠ

The pleasant university town of **NIŠ** (Ниш), 235km southeast of Belgrade, is a useful stopover point between Belgrade and Sofia or Skopje. Its inhabitants have a definite small-town pride, as well they might: this is the birthplace of Constantine, the Roman emperor responsible for the conversion of the whole empire to Christianity. Its collection of intriguing – if macabre – sights is a gritty reminder of the darker sides to Serbia's history, but the focus in the cafés and bars crammed with students is all on having a good time.

What to see and do

The city's centrepiece is its main square, **Trg Kralja Milana**, which sits across the Nišava from **Niš Fortress**. A Roman fortress once stood here – a circle of Roman tombstones remains inside – but the current fortifications date from the beginning of the eighteenth century. Enter from the main Istanbul Gate facing the bridge; inside, the town authorities have put real effort into making this a place residents can enjoy, with the beautiful **mosque of Bali Beg** converted into an exhibition space and the row of cafés in the shadow of the fortress's inner wall a cool spot to unwind. Each August the whole fortress is given over to the Nišville jazz festival (Ⓦwww.nisville.com).

The fortress apart, Niš does suffer from a surfeit of rather grim sights. The first, to your right as you leave the fortress, is the miniature blue-domed **memorial chapel** perched on the lawn, which commemorates the local people killed in the NATO bombings. East of the centre on Brače Taskoviča, **Ćele Kula** (The Skull Tower; Tues–Sun 9am–4pm; 100din; take any bus towards Niška Banja or a return taxi – 120din) is more gruesome still. It dates from 1809, when Stevan Sinđelić, commander of a nationalist uprising, found his men surrounded by the Turkish army on nearby Čegar Hill

VISITING THE MONASTERIES

While Žiča is easily accessible by bus from Kraljevo (every 30–45min; 50din), you'll probably need a **car** if you want to see more than one monastery in a day. Try Inter Rent-A-Car in Niš (T63/467-447 or 63/775-6741, Wwww.rentacarnis.rs) or Autotehna in Kraljevo (Karađorđeva 12/1; T36/319-944, Wwww.autotehna.com); prices should start at around €40–50 per day. If you have more time, you could try public **buses**: on the Kraljevo–Novi Pazar route, you can get off at Ušće, from where there are 2–3 daily buses to Studenica.

and took drastic action against his adversaries, firing into his gunpowder supplies and blowing up most of the Turks and all the Serbs around him. Following the battle, to deter future rebellion the ruling Pasha ordered that the heads of the Serbian soldiers killed in the battle be stuffed and mounted on the tower; 952 went into the making of this macabre totem pole, though today only 58 remain.

Even more evocative is the derelict **Crveni Krst** (Red Cross; Tues–Sun 9am–4pm; 120din) concentration camp, a ten-minute walk down busy Bulevar 12 Februar from the bus station, where the hand-painted German signs for the washroom, messroom and kitchen make it all seem very recent. The barbed-wire fences and watchtowers, so familiar from camps in Poland and Germany, are a reminder that the displacement and genocide of millions was a truly pan-European operation.

Arrival and information

Train The train station is 2km west of town on Dimitrija Tucovica.

Bus The bus station is a 5min walk from town, west of the fortress on Bulevar Februar 12.

Tourist office Voždova Karađorđa 7 (Mon–Fri 8am–7pm, Sat 9am–1pm; T18/523-118, Wwww.nistourism.org.rs).

Accommodation

Downtown Hostel Kej Kola Srpskih Sestara 3/2 T18/526-756, Wwww.downtownhostel.rs. Occupying a renovated apartment just yards from the riverfront, this enthusiastically run place conceals an eight-bed dorm and several doubles (all with a/c), as well as a well-equipped kitchen and lounge. Dorms €12, doubles €30.

Hostel Niš Dobrička 3a T18/513-703, Wwww.hostelnis.rs. Make this spotless hostel with engaging owners your first port of call; it's a few minutes' walk west from the fortress entrance. Breakfast not included. Dorms €12, doubles €35.

Eating and drinking

Cobbled Kazandžijsko Sokače (Tinker's Alley), just south of Trg Kralja Milana, is the town's social hub, thronging with café-bars.

Hamam Tvrđava bb. Named after the Turkish baths it's housed in (just inside the fortress entrance), this is the place to try some grilled lamb or oven-baked fish. There's often live music. Mains 400–500din.

Mamma Nade Tomić 10. Quirkily designed pizzeria with a terrific wood-fired oven; carnivores should have a stab at the house pizza, which comes topped with five types of meat. Pizzas 500din. Mon–Sat 10am–midnight, Sun noon–11pm.

Sinđelić Nikole Pašića 36. Named after the kamikaze general behind the Tower of Skulls episode, *Sinđelić* excels at simple, hearty Serbian food. Located near the Kalča shopping mall. Mains 500–700din. Daily 8am–1am.

Spark Strahinjića bana 2a. The city's most vibrant club, there's loads of great stuff going on here, such as live turbo-folk, gypsy bands, electronica parties and the occasional foreign act. A good time almost certainly guaranteed. Thurs–Sun 11pm–5am.

Moving on

Train Belgrade (7 daily; 4–5hr); Kraljevo (4 daily; 3hr 45min); Skopje (4 daily; 5–6hr); Sofia (2 daily; 5hr).

Bus Belgrade (every 30–45min; 3hr); Kraljevo (6 daily; 3hr); Skopje (6 daily; 5–6hr); Sofia (2 daily; 2hr 30min).

Slovakia

HIGHLIGHTS

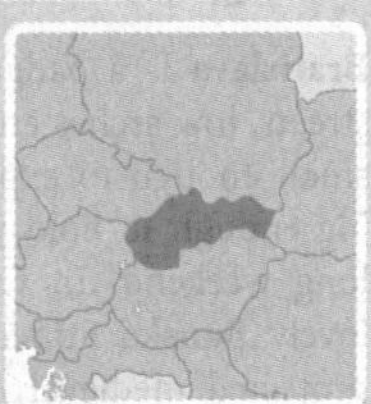

HIGH TATRAS: admire the majesty of Slovakia's highest peaks

LEVOČA: explore the crumbling backstreets of this beautiful walled town

SPIŠ CASTLE: step into the Middle Ages at this atmospheric pile

BANKSÁ ŠTIAVNICA: climb a volcano or swim in a mine

BRATISLAVA: try out the chic coffeehouses and cool underground bars

DANUBE: cruise to Vienna

ROUGH COSTS

DAILY BUDGET Basic €25 /occasional treat €35

DRINK Beer €1.40

FOOD Gnocchi with bacon €3

HOSTEL/BUDGET HOTEL €10/25

TRAVEL Train: Banska Štiavnica–Poprad €9

FACT FILE

POPULATION 5.4 million

AREA 49,037 sq km

LANGUAGE Slovak

CURRENCY Euro (€)

CAPITAL Bratislava (population: 431,000)

INTERNATIONAL PHONE CODE ⓣ421

Introduction

Hungarians and Turks came to Slovakia for its natural resources, and so does the modern tourist. Broad, sprawling mountains mean good skiing and snowboarding, Karst is for caving, and the rambling hilly midlands are a hiker's paradise.

Bratislava is a badger sett of cobbled streets, low arches and tiny squares. It's small enough to explore in a day, but big enough to hold your interest for a long weekend. In Central Slovakia is lovely **Banská Štiavnica**, a UNESCO-protected medieval mining town in a lunar landscape of dead volcanoes. East of that are the **High Tatras**, as decent a mountain range as any in Central Europe. They've long been the site of enthusiastic skiing, hiking and sonnet-writing. Heading east towards Ukraine is the wild, rocky **Spiš** region, home to medieval mammoth Spiš Castle and the twelfth-century walled town of **Levoča**.

Sharing borders with Poland, the Czech Republic, Austria and Ukraine, Slovakia is landlocked, with high mountains in the north, low mountains in the centre, hills to the west, and the Danube basin to the south. The popuation is fairly diverse, with over half a million ethnic **Hungarians**, hundreds of thousands of **Roma** (Gypsies), and several thousand Rusyns in the east.

CHRONOLOGY

450 BC Celts inhabit present-day Slovakia.
623 AD Samo becomes King of the Slavs after defeating the Avarians near Bratislava.
828 First Christian church consecrated in Slovakia.
863 First Slavic alphabet written in Greater Moravia by saints Cyril and Methodius.
895 The Magyars (Hungarians) gradually begin to conquer and occupy the territory.
1241 Mongol invasion of Slovakia results in heavy losses.
1526 Hungary loses Buda to the Turks; the Habsburgs move their capital to Bratislava.
1800s Growth in Slovak nationalism.
1895 Czechs and Slovaks form a strategy of mutual cooperation against dual monarchy Austria-Hungary.
1918 The independent republic of Czechoslovakia is established on the defeat of Austria-Hungary in World War I.
1939 Germany takes Sudetenland in Czechoslovakia, before occupying the rest of the country.
1945 Slovak National Uprising against German occupation is successful, but thousands of Slovakian Jews have already been sent to the camps.
1948 The Communist Party comes into power in Czechoslovakia.
1989 The Velvet Revolution heralds the end of Communism in Czechoslovakia.
1993 Czechoslovakia splits peacefully into two states.
2004 Slovakia joins NATO and the EU.
2009 The euro replaces the Slovak crown as the national currency.

ARRIVAL

Slovakia's main international airport is M.R. Štefánika, often referred to as **Bratislava Airport**, 9km northeast of central Bratislava. There are also international airports in **Košice**, operating flights to and from Prague, Vienna, London and Dublin, and in Poprad, operating mainly business flights to and from various European cities. Another option is to fly into Vienna; the two capitals are only 60km apart, flights to Vienna are often cheaper, and Eurolines (10 daily; 1hr 10min) and Postbus (18 daily; 1hr 30min–1hr 40min) both run shuttle bus connections for around €10 one-way. For a more romantic arrival, there's the Vienna–Bratislava hydrofoil (see p.1022).

Slovakia has good **rail connections** with Austria, Hungary, Poland and the Czech Republic. Most international trains terminate at Bratislava, but trains from Budapest, Krakow and Prague also run to Košice, and there's a direct service between Prague and Poprad.

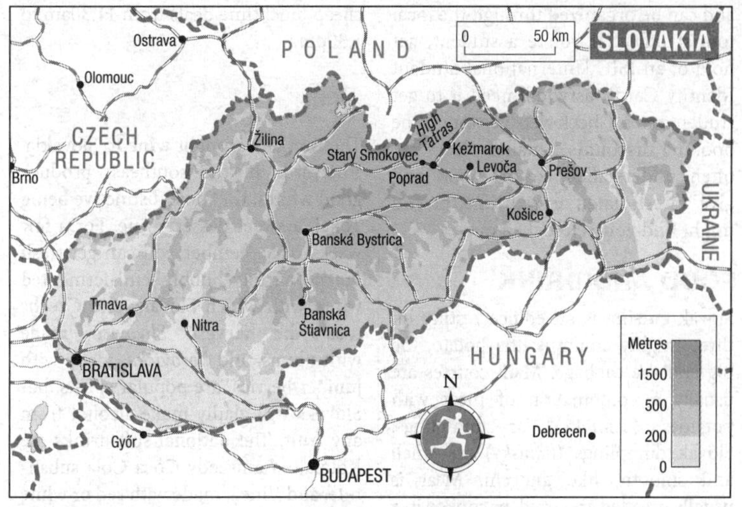

Eurolines buses connect European cities to Bratislava (Ⓦwww.eurolines.sk), and Student Agency's (Ⓦwww.studentagencybus.com) domestic and international coaches are cheap and comfortable.

GETTING AROUND

Train journeys are slow but scenic. Slovak Railways (Železnice Slovenskej republiky or ŽSR) runs fast *rýchlik* trains that stop at major towns; *osobný* (local) trains stop everywhere. You can buy **tickets** (*lístok*) for domestic journeys at the station (*stanica*) before or on the day of departure. Supplements are payable on all EuroCity (EC) trains, and occasionally for InterCity (IC) and Express (Ex) trains. ŽSR runs reasonably priced sleepers and couchettes. Book in advance no later than six hours before departure. **InterRail** is valid; **Eurail** requires supplements. Find train timetables online at Ⓦwww.zsr.sk, or Ⓦwww.cp.sk.

Buses (*autobus*) cover a more extensive network. The state bus company is Slovenská Autobusová Doprava or SAD. Buy your **ticket** from the driver or book in advance from the station if you're travelling at the weekend or early in the morning on one of the main routes.

Although much of Slovakia is mountainous and not ideal for **cyclists**, the countryside around Bratislava has well-maintained bike paths that stretch into Austria and Hungary. More demanding rides can take you into the Little Carpathians. Most trains allow bikes.

ACCOMMODATION

New B&Bs are opening all the time, and hostels are on the rise. There's no network of **hostels** in Slovakia, though a few are affiliated to HI (Ⓦwww.hihostels.com). Bratislava has plenty of good private hostels, and in the High Tatras you can find chalet-style **boarding houses** (*chata*) scattered over the mountains, with basic dorm beds from €8 per bed. There are plenty of **campsites** in Slovakia, which usually rent out basic wooden huts (*chata*), fun if you share with friends.

In summer the cheapest accommodation is university **halls**. You can book with CKM, the student travel agency (Ⓦwww.ckm.sk) or the local tourist office. **Private rooms** are also cheap, and can be organized through the local tourist office. If you're a student, get hold of an ISIC (International Student Identity Card), as you'll need it to get student rates. Check websites for online booking discounts. Smaller places are often understaffed so pre-book and give an estimated arrival time, or you might find yourself locked out.

FOOD AND DRINK

Slovak **cuisine** is an edifice resting on three mighty columns; the potato, the pig and the cabbage. Main courses are usually a combination of meat with potatoes (*zemiaky*), or dumplings. Slovak dumplings (*halušky*) are small and smooth, like gnocchi. Meat is usually breaded and fried, or cooked in a sauce. The main meal of the day is lunch, which starts with **soup** (*polievka*) – perhaps garlic (*cesnaková*) or sauerkraut (*kapustnica*). You can often find game meats like boar, rabbit and vension, on menus, as well as pork, beef, chicken, duck and goose.

A classic mid-morning **snack** is *párok*, a hot frankfurter. A Slovak delicacy is *jaternica*, made from pig's blood and rice. *Bryndza*, sheep's cheese made in the region since the Middle Ages, is light, salty and delicious. *Bryndzové halušky*, the national dish, is dumplings served with *bryndza* and bacon. Another favorite is *pirohy*; unleavened boiled dumplings stuffed with cheese, a little like ravioli. Hungarian goulash is popular, and so are *langoše* – deep-fried dough topped with crushed garlic, cheese or sour cream.

Some popular **desserts** are strudel (apple or curd cheese), *palacinky* (crepes filled with chocolate, fruit or jam, and usually cream) and *lievance*, which look like Scotch or American pancakes, and are served with hot fruit. An unusual Slovak speciality is sweet noodles (*rezance*), with poppy seeds and butter or curd cheese and sugar.

Outside the major cities, **closing time** is usually 9 or 10pm. Pubs often have cheap lunchtime deals from 11.30am to 1.30pm.

Drink

The Romans brought **wine** to Slovakia. Vineyards in the southeast produce good whites, the most distinctive being Tokaj, a sweet dessert wine. For a few weeks in September you can get fresh *burčák*, a fruity, bubbly semi-fermented white with which Slovaks and Czechs toast the harvest. *Slivovica*, made with plums, and *borovička*, made with juniper berries, are popular spirits, but Slovaks will gladly make alcohol from any fruit. The national soft drinks are Kofola, an aniseedy Coca Cola substitute, and Vinea, made with red or white grapes. The best-known bottled **beer** is Zlatý Bažant (Golden Pheasant). You'll find a pub krčma (*pivnica* is different) in every town, as well as a wine bar (*vináreň*), which will usually have later closing hours and often doubles as a nightclub. The legal drinking age is 18 and you may be asked for ID in shops, pubs or clubs. **Coffee** is traditionally served strong and black, but American-style coffeehouses are popularizing cappuccino, latte and the like. Teahouses (*čajovňa*) are popular, especially with young people, and stock dozens of types of **tea**.

CULTURE AND ETIQUETTE

Learning a few Slovak words helps break down Slovak reserve, even just "hello", "goodbye" and "thank you". If you've been travelling eastwards, your Czech will do fine, as all Slovaks understand Czech (an equation which doesn't work in reverse). When **tipping** Slovaks round up to the nearest euro or two, but as a foreigner it's courteous to tip ten percent. When you are introduced to strangers shake hands, and don't use first names when addressing older people. Casual greetings like *ahoj* are only for close friends. Wish fellow diners a good meal (*dobrú chuť*) before starting, and make a toast (*na zdravie*) before drinking. If you are invited to a Slovak home you must take off your shoes at the door, even when told not to (they're just being polite), and if you're invited to eat bring wine or chocolates.

SPORTS

Slovaks love football and **ice hockey**, which you can see live on screens in bars across the Republic. You can go to ice hockey games in stadiums from September to April (Ⓦwww.hcslovan.sk); tickets cost between €13 and €50 and can be bought from the arena on match days. There's plenty of **hiking**, **skiing**, **snowboarding** and **rafting** in the High Tatras (see Ⓦwww.tatry.sk) and caving in the Slovak Karst in east Slovakia (Ⓦwww.saske.sk/cave). Walking is a popular national pastime, and if there wasn't so much woodland, the woods would be full on Saturday afternoons.

COMMUNICATIONS

Most **post offices** (*pošta*) open Monday to Friday 8am to 5pm. You can also buy stamps (*známky*) from tobacconists (*trafika*) and street kiosks, and it's also worth asking in any place that sells postcards. Cheap local calls can be made from any **phone**, but for international calls it's best to buy a phonecard (*telefónna karta*) from a tobacconist or post office. You'll find an internet café in most towns; the average charge is €3 per hour.

SLOVAKIA ONLINE

Ⓦwww.slovakia.org Political, historical, cultural and economic information.
Ⓦwww.slovakia.travel Tourist information in a variety of languages with travel tips and event information.
Ⓦspectator.sme.sk English-language weekly with news and listings.
Ⓦwww.whatsonslovakia.com Events and attractions for the coming month, plus reviews and business news.

EMERGENCY NUMBERS

Police Ⓣ158; Ambulance Ⓣ155; Fire Ⓣ150; General emergency 112.

EMERGENCIES

Violent crime is fairly rare and pickpocketing or petty theft is the biggest danger. You should carry a photocopy of your passport with you, as ID is required by law. Small ailments can be dealt with by the **pharmacist** (*lekáreň);* for bigger problems go to the nearest **hospital** (*nemocnica*).

INFORMATION

Most towns have some kind of **tourist office** (*informačné centrum*) with English-speaking staff. In summer they're generally open Monday to Friday, 9am to 6pm, Saturday and Sunday 9am to 2pm; in winter they tend to close an hour earlier and all day Sunday. **Maps** are available from tourist offices, bookshops and some hotels. The Slovak for town plan is *plán mesta*.

MONEY AND BANKS

The euro was introduced in Slovakia in 2009. **Credit** and **debit cards** are accepted in upmarket hotels and restaurants and some shops, and there are plenty of **ATMs** in larger towns. **Exchange offices** (*zmenáreň*) can be found in big hotels, travel agencies and department stores, but it's usually better value to change your money in a bank.

OPENING HOURS AND HOLIDAYS

Opening hours for local shops are in the region of 9am to 6pm on weekdays and 9am to noon Saturdays, with

SLOVAK

	Slovak	Pronunciation
Yes	*Áno*	Uh-no
No	*Nie*	Nyeh
Please	*Prosím*	Pro-seem
Thank you	*Ďakujem*	Dya-koo-yem vam
Hello/Good day	*Dobrý deň/Ahoj*	Dob-rie den[y]/a-hoy
Goodbye	*Dovidenia*	Do-vid-en-ya
Excuse me	*Prepáčte*	Pre-patch-teh
Where	*Kde*	Gde
Good	*Dobrý*	Dob-rie
Bad	*Zlý*	Zlee
Near	*Blízko*	Bli-sko
Far	*Ďaleko*	D[y]a-lek-o
Cheap	*Lacný*	Lats-nie
Expensive	*Drahý*	Dra-hie
Open	*Otvorený*	Ot-vor-eh-nie
Closed	*Zatvorený*	Zat-vor-eh-nie
Today	*Dnes*	Dnes
Yesterday	*Včera*	Ftch-er-a
Tomorrow	*Zajtra*	Zuyt-ra
How much is...?	*Koľko stojí...?*	Kol-ko stat[y]...?
What time is it?	*Koľko je hodín?*	Kol-ko ye hod-in?
I don't understand	*Nerozumiem*	Ne-ro-zoom-yem
Do you speak English?	*Hovoríte po anglicky?*	Hov-or-i-te po ang-lits-ky?
Entrance	*Vchod*	FHod
Exit	*Východ*	VeeHot
Ticket	*Lístok*	Leestok
Hotel	*Hotel*	Hotel
Toilet	*Záchod*	ZaHod
Square	*Námestie*	Nahmestee
Station	*Stanica*	Stani-tza
Do you have a...?	*Máte...?*	Ma-te...?
Single room	*jednoposteľovú izbu*	yed-no-pos-tye-lyo-voo iz-bu
Open	*Otvorené*	Otvor-en-air
Closed	*Zatvorené*	Zatvor-en-air
Cheap	*Lacné*	Luhts-nair
One	*Jeden*	Yed-en
Two	*Dva*	Dva
Three	*Tri*	Tri
Four	*Štyri*	Shtir-i
Five	*Päť*	Pyat[y]
Six	*Šesť*	Shest[y]
Seven	*Sedem*	Sed-em
Eight	*Osem*	Oss-em
Nine	*Deväť*	Dev-yat[y]
Ten	*Desať*	Dess-at[y]

STUDENT DISCOUNTS

To get a student discount (which is often as much as fifty percent) you'll need an ISIC, as most places won't accept your university ID card.

supermarkets staying open later and sometimes on Sundays. Smaller rural shops close for an hour at lunchtime. Opening hours for **sights** and **attractions** are usually Tuesday to Sunday 9am to 5pm. Out of the season hours are often restricted to weekends and holidays. Most **castles** are closed in winter. When visiting a sight, ask for English (*anglický*) text. Admission rarely costs more than €4. **Public holidays** include January 1, January 6, Good Friday, Easter Monday, May 1, May 8, July 5, August 29, September 1, September 15, November 1, December 24, 25 and 26.

Bratislava

Sitting on both sides of the Danube in the southwest corner of Slovakia, **BRATISLAVA** is a festive city, with meandering streets and grand, tiny buildings. With its rural atmosphere, on a hot afternoon a flock of sheep wouldn't look out of place grazing on Františkánske Square. The Old Town showcases the skill of Slovak town planners, who crammed a city-worth of palaces, shops, cafés, pubs, restaurants, museums and churches into a few blocks.

The area has been settled since the Neolithic era (about 500 BC), making it centuries older than Prague or Budapest. It has always been an international city – Romans, Hungarians, Germans, Austrians, Turks, Czechs, Jews and Roma have all left their mark. The locals are less weary and cynical than the natives of most capitals, characterized by a friendly reserve.

What to see and do

Old Town (**staré mesto**) lies on the north bank of the Danube, 1km south of the train station, east of the stout **castle** and southwest of the shops and housing blocks of **new town** (**nové mesto**). A pedestrian zone stretches between Hodžovo námestie in the north down to the river in the south. South of the city is Hungary and west is Austria. Bratislava is the only capital city that borders two independent countries.

Old Town

You can enter the Old Town via the only surviving medieval gateway, **Michalská brána a veža** (St Michael's Gate and Tower; Tues–Fri 9.30/10am–4.30/5pm, Sat & Sun 11am–6pm; €1.50), which contains a military museum and a tower with a view. Michalská and Ventúrska, two halves of one street, are lined with stately **Baroque palaces**, the university library and dozens of places to eat. At number 10 is **Mozart House**, where the six-year-old Mozart performed for the Palffy clan, and at Michalská 1 is the former Hungarian parliament.

A little northeast are the adjoining squares of the **Old Town** – Hlavné námestie and Františkánske námestie. Hlavnè, dotted with street cafés, houses the Christmas and Easter markets, and a few stalls most weeks. On Františkánske, you'll find the Rococo **Mirbach Palace** (Františkánske nám. 11; Tues–Sun 11am–6pm; €3.50, students €2), home of the City Gallery's Baroque collection.

Primate's Palace

Neoclassical **Primate's Palace** (Primaciálne nám 1; Tues–Sun 10am–5pm; €2) contains the Hall of Mirrors, where Napoleon and Austrian Emperor Franz I signed the Peace of Pressburg (as Bratislava was then called) in 1805. In 1903 city authorities restored the palace, and discovered six seventeenth-century English tapestries concealed behind the plaster, which are now the palace's other main attraction.

ACTIVE BRATISLAVA

Cycling and **rollerblading** along the Danube, towards Austria (upstream) or Hungary (downstream), are popular activities. For information on bike rental see p.1023. The Small Carpathian mountains surrounding Bratislava are beautiful and make for a good day's **cycling** or **walking**; see ⓦwww.bratislavasightseeing.com or call ⓣ09/0768 3112 for suggested routes and guided tours.

By the time it reaches Bratislava the Danube is too gentle for **whitewater rafting** (ⓦwww.actionland.sk), but you can try the man-made rapids at Action Land (€26/90min).

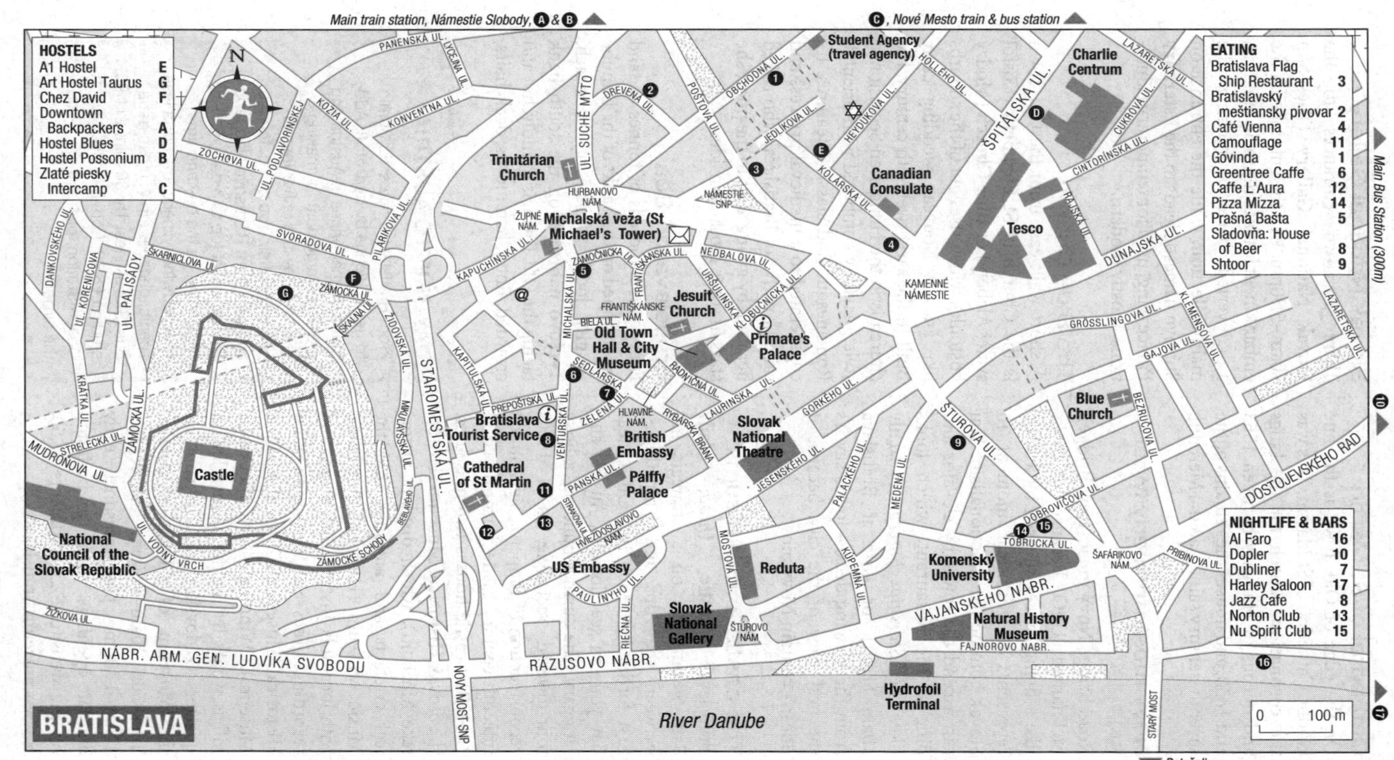
BRATISLAVA
Main train station, Námestie Slobody, A & B
C, Nové Mesto train & bus station
Main Bus Station (300m)
Petržalka
HOSTELS
A1 Hostel E
Art Hostel Taurus G
Chez David F
Downtown Backpackers A
Hostel Blues D
Hostel Possonium B
Zlaté piesky Intercamp C
EATING
Bratislava Flag Ship Restaurant 3
Bratislavský meštiansky pivovar 2
Café Vienna 4
Camouflage 11
Góvinda 1
Greentree Caffe 6
Caffe L'Aura 12
Pizza Mizza 14
Prašná Bašta 5
Sladovňa: House of Beer 8
Shtoor 9
NIGHTLIFE & BARS
Al Faro 16
Dopler 10
Dubliner 7
Harley Saloon 17
Jazz Cafe 8
Norton Club 13
Nu Spirit Club 15
Student Agency (travel agency)
Charlie Centrum
Trinitárian Church
Canadian Consulate
Tesco
Michalská veža (St Michael's Tower)
Jesuit Church
Old Town Hall & City Museum
Primate's Palace
Bratislava Tourist Service
Cathedral of St Martin
British Embassy
Pálffy Palace
Slovak National Theatre
Blue Church
Castle
National Council of the Slovak Republic
US Embassy
Reduta
Slovak National Gallery
Komenský University
Natural History Museum
Hydrofoil Terminal
River Danube
KAMENNÉ NÁMESTIE
HURBANOVO NÁM.
ŽUPNÉ NÁM.
NÁMESTIE SNP
FRANTIŠKÁNSKE NÁM.
HLVAVNÉ NÁM.
HVIEZDOSLAVOVO NÁM.
ŠTÚROVO NÁM.
ŠAFÁRIKOVO NÁM.
STAROMESTSKÁ UL.
ŠPITÁLSKA UL.
DUNAJSKÁ UL.
ŠTÚROVA UL.
VAJANSKÉHO NÁBR.
RÁZUSOVO NÁBR.
NÁBR. ARM. GEN. LUDVÍKA SVOBODU
FAJNOROVO NÁBR.
NOVÝ MOST SNP
STARÝ MOST
DOSTOJEVSKÉHO RAD
0 100 m

Cathedral of St Martin

On the edge of Old Town is the fine Gothic Cathedral of St Martin. This was the **coronation church** for the kings and queens of Hungary between 1563 and 1830, and houses the remains of the seventh-century saint Joan the Merciful.

Nový most (formerly Most SNP)

Road bridge **Nový most** (New Bridge), nicknamed UFO because it looks like a flying saucer speared by a twig, represents a whimsical moment in Slovak communist functionalism. You can ascend the tower by elevator and dine at the restaurant, which looks like the *Starship Enterprise* (daily 10am–11pm), or gaze at Bratislava from the viewing deck – locals say it's the best view of the city, because it doesn't contain Nový most.

The castle and museums

Bratislava's **castle** (*hrad*; daily 9am–6/8pm) sits on a strategic hill between the Alps and Carpathians, first fortified in 3500 BC. On a clear day you can see Slovakia, Austria and Hungary. The current building, a boxy four-towered rectangle, is a 1950s reconstruction of Emperor Sigismund's fifteenth-century castle, burnt down in 1811. The castle houses two museums: the **Slovak Historical Museum** (Historické Múzeum), which displays historical artefacts and antiques, and the Music Museum (Hudobné múzeum), with local folk instruments, scores and recordings (Tues–Sun 9am–5pm; €4 for Historical Museum, €2 for the Music Museum). Winding down the castle hill is what's left of the former Jewish quarter (Židovská), which contains the **Museum of Clocks** (Židovská; Tues–Sun 10am–4.30pm, Sat & Sun 11am–4.30pm, plus seasonal early and late openings, which can be found on the website; €2.50, students €1.50; ⓦwww.muzeum.bratislava.sk).

Slovak National Gallery

There are two entrances to the **Slovak National Gallery** (Tues–Sun 10am–5.30pm; €4): the entrance on the embankment leads to the main building, a converted barracks housing the main collection, while the entrance on Štúrovo námestie leads to the **Esterházy Palace** wing, used for temporary exhibitions, mostly modern.

The Blue Church

A short walk east from the Old Town is the Church of **St Elizabeth** (Kostol svätej Alžbety) or **Blue Church** (Modrý kostolík), which rises out of the suburbs like an Art Nouveau wedding cake. Built in the early twentieth century, the church is in the Hungarian Secessionist style, playfully combined with oriental, Romanesque and classical features. It's consecrated to a medieval princess and saint, a native of Bratislava, who risked her rank by giving alms to the poor; she stars in some mosaics inside.

Bratislava-on-Sea

Every year hundreds of tonnes of sand are dropped on the banks of the Danube to give locals a taste of the beach. **Tyršovo nábrežie**, on the south bank facing the Old Town, is friendly, hot and crowded. Entry, hammocks, deckchairs,

DAY-TRIP TO AUSTRIA

From Bratislava it takes 1hr 30min to get to Vienna by **hydrofoil**. Add that to higher prices in Austria and there's an argument for making Vienna a day-trip rather than an overnight affair. You can catch the hydrofoil from Rázusovo Nábriežie Embankment (up to 3 daily; €19–31 depending on the day and time; ⓦwww.twincityliner.com). For a less scenic, cheaper trip you can get a bus (Slovaklines; 1hr 30 min; €11.90, student €6.90; from Mlynské Nivy Coach Station, platform no. 12 or the airport).

parasols and sports equipment are free, there are cocktail bars, live music, table football, volleyball and snack bars.

Arrival and information

Air From Bratislava Airport, take bus #61 to the main train station, and from there walk or catch the tram into the centre. You can also take a taxi (see opposite).

Train Main station, Bratislava-Hlavná stanica, is within walking distance – 1km north – of the centre, or you can take tram #13 from the tram terminus just down from the main exit. Some trains, particularly those heading for west Slovakia, pass through Bratislava Nové Mesto station, 4km northeast of the centre, which is linked to town by tram #6.

Bus The main bus station is Bratislava autobusová stanica, on Mlynské nivy, just over 1km east of the centre. Trolleybuses #206 and #208 connect it to the main train station, stopping on the way in the centre at Hodžovo námestie.

Tourist office BKIS, Klobucnícká 2 (June–Sept Mon–Fri 8.30am–7pm, Sat 9am–5pm, Sun 10am–5pm; Oct–May Mon–Fri 8.30am–6pm, Sat 9am–4pm, Sun 10am–3pm; ⓣ02/5443 3715, ⓦwww.bkis.sk or ⓦwww.bratislava.sk).

Discount card The Bratislava City Card is available from BKIS tourist offices: it lasts for up to three days, costs up to €15, and gets you discounts to city attractions, a one-hour walking tour, and free transport (excluding night buses).

City transport

Walking is the only way to see pedestrianized Old Town (Staré Mesto), but it's less than five minutes end to end so you're unlikely to get tired.

Tram, bus and trolleybus Buy your ticket before you board and validate it in one of the orange machines inside. Inspectors target routes going to the airport and bus and train terminals; fines are €47. Buy one-way tickets from machines at the tram terminus and newsagents: €0.50/15min; €0.70/up to 60min. A day-pass costs €3.50 and a three-day pass €8; you can buy these from Bratislava Transport (Obchodná 14; ⓦwww.dpb.sk), and at the booth to the left of the train station's main exit. You also need a half-fare ticket for bulky luggage. Buses are slower than trams and trolleybuses. Public transport runs from 4.30am until approximately 11.30pm. Night buses run roughly every hour, you'll need a night ticket (€1.40), and to let the driver know where you're going, as the stops are by request only.

Bike See ⓦwww.bratislava.info/trips/bike for information on cycling in Bratislava. Bikes can be rented from Bratislava Sightseeing, also known as Luca Tours (ⓣ0907 683 112, ⓦwww.bratislava sightseeing.com; €4/hr; €18/day), and they also run bike tours. There are no designated bike paths in Bratislava.

Taxi Taxis are equipped with a meter, but even so it's normal to bargain the price in advance. It's best to order rather than taking a cab; try Happy Cab (ⓣ09/0222 2333) or Personal Express (ⓣ0948 506 064, ⓦwww.personalexpress.sk), which takes bookings by email.

Accommodation

You can book centrally located private rooms through the tourist office.

A1 Hostel Heydukova 1 ⓣ09/44 280 288, ⓦwww.a1hostelbratislava.com. Neat, and slightly characterless but the location is fantastic, prices are low and there's free wi-fi. Discounts if you stay more than 2 nights. Dorms €15, twins €42.

Art Hostel Taurus Zámocká 24–26 ⓣ01/2207 22401, ⓦwww.hostel-taurus.com. Gleaming white, central hostel with only eight rooms. There's free wi-fi, a dining area, sofas dotted around and a stage and musical instruments in case you want to jam. All rooms contain a private bathroom and locker. Breakfast included. Dorms from €13, doubles from €46.

Chez David Zámocká 13 ⓣ5441 3824, ⓦwww.chezdavid.sk. Quiet, family-run hotel close to the centre with traditional decor and a good restaurant (kosher) on site and free wi-fi. A perfect place to recoup from backpacker's fatigue. Breakfast included. Singles €56, doubles €79.

Downtown Backpacker's Hostel Panenská 31 ⓣ02/5464 1191, ⓦwww.backpackers.sk. Grand-looking HI-affiliated hostel on the edge of the Old Town with 24hr reception, a restaurant-bar, free wi-fi, common room with a tuneless old piano, books and games. Smoking allowed in the foyer, and there's a kitchen and laundry room. Dorms €14–18, twins €50 without bathroom.

Hostel Blues Špitálska 2 ⓣ09/0520 4020, ⓦwww.hostelblues.sk. Great concrete slab of a building which unexpectedly contains a warm, inviting hostel. The space given over to socializing (bar/reception, living room and a big kitchen (hosting free Slovak cookery classes), makes for a friendly atmosphere, and the staff are friendly and well informed. There's free internet (plus computers), rooms and dorms (single-sex or mixed) are clean and towels are provided. Dorms from €12, doubles from €54.

Hostel Possonium Šancová 20 ⓣ02/2072 0007, ⓦwww.possonium.sk. Great little hostel three minutes' walk from the station, which means a five-minute tram ride to the Old Town. Breakfast, wi-fi, washing machine and drier are included in the price. There's a popular horror-themed bar (inspired by the film *Hostel*) and a garden where guests chat and barbecue in the summer. The bunk beds are rickety though. Dorms €13, doubles €55.

Zlaté Piesky Intercamp ⓣ02/4425 7373, ⓦwww.intercamp.sk. Lakeside campsite 8km northeast of the city centre. Lifeguard services and a beach, as well as two restaurants on site. Take tram #2 from the main train station or #4 from town. Camping (May to mid-Oct) €3.50 per person, bungalow (sleeps three) €20.

Eating

Cafés

Café Vienna Nám. SNP. The place for breakfast on a sunny morning, with a central location, terrace and big, inexpensive breakfast menu (€2–5).

Caffe L'Aura Rudnayovo nám 4. Packed with creaking chairs, antique pitchers and cracked oil paintings this unruly café-bar is a good place to wait out a rainstorm. In better weather sit on the terrace overlooking the cathedral. Mon–Sat 10am–midnight, Sun 10am–10pm.

Greentree Caffe Ventúrska 20. Part of a likeable Italian-owned local chain. There are five dotted around town, and this is the newest and best, in an atmospheric vaulted cellar. Free wi-fi. Mon–Fri 8.30am–8.30pm, Sat & Sun 9am–8.30pm.

Shtoor Štúrova 8. Elegant but laidback café modelled on the glamorous coffeehouses of interwar Austro-Hungary. Freshly baked cakes, hearty sandwiches, and famous spiced home-made lemonade. There's a second branch on Panská. Daily 8am–10pm.

Restaurants

Bratislava Flag Ship Restaurant Nám SNP 8. Cavernous, echoing restaurant with decor that's half Charles Dickens half Las Vegas. The food is very decent and inexpensive, the atmosphere is warm and there's a terrace on the square. It's run by the same people as the ever-popular but increasingly shabby *Slovak Pub* (Obchodná 62). Mains €5–13. Daily 10am–midnight.

Bratislavský meštiansky pivovar Drevená 8. New old-style pub that brews its own beer and serves meaty Slovak staples. It can be hard to get a table on a Friday night. Mains €7–11, daily special €4.50. Sun–Thurs 11am–midnight, Fri & Sat 11am–1am.

Camouflage Ventúrska 1 ⓣ02/2092 2711. With a two-course lunch menu for €12, anyone can afford to eat at Bratislava's best restaurant. The head chef has cooked for royalty and presidents, the dining room is decorated with Andy Warhol originals from the *Camouflage* series (hence the name), and the food is excellent. Delicacies on the lunch menu include roast duck breast with honey-braised red onions, and lamb shoulder with cream-baked fennel. Sun–Thurs 11.30am–midnight, Fri & Sat 11.30am–1am.

Góvinda Obchodná 30. Good, inexpensive Indian vegetarian buffet on a busy shopping street. A plate of food is roughly €3.50. Mon–Fri 11am–8pm, Sat 11.30am–5.30pm.

Pizza Mizza Tobrucká 5. Reckoned to be the smartest pizza joint in Bratislava (though that's not saying much), *Pizza Mizza* is a decent place for a cheap, filling meal. They're dotted all over town and, if you don't feel like leaving your hotel you can get home delivery via the website (ⓦwww.pizzamizza.sk). Mon–Fri 10am–11pm, Sat & Sun 11am–11pm. Pizza €4–14.

Prašná Bašta Zámočnícka 11. Tucked in a quiet courtyard off Michalská gate is *Prašná Bašta*, an elegant, low-key restaurant loved by locals. The food deliciously combines Slovak and international flavours, there's a handsome vaulted interior, summer terrace and live jazz and classical music. Mains €6–16. Daily 11am–11pm.

Sladovňa: House of Beer Ventúrska 5. Decent local cuisine and good beer, outdoor seating (street or courtyard) in summer, and an atmospheric beer cellar in winter. Mains €8–18. Mon–Wed 11am–1am, Thurs–Sat 11am–2am, Sun 11am–11pm.

Drinking and nightlife

Al Faro Eurovea Shopping Compex, Pribinova 8/A. Strange to say, one of the nicest places for a cold drink on a hot evening is the mall. Eurovea, 15 minutes' walk from Old Town, has a row of bars, cafés and restaurants along the riverbank. *Al Faro* has a summer terrace on a pier over the river furnished with sofas and parasols, and serves food till late. Daily 11am–midnight.

Dopler Prievozská 18. Bratislava's biggest and most raucous nightclub is a taxi ride from the centre, popular with students and high schoolers. Fri & Sat 8pm–5am.

Dubliner Sedlárska 6. Busy Irish pub providing sports games and the occasional band. It's a great place to meet foreigners, but don't expect them to be sober. Daily 9am–3am.

Harley Saloon Rebarborová 1/a. Big place, heaving at weekends, with kitsch music (Bryan

Adams often reminisces about the summer of '69). It's on the edge of town so you'll need to take a trolley bus or taxi. Sun–Thurs 11am–2am, Fri & Sat 11am–6am.

Jazz Cafe Ventúrska 5. Crowded cellar pub with live jazz Thursday, Friday and Saturday nights. Arrive early if you want a table. Mon–Thurs 10am–midnight, Fri 10am–2am, Sat 11am–2am, Sun 11am–midnight.

Norton Club Panská 29. British motorcycle-theme bar, though you are unlikely to meet any bikers as it's on a pedestrian street. Mon–Thurs 11am–midnight, Fri–Sat 1pm–2am, Sun noon–midnight.

Nu Spirit Club Šafárikovo nám 7. Nudisco, drum'n'basse, funk, hip-hop, house and disco, DJ nights, stand-up comedy, live concerts and jam sessions. The owners also run a good bar on Medená St (same name). Mon–Sat 8pm–5am/6am.

Entertainment

The tourist office stocks *Kam do mesta* (free) and the English-language *What's on Bratislava & Slovakia* (€1.50; ⓦ www.whatsonslovakia.com). The weekly *Slovak Spectator*, available from kiosks and hotels, has news and listings.

Opera and ballet The Slovak National theatre has two sites, the New Slovak National Theatre (Pribinova 17), an impressive modern building completed four years ago, and the Historic Slovak National Theatre (Hviezdoslavovo nám). Tickets can be bought here one hour before the performance (€8–30). Some of the less well-known performances in the studio cost as little as €3, and you can also attend public rehearsals for €1.60. See ⓦ www.snd.sk.

Classical music Reduta Palace, on the corner of nám Štúra and Medená, is home to the Slovak Philharmonic Orchestra (ⓦ www.filharm.sk). There are open-air concerts in summer in courtyards and squares across the city, such as outside the Jesuit church by Michalská. Ask at the tourist office for details, or check out ⓦ www.whatsonslovakia.com or (in summertime) ⓦ www.bkis.sk.

Cinema Istropolis complex (ⓦ www.istropoliscinema.sk), Trnavské Mýto, Vajnorská 100 (tram #2 from the station; tram #4 or #6 from the centre) shows international current films; Charlie Centrum Špitálska 4 is an arthouse joint in the centre showing old and new Slovak, Czech and international films.

Shopping

Books Oxford Books Laurinská 9 (Mon–Fri 10am–7pm, Sat 10am–5pm; ⓣ 02/5262 2029, ⓦ www.oxfordbookshop.sk). Wide selection of English-language books and good browsing.

Malls AuPark, Einsteinova 18 (Mon–Fri 10am–10pm, Sat & Sun 9am–10pm; ⓦ www.aupark.sk). Large town mall with a Palace Cinema and foodcourt; Eurovea Galleria Pribinova 8 (daily 10am–9pm; ⓦ www.eurovea.sk), a 15min walk from the Old Town contains riverside bars and restaurants (see p.1024) and a multiplex cinema.

Souvenirs Michalská & Ventúrska sts in the Old Town are good for souvenir shopping.

Directory

Embassies and consulates Canada, Mostová 2 ⓣ 02/5920 4031; UK, Panská 16 ⓣ 02/5998 2258; US, Hviedoslavovo nám 5 ⓣ 02/ 5443 3338.

Hospital Poliklinika Ružinov, Ružinovská 10 (trams #8, #9, #14 and #50; ⓣ 02/4827 9111, ⓦ www.ruzinovskapoliklinika.sk) 24hr pharmacy on site.

Internet Wi-fi Cafe, Tatracentrum, Hodžovo nám. 4. Free use of computers when you buy a drink, plus wi-fi. Mon–Tues 9am–9pm, Sun 11am–8pm. There's

FESTIVALS

Bratislava hosts a raft of excellent festivals, especially for music-lovers. Here are a few of the best:

Cultural Summer ⓦ www.bkis.sk. Performance festival from June to September which floods Bratislava with theatre, opera, visual arts and dance.

Coronation Celebration ⓦ www.bratislava-info.sk. The first weekend in September history-lovers don their codpieces and stockings to celebrate the coronation of Ferdinand II (1612).

Jazz Days ⓦ www.bjd.sk. Brief but exuberant jazz festival which has been held every year in September since 1975.

Bratislava Music Festival ⓦ www.hc.sk. Classical music heavyweight organized by the Slovak Philharmonic every September and October, holding about 25 chamber and symphonic concerts each year.

free wi-fi access in certain parts of town, including Primaciálne nám, Hlavné nám and Františkánske nám.
Left luggage Main train station, daily 6.30am–11pm.
Pharmacies Lekáreň Pod Manderlom, nám SNP 20 ⓣ02/5443 2952, ⓦwww.lekarenpodmanderlom.sk. Lekáreň Pokrok, Račianske Mýto 1; 24hr; ⓣ02/4445 5291, ⓦwww.lekarenpokrok.sk.
Police Foreign police and passport services, Hrobáková 44 ⓣ09/6103 6866.
Post office Slovenská pošta, nám SNP 35. Mon–Fri 7am–8pm, Sat 7am–6pm, Sun 9am–2pm.

Moving on

Train Bánska Štiavnica (no direct service, 5 indirect trains daily; 3hr–4hr 20min); Brno (8 daily; 1hr 25min–2hr); Prague (to station Praha-Hlavní nádraží, every 2hr; 4hr 20min–6hr 30min); Poprad (the Košice train, approx 8 daily; 4hr–5hr).
Bus Bánska Štiavnica (2 direct buses daily; 3hr 25 min); Poprad (around 8 daily, the last stage of the journey is by train; 5hr 30min–8hr); Prague (Florenc station; hourly; 4hr 45 min).

Central Slovakia

If you're partial to an undulating hill or a winding mossy way, **Central Slovakia** is your kind of place. Quiet and agrarian, it's the heart of Slovakia; the cradle of Romantic Nationalism in the nineteenth century and the seat of the Slovak National Uprising in 1944. The way of life is slow, as are the trains, but what it lacks in zip it repays in beauty.

BANSKÁ ŠTIAVNICA

Lying in a great caldera created by the collapse of a volcano, **BANSKÁ ŠTIAVNICA** is Slovakia's oldest mining town. In the third century the Huns discovered precious metal here, and by the Middle Ages it was the largest source of gold and silver in the Hungarian Empire. During the Ottoman Wars the town sprouted fortifications, watch-towers and a castle to repel marauding Turks. As the metal reserves dwindled the inhabitants migrated, leaving the town unmodernized. Nowadays the population of about 10,000 is divided between the blue-collar descendants of mining families, and hotel-owning entrepreneurs from out of town, who tolerate each other grudgingly.

What to see and do

Main square **Námestie sv Trojice** is dominated by the Holy Trinity column, a red marble monolith marking the end of the plague in 1711. Southeast is Radničné Námestie, the Gothic Church of St Catherine and the Town Hall (Radnica), the latter with a clock that marks hours with its big hand and minutes with its little hand – according to an unusually credible local legend it was the work of a drunk clockmaker. Continuing southeast you'll come to the minimalist **New Castle** (Nový Zámok) and **Church of Our Lady of the Snows**.

The Old Castle

To the west of the main square is the **Old Castle** (Starý zámok; May–Sept daily 9am–6pm; Oct–April Tues–Sat 8am–4pm; €2) not a castle at all but a fortified Romanesque church used as a storage facility for municipal wealth. It's part of the Slovak Mining Museum, and exhibits Baroque sculptures, archeological remains and medieval blacksmithery.

Klopačka

Up A. Sládkoviča street is the **Clapping Tower** (Klopačka), home to a giant clapping contraption built for waking up miners. Today it claps for the amusement or irritation of tourists, and contains a teahouse (see p.1028).

Museums

Štiavnica is museum-rich. First up is the **Jozef Kollár Gallery** on Námestie sv Trojice, which exhibits everything from medieval madonnas to twentieth-century watercolours. A few doors down is the

Mineral Museum, which houses exhibits on the technical development of mining. **New Castle** contains a little museum about the Ottoman Wars in Slovakia. All of these museums are run by the **Slovak Mining Museum** (www.muzeum.sk) and have the same opening hours and prices (May–Sept daily 9am–6pm; Oct–April Tues–Sat 8am–4pm; €2).

At the **Open Air Mining Museum** (J. K. Hella 12; April–Oct; tours on oddly numbered hours 9am–5pm), 1.5km from town, you can take a trip down the old mines, while 3km from town the **Museum of St Anton** (72 Svätý Anton; always open Tues–Sun 9am–3pm, with some seasonal early opening and late closing - see www.msa.sk) is the kind of tapestry-heavy, trophy-stuffed manse which helps to while away a rainy morning.

Around Banská Štiavnica

The hills around Štiavnica are perfect for strolling, berry-picking and idling. Centuries of mining with gunpowder left the hills scarred with pits, which in time became lakes. On a hot day you can hike, swim, picnic, and be back by teatime. The most interesting walk is up to **Calvary** (Kalvária, 1km northeast of Old Town), a cluster of red and white Baroque chapels and churches perched on an inactive volcano, each one representing a stage in Christ's journey to the cross. Hiking maps are available at the tourist office and hotels.

Arrival and information

Train and bus The train station is a 2km walk through the suburbs from the old town. The bus stop is 100m closer, next to the big Billa supermarket at Križovatka, a steep climb up to the centre.

Tourist office Nám sv Trojice 3 (May–Sept Mon–Sat 8am–5.30pm; Oct–April Mon–Fri 8am–4pm, Sat 8am–2pm; 045/694 9653, www.banskastiavnica.sk, www.banskastiavnica.org). Go in through the gate and turn right.

Public transport You can walk from one side of the Old Town to the other in 10min. Cheap shuttle buses run through town; you can stop them anywhere by waving, and the fare is €0.50. Taxis are useful if you want to get out into the country but operators rarely speak English, so ask your hotel or hostel to order and agree the fee for you. Firms include Jo-Ma taxi (09/1018 0380) and Taxi Service Ivanič (09/05 85 233).

Internet Allcom, Radničné nám 11/1. Computer shop with internet, photocopying and printing (Mon–Sat 9am–5pm). There's free wi-fi at a number of cafés on Andreja Kmeťa st.

Accommodation

Archanjel Radničné nám 10b 421 915 365 371, archanjel.com. Smart rooms in an old townhouse above a local bar, with a shared kitchenette. The rooms aren't perfect (leaky showers, skimpy curtains), but paying hostel dorm prices for a single they're good value. Singles, doubles or triples €16.60 per person.

Hostel 6 Andreja Sladkovica 6 905 106 706 www.hostel6.sk. Neat, hostel with friendly staff and good views. 3-, 5- or 6-bed dorms. Dorms €16.

Hostel Juraj A. Pechá 2 0905 382 885, www.stiavnica.sk/hosteljuraj. Štiavnica's cheapest; a rambling, echoey hostel and campsite below the castle. Camping from €6, dorms from €7, doubles from €20.

Penzion Kachelman Kammerhofská 18 045/692 23 19, www.kachelman.sk. Pristine but characterless hotel with a restaurant, sauna and jacuzzi. Breakfast included. Singles €25, doubles €33.

Penzion Nostalgia Višňovského 3 0904 434 043, www.penzion-nostalgia.sk. Possibly the nicest B&B in Slovakia, *Nostalgia* is a seventeenth-century townhouse with a wood-burning stove, oak beams and linen sheets. It's

SPA

If the weather's bad, hop on a bus at Križovatka to **Sklené Teplice Spa** (Ul. A. Pechá 2; €7/hr; www.kupele-skleneteplice.sk). You'll be instructed to jump into hot springs and take cold showers alternately, an ordeal that leaves you exhausted to the point of relaxation. The spring is 42°C with high levels of magnesium and calcium, and the spa claims it heals visitors with muscle and locomotive conditions. There's also a pool, saunas and massage.

right in the centre of town, with views of the Old Town synagogue. Breakfast €3.90. Singles €25, doubles €35, apartments €45.

Eating and drinking

Art Café Akademicá 2. Bustling café, bar, exhibition space and sometime-cinema. It stocks a good range of local wines. Sun–Thurs 11am–11pm, Fri–Sat 11am–2am.

Čajovňa Klopačka A.Sládkoviča 7. Teahouse of the red cushion, smoky incense variety popular with Slovak students. There are 150 types of tea and water pipes. Mon 11am–11pm, Fri–Sun 10am–midnight.

Kaviareň Divná pani Andreja Kmeťa 8. Decorated like a flamboyant Roman library this café-bar is called "madwoman", but "charmingly eccentric lady" would be kinder. There's beer on tap, liquors, coffee and cakes, columns, statues and old books. The advertised closing times are often pushed back on busy nights. Mon–Fri 8am–10pm, Sat 9am–midnight, Sun 10am–midnight.

Pivovar ERB Novozámocká 2. Shiny tourist-orientated microbrewery and restaurant with specialities including smoked pork knuckles and sausages in vinegar brine. Mains €7–19. Sun–Thurs 11am–10pm, Fri & Sat 11am–midnight.

Terasa u Blažkov Jazero Počúvadlo. If you're in town on a balmy Friday or Saturday evening, take a long hike to *Terasa u Blažkov* (7km from Štiavnica). It's a traditional rustic night out with a whole pig roasted on a spit, fresh bread, salad and a folk band. Dinner is €5–7 and the taxi home around €7 more. It starts at 5pm, and if you arrive early you can swim in the adjoining lake. June–Sept daily 10am–11pm.

Tulsi Radničné nám 13. Banska's "sushi and chocolate bar" provides a break from *pirohy* and a sporting chance for vegetarians. Mains €3.50–9. Daily menu €3.30. Mon–Fri 11am–11pm, Sat & Sun noon–11pm.

U Mateja Akademicá 4. This small inn opposite *Grand Hotel Matej* is the place for a meat and dumpling binge. The food is popular with locals and there's terrace seating in the summer. Mains €4–8.

Moving on

Train No direct service to Bratislava (5 indirect daily; 3hr–4hr 20min).

Bus Bratislava (2 direct services daily; 3hr 30min–4hr 15min), Poprad (with multiple changes, 5 daily, 3hr 27min–4hr 10min).

THE TATRAS

Lying on the border with Poland, the **HIGH TATRAS** (Vysoké Tatry) are visible from space. The highest peak, pyramid-shaped Gerlach, is the tallest mountain in northern and eastern Central Europe at 2,655m high. The beauty and splendour of the mountains made them a magnet for Romantic and Nationalistic types in the eighteenth century, and in 1844 a student in Bratislava wrote a song beginning with the words "There is lightening over the Tatras" – today the national anthem. The mountains are awash with rare flora and fauna, and if you're lucky you might glimpse a lynx, wild boar, brown bear or Tatra chamois (goat-antelope).

Gloomy **Poprad** is an excellent transport hub, directly linking with Bratislava, Prague, Budapest and Krakow. From there you can catch a train or bus to the **Smokovec** resorts (divided into two adjoining halves, Nový (new) and Starý (old)), bustling ski resort **Tatranská Lomnica**, or spindly **Ždiar**, one endless street of painted wooden cabins. Wherever you stay you'll want to move between the villages; if you're using public transport you'll have to plan ahead a little because the trains and buses are erratically timed.

Arrival and information

Transport The main-line train station for the Tatras is Poprad-Tatry in Poprad. From there tiny red electrical trains (TEZ; hourly; 25min to Starý Smokovec; €2.40) trundle across the mountains, linking Poprad with Smokovec and Tatranská Lomnica. Ždiar isn't on the train line so you'll have to get the bus, which leaves Poprad twice hourly and takes an hour. There is also a small airport on the western outskirts of Poprad, Poprad-Tatry, which runs infrequent flights to and from a number of European countries including the UK.

Tourist office In Poprad: at the western end of námestie sv Egidia (Mon–Fri 9am–5pm, Sat 9am–noon; July & Aug Mon–Fri 8am–6pm, Sat 9am–1pm, Sun 1–4pm; ☎052/16 186, www.poprad.sk). In Starý Smokovec: down the road to your right as you face the *Grand Hotel* (Mon–Fri

9am–5pm; in summer also Sat & Sun 8am–2pm; ☎052/442 34 40, ⓦwww.tatry.sk). In Tatranská Lomnica it's on the main street opposite *Penzión Encián* (Mon–Fri 10am–6pm, Sat 9am–1pm; ☎4468118, ⓦwww.tatry.sk).

Accommodation

In high season (ski season and high summer) prices often double. All prices listed are for high season. The tourist offices in any of the resorts can help you arrange accommodation.

Ginger Monkey Hostel Ždiar 294 ☎05/2449 8084, ⓦwww.gingermonkey.eu. Many the eye of a hardened backpacker mists at the mention of *Ginger Monkey*, a wooden-cabin hostel on the edge of Ždiar. There are chickens in the garden, books in the kitchen, mountains out the window and a yellow dog for company. From Poprad, the bus stop is the fourth in Ždiar – keep an eye out for the sign that says "Petrol Station 500m" and alight at the next stop. Breakfast included. Dorms €13, doubles €32.

Grandhotel Praha Tatranská Lomnica ☎05/2446 7941, ⓦwww.ghpraha.sk. A stalwart remnant of the lost hotels of the nineteenth century, crammed with polished brass, carpet runners and nodding porters. If you've had enough of slumming it, blow a week's budget here. There are pools, saunas, spa treatments and massage for relaxing after skiing or hiking. Breakfast included. Doubles €145.

Mountain cabins For an authentic mountain experience hike to one of the wooden huts (*chata*) in the hills. Sleeping is often in dorms, and most huts offer dinner and breakfast. Try hotel-like *Bilíkova Chata* (☎52/442 2439, ⓦwww.bilikovachata.sk; €25/person, €28/person for en suite without breakfast), with single and double rooms, some en suite; or unpolished *Zbojnícka* (☎09/0363 8000, ⓦwww.zbojnickachata.sk; breakfast included; dorms €16.20), all oak beams and open fires, with one dorm sleeping 16.

Penzion Aqualand Štefánikova 893, Poprad ☎421 903 412 482, ⓦwww.aqualand.sk/en/pension. If you have to stay a night in Poprad, this *pension*, ten minutes' walk from the bus and train stations, is a neat and well-kept choice with friendly service. Guests get a discount at the waterpark. Doubles €45.

Penzion Mon Ami Nový Smokovec 31 ☎05/2442 3024, ⓦwww.monami.sk. Clean, comfortable B&B in a traditional wood-framed guesthouse on the high street in Smokovec, with views over the mountains. All rooms are doubles with en suite. €15/person, single or double.

Penzion Slalom Tatranská Lomnica 94 ☎05/2446 7216, ⓦwww.slalom.sk. Friendly little B&B close to the station. It looks like a retired couple's home, which it is. Doubles €39.

Penzión Ždiar Ždiar 460 ☎05/2449 8138, ⓦwww.penzionzdiar.sk. Big wooden guesthouse with equine equipment and painted plates on the walls. The prices are excellent. Rooms for 1–5 people. €8/person, €10/person with en suite.

Villa Kunerad Nový Smokovec 22, ☎090/535 0448, ⓦwww.penziongerlach.sk. Bright, spacious rooms in a large chalet behind the *Grand Hotel*. Doubles €35.

Eating and drinking

Cukráreň Tatra Starý Smokovec 66. Follow the warm scent of vanilla to this delightful *cukráreň* (the nearest translation is "sugary"), which serves great cakes, ice cream, chocolate and real coffee.

Hotel Atrium Bowling Bar Nový Smokovec 42. An amusing evening out in a village low on nightlife. Daily noon–midnight.

Humno Tatranská Lomnica 14640. Swish alpine chalet eatery that's also a bar, café, pub, and on Fridays and Saturdays a nightclub (the best in the mountains). There's an open fire, leather sofas, a snow plough coming out the wall (the DJ booth) and a cadillac once belonging to Madonna. Mains €5.50–18.50. Sun–Thurs 11am–midnight, Fri & Sat 11am–4am.

MOUNTAIN SAFETY

On average, twenty people a year die in the High Tatras. Keep safe by hiking with two or more friends and making sure someone knows where you are going. Wear layers, a waterproof and windproof coat, and hiking boots. Always take plenty of water and some food. Buy a whistle – the emergency signal is 6 blasts. Weather conditions change fast, so check the prognosis before you leave; the Mountain Rescue Service in Starý Smokovec will give you a forecast. If you get in trouble, call Mountain Rescue (☎18300) right away. Don't think of them as an easy fall-back though; they charge a large fee for call-outs.

Rustika Ždiar 334. Road-sign-strewn wood shack serving toothsome, inexpensive pizzas. Pizza €4.50, 50cm monster pizza €12.
Tatratom Ždiar 288. Traditional pub serving excellent, old-timey meals. The garlic soup was hot and piquant, and the fruit dumplings were dreamy. Mains €4–9.
Sabato Sobotské nám 6, Poprad. Medieval-style restaurants combine large slabs of meat and ludicrously dressed waiters, and this is a nice example of the genre. Mains €7–19.
Vila Park Tatranská Lomnica. Decent modern Slovak food with a sunny summer terrace overlooking the village green, three minutes from the train station. Mains €8–12.
Villa Siesta Nový Smokovec 88. Few non-guests eat at this bland-looking hotel restaurant, which is a shame because the food is great. Rumour has it the manager is the judge on a Slovak cookery show. Order *pirohy*. Mains €6.30–14. Daily noon–9pm.

Activities

AquaCity Športová 1, Poprad Ⓦwww.aquacity poprad.sk. AquaCity has outdoor thermal pools (30–38°C) and a 50m pool, toboganning, a beauty centre, massage, slides, restaurants, bars and a club. Perfect for a break after a few days skiing. €15–24 for a 3hr package. Daily 8am–10pm.
Belianska Cave The north slope of Kobylí Hill (near to Tatranská Kotlina) Ⓣ05/2446 7375, Ⓦwww.ssj.sk. A 70min tour of Belianska Cave, which was discovered by gold prospecteers in the 1700s, leads you past subterranean waterfalls, stalagmites and the Music Hall – so-called because of the melodious sound of water drops on the still pool. It's below freezing even in summer so dress warmly. The nearest bus stop is Tatranská Kotlina. Tour times 9.30am, 11.30am, 12.30pm & 2pm; times fluctuate so check beforehand. €7, students €6.
Climbing To go climbing you'll need a valid membership card for a recognized climbing club, or a guide. Certified guides are available at the Association of Mountain Guides (Spolok horských vodcov), but they're expensive, starting at €160/hike (Vila Alica, Starý Smokovec; Ⓣ052/442 20 66, Ⓦwww.tatraguide.sk).
Bikes, mountainboards, scooters and carts Tatry Motion rental, Starý Smokovec (Ⓣ09/0340 7413, Ⓦsport-smokovec@vt.sk) and Tatranská Lomnica (Ⓣ09/1144 2232, Ⓦsport@vt.sk). Scooter €4/ride, mountainboard €5, cart €6, bike €10/day. You can get a cable car up one of the peaks, and a scooter to ride back down on, for €9.There's also a bike park (Ⓦwww.vt.sk) at Hrebienok (accessible by funicular from Starý Smokovec) with easy and difficult routes; bikes €7/ride, €17/day (9am–6pm dependent on weather).
Rafting at Červený Kláštor Pieniny sport centrum, Červený Kláštor, Pieniny National Park, 45 Ⓣ09/0747 7412, Ⓦwww.rafting-pieniny.sk. It's almost two hours by bus to the Dunajec River in Pieniny National Park, on the Slovak–Polish border, but worth the trip. You can rent a raft, take a tour with a guide, or go in a traditional wooden punt helmed by folk in frilly costumes. May–Sept only; equipment rental 9am–6pm. Bus Poprad–Červený Kláštor two daily (1hr 45min).
Skiing and snowboarding The season is Dec–March. Tatranská Lomnica is an ideal place to ski and snowboard, with heated chairlifts and cable cars, long runs, routes for all abilities, good black runs plus off piste. Bachledova Dolina is a great affordable option – a day-pass is €16, ski hire is €7, and the restaurants on the slopes are cheap too. There's a 2km run, beginners' slopes in the villages (Strednica and Strachan) and blue, red and black routes at Bachledova. Štrbské Pleso hosts national and international skiing events and it's a beautiful place, but it's pricey and the skiing is pretty similar to Lomnica. See Ⓦwww.vt.sk and Ⓦwww.tatry.sk for more.
Tatrabob Tatranská Lomnica 29 Ⓣ09/4450 3069 Ⓦwww.tatrabob.com. Pint-sized mountainside roller coaster plus archery. €3/ride.

Moving on (from Poprad)

Air From Poprad-Tatry International Airport; Danube Wings and Czech Airlines fly to London, Dublin, Prague and Warsaw.
Train Bratislava (10 daily; 2hr 50min–3hr 40min); Košice (hourly; 1hr 7min–1hr 55min).
Bus Levoča (twice hourly; 15–45min); Prešov (hourly; 1hr 05min–2hr).

East Slovakia

Slovakia's **east** (východoslovenský kraj) has one foot in the past. Protected from the west by the Tatras, traditional dialects and folk customs thrive. The land is bleaker and grander than the west. Stretching northeast up the Poprad Valley to the Polish border, and east along the River Hornád towards Prešov, is the **Spiš** region, for centuries a semi-autonomous province in the Hungarian kingdom.

LEVOČA

What inspired the great Hungarian writer Kálmán Mikszáth to make **LEVOČA** the star of his 1910 revenge saga *The Black Town* is a mystery. The medieval town is as neat and respectable as a privet hedge, and if there are any passions seething they're well buried. The town's main attraction is the wonderful religious art at the Church of St James, but it's also a good base for visiting **Spiš castle** (see box, p.1032), and a gateway to beautiful Slovak Paradise National Park.

What to see and do

Levoča is a grid-plan town. The main streets run from **Námestie Majstra Pavla** (the main square) to the city walls, becoming darker and shabbier as they go. Churches, hotels and museums congregate in the main square, with the cheaper *pensions*, hostels and pubs scattered near the town walls. From the north side of **Námestie Majstra Pavla** you can see the graceful white church at Mariánska hora (Mary's Mountain), a Catholic pilgrimage.

Church of St James

The splendid **Church of St James** (Chrám sv Jakuba; Mon 11/11.30 am–4/5pm, Tues–Sat 8.30/9am–4/5pm, Sun 1–4/5pm; Nov–Easter closed Sun & Mon) soars above the north side of the main square. It houses a magnificent 18ft-high wooden altarpiece containing the Last Supper, and a baby-faced madonna, both the work of sixteenth-century master-carver Pavol of Levoča. The church can only be entered with a guide, and tours leave every 30min in summer, hourly in winter, from the ticket office opposite the main entrance, and cost €2.50. A small and uninspiring **museum** (daily 9am–5pm; €1.50) dedicated to Master Pavol, stands opposite the church and exhibits replicas of the art in the church.

Town Hall and Lutheran Church

Between St James and the squat, Neoclassical **Lutheran church** (*Evanjelický kostol*) is a wrought-iron contraption called the **Cage of Shame** (*klietka hanby*), built in a flourish of sixteenth-century misogyny: women caught on the streets after dark were imprisoned here overnight in their petticoats, heads shorn, as an example to other females. The third building on the square is the old **Town Hall** (daily 9am–5pm). **Spiš Museum** (daily 9am–5pm; Ⓦwww.snm.sk), which also exhibits paintings and icons.

ON YER HIKE

If you're not a hiker, there are plenty of shorter routes to leave the heel unblistered.

- **Štrbské pleso–Popradské pleso** A scenic stroll between two lakes that takes less than two hours. On the way you'll pass the Symbolic Cemetery, a memorial garden to those who died in the Tatras.
- **Biela voda–Chata pri Zelenom plese** Takes a little under 3 hours, and it ends on a high, with beautiful mountain panoramas around the chalet.
- **Kriváň peak** When you've got your mountain legs, hike up this high, hook-nosed peak (2495m – a hike for summer only), beloved of Slovak Romantic poets. It's one of the highest mountains in the Tatras and the walk takes a full day. You can start from Štrbské Pleso and follow the red trail towards Podbanské. Peruse our safety tips (see box, p.1029) before starting out.

SPIŠ CASTLE

An endless mass of ramshackle bone-white walls, roads and broken towers, **Spiš Castle** (Spišský hrad; March–April 10am–4pm, May–Oct 9am–7pm, last entry 6pm; €5, students €3; www.spisskyhrad.com) is a monumental twelfth-century fortress built over a much older castle. It's a bleak, dreamlike place, so isolated that the only sounds are birds and crickets. Inside are exhibits giving a clear picture of medieval life (short and dirty), audioguides and a tower to climb. You can catch a bus from Levoča to Spišské Podhradie for a euro (2 hourly; 30 min).

Arrival and information

Bus The bus station is 1km southeast of the old town. If you're coming from the east alight one stop earlier at the Košice gate.

Tourist office Nám Majstra Pavla 58 (Mon–Fri 9am–4pm; 053/451 37 63, www.levoca.sk).

Internet Levonet internet café, nám Majstra Pavla 38 (daily 10am–10pm; €2/hr).

Accommodation

Barbakan Košická 15 53 451 43 10, www.barbakan.sk. The kind of solid, old-fashioned hotel that smells of floor wax and pink soap. Breakfast €5. Singles €28, doubles €42.

Oaža Nová 65 053/451 4511, www.ubytovanieoaza.sk. Well-scrubbed, no-frills accommodation in a family-run boarding house a few minutes' walk from the main square. You can get a room or share (either with friends or strangers). A good option on a tight budget. Dorms €10.

Rekreačné zariadenie Levočská Dolina 421 53 4512705, www.rzlevoca.sk. Campsite with wooden bungalows and a *pension* 5km northwest of town with bike rental, a café, sauna and whirlpool. Price €3 per person plus €1.50 for the tent, bungalow rental €6.50 per person, *pension* €37 for a double.

U Leva Nám Majstra Pavla 24 4502311, www.uleva.sk. *U Leva* (At the Lion) has spacious, sunny rooms spread across two townhouses. There's a sauna, a fitness centre and restaurant (see opposite). Ask for one of the rooms at the front of the hotel, which overlook St James. In quiet weeks they give discounts. Singles €39, doubles €68.

Eating

Arkáda Nám Majstra Pavla 26. Vaulted cellar tavern stashed under one of the bigger hotels. Draught beer, local wine and Slovak staples. You'll also find similar food, decor and prices at *U Troch Apoštolov* (nám Majstra Pavla 11), further up the main square. Mains €4–14. Daily 7am–10pm.

Mama Mia Vetrová 4. Average small-town pizzeria with decent, cheap food. Pizza €3–8.

Planeta Nám Majstra Pavla 38a. Every sleepy provincial town needs a *Planéta*; a café at 4pm, a restaurant at 7pm and a bar at 10pm; opens early, closes late, and has free wi-fi. The menu is simple (pizza, salads, pasta) but fresh. Lunch menu €3, dinner menu €3.50. Oct–April Mon–Fri 8am–10pm, Sat & Sun 9.30am–10pm; May–Sept Mon–Fri 8am–11pm, Sat & Sun 11am–10.30pm.

Peko Spiš Košicka ulica. The town's best bakery. Mon–Fri 6am–6pm, Sat 6am–noon.

Restauracia U Leva Nám Majstra Pavla 24. *U Leva* earns a double-mention because it has the nicest mid-range restaurant in Levoča, combining Mediterranean (carpaccio, *insalata caprese*) and Slavic dishes (duck breast with cherry sauce, chicken liver with wild mushrooms), and doing both well. Mains €6–13.

Tatra Food Nám Majstra Pavla 54a. Pleasant snack bar with cheap baguettes, kebabs, milkshakes and desserts in the municipal theatre building. Sandwiches €1–2.50. Mon–Fri 8am–7pm, Sat 10am–10pm.

Moving on

Train Levoča is not on the train line, but you can get a taxi or catch a bus to Spišská Nová Ves (11 twice hourly; 20min) and from there catch the direct train to Bratislava (10 daily; 5hr 30min), which also stops at Poprad.

Bus Poprad (20 daily; 30 min).

Slovenia

HIGHLIGHTS

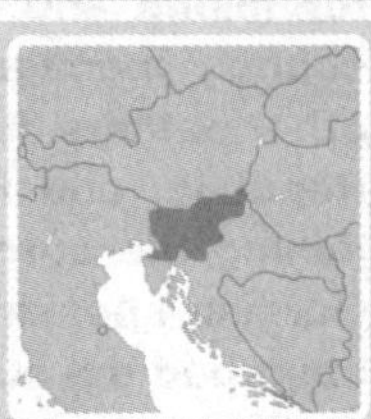

SOČA VALLEY: stunningly scenic location for hiking, rafting and skiing

PTUJ: Slovenia's oldest settlement is also its most endearing

OLD TOWN, LJUBLJANA: wonderful architecture, a hilltop castle and atmospheric riverside bars

ŠKOCJAN CAVES: magnificent underground canyon

PIRAN: historic coastal town with gorgeous Venetian Gothic architecture and pretty squares

ROUGH COSTS

DAILY BUDGET Basic €45 /occasional treat €65

DRINK *Pivo* (beer) €2.50 for half a litre

FOOD Pizza €5–7

HOSTEL/BUDGET HOTEL €15–25/€60–80

TRAVEL Ljubljana–Maribor €9 by train; Ljubljana–Bled €7 by bus

FACT FILE

POPULATION 2 million

AREA 20,273 sq km

LANGUAGE Slovenian

CURRENCY Euro (€)

CAPITAL Ljubljana (population: 280,000)

INTERNATIONAL PHONE CODE ⓣ386

Introduction

Stable, prosperous and welcoming, Slovenia is a charming and comfortable place to travel, with architecturally grand, cultured cities, and lush pine-forested countryside, perfect for hiking and biking in summer and skiing in winter. The country managed to avoid much of the strife that plagued other nations during the messy disintegration of the Yugoslav Republic, and has integrated quickly with Western Europe, joining the euro zone at the start of 2007. Administered by German-speaking Habsburg overlords until 1918, Slovenes absorbed the culture of their rulers while managing to retain a strong sense of ethnic identity through their Slavic language.

Slovenia's sophisticated capital, **Ljubljana**, is pleasantly compact and cluttered with fabulous Baroque and Habsburg buildings. Elsewhere, the Julian Alps provide stunning mountain scenery, most accessible at Lake Bled and **Lake Bohinj**, and most memorable along the **Soča Valley**. Further south are spectacular caves, including those at **Postojna** and Škocjan, while the short stretch of Slovenian coast is punctuated by two starkly different towns: Piran and Portorož. In the eastern wine-making regions, Ptuj is Slovenia's oldest and best-preserved town, while the country's second city, **Maribor**, is a worthwhile stopover point on the way to Austria.

CHRONOLOGY

181 BC The Romans conquer the area of present-day Slovenia.
550 AD Slavs begin to inhabit the area.
600s The first Slovenian state, the Duchy of Carantania, is established.
745 The Frankish Empire takes over Carantania, and converts the Slavs to Christianity.
1267 Coastal Istria officially becomes the territory of the Venetian Republic. It remains under Venetian rule until 1797.
1335 The Habsburgs take control of Slovenian regions through marriage.
1550 The first book is published in the Slovenian language.
1867 Slovenia is brought under the direct control of Austria.
Late 1800s Growth of Slovenian nationalism.
1918 Following the collapse of the Austro-Hungarian Empire after World War I, Slovenia is incorporated into the Kingdom of the Serbs, Croats and Slovenes.
1929 The Kingdom is renamed Yugoslavia.
1945 After being occupied by the Germans during World War II, a liberation force led by Slovenian General Tito incorporates Slovenia into the Republic of Socialist Yugoslavia.
1950s The industrialization of Slovenia leads to rapid economic development.
1980 General Tito dies; disintegration of Yugoslavia begins.
1990 Slovenians vote for independence in a referendum.
1991 Slovenia declares its independence from Socialist Yugoslavia, leading to a ten-day war with the Yugoslav army. The Slovenians win.
2003 The oldest wooden wheel in the world, thought to be 5000 years old, is discovered in Slovenia.
2004 Slovenia joins NATO as well as the EU.
2007 Slovenia is the first former Communist state to adopt the European single currency.
2012 Maribor is the European Capital of Culture.

ARRIVAL

Direct **flights** to Slovenia from the UK are increasing in number, with low-cost carrier easyJet (Ⓦwww.easyjet.com) flying daily to Ljubljana from London Stansted. Slovenia's location – surrounded by Austria, Croatia, Hungary and Italy – makes it easily approachable by road or rail; Ljubljana is well

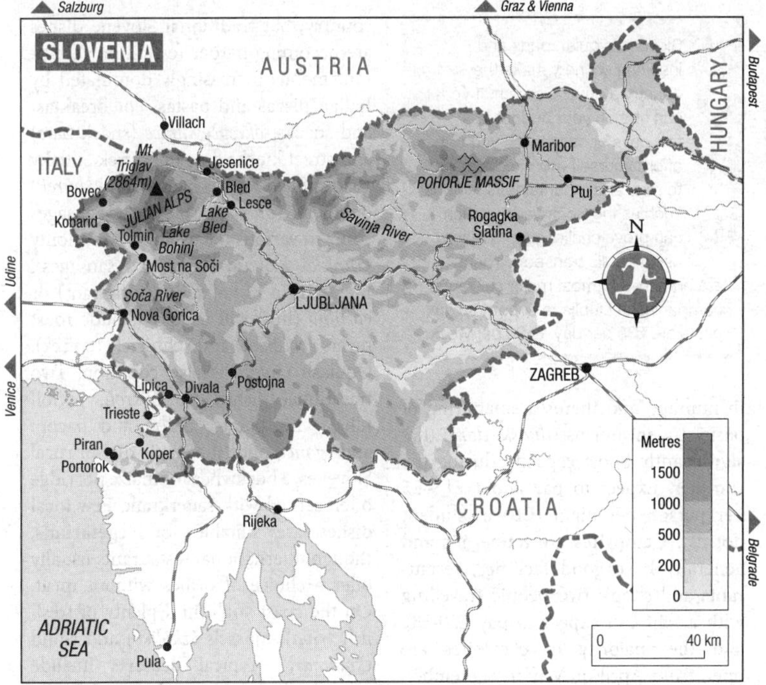

connected by bus and train with major cities in all four countries. Access to the Slovene coast is also straightforward: buses arrive daily from Trieste (Italy) and Pula (Croatia), and between April and October you can travel by **catamaran** between Venice and Piran/Izola.

GETTING AROUND

Slovene Railways (Slovenske železnice; ⓦwww.slo-zeleznice.si) is smooth and efficient. **Trains** (*vlaki*) are divided into slow (LP), and Intercity (IC) express trains, as well as the fast Inter City Slovenia trains (ICS) between Ljubljana and Maribor. Reservations (*rezervacije*) are obligatory, but free, on ICS trains, and there is a €5 booking fee for international trains to Italy. Most timetables have English notes; "departures" is *odhodi*, "arrivals" is *prihodi*. Eurail and InterRail passes are valid.

The **bus** network consists of an array of local companies offering a reliable service. Towns such as Ljubljana, Maribor and Koper have big bus stations, where you can buy your tickets in advance – recommended if you're travelling between Ljubljana and the coast in high season. Elsewhere, simply pay the driver or conductor. You'll be charged extra for cumbersome items of baggage. All public transport services are significantly reduced on Sundays.

Slovenia is a superb destination for **cycling**, with quiet roads, fabulous scenery and a well-established network of adventurous Alpine trails for mountain bikers. The lakes, the Soča Valley and the eastern wine roads are all pleasant places to explore on two wheels and many hotels and hostels rent bikes for free or a small charge. The website ⓦwww.mtb.si is a useful resource for mountain bikers.

ACCOMMODATION

Accommodation is universally clean and good quality. **Hostels** are growing

TREAT YOURSELF

Slovenia's quiet roads and inspiring scenery make the country a driver's dream. If you can stretch your budget to a few days of **car rental**, you will afford yourself unlimited access to rural and mountainous regions such as the Soča Valley, which can prove challenging to reach using public transport. There are branches of most major car rental companies at Ljubljana airport; typical costs are €35 per day, €120 per week.

in number, and there's a smattering of basic student dorms (*dijaški dom*) that significantly boost capacity during the summer. Expect to pay about €15–25 per person per night (€10 in student dorms). **Campsites** are numerous and generally have good facilities, restaurants and shops; two people travelling with a tent can expect to pay €20–30, and the majority of campsites are open from April or May to September. Camping rough without permission is punishable by a fine.

In the capital, double rooms at a two-star hotel start around €55. Family-run *pensions* and tourist farms in rural areas, especially the mountains, offer many of the same facilities as hotels but usually at a lower price. **Private rooms** (*zasebne sobe*) are available throughout Slovenia, with bookings often made by the local tourist office or travel agents like Kompas. Rooms are pretty good value at about €35–50 for a double, although stays of three nights or less can be subject to a surcharge in peak season. Self-catering **apartments** (*apartmaji*) are also plentiful in the mountains and on the coast.

FOOD AND DRINK

Slovene **cuisine** draws on Austrian, Italian and Balkan influences. There's a native tradition, too, based on age-old peasant recipes, which you may encounter at tourist farms across the country; but traditional Slovene dishes are becoming harder to find on restaurant menus increasingly dominated by Italian pizzas and pastas. For breakfast and snacks, *okrepčevalnice* (snack bars) and street kiosks dole out burek, a flaky pastry filled with cheese (*sirov burek*) or meat (*burek z mesom*). Sausages come in various forms, most commonly *kranjska klobasa* (big spicy sausages). Menus in a *restavracija* (restaurant) or *gostilna* (inn) will usually include roast meats (*pečenka*) and schnitzels (*zrezek*). Goulash (*golaž*) is also common. Two traditional dishes are *žlikrofi*, ravioli filled with potato, onion and bacon; and *žganci*, once the staple diet of rural Slovenes, a buckwheat or maize porridge often served with sauerkraut. Few local dishes are suitable for **vegetarians**, though international restaurants usually offer a choice of dishes without meat. On the coast you'll find plenty of fresh fish (*riba*), mussels (*žkoljke*) and squid (*kalamari*). Typical **desserts** include strudel filled with apple or rhubarb; *žtruklji*, dumplings with fruit filling; and *prekmurska gibanica*, a delicious local cheesecake.

Drinking

Daytime **drinking** takes place in small café-bars, or in a *kavarna*, where a range of cakes, pastries and ice cream is usually on offer. **Coffee** (*kava*) is generally served strong and black, as is tea (*čaj*), unless specified otherwise – ask

SLOVENIA ONLINE

Ⓦ**www.burger.si** Superb interactive maps and panoramic photos.
Ⓦ**www.inyourpocket.com/slovenia** Useful online listings compiled by locals.
Ⓦ**www.slovenia.info** Official tourist board site.
Ⓦ**www.visitljubljana.si** Detailed information on sights and events in the capital.

EMERGENCY NUMBERS

Police ⓣ113; Ambulance & Fire ⓣ112.

for *mleko* (milk) or *smetana* (cream). Slovene beer (pivo) is usually excellent (Laško Zlatorog is considered the best), although most breweries also produce *temno pivo* ("dark beer"), a Guinness-like stout. The superb local **wine** (vino) is either *črno* (red) or *belo* (white) and has an international reputation. Favourite aperitifs include *slivovka* (plum brandy), the fiery *sadjevec*, a brandy made from various fruits, and the gin-like *brinovec*.

CULTURE AND ETIQUETTE

Slovenes are welcoming people, who are only too willing to help tourists. The predominant religion is Catholicism, and respectful attire (no sleeveless tops or above-the-knee skirts) should be worn inside churches and around religious sites. **Tipping** is generally not required, though always welcome, and increasingly expected in the main tourist areas.

SPORTS AND OUTDOOR ACTIVITIES

Slovenia's dramatic and varied landscape provides ample opportunities for a whole host of sporting activities, be it **hiking**, **cycling** and **rafting** in summer, or **skiing** in winter. Most places cater well for adventure-seekers, especially in the mountains, with healthy competition generally keeping prices fair. Local tourist offices have comprehensive information on activities and sporting agencies.

COMMUNICATIONS

Most **post offices** (*pošta*) are open Monday to Friday 8am to 6/7pm and Saturday 8am to noon. Stamps (*znamke*) can also be bought at newsstands.

Public **phones** use cards (*telekartice* €2.92, €4.18, €7.09), available from post offices, kiosks and tobacconists. Make long-distance and international calls at a post office, where you're assigned to a cabin. It is also possible to buy a **SIM card** or a pre-paid phone from Slovenian mobile operators Mobitel and Simobil for around €10. **Wi-fi** access is widely available and many tourist information offices and hostels offer **free internet**.

EMERGENCIES

The **police** (*policija*) are generally easy-going and likely to speak some English. **Pharmacies** (*lekarna*) are typically open Monday to Friday from 7am to 7pm, Saturday 7am to 1pm, and a rota system covers night-time opening; details are in the window of each pharmacy.

INFORMATION

Most towns and resorts have a well-stocked and helpful **tourist information office**, which can usually arrange accommodation too. A very high standard of English is spoken almost everywhere.

MONEY AND BANKS

Slovenia adopted the euro in January 2007. **Banks** (*banka*) generally open Monday to Friday 9am to noon and 1 to 5pm, Saturday 8.30am to 11am/noon. You can also change money in tourist offices, post offices, travel agencies and exchange bureaux (*menjalnica*). **Credit cards** are accepted in a large number of

STUDENT & YOUTH DISCOUNTS

The EURO<26 card (ⓦwww.euro26.org; €14) is valid in Slovenia, and can be used to get discounts of up to 50 percent on many attractions. You can also purchase the affiliated SŽ-EURO<26 (€18; from most train stations) to get an additional 30 percent off train fares within Slovenia, and 25 percent off international rail travel.

SLOVENE

	Slovene	Pronunciation
Yes	*Ja*	Ya
No	*Ne*	Ne
Please	*Prosim*	Proseem
Thank you	*Hvala*	Huala
Hello/Good day	*Živijo/dober dan*	Zheeveeyoh/dohburr dhan
Goodbye	*Nasvidenje*	Nasveedehnye
Excuse me	*Dovolite mi, prosim*	Dovoleeteh mee, proseem
Where?	*Kje?*	Kye?
Good	*Dobro*	Dobro
Bad	*Slabo*	Slabo
Near	*Blizu*	Bleezoo
Far	*Daleč*	Daalech
Cheap	*Poceni*	Potzenee
Expensive	*Drago*	Drago
Open	*Odprto*	Odpurto
Closed	*Zaprto*	Zapurto
Today	*Danes*	Danes
Yesterday	*Včeraj*	Ucheray
Tomorrow	*Jutri*	Yutree
How much is...?	*Koliko stane...?*	Koleeko stahne...?
What time is it?	*Koliko je ura?*	Koleeko ye oora?
I don't understand	*Ne razumem*	Ne razoomem
Do you speak English?	*Ali govorite angleško?*	Alee govoreete angleshko?
One	*Ena*	Ena
Two	*Dve*	Dve
Three	*Tri*	Tree
Four	*Štiri*	Shteeree
Five	*Pet*	Pet
Six	*Šest*	Shest
Seven	*Sedem*	Sedem
Eight	*Osem*	Osem
Nine	*Devet*	Devet
Ten	*Deset*	Deset

hotels and restaurants, and **ATMs** are widespread.

OPENING HOURS AND HOLIDAYS

Most **shops** open Monday to Friday 8am to 7pm and Saturday 8am to 1pm; an increasing number open on Sunday mornings. Museum times vary, but many close on Mondays. All shops and banks are closed on the following **public holidays**: January 1 and 2, Febuary 8, Easter Monday, April 27, May 1 and 2, June 25, August 15, October 31, November 1, December 25 and 26.

Ljubljana

The vibrant Slovene capital **LJUBLJANA** gracefully fans out from its castle-topped hill, the old centre marooned in the shapeless modernity that stretches out across the plain. It's a dynamic and fast-growing capital packed with compelling sights, but they are only part of the picture; above all Ljubljana is a place to meet people and enjoy the nightlife.

What to see and do

Ljubljana's main point of reference is **Slovenska cesta**, a busy north–south thoroughfare that slices the city down the middle. Most of the sights are within easy walking distance of here, with the **Old Town** straddling the River Ljubljanica to the south and east and the **nineteenth-century quarter** situated to the west, where the principal museums and galleries are.

The Old Town

From the bus and train stations stroll south down Miklošičeva cesta for ten minutes and you'll reach **Prešernov trg**, the hub around which everything in Ljubljana's charming **Old Town** revolves. Overlooking the bustling square and the River Ljubljanica, the Baroque seventeenth-century **Church of the Annunciation** (daily 6.40am–noon & 3–8pm), blushes a sandy red; it's worth a look inside for Francesco Robba's marble high-altar, richly adorned with spiral columns and plastic figurines. Robba, an Italian architect and sculptor, was brought in to remodel the city in its eighteenth-century heyday. His best piece, a beautifully sculpted **fountain** that symbolizes the meeting of the rivers Sava, Krka and Ljubljanica, lies across the river, in front of the town hall on Mestni trg. To get there cross the elegant **Tromostovje** (Triple Bridge), one of many innovative creations by celebrated Slovene architect Jože Plečnik in Ljubljana, his birthplace. Plečnik made his mark on the city between the two world wars with his classically inspired designs.

St Nicholas' Cathedral and the market

A little east of Mestni trg, on Ciril-Metodov trg, **St Nicholas' Cathedral** (Mon–Fri 6–9am & 6.30–7pm; Sat 6–11am, 4–5pm & 6.30–7pm; Sun 6am–1pm, 4–5pm & 6.30–7pm) is the most sumptuous and overblown of Ljubljana's Baroque statements. Decorated with fabulous frescoes, this is the best preserved of the city's ecclesiastical buildings. Along the riverside, you can't fail to miss Plečnik's bustling **colonnaded market** (closed Sun). Just beyond the market is the striking Art Noveau **Dragon Bridge**, each corner plinth guarded by a copper dragon – the city's symbol.

The castle

Opposite the market, Študentovska ulica winds up the thickly wooded hillside to the **castle** (summer daily 9am–10pm; winter daily 10am–9pm), originally constructed in the twelfth century, its present appearance dates from the sixteenth century, following an earthquake in 1511. Climb the **clock tower** (daily 9am–9pm summer; 10am–6pm winter; €4 including entrance to the Virtual Museum) for a superlative view of the Old Town below and the magnificent Kamniške Alps to the north. A **funicular railway** (€3 return) provides a more sedate route up and down the castle hill.

Metelkova

The alternative face of Ljubljana, **Metelkova**, situated a five-minute walk east of both the bus and train stations, is the city's grungiest quarter. Concentrated in its graffitied streets

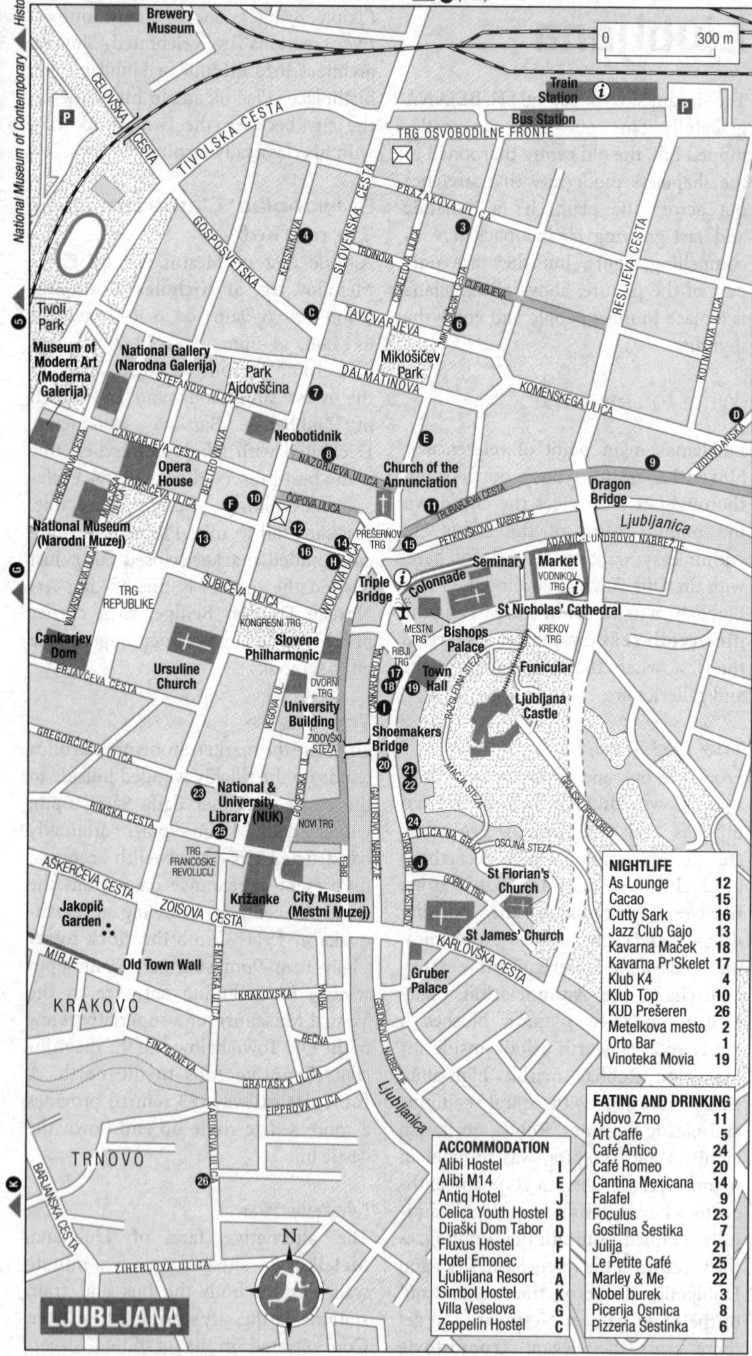
A (5km)
National Museum of Contemporary History
1
B, 2, Metelkova, Ethnographic Museum & Museum of Contemporary Art
5
G
K
0
300 m
Brewery Museum
Train Station
Bus Station
TRG OSVOBODILNE FRONTE
CELOVŠKA CESTA
TIVOLSKA CESTA
GOSPOSVETSKA
SLOVENSKA CESTA
KERSNIKOVA
PRAŽAKOVA ULICA
TRDINOVA
CIGALETOVA ULICA
MIKLOŠIČEVA CESTA
CUFARJEVA
RESLJEVA CESTA
KOTNIKOVA ULICA
TAVČARJEVA
DALMATINOVA
KOMENSKEGA ULICA
VIDOVDANSKA
Tivoli Park
Museum of Modern Art (Moderna Galerija)
National Gallery (Narodna Galerija)
ŠTEFANOVA ULICA
Park Ajdovščina
Miklošičev Park
Neobotidnik
CANKARJEVA CESTA
PRESERNOVA CESTA
BEETHOVNOVA
NAZORJEVA ULICA
Opera House
TOMŠIČEVA ULICA
MUZEJSKA ULICA
ČOPOVA ULICA
Church of the Annunciation
TRUBARJEVA CESTA
Dragon Bridge
Ljubljanica
PETKOVŠKOVO NABREŽJE
ADAMIČ-LUNDROVO NABREŽJE
National Museum (Narodni Muzej)
PREŠERNOV TRG
Seminary
Market
VODNIKOV TRG
Colonnade
Triple Bridge
St Nicholas' Cathedral
ŠUBIČEVA ULICA
WOLFOVA ULICA
TRG REPUBLIKE
VALVASORJEVA ULICA
KONGRESNI TRG
MESTNI TRG
Bishops Palace
KREKOV TRG
Cankarjev Dom
Ursuline Church
Slovene Philharmonic
RIBJI TRG
Town Hall
Funicular
ERJAVČEVA CESTA
DVORNI TRG
CANKARJEVO NA
RAZGLEDNA STEZA
Ljubljana Castle
University Building
VEGOVA UL.
ZIDOVSKI STEZA
Shoemakers Bridge
GREGORČIČEVA ULICA
MAČJA STEZA
GRAJSKI DREVORED
National & University Library (NUK)
GOSPOSKA UL.
NOVI TRG
GALLUSOVO NABREŽJE
RIMSKA CESTA
ULICA NA GRAD
OSOJNA STEZA
STARI TRG
TRG FRANCOSKE REVOLUCIJ
BREG
GORNJI TRG
AŠKERČEVA CESTA
Križanke
City Museum (Mestni Muzej)
St Florian's Church
LEVSTIKOV
Jakopič Garden
ZOISOVA CESTA
St James' Church
KARLOVŠKA CESTA
MIRJE
Old Town Wall
EMONSKA ULICA
Gruber Palace
KRAKOVO
KRAKOVSKA
VRTNA
GRUDNOVO NABREŽJE
REČNA
FINZGARJEVA
GRADAŠKA ULICA
EIPPROVA ULICA
Ljubljanica
KARUNOVA ULICA
TRNOVO
BARJANSKA CESTA
ZIHERLOVA ULICA
N
LJUBLJANA
NIGHTLIFE
As Lounge 12
Cacao 15
Cutty Sark 16
Jazz Club Gajo 13
Kavarna Maček 18
Kavarna Pr'Skelet 17
Klub K4 4
Klub Top 10
KUD Prešeren 26
Metelkova mesto 2
Orto Bar 1
Vinoteka Movia 19
EATING AND DRINKING
Ajdovo Zrno 11
Art Caffe 5
Café Antico 24
Café Romeo 20
Cantina Mexicana 14
Falafel 9
Foculus 23
Gostilna Šestika 7
Julija 21
Le Petite Café 25
Marley & Me 22
Nobel burek 3
Picerija Osmica 8
Pizzeria Šestinka 6
ACCOMMODATION
Alibi Hostel I
Alibi M14 E
Antiq Hotel J
Celica Youth Hostel B
Dijaški Dom Tabor D
Fluxus Hostel F
Hotel Emonec H
Ljubljana Resort A
Simbol Hostel K
Villa Veselova G
Zeppelin Hostel C

are a collection of underground clubs, bars and galleries, alongside a couple of more mainstream cultural attractions. The **Ethnographic Museum**, located in a grand building at Metelkova 2 (Tues–Sun 10am–6pm; €4.50; Ⓦwww.etno-muzej.si) houses an impressive collection of anthropological artefacts. Close by at Metelkova 22, the **Museum of Contemporary Art** (check the website for opening hours; €5; Ⓦwww.mg-lj.si), exhibits modern art from the 1960s onwards.

South of Prešernov trg

On bustling Slovenska cesta in western Ljubljana, the expanse of Kongresni trg slopes away from the early eighteenth-century **Ursuline Church** (daily 6.30–7.30am, 9–11am, 4–7pm), whose pillared Baroque exterior is one of the city's grandest. Vegova Ulica leads south from Kongresni trg towards Trg Francoske revolucije, passing the chequered pink, green and grey brickwork of the **National University Library** (€2), arguably Plečnik's greatest work. The **Illyrian Monument** on Trg Francoske revolucije was erected in 1929 in belated recognition of Napoleon's short-lived attempt to create a fiefdom of the same name centred on Ljubljana. Virtually next door is the seventeenth-century monastery complex of **Križanke**, originally the seat of a thirteenth-century order of Teutonic Knights, now an atmospheric concert venue.

Museums west of Slovenska

The town's leafy cultural quarter boasts several impressive museums and galleries. The grand **National Museum** (daily 10am–6pm, Thurs till 8pm; €5; Ⓦwww.nms.si), at Muzejska ul. 1, displays archeological finds and artefacts relevant to Slovene history. The building also houses the **Natural History Museum** (same hours and ticket), whose star exhibit is the only complete mammoth skeleton found in Europe. **The National Gallery** at Prešernova cesta 24 (Tues–Sun 10am–6pm; €7; Ⓦwww.ng-slo.si) is rich in local medieval Gothic work, although most visitors gravitate towards the halls devoted to the Slovene Impressionists, and in particular the outstanding paintings by Ivan Grohar. Diagonally across from here the **Museum of Modern Art** at Tomšičeva 14 (Tues–Sun 10am–6pm; €5; Ⓦwww.mg-lj.si) showcases more experimental work from the twentieth century onwards.

Tivoli Park

Beyond the galleries lies elegant **Tivoli Park**, an expanse of lawns and tree-lined walkways leading to dense woodland. It's a lovely retreat from the busy city centre. A Baroque villa at the edge of the park contains the **National Museum of Contemporary History** (Tues–Sun 10am–6pm; €3.50; Ⓦwww.muzej-nz.si) with interactive displays and carefully presented artefacts creating an evocative journey through Slovenia's conflict-riddled twentieth-century history.

Arrival and information

Air Jože Pučnik airport is 25km north of the city, and connected by hourly buses (45min; €4.10). Taxis should cost around €35–40; ask for a meter.

Train and bus stations Located side by side on Trg Osvobodilne fronte, a short walk north of the centre.

Tourist office The Slovenian Tourist Information Centre (STIC) is at Krekov trg 10 (June–Sept daily 8am–9pm; Oct–May Mon–Fri 8am–7pm, Sat & Sun 9am–5pm; Ⓣ01/306-4575), with the main Ljubljana Tourist Information Office (TIC) in the Old Town on Adamič-Lundrovo Nabrežje 2, next to the Triple Bridge (June–Sept daily 8am–9pm; Oct–May daily 8am–7pm; Ⓣ01/306-1215, Ⓦwww.visitljubljana.si); there's another branch at the train station (June–Sept daily 8am–10pm; Oct–May Mon–Fri 10am–7pm, Sat 9am–5pm, Sun closed; Ⓣ01/433-9475).

Discount pass The Ljubljana Tourist Card (€35), Urbana, is available from the tourist offices above and entitles you to three days' travel on Ljubljana's buses, free tours and entrance to selected sights.

Walking tours The Ljubljana Tourist Information Office organizes a range of pleasant walking tours (April–Sept; €10; 2hr) around the Old Town.

City transport

City transport Ljubljana's buses are cheap and frequent; buy a yellow Urbana public transport card (€2; €0.80/journey), available at tourist information offices, news kiosks and post offices, and top it up with credit for your journeys.

Bikes Bikes can be rented from various central docking stations including the Central Market and Tivoli Park through Ljubljana's "Bicike" scheme. Register at Ⓦen.bicikelj.si; free up to 1hr, €1/2hr, €2/3hr.

Accommodation

Early reservations are advised in the busy summer months.

Hostels

Alibi Hostel Cankarjevo Nabrežje 27 Ⓣ01/251-1244, Ⓦwww.alibi.si. Vibrant, sprawling hostel in the heart of the old town, with graffiti on the walls and large communal spaces. Dorms €12–19, doubles €30–50.

Alibi M14 Miklošičeva 14 Ⓣ01/232-2770, Ⓦwww.alibi.si. *Alibi*'s friendly sister hostel is small and centrally located with clean double rooms and a dorm. Dorms €15–20, doubles €36–70.

Celica Youth Hostel Metelkova 8 Ⓣ01/230-9700, Ⓦwww.souhostel.com. Brilliantly original hostel in a former military prison in the centre of artistic Metelkova, with bright dorms and two/three-bed "cells", each designed by a different architect or artist. Dorms €23, doubles €30.

Dijaški Dom Tabor Vidovdanska 7 Ⓣ01/234-8840, Ⓔddtaborlj@guest.arnes.si. Busy student hostel, with adequate rooms on offer in July and August only. Dorms €11.

Fluxus Hostel Tomšičeva 4 Ⓣ01/251-5760, Ⓦwww.fluxus-hostel.com. Deservedly popular hostel in a beautiful old building, with a friendly host and a stylish, yet homely feel. Dorms €21.

Simbol Hostel Gerbièeva 46 Ⓣ41/720-825, Ⓦwww.simbol.si. Comfortable and simply decorated option in quiet Trnovo with good-value dorms and a terrace. Dorms €15.

Villa Veselova Veselova 14 Ⓣ01/599-26721, Ⓦwww.v-v.si. Charming hostel in a historic villa bordering peaceful Tivoli Park. Large, bright dorms and one private room. Dorms from €21, double with private bathroom €68.

Zeppelin Hostel Slovenska 47 Ⓣ01/5919-1427, Ⓦwww.zeppelinhostel.com. A sociable and centrally located choice with friendly staff. Dorms from €18.

Hotels

Antiq Hotel Gornji trg 3 Ⓣ01/421-3560, Ⓦwww.antiqhotel.com. Charming Old Town hotel luxuriously decorated with period furniture. Singles from €115, doubles from €145.

Hotel Emonec Wolfova 12 Ⓣ01/200-1520, Ⓦwww.hotel-emonec.com. In the heart of town, with clean, comfortable rooms (singles from €64, doubles from €67) and an apartment sleeping 4 (€105).

Campsite

Ljubljana Resort Dunajska 270 Ⓣ01/568-3913, Ⓦwww.ljubljanaresort.si. Pleasant site 5km north of the centre, which also has a few mobile homes for hire. Bus #6 or #8 from Slovenska cesta. €7.50/person, plus €5.50/tent.

Eating and drinking

The streets of Ljubljana's Old Town are packed with restaurants to suit all budgets. The best choice for bargain snacks are the many kiosks and stands near the stations and scattered elsewhere throughout town, selling *burek*, hot dogs and the local *gorenjska* sausages. There's a lively food market on Vodnikov trg (closed Sun) where you can pick up tasty seasonal produce. On summer evenings the cafés and bars that line the Ljubljanica spill out onto the riverbanks.

Cafés and snacks

Art Caffe Tivoli Mansion. Located next to the International Centre for Graphic Arts in a beautiful mansion in the heart of Tivoli Park; the terrace is a lovely spot to enjoy an ice cream or coffee.

Café Antico Stari trg 27. Charming Old Town hangout with a pleasantly dated ambience serving coffee and wine alongside sandwiches and traditional Slovene dishes.

Falafel Trubarjeva 40. Generous servings of falafel (€3.50), surprisingly enough, as well as other Middle Eastern favourites such as hummus and *baklava*. Eat in or takeaway.

Le Petite Café Trg Francoske revolucije 4. Cosy Parisian-style café, perfect for a lazy brunch or a glass of wine in the evening. 7.30am–1am.

Nobel burek Miklošičeva cesta 30. Offering the greasy Slovene snack of choice – delicious, flaky

burek (€2) – on a 24hr basis, this takeaway near the train station is very popular.
Pizzeria Šestinka Miklošičeva cesta 22. Giant slices of thin-crust pizza to eat in or takeaway from just €1.80. 9am–midnight.

Restaurants

Ajdovo Zrno Trubarjeva 7. Excellent vegetarian canteen in a pleasant courtyard, with a self-service salad bar and daily specials like cannelloni, risotto or curry. Three-course lunch €6. Mon–Fri 10am–7pm.
Café Romeo Stari trg 6. Standing boldly opposite *Julija* (see below), this stylish place servescrêpes, salads and burritos alongside classy cocktails. Mains €6–10. Daily 11am–1am.
Cantina Mexicana Knafljev prehod. On a lively alleyway between Slovenska cesta and Wolfova ulica, this colourful restaurant serves decent Mexican fajitas and tortillas, as well as cocktails. Mains €8–12. Mon, Tues & Sun 9am–1am, Wed–Sat 10am–3am.
Foculus Gregorčičeva 3. Wonderfully decorated pizzeria with an enormous menu of cheap pizza and salad options from €6–9. Daily 11am–midnight.
Gostilna Šestika Slovenska cesta 40 ⓣ01/242-0855. Generous portions of traditional Slovenian cooking: plenty of sausages, schnitzels and fish. Mains from €7. Mon–Fri 10am–11pm, Sat noon–11pm, Sun noon–9pm.
Julija Stari trg 9 ⓣ01/1425-6463. Refined Old Town restaurant with a lovely atmosphere and a Mediterranean menu of delicious salads, pasta and risotto. Mains €8–12. Daily 11am–midnight.
Marley & Me Stari trg 9 ⓣ01/3135-8553. Friendly service and well-prepared Mediterranean classics such as tagliatelle with shrimp (€10.80) make this relaxed restaurant next to *Julija* an appealing option. Daily 9am–11pm.
Picerija Osmica Nazorjeva ulica 8. Comfortable, reliable pizzeria in a central location near Prešernov Trg. Pizzas €5–8. Mon–Fri 10am–11pm, Sat 11am–11pm, Sun noon–5pm.

Nightlife

Despite its diminutive size Ljubljana has an impressively varied and energetic choice of bars and clubs. The informative website Ljubljana In Your Pocket (ⓦwww.inyourpocket.com/slovenia/ljubljana) features nightlife listings.

Bars

Cacao Petkovškovo Nabrezje 3. Stylish riverside café-bar with an extensive cocktail menu.
Cutty Sark Knafljev prehod 1. English pub with draught beers and a daily happy hour from 4–6pm.
Kavarna Maček Krojaška 5. Lively and bohemian riverside café-bar. Its large outdoor terrace is an atmospheric spot for a glass of wine.
Kavarna Pr'Skelet Ključavničarska ulica 5. Cavernous themed bar with swinging skeletons and doors hidden in bookcases. 2-for-1 cocktails make the outdoor terrace the best value on the riverfront.
Vinoteka Movia Mestni trg 1. Traditional Old Town wine bar that's a charming place to sample Slovenia's exceptional wines.

Clubs and venues

As Lounge Čopova 5 (entrance on Knafljev prehod). The cellar beneath this upmarket restaurant transforms into a classy club with DJs and a refined crowd sipping cocktails.
Jazz Club Gajo Beethovnova 8 ⓦwww.jazzclubgajo.com. Suitably atmospheric venue for the genre, with quality live offerings and jam sessions every Mon.
Klub K4 Kersnikova 4 ⓦwww.klubk4.org. Legendary stalwart of Ljubljana's alternative scene, with eclectic music and a gay and lesbian night every Sun.
Klub Top Slovenska cesta (top of the Nama department store) ⓦwww.klubtop.si. Excellent people-watching and Old Town views at this fashionable rooftop club, reached by a glass elevator.
KUD Prešeren Karunova 14 ⓦwww.kud.si. Superb gig venue and cultural centre in Trvono that also hosts regular literary events, workshops and art exhibitions.
Metelkova mesto Metelkova cesta ⓦwww.metelkova.org. Ljubljana's counter-cultural quarter, consisting of a leftfield cluster of clubs, bars and galleries, is located in the former army barracks next to *Hostel Celica*.
Orto Bar Grablovičeva 1. Energetic rock venue and club east of the train station with regular gigs.

Entertainment and events

Ljubljana has a busy cultural calendar of dance, music and theatre at its purpose-built venues, as well as some exciting annual festivals.
Cankarjev Dom Prešernova cesta 10 ⓣ01/241-7100, ⓦwww.cd-cc.si. The city's cultural headquarters, hosting major orchestral and theatrical events, art exhibitions, and folk and jazz concerts.
Druga Godba ⓣ01/4308-260, ⓦwww.drugagodba.si. This annual world music festival

in May features concerts at atmospheric venues throughout the city.
International Summer Festival ⓣ01/241-6026, ⓦwww.ljubljanafestival.si. A programme of orchestral concerts at major venues. July to mid-Sept.
National Opera and Ballet Theatre Župančičeva 1 ⓣ01/241-1740, ⓦwww.opera.si. An impressive nineteenth-century Neoclassical theatre staging ballet and opera.

Shopping

BTC City Šmartinska 152. One of Europe's largest shopping centres; on the northeastern fringes of the capital. Buses #2, #7, #12 and #27.
Flea market Breg. Wonderful antiques market along the western riverbank (Sun 8am–2pm).
Iglu Sport Petkovškovo 31. Stocks camping gear and outdoors equipment; useful for trips to the lakes or mountains.

Directory

Embassies and consulates Australia, Železna cesta 14 ⓣ01/234-8675; Canada, Trg Republike 3 ⓣ01/252-4444; Ireland, Palaca Kapitelj, Poljanski nasip 6 ⓣ01/300-8970; UK, Trg Republike 3 ⓣ01/200-3910; US, Prešernova 31 ⓣ01/200-5500.
Exchange At the train station and at post offices.
Hospital Zaloška Cesta 2 ⓣ01/522-5050, ⓦwww.kclj.si.
Internet Slovenian Tourist Information Centre, Krekov trg 10 (June–Sept daily 8am–9pm; Oct–May Mon–Fri 8am–7pm, Sat & Sun 9am–5pm). Wi-fi is widely available.
Left luggage At the train station (€2–8/day depending on locker size).
Pharmacy Prisojne 7 ⓣ01/230-6230 (24hr).
Post office Slovenska cesta 32 and Pražakova ulica 3.

Moving on

Train Divača (hourly; 1hr 30min); Koper (3 daily; 2hr 30min); Maribor (hourly; 1hr 45min–2hr 30min); Postojna (hourly; 1hr); Ptuj (2 daily; 2hr 30min).
Bus Bled (hourly; 1hr 20min); Bohinj (hourly; 2hr); Bovec (4 daily; 3hr 30min–4hr 15min); Divača (7 daily; 1hr 30min); Kobarid (3 daily; 3–5hr); Koper (11 daily; 2hr); Maribor (3 daily; 2hr 30min–3hr); Piran (6 daily; 2hr 45min); Portorož (6 daily; 2hr 30min); Postojna (hourly; 1hr).

Southwest Slovenia

Not to be missed while you're in Ljubljana is a visit to either the **Postojna** or **Škocjan caves** – both spectacular, and both easily manageable either as a day-trip from the capital or en route south to Slovene Istria, to Croatia or to Italy. A trip easily combined with the caves is to **Predjama Castle**, near Postojna, a sombre fortress craftily embedded into the karst landscape. On the small stretch of Adriatic coastline are a number of charismatic towns, heavily influenced by a legacy of Venetian rule. Of these, **Piran** is by far the most rewarding, its fishing-village charm and gorgeous architecture contrasting starkly with the brash modernity of neighbouring **Portorož**.

POSTOJNA

Hourly trains run the 65km route from Ljubljana to **POSTOJNA**, but as the walk to the caves is shorter from the bus stop, most people opt for this mode of transport. Once in the town, signs direct you to the **caves** (May, June & Sept daily 9am–5pm; July–Aug daily 9am–6pm; April & Oct daily 10am–4pm; Jan, Feb, March, Nov & Dec daily 10am–3pm; tours every 1–2hr; 90min; €22). Inside, a train whizzes you through spectacular preliminary systems before the guided 1.5km walking tour starts. The vast and fantastic jungles of rock formations are breathtaking and there's also an opportunity to catch a rare glimpse of the cave-dwelling "human fish", a blind amphibian that can live for up to 100 years, before the climactic finale of the 40m high "concert hall". Bring a jacket and appropriate footwear; the air inside the caves is decidedly chilly. *Hostel Proteus* (Trzaska Cesta 36, ⓣ05/726-5291) has basic dorms (€14) in Postojna itself, while campers can stay at the large

Pivka Jama campsite (€9.90), 3.5km from the town in a peaceful spruce forest on the road towards Predjama Castle.

PREDJAMA CASTLE

9km northwest of the caves, but not served by public transport, is the precariously sited **Predjama Castle** (Jan–March, Nov & Dec daily 10am–6pm; April & Oct 10am–5pm; May, June & Sept 9am–6pm; July & Aug 9am–7pm; €9). Built into and around an elevated cave entrance in the midst of the dramatic karst landscape, this sixteenth-century fortress is a striking sight and affords excellent views of the surrounding countryside. Its damp, sparsely filled interior is less rewarding, though you can see weaponry and artefacts dating back to its heyday as the castle of the legendary knight Erazem Lueger. The easiest way to get here is to rent bikes from the *Hotel Sport* at Kolodvorska 1 in Postojna (€15/day).

ŠKOCJAN CAVES

Much less visited (but arguably more enchanting) than Postojna, the **Škocjan Caves** are a stunning system of echoing chambers, secret passages and collapsed valleys carved out by the Reka River, which begins its journey some 50km south near the Croatian border. Daily **tours** (June–Sept hourly, 10am–5pm; Oct–May 2–3 daily, 10am–3pm; €15; ⓦwww.park-skocjanske-jame.si) take you through several stalactite-infested chambers and halls, before you reach the breathtaking **Murmuring Cave**, reputedly the world's largest subterranean canyon. To get here follow the 3km footpath from Divača train station towards the caves (see map at the station). If you decide to stay, simple rooms are available in *Gostilna Malovec* (Kraška cesta 30a; ⓣ05/763-1225; singles €32, doubles €48) in Divača.

PORTOROŽ

Easily reached by bus from the train terminus in Koper, **PORTOROŽ** ("Port of Roses") sprawls at the beginning of a long, tapering peninsula that projects like a lizard's tail north into the Adriatic. Popular since the end of the nineteenth century for its mild climate and the health-inducing properties of its salty mud baths, today the resort's big draw is high-rise hotels, glitzy casinos and buzzing nightlife. The main "beach" is just a continuation of the concrete promenade and there's not a great deal of culture here, but the town's modernity and vibrant bars and clubs are unrivalled on this stretch of the coast.

The **tourist office** (daily: July & Aug 9am–9pm; Sept–June Mon–Sat 9am–5pm, Sun 10am–2pm; ⓣ05/674-2220, ⓦwww.portoroz.si) is on the main coastal strip, Obala Maršala Tita, just down from the bus terminal. The *Panorama Residence* is a pleasant **hostel** located halfway between Portorož and Piran with views of the Istrian coast (Šentjane 25; ⓣ04/674-7289, ⓦsi.hostel-portoroz.eu; dorms €23, doubles €50).

Restaurants in Portorož can be pricey, but the bright *Pizzeria Figarola* (Obala Maršala Tita 18) serves decent pizza from €5. Stylish *Cacao* and bamboo-clad *Alayah*, both on the main beachfront, are relaxed spots for a sunset drink; try the swanky *Club Paprika* on the same strip for cocktails and late-night dancing.

PIRAN

PIRAN, at the tip of the peninsula, 4km from Portorož, couldn't be more different. Its web of arched alleys, tightly packed ranks of historic houses and little Italianate squares is delightful. The centre, 200m around the harbour from the bus station, is **Tartinijev trg**, named after the eighteenth-century Italian violinist and composer Giuseppe Tartini, who was born in a cream villa on the square (irregular hours; ask at tourist office) and is commemorated by a weather-beaten bronze statue in the centre. With its striking oval shape, it's one of the loveliest squares on this coast, fringed by Venetian palaces and an imposing Austrian town hall. From the square's eastern edge, follow Rozmanova ulica all the way up to the commanding Baroque **Church of St George** (10am–4pm; closed Tues; €1), crowning a spectacular spot on the far side of Piran's peninsula.

Arrival and information

Bus station On Cankarjevo nabrežje, a 5min seafront walk from the main square, Tartinijev trg.
Tourist office Tartinijev trg 2 ⓣ05/673-4440. July & Aug daily 9am–1.30pm & 3–9pm; Sept–June Mon–Fri 9am–5pm & Sat 10am–2pm.

Accommodation

Private rooms can be booked through Maona, at Cankarjevo nabrežje 7, between the bus station and the square (ⓣ05/674-0363, ⓦwww.maona.si; €20–50).
Alibi Hostels Bonifacijeva 11 & 14, & Trubarjeva 60 ⓣ03/136-3666, ⓦwww.alibi.si. Three historic houses with clean rooms imaginatively decorated with a theme from a different region, town or attraction in Slovenia. No kitchens. Dorms from €15, double rooms from €40.
Fiesa Camping Fiesa 57b ⓣ05/674-6230. Decent site 1km past the church. €11.50/person.
Hostel Val Gregorčičeva 38a ⓣ05/673-2555, ⓦwww.hostel-val.com. Friendly and well run, with a homely guesthouse feel and a delightful restaurant. €22–25/person for bed and breskfast.

Eating and drinking

Though it's an atmospheric place for drinking and dining, things quieten down fairly early in Piran. For a proper night out head over to Portorož, where the beachside bars and clubs stay open until dawn.
Café Teater St Jenkova 1. Sophisticated cocktail bar overlooking the harbour.
Da Noi Prešernovo nabrežje. Popular, cellar-like bar on the seafront; open until 3am in the summer.
Fontana Trg 1 Maja. A local favourite on account of its excellent service and good choice of reasonably priced fresh fish; a filling plate of sardines is €6.
Pizzeria Petica Zupančičeva 6. Cosy pizzeria on a quiet alley with decent thin-crust pizzas €5–7.
Riva Gregorčičeva 35. Romantic seafront restaurant, serving classy meat and fish dishes. Mains €8–16.

Moving on

Bus Ljubljana (7 daily; 2hr 45min); Portorož/Koper (every 15–20min; 10/45min); Trieste (Mon–Sat 1 daily; 1hr 30min).

Northwest Slovenia

Within easy reach of Ljubljana are the stunning mountain lakes of **Bled** and **Bohinj**. The magnificent **Soča Valley**, on the western side of the Julian Alps, is much less touristed, and small towns such as **Kobarid** and **Bovec** are excellent bases for hiking and adventure sports.

BLED

The lake resort of **BLED** has all the right ingredients for a memorable visit – a placid mirror lake with a romantic island, a medieval cliff-top castle and a backdrop of snowcapped mountains. In summer, the lake is the setting for a whole host of watersports – including major rowing contests – and in winter the surface becomes a giant fairytale skating rink. Perhaps the most visited place outside of the capital, Bled manages to retain a magical calm despite the hordes of tourists.

What to see and do

A constant relay of stretched gondolas leaves from below the *Park Hotel*, the *Pension Mlino*, and the bathing resort below the castle, ferrying tourists back and forth to Bled's picturesque **island** (€12 return). With an early start (and by renting your own rowing boat from the Castle Boat House (€15/hr) or *Pension Pletna* (€10/hr); you can beat them to it. Crowning the island, the Baroque **Church of Sv Marika Božja** (€3) is the last in a line of churches on a spot that's

GETTING TO THE LAKES

Buses are the easiest way to get to the lakes (hourly from Ljubljana; 1hr 20min to Bled, 2hr to Bohinj). Direct **train** access to the region is via the main northbound line from Ljubljana (hourly; 40min–1hr; €4.80), which calls at Bled-Lesce, from where regular buses run to the lake. Trains on the Jesenice–Nova Gorica branch call at both Bled Jezero (5min walk from the northwest corner of Bled) and Bohinjska Bistrica (8 daily; 2hr–2hr 20min; €6–7). An old-fashioned steam train also sporadically plies the same route, providing a wonderful scenic option as it chugs steadily through the mountains towards Italy (see ⓦwww.slo-zeleznice.si; €38 return).

long held religious significance: under the present building lie remains of a pre-Roman temple.

From the north shore a couple of paths wind steeply uphill to **Bled Castle** (April–Oct daily 8am–8pm; Nov–March 8am–6pm; €8), originally an eleventh-century fortification whose present appearance dates from the seventeenth; the museum contains a well-presented collection of local artefacts relating to the settlement of Bled, and the lovely courtyard has magnificent views across the lake and towards the Alps. In the shade of the castle rock lies a clean, well-equipped **bathing area** with changing rooms (June to late Sept). **Bikes** can be rented cheaply from most guest-houses and tour agencies, providing an excellent way to see the surrounding area; the circumference of the lake can be cycled in thirty minutes.

Vintgar Gorge

The main attraction in the outlying hills is the **Vintgar Gorge** (April 20 to Oct daily 8am–7pm; €4), 4km north of town, an impressive defile accessed via a series of wooden walkways and bridges suspended from the rock face. To get here, take the morning tourist bus (10am; June–Oct) to the village of Zasip, climb to the hilltop chapel of **Sv Katarina** and pick up a path through the forest to the gorge entrance.

Arrival and information

Train Trains from Ljubljana stop at Bled-Lesce, 4km southeast of Bled itself and connected to the town by regular buses. Trains from Soča Valley arrive in Bled Jezero, a 5min walk from the western shore.

Bus station A 5min walk northeast of the lake on Grajska cesta.

Tourist office Cesta svobode 10, opposite the *Park Hotel* (Jan–March Mon–Sat 8am–6pm, Sun 8am–1pm; April–June Mon–Sat 8am–7pm, Sun 11am–7pm; Sept & Oct Mon–Sat 8am–7pm, Sun 11am–5pm; Nov & Dec Mon–Fri 8am–6pm, Sun 8am–1pm) ⓣ04/574-1122, ⓦwww.bled.si.

Accommodation

Private rooms are available through Kompas in the shopping centre at Ljubljanska 4 (ⓣ04/572-7501, ⓦwww.kompas-bled.si).

Bled campsite Kidričeva 10 ⓣ04/575-2000, ⓦwww.camping-bled.com. Beautifully located amid the pines at the western end of the lake, this family-friendly campsite has first-rate facilities. Wooden huts with double beds and hot tubs are on offer for glampers. €12.50/person camping; €50/hut.

Pension Bledec Grajska 17 ⓣ04/574-5250, ⓦwww.youth-hostel-bledec.si. Friendly hostel with comfortable dorms and double rooms, decked out with traditional furniture. Free bike rental and internet. Dorms €21, rooms €52.

Travellers Haven Riklijeva cesta 1 ⓣ05/904-4226, ⓦwww.travellershaven .com. The best hostel in Bled, with tastefully furnished dorms, a homely kitchen and common area, and free bike rental and laundry facilities. Dorms €19, doubles €48.

Eating and drinking

The best places for eating are in the hillside area between Bled's bus station and castle, though several *pensions* on the lake's perimeter offer decent food too. Bizarrely, the shopping centre on Ljubljanska is home to a few popular bars.

Chilli Cesta svobode 9. Popular bar and restaurant with a pleasant terrace and an appropriately spicy menu of Mexican and Mediterranean dishes (mains from €8).

Gostilna Pri Planincu Grajska 8. Historic pub and restaurant serving up hearty Slovene home cooking since 1903, plus plenty of pizzas and pasta. Mains €10.

Smon Grajska 3. The best place to try the ubiquitous Bled *Kremna Rezina* (cream cake; €2.50), this traditional café specializes in deliciously indulgent cakes and pastries.

LAKE BOHINJ

From Bled hourly buses make the 25km trip through the verdant, mist-laden Sava Bohinjka Valley to **Lake Bohinj**. In appearance and character Lake Bohinj is utterly different from Bled: the lake crooks a narrow finger under the wild mountains, evergreen woods slope gently down to the water, and in the relative absence of visitors, a lazy stillness hangs over all.

Ribčev Laz

RIBČEV LAZ (referred to as Jezero on bus timetables), at the eastern end of the lake, is where most facilities are based. **Walking trails** lead round both sides of the lake (the 12km circumference can be walked in 3 hours), or north onto the eastern shoulders of the Triglav range. One route leads north from the enchanting village of Stara Fužina into the Voje valley, passing through the dramatic **Mostnica Gorge**, a local beauty spot.

> **COUNTRY LIVING**
>
> Staying on one of the country's many excellent **tourist farms** is a memorable way to experience Slovene cooking and customs first-hand. Usually costing little more than an average dorm bed, you are provided with a comfortable room, generous hospitality, home-cooked food and top-quality Slovene wine. There's a comprehensive list of rural accommodation at Ⓦwww.slovenia.info, but the easily accessed **Mulej Tourist Farm** (Selo Ⓣ04/574-4617, Ⓦwww.mulej-bled.com), just 700m from Lake Bled, is one of the best, with superb food and spotless, comfortable rooms. Bed and breakfast €30 per person.

Ukanc, Mount Vogel and the Valley of the Seven Lakes

About 5km from Ribčev Laz at the western end of the lake is the hamlet of **UKANC** (sometimes referred to as Zlatorog), where a **cable car** (daily 8am–6pm, every 30min; closed Nov; €13 return) whizzes you vertiginously up to the summit of **Mount Vogel** (1540m) in no time – if the Alps look dramatic from the lakeside, from Vogel's summit they're breathtaking. Ukanc is also the starting point for a one-hour walk north to the photogenic **Savica Waterfalls** (Feb–Oct 8am–8pm; €2.50). From here, the serious hiking can commence, either as a day-trip to the **Valley of the Seven Lakes** – an area strewn with eerie boulders and hardy firs – or as an expedition to scale Mount Triglav itself.

Arrival and information

Train Trains on the Jesenice–Nova Gorica line call at Bohinjska Bistrica (4km from Bohinj Lake, connected by two morning shuttle buses).

Bus Buses from Ljubljana and Bled stop outside the tourist office in Ribčev Laz, terminating in Ukanc on the southwestern corner of the lake.

Tourist information Ribčev Laz 48 Ⓣ04/574-6010, Ⓦwww.bohinj-info.com. The excellent centre is 50m from the lake, next to the Mercator supermarket. July & Aug daily 8am–8pm; Sept–June Mon–Sat 8am–6pm, Sun 9am–3pm.

Accommodation

The tourist office offers a plentiful choice of private rooms and apartments (Ⓦwww.bohinj-info.com) around Ribčev Laz and in the idyllic villages of Stara Fužina and Studor, 1km and 3km north respectively.

Hostel Pod Voglom Ribčev Laz Ⓣ04/572-3461 Ⓦwww.hostel-podvoglom.com. Part of the PAC adventure sports complex, this basic hostel in a prime location on the lakeshore organizes winter and summer activities. Dorms €18, room with private bathroom €25/person.

Studor 13 Hostel Studor 13, Srednja Vas ⓣ03/146-6707, ⓦwww.studor13.si. Exceptional hostel in a tastefully renovated historic house 3km from the lake. A great base for hiking and horseriding. Free pick-up from Bohinj. €25/person.

Zlatorog Ukanc 2 ⓣ04/572-3482. Pleasant campsite on the western tip of the lake; conveniently located for trips up the mountains. May–Sept; €9/person.

Eating and drinking

Gostišče Erlah Ukanc 67. Good-value Slovene dishes such as fresh trout feature on the menu at this friendly inn at the western end of the lake. Mains from €7.

Pizzerija Ema Sredna Vas. The fabulous mountain views from the terrace and *Ema's* extensive menu of affordable, tasty pizzas and pasta dishes more than justifies the 4km hike from the lake to the pretty village of Sredna Vas.

THE SOČA VALLEY

On the other, less touristy side of the mountains from Bohinj, the brilliantly turquoise **River Soča** streaks through the western spur of the Julian Alps, running parallel with the Italian border. During World War I, the Soča marked the front line between the Italian and Austro-Hungarian armies; now memorial chapels and abandoned fortifications nestle incongruously amid awesome Alpine scenery. The valley is a major centre for activity-based tourism, with the river providing ideal **rafting** and **kayaking** conditions throughout the spring and summer, and the mountain slopes perfect for **skiing** and **snowboarding** in winter. The main tourist centres are **Kobarid** and **Bovec**, both small towns boasting a range of walking possibilities. The GZS 1:50,000 Zgornje Posočje **map** covers trails in the region.

Kobarid

It was at the little Alpine town of **KOBARID** that German and Austrian troops finally broke through Italian lines in 1917, almost knocking Italy out of World War I in the process. The **Kobarid Museum**, Gregorčičeva 10 (April–Sept Mon–Fri 9am–6pm, Sat & Sun 9am–7pm; Oct–March Mon–Fri 10am–5pm, Sat & Sun 9am–6pm; €5), presents a thoughtful account of the 29 months of fighting in the region through a collection of photographs, maps and mementoes. It's also the starting point for the superb **Kobarid Historical Trail** (3–5hr), a steep 5km loop where remote woodland paths are punctuated by forgotten wartime landmarks. From the town's main square you climb up to a striking three-tiered **Italian War Memorial**, opened by Benito Mussolini in 1938, before hiking further into the hills to see surviving military fortifications. At the trail's farthest point from town bubbles the **Kozjak waterfall** (40min walk), less impressive for its height than for the cavern-like space that it has carved out of the surrounding rock. Maps of the trail are available from the museum and the tourist office on Trg Svobode 16 (Mon–Fri 9am–1pm & 2–7pm, Sat & Sun 9am–1pm & 4–7pm; closed on Sun in winter ⓣ05/380-0490).

The tourist office can also arrange **private rooms** (from €20), while *Positive Sport Hostel* next door at Trg Svobode 15 (ⓣ04/0654-475) offers beds in clean, bright dorms for €16. Facing each other on opposite banks of the River Soča, 500m out of town near the

GETTING TO THE SOČA VALLEY

Four daily buses (4hr) travel from Ljubljana. Approaching the Soča Valley from the Bled–Bohinj area involves catching one of eleven daily trains from Bohinjska Bistrica to **Most na Soči** (40min; €2.40), where three buses daily run onwards up the valley. Getting here from the coast is an arduous task: from Koper, several bus changes are required to reach Kobarid, and expect a journey of 5–7hr.

end of the trail are two well-equipped **campsites**: the *Koren* (ⓣ05/389-1311, ⓦwww.kamp-koren.si; €11); and the *Lazar* (ⓣ05/388-5333, ⓦwww.lazar-sp.si; €11). Kobarid's reputation as a gastronomic centre was earned by the chefs at *Kotlar* (Trg svobode 11 ⓣ05/389-1110) and *Topli Val* (Trg svbode 1 ⓣ05/389-9300) – regarded as among Slovenia's best restaurants – but if you're on a tight budget, try the pizzas at *Fedrig* on Volaričeva 11 instead.

Moving on

Bus Bovec (3 daily; 35min); Ljubljana (3 daily; 3hr 30min); Nova Gorica (3 daily; 1hr 30min).

Bovec

25km up the valley from Kobarid, the village of **BOVEC** straggles between imperious mountain ridges. Thanks to its status as a winter ski resort, it has a greater range of accommodation options and sporting agencies than Kobarid, and as a result, a more vibrant atmosphere. The quickest route into the mountains from here is provided by the **gondola** that departs on the hour 1km south of the village (June–Sept 8am–4pm; €13 return), which ascends to the pasture-cloaked Mount Kanin over to the west.

The **tourist office** is around the corner from the bus stop at Trg Golobarskih žrtev 8 (Mon–Sat 9am–5pm, Sun 9am–2pm; ⓣ05/389-6444, ⓦwww.bovec.si), and can help with renting private **rooms**. Homely *Casa Rosa* (ⓣ05/187-9461, ⓦwww.casarosaslovenia.com) in the nearby village of Zaga, is a charming self-catering option for €25 per person. Europe's first sustainable outdoor **hostel**, *Eco Camp Canyon* (12km from Bovec, free pick-up; ⓣ04/138-3662, ⓦwww.adrenaline-check.com; camping €9 and dorms €15) offers camping, dorms and hammocks right on the river.

The best place to **eat** around the main square is *Stari Kovai*, at Rupa 3, with a long list of inexpensive pizzas and schnitzels. *Crna ovca* (The Black Sheep), at Ledina 8, is Bovec's most atmospheric bar, with dramatic valley views from the terrace.

ADVENTURE SPORTS

In Kobarid the main **adventure sports** company is X-Point (ⓣ05/388-5308, ⓦwww.xpoint.si), at Trg svobode 6; they organize rafting, paragliding and kayaking, among other activities guaranteed to raise your heart rate. Popular outfits in Bovec include Soča Rafting (ⓣ05/389-6200, ⓦwww.socarafting.si), opposite the tourist office at Trg Golobarskih žrtev 14, and Avantura (ⓣ41/718-317, ⓦwww.avantura.org), further down the same street, who specialize in tandem paragliding (€110).

Eastern Slovenia

The lush landscapes to the east of Ljubljana – where many of the country's most reputable vineyards are concentrated – are generally less explored by travellers. But as host to Slovenia's second city, **Maribor**, and oldest settlement, **Ptuj**, which lie on the main routes to Austria and Hungary respectively, the region can reward the passing visitor with its rich historical heritage, traditional culture and fine wine.

MARIBOR

Located 122km northeast of Ljubljana, **MARIBOR** is perched snugly on the Drava River between hillside vineyards and the Pohorje mountain range. Though beset by war and occupation, the old town's beautiful architecture preserves myriad historical and cultural influences, and the nightlife is unrivalled outside of Ljubljana.

What to see and do

Maribor's main attractions are condensed in a pedestrianized centre. Looming over Trg Svobode, the imposing, **St Mary's Franciscan church** (daily 6am–noon & 3–7.45pm) catches the eye first. Opposite the church, Maribor Castle houses the **regional museum** (Tues–Sat 9am–4pm, Sun 9am–2pm; €3; ⓣ02/228-3551). Nearby delve into the labyrinth of underground catacombs that make up the **Vinag Wine Cellar** (tours Mon–Fri at noon, 1pm & 2pm; 30min; €3.50; ⓣ02/220-8141), stopping to sample some of the acclaimed vintages. On the western fringe of the pedestrianized zone sits the photogenic **Slomškov trg**, a serene, leafy opening surrounded by a few landmarks, including the university building and the elegant **Slovene National Theatre**. Opposite the university, and mimicking its distinct yellow colour, is the sixteenth-century Gothic **Cathedral Church** (daily 10am–6pm; free), with a bell tower that offers fantastic views to the edges of the city and beyond. South of Slomškov, another charming square, **Glavni trg**, epitomizes the hopscotch architectural styles of the city. Its centrepiece is the Baroque **Plague Memorial**, erected after the deadly disease wiped out a third of the town's population in the seventeenth century.

Lent

Between Glavni and the Drava River, the streets become narrow and uneven, as you enter the oldest part of town, **Lent**, which hosts a myriad of open-air events during the Lent festival in late June and early July each year, comprising two entertaining weeks of street theatre, dance performances and jazz, rock and classical concerts. It is here that the world's oldest productive vine, a protected national monument, grows majestically outside the **Old Vine House** (May–Oct daily 10am–8pm; Nov–April daily 10am–6pm free). Inside, a small exhibition complements the range of top-quality, reasonably priced vintages from the area.

Pohorje

Just a short bus ride (#6; €1.10) or cycle southwest from the centre is the sprawling **Pohorje** mountain range. Take the hourly cable car (8am–8pm; €8 return) up the slope, where – depending on the season – you can hike, mountain bike, horseride and ski, or simply sit and admire the glorious views of Maribor and the countryside surrounding it. The website ⓦwww.pohorje.org has detailed information on activities in the area.

Arrival and information

Train station Partizanska cesta 50. Turn left out of the exit and the road curves directly into the town centre.

Bus station Mlinska ulica 1 (just off Partizanska cesta).

Tourist office Partizanska cesta 6a, opposite the Franciscan church (daily 9am–6/7pm; ⓣ02/234-6611, ⓦmaribor-pohorje.si). They rent out bikes for €5/day and provide helpful cycling maps to explore the vineyards.

Accommodation

The tourist office can book private accommodation (from €20/person).

Lollipop Hostel Maistrova ulica 17 ⓣ04/024-3160, ⓔlollipophostel@yahoo.com. Small, clean hostel 5min from the park with kitchen facilities and a homely common room. Free city tours given by the English owner. Dorms €20.

Uni Hotel Volkmerjev prehod 7 ⓣ02/250-6700, ⓦwww.termemb.si. Somewhat characterless but comfortable hostel right in the centre. All rooms have cable TV. Singles €32, doubles €54.

Eating and drinking

The best bars are located in Lent, on the banks of the Drava.

Ancora Jurčičeva 7. Generous portions of decent and affordable Mediterranean dishes at this atmospheric bar-restaurant. Mains €4–8.

KGB Vojašniški trg 5 ⓦklub-kgb.si. The most popular joint in Maribor, this lively underground cellar bar attracts all ages, with an eclectic programme of regular live music.

Satchmo Jazz Club Strossmayerjeva ulica 6. Hosts high-calibre jazz and rock sessions; see Ⓦwww.jazz-klub.si for programme.

Takos Mesarski prehod 3. Tucked away on a narrow cobbled alley, this cheap-and-cheerful Mexican restaurant also serves cocktails and turns into a club on Fri & Sat.

Toto Café Slomškov Trg 13. Popular, brightly painted courtyard café-bar with a studenty feel near the university.

Moving on

Train Ljubljana (10 daily; 2hr); Ptuj (8 daily; 1hr); Vienna (2 daily; 3hr 40min).

Bus Ljubljana (4 daily; 3hr); Ptuj (every 30min; 40min).

PTUJ

PTUJ is arguably Slovenia's most attractive town, rising up from the Drava valley in a flutter of red roofs, and topped by a charming castle. The streets themselves are the main attraction, with scaled-down mansions standing shoulder to shoulder on scaled-down boulevards and medieval fantasies crumbling next to Baroque extravagances.

What to see and do

Ptuj's main street is **Prešernova ulica**, an atmopspheric thoroughfare which snakes along the base of the castle-topped hill. At its eastern end is **Slovenski Trg**, home to a fine-looking sixteenth-century bell tower and the **Church of St George**, dating from the twelfth century, with an interior distinguished by some spectacular frescoes. From here Prešernova leads to the **Archeological Museum** (mid-April to Nov daily 10am–5pm; €4), housed in what was a Dominican monastery until the eighteenth century. Its likeably dishevelled cloisters now display medieval and modern stone carvings. At either end of Prešernova, cobbled paths wind up to the **castle** – featuring an agglomeration of architectural styles from the fourteenth to the eighteenth centuries – which now houses the carefully presented collections of the Ptuj Regional Museum (mid-Oct to April daily 9am–5pm; May to mid-Oct daily 9am–6pm; mid-Oct to April daily 9am–5pm).

Arrival and information

Train and bus stations Both on Osojnikova cesta, 5min walk northeast of town.

Tourist office Slovenski trg 5 (daily 9am–6/8pm; Ⓣ02/779-6011, Ⓦwww.ptuj.info), with free internet. The Centre for Free Time Activities (Mon–Thurs 9am–6pm, Fri 9am–11pm, Sat 7–11pm; Ⓣ2/780-5540, Ⓦwww.cid.si), also has free internet.

Accommodation

Apartments Silak Dravska ulica 13 Ⓣ02/787-7447, Ⓦwww.rooms-silak.com. Comfortable en-suite rooms in an attractive historic house near the river, all with TV. Singles €31, doubles €44.

Kurent Osojnikova cesta 9 Ⓣ02/771-0814, Ⓔyhptuj@csod.si. Large youth hostel offering functional twin and dorm rooms with private bathrooms (€22).

Terme Ptuj Pot v Toplice Ⓣ02/749-4100, Ⓦwww.sava-hotels-resorts.com. Across the river, 2km west of town, guests at this pleasant resort-style campsite can also use the Thermal Park pools and saunas. Camping €17/person; four-person cottages €110.

Eating and drinking

Café Evropa Mestni trg. This relaxed café transforms into an energetic, buzzing bar after dark.

Kitajski Vrt Dravska ulica. Ornately decorated Chinese restaurant serving up giant sizzling plates of noodles, meat and vegetarian dishes. Mains €5–7.

Musikafe Vrazov Trg. Excellent live music venue and café-bar with a carefully curated programme of events, an inviting stone terrace and stylish interior.

Ribič Dravska ulica 9 Ⓣ02/749-0635. The exceptional seafood at this riverside restaurant with a lovely terrace overlooking the Drava justifies the slightly higher price tag. From €10.

Moving on

Train Budapest (2 daily; 6hr 15min); Ljubljana (2 daily; 2hr 25min); Maribor (8 daily; 1hr).

Bus Maribor (every 1hr; 45min).

Spain

HIGHLIGHTS

MUSEO GUGGENHEIM, BILBAO: the building is as big an attraction as the art it houses

SAN SEBASTIÁN: stunning beaches and mouth-watering cuisine - the perfect pit stop

SANTIAGO DE COMPOSTELA: the end-point of Europe's most famous pilgrim trail

THE PYRENEES: some of Spain's best hiking and biking

BARCELONA: perhaps Europe's most alluring city

MADRID: world-class museums and legendary nightlife

ALHAMBRA, GRANADA: evocative Moorish palace atop this charming Andalucian city

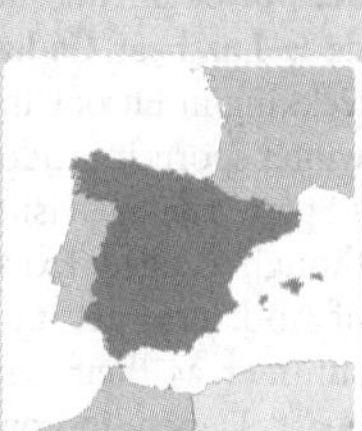

ROUGH COSTS

DAILY BUDGET Basic €55 /occasional treat €75

DRINK €1.50–2.50 per *caña* (small beer)

FOOD Three-course *menú del día* €10–12

HOSTEL/BUDGET HOTEL €16–28 /€25–50

TRAVEL Madrid–Barcelona: bus €42–65; train €65–120

FACT FILE

POPULATION 45.5 million

AREA 504,030 sq km

LANGUAGES Spanish, Catalan, Basque, Galician, Aranese

CURRENCY Euro (€)

CAPITAL Madrid

INTERNATIONAL PHONE CODE ⓣ34

Introduction

Spain has so much more to offer than the tourist brochure cliché of bullfights, crowded beaches, paella and flamenco. You don't have to travel for very long, or very far, to discover ancient castles, world-class museums, idyllic whitewashed villages, isolated coves and beaches, and a wealth of art and architecture. The separate kingdoms that made up the original Spanish nation are still very obvious today, encompassing a medley of languages, cultures and traditions.

Of the regions, **Catalunya** in the northeast is vibrant and go-ahead; **Galicia** in the northwest a verdant rural idyll; the **Basque country** around Bilbao a remarkable contrast between post-industrial depression and unbridled optimism; and **Castilla y León** and the **south** still, somehow, quintessentially "Spanish". There are definite highlights: the three great cities of **Barcelona**, **Madrid** and **Seville**; the Moorish monuments of **Andalucía** in the south and the Christian ones of **Castilla y León** in the west; beachlife on the islands of **Ibiza**, **Costa del Sol** or on the more deserted Costa de la Luz near **Cádiz**; some of the best trekking in Europe in the **Pyrenees,** and winter sports in Andorra.

Spain can be visited all year round, though Madrid, Extremadura and parts of Andalucía get unbearably hot in the summer as their residents flee for the coast. Depending on what you're after, you can party at numerous quirky local festivals, engage in all manner of outdoor pursuits, sample the seasonal and regional specialities, take in the splendid and varied architecture that traces Spain's multicultural heritage and enjoy some of Europe's best nightlife.

CHRONOLOGY

1000 BC Phoenicians colonize the Iberian Peninsula, establishing the cities of Cádiz and Málaga.
400s BC Carthaginians exert power over large parts of present-day Spain.
200s BC The Romans capture "Hispania" during the Punic Wars and rule it for over 500 years.
711 AD The Islamic Moors conquer Spain, and Moorish culture flourishes.
1085 With the capture of Toledo, Spanish Christians begin to diminish the influence of the Moors in Spain.
1480 The Spanish Inquisition persecutes non-Christians, leading to mass conversions and expulsion of Jews.
1492 Christopher Columbus discovers lands in the Americas for the Spanish Crown.
1605 The world's first "novel", *Don Quixote* by Cervantes, is published.
1714 The British capture Gibraltar.
1800s Spanish colonies in the Americas gain their independence.
1931 Surrealist artist Salvador Dalí completes his most famous painting, *The Persistence of Memory*.
1936 The Spanish Civil War breaks out as Nationalist forces led by General Franco defeat Republican forces.
1939 Spain remains neutral at the outbreak of World War II.
1975 Franco dies and is replaced by King Juan Carlos.
1977 First free elections are held in almost four decades.
2004 Bombs detonated on busy Madrid trains leave 191 people dead. An Islamic group takes responsibility.
2007 The government's struggle with Basque separatists, ETA, continues as the group end their ceasefire.
2008 Spain's construction boom brought to an end by international financial meltdown and unemployment soars from 6 percent to 20 percent. Spain wins the Euro Cup Final.
2010 Spain wins the FIFA World Cup.

ARRIVAL

The quickest – and cheapest – way to get to Spain is on one of the budget-airline

flights (try Barcelona-based Vueling as well as easyJet and Ryanair). All the major airlines serve Barcelona and Madrid. Other major airports include Alicante, Málaga, Valencia, Seville, the Balearic Islands and Gibraltar. **Trains** from France serve San Sebastían (from Biarritz), Barcelona (from Toulouse and Perpignan) and Girona (from Perpignan); while trains from Portugal run from Lisbon to Madrid via Cáceres and from Porto to Santiago de Compostela. **Ferries** also arrive in Bilbao and Santander from the UK, and regular ferries from Morocco serve the ports of Almería, Algeciras and Tarifa.

GETTING AROUND

Spain's public transport is backpacker friendly, offering safe and efficient travel options. While the high-speed trains are often more comfortable for longer journeys, they are also more expensive than buses.

By train

RENFE (Ⓦwww.renfe.es) operates three types of train: *cercanías* (local commuter trains); *media distancia* (intercity trains), and *larga distancia* (long-distance) express trains which include the high-speed *AVE* (Madrid–Barcelona and Madrid–Seville) and *Euromed* (Valencia–Barcelona) trains and the somewhat slower *Alaris* (Madrid–Valencia) and *Altaria* (Madrid–Alicante). To avoid queuing at the station, buy tickets online from the RENFE website and print the ticket out at the station using the code given. Return fares (*ida y vuelta*) often get a ten to twenty percent discount. **InterRail** and **Eurail** passes are valid on all RENFE trains and also on *Euromed*; additional supplements are charged on the fastest trains. Book well in advance, especially at weekends and holidays. The InterRail Spain Pass is only worth it if you're planning on a lot of train travel within a short space of time.

ON YOUR BIKE

Though few large Spanish cities (with the exception of Barcelona) have much in the way of cycle lanes, Spain is becoming more bicycle friendly, with **public bicycle** systems introduced in cities such as Seville, Valencia, Mérida and Zaragoza; dozens of pick-up/drop-off points are scattered around the streets. A small subscription fee allows you to borrow a bike in one location and drop it off at any other.

By bus

Alsa (Ⓦwww.alsa.es) is the biggest **bus** company, covering most of the country. Supplementary companies include Auto Rez (Ⓦwww.auto-res.net), Avanza (Ⓦwww.avanzabus.com) and Socibus (Ⓦwww.socibus.es). There are regular services between major cities and many smaller villages are accessible only by bus. Though they vary in quality, buses can be faster than regional trains. Frequency is drastically reduced on Sundays and holidays. For long-distance buses, you should buy your ticket in advance, whereas on short routes such as Madrid–Toledo, you can only purchase a ticket for the next bus due to leave.

By boat

Regular ferries and hydrofoils connect mainland Spain to the Balearic Islands and the Spanish enclaves of Ceuta and Melilla in Morocco. Acciona Trasmediterránea (Ⓦwww.trasmediterranea.es) is the main national ferry company; you can book seats or sleeping berths for its fast, modern passenger ferries on its website.

ACCOMMODATION

Book accommodation well in advance if planning on staying during a festival. Prices in popular areas often drop in low season.

Hotels and hostels

Budget travellers are best sticking to *pensiones* (*P*) – simple accommodation without breakfast, most rooms sharing a bathroom. Slightly more expensive are **hostales** (*H*) and *hostal-residencias* (*HsR*); both are budget hotels. They offer single and double rooms, mostly en-suite, with TV, heating, air-conditioning and, increasingly, with wi-fi. **Youth hostels** (*albergues juveniles*; Ⓦwww.reaj.com) can be inconveniently located, suffer from curfews and are often block-reserved by school groups. At €16–27 per person (HI card required), they offer basic accommodation in dorms, usually including breakfast, and are rarely cheaper than sharing a double room in a *pensión*. However, Madrid, Barcelona, and other popular destinations have a large network of popular, centrally located independent **hostels** with a full range of facilities, such as guest kitchen, lockers, free internet and wi-fi. Beds are €22–28; check Ⓦwww.hostels.com for lists of budget hotels and hostels.

Casas rurales, camping and refugios

Nationwide, **agroturismo** and **casa rural** programmes offer excellent cheap accommodation in rural areas. "*Camas y comidas*" ("beds and meals") in private houses cost around €40 for a double, and €20 for a single. Tourist offices have full lists. There are hundreds of **campsites** throughout Spain, charging about €5 per person plus the same for a tent; see Ⓦwww.vayacamping.net. In popular mountain areas you'll find *refugios* (mountain shelters) which comprise dorm-style accommodation and are on a first-come, first-served basis (€10–15 per night), some offering hot meals and a cooking area. Bring your own bedding and cooking equipment.

FOOD AND DRINK

Bars and cafés are best for **breakfast**, which can consist of *churros con chocolate* (long tubular doughnuts with thick drinking chocolate), *tostadas* (toast) *con mantequilla y mermelada* (butter and jam), or *tortilla* (omelette). **Coffee** and **pastries** are available at the many excellent *pastelerías* and *confiterías*, while *bocadillos* (sandwiches filled with sliced meats, cheese or *tortilla*), are available everywhere. *Tabernas*, *tascas*, *bodegas*, *cervecerías* and bars all serve **tapas** or *pintxos*: mini portions of meat, fish, *tortilla* or salad for €1.30–3.50 a plate. Their big brothers, **raciones** (€8–15), make a sufficient meal in themselves. Most restaurants offer a weekday lunchtime two- or three-course meal, *menú del día (*€10–12; from around €13 on weekends), or *platos combinados* (€7–10), a single dish such as meat with fries and a side of salad, drink included. **Fish** and **seafood** are excellent, particularly regional specialities such as Galician fish stew (*zarzuela*), paella (which can also contain meat) and *fideuá* (paella made with vermicelli instead of rice), especially popular in Valencia and Alicante. Andalucía's staples include *gazpacho* and *salmorejo* – cold summer soups, with Granada and Almería's culinary repertoire also incorporating North African food. Inland Spain is famous for its *carnes asados* (roasted meats), hearty stews and delicious cured meats – particularly *jamón iberico bellota*. The big cities, notably Madrid, Barcelona and Seville, are great for **vegetarians**, with scores of veggie restaurants, fusion cuisine and Asian specialities, while gourmets shouldn't miss San Sebastián on the north coast, with some of the most adventurous cuisine in the world.

Drink

Wine (*vino*) – either *tinto* (red), *blanco* (white) or *rosado/clarete* (rosé) – is usually very good. The best red is Rioja, and Catalunya produces the best whites, especially Penedès or Peralada. Vino de Jerez, Andalucían **sherry**, is served chilled and either *fino/jerez seco* (dry), *amontillado* (medium), or *oloroso/jerez dulce* (sweet). *Cerveza*, lager-type **beer**, includes San Miguel, Cruz Campo, Alhambra and Estrella del Galicia. In bars, you usually order a *caña* (small glass) of beer with your tapas. A shandy is a *corto con limón* (with fizzy lemon) or a *butano* (with fizzy orange); *tinto de verano* (red wine spritzers) are even more popular. **Sangría**, a red wine-and-fruit punch, and **sidra**, a dry farmhouse cider most typical in Asturia and the Basque Country, are well worth sampling. **Coffee** is invariably espresso, unless you specify *cortado* (with a drop of milk), *con leche* (a more generous dollop) or *americano* (weaker black coffee). **Tea** is drunk black, though you can order it *con leche*.

CULTURE AND ETIQUETTE

The main cultural difference between Spain and other European countries is its daily schedule. Lunch is usually eaten 2–4pm and dinner from 8pm. In the largest Spanish cities, a lot of shops, tourist offices and restaurants stay open all day, without a siesta break. However, in smaller towns and especially villages, don't expect much to be open 1–4pm. **Tipping** ten percent in restaurants is more than enough. When paying by credit/debit card in shops, you will need photo ID, so make sure you carry some with you at all times.

SPORTS AND ACTIVITIES

The beaches on the south coast are the best for **swimming**, while the north coast is ideal for watersports such as **windsurfing** and **surfing**: Playa de Zurriola in San Sebastián is a popular choice, as is Santander's Sardinero beach. Tarifa, at the southernmost tip of Spain, is a year-round paradise for kitesurfers and windsurfers. The Mediterranean waters of Costa Brava and Costa del Sol, as well as the Balearic Islands, offer numerous good scuba-diving and snorkelling spots. Whitewater junkies can head to Catalunya's Noguera Pallaresa River, or Cantabria's Carasa River for kayaking, hydrospeed and rafting. There are great paragliding destinations along the Mediterranean coast and in Aragón. The Aragonese Pyrenees, Picos de Europa and the Sierra Nevada, in Andalucía, are excellent in winter for **skiing** and equally good for **hiking** in summer. The **Camino de Santiago** (see p.1141) makes a superb long-distance walk or a shorter bike ride. Outside the main cities, Spain has numerous scenic and challenging cycling options throughout the country, including *bici todo terreno* (off-road tracks for mountain bikes).

Spectator sports

A match at Real Madrid's Estadio Santiago Bernabéu is a must for any **football** fan (tickets €25–100; ⓣ913 984 300, ⓦwww.realmadrid.es), as is a game at the Camp Nou, FC Barcelona's 100,000-seater stadium (tickets €30–200; ⓣ902 189 900, ⓦwww.fcbarcelona.com). For something a bit different, the Basque **jai alai** (or *pelota vasca*) is a fast-paced game where teams volley a ball within a three-walled court using wicker *cestas*; match details on ⓦwww.fipv.net. Another activity to witness from the safety of the sidelines is the electrifying spectacle of **bull runnings** (or *encierros*), the most famous of which take place every July in Pamplona during the week-long Fiesta de San Fermín (see p.1060). While **bullfighting** remains a subject of great passion in Madrid and Andalucía, its popularity is waning with the younger generation and it has been banned altogether in Catalonia.

COMMUNICATIONS

Post offices (*correos*) open Monday to Friday 8.30am to 2pm, Saturday 9am to noon; big branches in cities open until 9pm on weekdays. You can make international calls from blue public **payphones**. The prepaid phonecards (*tarjetas telefónicas*) for domestic and overseas calls are available from tobacconists, newspaper kiosks and internet cafés; in larger cities, there are lots of discount call centres (*locutorios*). International access code is ⓣ00, the Spain country code is ⓣ34 and local area codes are incorporated into the phone numbers. If you have an unlocked mobile phone, buying a prepaid SIM card is relatively inexpensive; and with roaming rates across the EU being reduced, using a mobile is now very affordable. **Internet** cafés are becoming rarer in big cities due to the proliferation of free wi-fi.

EMERGENCIES

Violent crime is rare, and as of January 2011, ETA have announced a permanent ceasefire, but watch out for pickpockets and scam artists. Petty thieves tend to work in groups and rely on distraction techniques; be particularly vigilant around market areas and during fiestas, and be discreet with your valuables. Report robberies to the **Policía Nacionál**; to avoid queuing at the police station (*comisaría*), you can report your loss by phone (ⓣ902 102112) or online under *Denuncias* at ⓦwww.policia.es. For minor **health** complaints, go to a pharmacy (*farmacía*). In more serious cases, head to *Urgencias* at the nearest **hospital**, or get the address of an English-speaking doctor from the nearest consulate, *farmacía*, local police or tourist office.

EMERGENCY NUMBERS

To summon the police, an ambulance or a fire brigade, call ⓣ112.

SPANISH

	Spanish	Pronunciation
Yes	*Si*	See
No	*No*	Noh
Please	*Por favor*	Por fahvor
Thank you	*Gracias*	Grath-yass
Hello/Good day	*Hola*	Ola
Goodbye	*Adiós*	Ad-yoss
Excuse me	*Con permiso*	Con pairmeeso
Sorry (strong)	*Lo siento*	Loh see-en-toh
Sorry (mild)	*Perdón*	Pear-don
Where?	*¿Donde?*	¿Donday?
Good	*Bueno*	Bwaynoh
Bad	*Malo*	Maloh
Near	*Próximo*	Prox-eemo
Far	*Lejos*	Layhoss
Cheap	*Barato*	Bar-ahto
Expensive	*Caro*	Cahro
Open	*Abierto*	Ahb-yairto
Closed	*Cerrado*	Thairrado
Today	*Hoy*	Oy
Yesterday	*Ayer*	A-yair
Tomorrow	*Mañana*	Man-yana
Toilet	*Aseo/baño*	Ahseyoh/ bahnio
I don't eat meat	*No como carne*	Noh cohmoh carnay
The bill	*La cuenta*	Lah kwentah
How much is...?	*¿Cuánto cuesta...?*	¿Kwanto kwesta...?
What time is it?	*¿Tiene la hora?*	¿Tee-eynay-la ora?
Do you speak English?	*¿Habla inglas?*	¿Ahblah eenglays?
Where is...?	*¿Dónde está...?*	¿Don-des-ta...?
I don't understand	*No entiendo*	Noh ent-yendo
I would like...	*Quisiera...*	Ki-si-yeah-ra...
One	*Un/Uno*	Oon/Oon-oh
Two	*Dos*	Doss
Three	*Tres*	Tress
Four	*Cuatro*	Kwatro
Five	*Cinco*	Theenko
Six	*Seis*	Say-eess
Seven	*Siete*	See-ettay
Eight	*Ocho*	Oh-cho
Nine	*Nueve*	Nwa-vay
Ten	*Diez*	Dee-yeth

INFORMATION

The **Spanish National Tourist Office** (*Información* or *Oficina de Turismo*) has a branch in virtually every major town, giving away detailed city maps and accommodation lists. There are also provincial or regional *Turismos*, which have information on the entire province, rather than just the city. Both types are usually open Monday to Friday 9/10am to 1pm and 4 to 7/8pm, Saturday 9am to 1/2pm.

MONEY AND BANKS

Currency is the euro (€). **Banks** have branches in all but the smallest towns, open Monday to Friday 8.30am to 2pm; some are also open Saturday 9am to

SPAIN ONLINE

ⓦ**www.spain.info** Comprehensive website of the Spanish tourist board.
ⓦ**www.guiadelocio.com** Nationwide restaurant and entertainment listings, updated weekly (in Spanish only).
ⓦ**www.gospain.org** Useful links directory.

1pm. The best exchange rates for foreign currencies are available from most banks and building societies. In tourist areas, you'll also find **casas de cambio**, with more convenient hours, but worse exchange rates. **ATMs** (*cajeros automáticos*) are widespread and all major credit cards (particularly Visa and MasterCard) are widely accepted in many shops, restaurants and hotels, especially in larger cities.

OPENING HOURS AND HOLIDAYS

In general, shops **open** Monday to Saturday 9am to 8pm and close (or open for a shorter time) on Sunday. Smaller towns take a **siesta** between 1 and 4pm. Tapas bars are often open at lunchtime and then from around 8pm and don't close before midnight. In nightclubs, things only kick off after midnight or so. Shops and banks are closed on the following public holidays: January 1 and 6, March 19, the week before Easter Monday, May 1, June 24, July 25, August 15, October 12, November 1, December 6, 8 and 24.

FESTIVALS

Each town and city celebrates their own annual **fiesta** in honour of their patron saint and local communities put an extraordinary amount of effort into their fiestas. Don't miss: Fiesta de **San Fermín** in Pamplona (second week of July) – the famous running of the bulls; **La Tomatina** in Buñol, near Valencia (second-last or last Wed in Aug) – messy fun with tomatoes; **Semana Santa** (week leading up to Easter Sunday) in Seville, Málaga and Córdoba – spectacular processions, feasting and fireworks, followed by Seville's **Feria de Abril** (late April); the decadent **Carnaval** in Cádiz (Feb/March); and Valencia's **Las Fallas** (March 15–19) – processions, fireworks and carousing around the clock.

Madrid

When Philip II moved the seat of government to **MADRID** in 1561 his aim was to create a symbol of Spanish unification and centralization. Given its lack of natural advantages, such as a sea port, and extreme temperatures in winter and summer, it was only the determination of successive rulers to promote a strong central capital that ensured its success.

What to see and do

Today, Madrid's streets are a beguiling mix of old and new, with narrow, atmospheric alleys and wide, open boulevards. It is also home to some of Spain's best art, from the Museo del Prado's world-renowned classical collection, to the impressive modern works at the Reina Sofía. Galleries and numerous sights aside, much of Madrid's charm comes from immersing yourself in the daily life of the city and tapping into its frenetic energy: hanging out in the traditional cafés and *chocolaterías* or the summer *terrazas*, packing the lanes of the Sunday Rastro flea market, or playing very hard and very late in a thousand bars, clubs and discos.

Puerta del Sol and the Plaza de Cíbeles

Central **Puerta del Sol** is officially the centre of the nation: a stone slab in the pavement outside the main building on the south side marks **Kilómetro Zero**, from where six of Spain's *Rutas Nacionales* (National Routes) begin. The city's emblem, a statue of a bear pawing a *madroño* bush, lies on the north side. To the west, c/Arenal heads directly towards the Teatro Real and Palacio Real, but there's more of interest along **c/Mayor**, one of Madrid's oldest thoroughfares, which runs southwest through the heart of the medieval city. The Cibeles fountain is the unofficial bathing spot for Real Madrid fans who congregate here to celebrate their team's victories.

Plaza Mayor

Plaza Mayor is one of the most important architectural and historical landmarks in Madrid and the centrepiece of Madrileño life for centuries. In this beautiful seventeenth-century square, *autos-da-fé* (trials of faith) and executions were held by the Inquisition, kings were crowned, demonstrations, festivals, and bullfights staged. These events were watched by up to 50,000 spectators and by royalty from the frescoed **Real Casa de la Panadería** (Royal Bakery). Today, the plaza is a pleasant place to have a drink or sprawl on the cobbles with young Madrileños and tourists. In summer, it's an outdoor theatre and music stage, in autumn, a book fair, and a Christmas market in mid-December.

Plaza de la Villa

About two-thirds of the way along c/ Mayor is the intimate **Plaza de la Villa**, almost a casebook of Spanish architectural development. The oldest survivor here is the **Torre de los Lujanes**, a fifteenth-century building in Mudéjar style where King Francis I of France was held prisoner by Carlos I after defeat in battle. Next in age is the **Casa de Cisneros**, built in 1537 by a nephew of Cardinal Cisneros in Plateresque style; and to complete the picture is the **Ayuntamiento** (Town Hall), begun in the seventeenth century, but later remodelled in Baroque mode.

Palacio Real

Palacio Real, or Royal Palace, on C de Bailén (Mon–Sat 9am–6pm, Sun 9am–3pm; €10, students €3.50; Ⓦwww.patrimonionacional.es; Ⓜ Ópera), built after the earlier Muslim Alcázar burned down on Christmas Day 1734,

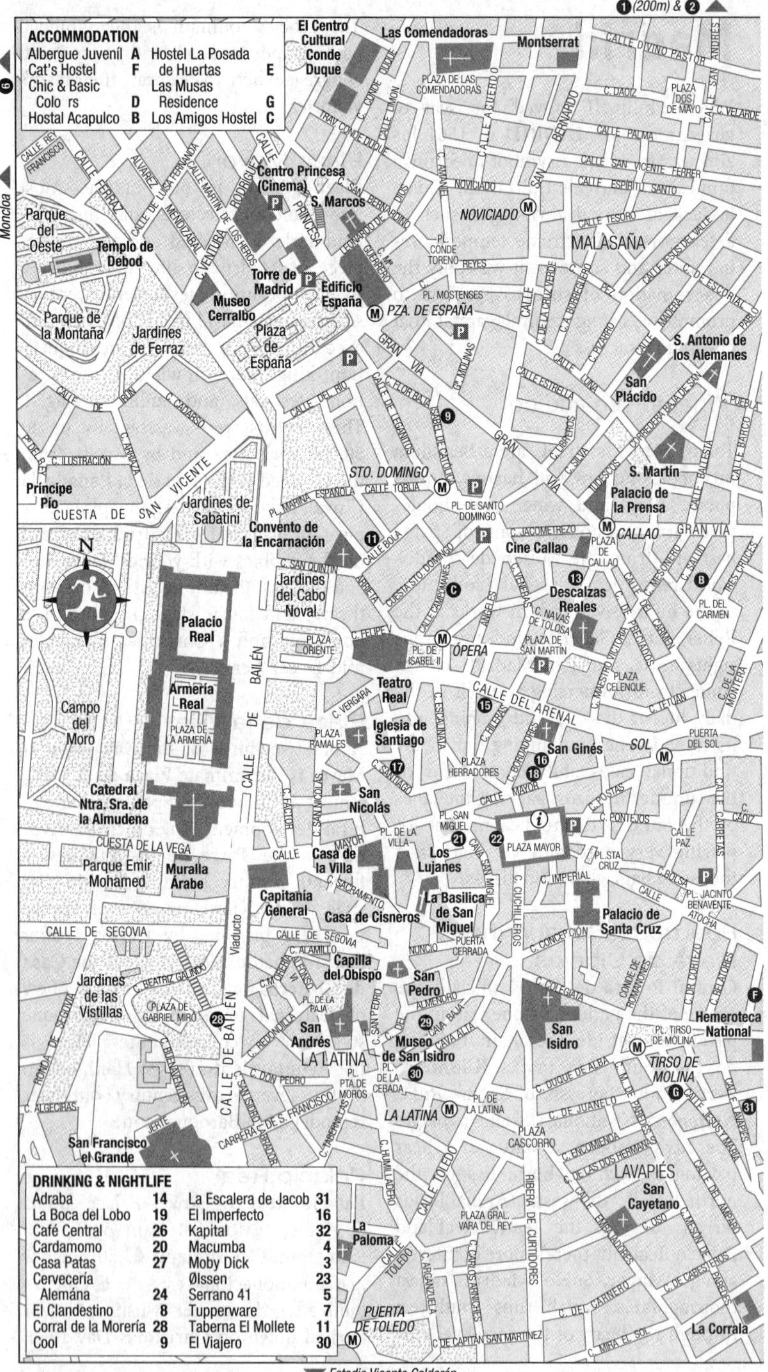
ACCOMMODATION
Albergue Juvenil A
Cat's Hostel F
Chic & Basic Colo rs D
Hostal Acapulco B
Hostel La Posada de Huertas E
Las Musas Residence G
Los Amigos Hostel C
DRINKING & NIGHTLIFE
Adraba 14
La Boca del Lobo 19
Café Central 26
Cardamomo 20
Casa Patas 27
Cervecería Alemána 24
El Clandestino 8
Corral de la Morería 28
Cool 9
La Escalera de Jacob 31
El Imperfecto 16
Kapital 32
Macumba 4
Moby Dick 3
Ølssen 23
Serrano 41 5
Tupperware 7
Taberna El Mollete 11
El Viajero 30
1 (200m) & 2
6
Moncloa
Estadio Vicente Calderón
El Centro Cultural Conde Duque
Las Comendadoras
Montserrat
Plaza de las Comendadoras
Centro Princesa (Cinema)
S. Marcos
Noviciado
Malasaña
Parque del Oeste
Templo de Debod
Torre de Madrid
Edificio España
Museo Cerralbo
Pza. de España
Parque de la Montaña
Jardines de Ferraz
Plaza de España
S. Antonio de los Alemanes
San Plácido
Gran Vía
Sto. Domingo
S. Martín
Palacio de la Prensa
Príncipe Pío
Cuesta de San Vicente
Jardines de Sabatini
Convento de la Encarnación
Cine Callao
Callao
Descalzas Reales
Jardines del Cabo Noval
Palacio Real
Plaza Oriente
Ópera
Teatro Real
Armería Real
Plaza de la Armería
Calle de Bailén
Campo del Moro
Iglesia de Santiago
Calle del Arenal
San Ginés
Sol
Puerta del Sol
San Nicolás
Catedral Ntra. Sra. de la Almudena
Plaza Mayor
Cuesta de la Vega
Parque Emir Mohamed
Muralla Árabe
Casa de la Villa
Los Lujanes
Capitanía General
Casa de Cisneros
La Basilica de San Miguel
Palacio de Santa Cruz
Calle de Segovia
Viaducto
Capilla del Obispo
San Pedro
Jardines de las Vistillas
Plaza de Gabriel Miró
San Andrés
Museo de San Isidro
San Isidro
La Latina
Hemeroteca National
Tirso de Molina
San Francisco el Grande
Lavapiés
San Cayetano
La Paloma
Puerta de Toledo
La Corrala

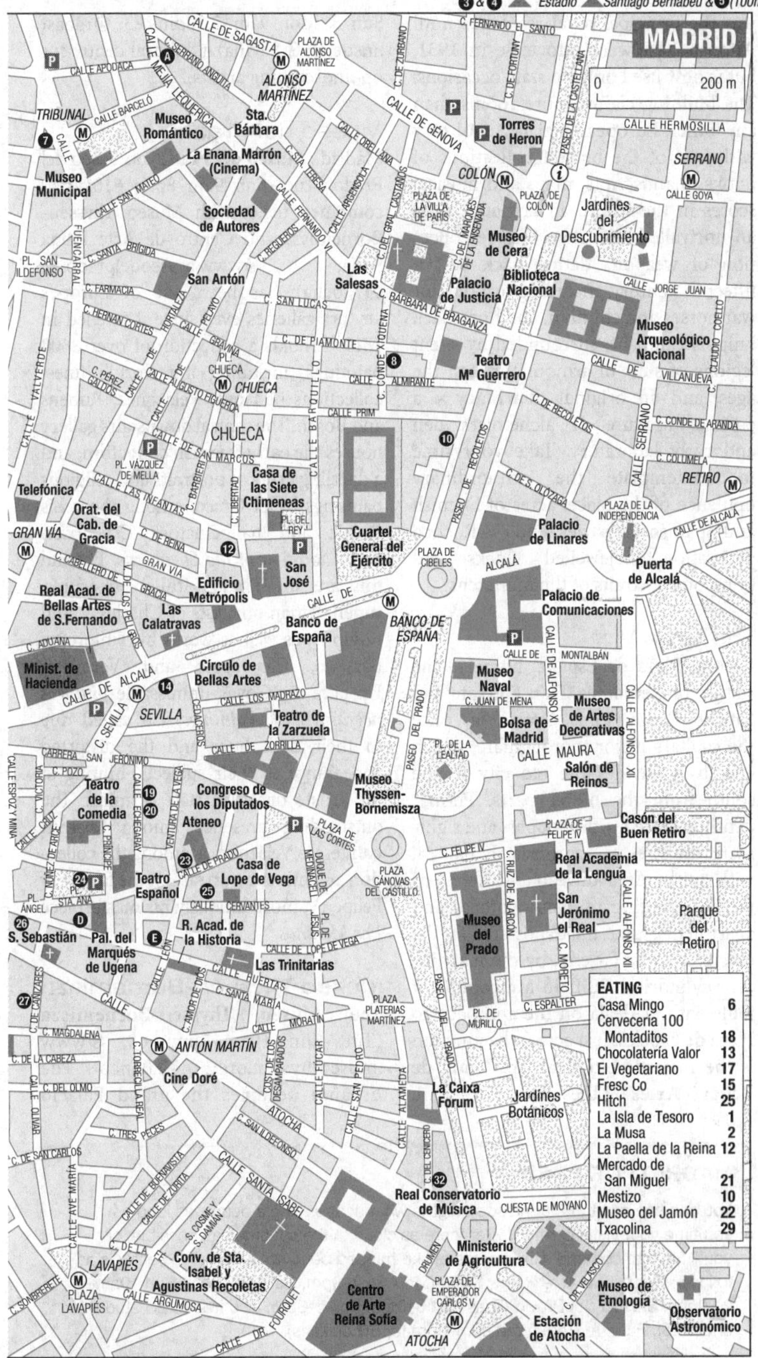

SPAIN

MADRID

was the principal royal residence until Alfonso XIII went into exile in 1931, but is now used only on state occasions. The building claims more rooms than any other European palace; a **library** with one of the biggest collections of books, manuscripts, maps and musical scores in the world; an **armoury** with an unrivalled and often bizarre collection of weapons dating back to the fifteenth century, including armour for war horses and children, and horseback knights rampant, surrounded by silent legions of suits of armour through the ages; and an original **pharmacy** – a curious mixture of alchemist's den and early laboratory. Take your time to contemplate the extraordinary opulence of the place: acres of Flemish and Spanish tapestries, endless Rococo decoration, bejewelled clocks and pompous portraits of the monarchs.

The Gran Vía

Central Plaza de España, home to the statues of Cervantes, Don Quixote and Sancho Panza, joins **Gran Vía**, once the capital's major thoroughfare, which effectively divides the old city to the south from the newer parts. Permanently crowded with shoppers and sightseers, the street is appropriately named, with quirky Art Nouveau and Art Deco facades fronting its banks, offices and apartments, and huge posters on the cinemas. At its far end, by the magnificent cylindrical **Edificio Metropolis**, it joins with c/Alcalá on the approach to Plaza de Cibeles. Just across the junction is the majestic old **Real Academia de Bellas Artes** (Tues–Sat 9am–5pm, Sun & Mon 9am–2.30pm; €3; Ⓦrabasf.insde.es; ⓂSevilla) a cultural centre for up-and-coming artists.

Museo del Prado

Madrid's **Museo del Prado**, on Paseo del Prado (Tues–Sun 9am–8pm; €10/14.40 combined ticket with Museo Thyssen-Bornemisza and Centro de Arte Reina Sofía; Ⓦwww.museodelprado.es; ⓂAtocha), has been one of Europe's key art galleries ever since it opened in 1819. It holds a collection of over 8600 paintings, including the world's finest collections of Goya, Velázquez, Rubens and Bosch. The central downstairs gallery houses the **early Spanish collection**, and a dazzling array of portraits and religious paintings by El Greco, among them his mystic and hallucinatory *Crucifixion* and *Adoration of the Shepherds.* Beyond this are the Prado's **Italian** treasures: superb Titian portraits of Charles V and Philip II, as well as works by Tintoretto, Bassano, Caravaggio and Veronese. Upstairs are Goya's unmissable *pinturas negras (Black Paintings)*, so called due to their dark hues and the distorted appearance of their subjects, hinting at the artist's unsettled state of mind. The outstanding presence among Spanish painters is Velázquez – among the collection are intimate portraits of the family of Felipe IV, most famously his masterpiece *Las Meninas.*

Museo Thyssen-Bornemisza

The **Museo Thyssen-Bornemisza** (Tues–Sun 10am–7pm; €8; Ⓦwww.museothyssen.org; ⓂBanco de España) occupies the grand Palacio

MADRID FOR FREE

You can see most of Madrid's top sights without spending a penny, as long as you time your visits carefully. Get there as close to the set times as possible, or you'll have to contend with crowds of like-minded penny-pinchers. Free entry is as follows: **Centro de Arte Reina Sofia** (Mon–Fri 7–9pm, Sat 2.30–9pm, Sun 10am–2.30pm); **Museo del Prado** (Tues–Sat 6–8pm, Sun 5–8pm; also free to EU students under 25); **Palacio Real** (Wed 9am–6pm for EU citizens).

de Villahermosa, diagonally opposite the Prado. In 1993, this prestigious site played a large part in Spain's acquisition of what was perhaps the world's greatest private art collection, belonging to the late Baron Thyssen-Bornemisza. There are important works from every major period and movement – from Duccio and Holbein, through El Greco and Caravaggio, to Schiele and Rothko; from a strong showing of nineteenth-century Americans to some very early and very late Van Goghs; and side-by-side hangings of parallel Cubist studies by Picasso, Braque and Mondrian.

Centro de Arte Reina Sofía

As well as the collection of twentieth-century art, the **Centro de Arte Reina Sofía**, c/Santa Isabel 52 (Mon & Wed–Sat 10am–9pm, Sun 10am–2.30pm; €6; Ⓦwww.museoreinasofia.es; Ⓜ Atocha) features a cinema, excellent art and design bookshops, a print, music and photographic library and edgy temporary exhibitions. However, it is **Picasso's Guernica** – his signature Cubism piece – that most visitors come to see, and rightly so. Superbly displayed along with its preliminary studies, this icon of twentieth-century Spanish art and politics – a response to the Fascist bombing of the Basque town of Guernica in the Spanish Civil War – carries a shock that defies all familiarity. Other halls are devoted to **Dalí** and Surrealism, early twentieth-century Spanish artists including **Miró** and post-World War II figurative art, mapping the beginning of abstraction through to Pop and avant-garde.

The Rastro

The **Rastro** flea market (Sun 8am–3pm) is as much a part of Madrid's weekend ritual as a Mass or a *paseo*. The stalls sprawl south from ⓂLa Latina to the Ronda de Toledo, selling everything from flamenco records to imitation designer gear to old photos of Madrid. Expect a great atmosphere, but you'll have to search hard for bargains among the junk. Keep a tight grip on your possessions. Afterwards, while away the afternoon in the bars and *terrazas* around Puerta de Moros.

Parque del Buen Retiro and Parque del Oeste

The most central and most popular of Madrid's parks is the **Parque del Buen Retiro** (ⓂRetiro or Ibiza; 6am–midnight May–Sept; until 11pm rest of the year) behind the Prado, a stunning mix of formal gardens and wilder spaces. You can row a boat, picnic, check out a travelling art exhibition at the beautiful **Palacio de Velázquez** and the nearby **Palacio de Cristal** and, above all, promenade like half of Madrid. You can also visit the "Hill of the Absents" – a mound constructed in memory of those who died in the Madrid bombing of 2004. Although charming by day, Retiro is best avoided at night. The **Parque del Oeste** on the city's western edge (ⓂVentura Rodríguez) boasts a genuine Egyptian temple – Templo de Debod, donated to Spain by Egyptian president Nasser in 1968 as a gesture of thanks to Spanish archeologists who saved it from the rising waters of Lake Nasser.

Arrival and information

Air Busy Barajas airport (Ⓦwww.aena.es), 12km north of the centre, is served by all major airlines from Europe, North and Latin America. Line #8 runs to ⓂNuevos Ministerios (6am–2am; 12min; €1; additional €1 supplement from Terminal 4). The fast, reliable 24hr Exprés Aeropuerto bus leaves terminals 1, 2 and 4 (every 15–35min; €2), stopping at c/O'Donnell, Plaza de Cibeles and Atocha (the last stop only between 6am and 11.30pm). AeroCITY minibuses (24hr; Ⓣ917 477 570, Ⓦwww.aerocity.com) drop passengers off door-to-door for €6–20.
Train Trains from the north and Portugal arrive at the Estación de Chamartín. Estación de Atocha serves the south, east and west of Spain. Local trains use the Estación de Príncipe Pío (Estación del Norte).

Bus Terminals are scattered throughout the city, but the largest – used by all international services and many national services – is the Estación del Sur (Ⓜ Méndez Alvaro) on c/Méndez Alvaro, south of Estación de Atocha.
Tourist office Centro de Turismo de Madrid, Plaza Mayor 27, Ⓜ Sol (daily 9.30am–8.30pm; ⓣ 91 588 163 651, ⓦ www.esmadrid.com). Branches at Plaza de Colón (Ⓜ Colón) and Terminal 4 at the airport (same hours). What's On listings are detailed in free English-language monthly *In Madrid* (ⓦ www.in-madrid.com) and *Guía del Ocio* (ⓦ www.guiadelocio.com).

City transport

Bus Buses (ⓦ www.emtmadrid.es) run from 6.30am to 11.30pm; there are also 26 night-bus *búhos* (owls) in the centre, from Plaza de Cibeles (midnight–6am; every 15min).
Metro ⓦ www.metromadrid.es. Runs 6.05am–2am; flat fare €1, €9 for a ten-journey ticket, also valid on buses.
Taxi Taxi ranks located throughout the city centre. Fares start from around €2.05 between 6am and 10pm during the week; higher fares at the weekends. Charges/kilometre are around €1–1.20, and supplementary charges apply to being dropped off at the airport, train and bus stations.

Accommodation

The best budget accommodation is in the area surrounding the buzzing, pedestrianized Plaza Santa Ana. Other good areas include Gran Vía and along noisy c/Fuencarral towards Chueca and Malsaña.

Hostels

Albergue Juvenil c/Mejia Lequerica 21 ⓣ 915 939 688, ⓦ www.ajmadrid.es Ⓜ Alonso Martínez or Tribunal. The stylish decor mixes ultra modern furnishings and graffiti murals and no dorm has more than 6 beds. Facilities include a gym, TV/DVD/games room and laundry. Breakfast buffet included. Dorms: under-26s €21–23, over-26s €27.
Cat's Hostel c/Cañizares 6 ⓣ 913 692 807, ⓦ www.catshostel.com Ⓜ Antón Martín. Huge backpackers' haven in a converted eighteenth-century palace with beautiful central patio. Rooms are a bit cramped but there's a lively cellar bar, nightly tapas bar crawls, free internet and wi-fi. Dorms €21–23, doubles €82.
Hostel La Posada de Huertas c/de las Huertas 21 ⓣ 914 295 526, ⓦ www.posadadehuertas.com Ⓜ Antón Martín. Spacious, secure, colourful dorms with lockers in the heart of Madrid's nightlife. Helpful staff, nightly tapas-bar tours, free breakfast, internet and kitchen facilities are just some of the perks. Dorms €20–22, doubles €80.
Las Musas Residence c/Jesus y María 12, 3rd floor ⓣ 915 394 984, ⓦ www.lasmusasresidence.com Ⓜ Tirso de Molina. Right in the heart of the nightlife, this spick-and-span hostel is a favourite with international backpackers who congregate in its large kitchen/lounge. Dorms €20.
Los Amigos Hostel Campomanes 6-4° ⓣ 915 471 707, ⓦ www.losamigoshostel.com Ⓜ Ópera. Popular, friendly hostel with bright dorms, lockers, kitchen and internet, on a quiet street near the Palacio Real. Separate branch at c/Arenal 26–24 ⓣ 915 592 472. Dorms €23–26, doubles €80.

Hotels

Chic & Basic Colors c/de las Huertas 14, 2nd floor ⓣ 914 296 935, ⓦ www.chicandbasic.com. Ⓜ Antón Martín. The name says it all: it's chic, sleek, and brightly coloured. Each minimalist, comfortable room comes with flat-screen TV and free wi-fi and the location is hard to beat. Singles €65, doubles €80.
Hostal Acapulco c/de la Salud 13, 4th floor ⓣ 915 311 945, ⓦ www.hostalacapulco.com Ⓜ Gran Vía. You're guaranteed not to go loco here: the spotless, sunny rooms with marble floors and balconies overlook cute little Plaza del Carmen. Singles €55, doubles €65.

Eating

Madrid has an incredible variety of restaurants, and it's easy to dine out on a tight budget.

Cafés and tapas

Some of the best areas to enjoy tapas are La Latína, Chueca, and Sol, with a myriad bars clustered along the little streets.
Cervecería 100 Montaditos c/Mayor 22 Ⓜ Sol. This chain is popular countrywide thanks to, as the name implies, its choice of a hundred sandwiches, at just €1.10–2.20 a pop. Simply fill in a menu form, pay at the counter and wait for your name to be called.
Chocolatería Valor Postigo de San Martín Ⓜ Callao. One of the best spots in town for *chocolate con churros*, with an incredible array of dipping chocolate for the *churros*.
Hitch c/Cervantes 8 Ⓜ Antón Martín. Café by day, arty bar by night, this versatile little spot screens classic films and football games, holds photography contests and makes to-die-for goat's cheese and caramelized onion tapas.

Museo del Jamón c/Mayor 7 Ⓜ Sol. Extraordinary place where hundreds of hams hang from the ceiling, and the *cañas* (€1.20) come with a free tapa. Plate of *jamón* €2.60–16, depending on the quality. Numerous other branches.
Txacolina c/de la Cava Baja 26 Ⓜ Latina. Renowned for its imaginative, elaborate Basque *pintxos* (tapas). Wash them down with *txacoli*, a dry Basque white wine.

Restaurants

Casa Mingo Paseo de la Florida 34 Ⓜ Príncipe Pío. Asturian cider house with a no-nonsense menu. If the roast chicken doesn't grab you, go for the *chorizo a la sidra* or the Madrid special – *callos a la madrileña El Vegetariano* (tripe, Madrid-style). Mains €3–8.
El Vegetariano c/Santiago 9 Ⓜ Bilbao. Stylish spot featuring imaginative salads and mains such as lasagna and vegetable curry (mains €8–10) as well as vegan options.
Fresc Co c/Las Fuentes 12 Ⓜ Ópera. All-you-can-eat extensive buffet of salads, pasta, pizza, and fresh fruit juices for under €10 at this popular chain restaurant.
La Isla de Tesoro c/de Manuela Malasaña 3 Ⓜ Bilbao. Worth seeking out for its eclectic decor and changing daily menu that features vegetable goulash, Thai vegetable curry and other internationally inspired dishes (*menú* €12).
La Musa c/Manuela Malasaña 18 Ⓜ Bilbao. Always heaving with a young clientele, the food here is sensational. Try the *bombas* (stuffed potatoes) or fried green tomatoes. *Menú del día* €12.
La Paella de la Reina c/de la Reina 39 Ⓜ Gran Vía. This is where Madrileños head to sate their rice-related cravings. Like any good *arrocería*, this place only cooks a variety of paellas for two people or more, so bring a friend. *Arroz negro* (€16/person) is delicious.
Mercado de San Miguel Plaza de San Miguel Ⓜ Sol. Transformed into a gleaming modern venue with numerous food counters and perpetually busy table, one of Madrid's oldest markets is now a top spot for tapas and light meals.
Mestizo c/Recoletos 13 Ⓜ Retiro. This authentic Mexican restaurant packs some proper heat, with an extensive menu of quesadillas, tamales, filled tacos and enchiladas, as well as excellent *mole poblano* and that hard-to-find-outside-Mexico special: tortillas stuffed with *cuitlacoche*, a black corn fungus. Mains €8–12.

Drinking and nightlife

Most tapas bars only really get going around 10.30pm and are known for a particular speciality and Madrileños have a drink and a tapa in one bar before moving on to another. Clubs open from midnight until well beyond dawn; the best areas are the student haunt of Malasaña, gay-area Chueca and multicultural Lavapiés/Antón Martín.

Bars

Cervecería Alemána Plaza Santa Ana 6 Ⓜ Sol. One of Hemingway's favourite haunts and consequently full of Americans; good traditional atmosphere and excellent German beers. Pricey but worth it. Closed Aug.
El Clandestino c/de Barquillo 34 Ⓜ Chueca. Immensely popular bar serving great mojitos to an accompaniment of indie/rock music, sometimes live.
El Imperfecto c/Coloreros 5 Ⓜ Sol. Far from being imperfect, this is an excellent bar for cocktails – sip on their great mojitos while admiring the topsy-turvy interior, and listening to live jazz on Tuesdays.
El Viajero Plaza de la Cebada 11 Ⓜ La Latina. Essential spot for a beer on a warm night, when you can watch the world pass by from the open-air rooftop *terraza*.
Ølssen c/del Prado 15 Ⓜ Antón Martín. Minimalist Nordic bar that tempts revellers with more than 80 kinds of vodka.
Taberna El Mollete c/de la Bola 4 Ⓜ Opera. Nab a table in the tiny loft dining space, sip your wine and savour the *morcilla* croquettes and the *huevos rotos* (fried potatoes with egg), or push your way to the bar (it fills up to the brim by 11pm) and have a beer with the friendly owner.

Clubs

Adraba c/de Alcalá 20 Ⓜ Seville. The heart of *la movida madrileña* until it burned down in 1983, this revived club attracts a sophisticated crowd, particularly on Thursdays. Friday and Saturday are dedicated to pumping dance tunes, courtesy of the city's top DJs. Entry €18. Wed–Sun midnight–6am.
Cool c/Isabel La Católica 6 Ⓜ Santo Domingo. Electronica and house dominate the dancefloor at this chic club filled with beautiful people; Sat nights are predominantly gay nights. Entry from €10. Thurs–Sat 11pm–6am.
Kapital c/Atocha 125 Ⓜ Atocha. One of the most popular megaclubs in town, with seven levels of different dancefloors – everything from hip-hop to salsa to r'n'b. The €20 admission includes one drink. Dress well. Fri & Sat midnight–6am.
Macumba Augustín de Foxá, above Estación Chamartín Ⓜ Chamartín. Weekend favourite for

hardcore clubbers, with a superb sound system and a half-naked, sweaty crowd, where the likes of Ministry of Sound hit the decks until 6am. Mostly gay crowd, but some nights are straight nights. Entry €25 (discounts with flyers). Thurs–Sat midnight–6am, Sun 4pm–midnight.

Serrano 41 c/de Serrano 41 Ⓦwww.serrano41.com Ⓜ Serrano. Chic venue playing a mix of pop, house and funk, where there's a good chance of spotting Real Madrid players and bullfighters strutting their stuff on the dancefloor. Strict door policy. Entry €10. Wed–Sun 11pm–5.30am.

Tupperware Corredora Alta de San Pueblo 26 Ⓜ Tribunal. This club is fun through-and-through, from its über-kitsch decor to its eclectic playlist – soul, indie and Sixties and Seventies classics, enjoyed by a 30-something crowd. Free entry. Daily 9pm–3am.

Entertainment

Big rock concerts are usually held at Palacio Vistalegre, Utebo 1 (Ⓜ Oporto), and La Peineta stadium, Avda Arcentales (Ⓜ Las Musas). Flamenco is at its best in the summer, especially at the Cumbre Flamenco, a week of free concerts held in a metro station in September.

Cinema

Cine Doré c/Santa Isabel 3 Ⓜ Antón Martín. Offers a bargain (€2.50) programme of classic films, a pleasant bar and, in summer, an outdoor *cine-terraza*; home to the Filmoteca Nacional (national film library).

Cines Princesa c/de la Princesa 3 Ⓜ Plaza de España. Films shown in their original language – from English-language Hollywood blockbusters to international art films.

La Enana Marrón Travesía de San Mateo 8 Ⓜ Alonzo Martínez. Artsy and independent Spanish-language films and alternative theatre.

Bullfighting

Plaza de Toros Monumental de las Ventas c/de Alcalá 237 Ⓜ Ventas. Hosts some of the year's most prestigious events, especially during the May/June San Isidro festivities; ticket prices start from around €7 for standing *sol* (sun) tickets, with *sombra* (shade) tickets from €15 and the most expensive ringside seats selling for around €100. Tickets for all but the biggest events are available at the box office (Ⓣ913 562 200, Ⓦwww.las-ventas.com).

Live music

Café Central Plaza del Ángel 10 Ⓦwww.cafecentralmadrid.com Ⓜ Sol. One of the best places in the world to hear live jazz; attracts big international musicians. Open from noon for drinks, with music nightly from 10pm; get here before 9pm to secure weekend tickets (€10–15).

La Boca del Lobo c/Echegaray 11 Ⓦwww.labocadellobo.com (in Spanish) Ⓜ Sevilla. Dark, atmospheric venue with a reputation for showcasing new rock and alternative acts, as well as funk, roots, ska and fusion. Live music from around 9.30pm, followed by DJs; entry free–€10.

La Escalera de Jacob c/de Lavapiés 11 Ⓦwww.laescaleradejacob.es Ⓜ Antón Martín. Intimate, multifaceted venue with fusion, soul, jazz, funk and indie nights, a loyal local following and some great live performances. Nightly from 10pm.

Moby Dick c/Avda de Brasil 5 Ⓦwww.mobydickclub.com Ⓜ Santiago Bernabéu. Popular, nautically themed venue attracting live rock bands, both local and international.

Flamenco

Cardamomo c/Echegaray 15 Ⓦwww.cardamomo.es Ⓜ Sevilla. This dark, smoky flamenco bar attracts a young, spirited local crowd and on Tuesdays and Wednesdays puts on a live flamenco jamming session that's not to be missed. Check website for flamenco show schedule. Daily 9pm–3.30am.

Casa Patas c/Cañizares 10 Ⓜ Antón Martín. Classic flamenco club with bar and restaurant, and incredible performances. Best nights Thurs & Fri from 8.30pm; can get rather crowded. Entrance €15, or €30–35 with dinner.

Corral de la Morería c/de la Morería 17 Ⓦwww.corraldelamoreria.com Ⓜ Ópera. Venerable flamenco venue that's been going strong for over 50 years, thanks to the quality of its nightly performers. Entrance €30–40. Daily 8.30pm–2.30am; check website for show schedules.

Shopping

Alternative shops Chueca and also c/Fuencarral and c/Hortaleza (off Gran Vía). There are several great places to find that quirky something, but particularly worth visiting are El Rastro (see p.1064) and Mercado de Fuencarral, c/Fuencarral 45 (Mon–Sat 10am–9pm), a three-storey mall with stores such as Black Kiss and Ugly Shop, selling grungy, outlandish clothes, accessories and more.

Bookshops Casa del Libro, Gran Vía 29 (Ⓜ Gran Vía), is a huge bookshop with a large selection in English. Petra's International Bookshop, c/de Compomanes 13 (Ⓜ Ópera), lets you swap your old books for other secondhand ones. Pasajes Librería Internacional, c/de Génova 3 (Ⓜ Alonso Martínez), is one of the better shops, with an extensive English section.

Traditional handicrafts The area from Plaza Mayor to Puerta de Toledo is filled with shops selling everything from religious icons to embroidered shawls – great for browsing and picking up the odd authentic souvenir, but often quite expensive.

Directory

Embassies Australia, Paseo de la Castellana 259d, 24th floor ⓣ913 536 600; Canada, Torre Espacio, Paseo de la Castellana 259d ⓣ913 828 400; Ireland, Paseo de la Castellana 46, 4th floor ⓣ914 364 093; New Zealand, c/de Pinar 7 ⓣ915 230 226; UK, Torre Espacio, Paseo de la Castellana 259d ⓣ917 146 300; US, c/Serrano 75 ⓣ915 872 200.

Exchange Large branches of most major banks on c/Alcalá and Gran Vía and ATMs all over the city centre. Round-the-clock currency exchange at the airport; Banco Central is best for AmEx travellers' cheques.

Hospitals Anglo-American Medical Unit (Unidad Médica), c/del Conde de Aranda 1 ⓣ914 351 823, ⓦwww.unidadmedica.com (Ⓜ Retiro), has Spanish- and English-speaking staff. Hospital General Gregorio Marañón, c/del Doctor Esquerdo 46 (Ⓜ Sáinz de Baranda) ⓣ915 868 000, is the main public hospital.

Left luggage Estación de Atocha has lockers (daily 6am–10pm); Estación de Chamartín also has lockers (daily 7am–11pm). There is also a *consigna* at the Estación Sur de Autobuses (6.30am–midnight). There are also 24hr *consignas* at the airport terminals 1, 3 and 4.

Pharmacies Farmacia Mayor, c/Mayor 13 ⓣ91 366 and Farmacia Velásquez, c/Velásquez 70 ⓣ915 756 028 are both open 24hr.

Post office Main post office at Paseo del Prado 1, Plaza de Cibeles (Ⓜ Banco de España).

Moving on

Train From Estación de Chamartín: Bilbao (2 daily; 5hr); Escorial (6 daily; 1hr); León (6 daily; 3hr 30min–4hr 30min); Segovia (13 daily; 30min–1hr 30min); Salamanca (7 daily; 2hr 30min); Santander (3 daily; 4hr 30min).

From Estación de Atocha: Barcelona (25 daily; 2hr 40min–3hr 30min); Cáceres (5 daily; 3hr 30min–4hr 30min); Cádiz (2 daily; 4hr 30min); Córdoba (every 30min; 1hr 40min–2hr); Escorial (hourly; 1hr); Granada (2 daily; 4hr 30min); Málaga (12 daily; 2hr 40min–3hr); Mérida (5 daily; 4hr 20min–6hr 40min); Pamplona (4 daily; 3hr); San Sebastián (2 daily; 5hr 20min); Santiago de Compostela (2 daily; 7–9hr); Segovia (13 daily; 30min–1hr 30min); Seville (22 daily; 2hr 30min); Toledo (11 daily; 30min); Valencia (13 daily; 3hr 45min).

Bus Alicante (5–10 daily; 5hr); Almería (5 daily; 7hr); Barcelona (20 daily; 7hr 30min–8hr); Bilbao (6 daily; 4hr 45min); Cáceres (7 daily; 4hr–4hr 30min); Cádiz (13 daily; 7hr); Córdoba (6 daily; 4hr 45min); El Escorial (hourly; 1hr); Granada (14 daily; 4hr 30min–5hr); León (12 daily; 4hr 15min); Málaga (4–8 daily; 6hr); Mérida (10 daily; 4–5hr); Pamplona (6 daily; 5hr); Salamanca (23 daily; 2hr 30min); San Sebastián (9 daily; 6hr); Santander (8 daily; 5hr 45min); Santiago de Compostela (5 daily; 8–9hr); Segovia (10am–11pm every 30min; 1hr 30min); Seville (8 daily; 6hr); Toledo (6.30am–10pm every 30min; 1hr 15min); Trujillo (17 daily; 3hr 30min); Valencia (16 daily; 4hr).

Day-trips from Madrid

Surrounding the capital are some of Spain's most fascinating cities, all an easy day-trip from Madrid or a convenient stopoff on the main routes out.

EL ESCORIAL

Fifty kilometres northwest of Madrid, nestled in the foothills of the Sierra de Guadarrama, are **SAN LORENZO DEL ESCORIAL** and the monastery of **El Escorial** (Tues–Sun: April–Sept 10am–6pm; Oct–March 10am–5pm; €10; free Wed for EU citizens). The city grew around this enormous, severe-looking building, which resembles a fortress rather than a palace. Start at the monastery's west gateway, which leads into the **Patio de los Reyes** and the impressive Basilica. Move on to the **Salas Capitulares**, outside and around to the left, to see works by El

Greco, Velázquez and Ribera. Nearby, the staircase next to the Sacristía leads down to the **Panteón de los Reyes**, the final resting place of virtually all Spanish monarchs since Charles V, where they lie in gilded tombs (guided/ audioguide visits only). You'll pass the **Prudería**, where corpses are left to rot for twenty years prior, and the eerie **Panteón de los Infantes**, with tiny marble coffins. The spartan Habsburg apartments inside the **Palace** itself, inhabited by Philip II, house the chair that supported his gouty leg and the deathbed from which he looked down into the church.

Arrival and information

Train From Madrid's Estación de Atocha, C8 cercanías run to El Escorial (hourly; 1hr; €1.25). Take a connecting local bus up to the town centre (€1.15); otherwise it's a 20min walk uphill.

Bus Routes #661 and #664 leaving from the Moncloa area, Madrid (every 15min weekdays, hourly on weekends; 50min), take you right to the monastery.

Tourist office c/Grimaldi 2 (Tues–Sat 10am–2pm & 3–6pm, Sun 10am–2pm; ⓣ918 905 313, ⓦwww.sanlorenzoturismo.org).

TOLEDO

Capital of medieval Spain until 1560, UNESCO World Heritage Site **TOLEDO** is the spiritual heart of Catholic Spain and a city redolent of past glories. Set in a desolate landscape, the haphazard maze of cobbled streets rests on a rocky mound isolated on three sides by a looping gorge of the Río Tajo. To see the city at its finest, lose yourself in the backstreets or stay the night; by 6pm, the tour buses have all gone home.

The Catedral

The **Catedral** is at the core of the city (Mon–Sat 10am–6.30pm, Sun 2–6.30pm; €7). This Gothic construction took almost three centuries to complete (1227–1493) and is bursting with treasures from numerous great artists. The Sacristía and New Museums are home to the most opulent paintings, most notably by Zurbarán, Velázquez and El Greco. Behind the Capilla Mayor's huge altarpiece is the Baroque *Transparente*, with marble cherubs and clouds, especially magnificent when the sun reaches through the strategically placed opening in the roof above.

The Alcázar and around

Inside the Alcázar fortress, the splendid cavernous interior of the Museo de Ejércitio (Army Museum; Tues–Sat 10am–7pm, until 9pm June–Sept, Sun 10am–3pm; €5, free Sun) does justice to its impressive collection of medieval weaponry and armour, model soldiers, scale models of fortifications, dioramas and much more, spread over four floors. In 1936, during the Civil War, six hundred barricaded Nationalists held out against relentless Republican attack for over two months until finally relieved by one of Franco's armies. North of here, the **Museo de Santa Cruz** (Mon–Sat 10am–6.30pm, Sun 10am–2pm; free), houses an excellent collection of works by El Greco. However, to see his masterpiece, *The Burial of the Count of Orgaz*, you need to visit the fourteenth-century **Iglesia de Santo Tomé**, west of the cathedral (daily 10am–6pm; €2.30).

The Judería

On c/Reyes Católicos in the **Judería**, the old Jewish Quarter, the beautifully restored **Sinagoga del Tránsito**, built along Moorish lines by Samuel Levi in 1366 and housing the **Sephardic Museum** (Feb–Nov Tues–Sat 9.30am–7pm; Dec & Jan Tues–Sat 10am–6pm; all year Sun 10am–2pm; €3) maps Jewish culture and tradition in Spain, exhibits including ceremonial artefacts and costumes.

Mezquita Cristo de la Luz

The tiny **Mezquita Cristo de la Luz** mosque (Cuesta de Carmelitas Descalzos 10; March–Sept 10am–6.45pm; until 5.45pm rest of the year; €2), built in 999 AD, is one of the oldest Moorish monuments surviving in Spain. Its original arches are still intact (as well as some Moorish graffiti).

Arrival and information

Train *Avant* trains run regularly from Estación de Atocha in Madrid (hourly; 30min; €10.60; last train back to Madrid at 9.25pm). Book tickets in advance on weekends. From Toledo's train station east of town, it's an uphill 20min walk to the central Plaza Zocódover (bus #5 or #6; €1.20).

Bus The bus station is on Avda de Castilla la Mancha in the modern part of the city, a 10min walk north of Plaza Zocódover via c/Armas. Buses depart from Madrid's Plaza Elíptica (every 30min between 6am and 10pm; 1hr–1hr 30min; €5.40), with the last bus back to the capital at 10.30pm (Sun 11.30pm).

Tourist office Plaza del Ayuntamiento (10am–2.30pm & 4–7pm; closed Mon pm; ⓣ925 254 030, ⓦwww.toledoturismo.com); you can book all manner of walking tours here (ⓦwww.toledopaisajes.com).

Accommodation

La Posada de Manolo c/Sixto Ramón Parro 8 ⓣ925 282 250, ⓦwww.laposadademanolo.com. Themed hotel with inviting rooms and the decor on each of its floors reflecting Toledo's cultural influences: Islamic, Jewish and Christian. Singles €42, doubles €66.

Eating and drinking

El Zoco Plaza Barrio Rey 7. Just off the touristy Plaza de Zocódover, *El Zoco* offers better value than the restaurants on its neighbouring square and serves the local speciality, *perdiz* (partridge). *Menú del día* from €10.

Mille Grazie c/de las Cadenas 2. The authentic Italian cuisine served at this brightly decorated restaurant includes delicious home-made pasta dishes, such as vegetarian spinach-filled ravioli, and a variety of thin and crispy pizzas. Mains €8.

SEGOVIA

Located 87km northwest of Madrid, **SEGOVIA** has a remarkable number of architectural achievements for a small city. Known to locals as the "stone ship", from a bird's-eye view the city resembles a boat, with its three most celebrated attractions at the stern, bow and mast: the Alcázar, Aqueduct and cathedral, respectively.

What to see and do

The **Aqueduct**, a magnificent structure that looms over the Plaza del Azoguejo, stretches over 800m and towers 30m high. And as if these dimensions weren't impressive enough, the entire structure stands up without a drop of mortar. No one knows exactly when it was built, but it was probably around the end of the first century AD under the Emperor Trajan. Dominating the Plaza Mayor in the heart of the old city, the **cathedral** (daily 9.30am–6.30pm; €3, free Sun am) takes the Gothic style to its logical extreme, with pinnacles and flying buttresses tacked on at every conceivable point. Beside the cathedral, c/Daoiz leads on to a small park in front of the **Alcázar** (April–Sept 10am–7pm; Oct–March 10am–6pm; €4.75, free for EU citizens third Tues of every month; tower access €2). This extraordinary castle with narrow towers and turrets, rebuilt in 1862 after the original was destroyed by fire, is said to have inspired Walt Disney's design for Sleeping Beauty's castle. Inside, you can admire the splendid Sala de Reyes, the three-dimensional frieze depicting all the monarchs of Asturias, Castilla and León, the peculiar "pine cones" decorating the ceiling in the Sala de Las Piñas, and, of course, the unsurpassed view of the city and the snow-tipped mountains behind it from the summit of the Torre de Juan II.

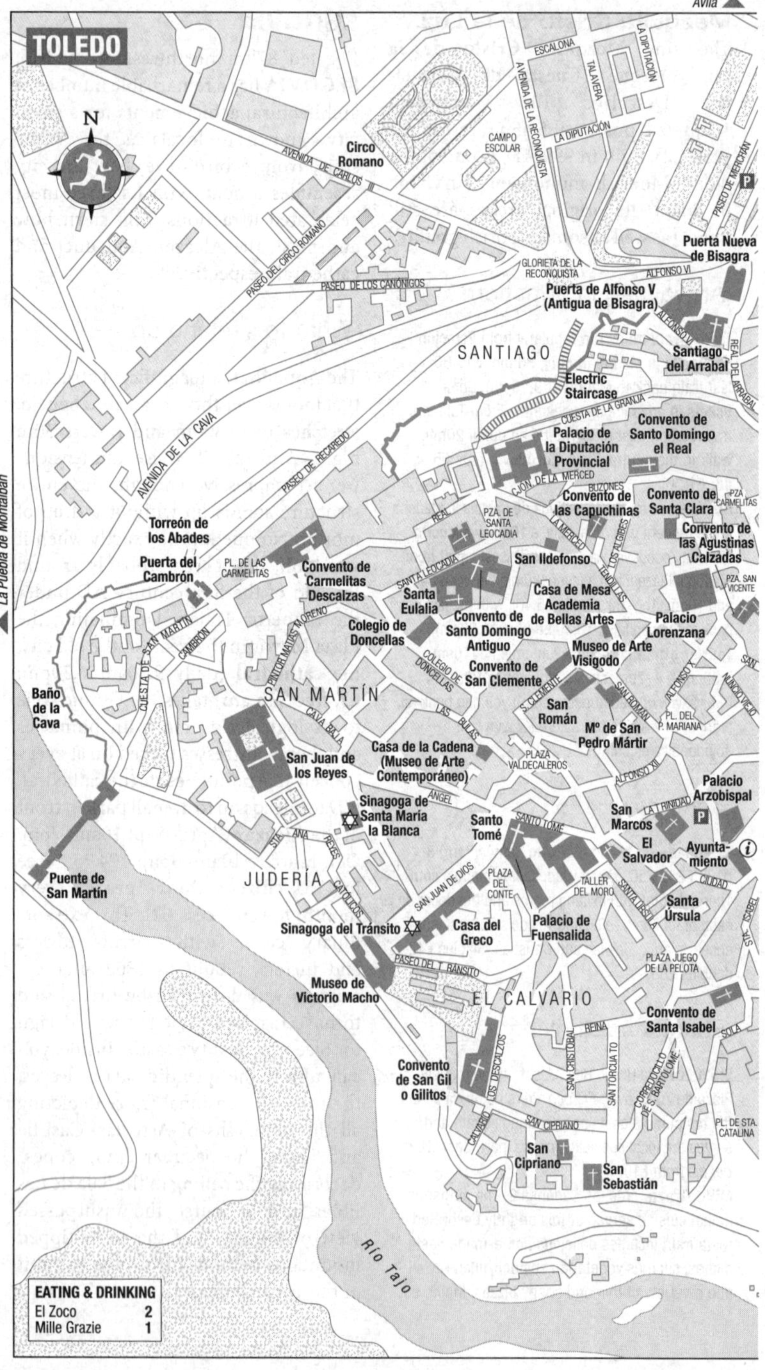
TOLEDO
Ávila
N
La Puebla de Montalbán
Circo Romano
AVENIDA DE CARLOS III
CAMPO ESCOLAR
ESCALONA
TALAVERA
LA DIPUTACIÓN
AVENIDA DE LA RECONQUISTA
PASEO DE MERCHÁN
P
Puerta Nueva de Bisagra
GLORIETA DE LA RECONQUISTA
ALFONSO VI
PASEO DEL CIRCO ROMANO
PASEO DE LOS CANÓNIGOS
Puerta de Alfonso V (Antigua de Bisagra)
SANTIAGO
Santiago del Arrabal
REAL DEL ARRABAL
Electric Staircase
CUESTA DE LA GRANJA
Palacio de la Diputación Provincial
Convento de Santo Domingo el Real
AVENIDA DE LA CAVA
PASEO DE RECAREDO
C.JON. DE LA MERCED
BUZONES
Convento de las Capuchinas
Convento de Santa Clara
PZA. CARMELITAS
REAL
PZA. DE SANTA LEOCADIA
LA MERCED
LOS ALJIBES
Convento de las Agustinas Calzadas
Torreón de los Abades
Puerta del Cambrón
PL. DE LAS CARMELITAS
Convento de Carmelitas Descalzas
SANTA LEOCADIA
San Ildefonso
TENDILLAS
PZA. SAN VICENTE
Santa Eulalia
Casa de Mesa Academia de Bellas Artes
Palacio Lorenzana
PINTOR MATÍAS MORENO
Colegio de Doncellas
Convento de Santo Domingo Antiguo
CUESTA DE SAN MARTÍN
CAMBRÓN
COLEGIO DE DONCELLAS
Museo de Arte Visigodo
Convento de San Clemente
ALFONSO X
NUNCIO VIEJO
Baño de la Cava
SAN MARTÍN
S. CLEMENTE
SAN ROMÁN
San Román
PL. DEL P. MARIANA
CAVA BAJA
LAS BULAS
Mº de San Pedro Mártir
Casa de la Cadena (Museo de Arte Contemporáneo)
PLAZA VALDECALEROS
San Juan de los Reyes
ALFONSO XII
Palacio Arzobispal
ÁNGEL
Sinagoga de Santa María la Blanca
Santo Tomé
SANTO TOMÉ
LA TRINIDAD
San Marcos
P
STA. ANA
REYES
El Salvador
Ayunta-miento
Puente de San Martín
JUDERÍA
SAN JUAN DE DIOS
PLAZA DEL CONDE
TALLER DEL MORO
SANTA ÚRSULA
CIUDAD
CATÓLICOS
Santa Úrsula
Sinagoga del Tránsito
Casa del Greco
Palacio de Fuensalida
PASEO DEL TRÁNSITO
PLAZA JUEGO DE LA PELOTA
Museo de Victorio Macho
EL CALVARIO
Convento de Santa Isabel
REINA
SOLA
Convento de San Gil o Gilitos
LOS DESCALZOS
SAN CRISTÓBAL
SAN TORCUATO
COBERTIZO DE S. BARTOLOMÉ
CALVARIO
SAN CIPRIANO
PL. DE STA. CATALINA
San Cipriano
San Sebastián
Río Tajo
EATING & DRINKING
El Zoco 2
Mille Grazie 1

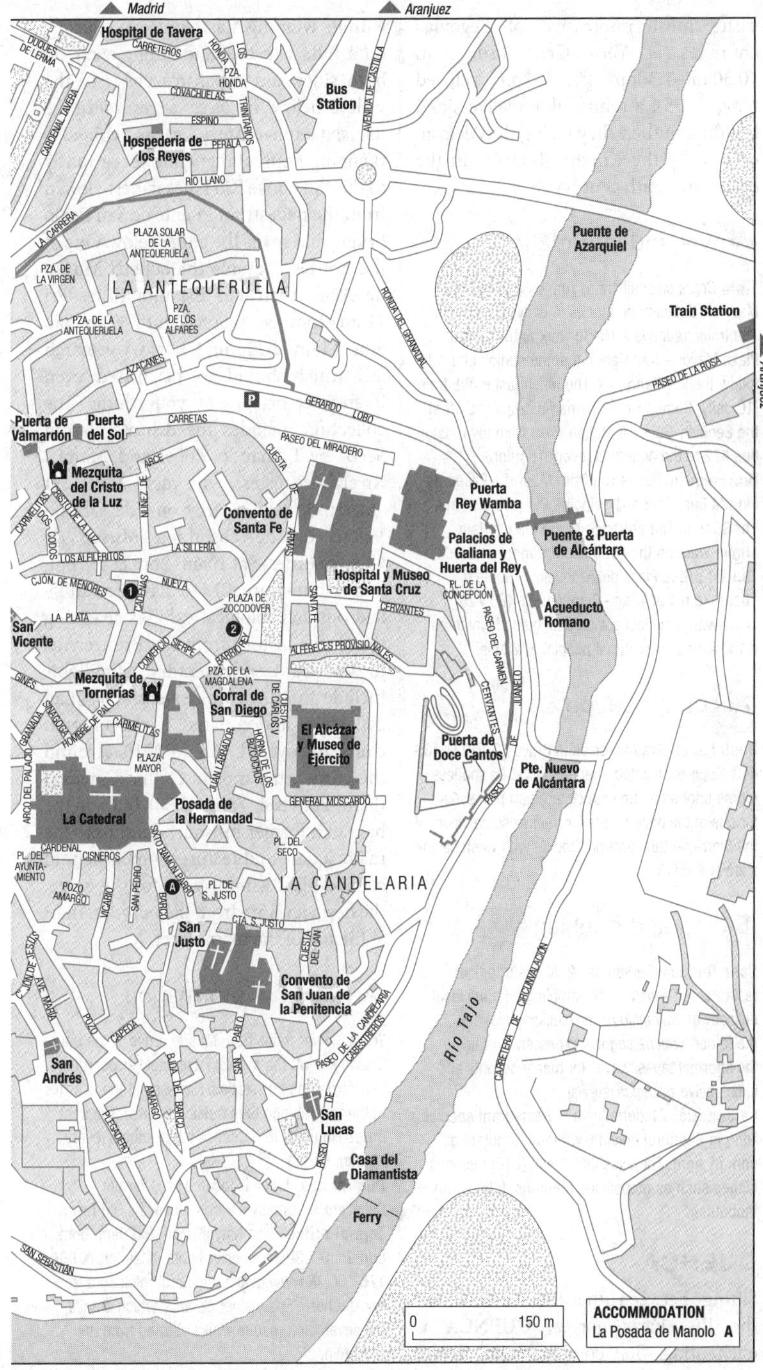
Madrid
Aranjuez
Hospital de Tavera
Bus Station
Hospedería de los Reyes
LA ANTEQUERUELA
Puente de Azarquiel
Train Station
Aranjuez
Puerta de Valmardón
Puerta del Sol
Mezquita del Cristo de la Luz
Convento de Santa Fe
Puerta Rey Wamba
Palacios de Galiana y Huerta del Rey
Puente & Puerta de Alcántara
Hospital y Museo de Santa Cruz
Acueducto Romano
San Vicente
Mezquita de Tornerías
Corral de San Diego
El Alcázar y Museo de Ejército
Puerta de Doce Cantos
Pte. Nuevo de Alcántara
La Catedral
Posada de la Hermandad
LA CANDELARIA
San Justo
Convento de San Juan de la Penitencia
Río Tajo
San Andrés
San Lucas
Casa del Diamantista
Ferry
0 150 m
ACCOMMODATION
La Posada de Manolo A

The most impressive of Segovia's churches is **Vera Cruz** (Tues–Sun 10.30am–1.30pm & 4–7pm; closed Nov; €1.75), a remarkable twelve-sided building in the valley facing the Alcázar, erected by the Knights Templar in the early thirteenth century.

Arrival and information

Train *Cercanía* snail-trains run to Segovia from Madrid's Estación de Atocha (9 daily; 1hr 45min). The train station is a 15min walk to the central Plaza Mayor – turn right out of the station and follow the left-hand fork. The much faster AVE train (10 daily; 35min) from Chamartín drops you off at the Segovia-Guiomar station, 7km from town; take bus #12 to the Aqueduct (every 15 min).
Bus Frequent buses run from Madrid's Paseo de Florida bus station Ⓜ Príncipe Pío (every 30min; 1hr 30min). The entrance to the old city is a 10min walk up the Avda de Fernández Ladreda.
Tourist office Plaza del Azoguejo 1 (Sun–Fri 10am–7pm, Sat 10am–8pm; Ⓣ 921 466 720, Ⓦ www.turismodesegovia.com); guided city tours (€14/person, minimum 4 people) available.

Accommodation

Hostal Juan Bravo c/de Juan Bravo 12 Ⓣ 921 463 413. Superbly located, friendly *hostal*, its spotless rooms brightened up with cheerful art prints. Ask for one of the back rooms for the awesome views of the Sierra de Guadarrama. Double with wash basin/shower €35/43.

Eating and drinking

Casa Duque c/Cervantes 12. At this traditional restaurant, it's well worth sampling both the local delicacy of *cochinillo asado* (suckling pig) and the famed *ponche segoviano* dessert. Or raid the informal tapas "cave" for meaty delights and inexpensive *cazuelas* (stews).
La Judería c/Judería Vieja 5. Restaurant specializing in Sephardi cuisine, with not a morsel of pork in sight. The excellent *menú* (€10) includes dishes such as moussaka, hummus, falafel and tabbouleh.

CUENCA

Sitting between the Río Huécar and the Río Júcar gorges, **CUENCA** is enchanting. Its compact Old Town, with its winding, narrow streets, clusters on a hill, with the land falling away on both sides and expansive views of the valleys below. Its *pièce de résistance* are its sixteenth-century **casas colgadas** (hanging houses) that cling precariously to the cliff above Río Huécar, best viewed from the pedestrian Puente de San Pablo bridge that spans the gorge below. One of the houses contains the superb **Museo de Arte Abstracto Español** (Tues–Fri 11am–2pm & 4–6pm, until 8pm Sat, Sun 11am–2.30pm; €3; Ⓦ www.march.es), which should not be missed, even if abstract art is not your thing. The collection includes the delicate "Jardín Seco" by Fernando Zóbel and Manuel Rivera's sinister wire-mesh-and-paint "Metamorfosis". Nearby, on c/del Obispo Valero 6, the absorbing **Museo de Cuenca** (Tues–Sat 10am–2pm & 4–7pm, Sun 11am–2pm; €1.50) has beautifully laid out archeological exhibits spanning the town's history from the Bronze Age to the eighteenth century. Highlights include the museum's extensive Roman collection and a large hoard of gold coins, uncovered only in 2010. Around the corner, the mostly Gothic **Catedral** (9am–2pm & 4–7pm; €2.80), built on the base of a former mosque, dominates the main square and features some splendid stained-glass windows. As for the gorge, the best views are from the *miradór*, right at the top of the main street.

Arrival and information

Train Slower trains from Madrid arrive at the train station just off the central Paseo del Ferrocarril, a block from the bus station. High-speed trains arrive at the train station 6km outside Cuenca; frequent buses connects it to Cuenca's bus station (every 15 min; €1.20).
Bus The bus station is located on C Fermín Caballero, a 10min walk from Cuenca's Old Town.
Tourist office Plaza Mayor (Mon–Sat 9am–9pm, Sun 9am–2.30pm; shorter hours in winter; Ⓣ 969 176 100, Ⓦ www.aytocuenca.org); pick up a free booklet here, *Paseos por Cuenca*, which details the seven picturesque walks starting from the Old Town.

Accommodation

Posada de San Julián c/de las Torres 1 ⓣ969 211 704. Just at the foot of the hill leading up into Old Town, this may be Cuenca's best bargain, with simple rooms with own toilets (but shared showers), wi-fi access and a popular restaurant on the ground floor. Singles €15–20, doubles €36.

Eating and drinking

La Bodeguita de Basilio c/Fray Luís de Léon 3. With photos of old Cuenca blanketing its cave-like walls, one of the town's best watering holes outdoes itself when it comes to tapas: each drink comes with a free plate, piled with salad, *jamón*, vegetable tempura and a quail's egg. Drinks €1.50.

Mesón Casas Colgadas c/de los Canónigos 3 ⓣ969 223 552. Treat yourself to some of the best food and views in Cuenca inside one of the *casas colgadas*. The *menú* (€30) features innovative takes on local specialities, such as suckling pig, sirloin with Manchego cheese and aubergine with crayfish. Reservations recommended.

Extremadura

The harsh environment of **Extremadura**, west of Madrid, is known as the "cradle of the conquistadors". Remote before and forgotten since, the area enjoyed a brief golden age when the conquerors of the Americas returned with their gold to live in a flourish of splendour. **Cáceres** preserves an entire town built with conquistador wealth, the streets crowded with the ornate mansions of returning empire-builders, as does **Trujillo**, the birthplace of Francisco Pizarro. An even more ancient past is tangible in the wonders of **Mérida**, the most completely preserved Roman city in Spain. The province attracts fewer tourists in June and July, as temperatures get unbearably hot.

TRUJILLO

Nicknamed the "Cradle of the Conquistadors", little **TRUJILLO** is the birthplace of key figures who shaped the fate of the New World; much of the town's wealth a direct result of the conquerors' plunders.

What to see and do

The town, a charming maze of russet-coloured houses and mansions topped with storks' nests, has at its heart the large, pedestrianized Plaza Mayor, just beneath the fortress walls of the Old Town and overlooked by a statue of Francisco Pizarro. In the southwestern corner of the plaza stands the elaborate **Palacio de la Conquista**, built for Hernando Pizarro, the brother of Francisco Pizarro – the swineherd turned conqueror of Peru – and his wife, the daughter of Francisco's union with Inés, his Incan consort; their carved images are on the corner. Across the plaza is the **Iglesia de San Martín** (Mon–Sat 10am–2pm & 4–7pm, Sun 10am–12.30pm; €1.40), which contains the family tombs of Francisco de Orellana, the first European to sail down the Amazon. West of the plaza is the **Palacio Juan Pizarro Orellana**, decorated with the coats of arms of the town's two most powerful families. In the Old Town uphill, encased within the crumbling medieval walls, head for the **Casa Museo Pizarro** (Mon–Sat 10am–2pm & 4.30–7.30pm; €1.40), a sixteenth-century house with well-laid out exhibits covering the history of the Pizarro family and the conquest of the Americas, using a mixture of maps, drawings and period artefacts. Nearby is the Gothic **Iglesia Santa María Mayor** (Mon–Sat 10am–2pm & 4–7pm; €1.40); from its Romanesque tower, you get all-encompassing views of the town, surrounded by arid plains. There's an even better view from the restored tenth-century Moorish **castle** (daily 10am–2pm & 4–7pm; summer 5–8pm; €1.40).

Arrival and information

Bus station In the Lower Town, 10min walk from the Plaza Mayor, and served by regular daily buses from Madrid (up to 10 daily; 3–4hr),

Cáceres (8 daily; 40min) and Merida (3–4 daily; 1hr 15min).

Tourist office Plaza Mayor (daily 10am–2pm & 5–8pm; ⓣ927 322 677, ⓦwww.trujillo.es); sells discounted combined tickets (€4.70–5.30) for Trujillo's top attractions.

Accommodation

Hostal Trujillo c/Francisco Pizarro 4–6 ⓣ927 322 274, ⓦwww.hostaltrujillo.com. A short walk from the Plaza Mayor, this simple guesthouse offers clean, a/c rooms. Good restaurant on site. Singles €40, doubles €50, triples €70.

Pensión Plaza Mayor Plaza Mayor ⓣ927 322 313. Light, bright singles and doubles with wi-fi access, superbly located right on the Plaza Mayor. Singles €25, doubles €40.

Eating and drinking

El Burladero Plaza Mayor 7. A large selection of tapas, including some excellent cured meats, at this popular bar. Wash it down with some great local wines.

Mesón La Troya Plaza Mayor 10. A local institution, decorated with photos of famous (and not-so-famous) patrons, *La Troya* serves up gargantuan portions of *extremeño* specialities, such as *migas* (breadcrumbs fried with chorizo) and hearty stews. If you go for the *menú del día* (€15), you better be ravenous.

CÁCERES

Old **CÁCERES** was built largely on the plunders of the New World and is home to the University of Extremadura. The Ciudad Monumental – a maze of tiny, winding streets, lined with immaculate historical buildings – is enclosed by medieval stone walls, with storks nesting on every rooftop.

What to see and do

Almost every building in the central **Plaza Mayor** is magnificent, featuring ancient walls pierced by the low **Arco de la Estrella**, the **Torre del Horno**, one of the best-preserved Moorish mud-brick structures in Spain, and the **Torre del Bujaco** – whose foundations date back to Roman times and which you can climb for a great view of the city (Mon–Sat 10am–2pm & 5.30–8.30pm, Sun 10am–2pm; €2.50). Another must-see is the **Museo de Cáceres** (Tues–Sat 9am–2.30pm & 5–8.15pm, Sun 10.15am–2.30pm; EU citizens free, non-EU €1.20), on the Plaza de las Veletas, which has jewellery, statuary, national costume and fine arts sections and whose highlight is the *aljibe* (cistern) of the original Moorish Alcázar, with rooms of wonderful horseshoe arches. The **Casa de Toledo-Montezuma** lies through the Estrella gate, and was where a follower of Cortés brought back a daughter of the Aztec emperor as his bride. Near the Plaza de San Jorge is the *judería* (former Jewish quarter) – narrow lanes of whitewashed houses and bright flowers. On c/Cuesta del Marqués 4, you'll find the entertaining **Casa Museo Árabe**, a traditionally decorated Moorish house (Tues–Sun 10.30am–2pm & 4.30–7.30pm; €1.50) complete with a harem and an original water cistern.

Arrival and information

Train and bus The stations face each other across the Carretera Sevilla, 2km out of town. Bus #L1 runs every 15min to Plaza de San Juan (€0.75), a central square, with signs leading on towards the Plaza Mayor.

Tourist office Regional tourist office, Plaza Mayor 3 (Mon–Fri 8.30am–2.30pm & 4–6pm, Sat & Sun 10am–2pm; ⓣ927 010 834, ⓦwww.turismocaceres.org and ⓦwww.turismoextremadura.com).

Accommodation

Albergue Las Veletas c/Margallo 36 ⓣ927 211 210. Bright, spacious dorms and rooms with modern furnishings and a/c. Friendly staff make it popular with groups of young Spaniards. Breakfast in on-site cafeteria for an additional €3. Dorms €18.

Pensión Carretero Plaza Mayor 22 ⓣ927 247 482. The large rooms with shared bathrooms are distinctly no-frills, but with little balconies overlooking the Plaza. Can be noisy, as it's right above a restaurant, but the location is as central as it gets. Singles €20.

Eating and drinking

Arabia Riad Plaza Mayor s/n. Lavishly decorated Arabic-style teahouse. Linger over a wide selection of exotic teas, fruit juices and smoothies or smoke a leisurely hookah. Teas €2.50–3.50.

Babel c/de Luís Sergios Sánchez 7. Arty café-bar where you can sip a coffee by day or a cocktail by night, with occasional art exhibitions.

Mesón Ibérico Plaza San Juan 10. Traditional restaurant serving local specialities. Try the excellent hams and cheeses, *migas* (chorizo-fried breadcrumbs), the *conejo al ajillo* (rabbit in garlic sauce) or the tasty *técula mécula* dessert. *Menú del día* €12.

Moving on

Train Madrid (5 daily, 4hr); Mérida (5 daily; 1hr).

Bus León (3 daily; 6hr); Madrid (8 daily; 4hr); Mérida (2–4 daily; 50min); Salamanca (4 daily; 3hr 30min); Seville (6 daily; 4hr); Trujillo (8 daily; 40min).

MÉRIDA

MÉRIDA, 70km south of Cáceres, contains one of Europe's most remarkable concentrations of Roman monuments, including two impressive aqueducts.

What to see and do

The beautiful **Teatro Romano** and **Anfiteatro** were presents to the city from Marcus Agrippa in around 15 BC. The stage is in a particularly good state of repair, and in July and August it's the scene for a season of classical plays (tickets from €10). In its day, up to fifteen thousand people would gather in the adjacent amphitheatre to watch gladiatorial combats and fights with wild animals. By the theatre's entrance, you'll find the vast, red-brick bulk of the superb **Museo Nacional de Arte Romano** (Tues–Sun 9.30am–3.30pm & 5.30–8.30pm; €3, free Sat pm & Sun am and for EU students), which does full justice to its superior collection, including portrait statues of Augustus, Tiberius and Drusus, some glorious mosaics, coins and other Roman artefacts. Further south, behind the Plaza de Toros, is the Casa de Mitreo – the remains of a Roman villa with an impressive mosaic. To the east of town you'll find the outline of the **Circo Romano**, which accommodated up to 30,000 people during chariot races. Also worth seeing is the magnificent **Puente Romano**, the pedestrian Roman bridge across the islet-strewn Guadiana on the city's west side – sixty arches long, and defended by an enormous Moorish **Alcazaba fortress**, built in 835 AD.

An **Entrada Conjunta** (combined ticket; €12) gives access to all the archeological sites (daily 9.30am–1.45pm & 5–7.15pm, 6.30pm in winter).

Arrival and information

Train station A 5min walk along c/Mártir Santa Eulalia from the main Plaza de la Villa and the tourist information office.

Bus station On Avda de la Libertad, a 15min walk across the Lusitania bridge or a short bus ride (bus #4 or #6) to the city centre.

Tourist office Paseo Sáenz de Buruaga (daily 9.30am–2pm & 5–7.30pm; ⓣ924 330 722, ⓦwww.turismomerida.org).

Accommodation

El Flor de Al-Andalus Avda Extremadura 6 ⓣ924 313 356, ⓦwww.laflordeal-andalus.es. Guesthouse with rooms decorated in Moorish style and sporting TVs and spick-and-span private bathrooms. Just a short walk from the train station and main attractions. Singles €36, doubles €49, triples €67.

Hostal El Alfarero c/Sagasta 40 ⓣ924 303 183, ⓦwww.hostalalfarero.com. The pick of the budget options in the centre, with simple, tastefully decorated en suites with TV and a/c. Enjoy good-quality local cuisine at the *Mesón El Alfarero* next door. Doubles €50, triples €70, quads €90.

Eating and drinking

Cervecería 100 Montaditos c/Felix Valverde Lillo 3. The ever-popular casual bar with a hundred different tiny sandwiches on offer; tick your selections and hand your form in at the bar. *Motaditos* €1.20–2.80.

Convivium c/de Sagasta 21. Thriving tapas bar specializing in *tortillinas* (mini potato omelettes) with fillings as varied as aubergine, prawns and chorizo. The *tortillina*, gazpacho and drink combo is a steal at only €2.50.

Mesón El Yantar Avda José Álvarez Saez de Buruaga 12. Snack on the best hams of the region, sample local *extremeño* dishes, or raid the shop for gourmet meats and cheeses to take home.

Moving on

Train Barcelona (1 daily at 7.55am; 13hr); Cáceres (5 daily; 1hr); Madrid (5 daily, 5hr–6hr 30min); Seville (1 daily; 4hr 10min).

Bus Cáceres (2–4 daily; 50min); Madrid (8 daily; 4–5hr); Salamanca (5 daily; 4hr 30min); Seville (5 daily; 2hr 30min); Trujillo (3 daily; 1hr 15min).

Castilla y León

The foundations of modern Spain were laid in the kingdom of **Castilla y León**, west and north of Madrid. A land of frontier fortresses – the *castillos* from which it takes its name – it became the most powerful and centralizing force of the Reconquest. The monarchs of this triumphant and expansionist age were enthusiastic patrons of the arts, endowing their cities with superlative monuments above which, quite literally, tower the great Gothic cathedrals of **Salamanca** and **León**.

SALAMANCA

SALAMANCA is home to arguably the oldest and what was once the most prestigious university in Europe. It's a small place, but with many golden sandstone monuments and an attractive Plaza Mayor. As if that weren't enough, Salamanca's student population ensures their town is lively at night during term time.

What to see and do

For a postcard-worthy view of Salamanca, cross the city's oldest surviving monument, the much-restored, four-hundred-metre-long **Puente Romano** (Roman Bridge) at the southern end of Old Town. To explore Salamanca, start at the grand **Plaza Mayor**, its bare central expanse enclosed by a four-storey refined Baroque building decorated with iron balconies and medallion portraits, the restrained elegance of the designs heightened by the changing strength and angle of the sun. Wander Salamanca's streets by night, when the glorious architecture is subtly lit by street lights; the pedestrian Calle de la Compañía has the best views.

Casa de las Conchas and the Universidad

The celebrated fifteenth-century **Casa de las Conchas**, or House of Shells, is so called because its facades are decorated with rows of carved scallop shells, symbol of the pilgrimage to Santiago de Compostela. It now houses the university library. From here, c/Libreros leads to the **Patio de las Escuelas Menores** and the Renaissance entrance to the **Universidad** (Mon–Sat 9.30am–1.30pm & 4–6.30pm, Sun 10am–1pm; €4). The ultimate achievement of Plateresque art, a Spanish style characterized by ornate decoration, this reflects the tremendous reputation of Salamanca in the early sixteenth century, when it was Europe's greatest university with the most important astronomy department in the world, consulted by Columbus before he set off on his sea voyage. Spotting the legendary "*rana de suerte*" (lucky frog) on its intricately sculpted facade allegedly brings you a year of good luck (spoiler: look closely at the skulls on the right column). The university's highlight is its incredible **library**, with its carved wooden ceiling and a collection of around 2800 manuscripts.

The cathedrals

Sumptuous and intricate, the late-Gothic **Catedral Nueva** (daily 9am–8pm) was begun in 1512, and acted as a buttress for the Catedral Vieja, which was in danger of collapsing. Entry to the **Catedral Vieja**

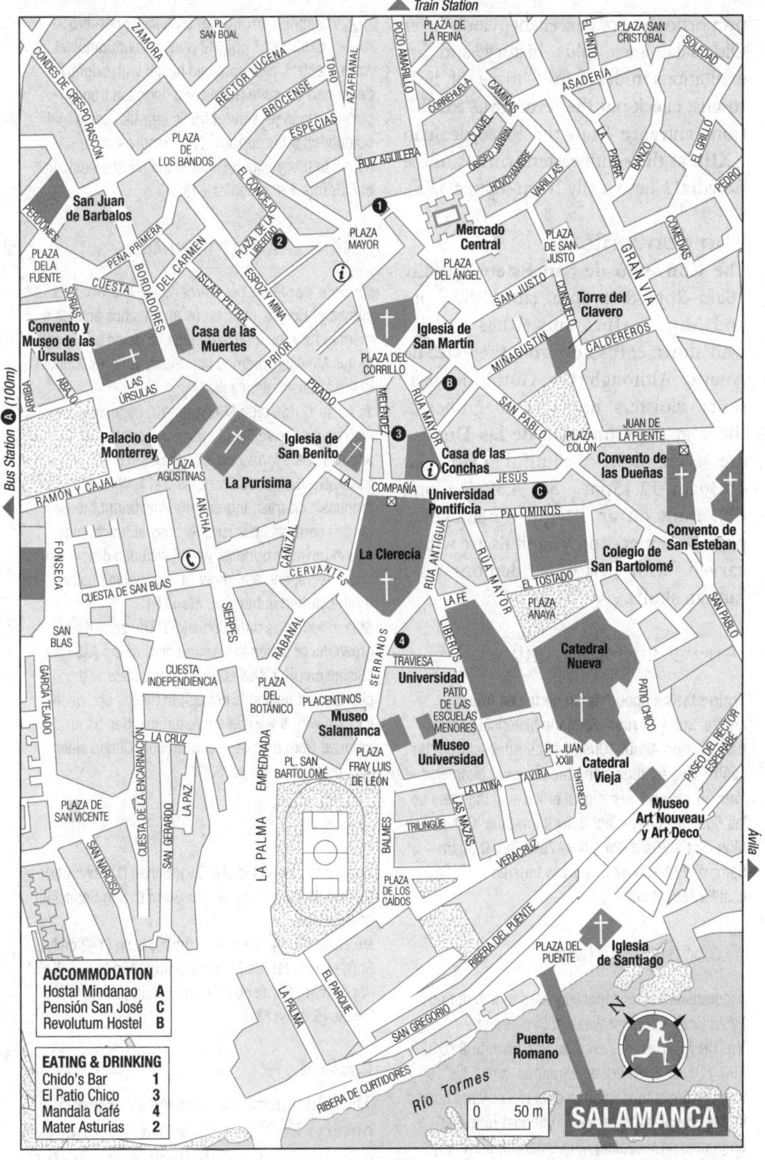

(daily 10am–7.30pm; €4.75) is inside the Catedral Nueva. Tiny by comparison and a stylistic hotch-potch of Romanesque and Gothic, its most striking feature is the fifteenth-century Renaissance altarpiece, its 54 tablets depicting the life of Christ. As you look at the Catedral Nueva from the Plaza de Anaya, try to spot the ice-cream cone and the astronaut, carved into the Puerta de Ramos during the last restoration. Inside the cathedral, you will find yourself dwarfed by its monolithic proportions. For excellent views over Old Salamanca, plus history and art exhibitions hidden in a maze of little rooms, check out the **Ieronimus exhibition** (entrance from the Plaza de Juan XXIII, at the southwestern corner of the Catedral Nueva; daily 10am–8pm; €3.75).

The convents

The **Convento de San Esteban** (daily 10am–2pm & 4–8pm, closed Sun pm and Mon & Tues am; €3) is a short walk down c/Tostado from the Plaza de Anaya. Although the Gothic-Renaissance cloisters here are magnificent, those at the **Convento de las Dueñas** are even more beautiful (Mon–Sat 10.30am–12.45pm & 4.30–7.30pm; €2). Built on an irregular pentagonal plan, its upper-storey capitals are wildly carved with writhing demons and human skulls.

Arrival and information

Train station About 15min northeast from the centre. Bus #11 runs along the historical centre.
Bus station About 10min walk northwest from the centre. Bus #4 runs along the old town perimeter.
Tourist office The regional office is in the Casa de las Conchas (July–Sept daily 9am–8pm; Oct–June Mon–Sat 9.30am–2pm & 4–7pm, Sun 9.30am–5pm; ⓣ923 268 571, ⓦwww.turismocastillayleon.com).

Accommodation

Accommodation is especially hard to find during fiesta time – the first week of September.
Hostal Mindanao Paseo de San Vicente 2 ⓣ923 100 114, ⓦwww.hostalmindanao.com. This friendly guesthouse with a cheerful colour scheme in the en-suite rooms has an almost religious emphasis on recycling. The bathrooms are tiny, but some proceeds support animal shelters in Madrid and Barcelona. Singles €32, doubles €40, triples €54.
Pensión San José c/Jesús 24 ⓣ923 265 461. Spotless, airy singles, doubles and triples, some en suite, located right near the cathedrals on a quiet street; the owners are friendly and helpful. Singles €25, doubles €40, triples €60.

Revolutum Hostel c/Sánchez Barbero 7 ⓣ923 217 656, ⓦwww.revolutumhostel.com. Central, chic boutique hostel with brightly decorated en-suite rooms and dorms, a trendy common lounge with futuristic egg-like seats and outdoor chill-out terrace. The friendly staff are happy to mix you a cocktail at the on-site bustling bar. Dorms €20, doubles €48.

Eating and drinking

Chido's Bar Plaza del Mercado 26. The Tex-Mex combo of Corona beer, tacos and nachos acts as a magnet for American exchange students and locals at this Mexican-themed bar. Nurse your drink down in the atmospheric vault.
El Patio Chico c/de Meléndez 13. Popular tavern with an extensive list of inexpensive tapas and sandwiches. *Platos combinados* €8–10.
Mandala Café c/de Serranos 9–11. With its emphasis on fresh ingredients, this bright Mediterranean spot gets particularly busy at lunchtimes due to its superb *menú,* which includes dishes like *arroz negro,* and a number of vegetarian choices – try the stuffed aubergine. *Menú* €12.
Mater Asturias c/de Consejo 3. The zany lime-green decor belies the seriousness of the Asturian cuisine on offer. The *fábada* (hearty stew with chorizo and beans) is enough to fill you up; wash it down with the excellent Asturian cider, hand-cranked from a strange contraption. Cheap cider-and-tapas offer for €2.50.

Moving on

Train Barcelona (1 daily; 8hr); Bilbao (1 daily; 6hr); Madrid (8 daily via Ávila; 2hr 30min); San Sebastián (2 daily; 6hr).
Bus Cáceres (4 daily; 3hr 30min); León (1–2 daily; 3hr); Madrid (16 daily; 2hr 30min); Mérida (5 daily; 4hr 30min); Santiago de Compostela (2 daily; 7hr); Seville (5 daily; 8hr).

LEÓN

The old *barrio* of **LEÓN** is steeped in history: in 914 A.D. as the Reconquest edged its way south from Asturias, the city became the Christian capital, and along with its territories it grew so rapidly that by 1035 the county of Castile had matured into a fully fledged kingdom. For the next two centuries, Castilla y León jointly spearheaded the war against the Moors, but by the thirteenth century

Castilla's power had eclipsed that of even her mother territory.

What to see and do

Historic sights aside – most notably its monumental Catedral – León has an attractive and enjoyable modern quarter and its Barrio Húmedo is where you'd head for a lively spot of tapas bar hopping.

The Catedral

León's enormous Gothic **Catedral** (July–Sept Mon–Sat 8.30am–1.30pm & 4–8pm, Sun 8.30am–2.30pm & 5–8pm; Oct–June until 7pm; ⓦwww.catedral deleon.org) dominates the Old Town. Dating back to the city's final years of greatness, it is perhaps the most beautiful of Spanish Gothic cathedrals. The kaleidoscopic stained-glass windows, which cover an amazing 19,375 square feet, present one of the most magical and harmonious spectacles in Spain, best appreciated from the inside.

Real Basílica de San Isidoro

The city's other great attraction is the **Real Basílica de San Isidoro**, a few minutes' walk west from the Catedral. It was commissioned by Ferdinand I, who united the two kingdoms in 1037, as a shrine for the bones of St Isidoro, and royal mausoleum. Its **Panteón Real** (Mon–Sat 10am–1.30pm & 4–6.30pm, Sun 10am–1.30pm; €4, free Thurs pm), a pair of twelfth-century, small crypt-like chambers, features some of the most imaginative and impressive paintings of Romanesque art, as well as a mummified finger of San Isidoro. It once contained the bones of eleven kings and twelve queens, but now lies empty, the French troops having destroyed the graves during the Napoleonic wars.

Convento de San Marcos

The opulent **Convento de San Marcos**, on the Plaza de San Marcos far west of the city's old pedestrianized quarter, was built in 1168 for the Knights of Santiago, one of several chivalric orders founded in the twelfth century to lead the Reconquest. It served as a resting point for weary pilgrims on their way to Santiago de Compostela, and is now part of a sumptuous hotel, though non-guests can visit the beautiful cloisters. The church's sacristy houses the small **Museo de León** (Tues–Sat 10am–2pm & 4–7pm, Sun 10am–2pm; €0.60), containing some beautiful statuary and portraits of the Knights of Santiago.

Museo de Arte Contemporaneo (MUSAC)

A short walk north of the Monasterio San Marcos is the award-winning **Museo de Arte Contemporaneo** (Tues–Fri 10am–3pm & 5–8pm, Sat & Sun 11am–3pm & 5–9pm; free; ⓦwww.musac.org.es), its exterior covered with 37 shades of glass, known for its excellent, thought-provoking exhibitions by contemporary artists, which include Spanish and international photography, sculpture and video installations.

Arrival and information

Train and bus stations The train station at the end of Avda de Palencia across the bridge from town, and the bus station on Paseo Ingeniero Saenz de Miera – from here, turn left onto the Paseo to reach the bridge. Casco Antiguo (the old city) is a 10min walk along Avda de Ordoño II.

Tourist office Plaza de la Regla 2 (July & Aug daily 9am–8pm; Sept–June Mon–Fri 9am–2pm & 5–8pm, Sat & Sun 10am–2pm & 5–8pm; ⓣ987 237 082, ⓦwww.turismocastillayleon.com).

Accommodation

Hostal Bayón c/del Alcázar de Toledo 6 ⓣ987 231 446. Basic rooms with a bright colour scheme, some en suite, some with wash basins, a 5min walk from the Old Town. Singles €17, doubles €32.

Hostal San Martín Plaza Torres de Omaña 1, 2º ⓣ987 815 187, ⓦwww.sanmartinhostales.com. Plain, bright rooms and spick-and-span bathrooms

presided over by a welcoming owner. Wi-fi available and Barrio Húmedo is nearby. Singles €24–30, doubles €42, triples €54.
Pensión La Torre de San Isídoro c/La Torre 3, 1° ⓣ987 225 594, ⓦwww.lahiguera.net/torresanisidoro. Spacious, good-quality rooms with private bathrooms. Friendly owner offers laundry service and free wi-fi. Singles €27, doubles €41.

Eating and drinking

Free tapas is the name of the game in the Barrio Húmedo around Plaza San Martín.
El Llar Plaza San Martín 9. Stalwart Leónese bar with dark wood interior and terracotta walls. The *patatas allioli* (potatoes with garlic mayonnaise) – free with every drink – are brilliant.
Estrella de Galicia c/de Ancha 22. Bustling Galician *restobar* specializing largely in seafood, but also serving excellent tapas, which include several variations on the traditional *tortilla.* Tapas platter €8.
La Bicha Plaza Tiendas s/n. Great place for all sorts of meaty tapas. This bar specializes in cured meats and *morcilla de León* – fried pig's blood with a slice of bread on the side.
Molly Malone c/Cardiles 2. Popular in equal measure with locals and visitors, this lively Irish pub has Guinness on tap and nightly live music.

Moving on

Train Barcelona (3 daily; 8hr–8hr 40min); Bilbao (daily at 3.22pm; 4hr 40min); Madrid (9 daily; 2hr 50min–4hr 45min); San Sebastián (daily at 3.22pm; 5hr); Santiago de Compostela (daily at 2.18pm; 5hr 40min).
Bus Barcelona (3 daily; 10hr); Bilbao (1–2 daily except Sat; 4–6hr); Cáceres (3 daily; 6hr); Madrid (10 daily; 3hr 30min–4hr); Santander (6 daily; 3hr 30min–7hr); San Sebastián (6 weekly; 6hr 40min); Seville (3 daily; 10hr 30min).

Andalucía

The southern region of **Andalucía** is likely to both meet and defy your preconceptions of Spain. It is the parched, passionate home of **flamenco** and the **bullfight**, tradition and fierce pride. But it's also much more than the cliché. Evidence of the **Moors**' sophistication remains visible to this day in **Córdoba**, in **Seville**, and, particularly, in **Granada's Alhambra**. Extending to either side of **Málaga** is the **Costa del Sol**, Europe's most developed resort area, but you can find unspoiled beaches even there, and along the **Costa de la Luz**, on the way to **Cádiz**, one of Spain's oldest cities. Andalucía is also where Europe stops and Africa begins: from **Tarifa**, the kitesurfer and windsurfer capital on the most southerly tip of Europe, the mountains of that great continent appear almost close enough to touch.

SEVILLE (SEVILLA)

SEVILLE (Sevilla) is the great city of the Spanish south, one of the earliest Moorish conquests (in 712 AD) and, as part of the Caliphate of Córdoba, the second city of al-Andalus. Under the Almohad dynasty, Seville became the capital of the last real Moorish empire in Spain from 1170 until 1212 before being conquered by Fernando III in 1248. With a monopoly on trade with the New World, the city grew in wealth and influence and, centuries on, still remains one of the most prosperous and beautiful of Spain's cities. Illustrious history aside, it is the city's life that remains the great attraction, expressed on a grand scale at the city's two great festivals: **Semana Santa**, the week before Easter, and the **Feria de Abril**, which lasts a week at the end of April. While thoroughly modern, the soul of the city lies in its historic latticework of narrow streets, patios and plazas, where minarets jostle for space among cupolas and palms, and in its atmospheric flamenco bars.

What to see and do

Seville's three architectural gems – the Alcázar, the Catedral and La Giralda – occupy the southern corner of the popular *barrio* of Santa Cruz, with a cluster of excellent restaurants and bars. To the north of this, the city centre lies in a curve of the Río Guadalquivir, on its eastern bank.

La Giralda and the Catedral

Topped with four copper spheres, the 90m tall **La Giralda** (Mon–Sat 11am–5.30pm, Sun 2.30–6.30pm; €8), erected by the Almohads between 1184 and 1198, still dominates the skyline today and you can ascend the former minaret for a remarkable view of the city. The Giralda was so venerated by the Moors that they wanted to destroy it before the Christian conquest of the city. Instead, in 1402 it became the bell tower of the **Catedral**, the world's largest Gothic church, and third largest cathedral after St Peter's and St Paul's. Its centre is dominated by a vast Gothic *retablo* composed of 45 carved scenes from the life of Christ, making up the largest altarpiece in the world. On your way out, linger inside the Patio de los Naranjas – the courtyard studded with orange trees where ritual ablutions would have been performed before entering the mosque. (To avoid the queues, book your ticket online with Ⓦwww.servicaixa.com for an extra €1).

The Alcázar

Across Plaza del Triunfo from the cathedral lies the **Alcázar** (April–Sept 9.30am–7pm; Oct–March Tues–Sat 9.30am–5pm, Sun 9.30am–1.30pm; €8), a site that rulers of Seville have occupied from the time of the Romans. Rebuilt and added to numerous times, under the Almohad dynasty, the complex was turned into an enormous citadel, forming the heart of the town's fortifications. Parts of the walls survive, but the palace was rebuilt in the Christian period by Pedro the Cruel (1350–69). His works, some of the best surviving examples of Mudéjar architecture, form the nucleus of the Alcázar today. The perfectly proportioned, sunny patios, beautiful tile work, the gilded ceilings, tranquil gardens and the calligraphy carved into the palace walls, reminiscent of Granada's Palacios Nazaríes, encourage wandering the complex for hours at leisure.

Torre del Oro and Hospital de la Caridad

By the river, west of the Catedral, stands the twelve-sided **Torre del Oro** (Tues–Fri 10am–1.30pm, Sat & Sun 10.30am–1.30pm; €2) built in 1220 as part of the Alcázar fortifications and named after the gold brought back to Seville from the Americas and stored here. It contains a small, nautically themed museum. Across from here is the **Hospital de la Caridad** (Mon–

SEMANA SANTA SURVIVAL

Semana Santa (Holy Week) is the most exciting time to be in Seville, with its eerie processions of robed and hooded faithful from different *hermanidades* (brotherhoods). But with the celebrations come the crowds. To navigate your way around the city during this frenetic time, here are some tips:

- Do all your sightseeing in the mornings, since most processions take place in the afternoons and evenings.
- Find out the day's procession routes and make sure you know how to get back to your guesthouse.
- Stock up on water and snacks, as many shops in the centre will be closed or difficult to reach.
- To push your way past a procession, shuffle along the side, NOT down the middle.
- Do buy yourself one of those collapsible walking-stick-cum-stools to perch on.
- Don't sit on the wooden chairs along the procession routes; the city's wealthiest residents will have paid up to €800 for each one.
- Do splurge on a balcony space (€60) for an unobstructed view of the processions.

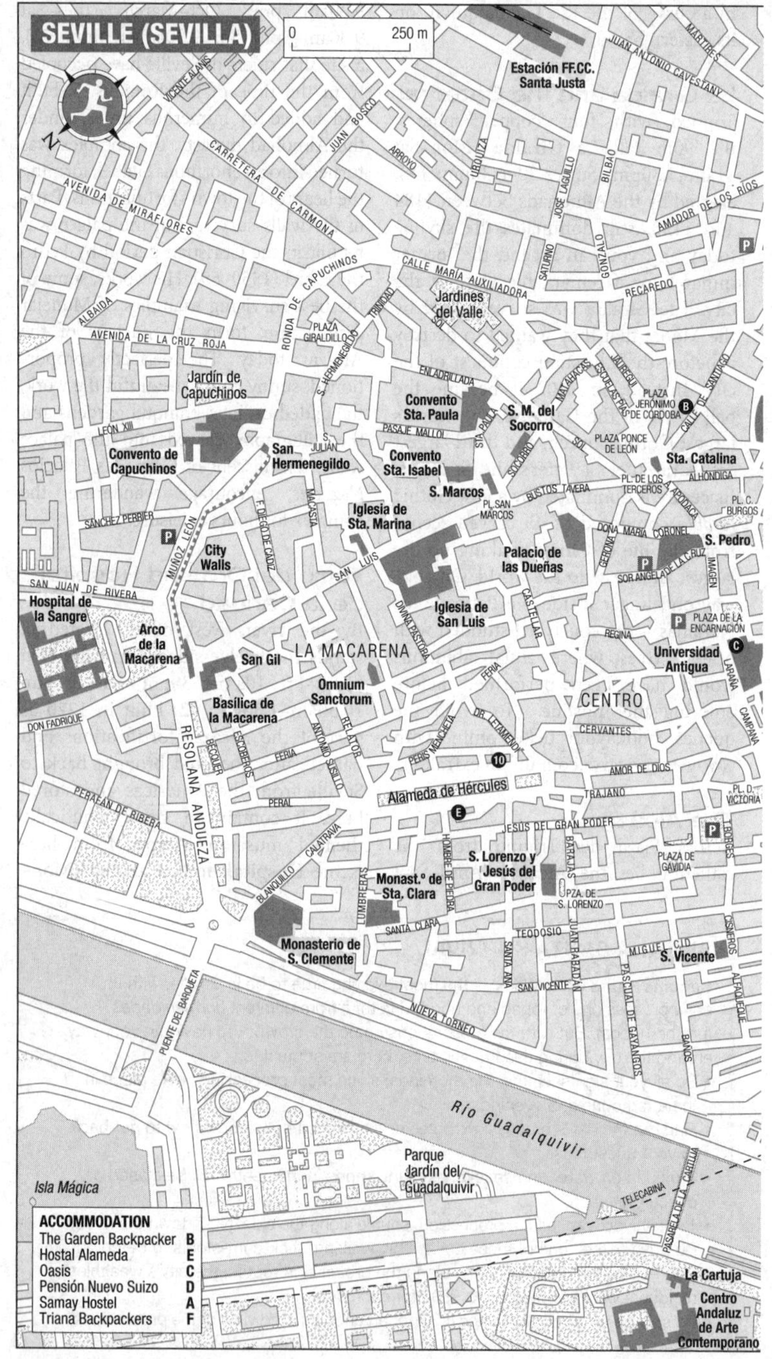
SEVILLE (SEVILLA)
0
250 m
N
Estación FF.CC.
Santa Justa
JUAN ANTONIO CAVESTANY
MARTIRES
VICENTE ALANIS
JUAN BOSCO
ARROYO
CARRETERA DE CARMONA
AVENIDA DE MIRAFLORES
URQUIZA
JOSÉ LAGUILLO
BILBAO
AMADOR DE LOS RÍOS
GONZALO
SATURNO
RECAREDO
CALLE MARÍA AUXILIADORA
RONDA DE CAPUCHINOS
TRINIDAD
SOL
Jardines
del Valle
ALBAIDA
AVENIDA DE LA CRUZ ROJA
PLAZA
GIRALDILLO
S. HERMENEGILDO
ENLADRILLADA
Jardín de
Capuchinos
Convento
Sta. Paula
S. M. del
Socorro
MATAHACAS
ESCUELAS PÍAS
JÁUREGUI
PLAZA
JERÓNIMO
DE CÓRDOBA
CALLE DE SANTIAGO
PASAJE MALLOL
STA PAULA
LEÓN XIII
Convento de
Capuchinos
San
Hermenegildo
S.
JULIÁN
Convento
Sta. Isabel
SOCORRO
SOL
PLAZA PONCE
DE LEÓN
Sta. Catalina
ALHÓNDIGA
S. Marcos
BUSTOS TAVERA
PL. DE LOS
TERCEROS
APODACA
PL. SAN
MARCOS
PL. C.
BURGOS
SÁNCHEZ PERRIER
MACASTA
F. DIEGO DE CÁDIZ
Iglesia de
Sta. Marina
DOÑA MARÍA CORONEL
S. Pedro
MUÑOZ LEÓN
City
Walls
SAN LUIS
Palacio de
las Dueñas
GERONA
SOR ÁNGELA DE LA CRUZ
IMAGEN
SAN JUAN DE RIVERA
Hospital de
la Sangre
Iglesia de
San Luis
DIVINA PASTORA
CASTELLAR
PLAZA DE LA
ENCARNACIÓN
Arco
de la
Macarena
San Gil
LA MACARENA
REGINA
Universidad
Antigua
FERIA
Omnium
Sanctorum
CENTRO
LARAÑA
Basílica de
la Macarena
DON FADRIQUE
RESOLANA
ANDUEZA
BÉCQUER
ESCOBEROS
FERIA
ANTONIO SUSILLO
RELATOR
PERIS MENCHETA
DR. LETAMENDI
CERVANTES
CAMPANA
AMOR DE DIOS
PERAFÁN DE RIBERA
PERAL
Alameda de Hércules
TRAJANO
PL. D.
VICTORIA
JESÚS DEL GRAN PODER
CALATRAVA
BLANQUILLO
LUMBRERAS
Monast.º de
Sta. Clara
HOMBRE DE PIEDRA
S. Lorenzo y
Jesús del
Gran Poder
BARATAS
PLAZA DE
GAVIDIA
T. BORGES
PZA. DE
S. LORENZO
SANTA CLARA
TEODOSIO
Monasterio de
S. Clemente
SANTA ANA
JUAN RABADÁN
MIGUEL CID
S. Vicente
CISNEROS
SAN VICENTE
PASCUAL DE GAYANGOS
ALFAQUEQUE
NUEVA TORNEO
PUENTE DEL BARQUETA
BAÑOS
Río Guadalquivir
Parque
Jardín del
Guadalquivir
Isla Mágica
TELECABINA
PASARELA DE LA CARTUJA
ACCOMMODATION
The Garden Backpacker B
Hostal Alameda E
Oasis C
Pensión Nuevo Suizo D
Samay Hostel A
Triana Backpackers F
La Cartuja
Centro
Andaluz
de Arte
Contemporano

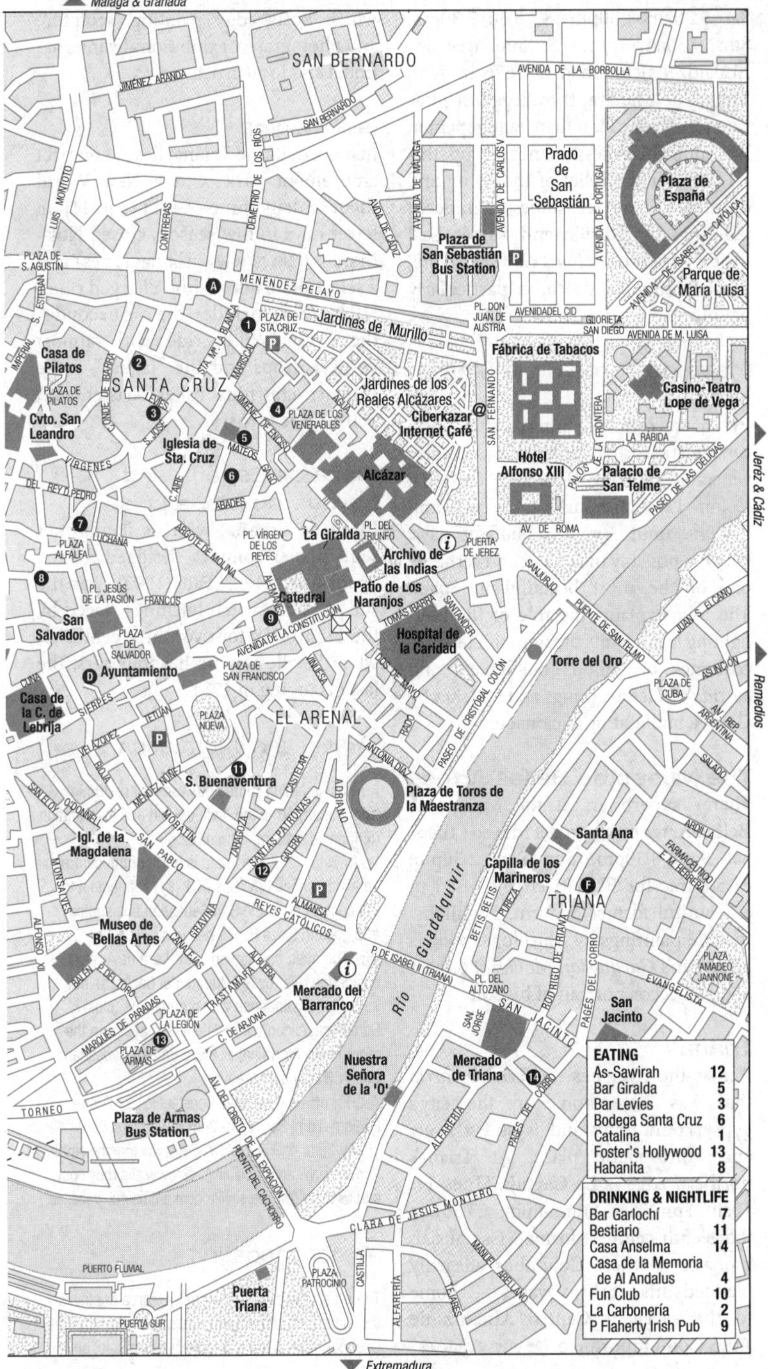
Málaga & Granada
SAN BERNARDO
Prado de San Sebastián
Plaza de España
Plaza de San Sebastián Bus Station
Parque de María Luisa
Jardines de Murillo
Fábrica de Tabacos
Casino-Teatro Lope de Vega
Jardines de los Reales Alcázares
Ciberkazar Internet Café
Casa de Pilatos
SANTA CRUZ
Cvto. San Leandro
Iglesia de Sta. Cruz
Alcázar
Hotel Alfonso XIII
Palacio de San Telmo
La Giralda
Archivo de las Indias
Patio de Los Naranjos
Catedral
San Salvador
Hospital de la Caridad
Torre del Oro
Ayuntamiento
Casa de la C. de Lebrija
EL ARENAL
S. Buenaventura
Plaza de Toros de la Maestranza
Igl. de la Magdalena
Santa Ana
Capilla de los Marineros
TRIANA
Museo de Bellas Artes
Río Guadalquivir
Mercado del Barranco
San Jacinto
Mercado de Triana
Nuestra Señora de la 'O'
Plaza de Armas Bus Station
Puerta Triana
Jeréz & Cádiz
Remedios
Extremadura
EATING
As-Sawirah 12
Bar Giralda 5
Bar Levíes 3
Bodega Santa Cruz 6
Catalina 1
Foster's Hollywood 13
Habanita 8
DRINKING & NIGHTLIFE
Bar Garlochí 7
Bestiario 11
Casa Anselma 14
Casa de la Memoria de Al Andalus 4
Fun Club 10
La Carbonería 2
P Flaherty Irish Pub 9

Sat 9.30am–1.30pm & 3.30–7.30pm, Sun 9.30am–1pm; €5, Sun free for EU citizens) founded in 1676 by Don Miguel de Manara, the alleged inspiration for Byron's Don Juan, who repented his youthful excesses and set up this hospital for the relief of the dying and destitute. There are some magnificent paintings by Murillo and Valdés Leal inside – the latter's *Finis Gloriae Mundi*, a meditation on death, is particularly haunting.

Plaza de Toros de la Maestranza

Even if you're not planning on attending a *corrida*, it's worth taking a tour of Seville's venerable **bullring** (Paseo de Cristóbal Colón 12; half-hourly tours 9.30am–8.30pm, until 3pm on bullfight days; €6.50) – possibly the oldest, and certainly one of the most beautiful in Spain. The tour explains the role of the bullfighting team, while the museum features costumes of famous bullfighters and *corrida*-related paintings and sketches by Goya, a bullfighting aficionado.

The Museo de Bellas Artes

There's superb art at the **Museo de Bellas Artes** on Plaza del Museo (Tues–Sat 9am–8.30pm, Sun 9am–2.30pm; €1.50, free for EU citizens), housed in a beautiful former convent. Highlights include paintings by Murillo, as well as Zurbarán's *Carthusian Monks at Supper* and El Greco's portrait of his son.

Triana

Across the river lies the **Triana** *barrio* that was once home to the city's gypsy community and is still a lively and atmospheric place. At Triana's northern edge is **La Cartuja** (Tues–Fri 10am–8pm, Sat 11am–8pm; €3.50), a fourteenth-century former Carthusian monastery, where Columbus allegedly planned his early voyages – home to the excellent **Centro Alnaluz de Arte Contemporáneo** (ⓦwww.caac.es) which hosts edgy painting, sculpture and photography exhibitions by international and local artists.

Isla Mágica

Just north of the Triana, lies, a compact amusement park with a New World theme (daily June–Aug 11am–11pm, fewer days in low season, closed Nov–March; €28; ⓦwww.islamagica.es) and a selection of adrenaline-charged rides. Highlights include the "Anaconda", the "Wet'n'Wild" ride with almost vertical drops and the "Jaguar" – the stomach-churning roller coaster with 360-degree turns.

Plaza de España and Parque de María Luisa

Plaza de España, with its flamboyant semicircular complex designed for the Spanish Americas Fair (1992), was the site of public witch burnings staged by the Inquisition for over three centuries, when Seville was its headquarters, the last occurring in 1781.

Arrival and information

Air Los Amarillos shuttle bus runs every 30min from the airport to the Avda del Cid and train station (5.45am–12.45am; 30min; €2.50).

Train Estación Santa Justa is north of the centre, on Avda Kansas City; bus #C1 (€1) connects it to the centre and to the San Sebastián bus station, #32 goes to Plaza Ponce de León.

Bus The main bus station is at Plaza de Armas, beside the river by the Puente del Cachorro, but buses for destinations within Andalucía (plus Barcelona, Alicante and Valencia) leave from the more central terminal at Plaza de San Sebastián. Bus #C3 connects the two.

Tourist office Avda de la Constitución 21 (Mon–Fri 9am–7pm, Sat 10am–2pm & 3–7pm & Sun 10am–2pm; ⓣ954 787 578, ⓦwww.turismo.sevilla.org, ⓦwww.andalucia.org). ⓦwww.eligirhoy.com and ⓦwww.discoversevilla.com are useful websites.

Accommodation

The most attractive – and pricey – area to stay is the maze-like Barrio Santa Cruz, near the Catedral. Cheaper options are available in c/Farnesio, on the periphery of the *barrio*, or slightly further out beyond Plaza Nueva, towards the river. During Easter Week and the Feria de Abril, prices double; book several months in advance.

The Garden Backpacker c/Santiago 19 ⓣ954 223 866, ⓦwww.thegardenbackpacker.com. With a tranquil back garden, sun-lounge area and a bustling bar serving up free sangría, this ever-popular central hostel has walking tours and tapas tours organized daily. Dorms €18–22, doubles €58.

Hostal Alameda Alameda de Hércules 31 ⓣ954 900 191, ⓦwww.hostalalameda.com. Quiet, central and friendly guesthouse featuring en-suite rooms with balconies and wi-fi. Singles €40, doubles €80, triples €100.

Oasis c/Compañia 1 ⓣ954 293 777, ⓦwww.hostelsoasis.com. Fantastic backpacker favourite, with helpful staff, clean dorms on several floors festooned with greenery. Rooftop pool, modern amenities and excellent breakfast included. Great for nightly tapas bar crawls. Dorms €22, doubles €56.

Pensión Nuevo Suizo c/Azofaifo 7 ⓣ954 229 147, ⓦwww.nuevosuizo.com. This friendly, creaky wooden house that's right on the procession route during Semana Santa offers free breakfast, teas and coffees, and trips to flamenco shows. Some rooms have shared bathrooms. Singles €39, doubles €68–72, triples €99.

Samay Hostel Avda. Menéndez Pelayo 13 ⓣ955 100 160, ⓦwww.samayhostels.com. Top backpacker choice in a modern, marble-floored building with light, spacious, secure en-suite dorms, breakfast, wi-fi and a large roof terrace. Ask for a dorm facing away from the busy main street. Dorms €19–24, doubles €58–62.

Triana Backpackers c/Rodrigo de Triana 69 ⓣ954 459 960, ⓦwww.trianabackpackers.com. Friendly and sociable place in the Triana, whose staff organize lots of guest events, such as a tapas night. Clean dorms inside the attractively tiled building have wi-fi and a/c. Dorms €18–22.

Eating

There are numerous choices in the Barrio Santa Cruz, the streets around Plaza Nueva and Triana.

As-Sawirah c/Galera 5. Excellent Moroccan restaurant near Triana serving light, fluffy couscous dishes and particularly good *tagines*. *Menú del día* €14.

Bar Giralda c/Mateos Gago 1. *Frituras* (fried fish platters) and *cazuela Tío Pepe* (meat stew with sherry) are among the specials at this top tapas bar, set in a former hammam.

Bar Levíes c/San José 15. Packed at night, this informal bar serves large portions of regional tapas, as well as pizza and beer. Try the *salmorejo* (thick, savoury gazpacho) or the *solomillo al whisky* (steak cooked in whisky). Tapas €2–4.50.

Bodega Santa Cruz c/Rodrigo Caro 1. Popular bar serving cheap tapas (€1.90–2.50). Try the *pringá*, a meaty sandwich and local speciality.

Catalina Paseo Catalina de Ribera 4. Vegetarians are welcome at this restaurant with an appealing outdoor terrace; the sumptuous aubergines with goat's cheese is one of the house specials. Mains €8–12.

Foster's Hollywood Plaza de Armas 1, 1st floor of the mall. Hankering for a giant burger, or perhaps some baby back ribs with 'slaw and fries followed by home-style apple pie or brownie sundae? Look no further than this popular American-style diner. Mains €8–14.

Habanita c/Golfo s/n, off c/Pérez Galdos. Informal Caribbean-style restaurant with good vegetarian options. Try the *moros y cristianos* (rice and beans) with fried plantain or the sweet potatoes with spicy sauce. Mains €8–12.

Drinking and nightlife

The Plaza Alfalfa area, north of the Catedral, is particularly lively at night. The other main area for nightlife, popular with tourists and Seville's gay population, is just across the river in Triana, on c/Betis.

Bar Garlochí c/Boteros 4. Weird and wonderful bar popular with *Sevillanos*, with a mock-religious theme and a sacrilegious house special – the Sangre de Cristo cocktail.

Bestiario c/Zaragoza 33. Rockin' club, popular with 20-something locals, that plays a retro 80s mix. Thurs–Sat from 11pm.

Fun Club Alameda de Hércules 86. It's a live music club that's definitely fun; most nights, live bands play a mix of funk, jazz and Latino. Entry €3–6 on live music nights. Thurs–Sun 11.30pm–late.

P Flaherty Irish Pub c/Alemanes 7. Lively expat haunt next to the Catedral, with Guinness on tap, a wide selection of beers, good pub grub and sports on TV nightly.

Flamenco

Flamenco – or more accurately Sevillanas – music and dance goes on at dozens of places in the city. Head to one of the following bars, or go to c/Rodrigo de Triana, the home of a handful of flamenco academies, to check out the students in action.

Casa Anselma c/Pagés de Corro 49. Thick with cigarette smoke and packed with local flamenco aficionados, all waiting for a spontaneous performance to break out. There's no sign; it's on the corner of c/Alfarería in the Triana neighbourhood. Mon–Sat from midnight.

Casa de la Memoria de Al Andalus c/Ximénez de Enciso 28 ☎954 560 670. Fantastic daily performances at this intimate cultural centre at 7.30/9/10.30pm, depending on the season. Book tickets in advance (€16).

La Carbonería c/Levíes 18. Tapas bar in an old coal merchant's building, packed to the rafters with locals and a few lucky tourists, with excellent flamenco performances at 11pm and midnight most nights.

Bullfighting

The season starts with the Feria de Abril and continues until October, with most *corridas* held on Sun evenings. Tickets from the Plaza de Toros de la Maestranza, Paseo de Colón 12 (☎902 5223 506), from as little as €15.

Directory

Exchange There are numerous banks, ATMs and *cambios* along Avda de la Constitución.

Hospital Hospital Universitario Virgen Macarena, Avda Dr Fedriani 3 (☎950 080 000) has English-speaking doctors. For an ambulance, call ☎061.

Internet Ciber Alcázar, c/San Fernando 35 (Mon–Fri 10am–11pm, Sat & Sun noon–11pm).

Left luggage Coin-operated lockers at the train station. *Consignas* at both bus stations.

Pharmacies Throughout the city centre.

Post office Avda de la Constitución 32.

Moving on

Train Almería (4 daily; 5hr 40min); Barcelona (5hr 30min–12hr 30min); Cádiz (11 daily; 1hr 30min–1hr 50min); Córdoba (every 30min; 40min–1hr 20min); Granada (4 daily; 3hr); Madrid (every 30min; 2hr 30min); Málaga (11 daily; 2hr–2hr 30min); Valencia (daily at 8.20am; 8hr 30min).

Bus Almería (3 daily; 5hr 45min); Cáceres (6 daily; 4hr); Cádiz (12 daily; 1hr 45min); Córdoba (12 daily; 2hr); Granada (12 daily; 3hr 30min); Madrid (14 daily; 6hr); Málaga (12 daily; 2hr 45min); Mérida (12 daily; 3hr); Ronda (6 daily; 2hr 30min); Tarifa (4 daily; 3hr 30min).

CÁDIZ

CÁDIZ is among the oldest settlements in Spain, founded about 1100 BC by the Phoenicans, and has long been one of the country's principal ports. In the eighteenth century it enjoyed a virtual monopoly on the Spanish-American trade in gold and silver. Central Cádiz, built on a peninsula island, entices with its grand open squares, narrow alleyways and high, turreted houses. It's also the spiritual home of flamenco, and has a tremendous atmosphere – slightly seedy, somewhat in decline, but still full of mystique. Cádiz's big party time is its annual **Carnaval**, complete with frenzied costumed revelry, normally held in February and early March.

What to see and do

With its winding alleys, backstreets and cafés, Cádiz is fascinating to wander around. For sweeping views of the city, climb the **Torre Tavira**, Marqués del Real Tesoro 10 (daily: June–Sept 10am–8pm; Oct–May 10am–6pm; €4.50), tallest of the 160 lookout towers in the city, with a *cámara oscura*, a device that uses mirrors to zoom in on any part of the city and project a live image onto a flat surface inside the tower (guided shows hourly). The huge white sea-facing **Catedral Nueva** (Mon–Sat 10am–6.30pm, Sun 1.30–6.30pm; €5, free Tues–Fri 7–8pm & 11am–1pm Sun) is a blend of High Baroque and Neoclassical styles as a result of it taking 116 years to build, decorated entirely in stone. Climb the adjacent **Torre de Poniente** (10am–6pm; €3) for a splendid panoramic view of the city. The spacious white interior at the **Museo de Cádiz** on Plaza de Mina (Tues 2.30–8.30pm, Wed–Sat 9am–8.30pm, Sun 9.30am–2.30pm; €1.50, free for EU citizens) perfectly showcases the Phoenician marble sarcophagi, Roman statuary and other archeological treasures. Upstairs are masterpieces by Zurbarán and Murillo, as well as temporary modern art exhibits. You can also enjoy a **coastal walk** that runs along the outside of Old Town, taking in two beautiful parks – the Alameda Apodaca, running along the Bay of Cádiz, and the large, sculpted Parque Genovés – home to numerous exotic plants. Cádiz also has two main **beaches**: the often-crowded little crescent Playa de la Caleta at its western end, and Playa de la Victoria's wide stretch of white sand (take bus #1 south along Avda del Puerto).

Arrival and information

Train The station is at the southeastern end of the old town, a 5min walk to the Plaza de San Juan de Dios.
Bus The bus station is opposite the train station.
Tourist office Turismo municipal office, Paseo de Canalejas (Mon–Fri 8.30am–6pm, Sat & Sun 9am–5pm; ⓣ956 241 001) and turismo regional, Avda Ramón de Carranza 1 (Mon–Fri 9am–7.30pm, Sat & Sun 10am–2pm; ⓣ956 203 191) have useful maps of the region.

Accommodation

Casa Caracol c/Suárez de Salazar 4 ⓣ956 261 166, ⓦwww.caracolcasa.com. This place has a chaotic vibe, laidback staff and open-plan dorms. You won't get much sleep, but you'll never lack for company during their rooftop parties. Dorms €20.

Melting Pot Hostel c/Rosario Cepeda 14 ⓣ956 070 207, ⓦwww.meltingpothostels.com. A super-central location, spacious, squeaky-clean dorms with lockers and helpful staff are just some of the bonuses at this hostel that's way ahead of the competition. Dorms €17.

Pensión España c/Marqués de Cádiz 9 ⓣ956 285 500, ⓦwww.pensionespana.com. This friendly, central guesthouse offers clean singles, doubles and triples, most with shared bathrooms. Wi-fi available. Singles €30, doubles €45–60, triples €60–70.

Eating and drinking

For drinks and seafood, head to c/Virgen de la Palma in the Barrio de la Viña, just east of Playa de la Caleta, or to Plaza de Las Flores.

Freiduría Las Flores Plaza Las Flores s/n. A Cádiz institution, this *freiduría* (fry shop) serves up large, cheap portions of all kinds of fish. Try the excellent *cazón adobo* (marinated shark) or the *tortilla de camarónes* (shrimp patty). Tapas €1.40–3.

La Gorda Te Da De Comer c/General Luque 1. Trendy spot with blood-red walls hung with old photos of Cádiz, serving cheap tapas. Try the *solomillo al whisky* or the *patatas bravas*. Tapas €2.

Taberna El Tío de la Tiza Plaza Tío de la Tiza s/n. *Bodega* with outdoor seating serving up excellent gazpacho, *salmorejo*, and cooked *gambas* (large prawns) by the pound.

Moving on

Train to: Córdoba (10 daily; 2hr 30min–3hr 30min); Madrid (3 daily; 4hr 30min); Seville (11 daily; 1hr 50min).
Bus to: Almería (1 daily at 3pm; 7hr); Granada (4 daily; 5hr); Málaga (4 daily; 4hr); Ronda (1–2 daily; 3hr); Seville (8–10 daily; 2hr); Tarifa (6 daily; 1hr 45min).

TARIFA

If there is one thing that defines **TARIFA**, it is the prevailing, massively powerful wind, which has made the most southerly point in mainland Europe one of the world's most popular wind- and kitesurfing destinations. There's a good feel to the place – with its funky, laidback atmosphere and compact maze of narrow streets. Africa feels very close, too, with the Rif mountains clearly visible – and easily accessible, via the ferry that runs to Tangier in Morocco.

What to see and do

The ten-kilometre white, sandy **beaches**, **Playa de los Lances** and **Ensenada de Valdevaqueros**, are the places to head for wind- and kitesurfing. To try any of the aquatic sports, you can book a course or rent equipment from a number of outfitters on c/Batalla del Salado, including Art of Kiting at no. 47 (ⓣ605 031 880, ⓦwww.artofsurfing.com) and the Wave Bandits Kite School out of town, on the N-340 at Km 82.7 (ⓣ619 471 735, ⓦwww.wavebandits.com); most charge similar prices, with a four-hour kitesurfing taster course costing around €135. Alternatively, go on a 2-hour **whale-watching** boat **trip** with Firmm, c/Pedro Cortéz 4 (April–Oct; €30; ⓣ956 627 008, ⓦwww.firmm.org), dedicated to research and conservation of the local population of pilot whales, sperm whales and dolphins. Finally, you can take a 1- or 2-day guided trip to Tangier, Morocco, with FRS (1-/2-day-trip €60/89; ⓣ956 681 830, ⓦwww.frs.es).

Arrival and information

Bus The bus stop is just off the main road, Batalla del Salado; the town centre is a 10min walk south.
Tourist office Paseo de la Alameda (10am–2pm; also 6–8pm Mon–Fri June–Sept; ⓣ956 680 993, ⓦwww.aytotarifa.com).

Accommodation

From July to mid-September, book accommodation well in advance. Campsites near the main windsurfing beaches include: *Tarifa* (ⓣ956 684 778) and *Paloma* (ⓣ956 684 203), both fully equipped and with their own pools.
Hostal Africa c/María Antonia Toledo 12 ⓣ956 680 220. Popular with kitesurfers, this central guesthouse has attractive marble-floored rooms, some en suite, and a covered roof terrace for lounging around and wi-fi use. Singles €35–50, doubles €50–65.
Melting Pot Hostel c/Turriano Gracil 5 ⓣ956 682 906, ⓦwww.meltingpothostels.com. Backpacker/kitesurfer haven with fully equipped kitchen, cosy lounge/bar with wi-fi and helpful staff. En-suite dorms are compact, but the ambience is great and kitesurfing courses can be arranged through the hostel. Dorms €23–26, doubles €56.

Eating and drinking

Bamboo c/Paseo Alameda 2 ⓣ956 627 304. Bob Marley on the stereo, deep sofas and fantastic breakfasts, smoothies and fresh juices. Turns into a hip bar after dark. Daily 10am–2am.
Chilimosa c/Peso 6. Fabulous vegetarian restaurant/takeaway serving up healthy food with an eastern twist. Try the excellent *plato degustación* (€7), featuring falafel, hummus, salad and more.
La Oca de Sergio c/General Copons 6. If you're lucky, friendly Sergio himself will serve you your pizza, fresh from the wood-fired oven, in this cosy, popular Italian joint. Pizzas €6–8.

Moving on

Bus Algeciras (6 daily; 30min); Cádiz (6 daily; 1hr 45min); La Línea de la Concepción (6 daily; 1hr 30min–2hr); Málaga (2 daily; 2hr); Seville (4 daily; 3hr).

GIBRALTAR

Long coveted for its strategic position at the entrance to the Mediterranean, the British territory of **GIBRALTAR**, at the southern tip of Spain, has been the source of tension between the two countries for nearly three hundred years since it was ceded to **Britain** under the Treaty of Utrecht. It is now a somewhat clichéd slice of Britain perched next to the Spanish mainland, complete with

MOROCCO-BOUND

The main reason to visit the gritty, busy post of **Algeciras** is to leave it again – by ferry to **Tangier** in Morocco, or the Spanish enclave of **Ceuta**. The best place to buy tickets is at the port, directly from the ferry companies. Wait until Tangier before buying any Moroccan currency as the exchange is better there (unless you'll be arriving after dark, in which case, pick up some dirhams at a bank in Algeciras). There are also ferries to Tangier from Tarifa.

From Algeciras: Ceuta (4 daily; 35min; €34 one-way); Tangier (8 daily; 1hr 10min; €38 one-way).

From Tarifa: Tangier (8 daily; 35min; €37 one-way).

If arriving in Algeciras, transport to other Spanish cities from the bus station on c/San Bernardo and the adjacent train station is as follows:

Bus Córdoba (2 daily; 6hr); Granada (6 daily; 3hr 45min–5hr 30min); La Línea (every 30min; 40min); Málaga (every 30min; 1hr 45min–3hr), Tarifa (13 daily; 30min).

Train Córdoba (2 daily; 3hr 10min); Granada (3 daily; 4hr 15min); Madrid (2 daily; 5hr 20min); Ronda (5 daily; 1hr 40min).

red postboxes, chippies, bilingual locals and, of course, the pound.

What to see and do

The town is dominated by the huge **Rock of Gibraltar**, the area's main attraction and thought, in antiquity, to be a pillar of Hercules. Take the cable car running from Red Sands Road (Mon–Sat 9.30am–8pm, Oct–April 9.30am–5pm; £6.50/8 one-way/return; £16 combined entry to nature reserve) to the top of the rock for spectacular views of the coastline and the distant African continent. Signs from the cable-car exit will lead you to the **nature reserve** (daily 9.30am–7.15pm; £10) on the Rock, which includes the immense **St Michael's Cave** – once home to the Rock's Neolithic inhabitants, the **Great Siege Tunnels**, carved out of the rock by the British during the siege of 1779–83, the **Gibraltar, A City Under Siege** exhibition (best viewed at twilight for the ultimate spooky effect) and the **Apes' Den** – the home of the peninsula's famous simian residents (get off at the middle station). The Barbary macaques are not afraid of humans, and may jump on you; remain calm and don't try to pet or feed them.

Arrival and information

Arrival Buses run to La Línea de la Concepción. To get to Gibraltar, simply walk across the border and follow Winston Churchill Ave into town (10min).
Tourist office Bilingual office on Grand Casemates Square (Mon–Fri 9am–5.30pm, Sat 10am–3pm, Sun 10am–1pm; ⓣ350 507 62).

Accommodation and eating

Clipper 78B Irish Town Rd. One of the better places to eat, serving fish and chips, a full English breakfast and other hearty pub grub. Mains £4–10.
Cannon Hotel 9 Cannon Lane ⓣ350 517 11, ⓦwww.cannonhotel.gi. Central, newly refurbished budget hotel with dated decor and an attractive patio. English breakfast included in the price. Singles £30, doubles £42–53, triples £52–60; the cheaper rooms share facilities.
Marrakech Restaurant 9 Governor's Parade. Serves tasty couscous and other Moroccan dishes.

Moving on

Bus La Línea de la Concepción to: Algeciras (every 30–45min; 40min); Cádiz (4 daily; 2hr 30min); Málaga (3–5 daily; 2hr 30min); Seville (4 daily; 5hr).

RONDA

Built on an isolated ridge of the sierra, and ringed by dark, angular mountains, the spectacular *pueblo blanco* of **RONDA**, a large cluster of attractive whitewashed houses, was made famous in Hemingway's *For Whom The Bell Tolls*. The town is split in two by a gaping river **gorge** with a sheer drop, spanned by an incredible eighteenth-century arched bridge from which hundreds of people were thrown to their deaths during the Spanish Civil War.

What to see and do

Most sights of interest lie in the tiny, atmospheric old quarter on the eastern side of the gorge. These include the well-preserved **Baños Árabes** (daily 10am–7pm, Sat & Sun 10am–3pm; €3, free Sun) and the **Palacio de Mondragón** (Mon–Fri 10am–7pm, Sat & Sun 10am–3pm; €3), probably once the palace of the Moorish kings and now home to the **Museo de Ronda** which charts the history of the area. Nearby, **Museo del Bandolero**, c/de Armiñán 65 (10.30am–8pm; €3) with its dashing bandit wax figures, explores the history of banditry in Andalucía, while the whimsical **Museo Lara**, c/de Armiñán 29 (10.30am–8pm; €3.50; ⓦwww.museolara.org) is home to an enormous private collection of antique objects and a cellar containing a macabre exhibit on witchcraft and the Inquisition. For that classic shot of the gorge, take the path down from the Plaza María Auxiliadora to the **viewpoint**. The principal gate of the town, through which the Christian conquerors passed, stands beside the **Alcázar**, destroyed by the French in 1809. In the modern Mercadillo quarter is Spain's oldest Plaza de Toros (**bullring**) where three generations of the Romero family shaped the rules of bullfighting into what they are today (daily 10am–8pm; €6 including the interesting museum of *corrida* memorabilia). Nearby, the **Jardínes de Forestier** ascend the gorge in a series of stepped terraces, offering superb views of the river, the bridge and the remarkable stairway of the **Casa del Rey Moro**, an early eighteenth-century mansion on the opposite side of the gorge.

Arrival and information

Bus and train stations The bus station is by Plaza Redondo, while the train station is several blocks north, along Avda Andalucía.

Tourist office Opposite the entrance to the bullring at Plaza de Toros (Mon–Fri 10am–7.30pm, Sat & Sun 10.15am–2pm & 3.30–6.30pm; ⓣ952 187 119, ⓦwww.turismoderonda.es). Sells the combined ticket that covers most sites of interest (€12) as well as booklets on eight easy hikes around Ronda (€5).

Accommodation

Hotel Andalucía c/Martínez Astein 19 ⓣ952 875 450, ⓦwww.hotel-andalucia.net. Clean, spacious en-suite rooms, directly across the street from the train station. Wi-fi available. Singles €27, doubles €42.

Hotel San Francisco c/María Cabrera 18 ⓣ952 873 299, ⓦwww.sanfranciscoronda.com. Elegant budget option, with Moorish archways in the dining room and cosy rooms equipped with a/c. Singles €44, doubles €63.

Eating and drinking

Bodega El Albero c/Pedro Romero 9. Old school tapas bar festooned with hams, serving regional specialities such as *rabo de toro* (oxtail) and the excellent *morcilla con arroz*. Tapas €1.50.

La Vita E Bella c/Nueva 5. Cheerful, home-style Italian joint serving up delicious home-made pasta dishes. Try the spaghetti marinera or the penne with cheese and truffles. Mains €8.

Moving on

Bus Cádiz (4 daily; 2hr 30min); Granada (2 daily; 3hr 30min); Málaga (7–10 daily; 3hr 30min); Seville (3–6 daily; 2hr 30min).

Train Algeciras (5–6 daily; 1hr 45min); Córdoba (twice daily; 2hr); Granada (3 daily; 2hr 30min); Madrid (2 daily; 4hr); Málaga (daily at 7.12am; 1hr 50min).

MÁLAGA

MÁLAGA is the second city of the south after Seville, one of the oldest in Spain, and also the main city on the Costa del Sol, the richest resort area in the Mediterranean.

What to see and do

While the clusters of high-rises are not attractive, the historic centre (Old Town) has plenty of charm. The most popular beach in town is the Playa de la Malagueta, ten minutes' walk from the Old Town, while the old fishing villages of El Palo and Pedregalejo, 4km east of the centre, boast a series of grey-sand **beaches** and a promenade lined with some of the best fish and **seafood restaurants** in the province; to get there, catch bus #11 along Paseo del Parque. Málaga's most famous native son, born here in 1881, is honoured in the immensely popular **Museo Picasso**, c/San Agustín 8 (Tues–Thurs & Sun 10am–8pm, Fri & Sat 10am–9pm; €8; ⓦwww.museopicassomalaga.org), which displays an intimate collection of works spanning Picasso's entire career. Don't miss the **Casa Natal de Picasso**, Plaza de la Merced 15 (9.30am–8pm; closed holidays; €1; ⓦwww.fundacionpicasso.es), where the artist was born, with choice works of his displayed upstairs. Just east of the Old Town rises Mount Gibralfaro where the Moorish citadels of **Alcazaba** (Tues–Sun: April–Oct 9.30am–8pm; Nov–March 9.30am–7pm; €2.60), built in 1057, and **Castillo de Gibralfaro** (daily: April–Oct 9am–8pm; Nov–March 9am–6pm;

> **TREAT YOURSELF**
>
> For an evening of relaxation, head for **El Hammam**, Málaga's traditional Arabic baths (Sun–Wed 11am–midnight; Thurs–Sat 11am–1am; shorter hours in winter; €20; Ⓦwww.elhammam.com). Sweat in the steam room, occasionally dousing yourself with water from your copper bowl, rub your arms and legs to remove the day's grit, shower off, then repeat the procedure until you are squeaky clean.

€2.10; joint ticket with Alcazaba €3.45), rebuilt in the fourteenth and fifteenth centuries, tower above the ruins of a Roman theatre. The viewpoint on the way to the castle offers spectacular views of the town and the glittering Mediterranean beyond.

Arrival and information

Air Charter and budget flights arrive at Málaga Airport, the hub of the south. From the airport, catch the electric train (every 30min; €2) to the main train station, or continue another stop to Málaga Centro: Alameda for the city centre. The airport bus (#19) leaves every 20–30min to the centre, via the main bus station (€1.10).
Train and bus The stations are across the road from each other, a 15min walk to Old Town; alternatively, take buses #3 and #4 from the train station, or buses #4 and #12 from the bus station along the Alameda Principal. There are ATMs and luggage storage at both.
Tourist office Plaza de la Marina (March–Sept Mon–Fri 9am–8pm, until 6pm otherwise; Ⓣ952 122 020, Ⓦwww.malagaturismo.com).

Accommodation

Casa Babylon c/Pedro de Quejana 3 Ⓣ952 267 228, Ⓦwww.casababylonhostel.com. Colourful, sociable and full of character, this is the place to meet fellow travellers. The staff are great, all mod cons are included, and it's a short walk from Málaga's historical centre. Dorms €18.
Melting Pot Hostel Avda del Pintor Joaquin Sorolla 30 Ⓣ952 600 571, Ⓦwww.meltingpothostels.com. A stone's throw from the beach, this friendly hostel has spotless dorms, there's an on-site café-bar serving affordable meals, and daily walking tours and nightly pub crawls encourage socializing between the guests. Dorms €18.

Eating and drinking

Málaga specialities – *fritura malagueña* (battered and fried fish and squid) and *espeto* – sardines grilled on bamboo spears – are best enjoyed at seaside restaurants along the El Palo and Pedregalejo beaches.
Clandestino c/Niño de Guevara 3. This chilled-out restaurant is simply bursting with imaginative dishes, from salad with smoked salmon, goat's cheese and honey to Thai-style pasta with prawns and coconut milk. Most dishes can be ordered as "Minis" – generous half-portions. Mains €8–10; Minis €5–6.
Mesón Lo Güeno c/Marín Garcia 9. Perch on a stool inside this little rustic bar – a Málaga institution for over thirty years, and order from a list of over 75 different tapas (€2.50–4.50).

Moving on

Train Barcelona (3 daily; 5hr 45min–13hr 40min); Córdoba (14 daily; 50min–2hr 25min); Madrid (10 daily; 2hr 30min–2hr 50min); Seville (8 daily; 2hr 30min); Valencia (1 daily at 7.10am; 9hr 40min).
Bus Almería (3 daily; 3hr–4hr 30min); Córdoba (5 daily; 2hr 30min); Granada (17 daily; 1hr 30min –2hr); Madrid (9 daily; 6hr); Ronda (9 daily; 2hr 30min); Seville (9 daily; 2hr 30min).

CÓRDOBA

CÓRDOBA was once the largest city of Roman Spain, and for three centuries the heart of the great medieval caliphate of the Moors. It's an engaging, atmospheric city, easily explored on foot.

What to see and do

For visitors, Córdoba's main attraction is a single building: **La Mezquita** – the grandest and most beautiful mosque ever constructed by the Moors in Spain. This stands right in the centre of the city, surrounded by the labyrinth of old Jewish and Moorish quarters, and is a building of extraordinary mystical and aesthetic power.

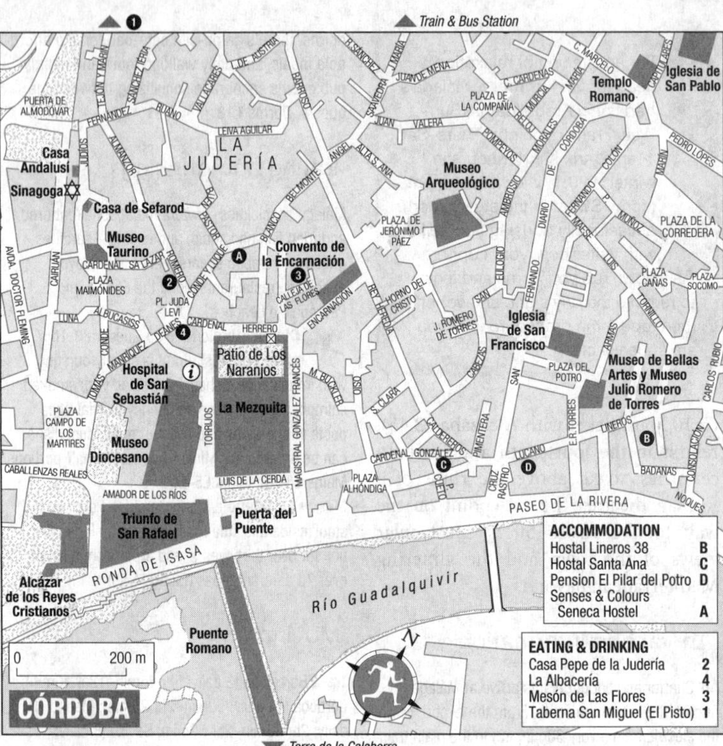

La Mezquita

Córdoba's domination of Moorish Spain began thirty years after the conquest, in 756 AD, when the city was placed under **Abd ar-Rahman I**, who established control over all but the north of Spain. He began the building of the Great Mosque – in Spanish, **La Mezquita** (Mon–Sat 8.30am–7pm, Sun 9–10.45am & 1.30–6.30pm; €8; free Mon–Sat 8.30–10am) – which is approached through the **Patio de los Naranjos**, a classic Islamic court preserving both its orange trees and fountains for ritual purification before prayer. Inside, a thicket of nearly a thousand twin-layered red and white archways combine to mesmerizing effect, the harmony culminating only at the foot of the beautiful **mihrab** (prayer niche), decorated with gold mosaic cubes – a gift from Nicephoras II Phocas, the Christian emperor of Byzantium. In the centre of what may be one of the most beautiful mosques in the world, you'll find the incongruous presence of a Renaissance cathedral, built in 1523, though it's the mihrab that commands most of the attention.

La Judería and around

North of La Mezquita lies **La Judería**, Córdoba's old Jewish quarter, a fascinating network of atmospheric lanes. Near the heart of the quarter, at c/Maimonides 18, is a tiny fourteenth-century **synagogue** with fine stuccowork (Tues–Sat 9.30am–2pm & 3.30–5.30pm, Sun 9.30am–1.30pm; €0.30, free for EU citizens), one of only three in Spain that survived the Jewish expulsion of 1492. Nearby, on the corner of c/Judíos and c/Averroes, the beautiful fourteenth-century **Casa de Sefarad** (Mon–Sat 10am–6pm, Sun 11am–2pm; €4; Ⓦwww.casadesefarad.es) explores the Sephardic-Judaic tradition. Its collections include weavings with gold thread and ceremonial objects; upstairs, exhibits are devoted to the contribution of Sephardic Jews to Islamic Córdoba and their persecution by the Inquisition.

Alcázar de los Reyes Cristianos

Near the Mezquita is the thirteenth-century **Castle of the Christian Monarchs** (Tues–Sat 10am–2pm & 5.30–7.30pm, Sun 9.30am–2.30pm €4; free on Fri), originally home to Alfonso X and then the headquarters of the Inquisition between 1490 and 1821. Highlights include the beautiful sculpted gardens, a third-century Roman sarcophagus and the view from one of the Alcázar's towers.

Torre de la Calahorra

Behind the Mezquita, across the attractive pedestrianized Roman Bridge (Puente Romano) stands the medieval **Torre de la Calahorra** (10am–6pm; €4.50), housing an entertaining high-tech museum; the talking dioramas bring the history of Córdoba to life. There's a great view of the Mezquita from the top of the tower, and also from across the bridge at night.

Arrival and information

Bus and train The bus and train stations are across the road from each other, 1km northwest of the old town. Bus #3 (€1.15) runs down c/San Fernández, just east of the Mezquita.

Tourist office c/Torrijos 10 (Mon–Fri 9am–7.30pm, Sat & Sun 9.30am–3pm; ⓣ957 355 179, ⓦwww.turismodecordoba.org).

Accommodation

Hostal Lineros 38 c/Lineros 38 ⓣ957 482 517, ⓦwww.hostallineros38.com. Live out your Arabian Nights fantasy at this Moorish-style guesthouse with luxurious four-poster beds and hammam-style bathrooms. Wi-fi available. Doubles €60.

Pension El Pilar del Potro c/Lucano 12 ⓣ957 492 966, ⓦwww.terracebackpackers.hostel.com. Extremely popular backpacker haunt with bright, cosy en-suite dorms (for no more than 3 people) and doubles, guest kitchen, wi-fi in lobby, and a chill-out rooftop terrace. 5min walk to the Mezquita. Dorms €21, doubles €52.

Senses & Colours Seneca Hostel c/Conde y Luque 7 ⓣ957 473 234, ⓦwww.sensesandcolours.com. Quiet hostel in the heart of the Judería with Moorish arches, a flowering courtyard and attractive terrace. En-suite dorms have a/c, but there is no kitchen or wi-fi. Dorms €24, singles €50, doubles €65.

Eating and drinking

Casa Pepe de la Judería c/Romero 1. Prop up the bar at this excellent Sephardic (Spanish-Jewish) restaurant; their *salmorejo* (a thicker, more savoury gazpacho) and *berenjenas con miel* (aubergines with honey) are delectable. Tapas €3.50.

La Albacería c/Deanes 1. This bar gets top marks for service, presentation, and very imaginative takes on traditional dishes. Try the melt-in-your-mouth lamb on a bed of couscous, the classic oxtail…but with chocolate, or the almond *salmorejo*. Tapas €2.60–4.80.

Mesón de Las Flores Calleja de las Flores s/n. This friendly little tapas bar adorned with bullfighting posters serves the best classic tapas around. Go for the *patatas bravas* (spicy potatoes), the *albóndigas* (meatballs) or the tortilla. Tapas €1.80–2.

Taberna San Miguel (El Pisto) Pl. San Miguel 1. Over a hundred years old, this Córdoba institution serves excellent Montilla wine, accompanied by regional tapas, such as *rabo de toro* (oxtail) or *callos en salsa picante* (tripe in spicy sauce). Tapas €3. Closed Sun & Aug.

Moving on

Train Barcelona (5 daily; 4hr 40min–11hr); Cádiz (9 daily; 2hr 30min–3hr 30min); Granada (2 daily; 2hr 20min); Madrid (every 30min between 8am and 10.30pm; 1hr 45min–2hr 20min); Málaga (14 daily; 50min–2hr 45min); Seville (every 30min between 8am and midnight; 40min–1hr 20min).

Bus Granada (7 daily; 2hr 30min); Madrid (7 daily; 4hr 50min); Málaga (5 daily; 2hr 45min); Seville (6 daily; 1hr 45min).

GRANADA

If you see only one town in Spain, it should be **GRANADA**, with its wonderful backdrop of the **Sierra**

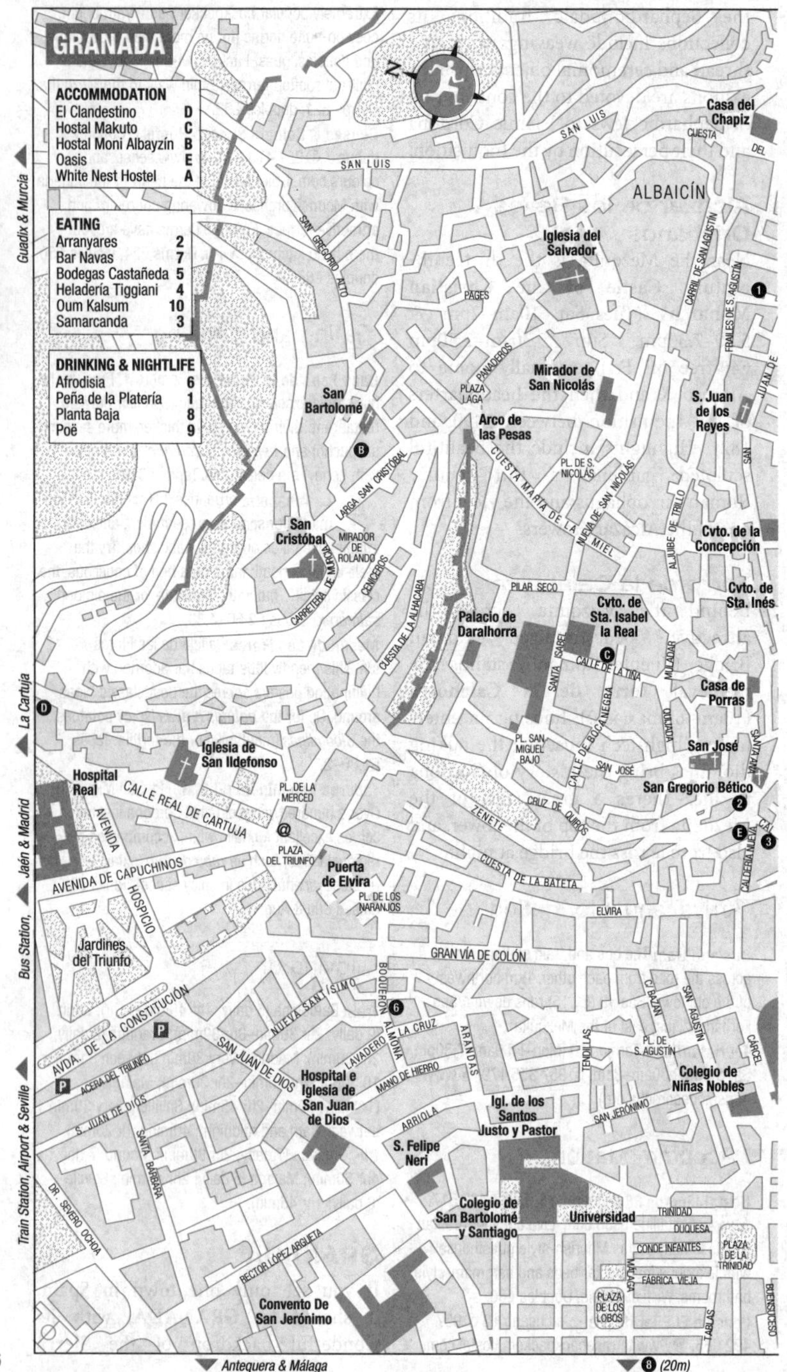
GRANADA
ACCOMMODATION
El Clandestino D
Hostal Makuto C
Hostal Moni Albayzín B
Oasis E
White Nest Hostel A
EATING
Arranyares 2
Bar Navas 7
Bodegas Castañeda 5
Heladería Tiggiani 4
Oum Kalsum 10
Samarcanda 3
DRINKING & NIGHTLIFE
Afrodisia 6
Peña de la Platería 1
Planta Baja 8
Poë 9
Guadix & Murcia
La Cartuja
Bus Station, Jaén & Madrid
Train Station, Airport & Seville
Antequera & Málaga
(20m)
ALBAICÍN
Casa del Chapiz
Iglesia del Salvador
Mirador de San Nicolás
S. Juan de los Reyes
San Bartolomé
Arco de las Pesas
San Cristóbal
Cvto. de la Concepción
Cvto. de Sta. Inés
Palacio de Daralhorra
Cvto. de Sta. Isabel la Real
Casa de Porras
San José
San Gregorio Bético
Iglesia de San Ildefonso
Hospital Real
Puerta de Elvira
Jardines del Triunfo
Hospital e Iglesia de San Juan de Dios
Igl. de los Santos Justo y Pastor
Colegio de Niñas Nobles
S. Felipe Neri
Colegio de San Bartolomé y Santiago
Universidad
Convento De San Jerónimo
SAN LUIS
CUESTA DEL
SAN GREGORIO ALTO
PAGES
PANADEROS
PLAZA LAGA
PL. DE S. NICOLÁS
CUESTA MARÍA DE LA MIEL
NUEVA DE SAN NICOLÁS
ALJIBE DE TRILLO
CARRIL DE SAN AGUSTÍN
FRAILES DE S. AGUSTÍN
JUAN DE
LARGA SAN CRISTÓBAL
MIRADOR DE ROLANDO
CARRETERA DE MURCIA
CENICEROS
CUESTA DE LA ALHACABA
PILAR SECO
SANTA ISABEL
CALLE DE LA TINA
MULADAR
OLIJADA
SANTA ANA
PL. SAN MIGUEL BAJO
CALLE DE BOCANEGRA
SAN JOSÉ
CRUZ DE QUIRÓS
ZENETE
CUESTA DE LA BATETA
CALDERERÍA NUEVA
PL. DE LA MERCED
CALLE REAL DE CARTUJA
AVENIDA
PLAZA DEL TRIUNFO
AVENIDA DE CAPUCHINOS
HOSPICIO
PL. DE LOS NARANJOS
ELVIRA
GRAN VÍA DE COLÓN
BOQUERÓN
NUEVA SANTÍSIMO
AVDA. DE LA CONSTITUCIÓN
SAN JUAN DE DIOS
ACERA DEL TRIUNFO
S. JUAN DE DIOS
SANTA BÁRBARA
DR. SEVERO OCHOA
LAVADERO
ALMONA
LA CRUZ
MANO DE HIERRO
ARANDAS
ARRIOLA
TENDILLAS
C/ BAZÁN
SAN AGUSTÍN
PL. DE S. AGUSTÍN
CÁRCEL
SAN JERÓNIMO
RECTOR LÓPEZ ARGUETA
TRINIDAD
DUQUESA
CONDE INFANTES
MÁLAGA
FÁBRICA VIEJA
PLAZA DE LA TRINIDAD
PLAZA DE LOS LOBOS
TABLAS
BUENSUCESO

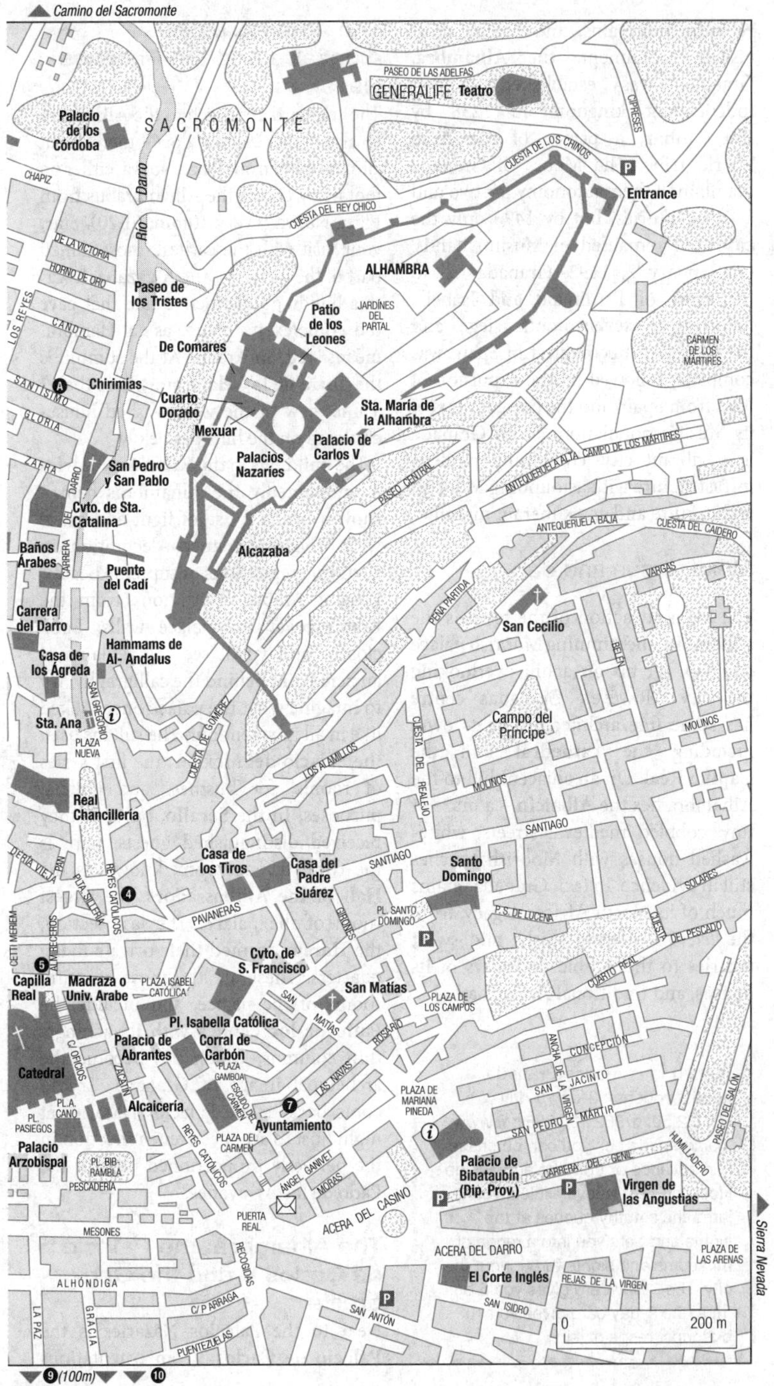

Camino del Sacromonte
PASEO DE LAS ADELFAS
GENERALIFE
Teatro
CIPRESES
Palacio de los Córdoba
SACROMONTE
CUESTA DE LOS CHINOS
Entrance
CHAPIZ
Río Darro
CUESTA DEL REY CHICO
DE LA VICTORIA
HORNO DE ORO
ALHAMBRA
Paseo de los Tristes
LOS REYES
CANDIL
Patio de los Leones
JARDÍNES DEL PARTAL
CARMEN DE LOS MÁRTIRES
De Comares
SANTISIMO
Chirimías
Cuarto Dorado
GLORIA
Mexuar
Sta. María de la Alhambra
Palacio de Carlos V
Palacios Nazaríes
ZAFRA
San Pedro y San Pablo
CAMPO DE LOS MÁRTIRES
ANTEQUERUELA ALTA
PASEO CENTRAL
Cvto. de Sta. Catalina
CARRERA DEL DARRO
ANTEQUERUELA BAJA
CUESTA DEL CAIDERO
Baños Árabes
Alcazaba
VARGAS
Puente del Cadí
PEÑA PARTIDA
Carrera del Darro
San Cecilio
Hammams de Al- Andalus
BELÉN
Casa de los Ágreda
SAN GREGORIO
Sta. Ana
PLAZA NUEVA
CUESTA DE GOMEREZ
CUESTA DEL REALEJO
Campo del Príncipe
MOLINOS
LOS ALAMILLOS
MOLINOS
Real Chancillería
SANTIAGO
DERÍA VIEJA
PAN
Casa de los Tiros
Casa del Padre Suárez
SANTIAGO
Santo Domingo
PLTA. SILLERÍA
REYES CATÓLICOS
SOLARES
PAVANERAS
GIRONES
PL. SANTO DOMINGO
P. S. DE LUCENA
CETTI MERIEM
ALMIBECEROS
CUESTA DEL PESCADO
Cvto. de S. Francisco
CUARTO REAL
Capilla Real
Madraza o Univ. Arabe
PLAZA ISABEL CATÓLICA
SAN MATÍAS
San Matías
PLAZA DE LOS CAMPOS
Pl. Isabella Católica
ROSARIO
Palacio de Abrantes
Corral de Carbón
C/ OFICIOS
ANCHA DE LA VIRGEN
CONCEPCIÓN
Catedral
ZACATÍN
PLAZA GAMBOA
ESCUDO DEL CARMEN
LAS NAVAS
SAN JACINTO
PL.A. CANO
Alcaicería
PLAZA DE MARIANA PINEDA
PASEO DEL SALÓN
PL. PASIEGOS
Ayuntamiento
MÁRTIR
SAN PEDRO
Palacio Arzobispal
PLAZA DEL CARMEN
HUMILLADERO
PL. BIB-RAMBLA
REYES CATÓLICOS
Palacio de Bibataubín (Dip. Prov.)
CARRERA DEL GENIL
PESCADERÍA
ÁNGEL GANIVET
MORAS
Virgen de las Angustias
PUERTA REAL
ACERA DEL CASINO
Sierra Nevada
MESONES
RECOGIDAS
ACERA DEL DARRO
PLAZA DE LAS ARENAS
ALHÓNDIGA
El Corte Inglés
REJAS DE LA VIRGEN
C/ P ARRAGA
SAN ISIDRO
SAN ANTÓN
LA PAZ
GRACIA
PUENTEZUELAS
0
200 m
9 (100m)
10

Nevada mountains, and Spain's most visited monument, the **Alhambra**. Granada was established as an independent kingdom in 1238 by **Ibn Ahmar**, a prince of the Arab Nasrid tribe. The Moors of Granada maintained their autonomy for two and a half centuries, but by 1490 only the city itself remained in Muslim hands. On January 2, 1492, Granada fell to the army of Ferdinand and Isabella following a seven-month siege and the Christian Reconquest of Spain was complete, followed by the expulsion of Jews from Spain and the persecutions of its Muslim population. Today Granada is a vibrant city, combining modern infrastructure with astounding Moorish architecture and an exuberant nightlife.

What to see and do

The main attraction of the town is the **Alhambra**, the stunning Moorish palace complex set up on a hill overlooking the city. However, Granada's centre has some fine architecture of its own, including the **cathedral** and the **Capilla Real**. On an adjacent hill to the Alhambra lies the **Albaicín** – a maze of tiny, cobbled medieval streets, whitewashed houses with Moorish touches still in evidence. In fact, Granada retains much of its North African legacy, from the *teterías* offering shisha and sweet pastries to the Arabic doorways of its houses, and traditional Arabic baths.

Buy a **bono turístico Granada** (tourist voucher; 3-day/5-day €27/32.50; ⓣ902 100 095, ⓦwww.cajagranada.es); you can purchase it in advance or from the audioguide kiosk in Plaza Nueva – it lets you jump the lengthy queues at top sights and gets you into a range of museums and sights throughout the city. The 3-day card gives you 5 bus trips; the 5-day card gives you 10 bus trips, respectively.

The Alhambra: the Alcazaba and the Palacios Nazaríes

The standard approach to the **Alhambra** is along the Cuesta de Gomérez that climbs uphill from Plaza Nueva, either on foot or by taking the Alhambrabus from Plaza Nueva (every 10min; €1.20). Start your visit with the earliest, most ruined part of the fortress – the **Alcazaba**. It was this building's distinctive hue that gave the complex its name, as "al-Hambra" means "red" in Arabic. At the summit is the **Torre de la Vela**, from where there's a fine view of the whitewashed houses clustered on the hillsides below.

The buildings in the **Palacios Nazaríes** – undoubtedly the Alhambra's gem – show a brilliant use of light and space with ornamental stucco decoration, in rhythmic repetitions of supreme beauty. Elegant Arabic inscriptions from the Koran cover the palace walls. Look closely, and you'll see the remains of ancient paint behind the calligraphy; try to imagine what the palace once looked like in all its splendour. The sultans used the **Palacio del Mexuar**, the first series of rooms, for business and judicial purposes. In the **Serallo**, beyond, they received distinguished guests: here is the royal throne room, known as the **Hall of the Ambassadors**, the largest room of the palace. The last section, the **Harem**, formed their private living quarters. These are the most beautiful rooms of the palace, and include the **Patio de los Leones** with its achingly thin columns, which has become the archetypal image of Granada. Try to come back to the Palacios Nazaríes at night, just to see the serene reflection in the perfectly proportioned pool of the Patio de los Arrayanes.

The Alhambra: the Palacio de Carlos V and the Generalife

Next to the Palacios Nazaríes is the **Palacio de Carlos V**, an ostentatious

ALHAMBRA PRACTICALITIES

Tickets for the Alhambra (daily: March–Oct 8.30am–2pm & 2–8pm; Nov–Feb until 6pm; €12) are limited, so buy well in advance by phone or online (lines open 8am–midnight, €1 booking fee; ⓣ902 888 001, ⓦwww.alhambra-tickets.es), and collect them from the Alhambra ticket office; bring ID and the credit card used to purchase the ticket. If online tickets are sold out, get to the ticket office no later than 5.30am on the day you want to visit. You can also buy advance tickets from the Servicaixa machines in the Alhambra grounds (March–Oct 8am–7pm; Nov–Feb 8am–5pm). You are given a 30-minute slot for the star attraction of **Palacios Nazaríes**; make sure not to miss it. Nocturnal visits to the Palacios Nazaríes (March–Oct Tues–Sat 10–11.30pm; Nov–Feb Fri & Sat 8–9.30pm; €12) also need to be booked in advance.

piece of Renaissance architecture, with a circular courtyard where bullfights once took place, which was built by its namesake Charles V, the grandson of Ferdinand and Isabella. A wing of the Palacios Nazaríes was demolished to make way for it. The palace's lower floor is home to Museo de la Alhambra (Tues–Sat 9am–2.30pm; free), which showcases an interesting collection of Islamic artefacts, while upstairs, the Museo de Bellas Artes (Tues 2.30–8pm; Wed–Sat 9am–2.30pm; Sun 9am–2.30pm; €1.50; free for EU citizens) features an absorbing collection of Hispano-Moorish paintings and sculpture. From here, a short walk takes you to the **Generalife**, the gardens and summer palace of the sultans.

The Albaicín

From just below the entrance to the Generalife, the **Cuesta del Rey Chico** winds down towards the Río Darro and the old Arab quarter of the **Albaicín**, where you'll find the well-preserved eleventh-century **Baños Árabes**, Carrera del Darro 31 (Tues–Fri 10am–2pm; €1.50, free with EU passport). From here, you can wind your way up the serpentine streets to the **Mirador de San Nicolás** for the quintessential Alhambra view, with the Sierra Nevada backdrop – it's particularly stunning (and crowded) at sunset.

The Capilla Real and the Cathedral

The **Capilla Real** in the city centre (April–Oct Mon–Sat 10.30am–1.30pm & 4–7.30pm, Sun 11am–1.30pm & 4–7pm; Oct–March closed Sun; €3.50) was built in the first decades of Christian rule as a mausoleum for Ferdinand and Isabella. Although their tombs are simple, above is the fabulously elaborate monument erected by their grandson, Charles V. Adjoining the Capilla Real, the stark Gothic-Renaissance bulk of Granada's **Cathedral** (Mon–Sat 10.45am–1.30pm & 4–8pm, Sun 4–8pm; Oct–March Sun until 7pm; €3.50), built on the site of the former mosque, has a simple, attractive interior.

Arrival and information

Airport 17km west of the centre; an Autocares J González bus runs to Gran Vía de Colón (5 daily; 30min; €3).

Train station 1km from town on Avda de Andaluces, connected to the centre by buses #4, #6, #7 and #11.

Bus station North of the city on Carretera de Jaén; bus #3 runs to Gran Vía de Colón (15min).

Tourist office Plaza Nueva (Mon–Sat 9am–7.30pm, Sun 9.30am–3pm; ⓣ958 247 128, ⓦwww.granadatur.com).

Internet Cyberlocutorio, Puerta Elvira, Plaza del Triunfo 5 (Mon–Thurs 9am–midnight, Fri 9am–2pm & 4pm–midnight, Sat & Sun 11am–midnight). Most hostels offer free internet and wi-fi.

TREAT YOURSELF

You can immerse yourself (literally) in the city's Moorish culture – at the oldest Arabic baths in Spain – the **Hammams de Al-Andalus** (c/Santa Ana 16; daily sessions every 2hr 10am–midnight; Mon–Fri only and shorter hours in low season; bath only €22, with massage €32–39; ⓣ958 229 978, ⓦwww.hammam.es). Book your session in advance, then alternate between the hot pools and the cold pool in the semi-darkness, not forgetting to take breaks to sip hot, sweet tea.

Accommodation

El Clandestino c/Miradór de Rolando ⓣ958 277 875, ⓦwww.makuto.net/clan. A mixed Spanish and international crowd congregate in the large guest kitchen or on the roof terrace with a fabulous view of the city. The rooms are simple, spotless and have wi-fi. Doubles €40–45, triples €54–60, quads €69–75; the higher prices are for en suite.

Hostal Makuto c/Tiña 18 ⓣ958 805 876, ⓦwww.makutoguesthouse.com. Colourful hostel popular with backpackers on a tiny street in the heart of the Albaicín, with a hippy vibe and hammocks strung up in the leafy common area. Dorms €18, doubles €55.

Hostal Moni Albayzín Plaza San Bartolomé 5 ⓣ958 285 284, ⓦwww.hostalalbayzin.com. This budget guesthouse offers stunning views of the Alhambra from its rooftop terrace, as well as cosy doubles, some en suite, some with a/c. The suites come with own kitchenettes. No wi-fi. Doubles €50, suites €60.

Oasis Placeta Correo Viejo 3 ⓣ958 215 848, ⓦwww.oasisgranada.com. Firm backpacker favourite, with spotless en-suite dorms arranged around a leafy central courtyard and a chill-out zone on the roof. The young, energetic staff do free tapas bar crawls several night a week. Dorms €20–22.

White Nest Hostel c/Santísimo 4 ⓣ958 994 714, ⓦwww.nesthostelsgranada.com. This friendly place distinguishes itself not just by its psychedelic colour scheme, but the helpfulness of its staff, rooftop terrace with great views of the Alhambra and multiple free daily tours on offer – from nightly tapas bar crawls to excursions outside the city. En-suite dorms €22, singles €35, doubles €49.

Eating

Arranyares c/Cuesta Marañas 4. Very popular Moroccan restaurant just off the main tourist drag. The couscous dishes are excellent, as are the fruity tagines. Mains €8–19. No alcohol served.

Bar Navas c/Navas 14. Try the great selection of *bocadillos*; *morcilla* (black pudding) with piquillo peppers and camembert with blueberries or dates are particularly tasty. Wash it down with a jug of sangría. Selection of *bocadillos* €7.50.

Bodegas Castañeda c/Almireceros 1. The oldest tapas bar in town, with rustic features and hams hanging from the ceiling. Go for the generous portions of home-made pâté, a selection of tasty *montaditos* (tiny sandwiches), or tuck into the tapa of paella which comes free with your drink. Tapas €2.50–4.50.

Heladería Tiggiani Plaza Nueva and c/Cuchilleros. The place for superb local ice cream; try the chocolate orange or pistachio. One scoop €2.

Oum Kalsum c/Jardines 17. Friendly and popular bar serving delicious tapas with an Arabic twist. The little chicken kebabs are great, as are the miniature tajines, though it's difficult to fault any of the dishes. Tapas €1.90–3.

Samarcanda c/Caldería Vieja 3. Vegetarians rejoice, for the falafel at this little Lebanese spot is very good, as is the *labneh* (thick yogurt) with flatbread. Mains €8.

Drinking and nightlife

Afrodisia Edificio Corona, c/Almona del Boquerón. If reggae, afro beats, hip-hop and funk are your thing, this laidback club is ideal. Tues–Sun from 11pm; free entry.

Peña de la Platería Placeta de Toqueros 7. Serious flamenco club hidden within the Albaicín for those with a genuine interest in the art. Excellent performances Thursdays or Saturdays at 9.30pm; entry €12 with drink.

Planta Baja c/Horno de Abad 11 ⓦwww.plantabaja.net. Attracting top DJs and playing a good mix of hip-hop, funk and electronica, this ever-popular club draws the all-nighter crowd. Tues–Sat 12.30am–6am; entry €5.

Poë c/Paz. This intimate British–Angolan bar has been a popular gathering spot for locals and visitors alike for years. It's also one of the few places in a spice-shy country where you can find truly fiery tapas, such as the spicy chicken livers or the pork stew with piri-piri peppers. Tapas €1.20. From 8pm; closed Mon.

Moving on

Train Almería (4 daily; 2hr 15min); Barcelona (1–2 daily; 11hr 30min); Córdoba (2 daily; 2hr 30min); Madrid (2 daily; 4hr 50min); Ronda (3 daily; 2hr 30min); Seville (4 daily; 3hr); Valencia (2 daily; 7–8hr). **Bus** Almería (5 daily; 2hr 15min); Cádiz (4 daily; 5hr 30min); Córdoba (9 daily; 2hr 45min); Madrid (10–13 daily; 5–6hr); Málaga (16 daily; 1hr 30min); Ronda (2 daily; 3hr 45min); Seville (8 daily; 3hr).

ALMERÍA

Founded by the Phoenicans, and having risen to prominence as the main port of Moorish Córdoba, **ALMERÍA** is an attractive, prosperous city sandwiched in between the Mediterranean and the barren mountain looming behind it.

What to see and do

The town is dominated by the grand, crumbling, tenth-century **Alcazaba** (Tues–Sun 9am–8.30pm; Nov–March 9am–6.30pm; €1.50 or free with EU passport), which was built by the Córdoba Caliph Abd-ar Rahman III. During its heyday, the fortress complex held up to 20,000 people and was said to rival Granada's Alhambra with the beauty of its palaces and sculpted gardens, though now little remains. The fabulous views of the coast are still well worth the climb, though. What looks like another fortress on Plaza de Catedral is, in fact, Almería's **cathedral** (Mon–Fri 10am–2pm & 4–5.30pm, Sat 10am–2pm; €3), built in 1524, and fortified to withstand the frequent pirate raids from North Africa and Turkey in the sixteenth century. Behind the cathedral, on c/Pintor Díaz Molina 9, the **Centro Andaluz de la Fotografía** (11am–2pm & 5.30–9.30pm; free) houses excellent temporary photography exhibitions by top international names.

Arrival and information

Train and bus Both buses and trains pull in at the combined Estación Intermodal on Carretera La Ronda, a 10min walk from the city centre. No luggage storage.
Tourist office c/Parque de Nicolás Salmarón at Martínez Campos (Mon–Fri 9am–7.30pm, Sat & Sun 9.30am–3pm; ⓣ950 274 355, ⓦwww.almeria-turismo.org).

Accommodation

Hostal Americano Avda de la Estación 4 ⓣ950 258 011. Friendly guesthouse located between Old Town and the bus/train station offering clean singles and doubles; en suite €2 extra. Singles €22, doubles €38.
Hotel Sevilla c/de Granada 23 ⓣ950 230 009; ⓦwww.hotelsevillaalmeria.es. Spick-and-span rooms with tiny but modern bathrooms in this centrally located hotel. The k/c is a godsend in summer. Singles €34, doubles €35.

Eating and drinking

Bodega Las Botas c/Fructuoso Pérez 3. This popular tapas bar festooned with hams is a great place to try the local speciality of oxtail stew, washed down with a glass of *tinto de verano*. Tapas €1.50.
La Encina c/Marín 16. Stop by for the imaginative tapas (€1.30) at Almería's top restaurant; *arroz negro* and the home-made pâté are delicious. Closed Sun night & Mon.

MINI HOLLYWOOD

Between the 1950s and the 1980s, the desert landscape around Almería was used as the set for such Hollywood classics as *Lawrence of Arabia* and *Indiana Jones and the Last Crusade*, as well as numerous "spaghetti westerns"; Clint Eastwood's career was launched here in *A Fistful of Dollars.* Visit the three Wild West sets and watch the spirited re-enaction of the capture of Jesse James (daily 5pm & 8pm mid-June to mid-Sept) at **Mini Hollywood** (April–Oct daily 10am–9pm; €19), 25km inland from Almería. To get there, take a Tabernas-bound bus which can drop you off by the entrance; to get back, walk back to the main road and flag down a bus.

EL CABO DE GATA

Only 15km east of Almería lies Cabo de Gata, a **national park** comprising dramatic cliffs, low-key fishing villages and some of the most beautiful unspoiled beaches in the south. You can explore the park on a bike, enjoy incredible views of the coast from Torre Vigia Vela Blanca – an eighteenth-century watchtower, camp at the seaside villages and enjoy the pristine beauty of Playa de los Genoveses – the cape's prettiest beach. The easiest village to reach by bus from Almería is San José, where you'll also find the greatest variety of accommodation and the National Park information office (Avda de San José 27, 10am–2pm & 5–8pm; Ⓦwww.degata.com).

Tetería Almedina c/Paz 2. A local legend, this cosy Moorish-themed restaurant really delivers when it comes to tagines and couscous dishes. Great selection of teas, too. Mains €8–10.

Moving on

Train Barcelona (1 daily on Wed, Fri & Sun; 13hr 15min); Granada (4 daily; 2hr 20min); Madrid (2 daily; 6hr 30min); Seville (4 daily; 5hr 30min); Valencia (1 daily on Wed, Fri & Sun; 9hr 15min). **Bus** Granada (10 daily; 2hr 15min); Madrid (5 daily; 7hr); Málaga (10 daily; 3hr 15min); Seville (3 daily; 5hr 45min); Valencia (5 daily; 8hr 30min).

Valencia and Alicante

Much of the coast around **Valencia** and further south on the **Costa Blanca** has been insensitively overdeveloped, suffering from mass package-tourism and its associated ills. The main cities, however – vibrant **Valencia** and relaxed **Alicante** – are appealing and worth a stop for anyone travelling down the east coast.

VALENCIA

VALENCIA has been working hard to shed its provincial reputation in recent years and is emerging as an exciting, cosmopolitan city to rival Madrid and Barcelona. The City of Arts and Sciences complex is the best example of this but Valencia's exuberance is also evident in its diverse nightlife. The city can also take pride in some good museums, a reasonable beach, and, of course, its festivals: the world-famous **Las Fallas**, international music festival **Benicassim** and the riotous **Tomatina**, held in nearby Buñol.

What to see and do

The Plaza del Ayuntamiento, a couple of blocks north of the train station, marks the centre of town with most of Valencia's key sights a short walk from here. However, the most interesting area for wandering is undoubtedly the maze-like **Barrio del Carmen**, with its arty, bohemian atmosphere. Stretching north of the Mercado Central up to the riverbed of the Río Turia, it's full of historic buildings being renovated and stylish cafés opening up next to crumbling townhouses.

The town centre

The **Palacio del Marqués de Dos Aguas** is an excellent example of traditional Valencian architecture. Hipólito Rovira, who designed its extraordinarily detailed alabaster doorway, died insane in 1740, which should come as no surprise to anyone who's seen it. On the **Plaza Patriarca** stands the Neoclassical former university, with beautiful cloisters. From here, up c/de la Paz, is the **Plaza de la Reina**, home to the impressive thirteenth-century **Catedral** (Mon–Sat 10am–5.30pm; €4.50), whose bell tower, the **Miguelete** (Mon–Sat 10am–7pm, Sun 10am–1pm & 5–7pm; €2), gives stunning city views. Just southwest of the cathedral lies the

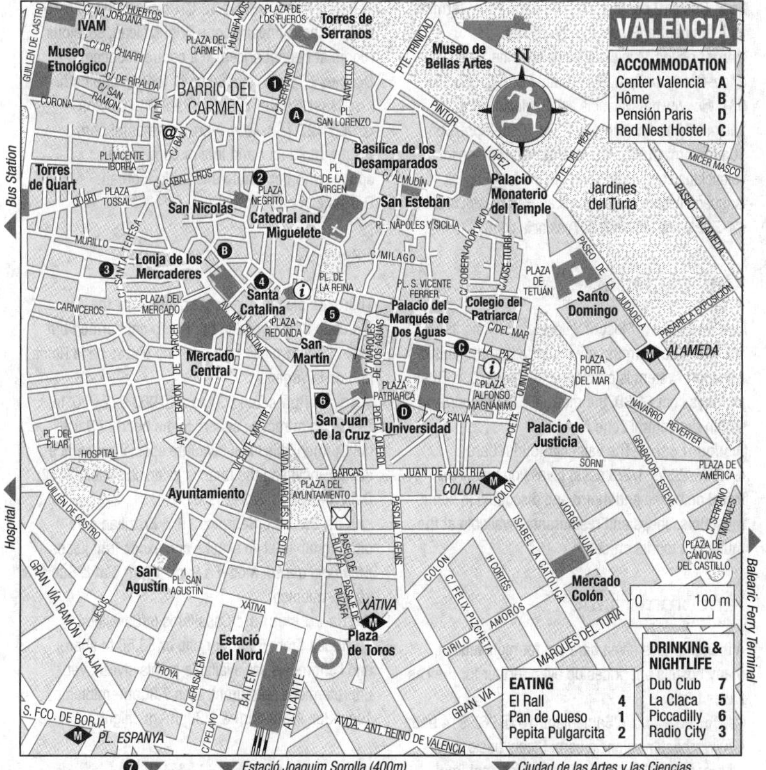

enormous **Mercado Central**, a huge iron and glass structure housing over one thousand stalls selling local fruit, vegetables and seafood until 2pm (closed Sun).

The museums

Art lovers will find **IVAM**, the modern art museum at c/Guillém de Castro 118 (Tues–Sun 10am–8pm; €2, free Sun; ⓦwww.ivam.es) a treat, but the real highlight of the city's museums is the **Ciudad de las Artes y las Ciencias** (City of Arts and Sciences; daily mid-Sept to June 10am–7pm, July to mid-Sept 10am–9pm; €32.40 for three-day pass; ⓣ902 100 031, ⓦwww.cac.es). Sitting in a huge landscaped park that was built in the old riverbed of the Río Turia, this breathtaking collection of futuristic concrete, steel and glass architecture comprises five main buildings, four of which were designed by local architect Santiago Calatrava. The complex includes an eyeball-shaped IMAX **cinema**, a vast **science museum**, a huge **oceanographic park** (with beluga whales, sharks and turtles) and a dramatic pistachio nut-shaped **arts centre**. Take bus #19 from Plaza del Ayuntamiento, or #35 from Avenida Marqués de Sotelo.

Arrival and information

Train station Trains from Alicante and Murcia arrive at the centrally located Estació del Nord on c/Játiva (c/Xàtiva; Ⓜ Xàtiva or Bailén). Most trains from Madrid and Barcelona arrive at the Estació Joaquim Sorolla, 500m further south.

Bus station Northwest of the centre, on the far bank of the Río Turia riverbed (Ⓜ Turia); bus #8 (or a 30min walk) to Pl. del Ayuntamiento.

Boat Bus #19 connects the Balearic Ferry Terminal with the central Pl. del Ayuntamiento.

Tourist office Municipal: Pl. de la Reina 19 (Mon–Sat 9am–7pm, Sun 10am–2pm; ⓣ963 153 931, ⓦwww.turisvalencia.es). Regional: c/Paz (c/ Pau) 48 (Mon–Fri 9am–8pm, Sat 10am–8pm, Sun 10am–2pm; ⓣ963 986 422, ⓦwww.comunitat valenciana.com). Both hand out the free English-language listings guides such as *Hello Valencia* and *24-7 Valencia* (ⓦwww.247valencia.com).

City transport

Bus and metro Most of Valencia's key sights are walkable from the town centre, but the public transport system is efficient and easy to use. Bus journeys cost €1.30, the metro €1.40 for journeys within the central zone A.

Discount cards The Valencia Tourist Card (€12/18/22 for 1/2/3 days) gives you unlimited travel on buses and metro and discounts in some museums, shops and restaurants. Available at the municipal tourist office.

Accommodation

Although prices given here are for high season, many hostels put prices up even further for the Las Fallas festival.

Center Valencia c/Samaniego 18 ⓣ963 914 915, ⓦwww.center-valencia.com. Clean, basic dorms with good facilities, including free internet, roof terrace, laundry service and breakfast. Dorm bed €22.50.

Hôme c/La Lonja 4 ⓣ963 916 229, ⓦwww.likeathome.net. One of two *Hôme* hostels in the city. Comfortable, relaxed accommodation, with kitchen, free internet and TV room, in a great central location. Book ahead in summer. €17 in three- or four-bed dorms. There are also double rooms for €46.

Pensión Paris c/Salvá 12 Ⓜ Colón ⓣ963 526 766, ⓦwww.pensionparis.com. Bright, clean, spacious rooms at budget prices, in a central location. Doubles €34 with shared bath, €42 private bath.

Red Nest Hostel c/Paz (c/Pau) 36 Ⓜ Colón ⓣ963 427 168, ⓦwww.rednesthostel.com. Bright, fun decor and lots of communal space, with pool table and table football. Dorms €21–25.

Eating

There are plenty of decent options near the Mercado Central and in the Barrio del Carmen but avoid touristy places too near the plazas de la Reina and de la Virgen.

El Rall c/Tundidores 2 ⓣ963 922 090. In an attractive square in the heart of Barrio del Carmen, this local favourite specializes in rice dishes, including the famous Valencian paella (€12). Daily 1–3.30pm & 8–11.30pm.

Pan de Queso c/Serranos 19. A Brazilian café offering tapas-style snacks and exotic fruit juices. *Menú del día* €6. Mon–Fri 9am–11pm, Sat & Sun 10am–midnight.

Pepita Pulgarcita c/Caballeros (c/Cavallers) 19. Tapas (from €5.50 for one or €6.50 to share) and light meals are available in this stylish, yet unpretentious restaurant. Mon 7.30pm–midnight, Tues–Sun 1.30–4pm & 7.30pm–midnight.

Drinking and nightlife

Valencia can seem dead at night, but only because the action is widely dispersed. The best of the city-centre nightlife is in the Barrio del Carmen (c/ Caballeros, c/Quart and c/Alta). For salsa, head to the bars on c/Juan Llorens. The best gay bars and clubs are in and around c/Quart.

Dub Club c/Jesús 91 Ⓜ Jesús. The emphasis is on reggae, but there's quality dance music of all

FESTIVALS

The famous **Las Fallas** (ⓦwww.fallasfromvalencia.com) are held annually from March 15 to 19, when hundreds of papier-mâché caricatures are installed and then burnt in the streets of Valencia amid a riot of fireworks in a tribute to St Joseph, the patron saint of carpenters. Summer heralds a host of festivals in and around Valencia: you can rock-on at the **Festival Internacional de Benicassim** (ⓦwww.fiberfib.com), a four-day music festival in the beach town of Benicassim, between Barcelona and Valencia, featuring well-known indie, pop and electronica acts; or indulge in some childhood fantasies at **La Tomatina** (ⓦwww.latomatina.es), essentially an enormous public tomato fight that takes place on the last Wednesday in August, in the tiny town of Buñol, one hour to the west of the city.

varieties at this spacious club, with live acts on Sundays and Tuesdays; entry usually free, but €9–12 for live concerts.

La Claca c/San Vicente Martir 3 ⓦ www.laclaca.com. A laidback spot to mingle with the locals, DJs play retro-pop most nights, with live flamenco on Sundays.

Piccadilly c/Embajador Vich 7 ⓦ www.groovelives.com. The range of theme nights and music, from electronica to retro Eighties and Nineties, make this one of the most eclectic clubs in town. Usually open midnight–3am, continuing to 7.30am Fri & Sat. Entry usually €10, including a drink, with discounts if you can find a flyer.

Radio City c/Santa Teresa 19 ⓦ www.radiocityvalencia.com. Lively and popular bar with exhibitions, theatre, dance and music performances. Free entry most nights; see website for programme. Tuesday is flamenco night, €7 including a drink.

Directory

Banks Main branches of most banks are around Pl. del Ayuntamiento or along c/Játiva (c/Xàtiva) near the train station. Outside banking hours, try Ria, c/Convento de Jerusalén 9, two blocks west of the train station.

Consulates US, c/Dr Romagosa 1 ⓣ 963 516 973.

Hospital Hospital General, Avda Tres Cruces 2, at Avda del Cid Ⓜ Nou d'Octubre; ⓣ 961 972 000.

Internet The L@undry Stop, c/Baja (c/Baix) 17 (Mon–Fri 9.30am–10pm, Sat & Sun 2.30–10pm; internet €1.50/hr).

Left luggage Lockers at the train station (by platform 6; daily 8am–9pm; €2.40–4/24hr) and the bus station (24/7; €3–4/24hr). You'll need the exact change.

Pharmacies Farmacia Baviera, c/Don Juan de Austria 30 (ⓣ 963 512 459). Pharmacies run a rota for night-time and Sunday opening, posted in all pharmacy windows.

Police c/ Los Maestres 2 (ⓣ 963 539 725).

Post office c/San Vicente Mártir 23.

Moving on

Train Alicante (11 daily; 1hr 35min–2hr); Barcelona (15 daily; 3hr–5hr 20min); Granada (1 daily; 7hr 50min); Madrid (20 daily; 1hr 40min–3hr 15min).

Bus Alicante (20 daily; 2hr 30min–5hr); Barcelona (10 daily; 4–5hr 45min); Denia (12 daily; 1hr 30min–2hr); Madrid (13–17 daily; 4hr); Seville (3 daily; 9hr 45min–11hr 40min).

Ferry Ibiza (4 weekly; 5–15hr 15min); Mahon (1 weekly; 14hr 30min); Palma (13 weekly; 7–8hr).

ALICANTE

ALICANTE is a thoroughly Spanish city, despite its proximity to a strip of package-holiday resorts. With good beaches nearby, lively nightlife and plenty of cheap hotels and restaurants, it's worth a day or two's stopover.

What to see and do

Wide esplanades give the town an elegant air, and around the Plaza de Luceros and along the seafront *paseo* you can relax beneath palm trees at terrace cafés. Try to time your visit to coincide with the **Hogueras fiesta** of processions, fire and fireworks, which culminates in an orgy of burning on the night of June 23/24. The towering fortress **Castillo de Santa Bárbara** (daily April–Sept 10am–10pm; Oct–March 10am–8pm; €2.40 for the lift, whose last ascent is at 7.30pm April–Sept, 7pm Oct–March), on the bare rock behind the town beach, is Alicante's only real sight, with pleasant park areas and a tremendous view from the top. Access to it is from Playa Postiguet via a tunnel, then a lift shaft cut straight up through the rock. For the best local **beaches**, head for **Playa San Juan**, ten minutes from the town, on the half-hourly #L3 tram.

Arrival and information

Air The airport is 12km south of town. The #L6 airport bus (6.10am–11.10pm; every 20min; €2.60) stops near the bus station (on c/Reyes Católicos northbound, c/Lorenzo Casanova southbound) and at Puerta del Mar.

Train The main train station is on Avda Salamanca, a twenty-minute walk from the town centre.

Tram Alicante's tram (or light railway) system includes L3 to El Campello and L1 to Benidorm (change there for Denia) from Pl. de los Luceros or the Central Market.

Bus Local and long-distance services arrive at the bus station on c/Portugal, a 15min walk from the town centre.

Tourist offices Municipal: Esplanada de España 1 (Mon–Fri 9am–2pm, Sat 10am–2pm, closed Sun; ⓣ 965 147 038, ⓦ www.alicanteturismo.com).

Regional: Avda Rambla Méndez Nuñez 23 (Mon–Fri 9am–8pm, Sat 10am–8pm, Sun 10am–2pm; ⓣ965 200 000, ⓦwww.comunitatvalenciana.com). There are also tourist offices inside the train and bus stations, and at the airport.

Accommodation

Outside July and August, you shouldn't have too much trouble finding accommodation, with the bulk of the options concentrated at the lower end of the old town, above the Esplanada de España – especially on c/San Fernando, c/Jorge Juan and c/ Castaño.

Albergue Juvenil La Florida Avda de Orihuela 59 ⓣ965 918 250, ⓦwww.ivaj.es. Pretty institutional HI hostel (card obligatory), with café and laundry facilities. From October to June many spaces are reserved for students, so booking ahead is essential. Under-25s €10.50, over-25s €14.50, full-board €20/23.50.

Camping Costa Blanca c/Convento 143, El Campello ⓣ965 630 670, ⓦwww.camping costablanca.com. In a small town, Campello, 10km to the north of Alicante, and close to the beach. Easy access by L1 or L3 tram, or bus #21. €5.95 for one person plus €5.95–8.75 one tent. Also has bungalows sleeping 4–6 people (from €91 late July to early Aug; €71 rest of July & Aug; €48 rest of year).

Hostal Les Monges Palace c/San Agustín 4 ⓣ965 215 046, ⓦwww.lesmonges.es. Elegant, stylishly decorated rooms, with excellent facilities for the price. Great central location too. En-suite double with TV €52.

Hostal Ventura c/San Fernando 10 ⓣ965 208 337. Fifth-floor hotel with tidy, en-suite rooms but rather small bathrooms. Doubles €45.

Eating and drinking

Known locally as El Barrio, the concentration of streets stretching north from the main Rambla to the castle contains an impressive 119 bars and is without a doubt the best place for eating and drinking, with the crisscross of streets around c/ Virgen de Belén and c/Santos Medicos (c/Sants Metges) probably best.

El Cisne de Oro c/César Elguezábal 23. Popular tapas bar full to the brim with locals sampling delicious Alicante specialities, such as *pulpo* and *pastel de tortilla*.

Desdén c/Labradores 22, El Barrio. A more sophisticated option than *La Banca*, this bar plays dance, jazz and funk music to an attractive crowd. Several similar options along the same strip.

La Banca c/Santos Medicos 1, El Barrio. Fun bar with cheap drinks that gets livelier in the small hours. Mojitos €3.50 on Fri and Sat, €3 on Thurs.

La Matanza Castellana c/Bailén 13. Forty different tapas on offer here, with a selection of any seven (for four people) at €45, and with a €9.40 lunchtime menu. Closed Mon.

Directory

Consulate UK, Pl. Calvo Sotelo 1–2 ⓣ965 216 022.
Internet Some *locutorios* (phone offices) have internet access, including c/San Fernando 7 (Mon–Fri 10am–9pm, Sat 11am–9pm, Sun closed).
Post office Junction of c/Alemania and c/ Arzobispo Loaces (Mon–Fri 8.30am–8.30pm, Sat 9.30am–2pm).

Moving on

Train Barcelona (8 daily; 4hr 45min–5hr 35min); Madrid (7 daily; 3hr–3hr 15min); Valencia (11 daily; 1hr 30min–2hr).
Bus Barcelona (9 daily; 7hr 45min–9hr 40min); Granada (6 daily; 5hr–6hr 40min); Madrid (9 daily; 4hr 15min–6hr 15min); Málaga (7 daily; 6hr 30min–9hr 24min); Valencia (1–2 hourly; 2hr 30min–4hr 20min).

The Balearic islands

The chief **Balearic islands** – Ibiza, Mallorca and Menorca – each maintain a character that is distinct from the mainland and from each other. **Ibiza**, firmly established among Europe's hippest resorts, has a floating summer population drawn from every corner of Europe, and beyond. **Mallorca**, the largest of the Balearics, still battles with its mass-market image, though in reality you'll find the worst clichés are crammed along the Bay of Palma and are easy to avoid. Away from these there are soaring pine-forested mountains, traditional villages, lively fishing ports, some beautiful coves and the Balearics' one real city, **Palma**. The farthest island from the mainland, **Menorca**, is relatively subdued by comparison, where limited nightlife is compensated for by an abundance of unspoilt coves lapped by waters turquoise enough to rival the Caribbean. Prices on all the Balearic islands are considerably above the mainland, and from mid-June to mid-September budget **rooms** are in short supply, so book in advance.

Getting there

Ferries from mainland Spain and inter-island connections are overpriced considering the distances involved and special **flight** deals mean it can be cheaper, as well as quicker, to fly. The three main ferry companies are Acciona **Trasmediterranea** (ⓦwww.trasmediterranea.es), **Balearia** (ⓦwww.balearia.com) and **Iscomar** (ⓦwww.iscomar.com) and they operate from Barcelona, Valencia and Denia (just south of Valencia) on the mainland and have connections to and between Ibiza, Palma, Port d'Alcúdia, Maó and Ciutadella on the islands. Ferry timetables and prices vary hugely and some services, particularly the fast boats, only run in summer. By way of example: a single journey for an under 25-year-old foot passenger with Acciona Trasmediterranea from Barcelona to Palma (7hr) costs €60; a single from Denia to Ibiza with Balearia costs €50 and takes 4hr 15min; and the 2hr 30min journey from Port d'Alcúdia on Mallorca to Ciutadella on Menorca costs about €47. For the latest fares and schedules, see ⓦwww.aferryto.com, a useful one-stop shop (in English) for all routes and services.

IBIZA

IBIZA (Eivissa in Catalan) is an island of excess. Internationally heralded as one of the world's top clubbing destinations, each summer Europe's best DJs play at its clubs, attracting large numbers of people looking to party 24/7. Yet it also has a quieter side, particularly in the north, with beautiful beaches and a bohemian vibe, a legacy from the 1960s when the island was a hippy hang-out.

What to see and do

In physical as well as atmospheric terms, **IBIZA TOWN** is the most attractive place on the island. Set around a dazzling natural harbour, it's one of the Mediterranean's most cosmopolitan small capitals. The old city walls enclose the ancient quarter of **Dalt Vila**, while the port area is a maze of small, whitewashed houses, market stalls and expensive boutiques specializing in boho fashions. Most **beaches** are easily accessible from the town – the best include **Ses Salines**, a long strip of sand surrounded by forests (bus #11; hourly 9.30am–7.30pm), and **Cala Bassa**, a cove on the west side of the island, roughly 9km west of the island's second clubbing town of **SANT ANTONI**; take bus #3 from Ibiza Town to Sant Antoni (every 30min; 7.30am–midnight), then bus #7 (hourly; 9.30am–6.30pm, except 1.30–2.30pm) from Sant Antoni to Cala Bassa. For celebrity spotting, head to the tiny **Platja de Benirràs** (no public transport), near San Miguel, a favourite of the Euro jet-set.

Just eleven miles south of Ibiza Town, the fourth Balearic island of Formentera (ferries leave Ibiza every 30min from the port at Avda Santa Eularia) is well worth a visit. It boasts even more beautiful beaches and a relaxed, rustic charm.

Arrival and information

Air The airport is 7km out of town; there are regular shuttle buses (daily 6.50am–11.50pm; €3.20), or you can take a taxi (€15–17).

Boat The terminal on Passeig des Moll serves ferries to and from the mainland and Mallorca; boats from Formentera arrive at the terminal on Avda Santa Eularia.

Tourist office On Passeig de Vara de Rey (June–Sept Mon–Fri 8.30am–7.30pm, Sat 9am–2pm; Nov–April Mon–Fri 8am–3pm, Sat 9.30am–1pm; ⓣ971 301 900). For a wealth of information about the island see ⓦwww.ibiza-spotlight.com.

Accommodation

Camping Cala Nova Platja Cala Nova ⓣ 971 331 774, ⓦ www.campingcalanova.com. Located 20km north of Ibiza Town – but only 50m from the beach. Good base for watersports. €8/tent, plus €8/person.

Hostal Giramundo c/Ramón Muntaner ⓣ 971 307 640, ⓦ www.hostalgiramundoibiza.com. Brightly coloured, backpacker-orientated *hostal* with an excellent in-house bar-café, just a block from Figueretes beach and a 10min walk from Ibiza Town. Dorms €28, doubles €80.

Camping La Playa Cala Martina, Es Canar ⓣ 971 338 526, ⓦ www.camping-laplaya-ibiza.com. East-coast camping among pine trees with direct access to the beach. Log cabins also available to rent. €13/tent, plus €11/person.

Hostal Sol y Brisa Avgda Bartomeu Vicent Ramon 15 ⓣ 971 310 818. Clean and friendly *hostal* with amiable owner just off the Passeig de Vara de Rey. €80.

Vara de Rey Guest House Passeig de Vara de Rey 7 ⓣ 971 301 376, ⓦ www.hibiza.com. Pleasant, artistically furnished rooms with shared toilets and showers. Just 5min from the port. €80.

Eating and drinking

Bide Bide c/Felipe II 13. Lively, modern tapas bar with a good wine selection and a superb choice of innovative tapas from €3. Try the steak with blue cheese. Daily 7pm–late.

Bon Profit Pl del Parque 5. Popular, reasonably priced Spanish restaurant with mains under €10. Grilled squid €8.40. Mon–Sat 1–3pm & 8–10pm. Closed Jan.

Comidas Bar San Juan c/Vicent Soler s/n. Family-run restaurant-bar, with a great Spanish menu. Arrive early to avoid queuing. Expect to share tables. Closed Sun. Spanish *tortilla* €4.

Lo Cura c/Antonio Mari Ribas 4. Tiny and welcoming place with cheaper drinks than the main portside bars and a DJ. Frozen Margarita €8. Mon–Sat from 9pm.

Los Pasajeros c/Lluis Tur i Palau 19. A bustling first-floor restaurant with a sociable atmosphere, serving bargain-priced and homely Spanish dishes. Mains about €7. May–Oct 6pm–2am.

Rock Bar c/Garijo 14. One of the cheaper portside bars, attracting many English-speakers and top DJs. A good place to meet fellow partygoers. Glass of red wine €4. Evenings only.

Sunset Café Pl del Parque 9. A meeting point of international visitors and the perfect spot for people watching over a coffee or a cocktail. Daily 8am–late.

Clubs

Ibiza's formidable club scene needs little introduction. The season is short, however (mid-June to Sept), with August particularly busy. Most of the main venues don't close until well past dawn. The handy Discobus links these clubs with the centre of town and runs through the night (€3 one-way). Be prepared to spend a lot of money, though, with entrance fees upwards of €35 and astronomical bar prices. Look out for touts selling discounted tickets around the port bars each night, and for club promoters handing out free invites on the beaches. Alternatively, head to Platja d'en Bossa to party day and night at the famous beach bar *Bora Bora* (free entry).

Amnesia Ibiza Town–Sant Antoni road, km6 ⓦ www.amnesia.es. A good mix of music across various nights. On Wednesdays, the island's most popular gay night, La Troya, is held here.

Las Dalias Ibiza Town–Sant Carles km 12, ⓦ www.lasdalias.es. A bar-cum-club with a legendary status, at the heart of Ibiza's hippy scene past and present. Namaste night on Wednesdays is a must.

Pacha Avda 8 d'Agost ⓦ www.pacha.com. A more commercial scene than some other Ibizan clubs, with a capacity of over three thousand. Playing a variety of music, including Spanish pop, jazzy house, soul and funk, but predominantly house – in different rooms.

Privilege Ibiza Town–Sant Antoni road, km7 ⓦ www.privilegeibiza.com. One of the biggest clubs in the world, with a capacity for 10,000 – and hosting extravagant club nights every day of the week.

Space Platja d'en Bossa ⓦ www.space-ibiza.es. Vast venue with a legendary terrace. Has a plethora of chill-out zones and alternative areas. Sunday sessions are a favourite.

Gay bars and clubs

Ibiza has one of the best gay scenes in Europe, with a lot of the action centred in the port and another cluster of bars on c/de la Virgen. Many mainstream Ibizan clubs hold a weekly gay night.

Anfora c/San Carlos 7, Dalt Vila ⓦ www.disco-anfora.com. Ibiza's only dedicated gay club. May to mid-Oct 11pm–6am; closed mid-Oct to April.

Dado c/Calle de la Virgen. One of the friendliest of the many trendy bars on Ibiza town's liveliest street. Cocktails from €6. Daily 9pm–late; Nov–Easter weekends only.

MALLORCA

MALLORCA has a split identity. There are sections of its coast where the concrete curtain of high-rise hotels, seedy bars and shopping centres is continuous, but the spread of development tends to be isolated, sectioned off into ugly ghettos that are easy to avoid. Elsewhere the island is as appealing as it gets in the Mediterranean, particularly in the northwest where several stunning coves and pretty villages are framed by the dramatic backdrop of the rugged Tramuntana mountains.

Palma

Much to the surprise of many visitors, **PALMA** is an attractive, historic and cosmopolitan city filled with quaint streets, stylish boutiques and lively bars and restaurants. The main sight is the **cathedral** (April–May & Oct Mon–Fri 10am–5.15pm, Sat 10am–2.15pm; June–Sept Mon–Fri 10am–6.15pm, Sat 10am–2.15pm; Nov–March Mon–Fri 10am–3.15pm, Sat 10am–2.15pm; €4), which was built in recognition of the Christian Reconquest of Mallorca, and later worked on by Gaudí. Nearby, within the old town quarter, are the **Arab baths** (daily: April–Nov 9am–7pm; Dec–March 9am–6pm; €2), while up the hill overlooking the bay lies the **Castell de Bellver** (April–Sept daily 8am–5.30pm; Oct–March daily 8am–7.30pm; €2.50, free Sun), offering spectacular views from its high point over the city. Several decent **beaches** are a bus ride away from the city centre. Bus #3 departs from the top of Plaça Rei Joan Carlos 1, outside C&A, and goes all the way to the attractive beach of Illetes, stopping off en route at the beaches at Cala Major and Portal Nous.

Arrival and information

Air Palma airport, 8km east of the city, is served by bus #1 (every 15min; €2) to the Passeig Mallorca.
Boat The large ferry port is 3.5km west of the city centre, connected to Palma by bus #1.

TREAT YOURSELF

Hidden amid the tourist trappings of La Lonja, behind a large wooden door, **Abaco** (c/Sant Joan 1, just off c/Apuntadores) is one of Palma's most decadent treats. The bar is dripping in excess, with fruit draped over the elegant staircase, copious flowers and even caged birds. Unsurprisingly the drinks aren't cheap but then the opulent surrounds are probably worth a €16 mojito.

Tourist office Plaça de la Reina 2 (Mon–Fri 9am–8pm, Sat 9am–2pm; ⓣ971 173 992, ⓦwww.infomallorca.net).
Internet Azul Computer Group, c/Soledad 4, just off the Plaça de la Reina; €3/hr.

Accommodation

The best areas to look for accommodation are around the Passeig Mallorca, on C/Apuntadores or C/Sant Feliu running west from Passeig d'es Born.
Hostal Apuntadores c/Apuntadores 8 ⓣ971 713 491, ⓦwww.palma-hostales.com. Not as much character as the *Ritzi* next door, but the rooms are slightly more comfortable. Doubles €55, with bath €50.
Hostal Brondo c/Ca'n Brondo 1 ⓣ971 719 043, ⓦwww.hostalbrondo.com. Stylish hotel, tastefully decorated in traditional Mallorcan style. Rooms are more enticing and quieter than the options on C/Apuntadores. Double with bath €68, without €55.
Hostal Ritzi c/Apuntadores 6 ⓣ971 714 610, ⓦwww.hostalritzi.com. Ramshackle Palma institution in a great location at the heart of La Lonja. Rooms are basic, and with no lift the rooms on the fourth floor are quite a climb. Basic breakfast included. Dorms €20, doubles with shared bath €55.

Eating and drinking

The best place to go strolling in search of food is the largely pedestrianized La Lonja.
Bar Dia c/Apuntadores 18. Cheap, delicious and popular with locals – always a good sign. Specializing in tapas, from tortilla for €3 to prawns in garlic for €12. Tues–Sun 1pm–late.
Celler Pagès Off c/Apuntadors at C/Felip Bauza 2. Small, inexpensive restaurant serving traditional Mallorcan food – try the stuffed marrows

with home-made mayonnaise. Good-value lunch menu at €13. Mon–Sat 1–3.30pm & 8–11pm.

La Taberna de la Bóveda Passeig de Sagrera 3. Hugely popular, elegant bar-restaurant, just off Plaça Llotja serving an excellent array of original tapas from €3.50. Also more elaborate dishes including mushrooms with roquefort €10. Always busy. Daily 1.30–4pm & 8pm–12.30am.

Nightlife

Most of the major clubs are along the Paseo Marítimo, though if you're expecting nightlife of Ibiza proportions, you'll be sorely disappointed.

Abraxas Avda de Gabriel Roca 42. Waterfront venue with guest DJs from Ibiza and the UK. Cover charge €12–15.

Tito's Plaça Gomila 3 www.titosmallorca.com. Arranged over three floors and with fantastic views across the bay of Palma. Music ranges from hardcore dance to pop. Cover charge €20.

Sóller

Set beneath the dramatic Tramuntana mountains, where the air is scented by orange and lemon groves, the beautiful town of **SÓLLER** is one of Mallorca's highlights. The town also makes a great base from which to explore the stunning northwest coast, including excursions to the nearby villages of **Fornalutx**, **Deià** and **Valdemossa**. You can also take the tram on to **Port Sóller** (every 30min in summer; €4 one-way), a little coastal town with a small, sandy cove that's good for bathing. The best way to get to Sóller from Palma is by train (see box below).

PALMA–SÓLLER TRAIN RIDE

The **train ride from Palma to Sóller** (7 daily; €10 one-way, €17 return; www.trendesoller.com) is definitely worth the trip. Built in 1912 to carry fruit to Palma, the line rattles and rolls in wooden carriages through the dusty outskirts of the capital before a cross-country climb up mountain passes and through tunnels, passing almond groves, unruffled lakes and craggy peaks topping a thousand metres.

Information

Tourist office In a converted train carriage next to the train terminal (Mon–Fri 9.45am–2pm & 3.15–5pm, Sat 9.15am–1pm; ☎971 638 008, www.sollernet.com).

Internet Cyber Phone, C/Metge Maiol 2, just off Plaça Constitució. €2/hr.

Accommodation

Casa Margarita c/Reial 3 ☎971 634 214. The best budget option in town with pleasant, basic rooms, some with terraces. Delightful Margarita, the owner, is a mine of information on the local area. Doubles with shared bath €33.

Hostal Nadal c/Romaguera 29 ☎971 631 180. Despite a rather unappealing exterior, rooms are clean and beds are comfy. Breakfast available. Double with shared bath €35.

Eating and drinking

Rino's Pizzeria c/Joan Baptista i Ensenyat. Tiny counter offering takeaway pizza and calzone. A cheaper option among the many nearby tourist-geared restaurants. Pizza €7.80. Daily July & Aug; April–Oct Tues–Sun noon–3pm & 8–11pm.

Sa Fabrica de Gelats c/Romaguera 12. Gelateria serving a wide range of delicious flavours, including orange cream, made with home-grown Mallorcan oranges. Two scoops €2.50. Mon–Sat 9am–7pm.

MENORCA

In 1993 **MENORCA** was declared a biosphere reserve and as such the island has largely avoided the ugly development seen elsewhere in the Balearics. Instead, idyllic coves and tranquil bays take their place. It's possible to get to some of the coastal resorts with local transport from the main towns of **Maó** or **Ciutadella**, but you'll need your own wheels if you want to discover the more isolated beauty spots. Cycling is a great option as the roads are flat and quiet. Unlike its larger neighbours, however, Menorca is not for those in search of a party – out of season, nightlife on the island is virtually nonexistent.

Maó

As most visitors stay in resorts along the coast, the Menorcan capital of **MAÓ** is relatively free from tourists and so retains an authentic feel and is a great place to stay. It has an impressive natural harbour, some lovely old streets and enough picturesque squares in which to while away a lazy afternoon or two. Local buses provide access to nearby attractions, such as the lunar landscape of the **Cap de Favaritx**, the lively town of **Fornells**, or the beach resorts in the southeast, such as **Cala en Porter**.

Arrival and information

Air Menorca's international airport is 5km southwest of Maó. Buses (€1.60) run every 30min from 6am to midnight to Maó's central bus station.

Boat Ferries from Palma and Barcelona arrive at Maó harbour, a short walk from the town centre.

Bicycle rental Bike Menorca, Avda Francesc Femenías, 44 ⓣ971 353 798.

Car rental Avis, Moll de Ponent 61 ⓣ971 364 778; Hertz, Maó airport ⓣ971 354 092.

Tourist office Moll de Llevant 2 (Mon–Fri 8am–8pm, Sat 8am–1pm; ⓣ971 355 952, ⓦwww.menorca.es).

Internet Locutorio Call Point II, c/Sant Elies 54.

Accommodation

Camping Son Bou Crta San Jaime ⓣ971 372 727, ⓦwww.campingsonbou.com. Located south of Alaior, a 30min bus ride from Maó. €7.94/person, plus one-person tent €4.51.

Hostal La Isla c/Santa Caterina 4 ⓣ971 366 492. More expensive than *Orsi*, but a few extra euros gets you a more comfortable room, a TV and private bath. Very friendly owner and decent bar downstairs. En-suite double €50.

Posada Orsi c/Infanta 19 ⓣ971 364 751. Brightly coloured rooms, sociable atmosphere and roof terrace make this a popular choice, but the colours can't quite hide the slightly institutional feel. Doubles with shared bath €47.

Eating and drinking

The best place for eating and drinking is down by the port, where there are plenty of bars and restaurants – open mainly in July and August.

Café Ars Plaça Príncipe. Restaurant-bar with a simple but superbly executed menu. Also hosts musical and cultural events. Mushroom risotto €10.50. Mon–Sat noon–4.30pm & 7.30–11.30pm, until 4am Fri & Sat.

Cristinal y Gradinata C/Isabel II. A collection of old radios, hats and beer bottles adorn the shelves of this delightful bistro bar. The delicious sandwiches are among the tastiest on the island and a snip at about €2. Mon–Sat 8.30am–3pm & 7.30–11.30pm.

Mirador Café Plaça Espanya 2. Café-bar with the usual range of drinks and tapas, but it's the great views across the harbour from the terrace that makes it such a popular choice. *Pomada* (gin and lemonade) €4. Mon–Sat 11am–late.

Ciutadella and around

Well-preserved **CIUTADELLA** has a lovely old quarter and harbour and is Menorca's prettiest town. Nearby are some of the most beautiful and secluded virgin beaches in the Mediterranean, such as **Cala Turqueta** and **Macarella** – both have soft white sand and turquoise waters and are about a twenty-minute drive from Ciutadella (also reachable by bike). There are no facilities at Turqueta, so bring your own lunch, while at Macarella, *Bar Susy* serves simple meals (pizzas from €8–10) and has toilets and showers. A

A wonderful exception to Menorca's limited nightlife is the fabulously located club, **Cova d'en Xoroi** in Cala en Porter (ⓦwww.covadenxoroi.com). Set in a large cave carved out of the cliff face, it's lit up to dramatic effect at night. The terraces give stunning views out to sea, especially at sunset or even sunrise (the club is open until dawn). Resident and top guest DJs match the ambient music to the tranquil setting. See website for event listings, gets going from 11pm; entrance €15–18, including one drink.

short walk from Macarella over the white stone gorge takes you to the even more picturesque bay of **Macarelleta**.

Arrival and information

Bus Buses arrive at Plaça dels Pins, a few minutes' walk from the centre of town.
Boat Ferries from Alcudia in Mallorca arrive at the ferry port about 4km south of the centre. Buses meet the boats to ferry passengers into town.
Bicycle and motorbike rental Velos Joan, Sant Isidre 78 ⓣ971 381 576.
Tourist office Plaça Catedral 5 (Mon–Fri 8.30am–8.30pm, Sat 9am–1pm; ⓣ971 382 693, ⓦwww.menorca.es).
Internet Locutori Rupit 18.Net, c/Castell Rupit 18.

Accommodation

Camping S'Atalaia Ctra Cala Galdana, Ferreries, ⓣ971 374 232, ⓦwww.campingsatalaia.com. Between the town of Ferreries and the resorts of Santa Galdana, a well-equipped site with several pools. €7.40 person, plus €4/tent.
Hostal Residencia Oasis c/Sant Isidre 33 ⓣ971 382 197. Comfortable, spacious rooms set back from a pretty courtyard and restaurant. Double with private bath €50. Closed June–Sept.

Eating and drinking

The charming market (Plaça Francesc Netto and Plaça Llibertat, Mon–Sat mornings) is a good place to pick up provisions for a picnic (there are no facilities at most of the isolated beaches). The best restaurants are off the side street of Plaça d'es Born. For nightlife, it's best to start the evening at the bars and cafés of the old town, then from midnight head down to the Port, where the bars and clubs (in high season) stay open until 6am.
Ca'n Nito c/Plaça d'es Born 11. A lively bar on the main square, popular for drinks and a fantastic range of tapas. *Platos combinados*, such as chicken and chips (€8.50), also available. Daily 9am–late.
Gabanna Plaça de Sant Joan 3. An attractive, bohemian bar in the trendy port area that becomes a club later in the evening, with alternative jazz, world and house music. Daily 11pm–4am.
La Guitarra c/Nostra Senyora dels Dolors 1. Family-run restaurant serving traditional Menorcan specialities, such as *caldereta de llagosta* (lobster stew) and *caracoles* (snails), in an atmospheric cellar. Mains from €14–20. Mon–Sat 12.30–3.30pm & 7.30–11pm.

Catalunya

With its own language, culture and, to a degree, government, **Catalunya** (Catalonia in English) has a unique identity. **Barcelona**, the capital, is very much the main event, one of the most vibrant and exciting cities in Europe. Inland, the monastery of **Montserrat**, Catalunya's premier sight, is perched on one of the most unusual rock formations in Spain and makes for a great day-trip. To the north, the rugged **Costa Brava** is slowly shedding its erstwhile unfortunate touristy image and boasts the best beaches in the region, along with some appropriately wacky and wonderful homages to surrealist artist Salvador Dalí.

BARCELONA

Cool and hip as they come, **BARCELONA** is Catalunya's elegant and self-confident modern capital. A thriving port, and the most prosperous commercial centre in the Iberian peninsula, its sophistication and cultural dynamism are way ahead of the rest of Spain – the city seems far more in tune with Milan and Paris than with Madrid or Lisbon. Barcelona also evolved a quirky and very individual identity of its own, most perfectly expressed in the eccentric Art Nouveau architecture of **Antoni Gaudí** and his contemporaries, but also evident in the huge diversity of the city's cultural events.

What to see and do

Though it boasts outstanding **Gothic** and **Art Nouveau** buildings, and some great museums – most notably those dedicated to Picasso, Miró and Catalan art – Barcelona's main appeal lies in getting lost in the narrow side streets of the **Barri Gòtic** (Gothic Quarter); rising, eating and drinking late; hitting the beach or lazing in the parks; and

CATALAN (CATALÀ)

	Catalan	Pronunciation
Yes	*Sí*	See
No	*No*	Noh
Please	*Si us plau*	See-uus-plow
Thank you	*Graciés*	Gra-see-ess
Hello/Good day	*Hola*	Oh-la
Goodbye	*Adéu*	A-day-uu
Excuse me	*Perdoni*	Perdoni
Where?	*On?*	On?
Good	*Bon/Bona*	Bon/Bonna
Bad	*Mal*	Mal
Near	*Aprop*	Aprop
Far	*Lluny*	Yoon
Cheap	*Barat*	Barat
Expensive	*Car*	Carr
Open	*Obert*	Oo-berrt
Closed	*Tancat*	Tun-cat
Today	*Avui*	A-boo-ee
Yesterday	*Ahir*	A-hear
Tomorrow	*Demà*	Du-maa
How much?	*Quant val?*	Kwant val?
What time is it?	*Quina hora és?*	Kina ora es?
I don't understand	*No ho entenc*	No oo antenk
Do you speak English?	*Parles anglès?*	Par-les ang-lays?
One	*Un/Una*	Oon/Oona
Two	*Dos/Dues*	Doss/Doo-guz
Three	*Tres*	Trays
Four	*Quatre*	Kwa-tra
Five	*Cinc*	Sing
Six	*Sis*	Seess
Seven	*Set*	Set
Eight	*Vuit*	Bweet
Nine	*Nou*	No
Ten	*Deu*	Dayoo

generally soaking up the atmosphere. As in any large city, keep an eye on your valuables

Las Ramblas

One of the most popular avenues in Europe, **Las Ramblas** has been overtaken by sightseers, tourist bars, postcard stalls and human statues; it's largely avoided by locals. However, as it bisects the city, Las Ramblas remains a useful point of reference, so it's worth strolling down to orient yourself before getting lost in the more interesting maze of side streets in the Barri Gòtic to the east or El Raval to the west. If you are walking down Las Ramblas towards the sea, just off to your right is the glorious **La Boqueria**, the city's main food market (Mon–Sat 8am–8.30pm; Ⓦwww.boqueria.info), a splendid gallery of sights and smells. A little further on, by the metro station, stands the **Liceu**, Barcelona's celebrated opera house (daily guided tours of the interior at 10am, €9; visit without guide daily at 11.30am, noon, 12.30pm and 1pm €4.20; Ⓣ934 859 914, Ⓦwww.liceubarcelona.cat). Further down still, positioned to the left off Las

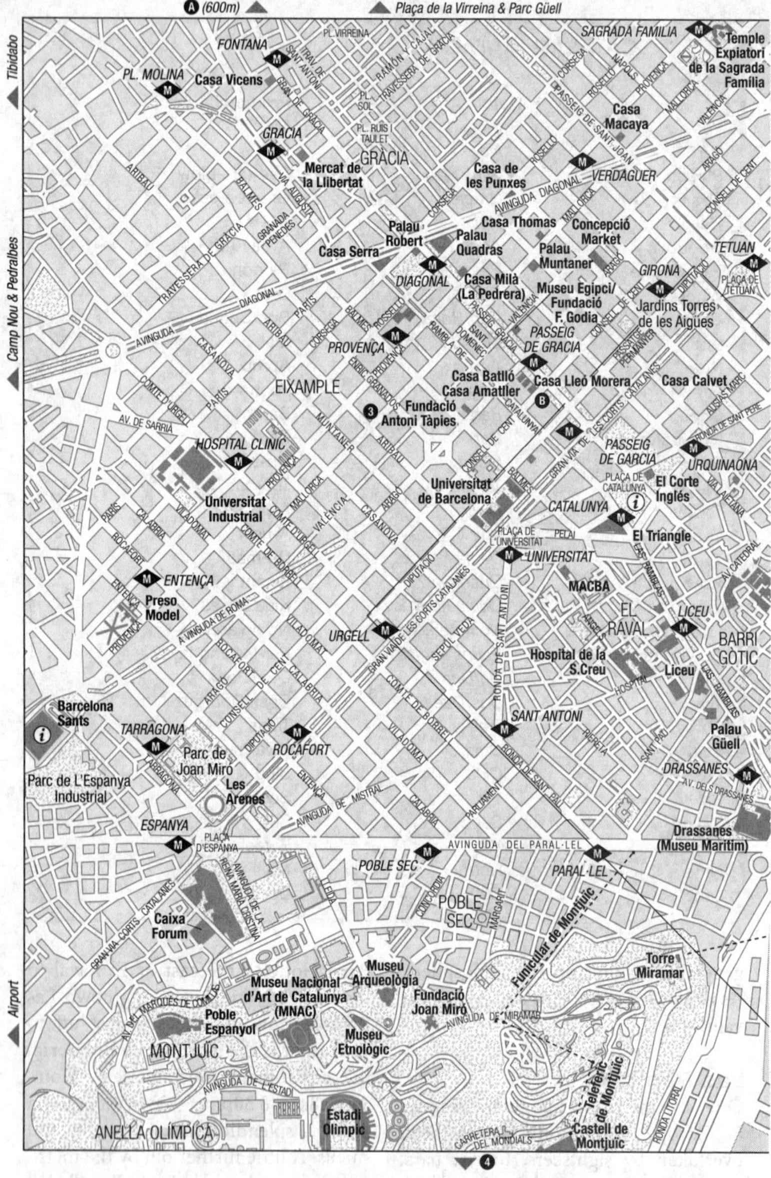

Ramblas and into the Barri Gòtic, is the elegant but seedy nineteenth-century **Plaça Reial**. Decorated with tall palm trees and iron lamps, it's the haunt of bohemians, eccentrics and hundreds of alfresco diners and drinkers. Right at the harbour end of Las Ramblas, Columbus stands perilously perched atop a tall, grandiose column, the **Mirador de Colom** (daily 8.30am–8pm; €4). Take the lift to his head for a fine view of the city.

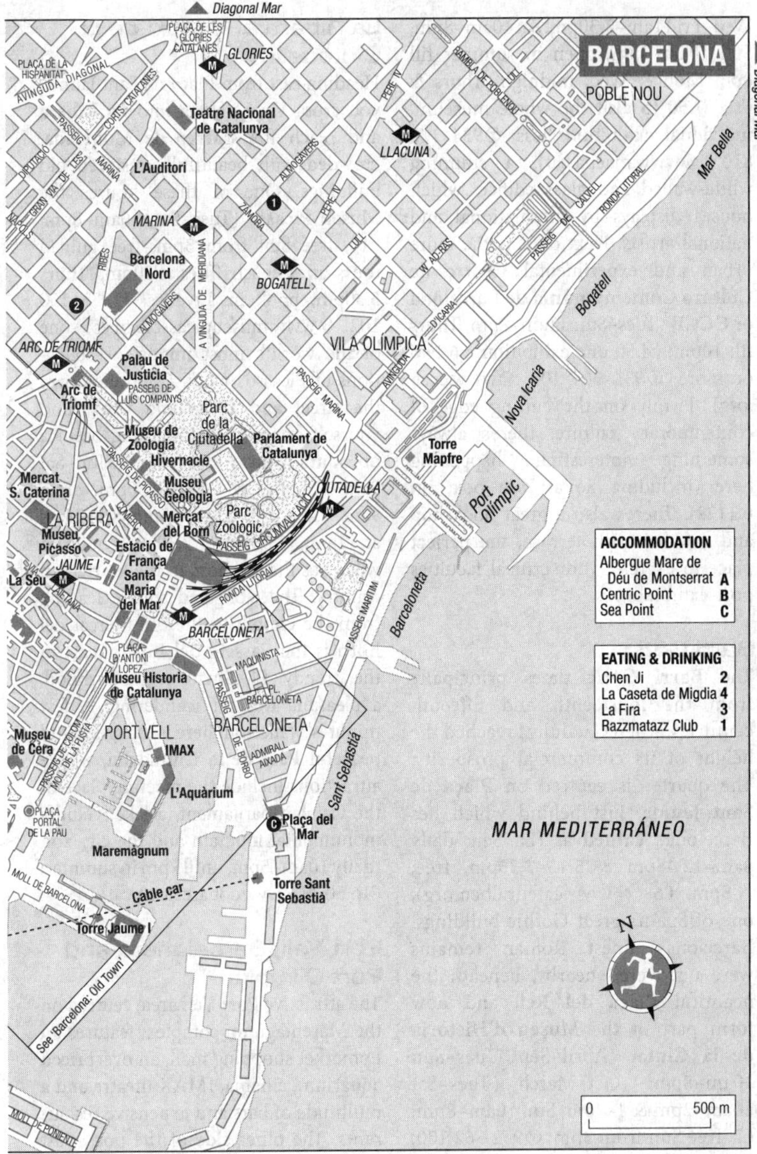

El Raval

The once-notorious red-light district of **El Raval** lies on the west side of Las Ramblas. With its two universities and numerous bars, clubs and arts centres, it is now one of the most exciting and authentic areas of the city. For a taste of the area's regeneration, walk up the **Rambla de Raval** – a boulevard with pavement cafés and bars – on your way to the **Museu d'Art Contemporani de Barcelona** or **MACBA** (Mon &

Wed–Fri 11am–7.30pm, Sat 10am–8pm, Sun 10am–3pm, open in summer till 8pm Mon & Wed, midnight Thurs & Fri; €7.50 to visit the whole museum, individual exhibitions less; ⓣ934 120 810, ⓦwww.macba.cat), a stunning white-walled and glass edifice, which houses displays by international and national artists. Next door is the more urban and experimental **Centre de Cultura Contemporània de Barcelona** or **CCCB** (Tues–Sun 11am–8pm, Thurs till 10pm; €4.50 one exhibition, €6 two or more; ⓣ933 064 100, ⓦwww.cccb.org). Firmly on the cutting edge of contemporary culture, there's always something interesting happening here (including Sónar; see box, on p.1122). There's also a great bookshop and café-bar with terrace, the perfect place to exercise your critical faculties post-exhibition.

Barri Gòtic

The **Barri Gòtic** dates principally from the fourteenth and fifteenth centuries, when Catalunya reached the height of its commercial prosperity. The quarter is centred on **Plaça de Sant Jaume**, just behind which lies Barcelona's **cathedral** (La Seu; daily 8am–12.45pm & 5.15–7.30pm, free; 1–5pm €6; ⓦwww.catedralbcn.org), one of Spain's great Gothic buildings. Barcelona's finest Roman remains were uncovered nearby, beneath the beautiful **Plaça del Rei**, and now form part of the **Museu d'Història de la Ciutat** (April–Sept Tues–Sun 10am–8pm; Oct–March Tues–Sat 10am–2pm & 4–7pm, Sun 10am–8pm; €7, free Sun from 3pm; ⓣ932 562 100, ⓦwww.museuhistoria.bcn.es). You'll also be able to see the interiors of the Plaça del Rei's finest buildings – including the famous **Saló del Tinell**, on whose steps Ferdinand and Isabella stood to receive Columbus on his triumphant return from his famous voyage of 1492.

La Ribera and Parc de la Ciutadella

Heading east from Plaça de Sant Jaume, you cross Vía Laietana into **La Ribera** and reach the **Carrer de Montcada**, crowded with beautifully restored old buildings. One of these houses the **Museu Picasso** (Tues–Sun 10am–8pm; €10, free Sun from 3pm, free guided tours in English Tues 4.30pm, Thurs 5.30pm, book in advance; ⓣ933 150 102, ⓦwww.museupicasso.bcn.es), one of the world's most important collections of Picasso's work. Continue down the street and at its end you'll find yourself opposite the stunning basilica of **Santa Maria del Mar** (Mon–Sat 9am–1.30pm & 4.30–8.30pm, Sun 9am–1.45pm & 4.30–8.45pm; Sun Mass at 11am, 12.30pm & 7.30pm), built on what was the seashore in the fourteenth century. The elongated square leading from the church to the old Mercat del Born is the **Passeig del Born**, heart of the trendy **El Born** neighbourhood, a pleasant area for wandering. A few minutes' walk from here is the green and peaceful **Parc de la Ciutadella**, whose attractions include the meeting place of the Catalan parliament, a lake, Gaudí's monumental fountain and the city **zoo** (daily 10am–5pm, until 7pm in summer; €16.50; ⓦwww.zoobarcelona.cat).

Port Vell, Barceloneta and Port Olímpic

The attractive **Port Vell** area, centred on the Maremàgnum complex, features an upmarket shopping mall, an overpriced aquarium, cinema, IMAX theatre and a multitude of bars and expensive restaurants. The other side of the port, past the marina, the **Barceloneta** district, in contrast, is one of the few remaining *barris* harbouring genuine local Catalan life: here, you'll find cleaned-up **beaches**, and the city's most famous **seafood** restaurants. A **cable car**, the **Trasbordador Aeri** runs from the tip of Barceloneta to Montjuïc (daily: late Oct to Feb 11am–5.30pm; March to early June & mid-Sept to late Oct 11am–7pm, early June to mid-Sept 11am–8.15pm; €9 one-way, €12.50 return). Walk 1km north along the beach promenade and you'll find **Port Olímpic** with its myriad bars and restaurants. At night, the tables are stacked up, dancefloors emerge and the area hosts one of the city's liveliest (and brashest) bar and club scenes.

Sagrada Família

Barcelona offers – above all through the work of **Antoni Gaudí** (1852–1926) – some of the most fantastic and exciting modern architecture anywhere in the world. Without doubt his most famous creation is the incomplete **Temple Expiatori de la Sagrada Família** (daily April–Sept 9am–8pm; Oct–March 9am–6pm; €12.50; Ⓦwww.sagradafamilia.cat; Ⓜ Sagrada Família), in the northeastern sector of the Eixample district. With construction still ongoing, the interior is a giant building site, but it's fascinating to watch Gaudí's last-known plans being slowly realized. The size alone is startling, with eight spires rising to over 100m. Take the lift, or climb up one of the towers, and you can enjoy a dizzy view down over the whole complex and clamber still further round the walls and into the towers.

More Art Nouveau

Barcelona's Eixample (the street-grid zone) abounds with wonderful modernista (Art Nouveau) buildings. The top two are Gaudí's Pedrera at Passeig de Gràcia 92 (daily March–Oct 9am–8pm; Nov–Feb 9am–6.30pm; €14; Ⓦwww.lapedreraeducacio.org), and very nearby, his Casa Batlló at Passeig de Gràcia 43 (daily 9am–8pm; €18.15; Ⓦwww.casabatllo.cat). Check out in particular the Casa Batlló's front window in the form of a dragon's mouth, with its roof like the dragon's back. Despite the outrageous entry fee, it's most definitely worth a look inside. It shares a block with two other great Art Nouveau buildings, the Casa Amatller at no. 41 and the Casa Lléo Morera at no. 35.

Barcelona's other great Art Nouveau masterpiece is the 1908 Palau de la Música Catalana concert hall in c/Sant Pere Més Alt, (guided tours in English at 10am, 11am, noon, 1pm, 2pm & 3pm, and in Aug also 4pm, 5pm & 6pm; €12, with limited places so worth buying in advance or on line; Ⓦwww.palaumusica.org; Ⓜ Urquinaona), where the multicoloured columns of the facade are just a taster for the wonders within, and in particular the amazing stained-glass roof.

Gràcia and Parc Güell

The residential neighbourhood of **Gràcia**, north of the centre, has a bohemian, village-like feel, and is a good place for an authentic night out. Popular with arty student types, the bars are best stumbled upon by chance – try your luck around the Plaça de la Virreina. Close by is the Verdi cinema, c/Verdi 32 (east along c/Asturies from Ⓜ Fontana; Ⓦwww.cines-verdi.com/barcelona), which shows art-house films, often in English.

In the eastern part of Gràcia, **Parc Güell** (daily: winter 10am–6pm, summer 10am–8pm; free) is Gaudí's most ambitious project after the Sagrada Família – and shouldn't be missed. This almost hallucinatory experience, with giant decorative lizards and a vast Hall of Columns, contains a small **museum** (daily 10am–6pm; €5.50) with some of the furniture Gaudí designed. To get here, take the metro to Vallcarca or Lesseps (15min walk from either) or bus #24 from Plaça de Catalunya to the eastern side gate.

Montjuïc

The hill of **Montjuïc** features the varied attractions of half a dozen museums, gardens, the Poble Espanyol, a superbly sited castle and spectacular views of the

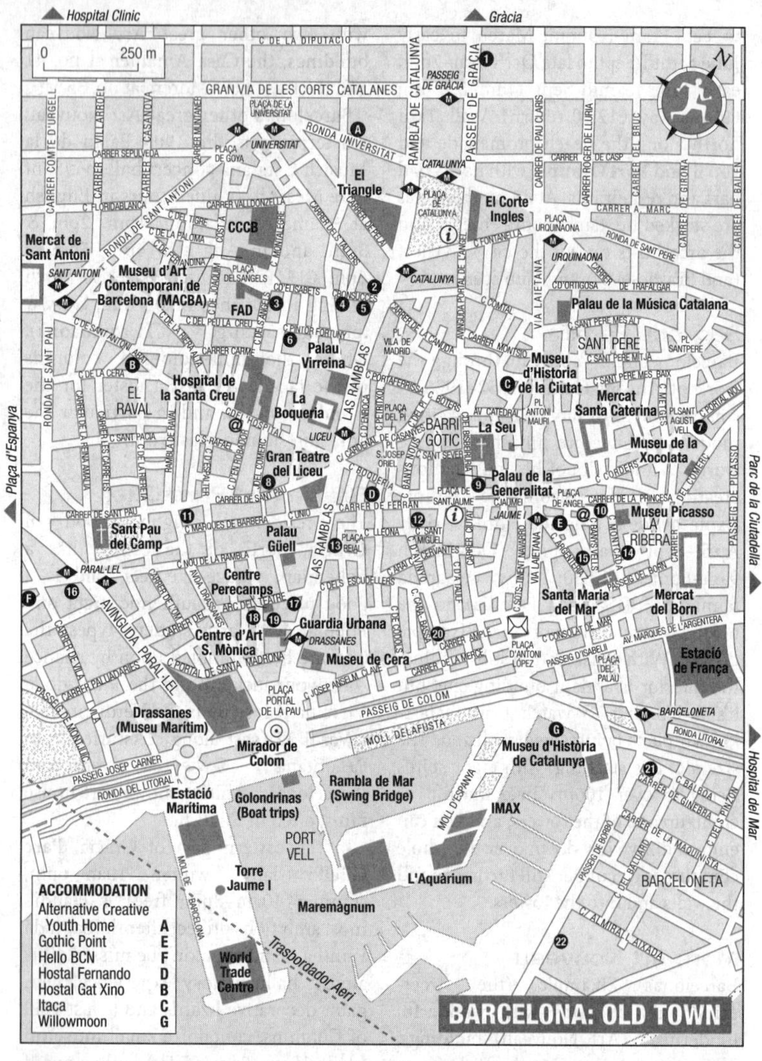

EATING							
Arc Café	20	Dhub	10	Gelaaati!	9	Organic	8
BioCenter	6	Divinus	1	Gran Café	12	Silenus	3
Buenas Migas	4	Euskal Etxea	14	Julivert Meu	5	Taller de Tapas	15
Can Manel	22			L'Economic	7	Vaso de Oro	21

DRINKING & NIGHTLIFE			
Ambar	11	Jamboree	13
Bar Pastis	19	Moog	17
Boadas	2	Sala Apolo/ Club Nitsa	16
Cangrejo	18		

sprawling city below. The most obvious approach is to take the metro to **Plaça d'Espanya** and walk from there up the imposing Avenida de la Reina María Cristina. If you'd rather start with the castle, take the **Funicular de Montjuïc** (daily, from 7.30am weekdays or 9am weekends until 10pm in summer, or 8pm in winter; every 10min; fare included in metro tickets), which runs from Paral.lel metro station to the start of the **Telefèric de Montjuïc** (daily: March–May & Oct

10am–7pm; June–Sept 10am–9pm; Nov–Feb 10am–6pm; €6.50 one-way, €9.30 return), which in turn leads to the **Castell de Montjuïc** (daily: April–Sept 9am–9pm, Oct–March 9am–7pm; free). This eighteenth-century fortress offers magnificent views across the city, has an outdoor café within its ramparts and a panoramic pathway into the surrounding woods. The alternative option to reach Montjuïc is to take bus #50 from Sagrada Familia or Gran Vía (for example, at Plaça de la Universitat, or just west of Rambla de Catalunya).

MNAC, the Poble Espanyol and the Fundació Joan Miró

The Palau Nacional, set at the back of Montjuïc, is the imposing peach-coloured home to one of Spain's great museums, the **Museu Nacional d'Art de Catalunya** or **MNAC** (Tues–Sat 10am–7pm, Sun 10am–2.30pm; €8.50, free first Sun of month; Ⓦwww.mnac.es). Its enormous bounty includes a Romanesque collection that is the best of its kind in the world and a substantial number of Gothic, Baroque and Renaissance works. Nearby is the **Fundació Joan Miró** (Tues, Wed, Fri & Sat: Oct–June 10am–7pm; July–Sept 10am–8pm, Thurs 10am–9.30pm, Sun 10am–2.30pm; €9; Ⓦwww.fundaciomiro-bcn.org), devoted to one of the greatest Catalan artists and the most adventurous of Barcelona's art museums. Downhill and to the west of MNAC is the **Poble Espanyol** or "Spanish Village" (Mon 9am–8pm, Tues–Thurs 9am–2am, Fri 9am–4am, Sat 9am–5am, Sun 9am–midnight; €8.90; Ⓦwww.poble-espanyol.com), consisting of replicas of famous or characteristic buildings from all over Spain, and with a lively club scene at night.

Arrival and information

Air The airport is 18km southwest of the city centre and is linked by train (daily 5.42am–11.38pm, approximately every 30min; €3.15) to the city's main station, Barcelona Sants, and Pg. de Gràcia in the city centre, both served by Ⓜ L3 to Liceu or Pl. de Catalunya. The Aerobús (6am–1am, every 5–10min from Terminal 1, every 10–20min from Terminal 2; €5.05; Ⓦwww.aerobusbcn.es) runs to Pl. d'Espanya and Pl. de Catalunya. A taxi to the centre will cost around €30.

Train Barcelona Sants (Ⓜ Sants) is the city's main train station, for national and some international arrivals – many national buses also stop here. Estació de França (Ⓜ Barceloneta), near Parc de la Ciutadella, is the terminal for long-distance Spanish and European express and intercity trains.

Bus The main bus terminal for international and long-distance services is the Estació del Nord (three blocks north of Parc de la Ciutadella; Ⓜ Arc de Triomf).

Ferry Balearics ferries dock at the Estació Marítima (metro Drassanes) at the bottom of Las Ramblas.

Tourist office Pl. de Catalunya (daily 8.30am–8.30pm; Ⓣ932 853 834, Ⓦwww.barcelonaturisme.com; Ⓜ Catalunya).

City transport

Metro and bus The quickest way of getting around is by metro (Mon–Thurs & Sun 5am–midnight, Fri till 2am, all night Sat); bus routes (roughly 6am–10.30pm, plus night-buses) are more complicated but every bus stop displays route maps. There's more information on Ⓦwww.tmb.cat, or pick up a free transport map at TMB customer service centres at Barcelona Sants, and at

DAY-TRIP: MONTSERRAT

The weird and bulbous mountains of **Montserrat**, 60km northwest of Barcelona, make for an interesting day-trip out of the city. As well as some short hikes (1–3hr) through the national park's unusual rock formations, the main attraction is the Benedictine monastery, with its well-preserved sixteenth-century basilica housing a twelfth-century image of La Moroneta, patron saint of Catalunya. To get here, take the R5 train from Plaça Espanya (every hour at 36min past; 1hr 05min) to Montserrat Aeri (for the cable car), or to Monistrol de Montserrat (for the rack railway to the town).

Universitat, Diagonal, La Sagrera and Sagrada Familia metro stations.

Tickets and discount cards Ticket prices for bus and metro are: zone 1 single (covers all major sights) €1.45; ten-ride *targeta* (a "T10") €8.25; two-day pass €11.50; three-day €16.50. The Barcelona Card, available from any tourist office (two days €27.50, five days €45), covers transport to and from the airport, all city transport, plus discounts at museums and a few shops and restaurants. The Articket (€22, available at ticket offices; Ⓦ www.articketbcn.org) covers entry to seven of the city's main art galleries. Note that student ticket prices in museums and galleries are often only available to those who are both a student and under 25.

Bus Turístic Links Barcelona's major sights, frequent services on three routes, which you can hop off and on at your leisure (€23 for one day, €30 for two days; Ⓦ www.barcelonabusturistic.cat); tickets are available at tourist offices or on the bus itself.

Bicycles Many hostels rent out bikes, or try Barcelona Rent a Bike, c/Tallers 45 (€6/2hr, €17/24hr; Ⓣ 933 171 970, Ⓦ www.barcelonarentabike.com).

Taxis Black-and-yellow taxis are plentiful and very useful late at night. There's a minimum charge of €2, plus €0.90/km 8am–8pm weekdays, €1.15 at other times, so a typical cross-town journey costs around €7–10.

Accommodation

Accommodation in Barcelona is among the most expensive in Spain, and in summer you'll be hard pushed to find a hostel bed for under €25, or a double room for under €65. You're also strongly advised to book ahead, at least for the first couple of nights. Most of the cheapest accommodation is in the side streets off and around Las Ramblas and in El Raval. The tourist office at Plaça de Catalunya can help find rooms (though not hostel space), or you can use Barcelona Online (Ⓣ 933 437 993, Ⓦ www.barcelona-on-line.es) or the hostel and budget-hotel reservation service Ⓦ www.hostelbarcelona.com. There are hundreds of campsites on the coast in either direction, but none less than 11km from the city. The following are on the map on p.1118, unless otherwise stated.

Hostels

Albergue Mare de Déu de Montserrat Pg. Mare de Déu del Coll 41–51, Vallarca Ⓣ 932 105 151, Ⓦ www.reaj.com. Ⓜ Vallcarca. See map, pp.1114–1115. A lovely HI mansion hostel with gardens and views, around 30min from the centre. Five-night maximum stay. Dorms from €21.75.

Alternative Creative Youth Home Ronda de la Universitat 17 Ⓣ 635 669 021, Ⓦ www.alternative-barcelona.com Ⓜ Catalunya. Self-consciously cool, but no less enjoyable for it, this well-organized hostel attracts the arty crowd its name suggests, with shared kitchen, wi-fi and helpful, informed staff. Dorms in very high season €32.70–35.70 (the higher price applies at weekends).

Centric Point Passeig de Gràcia 33, Eixample Ⓣ 932 156 538, Ⓦ www.equity-point.com Ⓜ Passeig de Gràcia. See map, pp.1114–1115. A beautiful, old mansion conversion in the smart Passeig de Gràcia. The smaller dorm rooms have en-suite bathrooms. Free wi-fi and shared kitchen. Book ahead, especially in summer. Breakfast included. Dorms €27.

Gothic Point c/Vigatans 5–9, La Ribera Ⓣ 932 687 808, Ⓦ www.equity-point.com Ⓜ Jaume I. Excellent location, featuring a sunny patio with deckchairs, plus bike rental, wi-fi and organized social events. Almost always full, so book ahead. Breakfast included. Dorms €25.

Hello BCN c/Lafont 8–10, Poble Sec Ⓣ 934 428 392, Ⓦ www.hellobcnhostel.com Ⓜ Paral.lel. A busy hostel 10min from Las Ramblas. Crowded dorms but great atmosphere; also has gym, kitchen, free internet, and a bar. Dorms €24, doubles with bathroom €70.

Itaca c/Ripoll 21, Barri Gòtic Ⓣ 933 019 751, Ⓦ www.itacahostel.com Ⓜ Jaume I. Jolly little hostel near La Seu (the Cathedral), with spacious mixed dorms (women-only dorm also available), plus plenty of communal spaces and a kitchen. No smoking. Dorms €26 (not including breakfast), doubles €65 (with breakfast).

Sea Point Pl. del Mar 1–4, Barceloneta Ⓣ 932 213 045, Ⓦ www.equity-point.com Ⓜ Barceloneta. See map, pp.1114–1115. Not so hot on facilities but the excellent beachside location is popular with the surfers. En-suite dorms, but no kitchen. The organized social activities join up with sister hostels *Gothic* and *Central*. Breakfast included. Dorms €26.

Hotels

Hostal Fernando c/Ferran 31, Barri Gòtic Ⓣ 933 017 993, Ⓦ www.hfernando.com Ⓜ Liceu. Well-kept *hostal* a cut above the norm, plus top-floor dorm accommodation. Breakfast included. Dorms €24, rooms €78.

Hostal Gat Xino c/Hospital 155, El Raval Ⓣ 933 248 833, Ⓦ www.gatrooms.com Ⓜ Sant Antoni. Rooms are small but stylish and comfortable, with double glazing, wi-fi access, a/c and TV. The attractive roof terrace opens in summer for drinks and music. Breakfast included. Doubles with private bath €65 weekdays, €70 weekends.

TREAT YOURSELF

For a night away from the hubbub and hordes of downtown Barcelona, head to sea. **Willowmoon**, a sailing boat moored in Marina Port Vell, close to the city centre, offers unique B&B accommodation in its cosy en-suite cabin. With only one set of guests allowed at a time, the deck is all yours, a secluded spot to catch some rays or watch the sun set. €75 per person per night; see ⓦwww.willowmoon.uk.com for details.

Eating

Barcelona is a reasonably expensive place to eat out. Awash as it is with trendy new restaurants, the best bet for a cheap meal is to take advantage of the lunchtime *menú del día* many places offer from Monday to Friday – you can get three courses with wine and bread for as little as €10. For picnics, head for La Boqueria market off Las Ramblas, or stop in at one of the many bakeries. Tapas are another option, and there are hundreds of excellent tapas bars in the old town, although these can end up being costly, depending on the portion size. The following are on the map on p.1118, unless otherwise stated.

Cafés

Buenas Migas Pl. Bonsuccés 6, El Raval Ⓜ Catalunya or Liceu. Small café in the heart of arty Raval, serving delicious pizza or quiche slices for under €5. Pasta of the day €3.90. Set menus from €7.45.

Dhub c/Montcada 12, La Ribera Ⓜ Jaume I. In the atmospheric medieval courtyard of the textile museum, with braziers in winter. *Plato del día* €11.20. Closed Mon.

Gelaaati! c/Llibreteria 7 Ⓜ Jaume I. Home-made Italian ice creams, in an array of delicious – and sometimes unusual – flavours. Two scoops €2.50, three scoops €3.50.

Silenus c/Angels 8, El Raval Ⓜ Liceu. The full set lunch isn't cheap (€14) but there's a cheaper, no-puddings menu (€10), and it's worth stopping here for at least a coffee to enjoy the shabby-chic decor. Free wi-fi.

Tapas bars

Divinus Pg. de Gràcia 28, Eixample Ⓜ Passeig de Gràcia. Delicious range of tapas, all at reasonable prices (€4.50–10.50), and €11.70 lunchtime set menu. Open until 2am.

Euskal Etxea Pl. Montcada 1–3, La Ribera Ⓜ Jaume I. Specializing in mouthwatering *pinchos* (Basque tapas) from €1.80 each.

Taller de Tapas c/de l'Argenteria 51 Ⓜ Jaume I. One of several city-centre branches of this popular chain of tapas bars/restaurants offering simple, quality food in elegant, relaxed surroundings. Tapas €3.95–17.45.

Vaso de Oro c/Balboa 6, Barceloneta Ⓜ Barceloneta. A tiny but lively bar, packed with locals, noise and character. Excellent tapas, at around €5. Closed Sept.

Restaurants

Arc Café c/Carabassa 19, Barri Gòtic ⓦwww.arccafe.com Ⓜ Drassanes. Bohemian brasserie-bar with attractive split-level interior. Set lunch €9.90. Popular Thai food nights on Thurs and Fri with curries at €10–11.

BioCenter c/Pintor Fortuny 25 ⓦwww.restaurantebiocenter.es Ⓜ Catalunya. One of the best-value lunchtime menus in town at this bright vegetarian restaurant including a soup, unlimited salad bar, main course and puddings, all for €9.95 weekdays, €12.10 weekends.

Can Manel Pg. Joan de Borbó 60, Barceloneta Ⓜ Barceloneta. Probably the best-value place by the harbour, with a weekday €11.25 *menú del día*. Closed Mon.

Chen-Ji c/Ali Bei 65, Poble Nou ⓂArc de Triomf. See map, pp.1114–1115. An excellent-value Chinese in what's become Barcelona's mini-Chinatown, by the Estació del Nord bus station. The lunchtime set menu is a real bargain, with four dishes plus rice and soup for just €5.

Gran Café c/Avinyó 9, Barri Gòtic Ⓜ Jaume I. Elegant Barcelona institution offering exceptional service and good Catalan/French food. Weekday *menú del día* €11.25.

Julivert Meu c/ Bonsuccés 7, El Raval ⓣ933 180 343, ⓦwww.julivertmeu.com Ⓜ Catalunya. Excellent selection of traditional Catalan dishes. Eat well for €15–20.

L'Economic Pl. Sant Agustí Vell 13, La Ribera Ⓜ Jaume I ⓣ933 196 494. The beautiful tiled dining room is the backdrop for one of the city's bargains – an excellent three-course lunch for €12.90, wine included. Tues–Sun 1–4pm (Thurs–Sat also 9–11pm).

Organic c/Junta de Comerc 11, El Raval Ⓜ Liceu. Bright little organic vegetarian restaurant with a hippy vibe. Three courses for €10. There's another branch at the back end of La Boqueria market that does takeaways.

Drinking and nightlife

Barcelona's nightlife is some of Europe's best, though it's not cheap. The high-tech theme palaces

SÓNAR

If electronica is your thing, make sure you're in town for **Sónar** (ⓦ www.sonar.es), an internationally recognized multimedia art and progressive music festival, held every June in Barcelona. Day-tickets bought on line cost €39, night-tickets €60, while a three-day, two-night pass will set you back €155.

are concentrated mainly in the Eixample, especially around c/Ganduxer, Avda Diagonal and Vía Augusta. Laidback and/or alternative places can be found in the streets of El Raval, while the waterfront Port Olímpic area is a more mainstream summer-night playground, where big, brash identikit clubs lure in large groups of fun-seeking tourists and stag and hen parties with cheap two-for-one drinks deals. Music bars close at 3am, the clubs at 4 or 5am, though later at weekends. For listings, pick up a copy of *Butaxaca*, a free weekly guide available in most bars and clubs (ⓦ www.butxaca.com), or buy the weekly *Guía del Ocio* from any newsstand (ⓦ www.guiadelociobcn.com). The thriving gay scene in Barcelona (ⓦ www.gaybarcelona.net) is prevalent in the so-called Gaixample, a few square blocks northwest of the main university: *Sestienda*, at c/Rauric 11 (near Plaça Reial), supplies free maps of gay Barcelona with a list of bars, clubs and contacts. The following are marked on the map on p.1118, unless otherwise stated.

Bars

Ambar c/Sant Pau 77 (at Rambla del Raval) Ⓜ Paral.lel or Liceu. Retro lamps, shabby sofas and quirky artwork make this café-bar a stylish place to while away an afternoon/evening. Cocktails €6–9. Open till 3am with DJs at weekends.

Bar Pastis c/Santa Mònica 4, El Raval Ⓜ Drassanes. Opened in 1946 to cater to French sailors and judging by the Gallic music and weary oil paintings, it hasn't changed much since. A small gem. Sun–Wed 7.30pm–2am, Fri & Sat 7.30pm–3am.

Boadas c/Tallers 1, El Raval Ⓜ Catalunya. A popular old-fashioned cocktail bar just off Las Ramblas. Mon–Thurs noon–2am, Fri & Sat noon–3am.

Cangrejo c/Montserrat 7, El Raval Ⓜ Drassanes. Fun bar playing Spanish music; becomes a lively club later in the evening. Thurs–Sat 10.30pm–3am.

La Caseta del Migdia Mirador de Migdia, Pg. de Migdia, Montjuïc ⓦ www.lacaseta.org. See map, pp.1114–1115. Deckchairs, DJs and alfresco drinking make this the perfect place in Barcelona to watch the sun set. Open in summer from 8pm Wed–Fri, noon Sat & Sun, until 2.30am on Fri and Sat, 1am other days (also open weekends in winter, noon–sunset only). Check website for programme. Bus or funicular to Montjuïc (see pp.1114–1115).

La Fira c/Provença 171, Eixample Ⓜ Provença. See map, pp.1114–1115. Only in Barcelona – fairground rides and circus paraphernalia adorn this long-standing theme bar. Tues–Sat from 11pm till late.

Clubs

Jamboree Pl. Reial 17, Barri Gòtic Ⓜ Liceu. Cavernous (and smoky) basement club with an international crowd dancing to hip-hop or funky jazz 11.30pm–5.30am (cover charge €10), with live jazz acts earlier in the evening (9–11pm). See ⓦ www.masimas.com/jamboree for details.

Moog c/Arc del Teatre 3, El Raval Ⓜ Drassanes. From disco to drum'n'bass with regular appearances from top UK and Euro DJs. Despite the large, industrial setting the atmosphere is relaxed and both gay- and straight-friendly. See ⓦ www.masimas.com/moog for line-up. Cover charge €10. Midnight–5am.

Razzmatazz Club c/Amogàvers 122, Poble Nou ⓦ www.salarazzmatazz.com Ⓜ Marina. See map, pp.1114–1115. Well worth the taxi or metro ride out of town – Barcelona's music scene happens here. Five rooms, each dedicated to a different sound. Cover charge €15–25, includes drink. Fri & Sat 1pm–6am.

Sala Apolo/Club Nitsa c/Nou de la Rambla 113, Poble Sec ⓦ www.sala-apolo.com Ⓜ Paral.lel. Regular live gigs by biggish names and burgeoning stars from the worlds of alternative electronica, rock and techno – *Nitsa* club night rules the roost at weekends. Cover charge varies. Hours vary depending what's on (the website has full details).

Shopping

Barcelona has a well-deserved reputation for great shopping. The big names of the fashion industry occupy the smart Passeig de Gràcia, but if this breaks your budget head to the oceanic shopping centre Maremagnum which has many high-street brands under one roof. For more unusual purchases, the crooked passages of La Ribera and El Born are home to dozens of little boutiques, while in El Raval, numerous trendy vintage shops lie along the Carrer de la Riera Baixa. There are also a number of excellent speciality food retailers in the city, and chocolate shops are scattered throughout the Ciutat Vella. Note that all prices are fixed, with the exception of Els Encants flea market.

La Botifarrería de Santa María c/Santa María 4, El Born Ⓜ Barceloneta or Jaume I. Sells fabulous speciality hams, cheeses and their famous *botifarras* (Catalan sausages).
Gispert c/Sombrerers 23, La Ribera Ⓦ www.casagispert.com Ⓜ Barceloneta or Jaume I. Freshly roasted nuts, dried fruits, speciality chocolates and *turrons* (marzipan and nougat bars, originally for Christmas, but sold here year-round) make this a top address for anyone with a more sophisticated than average sweet tooth.
Papabubble c/Ample 28, Barri Gòtic Ⓜ Drassanes or Barceloneta. Sweet-smelling candy store, where you can watch confectionery taking shape before your eyes. Closed Aug.
Produit National Brut c/Avinyó 29, Barri Gòtic Ⓜ Drassanes. Vintage and customized clothes for men and women, plus retro sunglasses.

Directory

Consulates Australia, Diagonal 458, 3º, Gràcia Ⓣ 934 909 013; Canada, Pl. de Catalunya 9 Ⓣ 934 127 236; Ireland, Gran Vía Carles III 94, Les Corts Ⓣ 934 915 021; New Zealand, Trav. de Gràcia 64, Gràcia Ⓣ 932 090 399; UK, Avda Diagonal 477, Eixample Ⓣ 933 666 200; US, Pg. Reina Elisenda 23, Sàrria Ⓣ 932 802 227.
Emergency numbers General emergencies Ⓣ 112; ambulance Ⓣ 061; police Ⓣ 092; fire Ⓣ 080.
Exchange Most banks are located in Pl. de Catalunya and Pg. de Gràcia. ATMs and money exchange available at the airport; Barcelona Sants; the tourist office at Pl. Catalunya; and at *casas de cambio* throughout the centre.
Hospitals 24hr accident and emergency centres at: Centre Perecamps, Avda Drassanes 13, El Raval Ⓣ 934 410 600; Hospital Clínic, c/Villaroel 170, Eixample Ⓣ 932 275 400; Hospital del Mar, Pg. Marítim 25–29, Vila Olímpica Ⓣ 932 483 000.
Internet El Raval has the cheapest places (mostly €1/hr); try Raval Centre, Hospital 103, or Ria, Hospital 143. Otherwise, there's Bornet, Barra de Ferro 3, La Ribera (€2.80/hr).
Left luggage Lockers at Sants station (daily 5.30am–11pm; €3–4.50/day), and at Consignas, Estruc 36, Barri Gòtic Ⓜ Catalunya (daily 9am–9pm; €5.50/day).
Pharmacies At least one *farmacía* in each neighbourhood is open nights and weekends.
Police Guàrdia Urbana (City Police), Ramblas 43 Ⓣ 092 or 932 562 457, Ⓜ Deassanes; open 24hr for emergencies.
Post office Pl. Antoni López, Barri Gòtic Ⓜ Barceloneta (Mon–Fri 8.30am–9.30pm, Sat 8.30am–2pm).

Moving on

Train Girona (1–2 hourly; 1hr 10min–1hr 45min); Madrid (1–2 hourly; 2hr 40min–9hr); Tarragona (2–4 hourly; 35min–1hr 45min); Valencia (15 daily; 3–4hr); Zaragoza (1–2 hourly; 1hr 30min–5hr 30min).
Bus Alicante (9 daily; 7hr–9hr 45min); Madrid (17 daily; 7hr 20min–8hr 05min); Valencia (9 daily; 4hr–4hr 30min); Zaragoza (20 daily; 3hr 30min–4hr).
Ferry Acciona Transmediterranea (Ⓦ www.trasmediterranea.es; British agents at Ⓦ www.southernferries.co.uk) and Balearia (Ⓦ www.balearia.com) are the main ferry companies with regular services from Barcelona to Palma de Mallorca, Maó on Menorca and Ibiza Town. Journey times and frequencies vary hugely depending on routing and the time of year. For the latest schedules and prices, see Ⓦ www.aferryto.com.

THE COSTA BRAVA

Stretching for 145km from the French border to the town of Blanes, the **Costa Brava** (Rugged Coast) boasts wooded coves, high cliffs, pretty beaches and deep blue water. The more rugged northern part, dominated by the spectacular **Cap de Creus** headland and park, and the bohemian town of **Cadaqués**, is the most attractive yet least crowded, with a natural appeal all its own. Inland are the twin hubs of **Girona**, the beautiful medieval capital of the region, and **Figueres**, Dalí's birthplace and home to his outrageous **museum**. **Buses** in the region are almost all operated by SARFA (Ⓣ 902 302 025, Ⓦ www.sarfa.es), with an office in every town. To visit the smaller and more picturesque coves, a car or bike is useful, or you could walk the fabulous Camí de Ronda necklace of footpaths running along the coastline.

Figueres

The northernmost parts of the Costa Brava are reached via **FIGUERES**, a provincial Catalan town with a lively *rambla* and plenty of cheap food and accommodation. The place would pass almost unnoticed, however, were it not for the most visited museum in Spain after El Prado, the surreal **Teatre-Museu Dalí** (March–June & Oct 9.30am–6pm; July–Sept 9am–8pm; Nov–Feb 10.30am–6pm; Oct–May closed Mon; €12; ⓣ972 677 500, ⓦwww.salvador-dali.org). Born in Figueres, Dalí also died here and the museum showcases some of his most eccentric work. The extraordinary pink facade, topped with enormous eggs and bronze mannequins, sets the tone for the exhibitions inside, which include collages, sculptures and mechanical contraptions requiring audience participation, as well as more conventional art.

Arrival and information

Train To make your way into the centre of town (about 600m), simply follow the "Museu Dalí" signs from the train station.

Tourist office In front of the post office building by the Pl. del Sol (July–Sept Mon–Sat 9am–8pm, Sun 10am–3pm; Jan–Feb Mon–Fri 10am–2pm; spring and autumn hours vary; ⓣ972 503 155, ⓦwww.figueres.cat). It runs English-language guided walks of the town in summer.

Accommodation

Camping Pous Cra. Nacional 2, 8.5km ⓣ972 670 254. Offers more expensive rooms but also has year-round camping (€16 for two people and a tent) and a restaurant-bar. Breakfast included. Singles €35, doubles €45.

Pensión San Mar c/Rec Arnau 31 ⓣ972 509 813. Good, comfortable rooms. Singles €22, doubles €34.

FESTIVAL CASTELL DE PERALADA

Every July and August, the **Festival Castell de Peralada** (ⓦwww.festivalperalada.com) attracts internationally acclaimed musicians and artists, mostly classical, to perform in the gardens of this medieval castle just outside of Figueres. Ticket prices vary enormously depending on the event, but start at €15, going up as high as €140.

Eating

There's a gaggle of cheap tourist restaurants in the narrow streets around the Museu Dalí and some nice, but pricier, pavement cafés lining the *rambla*.

Creperie Bretonne Annaick c/Cap de Creus 6. Continuing the absurdist theme, this restaurant is worth a visit for the decor alone, though their wide range of salads, and sweet and savoury stuffed-crêpes and salads (set lunch menu from €6) is equally enticing.

Moving on

Train Barcelona (1–2 hourly; 1hr 50min–2hr 20min); Girona (1–2 hourly; 28–37min); Madrid (daily; 11hr 15min).

Bus Barcelona (3–4 daily; 2hr 20min); Cadaqués (4 daily; 1hr); Girona (2–6 daily; 50min).

Cadaqués

The beautiful fishing village of **CADAQUÉS**, an hour by SARFA bus (4 daily) from Figueres, was Dalí's home from 1930 until his death, and has attracted an arty crowd ever since. The stunning **Casa-Museu Dalí** (mid-June to mid-Sept daily 9.30am–9pm; mid-Sept to early Jan & mid-Feb to mid-June Tues–Sun 10.30am–6pm; closed early Jan to mid-Feb; €11; booking required ⓣ972 251 015, ⓦwww.salvador-dali.org), the museum set up in his jumble of a home, lies 1km northeast in the tiny Portlligat cove and offers an enthralling glimpse into his private life. Cadaqués itself is a picture-postcard, whitewashed village with tiny beaches and narrow cobbled streets straddling a hill topped by an imposing church.

Information

Bike and scooter rental Rent@Bit on Avda Caritat Serinyana 9 (ⓣ972 258 226, ⓦwww.rentabit.net; scooter €45/day; bike €20/day; March–Nov) – internet access (€4/hr) also available here.

Acommodation

Accommodation is expensive. These are the cheapest options.

SPRING AND SUMMER IN GIRONA

For a fortnight from the second Saturday in May each year, Girona decks itself out in its floral finest to celebrate the **Tems de Flors**. Many houses in the historic centre, elaborately wreathed in fragrant blooms, open to the public. From the end of June until mid-September, open-air bars set up shop in the **Parc de la Devesa** to the north of the city centre, quenching the thirst of young people who flock there to enjoy live music and the long summer evenings.

Hostal Marina La Riera 3 ⓣ972 159 091. There's a choice of en-suite rooms, or cheaper rooms with shared bathroom facilities, at this simple *pension*, which is open April–Oct only. Singles from €35, doubles from €45.

Camping Cadaqués Ctra Port-Lligat 17 ⓣ972 258 126. Well-equipped campsite with a large pool and good facilities. Open April–Sept. €8.20/person, plus €10.40/tent.

Eating and drinking

For a drink or a meal, the areas around c/Miguel Rosset and below the church are the liveliest.

Girona

GIRONA, 37km south of Figueres and 100km from Barcelona, is one of Spain's loveliest unsung cities, with alleyways winding around its compact old town, the **Barri Vell**, through the atmospheric streets of **El Call**, the beautifully preserved medieval Jewish quarter. The city was fought over every century since the Romans first set foot here, and is dominated by its towering **cathedral** (daily: April–Oct 10am–8pm; Nov–March 10am–7pm; €5, free Sun; services Sat from 4.30pm, Sun 10am–2pm, at which time only part of the cathedral can be visited). Girona's eclectic past is tangible in its **medieval walls**, which provide a great afternoon's walk.

Girona is also popular with hikers and cyclists who use the city as a base for the many great routes in the area, details of which are available at the tourist office.

Arrival and information

Bus and train The bus and train stations, located next to one another off the. Barcelona, Crta are a 10min walk southwest from the centre.

Tourist office c/Joan Maragall 2 (Mon–Sat 9am–8pm, Sun 9am–2pm; ⓣ872 975 975, ⓦwww.ajuntament.gi/turisme). In summer, there's also an information stand at the train station.

Accommodation

Alberg Cerverí de Girona c/Ciutadans 9 ⓣ934 838 363. HI hostel in a central location. Dorms for under-25s €15.95 with a HI card, including breakfast.

Pensió Margarit c/Ultònia 1 ⓣ972 201 066, ⓦwww.hotelmargarit.com. A good option slightly out of the centre but not far from the station. Doubles and twins from €53.

Pensión Massó Pl. Sant Pere 12 ⓣ972 207 175. In a quiet location on the other side of town to the train station. Doubles €34.

Eating and drinking

For evening drinking it's best to head into the Barri Vell or the area around Pl. Independència, where you'll find most of the bars and clubs.

Alberg Ceverí de Girona c/dels Ciutadans 9. During term time, when it's a popular eating-place for students, the hostel offers a great set-lunch menu for €6.50, a real bargain compared to what's on offer elsewhere.

La Terra c/Ballesteries 23. An attractive tiled café-bar by day – serving good-value quiches, salads and burgers – and a trendy, buzzing bar by night. Open till around 2am.

Moving on

Train Barcelona (1–2 hourly; 1hr 05min–1hr 40min); Figueres (1–2 hourly; 26–39min); Madrid (1 daily; 10hr 40min).

Bus Barcelona (3–5 daily; 1hr 20min); Figueres (2–6 daily; 50min).

Andorra

A tiny country nestled in the Pyrenees, Andorra is one of the oldest nations in Europe. Set up by Charlemagne in the eighth century as a buffer between France and the Islamic Moors, it became an independent, democratic principality in 1993. It's the only country in the world with Catalan as its official language although Spanish is also widely spoken, as is basic English in some touristy places.

The capital, **Andorra la Vella**, offers a few sights and some good shopping, while next-door **Escaldes-Engordany** lays claim to the biggest thermal spa in Europe. Duty-free shopping, winter sports and summer hiking are the main attractions of this picturesque alpine nation: to the northwest is the popular ski resort of **Pal-Arinsal**, while the hills around **Ordino** boast excellent trails and breathtaking valley views. East of Ordino, a road weaves through jaw-dropping mountainscapes to **Canillo**, home to a captivating Romanesque chapel, and near the French border are sleepy **Soldeu** and the busy ski slopes of **Grandvalira**.

ARRIVAL

Andorra doesn't have an airport, but regular buses link the tiny nation to the nearest international ones three to four hours' drive away, in Barcelona (225km) and Toulouse (180km). Alsina Graells (ⓣ902 335 533, ⓦwww.movelia.es) has several daily services from Barcelona (€25.70), as does Nadal Autocars (Andorra ⓣ805 151, ⓦwww.autocarsnadal.com; from €26.50), while Novatel (ⓣ804 010, ⓦwww.andorrabybus.com) does airport transfers from both Barcelona and Toulouse (from €32/35). Alternatively, you can travel by rail from Barcelona (Sants or Arc de Triomf) to La Tour de Carol, just over the French border, also served by SNCF trains from Perpignan and Toulouse, and then take a local bus from there (or from L'Hospitalet, two stops up the line) to Pas de la Casa in eastern Andorra, where there are regular buses to Andorra la Vella. The international phone code for Andorra is ⓣ376 and the currency is the euro.

ENTRY REQUIREMENTS

Passports are required to cross the Andorran border. If entering by bus, you may not be inspected, but it's possible you'll be asked to show your passport when buying a bus ticket.

GETTING AROUND

Its small size makes Andorra easy to get around – most places can be visited as day-trips. Touring on foot takes advantage of the wonderful hiking trails, while the cheap fuel makes renting a car in the capital a good option for the less energetic. The reliable, cost-effective network of public buses links all the main towns.

ACCOMMODATION

Good **budget hotels** are scarce, and most of the cheapest, located in the capital, have zero charm. Prices peak in high season – July to August (when reservations are a must) and December to March – expect to pay at least €40 for a double room in most places. As a lower-priced alternative, there are many low-priced, well-equipped **campsites** throughout Andorra, and in summer you can stay for free in one of the 26

EMERGENCY NUMBERS

Police ⓣ110; Ambulance and Fire ⓣ118; Medical ⓣ116; Mountain Rescue ⓣ112.

state-run **refugis** – simple mountain cabins – information is available at tourist offices. Camping in the wild is illegal except around *refugis*.

ANDORRA LA VELLA

The name of the national capital **ANDORRA LA VELLA** is a bit of a misnomer: "Old Andorra" is for the most part a collection of neon-lit, soulless tourist restaurants and ageing storefronts. Where once the streets bustled with shepherds and their livestock – most of the capital was farmland until a few decades ago – today it exists more or less as a base for duty-free shoppers and skiers. However, since most buses arrive here you'll probably end up passing through during your stay, and the often quickly dismissed city does have some appeal. Lying at the confluence of three mountain rivers, it's framed by a stunning backdrop of towering mountains. As well as a few lively bars it holds enough sights to while away an agreeable afternoon – and enough bargain hunting to while away a few lifetimes.

What to see and do

The capital is bisected by the Avinguda del Príncep Benlloch, which further east becomes the shop-filled Avinguda de Meritxell and then, on towards neighbouring Escaldes-Engordany, Avinguda de Carlemany. The old quarter lies just south of Príncep Benlloch.

Barri Antic and the Casa de la Vall

Towards the western end of town, **Barri Antic** is the capital's old quarter and, with its cobbled streets and quiet *plaças*, a great escape from the shopping mall that is the rest of the city. In the centre is one of the oldest parliaments in Europe – and certainly the smallest – the **Casa de la Vall** (Tues–Sat 10am–1pm & 3–6pm, Sun 10am–1pm, closed Mon; free compulsory guided tours; bookings required on ⓣ839 760 or ⓔreserves.museus@andorra.ad). Built in 1580 and complete with towers, battlements and steel-barred windows, it provides an appropriately historical base for the courts and the Sindic, Andorra's representative house. South of here,

Plaça del Poble makes a great hangout in the evenings and houses the **Centre de Congresos**, one of the country's only theatre and music venues; see Ⓦwww.andorralavella.ad for more details.

Grans Magatzems Pyrénées

Avinguda Meritxell and the streets around have the highest concentration of shops, including Andorra's largest department store, the **Grans Magatzems Pyrénées**, at no. 11 (Mon–Fri 9.30am–8pm, Sat 9.30am–9pm, Sun 9.30am–7pm; Aug weeknights until 9pm), which also houses several cafeteria-style restaurants on the top floor.

Arrival and information

Bus Most international buses arrive and depart at the Central d'Autobusos, located just southeast of the small Parc Central, 5min south of the city centre. Llieda buses run by Viatges Montmantell (Ⓣ807 444, Ⓦwww.montmantell.com) leave from Caldea but stop on c/Prat de la Creu in front of the Spanish embassy. Domestic buses leave from just west of Pl. Benlloch.

TREAT YOURSELF

The **Caldea Spa** (opening hours vary, check website for details; bus #L1 from Avda. Princep Benlloch; €34.50 for 3hr, €28 for 2hr evening session; Ⓣ800 999, Ⓦwww.caldea.com), 1km east of Casa de la Vall, in Escaldes-Engordany, is the largest health centre on the continent, pumping in water from the nearby thermal springs to offer everything from Turkish baths to exfoliating hydro-massages. The mountain views from the outdoor lagoon are particularly spectacular. The thermal water is rich in sodium, silica and sulphur and is reputed to have considerable therapeutic effects for skin and respiratory ailments. Even if the spa is not your cup of tea, the eleventh-floor bar offers some nice views.

Tourist office Municipal: Avda. Meritxell at Pl. de la Rotonda (July & Aug Mon–Sat 9am–9pm, Sun 9am–7pm; Sept–June Mon–Fri 9am–1pm & 3–7pm, Sat 9am–1pm & 3–8pm, Sun 9am–1pm; Ⓣ873 103). National: c/Dr Vilanova 13 (Mon–Sat 9am–7pm, July and Aug also Sun 10am–1pm; Ⓣ820 214, Ⓦwww.andorra.ad).

Accommodation

Camping Valira Avda. de Salou Ⓣ722 384, Ⓦwww.campvalira.com. 10min from the city centre; the not-quite-in-the-wild camping facilities are good and there is a pool and restaurant. Open all year round. €6 one adult plus €6 tent, bungalows €75 for two people.

Pensió Garcia Avda. Príncep Benlloch 51 Ⓣ820 868. More like a hotel than a *pension*, its rooms are small but bright, with free wi-fi, and it's worth paying the €2 extra for a private bathroom. Singles (with shared bathroom) €26, doubles €36–38.

Pensió La Rosa Antic Carrer Major 18 Ⓣ821 810, Ⓔpensiolarosa@andorra.ad. Just inside the old quarter, the 24 simple rooms with outside bathroom are excellent value and there's free wi-fi. Singles €19, doubles €30.

Eating

The cheapest eats in town are from supermarkets; Punt Fresc, at Príncep Benlloch 22 in the Barri Antic, is small but convenient.

Don Quixot Passatge Antònia Font Caminal, Escaldes-Engordany. Off Av. Carlemany, the eastward continuation of Av. Meritxell, about 1km from the Barri Antic, in a little square with several other budget eating locales, this modern bar-restaurant has set menus at from €7.50, and football on three large screens.

L'Espiga d'Or Avda. Príncep Benlloch 27, opposite Punt Fresc. This pleasant bakery has a wide selection of sweet treats to take away or to eat in their small café at the back.

Lizarran Avda. Meritxell 86. Set just off the shopping thoroughfare, this popular, traditional restaurant-bar has a terrace and serves a large selection of small tapas from €1.45, bigger ones from €5.45, and main dishes from €7.50.

Mama Maria Avda. Meritxell 25 Ⓣ869 996. Large, attractive bar-restaurant serving tapas from €3.95 and *platos combinados* from €11.95. Or try one of their large pizzas for €9.90. Daily until 11pm.

Papa Nico Avda. Príncep Benlloch 4 Ⓣ867 333. Busy, bustling bar-restaurant serving good range of tapas from around €3.20 and *platos combinados* from €9. Similar to *Mama Maria* but with more atmosphere.

Drinking and nightlife

Party animals be warned, nightlife in the capital leaves much to be desired, especially out of ski season.

Cerveseria L'Abadia Cap del Carrer 2. Up the stairs from the Pl. Guillemó, this popular local pub has Leffe, Hoegaarden and Becks on draught. Daily till 1–2am, or 3am at weekends and in summer.

La Mafia Av. Tarragona 36 ⓣ868 691. Just around the corner from the bus station, a happening club in season, but social rigor mortis otherwise. Sun–Wed midnight–3am, Thurs 11pm–3am, Fri & Sat 11pm–4am.

Directory

Car rental Avis, Edifici Becier, Avda d'Enclar 142 ⓣ871 855.

Cinema MDRN Cinemes, Avda Meritxell 26. Offers good discounts weekday afternoons with tickets at €3.30. Most films dubbed into Spanish.

Embassies The closest UK, Irish, US, Canadian, Australian and New Zealand representatives are in Barcelona.

First aid centre c/la Llacuna 16 at c/Mossè Enric Marfany, just off Pl. Guillemó (Mon–Fri 8.30am–8.30pm, Sat, Sun and public hols 9–11am & 6–7pm).

Hospital Hospital Nostra Senyora de Meritxell, just next to Caldea spa (ⓣ871 000).

Internet Selenites, c/l'Alziranet 5, at c/Mossè Enric Marfany, off Pl. Guillemó (€3/hr).

Pharmacy Les Tres Creus, c/Canals 5 (ⓣ820 212, ⓦwww.farmacialestrescreus.com), usually has someone who speaks English.

Post offices Spanish PO at c/Joan Maragall 10 (Mon–Fri 8.30am–2.30pm, Sat 9.30am–1pm); French PO at c/Pere d'Urg 1 (Mon–Fri 8.30am–2.30pm, Sat 9.30am–noon).

Moving on

Domestic bus services connect the capital to all the main towns. Check ⓦwww.transportpublic.ad for schedules.

Buses Barcelona (16 daily; 3–4hr); Llieda (for Zaragoza and Madrid) (6–8 daily; 2hr 30min); Toulouse (2 daily; 3hr 15min).

LA MASSANA

Ascending northwest out of Andorra la Vella, the CG3 follows the Valira del Nord through a verdant valley, arriving at **LA MASSANA** 5km or so on (bus #L5 or #L6 from Avenida. Princep Benlioch, every 15min 7am–9pm, €1.50). The town itself, presided over by a modern church clock-tower, has little to detain you and the real joy is in the hiking or skiing – check with the helpful tourist office for specifics.

Information

Tourist office c/Avda. Sant Antoni 1, Pl. les Fontetes, (Mon–Sat 9am–1pm & 3–7pm, Sun same hours when the ski station is open; ⓣ835 693, ⓦwww.lamassana.ad). The book *36 Interesting Itineraries of Ordino and La Massana*, which covers all the walks in great detail, is available at the tourist office (€2).

Internet Porquets, Av. el Traves 4 (€1.50/30min; €3/hr).

Accommodation

Borda Jovell Hostel Avda. Jovell 18 ⓣ836 520. Up the steep hill in Sispony, this basic hostel has a hundred cheap bunks – even less if you bring your own sleeping bag. Dorm bed with own sleeping bag plus breakfast €17; €19.70 without your own sleeping bag.

Camping Xixerella Carretera de Pal ⓣ738 613, ⓦwww.xixerellapark.com. Campsite with great facilities, and activities from mini-golf to volleyball. €6.30/person, plus €6.30/tent.

Eating

Versió Original Carrer Josep Rossell. This trendy establishment has great Pop Art decor. The menu comprises fresh, modern cuisine, from salads to risottos. Set lunches and dinners available.

PAL AND ARINSAL

At the western end of the La Massana commune lies **PAL** (bus #M2 from La Masana, 4 daily), one of the best-preserved villages in Andorra, hugging the slopes that veer up to Pal-Arinsal, part of the popular Vallnord ski complex (ⓦwww.vallnord.com). Pal is also a great base for summertime activities – ask at the tourist office in Massana for details. Head back down to La Massana to take the road up to **ARINSAL** 2km northwest (bus #L5 from Avda. Princep Benlloch in Andorra la Vella via La Massana, every 30min 7.15am–8.45pm, €2.90), much bigger than Pal and also a great base for summer treks and known for its lively **nightlife**. *Surf* (next to the cable-car station), the most popular place in town, is an Argentinian steak-house until 11.30pm before becoming a raucous bar-club until 4am during the ski season. Or try *El Cau* at c/Arinsal 5, a popular restaurant, bar and club with themed nights such as "beach party" and "Seventies disco" (open till 3am). For **accommodation** try *Hotel Aymà*, c/Arinsal 6 (ⓣ835 295, ⓔhotelayma@andorra.ad; doubles with bath €40). The *360° Restaurant* next door does not offer the views its name suggests, but it does have €11.50 set lunches, with cheaper snacking menus.

The Pyrenees

The area around the Spanish Pyrenees is little visited – most tourists who come here travel straight through, but in so doing they miss out on some of the most wonderful scenery in Spain, and some of the country's most attractive trekking, with several beautiful **national parks** as a focus for exploration. To the south lies Aragón, and most especially its capital, **Zaragoza**, with its fine Moorish architecture and stately pace of life. One place that attracts tourists is **Pamplona**, the capital of **Navarra** and famous for its bull-running fiesta, but a great place to visit at any time of the year.

ZARAGOZA

ZARAGOZA is the capital of Aragón, and easily its largest and liveliest city, with over half the province's one million people and the majority of its industry. There are some excellent bars and restaurants tucked in among its remarkable monuments, and it's also a handy transport centre, with good connections into the Pyrenees and east towards Barcelona.

What to see and do

Many places of interest are clustered around the rectangular Plaza del Pilar, near the Río Ebro. Other beautiful medieval monuments are a short walk away. Try and be in town for **Semana Santa** – the week before Easter – for the spectacular street processions.

Aljafería

Zaragoza's highlight, the **Aljafería** (April–Oct daily 10am–2pm & 4.30–8pm; Nov–March Mon–Sat 10am–2pm & 4.30–6.30pm, Sun 10am–2pm; €3, free on Sun; ⓦwww.cortesaragon.es), was built in the eleventh century by the independent dynasty of Beni Kassim, and is the city's only surviving legacy from Moorish times. After Zaragoza was reconquered in 1118, the palace was Christianized and used by the *reconquista* kings of Aragón. From the original design, the foremost relic is a tiny and beautiful mosque adjacent to the ticket office. Further on is an intricately decorated court, the **Patio de Santa Isabella**. Across from here, the **Grand Staircase** (added in 1492) leads to a succession of rooms remarkable chiefly for their carved ceilings.

Basílica de Nuestra Señora del Pilar

The most imposing of the city's churches, majestically fronting the Río Ebro, is the **Basílica de Nuestra Señora del Pilar** (daily: summer 6.45am–9.30pm; winter 6.45am–8.30pm), one of Zaragoza's two cathedrals. It takes its name from the column that the Virgin is said to have brought from Jerusalem during her lifetime to found the first Marian chapel in Christendom. Topped by a diminutive image of the Virgin, the pillar forms the centrepiece of the Holy Chapel and is the focal point for pilgrims, who line up to kiss an exposed section encased in a silver sheath.

San Salvador

In terms of beauty, the Basilica de Nuestra Señora del Pilar can't compare with the nearby Gothic-Mudéjar old cathedral, **San Salvador,** or **La Seo** (summer Tues–Fri 10am–6.30pm, Sat 10am–12.30pm & 4–6.30pm, Sun 10am–noon & 4–6.30pm; winter Tues–Fri 10am–2pm & 4–6.30pm, Sat 10am–12.30pm & 4–6.30pm, Sun 10am–noon & 4–6.30pm; €4), at the far end of the pigeon-thronged Plaza del Pilar.

Roman remains

The city has brought to light its Roman past in several underground excavations: the **Forum** and **River Port** (close by La Seo), and the **Roman Baths** (all Mon–Sat 9am–9pm, Sun 9am–2pm; €3) and the **amphitheatre** on c/San Jorge (same hours; €4). You can visit all of them with a combined ticket (€7). Following the semicircle of c/Coso and c/Cesar Augusto, the **Roman walls** are steadily being excavated; the best place to view them is at c/Echegaray at the junction with c/Coso, where remains of towers and ramparts can be seen.

Arrival and information

Train and bus Zaragoza's stunning modern station, Intermodal Delicias, serves all train and bus destinations. It's on Avda. Navarra, about a 30min walk from the centre and connected by bus #51 to Paseo de Pamplona, at the southern end of Avda. de la Independencia (every 10min).

Tourist office Pl. del Pilar (daily: summer 10am–9pm; winter 10am–8pm; ⓣ976 201 200, ⓦwww.zaragozaturismo.es); also at Torreón de la Zuda, and in the train station and airport (all same hours and phone). There's an English information line on ⓣ902 142 008.

Discount card The Zaragoza Card, available at the tourist office (24hr €15/48hr €20, with discount if bought on line; ⓦwww.zaragozacard.com), includes entrance to all the city's museums and monuments, unlimited travel on the tourist bus, and various discounts in hotels, bars and restaurants.

Internet Conecta-T (Mon–Fri 10am–11pm, Sat & Sun 11am–11pm; €1.60/hr), c/Murallas Romanas 4, opposite the Mercado Central

Accommodation

Albergue Juvenil Baltasar Gracián c/Franco y López 4 ⓣ902 088 905 (note that this is a premium-rate number and you can expect to be left on hold for quite a while), ⓔbalta@aragob.es. Very institutional youth hostel behind the city's main police station, 30min walk from the centre. HI card necessary. Breakfast included. Under-26s €13.50, over-26s €17.83.

Hostal Descanso c/San Lorenzo 2 ⓣ976 291 741. Light, bright and cheerful rooms, each with basin and some overlooking the attractive Pl. de San Pedro below. Shared bathroom. Singles €20, doubles €30.

Pensión Iglesias c/Verónica 14-2º ⓣ976 293 161, ⓦwww.pensioniglesias.com. In a great location with some rooms overlooking the Roman amphitheatre. Double rooms have TVs and a basin and shower behind glass partitions; loos and bathrooms separate. Singles (with shared bathroom) €20, doubles €30.

Eating and drinking

El Tubo, the name given to the streets around c/Estébanes and c/Libertad, is the best place for bar-hopping and tapas, while the bars around the church of Santa María de Magdalena have a more bohemian and alternative vibe. The districts of El Casco, La Paz and Bohemia are best for late-night bars and dancing. Those on a self-catering budget can try Zaragoza's main fresh-food market, Mercado Central, on c/Caesar Agosto (daily until 2pm).

Bodegas Almau c/Estébanes 10. Right in the heart of El Tubo, this deservedly popular joint has been feeding the crowds since 1870. Usually has a bargain-rate happy hour early evenings in summer.

Café Tertulia Actual c/Don Jaime I 28. Great lunchtime menu for €8.90 (€11.90 on weekends), and art exhibitions inside. Also open until late for drinks.

Fantoba c/Don Jaime I 21. A beautiful bakery dating back to 1856 and specializing in Aragonese *dulces*. Each sugary treat is small but perfectly turned out. Pay by weight.

Gran Café Zaragozano c/Coso 35. A lively place for breakfast or drinks throughout the afternoon and evening. Quirky decor, from barbers' chairs to transparent flooring.

Mejillonera c/Moneva 3. *Mejillones* (mussels) are the speciality here. Get them *a la marinera* (in white wine and garlic) for €2.50 a tapa, or try the *calamares bravos* (fried squid in mayonnaise and chilli sauce) for €3.

Wok Japonés c/Don Jaime I 34. Stylish Japanese restaurant done out in black with an impressive all-you-can-eat buffet featuring sushi, tempura, salad and seafood, €10.75 at lunchtime (noon–4pm), €16.15 at dinner (8pm–midnight).

Moving on

Train Barcelona (1–2 hourly; 1hr 30min–4hr 45min); Bilbao (2 daily; 4hr 15min–4hr 20min); Madrid (21 daily; 1hr 20min–4hr 10min); Pamplona (5 daily; 1hr 45min–2hr 15min).

Bus Barcelona (20 daily; 3hr 30min–4hr); Madrid (22 daily; 4hr); Pamplona (8–10 daily; 2hr–2hr 45min).

PARQUE NACIONAL DE ORDESA

For summertime walking, there's no better destination than the **Parque Nacional de Ordesa** (www.ordesa.net), focused on a vast, trough-like valley flanked by imposingly striated limestone palisades. From Zaragoza's Estación Central you'll need to take an 8.30am bus (6.30am Sat) to reach the town of **Sabiñánigo** in time to connect with the 11am service (9.15am Sat) to **Torla**, the best base for the park. Note that bus services between Torla and Sabiñánigo are very limited, so plan your journey well: see www.alosa.es more details. At Torla, a regular shuttle bus takes you to and from the park (the park is not accessible by car) but trekkers should opt instead for the lovely trail (1hr 30min) on the far side of the river, well marked as the GR15.2. Further **treks** can be as gentle or as strenuous as you like, the most popular outing being an all-day trip to the **Circo de Soaso** waterfalls. For detailed information on the park, contact either Torla's tourist office (July–Sept daily except Wed 9.30am–1.30pm & 5–9pm; ⓣ974 486 378) or the park's **Centro de Visitantes**, which is also in Torla (daily 9am–2pm & 4–6pm; ⓣ974 486 472).

Accommodation

Reserve well in advance for accommodation in July and August; even the three campsites, *San Antón* (ⓣ974 486 063), *Río Ara* (ⓣ974 486 248), and *Valle de Bujaruelo* (ⓣ974 486 348), strung out between 1km and 3km north, often fill up.

Refugio Lucien Briet c/A'rruata ⓣ974 486 221, www.ordesa.net/refugio-lucienbriet. Simple *refugio* in the middle of Torla offering good-value meals. Dorms €10, double with private bath €40.

SAN FERMÍN: THE RUNNING OF THE BULLS

From midday on July 6 until midnight on July 14, Pamplona embraces the riotous nonstop celebration of the **Fiestas de San Fermín**. The focus is the **encierro**, or running of the bulls – in which the animals decisively have the upper hand. Six bulls are released each day at 8am to run from their corral near the Plaza San Domingo to the bullring. In front, around and occasionally under them scramble the hundreds of locals and tourists who are foolish or drunk enough to test their daring against the horns. To watch the *encierro* it's essential to arrive early – crowds form an hour before it starts. The best vantage points are near the start or on the wall leading into the bullring. The event has two parts: first the bull runnings; then bullocks with padded horns are let loose on the crowd inside the bullring. If you watch the actual running, you won't be able to get into the bullring, so go on two separate mornings to see both. At midnight on July 14, there's a mournful candlelit procession, the **Pobre De Mi**, to wind up the festivities. See www.sanfermin.com for more details. There's also an anti-bullfighting alternative, the **Running of the Nudes** (www.runningofthenudes.com), held two days before the first bull run; participants mostly wear a red scarf and plastic horns, but nothing else.

PAMPLONA

PAMPLONA (Iruña in Basque) has been the capital of the old kingdom of Navarra since the ninth century, and long before that was a powerful fortress town defending the northern approaches to Spain. Even now it has something of the appearance of a garrison city, with its hefty walls and elaborate pentagonal citadel.

What to see and do

The compact and lively streets of the old town have plenty to look at: the elaborately restored **cathedral** with its magnificent cloister and interesting **Museo Diocesano** (mid-June to mid-Nov Mon–Sat 10am–7pm; mid-Nov to mid-June Mon–Sat 10am–5pm; €4.40; Ⓦwww.catedraldepamplona.com); the colossal **city walls** and **citadel**; the display of regional archeology, history and art in the **Museo de Navarra** (Tues–Sat 9.30am–2pm & 5–7pm, Sun 11am–2pm; €2, free Sat pm & all Sun; Ⓦwww.cfnavarra.es/cultura/museo), and much more – but most visitors come here for just one thing: the thrilling week of the Fiestas de San Fermín (see box opposite).

Arrival and information

Train station 800m from the old part of town; bus #9 runs every 15min to the end of Paseo de Sarasate, a short walk from the central Pl. del Castillo – there is a RENFE ticket office at c/Estella 8.
Bus station c/Yanguas Miranda in front of the citadel.
Tourist office Avda. Roncesvalles 4 (summer Mon–Sat 10am–7pm, Sun 10am–2pm; winter Mon–Sat 10am–2pm & 4–7pm, Sun 10am–2pm; Ⓣ848 420 420, Ⓦwww.turismo.navarra.es). Pick up the monthly *Factoría* for detailed events listings.
Internet A *locutorio* at c/San Antón 4 has internet access (daily 11am–midnight; €1.50/hr). The train and bus stations have free wi-fi zones.

Accommodation

Rooms are in short supply during summer, and at fiesta time you've virtually no chance of a place without booking. Most hotels double their prices during San Fermín, so you're better off staying nearby (San Sebastián is a viable option) and travelling to Pamplona to enjoy the night-long festivities and early morning running of the bulls. If you end up sleeping rough, remember that there is safety in numbers – head for one of the many parks such as Vuelta del Castillo or Media Luna and bring a sleeping bag, as the nights are cool. For a hot shower or bath, there are public baths at c/Eslava 9 (Tues–Sat 8.30am–8pm, Sun 9am–1pm; shower €1.05, towel and soap €0.80). All prices below are high season, outside of fiesta time.
Ezcaba Camping Ⓣ948 330 315, Ⓦwww.campingezcaba.com. Located 7km out of town, on the road to France, reached by bus #4. Fills up several days before the fiesta. €5.50/person plus €6/tent.
Pensión Escaray Lozano c/Nueva 24-1° Ⓣ948 227 825, Ⓔjescaray@pnte.cfnavarra.es. A variety of rooms (so best check a few before choosing) with wooden floors and high ceilings in a rambling old building. Doubles €36, singles €18.
Pensión Eslava c/Hilarión Eslava 13-1° Ⓣ948 221 558. Don't let the building's peeling facade put you off, the rooms inside (albeit weathered) are clean enough with bright tartan bedspreads. Doubles €30, singles €15.
Pensión Otano c/San Nicolás 5 Ⓣ948 227 036 or 948 225 095, Ⓦwww.casaotano.com. This bar-cum-*pensión* is in a great location and the rooms are comfortable. Doubles €30 with shared bath, €45 with private shower, singles €15.

Eating and drinking

Pamplona has a number of great little restaurants, but the cheapest food is available at the Caprabo supermarket (daily 9.30am–9.30pm), upstairs in the Mercado de Santo Domingo, the town's main food market (Tues–Sat 9.30am–2pm & 5–7pm), worth a browse in its own right. The best areas for nightlife are the Casco Antiguo and San Juan.
Bodegón Sarria c/Estafeta 50–52. Immaculate modern tapas bar and restaurant, specializing in home-style Navarrese dishes and iberico cold cuts. Daily 9am–12.30pm.
Dom Lluis c/San Nicolás 1. Tapas bar downstairs, with a restaurant upstairs serving Castilian dishes; the €10 set menu is an excellent bargain. Restaurant: Mon–Sat 1–4pm & 8–11pm, Sun 1–4pm; bar: Mon–Sat 8am–midnight, Sun 8am–4pm.
Otano c/San Nicolás 5. Popular bar, and deservedly so. Excellent *pinchos* for €2.50 and *raciones* from €4.30. Daily 9.30am–3pm & 6.30–11pm or later.

Sarasate c/San Nicolás 19. A great vegetarian restaurant that could convert even the most committed carnivores. There's a weekday €14.50 set menu (€16.50 at weekends). Daily 1–4pm, also open Fri & Sat 8.30am–11pm.

Moving on

Train Barcelona (3 daily; 4hr); Madrid (4 daily; 3hr–3hr 20min); San Sebastián (2 daily; 1hr 45min); Zaragoza (4 daily; 2hr).
Bus Santander (2 weekly; 3hr 30min); San Sebastián (11–16 daily; 1hr–1hr 30min); Zaragoza (7–12 daily; 2hr–2hr 55min).

The north coast

Spain's **north coast** veers wildly from the typical conception of the country, with a rocky, indented coastline full of cove beaches and fjord-like *rías*. It's an immensely beautiful region – mountainous, green and thickly forested, with frequent rains often shrouding the countryside in a fine mist. In the east, butting against France, is the **País Vasco** (**Euskadi**, or **Basque Country**) which, despite some of the heaviest industrialization on the peninsula, remains remarkably unspoiled. **San Sebastián** is the big seaside attraction, a major resort with superb but crowded beaches, but there are any number of lesser-known, equally attractive coastal villages all the way to **Bilbao** and beyond. Note that the Basque language, Euskera, bears no relation to Spanish, or any other known language (we've given the alternative Basque names where popularly used) – it's perhaps the most obvious sign of Spain's strongest separatist movement. To the west lies **Cantabria**, centred on the port of **Santander**, with more good beaches and superb trekking in the mountains of the **Picos de Europa**. In the far west, **Galicia** is green and lush but, despite its fertile appearance, has a history of famine and poverty. This province also treasures its independence, and Gallego is still spoken by around 85 percent of the population. For travellers, the obvious highlight here is the world-class city of **Santiago de Compostela**, the greatest goal for pilgrims in medieval Europe.

SAN SEBASTIÁN

The undisputed queen of Basque resorts, **SAN SEBASTIÁN** (Donostia) has excellent beaches and is acknowledged by Spaniards as an unrivalled gastronomic centre. Along with Santander, San Sebastián has always been a fashionable place to escape the heat of the southern summers, and in July and August it's packed with well-to-do families. Its summer **festivals** include annual rowing races between the villages along the coast, and an International Jazz Festival (late July; www.jazzaldia.com) that attracts top performers to play in different locations around town.

What to see and do

San Sebastián is beautifully situated around the deep, still bay of **La Concha**. The **Parte Vieja** (old quarter) sits on the eastern promontory, while newer development has spread inland along the banks of the River Urumea and around the edge of the bay to the foot of **Monte Igeldo**.

Parte Vieja

The **Parte Vieja**'s cramped and noisy streets are where crowds congregate in the evenings to wander among the small bars and shops or sample the shellfish from the traders down by the fishing harbour. Here, too, are the town's chief sights: the gaudy Baroque facade of the church of **Santa María** and the more elegant and restrained, sixteenth-century **San Vicente**. The centre of the old town is the Plaza de la Constitución, known locally as "La

Consti"; the numbers on the balconies of the buildings around the square date back to the days when it was used as a bullring. Behind La Consti, winding footpaths crisscross up to the top of **Monte Urgull**. From the mammoth figure of Christ on its summit, there are great views out to sea and back across the bay to town.

Monte Igeldo

For wonderful views across the bay head to the top of **Monte Igeldo**: take bus #16 or walk around the coastline to its base, from where a **funicular** (variable hours, but at least 11am–6pm, and in Aug 10am–10pm, for full details see ⓦwww.monteigeldo.es; €2.70 return) will carry you to the summit.

City beaches

La Concha beach is the most central and most celebrated, a wide crescent of yellow sand stretching round the inlet from the town. Out in La Concha bay is a small island, **Isla de Santa Clara**, which makes a good spot for picnics; a boat leaves from the Paseo Mollaberria (June–Sept 10am–8pm; every 30–60min; €3.80; ⓦwww.motorasdelaisla.com).

Ondarreta, considered the best beach in San Sebastián for swimming, lies beyond the rocky outcrop that supports the **Palacio Miramar** (gardens open summer 8am–9pm, winter 9am–6pm; free), once a summer home of Spain's royal family. The beach's facilities are good (showers €0.80, towels €0.90 and lockers €1.20) but the atmosphere here is more staid – it's known as La Diplomática for the number of Madrid's "best" families who holiday here. Far less crowded, and popular with surfers, **Playa de Zurriola** and the adjacent **Playa de Gros** have breakwaters to shield them from dangerous currents.

Arrival and information

Train The main-line train station is across the Río Urumea on Paseo de Francia, although local lines to Hendaye and Bilbao (rail passes not valid) have their terminus on c/Easo.

Bus National buses arrive at Pl. Pío XII, 20min walk or a bus journey (#28) from the Parte Vieja. The terminal is really just a bus stop. Buy tickets from the appropriate *taquilla* along Paseo de Bizkaia or Avda de Sancho El Sabio at least 30min before boarding (and note that some close for lunch). There are no luggage lockers, but the *locutorio* one block north may let you leave baggage if open, and Locutorio Navinet (see p.1136) definitely will.

Tourist office Alameda del Boulevard 8 (summer Mon–Sat 9am–8pm, Sun 10am–7pm; winter Mon–Fri 9am–1.30pm & 3.30–7pm, Sat 10am–7pm, Sun 10am–2pm; ⓣ943 481 166, ⓦwww.sansebastianturismo.com). Also has an online reservations service at ⓦwww.sansebastianreservas.com.

Listings guide The free, monthly *Donostiaisia* is in Spanish, available at tourist offices.

Accommodation

During busy July and August prices are inflated. High season extends to September when the popular cinema festival takes place.

Albergue Juvenil Ondarreta Paseo de Igüeldo 25 ⓣ943 310 268, ⓦwww.donostialbergues.org. Fantastic location, just 200m from Ondarreta beach, in a great Swiss-cottage-style building. Kitchen facilities, free internet access and laundry available. Book in advance, especially in summer. HI card required. Dorms under-30s €17.60, over 30 €20.70.

Pensión Amaiur c/31º de Agosto 44 ⓣ943 429 654, ⓦwww.pensionamaiur.com. Incredible attention to detail marks out the *Amaiur*: the charming owners have thought of everything, from lending beach towels to organizing book-exchanges. All rooms – especially the kitchens – are well equipped and stylish. Internet and wi-fi access. Singles €42, doubles €50.

TREAT YOURSELF

Bodegón Alejandro (c/Fermín Calbetón 4 ⓣ943 427 158, ⓦwww.bodegonalejandro.com). This is the most affordable of the three great restaurants established in San Sebastián by the Michelin-starred chef, Martín Berasategui. The tasting menu, at €41.58, is a not-to-be-missed chance to sample world-class food. Closed Sun & Tues night & Mon.

Pensión Arsuaga c/Narrica Kalea 3-3º ⓣ943 420 681. Colourful rooms, some with balconies and each cheerfully decorated with paintings, books and plants. Not as slick as *Amaiur* or *Larrea*, but a good budget option. Singles €22, doubles €44.

Pensión Larrea c/Narrica Kalea 21-1º ⓣ943 422 694, ⓦwww.pensionlarrea.com. As well as having a friendly owner, the rooms here are excellent, and bathrooms have powerful, spacious showers. Every room has balcony, soundproof windows and wi-fi access. Doubles €60.

Eating and drinking

Food in the Basque country is generally considered the best in Spain and it's easy to see why in San Sebastián. The Parte Vieja, especially along c/Fermín Calbetón, is crammed with bars serving gourmet *pinchos* and tapas. Don't forget to sample the excellent Rioja.

Bidebide c/31 de Agosto 22. Minimalist, sleek furnishings, chill-out music and great food that isn't as expensive as you'd expect. Burgers from €5.40, salads from €6.30 and *platos combinados* from €7.95.

Bokado Pl. Carlos Blasco de Imaz. Located above the aquarium, this bar-restaurant serves overpriced food, but it's a great spot to have a drink (and a *pincho*) and take in the magnificent views across the bay. Come here for sunset.

Fuego Negro c/31º Agosto 31. A couple of doors up from *Gandarias*, serving more modern and experimental *pinchos* from €3.10.

Gandarias c/31 de Agosto 23. Traditional bar and restaurant, serving excellent *pinchos* at great prices, starting from €1.60.

Nightlife

Etxe Kalte c/Mari 11. Jazz, urban soul and hip-hop in a relaxed, low-key bar with DJs. Free entry. Tues–Thurs & Sun 6pm–4am, Fri & Sat 6pm–5am.

Tas-Tas c/Fermín Calbetón 35. The happy hour (9pm–1am), drinks promotions and group discounts make this a popular backpacker choice. Great for a fun night. Free entry. Daily until around 3am.

Zibbibo Pl. Sarriegi 8. This mini-club plays dance music, serves good sangría and has happy hours and themed nights, attracting an international crowd. Free entry.

Directory

Internet Locutorio Navinet, c/Fermín Cabeltón 39 (Mon–Fri 9.30am–10pm, Sat 10am–10pm, Sun 11am–10pm; €2/hr; left luggage €3/3hr); Zarr@net, c/San Lorenzo 6 (daily 10am–10pm; €2/hr).

Pharmacy c/Legazpi 7 ⓣ943 424 826. Check any pharmacy window to see which will be on duty lunchtime, night-time and Sunday.

Post office c/Urdaneta 7 (Mon–Fri 8.30am–8.30pm, Sat 9.30am–2pm).

Moving on

Train Barcelona (2 daily; 5hr 45min–5hr 50min); Madrid (2 daily; 5hr 20min); Pamplona (2 daily; 1hr 42min); Salamanca (2 daily; 6hr); Zaragoza (2 daily; 3hr 40min).

Bus Bilbao (13–28 daily; 1hr 10min); Madrid (7–9 daily; 5hr–6hr 45min); Pamplona (11–16 daily; 1hr–1hr 30min).

BILBAO

Although traditionally an industrial city, **BILBAO** (Bilbo) has given itself a makeover and is now a priority destination on any Spanish tour. A state-of-the-art metro, designed by British architect Norman Foster, links the city's widely spread attractions: the breathtaking Museo Guggenheim by Frank Gehry – along with Jeff Koons' puppy sculpture in flowers – is a major draw; the airport and one of the many dramatic river bridges are Calatrava-designed; and there are various bids to further

FEVE RAIL LINE

If you're not in a great hurry, you may want to make use of the independent **FEVE rail line** (ⓣ944 250 615, ⓦwww.feve.es; rail passes not valid). The 650-kilometre track begins at Bilbao and follows the coast west, with inland branches to Oviedo and León, all the way to El Ferrol in Galicia. Despite recent major repairs and upgrading, it's still slow but it's cheap and a terrific journey, skirting beaches, crossing rivers and snaking through a succession of limestone gorges.

develop the riverfront with university buildings and public parks. The city's vibrant, friendly atmosphere, elegant green spaces and some of the best cafés, restaurants and bars in Euskadi, combine to make it an appealing destination. From the first Saturday after August 15, the whole city goes totally wild during the annual bullfighting extravaganza, **La Semana Grande**, with scores of open-air bars, live music and impromptu dancing.

What to see and do

The **Casco Viejo**, the old quarter on the east bank of the river, is focused on the beautiful **Teatro Arriaga**, the elegantly arcaded **Plaza Nueva** and the fourteenth-century Gothic **Catedral de Santiago** (Mon–Sat 10am–1pm & 5–7.30pm). Along the the Río Nervión a number of exciting new buildings have appeared.

Museo Guggenheim

A good route leads from the Casco Viejo down the river past the Campo Volantín footbridge and the more imposing Puente Zubizuri to the sensual, billowing titanium curves of the **Museo Guggenheim** (daily 10am–8pm; Sept–June closed Mon; €11, ticket office shuts 30min before closing; Ⓦwww.guggenheim-bilbao.es), described as "the greatest building of our time" by architect Philip Johnson. The building and exterior sculptures are arguably more of an attraction than most of the art inside: the permanent collection, which includes works by Kandinsky, Klee, Mondrian, Picasso, Chagall and Warhol, to name a few, is housed in traditional galleries; temporary exhibitions and individual artists' collections are displayed in the huge sculpted spaces nearer the river.

Museo de Bellas Artes

Further along from the Guggenheim, on the edge of the Parque de Doña Casilda de Hurriza, is the **Museo de Bellas Artes** (Tues–Sun 10am–8pm; €6, combined ticket with the Guggenheim €13.50, free on Wed; Ⓦwww.museobilbao.com), which houses works by Goya, one by El Greco, and some fine temporary exhibitions.

Arrival and information

Air From the airport 12km north of town (Ⓣ902 404 704), the Bizkaibus #A3247 runs to Pl. Moyúa in the centre (daily 6.15am–midnight; every 30min; €1.30).
Train The FEVE and RENFE train stations are located just over the river from the Casco Viejo; trains from San Sebastián arrive at Atxuri station, just south of the Casco Viejo.
Bus Most buses arrive at Estación Termibús in San Mamés, a 20min walk or three stops by metro from the Casco Viejo.
Ferry P&O ferries from Portsmouth arrive at Santurtzi, 14km north of the city centre and connected by train and metro.
Tourist office Pl. Ensanche 11 (Mon–Fri 9am–2pm & 4–7.30pm; Ⓣ944 795 760, Ⓦwww.bilbao.net), with branches in the basement of the theatre at Pl. Arriaga 1, near the Guggenheim at c/Abandoibarra Etorbidea 2, and at the airport. All provide a good listings guide called *Bilbao*.

City transport

Metro €1.45 for a single journey in the central zone, €4.50 for a day-pass.
Tram Offering better views than the metro, the swish EuskoTran tram line costs €1.30 for a single, €3.65 for a day-pass. Make sure you validate your ticket in the platform's machine before boarding the tram or you could face a hefty fine.
Bilbaocard Good value if you're planning on covering the city in a short space of time, as it can be used on all transport systems in the city centre (€6/10/12 for 1/2/3 days). It also provides discounts on some museums – check at the tourist office for details.

Accommodation

In summer and at weekends, booking ahead is advisable.
Albergue Bilbao Ctra. Basurto-Kastrexana Errep 70 Ⓣ944 270 054, Ⓔalbergue.bilbao.net. Ten minutes from the city centre, connected by #58 and #80 bus, this eight-storey building has a TV room, internet and laundry. HI card required. Dorms

€16.75–20.10 for under-25s, €18.50–21.80 for over-25s.

Pensión de la Fuente c/Sombrerería 2-2º ⓣ944 169 989. Good-value *pensión* in a beautifully renovated building with wi-fi. Communal sitting area, and laundry service for €7. Singles without bath €24, doubles with bath €44, without €30–33.

Pensión Mendez c/Santa María 13-4º ⓣ944 160 364, ⓦwww.pensionmendez.com. Attractive rooms, all with balcony and wi-fi. Popular so book ahead. Fourth-floor doubles without bath €30–35, first-floor doubles with bath €45–50.

Pensión Serantes c/Somera 14-2º ⓣ944 151 557. With friendly owners, the *Serantes* is in a great location. The hall is in painted fluorescent colours, but the rooms themselves are spacious and tranquil. Doubles without bath €35.

Residencia Manoli c/Libertad 2-4º ⓣ944 155 636, ⓦwww.pensionmanoli.com. Don't let the slightly musty interior put you off, the rooms are clean enough. All come with bathroom, balcony and wi-fi. Doubles without bath €35.

Eating and drinking

Bar Bizitza c/Torre 1. Quirky, alternative bar with a great vibe and cool music. Open plan but with an intimate feel. Open daily from 5pm until 1.30am or later.

Café Iruña c/Barrastegui 5 Ⓜ Abando. Dating back to 1903, this atmospheric, bustling café has separate smoking and non-smoking areas, both decorated with ornate tiles and murals. *Pinchos* from €2.20, *menú del día* €13.75.

Gatz c/Sta María 10. Lively bar known for its award-winning "fusion" tapas. Sample the creative *pinchos* for €1.60 a pop and wash them down with *txakoli* (Basque white wine) for €1.60. Closed Sun.

Rio-Oja c/Perro 4. Basque restaurant, specializing in grilled meats (€8–15), fish (€12–15) and stews (€6.50–9.50). Portions are filling and good value.

Directory

Consulate UK, Alameda Urquijo 2-8º, Ensanche ⓣ944 157 722.

Currency exchange Bureau de change in the basement of El Corte Inglés, Gran Vía 7–9.

Hospital Santa Marina, Ctra. Santa Marina 41 ⓣ944 006 900.

Internet Cyber Locutorio Ariani, c/Hurtado de Amezaga 7, Ensanche (daily 10am–10pm; €1.50/hr).

Lost property Luis Briñas 14, one block from the bus station ⓣ944 204 981.

Pharmacy Farmacia Zaballa, Gran Vía 56 (Mon–Fri 9am–10pm, Sat 9am–1.30pm; ⓣ944 424 177).

Post office Alameda Urquijo 19, Ensanche (Mon–Fri 8.30am–8.30pm, Sat 9.30am–2pm).

Moving on

Train Barcelona (2 daily; 6hr 28min–6hr 40min); Madrid (2 daily; 4hr 50min–5hr); Santander (FEVE; 3 daily; 2hr 45min–3hr).

Bus San Sebastián (13–27 daily; 1hr 10min); Santander (21–26 daily; 1hr 30min); Santiago de Compostela (3 daily; 8hr 45min–11hr 30min).

SANTANDER

Long a favourite summer resort of Madrileños, **SANTANDER** has an elegant, reserved, almost French feel. Some people find it a clean, restful base for a short stay; for others, it is dull and snobbish. On a brief visit, the balance is tipped in its favour by its excellent beaches and the sheer style of its setting. Be aware that some establishments close after the summer season (mid-June to mid-September).

What to see and do

The narrow **Bahía de Santander** is dramatic, with the city and port on one side, in clear view of open countryside, and high mountains on the other; it's a great first view of Spain if you're arriving on the ferry from England. Santander was severely damaged by fire in 1941 and what's left of the city divides into two parts: the **town and port**, clumsily reconstructed on the old grid around a mundane cathedral; and the beach suburb of **El Sardinero**, a twenty-minute walk from the centre (or bus #4 or #15 from the train and bus stations to Pl. de Italia; €1.10). There are few real sights to distract you, and it's for the glorious beaches that most people come. The first of these, **Playa de la Magdalena**, begins on the near side of the wooded headland of the same name. This beautiful yellow strand, sheltered by cliffs and flanked by a summer windsurfing school, is deservedly popular. If you find these beaches too crowded, head for **Somo** (which has a surf school, boards to rent and a summer campsite) or **Pedreña**; jump on a *lancha*, a cheap taxi-ferry (every 15–60min; €4.30 return; Ⓦwww.losreginas.com) from Los Reginas, on the waterfront by Palacete del Embarcadero.

Arrival and information

Train and bus The RENFE and FEVE train stations, and the bus station are centrally located, side by side near the waterfront at Pl. de las Estaciones.

Ferry Ferries from Plymouth and Portsmouth dock in the middle of the Bahía de Santander, right opposite the Jardines de Pereda and the tourist office (see Ⓦwww.brittany-ferries.co.uk for more information).

Bicycle rental The local council offers free bikes for loan – check the tourist office for details, or see Ⓦwww.tusbic.es (in Spanish only).

Tourist office The best is in the Jardines de Pereda (daily: mid-June to mid-Sept 9am–9pm; mid-Sept to mid-June Mon–Fri 9am–7pm, Sat 10am–7pm, Sun 10am–2pm; Ⓣ942 203 000 or 001, Ⓦwww.santander.es).

Accommmodation

Some places shut down outside the peak summer season of mid-June to mid-September.

Hospedaje Magallanes c/Magallanes 22 Ⓣ942 371 421, Ⓦwww.hospedajemagallanes.com. Located in the city centre, this little place is simple but bright, clean and good value. Doubles €58 with bathroom, €38 without, singles €30/39.

Pensión La Corza c/Hernán Cortés 25 Ⓣ942 212 950. Great central location – modern, spacious rooms, all with TV – in a friendly house. Doubles with bath €60, without €47.

Pension Lusito Avda de los Castros 17 Ⓣ942 271 971. A sound option just minutes away from El Sardinero beach, with a very welcoming owner, but open summer only, with the very similar *Soledad* at no.17 (Ⓣ942 270 936), and Margarita at no.19 (Ⓣ942 270 973), both on hand if it's full. Doubles at all of these €50–55.

Pensión Madrid c/Madrid 21-1º Ⓣ942 214 494. Bright little rooms and free wi-fi, but shared bathrooms, located very close to the train and bus stations. Doubles €40.

Eating and drinking

Bodega Cigaleña c/Daoiz y Velarde 19. Traditional, atmospheric *bodega*. The straightforward *pinchos*, such as regional cheeses or dried hams for €2.50, are very popular with locals.

Bodega la Conveniente c/Gómez Oreña 9. Curious yet successful mix of traditional *bodega* and chic piano-bar. Elegant, spacious interior and great food too. Definitely worth the inevitable wait for a table (no reservations).

California Café c/Casimiro Sainz 3, just off the sea front. Baguettes (€4), burgers (€3–5.50), *platos combinados* (€7.50–8). Not much atmosphere, but good for relatively cheap, filling food.

El Solecito c/Bonifaz 19. Fun decor, and excellent pizzas (€5.50–13) and pasta (€7–10).

La Rana Verde c/Daoiz y Velarde 30, Ⓦwww.laranaverde.es. Famed for its many varieties of *patatas bravas* ranging from the mild to the "nuclear" (portion €2.70). Sandwiches and *bocadillos* from €2.40.

Rocambole c/Hernán Cortes 35. Very popular late-night subterranean bar, with live music on Thursdays. Start your evening elsewhere but make sure you end it here. Open till 5am, 6am on weekends and every day in summer. Free entry.

Directory

Currency exchange Banco Santander, Avda Calvo Sotelo 19, across from the post office.

Internet Pak Telecom, c/Castilla 9 (daily 10am–midnight; €1/hr).

Pharmacy Farmacia Valdés, c/Calvo Sotelo 2 (at Pl. del Ayuntamiento) Ⓣ942 071 932 (24hr).

Moving on

Train Madrid (3 daily; 4hr 30min); Bilbao (FEVE; 3 daily; 2hr 45min); Oviedo (FEVE, see box, p.1136; 2 daily; 4hr 30min).

Bus Bilbao (21–26 daily; 1hr 30min); Oviedo (10–11 daily; 2hr 10min–2hr 45min); Santiago de Compostela (2–3 daily; 7hr 15min–9hr 45min).

Ferry Plymouth, UK (once weekly; 20hr); Portsmouth, UK (twice weekly; 24hr).

PARQUE NACIONAL PICOS DE EUROPA

The **Picos de Europa** (Ⓦwww.picosdeeuropa.com) offers some of the finest hiking, canoeing and other mountain activities in Spain. The densely forested national park boasts two glacial lakes, a series of peaks over 2400m high, and wildlife including otters and bears. From Santander, about 80km to the east, the park is reached by car by passing through San Vicente de la Barquera, Unquera and Cares; alternative access is from Oviedo in the south, a spectacular drive of 80km along winding, narrow roads. **CANGAS DE ONÍS**, a major gateway to the park, has a **tourist office** (June–Sept daily 10am–9pm; Oct–May Mon–Sat 10am–2pm & 4–7pm, Sun 10am–2pm; ⓣ985 848 005, ⓦwww.cangasdeonis.com/turismo) and **accommodation**, at *Pensión Torreón* (ⓣ985 848 211, July €40, Aug €50, rest of year €35). There's also a private hostel, *La Posada del Monasterio* (ⓣ985 848 553, ⓦwww.posadamonasterio.com; dorms €18–22) in an atmospheric old monastery in La Vega-Villanueva, 2km northwest of Cangas de Onís; the management organizes canoeing, hiking and other activities in the park. Alternatively, you can stay at **COVADONGA** in the park at the *Hospedería del Peregrino* (ⓣ985 846 047, ⓦwww.picosdeuropa.net/peregrino; Aug & Easter €40, rest of year €25).

OVIEDO

The fresh and unpretentiously arty capital of the ancient principality of Asturias, OVIEDO is best known for its *sidrerías* (cider bars), whose waiters artfully sling the tasty local brew (more like scrumpy than commercial cider) from above head height into glasses held at waist level, without looking. The *sidrerías* are concentrated in (but not confined to) the old quarter in the heart of the city, a warren of beautiful squares and quaint narrow streets.

What to see and do

Oviedo has a couple of unusual ninth-century churches, dating from a time when Asturias was an independent kingdom, and the only part of Spain under Christian rule. One of these churches, the Cámara Santa, now forms part of the city's otherwise Gothic Cathedral (Jan–Feb Mon–Fri 10am–1pm & 4–6pm; July to mid-Sept Mon–Fri 10am–2.30pm & 4–8pm, Sat 10am–2.30pm & 4–6pm; entry to Cámara Santa and Diocesan Museum €3.50). Another ninth-century Asturian church, San Julian de los Prados (May–Sept Mon 10am–12.30pm, Tues–Fri 10am–12.30pm & 4–5.30pm, Sat 9.30am–noon & 3.30–5pm; Oct–April Mon 10am–12.30pm, Tues–Sat 9.30–11.30am; €1.20, Mon free) is on c/Selgas, ten minutes' northeast of the old quarter, next to the Oviedo–Gijón highway, with colourful frescoes, and a "secret chamber" in the walls.

Fine arts are free in Oviedo, and the Museo de Bellas Artes at c/Santa Ana 1 (July & Aug Tues–Sat 10.30am–2pm & 4.30–8.30pm, Sun 10.30am–2.30pm; Sept–June Tues–Fri 10.30am–2pm & 4.30–8.30pm, Sat 11.30am–2pm & 5–8pm, Sun 11.30am–2.30pm, Mon closed; free; ⓦwww.museobbaa.com) is not to be missed. Its fine collection of Old Masters and modern masterpieces features portraits of the twelve apostles by El Greco, a couple of Goyas, a Rubens or two, a Picasso and a Dalí, plus paintings by local Asturian artists. Also free are the profusion of street sculptures strewn across the city, which include a statue of Woody Allen (who expressed a fondness for Oviedo) on c/Milicias Nacionales, and a monumental bottom on c/Pelayo.

Arrival and information

Train stations RENFE and FEVE trains, one atop the other, are on Avda. de Santander, ten minutes' walk northwest of the old quarter.
Bus station On c/Pepe Cosmen, 200m north of the train stations.
Tourist office Municipal: Pl. de la Constitución 4 (daily: June 10am–7pm, July & Aug 9.30am–7.30pm, Sept–May 10am–2pm & 4.30–9pm; ⓣ985 086 060, ⓦturismo.ayto-oviedo.es), with booths

at c/Marquéz de Santa Cruz 1 (daily 10am–2pm & 4–7pm) and in the bus station (daily 10am–2pm & 4–7pm). Regional: c/Cimadevilla 4 (July to mid-Sept Mon–Fri 10am–8pm, Sat 10am–7pm, Sun 10am–5pm; mid-Sept to June Mon–Sat 10am–6pm; ⓣ985 213 385, ⓦwww.infoasturias.com).

Accommodation

Hostal Arcos c/Magdalena 3-2° ⓣ985 214 773, ⓦwww.hostal-arcos.com. Clean and welcoming, in an unbeatable location in the heart of the old quarter. Free wi-fi but shared bathrooms. Doubles €55.
Hostal Oviedo c/Uría 43-2° ⓣ985 241 000, ⓔhostaloviedo@hotmail.com. Directly opposite RENFE, a cool place with big rooms, attached bathrooms and free wi-fi. Singles €32, doubles €43.
Pensión la Armonia c/9 de Mayo 14-3° ⓣ985 220 301. Some rooms here are lacy and chintzy, others brighter with a street view, but they're the same price, so get in quick if you want first choice. Singles €20, doubles €30.
Pensión Riesgo c/9 de Mayo 16-1° ⓣ985 218 945, ⓔpensionriesgo@hotmail.com. A homely little place where the rooms are small but jolly and modern, in pastel colours with parquet floors. Singles €18, doubles €34.

Eating and drinking

Los Lagos Pl. de Carbayón 4. Old-school *sidrería* where they sling the cider about and serve anything from *pinchos* to full-blown meals, with the emphasis on Asturian meat dishes.
Marcelino Pan y Vino Bustling *sidrería* serving good food in generous portions (set menus €10–16); the house speciality is *navajas* (razor clams), at €10 for a dozen with a bottle of cider.
Pinchín c/Caveda 19 ⓦwww.pinchin.es. A stylish, modern bar specializing in wines and cocktails, where the *pinchos* are mostly €2 – try the four cheeses with raspberry, or the goat's cheese with *cecina* (beef ham). There's also a €10 set menu lunchtime and evenings.
Rubial c/Rio de San Pedro 9. The €8 set menu at this easy-going little bar is a great-value lunchtime fill-up and usually includes a delicious *fabada* (Asturian bean stew with pork and sausage).

Directory

Internet Locutorio Telefónica. 77b c/General Elorza (Mon–Sat 10am–9pm; €1.90/hr).
Pharmacy Farmacia Mijoya, Jovellanos 2 (Mon–Fri 9am–9pm, Sat 10am–1.30pm).
Post office c/Santa Susana 18 (temporary address while the main office at c/Alfonso Quintanilla 1 is closed for renovation), Mon–Fri 8.30am–8.30pm, Sat 9.30am–2pm.

Moving on

Train León (7 daily; 2–3hr); Madrid (4 daily; 5hr–5hr 45min); Santander (FEVE, see box, p.1136; 2 daily; 4hr 40min); Zaragoza (2 daily; 8hr 30min).
Bus Bilbao (9–11 daily; 3hr 35min–5hr 30min); Madrid (16–21 daily; 5hr 15min–6hr); Santander (8–12 daily; 2hr 20min–3hr 45min).

SANTIAGO DE COMPOSTELA

SANTIAGO DE COMPOSTELA, built in warm golden granite, is one of the most beautiful of all Spanish cities and has been declared a national

THE CAMINO DE SANTIAGO

The most famous Christian pilgrimage in the world, the **Camino de Santiago** – or Way of St James – traces a route through France and Spain to Santiago de Compostela (Saint James of the Field of Stars), the supposed burial place of St James the Apostle and the third-holiest site in Christendom after Jerusalem and Rome. Pilgrims identify themselves by attaching a large scallop shell to their backpack. Many carry a "pilgrim passport" that permits overnight stay in some mountain refuges, and collect stamps along the way in order to receive a Compostela (certificate of completion) from the Church authorities. To be eligible, you must walk at least 100km or cycle 200km. Aside from those motivated by faith, people are drawn by the physical challenge of the long hike, the stunning countryside, and the spiritual benefits of a temporary retreat from hectic urban life. Begin from your own doorstep, or from one of the popular starting points in France and Spain. For more details, see ⓦwww.xacobeo.es.

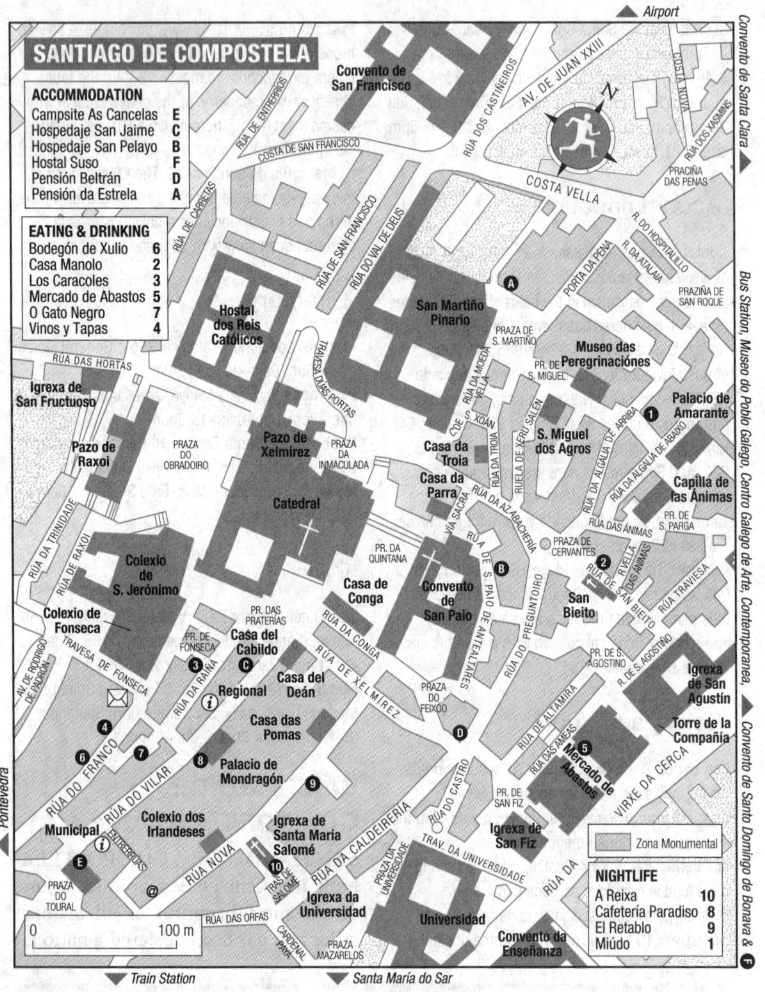

monument. The **pilgrimage to Santiago** (see box, p.1141) captured the imagination of medieval Christian Europe on an unprecedented scale, peaking at half a million pilgrims each year during the eleventh and twelfth centuries. The route continues to be well trodden by the faithful, with around 100,000 visitors claiming their Compostela offical certificate annually. Santiago retains some of its ancient political and cultural importance – it's the seat of Galicia's regional government, and home to a great contemporary art gallery as well as a large student population and buzzing nightlife.

What to see and do

Manageable in size, with many pedestrianized areas, Santiago is ideal to discover on foot. Most sights are grouped near each other in the historic **old town**; make your way down narrow, winding streets to visit the impressive cathedral and other religious attractions and monuments, such as the Monastery of San Martín Pinario and the Centro Galego art gallery. Santiago's **university** is worth seeing – parts of the eighteenth-century faculty of geography and history are open to the public. The large **Parque de Alameda** separates the old centre from the modern new town, which boasts many bars and cafés.

Catedral de Santiago

All roads lead to the **cathedral** (daily 7am–9pm, visits allowed outside Mass), on Praza do Obradoiro. The fantastic granite pyramid adorned with statues of St James was built in the mid-eighteenth century by an obscure Santiago-born architect, Fernando Casas y Novoa. Just inside this facade is the building's original west front: the **Pórtico de Gloria**. So many millions have pressed their fingers into the roots of its sacred Tree of Jesse that five deep holes have been worn into the solid marble. Behind, the **High Altar** symbolizes the spiritual climax of the pilgrimage. Visitors climb steps behind the altar, embrace the *Most Sacred Image of Santiago*, kiss his bejewelled cape, and receive a Latin certificate called a Compostela – a procedure that's seven centuries old. The elaborate pulley system in front of the altar is for moving the immense incense-burner – **El Botafumeiro** – which, operated by eight priests, is swung in a vast ceiling-to-ceiling arc across the transept. It is stunning to watch, but takes place only during certain festival services – check with the tourist office. You can also visit the cathedral museum, which includes the treasury, cloisters and crypt (June–Sept Mon–Sat 10am–2pm & 4–8pm, Sun 10am–2pm; Oct–May Mon–Sat 10am–1.30pm & 4–6.30pm, Sun 10am–1.30pm; €5).

San Martín Pinario monastery and around

The enormous Benedictine **San Martín Pinario monastery** stands close to the cathedral, the vast altarpiece in its church depicting its patron riding alongside St James. Nearby is the **Convento de San Francisco**, reputedly founded by the saint himself during his pilgrimage to Santiago. In the north of the city are Baroque **Convento de Santa Clara**, with a unique curving facade, and a little southwards, **Convento de Santo Domingo de Bonaval**. This last is perhaps the most interesting of the buildings, featuring a magnificent seventeenth-century triple stairway, each spiral leading to a different storey of a single tower. The adjacent **Museo do Pobo Gallego** is a fascinating museum of Galician culture (Tues–Sat 10am–2pm & 4–8pm, Sun 11am–2pm; free). Just next door is the **Centro Galego de Arte Contemporánea** (Tues–Sun 11am–8pm; free), a beautiful gallery designed by Portuguese architect Álvaro Siza and host to changing exhibition cycles.

Arrival and information

Air The airport, 1km northeast of town (Ⓣ981 547 501), is linked to the centre by half-hourly buses (€3).

Train The train station is a walkable distance south of the plaza along Rúa do Horreo.

Bus station 1km or so north of the town centre; bus #5 runs every 16–30min to Pr. Galicia at the old city's southern edge.

Tourist office Rúa do Vilar 63 (Easter & June–Sept daily 9am–9pm; rest of year Mon–Fri 9am–7pm, Sat & Sun 9am–2pm & 4–7pm; Ⓣ981 555 129, Ⓦwww.santiagoturismo.com); it has an accommodation booking system (Ⓣ981 568 521, Ⓦwww.santiagoreservas.com). The local hoteliers' association have an information desk at the airport. Spanish guided tours leave from Pl. de Platerías daily at noon (April to mid-Oct also at 6pm; €10). Regional: Rúa do Vilar 32 (Mon–Fri 8am–8pm, Sat 11am–2pm & 5–7pm, Sun 11am–2pm; Ⓣ981 584 081, Ⓦwww.turgalicia.es).

Listings guide *Culturall* is a very comprehensive monthly guide. Available at tourist offices and downloadable at Ⓦwww.santiagoturismo.com.

Accommodation

You should have no difficulty finding inexpensive accommodation; note that *pensiones* here are often called *hospedajes*.

Campsite As Cancelas Rúa do 25 de Xulio 35 ⓣ981 580 266, ⓦwww.campingascancelas.com. 2km northeast of the cathedral; take city bus #4 or #6 from Praza de Galicia. Located in a tranquil green zone, this campsite offers good facilities, including an outdoor swimming pool. €6.50/person, plus tent €6.80.

Hospedaje San Jaime Rúa do Vilar 12-2º ⓣ981 583 134. Creaky but decent central budget accommodation. Some rooms are quite spacious. Ask for one with a balcony and great views of the cathedral. Singles €15, doubles €30.

Hospedaje San Pelayo Rúa San Paio 2 ⓣ981 565 016. Basic, standard *pensión* rooms with a couple of extras thrown in: free laundry service and kitchen access. Just 3min from the cathedral. Singles €25, doubles without bath €30–36, with €40.

Hostal Suso Rúa do Vilar 65 ⓣ981 586 611, ⓔhostalsuso@gmail.com. Clean, modern rooms with attached bathrooms and free wi-fi access. Doubles €49.

Pensión Beltrán c/Preguntoiro 36-2º ⓣ981 582 225. Beautiful *pensión*, set in an old converted palace with stunning views and at absolute bargain rates. Rooms have modern furnishings but the large *salón* maintains gorgeous antiques. July–Sept only. Singles €15, doubles €22.

Pensión da Estrela Plazuela de San Martín Pinario 5-2º ⓣ981 576 924, ⓦwww.pensiondaestrela.com. Spotless, inviting rooms with warm-coloured decor. All have private bathrooms. Ask for one with a view of the square below. Singles €30, doubles €50.

Eating and drinking

Thanks, perhaps, to the students, there are plenty of cheap restaurants and excellent bars. For tapas and *pinchos* it's best to wander the lively streets of the historic centre, particularly Rúa do Franco and Rúa da Raíña.

Bodegón de Xulio Rúa do Franco 24. Good choice for fish on a street that's full of seafood restaurants. Portion of *pulpo a la feria*, the Galician octopus speciality, €8.95.

Casa Manolo Pr. de Cervantes 25 ⓣ981 582 950, ⓦwww.casamanolo.es. The modern, elegant interior and central location make it seem more expensive than it actually is – the excellent set menu is just €9. Daily 1–4pm & 8–11.30pm, closed Sun evening.

Los Caracoles Rúa da Raíña 14 ⓣ981 561 498. Cosy interior with low-hanging lamps and stone brick walls. Try their snail speciality. Also serves a hearty three-course lunch menu for €10.80. Daily 11am–4pm & 8pm–midnight.

Mercado de Abastos Pl. de Abastos. Well-maintained food market built around an attractive granite structure. Quality fresh, local produce at cheap prices. Mon–Sat 8am–2pm.

O Gato Negro Rúa da Raíña s/n. Very basic decor means this bar easily goes unnoticed. It shouldn't – its traditional Galician food is first class.

Vinos y Tapas Rúa do Franco 10. Wide range of cheap, tasty *pinchos* on display, starting from €1.10. A great place to start the evening before heading off to one of the late-night bars. Glass of *cava* €1.80, jug of sangría €11.

Nightlife

A Reixa Rúa de tras Salomé 3. Basement bar with low lighting and a chilled-out vibe. The huge CD collection behind the bar means an eclectic playlist. Daily till 2.30am.

Cafetería Paradiso Rúa do Vilar 29. This gorgeous green-tiled, mirrored bar is a good place to start the night. *Raciones*, such as the fiery *pimientos de padrón*, from €3; set lunch menu €12.

El Retablo Rúa Nova 13 ⓣ981 564 851. Very large bar with dancefloor. Warms up after midnight.

Miúdo Rúa dos Troques 3 ⓣ617 082 447. Same laidback vibe as *A Reixa*, but friendlier. Interesting prints adorn the stone walls; cool, relaxed clientele populate the bar. Open until 3am on weekends.

Directory

Internet Cibernova, Rúa Nova 50 (Mon–Fri 9.30am–11pm, Sat 10am–10pm; €2/hr).

Lost property c/o local police, north end of Rúa da Trindade ⓣ981 543 027.

Pharmacy Pr. do Toural 11 (24hr); Cantón do Toural 1 (daily 8am–midnight).

Post office Rúa do Franco 4. Mon–Fri 8.30am–8.30pm, Sat 9.30am–2pm.

Moving on

Train Bilbao (daily; 10hr 35min); León (daily; 5hr 40min); Madrid (2 daily; 7hr 15min–9hr 30min); Porto (2 daily, changing at Vigo; 5hr 10min–6hr 20min).

Bus Bilbao (3 daily; 9hr 30min–11hr 15min); Lisbon (1 daily; 9hr 45min); Madrid (4–5 daily; 7hr 45min–9hr); Oviedo (2–3 daily; 4hr 45min–6hr 45min); Porto (1–2 daily; 3hr 45min–4hr); Santander (2 daily; 9hr 30min–10hr 10min).

Sweden

HIGHLIGHTS

THE ICE HOTEL: the original and best - a chilly treat worth breaking the budget for

INLANDSBANAN: whistle past virgin forest and crystal-clear streams en route to Lapland

STOCKHOLM: edgy fashion, cool cafés and perhaps the most beautiful setting of any European capital

GOTHENBURG: hop on a tram and explore Sweden's second city

GOTLAND: join the summer exodus to Sweden's party island

MALMÖ: fun-sized city offering beaches, bars and a towering skyscraper

ROUGH COSTS

DAILY BUDGET Basic €50 /occasional treat €75

DRINK *Akvavit* (schnapps) €5

FOOD *Tunnbrodsrulle* (Swedish kebab) €4

HOSTEL/BUDGET HOTEL €28/€60

TRAVEL Train: Stockholm–Gothenburg €70; bus: Stockholm–Gothenburg €33

FACT FILE

POPULATION 9 million

AREA 449,964 sq km

LANGUAGE Swedish

CURRENCY Swedish krona (kr)

CAPITAL Stockholm (population: 851,000)

INTERNATIONAL PHONE CODE ⓣ46

Introduction

Sweden combines stylish, sophisticated cities with a vast wilderness of dense forests and crystal-clear mountain lakes. Quality of life is high, almost everyone speaks fluent English, and even a short visit here leaves you with the impression that the Swedes have somehow got things "right". While the country is not entirely populated by blonde, blue-eyed sauna-loving eco-warriors, you'll find plenty to reinforce the stereotype.

As with the rest of Scandinavia, Sweden can prove a challenge for the budget traveller. However, it's still behind Norway and Denmark in terms of travel costs. If you stick to hostels, eat out only at lunch and resist the temptation to buy a round of drinks, you can still manage to explore beyond a flying visit.

First on the list for almost any traveller is **Stockholm**. One of Europe's most beautiful capital cities, it's a bundle of islands hosting a picture-postcard old town, fine museums and the country's most active nightlife. After Stockholm, Sweden's other main cities **Gothenburg** and **Malmö** can seem like also-rans, yet they are both eminently likeable places worthy of at least a couple of nights' stay. Similarly, the two university towns, **Lund** and **Uppsala** make excellent day-trips.

During summer Sweden's interior beckons with the opening of the 1300-kilometre **Inlandsbanan** rail line running along the spine of the country through lakeland and bear country as far as the **Arctic Circle**. Summer is also the time to join the rush to **Gotland**, Sweden's Baltic island escape. If you're here in winter you shouldn't miss a trip to Swedish Lapland and consider taking a splurge on a night at the *ICEHOTEL* near **Kiruna** in the far north.

CHRONOLOGY

98 AD Tacitus refers to a Scandinavian tribe known as the "Suiones".

800s The Swedish Vikings become a powerful force in Europe over the following few centuries.

1255 City of Stockholm founded.

1397 The Kalmar Union unites Sweden with Denmark and Norway through a marriage arrangement.

1520 Hundreds of nobles are killed by Danish forces during the "Stockholm Bloodbath". A counter-attack is led by Swede Gustav Vasa.

1523 Gustav is crowned King Gustav I and leads the Protestant Reformation of Sweden.

1536 Sweden leaves the Kalmar Union, asserting independence.

1628 The *Vasa* battleship sinks in Stockholm harbour – a national embarrassment now turned into a money-spinning tourist attraction.

1721 Sweden is defeated by a coalition led by Russia in the Great Northern War, ending the success of the Swedish Empire.

1814 Sweden invades and conquers Norway.

1901 First Nobel Prize ceremony held, as part of the will of Swedish inventor Alfred Nobel.

1905 Sweden peacefully concedes Norwegian independence.

1914 Sweden remains neutral during World War I.

1939 Sweden declares neutrality during World War II, and is one of only five countries to maintain it.

1943 The first IKEA store is opened by founder Ingvar Kamprad.

1974 ABBA top the charts after winning the Eurovision Song Contest with "Waterloo".

1986 Prime Minister Olof Palme is assassinated in Stockholm; the crime is still unresolved.

1995 Sweden joins the EU after a closely fought referendum.

2003 Swedish voters reject the adoption of the euro.

2006 After seventy years of rule, the Social Democrats finally lose an election to the centre-right Alliance for Sweden.

2010 A four-day celebration ends with Crown Princess Victoria marrying a "commoner" at Stockholm Cathedral.

ARRIVAL

Most travellers arrive at one of Stockholm's three international **airports**. The

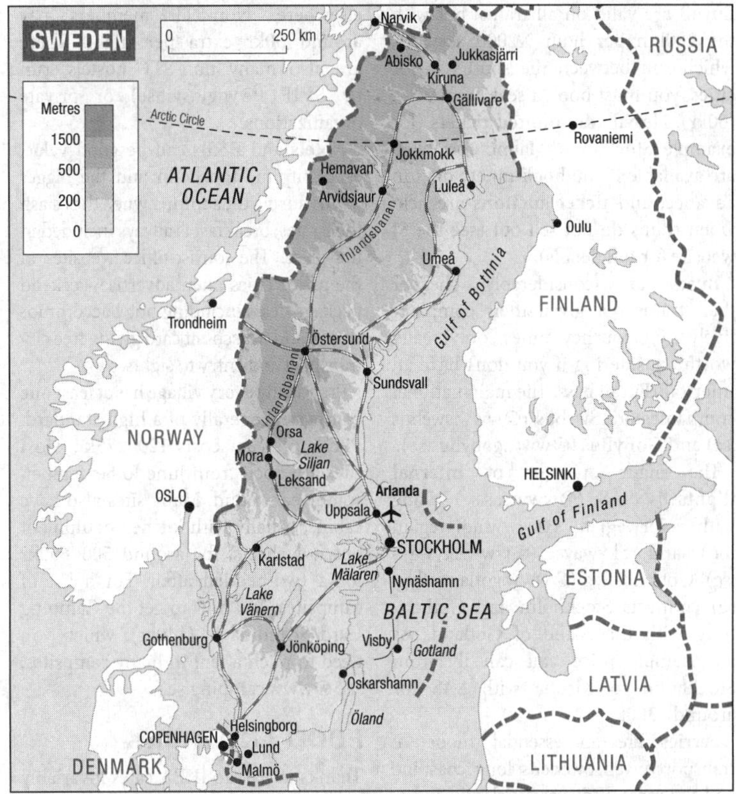

largest and most convenient, Arlanda, is served by the big international carriers including Sweden's SAS as well as a few budget airlines such as easyJet and Norwegian. Ryanair uses Skavsta and Västerås airports, both a long way from Stockholm (around 90km); the budget airline also flies into Gothenburg, a three-hour train ride away from Stockholm, as does easyJet.

International **trains** arrive in Stockholm, Malmö and Gothenburg from Norway, Denmark and Germany; in the north, Kiruna is the first stop in Sweden for visitors arriving from northern Norway.

International **ferry routes** include: Stockholm–Tallinn (Estonia), Stockholm–Helsinki and Turku (Finland); Helsingborg–Helsingør (Denmark) and Oslo (Norway); Gothenburg–Kiel (Germany) and Newcastle (UK).

GETTING AROUND

The best way to explore Sweden is by train. **Swedish State Railways'** extensive network (SJ; Ⓦwww.sj.se) runs as far north as Abisko, 250km inside the Arctic Circle, and there are also other companies in charge of regional routes (all of them are visible on the SJ website). The famous **Inlandsbanan** line (Ⓦwww.inlandsbanan.se), which travels through central and northern Sweden, is privately run and only operates from June to August (see box, p.1171). **InterRail** and

Eurail are valid on all trains, but with the 200km per hour X2000 services, which run between the south's major cities, you must book a seat in advance (60kr). Heavily **discounted tickets** (for example Stockholm–Malmö for 99kr) are available if you book ninety days in advance, and **ticket auctions** are held when trains do not sell out (see the SJ website for full details).

Buses are considerably cheaper than trains but given their comparatively long journey times, only really worth considering if you don't have an InterRail/Eurail pass. The main national companies are Swebus (Ⓦwww.swebus.se) and GoByBus (Ⓦwww.gobybus.se).

The main operator of **internal flights** is SAS (Ⓦwww.sas.se) along with Norwegian (Ⓦwww.norwegian.no) and Skyways (Ⓦwww.skyways.se). Gotlandsflyg (Ⓦwww.gotlandsflyg.se) connects Stockholm and Gothenburg with the island of Gotland. As an example price you can fly from Stockholm to Kiruna with SAS for around 1300kr.

Ferries are an essential mode of transport given Sweden's long coastline and the mass of disparate islands. Information on accessing the islands of Stockholm's archipelago and Gotland is given later in the chapter (see box, p.1170).

ACCOMMODATION

Sweden has an excellent network of **hostels** (*vandrarhem*) mostly operated by STF (Ⓦwww.svenskaturistforeningen.se). They are found all over the country, often in incongruous surroundings, such as prisons or ships. Double rooms are usually available as well as dorms, and virtually all hostels have self-catering kitchens and serve a buffet breakfast. Prices are low (250kr–350kr for a bed), but you have to pay extra for sheets and breakfast (usually 70kr–100kr extra each), so it can be worth bringing a sleeping bag and seeking out cheaper breakfasts elsewhere. Non-STF members pay around 50kr extra per night. There are also many non-STF hostels, run by SVIF (Ⓦwww.svif.se) or private organizations.

Hotels and **B&Bs** can be good value, especially in Stockholm and the bigger towns during the summer when they slash their rates; breakfast is always included in the price. The tourist-office websites of the major cities often advertise weekend package deals including hotel accommodation and a discount card giving free city transport and entry to sights.

Practically every village has at least one **campsite**, generally of a high standard. Pitching a tent costs 120–275kr. Most sites are open from June to September, some year-round. Many sites also have cabins, usually with kitchen equipment but not sheets, for around 500–600kr for a two-bedded affair. For a list of campsites, and how to get the Camping Card Scandinavia (140kr), which you need to pitch a tent in many campsites, see Ⓦwww.camping.se.

FOOD AND DRINK

Thanks in part to IKEA cafés invariably dishing them up, Swedish meatballs (*köttbullar*) are familiar across the world. However, there is rather more to the national cuisine than this. **Seafood** is particularly good with marinated salmon (*gravlax*) and herring (*strömming*), the latter pickled, smoked and even fermented, being served everywhere; you'll often find them offered as part of a classic **smörgåsbord** buffet with potato salad, rye bread, cheeses and fruit. Other specialities include reindeer and elk – both surprisingly tasty – and sweet cloudberries (delicious with ice cream).

Breakfast (*frukost*) is invariably a help-yourself buffet of juice, cereals, bread, boiled eggs, jams, salami and coffee or tea. For **snacks**, a *gatukök* (street kitchen) or *korvstånd* (hot-dog stall) will serve hot dogs, burgers, chips and the like for around 40kr. Coffee shops always display a range of freshly baked pastries (coffee and cake for 40–60kr), and also serve *smörgåsar* – open sandwiches piled high with toppings (40–70kr) – and usually a good range of salads.

Lunch (*lunch*; usually served around noon) is the main meal of the day for many Swedes. Restaurants tend to be great value at lunchtime, with most places offering a **set meal** (*dagens rätt*) of a main dish with bread, salad and coffee at 80–100kr. Otherwise meals in restaurants, especially at **dinner** (*middag*), can be expensive: 250–350kr for two courses, plus drinks. Better value are kebab shops, pizzerias and Thai restaurants. Swedes tend to eat early, tucking into dinner from around 6pm.

Drinking

Although the costs have come down in recent years, Sweden remains one of the most expensive places in Europe to **drink**. In a bar or pub you'll pay around 50kr for half a litre (or less) of one of the main national brands, Spendrups or Falcon. Unless you specify, it will be *starköl*, the strongest beer, or the slightly weaker *mellanöl*; *folköl* is the cheaper and weaker brew; cheapest (around half the price) is *lättöl*, a concoction that is virtually non-alcoholic. With the exception of the latter, the only outlets where you can buy alcohol outside of bars and restaurants are the government-run **Systembolaget** (known informally as Systemet) shops, where alcohol costs around a third of what you'll pay in a bar. There are at least one or two branches in even the smallest towns. A glass of **wine** in a bar or restaurant costs around 60kr, while you can buy a whole bottle for a little more at Systembolaget.

CULTURE AND ETIQUETTE

Swedes are a mix of apparent contradictions: fiercely patriotic yet globally minded, confident yet self-deprecating, orderly yet creative. Throughout the country you'll find the small ritual of *fika* – a verb that means something like "to have a coffee and a bun and a chat with a friend or two" – is a common pastime, along with singalongs and complaining about winter. **Traditional festivities** like Midsummer's Day and Easter inspire enormous enthusiasm, and on holidays young and old alike head for the countryside to celebrate. The vast majority of Swedes speak some **English** and most speak it with disarming fluency, so Anglophone travellers will have no problem striking up conversations.

SPORTS AND OUTDOOR ACTIVITIES

Football is Sweden's national sport, with a club or two in most of the main cities. Naturally enough, **winter sports** are where the Swedes excel on the world stage and skiing, snowboarding and ice hockey are all very popular. The best ski resorts are in Åre, Kittelfjäll, Riksgränsen and Ramundberget. In summer, everyone flocks to Sweden's exquisite, unpolluted lakes and to Stockholm's archipelago for **swimming**, **kayaking** and **sailing**. Sweden is a

SWEDEN ONLINE

www.cityguide.se Up-to-date events listings in the main Swedish cities.

www.thelocal.se English-language news, views, listings and blogs on life in Sweden.

www.visitstockholm.com Everything you ever wanted to know about the Swedish capital.

www.svenskaturistforeningen.se Tips and ideas on where to visit in Sweden, courtesy of STF (the Swedish Youth Hostel Association).

www.visit-sweden.com Slick tourist board website with plenty of themed ideas and itineraries.

fantastic place for **hiking**, with some of Europe's most unspoilt wildernesses to explore. The most trekked path is the 500-kilometre Kungsleden (King's Trail; see p.1174).

COMMUNICATIONS

The Swedish **postal service** scrapped normal post offices in 2001. Instead, you can send and receive mail and buy stamps at supermarkets, newsagents and tobacconists (look for the blue postal sign). **Public phones** usually only take pre-paid cards (*telefonkort*), available from newsagents and kiosks. **Internet** access is free in local libraries. Otherwise, **wi-fi** is widely available in cafés, bars and restaurants across the country.

EMERGENCIES

The **police** are courteous and fluent in English. Medical treatment is free for anyone with a European Health Insurance Card (EHIC), although a small administration fee may be charged. **Pharmacies** operate normal shop opening hours with a rota system for late opening. Stockholm has a 24-hour pharmacy (see p.1159).

SWEDISH

	Swedish	Pronunciation
Yes	*Ja*	Ya
No	*Nej*	Nay
Please	*Var så god*	Vaa-show-go
Thank you	*Tack*	Tak
Hello/Good day	*Hej*	Hay
Goodbye	*Hejdå*	Hay-dor
Excuse me	*Ursäkta*	Urh-shekta
Where?	*Var?*	Vaar?
Good	*Bra*	Braa
Bad	*Dålig*	Doo-ah-lig
Near	*Nära*	Nehra
Far	*Avlägsen*	Arv-lessen
Cheap	*Billig*	Billi
Expensive	*Dyr*	Deyur
Open	*Öppen*	Upp-en
Closed	*Stängd*	Stengd
Today	*I dag*	Ee daa
Yesterday	*I går*	Ee gor
Tomorrow	*I morgon*	Ee morron
How much is...?	*Vad kostar det…?*	Vaa kostar day…?
What time is it?	*Hur mycket är klockan?*	Hoor mucker er clockan?
I don't understand	*Jag förstår inte*	Yaa fur-stor int-eh
Do you speak English?	*Talar du engelska?*	Taalar doo eng-ul-ska?
One	*Ett*	Ett
Two	*Två*	Tvo
Three	*Tre*	Tray
Four	*Fyra*	Feera
Five	*Fem*	Fem
Six	*Sex*	Sex
Seven	*Sju*	Shoo
Eight	*Åtta*	Otta
Nine	*Nio*	Nee-o
Ten	*Tio*	Tee-o

EMERGENCY NUMBERS

All emergencies ⓣ112.

INFORMATION

Almost all towns have a **tourist office**, giving out good-quality maps and timetables; they are also usually able to book accommodation, rent out bikes and change money. Information on regional tourist offices can be found at ⓦwww.visitsweden.com. You're only likely to buy a map if you are going hiking – if so try ⓦwww.kartbutiken.se, which stocks a wide range.

MONEY AND BANKS

Sweden's currency is the **krona** (abbreviated to kr; plural: kronor). There are coins of 1kr, 5kr and 10kr, and notes of 20kr, 50kr, 100kr, 500kr and 1000kr. At the time of writing €1 was worth 9kr, US$1 was 6.3kr, and £1 was 10.3kr. **Banks** are generally open Monday to Friday 9.30am to 3pm, but most have later opening hours (until around 6pm) at least one day per week. Outside these hours you can **change money** at airports and ferry terminals, as well as at Forex offices, which usually offer good rates (minimum 45kr commission). **ATMs** are plentiful and paying with credit and debit cards is the norm.

STUDENT AND YOUTH DISCOUNTS

The main cities all have **tourist cards** or passes, which offer either free or discounted entry to museums, unlimited use of local transport (often including ferries), and sometimes other goodies, such as discounts in cafés and restaurants. An **ISIC card** can halve the price of museums, and attract variable discounts on accommodation, shops, restaurants and transport (for example 20 percent off at Swebus and 30 percent off train journeys with SJ).

OPENING HOURS AND HOLIDAYS

Generally, **shops** open Monday to Friday 9am to 6pm, and on Saturday from 9am to 1/4pm. Most larger stores stay open until 8/10pm, and the majority are also open until 8/10pm on Sundays. Banks, offices and shops close on **public holidays** (Jan 1, Jan 6, Good Fri, Easter Sun & Mon, May 1, Ascension, Whit Sun & Mon, June 20 & 21, Nov 1, Dec 24–26 & 31). They may also close early the preceding day.

Stockholm

With the air of a grand European capital yet on a small, Scandinavian scale, **STOCKHOLM** is a vibrant and instantly likeable city. Built on fourteen islands, water and green space dominate the landscape, but there are still plenty of distinctly urban attractions to fill your days, from elegant museums and royal palaces to achingly cool bars and clubs.

What to see and do

Taking a **boat tour** is the classic way to see Stockholm. Once you've checked into your accommodation, head straight to the harbour fronting the *Grand Hotel* from where you can pick one up from any number of operators (see p.1156). Once you have a fix on the city's layout you can cover most ground on foot or take the T-bana **metro** for cross-city trips.

The key **sights** to tick off are the Gamla Stan (Old Town), Vasa Museum, the National and Modern art museums as well as Sodermalm's SoFo neighbourhood. Aside from these it's best, in summer at least, to stroll around the parks and gardens (especially Djurgården) and take a trip to the Stockholm Archipelago. In winter the city's ice rinks and cosy coffee-houses come into their own.

Central Station and the Stadshuset

The first impression of Stockholm for most people is the vast yet elegant **Central Station**, the transport hub for the city with the bus terminal next door and metro underneath. A short walk south across the bridge to Kungsholmen is one of the city's main attractions: the **Stadshuset** (Town Hall) at Hantverkargatan 1, Ⓜ Centralen (guided tours only, tours in English hourly from 10am–3pm; April–Oct; 90kr; Jan–March & Nov–Dec; 60kr). Climbing its gently tapering 106-metre-high red-brick **tower** (May–Sept daily 10am–4/5.15pm; 40kr) is well worth the effort for the unrivalled views of the city.

Gamla Stan

One of the best-preserved medieval towns in Europe, **Gamla Stan** is packed with sights to explore. However, its main appeal is simply strolling around, particularly in the evening after the tourists depart and the lamp-lit streets become more intimate.

Stortorget, the main square, is surrounded by beautiful terracotta and saffron-coloured eighteenth-century buildings – look out for no. 7 where you'll see a cannon ball lodged into the wall, supposedly fired during the Stockholm Bloodbath of 1520. The surrounding narrow streets are clogged with arts and craft shops, restaurants and bars. The excellent **Nobelmuseet** on Stortorget (mid-May to mid-Sept daily 10am–6pm; mid-Sept to mid-May Wed–Sun 11am–5pm; closes 8pm Tues; 70kr) showcases the work of various Nobel Prize winners.

Gamla Stan: Kungliga Slottet

Stockholm's most distinctive monumental building, the **Kungliga Slottet** (Royal Palace; Ⓜ Gamla Stan), is a beautiful Renaissance successor to Stockholm's original castle. The Swedish Royals don't actually live here, having relocated to the Drottningholm Palace 10km west of the city, but no one seems to have told the royal guards who put on a display of pomp, pageantry and shouting at the daily changing of the guard (Mon–Sat 12.15pm, Sun 1.15pm). Inside are the royal **apartments** (mid-May to mid-Sept daily 10am–5pm; mid-Sept to early May Tues–Sun noon–4pm; 100kr), a dazzling collection of regal furniture, tapestries and Rococo decoration, while the **Treasury** (same times as apartments; 90kr) displays ranks of regalia, including jewel-studded crowns and a sword belonging to Gustav Vasa.

Gamla Stan: Storkyrkan

Close to the royal palace, Stockholm's cathedral, the **Storkyrkan** (daily 9am–4/6pm; 40kr), was consecrated in 1306 and is where the monarchs of Sweden are married and crowned. Look out inside for the animated fifteenth-century sculpture of St George and the Dragon, which incorporated elk horns into the design, and for the royal pews – more like golden billowing thrones.

Gamla Stan: Riddarholmen

Across the bridge from Gamla Stan, Riddarholmen or "Nobles Island" is often less crowded but just as pretty. It's also home to a Stockholm landmark, the thirteenth-century **Riddarholmskyrkan** (mid-May to end Sept daily 10am–5pm; 30kr), with its iron latticework spire. Originally a thirteenth-century monastery, the church is now the burial place of Swedish monarchs.

Nationalmuseum

The **Nationalmuseum** (Tues 11am–8pm, Wed–Sun 11am–5pm, also open until 8pm on Thurs between Sept–May; 100kr; Ⓜ Kungsträdgården), next to the *Grand Hotel*, houses an impressive collection of paintings, from Rembrandts to Renoirs as well as exhibiting local talent like Swedish artists Carl Larsson, Ernst Josephson and C.F. Hill. Perhaps less expected is the eclectic applied-arts collection which includes beds slept in by kings and examples of Swedish furniture design.

STOCKHOLM BY KAYAK

Seeing Stockholm by boat is one thing but getting right down to water level on a kayak gives you a terrific sense of freedom – you can stop off just about anywhere – and a unique vantage point on the city. The best place to rent kayaks is the **Kafé Kajak** at Smedsuddsvägen 23 on Kungsholmen (150kr for two hours).

THE MILLENNIUM BUG

The runaway success of Stieg Larsson's Millennium trilogy has helped stoke a worldwide interest in all things Swedish. Nowhere is this more apparent than on the streets of Stockholm, where you'll find some of the main characters' favourite haunts. If you'd like someone to guide the way, the **Millennium Tour** (Saturdays at 11.30am & Wednesdays at 6pm; 120kr; book through the tourist office) is a nice, sociable option. A cheaper alternative is to buy the *Millennium Tour* map (available at Arlanda Airport and the tourist office on Vasagatan; 40kr) and go it alone.

Moderna Muséet

Stockholm's answer to London's Tate Modern or Bilbao's Guggenheim, the **Moderna Muséet** (Tues 10am–8pm, Wed–Sun 10am–6pm; 80kr) on Skeppsholmen certainly keeps up with its rivals in terms of grand modernist architecture though the art collection plays second fiddle in some respects. Connoisseurs will appreciate the large selection of Cubist painting as well as lesser-known works by Picasso and Dalí, plus a peppering of American Pop Art. There's also a restaurant with great views over the city.

Norrmalm and Östermalm

Modern Stockholm lies immediately north of Gamla Stan. It's split into two distinct sections: the central **Norrmalm** and the classier, residential streets of Östermalm to the east. Norrmalm was redeveloped in the 1970s and is dominated by high-rises and the huge public-square-cum-roundabout, Sergels

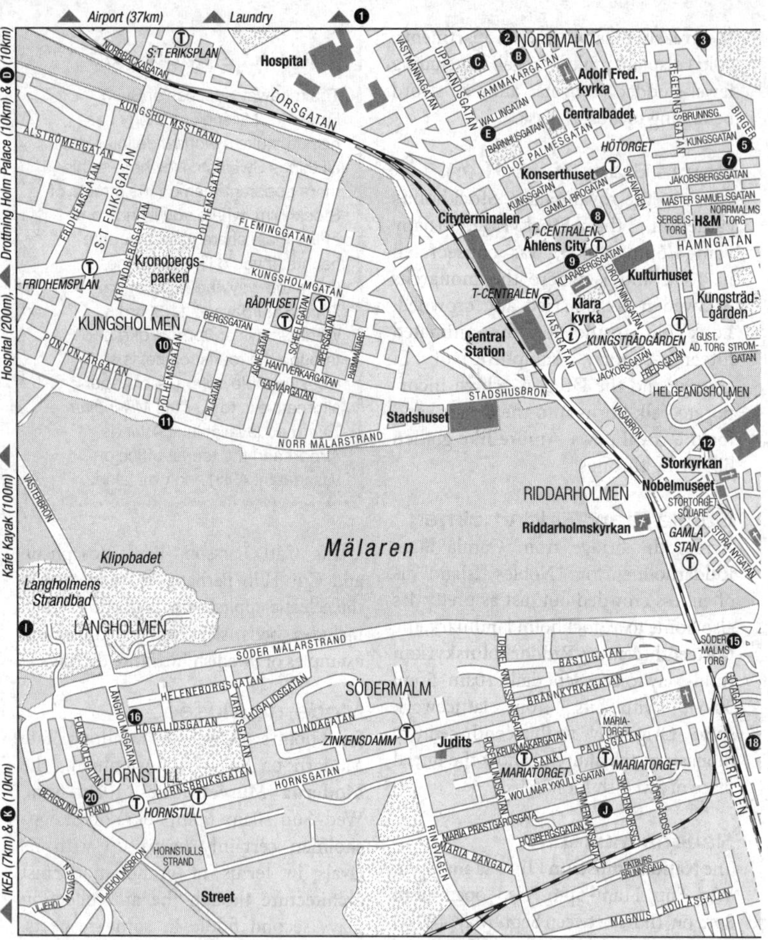

Torg. Taking up most of the east side of the square is the **Kulturhuset** (Tues–Fri 9am–7pm, Sat & Sun 11am–5pm; free), an interesting mix of exhibition space/art gallery/cinema/theatre and meeting place. Norrmalm is also home to Stockholm's biggest department stores, Åhlens and NK, as well as H&M's flagship store on Hamngatan. The eastern boundary is marked by **Kungsträdgården**, the most central of the city's numerous parks

Ostermalm, west of Norrmalm, is the address of choice for upmarket Stockholmers. It also hosts the city's most exclusive nightlife – particularly on Stureplan, where you'll find legions of designer-clad revellers queuing round the block for ultra-expensive nightclubs. The main attractions during the day are the **Östermalms Saluhall** food market (see p.1164) and the **Historiska Muséet** (May–Sept daily 10am–5pm, Oct–April same hours but closed Mon; 70kr; Ⓜ Karlaplan). Highlights here include a Stone Age household and a mass of Viking weapons, boats and most interestingly gold, over 52kg of the stuff.

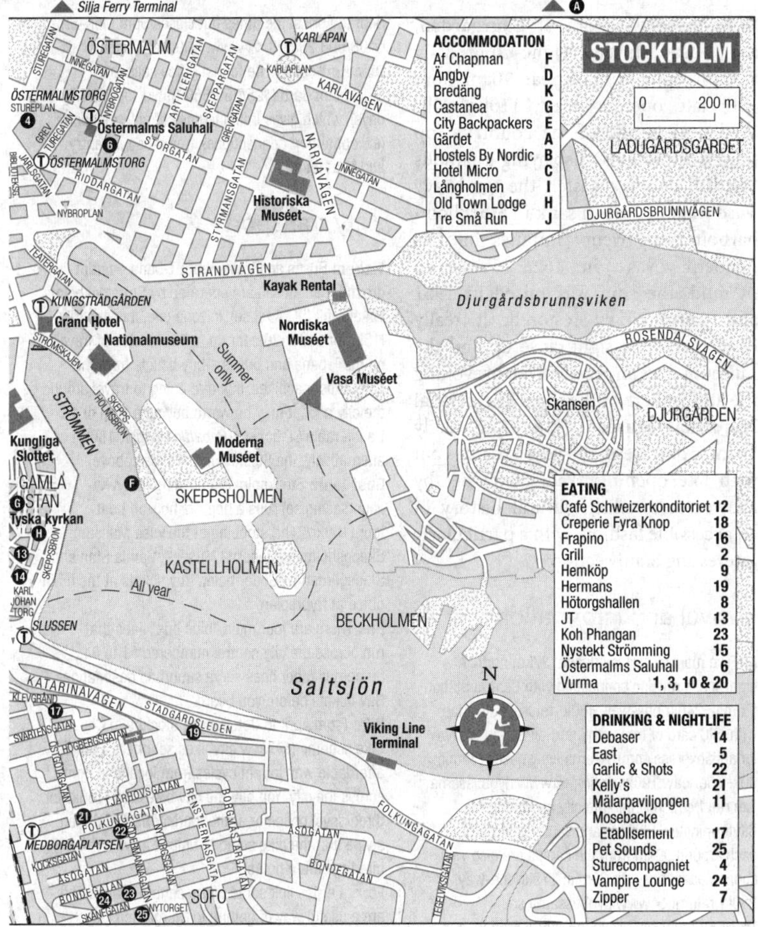

Södermalm and Långholmen

Stockholm's hippest island has to be **Södermalm**, just south of Gamla Stan. Head south from the traffic hub of Slussen along Götgatan, past Medborgarplatsen, lined with shops and bars, to arrive at the central district of **SoFo** (South of Folkungagatan), which bristles with cool bars, clubs and boutiques. To the west of Södermalm, **Hornstull** is SoFo's quieter cousin, with a cluster of bars and restaurants along Hornsgatan and around Bergsundstrand. It's a short walk from here to the lovely green island of **Långholmen**, perfect for picnics or summertime beach-lazing at the small stretch of sand on the north shore.

Djurgården

A former royal hunting ground, **Djurgården** is the nearest large expanse of park to the city centre and home to several interesting museums. You could walk to the park from Central Station, but it's quite a hike: it's quicker to take a bus or ferry instead. Bus #44 makes the journey from Karlaplan, while the #47 and #69 run from Nybroplan. Ferries leave in summer from Nybroplan, and all year round from Slussen.

On the west shore of **Djurgården**, the **Vasa Muséet** (June–Aug daily 8.30am–6pm; rest of year 10am–5pm with late opening Wed; 110kr, 80kr Wed pm) is one of the country's top tourist attractions, displaying a famous Swedish design disaster: the top-heavy *Vasa* warship, which sank in Stockholm harbour just twenty minutes into its maiden voyage in 1628. Preserved in mud, the ship was raised in 1961 and painstakingly restored. It really is an incredible sight close up and the museum does an excellent job of evoking the atmosphere of the time. The palatial **Nordiska Muséet** (June–Aug daily 10am–5pm; rest of year 10am–4pm with late opening Wed; 80kr) nearby showcases Swedish cultural history in an accessible fashion, with a particularly interesting Sámi section.

Arrival and information

Air The main airport is Arlanda, 37km north. A high-speed rail line connects it with Central Station (20min; 240kr one-way, 460kr return; half-price with ISIC card or free with InterRail/Eurail; Ⓦwww.arlandaexpress.com). Alternatively buses (45min; 99kr one-way. 198kr return; Ⓦwww.flygbussarna.se) run frequently into the city arriving at the Cityterminalen. Skavsta and Västerås airports, each around 90km from the capital are also well connected by bus (1hr 20min; 119kr one-way, 238kr return; Ⓦwww.flygbussarna.se).

Train By train, you arrive at Central Station, a cavernous structure on Vasagatan in Norrmalm. All branches of the Tunnelbana, Stockholm's metro, meet at T-Centralen, the station directly below Central Station.

Bus Cityterminalen, adjacent to Central Station, handles almost all bus services, both domestic and international.

Ferry Viking Line ferries arrive at Tegelvikshamnen in Södermalm, in the south of the city. The terminal is a 30min walk from the centre, or connected by bus to Ⓜ Slussen. The main terminal for Tallink Silja Line ferries is in the northeastern reaches of the city, a short walk from Gärdet and Ropsten T-bana stations.

Tourist office The main tourist office is at Vasagatan 14 in Norrmalm, just across from the Central Station (May to mid-Sept Mon–Fri 9am–7pm, Sat 10am–5pm, Sun 10am–4pm, late Sept to April same times but closes 6pm Mon–Fri; Ⓣ08/508 28 508, Ⓦwww.visitsweden.com).

Discount cards The tourist office sells the Stockholm Card (425/550/650/895kr for 1/2/3/5/ days), which gives unlimited use of city transport (except airport connections), free museum entry and boat tours.

City transport

Tickets Buses and trains (both T-bana – underground – and local) are operated by Storstockholms Lokaltrafik (SL; Ⓦsl.se). In zone one, it costs 30kr (18kr for under-20s) for up to 75 minutes of travel on the T-bana and buses – buy tickets from the automatic machines. If you're going to travel around the city a lot, it may be worth buying a strip of 16 transferable SL tickets (*Rabattkuponger*, 180kr) or, alternatively, the Stockholm Card (see above).

Boat tours Stockholm Sightseeing (Ⓦwww.sightseeing.se) runs a hop-on, hop-off boat tour (100kr/24hr) stopping at the Vasa Museum, Skeppsholmen (Moderna Muséet), Gamla Stan and Stadsgården on Södermalm. Buy tickets at the main office at Nybroplan.

Bus There are four main "blue bus" lines that run across the city centre, numbered #1 to #4; numerous other lines serve suburban destinations. Buy tickets before you board.

Bike From April to October the Stockholm City Bike scheme (Ⓦwww.citybikes.se) offers a quick, affordable way to rent cycles from locations right across the city. You buy the city bike card (165kr for three days) online or at the tourist office and then swipe it at the bike stand to unlock a cycle (max hire time three hours).

Ferry Ferries link some of the central islands and are a useful way of getting to Djurgården (see p.1155). Individual tickets are relatively expensive but the Stockholm Card is valid.

Metro The clean, efficient Tunnelbana (T-bana) is worth considering once you've tired of walking. There are three lines (red, green and blue) and trains run Sun–Thurs 5am–midnight, Fri & Sat 24hr.

Taxi Taxis are expensive (the meter starts at 45kr) and only really a good option if you are in a group. You can hail taxis in the street or try Taxi Stockholm (Ⓣ08/15 0000).

Accommodation

Hostels

Af Chapman Flaggmansvägen 8, Skeppsholmen Ⓣ08/463 22 66, Ⓦwww.stfchapman.com. A Stockholm landmark, the

Af Chapman is a tall sailing ship converted into probably the world's most elegant hostel. If you can't get a bed on board there are more rooms on dry land in the hostel building, which houses the reception and a breakfast room plus a decent café. Dorms 310kr, rooms 690kr.

Castanea Kindstugatan 1, Gamla Stan ⓣ08/22 35 51, ⓦwww.castaneahostel.com. The Old Town location of this quiet, non-STF hostel (just 150m from the Royal Palace) takes some beating while inside are clean and brightly decorated dorms. Dorms 195kr, rooms 600kr.

City Backpackers Upplandsgatan 2a, Norra Bantorget ⓣ08/20 69 20, ⓦwww.citybackpackers.se. Fun, sociable hostel with everything from private rooms to 12-bed dorms. Free pasta, internet, bike rental, wi-fi and, this being Sweden, sauna. Dorms 190kr, rooms 650kr.

Gärdet Sandhamnsgatan 59 ⓣ08/463 22 99, ⓦwww.stfturist.se/gardet. Modern-feeling hotel/hostel set in quiet parkland northeast of the centre and within walking distance of Djurgården and the Vasa Museum. T-bana to Gärdet, then a 10-minute walk. Singles 525kr, doubles 820kr.

Hostels By Nordic Drottninggatan 83 ⓣ07/6021 71 01, ⓦwww.hostelsbynordic.se. The building itself is hardly inspiring, but the dorm rooms are clean and secure, and there's no denying that the location on Stockholm's main shopping street is very handy indeed. Free wi-fi included. Dorms 250kr, rooms 800kr.

Långholmen Kronohäktet, Långholmen ⓣ08/720 85 00, ⓦwww.langholmen.com. Located within an old prison on leafy Långholmen island. Spend the night in a converted cell: there are dorms with shared bathroom as well as en-suite doubles. To reach it take the T-bana to Hornstull, turn left and follow the signs. Dorms 260kr, singles 550kr.

Hotels and pensions

Hotel Micro Tegnerlunden 8 (near Drottninggatan) ⓣ08/545 455 69, ⓦwww.hotelmicro.se. Bargain prices for central Stockholm. The rooms are windowless but pleasant enough and there are clean men's and women's bathrooms along each corridor. Single room 545kr, plus 100kr for each additional person.

Old Town Lodge Baggensgatan 25, Gamla Stan ⓣ08/20 44 55, ⓦwww.oldtownlodge.se. This cosy little place in the heart of the Old Town dates back to the 1600s. As a result its 19 rooms are a little small, but they feel modern inside and are most certainly comfortable. Single room 572kr, double (without windows) 557kr.

Tre Små Rum Högbergsgatan 81 ⓣ08/641 23 71, ⓦwww.tresmarum.se Ⓜ Mariatorget The name means "three small rooms" but there are now seven at this good-value hotel in the heart of Södermalm. Delicious buffet breakfast is served in the lovely kitchen area and there are cycles for rent for 150kr/day. Rooms 795kr.

Campsites

Ängby Blackebergsvägen 25 ⓣ08/37 04 20, ⓦwww.angbycamping.se. Pretty, well-organized site west of the city on Lake Mälaren and near the beach. T-bana to Ängbyplan, then a 300-metre walk. Open all year. Camping spot 140kr/pitch. Family tent 225kr.

Bredäng Stora Sällskapets Väg ⓣ08/97 70 71, ⓦwww.bredangcamping.se. Decent spot with hostel and restaurant on site, 10km southwest of the centre by Lake Mälaren. Take T-bana to Bredäng from where it's a 700m walk. April–Oct only. Camping 135kr for a one-man tent. Bigger tents 265kr. Dorm bed 220kr, room 400kr.

Eating

Food courts and markets

Hemköp Below Åhléns, Mästersamuelsgatan 57. Convenient supermarket with an excellent deli counter and in-house bakery. Mon–Fri 7am–10pm, Sat & Sun 10am–9pm.

Hötorgshallen Hötorget. A varied indoor market, awash with small cafés and ethnic snacks. To the north is the Kungshallen food court. Mon–Thurs 10am–6pm, Fri 10am–6.30pm, Sat 10am–4pm.

Östermalms Saluhall Östermalmstorg. Pig out in style at this stylish indoor market packed with discerning foodie types. Wine bars and restaurants surround the stalls. Mon–Thurs 9.30am–6pm, Fri 9.30am–6.30pm, Sat 9.30am–4pm.

Cafés and food stands

Café Schweizerkonditoriet Västerlånggatan 9, Gamla Stan. The most homely and welcoming café in a very touristy part of the old town. Coffee is served in great big cereal bowls, and the sandwiches are packed with healthy fillings like smoked salmon and sun-dried tomatoes.

Nystekt Strömming Södermalmstorg, just outside Ⓜ Slussen. This tiny but well-known takeaway cart serves fried herring on oatmeal crackers. It's always busy, and rumour has it that the food works wonders on a hangover.

Vurma Polhemsgatan 15, Kungsholmen; Birger Jarlsgatan 36, Östermalm; Gästrikegatan 2, Vasastan & Bergsundstrand 31, Södermalm. Kitsch and cosy cafés that double as bakeries. *Vurma* has become something of a Stockholm institution with four branches now open across the city.

Restaurants

Creperie Fyra Knop Svartensgatan 4, Södermalm ⓣ08/640 77 27. Good-value crêpes are served in this dark, evocative restaurant, which is fashionably tatty and often packed.

Grill Drottninggatan 89, Normalm ⓣ08/31 45 30. It's the lavish boudoir-style decor (with rich velvety sofas and dressed mannequins standing in the windows) that first entices people to *Grill*. But the daily lunch buffet (110kr), with tasty treats like lime-marinated chicken, also happens to be unbeatable value.

Frapino Långholmsgatan 3, Hornstull. Fantastic pick'n'mix salads and good-value lunch deals.

Hermans Fjällgatan 23b. Join the locals for a guilt-free feast at this veggie restaurant which also boasts some of the best views of Stockholm. You may need a taxi back after the all-you-can-eat dinner buffet (150kr).

Koh Phangan Skånegatan 57, Södermalm ⓣ08/642 50 40. Thai restaurant-bar with an interior resembling a tropical forest strewn with fairy lights. The food – green curries, *pad thai* and the like – struggles to compare with the decor but it's competently put together. Listen out for the hourly "thunderstorm" noises that rattle through the restaurant.

JT Järntorget 78, Gamla Stan. Refined Swedish food in the heart of the old town – one of the best places to try classics like meatballs and lingonberries.

Drinking and nightlife

Bars and pubs

East Stureplan 13, Östermalmstorg. Lively Japanese bar-restaurant with a heated outdoor area. Always packed at weekends, when DJs play late into the night. Mon–Fri lunchtime only, weekends 5pm–1am.

Garlic & Shots Folkungagatan 84. Garlic is offered with just about everything at this American-style bar-restaurant – including the draught beer. For something a little sweeter, check out the excellent list of long and short drinks. Daily 4pm–late.

Kelly's Folkungagatan 49, Södermalm. Big, brash and student-friendly rock bar right near ⓜMedborgarplatsen, serving what must be some of the city's cheapest beer (24kr). If you don't have a coat to hang up (20kr) it's free to get in, too. Daily 4pm–3am.

Pet Sounds Skån egatan 80, Södermalm. Cool bar-restaurant that plays host to a mixed crowd of indie kids and older SoFo regulars. DJs play sets in the basement area and you can buy what you hear at the Pet Sounds music shop across the road. Daily 5pm–midnight.

Vampire Lounge Östgötagatan 41, Södermalm. Subterranean cocktail bar – comfy red sofas, bare stone walls and hip clientele. Try the Vlad the Impaler if you want to kick-start your evening. Daily 5pm–1am except Sat, 7pm–1am.

Live music and clubs

Debaser Karl Johans Torg 1 ⓦwww.debaser.se ⓜSlussen/Gamla Stan Legendary live music and DJ venue, attracting great local and international bands and packing in hundreds of energetic clubbers.

Mosebacke Etablisement Mosebacke Torg 3 ⓦwww.mosebacke.se ⓜSlussen. This gig venue/club/bar has an incredibly varied music programme from jazz to electro. The sprawling terrace is one of the best places in town to hang out in summer, with barbecues and live music. Daily 9pm–2am.

Sturecompagniet Sturegatan 4 ⓦwww.sturecompagniet.se ⓜÖstermalmstorg. This Stockholm staple boasts a terrific light-show with house and techno sounds blaring long into the night. Dress to impress and start queuing early. Over-23s only. Thurs–Sat 10pm–3am.

Gay Stockholm

Mälarpaviljongen Norr Mälarstrand 64, ⓦwww.malarpaviljongen.se. Open-air bar-restaurant down by the water with great views of Gamla Stan. It attracts a mixed gay/straight crowd and puts on events during the annual Stockholm Pride. Daily 11am–12am.

Zipper Lästmakargatan 8. ⓦwww.zippersthlm.com. Pumping house music and Eurovision-style pop played across three dancefloors and four bars. Sat 10pm–3am.

Shopping

Åhlens City Klarabergsgatan 50, T-Centralen. Stockholm's biggest department store – the place to stock up on Bjorn Borg underkecks or, if you can fit into them, skinny Acne jeans.

H&M Hamngatan 37. The main Stockholm branch of one of Sweden's biggest retail success stories; floor-to-ceiling cut-price fashion.

IKEA Modulvägen 1, Skärholmen (7km southwest of Stockholm). If you're dying to see the world's largest IKEA then hop on one of the free shuttle buses leaving from Vasagatan 18 (Mon–Fri on the hour 10am–7pm).

Judits Hornsgatan 75 ⓦwww.judits.se Truly fantastic secondhand clothes emporium with a wealth of great shoes and accessories at affordable prices. The menswear equivalent is just up the road.

Street Hornstulls Strand 4. Inspired by London's Camden Market, Street has transformed a run-down area of Stockholm into a vibrant weekend meeting and browsing spot (April–Sept) packed with arty types.

Directory

Embassies Australia, Klarabergsviadukten 63, 8th floor ⓣ08/613 29 00; Canada, Klarabergsgatan 23, 6th floor ⓣ08/453 30 00; Ireland, Hovslagargatan 5 ⓣ08/5450 40 40; UK, Skarpögatan 6–8 ⓣ08/671 30 00; US, Dag Hammarskjöldsväg 31 ⓣ08/783 53 00.
Hospital St Görans Sjukhus, St Göransplan 1 ⓣ08/5870 10 00, ⓦwww.stgoran.se/in-english. 24hr.
Internet Free wi-fi at cafés and bars across the city. Otherwise, good-value wired internet access is offered at Sidewalk Express (19kr/hr; ⓦwww.sidewalkexpress.com) with branches at Arlanda Airport, Central Station, City Terminalen and Kulturhuset.
Left luggage Lockers in Central Station (30kr, 50kr or 90kr/24hr, depending on size).
Pharmacy Apoteket C.W. Scheele, Klarabergsgatan 64 ⓣ07/7145 04 50 (24hr).
Post office There's no central post office, but you can send packages from Posten counters in branches of Hemköp and Ica.

Moving on

Train Copenhagen (5 daily; 5hr); Gothenburg (hourly; 3hr by X2000, 5hr by Intercity); Helsingborg (hourly, change at Lund; 5hr 30min); Kiruna (1 nightly; 16hr 25min); Lund (hourly; 4hr 10min); Malmö (hourly; 4hr 30min); Oslo (1 daily; 6hr); Östersund (4 daily; 6hr); Uppsala (every 30min; 40min).
Ferry Helsinki (Helsingsfors) (1 daily; 16hr); Tallinn, (1 daily; 15hr); Turku (Åbo) (1 daily; 11hr).

Around Stockholm

One of the key excursions from Stockholm is to the royal palace of Drottningholm, on the shores of Lake Mälaren, west of the capital. In summer the pine-clad islands of Stockholm's **archipelago** make an enticing escape from the city while history buffs should head to the elegant town of **Uppsala**, a short train ride away.

DROTTNINGHOLM PALACE

Just 10km west of Stockholm, the **Drottningholm Palace** (April & Oct Sat & Sun 11.30am–3.30pm; May–Aug daily 10am–4.30pm; Sept daily 11am–3.30pm; Nov–March Sat & Sun noon–3.30pm; 80kr; ⓦwww.royalcourt.se) is a Versailles-like monument to excess dating from the mid-seventeenth century. The Swedish royal family made it their permanent residence in 1981, and, while you're unlikely to spot any of them, you are free to wander through sections of the palace on guided tours and visit the manicured gardens. The best way to get here is on one of the majestic old steam ships which leave from the quay near Stadshusbron five times a day (165kr return; ⓦwww.stromma.se), although you can also reach it on the less regal combination of T-bana to Brommaplan followed by the #177 bus.

THE STOCKHOLM ARCHIPELAGO

For 80km east of the capital stretches the **Stockholm archipelago**, made up of 30,000 islands, most of which are little more than lumps of rock rising up from the sea. In summer, the area bristles with tourists, day-trippers, sailing boats and locals making use of their summer homes. Boats to the islands leave from Strömkajen near Slussen and are run by Waxholmbolaget (ⓣ08/614 64 50, ⓦwww.waxholmsbolaget.se). If you're sticking around for a while, invest in a Båtluffakortet (island-hopping card, 420kr), a **pass** that entitles you to five days of unlimited transport; it's available at the tourist office, where you can also pick up a boat timetable. Alternatively, single tickets start at 75kr one-way.

Vaxholm

Just an hour's scenic boat ride from Stockholm and also connected by road, **Vaxholm** is the most easily accessible of the archipelago islands, which means it can be swamped with visitors in summer. However, it's still a charming spot, only two miles long, and boasts an elegant harbourside packed with restaurants, cafés and shops. Throughout July and August there are frequent concerts and outdoor events held here.

The **tourist office** is in the quaint Rådhuset (ⓣ08/541 314 80). If you decide to **stay** overnight on the island there's a peaceful STF hostel (ⓣ08/541 750 60, ⓔinfo@bogesundsslottsvandrarhem.se; single rooms 295kr, doubles 390kr) at Per Brahesväg 1, about 3km from the harbour.

Siaröfortet

Locals rave about this cute little island, an hour's ferry ride north of Vaxholm (2hr 10min from Stockholm). It's known as **Siaröfortet** after its small naval fort, built during World War I. The fort has been turned into a museum but the real attraction is the island's indented coastline perfect for kayaking and swimming. There's also a lovely STF **youth hostel** with a wood-fired sauna (ⓣ08/243 090, ⓦwww.svenskaturistforeningen.se; dorms 250kr, twin rooms 425kr; May to mid-Oct only).

UPPSALA

Forty minutes' train ride north of Stockholm, the pretty university town of **UPPSALA** makes an excellent day-trip. Just north of the restaurant- and bar-lined River Fyris, which bisects the town, you'll find the vast Gothic **Domkyrkan** (daily 8am–6pm), Scandinavia's largest cathedral. Poke around and you'll find the tombs of Reformation rebel monarch Gustav Vasa and his son Johan III, as well as local hero Carl Linnaeus, the famous botanist.

The other key sights to see are the remarkable royal burial mounds at **Gamla (Old) Uppsala**. Thought to have been created by the Svea tribe some 1500 years ago they were once the site of gruesome human sacrifices – with unfortunate victims strung up from a tree. The place where this took place is marked by the **Gamla Uppsala Kyrka** (daily 9am–4/6pm), a church built when the Swedish kings first took baptism in the new faith. The worthwhile **Gamla Uppsala Museum** (April & Sept–Oct, Mon, Wed, Sat & Sun noon–3pm; May–Aug daily 10am–4pm; 60kr) fills you in on all the background.

Uppsala's **train** and **bus stations** are a couple of blocks east of the river. Signs indicate the way to the cathedral and **tourist office** (Mon–Fri 10am–6pm, Sat 10am–3pm; mid-June to mid-Aug also Sun 11am–3pm; ⓣ018/727 48 00, ⓦwww.uppland.se). For cheap **eats** try *Max* on Stora Torget, the city's main square. It's part of a nationwide environmentally conscious hamburger chain, which lets customers know the carbon footprint of their burger before they order. Otherwise, *Ekocaféet* at Drottninggatan 5 does a nice line in organic ales and veggie mains (around 220kr for lunch and a drink). The most convenient and best-value **place to stay** is the *Uppsala City Hostel* (ⓣ018/10 00 08, ⓦwww.uppsalacityhostel.se; dorms 170kr, single rooms 350kr, doubles 400kr) at St Persgatan 16, four blocks north of the station along Kungsgatan.

Southern Sweden

Southern Sweden is dominated by endless expanses of farmland while its coastline is famous for its superb beaches. Local dialects are strong and cause much mirth among metropolitan

Stockholmers. Yet to portray the area as a rural backwater would do it a disservice. Here you'll find the grand port city of **Gothenburg**, well deserving of exploration. South of here, the cosmopolitan city of **Malmö** is worth a day or two, while **Lund**, a medieval cathedral and university town is an essential day-trip. Lying 90km off the southern coast in the Baltic Sea is the attractive island of **Gotland**, whose beaches and bars are awash with visitors over the summer.

GOTHENBURG

Sweden's second city, **GOTHENBURG** (Göteborg, pronounced *Yuh-teh-borr*) is Scandinavia's largest seaport and home to some of Sweden's biggest brands, including Volvo and Ericsson. Beyond the industrial gloom of its shipyards you'll find an attractive and distinctly continental city with broad avenues, beautiful parks and several outstanding museums and galleries. With students making up an eighth of the population it's also a fun, youthful city with plenty of quirky bars, nightclubs and coffee shops.

What to see and do

Exploring Gothenburg by tram is one of the great pleasures of the city, but almost all of its sights can be covered on foot. Most visitors head straight towards the main shopping street, Avenyn, which leads uphill towards the Konstmuseum, but from here it's only a short stroll to Liseberg, Scandinavia's biggest theme park, and the Universeum science centre. If you have time, dedicate a lazy afternoon to Slottskogen, the city's most attractive swathe of green space, or head out to the beaches of the Southern Archipelago.

Maritiman and the Opera House

A short walk north from the station, **Maritiman** (May–Sept daily 10am–6pm; April & Oct Fri–Sun only 10am–4pm; 75kr) offers you the chance to clamber aboard a destroyer and descend into a submarine moored at the quayside. It's worth coming down here just to look at the dockyards beyond, which frame the ship-shaped **Gothenburg Opera House** (open daily; Ⓦwww.en.opera.se).

The Wheel of Gothenburg

Gothenburg has long been nicknamed Little London, and now the city has its very own version of the London Eye. The 60m-high **Wheel of Gothenburg** (Fri, Sat & Sun 11am–9pm, daily during summer; 85kr) is currently next to the Opera House, with magnificent views over the waterfront.

Avenyn and the Röhsska Museet

Running southeast from the central area around the Nordstan shopping centre, Kungsportsavenyn is Gothenburg's showiest thoroughfare. Known simply as **Avenyn**, this wide strip was once flanked by private houses fronted by gardens and is now lined with some of the city's most popular – and overpriced – restaurants and bars. About halfway down, the excellent **Röhsska Museet** at Vasagatan 37–39 (Tues noon–8pm, Wed–Fri noon–5pm, Sat & Sun 11am–5pm; 40kr; Ⓦwww.designmuseum.se) traces the history of design from 1850 to the present day as well as

THE FULL PACKAGE

Gothenburg can be an affordable place to treat yourself to a proper a hotel room, thanks to the **Gothenburg Package** (from 620kr/person), run by the city tourist board. This deal gets you a double room in a central hotel, with breakfast and a free Gothenburg City Card worth 285kr – book ahead at Ⓦwww.goteborg.com.

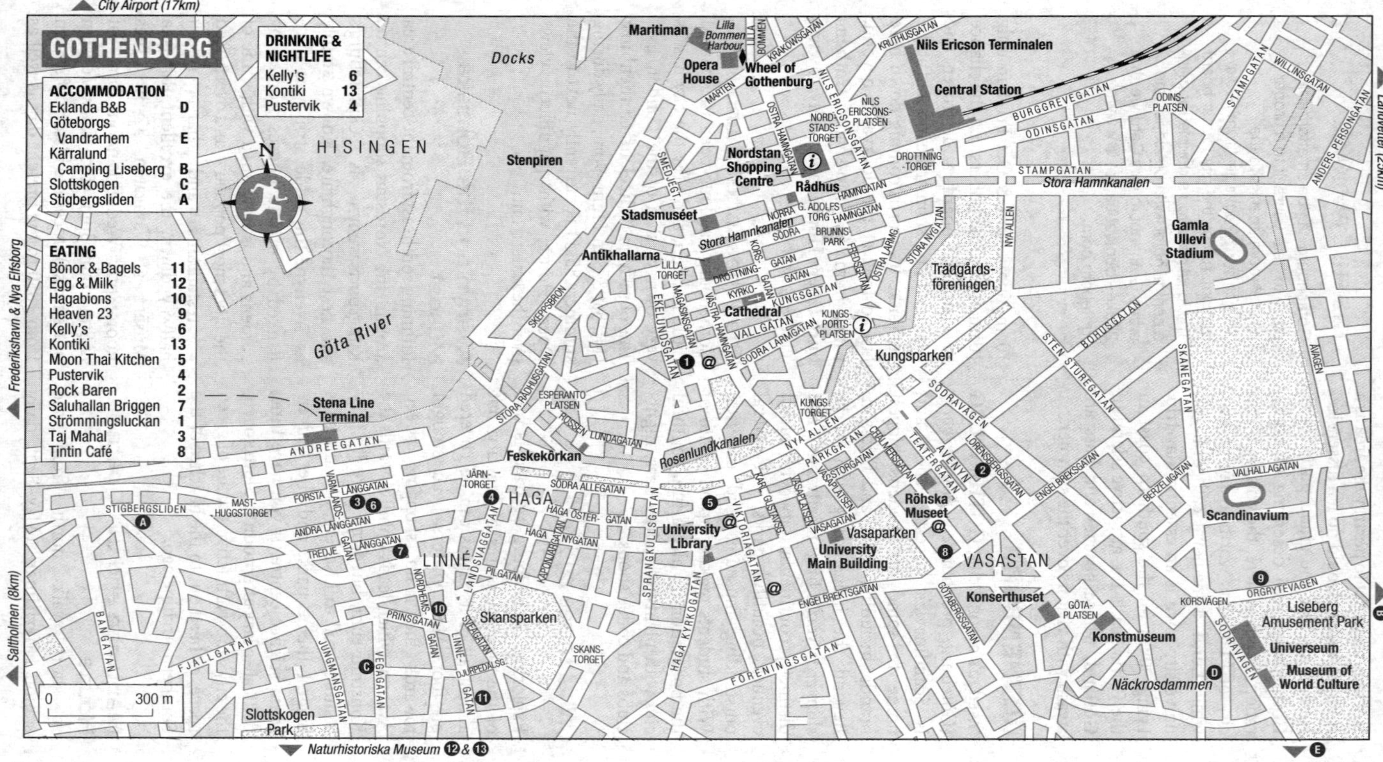
GOTHENBURG
ACCOMMODATION
Eklanda B&B D
Göteborgs Vandrarhem E
Kärralund Camping Liseberg B
Slottskogen C
Stigbergsliden A
EATING
Bönor & Bagels 11
Egg & Milk 12
Hagabions 10
Heaven 23 9
Kelly's 6
Kontiki 13
Moon Thai Kitchen 5
Pustervik 4
Rock Baren 2
Saluhallan Briggen 7
Strömmingsluckan 1
Taj Mahal 3
Tintin Café 8
DRINKING & NIGHTLIFE
Kelly's 6
Kontiki 13
Pustervik 4
City Airport (17km)
Landvetter (25km)
Frederikshavn & Nya Elfsborg
Saltholmen (8km)
Naturhistoriska Museum 12 & 13
HISINGEN
Docks
Göta River
Stenpiren
Stena Line Terminal
Maritiman
Lilla Bommen Harbour
Opera House
Wheel of Gothenburg
Nils Ericson Terminalen
Central Station
Nordstan Shopping Centre
Rådhus
Stadsmuséet
Antikhallarna
Cathedral
Kungsparken
Trädgårdsföreningen
Gamla Ullevi Stadium
Scandinavium
Feskekôrkan
Rosenlundkanalen
Stora Hamnkanalen
HAGA
LINNÉ
VASASTAN
University Library
Vasaparken
University Main Building
Röhska Museet
Konserthuset
Konstmuseum
Näckrosdammen
Liseberg Amusement Park
Universeum
Museum of World Culture
Skansparken
Slottskogen Park
ANDREEGATAN
STIGBERGSLIDEN
MAST-HUGGSTORGET
FÖRSTA LÅNGGATAN
ANDRA LÅNGGATAN
TREDJE LÅNGGATAN
VÄRMLANDSGATAN
JÄRNTORGET
SÖDRA ALLEGATAN
HAGA ÖSTERGATAN
HAGA NYGATAN
KAPONJÄRGATAN
LANDSVÄGGATAN
PILGATAN
SPRANGKULLSGATAN
HAGA KYRKOGATAN
VIKTORIAGATAN
KARL GUSTAVSG.
VASAPLATSEN
VASAGATAN
ENGELBREKTSGATAN
FÖRENINGSGATAN
GÖTABERGSGATAN
GÖTAPLATSEN
KORSVÄGEN
ORGRYTEVÄGEN
SÖDRAVÄGEN
VALHALLAGATAN
BERZELIIGATAN
LORENSBERGSGATAN
AVENYN
TEATERGATAN
CHALMERSGATAN
VASASTORGATAN
PARKGATAN
NYA ALLÉN
KUNGSTORGET
STORA RADHUSGATAN
ESPERANTOPLATSEN
RUSSEN
LUNDAGATAN
SKEPPSBRON
EKELUNDSGATAN
MAGASINSGATAN
VÄSTRA HAMNGATAN
SÖDRA LARMGATAN
VALLGATAN
KUNGSGATAN
KUNGSPORTSPLATSEN
KYRKOGATAN
DROTTNINGGATAN
KORSGATAN
LILLA TORGET
SÖDRA HAMNGATAN
NORRA HAMNGATAN
G. ADOLFS TORG
BRUNNS PARK
FREDSGATAN
ÖSTRA LARMG.
STORA NYGATAN
SMEDJEGT.
ÖSTRA HAMNGATAN
NORDSTADSTORGET
NILS ERICSONSGATAN
NILS ERICSONSPLATSEN
DROTTNINGTORGET
STAMPGATAN
ODINSGATAN
BURGGREVEGATAN
ODINSPLATSEN
WILLINSGATAN
ANDERS PERSONGATAN
KRUTHUSGATAN
KRAKOWSGATAN
MARTEN
LILLA BOMMEN
STEN STUREGATAN
BOHUSGATAN
SKANEGATAN
ÅVÄGEN
NYA ALLEN
SKANSTORGET
LINNÉGATAN
DJURPEDALSG.
SVEAGATAN
PRINSGATAN
NORDHEMSGATAN
VEGAGATAN
JUNGMANSGATAN
FJÄLLGATAN
BANGATAN
0 300 m

hosting regular fashion shows by young designers from Gothenburg University.

The Konstmuseum

Gothenburg's museum of art, the **Konstmuseum** (daily except Mon 11am–5/6pm, Wed till 9pm; 40kr, free for under-25s), houses a unique collection of Nordic masterpieces. Among the highlights are paintings by Edvard Munch, P.S. Krøyer and Carl Larsson, but there are also works by Picasso, Van Gogh and Rembrandt. The square outside the museum, **Götaplatsen,** is home to a city icon – Carl Milles' seven-metre-high bronze statue of Poseidon in all his naked glory.

Liseberg Amusement Park

Liseberg, five minutes' walk southeast of Götaplatsen, is a gorgeous inner-city amusement park (late April to early Oct; opening times vary; Åkpass 310kr for unlimited rides all day; Ⓦwww.liseberg.com) with restaurants, bars and adrenaline-pumping rides set among acres of landscaped gardens. It's the biggest theme park in Scandinavia, and Balder, the rickety wooden roller coaster, is one of the best of its kind in the world.

Universeum and the Museum of World Culture

Nearby, **Universeum** (daily: mid-June to mid-Aug 9am–8pm; rest of year 10am–6pm; Ⓦwww.universeum.se; 160kr), is a fun yet expensive "science discovery centre" (it's worth getting a Gothenburg City Card just to visit here). The main attraction is a huge, climate-controlled tropical forest and there's also a large seawater aquarium.

Adjacent to the Universeum, the **Museum of World Culture** (Tues–Sun noon–5pm, late opening Wed & Thurs; free; Ⓦwww.varldskulturmuseet.se) features imaginative exhibits on global issues such as HIV/Aids, human trafficking and fair trade as well as more upbeat topics such as Bollywood and hip-hop.

Haga and Linnégatan

The old working-class district of **Haga**, a few minutes' walk west of Avenyn is now a picturesque area of cobbled streets lined with cafés, boutiques and antique shops. **Linnégatan**, further west still, is a more charismatic and cosmopolitan version of Avenyn, with offbeat cafés and restaurants leading almost all the way to Slottskogen.

Slottskogen Park and the Naturhistoriska Museum

Slottskogen (tram #13 or #2 to Linnéplatsen) is the city's largest park, a lovely expanse of woodland, lakes and wide avenues perfect for joggers and cyclists. Several vantage points offer sweeping views over the city and there's also a small zoo area with penguins and a seal pond. The nearby **Naturhistoriska Museum** (Tues–Sun 11am–5pm; 40kr, under-25s free; Ⓦwww.gnm.se) houses the world's only stuffed blue whale.

Southern Archipelago

Saltholmen (the southernmost stop on tram #11) is the jumping-off point for trips to Gothenburg's craggy **Southern Archipelago**. Ferries run from here to inhabited islands like Vargö, Bränö and Styrsö, which make great spots for swimming and sunbathing in the summertime. Tram tickets are valid for ferry journeys, too.

Arrival and information

Air The main airport, Gothenburg Landvetter, is 25km east of the city; buses (every 20min; 30min; 80kr; Ⓦwww.flygbussarna.se) connect to the Nils Ericson terminal next to Central Station. Gothenburg City airport, used by budget airline Ryanair, is a corrugated steel building 17km north of the city; bus departures are synchronized with flight arrivals (30min; 60kr).
Train Trains arrive at Central Station on Drottningtorget, just north of the centre; an underground

walkway leads into Nordstan, the city's biggest shopping mall.

Bus Buses from all destinations use the Nils Ericson bus terminal, which adjoins Central Station.

Ferry Stena Line ferries from Frederikshavn in Denmark and Kiel in Germany dock within 20min walk of the centre. Trams #3 and #9 run from here to the centre.

Information Gothenburg has two tourist offices: a glass kiosk (Mon–Fri 10am–8pm, Sat 10am–6pm, Sun noon–5pm) in the middle of Nordstan, and a main office on the canal front at Kungsportsplatsen 2 (June–Aug daily 9.30am–6/8pm; rest of year Mon–Sat 9.30am–2/5pm; ⓣ031/61 25 00, ⓦwww.goteborg.com).

Discount passes The tourist office sells the Gothenburg City Card (285/395kr for 24/48hr), giving unlimited bus and tram travel, free or half-price museum and attraction entry, free Paddan boat tours and a fifty percent discount on a day-trip to Frederikshavn in Denmark.

Internet Some branches of the *Condeco* coffee shop including the one on Avenyn have free wi-fi, but you'll have to at least buy a coffee. If you need a computer, try Game Net at Viktoriagatan 22, or head to the library nearby.

City transport

Trams There are 12 colour-coded tram routes – pick up a map from the tourist office. Tickets (25kr or free with Gothenburg City Card) can usually be bought from the on-board vending machines. A more reliable option is the Västtrafikkort, which can be purchased at any branch of Pressbyrån. You pay a 100kr deposit for the card, and can then top it up with 100, 200 or 500kr at a time. Touch the card against the on-board scanner when you start each journey, and you'll only pay 16.50kr for inner-city trips.

Boat tours Paddan boats (ⓦwww.stromma.se) offer open-topped boat tours (April–Oct; 145kr or free at certain times with Gothenburg City Card) along the city's canal network. Boats depart from Kungsportsplatsen.

Cycling The city is packed with cycle paths. You can rent bikes (150kr/day) from Cykelkungen at Chalmersgatran 19 (ⓦwww.cykelkungen.se) or buy a three-day pass for the city's bike rental scheme, Styr & Ställ (10kr). The first half an hour of every journey is free.

Accommodation

Eklanda B&B Lilla Regementsvägen 35 ⓣ031/43 50 55, ⓦwww.vandrarhem.com. A 10-minute tram ride from the centre (take #6 or #7 to Kviberg), this quiet place offers a range of decent accommodation, from dorms with shared bathrooms to self-contained cabins with their own kitchens. Recommended for bigger groups. Dorm beds from 325kr, singles 490kr, doubles 690kr.

Göteborgs Vandrarhem Mölndalsvägen 23 ⓦwww.goteborgsvandrarhem.se. Not the cheapest hostel in town, but it's hard to argue with the location, a short walk from Liseberg. Take tram #4 towards Mölndal (stop: Getebergsäng). Dorms 300kr, singles and doubles 600kr.

Kärralund Camping Liseberg Olbergsgatan ⓦwww.liseberg.se. Busy campsite 4km from the centre aimed mostly at families visiting the Liseberg Amusement Park. There is also a youth hostel (dorms only) on site. From the city centre, hop on tram #5 to Welandergatan (direction: Torp). Tents 275kr (for up to 4 people), dorms 595kr.

Slottskogen Vegagatan 21 ⓣ031/42 65 20, ⓦwww.sov.nu. This huge, recently upgraded hostel is in a great location near Slottskogen park. There's a sauna, free internet and a chill-out area for meeting other travellers, and dorms come with lockers built into the bunks. Two minutes' walk from Linnégatan; take tram #1 or #6 to Olivedalsgatan. Dorms 215kr, singles 360kr.

Stigbergsliden Stigbergsliden 10 ⓣ031/24 16 20, ⓦwww.hostel-gothenburg.com. Comfortable hostel in a charming old sailor's mission, close to Linné, the Stena ferry terminal and the bars of Andra Långgatan. Tram lines #3, #9 and #11 from the city centre. Dorms 225kr, singles 550kr. No check-in noon–4pm.

Eating

Shops and market stalls

Saluhallan Briggen Nordhemsgatan near Linnégatan. Indoor food market with plenty of cheap ethnic stalls as well as high-quality deli counters.

Strömmingsluckan On the car park near Magasinsgatan 17. Insanely popular takeaway van serving a truly Swedish take on fast food: fried herring with mashed potatoes and lingonberries. Mon–Fri 11am–3pm and Sat noon–4pm; 50kr.

Cafés

Bönor & Bagels Linnégatan 48. Cracking little café on one of the city's most attractive streets. Grab a coffee, some soup and a bagel, then sit outside and watch the trams roll by.

Egg & Milk Carl Skottsbergs Gata 6. A quirky, American-style diner complete with chequerboard floor tiles and green, vinyl-covered seats. The syrup-drizzled pancakes are delicious.

Hagabions Linnégatan 21. Sample some imaginative vegetarian food at this lovely café before catching a film in the attached arthouse cinema.

Restaurants

Heaven 23 Mässans Gata 24, inside the *Gothia Towers* hotel. Certainly not the cheapest place in town, but the view from the 23rd floor is worth paying a little extra for. The huge shrimp sandwiches (more like a full meal) are divine.

Moon Thai Kitchen Storgatan 1. The best Thai restaurant in town, with a cool tropical vibe and dishes grouped according to spiciness and cost. Closed Mon.

Taj Mahal Första Långgatan 24. Reliable Indian food right through the day. The 70kr lunch menu is great value, with naan bread, a salad buffet, rice and water included with your main dish.

Tintin Café Engelbrektsgatan 22, off Avenyn. This 24-hour, Tintin-themed diner is popular among students and late-night drinkers. A fun experience at 4am on a Saturday.

Drinking and nightlife

For cheap beer and good times, Andra Långgattan ("second long street") is a safe bet – it's one of the few places in Sweden you can buy a beer for under 40kr and there are plenty of cheap Indian and Thai restaurants.

Kelly's Andra Långgatan 20. Not the most stylish bar in town but wildly popular with students, attracted by cheap beer and vegan food.

Kontiki Storängsgatan 2. This cosy Polynesian-style hangout, complete with little bamboo "huts" for diners, is a welcome escape on those long winter nights. Expect live music and long, fruity cocktails. Nearest tram stop Botaniska Trädgården. Wed–Sat 5pm–1/2am (weekends only in winter).

Pustervik Järntorgsgatan 14. A fun and friendly bar-club that attracts hordes of local students. Live music and/or DJs most nights. Try to visit on a Monday (free entry) when you can take part in the rather surreal ping pong competition.

Rock Baren Kristinelundsgatan 14. Two floors of noisy rock 'n' roll action, just steps from the swanky clubs of Avenyn. Head in between 5–9pm for the daily happy hour, when a draught beer costs just 25kr.

Moving on

Train Copenhagen (hourly; up to 3hr 45min); Lund (hourly; 2hr 45min); Malmö (hourly; 3hr 10min); Oslo (3 daily; 4hr); Stockholm (hourly; 3hr by X2000, 5hr by Intercity).

Ferry Frederikshavn, Denmark (3–8 daily; 3hr 15min); Kiel, Germany (1 daily; 14hr).

MALMÖ

Linked to continental Europe by the impressive Öresund Bridge, **MALMÖ** is Sweden's most cosmopolitan city. More than a hundred languages are spoken on its streets and you'll find Turkish and Thai food as popular as meatballs and herring. In fact, Malmö didn't even become Swedish until 1658 having been Denmark's second city for generations. Today it's the country's third largest town, an attractive mix of chocolate-box medieval squares and striking modern architecture, most notably the Turning Torso skyscraper, Scandinavia's tallest building.

What to see and do

Mostly flat and home to an extensive cycle network, Malmö is the perfect place to rent a bike and explore at leisure. Most of the sights are squeezed into the compact medieval centre although the **beaches** and modern **docklands** to the north make a tempting excursion. South of the old centre is the bohemian district of **Möllevångstorget**, where you'll find many of the best places to eat and drink.

Stortorget

The city's main square, **Stortorget** is as impressive today as it must have been when it was first laid out in the sixteenth century. It's flanked on one side by the imposing **Rådhus**, built in 1546 and covered with statuary and spiky accoutrements. To its rear stands the fine Gothic **St Petri Kyrka** (daily 10am–6pm) while to the south runs **Södergatan**, Malmö's main pedestrianized shopping street.

Lilla Torg

A late sixteenth-century spin-off from Stortorget, **Lilla Torg** is everyone's

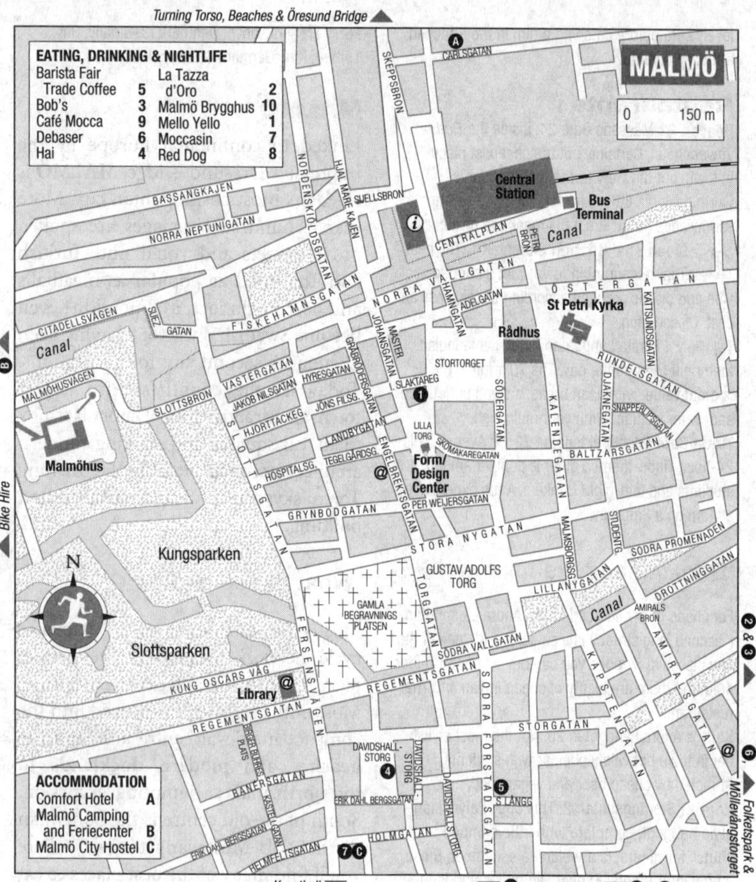

favourite part of the city. Lined with cafés and restaurants, it's usually pretty crowded at night, with drinkers kept warm under patio heaters and bars handing out free blankets. On the south side of the square, through an archway, is the **Form/Design Centre** (Tues–Fri 11am–5/6pm, Sat 11am–4pm, Sun noon–4pm; free; ⓦwww.formdesigncenter.com) a showcase for cutting-edge Swedish furniture, textiles and lighting with a pleasant "literary café" upstairs.

Malmöhus

The princely **Malmöhus** (June–Aug 10am–4pm; Sept–May 10am–4pm weekdays and noon–4pm Sat and Sun; 40kr) is a low fortified castle defended by a wide moat and two circular keeps. Built by Danish king Christian III in 1536, the castle was later used for a time as a prison, but it now houses the **Malmö Museer**, a disparate but fascinating collection of exhibitions on everything from geology to photography – and an aquarium, too. The pleasant grounds, the **Kungsparken**, are peppered with small lakes and an old windmill.

The Turning Torso and Öresund Bridge

A good twenty-minute walk or five-minute cycle ride north of the station is Malmö's most iconic sight, the 190-metre-high **Turning Torso** skyscraper. A spiralling helix of glass and steel, the structure was completed in 2005 and now lords it over the sea towards Denmark. A small museum next door shows a short film on the tower and its architect, Santiago Calatreva. Surrounding the tower are lots of modern apartments and cycle pathways. Heading coastwards takes you to a viewpoint of the **Öresund Bridge**, the seventeen-kilometre engineering marvel that links the city with Copenhagen, a journey of just 20min by train.

The beach

Ribersborgsstranden or "Ribban", as city residents call it, is Malmö's artificial sandy beach, created in the 1920s. A long access path, busy in summer with rollerbladers and cyclists, leads down to the sections of beach, each indicated by a jetty.

Möllevångstorget

Known as **Möllan**, this giant cobbled square towards the south of the city was once the heart of working-class Malmö. By day it hosts a busy market with everything from cassava to Arabic sweets on sale while by night it becomes the alternative hangout of choice for the city's student population.

Arrival and information

Air Copenhagen/Kastrup Airport is just 20min by train from Malmö's Central Station; trains leave round the clock and cost 105kr. Malmö's own airport Sturup, is used mostly by Swedish airlines flying to domestic destinations and the odd Ryanair service to Spain. It's 30km southeast of the city; buses to the centre are timed to coincide with arrivals (40min; 99kr one-way; Ⓦwww.flygbussarna.se).

Train All trains terminate at Central Station, including the local Pågatåg services that run from Helsingborg and Lund (rail passes are valid). Underground trains bound for the Öresund Bridge, which connects Malmö with Copenhagen, also depart from here.

Bus The main bus terminal is outside Central Station, on Centralplan.

Tourist office The main tourist office is opposite the train station at Skeppsbron 2 (July and Aug 9am–7pm and Sat and Sun 9am–4pm; otherwise Mon–Fri 9am–5pm, Sat and Sun 10am–2.30pm; Ⓣ040/34 12 00, Ⓦwww.malmotown.com). They sell the Malmö Card.

Discount passes The Malmö Card (170kr/200kr for one/two days) gives free museum entry, free travel on city buses, free parking, plus discounts at shops and cafés across the city.

Internet The city library at Kung Oscars Väg 11 offers free internet access.

City transport

Bus City buses are run by Ⓦwww.skanetrafiken.se; tickets start at 19kr and route maps are available at the tourist office.

Bike rental Fridhems Cykelaffär, Tessins Väg 13. Bikes 150kr for the first day, then 100kr/day thereafter. They're located about two blocks along Tessins Väg which runs west from the castle.

Accommodation

Comfort Hotel Carlsgatan 10c Ⓣ040/33 04 40, Ⓔco.malmo@choice.se. Malmö's biggest hotel has bright, modern rooms just two minutes' walk from the Central Station. Room rates include free breakfast, wi-fi and access to the on-site gym. Book ahead for the best deal. Doubles and singles from 580kr.

Malmö Camping and Feriecenter Strandgatan 101 Ⓣ040/15 51 65, Ⓦwww.malmocamping.se. Idyllic beachside campsite with views of the Öresund bridge. Bus #4 from Central Station. 150kr/person.

Malmö City Hostel Rönngatan 1 Ⓣ040/611 62 20. Comfortable, clean and very popular STF hostel 1km south of the centre in a great location for nightlife and shops; take bus #2, #5, #7 or #8 to Davidshall. Dorms 240kr, doubles 560kr.

Eating

Barista Fair Trade Coffee Södra Förstadsgatan 24. Chow down on lactose-free vegan muffins and drink certified organic espresso at this do-gooding café chain, now with branches across Sweden.

Café Mocca Friisgatan 4. It's worth making a stop here to try one of the huge healthy salads (69kr). Fresh filter coffee and stylish surroundings are included in the price.

Hai Davidshallstorg 5 Ⓣ040/50 50 05. The best sushi in town is served in this buzzing restaurant on elegant Davidshallstorg. Try the lunch menu (85kr) which changes every day.

La Tazza D'oro Corner of Claesgatan and Ystadsgatan, off Möllevångstorg. Intimate little student hangout serving tasty Italian-style focaccias (50kr).

Red Dog Södra Förstadsgatan 84a. Cheap-and-cheerful gallery-cum-café with decent home-made sandwiches and friendly staff.

Drinking and nightlife

Bob's Möllevångstorget 6b. One of the cheapest places for beer and banter on Möllevångstorget. The outside area can get lively on spring and summer evenings. Daily until 11/noon.

Debaser Norra Parkgatan 2 ⓦwww.debaser.se. The Malmö branch of the popular Stockholm club/venue. Live music, DJ nights, dancing and drinking. Check website for specific opening hours.

Mello Yello Lilla Torg 1. The best of Lilla Torg's many bar-restaurants, though there's not so much to choose between them. Noon–1am Sat & Sun, 3.30pm–1am on weekdays.

Malmö Brygghus Bergsgatan 33. Sup pale ales, pilsners and porters at the city's only microbrewery. There's a pub that's open until 1am every day, and on Fridays and Saturdays you can take a tour of the brewery itself (195kr).

Moccasin Fersensväg 14. Loungey hangout just south of the centre with comfy sofas and a nice relaxed vibe; drinks are pricey but the scrummy snacks and cheeses are hard to beat. Fri–Sun 10am–5pm, Mon–Thurs 10am–8pm.

Moving on

Train Copenhagen (every 20min; airport 21min, city 35min); Gothenburg (10 daily; 3hr); Helsingborg (at least hourly; 50min); Lund (at least hourly; 15min); Oslo (1 daily; 7hr 30min); Stockholm (hourly; 4hr 30min).

LUND

Just a short hop inland from Malmö, the pretty university town of **LUND** makes for a pleasant afternoon wander. A recent survey named it the best place to live in Sweden and it's not hard to see why with its quaint cobbled streets, relaxed pace of life and mix of well-heeled residents and students from across the world. The high student population may account for the huge number of **bikes** you'll see across the city. To get your own wheels, head to Lundahoj, next to the train station, which has very cheap bikes for rent (Bangatan 17, ⓣ046/35 57 42; 20kr/day).

The main sight in town is the impressive, twin-towered **cathedral** (Mon–Fri 8am–6pm, Sat & Sun 9.30am), one of Scandinavia's finest medieval buildings. Inside is a quirky attraction: a fifteenth-century astronomical clock from which two mechanical knights pop out and clash swords as the clock strikes (daily Mon–Sat noon & 3pm, Sun 1pm & 3pm). Surrounding the cathedral are several grand nineteenth-century buildings belonging to the university. Also nearby is the entrance to the vast **Kulturen** open-air museum (May–Aug daily 11am–6pm; 120kr; Sept–April Tues–Sun noon–4pm; 90kr), a village in itself full of perfectly preserved cottages and permanent exhibitions covering everything from Viking weapons to modernist design. Discounts are available for students.

The **train station** is towards the west of town, an easy walk from the centre. The **tourist office** (May–Sept Mon–Fri 10am–6pm, Sat & Sun 10am–2pm; Oct–April Mon–Fri 10am–5pm, Sat 10am–2pm; ⓣ046/35 50 40, ⓦwww.lund.se) is opposite the cathedral at Kyrkogatan. The cheapest option for food is to put together a picnic at the Saluhallen on Mårtenstorget. Otherwise there are plenty of kebab and falafel stands around the old centre, selling hearty snacks for around 30kr. Cafés include the historic *Conditori Lundagård* at Kyrkogatan 17. Rail buffs may be enticed to spend the night onboard *Tåget*, a 1930s express train converted in inimitable Swedish style into a **youth hostel** (ⓣ046/14 28 20, ⓦwww.trainhostel.com; dorms 250kr, double/twin rooms 960kr). Located just behind the station, the sleeper carriages are very basic, a little poky but a lot of fun.

GOTLAND

Sweden's largest island, **GOTLAND** is packed with historical intrigue, lined with great beaches, and, in summer at least, full of partying students. The star attraction is the beautifully preserved medieval town of **Visby** though the rest of the island is also well worth exploring, especially by bike or car.

What to see and do

Once the main trading centre of the Baltic, **VISBY** is an unspoilt gem of a town, full of crumbing medieval churches and cute half-timbered houses. The best approach is to simply get lost in its warren of cobbled alleyways, using the thirteenth-century walls circling the town as a reference point. After a while you'll find your way to the main open space, **Stora Torget**, lined with bars and restaurants.

Visby's museums

The truly fascinating **Gotlands Fornsal** (daily except Mon 11am–4pm; 100kr, free for visitors under 20), houses exhibitions about everything from Viking rune stones and gold to the macabre discovery of shallow graves that held the bones of townsfolk executed in the Middle Ages.

Behind the museum is Visby's art gallery or **Konstmuseum** (Tues–Sun noon–4pm; 50kr, or free on same day with entry to Gotlands Fornsal), mostly focused on paintings depicting the island by residents themselves.

Visby cathedral and church ruins

Visby's graceful **cathedral**, St Maria (daily 9am–5pm), is a short walk west of Stora Torget. Its three towers, two octagonal and one square, can be seen for kilometres around. Of the town's ruined churches, the most impressive and photogenic are **St Hans** on St Hansgatan and **St Katarina** on the eastern side of Stora Torget.

The rest of the island

Tofta Strand, 20km south of Visby (take bus #10 or rent a car; see below), is one of the island's most picturesque sandy beaches. It's packed out in summertime, especially during week 29 (known as Stockholm Week) when rich kids from the capital invade the island, sending prices sky-high. To avoid the crowds it's often worth checking out the beaches on the eastern side of the island instead. Buses are infrequent on the island, so renting a car (see below) makes things easier. With your own wheels you can also take a trip up to **Fårö**, Gotland's tiny sister island (the ferry is free, with frequent crossing), where you'll find the beach resort of Suder-sandsviken, and the mysterious-looking sea stacks known as Langhammers on the wind-battered north coast. Halfway there, the caves at **Lummelunda**, a short drive north of Visby (May–Sept only, 130kr) make for an interesting stop.

Arrival and information

Air The airport is 4km north of Visby. An infrequent bus service runs into the centre of town during high season. Otherwise, a taxi costs 120–150kr.
Ferry Ferries arrive at the harbour, a 10min walk west of Visby.
Tourist office Skeppsbron 4–6, near the ferry terminal (mid-June to mid-Aug daily 8am–7pm; mid-Aug to mid-June Mon–Fri 8am–4pm; ⓣ0498/20 17 00, ⓦwww.gotland.info).

Island transport

Bus The main bus terminal is beyond the town wall to the southeast, on Kung Magnus Väg.
Car rental Mickes Biluthyrning, down by the ferry terminal (ⓣ0498/26 62 62, ⓦwww.mickes biluthyrning.se; 250kr/day). Good selection of old VWs and the like at bargain prices.
Bike rental Gotlands Cykeluthyrning, Skeppsbron 2, near to the tourist office (ⓣ0498/21 41 33, ⓦwww.gotlandscykeluthyrning.se; from 85kr/day).

Accommodation

Hotel Stenugnen Korsgatan 4–6, one street back from the tourist office ⓣ498/21 02 11 ⓦwww.stenugnen.nu. A smart, maritime-themed hideaway just inside the old town. A good option for couples, with breakfast served next to a stretch of the ancient city wall. Singles from 700kr, doubles from 850kr.

Visby Logi St Hansgatan 31/Hästgatan 1430 ⓣ070/752 20 55, ⓦwww.visbylogi.se. Two beautiful historic homes in the heart of Visby converted into double and single rooms (shared bathroom). No breakfast but kitchen facilities available. Singles 550kr, doubles 650kr.

Visby Fängelse Skeppsbron 1 ⓣ0498/20 50 60, ⓦwww.visbyfangelse.se. Striking but shabby youth hostel in a converted prison near the waterfront, with beds in "cells" that sleep between 2 and 6 guests. Book ahead in summer. Dorms from 290kr.

Visby Strandby & Snäcks Camping Holiday houses and a pleasant campsite just beside Snäckviken beach, about 4km from the town centre. Camping 275kr/tent, holiday homes 995kr/night.

Eating, drinking and nightlife

Black Sheep Arms St Hansgatan 51. English-style pub serving up tasty if expensive (mains 140kr) food and a wide selection of beers; a favourite with locals and tourists alike.

Gutekällaren Stora Torget ⓦwww.gutekallaren.com. Housed in a historic building, this club/bar complex is heaving with bronzed, dressed-up twenty-somethings in summer and attracts Sweden's top DJ talent. Daily 10pm–2am.

Hedbergs Bok & Musikkafe Södra Kyrkogatan 4b. Part book shop, part art gallery and part cosy café, this quirky little place has all the charm of your granny's front room. Pop in for a sandwich and a piece of home-made cake. Fast wi-fi, plus occasional live music.

Munkkallaren Stora Torget ⓦwww.munkkallaren.se. Visby nightlife stalwart with live bands and a big party vibe later in the evening, particularly on Thursdays and Fridays. The restaurant serves up decent grub. Mon–Sat 4pm–2am, closed Sun.

Strykjärnet Wallersplats 3 ⓦwww.creperielogi.se. Quality crêpes (around 100kr) served in a narrow iron-shaped building on the corner of Adelgatan and Hästgatan. There's a lovely terrace outside and a slick but expensive apartment (2250kr) for rent upstairs.

Central Sweden

The rural Sweden of most visitors' imaginations begins in the central areas of the interior: vast tracts of forest, peaceful lakes and log cabins. Deep-blue **Lake Siljan**, at the heart of the province of Dalarna, is a major draw, particularly in midsummer when it's a focus of festivities celebrating the long days and warm weather. From here one of Europe's classic rail journeys, the **Inlandsbanan**, begins its slow route north to the Arctic Circle via the towns of Orsa and Östersund.

GETTING TO GOTLAND

Visby is accessible by **ferry** from the mainland ports of **Nynäshamn**, a one-hour train ride south of Stockholm, and **Oskarhamn**, five hours by train from Gothenburg. Both crossings take around three hours and are run by Destination Gotland (ⓣ0771/22 33 00, ⓦwww.destinationgotland.se). For the cheapest fares (one-way tickets start at 230kr for adults and 185kr for under-25s), book at least 21 days in advance; regular fares cost around 25 percent more. If you have an InterRail pass you're eligible for a discount, but you'll need to call ahead to get it.

Several **airlines**, including Gotlandsflyg (ⓦwww.gotlandsflyg.se), Golden Air (ⓦwww.goldenair.se) and Skyways (ⓦwww.skyways.se) fly to Gotland, with services all year round from Stockholm and summer flights from Gothenburg, Helsingborg and cities as far afield as Oslo and Hamburg. From Stockholm you're looking at a minimum of 470kr one-way.

THE INLANDSBANAN

The **Inlandsbanan** (Inland Railway), which cuts a route through 1300km of Sweden's best-looking scenery, ranks amongst the most enthralling of European train journeys. The quaint, toy-like line links central Sweden with Gällivare in the north, a two-day trip if attempted without a break. The railway (Ⓣ0771/53 53 53, Ⓦwww.inlandsbanan.se) operates from June to the end of August only.

Ticket fares are calculated per kilometre – for example, Mora to Östersund costs 414kr, Östersund to Gällivare is 962kr; reserving a seat costs 50kr per journey.

Discounts and rail cards InterRail and Eurail pass holders travel for free apart from seat reservation fees. Students receive a 25 percent discount. The Inlandsbanan Card (1595kr) offers unlimited travel on the line for fourteen days.

LAKE SILJAN

Lake Siljan (Ⓦwww.siljan.se) holds a special, misty-eyed place in the Swedish heart. Thousands head here in summer to stay at its iconic red lakeside cabins, potter around in canoes and kayaks and hike in the surrounding countryside. If you happen to be here around Midsummer's Night, head to the town of **Leksand** at the south end of the lake, which holds a huge festival with maypole dances and longboat races.

Mora, at the north end of Siljan, has more facilities and is the starting point for the Inlandsbanan rail route (see box above). The **tourist office** (Mon–Fri 10am–5pm, Sat 10am–2pm, closed Sun; Ⓣ0250/59 20 20) at the train station gives out information on activities around the lake, and the rustic but welcoming STF **hostel** is 600m northeast at Vasagatan 19 (Ⓣ0250/381 96, Ⓦwww.maalkullann.se; dorms 250kr, singles 250kr, doubles 350kr).

ORSA

The Inlandsbanan, having begun in Mora (see above), makes its first stop at **ORSA**, fifteen minutes up the line, where the nearby **Grönklitt Bear Park** (mid-May to mid-Sept daily 10am–3/6pm; 160kr; Ⓦwww.orsagronklitt.se; bus #118) provides the best chance to see the brown bears that roam over large swathes of central Sweden. In winter, there's some great skiing, snowshoeing and walking to be done here and the on-site hostel, *Grönklitts Vandrahem* (Ⓣ0250/462 00; dorm beds 350kr), has nice clean rooms in a building at the foot of one of the slopes.

ÖSTERSUND

ÖSTERSUND, halfway point on the Inlandsbanan, is a very provincial but welcoming town on the shores of **Lake Storsjön**. It's most famous for the Loch Ness-style monster, the Storsjöodjur, said to inhabit the lake. More prosaically the town is also a major inland rail junction: as well as the Inlandsbanan, routes head west to Stockholm and east to Trondheim in Norway.

What to see and do

Apart from monster-spotting (there are eight "observation points" along the lakeshore), the main thing to do is visit **Jamtli** (11am–5pm; closed Mon Sept–May; 90kr), an impressive, partly open-air **museum,** fifteen minutes' walk north from the centre along Rådhusgatan. The key exhibits are the ninth-century **Överhogdal Viking tapestries**, whose simple hand-woven patterns of horses, dogs and other beasts are quite breathtaking.

From the **harbour** you can take the bridge over the lake to **Frösön** island, site of the original Viking settlement here. In winter, when the lake freezes, it's possible to skate or walk from one side to the other.

Arrival and information

Train It's a 5 min walk north into the centre from Ostersund Central train station.
Bus The main bus station is on Gustavs III Torg, off Rådhusgatan.
Tourist office Rådhusgatan 44 (Mon–Fri 9am–5pm; June–Aug until 5/7pm and also Sat & Sun 10am–3/5pm; ⓣ063/14 40 01, ⓦwww.turist.ostersund.se). They sell the Östersundskort, valid for three days (June–Aug; 295kr), giving free access to the town's sights, free bike rental and other discounts.

Accommodation

Frösö Camping ⓣ063/432 54. The most picturesque of Östersund's campsites. June to early Aug only; bus #3 or #4 from the centre. 160kr/person.
Jamtli Hostel ⓣ063/12 20 60, ⓦwww.jamtli.com. Quaint, appealing hostel in the grounds of Jamtli museum. Booking ahead is essential in summer. Dorms 225kr.
Östersund Ledkrysset Biblioteksgatan 25 ⓣ063/10 33 10, ⓦwww.ostersundledkrysset.se. The most modern and sociable of the city's hostels, with immaculate dorms and private rooms housed in an attractive former fire station near the centre. Free wi-fi. Dorms 210kr, single and double rooms 350kr/person.

Eating and drinking

Captain Cook Hamngatan 9. Australian-themed drinking haunt with decent food to boot – mains around 100kr. Head over on a Wednesday night for live music and a glass of cold beer. Daily 4pm–12am.
Starlanders Prästgatan 43. The best budget choice in town for mid-morning coffee and cake. The seats by the window are great for people watching.
Wedemarks Konditori Prästgatan 27. Popular bakery with a cosy downstairs lunch bar and some delicious prawn-topped open sandwiches (50kr).

Moving on

Train Stockholm (5 daily; 6hr); Trondheim (2 daily; 4hr); Uppsala (3 daily; 4hr 30min).

Northern Sweden

Northern Sweden – Swedish Lapland – is the wildest, strangest part of the country. The region is famous for the northern lights and midnight sun as well as the Sámi people – reindeer herders who were once the sole inhabitants here. The Sámi are still visible, especially in the small town of **Jokkmokk**, which almost straddles the Arctic Circle. A couple of hundred kilometres further north, **Kiruna** is the access point for the celebrated **ICEHOTEL**, a once-in-a-lifetime stay if you're feeling rich.

The most atmospheric way to reach the far north of the country is the Inlandsbanan rail line (see box, p.1171) although you can also get here via regular rail services from Stockholm and by air to Kiruna. Flights also run to the east coast city of Luleå, which has a direct train to Kiruna and Abisko.

THE ARCTIC CIRCLE AND JOKKMOKK

After a brief stop at Arvidsjaur, the Inlandsbanan finally crosses the **Artic Circle** at a point 7km south of Jokkmokk. Painted white rocks indicate this latitudinal milestone making it an essential photo stop; killjoys will point out that the real Arctic Circle (66°33) has shifted a further kilometre north owing to changes in the earth's orbit but no one seems to care. **JOKKMOKK** itself is a welcome oasis after hours on a tiny train. The town is a renowned handicraft centre, with a Sámi educational college keeping the language and culture alive and a lively winter market. The **Ájtte Museum** (end April to end Sept Mon–Sat 9am–6pm & Sun 10am–4pm; otherwise Tues–Fri 10am–4pm & Sat 10am–2pm; 70kr) on Kyrkogatan is the place to bone up on Sámí culture. The permanent exhibitions house vivid Sámi costumes and a fascinating section on how the industrial age has affected the region and its people. Jokkmokk's **Great Winter Market** (first Thurs, Fri & Sat of Feb) is the best and busiest time to visit; you'll need to book accommodation a good six months in advance.

Information about the town is in the **tourist office** at Stortorget 4 (mid-June to mid-Aug daily 9am–6pm; mid-Aug to mid-June Mon–Fri 8.30am–noon & 1–4pm; ⓣ0971/222 50, ⓔturist@jokkmokk.se, ⓦwww.turismjokkmokk.se). If you're washed out from the long journey to get here, try Jokkmokk Camping Center (ⓣ0971/12370, ⓦwww.jokkmokkcampingcenter.com, camping 120kr, cabins 500kr), which has family-friendly cabins and heated swimming pools in a lakeside location 3km east of Jokkmokk. A good alternative is the STF **hostel** at Åsgatan 20 (ⓣ0971/559 77, ⓦwww.jokkmokkhostel.com), housed in a rather grand 1920s house with a sauna in the basement. Dorms 175kr, rooms 365kr. The new camping spaces here are charged at just 75kr per person per night, but there's only room for four tents.

KIRUNA

With its nearby airport, rail connections to Norway and proximity to the *ICEHOTEL* (see box below), **Kiruna**, 145km north of the Arctic Circle has become the unlikely tourist hub for Swedish Lapland. The town is dominated by its iron ore mine, the world's largest, and became a focus during World War II, when the supply of iron was fought over by the Germans and Allies. More recently, Kiruna achieved modest international fame after it was announced that portions of the town would have to be moved 4km northwest, to avoid them collapsing into the **mine** beneath.

What to see and do

Guided tours of the **mine** (daily 3pm; book at the tourist office; 295kr), run by mining company LKAB, are truly fascinating. Descending more than 500m below the surface, you'll learn about the mine's history and the techniques used for extracting iron ore.

Another unusual day-trip from Kiruna is to **Esrange**, a civilian space centre that launches and monitors satellites, and conducts research into climate change (daily tours in English, 8.30am; book at the tourist office; adults 650kr, students 600kr). Time your visit right and you might even see a rocket launch.

Arrival and information

Air Kiruna's airport is 10km from the city. An airport bus (50kr, cash only) runs during the summer and winter seasons; otherwise take a shared taxi (350kr/car).

Train The train station is at the western edge of town, on Bangårdsvägen. It's a 10min uphill walk into the centre from here.

Bus The bus station is at the top of Skolgatan, just across the road from the tall clock tower.

THE ICEHOTEL

If you've made it this far north, a visit to Sweden's world-famous **ICEHOTEL** (ⓦwww.icehotel.com; bus #501) 17km west of Kiruna in the small village of Jukkasjärvi, is a tempting prospect. Although the hotel operates year-round, the obvious time to come is December to April when the fairytale-like ice structure is in place; a visitor pass (325kr) allows you a look inside the rooms.

If you can stump up around 4000kr for a room, you could consider spending a night in its igloo-like conditions; temperatures hover around –5°C to –8°C although you'll be toasty warm, wrapped up tight in an army sleeping bag and lying on reindeer skins. You can also stay in the hotel's regular, heated chalets (winter prices start at 1250kr per person per night with large discounts in summer).

Tourist office Right in the town centre, on the main square at Lars Janssonsgatan 17 (Mon–Fri 8.30am–5/6pm, Sat till 3/4pm, Sun till 4pm; ⓣ0980/188 80, ⓦwww.lappland.se).

Accommodation

Camp Ripan Campingvägen 5 ⓣ0980/630 00, ⓦwww.ripan.se/en. Family-oriented campsite with an on-site restaurant, sauna and swimming pool. Between December and April you can even rent an igloo for the night. Camping 155k/person, doubles 995kr.

Kiruna Vandrarhem Bergmästaregatan 7 ⓣ0980/171 95, ⓦwww.kirunahostel.com. Sociable STF hostel just around the corner from the bus station, with TV, sauna and kitchen facilities. Breakfast costs 70kr. Dorms 200kr, singles 440kr, doubles 500kr.

Yellow House Hantverkaregatan 25 ⓣ0980/137 50, ⓦwww.yellowhouse.nu. Popular independent hostel across not one but two yellow houses. Advance booking recommended in summer. Dorms 170kr, singles 350kr.

Eating and drinking

Manuella Vänortsgatan 2. The pizzas here are good, but the huge falafel wraps (drizzled in garlic sauce) are the best reason to visit.

Momma's Steakhouse Lars Janssonsgatan 15. Rowdy bar-restaurant in the *Scandic Hotel* with live music on Wed. Busy on weekends, so show up early if you want a seat. Until midnight on weekdays, 2am on Fri & Sat, 11pm on Sun.

Thai Kitchen Vänortsgatan 8. A friendly little Thai place near the tourist office, where you can enjoy a fresh green curry for less than 80kr.

Moving on

Train Narvik, Norway (3 daily; 3hr); Stockholm (2 daily; 17hr).

ABISKO AND THE KUNGSLEDEN TRAIL

Sweden's premier trek, the **Kungsleden** (King's Trail) winds through 500km of wilderness from Abisko, 98km west of Kiruna, south to Hemavan. Mountain huts are spaced every 10–20km along the route to allow for a day's walk between them. The northern section of the trail between Abisko and Kebnekaise (86km) is the most popular and well worth tackling if you have around a week to spare. **Absiko**, just an hour and twenty minutes by train from Kiruna on the Narvik line, is considered one of the world's best places for watching the Northern Lights. The eco-conscious *Abisko Turiststation* (ⓦwww.abisko.nu; dorms 260kr, double rooms 139kr), is the starting point for the trail, and the slopes around the outpost are popular with skiers and snowboarders alike. For more information on each section of the trail visit ⓦwww.stfturist.se.

Switzerland

HIGHLIGHTS

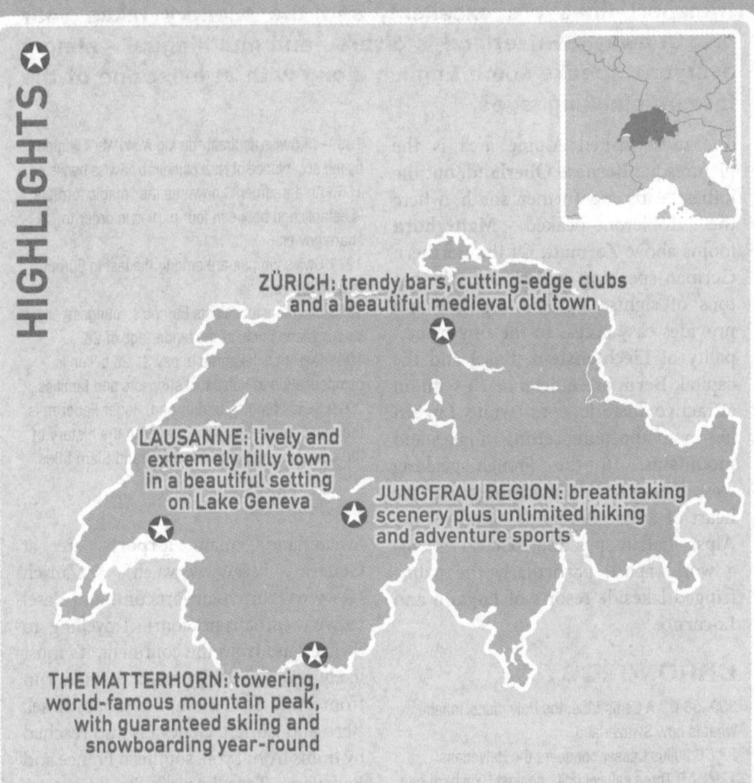

ROUGH COSTS

DAILY BUDGET Basic €45 /occasional treat €70

DRINK Beer €5

FOOD Fondue €20

HOSTEL/BUDGET HOTEL €20/€70

TRAVEL Train: Geneva–Zürich €63; bus St Moritz–Lugano €54

FACT FILE

POPULATION 7.5 million

AREA 41,293 sq km

LANGUAGES German, French, Italian, Romansch

CURRENCY Swiss Franc (Fr.)

CAPITAL Bern (population: 131,791)

INTERNATIONAL PHONE CODE ⓣ41

Introduction

All the quaint stereotypes are true – cheese, chocolate, clocks, obsessive punctuality – but there's much more to Switzerland than this. The major cities are cosmopolitan and vibrant, transport links are excellent, and the scenery takes your breath away. Switzerland is diverse and multilingual – almost everyone speaks some English along with at least one of the four official languages.

The most visited Alpine area is the picturesque **Bernese Oberland**, but the loftiest Alps are further south, where the Toblerone-peaked **Matterhorn** looms above **Zermatt**. Of the northern German-speaking cities, **Zürich** has tons of sightseeing and nightlife and provides easy access to the tiny principality of **Liechtenstein. Basel** and the capital, **Bern**, are quieter, each with an attractive historic core, while **Luzern** lies in an appealing setting of lakes and mountains. In the French-speaking west, **Geneva** and **Lausanne** are at the heart of Suisse-Romande. South of the Alps, Italian-speaking **Ticino** seems a world apart, particularly the palm-fringed lakeside resorts of **Lugano** and **Locarno**.

CHRONOLOGY

800–58 BC A Celtic tribe, the Helvetians, inhabit what is now Switzerland.
58 BC Julius Caesar conquers the Helvetians.
1291 AD Three valleys unite against Habsburg rule, forming the basis of the Swiss Confederation.
1388 The Swiss Confederation defeats the Habsburgs.
1536 Protestant Reformation in Switzerland led by Calvin.
1719 Liechtenstein becomes an independent principality of the Holy Roman Empire.
1803 The Swiss start to produce chocolate.
1803–15 Nine cantons join the confederation, including most of the non-German-speaking ones, giving the country's present frontiers.
1864 Red Cross founded in Geneva.
1914 Switzerland remains neutral during World War II.
1920 The League of Nations headquarters are based in Geneva.
1921 Liechtenstein adopts Swiss currency.
1939–45 Swiss neutrality during World War II tainted by the acceptance of Nazi plunder by Swiss banks.
1959 An agreement known as the "magic formula" is established between four parties in order to share power.
1971 Swiss women are among the last in Europe to gain the vote.
1993 Liechtenstein elects Europe's youngest leader, Mario Frick, at the tender age of 28.
1998 Swiss banks agree to pay $1.25 billion in compensation to Holocaust survivors and families.
2010 Swiss tennis number one, Roger Federer, is the most successful male player in the history of the game, having won sixteen Grand Slam titles.

ARRIVAL

Switzerland's main **airports** are at Geneva (Ⓦwww.gva.ch), Zürich (Ⓦwwww.zurich-airport.com) and Basel (Ⓦwww.euroairport.com). Travelling to Switzerland from the continent, it's most likely you'll arrive by **train**. Services run from Paris to Geneva, Lausanne, Basel, Bern and Zürich. Geneva is also reached by trains from Lyon, southern France and Barcelona. Travelling via Strasbourg, or southwestern Germany, you'll probably arrive at Basel. Zürich is the main hub for trains from Bavaria, Austria, Italy and Eastern Europe. The most scenic way to arrive is by **ferry**, crossing Lake Maggiore from Italy, Lake Geneva from France or Lake Constance from Germany.

GETTING AROUND

Public transport is comprehensive. **Train** travel is comfortable, hassle-free and extremely scenic, with many mountain routes attractions in their own right. The national network, run by

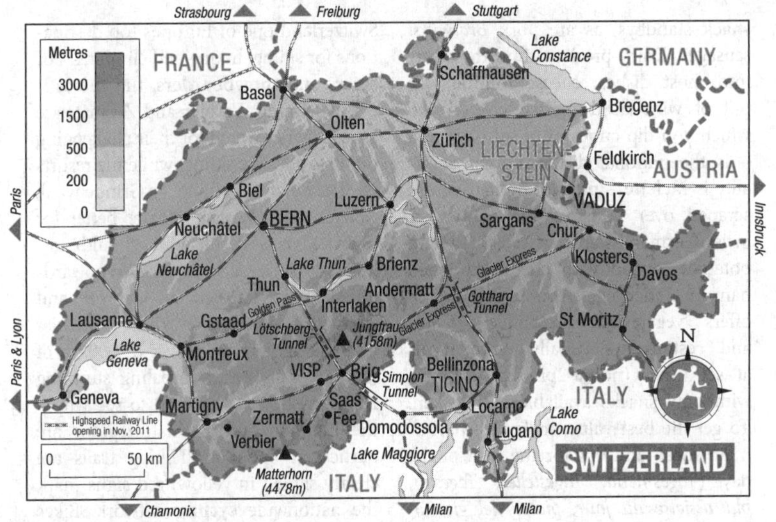

SBB-CFF-FFS, is seamlessly integrated with the many routes, especially Alpine lines, operated by local companies. **Buses** take over where the rails run out – generally yellow postbuses, departing from train station forecourts. InterRail, Eurail and various Swiss Passes give free travel on SBB and most minor lines, plus discounts on boats, cable cars and mountain railways (specified in the text as "IR", "ER" and "SP" respectively). Bargain Supersaver tickets are available up to two weeks in advance at Ⓦwww.rail.ch. Postbuses are free with Swiss Passes – although some routes over Alpine passes command a supplement – but not with Eurail or InterRail. There are also regional passes such as the Tell Pass in central Switzerland (Ⓦwww.tell-pass.ch) or the Léman-Alpes Regional Pass (Ⓦwww.goldenpass.ch), both giving some days of free travel and others at half-price. Most lake **ferries** run only from April to October, and may duplicate routes covered more cheaply and quickly by rail.

ACCOMMODATION

Accommodation, though admittedly expensive, is nearly always excellent. Tourist offices can often book rooms for free; some have boards (with a courtesy phone) on the street or at the train station, giving hotel details. When you check in, ask for a **guest card**, giving free local transport and other discounts. A **hostel** (*Jugendherberge*; *Auberge de Jeunesse*; *Albergo/Ostello per la Gioventù*) represents great value for money (book ahead June–Sept). **HI hostels** (Ⓦwww.youthhostel.ch) are universally excellent, with doubles as well as small dorms. Non-HI members pay Fr.6 extra. A rival group known as Swiss Backpackers (Ⓦwww.backpacker.ch) has lively hostels that are less institutional, often centrally located and priced to compete; they're specified "SB" in the text. Typically a dorm bed costs around Fr.30. **Campsites** are clean and well equipped, charging about Fr.8 per person plus Fr.8–12 per pitch and per vehicle. Many require an international camping carnet. Camping outside official sites is illegal. **Hotels** are first-rate, but will stretch your budget; shared-bath doubles start around Fr.90 (average Fr.110), en suites around Fr.135.

FOOD AND DRINK

Eating out in Switzerland can punch a hole in your wallet. Burgers, pizza slices, kebabs and falafel are universal

snack standbys, as are pork *Bratwürst* sausages. Dairy products find their way into most dishes: cheese **fondue** – a pot of wine-laced molten cheese into which you dip cubes of bread or potato – is the national dish. Another speciality is **raclette** – piquant molten cheese scraped over potatoes and pickles. A Swiss-German staple is **rösti**, grated potatoes topped with cheese, chopped ham or a fried egg. Almost everywhere offers vegetarian alternatives. **Cafés** and **restaurants** usually serve meals at set times (noon–2pm & 6–10pm), with only snacks available in between. To get the best value, make lunch your main meal, and opt for the dish of the day (*Tagesmenu*, *Tagesteller*, *Tageshit*; *plat/assiette du jour*; *piatto del giorno*) – substantial nosh for around Fr.18 or less. The same meal in the evening, or choosing à la carte anytime, can cost double. Manor department stores, and some Coop or Migros supermarkets have excellent-value self-service restaurants: a small/large plate costs about Fr.9/15, with as much fresh salad or hot food as you can pile onto it. There are supermarkets in most large stations, which open late seven days a week. Cafés are open from breakfast till midnight or 1am and often sell alcohol; **bars** and **pubs** tend to open for late-afternoon and evening business only. **Beers** are invariably excellent, at Fr.5–8 for a glass (*e'Schtange*, *une pression*, *una birra*). Even the simplest places have **wine**, most affordably as *Offene Wein*, *vin ouvert*, *vino aperto* – a handful of house reds and whites chalked up on a board (small glass Fr.4–5).

CULTURE AND ETIQUETTE

It's not customary to **tip**; if you're impressed by the service, just round up your bill to the nearest franc.

SPORTS AND ACTIVITIES

Spectacular scenery and an excellent transport infrastructure combine to make Switzerland one of Europe's top destinations for skiing, hiking and climbing. For **skiers and snowboarders,** the choice is overwhelming: Verbier and Zermatt are especially renowned for their challenging on- and off-piste skiing, while the resorts of the Jungfrau region – Grindelwald, Mürren and Wengen – cater better for intermediates. A lift pass should cost Fr.50–65 for a day or Fr.275 upwards for six days. Glaciers at Saas Fee and Zermatt allow summer skiing. The Swiss love hiking, and with over 65,000km of marked trails, most revealing stunning Alpine vistas, it's not hard to see why – the Jungfrau and Zermatt regions are particularly popular. Hiking trails are clearly signed in yellow; red signs mark the nationwide **cycling** network. Bikes (and trailers, e-bikes etc) can be rented from main stations, and in summer the largest cities also have free bike schemes (such as Zuri-rollt and Genèveroule). Ask at tourist offices or consult Ⓦwww.myswitzerland.com for routes and tips.

COMMUNICATIONS

Main **post offices** open Monday to Friday 7.30am to noon and 1.30 to 6.30pm,

ADVENTURE SPORTS IN SWITZERLAND

With its landscape of mountains, glaciers, deep gorges and fast-flowing rivers, Switzerland is ideal for **adventure sports.** Dozens of companies, in all the main resorts, offer activities through the summer, such as **canyoning** (Fr.110/half-day), **river-rafting** (Fr.100/half-day), **bungee-jumping** (Fr.130 from 85m; Fr.170 from 134m), **zorbing** (rolling down a mountainside strapped inside a giant plastic sphere; Fr.125) and **flying fox** (gliding across a chasm on a rope; Fr.40). **Hang-gliding** (Fr.220), **paragliding** (Fr.160) and **skydiving** from 4000m (Fr.400) can all be done alone or in tandem with an instructor.

SWITZERLAND AND LIECHTENSTEIN ONLINE

Ⓦwww.myswitzerland.com Tourist office site – vast, detailed and authoritative.
Ⓦwww.postbus.ch Details of the postbus network, including Alpine routes.
Ⓦwww.swissinfo.org News database in English, with good links.
Ⓦwww.tourismus.li The Liechtenstein tourist board.

Saturday 8 to 11am. Most **public phones** take phonecards (*taxcards*), available from post offices and news kiosks, as well as credit cards; some take Swiss and euro coins. Kiosks sell discount cards for cheap international calls. **Wi-fi** internet access (known as WLAN) is widespread, at cafés (Fr.4–12/hr) or free at many hotels and hostels.

EMERGENCIES

You'll have to pay **hospital** (*Spital, hôpital, ospedale*) bills up-front and claim expenses back later. Every district has one local **pharmacy** (*Apotheke, pharmacie, farmacia*) open outside normal hours; each pharmacy has a sign telling you where the nearest open one is.

INFORMATION

Tourist offices (*Verkehrsverein* or *Tourismus*; *Office du Tourisme*; *Ente Turistico*) are invariably located near the train station and always extremely useful. Most staff speak English. Opening hours in smaller towns involve a long lunch and can be limited at weekends and out of season. All have accommodation and transport lists, and maps. *Swiss Backpacker News* (Ⓦwww.backpacker.ch) is an excellent free paper, widely available.

MONEY AND BANKS

Both Switzerland and Liechtenstein use the **Swiss franc** (CHF or Fr.), divided into 100 Rappen (Rp), centimes or centisimi (c). There are coins of 5c, 10c, 20c, 50c, Fr.1, Fr.2 and Fr.5, and notes of Fr.10, Fr.20, Fr.50, Fr.100, Fr.200 and Fr.1000. It's easiest to **change money** in train stations. **Banks** usually open Monday to Friday 8.30am to 4.30pm; some in cities and resorts also open Saturday 9am to 4pm. **Post offices** give a similar exchange rate to banks, and **ATMs** are everywhere. Many shops and services, especially in tourist hubs, accept euros. At the time of writing, €1 was roughly equal to Fr.1.20, US$1 to Fr.0.85 and £1 to Fr. 1.37.

EMERGENCY NUMBERS

Police Ⓣ117; Fire Ⓣ118; Ambulance Ⓣ144.

OPENING HOURS AND HOLIDAYS

Shop hours are Monday to Friday 9am to 7pm, Saturday 8.30am to 4pm, sometimes with a lunch break and earlier closing in smaller towns. **Museums** and attractions generally close on Monday. Almost everything is closed on **public holidays**: January 1, Good Friday and Easter Monday, Ascension Day, Whit Monday, December 25 and 26. In Switzerland, shops and banks close for all or part of the national holiday (Aug 1) and on a range of local holidays. Liechtenstein keeps May 1 as a public holiday, and August 15 as the national holiday.

STUDENT AND YOUTH DISCOUNTS

With an ISIC card, you can take advantage of student discounts (up to 50 percent) at almost all **museums** and galleries. Although there is no student discount on cable-car tickets, during the winter season many resorts offer a youth discount on **lift passes**.

Lake Geneva

French-speaking Switzerland, or Suisse Romande, occupies the western third of the country, comprising the shores of **Lake Geneva** (Lac Léman) and the hills and lakes to the north. **Geneva**, at the southwestern tip of the lake, was once a haven for freethinkers from cross Europe; now it's a city of diplomats and big business, but you'll see its more relaxed side by the lake on a warm day. Halfway around the lake, **Lausanne** is full of young people; it's a cultured, energetic town acclaimed as the skateboarding capital of Europe. Further east is the stunning medieval **Château de Chillon**, which drew Byron and the Romantic poets. **Mont Blanc**, Western Europe's highest mountain (4807m), is visible from Geneva, while **Lausanne** has breathtaking views across the water to the French Alps. On a sunny day, the train ride around the beautiful northern shore is memorably scenic, but the excellent boat service (ER & SP free, IR 50 percent discount; Ⓦwww.cgn.ch) brings home the full grandeur of the setting.

GENEVA

The struggle of **GENEVA** (Genève) for independence is inextricably linked with Puritanism. By 1602, when it won independence from Savoy, the city's religious zeal had painted it as the "Protestant Rome". Geneva joined the Swiss Confederation only in 1815, with a reputation for joylessness which it still struggles to shake off. Today, there is plenty for budget travellers, with its beautiful Old Town and many galleries.

What to see and do

The **Rive Gauche**, on the south bank, takes in a grid of waterfront streets comprising the main shopping and business districts, and above them the Old Town. Further south is **Carouge**, characterized by artisans' shops and picturesque Italianate architecture. Behind the grand hotels lining the northern **Rive Droite** waterfront is the main station and the cosmopolitan (and in places sleazy) **Les Pâquis** district, full of cheap ethnic eateries. Further north are the dozens of international bodies headquartered in Geneva, including the UN.

Jet d'Eau and the Old Town

On the Rive Gauche, beyond the ornamental flowerbeds of the Jardin Anglais, erupts the roaring 140-metre-high plume of Geneva's trademark **Jet d'Eau**. Nearby is the main thoroughfare of the **Old Town**, the steep, cobbled Grande Rue. Here, among the jewellery shops and galleries, you'll find the atmospheric seventeenth-century **Hôtel de Ville** and the arcaded armoury. A block away is the late-Romanesque **Cathédrale St-Pierre** (June–Sept Mon–Sat 9.30am–6.30pm Sun noon–6.30pm; Oct–May Mon–Sat 10am–5.30pm Sun noon–5.30pm), with an incongruous Neoclassical portal and a plain, soaring interior. Tucked behind the cathedral in the eighteenth-century Maison Mallet, the **Musée Internationale de la Réforme** (Tues–Sun 10am–5pm; Fr.13; Ⓦwww.musee-reforme.ch), documents Geneva's contribution to the Reformation. Just beyond is the hub of the Old Town, **Place du Bourg-de-Four**, a picturesque split-level square ringed by cafés. Alleys wind down from here to a lovely terrace, the Promenade de la Treille, with the world's longest wooden bench (126m). Beneath this is the austere **Wall of the Reformation** (1909–17), with statues of the leading reformist preachers, in the university park.

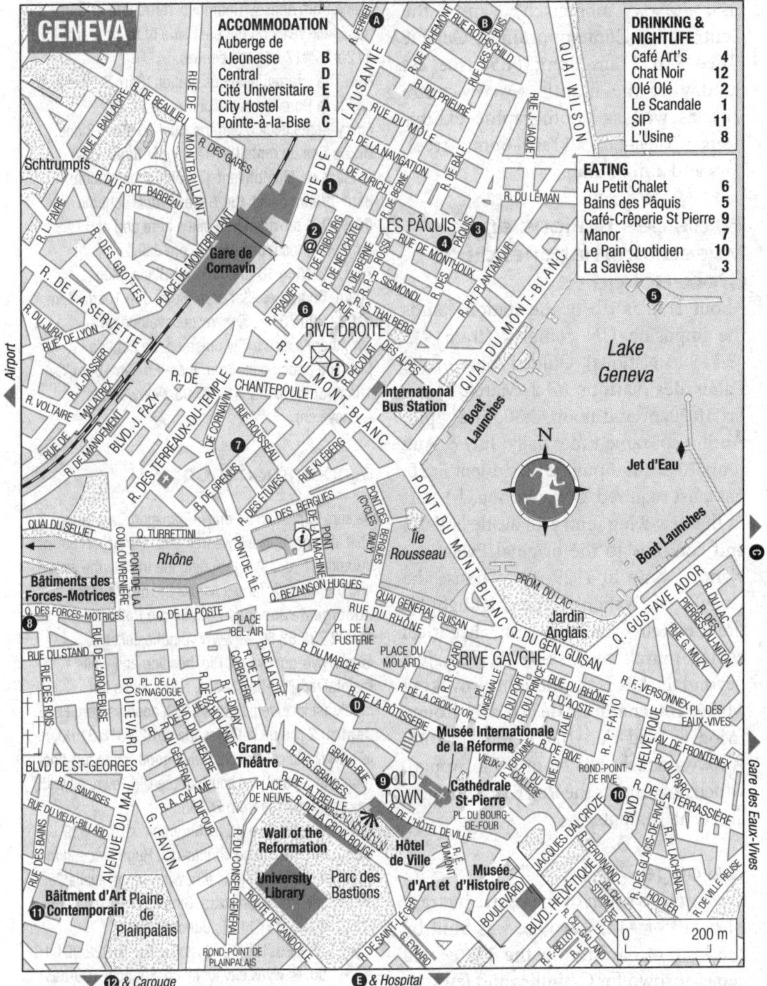

The Musée d'Art et d'Histoire

Just east of the Old Town is the gigantic **Musée d'Art et d'Histoire**, 2 rue Charles Galland (Tues–Sun 10am–6pm; free; Ⓦwww.ville-ge.ch/mah). The first floor houses a superb collection of armour and weaponry, fine panelled interiors and silverware; upstairs the art collection includes Konrad Witz's famous altar-piece, made for the cathedral in 1444, with Christ and the fishermen transposed to Lake Geneva. The basement holds a huge archeological collection.

Bâtiment d'Art Contemporain

A former factory west of the Old Town at 10 rue des Vieux-Grenadiers, the **Bâtiment d'Art Contemporain** now houses top-quality contemporary art galleries, notably **MAMCO** (Tues–Fri noon–6pm, Sat & Sun 11am–6pm; first Sunday of month free; Fr.8, students

Fr.6; ⓦwww.mamco.ch) and the Centre d'Art Contemporain de Genève (Tues–Sun 11am–6pm; Fr.5, free 1st Sunday of the month; ⓦwww.centre.ch), as well as photographic exhibitions (Tues–Sun 11am–6pm; free), bars and a nightclub.

Palais des Nations and Museé International de la Croix-Rouge

About 1km north of the station stands the imposing UN complex (tram #13 or #15 to Nations). Guided tours of the **Palais des Nations** (Oct–March Mon–Fri 10.30am and noon, 2.30pm & 4pm; April–Sept same times daily; July & Aug tours 10.30am–5pm; Fr.12, student Fr.10; passport required; ⓦwww.unog.ch) start in the new wing (entry 14 av. de la Paix) and continue to the original Palais des Nations, built in 1929–38 to house the League of Nations. The highlight is the Council Chamber, with allegorical ceiling murals by José-Maria Sert. Just beyond the UN is the thought-provoking **Musée International de la Croix-Rouge** (Mon & Wed–Sun 10am–5pm; Fr.10/5; ⓦwww.micr.ch; bus #8 or #F to Appia), which documents the Red Cross's origins and achievements.

Carouge

Ten minutes south of the centre by tram #12, #13 or #14, **Carouge** was built by the king of Sardinia in the 1750s as a separate town for Catholics and Jews. Its low Italianate houses and leafy streets now house fashion designers and small galleries, and the area's reputation as an outpost of tolerance and hedonism lives on in its numerous cafés and music bars.

Arrival and information

Air From the airport, 5km northwest, trains and buses #5 and #10 run into the city.
Train The main station, Cornavin, lies at the head of rue du Mont-Blanc in the city centre. Trains from Paris, Lyon and southern France arrive in a separate French section, while local French trains from Annecy/Chamonix terminate at Gare des Eaux-Vives on the east side of town (tram #12/#16/#17 into the centre).
Bus The international bus station (Gare Routière) is on Place Dorcière in the centre
Ferry Boats dock along the Quai du Mont-Blanc.
Bikes Can be rented (Fr.12/day, Fr.8/half-day) at Place de Montbrillant 17 behind the station; 8am–6/9pm daily); the *Genève'roule* scheme (May–Oct) provides free bikes here and at temporary locations (9am–7pm daily).
Tourist office 18 rue du Mont-Blanc (Mon 10am–6pm, Tues–Sat 9am–6pm, Sun 10am–4pm; ⓣ022 909 70 00, ⓦwww.genevatourism.ch); there's also a city office on the Pont de la Machine (Mon noon–6pm, Tues–Fri 9am–6pm, Sat 10am–5pm; ⓣ022 418 20 00, ⓦwww.ville-geneve.ch).

Accommodation

Be sure to pick up a Geneva Transport Card when checking in – this allows free public transport for the duration of your stay including the train to the airport and the *mouette* ferries across the mouth of the lake.
Auberge de Jeunesse (HI) 30 rue Rothschild ⓣ022 732 62 60, ⓦwww.youthhostel.ch & ⓦwww.yh-geneva.ch. Big, bustling and well-maintained 360-bed hostel. No kitchens but breakfast included. Dorms Fr.29, doubles from Fr.85.
Central 2 rue de la Rôtisserie ⓣ022 818 81 00, ⓦwww.hotelcentral.ch. Quiet, good-value top-floor rooms in a hotel just south of the Old Town, all with balcony. Doubles from Fr.105.
Cité Universitaire 46 av Miremont ⓣ022 839 22 22, ⓦwww.unige.ch/cite-uni. Huge place 3km south of the centre (bus #3), with rooms available July–Sept. Breakfast extra. Singles Fr.62 (student Fr.52); doubles Fr.110 (student Fr.100).
City Hostel (SB) 2 rue Ferrier ⓣ022 901 15 00, ⓦwww.cityhostel.ch. Friendly 100-bed backpacker place near the station. No meals, but each corridor shares a kitchen. Dorm beds Fr.32–37.50, doubles Fr.88.
Pointe-à-la-Bise ⓣ022 752 12 96, ⓦwww.campingtcs.ch. Lakeside site in Vésanaz, 7km northeast (by a charming nature reserve); bus #E or #G. April–Sept. Fr.9.20/person, plus Fr.14.20/tent; also bungalows (Fr.120 for four, Fr.80 for two out of peak).

Eating

Au Petit Chalet 17 rue de Berne. Unpretentious place for fondues and rösti (Fr.19); also good pizzas for Fr.22. Closed Mon.

Bains des Pâquis 30 quai du Mont-Blanc. Popular café-bar at the lakefront swimming area. Great spot to soak up some sun. Breakfast 8–11.30am, then *plat du jour* (Fr.12). Daily 8am–9pm.
Café-Crêperie St Pierre place de la Taconnerie 6. With a terrace facing the cathedral, this little place serves crêpes (Fr.15.50–19.50), salads (Fr.8–18), or simply enjoy a beer or coffee.
Manor 6 rue Cornavin. Deli counters on the ground floor of this department store sell good takeaway panini and ciabattas (Fr.6.50), pizza slices (Fr.4) and curries (Fr.4). Mon–Sat 8.30am–6/9pm.
Le Pain Quotidien 21 bd Helvétique. Homely café with delicious pastries (Fr.4), sandwiches (Fr.9–16), salads, quiche or pasta, plus a range of newspapers. To 6pm daily.
La Savièse 20 rue des Pâquis ⓣ022 732 8330. You can choose from lasagne and vegetarian dishes for Fr.22, but the speciality here is fantastic fondues at Fr.23. This friendly restaurant is great for groups; book for weekend nights. Mon–Fri all day, Sat & Sun evenings only.

Drinking and nightlife

Bars

Café Art's 17 rue des Pâquis. Café-bar with a relaxed bohemian feel. Good simple food, beer Fr.8 for half a litre, cocktails Fr.15. Open until 2am daily.
Chat Noir 13 rue Vautier, Carouge ⓦwww.chatnoir.ch. Bar and cellar venue with DJs and live music (anything from world to techno). Tues–Sat 6pm–4am.
Olé Olé 11 rue de Fribourg. Tapas bar with personality, offering cocktails at Fr.15, glasses of wine at Fr.5 and bottles of beer at Fr.8. Chalk boards list a host of tapas dishes for Fr.10 plus salads and burgers. Open until 2am; closed Sun.
Le Scandale 24 rue de Lausanne ⓦwww.lescandale.ch. Funky bar with comfy armchairs and DJs several nights a week. It also serves food; dish of the day Fr.17 and drinks from Fr.5. Tues–Fri 11am–2am, Sat & Mon 5pm–2am.

Clubs

SIP 10 rue des Vieux Grenadiers ⓦwww.lasip.ch. Former factory with hip interior and dynamic, wide-ranging programme; Thurs–Sat 10pm–4/5am.
L'Usine 4 Place des Volontaires ⓦusine.ch. Converted factory hosting a plethora of arts and music events. *Zoo* (ⓦwww.lezoo.ch) runs club nights (hip-hop, breakbeat, electronica) and *leREZ* puts on gigs.

Entertainment

Cinema In July and Aug films are screened on the lakeside Quai Gustave-Ador (Fr.17; ⓦwww.orangecinema.ch). Two multiplexes, Rialto at bd James-Fazy 33 and Rex at rue Confedération 8, show recent blockbusters for Fr.18. Cine Bio on Place du Marché, Carouge is a charming arthouse cinema (Fr.11–16.50; ⓦwww.cinema-bio.ch).

Shopping

Carouge A good choice for affordable and whimsical shopping; it's crammed with cute boutiques and hosts a colourful market (Wed & Sat).
Flea market At Plainpalais near the Old Town pick up anything from old records and retro kitchenware to gemstones (Wed & Sat).

Directory

Consulates Australia, 2 chemin des Fins ⓣ022 799 91 00; Canada, 5 av. de l'Ariana ⓣ022 919 92 00; New Zealand, 2 chemin des Fins ⓣ022 929 03 50; US, 7 rue Versonnex ⓣ022 840 51 60. Embassies are in Bern.
Exchange At the train station (Mon–Sat 7am–8pm, Sun 8am–5.50pm).
Hospital Hôpitaux Universitaires, 2 rue Gabrielle-Perret-Gentil ⓣ022 372 81 20.
Internet Charly's Checkpoint, 7 rue de Fribourg; 15min Fr.1 (Mon–Sat 9am–midnight, Sun 1–11pm).
Left luggage At the train station (4.30am–12.45am; Fr.4/7); lockers 24hr, Fr.5.
Post office 18 rue du Mont-Blanc. Mon–Fri 7.30am–6pm, Sat 9am–4pm.
Pharmacy Amavita, at the train station (Mon–Sat 7am–11pm, Sun 10am–11pm).

Moving on

Train Barcelona (1 daily; 9hr 30min); Basel (hourly; 2hr 40min); Bern (every 30min; 1hr 45min); Lausanne (every 15min; 35min); Lyon (10 daily; 1hr 40min); Marseille (2 daily; 3hr 45min); Milan (4 daily; 4hr); Paris (6–9 daily; 3hr 5min); Zürich (every 30min; 2hr 45min).
Ferry Lausanne (1–2 daily; 3hr 35min).

LAUSANNE

LAUSANNE is attractive and vibrant, set on a succession of south-facing terraces above Lake Geneva, with the Old Town at the top, the train station and commercial districts in the middle, and the former fishing village of **Ouchy**, now prime territory for waterfront café-lounging and strolling, at the bottom.

Switzerland's biggest university makes this a lively, fun city. For chilled-out bars, head for the trendy **Flon** district.

What to see and do

To reach the central **Place St-François** from the train station, walk up the steep **rue du Petit-Chêne**, or take the metro to **Flon**; from the metro platforms, lifts raise you to the level of the giant Grand Pont, between **Place Bel-Air** on the left and Place St-François on the right. From here, Rue St-François drops down into a valley and up again to the cobbled **Place de la Palud**, an ancient, fountained square flanked by the Renaissance town hall.

The Cathedral and around

From Place de la Palud the medieval Escaliers du Marché lead up to the **Cathedral** (Mon–Fri 7am–7pm, Sat & Sun 8am–7pm, winter closes 5.30pm; Ⓜ Bessières), a fine Romanesque-Gothic jumble. Opposite, in the former bishop's palace, is the **Musée Historique** (Tues–Thurs 11am–6pm, Fri–Sun 11am–5pm; also Mon July & Aug; Fr.8/ students free, 1st Sat of month free for all; Ⓦ www.lausanne.ch/mhl), covering the history of the canton of Vaud. Next door is the **MUDAC Musée de Design et d'Arts Appliqués Contemporains** (same hours as Musée Historique; Fr.10, students Fr.5; Ⓦ www.mudac.ch) displaying contemporary glass and temporary exhibitions upstairs. Lausanne suffered many medieval fires, and is the last city in Europe to keep alive the tradition of the **nightwatch**: every night, on the hour (10pm–2am), a sonorous-voiced civil servant calls from the cathedral tower "*C'est le guet; il a sonné l'heure*" ("This is the nightwatch; the hour has struck").

Collection de l'Art Brut

Ten minutes' walk west of Palud on Avenue Vinet (or bus #2, #3 or #21 to Beaulieu) is the **fascinating Collection de l'Art Brut**, 11 av des Bergières (Tues–Sun 11am–6pm; July & Aug also Mon same hours; Fr.10, students Fr.5; Ⓦ www.artbrut.ch). This unique gallery is devoted to utterly absorbing "outsider art".

Ouchy, the Olympic Museum and Museé de l'Elysée

Ouchy's waterfront hosts regular free music events all summer, and people come down here to do a spot of café sunbathing or blading (rent blades or skates from beside Ouchy metro). In a waterfront park just to the east sits Lausanne's vacuous **Olympic Museum** (daily 9am–6pm; Nov–March closed Mon; Fr.15, students Fr.10; Ⓦ www.olympic.org). Bypass it for the **Musée de l'Elysée**, an excellent photography museum in the same park (Tues–Sun 11am–6pm; Fr.8, students Fr.4, free on first Sat of month).

Information

Tourist office Lausanne has two tourist offices (Ⓣ 021 613 73 92, Ⓦ www.lausanne-tourisme.ch): one in the train station (daily 9am–7pm), the other facing Ouchy metro station (daily 9am–7pm; Oct–April closes 6pm; Ⓣ 021 013 73 01).

Accommodation

Camping Vidy Ⓣ 021 622 50 00, Ⓦ www.campinglausannevidy.ch. Bus #1/#2/#6 west to Maladière and walk 5min to this decent lakeside campsite

LAUSANNE FESTIVALS

Lausanne's big party is the free **Festival de la Cité** in early July (Ⓦ www.festivaldelacite.ch), featuring music, dance and drama on open-air stages in the Old Town. Late June is also a great time to visit, with the **Fête à Lausanne**, a weekend of fairground attractions, the **Chocolate Festival** (Ⓦ chocolate-festival.ch) of electronic music, and **the Fête de la Musique** (Ⓦ lausanne.ch/fetedelamusique).

with restaurant and supermarket. Bungalows available from Fr.56. Fr.8.50/person, plus Fr.15/tent. Open all year.

Jeunotel (HI) 36 chemin du Bois-de-Vaux ⓣ021 626 02 22, ⓦwww.youthhostel.ch/lausanne. Huge place beside *Vidy* campsite with four-bed dorms and rooms, plus cheap meals on request (Fr.13.40). Dorms Fr.36, doubles Fr.93.

Lausanne Guest House (SB) 4 chemin des Epinettes ⓣ021 601 80 00, ⓦwww.lausanne-guesthouse.ch. Fabulous, friendly hostel with lake views, kitchen, garden, four-bed dorms and rooms. Dorms Fr.37, rooms Fr.106.

Pension Bienvenue 2 rue du Simplon ⓣ021 616 29 86, ⓦwww.pension-bienvenue.ch. Respectable, women-only guesthouse behind the station. Long stays available. Singles Fr.55, doubles Fr.85.

Eating and drinking

Le Barbare 27 Escaliers du Marché. Perfect little café among the Old Town's rooftops. There's a sun-trap terrace for summer and it's cosy inside in winter. Pizza Fr.15, sandwich Fr.6.

Café Romand Place St-François (under Le Dynasty). Bustling, heartwarming place with cosy alcoves for beer, coffee or heavy Swiss fare. Mains Fr.17–30. Closed Sun.

Café Saint Francois Place St-François. Soak up the sun at this French-style café by the church; choose from its ever-changing lunch menu. Fr.17.50 and Fr.19, takeaway pastries for Fr.4. Until 7pm daily.

Laxmi 5 Escaliers du Marché. Indian restaurant offering all-you-can-eat buffet lunches for Fr.20 (vegetarian Fr.17); evening mains cost a little more. Closed Mon lunch & Sun.

Manora 17 Place St-François. Excellent self-service cafeteria, with a wide range of wholesome hot and cold food for Fr.12 or under. To 10pm daily.

Nightlife

Bars

Bleu Lézard 10 rue Jenni Enning ⓦwww.bleu-lezard.ch. Fashionable, lively café-bar with regular live music sets downstairs. Sun–Tues until 1am, Wed–Sat 3pm–5am.

Brasserie Au Château 1 Place du Tunnel ⓦwww.biereduchateau.ch. Bar with funky music and some tasty home-brewed beers. Daily 5pm to 2/4am.

Clubs

All clubs listed below are located in Flon.

D! Club Place Centrale ⓦwww.dclub.ch. Popular basement club playing house and drum 'n' bass. Wed–Sat, 11pm/midnight–5am.

Le Loft 1 Escaliers Bel-Air ⓦwww.loftclub.ch. Bar and club with a mixed programme, including popular electro nights. Free entry for women before midnight. Wed–Sat until 5am.

MAD (Moulin à Danse) 23 rue de Genève ⓦwww.mad.ch. Cutting-edge dance club with well-known DJs, plus a theatre, art galleries and alternative-style café; hub of the trendy Flon district. Daily 11pm–5am.

Le V.O. 11 Place du Tunnel. Unpretentious café-bar and live venue with regular jazz and DJ nights. Sun–Thurs 5pm–4am, Fri–Sat 5pm–5am.

Moving on

Train Basel (every 30min; 2hr 10min); Bern (every 30min; 1hr 10min); Geneva (every 15min; 35min); Milan (4 daily; 3hr 20min); Paris (5 daily; 3hr 40min); Zermatt (hourly, change at Visp; 3hr); Zürich (every 30min; 2hr 10min).

Ferry (mid-April to mid-Dec) Chillon (1 daily; 1hr 45min); Geneva (1–2 daily; 3hr 35min); Montreux (2–4 daily; 1hr 30min).

CHÂTEAU DE CHILLON

The highlight of a journey around Lake Geneva, or en route to Zermatt, is the spectacular thirteenth-century **Château de Chillon** (daily April–Sept 9am–7pm; March & Oct 9.30am–6pm; Nov–Feb 10am–5pm; Fr.12, students Fr.10; ⓦwww.chillon.ch), one of the best-preserved medieval castles in Europe. Take the hourly train to Veytaux-Chillon, or it's a 45-minute walk or a short ride on bus #1 east from

MONTREUX JAZZ FESTIVAL

The sleepy lakeside town of Montreux livens up during its star-studded **Montreux Jazz Festival** (ⓦwww.montreuxjazz.com), held in the first half of July. Over 45 years it's pulled in the likes of Miles Davis and Ray Charles, but "jazz" is now something of a misnomer; these days the festival features big-name acts from all types of popular music. Check online for tickets (Fr.65–240), or just join the street parties and free entertainment around the lake.

Montreux station (every 10min). Your first glimpse of the castle, jutting into the water and framed by craggy mountains, is simply unforgettable. A pamphlet directs you to gloomy dungeons where François Bonivard, a Genevan priest, was imprisoned from 1530 to 1536; the story captured the imagination of Lord Byron, who wrote his poem *The Prisoner of Chillon* after sailing here with Shelley in 1816. Upstairs you'll find grand halls, lavish bedchambers and dreamy lake views.

The Swiss heartland

The Mittelland – between Lake Geneva and Zürich, flanked by the Jura range to the north and the high Alps to the south – is a region of lakes, gentle hills and some higher peaks. There's a wealth of cultural and historical interest in the cities of **Basel**, **Luzern** and the federal capital, **Bern**. Wherever you are, the mountains are never more than a couple of hours away by train.

BASEL

Astride the Rhine where Switzerland, France and Germany touch, **BASEL** (Bâle in French) is a logical staging post en route north. Despite its pan-European location, the city has gained a reputation for insularity. Certainly, Basel feels like a working city; it's neither as picturesque as Bern or Luzern, nor as vibrant as Zürich. Yet it's a wealthy place and boasts first-rate museums and galleries, in addition to some superb contemporary architecture. It also holds a massive three-day **carnival** in February (ⓦwww.fasnacht.ch), beginning at 4am on the Monday after Mardi Gras.

TREAT YOURSELF

Au Violon Im Lohnhof 4 (ⓣ061 269 87 11, ⓦwww.au-violon.com). Comfortable, stylish Old Town hotel (once a prison), next to St Leonhard's Church. There are fourteen converted "cell rooms" (all en suite) or you can opt for a grander "police office" with great views over the Old Town. Single/double without breakfast, Fr.120/Fr.160.

What to see and do

The River Rhine curves through the city, flowing from east to north. On the south/west bank (1km north of the main station) is the historic Old Town, centred on **Barfüsserplatz**. Across the river, on the north bank lies **Kleinbasel**, historically scorned by the city's merchants as a working-class quarter. Nowadays, the steps down to the Rhine are a popular place to catch the sun.

Historisches Museum and the Münster

The city's pre-eminence in the fifteenth and sixteenth centuries is amply demonstrated in the **Barfüsserkirche**, home since 1894 to the **Historisches Museum** (Tues–Sun 10am–5pm; Fr.7, students Fr.5; free for the last hour daily and first Sun of the month); don't miss the sumptuous medieval tapestries hidden behind protective blinds. On a terrace between the river and the Historisches Museum the **Münster** (summer sits Mon–Fri 10am–5pm, Sat 10am–4pm, Sun 11.30am–5pm; winter Mon–Sat 11am–4pm, Sun 11.30am–4pm). Inside, in the north aisle, is the tomb of the Renaissance humanist Erasmus, and behind the church is the Pfalz terrace, perfect for a picnic.

Kunstmuseum and Museum für Gegenwartskunst

Just east of the Old Town at St Alban-Graben 16, you'll find Basel's

Kunstmuseum (Tues–Sun 10am–5pm; Fr.12 includes entry to Museum für Gegenwartskunst; free on 1st Sun of month), which has a dazzling array of twentieth-century art, plus an outstanding medieval collection, including many works by the Holbein family. Tucked away by the river, the **Museum für Gegenwartskunst** (Museum of Contemporary Art; Tues–Sun 11am–5pm; joint admission with Kunstmuseum) contains installations by Frank Stella and Joseph Beuys.

Museum Jean Tinguely

On the north bank of the Rhine at Paul Sacher-Anlage 2, the beautiful **Museum Jean Tinguely** (Tues–Sun 11am–7pm; Fr.15, students Fr.10; ⓦwww.tinguely.ch) is dedicated to one of Switzerland's best-loved artists. Tinguely used scrap metal, plastic and everyday junk to create room-sized Monty Pythonesque machines, veering between grotesque and comical, that – with the touch of a button – judder into life, clanking and squeaking.

Eating

Mr Wong Steinenvorstadt 3. Popular Asian fast-food joint just off Barfüsserplatz with noodle dishes from Fr.12.

Parterre Klybeckstr. 1. Lively Kleinbasel hangout, with busy outside terrace and a creative, vegetarian-friendly menu; mains Fr.19–23. Mon–Wed 10am–11pm, Thurs–Sat 10am–midnight, closed Sun.

Zum Roten Engel Andreasplatz. Busy little café serving cakes and light meals, in a pedestrianized cobbled square. It attracts a studenty clientele. Mon–Sat 9am–midnight, Sun 10am–10pm.

Drinking and nightlife

Bars

Eoipso Dornachstr. 192. Trendy, spacious industrial bar in a buzzing factory complex behind the train station. Closed Sun.

Fischerstube Rheingasse 45. Atmospheric Kleinbasel beer hall with an older clientele.

Clubs and live music

Atlantis Klosterberg 10 ⓦwww.atlan-tis.ch. Lounge-bar and restaurant; club nights Fri and Sat 11pm–4am. Closed Sun & Mon.

Bird's Eye Kohlenberg 20 ⓦwww.birdseye.ch. Basel's main jazz venue. Entry Fr.12. Tues–Sat from 8pm.

Kaserne Klybeckstr. 1b ⓦwww.kaserne-basel.ch. Alternative hangout with varied live music, theatre and dance programme. Becomes Basel's premier gay/lesbian meeting point on Tues. Events mainly on Thurs–Sat nights; closed July.

Moving on

Train Frankfurt (11 daily; 2hr 50min); Geneva (hourly; 2hr 45min); Interlaken (every 30min; 2hr); Lausanne (every 30min; 2hr 5min); Lugano (hourly; 3hr 45min); Luzern (2 hourly; 1hr 10min); Paris (5 daily; 3hr); Strasbourg (hourly; 1hr 10min–1hr 40min); Zürich (every 15min; 1hr).

LUZERN (LUCERNE)

An hour south of Basel is beautiful **LUZERN** (Lucerne), offering captivating mountain views, lake cruises and a picturesque medieval quarter.

What to see and do

To the right of the train station, you're greeted by the striking KKL concert hall; busy Pilatusstrasse is to the left with 100m along it the **Sammlung Rosengart gallery** (April–Oct daily 10am–6pm; Nov–March daily 11am–5pm; Fr.18, students Fr.10) with a superb collection of twentieth-century art, notably by Picasso and Klee. The alleyways of the Old Town span both riverbanks, linked by the fourteenth-century **Kapellbrücke**, a covered wooden bridge rebuilt after a fire in 1993; some of the seventeenth-century paintings fixed to its roof beams have been replaced by facsimiles. Northeast of the Old Town is **Löwenplatz**, dominated by the absorbing **Bourbaki Panorama** (Mon 1–5 pm, Tues–Sun 10am–5pm; Nov–March April–Oct; Mon 1–6pm, Tues–Sun 9am–6pm; Fr.8), a 110m by 10m circular mural, depicting the flight of General Bourbaki's 87,000-strong army into Switzerland during the Franco-Prussian War. Just off the square is the **Löwendenkmal**, a dying lion hewn out of a cliff-face to commemorate seven hundred Swiss mercenaries killed by French revolutionaries in 1792.

A pleasant 2km stroll east along the lakeside (or train, boat, or bus #6/#8/#24) lies the **Verkehrshaus** (summer daily 10am–6pm; winter daily 10am–5pm; Fr.28, or Fr.38 including IMAX cinema; ER 25 percent off; Ⓦwww.verkehrshaus.ch). This is the transport museum, a vast complex containing original space capsules, railway locomotives, cable cars and a planetarium.

Lake Luzern

You shouldn't leave Luzern without taking a trip on the lake (ER & SP free, IR 50 percent reduction; Ⓦwww.lakelucerne.ch), Switzerland's most beautiful and dramatic by far, the thickly wooded slopes rising sheer from the water.

Arrival and information

Train The station sits at the south end of the Seebrücke, facing the docks for boats on Lake Luzern.

Tourist Office Zentralstr. 5 (Mon–Fri 8.30am–5.30pm, Sat 9am–5pm, Sun 9am–1pm, May–Oct to 6.30pm daily, mid-June to mid-Sept to 7.30pm daily; Ⓣ041 227 17 17, Ⓦwww.luzern.org), on the west side of the railway station.

City transport Everything in the centre is easily reached on foot, but the Luzern Card (Fr.19/27/33 1/2/3 days), gives free bus and train travel within the city plus half-price admission to eleven museums. Bikes can be rented at the station (9.30am–7pm; Fr.25/half-day Fr.33/day) or at *Backpackers Lucerne*.

Accommodation

Backpackers Lucerne 42 Alpenquai Ⓣ041 360 04 20, Ⓦwww.backpackerslucerne.ch. A friendly place, with no breakfast but kitchen and bike rental, ten minutes' walk east from the station along the lake. Dorms Fr.32, doubles Fr.74.

Lido 19 Lidostr. Ⓣ041 370 2146 Ⓦwww.camping-international.ch. A shady lakeside site, open all year. Fr.10/person, plus Fr.10–25/tent; dorms Fr.25.

Tourist Hotel 12 Karliquai Ⓣ041 410 24 74, Ⓦwww.touristhotel.ch. Simple but clean and ideally sited. Rooms for up to six, most with balcony; washing machines. Singles Fr.118, doubles Fr.120.

Eating and drinking

There's a good range of cafés and restaurants on both sides of the river; Coop at the station sells picnic supplies (to 10pm daily).

Bourbaki Löwenplatz 11 As well as an arthouse cinema, there's a café-bar (serving panini and salads from Fr.7.50; 9am–6pm), and the *Angola* pasta & pizza restaurant, with a Fr.14 lunch menu (Mon–Sat 11am–10pm, Sun noon–9pm).

Café La Suisse Gerbergasse 11. A splendidly traditional café, with a dish of the day for Fr.16.50. Open daily 9/10am to midnight.

Café LUZ Bahnhofplatz. On the lake by the station, a lovely café with cheap food, such as würst, baked potatoes or salads (all from Fr.7), or ciabattas from Fr.10. From 7.30am daily.

Manora Weggisgasse 5. Excellent self-service cafeteria with a wide range of hot and cold food for Fr.12 or under. Mon–Wed 9am–6.30pm, Thurs & Fri 9am–9pm, Sat 8am–4pm.

Roadhouse Pilatusstr. 1. A lively pub facing the west side of the station. 7am–4/5am daily.

World Café In the KKL building, this has changing specials with a global twist from Fr.18. Daily 9am–8pm.

Moving on

Train Basel (2 hourly; 1hr 10min); Bern (hourly; 1hr); Interlaken (hourly; 2hr); Lausanne (hourly; 2hr 15min); Zürich (every 30min; 45min).

ENGELBERG

Under 50 minutes from Luzern by train is the picturesque Alpine resort of **ENGELBERG**, from where a revolving cable car (Fr.86 return; ER, IR & SP 50 percent reduction) serves the snowbound summit of Mount Titlis (3239m), the highest point in Central Switzerland (Ⓦwww.titlis.ch). Here you can hit the snow year-round, with countless rental deals for snowboards, as well as for mountain bikes, scooters and DevilBikes.

BERN

Of all Swiss cities, **BERN** is the most immediately charming. Crammed onto a steep-sided peninsula in a crook of the River Aare, the city's quiet, cobbled lanes, lined with sandstone arcaded buildings, have changed little in five hundred years. It's sometimes hard to remember that this petite town of just 130,000 people is the nation's capital.

What to see and do

The heart of Bern's compact old town is **Spitalgasse**. Heading east from the Bahnhofplatz, this becomes **Marktgasse**, Kramgasse and then Gerechtigkeitsgasse, before crossing the river to the **Bärengraben** (bear pits). The main museums are on Helvetiaplatz, on the south bank of the river, across the Kirchenfeldbrücke.

The Old Town and the Münster

Marktgasse, lined with attractive seventeenth- and eighteenth-century buildings and arcaded boutiques, leads you past various landmarks, such as the distinctively top-heavy Zytglogge, a medieval city gate converted to a clock tower in the sixteenth century. To the left in Kornhausplatz, the most notorious of Bern's fountains, the horrific **Kindlifresserbrunnen**, depicts an ogre devouring a baby. Münstergasse, one block south, takes you to the fifteenth-century Gothic **Münster** (Mon–Sat 10am–5pm, Sun 11.30am–4pm), with a magnificently gilded high-relief *Last Judgement* above the main entrance. Its 444-stepped tower (closes 30min earlier; Fr.5), the tallest in Switzerland, offers terrific views. Munsterplattform, nearby, hosts a craft market on the first Saturday of the month from March to November.

The Bärengraben

At the eastern end of the centre, the Nydeggbrücke crosses the river to the **Bärengraben**, Bern's famed bear pits, which held generations of morose shaggies from the early sixteenth century to 2009. The new Bear Park (open access), sloping down to the river, houses four bears in far better conditions than before. Legend has it that the town's founder, Berchtold V of Zähringen, named Bern after killing one of the beasts during a hunt.

The Kunstmuseum

Bern's **Kunstmuseum**, near the station at Hodlerstrasse 8 (Tues 10am–9pm, Wed–Sun 10am–5pm; Fr.7, more for temporary exhibitions; ⓦwww.kunstmuseumbern.ch), is especially strong on twentieth-century art, notably Matisse, Kandinsky, Braque and Picasso.

The Historisches Museum

The vast Historisches Museum (Tues–Sun 10am–5pm; Fr.13; ⓦwww.bhm.ch), on Helvetiaplatz, south of the river, details the country's history and also houses the superb Einstein Museum (same hours, Fr.18), documenting the physicist's eventful family life and his chequered early career. Exhibits include examples of young Albert's schoolwork, complete with scathing marginalia.

Zentrum Paul Klee

East of the centre at Ostring, the **Zentrum Paul Klee** (Tues–Sun 10am–5pm; Fr.22; ⓦwww.paulkleezentrum.ch; bus #12) has the world's largest collection of works by the artist, who spent much of his life in Bern. The building is a stunning, triple-arched design by the star Italian architect Renzo Piano.

Arrival and information

Train station On Bahnhofplatz, to the west of the Old Town.

Tourist office In the train station ⓣ031 328 12 12, ⓦwww.berninfo.com (June–Sept Mon–Sun 9am–8.30pm; Oct–May Mon–Sat 9am–7pm, Sun 10am–6pm). Staff sell the Bern Card (Fr.20/31/38 for 24/48/72 hr), which allows free public transport and discounts.

City transport

Bern's Old Town is compact and can easily be covered on foot.

Bike Bern rollt, ⓦwww.bernrollt.ch. Available all year at the Velostation in the Bahnhof (daily 7.30am–9.30pm), also May–Oct at Hirschengraben and Zeughausgasse. Rental is free for the first 4 hours, but you need photo ID and Fr.20 deposit and must return bikes the same day.

Bus #12 runs from the train station, through the Old Town to the Bärengraben and then to the Zentrum Paul Klee.

Accommodation

Bern Backpackers/Hotel Glocke (SB) Rathausgasse 75 ⓣ031 311 37 71, ⓦwww.bernbackpackers.com. Very central hostel (if a little noisy) with a large common room and kitchen area. Dorms Fr.35, rooms Fr.94–142.

Eichholz campsite Strandweg 49 ⓣ031 961 26 02, ⓦwww.campingeichholz.ch; tram #9 to Wabern. Good-value campsite. April–Sept. Fr.7.50/person, plus Fr.7/tent.

HI Hostel Weihergasse 4 ⓣ031 311 63 16, ⓦwww.youthhostel.ch/bern. Good hostel in a quiet location by the river, just below the Bundeshaus. Breakfast included. Dorms Fr.33, doubles Fr.51.

Landhaus (SB) Altenbergstr. 4 ⓣ031 331 41 66, ⓦwww.landhausbern.ch. Excellent hostel in an old house near the Bärengraben. Full of character, with wonky wooden stairs leading to a modern extension, and a lively downstairs bar (live jazz on Thurs). Dorms have neat 2-bed cubicles. Dorms from Fr.33, doubles Fr.120.

Eating and drinking

For picnic supplies and takeaways, Migros supermarket at the train station is open until 9pm, or visit the produce market in Bärenplatz (every Tues & first Sat each month 7am–noon).

Altes Tramdepot Grosser Muristalden 6 ⓦwww.altestramdepot.ch. Microbrewery with fantastic views across the river to the Old Town, serving Swiss cuisine such as rösti from Fr.17 (plus ciabattas from Fr.15.50). Daily from 10am summer & 11am winter until midnight.

Le Lötschberg Zeughausgasse 16. Relaxed, trendy wine bar and deli serving a range of cheese platters and substantial salads for Fr.9–15. Mon–Thurs 9am–midnight, Fri & Sat 9am–1.30am, Sun 11am–11pm.

Markthalle Bubenbergplatz 9. Large hall offering different world foods. Grab a pizza slice for Fr.8 or stick around for soup or noodles from Fr.15. Closed Sun.

Tibits Bahnhofplatz. Excellent vegetarian self-service place, with a great selection of salads and hot dishes. Pay by weight. Mon–Wed 6.30am–11.30pm, Thurs–Sat 6.30am–midnight, Sun 8am–11pm.

Nightlife and live music

Bern hosts a huge open-air rock event (ⓦwww.gurtenfestival.ch) in July.

Dampfzentrale Marzilistr. 47 ⓣ031 310 05 40, ⓦwww.dampfzentrale.ch. Bern's premier venue for live music, hosting a range of acts. Mon–Sat 5–11.30pm.

Reitschule Neubrückstr. 8 ⓦwww.reitschule.ch. Cultural and political arts squat at the heart of the alternative clubbing scene.

Directory

Embassies Australia, consulate in Geneva ⓣ022 799 91 00; Canada, Kirchenfeldstr. 88 ⓣ031 357 32 00; Ireland, Kirchenfeldstr. 68 ⓣ031 352 14 42; New Zealand, consulate in Geneva ⓣ022 929 03 50; UK, Thunstr. 50 ⓣ031 359 77 00; US, Sulgeneckstr. 19 ⓣ031 357 70 11.

Hospital Inselspital, Freiburgstr. ⓣ031 632 24 64.

Internet Weblane, Kramgrasse, 47. Daily 9am–11pm, Fr.4/30min.

Left Luggage in the station (6am–midnight; lockers Fr.5-8).

Pharmacy Bahnhof Apotheke, in the station (daily 6.30am–10pm).

Post office Schanzenstr. 4, behind the station.

Moving on

Train Basel (every 30min; 55min); Geneva (every 30min; 1hr 45min); Interlaken (every 30min; 55min); Lausanne (every 30min; 1hr 10min); Luzern (hourly; 1hr); Milan (3 daily; 3hr); Paris (2 daily; 4 hr); Zermatt (hourly, change at Visp; 2hr 10min); Zürich (every 30min; 1hr).

The Swiss Alps

South of Bern and Luzern, and east of Lake Geneva, lies the grand Alpine heart of Switzerland, a massively impressive region of classic Swiss scenery – high peaks, sheer valleys and cool lakes – that makes for great summer hiking and world-class winter sports. The Bernese Oberland, centred on the **Jungfrau Region**, is the most accessible and touristed area, but beyond this first great wall of peaks is another even more daunting range on the Italian border in which the **Matterhorn** is the star attraction.

THE JUNGFRAU REGION

The spectacular **Jungfrau Region** is named after a grand triple-peaked ridge – the Eiger, Mönch and Jungfrau – which crests 4000m. Switzerland's most popular **mountain railway**, celebrating its centenary in 2012, trundles south from **Interlaken** before coiling up across mountain pastures, and tunnelling clean through the Eiger to emerge at the **Jungfraujoch** (3454m), an icy, windswept col just beneath the Jungfrau summit. Touted relentlessly as the "Top of Europe", it's a scenic but very long journey (2hr 20min from Interlaken, with two changes to progressively smaller trains) and also extremely pricey; it's only worthwhile on a clear day, for the spectacular panoramic views from the Sphinx Terrace (3571m) to Germany's Black Forest in one direction and across a gleaming wasteland to the Italian Alps in the other. Bring your sunglasses.

The cable-car ride up the **Schilthorn** (2970m) gets second billing, but is in fact quicker, cheaper, offers a more scenic ride up, and has better views from the top. A return trip from Interlaken takes six hours to the Jungfraujoch, or four hours to the Schilthorn (both allowing an hour at the summit). Taking the first train of the day (6.30am) brings discounts on both routes.

The most beautiful countryside is the **Lauterbrunnen valley**, overlooked by the village of **Mürren**, which makes an excellent base for winter skiing and summer hiking, as does **Grindelwald**, in the next valley east. Interlaken is the region's transport hub, but the sheer volume of tourists passing through can make it a less than restful place to stay.

INTERLAKEN

INTERLAKEN is centred on its long main street, Höheweg, which is lined with cafés and hotels and has a train station at each end, though the best way to arrive is by boat. The town lies on a neck of land between two of Switzerland's loveliest lakes, and it exists chiefly to amuse the trippers on their way to the mountains. Interlaken Ost station is the terminus for both main-line trains and those into the mountains coming from Luzern, you could get out at Brienz and do the last stretch to Interlaken Ost by boat (ER & SP free, IR 50 percent discount). Likewise, from the Bern/Zürich direction, you could take a boat from Thun to Interlaken West.

TREAT YOURSELF

Interlaken is a real hub for extreme sports; paragliders spiral above, landing right in the town centre. If you decide to splash out on an adventure, **Skywings** (☎033 266 8228, Ⓦwww.skywings.ch) will take you paragliding for Fr.160; agencies such as **Alpin Raft** (Hauptstr. 7, Matten; ☎033 823 41 00, Ⓦwww.alpinraft.com) can arrange everything from rafting (Fr.110) to ice climbing (Fr.180) or canyon jumping (Fr.129), and can be booked direct or through hostels.

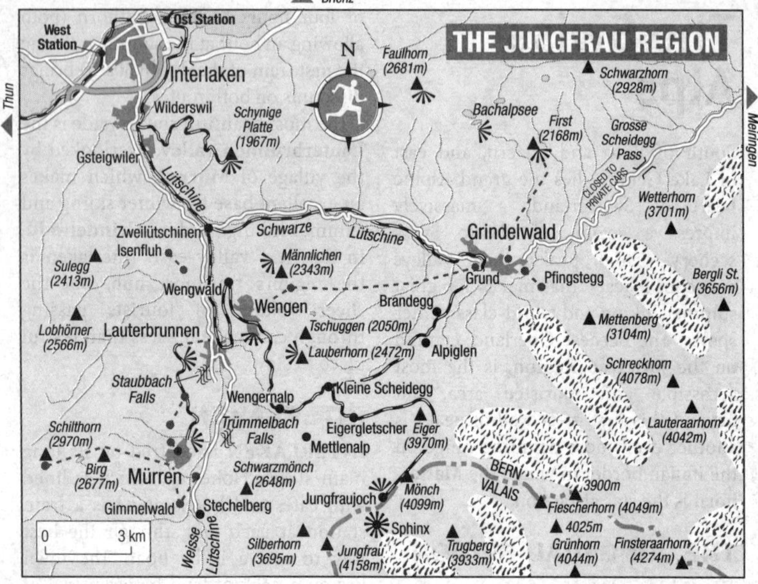

Arrival and information

Train From Interlaken West station Bahnhofstrasse leads east, becoming the main street, Höheweg, with Interlaken Ost station at its far end.

Tourist office Beneath the town's tallest building at Höheweg 37 (May–Sept Mon–Fri 8am–6pm & Sat 8am–4pm; July & Aug closes one hour later, also Sun 10am–noon & 5–7pm; Oct–April Mon–Fri 8am–noon, 1.30–6pm, Sat 9am–noon; ⓣ 033 826 53 00, ⓦ www.interlaken.ch).

Accommodation

Accommodation fills up quickly in the high seasons, so it really is essential to book ahead. There are hotel lists and courtesy phones at both stations.

Hostels

Backpackers Villa Sonnenhof (SB) Alpenstr. 16 ⓣ 033 826 71 71, ⓦ www.villa.ch. Excellent hostel with a superb new extension; peaceful, well equipped and friendly. Excellent deals with local restaurants. Dorms Fr.37, doubles Fr.98.

Balmer's Herberge (SB) Hauptstr. 23–33, Matten ⓣ 033 822 19 61, ⓦ www.balmers.com. Sociable hostel 10min south of town, its DJ bar and summer beer garden are the hub of Interlaken's lively backpacker scene. Dorms Fr.28.50, doubles Fr.77.

Camping Jungfraublick Gsteigstr. 80, Matten ⓣ 033 822 4414, ⓦ www.jungfraublick.ch. At the southern exit from town, a clean, modern site with a solar-heated outdoor pool and a view to die for. Fr.9/person, plus Fr.10–30/pitch.

Jugendherberge Bahnhofplatz Ost ⓣ 033 82610 90, ⓦ www.youthhostel.ch/interlaken A big, brand-new HI hostel right by Interlaken Ost station, with rooms for up to six, many en suite and some with balcony, plus internet access, billiards and good food.

Eating, drinking and nightlife

In the evenings most backpackers congregate at one of the busier hostel bars: *Balmer's* is the most popular and has cheap beer; *Funny Farm* (Hauptstr. 36, Matten) is a maverick hostel attracting party-goers with DJs at its *Club Caverne* till 1.30am (ⓦ www.caverne.ch).

Coop Opposite Interlaken Ost station. Huge supermarket with a restaurant; a smaller Coop at Höheweg 26 is open until 10.30pm.

Migros Opposite Interlaken West station. Cheap self-service staples. Closed Sun.

PizPaz Centralstr. Large place serving affordable pizza and pasta (from Fr.14.50; 20 percent less for takeaway). Closed Mon.

Restaurant des Alpes Höhenweg 115 ⓣ 033 822 23 23. A friendly and hectic place serving Swiss and Italian food; good salad bar. To 10.30/11pm daily.

Sandwich Bar Rosenstr. 5. Decent English-style sandwiches for Fr.4–9; daytime only.

Moving on

Train Bern (every 30min; 55min); Grindelwald (every 30min; 35min); Jungfraujoch (every 30min; 2hr 20min – change at Grindelwald or Lauterbrunnen, then Kleine Scheidegg); Lauterbrunnen (every 30min; 20min); Luzern (hourly; 2h); Zürich (every 30min; 1hr 55min).

LAUTERBRUNNEN

It's hard to overstate the impact of the **Lauterbrunnen valley**. An immense U-shaped cleft with bluffs on either side rising 1000m sheer, doused by some 72 waterfalls, it is utterly spectacular. The **Staubbach falls** – Switzerland's highest at nearly 300m – tumble just beyond the village of **LAUTERBRUNNEN** at the valley entrance, whose station (served by trains from Interlaken Ost) is opposite both the cable-car station for Mürren and the **tourist office** (Mon–Fri 9am–noon, 1.30–5pm; June–Sept daily 8.30am–noon, 1.30–6pm; ⓣ033 856 85 68, ⓦwww.lauterbrunnen.ch). **Accommodation** is just beyond the tourist office at the cosy *SB Valley Hostel* (ⓣ033 855 20 08, ⓦwww.valleyhostel.ch; dorms Fr.28, doubles Fr.66) or up at the excellent *Mountain Hostel* in Gimmelwald (see opposite). Pitch your tent at *Camping Jungfrau* (ⓣ856 2010, ⓦwww.camping-jungfrau.ch; Fr.10 per person, plus Fr.11 per tent), which also rents chalets by the week.

From Lauterbrunnen, it's a scenic half-hour walk, or an hourly postbus, 3km up the valley to the spectacular **Trümmelbach falls** (April–June & Sept–Oct 9am–5pm; July & Aug 8.30am–6pm; Fr.11), a series of thunderous waterfalls – fed by the glaciers above – which have carved corkscrew channels inside the valley walls. The bus continues 1.5km to the end of the road at **STECHELBERG**; the **cable-car** station for Gimmelwald, Mürren and the Schilthorn is 1km before the hamlet.

MÜRREN AND UP TO THE SCHILTHORN

The cable car from Stechelberg leaps the valley's west wall to reach the little-visited hamlet of **GIMMELWALD**, with the superb self-catering *Mountain Hostel* (ⓣ033 855 17 04, ⓦwww.mountainhostel.com; mid-April to Nov; Fr.28), continuing to the car-free village of **MÜRREN**. It's worth the journey for the views: from here, the valley floor is 800m straight down, and a dazzling panorama of snowy peaks fills the sky. Mürren is also accessible from Lauterbrunnen by taking a cable car to **Grütschalp** and a spectacular little cliff-edge train from there (one-way Fr.10.40/return Fr.20.80; IR no discount; ER 25 percent discount; SP free). It's easy to do a loop by cable car and train. A cable car continues from Mürren on a breath-taking ride (20min) to the 2970m peak of the Schilthorn (ⓦwww.schilthorn.ch), where you can enjoy exceptional panoramas and sip cocktails in the revolving *Piz Gloria* restaurant, famed as Blofeld's hideout in the Bond film *On Her Majesty's Secret Service*. Schilthornbahn prices, compared to the Jungfraujoch ride, are a bargain. From Stechelberg to the top is Fr.94.80 return trip, from Mürren Fr.74 (IR no discount; ER 25 percent discount; SP free to Mürren, then 50 percent). Going up before 8.55am or after 3.25pm (or in May/Oct) knocks the fare down to Fr.71.20 (Fr.55.60 from Mürren).

GRINDELWALD

Valley-floor trains from Interlaken Ost also run to the more popular resort of **GRINDELWALD**, nestling under the craggy trio of the Wetterhorn, Mettenberg and Eiger. Numerous trails around **Pfingstegg** and especially **First** – both reached by gondolas from Grindelwald

– offer excellent hiking. The **tourist office** (daily 8am–6pm) ⓣ033 854 12 12, ⓦwww.grindelwald.com) is 200m east of the station. A steep ten-minute walk brings you to the excellent *Die Weid* **HI hostel** (ⓣ033 853 10 09, ⓦwww.youthhostel.ch/grindelwald; dorms Fr.35.70, doubles Fr.120; closed mid-April to mid-May & mid-Oct to early Dec) on Terrassenweg, a quiet lane above the village. The well-run SB *Mountain Hostel* (ⓣ033 854 3838, ⓦwww.mountainhostel.ch; dorms Fr.37, doubles Fr.94) is on the valley floor beside Grindelwald-Grund station (where trains from Grindelwald call on their way up to Kleine Scheidegg). *Camping Gletscherdorf*, a quiet site by a stream to the east of the village (ⓣ033 853 14 29 ⓦwww.gletscherdorf.ch; Fr.8 per person, plus Fr.17 per pitch), is open from May to late October.

Mountain transport

Train There are two routes up the Jungfrau from Interlaken, changing trains at either Lauterbrunnen or Grindelwald (it's normal to go up one way and down the other). The routes meet at the spectacularly sited station of Kleine Scheidegg, where you change for the final pull to the Jungfraujoch.

Fares and tickets The adult return-trip fare from Interlaken to the Jungfraujoch is a budget-crunching Fr.186 (IR no discount; ER 25 percent discount; SP free to Grindelwald and Lauterbrunnen, then half-price to Kleine Scheidegg and 25 percent off to the top) – but the discounted "Good Morning" and "Good Afternoon tickets", valid if you travel up on the first or second trains of the day (at 6.30am & 7.20am from Interlaken Ost), or leave Kleine Scheidegg after 3.30pm, cost Fr.140 from Interlaken, and Fr.130 from Lauterbrunnen or Grindelwald.

Walking Hiking some sections, up or down, is perfectly feasible in summer, and can save a great deal on train tickets. Excellent transport networks and vista-rich footpaths linking all stations mean that with a hiking map – such as the *Wanderkarte Wengen-Mürren-Lauterbrunnental* (1:40,000) – you can see and do a great deal in a day.

ZERMATT AND THE MATTERHORN

The shark's-tooth **Matterhorn** (4478m) is the most famous of Switzerland's mountains; for most people, the Matterhorn stands for Switzerland like the Eiffel Tower stands for France. One reason it's so famous is that it stands alone, its impossibly pointy shape sticking up from an otherwise uncrowded horizon above **ZERMATT**; another is that the quintessential Swiss chocolate, Toblerone, was modelled on it.

What to see and do

Zermatt's main street is thronged year-round with an odd mix of professional climbers, glacier skiers, tour groups, backpackers and fur-clad socialites. No cars are allowed in the town; electric buses ferry people between the train station at the town's northern end and the cable-car terminus 1km south. All Zermatt's cable cars and trains bring you to trailheads and spectacular views: opposite the station, Gornergrat-Bahn trains (ER 25 percent discount, IR Youth Pass & SP 50 percent discount) give spectacular Matterhorn views (sit on the right) as they climb all the way to the **Gornergrat**, a vantage point with a magnificent panorama including Switzerland's highest peak, the **Dufourspitze** (4634m). Once a week in summer, GGB trains leave Zermatt at dawn for a breathtaking Alpine sunrise and a wildlife hike (Fr.79, SP Fr.59). At the south end of Zermatt a cable car climbs to the **Schwarzsee** (2583m), in summer, the start of a zigzag walk (2hr) to the *Hörnli Hut* (3260m), on the flank of the mountain itself. Lifts to **Trockener Steg** give access to 21km of ski runs and a snowboard half-pipe that are open all summer long (day pass Fr.74; SP 50 percent discount).

Arrival and information

Train The only access to Zermatt is on the spectacular narrow-gauge MGB train line (ER no discount, IR 50 percent discount, SP free; ⓦwww.mgbahn.ch); change at Visp from main-line trains. The most celebrated way to arrive is on the *Glacier Express*, a day-long journey from St Moritz by panoramic train (reserve at any train station; ER 25 percent discount, IR Youth Pass 50 percent discount, SP free; ⓦwww.glacierexpress.ch).
Tourist office Outside the station (Mon–Sat 8.30am–6pm; June–Sept & Dec–April also Sun 9.30am–noon & 4–6pm). There's a hotel list and courtesy phone here.
Snow and Alpine Centre Bahnhofstr. 58 ⓣ027 966 24 60, ⓦwww.alpincenter-zermatt.ch (daily 8am–noon & 4–7pm). Runs fixed-rope courses for Fr.135 and ice climbing for Fr.190. The place to book climbing guides; also ski/snowboard lessons (ⓣ027 966 24 64; Mon–Fri 8am–noon & 3–7pm, Sat & Sun 5am–9pm).

Accommodation

Hotel Tannenhof Englischer Viertel 3 ⓣ027 967 31 88, ⓦwww.rhone.ch/tannenhof. Good-value hotel that's popular with climbers. Cosy doubles, with or without private bathroom. Singles Fr.90/80 & doubles Fr.130/Fr.110 with/without bathroom.
Matterhorn campsite Bahnhofstr. ⓣ027 967 39 21, ⓦcampingzermatt.ipeak.ch. Just north of the train station. June–Sept. Fr.11/person
Matterhorn Hostel (SB) Schluhmattstr. 32 ⓣ027 968 19 19, ⓦwww.matterhornhostel.com. Friendly staff and a lively bar with food, but rather cramped and in need of a re-vamp. Dorms Fr.36, doubles Fr.92.
Zermatt Youth Hostel Staldenweg. 5, Winkelmatten ⓣ027 967 23 20, ⓦwww.youthhostel.ch/zermatt. Excellent hostel on the east side of town. Half-board only. Dorms Fr.51, doubles Fr.142.

Eating and drinking.

Brown Cow Bahnhofstr. 41, in the *Hotel Post*. Popular pub, serving reasonably priced snacks: sandwiches (from Fr.6) and burgers (Fr.12). Until 2am daily; food till 10.30pm.
North Wall Steinmattstr. 71. Lively British-run bar. Open 6pm–1am daily, pizza served until 10pm.
Papperla Pub Steinmattstr. 34 ⓦwww.papperlapub.ch. Zermatt's busiest après-ski spot. Daily 11am–4am.

Moving on

Train Brig (hourly; 1hr 24min); St Moritz (1–4 daily; 7hr 50min); Visp (hourly; 1hr 10min).

ZÜRICH

A beautiful city, set astride a river and turned towards a crystal-clear lake and distant snowy peaks, **ZÜRICH** has plenty to recommend it. Niederdorf's steep cobbled alleys are great to wander around, with an engaging café culture and a wealth of nightlife, whereas to the northwest of the centre the city's former industrial quarter, known as "Züri-West", has become home to many of the city's trendiest clubs. Whether wandering the streets of the Old Town, window shopping in Bahnhofstrasse or day-tripping to the Rhine Falls, you may end up spending longer here than originally planned.

What to see and do

Across the River Limmat from the station, the narrow lanes of the medieval **Niederdorf** district stretch south, quiet during the day and bustling after dark. The waterfront is lined with fine Baroque *Zunfthäuser* (guildhalls), arcaded lower storeys fronting the quayside, now mostly upmarket restaurants. One block in is **Niederdorfstrasse**, initially tacky, but offering plenty of opportunities to explore atmospheric cobbled side alleys and secluded courtyards: Lenin lived at Spiegelgasse 14 in 1917 (pre-Revolution). Just south is Zürich's trademark **Grossmünster** (Great Minster; March 15 to Oct daily 9am–6pm; Nov–March 14 daily 10am–5pm), where Huldrych Zwingli, father of Swiss Protestantism, began preaching the Reformation in 1519. Its exterior is largely fifteenth-century, while its twin towers were topped with distinctive octagonal domes in the seventeenth century. The interior is austere apart from the intensely coloured choir windows (1933) by

Augusto Giacometti and the Romanesque crypt which contains an oversized fifteenth-century statue of Charlemagne.

The Kunsthaus

Switzerland's best gallery, the **Kunsthaus** (Sat, Sun & Tues 10am–6pm, Wed–Fri 10am–8pm; Fr.16, students Fr.11, more for temporary exhibits, free Wed; Ⓦwww.kunsthaus.ch), is up the hill from the Grossmünster via several alleys. Some fascinating Gothic paintings are followed by Venetian masters, fine Flemish pieces, and the greatest Swiss artists, Fuseli, Böcklin, Hodler, Segantini, Vallotton and Klee. The collection of international twentieth-century art is also stunning.

West of the centre

The **west bank** is the main commercial district, while further west are the coolest hangouts and the best streetlife. Tram #8 towards Hardplatz will deliver you to relaxed **Helvetiaplatz**, from where funky **Langstrasse** heads north – lowlife bars rubbing shoulders with avant-garde galleries, the smells of kebabs and pizza mixing with the aroma of marijuana. This fascinating street is a mixture of styles and cultures – Swiss-German blending with French-African, Turkish, Balkan, East Asian and Latin American.

The Landesmuseum

Immediately north of the main station, the **Landesmuseum** or Federal History Museum (Museumstr. 2; Tues–Sun 10am–5pm, Thurs till 7pm; Fr.10; Ⓦwww.nationalmuseum.ch;) gives the definitive account of Switzerland's tortuous development and its cultural context.

Bahnhofstrasse

Leading south from the station, **Bahnhofstrasse** is one of Europe's most prestigious shopping streets. This is the gateway into the modern city, and where all of Zürich strolls, to browse at the inexpensive department stores that crowd the first third of the street, or to sign away Fr.25,000 on a Rolex watch or a Vuitton bag at the super-chic boutiques further south.

Lindenhof and St Peterkirche

The narrow lanes between Bahnhofstrasse and the river lead up to the Lindenhof, site of a Roman fort that now offers fine views. James Joyce wrote *Ulysses* in Zürich (1915–19), and the **James Joyce Foundation**, nearby at Augustinergasse 9 (Mon–Fri 10am–5pm; free), can point you to his various hangouts, and his grave. Steps away is **St Peterkirche** (Mon–Fri 8am–6pm, Sat 8am–4pm, Sun 11am–5pm), renowned for its enormous sixteenth-century clock faces – the largest in Europe. Immediately south rises the slender-spired Gothic **Fraumünster** (Mon–Sat 10am–4/6pm Sun 11.30am–6pm), which began life as a convent in the ninth century; its spectacular stained glass by Marc Chagall is unmissable.

Arrival and information

Air Zürich's airport (Flughafen) lies 11km northeast of the city centre. Frequent trains leave for the city stations.

Train Zürich's giant Hauptbahnhof (HB) is served by trains from all over Europe. Extending three storeys below ground, it includes a shopping mall, supermarket and some decent places to eat; beware of pickpockets and bag-snatchers on the main concourse.

Bus 50m north of the train station, on Sihlquai.

Tourist office On the train station concourse Ⓣ044 215 40 00, Ⓦwww.zuerich.com (May–Oct Mon–Sat 8am–8.30pm, Sun 8.30am–6.30pm; Nov–April Mon–Sat 8.30am–7pm, Sun 9am–6pm). Staff will book rooms for free, and sell the Zürich Card (Fr.19/38 one/three days), allowing free public transport and free entry to museums.

City transport

Bike rental Free bikes (Fr.20 deposit) are available at the Velostation Nord and Sud, on either side of

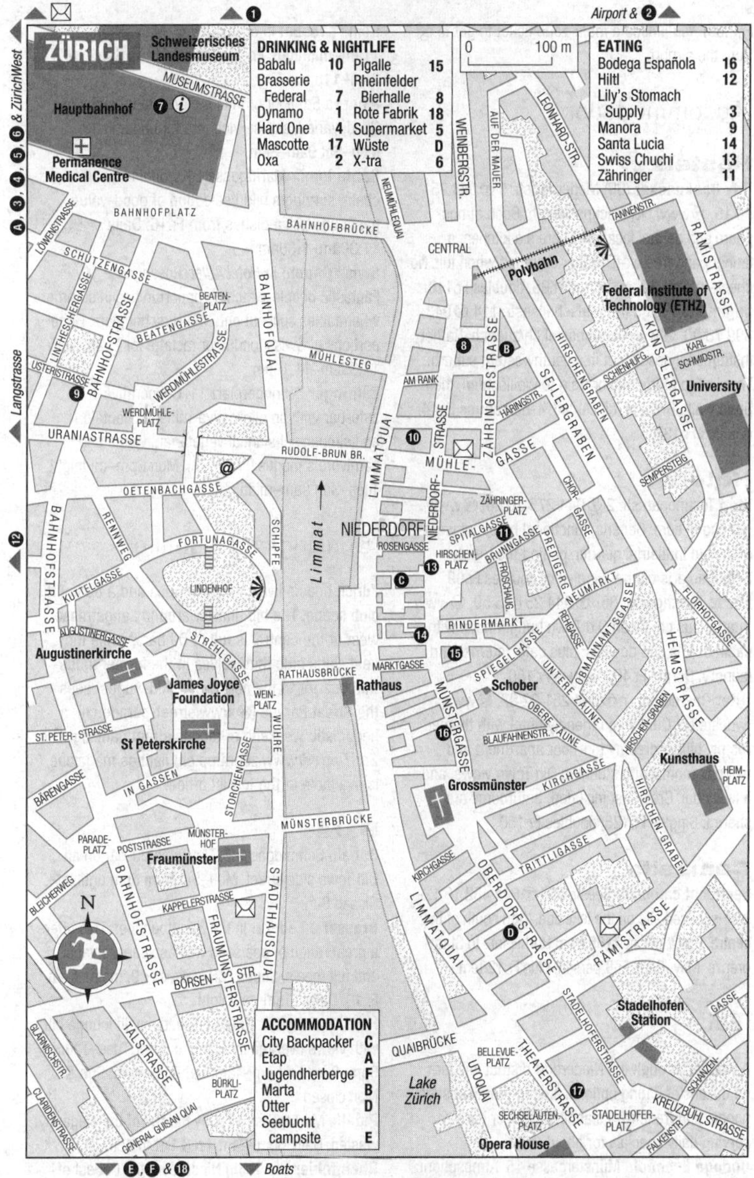

the Hauptbahnhof (daily 8am–9.30pm), and May–Oct elsewhere in the city (Mon–Fri 11am–9.30pm, Sat & Sun 9am–9.30pm).

Boats Cruises on the Zürichsee leave from Bürkliplatz (Ⓦ www.zsg.ch); the shortest trips (1hr 30min; Fr.8.20; IR 50 percent discount) are covered by public transport tickets.

Tram and bus Although most sites can be covered on foot, the tram and bus system is easy to use (Ⓦ www.zvv.ch), with all tickets valid on trams, buses, some boats and "S-Bahn" city trains.

Tickets Buy tickets from machines at every stop: either the green button (24hr; Fr.8.20); blue button (1hr; Fr.4.10); or yellow button (short one-way hop;

Fr.2.60). You'll need a multi-zone ticket to get to or from the airport.

Accommodation

Hostels

City Backpacker (SB) Niederdorfstr. 5 ⓣ044 251 90 15, ⓦwww.city-backpacker.ch. Good atmosphere and central location. There's a kitchen, a laundry and free wi-fi. Rather cramped when full. No check-in after 10pm. Dorms Fr.35, doubles Fr.110.
Jugendherberge (HI) Mutschellenstr. 114 ⓣ043 399 78 00, ⓦwww.youthhostel.ch/zuerich. Rather institutional hostel, out in a southwestern suburb. Tram #7 to Morgental or train to Wollishofen, then 5min walk. Breakfast included. 4-bed dorms Fr.44, doubles Fr.137.

Hotels

Etap Technoparkstr. 2 ⓣ044 276 20 00, ⓦwww.etaphotel.com. Generic, functional hotel out west in the old industrial quarter, behind the trendy Schiffbau arts centre. Singles or doubles Fr.99.
Marta Zähringerstr. 36 ⓣ044 251 45 50, ⓦwww.martahaus.ch. Clean Old Town budget hotel with cabin dorms and doubles, plus café, internet and laundry. Dorms Fr.40, doubles Fr.150.
Otter Oberdorfstr. 7 ⓣ044 251 22 07, ⓦwww.wueste.ch. Quirky and friendly hotel with themed rooms, plus a dreamy top-floor apartment and balcony rooms with stunning Old Town views, and a lively bar. Breakfast included; bathrooms are shared. Singles Fr.125, doubles Fr.150.

Campsite

Seebucht campsite Seestr. 559 ⓣ044 482 16 12. Well-serviced site on the lakeside, 2km south of the centre. Bus #161 or #165 from Bürkliplatz to Stadtgrenze. May–Sept. Fr.8/person, plus Fr.12/tent.

Eating

A wander through the Niederdorf district will turn up dozens of eating options, among them sausage, noodle and french-fry stands, plus beer halls serving daily specials for about Fr.13.
Bodega Española Münstergasse 15. Atmospheric tapas bar and paella restaurant. Tapas from Fr.10. Daily 10am–midnight.
Hiltl Sihlstr. 28 Top-quality vegetarian buffet, with budget takeaway prices. Daily specials Fr.16.50. Mutates into a trendy cocktail bar with DJs most nights. Sun–Thurs 6am–midnight, Fri & Sat to 4am.
Lily's Stomach Supply Langstr. 197. Bustling pan-Asian noodle-bar, serving huge stir-fries from Fr.15. Eat in or takeaway. Mon–Thurs 11am–midnight, Fri–Sat 11am–1am, Sun 3pm–11pm.
Manora 5th floor of Manor store, Bahnhofstr. 75. Good, varied, self-service fare for under Fr.13. Mon–Sat 9am–8pm.
Santa Lucia Marktgasse 21. Popular local chain, serving a wide selection of good-value pasta and pizza dishes from Fr.16. Daily 11.30am–1.30am.
Swiss Chuchi in *Hotel Adler*, Rosengasse 10. Fantastic people-watching opportunities in summer when tables spill out onto the Hirschenplatz. Huge portions of Swiss fondue or raclette for Fr.25. Daily 11.30am–11.15pm.
Zähringer Zähringerplatz 11. Cooperative-run café-bar with an alternative-minded clientele and simple, substantial vegetarian, vegan and carnivore's menus (Fr.22–28). Mon 6pm–midnight, Tues–Sun 9am–midnight.

Drinking and nightlife

Zürich boasts lively music venues and a booming club scene. The hip quarter around Langstrasse, west of the centre, is full of DJ bars, while the best clubs hide themselves in the former industrial quarter to the northwest. Mid-August sees the Street Parade (ⓦwww.street-parade.ch), a hedonistic weekend of techno street dancing. The *ZüriTipp* (ⓦwww.zueritipp.ch) listings magazine is available at the tourist office.

Bars

Babalu Schmidgasse 6. Tiny, chic DJ-bar on an Old Town side street. Mon–Sat from 5pm until late. Closed Sun.
Brasserie Federal In the Hauptbahnhof. This offers a great range of beers, as well as soups, salads and full meals. Soups Fr.8, salads Fr.9, mains from Fr.18. Daily 11am–midnight.
Hard One Hardstr. 260. Stylish, dimly lit lounge bar with views over the industrial quarter. Tues–Thurs 6pm–2am, Fri 6pm–4am, Sat 9pm–4am, Sun & Mon closed.
Pigalle Marktgasse 14. Gay bar full of the elegantly wasted. Daily 6pm–2am, Fri & Sat to 4am.
Rheinfelder Bierhalle Niederdorfstr. 76. Best of the beerhalls, filled with locals and serving cheap daily specials. Daily 9am–midnight.
Wüste In *Hotel Otter*, Oberdorfstr. 7. Mellow, relaxed bar near the Grossmünster. Open until 2am at the weekend.
X-tra Limmatstr. 118 ⓦwww.x-tra.ch. Spacious modern bar-restaurant, with popular upstairs DJ club (from 10pm) and gigs.

Clubs

Dynamo Wasserwerkstr. 21 ⓦwww.dynamo.ch. Alternative, punkish bands and dance nights for a young crowd.
Mascotte Theaterstr. 10 ⓦwww.mascotte.ch. Most popular of the Old Town clubs. Renowned for its Tuesday rock/metal "Karaoke from Hell" night. Mon–Sat from 11pm until late.
Oxa Andreasstr. 70. Techno and house music, plus famed after-hours parties (Sat & some Fri 10pm–5am, Sun 5am–noon).
Rote Fabrik Seestr. 395 ⓦwww.rotefabrik.ch. Alternative bands, big-name DJs, a cheap and funky restaurant (closed Mon) and a great riverside bar.
Supermarket Geroldstr. 17 ⓦwww.supermarket.li. Popular Züri-West club, attracting international DJs. Thurs–Sat from 8pm.

Shopping

Flea market Bürkliplatz (May–Oct Sat 8am–4pm).
Jelmoli Bahnhofstrasse/Seidengasse. Zürich's largest department store.
Kirchgasse has a high concentration of second-hand bookshops, antiques shops and galleries.
Niederdorfstrasse and **Viaduktstrasse** are crammed with boutiques from grungy indie fashions to fabulous jewellery.
Schober Napfgasse 4 or Bellevueplatz 5. Good option for chocolate and cakes.
Travel Book Shop Rindermarkt 20. Good selection of maps and travel guides. Open Tues–Sat.

Directory

Consulates Ireland, Claridenstr. 25 ⓣ044 289 25 15; UK, Hegibachstr. 47 ⓣ044 383 65 60; US, Dufourstr. 101 ⓣ044 422 25 66. Embassies are in Bern.
Exchange/bank At the station (6.30am–9.30pm daily) or UBS, Bahnhofstr. 45 (Mon–Fri 8.15am–4.15pm).
Hospital Permanence Medical Centre, Bahnhofplatz 15 ⓣ044 215 44 44 (7am–10pm daily).
Internet Urania, Uraniastr. 3 (Mon–Sat 7/8am–11pm & Sun 10am–10pm).
Left luggage North side of the station 7am–9pm daily.
Pharmacy Bellevue, Theaterstr. 14 (24hr) ⓣ044 266 62 22; and at the station.
Post office Sihlpost, Kasernenstr. 95, beside the station. Mon–Fri 6.30am–10.30pm, Sat 6.30am–8pm, Sun 10am–10.30pm.

Moving on

Train Basel (every 15min; 1hr); Bern (every 30min; 1hr); Geneva (every 30min; 2hr 45min); Innsbruck (7 daily; 3hr 30min); Interlaken (every 30min; 1hr 55min); Lausanne (every 30min; 2hr 10min); Lugano (hourly; 2hr 40min); Luzern (every 30min; 45min); Milan (7 daily; 3hr 40min); Munich (5 daily; 4hr 12min); Paris (6 daily; 4hr); Sargans (every 30min; 55min); Schaffhausen (hourly; 40min); St Moritz (hourly; 3hr 20min–change at Chur); Stuttgart (7 daily; 3hr); Vienna (4 daily; 8hr).

THE RHINE FALLS

A great excursion from Zürich is the half-day trip north to the **Rhine Falls** (ⓦwww.rhinefalls.com), Europe's largest waterfalls, 3km west of **SCHAFFHAUSEN**. They are magnificent, not so much for their height (just 23m) as for their impressive breadth (150m) and sheer drama, with spray rising in a cloud of rainbows above the forested banks and the turreted castle, **Schloss Laufen**, on the south bank. Come on the national holiday, August 1, for the famous fireworks display. In summer, the best views are from daredevil boats (Fr.4–14; ⓦwww.maendli.ch), which scurry about in the spray from Schloss Laufen or Schlössli Wörth, across the river, from where a restaurant gives a great view of the falls.

Take a train to Schaffhausen then bus #1 to Neuhausen Zentrum, or a local train to either Laufen am Rheinfall (below the castle; April–Oct) or Neuhausen; you can also walk in 30min from Schaffhausen to the bridge above the falls.

Ticino

Italian-speaking **Ticino** (Tessin in German and French) occupies the balmy, lake-laced southern foothills of the Alps. It's a little pocket of Italy in Switzerland and radically different in almost every way: culture, food, architecture, attitude and driving style owe more to Milan than Zürich, although Switzerland has controlled the area since the early 1500s. The main attractions are the lakeside resorts of **Locarno** and **Lugano**, where mountain scenery meets subtropical flora. The best way to enjoy these chic towns is to join the locals promenading with ice creams.

Unless you approach from Italy, there's only one train line in – through the 15km **Gotthard Tunnel**. The climb to the tunnel is famous for its spiralling contortions: trains pass Wassen's onion-domed church three times, first far above, then on a level, and finally far below.

LOCARNO

A branch line heads west from Bellinzona (whose three superb castles are on UNESCO's World Heritage list) to **LOCARNO**. It's a charming town on **Lake Maggiore**, its piazzas overhung by subtropical shrubbery. Overrun with the rich and wannabe-famous on summer weekends and during its world-class film festival (early August), it manages to retain a sun-drenched cool.

What to see and do

The **Piazza Grande**, where exquisitely groomed locals parade on warm summer nights, is near the lake, with the Renaissance Old Town rising gently behind. The fifteenth-century church of **Madonna del Sasso** (daily 6.30am–6.45pm) is an impressive ochre vision high on a crag. It's a glorious walk up (or down); or take the funicular (Fr.6.60 return) from just west of the station to Ticino's greatest photo-op, looking down on the church and lake.

From the top station, a cable car climbs steeply to **Cardada**, amid fragrant pine woods with walking routes; a spectacular chairlift whisks you further up to **Cimetta**, where the restaurant terrace offers a view you won't forget in a hurry.

A short bus ride east of Locarno is Valle Verzasca, where you can re-enact the opening of the James Bond film *Goldeneye* by bungee-jumping a world-record 220m off the Verzasca Dam (April–Oct daily; Fr.255; book on ⓣ091 780 78 00, ⓦwww.trekking.ch) – in July & August, you can jump by moonlight.

Arrival and information

Train Locarno's train station is 150m northeast of Piazza Grande.

Boat The landing stage is between the train station and Piazza Grande; in summer boats (ⓦwww.navigazionelaghi.it) sail to nearby Swiss resorts such as Ascona (Fr.9), and south to Italian ones such as Stresa (on the main line to Milan; Fr.33).

Tourist office In the Casino opposite the landing stage (Mon–Fri 9am–6pm; April–Oct also Sat 10am–6pm, Sun 10am–1.30pm & 2.30–5pm; ⓣ091 791 00 91, ⓦwww.ascona-locarno.com).

Accommodation

Delta campsite Via Respini 7 ⓣ091 751 60 81, ⓦwww.campingdelta.com; March–Oct. Expensive but well-equipped campsite 20min walk south by the lake (just past the lido). From Fr.37/pitch plus Fr.20/person; caravans Fr.69.

HI hostel "Palagiovani" Via Varenna 18 ⓣ091 756 15 00, ⓦwww.youthhostel.ch/locarno; bus #1/#2/#7 from opposite the station to Cinque Vie. Friendly hostel 10min walk from the centre with six-bed dorms Fr.41 and doubles Fr.130.

Eating and drinking

Cantina Canetti Little place at the west end of the Piazza Grande with simple local cooking (from Fr.14) and live accordion on weekend nights. Closed Sun evening.

Manora Branch of the self-service chain facing the train station, with good, cheap meals for Fr.14 or under. Daily 7.30am–9/10pm.

Moving on

Train Basel (every 2hr; 4hr 10min); Bellinzona – change for Lugano (3 hourly; 20min); Domodossola – change for Brig and southwestern Switzerland (7–10 daily; 1hr 45min); Luzern (every 2hr; 3hr); Zürich (every 2hr; 3hr 10min).

LUGANO

With its tree-lined promenades and piazzas, **LUGANO** is Ticino's most alluring resort, less touristy than Locarno but twice as chic.

What to see and do

The centre of town is **Piazza della Riforma**, a café-lined square by the exceptionally beautiful **Lago di Lugano**. Through the maze of steep lanes northwest of Riforma, Via Cattedrale dog-legs up to the **Cattedrale San Lorenzo**, with its fine Renaissance facade, fragments of interior frescoes and spectacular views from its terrace. Also from Riforma, narrow Via Nassa – home to big-name boutiques – heads southwest to the medieval church of **Santa Maria degli Angioli**, home to a stunning wall-sized fresco of the Crucifixion. A little further south is the **Museo d'Arte Moderna**, Riva Caccia 5 (Tues–Sun 10am–6pm; Fr.12, students Fr.8; ⓦwww.mdam.ch), with world-class exhibitions; a little further still is the modestly named district of Paradiso, from where a funicular rises 600m to San Salvatore, a rugged sugarloaf pinnacle offering fine views of the lake and surrounding countryside. The best of the lake is behind (south of) San Salvatore on the Ceresio peninsula, accessed by boats or buses.

Arrival and information

Train Lugano's train station overlooks the town from the west, linked to the centre by a short funicular or by steps down to Via Cattedrale.
Tourist office Palazzo Civico, off Riforma ⓣ091 913 32 32, ⓦwww.lugano-tourism.ch (Mon–Fri 9am–7pm, Sat 9am–5pm, Sun 10am–5pm). Boats around the lake (ⓦwww.lakelugano.ch; April–Oct; Fr.4–22, SP free) depart from directly opposite.

Accommodation

HI hostel Via Cantonale 13, Savosa ⓣ091 966 27 28, ⓦwww.youthhostel.ch/lugano. Excellent, quiet hostel with a large garden and swimming pool. Bus #5 to Crocifisso from 200m north of the train station. Dorms Fr.37, doubles Fr.96.
Hotel Pestalozzi Piazza Indipendenza ⓣ091 921 46 46, ⓦwww.pestalozzi-lugano.ch. More central (150m from the lake) with a great (alcohol-free) restaurant and friendly staff. Single room from Fr.68, double from Fr.116.
La Piodella campsite ⓣ091 994 77 88, ⓦwww.campingtcs.ch. One of several lakeside campsites in Muzzano, 3km west. Take a train from the FLP station (direction Ponte Tresa). Fr.8.40/person, plus Fr.14.40/tent.

Eating and drinking

Manora Salta Chiattone. Inexpensive self-service staples for under Fr.12, plus pizza (Fr.11–14) in the evening. There's an outside terrace. Daily to 10pm.
La Tinèra Via dei Gorini, behind Riforma. Great for pasta and tasty Ticinese chicken stews (Fr.19). Closed Sun & Mon.

Moving on

Train Luzern (hourly; 2hr 30min); Milan (every 2 hours; 1hr); Zürich (hourly; 2hr 40min).
Bus St Moritz (mid-June to mid-Oct daily, otherwise 3 weekly; 4hr); book at the train station.

Liechtenstein

Barely larger than Manhattan, **Liechtenstein** is the world's sixth-smallest country. It's an unassuming place squashed between Switzerland and Austria, ruled over by His Serene Highness Prince Hans Adam II, and has made a mint from nursing some Fr.90 billion in numbered bank accounts. The main reason to visit is the novelty value – you can see the whole country in an easy day-trip from Zürich, less than two hours away by train. Swiss francs are legal tender, but the phone system is separate (country code ⓣ423).

VADUZ

From Sargans train station on the Zürich–Chur line, bus #1 shuttles over the Rhine (no border controls) in half an hour to the capital **VADUZ**, a tiny town bulging with glass-plated **banks** and squadrons of aimless visitors. The central hub is the post office, where all buses stop, midway between the main highway, Äulestrasse, and pedestrianized Städtle. On either side are the sleek **Kunstmuseum** (Tues–Sun 10am–5pm, Thurs till 8pm; Fr.12, students Fr.8, Fr.15/10 combined ticket with Landesmuseum), displaying temporary art exhibitions drawing on the prince's private collection and other donations, and the **Landesmuseum** (Tues–Sun 10am–5pm, Wed to 8pm, Fr.8, students Fr.5), with excellent coverage of local history. Perched on the forested hillside above is the prince's sixteenth-century **castle** (no public access).

Buses from Vaduz serve all points in Liechtenstein, as well as connecting to Feldkirch just across the border in Austria, from where trains run on to Bregenz, Innsbruck and Vienna.

Arrival and information

Arrival Buses stop on Vaduz's main street, by the post office.

Tourist office Städtle 37 (daily 9am–5pm; Nov–April closed Sat & Sun; ⓣ00423 239 63 00, ⓦwww.tourismus.li). They can bang a stamp into your passport as a memento (Fr.3/€2).

Accommodation

HI hostel Schaan-Vaduz Untere Rüttigasse 6 ⓣ232 50 22 (March–Oct). Quiet rural location, looking out over fields and mountains. 5min walk from the Mühleholz bus stop in Schaan (2km north of Vaduz). Dorms Fr.33.60, doubles Fr.85.

Mittagsspitze campsite ⓣ392 36 77, ⓦwww.campingtriesen.li. Tranquil rural campsite with swimming pool, 5km south near Triesen. Fr.9/person, plus Fr.6–8/tent.

Eating and drinking

Café im Kunstmuseum Städtle 32 Stylish café and sushi bar in the art museum. Wed–Fri 9am–11pm, Sat–Tues 9am–6pm.

Potenza Städtle 29. Pavement café serving up crispy thin-crust pizzas, as well as tapas and salads.

Moving on

Bus Feldkirch (Austria) (hourly; 30min); Sargans (Switzerland) (every 30min; 25min).

Turkey

HIGHLIGHTS

İSTANBUL: a sensory overload with historical sights, fantastic nightlife and delicious cuisine

CAPPADOCIA: a lunar landscape, complete with eerie caves and underground cities

EPHESUS: one of the world's best-preserved ancient cities

BODRUM: Turkey's party town. Spend your days on the beach and dance under the stars in an open-air nightclub

KAS: a great base for beaches, ancient sites, and adventure sports

ROUGH COSTS

DAILY BUDGET Basic €25 /occasional treat €40

DRINK *Rakí* €3, beer (*Efes*) €2.50

FOOD Kebab with side order €5

HOSTEL/BUDGET HOTEL €11 (dorm)/€25–50

TRAVEL Bus: Istanbul–Ankara €12

FACT FILE

POPULATION 75.8 million

AREA 780,580 sq km

LANGUAGE Turkish

CURRENCY Turkish lira (TL)

CAPITAL Ankara (population: 4.3 million)

INTERNATIONAL PHONE CODE ⓣ90

Introduction

Turkey has multiple identities. Poised between East and West, mosques coexist with churches, and Roman remnants crumble alongside ancient Hittite sites. The country is politically secular, though the majority of its people are Muslim, and is an immensely rewarding place to travel, not least because of the people, whose reputation for friendliness and hospitality is richly deserved.

Much of the country's delights are inexpensive pleasures. Whether it's indulging in tasty *börek* pastries or dancing in backstreet bars, there are plenty of activities to consume your time but not your budget.

Most visitors begin their trip in **İstanbul**, a heady mixture of European shopping districts, Ottoman architecture and Anatolian cultural influences. South from here, small country towns are swathed in olive groves, while the area is littered with ancient sites, most notable of all **Ephesus**. Beyond the functional city of **İzmir**, the **Aegean coast** is Turkey at its most developed, with large numbers drawn to hedonistic party resorts such as **Bodrum** and **Marmaris**. Beyond here, the aptly named Turquoise Coast is home to resorts such as **Fethiye** and **Kaş**, famous for their fabulous water- and adventure-sports facilities. Inland from here is spectacular **Cappadocia**, with its well-known rock churches, subterranean cities and landscape studded with cave dwellings. Further north, **Ankara**, Turkey's capital, is a planned city whose contrived Western feel gives some indication of the priorities of the modern Turkish Republic. Further south, **Konya** is best known as the birthplace of the Sufi sect.

CHRONOLOGY

1250 BC According to Homer's *Iliad* Troy is cleverly taken by the Greeks who sneak into the city in a wooden horse.
334 BC Alexander the Great marches through Anatolia, present-day Turkey.
129 BC Romans conquer Anatolia.
47 AD St Paul brings Christianity to Anatolia.
330 Emperor Constantine founds Constantinople, calling it the new Rome and establishing the Byzantine Empire.
1288 The Islamic Ottoman Empire starts to expand across present-day Turkey.
1526 The Ottomans defeat the Habsburgs taking large areas of Europe.
1832 Following heavy fighting, the Greeks gain independence from Ottoman Turkey.
1918 The Ottomans enter World War I on the side of the Germans and are defeated by the Allies.
1923 After its War of Independence, Turkey is declared a Republic led by President Kemal Atatürk.
1928 The Turkish constitution declares Turkey to be a secular state.
1938 Atatürk dies.
1945 Turkey remains neutral during World War II, lending nominal assistance to the Nazis while outwardly supporting the Allies.
1960 Army takes power in a coup that encounters minimal resistance, dismissing the ruling Democrat Party and hanging its leaders.
1980 Once more the army overthrows government and takes control. Governance is given back to civilians a couple of years later.
1993 Tansu Cillar becomes Turkey's first female Prime Minister.
2005 Talks about Turkish accession to the EU are held.
2007 Tens of thousands of secularists protest in Ankara against Islamist Prime Minister Erdogan's proposed run for president.
2009 Rare meeting between Prime Minister Erdogan and Ahmet Türk, leader of the pro-Kurdish Democratic Society Party.
2010 İstanbul named European Capital of Culture.

ARRIVAL AND VISAS

Tourist **visas** (€15–45 depending on nationality) are required for individuals from most countries and can be obtained

upon arrival; you'll need to pay in cash. Visas usually last for three months and enable visitors to travel between Turkey and neighbouring countries.

The most common point of **arrival** is İstanbul with overland travellers arriving at the bus station or Sirkeci train station located near the pier in Eminönü. International air arrivals fly into one of İstanbul's two **airports**: Atatürk (Ⓦwww.ataturkairport.com) on the European side or Sabiha Gökçen (Ⓦwww.sgairport.com), where many budget airlines arrive, on the Anatolian side. For travellers heading to Turkey's Turquoise Coast, Antalya's international airport is a good bet for the region's many resorts. If you're travelling to Turkey by sea you're likely to arrive at either Kuşadasi or Marmaris where ferries connect Turkey with the Greek islands.

GETTING AROUND

The **train** system, run by TCDD (Ⓦwww.tcdd.gov.tr) is limited. The most useful services are the express routes between İstanbul and Ankara, and other long-distance links to main provincial cities such as Edirne, Konya, Denizli and İzmir. Cheap sleeper cabins are available on overnight services. Reservations are only necessary at weekends or on national holidays. An ISIC card gets a twenty percent discount. InterRail passes are valid, Eurail aren't.

The **long-distance bus** network is extensive, reliable and affordable. Most destinations are served by several competing firms, which all have ticket booths at the bus station (*otogar* or terminal) from which they operate, as well as an office in the town centre. Book ahead if you're travelling in high season or on a public holiday. **Fares** vary only slightly between companies: expect to pay about 10TL per 100km. Bus companies usually provide a free shuttle bus between the *otogar* and town centre. For short hops you're most likely to use a **dolmuş** (shared taxi), a **car** or **minibus** that follows a set route, picking up and dropping off along the way. Sometimes the destination will be posted on a sign at the kerbside, and sometimes within the *dolmuş* itself, though you'll generally have to ask. Fares are very low. Vehicle and passenger **ferries** that cross the Sea of Marmaris are run by İstanbul Deniz Otobüsleri (Ⓦwww.ido.com.tr). Buy tickets in advance from official outlets.

ACCOMMODATION

Finding **accommodation** is generally no problem, except in high season in İstanbul, at the busier coastal resorts and in the larger towns. Basic ungraded **hotels** or **pansiyons** (*pensions*) offer fairly spartan rooms, with or without bathroom, for €30–60 for a double room. There's also a well-established network of **backpacker hotels** that generally cost €8–18 for a dorm bed, €20–60 for a private double room (some are en suite). Many resort-based places close in winter, so it's wise to call ahead. **Campsites** are common only on the coast and in national parks. Per-person charges are around €8–13. Campsites sometimes rent out tents.

FOOD AND DRINK

At its finest, Turkish food is one of the world's great cuisines, yet prices are on the whole affordable. **Breakfast** (*kahvaltı*) served at hotels and *pansiyons* is usually a buffet (approximately 5TL though often included in the price), offering bread with butter, cheese, jam, honey, olives and tea or coffee. Many workers start the morning with a *börek* (1.50TL) or a *poça*, pastries filled with meat, cheese or potato that are sold at a tiny *büfe* (stall/café) or at street carts. Others make do with a simple *simit* (sesame-seed bread ring). Snack vendors hawk *lahmacun*, small "pizzas" with meat-based toppings, and, in coastal cities, *midye dolma* (stuffed mussels). Another option is *pide*, or Turkish pizza – flat bread with various toppings.

NARGILES

Any visitor to Turkey will soon observe the nation's love affair with smoking. Smoke-free zones in restaurants and other public places are virtually nonexistent. Instead, a variety of bars exist specializing in **nargile** (waterpipe) smoking. *Nargiles* use special flavoured tobacco with varieties ranging from chocolate to strawberry. In touristy cafés smoking a *nargile* can cost about 16TL compared with 7TL in a locals' joint.

Meat dishes in **restaurants** include several variations on the kebab (*kebap*). Fish and seafood are good, if usually pricey. **Meze** – an extensive array of cold appetizers – come in all shapes and sizes, the most common being *dolma* (peppers or vine leaves stuffed with rice), *patlícan salata* (aubergine in tomato sauce), and *acılı* (a mixture of tomato paste, onion, chilli and parsley). Most budget restaurants are alcohol-free; some places marked *içk ili* (licensed) may be more expensive.

For **dessert**, there's every imaginable concoction at a *pastane* (sweet shop): best are the honey-soaked baklava, and a variety of milk puddings, most commonly *sütlaç*. Other sweets include *aşure* (Noah's pudding), a sort of rosewater jelly laced with pulses, raisins and nuts: and *lokum* or Turkish delight.

Restaurant opening hours vary widely but in general are open all day; some open as early as 7am, others open for lunch at around 11am and close between 11pm and 1am. Bars are generally open 11am or noon–2am. Clubs are usually open after 11pm until 5am–6am.

Drinks

Tea (*çay*) is the national drink, with sugar on the side but no milk. **Turkish coffee** (*kahve*) is strong and served in tiny cups, instant coffee is losing ground to fresh filter coffee in trendier cafés. **Fruit juices** (*meyva suyu*) can be excellent but are usually sweetened. You'll also come across **ayran**, watered-down yogurt, which makes a refreshing drink. The main locally brewed brands of **beer** (*bira*) are Efes Pilsen and Tuborg. The national aperitif is anis-flavoured *rakí* – a strong spirit consisting of 45 percent alcohol. It's usually topped up with water and enjoyed with meze or a *nargile* (see box opposite).

CULTURE AND ETIQUETTE

Turkey's unspoken codes of conduct can catch the first-time visitor off guard. Away from the main cities you should **dress modestly** and avoid shorts and revealing attire – this is particularly important the further east you travel. If you are a female traveller, it is essential to take a headscarf or shawl if you plan on visiting a mosque.

In almost every sphere of social interaction, **tea drinking** plays an important role. You'll notice shop salesmen commonly invite you to peruse their goods over tea.

Although interaction between Turkish men and women is quite formal, single female travellers may experience harassment and should take care, particularly in the evenings. Note also that while many young Turkish women visit bars and clubs few of them go out unaccompanied at night and you should observe this rule away from tourist areas.

HAGGLING

Shopping in Turkey requires more than just money. In bazaars, market stalls and independent shops, you should try **haggling** – the original price quoted can be three times the price of the item's actual value. Avoid displaying too much enthusiasm over your desired item and if the price quoted sounds expensive, inform the shopkeeper that you would like to shop around for a better deal – this might result in a better offer.

TURKEY ONLINE

ⓦ**www.roughguides.com** Information, travel deals and offers.
ⓦ**www.goturkey.com** Turkey's official tourism portal.
ⓦ**www.turkeytravelplanner.com** Turkey expert's personal guide to the country.

SPORTS AND ACTIVITIES

Undoubtedly the most popular sport enjoyed by locals is **football**, with Galatasaray, Beşiktaş and Fenerbahçe (all from İstanbul) being three of the nation's favourite teams. Major stadiums for national games include 19 Mayıs stadium, located in Ankara. To find out about games and buy tickets, visit ⓦwww.biletix.com. Most tour operators in the established resorts have information about both summer and winter adventure sports. Turkey specialists **IAH Holidays** (ⓦwww.iah-holidays.co.uk) will help you organize activities from horseriding and quad biking to canyoning and kayaking.

COMMUNICATIONS

Most **post offices** (PTT) open Monday to Saturday 8.30am to 5.30pm, with main branches open till 7/8pm and also on Sun. Use the *yurtdışı* (overseas) slot on postboxes. **Phone calls** can be made from Turk Telecom booths and the PTT. Post offices and kiosks sell phonecards (30, 60 and 100 units) and also have metered phones. Some payphones accept credit cards. Numerous private phone shops (Köntürlü telefon) offer metered calls at dubious, unofficial rates. The international operator is on ⓣ115. There are **internet** cafés in most towns, charging 1.50–3.50TL per hour. You'll find that most hostels and hotels have wi-fi or a computer for use by residents. Many bars, cafés, restaurants

– and even the long-distance buses – have free **wi-fi**.

INFORMATION

Most towns of any size have a **tourist office** (Turizm Danışma Bürosu) generally open Monday to Friday 8.30am to 12.30pm and 1.30 to 5.30pm. Staff usually speak English, and should be able to help you with accommodation and you'll generally find a good range of brochures and maps.

MONEY AND BANKS

Currency is the **Turkish lira** (TL), divided into 100 kuruş. There are coins

TURKISH

English	Turkish	Pronunciation
Yes	*Evet*	Evet
No	*Hayır/yok*	Hi-uhr/yok
Please	*Lütfen*	Lewtfen
Thank you	*Teşekkürler/mersi/sağol*	Teshekkewrler/sa-ol
Hello/Good day	*Merhaba*	Merhabuh
Goodbye	*Hoşçakalın*	Hosh-cha kaluhn
Excuse me	*Pardon*	Pardon
Where?	*Nerede?*	Neredeh?
Good	*İyi*	Eeyee
Bad	*Kötü*	Kurtew
Near	*Yakın*	Yakuhn
Far	*Uzak*	Oozak
Cheap	*Ucuz*	Oojooz
Expensive	*Pahalı*	Pahaluh
Open	*Açık*	Achuhk
Closed	*Kapalı*	Kapaluh
Today	*Bugün*	Boogewn
Yesterday	*Dün*	Dewn
Tomorrow	*Yarın*	Yaruhn
How much is...?	*Ne kadar...?*	Ne kadar...?
What time is it?	*Saatiniz var mı?*	Saatiniz var muh?
I don't understand	*Anlamıyorum*	Anlamuh-yoroom
Do you speak English?	*İngilizce biliyor musunuz?*	Eengeeleezjeh beeleeyor moosoonooz?
Sorry	*Özür dilerim*	Erzer delereem
Do you have...?	*...var mı?*	...va mur?
I would like...	*...istiyorum*	...e-stee-yo-rum
What is your name?	*Adınız ne?*	A-denurz nay?
I'd like the bill	*Hesabı Istiyorum*	hes-ab ee-stee-yo-rum
One	*Bir*	Bir
Two	*İki*	Iki
Three	*Üç*	Ewch
Four	*Dört*	Durt
Five	*Beş*	Besh
Six	*Altı*	Altuh
Seven	*Yedi*	Yedi
Eight	*Sekiz*	Sekiz
Nine	*Dokuz*	Dokuz
Ten	*On*	On

of 1, 5, 10, 25, 50 kuruş and 1TL, and notes of 1, 5, 10, 20, 50 and 100TL. £1 = 3TL, €1 = 2.5TL, US$1 = 2TL. Exchange rates for foreign currency are always better inside Turkey. Many *pensions* and hotels, particularly in the popular destinations, also quote prices in **euros**, particularly for more expensive options, and you can usually pay in either euros or Turkish lira.

Banks open Monday to Friday 8.30am to noon and 1.30pm to 5pm; some, notably Garanti Bankasi, are open at lunchtimes and on Saturday. Some of the **exchange booths** run by banks in coastal resorts, airports and ferry docks charge a small commission. Private exchange offices have competitive rates and no commission. Almost all banks have ATMs. **Post offices** in sizeable towns also sometimes change cash and cheques, for a one percent commission.

OPENING HOURS AND HOLIDAYS

Shops are generally open Monday to Saturday 9am to 7/8pm, and possibly Sunday, depending on the owner. There are two **religious holidays**. **Kurban Bayramı** (the Feast of the Sacrifice) falls on October 25 to 28 in 2012, on October 15 to 18 in 2013, and October 4 to 7 in 2014. **Şeker Bayramı** (Sugar Holiday), which marks the end of the Muslim fasting month of Ramadan falls August 18 to 20 in 2012, and August 8 to 10 in 2013. If either falls midweek, the government may choose to extend the holiday period to as much as nine days. Many shops and restaurants close as their owners return to their home towns for the holiday. Banks and public offices are also closed on the **secular holidays**: January 1, April 23, May 19, August 30, October 28 and 29.

STUDENT AND YOUTH DISCOUNTS

Finding places that consistently offer **student discounts** in Turkey is a task in itself. Despite the presence of a large student population in many of the major cities, few shops or bars offer student discounts. Nevertheless, an ISIC card can get you a small discount on bus travel with some of the major firms such as Kamil Koç, Pamukkale, Uludag and Varan. It's also worth asking about student discounts before you book into a hotel, as many may be willing to offer a discount but reluctant to publicize the fact.

EMERGENCY NUMBERS

Police ☎155; Ambulance ☎112; Fire ☎110.

EMERGENCIES

Street **crime** is uncommon and theft is rare, however, lone women should pay attention and be very wary of going out alone after dark. Police wear dark blue uniforms with baseball caps, with their division – *trafik*, *narkotik*, etc – clearly marked. In rural areas, you'll find the camouflage-clad Jandarma, a division of the regular army. For minor **health** complaints, head for the nearest pharmacy (*eczane*). Night-duty pharmacists are known as *nöbetçi*; the current rota is posted in every pharmacy's front window. For more serious ailments, go to a hospital (*klinik*) – either public (Devlet Hastane or SSK Hastanesi), or the much higher quality and cleaner private (Özel Hastane).

İstanbul

Arriving in **İSTANBUL** can result in sensory overload: backstreets teem with traders pushing handcarts, the smell of grilled food from roadside vendors lingers in the air and the sales patter of hawkers reverberates through the streets. Yet this is merely one aspect of modern İstanbul. With the hip bars, cafés, boutiques and art galleries in Beyoğlu, a distinctly continental influence also pervades.

İstanbul is the only city in the world to have played capital to consecutive Christian and Islamic empires, and retains features of both. Named **Byzantium** after the Greek colonists' Byzas, the city was an important trading centre. In the fourth century it was renamed **Constantinople** when Constantine chose it as the new capital of the Roman Empire. The city later became an independent empire, adopting the Greek language and Christianity as its religion. The region gradually became ruled by the Islamic **Ottomans** and in 1453 the city was captured by the Ottoman Conqueror Mehmet. By the nineteenth century, the glory days of Ottoman domination were over. After the War of Independence, the territorial boundaries of modern-day Turkey were set and the country's leader, Mustafa Kemal Atatürk, created a new capital in Ankara.

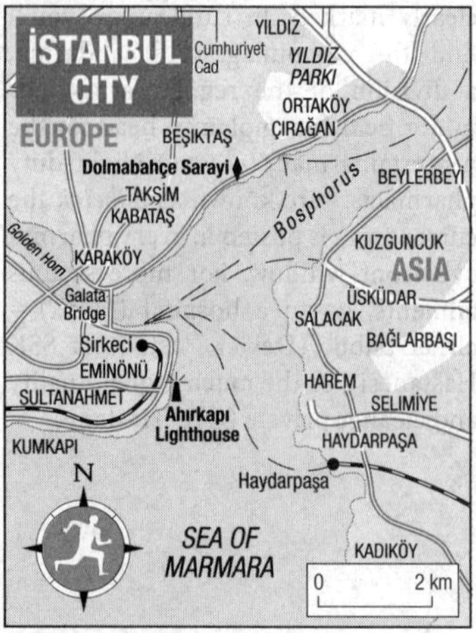

What to see and do

The city is divided in two by the **Bosphorus**, a stretch of water that runs between the Black Sea and the Sea of Marmara, dividing Europe from Asia. At right angles to it, the inlet of the **Golden Horn** cuts the European side in two. It is this European section where most visitors spend their time, wandering around the cobbled streets and tourist sites in **Sultanahmet** or exploring the arty district of **Beyoğlu**. Sandwiched between the two is **Eminönü** and the old Levantine area of Galata, now **Karaköy**, home to one of the city's most famous landmarks, the Galata Tower. **Taksim** is a convenient base, and comes into its own at night as a centre of cultural and culinary activity; take bus #T4 from Sultanahmet, which runs via Karaköy.

Aya Sofya

The former Byzantine cathedral of **Aya Sofya** (May–Nov Tues–Sun 9am–7pm 9am–6pm; Nov–April Tues–Sun 9am–4.30pm; 20TL), readily visible thanks to its massive domed structure, is perhaps the single most compelling sight in the city. Commissioned in the sixth century by the Emperor Justinian, it was converted to a mosque in 1453, after which the minarets were added; it's been a museum since 1934. For centuries this was the largest enclosed space in the world, and the interior – filled with shafts of light from the high windows around the dome – is still profoundly impressive. There are a few features left over from its time as a mosque – a mihrab (niche indicating the direction of Mecca), a mimber (pulpit) and the enormous wooden plaques which bear sacred names of God, the Prophet

Mohammed and the first four Caliphs. There are also remains of abstract and figurative mosaics.

Topkapı Palace

Immediately north of Aya Sofya, **Topkapı Palace** (daily except Tues 9am–7pm, last admission 6pm; 20TL) is İstanbul's second unmissable sight. Built between 1459 and 1465, the palace was the centre of the Ottoman Empire for nearly four centuries. The ticket office is in the first courtyard, followed by the beautifully restored Divan, containing the Imperial Council Hall in the second courtyard. Around the corner is the Harem, well worth the additional 15TL (9am–4pm; tickets sold outside Harem entrance). The only men once allowed in here were eunuchs and the imperial guardsmen, who were only employed at certain hours and even then blinkered. Back in the main body of the palace, in the third courtyard, the throne room was where the sultan awaited the outcome of sessions of the Divan.

The Blue Mosque

With its six minarets, the **Camii Sultanahmet**, or Blue Mosque (daily 9am–one hour before dusk prayer call), is instantly recognizable; inside, its four "elephant foot" pillars obscure parts of the building and dwarf the dome they support. It's the 20,000-odd blue tiles inside that lend the mosque its name. Outside the precinct wall is the Tomb of Sultan Ahmet (daily 8.30am–5pm), where the sultan is buried along with his wife and three of his sons. Behind the mosque is the **Vakıf Carpet Museum** (Tues–Sat 9am–4pm; 2TL), which houses antique carpets and kilims from all over Turkey.

The Museum of Turkish and Islamic Art

Located in the former palace of Ibrahim Paşa, the **Museum of Turkish and Islamic Art** (Tues–Sun 9am–4.30pm; 10TL) houses one of the best-exhibited collections of Islamic artefacts in the world. Ibrahim Paşa's magnificent audience hall is devoted to a collection of Turkish carpets, while on the ground floor, in rooms off the central courtyard, is an exhibition of the folk art of the Yörük tribes of Anatolia.

The Archeological Museum and around

Just west of Topkapkı, **Gülhane Parkı**, once the palace gardens, houses three museums (May–Sept Tues–Sun 9am–6pm; Nov–April Tues–Sun 9am–4pm) all covered by one ticket (10TL). In the **Archeological Museum** is a superb collection of sarcophagi, sculptures and other remains of past civilizations. The adjacent **Çinili Köşk** is the oldest secular building in İstanbul, now a Museum of Ceramics housing a select collection of İznık ware and Selçuk tiles. Nearby, the **Museum of the Ancient Orient** contains a small but dazzling collection of Anatolian, Egyptian and Mesopotamian artefacts.

The Covered Bazaar

Off the main street of Divan Yolu Caddesi lies the district of Beyazıt, centred on the Kapalı Çarşı or **Covered Bazaar** (Mon–Sat 8.30am–7.30pm; Beyazıt tram stop), a huge web of passageways housing more than four thousand shops, each with chatty, persuasive salesmen. Give yourself an hour or two to negotiate its network of alleyways and to soak up the bustling atmosphere. There are carpet shops everywhere catering for all budgets, shops selling leather goods, gold jewellery, slippers, ceramics and mass-made souvenirs. If you do decide to buy something, don't forget to haggle (see box, p.1207).

Kadiköy

On the Asian (or Anatolian) side of the city, **Kadiköy** makes a great day-trip or base for a few days. It's a fun residen-

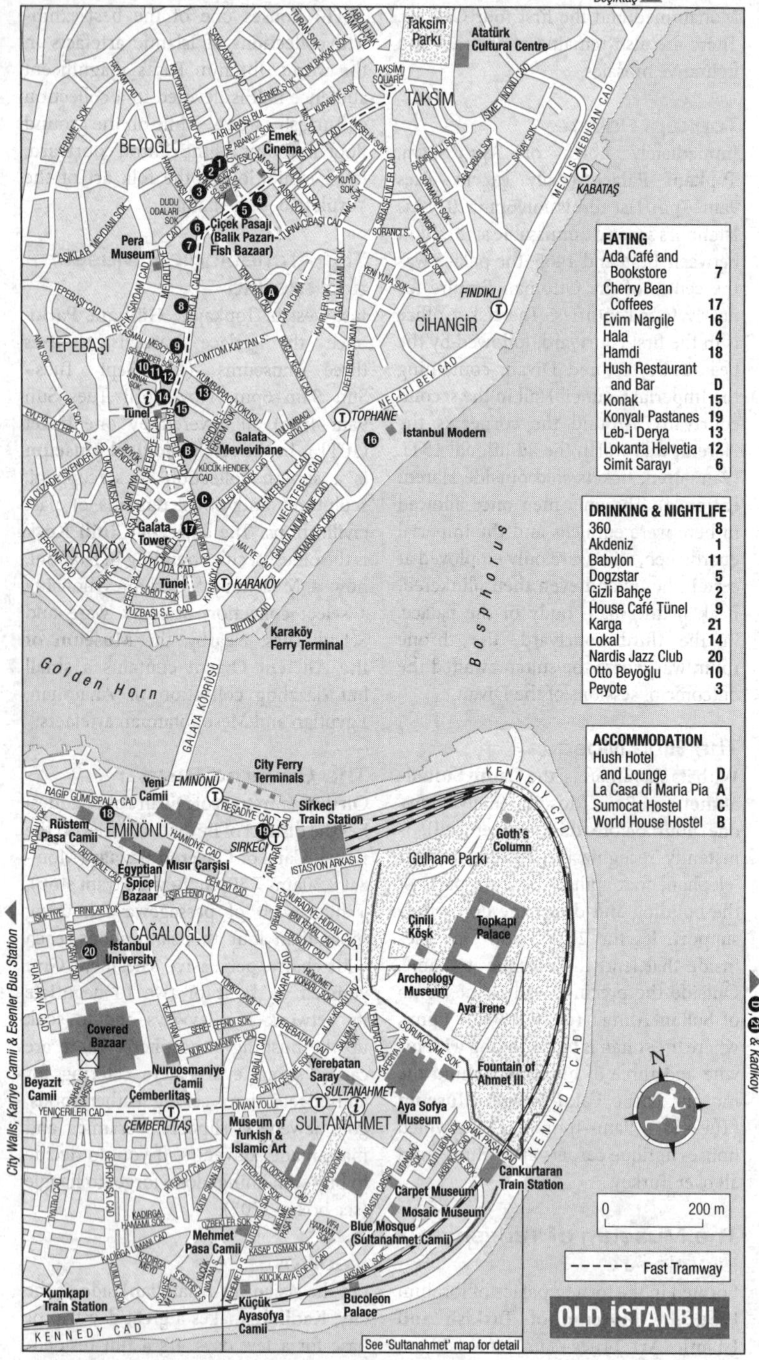
OLD İSTANBUL
EATING
Ada Café and Bookstore 7
Cherry Bean Coffees 17
Evim Nargile 16
Hala 4
Hamdi 18
Hush Restaurant and Bar D
Konak 15
Konyalı Pastanes 19
Leb-i Derya 13
Lokanta Helvetia 12
Simit Sarayı 6
DRINKING & NIGHTLIFE
360 8
Akdeniz 1
Babylon 11
Dogzstar 5
Gizli Bahçe 2
House Café Tünel 9
Karga 21
Lokal 14
Nardis Jazz Club 20
Otto Beyoğlu 10
Peyote 3
ACCOMMODATION
Hush Hotel and Lounge D
La Casa di Maria Pia A
Sumocat Hostel C
World House Hostel B
Beşiktaş
Taksim Parkı
Atatürk Cultural Centre
TAKSIM SQUARE
TAKSİM
BEYOĞLU
Emek Cinema
Çiçek Pasajı (Balik Pazarı-Fish Bazaar)
Pera Museum
KABATAŞ
FINDIKLI
CİHANGİR
TEPEBAŞI
Tünel
TOPHANE
İstanbul Modern
Galata Mevlevihane
Galata Tower
KARAKÖY
Karaköy Ferry Terminal
Golden Horn
Bosphorus
GALATA KÖPRÜSÜ
City Ferry Terminals
Yeni Camii
EMİNÖNÜ
Sirkeci Train Station
SIRKECI
Rüstem Pasa Camii
Egyptian Spice Bazaar
Mısır Çarşisi
Goth's Column
Gulhane Parkı
CAĞALOĞLU
Istanbul University
Çinili Köşk
Topkapı Palace
Archeology Museum
Aya Irene
Covered Bazaar
Nuruosmaniye Camii
Beyazit Camii
Çemberlitaş
ÇEMBERLITAŞ
Yerebatan Saray
SULTANAHMET
Fountain of Ahmet III
Aya Sofya Museum
Museum of Turkish & Islamic Art
Cankurtaran Train Station
Carpet Museum
Mosaic Museum
Blue Mosque (Sultanahmet Camii)
Mehmet Pasa Camii
Kumkapı Train Station
Küçük Ayasofya Camii
Bucoleon Palace
KENNEDY CAD
City Walls, Kariye Camii & Esenler Bus Station
D, 21 & Kadiköy
0 200 m
Fast Tramway
See 'Sultanahmet' map for detail

tial district where you can escape the backpacker hordes of Sultanahmet; many residents live here and commute to work on the Euro side. Ferries between Asia and European sides are cheap and frequent, take twenty minutes and operate from around 6am to 11.30pm.

Karaköy and Beyoğlu

Across the Galata Bridge from Eminönü is **Karaköy** (formerly Galata) and **Beyoğlu.** Karaköy was previously the capital's "European" quarter, and has been home to Jewish, Greek and Armenian minorities. Today you'll find boutiques, one-off crafts shops and small art galleries, and it's where locals and clued-up overseas visitors meet in hip café-bars, restaurants and clubs; this is the place to come for a night out without the tourist hordes you get in Sultanahmet. The **Galata Tower** (daily 9am–7pm; 11TL), built in 1348, is the area's most obvious landmark; its viewing galleries, café (Turkish coffee 5TL, beer 8TL) and ridiculously expensive restaurant offer the best panoramas of the city.

Up towards Istiklâl Caddesi, Beyoğlu's main boulevard, an unassuming doorway leads to the courtyard of the **Galata Mevlevihane** (9am–4.30pm, closed Wed; 5TL), a former monastery and ceremonial hall of the Whirling Dervishes, a sect founded in the thirteenth century. Staged dervish ceremonies take place at the Sirkeci Central Train Station Exhibition Hall (check at the Mevlevihane for details). Pay a visit to the **Pera Museum** (Tues–Sat 10am–7pm; Sun noon–6pm; 7TL) on Meişrutiyet Cad 65, housed in a beautiful nineteenth-century building and displaying changing exhibitions of contemporary art, historical oil paintings of old İstanbul, ceramic tiles and a collection of historical weights and measures.

Arrival and information

Air İstanbul's Atatürk airport is 24km west of the city. The cheapest option to get to Sultanahmet or Beyoğlu (if you arrive in the daytime) is to take the metro from the airport; it runs to the city centre at Aksaray, but for Sultanahmet or Taksim it's best to change onto the tramway at Zeytinburnu; this entire journey costs around 4TL and takes about an hour. A taxi will cost around 35TL to Sultanahmet or 40TL to Taksim; make sure they use the meter. Be wary of trusting a shuttle bus tout at the airport, although the Havaş bus (4am–1am every 30min; 10TL; 40min) is a reliable option; the bus terminates at Taksim but get off at Aksaray and take the tram (1.75TL) for Sultanahmet.

İstanbul's Sabiha Gökçen airport is in Asia. The Havaş bus (every 30min; 4am–midnight, thereafter when flights land; 14TL; 1hr 30min) terminates at Taksim (a taxi from Taksim to Sultanahmet is around 12TL). A taxi from Sabiha Gökçen airport to Sultanahmet will cost around 90TL.

Train Trains from Europe terminate at Sirkeci station, linked to Sultanahmet by a short tram ride

HISTORICAL ÇEMBERLITAŞ HAMMAM

No trip to Turkey is complete without a trip to a traditional Turkish bath. In İstanbul, a short walk from the Grand Bazaar is one of İstanbul's finest historical public baths, **Çemberlitaş Hammam** at Vesir Hanı Cad 8, Çemberlitaş. At the entrance you'll be given a *peştamal* (cotton towel) to wrap yourself in, and a scrubbing mitt; ladies will also be given a pair of disposable underwear. Men and women bathe in separate areas. Once you've changed and put any personal items in a locker you'll be led into the *sıcakılk*, a hot room with a heated marble platform on which you lie down and relax for 15 minutes or so until you start to sweat. If you've opted for a soap scrub, your attendant will spend fifteen minutes washing, scrubbing and rinsing you, removing grime and dead skin cells. Otherwise you wash yourself. Afterwards, take a dip in the hot tub or relax in the cool lounge afterwards with a cup of tea or fresh fruit juice. Allow at least an hour for the entire process. Basic entry 39TL; entrance plus soap scrub by an attendant 59TL; discount for ISIC cardholders.

(1.75TL); trains from Asia terminate at Haydarpaşa station on the east bank of the Bosphorus, from where you can get a ferry (1.75TL) to Eminönü and a tram from there to Sultanahmet.

Bus From İstanbul's bus station (*otogar*) at Esenler, 15km northwest, the better bus companies run courtesy minibuses to various points in the city, although if you're heading for Sultanahmet it's often quicker to take the metro (actually an express tramway; 1.75TL). Some buses also stop at the Harem bus station on the Asian side, from where there are regular *dolmuşes* to Haydarpaşa station. Taxis to Sultanahmet cost approximately 20TL from the main *otogar*. Watch out for drivers who offer their services near to the departure area. These are usually unlicensed and do not operate a meter.

Tourist office The most central office is in Sultanahmet, near the Hippodrome on Divan yolu Cad (daily 9am–5pm; ⓣ0212/518 8754). Smaller branches are at the airport (24hr) and the two train stations. The branch at Sirkeci is especially helpful.

City transport

Train There's a municipal train network running along the Marmara shore – west from Sirkeci station on the European side, and east from Haydarpaşa on the Asian (allow at least 1hr to get to the Asian station from the centre). On the European side you buy a token (1.75TL) to let you through the turnstile onto the platform, while on the Asian side you buy a ticket (same price).

Bus Two bus services operate on the same city routes, either the private Halk Otobus service (pay conductor; 1.50TL) or the more common municipality buses (marked IETT), for which you have to buy tickets (1.50TL) in advance from bus stations, newspaper kiosks or fast-food booths; some longer routes, usually served by double-deckers, require two advance tickets (look for the sign *iki bilet geçerlidir*). There are route maps at main bus stops.

Tram The European side has two tram lines, one running from Kabataş through Sultanahmet to outlying suburbs; buy tokens (*jetons*; 1.75TL) from a booth before you enter the platform. The other "toy" tram runs along Istiklâl Cad from Beyoğlu to Taksim using an antique tram; pay on board (1.75TL). The funicular between Tünel in Beyoğlu to Karaköy takes three minutes and costs 2.50TL.

Dolmuş *Dolmuşes* have their point of departure and destination displayed somewhere about the windscreen or painted on the bonnet.

Boat Regular ferries run between Eminönü and Karaköy on the European side, and Üsküdar, Kadiköy and Haydarpaşa in Asia; buy your ticket (1.75TL one-way) from the dockside kiosks. Ferries depart every 15–20min from around 6am to 11.30pm; crossings take 20min. There are also sightseeing hop-on-and-off boats that cruise the Bosphorus. These leave from the Boğaz Iskelesi terminal near the Eminönü tram stop and stop at either Anadolu Hisarı or Anadolu Kavağı. The trip on a government-run boat costs between 6 and 10TL, whereas private boat tours can cost up to 45TL (including hotel pick-up and guided tour). The cruise takes approximately 1hr 45min each way and the last return boat from Anadolu Kavağı in summer is at 5pm, after which you'll need to take a bus or *dolmuş*.

Travel passes The handy Akbil travel pass (from kiosks at most bus, tram, train and metro stations; deposit 6TL – get a receipt so you can claim the money back; then charge it with as much as you like), once charged with money, provides travellers with a marginal discount (approx 10 percent) on travel and makes it easier to hop on and off the metro, tram and bus. It looks like a large watch battery on a small piece of plastic that can be attached to a key ring. Any changes between modes of transport made within 45min of your first touch-in will not be charged, whereas if you were using *jetons* (1.75TL) then you would need one each time. To use it, touch it to the small button, usually marked, on turnstiles at stations or next to the driver on buses. The İstanbulkart is similar to London's Oyster card and was launched with a view to phasing out the Akbil. Buy an İstanbulkart for 10TL then charge it (like a pay-as-you-go phone) at machines at stops or stations. To use, swipe the card as you board a bus, ferry or tram.

Accommodation

There are numerous small hotels and *pansiyons* in Sultanahmet, particularly around Yerebatan Cad and the backstreets between the Blue Mosque and the sea. Taksim is a great base, and is handy for nightlife and boutique shopping and hip cafés. From Eminönü and Aksaray, many buses pass through either Karaköy or Taksim, or both. To escape the backpacker hordes and experience the city as a local, stay in Kadiköy on the Asian side. Most hotels include breakfast in the price and some have a/c, cable TV and free internet access.

Sultanahmet

Antique Hostel Kutlugün Sok 51 ⓣ0212/638 1637, ⓦwww.antiquehostel.com. The rooms are a little stuffy but good looking nonetheless. The sea-view terrace is perched atop the city like an eyrie with an island bar and decent food available (mains 12–15TL). Wi-fi and breakfast included. All rooms have a/c. Dorms €18, singles €45, doubles €58, triples €73, quads €85.

Big Apple Akbıyık Cad Bayram Fırını Sok No 12 ⓣ0212/517 7931, ⓦwww.hostelbigapple.com. The place as a whole has a slightly sombre feel but the dorms are clean and bright and there's a great view from the roof terrace where there's a bar, music and belly dancing in the evenings. No kitchen. Breakfast and wi-fi included. Dorms €15, doubles from €50, singles from €40.

İstanbul Hostel Kutlugün Sok 35 ⓣ0212/516 9380, ⓦwww.istanbulhostel.net. Friendly long-running hostel, with 68 beds in clean, bright rooms, free wi-fi and internet access, terrace and bar. Hostel guests get ten percent discount in the restaurant. Ground-floor rooms are noisy. Dorms €13, doubles €30–70.

Moonstar Hostel Akbıyık Cad 33 ⓣ0212/458 7471, ⓦwww.moonstarhostel.com. Small and friendly 18-bed place. Breakfast and wi-fi included. Pretty rooftop terrace serves food – on Fridays fish supper and a beer is a bargain 12TL. Dorms €8–23, doubles €50, singles €40.

Orient International Youth Hostel Akbıyık Cad 13 ⓣ0212/518 0789, ⓦwww.orienthostel.com. A large hostel with 150 beds in clean and bright rooms with fresh bathrooms. A good atmosphere, a spacious rooftop bar, and free wi-fi and laptops. Breakfast included. Dorms €10, doubles €40.

Sultan Hostel Akbıyık Cad 21 ⓣ0212/516 9260, ⓦwww.sultanhostel.com. The friendly bar-restaurant is a social focal point on this, the main hostel street, with dorm beds empty until the early hours. Despite the attempt at soundproofing the music makes it through from the bar. Fine views from the terrace and top-floor 20-bed dorm. Decent food with mains around 10TL. Breakfast, tea and coffee (till 6pm) and wi-fi included. No a/c. Dorms from €9, doubles €48–60.

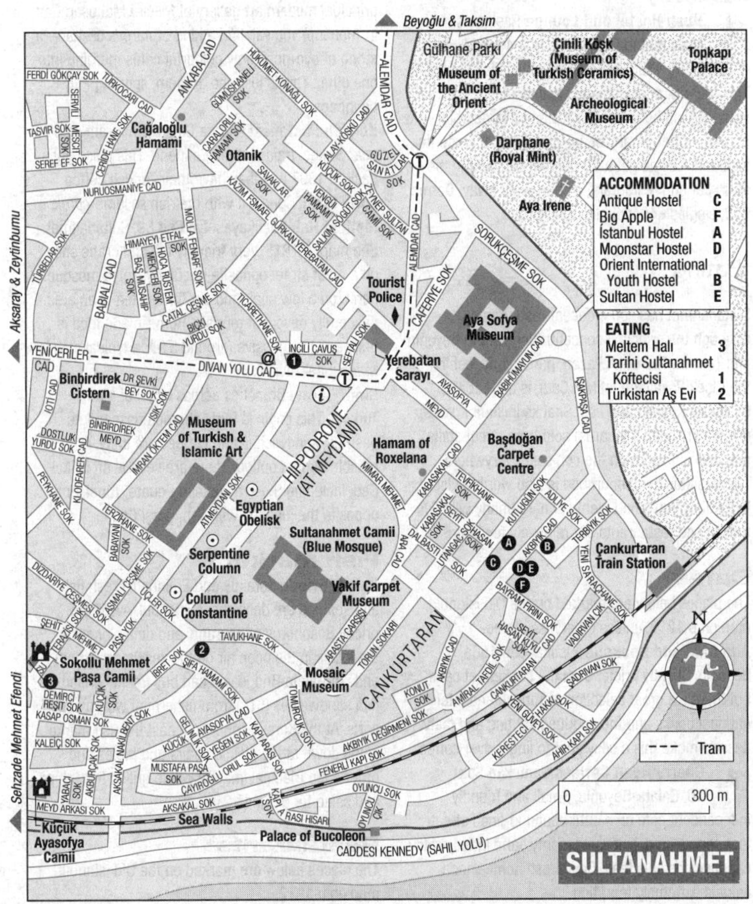

Beyoğlu and Taksim

Sumocat Hostel Alı Hoca Aralık Sok 9 ⓣ0212/292 7866, ⓦwww.sumocathostel.com. A small friendly hostel in Galata housed in a renovated nineteenth-century building with funkily decorated rooms. Close to the bars and nightlife of Beyoğlu. Breakfast and wi-fi included. All rooms have a/c. Kitchen. Dorms €10–16, doubles €50–60.

World House Hostel Galipdede Cad No 85, Kadiköy ⓣ0212/293 5520, ⓦwww.worldhouseistanbul.com. Just round the corner from Galata Tower, a nice alternative to the Sultanahmet hostels. The best dorm is at the top with great views of the tower. Wi-fi available and breakfast included. The mosque next door means there is no bar, but booze can be taken in. Dorms €17, doubles from €50, triples from €60.

Kadiköy

Hush Hostel and Lounge Rasimpaşa Mah, Rıhtım Cad, İskele Sok 46, Kadiköy ⓣ0216/450 4363, ⓦwww.hushhostelistanbul.com. This friendly, spacious and clean hostel has a well-equipped kitchen, roof terrace and a large back garden. Buffet breakfast, wi-fi and use of computer included. Guests get a 20 percent discount in the *Hush* bar and restaurant, a short walk away. Dorms €12, singles €40, doubles €34–50.

Eating

Sultanahmet has some decent restaurants, although the principal concentrations are in Beyoğlu and Taksim. The Balık Pazarı, particularly, behind the Çiçek Pasajı (off Istiklâl Cad), is a great area for meze, kebabs and fish. Snacks include *kokoreç* (skeins of sheep's innards) sold from street stalls and delicious corn on the cob sold everywhere. The Beşiktaş neighbourhood is also worth a visit. In Kadiköy you'll find plenty of bars (many with live music) and restaurants but relatively few tourists.

Cafés

The places below are marked on the Old İstanbul map on p.1212, unless otherwise stated.

Ada Café and Bookstore İstikal Cad 158a, Beyoğlu. Slightly pricier than the backstreet caffs but there's a great selection of Turkish and international books and the subdued lighting and tasty deserts make this a cosy spot to linger over coffee.

Cherry Bean Coffees Camekan Sok 10, Galata-Beyoğlu. Small and friendly independent café on a cute boutique-lined street that serves up deliciously creamy caffe lattes, frothy cappuccinos plus teas. Daily fresh home-made cake is extremely tempting.

LIVE LIKE A LOCAL

La Casa di Maria Pia Yeni Carsi Cad 37, Beyoğlu (ⓣ0541/624 5462, ⓦwww.lacasadimariapia.com). If you're planning on staying for a week or so in İstanbul then renting an apartment is a good, affordable option. The five apartments, small guestroom and studio flat are quirkily decorated with *objets* collected by the owner. Fully equipped kitchenettes in the apartments. Guestroom €40 per night, apartments from €75 per night.

Evim Nargile In front of İstanbul Modern (the city's principal modern art gallery at Mecli-i Mebusan Cad in Tophane) you will find a kind of *nargile* bazaar – a string of eye-poppingly colourful cafés merging into one other. This is just one of them, sporting PVC beanbags.

Konyalı Pastanesi Ankara Cad, by the tram stop near Sirkeci train station, Eminönü. This place goes back to 1897 and they have their Turkish coffee down to a T. Couple it with the rich sesame *çörek*.

Meltem Halı Küçükayasofya Cad 89, Sultanahmet. See map, p.1215. Very friendly tea and crafts shop on a quiet street opposite Küçük Ayasofya mosque. Perch on a low chair and sip Turkish tea in an area peacefully devoid of tourists. Home-made food is tasty and inexpensive (around 5TL); a typical dish is *mantı* (beef ravioli).

Simit Sarayı Branches across İstanbul (and Turkey). This chain is fairly characterless but its pastries, sandwiches and coffees are tasty. A reliable budget option. There are several on İstikal Cad, including those at Taksim Square, Tünel, and opposite the junction with Yeni Çarşi Cad.

Fish market

Galate Brigde Karaköy and Eminönü. Fresh fish and seafood are delicious in İstanbul. Avoid the pricey Bosphorus restaurants and dine alongside the locals in the open air on the seashore. At both ends of Galata Bridge you can buy freshly grilled fish sandwiches (5TL) from fishermen with mobile carts. At the Karaköy end walk past the fish market, settle down at the plastic chairs and tables and order crisp fried calamari, a whole grilled fish, chips and salad for around 12TL.

Restaurants

The places below are marked on the Old İstanbul map on p.1212.

Hala Istiklâl Cad 211, near Turnacıbaşı Cad, Beyoğlu. If you don't want to wander too far from the main Beyoğlu thoroughfare then this is the most authentic purveyor of *mantı* and *gözleme* nearby. You'll see the women making the pancakes in the window – maybe it is auntie, which is what "hala" means. *Gözleme* 5–6.50TL.

Hamdi Tahmis Cad Kalçin Sok 17, Eminönü ⓣ0212/528 0390. Third-floor restaurant next to the spice bazaar. Fresh meze and *köfte* are all served to a high standard. Highly popular and touristy but the views of the Golden Horn are irresistible. Reservations advised. Mains 12–18TL.

Hush Restaurant and Bar Caferağa Mah, Miralay Nazim Sok 20, Kadıköy. Housed in a beautiful 140-year-old Greek house that retains original features like high ceilings, tiles and plasterwork, this bar and restaurant is very popular with locals. There are several rooms over three floors, a large outdoor terrace garden and a small contemporary art gallery in the basement. Food is Italian and includes pizza (11–22TL), home-made gnocchi (11TL) and American dishes such as nachos (10TL) and cheeseburger with chips (12.50TL). The bar stays open till 4am on weekends.

Konak Istiklâl Cad, near Tünel. Very fresh salads and light, scorchingly hot flatbread accompany the excellent food such as *beyti kebap* for 10TL and *lahmacun* for just 2.50TL – surprising prices for such a smart place.

Leb-i Derya Kumbaracı Yokuşu 57/6, Tünel. This is one of the best bar-restaurants from which to see the city from up high. The food and the cocktails are as good as the view, though prices are not budget. The street is steep and narrow, leading off from the main drag, Istiklâl Cad.

Lokanta Helvetia General Yazgan Sok 8/a, Beyoğlu. It may be small but the buffet-style lunches and dinners make this one of Beyoğlu's best bargains (it's 10TL/plate). Soups (4TL) are tasty too.

Tarihi Sultanahmet Köftecisi Divanyolu Cad 12, Sultanahmet. See map, p.1215. Join local workers, who queue at lunchtimes outside this İstanbul institution. Service is speedy and the food is delicious. *Köfte* (meatballs), fresh salad and basket of bread with a glass of *ayran* or Coke will cost around 15TL.

Türkistan Aş Evi Tavukhane Sok 36, Sultanahmet. See map, p.1215. A restored Ottoman house restaurant serving set three-course meals of Turkish dishes. Try the "Harput Marriage Feast Soup" of meat, chickpeas, potatoes, yogurt and saffron for 8TL. Live music at night. Mains 15TL.

Drinking and nightlife

Backpackers tend to gather in the bars on Akbıyık Cad in Sultanahmet, but Beyoğlu is a much better choice, especially around Nevizade Sok where you'll find a hip arty international crowd hanging out. In Kadıköy go to Kadife Sok, aka "bar street", for the liveliest places. The places below are marked on p.1212.

Bars

360 Misir Apartmani 32/309, Istiklâl Cad, Tünel ⓦwww.360istanbul.com. Actually a restaurant, bar and club, as its name suggests this place has panoramic views best appreciated at night. At weekends the place rocks till the small hours.

Akdeniz Nevizade Sok 25, Beyoğlu. Rambling, multistorey student bar, with rock music and cheap drinks. A nice one for aimless sitting around.

Gizli Bahçe Nevizade Sok 27, Beyoğlu. Cutting-edge dance music in a dilapidated Ottoman town-house bar. Probably looks like a squat in daylight. This is hipster İstanbul, with languidly cool staff. No sign on the door, but the street is tiny and anybody will point you to it.

House Café Tünel Asmalı Mescit 9/1-2, Tünel. If you are not hipstered-out and stony broke then you might squeeze in one more cocktail outside this café-bar. There are loads of places to eat nearby if you develop a beer hunger.

Karga Kadife Sok 16, Kadıköy. A hip yet friendly bar spread across several floors and furnished with lots of dark chunky wood tables. DJs and live music.

Lokal 4 Tünel Meydanı, Tünel. Formerly *Kaffeehaus*, this place has turned to the drink, and its new persona suits it very well. With high ceilings and a raucous atmosphere, its location means new faces are constantly arriving. Beers 10TL.

Otto Beyoğlu Şehbender Sok 5, Beyoğlu. The thick graffiti in the main room is a kind of testament to its huge popularity. It has a vibrant and edgy atmosphere. Perhaps the delicious hazelnut vodka is the secret of its success. Towards midnight it turns clubby. Its sister bar *Otto Sofyalı* is just round the corner.

Clubs

Babylon Şehbender Sok 3, Asmalı Mescıt Tünel, Beyoğlu ⓦwww.babylon.com.tr. More of a gig and performance venue than a club, it attracts the most exciting, alternative Turkish and international acts.

Dogzstar Kartal Sok 3, Kat 3 ⓦwww.dogzstar.com. A pioneering club on the city's music scene, which seeks out innovative, genre-bending musicians and bands. There is currently a trend for electronic rock. Sometimes charges a small entrance fee.

Peyote Sahne Sok 24, Beyoğlu ⓦwww.peyote.com.tr. Sweaty folk cool off on the godsend of a roof terrace before delving back into this deep/hard house hothouse.

Shopping

İstanbul is famous for its bazaars, where you can pick up pretty much anything, from mass-produced trinkets and souveniers to megabucks hand-woven carpets. Shops lining Istiklâl Cad are the place to head for clothes (you'll find European and American brands here) and the network of narrow streets in Beyoğlu are home to numerous boutiques, second-hand and vintage shops, as well as owner-maker artist studios where you can buy one-off craft items for affordable prices.

Bazaars

Arasta Bazaar Mimar Mehmet Ağa Cad 14, Sultanahmet. Good for handmade crafts and carpets.
Mısır Çarşısı (Egyptian Spice Bazaar). Çiçek Pazarı Sok, 5min southwest of Eminönü tram stop. Everything from spices to jewellery, natural apple tea and aphrodisiacs including chewy sweet-like blocks of Viagra.

Entertainment

For listings pick up monthly *Time Out İstanbul* (5TL) from newsstands, bookshops, hotels and hostels.
Atatürk Cultural Centre Taksim Square, Beyoğlu. Concert and exhibition venue. Principal centre for events during the International Music Festival (June–July).
Emek Cinema Yeşilçam Sok 5, Istiklâl Cad. Popular cinema regularly screening international releases. Student discount available.
Nardis Jazz Club Galata Kulesi Sok. Small, dimly lit jazz club where music rather than conversation takes centre stage. Performances by international artists during the İstanbul Jazz Festival (July).

Directory

Consulates Australia, 16 Floor Süzer Plaza, Elmadag Askerocagi Cad 15, Şişli 34367 ⓣ0212/243 1333; Ireland, Ali Rıza Gürcan Cad, Meridyen İş Merkezi Kat:4 No 417, Merter ⓣ0212/482 1862; New Zealand, İnönü Cad No 48/3, Taksim 80090 ⓣ0212/244 0272; US, Kaplıcalar Mevkii Sok 2, Istinye 34460 ⓣ0212/335 9000.
Hospitals American Hospital, Güzelbahçe Sok 20, Nişantaşı ⓣ0212/231 4050; International Hospital, İstanbul Cad 82, Yeşilköy ⓣ0212/663 3000.
Internet Blue Internet Café, Yerebatan Cad 54; Seycom, Divan Yolu Cad 54/4, Sultanahmet; Net A Net, Divan Yolu Cad İncili Çavuş Sok 33, Sultanahmet; A Çayevi, Ebussuud Cad 37, Sirkeci.
Left luggage Sirkeci and Haydarpaşa train stations.
Police Tourist Police, Yerebatan Cad, Sultanahmet ⓣ0212/527 4503.
Post office Yeni Posthane Cad, Sirkeci; corner of Istiklâl Cad and Yeniçarşi Cad, Beyoğlu.
Telephone International Cheap Call, Dr Eminpaşa Sok 2, Divan Yolu Cad, Sultanahmet, or Net A Net, Divan Yolu Cad İncili Çavuş Sok 33, Sultanahmet.
Travel agents Road Runner Travel Agency (Alemdar Cad 2/b, Sultanahmet ⓦwww.roadrunnertravel.net) is a well-run company offering tours in İstanbul and the rest of the country.

Moving on

Train Ankara (6 daily; 8–9hr 30min); Budapest, Hungary (26hr); Edirne (1 daily; 5hr 30min); İzmir (1 daily; 7hr 30min); Konya (1 daily; 12hr); Sofía, Bulgaria (15hr).
Bus/dolmuş Alanya (hourly; 14hr); Ankara (hourly; 6hr); Antalya (4 daily; 12hr); Bodrum (5 daily; 12hr); Bursa (hourly; 5hr); Çanakkale (hourly; 5hr 30min); Datça (1 daily; 17hr); Denizli (hourly; 15hr); Edirne (hourly; 3hr); Fethiye (hourly; 15hr); Göreme (5 daily; 12hr 30min); İzmir (hourly; 10hr); İznık (Orhangazi; hourly; 5hr); Kaş (2 daily; 12hr); Konya (7 daily; 11hr); Kuşadası (3 daily; 11hr); Marmaris (4 daily; 13hr); Nevşehir (3 daily; 12hr); Sofía, Bulgaria (12hr); Ürgüp (5 daily; 12hr 30min).
Ferry Yalova (for Bursa or İznık, 8 daily; 1hr 30min).

The Sea of Marmara

Despite their proximity to İstanbul, the shores and hinterland of the Sea of Marmara are relatively neglected by foreign travellers – but there are good reasons to come: not least the border town of **Edirne** which was once the Ottoman capital, while nearby **Bursa**, the first Ottoman capital, has some of the finest monuments in the Balkans. Many visitors also stop off at the extensive World War I battlefields and cemeteries of the **Gelibolu** peninsula (Gallipoli), using either the port of **Eceabat** as a base, or, more commonly, **Çanakkale**.

EDIRNE

Bordering both Greece and Bulgaria, the small sleepy town of **EDIRNE**, where few of the locals speak English, boasts an impressive number of elegant monuments. It springs to life for the week-long oil-wrestling festival of Kırkpınar (end of June).

What to see and do

You can see the sights on foot in a day. The best starting point is the **Eski Camii** bang in the centre, the oldest mosque in town, begun in 1403. Just across the way, the **Bedesten** was Edirne's first covered market. The beautiful **Üç Şerefeli Camii** mosque dates from 1447 and has four idiosyncratic minarets, the tallest of which has three galleries for the muezzin. A little way east of here, the masterly **Selimiye Camii** was designed by Minar Sinan. Its four slender minarets, among the tallest in the world, also have three balconies; the interior is most impressive, its dome planned to surpass that of Aya Sofya in İstanbul. The main **Archeological Museum** (Tues–Sun 9am–5pm; 5TL), just northeast of the mosque, contains an assortment of Greco-Roman fragments and some Neolithic finds.

Arrival and information

Train The train station is 5km southeast of the centre. *Dolmuşes* run into town from here (0.50TL).
Bus The bus station is 8km southeast of the centre. When you arrive, walk through the terminal to the car park on the other side – here you'll find *dolmuşes* that go to the centre of town (0.50TL). Get off either near the main shopping area or the Eski Camii mosque.
Tourist office Talat Paşa Cad (daily 8.30am–5.30pm; ⓣ0284/213 9208).
Internet Eska Internet Café, Ilk Kapalıhan Cad 5.

Accommodation

Efe Hotel Maarif Cad 13 Kaleiçi ⓣ0284/213 6166, ⓦwww.efehotel.com. Smart boutique hotel with impressive rooms and an English pub. Breakfast Included. Singles 85TL, doubles 125TL.
Hotel Aksaray Alipaşa Ortakapı Cad ⓣ0284/212 6035. A small *pension* with a friendly welcome but the rooms are slightly scruffy. Breakfast not included. Singles 40TL, doubles 75TL.

Eating and drinking

Meşhur Edirne Ciğercisi Balıkpazarı Osmaniye Cad 43. You can have anything you want as long as it's liver, freshly floured and quickly deep-fried. Proper fast food, served with lots of onion and salad. An Edirne delicacy.
Pena Cafe Pub Alipaşa Ortakapı Cad 6. Sash windows usher cool breezes into this café-bar made up of small rooms with wooden floorboards and panelling. A youthful atmosphere in a middle-aged-feeling town.
Polat Lokantası Tahmis Çarşısı 8. The friendly English-speaking owner keeps his simple place spotless and smoke-free – a rare thing in Turkey. Offers a fine variety of desserts (try the *kabak tatlısı*).

Moving on

Train İstanbul only at 7.35am and 3.50pm (5hr).
Bus/dolmuş Ankara (10pm & 11am; 10hr); Çanakkale (4 daily; 4hr 30min); İstanbul (hourly; 4hr 30min); İzmir (4 daily; 10hr); Plovdiv (take Sofía bus, get off at Plovdiv 7hr); Selçuk (one bus at 11.30pm; 7hr).

ÇANAKKALE

ÇANAKKALE is a progressive, modern city celebrated for its setting on the Dardanelles and is a popular base for visiting Gelibolu (Gallipoli) and Troy. There's a big university here and the 15,000-odd students, together with Aussie and Kiwi backpackers visiting Gallipoli, make for a busy nightlife scene and you'll find no shortage of bars, clubs and budget places to eat. Almost everything of interest – park, **Naval Museum** (Tues, Wed & Fri–Sun 9am–noon & 1.30–5pm; 4TL) and **Archeological Museum** (daily 8am–noon & 1–5.30pm; 5TL) – is within walking distance of

CROSSING TO BULGARIA

Edirne is a popular base for travellers crossing the border into **Bulgaria**. Regular buses leave from Edirne to Plovdiv and tickets cost 30–35TL. If visiting Edirne for the day, bring your passport along even if you don't intend to cross the border. When departing, officials at the bus station may ask to see your passport in order to verify that you haven't crossed over the border from Bulgaria illegally.

the ferry docks, close to the start of the main Demircioğlu Caddesi. Stroll past the Trojan horse on the seafront promenade near the ferry terminal; you might recognize the enormous wooden structure from the 2004 film *Troy*.

Arrival and information

Bus station On the coastal highway, Atatürk Cad, a 15min walk from the waterfront; if you're arriving on the bus from İstanbul, get off at the ferry rather than going out to the bus station.

Ferry Ferries run every 30min between Çanakkale and Eceabat (hourly out of season). Tickets can be bought at the ferry terminal for 2TL.

Tourist office Beside the ferry docks (daily 8.30am–5.30/7pm depending on season; ⓣ0286/217 1187).

Accommodation

Except for a crowded couple of weeks during the Çanakkale/Troy Festival (mid-Aug), or on ANZAC Day (April 25), when the town is inundated with Antipodeans, you'll have little trouble finding budget accommodation.

Anzac House Hostel Cumhuriyet Meydanı 61 ⓣ0286/213 5969, ⓦwww.anzachouse.com. Clean, good-sized rooms with shared bathrooms. Roof terrace. Breakfast excluded. Dorms 22–25TL, singles 32TL, doubles/twins 55TL.

Crowded House Hostel İsmetpaşa Mah Hüseyin Avni Sok 4, Eceabat ⓣ0286/814 1565, ⓦwww.crowdedhousegallipoli.com. A 30min ferry ride from Çanakkale in Eceabat (on the Gallipoli peninsula) is this hostel, fresh-faced and keen to please. Attractive natural light and crisp linen in the bedroom, LCD TVs, a/c and a buffet breakfast (included) make it a winner. Dorms €7, singles €23, doubles/twins €30, triples €39.

Grand Anzac Hotel Slick new hotel (sister hotel to the plush *Kervansaray*, below) with clean, modern decor. It's excellent value for money, with each of the 37 rooms spotless and equipped with flat-screen TV. Three rooms have four beds; a good option for budget travellers/families. Free wi-fi. Breakfast included. Singles €40, doubles €50, triples €60, quads €70.

Kervansaray Hotel Fetvane Sok No 13 ⓣ0286/217 7777, ⓦwww.otelkervansaray.com. The former home of an Ottoman judge: you'll find big plush rooms, a pretty garden and a quality buffet breakfast waiting in the morning. Be sure to get a room in the main, old building, as the annexe at the back of the garden has far less character. Singles €45, doubles €60.

Yellow Rose Yeni Sok 5 ⓣ0286/217 3343, ⓦwww.yellowrose.4mg.com. Pretty bland, but good prices and you can economize further by using the kitchen. Breakfast is included and can be taken in the attractive garden. Dorms 16TL, doubles 20TL/person, 25TL with bathroom, singles 30TL with bathroom.

Eating and drinking

You will find stuffed mussels – *midye dolma* – sold on the streets, as well as other snacks such as delicious grilled corn on the cob (2TL), candyfloss, ice cream and *simit*. Be sure also to seek out the *peynir helvası* – Çanakkale's famous cheese dessert – it's much tastier than it sounds.

Cevahir Fetvane Sok 15/a. Small, family-run corner café serving tasty home-style Turkish food. Buffet-style food served on small (4TL) medium (5TL) or large (6TL) plates; salad and bread included. Dishes might include aubergine and chicken, sweet grated carrot with yogurt, or bean salad.

Gülen Pide Cumhuriyet Meydanı 27/a. Popular kebab and pizza joint on the main road leading from the ferry dock. Try the *Gülen* kebab (22TL) or a *pide* pizza (5.50–8.50TL). Their sister restaurant across the road, *Gülen Pizza* serves conventional pizza as well as french fries and cheeseburgers.

Sarap Evi Vino Kordon Boyu 42/b. Beer, wine, cocktails and a lively atmosphere at this waterfront bar keep the local uni students coming back. Beer 6TL.

Secret Benzin Station Eski Balıkhane Sok 11. A long Antipodean-influenced bar on the seafront, stacked with tables of people gazing into laptops (free wi-fi). Pizzas 8–11TL, beer 4TL, caffe latte 5.50TL and cocktails 8–10TL.

Yalı Hanı no dot 1889' beri Fetvane Sokak 26. A peaceful and atmospheric little courtyard, home to a bookshop, café and gig venue (less peaceful during gigs).

Moving on

Bus İstanbul (6 daily; 5hr); İzmir (4 daily; 6hr); Selçuk (4 daily; 7hr).
Ferry Eceabat (hourly winter, every 30min in summer; 30min).

THE GELIBOLU (GALLIPOLI) PENINSULA

Though endowed with splendid scenery and beaches, the slender **Gelibolu** (Gallipoli) peninsula, which forms the northwest side of the Dardanelles, is known chiefly for its grim military history. In April 1915 it was the site of a plan, devised by Winston Churchill, to land Allied troops, many of them Australian and New Zealand units, with a view to putting Turkey out of the war. Huge strategic mistakes, as well as a fierce opposition headed by the gifted officer Mustafa Kemal (Atatürk), led to the dismal failure of the operation, incurring massive casualties. This was the first time Australians and New Zealanders had seen action under their own commanders, and the date of the first landings, April 25, is celebrated as ANZAC Day.

What to see and do

The World War I battlefields and Allied cemeteries are by turns moving and numbing in the sheer multiplicity of graves, memorials and obelisks. The first stop on most tours is the **Kabatepe Orientation Centre and Museum** (daily 8am–6pm; 3TL), beyond which are the **Beach**, **Shrapnel Valley** and **Shell Green** cemeteries, followed by **Anzac Cove** and **Arıburnu**, site of the ANZAC landing. Most tourists then bear right for **Büyük Anafartalar** village and **Çonkbayırı Hill**, where there's a massive New Zealand memorial and a Turkish memorial detailing Atatürk's words and deeds. Working your way back down towards the orientation centre, you pass **The Nek**, **Walker's Ridge** and **Quinn's Post**, where the trenches of the opposing forces lay within a few metres of each other: the modern road corresponds to no-man's-land.

BURSA

Draped along the leafy lower slopes of Uludağ, which towers more than 2000m above, **BURSA** – first capital of the Ottoman Empire and the burial place of several sultans – does more justice to its setting than any other Turkish city besides İstanbul. Gathered here are some of the finest early Ottoman monuments in Turkey, in a tidy and appealing city centre.

What to see and do

Flanked by the busy Atatürk Caddesi, the compact **Koza Parkı**, with its

BATTLEFIELD TOURS

Various companies offer **battlefield tours**. The best include those operated by Fez Bus (Ⓦwww.fezbus.co.uk), which runs a one-day Trooper Tour to Gallipoli starting and finishing in İstanbul for €99 (£89) and includes visits to Lone Pine, ANZAC Cove and the Gallipoli Museum, and lunch in a local restaurant. Tours run daily from May to September and several days a week during the winter months and there are special tours to coincide with the ANZAC Day service. If you're starting a tour from Çanakkale, recommended operators include the *Crowded House Hostel* in Eceabat (Gallipoli tour €25; see opposite) or the Hassle Free Travel Agency in Çanakkale (half-day Gallipoli tour €40 includes lunch; one-day Gallipoli and Troy tour €72 includes lunch; in the *Anzac House Hostel*, see opposite).

fountains, benches and cafés, is the heart of Bursa. On the far side looms the fourteenth-century **Ulu Camii**, whose interior is dominated by a huge *şadırvan* pool for ritual ablutions. A little way north is Bursa's covered market, the **Bedesten**, given over to the sale of jewellery and precious metals, and the **Koza Hanı**, flanking the park, still entirely occupied by silk and brocade merchants.

Yeşil Camii, Yeşil Türbe and the Museum of Turkish and Islamic Art

Across the river to the east, the **Yeşil Camii** (daily 8am–8.30pm) is easily the most spectacular of Bursa's imperial mosques. The nearby hexagonal **Yeşil Türbe** (daily 8am–noon & 1–7pm) contains the sarcophagus of Çelebi Mehmet I and assorted offspring. Just north of Yeşil Türbe is the small **Museum of Turkish and Islamic Art** (Tues–Sun 8.30am–noon & 1–5.30pm; 3TL), with Çanakkale ceramics, glass items and clothing. The peaceful courtyard is a nice place to chill out.

The Hisar and around

West of the centre, the **Hisar** ("citadel") district was Bursa's original nucleus. Narrow lanes wind up past dilapidated Ottoman houses, while walkways clinging to the rock face offer fabulous views. The best-preserved dwellings are a little way west in medieval **Muradiye**, where the Muradiye Külliyesi mosque and *medrese* complex was begun in 1424. This is the last imperial foundation in Bursa, although it's most famous for its tombs, set in lovingly tended gardens.

THE EVIL EYE

Take a short stroll around any Turkish town and it won't be long until you spot one of the ubiquitous evil eye symbols. This circular blue and white emblem with a dot in the middle is a good luck charm designed to ward off evil spirits. As well as being proudly displayed in homes and businesses, the symbol is also printed on pendants, bracelets and brooches.

Arrival and information

Bus station 5km north on the main road to İstanbul, from where bus #38 (every 15min) runs to Koza Parkı.

Tourist office Corner of Koza Parkı (Mon–Fri 8.30am–5.30pm; ⓣ0224/220 1848).

Accommodation

Hotel Çeşmeli Gümüşçeken Cad 6 ⓣ0224/224 1511. Female-run place with a handy location that makes up for its old-fashioned look. Centrally located with an excellent self-service breakfast. Singles 60TL, doubles 100TL.

Hotel Günes İnebey Cad 75 ⓣ0224/222 1404. Cheap, clean and friendly. Singles 30TL, doubles 50TL.

Kitap Evi Kavaklıdere Cad, Burçüstü Sok 21 ⓣ0224/225 4160, ⓦwww.kitapevi.com.tr. This one-time bookshop has been turned into a swish boutique hotel. The place to come if you need pampering – one room boasts a private hammam. Singles from €90, doubles from €120.

Eating and drinking

Sakarya Cad. A pretty cobbled street filled with fish and seafood restaurants that fill with post-work locals after dark. The food's reasonably priced and the restaurants all serve beer and, of course, *rakı*. Mains around 15TL.

Çiçek Izgara Belediye Cad 15. Elegant restaurant with a decent take on Ottoman dishes. Try the *köfte* and *sütlü tel kadayıfı*. Mains 9TL.

Kebapçi İskender Ünlü Cad 7 ⓦwww.kebapci iskender.com.tr. A great choice for trying Bursa's speciality, the *İskender kebap* – lamb with tomato sauce and yoghurt (15TL).

Resimli Bar Ünlü Cad. American-style bar with frequent live music, often hard/alt rock.

Moving on

Bus Çanakkale (hourly; 5hr); İstanbul (hourly; 3hr); İznık (hourly; 2hr).

The Aegean coast

The **Aegean coast** is, in many ways, Turkey's most enticing destination, home to some of the best of its antiquities and the most appealing resorts. The city of **İzmir** serves as a base for day-trips to nearby sights and beaches. Visitors continuing south will be spoilt for sightseeing choices as the territory is rich in Classical, Hellenistic and Roman ruins, notably **Ephesus** and the remains inland at **Hierapolis** – sitting atop the famous pools and mineral formations of **Pamukkale**. The coast itself is better down south, too, and although the larger resorts, including **Kuşadası** and **Marmaris**, have been marred by the developers, **Bodrum** still has a certain charm and is the seaside holiday spot of choice for İstanbulites.

İZMIR

İZMIR – ancient Smyrna – was mostly burned down in the Turkish–Greek war of 1922, and was built pretty much from scratch afterwards. Nowadays it's Turkey's third largest city, a booming, cosmopolitan and relentlessly modern place that's home to nearly three million people. Orientation can be confusing – many streets are unmarked – but most points of interest lie near each other and walking is the most enjoyable way of exploring. Be warned: attacks and muggings are not unheard of in izmir – take particular care, especially if you are a woman travelling alone.

What to see and do

İzmir doesn't have a single centre, although **Konak**, the busy park, city bus terminal and **Konak Pier** on the waterfront, is where visitors spend most time. It's marked by the ornate **Saat Kulesi** (clock tower), the city's official symbol. Head north and you'll reach the **Kūltur Parkı**, a large park with regular outdoor entertainment particularly in the summer. Continue in the same direction and you'll soon reach the district of **Alsançak** – the hub of evening entertainment with alfresco bars and restaurants and, on the seafront, the **Atatūrk Museum** on Atatürk Caddesi. This beautiful nineteenth-century seafront house is where Atatürk stayed when he visited the city in the 1930s. If you fancy a walk, head south along the waterfront for about twenty minutes to the city's free elevator, **Asansör**, which has wonderful views over the city and Gulf of İzmir.

Archeological Museum and Ethnography Museum

Southwest of the Konak Camii is İzmir's **Archeological Museum** (Tues–Sun 9am–noon & 1–5pm; 8TL). The collection consists of finds from all over İzmir province, including some stunning marble statues and sarcophagi. Next door in an old Turkish house is the charming **Ethnography Museum** (Tues–Sun 9am–noon & 1–5pm; free) where you can learn about the local tradition of camel wrestling and see examples of Anatolian crafts such as clog-making, lacemaking and the ubiquitous "evil eye" beads.

Kemeraltı Bazaar

Immediately east of Konak is **Kemeraltı**, İzmir's bazaar. The main drag, Anafartalar Caddesi, is lined with clothing, jewellery and shoe shops; Fevzipaşa Bulvarı and the alleys just south are strong on leather garments. A pleasant, relaxed alternative to the bazaar is the street market at the northernmost end of Sevgi Yolu, where you can browse jewellery, scarves, leather bracelets and lots of books, including English ones. When you've finished shopping, enjoy a Turkish coffee (2.50TL) at one of the many street cafés.

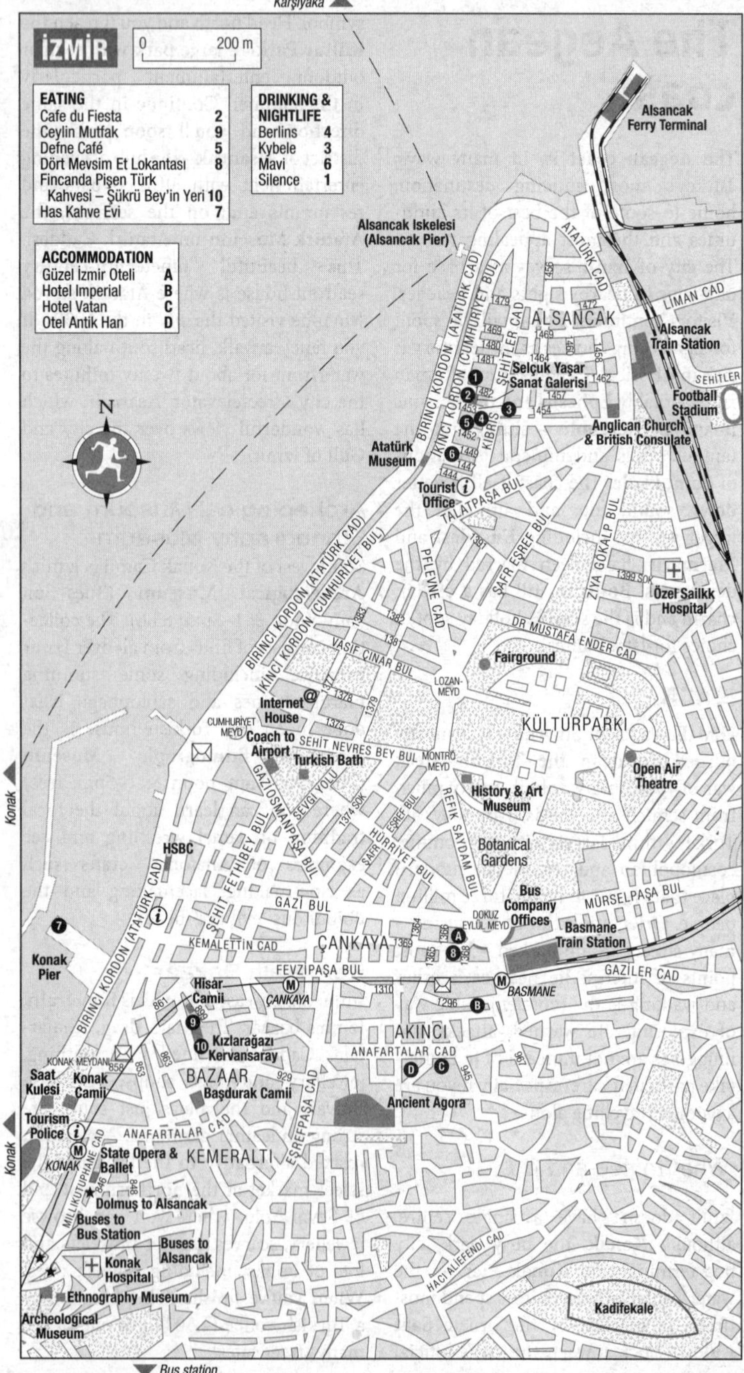
İZMİR
0 200 m
EATING
Cafe du Fiesta 2
Ceylin Mutfak 9
Defne Café 5
Dört Mevsim Et Lokantası 8
Fincanda Pişen Türk Kahvesi – Şükrü Bey'in Yeri 10
Has Kahve Evi 7
DRINKING & NIGHTLIFE
Berlins 4
Kybele 3
Mavi 6
Silence 1
ACCOMMODATION
Güzel İzmir Oteli A
Hotel Imperial B
Hotel Vatan C
Otel Antik Han D
Karşiyaka
Alsancak Ferry Terminal
Alsancak Iskelesi (Alsancak Pier)
ALSANCAK
Alsancak Train Station
Selçuk Yaşar Sanat Galerisi
Football Stadium
Anglican Church & British Consulate
Atatürk Museum
Tourist Office
Özel Sailkk Hospital
Fairground
KÜLTÜRPARKI
Internet House
Coach to Airport
Turkish Bath
Open Air Theatre
History & Art Museum
Botanical Gardens
HSBC
Bus Company Offices
Basmane Train Station
Konak Pier
ÇANKAYA
BASMANE
Hisar Camii
Kızlarağazı Kervansaray
AKINCI
Saat Kulesi
Konak Camii
BAZAAR
Başdurak Camii
Ancient Agora
Tourism Police
State Opera & Ballet
KEMERALTI
KONAK
Dolmuş to Alsancak
Buses to Bus Station
Buses to Alsancak
Konak Hospital
Ethnography Museum
Archeological Museum
Kadifekale
Konak
Bus station

Kadifekale

A symbol of İzmir's historic past, the castle ruins of **Kadifekale** (always open; free) provide great views of İzmir's metropolitan expanse. To get to the castle, take a red-and-white city bus #33 from Konak and get off shortly after you see the national flag flying from the top of the hill. Buses back to Konak are from the bus shelter at the corner of the road approaching the castle.

Arrival and information

Air İzmir's Adnan Menderes airport is approximately 15km outside of the city. A taxi from the airport to Çankaya is about 50TL. A cheaper alternative is to catch a Havaş shuttle bus (30min; 10TL). The Havaş service to the airport runs hourly 3.30am–11.30pm every day from the northern end of Gaziosmanpaşa Bul.

Train Intercity trains pull in at Basmane station, 1km from the seafront at the eastern end of Fevzipaşa Bul.

Bus The bus station is way out on the east side of the city, from where buses #64 and #54 run to Basmane station and Konak. Buses to and from Çeşme depart from the Uçkuyular bus station: bus #169 from Konak.

Tourist office 1344 Sok 2. Housed in a grand building near the seafront just off Atatürk Cad near the junction with Gazi Bul. The helpful, friendly staff speak English and other European languages (daily 8am–7pm; ⓣ0232/445 7390).

Internet Numerous internet cafés across the city.

Post office The PTT near Cumhuriyet Med; open for postal services Mon–Sat 8am–8pm, Sun 8.30am–5pm; for money services including exchange, daily 8.30am–5pm.

City transport

Bus Intercity bus tickets can be bought from the bus ticket offices near the Basmane train station, and a free shuttle bus to the main bus terminal leaves from outside the offices. To get to Alsancak from Konak (2TL) take the #169, #554 or #8 all from the same bus stop on the opposite side of the road from Atatürk Kültur Merkezi (Mithatpaşa Cad). To get to the *otogar* from Konak you need the #54 or #64. Take them from the bus stop sandwiched between the Atatürk Kültür Merkezi and the flyover.

Dolmuş The city's *dolmuşes* (silver or white cars that gather alongside taxis and have their destination in the windscreen) cost 2TL/ride. Find one to head down to Konak from the Alsancak area on Talatpaşa Bul north of the junction with 1407 Sok. Heading in the opposite direction pick one up just south of the Devlet Opera Balesi/State Opera and Ballet.

Metro The handy metro system (2TL) links Basmane station (the metro is located at the bottom of the escalators behind the station), Çankaya (the hotel district) and Konak. Ticket office 7am–9.30pm.

Accommodation

Although İzmir is one of Turkey's major cities, its tourism industry is only just developing. Consequently, good-quality budget hotels are hard to come by and *pansiyons* within the centre are nonexistent. There's a street (1296 Sok) lined with dingy-looking budget hotels near Basmane train station.

Güzel İzmir Oteli 1368 Sok 8 ⓣ0232/483 5069, ⓦwww.guzelizmirhotel.com. Very bright and airy rooms with none of the staleness that other, similar-looking hotels around here suffer from. Friendly welcome and professional attitude. Includes breakfast and wi-fi. Singles €26, doubles €48, triples €73.

Hotel Imperial 1296 Sok 54 ⓣ0232/425 6883. A museum piece from the 1970s. The rooms are mournful but well looked after. Singles 25TL, doubles 50TL.

Hotel Vatan Anafartalar Cad 626 ⓣ0232/425 3461, 483 0637 & 484 5681, ⓦwww.vatanotel.com. Clearly aimed for sleek and modern but ended up with an interior design calamity. The owner is ever-so-slightly overbearing but endearing with it. Comfortable and good value. Breakfast included. Singles 40TL, doubles 80TL.

Otel Antik Han Anafartalar Cad 626 ⓣ0232/489 27 50, ⓦwww.otelantikhan.com. Friendly, with a pretty courtyard where you can enjoy breakfast. Close to the ancient agora. Singles €40, doubles €80.

Eating and drinking

Head to Sok numbers 1482, 1453 and 1452 in Alsancak for a night out. 1482 and 1453 have a certain grunginess about them, while narrow 1452 is a little smarter, though still young.

Cafe du Fiesta Sok 1482. A café that feels like it is squatting in a 150-year-old mansion, packed out with teenagers, students and musicians. Nab the one-table balcony. Americano 4TL and cheeseburger 4TL.

Ceylin Mutfak Near Hisar Camii. At the heart of the bazaar on a street leading from the mosque is this atmospheric place run by a husband-and-wife team. There are only three tables outside. The *köfte* (5TL) is grilled to perfection.

Defne Café 1452 Sok. Cosy little place on a cute side street where Efes is 6TL and a steak sandwich is just 9TL.

Dört Mevsim Et Lokantası 1369 Sok 51a. A *lokanta* par excellence with mains running 10–17TL.

Fincanda Pişen Türk Kahvesi – Şükrü Bey'in Yeri Where Sok 905 meets Bazaar entrance "876 Sok 62". Come for Turkish coffee while relaxing on carpet-covered seating in the beating heart of the bazaar.

Has Kahve Evi Konak Pier. A lovely setting on a breezy terrace at the far end of the pier. Take a look and weigh up whether the view merits the 6–8TL coffee.

Bars and clubs

Berlins Sok 1453. Combating the pervading scruffiness with bling, reggae and r'n'b.

Kybele 1453 Sok 28. Live music and alt rock club with a tiny stage and super-speedy bar staff. Entrance is 15TL, which includes one drink. Beers thereafter run 10TL.

Mavi Cumhuriyet Bul 206, Alsançak. Music venue in an atmospheric old building. People head here around 10pm for live music – jazz on Mondays, general rock cover bands rest of the week.

Silence 1482 Sok 24. Slightly cheaper music and alt rock club: entrance is 10TL with one free drink, then beers are 6TL after that.

Entertainment

Bostanlı Karşıyaka Açıkhava Tiyatrosu Saat Taşer Tiyatrosu, İzmir. Large concert hall hosting regular pop concerts in Konak Pier. Daily 10.30am–9.30pm.

Cinebonus Konak Pier, İzmir. Cinema with recent Hollywood releases. Student discount available.

State Opera and Ballet Milli Kütüphane Cad, Konak ☎0232/484 3692. A diverse programme of concerts ranging from classical to jazz and pop.

Moving on

Train Basmane station to: Denizli (3 daily; 5hr); İstanbul by way of a ferry from Bandirma (2 daily; 8hr); Selçuk (5 daily; 1hr 30min).

Bus/dolmuş Ankara (every 30min; 8hr); Bergama (hourly; 2hr); Bodrum (hourly; 4hr); Bursa (6 daily; 6hr); Çanakkale (8 daily; 5hr); Datça (hourly; 7hr); Denizli (hourly; 4hr); Fethiye (12–18 daily; 7hr); İstanbul (hourly; 9hr); Konya (1 daily; 8hr); Kuşadası (every 30min; 1hr 40min); Marmaris (hourly; 5hr); Nevşehir (1 daily; 12hr); Selçuk (every 40min; 1hr).

KUŞADASI

KUŞADASI is Turkey's most bloated resort, yet the old town has its charms even when the town centre is heaving with football shirts. Ferry services link it with the Greek island of Sámos, while the resort is a port of call for Aegean cruise ships, which disgorge vast numbers in summer.

Liman Caddesi runs from the ferry port up to Atatürk Bulvarı, the main harbour esplanade, from which pedestrianized Barbaros Hayrettin Bulvarı ascends the hill. To the left of here, the **Kale** district, huddled inside the town walls, is the oldest and most appealing part of town, with a mosque and some fine traditional houses. Kuşadası's most famous beach, **Kadınlar Denizi**, 3km southwest of town, is a popular strand, usually too crowded for its own good in season. Much the best beach in the area is **Pamucak**, at the mouth of the Kücük Menderes River, 15km north, an exposed 4km stretch of sand that is as yet little developed; in season it's served by regular *dolmuşes* from both Kuşadası and Selçuk.

The combined *dolmuş* and long-distance **bus station** is about 2km out, past the end of Kahramanlar Caddesi on the ring road to Söke, while the *dolmuş* stop is closer to the centre on Adnan Menderes Bulvarı. The **tourist office** (Mon–Fri 8am–5.30pm; summer also Sat & Sun; ☎0256/614 1103) is right by the ferry port. For somewhere to **stay**, try *Sezgin Hotel and Guesthouse* (☎0256/614 4225, Ⓦwww.sezginhotel.com; doubles €35) at Arsanlar Cad 68, which has a lovely garden and swimming pool. **Food** options include *Avlu*, at Cephane Sok 15/a, which serves a wide range of kebabs, stews, steamed vegetables and meze in an outdoor courtyard (mains 7TL).

SELÇUK

SELÇUK has been catapulted into the limelight of premier-league tourism by its proximity to the ruins of Ephesus, which are an easy twenty-minute walk away. Pleasant Pamucak beach (see opposite) is easily accessible by a *dolmuş* ride or by bike (9km).

What to see and do

The sights and attractions in this small, friendly farming town can easily be seen in a day; allow an additional day to visit Ephesus. **Ayasoluk** hill (daily 8.30am–5.30pm; 5TL) to the north-west of the centre is the traditional burial place of St John the Evangelist, who died here around 100 AD; it boasts the remains of a basilica built by Justinian that was one of the largest Byzantine churches in existence. Just behind the tourist office, the **Efes Archeological Museum** (Tues–Sun 8.30am–5pm; 5TL) has galleries of finds from Ephesus, while beyond the museum, 600m along the road towards Ephesus, are the scanty remains of the **Artemision** or sanctuary of Artemis.

Some 9km southwest of Selçuk lies **Meryemana** (daily dawn–dusk; 10TL), a tiny Greek chapel (Mass, summer daily 7.15am, Sun also 10.30am) where some Orthodox theologians believe the Virgin Mary passed her last years.

Şirince

A pleasant day-trip from town is the pretty hillside village of **Şirince**. Despite being overrun with tourist buses the village is stunning, full of nineteenth-century houses – some in a sorry state of disrepair – lining higgledy-piggledy, steep cobbled passageways. Wander upwards out of the village through olive groves and orchards, though you'll have to follow your nose as maps of the area don't exist. Spending a night here is a treat (if you like peace and quiet; there's little in the way of nightlife here) and if you've got money to burn, undoubtedly the best place to kip is *Nişanyan House* (see p.1228).

Arrival and information

Train and bus The train station lies a little east of the aqueduct. The bus and *dolmuş* terminal is a few minutes' walk south from the centre of town.
Tourist office Opposite the bus terminal (daily 8.30am–noon & 1–5.30pm; winter closed Sat & Sun; ⓣ0232/892 6945).

Accommodation

ANZ Guesthouse 1064 Sok 12 ⓣ0232/892 6050, ⓦwww.anzguesthouse.com. Popular backpacker choice with free use of bicycles. Check rooms as some are better than others. Dorms €8 (shared bathroom), doubles €22, triples €25.
Atilla's Getaway Acarlar Köyü ⓣ0232/892 3847, ⓦwww.atillasgetaway.com. They know how to throw a party here but the setting – peaceful, almost rural – is conducive to sloth-like relaxation too. A little out of town but the management shuttle to and from Selçuk centre several times daily. En-suite dorms €12 (with breakfast and dinner €17), en-suite single €24, single with shared bathroom €21, en-suite doubles €40, camping €13.
Boomerang Guest House 1047 Sok 10 ⓣ0232/892 4879, ⓦwww.boomerangguesthouse.com. Handily located adjacent to the Efes Archeological Museum. Clean rooms, all en suite and some with balconies and a decent 10-bed dorm. Breakfast is included. All rooms have a/c. There's a

FERRIES TO GREECE

Every day in high season a morning (8.30am) and afternoon (5pm) ferry leaves from Kuşadası to the Greek island of **Sámos** (€30 one-way, €40 day return, €55 open return; 1hr 15min). Returning ferries depart from Greece at the same times. Meander on Kıbrıs Cad (right by the ferry port ⓣ0256/614 3859, ⓦwww.meandertravel.com) runs up to two boats daily in summer. From Sámos, a popular follow-on destination is the party island **Íos** (see p.558). Tickets from Sámos to Íos can be bought from ITSA or By Ship travel agents located near the pier.

roof terrace and residents get ten percent discount in the restaurant. Dorms 20TL, singles 50TL, doubles/twin 80TL, triples 120TL, quads 140TL.

Homeros Pansiyon Atatürk Mah Asmalı/1048 Sok 17 ⓣ0232/892 3995, ⓦwww.homerospension.com. This super-friendly family-run *pension* is one of the best places to stay in the area. The bedrooms (some with a balcony, all with a/c) are cosy and are richly decorated with colourful carpets, blankets and knick-knacks. Breakfast and wi-fi included. Roof terrace has fabulous views of the town. Free home-made wine served at 7pm every day. Home-cooked dinner 16TL. Free pick-up from the bus station and free use of bikes. Singles 45–55TL, doubles/twin 70–80TL/person, triples 120TL.

Nişanyan House Şirince village ⓣ0232/898 3208, ⓦwww.nisanyan.com. A peaceful boutique hotel high on the hillside with a private hammam and spectacular views. Rooms are individually decorated and the traditional Turkish breakfast, made on site by the talented kitchen staff, is one of the best in the country. Doubles from 120TL.

Wallabies Hostel Cengiz Topel Cad 2 ⓣ0232/892 3204, ⓦwww.wallabieshostel.com. A family affair, headed up by Mehmet (aka Geoff). Some rooms have views of the Roman aqueduct and nesting storks (the best is room 305). Includes breakfast. Singles 30TL, doubles 50TL.

Eating and drinking

Mehmet and Alibaba Kebab House 1047 Sok 4/a ⓣ0232/892 3872. Finger-licking Turkish fare ranging from trad kebabs (13TL) and *köfte* (9TL) to generous plates of mixed veg meze (10TL) and *gözleme* (5TL). The meatballs are particularly succulent, apple tea, orange tea and regular tea are free to diners. The menu is translated into seven languages and if you eat here the brothers will give you a free ride to Ephesus.

Mosaik Atatürk Mah 1005 Sok 6/b. Low tables and kilim conducive to a *nargile* session. *Nargile* 10TL, beer 4TL.

Old House Opposite *Mosaik*. Carefully prepared mains between 7 and 12TL served up in a shady little garden courtyard.

Selçuk Köftecisi Şahabettin Dede Cad. Easily overlooked because of its basic, rather bland appearance but, with forty years' experience behind it, this place is all about the food. Smoky bread cooked in a wood oven, known as Şirince bread, accompanies mains. Soups 4–5TL, meaty mains 6–9TL.

Moving on

Train Denizli (5 daily; 4hr); İzmir (6 daily 1hr 30min).
Bus Bodrum (3/4 direct daily; 3hr); Marmaris (one direct daily; 4 hr).
Dolmuş Kuşadası (regular until 8/9pm; 30min); Pamucak beach (hourly; 15min); Şirince (every 45min until 7pm).

EPHESUS

With the exception of Pompeii, **EPHESUS** (Efes in Turkish) is the largest and best-preserved ancient city around the Mediterranean. You'll need at least three partly shady hours, and a water bottle. Your best hope of avoiding the crowds is to visit early morning.

Originally situated close to a temple devoted to the goddess Artemis, Ephesus' location by a fine harbour was the secret of its success in ancient times, eventually making it the wealthy capital of Roman Asia, ornamented with magnificent public buildings.

What to see and do

Approaching **from Kuşadası**, get the *dolmuş* to drop you at the *Tusan Motel* junction, 1km from the gate. **From Selçuk**, it's a 3km walk (although most hotels and hostels offer free rides). In the centre of the site (daily 8am–5.30pm; 20TL; it's worth spending the additional 15TL for entrance into the Terrace House) is the **Arcadian Way**, which was once lined with hundreds of shops and illuminated at night. The nearby theatre has been partly restored to allow its use for open-air concerts and occasional summer festivals; climb to the top for views of the surrounding countryside. About halfway along Marble Street is a footprint, a female head and a heart etched into the rock – an alleged signpost for a brothel. Across the intersection looms the elegant **Library of Celsus**, erected by the consul Gaius Julius Aquila between 110 and 135 AD. Just uphill, a Byzantine fountain looks across the Street of the Curetes to the public latrines, a favourite with visitors. Note there's not much in the way of information boards on the site, and be wary of hiring one of the sharks masquerading as guides near the entrance; guides worth their salt are pricey and should be booked via the tourist office in town.

BODRUM

In the eyes of its devotees, **BODRUM** – ancient Halicarnassos – with its whitewashed houses and subtropical gardens, is the most attractive Turkish resort, a quality outfit in comparison to its upstart Aegean rivals.

What to see and do

The town's centrepiece is the **Castle of St Peter** (Tues–Sun 9am–noon & 1–5pm; summer open until 7pm; 10TL), built by the Knights of St John over a Selçuk fortress between 1437 and 1522. Inside, the various towers house a **Museum of Underwater Archeology**, which includes coin and jewellery rooms, Classical and Hellenistic statuary, and Byzantine relics retrieved from two wrecks. The **Carian Princess Hall** (Tues–Fri 10am–noon & 2–4pm; 5TL extra) displays the skeleton and sarcophagus of a fourth-century BC noblewoman unearthed in 1989. There is also the **Glass Wreck Hall** (Tues–Fri 10am–noon & 2–4pm; 5TL extra) containing the wreck and cargo of an ancient Byzantine ship, which sank near Marmaris. Note that some of these displays may be closed without warning, though you can always bank on enjoying the fantastic views of the water from various vantage points in the castle. Immediately north of the castle lies the bazaar, from where you can stroll up to Türkkuyusu Caddesi to see what's left of the **Mausoleum** (Tues–Sun 8.30am–5.30pm; 8TL), the burial place of Mausolus, ruler of Halicarnassos from 376–353 BC and the origin of the word mausoleum.

Arrival and information

Bus The bus station is 500m up Cevat Şakir Cad, which divides the town roughly in two.
Ferry Ferries dock at the jetty west of the castle.
Tourist office Baris Square 48, close to the jetty (Mon–Fri 8am–noon, 1–5pm; summer daily 8.30am–6.30pm ⓣ0252/316 1091). Friendly staff will help you book accommodation and boat trips.

Accommodation

Bodrum Backpackers Atatürk Cad 37/b ⓣ0252/313 2762, ⓦwww.bodrumbackpackers.net. Lively and friendly backpackers' hostel regularly hosting both budget travellers and the English party crowd – not the place to go if you want to get your beauty sleep. When all the beds are full you can sleep on the terrace for 15TL. Breakfast and wi-fi included. Dorms 20TL, singles 25TL.
Hotel Güleç Üçkuyular Cad 22 ⓣ0252/316 5222, ⓦwww.hotelgulec.com. Lovely flower-filled garden and cool, wood-trimmed bedrooms. It's on a quiet street a short walk from the beach and bars. Breakfast included. Singles €55, doubles €55, triples €66, quads €72.
Hotel Kalender Cevat Şakir Mah İnönü Cad Bitez Sok 15 ⓣ0252/319 5229, ⓦwww.hotelkalender.com. In the Gumbet neighbourhood, a little way out, but free pick-up from the bus station is offered. Bright, simple rooms with chairs and tables set outside around a central swimming pool. Breakfast included. Singles €40, doubles €60.
Mars Otel Turgut Reis Cad, İmbat Çıkmazi 29. ⓣ0252/316 6559, ⓦwww.marsotel.com. Clean, friendly and great value – and quiet, despite its central location. Free rides to the *otogar* and free Turkish bath if you stay for at least three nights. Small swimming pool and bikes for rent. Breakfast included. Singles from €45, doubles €50, triples €65, quads €85.

Eating and drinking

Berk Balık Cumhuriyet Cad 167. An excellent fish and meze restaurant at the far end of the bar strip. Try the 10TL mixed meze on the shady first-floor sea-facing terrace. Mains 10–18TL.
Hadigari 1025 Sok 2. A Bodrum stalwart that still pulls in 2000-odd punters on summer nights. Find it at the marina near Bodrum Castle and dance till 5am under the stars.
Halikarnas Far end of bar strip, near *Mavi* and *Berk Balık*. Fancies itself as the biggest nightclub in Europe. It'll cost you 30TL and pricey drinks to party

like it's 1999, but if you're in the mood then the laser show, loved-up atmosphere and superb view of the bay can make it worth the money.

Mavi Cumhuriyet Cad 175. Tiny bar with an outdoor terrace and live music every day. A cut above the rest in town. Open till the early hours.

Otantik Ocabaşı Atatürk Cad Çarşı Mah 46. Decent prices considering the location (opposite *Bodrum Backpackers*) probably thanks to the very high turnover. Its wood-burning oven assures succulence.

Moving on

Bus/dolmuş Denizli (1 daily; 5hr); Fethiye (6 daily; 4hr 30min); İzmir (hourly; 4hr); Kaş (3 daily; 6hr); Kuşadası (3 daily; 3hr); Marmaris (14 daily; 3hr 15min); Selçuk (hourly; 3hr).

Domestic ferry Datça (April–Oct 1 or 2 daily; 1hr 30min).

International ferry Bodrum Ferryboat Association (☎0252/316 0882, ⓦwww.bodrumferryboat.com) runs ferries to Kos, as well as domestic services to Datça, while Bodrum Express Lines (☎0252/316 1087, ⓦwww.bodrumexpresslines.com) handles hydrofoils to Kos, Rhodes and domestic services to Marmaris. Check websites for current prices.

PAMUKKALE

The rock formations of **PAMUKKALE** (literally "Cotton Castle"), 140km northeast of Marmaris, are the most-visited attraction in this part of Turkey, a series of white terraces saturated with dissolved calcium bicarbonate, bubbling up from the feet of the Çal Dağı mountains beyond. The spring emerges in what was once the ancient city of **Hierapolis**, the ruins of which would merit a stop even if they weren't coupled with the natural phenomenon. Access to the travertine terraces is 5TL while up on the plateau is what is spuriously billed as the sacred pool of the ancients (daily 8am–6.30pm; 25TL) open for bathing in the 35°C mineral water.

Hierapolis

The archeological zone of **HIERAPOLIS** lies behind the Pamukkale terraces and is admissible by the same entrance fee. Its main features include a **Temple of Apollo** and the infamous, albeit inconspicuous, **plutonium cavern**, where a toxic mixture of sulphur dioxide and carbon dioxide brews. The site has been firmly sealed off following the deaths of two German tourists. Perhaps the most interesting part of the city is the colonnaded street which once extended for almost 1km, terminating in monumental portals a few paces outside the walls – of which only the most northerly, a triple arch, still stands.

Moving on

Bus and dolmuş Buses run directly from Pamukkale village to Selçuk, Fethiye and Bodrum. Otherwise head to Denizli and change there. *Dolmuşes* run every 20min until 7pm then less regularly until 10pm.

Mediterranean coast

The first stretch of Turkey's Mediterranean coast, dominated by the Akdağ and Bey mountain ranges of the Taurus chain and known as the "Turquoise Coast", is its most popular, famed for its pine-studded shore, minor ruins and beautiful scenery. In the west, **Fethiye** is a perfect base for visits to **Ölüdeniz**, **Kaya Köyü** and **Butterfly Valley**. The scenery becomes increasingly spectacular as you head towards the site of **Olympos**, and **Kaş**, which offers great scuba-diving, before reaching the port and major city of **Antalya**.

FETHIYE

FETHIYE is well sited for access to some of the region's ancient sites, many of which date from the time when this area was the independent kingdom of Lycia. The best beaches, around the Ölüdeniz lagoon, are now much too crowded for comfort, but Fethiye is still a market town and has been able to spread to accommodate increased tourist traffic.

What to see and do

Fethiye itself occupies the site of the Lycian city of Telmessos, little of which remains other than the impressive ancient theatre, and a number of Lycian rock tombs on the hillside. You can also visit the remains of the medieval fortress behind the harbour area of town. In the centre of town the small **museum** (Tues–Sun 8.30am–5pm; 5TL) has some fascinating exhibits from local sites and a good ethnographic section. There are numerous boats on the harbour offering island-hopping trips. (around 25TL/day including lunch and stops for swimming).

Kaya Köyü and Ölüdeniz

One of the most dramatic sights in the area is the ghost village of **KAYA KÖYÜ** (Levissi), 7km out of town, served by *dolmuşes* from the old bus station. The village was abandoned in 1923, when its Anatolian-Greek population was relocated, and all you see now is a hillside covered with more than two thousand ruined cottages and an attractive basilica. **Ölüdeniz** is about two hours on foot from Kaya Köyü or a *dolmuş* ride from Fethiye. The warm waters of this lagoon make for pleasant swimming although the crowds can reach saturation level in high season – in which case the nearby beaches of Belceğiz and Kidrak are better bets.

Arrival and information

Bus Fethiye's bus station is 2km east of the centre; *dolmuşes* to and from Ölüdeniz, Çalış Beach and Kaya Köyü leave from near the mosque (Yeni Camii), which is beyond the town hall and the PTT on Atatürk Cad.

Tourist office Close to the theatre, near the harbour at Fevzi Kakmak Cad 9/d (summer: Mon–Fri 8am–8pm & Sat 10am–5pm; winter: Mon–Fri 8am–noon, 1–5pm; ⓣ0252/612 1527). Very helpful and friendly. English spoken.

Tours Daily boat tours generally run 35–55TL, lasting from 10.30am to 6.30pm. Tickets can be bought through your accommodation.

Activities Divers Delight (ⓦwww.diversdelight.com) runs several diving courses including PADI on a liveaboard *gület*, and try-a-dive day-trips for complete beginners inclusive of equipment, tuition and freshly cooked lunch for 100TL (there's a snorkelling option charging 30TL for non-diving partners). They can also arrange jeep safaris to Saklıkent Gorge and the ancient Lycian sites of Xanthos and Patara for around 50TL/person.

Accommodation

Ceylin Pansiyon Fevzi Çakmak Cad ⓣ0252/614 0031. No English spoken but a warm welcome nonetheless. The rooms are basic but clean and well presented. Breakfast included. 5min walk from the centre of town. 30TL/person.

Duygu Pension Karagözler Ordu Cad 54 ⓣ0252/614 3563, ⓦwww.duygupension.com. Eleven rooms, some with amazing views of the bay, kept in great condition. Swimming pool and free bus station pick-up. May not be open off-season so call ahead. Singles 40TL, doubles 60TL, triples 90TL.

Ferah Pension (Monica's Place) Karagözler Orta Yol 21 ⓣ0252/614 2816, ⓦwww.ferahpension.com. Waking up to a view of the bay and one of Monica's excellent breakfasts is a rare treat, as are her dinners (€7.50). The upstairs dorm has a huge sea-facing window. Free transfer from the bus station. Dorms €16, singles €30, doubles €38, triples €50, quads €55.

Irem Pansiyon Fevzi Çakmak Cad 61 ⓣ0252/614 3985, ⓦwww.irempansiyon.com. A rather hotel-like *pansiyon*, the rooms are bland but fine, with a/c and en suite. 25TL/person.

Eating and drinking

The town's main roads, Atatürk Cad and Cumhuriyet Cad, are minutes away from the harbour and are the focus for most of the town's amenities, bars and restaurants.

Capkin B Hamam Sok 16. This place is heaving after 11pm with locals, expats and in-the-know tourists. It's an upstairs bar accessed by a stairs leading off a side street and rocks with live music most nights. You'll probably hear the noise from the balcony as you stroll past.

Car Cemetery Bar Hamam Sok 33. Hip, lively and tasty cocktails. Open until the (very) early hours.

The Duck Pond Eski Cami Sok 41. Bag a table next to the pond in welcome shade, sip on a beer (5TL) and nibble on a plate of the best mixed meze in town (20TL for 2/3 people) or treat yourself to a trade Turkish casserole.

Meğri Lokantasi Carşı Cad near the duck pond. This *lokanta*, a humbler version of *Meğri Restaurant* round the corner, has a nice setting by the duck pond and delivers good traditional Turkish grub. Mains 8–13TL.

Mercan Balık Restaurant Hal ve Balık Pazarı, Zabıta Bürosu Yanı. One of numerous restaurants surrounding the little fish market which will cook the fish you buy and give you salad and bread into the bargain. The fish market can get popular with tourists so arrive early.

Moving on

Bus Kaş (hourly; 4hr); Marmaris (every 30min; 3hr); Patara (10 daily; 1hr 30min).

Dolmuş Leave from near the mosque (Yeni Camii) which is beyond the town hall and the PTT on Atatürk Cad to: Kaya Köyü (30min; hourly) and Saklıkent (every 15min; 1hr); Ölüdeniz (hourly; 30min).

KAŞ

KAŞ sprang to prominence after about 1850, when it established itself as a Greek fishing and timber port. It is beautifully located, nestled in a small curving bay below rocky cliffs. But what was once a sleepy fishing village is fast becoming an **adventure-sports centre** for backpackers, with nightlife to match, and provides a handy base for paragliding, mountain biking and some of the cheapest and best scuba-diving in Turkey. Many of the *pansiyons* listed can organize these activities, or try one of the numerous operators in town, such as Bougainville (Ⓣ0242/836 3737, Ⓦwww.bt-turkey.com). Scattered around the streets and to the west are the remains of ancient **Antiphellos**, one of the few Lycian cities to bear a Greek name, small in number but nevertheless impressive. Five hundred metres west of town lies an almost complete **Hellenistic theatre**, behind which is a unique Doric tomb named Kesme Mezar, again almost completely intact. Kaş is also well situated for the nearby ruins of Kekova and Patara. On Fridays there is a big market behind the bus station.

Arrival and information

Bus All buses and *dolmuşes* arrive at the small bus station just north of the town at the top of Elmalı Cad.

Tourist office In the town square at Cumhuriyet Maydanı 5 (April–Oct Mon–Fri 8.30am–7pm, Sat & Sun 10am–7pm; Ⓣ0242/836 1238).

Accommodation

Most *pansiyons* are located in the streets close to the bus station, particularly around Recep Bilgin Cad and immediately beyond.

Ateş Pension Yeni Cami Sok 3 Ⓣ0242/836 1393, Ⓦwww.atespension.com. Meals can be eaten up on the pleasant rooftop terrace, with up to fifteen meze on offer in summer. Check the rooms – prices are negotiable on the less pleasant ones. You can use the pool at the *Hideaway Hotel* across the road (also worth checking out though a notch up price-wise). Breakfast included. Dorms 30TL, singles 65TL, doubles 80TL.

Hilal Pension Süleyman Yıldırım Cad Ⓣ0242/836 1207, Ⓦwww.korsan-kas.com. The really helpful

BUTTERFLY VALLEY

Popularized in the 1980s by hippies, Butterfly Valley (Kelebek Vadisi) is a peaceful spot to spend a couple of days. Reached by boat from Ölüdeniz (3 return trips daily), and usually open from March to October, it's home to a colony of butterflies, including the Jersey Tiger. There are no mod cons here; electricity is sparse and accommodation is basic – in tents (50TL), bungalows (60TL) or wood huts with a roof terrace (70TL); prices include a buffet breakfast and dinner. Lazy days drift into a cycle of sleeping, eating, swimming and night-time campfires. Book via Ⓦwww.butterflyvalley.org.

owner here can help with all manner of excursions and activities. The rooms are decent and you can often feast on reasonably priced fish from the barbecue in the evening. Breakfast included. Singles €22, doubles €35, triples €45; rooms without a/c are slightly cheaper.

Oreo Hotel Cukarbagli Sok 10 ⓣ0242/836 2220, ⓦwww.oreohotel.com. Friendly hotel near the town centre and beach. Swimming pool, bar and pretty garden. Includes breakfast. Singles €45, doubles €60, triples €79.

Meltem Atatürk Buluari Meltem Sok ⓣ0242/836 18 55, ⓦwww.kasmeltempansion.com. Very nice, airy bedrooms, with cooling tiled floors – ten out of the fourteen have balconies. Buffet breakfast included. Call for pick-up from the bus station. Singles 60TL, doubles 70TL.

Eating and drinking

Bar Celona Uzunçarşı Gürsoy Sok 2/a. The beer flows endlessly here and the little outdoor seating area on a small side street makes it difficult not to partake.

Bi Lokma (Mama's Kitchen) Hükümet Cad 2. A charming little place with good views of the harbour from the terrace and a reassuringly brief menu. The highlight is probably Mama's home-made *mantı* for 8TL.

Kas'ım Oztürk Sok 15. Chicken stew, pied pizzas and good old kebabs are all cooked to delicious perfection.

Mavi Cumhuriyet Medanı. A well-loved bar on the square that rivals *Bar Celona* for its drunk-making properties.

Smiley's Yat Limanı Girişi. Smiley is the twinkly-eyed owner. She makes fresh meze every day and has fostered an atmosphere conducive to both splurging and eating frugally. Fish soup is 7TL or go for delicious sea bream for around 20TL.

Sultan Garden Hükümet Cad. Marvellous, atmospheric spot and excellent meze.

OLYMPOS AND ÇIRALI

The Lycian site of **OLYMPOS**, 50km before Antalya, is located on a beautiful sandy bay and the banks of a largely dry river. It's an idyllic location with a small village that is now firmly on the backpacker circuit. You can while away several hours rambling among the overgrown ruins of Olympos (3TL, including access to the beach) before chilling out on the beach. The ruins include some recently excavated tombs, the walls of a Byzantine church and a theatre, though most seats are long gone. On the north side of the river are more striking ruins, including a well-preserved marble temple entrance. Beyond is a Byzantine bathhouse, with mosaic floors, and a Byzantine canal that would have carried water to the heart of the city. A 1.5km walk along the pebbly beach is the quieter holiday village of **ÇIRALI**. About an hour's well-marked stroll above the village's citrus groves flickers the dramatic **Chimaera** (open 24hr; 4TL), a series of eternal flames issuing from cracks in the bare rock, which is particularly beautiful at night (take a torch for the walk there and back); many hostels in Olympos organize transport for residents for a small fee. The Chimaera fires have been burning since antiquity, and inspired the Lycians to worship the god Hephaestos (or Vulcan to the Romans). The mountain was associated with a fire-breathing monster, also known as the Chimaera, with a lion's head, a goat's rear and a snake for a tail.

Arrival and information

Bus Catch any Kaş–Antalya bus to the minibus stop on the main highway, 8km up from the shore; in season a minibus departs every 15min from the main road to Olympos. In winter minibuses run but there are fewer of them so be prepared to take a taxi from the main road to Olympos village. You could walk but it's 11km down a steep twisty road. There are also one or two minibuses a day from Antalya to Çıralı in season.

Money Note that there are no banks or ATMs in Olympos or Çıralı, so make sure you have enough cash before arriving. Many of the *pansiyons* can accept card payment for accommodation.

Accommodation

With few road names around Olympos – where all the following accommodation is – it's best to ask at the bus station ticket office for directions or arrange pick-ups. It's best to book ahead. See also *Cactus Café*, p.1234.

Bayram's ⓣ0242/892 1243, ⓦwww.bayrams.com. Accommodation ranges from bungalow shacks to tree-house dormitory rooms. Organizes trips to Chimaera. Excellent facilities include laundry service and internet access. Prices include breakfast and dinner. Dorms €15, tree-house dorms €17, bungalows (with en suite and a/c) €27/person.

Kadir's ⓣ0242/892 1250, ⓦwww.kadirstreehouses.com. With 338 dorm and bungalow beds plus space for campers, a volleyball court, the eclectic *Hangar Bar* for cocktails and the lively *Bull Bar* alfresco nightclub (from midnight till very late) it's no surprise this is the backpacker hangout of choice. Organizes trips to Chimaera, beach and ruins 20min walk away. Includes breakfast and hearty buffet dinner. Bungalows with en suite and a/c for 2/3 people 40–60TL or without a/c 35–45TL, dorms from 20TL, campers with own tent 15TL.

Orange ⓣ0242/892 1317, ⓦwww.olymposorangepension.com. Professionally run and good wholesome grub. Bungalow with shared bathroom 40TL, bungalow with en suite 60TL.

Şaban ⓣ0242/892 1265, ⓦwww.sabanpansion.com. Tranquil, treehouse-style *pansiyon* with excellent home-made food and a friendly, relaxed atmosphere. Accommodation is in bungalows, tree houses and dorms. English and German spoken. Dorms 30TL, tree houses 35TL, bungalows 45TL/person including breakfast and tasty Turkish buffet at dinner.

Sheriff Pension ⓣ0242/892 1301, ⓦwww.olympos.biz. A friendly *pension* with 40 clean bungalows on stilts (some with a/c, all with small veranda) accommodating 100 people. Orange and pomegranate trees provide shade from the summer sun; in the evenings you can chat and dance around the campfire outside the bar. Includes breakfast and dinner. Free wi-fi and hot drinks. Singles 60TL, doubles 60TL/person; cabins without en suite 35TL/person.

Eating and drinking

Be sure to ask for a menu with prices, as seafood can be very expensive.

Cactus Café Chilled-out place playing reggae in Olympos village set amid a shady orange grove. Basic fare such as omelette (5TL), salads, sandwiches and pasta dishes. Beer 7TL. Camping space for those with own tents also available (20TL incl breakfast and dinner).

Çirali Gözleme Çıralı village between the Orange Market and Olympos Rent A Car, close to the *Orange Motel*. The most succulent specimens of *gözleme* hereabouts.

Yörükoğlu On the Çıralı end of the beach right next to the *Olympos Lodge Hotel*. Fine meze and a friendly owner.

ANTALYA

ANTALYA is blessed with an ideal climate and a stunning setting, and, despite the grim appearance of its concrete sprawl, it's an agreeable place – although the main area of interest for visitors is confined to the relatively small old quarter; its beaches don't rate much consideration. A short bus ride away are the charming **Düden** falls where tourists and locals flock on hot summer days. Antalya's principal attraction, however, is situated on the outskirts of the city – **Aspendos**, a Roman theatre that still holds live performances.

What to see and do

Antalya is dominated by the **Yivli Minare** or "Fluted Minaret", erected in the thirteenth century. Downhill from here is the old **harbour**, recently restored and site of the evening promenade. North is the **bazaar**, while south, beyond the Saat Kalesi (clock tower), lies Kaleiçi or the **old town**, with every house now a carpet shop, café or *pansiyon*. On the far side, on Atatürk Caddesi, the triple-arched **Hadrian's Gate** recalls a visit by the emperor in 130 AD; Hesapçı Sokak leads south past the Kesik Minare to a number of tea gardens.

The Antalya Museum

The one thing you shouldn't miss is the **Antalya Museum** (Tues–Sun 9am–6.30pm; 15TL), one of the top five archeological collections in the country; it's on the western edge of town at the far end of Kenan Evren Bulvarı, easily reachable by a tram that departs from the clock tower in Kaleiçi.

Düden falls

A small but nonetheless enchanting waterfall, **Düden falls** attracts a large number of visitors. The upper falls provide the best visual spectacle and are situated in the middle of a park. There is even a precarious walkway carved out to enable visitors to walk behind the falls. To get to the falls from Kaleiçi, get a #14 bus from the *dolmuş otogar* (25min; 2TL). Ask the driver for Düden falls and you'll be dropped near the entrance.

Arrival and information

Air The airport is 12km northeast; Havaş buses into town depart from the domestic terminal, 5min walk from the international terminal, while city-centre-bound *dolmuşes* pass nearby.

Bus Antalya's main bus station is 7km north of town. From the bus station take bus #93 to Hadrian's Gate (*Üçkapılar*) then walk into the old town.

Tourist office A 15min walk west from the clock tower on Cumhuriyet Cad (daily 8am–6/7pm; ⓣ0242/241 1747).

City transport

Bus Buses and *dolmuşes* can be caught throughout the city though the system is currently in flux.

Tram The tram runs along Atatürk Cad, ending its route at the Museum. Tickets (1.75TL) can be bought on board.

Accommodation

Most budget accommodation is in the area sandwiched between Hadrian's Gate and the back of the bazaar.

Blue Sea Garden Hotel Kılçarslan Mah Hesapçı Sok 65 ⓣ0242/248 8213, ⓦwww.hotelblueseagarden.com. The rooms are not exactly a knockout but most guests spend their time in the hotel's garden anyway, which has a pool and a small restaurant area. Includes breakfast. Singles €35, doubles/twin €50, triples €75.

Lazer Pension Hesapçı Sok 61 ⓣ0242/242 7194, ⓦwww.lazerpansiyon.com. Friendly and good location, but room quality varies; those upstairs are less dingy. Includes (slightly meagre) breakfast in the pleasant garden. Free wi-fi. Private rooms have en suite and a/c. Dorms €10, singles €19, doubles €35, triples €50.

Sabah Pansiyon Hesapçı Sok 60/a ⓣ0242/247 5345, ⓦwww.sabahpansiyon.com. Backpacker-friendly place with decent rooms and a sleepy courtyard. Price includes breakfast. Singles €28, doubles/twin €35, triples €48, quads €60.

White Garden Kaleiçi Kılıçaslan Hesapçı Geçidi 9 ⓣ0242/241 9115, ⓦwww.whitegardenpansion.com. Charming Ottoman restoration; fifteen immaculate rooms with large en suites. Buffet Turkish breakfasts included. Singles 35TL, doubles 55TL.

Eating and drinking

Art Café and Meyhane Hesapçi Sok 51. In a refurbished Ottoman building with wood floors, exposed bricks and assorted chairs and tables. The atmosphere is laidback and clientele includes students from Antalya's uni. There's live music every night, an open-mic music night on Fridays and film screenings on Sundays. Mains might include fresh grilled fish or chicken stew for 10TL, beer 5TL, tasty bar snacks 4TL/plate.

Gül Restoran Kocetepe Sok 1/1. In the old town not far from Hadrian's Gate, this friendly restaurant has a pretty outdoor garden bordered with huge Byzantine walls blocking the traffic from the adjacent Atatürk Cad. Delicious mixed meze 10TL.

Parlak Restaurant Kazım Özalp Cad Zincirlihan 7. Courtyard dining popular with locals. Try

ACTIVE OLYMPOS

Olympos, with its beautiful scenery, calm warm sea and plenty of sunshine, is perfect for anyone who likes outdoor life. Most hostels can organize day-trips on the sea: Kadir's (bookings via ⓦwww.iah-holidays.co.uk) runs courses and day-trips for all levels from beginner to expert, all including lunch. You could try scuba diving (70TL for one-day beginner session), trekking part of the Lycian Way to Mount Musa (45TL), a half-day sea kayak tour (45TL), an introduction to rock climbing on natural rock (45TL) or a mountain biking tour (25TL). If you're heading to Fethiye, opt for the three-night *gület* boat trip with V-Go (ⓣ0252 612 2113, ⓦwww.boatcruiseturkey.com; from €129 per person), which stops en route at archeological sites, small villages and Butterfly Valley (see box, p.1232).

the slow-roasted chicken. Lovely fresh meze thanks to the high turnover. Meze 4–8TL, mains 12–25TL.

Sim Reasaurant Kaledibi Sok 7. Charming husband-and-wife-run place; tables are either upstairs in a small dining room decorated with antiques or outdoors on the quiet street beneath shady vines. Mains 12–15TL.

Salman Patisserie Fevzi Çakmak Cad. Uluç Apt 7 ⓣ0242/316 7738, ⓦwww.salmanpatisserie.com. Treat yourself to a sumptuous breakfast buffet or baklava and a top-notch cappuccino.

Seraser Karanlik Sok 18 ⓣ0242/247 6015. A cut above the budget joints in town serving well-presented fresh fish and other Turkish delights. Good for a special night out.

Topçu Kebap 1885 Kazım Özalp Cad 21. They have been honing their kebabs since 1885, and hordes descend every lunchtime to enjoy them. Near the square by the tram stop. Kebabs 12TL.

Moving on

Bus/dolmuş Antalya (3 daily; 12hr); Denizli (6 daily; 5hr 30min); Fethiye, by inland route (6 daily; 4hr); İstanbul (4 daily; 12hr); İzmir (6 daily; 9hr 30min); Kaş (6 daily; 5hr); Konya (6 daily; 5hr 30min); Side (3 hourly; 1hr 15min); Nevşehir (1 daily; 11hr); Olympos (every 30min; 2hr).

Central Turkey

When the first Turkish nomads arrived in Anatolia during the tenth and eleventh centuries, the landscape must have been strongly reminiscent of their Central Asian homeland. **Ankara** grew as a result of immigration from the Anatolian villages to become the metropolis it is now. The south-central part of the country draws more visitors, not least for **Cappadocia** in the far east of the region, where water and wind have created a land of fantastic forms from the soft tufa rock, including forests of cones, table mountains and canyon-like valleys. Further south still, **Konya** is best known as the birthplace of the mystical Sufi sect and makes an interesting place to stop over between Cappadocia and the coast.

ANKARA

Modern **ANKARA** is really two cities, a double identity that is due to the breakneck pace at which it has developed since being declared capital of the Turkish Republic in 1923. Until then Ankara – known as Angora – had been a small provincial city, famous chiefly for the production of soft goat's wool. This city still exists, in and around the old citadel that was the site of the original settlement. The other Ankara is the modern metropolis that has grown up around a carefully planned attempt to create a seat of government worthy of a modern, Western-looking state.

What to see and do

The city is bisected north–south by **Atatürk Bulvarı**, and everything you need is in easy reach of this broad and busy street. At the northern end, **Ulus Meydanı**, a large square and an important traffic intersection marked by a huge equestrian Atatürk statue, is the best jumping-off point for the old part of the city – a village of narrow cobbled streets and ramshackle wooden houses centring on the **Hisar**, Ankara's old fortress and citadel. To the south, the modern shopping district of **Kızılay** sees Turkish students congregate on its streets and aspiring authors sell and sign their books on street corners. At night, the area is awash with entertainment, bars and restaurants, as are the neighbouring districts of **Kavaklidere** and **Çankaya**.

The Museum of Anatolian Civilizations

Located in Ulus, at the end of Kadife Sokak, is the **Museum of Anatolian Civilizations** (Tues–Sun 9am–5.30pm;

15TL), which boasts an incomparable collection of archeological objects housed in a restored Ottoman *bedesten*, or covered market. Hittite carving and relief work form the most compelling section of the museum, mostly taken from Carchemish, near the present Syrian border. There are also Neolithic finds from Çatal Höyük, the site of one of Anatolia's oldest settlements and widely regarded as the world's first "city".

Hisar

A steep walk up Hisarpark Cad brings you to the **Hisar**, a small citadel amid the old city walls. Most of what can be seen today dates from Byzantine times, with substantial Selçuk and Ottoman additions. Inside the confines, follow the steps leading up the hill and look out for the flag flying in the distance and you'll soon reach **Ak Kale**, a castle ruin which provides a perfect perch for viewing Ankara from above. A walk around the rest of the Hisar will let you amble in and out of the narrow alleys that intersect the ramshackle houses. Continue to head south and you'll find the twelfth-century mosque, **Alâeddin Camii**, along with a series of touristy souvenir stalls selling handmade carpet bags, jewellery and crockery.

Roman Ankara

What's left of Roman Ankara lies north of Ulus Meydanı. First stop is the **Column of Julian** on Hükümet Meydanı. Close by are the ruins of the **Temple of Augustus and Rome** built in honour of Augustus around 20 BC. Northeast of here are the remains of Ankara's **Roman baths** (daily 8.30am–12.30pm & 1.30–5.30pm; 3TL). Only the foundation stones that supported the heating and service areas remain.

Arrival and information

Air Esenboğa airport is 33km north of town. Havaş buses (10TL) meet incoming Turkish Airlines flights; a taxi will set you back 60TL.

Train station At the corner of Talat Paşa Cad and Cumhuriyet Bul, from where frequent buses run to Kızılay and Ulus. The high-speed line linking Ankara with Istanbul is due to be completed in 2013; until then you'll have to travel part of the way on the high-speed route and the rest on the old, slower route.

Bus station 5km to the southwest; some companies run service minibuses to the centre, otherwise take a *dolmuş* or the Ankaray rapid transit system (2.50TL) to Kızılay (10min) and change onto the metro (same ticket) for Ulus (red line towards Batıkent), where most of the budget hotels are located.

Tourist office There's a helpful tourist office across from the train station at Gazi Mustafa Kemal Bul 121, just outside Maletepe station on the Ankaray (Mon–Fri 9am–5pm, Sat & Sun 10am–5pm; winter closed Sun; ⓣ0312/231 5572).

City transport

Bus As well as displaying numbers, buses in Ankara also display the names of their destinations, so it's easy to work out which one to catch. For buses heading from Ulus to Çankaya try catching #413, #228 or the GOP although a multitude of other buses also head in this direction. Buy bus tickets in advance from kiosks next to the main bus stops (it's a good idea to stock up, as some areas have no kiosks). Tickets cost 1.30TL and should be inserted into the machine next to the driver. However, on some buses you can buy your ticket on board from the conductor. Most buses stop running between midnight and 1am.

Metro/Ankaray The metro runs from Batıkent in the northwest and splits at Kızılay where the metro becomes the Ankaray (light railway). The Ankaray heads to either Aşti (where the bus station is based) or Dikimevi in the east. Tickets (1.50TL one-way) can be bought from the ticket offices inside the station. In the summer, the metro stops running at midnight and in the winter it terminates at 11pm.

Accommodation

Most of the cheaper hotels are in the streets east of Atatürk Bul between Ulus and Opera Meydanı.

And Hotel Istek Sok 2, Ulus ⓣ0312/310 2304, ⓦwww.andbutikhotel.com. Smart hotel with clean and pleasant rooms. Singles 60TL, doubles 120TL.

Devran Opera Meydanı, Ulus ⓣ0312/311 0485. Friendly welcome and professional feel. Tidy and cool though very basic. Bathrooms are clean and rooms have TVs. Free internet and wi-fi. Singles 25TL, doubles 45TL, breakfast 5TL.

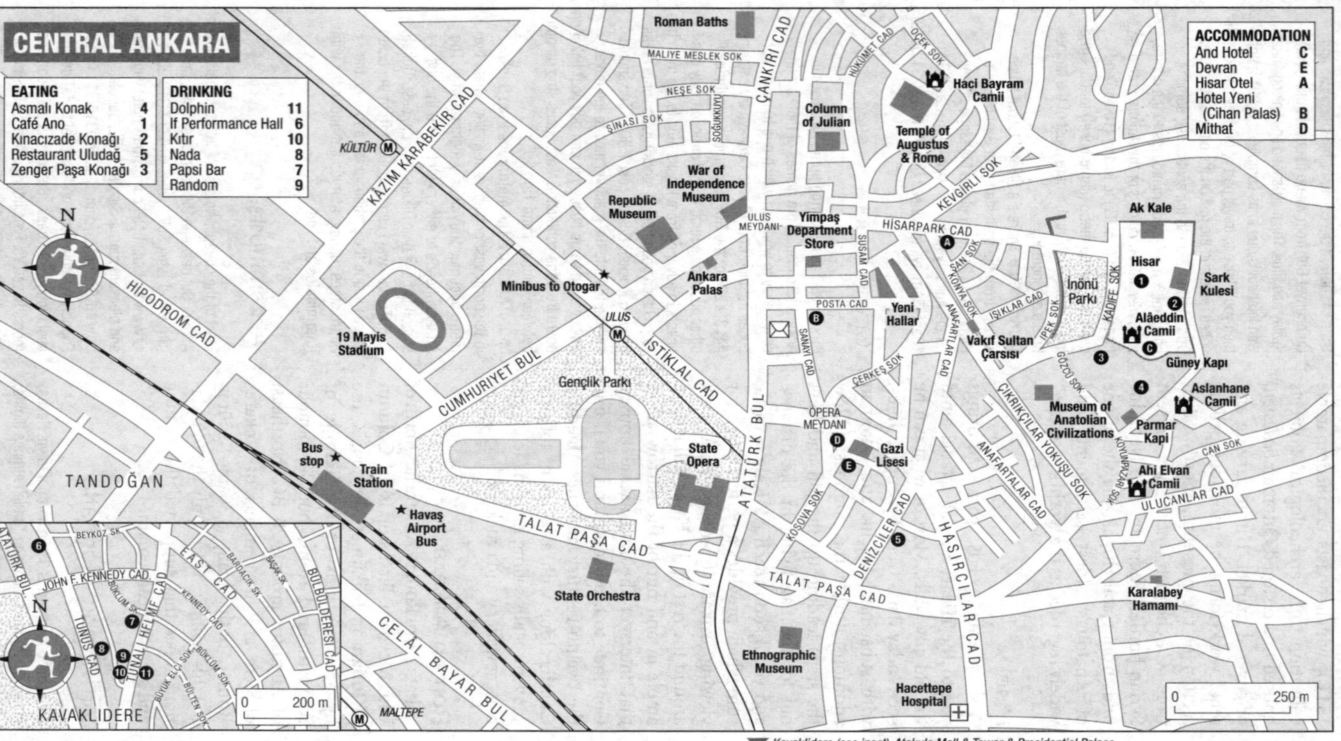
CENTRAL ANKARA
EATING
Asmalı Konak 4
Café Ano 1
Kınacızade Konağı 2
Restaurant Uludağ 5
Zenger Paşa Konağı 3
DRINKING
Dolphin 11
If Performance Hall 6
Kıtır 10
Nada 8
Papsi Bar 7
Random 9
ACCOMMODATION
And Hotel C
Devran E
Hisar Otel A
Hotel Yeni (Cihan Palas) B
Mithat D
Roman Baths
Column of Julian
Haci Bayram Camii
Temple of Augustus & Rome
War of Independence Museum
Republic Museum
Yimpaş Department Store
Ak Kale
Hisar
Sark Kulesi
Alâeddin Camii
Güney Kapı
Aslanhane Camii
İnönü Parkı
Minibus to Otogar
Ankara Palas
Yeni Hallar
Vakıf Sultan Çarsısı
19 Mayis Stadium
Gençlik Parkı
Museum of Anatolian Civilizations
Parmar Kapi
Ahi Elvan Camii
State Opera
Gazi Lisesi
Bus stop
Train Station
Havaş Airport Bus
State Orchestra
Karalabey Hamamı
Ethnographic Museum
Hacettepe Hospital
TANDOĞAN
KAVAKLIDERE
MALTEPE
KÜLTÜR
ULUS
ULUS MEYDANI
OPERA MEYDANI
KÂZIM KARABEKİR CAD
HİPODROM CAD
CUMHURİYET BUL
İSTİKLAL CAD
ATATÜRK BUL
TALAT PAŞA CAD
CELÂL BAYAR BUL
HASIRCILAR CAD
DENİZCİLER CAD
ANAFARTALAR CAD
ÇIKRIKÇILAR YOKUŞU SOK
HİSARPARK CAD
ÇANKIRI CAD
KEVGİRLİ SOK
ULUCANLAR CAD
0 250 m
0 200 m
Kavaklidere (see inset), Atakule Mall & Tower & Presidential Palace

Hisar Otel Hisarpark Cad 6, Ulus ⓣ0312/ 311 9889. Rooms in a much better state than similarly priced options, some with better views than others. Shower cubicles, TV and firm beds. 20TL no shower, 25TL with shower.
Hotel Yeni (Cihan Palas) Sanayi Cad 5/b, Ulus ⓣ0312/310 4720 (5 Hat), ⓦwww.hotelyeni.com. A good couple of notches up from the rest of the town's more affordable hotels. Breakfast €3. Singles €25, doubles €40, triples €55.
Mithat Opera Meydanı, Tavus Sok 2, Ulus ⓣ0312/311 5410, ⓦwww.otelmithat.com.tr. Professionally run, the rooms are sombre but the bed linen is clean and the bathrooms inviting. Proper bellboys and sexy lift music. Breakfast included. Singles €25, doubles €40, triples €50.

Eating

Standard *pide* and kebab places are on just about every street in Ankara and there's an abundance of good sweet and cake shops. Ulus, particularly along Çankırı Cad, is the place to look for cheap lunchtime venues. Come evening, head south to Kavaklıdere.
Asmalı Konak Kalekapısı Sok 14, Hisar. Great range of fresh meze (5TL) in an atmospheric old building. Affable owner Osman is a big belly-dancing fan and organizes regular shows.
Café Ano Demirfırka Mahallesi 29, Hisar. A lovely café in the citadel serving coffee, tea and sandwiches.
Kınacızade Konağı Hisar. A nice down-to-earth and warm atmosphere, with a cute two-table balcony and a fine range of breakfast choices. One room is a kind of mini-museum/shrine to the Ottoman period. Mains 10–12TL.
Restaurant Uludağ Denizciler Cad 54, Ulus. Look no further for the finest *Iskender kebab* in Ankara.
Zenger Paşa Konağı Doyran Sok 13, Hisar. Just climbing up to the restaurant is a treat. On the way up you will see women sitting by a fire making breads. Reasonable prices considering the wonderful views and delicious *pide* and grilled meats.

Drinking

Dolphin Tunalı Hilmi Cad 99, Kavaklıdere. Long and narrow, low-lit drinking joint, with the atmosphere of a classic American bar.
If Performance Hall Tunus Cad 14/a, Kavaklıdere ⓣ0312/418 9506, ⓦwww.ifperformance.com. Bands perform nightly – a stalwart of the Ankara music scene.
Kıtır Tunalı Hilmi Cad 114/24, Kavaklıdere. Small, buzzy pub with a little fast-food window at the entrance – outdoor seating, too.
Nada Tunus Cad 85/a, Kavaklıdere ⓦwww.nada.com.tr. Smart and sleek but nevertheless friendly.
Papsi Bar Tunalı Hilmi Cad 68/c, Kavaklıdere. Lively outdoor spot with an accordion player serenading drinkers.
Random Tunalı Hilmi Cad 114, Kavaklıdere (below *Kıtır*). Busy, intimate bar popular with a young crowd.

Entertainment

Anadolu Gösteri Kongre Merkezi Türkocağl Cad Balgat. Large performance hall for theatre or music concerts. See ⓦwww.biletix.com for tickets.

Directory

Embassies Australia, Nenehatun Cad 83, Gaziosmanpaşa ⓣ0312/459 9500; Canada, Cinnah Cad 58, Çankaya ⓣ0312/409 2700; New Zealand, Iran Cad 13/4, Kavaklıdere ⓣ0312/467 9054; UK, Şehit Ersan Cad 46/a, Çankaya ⓣ0312/468 6230; US, Atatürk Bul 110, Kavaklıdere ⓣ0312/455 5555.
Hamam Karacabey Hamami, Talat Paşa Bul 101 (men 6am–11pm; women 7am–7pm; from 15TL).
Hospital Hacettepe University Medical Faculty, west of Hasırcılar Sok, Sıhhıye ⓣ0312/305 5000.
Internet Intek Internet Café, Karanfil Sok 47/a, Kızılay; Internet Café, next to PTT, Maltepe.
Left luggage At the bus and train stations.
Post office Merkez Postahane, on Atatürk Bul, Ulus.

Moving on

Train İstanbul (3 high-speed daily, changing at Eskisehir, 5hr 30min; 1 sleeper daily 10.30pm; 9hr 30min); İzmir (2 daily; 10hr).
Bus/dolmuş Antalya (12 daily; 10hr); Bodrum (10 daily; 10hr); Bursa (hourly; 7hr); Fethiye (2 daily; 12hr); İstanbul (every 30min; 7hr); İzmir (hourly; 8hr); Konya (14 daily; 3hr 30min); Marmaris (14 daily; 13hr); Nevşehir (12 daily; 4hr 30min).

CAPPADOCIA

A land created by the complex interaction of natural and human forces over vast spans of time, **CAPPADOCIA**, around 150km southeast of Ankara, is a superlative visual experience. Its weird formations of soft, dusty rock have been adapted into caves and even underground cities over centuries by many cultures. Cappadocia scores highly on value for money thanks to the wide selection of competitively priced accommodation, restaurants and activities on offer. Long-distance buses arrive into the unappealing working city of Nevşehir, so you'll need to either arrange a transfer from your hotel or take a *dolmuş* to your destination. Many backpackers choose to stay in the touristy hotspot of **Göreme**, but alternatives include **Uçhisar**, which has a spectacular castle (8am–8pm; 5TL), or **Ürgüp**, a small town where many of the old abandoned cave dwellings are being renovated into smart guesthouses and private homes. *Dolmuşes* operate regularly between Cappadocia's villages.

What to see and do

About 2km outside Göreme village, the **Göreme Open-Air Museum** (daily 8am–5/6pm; 15TL) is the site of more than thirty churches, mainly dating from the ninth to the end of the eleventh century and containing some of the best of all the frescoes in Cappadocia.

Outdoor pursuits include walking in the valleys, in particular **Ihlara Valley** – which is often on the tour itineraries offered by the hostels; allow two to four hours per walk and don't miss a stop at one of the rustic farmer-run teashops en route. Note that there are no detailed maps of the area and waymark signs tend to be arrows painted on rocks. The best routes are Pigeon Valley between Göreme and Uçhisar, and the Red Valley from Ortahisar to the village of Çavuşin. Don't miss a visit to the city of **Zelve** (8am–5pm, 8TL), which was occupied for some 4000 years and was the site of a monastery from the ninth to the thirteenth centuries.

Arrival and information

Bus When buying your bus ticket to Göreme or another village, be sure to check the end destination. Direct services arrive at the Göreme bus station, located in front of Müze Cad, in the centre of town. However, some firms will drop you off in Nevşehir, from where you'll have to continue by local bus or *dolmuş* (the last of which leaves Nevşehir at about 6pm). *Dolmuş* to Nevşehir runs hourly on Sundays, half-hourly otherwise.

Tourist office In Nevşehir bus station (daily 5am–9pm). Has a useful accommodation list and maps of the local area.

Tour operators TravelAtelier (Ⓦwww.travelatelier.com) offers one-day tours (€49/person for a group of 10) which take in Göreme Open-Air Museum and the underground city of Kaymakli, plus wine-tasting seminars (€35/person).

Argeus Travel Agency (Ⓦwww.argeus.com.tr) specialize in cycling trips: bike rental is €30/day and a guide is €110/day. Royal Balloons (Ⓣ0384 271 3300, Ⓦwww.royalballoon.com; 1hr €175, 90min €240) is the best choice for a hot-air balloon ride.

Accommodation

Cave hotels are the most popular form of accommodation in Cappadocia but there are alternatives – often with great views – for those with claustrophobia. Some hostels/hotels can be tricky to find, though most are walkable from bus stations. In Göreme, the accommodation office will arrange free pick-ups. If you're staying in another village, ask your accommodation as many will arrange a free transfer from the bus station.

Esbelli Evi Esbelli Sok 8, Ürgüp Ⓣ0384/341 3395, Ⓦwww.esbelli.com. Magnificent views and sumptuous boutique rooms in caves with private terraces and secret gardens at one of Cappadocia's finest hotels. Well worth stretching your budget for. Includes breakfast. Doubles €120.

Kale Konak Kale Sok 9, Uçhisar Ⓣ0384/219 2828, Ⓦwww.kalekonak.com. A wonderfully cosy labyrinthine hotel at the foot of Uçhisar Castle. All fifteen rooms are tastefully furnished with antiques; a private session in the marble hammam is the ultimate indulgence. Excellent value for money. Doubles €120, triples €130.

Köse Pansion Ragıp Üner Cad, Göreme. Ⓣ0384/271 2294, Ⓦwww.kosepension.com. Large, homely *pansiyon* near the bus station with swimming pool and clean rooms. The mattress-strewn dorm (sleeping bag hire 2.50TL) is in a large, atmospheric wooden hall on the rooftop. Free wi-fi. Breakfast not included. Dorms 15TL, doubles 80TL, triples 90TL.

Rock Vlalley Hostel Iceri Dere Sok, Göreme Ⓣ0384/271 2153, Ⓦwww.rockvalleycappadocia.com. Attractive wooden dorm with heating chimney for snugness. Big pool with the valley looming up all around – very atmospheric. A pleasant, low-key option. Breakfast included. Dorms 25TL, doubles/twins 80TL.

Shoestring Kazım Erin Sok 23, Göreme ⓣ0384/271 2450, ⓦwww.shoestringcave.com. A warm, sociable atmosphere. Quality beds and bedding make these cave rooms very cosy indeed. Dorms €8, doubles (shared bathroom) €25, doubles (private bath) €35, additional bed €10/person/night.

Eating and drinking

In Göreme, several restaurants and bars are on Müze Cad, behind the bus station.

Anatolia Kitchen Müze Cad 1, Göreme. Offers local wine as well as beer. A quality mixed meze with pizza-like bread is 10TL, vegetable kebab of mushrooms, aubergine, tomato and peppers 12TL and *pide* 5–10TL. A lovely shady terrace in the middle of town, a minute or two from the bus station.

Dibek Hakkı Paşa Meydanı, Göreme. It won't take long for someone to tell you about this place's *testi kebab* but it takes the restaurant a long time to cook it – you need to order it at least three hours in advance.

Flintstones Bar Müze Cad, Göreme. Local hub for low-key nocturnal entertainment. Plays good old-time and rock'n'roll. Beer 5TL, spirits 10TL.

Göreme Restaurant With kilim and cushions on the floor this place has a warm feel (welcome in sometimes chilly Göreme). Tasty sun-dried tomato and pomegranate molasses starter 5TL. *Kuzu şiş* with a herby salad 12TL.

Ziggy's Yunak Mah, Tevfik Fikret Cad 24, Ürgüp. Delicious meze, an outdoor terrace and cosy indoor seating ensure locals and travellers return again and again.

Moving on

Bus/dolmuş Ankara (daily; 6hr); Konya (4 daily; 3hr); Nevşehir (Sun every hour, Mon–Sat every 30min; 30min).

Derinkuyu and Kayamaklı underground cities

Among the most extraordinary phenomena of the Cappadocia region are the remains of a number of underground settlements, some of them large enough to have accommodated up to 30,000 people. The cities are thought to date back to Hittite times, though the complexes were later enlarged by Christian communities. Most thoroughly excavated is **DERINKUYU** (daily 8am–5.30pm; 15TL), 29km from Nevşehir and accessible by *dolmuş*. The city is well lit, and the original ventilation system still functions remarkably well, though some of the passages are small and cramped. The excavated area (only a quarter of the total) consists of eight floors and includes stables, wine presses and a dining hall or schoolroom with two long, rock-cut tables, plus a cruciform church and dungeon. Some 10km north of Derinkuyu is **KAYMAKLI** (daily 8am–5.30pm; 15TL), where only five of its underground levels have been excavated to date.

KONYA

Roughly midway between Antalya and Nevşehir, **KONYA** is a place of pilgrimage for the Muslim world – the home of Celalledin Rumi or the Mevlâna ("Our Master"), the mystic who founded the Mevlevî or Whirling Dervish sect, and the centre of Sufic mystical practice and teaching.

The Mevlâna Museum

The **Mevlâna Museum** (Mon 10am–5pm, Tues–Sun 9am–5pm; 3TL) is housed in the first lodge (*tekke*) of the Mevlevî dervish sect, at the eastern end of Mevlâna Bulvarı, recognizable by its distinctive fluted turquoise dome. The main building of the museum holds the mausoleum containing the tombs of the Mevlâna, his father and other notables. The original *semahane* (ceremonial hall) exhibits some of the musical instruments of the first dervishes, the original illuminated poetical work of the Mevlâna, and a 500-year-old silk carpet from Selçuk Persia that is supposedly the finest ever woven. In the adjoining room, a casket containing hairs from the beard of the Prophet Mohammed is displayed alongside illuminated medieval Korans.

Karatay Tile Museum

Built by Emir Celaleddin Karatay in the thirteenth century, the interior of the **Karatay Tile Museum** (Alâeddin Bulvarı; daily 8am–noon & 1–5pm; 3TL) is equally as fascinating as the ceramics on show, with a beautifully decorated domed central ceiling and ornamental green tiles.

Arrival and information

Train station 2km out of the centre at the far end of Istasyon Cad, connected to the centre by regular *dolmuş*.

Bus station 10km out of town, from where the *otogar dolmuş* and tramway connects with the town centre.

Tourist office Mevlâna Cad No 73 (May–Sept Mon–Sat 8.30am–5.30pm; Oct–April Mon–Fri 8am–5pm; ⓣ0332/353 4021 extension 115).

Internet Internet cafés are around Alâeddin Hill, next to the *McDonalds* or Ince Minare Medresesi.

Accommodation

Deluxe Otel Ayanbey Sok 22 ⓣ0332/351 1546. All 25 rooms are en suite with a/c, minibar and flat-screen TV at this hotel, with a business-style feel but impressive for the money. Singles 80TL, doubles 150TL.

Otel Mevlana İstanbul Cad Cengaver Sok 2 ⓣ0332/352 0029, ⓦwww.otelmevlana.com. Friendly, helpful and warm place. En-suite rooms with satellite TV and a/c. Price includes open buffet breakfast. Singles 40TL, doubles 60TL.

Rumi Hotel Durakfakih Sok 5 ⓣ0332/353 1121, ⓦwww.rumihotel.com. A comfortable and very centrally located hotel opposite the Mevlâna Museum, and with a hammam. Large rooms and decent bathrooms. Breakfast included. Singles 100TL, doubles 150TL, triples 250TL.

Ulusan Off Alâeddin Cad on side road behind the PTT ⓣ0332/351 5004. Kind of a smoky, sterile atmosphere but a solid choice nonetheless. Unusual breakfast area – a tiny impromptu lounge on an upper-floor landing. Singles 40TL, doubles 70TL.

Eating and drinking

There is a limited selection of restaurants and no reputable bars or pubs. The nightlife scene is underground and few women venture out at night alone. The area around Alâeddin Parkı is where younger people hang out.

Ali Baba Eski Avukatlar Sok 5/a. Everything is about the *konya firin kebap*, lamb cooked for hours in a wood-fired oven, eaten with bread and a plateful of raw onion to cut through the richness. Near the Şerafettin mosque. A bit tricky to find.

Köşk Konya Mutfağı Mengüç Cad 66. A fantastic place that looms up, a 10min walk from the town centre. The dining rooms scattered throughout the house are smart yet a nice ramshackle feel endures. Really good prices – barely anything exceeds 10TL – and excellent, traditional food. Try the *patlican orta* and, for dessert, the *höşmerim helvası*. To find it head down Topraklık Cad then bear right down Sokullu Mehmet Paşa Sok. You should spot it at the end of this road. Locals can direct you.

Mevlevi Sofrası Nazimbey Cad 1/a. Smart, spacious terrace with sweeping views of the museum garden. If you're hungry after a museum visit try the *adana kebap* 8TL.

Osmanlı Çarsisi A classic *nargile* and coffee place with Ottoman-style rooms. It is behind the Ince Minare Medresesi.

WHIRLING DERVISH CEREMONY

This meditational ceremony, where worshippers spin around to draw closer to God, is held at the Mevlâna Cultural Centre close to the museum. The ceremony is free and takes place every Saturday night. Tickets can be booked through most hotels or the tourist information office. You'll find plenty of background reading on ⓦwww.mevlana.net.

Moving on

Airport Havaş has started an 8TL transfer to the airport (35TL by cab). Catch it from outside the Turkish Airlines office at Feritpaşa Cad 10/b.

Bus Buy bus tickets from the offices on Mevlâna Cad. Ankara (every 20min; 3hr 20min); Antalya (25 daily; 5hr 30min); Göreme (5 daily; 3hr 45min); İstanbul (every 40min; 9hr); Nevşehir (10 daily; 3hr 30min).

Ukraine

HIGHLIGHTS

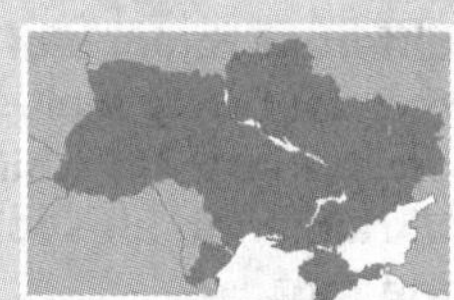

(KYIV) CHORNOBYL MUSEUM, KYIV: Learn about the world's worst nuclear accident and the heroism of those who cleared it up

(KYIV) PECHERSKA LAVRA, KYIV: experience orthodox-christian spirituality firsthand in this centuries-old religious site

L'VIV OLD TOWN: lose yourself in the café-filled alleys and courtyards of this central european jewel

ODESA: soak up the sun then party the night away at Arkadia beach

ROUGH COSTS

DAILY BUDGET Basic €30 /occasional treat €50

DRINK *horilka* (vodka; 50ml shot) €1

FOOD Ukrainian borscht €1

HOSTEL/BUDGET HOTEL €8/€30

TRAVEL Train: Kiev–Odessa €10; bus €18

FACT FILE

POPULATION 45.8 million

AREA 603,628 sq km

LANGUAGES Ukrainian, Russian

CURRENCY Hryvnia (Hr/UAH)

CAPITAL Kyiv (population: 2.8 million)

INTERNATIONAL PHONE CODE ⓣ380

Introduction

The second largest country in Europe, Ukraine has not always had clearly defined frontiers and has spent large tracts of its history under foreign rule. Even today the issue of "Ukrainianness" is viewed differently by people living in different regions of the country: Ukrainians living in Kyiv and the east may well speak the Russian language at home and on the streets; while those living in L'viv and the west speak Ukrainian in all social situations and are enormously proud of the fact.

Despite being a country of large distances and time-consuming travel, Ukraine is not as far away as you might think, and its three key cities are well worth fitting in to a wider European trip. Ukraine's fast-paced capital **Kyiv** offers a fascinating insight on a country in the throes of transformation, with chic boutiques and slick bars sprouting up along broad, cobbled boulevards. Glittering church domes and steeples show off the city's medieval glories. One of Europe's great maritime cities, **Odesa** exudes a sense of Tsarist-Empire grandeur, while its bars and beaches provide a vibrant hedonistic edge. In total contrast is the western city of **L'viv**, a Central European city that looks like an estranged cousin of Vienna or Prague, and has the cultural attractions and café life to match. Situated within easy travelling distance of Central European cities, L'viv is the one Ukrainian city that you should squeeze into your itinerary.

CHRONOLOGY

Tenth century AD A strong Slav state known as "Rus" emerges, centred on Kyiv.
988 Prince Vladimir of Kyiv accepts Christianity.
1240 Kyiv is sacked by the Tatars.
1362 After the Battle of the Blue Waters, much of Ukraine is absorbed into the Grand Duchy of Lithuania.
1569 The Union of Lublin creates the Polish–Lithuanian Commonwealth, with most of Ukraine falling under direct Polish rule.
1648 Cossack leader Bohdan Khmelnitskyi leads an uprising against the Commonwealth.
1654 Khmelnitskyi swears allegiance to Tsarist Russia, bringing Ukraine into the orbit of Moscow.
1709 An anti-Russian revolt under Ivan Mazepa is defeated.
1780s Russia drives the Ottoman Turks from southern Ukraine and the Crimea.
1794 Russian Empress Catherine the Great founds the Black Sea port of Odesa.
1917–21 The Russian Revolution sparks failed attempts to recreate an independent Ukrainian state. Central and Eastern Ukraine are absorbed into the Soviet Union, while Western Ukraine becomes part of Poland.
1932–33 Stalinist collectivization policies lead to the Holodomor or Great Famine, resulting in anything between 2.5 and 7.5 million deaths.
1941 Nazi Germany invades the Ukraine, meeting fierce resistance in Kyiv and Odesa.
1945 International borders are redrawn: Western Ukraine is absorbed into the Ukrainian Soviet Republic.
1986 A fire at the Chornobyl power plant leads to the world's worst nuclear accident.
1991 The USSR is dissolved and Ukraine becomes an independent republic
2004 Viktor Yanukovych wins a presidential election regarded by many as fraudulent. Popular protests spark the so-called Orange Revolution. A re-vote ordered by the Supreme Court is won by pro-Western Viktor Yushchenko.
2005 The Orange Revolution runs out of steam: President Yushchenko falls out with Prime Minister Yulia Tymoshenko.
2009 Old-style conservative Viktor Yanukovych is elected president.
2012 Ukraine hosts the European Football Championships together with Poland.

ARRIVAL

The main hub for arrivals **by air** is Kyiv Borispil, which is served by major European and transatlantic airlines. The smaller Kyiv Zhulyany is used by the budget carrier Wizz Air, while the airports at Odesa and L'viv receive a limited number of flights from other European cities. Kyiv Pasazhirs'kyi is the main international **train station**, served by overnight trains from Budapest, Kraków and Warsaw. The western Ukrainian city of L'viv is by far the easiest to reach from Central Europe, served by trains from Bucharest, Budapest and Kraków, and **buses** from Kraków, Warsaw and Prague.

GETTING AROUND

Ukraine's principal cities are a long distance apart and travelling between them usually takes a whole day or night. Trains and buses are frequently booked solid days in advance so it is wise to plan ahead.

Train is the cheapest way to travel. However, there is only one daytime train each way between Kyiv–L'viv and Kyiv–Odesa; all other services are overnight. The cheapest tickets are for so-called *platskart* or third class, a cramped open carriage in which the (relatively hard) seats are turned into bunks at night. The next step up is *kupe*, a second-class compartment with four bunks; while *luks* are private one- or two-person sleeping compartments that are three times more expensive. Whichever class you travel in, your carriage will be controlled by an attendant (*provodnitsa*) who serves you tea but who also prevents you from wandering around from carriage to carriage. Dining cars are rare so bring your own food and drink. **Train stations** (*vokzal*) are confusing places with little in the way of Latin-script labelling and a proliferation of counters selling different types of ticket. Counters selling tickets for today are marked "Dobovoho prodazhu"; those for advance bookings are marked "Poperednyoho prodazhu". International tickets are brought from counters marked "Mizhnarodnoho spolucheniya".

Intercity bus services are slightly quicker than trains and usually run during daylight hours, although tickets are more expensive. Companies such as Avtolyuks (Ⓦwww.autolux.ua) and Gunsel (Ⓦwww.gunsel.com.ua) operate services between Kyiv–Odesa and Kyiv–L'viv. They have booking

offices at the main bus stations (*avtovoksal*) in each city. Avtolyuks operate "VIP" services between Kyiv and Odesa that are quicker and slightly more expensive than the regular buses; tickets sell out fast and should be booked well in advance.

Public transport in Ukraine's cities is cheap, with flat fares rarely exceeding 2Hr. Many urban transport routes are operated by privately owned **minibuses** known as *marshrutki*. They are speedier than regular buses and trams, but can be overcrowded.

ACCOMMODATION

Backpacker **hostels** are common in the main cities. They're often rough-and-ready affairs in converted apartments, although most will offer a mixture of multi-bed dorms and private doubles, with a kitchen and/or common room to lounge around in and socialize.

Hotels are the most unpredictable category of accommodation, with informal B&Bs, Soviet-era concrete blocks and modern business-oriented establishments all charging similar prices for hugely varying levels of comfort. In Kyiv it is difficult to find an acceptably habitable double room for less than $100/800Hr; prices are cheaper in Odesa and L'viv.

Local agencies rent out **private rooms** and apartments to tourists in Odesa, where a small self-catering apartment can work out cheaper than a double room in a hotel.

FOOD AND DRINK

Ukrainian cities are well supplied with restaurants (*restoran*), and cafés and pubs frequently have a full menu of food. Cheap and convenient are the self-service **canteens** (*stolova*), which serve local food and help-yourself salads at hard-to-resist prices.

Ukraine is one of the original homelands of **borshch**, the pinky-hued beetroot soup. Ukrainian *borshch* often includes cabbage, along with bits of pork or other meat. A summer alternative to *borshch* is *okroshka*, a cold soup consisting of sour milk, cucumber, bits of ham and boiled egg. Other staples include *varenyky*, ravioli-like parcels of dough with potato, cottage cheese or minced-meat fillings; *sirniki*, cylindrical little cheese cakes with a sweet-and-savoury taste; and a whole range of pancakes (*mlintsi*) stuffed with a variety of ingredients. Pork, beef and chicken figure prominently among the main courses; fish (particularly anchovy and mackerel) is common on the Black Sea coast. Buckwheat (*hrechka*) is a staple side-order; while bread with *salo* (pork fat) is a traditional snack. Central Asian dishes once popular across the Soviet Union and still ubiquitous in the Ukraine include *shashlik* (shish-kebab) and *cheburek* (a deep-fried meat pasty).

Drink

Horilka (vodka) is very much the national drink. It usually comes in classic, clear form, although flavoured varieties are also available – *medova s pertsem* (honey vodka with hot red pepper) is the one you must try at least once. The standard measure for spirits is 0.50cl (almost a double by Western standards), so consume in moderation. Ukrainian **beer** (*pivo*) is on the whole excellent, with Obolon, Slavutich, L'vivske and Chernihivske among the main mass-market brewers. Most produce a regular lager-type brew (*svitle*) alongside a dark porter (*tamne*) and a "white" unfiltered beer (*bile*). In addition, an increasing number of brewpubs serve up their own-brand ales, and a good number of small-scale breweries (notably Stare Misto in western Ukraine) are producing a cracking range of tasty beers.

> **EMERGENCY NUMBERS**
>
> Fire ⓣ101; Police ⓣ102; Ambulance ⓣ103.

There are a handful of domestic red and white **wines** from the Crimea, although most bars and restaurants in Kyiv and L'viv tend to serve European, Australian and American imports.

Hookah pipes (kalyan) with flavoured tobaccos are very popular among young adults and are a regular feature of Ukrainian bars.

CULTURE AND ETIQUETTE

The majority of Ukrainians are Orthodox Christians. In churches and monasteries, women should cover their heads and shoulders (there may well be stalls outside selling cheap scarves and shawls for precisely this purpose), while men should don long trousers. A ten percent **tip** is common in restaurants. **Tipping** is not required if you are just having a drink in a café, but ten percent is common in restaurants.

SPORTS AND OUTDOOR ACTIVITIES

Football is the most popular spectator sport, with Shakhtar Donetsk (UEFA Cup winners in 2009) and Dinamo Kyiv enjoying mass support. Karpaty L'viv have had their moments, playing in the group stages of the Europa League in 2010 Ukraine is set to co-host the 2012 European Football Championship together with Poland; there has been a massive investment in facilities, with a brand-new stadium on the outskirts of L'viv and the total reconstruction of the national stadium in downtown Kyiv.

Ukraine's main **hiking** area is in the smooth green hills of the Carpathian range, with the 2061m Mount Hoverla (Ukraine's highest) the main target. The trailheads are a good 3 to 4 hours' drive southeast of L'viv so you will need to plan a 2- to 3-day trip to make the most of it.

COMMUNICATIONS

Post offices (*Poshta*) in major cities are open Monday to Saturday 9am–9pm, Sunday 10am–5pm. Public phones on the street are increasingly rare and can only be used for local calls. They take phonecards (purchased at the post office). Long-distance and international calls are best made from a **telephone office** (usually attached to the main post office), where you pay a deposit before being assigned a cabin to make your call. Cheap international calls are also available at many of the internet cafes spread throughout city centres. If you are travelling with a laptop, wi-fi internet access is free of charge in many a hostels, hotels and city-centre cafés.

EMERGENCIES

Ukraine is a relatively safe country to travel in, although tourists are frequently the target of pickpockets and petty thieves. Ukrainian **police** occasionally carry out spot checks on foreigners so always carry your passport with you. They rarely speak English.

High-street **pharmacies** (*apteka*) sell familiar medicines over the counter. Each city has a 24hr pharmacy in the centre. Staff in Ukrainian public **hospitals** are unlikely to speak English and you are advised to seek private treatment in the event of illness or injury – so make sure you are insured before you travel.

INFORMATION

L'viv is the only Ukrainian city that has a **tourist information office** and Latin-alphabet signage in the streets. In Kyiv and Odesa, hostel staff and private

UKARAINE

	Ukrainian	Pronunciation
Yes	*ak*	Tak
No	*Hi*	Nyi
Please	*Будь ласка*	bood-la-ska
Thank you	*Дякую*	dya-koo-yoo
Hello/Good day	*Доброго дня*	do-bro-ho dnya
Goodbye	*До побачення*	do po-ba-che-nya
Excuse me/sorry	*Вибачте*	vee-bach-teh
Today	*Сьогодні*	syo-hod-nyi
Yesterday	*Вчора*	Fcho-ra
Tomorrow	*Завтра*	Zaf-tra
I don't understand	*Я не розумію*	Ya ne roz-um-i-yoo
How much?	*Скільки?*	Skil-ki?
Do you speak English?	*Ви розмовляєте англійскою мовою?*	Vi roz-mov-lya-ee-tee an-hlee-sko-yoo mo-vo-yoo?
Where is the..?	*Де?*	Deh?
Hotel	*Готель*	Hotel
Bus	*Автобус*	Af-to-boos
Plane	*Літак*	Li-tak
Train	*Поїзд*	Po-yizd
I would like a...	*Я хочу*	Ya ho-chu
Open	*Відчинено*	Vid-chi-ne-no
Closed	*Зачинено*	Za-chi-ne-no
One	*Один*	O-din
Two	*Два*	Dva
Three	*Три*	Tri
Four	*Чотири*	Cho-ti-ri
Five	*П'ять*	Pyat
Six	*Шість*	Shist
Seven	*Сім*	Sim
Eight	*Вісім*	Vi-sim
Nine	*Дев'ять*	Dev-yat
Ten	*Десять*	Des-yat

tourist agencies are the most likely sources of information.

MONEY AND BANKS

Currency is the **hryvnia** (Hr/UAH), divided into 100 kopinky. Coins come in 1, 2, 5, 10, 25 and 50 kopinky denominations; and notes in 1, 2, 5, 10, 20, 50, 100 and 200 hryvnias. At the time of writing, £1 = 13Hr, €1 = 11.50Hr, US$ = 8Hr. Banks (Mon–Fri 9am–6pm, Sat 9am–noon) and exchange offices (*obmin valyut*) offer similar exchange rates. Credit cards are accepted in larger hotels and city-centre shops, but will be refused elsewhere. ATMs are fairly widespread.

OPENING HOURS AND HOLIDAYS

An increasing number of shops in Ukrainian cities are open 10am–6pm daily, although some have restricted hours on Saturdays and are closed on Sundays. Most museums and historic sights are closed one day a week, and one day at the end of the month for cleaning. **Public holidays** are January 1, January 7, March 8, Easter Sunday & Monday, May 1, May 9, June 28 and August 24.

Kyiv

Sprawling, energetic but never overwhelming, **KYIV** (Київ) combines the stately aura of a great historical city with the raw vigour of a rapidly changing society. Golden-domed churches recall the city's role as the birthplace of Christian Rus – the medieval Slav civilization that subsequently gave rise to both the Ukrainian and Russian nations. Designer-label boutiques, flashy bars and top-of-the-range jeeps offer a jarringly contemporary contrast. With attractions aplenty and a fast-developing nightlife scene it's a city that is easy to enjoy. It also remains an easy-to-explore capital despite its scale: walking distances between the main sights are not too taxing, and the city's metro system provides quick and cheap transport from one neighbourhood to the next.

What to see and do

At the heart of the city is **Khreschatyk**, a broad, tree-lined boulevard bordered by fashion stores, glitzy cafés and imposing government buildings. A brace of historic churches occupy the high ground above, while downhill to the northeast is Podil, an area of serene Neoclassical buildings bordered by residential streets. Linking the two is **Andriivs'kyi uzviz**, the winding cobbled street that most captures the atmosphere of nineteenth-century Kyiv. A short southbound hop on the metro is **Pecherska Lavra**, a rambling monastery complex famous for its icon-rich churches and candlelit catacombs. Bordering the monastery complex to the south, a swathe of riverside park is dominated **by Rodina Mat'**, the imperious statue that symbolizes the Soviet Ukraine's struggles against Nazi Germany during the "Great Patriotic War" of 1941–45.

Khreschatyk and around

Lined by shops and cafés, Khreschatyk is the place where many Kievans come to sip coffee during the day and stroll on summer evenings. At its south-western end, the boutiques of the Metrograd underground shopping centre provide a contemporary contrast to the pre-World War I Besarabs'kyi Rynok, the indoor market hall that fills daily with fresh produce.

Opposite the Rynok on the corner of Velyka Vasylkivs'ka and Baseina, the **PinchukArtCentre** (Tues–Sun noon–9pm; free) displays contemporary art on four storeys, with major international names featuring heavily in the programme. The top-floor café is decked out in minimalist all-white style and comes with roofline views of downtown Kyiv.

Maidan nezalezhnosti

A horseshoe-shaped square at the eastern end of Khreschatyk, Maidan nezalezhnosti or "Independence Square" has long served as the symbolic heart of the city. During the Soviet period it hosted a statue of Lenin, removed by pro-independence protesters in 1991 and replaced in 2001 with a gilded **statue of Berehynia**, the pre-Christian spirit adopted by romantically inclined Ukrainians as some kind of all-protecting mother-goddess. In December 2004 the square was the scene of mass demonstrations that presaged the so-called Orange Revolution.

St Sofia's Cathedral

Beckoning visitors with its vivacious cluster of green and golden domes, **St Sofia's Cathedral** at Volodymyrs'ka 24 (daily 10am–5pm; entry to complex 2Hr; entry to cathedral and museums 30Hr) was founded by Prince of Rus Yaroslav the Wise in 1037. Inside the church are Kyiv's most stunning collection of medieval frescoes and mosaics, with scenes in the central dome including Christ the Pantocrator surrounded by angels, and a resplendent Virgin with outstretched arms lower down.

St Michael's Golden-Domed Cathedral

Standing opposite St Sofia's at the far end of a long square, **St Michael's** (daily 8am–6pm) was demolished by the Soviets in the 1930s and faithfully reconstructed six decades later. A medieval church given a thorough Baroque makeover in the eighteenth century, it was the first church in Kyiv to sport gilded domes, a practice later picked up by most of the other churches in the city. The church interior contains fragments of original twelfth-century mosaics and frescoes, taken to St Petersburg in 1937 and returned to Kyiv in 2008.

Andriivs'kyi uzviz

Still paved with its original cobblestones and lined with nineteenth-century houses, the steep and winding **Andriivs'kyi uzviz** ("St Andrew's Descent") is one of the few streets to have preserved its pre-Revolutionary appearance. It is also Kyiv at its most tourist-laden, lined with stalls selling Ukrainian embroidered shirts, Soviet-era collectables and souvenir tat. At the top of the street is St Andrew's Church (closed for restoration), designed by Baroque master Bartolomeo Rastrelli, its slender dome-topped towers spearing skywards like a gargantuan clump of asparagus. Halfway down, the **Mikhail Bulgakov Museum** at no. 13 (10am–5pm, closed Wed; 20Hr) fills the novelist's former home with a theatrically arranged collection of exhibits, drawing attention to the more fantastical elements of the author of *The Master and Margarita*'s work. At the bottom of the street, the **One Street Museum** at no. 2 (Tues–Sun noon–6pm; 30Hr) recalls the area's Tsarist-era heyday through a collection of period costumes, and sepia photographs.

The Chornobyl Museum

Main sight of the Podil area is the **Chornobyl Museum** at proulok Khoreviy 1 (Natsionalniy Muzei Chornobyl; Mon–Fri 10am–5pm, Sat 10am–4.30pm; 10Hr; English-language audioguide 50Hr), an informative and frequently moving account of the events of April 1986 – when an explosion at Chornobyl nuclear power station, 100km north of Kyiv, released a radioactive plume of smoke that travelled over much of Central Europe. The 50,000-strong city of Pripyat was evacuated, and a 30km exclusion zone established – it still exists today. The museum is mostly labelled in Ukrainian, although the photographs and newsreels on display tell the story

CHORNOBYL TOURS

Tours of the 30km exclusion zone around the Chornobyl reactor have been offered on a semi-official, at-your-own-risk basis by local tour agencies for the last few years. The Ukrainian authorities appeared ready to officially sanction the tours in 2011, although a final decision had not been taken at the time of going to press. In the event of local agencies offering tours, the **day-long trip** will visit the ghost town of Pripyat alongside other eerily deserted sites within the exclusion zone. Despite the high levels of radiation within the zone, one day's exposure is thought to be too insignificant to have an adverse effect on a visitor's health. Per-person prices range from $150–450 depending on how many individuals have signed up for the tour. Tours are likely to be advertised by hostels in Kyiv; otherwise contact one of the agencies listed under "Directory" on p.1254.

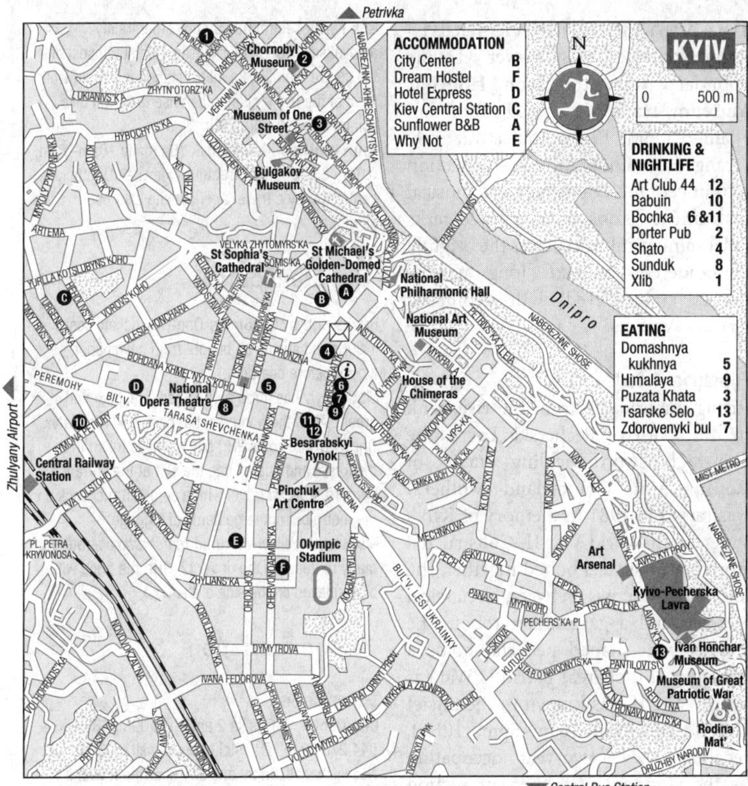

eloquently enough. It's certainly an affecting tribute to the emergency crews who risked their lives in the aftermath of the disaster.

Kyivo-Pecherska Lavra

Few sights in Kyiv pack the historical and spiritual punch of **Pecherska Lavra**, the "Cave Hermitage" founded on a bluff overlooking the River Dnipro in the eleventh century. Located 1.5km southeast of Khreschatyk, just beyond the Arsenal'na metro station, this sprawling complex of churches, monastery buildings and museums is regarded as the birthplace of Ukrainian and Russian Orthodoxy, and is swarming with pilgrims all year round.

The Lavra is divided into two parts, the **Upper Lavra** to the northwest and the Lower Lavra to the southeast. The Upper Lavra centres on the **Cathedral of the Dormition** and its accompanying bell tower, a five-storey Baroque beauty topped by a gilded dome. The **Museum of Ukrainian Folk Art** (10am–6pm; closed Tues; 10Hr) is worth visiting, containing the fantasmagorical paintings of self-taught village artist Mariya Pryimachenko.

Highlight of the **Lower Lavra** is the system of caves used by medieval monks as burial vaults, the dry subterranean air helping to mummify many of the bodies laid to rest there. Entrance to the largest group of catacombs, the **Near Caves**, is inside the **Church of the Raising of the Cross** (daily 9am–6pm). Among the coffins stored in niches are the Lavra's founder, Anthony of Athos, eleventh-century folk hero Ilya Muromets, and twelfth-century chronicler Nestor.

The Ivan Honchar Museum

Right outside the Lower Lavra's boundary wall, the **Ivan Honchar Museum**, Ivana Mazepy 29 (Tues–Sun 10am–5.30pm; 15hr) is an attractively arranged ethnographical collection rich in ceramics, costumes and musical instruments. Look out for trademarks of Ukrainian culture such as the brightly embroidered *rushniki*, long narrow drapes embroidered with geometric fertility symbols.

Rodina Mat'

Rising imperiously from the riverbank to the south of Pecherska Lavra, the 68m-high sword-wielding statue of **Rodina Mat'** ("Homeland Mother") was raised in 1981 in memory of Kyiv's suffering in World War II. Constructed from plates of steel bolted together, she looks like a cross between a classical goddess and a gargantuan robot. The statue's cone-shaped pedestal holds a Museum of the Great Patriotic War (as World War II was known in the Soviet Union; Tues–Sun 10am–5pm; 10Hr), recalling Kyiv's two-year occupation by the Germans. An open-air section of the museum (daily 9am–7pm; 2Hr) is packed with post-World War II Soviet hardware, MIG jets and rocket launchers included.

Arrival and information

Air Most international flights arrive at Boryspil 29km southeast of the city, which has four terminals (A, B, C and D). The terminals are within a 5–10min walk from each other, and there is also a shuttle bus connecting them all. Polit buses from the stop in front of terminal D run to the central train station every 15 minutes from 6am till 8pm, then every 30 minutes (50min; 25Hr).

Some budget flights arrive at Zhulyani airport, which is 8km west of the centre (bus #9 runs to the central train station).

Train International trains terminate at the Central Railway Station (Tsentralniy vokzal) on the western fringes of the centre. Leave the main exit and turn left to find the Voksal'na metro station: downtown Khreschatyk is only two stops from here.

Bus Kyiv's Central Bus Station (Tsentralniy avtovoksal) is at pl. Moskovska 4km southwest of the centre. Demiivs'ka metro station is a 5min walk west of the bus station; otherwise taxis will take you into town for 50–60Hr.

Tourist office Khreschatyk 19a (daily 10am–7pm; ⓣ066 851 8558, ⓦfreetours.kiev.ua). Unofficial centre run by a travel agency who also book city tours.

City transport

Buses and trolleybuses One-way tickets cost 1.50Hr and should be bought from newspaper kiosks before boarding.

Metro Kyiv has three metro lines (red, blue and green). All of them intersect at central Khreschatyk. One-way fare costs 2Hr; buy a plastic token from the *kassa* and push it into the slot at the entrance barriers. You can travel with a compact rucksack on the metro but not large items of luggage.

Minibuses Yellow-coloured *marshrutki* operate on many routes. Pay the driver (2–3Hr; the price will be displayed on the side of the bus).

Accommodation

Hostels

City Center Sofiivs'ka 2 apt 10 ⓣ098 263 6506 & 044 278 5246, ⓔhostel.happy@mail.ru Ⓜ Maidan Nezalezhnosti. Bright and airy apartment with a mixture of social space, dorms and privates rooms. Not the quietest of locations but it does come with a balcony overlooking the main square. Dorms from 140Hr, doubles from 430Hr.

Dream Hostel Chervonoarmiys'ka 47 ⓣ066 244 1447, ⓦdream-hostel.com Ⓜ L. Tolstoho. Bright and pleasant hostel with two dorms, a quad and a double, within striking distance of both Khreschatyk and the national football stadium. There's a slump-in-a-beanbag common room, and breakfast for a few extra hryvnia. Dorms from 80Hr, doubles 220Hr.

Kiev Central Station Hoholivs'ka 25, apt 11 ⓣ098 669 4783, ⓦwww.kievcentralstation.hostel.com Ⓜ Universytet. In a nicely kept apartment with parquet floors and cheerful colours, this is the most convenient hostel for early-morning getaways, with the central train station a 15- to 20-minute walk away. The usual mix of doubles and dorms, plus kitchen-diner chill-out zone. Dorms from 120Hr, doubles from 370Hr.

Why Not Saksahanskoho 30/3a ⓣ063 867 7828, ⓦwww.whynothostels.com Ⓜ L. Tolstoho. A colourful collection of rooms ranging in size from

from 10-bed dorm to quads and doubles, a short 1km walk southwest of Khreschatyk. Kitchen and chill-out room. Dorms from 70hr, doubles 250hr.

Hotels

Hotel Express Shevchenko 38/40 ⓣ044 234 2113, ⓦwww.expresskiev.com Ⓜ Universytet. This ungainly tower block is a perfectly situated 10-minute walk from the train station and has neat, acceptably clean en-suite rooms with TV and tiny balcony. The top-floor breakfast room (complete with tropical fish) is a major plus. Doubles 890Hr.

Sunflower B&B Kostel'na 9–41 ⓣ044 279 3846, ⓦwww.sunflowerhotel.kiev.ua Ⓜ Maydan Nezalezhnosti. Superbly central but secretively tucked away in a courtyard, this intimate B&B offers bright rooms, warm colours and friendly customer service. Doubles from 1000hr.

Eating

Domashnya kukhnya Khmel'nyts'koho 16 Ⓜ Teatral'na. A self-service canteen with a long line of dishes laid out on hotplates, this is a good place to sample local favourites such as *kievski kotlet* (chicken kiev), *vareniki* (ravioli-like dumplings stuffed with savoury fillings), and more. Main courses 15–25Hr.

Himalaya Khreschatyk 23 Ⓜ Khreschatyk. Occupying a glassy pavilion set back from the main boulevard, this well-established Indian restaurant serves authentic food with plenty of spice – and a good range of vegetarian options. Mains from 80Hr.

Puzata Khata Sahaidachnoho 24 Ⓜ Kontraktova. Cafeteria with roomy second-floor dining room overlooking Kontraktova pl, with a broad range of Ukrainian dishes (*borshch*) and staff dressed in folksy costumes, this is a convenient place to grab a bite in Podil. Ukrainian *borshch* from 6Hr.

Tsarske Selo Ivana Mazepy 42/1 Ⓜ Arsenal'na. Ukrainian food, wait-staff dressed in traditionally embroidered blouses, and an interior strong on wooden benches and wall-mounted textiles. Hearty pork and chicken dishes from 60Hr.

Zdorovenyki buli Luteran'ska 3 Ⓜ Kheschatyk. Through the archway at Hreschatyk 21 and up the steps, this popular self-service restaurant always has a good choice of fish and meat main courses and a well-stocked salad bar. Dining rooms are gaudily decorated with murals depicting Ancient Greece, China and other civilizations. Mains 10–30hr.

Drinking and nightlife

Art Club 44 Khreschatyk 44b ⓦwww.club44.com.ua Ⓜ Khreschatyk. Live rock, jazz, blues and world music with acts ranging from local cover bands to cutting-edge alternative acts. Face control, but not as strict as in some of the other clubs. Admission 40–50Hr.

Babuin Simona Petlyura 10 Ⓜ Universytet. A bookshop, café and drinks bar rolled into one, the "baboon" is a mellow and rather chic place decked out in orangey colours and oriental-looking lanterns. Long popular with an arty crowd, there's a menu that takes in everything from salads to steaks, and a functions room that hosts literary events and live jazz. Daily 10am–1am.

Bochka Khmelnyts'koho 3 Ⓜ Teatral'na. Popular microbrewery pub serving their own brew on tap alongside plenty of other Ukrainian beers. There's also an extensive menu of main meals and snacks. Set in a courtyard with a colonnaded terrace decorated with hanging baskets, it's a relaxing spot for a beer. The other branch of *Bochka*, in the courtyard behind Khreshchyatyk 21, has a more raucous beer-hall feel. Both are open 24hr.

Porter Pub Spas'ka 13 Ⓜ Kontraktova. Best of the drinking venues in the Podil district, with a good choice of Ukrainian and Czech beers on tap, and outdoor seating on the street-facing wooden decking. Live cover bands at weekends. Daily 11am–1am.

Shato Khreschatyk 24 Ⓜ Khreschatyk. Pricier than most and occasionally slightly snobbish, this roomy brewpub is still one of the few spots along Khreschatyk that has a street-side terrace. Excellent own-brand beer, and traditional snacks such as cheese platters, sausages and pigs' ears. Open 24hr.

Sunduk Mykhailivs'ka 16 Ⓜ Universytet. A laidback and cosy pub on a quiet but central street, serving up its own-brew lager beer as well as more mainstream names. The food menu ranges from pizza to ribs, and there's a pleasant outdoor terrace under the trees. Daily 11am–11pm.

Xlib (pronounced "hlib") Frunze 12 Ⓜ Kontraktova. Minimally decorated warehouse-style space that concentrates on quality of music (house, trance, techno, jungle) rather than kitsch decor and bad-attitude bouncers. Occasional live gigs too. Admission 40–50Hr.

Shopping and markets

Besarabskyi rynok. A pungent collection of fresh fruit, vegetables, fish and flowers in a nineteenth-century covered market hall. Tins of caviar 200Hr Ⓜ L. Tolstoho.

Petrivka Book Market pr. Moskovsky. A warren of stalls selling new and secondhand books, maps, stationery and computer software Ⓜ Petrivka.

Directory

Embassies Canada, Yaroslaviv val 31 ⓣ590 3100, ⓦwww.kyiv.gc.ca; Ireland, Schorsa 44 ⓣ285 5902, ⓦirishconsulate.kiev.ua; UK, Desyatynna 9 ⓣ490 3660, ⓦukinukraine.fco.gov.uk; US, Y. Kotsyubins'koho 10 ⓣ490 4000, ⓦkyiv .usembassy.gov.
Hospital American Medical Center Berdychivs'ka 1 ⓣ044 490 7600 ⓜLuk'yanivs'ka.
Internet At the Post Office, Khreschatyk 22 (24hr).
Left Luggage At the train station: luggage lockers in the basement (buy a token from the cashier; 24hr/14Hr). At the bus station (6am–10.30pm; 7–10Hr/item).
Pharmacy Apteka no. 24 Chervonoarmiys'ka 10; 24hr.
Post office Khreschatyk 22 (Mon–Sat 8am–8pm, Sun 9am–5pm).
Tours Free Tours, Khreschatyk 19a ⓣ066 851 855, ⓦfreetours.kiev.ua (daily 10am–7pm), free walking tour of the city centre and paid city tours; New Logic Khme'nyts'koho 17/52 ⓣ044 206 2200, ⓦwww.newlogic.ua (Mon–Fri 9am–9pm, Sat & Sun 10am–7pm), city tours and Chornobyl tours; Solo East, Prorezna 10 ⓣ044 279 3505 ⓦwww .tourkiev.com (Mon–Fri 9am–6pm), Chornobyl tours.

Moving on

Train to Budapest (1 daily; 25hr); Kraków (1 daily; 20hr); L'viv (8 daily; 6hr 30min–9hr 30min); Moscow (3 daily; 14hr); Odesa (4 daily; 8hr 30min–11hr); Warsaw (1 daily; 15hr).
Bus to L'viv (4 daily; 8hr); Odesa (8 daily; 5hr 30min–7hr 30min); Warsaw (4 weekly; 16hr).

Odesa

Founded by Russian Empress Catherine the Great in 1794, **ODESA** (Одеса) is both busy port and beach resort, exuding a seductive blend of commercial swagger and riviera-town style. Well-preserved nineteenth-century buildings provide a sense of historical grandeur, while the bars of Deribasivs'ka and nightclubs at the nearby beaches ensure that you're never too far away from a party. It's a town popular with tourists all over the Russian-speaking world, and a holiday atmosphere reigns for much of the spring and summer.

What to see and do

With a grid of predominantly nineteenth-century streets Odesa is a welcoming and easily strollable city. The pedestrianized, café-lined strip of Deribasivs'ka is the centre's main focal point, with a deliciously pink-and-cream Art Nouveau shopping arcade at its western end providing an irresistible architectural flourish. From Deribasivs'ka, Yekaterynyns'ka curves down towards the Potemkin Stairs and the port area, passing stately rows of Neoclassical buildings on the way. Odesa's sandy beaches spread for several kilometres along the eastern side of the city; the most famous of them is Arkadia, a 20-minute tram ride from the centre.

The Potemkin Stairs

Completed in 1841, the 192-step sweep of the Potemkin Stairs was immortalized in Sergei Eisenstein's 1925 film *Battleship Potemkin* – in which Tsarist troops march remorselessly down the steps firing on demonstrators, famously upsetting a baby's pram on the way. It remains one of the most iconic locations in the whole Ukraine, and it's here that every visitor to Odesa comes to be photographed.

The tree-lined Prymors'ka promenade runs either side of the top of the steps. At the eastern end of the promenade a statue of Alexander Pushkin (resident here 1823–24) stands in front of **Odesa City Hall**, a Neoclassical building boasting a Corinthian columned portico.

Beaches

Stretching east of town is a string of sandy beaches, each backed by a clutch of cafés and restaurants. They are linked by Trasa zdoroviya ("The Path of Health"), a tree-shaded path that runs along the coast from central Odesa – pick it up from the Monument to the Unknown

Sailor in Shevchenko Park. Nearest to the centre is **Lanzheron**, packed with city folk on summer weekends. One kilometre further on is **Otrada**, famous for the rudimentary cable car (each car resembling a metal bucket) that links the beach to bul. Frantsuzsky, the main street that runs along the high ground above.

Best known of the beaches is **Arkadia**, 5km from the centre (near the terminus of tram #5 if you don't fancy the walk), and main focus of the city's party life. It's a small but undoubtedly beautiful crescent of sand, much of which is administered by beach-side cafés renting out sun loungers and parasols (70–80Hr for the day). On the edges are "free" stretches of beach where you can lay your towel – although they are crowded at weekends.

Odesa catacombs

Stay at one of Odesa's backpacker hostels and you'll inevitably be offered the chance to go on a tour of Odesa's so-called **catacombs**, the honeycomb of tunnels carved by nineteenth-century limestone miners and used by anti-Nazi partisans during World War II. Led by local speleologists, the tours are unofficial, at-your-own-risk affairs that pay scant regard to health-and-safety regulations – you may get a pair of overalls but you're unlikely to be issued a hard hat. The tours usually focus on the catacombs near Nerubays'ke, 10km north of Odesa, and frequently include a visit to the **Partizanska Slava** memorial complex, where a few short stretches of tunnel have been opened as an official museum. Expect to pay 180–220Hr per person for the guided tour and taxi transfer.

Arrival and information

Air Odesa airport is 12km south of the centre. Marshrutka #117 runs from here to the central Yekaterins'ka.

Train Odesa train station is 2km south of the main downtown area. Bus #220 runs from here to Hrets'ka, a stone's throw from the main Deribasivs'ka.

Bus Odesa's central bus station is 4km west of the centre at Kolontaevs'ka 58. Tram #5 runs from here to the train station.

Bookshop Empik, Deribasivs'ka 14, sells maps of Odesa and surrounding region.

City transport

By bus, trolleybus and tram Tickets (1Hr) are bought from conductors on board.

Accommodation

Private rooms The Kvartirne byuro at Odesa train station (opposite platform 4; daily 8am–noon & 1–5pm; ⓣ048 727 4133) has a choice of private rooms (60–100Hr) and apartments (from 300Hr) in locations across the city. Outside the train station, unofficial landladies hawk rooms ("kvartiri") at cheaper prices – have a map handy to check locations before accepting any offers.

Hostels

Babushka Grand Mala Arnauts'ka 60 ⓣ630 705 535. Conveniently close to the train station *Babushka* offers a taste of Odesa's faded glories, with nineteenth-century chandeliers and ceiling mouldings presiding over a snug collection of dorm beds and privates. It's a good place for mellow socializing and staff have good local knowledge. Dorms from 95Hr, doubles 310Hr.

Magic Bus Backpackers Hreches'ka 50, apt 7 ⓣ978 333 358, ⓦmagicbushostel.com. Central, converted apartment comprising private doubles, 8- to 10-bed dorms, homely kitchen and common room. Dorms 95Hr, doubles from 265Hr.

TUI Front Page Koblevs'ka 42 ⓣ968 344 074. A fine old apartment with creaky floors, high ceilings, and a welcoming living room and kitchen-diner, *Front Page* has a good mix of dorms and private doubles. Friendly staff and a family atmosphere. Dorms 165Hr, doubles from 350Hr.

Hotels

Deribas Deribasivs'ka 27 ⓣ048 794 4364 or 675 590 101, ⓦwww.hotel-deribas.com. Apartment-hotel offering pristine modern doubles and 3- to 4-person studios in a superbly central spot. Free wi-fi, but no breakfast. Hidden behind a badly signed door in an alleyway linking Deribasivs'ka with pl. Hrets'ka, it's initially difficult to find. Doubles from 450Hr.

Eating

Chaynaya Roza Koblevs'ka 46. Cool design-magazine decor and laidback vibe make this café an ideal choice for a light lunch, with salads (30–35Hr), toasted sandwiches (30Hr) and pancakes (28Hr) complementing the selection of strong coffee and leaf teas. Daily 9am–10pm.

Fat Mozes Yekateryns'ka 8/10. Cosy restaurant with booth-seating inside and a 4-table terrace overlooking the street, with a short but varied menu of regional cuisine taking in Moldavian mincemeat kebabs, local fish and meaty stews. Mains in the 70Hr range. Daily 11am–11pm.

Pizza Olio Gavanna 7 and Bunina 35. Justifiably popular Mediterranean-themed place serving up speedy and reliable thin-crust pizzas and a range of pasta dishes, with mains in the 40–55Hr bracket. Daily 9am–11pm.

Robin Bobin Saborna 2. Occupying a comfy timber porch facing a leafy park, *Robin Bobin* offers traditional Ukrainian dishes and also plenty of salt- and freshwater fish. Try the pan-fried fillets of pike-perch (*sudak*) for 70Hr. Daily 11am–11pm.

Tavriya Galereya Afina, pl. Hrets'ka 3–4. Smart self-service restaurant with passable main courses and good pastries and cakes, in the basement of the Afina shopping mall. There's also an express pizzeria, sushi bar and supermarket on the same floor. Pile your tray high for under 40hr. Daily 8am–10pm.

Drinking and nightlife

Fanconi Katerynyns'ka 15. Swish café-bar whose street-facing terrace is hugely popular with the mid-evening cocktail-sipping crowd. The menu takes in sushi, cakes, ice cream and other fancy food. Open 24hr.

Ibiza Arkadia ⓦibiza.ua. Popular beach club with a dancefloor right by the sea and bizarre-looking white pods that serve as "VIP" boxes, with a busy programme of DJs and Ukrainian pop stars throughout the summer. May–Sept 10pm–5am.

Itaka Arkadia ⓦitaka.com.ua. With palm trees, swimming pools and fluted columns reminiscent of a classical Greek temple, this is an enjoyably kitsch beach club pulling in international DJs and party-hungry locals. May–Sept 9pm–5am.

Pivnoy sad Havanna 6. Brewpub with a big subterranean dining hall and a terrace facing the lush lawns of the city garden. With a couple of own-brand lagers and porters there's plenty of ale to sample, plus a food menu taking in soups, grilled sausages and other pub grub. Daily 11am–midnight.

Rock and Roll Dvoryans'ka 7. One of several local bars squeezed into the streets west of pl. Soborna, with inexpensive draft beer, quirky-but-cool pop rock sounds, and an odd mixture of comfy chairs and sofas. Live bands at weekends. Daily 10am–midnight.

Entertainment

Opera Chaikovs'koho 1 ⓣ048 722 2230, ⓦwww.opera-ballet.tm.odessa.ua. Nothing sums up Odesa's belle époque more than the grandeur of its opera house, erected in 1883. It hosts top-quality performances from the classic opera and ballet repertoire, and tickets are comparatively cheap.

Markets

Novy rynok Torhova. Not the biggest of Odesa's markets but certainly the handiest central place to stock up on picnic provisions, with smoked Black Sea mackerel, fresh cheese and other scrumptious local produce. Daily 7am–6pm.

Pl. Soborna This centrally located square fills up daily with stalls selling crafts and souvenirs in spring and summer. Daily 9am–9pm.

Starokonny rynok Starokonny pereulok. A neighbourhood market near the bus station that hosts a huge flea market on Sundays, with vendors laying out their wares on the pavements of several surrounding streets. Old clothes, crockery, kids' toys, Soviet-period junk and more. Tram #5 to Kosvenna. Sun 7am–3pm.

L'viv

Home to a burgeoning café scene and an ever-growing stock of backpacker hostels, forward-looking **L'VIV** (Львів) represents the Ukraine at its most tourist-friendly. For centuries subject to Polish then Habsburg overlords, L'viv still looks and feels like a slice of Central Europe, its welter of Catholic, Orthodox and Armenian churches attesting to a multicultural past. Historically the centre of the Ukrainian national movement, L'viv remains an avowedly Ukrainian-speaking city. With uneven cobbled streets, creaky-floored art galleries and trams screeching their way around tracks that were laid generations ago, the city has the look of a well-preserved nineteenth-century survivor. A night spent exploring the city's addictively eccentric bars will soon dispel any ideas that this is just a museum piece.

What to see and do

A fistful of churches and palaces lie within a pedestrian-friendly Old Town, its neat grid of streets arranged around the spacious Rynok (Market Square). An irregular circle of broad boulevards and park-like greenery separate the Old Town from the nineteenth-century suburbs beyond. A short hike up Visokyi Zamok hill, just north of the Old Town, provides an expansive panorama of central L'viv and is a good way to get your bearings.

The Rynok

Surrounded by stately mansions and a warren of courtyards, the Rynok is the centre of L'viv's social life, abuzz with outdoor cafés in the summer. At its centre is the Neoclassical **Town Hall** or Ratusha, its castellated **tower** (Tues–Sun 10am–6pm; 10Hr) a nineteenth-century copy of an earlier medieval version. Most eye-catching of the buildings on the Rynok's eastern side is the **Black House** at no. 4, with statues of saints protruding from its grime-encrusted sixteenth-century facade. Next door at no. 6 is the **Kornyakt Palace**, famous for its arcaded Renaissance courtyard (nowadays a daytime café).

Around the Old Town

Just off the southwestern corner of the Rynok, the fourteenth-century **Latin Cathedral** (the city's main Catholic church) contains a show-stopping sequence of Baroque altarpieces. Have your camera at the ready for the next-door **Boim Chapel**, at Katedral'na 1 (Tues–Sun 10am–5pm; 10Hr), encrusted both inside and out with an animated collection of seventeenth-century statuettes. The **Armenian Cathedral**, a block north of the square on Virmens'ka, was built on the model of medieval Armenian churches and contains a delicious collection of Art Nouveau frescoes by Józef Mehoffer and Jan Henryk Rosen.

Arguably the finest of L'viv's churches, the Bernardine Cathedral on pl. Soborna boasts a Dutch-Renaissance facade and bulbous belfry, its profile recognizable from countless tourist brochures.

Fragments of L'viv's fortifications still survive along Pidval'na, where the sixteenth-century Arsenal at no. 5 (daily except Wed 10am–5pm; 15Hr) contains a display of helmets, breastplates, pikes and early firearms.

Prospekt Svobody

Running along L'viv's Old Town to the west is **Prospekt Svobody** ("Freedom Avenue"), a broad two-lane street with a strip of fountain-splashed park running up the middle. Presiding haughtily over the scene is L'viv Opera House, dating from 1900 and topped with a trio of winged statues symbolizing the arts. Diagonally opposite at Svobody 20, the **National Museum** (Tues–Sun 10am–6pm; 30Hr) holds an impressive collection of Ukrainian Orthodox icons.

The Brewery Museum

Two kilometres northwest of the centre at bul. Kleparivs'ka 18, L'viv's brewery was a highly respected brand throughout the Habsburg and Soviet eras, and (although now owned by a well-known multinational) continues to churn out well-regarded local-recipe brews. Right beside the brewery gate is the Brewery Museum (admissions at 10.30am, noon, 1.30pm, 3pm, 4.30pm & 5.30pm; closed Tues; museum only 10Hr, museum and beer tasting 20Hr), a small but entertaining display that tells the history of beer brewing from its origins in the ancient Middle East to the present day. There's a diorama of ale-making friars (beer brewing in L'viv was actually founded by the Jesuits in 1715), and a model of L'viv brewery as it looked in 1860.

Occupying the huge barrel-vaulted cellars underneath the museum, the

Robert Doms House of Beer (daily noon–midnight) is named after the Swiss entrepreneur who owned the brewery in the mid-nineteenth century, and serves up draught Lvivs'ke by the litre.

Lychakivs'ke Cemetery

Entered from Mechnikova 3km southeast of the centre, **Lychakivs'ke Cemetery** (tram #7 or #8 to Pekars'ka; daily 10am–6pm; 10Hr) is one of Central Europe's classical burial grounds, park-like in its landscaped beauty and brimming with over two centuries' worth of fine funerary monuments. Originally laid out in 1786 it is now a museum reserve: indeed the sheer profusion of ornate family chapels, sculpted angels and statues of the deceased gives the place the appearance of an outdoor art gallery. The southeastern corner of the cemetery is dominated by the so-called **Cemetery of the Eagles**, a memorial complex built by the interwar Polish state to commemorate the (mostly very young) volunteers who beat off pro-independence Ukrainian forces in the winter of 1918/1919. Right next to it is a towering, pillar-top statue of the **Archangel Michael**, honouring the Ukrainians who fell in the very same conflict.

Folk Architecture Museum

Spread over a forested hillside to the north of Lichakivs'ke Cemetery at Chernecha Hora 1 (Tues–Sun 10am–5pm; 10Hr), this collection of timber-built houses and barns from all over western Ukraine provides the ideal introduction to the region's much-cherished rural traditions. The most spectacular buildings are the fairytale Carpathian churches, their belfries raised in pagoda-like tiers. Take tram #2, #7 or #8 to Mechnikova then walk uphill.

Arrival and information

Air L'viv airport is 6km southwest of the city centre. Trolleybus #9 (40min; 1Hr) and *marshrutka* 95 (35min; 2Hr) run into town; otherwise a taxi costs 80–120Hr.

Train The train station is 2km west of the centre at the top of Chernivets'ka. ATMs are in the arrivals hall, and the "lux" waiting room (3Hr/hr) offers free wi-fi. Trams #1 & #9 run to the centre. Taxis vary between 30–60Hr depending on how gullible you look.

Bus The main bus station is at bul. Striys'ka 109, 6km southeast of the centre. Trolleybus #4 runs to Shota Rustaveli, 10min walk south of the main square. A taxi will set you back 50–60Hr. *Marshrutki* from Medyka-Shehyni (the Polish–Ukraine border) arrive at the train station.

Tourist office In the town hall, Rynok 1 (Mon–Fri 10am–8pm, Sat 10am–7pm, Sun 10am–6pm; ⓣ032 254 6079, ⓦwww.touristinfo.lviv.ua) has free town maps and can advise on accommodation.

Bookshop Knigarnya E, pr. Svobodi 7 (Mon–Fri 10am–8pm, Sat 10am–3pm) is the place to stock up on maps.

City transport

Almost everything in central L'viv is walkable but you will need to use the city's mixture of trams, buses and trolleybuses to get to train and bus stations as well as outlying attractions such as Lychakivs'ke Cemetery and the Folk Architecture Museum. Buy single-journey tickets (1Hr) from kiosks or from the driver.

Accommodation

Hostels

Art Hostel Rynok 3 apt. 4 ⓣ032 297 5195, ⓦarthostel.lviv.ua. Located up several flights of magnificently creaky stairs, this hostel looks directly out onto the main square. A multi-bed dorm, a private double and a small kitchen. Breakfast available for an extra few hryvnia. Dorms 85Hr, doubles 220Hr.

Central Square Hostel Rynok 5 ⓣ095 225 6654, ⓦcshostel.com. Historical building in a square-side location, with two bunk-bed dorms, a very spacious private double, a social room and a kitchen. Dorms from 95Hr, doubles 350Hr.

Kosmonaut Sichovych striltsiv 6 ⓣ032 260 1602, ⓦthekosmonaut.com. A bit tatty round the edges but superbly welcoming, *Kosmonaut* continues to lead the way when it comes to cultivating a friendly, sociable and informative hostel environment. A range of 12- to 4-bed dorms in an off-street courtyard, and breakfast is included in the price. Dorms from 100Hr.

Old City Hostel Beryndy 3 ⓣ032 294 9644, ⓦoldcityhostel.lviv.ua. This new hostel in a nineteenth-century apartment block with plush furnishings and parquet floor will suit those who prefer their accommodation to be squeaky clean. There's a fully equipped kitchen. Dorms 100Hr, doubles from 320Hr.

Hotels

George Mitskievycha 1 ⓣ032 232 6236, ⓦgeorgehotel.com.ua. A charming Habsburg-era hotel that has retained many of its interior features, the *George* offers high ceilings, sturdy furnishings and parquet floors at decidedly old-school prices. "Tourist Class" rooms with shared facilities 350Hr; en-suite doubles 700Hr.

Eating

Amadeus Katedral'na pl. 7. For quality pan-European cuisine on a picturesque city-centre square, you can't do much better than *Amadeus*. The food ranges from humble *varenyky* to fancy Adriatic seafood with plenty of pork-chop fare in between; expect to fork out 100–150Hr for mains. Daily 11am–11pm.

Kumpel Vynnychenka 6. Microbrewery and restaurant whose huge copper vats form an attractive centerpiece to the dining room. Steaks, stews, sausages and schnitzels are the main items on the menu. Wash it down with *Kumpel*'s own-brand *svitle* (a pale refreshing lager) or *burshtinove* (a more rounded brown-coloured ale). Mains 50–90Hr. Daily 10am–midnight.

Myasa ta spravedlivost Bernardine Monastery courtyard (access from Halyts'ka pl). An open-sided barn with medieval torture masks hanging from the beams, "Meat and Justice" serves up sausage, chicken, steak and other grilled fare, with staff dressed in serving-wench garb and food arriving on wooden platters. Theatrical it may be but young locals love it. Mains 35–70Hr. Daily 11am–11pm.

Pid zolotoyu rozoyu Staroevreyska. Ukrainian-Jewish restaurant named after the Golden Rose synagogue (which stood nearby until destroyed during World War II), offering a good range of traditional dishes like *cholent* (meat and barley stew) and stuffed carp. The interior is dark, woody and atmospheric, and the outdoor terrace comes with views of the town walls. There are no prices on the menu, and you are invited to bargain your bill at the end of your meal. Daily noon–midnight.

Puzata Khata Sichovykh Striltsiv 12. City-centre branch of the trusty self-service canteen chain, especially strong on *vareniki*, *mlintsi* and other Ukrainian staples. Frequently packed with Polish tour groups, who know a good culinary bargain when they see one. Fill up your plate for under 40Hr. Daily 8am–11pm.

Drinking

Bilya Diani Rynok. With chairs and tables scattered around the statue of Diana in the Rynok's south-western corner, this outdoor café is the ideal place for a thirst-quenching beer, serving up own-brand light and dark ales as well as a range of nibbles – the *sudzhuk* (spicy beef sausage) platter goes down a treat. May–Sept 10am–11pm.

Dim lehend Staroevreyska 48. The five-storey "House of Legends" begins with a souvenir shop on the ground floor and a sequence of wackily decorated drinking rooms above, culminating with a dizzying roof terrace. Fills nightly with young L'vivians enjoying draught beers and a menu of snacks. Daily 11am–2am.

Dveri v... Ivana Fedorova 16. A large table-filled courtyard hung with chandeliers and the odd hanging basket, this is one of the city centre's most popular outdoor drinking spots. The name means "The Doors to...", menus are decorated with door handles and doors leading nowhere are placed in the middle of the yard. Daily 11am–midnight.

Dzyha Virmens'ka 35. Cult art centre comprising a gallery, a café-pub (*Pid Klepsydroyu*) with a varied food menu, and an upstairs performance space (*Kvartyra 35*) that hosts folk and jazz concerts as well as being a cool place to drink. Daily 11am–midnight.

Gasova Lyampa Virmens'ka 20. Head down the steps and then up a spiral staircase to reach this characterful bar occupying four cramped storeys of a tall and narrow house. Draught beers and meaty snacks are served up in rooms decorated with pictures of gas lamps and oil derricks: a statue of Ignacy Lukasiewicz, oil pioneer and inventor of the kerosene lamp, sits outside. Daily 11am–2am.

Kabinet Vynnychenka 12. Literary café with book-filled shelves and a programme of cultural events, *Kabinet's* collection of armchairs and sofas make it an ideal venue for a relaxing evening drink. Also menu of inexpensive eats. Daily 10am–11pm.

L'vivs'ka maysternya shokoladu Serbs'ka 13. Strong coffee, velvety drinking chocolate and in-house ice creams. The delectable range of own-brand, hand-made chocolates makes repeat visits a near-certainty. Daily 10am–9pm.

Nightlife

Metro Zelena 14. Big city-centre club with a dance-floor policy ranging from commercial Euro-pop to cutting-edge trance and techno. Good social mix of local youngsters and international students. Cover 25–50Hr. Daily 9pm–6am.

Picasso bul. Zelena 88. Fifteen years old and still going strong, *Picasso* is the place to catch incoming DJs and live jazz & rock acts. Open as a café during the daytime, gigs and club nights kick off at 8–10pm. Cover 30–100Hr depending on event.

Shopping

Krakivsky rynok ul. Bazarna. Covered market with fruit, veg and dairy products, bordered by a lively strip of outdoor clothes stalls.

Souvenir market cnr Teatral'na and Lesi Ukrainky. Open-air stalls selling embroidered tablecloths and blouses, near-antique collectables and kitschy souvenir trash by the bag-load.

Listings

Exchange ATMs and exchange offices are scattered throughout the centre.

Hospital Emergency dept, Mykolaychuka 9 (Ⓣ032 252 7590).

Internet Chorna Medea, Doroshenka 50 (24hr). There is a wi-fi zone on the main square.

Left luggage At the train station (24hr with breaks at 11am–noon & 2–3am; 10Hr/item).

Pharmacy Apteka, cnr Brativ Rohatyntsiv & Halyts'ka (24hr).

Post office Slovats'koho 1 (Mon–Fri 9am–7pm, Sat 10am–4pm, Sun 10am–3pm).

Moving on

Train Bucharest (1 daily; 17hr); Budapest (1 daily; 13hr); Kraków (2 daily: 8hr); Odesa (1 daily; 12hr); Wrocław (2 daily; 12hr).

Bus Prague (5 weekly; 17hr); Rīga (4 weekly;16hr).

Travel store

Small print and

Index

A Rough Guide to Rough Guides

Published in 1982, the first Rough Guide – to Greece – was a student scheme that became a publishing phenomenon. Mark Ellingham, a recent graduate in English from Bristol University, had been travelling in Greece the previous summer and couldn't find the right guidebook. With a small group of friends he wrote his own guide, combining a highly contemporary, journalistic style with a thoroughly practical approach to travellers' needs.

The immediate success of the book spawned a series that rapidly covered dozens of destinations. And, in addition to impecunious backpackers, Rough Guides soon acquired a much broader and older readership that relished the guides' wit and inquisitiveness as much as their enthusiastic, critical approach and value-for-money ethos.

These days, Rough Guides include recommendations from shoestring to luxury and cover more than 200 destinations around the globe, including almost every country in the Americas and Europe, more than half of Africa and most of Asia and Australasia. Our ever-growing team of authors and photographers is spread all over the world, particularly in Europe, the US and Australia.

In the early 1990s, Rough Guides branched out of travel, with the publication of Rough Guides to World Music, Classical Music and the Internet. All three have become benchmark titles in their fields, spearheading the publication of a wide range of books under the Rough Guide name.

Including the travel series, Rough Guides now number more than 350 titles, covering: phrasebooks, music guides from Opera to Heavy Metal, reference works as diverse as Conspiracy Theories and Shakespeare, and popular culture books from iPods to Poker. Rough Guides also produce a series of more than 120 World Music CDs in partnership with World Music Network.

Visit www.roughguides.com to see our latest publications.

Rough Guide credits

Text editors: Lucy White and Lucy Cowie
Layout: Sachin Tanwar
Cartography: Jasbir Sandhu
Picture editor: Michelle Bhatia
Production: Rebecca Short
Proofreader: Karen Parker
Cover design: Nicole Newman, Jess Carter and Sachin Tanwar
Editorial: **London** Andy Turner, Keith Drew, Edward Aves, Alice Park, James Smart, Natasha Foges, James Rice, Emma Beatson, Emma Gibbs, Kathryn Lane, Monica Woods, Mani Ramaswamy, Harry Wilson, Alison Roberts, Lara Kavanagh, Eleanor Aldridge, Ian Blenkinsop, Charlotte Melville, Joe Staines, Matthew Milton, Tracy Hopkins, Lorna North; **Delhi** Madhavi Singh, Jalpreen Kaur Chhatwal, Dipika Dasgupta, Prema Dutta
Design & Pictures: **London** Dan May, Diana Jarvis, Mark Thomas, Rhiannon Furbear; **Delhi** Umesh Aggarwal, Ajay Verma, Jessica Subramanian, Ankur Guha, Pradeep Thapliyal, Anita Singh, Nikhil Agarwal, Sachin Gupta
Production: Liz Cherry, Louise Minihane, Erika Pepe
Cartography: **London** Ed Wright, Katie Lloyd-Jones; **Delhi** Rajesh Chhibber, Ashutosh Bharti, Rajesh Mishra, Animesh Pathak, Swati Handoo, Deshpal Dabas, Lokamata Sahu
Marketing, Publicity & roughguides.com: Liz Statham
Design Director: Scott Stickland
Rough Guides Publisher: Jo Kirby
Digital Travel Publisher: Peter Buckley
Reference Director: Andrew Lockett
Operations Coordinator: Becky Doyle
Operations Assistant: Johanna Wurm
Publishing Director (Travel): Clare Currie
Commercial Manager: Gino Magnotta
Managing Director: John Duhigg

SMALL PRINT

Publishing information

This third edition published February 2012 by

Rough Guides Ltd,
80 Strand, London WC2R 0RL
11, Community Centre, Panchsheel Park, New Delhi 110017, India

Distributed by the Penguin Group

Penguin Books Ltd,
80 Strand, London WC2R 0RL

Penguin Group (USA)
375 Hudson Street, NY 10014, USA

Penguin Group (Australia)
250 Camberwell Road, Camberwell, Victoria 3124, Australia

Penguin Group (NZ)
67 Apollo Drive, Mairangi Bay, Auckland 1310, New Zealand

Rough Guides is represented in Canada by Tourmaline Editions Inc. 662 King Street West, Suite 304, Toronto, Ontario M5V 1M7

Cover concept by Peter Dyer.

Typeset in Bembo and Helvetica to an original design by Henry Iles.

Printed in Italy by L.E.G.O. S.p.A, Lavis (TN)

1280pp includes index

A catalogue record for this book is available from the British Library

ISBN: 978-1-40538-692-0

11 12 13 14 8 7 6 5 4 3 2 1

Help us update

We've gone to a lot of effort to ensure that the third edition of **The Rough Guide to Europe on a Budget** is accurate and up-to-date. However, things change – places get "discovered", opening hours are notoriously fickle, restaurants and rooms raise prices or lower standards. If you feel we've got it wrong or left something out, we'd like to know, and if you can remember the address, the price, the hours, the phone number, so much the better.

Please send your comments with the subject line "**Rough Guide Europe on a Budget Update**" to Ⓔmail@uk.roughguides.com. We'll credit all contributions and send a copy of the next edition (or any other Rough Guide if you prefer) for the very best emails.

Find more travel information, connect with fellow travellers and book your trip on Ⓦwww.roughguides.com

Acknowledgements

Lucy White would like to thank all the contributors for their hard work in updating this edition: Jonathan Bousfield (Ukraine), Tim Burford (Switzerland), Caroline Daly (France), Kiki Deere (Morocco and Russia), Jen Foster (Balearics), Nick Harrison (Italy), Hilary Heuler (Poland), Daniel Jacobs (Spain), Anna Kaminski (Estonia, Latvia, Norway and Spain), Ciara Kenny (Ireland), Norm Longley (Romania and Serbia), John Malathronas (Greece), Neil McQuilian (France), Sophie Middlemiss (Hungary), Kathryn Miller (Turkey), Suzanne Morton-Taylor (Netherlands), Roger Norum (Finland), Alice Park (Austria), Georgia Platman (Britain), Natalia O'Hara (Czech Republic and Slovakia), James Rice (Lithuania), Alison Roberts (Croatia), Rmishka Singh (Italy), James Stewart (Germany), Emma Thomson (Belgium and Luxembourg), Kate Turner (Portugal), Steven Vickers (Sweden), Neville Walker (Germany), Luke Waterson (Britain and Denmark), Christian Williams (Germany), Matt Willis (Bulgaria) and Martin Zatko (Albania, Bosnia and Herzegovina, Macedonia and Montenegro). Thanks also to Lucy Cowie (who also updated Slovenia) for stepping into the editorial breach, and last but not least, Sachin, for being my typesetting teammate for most of 2011.

Kiki Deere would like to thank her dear friend Charlotte Aitken for her endless hospitality, true friendship and help in Tangiers and Chaouen; Paul O'Grady, as ever, for his magnificent help, support and superb company; Sam Bhiri and his family for their kindness in Casablanca; Nicole, Ory Gandini and Jamila for pointing me in the right direction in Marrakesh; Jack Coleman, Alex Snelling, Alina Solotarov and Beatrice Randall for all the fun and friendship in snowy Moscow.

Kate Turner thanks Rachael for the company and opinions.

SMALL PRINT

Photo credits

All photos © Rough Guides except the following:

Cover
Venice canal © Pictures Colour Library
Grindelwald, Wetterhorn and Schreckhorn, Switzerland © Slow Images/Getty

Back cover
La Tomatina, Spain © Demetrio Carrasco/Rough Guides
Pantheon at night, Rome © Roger Mapp/Rough Guides
Komiža, Croatia © Tim Draper/Rough Guides

Full page
Snorkelling at Lalaria Beach, Skiathos, Greece © SuperStock

Ideas: Art & Culture
Bolshoi Ballet, Moscow © SERGEI ILNITSKY /epa/Corbis
Guggenheim Museum, Bilbao © Allan Baxter /Getty Images

Ideas: Festivals & Events
Camp Nou, Barcelona © Gregorio/Alterphotos /EXPA/NewSport/Corbis
Oktoberfest, Munich © Steven Vidler/Eurasia Press/Corbis
EXIT Festival, Novi Sad © BALAZS MOHAI/epa /Corbis

Ideas: Outdoor Activities
Sauna, Finland © Patrick Pleul/dpa/Corbis
Skiers on the Argentiere Glacier, Chamonix, France © Julian Love/JAI/Corbis
Edinburgh Fringe Festival © Ken Jack/Demotix /Demotix/Corbis
Hikers in the High Tatras, Slovakia © LOOK Die Bildagentur der Fotografen GmbH/Alamy
Windsurfing, Essaouira, Morocco © Nicholas Pitt/Alamy

Index

Map entries are in colour.

A

Å ... 876
Aachen ... 494
Aalborg ... 329
Aarhus ... *see Århus*
Abergavenny ... 199
Aberystwyth ... 200
Abri de Cap Blanc ... 413
accommodation ... 8, 38, *see also individual chapters*
Acrocorinth ... 538
activities ... *see individual chapters*
Aegean islands, northeastern ... 565
Aerodium (Latvia) ... 733
Agnóndas ... 567
Agrigento ... 714
Aix-en-Provence ... 428
Ajaccio ... 444–446
ALBANIA ... 53–66
Albania ... 55
Alcobaça ... 930
Alentejo coast ... 943–946
Ålesund ... 872
Algarve, the ... 941–943
Algeciras ... 1090
Alghero ... 718
Alicante ... 1105
Almería ... 1101
Alps (France) ... 442
Alps (Germany) ... 515–517
Alps (Switzerland) ... 1191–1199
Alsace ... 404
Alvão, Parque Natural do ... 941
Amalfi ... 704
Amarante ... 941
Ambleside ... 189
Amboise ... 401
Amsterdam ... 828–838
Amsterdam ... 829
Amsterdam, Central ... 831
- accommodation ... 834
- arrival ... 834
- coffeeshops ... 836
- eating and drinking ... 835
- entertainment ... 837
- nightlife ... 836
- sights ... 828–834
- tourist information ... 834
- tours ... 834
- transport ... 834

Anacapri ... 704
Ancona ... 696
Åndalsnes ... 873
Andalucía ... 1082–1102
Andorra ... 1126–1129
Andorra la Vella ... 1127–1129
Andorra la Vella ... 1127
Angla ... 348
Anglesey ... 200, 201
Ankara ... 1236–1239
Ankara, Central ... 1238
Antalya ... 1234
Antwerp ... 108–112
Antwerp ... 109
Apollonía ... 554
Aran Islands ... 629–631
Arctic Circle (Norway) ... 875
Arctic Circle (Sweden) ... 1172
Ardennes ... 117
Areópoli ... 544
Argostóli ... 570
Arhéa Kórinthos ... 539
Århus ... 326–329
Århus ... 327
Arinsal ... 1129
Arles ... 425
Arnhem ... 848
Assisi ... 695
Athens ... 529–537
Athens ... 530–531
- accommodation ... 534
- arrival ... 533
- eating and drinking ... 535
- entertainment ... 536
- excursions ... 537
- nightlife ... 536, 547
- ports ... 534
- shopping ... 536
- sights ... 529–533
- tourist information ... 533
- transport ... 534

ATMs ... 48
Aurlandsfjord ... 870
Auschwitz-Birkenau ... 905
AUSTRIA ... 67–94
Austria ... 69
Austvågøy ... 875
Avebury ... 166
Aviemore ... 216
Avignon ... 427–430
Avignon ... 429
Áyios Nikólaos ... 544

B

Bacharach ... 496
Bachkovo Monastery ... 238
Bad Gastein ... 90
Badacsony ... 595
Baden-Baden ... 504
Baden-Württemburg ... 501–509
Bakken ... 320
Balaton, Lake ... 593
Bâle ... *see Basel*
Balearic islands ... 1106–1112
Balestrand ... 870
Balloch ... 214
Banat, the ... 969
banks ... 48, *see also individual chapters*
Banská Štiavnica ... 1026
Bansko ... 233
Bar ... 781
Barcelona ... 1112–1123
Barcelona ... 1114–1115
Barcelona Old Town ... 1118
- accommodation ... 1120
- arrival ... 1119
- eating and drinking ... 1121
- festivals ... 1104, 1122
- nightlife ... 1121
- shopping ... 1122
- sights ... 1112–1119
- tourist information ... 1119
- transport ... 1119

Barèges ... 417
Basel ... 1186
Basilicata ... 706
Basque Country ... 1134–1144
Bastia ... 444, 446
Bath ... 167
Bavaria ... 509–520
Bay of Kotor ... 779
Bayeux ... 396
Bayonne ... 415
Beatles, The ... 185
Beaumaris Castle ... 201
Beaune ... 403
Belfast ... 632–636
Belfast ... 633
BELGIUM ... 95–120
Belgium and Luxembourg ... 97
Belgium's provincial and linguistic borders ... 101
Belgrade ... 1001–1007
Belgrade ... 1002
Benicassim ... 1104
Berati ... 63
Berchtesgaden ... 516
Bergen ... 867–870
Bergen ... 868
Berlin ... 459–471
Berlin, Central ... 460–461
Berlin: Kreuzberg & Friedrichshain ... 466
Berlin: Mitte & Prenzlauerberg ... 463

accommodation 467
arrival.............................. 466
drinking and nightlife 470
eating 468–470
entertainment.................. 470
shopping 470
sights.......................459–466
tourist information........... 466
transport.......................... 467
Bern 1188
Biarritz 413
Bihać 132
Bilbao............. 1136–1138
Bingen 496
Bitola 767
Black Forest, the 504
Black Mountains...........199
Black Sea coast (Bulgaria) 241–246
Black Valley 624
Blagaj.........................135
Blasket Islands 626
Bled 1046
Blue Grotto 704
Bodensee (Germany)....508
Bodø 875
Bodrum......................1229
Bohemia 292–298
Bohinj, Lake...............1048
Bol 267
Bologna 677–679
Bonifacio 449
Bonn 493
Bordeaux 408–412
Bordeaux 410
Borrowdale.................190
BOSNIA-HERZEGOVINA 112–136
Bosnia-Herzegovina....124
Boulogne 393
Bovec 1050
Bowness.....................188
Brač 266
Braga 938
Brajčino 768
Bran 965
Braşov................. 963–965
Braşov.........................964
Bratislava........ 1020–1026
Bratislava 1021
Brecon (town) 199
Brecon Beacons...........199
Brighton............. 162–165
Brighton 163
Brindisi........................705
Bristol 168–170
BRITAIN 137–218
Britain..........................139
Brittany 397
Brno 298–300
Brno 299
Bruges 114–116
Bruges.........................115
Brugge............*see Bruges*
Brussels............. 102–108
Brussels 104–105
Bruxelles.........*see Brussels*
Bucharest........... 956–962
Bucharest....................957
Bucharest, Central.......960
Bucureşti .....*see Bucharest*
Budapest 584–592
Budapest 585
accommodation 589
arrival.............................. 588
baths 587
drinking and nightlife 590
eating 590
entertainment.................. 591
festivals........................... 591
shopping 591
sights.......................584–588
tourist information........... 588
transport.......................... 589
budget airlines 30
budget tips 45
Budva................. 779–781
Budva old Town...........779
bulbfields (Netherlands) 839
BULGARIA.......... 219–246
Bulgaria.......................221
bullfighting.................1058
bulls, running of the (Pamplona)..............1132
bunkers, Albania............64
Burgas 243
Burgundy............ 402–404
Burren, The..................627
Bursa 1221
buses.........30, 37, *see also individual chapters*
passes............................. 37
from Britain and Ireland 30
within Europe 37
bus journey times.... 34–35
Busabout 37
Butrinti 63

C

Cáceres 1076
Cadaqués 1123
Cádiz 1088
Caernarfon................. 201
Cagliari 715–717
Cahersiveen.................625
Cairngorms..................216
Calais 394
Calvi............................446
Camargue....................426
Cambridge.......... 178–180
Cambridge 179
Camino de Santiago...1141
Campania 697–708
camping..........39, *see also individual chapters*
Çanakkale..................1219
Canillo.......................1126
cannabis 825
Cannes 433
Canterbury...................161
Caparica, Costa de 928
Cape Sounion..............537
Cappadocia..... 1239–1241
Capri 704
Carcassonne 420
Cardiff 197
Carpathian Mountains 953, 962
Carrick-a-Rede............637
Casablanca 810–813
Casablanca......... 812–813
Cascais........................928
Cashel 620
Cashel, Rock of...........620
Castilla y León 1078–1082
Catalunya 1112–1123
cell phones 49
Cēsis...........................735
Český Budějovice........293
Český Krumlov 294
Cetinje 782
Ceuta 797
Chamonix 443
changing money..... 48, *see also individual chapters*
Chartres 393
Chefchaouen 798
Chenonceaux, Château de.............................400
Chepstow 198
Chia 717
Chillon, Château de....1185
Chinon 400
Cinque Terre 666
Çıralı 1233
Ciutadella 1111
Cliffs of Moher.............627
climate change..............30
clothing sizes.................50
Cognac 409
Coimbra............... 930–933
Collioure 423
Cologne 489–493
Cologne.......................491
Combarelles, Grotte de 413
comics, Brussels 103
Como, Lake 663
Constance, Lake 508
contraceptives................47
Conwy 202
Copenhagen........ 310–319
Copenhagen 312–313
accommodation 316
arrival.............................. 315
drinking and nightlife 317
eating 316
entertainment.................. 319
shopping 318
sights.......................310–315
tourist information........... 315

tours.................................315
transport...........................315
Córdoba.......... 1093–1095
Córdoba 1094
Corfu...............................568
Cork..................... 620–623
Cork City............. 622–623
Corsica............... 444–450
Corte...............................448
Costa Brava.... 1123–1126
costs...............44, *see also individual chapters*
Côte d'Azur......... 423–437
Côte Vermeille.............423
couchsurfing..................39
Craignure.......................217
Crete.................... 571–574
Crete.................... 572–573
Crickhowell..................199
crime...............44, *see also individual chapters*
CROATIA............. 247–276
Croatia..........................249
Cuillin hills....................218
culture and etiquette.... *see individual chapters*
Curonian Spit...............755
customs..........................45
Cyclades islands, the 553–560
CZECH REPUBLIC 277–302
Czech Republic...........279

D

Dachau concentration camp..........................515
Dalmatian Coast (Croatia) 261–276
Dartmoor.......................170
D-Day beaches.............397
De Koog........................848
Delft..............................843
Delos.............................553
Delphi............................546
Den Burg.......................848
Den Haag............ 840–843
Den Haag.......................841
DENMARK........... 303–332
Denmark........................305
Derinkuyu....................1241
Derry.............................637
Derwent Water.............190
Dhiakoftó–Kalávryta Railway.........................439
Dijon.............................402
Dingle............................625
disabled travellers..........52
Dodecanese islands, the 561–565
Donegal Town...............630
Doolin............................626
Dordogne............ 412–414
Douro valley.................940
Dover.............................161
Dracula, Count.....965, 966
Dresden............... 472–476
Dresden.........................473
drink ....*see individual chapters*
Drottningholm Palace 1159
drugs.....................46, 837
Drumnadrochit.............216
Duart Castle.................217
Dublin.................. 610–618
Dublin............................611
Dubrovnik........... 272–276
Dubrovnik.....................274
Dunquin.........................626
Durham..........................193
Durmitor National Park 784
Durrësi............................63

E

Eden Project.................172
Edinburgh........... 202–209
Edinburgh.....................203
Edirne..........................1219
Eger...............................599
EHIC................................46
Eisenach........................480
Eisriesenwelt ice caves...89
electricity........................46
Elgol..............................218
Elterwater.....................189
email..............48, *see also individual chapters*
emergencies................ *see individual chapters*
Emilia-Romagna.........666
Engelberg...................1188
Ennis.............................626
Ephesus.......................1228
Epidaurus......................541
Ercolano........................702
Ermoúpoli......................554
Esbjerg..........................326
Essaouira............ 818–820
ESTONIA.............. 333–352
Estonia..........................335
Etna, Mount..................712
euro, the.........................49
EURO<26 youth card.....50
Eurolines..................31, 37
European Health Insurance card..............................46
European Union (EU)......31
Eurostar..........................30
Évora.............................942
EXIT Festival..............1008
Extremadura.... 1075–1078

F

Faro...............................944
Faroe Islands, The........330
ferries...............31, 37, *see also individual chapters*
from Britain and Ireland.....31
operators...........................31
within Europe....................37
Fes (Fez)............. 802–807
Fes El Bali.....................803
Fes Ville Nouvelle........804
festivals..........40, *see also individual chapters*
Fethiye............ 1230–1232
FEVE rail line..............1136
Fez..........................*see Fes*
Fiesta of San Fermín...1132
Figueres.......................1123
FINLAND............. 353–372
Finland..........................355
Fíra................................560
Firenze........... *see Florence*
fjords (Norway)... 866–870
Flakstadøya..................876
Flåm..............................870
flights....29, 30, 32, 37, *see also individual chapters*
from Australia and New Zealand..........................32
from Britain and Ireland.....29
from South Africa..............32
from the US and Canada...32
within Europe....................37
Florence.............. 682–687
Florence............. 684–685
Fnideq...........................797
Font de Gaume, Grotte de 413
food ....*see individual chapters*
Formentera..................1107
Fort William..................216
FRANCE.............. 379–454
France...........................375
Frankfurt............. 498–501
Frankfurt.......................499
Frederikshavn...............326
Freiburg im Breisgau.....505
Fruška Gora................1008
Funen.................. 323–325
Füssen...........................520

G

Galičica National Park...769
Gallipoli.......................1221
Galway................ 627–629
Galway City.................628
Gap of Dunloe..............624
Gateshead.....................194
Gavarnie........................417
gay travellers..................46

INDEX

Gdańsk 894–897
Gdańsk 895
Geirangerfjord 872
Geliboli peninsula 1221
Geneva 1180–1186
Geneva 1181
Genoa 663–665
Genova ....*see Genoa*
Gent .... *see Ghent*
GERMANY 451–520
Germany 453
Ghent 112–114
Ghent 112
Giant's Causeway 636
Gibraltar 1090
Gimmelwald 1193
Girona 1125
Giverny 393
Gjirokastra 65
Glasgow 209–213
Glasgow 210
Glastonbury 170
Glenbrittle 218
Glencolmcille 641
Glendalough 618
Golfe de Porto 446
Göreme 1240
Górtys 573
Goslar 491
Gothenburg 1161–1165
Gothenburg 1162
Gotland 1169
Gouda 844
GR20 449
Granada 1095–1101
Granada 1096–1097
Grandvalira 1126
Graz 82–84
Graz 83
Great Plain (Hungary) 600–602
GREECE 521–576
Greece 523
Greek ferries, catamarans and hydrofoils 524
Grenen 332
Grenoble 442
Grindelwald 1193
Guaja National Park 735
guesthouses ....39, *see also individual chapters*
Guimarães 940

H

Haarlem 838
Hadrian's Wall 195
Hague, The 840–843
Hague, The 841
Hallstatt 89
Hamburg 481–485
Hamburg 482
Haniá 575
Hannover 486–488
Haráki 562
Haverfordwest 203
Hay-on-Wye 199
health ....46, *see also individual chapters*
Heidelberg 502–505
Heidelberg 503
Helsingør 320
Helsinki 360–365
Helsinki 361
Herceg Novi 776
Herculaneum 702
Hersónissos 573
Herzegovina 132–136
HI hostels 39
Hierapolis 1230
Hill of Crosses 752
history .... *see individual chapter chronologies*
Hoge Veluwe National Park 848
Hohenschwangau Castle 520
Holyhead 200
Honningsvåg 880
Hóra (Íos) 558
Hóra (Pátmos) 564
hostels ....8, 38, *see also individual chapters*
hotels ....39, *see also individual chapters*
Humlebæk 325
HUNGARY 577–602
Hungary 579
Hungerburg plateau 92
Hvar 268

I

Ía 560
Ibiza 1107
Ihlara Valley 1240
Inari 372
Inisheer 630
Inishmaan 630
Inishmore 630
Inlandsbanan, the 1171
Innsbruck 92–94
Innsbruck 93
insurance 47
Interlaken 1191
International Youth Travel Card 50
internet ....48, *see also individual chapters*
InterRail passes 33
Inverness 215
Ioánnina 548
Iona, Isle of 217
Ionian Coast (Albania) 63
Ionian islands 568–571
Íos 558
Iráklion 575
IRELAND 603–638
Ireland 605
Ireland, Northern 632–638
ISIC 50
İstanbul 1210–1218
İstanbul City 1210
İstanbul, Old 1212
İstanbul: Sultanahmet 1215
accommodation 1214
arrival 1213
drinking and nightlife 1217
eating 1216
entertainment 1218
shopping 1218
sights 1210–1213
tourist information 1213
transport 1214
Istria 259–261
ITALY 639–718
Italy 641
itineraries 17–26
İzmir 1223–1226
İzmir 1224

J

Jajce 131
Jarve 348
Jokkmokk 1172
Jostedalsbreen 872
Jungfrau Region 1191
Jungfrau Region 1192
Jūrmala 732
Jutland 325–332

K

Kaali 348
Kafka, Franz 287
Kalambáka 547
Kamáres 554
Kamári 560
Kardhamýli 544
Karlovy Vary 296
Kaş 1232
Kastráki 547
Kástro 554
Kaunas 750–754
Kaunas 751
Kaymaklı 1241
Kecskemét 600
Kefalloniá 570
Kérkyra 568–570
Keswick 190
Keszthely 594
Keukenhof 839
Kilkenny 619
Killarney 624
Kilronan 629

Kiruna........................1173
Klaipėda........................754
Knossós........................571
Kobarid........................1049
København.............. *see Copenhagen*
Koblenz........................4969
Köln...............*see Cologne*
Komiža........................270
Konstanz........................508
Konya........................1241
Koprivshtitsa........................238
Korčula........................271
Kós........................564
Košice........................1014
Kotor........................776–779
Kotor........................777
Kraków........................900–905
Kraków........................901
Kravice Waterfalls........................136
Kristiansand........................865
Kruja........................63
Kungsledden Trail........................1174
Kuopio........................369
Kuressaare........................347
Kuşadası........................1226
Kutná Hora........................292
Kyiv........................1249–1254
Kyiv........................1251
Kyle of Lochalsh........................218

L

La Massana........................1129
La Roche-en-Ardenne........................118
La Rochelle........................407
La Tomatina........................1104
Lacanau........................412
Lagos........................945
Lahemaa National Park 346
Lahinch........................627
Lake Bohinj........................1057
Lake Constance.......... *see Bodensee*
Lake District (England) 187–190
Lake District, central........................188
Lake Geneva........................1180–1186
Lake Luzern........................1188
Lake Matka........................766
Lake Region (Finland) 367–370
Lake Siljan........................1171
Lake Skadar........................784
Lake Storsjön........................1171
Land's End........................172
Langdale........................189
language
- Albanian........................57
- Arabic (Moroccan)........................791
- Bosnian........................126, 252
- Bulgarian........................225
- Catalan........................1113
- Croatian........................252
- Czech........................281
- Danish........................309
- Dutch........................826
- Estonian........................336
- Finnish........................358
- Flemish........................101
- French........................101, 378
- German........................71, 101, 457
- Greek........................527
- Hungarian........................582
- Irish........................609
- Italian........................645
- Latvian........................722
- Letzebuergesch........................101
- Lithuanian........................741
- Macedonian........................761
- Montenegrin........................775
- Norwegian........................856
- Polish........................886
- Portuguese........................916
- Romanian........................954
- Russian........................976
- Serbian........................1000
- Slovak........................1018
- Slovene........................1038
- Spanish........................1059
- Swedish........................1150
- Turkish........................1208
- Ukrainian........................1248
- Welsh........................197

Lapland (Finland) 370–372
Lapland (Sweden) 1172–1174
Las Fallas........................1104
Lascaux........................413
LATVIA........................719–736
Latvia........................721
Lausanne........................1183
Lauterbrunnen........................1193
Le Corbusier........................433
Le Puy-en-Velay........................437
Lecce........................707
left luggage........................48
Leiden........................839
Leipzig........................477–479
León........................1080–1082
Les Calanques........................431
Les Eyzies........................413
lesbian travellers........................46
Lésvos........................565
Levoča........................1031
Liechtenstein........................1201
Liepāja........................745
Liguria........................656
Lille........................394
Líndhos........................563
Lindisfarne........................196
Linz........................81
Lisboa...............*see Lisbon*
Lisbon........................918–928
Lisbon........................920–921
Lisbon, Central........................923
- accommodation........................925
- arrival........................924
- beaches........................928
- eating and drinking........................926
- entertainment........................927
- fado........................927
- nightlife........................927
- shopping........................928
- sights........................912–924
- tourist information........................924
- transport........................924

Lisse........................839
LITHUANIA........................737–756
Lithuania........................739
Litóhoro........................553
Liverpool........................184–187
Ljubljana........................1039–1044
Ljubljana........................1040
Llanberis........................201
Locarno........................1200
Loch Lomond........................214
Loch Ness........................216
Lofoten Islands........................875
Loire Valley........................399–402
Lokrum........................275
London........................145–160
London........................146–147
London, West End........................149
- accommodation........................155
- arrival........................153
- drinking and nightlife........................157
- eating........................156
- entertainment........................158
- shopping........................159
- sights........................145–153
- tourist information........................154
- transport........................154

Londonderry........*see Derry*
Lorraine........................404
Lourdes........................416
Lübeck........................485
Lucerne...........*see Luzern*
Lugano........................1201
Lumbarda........................272
Luxembourg........................118
Luxembourg City........................118
Luxembourg City........................119
Luzern........................1187
L'viv........................1256–1260
Lyon........................438–441
Lyon........................440

M

MACEDONIA........................757–770
Macedonia........................760
Madrid........................1061–1069
Madrid........................1062–1063
- accommodation........................1066
- arrival........................1065
- drinking and nightlife........................1067
- eating........................1066
- entertainment........................1068
- excursions........................1069–1075
- shopping........................1068
- sights........................1061–1065
- tourist information........................1065
- transport........................1066

INDEX

Magaziá 567
Magerøya 880
Magură 966
mail .... 48, *see also individual chapters*
Mainz 495
Málaga 1092
Malbork 897
Mália 573
Mallaig 218
Mallorca 1109
Malmö 1165–1168
Malmö 1166
Malovište 768
Manchester 181–184
Manchester 182
Manganári 559
Máni peninsula 544
Mantova .... *see Mantua*
Maó 1111
maps 48
Marathoníssi 543
Maribor 1050
Marrakesh 813–818
Marrakesh 815
Marseille 430–433
Marseille 432
Matera 706
Matka, Lake 766
Matterhorn 1194
Mavrovo National Park 767
Međugorije 135
Meissen 476
Meknes 798–802
Meknes 800
Melk 80
Menorca 1110
Mérida 1077
Metéora 547
midges 215
Midnight Sun (Norway) 877
Milan 658–663
Milan 660–661
Mini Hollywood 1101
Mittenwald 516
mobile phones 49
Mólyvos 565
Monaco 437
Monemvasiá 542
money .... 48, *see also individual chapters*
Mont Blanc 443
Mont St-Michel 398
Monte Carlo 437
MONTENEGRO 771–784
Montenegro 773
Montignac 413
Montpellier 421
Montreux Jazz Festival 1185
Montserrat 1119
Moravia 298–302
MOROCCO 785–820
Morocco 787
Moscow 978–986
Moscow 980–981
accommodation 984
arrival 983
drinking and nightlife 985
eating 984
entertainment 985
shopping 986
sights 978–983
tourist information 983
transport 983
Mosel, River 497
Moskenesøya 876
Moskva .... *see Moscow*
Mostar 133–135
Mount Dajti 62
Mount Etna 712
Mount Olympus (Greece) 552
Mourne Mountains 636
Mull, Isle of 218
München .... *see Munich*
Munich 509–515
Munich 510
Mürren 1193
Mycenae 540
Mykínes 540
Mýkonos 554–556
Mýkonos Town 555
Mylopótas 559
Myrdal 870
Mystra 541
Mytilíni 565

N

Náfplio 541
Namur 117
Nancy 404
Nantes 398
Náoussa 557
Naples 697–701
Naples, Centro Storico 698
Naples, Bay of 701–704
Napoli .... *see Naples*
Náxos 557
Neringa 755
Nesebar 244
NETHERLANDS, THE 821–850
Netherlands, The 823
Neuschwanstein Castle 520
Newcastle upon Tyne 194
Newgrange 618
Newquay 173
newspapers 48
Nice 434–436
Nice 435
Nida 756
Nîmes 424–426
Niš 1012
Nora 717
Nordkapp 880
Nordpark 92, 94
Normandy 396–398
Northern Lights (Norway) 877
NORWAY 851–880
Norway 853
Novi Sad 1007–1011
Nuremberg 518
Nuremberg 519
Nürnberg ... *see Nuremberg*
Nymphenburg Castle ... 515
Nynäshamn 1170

O

Odense 323–325
Odense 324
Odesa 1254–1256
Ohrid 768–770
Okehampton 171
Oktoberfest 514
Old Man of Storr 218
Old Sarum 165
Olhão 946
Olomouc 300
Olympia 545
Olympos (Turkey) 1233
Olympus, Mount (Greece) 552
opening hours .... *see individual chapters*
Oporto .... *see Porto*
Ordesa, Parque Nacional de 1132
Ordino 1126
Orléans 402
Orsa 1171
Ósios Loukás 546
Oslo 858–865
Oslo 858–859
Östersund 1171
Oświęcim 905
Oudeschild 848
Oulu 370
Oxford 174–176
Oxford 175

P

Padova .... *see Padua*
Padua 668
Pakleni otoci 268
Pal 1129
Palanga 754
Palermo 708–711
Palermo, Central 710
Palio, Siena 689
Palma 1109
Pamplona 1133

Pamukkale 1230
Parikia 557
Paris 380–393
Paris 382–383
Paris, central 386–387
accommodation 388
arrival 385
drinking and nightlife 391
eating 389
entertainment 392
excursions 393
shopping 392
sights 380–385
tourist information 385
transport 385
Parma 679
Pärnu 348
Páros 556
Parque Nacional de Ordesa 1132
Parque Natural do Alvão 941
Pátmos 564
Pátra 538
Pavlovsk 994
Pécs 597
Pélekas 569
Pelister National Park 767
Peloponnese, the 538–546
Pembrokeshire 200
Peneda-Gerês, Parque Nacional da 939
Penzance 171
Périgueux 412
Períssa 560
Perpignan 422
Perugia 693–695
Peso da Régua 941
Peterhof, the 994
Petrčane 263
phones 48, *see also individual chapters*
Picos de Europa 1139
Pilsen *see Plzeň*
Piran 1044
Pisa 687–689
Plakiás 575
Plomári 565
Plovdiv 234–238
Plovdiv, Old 235
plugs 46
Plzeň 295
Počitelj 136
Podgorica 783
POLAND 881–910
Poland 883
police 45, *see also individual chapters*
Pompeii 702
Pont du Gard 424
Ponte de Barca 939
Poprad 1028
port 935
Porto (Corsica) 446
Porto 933–938
Porto 934
Portorož 1044
Portree 218
Portstewart 637
PORTUGAL 911–948
Portugal 913
Porvoo 365
post 48, *see also individual chapters*
Postbridge 171
Postojna 1044
Potsdam 471
Potter, Beatrix 189
Poulnabrone Dolmen 627
Powercourt 618
Poznań 909
Prague 283–291
Prague 284–285
accommodation 288
arrival 287
drinking and nightlife 290
eating 289
entertainment 290
shopping 291
sights 283–287
tourist information 287
transport 288
Praha *see Prague*
Predjama Castle 1044
Prešov 1030
Provence 427–437
Ptuj 1052
public holidays *see individual chapters*
Pula (Croatia) 259
Pula (Italy) 717
punting 174
Pyrenees (France) 417
Pyrenees (Spain) 1126–1134

R

Rabat 807–810
Rabat 808
rail passes 33
Randstad 838–847
Rapallo 665
Râşnov 966
Ravello 706
Ravenna 681
Regensburg 517
Reims 395
Republika Srpska 136
Réthymnon 574
Rhine Falls 1199
Rhine Gorge 496
Rhodes 561–563
Rhodes Town 561
Ria Formosa 946
Ribčev Laz 1048
Rīga 725–732
Rīga 728
Rīga, Old 726
Rijeka 260
Rila Monastery 232
Ring of Kerry 624
Riviera di Levante 665
Rock of Cashel 620
ROMANIA 949–970
Romania 951
Romantic Road 511
Rome 647–656
Rome, Central 648–649
accommodation 653
arrival 652
drinking and nightlife 654
eating 653
entertainment 655
festivals 655
shopping 656
sights 647–652
tourist information 652
transport 653
Ronda 1091
Roskilde 321
Rothenburg ob der Tauber 520
Rotterdam 844–847
Rotterdam 844
Rouen 396
Rovaniemi 371
Rovinj 260
Royal Shakespeare Company (RSC) 177
Rundāle Palace 733
Ruskin, John 189
RUSSIA 971–994
Russia 973

S

Saaremaa 347
Sachsehausen concentration camp 471
Sächsische Schweiz 476
safety 44, *see also individual chapters*
St Andrews 214
St David's 200
St Ives 173
St-Malo 397
St Petersburg 986–994
St Petersburg 987
accommodation 991
arrival 991
drinking and nightlife 993
eating 992
entertainment 993
excursions 994
shopping 993
sights 986–991
tourist information 991
transport 991
St Wolfgang 89
Saintes-Marie-de-la-Mer 427
Salamanca 1078–1080
Salamanca 1079

INDEX

Salaspils 733
Salisbury........................165
Salzburg 84–88
Salzburg 86
Samarian Gorge 575
Sámi 570
San Gimignano............692
San Sebastián
........................1134–1136
Sant Antoni................1107
Santa Margherita Ligure
..................................665
Santander..................1138
Santiago de Compostela
.....................1141–1144
Santiago de Compostela
................................1142
Santoríni 559
Sarajevo..............127–131
Sarajevo.......................128
Saranda 65
Sardinia...............715–718
Saumur 401
Savonlinna 368
Schaffhausen.............1199
Scheveningen 843
Schwangau...................520
SCOTLAND.........202–218
Scottish Highlands 216
Segovia.......................1071
Selçuk.........................1227
SERBIA 995–1012
Serbia 997
Seville 1082–1089
Seville..............1084–1085
sexual harassment 52
Shakespeare, William
..................................177
shoe size conversions....50
shopping.........................49
Siaröfortet...................1160
Sibiu 967–969
Sicily......................708–715
Siena 689–692
Siena 690
Sífnos 555
Sighişoara....................966
Sigulda 734
Siljan, Lake 1171
Sintra 928
Siófok 593
Siracusa.......................713
Sitía..............................573
Skadar, Lake................784
Skagen 331
Skála.............................564
Škocjan Caves 1044
Skoji islands 271
Skópelos.......................566
Skopje.................763–767
Skopje 764
Skye, Isle of.................218
Skýros...........................567
Slea Head 626
Slieve League..............631
Sligo 626
SLOVAKIA........1013–1032
Slovakia......................1015
SLOVENIA 1033–1052
Slovenia 1035
Snowdonia...................200
Soča valley 1049
Sofia...................226–232
Sofia 227
Sognefjord....................870
Soldeu 1126
Sóller 1110
Sopoćani 1011
Sopot............................896
Sopron 596
Sorrento........................703
Sound of Music, The
....................................87
Sozopol 245
SPAIN.............1053–1144
Spain 1055
Spárti 542
Split......................264–266
Spoleto 695
Sporades islands
.........................566–568
sports ....*see individual chapters*
Sremski Karlovci.........1008
Staffa, Isle of 218
Stamsund 876
Stavanger 865
Stechelberg 1193
Stirling 213
Stockholm 1152–1159
Stockholm........1154–1155
Stockholm archipelago
..................................1159
Stonehenge 166
Stoúpa 544
Strasbourg...................405
Strasbourg 406
Stratford-upon-Avon 176
Studenica 1011
student discounts... 50, *see also individual chapters*
study..............................43
Stuttgart 507
Subotica 1009
Supetar 266
Sveti Jovan Bigorski.....769
Sveti Stefan 781
Svolvær 875
SWEDEN..........1145–1174
Sweden 1147
SWITZERLAND
.......................1175–1202
Switzerland 1177
Sýros 553
Szeged 601
Szentendre 592
Szépasszonyvölgy........601

T

Tallinn..................339–346
Tallinn 340
Tampere........................367
Tangier................793–797
Tangier 794–795
Taormina.......................711
Tara Canyon 784
Tarifa...........................1089
Tartu.......................350–352
Tartu, Central 351
Tatras Mountains (Poland)
..................................905
Tatras Mountains (Slovakia)......1028–1030
Tavira 947
Teelin Bay 631
telephones...... 48, *see also individual chapters*
Tetouan 798
Texel 848
Thessaloníki........ 549–552
Thessaloníki 550
Thíra....... 559, *see Santoríni*
Ticino 1199–1201
time zones 50
Timişoara....................969
Tintern Abbey...............198
tipping .... *see individual chapters*
Tirana......................59–62
Tirana 60
Tirol.......................*see Tyrol*
Tobermory 221
Toledo.........................1070
Toledo 1072–1073
Tomar...........................930
Torino......................*see Turin*
Toruń............................899
Toulouse..............417–421
Toulouse.......................419
tourist information ... 50, *see also individual chapters*
Tours 399
trains.............................30, 33–37, *see also individual chapters*
from Britain and Ireland 30
in Europe.......................33–36
passes 33
train journey times... 34–35
Trakai 749
Transylvania 962–969
Travnik 131
Trebinje 136
Trier..............................497
Trollstigen Highway 872
Tromsø..................877–879
Trondheim 873–875
Trossachs 214
Trujillo 1075
Tsarkoe Selo 994

INDEX

Turaida Castle 734
Turin 656–658
TURKEY 1203–1242
Turkey 1205
Turku 365–367
Tuscany 682–696
Tyrol 92–94

U

Uig 218
Ukanc 1048
Ukraine 1243–1260
Ukraine 1245
Umbria 693–696
Uppsala 1160
Urbino 696
Utrecht 846

V

Vaduz 1201
Valencia 1102–1105
Valencia 1103
Van Gogh, Vincent 426
Varna 242
Vathý 554
Vatican 652
Vátos 569
Vaxholm 1160
Veliko Tarnovo 240
Veneto 666–681
Venezia .... *see Venice*
Venice 670–677
Venice 671
Venice, Central 674–675
accommodation 676
arrival 673
drinking and nightlife 677
eating 676
entertainment 677
sights 670–673
tourist information 673
transport 673
Vergina 552
Vermilion Coast 423
Verona 666–668
Versailles 393
Vestvågøy 876
Vesuvius 702
Vézère Valley 413
Vienna 72–80
Vienna 74–75
Vila do Gerês 939
Vila Nova de Gaia 933
Vila Nova de Milfontes 943
Vila Real 941
Villandry, Château de 400
Vilnius 743–749
Vilnius 744
Vintgar Gorge 1047
Virpazar 784
Vis 269
visas 45, 46
Visby 1169
Vojvodina 1007

W

WALES 196–202
Warsaw 888–894
Warsaw 889
Wartburg Castle 480
water 47
Weimar 479
Werfen 88
Westport 624
wheelchair access 52
Wicklow 618
Wien .... *see Vienna*
wi-fi 48
Windermere 188
women travellers 52
Wordsworth, William 189
work 42
Wrocław 907–909

Y

Yíthio 543
York 190–193
York 191
youth discounts .... 50, *see also individual chapters*
youth hostels .... 38, *see also individual chapters*

Z

Žabljak 784
Zadar 262
Zagreb 254–259
Zagreb 254
Zakopane 905
Zambujeira do Mar 943
Zaragoza 1130–1132
Zare Lazarevski 767
Zărneşti 966
Zdiar 1028
Zealand 320–322
Zeebrugge 108
Zermatt 1194
Žiča 1011
Zürich 1195–1199
Zürich 1197

Map symbols

maps are listed in the full index using coloured text

International boundary
Province boundary
Railway
Funicular
Cable car
Motorway
Tolled motorway
Road
Pedestrianized street
Steps
Path
Ferry route
Waterway
Wall
Mountains
Peak
Hill
Rocks
Ruins
Cave
Waterfall
Fountain
Viewpoint
Lighthouse
Point of interest
Museum
Stately home
Monastery
Church (regional)

Synagogue
Mosque
Hospital
Post office
Tourist information
Telephone office
Internet access
Bus stop
Metro station
RER station
S-Bahn
Tram stop
U-Bahn
London Underground Station
FGC station
Parking
Gate
Swimming pool
Statue
Building
Church (town)
Stadium
Park/forest
Christian cemetery
Muslim cemetery
Jewish cemetery
Beach
Glacier